THE CAPITOL OF THE UNITED STATES AT WASHINGTON, MORE THAN ANY OTHER BUILDING IS SYMBOLIC OF OUR GOVERNMENT AND OUR NATIONAL LIFE. IT IS THE SEAT OF THE JOINT HOUSES OF LEGIS-
LATURE—THE CONGRESS OF THE UNITED STATES. IN THE NORTH WING (RIGHT) IS THE SENATE CHAMBER, WHILE IN THE SOUTH WING (LEFT) IS THE HOUSE OF REPRESENTATIVES. THE
CORNERSTONE WAS LAID IN 1793 BY GEORGE WASHINGTON. STANDING ON A LOW HILL AT THE EAST END OF PENNSYLVANIA AVENUE, THE CAPITOL IS THE CENTRAL
POINT FROM WHICH TWELVE OF THE PRINCIPAL STREETS OF WASHINGTON RADIATE

Collier's

WORLD ATLAS
and
GAZETTEER

PUBLISHED IN NEW YORK BY

P. F. COLLIER & SON CORPORATION

General Contents

Full-page Colored Maps

Star Map and Economic Maps

General Map Index of the World

List of Illustrations

List of City Maps

Map Keys and How to Use Them

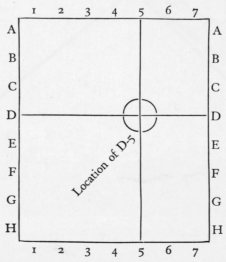

The maps in this atlas are so indexed as to serve the convenience of the reader or student in finding the location of any city, town, or physical feature. If the point he is seeking is indexed as at D-5, it means that the location is represented at or not far from the point of intersection of a line drawn from D to D (usually right to left)

and one drawn from 5 to 5 (usually from top to bottom) as indicated in the accompanying diagram. For example, Jerusalem, page 100, is keyed as at N-10. A line drawn from 10 at the top to 10 at the bottom will intersect a line drawn from N at the left to N at the right close to the word Jerusalem, accurately revealing the city's position.

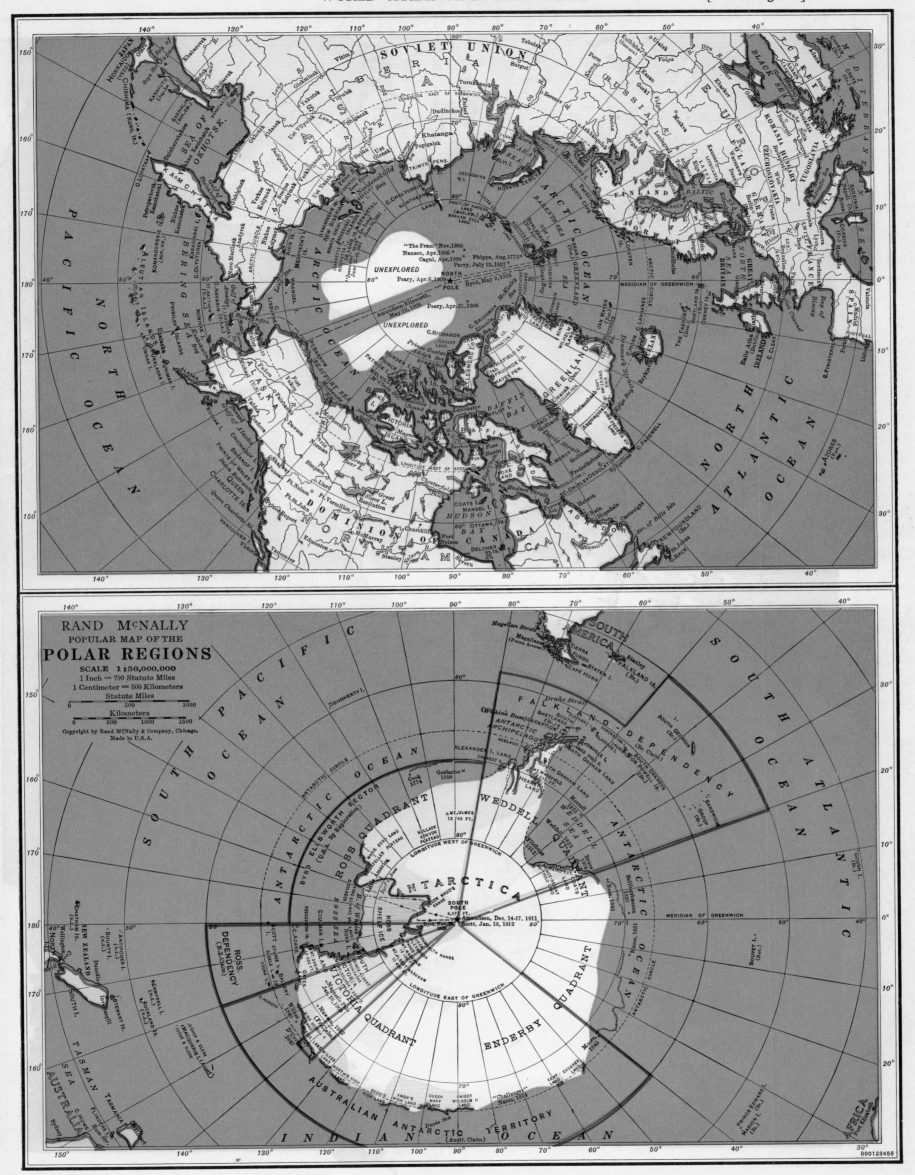

THE WORLD
PRINCIPAL COUNTRIES

ARGENTINA..N 16
Ar.1,079,965 sq. m.
Pop....12,564,301
AUSTRALIA....N 5
Ar.2,974,581 sq. m.
Pop.....6,806,752
BELGIUM..H 21
Area 11,752 sq. m.
Pop.....8,299,940
BOLIVIA......M 16
Area 581,785 sq. m.
Pop.....3,282,736
BRAZIL......L 17
Ar.3,285,319 sq. m.
Pop....47,795,000
BULGARIA....I 22
Area 39,814 sq. m.
Pop.....6,319,232
CANADA......F 14
Ar.3,694,863 sq. m.
Pop....11,120,000
CHILE........O 15
Area 286,322 sq.m.
Pop.....4,597,254
CHINA........I 3
Ar.3,756,102 sq. m.
Pop...422,527,000
COLOMBIA....L 15
Area 441,651 sq.m.
Pop.....8,390,950
CZECHOSLOVAKIA
H 21
Area 38,252 sq.m.
Pop....10,285,900
DENMARK....G 21
Area 16,571 sq. m.
Pop.....3,749,000
ECUADOR....L 15
Area 176,155 sq.m.
Pop.....2,758,505
EGYPT........J 22
Area 383,000 sq.m.
Pop....15,904,525
FINLAND....F 22
Area 149,954 sq.m.
Pop.....3,807,163
FRANCE......H 21
Area 212,681 sq.m.
Pop....41,905,968
FR. EQ. AFRICA
K 22
Area 912,049 sq.m.
Pop.....3,422,815
FR. W. AFRICA K 20
Ar.1,814,810 sq.m.
Pop....14,713,748
GERMANY....H 21
Area 224,973 sq.m.
Pop....77,028,433
GREAT BRITAIN
G 20
Area 89,041 sq.m.
Pop....45,419,061
GREECE......I 22
Area 54,092 sq. m.
Pop.....7,020,000
HUNGARY....H 22
Area 40,510 sq.m.
Pop....10,076,315
INDIA........J 1
Ar.1,575,107 sq. m.
Pop...338,170,632
IRAN........I 24
Area 628,000 sq.m.
Pop....15,055,115
IRELAND....G 20
Area 26,592 sq. m.
Pop.....2,944,000
ITALY........I 21
Area 119,703 sq.m.
Pop....43,691,000
JAPAN (Total)..I 5
Area 263,357 sq.m.
Pop....99,698,779
MEXICO......J 13
Area 760,290 sq.m.
Pop....18,852,086
NETHERLANDS
H 21
Area 13,202 sq. m.
Pop.....8,639,595
NETH. INDIES..L 3
Area 733,790 sq.m.
Pop....60,727,233
NEW ZEALAND O 7
Area 103,862 sq.m.
Pop.....1,591,974
NORWAY....F 21
Area 124,984 sq.m.
Pop.....2,908,000
PARAGUAY..M 16
Area 155,000 sq.m.
Pop......931,800
PERU........L 15
Area 482,133 sq.m.
Pop.....6,500,000
PHILIPPINE IS.K 4
Area 114,400 sq.m.
Pop....16,000,000
POLAND......H 22
Area 150,290 sq.m.
Pop....34,769,400
PORTUGAL..I 20
Area 35,894 sq. m.
Pop.....6,825,883
ROMANIA....H 22
Area 122,282 sq.m.
Pop....19,535,398
SOVIET UNION G 25
Ar.8,073,155 sq.m.
Pop...165,768,400
SPAIN........I 20
Area 195,010 sq.m.
Pop....24,583,096
SWEDEN....F 22
Area 173,105 sq.m.
Pop.....6,266,888
SWITZERLAND H 21
Area 15,940 sq. m.
Pop.....4,167,100
TANGANYIKA..L 23
Area 363,548 sq.m.
Pop.....5,146,886
TURKEY......I 23
Area 294,415 sq.m.
Pop....16,200,694
UN. OF S. AFRICA
N 22
Area 472,550 sq.m.
Pop.....8,488,300
UNIT. STATES..H 14
Ar.3,026,789 sq.m.
Pop...129,257,000
URUGUAY....N 16
Area 72,153 sq. m.
Pop.....2,082,367
VENEZUELA..K 16
Area 352,051 sq.m.
Pop.....3,491,159
YUGOSLAVIA..H 22
Area 95,551 sq. m.
Pop....15,400,177
(COL. AT. 89)

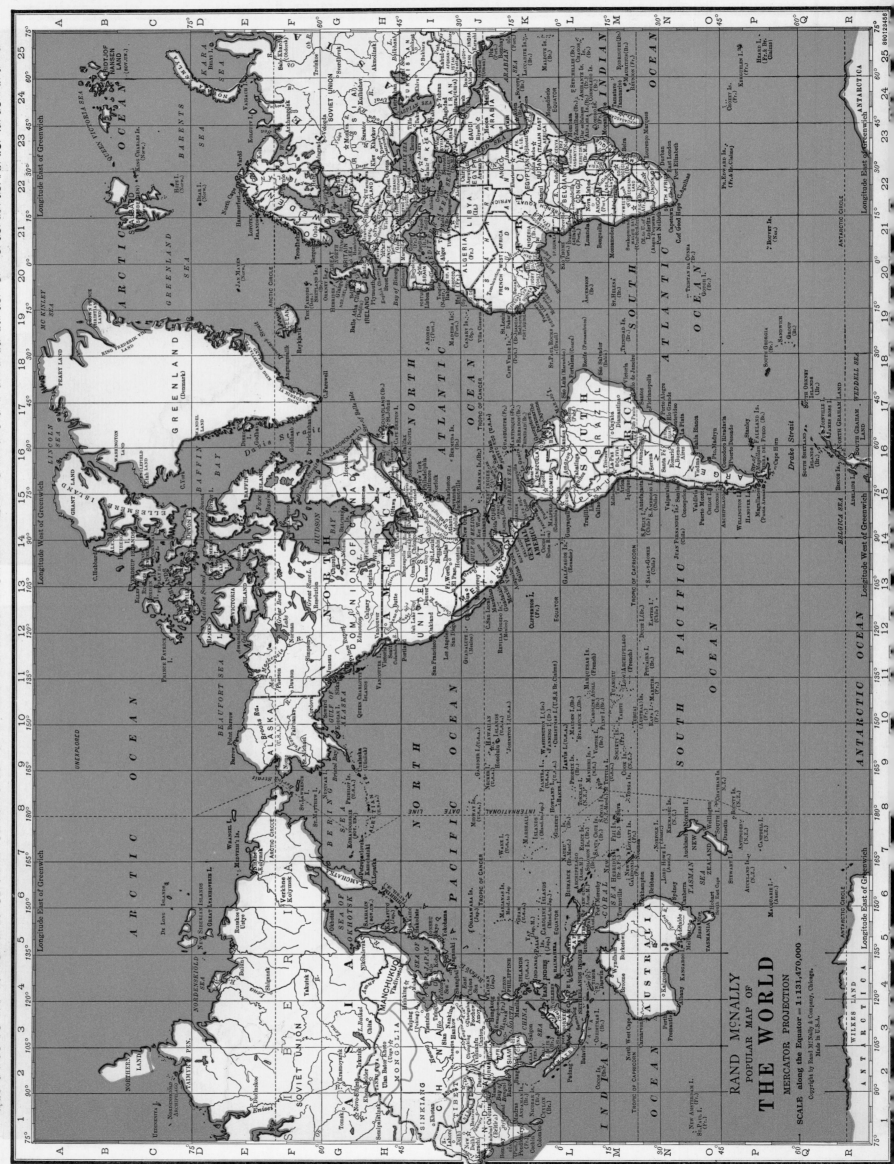

RAND McNALLY
POPULAR MAP OF
THE WORLD
MERCATOR PROJECTION
SCALE along the Equator = 1:131,470,000
Copyright by Rand McNally & Company, Chicago.
Made in U.S.A.

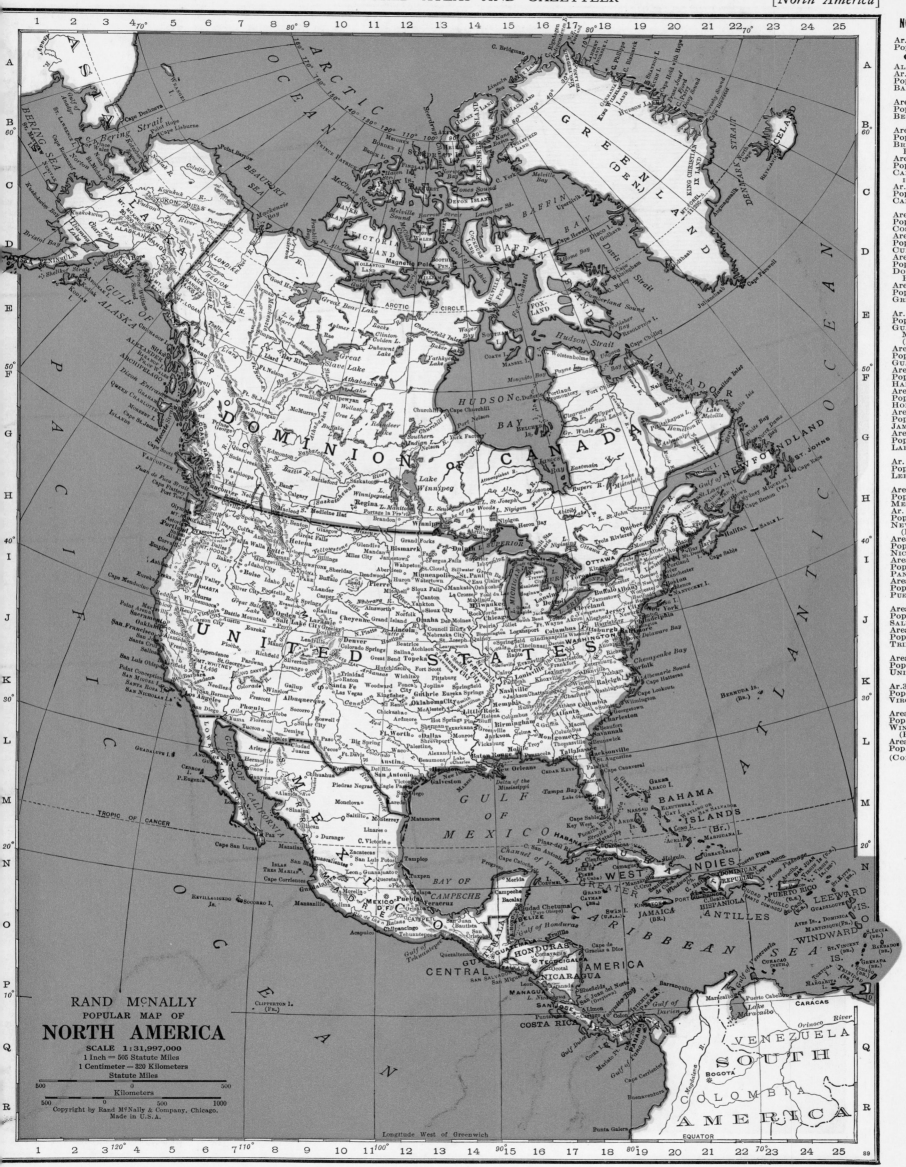

UNITED STATES
—
Ar.3,026,789 sq. m.
Pop. 129,257,000
(Capital)
WASHINGTON,D.C.
Pop.627,000H 22

ALABAMA....M 18
Area . 51,998 sq. m.
Pop.....2,895,000
Cap. Montgomery
Pop.66,079M 18

ARIZONA.....L 5
Area 113,956 sq. m.
Pop.....412,000
Cap. Phoenix
Pop.48,118..L 5

ARKANSAS.....L 15
Area.53,335 sq. m.
Pop.....2,048,000
Cap. Little Rock
Pop. 81,679.L 15

CALIFORNIA...I 2
Area 158,297 sq. m.
Pop....6,154,000
Cap. Sacramento
Pop. 93,750 H 1

COLORADO.....I 9
Area 103,948 sq. m.
Pop.....1,071,000
Cap. Denver
Pop.287,861 H 9

CONNECTICUT.F 24
Area..4,965 sq. m.
Pop.....1,741,000
Cap. Hartford
Pop.164,072F 24

DELAWARE.....H 23
Area..2,370 sq. m.
Pop.....261,000
Cap. Dover
Pop. 4,800.H 23

DISTRICT OF
COLUMBIA.....
Area.....70 sq. m.
Pop.....627,000
Cap. Washington
Pop. 497,000H22

FLORIDA.....P 21
Area 58,666 sq. m.
Pop.....1,670,000
Cap. Tallahassee
Pop. 11,725 O 19

GEORGIA.....M 19
Area.59,265 sq. m.
Pop.....3,085,000
Cap. Atlanta
Pop. 270,366
L 19

IDAHO.......E 5
Area 83,888 sq. m.
Pop.....493,000
Cap. Boise
Pop. 21,544. E 5

ILLINOIS.....H 16
Area 56,665 sq. m.
Pop.....7,878,000
Cap. Springfield
Pop. 71,864. I 16

INDIANA.....I 18
Area. 36,354 sq. m.
Pop.....3,474,000
Cap. Indianapolis
Pop.364,161.I 18

IOWA.......G 14
Area. 56,147 sq. m.
Pop.....2,552,000
Cap. Des Moines
Pop.142,559H 14

KANSAS.....J 12
Area.82,158 sq. m.
Pop.....1,864,194
Cap. Topeka
Pop. 68,870 I 13

KENTUCKY...J 18
Area.40,598 sq. m.
Pop.....2,920,000
Cap. Frankfort
Pop.11,626.. I 18

LOUISIANA...O 15
Area.48,506 sq. m.
Pop.....2,132,000
Cap. Baton Rouge
Pop. 30,729 O 16

MAINE.......C 25
Area.33,040 sq. m.
Pop.....856,000
Cap. Augusta
Pop.17,198 D 24

MARYLAND...H 22
Area.12,327 sq. m.
Pop.....1,679,000
Cap. Annapolis
Pop.12,531.H 22

MASSACHUSETTS
F 24
Area..8,266 sq. m.
Pop.....4,426,000
Cap. Boston
Pop.817,713E 24

MICHIGAN...F 17
Area. 57,980 sq. m.
Pop.....4,830,000
Cap. Lansing
Pop.78,397.F 18

MINNESOTA...E 14
Area.84,682 sq. m.
Pop.....2,652,000
Cap. St. Paul
Pop.271,606E 14

MISSISSIPPI..N 16
Area.46,865 sq. m.
Pop.....2,023,000
Cap. Jackson
Pop.48,282.N 16

MISSOURI.....J 15
Area. 69,420 sq. m.
Pop.....3,989,000
Cap. Jefferson City
Pop.21,596.. I 15

(Col. At. 7 R 35)

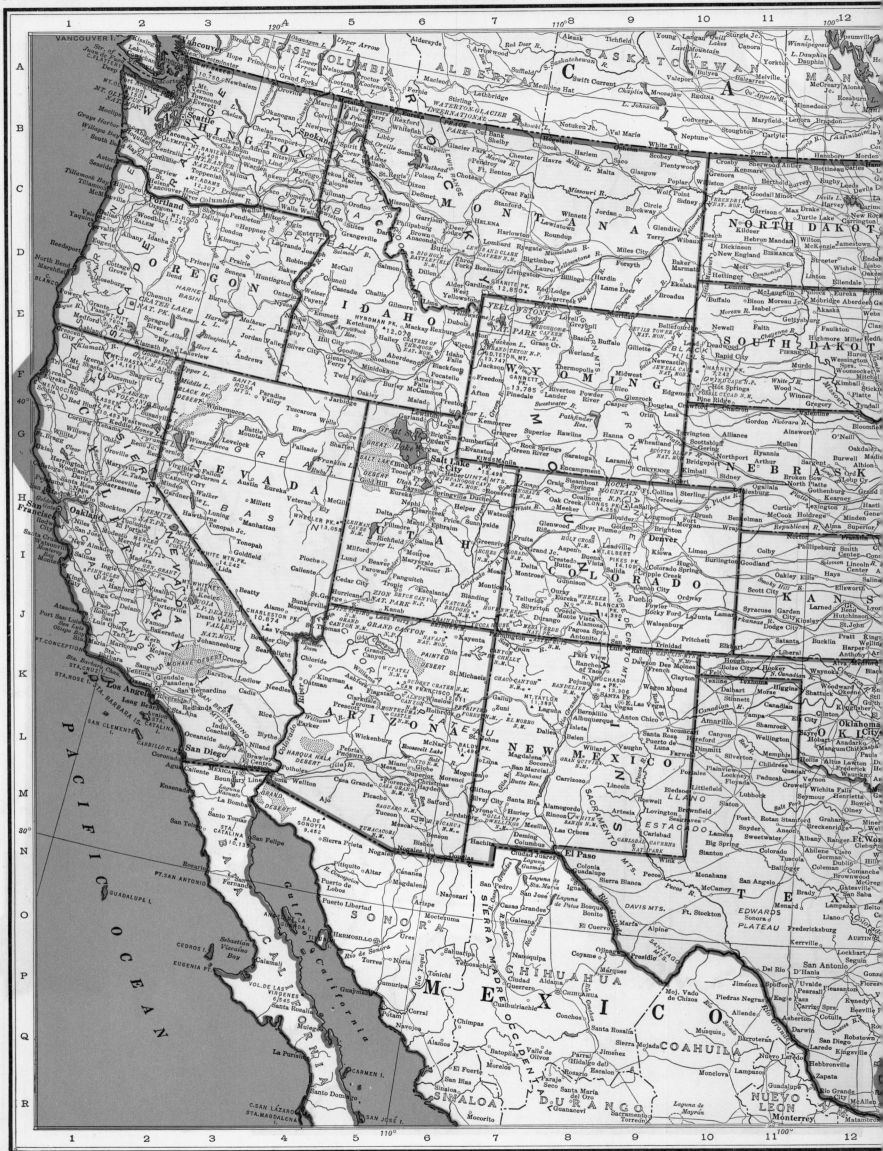

RAND McNALLY
14 x 21 INCH MAP OF
UNITED STATES
SCALE 1:9,757,000
1 Inch = 154 Statute Miles
1 Centimeter = 97 Kilometers

Statute Miles

Kilometers

Copyright by Rand McNally & Company, Chicago,
Made in U.S.A.

No.101 PP

7R35

GULF OF MEXICO

ATLANTIC OCEAN

ALABAMA

Area, 51,998 sq. m.
Pop.....2,895,000

PRINCIPAL CITIES

Pop.—Thousands

2	Abbeville	M 22
9	Alabama City	D 17
3	Albertville	O 16
6	Alexander City	H 18
1	Aliceville	H 5
1	Altoona	D 16
5	Andalusia	N 15
22	Anniston	F 19
2	Ashland	G 19
3	Athens	A 12
3	Atmore	O 8
3	Attalla	D 17
1	Auburn	J 21
2	Bay Minette	P 7
21	Bessemer	G 12
1	Bevelle	I 18
260	Birmingham	F 13
1	Blocton	H 11
1	Blue Mountain	F 19
2	Boaz	D 17
1	Boothton	G 12
1	Brantley	M 16
3	Brewton	O 11
2	Bridgeport	A 19
1	Brighton	G 12
1	Brundidge	M 19
1	Calera	H 13
1	Camp Hill	I 20
1	Carbon Hill	E 9
2	Chapman	M 13
1	Chickasaw	P 5
1	Citronelle	O 4
2	Clanton	I 14
1	Clayton	L 21
1	Columbiana	G 14
2	Cordova	E 11
1	Crichton	Q 5
3	Cullman	D 13
2	Dadeville	I 19
2	Dallas Mills	B 14
16	Decatur	B 12
4	Demopolis	J 6
3	Dixiana	E 14
1	Dora	E 11
16	Dothan	O 21
1	E. Brewton	O 11
1	E. Tallassee	J 19
1	Elba	N 17
4	Enterprise	N 18
5	Eufaula	L 23
2	Eutaw	I 7
1	Evergreen	N 12
1	Fairfax	I 23
11	Fairfield	F 12
1	Fairhope	Q 6
1	Fayette	F 7
3	Fivepoints	H 22
2	Florala	O 16
12	Florence	A 8
1	Ft. Deposit	L 14
1	Fort Payne	O 19
1	Frisco City	N 9
24	Gadsden	D 18
2	Geneva	O 18
2	Georgiana	M 13
1	Good Water	H 17
1	Graselli	F 12
1	Greensboro	I 8
4	Greenville	L 14
1	Guin	D 6
2	Guntersville	C 16
2	Haleyville	D 8
1	Hartford	O 19
3	Hartselle	C 12
2	Headland	N 21
1	Heflin	F 20
12	Huntsville	B 14
3	Irondale	F 13
1	Jackson	N 6
3	Jacksonville	E 19
5	Jasper	E 10
2	Lafayette	I 21
5	Lanett	I 22
3	Leeds	F 14
5	Linden	K 7
2	Lineville	G 19
2	Lipscomb	G 12
2	Livingston	J 5
2	Luverne	M 16
3	Marion	J 10
2	Mignon	H 16
68	Mobile	Q 5
1	Monroeville	N 10
1	Montevallo	H 13
66	Montgomery	J 16
2	Mt. Hope	C 9
2	Northport	G 8
1	Oneonta	E 15
8	Opelika	I 21
3	Opp	N 16
1	Oxford	F 19
3	Ozark	N 19
1	Parrish	E 10
14	Phenix City	J 24
4	Piedmont	E 20
1	Piper	H 11
2	Prattville	J 15
5	Prichard	P 5
1	Ragland	E 17
1	Red Bay	C 5
2	Roanoke	H 21
3	Russellville	B 8
2	Samson	O 17
2	Scottsboro	B 17
18	Selma	J 12
3	Sheffield	B 8
1	Slocomb	O 20
1	Stockton	O 6
1	Sulligent	E 5
4	Sylacauga	G 16
8	Talladega	F 17
7	Tarrant City	F 13
2	Thomasville	L 7
7	Troy	M 18
21	Tuscaloosa	G 8
5	Tuscumbia	B 8
3	Union Springs	K 19
1	Uniontown	J 9
1	Vincent	G 15
1	W. Blocton	H 11
2	Wetumpka	J 16
2	Whistler	P 5
2	Wilson Dam	B 8
1	Winfield	E 7
2	York	J 4

(Col. At. 7 R 35)

RAND McNALLY POPULAR MAP OF ALABAMA

SCALE 1:1,774,000
1 Inch = 28 Statute Miles
1 Centimeter = 17.7 Kilometers

Copyright by Rand McNally & Company, Chicago.
Made in U.S.A.

RAND McNALLY
POPULAR MAP OF
ARIZONA

SCALE 1:2,470,000
1 Inch = 39 Statute Miles
1 Centimeter = 24.7 Kilometers
Statute Miles

Kilometers

Copyright by Rand McNally & Company, Chicago
Made in U.S.A.

ARIZONA

Area, 113,956 sq. m.
Pop. 412,000.

PRINCIPAL CITIES

Pop.—Thousands

1 Ajo	N 9
8 Bisbee	P 22
1 Buckeye	K 11
1 Casa Grande	L 14
1 Chandler	K 14
1 Claypool	K 18
3 Clarkdale	H 13
2 Clifton	L 24
1 Coolidge	L 15
10 Douglas	P 23
1 Duncan	M 25
4 Flagstaff	G 14
1 Florence	L 15
Ft. Huachuca	P 20
4 Glendale	K 12
7 Globe	K 18
2 Hayden	L 18
1 Holbrook	G 20
1 Jerome	H 13
2 Kingman	G 5
4 Mesa	K 14
8 Miami	L 17
1 Morenci	L 24
4 Nogales	P 17
48 Phoenix	K 13
1 Pima	L 22
1 Prescott	H 11
1 Ray	L 17
1 Safford	M 22
1 St. Johns	H 24
1 Scottsdale	K 13
1 Sonora	L 17
4 Superior	K 17
2 Tempe	K 13
33 Tucson	N 17
2 Warren	P 22
4 Williams	F 12
4 Winslow	G 18
5 Yuma	M 2

Pop.—Hundreds

4 Blackwater	L 15
1 Blalack	M 3
5 Bylas	L 21
3 Chino Valley	H 11
8 Clemenceau	H 13
1 Copper	H 11
1 Dome	M 3
2 Duquesne	P 18
4 Fort Apache	J 21
6 Fort Defiance	E 24
1 Geronimo	L 21
8 Gilbert	K 14
2 Glenbar	L 22
4 Inspiration	K 17
4 Joseph Cy.	G 20
2 Lakeside	L 21
1 Peoria	K 12
2 Pinedale	I 20
6 Pirtleville	P 23
6 Polacca	E 19
2 Rowood	N 9
3 Sacaton	L 14
6 San Simon	N 24
7 Snowflake	H 21
8 Solomon	L 23
4 Somerton	M 1
4 Taylor	H 21
7 Thatcher	L 22
1 Theba	L 9
8 Tolleson	K 12
1 TollesonO	21
1 Valentine	F 7
7 Wickenburg	J 10
8 Willcox	N 22
7 Winkelman	L 18

(Col. AT. 7 R 35)

RAND McNALLY
POPULAR MAP OF
ARKANSAS

SCALE 1:1,774,000
1 Inch = 28 Statute Miles
1 Centimeter = 17.7 Kilometers

Copyright by Rand McNally & Company, Chicago.
Made in U.S.A.

RAND McNALLY
POPULAR MAP OF
CALIFORNIA

SCALE 1:3,909,000
1 Inch = 61.7 Statute Miles
1 Centimeter = 39 Kilometers
Statute Miles

Kilometers

Copyright by Rand McNally & Company, Chicago,
Made in U.S.A.

COLORADO

Area 103,948 sq.m.
Pop. 1,071,000

PRINCIPAL CITIES

Pop.—Thousands

1 Aguilar	O 16
1 Akron	E 20
5 Alamosa	O 12
1 Arvada	F 14
2 Aurora	F 15
11 Boulder	E 14
3 Brighton	E 15
2 Brush	D 19
1 Burlington	H 23
6 Canon City	K 14
1 Center	N 11
33 Colorado Springs	J 15
1 Craig	C 7
1 Crested Butte	J 8
1 Cripple Creek	J 14
1 Delagua	P 16
1 Del Norte	N 10
3 Delta	J 5
288 Denver	F 15
5 Durango	P 5
2 Eaton	C 16
1 Edgewater	F 15
8 Englewood	G 15
2 Florence	K 14
11 Ft. Collins	C 14
1 Ft. Lyon	M 20
2 Ft. Morgan	D 18
1 Fowler	M 18
1 Fruita	H 3
2 Glenwood Springs	G 7
2 Golden	F 14
10 Grand Junction	I 4
12 Greeley	D 16
1 Gunnison	K 8
1 Haxtun	C 22
1 Holly	M 24
1 Holyoke	C 23
1 Idaho Springs	F 13
1 Julesburg	A 23
1 Lafayette	E 14
7 La Junta	M 19
1 Lamar	M 22
3 Las Animas	M 20
4 Leadville	H 11
1 Limon	H 19
1 Littleton	G 15
6 Longmont	E 14
10 Louisville	E 14
1 Loveland	D 14
2 Lupton	E 15
1 Manassa	P 12
1 Manitou	J 15
1 Meeker	E 6
3 Monte Vista	O 11
4 Montrose	K 6
1 Mt. Harris	C 8
1 Oak Creek	D 9
1 Ordway	L 19
2 Paonia	J 6
2 Primero	P 15
50 Pueblo	L 16
1 Rifle	G 6
1 Rocky Ford	M 19
1 Saguache	M 11
5 Salida	K 12
1 Silverton	N 5
1 Springfield	O 22
1 Steamboat Springs	C 9
1 Sterling	C 20
12 Trinidad	O 17
1 Victor	J 14
4 Walsenburg	O 15
2 Windsor	C 15
2 Wray	C 23
1 Yuma	Q 15

Pop.—Hundreds

9 Antonito	Q 11
7 Aspen	H 9
7 Ault	D 16
8 Berthoud	D 14
8 Buena Vista	J 11
5 Castle Rock	H 15
5 Cedaredge	I 6
6 Central City	F 13
6 Cheyenne Wells	J 23
9 Cortez	P 3
5 Dolores	O 3
8 Eads	K 22
8 Erie	E 15
8 E. Canon	K 14
3 Evans	D 16
5 Flagler	H 21
8 Ft. Logan	G 14
3 Fountain	J 16
8 Frederick	E 15
7 Hayden	C 8
7 Hotchkiss	J 6
7 Hugo	I 19
8 Ignacio	Q 6
9 Johnstown	D 15
6 La Jara	P 11
5 La Salle	D 16
3 La Veta	O 14
7 Lyons	D 14
4 Mancos	P 4
4 Manzanola	M 18
5 Milliken	D 15
7 Mountain View	F 14
5 New Castle	G 7
8 Olathe	K 5
8 Otis	E 21
7 Ouray	N 5
8 Ovid	B 23
8 Pagosa Springs	P 8
9 Palisade	I 4
5 Platteville	D 15
5 Pritchett	Q 23
7 Red Cliff	G 10
7 Rockvale	L 14
6 Sanford	P 12
7 San Luis	P 13
9 Segundo	P 15
6 Somerset	I 7
7 Stratton	H 22
5 Starkville	P 16
6 Sugar Cy.	L 19
5 Telluride	N 4
5 Wellington	C 15
3 Weston	O 15
6 Wiley	L 22

(Col. At. 7 R 35)

RAND McNALLY POPULAR MAP OF **COLORADO**

SCALE 1:2,304,500
1 Inch = 36.4 Statute Miles
1 Centimeter = 23 Kilometers

Copyright by Rand McNally & Company, Chicago.
Made in U.S.A.

RAND McNALLY
POPULAR MAP OF
FLORIDA

SCALE 1:2,471,000
1 Inch = 39 Statute Miles
1 Centimeter = 24.7 Kilometers
Statute Miles

Copyright by Rand McNally & Company, Chicago.
Made in U.S.A.

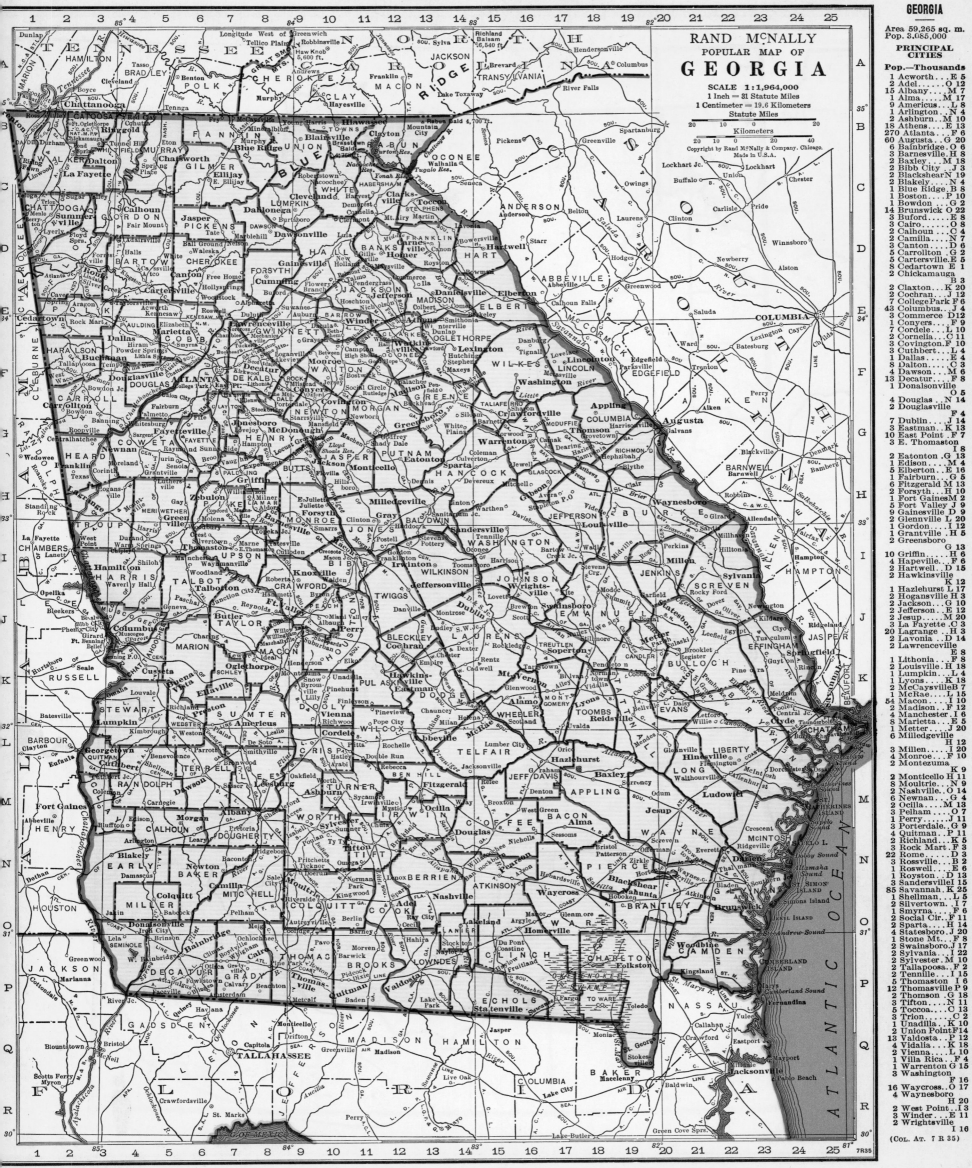

RAND McNALLY
POPULAR MAP OF
GEORGIA
SCALE 1:1,964,000
1 Inch = 31 Statute Miles
1 Centimeter = 19.6 Kilometers
Statute Miles

Copyright by Rand McNally & Company, Chicago.
Made in U.S.A.

GEORGIA

Area 59,265 sq. m.
Pop. 3,085,000

**PRINCIPAL
CITIES**

Pop.—Thousands

1 Acworth	E 5
2 Adel	O 12
15 Albany	M 7
1 Alma	M 17
9 Americus	L 8
1 Arlington	N 4
2 Ashburn	M 10
18 Athens	E 13
270 Atlanta	F 6
60 Augusta	G 20
2 Bainbridge	O 6
3 Barnesville	H 8
2 Baxley	M 18
2 Bibb City	J 3
2 BlackshearN	19
2 Blakely	N 4
1 Blue Ridge	B 8
1 Boston	P 10
1 Bowdon	G 2
14 Brunswick	O 22
3 Buford	E 8
3 Cairo	O 8
3 Calhoun	C 4
2 Camilla	N 7
3 Canton	D 6
5 Carrollton	G 2
5 Cartersville	E 5
2 Cedartown	E 1
2 Chickamauga	
	J 3
2 Claxton	K 20
2 Cochran	J 12
1 CollegePark	F 6
43 Columbus	J 4
2 Commerce	D 12
1 Conyers	F 7
2 Cordele	L 10
1 Cornelia	C 11
2 Covington	F 10
2 Cuthbert	L 4
1 Dallas	E 4
3 Dalton	O 3
2 Dawson	M 6
13 Decatur	F 8
1 Donalsonville	
	O 5
4 Douglas	N 14
2 Douglasville	
	F 4
7 Dublin	J 14
3 Eastman	K 13
10 East Point	F 7
3 E. Thomaston	
	I 8
2 Eatonton	G 13
2 Edison	M 4
5 Elberton	E 16
1 Fairburn	G 5
6 Fitzgerald	M 13
1 Forsyth	H 10
1 Fort Gaines	M 2
3 Fort Valley	J 9
9 Gainesville	D 9
2 Glennville	L 20
1 Gordon	I 12
1 Grantville	H 5
2 Greensboro	
	G 13
10 Griffin	H 6
1 Hapeville	F 6
3 Hartwell	D 15
2 Hawkinsville	
	K 12
1 Hazlehurst	L 17
1 Hogansville	H 3
2 Jackson	G 10
2 Jefferson	E 12
2 Jesup	M 20
3 La Fayette	C 3
20 Lagrange	H 3
2 Lavonia	D 14
2 Lawrenceville	
	E 8
1 Lithonia	F 8
5 Louisville	H 18
1 Lumpkin	L 4
1 Lyons	K 18
2 McCaysville	B 7
1 McRae	L 15
54 Macon	I 10
2 Madison	F 12
1 Manchester	I 6
5 Marietta	E 5
1 Metter	J 20
6 Milledgeville	
	H 12
3 Millen	G 19
2 Monroe	F 10
4 Moultrie	N 10
1 Montezuma	
	K 9
2 Monticello	H 11
8 Moultrie	N 10
3 Nashville	O 14
2 Newnan	G 4
2 Ocilla	M 13
2 Pelham	O 7
2 Perry	J 10
3 Porterdale	G 9
3 Quitman	P 11
2 Richland	L 4
3 Rock Mart	F 3
22 Rome	N 2
3 Rossville	B 2
4 Roswell	E 6
2 Royston	D 13
15 Sandersville	
	H 15
85 Savannah	K 25
2 Shellman	L 5
2 Silvertown	B 7
2 Smyrna	F 6
2 Social Cir.	F 11
2 Sparta	H 14
20 Statesboro	J 20
1 Stone Mt.	F 8
3 Swainsboro	J 17
2 Sylvania	J 22
2 Sylvester	M 10
2 Tallapoosa	F 2
5 Tennille	H 15
12 Thomasville	P 9
2 Thomson	G 18
5 Tifton	N 11
5 Toccoa	C 13
3 Trion	C 2
1 Unadilla	K 10
1 Union Point	F 14
2 Valdosta	P 11
4 Vidalia	K 18
2 Vienna	K 10
1 Villa Rica	F 4
1 Warrenton	G 15
3 Washington	
	F 16
16 Waycross	O 17
4 Waynesboro	
	H 20
2 West Point	I 3
2 Winder	E 11
2 Wrightsville	
	I 16

(Col. At. 7 R 35)

IDAHO

Area 83,888 sq. m.
Pop. 493,000

PRINCIPAL CITIES

Pop.—Thousands

2 Alameda.....P 19
1 American Falls
       ....P 17
1 Ashton.....M 21
3 Blackfoot..O 19
22 Boise.......N 6
1 Bonners Ferry
       ....A 5
2 Buhl........Q 10
4 Burley......Q 14
5 Caldwell...N 3
8 Coeur d'Alene
       ....D 4
3 Emmett......N 4
1 Filer.......Q 11
1 Glenns Ferry
       ....P 8
2 Gooding....P 11
1 Grangeville H 6
1 Hailey......N 12
9 Idaho FallsO 20
2 Jerome.....P 11
2 Kellogg-
    Wardner..D 6
9 Lewiston...G 3
3 Malad City
       ....R 18
1 Meridian...N 5
2 Montpelier.Q 22
4 Moscow.....F 13
1 Mountain
    Home......O 8
2 Mullan.....E 7
8 Nampa......N 4
1 Orofino....G 6
3 Payette....M 3
16 Pocatello..P 19
2 Preston....R 20
3 Rexburg....M 20
2 Rigby......M 20
2 Rupert.....P 13
2 St. Anthony
       ....M 22
2 St. Maries..E 5
1 Salmon......J 13
3 Sandpoint..B 4
1 Shelley....O 19
3 Shoshone...P 11
1 Spirit Lake C 3
9 Twin Falls Q11
1 Wallace....E 6
3 Weiser......L 3

Pop.—Hundreds

6 Aberdeen...P 17
1 Albion.....Q 14
4 Ammon......N 20
4 Archer.....N 20
6 Arco.......N 16
4 Bancroft...P 20
4 Barber......N 6
3 Basalt.....O 19
4 Bellevue...N 12
8 Bloomington
       ....R 22
6 Bovill......F 5
2 Bruneau.....P 7
8 Burke.......D 7
3 Cambridge L 4
6 Carey......O 14
5 Cascade....L 6
4 Challis....L 12
3 Clark Fork C 6
3 Clifton....Q 20
7 Cottonwood
       ....H 5
4 Council....K 5
5 Craigmont..H 5
3 Culdesac...G 4
3 Dayton.....R 20
3 Deary......F 5
3 Downey.....Q 19
3 Driggs.....N 23
3 Dubois.....M 19
3 Eagle......N 5
4 Eden.......Q 12
9 Elk River..F 6
2 Fairfield..O 10
2 Ferdinand..H 5
3 Franklin...R 21
6 Genesee....G 3
8 Georgetown
       ....Q 22
6 Grace......Q 20
5 Hagerman...P 9
4 Hansen.....O 12
4 Harrison...E 4
6 Hazelton...Q 12
4 Heyburn....Q 14
4 Homedale...N 3
4 Iona.......N 20
6 Juliaetta..G 4
5 Kamiah.....H 6
4 Kendrick...G 4
6 Kimberly...Q 11
5 Kooskia....H 7
4 Kuna.......N 5
4 Lapwai.....G 3
5 Lava Hot
    Springs...P 20
3 Lewisville.N 19
7 McCall.....K 6
5 McCammon
       ....P 19
8 Mackay.....M 14
2 Menan......N 20
4 Middleton..N 4
4 Midvale....L 4
4 Minkcreek..Q 20
4 Newdale....M 21
2 New Meadow
       ....K 5
5 New Plymouth
       ....M 3
4 Nezperce...H 6
5 Oakley.....Q 13
8 Paris......Q 21
4 Parker.....M 20
4 Parma.......N 3
4 Paul.......Q 13
5 Plummer....E 4
8 Post Falls..D 3
4 Priest River C 3
4 Rathdrum...D 3
4 Ririe......N 20
3 Roberts....N 19
4 Rockland...Q 19
4 St. John...M 20
4 Salem......M 20
8 Soda Springs
       ....Q 21
4 Star.......N 4
3 Stites......H 7
6 Sugar......N 21
4 Teton......N 21
4 Troy.......F 4
7 Ucon.......N 23
4 Victor.....N 23
9 Wardner....D 6
7 Wendell....P 11
4 Weston.....R 20
4 Wilder.....N 3
7 Winchester.H 4

(Col. AT. 7 R 35)

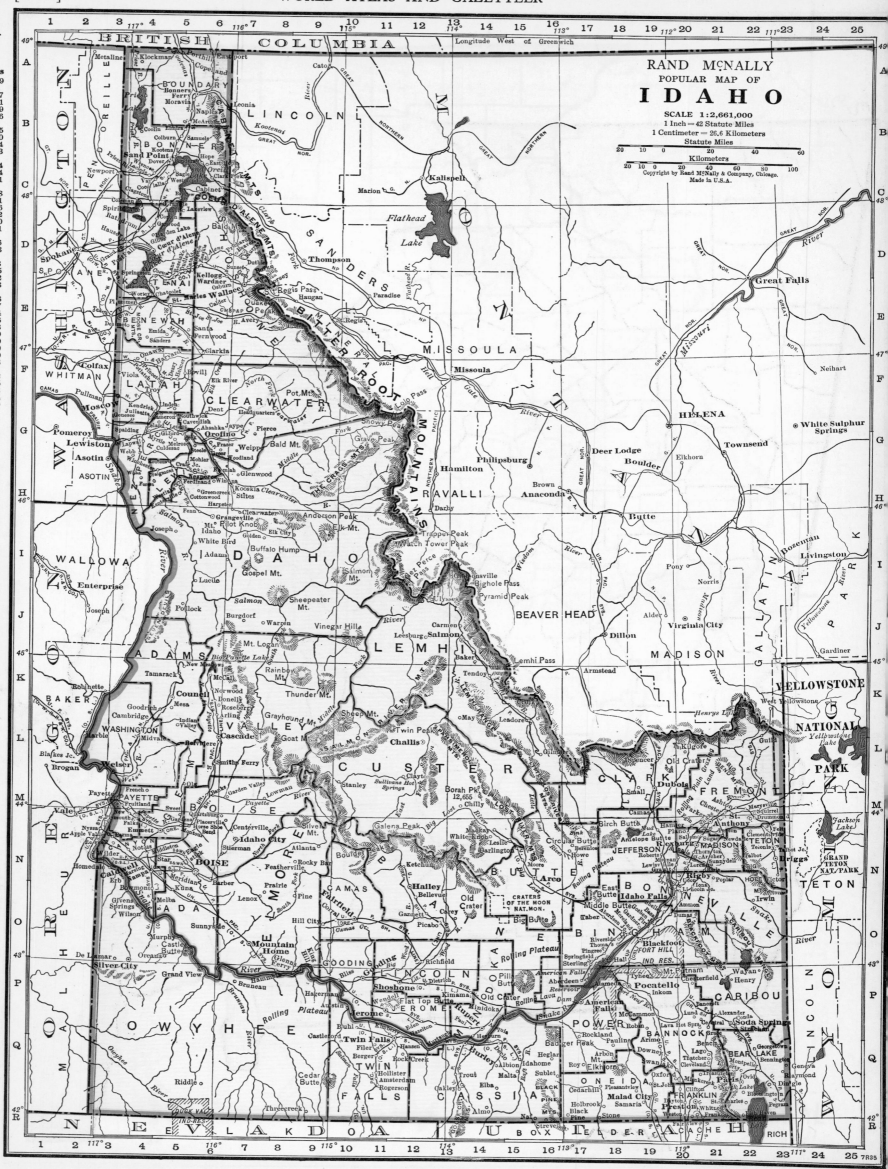

RAND McNALLY
POPULAR MAP OF
IDAHO
SCALE 1:2,661,000
1 Inch = 42 Statute Miles
1 Centimeter = 26.6 Kilometers
Statute Miles
Kilometers
Copyright by Rand McNally & Company, Chicago.
Made in U.S.A.

7R35

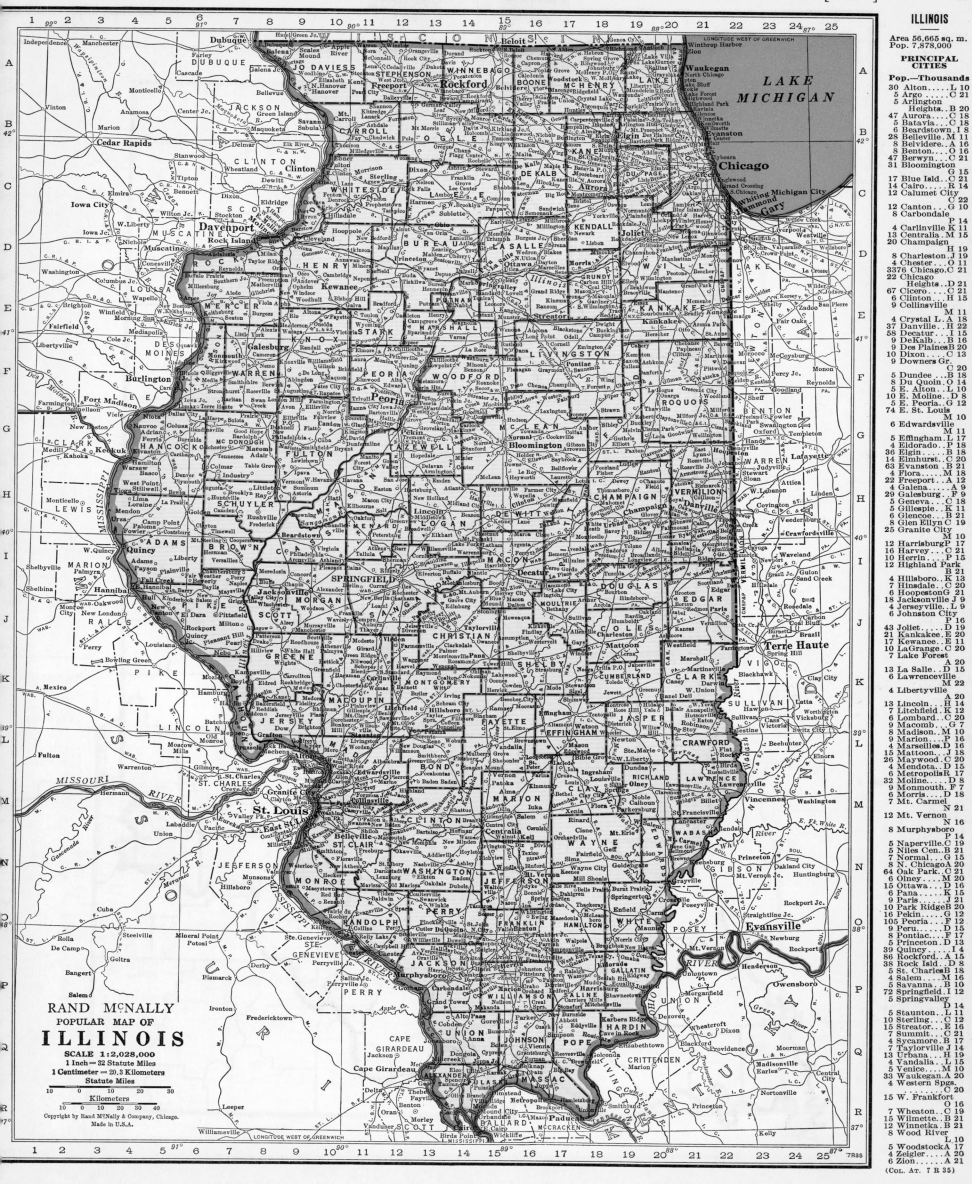

RAND McNALLY
POPULAR MAP OF
ILLINOIS

SCALE 1:2,028,000
1 Inch = 32 Statute Miles
1 Centimeter = 20.3 Kilometers
Statute Miles
Kilometers

Copyright by Rand McNally & Company, Chicago.
Made in U.S.A.

ILLINOIS

Area 56,665 sq. m.
Pop. 7,878,000

PRINCIPAL CITIES

Pop.—Thousands

30	Alton	L 10
5	Argo	C 21
5	Arlington Heights	B 20
47	Aurora	C 18
5	Batavia	C 18
6	Beardstown	I 8
28	Belleville	M 11
8	Belvidere	A 16
6	Benton	O 16
47	Berwyn	C 21
31	Bloomington	G 15
17	Blue Isld.	C 21
14	Cairo	R 14
12	Calumet City	C 22
12	Canton	G 10
8	Carbondale	P 14
4	Carlinville	K 11
13	Centralia	M 15
20	Champaign	H 19
8	Charleston	J 19
4	Chester	O 11
3376	Chicago	C 21
22	Chicago Heights	D 21
67	Cicero	C 21
6	Clinton	H 15
	Collinsville	M 11
4	Crystal L.	A 18
37	Danville	H 22
58	Decatur	I 15
9	De Kalb	B 16
9	Des Plaines	B 20
10	Dixon	C 13
9	Downers Gr.	C 20
3	Dundee	B 18
8	Du Quoin	O 14
5	E. Alton	L 10
10	E. Moline	D 8
5	E. Peoria	G 12
74	E. St. Louis	M 10
4	Edwardsville	M 11
12	Effingham	L 17
5	Eldorado	P 18
36	Elgin	B 18
14	Elmhurst	C 20
63	Evanston	B 21
4	Flora	M 18
14	Freeport	A 12
4	Galena	A 9
29	Galesburg	F 9
5	Geneva	C 18
6	Gillespie	K 11
6	Glencoe	B 21
6	Glen Ellyn	C 19
25	Granite City	M 10
12	Harrisburg	P 17
16	Harvey	C 21
7	Herrin	P 15
12	Highland Park	B 21
5	Hillsboro	K 13
7	Hinsdale	C 20
6	Hoopeston	G 21
18	Jacksonville	J 9
4	Jerseyville	L 9
6	Johnston City	P 16
43	Joliet	D 19
21	Kankakee	E 20
17	Kewanee	E 11
4	LaGrange	C 20
7	Lake Forest	B 21
3	La Salle	D 15
5	Lawrenceville	M 22
4	Libertyville	A 20
13	Lincoln	H 14
7	Litchfield	K 12
4	Lombard	C 20
9	Macomb	G 7
8	Madison	M 10
9	Marion	M 16
4	Marseilles	D 16
15	Mattoon	J 18
26	Maywood	C 21
32	Moline	D 8
5	Monmouth	F 7
9	Morris	D 18
7	Mt. Carmel	N 21
12	Mt. Vernon	N 16
8	Murphysboro	P 14
5	Naperville	C 19
5	Niles Cen.	B 21
3	Normal	G 15
8	N. Chicago	A 20
64	Oak Park	C 21
6	Olney	M 20
15	Ottawa	D 16
9	Pana	K 15
9	Paris	J 21
10	Park Ridge	B 20
16	Pekin	G 12
105	Peoria	F 12
9	Peru	D 15
6	Pontiac	F 17
5	Princeton	D 13
39	Quincy	I 4
86	Rockford	A 15
35	Rock Isl.	D 8
5	St. Charles	B 18
4	Salem	M 16
5	Savanna	B 10
72	Springfield	I 12
	Springvalley	
8	Staunton	L 11
5	Sterling	C 12
15	Streator	E 16
5	Summit	C 21
4	Sycamore	B 17
7	Taylorville	J 14
13	Urbana	H 19
4	Vandalia	L 15
5	Venice	M 10
33	Waukegan	A 20
	Western Spgs.	C 20
15	W. Frankfort	O 16
7	Wheaton	C 19
5	Wilmette	B 21
12	Winnetka	B 21
8	Wood River	L 10
5	Woodstock	A 18
4	Zeigler	A 20
6	Zion	A 21

(Col. At. 7 R 35)

INDIANA

Area 36,354 sq. m.
Pop. 3,474,000

PRINCIPAL CITIES

Pop.—Thousands

4 Alexandria . . H17
40 Anderson . . H 17
3 Angola . . . . B 21
4 Attica . . . . . H 7
4 Auburn . . . C 21
4 Aurora . . . M 22
3 Batesville . . L 20
13 Bedford . . . N 12
18 Bloomington . . M 11
5 Bluffton . . . F 20
4 Boonville . . . Q 7
9 Brazil . . . . K 8
3 Bremen . . . . C 14
5 Brookville . K 21
2 Brownstown . . N 14
2 Butler . . . . C 22
2 Cambridge
     City . . . . J 20
5 Cannelton . R 10
3 Chesterton . . B 8
3 Clarksville . P 17
8 Clinton . . . . J 6
3 Columbia City
     . . . . . . D 18
10 Columbus . . L 16
13 Connersville . . J 21
2 Corydon . . Q 14
2 Covington . . H 6
10 Crawfordsville
     . . . . I 9
4 Crown Pt. . . C 6
4 Danville . . . J 12
5 Decatur . . . E 22
4 Delphi . . . F 11
3 Dunkirk . . . G 20
55 E. Chicago . . B 6
2 E. Gary . . . B 7
33 Elkhart . . . B 15
11 Elwood . . . H 16
102 Evansville . R 5
2 Fairmount . G 17
115 Ft. Wayne D20
12 Frankfort . H 12
5 Franklin . . . K 15
2 French Lick
     . . . . O 11
4 Garrett . . . C 20
100 Gary . . . . B 7
3 Gas City . . G 17
10 Goshen . . . B 16
6 Greencastle J 10
6 Greenfield . J 17
6 Greensburg L 18
6 Greenwood K 14
65 Hammond . B 5
7 Hartford City
     . . . . G 19
6 Hobart . . . B 7
4 Huntingburg
     . . . . P 9
13 Huntington . F 19
364 Indianapolis
     . . . . J 14
4 Jasonville . . M 7
4 Jasper . . . . P 9
12 Jeffersonville
     . . . . P 17
5 Kendallville
     . . . . C 20
2 Knightstown
     . . . . J 18
2 Knox . . . . C 11
33 Kokomo . . G 14
26 LaFayette . G 9
4 La Porte . . B 10
4 Lawrenceburg
     . . . . M 22
6 Lebanon . . I 12
6 Ligonier . . C 18
5 Linton . . . . M 7
19 Logansport F 13
2 Loogootee . O 9
7 Madison . . N 19
25 Marion . . . F 17
5 Martinsville
     . . . . K 12
27 Michigan City
     . . . . B 9
29 Mishawaka B 14
3 Mitchell . . N 12
2 Monticello . F 10
2 Montpelier G 20
2 Mooresville
     . . . . K 12
5 Mt. Vernon. R 3
47 Muncie . . . H 19
26 New Albany P 16
14 Newcastle . I 19
2 New Haven
     . . . . E 16
5 Noblesville I 15
3 N. Manchester
     . . . . E 16
3 N. Vernon M 18
3 Oakland City P 6
2 Paoli . . . . O 12
13 Peru . . . . F 14
3 Petersburg . O 7
5 Plymouth . C 13
2 Portland . . G 22
5 Princeton . . P 5
2 Rensselaer . E 8
32 Richmond . . J 22
4 Rochester . D 14
4 Rockville . . K 7
6 Rushville . K 19
3 Salem . . . . O 14
3 Scottsburg O 16
5 Seymour . . M 16
11 ShelbyvilleK 17
2 Sheridan . . H 14
104 South Bend
     . . . . B 13
5 Sullivan . . M 6
5 Tell City . R 10
63 Terre Haute
     . . . . K 6
5 Tipton . . . H 15
3 Union City H 23
8 Valparaiso . C 8
5 Vincennes . O 5
9 Wabash . . F 16
6 Warsaw . . C 16
3 Washington
     . . . . O 7
5 West Lafay-
     ette . . . . G 9
4 West Terre
     Haute . . . K 6
11 Whiting . . B 6
4 Winchester H 21

(Col. At. 7 R 35)

RAND McNALLY
POPULAR MAP OF
INDIANA

SCALE 1:1,521,000
1 Inch = 24 Statute Miles
1 Centimeter = 15.2 Kilometers
Statute Miles

Kilometers

Copyright by Rand McNally & Company, Chicago.
Made in U.S.A.

7R35

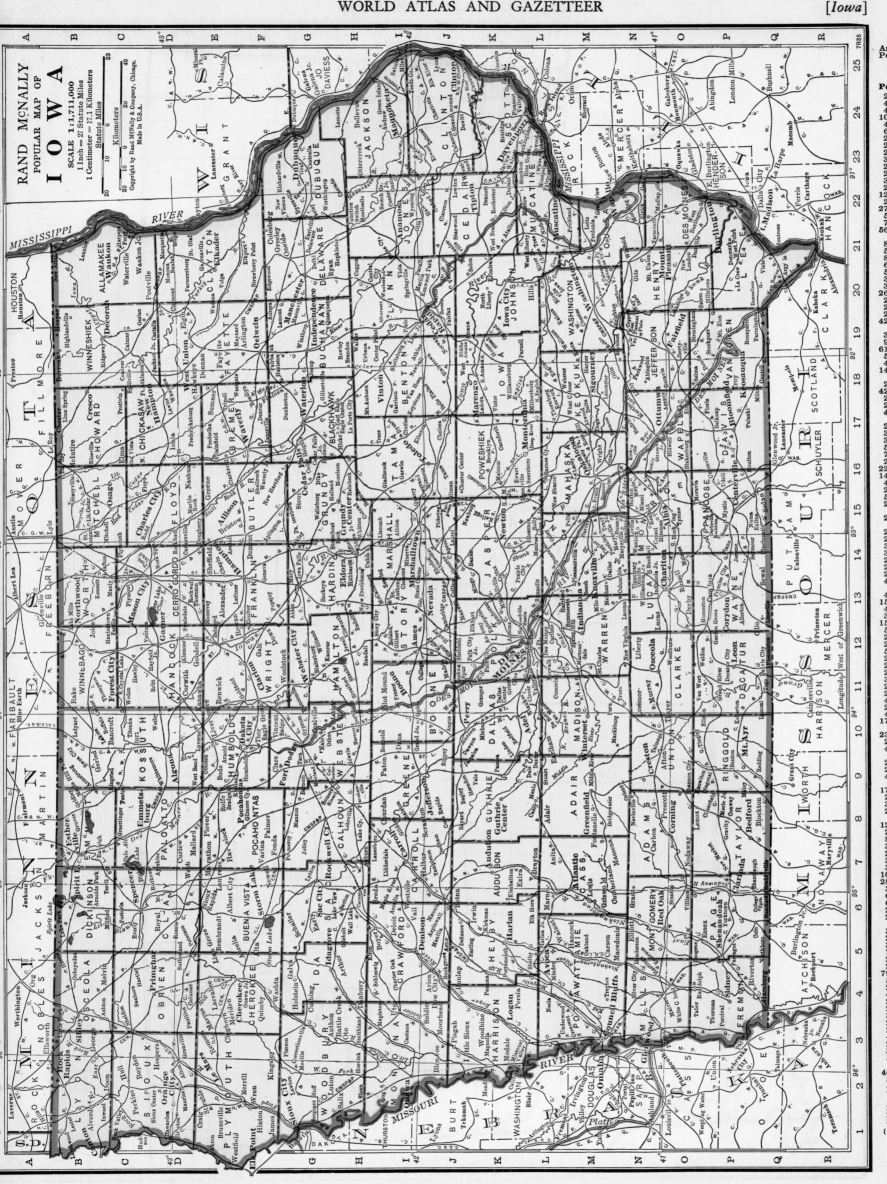

RAND McNALLY
POPULAR MAP OF
IOWA

SCALE 1:1,711,000
1 Inch = 27 Statute Miles
1 Centimeter = 17.1 Kilometers

Copyright by Rand McNally & Company, Chicago.
Made in U.S.A.

IOWA

Area 56,147 sq. m.
Pop. 2,552,000

PRINCIPAL CITIES

Pop.—Thousands

2 Adel	K 10
5 Albia	O 15
4 Algona	D 10
10 Ames	I 12
4 Anamosa	I 21
6 Atlantic	M 6
2 Audubon	K 7
2 Avoca	L 5
2 Bedford	P 8
3 Belle Plaine	J 17
2 Bellevue	H 24
2 Belmond	F 12
4 Bettendorf	I 24
2 Bloomfield	P 17
12 Boone	I 11
2 Britt	D 11
27 Burlington	P 22
7 Carroll	J 8
7 Cedar Falls	G 16
56 Cedar Rapids	J 20
8 Centerville	P 15
5 Chariton	O 13
3 Charles Cy.	D 16
6 Cherokee	E 4
4 Clarinda	P 6
3 Clarion	F 12
3 Clear Lake	D 13
26 Clinton	I 25
2 Colfax	N 11
2 Corning	O 8
2 Corydon	P 13
42 Council Bluffs	M 3
3 Cresco	B 18
5 Creston	N 9
61 Davenport	I 24
5 Decorah	C 19
4 Denison	I 5
143 Des Moines	L 12
2 Dewitt	J 24
42 Dubuque	G 23
4 Dunlap	J 4
2 Dyersville	G 22
4 Eagle Grove	F 11
2 Eldon	O 18
3 Eldora	H 14
2 Emmetsburg	C 8
5 Estherville	B 7
7 Fairfield	O 19
2 Forest City	C 12
22 Ft. Dodge	G 10
14 Ft. Madison	Q 21
3 Glenwood	N 3
2 Greenfield	M 9
3 Grinnell	K 16
2 Grundy Center	H 15
2 Guthrie Center	K 8
2 Guttenberg	E 22
2 Hamburg	Q 4
3 Hampton	F 13
3 Harlan	K 5
2 Hawarden	E 2
2 Humboldt	F 10
2 Ida Grove	G 5
4 Independence	G 19
4 Indianola	M 12
15 Iowa City	K 20
4 Iowa Falls	G 14
3 Jefferson	I 9
15 Keokuk	R 21
3 Knoxville	M 13
2 Lake City	H 8
2 Lamoni	Q 11
5 Le Mars	F 3
2 Leon	P 12
2 Logan	K 3
3 Madrid	J 11
3 Manchester	G 20
2 Manning	J 7
2 Mapleton	H 4
3 Maquoketa	I 23
2 Marengo	K 18
4 Marion	I 20
17 Marshalltown	J 15
23 Mason City	D 13
2 Melcher	M 13
4 Missouri Valley	L 4
2 Monticello	H 21
2 Mount Ayr	P 10
4 Mount Pleasant	O 20
17 Muscatine	L 22
2 Mystic	P 15
2 Nevada	I 13
2 New Hampton	D 17
12 Newton	J 14
2 Northwood	B 14
2 Oelwein	F 18
3 Onawa	I 2
2 Orange City	D 4
2 Osage	C 15
3 Osceola	N 11
10 Oskaloosa	M 16
28 Ottumwa	O 17
5 Pella	M 15
6 Perry	J 10
2 Red Oak	O 8
2 Rock Rapids	B 2
2 Rockwell City	G 8
3 Sac City	G 7
2 Seymour	P 14
3 Sheldon	D 4
7 Shenandoah	P 7
2 Sibley	B 4
3 Sigourney	M 18
79 Sioux City	G 1
5 Spencer	C 6
2 Spirit Lake	B 6
4 Storm Lake	F 6
2 Stuart	L 9
3 Sumner	E 18
3 Tama	J 16
2 Tipton	K 22
2 Toledo	J 16
2 Valley Junc.	L 11
2 Villisca	O 8
2 Vinton	I 18
5 Washington	M 20
46 Waterloo	G 17
3 Waukon	C 20
4 Waverly	E 16
7 Webster City	G 11
2 W. Liberty	L 21
2 W. Union	D 19
3 Winterset	M 10

(COL. AT. 7 R 35)

KANSAS

Area 82,158 sq. m.
Pop. 1,864,000

PRINCIPAL CITIES

Pop.—Thousands

6 Abilene...H 16
3 Anthony...O 14
13 Arkansas City...O 18
2 Arma....M 25
1 Ashland...O 8
13 Atchison...E 23
3 Augusta...M 18
4 Baldwin...H 23
4 Baxter Springs...O 24
3 Belleville...D 15
2 Beloit...F 13
1 Blue Rapids...E 18
2 Bonner Springs...G 24
1 Burlingame...H 21
3 Burlington...J 21
2 Caldwell...O 15
9 Caney...O 23
9 Chanute...N 24
1 Cherokee...N 24
1 Cherryvale...N 22
2 Chetopa...O 24
4 Clay Cen...F 16
1 Clyde...E 16
18 Coffeyville...O 22
1 Colby...E 4
1 Coldwater...O 10
1 Columbus...O 24
3 Concordia...E 15
1 Council Gr...I 18
9 Dodge City...L 8
1 Downs...E 12
9 Eldorado...L 18
1 Ellinwood...J 12
1 Ellis...H 9
1 Ellsworth...H 13
13 Emporia...J 20
1 Erie...M 22
1 Eureka...L 19
1 Florence...J 17
5 Fort Leaven-
worth...F 24
2 Ft. Riley...G 18
10 Fort Scott...K 25
4 Frankfort...D 19
4 Fredonia...M 21
4 Frontenac...M 25
6 Galena...O 25
6 Garden Cy...K 5
2 Garnett...J 24
3 Girard...M 24
1 Goodland...F 2
6 Great Bend...J 11
2 Greensburg...M 10
1 Halstead...K 16
1 Harper...N 14
5 Hays...H 10
2 Herington...I 17
3 Hiawatha...D 21
1 Hill City...F 9
2 Hillsboro...J 17
3 Hoisington...I 11
3 Holton...E 21
4 Horton...D 22
1 Hugoton...O 3
1 Humboldt...L 23
33 Hutchinson...K 14
11 Independence...L 21
7 Iola...L 23
8 Junction City...G 18
123 Kansas City...F 25
3 Kingman...M 14
2 Kinsley...L 9
3 La Crosse...I 9
3 Larned...J 10
4 Lawrence...H 23
19 Leavenworth...F 23
5 Liberal...O 4
2 Lincoln
Center...G 13
2 Lindsborg...I 16
2 Lyons...J 13
2 McPherson...J 15
11 Manhattan...G 18
2 Mankato...D 13
2 Marion...J 17
2 Marysville...D 18
2 Medicine
Lodge...N 12
2 Minneapolis...G 16
1 Mulberry...M 25
2 Neodesha...M 22
2 Ness City...I 8
10 Newton...K 16
3 Nickerson...K 13
3 Norton...D 8
1 Oakley...E 5
2 Oberlin...D 6
3 Olathe...G 24
2 Osage City...I 21
1 Osawatomie...I 24
2 Osborne...E 11
2 Oswego...O 23
10 Ottawa...H 23
14 Paola...I 25
14 Parsons...N 23
2 Peabody...K 17
2 Phillipsburg...D 9
19 Pittsburg...N 24
1 Plainville...F 10
1 Pleasanton...J 25
6 Pratt...M 11
2 Russell...M 12
2 Sabetha...C 21
2 St. John...K 11
1 St. Marys...F 20
20 Salina...H 15
2 Scott City...H 4
2 Sedan...O 20
2 Seneca...D 20
2 Smith Cen...D 11
2 Stafford...L 12
2 Sterling...J 14
2 Stockton...K 9
1 Syracuse...K 2
1 Tonganoxie...G 23
69 Topeka...G 21
1 Valley Falls...F 22
3 Veterans
Administration
Home...F 24
2 Wakeeney...G 8
2 Wamego...F 19
2 Washington
D 17
2 Weir City...N 25
2 Wellington...N 15
103 Wichita...M 16
9 Winfield...N 18
2 Yates Cen...L 21
(COL. AT. 7 R 35)

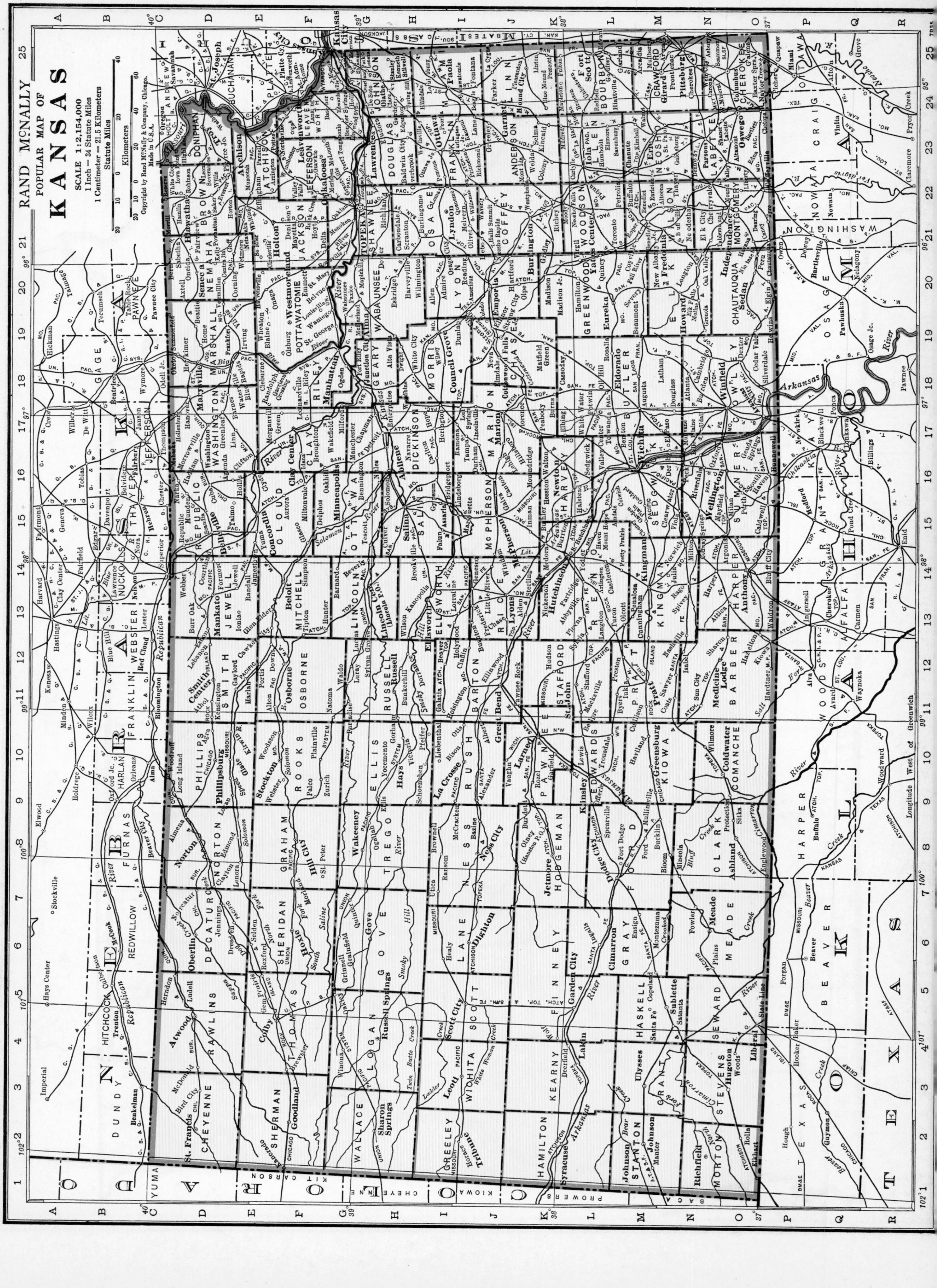

RAND McNALLY
POPULAR MAP OF
KANSAS

SCALE 1:2,154,000
1 Inch = 34 Statute Miles
1 Centimeter = 21.5 Statute Miles
Statute Miles

Copyright by Rand McNally & Company, Chicago

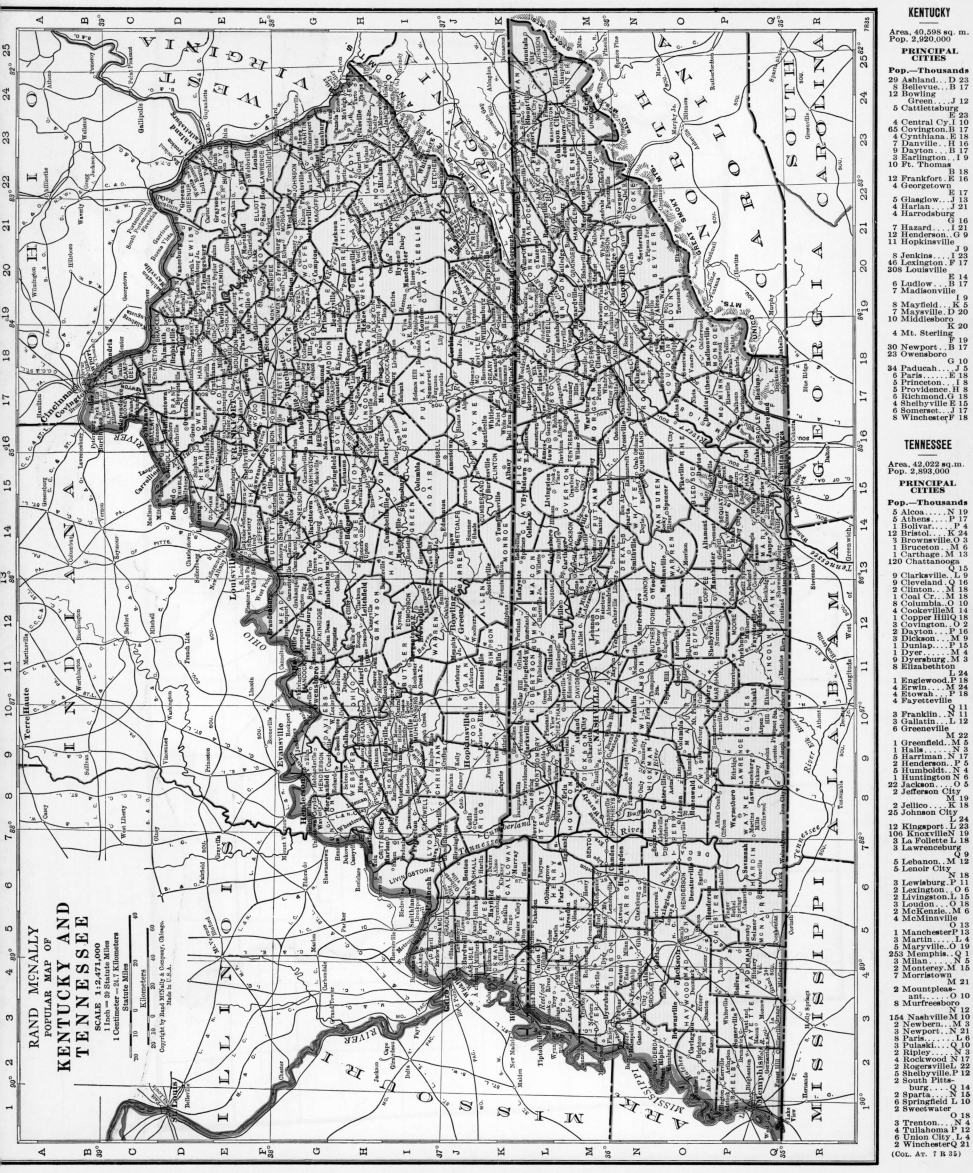

RAND McNALLY
POPULAR MAP OF
KENTUCKY AND
TENNESSEE

SCALE 1:2,471,000
1 Inch = 39 Statute Miles
1 Centimeter = 24.7 Kilometers

Statute Miles

Copyright by Rand McNally & Company, Chicago.
Made in U.S.A.

KENTUCKY

Area, 40,598 sq. m.
Pop. 2,920,000

PRINCIPAL
CITIES

Pop.—Thousands

29	Ashland...	D 23
8	Bellevue..	B 17
12	Bowling	
	Green..	J 12
5	Cattlettsburg	
		E 23
4	Central Cy.	I 10
65	Covington.	B 17
7	Cynthiana.	E 18
7	Danville..	H 16
9	Dayton...	B 17
3	Earlington.	I 9
10	Ft. Thomas	
		B 18
12	Frankfort.	E 16
4	Georgetown	
		E 17
5	Glasgow..	J 13
4	Harlan...	J 21
4	Harrodsburg	
		G 16
7	Hazard...	I 21
12	Henderson.	G 9
11	Hopkinsville	
		J 9
8	Jenkins...	I 23
46	Lexington.	F 17
308	Louisville	
		E 13
6	Ludlow...	B 17
7	Madisonville	
8	Mayfield...	K 5
7	Maysville.	D 20
10	Middlesboro	
		K 20
4	Mt. Sterling	
		F 19
30	Newport..	B 17
23	Owensboro	
		G 10
34	Paducah...	J 5
6	Paris....	E 18
5	Princeton..	I 8
5	Providence.	H 8
6	Richmond.	G 18
4	Shelbyville	E 15
8	Somerset..	I 17
8	Winchester	F 18

TENNESSEE

Area, 42,022 sq.m.
Pop. 2,893,000

PRINCIPAL
CITIES

Pop.—Thousands

5	Alcoa.....	N 19
8	Athens...	P 17
1	Bolivar....	P 4
12	Bristol...	K 24
3	Brownsville	O 3
1	Bruceton..	M 6
1	Carthage..	M 13
120	Chattanooga	
		Q 15
9	Clarksville.	L 9
9	Cleveland..	Q 16
2	Clinton...	M 18
1	Coal Cr..	M 18
8	Columbia..	O 10
1	CookevilleM 14	
1	Copper HillQ 18	
3	Covington..	O 2
2	Dayton...	P 16
3	Dickson..	M 9
1	Dunlap....	P 15
1	Dyer.....	M 4
9	Dyersburg.	M 3
8	Elizabethton	
		L 24
1	EnglewoodP 18	
4	Erwin....	M 24
4	Etowah...	P 18
4	Fayetteville	
		M 12
3	Franklin..	Q 11
3	Gallatin..	L 12
6	Greeneville	
		M 22
1	Greenfield.	M 5
1	Halls.....	N 3
5	Harriman..	N 17
5	Henderson.	P 5
5	Humboldt..	N 4
1	Huntington	N 6
22	Jackson...	O 5
3	Jefferson City	
		M 19
2	Jellico...	K 18
25	Johnson City	
		L 24
12	Kingsport.	L 23
106	KnoxvilleN 19	
3	La Follette	L 18
1	Lawrenceburg	
		O 9
5	Lebanon..	M 12
1	Lenoir City	
		N 18
3	Lewisburg.	P 11
2	Lexington.	O 6
2	Livingston.	L 15
2	Loudon...	O 18
2	McKenzie..	M 6
4	McMinnville	
		O 13
1	ManchesterP 13	
3	Martin....	N 5
5	Maryville.	O 19
253	Memphis..	Q 1
3	Milan....	N 5
2	Monterey.	M 15
7	Morristown	
		M 21
2	Mountpleas-	
	ant......	O 10
8	Murfreesboro	
		N 12
154	Nashville	M 10
2	Newbern..	N 3
2	Newport..	N 21
8	Paris....	L 6
3	Pulaski...	Q 10
3	Ripley....	N 3
4	Rockwood.	N 17
2	RogersvilleL 22	
5	Shelbyville.P 12	
2	South Pitts-	
	burg....	Q 14
2	Sparta...	N 15
9	Springfield L 10	
2	Sweetwater	
		O 18
3	Trenton...	N 4
4	Tullahoma.	P 12
6	Union City,	L 4
2	WinchesterQ 21	

(Col. At 7 B 35)

LOUISIANA

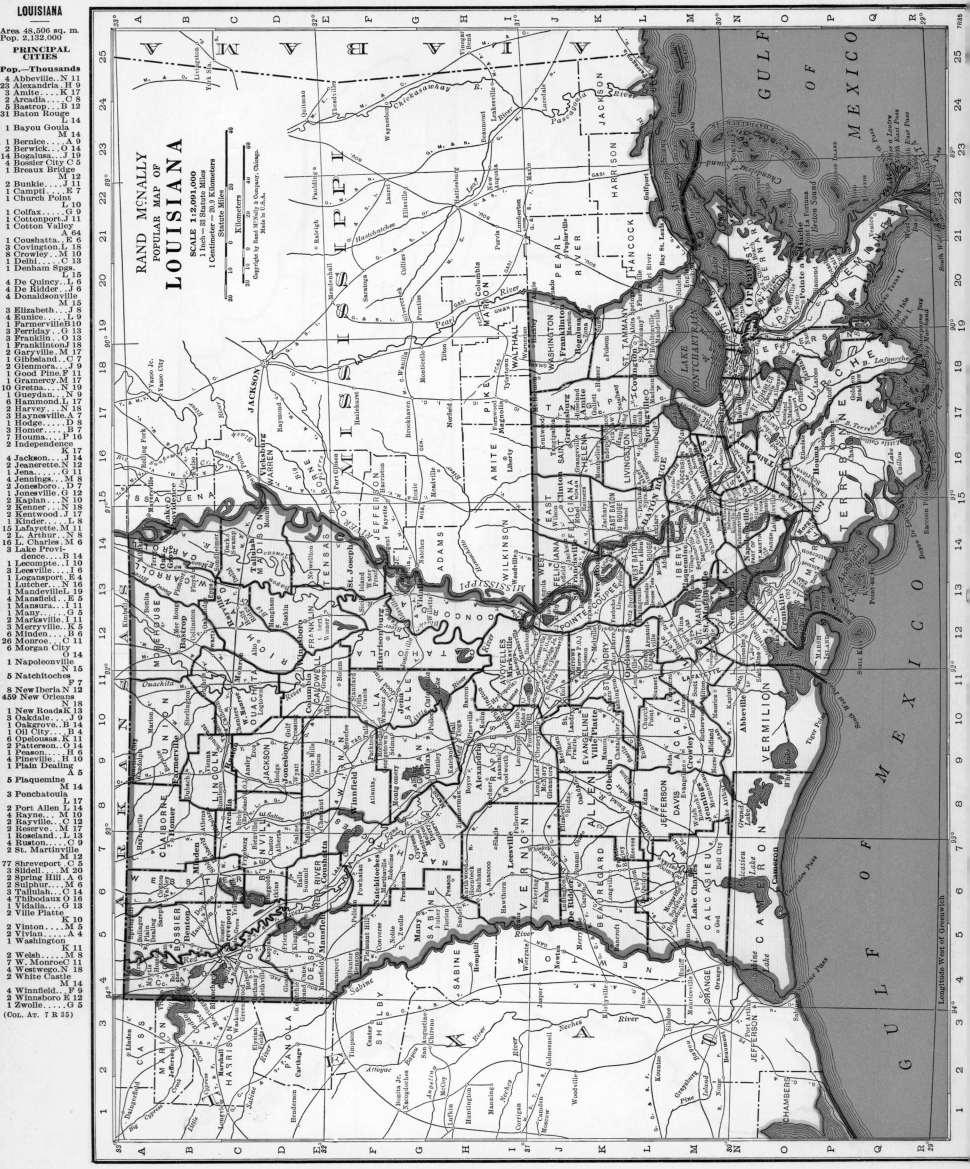

RAND McNALLY
POPULAR MAP OF
LOUISIANA
SCALE 1:2,091,000
1 Inch = 33 Statute Miles
1 Centimeter = 20.9 Kilometers

Copyright by Rand McNally & Company, Chicago.
Made in U.S.A.

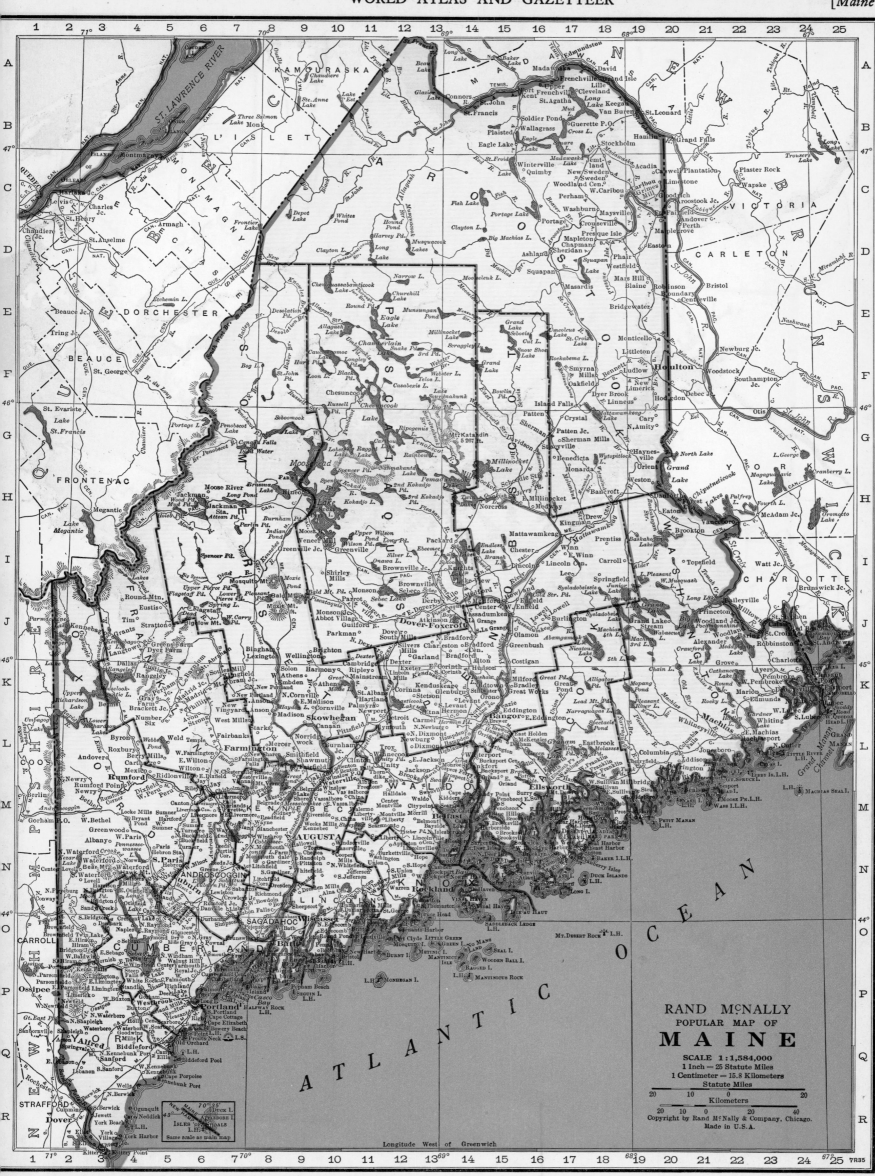

RAND McNALLY
POPULAR MAP OF
MAINE

SCALE 1:1,584,000
1 Inch = 25 Statute Miles
1 Centimeter = 15.8 Kilometers
Statute Miles

Copyright by Rand McNally & Company, Chicago.
Made in U.S.A.

ATLANTIC OCEAN

MAINE

Area 33,040 sq. m.
Pop. 856,000

PRINCIPAL CITIES

(▲ Township Pop.)
Pop.—Thousands

2 Ashland	D 16
19 Auburn	N 6
17 Augusta	N 9
29 Bangor	L 14
4 Bar Harbor	M 18
9 Bath	O 8
5 Belfast	M 13
1 Berwick	R 2
1 Bethel	M 3
18 Biddeford	Q 5
2 Boothbay Harbor	O 10
6 Brewer	L 14
2 Bridgton	O 3
1 Brownville	I 13
6 Brunswick	O 8
1 Bucksport	L 14
2 Buxton	P 4
5 Calais	J 23
2 Camden	N 13
8 Caribou	C 20
1 Cherryfield	L 19
1 Chisholm	M 6
1 Corinna	K 12
1 Danforth	H 19
3 Dexter	K 12
4 Dover-Foxcroft	J 12
1 Eagle Lake	B 15
4 E. Machias	L 22
1 E. Millinocket	H 16
3 Eastport	K 24
1 Eliot	R 3
4 Ellsworth	M 16
1 Ellsworth Falls	M 16
1 Enfield	J 15
4 Fairfield	L 10
2 Farmington	L 7
1 Ft. Fairfield	C 20
2 Fort Kent	A 15
1 Frenchville	A 17
6 Gardiner	N 9
1 Gorham	P 5
1 Greenville	I 10
1 Guilford	I 11
3 Hallowell	N 9
6 Houlton	F 19
1 Jonesport	M 21
2 Kennebunk	Q 4
1 Kingfield	K 6
3 Kittery	R 3
1 Kittery Point	R 3
35 Lewiston	N 6
2 Lincoln	I 16
3 Lisbon Falls	O 7
2 Livermore Falls	M 7
1 Lubec	K 24
2 Machias	L 22
3 Madawaska	A 17
3 Madison	K 8
1 Mars Hill	D 19
2 Mechanic Falls	N 5
2 Mexico	L 4
1 Millbridge	M 19
3 Millinocket	H 15
2 Milo	J 13
1 Monson	J 10
1 Monticello	E 19
1 N. Anson	K 8
1 N. Berwick	R 3
1 Norway	M 4
2 Oakland	M 9
1 Old Orchard Beach	Q 5
5 Old Town	K 15
2 Orono	K 15
2 Pittsfield	L 11
71 Portland	P 6
5 Presque Isle	D 19
2 Ridlonville	M 4
9 Rockland	N 13
1 Rockport	N 13
4 Rumford	M 4
7 Saco	Q 5
1 St. Agatha	A 17
1 St. David	A 17
1 St. Francis	A 14
2 St. George	O 12
3 Sanford	Q 3
2 Scarboro	Q 5
1 Searsport	M 13
1 Sherman Mills	G 16
6 Skowhegan	L 9
2 S. Berwick	R 3
1 S. Eliot	R 3
2 S. Paris	N 5
14 S. Portland	P 6
2 Springvale	Q 3
2 Thomaston	O 12
2 Togus	N 9
1 Topsham	O 8
1 Upper Frenchville	A 16
3 Van Buren	B 19
2 Vinalhaven	O 15
2 Waldoboro	N 11
15 Waterville	M 10
11 Westbrook	P 5
1 W. Jonesport	M 21
1 Wilton	L 6
3 Winslow	L 10
2 Winthrop	N 8
1 Woodland	P 6
2 Yarmouth	P 6
1 Yarmouth Junction	P 6

(COL. AT. 7 R 35)

MARYLAND

Area, 12,327 sq. m.
Pop. 1,679,000

PRINCIPAL CITIES

Pop.—Thousands

1	Aberdeen	D 17
1	Abingdon	D 16
13	Annapolis	J 15
805	Baltimore	F 14
2	Bel Air	F 16
2	Berlin	O 24
1	Berwyn	H 12
2	Brentwood	I 11
4	Brunswick	F 7
9	Cambridge	L 18
2	Capitol Heights	I 12
1	Centerville	H 18
1	Chesapeake City	C 20
3	Chestertown	G 18
8	Chevy Chase	H 11
1	Churchton	J 15
2	Cockeysville	D 13
4	Crisfield	R 20
38	Cumberland	L 6
2	Denton	I 20
1	Dundalk	F 15
4	Easton	J 18
3	Elkton	C 19
1	Ellicott City	F 13
1	Emmittsburg	B 9
2	Essex	E 15
1	Federalsburg	
1	Ferndale	G 14
2	Forest Hill	C 16
14	Frederick	E 8
1	Frostburg	M 5
2	Fullerton	E 15
1	Gaithersburg	G 10
1	Glen Burnie	G 14
2	Grasonville	I 17
31	Hagerstown	B 6
2	Halethorpe	F 14
3	Havre de Grace	C 18
4	Hyattsville	I 12
1	Indianhead	M 10
2	Lansdowne	F14
3	Laurel	H 12
1	Linthicum	G 14
2	Lonaconing	M 5
1	Luke	N 4
4	Mt. Ranier	I 11
2	Mt. Savage	L 5
1	North East	C 19
1	Oakland	O 1
2	Orangeville	F 14
3	Pocomoke	Q 22
1	Port Deposit	C 18
1	Princess Anne	P 21
2	Reisterstown	D 12
1	Riverdale	I 12
1	Rockville	H 10
1	St. Michaels	K 17
11	Salisbury	N 22
1	Savage	G 12
2	Seat Pleasant	I 12
5	Silver Springs	H 11
2	Snow Hill	P 23
6	Takoma Park	I 11
1	Texas	D 14
1	Thurmont	C 7
2	Towson	E 14
3	Westernport	N 5
4	Westminister	C 12
2	Williamsport	C 5

DELAWARE

Area, 2,370 sq. m.
Pop. 261,000.

PRINCIPAL CITIES

Pop.—Thousands

1	Bridgeville	K 21
6	Claymont	A 22
1	Delaware City	C 21
2	Delmar, Md. and Del.	M 22
5	Dover	G 22
1	Elsmere	B 21
2	Georgetown	K 23
2	Harrington	I 22
1	Laurel	L 22
2	Lewes	J 25
2	Marshallton	B 21
1	Middletown	D 20
4	Milford	I 23
1	Milton	J 24
4	Newark	B 20
4	New Castle	B 21
1	Newport	B 21
4	Richardson Park	B 22
2	Seaford	L 22
2	Smyrna	F 21
107	Wilmington	B 22

DIST. OF COLUMBIA

Area....70 sq. m.
Pop. 627,000.

CITY

Pop.—Thousands

497 Washington
           J 11
(COL. AT. 7 R 35)

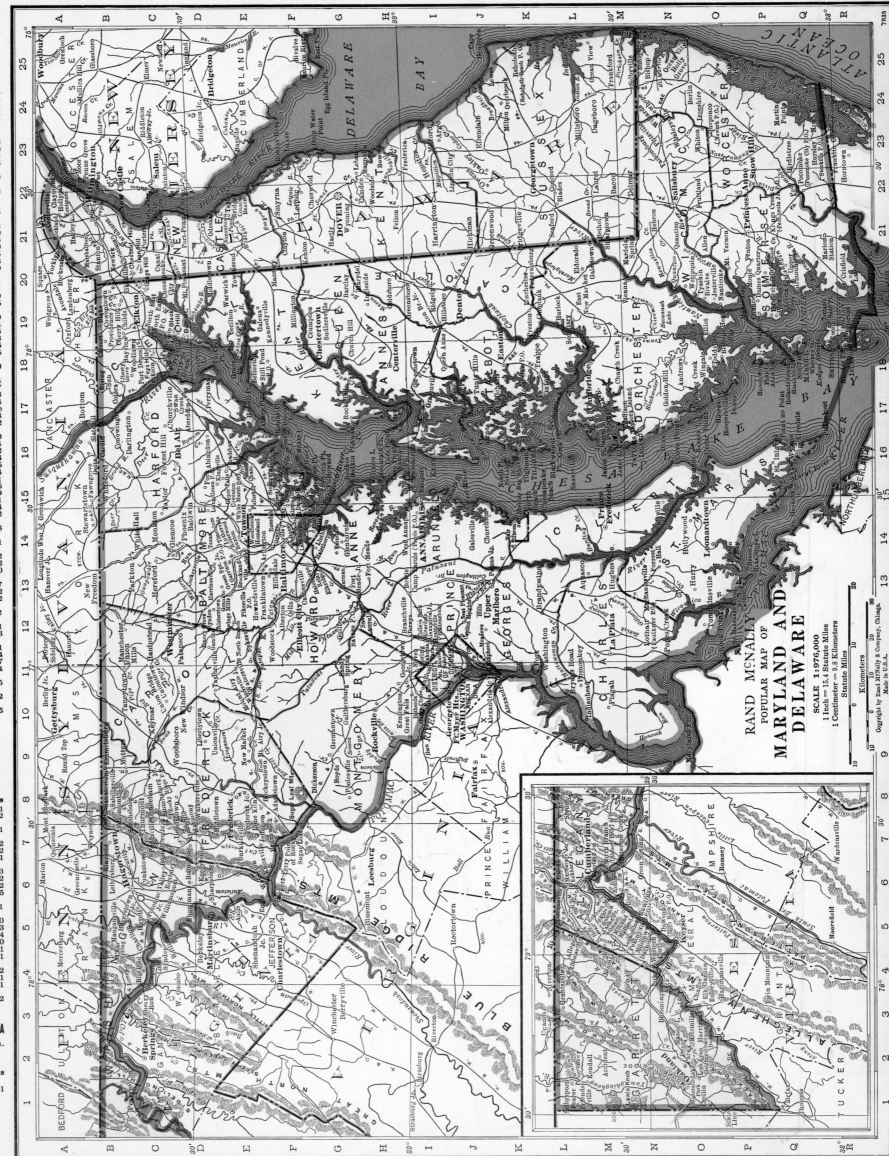

RAND McNALLY
POPULAR MAP OF
MARYLAND AND DELAWARE

SCALE 1:1,976,000
1 inch = 15.4 Statute Miles
1 Centimeter = 9.8 Kilometers

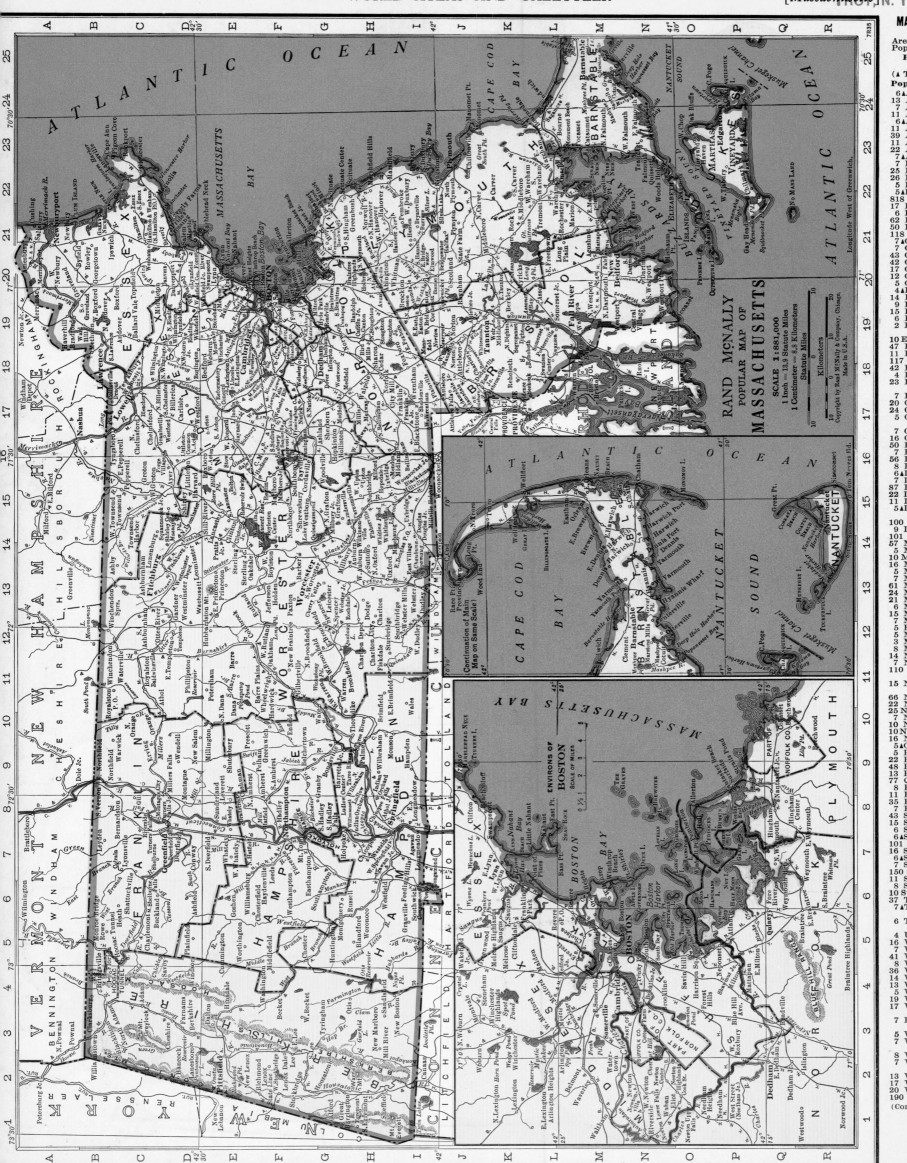

RAND McNALLY
POPULAR MAP OF
MASSACHUSETTS

SCALE 1:881,000
1 Inch = 13.9 Statute Miles
1 Centimeter = 8.8 Kilometers
Copyright by Rand McNally & Company, Chicago.
Made in U.S.A.

MASSACHUSETTS

Area 8,266 sq. m.
Pop. 4,426,000

PRINCIPAL CITIES

(▲ Township Pop.)
Pop.—Thousands

Pop.	City	Ref.
6	▲Abington	H 20
13	Adams	C 4
7	Agawam	I 7
11	Amesbury	A 20
6	▲Amherst	F 8
11	Andover	C 19
39	Arlington	E 18
11	Athol	C 10
22	Attleboro	J 17
7	▲Auburn	H 14
7	Barnstable	M 25
25	Belmont	E 18
26	Beverly	C 21
5	Billerica	D 17
5	Blackstone	I 15
818	Boston	F 20
17	Braintree	G 20
6	Bridgewater	J 20
62	Brockton	H 20
50	Brookline	F 19
118	Cambridge	E 18
7	▲Canton	H 19
7	Chelmsford	C 17
43	Chelsea	E 19
42	Chicopee	H 7
17	Chicopee Fs.	H 8
12	Clinton	E 14
5	Concord	E 17
4	Dalton	D 3
14	Danvers	C 20
9	Dartmouth	N 20
15	Dedham	G 18
3	Dracut	C 17
2	E. Bridgewater	I 20
10	Easthampton	G 6
47	Everett	E 19
11	Fairhaven	M 20
117	Fall River	M 19
42	Fitchburg	C 13
4	Foxboro	I 18
23	Framingham	G 16
7	Franklin	I 17
20	Gardner	D 13
22	Gloucester	C 23
5	Gt. Barrington	G 1
7	Grafton	G 15
16	Greenfield	C 7
50	Haverhill	A 19
8	Hingham	G 21
56	Holyoke	G 7
8	Hudson	F 16
6	Ipswich	B 21
11	IndianOrch.	H 8
87	Lawrence	B 18
22	Leominster	D 14
11	Lexington	E 18
5	Longmeadow	I 7
100	Lowell	C 17
9	Ludlow	H 8
101	Lynn	E 20
57	Malden	E 19
5	Mansfield	I 18
10	Marblehead	D 21
16	Marlboro	F 15
5	Mattapan	G 20
7	Maynard	E 17
61	Medford	E 19
24	Melrose	E 20
21	Methuen	B 19
6	Middleboro	J 21
15	Milford	G 16
9	Millbury	H 14
5	E. Milton	P 5
8	Milton	G 19
5	Monson	H 9
8	Montague	D 8
14	Natick	F 17
7	Needham	G 18
110	New Bedford	M 20
15	Newburyport	A 21
66	Newton	E 18
22	N. Adams	B 3
25	Northampton	F 8
7	N. Andover	B 19
10	N. Attleboro	J 18
10	Northbridge	H 15
16	Norwood	G 19
5	Orange	C 10
7	Palmer	H 9
22	Peabody	D 20
48	Pittsfield	E 2
13	Plymouth	J 23
77	Quincy	G 20
7	Randolph	H 19
11	Reading	D 19
35	Revere	E 20
21	Rockland	H 21
43	Salem	D 21
15	Saugus	K 5
8	Shrewsbury	F 15
5	Somerset	L 19
101	Somerville	F 19
16	Southbridge	I 12
6	Spencer	G 12
7	S. Hadley	G 8
150	Springfield	H 8
11	Stoneham	D 19
6	Stoughton	H 19
10	Swampscott	D 20
37	Taunton	K 19
7	▲Tewksbury	C 18
6	Turners Falls	C 8
4	Uxbridge	I 15
16	Wakefield	D 19
7	Walpole	H 18
41	Waltham	E 18
8	Ware	G 10
36	Watertown	M 2
14	Webster	I 13
13	Wellesley	F 17
5	Westboro	G 15
19	Westfield	H 6
17	West Springfield	I 7
7	E. Weymouth	G 21
5	Weymouth	G 20
7	Whitinsville	H 14
8	Whitman	H 20
7	Winchendon	B 11
8	Winchester	E 18
17	Winthrop	M 6
20	Woburn	D 18
190	Worcester	G 13

(COL. AT 7 R 35)

MICHIGAN

Area, 57,980 sq. m.
Pop. 4,830,000

PRINCIPAL CITIES
Pop.—Thousands

13 Adrian....R 19
8 Albion....Q 16
4 Allegan....P 12
7 Alma....N 17
7 Alpena....J 21
27 Ann Arbor Q 20
2 Bad Axe...L 23
44 Battle Creek
....Q 15
47 Bay City. M 20
15 Belding...N 15
15 Benton Harbor
....Q 10
2 Berkley..P 23
4 Bessemer..B 21
5 Big RapidsM14
10 Birmingham
....P 23
2 Blissfield..R 20
5 Boyne City..I 16
2 Buchanan..R 10
10 Cadillac...K 14
2 Calumet...C 3
3 Caro....M 22
5 CharlevoixH 15
5 Charlotte..P 16
5 Cheboygan H 18
2 Chelsea...Q 19
3 Clawson..P 22
7 Coldwater..R 16
2 Corunna..N 18
1 Crystal Fs..F 3
50 Dearborn..Q 22
1569 Detroit..Q 23
2 Dowagiac..R 11
3 Durand....O 20
6 E. Detroit P 24
4 E. Gd. Rapids
....N 11
3 E. LansingO 20
3 Eaton Rapids
....P 17
13 Ecorse....Q 23
15 Escanaba..G 8
21 Fenton....O 21
156 Flint....O 21
5 Fremont..M 12
4 Garden CyG 10
3 Gladstone..G 8
6 Grand Haven
....O 11
4 Grand Ledge..O 17
169 Grand Rapids
....O 13
2 Grayling...J 17
5 Greenville..N 15
11 Grosse Pointe
Park....P 24
....P 23
6 Hancock...C 3
5 Hastings..P 15
53 Highland Park
....P 23
14 Hillsdale..R 17
10 Holland..O 11
2 Holly....O 21
6 Houghton..C 3
4 Howell....P 20
2 Hudson...R 18
1 Inkster..Q 22
7 Ionia....O 15
12 Iron Moun-
tain....G 4
5 Iron River..F 2
14 Ironwood..B 21
6 Ishpeming..E 6
5 Jackson..Q 18
55 Kalamazoo Q 13
4 Kingsford..G 4
78 Lansing..O 17
5 Lapeer....O 22
2 Laurium...C 3
12 Lincoln PkQ 23
5 Ludington L 10
2 Manistee..K 11
3 ManistiqueG 11
2 Marine City
....O 25
15 Marquette..E 7
4 Marshall..Q 16
3 Mason....P 18
10 Menominee I 6
12 Midland..M 18
3 Milan....Q 20
3 Monroe...R 22
13 Mt. Clemens
....P 24
2 Mt. Morris N 21
5 Mount
Pleasant.M 16
4 Munising..E 10
47 Muskegon N 11
16. Muskegon
Heights..N 11
7 Negaunee..E 6
2 Newberry F 14
11 Niles....R 11
5 Northville P 22
4 Norway...G 5
3 Ontonagon B 4
2 Otsego...O 13
14 Owosso..O 19
2 Oxford...Q 21
5 Petoskey..H 16
2 Plainwell..P 13
7 Plymouth..P 22
65 Pontiac..P 22
31 Port HuronO 25
17 River Rouge
....P 23
4 Rochester..P 23
4 Rogers City
....H 20
2 Romeo...O 23
3 Roseville..P 23
11 Royal Oak P 23
81 Saginaw..N 20
3 St. Clair..O 25
2 St. Clair
Shores..P 24
2 St. Ignace..G 17
3 St. Johns..O 17
8 St. Joseph Q 10
3 St. Louis..N 17
14 Sault Sainte
Marie..E 18
5 S. Haven..P 11
3 Sparta...N 13
1 Stambaugh..F 2
7 Sturgis..R 14
2 Tecumseh..Q 20
3 Three Rivers
....R 13
13 Traverse City
....J 13
4 Trenton...Q 22
4 Wakefield..B 21
3 Wayne...P 21
28 Wyandotte Q 23
10 Ypsilanti Q 21
3 Zeeland....Q 12
(Col. at 7 R 35)

RAND McNALLY
POPULAR MAP OF
MICHIGAN
SCALE 1:2,408,000
1 Inch = 38 Statute Miles
1 Centimeter = 24 Kilometers
Statute Miles
Copyright by Rand McNally & Company, Chicago.
Made in U.S.A.

RAND McNALLY
POPULAR MAP OF
MINNESOTA
SCALE 1:2,154,000
1 Inch = 34 Statute Miles
1 Centimeter = 21.5 Kilometers
Statute Miles

Copyright by Rand McNally & Company, Chicago.
Made in U.S.A.

ST. PAUL—MINNEAPOLIS AND VICINITY
SCALE 1 Inch = 19.5 Statute Miles

MINNESOTA
Area 84,682 sq. m.
Pop. 2,652,000
PRINCIPAL
CITIES
Pop.—Thousands

1 Ada..... G 3
2 Aitkin..... I 14
10 Albert Lea R 15
4 Alexandria. K 7
5 Anoka.... M 15
1 Appleton.. M 5
1 Aurora... P 20
12 Austin... R 17
1 Barnesville. I 3
3 Bayport.. N 18
7 Bemidji.. F 9
2 Benson... M 6
1 Biwabik.. F 19
3 Blue Earth R 13
1 Bovey... G 15
10 Brainerd.. J 12
2 Breckenridge
J 3
1 Buffalo.. M 13
1 Buhl.... F 18
2 Caledonia. R 23
1 Canby.... O 4
1 Cannon FsO 17
1 Cass Lake F 11
2 Chaska... N 15
1 Chatfield.. Q 20
1 Chisholm.. F 17
7 Cloquet.. I 19
1 Coleraine. G 15
6 Columbia
Heights.. M 23
1 Crookston.. E 3
4 Crosby.. I 13
2 Crystal... M 22
1 Dawson... N 5
1 Detroit Lakes
H 6
101 Duluth .. H 21
3 East Grand
Forks.... E 1
3 Edina.... N 22
6 Ely.... E 21
8 Eveleth.. F 19
1 Fairmont.. R 11
13 Faribault.. P 16
9 Fergus Fs.. J 5
1 Frazee... H 6
3 Gilbert.. F 19
2 Glencoe.. N 12
2 Glenwood.. L 7
3 Grand Rapids
G 15
1 Granite Fs.. N 7
5 Hastings.. O 18
16 Hibbing.. F 17
4 Hopkins.. N 15
1 HutchinsonN11
5 International
Falls.... C 15
1 Ironton.. I 13
1 Jackson.. R 9
1 Janesville. P 14
1 Kasson... Q 18
1 Keewatin.. G 17
1 Kenyon... P 17
3 Lake City.. O 20
2 Le Sueur.. O 15
3 Litchfield. M 11
1 Little FallsK 12
2 Long Prairie
K 10
5 Luverne... R 4
1 Madelia.. Q 11
2 Madison... N 4
14 Mankato.. P 13
1 Marshall.. O 6
2 Melrose.. L 10
N 16
464 Minneapolis
4 MontevideoN 6
2 Montgomery
O 15
8 Moorhead.. H 2
3 Morris... L 5
1 Mountain
Iron.... F 18
3 Nashwauk G 16
1 New Prague
O 15
7 New Ulm.. P 11
6 Northfield.O 16
3 N. Mankato
P 13
3 North St. Paul
M 25
1 Olivia... N 9
1 Ortonville.. M 3
8 Owatonna.. P 16
2 Park RapidsH 9
1 Perham... I 7
1 Pine City.. K 17
1 Pipestone.. Q 3
1 Plainview.. P 20
1 Preston... R 21
1 Princeton.. L 15
1 Proctor (Proc-
torknott) H 20
1 Red Lake Fs.
E 4
10 Red Wing. O 19
3 Redwood
Falls.... O 8
1 Richfield.. N 23
4 Robbinsdale
N 22
21 Rochester.. Q 19
21 St. Cloud.. L 12
3 St. James.. Q 10
5 St. Louis Pk.
N 22
272 St. Paul.. N 24
5 St. Peter.. P 13
1 Sandstone.. I 17
9 Sauk CenterL 9
1 Sauk RapidsL12
2 Shakopee.. N 15
1 Sleepy EyeP 10
5 South St. Paul
N 17
3 Springfield. P 9
2 Spring Valley
R 20
3 Staples.. J 10
7 Stillwater.. N 18
4 Thief River
Falls.... D 4
1 Tracy.... Q 6
2 Two Harbors
H 22
12 Virginia.. F 19
2 Wabasha.. P 21
3 Wadena.. I 8
1 Warren... D 2
4 Waseca.. Q 14
2 Wells.... Q 13
5 W. St.PaulN 24
3 White Bear
Lake.... M 25
6 Willmar.. M 9
2 Windom.. Q 8
21 WinnebagoQ 12
21 Winona.. Q 23
4 WorthingtonR 6
1 Zumbrota.. P 18
(COL. AT. 7 R 35)

MISSISSIPPI

Area..46,865 sq.m.
Pop. 2,023,000

PRINCIPAL CITIES
Pop.—Thousands

4 Aberdeen..E 21
1 Ackerman..G 17
1 Amory....D 21
1 Baldwyn..B 20
1 Batesville..C 12
4 Bay St. Louis
        R 17
3 Belzoni...G 9
15 Biloxi....R 19
2 Booneville.R 21
2 Brookhaven
        N 9
1 Bude.....E 16
1 Calhoun City
        E 16
5 Canton....J 12
1 Carthage..J 15
1 Centreville..P 5
2 Charleston D 12
10 Clarksdale..C 9
3 Cleveland..E 8
1 Cohay....L 14
5 Columbia..O 13
11 Columbus.F 22
6 Corinth..A 21
2 Crystal Springs
        L 10
1 Drew.....E 9
1 Durant...H 13
1 Electric Mills
        I 22
2 Ellisville..N 17
1 Eupora...F 17
1 Finkbine..K 13
2 Forest...K 15
1 Friar Point.C 8
1 Gloster...O 6
15 Greenville..F 6
11 Greenwood F 11
4 Grenada..E 13
13 Gulfport..R 18
1 Handsboro R 19
19 Hattiesburg
        O 17
2 Hazlehurst
        M 10
1 Hollandale.G 7
2 Holly Springs
        A 16
1 Houston..E 18
1 Indianola..F 8
1 Itta Bena.F 10
1 Iuka.....A 23
48 Jackson...J 11
3 Kosciusko.H 15
18 Laurel...M 18
2 Leland...F 7
2 Lexington.H 12
1 Long Beach
        R 18
1 Louisville.H 18
2 Lumberton P 16
10 McComb..O 9
2 Macon...H 21
2 Magee...L 14
2 Magnolia..O 9
1 Marks....C 9
32 Meridian..K 20
1 Mississippi City
        R 19
2 Moorhead.F 9
1 Morton..K 14
2 Moss Point R 22
13 Natchez...N 3
3 New Albany
        B 18
5 Newton...K 17
1 Norfield..N 9
2 Ocean Springs
        R 20
2 Okolona..D 20
3 Oxford...C 15
4 Pascagoula
        R 22
3 Pass Christian
        R 17
2 Pelahatchee
        K 13
3 Philadelphia
        I 18
1 Piave....N 20
5 Picayune..R 14
2 Pontotoc..C 18
6 Poplarville Q 15
2 Port GibsonL 6
2 Quitman..L 20
1 Ripley...A 18
2 Rosedale..E 8
5 Ruleville..E 9
1 Sardis...B 13
1 Senatobia.B 12
2 Shaw....F 7
2 Shelby...D 8
4 Starkville.F 19
2 Stonewall.K 20
1 Summit...O 9
1 Sumrall..N 15
1 Tunica...A 10
6 Tupelo...C 20
1 Tylertown.O 11
2 Union....J 18
23 Vicksburg.K 7
4 Water Valley
        D 14
1 Waynesboro
        M 21
5 West Point F 20
1 Wiggins...P 18
3 Winona...F 14
1 Woodville.P 4
6 Yazoo City.I 10

Pop. Hundreds.

9 Bay Springs
        L 17
7 Boyle....E 8
3 Brandon..K 12
9 Brookville.G 21
9 Bruce....D 16
9 Clinton...K 10
9 Collins...M 15
9 Como....B 13
9 DeKalb...I 20
6 Fayette...M 5
9 Fulton...C 22
9 Hernando.A 12
9 Lambert..B 11
8 Lucedale..P 21
9 Mendenhall
        L 13
8 Merigold..E 8
8 Mound Bayou
        E 8
8 Mt. Olive.M 14
8 Nettleton.D 21
9 Osyka....P 9
9 Purvis...O 16
9 Rolling Fork
        H 7
9 Scooba...I 22
8 Shuqualak.H 21
9 Tchula...G 11
9 Tutwiler..D 10
8 Wesson...M 10

(Col. At 7 R 35)

RAND McNALLY
POPULAR MAP OF
MISSISSIPPI

SCALE 1:1,774,000
1 Inch = 28 Statute Miles
1 Centimeter = 17.7 Kilometers

Statute Miles

Kilometers

Copyright by Rand McNally & Company, Chicago.
Made in U.S.A.

7R35

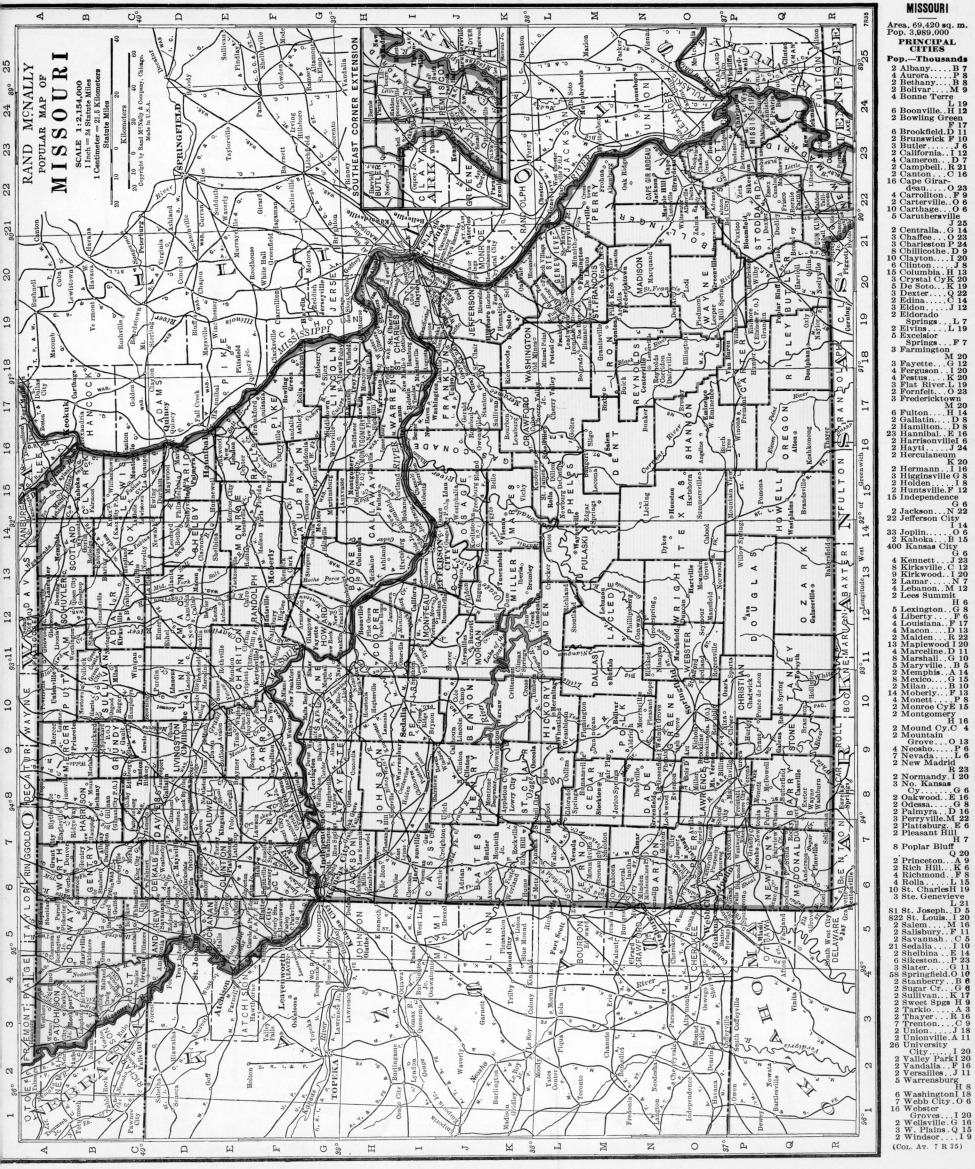

MISSOURI
Area, 69,420 sq. m.
Pop. 3,989,000
PRINCIPAL CITIES
Pop.—Thousands

2 Albany	B 7
4 Aurora	P 8
2 Bethany	B 8
2 Bolivar	M 9
4 Bonne Terre	L 19
6 Boonville	H 12
2 Bowling Green	F 17
6 Brookfield	D 11
3 Brunswick	F 10
2 Butler	I 12
2 California	D 7
2 Cameron	R 21
2 Campbell	C 16
2 Canton	
16 Cape Girardeau	O 23
2 Carrollton	F 9
6 Carterville	O 6
10 Carthage	O 6
5 Caruthersville	J 25
2 Centralia	G 14
3 Chaffee	O 23
3 Charleston	P 24
9 Chillicothe	D 9
10 Clayton	I 20
6 Clinton	J 8
16 Columbia	H 13
3 Crystal City	E 20
5 De Soto	K 19
2 Dexter	Q 22
2 Edina	C 14
3 Eldon	J 12
2 Eldorado Springs	L 7
2 Elvins	L 19
5 Excelsior Springs	F 7
2 Farmington	M 20
3 Fayette	G 12
4 Ferguson	I 20
3 Festus	K 20
4 Flat River	L 19
2 Fornfelt	O 23
3 Fredericktown	M 20
6 Fulton	H 14
2 Gallatin	D 8
2 Hamilton	D 8
23 Hannibal	E 16
6 Harrisonville	I 6
2 Hayti	J 24
2 Herculaneum	K 20
2 Hermann	I 16
2 Higginsville	G 8
2 Holden	I 8
15 Independence	F 6
2 Jackson	N 22
22 Jefferson City	I 14
33 Joplin	O 6
2 Kahoka	B 15
400 Kansas City	G 6
4 Kennett	J 23
8 Kirksville	C 12
9 Kirkwood	I 20
2 Lamar	N 7
4 Lebanon	M 12
2 Lees Summit	H 6
5 Lexington	G 8
4 Liberty	F 6
4 Louisiana	F 17
3 Macon	D 13
2 Malden	J 23
13 Maplewood	I 20
4 Marceline	D 11
5 Marshall	G 10
3 Maryville	B 6
6 Memphis	B 14
8 Mexico	G 15
2 Milan	B 10
14 Moberly	F 13
2 Monett	O 8
2 Monroe City	E 15
2 Montgomery	G 16
2 Mound City	C 4
2 Mountain Grove	O 13
4 Neosho	P 6
7 Nevada	L 6
2 New Madrid	R 23
2 Normandy	I 20
3 No. Kansas City	G 6
2 Oakwood	E 16
2 Odessa	G 8
2 Palmyra	D 16
2 Perryville	M 22
2 Plattsburg	E 6
2 Pleasant Hill	H 7
8 Poplar Bluff	Q 20
2 Princeton	A 9
2 Rich Hill	K 6
4 Richmond	F 8
4 Rolla	L 15
10 St. Charles	H 19
3 Ste. Genevieve	L 21
81 St. Joseph	D 5
822 St. Louis	I 20
2 Salem	M 16
2 Salisbury	F 11
2 Savannah	C 5
21 Sedalia	I 10
3 Shelbina	E 14
6 Sikeston	P 23
2 Slater	G 11
55 Springfield	O 10
2 Stanberry	B 7
2 Sugar Cr.	G 6
2 Sullivan	K 17
2 Sweet Spgs	H 9
2 Tarkio	A 3
2 Thayer	R 16
7 Trenton	C 9
2 Union	A 11
2 Unionville	A 11
26 University City	I 20
2 Valley Park	I 20
2 Vandalia	F 16
2 Versailles	I 11
5 Warrensburg	H 8
6 Washington	I 18
7 Webb City	O 6
16 Webster Groves	I 20
2 Wellsville	G 16
3 W. Plains	Q 15
2 Windsor	I 9

(COL. AT. 7 R 35)

MONTANA

Area 146,997 sq. m.
Pop. 539,000

PRINCIPAL CITIES

Pop.—Thousands

12 Anaconda...K 6
1 Baker.......J 25
1 Big Timber..L 13
16 Billings....L 16
1 Black Eagle.
          F 10
7 Bozeman...L 10
1 Browning...C 6
40 Butte.......K 7
1 Chinook....C 14
1 Choteau....F 8
1 Conrad.....E 9
4 Deer Lodge.J 7
1 Dillon.....N 7
1 E. Helena..J 9
1 Forsyth....K 20
1 Ft. Benton F 11
1 Fort Peck..E 20
2 Glasgow....B 19
2 Glendive...H 24
29 Great Falls.G 10
2 Hamilton...J 4
1 Hardin.....L 18
1 Harlowton..J 13
1 Havre......D 13
12 Helena.....J 8
6 Kalispell..E 4
5 Laurel.....M 15
5 Lewistown..H 14
1 Libby......D 1
6 Livingston.M 12
1 Malta......D 17
7 Miles City.J 22
15 Missoula...H 4
1 Phillipsburg.J 5
1 Plentywood.C24
1 Polson.....F 4
6 Poplar.....E 23
1 Red LodgeN 14
1 Roundup....J 15
1 Scobey.....C 22
2 Shelby.....D 9
2 Sidney.....F 24
1 Somers.....E 4
1 Walkerville.K 7
1 Warmsprings.
          J 7
3 Whitefish..D 4
2 Wolf PointE 22

Pop.—Hundreds

4 Absarokee.M14
1 Alberton...H 3
2 Arlee......H 4
3 Augusta....G 8
5 Bainville..D 25
5 Bearcreek..N 15
6 Belgrade...B 10
8 Belt.......G 11
2 Bigfork....E 4
6 Big Sandy.E 13
6 Bridger....N 15
2 Broadview K 15
9 Boulder....K 8
6 Brockton...E 23
5 Cascade....H 9
1 Chester....D 11
5 Circle.....G 22
1 Clyde ParkL 11
6 Columbia Falls
          D 4
8 Columbus.M 14
3 Corvallis..J 4
2 Crow Agency
          L 18
5 CulbertsonD 24
8 Cut Bank...C 8
1 Darby......K 4
1 Denton.....G 13
5 Dodson.....D 16
2 Dutton.....E 9
1 Ekalaka....K 24
1 Ennis......M 9
1 Eureka.....B 3
3 Fairview...E 25
3 Frazer.....E 21
3 FrenchtownH 4
6 Froid......D 24
6 Fromberg..M 15
3 Geraldine..F 13
7 Harlem.....D 15
6 Hays.......E 15
3 Hingham....D 12
3 Hobson.....H 13
7 HomesteadD 24
3 Hot SpringsF 3
3 Hysham.....K 19
3 Ismay......J 24
6 Joliet.....M 15
1 Joplin.....D 11
5 Judith Gap H 13
6 Kevin......C 9
5 Lima.......P 7
4 Lodge Grass
          M 18
5 ManhattanL 10
4 Medicine
   Lake....C 24
2 Melstone..I 17
3 Moore......H 13
4 Nashua.....E 20
2 Neihart....I 11
3 Opheim....C 20
5 Outlook....B 23
5 Plains.....G 3
5 Plevna.....J 4
4 Richey.....F 23
5 Ronan.....G 4
3 Rygate.....J 15
5 Saco.......D 18
5 St. Ignatius G 4
3 St. Regis..G 2
5 SandcouleeG 10
5 Sheridan...M 8
4 Southern
   Cross....K 6
5 Stanford...H 12
5 Stevensville.J 4
5 Stockett...G 10
5 Sunburst...C 9
3 Sweetgrass.B 9
5 Terry......I 22
5 Thompson
   Falls.....F 2
9 Three Forks L 9
7 Townsend...J 10
4 Troy.......C 1
7 Twin Bridges
          M 8
6 Valier.....D 8
3 Victor.....J 4
3 Westby.....B 25
6 Whitehall..L 8
6 White Sulphur
   Springs...J 11
6 Wibaux.....H 25
6 Wilsall....K 11
5 Winifred...G 14
4 Winnett....H 16
4 Wisdom....L 5
(Col. At. 7 R 35)

RAND McNALLY POPULAR MAP OF
MONTANA

SCALE 1:3,041,000
1 Inch = 48 Statute Miles
1 Centimeter = 30.4 Kilometers

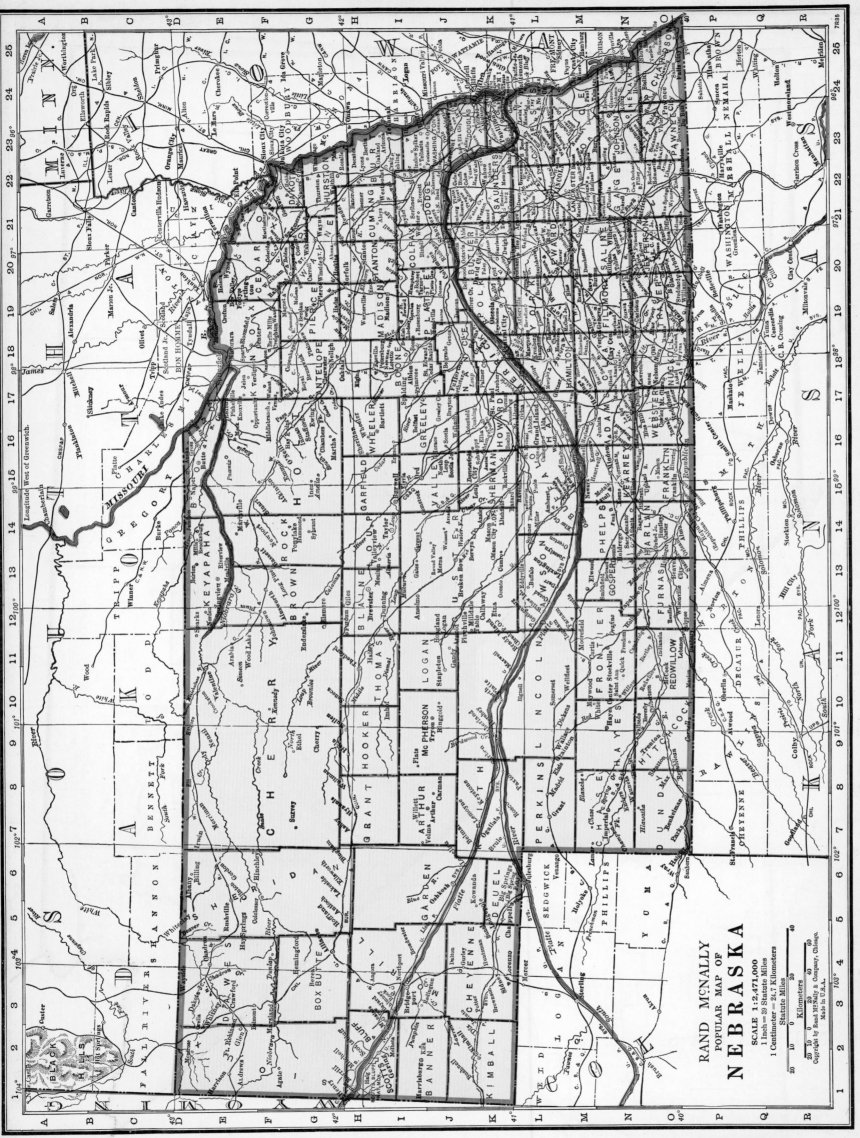

RAND McNALLY
POPULAR MAP OF
NEBRASKA

SCALE 1:2,471,000
1 Inch = 39 Statute Miles
1 Centimeter = 24.7 Kilometers
Statute Miles

Copyright by Rand McNally & Company, Chicago.
Made in U.S.A.

NEBRASKA

Area 77,520 sq. m.
Pop. 1,364,000

PRINCIPAL CITIES

Pop.—Thousands

1 Ainsworth	F 13
2 Albion	I 18
7 Alliance	G 4
1 Alma	N 14
2 Arapahoe	N 13
1 Ashland	K 23
3 Atkinson	F 15
3 Auburn	N 24
1 Aurora	L 18
2 Bayard	I 3
10 Beatrice	N 22
1 Beaver City	O 13
1 Bellevue	K 24
1 Benkleman	O 8
3 Blair	J 23
1 Bloomfield	F 19
1 Bridgeport	I 3
3 Broken Bow	J 13
1 Burwell	I 15
1 Cambridge	N 12
2 Central City	K 18
5 Chadron	E 4
1 Chappell	K 5
7 Columbus	J 20
2 Cozad	L 12
2 Crawford	E 3
1 Creighton	F 18
3 Crete	M 21
1 Curtis	M 11
2 David City	K 20
1 Deshler	O 19
1 Edgar	N 18
6 Fairbury	O 20
6 Falls City	O 25
1 Franklin	O 15
11 Fremont	J 22
1 Friend	M 20
2 Fullerton	J 18
1 Geneva	M 19
1 Genoa	J 19
2 Gering	H 2
2 Gordon	E 6
2 Gothenburg	L 12
18 Grand Isld.	L 17
2 Hartington	F 20
15 Hastings	M 17
2 Hebron	O 19
1 Hemingford	G 4
1 Hooper	I 21
1 Howell	I 21
1 Humboldt	O 24
9 Kearney	M 15
1 Kimball	K 2
2 Lexington	M 13
80 Lincoln	L 22
1 Louisville	L 23
1 Loup City	K 15
1 Lyons	G 21
1 McCook	O 10
2 Madison	J 19
1 Minatare	I 2
2 Minden	N 15
1 Mitchell	H 2
7 Nebraska City	M 24
2 Neligh	G 18
1 NewmansGrove	H 19
11 Norfolk	H 20
12 N. Platte	K 10
1 Oakland	I 22
2 Ogallala	K 7
214 Omaha	K 24
2 O'Neill	F 16
2 Ord	I 15
1 Orleans	O 14
1 Osceola	K 19
1 Oxford	N 13
2 Pawnee Cy	O 23
1 Pender	G 21
1 Pierce	G 19
1 Plainview	F 19
4 Plattsmouth	L 24
2 Randolph	G 19
2 Ravenna	L 15
1 Red Cloud	O 16
1 Rising City	K 20
1 Rushville	E 5
1 St. Edward	J 18
3 St. Paul	K 17
8 Scottsbluff	H 2
1 Scribner	I 22
3 Seward	L 20
1 Sidney	K 4
4 South Sioux City	F 22
1 Stanton	H 20
1 Stromsburg	K 19
3 Superior	O 18
1 Sutton	M 18
2 Tecumseh	N 23
2 Tekamah	I 23
1 Tilden	H 18
2 Valentine	E 11
1 Valley	J 23
3 Wahoo	K 22
1 Wakefield	G 21
1 Walthill	G 21
1 Wayne	G 21
1 Weeping Water	L 23
2 Westpoint	I 21
1 Wilber	N 21
1 Wisner	H 21
3 Wymore	O 22
6 York	L 19

Pop.—Hundreds

9 Arnold	J 12
9 Clarkson	I 20
9 Clay Center	N 18
9 Elgin	H 18
9 Emerson	G 21
9 Exeter	M 19
9 Greeley (Greeley Center)	J 16
9 Harvard	M 18
9 Hay Springs	E 5
9 Humphrey	I 19
9 Imperial	N 7
9 Laurel	F 20
9 Long Pine	F 13
9 Nelson	O 18
9 Ponca	F 21
9 Shelton	M 16
9 Trenton	O 9

(Col. at 7 R 35)

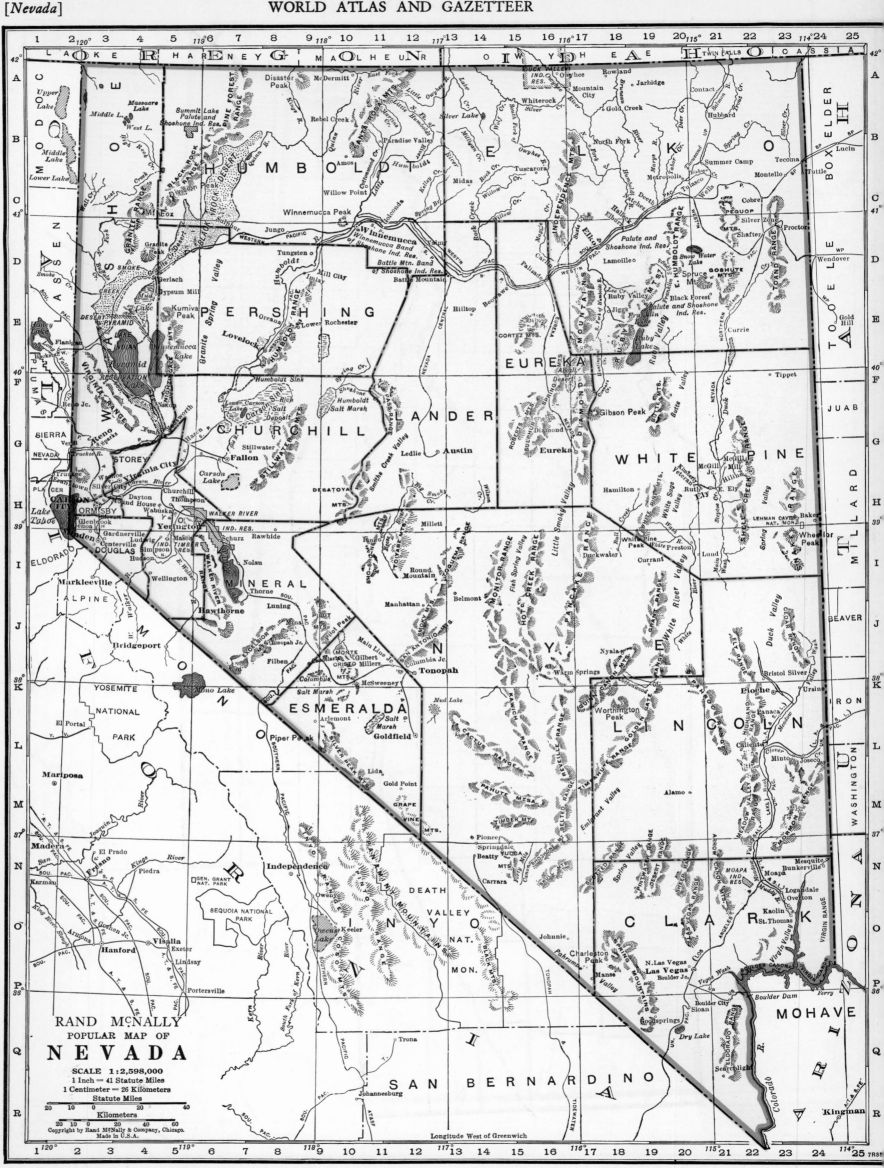

RAND McNALLY
POPULAR MAP OF
NEVADA

SCALE 1:2,598,000
1 Inch = 41 Statute Miles
1 Centimeter = 26 Kilometers
Statute Miles

Copyright by Rand McNally & Company, Chicago.
Made in U.S.A.

Longitude West of Greenwich

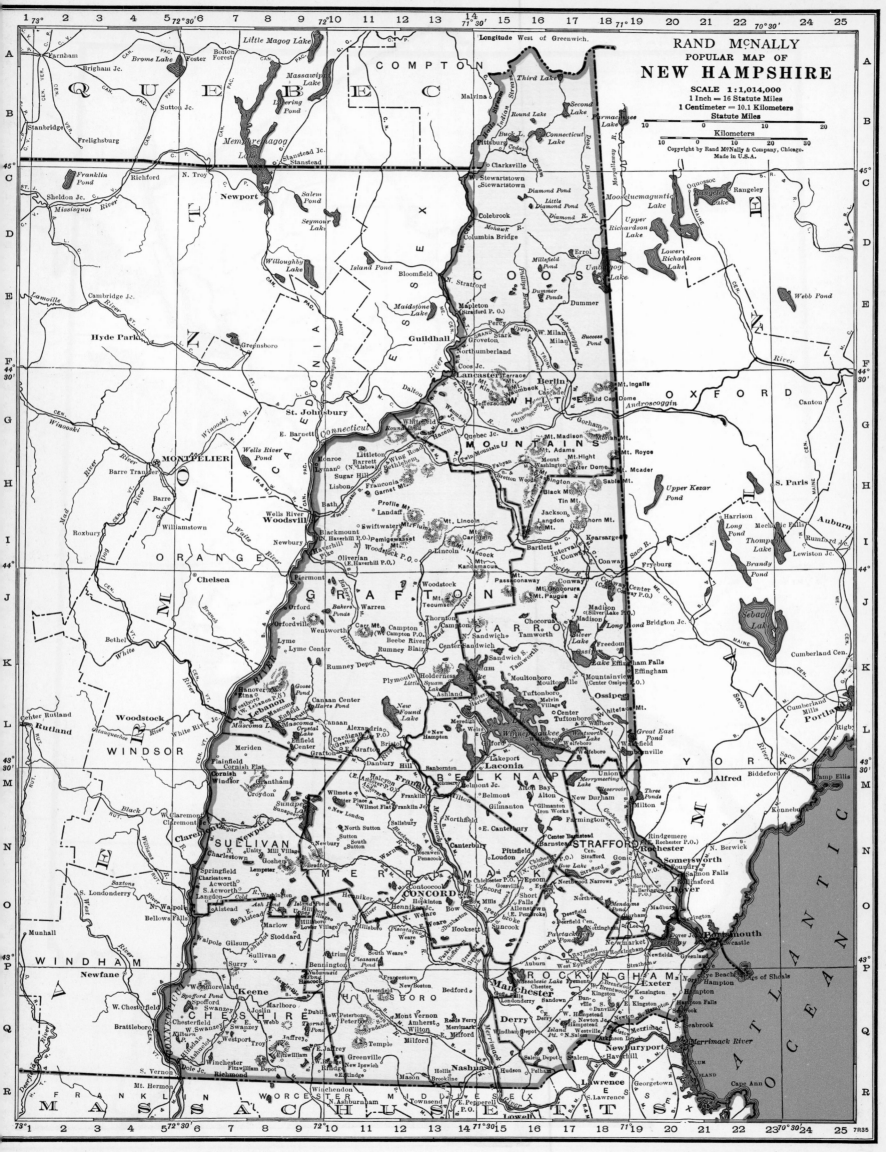

RAND McNALLY
POPULAR MAP OF
NEW HAMPSHIRE
SCALE 1:1,014,000
1 Inch = 16 Statute Miles
1 Centimeter = 10.1 Kilometers
Statute Miles
Kilometers
Copyright by Rand McNally & Company, Chicago. Made in U.S.A.

NEW HAMPSHIRE

Area, 9,341 sq. m.
Pop. 510,000.

PRINCIPAL CITIES
(▲ Township Pop.)

Pop.—Thousands

2	Allenstown	O 15
1	Antrim	P 11
1	Ashland	K 13
1	Bedford	P 14
20	Berlin	F 17
1▲	Boscawen	N 13
1	Bristol	L 12
1	Cascade	F 17
1	Charlestown	N 6
12	Claremont	N 7
1	Colebrook	D 14
25	Concord	O 14
1	Conway	J 18
4	Derry	Q 16
14	Dover	O 20
1	Durham	O 19
2	E. Jaffrey	Q 10
2	East Pembroke	O 15
1	E. Rochester (Rindgemere)	N 19
5	Exeter	P 19
2	Farmington	N 18
7	Franklin	M 13
2	Gorham	G 17
2	Greenville	R 12
1	Groveton	F 14
1	Hampton	P 20
2	Hanover	K 7
1	Henniker	O 11
1	Hillsboro	O 11
1	Hinsdale	Q 5
1	Hooksett	O 14
1	Hudson	R 15
14	Keene	P 7
12	Laconia	M 15
2	Lancaster	F 14
5	Lebanon	L 8
1	Lincoln	I 13
2	Lisbon	H 11
2	Littleton	G 12
77	Manchester	P 15
1	Marlboro	Q 8
1	Meredith	L 14
3	Milford	Q 13
31	Nashua	R 15
2	Newmarket	P 19
4	Newport	N 8
1▲	Northfield	M 13
2▲	Northumber-land	F 14
1	N. Walpole	O 6
2	Peterboro	Q 10
1	Pittsfield	N 16
2	Plymouth	K 12
14	Portsmouth	O 21
1	Ringemere (E. Rochester)	N 19
10	Rochester	N 19
1▲	Rye	P 21
1	Seabrook	Q 20
6	Somersworth	N 20
3	Suncook	O 15
1	Tilton	M 13
1	Troy	Q 8
2	Westboro (W. Lebanon)	L 7
1	Whitefield	G 13
1	Wilton	Q 12
2	Wolfboro	L 17
1	Woodsville	I 10

Pop.—Hundreds

7	Alton	M 17
4	Andover	M 11
4	Bath	H 10
4	Belmont	M 14
5	Bethlehem	H 12
8	Bow	O 14
5	Canaan	L 10
3	Candia	P 17
5	Contoocook	O 12
8	Enfield	L 8
5	Epping	P 18
7▲	Gilmanton	M 15
8	Goffstown	P 13
2	Hampstead	Q 18
2	Hopkinton	O 13
4	Kingston	P 18
7	Londonderry	O 15
7	Loudon	N 15
7	Milton	M 19
5	New Boston	P 12
4	New Ipswich	R 11
8	New London	M 10
9	N. Conway	I 18
6	North Haver-hill	I 10
1	N. Stratford	E 13
5	N. Woodstock	I 13
1	Pelham	R 16
2	Pittsburg	B 15
7	Plaistow	Q 18
7	Raymond	P 17
5	Rollinsford	N 20
4	Rummy	K 11
6	Salem	Q 17
8	Salem Depot	Q 17
5	Salmon Fs	N 20
8	Sanbornville	L 19
5	Walpole	O 6
9	Winchester	R 6

(Col. at 7 R 35)

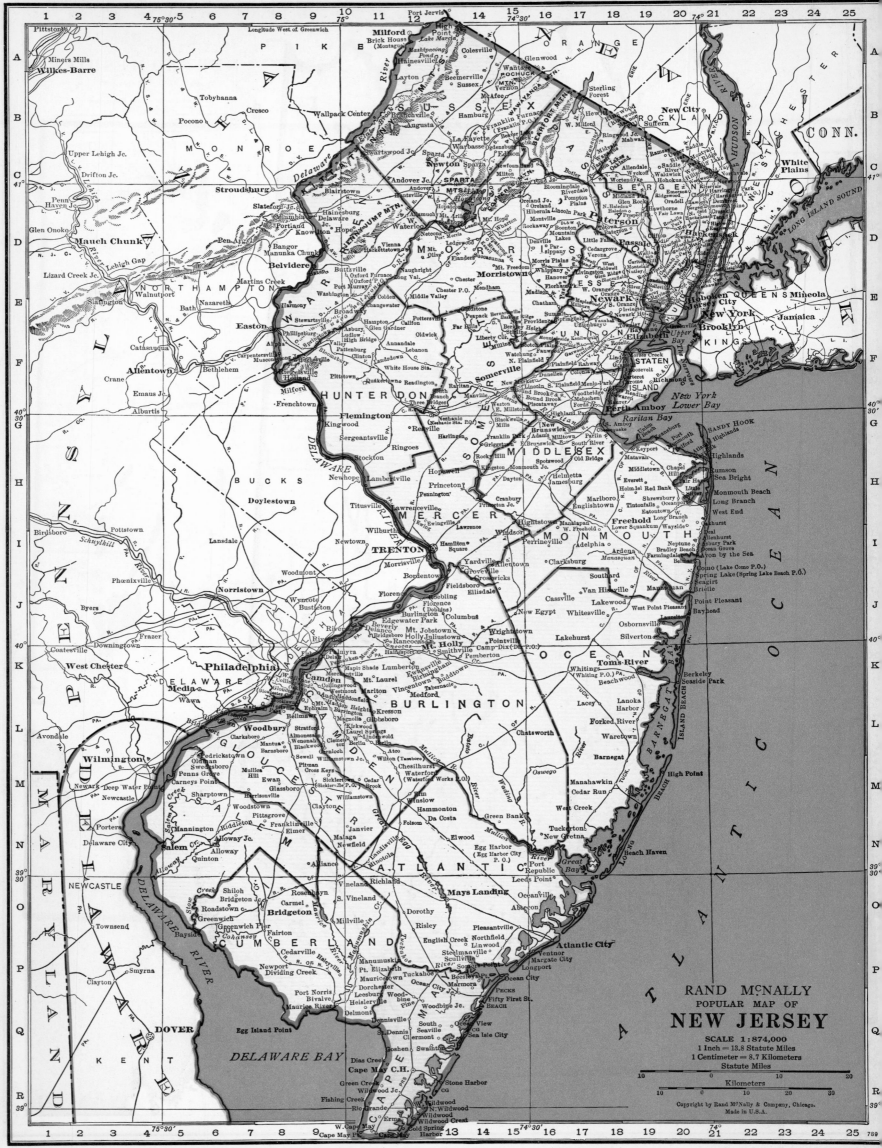

RAND McNALLY
POPULAR MAP OF
NEW JERSEY

SCALE 1:874,000
1 Inch = 13.8 Statute Miles
1 Centimeter = 8.7 Kilometers
Statute Miles

Copyright by Rand McNally & Company, Chicago.
Made in U.S.A.

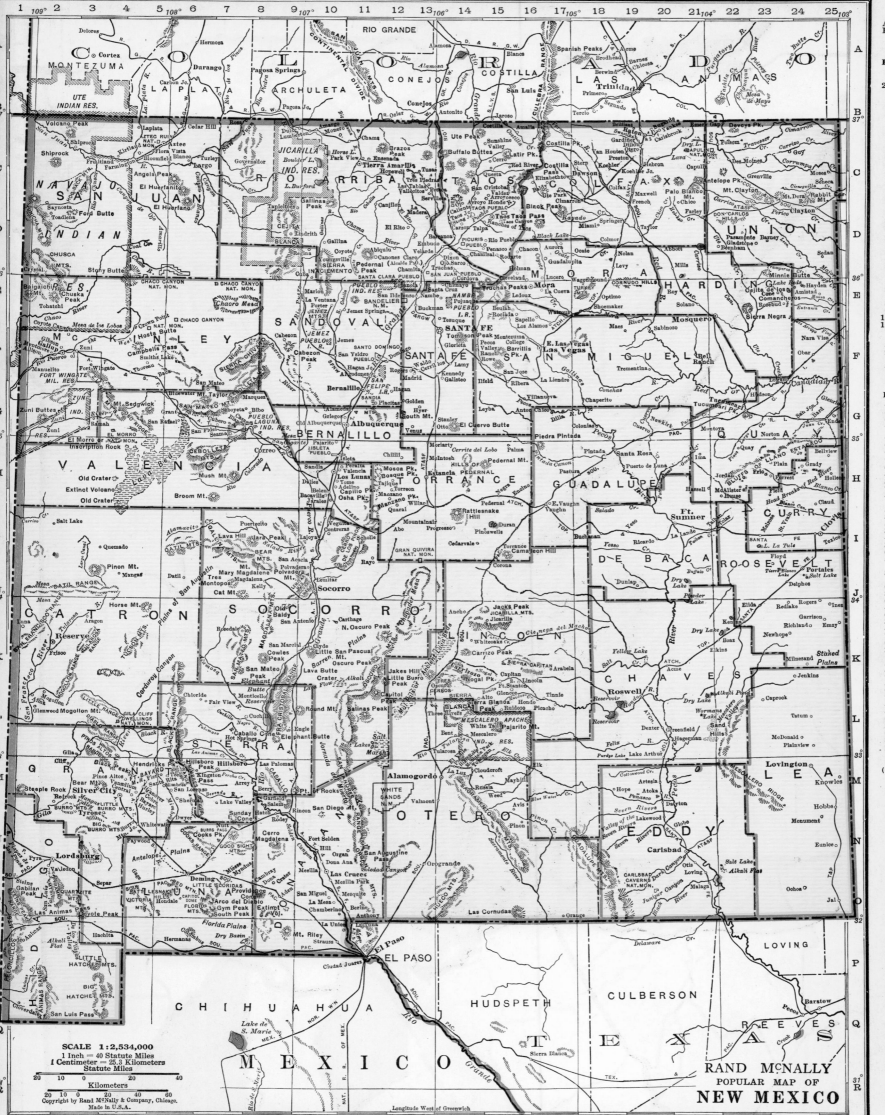

NEW MEXICO

Area 122,634 sq.m.
Pop. 422,000.

PRINCIPAL CITIES

Pop.—Thousands

3	Alamogordo	M 12
27	Albuquerque	G 11
2	Artesia	M 20
2	Belen	H 10
1	Bernalillo	G 10
4	Carlsbad	N 20
3	Carrizozo	K 14
1	Clayton	D 24
8	Clovis	I 25
2	Dawson	C 18
4	Deming	O 6
4	East Las Vegas (Las Vegastown)	F 17
1	Farmington	C 4
1	Ft. Bayard	M 4
6	Gallup	F 2
1	Hot Springs	L 7
4	Hurley	M 4
1	Isleta	H 11
10	Las Cruces	N 10
5	Las Vegas	F 16
1	Lordsburg	N 2
1	Lovington	M 23
1	Magdalena	J 8
1	Mesilla	N 9
1	Mora	E 16
1	Mountainair	I 13
2	Old Albuquerque	G 9
3	Portales	J 25
2	Raton	B 19
11	Roswell	L 19
11	Santa Fe	E 14
1	Santa Rosa	H 19
4	Silver City	M 3
5	Socorro	J 10
1	Springer	D 18
4	Tucumcari	G 22
1	Tularosa	M 13
1	Vaughn	H 17

Pop.—Hundreds

4	Adelino	H 11
5	Alameda	G 10
5	Allison	F 1
2	Anton Chico	G 16
7	Aztec	C 5
7	Central	M 4
7	Chama	B 11
3	Cimarron	C 17
6	Cleveland	E 16
6	Columbus	P 6
8	Cordova	E 14
7	Cuba	E 9
4	Des Moines	C 22
5	Dexter	L 20
4	Dixon	D 14
5	Dona Ana	N 10
4	Elida	J 22
6	Ensenada	C 12
5	Espanola	E 14
6	Estancia	H 13
5	Ft. Stanton	K 15
8	Ft. Sumner	I 21
6	Glencoe	L 15
6	Grants	G 15
6	Hagerman	L 21
4	Hatch	N 8
5	Hobbs	M 25
6	Hope	M 19
4	Jal	O 25
7	Jarales	H 10
6	Jemes	F 7
4	Lake Arthur	M 19
4	Los Lunas	H 11
4	Maxwell	C 19
4	Melrose	I 23
4	Mosquero	E 21
6	Questa	C 15
7	Roy	E 20
6	San Jose	F 15
4	San Marcial	K 9
6	Santa Cruz	E 14
6	Sugarite	B 20
4	Texico	I 25
8	Truchas	E 14
9	Wagon Mound	E 18
5	Willard	H 13

(Col. At. 7 R 35)

NEW YORK

Area 49,204 sq. m.
Pop. 12,959,000

PRINCIPAL CITIES

Pop.—Thousands

127 Albany . . N 23
35 Amsterdam M 22
37 Auburn . . . M 13
17 Batavia . . . M 7
12 Beacon . . . . D 5
77 Binghamton O 16
573 Buffalo . . . N 4
8 Canandaigua M 10
23 Cohoes . . . N 23
16 Corning . . . Q 11
15 Cortland . . O 15
7 Depew . . . . M 5
18 Dunkirk . . . O 2
47 Elmira . . . . Q 12
16 Endicott . . Q 15
10 Floral Park . H 6
15 Freeport . . . . I 7
12 Fulton . . . . K 13
7 Garden City H 7
16 Geneva . . . M 11
11 Glen Cove . . G 6
19 Glens Falls K 24
23 Gloversville M 21
7 Hastings-upon-Hudson . . G 5
13 Hempstead . H 7
10 Herkimer . . L 19
16 Hornell . . . . P 9
12 Hudson . . . P 24
10 Ilion . . . . . M 19
21 Ithaca . . . . P 13
45 Jamestown . Q 3
14 Johnson Cy R 15
11 Johnstown M 21
16 Kenmore . . M 4
28 Kingston . . R 22
24 Lackawanna N 4
7 Lancaster . . M 5
11 Little Falls L 20
23 Lockport . . . L 5
12 Lynbrook . . H 7
9 Malone . . . C 21
12 Mamaroneck G 6
11 Massena . . C 19
8 Mechanicville M 23
21 Middletown E 3
8 Mineola . . . H 6
62 Mt. Vernon . G 6
8 Newark . . M 11
31 Newburgh . . D 5
54 New Rochelle G 6
6930 New York I 5
1265 Bronx
2560 Brooklyn
1867 Manhattan
1079 Queens
158 Richmond
75 Niagara Falls L 4
19 North Tonawanda . . . L 5
8 Norwich . . O 17
17 Ogdensburg D 17
22 Olean . . . . . . R 6
11 Oneida . . . . L 16
13 Oneonta . . . P 19
15 Ossining . . . . F 6
23 Oswego . . . K 13
7 Patchogue . . H 9
17 Peekskill . . . E 5
13 Plattsburg D 24
23 Port Chester G 7
10 Port Jervis . E 3
40 Poughkeepsie C 6
11 Rensselaer . O 24
328 Rochester . L 9
14 Rockville Center . . . I 7
32 Rome . . . . . L 17
9 Rye . . . . G 6
3 Sag Harbor F 12
10 Salamanca . . Q 5
8 Saranac L . . F 22
13 Saratoga Springs . . L 23
96 Schenectady N 22
7 Scotia . . . . M 23
8 Solvay . . . M 14
209 Syracuse . M 15
7 Tarrytown . . F 6
13 Tonawanda M 4
73 Troy . . . . . N 24
102 Utica . . . . L 18
12 Valley Stream H 6
32 Watertown H 15
16 Watervliet N 23
36 White Plains G 6
135 Yonkers . . . G 5

(COL. AT. 7 R 35)

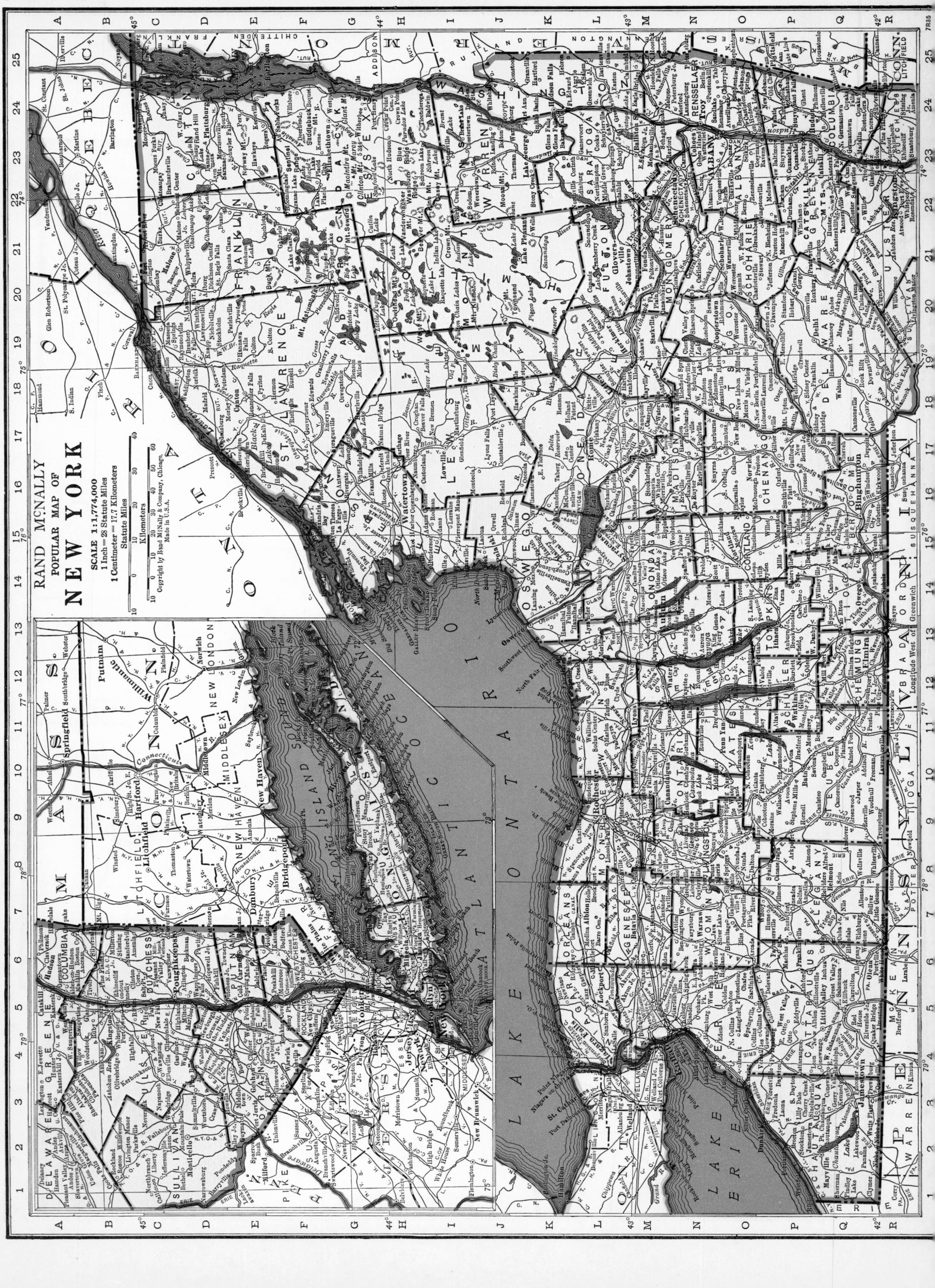
RAND McNALLY
POPULAR MAP OF
NEW YORK
SCALE 1:1,774,000
1 Inch = 28 Statute Miles
1 Centimeter = 17.7 Kilometers
Statute Miles
Kilometers
Copyright by Rand McNally & Company, Chicago.
Made in U.S.A.
LAKE ONTARIO
LAKE ERIE
ATLANTIC OCEAN
LONG ISLAND SOUND

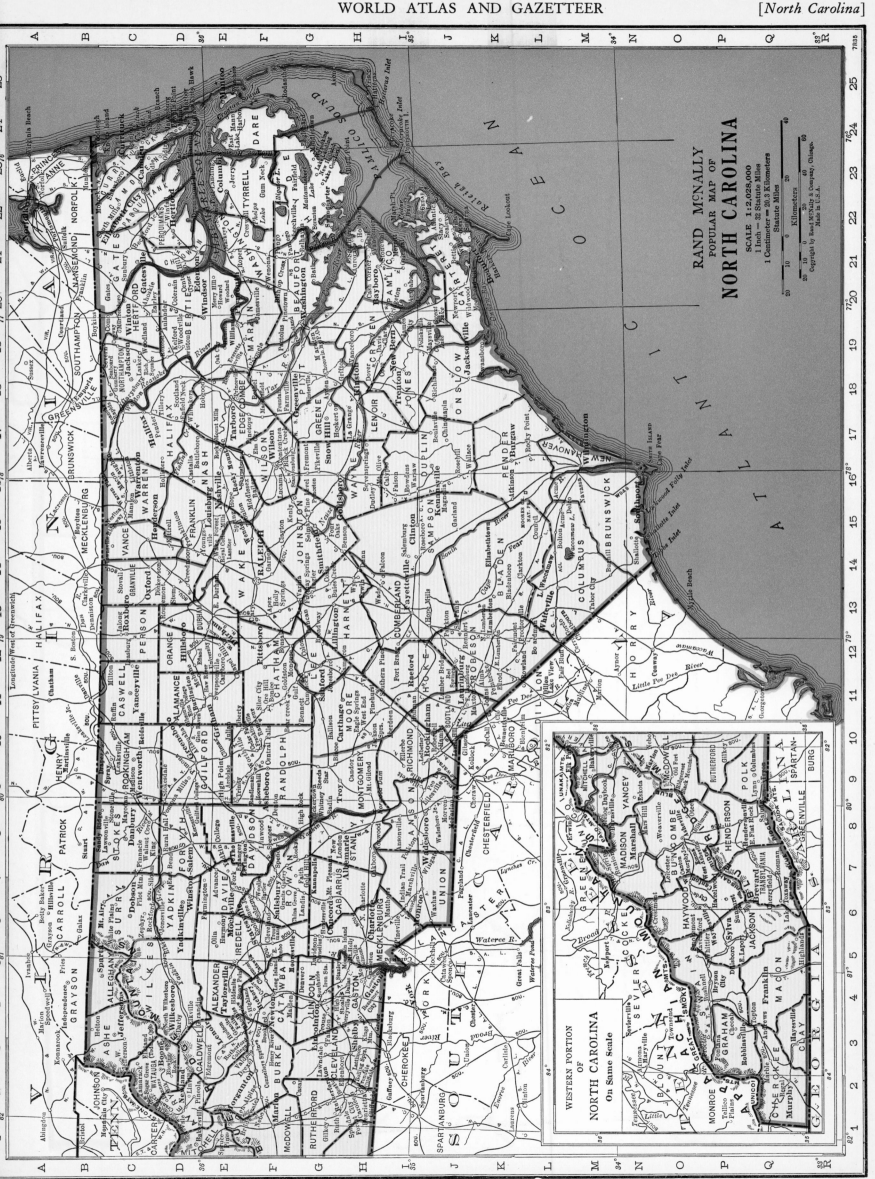

RAND McNALLY
POPULAR MAP OF
NORTH CAROLINA

SCALE 1:2,028,000
1 Inch = 32 Statute Miles
1 Centimeter = 20.3 Kilometers
Statute Miles

Kilometers

Copyright by Rand McNally & Company, Chicago.
Made in U.S.A.

WESTERN PORTION
OF
NORTH CAROLINA
On Same Scale

NORTH CAROLINA

Area, 52,426 sq. m.
Pop. 3,492,000.

**PRINCIPAL
CITIES**

Pop.—Thousands

2	Ahoskie	C 20
3	Albemarle	H 8
2	Andrews	Q 3
5	Asheboro	F 9
50	Asheville	O 8
2	Ayden	G 18
3	Badin	H 8
2	Beaufort	J 21
2	Belhaven	G 21
4	Belmont	H 5
2	Benson	H 15
4	Bessemer Cy.	H 4
2	Brevard	Q 7
2	Bryson City	P 4
1	Burgaw	H 17
10	Burlington	D 11
5	Canton	O 7
1	Carrboro	E 12
1	Chadbourn	L 13
3	Chapel Hill	E 12
83	Charlotte	H 6
3	Cherryville	H 4
2	Clayton	F 15
2	Cliffside	H 2
1	Clinton	I 15
12	Concord	G 6
1	Cooleemee	F 6
1	Cornelius	G 5
1	Cramerton	H 5
1	Dallas	H 4
1	Davidson	G 5
3	Dunn	H 14
52	Durham	E 13
1	East Flat Rock	Q 8
2	East Spencer	F 8
4	Edenton	D 21
10	Elizabeth City	C 22
3	Elkin	D 5
2	Enfield	D 17
3	Erwin	H 14
2	Farmville	H 18
13	Fayetteville	I 13
2	Forest City	H 1
1	Fremont	G 16
17	Gastonia	H 4
2	Gibsonville	D 10
10	Goldsboro	G 16
2	Graham	E 11
1	Granite Fs.	E 4
54	Greensboro	D 10
9	Greenville	G 18
1	Hamlet	J 10
6	Henderson	C 15
5	Hendersonville	P 8
1	Henrietta	H 2
1	Hertford	D 22
7	Hickory	F 4
1	Highland	F 4
37	High Point	F 9
7	Kannapolis	G 7
2	Kernersville	D 8
6	Kings Mountain	H 3
11	Kinston	H 18
1	La Grange	H 17
3	Laurinburg	J 11
2	Leaksville	C 10
1	Lenoir	E 3
10	Lexington	E 7
3	Lincolnton	G 4
5	Louisburg	D 15
2	Lowell	H 4
4	Lumberton	K 12
1	Madison	C 9
1	Maiden	G 4
2	Marion	F 1
1	Maxton	J 11
2	Mayodan	C 9
2	Mebane	D 12
2	Mocksville	E 6
2	Monroe	H 6
5	Mooresville	F 5
3	Morehead City	K 20
6	Morganton	F 2
6	Mount Airy	B 7
2	Mt. Holly	H 5
3	Mt. Olive	H 16
2	Murphy	Q 2
12	New Bern	I 19
4	Newton	F 4
4	North Wilkesboro	D 4
2	Oxford	C 14
2	Plymouth	E 20
37	Raleigh	F 14
2	Randleman	F 9
7	Reidsville	C 10
3	Roanoke Rapids	C 17
	Rockingham	I 10
21	Rocky Mt.	E 16
2	Roxboro	C 13
2	Rutherfordton	G 2
1	St. Paul	J 13
21	Salisbury	F 6
3	Sanford	G 12
2	Scotland Neck	D 18
2	Selma	G 15
14	Shelby	H 3
2	Siler City	F 10
3	Smithfield	G 14
2	Southern Pines	H 11
2	Southport	N 15
2	Spencer	F 7
1	Spindale	H 1
2	Spray	C 10
2	Spruce Pine	E 1
10	Statesville	F 6
6	Tarboro	E 17
10	Thomasville	E 8
2	Troy	H 9
2	Tryon	Q 9
2	Valdese	F 3
2	Wadesboro	I 8
2	Wake Forest	E 15
7	Washington	G 19
9	Waynesville	O 6
2	Weldon	C 17
	West Hickory	F 4
2	Whiteville	L 13
3	Williamston	E 19
32	Wilmington	M 16
13	Wilson	F 16
75	Winston-Salem	D 8

(Col. At. 7 R 35)

NORTH DAKOTA

Area.70,837 sq. m.
Pop. 706,000.

PRINCIPAL CITIES

Pop.—Thousands

1 Ashley....Q 16
1 Beach.....M 1
11 Bismarck..N 11
1 Bottineau..D 12
1 Cando.....K 15
2 Carrington.K 17
1 Casselton.M 23
1 Cooperstown
    K 20
1 Crosby....D 4
5 Devils Lake
    H 18
5 Dickinson..M 5
1 Ellendale..L 18
2 Enderlin..O 22
29 Fargo.....M 25
1 Garrison...J 8
3 Grafton...P 22
17 Grand Forks 2
    H 24
1 Hankinson Q 24
2 Harvey....I 14
1 Hebron....M 7
1 Hettinger..Q 5
1 Hillsboro..K 23
2 JamestownM 18
1 Kenmare...E 7
1 Langdon...D 19
1 Larimore...H 22
1 Lidgerwood
    Q 24
1 Linton....P 13
1 Lisbon....O 22
5 Mandan...N 11
1 Mayville..J 23
16 Minot.....G 10
1 Mott.....P 6
2 New Rockford
    J 17
1 Northwood.I 22
2 Oakes....Q 20
1 Park River F 21
1 Rugby....F 14
5 ValleyCityM 21
5 Wahpeton.M 25
5 Williston..G 2
1 Wilton...L 11
1 Wishek....P 15

Pop.—Hundreds

6 Anamoose..I 13
1 Aneta....I 21
7 Belfield....M 4
5 Berthold..G 8
9 Beulah....L 8
5 Bisbee....E 16
7 Bowbells..D 7
5 Bowman...P 3
4 Buxton....D 21
8 Cavalier..D 21
4 Cogswell..D 21
5 Columbus..P 3
6 Drake....I 13
5 Drayton...E 23
4 Dunseith..D 14
8 Edgeley...P 18
4 Edmore...F 19
4 Elgin.....P 8
4 Fairmount Q 25
2 Fessenden.J 15
4 Finley....D 21
4 Flaxton...D 7
6 Fordville..G 21
4 Forman...Q 22
4 Ft. Yates..P 12
4 Fredonia..P 17
2 Gackle...N 17
9 Glenullen (Glen
    Ullin)...N 8
5 Goodrich..K 13
2 Granville..E 11
5 Grenora...E 2
4 HannafordK 21
8 Hatton...J 22
4 Hazelton..O 13
7 Hazen....K 9
5 Hope....K 21
7 Hunter...I 23
4 Kensal...K 18
5 Killdeer...K 5
4 Kindred...N 24
4 Kulm....P 18
4 Lakota...H 19
9 La Moure I 19
7 Lansford..E 10
7 Leeds....G 16
5 Lehr....P 16
17 Litchville.N 20
7 McClusky K 12
5 McVille...L 20
8 Maddock..H 16
5 Marmarth..P 1
5 Max....I 10
4 Medina...M 16
8 Michigan.H 20
6 Milnor...P 22
5 Minnewaukan
    H 16
6 Minto....F 22
7 Mohall...C 9
7 Napoleon..O 15
5 Neche....C 21
9 New England
    O 5
4 New LeipzigP 8
8 New Salem N 9
4 Noonan...D 5
4 Page.....L 22
7 Parshall...H 7
6 Pembina..C 22
4 Plaza....G 8
5 Portal....C 6
7 Portland..J 22
5 Ray.....F 4
4 RichardtonM 6
6 Rolette...E 14
9 Rolla....D 15
5 Ryder....I 9
4 St. John...D 15
5 St. ThomasE 22
5 Sherwood..D 9
4 Sheyenne..I 17
5 Stanley...G 6
5 Steele....N 14
5 Strasburg..Q 14
7 Streeter...M 16
4 Tioga....F 5
4 Tower City
    M 22
6 Towner...G 13
6 Turtle LakeJ 11
5 UnderwoodK 10
4 Van Hook..H 7
4 Velva....H 11
8 Walhalla..D 20
8 Washburn.K 11
8 WatfordCityI 4
5 Westhope..D 11
4 Wildrose..E 4
5 WillowCityE 13
4 WimbledonL 19
4 Wyndmere P 23
4 Zap.....K 8
4 Zeeland..Q 15
(Col. At. ꚍ R 35)

RAND McNALLY
POPULAR MAP OF
NORTH DAKOTA
SCALE 1:1,913,000
1 Inch = 30.2 Statute Miles
1 Centimeter = 19.1 Kilometers
Copyright by Rand McNally & Company, Chicago.
Made in U.S.A.

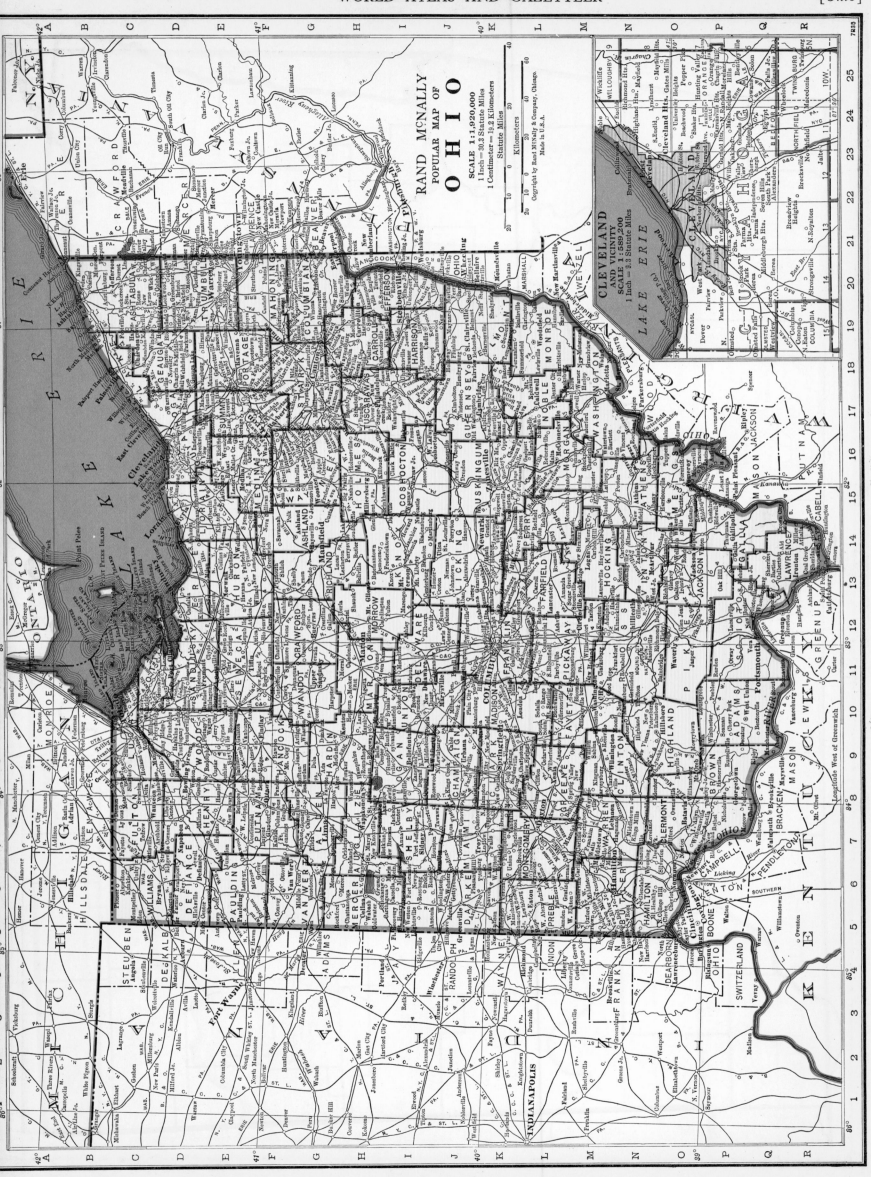

RAND McNALLY
POPULAR MAP OF
OHIO

SCALE 1:1,920,000
1 Inch = 30.3 Statute Miles
1 Centimeter = 19.2 Kilometers

Statute Miles

Kilometers

Copyright by Rand McNally & Company, Chicago.
Made in U.S.A.

CLEVELAND
AND VICINITY
SCALE 1,589,200
1 Inch = 9.3 Statute Miles

OHIO

Area 41,040 sq. m.
Pop. 6,733,000
**PRINCIPAL
CITIES**

Pop.—Thousands

255 Akron....E 17
23 Alliance...F 19
11 Ashland...G 14
23 Ashtabula.B 19
5 Athens....N 15
24 Barberton..P 17
27 Bedford...D 17
5 Bellaire...K 20
10 Bellefontaine I 9
6 Bellevue..E 13
6 Berea.....D 16
7 Bexley....K 12
7 Bowling Green
        D 9
10 Bucyrus..G 12
11 Cambridge K 17
51 Campbell..F 20
105 Canton...G 18
6 Celina....H 10
5 Cheviot...O 5
18 Chillicothe N 12
451 Cincinnati.O 5
7 Circleville.M 12
900 Cleveland C 16
51 Cleveland Hts.
        O 24
291 Columbus K 11
10 Conneaut..A 21
11 Coshocton.J 16
20 Cuyahoga Falls
        P 18
201 Dayton....K 7
9 Defiance...D 6
9 Delaware..I 11
6 Delphos...G 7
9 Dover.....H 17
40 East Cleveland
        O 17
23 E. Liverpool G 21
26 Elyria....D 15
12 Euclid....C 17
19 Findlay...F 10
13 Fostoria..F 10
13 Fremont...E 11
8 Galion....H 12
7 Gallipolis..P 14
16 Garfield Hts.
        P 23
10 Girard....E 20
7 Greenville..J 6
52 Hamilton..N 6
17 Ironton...R 13
6 Jackson...O 13
16 Kent......E 18
6 Kenton....H 10
70 Lakewood..C 16
19 Lancaster..L 13
42 Lima......H 9
6 Logan.....M 14
45 Lorain....D 15
34 Mansfield..G 14
6 Maple Hts. P 24
14 Marietta..M 18
31 Marion....H 11
15 Martins Ferry
        J 20
26 Massillon..G 18
5 Miamisburg M 7
30 Middletown M 7
9 Mt. Vernon I 13
31 Newark....K 14
6 New Boston Q 12
12 New Philadel-
        phia.....H 18
16 Niles.....E 20
6 Norwalk...E 13
33 Norwood...O 7
6 Oakwood...E 7
11 Painesville B 18
13 Parma.....D 17
7 Piqua.....J 7
43 Portsmouth Q 11
9 Ravenna...E 18
5 Rocky Riv. C 16
11 Salem.....F 20
25 Sandusky..D 13
5 Shaker Hts. P 24
9 Shelby....G 13
5 Sidney....I 7
69 Springfield..K 9
35 Steubenville J 20
11 Struthers..F 20
8 Tiffin.....F 11
291 Toledo....C 10
7 Toronto...H 20
9 Troy......K 7
9 Uhrichsville J 18
8 Urbana....J 9
5 Van Wert..F 6
6 Wadsworth F 16
41 Warren....E 20
8 Washington
        C. H...M 10
6 Wellsville..H 20
11 Wooster...G 15
11 Xenia.....L 9
170 Youngstown
        E 21
36 Zanesville K 16
(COL. AT 7 R 35)

OKLAHOMA

Area 70,057 sq. m.
Pop. 2,548,000

RAND McNALLY
POPULAR MAP OF
OREGON
SCALE 1:2,186,000
1 Inch = 34.5 Statute Miles
1 Centimeter = 21.9 Kilometers
Statute Miles
Kilometers
Copyright by Rand McNally & Company, Chicago.
Made in U.S.A.

OREGON
Area..96,699 sq.m.
Pop. 1,027,000
PRINCIPAL CITIES
Pop.—Thousands

5	Albany	G 6
5	Ashland	Q 7
10	Astoria	A 4
8	Baker	G 22
2	Bandon	M 2
9	Beaverton	D 7
9	Bend	J 11
3	Burns	L 18
3	Coquille	M 2
5	Corvallis	G 5
2	Cottage Grove	K 6
3	Dallas	F 5
1	Enterprise	D 23
19	Eugene	J 6
2	Forest Grove	D 6
1	Gladstone	D 8
4	Grants Pass	P 5
3	Gresham	D 8
1	Heppner	D 16
3	Hillsboro	D 6
3	Hood River	C11
1	Independence	F 6
16	Klamath Falls	P 9
8	La Grande	E 21
2	Lakeview	Q 14
2	Lebanon	H 7
3	McMinnville	E 6
5	Marshfield	L 2
11	Medford	Q 6
2	Milton	B 20
2	Milwaukie	D 7
1	Mount Angel	D 7
1	Multnomah	D 7
1	Myrtle Point	N 3
3	Newberg	E 6
2	Newport	G 3
4	North Bend	L 2
2	Ontario	J 24
6	Oregon City	D 7
1	Oswego	D 7
7	Pendleton	C 19
302	Portland	D 7
2	Prineville	J 13
1	Rainier	A 6
1	Redmond	I 12
1	Reedsport	K 3
4	Roseburg	M 5
3	St. Helens	M 5
26	Salem	F 6
2	Seaside	A 4
1	Sheridan	E 5
2	Silverton	F 7
3	Springfield	J 6
6	The Dalles	C 12
3	Tillamook	D 4
2	Toledo	G 3
1	Union	E 22
2	Vernonia	B 6
1	West Linn	D 7
1	West Salem	F 6
1	Willamette	F 8
2	Woodburn	E 7

Pop.—Hundreds

4	Amity	E 6
6	Arlington	C 15
3	Athena	C 20
6	Bay City	C 4
7	Brownsville	H 7
3	Canby	E 7
3	Canyon City	H 18
7	Carlton	E 6
5	Cascade Locks	C 10
8	Central Point	Q 7
5	Chiloquin	D 10
5	Clackamas	D 8
7	Clatskanie	B 6
6	Condon	E 14
5	Cornelius	D 6
5	Drain	K 5
9	Elgin	C 21
5	Empire	L 2
5	Estacada	D 9
5	Falls City	F 5
2	Fossil	F 15
7	Freewater	P 20
5	Glendale	O 5
6	Gold Beach	P 2
6	Gold Hill	P 6
6	Harrisburg	I 6
6	Hermiston	B 17
8	Hubbard	E 7
8	Huntington	H 23
7	Jacksonville	Q 6
4	Jefferson	G 6
4	John Day	H 18
5	Joseph	D 23
5	Junction City	I 5
3	Lafayette	E 6
5	Lake Grove	H 9
5	Marcola	I 7
4	Merrill	R 16
4	Millington	L 4
5	Molalla	E 8
5	Monmouth	F 5
4	Moro	D 13
4	Myrtle Creek	N 5
6	N. Powder	F 21
8	Nyssa	J 24
6	Oakland	L 5
7	Philomath	H 5
6	Phoenix	Q 6
5	Pilot Rock	D 18
4	Prairie (Prairie City)	H 19
3	Sandy	D 9
5	Scio	G 7
4	Sherwood	D 7
4	Stayton	G 7
5	Sutherlin	L 5
4	Talent	Q 6
7	Tigard	D 7
9	Vale	J 23
7	Waldport	H 3
7	Wallowa	C 22
4	Warrenton	A 4
5	Wasco	C 13
5	Wendling	I 7
5	Westfir	J 5

(Col. At. 7 R 35)

PENNSYLVANIA

Area 45,126 sq. m.
Pop. 10,176,000

PRINCIPAL CITIES

Pop.—Thousands

27	Aliquippa	L 2
93	Allentown	L 22
82	Altoona	M 10
20	Ambridge	L 2
10	Archbald	F 22
18	Ardmore	P 23
11	Arnold	L 4
17	Beaver Falls	K 2
10	Bellevue	M 3
13	Berwick	J 19
58	Bethlehem	L 23
19	Braddock	M 4
19	Bradford	E 9
11	Bristol	O 25
10	Bryn Mawr	P 23
24	Butler	K 4
13	Canonsburg	N 2
20	Carbondale	F 22
13	Carlisle	O 15
12	Carnegie	M 3
14	Chambersburg	P 12
11	Charleroi	O 3
59	Chester	Q 23
15	Clairton	N 4
15	Coatesville	P 20
12	Columbia	P 18
11	Connellsville	P 5
11	Conshocken	O 23
11	Coraopolis	M 2
10	Darby	P 23
12	Dickson	G 21
14	Donora	O 4
12	Du Bois	I 9
21	Dunmore	H 22
21	Duquesne	N 4
34	Easton	L 23
12	Ellwood Cy.	K 2
116	Erie	C 3
14	Farrell	I 1
10	Franklin	H 4
16	Greensburg	N 5
12	Hanover	Q 16
80	Harrisburg	N 16
37	Hazleton	J 20
37	Homestead	M 3
10	Indiana	L 7
15	Jeannette	N 5
67	Johnstown	N 7
22	Kingston	H 20
60	Lancaster	P 18
10	Lansford	K 21
11	Latrobe	N 6
15	Lebanon	M 18
13	Lewistown	L 13
10	Lock Haven	I 14
55	McKeesport	N 4
18	McKees Rocks	M 3
15	Mahanoy City	K 19
17	Meadville	F 3
20	Monessen	O 3
18	Mt. Carmel	K 18
11	Munhall	N 3
26	Nanticoke	I 19
10	New Brighton	K 2
49	New Castle	J 2
17	New Kensington	M 4
36	Norristown	O 23
10	Northampton	L 22
22	Oil City	G 4
13	Old Forge	H 21
11	Olyphant	G 21
1951	Philadelphia	P 24
12	Phoenixville	O 22
670	Pittsburgh	M 3
18	Pittston	H 21
17	Plymouth	I 20
19	Pottstown	N 22
24	Pottsville	L 19
111	Reading	N 20
143	Scranton	H 21
20	Shamokin	K 18
26	Sharon	I 1
22	Shenandoah	K 19
13	Steelton	N 16
16	Sunbury	K 16
16	Swissvale	M 4
14	Tamaqua	K 20
10	Tarentum	M 4
10	Taylor	H 21
20	Turtle Cr.	N 4
11	Uniontown	P 4
11	Vandergrift	L 5
15	Warren	E 7
25	Washington	O 2
12	W. Chester	P 22
87	Wilkes-Barre	I 21
30	Wilkinsburg	M 4
46	Williamsport	H 16
55	York	P 17

(COL. AT. 7 R 35)

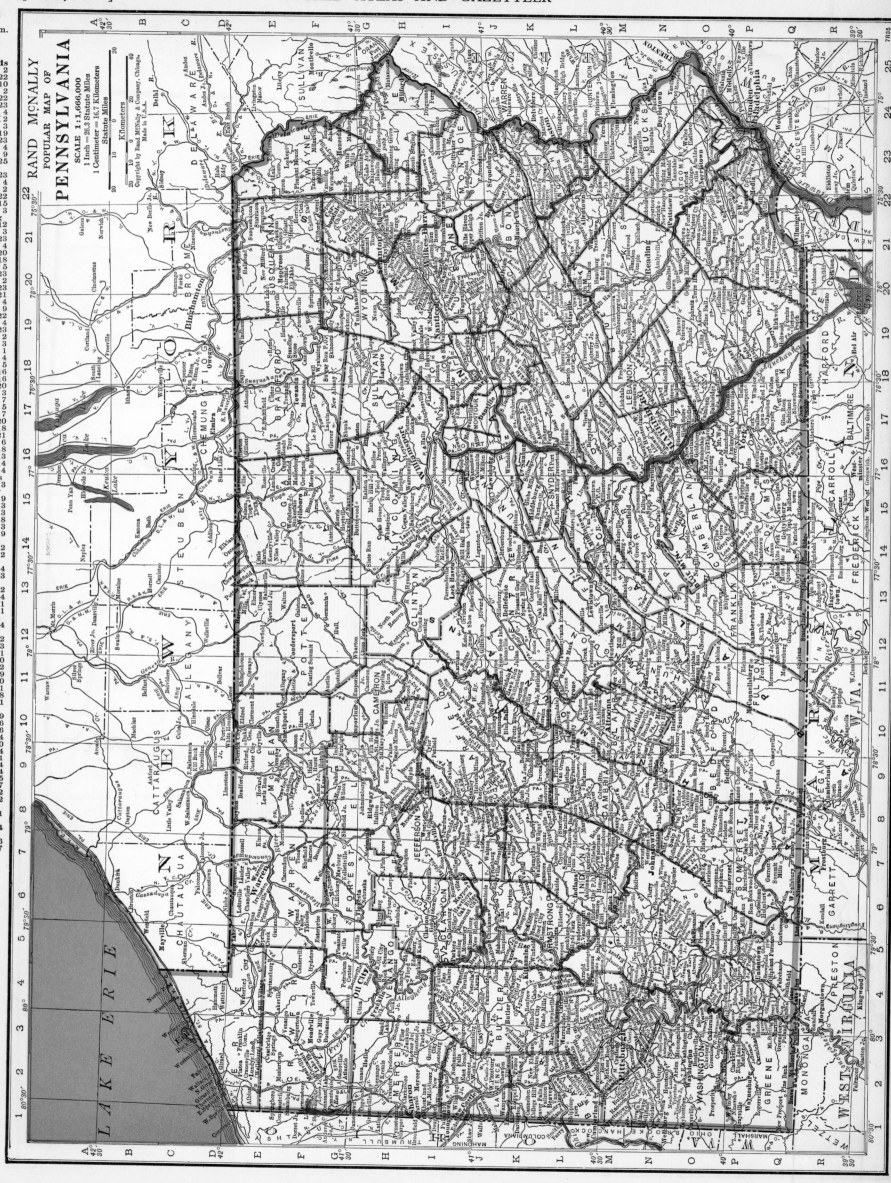

RAND McNALLY
POPULAR MAP OF
PENNSYLVANIA

SCALE 1:1,666,000
1 Inch = 26.3 Statute Miles
1 Centimeter = 16.7 Kilometers
Statute Miles
Kilometers

Copyright by Rand McNally & Company, Chicago.
Made in U.S.A.

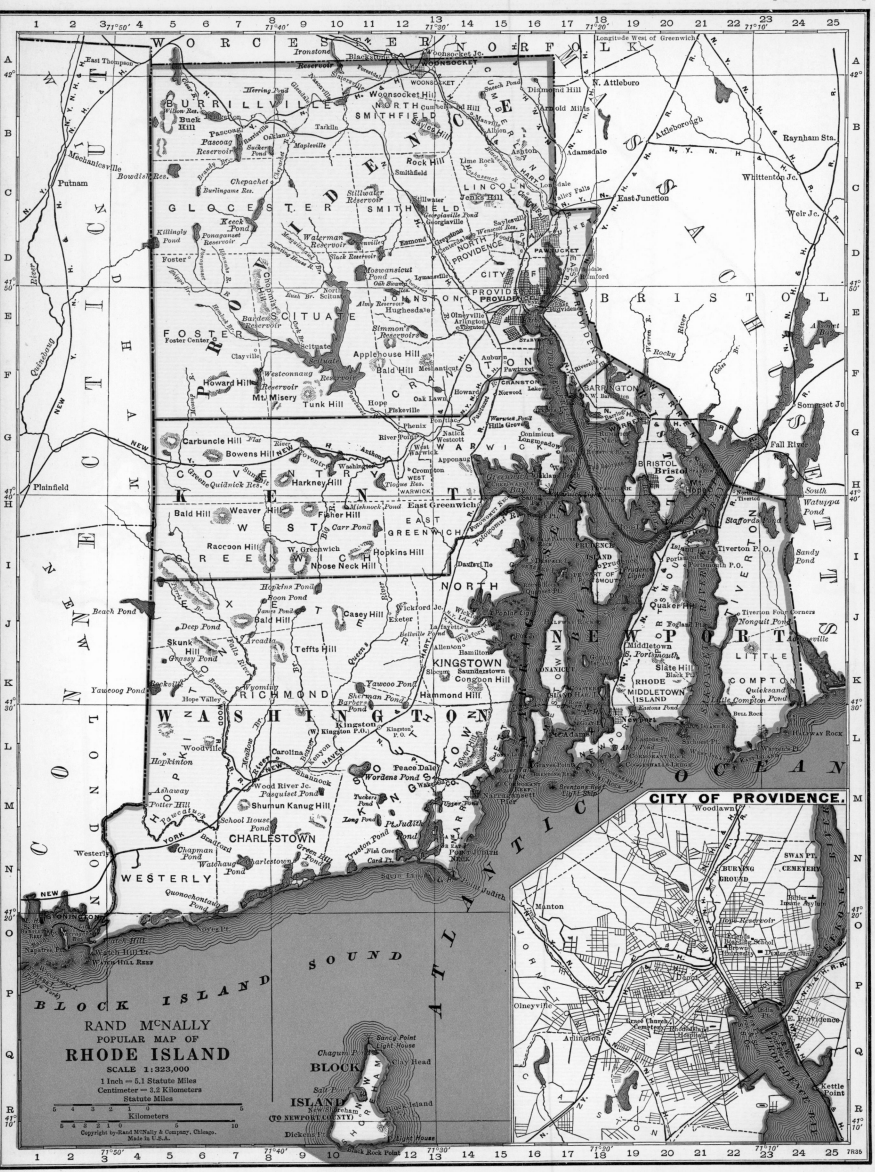

RHODE ISLAND

Area 1,248 sq. m.
Pop. 681,000

PRINCIPAL CITIES

(▲ Township Pop.)

Pop.—Thousands

1 Albion	B 15
1 Allenton	J 13
3 Anthony	G 11
2 Apponaug	G 14
8 Arctic (W. Warwick)	G 12
1 Arkwright (Fiskeville)	G 12
2 Arlington	E 14
1 Ashton	B 16
3 Auburn	F 15
6 ▲Barrington	G 19
1 Block Island	R 12
1 Bradford	N 6
10 Bristol	H 20
2 Centerdale	D 13
1 Centerville	G 12
24 Central Falls	C 16
1 Chepachet	C 7
1 Conimicut	G 16
45 Cranston	F 14
1 Cumberland Hill	B 15
4 ▲E. Greenwich	H 13
30▲E. Providence E 17, P 24
1 Esmond	D 12
1 Fiskeville (Arkwright)	G 12
1 Greenville	D 11
1 Greystone	D 13
1 Harrisville	B 7
1 Hills Grove	G 15
6 Howard	F 14
2 Jamestown	K 17
1 Kingston	L 12
1 Lakewood	F 16
4 Lonsdale	C 16
1 Lymansville	D 13
5 Manville	B 15
1 Narragansett	K 21
1 Narragansett Pier	M 15
5 Natick	G 14
29 Newport	L 20
2 North Tiverton	H 22
1 Norwood	F 15
2 Oakland Beach	H 16
1 Pascoag	B 7
73 Pawtucket	D 16
2 Pawtuxet	F 16
2 Peace Dale	L 12
2 Phenix	G 12
2 Pontiac	G 13
2 Portsmouth	I 21
243 Providence	E 15
3 River Point	G 12
2 Riverside	F 17
1 Saylesville	C 15
2 Slatersville	A 10
4 Thornton	E 14
4 Tiverton	I 22
2 Valley Falls	C 17
4 Wakefield	M 13
7 ▲Warren	G 19
27▲Warwick	H 17
1 Washington	H 11
2 West Barrington	F 18
11▲Westerly	N 3
8 West Warwick (Arctic)	G 12
1 Wickford	G 15
47 Woonsocket	A 13

Pop.—Hundreds

2 Adamsville	J 24
4 Carolina	L 8
2 Davisville	I 14
4 Forestdale	A 11
4 Glendale	A 9
1 Greene	H 6
4 Hamilton	J 14
1 Hughesdale	E 12
6 Lafayette	J 13
5 Lime Rock	B 14
8 Mapleville	B 9
3 Nasonville	A 9
5 Oakland	B 8
7 Oak Lawn	F 13
5 Phillipsdale	D 17
4 Potter Hill	M 2
6 Rumford	D 17
2 Saunderstown	K 14
2 Slocum	K 13
2 Tarkiln	B 10
6 Tiverton Four Corners	J 24
2 Woodville	L 6
3 Wyoming	K 8

(COL. AT. 7 R 35)

SOUTH CAROLINA

Area 30,989 sq. m.
Pop. 1,875,000.

PRINCIPAL CITIES
Pop.—Thousands

RAND McNALLY
POPULAR MAP OF
SOUTH CAROLINA

SCALE 1:1,565,000
1 Inch = 24.7 Statute Miles
1 Centimeter = 15.6 Kilometers
Statute Miles
Kilometers
Copyright by Rand McNally & Company, Chicago. Made in U.S.A.

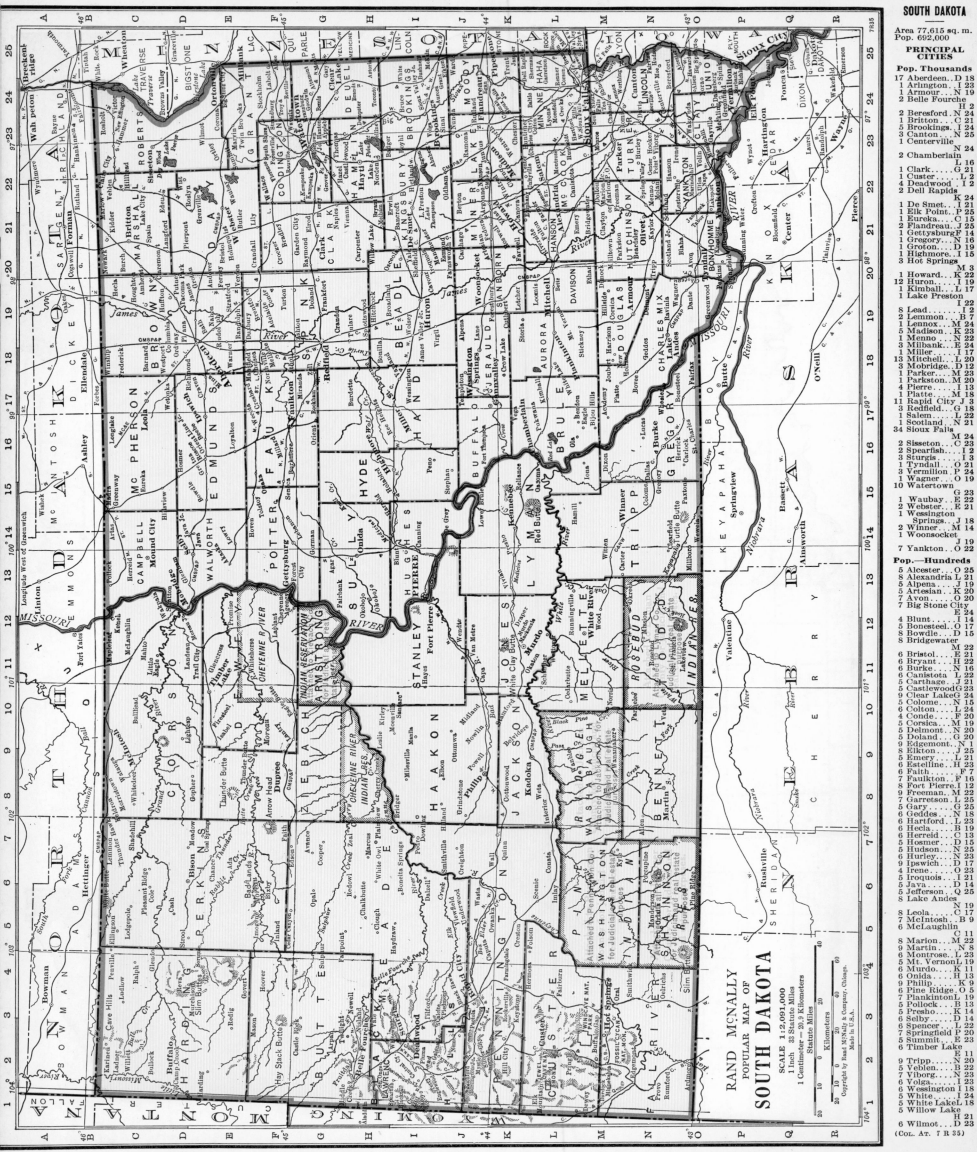

RAND McNALLY
POPULAR MAP OF
SOUTH DAKOTA

SCALE 1:2,091,000
1 Inch 33 Statute Miles
1 Centimeter = 20.9 Kilometers

Statute Miles
Kilometers

Copyright by Rand McNally & Company, Chicago.
Made in U.S.A.

TEXAS

Area 265,896 sq.m.
Pop. 6,172,000

PRINCIPAL CITIES

Pop.—Thousands

23 Abilene....E 14
43 Amarillo...D 3
53 Austin....J 17
58 Beaumont.K 25
5 Beeville...O 18
14 Big Spring.F 10
6 Bonham...C 20
7 Borger....C 4
8 Breckenridge
　 E 15
6 Brenham..K 20
22 Brownsville R 5
13 BrownwoodG15
8 Bryan....I 20
7 Cameron..I 19
7 Childress..A 13
6 Cisco....F 15
12 Cleburne..F 18
6 Coleman..G 14
5 Colorado..F 11
28 Corpus Christi
　 P 18
15 Corsicana..F 20
7 Crystal CyN 13
5 Cuero....M 18
5 Dalhart...B 2
260 Dallas...E 19
12 Del Rio..M 11
14 Denison..B 19
10 Denton...D 18
5 Eagle Pass N 12
5 Eastland..F 14
7 Edinburg..P 4
7 Electra...B 15
102 El Paso..F 1
7 Ennis....F 19
163 Ft. WorthE 18
9 Gainesville C 18
53 Galveston.M 23
8 Gladewater E 23
5 Goose Ck..L 23
5 Graham...D 16
9 Greenville.D 21
12 Harlingen..Q 5
8 Henderson F 23
8 Highland Pk.
　 D 19
8 Hillsboro..F 19
292 Houston..K 22
7 Huntsville.I 22
7 Jacksonville F22
7 Kerrville..K 15
7 Kingsville.Q 18
33 Laredo...Q 14
21 Longview..E 23
21 Lubbock..C 10
7 Lufkin...H 23
8 Luling...L 18
9 McAllen..P 3
7 McKinney D 19
5 Marlin...H 19
16 Marshall..E 24
7 Mercedes..Q 4
11 Mexia...G 20
7 Midland..F 9
6 Mineral Wells
　 E 17
5 Mission....P 3
6 Nacogdoches
　 G 23
5 Navasota..J 21
6 New Braunfels
　 L 17
4 Olney.....C 15
8 Orange...K 25
11 Palestine..G 21
5 Pampa....C 5
16 Paris.....C 21
10 Plainview..A 10
51 Port ArthurK25
7 Quanah...A 14
6 Ranger...E 16
4 Rusk.....G 22
25 San AngeloH 12
232 San Antonio
　 L 16
11 San Benito..P 5
7 San MarcosK17
5 Seguin...L 17
16 Sherman..C 19
4 Slaton...C 10
4 Stephenville
　 F. 10
5 Sulphur Spgs.
　 D 21
11 Sweetwater E12
7 Taylor....J 18
15 Temple..H 18
7 Terrell...E 20
17 Texarkana C 24
4 Texas City L 23
30 Tyler....F 22
4 University Pk.
　 D 19
5 Uvalde...M 14
9 Vernon...B 14
9 Victoria...N 19
53 Waco...G 19
8 WaxahachieF19
5 WeatherfordE17
4 Wellington. E 6
4 Weslaco...P 4
44 Wichita Fs.B 16
6 Yoakum..M 19

(Col. AT. 7 R 35)

RAND McNALLY POPULAR MAP OF **TEXAS**

SCALE 1:3,992,000
1 Inch = 63 Statute Miles
1 Centimeter = 40 Kilometers

Statute Miles

Kilometers

Copyright by Rand McNally & Company, Chicago
Made in U.S.A.

RAND McNALLY
POPULAR MAP OF
UTAH
SCALE 1:2,028,000
1 Inch = 32 Statute Miles
1 Centimeter = 20.3 Kilometers
Statute Miles
Kilometers
Copyright by Rand McNally & Company, Chicago.
Made in U.S.A.

UTAH
Area 84,990 sq. m.
Pop. 519,000.

PRINCIPAL CITIES

Pop. Thousands
3 American Fork . G 12
2 Beaver . . . . M 7
3 Bingham Canyon . F 10
5 Bountiful . E 11
5 Brigham . . C 11
4 Cedar City . O 5
1 Delta . . . . J 8
3 Draper . . F 11
3 Ephraim . J 13
4 Eureka . H 10
1 Fairview . I 14
1 Farmington E 11
1 Fillmore . . K 9
1 Fountain Green . . I 13
3 Garfield . F 10
1 Grantsville . F 9
2 Gunnison . K 12
2 Heber . . I 14
1 Helper . . I 16
1 Hooper . . D 10
1 Hurricane . Q 4
2 Hyrum . . . . B 11
1 Kanab . . . . Q 8
1 Kaysville . E 11
2 Lehi . . . . G 12
1 Lewiston . . A 12
10 Logan . . . B 12
4 Magna . . . F 10
1 Manti . . . J 13
2 Midvale . . F 11
3 Milford . . M 5
2 Monroe . . L 10
1 Morgan . . D 12
1 Moroni . . I 13
2 Mt. Pleasant . G 12
5 Murray . . F 11
2 Nephi . . . I 12
40 Ogden . . . D 11
1 Orem . . . G 12
1 Panguitch . O 8
1 Park City . F 13
1 Parowan . . O 5
1 Payson . . G 12
2 Pleasant Grove . G 12
4 Price . . . . I 17
1 Providence B 12
15 Provo . . . G 12
3 Richfield . L 10
1 Richmond . B 12
1 Riverton . F 11
1 Roosevelt . G 21
2 St. George . Q 2
1 Salina . . . K 11
140 Salt Lake City . E 11
1 Sandy . . . F 11
1 Santaquin . H 12
2 Smithfield . B 12
4 Spanish Fork . H 12
1 Spring Canyon . I 16
1 Spring City J 13
4 Springville G 13
2 Tooele . . . F 9
1 Tremonton B 10
2 Vernal . . F 23
1 Wellsville . B 11
1 Woods Cross . E 11

Pop.—Hundreds
5 Alpine . . . F 12
6 Aurora . . . K 11
4 Bear River C 10
8 Blanding . . O 23
7 Castle Dale I 16
2 Castlegate . I 16
6 Centerfield K 12
5 Centerville E 11
5 Circleville . N 3
6 Clarkston . B 11
8 Clearfield . D 11
5 Cleveland . J 17
3 Coalville . E 14
5 Columbia . I 19
4 Corinne . . C 10
4 Deseret . . . J 8
6 Duchesne . G 19
5 Elsinore . L 10
4 Emery . . K 15
5 Enterprise . P 2
Pop. Escalante . O 13
5 Ferron . . . K 15
3 Fielding . B 11
6 Garland . . B 10
5 Glenwood . L 11
5 Goshen . . H 11
5 Greenriver K 20
4 Henefer . . E 13
9 Hiawatha . J 16
5 Hinckley . . J 7
5 Holden . . . K 9
5 Honeyville C 10
5 Huntington J 16
5 Huntsville . D 12
5 Hyde Park E 12
4 Junction . . N 10
5 Kamas . . . F 14
6 Kanosh . . L 9
3 Koosharem M 11
6 Layton . . . D 11
4 Levan . . . . I 11
6 Lindon . . . G 12
6 Mammoth . H 10
4 Mantua . . C 11
5 Mapleton . H 13
5 Marysvale . M 9
5 Mayfield . . K 12
4 Meadow . . K 9
4 Mendon . . B 11
5 Midway . . F 13
5 Millville . . B 12
5 Minersville N 6
9 Moab . . . . L 23
5 Moriland . . J 16
5 Monticello . O 24
6 Myton . . . G 20
6 Newton . . B 11
6 Orangeville J 15
4 Orderville . C 12
4 Paradise . . C 12
4 Paragonah O 7
5 Portage . . A 10
4 Randolph . B 15
6 Redmond . K 11
6 Roy . . . . D 10
5 Salem . . . H 12
5 Scipio . . . . J 9
6 Stockton . . F 9
5 Sunnyside . I 19
6 Sunset . . . D 11
5 Syracuse . D 11
5 Tropic . . . . P 10
4 Washington Q 3
6 Willard . . . C 11
4 Winterquarters . I 15
4 Woodruff . . C 15
(Col. AT. 7 R 35)

VERMONT

Area 9,564 sq. m.
Pop. 383,000.

PRINCIPAL CITIES

(▲ Township Pop.)

Pop.—Thousands

2 Alburg....	A 5
11 Barre....	G 13
1 Barton....	C 16
4 Bellows Falls	
	O 14
7 Bennington	Q 6
1 Bethel....	J 12
1 Brandon....	J 7
9 Brattleboro	
	Q 12
1 Bristol....	H 7
25 Burlington..	E 6
2 Colchester..	C 16
1 Enosburg Falls	
	B 10
2 Essex Junction	
	E 7
2 Fair Haven..	L 5
1 Graniteville	
	G 13
2 Hardwick..	E 14
2 Island Pond	
	C 20
2 Ludlow....	M 12
2 Lyndonville	
	E 18
2 Middlebury	
	H 6
1 ▲Montgomery	
	B 12
8 Montpelier	G 12
2 Morrisville	
	D 12
5 Newport..	B 16
2 Northfield	H 11
1 N. Troy..	A 14
1 Norwich..	K 15
1 Orleans..	C 16
2 Poultney..	L 6
1 ▲Pownal..	R 6
3 Proctor..	K 8
1 Randolph..	I 11
1 Richford..	A 11
17 Rutland..	L 8
1 ▲Ryegate..	G 17
8 St. Albans.	C 7
8 St. Johnsbury	
	E 18
5 SpringfieldN	13
3 Swanton..	B 7
2 Vergennes..	G 5
2 WaterburyF	11
1 West Pawlet	
	M 5
2 West Rutland	
	L 8
1 White River	
Junction K	15
1 Wilder...	K 15
4 Windsor..	M 14
2 Winooski..	E 6
1 WoodstockL	13

Pop.—Hundreds

5 Arlington..	P 7
5 Benson...	K 5
6 Bradford..	I 17
8 Castleton..	L 6
5 CavendishM	12
7 Center Rutland	
	L 8
4 Centervale	E 18
5 Chester...	N 12
7 Derby Line	A 17
4 Dorset....	N 7
5 Duxbury..	F 9
8 E. Arlington	
	P 7
2 E. Berkshire	
	B 11
5 Fairfax....	C 8
5 Georgia...	C 7
8 Grand Isle..	C 5
5 Greensboro	
	D 15
4 Groton...	G 16
5 Hartford..	K 15
4 Highgate..	B 8
2 Hinesburg..	F 7
5 Hydeville..	L 6
4 Irasburg..	C 15
2 Johnson...	D 11
6 LunenburgE	21
8 Manchester	
Center...	O 7
8 ▲Middlesex.F	11
6 Milton....	D 7
4 Montgomery	
Center...	B 12
2 New HavenH	7
9 N. Bennington	
	Q 5
8 North Ferrisburg....	G 6
7 North Pownall	
	Q 5
4 N. Springfield	N 13
5 Orwell....	J 5
9 Pittsford..	K 8
7 Proctorville	
	M 12
7 Readsboro..	R 8
7 Richmond..	F 8
4 Rochester..	J 10
4 Sheldon...	B 9
8 S. Royalton	
	J 13
1 Thetford..	J 16
7 Waitsfield.G	10
7 Wallingford	
	M 8
5 Williamstown	H 12

(Col. at 7 R 35)

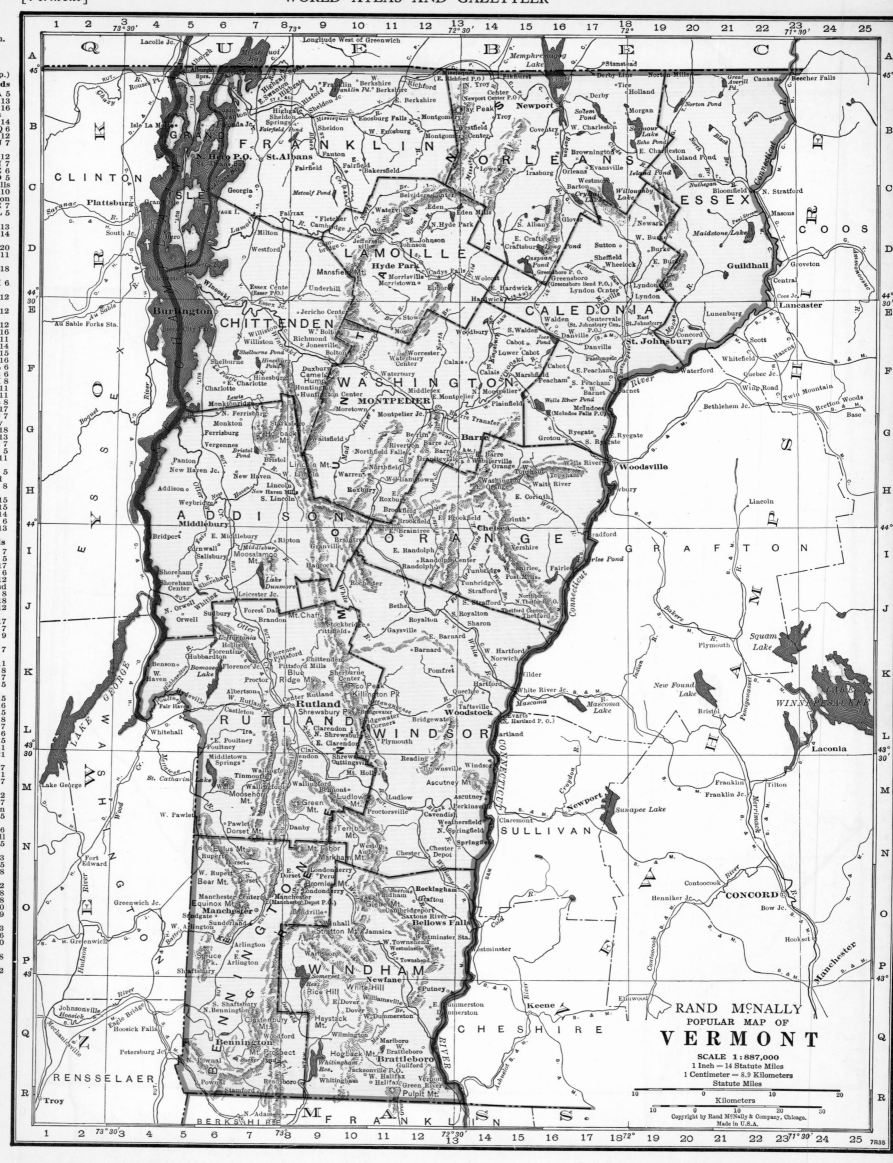

RAND McNALLY
POPULAR MAP OF
VERMONT

SCALE 1:887,000
1 Inch = 14 Statute Miles
1 Centimeter = 8.9 Kilometers
Statute Miles

Kilometers

Copyright by Rand McNally & Company, Chicago.
Made in U.S.A.

7R35

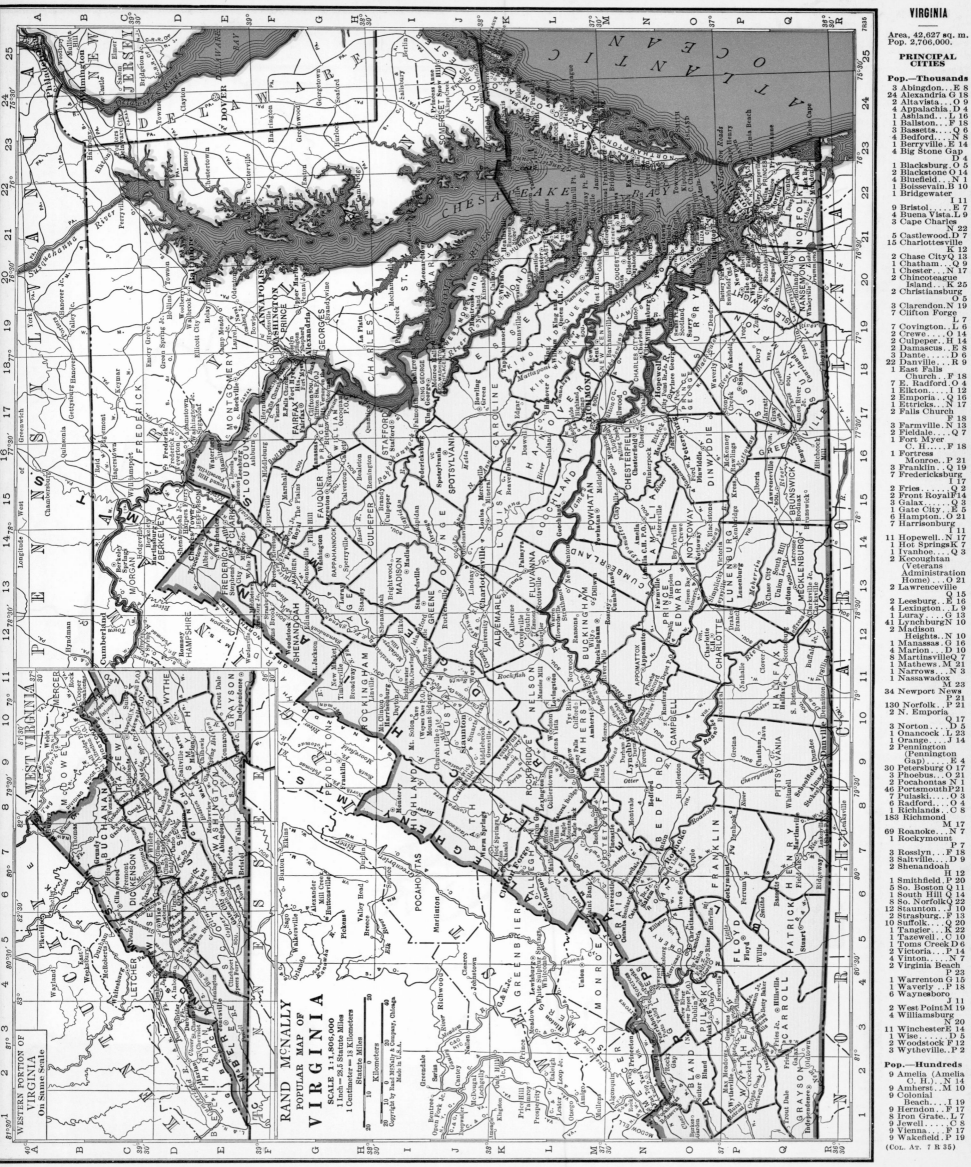

VIRGINIA

Area, 42,627 sq. m.
Pop. 2,706,000.

PRINCIPAL CITIES

Pop.—Thousands

3	Abingdon...	E 8
24	Alexandria	G 18
2	Altavista...	O 9
4	Appalachia.	D 4
4	Ashland...	L 16
1	Ballston...	P 18
3	Bassetts...	Q 6
8	Bedford...	N 8
1	Berryville.	E 14
4	Big Stone Gap	
		D 4
1	Blacksburg.	O 5
2	Blackstone	O 14
4	Bluefield...	N 1
1	Boissevain.	B 10
1	Bridgewater	
		I 11
9	Bristol...	E 7
4	Buena Vista	L 9
3	Cape Charles	
		N 22
5	Castlewood.	D 7
15	Charlottesville	
		K 12
2	Chase City	Q 13
1	Chatham...	Q 9
2	Chester...	N 17
2	Chincoteague	
	Island...	K 25
2	Christiansburg	
		J 5
3	Clarendon.	N 19
7	Clifton Forge	
		L 8
7	Covington.	L 6
2	Crewe...	O 14
2	Culpeper..	H 14
2	Damascus.	E 8
1	Dante...	D 6
22	Danville...	R 9
1	East Falls	
	Church..	F 18
7	E. Radford.	O 4
2	Elkton...	I 12
2	Emporia..	Q 16
1	Ettricks...	N 17
2	Falls Church	
		F 18
3	Farmville..	N 13
1	Fieldale...	Q 7
1	Fort Myer	
	C. H...	F 18
1	Fortress	
	Monroe..	P 21
3	Franklin...	Q 18
7	Fredericksburg	
		H 16
1	Fries...	Q 2
2	Front Royal	F 14
2	Galax...	Q 3
1	Gate City.	E 5
6	Hampton...	P 21
7	Harrisonburg	
		I 11
11	Hopewell..	N 17
3	Hot Springs	K 7
2	Ivanhoe...	Q 3
2	Kecoughtan	
	(Veterans	
	Administration	
	Home)...	O 21
2	Lawrenceville	
		Q 15
2	Leesburg..	E 16
4	Lexington.	L 9
1	Luray...	G 13
41	Lynchburg	N 10
2	Madison	
	Heights..	N 10
9	Manassas	G 16
2	Marion...	D 10
8	Martinsville	Q 7
1	Mathews..	M 21
1	Narrows...	N 3
1	Nassawadox	
		M 23
34	Newport News	
		P 21
130	Norfolk..	P 21
2	N. Emporia.	
		Q 17
3	Norton...	D 5
1	Onancock.	L 23
2	Orange...	J 14
2	Pennington	
	(Pennington	
	Gap)...	E 4
30	Petersburg	O 17
2	Phoebus..	O 21
1	Pocahontas	N 1
46	Portsmouth	P 21
7	Pulaski...	O 3
6	Radford...	O 4
1	Richlands.	C 8
183	Richmond..	
		M 17
69	Roanoke...	N 7
1	Rockymount	
		P 7
3	Rosslyn...	F 18
3	Saltville...	D 9
2	Shenandoah	
		H 12
1	Smithfield.	P 20
11	So. Boston	Q 11
4	South Hill	Q 14
8	So. Norfolk	Q 21
12	Staunton..	J 10
2	Strasburg.	F 13
10	Suffolk...	Q 20
1	Tangier...	K 22
2	Tazewell..	C 10
2	Toms Creek	D 6
2	Victoria...	O 14
1	Vinton...	N 7
2	Virginia Beach	
		P 23
1	Warrenton	G 15
2	Waverly...	P 18
6	Waynesboro	
		J 11
2	West Point	M 19
4	Williamsburg	N 20
11	Winchester	E 14
1	Wise...	D 5
1	Woodstock	F 12
1	Wytheville.	P 2

Pop.—Hundreds

9	Amelia (Amelia	
	C. H.)..	N 14
9	Amherst..	M 10
9	Colonial	
	Beach...	I 19
9	Herndon..	F 17
1	Iron Grate.	L 7
9	Jewell...	N 2
9	Vienna....	F 17
9	Wakefield.	P 19
		(Col. At. 7 R 35)

RAND MCNALLY
POPULAR MAP OF
VIRGINIA

SCALE 1:1,806,000
1 Inch = 28.5 Statute Miles
1 Centimeter = 18 Kilometers

Statute Miles

Kilometers

Copyright by Rand McNally & Company, Chicago
Made in U.S.A.

WESTERN PORTION OF
Virginia
On Same Scale

WASHINGTON

Area, 69,127 sq. m.
Pop. 1,658,000.

PRINCIPAL CITIES

Pop.—Thousands

22 Aberdeen	K 3
7 Anacortes	D 7
1 Arlington	F 9
4 Auburn	J 8
31 Bellingham	C 7
1 Black Diamond	I 9
2 Blaine	B 7
10 Bremerton	H 6
1 Buckley	J 9
1 Burlington	D 8
1 Camas	Q 8
1 Cashmere	I 13
1 Castle Rock	N 6
8 Centralia	L 6
5 Chehalis	L 6
1 Chelan	G 16
1 Cheney	J 22
3 Chewelah	E 23
3 Clarkston	M 24
3 Cle Elum	J 12
3 Colfax	K 24
1 College Place	O 21
2 Colville	D 22
1 Cosmopolis	K 3
1 Davenport	H 21
3 Dayton	N 22
1 Deer Park	F 23
1 Edmonds	G 8
5 Ellensburg	K 14
1 Elma	K 4
2 Enumclaw	J 9
31 Everett	F 8
1 Goldendale	P 13
1 Grandview	N 16
1 Greenacres	H 24
13 Hoquiam	K 3
1 Juanita	H 8
2 Kelso	O 6
2 Kennewick	O 18
2 Kent	J 8
1 Kirkland	H 8
1 Leavenworth	H 13
11 Longview	O 5
1 Lynden	B 7
1 McCleary	J 4
2 Marysville	F 8
2 Medical L.	H 22
3 Monroe	G 9
2 Montesano	K 3
4 Mt. Vernon	E 7
1 Newport	E 24
1 Okanogan	E 17
12 Olympia	K 5
3 Omak	E 17
1 Onalaska	M 7
2 Opportunity	G 24
1 Orting	K 8
1 Palouse	K 25
3 Pasco	N 18
2 Pomeroy	M 23
10 Port Angeles	F 5
4 Port Orchard	I 6
1 Port Townsend	F 6
2 Prosser	O 16
3 Pullman	L 24
7 Puyallup	J 8
1 Raymond	L 4
4 Renton	J 8
1 Ritzville	J 20
2 Roslyn	J 12
366 Seattle	H 8
3 Sedro Woolley	D 8
3 Shelton	J 5
2 Snohomish	G 9
2 South Bend	L 3
116 Spokane	H 23
2 Sumner	J 8
5 Sunnyside	N 15
107 Tacoma	J 7
1 Tekoa	J 24
5 Toppenish	N 14
16 Vancouver	Q 7
16 Walla Walla	O 21
1 Wapato	M 14
1 Washougal	Q 8
12 Wenatchee	I 14
1 Woodland	P 6
22 Yakima	M 14

Pop.—Hundreds

9 Asotin	N 24
8 Bingen-White Salmon	Q 11
8 Bothell	H 8
7 Bucoda	L 6
7 Concrete	D 10
9 Eatonville	K 8
9 Endicott	K 22
3 Ephrata	J 17
8 Ferndale	C 7
5 Friday Hbr.	D 5
7 Garfield	K 24
6 Granger	N 15
7 Harrington	I 20
4 Ilwaco	N 2
6 Ione	C 23
5 Issaquah	H 9
4 Kalama	O 6
5 La Conner	D 7
6 Lind	K 20
6 Lowell	G 8
6 Marcus	C 21
6 Milton	J 8
8 North Bend	I 10
6 Oakesdale	J 23
8 Odessa	I 19
8 Oroville	B 17
9 Pe Ell	M 4
9 Poulsbo	H 7
6 Redmond	H 9
5 Republic	D 19
6 Ridgefield	P 7
6 Ronald	J 12
6 Rosalia	J 23
8 Ruston	J 7
4 Selah	L 14
8 Sequim	F 5
6 Skykomish	G 11
8 Snoqualmie	I 9
5 Sprague	I 21
7 Stanwood	E 8
8 Steilacoom	J 7
9 Sultan	G 10
4 Sumas	B 8
5 Toledo	M 6
5 Tonasket	C 17
4 Tumwater	K 5
6 Union Gap	M 14
9 Waitsburg	N 21
9 Waterville	H 15
5 White Salmon	P 11
7 Wilbur	G 19
9 Winlock	M 5
7 Zillah	M 15

(Col. At. 7 R 35)

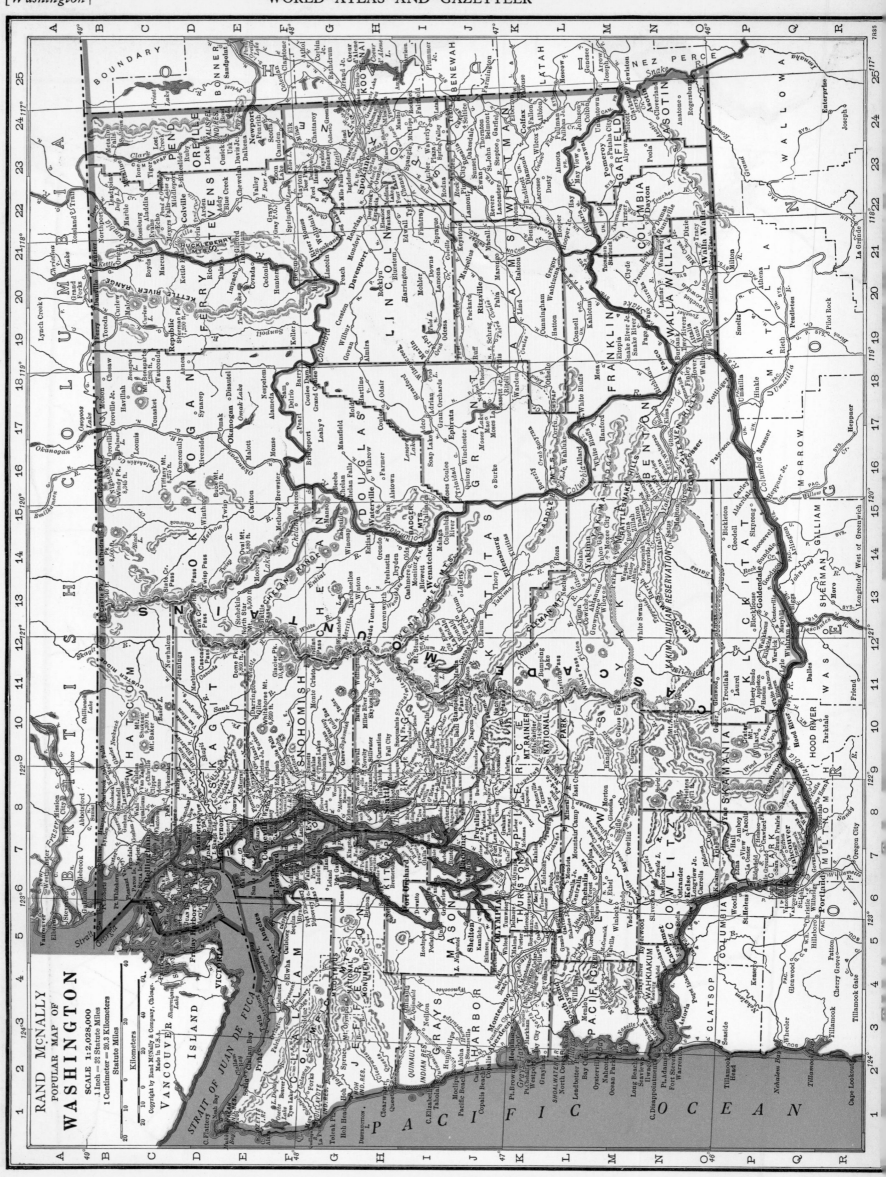

RAND McNALLY
POPULAR MAP OF
WASHINGTON

SCALE 1:2,028,000
1 Inch = 32 Statute Miles
1 Centimeter = 20.3 Kilometers

Copyright by Rand McNally & Company, Chicago.
Made in U.S.A.

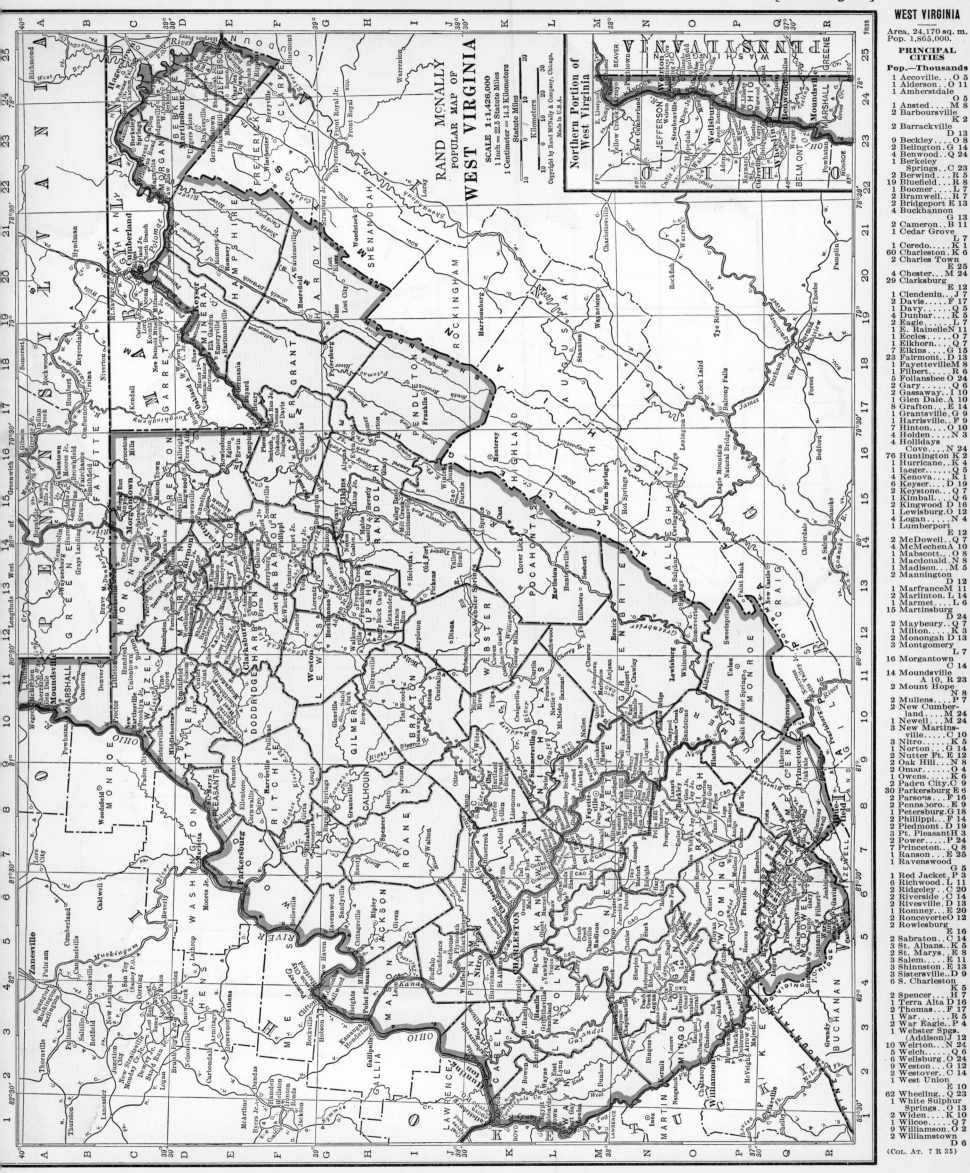

RAND MCNALLY
POPULAR MAP OF
WEST VIRGINIA

SCALE 1:1,426,000
1 Inch = 22.5 Statute Miles
1 Centimeter = 14.3 Kilometers

Copyright by Rand McNally & Company, Chicago.
Made in U.S.A.

Northern Portion of West Virginia

WEST VIRGINIA

Area, 24,170 sq. m.
Pop. 1,865,000.

PRINCIPAL CITIES

Pop.—Thousands

1	Accoville	O 5
1	Alderson	O 11
1	Amherstdale	O 5
1	Ansted	M 8
2	Barboursville	K 2
2	Barrackville	D 13
9	Beckley	O 8
1	Bellington	G 14
4	Benwood	Q 24
1	Berkeley Springs	C 23
2	Berwind	N 3
19	Bluefield	R 8
1	Boomer	L 7
2	Bramwell	R 7
2	Bridgeport	E 13
4	Buckhannon	G 13
2	Cameron	B 11
1	Cedar Grove	
		L 7
1	Ceredo	K 1
60	Charleston	K 6
2	Charles Town	E 25
4	Chester	M 24
29	Clarksburg	E 12
1	Clendenin	J 7
2	Davis	F 17
1	Davy	Q 5
4	Dunbar	K 5
2	Eagle	L 7
1	E. Rainelle	N 11
1	Eccles	O 7
1	Elkhorn	Q 5
7	Elkins	G 15
23	Fairmont	D 13
1	Fayetteville	M 8
1	Filbert	R 6
5	Follansbee	O 24
1	Gary	Q 6
1	Gassaway	I 10
1	Glen Dale	A 10
8	Grafton	E 14
1	Grantsville	G 9
1	Harrisville	F 9
1	Hinton	O 10
1	Holden	N 3
1	Hollidays Cove	N 24
76	Huntington	K 2
1	Hurricane	K 4
1	Iaeger	Q 5
1	Kenova	K 1
1	Keyser	D 19
2	Keystone	Q 7
1	Kimball	Q 7
1	Kingwood	D 16
1	Lewisburg	O 12
1	Logan	N 4
1	Lumberport	E 12
2	McDowell	Q 7
4	McMechen	A 10
1	Mabscott	O 8
1	Macdonald	S 8
1	Madison	M 5
1	Mannington	D 12
1	Marfrance	M 11
1	Marlinton	L 14
1	Marmet	L 6
15	Martinsburg	D 24
2	Maybeury	Q 7
1	Milton	K 3
2	Monongah	D 13
3	Montgomery	L 7
16	Morgantown	C 14
14	Moundsville	A 10, R 23
2	Mount Hope	N 8
2	Mullens	P 7
2	New Cumberland	M 24
1	Newell	M 24
3	New Martinsville	C 10
3	Nitro	K 5
1	Norton	G 14
1	Nutter Ft.	E 12
1	Oak Hill	N 8
2	Omar	O 4
2	Owens	K 6
2	Paden City	C 9
30	Parkersburg	E 6
1	Parsons	F 16
2	Pennsboro	E 9
1	Petersburg	G 18
1	Phillippi	F 14
2	Piedmont	D 19
3	Pt. Pleasant	H 3
2	Power	P 24
7	Princeton	Q 8
1	Ranson	E 25
1	Ravenswood	G 5
1	Red Jacket	P 3
6	Richwood	L 11
2	Ridgeley	C 20
2	Riverside	C 14
3	Rivesville	D 13
1	Romney	E 20
1	Ronceverte	O 12
1	Rowlesburg	E 16
2	Sabraton	C 14
3	St. Albans	K 5
2	St. Marys	E 8
3	Salem	E 11
3	Shinnston	E 13
1	Sistersville	D 9
6	S. Charleston	K 5
2	Spencer	H 7
1	Terra Alta	D 16
3	Thomas	F 17
1	War	R 5
2	War Eagle	P 4
1	Webster Spgs. (Addison)	J 12
10	Weirton	N 24
2	Welch	N 6
6	Wellsburg	O 24
9	Weston	G 12
2	Westover	C 14
1	West Union	E 10
62	Wheeling	Q 23
1	White Sulphur Springs	O 13
2	Widen	K 10
1	Wilcoe	Q 7
1	Williamson	O 2
2	Williamstown	D 6

(Col. At. 7 R 35)

RAND McNALLY
POPULAR MAP OF
WISCONSIN

SCALE 1:2,154,000
1 Inch = 34 Statute Miles
1 Centimeter = 21.5 Kilometers
Statute Miles

Copyright by Rand McNally & Company, Chicago.
Made in U.S.A.

7R35

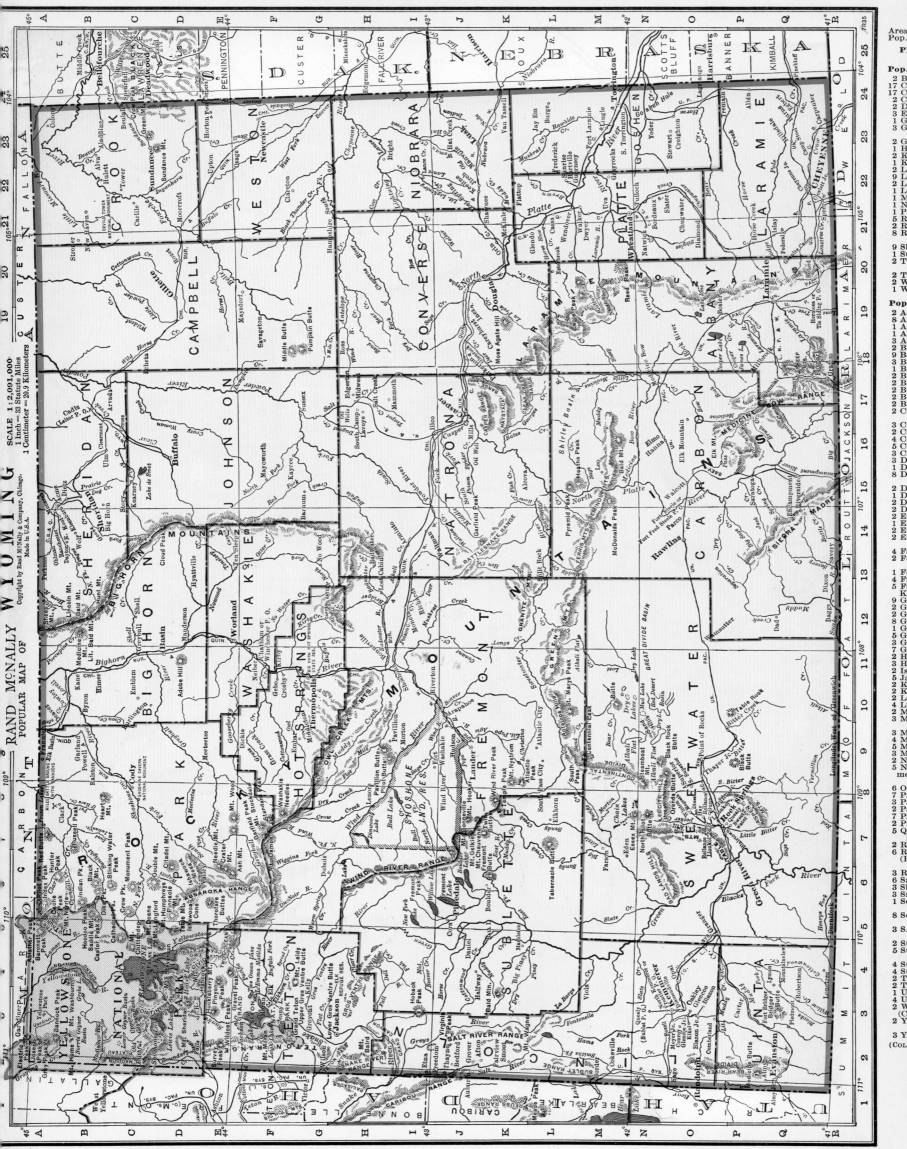

RAND McNALLY **WYOMING**
SCALE 1 : 2,091,000
1 Inch = 33 Statute Miles
1 Centimeter = 20.9 Kilometers
POPULAR MAP OF
Copyright by Rand McNally & Company, Chicago.
Made in U.S.A.

WYOMING

Area, 97,914 sq. m.
Pop. 235,000

PRINCIPAL CITIES

Pop.—Thousands

2 Buffalo...	D 16
17 Casper...	J 17
17 Cheyenne.	R 22
2 Cody...	C 8
2 Douglas...	K 19
1 Evanston..	Q 2
1 Gillette...	D 20
3 Green River	
	P 6
2 Greybull...	C 12
1 Hanna...	N 14
2 Kemmerer..	N 4
1 Kleenburn.B	14
2 Lander...	J 9
9 Laramie...	Q 20
2 Lovell...	A 11
1 Lusk...	J 23
1 Midwest...	H 17
1 Newcastle.	F 23
1 Powell...	B 9
5 Rawlins...	N 14
2 Riverton...	I 11
2 Rock Springs	
	P 8
9 Sheridan...	B 14
1 Superior...	O 8
2 Thermopolis	
	G 10
2 Torrington N	23
2 Wheatland N	21
1 Worland...	E 12

Pop.—Hundreds

2 Acme...	A 15
8 Afton...	J 2
1 Aladdin...	B 23
3 Arvada...	B 17
3 Auburn...	J 1
5 Baggs...	R 12
2 Basin...	D 12
3 Bedford...	J 2
1 Big Horn..B	14
2 Big Piney..	K 4
2 Blazon...	O 3
1 Burlington C	10
3 Burns...	Q 24
2 Byron...	B 10
2 Chatham (Winchester).F	11
3 Chugwater O	21
6 Clearmont.B	16
5 Cokeville..	M 2
2 Cowley...	A 10
3 Crosby...	F 10
5 Dayton...	B 14
2 Deaver...	A 10
8 Diamondville	
	O 3
2 Dines...	O 8
1 Dixon...	R 13
3 Dubois...	F 6
2 Du Noir...	F 6
2 Eden...	N 7
1 Elk Basin..	A 9
2 Emblem...	C 11
2 Encampment	
	Q 15
4 Fairview...	K 2
2 Fort Laramie	
	M 23
1 Foxpark...	R 18
1 Freedom...	I 2
5 Frontier (North Kemmerer)	N 3
2 Gebo...	F 10
2 Glencoe...	O 3
3 Glendo...	K 21
5 Glenrock...	J 18
1 Granger...	O 5
5 Grass Creek F	9
3 Grover...	J 2
2 Guernsey.M	22
3 Hartville..L	22
3 Hudson...	J 9
2 Ishawooa...	D 7
5 Jackson...	G 3
2 Kaycee...	F 15
3 Kirby...	F 11
3 Lagrange..	Q 24
2 Lingle...	M 23
2 Manville...	J 23
3 Medicine Bow	
	N 18
3 Meeteetse.	B 9
3 Mills...	J 16
5 Monarch...	A 15
2 Moorcroft.D	21
2 Node...	K 23
5 North Kemmerer (Frontier)	N 3
6 Oakley...	O 10
3 Parco...	O 14
3 Parkman...	A 15
2 Pavillion...	I 10
5 Pine Bluffs Q	25
1 Pinedale...	J 6
5 Quealy (Sublet)...	N 3
4 Ranchester A	14
5 Reliance (Reliance Mine)	
	O 7
3 Rock River O	18
6 Saratoga...	P 15
3 Shoshoni..	I 11
3 Smoot...	K 2
1 South Camp	
	H 17
8 South Superior	
	O 9
3 S. Torrington	
	M 24
2 Story...	C 15
2 Sublet (Quealy)..	N 3
4 Sundance..C	22
2 Sunrise....L	22
2 Ten Sleep.	E 14
2 Thayne...	J 2
1 Tim...B	16
1 Upton...	E 22
2 Winchester (Chatham).F	11
2 Yellowstone Pk.	
	A 2
3 Yoder...	N 23
(COL. AT. 7 R 35)	

ALASKA

Area, 586,400 sq.m.
Pop........75,000

PRINCIPAL CITIES

(Including Figures
from Latest Population Estimates)

Pop.—Thousands

2 Anchorage L 13
1 Cordova....L 5
2 Fairbanks. H 14
1 Juneau....N 22
4 Ketchikan..P 25
1 Nome......G 6
1 Petersburg O 23
1 Sitka.....O 22
1 Wrangell..O 24

Pop.—Hundreds

3 Afognak...O 12
2 Akiak.....K 7
1 Alitak....P 10
3 Angoon...O 22
2 Anvik.....J 8
3 Barrow...A 11
3 Bayview...P 24
1 Belkofsky..R 5
2 Bethel....L 7
3 Brook....G 13
1 Candle.....F 8
1 Chatanika G 14
1 Chichagof..O 21
5 Chignik...Q 8
1 Chitina...K 16
2 Craig....Q 23
2 Deering...F 7
2 Douglas. N 22
3 Ester....H 14
2 Eyak.....L 15
2 Flat......J 9
3 Ft. Yukon. F 15
3 Golovin...G 7
1 Haines...M 21
1 Haycook...G 8
3 Holy Cross J 8
3 Hoonah...N 21
3 Hydaburg Q 24
3 Hyder....P 25
1 Igloo.....G 6
4 Kake.....O 23
4 Kanatak...P 9
1 Karluk...P 10
1 Kassan...P 24
2 Kenai....L 12
2 Kennecott K 17
1 Kiana.....E 8
1 Klukwan. M 21
2 Kodiak...O 12
1 Kotzebue..E 7
1 Koyukuk .G 10
1 Latouche. M 14
1 McCarty..K 17
2 Metlakatla Q 25
2 Naknek...N 9
3 Nenana...H 13
2 Noatak...D 7
2 Noorvik...E 8
1 Nulato...H 9
1 Pilot Sta...O 8
1 Quinhagak M 7
2 Rampart..G 13
1 Ruby.....H 10
1 St. Michael I 7
2 Saxman...Q 25
2 Selawik...E 9
4 Seldovia..N 12
8 Seward...M 13
1 Shageluk..J 8
2 Shishmaref. E 6
2 Shungnak. E 10
5 Skagway..M 21
2 Stevens...H 13
1 Takotna..I 10
2 Tanana..G 12
1 Tanana Crossing......I 16
1 Tatitlek..L 15
2 Tenakee..N 22
3 Thane...N 22
1 Tigara....C 6
2 Togiak...N 7
3 Unalakleet. H 8
2 Unalaska..R 2
1 Unga....R 7
4 Valdez...L 15
1 Wainwright A 9
2 Wales....F 5
1 Wasilla..K 13
2 White Mountain ....G 7
1 Wiseman..D 13
3 Yakutat..M 19

(Col. At. 11 R 33)

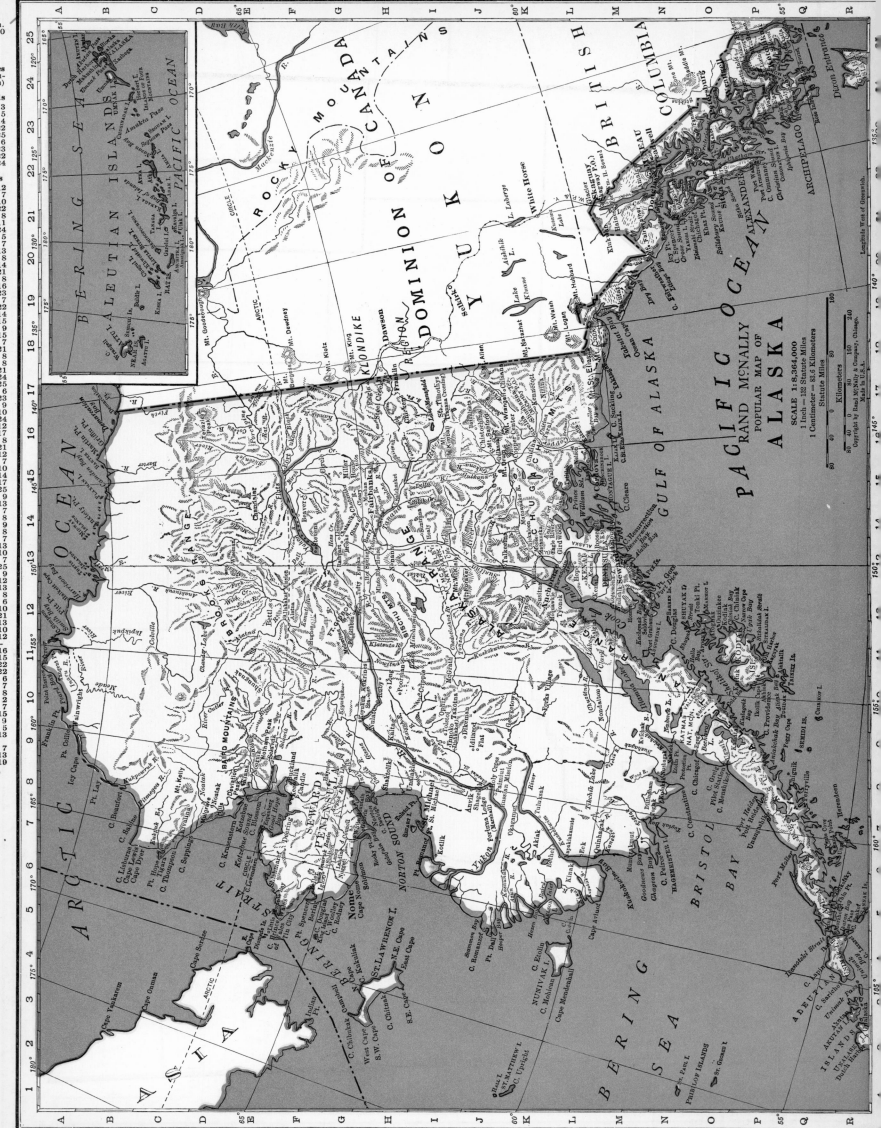

PACIFIC OCEAN

RAND McNALLY
POPULAR MAP OF
ALASKA

SCALE 1:8,364,000
1 Inch = 132 Statute Miles
1 Centimeter = 83.6 Kilometers
Copyright by Rand McNally & Company, Chicago.
Made in U.S.A.

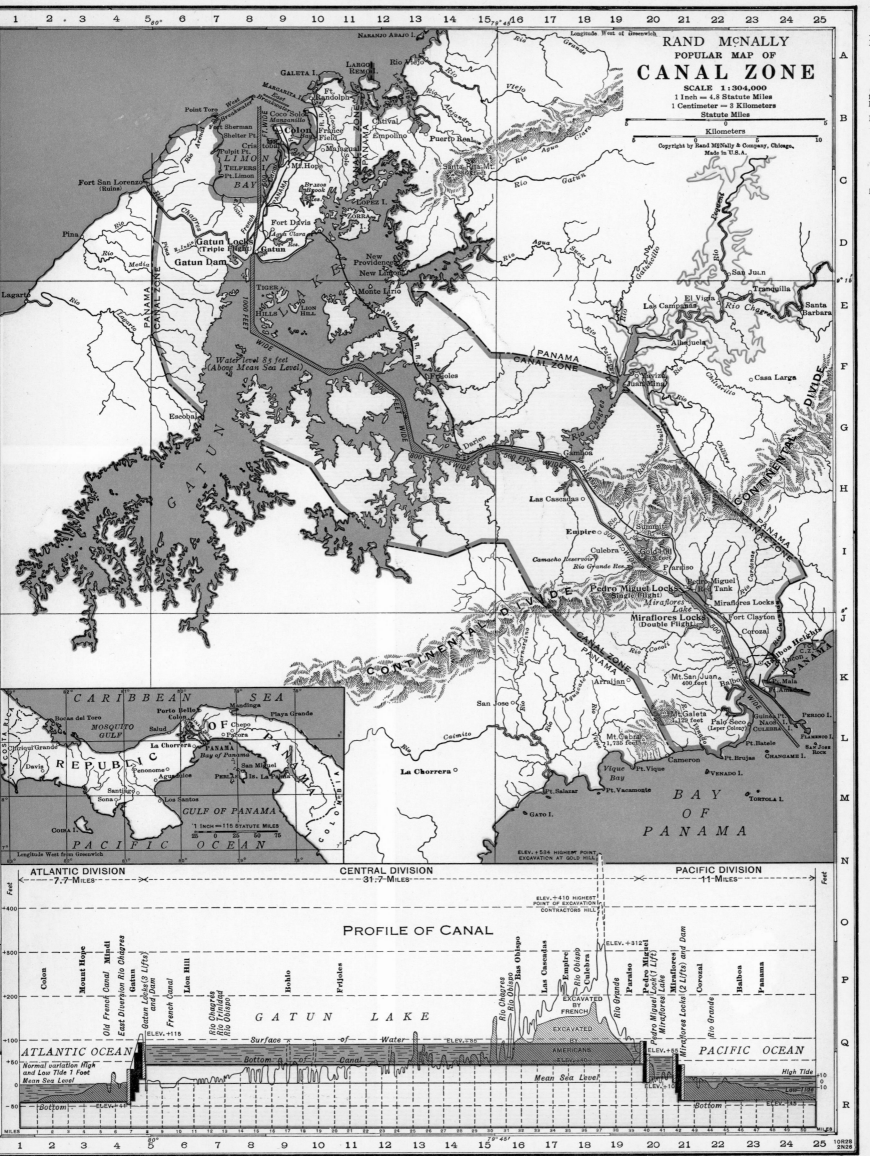

RAND McNALLY
POPULAR MAP OF
CANAL ZONE
SCALE 1:304,000
1 Inch = 4.8 Statute Miles
1 Centimeter = 3 Kilometers
Statute Miles

Copyright by Rand McNally & Company, Chicago.
Made in U.S.A.

PROFILE OF CANAL

ATLANTIC DIVISION
7.7 Miles

CENTRAL DIVISION
31.7 Miles

PACIFIC DIVISION
11 Miles

CANAL ZONE

Area...554 sq. m.
Pop........29,636

PRINCIPAL CITIES

(Including Figures
from Latest Popu-
lation Estimates)

Pop.—Thousands

1 Ancon....K 24
3 Balboa....K 23
1 Fort Amador....K 23
2 Fort Clayton....J 22
1 Paraiso....I 20
2 Red Tank.J 21

Pop.—Hundreds

7 Balboa Heights....K 23
6 Cristobal...B-9
Darien.....G 14
6 Empire....I 18
1 Frijoles....F 13
3 Gamboa..G 17
5 Gatun.....D 8
Las Cascades....H 18
1 Miraflores Locks..J 22
7 Pedro Miguel....I 21
1 Summit...I 20
(COL. AT. **10 R 28**)

HAWAII

Area..6,407 sq. m.
Pop. est...384,437

**PRINCIPAL
CITIES**

(Including Figures
from Latest Popu-
lation Estimates)

Pop.—Thousands

3 Aiea	F 11
5 Ewa	F 11
2 Haiku	H 18
1 Hanapepe	C 4
5 Hawi	K 20
19 Hilo	M 23
1 Honokaa	L 22
137 Honolulu	F 11
2 Honomu	L 23
2 Kahuku	D 11
2 Kakului	H 17
1 Kilauea	B 5
2 Koloa	C-5
2 Lahaina	H 17
1 Paauilo	L 22
1 Pearl City	E 11
1 Puunene	H 18
4 Schofield Barracks	E 10
3 Wahiawa	E 11
5 Waialua	E 10
1 Waianae	E 10
7 Wailuku	H 17
2 Waimea	C 4
6 Waipahu	F 11

Pop.—Hundreds

1 Anahola	B 5
2 Eleele	C 4
5 Hakalau	L 23
1 Halawa	K 20
3 Haleiwa	E 10
3 Hana	H 20
1 Hanalei	B 4
1 Hanamaulu	C 5
1 Hauula	E 11
1 Holualoa	N 20
1 Honouliuli	F 11
2 Hookena	O 20
1 Hoopuloa	O 20
2 Kaanapali	H 16
4 Kailua	M 20
2 Kalaheo	C 4
6 Kalapana	O 24
1 Kamuela	L 21
3 Kapaa	B 5
3 Kapoho	N 25
2 Kaunakakai	G 15
1 Kaupo	I 19
1 Kawaihae	L 20
4 Kealakekua	N 20
1 Kealia	B 5
1 Keanae	H 19
1 Keei	N 20
1 Kekaha	C 4
8 Keokea	H 17
7 Keokea	K 20
2 Kohala	L 22
1 Kukaiau	K 21
1 Kukuihaele	
5 Kurtistown	N 24
4 Laupahoehoe	L 23
4 Lihue	C 5
5 Makawao	H 18
9 Makaweli	C 4
1 Mana	C 3
2 Maunawai	D 10
1 Mokuleia	E 10
1 Mountainview	N 23
1 Naalehu	P 21
2 Napoopoo	N 20
2 Nawiliwili	C 5
4 Ninole	L 23
1 Niulii	K 21
6 Olaa	M 24
5 Paauhau	K 22
3 Pahala	O 22
2 Pahoa	N 24
3 Paia	H 18
1 Pakala	C 4
1 Papaaloa	L 23
5 Papaikou	M 23
6 Pauwela	H 18
3 Peahi	H 18
5 Pepeekeo	M 23
1 Pukoo	G 16
1 Waiakoa	H 18
1 Waihee	H 17
1 Waikane	E 11
7 Waimanalo	F 12
1 Wainiha	B 4
1 Waiohinu	P 21
1 Watertown	F 11

(COL. AT. 11 R 33)

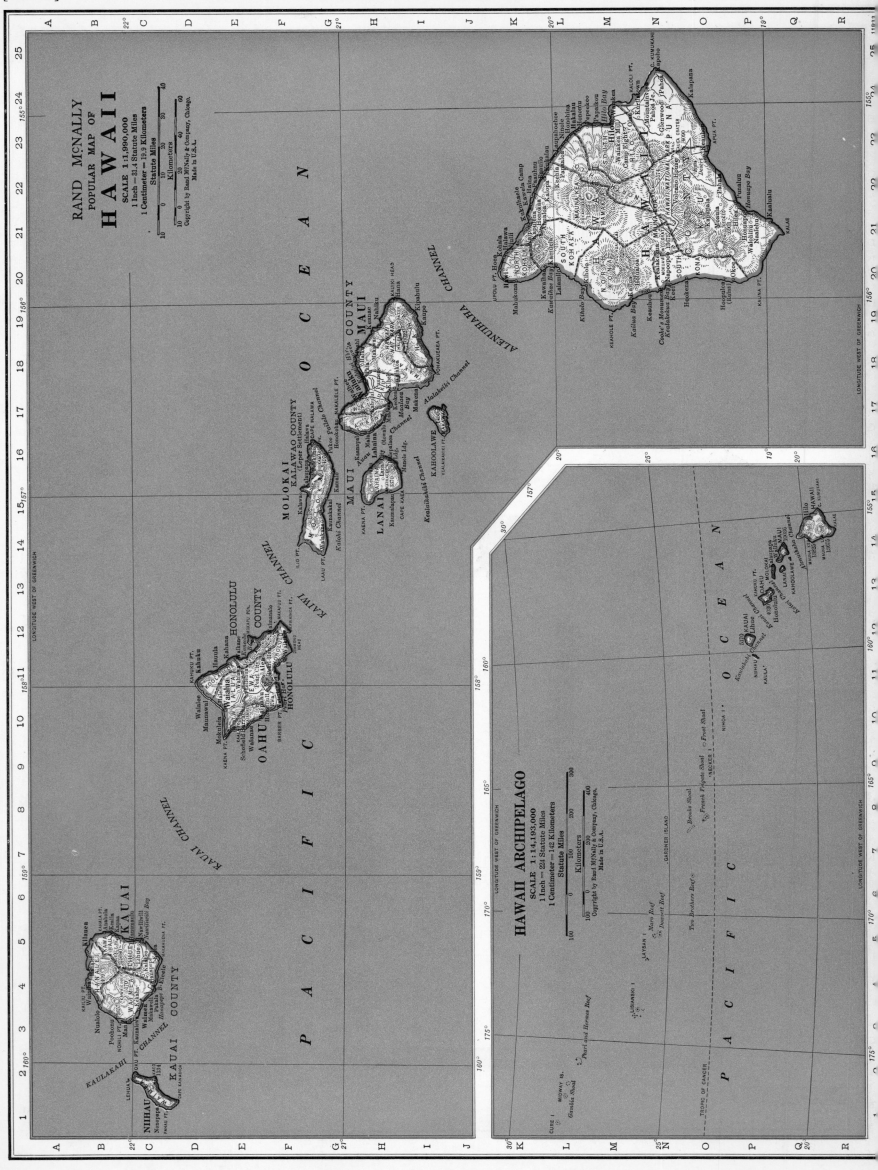

RAND McNALLY
POPULAR MAP OF
HAWAII

SCALE 1:1,990,000
1 Inch = 31.4 Statute Miles
1 Centimeter = 19.9 Kilometers

Copyright by Rand McNally & Company, Chicago.
Made in U.S.A.

HAWAII ARCHIPELAGO

SCALE 1:14,193,000
1 Inch = 224 Statute Miles
1 Centimeter = 142 Kilometers

Copyright by Rand McNally & Company, Chicago.
Made in U.S.A.

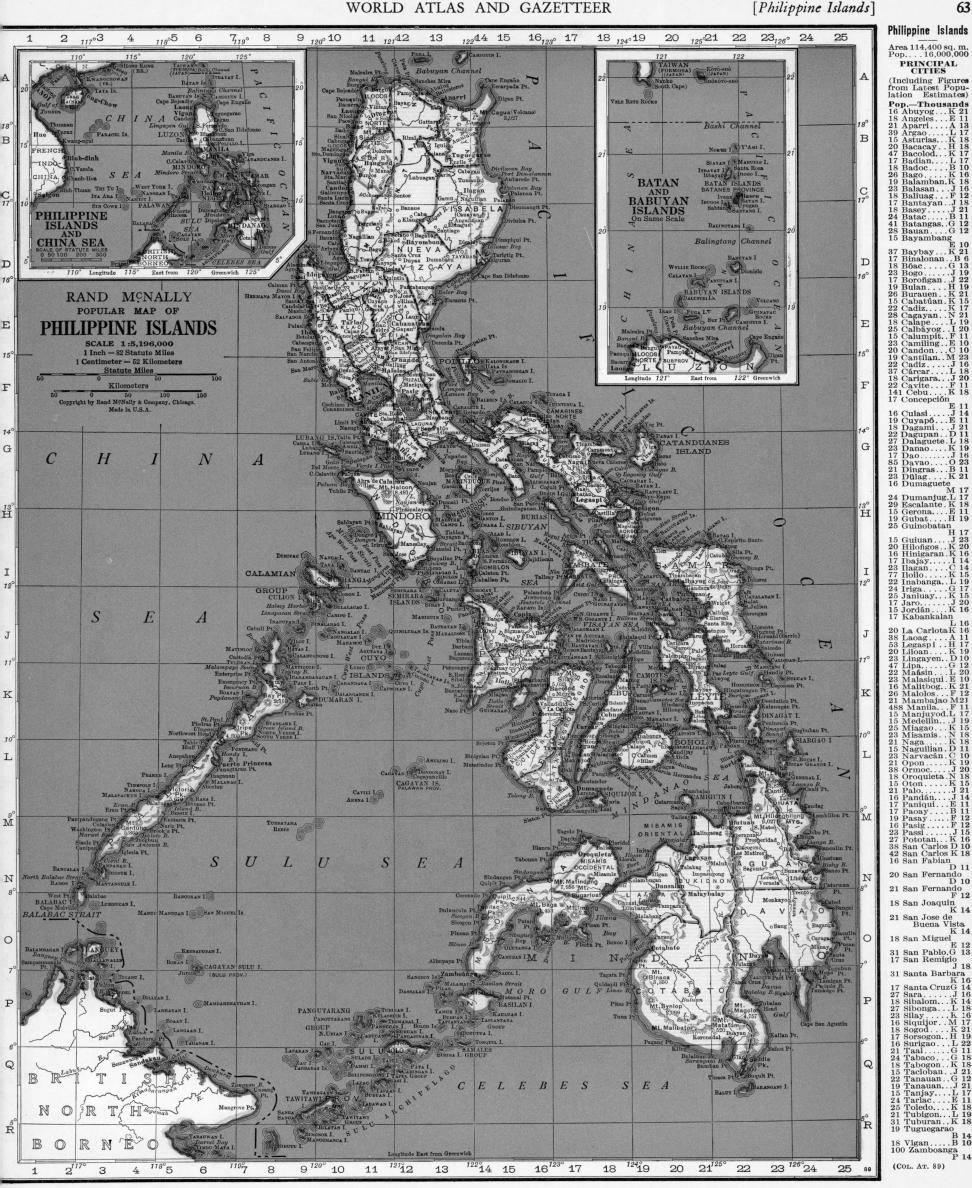

RAND McNALLY
POPULAR MAP OF
PHILIPPINE ISLANDS

SCALE 1:5,196,000
1 Inch = 82 Statute Miles
1 Centimeter = 52 Kilometers

Statute Miles

Kilometers

Copyright by Rand McNally & Company, Chicago.
Made in U.S.A.

BATAN
AND
BABUYAN
ISLANDS
On Same Scale

Philippine Islands

Area 114,400 sq. m.
Pop.... 16,000,000

**PRINCIPAL
CITIES**
(Including Figures
from Latest Popu-
lation Estimates)

Pop.—Thousands

16	Abuyog.......	K 21
18	Angeles......	E 11
21	Aparri.......	A 13
39	Argao........	L 17
15	Asturias.....	K 18
20	Bacacay......	H 18
47	Bacolod......	K 17
17	Badian.......	L 17
18	Badoc........	B 10
25	Bago.........	K 16
19	Balamban.....	K 18
23	Balasan......	J 16
18	Baliuag......	F 12
18	Bantayan.....	J 18
18	Basey........	J 21
24	Batac........	B 10
41	Batangas.....	G 12
18	Bauan........	G 12
15	Bayambang....	
		E 10
37	Baybay.......	K 21
17	Binalonan....	B 6
15	Böac........	G 13
23	Bogo........	J 18
17	Borongan.....	J 22
19	Bulan.......	H 19
26	Burauen.....	K 21
15	Cabatuan....	K 15
22	Cadiz........	J 17
28	Cagayan.....	N 21
19	Calape......	L 19
25	Calbáyog....	J 20
15	Calumpit....	F 11
23	Camiling....	E 11
20	Candon......	C 10
22	Cantilan....	M 23
22	Cadiz........	J 16
37	Cárcar......	L 18
18	Carigara....	J 20
22	Cavite......	F 11
141	Cebu........	K 18
17	Concepción...	
		E 10
16	Culasi......	J 14
19	Cuyapó......	E 11
18	Dagami......	J 21
22	Dagupan.....	D 11
27	Dalaguete...	L 18
23	Danao.......	K 19
17	Dao.........	J 16
85	Davao.......	O 23
21	Dingras.....	B 11
23	Dúlag.......	K 21
16	Dumaguete...	
		M 17
24	Dumanjug....	L 17
29	Escalante...	K 18
15	Gerona......	E 11
19	Gubat.......	H 19
25	Guinobatan..	
		H 17
15	Guiuan......	J 23
20	Hilongos....	K 20
16	Hinigaran...	K 16
17	Ibajay......	J 15
23	Ilagan.....	C 14
77	Iloilo......	K 15
22	Inabanga....	L 19
21	Iriga.......	G 17
25	Januiay.....	K 15
17	Jaro........	J 20
15	Jordán......	K 16
17	Kabankalan..	
		L 16
20	La Carlota..	K 16
38	Laoag......	A 11
53	Legaspi.....	H 17
19	Liloan.....	K 19
23	Lingayen....	D 10
47	Lipa........	G 12
22	Maasin.....	L 20
23	Malasiqui...	E 10
26	Malitbog...	K 21
26	Malolos.....	F 12
21	Manbajao....	M 21
488	Manila.....	F 11
15	Manjuyod....	L 17
16	Medellin...	J 18
23	Miagao.....	K 15
23	Misamis....	N 18
21	Naga.......	K 18
18	Naguilian..	D 11
21	Narvacán...	C 10
21	Opon.......	K 19
38	Ormoc......	K 20
18	Oroquieta..	N 18
15	Oton.......	K 15
21	Palo.......	J 21
16	Pandán.....	J 14
17	Paniqui....	E 11
17	Pacay......	K 18
19	Pasay......	F 12
16	Pasig......	F 12
23	Passi......	J 15
22	Pototan....	K 16
38	San Carlos	D 10
42	San Carlos	K 18
16	San Fabian	
		D 11
20	San Fernando	
		D 10
21	San Fernando	
		F 12
18	San Joaquin	
		K 14
21	San Jose de	
	Buena Vista	
		K 14
18	San Miguel	
		E 12
31	San Pablo.	G 13
17	San Remigio	
		J 18
31	Santa Barbara	
		K 16
17	Santa Cruz	K 14
25	Sara.......	K 16
17	Sibalom....	J 14
27	Sibonga....	L 18
23	Silay......	K 17
16	Siquijor..	M 17
18	Sogod......	K 21
17	Sorsogon..	H 19
16	Surigao...	L 22
21	Taal.......	G 11
18	Tabaco....	G 18
18	Tabogon...	K 18
15	Tacloban..	J 21
28	Tanauan...	J 21
22	Tanauan...	J 21
19	Tanjay....	M 17
24	Tarlac....	E 11
25	Toledo....	K 18
15	Tubigon...	L 19
25	Tuburan...	K 18
19	Tuguegarao	
		B 14
18	Vigan.....	B 10
100	Zamboanga	
		P 14

(COL. AT. 89)

PUERTO RICO

Area, 3,435 sq. mi.
Pop.....1,723,534

PRINCIPAL CITIES

(Including Figures
from Latest Popu-
lation Estimates)

Pop.—Thousands

3	Adjuntas..	F 7
2	Aguada....	C 2
11	Aguadilla ..	C 2
3	Aguas Buenas	
		E 15
4	Aibonito..	F 13
3	Anasco	E 3
14	Arecibo....	B 7
4	Arroyo....	I 15
2	Barceloneta	
		B 10
2	Barranquitas	
		F 13
14	Bayamon .	C 14
5	Cabo Rojo..	G 2
23	Caguas ...	E 16
2	Canuy...	B 6
5	Carolina .	C 17
7	Catano...	B 14
6	Cayey....	G 14
2	Ceiba....	G 20
3	Ciales...	D 11
2	Cidra....	F 14
8	Coamo ...	G 12
2	Comerio..	E 14
2	Corozal..	D 12
2	Dorado...	B 13
7	Fajardo ..	D 20
3	Guanica...	H 6
16	Guayama.	H 14
2	Guayanilla	H 7
1	Guaynabo..	D 13
3	Gurabo...	E 16
2	Hatillo...	B 7
2	Hormigueros	
		F 3
8	Humacao .	F 18
3	Isabela ...	B 4
6	Jayuya...	E 9
3	Juana Diaz	
		G 10
6	Juncos....	E 17
5	Lajas....	G 3
3	Lares....	D 6
2	Las Marias..	E 5
2	Las Piedras	
		F 18
2	Luquillo .	C 20
8	Manati ..	B 10
1	Maricao ..	F 5
1	Maunabo..	H 18
45	Mayaguez.	F 3
3	Moca....	C 3
2	Morovis .	D 11
4	Naguabo..	D 19
2	Naranjito..	E 13
2	Patillas...	H 16
1	Penuelas..	G 8
60	Ponce.....	H 9
2	Quebradillas	
		C 18
2	Rincon....	D 1
2	Rio Grande	
17	Rio Piedras.	C 16
4	Sabana Grande	
		G 5
3	Salinas...	G 12
6	San German	
		G 4
137	San Juan.	B 15
5	San Lorenzo	
		F 17
4	San Sebastian	
		D 5
2	Santa Isabel	
		H 11
1	Toa Alta..	C 13
2	Toa Baja..	B 13
1	Trujillo Alto	
		C 10
6	Utuado ...	E 8
3	Vega Alta.	C 12
5	Vega Baja.	C 11
4	Vieques...	F 23
4	Villalba ..	F 10
4	Yabucoa..	G 17
9	Yauco.....	G 6

VIRGIN ISLANDS

Area...133 sq. mi.
Pop........22,012

PRINCIPAL CITIES

(Including Figures
from Latest Popu-
lation Estimates)

Pop.—Thousands

4	Christiansted	
		Q 22
3	Frederiksted	
		R 20
7	Charlotte	
	Amalie (St.	
	Thomas)	J 20

(COL. AT. 7890)

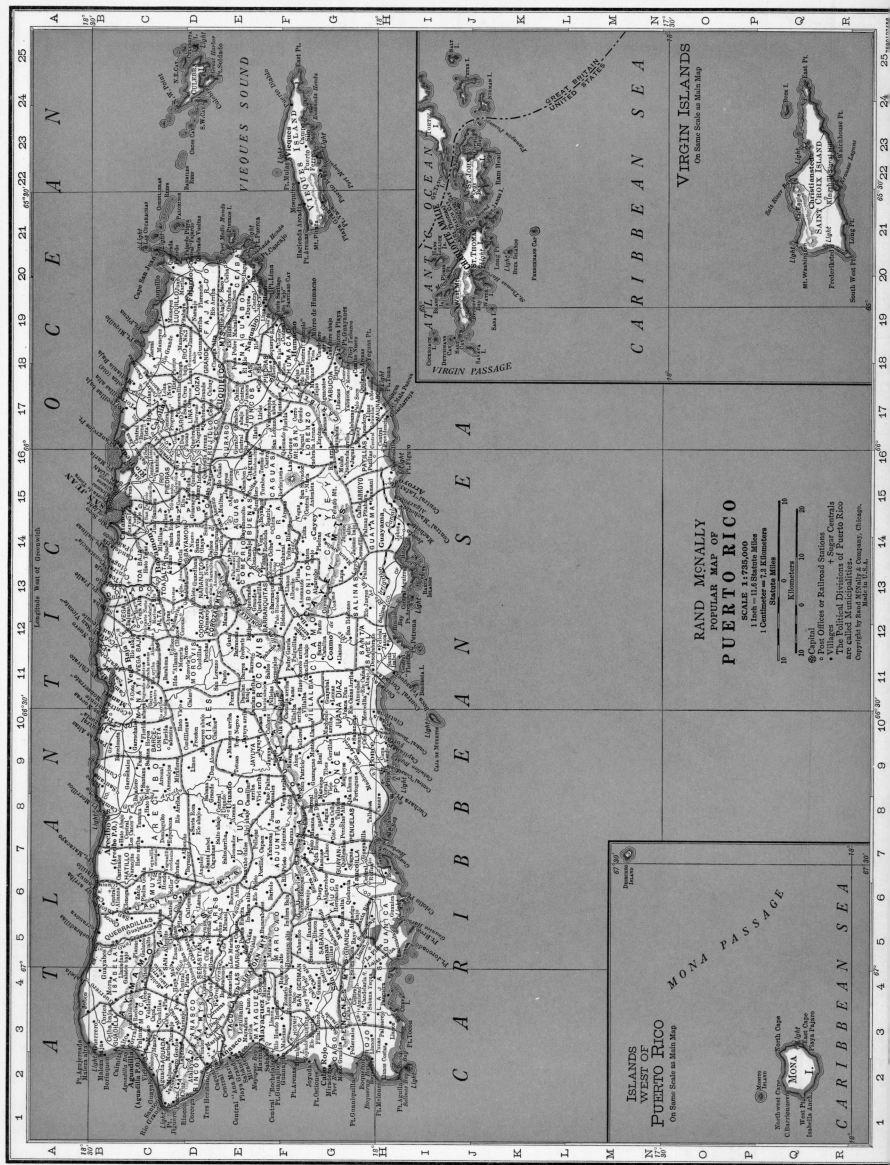

RAND McNALLY
POPULAR MAP OF
PUERTO RICO

SCALE 1:735,000
1 Inch = 11.6 Statute Miles
1 Centimeter = 7.3 Kilometers

The Political Divisions of Puerto Rico
are called Municipalities.

Copyright by Rand McNally & Company, Chicago.
Made in U.S.A.

VIRGIN ISLANDS
On Same Scale as Main Map

ISLANDS
WEST OF
PUERTO RICO
On Same Scale as Main Map

RAND MCNALLY
POPULAR MAP OF
DOMINION OF CANADA
AND
NEWFOUNDLAND

SCALE 1:18,058,000
1 Inch = 285 Statute Miles
1 Centimeter = 181 Miles

Copyright by Rand McNally & Company, Chicago.
Made in U.S.A.

DOMINION OF CANADA

Ar.3,694,863 sq. m.
Pop.....11,120,000

PRINCIPAL CITIES
(Including Figures from Latest Population Estimates)

Pop.—Thousands

7	Amherst...N 22
1	Assiniboia..O 9
14	Belleville..P 19
1	Battleford.M 8
16	Brandon...O 11
10	Brockville.P 19
5	Buckingham O 19
83	Calgary....N 6
7	Campbelltown M 21
2	Cardston...O 6
1	Carman...O 11
12	Charlottetown M 23
15	Chatham..R 17
4	Chatham..M 22
12	Chicoutimi M 20
4	Cochrane..N 17
2	Cumberland M 3
4	Dauphin..N 11
1	Dawson....E 2
4	East AngusO 20
86	Edmonton..L 7
3	Estevan..O 10
3	Fernie.....N 6
26	Ft. William O 14
9	Fredericton N 22
21	Guelph....Q 17
59	Halifax...N 23
156	Hamilton Q 18
1	Hanna....M 7
29	Hull.....O 19
2	Humbolt..M 9
7	Kenora...O 12
23	Kingston..P 19
2	La Malbaie N 20
8	La Tuque..N 20
14	Lethbridge.N 7
12	Levis.....O 20
3	Liverpool..O 23
71	London...Q 17
1	Macleod...O 6
10	Medicine Hat N 7
4	Megantic..O 20
4	Melville...N 10
1	Merritt....N 4
21	Moncton..N 22
2	Mont Laurier O 19
819	Montreal.O 19
20	Moose Jaw.N 9
7	Nanaimo...N 5
6	Nelson....N 5
3	Newcastle.M 22
18	New West- minster...N 3
19	Niagara Falls Q 18
5	North Battle- ford....M 8
16	North Bay O 17
9	North Van- couver...M 4
127	Ottawa...O 19
13	Owen Sound P 17
9	Pembroke..O 18
22	Peterboro..P 18
2	Portage la Prairie..N 11
20	Port Arthur O 14
11	Pr. Albert..M 9
6	Pr. Rupert..K 2
131	Quebec....N 20
2	Red Deer..M 6
53	Regina....N 9
5	Revelstoke.M 5
8	Riviere du Loup...M 20
48	Saint John N 22
42	Saskatoon..M 8
23	Sault Ste. Marie..P 16
15	Shawinigan Falls....O 20
29	Sherbrooke O 20
10	Sorel.....O 20
2	Souris....O 10
1	Stettler...M 7
19	Sudbury...O 17
2	Sussex....N 22
5	Swift Current N 8
23	Sydney...N 23
3	The Pas...M 10
631	Toronto..Q 18
1	Trail.....N 5
8	Truro....N 23
247	Vancouver N 3
2	Vegreville..L 7
39	Victoria...N 3
2	Wetaskiwin M 7
63	Weyburn..O 9
63	Windsor...R 17
216	Winnipeg.O 11
11	WoodstockN 21
7	Yarmouth..O 22
3	Yorkton...N 10

NEWFOUNDLAND AND LABRADOR

Area 155,134 sq. m.
Pop.......293,216

PRINCIPAL CITIES

Pop.—Thousands
(Including Figures from Latest Population Estimates)

4	Bonavista.J 25
4	Carbonear.K 25
2	Harbor Grace K 25
1	St. GeorgesL 23
40	St. John's.K 25
3	Twillingate J 24

(COL. AT. 6789)

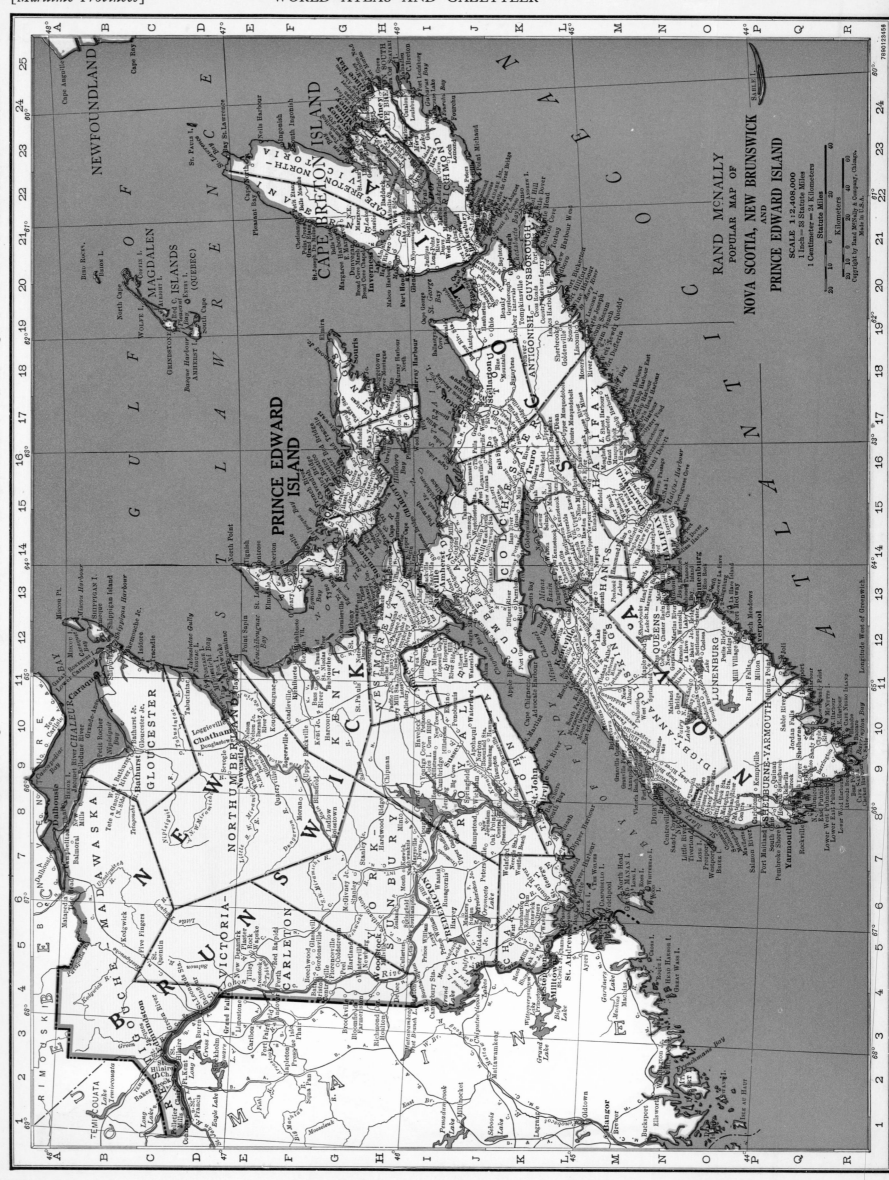

RAND McNALLY
POPULAR MAP OF
NOVA SCOTIA, NEW BRUNSWICK
AND
PRINCE EDWARD ISLAND

SCALE 1:2,408,000
1 Inch = 38 Statute Miles
1 Centimeter = 24 Kilometers

Statute Miles

Kilometers

Copyright by Rand McNally & Company, Chicago.
Made in U.S.A.

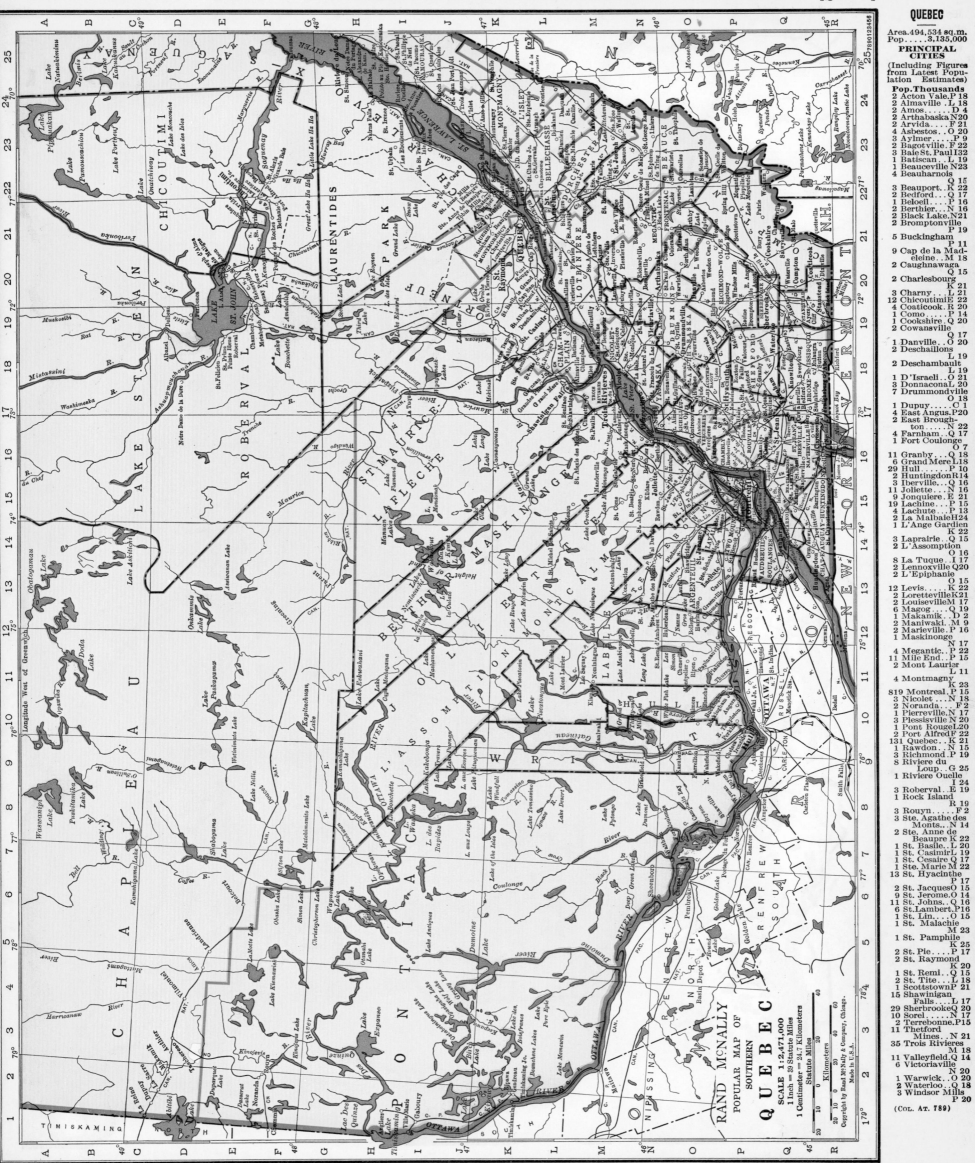

RAND McNALLY
POPULAR MAP OF
SOUTHERN
QUEBEC
SCALE 1:2,471,000
1 Inch = 39 Statute Miles
1 Centimeter = 24.7 Kilometers

Copyright by Rand McNally & Company, Chicago.
Made in U.S.A.

QUEBEC

Area.494,534 sq.m.
Pop....3,135,000

PRINCIPAL CITIES
(Including Figures
from Latest Popu-
lation Estimates)

Pop.Thousands
2 Acton Vale.P 18
2 Almaville . L 18
2 Amos......D 4
2 Arthabaska N20
4 Arvida....P 22
4 Asbestos . O 20
3 Aylmer....P 9
2 Bagotville. F 22
1 Baie St. Paul I32
1 Batiscan . L 19
1 Beauceville N23
4 Beauharnois
          Q 15
3 Beauport. K 22
1 Bedford...Q 17
2 Beloeil...P 16
2 Berthier..N 16
2 Black Lake.N21
2 Bromptonville
          P 19
5 Buckingham
          P 11
9 Cap de la Mad-
    eleine..M 18
2 Caughnawaga
          Q 15
2 Charlesbourg
          K 21
3 Charny...L 21
12 ChicoutimiE 22
2 Coaticook.R 20
2 Como....P 14
1 Cookshire .Q 20
2 Cowansville
          Q 17
1 Danville..O 20
1 Deschaillons
          L 19
2 Deschambault
          L 19
1 D'Israeli..O 21
2 DonnaconaL 20
7 Drummondville
          O 18
1 Dupuy....C 1
4 East Angus.P20
2 East Brough-
    ton.....N 22
2 Farnham .Q 17
1 Fort Coulonge
          O 7
11 Granby...Q 18
6 Grand Mere L18
29 Hull.....P 10
2 Huntingdon14
2 Iberville..Q 16
11 Joliette..N 16
9 Jonquiere. E 21
19 Lachine..P 15
4 Lachute..P 13
2 La MalbaieH24
1 L'Ange Gardien
          K 22
1 Laprairie .Q 15
2 L'Assomption
          O 16
8 La Tuque . I 17
2 LennoxvilleQ20
2 L'Epiphanie
          O 15
12 Levis....K 22
1 LorettevilleK21
2 LouisevilleM 17
6 Magog...Q 19
2 MakamikD 2
2 Maniwaki. M 9
2 Marieville. P 16
1 Maskinonge
          N 17
4 Megantic. P 22
11 Mile End..P 15
2 Mont Laurier
          L 11
4 Montmagny
          K 23
819 Montreal. P 15
3 Nicolet ...N 18
2 Noranda...F 2
1 Pierreville.N 17
3 Plessisville N 20
2 Pont RougeL20
2 Port AlfredP 22
131 Quebec...K 21
1 Rawdon.. N 15
3 Richmond.P 19
8 Riviere du
    Loup..G 25
1 Riviere Ouelle
          I 24
1 Rock Island
          R 19
3 Rouyn....F 2
3 Ste. Agathe des
    Monts.. N 14
2 Ste. Anne de
    Beaupre K 22
1 St. Basile. L 20
1 St. CasimirL 19
1 St. Cesaire Q 17
1 Ste. Marie M 22
13 St. Hyacinthe
          P 17
2 St. JacquesO 15
9 St. Jerome.O 14
11 St. Johns. O 16
6 St. Lambert.P16
1 St. Lin.... O 15
1 St. Malachie
          M 23
1 St. Pamphile
          K 25
2 St. Pie...P 17
2 St. Raymond
          K 20
1 St. Remi.. Q 15
1 St. Tite...L 18
2 ScottstownP 21
15 Shawinigan
    Falls....L 17
29 SherbrookeQ 19
10 Sorel....N 17
11 Thetford
    Mines...N 21
35 Trois Rivieres
          M 18
11 Valleyfield.Q 14
6 Victoriaville
          N 20
1 Warwick. .O 20
2 Waterloo .Q 18
3 Windsor Mills
          P 20

(COL. AT. 789)

ONTARIO

Area 412,582 sq.m.
Pop.....3,711,000

PRINCIPAL CITIES
(Including Figures from Latest Population Estimates)
Pop.—Thousands

2 Acton....L 10
2 Alexandria E 25
2 Almonte...E 20
2 Amherstburg R1
4 Arnprior..D 20
2 Aurora....J 12
2 Aylmer....O 7
8 Barrie....I 11
14 Belleville..I 17
2 Blenheim..Q 4
2 Blind River.A 2
4 Bowmanville
  K 14
2 Bracebridge F12
2 Brampton.K 11
32 Brantford..N 9
10 Brockville.H 22
5 Burlington M 10
3 Campbellford
  I 16
4 Carleton Place
  F 21
2 Chapleau..Q 22
15 Chatham...P 3
2 Chesley....I 7
2 Clinton....L 6
2 Cobalt....Q 15
2 Cobourg..J 15
2 Cochrane..O 24
7 Collingwood
  H 9
11 Cornwall..F 25
2 Deseronto. I 18
3 Dunnville..O 11
2 Durham....I 8
7 Eastview..D 22
2 Elmira....L 8
2 Essex.....Q 2
2 Fergus....R 9
5 Ft. Frances.P 15
26 Ft. William.P 18
14 Galt.....M 9
2 Gananoque I 21
2 Georgetown
  K 10
4 Goderich...K 5
2 Gravenhurst
  G 12
2 Grimsby...M11
21 Guelph....L 9
3 Haileybury Q 24
156 Hamilton M 10
3 Hanover...J 7
5 Hawkesbury
  C 25
2 Hespeler..L 9
2 Humberstone
  O 12
3 Huntsville.E 12
5 Ingersoll..N 7
7 Kenora....O 15
2 Kincardine..I 5
23 Kingston...I 20
2 Kingsville..R 2
2 Kirkland Lake
  Q 24
31 Kitchener..L 8
2 Leamington R 2
8 Lindsay...I 14
3 Listowel...K 7
71 London....N 6
2 Meaford...H 8
5 Merritton..N 12
7 Midland...G 10
2 Milton....L 10
7 Mimico....L 11
3 Mitchell...L 6
3 Mt. Forest..J 8
2 Napanee..I 19
2 New Liskeard
  Q 24
4 Newmarket J 12
19 Niagara Falls
  N 13
16 North Bay A 12
4 Oakville..M 11
4 Orangeville J 10
28 Orillia....H 12
23 Oshawa...J 13
127 Ottawa..D 22
13 Owen Sound
  H 7
2 Palmerston.K 8
4 Paris.....M 9
2 Parry Sound
  E 10
9 Pembroke. C 18
4 Penetanguish-
  ene...G 10
4 Perth.....E 21
9 Peterboro..I 15
4 Petrolia...N 4
4 Picton....J 18
20 Port Arthur P18
7 Port Colborne
  O 12
2 Port Dover.O 9
5 Port Hope..J 15
3 Portsmouth I 20
3 Prescott...G 23
2 Preston....M 9
5 Renfrew...D 19
2 Ridgetown.Q 5
2 Rockland..D 23
25 St. Catharines
  M 12
4 St. Marys..M 6
15 St. Thomas.O 6
11 Sandwich...O 1
18 Sarnia....N 3
23 Sault Ste. Marie
  R 21
2 Seaforth...L 6
2 Simcoe....O 9
2 Smiths Fs. G 21
1 Southampton
  H 6
18 Stratford..M 7
2 Strathroy..N 5
5 Sturgeon Falls
  R 24
19 Sudbury...R 23
2 Thessalon..R 22
5 Thorold...N 12
2 Tilbury....O 3
3 Tillsonburg.O 8
14 Timmins...P 23
631 Toronto...L 12
6 Trenton...J 17
2 Walkerton..J 7
10 Walkerville Q 1
2 Wallaceburg P 2
11 Welland...N 12
2 Westor....K 11
5 Whitby...K 13
2 Wiarton....G 7
63 Windsor...Q 1
2 Wingham..K 6
11 Woodstock .N 7

(Col. At. 789)

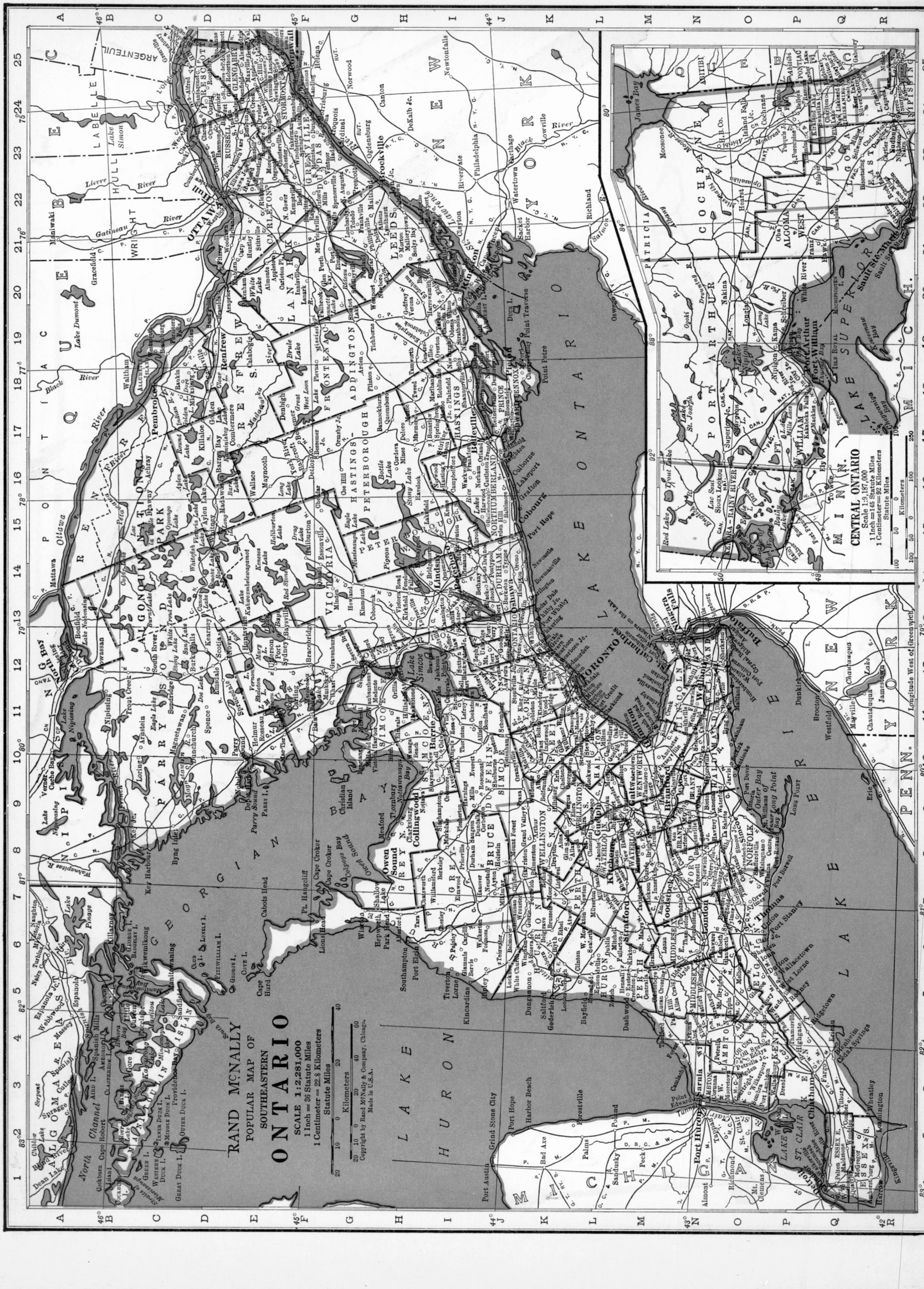

RAND McNALLY
POPULAR MAP OF
SOUTHEASTERN
ONTARIO
SCALE 1:2,281,000
1 Inch = 36 Statute Miles
1 Centimeter = 22.8 Kilometers
Statute Miles
Kilometers
Copyright by Rand McNally & Company, Chicago.
Made in U.S.A.

CENTRAL ONTARIO
Scale 1:9,187,000
1 Inch = 145 Statute Miles
1 Centimeter = 92 Kilometers
Statute Miles
Kilometers

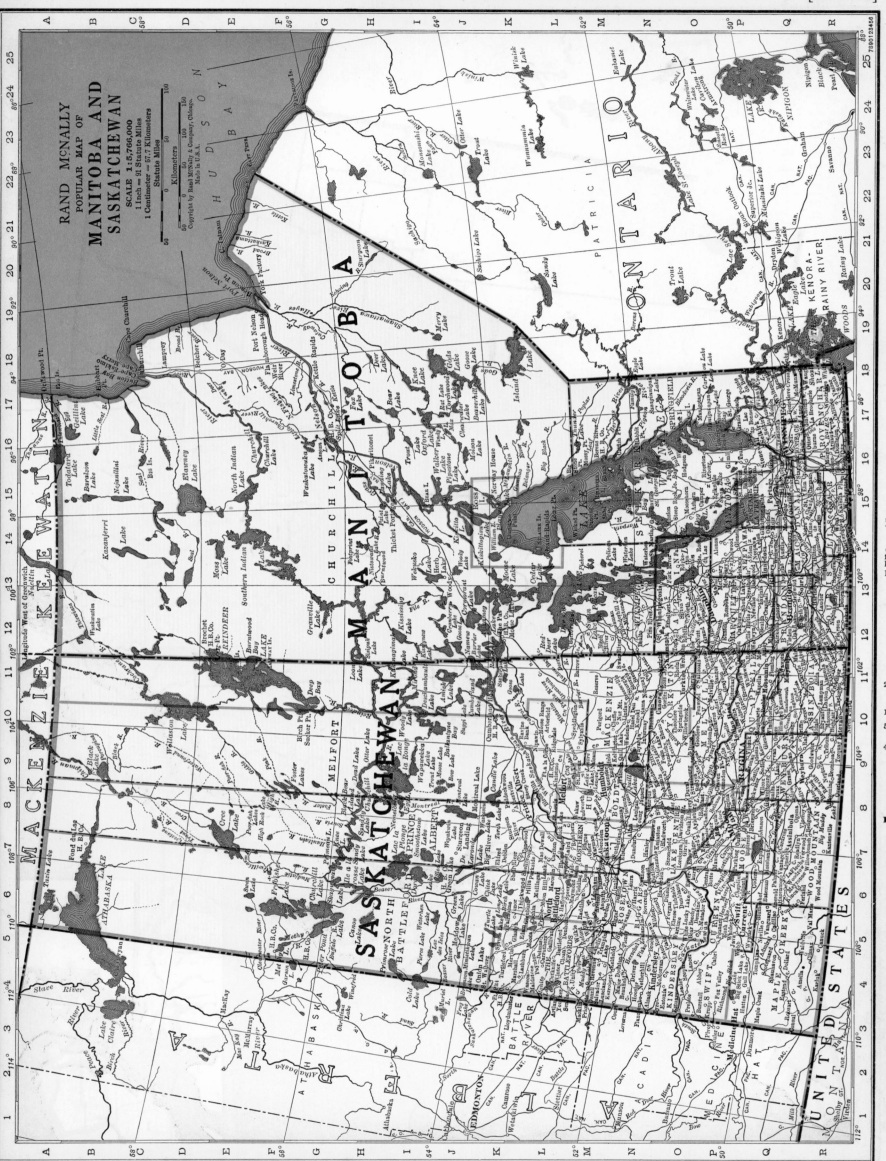

RAND McNALLY
POPULAR MAP OF
MANITOBA AND
SASKATCHEWAN

SCALE 1:5,766,000
1 Inch = 91 Statute Miles
1 Centimeter = 57.7 Kilometers
Made in U.S.A.
Copyright by Rand McNally & Company, Chicago.

MANITOBA

Area 246,512 sq.m.
Pop.......717,000

PRINCIPAL
CITIES
(Including Figures
from Latest Popu-
lation Estimates)

Pop.—Thousands

1 Beausejour	Q 17
16 Brandon	Q 13
1 Carman	R 15
2 Dauphin	P 13
1 Emerson	R 16
2 Minnedosa	Q 13
2 Neepawa	P 14
7 Portage la Prairie	Q 15
5 Selkirk	Q 16
2 Souris	Q 13
1 Stonewall	Q 16
1 Swan River	N 12
3 The Pas	K 12
6 Transcona	Q 16
2 Virden	Q 12
216 Winnipeg	Q 16
1 Winnipegosis	N 13

Pop.—Hundreds

3 Austin	Q 14
6 Birtle	P 12
6 Boissevain	R 13
8 Carberry	Q 14
4 Cartwright	R 14
8 Deloraine	R 13
4 Elm Creek	Q 15
7 Gilbert Plains	O 13
7 Gimli	P 16
7 Gladstone	Q 14
7 Glenboro	Q 14
6 Grand View	O 12
5 Hamiota	Q 12
3 Hartney	R 13
5 Lyleton	R 12
6 MacGregor	Q 14
5 Miami	R 15
3 Miniota	Q 12
8 Morris	R 16
4 Newdale	Q 13
6 Oak Lake	Q 12
5 Plum Coulee	R 15
4 Reston	R 12
7 Rivers	Q 13
7 Roblin	O 12
6 Roland	R 15
4 Rossburn	P 12
8 Russell	P 12
6 St. Laurent	P 16
3 Ste. Anne des Chenes	Q 17
3 Starbuck	Q 16
7 Shoal Lake	P 13

SASKATCHEWAN

Ar. .251,700 sq. m.
Pop.......939,000

PRINCIPAL
CITIES
(Including Figures
from Latest Popu-
lation Estimates)

Pop.—Thousands

1 Assiniboia	Q 7
1 Battleford	L 5
2 Biggar	M 5
1 Canora	N 11
3 Estevan	R 10
1 Herbert	P 6
2 Humboldt	M 8
1 Indian Head	P 9
2 Kamsack	O 11
1 Kindersley	N 5
1 Lloydminster	K 4
1 Maple Creek	P 4
2 Melfort	N 8
4 Melville	O 10
20 Moose Jaw	P 8
1 Moosomin	Q 11
5 North Battleford	L 6
11 Prince Albert	L 8
1 Radville	R 9
53 Regina	P 9
2 Rosetown	N 5
1 Rosthern	M 7
42 Saskatoon	M 7
2 Shaunavon	P 4
3 Sutherland	N 7
5 Swift Current	P 5
1 Tisdale	N 9
1 Watrous	N 8
9 Weyburn	Q 9
1 Wilkie	M 5
1 Wynyard	N 9
5 Yorkton	O 11

Pop.—Hundreds

6 Arcola	R 11
4 Balcarres	P 10
4 Big River	K 7
2 Broadview	P 10
6 Cabri	P 5
9 Carlyle	Q 11
5 Carnduff	R 11
6 Craik	O 7
2 Cupar	O 9
2 Davidson	O 7
6 Duck Lake	L 7
4 Esterhazy	P 11
5 Foam Lake	N 10
5 Ft. Qu'Appelle	P 9
4 Govan	O 8
2 Grenfell	P 10
9 Gull Lake	P 5
5 Kerrobert	M 4
5 Kinistino	L 8
4 Langham	M 6
4 Lanigan	N 8
4 Leader	O 4
8 Lumsden	P 8
4 Morse	P 6
3 Mortlach	P 7
5 Neudorf	P 10
4 Nokomis	O 8
5 Outlook	N 6
8 Oxbow	R 11
9 Qu'Appelle	P 9
3 Radisson	M 6
4 Rocanville	P 11
5 Saltcoats	O 11
3 Star City	N 9
8 Strasbourg	P 9
8 Unity	M 4
4 Wadena	N 9
5 Wapella	Q 11
4 Watson	N 9
9 Whitewood	P 11
3 Wilcox	Q 9
9 Wolseley	P 10

(COL. AT. 789)

ALBERTA

Ar..255,285 sq. m.
Pop......778,000

**PRINCIPAL
CITIES**
(Including Figures
from Latest Population Estimates)

Pop.—Thousands
3 Banff.....N 19
2 Blairmore..P 20
83 Calgary...N 20
2 Camrose..K 21
2 Cardston..Q 21
2 Claresholm.P 21
2 Coleman...P 20
3 Drumheller
         N 22
86 Edmonton.K 20
1 Ft. Saskatchewan..J 21
1 Grande Prairie
         I 16
1 Hanna....M 22
1 High RiverO 21
1 Innisfail..M 20
1 Lacombe..L 21
14 Lethbridge P 22
1 Macleod..P 21
1 Magrath..P 22
10 Medicine Hat
         O 24
1 Olds.....M 20
1 Pincher P.P21
2 Raymond.P 22
1 Redcliff..O 24
2 Red Deer.M 20
1 Stettler...L 21
1 Taber.....P 22
2 Vegreville.K 22
2 Vermilion.K 23
1 WainwrightK23
2 WetaskiwinK21

Pop.—Hundreds
4 Bashaw...L 21
6 Bassano..M 22
5 Big ValleyM 21
8 Bow IslandP 23
7 Brooks....O 22
8 Canmore..N 19
6 Castor....L 22
6 CoronationO23
4 Daysland..L 21
8 Didsbury.M 20
6 Gleichen..N 21
4 Hardisty..L 23
5 Lamont...J 21
9 Leduc....K 20
6 Morinville P 20
8 Mundare..K 21
7 Nanton...O 21
7 Ogden....N 21
8 Okotoks..O 21
9 PeaceRiverG17
6 Ponoka..L 21
8 Provost...L 23
8 St. Albert.K 20
9 St. Paul...J 22
5 Strathmore N 21
3 Three Hills M 21
5 Tofield...K 21
5 Trochu...M 21
8 Vulcan...O 21

BRITISH
COLUMBIA

Area 366,255 sq.m.
Pop.......751,000

**PRINCIPAL
CITIES**
(Including Figures
from Latest Population Estimates)

Pop.—Thousands
1 Armstrong O 16
2 Chilliwack Q 13
2 Courtenay Q 11
3 Cranbrook.Q 19
2 Cumberland
         Q 11
2 Duncan...Q 12
3 Fernie....Q 20
1 Grand Forks
         Q 17
6 Kamloops.O 15
5 Kelowna..P 16
1 Ladysmith Q 12
1 Merritt....P 15
1 Mission...Q 13
6 Nanaimo..Q 12
6 Nelson....Q 18
18 New Westminster..Q 13
9 North Vancouver..Q 12
2 Port Alberni
         Q 11
1 Port Moody.O 3
2 Prince George
         K 13
6 Prince Rupert
         J 7
3 Revelstoke O 17
3 Rossland..O 17
1 Smithers...I 9
8 Trail.....Q 18
245 Vancouver
         Q 12
4 Vernon...P 16
39 Victoria..R 12

Pop.—Hundreds
6 Agassiz....O 6
7 Alberni....Q 11
8 Ashcroft..O 14
5 Atlin.....B 5
7 Comox....P 11
6 Creston...Q 19
6 Enderby...O 16
5 Hazelton..I 9
4 Hope.....Q 14
2 Kimberley P 19
5 Michel....P 20
8 Peachland P 15
3 Princeton..Q 15
4 Quesnel..L 13
8 Salmon Arm
         O 16
5 Union Bay Q 11
3 VanderhoofJ 12

(Col. At. 7890)

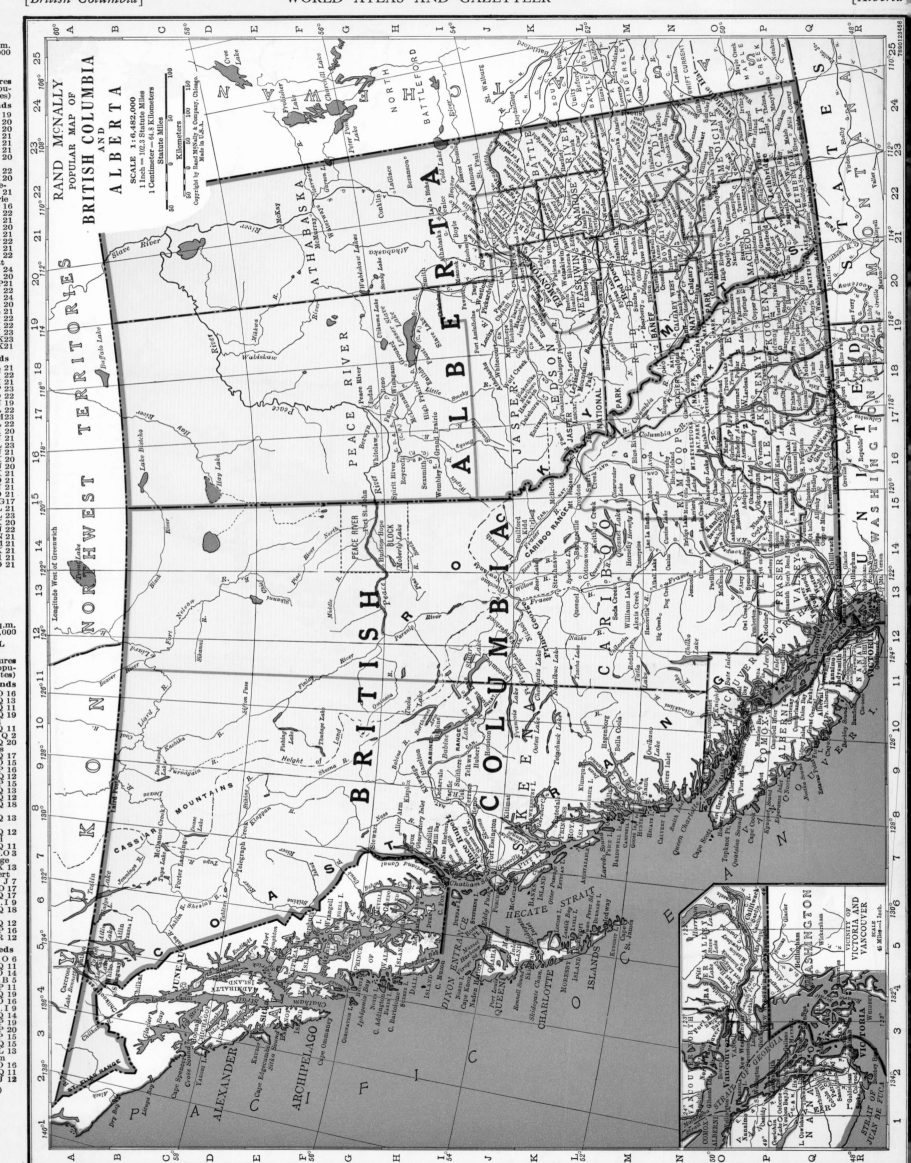

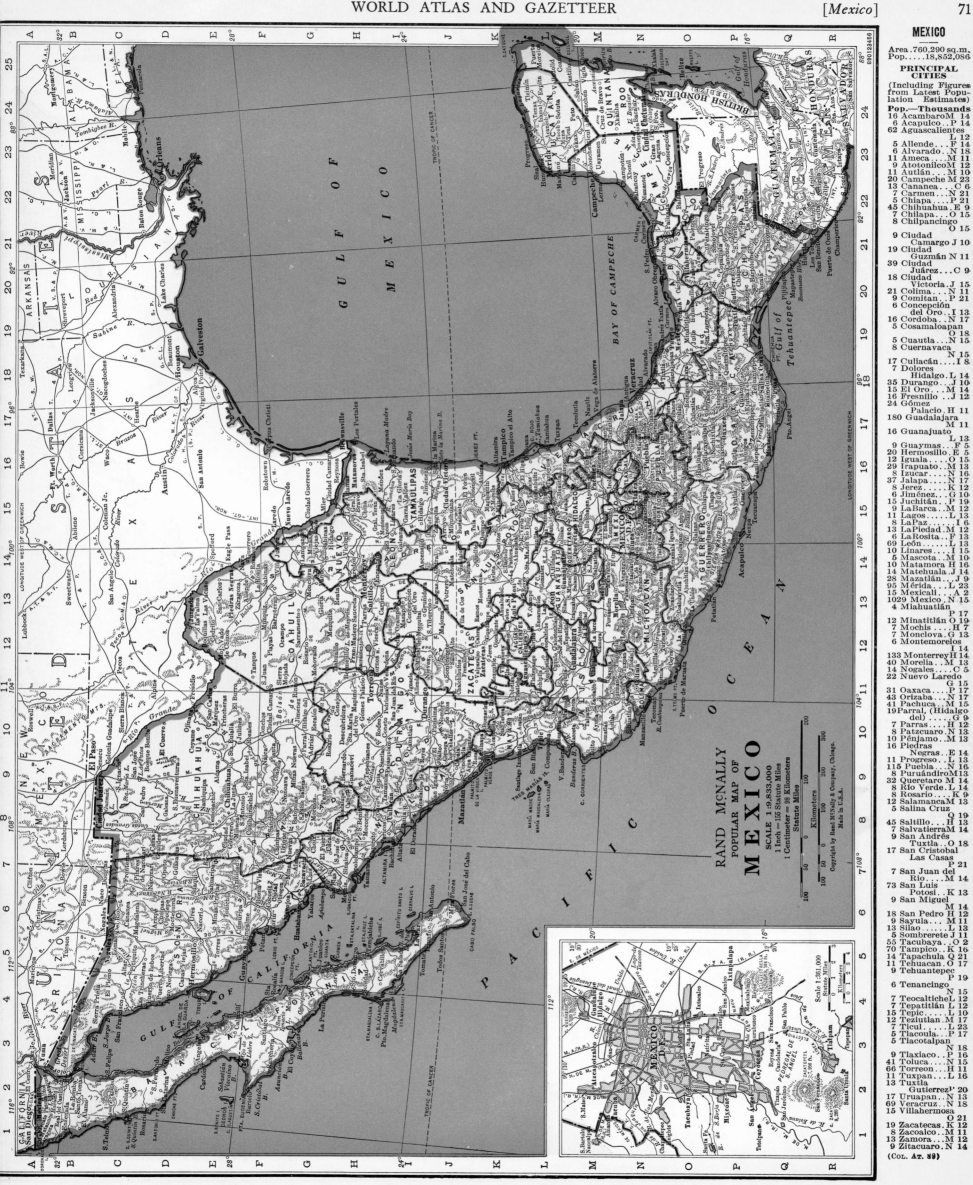

RAND McNALLY
POPULAR MAP OF
MEXICO

SCALE 1:9,833,000
1 Inch = 156 Statute Miles
1 Centimeter = 98 Kilometers

Copyright by Rand McNally & Company, Chicago.
Made in U.S.A.

MEXICO
Area .760,290 sq.m.
Pop.....18,852,086

PRINCIPAL CITIES
(Including Figures
from Latest Population Estimates)
Pop.—Thousands
16 AcambaroM 14
6 Acapulco..P 14
62 Aguascalientes
L 12
5 Allende...F 14
6 Alvarado..N 18
11 Ameca....M 11
4 AtotonilcoM 12
11 Autlán...M 10
20 Campeche M 23
13 Cananea..C 6
2 Carmen...N 21
5 Chiapa...P 21
45 Chihuahua..E 9
7 Chilapa...O 15
8 Chilpancingo
O 15
9 Ciudad
Camargo J 10
19 Ciudad
Guzmán N 11
39 Ciudad
Juárez...C 9
18 Ciudad
Victoria.J 15
21 Colima...N 11
9 Comitan..P 21
6 Concepción
del Oro..I 13
16 Cordoba..N 17
5 Cosamaloapan
O 18
5 Cuautla...N 15
8 Cuernavaca
N 15
17 Culiacán....I 8
7 Dolores
Hidalgo..L 13
35 Durango..J 10
15 El Oro...M 14
16 Fresnillo ..J 12
24 Gómez
Palacio. H 11
180 Guadalajara
M 11
16 Guanajuato
L 13
9 Guaymas..F 5
20 Hermosillo.E 5
12 Iguala...O 15
29 Irapuato..M 13
8 Izucar...N 16
37 Jalapa...N 17
6 Jerez...M 12
8 Jiménez..G 10
15 Juchitán .P 19
9 LaBarca..M 12
11 Lagos...L 13
8 LaPaz....I 6
13 LaPiedad..M 12
5 LaRosita..P 13
69 León...L 13
10 Linares ...I 15
5 Mascota..M 10
10 Matamora H 16
24 Matehuala .J 14
28 Mazatlán..J 8
95 Mérida...L 23
15 Mexicali...A 2
1029 Mexico..N 15
4 Miahuatlán
P 17
12 Minatitlán O 19
7 Mochis ....H 7
7 Monclova.G 13
6 Montemorelos
I 14
133 Monterrey H 14
40 Morelia...M 13
14 Nogales ..C 5
22 Nuevo Laredo
G 15
31 Oaxaca...P 17
43 Orizaba...N 17
41 Pachuca..N 16
19 Parral, (Hidalgo
del) ....G 9
7 Parras...H 12
8 Patzcuaro .N 13
10 Pénjamo..M 13
16 Piedras
Negras..E 14
11 Progreso .L 13
115 Puebla...N 16
8 Puruándiro M 13
32 Queretaro M 14
8 Rio Verde.L 14
5 Rosario...K 9
12 SalamancaM 13
5 Salina Cruz
Q 19
45 Saltillo...H 13
7 SalvatierraM 14
9 San Andrés
Tuxtla ..O 18
17 San Cristobal
Las Casas
P 21
8 San Juan del
Rio.....M 14
73 San Luis
Potosi...K 13
9 San Miguel
M 14
18 San Pedro H 12
9 Sayula...M 11
13 Silao...M 13
5 Sombrerete J 11
55 Tacubaya...O 2
70 Tampico..M 17
14 Tapachula Q 21
11 Tehuacan .O 17
7 Tehuantepec
P 19
6 Tenancingo
N 15
7 Teocaltiche L 12
7 Tepatitlán L 12
15 Tepic...L 10
12 Teziutlán .M 17
7 Ticul...L 23
5 Tlacoula...L 7
5 Tlacotalpan
N 18
9 Tlaxiaco..N 15
41 Toluca...N 15
66 Torreon...H 11
11 Tuxpan..L 16
5 Tuxtla
Gutierrez¹.20
17 Uruapan..N 13
69 Veracruz..N 17
15 Villahermosa
O 21
19 Zacatecas..K 12
8 Zacoalco..M 11
13 Zamora...M 12
9 Zitacuaro..N 14
(Col. At. 89)

CENTRAL AMERICA

BRITISH HONDURAS

Area..8,598 sq. m.
Pop.......56,893

PRINCIPAL CITY

(Including Figures
from Latest Population
Estimates)

Pop.—Thousands

15 Belize......B 8

CANAL ZONE

Area...554 sq. m.
Pop.......29,636

COSTA RICA

Area...23,000 sq. m.
Pop.......591,862

PRINCIPAL CITY

(Including Figures
from Latest Population
Estimates)

Pop.—Thousands

14 Cartago...N 15
17 Limón....N 15
64 San Jose..N 14

GUATEMALA

Area 42,353 sq. m.
Pop.......2,466,227

PRINCIPAL CITIES

(Including Figures
from Latest Population
Estimates)

Pop.—Thousands

21 Chiquimula F 6
25 Coban.....E 5
22 Escuintla...G 4
144 GuatemalaG 4
17 Jalapa.....F 5
14 Jocotan....F 5
14 Joyabaj....F 4
19 Jutiapa....G 6
26 Momostenango
........F 3
23 Quezaltenango
........F 3
12 Quiche....F 3
12 Retalhuleu G 2
14 Salamá....F 5
30 Totonicapam
........F 3
18 Zacapa.....F 6

HONDURAS

Area..44,275 sq. m.
Pop.......962,700

PRINCIPAL CITIES

(Including Figures
from Latest Population
Estimates)

Pop.—Thousands

12 Choluteca..I 9
10 Danli....H 12
11 Juticalpa..G 12
10 Nacaome..H 9
17 San Pedro E 8
11 Santa Rosa F 7
23 Tegucigalpa
........G 10

NICARAGUA

Area..51,660 sq. m.
Pop.......1,133,500

PRINCIPAL CITIES

(Including Figures
from Latest Population
Estimates)

Pop.—Thousands

8 Bluefields..K 15
14 Boaco.....J 12
14 ChinandegaJ 10
27 Granada...K 11
20 Jinotega...I 12
59 Leon.....J 10
62 Managua..K 11
18 Masaya...K 11
39 Matagalpa.I 12
9 Rivas.....L 12

PANAMA

Area..29,065 sq. m.
Pop.......534,631

PRINCIPAL CITIES

(Including Figures
from Latest Population
Estimates)

Pop.—Thousands

2 Bocas del Toro
........O 17
30 Colon.....O 21
5 David.....P 17
11 Las Palmas
........P 19
74 Panamá...P 22
3 Penonomé.P 21

SALVADOR

Ar...13,176 sq. m.
Pop......1,597,549

PRINCIPAL CITIES

(Including Figures
from Latest Popu-
lation Estimates)

Pop.—Thousands

32 Ahuachapán
........H 5
21 Izalco.....H 6
41 San Miguel H 8
97 San Salvador
........H 6
77 Santa Ana..C 6
29 Santa Tecla H 6
33 San Vicente
........H 7
24 Zacatecoluca
........H 7

(Col. At. 89)

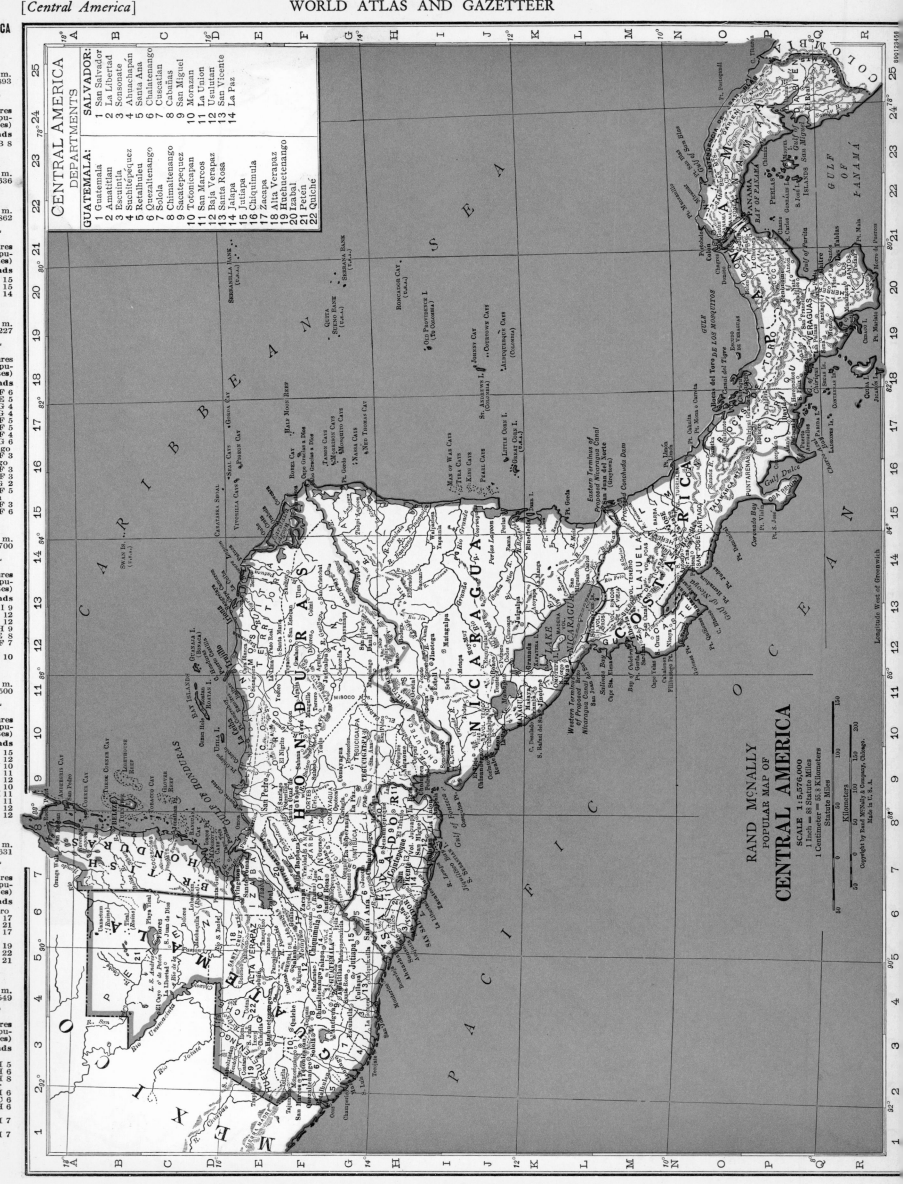

CENTRAL AMERICA
DEPARTMENTS

GUATEMALA:
1 Guatemala
2 Amatitlan
3 Escuintla
4 Suchitepéquez
5 Retalhuleu
6 Quezaltenango
7 Solola
8 Chimaltenango
9 Sacatepequez
10 Totonicapan
11 San Marcos
12 Baja Verapaz
13 Santa Rosa
14 Jalapa
15 Jutiapa
16 Chiquimula
17 Zacapa
18 Alta Verapaz
19 Huehuetenango
20 Izabal
21 Petén
22 Quiché

SALVADOR:
1 San Salvador
2 La Libertad
3 Sonsonate
4 Ahuachapán
5 Santa Ana
6 Chalatenango
7 Cuscatlan
8 Cabañas
9 San Miguel
10 Morazan
11 La Union
12 Usulutan
13 San Vicente
14 La Paz

RAND McNALLY
POPULAR MAP OF
CENTRAL AMERICA

SCALE 1:5,576,000
1 Inch = 88 Statute Miles
1 Centimeter = 55.8 Kilometers

Copyright by Rand McNally & Company, Chicago.
Made in U.S.A.

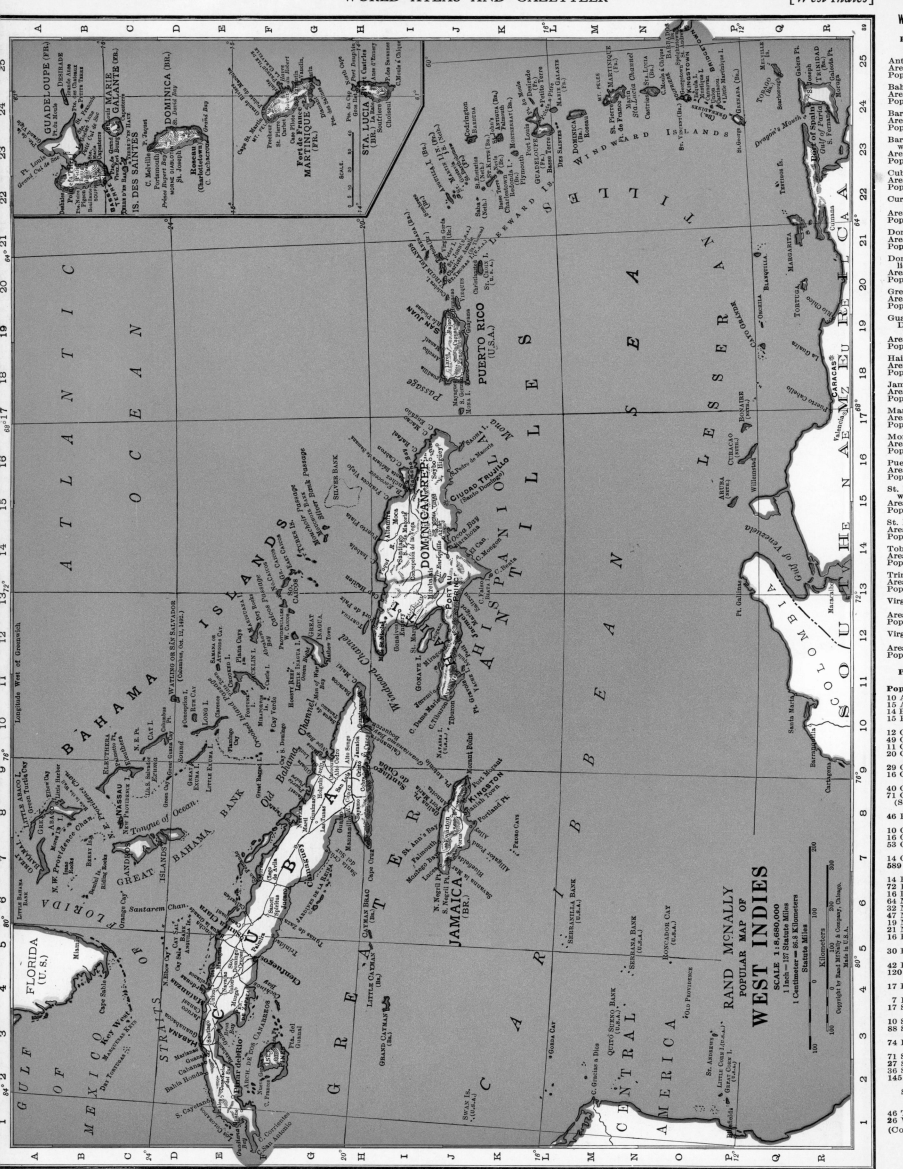

RAND McNALLY
POPULAR MAP OF
WEST INDIES
SCALE 1:8,680,000
1 Inch=137 Statute Miles
1 Centimeter=86.8 Kilometers
Statute Miles
Kilometers
Copyright by Rand McNally & Company, Chicago.
Made in U.S.A.

WEST INDIES

PRINCIPAL ISLANDS

Antigua.....K 23
 Area...108 sq. m.
 Pop......33,060
Bahama Is...E 11
 Area..4,404 sq. m.
 Pop......66,908
Barbados....O 25
 Area...166 sq. m.
 Pop......188,294
Barbuda....J 23
 with Redonda
 Area.....62 sq. m.
 Pop......926
Cuba........F 6
 Area 44,164 sq. m.
 Pop....4,046,706
Curaçao....P 16
 (Colony)
 Area...403 sq. m.
 Pop......90,870
Dominica....M 24
 Area...305 sq. m.
 Pop......48,280
Dominican Repub-
 lic.........I 14
 Area 19,332 sq. m.
 Pop....1,567,708
Grenada....P 24
 Area...133 sq. m.
 Pop......87,105
Guadeloupe and
 Dependencies
 L 24
 Area...688 sq. m.
 Pop......304,239
Haiti........I 13
 Area 11,069 sq. m.
 Pop....3,000,000
Jamaica.....J 8
 Area..4,450 sq. m.
 Pop....1,138,558
Martinique..M 25
 Area...385 sq. m.
 Pop......246,712
Montserrat..K 23
 Area....32 sq. m.
 Pop......13,161
Puerto Rico.J 18
 Area..3,435 sq. m.
 Pop....1,723,534
St. Kitts.....K 22
 with Nevis
 Area...150 sq. m.
 Pop......37,521
St. Lucia....N 24
 Area...233 sq. m.
 Pop......66,230
Tobago....Q 25
 Area...114 sq. m.
 Pop......25,358
Trinidad....R 25
 Area..1,862 sq. m.
 Pop......430,642
Virgin Is.....J 20
 (British)
 Area....58 sq. m.
 Pop......5,488
Virgin Is.....J 20
 (U. S.)
 Area...133 sq. m.
 Pop......22,012

PRINCIPAL CITIES
Pop.—Thousands

10 Arecibo....J 18
15 Aux Cayes.J 11
14 Basse TerreB 22
15 Bridgetown
 O 25
12 Caibarien..F 6
49 Camaguey..G 7
11 Capesterre.B 23
20 Cap Haitien
 H 13
29 Cardenas...E 4
16 Ciego de Avila
 F 6
40 Cienfuegos.F 5
71 Ciudad Trujillo
 (Santo Domingo)
 J 15
46 Fort de France
 M 24
10 Gonaives...I 12
16 GuanabacoaE 3
53 Guantanamo
 H 10
14 Guines....E 3
589 Habana
 (Hayana) E 3
14 Holguin....G 9
72 Kingston...J 8
16 Lamentin. G 24
64 Manzanillo.H 8
47 Matanzas..E 4
19 Mayaguez.J 18
21 Nassau....D 2
16 Pinar del Rio
 E 2
30 Pointe à Pitre
 L 24
42 Ponce.....J 18
120 Port au Prince
 J 13
17 Port du Moule
 L 24
7 Roseau....D 23
17 Sagua la Grande
 E 5
10 St. Johns. K 23
88 Sancti-Spiritus
 F 6
74 Port of Spain
 R 24
71 San Juan..J 19
27 Santa Clara.E 5
36 Santiago...I 14
145 Santiago de
 Cuba....H 9
SantoDomingo,
 see Ciudad
 Trujilo.
46 Trinidad...F 5
26 Willemstad P16
(Col. At. 89)

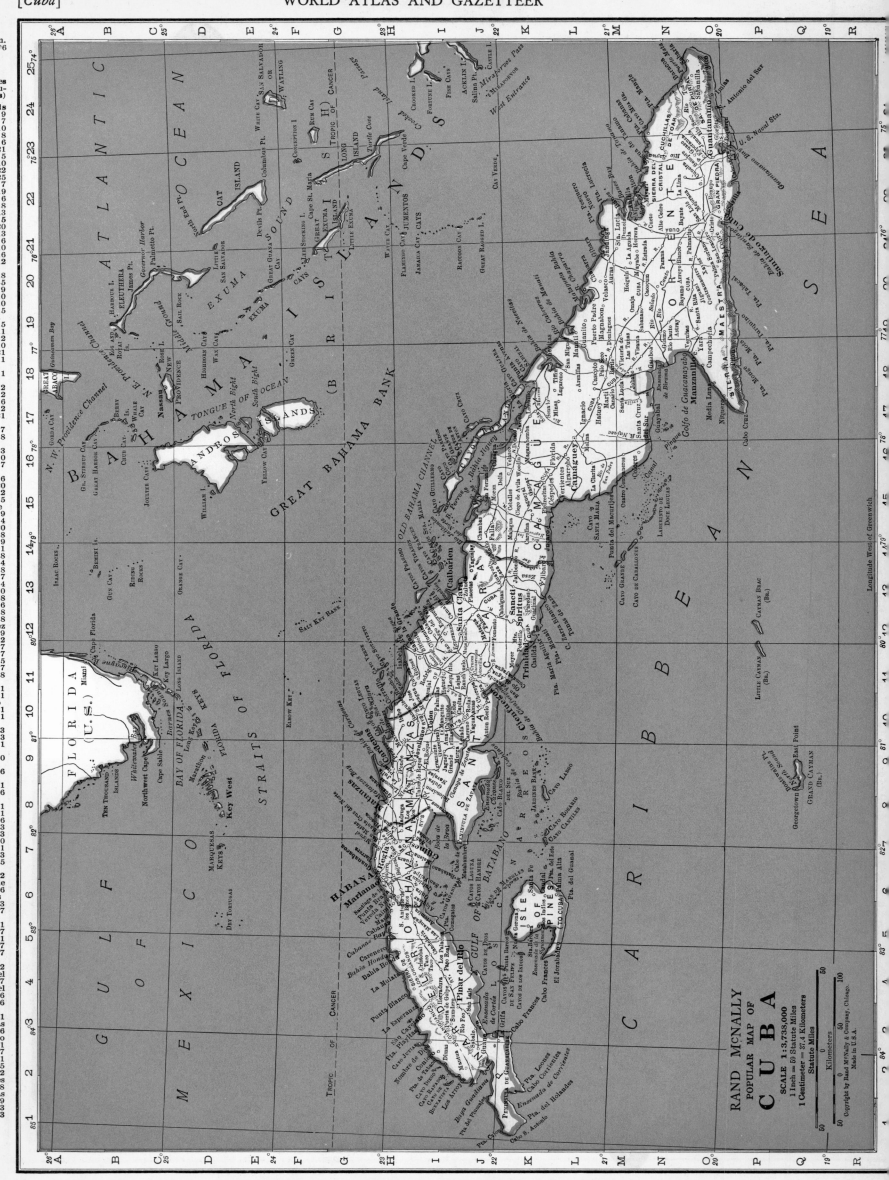

CUBA

Area..44,164 sq. m.
Pop.....4,046,706

PRINCIPAL CITIES

(Including Figures from Latest Population Estimates)

Pop.—Thousands

3	Agramonte	I 9
3	Aguacate	H 7
4	Aguada	I 10
4	Alacranes	I 8
5	Alquizar	H 6
7	Alto Cedro	N 21
7	Artemisa	H 5
2	Banagulses	I 10
10	Banes	M 22
2	Baracoa	N 25
2	Batabanó	I 7
2	Bayamo	N 19
5	Bejucal	H 6
4	Bolondron	I 8
2	Cabaiguan	J 13
2	Cabañas	H 5
4	Cacocum	N 20
12	Caibarién	I 13
2	Caimito	H 6
2	Calimete	I 10
49	Camaguey	L 16
2	Camajuani	I 12
5	Campechuela	O 18
2	Candelaria	I 5
29	Cardenas	H 9
2	Carreno	J 10
2	Cascajal	I 10
2	Ceballos	K 15
16	Ciego de Avila	K 15
40	Cienfuegos	J 11
2	Cifuentes	I 12
2	Colon	I 10
2	Cristo	O 21
2	Cruces	J 11
3	Cumanayagua	J 11
4	Encrucijada	I 12
4	Esperanza	I 12
2	Florida	L 16
3	Fomento	J 12
7	Gibara	M 21
16	Guanabacoa	H 7
3	Guanabana	H 8
53	Guantánamo	O 23
2	Guareiras	I 10
14	Güines	H 7
589	Habana (Havana)	H 6
14	Holguin	M 20
3	Isabela	H 12
3	Jagueyal	K 15
3	Jaguey Grande	I 9
5	Jatibonico	K 14
2	Jiguani	O 20
2	Jobabo	M 18
7	Jovellanos	H 9
2	Lajas	J 11
2	Limonar	H 8
2	Los Palacios	I 4
3	Lugareño	L 18
2	Madruga	H 7
2	Majagua	K 14
2	Manguito	I 10
64	Manzanillo	O 18
32	Marianao	H 6
2	Martí	M 18
47	Matanzas	H 8
3	Maximo Gomez	H 9
3	Mayari	N 22
2	Melena	L 17
2	Minas	L 17
10	Moron	O 15
3	Niquero	O 17
6	Nuevitas	K 18
2	Ojo de Agua	J 11
2	Palmarito	O 21
7	Palma Soriano	O 21
2	Palmira	J 11
16	Pinar del Rio	I 3
9	Placetas	J 13
2	Potrerillo	J 11
4	Puerto Padre	L 20
2	Punta Brava	H 6
3	Quemados de Guines	I 11
2	Quivican	H 6
2	Rancho Veloz	H 11
3	Ranchuelo	J 11
14	Regia	H 6
9	Remedios	I 13
2	Rio Feo	I 3
3	Rodas	J 10
2	Rodrigo	J 11
2	Sabalo	J 3
2	Sabanilla	O 25
17	Sagua la Grande	I 12
11	San Antonio de los Baños	H 6
88	Sancti Spiritus	K 13
2	San Felipe	I 7
2	San Fernando	J 11
4	San Jose	H 7
6	San Luis	O 21
3	San Miguel	H 7
3	San Nicolas	I 7
27	Santa Clara	I 12
3	Santa Cruz del Norte	H 7
2	Santa Cruz del Sur	N 16
2	Santa Fe	K 6
145	Santiago de Cuba	O 21
6	Santiago de las Vegas	H 6
3	Santo Domingo	I 11
4	Senado	K 17
3	Sitiecito	H 11
5	Taco Taco	I 5
46	Trinidad	K 12
5	Union de Reyes	H 8
4	Victoria de las Tunas	M 19
3	Yaguajay	J 13
3	Zulueta	J 13

(Col. At. 8901)

RAND McNALLY
POPULAR MAP OF
CUBA

SCALE 1:3,738,000
1 inch = 59 Statute Miles
1 Centimeter = 37.4 Kilometers

Statute Miles

Kilometers

Copyright by Rand McNally & Company, Chicago.
Made in U.S.A.

RAND McNALLY
POPULAR MAP OF
SOUTH AMERICA
SCALE 1:25,724,000
1 Inch = 406 Statute Miles
1 Centimeter = 257 Kilometers
Statute Miles
Kilometers
Copyright by Rand McNally & Company, Chicago.
Made in U.S.A.

SOUTH AMERICA
(Including Figures
from Latest Popu-
lation Estimates)
Ar.7,096,656 sq. m.
Pop....93,500,000

ARGENTINA
Ar.1,079,965 sq. m.
Pop....12,564,301
PRINCIPAL
CITIES
Pop.—Thousands
100 Bahia Blanca
N 11
2291 Buenos Aires
M 13
309 Cordoba..L 10
180 La Plata.M 13
509 Rosario..L 12
138 Santa Fe.L 12

BOLIVIA
Area 581,785 sq.m.
Pop....3,282,736
PRINCIPAL
CITIES
Pop.—Thousands
202 La Paz....H 8
30 Sucre.....I 10

BRAZIL
Ar.3,285,319 sq. m.
Pop....47,795,000
PRINCIPAL
CITIES
Pop.—Thousands
311 Belém...D 18
60 Campos..J 20
137 Caratinga.I 20
328 Porto Alegre
L 16
473 Recife (Per-
nambuco.F 24
1700 Rio de Janeiro...J 20
105 Santos...J 18
1151 São Paulo J18
364 São Salvador
(Bahia) G 22

CHILE
Area 286,322 sq.m.
Pop....4,597,254
PRINCIPAL
CITIES
Pop.—Thousands
844 Santiago..M 8
263 Valparaiso.L 7

COLOMBIA
Area 441,651 sq.m.
Pop....8,390,950
PRINCIPAL
CITY
Pop.—Thousands
252 Bogotá....C 5

ECUADOR
Area 176,155 sq.m.
Pop....2,758,505
PRINCIPAL
CITIES
Pop.—Thousands
131 Guayaquil.D 2
118 Quito....D 3

GUIANA
(British)
Area .89,480 sq. m.
Pop....332,898
PRINCIPAL
CITY
Pop.—Thousands
65 Georgetown
B 13

GUIANA
(Neth.)
Area .54,291 sq. m.
Pop....171,396
PRINCIPAL
CITY
Pop.—Thousands
52 Paramaribo
B 14

GUIANA & ININI
(French)
Area .34,354 sq. m.
Pop....36,975
PRINCIPAL
CITY
Pop.—Thousands
11 Cayenne..C 16

PARAGUAY
Area .155,000 sq.m.
Pop....931,800
PRINCIPAL
CITY
Pop.—Thousands
96 Asuncion..J 13

PERU
Area 482,133 sq.m.
Pop....6,500,000
PRINCIPAL
CITY
Pop.—Thousands
300 Lima.....G 4

URUGUAY
Area .72,153 sq.m.
Pop....2,082,367
PRINCIPAL
CITY
Pop.—Thousands
674 Montevideo
M 14

VENEZUELA
Area 352,051 sq.m.
Pop....3,491,159
PRINCIPAL
CITY
Pop.—Thousands
203 Carácas..A 9
(Col. At. 890)

890123456

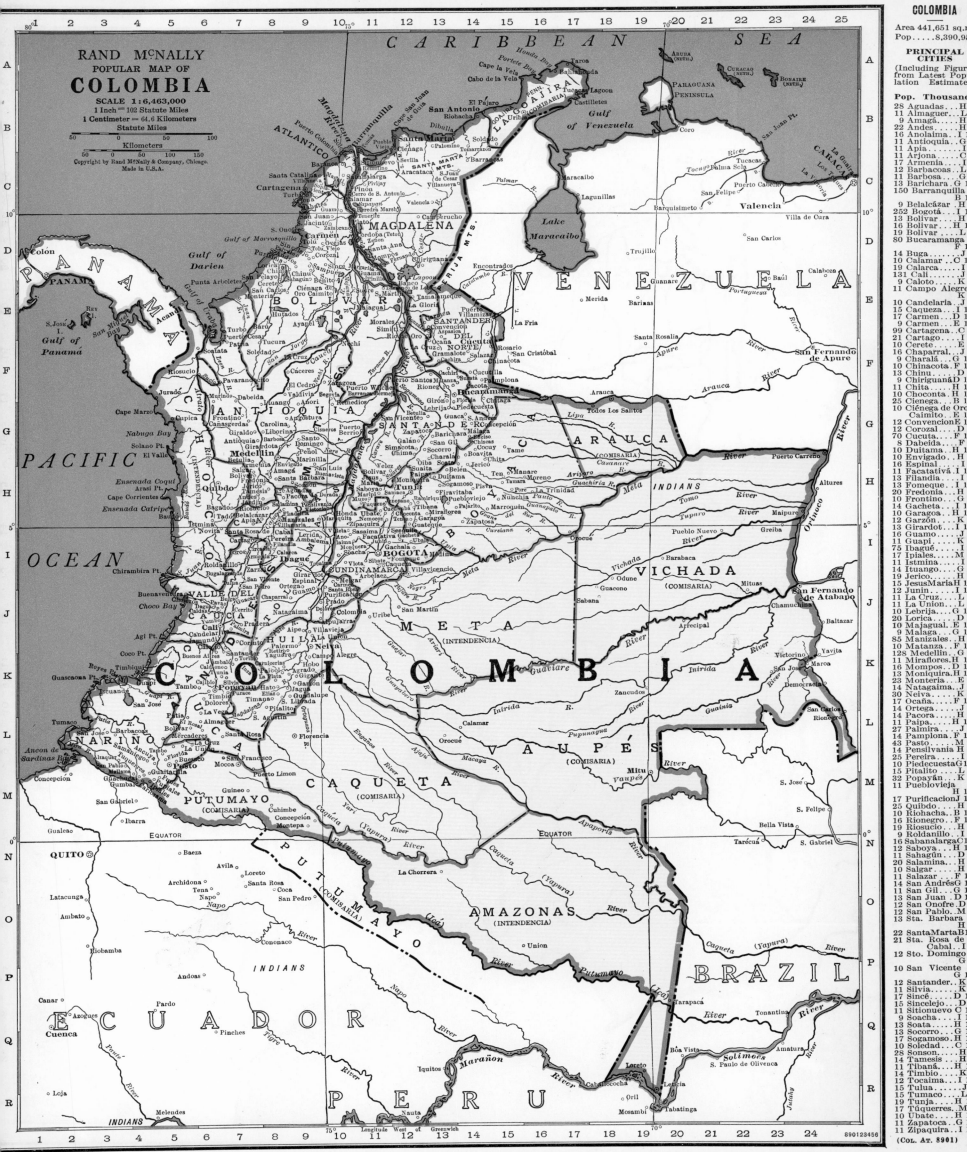

RAND McNALLY
POPULAR MAP OF
COLOMBIA
SCALE 1:6,463,000
1 Inch = 102 Statute Miles
1 Centimeter = 64.6 Kilometers
Statute Miles
Kilometers
Copyright by Rand McNally & Company, Chicago.
Made in U.S.A.

COLOMBIA

Area 441,651 sq.m.
Pop.....8,390,950

PRINCIPAL CITIES
(Including Figures
from Latest Popu-
lation Estimates)

Pop. Thousands

28	Aguadas	H 8
11	Almaguer	L 6
9	Amagá	H 8
22	Andes	H 8
16	Anolaima	I 10
11	Antioquia	G 8
11	Apia	H 8
11	Arjona	C 9
17	Armenia	I 8
12	Barbacoas	L 3
11	Barbosa	G 8
13	Barichara	G 13
150	Barranquilla	
		B 10
9	Belalcázar	H 8
252	Bogotá	I 11
13	Bolivar	H 7
15	Bolivar	H 4
19	Bolivar	I 5
80	Bucaramanga	
		F 14
14	Buga	J 7
10	Calamar	C 10
13	Calarca	I 10
131	Cali	J 6
9	Caicto	K 7
11	Campo Alegre	
		K 9
10	Candelaria	J 7
11	Caqueza	J 11
17	Carmen	D 10
99	Cartagena	C 9
21	Cartago	I 8
10	Cerete	E 9
16	Chaparral	J 8
9	Charalá	G 13
10	Chinacota	F 14
13	Chinu	D 9
9	Chiriguaná	D 12
11	Chita	H 14
10	Choconta	H 12
25	Cienaga	B 12
10	Cienega de Oro	
	Caimto	E 10
12	Convencion	E 13
12	Corozal	D 9
70	Cucuta	F 14
8	Dabeiba	P 7
13	Duitama	I 13
8	Envigado	H 8
16	Espinal	I 9
11	Facatativá	I 11
13	Filandia	I 8
13	Fomeque	I 12
20	Fredonia	H 8
10	Frontino	G 7
14	Gacheta	I 12
10	Garagoa	H 13
12	Garzón	K 9
15	Giradot	I 10
16	Giraron	I 9
10	Guapi	K 4
75	Ibagué	I 9
17	Ipiales	M 4
11	Istmina	I 6
19	Ituango	G 8
19	Jerico	H 8
12	JesusMarial	I 11
12	Junin	I 11
11	La Cruz	L 6
11	La Union	L 5
10	Lebrija	G 13
26	Lorica	D 8
9	Magagui	K 11
9	Malaga	G 14
85	Manizales	H 8
11	Matanza	F 14
128	Medellin	G 8
13	Miraflores	H 13
11	Mompox	H 12
23	Monteria	E 8
14	Natagaima	K 9
10	Neiva	K 9
10	Ocaña	D 13
14	Ortega	J 9
14	Pacora	H 8
11	Paipa	H 13
27	Palmira	J 7
11	Pamplona	F 14
43	Pasto	M 5
14	Pensilvania	H 9
25	Pereira	I 8
12	PiedecuestaG	13
15	Pitalito	L 6
52	Popayán	K 7
11	Pueblovieja	
		H 13
17	Purificacion	J 10
25	Quibdo	I 6
10	Riohacha	B 14
10	Rionegro	F 13
19	Riosucio	H 8
9	Roldanillo	I 7
16	SabanalargaC	10
12	Saboya	H 12
11	Sahagún	D 9
20	Salamina	H 8
11	Salazar	H 7
11	Salazar	F 14
11	San AndrésG	14
11	San Gil	G 13
13	San Juan	D 10
12	San Onofre	D 9
12	San Pablo	M 4
13	Sta. Barbara	
		H 8
22	SantaMarta	B 12
21	Sta. Rosa de	
	Cabal	I 8
12	Sto. Domingo	
		G 12
10	San Vicente	
		G 12
12	Santander	K 7
11	Silvia	K 7
12	Sincé	D 10
11	Sincelejo	D 9
11	Sitionuevo	C 11
9	Soacha	I 11
13	Soata	H 14
17	Socorro	G 13
17	Sogamoso	H 13
10	Soledad	C 10
20	Sonson	H 9
14	Tamesis	H 8
12	Tibaná	H 12
14	Timbio	K 6
12	Tocaima	I 10
7	Tulua	J 7
15	Tumaco	L 2
17	Túquerres	M 4
10	Ubate	H 11
11	Zapatoca	G 13
11	Zipaquira	I 11

(COL. AT. 8901)

PERU

Area 482,133 sq.m.
Pop.....6,500,000

PRINCIPAL CITIES
(Including Figures
from Latest Population Estimates)

Pop.—Thousands

7 Abancay...N 15	
70 Arequipa...P 17	
4 Ascope...H 4	
20 Ayacucho..M 13	
14 Callloma..O 16	
15 Cajamarca..H 5	
75 Callao....L 8	
7 Camaná...P 15	
5 Cañete...M 9	
6 Casma...J 6	
2 Castrovirreina...M 11	
12 Catacaos...F 2	
1 Cerro Azul..M 8	
18 Cerro de Pasca...K 9	
4 Chala....O 13	
9 Chepén...H 4	
35 Chiclayo...H 3	
1 Chimbote...J 5	
20 Chincha Alta...M 10	
5 Chorrillos..L 8	
40 Cuzco....M 16	
3 Eten...H 3	
6 Guadalupe..H 4	
5 Huacho...K 7	
5 Hualgayoc..H 5	
9 Huancavelica...M 11	
25 Huancayo..L 11	
6 Huanuco...J 9	
20 Huarás...J 7	
20 Ica....N 11	
1 Ilo...N 17	
25 Iquitos...E 13	
1 Jauja...L 11	
3 Juliaca...O 19	
8 Lambayeque...H 3	
300 Lima...L 8	
2 Locumba...Q 18	
9 Mollendo..P 16	
4 Moquegua..Q18	
8 MoyobambaG 8	
4 Oroya....L 10	
4 Pacasmayo..H 4	
4 Paita...F 1	
1 Pampas...L 11	
1 Pisco...N 9	
20 Piura...F 2	
1 Puerto Maldonado...M 20	
2 Puerto Pizarro...E 1	
15 Puno...O 19	
9 Quilca...P 16	
3 Salavery...I 5	
4 San Pedro de Lloc...H 4	
4 Santa Ana...M 15	
3 Santo Tomás...N 16	
5 Sicuani...N 17	
10 Sullana...F 2	
1 Supe...K 7	
17 Tacna...Q19	
4 Talara...F 1	
1 Tamba de Mora...M 10	
6 Tarmo...L 10	
30 Trujillo...I 5	
3 Tumbes...E 2	
1 Yurimaguas G 9	

ECUADOR

Area 176,155 sq.m.
Pop.....2,758,505

PRINCIPAL CITIES
(Including Figures
from Latest Population Estimates)

Pop.—Thousands

5 Alausi.....D 5	
17 Ambato...D 5	
2 Archidona..B 8	
12 Azogues...D 4	
11 Babahoyo..C 3	
5 Bahia de Carácquez.B 2	
5 Cayambe...B 6	
10 Chone...B 3	
45 Cuenca...D 4	
3 Daule...C 3	
9 Esmeraldas..A 3	
5 Gualaceo...D 5	
11 Guaranda..C 4	
131 Guayaquil.D 3	
11 Ibarra...B 6	
3 Jipijapa...C 2	
16 Latacunga..C 5	
17 Loja...E 4	
7 Machala...E 3	
4 Manta...C 1	
2 Montecristi.C 2	
4 Naranjal...D 3	
10 Otavalo...B 5	
8 Portoviejo..C 2	
118 Quito...B 5	
22 Riobamba..C 5	
2 Santa Rosa.C 9	
2 Taura...D 3	
9 Tulcan...A 6	
5 Zamborondon...D 3	

WESTERN BRAZIL

(For area and pop.
see Brazil)

PRINCIPAL CITIES
(Including Figures
from Latest Population Estimates)

Pop.—Thousands

15 Cruzeiro do Sul..H 15	
12 FlorianoPeixoto...J 23	
11 Fonte Bôa..D 25	
12 Humaytá...I 16	
12 São FelippeH19	
4 S. Paulo de Olivença E 20	
18 Senna Madureira...J 21	
17 Villa Seabra I 18	
12 Xapury..K 21	

(COL. AT. 590)

RAND McNALLY
POPULAR MAP OF
PERU ECUADOR
AND WESTERN BRAZIL
SCALE 1:7,920,000
1 Inch = 125 Statute Miles
1 Centimeter = 79 Kilometers
Statute Miles
Kilometers
Copyright by Rand McNally & Company, Chicago.
Made in U.S.A.

COLOMBIA

ECUADOR

PERU

BRAZIL

AMAZONAS

ACRE

PACIFIC OCEAN

CHILE

BOLIVIA

DISPUTED AREAS
ECUADOR
PERU

GALÁPAGOS ISLANDS
(To Ecuador)
Same scale as main map.

Longitude West of Greenwich

890123456

BRAZIL
Ar.3,285,319 sq.m.
Pop....47,795,000
PRINCIPAL
CITIES
(Including Figures
from Latest Popu-
lation Estimates)
Pop.—Thousands
63 Alagoinhas.I 21
48 Amargoza..J 21
34 Aracati....F 23
108 Arassuahy
                K 19
41 Araxá.....L 15
Bahia, see São
Salvador.
100 Barbacena
                M 17
311 Belém..E 14
168 Bello Hori-
zonte..M 17
112 BlumenauP 13
62 Cachoeira..I 21
62 Cachoeira..Q 10
71 Campina
Grande..G 22
80 Campinas
                N 15
60 Campos..N 19
137 Caratinga
                M 19
40 Catalao..L 15
42 Caxias....P 12
Ceara, see
Fortaleza.
62 Conceicao do
Serro..L 18
60 Condeúba..J 19
84 Conquista..J 20
53 Crato....G 21
44 Cuiabá...K 8
117 Curityba..O 13
76 Curvello..L 17
69 DiamantinaL 18
78 Feira de Sant'
Anna..I 21
48 Florianopolis
                P 14
143 Fortaleza..F 22
64 GaranhunsH 24
67 Grão-Mogol
                K 18
55 Guaratingueta
                N 16
63 Ilheos....M 19
116 Itaperuna
                M 19
44 Januaria..K 17
101 João Pessoa
(Parahiba)
                G 25
70 Juiz de Fora
                M 18
45 LeopoldinaM 18
60 Macahé...M 19
129 Maceió...H 25
86 Manaus
(Manáos)..E 5
67 Marianna.M 18
4 Minas Novas
                K 19
54 Montes Claros
                K 18
113 Nazareth.G 25
125 Niteroi
(Nictheroy)
                N 18
39 Para.....M 17
113 Passo Fundo
                P 11
66 Patrocinio.L 15
85 Pecanha..L 19
60 Pelotas...Q 11
63 Ponte Nova
                M 18
328 Porto Alegre
                Q 12
67 Pouso AlegreI 7
473 Recife...H 25
50 Ribeirão Preto
                M 14
1700 Rio de
Janeiro..N 18
43 Rio Pardo.K 19
61 Sta. Barbara
                M 18
105 Santo Amaro
                G 22
105 Santos...N 15
48 São Carlos do
Pinhal..M 14
67 São João d'el
Rey...M 17
66 São Luiz
(Maranhao) E 18
96 São Miguel dos
GuanhãesL18
1151 São Paulo
                N 15
364 São Salvador
(Bahia)..J 22
39 Soledade..P 12
66 Serro....K 18
126 Theophilo-
Ottoni..L 19
58 Teresina..F 19
50 União....H 24
54 Vicosa...M 18

GUIANA
(British)
Area.89,480 sq. m.
Pop....332,898
PRINCIPAL
CITIES
(Including Figures
from Latest Popu-
lation Estimates)
Pop.—Thousands
65 Georgetown A 7
9 New Amster-
dam......B 7

GUIANA
(Neth.)
Area.54,291 sq. m.
Pop....171,396
PRINCIPAL
CITY
(Including Figures
from Latest Popu-
lation Estimates)
Pop.—Thousands
52 Paramaribo.B 9

GUIANA & ININI
(French)
Area.34,354 sq. m.
Pop....36,975
PRINCIPAL
CITY
(Including Figures
from Latest Popu-
lation Estimates)
Pop.—Thousands
11 Cayenne..B 11
(COL. AT. 326)

BOLIVIA

Area 581,785 sq.m.
Pop....3,282,736

PRINCIPAL CITIES

(Including Figures from Latest Population Estimates)

Pop.—Thousands

6 Acacio.....J 8
4 Achacachi.H 3
4 Achiri.....I 3
3 Achocallo.H 4
7 Aigachi...H 3
6 Aiquile....J 9
4 Alcalá....K 11
9 Ancoraimes
    .....G 2
11 Anzaldo...I 8
4 Araca.....I 5
5 Arani.....I 8
6 Aromaó Sica-
    sica......I 5
5 Ascención.G 14
5 Ayata....G 3
6 Ayoayo...I 4
6 Azurduy..L 12
5 Betanzos..K 9
3 Bolivar...I 7
6 Caiza....L 9
3 Calacoto..I 3
7 Calamarca.H 4
5 Calcha....L 10
5 Callapa...I 4
3 Camata...G 3
6 Capinota..I 3
4 Caquiviri..I 3
4 Caracolla.I 6
4 Cavari....I 6
5 Challacollo..J 5
4 Challapata.K 6
5 Charagua..K 13
4 Charazani..J 2
5 Chayanta..J 7
4 Chuma....G 3
4 Cliza....I 8
38 Cochabamba.I 7
4 Coloni...I 8
8 Colquechaca.J 8
6 Comarapa.J 11
6 Concepcion
    .....H 16
8 CopacabanaH 2
4 Corque...J 5
6 Cotagaita..M 9
4 Cotoca....I 14
4 Escoma....G 2
4 General
    Saavedra.I 13
5 Huanchaca.L 7
6 Huaqui...H 3
6 Huarina...H 3
6 Independencia
    .....I 7
4 Italaque...G 2
4 Izozog....K 14
4 Junchara.N 10
9 Lagunillas K 13
7 Laja....H 3
4 La Loma..M 11
202 La Paz..H 4
4 Livilivi...M 10
6 Macha....J 8
3 Machaca..I 7
6 Mocomoco..G 2
4 Molinero...J 9
4 Monteagudo
    .....K 12
5 Morachata..I 7
3 Moromoro.J 12
41 Oruro.....J 6
7 Padilla...K 11
4 Parapiti Grande
    .....L 13
6 Pária....I 6
5 Peñas....H 3
5 Pescado..K 11
5 Pitantora..I 8
3 Popo.....J 9
7 Pojo.....I 10
5 Poopo....J 6
7 Portachuelo
    .....I 13
36 Potosi...K 8
3 Presto...K 11
4 Pucará...J 12
8 Pucarani.H 3
4 Pulacayo..L 7
8 Punata...I 8
4 Quillacollo.I 7
6 Riberalta..H 7
18 Sacaba...I 8
11 Sacaca...J 7
5 Salinas...K 5
5 Salinas de
    Yocalla..K 8
5 Samaipata.J 12
6 San Benito..I 8
3 San IgnacioI 12
4 San José..I 17
11 San Lucas L 10
7 Sta. Ana de
    Calacala.I 7
21 Sta. Cruz..I 13
8 Santiago de
    Haute..H 3
4 Santiago de
    Machaca..I 2
8 Santibanez..I 7
8 Sipesipe..I 7
3 Sococha...N 9
30 Sucre....K 9
5 Talabera ó
    Puna....K 9
8 Talina....M 8
4 Tapacari..I 7
4 Tarabuco.K 10
4 Tarata...I 8
17 Tarija...M 11
5 Tiaguanaco.H 3
10 Tinguipaya.K 8
4 Tintin....J 9
7 Tiraque...I 8
7 Toco....I 8
6 Tomabe...L 7
4 Toropalca.L 9
7 Totora....I 9
7 Trinidad..F 10
4 Tupiza...M 8
3 Turóchipa K 10
4 Ulloma....I 3
3 Umala....I 4
5 Uyuni....L 8
6 Vacas....I 9
4 VallegrandeJ 12
3 Ventila....I 7
4 Vilavila...I 7
3 Villar....K 11
5 Vitichi....L 10
7 Warnes...I 13
5 Yamparaez
    .....K 10
4 Yura.....L 8

(Col. At. 890)

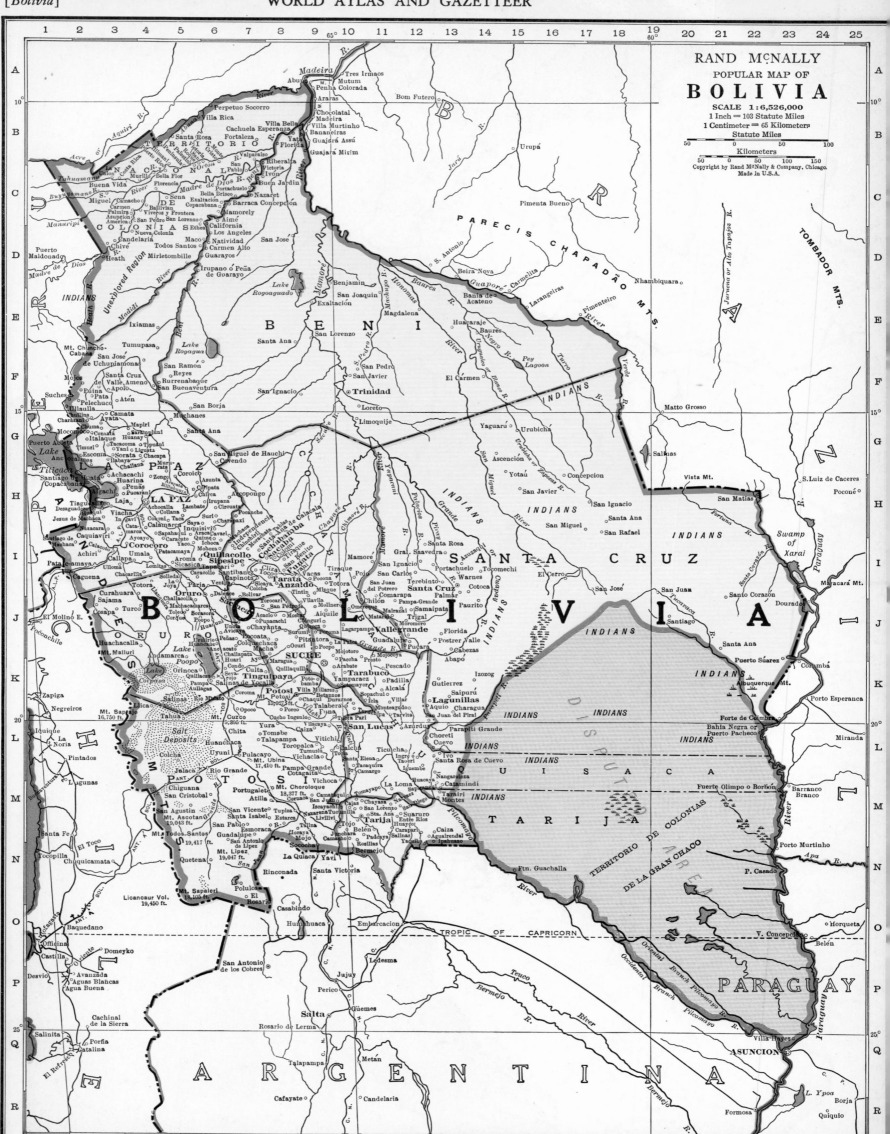

RAND McNALLY
POPULAR MAP OF
BOLIVIA
SCALE 1:6,526,000
1 Inch = 103 Statute Miles
1 Centimeter = 65 Kilometers
Statute Miles
Kilometers
Copyright by Rand McNally & Company, Chicago.
Made in U.S.A.

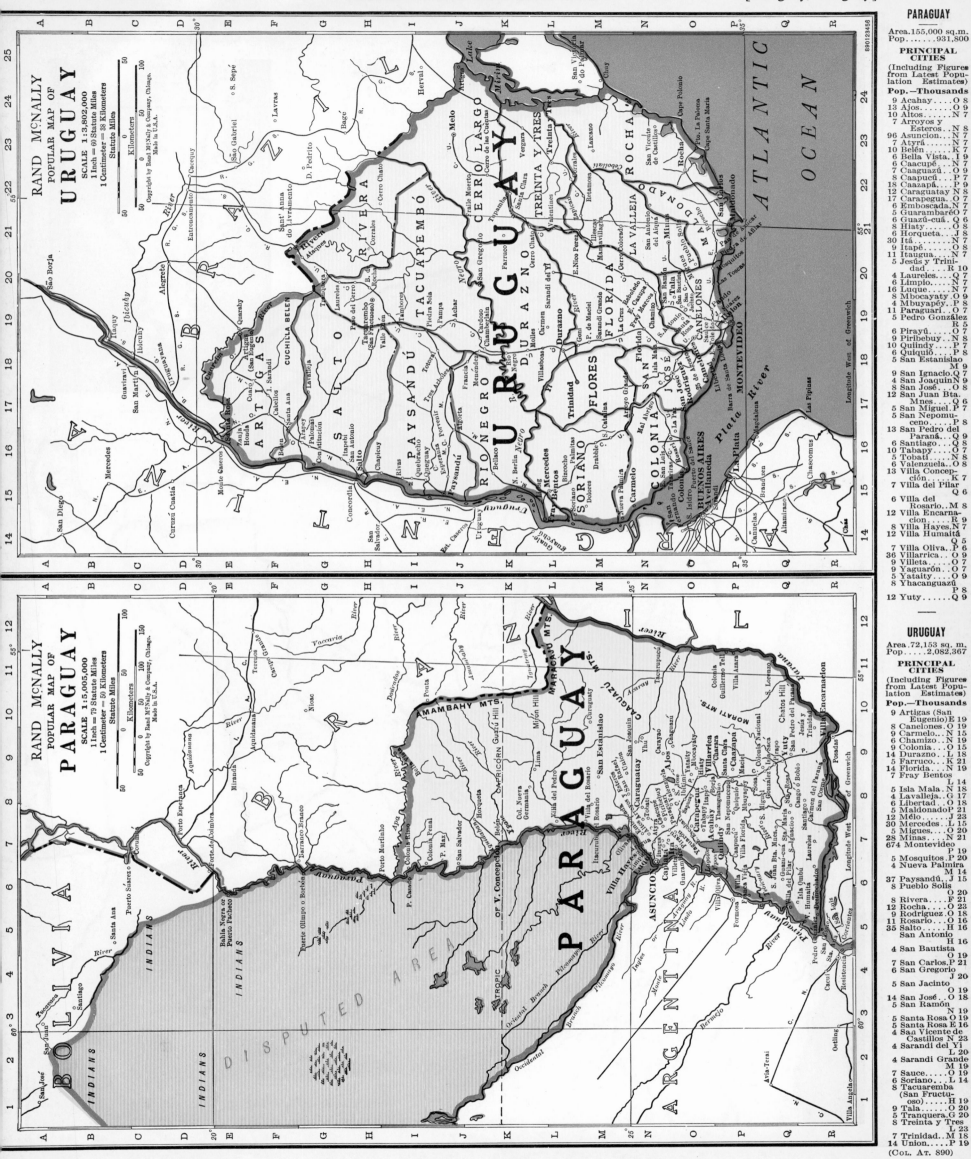

PARAGUAY

Area. 155,000 sq. m.
Pop. 931,800

PRINCIPAL CITIES

(Including Figures from Latest Population Estimates)

Pop.—Thousands

9 Acahay . . . . O 8
13 Ajos . . . . . . O 9
10 Altos . . . . . . N 7
7 Arroyos y
Esteros . . N 8
96 Asuncion . . N 7
7 Atyrá . . . . N 7
10 Belén . . . . N 7
6 Bella Vista . I 9
6 Caacupé . . O 7
7 Caaguazú . . O 7
8 Caapucú . . . P 7
18 Caazapá . . . P 9
6 Caraguatay N 8
17 Carapeguá . O 7
6 Emboscada, N 7
7 Guarambaré O 7
6 Guazú-cuá . Q 6
8 Hiaty . . . . O 8
7 Horqueta . . N 7
30 Itá . . . . . . N 7
9 Itapé . . . . O 7
11 Itauguá . . . N 7
5 Jesús y Trini-
dad . . . . R 10
4 Laureles . . Q 7
6 Limpio . . . N 7
6 Luque . . . . N 7
8 Mbocayaty O 9
4 Mbuyapéy . . P 8
11 Paraguari . . O 7
6 Pedro
González . . R 5
6 Pirayú . . . . O 7
9 Piribebuy . . N 8
10 Quindy . . . P 7
6 Quiquió . . . O 7
5 San Estanislao
M 9
9 San Ignacio. Q 7
4 San Joaquín N 9
8 San José . . O 8
12 San Juan Bta.
Mnes. . . . O 8
5 San Miguel. P 7
5 San Nepomu-
ceno . . . . P 8
13 San Pedro del
Paraná . . Q 9
6 Santiago . . Q 8
10 Tabapy . . . O 7
5 Tobatí . . . . N 7
6 Valenzuela. O 8
13 Villa Concep-
ción . . . . K 7
7 Villa del Pilar
Q 6
6 Villa del
Rosario . . M 8
12 Villa Encarna-
cion . . . . R 9
8 Villa Hayes, N 7
12 Villa Humaitá
Q 6
7 Villa Oliva . P 6
36 Villarrica . . O 7
9 Villeta . . . . O 7
9 Yaguarón . . O 7
5 Yataity . . . O 9
8 Yhacanguazú
P 8
12 Yuty . . . . . Q 9

URUGUAY

Area . 72,153 sq. m.
Pop 2,082,367

PRINCIPAL CITIES

(Including Figures from Latest Population Estimates)

Pop.—Thousands

9 Artigas (San
Eugenio) E 19
8 Canelones . O 19
9 Carmelo . . N 15
6 Chamizo . . O 19
4 Colonia . . . O 15
14 Durazno . . L 18
5 Farruco . . . K 21
14 Florida . . . N 19
7 Fray Bentos
J 14
5 Isla Mala . N 18
4 Lavalleja . . G 17
6 Libertad . . O 18
5 Maldonado P 21
3 Mélo . . . . . J 23
30 Mercedes . I 15
7 Migues . . . O 20
28 Minas . . . . N 21
674 Montevideo
P 19
5 Mosquitos . P 20
4 Nueva Palmira
M 15
37 Paysandú . J 15
5 Pueblo Solís
O 20
8 Rivera . . . . F 21
12 Rocha . . . . O 23
9 Rodriguez . O 19
11 Rosario . . . N 16
35 Salto . . . . . H 16
San Antonio
H 16
4 San Bautista
O 19
7 San Carlos. P 21
6 San Gregorio
J 20
5 San Jacinto
O 19
14 San José . . O 18
5 San Ramón
N 19
5 Santa Rosa O 19
5 Santa Rosa E 16
5 Saa Vicente de
Castillos N 23
4 Sarandí del Yi
L 20
4 Sarandí Grande
M 19
7 Sauce . . . . O 19
6 Soriano . . . L 14
Tacuaremba
(San Fructu-
oso) . . . . H 19
9 Tala . . . . . O 20
5 Tranquera. G 20
5 Treinta y Tres
L 23
7 Trinidad . . M 18
14 Union . . . . . P 19

(COL. AT. 890)

ARGENTINA

Ar. 1,079,965 sq.m.
Pop.....12,564,301

PRINCIPAL
CITIES
(Including Figures
from Latest Popu-
lation Estimates)

Pop.—Thousands
215 Avellaneda
................N 19
40 Azul......P 17
100 Bahía Blanca
................Q 15
42 Balcarce..Q 19
30 Baradero. M 18
20 Bell-Ville. M 14
50 Bolivar...O 16
25 Bragado..N 17
2291 Buenos Aires
................N 19
28 Campana. N 18
21 Canada de
Gomez.. M 16
13 Canuelas..N 19
30 Carlos Casares
................O 16
11 Carmen de
Areco...N 18
20 Catamarca. I 10
57 ChacabucoN 17
29 Chascomus O 20
22 Chivilcoy..N 17
9 Concepcion del
Uruguay
(Uruguay)
................L 19
30 Concordia. L 20
309 Cordoba. L 12
53 Corrientes. I 19
11 Curuzú Cuatiá
................J 20
27 Dolores...O 20
309 Esperanza. L 16
33 Goya.....J 20
13 Gualeguay M 18
25 Gualeguaychú
................M 19
14 Jujuy....F 10
16 Junin....N 16
11 La Banda. I 12
10 La Paz...K 18
180 La Plata. N 20
13 La Rioja..J 9
33 Las Flores .O 18
46 Lincoln...N 15
31 Lobos....N 18
11 Luján....N 18
50 Mar del Plata
................Q 20
77 Mendoza.. M 7
11 Mercedes. J 20
32 Mercedes. N 18
41 Necochea. .Q 19
57 Nuevo de Julio
................O 16
49 Olavarria. .P 17
66 Paraná...L 17
70 PergaminoN 17
10 Posadas..I 22
16 Pringles...Q 16
15 Rafaela...L 15
35 Resistencia. I 18
90 Rio CuartoM12
509 Rosario. M 16
36 Saladillo. .O 18
34 Salta....G 10
49 San Fernando
................N 18
30 San Francisco
................L 15
39 San Isidro. N 19
50 San Juan... J 7
25 San Luis.. M 10
85 San MartinM 7
50 San Nicolas
................M 17
40 San Pedro. M 18
138 Santa Fe. L 16
46 Santiago...I 12
53 Tandil....P 18
46 Tres Arroyos
................Q 17
126 Tucumán H 10
10 25 de MayoO 17
12 Victoria. M 17
20 Villa MariaL 13
18 Villa Mercedes
................M 11
43 Zarate....N 18

CHILE

Area 286,322 sq.m.
Pop.....4,597,254

PRINCIPAL
CITIES
(Including Figures
from Latest Popu-
lation Estimates)

Pop.—Thousands
10 Angol....Q 3
54 Antofagasta F 3
13 Arica....B 3
2 Cauquénes. O 3
55 Chillán....P 3
1 Chuquicamata
................E 5
86 Concepcion. P 2
8 Constitucion O 3
11 Copiapo...I 4
9 Coquimbo. K 3
19 Curico....N 4
52 Iquique...C 3
15 Linares...O 4
12 Los Andes. M 4
6 Los Angeles. P 3
7 Lota.....P 2
31 Magallanes E 21
4 Melipilla. M 4
16 Osorno...A 19
12 Ovalle....K 3
2 Parral....O 3
16 Puerto Montt
................B 19
Punta Arenas,
see Magallanes.
15 Quillota...M 3
32 Rancagua. N 5
14 San Bernardo
................M 4
9 San Carlos. O 3
12 San Felipe. M 4
13 San Fernando
................N 4
844 Santiago.. M 4
33 Serena, La.. J 3
33 Talca....O 3
8 Talcahuano. P 2
81 Temuco...Q 3
5 Traiguen...Q 3
51 Valdivia...R 2
263 Valparaiso M 3
49 Viña del Mar
................M 3

(Col. At. 890)

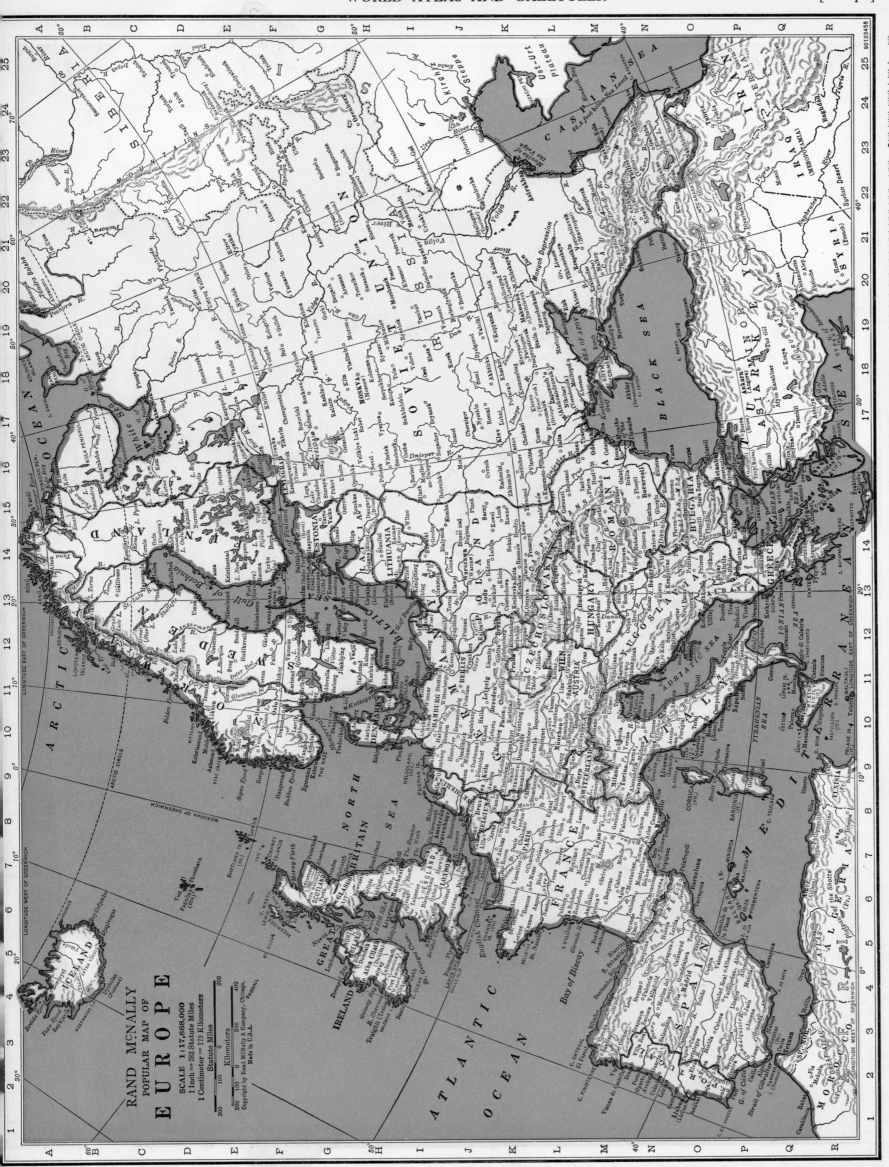

RAND McNALLY
POPULAR MAP OF
EUROPE

SCALE 1:17,868,000
1 Inch = 282 Statute Miles
1 Centimeter = 179 Kilometers
Statute Miles
Kilometers
Copyright by Rand McNally & Company, Chicago.
Made in U.S.A.

BRITISH ISLES

DIVISIONS

ENGLAND AND WALES
Area..58,340 sq. m.
Pop.....40,350,000

IRELAND
Area 26,592 sq. m.
Pop.....2,944,000

Northern Ireland
Area..5,237 sq. m.
Pop.....1,279,753

SCOTLAND
Area..30,405 sq. m.
Pop....4,916,000

PRINCIPAL CITIES
(Including Figures from Latest Population Estimates)

Pop.—Thousands

167 Aberdeen..F 17
42 Accrington K 17
468 Baile Atha Cliath (Dublin)..L 10
72 Barnsley..L 19
73 Barrow...K 15
69 Bath.....O 17
415 Belfast...J 10
148 Birkenhead L 16
1013 Birmingham M 18
125 Blackburn K16
102 Blackpool K 16
177 Bolton....L 16
85 Bootle...L 16
117 Bournemouth P 18
301 Bradford..K 18
147 Brighton..P 22
411 Bristol....O 17
98 Burnley...K 17
49 Burton-on-Trent..M 18
56 Bury.....K 17
67 Cambridge N 22
224 Cardiff....O 16
57 Carlisle...J 16
43 Chatham..O 23
49 Cheltenham N 18
61 Chesterfield L19
81 Cork......N 6
180 Coventry N 18
46 Crewe....L 17
240 Croydon..O 23
72 Darlington.J 18
142 Derby....M 19
82 Devonport Q 14
58 Doncaster L 19
60 Dudley...M 18
176 Dundee..G 16
57 Eastbourne P22
439 Edinburgh H15
66 Exeter....P 15
61 Gillingham P 17
1088 Glasgow H 13
53 Gloucester N 17
90 Govan....H 13
79 Greenock..H 13
92 Great Grimsby K 21
101 Greenwich O23
98 Halifax...K 18
62 Hanley...L 17
65 Hastings..R 23
113 Huddersfield K 18
313 Hull......K 21
89 Ipswich..N 24
43 Lancaster..K 16
483 Leeds.....K 18
239 Leicester M 19
46 Leigh....L 17
80 Leith....H 15
66 Lincoln...L 20
863 Liverpool L16
4299 London...O 21
19 Luimneach M 5
42 Lowestoft M 25
69 Luton....O 21
758 Manchester L 17
71 Merthyr Tydfil...O 15
138 Middlesbrough..J 19
70 Motherwell H 13
283 Newcastle I 19
89 Newport...O 16
92 Northampton N 20
126 Norwich..M 24
283 Nottingham M 19
140 Oldham...L 17
81 Oxford....N 19
120 Paisley...H 13
208 Plymouth Q 14
249 Portsmouth P 20
119 Preston..K 16
97 Reading...O 20
90 Rochdale..K 17
70 Rotherham L 19
25 Rutherglen H 13
517 Sheffield..L 19
176 Southampton P 18
120 Southend O 23
79 Southport..K 16
113 S. Shields I 18
126 Stockport L 17
68 Stockton..J 18
277 Stoke...M 17
186 Sunderland I 18
165 Swansea..O 16
62 Swindon..O 18
158 Tottenham O 22
65 Tynemouth I 18
56 Wakefield..K 18
103 Walsall..M 18
79 Warrington L17
57 Watford ..O 21
81 W. Bromwich M 18
294 Westham..O 22
68 West Hartlepool.....J 19
85 Wigan....L 16
184 Willesden O 21
133 Wolverhampton....M 17
50 Worcester..N 17
85 York......K 19

(Col. At. 89)

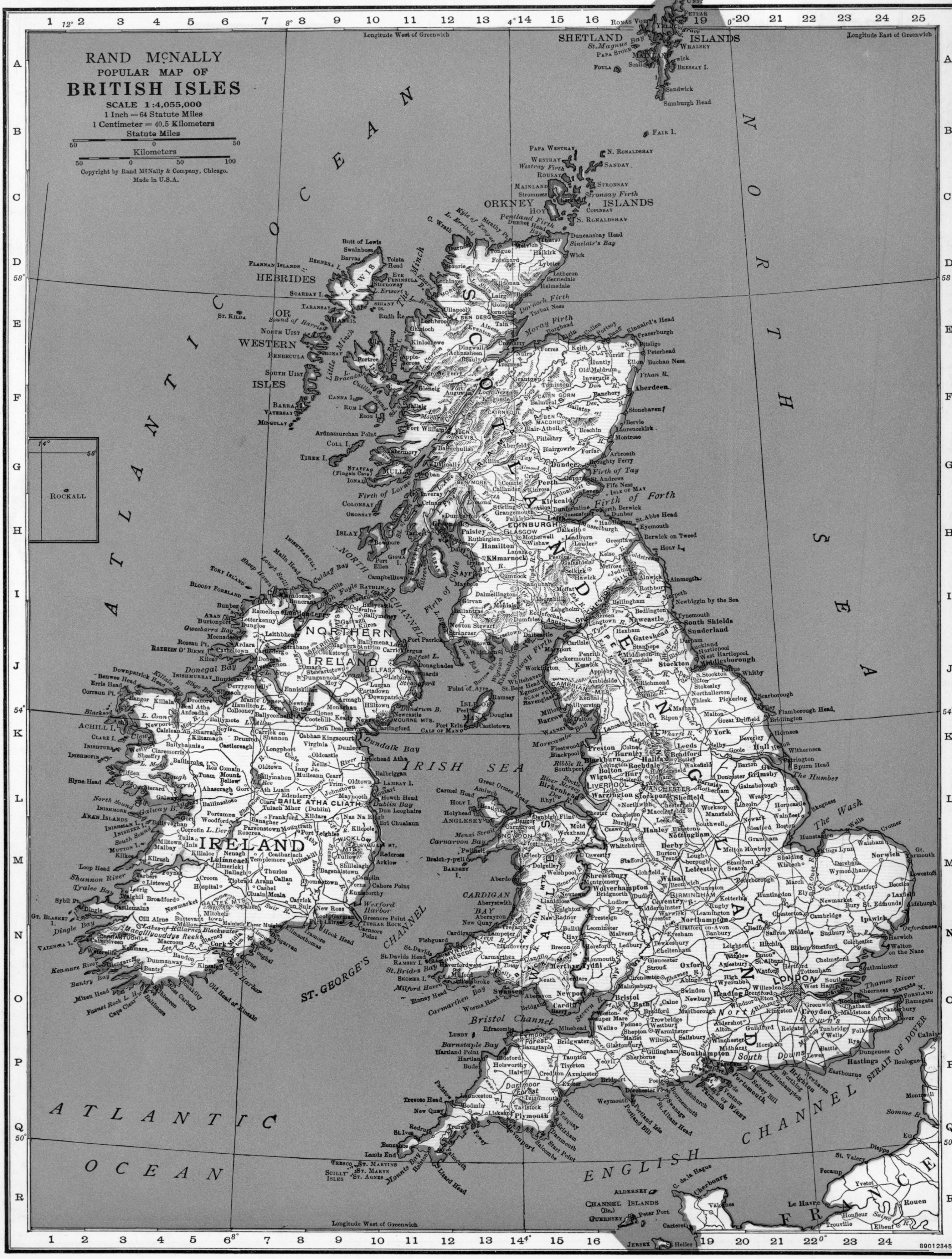

RAND McNALLY POPULAR MAP OF BRITISH ISLES

SCALE 1:4,055,000
1 Inch = 64 Statute Miles
1 Centimeter = 40.5 Kilometers

Statute Miles

Kilometers

Copyright by Rand McNally & Company, Chicago.
Made in U.S.A.

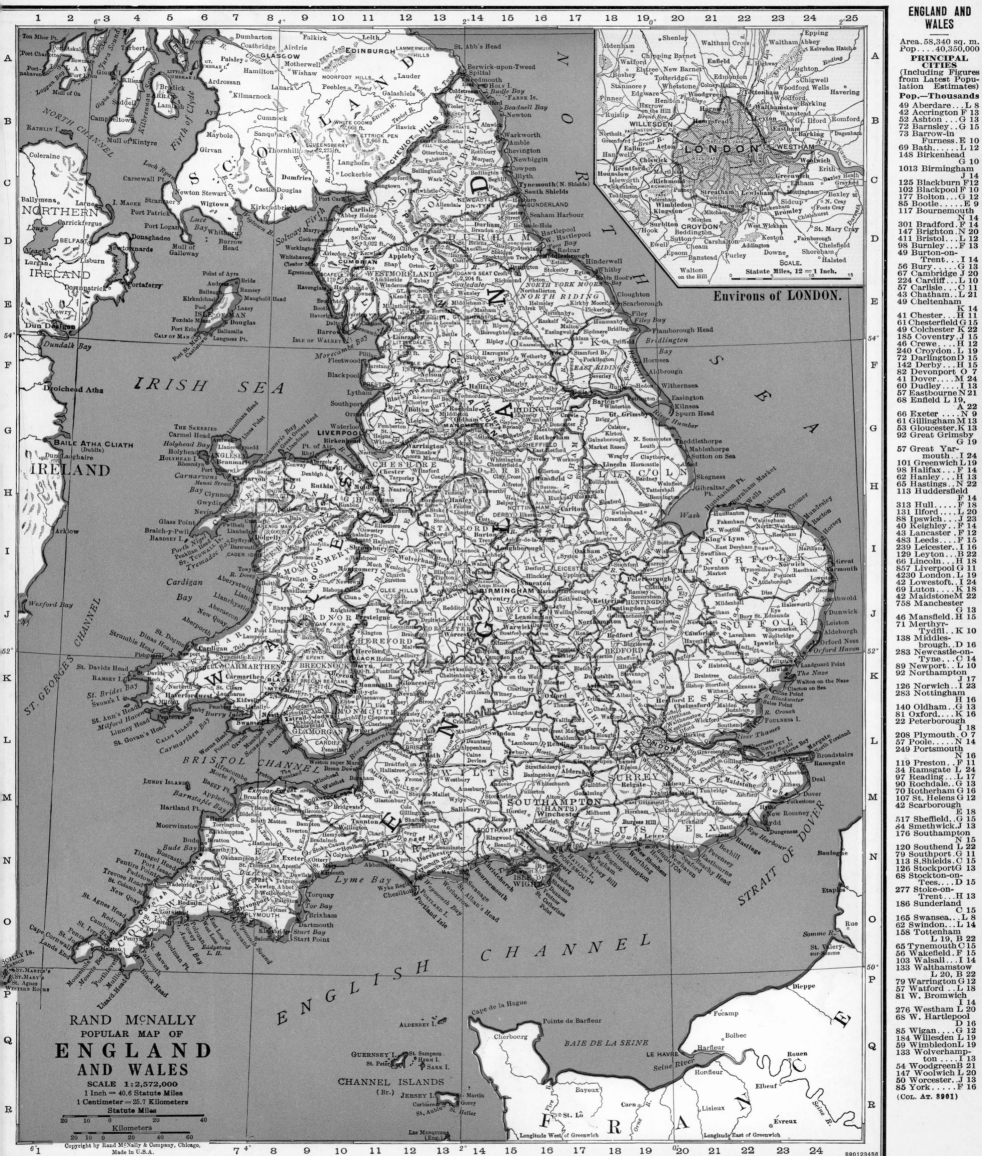

Environs of LONDON.

RAND McNALLY
POPULAR MAP OF
ENGLAND
AND WALES
SCALE 1:2,572,000
1 Inch = 40.6 Statute Miles
1 Centimeter = 25.7 Kilometers
Statute Miles
Kilometers

Copyright by Rand McNally & Company, Chicago.
Made in U.S.A.

SCOTLAND

Area .30,405 sq. m.
Pop.....4,916,000

PRINCIPAL CITIES

(Including Figures from Latest Population Estimates)

Pop.—Thousands

167	Aberdeen . I 23
2	Aberfeldy . K 16
26	Airdrie.... N 16
18	Alloa......M 17
5	Alva......M 17
3	Alyth.....K 16
5	Annan.....Q 19
18	Arbroath..K 22
14	Ardrossan .O 13
4	Armadale .M 17
40	Ayr.......O 14
4	Banff.....G 22
11	Barrhead..N 14
18	Bathgate. M 18
5	Blairgowrie K 19
10	Borrowstoun-
	ness..... M 18
8	Brechin..J 21
6	Buckie....G 20
6	Burntisland M 19
2	Callander . L 15
5	Campbelltown O 9
5	Carnoustie K 21
47	ClydebankM 14
43	CoatbridgeN 16
2	Coupar Angus K 19
13	Cowdenbeath M 19
6	Crieff.....L 17
5	Cupar....L 20
3	Dalbeattie.Q 17
8	Dalkeith. M 20
3	Darvel...N 15
3	Dingwall . G 14
22	Dumbarton M 14
19	Dumfries .Q 18
5	Dunbar...M 21
3	Dunblane. L 16
176	Dundee. .K 20
41	Dunfermline M 18
439	Edinburgh M 19
10	Elgin.....G 19
36	Falkirk...M 17
11	Forfar....K 20
8	Forres....G 17
10	Fraserburgh G 23
13	Galashiels .O 21
6	Galston...O 14
8	Girvan....P 13
1088	Glasgow N 15
21	Grangemouth M 17
79	Greenock. N 13
6	Haddington M 21
44	Hamilton. N 16
18	Hawick...O 21
9	Helensburgh M 13
5	Huntly....G 21
5	Inverkeithing M 19
23	Inverness. H 15
2	Inverurie. .H 22
9	Irvine.....O 14
4	Jedburgh .O 22
13	Johnstone. N 14
6	Keith.....G 20
6	Kelso....O 22
36	Kilmarnock O 14
10	Kilsyth...N 16
6	KilwinningN 13
3	Kinross...L 18
46	Kirkcaldy M 19
17	Kirkintilloch N 15
4	Kirkwall. .B 20
6	Kirriemuir K 20
9	Lanark...N 17
3	Langholm P 20
12	Largs....N 12
80	Leith....M 19
6	Lerwick...C 4
7	Leven....L 20
7	LinlithgowM 18
2	Lockerbie P 19
4	Lossiemouth F 19
6	Maybole . .P 13
5	Melrose...O 21
5	Milngavie M 15
4	Moffat....P 18
2	Monifieth .K 21
12	Montrose . J 21
65	Motherwell N 16
17	Musselburgh M 20
6	Nairn....G 16
3	Newport. .K 20
4	North Berwick M 21
6	Oban.....L 12
120	Paisley...N 14
6	Peebles...N 19
35	Penicuik . P 19
35	Perth.....L 18
15	Peterhead. G 25
20	Port Glasgow M 13
9	Rothesay. N 12
25	Rutherglen N 15
8	St. Andrews L 21
7	Selkirk...O 21
23	Stirling...M 16
5	Stonehaven I 23
4	Stornoway .E 7
3	Stranraer. Q 12
2	Stromness B 18
8	Tain......F 15
7	Turriff....G 22
4	Whitburn M 18
10	Wick.....D 19

(Col. At. 8901)

SHETLAND ISLANDS

RAND McNALLY
POPULAR MAP OF
SCOTLAND

SCALE 1:1,736,000
1 Inch = 27.4 Statute Miles
1 Centimeter = 17.4 Kilometers
Statute Miles

Kilometers

890123456

RAND McNALLY
POPULAR MAP OF
IRELAND
AND NORTHERN IRELAND
SCALE 1:1,521,000
1 Inch = 24 Statute Miles
1 Centimeter = 15.2 Kilometers
Statute Miles

Copyright by Rand McNally & Company, Chicago.
Made in U.S.A.

DENMARK

Area..16,571 sq. m.
Pop.....3,749,000

PRINCIPAL CITIES
(Including Figures from Latest Population Estimates)
Pop.—Thousands

10 Aabenraa
   (Apenrade)M 7
2 Aal........J 2
48 Aalborg....D 10
96 Aarhus....H 12
2 Aars.......E 9
2 Allinge-Sandvig
             Q 23
5 Assens....L 10
3 Bogense...K 11
2 Bramminge.K 5
6 Brönderslev
             C 10
2 Brande....I 7
2 Dragör....K 23
2 Ebeltoft..H 14
29 Esbjerg...K 3
5 Faaborg...M 12
2 Fakse.....L 21
20 Fredericia K 10
109 Frederiksberg
             J 23
10 Frederikshavn
             B 13
3 Frederikssund
             J 21
62 Gentofte..J 22
3 Glostrup..J 22
5 Grenaa...G 15
2 Grindsted.J 5
16 Haderslev
   (Haderslben)
             L 8
2 Hadsund..F 11
3 Haslev....L 20
16 Helsingör.I 22
11 Herning...H 5
7 Hilleröd..I 22
11 Hjörring..B 10
6 Hobro.....F 9
12 Holbaek...J 19
10 Holstebro..G 4
28 Horsens...J 9
7 Kalundborg
             J 16
3 Kerteminde
             K 14
686 Köbenhavn
             J 23
6 Köge......K 21
22 Kolding...K 8
2 Korsör....L 16
5 Lemvig....F 3
3 Lögstör...E 8
2 Lögumkloster
             M 6
7 Lyngby...J 23
5 Maribo....N 18
2 Marstal...N 13
14 Middelfart K 10
11 Naestved..L 20
15 Nakskov...N 16
5 Neksö.....R 24
2 Nibe......D 9
7 Nörresundby
             D 11
10 Nyborg...L 15
5 Nyköbing..E 5
4 Nyköbing..I 18
2 Nysted....O 19
14 Nyköbing N 20
5 Odder.....I 11
76 Odense....L 13
30 Randers...G 10
4 Ribe......L 5
2 Ringe.....L 13
4 Ringköbing
             H 3
6 Ringsted..J 19
3 Rödby....O 18
2 Rönne.....R 23
14 Roskilde..J 20
2 Rudkjöbing
             N 14
3 Saeby....C 13
2 Saltum....C 9
11 Silkeborg..H 9
4 Skagen....A 13
2 Skanderborg
             I 11
5 Skelskör..L 17
3 Skern.....I 3
10 Skive.....F 6
12 Sönderborg
             N 10
3 Sorö......K 18
2 Stege.....M 21
2 Storeheddinge
             L 22
14 Struer....G 4
5 Stubbeköbing
             N 20
SvendborgM 13
8 Thisted...D 5
3 Thorshavn
6 Tönder...M 5
2 Usseröd..I 22
2 Vamdrup..K 8
7 Varde.....J 3
3 Vejen.....K 6
23 Vejle.....J 8
17 Viborg....G 8
6 Vordingborg
             M 19

ICELAND

Area..39,709 sq. m.
Pop.......116,948

PRINCIPAL CITIES
(Including Figures from Latest Population Estimates)
Pop.—Thousands

4 Akureyri..B 21
34 Reykjavik.C 18
(Col. At. 789)

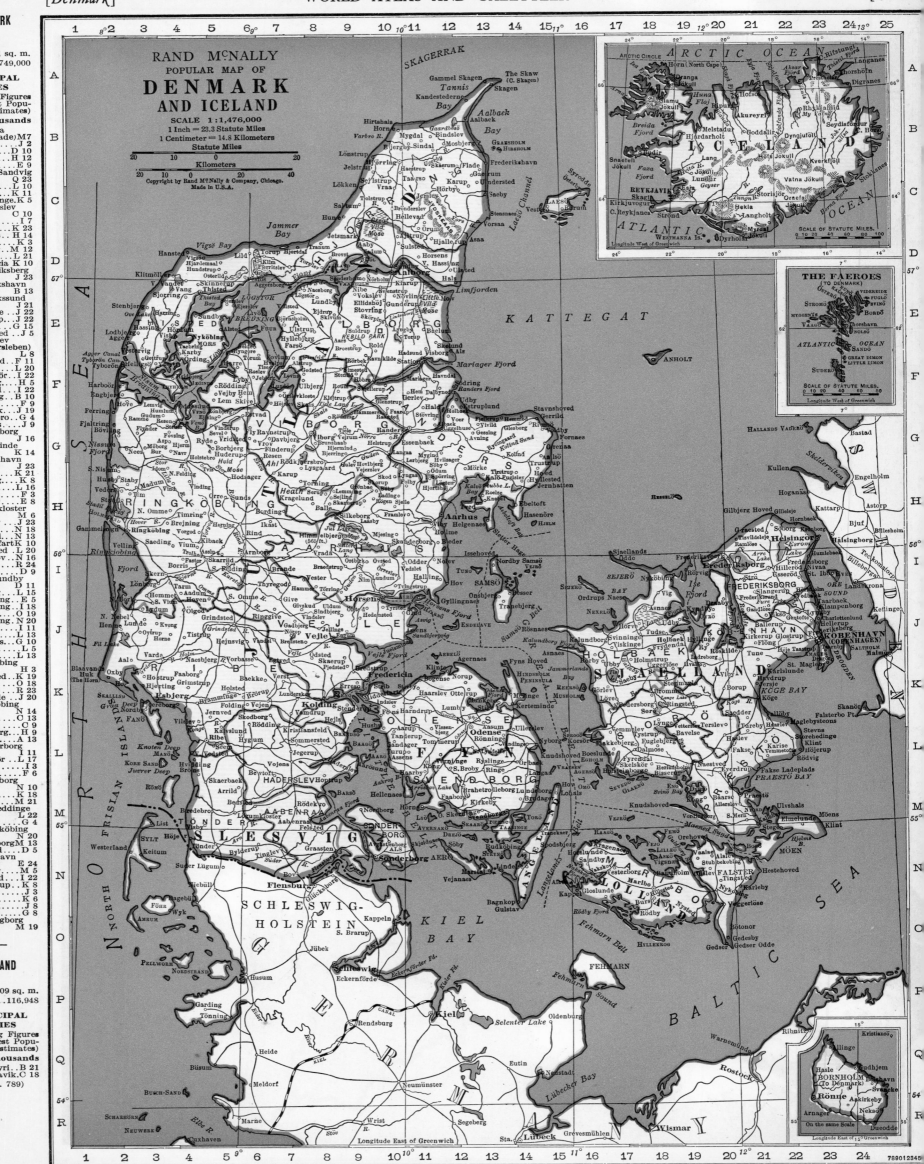

RAND McNALLY
POPULAR MAP OF
DENMARK
AND ICELAND
SCALE 1:1,476,000
1 Inch = 23.3 Statute Miles
1 Centimeter = 14.8 Kilometers
Statute Miles

Copyright by Rand McNally & Company, Chicago.
Made in U.S.A.

THE FAEROES
(TO DENMARK)

BORNHOLM
(To Denmark)

RAND McNALLY
POPULAR MAP OF
**NETHERLANDS
BELGIUM
AND LUXEMBOURG**
SCALE 1:1,609,000
1 Inch = 25.4 Statute Miles
1 Centimeter = 16.1 Kilometers
Statute Miles

Copyright by Rand McNally & Company, Chicago.
Made in U.S.A.

ZUIDER ZEE LAND
RECLAMATION PROJECT

AMSTERDAM
AND ITS
ENVIRONS.
SCALE OF MILES

ANVERS (ANTWERP), GAND (GHENT), AND THE LOWER SCHELDT.

NETHERLANDS

Area .13,202 sq. m.
Pop.....8,639,595

PRINCIPAL CITIES
(Including Figures from Latest Population Estimates)
Pop.—Thousands

28 Alkmaar..	E 13
23 Almelo....	F 23
39 Amersfoort	G 17
782 Amsterdam	
	F 14
67 Apeldoorn	G 19
84 Arnhem....	I 18
18 Assen.....	D 22
45 Breda.....	J 13
51 Delft.....	H 11
36 Deventer..	G 20
57 Dordrecht.	I 13
31 Ede.......	H 18
100 Eindhoven	
	J 16
41 Emmen....	D 24
87 Enschede..	H 24
Flushing, see Vlissingen.	
29 Gouda.....	H 13
115 Groningen	
	C 22
129 Haarlem..	F 14
47 Heerlen...	N 19
25 Helder....	D 13
34 Helmond..	J 18
34 Hengelo..	G 23
67 Hilversum.	G 15
20 Kampen...	F 19
16 Katwijk aan Zee..	G 11
37 Kerkrade..	L 19
48 Leeuwarden	
	C 18
71 Leiden....	G 12
31 Lonneker..	G 24
61 Maastricht	
	M 18
18 Middelburg	J 9
89 Nijmegen..	I 18
25 Rheden...	H 19
22 Roosendaal-en-Nispen..	J 12
595 Rotterdam	
	H 12
61 Schiedam.	H 12
482 's Gravenhage	
	H 11
42 's Hertogen-bosch..	I 16
The Hague, see 's Gravenhage.	
87 Tilburg...	I 15
161 Utrecht..	H 15
41 Velsen...	F 13
24 Venlo.....	J 20
28 Vlaardingen	
	H 11
22 Vlissingen.	J 7
33 Zaandam..	F 14
41 Zwolle....	F 20

BELGIUM

Area .11,752 sq. m.
Pop.....8,299,940

PRINCIPAL CITIES
(Including Figures from Latest Population Estimates)
Pop.—Thousands

38 Alost.....	L 10
278 Anvers (Antwerp)	
	K 11
44 Berchem..	K 12
19 Boom.....	L 11
54 Borgerhout	K 12
51 Bruges...	K 6
194 Bruxelles (Brussels)	M 12
28 Charleroi.	N 12
18 Courcelles	N 12
39 Courtrai..	M 6
8 Furnes....	L 3
167 Gand.....	L 9
16 Gentbrugge	L 9
19 Gheel.....	L 14
Ghent, see Gand.	
25 Gilly.....	N 12
17 Hal.......	M 11
26 Hasselt...	L 16
35 Herstal...	M 17
33 Hoboken..	R 8
30 Jumet....	N 12
22 Laeken...	L 11
24 La Louvière	
	N 11
166 Liège....	M 17
28 Lierre....	L 12
24 Lokeren..	L 9
40 Louvain..	M 13
60 Malines..	L 12
22 Marcinelle	O 12
20 Menin....	M 5
27 Merxem..	K 12
28 Mons.....	N 10
32 Mouscron.	M 6
30 Namur....	N 13
49 Ostend...	K 4
20 Ougrée...	N 17
24 Renaix...	M 7
24 Roulers...	L 5
42 St. Nicolas	K 11
123 Schaerbeek	
	M 12
45 Seraing...	M 17
21 Tirlemont.	M 14
38 Tournai...	M 7
27 Turnhout..	K 14
50 Uccle....	M 11
41 Verviers..	N 18
Veurne, see Furnes.	
23 Vilvorde..	L 12
18 Wetteren.	L 9

LUXEMBOURG

Area....998 sq. m.
Pop....296,913

PRINCIPAL CITIES
(Including Figures from Latest Population Estimates)
Pop.—Thousands

4 Diekirch..	Q 21
3 Echternach	
	Q 22
29 Esch......	P 19
4 Ettelbrück	Q 20
3 Grevenmacher	
	Q 21
58 Luxembourg	
	R 20

(COL. AT. 789)

FRANCE

Area 212,681 sq.m.
Pop.... 41,905,968

PRINCIPAL CITIES

(Including Figures from Latest Population Estimates)

Pop.—Thousands

19 Abbeville....F 13
27 Agen.....O 10
43 Aix......P 21
37 Ajaccio...Q 2
30 Albi.....O 14
41 Alès.....O 18
30 Alfortville..B 7
94 Amiens....F 13
88 Angers....J 8
39 Angouleme M 10
59 Argenteuil..A 3
29 Arles.....P 19
31 Arras....E 15
72 Asnières...A 4
56 Aubervilliers A 6
24 Auxerre...I 16
59 Avignon...O 20
52 Bastia....P 4
31 Bayonne...P 8
46 Belfort...I 23
73 Besançon..I 22
73 Béziers...P 16
26 Blois.....I 12
258 Bordeaux..N 7
52 Boulogne..E 12
97 Boulogne sur
Seine....B 4
49 Bourges...J 14
79 Brest.....H 1
29 Brive....M 13
61 Caen.....G 9
68 Calais....D 13
30 Cambrai..F 15
49 Cannes...P 24
33 Carcassonne
P 14
29 Castres....P 14
33 Chalon-sur-
Saone...K 19
36 Chalons-sur-
Marne..G 18
28 Chambery M 21
27 Chartres..H 12
33 Chateauroux
K 12
39 Cherbourg..F 7
23 Cholét....I 9
101 Clermont-
Ferrand..L 15
45 Clichy....A 5
49 Colmar...I 23
52 Colombes..A 4
59 Courbevoie..A 3
26 Denain....E 15
26 Dieppe...F 12
46 Dieppe...I 2
24 Dijon....I 19
96 Dijon....I 19
42 Douai....E 15
43 Drancy...A 7
31 Dunkerque
(Dunkirk) D 14
17 Epernay...G 17
33 Epinal....I 22
20 Fougeres..H 7
29 Gennevilliers
A 5
96 Grenoble..M 21
44 Issy-les-Mouli-
neaux....B 4
45 Ivry-sur-Seine
B 5
48 La Rochelle..L 8
28 Laval....I 8
165 Le Creusot K 18
85 Le Havre..G 9
83 Le Mans...I 10
53 Lens.....E 14
65 Levallois-
Perret....A 5
201 Lille.....E 15
95 Limoges...L 12
46 Lorient...I 2
24 Luneville..H 22
571 Lyon....L 19
914 Marseille.P 20
24 Maubeuge.E 16
83 Metz....G 21
43 Montlucon K 14
91 Montpellier
P 17
72 Montreuil-
sous-Bois..B 7
33 Montrouge..B 5
97 Mulhouse..I 23
121 Nancy....H 22
46 Nanterre...B 3
195 Nantes....J 7
30 Narbonne..P 16
34 Nevers....J 16
242 Nice.....O 25
94 Nimes....O 18
28 Niort....K 9
73 Orleans...I 13
38 Pantin....A 7
2830 Paris....H 14
40 Pau......P 8
29 Perigueux.M 11
72 Perpignan.Q 16
44 Poitiers..K 10
44 Puteaux...B 3
117 Reims....G 17
89 Rennes...I 6
29 Roanne...L 17
29 Rochefort..L 8
107 Roubaix..E 15
123 Rouen....G 12
32 St. Brieuc..H 4
78 St. Denis..G 14
190 St. Etienne
M 19
57 St. Maur-des-
Fosses....B 8
43 St. Nazaire..J 4
51 St. Ouen sur
Seine....A 5
49 St. Quentin
F 15
37 Sète......P 17
193 Strasbourg
H 24
35 Tarbes...P 10
150 Toulon...P 21
213 Toulouse..P 12
78 Tourcoing..E 15
84 Tours....J 11
58 Troyes...I 17
37 Valence...N 20
43 Valenciennes
E 16
74 Versailles..H 13
25 Vienne...M 19
49 Vincennes..B 6
47 Vitry-sur-Seine
C 6

(Col. At. 890)

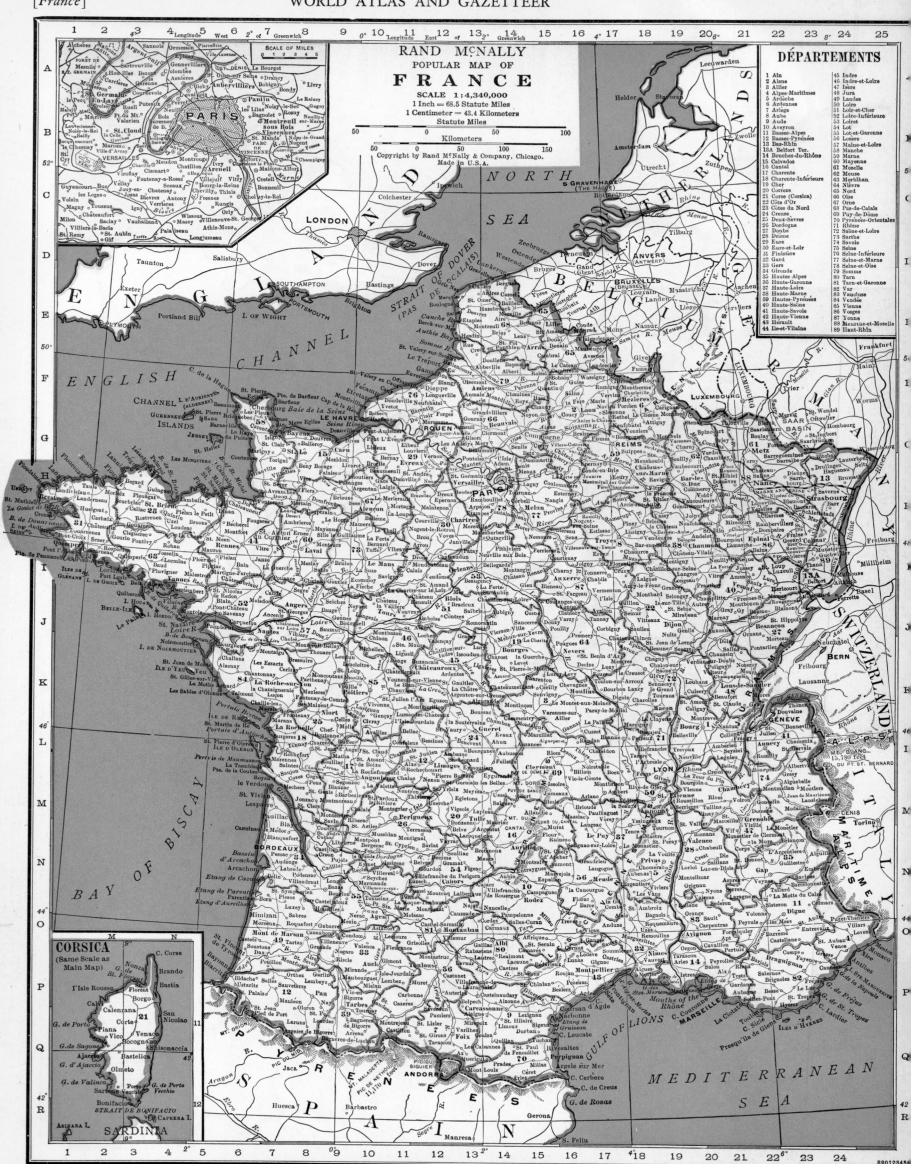

RAND McNALLY
POPULAR MAP OF
FRANCE
SCALE 1:4,340,000
1 Inch = 68.5 Statute Miles
1 Centimeter = 43.4 Kilometers
Copyright by Rand McNally & Company, Chicago.
Made in U.S.A.

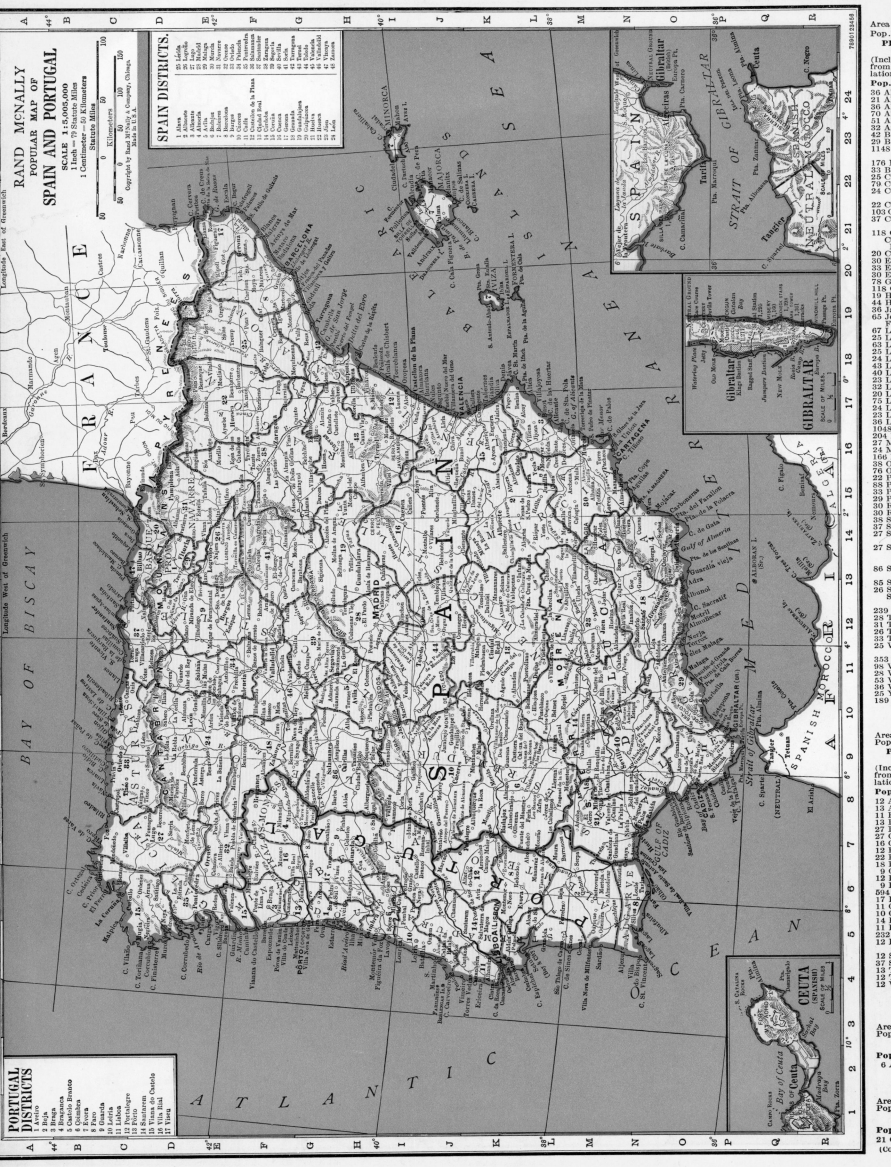

SPAIN
Area 195,010 sq.m.
Pop....24,583,096
PRINCIPAL CITIES
(Including Figures from Latest Population Estimates)
Pop.—Thousands

36	Albacete	K 14
21	Alcira	K 16
36	Alcóy	L 17
70	Alicante	L 17
51	Almeria	O 14
32	Antequera	O 11
42	Badajoz	H 8
29	Badalona	G 21
1148	Barcelona	G 20
176	Bilbao	C 13
32	Burgos	E 12
25	Cáceres	J 9
79	Cadiz	O 8
5	Cangas de Tineo	C 8
22	Carmona	N 9
103	Cartagena	M 16
37	Castellon de la Plana	J 17
118	Córdoba	M 10
	Coruña, see La Coruña	
20	Cuevas	N 14
30	Ecija	N 10
33	Elche	L 16
10	El Ferrol	C 6
78	Gijón	C 8
118	Granada	N 12
19	Hellin	N 14
44	Huelva	N 7
36	Jaén	M 12
65	Jerez de la Frontera	O 9
67	La Coruña	C 6
25	La Estrada	D 6
8	La Linea	N 11
25	La Unión	N 16
24	Léon	D 10
18	Lérida	F 18
40	Lináres	M 12
5	Llanes	C 11
32	Logrono	E 14
75	Lorca	M 15
9	Luarca	C 9
36	Lucena	N 11
36	Lugo	D 7
1048	Madrid	I 12
204	Malaga	O 11
27	Manresa	F 20
24	Mataro	G 21
166	Murcia	M 16
38	Orihuela	L 16
70	Oviedo	C 9
22	Palencia	F 11
88	Palma	J 21
50	Pamplona	D 15
67	Pontevedra	E 6
30	Réus	G 19
15	Ronda	O 10
39	Sabadell	F 20
65	Salamanca	H 9
27	San Fernando	P 8
27	Sanlúcar de Barrameda	O 8
86	San Sebastian	C 15
65	Santander	C 12
26	Santiago	D 6
	Saragossa, see Zaragoza	
239	Sevilla	N 9
32	Tarragona	G 19
31	Tarrasa	F 20
26	Toledo	I 11
33	Tortosa	H 18
25	Valdepeñas	
353	Valencia	J 17
98	Valladolid	F 11
15	Vallecas	I 12
53	Vigo	E 5
39	Vitoria	D 14
25	Yecla	L 16
189	Zaragoza	G 16

PORTUGAL
Area..34,894 sq.m.
Pop....6,825,883
PRINCIPAL CITIES
(Including Figures from Latest Population Estimates)
Pop.—Thousands

12	Almada	K 4
12	Aveiro	H 5
11	Barreiro	K 4
8	Beja	L 6
27	Braga	F 6
27	Coimbra	H 5
12	Covilhã	H 7
12	Elvas	K 7
12	Evora	L 6
18	Faro	N 6
6	Guimarães	F 6
15	Ilhavo	H 5
9	Lamego	G 6
594	Lisboa	K 5
11	Loulé	N 6
11	Olhão	N 6
12	Ovar	G 5
14	Palmella	K 5
11	Portalegre	J 7
232	Porto	G 5
12	Povoa de Varzim	F 5
12	Santarem	J 5
37	Setubal	L 5
13	Tavira	N 6
12	Torres Novas	J 6
12	Viana do Castello	F 5

ANDORRA
Area....191 sq.m.
Pop......5,231
CITY
Pop.— Hundreds
6 Andorra ..D 19

GIBRALTAR
Area......2 sq. m.
Pop........21,372
CITY
Pop.—Thousands
21 Gibraltar..P 18
(Col. At. 789)

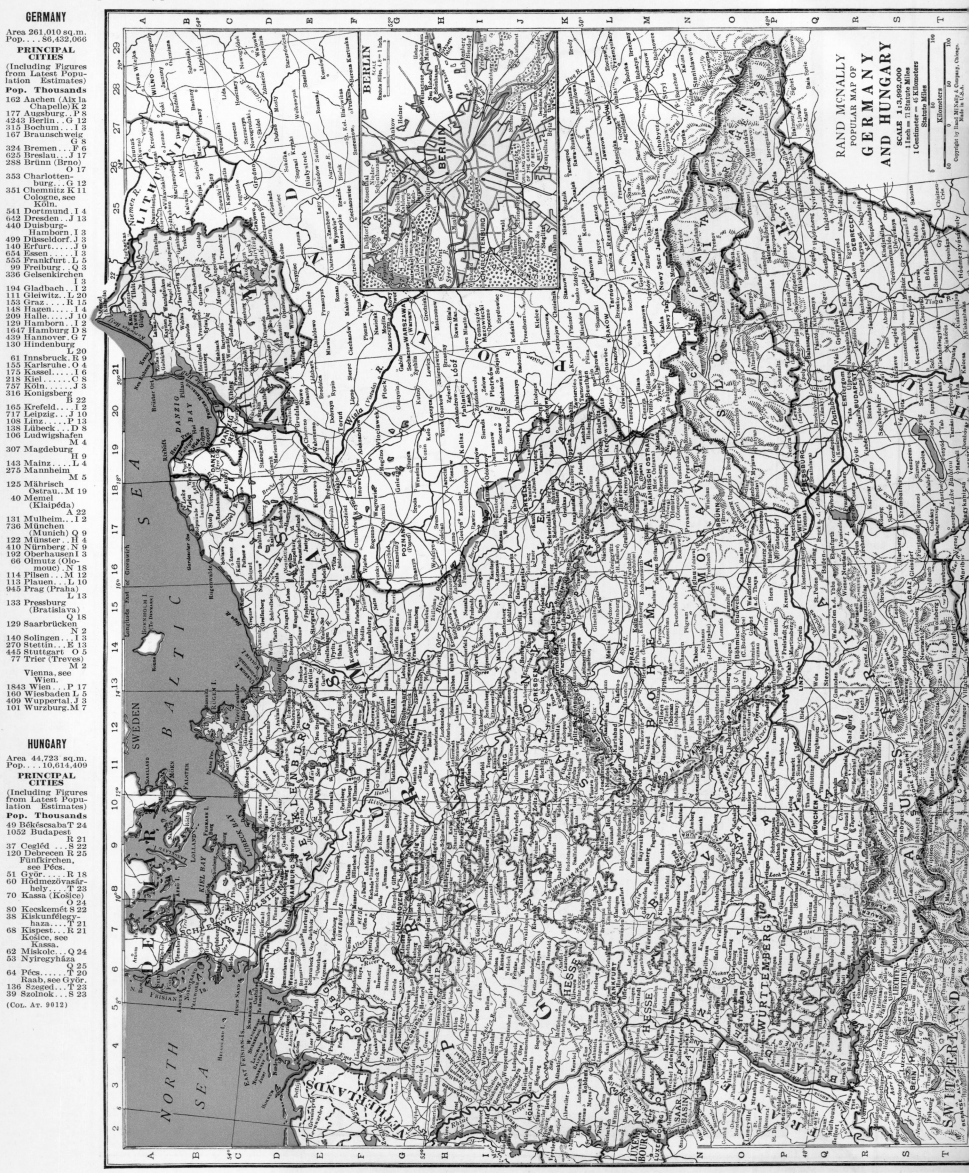

RAND M?NALLY
POPULAR MAP OF
GERMANY
AND HUNGARY

SCALE 1:3,992,000
1 Inch = 71 Statute Miles
1 Centimeter = 45 Kilometers

Copyright by Rand M?Nally & Company, Chicago.

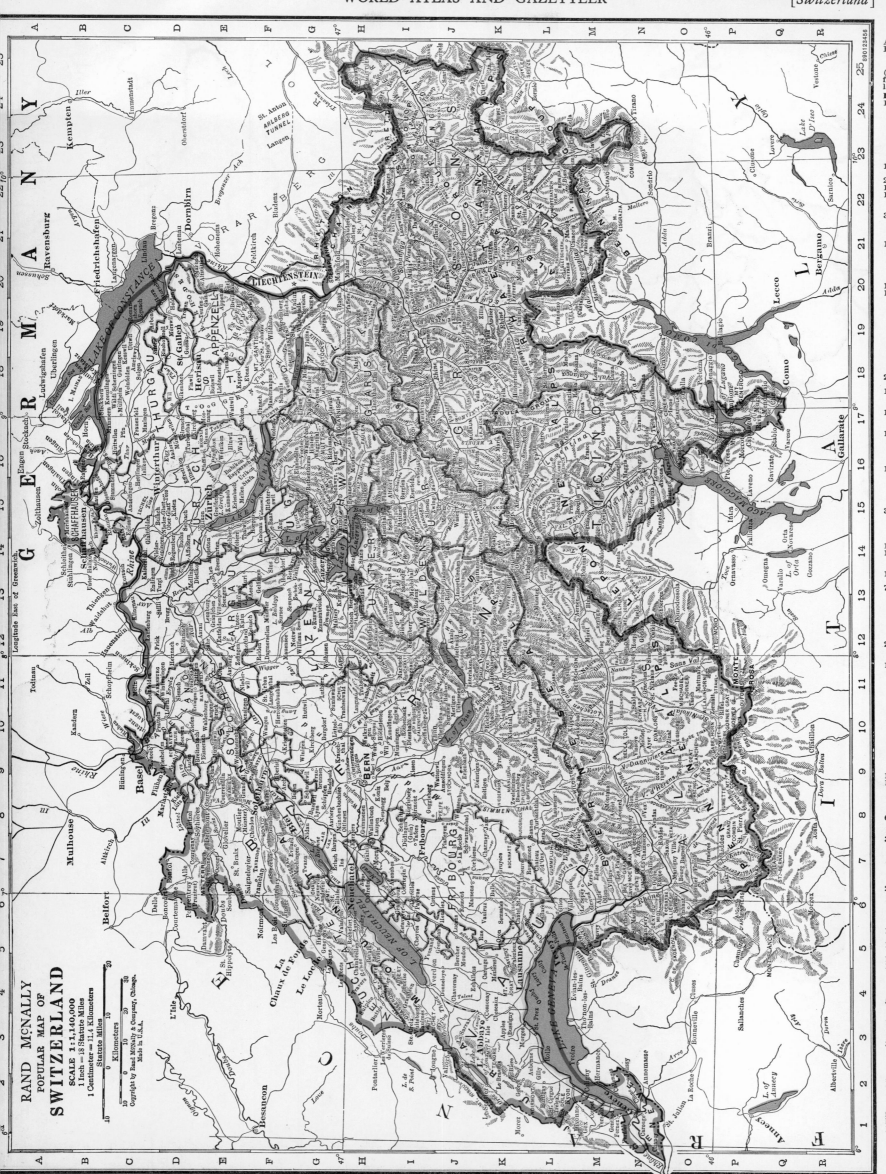

RAND McNALLY
POPULAR MAP OF
SWITZERLAND
SCALE 1:1,140,000
1 Inch = 18 Statute Miles
1 Centimeter = 11.4 Kilometers
Statute Miles

Kilometers

Copyright by Rand McNally & Company, Chicago.
Made in U.S.A.

ITALY

Area 119,703 sq. m.
Pop....43,691,000

PRINCIPAL CITIES

(Including Figures
from Latest Popu-
lation Estimates)
Pop.—Thousands

MALTA and GOZO

Area...122 sq. m.
Pop......264,663

PRINCIPAL CITY

(Including Figures
from Latest Popu-
lation Estimates)
Pop.—Thousands

SAN MARINO

Area...38 sq. m.
Pop......14,170

PRINCIPAL CITY

(Including Figures
from Latest
Estimates)
Pop.—Thousands

(Col. At. 89)

Environs of ROMA

RAND McNALLY
POPULAR MAP OF
ITALY

SCALE 1:4,815,000
1 Inch = 76 Statute Miles
1 Centimeter = 48 Kilometers
Statute Miles

Kilometers

Copyright by Rand McNally & Company, Chicago.
Made in U.S.A.

RAND McNALLY
POPULAR MAP OF
CENTRAL EUROPE
SCALE 1:7,667,000
1 Inch = 121 Statute Miles
1 Centimeter = 77 Kilometers
Statute Miles
Kilometers
Copyright by Rand McNally & Company, Chicago.
Made in U.S.A.

CENTRAL EUROPE
(Including Figures
from Latest Popu-
lation Estimates)

ALBANIA
Area 10,629 sq. m.
Pop.....1,050,000
PRINCIPAL
CITY
Pop.—Thousands
31 Tiranë...M 13

BULGARIA
Area 39,814 sq. m.
Pop.....6,319,232
PRINCIPAL
CITY
Pop.—Thousands
321 Sofija (Sofia)
........L 17

CZECHOSLOVAKIA
Area 38,252 sq. m.
Pop.....10,285,900
PRINCIPAL
CITIES
Pop.—Thousands
125 Moravská-
Ostrava, F 11
945 Praha
(Prague).F 7

GREECE
Area 54,092 sq. m.
Pop.....7,020,000
PRINCIPAL
CITIES
Pop.—Thousands
495 Athēnai
(Athens) P 18
265 Thessalonikē
........N 17

HUNGARY
Area 40,510 sq. m.
Pop.....10,076,315
PRINCIPAL
CITY
Pop.—Thousands
1052 Budapest
........H 12

POLAND
Area 150,290 sq.m.
Pop....34,769,400
PRINCIPAL
CITY
Pop.—Thousands
1261 Warszawa
(Warsaw)
........D 14

ROMANIA
Area 122,282 sq.m.
Pop....19,535,398
PRINCIPAL
CITIES
Pop.—Thousands
77 Arad......I 14
640 Bucuresti
(Bucharest)
........K 20

YUGOSLAVIA
(Serb-Croat-
Slovene Kingdom)
Area 95,551 sq. m.
Pop....15,400,177
PRINCIPAL
CITY
Pop.—Thousands
289 Beograd
(Belgrade) J 14
(Col. At. 89)

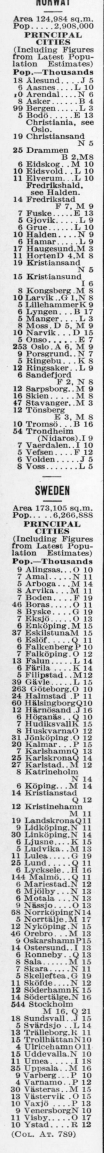

NORWAY

Area 124,984 sq.m.
Pop.....2,908,000

PRINCIPAL CITIES
(Including Figures from Latest Population Estimates)

Pop.—Thousands

18 Alesund....J 5
6 Aasnes....L 10
10 Arendal....N 6
8 Asker....B 4
99 Bergen....L 3
5 Bodö....E 13
Christiania, see Oslo.
19 Christiansand N 5
25 Drammen B 2,M8
6 Eidskog...M 10
10 Eidsvold...L 10
11 Elverum...L 10
Fredrikshald, see Halden.
14 Fredrikstad F 7, M 9
7 Fuske....E 13
5 Gjøvik....L 9
6 Grue....L 10
10 Halden....N 9
6 Hamar....L 9
17 Haugesund.M 3
11 HortenD 4,M 8
5 Kristiansand N 5
15 Kristiansund I 6
8 Kongsberg.M 8
10 Larvik...G 1,N 8
5 Lillehammer K 9
6 Lyngen...B 17
5 Manger....L 2
8 Moss.D 5, M 9
5 Narvik...D 15
5 Onso....D 7
253 Oslo A 6, M 9
9 Porsgrund..N 7
5 Ringebu....K 8
12 Ringsaker..L 9
6 Sandefjord F 2, N 8
12 Sarpsborg..M 9
16 Skien....M 8
47 Stavanger..M 3
12 Tönsberg E 3, M 8
10 Tromsö....B 16
54 Trondheim (Nidaros) I 9
7 Vaerdalen..I 10
5 Vefsen....F 12
6 Volden....J 5
8 Voss.......L 5

SWEDEN

Area 173,105 sq.m.
Pop.....6,266,888

PRINCIPAL CITIES
(Including Figures from Latest Population Estimates)

Pop.—Thousands

9 Alingsas..O 10
7 Amal....O 11
7 Arboga...M 14
8 Arvika...M 11
7 Boden....P 19
46 Boras....O 11
8 Byske....G 19
7 Eksjö....O 13
8 Enköping..M 15
37 Eskilstuna M 15
6 Eslöf....O 11
7 Falkenberg P 10
7 Falköping O 12
13 Falun....L 14
5 Färila....K 14
5 Filipstad..M 12
39 Gävle....L 14
263 Göteborg.O 10
24 Halmstad..P 11
60 Hälsingborg Q 10
12 Härnösand .J 16
7 Höganäs..Q 10
7 Hudiksvall K 15
8 Huskvarna O 12
31 Jönköping.O 12
20 Kalmar...P 15
7 Karlshamn Q 13
25 Karlskrona Q 14
27 Karlstad..M 12
8 Katrineholm N 14
6 Köping....M 14
14 Kristianstad Q 12
12 Kristinehamn M 11
19 Landskrona Q 11
9 Lidköping.N 11
30 Linköping.N 14
5 Ljusne....K 15
5 Ludvika..M 13
11 Lulea....G 19
25 Lund....Q 11
6 Lycksele..H 11
144 Malmö...Q 11
8 Mariestad.N 12
6 Mjölby....O 13
8 Motala....N 13
9 Nässjö....O 13
68 Norrköping N 14
5 Norrtälje .M 17
12 Nyköping .N 14
46 Orebro...M 13
9 Oskarshamn P 15
14 Ostersund..I 13
6 Ronneby..Q 13
8 Sala....M 15
7 Skara....M 11
5 Skelleftea.G 19
11 Skötde...N 12
12 SöderhamnK 15
14 Södertälge.N 16
544 Stockholm M 16, Q 21
18 Sundsvall..J 16
5 Svärdsjö ..L 14
13 Trälleborg.R 11
11 Trollhättan N 10
4 Ulricehamn O 11
15 Uddevalla.N 10
11 Umea....I 18
35 Uppsala..M 16
5 Varberg..P 10
4 Varnamo..P 12
30 Västeras..M 15
13 Västervik .O 15
10 Vaxjö....P 13
9 Venersborg N 10
11 Visby....O 17
10 Ystad....R 12

(Col. At. 789)

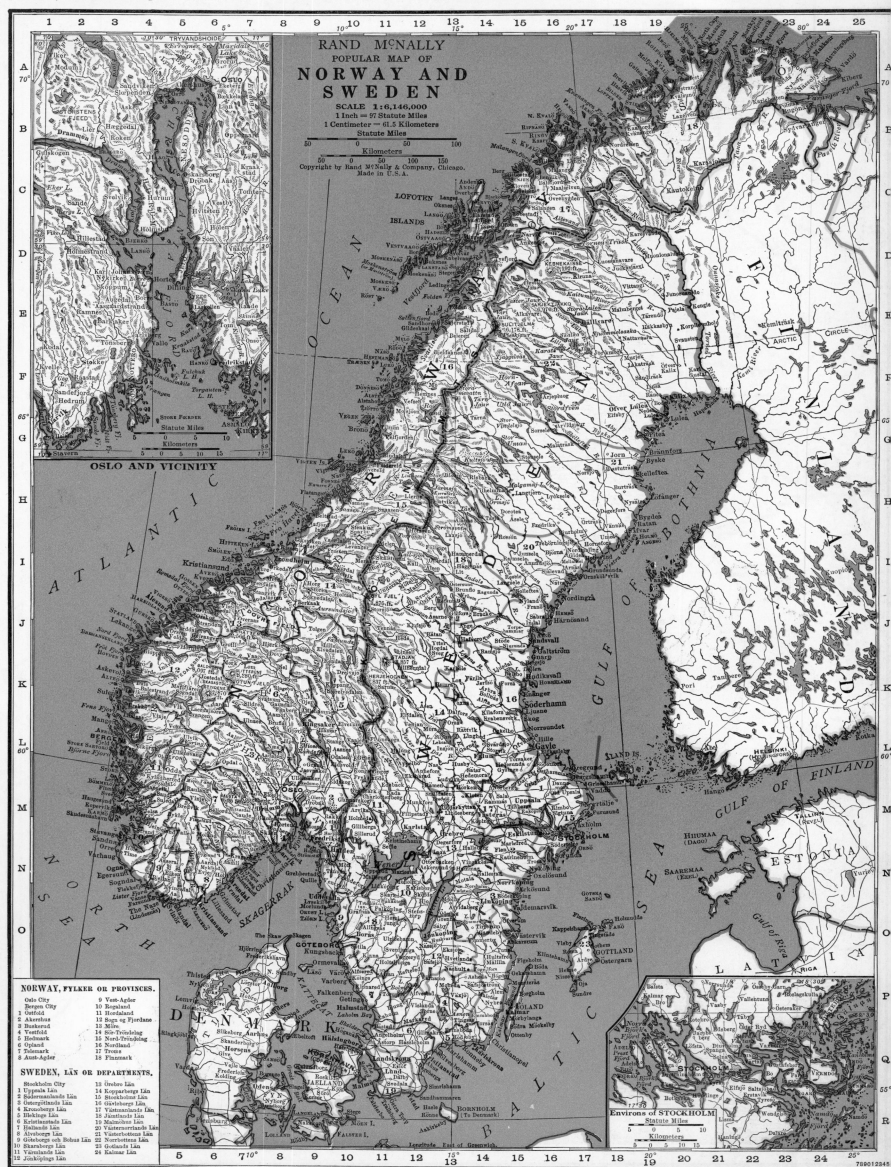

RAND McNALLY
POPULAR MAP OF
EASTERN EUROPE

SCALE 1:11,405,000
1 Inch = 180 Statute Miles
1 Centimeter = 114 Kilometers

Statute Miles
100   50   0   100   200
Kilometers
100   50   0   100   200   300

Copyright by Rand McNally & Company, Chicago.
Made in U.S.A.

LONGITUDE EAST OF GREENWICH

ESTONIA

Area .18,354 sq. m.
Pop.....1,131,200
PRINCIPAL CITIES
(Including Figures from Latest Population Estimates)
Pop.—Thousands
25 Narva.....G 6
21 Pärnu
(Pernau)...G 3
146 Tallinn
(Revel)...F 4
59 Tartu.....G 5

FINLAND

Area.149,954 sq.m.
Pop.....3,807,163
PRINCIPAL CITIES
(Including Figures from Latest Population Estimates)
Pop.—Thousands
Abo, see Turku.
284 Helsinki
(Helsingfors)
.....F 4
24 Kuopio....E 6
59 Tampere...E 3
68 Turku....F 3
72 Viipuri.....F 6

Latvia

Area .25,395 sq. m.
Pop.....1,950,502
PRINCIPAL CITIES
(Including Figures from Latest Population Estimates)
Pop.—Thousands
43 Daugavpils
(Dvinsk)..H 4
57 Liepaja
(Libau)...H 1
385 Riga.....H 3

LITHUANIA

Area.21,683 sq. m.
Pop.....2,549,668
PRINCIPAL CITIES
(Including Figures from Latest Population Estimates)
Pop.—Thousands
130 Kaunas
(Kovno)...I 2
40 Klaipéda
(Memel)...H 1
27 Siauliai...H 2

Soviet Union

(Europe)
Ar. 1,707,496 sq.m.
Pop...122,114,545
PRINCIPAL CITIES
(Including Figures from Latest Population Estimates)
Pop.—Thousands
194 Arkhangelsk
.....D 13
225 Astrakhan
.....N 19
709 Baku....Q 21
379 Dnepropetrovsk (Ekaterinoslav)..M 9
Ekaterinodar, see Krasnodar
Elisavetgrad, see Zinovevsk.
Elisavetopol, see Grandzha
451 Gorki....I 15
201 Grozni..P 17
188 Ivanovo..H 13
146 Kalinin..H 10
259 Kazañ...I 18
654 Kharkov..L 9
539 Kiev.....L 6
69 Kirovo (Zinovevsk)...M 7
219 Krasnodar O12
183 Kuibishev
(Samara)..J 19
102 Kursk...K 10
2776 Leningrad.F 7
181 Minsk...J 4
3663 Moskva
(Moscow)..I 11
141 Nikolaev
(Vernoleninsk)
.....N 7
Nizhnii-Novgorod,see Gorki
100 Novorossiisk
.....O 11
459 Odessa....N 5
113 Ordzhonikidze..P 16
145 Orenburg K 23
119 Penza...J 16
Petrograd, see Leningrad.
521 Rostov..N 12
Samara, see Kuibishev
327 Sarátov..K 17
78 Sevastopol..O 7
Simbirsk, see Ulyanovsk.
99 Simferopol..O 8
285 Stalin (Yuzovka)
.....M 11
383 Stalingrad
149 Taganrog N 12
102 Tambov..K 13
406 Tiflis....Q 17
Tsaritsin, see Stalingrad.
199 Tula....J 11
Tver, see Kalinin
168 Ufa....I 23
74 Ulyanovsk .J 18
127 Vitebsk...I 6
Vladikavkaz, see Ordzhonikidze
212 Voronezh.K 12
167 YaroslaviH 13
Zinovevsk, see Kirovo
(Col. At. 89)

ASIA
Ar.16,494,217sq.m.
Pop..1,092,000,000
COUNTRIES
Aden..........N 4
Area..42,080 sq.m.
Pop.....100,000
Afghanistan..L 9
Area 245,000 sq.m.
Pop...12,000,000
Bahrein Is....L 6
Area.....250 sq. m.
Pop.....120,000
Bhutan......M 13
Area.18,000 sq. m.
Pop.....300,000
British North
    Borneo....Q 19
Area.31,106 sq.m.
Pop.....290,526
Brunei......R 19
Area..2,500 sq. m.
Pop......33,500
Burma......N 15
Area.233,492 sq.m.
Pop...14,667,146
Ceylon......R 11
Area.25,332 sq.m.
Pop....5,712,000
China........L 17
Ar.3,756,102 sq.m.
Pop..422,527,000
Chosen (Korea)
...............J 20
Area.85,206 sq.m.
Pop...22,047,836
Cyprus........I 4
Area..3,584 sq. m.
Pop.....369,000
Damao and Diu
...............O 10
Area....169 sq. m.
Pop......32,700
FederatedMalay
    States....R 16
Area.27,506 sq.m.
Pop....2,052,729
French Indo-
    China....P 17
Area.284,522 sq.m.
Pop...23,250,000
Goa...........P 10
Area..1,516 sq. m.
Pop.....579,969
Hong Kong.N 18
Area....391 sq. m.
Pop.....988,190
India........M 12
Ar.1,575,107 sq.m.
Pop..338,170,632
Iran (Persia).K 7
Area.628,000 sq.m.
Pop...15,055,115
Iraq (Meso-
    potamia)....J 5
Area.143,240 sq.m.
Pop....4,000,000
Japan(Empire)J21
Area.263,357 sq.m.
Pop...99,698,779
Karafuto....G 20
Area.13,931 sq. m.
Pop.....295,196
Kuwait......K 6
Area..........
Pop......80,000
Kwangchowan
...............N 18
Area....325 sq. m.
Pop.....220,000
Macau......N 18
Area......4 sq. m.
Pop.....157,805
Maldive Is..R 10
Area....115 sq. m.
Pop......79,000
Manchukuo..I 19
Area.503,013 sq.m.
Pop...34,200,900
Nepal.......M 12
Area.54,000 sq. m.
Pop....5,600,000
Netherlands
    Indies....R 21
Area.733,790 sq.m.
Pop..60,727,233
New Guinea
    Territory.Q 25
Area.91,000 sq. m.
Pop.....765,582
Nicobar Is..R 14
Area...635 sq. m.
Pop......10,240
Oman........M 7
Area.82,000 sq. m.
Pop.....500,000
Palestine.....J 4
Area.10,155 sq. m.
Pop...1,401,794
Papua Terri-
    tory.....R 25
Area.90,540 sq. m.
Pop.....276,366
Philippine Is.P 21
Area.114,400 sq.m.
Pop...16,000,000
Sarawak....R 19
Area.42,000 sq. m.
Pop.....442,900
Saudi Arabia.L 5
Area...413,792
Pop....4,500,000
Siam.........P 16
Area.200,148 sq.m.
Pop...14,464,489
Soviet Union
    in Asia....F 14
Ar.6,365,689 sq.m.
Pop..43,653,855
Straits Setr.R 16
Area...1,600 sq. m.
Pop...1,310,969
Syria & Lebanon
...............I 5
Area.77,972 sq. m.
Pop....3,444,322
Taiwan
    (Formosa).M 19
Area.13,836 sq. m.
Pop....5,315,642
Transjordan..J 4
Area...16,220
Pop.....325,000
Turkey......H 5
Area.294,415 sq.m.
Pop...16,200,694
Yemen......N 4
Area..23,932 sq. m.
Pop.....875,000
(Col. At. 89)

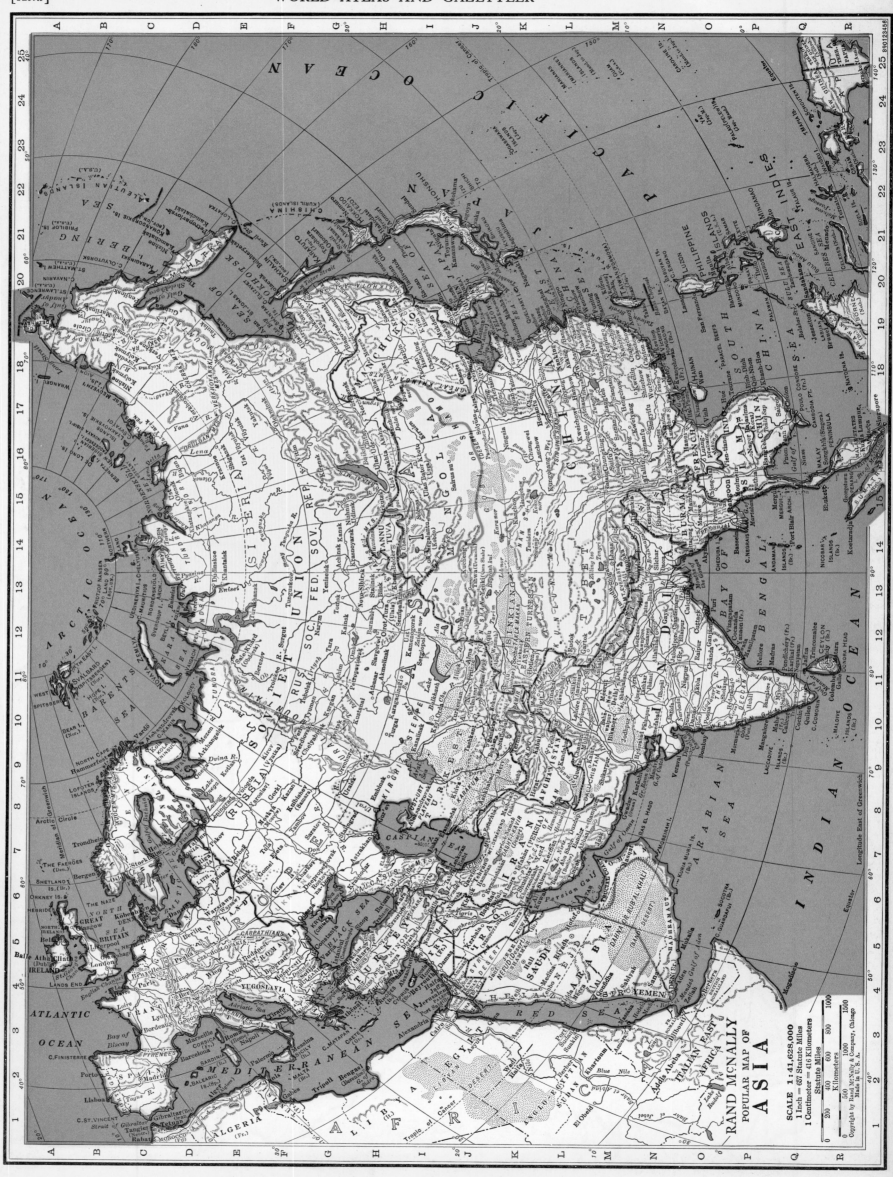

SCALE 1:41,628,000
1 Inch = 657 Statute Miles
1 Centimeter = 416 Kilometers

RAND McNALLY
POPULAR MAP OF
ASIA

Copyright by Rand McNally & Company, Chicago
Made in U.S.A.

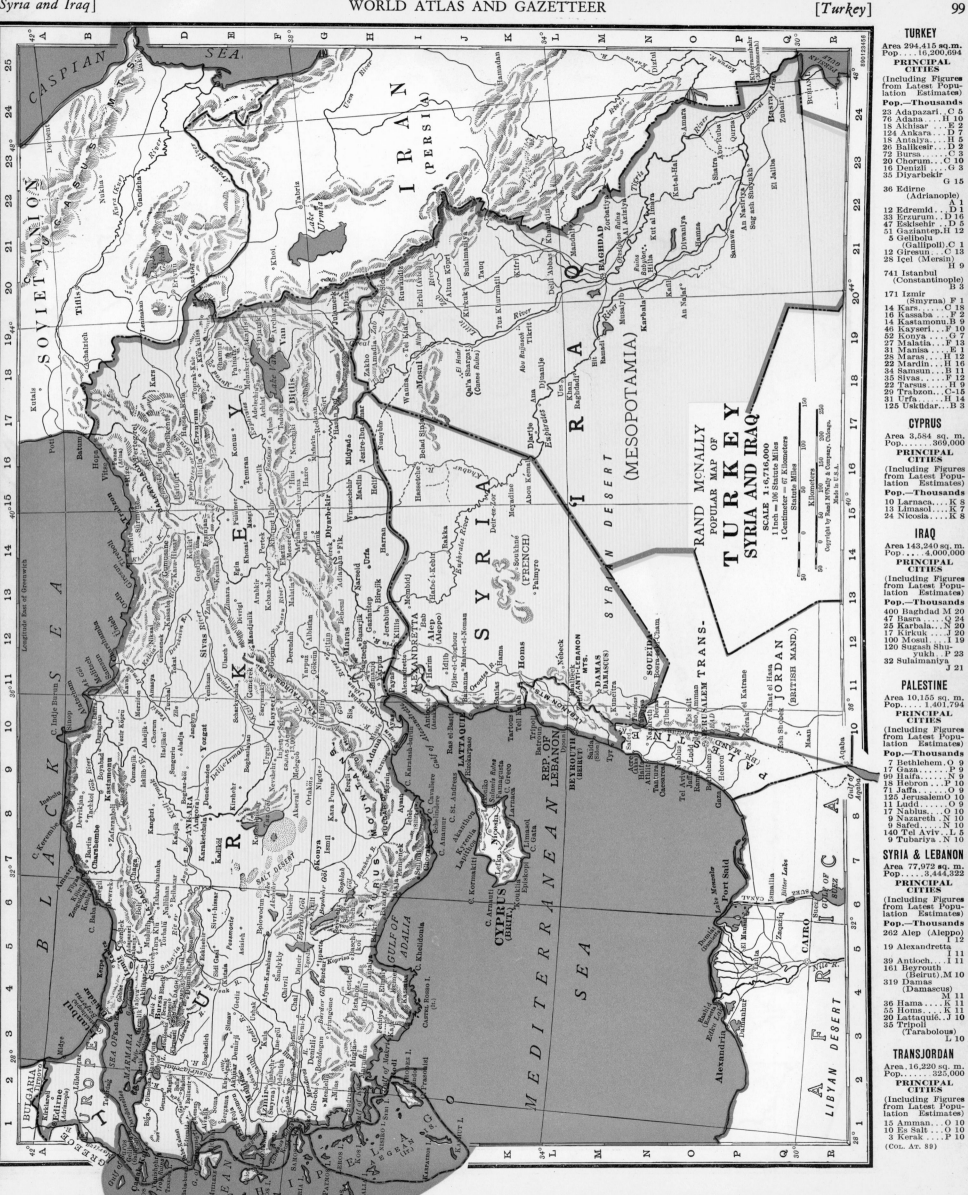

RAND McNALLY
POPULAR MAP OF
TURKEY
SYRIA AND IRAQ

SCALE 1:6,716,000
1 Inch = 106 Statute Miles
1 Centimeter = 67 Kilometers
Statute Miles
Kilometers
Copyright by Rand McNally & Company, Chicago.
Made in U.S.A.

TURKEY

Area 294,415 sq. m.
Pop.....16,200,694

PRINCIPAL CITIES
(Including Figures from Latest Population Estimates)
Pop.—Thousands
23 Adapazari...C 5
76 Adana......H 10
18 Akhisar....E 2
124 Ankara....D 7
18 Antalya....H 5
26 Balikesir..D 2
72 Bursa......C 3
20 Chorum....C 10
16 Denizli....G 3
35 Diyarbekir.....G 15
36 Edirne
(Adrianople)....A 1
12 Edremid...D 1
33 Erzurum...D 16
47 Eskisehir..D 5
51 Gaziantep.H 12
5 Gelibolu
(Gallipoli).C 1
12 Giresun...C 13
28 Içel (Mersin)....H 9
741 Istanbul
(Constantinople)....B 3
171 Izmir
(Smyrna) F 1
14 Kars......C 18
16 Kassaba...F 2
14 Kastamonu.B 9
46 Kayseri...F 10
52 Konya....G 7
27 Malatia...F 13
31 Manisa...E 1
17 Maras....H 12
22 Mardin...B 16
34 Samsun...B 11
35 Sivas.....F 12
22 Tarsus...H 9
29 Trabzon..C 15
31 Urfa.....H 14
125 Usktüdar...B 3

CYPRUS

Area 3,584 sq. m.
Pop.....369,000

PRINCIPAL CITIES
(Including Figures from Latest Population Estimates)
Pop.—Thousands
10 Larnaca...K 8
13 Limasol...K 7
24 Nicosia...K 8

IRAQ

Area 143,240 sq. m.
Pop.....4,000,000

PRINCIPAL CITIES
(Including Figures from Latest Population Estimates)
Pop.—Thousands
400 Baghdad M 20
47 Basra....Q 24
25 Karbala..N 20
17 Kirkuk...J 20
100 Mosul...I 19
120 Sugash Shu-
yukh..P 23
32 Sulaimaniya
J 21

PALESTINE

Area 10,155 sq. m.
Pop.....1,401,794

PRINCIPAL CITIES
(Including Figures from Latest Population Estimates)
Pop.—Thousands
7 Bethlehem.O 9
17 Gaza.....P 9
99 Haifa....N 9
71 Hebron...O 10
71 Jaffa....O 10
125 JerusalemO 10
11 Ludd.....O 9
1 Nablus....O 10
9 Nazareth.N 10
9 Safed....N 10
140 Tel Aviv..L 5
9 Tubariya.N 10

SYRIA & LEBANON

Area 77,972 sq. m.
Pop.....3,444,322

PRINCIPAL CITIES
(Including Figures from Latest Population Estimates)
Pop.—Thousands
262 Alep (Aleppo)....I 12
19 Alexandretta....I 11
39 Antioch..I 11
161 Beyrouth
(Beirut).M 10
319 Damas
(Damascus)....M 11
36 Hama....K 11
55 Homs....K 11
20 Lattaquié.J 10
35 Tripoli
(Tarabolous)
L 10

TRANSJORDAN

Area 16,220 sq. m.
Pop.....325,000

PRINCIPAL CITIES
(Including Figures from Latest Population Estimates)
Pop.—Thousands
15 Amman...O 10
10 Es Salt..O 10
3 Kerak....P 10
(COL. AT. 89)

PALESTINE

Area. 10,155 sq. m.
Pop. 1,401,794

PRINCIPAL CITIES

(Including Figures from Latest Population Estimates)

Pop.—Thousands

8 Acre . . . . . . G 8
7 Bethlehem . N 9
1 Bittir . . . . . N 9
17 Gaza . . . . . O 2
99 Haifa . . . . . H 7
18 Hebron . . . . O 8
71 Jaffa . . . . . . L 5
3 Jenin . . . . . J 10
125 Jerusalem N 10
11 Ludd . . . . . M 6
17 Nablus (Shechem) K 10
9 Nazareth . . H 10
9 Safed . . . . G 12
4 Seffurieh . . H 10
Shechem, see Nablus.
140 Tel Aviv . . L 5
9 Tubariya . . H 12

SYRIA & LEBANON

Area . . 77,972 sq. m.
Pop 3,444,322

PRINCIPAL CITIES

(Including Figures from Latest Population Estimates)

Pop.—Thousands

5 Baalbek . . A 18
161 Beyrouth (Beirut) . . A 12
319 Damas (Damascus) D 20
6 Sour (Tyre) E 9
15 Zahle . . . . A 16

TRANSJORDAN

Area. 16,220 sq. m.
Pop. 325,000

PRINCIPAL CITIES

(Including Figures from Latest Population Estimates)

Pop.—Thousands

15 Amman . . M 16
10 Es Salt . . . L 14
3 Kerak . . . . Q 13
(Col. At. 789)

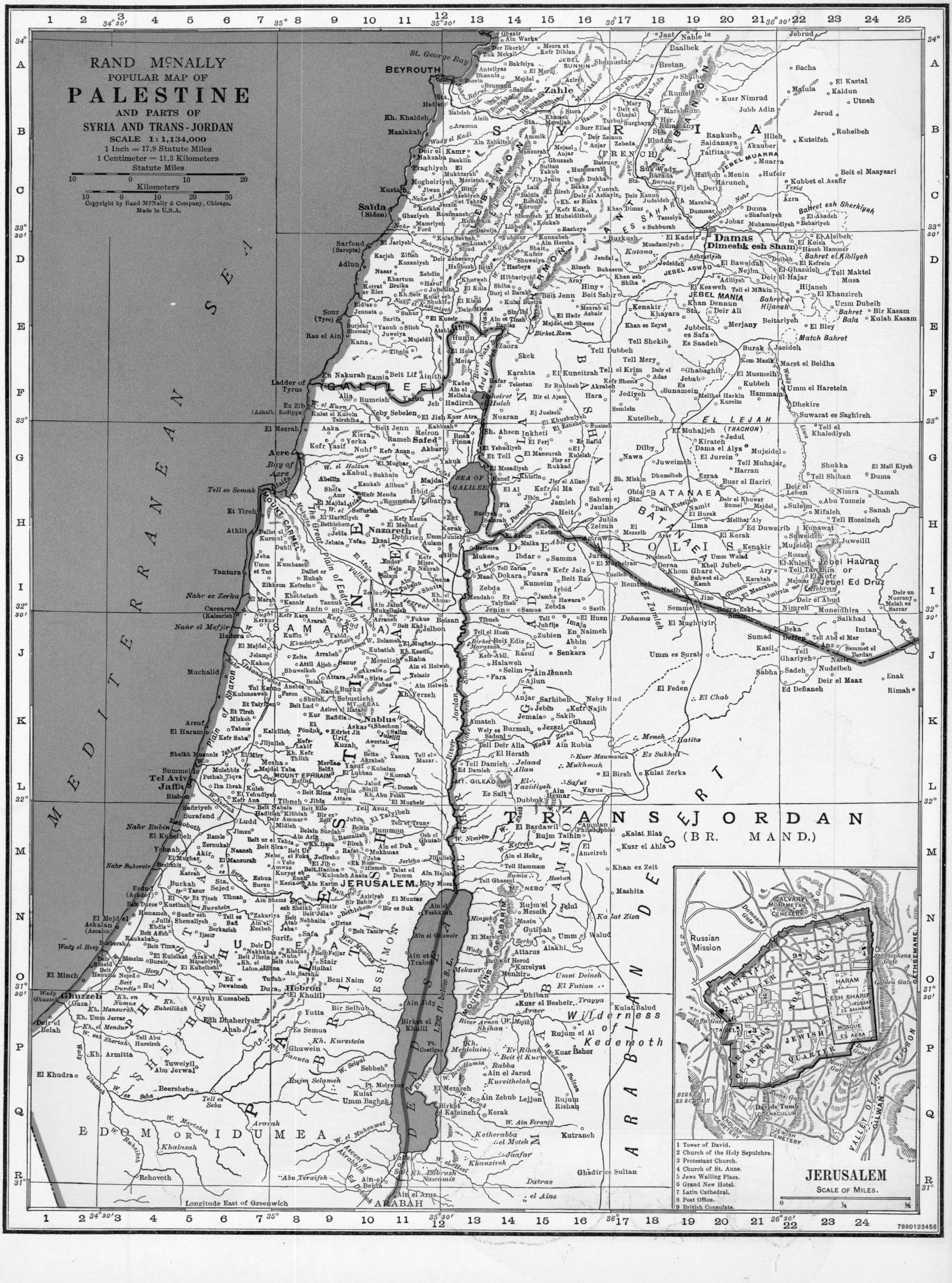

RAND McNALLY
POPULAR MAP OF
PALESTINE
AND PARTS OF
SYRIA AND TRANS-JORDAN
SCALE 1 : 1,134,000
1 Inch = 17.9 Statute Miles
1 Centimeter = 11.3 Kilometers
Statute Miles
Kilometers
Copyright by Rand McNally & Company, Chicago. Made in U.S.A.
MEDITERRANEAN SEA
SYRIA (FRENCH)
TRANSJORDAN (BR. MAND.)
ARABIAN DESERT
GALILEE
SAMARIA
JUDEA
PHILISTIA
DECAPOLIS
BATANAEA
EDOM OR IDUMEA
DEAD SEA
SEA OF GALILEE
BEYROUTH
Damas (Dimeshk esh Sham)
Saida (Sidon)
Sour (Tyre)
Acre
Haifa
Nazareth
Nablus (Shechem)
JERUSALEM
Tel Aviv
Jaffa
Hebron
Ghuzzeh (Gaza)
Beersheba
Amman (Philadelphia)
Es Salt
Kerak
Longitude East of Greenwich
JERUSALEM
SCALE OF MILES
1 Tower of David.
2 Church of the Holy Sepulchre.
3 Protestant Church.
4 Church of St. Anne.
5 Jews Wailing Place.
6 Grand New Hotel.
7 Latin Cathedral.
8 Post Office.
9 British Consulate.
7890123456

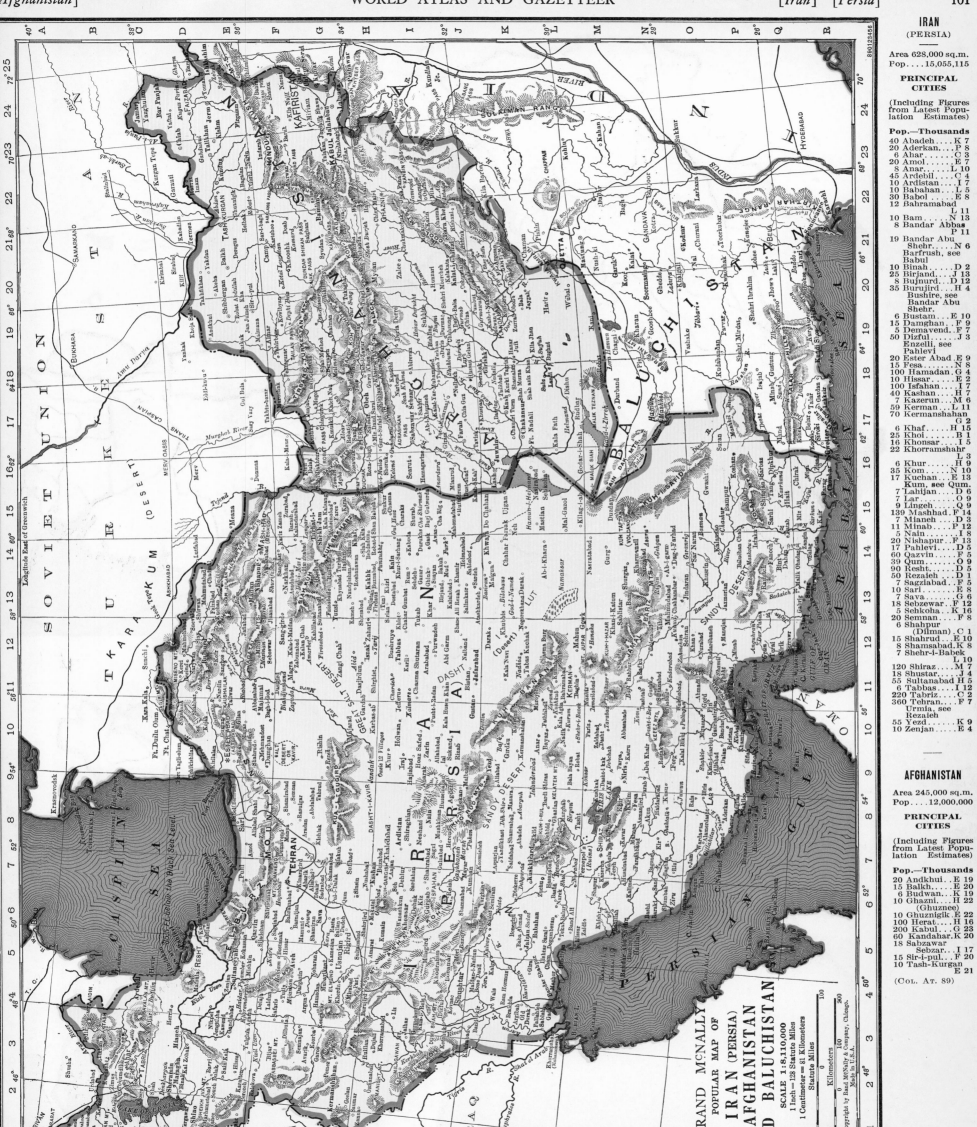

RAND McNALLY
POPULAR MAP OF
IRAN (PERSIA)
AFGHANISTAN
AND BALUCHISTAN

SCALE 1:8,110,000
1 Inch = 128 Statute Miles
1 Centimeter = 81 Kilometers

Statute Miles

Kilometers

Copyright by Rand McNally & Company, Chicago.
Made in U.S.A.

IRAN
(PERSIA)

Area 628,000 sq.m.
Pop....15,055,115

PRINCIPAL CITIES

(Including Figures from Latest Population Estimates)

Pop.—Thousands

40 Abadeh	K 7
20 Aderkan	P 8
6 Ahar	C 3
20 Amol	E 7
8 Anar	L 10
45 Ardebil	C 4
10 Ardistan	I 7
10 Babahan	L 5
50 Babol	E 8
12 Bahramabad	L 11
10 Bam	N 13
8 Bandar Abbas	P 11
19 Bandar Abu Shehr	N 6
Barfrush, see Babul	
10 Binah	D 2
25 Birjand	J 13
12 Bujurd	D 12
35 Burujird	H 4
Bushire, see Bandar Abu Shehr.	
6 Bustam	E 10
15 Damghan	F 9
5 Demavend	F 7
50 Dizful	J 3
Enzelli, see Pahlevi	
20 Ester Abad	E 9
15 Fesa	N 8
100 Hamadan	G 4
10 Hissar	E 2
100 Isfahan	I 7
40 Kashan	H 7
7 Kazerun	M 6
59 Kerman	L 11
70 Kermanshahan	G 2
6 Khaf	H 15
25 Khoi	B 1
16 Khonsar	I 5
22 Khorramshahr	J 3
6 Khur	H 9
35 Kom	N 10
17 Kuchan	E 13
Kum, see Qum.	
6 Lahijan	D 6
7 Lar	O 9
9 Lingeh	Q 9
139 Mashhad	F 14
7 Mianeh	D 3
11 Nahin	P 12
7 Nain	I 8
20 Nishapur	F 13
17 Pahlevi	D 5
60 Qazvin	F 5
39 Qum	O 9
90 Resht	D 5
50 Rezaieh	I 1
8 Sagzíabad	F 5
10 Sari	E 8
7 Sava	L 11
18 Sebzewar	F 12
5 Sehkoha	K 16
20 Semnan	F 8
6 Shahpur (Dilman)	C 1
15 Shahrud	E 10
8 Shamsabad	K 8
7 Shehr-i-Babek	L 10
120 Shiraz	M 7
18 Shustar	J 4
55 Sultanabad	H 5
6 Tabbas	I 12
220 Tabriz	C 2
360 Tehran	F 7
Urmia, see Rezaieh	
55 Yezd	K 9
10 Zenjan	E 4

AFGHANISTAN

Area 245,000 sq.m.
Pop....12,000,000

PRINCIPAL CITIES

(Including Figures from Latest Population Estimates)

Pop.—Thousands

20 Andkhui	E 19
15 Balkh	E 20
6 Budwan	K 19
10 Ghazni	H 22
(Ghuznee)	
10 Ghuznigik	E 22
100 Herat	H 16
200 Kabul	G 23
60 Kandahar	K 20
18 Sabzawar	I 17
15 Sir-i-pul	F 20
10 Tash-Kurgan	E 21

(Col. At. 89)

INDIA

Ar.1,575,107 sq. m.
Pop...338,170,632

PRINCIPAL CITIES

(Including Figures from Latest Population Estimates)

Pop.—Thousands
205 Agra.....F 11
310 Ahmedabad..G 16 H 6
114 Ajmer....F 8
67 Aligarh....F 11
(Koil)
174 Allahabad ..G 15
76 Ambala ...D 10
265 Amritsar...C 8
306 Bangalore ..N 11
144 Bareilly...E 13
113 Baroda...I 6
205 Benares ..G 16
84 Bhagalpur.G 20
76 Bhaunagar..I 5
86 Bikaner...F 6
1161 Bombay..K 6
1194 Calcutta.I 21
99 Calicut...O 9
219 Cawnpore F 13
95 Coimbatore ..O 10
139 Dacca...H 23
348 Delhi...E 10
346 Emphal..L 19
88 Gaya...G 18
22 Gwalior...F 11
225 Howrah..I 21
69 Hubli...M 8
96 Hyderabad G 1
346 Hyderabad..L 11
127 Indore...I 9
144 Jaipur...F 9
64 Jamkhandi..L 8
66 Jhansi ..G 12
95 Jodhpur..F 6
104 Jubbulpore I 13
248 Karachi...G 1
83 Koil AigarhF 11
70 Kolhapur...L 7
400 Lahore...C 8
251 Lucknow..F 14
647 Madras ..N 13
182 Madura..P 11
91 Meerut...F 11
111 Moradabad.E 2
108 Multan ...D 5
107 Mysore...O 10
215 Nagpur...I 12
160 Patna...G.18
87 Peshawar...B 5
198 Poona ...K 7
73 Rampur...D 11
76 Rawal Pindi B 6
79 Saharanpur ..E 11
121 Secunderabad ..L 11
73 Shahjahanpur F 13
145 Sholapur..L 9
85 Sialkot...C 8
174 Srinagar...B 8
99 Surat...I 6
67 Tanjore ..P 12
142 Trichinopoly ..P 12
73 Trivandrum ..Q 10

FRENCH INDIA

Area...196 sq. m.
Pop......290,460

PRINCIPAL CITIES

(Including Figures from Latest Population Estimates)

Pop.—Thousands
26 Chandernagore ..H 21
19 Karikal ..P 13
11 Mahé ...O 8
47 Pondichéry ..O 13
5 Yanaon...L 15

PORTUGUESE INDIA

Area..1,516 sq. m.
Pop......579,969

PRINCIPAL CITIES

(Including Figures from Latest Population Estimates)

Pop.—Thousands
7 Damao.....J 6
13 Diu......J 4
308 GOA (Port.) ..

CEYLON

Area.25,332 sq. m.
Pop.....5,712,000

PRINCIPAL CITIES

(Including Figures from Latest Population Estimates)

Pop.—Thousands
308 Colombo..R 13
38 Galle....R 13
46 Jaffna ...P 13
37 Kandy....R 14

BURMA

Area.233,492 sq. m.
Pop....14,667,146

PRINCIPAL CITIES

(Including Figures from Latest Population Estimates)

Pop.—Thousands
135 Mandalay ..N 22
61 Moulmein ..P 23
400 Rangoon..P 22

BHUTAN

Area..18,000 sq. m.
Pop......300,000

NEPAL

Area..54,000 sq. m.
Pop.....5,600,000
(Col. At. 890)

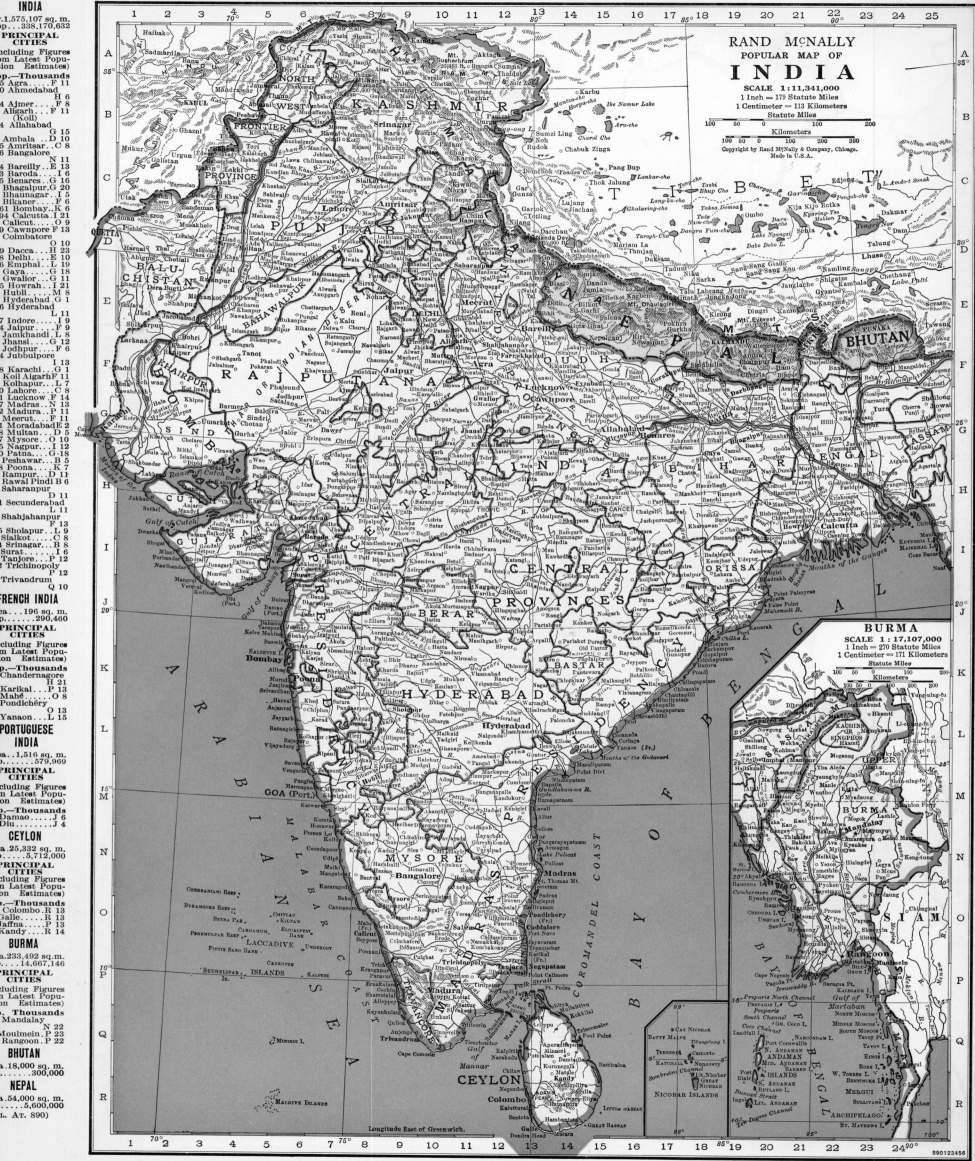

RAND McNALLY
POPULAR MAP OF
INDIA
SCALE 1:11,341,000
1 Inch = 179 Statute Miles
1 Centimeter = 113 Kilometers
Statute Miles

Copyright by Rand McNally & Company, Chicago.
Made in U.S.A.

BURMA
SCALE 1:17,107,000
1 Inch = 270 Statute Miles
1 Centimeter = 171 Kilometers
Statute Miles

890123456

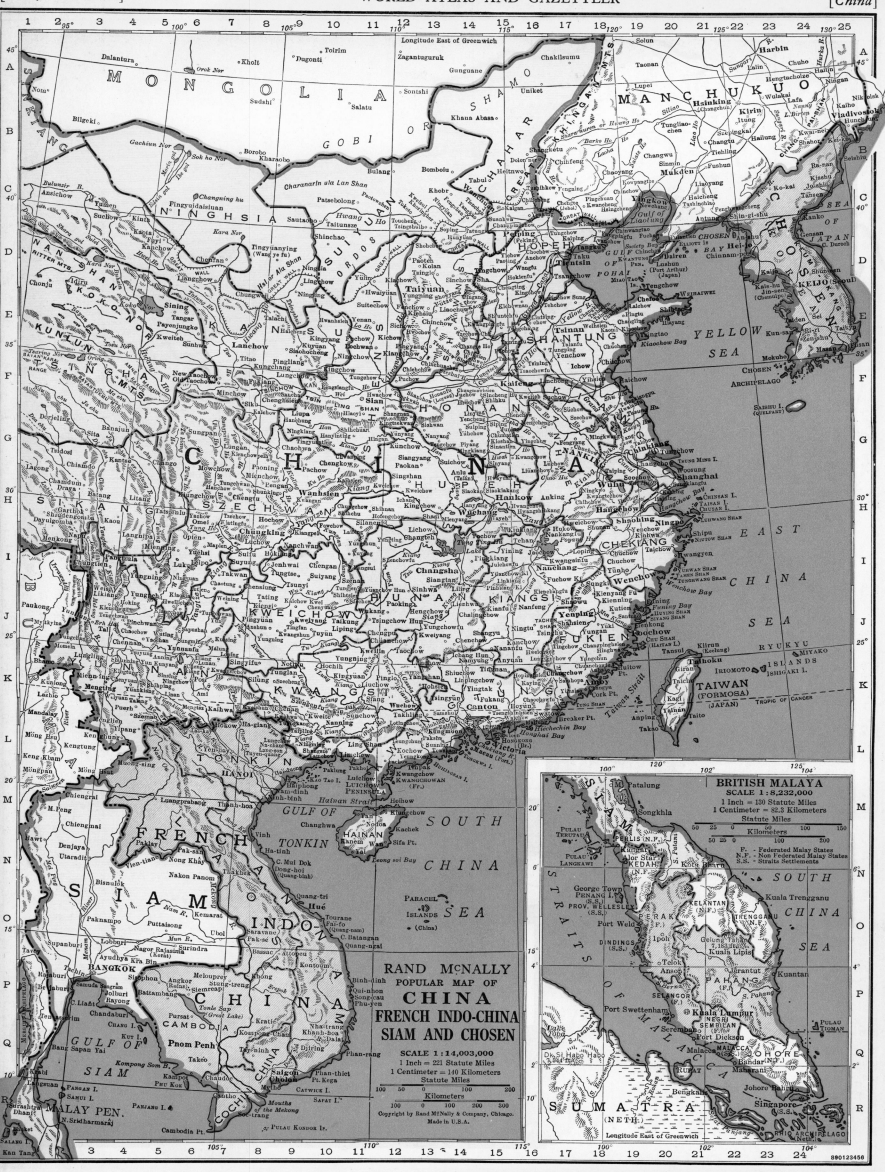

RAND McNALLY
POPULAR MAP OF
CHINA
FRENCH INDO-CHINA
SIAM AND CHOSEN

SCALE 1:14,003,000
1 Inch = 221 Statute Miles
1 Centimeter = 140 Kilometers
Statute Miles

Kilometers

Copyright by Rand McNally & Company, Chicago.
Made in U.S.A.

BRITISH MALAYA
SCALE 1:8,232,000
1 Inch = 130 Statute Miles
1 Centimeter = 82.3 Kilometers
Statute Miles

Kilometers

F. = Federated Malay States
N.F. = Non Federated Malay States
S.S. = Straits Settlements

CHINA
(Entire Republic)
Ar. 3,756,102 sq. m.
Pop...422,527,000
PRINCIPAL CITIES
(Including Figures
from Latest Popu-
lation Estimates)
Pop.—Thousands
234 Amoy...K 18
861 Canton..K 14
100 Changchow
...K 18
388 Foochow.J 19
507 Hangchow.H19
778 Hankow.H 15
400 Hanyang.H 15
500 Lanchow..E 7
633 Nanking.G 18
213 Ningpo..H 21
811 Peiping
(Peking).D 16
3259 Shanghai H20
500 Sian...F 11
260 Soochow.H 20
1389 Tientsin.D 17
250 Tsinan...E 17
390 Tsingtao.E 19
500 Victoria.L 15
(Hong Kong)
631 Wenchow.I 20
610 Wuchang.H 15
607 Changsha.I 14
800 Chengtu..H 7
635 Chungking H 9

MANCHUKUO
Area 503,013 sq. m.
Pop...34,200,900
PRINCIPAL CITIES
(Including Figures
from Latest Popu-
lation Estimates)
Pop.—Thousands
650 Chengte . C 17
482 Harbin
(Pingkiang)A 23
201 Hsinking.B 22
143 Kirin (Chilin)
B 23
412 Mukden
(Shenyang)
B 21
135 Yingkow
(Newchwang)
C 19

MONGOLIA
Ar...558,054 sq. m.
Pop.....6,160,000

SINKIANG
Area 550,050 sq. m.
Pop.....2,552,000

TIBET
Area 443,900 sq. m.
Pop.....3,722,000

SIAM
Area 200,148 sq. m.
Pop...14,464,489
PRINCIPAL CITIES
(Including Figures
from Latest Popu-
lation Estimates)
Pop.—Thousands
745 Ubon...O 7
681 Bangkok..P 4

FRENCH INDOCHINA
Area 284,522 sq. m.
Pop...23,250,000
PRINCIPAL CITIES
(Including Figures
from Latest Popu-
lation Estimates)
Pop.—Thousands
145 Cholon...R 8
80 Haiphong.M 9
149 Hanoi.....L 8
122 Saigon...Q 8

TAIWAN (FORMOSA)
Area.13,836 sq. m.
Pop.....5,315,642
PRINCIPAL CITIES
(Including Figures
from Latest Popu-
lation Estimates)
Pop.—Thousands
81 Kiirun
(Keelung)
K 21
288 Taihoku.J 21
112 Tainan...L 20
76 Takao...L 20

CHOSEN (KOREA)
Area.85,206 sq. m.
Pop...22,047,836
PRINCIPAL CITIES
(Including Figures
from Latest Popu-
lation Estimates)
Pop.—Thousands
206 Fusan...E 25
173 Heijo...D 23
677 Keijo...E 24

BRITISH MALAYA
Area.52,592 sq. m.
Pop.....5,137,494
PRINCIPAL CITIES
(Including Figures
from Latest Popu-
lation Estimates)
Pop.—Thousands
148 George Town
N 19
112 Kuala Lumpur
Q 22
45 Malacca.Q 22
550 SingaporeR 24

(Col. At. 89)

JAPAN

Area 263,357 sq. m.
Pop.... 99,698,779

PRINCIPAL CITIES

(Including Figures from Latest Population Estimates)

Pop.—Thousands

TAIWAN (FORMOSA)

Area..13,836 sq. m.
Pop.....5,315,642

PRINCIPAL CITIES

(Including Figures from Latest Population Estimates)

Pop.—Thousands

RAND McNALLY
POPULAR MAP OF
JAPAN

SCALE 1:4,372,000
1 Inch = 69 Statute Miles
1 Centimeter = 43.7 Kilometers
Statute Miles
Kilometers
Copyright by Rand McNally & Company, Chicago.
Made in U.S.A.

HOKKAIDO (YEZO) AND CHISHIMA (KURIL IS.)
Scale
190 Statute Miles to one inch

TAIWAN (FORMOSA) AND RYUKYU ISLANDS
Scale
173 Statute Miles to one inch

OUTLINE MAP OF JAPAN
Scale
575 Statute Miles to one inch

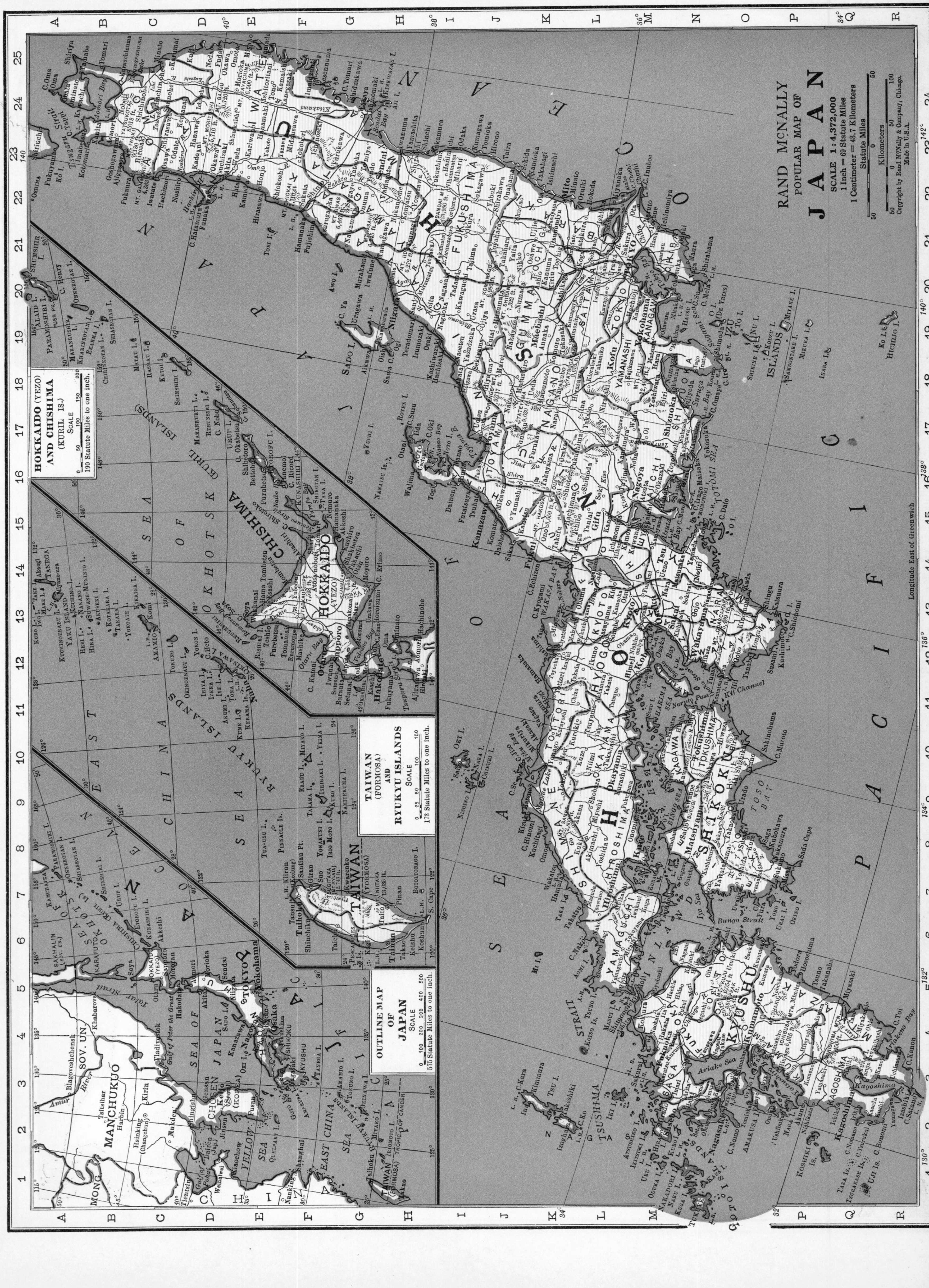

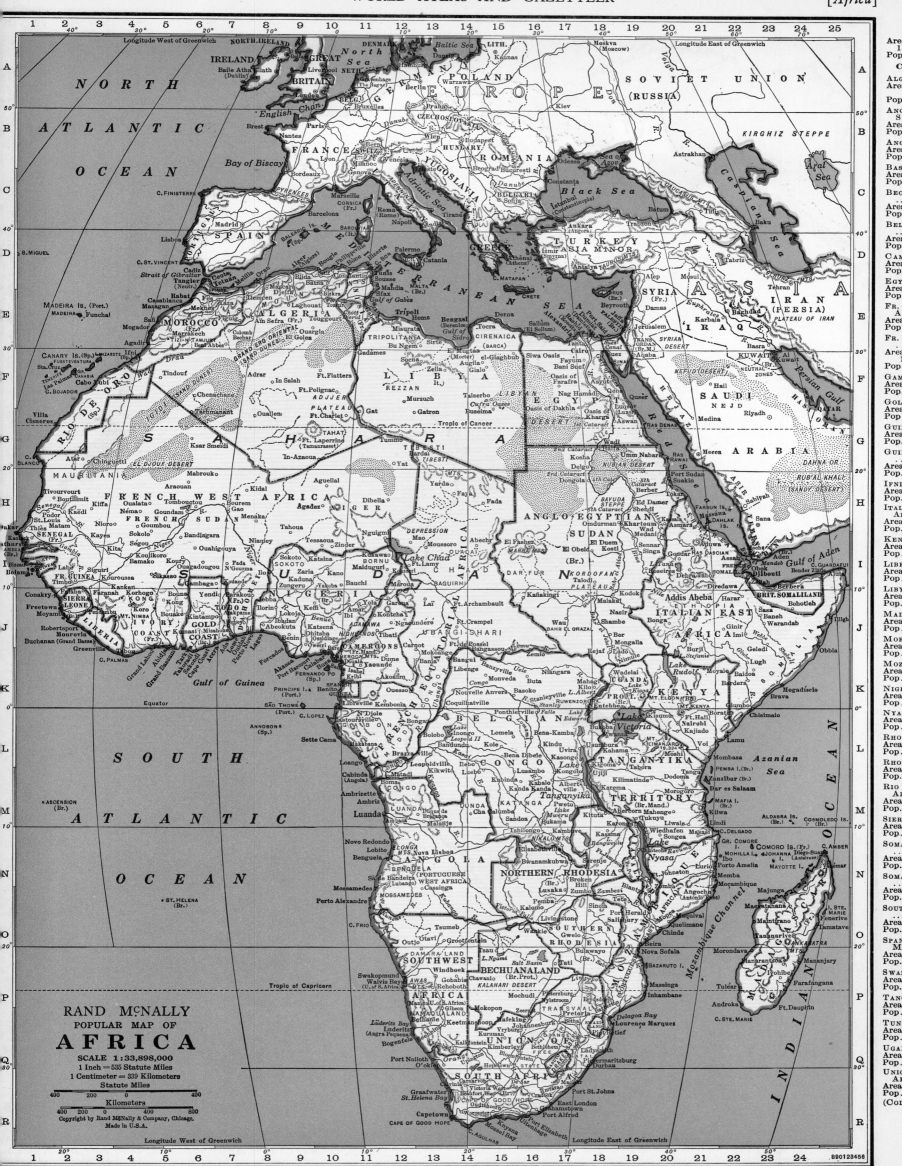

RAND McNALLY
POPULAR MAP OF
AFRICA
SCALE 1:33,898,000
1 Inch = 535 Statute Miles
1 Centimeter = 339 Kilometers
Statute Miles
Kilometers
Copyright by Rand McNally & Company, Chicago.
Made in U.S.A.

AFRICA

Area
11,529,480 sq.m.
Pop....151,000,000

COUNTRIES

ALGERIA......E 9
  Area
  847,818 sq.m.
  Pop....7,234,684
ANGLO-EGYPTIAN
  SUDAN...H 18
  Area.969,600 sq.m.
  Pop....6,000,000
ANGOLA...N 13
  Area.484,729 sq.m.
  Pop....3,225,015
BASUTOLAND.Q 17
  Area...11,716 sq.m.
  Pop....562,311
BECHUANALAND
  ....P 16
  Area.275,000 sq.m.
  Pop....265,756
BELGIAN CONGO
  ....L 15
  Area.941,809 sq.m.
  Pop...13,740,499
CAMEROONS...J 11
  Area.166,489 sq.m.
  Pop....2,516,623
EGYPT....F 17
  Area.383,000 sq.m.
  Pop...15,904,525
FR. EQUATORIAL
  AFRICA...J 13
  Area.912,049 sq.m.
  Pop....3,422,815
FR. WEST AFRICA
  ....H 7
  Area
  1,814,810 sq.m.
  Pop...14,713,748
GAMBIA....I 1
  Area...4,068 sq.m.
  Pop....199,520
GOLD COAST....J 6
  Area..91,843 sq.m.
  Pop....3,700,267
GUINEA, PORT..I 1
  Area..13,944 sq.m.
  Pop....390,400
GUINEA, SPANISH
  ....K 10
  Area..10,860 sq.m.
  Pop....140,000
IFNI.........F 4
  Area....965 sq.m.
  Pop....20,000
ITALIAN EAST
  AFRICA...J 22
  Area.585,783 sq.m.
  Pop....9,331,776
KENYA....K 21
  Area.224,960 sq.m.
  Pop....3,267,478
LIBERIA....J 3
  Area..43,000 sq.m.
  Pop....1,500,000
LIBYA....F 14
  Area.633,040 sq.m.
  Pop....717,000
MADAGASCAR.O 24
  Area.228,707 sq.m.
  Pop....3,797,936
MOROCCO....E 6
  Area.200,000 sq.m.
  Pop....5,874,888
MOZAMBIQUE.O 19
  Area.297,917 sq.m.
  Pop....4,006,000
NIGERIA....I 10
  Area.372,374 sq.m.
  Pop...20,190,771
NYASALAND..N 19
  Area..37,596 sq.m.
  Pop....1,639,329
RHODESIA, N.N 17
  Area.290,320 sq.m.
  Pop....1,383,000
RHODESIA, S..O 16
  Area.150,354 sq.m.
  Pop....1,305,635
RIO DE ORO &
  ADRAR....F 3
  Area.109,200 sq.m.
  Pop....32,000
SIERRA LEONE.J 2
  Area..31,000 sq.m.
  Pop....1,672,057
SOMALILAND, BR.
  ....I 24
  Area..68,000 sq.m.
  Pop....344,768
SOMALILAND, FR.
  ....I 22
  Area...5,790 sq.m.
  Pop....69,782
SOUTHWEST AFRICA
  ....P 13
  Area.322,393 sq.m.
  Pop....212,187
SPANISH
  MOROCCO...E 7
  Area...8,880 sq.m.
  Pop....795,000
SWAZILAND.P 18
  Area...6,705 sq.m.
  Pop....156,715
TANGANYIKA.L 19
  Area.363,548 sq.m.
  Pop....5,146,886
TUNISIA....E 11
  Area..48,300 sq.m.
  Pop....2,608,300
UGANDA...K 19
  Area..94,204 sq.m.
  Pop....3,711,494
UNION OF SOUTH
  AFRICA...Q 15
  Area.472,550 sq.m.
  Pop....8,488,300
  (Col. At. 89)

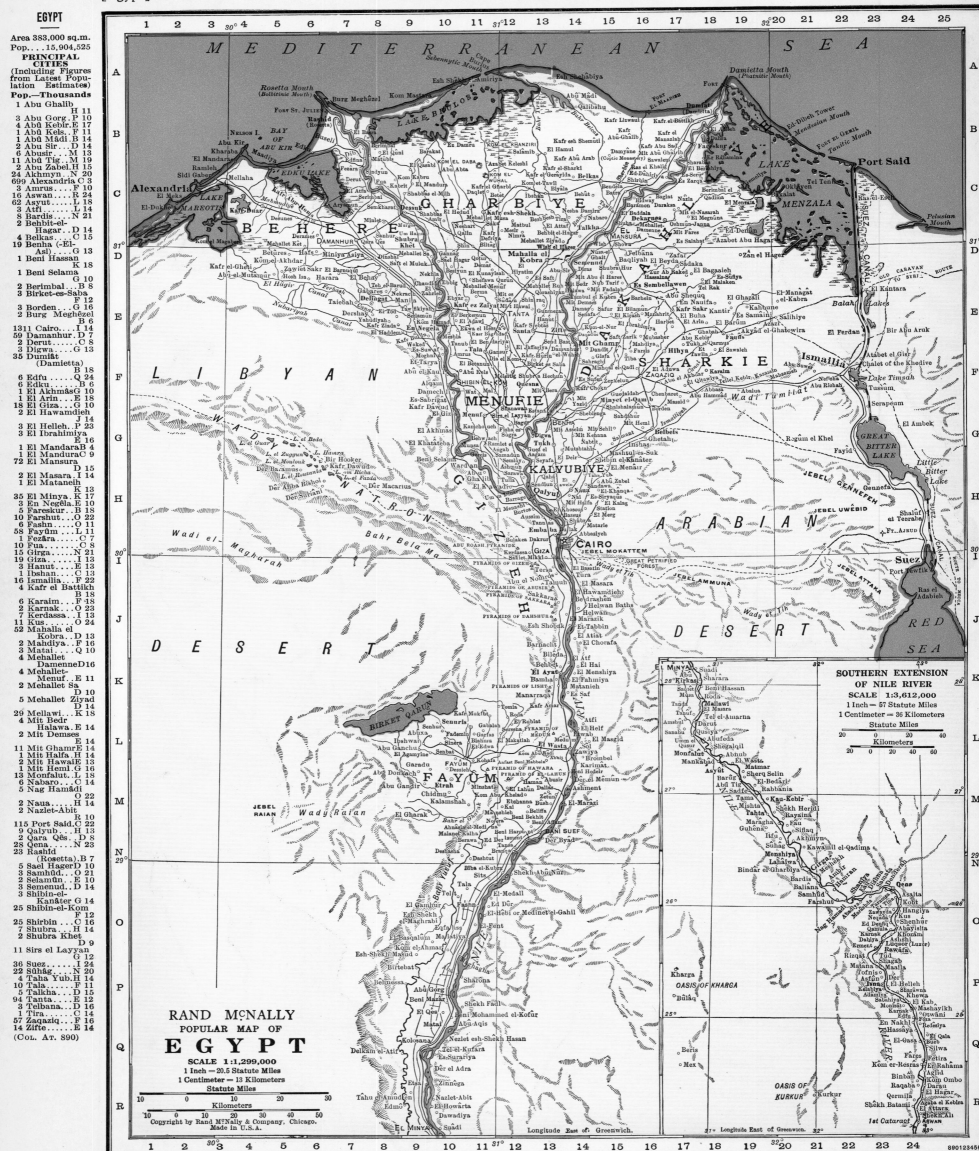

RAND McNALLY
POPULAR MAP OF
EGYPT

SCALE 1:1,299,000
1 Inch = 20.5 Statute Miles
1 Centimeter = 13 Kilometers
Statute Miles

Copyright by Rand McNally & Company, Chicago.
Made in U.S.A.

SOUTHERN EXTENSION OF NILE RIVER
SCALE 1:3,612,000
1 Inch = 57 Statute Miles
1 Centimeter = 36 Kilometers
Statute Miles

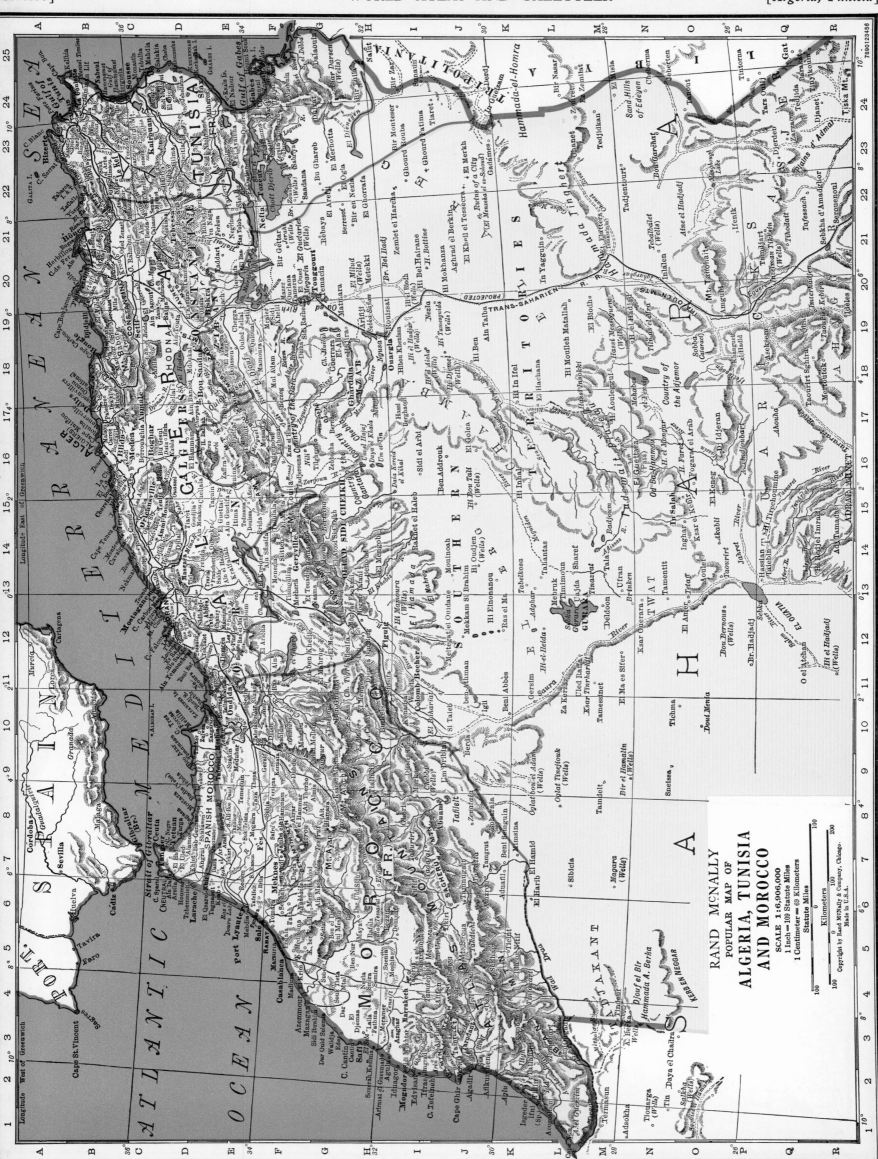

RAND MCNALLY
POPULAR MAP OF
ALGERIA, TUNISIA
AND MOROCCO
SCALE 1:6,906,000
1 Inch = 109 Statute Miles
1 Centimeter = 69 Kilometers
Statute Miles
100   0   100   200
Kilometers
100   0   100   200
Copyright by Rand McNally & Company, Chicago.
Made in U.S.A.

ALGERIA

Area 847,818 sq.m.
Pop.....7,234,684

PRINCIPAL CITIES
(Including Figures from Latest Population Estimates)
Pop.—Thousands

7 Affreville....C 16
14 Ain Beida..C 21
17 Ain Temou-
chent.....D 11
264 Alger
(Algiers) B 16
5 Arzeu.....C 12
7 Aumale....C 17
14 Batna.....D 19
11 Biskra....E 19
30 Blida.....C 16
86 Bône......B 21
15 Boufarik..C 16
25 Bougie....B 19
7 Bou Saada D 18
13 Cherchel..B 15
114 Constantine
           C 20
5 Daya......E 12
11 Djidjelli,
(Jijelli)..B 19
6 Douera....B 16
5 Doussen...E 18
8 El Affroun C 16
12 El Oued...G 20
5 Géryville..F 14
12 Ghardaia..H 18
9 Guelma....B 21
5 Guerrara..G 18
Khenchela.D 21
10 Laghouat..F 16
24 Maison Carree
           B 17
31 Mascara...D 13
16 Medea.....C 16
9 Mogador...G 20
13 Miliana...C 15
7 MograrFoukani
           H 13
5 Mondovi...B 21
38 Mostaganem
           C 13
6 Nedroma..D 11
201 Oran.....D 12
9 Orleansville
           C 15
6 Ouargla...H 19
18 Perregaux.D 13
51 Philippeville
           B 20
9 Randon....B 21
15 Relizane..D 14
9 Rio Salado D 12
5 Rouiba....B 17
5 Saida.....E 13
11 St. Denis-du-
Sig.......D 13
32 Setif.....C 19
53 Sidi Bel Abbes
           D 12
14 Souk-Ahras
           B 22
5 Stitten...F 14
8 Tebessa...D 21
7 Temacin...G 20
7 Tenez.....C 15
24 Tiaret....D 15
5 Timimoun..L 13
26 Tlemçen...E 12
12 Touggourt.G 20

MOROCCO

Area 200,000 sq.m.
Pop.....5,874,888

PRINCIPAL CITIES
(Including Figures from Latest Population Estimates)
Pop.—Thousands

259 Casablanca
           E 5
144 Fés (Fez)..F 8
15 Figuig....H 12
192 Marrakech
(Morocco).I 4
21 Mazagan...G 3
75 Meknes
(Mekines) F 7
50 Melilla...D 10
14 Mogador...E 2
20 Oujda.....E 11
84 Rabat.....F 5
26 Safi......H 3
26 Sale......F 5
60 Tangier...D 7

TUNISIA

Area .48,300 sq. m.
Pop.....2,608,300

PRINCIPAL CITIES
(Including Figures from Latest Population Estimates)
Pop.—Thousands

23 Bizerte...A 23
10 Gabes....F 24
22 Kairouan..C 24
8 Monastir.C 25
8 Nabeul...B 25
40 Sfax.....D 25
8 Sousse...C 24
202 Tunis....B 24
(COL. AT. 789)

UNION OF SOUTH AFRICA

Area 472,550 sq. m.
Pop.....8,488,300

PRINCIPAL CITIES

(Including Figures from Latest Population Estimates)

Pop.—Thousands

20 Beaconsfield
         J 15
8 Beaufort West
         O 12
6 Bethlehem. I 18
43 Bizana...M 20
51 Bloemfontein
         J 16
9 Bredasdorp. R 9
17 Bridgetown P 7
352 Capetown. Q 7
9 Cradock..O 15
270 Durban..L 21
47 East London
         P 18
68 Germiston.F 18
12 Graaf Reinet
         O 13
9 Graafwater O 7
20 Grahamstown
         P 16
9 Harrismith.I 19
10 Impendhle.L 19
554 Johannesburg
         F 18
39 Kimberley.J 14
10 King Williams
    Town.....P 17
6 Klerksdorp
         G 16
14 Kroonstad.I 17
55 Krugersdorp
         F 17
25 Kuruman.H 12
10 Ladysmith.J 20
26 Libode....N 19
4 Maclear..M 18
27 Marico...F 16
7 Mossel Bay
         Q 11
35 Mquanduli N18
13 Oudtshoorn
         Q 11
19 Paarl......Q 7
47 Pietermaritz-
    burg....K 21
118 Port Elizabeth
         Q 15
19 Potchefstroom
         G 16
138 Pretoria..F 18
7 Prieska...K 11
18 Queens Town
         N 16
34 Qumbu...M 18
23 Taungs...H 14
15 Ubombo..I 22
21 Uitenhage.Q 15
37 Umzimkulu
         L 19
8 Witbank..F 19
13 Wolmarans-
    stadt...H 15
13 Worcester.Q 8
12 Zwart Kop L 10

BASUTOLAND

Area..11,716 sq. m.
Pop......562,311

PRINCIPAL CITY

(Including Figures from Latest Population Estimates)

Pop.—Thousands

2 Maseru...K 18

BECHUANALAND

Area 275,000 sq. m.
Pop.......265,756

PRINCIPAL CITIES

(Including Figures from Latest Population Estimates)

Pop.—Thousands

8 Mochudi .D 15
20 Serowe ..A 17

SOUTHWEST AFRICA

Area 322,393 sq.m.
Pop.......212,187

PRINCIPAL CITIES

(Including Figures from Latest Population Estimates)

Pop.—Thousands

14 Grootfontein
         E 4
4 Keetmanshoop
         G 7
3 Lüderitz..G 3
9 Rehoboth..C 5
3 Swakopmund
         B 1
1 Walvis Bay C 1
20 Windhoek..B 5

SWAZILAND

Area..6,705 sq. m.
Pop.......156,715

PRINCIPAL CITIES

(Including Figures from Latest Population Estimates)

Pop.— Hundreds

1 Bremersdorp
         G 22
2 Mbabane .G 22

(COL. AT. 7890)

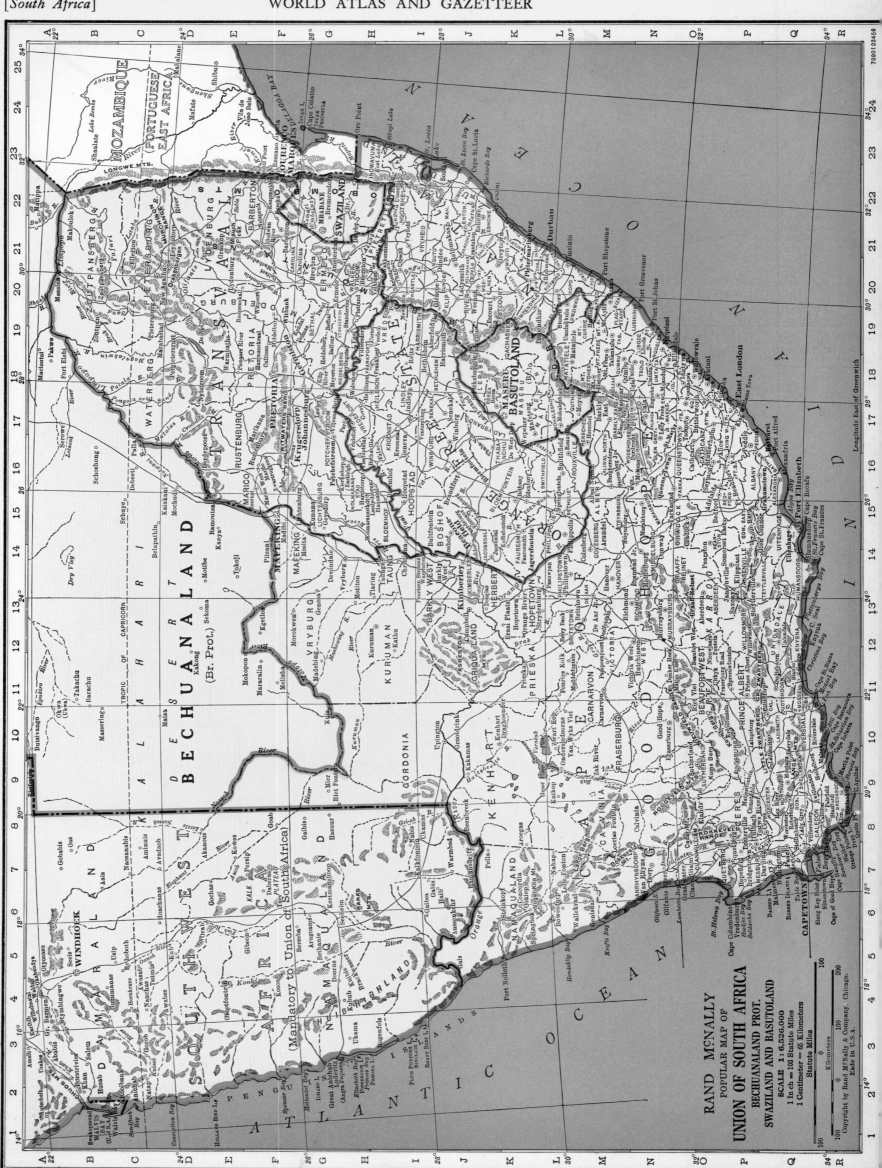

RAND M°NALLY
POPULAR MAP OF
UNION OF SOUTH AFRICA
BECHUANALAND PROT.
SWAZILAND AND BASUTOLAND

SCALE 1:6,526,000
1 Inch = 103 Statute Miles
1 Centimeter = 65 Kilometers

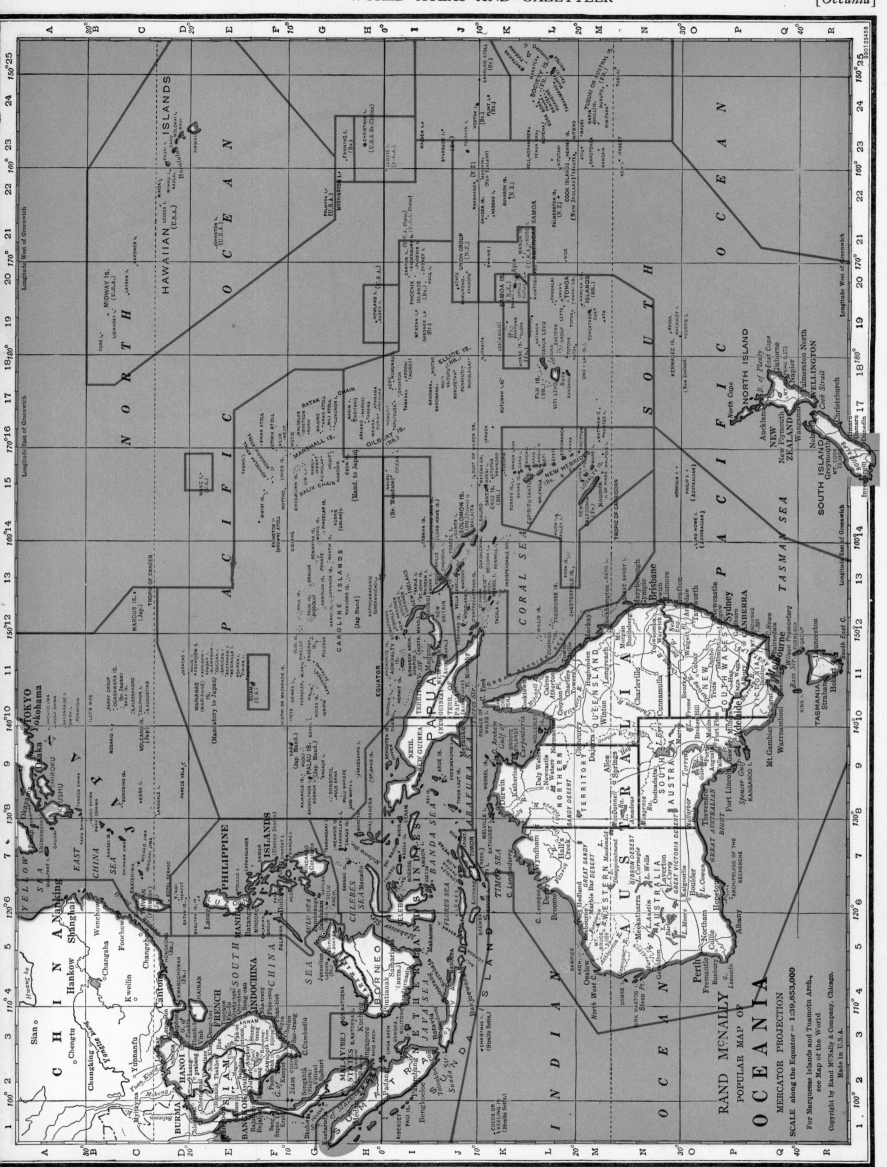

RAND McNALLY
POPULAR MAP OF
OCEANIA
MERCATOR PROJECTION
SCALE along the Equator = 1:39,853,000
For Marquesas Islands and Tuamotu Arch.,
see Map of the World
Made in U.S.A.
Copyright by Rand McNally & Company, Chicago.

AUSTRALIA

Ar. 2,974,581 sq.m.
Pop.....6,806,752

PRINCIPAL CITIES
(Including Figures from Latest Population Estimates)
Pop.—Thousands

(Col. At. 789)

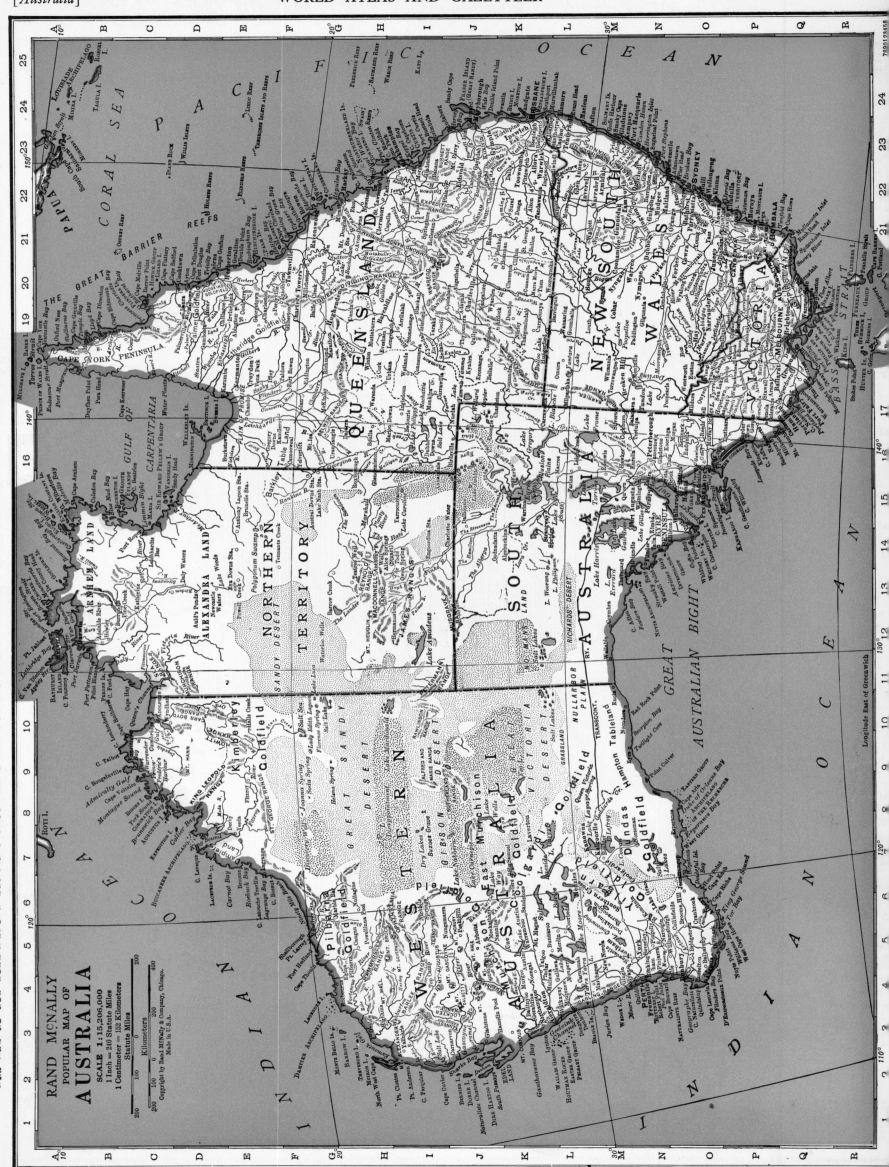

RAND McNALLY
POPULAR MAP OF
AUSTRALIA

SCALE 1:15,206,000
1 Inch = 240 Statute Miles
1 Centimeter = 152 Kilometers

Copyright by Rand McNally & Company, Chicago.
Made in U.S.A.

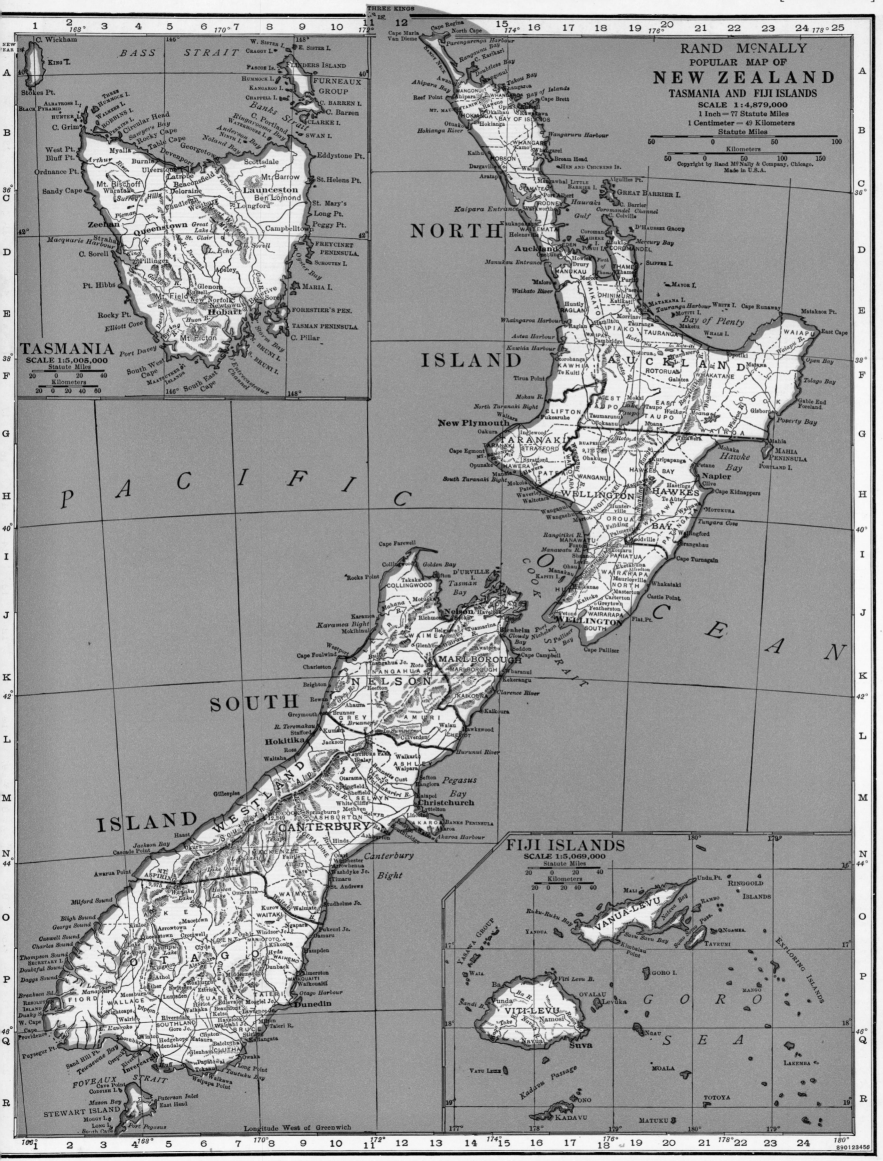

NEW ZEALAND

Area 103,862 sq. m.
Pop.....1,591,974

PRINCIPAL CITIES

(Including Figures from Latest Population Estimates)

Pop.—Thousands

1 Ahaura...K 11
5 Ashburton N 11
103 Auckland D 17
2 Balclutha...Q 7
1 Belgrove...J 13
5 Blenheim...J 15
2 Cambridge E 18
2 Carterton...J 18
93 Christchurch
   M 12
2 Dargaville..C 15
2 Drury.....D 17
65 Dunedin...P 9
1 FeatherstonJ 18
1 Feilding...I 18
2 Foxton...I 18
14 Gisborne..G 23
4 Gore Junction
   Q 6
6 Greymouth L10
1 Greytown..J 18
18 Hamilton..E 18
13 Hastings...H 21
1 Havelock..J 15
5 Hawera...H 16
1 Helensville
   D 16
3 Hokitika...L 9
2 Huntly....E 18
1 Inglewood.G 16
21 Invercargill Q 5
2 Kaiapoi...M 12
1 Kaitangata.Q 7
1 Kelso.....Q 6
2 Levin...I 18
4 Lyttelton.M 13
2 Marton...H 18
1 Masterton.J 18
1 Mataura...Q 6
1 Mauriceville
   J 18
1 Methven..M 11
2 Milton....Q 8
2 Morrinsville
   E 18
2 Mosgiel Jc..P 8
4 Motueka..J 13
15 Napier...H 21
12 Nelson....J 14
18 New Plymouth
   G 15
8 Oamaru...O 9
2 Ohakune...G 18
11 Onehunga..D 17
1 Opotiki...F 22
1 Orari.....N 10
2 Paeroa....E 19
23 Palmerston,
   North...H 18
1 Patea....H 16
10 Petone....J 18
1 Picton...J 15
2 Rangiora.M 12
2 Reefton...K 11
1 Richmond.J 13
5 Rotorua..F 20
1 Selwyn...M 12
1 Shannon..I 18
2 Sheffield..M 11
4 Stratford..G 16
2 Taumarunui
   G 18
3 Tauranga..E 19
2 Te Aroha..E 19
2 Te Kuiti..F 17
5 Thames...D 18
18 Timaru...N 10
2 Wainate..O 10
1 Waipawa..H 20
1 Wallingford
   I 20
23 Wanganui.H 17
117 Wellington
   J 17
4 Westport..K 10
8 Whangarei B 16
1 Woodville..I 19

TASMANIA

Area .26,215 sq. m.
Pop.......227,599

PRINCIPAL CITIES

(Including Figures from Latest Population Estimates)

Pop.—Thousands

4 Burnie.....B 5
6 Deloraine..C 6
5 Devonport..C 6
47 Hobart.....E 7
1 Latrobe...C 6
28 Launceston.C 7
1 Longford...C 7
2 New Norfolk
   E 7
4 Queenstown 4
1 St. Mary's.C 9
3 Scottsdale..C 8
1 Ulverstone..C 5
1 Westbury...C 6
2 Zeehan.....C 4

FIJI ISLANDS

Area ..7,083 sq. m.
Pop.......198,379

PRINCIPAL CITY

(Including Figures from Latest Population Estimates)

Pop.—Thousands

.. Suva.....Q 17

(COL. AT. 890)

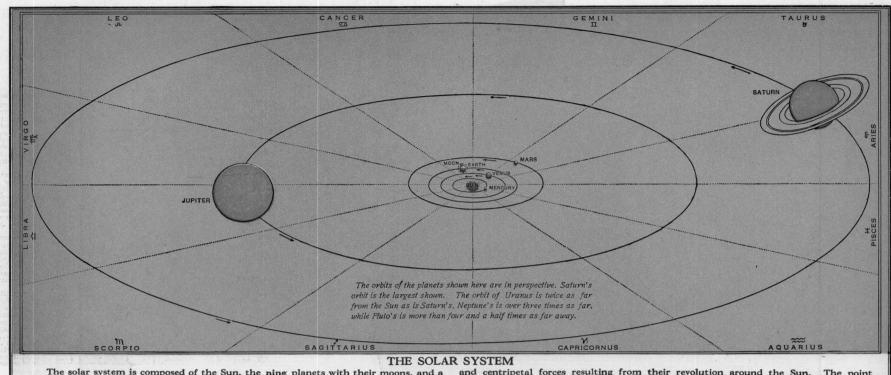

The orbits of the planets shown here are in perspective. Saturn's orbit is the largest shown. The orbit of Uranus is twice as far from the Sun as is Saturn's, Neptune's is over three times as far, while Pluto's is more than four and a half times as far away.

THE SOLAR SYSTEM

The solar system is composed of the Sun, the nine planets with their moons, and a number of comets and asteroids. The planets rotate on their axes, and at the same time revolve around the Sun in a counter-clockwise direction, along their paths, or orbits, at varying distances from the Sun. They are held in their orbits by the centrifugal and centripetal forces resulting from their revolution around the Sun. The point nearest the Sun in the orbit of a planet is its Perihelion; the farthest, its Aphelion. The orbits of Uranus, Neptune and Pluto are too large to be shown in their true proportions on this diagram.

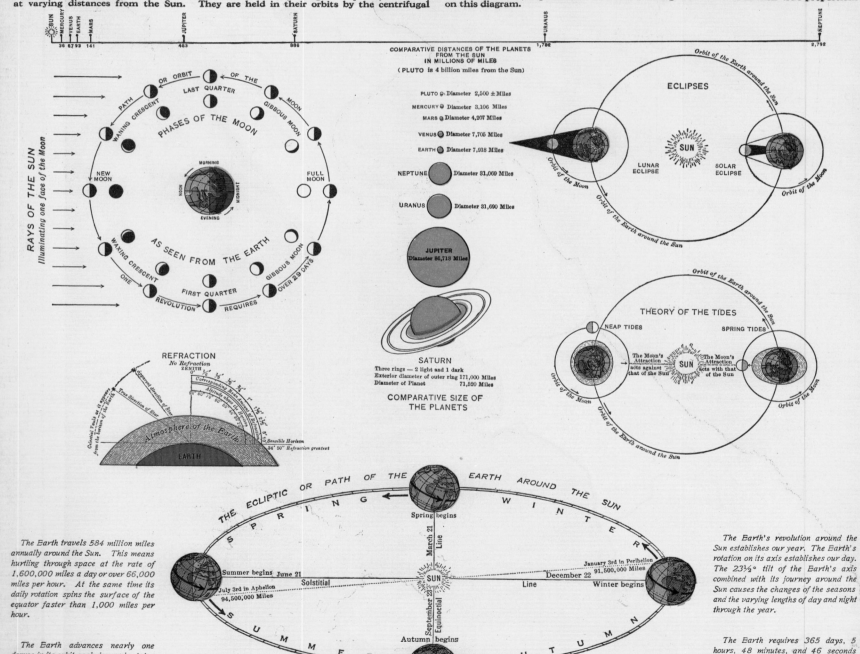

The Earth travels 584 million miles annually around the Sun. This means hurtling through space at the rate of 1,600,000 miles a day or over 66,000 miles per hour. At the same time its daily rotation spins the surface of the equator faster than 1,000 miles per hour.

The Earth advances nearly one degree in its orbit each day and rotates nearly 361 degrees each day on its axis. This extra degree of rotation is necessary to compensate for the daily advance in its orbit and to complete a solar day.

The Earth's revolution around the Sun establishes our year. The Earth's rotation on its axis establishes our day. The 23½° tilt of the Earth's axis combined with its journey around the Sun causes the changes of the seasons and the varying lengths of day and night through the year.

The Earth requires 365 days, 5 hours, 48 minutes, and 46 seconds to complete one revolution of 360 degrees around the Sun. This is a Solar Year. Our calender year is 365 days. One day is added every fourth year to make up for the extra hours in the Solar Year.

THE ORBIT OF THE EARTH

The Earth's yearly journey around the Sun, showing the Earth's position on the four important days of the year when the northern seasons begin.

A Physical and Commercial Analysis of the World

THE UNIVERSE.—In the strict sense of the word, the universe is the whole sum of existing things to the farthest extremity of space, and in it our earth, for all its apparent size, diversity and interest, is less than the smallest grain of dust compared to the earth. Not many years ago it was still supposed that the lens-shaped aggregation of stars in which our solar system is located and which we see, as the Milky Way or Galaxy, overhead at night from any part of the earth, contained a large part of the stars and material of the universe. It is now evident that there are many "galaxies" comparable in size to this one. Modern scientists think of the universe as boundless, in the sense that a sphere is boundless. It is not of infinite extent, for if it were our sky would be entirely bright—brighter than the sun. There is, as yet, no method of measuring it, but instruments now available give information about a magnitude with a diameter of approximately 500,000,000 light years, using for the unit of measurement the distance that light, which travels approximately 186,300 miles a second, would move in a year.

The general conception of the mechanics and mathematics of the universe was based for at least two centuries on the work of Sir Isaac Newton (1642-1727). His Laws of Motion and Gravitation account for most of the phenomena connected with the movements of the sun and planets. In recent times the Newtonian laws have been supplemented and to some extent superseded by the work of other physicists, one of the most prominent being Albert Einstein, whose special contribution is usually called the Theory of Relativity, or the Einstein Theory.

Ether had long been assumed to be an all-pervading entity, weightless and extremely elastic, filling the universe and permeating solids, liquids and gases. Light and electro-magnetic radiations were assumed to be transmitted through the ether as undulations. If the earth, in addition to its rotation and revolution, is also rushing through space along with the sun, it should be possible to detect and measure this movement by the use of light reflections to determine the apparent drag of the ether, assuming the ether to be stationary. Such experiments were made by A. A. Michelson in 1887 and continued in collaboration with E. W. Morley. Only negative results were obtained. Other scientists tried different methods, with no positive results. The failure to detect any ether drift was a basis for the Einstein Theory announced in 1905, that "it is of necessity impossible to determine absolute motion by any experiment whatsoever." According to Einstein neither *space* nor *time* is absolute. Both are relative and relate to moving systems. This is the Theory of Relativity. Einstein declares also that light has mass and that light beams are affected by gravitational influence. As the sun is the center of immense gravitational force, beams of light passing near the sun must be bent toward it by gravitation. He predicted that the light from a distant star, passing close to the sun, would, if just grazing the sun's limb, be bent by an angle of 1.745″. Parties from the observatories of Greenwich and Cambridge tested this in the eclipse of 1919. The Greenwich party reported an average deviation of 1.98″ for light beams from seven stars; the Cambridge party, an average of 1.61″. In 1922, a Lick observatory party, with better weather, made the same experiment and obtained a value of 1.72″, near enough to Einstein's prediction to have the difference charged to likely error. Other tests further confirmed the theory.

During the past few years an intensive study of cosmic radiation has been carried on by A. H. Compton and R. A. Millikan, American physicists. A phase of this study has been carried on by stratosphere flights in large balloons, the first being made by Auguste Piccard, a Belgian physicist, who took off on May 27, 1931, from Augsburg, Germany, and landed at Ober Gurgl, Austria, after reaching an altitude of 51,775 feet. Captains Albert W. Stevens and Orvil A. Anderson of the U. S. Army reached a height of 72,395 feet in the "Explorer II" on November 11, 1935. Unmanned small balloons carrying self-recording instruments have ascended to considerably greater heights.

THE SOLAR SYSTEM.—There are nine known major planets in the solar system, Mercury, Venus, the Earth, Mars, Jupiter, Saturn, Uranus, Neptune, Pluto. Our planet is the third in distance from the sun, the vast central body around which they all revolve. Besides these larger celestial bodies about eighteen hundred minor planets, or asteroids, have been discovered between the orbit of Mars and Jupiter. Most of the miniature planets range in diameter probably from 10 miles to 20 miles. Undoubtedly many more await discovery. The largest four (Ceres, in diameter, 485 miles; Pallas, 304 miles; Vesta, 243 miles, and Juno, 118 miles) were first noted in the early years of the 19th century.

The periodic comets—those that return at regular intervals—are also members of our solar system.

THE SUN.—The Sun is regarded as an immense globe of matter, not different in kind from that of the earth, but so extremely hot as to remain completely or almost completely gaseous.

Diameter of the sun........ 864,100 miles
Mean distance from the earth 92,870,000 miles
Period of rotation (Equat.).. 24.65 days
Mass of sun............... 331,350 × mass of the earth
Mean density.............. 1.415
Solar constant............ 1.95 calories
Effective temperature..... 6,000° minimum
Contraction of volume..... 250 feet per annum

THE MOON.—Our earth has but one satellite—the moon. Its surface exhibits evidence of volcanic action in ages past. Several of the mountain chains are 20,000 feet high and there are depressions of corresponding depth. But all the volcanoes have long since been extinct. The moon having neither atmosphere nor water cannot support animal or vegetable life. It is a dead world.

Moon's greatest distance from the
  earth .... 252,700 miles
Least distance from the earth...... 221,460 miles
Diameter of moon................ 2,163 miles
Moon's area .... 14,652,400 sq. miles
Inclination of the moon's axis to
  the plane of the moon's orbit.... 6° 41′
On the moon gravitation is only 1-6 that of our globe.
Moon's volume 1-49 the volume of the earth.
Moon's density 3-5 that of the earth.
Moon's mass 1-81 the earth's mass.

As the moon's period of axial rotation, 27 days, 7 hours, 43.2 minutes, is exactly equal to her time of revolution around the earth, she always presents the same side toward us.

THE EARTH.—As our earth cooled, much of the water vapor in the atmosphere was turned into rain and fell on the surface. There the half-molten rock changed the rain water back to vapor. Thousands of

THE SOLAR ECLIPSE OF JUNE 8, 1937, SHOWING—IN PART FAINTLY—THE GLOBULAR CORONA OF THE SUN. THE PHOTOGRAPH WAS TAKEN FROM AN AIRPLANE FLYING IN THE LOWER STRATOSPHERE BY MAJOR ALBERT W. STEVENS

centuries must have elapsed before the water finally remained on the earth, completely covering its surface of rock.

But the cooling of the globe caused the rock crust to shrink, thus producing in it stupendous folds or heights. These were the beginnings of dry land areas of geological times. Gathering in the depressions, the water formed oceans. For ages the shrinking of the interior rock continued, and the early surface underwent numerous upheavals and subsidences before the principal land masses assumed their present outlines.

FORM AND SIZE OF THE EARTH.—The earth is a sphere slightly flattened at the poles—an oblate spheroid. Recent measurements indicate that the equatorial section of the earth, hitherto supposed to be circular, is in fact somewhat elliptical.

Equatorial diameter .... 7,926.68 miles
Polar diameter .... 7,899.99 "
Difference .... 26.69 "
Mean diameter .... 7,918.0 "
Equatorial circumference .... 24,902.37 "
Meridional circumference .... 24,860.44 "
Difference .... 41.83 "
Area of surface .... 196,940,400 square miles
Water area .... 141,055,400 " "
Land area .... 55,885,000 " "
Volume .... 260,000,000,000 cubic miles

The equatorial semidiameter is to the polar semidiameter as 300 is to 299.

THE SOLAR SYSTEM

Sun and Planets	Mean Distance from the Sun in Miles	Sidereal Revolution Days	Orbital Velocity. Miles per Second	Diameter in Miles	Mass Compared with Earth (Earth = 1)	Period of Axial Rotation				Gravity at Surface of the Earth (Earth = 1)
						Days	Hrs.	Mins.	Secs.	
Sun				864,080	331,950	25	15	36		27.98
Mercury ☿	35,950,000	87.97	29.73	3,106	0.045	±24	0			0.27
Venus ♀	67,170,000	225.00	21.75	7,705	0.81	±24	0			0.88
Earth ⊕	92,900,000	365.26	18.50	7,918	1.00	23	56			1.00
Mars ♂	141,498,000	686.98	14.98	4,207	0.107	24	37	5		0.38
Jupiter ♃	483,177,000	4,332.63	8.11	86,718	317.00	9	50			2.64
Saturn ♄	885,825,000	10,759.22	5.99	71,520	95.00	10	14	24		1.17
Uranus ♅	1,782,151,000	30,685.93	4.22	31,690	14.7	10	7			0.92
Neptune ♆	2,792,499,000	60,187.64	3.36	31,069	17.16	±15				1.12
Pluto PL	3,700,000,000	90,469.31	2.90	3,800	0.66					2.70

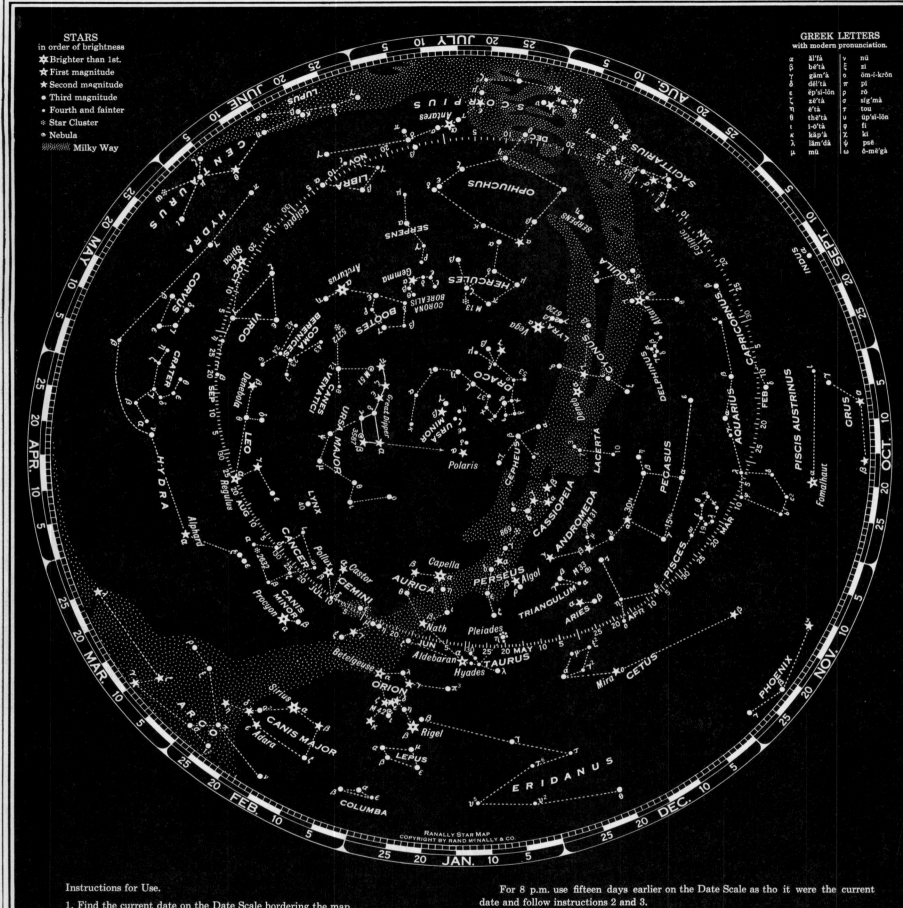

Ranally Star Map
COPYRIGHT BY RAND McNALLY & CO.

Instructions for Use.

1. Find the current date on the Date Scale bordering the map.

2. Face South and hold the map upright, with the current date at the bottom of the sheet. The stars and constellations just above this part of the Date Scale will correspond with the stars above the Southern Horizon in the night sky, at 9 p.m. on that date. The stars on the map midway between the current date and the center of the map will be found approximately overhead in the sky.

3. Face North, holding the map upright, with the current date at the top. The stars in the center of the map will then correspond with the stars to be seen in the sky above the Northern Horizon at 9 p.m. (10 p.m. daylight saving time).

For 8 p.m. use fifteen days earlier on the Date Scale as tho it were the current date and follow instructions 2 and 3.

For 10 p.m. use fifteen days later on the Date Scale instead of the current date.

For 11 p.m. use one month later, etc., adding fifteen days later for each later hour. The moon and the planets will be seen near the Ecliptic circle when above the Horizon.

The map is constructed for the mean latitude of the United States, 40° north. From the northern limits of this country the stars within one-third of an inch of the date scale will be below the southern horizon and therefore not visible. From the southern parts of the country the stars along the date scale will appear slightly above the southern horizon.

LOCATION OF STARS AND CONSTELLATIONS

Map identifying the stars and constellations visible in the night sky. The brightness of the stars is expressed in magnitudes, the brightest stars being of the first magnitude. Astronomers have been successful in reaching stars of the twenty-first magnitude with large telescopes. The naked eye can see stars up to the sixth magnitude. The number of stars steadily increases with the increasing magnitude. There are only about twenty stars of the first magnitude and over a billion of the twenty-first magnitude. The colors of the stars range from bluish white to yellow and red. These colors depend on the different temperatures of the stars, the hottest stars being bluish white and the coldest stars red.

DENSITY AND MASS.

Our globe's density is 5.5, the density of water being taken as unity, or 1. As the surface rock is only 2.5 denser than water, the interior must have a density of about 11.2. The earth's weight is computed to be 6,660,000,000,000,000,000,000 tons (six sextillion six hundred and sixty quintillion tons), a figure so great as to be meaningless to most of us. Yet it would take nearly 1,300,000 globes like our earth in size to equal the volume of the sun.

Experiments made in deep mines show that the earth's temperature generally increases about 1° F. for every seventy feet of descent. If this temperature were maintained, water, at 8,000 feet below the surface would boil and the hardest rock would melt. It is improbable, however, that this increase in temperature continues to the earth's center. Were the rate of increase kept up for even a thousand miles, the resulting temperature of the earth would be inconceivably high.

What is the condition of the earth's interior? Many geophysicists believe that the inner core (of iron and nickel and four thousand miles or more in diameter) is far more rigid than steel, the rigidity resulting from the enormous pressure of the earth's crust.

MOTIONS OF THE EARTH.

With the other planets of the solar system our globe revolves around the sun in a slightly elliptical orbit, the sun being at one of the foci. The longer diameter of the ellipse is to the shorter as 60 is to 50. To complete a revolution requires a year of 365 days, 5 hours, 48 minutes, and 46 seconds. Such a year is 20 minutes shorter than the true or sidereal year. On January 3 the earth is in perihelion, or nearest the sun, being then distant from it about 91,000,000 miles. On July 2 the earth is in aphelion, or farthest from the sun, which is then nearly 94,000,000 miles away. As the earth's orbit is 560,000,000 miles in length, our planet is speeding around the sun at the rate of about a thousand miles a minute.

INCLINATION OF THE EARTH'S AXIS.

The earth's *axis* is an imaginary straight line passing through the earth's center and terminating at the poles. There would be no change of seasons, and day and night would be everywhere of equal length throughout the year, if the axis were perpendicular to the plane of the earth's orbit. But the axis always inclines 23° 27' 3.3". The north terminal point of the axis—that is, the north pole—always points to a spot in the sky very near the North Star. The axis oscillates about 0.3" periodically.

ROTATION OF THE EARTH.

Our globe is always rotating from west to east on its shortest diameter. A day of 23 hours, 56 minutes, and 4.09 seconds is required for one complete rotation. It should be noted that axial rotation increases in speed from the poles, where it is zero, to the equator on which a point moves about 1,038 miles an hour.

SURFACE OF THE EARTH.

About one-fourth of the earth's surface is dry land. The remaining three-fourths is covered with water. Most of the land above the ocean lies in five great masses, the rest consisting of many smaller masses, known as islands. Europe, Asia, Africa, and the great island of Australia are the continents which make up the large land masses of the eastern hemisphere. In the western hemisphere are the continents of North America and South America. The land mass covering the South Pole is sometimes termed the continent of Antarctica.

The equator, which is an imaginary circle described around the earth at an equal distance from the poles, divides the earth's surface into a northern hemisphere and a southern. The plane of this circle passes through the center of the earth and is at right angles to the axis. All Europe, continental Asia, North America, and most of Africa lie north of the equator. Australia, the southern part of Africa, and most of South America are in the southern hemisphere and are mainly tropical in climate and product. Three-fourths of the earth's land lies north of the equator, while the larger part of the southern hemisphere is occupied by the ocean. This hemisphere's coasts lack the numerous deep indentations which furnish so many capacious harbors in all northern continents. Hence the northern half of the globe is the home of civilization, commerce, and power.

Plains and plateaus, high and low, occupy almost two-thirds of the land surface. A few mountains rear their summits four miles above sea level. Most of the land surface, however, averages only a tenth of that height. Land below half a mile high is termed *lowland*. All land above that level is called *highland*.

The great highland section of the globe forms a horseshoelike curve sweeping from Cape Horn around to the Cape of Good Hope. One side slopes abruptly to the Pacific and Indian Oceans. On the other side the slope is long and gradual to the Atlantic and Arctic Oceans and includes most of the continental lowland. Part of this lowland slope passes under the sea and is called the *continental shelf*. Over it the sea averages about 600 feet in depth. All the large islands and hundreds of lesser size are located on this submerged slope. They are called *continental* or *littoral* islands. Smaller ones farther out in the ocean and surrounded by deeper water are termed *oceanic* or *pelagic* islands.

For example, the British Isles rise from the continental shelf of Europe. Once they formed part of the continent, and they would be united to it again if the floor of the North Sea were to rise 150 feet. A large area of that body of water is not over 95 feet deep. Along the Atlantic Coast of North America the continental shelf extends out for 110 miles at an average depth of 600 feet. Around Newfoundland the shelf is

over 500 miles wide. Shelves occur also on the northern and eastern coasts of South America. Along the Pacific shores of both Americas the continental shelf is quite narrow. Off California it is only 10 miles wide. At its edge there is an abrupt dip of 3,600 feet, and then for 40 or 50 miles there is a slope deepening from 9,600 to 14,400 feet.

From continental Europe a broad shelf passing under the North Sea extends from the British Isles far out into the Atlantic. Almost all the East India islands are situated on a wide shelf stretching southeastward from Asia. Papua (New Guinea) and several smaller islands rise from a shelf which extends north from Australia.

HEIGHTS OF LAND.

The elevation of the land above sea level varies from 0 to 29,000 feet (5½ miles).

The following table shows the percentage of the earth's surface above and below indicated levels in feet:

Over 6,000 feet above sea level	2.3 per cent
Over sea level to 6,000 feet	25.5 " "
Under sea level to 6,000 feet	14.8 " "
From 6,000 to 12,000 feet below	14.8 " "
From 12,000 to 18,000 feet below	39.4 " "
More than 18,000 feet depth	3.2 " "

The immense heights and depths thus represented are insignificant compared with the total bulk of the earth. On a globe of 15 feet in diameter the highest mountain would be represented by an elevation of no

more than one-eighth inch, and a depth of one-seventh inch would represent the deepest abyss in the ocean bed. The greatest heights, therefore, being no more than .0007 of the diameter, are mere roughnesses of the surface. On a globe reduced to the size of a large orange they would be insignificant. Between the lowest sea depth, 35,400 feet, which is near Mindanao, and the top of the highest mountain, Mt. Everest in the Himalayas, 29,141 feet, the vertical distance is about 12 miles.

The surface of the earth above sea level is diversified into plains, hills, ridges, mountains, valleys, table-lands, plateaus, and basins.

In general, a mountain is any height of land, sloping on either side, that rises above 1,000 feet. A hill is any sloping rise of less than 1,000 feet. A plateau or table-land is an extended elevated surface. Mountains—elevations of land other than plateaus—generally occur in chains or systems.

According to the most recent authorities, about two-thirds of the dry land lies at an elevation of 1,000 feet above sea level, leaving about one-third below that height. About 8.3% lies above 6,000 feet elevation;

THE ADLER PLANETARIUM IN CHICAGO

about 2.5% above 12,000 feet; about 0.3% above 18,000 feet; about 0.01% above 24,000 feet.

HIGH AND LOWLAND LEVELS.

The lowest levels in the land are:

The Dead Sea, 1,290 feet below the level of the sea, in the Jordan Valley; Death Valley, 280 feet below sea level, in southeastern California; and in Sahara Desert, in northern Africa, about 150 feet below sea level.

The mean approximate height of the several continents is as follows:

North America	2,000	feet
South America	1,800	"
Europe	980	"
Asia	3,000	"
Africa	1,900	"
Australia	1,000	"
Antarctica	6,000	"

The great lowlands are found in the interior regions; as, in North America, the Mississippi Valley; and in South America the plains of the Amazon and La Plata, and in northern Europe and Asia the vast plains and steppes on each side of the Ural Mountains.

The great plateaus or extensive areas of elevated land over 1,000 feet are:

In North America.—The Laurentian plateau, mainly in the Province of Quebec. The Appalachian plateau extending from southern New York to Georgia. Between the Rocky Mountains and the Cascade and Sierra Nevada ranges is the largest plateau on this continent.

ROYAL GORGE, COLORADO, SHOWING AN AUTOMOBILE BRIDGE HIGH ABOVE THE CANYON AND A TRAIN CREEPING ALONG THE RIVER'S EDGE

The northern part is known as the Columbia plateau, and the southern part as the Great Basin. The average height is about 5,000 feet. The Mexican plateau, 7,500 feet high, is also part of the Rocky Mountain highland.

In Asia.—The plateau of Tibet, an intermontane plateau between the main range of the Himalayas and the Kunlun Mountains, is about 13,000 feet high. There are also the Mongolian plateau, 3,000 feet in height, and the Deccan plateau, 2,000 feet high. The Iran plateau comprises most of Iran (Persia). It has an average height of 3,000 feet.

In South America.—The plateau of Quito, 10,000 feet above sea level, 300 miles long, 40 miles wide, is part of the Andean highland, and has on it the high peaks Cayambe (19,023 feet), Antisana (18,885 feet), Cotopaxi (19,347 feet), Sangay (17,465 feet), Chimborazo (20,702 feet), and Altar (17,730 feet). The plateau of Bolivia has an elevation of 12,000 feet, with Lake Titicaca at 12,507 feet, and the city of Potosi 13,325 feet above sea level. The Brazilian plateau averages about 3,500 feet in height, and the plateau of Guiana has about the same altitude.

In Europe.—Spain has a plateau of 2,250 feet mean elevation; Auvergne, France, has another of 2,100 feet; Bavaria another of 1,660 feet. The Swiss plateau is much higher, and a short distance east of the Adriatic Sea is a highland region forming a narrow plateau extending from the Gulf of Trieste to Cape Matapan.

In Africa.—The Abyssinian plateau with a mean elevation of 7,000 feet, and in South Africa a plateau 3,000 to 4,000 feet high. The Sahara Desert is about 1,500 feet above sea level. There are also the Morvean, the Kong, and the Desert plateaus. Beginning near the Angola coast and extending thence eastward to Lake Nyasa and from there north to the Red Sea, the African highland forms a low rolling plateau, 3,000 miles long and 300 miles wide.

Other famous volcanoes than those that have been mentioned above are Vesuvius, Etna, and Stromboli in Italy; Hekla and Oraefa Jökul in Iceland; Mauna Loa, Mauna Kea, and Hualalai in Hawaii, and Soufrière and Mount Pelée in the West Indies. Mt. Lassen in California has displayed volcanic action in recent years, and Alaska has several volcanoes intermittently active.

LAND CHANGES.—In geological times portions of the present sea floor stood above the water and joined together certain land masses now separate. North America was connected with Europe's Arctic regions, and Australia with southeastern Asia. The Gulf of Mexico covered a large part of the present Mississippi Valley.

Rising and sinking land movements are still taking place throughout the world, though most of them are so slight they are not felt. Norway's east coast is rising at the rate of 3 feet a century, and the Italian coast near Naples has sunk and risen within historic times. A sinking or a rising movement violent enough to break layers of rock occasions an earthquake.

CORAL ISLANDS AND REEFS.—In warm and shallow seas great colonies of coral polyps, tiny jelly-like animals, extract lime from the sea water and build up out of the lime the stony skeletons by which they are attached to the colony's rocky base, which rests on the sea floor. Countless millions of these little limestone skeletons are piled on one another till finally a reef rises above the water. Coral polyps cannot live at a greater depth than thirty fathoms. Reefs that rise from lower depths were originally started on some submarine mountain top, which slowly sank while the polyps continued to build.

Many of the islands in the Pacific and Indian Oceans are of coral formation and are raised only as high as the waves can throw up the coral fragments, and the winds can pile up sand. The *atoll* is the most common form of coral land. It is simply a narrow reef inclosing a shallow lagoon.

Barrier reefs either extend in nearly straight lines almost parallel to a shore of a continent or large island or else surround smaller islands. In both cases they are separated from the land by water. The great barrier reef off the northeast coast of Australia is 400 miles long. Coral reefs often become part of the shores they fringe. The channels of water separating the reefs from the shores fill up with sand, sediment, and rock fragments. In a similar manner barrier reefs are sometimes joined to the coast.

CHEMICAL ELEMENTS.—On analysis all chemical compounds reduce to a small group of substances known as *elements*. Recent developments in science prove that the atomic structure of these elements is electrical, each atom consisting of a central nucleus around which one or more electrons revolve. The *hydrogen* atom has only one of these free electrons. The atom of *uranium* has 92. The 92 elements have all been reported discovered.

SOIL.—Soil is composed principally of humus, clay, chalk, and sand. Humus is decaying animal or vegetable matter. All these substances are composed of chemical elements, principally oxygen, hydrogen, carbon, sulphur, phosphorus, potassium, magnesium, nitrogen, iron, calcium, chlorine, sodium, and silicon. These are found in the soil in chemical combinations—sulphates, phosphates, silicates, carbonates, and other compounds. Some plants, as peas, lentils, and beans, get from the air some of the nitrogen they require, but most crops obtain it from nitrates—nitrogen compounds—present in the soil.

MINERALS.—Minerals are combinations of chemical elements. There are more than 2,000 species of minerals; but nine-tenths of them are rare.

Rocks are formed of minerals combined in various ways. According to their formation rocks are classified as igneous—that is, fire-formed; metamorphic, derived from other rocks altered by heat and pressure, and sedimentary, resulting from sediments in water.

THE OCEAN.—Sea water contains about 3.5 per cent of solids. Of the solids about 75 per cent are common salt and 10 per cent are chloride of magnesium.

Mud or slime overlies all the sea bottom. Most of the sea floor is fairly level, but there are many ridges, extensive plateaus and vast mountain ranges. The tops of many of these ranges projecting above water form islands. There are numerous valleys and deep abysses.

Pacific Ocean.—The greatest depth is 35,400 feet; area, 63,985,000 square miles.

Atlantic Ocean.—Greatest depth, 27,972 feet; area, 31,529,000 square miles.

Indian Ocean.—Greatest depth, 22,968 feet; area, 28,357,000 square miles.

Arctic Ocean.—Greatest depth, 17,848 feet; area, 4,780,000 square miles.

Antarctic Ocean.—Greatest depth, 18,804 feet; area, 5,731,400 square miles.

The Caribbean Sea.—Greatest depth, 20,568 feet; with deepest Atlantic connection between Santa Cruz and Puerto Rico, 5,400 feet.

The Gulf of Mexico.—Greatest depth, 12,714 feet; area, 716,000 square miles.

The Mediterranean Sea.—Greatest depth, 14,448 feet; area, 1,145,000 square miles.

Black Sea (connected with the Mediterranean).—Greatest depth, about 7,000 feet; area, 165,000 square miles.

Bering Sea.—Greatest depth, 12,516 feet; area, 878,000 square miles.

North Sea.—Greatest depth, 2,226 feet (in Skagerrak); area, 221,000 square miles.

Red Sea.—Greatest depth, 6,324 feet; area, 178,000 square miles.

If the ocean's surface were one mile lower all the continents would be united by bridges of dry land, leaving a sea averaging a mile and a half deep. Were the earth's surface smooth, the waters of the ocean would cover it to a depth of 9,000 feet.

Ocean currents are horizontal, caused by winds, or vertical, caused by differences of temperature.

HITLER INSPECTING DEFENSES IN CZECHOSLOVAKIA, ANNEXED BY GERMANY IN 1938 AND 1939

HORIZONTAL OR SURFACE CURRENTS.—In the Atlantic, Pacific, and Indian Oceans the direction of the winds is generally westward on the equatorial side of the tropical wind belts of high pressure. These are the trade winds, turning northeast in the northern hemisphere and southeast in the southern hemisphere.

The surface waters respond to the winds in both tropical latitudes by movements toward the west, called the north and south equatorial drifts, which drive the Atlantic waters toward the American shores and the Pacific waters toward the shores of Africa and Australia at a rate of 12 to 24 miles a day. Between the two drifts are compensation currents, which first spread out in a sheaflike form, then reverse their direction and flow to the east, those on the equatorial side of the main drifts uniting to form the counter-equatorial current, flowing east during July, August, September, driven by the southwest monsoon winds blowing off the African and Asiatic coasts.

On the polar side of the tropical belt the ocean winds have generally an easterly direction. The equatorial drifts bank up on the eastern continental shores, causing a disturbance of equilibrium. This is adjusted by a "stream" or gravity current which follows the coast line away from the equator until it is turned off shore by west winds and by the earth's diurnal rotation, and is lost in the general easterly drift of temperate-zone ocean waters. Thus are formed the Gulf Stream in the North Atlantic, the Kuro Siwo stream in the North Pacific, the Australian current in the South Pacific, the Mozambique current in the Indian Ocean.

In extra-tropical latitudes the easterly drift is as variable as the winds themselves. In the North Atlantic Ocean it divides northwest of the Azores. One part, turning to the south along the African shore, blends with the north equatorial current, thus forming a vast eddy, obedient to the prevailing winds. The other part turns northeast toward Great Britain, Norway, and Iceland. The winds, warmed by contact with these currents, carry heat and moisture to the land and make the climates of those countries much warmer than the climates of places in the same latitude in North America. Thus Great Britain has a far milder climate than Labrador, and Norway, though as far north as Greenland, has even in winter open ports on the Arctic Ocean.

Antarctic currents flow into the Atlantic, Pacific, and Indian Oceans and drift against the shores of Australia, Africa, and South America. Winds sweeping over them become cooled and, reaching land, cool the air over it.

VERTICAL CURRENTS.—These are caused by differences of temperature. The bottom water of every ocean (even in the equatorial regions) has a temperature differing but slightly from the temperature of the sea-bottom water of polar regions. The North Atlantic has a bottom temperature of 35° F.; the South Atlantic, 32° F.; the Pacific 34.6° F.; the Arctic, 28° F.; the Caribbean Sea, 39.5° F. Free from inflowing cold waters, the Mediterranean maintains below 600 feet a temperature of 55° F.

At 500 fathoms deep the waters of the sea have an average temperature of 43° F.; at 600 fathoms, 40° F.; at 1,000 fathoms, 38° F.; and at 2,000 fathoms the temperature is 34° F.

THE TIDES.—Twice each day the sea rises and falls. Flood, or high, tide is the name given to the rising of the sea, and its highest reach is called high water. The falling of the sea is termed ebb, or low tide, and its lowest line is low water.

Tides are caused by the attraction of the moon and the sun. Though the attraction of the sun is much stronger than that of the moon, yet the moon is so much nearer to us that its effect is more apparent. It causes the surface of the sea to rise in two low but broad tidal waves, each on the side of the earth opposite the other. As the earth rotates, these waves travel over the ocean's surface, but the crest of each keeps a little behind the moon. Therefore, high tide occurs about 50 minutes later each day. While the earth is rotating, the moon is moving forward, so that the earth has to turn nearly 25 hours to bring the same meridian again under the moon, and during that time two complete tidal waves pass the meridian. Hence there are two high tides and two low ones every 25 hours. High tide occurs at any place where the moon is over it or on the side of the earth opposite it. For

PHOTO. E. GYGER, ADELBODEN

ZERMATT, SWITZERLAND, WITH ITS MAJESTIC GUARDIAN, THE MATTERHORN

about six hours the tide rises, and it falls for six hours more.

Twice each month the sun, earth, and moon are in the same line, and then sun and moon, acting together on the ocean's surface, produce a very high tide called *spring tide.* About a week after each spring tide the sun and moon act at right angles on the earth. The resultant is a very low tide called *neap tide.*

In the open sea the tidal wave is so low that its passage is imperceptible; but, as it advances into a bay or harbor, the shallowing water and the converging of the land sides raise the height of the wave. In a narrowing bay, as the Bay of Fundy, the tide may rise 50 or 60 feet; but on open coasts heights of 6 to 12 feet are more usual.

Tides dash waves with great force against the land. If the shore is high and rocky, the waves break off pieces of rock and hurl them against the cliff, thus breaking off more rock fragments. In time the ceaseless action of the waves reduces the pieces to pebbles and then to sand.

On low and gently sloping shores tidal waves break at some distance out from them. Sand rolled shoreward often piles up into banks and forms bars across the mouths of navigable streams. In the course of years narrow sandy islands or barrier beaches may be thus built up.

Tidal currents carrying sand are constantly flowing along the coast. Meeting them, ebb currents from harbors are turned to one side. Sand from the meeting currents is deposited in a section of still water, and thus gradually there rise, stretching out from shore to shore, long narrow hooks or spits. Many low capes are formed in this way.

THE ATMOSPHERE.—The air ocean enveloping our planet weighs less than the ocean of water, but is much greater in volume. There is no doubt that air exists a hundred miles above us, and it is possible that the atmosphere's upper limit may be five times that height. But even ten miles above the earth the air is so rarefied that microorganisms are the only life it supports. The lowest layer of the atmosphere is called the troposphere; it has an average thickness of about six miles. Above the troposphere is the stratosphere.

As any layer of air is pressed down by all the atmosphere above it, the air on the sea's surface is the densest. At sea level, nineteen cubic yards of air weigh one pound. But a pound of air will fill 38 cubic yards 18,000 feet above the earth. Hence one-half the earth's atmosphere, by weight, must be below that height.

Like the ocean, the atmosphere has a complex circulation. There are upper and lower currents of air constantly flowing in opposite directions. There are atmospheric eddies powerful enough to whirl aviators to death.

Air is a mixture of gases. It is not a chemical compound. Oxygen and nitrogen are the chief constituents of the air. These gases are mixed in the ratio of about four parts of nitrogen to one part of oxygen.

Air also contains about 0.9 per cent (by volume) of argon; about 0.3 per cent of carbon dioxide (carbonic acid gas) and minute quantities of helium, krypton, neon, and xenon. There are traces of ammonia and nitrous and nitric acids; of sulphurous and sulphuric acids. Bacteria, yeast spores, and suspended particles of dust are also found. Water vapor is present in varying amounts. It is the source of clouds, fogs, mists, dew, frost, rain, hail, sleet, and snow.

WINDS.—Winds are caused by differences of temperature in different parts of the atmosphere. Moisture and heat from tropical seas are borne to the land by winds, and much of the globe's habitability is due to their influence.

In the torrid zone the air is always warmer and lighter than the air in the polar regions. Hence currents of air are constantly streaming from the frigid zones toward the tropics. As these air streams advance, the rotation of the earth turns them to the right north of the equator, but to the left south of that circle. Therefore the winds which blow constantly in the same direction over the ocean come from the northeast in the northern hemisphere and from the southeast in the southern hemisphere. From their value to commerce they are known as trade winds.

Along the heat equator, where the northeast and southeast trade winds meet, there is a narrow region where they either die away or become very light and fitful. This is the belt of *equatorial rains,* so called because heavy showers fall there almost every afternoon or evening. Near both the Tropic of Cancer and the Tropic of Capricorn, each on the outer side of a trade wind circuit, there is a narrow belt in which the heated air, which rose near the equator, sinks slowly again to the sea surface. These are the belts of *tropical calms.*

Beyond this belt the air moves generally toward the polar regions. In the north temperate zone air currents blow from the southwest, but from the northwest in the south temperate. These winds are known as the *prevailing westerlies,* or antitrades. They differ from the trade winds in being quite variable in direction and in frequently forming cyclones which, in the United States, usually move northeastward.

In temperate latitudes, where the westerlies occur,

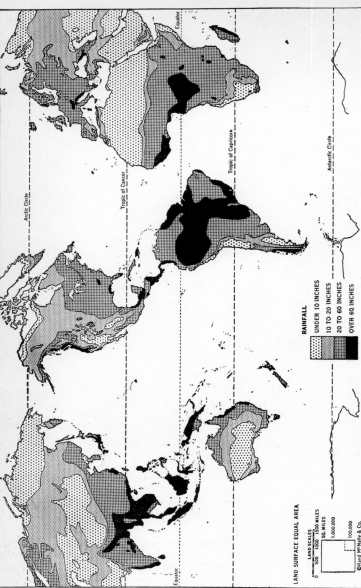

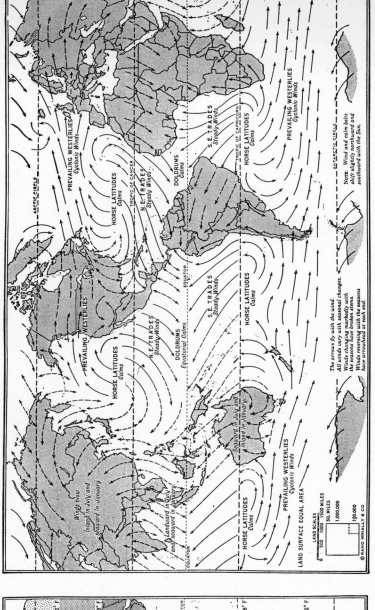

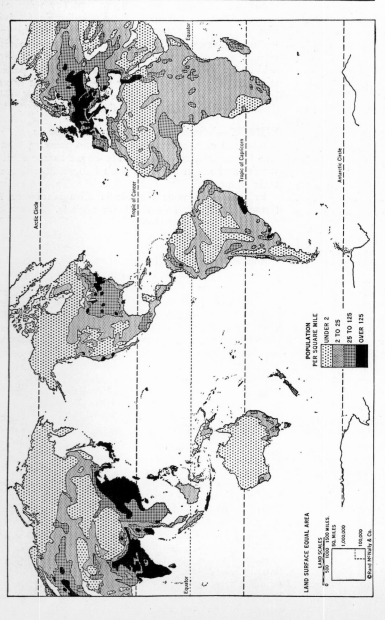

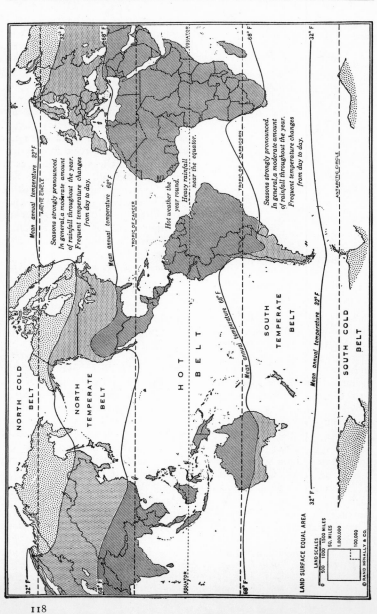

MAPS SHOWING THE PHYSICAL FEATURES OF THE WORLD

Top left. **The density of population of the world.** The total population is approximately 2,000,000,000 people, of which Asia has nearly one-half; Europe, 550,000,000; North America and South America, 230,000,000; Africa, 15,000,000; and Oceania (including Australia, New Zealand and the Pacific Islands), 9,000,000.

Lower left. **Temperature belts of the world.** There are five main climatic zones: the torrid zone (hot belt), the two temperate zones (north and south temperate belts), and the arctic and antarctic zones (north and south cold belts). In addition there are two subtropical zones, one boreal zone in the northern hemisphere.

Top right. **Average annual rainfall in the world.** The rainiest regions are in the torrid zone, such as equatorial Africa, South America (south of the equator), southeastern Asia and the East Indies, where the average annual rainfall reaches as high as one hundred inches. The driest regions are for the most part in the arctic and temperate zones.

Lower right. **Prevailing winds of the world.** Calms, called the doldrums, prevail near the equator. On the northern hemisphere the trade winds blow in a northeasterly direction; on the southern hemisphere, in a southeasterly direction. The two temperate belts are comparatively calm near the torrid zone, but are cyclonic near the polar regions.

the land is in winter cooler than the sea, and warmer in the summer. Winds take the temperature of the surface they move over, and the westerlies, coming from the ocean, cool the west coast of temperate-zone lands in summer and warm them in winter. In those lands also storm winds sometimes blow from the polar regions. They are called polar winds, but they vary in direction.

All the wind currents move north and south with the shifting of the heat zone, thus following the sun's apparent course from one tropic to the other.

The trades strike the east side of a continent, and sweeping around from it and from the equator, become the westerly winds. Conversely, the wind from the west strikes the west side of a continent and divides— one part, deflected toward the equator, becoming warm, the other curving around toward the poles loses its heat. In the Indian Ocean, however, north of the equator, these conditions are modified by the great continent of Asia, which turns the wind circuit to the south, so that the winds from the east correspond to the trades over other oceans.

In the South Pacific the cold, moist wind from the west divides on striking South America. A northern branch passing into warmer regions expands and thereby increases its capacity for absorbing moisture, and thus causes the desert of Atacama and the dry-shore region northward through Peru. The southern branch passes into colder regions, where it loses heat and condenses out its moisture. The annual rainfall at Valdivia, Chile, is 115 inches. The west branches behave in a similar manner on much of the western border of North America, North Africa, and Europe, as well as in the western regions of South Africa and in western Australia.

The warm, moist wind from the east over the tropics, as it strikes America, curves away from the equator into cooler latitudes, and carries rain into eastern North America and South America; also the great Andes Mountain range causes condensation of the water vapor brought by the winds that blow from the east against the snow-covered heights. Trade winds, laden with moisture from the Pacific, bring heavy rains to the eastern side of Asia.

All mountain chains with their cold summits cause vapor-carrying winds to precipitate moisture and, therefore, modify the system of rainfall both locally and generally. But as a high range prevents clouds from passing over it, the rainfall, though possibly heavy on one side, will be limited on the other.

LAND AND SEA BREEZES.—As land heats and cools more rapidly than water, the air over the land becomes lighter in daytime than the air over the ocean. Therefore, during the day a current of cool air sets landward from the sea. At night, the land being cooler than the sea, a wind blows seaward from the land. When land and sea breezes occur on a large scale, and alternate with summer and winter instead of day and night, they are called *monsoons* (seasonal winds).

MONSOONS.—Over the northern Indian Ocean the trade winds blow in one direction in summer and in another in winter. They blow in a curve toward the calms, and these move north and south with the change of seasons, thus leaving much land in the torrid zone south of the calms belt in hot weather and north of it in the cooler half of the year.

When the heat equator is south of the true equator, as in January, the regular trade wind is called the northeast monsoon. But the summer monsoons come from the southwest, southeast, or south. The most noted of these seasonal winds, the Indian monsoon, blows from the southwest. Surcharged with vapor from the torrid-zone part of the Indian Ocean, this wind, reaching the highlands of India, deluges them with warm rains daily for half a year. The air in those districts, cooled by the eternal snows of the Himalayas, chills the monsoons and thus precipitates their vapor. Certain small areas in Assam, a province at the foot of the mountains, have in some years received from 3 inches to 4 inches of rain a day for four consecutive months.

CLIMATE.—Climate is the aggregate of weather conditions. The most important elements of climate are temperature, moisture, and wind. Latitude, topography, altitude, and location relative to the path of storms are the controlling factors of climate. Latitude is the most important of these factors; for with change

of latitude the amount of heat received from the sun varies. Altitude has a somewhat similar effect on temperature. Usually the thermometer falls one degree for every 300-foot increase in the elevation to which it is carried. Hence the summits of high mountains are covered with snow throughout the year even in tropical climates.

CLIMATIC CHANGES.—Our globe has experienced extraordinary mutations in climate, even in its modern geological history. Greenland is now covered with ice hundreds of feet thick. Yet large seams of coal crop out in certain hillsides near the sea. As coal is the mineralized remains of vegetation—of tropical forests —Greenland must have had a warm climate even after the end of the Carboniferous era. Walrus bones have been dug up several feet below the surface of New Jersey soil. As the walrus lives only in icy seas, those fossil remains are acceptable proof that an arctic temperature once prevailed over the Middle Atlantic States.

In the Glacial epoch a vast ice sheet, which must have been over a mile in thickness, moved from the north polar region southward till it covered most of northern Europe and North America. In its progress it ground off hilltops, grooved out valleys, transported huge bowlders many miles and, melting, left detritus and rock waste over thousands of square miles. All life, plant and animal, retreated before it. Yet this ice age closed so recently, from the point of view of geology, that prehistoric man may have seen the glacier's remnants disappear from the temperate zone.

ISOTHERMS.—Lines drawn on maps through all places having, for a certain period, the same average temperature, are called *isotherms*. The bends in these lines are caused by various agencies—winds, ocean currents, altitude, and moisture in the atmosphere being the principal ones.

ISOBARS.—Isobars are lines drawn on maps connecting points on the globe's surface where the barometric height at each point, reduced to sea level, is the same for a given period. As the height of the barometer indicates the atmosphere's pressure, the distances between consecutive isobars widen in proportion as winds grow weak. When winds are strong, the distances are smaller.

RAINFALL.—Most of our rainfall comes from the ocean. When water evaporates it leaves all impurities behind; hence rain from sea water is fresh, the salt being left in the ocean.

The amount of vapor in the air varies with the temperature. Warm air holds more moisture than cold

air. When air has absorbed all the vapor it can hold, it is said to be saturated.

Some Saturation Degrees and Weights

10° F.	30° F.	50° F.	70° F.	90° F.
0.84 gr.	1.97 gr.	4.09 gr.	7.99 gr.	14.81 gr.

The second line records the weight in grains which a cubic foot of air will hold at the temperature given. Water vapor turns into rain when the air is cooled below the saturation point. Nuclei in solid or liquid particles, or else ions of dissociated air molecules are necessary as bases for raindrops. Air is cooled in various ways—by radiation, by contact with colder, drier air, and by expansion, as when air ascends into regions of lower atmospheric pressure. Rainfall distribution is influenced by winds, storms, by the configuration of the land, and by the relative position of land and water areas.

In temperate climes a rainfall of less than 12 inches annually results in semidesert conditions of the land. If over 20 inches of rain falls, agriculture becomes possible. In cold climates a rainfall higher than 50 inches yearly, or above 70 inches in the tropics, may result in the destruction of field crops.

As crops must have rain in their growing period, the *seasonal* distribution of rain is of great importance.

COURTESY OF THE AMERICAN MUSEUM OF NATURAL HISTORY
A TYPICAL SCENE IN A NATIVE VILLAGE, APIA, SAMOA

LENGTH OF CROP-GROWING SEASON IN THE VICINITY
OF VARIOUS NORTH AMERICAN CITIES

Edmonton	114 days
Winnipeg	121 "
Bismarck	130 "
St. Paul	159 "
Des Moines	172 "
Boston	185 "
Albany	177 "
Buffalo	173 "
Chicago	183 "
Little Rock	240 "
Atlanta	225 "
Shreveport	252 "
Charleston	295 "
Jacksonville	298 "
Mobile	291 "
New Orleans	310 "
Galveston	331 "
San Antonio	276 "

Colored rains are usually due to an admixture of brown, red, or yellow dust, or else to the presence of colored microscopic forms of life. Such rains in more superstitious times used to be considered portents of dire evils about to befall mankind.

Many attempts have been made to produce rain artificially. They all have resulted in failure. Cannon firing and the exploding of bombs high in the air have been the principal agencies employed. In France and

PHOTO. J.-E. AUCLAIR-MELOT FROM RAILWAYS OF FRANCE

MORLAIX, FRANCE, A QUAINT, PICTURESQUE TOWN TYPICAL OF THE FRENCH PROVINCES

Italy some years ago somewhat similar experiments were made for an opposite purpose—to dissipate rain clouds when atmospheric conditions indicated the probability of hail coming. No success attended these efforts which were made in the hope of safeguarding grape crops in those countries. Intense and prolonged artillery fire in the World War caused neither rainfall nor cloud dissipation.

RIVERS.—Springs, lakes, swamps, and glaciers are common sources of rivers. As a river advances, it is usually increased in volume by smaller streams—tributaries—flowing into it. A river with all its tributaries is called a *river system;* and the area drained by the system is termed the river's *basin.*

The waters of all large rivers finally reach the ocean. Corroding their beds and banks, they carry with them immense quantities of mud or silt. This silt may form flood plains or, deposited at a river's mouth, may slowly build up a delta.

In the interior of a country the river beds are few but large. In North America there are three great river systems. (1) The Mississippi system, which drains southward into the Gulf of Mexico; (2) the St. Lawrence system, draining eastward into the Gulf of St. Lawrence; and (3) the Mackenzie system, whose basin slopes north to the Arctic Ocean. South America has a somewhat similar arrangement of interior river basins. The La Plata system flows southward, the Amazon eastward, and the Orinoco toward the north. In Asia three large river systems, whose main streams have their sources in the continent's interior, drain southward—the Euphrates-Tigris, the Indus, and the Mekong. Three drain eastward—the Ganges, the Yangtze, and the Hwang. One large river, the Amur, flows north during most of its course. Three river systems drain into the Arctic Ocean—the Lena, the Yenisei, and the Ob.

Africa's longest river, the Nile, flows north; the Congo drains generally westward, and the Niger flows east and south. The Zambezi is the sole great African stream whose course is wholly eastward. The Orange River flows toward the west.

In Europe the systems of the Volga, the Dnieper, and the Rhone flow south; the Danube is the only large river flowing eastward; the Elbe and the Rhine drain to the northwest.

PLANTS.—There are but few parts of the globe without any plant life. Vegetation is most luxuriant, however, in the tropical lowlands where heat and rain are greatest. From these regions plant life decreases gradually, though irregularly, toward the frigid zones. Jungles and dense forests of huge trees standing close together and interlaced with thick vines are common in the rainy portions of the torrid zone. In the cooler temperate zones the forests are generally more open;

yet in some sections of these zones the trees are larger but of less varied species. The farther toward the frigid zones that tree life advances, the smaller become the trees; and finally, within the Arctic circle, plants with woody stems disappear, and mosses and lichens are the only representatives left of the vegetable world.

Arid regions, even if warm, have but little vegetation. A few plant species have, however, adapted themselves to semi-desert life. Some are shrubs with hard close bark and leaves so small that only a minimum of transpiration can take place; others are thorny, leafless plants with leathery stems.

Every plant has its own geographical range. Outside that area it will not thrive in the open air. Certain plants, as the cinchona (quinine) tree, or the rubber tree, will grow only in hot moist lands, while such plants as the hemp and the apple tree prefer temperate climates.

Still, nowhere are the boundaries of plant life rigidly fixed. Culture often enables plants that are native to one belt to flourish in another. To-day wheat is a farm crop on the banks of the Peace River in northern Alberta, and kitchen vegetables are grown in gardens at Dawson in the Klondike, 500 miles farther north. Such plant growth in those frozen districts would, some years ago, have been regarded as impossible.

In the torrid and temperate zones there are large areas in which the rainfall is less than 12 inches per annum. Agriculture cannot be practiced successfully with so small an amount of precipitation; but under certain conditions grazing may be profitable. "Dry" farming has succeeded in districts receiving only 20 inches of rain yearly. About 35 inches per annum, while not the maximum amount that could be utilized for field crops, may be considered sufficient to insure the farmer against loss by drought. Grasslands, such as prairies, pampas, llanos, and steppes, will afford abundant pasturage if an annual rainfall of as much as 25 inches is properly distributed over them in the growing season.

ANIMALS.—Thousands of species of animals, large and small, have appeared on the earth, flourished for many generations, and then have become extinct. As a rule they were simpler forms of life than the highly organized ones of to-day.

Peculiar to North America are the otter, raccoon, skunk, opossum (the only marsupial outside of Australia), prong-horned antelope, muskrat, prairie dog, and musk ox. Wild turkeys, blue jays, humming birds, orioles, and mocking birds are also North American. Among the venomous snakes are the rattlesnake, the moccasin, and the copperhead.

South America has many life forms found nowhere else. Included among them are tapirs, jaguars, peccaries, guinea pigs, armadillos, sloths, alpacas, and llamas. The avi-fauna comprises macaws, rheas, curas-

sows, condors (the largest of the flying birds), and hundreds of other species.

There is much resemblance between Eurasian life forms and those of North America, resulting probably from the fact that both continents were once connected by land.

Wolves, foxes, bears, beavers, and squirrels are found in both portions of the globe. Common also to both are hawks, owls, and eagles. But vultures, starlings, pheasants, magpies, and nightingales are native to Europe and Asia. Useful animals in Asia are the yak, water-buffalo, and two-humped camel. In Europe chamois, ibexes, and wild boars afford sport to the hunter.

The Orient life realm is remarkable for its numerous carnivora, including lions, tigers, leopards, and hyenas. Elephants, rhinoceroses, and wild buffalos are common in the jungles. Bears, deer, wild cattle, the domesticated zebu, and the large crocodiles, called gavials, are also found. The orang-outang, a huge ape, lives in the forests of the large islands of the East Indies. Bird life is very varied. It includes the birds of paradise, the bulbul, famed in Oriental poetry, the peacock, and the jungle fowl, the ancestor of our domestic hen. Southern Asia is the home of the venomous cobra.

Many Australian life forms are examples of arrested development, as the marsupials, of which the kangaroos are the best-known examples. It is probable that many species of mammals were of that type many thousands of years ago. Other strange Australian creatures are: the duck mole, a furred animal which lays eggs, and the echidna, also an egg layer, which resembles a porcupine, but is a water animal.

Africa has many remarkable native animals—lions, gorillas, chimpanzees, giraffes, zebras, and jackals. Others are cape buffalos, various species of antelopes, hippopotamuses, wild asses, rhinoceroses, and hyenas. In many respects African elephants differ from their Asian congeners, the former being smaller and less intelligent. Among the birds are the ostrich, the beautiful plantain eaters, various guinea-fowl, and the noted secretary vulture. Few snakes are more deadly than the African asp.

SEA ANIMALS.—There are thousands of different kinds of sea animals but only comparatively few species of mammals living in the ocean. The most common sea mammals are the whale, walrus, manatee, and dugong. In the ocean the temperature is more uniform than on land, and the food supply is more evenly distributed. Hence the sea shows less variety in life forms than the land.

RACES OF MANKIND.—Ethnologists are not agreed as to the most satisfactory racial classification of mankind. Perhaps the most generally recognized is Blumenbach's division of the human race into five leading families, the color of the skin being the chief basis of classification: (1) Caucasian, (2) Mongolian, (3) Negro, (4) Malay, and (5) American Indian. Principal differentiating criteria in more modern ethnological systems are feature characteristics, the shape of the skull, the character of the hair, and the facial angle. (See Table of Races, page 121.)

Some ethnologic authorities class the Malay and Mongolian together. A few prominent ethnologists recognize only three primary races of mankind—the Caucasic, or White race; the Ethiopic, or Black race; and the Mongolic, or Yellow race, including in this last division the Malay or Brown type and the American or Red type.

There is no specific difference between the various branches of the human family—no difference, that is, which implies anything in contradiction to the assumption of a common origin. The order *Bimana* (Latin, two-handed) to which, in scientific classification, man is referred, contains only a single genus and a single species (*Homo sapiens*).

THE CAUCASIC OR WHITE RACE.—This race is characterized by an oval skull and face also oval, the features moderately prominent, the forehead arched, the cheek bones only slightly projecting, the chin full and round. The eyes and hair may vary from the lightest blond to deep blue-black.

The Caucasic (or Caucasian) is usually described as the *white* variety of the human family, but this characteristic must be considered applicable only in a general sense, for numerous shades of color intervene between the Hindu's complexion, almost black, to the

Race	Color	Skull	Hair	Eyes	Nose	Jaws
Caucasic	White or swarthy	Two types: the long, index 74, and short 80 to 90	Straight or wavy; black, brown, flaxen, red	Blue, gray, brown, black; straight; large; round	Narrow; straight, or arched	Orthognathous
Mongolic	Yellowish or brown	Short; index 82 to 90	Black; Coarse, lank	Oblique; small, black	Snub or medium	Mesognathous, or orthognathous
Ethiopic	Black or brown	Long; index 72 to 75	Woolly, Black; flat in transverse section	Round, black, yellowish cornea	Flat or aquiline; broad at base	Prognathous
Malayan	Dark	Short; index 80 to 90	Black, lank	Black or dark brown, round	Straight or snub, small	Prognathous
American Indian	Coppery or dark brown	Variable; index from 74 to 90	Coarse, lank, black	Small, round, black	Long, arched or aquiline	Mesognathous or prognathous

blond complexions of the people of northern Europe. These differences seem to be in some measure determined by differences in climate.

The white race comprises the most enlightened and powerful nations of the world, including not only Europeans, wherever found, but also Hindus, Hebrews, and Arabs.

The geographical distribution of the Caucasic family in the present day is nearly coextensive with the cultivable land area of the globe; but it is most numerous within the temperate latitudes of the northern hemisphere. White people have colonized nearly every part of the New World as well as much of Southern Africa, Australia, and New Zealand.

In the Americas the Caucasic family has virtually supplanted the indigenous races.

MONGOLIAN OR YELLOW RACE.—The *Mongolic* or yellow variety of man is distinguished by an approximate squareness of the skull (viewed from above) and with greater prominence in the cheek bones. The forehead is usually slanting; the face and nose are broad and flat; the eyes small, black and apparently obliquely set; the complexion is yellowish or olive; the hair, lank and black; the beard scanty; the frame generally square and robust, with high shoulders; the neck thick and strong.

The term Mongolic, or Mongolian, is derived from the nomad races who inhabit central Asia. It comprehends, besides the Mongols proper, the vast population of China, together with the Burmese, Siamese, and other tribes of the Siberian lowlands. The Turks; the Magyars in central Europe; and the Finns, Samoyeds, and Laplanders in the northern part of the same continent are regarded as Mongolic. But in the cases of the Finns and Magyars, intermarriage with branches of the white race has obliterated most traces of Mongolian descent.

THE ETHIOPIC OR BLACK RACE.—The *Negro* is distinguished in a general way by the elongated form of the skull. The eyes, as well as the skin, are black; the nose is generally broad and flat, the cheek bones are prominent; the lips thick; the jaws (especially the lower one) projecting; the hair is black, short and woolly; the palms of the hands and soles of the feet are often flat. These attributes, however, vary somewhat in the different Negro tribes. Africa is the home of the Negro race. Tribes of true Negro stock occupy by far the larger portion of that great continent south of the Sahara.

The slave trade transplanted from Africa to the other side of the Atlantic many thousands of Negroes, and their descendants now form a considerable part of the population of the New World.

THE MALAY OR BROWN RACE.—The *Malay* is distinguished by brown skin, lank, coarse black hair, flat face, and slanting eyes. The height is below the average of either Caucasian or Negro, and the figure is generally square and robust. The Brown type is found in eastern and southeastern Asia.

Some ethnological authorities claim that the Malay family must be regarded as a variety either of the Mongol or the Negro stock.

THE AMERICAN INDIAN OR RED RACE.—The *American* race, commonly called the Indian, has its home in the two great continents which are together known as the New World. Its distinguishing attributes are a reddish, or copper-colored, skin, with coarse, straight, black hair. The cheek bones are prominent, but more arched and rounded than those of the Mongol, and the eyes are black and usually small. In temperament the Indian is phlegmatic. His sight, hearing, and smell are remarkably acute. These,

and other attributes of his race, have probably resulted from conditions of the hunter's life.

The above characteristics, however, are exhibited in widely different degrees among the numerous native tribes found throughout the American continent.

The Eskimos are classified by the majority of anthropologists as American Indians, although some still hold that they more properly belong to the Mongolian race. The Eskimos have the light brownish yellow skin characteristic of the Mongols, but this complexion is also found in the American Indian of the northwest coast. They have long skulls, wide faces and narrow noses.

The Indian family makes, perhaps, a nearer approach to the Mongol than to any of the other great divisions of mankind.

RACES OF MANKIND.—ETHNIC CRITERIA.—In some ethnological systems craniometry plays a prominent part, and the importance of the cranial index in the genus *Homo,* or man, is emphasized. This index is found by comparing the breadth of the skull with its length as seen from above. Craniologists recognize three racial types: the long headed, or dolichocephalic; the round-headed, or mesocephalic, and the brachycephalic, or broad-headed. The ratios of breadth to length in the above types are, respectively: 70 : 100, dolichocephalic; 80 : 100, mesocephalic, and 85 : 100, brachycephalic.

LANGUAGES OF THE WORLD.—The languages of the world may conveniently be treated under the following twelve groups:

1. THE INDO-GERMANIC OR ARYAN FAMILY.—This family contains many separate subdivisions, as follows: *Indian group,* including Sanskrit (dead) and many spoken Indian languages.

BY BURTON HOLMES, FROM EWING GALLOWAY

THE HISTORIC TORII OF MIYAJIMA, JAPAN. A CLASSIC IN TORII DESIGNING

Iranian group, including Old Persian (Zend), Pahlevi, Parsi, and modern Iranian (Persian).

Armenian.

Hellenic: All varieties of Greek.

Italic group: Latin and the Romance languages—French, Italian, Spanish, Portuguese, Rumanian, etc.

Celtic group: Cornish, Armorican or Breton, Welsh, Irish (Erse), Scotch Gaelic, and Manx.

Teutonic group: Scandinavian (Norwegian, Swedish, Danish, and Icelandic), Low German (English, Dutch, Plattdeutsch, and Frisian), High German or modern German.

Slavonic group: Russian, Polish, Bohemian (Czech).

Baltic group: Lithuanian, Old Prussian.

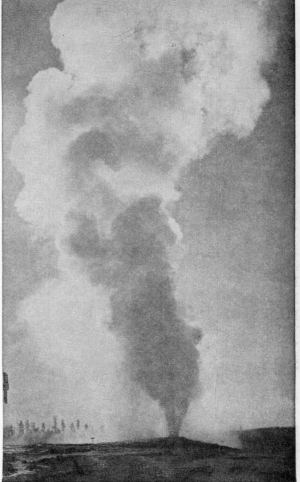

© ASAHEL CURTIS

OLD FAITHFUL GEYSER, WHICH SPOUTS EVERY HOUR, YELLOWSTONE NATIONAL PARK

2. SEMITIC FAMILY.—The two most important members of this family are the Hebrew and the Arabic. Besides these there are the extinct Babylonian, Assyrian and Phœnician, and the Syriac.

3. HAMITIC FAMILY.—The most important member of this family is the Egyptian, of which the ancient Egyptian and the Coptic are forms.

4. MONOSYLLABIC FAMILY.—The Chinese is the leading member of this family. It appears to have had substantially its present form for thousands of years. The Tibetan and Burmese are allied languages.

5. URAL-ALTAIC GROUP.—All these languages are distinguished by a highly agglutinative structure. They are spoken from the eastern coast of Asia to Finland and Lapland. It is convenient to divide them into six groups—the Finnic, the Ugric, the Turkic, the Mongolic, the Tungusic, and the Samoyedic.

6. DRAVIDIAN GROUP.—These languages are spoken in the Deccan and in Ceylon. They are believed to represent the languages spoken in India before the Aryans came.

7. MALAY-POLYNESIAN GROUP.—This group is characterized by great simplicity of structure. It may be divided into three—the Malay, the Polynesian, and the Melanesian. The Malay is spoken in the Malacca Peninsula (whence its name) and in Sumatra, Java, Borneo, the Philippines, and Taiwan (Formosa). The Polynesian includes the other languages spoken in the scattered groups of Pacific islands, the Melanesian in the Melanesian Islands. The Australian, Tasmanian, and Papuan dialects have not been much studied, and some of them may constitute another distinct group.

8. CAUCASIAN GROUP.—This is a group of apparently unrelated languages of elaborate structure spoken in the highlands between the Black and Caspian Seas. The principal are the Georgian, the Circassian, and the Leshghian.

9. BASQUE.—This is still spoken in the region of the Pyrénées, near the Bay of Biscay.

10. BANTU OR SOUTH AFRICAN GROUP.—Zulu is a typical member of the group. The dialects of this group are very numerous.

11. CENTRAL AFRICAN GROUP.—These languages are spoken in the remainder of Africa.

12. AMERICAN INDIAN GROUP.—The languages of the North American Indians. A collection of different dialects. They seem, however, to agree in structure.

Great Rivers of the World

Streams and Drainage Basins Important in Political, Industrial and Commercial Development

River	Location	Length in Miles	Flows Into	Area of Drainage in Square Miles
Mississippi-Missouri	United States	4,221	Gulf of Mexico	1,240,000
Nile	Egypt	4,000	Mediterranean Sea	1,050,000
Amazon	Brazil	3,900	Atlantic Ocean	2,700,000
Ob	Soviet Union	3,200	Gulf of Ob	1,125,000
Yangtze-Kiang	China	3,100	Yellow Sea	700,000
Amur	Asia	2,900	Tatar Strait	Navigable for 1,800 miles
Congo	Africa	2,900	Atlantic Ocean	1,430,000
Lena	Soviet Union	2,860	Arctic Ocean	856,000
Yenisei	Soviet Union	2,800	Bay of Yenisei	1,000,000
Hwang Ho	China	2,700	Gulf of Pohai	376,400
Mekong	Indo-China	2,600	China Sea	Navigable for 200 miles
Niger	Africa	2,600	Atlantic Ocean	808,000
Mackenzie	Canada	2,525	Arctic Ocean	676,000
Plata-Parana	Argentina and Brazil	2,450	Atlantic Ocean	2,300,000
Volga	Soviet Union	2,300	Caspian Sea	560,000
Yukon	Alaska	2,300	Bering Sea	500,000
St. Lawrence	United States and Canada	2,150	Gulf of St. Lawrence	300,000
Indus	India	1,800	Arabian Sea	Navigable for 1,100 miles
Brahmaputra	India	1,800	Bay of Bengal	Navigable for 800 miles
São Francisco	Brazil	1,800	Atlantic Ocean	249,000
Syr Darya	Turkestan	1,800	Sea of Aral	175,000
Saskatchewan-Nelson	Canada	1,732	Hudson Bay	730,000
Danube	Austria and Hungary	1,725	Black Sea	311,000
Euphrates	Turkey	1,700	Persian Gulf	260,000
Colorado	United States	1,650	Gulf of California	244,000
Rio Grande	United States and Mexico	1,650	Gulf of Mexico	248,000
Orinoco	Colombia and Venezuela	1,600	Atlantic Ocean	364,000
Zambezi	Africa	1,600	Indian Ocean	800,000
Amu Darya	Turkestan	1,500	Sea of Aral	174,000
Arkansas	United States	1,460	Mississippi River	175,000
Ganges	India	1,455	Bay of Bengal	409,000
Murray	Australia	1,450	Indian Ocean	351,000
Dneiper	Soviet Union	1,400	Black Sea	203,000
Ural	Soviet Union	1,400	Caspian Sea	85,000
Ohio	United States	1,283	Mississippi River	203,900
Columbia	United States	1,270	Pacific Ocean	259,000
Irrawaddy	India	1,250	Bay of Bengal	Navigable for 800 miles
Tigris	Turkey	1,150	Euphrates to Persian Gulf	Navigable generally for small boats
Don	Soviet Union	1,100	Sea of Azov	166,000
Orange	Africa	1,100	Atlantic Ocean	370,000
Senegal	Africa	1,100	Atlantic Ocean	270,000
Churchill	Canada	1,000	Hudson Bay	Navigable by canoes
Magdalena	Colombia	950	Caribbean Sea	Navigable for 600 miles
Elbe	Germany	700	North Sea	57,000
Rhine	Germany	700	North Sea	76,000
Fraser	British Columbia	695	Gulf of Georgia	Navigable generally for small boats
Loire	France	650	Bay of Biscay	25,000
Vistula	Germany and Poland	630	Gulf of Danzig	120,000
Tagus	Portugal	550	Atlantic Ocean	32,000
Oder	Germany	550	Baltic Sea	43,000
Parnahiba	Brazil	530	Atlantic Ocean	Navigable for 400 miles
Gambia	Africa	500	Atlantic Ocean	Navigable for 300 miles
Rhone	France	500	Gulf of Lion	38,000
Seine	France	475	English Channel	30,000
Po	Italy	420	Adriatic Sea	29,000
Potomac	United States	420	Chesapeake Bay	14,650
Susquehanna	United States	420	Chesapeake Bay	27,400
Ebro	Spain	400	Mediterranean Sea	32,000
Guadiana	Spain	400	Mediterranean Sea	32,000
Sacramento	United States	400	Pacific Ocean	27,100
Garonne	France	385	Bay of Biscay	33,000
Connecticut	United States	380	Long Island Sound	11,345
Hudson	United States	315	New York Bay	13,400
Thames	England	215	North Sea	5,250

The Great Lakes
According to Latest Government Figures

Lake	Coast Line Length Miles	Extreme Dimensions in Miles			Water Surface Sq. Miles	Drainage Basin Sq. Miles	Maximum Depth Feet	Average Elevation above Sea Level 1860-1934. Feet	Discharge at Average Height Cu. Ft. per Second	Average Yearly Rainfall Inches
		Length Steamer Track	Length Right Line	Width						
Superior	1,900	383	350	160	31,820	80,900	1,290	602.24	† 70,900	28
Michigan	1,300	340	307	118	22,400	69,040	923	580.79	‡ 50,800	32
* Huron	2,400	247	206	183	23,010	72,420	750	580.79	202,000	30
St. Clair	200	18	26	24	460	6,420	21	575.33	202,000	34
Erie	800	236	241	57	9,940	34,680	210	572.35	203,000	34
Ontario	850	180	193	53	7,540	34,640	774	246.03	238,000	33

* Including Georgian Bay.   † Outflow is regulated by gates.   ‡ Estimated from supply factors.

Principal Salt Water Lakes of the World

Name	Location	Area in Square Miles	Mean Elevation in Feet	Tributaries	Outlets
Caspian Sea	Asia	169,383	83 below sea level	Ural, Volga, Terek, Kura, Aras	None
Sea of Aral	Asia	26,160	157 above sea level	Syr Darya (Jaxartes), Amu Darya (Oxus)	None
Balkash	Asia	7,115	899 above sea level	Ili	None
Maracaibo	South America	6,315	0 above sea level	Catatumbo, Motatán, Bravo, Chama, Zulia	Channel to sea
Titicaca (slightly saline)	South America	3,800	12,507 above sea level	Asangaro, Lagunillas	Desaguadero to Lake Poopo
Eyre	Australia	3,700	39 above sea level	Barcoo, Macumba, Diamantina	None
Great Salt Lake	North America	1,750	4,218 above sea level	Bear, Jordan, Weber	None
Issykkul	Asia	2,250	5,300 above sea level	Various streams	Tchu (high water only)
Koko-nor	Asia	1,850	10,300 above sea level	Bukhain-gol	None
Urmia	Asia	1,795	4,100 above sea level	Aji-chai, Jaghatucht	None
Van	Asia	1,400	5,200 above sea level	Small streams	None
Dead Sea	Asia	340	1,290 below sea level	Jordan	None
Ngami (nearly dried up)	Africa		2,930 above sea level	Tioge (practically dry)	None

Principal Fresh Water Lakes of the World

Name	Location	Area in Square Miles	Mean Elevation in Feet	Tributaries	Outlets
Superior	North America	31,820	602 above sea level	St. Louis and others	St. Mary's River, Sault Ste. Marie
Victoria	Africa	26,000	3,720 above sea level	Kagera	Branch of the Nile
Huron	North America	23,010	581 above sea level	St. Mary's River, Sts. of Mackinac	St. Clair River, canals
Michigan	North America	22,400	581 above sea level	Fox, St. Joseph, Grand	Straits of Mackinac to L. Huron
Great Bear	North America	14,000	391 above sea level	Various streams	Great Bear River to Mackenzie
Baikal	Asia	13,200	1,601 above sea level	Upper Angara, Barguzin, Selenga	Lower Angara to Yenesei
Tanganyika	Africa	12,700	2,588 above sea level	Rusisi from L. Kivu	Lukuga to Congo
Great Slave	North America	10,719	391 above sea level	Great Slave River	Mackenzie River to Arctic
Chad	Africa	10,400	1,150 above sea level	Shari, Yeu	No regular outlet
Nyasa	Africa	10,231	1,545 above sea level	Mountain streams	Shiré to Zambezi
Erie	North America	9,940	572 above sea level	Detroit River from Lake Huron	Niagara River
Winnipeg	North America	9,400	710 above sea level	Red, Saskatchewan, Winnipeg	Nelson to Hudson Bay
Ontario	North America	7,540	246 above sea level	Niagara River from Lake Erie	St. Lawrence to Atlantic
Ladoga	Europe	7,000	49 above sea level	Svir, Sias	Neva to Gulf of Finland
Onega	Europe	3,700	237 above sea level	Migra, Shuya, Vodla	Svir to L. Ladoga
Rudolf	Africa	3,000	1,335 above sea level	Omo	None
Nicaragua	Central America	2,975	108 above sea level	Tipitapa from L. Managua	San Juan to Caribbean Sea
Athabasca	North America	2,850	697 above sea level	Athabasca River	Slave River
Wener	Europe	2,200	147 above sea level	Klar	Göta
Bangweulu	Africa	2,000	3,740 above sea level	Chambezi	Luapula
Albert Nyanza	Africa	1,800	2,230 above sea level	Semlik, Kari	Nile
Lake of the Woods	North America	1,500	1,060 above sea level	Rainy River	Winnipeg River
Dembea (Tsana)	Africa	1,000	6,100 above sea level	Little Abai, Reb, Gumara	Abai (Upper Blue Nile)
Wetter	Europe	733	288 above sea level	Small streams	Motala to Baltic Sea
Okeechobee	North America	680	21 above sea level	Kissimee	Canals and streams
Managua	North America	560	154 above sea level	Small streams	Tipitapa to L. Nicaragua
Champlain	North America	436	96 above sea level	Lamoille, Winooski	Richelieu to St. Lawrence
Balaton (Platten See)	Europe	420	426 above sea level	Small streams	Sió, Kapos, into Danube
St. Clair	North America	410	576 above sea level	St. Clair from L. Huron	Detroit River to L. Erie
Geneva (Leman)	Europe	224	1,220 above sea level	Rhone	Rhone
Constance (Boden See)	Europe	208	1,308 above sea level	Rhine	Rhine
Garda	Europe	136	213 above sea level	Sarka	Mincio
Neuchâtel	Europe	90	1,424 above sea level	Thièle	Thièle
Maggiore	Europe	78	646 above sea level	Ticino	Ticino to Po
Cayuga	North America	76	381 above sea level	Taughannock Creek	Seneca River
George	North America	61	323 above sea level	Small streams	Channel to L. Champlain
Como	Europe	56	649 above sea level	Adda, Maira	Adda
Lucerne	Europe	40	1,435 above sea level	Reuss	Reuss
Zürich	Europe	37½	1,340 above sea level	Walensee through canal	Limmat

Leading Countries of the World

Countries	Area in Sq. Miles	Population
United States (continental)	3,026,789	122,775,046
Alaska	586,400	59,278
Philippine Islands	114,400	13,099,405
Puerto Rico	3,435	1,723,534
Hawaii	6,407	368,336
American Samoa	76	10,055
Guam	206	18,509
Canal Zone	554	39,467
Virgin Islands	133	22,012
Afghanistan	245,000	9,000,000
Albania	10,629	1,003,077
Argentina	1,079,965	12,228,000
Austria (annexed by Germany, 1938)	32,369	6,760,233
Belgium	11,752	8,275,552
Belgian Congo	920,656	10,000,000
Bhutan	18,000	300,000
Bolivia	514,464	3,077,531
Brazil	3,285,319	45,332,660
British Empire	13,355,426	495,764,000
England	50,874	38,173,950
Scotland	30,405	4,916,000
Wales	7,466	2,176,050
Northern Ireland	5,237	1,280,000
Ireland (Eire)	26,592	3,033,000
Other European Possessions	124	259,139
Canada	3,694,863	10,376,786
Newfoundland and Labrador	155,134	293,951
British Guiana	89,480	323,171
Other American Possessions	26,443	2,126,000
Australia	2,974,581	6,706,438
New Zealand	103,862	1,573,810
Papua	90,540	276,366
New Guinea	91,000	462,571
Other Australasian Possessions	19,765	494,540
Union of South Africa	472,550	9,479,985
Anglo-Egyptian Sudan	972,600	5,816,376
Bechuanaland	275,000	152,983
Northern and Southern Rhodesia	440,674	2,652,118
Tanganyika	363,548	4,988,338
Nigeria	372,674	19,928,171
Kenya	224,960	3,094,300
South West Africa	322,393	266,930
Other African Possessions	394,410	12,424,000
India	1,808,679	352,837,778
Palestine	10,155	1,261,000
Ceylon	25,332	5,306,000
Other Asiatic Possessions	143,000	6,197,000
Bulgaria	39,814	6,090,215
Chile	286,322	4,465,447
China	3,806,051	428,687,000
Colombia	441,651	9,018,000
Costa Rica	23,000	577,833
Cuba	44,164	4,011,088
Czechoslovakia (before partition)	54,192	15,096,025
Danzig, Free City of	754	407,517
Denmark	16,571	3,656,000
Faroes, The	540	24,200
Greenland	837,620	17,486
Dominican Republic	19,332	1,478,121
Ecuador	176,155	2,646,645
Egypt	383,000	15,546,000
Estonia	18,354	1,126,413
Ethiopia	350,000	7,500,000
Finland	149,954	3,762,000
France and Possessions	4,830,646	99,882,968
France	212,681	41,905,968
Algeria	847,818	6,553,451
Madagascar	228,707	3,853,300
French Equatorial Africa	912,049	3,226,940
French West Africa	1,604,159	14,468,828
Other African Possessions	289,129	5,436,591
French Indo-China	284,522	21,452,000
Syria	57,460	3,130,100
Other Asiatic Possessions	196	286,410
French Guiana and Inini	34,740	32,596
Other American Possessions	1,166	504,083
Oceanic Possessions	10,068	93,065
Germany (not including 1938 additions)	181,683	66,616,000
Greece (with islands)	54,092	6,750,000
Guatemala	45,452	2,245,553
Haiti	10,204	2,550,000
Honduras	44,275	859,761
Hungary	35,875	8,898,367
Iceland	39,709	114,743
Iran (Persia)	628,000	15,055,115
Iraq (Mesopotamia)	143,240	3,300,000
Italy and Possessions	869,053	43,693,807
Italy	119,703	41,176,671
Eritrea	45,783	621,776
Italian Somaliland	190,000	1,210,000
Libya	632,500	717,000
Japanese Empire	260,911	98,219,812
Japan proper	147,889	69,251,900
Chosen (Korea)	85,206	22,898,695
Taiwan (Formosa)	13,836	5,212,719
Karafuto	13,931	331,949
Latvia	25,395	1,950,502
Liberia	43,000	2,250,000
Liechtenstein	65	10,213
Lithuania	21,683	2,451,200
Luxembourg	998	304,900
Manchukuo	446,000	30,290,000
Mexico	760,290	16,552,722
Monaco	½	22,994
Morocco	213,350	5,867,271
Nepál	54,000	5,600,000
Netherlands, The	13,202	8,392,102
Netherland India	733,642	60,731,025
Java and Madura	50,745	43,521,670
Sumatra	163,138	8,238,490
Dutch Borneo	206,810	2,194,531
Celebes	72,679	4,226,586
New Guinea	160,692	249,131
Other Islands	78,978	2,300,617
Netherland West Indies	54,694	237,340
Dutch Guiana (Surinam)	54,291	164,100
Curaçao	403	83,254
Nicaragua	51,660	829,700
Norway	124,984	2,871,400
Svalbard	24,142	2,415
Oman	82,000	500,000
Panama	29,065	483,800
Paraguay	173,700	901,768
Peru	482,258	6,237,000
Poland	149,915	33,418,000
Portugal and Possessions	848,096	15,741,705
Portugal	35,490	6,826,000
African Possessions	798,663	7,162,414
Asiatic Possessions	8,804	1,198,583
Rumania (România)	122,282	19,033,363
Salvador	13,176	1,574,500
San Marino	38	14,170
Saudi Arabia	413,792	3,000,000
Siam	200,148	14,464,489
Soviet Union	8,241,921	165,768,400
Russian S.F.S.R.	7,626,717	113,983,200
White Russian S.S.R.	48,751	5,439,400
Ukrainian S.S.R.	174,201	31,901,400
Tadzhik	56,608	1,183,100
Transcaucasian F.S.S.R.	71,255	7,074,000
Turkoman S.S.R.	189,603	1,268,900
Uzbek S.S.R.	74,786	4,918,400
Spain	195,010	24,583,096
Sweden	173,105	6,233,100
Switzerland	15,940	4,066,400
Turkey	294,415	16,188,800
Uruguay	72,153	2,020,040
Vatican City	0.17	1,025
Venezuela	352,051	3,291,442
Yugoslavia	95,551	15,173,608

A Physical and Commercial Analysis of the United States

AREA AND BOUNDARIES.—The *area* of the United States, including Alaska, is 3,613,189 square miles; of the dependencies, the area of Hawaii is 6,407 square miles; of the Philippine Islands, 114,400 square miles; of Puerto Rico, 3,435 square miles; of Guam, 206 square miles; of Tutuila and other Samoan Islands, 76 square miles; of the Panama Canal Zone, 554 square miles; of the Virgin Islands, 133 square miles.

The United States west of the 95th meridian of west longitude is bounded by parallel 49° north latitude, which divides it from western Canada; east of this point it is irregular, following in greater part the median line of the Great Lakes (Superior, Huron, Erie, and Ontario) and the St. Lawrence River, which latter it leaves at the 45th parallel of north latitude; from Lake Ontario the line follows the northern frontiers of the States of New York, Vermont, New Hampshire, and the western and northern boundary of Maine, its course forming the dividing line with eastern Canada. On the east the boundary line is formed by the Atlantic Ocean; on the south by Mexico and the Gulf of Mexico; on the west by the Pacific Ocean. The most southern mainland point is Cape Sable (in Florida), lat. 25° 10′ N., but since Key West is now linked with the mainland by a highway extending across the intervening keys or islands, this point may really be said to be lat. 24° 32′ N.; the most western point is Cape Alva, about 15 miles south of Cape Flattery, long. 124° 36′ W. in Washington; the most northern point is a small detached land area of Minnesota on the Lake of the Woods, ending in lat. 49° 23′, and long. 95° 9′; the most eastern point is West Quoddy Head, near Eastport, the eastern extremity of Maine, long. 66° 58′ W.

LENGTH OF SEA COAST (TIDAL SHORE LINES) OF
UNITED STATES (INCLUDING ISLANDS)

North Atlantic States:

	Miles of Coast
Maine	1,319
New Hampshire	20
Massachusetts	671
Rhode Island	218
Connecticut	144
New York	829
New Jersey	760
Pennsylvania	13
Delaware	154
Maryland	1,045

South Atlantic States:

Virginia	1,280
North Carolina	1,871
South Carolina	1,241
Georgia	893
Florida (east coast)	1,221

Mexican Gulf States:

Florida (west coast)	2,530
Alabama	291
Mississippi	202
Louisiana	1,713
Texas	1,682

Pacific States:

California	1,555
Oregon	489
Washington	1,721
Total	21,862

Alaska's most northern extremity, Point Barrow, projects into the Arctic Ocean at 71° 23′ 31″ N. lat.; and Attu Island, the westernmost of the Aleutian chain of islands, reaches the meridian of 187° 34′ W. long.

The gross area of the United States, exclusive of Alaska, is 3,026,789 square miles.

The land area is 2,973,774 square miles.

The water area, exclusive of the Great Lakes, the Atlantic, the Pacific, and the Gulf of Mexico within the 3-mile limit, is 53,015 square miles.

From the easternmost point, West Quoddy Head, due west to the Pacific Ocean the distance is 2,807 miles.

The shortest distance from Atlantic to Pacific, between points near Charleston, S. C., and San Diego, Cal., is 2,152 miles.

The distance from the most northern point of Minnesota to the most southern point in Texas is about 1,600 miles.

COURTESY BEAUMONT AND HOHMAN

WITH A BACKGROUND OF ALPINE GRANDEUR, GLACIER-FED STREAMS WEND THEIR WAY THROUGH FERTILE
AND BEAUTIFUL VALLEYS OF ALASKA

The Canadian boundary is 3,898 miles long.

The Mexican boundary is 1,744 miles long.

The Atlantic coast line is 5,565 miles long.

The Pacific coast line is 2,730 miles long.

The Gulf of Mexico coast line is 3,641 miles long.

TOPOGRAPHICAL FEATURES.—There are in the United States two great uplands with a broad lowland lying between. On the east the Appalachian Mountain System extends from Alabama to the Gulf of St. Lawrence. The western Cordilleras, much higher and broader than the Appalachian, begin in Central America, rise high in Mexico, become higher and wider in the western United States and continue through western Canada to Alaska. The broad lowlands are the Mississippi plains, continuous with the Hudson Bay region and the central plains of Canada as far as the Arctic Ocean.

The Blue Ridge Mountains, extending from New York southwest through Pennsylvania, rise at Harper's Ferry to 1,500 feet above sea level; at White Top, Virginia, to 5,530 feet. In western North Carolina the mountain chain broadens out into a plateau on whose western slope there are many ridges trending north, east, and southwest. Among these is the Black Ridge group, which contains the highest peak east of the Rocky Mountains—Mt. Mitchell, 6,684 feet high.

The Appalachian Valley, stretching from Pennsylvania to Alabama, is intersected throughout by abrupt ridges, with level tops cut by occasional water gaps. Rising from the northwest limit of this valley, the Allegheny Mountains extend through Maryland, West Virginia (here called the Greenbrier Mountains), southwest Virginia, and eastern Tennessee (here called the Cumberland Mountains). These heights slope gently toward the north, terminating in the Ohio Valley.

The Mississippi Valley lies between the Appalachian System and the Rocky Mountains; the greater part is drained by the Mississippi River and other streams into the Gulf of Mexico; the northern part in general drains into the Great Lakes, but there is a small area draining into Hudson Bay by way of the Red River

of the North. In western Arkansas and southern Oklahoma the serpentine Ozark Hills rise from 2,500 feet to 3,000 feet above sea level.

From the Mississippi and lower Missouri Rivers the land inclines gradually upward to the base of the Rocky Mountains. This great incline, called the Great Plains, extends from the northern to the southern boundary of the country. The eastern base has an altitude ranging from sea level to 2,000 feet high, and at the base of the Rocky Mountains it rises from 4,000 feet to 8,000 feet above sea level.

From Alaska to Cape Horn the Cordilleran System borders the Pacific Coast of North America and South America. The mountain ranges stand upon a plateau which rises from 4,000 feet high in the north to 10,000 feet in Colorado. The region is divided into a number of districts—viz., Bitter Root Mountain district, the Park Range district, the Plateau district, the Great Basin, the Cascades and the Sierra Nevada sections, the Pacific Valley and the Coast Range district.

The Plateau Region, the region of canyons and horizontal plateaus terminated by cliffs, is drained by the Colorado River. Besides the canyons cut by the living streams, there are many huge trenches in which ordinarily no water flows, so that much of the plateau is a series of flat ridges between narrow, precipitous gorges. The most remarkable of these gorges is the Grand Canyon of the Colorado in northern Arizona—a gorge that exceeds 6,000 feet at its deepest part and is about 250 miles long. It is from 5 miles to 12 miles broad at the top. The walls of the canyon are eroded into a series of irregular steps.

West of the Wasatch Range is the Great Basin comprising parts of Utah, Nevada, California, and Oregon. It consists practically of a large number of smaller basins, unconnected for the most part by drainage with other basins; for the rainfall here is very deficient, and the mountain streams either sink into the earth or else evaporate. The principal smaller basins are the basins of the Great Salt Lake and of the Carson and Humboldt Lakes.

MEAN ALTITUDE.—The mean elevation of the United States, excluding Alaska, is about 2,500 feet.

SOILS.—The soils of the United States may be divided into two main classes. Outside of the glacial region they are known as residual soils, as they are mostly the product of local rock disintegration. Such soils are found along river courses. An illustration is the soil of the lower Mississippi. The other class is made up of glacial soils. The ice sheet plowed up the residual soils of preglacial time, pushed and carried them forward varying distances and mingled with them a variety of new materials derived from the rocks over which the glacier passed.

LAKES AND DRAINAGE SYSTEMS.—The rivers of the United States form generally four great groups: the Great Lakes, the Atlantic, the Gulf, and the Pacific. **The Great Lakes.**—The Lake Region, including the five lakes, Superior, Michigan, Huron, Erie, and Ontario, with their connecting channels and tributaries are the center of a great system of elevated fresh-water lakes extending through Maine, through New York, including the "finger lakes" and through Michigan, Wisconsin, and Minnesota, and in Canada through Quebec, Ontario, Manitoba, Saskatchewan, and the Northwest Territories.

These lakes cover a total area of over 90,000 square miles, forming the largest collective mass of fresh water in the world. They form the northerly boundaries of the United States from Jefferson County, N. Y., to Cook County, Minn.

Lake Superior.—The northern shores of Superior are mostly precipitous cliffs of Archæan, or basalt, rock, ranging from 300 to 1,000 feet in height. On the southeast, sandy coasts prevail. The coast of the northern counties of Michigan, Wisconsin, and Minnesota are composed largely of Cambrian sandstone cliffs, rich in iron and other metal deposits, veins of copper and iron ore crossing its bottom from the southern shore.

The bed of Superior is supposed to be an ancient volcanic crater, lying within the Archæan or earliest rock formations. Its depth of 1,250 feet represents a depression extending 600 feet below sea level. Superior is, therefore, distinct in origin from the other lakes of the group, whose beds represent ancient river systems. Area, 31,820 square miles.

Lake Huron, the second of the Great Lakes, is bounded north, east, and south by the Province of Ontario, and south and west by the State of Michigan. The area of Lake Huron is 23,010 square miles, including Georgian Bay (5,626 square miles), and North Passage, 1,556 square miles. It is connected with Lake Michigan by the Straits of Mackinac, 3½ miles broad and 135 feet deep.

From Lake Superior, which is 20 feet higher, the St. Mary's River flows down into Lake Huron, while from the Canadian side flow numerous smaller streams. From the city of Port Huron, at the lake's southern extremity, the St. Clair River flows almost due south about 25 miles into Lake St. Clair. From Detroit, at the southwest extremity of this small lake, the Detroit River falls in the same general direction into Lake Erie.

The discharge of Lake Huron is about 217,000 cubic feet per second. By reason of evaporation and rainfall, the level of the lake varies annually between 4 and 5 feet, but much greater local variation is caused by the strong winds. The densely wooded northeast is broken by many low islands of limestone and glacial débris. Elsewhere the shores are generally low, except on the northeast border, where rise numerous cliffs of 100 or 150 feet high. Nearly all the harbors on this coast are protected by breakwaters. Far inland there are traces of ancient lake beaches, proving that Huron, like all the other Great Lakes, has shrunken in area. In summer the surface temperature of the lake varies from 52° to 58° F.

Lake Michigan.—This, the third of the Great Lakes, is bounded on the north and west by Wisconsin, on the west and south by Illinois and Indiana, and on the east by Michigan. This is the only one of the Great Lakes wholly within the United States borders. The shores are generally low and sandy, with rocks of sandstone and limestone.

The area of Lake Michigan is 22,400 square miles, including Green Bay on the northwestern shore, and Grand Traverse Bay on the eastern shore. Many islands lie in the lake between these two breaks in the shore, which elsewhere is low and unbroken.

The level of Lake Michigan varies according to the direction and force of the winds, the changes in rainfall, evaporation, and atmospheric pressure. Except when caused by protracted gales blowing steadily in one direction, this variation rarely exceeds 1.3 feet. The lake has a lunar tide with accompanying variation of from 1½ inches neap to about 3 inches spring tide.

The principal rivers which empty into it are the St. Joseph, Muskegon, Grand, Kalamazoo, Manistee, all in Michigan; the Fox in Wisconsin, and the Menominee, between Michigan and Wisconsin.

Lake Erie, the fourth of the Great Lakes, and the most southern, has a northeast and southwest direction, bounded on the entire upper shore by the Province of Ontario, and on the southern and eastern shores by Ohio, Pennsylvania, and New York. At its southwestern end it is connected with Lake St. Clair by the Detroit River. At its northeastern end it discharges into Lake Ontario through the Niagara River. It is connected by the Welland Canal with Lake Ontario, and by other canals with the Hudson and Ohio Rivers.

Besides the drainage from the Lake Superior system, Lake Erie receives the Grand River, the Maumee from the west, and the Sandusky, Huron, and Cuyahoga from the south. Its area is 9,940 square miles.

Lake Ontario, the fifth of the Great Lakes, is the most eastern, with a northeast and southwest direction. It is connected with Lake Erie by the Niagara River. It is the lowest of the Great Lakes, and has the largest discharge, 300,000 cubic feet per second. The shores are flat, except in the Bay of Quinte, which extends on the northeast 50 miles inland. There are many harbors and flourishing ports. The waters have a surface current due to the fact that the longer axis of the lake coincides with the direction of the prevailing westerly winds. This, added to frequent violent storms, keeps the lake from freezing, except in an area of a few miles in width along the shores. Area, 7,540 square miles.

Lake Ontario is connected with the Erie Canal and Hudson River by the Oswego Canal and with the Ottawa River by the Rideau Canal.

From the mouth of the St. Lawrence to the head of Lake Superior it is nearly 2,400 miles, a navigable system exceeded in the United States only by the Mississippi and its tributaries.

The entire system of the Great Lakes, including their tributary streams and outlets, covers 175,340 square miles. Commercially, it is of the first importance, the amount of its shipping exceeding that of all the Atlantic ports, or of all the Pacific and Gulf ports together.

RIVER SYSTEMS OF THE UNITED STATES.—The river systems of the United States may be classified according to the areas drained and the bodies of water into which their rivers flow, as follows:

Atlantic Region, draining an area of about 276,890 square miles, through a total river length of about 6,100 miles.

Gulf Region, draining an area of about 1,725,980 square miles, through a total river length of about 25,000 miles.

Pacific Region, draining an area of 619,240 square miles, through a total river length of about 4,100 miles.

The total drainage area of the entire country includes over 2,600,000 square miles of territory, and the total river length, nearly 35,200 miles of channel.

THE ATLANTIC RIVER REGION.—From the north in the State of Maine to the south in the State of Florida, nineteen streams worthy to rank as rivers, and most of them navigable, flow into the Atlantic Ocean. They are as follows:

1. *The Penobscot River,* having its headwaters in Lake Chesuncook, Piscataquis County, Maine, and numerous branches in the northeast region of Maine, flows through 350 miles of channel into Penobscot Bay. It is navigable through 60 miles from its mouth to Bangor, and for small boats still farther up.

2. *The Kennebec River,* having its headwaters in Oxford County, Maine, flows through about 190 miles of channel to the Atlantic Ocean, east of Casco Bay. It is navigable for river craft as far as Augusta, but for seagoing ships, as far as Bath only. Navigation is impeded by ice during the winter months. Large towns and cities are Bath, Gardiner, and Augusta.

3. *The Connecticut River,* having its headwaters in Coos County, in the northern extremity of New Hampshire, flows through 390 miles of channel into Long Island Sound near Saybrook, Conn. It drains a total area of about 11,000 square miles. Navigation by large steamboats is possible as far north as Hartford, Conn., and for smaller craft as far as Holyoke, Mass. Important cities along its course are Hartford and Middletown, Conn.; Springfield, Holyoke, and Northampton, Mass.; Brattleboro and Bellows Falls, Vt., and Lebanon, N. H.

4. *The Hudson River,* having its headwaters in an Adirondack Mountain lake in northeastern New York, flows through 315 miles of channel into New York Bay. It receives three large tributaries from the west, the Mohawk, the Sacondaga, and the Wallkill. Navigation for seagoing ships is possible as far north as Hudson, 117 miles from its mouth, and for river steamboats, as far north as Troy, 150 miles. The Hudson River is noted for the beauty of its scenery, which has won for it the title "Rhine of America." Important cities along its course are New York, Yonkers, Newburgh, Poughkeepsie, Kingston, Hudson, Albany, Troy, Cohoes, and Glens Falls, N. Y., and Jersey City and Hoboken, N. J.

5. *The Delaware River,* rising in the Catskill Mountains, N. Y., flows through 350 miles of channel into Delaware Bay.

It cuts its way to the Atlantic through the Delaware Water Gap, two miles long; forms the entire boundary between New Jersey and Pennsylvania. It is navigable for large ships to Philadelphia; for steamboats to Trenton at high tide; from Bristol to Easton by a 60-mile canal.

Important cities along its course are: Philadelphia, Chester, Easton, and Bristol, Pa.; Wilmington and Newcastle, Del.; Camden, Trenton, and Burlington, N. J.

6. *The Susquehanna River,* having its headwaters in Otsego Lake, Otsego County, New York, flows through 420 miles of channel into the northern end of Chesapeake Bay at Havre de Grace. It drains the greater part of Pennsylvania, receiving three large tributaries from the west, the Chemung, which joins it near the New York boundary, the large West Branch, 200 miles long, and the Juniata. Flowing through very picturesque country and gapping several ridges of the Appalachian Mountains, it is almost throughout a swift-flowing, but shallow and unnavigable stream, its only importance as a waterway being for floating lumber. Chief cities along its course are Binghamton and Owego, N. Y.; Pittston, Wilkes-Barre, and Harrisburg, Pa.; and Port Deposit, Md.

7. *The Potomac River,* rising in the western Alleghenies, flows through 420 miles of channel into Chesapeake Bay, and forms throughout its course the boundary between Maryland on the north and east, and West Virginia and Virginia on the south and west. Its chief tributaries, besides the South Branch which joins the headstream, 14 miles southeast of Cumberland, Md., are the Shenandoah from the south and the Monocacy from the north. Its upper course is through remarkably picturesque scenery, and there are several falls in its passage through the mountains and the Piedmont Plain, the Great Falls being 11 miles above Washington. Navigable for the largest ships as far as Washington, 125 miles from its mouth, this tidal stream is for 100 miles a magnificent estuary from two to seven miles wide. The leading cities and towns along its course are Hancock, Md.; Harper's Ferry, W. Va.; Alexandria, Va.; and Washington, D. C.

8. *The Rappahannock River,* formed by several small headstreams rising in the Blue Ridge in northwest Virginia, flows through 200 miles of channel into Chesapeake Bay, which it enters by a broad and long estuary running parallel with that of the Potomac and about 20 miles south of it. A navigable tidal stream for nearly 100 miles to Fredericksburg, which is the only important city along its course, the Rappahannock there has a fall supplying good water power.

9. *The James River,* formed near the middle of the western boundary of Virginia by the union of the Jackson and Cowpasture Rivers, which rise in the Alleghenies, flows through 420 miles of channel into Chesapeake Bay through Hampton Roads near Norfolk. Its chief tributaries are the Appomattox and the Chickahominy Rivers. For the last 66 miles of its source it is a broad and deep tidal estuary, and is navigable for vessels of 130 tons as far as Richmond, 150 miles from the sea, where it is obstructed by rapids having a fall of 100 feet in six miles and affording enormous

water power. The important cities along its course are Richmond and Lynchburg.

10. *The Roanoke River,* formed in southern Virginia by the union of the Dan and the Staunton, which rise in the Blue Ridge, flows through 250 miles of channel into Albemarle Sound. Its length, including the Staunton, is 450 miles, and it is navigable for steamboats to Weldon, N. C., which is the principal town along its course.

11. *The Neuse River,* rising in Person County, the middle county of the northern tier of North Carolina, flows through 300 miles of channel into Pamlico Sound. At Newbern, 30 miles from its mouth, it widens into a broad estuary. It is navigable by steamboats to Goldsboro, 100 miles from its mouth. The principal towns along its course are Newbern, Kingston, and Goldsboro.

12. *The Cape Fear River,* rising in the central northern part of North Carolina, flows through 300 miles of channel into the Atlantic Ocean. It is the longest river wholly within the State of North Carolina, the whole central part of which it drains. Its largest tributaries are Deep River, from the west; South River, from the east; and Northeast Cape Fear River from the northeast. It is navigable for steamboats at all seasons as far as Fayetteville, 120 miles from the sea. The important cities along its course are Wilmington and Fayetteville.

13. *The Pedee River,* rising in the Blue Ridge in northwestern North Carolina (where it is known as the Yadkin River; being called the Great Pedee after it enters South Carolina), flows through 400 miles of channel into Winyaw Bay. The Yadkin from its source to the boundary line between North and South Carolinas is 300 miles long. The Pedee is navigable for small vessels for about 150 miles. The only city of importance on this river is Georgetown, S. C.

14. *The Santee River,* formed near the center of South Carolina by the junction of the Congaree and Wateree or Catawba, both of which rise in the Blue Ridge in North Carolina, flows through 150 miles of channel into the Atlantic by two arms south of Winyaw Bay. The length of the stream from its mouth to the source of the Wateree, its longer branch, is 450 miles. It is navigable for steamboats to Columbia on the Congaree branch, and to Camden on the Wateree branch. The important towns in its course are Columbia and Camden.

15. *The Edisto River,* formed near Branchville, South Carolina, by the union of its north and south forks, both of which rise in the western part of that State, flows through 150 miles of channel and divides into the North and South Edisto 15 miles from the Atlantic, which these arms enter southwest of Charleston Harbor and just north of Saint Helena Sound. It is navigable for about 100 miles.

16. *The Savannah River,* rising in the Blue Ridge, flows through 450 miles of channel into the Atlantic Ocean through the Tybee Roads, and forms the boundary line between Georgia and South Carolina. It is navigable for large vessels as far as Savannah, 18 miles inland; for smaller steamboats as far as Augusta, 230 miles from the coast; and for still smaller boats 150 miles higher. The important cities along its course are Savannah and Augusta.

17. *The Ogeechee River,* having its headwaters in Greene County in central eastern Georgia, flows through 250 miles of channel into the Atlantic through Ossabaw Sound, 18 miles south of Savannah. It is navigable for small steamers for about 40 miles from the sea.

18. *The Altamaha River,* formed by the confluence of the Oconee and Ocmulgee Rivers at the boundary line of Montgomery and Appling Counties, Georgia, flows through 150 miles of channel into the Atlantic. It drains an area of 14,400 square miles, and is navigable for steamboats as far as Macon, on the Ocmulgee branch, 300 miles from the ocean. The important cities and towns along its course are Macon, Milledgeville, and Darien.

19. *The St. John's River,* rising in the swamps of Brevard and Osceola Counties, Florida, flows northward through 400 miles of channel, parallel with and 20 miles from the Atlantic Coast, and empties into the Atlantic 25 miles south of the Georgia boundary. From its source it passes through a chain of lakes, and from the largest of these, Lake George, 200 miles from its mouth, the river expands into a lagoon from one to five miles wide. It has been dredged to a depth of

24 feet to Jacksonville, about 20 miles; and is navigable for small steamboats as far as Enterprise, 230 miles from its mouth. The only city of importance on the river is Jacksonville.

THE GULF RIVER SYSTEM.—From the east in the State of Florida to the west in the State of Texas, counting the Mississippi, eleven rivers, eight of them important in navigation, flow into the Gulf of Mexico. They are the following:

1. *The Suwanee River,* having its headwaters in the Okefinokee Swamp in southern Georgia, flows through 250 miles of channel into the Gulf 12 miles north of Cedar Keys, Florida. It is navigable for steamboats for about 65 miles, to the post village of New Troy, which is the largest settlement along its course.

2. *The Apalachicola River,* formed by the junction of the Chattahoochee and Flint Rivers at the southwestern corner of the State of Georgia, flows through 90 miles of channel into Apalachicola Bay, an arm of the Gulf of Mexico. It is navigable for steamboats throughout its whole length. Its port of entry, and the only important town along its course, Apalachicola, has naval stores and lumber manufacturing interests.

3. *The Mobile River,* formed by the union of the Alabama and Tombigbee Rivers, which rise in central and western Alabama, flows through 50 miles of channel into Mobile Bay. At several points it communicates with the Tensas, or eastern channel, through which the same rivers discharge, and the two enter the bay through a common delta at the city of Mobile. It is navigable for large steamboats. The only important town on the river is Mobile.

4. *The Pearl River,* having its headwaters in Winston County, in the east central part of Mississippi, flows through 300 miles of channel into Mississippi Sound, after having formed for some distance the boundary between Mississippi and Louisiana. Its navigation is impeded by shoals and sand bars. The only city of importance along its course is Jackson.

5. *The Mississippi River.*—See *The Mississippi River System,* below.

6. *The Sabine River,* rising in northeastern Texas, flows through 400 miles of channel into the Gulf through Sabine Lake and Sabine Pass, after forming for 150 miles the boundary between Texas and Louisiana. For a short distance only it is navigable for small steamboats. Navigation of the pass has been improved by dredging and jetty building.

7. *The Trinity River,* formed by the union, near Dallas, of the two forks which rise near the northern boundary of Texas, flows through 535 miles of channel into Galveston Bay, about 40 miles north of Galveston. It is navigable for steamboats, at high water, for 300 miles. The principal city along its course is Dallas.

8. *The Brazos River,* formed by the junction of Clear and Salt forks, in Young County, north central Texas, flows through 950 miles of channel into the Gulf of Mexico, about 40 miles southwest of Galveston. It drains a large area, winding in a tortuous course. It is navigable for steamboats during high tide for 300 miles, and at all times as far as Columbia, 40 miles from the Gulf. The principal towns along its course are Waco and Columbia.

9. *The Colorado River,* rising in the western part of Texas, near the southeastern boundary of New Mexico, flows through 650 miles of channel into the Gulf through Matagorda Bay. It receives several tributaries, chiefly from the south. It is navigable in winter for river steamers as far as Austin, 200 miles from its mouth. The principal towns along its course are Bay City, Ballinger, Wharton, Columbus, Lagrange, Bastrop, and Austin.

10. *The Nueces River,* having its headwaters in a range of low mountains in Edwards County, in southern Texas, flows through 400 miles of channel into Corpus Christi Bay. The chief towns on its course are Oakville and Nuecestown.

11. *The Rio Grande,* rising in the Rocky Mountains in southwestern Colorado, flows through 1,650 miles of channel into the Gulf, after having formed for about 800 miles the boundary between Texas and Mexico. It drains some 248,000 square miles, in its upper course passing through rocky gorges and forming rapids and cataracts, but lower down becoming a shallow stream obstructed by sand bars. Its waters are used for irrigation in New Mexico, so that in the dry season the river dries up for a considerable distance above and below El Paso. In its lower course

it is subject to serious floods. It is navigable for small steamboats for about 450 miles. The leading towns along its course are El Paso, Laredo, and Brownsville, Texas, and Matamoras, Mexico.

THE MISSISSIPPI RIVER.—The Mississippi River System, draining an area of 1,240,000 square miles, through the Mississippi proper and its tributaries, forms the largest river drainage system in the world and the longest continuous length of river channel.

The Mississippi River rises in Itasca Lake, Minnesota, 1,462 feet above sea level. The river winds southward for 2,495 miles into the Gulf. Including the Missouri branch and the Jefferson, rising in southwest Montana, it is 4,221 miles long. The Mississippi and its branches drain the entire eastern slope of the Rocky Mountain System within the United States. It is navigable from the Gulf of Mexico to the Falls of St. Anthony at Minneapolis, 3,161 miles. The total navigable length of the Mississippi system is 14,000 miles, following its windings. Near its source the river is about 12 feet wide and 2 feet deep. It winds for 270 miles down to the Falls of Pokegama, below which it first becomes navigable for small steamers. Farther down, the river is interrupted by the Falls of St. Anthony. From here, by the aid of a canal at Rock Island and another at the rapids near the mouth of the Des Moines River, navigation of the upper Mississippi is uninterrupted. For about 30 miles north of the mouth of the Ohio, the flood plains are above the level of the river. Below Cape Girardeau the west side down to the Gulf is bottom land for a width of 50 miles.

From Cairo at the mouth of the Ohio to the Gulf the river flows in a channel on the summit of a low ridge, the land sloping gradually away from the banks on each side, so that these flood plains lie below the level of the river. In the lowland near the "delta" district, the river divides into "passes," the principal of which are the Southwest and South Passes and the Pass a Loutre. At the mouth of each pass (except the South Pass where jetties have been built) there is a bar formed by the deposit of silt from the river. The area of the delta is about 12,000 square miles.

In the navigable part of the Mississippi River, above the mouth of the Ohio, where the banks are higher and the depth is nearly uniform, the river falls about 6 inches per mile, except at the Des Moines Rapids, where the descent is 24 feet in a mile and at the Rock Island Rapids, 22 feet. At the Falls of St. Anthony the drop is 78 feet in a mile.

The width of the river above the mouth (where it is dotted with many islands) as far as Lake Pepin is about 1 mile. Lake Pepin averages 2½ miles wide and is about 20 miles long. Below the Missouri to the Red River the Mississippi's width varies from one-half mile to 1 mile, with occasional widths of 1½ miles. Below the Red River to the passes the width is about one-half mile.

The mean annual outflow of the Mississippi River is estimated to be 21,000,000,000,000 cubic feet. The average annual amount of solid matter discharged by the river into the Gulf of Mexico is about 400,000,000 tons. Among the important cities along the course of the Mississippi are Minneapolis and St. Paul, Minn.; La Crosse, Wis.; Dubuque, Iowa; St. Louis, Mo.; Rock Island, Ill.; Quincy, Ill.; East St. Louis, Ill.; Memphis, Tenn.; Vicksburg, Miss.; and Baton Rouge and New Orleans, La.

From its mouth to the confluence with the Ohio, the Mississippi flows over silt brought down by its own current. The south central section of the United States was once an alluvial basin covered by part of the Gulf of Mexico. Upheavals in geological times raised the land to nearly its present height. The constant deposits of river sediment are slowly raising the river bed still higher, and this steady upbuilding of the river's channel must be met with higher levees in order to protect the farm land on each side.

TRIBUTARIES OF THE MISSISSIPPI.—Of the numerous tributaries of the Mississippi the most important navigable streams are the following seven:

1. *The Missouri River,* the longest river in the United States, formed in southwestern Montana by the confluence of the Jefferson, Madison, and Gallatin Rivers, and having a total length, from the source of the Jefferson, of 2,945 miles, flows north and east across Montana, turns southeastward in North Dakota, crosses South Dakota, divides Nebraska from Iowa and Mis-

souri, forms the northeastern boundary of Kansas, and finally crosses Missouri in an easterly course and enters the Mississippi 20 miles above St. Louis. It drains 528,000 square miles and is a swift, turbulent stream, navigable only by flat-bottomed steamboats. During the flood period in early summer it can be ascended 2,300 miles to Great Falls, Mont.; but in low water navigation is suspended above the junction of the Yellowstone. The principal cities along its course are Great Falls, Mont.; Bismarck, N. D.; Pierre and Yankton, S. D.; Sioux City and Council Bluffs, Iowa; Omaha and Nebraska City, Neb.; Atchison, Leavenworth, and Kansas City, Kans.; St. Joseph, Kansas City, and Jefferson City, Mo.

2. *The Ohio River,* formed by the junction at Pittsburgh of the Alleghany and Monongahela Rivers, flows through 1,283 miles of channel between Ohio, Indiana, and Illinois on the right, and West Virginia, and Kentucky on the left, joining the Mississippi at the southernmost part of Illinois. It drains an area of 203,900 square miles, having an average rainfall of 43 inches a year; and the Ohio's discharge of water averages 158,000 cubic feet a second, nearly 40,000 cubic feet more than that of the Missouri. It is navigable for large steamboats to Pittsburgh, except when frozen over or when a period of drought greatly reduces its current. The total length of navigation on the river and its several large tributaries is about 2,300 miles; and on it more than 15,000,000 tons of freight are carried annually. The more important cities along its course are Pittsburgh, Pa.; Wheeling, W. Va.; Marietta, Portsmouth, and Cincinnati, Ohio; Newport, Covington, Louisville, and Paducah, Ky.; and Madison, New Albany, and Evansville, Ind. Cairo, Ill., is at the confluence of the Ohio and the Mississippi.

3. *The Arkansas River.* This stream, rising in central Colorado, flows through 1,460 miles of channel, crossing Kansas, Oklahoma, and Arkansas, into the Mississippi 60 miles north of the Louisiana line. It drains about 175,000 square miles. Much of the water in the upper course is used for irrigation. The river is navigable for steamboats to Wichita, 600 miles from its mouth. The principal cities along its course are Pueblo, Col.; Wichita and Arkansas City, Kans.; Fort Smith and Little Rock, Ark.

4. *The Red River,* rising in the northern part of Texas, flows through 1,275 miles of channel, crossing Arkansas, and Louisiana, into the Mississippi, 340 miles above the mouth of the latter and opposite the southwestern corner of the State of Mississippi. For the first 60 miles it flows between deep banks, after which it enters a sandy plain where it broadens out to a width of nearly 3,000 feet, but the depth is very shallow. Farther down it enters fertile alluvial bottom land. It drains about 90,000 square miles. In seasons of drought it is wholly cut off from the Mississippi, emptying into the Gulf through the Atchafalaya, the chief of several bayous formed in the Red River's lower course in Louisiana. The National Government has spent large sums on this river and has made it navigable for steamers drawing four feet as far as Shreveport, 350 miles at all seasons except in extreme low water, and almost to the Texan boundary at high water. The leading towns on its course are Shreveport and Alexandria, La.

5. *The Des Moines River,* having its headwaters in a chain of lakes in southwestern Minnesota, flows through 500 miles of channel, southeasterly across Iowa, entering the Mississippi 3 miles below Keokuk. It drains an area of 14,500 square miles and is navigable for steamboats to Des Moines, 150 miles. The principal cities along its course are Ottumwa, Des Moines, and Fort Dodge.

6. *The Illinois River,* formed by the junction of the Des Plaines and the Kankakee 45 miles southwest of Chicago, flows through 433 miles of channel into the Mississippi near the mouth of the Missouri. It is navigable for steamboats 250 miles to La Salle, whence a ship canal connects it with the south branch of the Chicago River, thus affording uninterrupted water communication between Lake Michigan and the Mississippi. The chief cities on its banks are Peoria, Ottawa, La Salle, and Pekin.

7. *The Yazoo River,* originating in several bayous sent out by the Mississippi River near Friar Point in northwestern Mississippi, and reinforced by the waters of several streams from the northeast, flows through 300 miles of channel in a sluggish and winding south-

west course and rejoins the Mississippi 12 miles above Vicksburg. It is deep and navigable in all seasons.

THE PACIFIC RIVER SYSTEMS.—The large rivers of the Pacific States flowing into the Pacific Ocean or into the Gulf of California are three in number, representing a total drainage area of 610,240 square miles and about 4,100 miles of channel. From the north in Washington and Oregon to the south in California they are as follows:

1. *The Columbia River* which, rising in the Rocky Mountains of British Columbia, flows through a channel nearly 1,270 miles in length into the Pacific Ocean, where the mouth is widened into a deep bay between Pacific and Wahkiakum Counties, Wash., and Clatsop County, Ore. Its course after crossing the American border is first nearly due south, then westward, later southeasterly, and finally in a general westerly direction to its mouth. It receives three important tributaries: the Pend Oreille, the Spokane, and the Snake Rivers. The Columbia River System drains an area of about 259,000 square miles. The total navigable length of the Columbia is 756 miles, but this is broken by falls and rapids into many separate parts; the first navigable stretch is that from its mouth to The Dalles, 190 miles; from Celilo, 13 miles above The Dalles, it is navigable 198 miles to Priest Rapids, and from Colville up, 250 miles, and for other shorter reaches. The total navigable length of the river and its tributaries is 2,132 miles. The entrance to the mouth of the Columbia is obstructed by a bar, lessening its value as a waterway; but large vessels ascend the Columbia to Vancouver, Wash., and thence the Willamette to Portland, Ore. The tide flows to the Cascades, 160 miles from the sea. These falls are overcome for vessels by means of a lock built by the United States Government. The principal towns on the Columbia are Pasco, Vancouver, and Kalama, Wash.; and The Dalles and Astoria, Ore.

a. *The Snake River,* also called the Shoshone, the largest tributary of the Columbia, rising in the Rocky Mountain Divide in the southern part of the Yellowstone Park, flows through 940 miles of channel, first southeast, turning gradually west and then northwest in a great curve through southern Idaho and Oregon, and finally westward through southeastern Washington, and enters the Columbia about 20 miles north of the Oregon line. For much of its length the river has worn its course in narrow canyons from 1,000 to 4,000 feet deep, at the bottom of which the stream flows sometimes for 100 miles in tumultuous rapids, and in several places plunges in great cataracts, of which the most famous are the Shoshone Falls. The Snake is navigable for steamboats 100 miles to the Idaho boundary at Lewiston, and in several isolated stretches in its middle course. Lewiston is the only town of importance on its course.

2. *The Sacramento River,* rising on the southern slope of Mount Shasta in the northern part of California and soon receiving the Pitt River, which has its headwaters in Oregon, flows northward through 400 miles of channel into San Francisco Bay. The length of the stream to the source of the Pitt is more than 600 miles. It drains the northern half of the great central California valley, receiving tributaries originating in the Sierra Nevada and the Coast Range. It is navigable for small steamers only to Sacramento, 80 miles. The principal towns along its course are Sacramento, Redding, and Red Bluff.

3. *The Colorado River,* formed in southwestern Utah by the junction of the Green River, which rises in southwestern Wyoming, and the Grand River rising in north central Colorado, flows through about 1,650 miles of channel, southwesterly across the northwest corner of Arizona, turns south to form the western boundary of that State, and leaving United States territory near its mouth pours its waters into the Gulf of California. Its total length to the source of the Green River is 2,000 miles. It drains about 244,000 square miles and passes through what is now in some respects the most remarkable region on the earth, both scenically and geologically. The river has cut several large canyons deeply into the rock foundations through which it passes, the largest and deepest of which is the famous Grand Canyon in northern Arizona. This is 200 miles long, and in the middle is the narrow and gloomy canyon proper, with a sheer depth of 2,000 to 3,000 feet, along the bottom of which rushes the river. Below this canyon the river flows through a low desert

region, receiving almost no tributaries and diminishing in volume by evaporation and absorption. It is navigable for light steamboats 500 miles, but navigation is much impeded by rocks and sand-bars as well as by the ever-changing volume of water and the shifting of the river bed.

MINERALS.—The United States has great mineral wealth, including an abundance of the leading industrial minerals. In 1937, the United States ranked first in the production of coal, copper, petroleum and zinc and regained leadership in the output of iron. In gold production, the United States is surpassed by South Africa, the U.S.S.R. and Canada; in silver, it is second to Mexico. Lead and aluminum are largely produced. Tin is found, but in small quantity and chiefly from Alaska. Mercury, talc, salt, lime, gypsum, asphalt, potash, sand, slate, sulphur, fluorspar, building stones, borax, fictile clays, phosphate rock, natural gas, mineral waters and cement rock are other mine and quarry products of importance.

Deposits of most of the lesser-known minerals or their ores are worked either in the United States proper or in the dependencies. Among them are the useful items of manganese, molybdenum, tungsten, vanadium, chromium, platinum, radium (in connection with uranium), and helium gas (used for inflating dirigibles, balloons, etc.).

The presence of large conveniently located deposits of iron, coal, oil and copper has been a determining factor in causing the development of vast and varied manufacturing industries in the United States.

Precious stones do not figure largely in the mineral output of the United States. Corundum, sapphires, agate, beryl, turquoise, opal, garnet, topaz, tourmaline and quartz are found. A few diamonds are found in Pike County, Arkansas. Fresh-water pearls occur in the shellfish of rivers of the Middle West.

The United States leads in petroleum production. Total world production in 1937 was 2,040,500,000 barrels of 42 gallons each; that of the United States, 1,277,653,000 barrels. There are seven main fields in this country: Mid-Continent, California, Gulf Coast, Rocky Mountain, Appalachian, Illinois and Southwestern Indiana, and Lima-Indiana. Oklahoma, California, Texas and Kansas are the chief producing states. Production of petroleum in commercial quantities began in Pennsylvania in 1859. Consumption has constantly increased, and to-day, when industrial greatness and naval strength depend to a considerable degree upon oil, it is hardly possible for supply to exceed demand. New wells are sought in many parts of the world. The Soviet Union, the second country in production, is followed by Venezuela, Rumania, Iran (Persia), Netherland India, Mexico, Iraq, Colombia, Peru, Argentina, Trinidad, India, Borneo, Poland, Germany, Japan, Ecuador, Canada and Egypt.

MINERAL SPRINGS.—Some of the most noted mineral springs in the world are to be found in this country. Among them are the Hot Springs, Ark.; White Sulphur Springs, W. Va.; French Lick Springs, Ind.; West Baden Springs, Ind.; Saratoga Springs, N. Y.; Poland Springs, Me.; Waukesha Springs, Wis.; Clifton Springs, N. Y.; Las Vegas Springs, N. Mex.; the Medical Lake Springs, Wash.; and the Berkeley Springs, Va. The waters of many of these springs are bottled in immense quantities and sold all over the globe, and the localities in which the springs occur receive many tourists.

VALUE OF MINERAL INDUSTRIES.—Mineral industries in the United States are again increasing. The total output of mine and quarry products for 1937 was valued at about $5,440,000,000, greater than in 1936, but still considerably less than the value for 1920, which was the year when high prices were at their peak. Mineral fuel production accounted for more than half the sum. Aluminum industries are on the increase. Aluminum uses include car bodies, alloys, dirigible frames, aluminum paint, electric power cables. Phosphate-rock products for agricultural purposes are developing.

COAL.—It is estimated that the coal fields of the coal-producing countries of the world hold 7,685,000,000,000 tons of unmined coal. Of this great reserve of power and heat, by far the greater part is bituminous, or other "soft" coals. The United States has some 16,000,000,000 tons of anthracite; China's anthracite is estimated at about 427,000,000,000 tons.

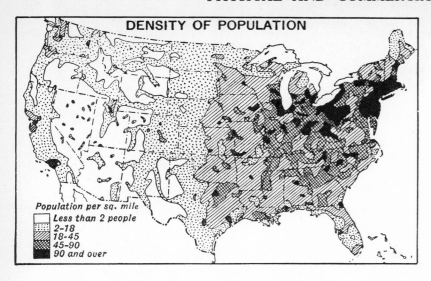

DENSITY OF POPULATION

Population per sq. mile
Less than 2 people
2–18
18–45
45–90
90 and over

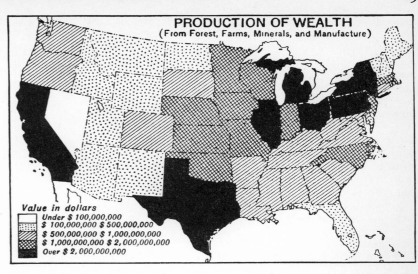

PRODUCTION OF WEALTH
(From Forest, Farms, Minerals, and Manufacture)

Value in dollars
Under $100,000,000
$100,000,000 $500,000,000
$500,000,000 $1,000,000,000
$1,000,000,000 $2,000,000,000
Over $2,000,000,000

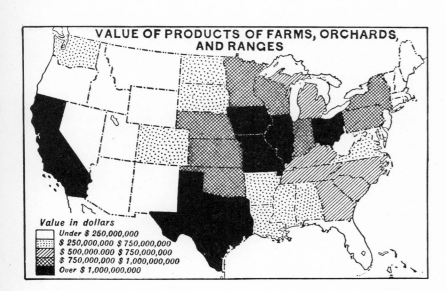

VALUE OF PRODUCTS OF FARMS, ORCHARDS, AND RANGES

Value in dollars
Under $250,000,000
$250,000,000 $750,000,000
$500,000,000 $750,000,000
$750,000,000 $1,000,000,000
Over $1,000,000,000

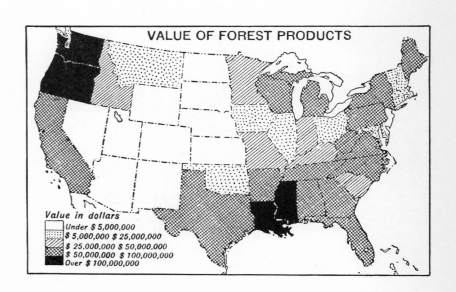

VALUE OF FOREST PRODUCTS

Value in dollars
Under $5,000,000
$5,000,000 $25,000,000
$25,000,000 $50,000,000
$50,000,000 $100,000,000
Over $100,000,000

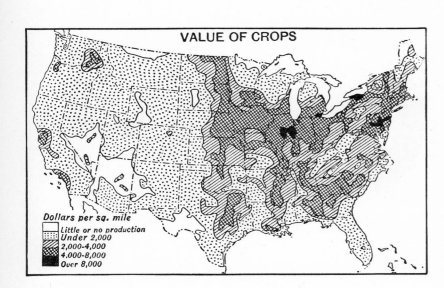

VALUE OF CROPS

Dollars per sq. mile
Little or no production
Under 2,000
2,000–4,000
4,000–8,000
Over 8,000

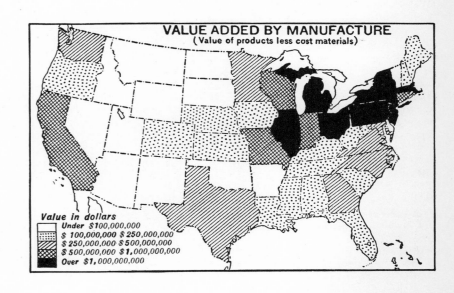

VALUE ADDED BY MANUFACTURE
(Value of products less cost materials)

Value in dollars
Under $100,000,000
$100,000,000 $250,000,000
$250,000,000 $500,000,000
$500,000,000 $1,000,000,000
Over $1,000,000,000

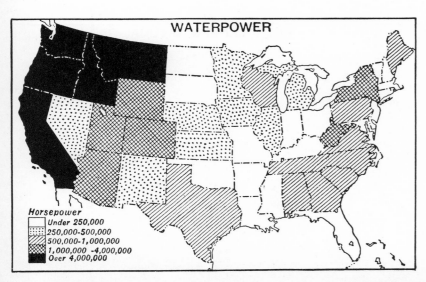

WATERPOWER

Horsepower
Under 250,000
250,000–500,000
500,000–1,000,000
1,000,000 –4,000,000
Over 4,000,000

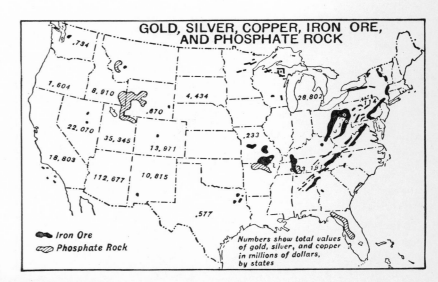

GOLD, SILVER, COPPER, IRON ORE, AND PHOSPHATE ROCK

Iron Ore
Phosphate Rock

Numbers show total values
of gold, silver, and copper
in millions of dollars,
by states

ECONOMIC MAPS OF THE UNITED STATES

FARM ANIMALS

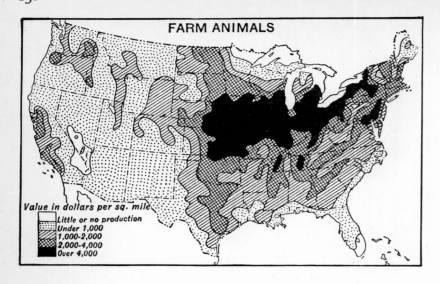

Value in dollars per sq. mile
Little or no production
Under 1,000
1,000-2,000
2,000-4,000
Over 4,000

HORSES AND MULES

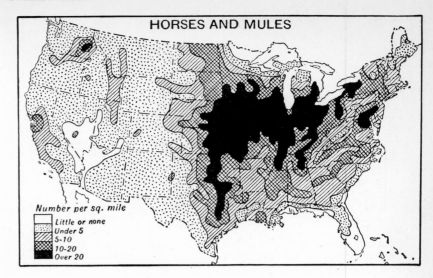

Number per sq. mile
Little or none
Under 5
5-10
10-20
Over 20

CATTLE

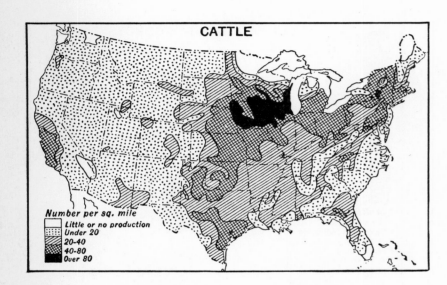

Number per sq. mile
Little or no production
Under 20
20-40
40-80
Over 80

SHEEP

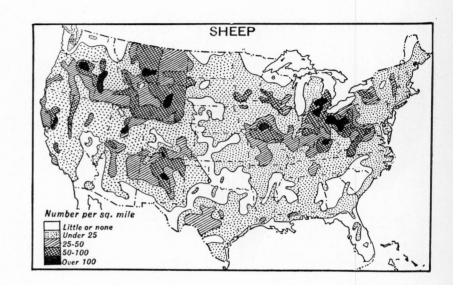

Number per sq. mile
Little or none
Under 25
25-50
50-100
Over 100

SWINE

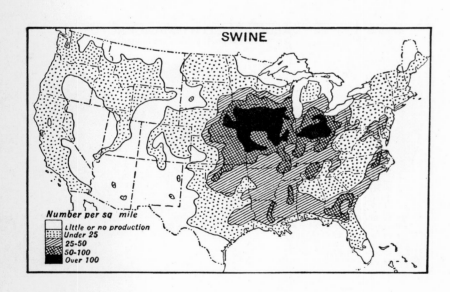

Number per sq. mile
Little or no production
Under 25
25-50
50-100
Over 100

AUTOMOBILES

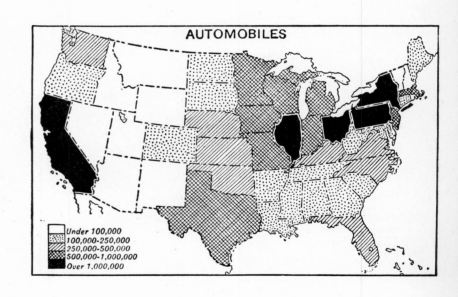

Under 100,000
100,000-250,000
250,000-500,000
500,000-1,000,000
Over 1,000,000

COAL FIELDS

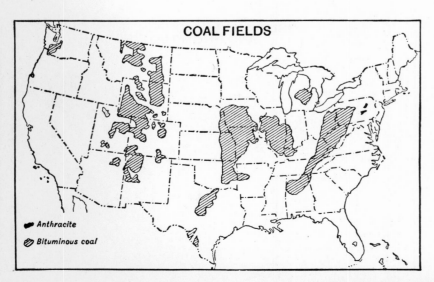

Anthracite
Bituminous coal

PETROLEUM & NATURAL GAS

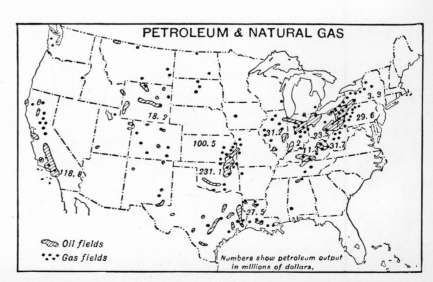

Oil fields
Gas fields

Numbers show petroleum output
in millions of dollars.

ECONOMIC MAPS OF THE UNITED STATES

HAY AND FORAGE

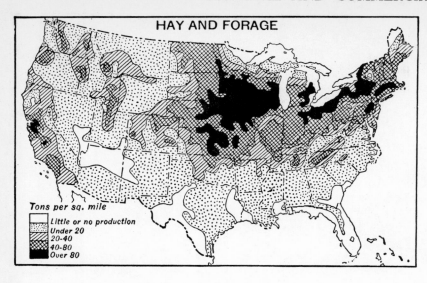

Tons per sq. mile
Little or no production
Under 20
20-40
40-80
Over 80

FRUITS AND NUTS

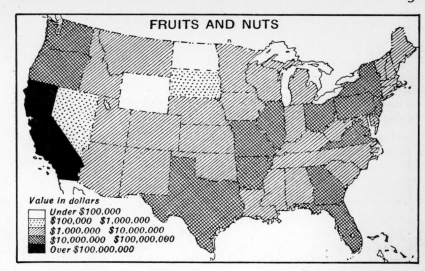

Value in dollars
Under $100,000
$100,000 $1,000,000
$1,000,000 $10,000,000
$10,000,000 $100,000,000
Over $100,000,000

OATS

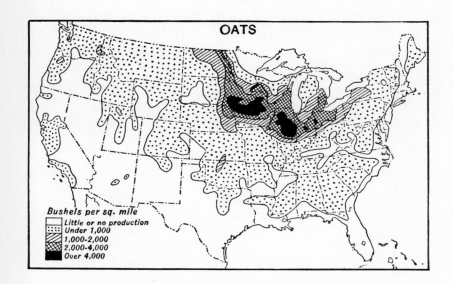

Bushels per sq. mile
Little or no production
Under 1,000
1,000-2,000
2,000-4,000
Over 4,000

CORN

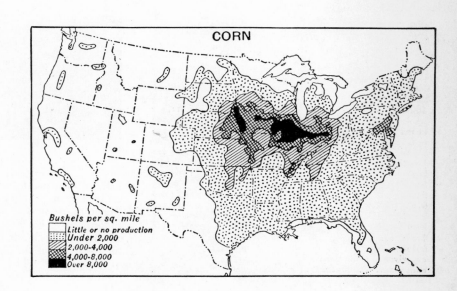

Bushels per sq. mile
Little or no production
Under 2,000
2,000-4,000
4,000-8,000
Over 8,000

WHEAT

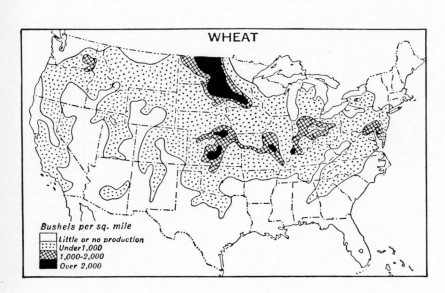

Bushels per sq. mile
Little or no production
Under 1,000
1,000-2,000
Over 2,000

POTATOES

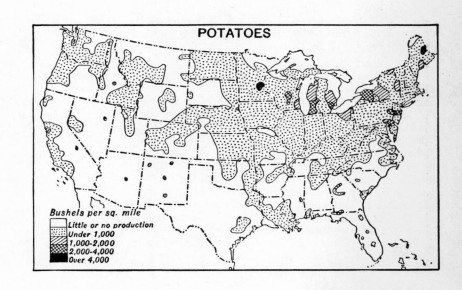

Bushels per sq. mile
Little or no production
Under 1,000
1,000-2,000
2,000-4,000
Over 4,000

TOBACCO

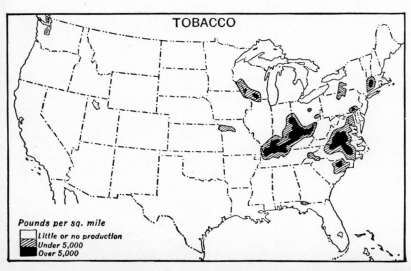

Pounds per sq. mile
Little or no production
Under 5,000
Over 5,000

COTTON

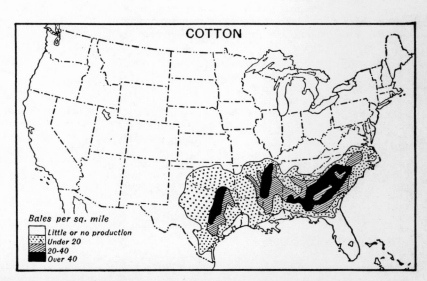

Bales per sq. mile
Little or no production
Under 20
20-40
Over 40

ECONOMIC MAPS OF THE UNITED STATES

United States coal fields comprise about 311,000 square miles, exclusive of Alaska, and geologists declare Alaskan coal fields to be very extensive.

As far back as 1750 soft coal was occasionally used in blacksmiths' forges here, and attempts were made to utilize it in smelting iron. The exceedingly rapid increase in the production of coal is shown in the following table:

BITUMINOUS COAL PRODUCTION IN UNITED STATES

Year	Tons	Year	Tons
1807-1820	3,000	1890	111,302,322
1830	104,800	1910	417,111,142
1850	2,880,017	1920	556,563,000
1870	17,371,305	1930	467,526,299
		1936	439,087,903

The total number of tons of coal, bituminous and anthracite produced in the United States in 1937 was estimated at 447,575,000 net tons of 2,000 pounds.

COAL PRODUCTION BY STATES
Net tons

State	Year 1930	Year 1936
Alabama	15,570,058	12,229,287
Arkansas	1,533,434	1,622,787
Colorado	8,196,910	6,811,802
Illinois	53,731,230	50,926,599
Indiana	16,489,962	17,822,536
Iowa	3,892,571	3,960,700
Kansas	2,429,929	2,944,028
Kentucky	51,208,995	47,521,950
Maryland	2,270,593	1,703,589
Michigan	661,113	626,145
Missouri	3,853,150	3,984,999
Montana	2,002,004	2,988,524
New Mexico	1,969,433	1,596,775
North Dakota	1,700,157	2,215,335
Ohio	22,551,978	24,110,078
Oklahoma	2,793,954	1,540,303
Pennsylvania (bituminous)	124,462,787	109,887,470
Pennsylvania (anthracite)		54,579,535
South Dakota		41,331
Tennessee	5,130,428	5,108,195
Texas	833,872	842,624
Utah	4,257,541	3,246,565
Virginia	10,907,377	11,661,636
Washington	2,301,928	1,812,104
West Virginia	121,472,638	117,925,706
Wyoming	6,088,133	5,780,590

IRON.—Iron ore is widely distributed in the United States, with the Lake Superior region leading in production. Ore mining began in early colonial days, but did not rise in importance till near the middle of the 19th century. From a total output at that time of 1,560,442 long tons, there was a steady increase year by year, the production in 1910 reaching 56,889,734 long tons, valued at $140,735,607. In 1920, the output was 69,558,000, valued at $290,607,000. In 1937 the production of iron ore was 72,093,548 gross tons. In pig iron production the United States had long since outranked Great Britain. In 1920 the output was 35,710,227 long tons with a value of $1,140,904,096. The output in 1937 36,145,095 gross tons, an increase of more than 6,000,000 gross tons over 1936.

GOLD AND SILVER.—The mining of gold began practically with the discovery of the placer gold in California in 1848. In 1850 the output was $50,000,000; in 1860 it fell. With the introduction of quartz and

UNITED STATES GOLD AND SILVER PRODUCTION SINCE 1845

Year	Gold Troy Ozs.	Gold Value	Silver Troy Ozs.	Silver Value
1845	48,762	$1,008,000	38,700	$50,200
1848 *	483,750	10,000,000	38,700	50,500
1850	2,418,750	50,000,000	38,700	50,900
1880	1,741,500	36,000,000	30,318,000	34,717,000
1900	3,829,897	79,171,000	57,647,000	35,741,000
1920	2,476,166	51,186,900	55,361,573	60,801,955
1930	2,285,603	47,247,600	50,748,127	19,538,029
1937	4,822,775	168,797,125	71,643,863	55,416,528

* Gold discovered in California.

hydraulic mining California has continued to be an important gold mining State. In Montana placer mines were worked in 1860. Nevada, with its Comstock

OIL TANKS AND REFINERIES, WHITING, INDIANA

lode (which has since declined), and other States, especially Arizona, Colorado, South Dakota, Utah, and the Territory of Alaska, have also contributed much to the production of gold.

The first great impetus to silver mining came with the discovery of the Comstock lode in western Nevada in 1859, after which the United States became the leading silver-mining country of the world. Mexico is now first. Idaho, Montana and Utah now lead as silver States, with Arizona, Colorado, and Nevada following. Other metals are often obtained from the same mines.

FROM THE YEAR 1792-1937

Gold Troy Ozs.	Gold Value	Silver Troy Ozs.	Silver Value
239,940,131	$5,118,435,700	3,387,660,989	$2,632,195,924

UNITED STATES, GOLD AND SILVER PRODUCTION, 1937, WESTERN STATES, ALASKA AND PHILIPPINE IS.

State or Territory	Gold Troy Ozs.	Gold Value	Silver Troy Ozs.	Silver Value
Alaska	627,940	$21,977,900	494,340	$382,372
Arizona	338,500	11,847,500	9,000,000	6,961,500
California	1,174,578	41,110,230	2,888,265	2,234,073
Colorado	368,905	12,911,675	6,260,693	4,842,646
Idaho	81,861	2,865,135	19,587,766	15,151,137
Montana	202,252	7,078,820	11,812,093	9,136,654
Nevada	281,332	9,846,620	4,864,750	3,762,884
New Mexico	41,171	1,440,985	1,243,766	962,053
Oregon	52,662	1,843,170	60,564	46,846
Philippine Islands	699,873	24,495,578	657,789	508,800
So. Dakota	581,544	20,354,040	139,638	108,010
Texas	562	19,670	1,325,660	1,025,398
Utah	322,759	11,296,565	12,869,117	9,954,262
Washington	36,310	1,270,850	126,304	97,696
Wyoming	1,776	62,160	203	157

COPPER AND LEAD.—The mining of copper began practically with the development of the Lake Superior copper mines in Michigan in 1845. In 1866 the Calumet and Hecla mine, the richest of the Lake Superior region, was opened. In 1880, Arizona began to yield, and this State is still far in the lead in copper production. In 1937 Arizona produced 580,493,036 pounds (fine) of copper, while Utah produced 404,168,742 pounds (fine), Montana produced 280,662,270 pounds (fine), and Nevada produced 149,963,847 pounds (fine). Michigan produced 84,751,478 fine pounds.

Lead is largely produced from the silver mines. Galena is its principal ore, and is found in numerous localities along the Atlantic border. One of the most productive mining regions is in southeastern Missouri. Galena in association with zinc blende is found in Illinois, Wisconsin, and Iowa in proximity with the Mississippi River and also in southwestern Missouri. Lead-silver mines are operated in Idaho (the Coeur d'Alene district), Colorado, and Utah. In 1937 the output of lead in Missouri was 157,631 short tons, and that of Idaho 103,711 tons.

COPPER AND LEAD PRODUCTION IN THE UNITED STATES SINCE 1840

Year	Copper		Lead	
1840	100	Long Tons	17,000	Short Tons
1870	12,600	" "	17,850	" "
1900	270,588	" "	270,824	" "
1920	539,759	" "	476,849	" "
1930	663,810	" "	580,013	" "
1937	745,233	" "	465,038	" "

PLANT LIFE.—The United States has a flora of far greater variety than is found in Europe. Its trees, including most of the European genera, number about 400 species, many of them, such as hickories and the sassafras genus of the bay laurel family, not being found in Europe. Numerous trees, shrubs, and herbs of the Eastern States, however, are unknown on the Pacific Coast, and many plants of that section are not native to the East. On the plains west of the Mississippi, the forests practically become non-existent until the mountains are reached when they again appear, in varying density, and finally culminate in the world's greatest timber region along the Pacific Coast.

The country has been divided into eight floral regions, as follows:

1. **Southern Florida** (tropical).—The vegetation is closely related to the regional flora of the West Indies and more remotely to that of South America. Mangrove swamps, palm woods, and a profusion of vines and epiphytes, including some 400 tropical species, flourish here that are found in no other part of the country.

2. **Southwestern Texas** (tropical).—A semidesert area regarded botanically as a part of the Mexican zone. Among the typical plants are, mesquite, greasewood, and other shrubs, herbs, cacti and nut pines.

3. **Southeastern Coast Region** (sub-tropical or austral).—Including the coast States from Texas to Virginia. Here are large belts of yellow pine forests, chiefly long-leaf, short-leaf, slash, and loblolly; also juniper, southern white cedar, swamp cypress, palmetto (the northernmost palm, ranging as far north as North Carolina), magnolia, live oak, as well as hickory, maple, gum and other common hardwoods.

4. **The Appalachian** (temperate).—Including all

the Northeastern States north of the southeastern coast region and east of the Mississippi. This section has a very varied and luxuriant vegetation due to abundant rainfall and long summer heat and also to the existence of plants which first appeared ages ago, but survive here with more recently evolved species. The region has vast deciduous, or leaf-shedding, forests, many containing representatives of nearly all European genera of trees, such as oak, maple, ash, chestnut, birch, elm, walnut, linden, poplar, and beech, and one of the finest of North American trees, the tulip tree. On the higher mountains are found conifers such as growths of hemlock, white pine, and fir, with an admixture of the hardier deciduous species. In some places the undergrowth shows a wealth of vines and also a great variety of flowering plants—such as rhododendrons, honeysuckles, mountain laurels, viburnums, and dogwoods.

5. **The Great Plains** (temperate).—From central Texas northward between the Mississippi and the Rocky Mountains. Grass predominates, but asters, daisies, and other well-known flowers are common. Along the streams grow cottonwood and willows. On the western desert plains instead of grass are sage brush and greasewood, and in the south on the Llano Estacado and in southern New Mexico and Arizona yuccas and cacti are found.

6. **The Rocky Mountains.**—This great floral region differs widely from the Appalachian, scarcely 20 per cent of the mountain section's plants being found in the east. The upper limit of tree growth rises toward the south, climbing from 9,000 feet on the Canadian boundary to 12,000 feet in Colorado. South in the Bitter Root and Park Mountain regions the limit is lower on account of decreased rainfall. In Idaho and in southern Wyoming the larger valleys are below this dry timber line. Throughout this richly coniferous area few of the trees are common to the Appalachian region. The most characteristic trees are the western white and yellow pine, lodgepole pine, piñon pine and Chihuahua pine in the south. The Engelmann spruce is common throughout seeking high altitudes. Other trees common in the north are firs, western hemlock, and tamarack; in the dry southwestern ranges shrubby conifers, such as junipers, above the timber line. The deciduous forests are of small extent and poor in species, like the six species of small and scrubby oak. Sycamores, the Mexican locust, and mulberries grow in the south. Throughout the region the rivers are lined with cottonwood, poplar, and willows. On the plateaus are found sage brush, greasewood and rabbit brush. In the southwest the plains have the characteristic desert flora. Above the timber line the flora is much like that of the Arctic region. Among the flowering plants of this colder area the most common are asters, daisies, buttercups, and species of the sweet pea and evening primrose families. There are also many species of grasses and sedges.

7. **California Region** (temperate).—Isolated by the lofty Sierras, the vegetation here is peculiar. The almost wholly coniferous forests, confined, except in the north, to the mountain slopes, or to the central river valley, are noted for their gigantic trees, the sequoia, a species of redwood ranking as the largest forest tree in the world. The Douglas fir, the sugar pine and the cedar also attain huge proportions. Of non-coniferous trees, the few represented are largely evergreen. Of Eastern trees there are few, except oaks. In the arid sections the vegetation is of the desert type with its sage brush, greasewood and cacti.

8. **Cascade Mountains** (temperate).—A northward continuation of the California region. The forests are of greater extent than in California and reach down to the coast. Douglas fir, white fir, western hemlock, noble fir, Sitka spruce, Port Orford cedar, and western red cedar reach their largest growth here. Hardwoods are limited to a few unimportant species.

FORESTRY.—Forestry is a science which aims at the preservation of forests, the reforestation of denuded lands, and the proper management of forests as a national resource. Besides their use as a timber and fuel supply, forests offer protection against winds, conserve moisture by eliminating fast run-off, minimizing erosion, and providing parks and game cover.

The act of March 3, 1891, authorized the President to set aside public lands "wholly or in part covered with timber or undergrowth" as natural reserves, now called national forests. During the next few years over 17,000,000 acres were set aside and many million acres have since been added.

The net area of national forest land in 1938 was 175,238,168 acres. The Clarke-McNary Act, passed in June, 1924, provides for coöperation between Federal and private owners against fire; for study of forest taxation; for forest planting on farms; for instruction of farmers in forestry. The following are some of the national forests:

Alaska.—Chugach, Tongass.

Arizona.—Prescott, Coconino, Tonto, Apache, Kaibab, Tusayan; Coronado, Crook, Sitgreaves.

Arkansas.—Ouachita, Ozark.

California.—Angeles, Cleveland, Eldorado, Inyo, Klamath, Lassen, Mendocino, Modoc, Mono, Plumas, Rogue River, Santa Barbara, Sequoia, Shasta, Sierra, Stanislaus, Tahoe, Trinity.

Colorado.—Arapaho, Cochetopa, Grand Mesa, Gunnison, Holy Cross, La Sal, Montezuma, Pike, Rio Grande, Roosevelt, Routt, San Isabel, San Juan, Uncompahgre, White River.

Florida.—Choctawhatchee, Ocala, Osceola.

Georgia.—Cherokee, Nantahala.

Idaho.—Boise, Cache, Caribou, Challis, Clearwater, Coeur d'Alene, Idaho, Kaniksu, Lemhi, Minidoka, Nezperce, Payette, Pend Oreille, St. Joe, Salmon, Sawtooth, Selway, Targhee, Weiser.

Illinois.—Bellevue-Savanna.

Louisiana.—Kisatchie.

Michigan.—Hiawatha, Huron, Marquette, Ottawa.

Minnesota.—Chippewa, Superior.

Montana.—Absaroka, Beaverhead, Bitter-root Blackfeet, Cabinet, Custer, Deerlodge, Flathead, Gallatin, Helena, Kootenai, Lewis and Clark, Lolo.

Nebraska.—Nebraska.

Nevada.—Dixie, Humboldt, Mono, Nevada.

New Hampshire.—White Mountain.

New Mexico.—Carson, Cibola, Coronado, Gila, Lincoln, Santa Fe.

North Carolina.—Nantahala, Pisgah, Unaka.

Oklahoma.—Wichita.

Oregon.—Cascade, Deschutes, Fremont, Malheur, Mt. Hood, Ochoco, Rogue River, Siskiyou, Siuslaw, Umatilla, Umpqua, Wallowa, Weiser, Whitman.

Pennsylvania.—Allegheny.

South Carolina.—Nantahala.

South Dakota.—Black Hills, Custer, Harney.

Tennessee.—Cherokee, Pisgah, Unaka.

Utah.—Ashley, Cache, Dixie, Fishlake, La Sal, Manti, Powell, Uinta, Wasatch.

Vermont.—White Mountain.

Virginia.—George Washington, Monongahela, Natural Bridge, Unaka.

Washington.—Chelan, Columbia, Colville, Kaniksu, Mt. Baker, Olympic, Rainier, Snoqualmie, Wenatchee.

Wisconsin.—Nicolet.

Wyoming.—Ashley, Bighorn, Black Hills, Medicine Bow, Shoshone, Teton, Wyoming, Washakie.

The public forests contain only about one-fifth of all the timber standing in the United States. The remaining four-fifths is contained in forests privately owned, the timber of which is generally more valuable. The present rate of cutting timber for all purposes in the private forests largely exceeds the annual growth. For some years past the waning timber supply and means of conserving and extending it have occupied public attention. Reforestation by Government agencies has been regarded as inadequate to meet the situation and the real solution lies in farming and putting into effect a scientific management plan for public and private forests, by which a future supply of timber is assured by proper utilization. The timber taken from privately owned forests comprises nearly the entire supply of such important commercial species as eastern white pine and spruce, southern pine, cypress, redwood, and most of the hardwoods. Private holdings generally are not reforested after being cut over.

The situation which is unlikely to be materially changed for some years to come has been thus surveyed:

Three-fifths of the original forests of the United States have disappeared. In 1933 the Forest Service reported that timber was being cut in the remaining forests at the rate of 16.3 billion cubic feet a year, and by way of replenishment to make good that loss by reforestation, less than 60 per cent of the wood used was being grown; that is, the provision for replacement was only at the rate of 9 billion cubic feet a year as against the 16.3 billions cut. The depletion of the timber resources has not resulted primarily from the use of the forests, but from their devastation. Vast areas of forest lands, the Forest Service ascertained, are not producing the timber crops which they could produce. In fact, the lumber jack and the sawmill have passed through no less than 326 million acres of timber land of which to-day about 80 million acres is more or less completely devastated. The remedies proposed embrace coöperation with the States in fire prevention and forest renewal, further extension of Federal forest holdings, reforestation of denuded Federal land, a study of the question of forest taxation and insurance, a survey and classification of forest resources, utilization under a system of sustained yield, and appropriations for forest research.

The following list shows the principal American woods and the States in which they are mostly produced:

Red Gum	South Carolina, Mississippi, Louisiana.
Yellow Poplar	West Virginia, Tennessee.
Chestnut	West Virginia, Virginia, North Carolina.
Yellow Pine, Southern	Louisiana, Mississippi, Texas, North Carolina, Alabama, Arkansas, Florida, Georgia, South Carolina, Virginia.
Aspen	Northeastern and Northern Rocky Mountain States.
Sycamore	Arkansas, Indiana, Tennessee.
Lodgepole Pine	Colorado, Wyoming.
Balsam Fir	Maine, Minnesota, Michigan, Wisconsin.
Walnut	Missouri, Ohio, Kentucky, Indiana.
Sugar Pine	California, Oregon.
Hickory	Arkansas, Tennessee.
Cottonwood	Mississippi, Minnesota, Arkansas.
White Fir	California, Nevada, Oregon.
Ash	South Carolina, Mississippi, Texas, Louisiana, Tennessee.
Basswood	Wisconsin, Michigan, Tennessee, North Carolina, West Virginia.
Elm	Wisconsin, Michigan, Ohio.
Cedar	Washington, Oregon, Idaho.
Beech	Michigan, Pennsylvania, Indiana, West Virginia, New York.
Tupelo Gum	Louisiana, South Carolina, Alabama.
Redwood	California.
Larch, Western	Montana, Idaho, Washington.
Birch	Wisconsin, Michigan, Maine, New Hampshire.
Cypress	Louisiana, Florida.
Magnolia	Louisiana.
Maple	Michigan, Wisconsin, West Virginia, New York.
Spruce	Maine, Washington, West Virginia, Oregon, Vermont.
Yellow Pine, Western	California, Oregon, Idaho, Washington, Montana, Arizona, New Mexico.
White Pine	Minnesota, Idaho, Washington, Maine, Wisconsin, New Hampshire, Massachusetts.
Hemlock	Wisconsin, Michigan, Washington, Pennsylvania, West Virginia, Maine, New York.
Douglas Fir	Washington, Oregon, California, Nevada, Idaho, Montana.
Oak	West Virginia, Arkansas, Tennessee, Louisiana, Kentucky, Virginia, Mississippi, North Carolina, Texas, Missouri, Pennsylvania, Ohio.

In 1933, at the suggestion of President F. D. Roosevelt, Congress authorized the launching of a national conservation program on a large scale,—partly to alleviate the sufferings of unemployment and partly because it was felt necessary to take active measures in conserving forest resources. Since that time thousands of young men have been profitably engaged in reforestation, trail-building, erosion control, fire suppression, and the numerous other activities connected with the perpetuation of our timber supply.

The principal lumber-producing States are Washington, Louisiana, California and Oregon, with Mississippi, Alabama, Florida, Texas, Arkansas, North Carolina, Idaho, Georgia, and South Carolina following.

AGRICULTURE.—Agriculture in the United States employs more than ten million people, with 31,819,000 living on farms in 1938. Owing to the country's great variety of physical and climatic conditions, most of the world's staple products can be raised in the United States.

The Mississippi Valley is preeminent in agricultural production, though much of the vast plateau region west of the one-hundredth meridian seldom has rainfall enough to make tillage profitable. Throughout the eastern half of the United States the rainfall is usually sufficient for crop growing. Most of the land here is fertile, but the Appalachian region is generally rocky, and the soil of much of the Atlantic seaboard is poor.

Westward from central Kansas the rainfall decreases, and grazing lands appear. In the Gulf States the rainfall is heavy, but there is no mountain barrier against cold winds from the north, though the Gulf of Mexico moderates the climate, particularly in Florida.

The climate of the Atlantic section is tempered by the Atlantic Ocean and the Appalachian Mountains, so that some products, especially fruits, grow to better advantage there than in the Middle West. The Great Lakes region is also well adapted to fruit growing, as well as to the production of grain and the grazing of cattle.

The Pacific Coast, protected by mountains on the east and favored by ocean breezes on the west, is unequaled for the culture of various fruits. Apple orchards are numerous in Washington and Oregon, especially the Hood River valley, and citrus fruit groves, olive trees, almond and walnut trees, grapes, and date palms flourish in southern California.

In 1938 the total area harvested of the principal crops in the United States was placed at 341,846,100 acres.

On the basis of prices then current, the cash income from such crops produced in the United States in 1938 was estimated by the Department of Agriculture at $3,160,025,000.

In 1938 the great wheat-producing States were: Kansas, North Dakota, Nebraska, Oklahoma, Montana, Ohio, Illinois, Minnesota, Indiana, South Dakota, Washington, Texas, Missouri, Pennsylvania, Michigan, Colorado, Idaho, Oregon, Virginia, Maryland, California; the chief corn-producing States were Iowa, Illinois, Nebraska, Missouri, Kansas, Indiana, Minnesota, Ohio, Texas, Kentucky, and Tennessee.

The following table shows the area harvested of leading crops in 1938 with estimated production and value:

Crop	Acreage Harvested	Production	Cash Farm Income
Corn	91,792,000	2,542,238,000 bu.	$271,657,000
Cotton	25,346,000	12,008,000 bales	575,741,000
Hay	68,083,000	90,743,000 tons	80,218,000
Wheat	70,221,000	930,801,000 bu.	432,691,000
Potatoes	3,007,600	369,297,000 bu.	136,109,000
Oats	35,477,000	1,053,839,000 bu.	41,608,000
Tobacco	1,626,700	1,455,970,000 lbs.	294,063,000
Apples	....	131,882,000 bu.	92,231,000
Cottonseed	....	5,339,000 tons	91,494,000
Barley	10,513,000	252,139,000 bu.	37,586,000
Sugar Beets....	931,000	11,292,000 tons	51,741,000
Grain Sorghums....	7,792,000	100,816,000 bu.	4,829,000
Peanuts	1,887,000	1,424,825,000 lbs.	39,951,000
Beans	1,671,000	15,268,000 bags	31,748,000
Sweet Potatoes..	883,000	76,647,000 bu.	15,958,000
Grapes	....	2,503,000 tons	37,012,000
Rice	1,068,000	52,303,000 bu.	32,879,000
Cowpeas	1,362,000	8,474,000 bu.	3,361,000
Rye	3,979,000	55,039,000 bu.	9,455,000
Soybeans	2,898,000	57,665,000 bu.	31,933,000
Hops	31,500	35,261,000 lbs.	5,546,000
Flaxseed	954,000	8,171,000 bu.	9,472,000
Clover Seed....	1,876,000	2,204,000 bu.	15,664,000
Alfalfa Seed...	584,000	998,000 bu.	9,804,000
Sorghum Sirup.	190,000	11,467,000 gals.	1,533,000
Velvetbeans ...	2,372,000	966,000 tons	....
Broomcorn	263,000	37,000 tons	2,274,000
Maple Sirup ..	*11,672,000	2,777,000 gals.	} 4,281,000
Maple Sugar...	*11,672,000	1,084,000 lbs.	}
Buckwheat	453,000	6,682,000 bu.	1,640,000

* 1,000 trees tapped.

Live stock on American farms on January 1, 1939 was estimated by the Department of Agriculture as follows: 66,821,000 cattle valued at $2,569,793,000, against 66,083,000 cattle valued at $2,417,235,000 in 1938; 49,011,000 swine valued at $547,461,000, against 44,218,000 swine valued at $498,070,000 in 1938; 10,800,000 horses valued at $911,572,000, against 11,128,000 horses valued at $1,012,217,000 in 1938; and 4,382,000 mules valued at $515,869,000, against 4,428,000 mules valued at $543,092,000 in 1938; 53,762,000 sheep valued at $309,180,000, against 52,682,000 sheep valued at $322,525,000 in 1938. The cattle figure includes 25,093,000 milk cows, valued at $1,397,280,000.

The cash income from farm products in 1938 including crops and animal products was $7,149,588,000. The cash income from animal products was estimated at $3,989,563,000. As part of the crops feed the livestock, some duplication exists. In 1919 the total value of important farm products reached the enormous sum of $22,646,597,000, of which $13,689,597,000 covered the chief crops, and $8,957,000,000 animals and animal products. The figures of 1919 reflect the increased production and high prices due to war con-

ditions; those of 1920 show the status of agriculture at the beginning of readjustment. Conditions had changed greatly by 1939.

In the production of tobacco the war period stimulated the growth of four large crops in succession (1916-1919), and the domestic manufacture of leaf tobacco showed a great increase due mainly to the enlarged production of cigarettes. The South, especially Kentucky, the Carolinas, Tennessee, and Virginia, continue to make the largest contribution of this product, with Wisconsin leading among tobacco-bearing States outside that section. The 1919 value, like the value of almost all American products during the war and immediately after, was greatly in excess of the tobacco values of the pre-war period, and an acreage of 1,951,000 produced 1,465,481,000 pounds with a total value of $570,868,000. The 1930 acreage was the largest ever harvested, being 2,124,300 acres, which produced 1,648,229,000 pounds of tobacco, with a value of $210,860,000. The total area harvested in 1938 was 1,626,700 acres, which produced 1,455,970,000 pounds, with a cash farm income of $294,063,000.

In the production of cotton Texas leads with Mississippi, Arkansas and Oklahoma following. Other leading cotton-producing states are Alabama, Georgia, South Carolina and Louisiana. The total production for 1938 on an acreage of 25,346,000 was 12,008,000 bales with a cash income of $575,741,000. This year's crop showed the second highest yield on record and was harvested from the smallest acreage picked since 1900.

Louisiana is the only state producing cane sugar in very considerable amounts, the output for 1938 being 5,832,000 short tons.

The production of sugar beets in 1938 amounted to 11,292,000 short tons, California, Colorado and Nebraska being the chief producers. This crop yielded 1,619,000 short tons of beet sugar. European shortage during the World War has stimulated the growing of sugar beets and the 1938 harvest is the largest on record.

FISHERIES.—On the basis of canvasses made in the course of ten years, the annual production of fishery products in the United States was estimated by the Bureau of Fisheries of the Department of Commerce at about 2,657,317,000 pounds, valued approximately at $77,344,000 to the fishermen, representing an industry employing more than 200,000 persons.

The chief fishery centers are on the New England coast, the Great Lakes, Pacific Coast (Seattle), and along the South Atlantic and Gulf States. At Boston and Gloucester, Mass., and Portland, Me., the fishing fleet of over 600 vessels, sail, steam, and gasoline, in 1936 landed from various grounds off the coast of the United States, Newfoundland, and the Canadian Provinces, 414,767,000 pounds of fresh and salted fish, having a value to the fishermen of $11,144,000. At Seattle, Wash., fish taken from Puget Sound and from the grounds along the Pacific Coast from Oregon to Alaska (especially Flattery Banks, Hecate Strait, and the Yukatat Grounds) were landed to the amount of 1,925,342,000 pounds in 1936, of a value to the fishermen of $24,882,000. The products of the Great Lakes fisheries (Lakes, Superior, Michigan, Huron, Erie, Ontario, Lake St. Clair and the St. Clair River, and the

St. Lawrence and the Niagara Rivers) amounted to 94,277,000 pounds in 1936, having a value to the fishermen of $6,389,000. The South Atlantic and Gulf States' fisheries had a production in 1936 of 556,993,000 pounds, valued at $13,542,000. Mussel shells for the pearl-button industry are an important item in this district. There are sponge fisheries off the Florida coast and alewife and shad fisheries on the Potomac. The principal catches are as follows:

North Atlantic.—Haddock, cod, pollock, herring, hake, mackerel, swordfish, halibut, and cusk.

COURTESY OF THE CUNARD WHITE STAR LIMITED

"QUEEN MARY," THE CUNARD WHITE STAR LINE'S RECORD-BREAKING PASSENGER SHIP

Pacific (Seattle).—Salmon, halibut, sablefish, "lingcod," and rockfish.

Great Lakes.—Carp, ciscoes (including lake herring, chub, longjaw, bluefin or blackfish, and tullibee), pike, perch (including blue pike and wall-eyed or yellow pike), sauger, sheepshead or drum suckers, lake trout, whitefish (common, including caviar), and yellow perch. Various other kinds were also found in considerable quantities. Other species of the Great Lakes regions are: Bowfin, burbot, catfish, eels, gold eye, muskellunge, rock bass, sturgeon, sunfish, and white bass.

Gulf States.—Black drum, catfish, croaker, groupers, menhaden, mullet (including roe), redfish or red drum, red snapper, Spanish mackerel, squeteagues or "sea trout," shrimp (green and dried), and oysters. The Gulf States' fishery grounds also contain the following species: Amberfish, angelfish, barracuda, bluefish, blue runner or hardtail, bonito, cero or kingfish, cowfish or "shellfish," crevalle, elops or ten-pounder, flounders, grunts, hogfish, jewfish, king whiting, leather jacket or "turbot," moonfish, permit, pigfish, pompano, porgies, porkfish, sailor's choice, scamp, sea bass, sea gar, sergeant fish or snook, sharks, sheepshead, mangrove and mutton snappers, spotfish, sturgeon, tang, tarpon and yellow tail.

The oyster production of the United States yields a crop of about 19,000,000 bushels annually. The principal beds are on the Atlantic Coast and are to be found from Cape Cod to Mexico, in coves, bays, estuaries, and the mouths of rivers, but reckless overfishing has destroyed most of them, and the oyster crop is becoming more and more derived from planted or cultivated grounds than from natural beds. In New England natural beds are practically exhausted, production being dependent on cultivation, and even in Chesapeake Bay extensive areas formerly prolific of oysters are now barren. Nevertheless Chesapeake Bay produces more oysters than any other body of water in the world, enabling Virginia and Maryland to lead in oyster production with an output of more than five million bushels each, annually.

RECLAMATION OF ARID LANDS.—Wherever the rainfall is deficient—that is, less than 20 inches annually—an artificial supply of water is necessary for successful farming. Even in ancient times works for the storage and distribution of water for irrigating purposes were constructed; as in Egypt, 2000 B. C., and in Assyria, Mesopotamia, Iran, India, Ceylon, China, Peru, and Mexico. There are evidences of ancient irrigating works also in our own southwest, particularly in New Mexico and Arizona.

Water for artificial irrigation is supplied from rivers, springs, or lakes; usually it is conducted by canals. The most common method is to divert the water from a stream by means of a dam in a canal running with the stream and at a lower level. In many parts of the West artesian wells are used.

The arid lands of the United States comprise about one-third of the country's entire surface. These lands, rich in precious metals, are deficient in water. Irrigated lands have one advantage over others—water can be supplied at the times and in the amounts needed. Dry countries are likely to have an unusual number of sunny days during the year, thus stimulating the growth of crops whenever water can be provided. For this reason irrigated lands usually produce an unusual number of crops per acre.

By 1870 the practice of irrigating arid land had become more familiar to Western farmers, and about 20,000 acres were under irrigation at the end of that year. Irrigation development by the construction of small ditches had brought the number of artificially watered acres up to 1,000,000 by 1880. Then canals for conveying water from rivers were introduced. Trenches, leading from the canals, conducted the water to the cultivated fields.

The construction of the gigantic reservoirs proved too costly an undertaking for private enterprise, and the Federal Government was forced to act. Congress established the Reclamation Service in 1902.

Prior to the enactment of the law authorizing the establishment of the Reclamation Service, the Hydrographic Bureau had made extensive surveys in the vast arid region and had collected much valuable information. There being millions of acres of Government land in the Rocky Mountain States and Territories, Congress directed that the proceeds of the sales

irrigation. It is simple and cheap. Supply ditches are usually constructed about 40 rods apart.

The furrow-irrigating method was adopted for the second great irrigation project, the Minidoka, in southern Idaho. This can provide for 121,570 acres on both sides of the Snake River.

In Colorado a divide separated the Uncompahgre Valley from the Gunnison River. The Reclamation Service decided to tunnel the divide and then turn the river into the valley. A tunnel 6 miles long was dug through the divide, and the water from the river poured through to fertilize the valley land. As in the case of most rivers in the Rocky Mountain States the flow of water varies with the season. In dry seasons the Gunnison has only 700 feet, but in flood times it pours 20,000 feet along its canyon bed. The tunnel can convey 13,000 feet per second, and when the river exceeds this amount the rest flows in its old channel.

The Salt River Project, Arizona, making use of the waters of the Salt and Verde Rivers, contains six large dams. One of them, Roosevelt Dam, 1,125 feet long and 284 feet high, is one of the largest structures of the kind in the world. It is about sixty miles from Phoenix, with which it is connected by a broad macadamized road. Not including townsite areas, the project supplies irrigation for 242,000 acres of farm land.

Another large undertaking of the Reclamation Service was the building of Elephant Butte Dam, located at Engle, N. Mex. The reservoir formed covers 40,080 acres and has a capacity of 2,638,000 acre-feet.

An immense soil conservation and power project in process of development in Tennessee is directed by the Tennessee Valley Authority (TVA). A project in the state of Washington includes Grand Coulee Dam, 550 feet in height. This development also provides for flood control, irrigation of land, and power.

tures in the drier portions of Texas and Arizona is from 115° F. to 120° F., and in northern Minnesota the minimum falls as low as —40° F.

The winds in January are from the west; but in July southeast winds prevail in the southern States. The Pacific coast is visited by frequent south and west winds. These bring abundant winter rains to northern California, Oregon, and Washington.

Storm centers originate in both the Pacific and the Atlantic. From the Pacific they move southeasterly to the Mississippi and then turn northeastward to the Great Lake section. From the Atlantic they move westward over the West Indies and turn northward toward the lower lake district. Some storms originate on the eastern slope of the Rocky Mountains in both the United States and Canada and move eastward toward the lake region. This region is therefore the stormiest portion of the continent. The passage of every storm center is accompanied by a shifting of warm southerly winds to cold northwesterly ones, thus giving the interior of the United States its variable climate.

Cold waves originate in the cold air that blows behind the storm centers. These waves move usually eastward, but sometimes southward toward the Gulf, while the areas of low pressure of cyclones move northeast over the lake region and beyond it. The range of temperature is greatest in the interior of the country. Sometimes it reaches 150° F. in the upper portion of the Missouri Valley and falls to 60° F. in southern Florida and southwestern Arizona. The latest spring frost occurs about May 15 from Idaho to Lake Superior and about February 15 along the south Atlantic and east Gulf coasts. Between the latest spring frost and the first autumn one there is an average daily temperature not below 40° F. This growing season shortens northward until it is only about 120 days at our northern border. The warmer portion of the year in the United States is longer than the colder portion. A striking characteristic is the contrast between the climate of the Mississippi Valley and the warmer climate of our Pacific Coast section. The difference is due largely to the fact that the cold, dry air (following each area of low pressure) is confined between the Rocky Mountains and the Appalachian system.

RAINFALL.—The heaviest precipitation prevails along the coasts of Oregon and Washington. Next to the rainfall of the north Pacific section, the rains are heaviest along the coasts of Florida and adjacent States. Throughout the Mississippi Valley and along the Atlantic Coast from South Carolina to Nova Scotia there is great fluctuation in moisture and evaporation. The driest portion of the United States extends from southern California to Texas. Irrigation is essential here for successful agriculture. Even the summits of the mountains in this region have but little permanent snow, the dry air rapidly evaporating precipitation.

Rainfall over the eastern half of our country is abundant; over the western half, scanty; but on the northern part of the Pacific Coast the annual rainfall is in some areas 100 inches. The south Atlantic and Gulf coasts receive annually a rainfall exceeding 60 inches, which diminishes northward toward the Great Lakes, where it is seldom exceeds 40 inches, and is still less on the Great Plains and over most of the Rocky Mountain region. There it ranges from 10 inches to 20 inches a year. In the Great Basin and in southwestern Arizona there is less than 10 inches, and in some localities no rain falls for months. The winter rainfall exceeds the summer on the Pacific Coast, but in the Rocky Mountain region this condition is reversed.

WINDS.—Wind is air in motion. Windstorms are known as gales, cyclones, typhoons, hurricanes, or tornadoes.

A cyclone is an ordinary windstorm resulting from the disturbance of the equilibrium of the atmosphere considered horizontally. In the United States cyclones move usually from the northwest or the southwest.

Hurricanes usually enter the United States from the south or the southeast—never from the northwest. They occur late in summer or in early autumn and are very violent, often reaching a velocity of 60 miles an hour.

Typhoon is the name usually given to a wind of cyclonic force which occurs in the China seas.

A tornado is the most violent of all storms. It is characterized by a pendent, funnel shaped cloud, having a swift rotary motion of 100 miles to 500 miles an

COURTESY OF THE UNION PACIFIC-CHICAGO & NORTH WESTERN

THE LATEST TYPE OF STREAM-LINE TRAIN ON THE UNION PACIFIC-CHICAGO & NORTH WESTERN

of those lands should be devoted to irrigation projects under the Reclamation Service Bureau.

During the first four years of the Reclamation Service work many surveys were made, and various locations were examined with a view to constructing the first large irrigation works.

The Truckee-Carson project, now Newlands, was one of the first large projects to be carried out. The plan was to conduct the Truckee River 30 miles across country in Nevada and then turn it into the Carson River basin. The project proved so successful that the Government embarked on an elaborate reclamation scheme which is still under way.

Fields are irrigated in several ways, the method used being determined by various circumstances. The oldest and simplest way is to run the water from the ditch in which it flows. The ditch is located on the highest part of the field, and, in some cases, the water is let out by spade cuts in the banks, or else dams across the ditches cause the water to overflow the banks. This plan is used to irrigate crops of grain as well as of clover and other forage plants. But as this free flooding method calls for considerable labor and does not readily yield uniform results, it is less used to-day than the furrow irrigation and the subirrigation methods.

Furrow irrigating, in which water is run between rows of crops, is the most generally used method of

The Service is developing or planning development of some thirty irrigation projects for making fertile farms out of semi-arid lands in 18 States—Arizona, California, Colorado, Idaho, Kansas, Louisiana, Montana, Nebraska, Nevada, New Mexico, North Dakota, Oklahoma, Oregon, South Dakota, Texas, Utah, Washington, and Wyoming. Largest of them is the Boulder Dam project on the Colorado River in Arizona-Nevada. The dam is 726 feet high with a crest 1,232 feet long. It creates a reservoir with a capacity of 30,500,000 acre-feet, making a lake (Lake Mead) 151 miles long and 40 miles in width, the largest artificial lake in the world. Its eventual capacity will be 44,858,800 acre-feet. The dam was nearly five years in building. The Reclamation Service built canals, ditches, drains, storage and diversion dams, roads, tunnels, railroad, etc., erected telephone and power transmission lines, mined coal and manufactured the cement used. The development will supply flood control, navigation improvement, irrigation, and hydroelectric power.

CLIMATE.—As the United States extends through many degrees of the temperate zone, the climate varies with the locality. On the northern border the average temperature is about 60° F. for July and 20° F. for January. The average annual temperatures vary from 60° F. in the northern tier of States to 75° F. in southern Florida. The average of the maximum tempera-

hour and lasts from a few minutes to several hours. The middle States have suffered most from cyclones and tornadoes.

FLOODS.—Many large areas of low ground near rivers are sometimes inundated by spring floods, generally caused by melting snow. Heavy rains in January, 1937, caused terrific floods in the Ohio and Mississippi valleys, with estimated property loss of $550,000,000 and 800,000 people left homeless.

An area of 30,000 square miles, inhabited by a million people, is safeguarded from the Mississippi River floods by means of low natural embankments, built by past floods, or by artificial levees constructed from the Gulf to Cairo. But these are sometimes broken through.

During the passage of tropical hurricanes originating in the West Indies, those islands, the Gulf Coast, and the coast of the Middle Atlantic States are subjected to a rise of the sea from 10 feet to 15 feet higher than normal. The harbors of New York and Boston have felt it. At Galveston on September 8, 1900, thousands of lives were lost. The sea islands on the Georgia coast are sometimes overflowed during these terrible storms. Sea floods are caused by a combination of the ordinary tides with violent winds. In the Pacific these combination storms, there called typhoons, often cause great destruction of life and property.

ANIMALS.—The fauna of the United States is very comprehensive. Zoölogists have identified 2,240 species of vertebrates, viz.:

Mammals	310
Birds	756
Reptiles	257
Amphibians	101
Fishes	816

The mollusks comprise about 1,430 species.

NATIVE ANIMALS

Bison, or Buffalo.—The bison is now very limited in numbers, there being but a few small herds in captivity in the United States and Canada. (The true buffalo has no hump.)

Rocky Mountain Sheep, or Big Horn.—Found in Wyoming and in other plateau States.

Rocky Mountain Goat.—A goat-like antelope, found in the Rocky Mountains and in the Coast Range.

Prong-Horn Antelope.—The only antelope known with deciduous and forked horns, found only in a few isolated spots in Montana, Wyoming, Colorado, New Mexico, Idaho, and Utah.

Elk.—In small numbers in the mountains of Washington, Oregon, Colorado, Montana, Idaho, central California, and in Maine.

Moose.—Found principally in Minnesota and Maine, but also in Idaho, Montana and Washington.

Caribou, or American Reindeer.—Maine (northern), arctic regions, Labrador and Newfoundland.

The Grizzly Bear.—Ranges the Cordilleran Highland from Mexico to Alaska.

Raccoon.—Timbered regions of the Southeastern States from Arizona to British Columbia.

Cougar (Panther, Mountain Lion, or Puma).—In all the great western mountain ranges of the United States.

Jaguar.—Handsomest of American cat family. Is found from our Southwestern States southward through Mexico.

Ocelot, or Tiger Cat.—In the southwest and in Mexico.

Lynx.—In forests west of Mississippi. In northern New England, the Carolinas, Florida, Virginia, Tennessee, Montana, Wyoming, Colorado, and Texas.

Wolves.—In our northern tier of States, in the Great Plains, and the Rocky Mountain districts.

Foxes.—Several species scattered over the United States.

Weasel.—Throughout the United States.

Marten.—In rocky, forest-covered mountains in our Northern States. Very rare.

Skunk.—Confined to the United States and Mexico. Most abundant in the North.

Polecat.—Widely distributed.

Otter.—Florida, the Carolinas, and a few localities in the Rocky Mountain region, and in Alaska.

Mink.—Throughout the country.

Beaver.—From Rio Grande in Texas through the western highland to the arctic limit of trees, and southwest through Canada to New England.

Muskrat.—Alaska, south to Arizona and Louisiana.

Woodchuck.—Eastern United States from New York

to Georgia; Western United States anywhere east of the Rocky Mountain section.

Prairie Dog.—From Texas, New Mexico, Arizona, north to the Canadian border.

Sewellel (Mountain "Beaver").—Found in the Northwest. Rare now.

Hare.—Several species scattered through the country.

Porcupine.—New England, New York, Pennsylvania, Ohio, and thence north to Hudson Bay.

Squirrels and Gophers.—Widely distributed.

Opossum.—From New York to Florida, and west through the Southern States to Texas.

Armadillo.—In Texas.

Rats and Mice.—Everywhere.

NATIVE BIRDS

Wild Turkey.—Timbered region. Once inhabited half the United States, now rare and found only in Florida, Missouri, Arkansas, the Virginias, and Pennsylvania.

Grouse.—Several kinds. Maine and Florida to Texas, western border of Oklahoma, and South Dakota.

Cranes and Herons.—Several species. Throughout the United States, but most common in the Gulf States.

Pigeon.—Several species. Throughout the United States.

Mocking Bird.—States south of Ohio River.

Parrot.—Only one species in United States, the Carolina parrakeet, in a few localities in Florida.

Humming Bird.—Several species. Thoroughly tropical, but migrates in summer as far north as Alaska and south as Patagonia. The ruby-throat is found in the eastern half of the United States; all other species west of Arkansas and the Rocky Mountains.

Song Thrushes (Robin, Thrush, Bluebird).—Eastern half of United States to Great Plains, beyond the Mississippi.

Sparrows and Flycatchers.—Widely distributed.

Eagles.—Many kinds. Bald: North America from Mexico to Alaska, along rivers. Golden: Throughout the country, but most abundant in the great mountain ranges of the West. A bird of the mountains.

Buzzard Vultures.—Black vulture, Gulf States and southward; California vulture, coast ranges of southern California from Monterey Bay south to Lower California and southeast to Arizona.

Hawks.—Many kinds.

Owls.—Many kinds. Scattered throughout the country.

Flamingo.—Bright scarlet all over. Bahamas, Cuba, and Cape Sable, Florida.

Ibises.—White, in Florida; glossy, in Florida and in Texas and southward.

Geese.—Variously throughout the country.

Ducks.—Variously throughout the country.

REPTILES

Alligator.—In southern waters.

Crocodile.—Southeast coast of Florida and a species in Cuba.

Gila (pronounced he'la) *Monster.*—Or lizard (poisonous), desert regions of Arizona and Mexico.

Horned Toad.—Arid regions of Southwest.

Chameleon.—A green lizard of Florida.

Rattlesnake.—Poisonous. Various species throughout the country.

Moccasin.—Poisonous. Gulf States as far north as North Carolina and south Illinois, and west of Texas.

Copperhead.—Poisonous. South from Indiana, east to Atlantic Coast, and well up into New England and southward to Texas.

FISHES

Fresh-Water Bass.—Black: Manitoba, south to Gulf States. Through the latter to Texas and Florida. Rock: Great Lake region and Missouri Valley. Calico: Great Lakes, Mississippi Valley to Florida, the Carolinas and Georgia. A few other species of fresh-water bass are found.

Sea Bass.—Black: Southern California. "Jew Fish": Atlantic Coast, Charleston to Brazil. Striped: Fire Island, New York, to Albemarle Sound, North Carolina. Less abundant in Gulf. Introduced into coast waters of California in 1879.

Perch.—Yellow: from Maine to Iowa and Minnesota.

Yellow Pike Perch.—Lakes Ontario, Erie, and Huron, and elsewhere.

Bluefish.—Common in Atlantic coast waters, from Florida to northern Maine.

Spanish Mackerel.—Florida, Cuba, the sea.

Tuna.—In the coast waters of southern California. Known as "tuny" on the Atlantic Coast.

Pompano.—New River, Florida, and northern half of Gulf of Mexico. Sea.

Mullets.—Sounds, bays, and half-salt rivers of the Carolinas, Florida, Gulf States.

Snappers.—Cedar Keys, toward delta of Mississippi. Well-populated banks near Jacksonville, Florida. Sea.

Remora.—Gulf of Mexico; in the waters around the West Indies, and along the Atlantic Coast.

Swordfish.—Atlantic Coast waters.

Lobster.—Shore waters from Maine to Delaware.

Oysters.—More on the Atlantic Coast than in any other part of the world.

Pikes.—From Alaska, south through upper Mississippi Valley and Great Lake region.

Mississippi Catfish.—Mississippi River and Gulf States.

Maskinonge.—Great Lakes and Chautauqua Lake, and in parts of Ohio Valley.

Pickerel.—In the region bounded by Maine, Florida, Arkansas, Minnesota.

Trout.—Mountain: Rocky Mountain region. Rainbow: Pacific Coast ranges. Salmon: Coast ranges (Pacific). Lake: Great Lakes to northern Alaska. Brook: Once abundant in northeastern United States; is becoming scarce.

Salmon.—Quinnat: Monterey Bay, Cal., up the Pacific Coast to Bering Strait. Blueback: Columbia River and Alaska. Silver: California to Alaska Peninsula. Introduced into Maine coast waters in 1913. Humpback: from the Sacramento River to Bering Strait. Dog: Pacific Coast. Off the New England coast. Fresh-water: Penobscot River, Maine.

Tarpon.—Florida coast.

Shad.—Atlantic Coast from Florida to Newfoundland, but most abundant from Hudson River to the Potomac. Introduced into Pacific waters in 1871, and in 1885 and 1886 into Columbia and Willamette Rivers, and now range from southern California to southern Alaska on Pacific Coast.

Whitefish.—Upper Mississippi Valley and Great Lakes.

Flying Fish.—Cape Cod to Brazil.

Trigger Fish.—Gulf Coast, and Atlantic to mouth of Potomac.

Suckers.—Widely distributed.

Carp.—Introduced between 1877 and 1885 into nearly all streams of Pacific Coast. They are found also in Lake Erie.

Bullhead.—From the Atlantic to the Great Plains. From Great Lakes to the Gulf.

Flounders.—Extensively propagated by United States Fish Commission. Now found in both Atlantic and Pacific waters.

Halibut.—On the Atlantic Coast north of Delaware River, especially Maine and Massachusetts coasts. Also on the Pacific Coast from Farallone Islands to Bering Strait.

Dogfish.—Great Lakes, Mississippi Valley, and in fresh-water streams on southern Atlantic Coast.

Garfish.—Large streams and lakes from New Jersey to Mexico, and northward in Mississippi Valley to Minnesota. In the Gulf States and Cuba.

Sturgeon.—Short-nosed: Atlantic and Gulf Coasts from Cape Cod to Texas (sea). White: Pacific from southern California to Alaska (sea). It has been taken also in the Snake River, Idaho. Also lake variety.

Paddlefish.—Mississippi, Arkansas, Tennessee, Illinois, Missouri, and other Central States.

Chimeras.—Northwest coast of United States in blue waters.

Sharks.—The Man-eater: in the Atlantic and the Pacific. The Mackerel: both coasts of United States. Hammer-head: sometimes as far north as New Jersey.

Sawfish.—Florida.

Sting Ray ("Stingaree").—From Cape Cod to Orinoco River.

Devilfish.—Gulf Coast to Florida.

Lampreys.—Merrimac River, nearly extinct.

THE INDIANS.—What is now the United States was originally inhabited by so-called Indians. In 1930, the Indians in the United States numbered 332,397.

STATES HAVING MORE THAN 1,000 INDIANS

Arizona	43,726
California	19,212
Colorado	1,395
Idaho	3,638
Kansas	2,454
Louisiana	1,536
Maine	1,012
Michigan	7,080
Minnesota	11,077
Mississippi	1,458
Montana	14,798
Nebraska	3,256
Nevada	4,871
New Mexico	28,941
New York	6,973
North Carolina	16,579
North Dakota	8,387
Oklahoma	92,725
Oregon	4,776
South Dakota	21,883
Texas	1,001
Utah	2,869
Washington	11,253
Wisconsin	11,548
Wyoming	1,845

While the Indian inhabitants of North America conform to a very definite type, the languages of the various tribes differ widely. So far as language similarities indicate unity of origin, they furnish a convenient basis for the classification of the Indian tribes. The number of linguistic stocks north of Mexico is 57, and these represent 779 distinct tribes, according to the researches of the Smithsonian Institution, as shown in the following table, where each name appears with the number of tribes belonging to it:

INDIAN LINGUISTIC STOCKS
(Handbook of American Indians)

Algonkian	36	Muskhogean	9
Athapascan	53	Natchesan	2
Attacapan	2	Palaihnihan	8
Beothukan	1	Piman	7
Caddoan	9	Pujunan	26
Chimakuan	2	Quratean	3
Chimarikan	2	Salinan	2
Chimmesyan	8	Salishan	64
Chinookan	11	Sastean	1
Chitimachan	1	Shahaptian	7
Chumashan	6	Shoshonean	12
Coahuiltecan	22	Siouan	68
Copehan	22	Skittagetan	17
Costanoan	5	Takilman	1
Eskimoan	70	Tañoan	14
Esselenian	1	Timuquanan	60
Iroquoian	13	Tonikan	3
Kalapooian	8	Tonkawan	1
Karankawan	1	Uchean	1
Keresan	17	Waiilatpuan	2
Kiowan	1	Wakashan	37
Kitunahan	4	Washoan	1
Kolushan	12	Weitspekan	6
Kulanapan	30	Wishoskan	3
Kusan	4	Yakonan	4
Lutuamian	4	Yanan	1
Mariposan	24	Yukian	5
Moquelumnan	35	Yuman	9
Zunian	1		

The problem of the origin of the Indians is unsolved. Though the members of the tribes in both North America and South America have many characteristics in common, nevertheless there are indications of separate origins. American aborigines may have come from Asia by way of Bering Strait, or they may have drifted across the Pacific from Polynesia. North American Indians are copper colored, with reddish tints. South American Indians are dark brown. All have the hair glossy black, straight, or slightly wavy; baldness is almost unknown; the beard is scanty; the cheek bones are prominent; the nose is aquiline; the eyes are dark and small.

The Cherokees alone of all the Indian tribes have a literature recorded in an alphabet which was developed by a gifted Cherokee half-breed, Sequoia, in the first quarter of the 19th century.

TERRITORIAL GROWTH OF UNITED STATES.—At the adoption of the Constitution in 1789 the combined areas of the thirteen (original) States totaled 845,882 square miles. The population was nearly 3,930,000. Different sections of the territory west of the Allegheny Mountains and extending to the Mississippi River were claimed by Virginia, Connecticut, Massachusetts, New York, South Carolina, North Carolina, and Georgia. Trouble on account of claims that overlapped and questions as to area and proprietory rights created much confusion. Final settlement was made by each State ceding to the United States its rights in all western lands. By 1802 all the States had relinquished their claims, and out of the vast region thus added to its original area the United States carved the territories which afterward became the great States now situated between the Alleghenies and the Mississippi.

In 1818 the *Red River Basin* was obtained from England by treaty which added 46,253 square miles to the Nation's area.

The next addition was the **Louisiana Purchase,** which cost $15,440,000. This region, containing 827,987 square miles, was bought from France, Napoleon being then the ruler of that country. The vast territory comprising Alabama, Arkansas, Colorado, part of Florida, Iowa, Kansas (in part), Louisiana, Minnesota, Mississippi, Missouri, Montana, Nebraska, North Dakota, Oklahoma, South Dakota, and Wyoming passed to the United States in that purchase, which was completed in 1803.

The Florida Purchase.—A portion of west Florida had passed to this country in the Louisiana Purchase; another section was taken possession of by the United States in 1813. Spain transferred the remainder of Florida under the provisions of a treaty negotiated in 1819. In that treaty the United States settled certain Spanish claims to Northwest Territory, including Washington, Oregon, Idaho, and portions of western Montana and Wyoming. This purchase cost the United States about $5,500,000. It added 72,101 square miles to our domain.

The Annexation of Texas.—Texas, once a part of Mexico, freed itself from the domination of that country and established a republican form of government in 1836. It was admitted as a State into the Union in 1845. Texas had claims to territory lying beyond her present borders, and in 1850 these claims were settled by the United States for $10,000,000. The total area gained by this annexation was 389,166 square miles, and now forms, besides Texas, the eastern half of New Mexico and portions of Oklahoma, Kansas, Colorado, and Wyoming.

The Oregon Addition.—In 1846 the United States and Great Britain selected by treaty the parallel of 49° N. lat. as the boundary between the United States and Canada west of the Rocky Mountains. This treaty settled a territorial dispute of long standing and represented an acknowledgment by Great Britain of the American claim to 58,800 square miles of territory north of the Columbia River, and brought what was then known as the Oregon addition to 286,541 square miles.

The Mexican Cession.—An immense area comprising New Mexico (claimed by Texas up to 1850), California, Utah, Nevada, and parts of Colorado, Wyoming, and Arizona were ceded by Mexico in 1848 for the sum of $18,250,000, including the payment by the United States of certain debts due to American citizens by Mexico. These debts aggregated $3,250,000. The total area ceded contained 529,189 square miles.

The Gadsden Purchase.—A strip of land was purchased in 1853 from Mexico for the sum of $10,000,000. It is included in the present State of New Mexico and Arizona, and has an area of 29,670 square miles.

The Alaska Purchase.—In 1867 Alaska (then called Russian America) was ceded to the United States by Russia for $7,200,000. The area purchased comprised 586,400 square miles.

The Hawaii Annexation.—The Republic of Hawaii was formally annexed by the United States in 1898 and was formed into the Territory of Hawaii in 1900. Total area of all the islands estimated at 6,407 square miles.

Annexation of Puerto Rico.—The Treaty of Paris, concluded in 1898 between Spain and the United States, transferred the island of Puerto Rico from Spanish rule to the Government of this country. Thus 3,435 square miles were added to the area of the United States.

The Island of Guam.—Guam was ceded to the United States by Spain at the conclusion of the Spanish-American War in 1898. Area, 206 square miles.

Philippine Islands' Cession.—The transference of these islands from Spain to the United States was one of the articles in the Treaty of Paris of December 10, 1898, which terminated our war with Spain. The area of the islands is 114,400 square miles.

A few small rocky Philippine Islands lying near Bashi Strait, which are known as the *Batan Islands,* accidentally omitted from cession by the Treaty of Paris of December 10, 1898, were sold by Spain for $100,000 to the United States in 1901. Their area is about 68 square miles.

For Spain's relinquishment of Guam, Puerto Rico, and the Philippines the United States paid Spain $20,000,000. The United States has promised the Philippines full independence, to begin July 4, 1946.

Samoa Islands.—Samoa, area 76 square miles, was taken formal possession of by the United States in 1899 in order to protect American interests.

Panama Canal Zone Purchase.—In 1904 a strip of land, 10 miles wide and extending across the Republic of Panama, was delivered over by that country to the perpetual control of the United States for the sum of $10,000,000 and the payment of $250,000 annually from 1913. The Canal Zone contains 554 square miles.

The Virgin Islands Purchase.—These islands (formerly Danish West Indies), area 133 square miles, were bought from Denmark in 1917 for $25,000,000.

Small Pacific Islands.—These are: Baker, Howland, Jarvis, Palmyra, Johnston, Marcus, Wake islands; also Midway Islands, Canton Island and Enderbury Island.

NATIONAL PARKS OF THE UNITED STATES.—National parks are extensive tracts of public land reserved by special act of Congress from sale or other disposition and set apart for the enjoyment and instruction of the public. They are under the control of the Secretary of the Interior.

At present there are 27 national parks, covering a total area of 14,835 square miles, and 2 national historical parks, covering a total area of 11 square miles.

Three new projects are: *Isle Royale National Park,* largest island in Lake Superior; *Everglades National Park,* in Florida; *Big Bend National Park,* in Texas, part of a proposed international park.

1. *Hot Springs National Park,* established as a special reservation in 1832 and given national park status in 1921, in middle Arkansas. Area, 1½ square miles. The hot springs possess curative properties.

2. *Yellowstone National Park,* established in 1872, in parts of Wyoming, Montana, and Idaho, comprises 3,438 square miles. It has more geysers than all the rest of the world put together. It contains the famous Grand Canyon of the Yellowstone, boiling springs, mud volcanoes, petrified forests, and is one of the greatest wild animal and bird preserves in the world.

3. *Sequoia National Park,* established 1890, in California. Area, 604 square miles. Includes the Giant Forest, famous for its gigantic sequoia trees.

4. *Yosemite National Park,* established 1890, in eastern California, comprises 1,176 square miles. It is famous for its wonderful valley, lofty cliffs, waterfalls, and groves of large trees.

5. *General Grant National Park,* established 1890, in eastern California. Area, 4 square miles. Created to preserve the General Grant Tree, 35 feet in diameter.

6. *Mount Rainier National Park,* established 1899, in west central Washington. Area, 378 square miles. Contains snow-clad peak of Mount Rainier, and a glacier field 48 square miles in area.

7. *Crater Lake National Park,* established 1902, in southern Oregon. Area, 251 square miles. Contains a lake formed by the crater of an extinct volcano. The sides of the crater are 1,000 feet high, and the lake is one of the most beautiful in the world.

8. *Platt National Park,* established 1902, 1904 and 1906, in southern Oklahoma. Area, 1⅓ square miles. It contains sulphur and other springs of medicinal value.

9. *Wind Cave National Park,* established 1903, in South Dakota. Area, 19 square miles. The park is famous for its cavern with many miles of galleries and numerous chambers of great size and peculiar formations.

10. *Mesa Verde National Park,* established 1906 and 1913, in southwestern Colorado. Area, 80 square miles. Contains the most notable and best preserved prehistoric cliff dwellings in the United States.

11. *Glacier National Park,* now *Waterton-Glacier International Peace Park,* established 1910, in northwestern Montana. Area, 1,534 square miles. In a rugged mountain region of unsurpassed Alpine character. Contains 250 glacier-fed lakes, and 60 small glaciers.

12. *Rocky Mountain National Park,* established 1915 and 1917, in northern Colorado. Area, 405 square miles. It is noted for its rugged mountain scenery.

13. *Hawaii National Park,* established 1916, in Hawaiian Islands. Area, 245 square miles. Contains the

active volcanoes of Mauna Loa and Kilauea, on the island of Hawaii, and the great crater Haleakala, on the island of Manu.

14. *Lassen Volcanic National Park,* established 1916, in northern California. Area, 163 square miles. Only active volcano in United States proper. It contains hot springs, mud geysers, ice caves, canyons, and lakes.

15. *Abraham Lincoln National Park,* established 1916, in Kentucky. Area, 110 acres. Embraces the homestead of Abraham Lincoln and log cabin in which he was born.

16. *Mount McKinley National Park,* established 1917, in south central Alaska. Area, 3,030 square miles. The Alaska Range, which occupies much of this area, has for its most remarkable feature Mount McKinley, the loftiest mountain on the North American continent.

17. *Grand Canyon National Park,* established 1908 and 1919, in north central Arizona. Area, 1,009 square miles. One of the most remarkable and unusual scenic areas of the world, including some 56 miles of the length of the Grand Canyon of the Colorado, with its deep, brilliantly colored walls at the foot of which the Colorado River flows.

18. *Acadia National Park,* established 1916 and 1919.

Area, 19 square miles. A group of granite mountains upon Mount Desert Island, off the coast of Maine.

19. *Zion National Park,* established 1909, 1918, and 1919, in southwestern Utah. Area, 148 square miles. The magnificent gorge (Zion Canyon) has a depth from 800 to 2,000 feet, with precipitous walls.

20. *Bryce Canyon National Park,* established 1924 and 1928, in southwestern Utah. Area, 55 square miles. A box canyon filled with countless array of fantastically eroded pinnacles.

21. *Fort McHenry National Park,* established 1925, in Maryland. Area, 47 acres. The defense of this fort inspired the composition of our national anthem.

22. *Grand Teton National Park,* established 1929, in northwestern Wyoming. Area, 150 square miles. In-cludes most spectacular portion of Teton Mountains, an uplift of unusual grandeur.

23. *Carlsbad Caverns National Park,* established 1930, in southeastern New Mexico. Area, 1⅛ square miles. Contains stupendous caverns, not yet wholly explored, with magnificent limestone decorations.

24. *Great Smoky Mountains National Park,* estab-lished 1930, in North Carolina and Tennessee. Area, 617 square miles. This area is not to be developed

as a national park until at least 427,000 acres have been donated to the United States, as specified in the or-ganic act. Meanwhile the park area of 394,883 acres already in Federal ownership is being protected by the National Park Service.

25. *Shenandoah National Park,* established 1935, in Virginia's Blue Ridge Mountains. Area, 80 square miles. Through its length runs the scenic Skyline Drive.

26. *Mammoth Cave National Park,* established 1936, in southwestern Kentucky. Area, 38⅓ square miles. A series of caverns, with spectacular onyx cave formations.

27. *Olympic National Park,* established in 1938, com-prises 892,292 acres, in a scenic region on the Olympic Peninsula in the state of Washington.

The two National Historical Parks are:

1. *Morristown National Historical Park,* established in 1933, near Morristown, New Jersey. Area, 1½ square miles. The area was set aside to preserve the area upon which Baron Von Steuben drilled the colonial army during the Revolutionary War.

2. *Colonial National Historical Park,* established 1936, in southeastern Virginia. Area, 9.61 square miles. Includes three areas of importance in our colonial his-tory—Jamestown, Williamsburg, and Yorktown.

Area, Population and Rank of the States, Territories and Possessions of the United States

State, Territory or Possession	Population 1930	Land Surface		Water Surface		Total Areas		Rank		Population per Sq. Mile 1930
		Sq. Miles	Acres	Sq. Miles	Acres	Sq. Miles	Acres	Population	Area	
Alabama	2,646,248	51,279	32,818,560	719	460,160	51,998	33,278,720	15	28	51.6
Arizona	435,573	113,810	72,838,400	146	93,440	113,956	72,931,840	44	5	3.8
Arkansas	1,854,482	52,525	33,616,000	810	518,400	53,335	34,134,400	25	26	35.3
California	5,677,251	155,652	99,617,280	2,645	1,692,800	158,297	101,310,080	6	2	36.5
Colorado	1,035,791	103,658	66,341,120	290	185,600	103,948	66,526,720	33	7	10.0
Connecticut	1,606,903	4,820	3,084,800	145	92,800	4,965	3,177,600	29	46	333.4
Delaware	238,380	1,965	1,257,600	405	259,200	2,370	1,516,800	47	47	121.3
District of Columbia	486,869	62	39,640	8	5,120	70	44,800	41	49	7,852.7
Florida	1,468,211	54,861	35,111,040	3,805	2,435,200	58,666	37,546,240	31	21	26.8
Georgia	2,908,506	58,725	37,584,000	540	345,600	59,265	37,929,600	14	20	49.5
Idaho	445,032	83,354	53,346,560	534	341,760	83,888	53,688,320	43	12	5.3
Illinois	7,630,654	56,043	35,867,520	622	398,080	56,665	36,265,600	3	23	136.2
Indiana	3,238,503	36,045	23,068,800	309	197,760	36,354	23,266,560	11	37	89.8
Iowa	2,470,939	55,586	35,575,040	561	359,040	56,147	35,934,080	19	24	44.5
Kansas	1,880,999	81,774	52,335,369	384	245,760	82,158	52,581,120	24	13	23.0
Kentucky	2,614,589	40,181	25,715,840	417	266,880	40,598	25,982,720	17	36	65.1
Louisiana	2,101,593	45,409	29,061,760	3,097	1,982,080	48,506	31,043,840	22	30	46.3
Maine	797,423	29,895	19,132,800	3,145	2,012,800	33,040	21,145,600	35	38	26.7
Maryland	1,631,526	9,941	6,362,240	2,386	1,527,040	12,327	7,889,280	28	41	164.1
Massachusetts	4,249,614	8,039	5,144,960	227	145,280	8,266	5,290,240	8	44	528.6
Michigan	4,842,325	57,480	36,787,200	500	320,000	57,980	37,107,200	7	22	84.2
Minnesota	2,563,953	80,858	51,749,120	3,824	2,447,360	84,682	54,196,480	18	11	31.7
Mississippi	2,009,821	46,362	29,671,680	503	321,920	48,865	29,993,600	23	31	43.4
Missouri	3,629,367	68,727	43,985,280	693	443,520	69,420	44,428,800	10	18	52.8
Montana	537,606	146,131	93,523,840	866	554,240	146,997	94,078,080	39	3	3.7
Nebraska	1,377,963	76,808	49,157,120	712	455,680	77,520	49,612,800	32	15	17.9
Nevada	91,058	109,821	70,285,440	869	556,160	110,690	70,841,600	49	6	0.8
New Hampshire	465,293	9,031	5,779,840	310	198,400	9,341	5,978,240	42	43	51.5
New Jersey	4,041,334	7,514	4,808,960	710	454,400	8,224	5,263,360	9	45	537.8
New Mexico	423,317	122,503	78,401,920	131	83,840	122,634	78,485,760	45	4	3.5
New York	12,588,066	47,654	30,498,560	1,550	992,000	49,204	31,490,560	1	29	264.2
North Carolina	3,170,276	48,740	31,193,600	3,686	2,359,040	52,426	33,552,640	12	27	65.0
North Dakota	680,845	70,183	44,917,120	654	418,560	70,837	45,335,680	38	16	9.7
Ohio	6,646,697	40,740	26,073,600	300	192,000	41,040	26,265,600	4	35	163.1
Oklahoma	2,396,040	69,414	44,424,960	643	411,520	70,057	44,836,480	21	17	34.5
Oregon	953,786	95,607	61,188,480	1,092	698,880	96,699	61,887,360	34	9	10.0
Pennsylvania	9,631,350	44,832	28,692,480	294	188,160	45,126	28,880,640	2	32	214.8
Rhode Island	687,497	1,067	682,880	181	115,840	1,248	798,720	37	48	644.3
South Carolina	1,738,765	30,495	19,516,800	494	316,160	30,989	19,832,960	26	39	57.0
South Dakota	692,849	76,868	49,195,520	747	478,080	77,615	49,673,600	36	14	9.0
Tennessee	2,616,556	41,687	26,679,680	335	214,400	42,022	26,894,080	16	34	62.8
Texas	5,824,715	262,398	167,934,720	3,498	2,238,720	265,896	170,173,440	5	1	22.2
Utah	507,847	82,184	52,597,760	2,806	1,795,840	84,990	54,393,600	40	10	6.2
Vermont	359,611	9,124	5,839,360	440	281,600	9,564	6,120,960	46	42	39.4
Virginia	2,421,851	40,262	25,767,680	2,365	1,513,600	42,627	27,281,280	20	33	60.2
Washington	1,563,396	66,836	42,775,040	2,291	1,466,240	69,127	44,241,280	30	19	23.4
West Virginia	1,729,205	24,022	15,374,080	148	94,720	24,170	15,468,800	27	40	72.0
Wisconsin	2,939,006	55,256	35,363,840	810	518,400	56,066	35,882,240	13	25	53.2
Wyoming	225,565	97,548	62,430,720	366	234,240	97,914	62,664,960	48	8	2.3
	122,775,046	2,973,774	1,903,216,600	53,015	33,928,360	3,026,789	1,937,144,960			
Alaska	59,278					586,400	378,165,760			
Guam	18,509					206	134,400			
Hawaii	368,336					6,407	4,127,360			
Canal Zone	39,467					554	282,880			
Philippine Islands	12,082,366					114,400	73,616,640			
Puerto Rico	1,543,913					3,435	2,198,400			
American Samoa	10,055					76	49,280			
Virgin Islands	22,012					133	88,320			
U. S. Services abroad	89,453									
Pacific Islands						12				
Total	137,008,435					3,738,412	2,395,808,000			

The States and Possessions of the United States

ALABAMA.—**Physiography.**—The Allegheny plateau, entering the State in the northeast, extends to the central portion. There it sinks into low hills. In the mountainous part the climate is agreeable. Severe frost is unusual. The coast district has a summer temperature, high and uniform, but endurable. The annual rainfall in the State is 52 inches. South of the hilly region lies the "Black Belt," a tract of rich, dark earth which crosses the State. Here is also the cane-brake region. Both sections are noted for their remarkably fertile soil and are regarded as the best cotton-growing lands in the United States. Farther south are many million acres of lowland covered with pine forests. Hardwood timber is found in the northern part of the State. There stock raising, as well as farming, is an important industry. Most of the State drains into the Gulf of Mexico through the Mobile River. All the largest rivers of the State, the Mobile, Tombigbee, Alabama, Coosa, Warrior, and Tallapoosa are navigable for many miles.

Minerals.—Alabama has immense deposits of coal and iron ores. Mining has become a very important industry. Limestone is abundant. There are extensive beds of clays—potter's, porcelain, and fire brick. Manganese, mica, graphite, asbestos, and cement are found in paying quantities. Lithographic stone and building stone, including granite, are procured in several counties. Bauxite has been mined for several years.

Agriculture.—Alabama is one of the leading States in the production of peanuts, sorghum sirup, and in the yield of sweet potatoes. Cotton is the most valuable agricultural product. Corn, oats, white potatoes, velvet beans, soy beans, and hay are other standard crops. Garden truck raising and the cultivation of berries and small fruits are lucrative industries.

Manufactures.—The principal manufactures are pig-iron, coke, steel, heavy castings, machinery, and iron piping. Cotton goods, yarns and thread, flour, and fertilizers are steadily increasing in importance.

More cane sirup is made in Alabama than in any other State except Louisiana and Florida. The annual lumber cut is about 1,200,000,000 feet. Large quantities of naval stores are produced.

Commerce.—Cotton is the chief export. Lumber, cereals, flour, and lard are shipped to the North and to foreign countries. Mobile, the largest port, has an extensive trade; being the outlet for the products of neighboring sections of other States as well as of Alabama. Sisal grass and tropical fruits from Mexico are imported in large quantities.

History.—De Soto's expedition crossed the State in 1540. Frenchmen made a settlement near Mobile Bay in 1702 and founded Mobile in 1711. In 1763 France ceded all her possessions (including Alabama, except for the southern part which was claimed by Spain as part of Florida) east of the Mississippi to Great Britain. During the Revolutionary War Spain seized the coast strip. The rest of the region passed to Georgia after the adoption of the Constitution. Congress set off the Mississippi Territory in 1798. This Territory included part of what is now Alabama. In 1804 the Territory was extended northwest and in 1813 southwest to the Gulf, thus taking in all the region now called Alabama. Four years later, however, Alabama was made a Territory. It became a State in 1819. In 1861 Alabama seceded from the Union, and Montgomery was chosen as the temporary capital of the Confederacy. A new constitution having been adopted in 1868, the State was readmitted into the Union.

ARIZONA.—Physiography.—Broken plateaus, rising in step-like formations from Mexico to Utah, constitute the larger part of the State's surface. Much of northern Arizona is 5,000 feet above sea level. Everywhere the surface is arid, hilly and cut by numerous canyons. These are eroded river channels, some of them a mile deep. The southern part of the State has many shallow water courses which, when swollen by rains, become affluents of the permanent rivers.

During its 400-mile course through Arizona to the Gulf of California, the Colorado River descends 3,000 feet. The Grand Canyon, which the river has cut through successive strata of rock, is one of the world's greatest natural wonders. For over 250 miles its cliff walls rise from 3,000 feet to 5,000 feet above the river. At the top the canyon is from 5 miles to 15 miles wide. Within the canyon's limits the Colorado is unsafe for navigation even by small boats.

Minerals.—Arizona has vast mineral wealth. The leading minerals are copper, silver, gold, zinc, and lead, the value of these minerals produced in 1936 being $56,116,940. There are also large deposits of iron, coal, sulphur, tungsten, borax, salt, cinnabar, and other valuable minerals.

Climate.—The climate is dry and healthful. Catarrhal and respiratory diseases are almost unknown. In the northern part of the State a delightfully temperate climate prevails in the valleys.

Yuma, 100 feet above sea level, is the driest place in the United States. There the average annual rainfall is 4 inches, while at Flagstaff, which has an elevation of 12,611 feet, it is 24 inches. For the whole State the yearly rainfall averages about 15 inches.

Vegetation.—Characteristic Arizona plants are the greasewoods, mesquites, sage brushes, agaves, yuccas, creosote brushes (stinkweeds), and candelabras, or giant cactuses.

In the northeast there are about 3,000 square miles of forest under control of the United States Government. Most of the trees are coniferous. These yield about 80,000,000 feet of lumber every year. Cottonwood trees flourish along the banks of the streams.

Agriculture.—The soil is very fertile and, if watered, a succession of crops can be grown all the year round. Large dams, which have been constructed across several rivers in order to form reservoirs, insure the irrigation of over 1,000,000 acres. Boulder Dam (completed in 1935) will later make irrigation possible for several million acres more. Hay has proved to be the most profitable crop. Cotton, wheat, and corn follow in order of value. Barley and oats are extensively cultivated. Figs, grapes, dates, almonds, and citrus fruits thrive in the south, while in the northern part all the fruits and vegetables of the temperate zone can be grown successfully. No irrigation is needed on the bottom lands of the Gila and Colorado rivers, and in those sections abundant crops are raised throughout the year. There are millions of acres of natural pasture lands, and many cattle, sheep, and horses are raised. The wool clip was 4,740,000 pounds in 1936.

Manufacturing.—Copper smelting and refining is the most important manufacturing industry. Meat packing, making of cottonseed products, lumber working, ice manufacture, dairying, flour and grist milling and baling of raw cotton are important industries.

History.—Early Spanish explorers found here many ruins of large irrigation aqueducts and Pueblo communal structures. These were undoubtedly the remains of works executed by Indian tribes who had attained a considerable degree of civilization. The buildings were practically huge tenement houses, several stories high, built of undressed stone or of sun-dried brick. They must have afforded room for hundreds of occupants and, it is believed, were erected for purposes of defense as well as for dwelling places.

Marcos de Niza was probably the first Spaniard to visit this region, and in the following year, 1540, Coronado led an expedition. Attempts at colonization were few, due largely to the extremely hostile attitude of the Apache Indians. The first permanent settlement was made at the present site of Tucson in 1580.

In 1848 the whole region, then part of New Mexico, was ceded by Mexico to the United States.

A large section of southern Arizona was part of the Gadsden Purchase made by the United States from Mexico in 1853. For several years the State was the theater of savage Indian warfare and the resort of Mexican outlaws. Peace and order were finally established. Arizona was organized as a Territory in 1863 and admitted to statehood in 1912.

ARKANSAS.—Physiography.—Much of the surface is low and nearly level. There is considerable swampy land, some of which is heavily forested. There are many dense pine forests, and there is also an abundance of such useful trees, as the oak, hickory, cypress, walnut, cedar, pecan, and cottonwood. The Boston Mountains which extend from the Ozarks of Missouri to the Arkansas River have, as branches, the Black Hills in the north, the Cane Hills in the northwest, and the Ouachita Mountains in the south.

In the central part the surface is undulating, and hilly in the west and southwest. The chief rivers, the Mississippi, Arkansas, Washita, St. Francis, and Red are navigable for many miles. The Arkansas bisects the State. All the river bottoms are very fertile, and the marshy land, when drained, will grow any crop. An extensive system of levees and dikes prevents flooding of the Mississippi bottoms. The climate is mild and healthful in the higher parts. The rainfall ranges from 45 inches to 55 inches annually.

Minerals.—Arkansas has much mineral wealth. Coal—semi-anthracite, bituminous, and lignite—is mined. Ores of lead, zinc, iron, copper, and manganese have been found, the manganese deposits being exclusively worked in the Batesville district. Natural gas, marble, slate, honestone, burr millstone, granite, fuller's earth, lithograph stone, cement rock, and kaolin are also among the State's mineral treasures. Bauxite, from which aluminum is made, is obtained in large amounts. Pike County, Arkansas, is the only place in North America where diamonds are found. The mineral springs, particularly those of Hot Springs, Eureka Springs, Heber, and Searcy, are among the most noted in the country. Millions of gallons of mineral waters are shipped out of the State every year. The total value of the State's mineral output is steadily increasing. Petroleum is now chief in order of value.

Agriculture.—Soil and climate make it possible to grow any crop of the temperate zone. Cotton is the chief product, grown like corn, and sweet potatoes on the fertile river bottom lands. Arkansas holds third place in the production of rice. Hay, white potatoes, oats, alfalfa, wheat, cowpeas, and peanuts are important crops. Stock raising is a growing industry. Apples, peaches, grapes, strawberries and other fruits are profitably cultivated.

Manufacturing.—Lumber articles constitute the most valuable manufacture, Arkansas being one of the few States having a large supply of hardwoods left. Petroleum refinery products come next in value.

There are numerous establishments for manufacturing leather, furniture, cotton goods, wagons, and flour.

History.—The first explorers of Arkansas were the Spaniards under De Soto, who crossed the northern portion of it in 1541. Marquette reached it in 1673. It was first settled by Frenchmen at Arkansas Post in 1686, but was held by Spain as part of the Louisiana territory from 1762 to 1800 when it was restored to France. With the rest of the Louisiana Territory it was bought from France by President Jefferson in 1803. In 1812 it became a part of Missouri Territory, but was organized as Arkansas Territory in 1819. In 1828 the present boundaries were established and it was admitted as a State into the Union in 1836. It joined the Confederacy in 1861 and became the theater of several military campaigns. In 1868 the State was readmitted into the Union.

CALIFORNIA.—Physiography.—California is the largest State in the Union, except Texas. It is about 750 miles long and has an average breadth of 230 miles. Two great mountain ranges, the Sierra Nevada and the Coast Range, traverse the State lengthwise. Between them lie the immense fertile valleys of the San Joaquin and the Sacramento which form practically one vast basin, known as the Great Valley. It is about 400 miles long and is from 50 to 60 miles wide. The small rift or glacial valleys, Yosemite, Kings, and Tuolumne, famous for their magnificent scenery, are on the western slope of the Sierra Nevada range.

In the southeast of the State is a vast low-lying arid area containing the Mohave and Colorado deserts, Death Valley, and Owens Lake. The north of the State is a mountainous region, heavily timbered.

The highest peak in the United States, excluding Alaska, is Mt. Whitney (14,496 feet), in California, and the lowest land area is Death Valley (276 feet below sea level). Much of the southwest has a desertlike surface, and irrigation is indispensable to farming, but the central and northern sections have soil noted for fertility. In some other districts, however, the land has to be irrigated to obtain full crops. Climatic conditions vary. In the north among the mountains the weather is severe, and the rainfall is heavy. West of the Cascade Mountains the climate is cool and damp and fogs prevail, but east of that range in the Great Valley the climate is delightful.

Minerals.—California has long been noted for its yield of gold, and the metal is still extensively mined

The State leads in the production of oranges, hay, peaches, pears, and hops. An immense wheat harvest is reaped in the Great Valley every year. Corn, oats, and rice are raised. The wool clip was 28,901,000 pounds in 1938. Ostrich farming is practiced very successfully in the south. Cotton of good quality is grown in several of the valleys. Barley, the largest of the State's grain crops, is raised principally in the Sacramento and San Joaquin Valleys. Milo maize, Egyptian, and Kaffir corn and feterita are largely grown for stock feed and ensilage. Alfalfa, raised in every county

California having vast water-power resources was the first State to utilize hydroelectric power in manufacturing. Official estimates give 2,448,000 horsepower available.

Fisheries.—Many food fish are caught along the coast. Among them are halibut, tuna, bass, sole, rock cod, and sardine. Salmon is the most valuable of the fishes taken. The total catch of fisheries for California in 1936 amounted to about 1,760,182,500 pounds.

Commerce.—California's chief commercial ports are San Francisco and Los Angeles. Lines of steamers connect those cities with the principal seaports of Asia and Australia as well as with United States centers of commerce on the Atlantic and with several European ports. The coasting trade is also important and many ships, in cases where using the Panama Canal is not advantageous, still make the trip around Cape Horn. The all-rail routes across the continent carry still more of California's products to Eastern markets.

History.—The coast was visited in 1542-43 by the Spanish explorer, Cabrillo; in 1579 by Sir Francis Drake, who named the region New Albion, and in 1602-3 by Sebastian Viscaino. The first settlement by whites was made near the present site of San Diego by a company of Franciscan friars in 1769. Until 1822 the country was under Spanish rule, when at the close of the Mexican Revolution, it declared its allegiance to Mexico. In 1776 members of the same religious order planted a colony on San Francisco Bay. In several parts of the State they established agricultural stations for the benefit of the Indian tribes. A large trade in wool and hides was developed, and immigrants came in large numbers after Mexico shook off the Spanish yoke. Fremont's expedition, which reached northern California in 1845, called attention to this new and rich region, and thousands of Americans emigrated thither. During our war with Mexico, Commodores Stockton and Sloat seized the best harbors, and General Kearney and Colonel Fremont raised the American flag and established military posts in the interior of the county. By the treaty of Guadalupe Hidalgo, executed in 1848, Mexico ceded upper California to the United States. In the same year the discovery of gold in Sutter's millrace resulted in an unexampled rush of fortune-seekers into the territory. The next year a State constitution was adopted, and California was admitted into the Union in 1850.

COLORADO.—Physiography.—The surface presents two general divisions—one, the eastern half of the State, a region of plains broken by low ridges, and the other, or western division, containing foothills and ranges of the Rocky Mountains. Between the Front range and the Park range are three of the State's great "parks." These are basins of former lakes. Although high above sea level, they have a mild climate and are well wooded. Volcanic action raised much of the State, and through this section the rivers cut for themselves deep canyons. Fantastically carved rock pillars, like those in the "Garden of the Gods" near Colorado Springs, attest the power of eroding agencies on the land surface.

In some of the gorges are remains of cliff dwellings, located on edges extremely difficult of access and hewed out of the solid rock.

Rocky Mountain National Park, having an area of 405 square miles, created a park by Congress in 1915, lies in the north central part of the State and is much visited by tourists. Mesa Verde National Park is located in the southwestern corner of Colorado. It is noted for its large numbers of ruins of former community buildings constructed by the cliff dwellers. This park contains 80 square miles and was established by Act of Congress in 1906. The Colorado National Monument and the Wheeler National Monument are noted for their picturesque rock formations.

Minerals.—Colorado is one of the richest of the States in metallic ores. The mountain districts are seamed with gold, silver, zinc, lead, iron, tungsten, and copper. Coal is extensively mined. Petroleum occurs in several counties. There are numerous mineral springs, some of them of proved medicinal value. The mining industry is the most important one in the State. Building stone is abundant, especially granite, marble, sandstone, limestone, and slate. Fluorspar is important and there are immense deposits of oil shale. The mineral production of Colorado for 1936 was estimated at $56,901,366.

Among the rarer mineral products are uranium, ra-

HIGHEST AND LOWEST ALTITUDES IN THE UNITED STATES

(From the United States Geological Survey)

State or Territory	Highest		Lowest	
	Place	Alt. ft.	Place	Alt. ft.
Alabama	Cheaha Mountain	2,407	Gulf of Mexico	Sea level
Alaska	Mount McKinley	20,300	Pacific Ocean	Sea level
Arizona	Humphreys Peak	12,611	Colorado River	100
Arkansas	Blue Mountain	2,800	Ouachita River	55
	Magazine Mountain	2,800		
California	Mount Whitney	14,495	Death Valley	280 (below sea)
Colorado	Mount Elbert	14,431	Arkansas River	3,350
Connecticut	Bear Mountain	2,355	Long Island Sound	Sea level
Delaware	Centerville	440	Atlantic Ocean	Sea level
District of Columbia	Tenleytown	420	Potomac River	Sea level
Florida	Iron Mountain	325	Atlantic Ocean	Sea level
Georgia	Brasstown Bald	4,768	Atlantic Ocean	Sea level
Idaho	Borah Peak	12,655	Snake River	720
Illinois	Charles Mound	1,241	Mississippi River	279
Indiana	Greensfork tp.	1,240	Ohio River	316
Iowa	West Boundary	1,675	Mississippi River	477
Kansas	On west boundary	4,135	Verdigris River	700
Kentucky	Big Black Mountain	4,150	Mississippi River	257
Louisiana	B. M. at Athens (old)	469	New Orleans	5 (below sea)
Maine	Mount Katahdin	5,268	Atlantic Ocean	Sea level
Maryland	Backbone Mountain	3,340	Atlantic Ocean	Sea level
Massachusetts	Mount Greylock	3,505	Atlantic Ocean	Sea level
Michigan	Porcupine Mountains	2,023	Lake Erie	572
Minnesota	Misqua Hills	2,230	Lake Superior	602
Mississippi	Near Iuka	806	Gulf of Mexico	Sea level
Missouri	Taum Sauk Mountain	1,772	St. Francis River	230
Montana	Granite Peak	12,850	Kootenai River	1,800
Nebraska	S. W. part, Banner Co.	5,300	Southeast corner of State	825
Nevada	Boundary Peak, White Mts.	13,145	Colorado River	470
New Hampshire	Mount Washington	6,288	Atlantic Ocean	Sea level
New Jersey	High Point	1,801	Atlantic Ocean	Sea level
New Mexico	North Truchas Peak	13,306	Red Bluff	2,876
New York	Mount Marcy	5,344	Atlantic Ocean	Sea level
North Carolina	Mount Mitchell	6,684	Atlantic Ocean	Sea level
North Dakota	Black Butte	3,468	Pembina	790
Ohio	Campbell Hill	1,550	Ohio River	425
Oklahoma	Black Mesa	4,978	Red River	300
Oregon	Mount Hood	11,253	Pacific Ocean	Sea level
Pennsylvania	Negro Mountain	3,213	Delaware River	Sea level
Rhode Island	Durfee Hill	805	Atlantic Ocean	Sea level
South Carolina	Sassafras Mountain	3,548	Atlantic Ocean	Sea level
South Dakota	Harney Peak	7,242	Big Stone Lake	962
Tennessee	Clingmans Dome	6,643	Mississippi River	182
Texas	Guadalupe Peak	8,751	Gulf of Mexico	Sea level
Utah	Kings Peaks	13,498	Beaverdam Creek	2,000
Vermont	Mount Mansfield	4,393	Lake Champlain	95
Virginia	Mount Rogers	5,719	Atlantic Ocean	Sea level
Washington	Mount Rainier	14,408	Pacific Ocean	Sea level
West Virginia	Spruce Knob	4,860	Potomac River	240
Wisconsin	Rib Hill	1,940	Lake Michigan	581
Wyoming	Gannett Peak	13,785	Belle Fourche River	3,100

there. About 1,049,000 fine ounces were mined in 1936. Copper, lead, silver, and zinc are also found in large quantities. The State is the world's chief supply of mercury. There are valuable deposits of tungsten, platinum, molybdenum, chromite, cadmium, and soda. California has been for some years a leading State in petroleum production. Granite, marble, limestone, soapstone, and fictile clays occur in considerable amounts. Cement rock, natural gas, sulphur, clay products, potash, and borax are important.

Agriculture.—The State is famous for its fruits—oranges, lemons, olives, grapefruits, dates, figs, apples, prunes and other plums, peaches, pears, and grapes. Every kind of fruit grown in temperate and subtropical climes can be grown in California.

Record potato yields have come from irrigated fields intensively cultivated.

of the State, is regarded as the chief field crop. The yield is over 2,500,000 tons yearly. The hay harvest is also heavy, being about 4,595,000 tons in 1938. The truck-crop industry is very large. Refrigeration processes enable millions of pounds of fruits and vegetables to reach Eastern markets in available condition. Tomatoes, lettuce, cantaloupes, and carrots form the most important of these crops. California now ranks second among the States in the production of barley, Minnesota being first.

Manufacturing.—Manufacturing industries include petroleum refining, canning and preserving, meat packing, aircraft and motor vehicle construction. Most of the lumber sawed for the market is redwood, western yellow pine, Douglas fir, sugar pine, and white fir. The State ranks high in the production of beet sugar and is the leading state in the production of wine.

dium, arsenic, barium, bismuth, mercury, molybdenum, platinum, vanadium, yttrium, and zircon. Kaolin, and potter's and brick clays are widely distributed. Colorado is first among the States in yield of radium, tungsten, and molybdenum; second in gold and lead, and fifth in zinc and silver. The value of Colorado's total output of gold, silver, lead, copper, and zinc in 1936 was $19,819,869.

Climate.—The State has a high reputation as a resort for invalids afflicted with lung disease. Its elevation and dry soil give it a delightful climate and freedom from malaria. The rainfall seldom exceeds 20 inches annually. Snowfall is light in most areas.

Agriculture.—Where irrigation is in use, the soil produces heavy crops. Wheat, corn, and oats are grown. Some of Colorado's garden-truck specialties bring the highest prices in Eastern markets. Cattle raising and sheep husbandry are occupations favored by natural conditions on the plains, the grass there being abundant and nutritious. Colorado leads in the production of sugar beets. The plums, apples, peaches, pears, cherries, and grapes grown are of the highest quality; although the amount produced small.

Manufacturing.—The refining of various ores, the making of beet sugar, slaughtering, and meat packing, flour milling, the production of iron and steel and of chemicals form the principal manufacturing industries. Colorado's wealth of raw materials, including coal, insures a steady increase of manufactures.

History.—Remains of Indian pueblos are found in the south. Colorado was probably first visited by Spanish explorers under Coronado in the 16th century, but the first authenticated exploration was made by Francisco Escallante in 1776. The Spaniards, however, made no attempt at colonization. Parts of it have, at times, belonged to the Territories of Kansas, Nebraska, New Mexico, and Utah. The region east of the Rocky Mountains was comprised in the Louisiana Purchase in 1803, after which fortified posts were established and American exploration and settlement began. The first permanently established place was Denver in 1858. A large section south of the Arkansas River was claimed by the Republic of Texas on winning its independence from Mexico. The western part of what is now Colorado was ceded to the United States by Mexico in 1848. Gold discoveries in 1858 brought a large number of adventurers into this region, and since that time the history of the State's development has been largely that of its mines. Most of the eastern half of the State was, under the name of Arapahoe county, included in Kansas Territory in 1858. In 1861 the Territory of Colorado was organized. It became a State in 1876.

CONNECTICUT.––Physiography.—The chief topographical features of Connecticut are the three great river valleys—the Thames, the Connecticut, and the Housatonic—which occupy most of the State. The Berkshire Hills of Massachusetts are continued through the northwestern part of Connecticut, but sink into rolling plains before reaching Long Island Sound. The northeastern part is also hilly. The coast is broken by a number of rocky points. Sandy beaches are common, and the shore is skirted by a succession of small islands.

Most of the valley soil is very fertile. The hill sections are traversed by numerous small streams and comprise much rich pasture land.

Minerals.—Building stone is quarried in several places. Iron mines have been worked at Salisbury since 1732. Other mineral products are feldspar, clay products, lime, slates, cement rock, and flagstone, sand and gravel. Generally speaking, however, Connecticut's mineral products are relatively unimportant.

Agriculture.—Tobacco is the most valuable crop. Hay is next in value. Tobacco is grown chiefly in the Connecticut and Housatonic valleys and is of high grade. Market gardening is a profitable industry. Corn, oats, rye, and potatoes are the principal field crops. In 1938 the yield of corn was 1,764,000 bushels, of potatoes 2,310,000 bushels; the tobacco crop 4,716,000 pounds, and the hay crop 528,000 tons. Apples, peaches and strawberries are the chief fruits produced.

Manufacturing.—Connecticut has long been noted for the variety of its manufactures. It is the leading State in brass and brass goods and builders' hardware. Other important industries are the manufacturing of rubber articles; firearms, cotton, ammunition, woolen, paper, and silk goods; machinery, automobile parts,

typewriters, rayon, clothing, and electrical apparatus. Each city is a manufacturing center.

Commerce.—The State has ample transportation facilities by both rail and water. The Connecticut River is navigable for steamboats as far as Hartford. New Haven, New London, and Bridgeport are centers of an active coast-line commerce. Along the shore there are about 100,000 acres of oyster beds.

History.—The English claimed the region by virtue of Cabot's discoveries in 1497-98. The first settlement was made in 1633 near the present site of Hartford by Dutch colonists from New Amsterdam. Shortly afterward a trader from Plymouth, Mass., established a post near the site of Windsor. Wethersfield was founded in 1634 by emigrants from Massachusetts Bay, and Hartford in 1636 by settlers from the same colony. They leased their claim to the land on the English Crown's patent granted to Lord Say and Sele in 1631. A colony was planted at Saybrook at the mouth of the Connecticut in 1635. A Pequot Indian uprising, which threatened the safety of the Connecticut colonies for a time, was suppressed in 1637. New Haven, an independent Puritan colony, was established in 1638. King Charles II granted in 1662 a charter permitting autonomous government to the Connecticut colonists. Connecticut took a prominent part in the Revolution, and in 1776, was organized as an independent State. For many years it was engaged in boundary disputes, the last of which was not settled until 1881. A constitution was adopted in 1818, the year in which it actually became part of the Union.

DELAWARE.—Physiography.—In the north the surface is hilly, but level elsewhere. Along the Delaware Bay shore much of the land is marshy. Some of it, however, has been reclaimed. In general the soil is a light, sandy loam easily worked and, when fertilized, capable of producing large crops.

Minerals.—Granite, glass sand, pottery clays and building clays, besides mineral waters, are the most valuable of the limited mineral products of the State.

Agriculture.—Fruit growing, especially of peaches and strawberries, is the principal agricultural industry. Apples, pears, tomatoes, and cantaloupes are also grown in large quantities. The State produces much corn and wheat; and market gardening and the raising of early spring vegetables for northern cities receive much attention. In the southern part, along the Delaware Bay shore, there are extensive oyster fisheries. Menhaden also are taken in large numbers.

Manufactures.—Canning and preserving of fruits and vegetables, leather tanning and finishing and the manufacture of synthetic plastics and allied products are prominent industries. Shipbuilding is carried on at Wilmington. Iron and steel goods, cars, gunpowder, machinery, cottons, woolens, flour, and chemicals are the important products.

Commerce.—Wilmington, the chief port, has an active coastwise trade and is connected with New York by steamers. The city has also some foreign commerce.

History.—Delaware Bay was discovered by Hudson in 1609. Two years later it was visited by Lord de la Warr after whom the State was named. In 1623, Mey, a Dutch explorer, built Fort Nassau, and eight years later a Dutch company established a colony on Lewes Creek, which was later destroyed. Some Swedes and Finns established in 1638 on the Delaware River the colony of New Sweden. New Amsterdam's Governor claimed the land along the river and declared war on the Swedes. He captured New Sweden, but it was surrendered to the English when they took New Amsterdam in 1664. In 1681 it became part of the territory granted to William Penn by Charles II. Penn subsequently purchased it from the Duke of York who later became James II, and for twenty years it was governed as part of Pennsylvania. Delaware became a State in 1776 and was the first to adopt the Federal Constitution in 1787.

COURTESY OF THE DENVER AND RIO GRANDE WESTERN R.R.
GATEWAY TO THE GARDEN OF THE GODS WITH PIKE'S PEAK IN THE DISTANCE

DISTRICT OF COLUMBIA.—Physiography.—The District of Columbia, coextensive with the city of Washington, has an area of approximately 70 square miles, about 8 of which are water. The Potomac River is on the southwest; otherwise the District is inclosed by Maryland. The surface is rolling, with low hills.

Agriculture.—The soil of the District of Columbia is loamy and fertile. Market gardening, dairying and floriculture are important in the areas outlying the city proper, and the city of Washington is notable for the number and beauty of its trees.

Manufacturing.—The manufactured products comprise pottery, ice, bricks, planing-mill products, marble, flour, and bottled mineral waters. About 66,000 persons are employed in the United States Government Offices in Washington.

History.—Congress had no permanent meeting-place until 1788, when Maryland gave the United States the present district in which the new nation's capital was to be established. In 1789 Virginia added 30.75 square miles on the southwest side of the Potomac. In 1800 Congress removed from Philadelphia to the new town. This was incorporated in 1802 and called Washington. In 1846 the section of the district southwest of the Potomac was ceded back to Virginia.

For three years, from 1871 to 1874, a territorial government was in operation, and a delegate represented the district in the House of Representatives. In 1878 Congress abolished that system of government. The district is now governed by three commissioners appointed by the President of the United States. Citizens of the district cannot vote in either local or national elections.

FLORIDA.—Physiography.—Most of Florida has a low level surface. Nowhere is it more than 325 feet above sea level. It is curiously diversified with numerous lakes and with swamps, savannahs and hummocks. Various kinds of soil are found. The pine barrens furnish only forest products. A marshy district, called the Everglades, about 150 miles long by 55 miles wide, overgrown with sawgrass, 8 feet to 10 feet high and almost impenetrable, is a feature of southern Florida. This vast swamp is dotted with islands covered with jungle-like growths of vines, evergreens, palmettos and pines. Remnants of the tribe of Seminole Indians inhabit parts of the region. The State of Florida has a vast reclamation scheme to drain the Everglades lands for cultivation.

Numerous rivers, some navigable, flow through extensive marshes before reaching the Gulf or the Atlantic. Okeechobee is the largest lake.

The coast line, which is 3,751 miles long (including islands), is indented by bays, harbors and lagoons.

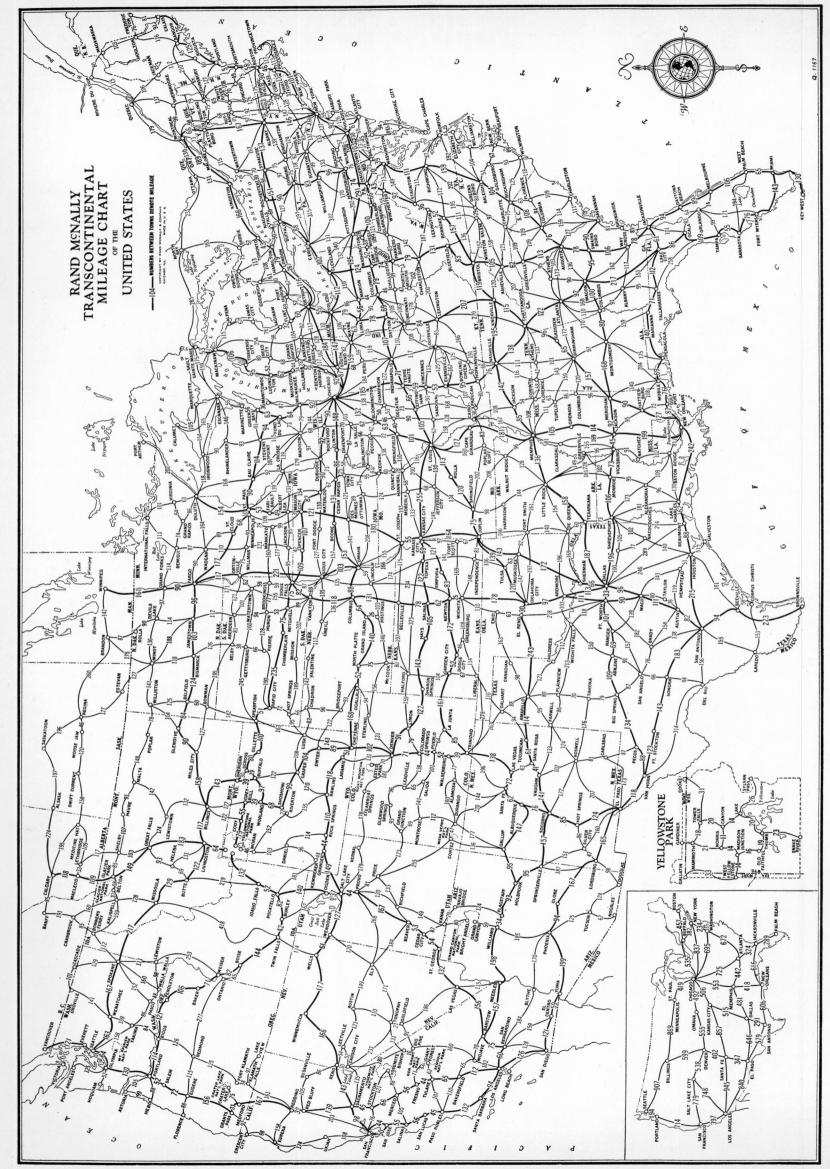

RAND McNALLY
TRANSCONTINENTAL
MILEAGE CHART
OF THE
UNITED STATES

—104— NUMBER BETWEEN TOWNS DENOTE MILEAGE

MAP SHOWING THE AUTOMOBILE ROUTES IN THE UNITED STATES, WITH THE DISTANCES BETWEEN THE CITIES GIVEN IN STATUTE MILES. THE HEAVY LINES INDICATE THE PRINCIPAL HIGHWAYS, WHEREAS THE LIGHT LINES SHOW THE MINOR ROADS. THE SMALL MAP IN THE LEFT CORNER GIVES AT A QUICK GLANCE THE TOTAL MILES BETWEEN THE LARGER CITIES ON THE MAIN ROUTES

YELLOWSTONE PARK

Most of these, however, are barred off from the sea by sandpits or by islands called "keys" (Spanish, *cayo,* an island). Springs are abundant. Many have medicinal value.

There are numerous stretches of seabeach (notably Daytona), wide, hard and level, for miles. Some of them, as Palm Beach, Miami Beach, and Vero Beach, are noted winter resorts. The climate is mild. Even in the summer months the heat never becomes oppressive, although Florida extends farther south than any other State.

Minerals.—Phosphate rock is the most important mineral, the State leading in production among the states with 2,624,900 long tons in 1936. Fuller's earth, shell limestone and coral limestone, clay for pottery and brick making, and coquina, a shell conglomerate used for building purposes, are other minerals of industrial use.

Vegetation.—No other state can rival Florida in the extent and variety of its plant life. Among the rare trees found here are the mahogany, torreya (stinking yew), cachibon, satinwood, cocoanut, manchineel, kino, lignum vitæ, canella, ironwood, and sea grape. Cabbage palms of several species flourish in all parts of the State. Thick growths of mangrove fringe the shores of bays and islands. Abundant supplies of timber are furnished by forests of long-leaf pine, red cedar, hickory, live oak, cypress and other valuable woods.

Agriculture.—Citrus fruits are the most valuable individual crop; corn next. Potatoes, sweet potatoes, and peanuts follow. Market gardening is a highly profitable pursuit, over 15 million dollars' worth of early vegetables being shipped north each year. Citrus fruits (oranges, grape fruit, lemons, limes), figs, pomegranates, guavas, dates, olives and avocado pears are raised. Cotton and hay and tobacco are extensively cultivated. In the south pineapples and bananas grow readily. Cattle and hogs are raised in large numbers for the markets of Cuba and other West India islands.

Manufacturing.—Naval stores are produced in immense quantities. Tar, resin and turpentine are exported to our Atlantic coast cities and also to European ports. The lumber cut amounts to nearly 1,000,000 feet a year. Cigars and cottonseed oil are important manufactures. Tampa and Key West rival Habana in the production of tobacco goods. Key West is the center of the sponge trade, sponge fishing being a lucrative Florida industry.

Fisheries.—The chief products of the long coast-line fisheries are shad, mullet, red snapper and turtles. Pensacola is the most important fresh fish market on the Gulf.

Commerce.—The State's principal exports are fruits, resin, tar, turpentine, and phosphate rock. Immense quantities of tobacco articles are sent into other States. Raw cotton is also an important export. Pensacola, Miami, Key West, Jacksonville and Tampa are the chief ports. From these are shipped cotton, lumber, naval stores, phosphate rock, wheat and tobacco goods.

History.—Juan Ponce de Leon, heading an expedition in search of the fabled Fountain of Youth, discovered Florida in 1513. Because he saw the country on Easter Sunday, he gave it the name of *Florida* (Spanish, *Pascua Florida*). In 1539 Hernando de Soto crossed the region. The French founded the first colony at the mouth of the St. Johns River in 1564. The following year the Spaniards destroyed this colony, however, and founded St. Augustine, the first permanent settlement. In 1586 this city was burned by Sir Francis Drake and great rivalry continued until the Peace of Paris in 1763 took the region from Spain and gave it to England. In 1783 England was compelled to return it to Spain. In 1819 the United States made a treaty with Spain for the cession of Florida. A territorial government was organized in 1822. War with the Seminole Indians lasted from 1835 to 1846. Florida became a State in 1845. It joined the Confederacy, but was readmitted to the Union in 1868.

GEORGIA.—Physiography.—Three great natural divisions, Upper, Middle and Lower Georgia, comprise the surface, which rises from the coast to 5,000 feet in the northwest. Lower Georgia occupies more than half the State. It includes the coast belt, about 20 miles wide, with an average elevation of 12 feet, and contains numerous swamps. The best known is the immense Okefenokee Swamp in the south. Skirting the coast are numerous islands, heavily timbered. Farther inland is the higher pine-barrens region. Middle Georgia is an extensive plateau, broken in the north by

hills. This section has an average elevation of 1,000 feet and extends to the foothills of the Alleghenies. Upper Georgia contains the Blue Ridge Mountains, which terminate here. At the eastern limits of the island plateau the slope is abrupt, and here the eastward flowing rivers are broken by falls. These furnish abundant water power. The mountain valleys are fertile and have an agreeable climate. Most of the State has a loamy soil, very productive.

The climate is varied. In the north the summers are cool and the winter weather is mild. The pine barrens are warmer and are much resorted to in winter by invalids. Snow sometimes falls in the northern and central parts of the State, but does not remain long. The swampy region is malarious.

Minerals.—Coal is mined in the northwest. Marble of high grade is extensively quarried, as well as granite, slate, and gypsum. In several counties the working of deposits of iron ore, gold, bauxite, barytes, mineral paints, manganese, fuller's earth, and asbestos furnish employment to thousands of hands. There are numerous mineral springs, some widely known. Clay products are important, the State leading the United States in production. Cement is also produced.

Agriculture.—Georgia ranks high among the agricultural States. Cotton is grown in the central and southern parts, and is the most important crop. The islands produce the famous "sea-island" variety. Corn is the crop second in value. Live stock forms an important element in the State's wealth. Wheat, oats, sweet potatoes, peanuts, tobacco, fruits and field vegetables are produced. Much hay is harvested. Georgia peaches and melons are well known for their flavor in northern markets. In the production of cane sirup the State is exceeded only by Louisiana. Market gardening has of late years become an important industry.

Forests occupy large areas and yield annually about half a billion feet of lumber. Live oak and yellow pine are the principal trees. There are also valuable species of ash, cedar, cypress, hickory and other timber trees.

Manufactures.—Manufacturing is favored by the readiness with which water power is obtained and by the abundance of raw materials. Georgia is the leading State in the production of naval stores. Among the principal manufactures are cotton goods, lumber, flour, woolen goods, furniture, farm implements and cottonseed oil. The output of tobacco goods is large. There are numerous tanneries, machine shops and flour mills. The clay-working industries are important, brick, tiles and pottery being produced to the value of about $2,000,000 yearly.

Commerce.—There are ample transportation facilities by both sea and land. Savannah, the chief port, has eight miles of river frontage and is accessible to steamers of large tonnage. The principal exports are raw cotton, cottonseed products, sugar, rosin, naval stores and lumber.

History.—The State was named after George II, King of England. De Soto, a Spaniard, explored the interior in 1540; and Ribault, a Frenchman, visited the coast in 1562. A greater part of the region was included in the Carolina grants of 1663 and 1665. The first white settlement was made in 1733 at Savannah by James Oglethorpe of England and his associates, as a refuge for poor debtors and other distressed persons. Within a few years large numbers of Methodists, then persecuted in the British Isles, emigrated to Georgia. In 1752 the colony became a royal province. Georgia sided with her sister colonies at the outbreak of the Revolutionary War. In 1777 the first State Constitution was adopted, and in 1788 it became part of the Union. Up to 1798 Georgia was bounded on the west by the Mississippi River, but in that year the Mississippi Territory was organized. By the removal of the last remnants of the hostile Cherokee Indian tribes to Indian Territory in 1838, the rapid and peaceful progress of the State was insured. In 1861 Georgia seceded from the Union. Readmission was effected in 1870.

IDAHO.—Physiography.—Vast lava sheets have built up much of the surface, which rises from 720 feet in the west to 12,655 feet at Mt. Borah, Custer County. These reach their highest altitudes in the east. Most of the State drains into the Pacific through the Snake River. Plains and valleys of fertile land are interspersed among the many small ranges which are found in the State. There are many dense forests of white and lodge-pole pines. Forests of the larger

trees, such as red cedar, spruce and fir abound, but hardwood timber is scarce.

Minerals.—Idaho has great mineral wealth. Lead and silver are the most important metals, and are produced in enormous quantities. Zinc, gold, and copper are also extensively mined. Deposits of coal, iron, nickel, cobalt, mica, tungsten, salt and phosphate rock are worked. Building stones, including granite, sandstone and limestone, are quarried. The value of gold, silver, copper, lead, and zinc mined in 1936, was about $26,981,000.

Agriculture.—Nearly all farm products of the Temperate Zone can be grown, the soil being exceedingly fertile. Farms are rapidly increasing in number. Hay, wheat, barley, oats, and corn are standard crops. Vegetables and fruits of the highest grade are produced abundantly. Idaho is one of the important States in wool production, the clip in 1938 being 17,463,000 pounds. Dry farming is successfully practiced. There are large areas of rich land that need only irrigation to repay the agriculturist manyfold. It is estimated that about 10,000,000 acres can be turned by irrigation into fruitful farm lands. Abundant water can be obtained from the State's rivers. Stock raising is a highly profitable industry, and much capital is invested in it. Cattle, horses, hogs, and sheep feed the year around on the nutritious natural grasses. In the fall these grasses dry into self-cured hay, and but little else is needed to carry the live stock through the winter. The State contains about 19,000,000 acres of National Forest.

Manufactures.—There is immense water power for manufacturing purposes. Lumber and other timber products are at present the chief manufactures. Over one hundred tons of beet sugar are made annually. Dairying and flour and grist milling are important industries. Manufacturing to supply local needs is increasing with the extension of transportation facilities and the rapid advance in population.

Commerce.—Idaho has 2,880 miles of railroad and about 36 miles of track for electric cars. Trunk lines crossing the State are the Northern Pacific, the Great Northern, the Chicago, Milwaukee, St. Paul and Pacific, and the Union Pacific. The opening of the Celilo Canal on the Oregon side of the Columbia River enables vessels to pass from Lewiston to the Pacific Ocean, a distance of 480 miles.

History.—Lewis and Clark were the first white men to visit the territory, in 1805-06. The first permanent settlement was made at Fort Hall. The Oregon country, of which Idaho originally formed a part, was claimed by the United States, Great Britain, Spain, and Russia. At the time of the Florida Purchase in 1819, Spain transferred her rights to the United States. Russia did likewise in 1824. In 1818 a treaty had been concluded between the United States and England, under which they were to occupy the Oregon region jointly. In 1846 this joint occupation was terminated by the establishment of the International Boundary at approximately 49° N. In March, 1863, Idaho Territory was organized from parts of the Territories of Washington, Dakota, and Nebraska. It included the area now comprising Idaho, Montana, and part of Wyoming. The organization of Montana and Wyoming as territories, in 1864 and 1868 respectively, left Idaho with its present boundaries. On July 3, 1890, Idaho was admitted into the Union.

ILLINOIS.—Physiography.—Most of the surface is nearly level, with a slight declination toward the south, varied by bluffs along the principal rivers and by low grassy hills. From the site of Cairo, at the confluence of the Ohio and Mississippi Rivers, 279 feet above sea level, to the northwest corner of the State the surface rises to a mean altitude of about 850 feet. The highest point is Charles Mound in Jo Daviess County, 1,241 feet. In the central portion of the State lies the Great Prairie, 200 miles in length. Illinois is noted for its soil—a rich, deep loam, unexcelled for the growing of cereals. In the south is the well-known "Egypt" district, a low plateau of remarkable fertility. The river bottom lands are unsurpassed anywhere for farming purposes. The Mississippi River, the Illinois, the Rock, the Fox, the Kankakee, and the Des Plaines are the principal streams. From the immense prairies, or natural meadows, occupying most of its surface, Illinois derives a great portion of its wealth.

Minerals.—Illinois ranks seventh among the States in mineral output. Bituminous coal forms the chief prod-

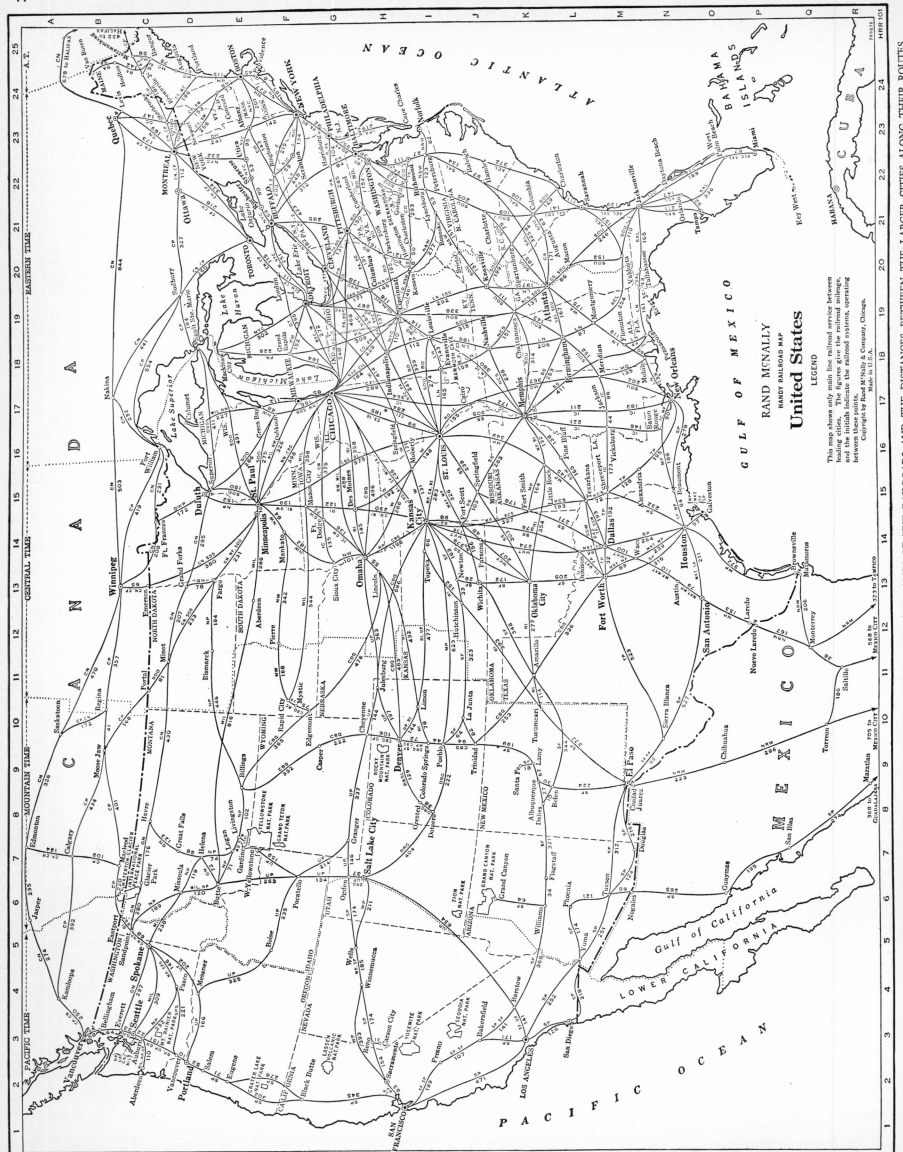

RAND McNALLY
HANDY RAILROAD MAP

United States

LEGEND

This map shows only main line railroad service between leading cities. The figures give the railroad mileage, and the initials indicate the railroad systems, operating between these points.

Copyright by Rand McNally & Company, Chicago.
Made in U.S.A.

THE ABOVE MAP SHOWS THE PRINCIPAL RAILROAD SYSTEMS OF THE UNITED STATES, WITH THE NAMES OF THE RAILROADS AND THE DISTANCES BETWEEN THE LARGER CITIES ALONG THEIR ROUTES. IT IS INTERESTING TO NOTE THE FEW RAILROAD LINES IN THE WEST COMPARED WITH THE LARGE NUMBER OF LINES EAST OF THE MISSISSIPPI

Principal Railroads of the United States

A List that Includes the Largest and Most Important of the Railroad Systems in the United States

Showing Routes of the Main Lines and the Chief Branches

Alaska Railroad
Seward, Alaska, to Fairbanks, and Chatanika, and other branches.

Alton (The)
(*Baltimore & Ohio*)
Chicago, Ill., to St. Louis, Mo.
Bloomington, Ill., via Roodhouse, to Kansas City, Mo., and branches.

Atchison, Topeka & Santa Fe
(*Santa Fe Route*)
Chicago, Ill., via Kansas City, Mo., Topeka, Kan., La Junta, Colo., to Albuquerque, N. M., and to San Francisco, Calif., via coast lines.
Albuquerque, N. M., to El Paso, Tex.
Clinton, Okla., to Pampa, Tex.
Wichita, Kan., to Altus, Okla., and branches.

Atlantic Coast Line
Richmond, Va., via Fayetteville, N. C., Charleston, S. C., Savannah, Ga., Jacksonville, Fla., Haines City, Fla., to Port Tampa, Fla., and Punta Gorda, and Everglades, Fla.

Baltimore & Ohio
Chicago, Ill., via Auburn Junction, Ind., Akron, Ohio, Pittsburgh, Pa., Harpers Ferry, W. Va., Washington, D. C., to Baltimore, Md., Philadelphia, Pa., and to New York, N. Y.
Pittsburgh, Pa., via Wheeling, W. Va., and Columbus, Ohio, to Benwood, W. Va.
Cincinnati, Ohio, via Dayton to Toledo, Ohio.
Buffalo, N. Y., to Pittsburgh, Pa.
Rochester, N. Y., to Ashford and branches.
Cincinnati, Ohio, to Springfield, Ill.

Bangor & Aroostook
Searsport, Me., via Oakfield and Ft. Kent to St. Francis.
South Lagrange, Me., via Derby to Greenville.
Ft. Kent, Me., via Van Buren and Stockholm to Squa Pan and Oakfield, also other branches.

Boston & Albany
(*New York Central*)
Boston, Mass., to Albany, N. Y., with branches.

Boston & Maine
Boston, Mass., via Portsmouth, N. H., to Portland, Me.
Boston, Mass., via Lawrence to Portland, Me.
Worcester, Mass., via Rochester, N. H., to Portland, Me.
Boston, Mass., via Concord, N. H., to Wells River, Vt., and other branches.
Springfield, Mass., via Brattleboro, Vt., to Windsor, Vt.
Boston, Mass., to Rotterdam Junction, N. Y.

Canadian National
Halifax, N. S., via Montreal, Que., Ottawa, Ont., and Winnipeg, Man., to Vancouver, B. C.

Canadian Pacific
Montreal, Que., via Ottawa, Ont., Winnipeg, Man., Moose Jaw, Sask., Calgary, Alta, to Vancouver, B. C.

Central of Georgia
Savannah, Ga., to Atlanta.
Griffin, Ga., to Chattanooga, Tenn.
Macon, Ga., to Lockhart, Ala.
Fort Valley, Ga., via Columbus to Birmingham, Ala., and branches.

Central Railroad of New Jersey
New York, N. Y., via Jersey City, N. J., Elizabethport and Bound Brook, to Scranton, Pa.
Highland Beach, N. J., via Branchport, to Bay Side, and other branches.

Central Vermont, Inc.
(*Canadian National*)
St. Johns, Que., via St. Albans, Vt., Palmer, Mass., to New London, Conn.
Fonda, Vt., to Rouses Point, N. Y., and branches.

Chesapeake & Ohio
Washington, D. C., via Gordonsville, Va., Charleston, W. Va., Ashland, Ky., Cincinnati, Ohio, and Muncie, Ind., to Chicago, Ill.
Toledo, Ohio, to Pomeroy, with branches.
Meadow Creek, W. Va., via Nallen to Swiss, and branches.
Louisville, Ky., via Ashland, to Elkhorn City, Ky., with branches.
Old Point Comfort, Va., via Richmond to Gordonsville, and Clifton Forge, Va.

Chicago, Burlington & Quincy
Chicago, Ill., via Council Bluffs, Iowa, and Omaha, Neb., to Denver, Colo.
Minneapolis, Minn., via Savanna, Ill., and Galesburg, to East St. Louis, Ill., and Palmyra, Neb.
St. Louis, Mo., via Kansas City, Mo., to Omaha, Neb.
Denver, Colo., via St. Joseph, Mo., to St. Louis, Mo., and other branches.

Chicago Great Western
Chicago, Ill., via Oelwein, Iowa, to Minneapolis, Minn., and St. Paul, Minn.
Oelwein, Iowa, via St. Joseph, Mo., to Kansas City, Kan.
Oelwein, Iowa, to Council Bluffs, Iowa, and Omaha, Neb., and other branches.

Chicago, Milwaukee, St. Paul & Pacific
Chicago, Ill., via Milwaukee, Wis., to Green, Mich.
Chicago, Ill., via Council Bluffs, Iowa, to Omaha, Neb.
Milwaukee, Wis., to Wessington Springs, S. D., and Milwaukee, Wis., via Waukesha, Wis., and Mason City, Iowa, to Rapid City, S. D.
Minneapolis, Minn., via Aberdeen, S. D., Miles City, Mont., to Seattle, Wash.
Chicago, Ill., to Westport, Ind., and other branches.

Chicago, Rock Island & Pacific
Chicago, Ill., via Council Bluffs, Iowa, Lincoln, Neb., Belleville, Kan., to Colorado Springs, Colo.
Vinton, Iowa, via Dows, Iowa, and Ellsworth, Minn., to Watertown, S. D.
Davenport, Iowa, via St. Joseph, Mo., and Topeka, Kans., to Santa Rosa, N. Mex.
Burlington, Iowa, to Minneapolis, Minn.
St. Louis, Mo., via Kansas City, Mo., and Topeka, Kans., to Belleville, Kans.
Memphis, Tenn., via Little Rock, Ark., to Texola, Okla.

Chicago & North Western
Chicago, Ill., via Belle Plaine, Iowa, and Omaha, Neb., to Lander, Wyo.
Chicago, Ill., via Milwaukee, Wis., and Fond du Lac, Wis., to Hurley, Wis.
Chicago, Ill., via Madison, Wis., and Rochester, Minn., to Blunt, S. D.
Spring Valley, Ill., via Belvidere, Ill., and Fond du Lac, Wis., to Michigamme, Mich.
Tracy, Minn., via Pierre, S. D., to Rapid City and other branches.

Cleveland, Cincinnati, Chicago & St. Louis
(*Big Four Route*) (*New York Central*)
Chicago, Ill., via Indianapolis, Ind., to Cincinnati, Ohio.
St. Louis, Mo., via Paris, Ill., Indianapolis, Ind., to Cleveland, Ohio.
Peoria, Ill., via Indianapolis, Ind., to Springfield, Ohio.
Louisville, Ky., via North Vernon, Ind., to Benton Harbor, Mich.
Cincinnati, Ohio, to Sandusky, and other branches.

Delaware, Lackawanna & Western
Buffalo, N. Y., via Scranton, Pa., and Hoboken, N. J., to New York, N. Y., with branches.

Delaware & Hudson
Albany, N. Y., to Rouses Point, Binghamton, and Wilkes-Barre, Pa., also other branches.

Denver & Rio Grande Western
Denver, Colo., via Pueblo to Trinidad, and Grand Junction, Colo., Salt Lake City, Utah, and Ogden, Utah, also other branches.

Erie
New York, N. Y., and Jersey City, N. J., via Jamestown, N. Y., to Chicago, Ill.
Cincinnati, O., via Marion, O., and Leavittsburg, O., to Cleveland, O., and Buffalo, N. Y.

Grand Trunk Railway (in United States)
(*Canadian National*)
Portland, Me., to Norton Mills, Vt., with branches.
Chicago, Ill., via South Bend, Ind., to Port Huron, Mich.

Great Northern
St. Paul, Minn., via Fargo, N. D., Glasgow, Mont., Bonners Ferry, Idaho and Spokane, Wash., to Seattle, Wash., and Vancouver, B. C.
Duluth, Minn., via Grand Forks, N. D., to Surrey, N. D.
Seattle, Wash., to Portland, Ore.
Spokane, Wash., via Curlew, to beyond Brookmere, B. C., and other branches.

Illinois Central
Chicago, Ill., via Cairo, Ill., Memphis, Tenn., and Jackson, Miss., to New Orleans, La.
Chicago, Ill., to Omaha, Neb.
Centralia, Ill., via Clinton, Iowa, to Madison, Wis.
Peoria, Ill., via Evansville, Ind., to Hopkinsville, Ky.
Louisville, Ky., via Paducah, Ky., Fulton, Ky., and Jackson, Tenn., to Birmingham, Ala.

Kansas City Southern
Kansas City, Mo., via Pittsburg, Kan., Joplin, Mo., Spiro, Okla., to Shreveport, La., with branches.

Lehigh Valley
Buffalo, N. Y., via Pittston, Pa., to Jersey City, N. J.
Sayre, Pa., to Fair Haven, N. Y., and other branches.

Louisville & Nashville
Cincinnati, Ohio, via Louisville, Ky., Nashville, Tenn., and Birmingham, Ala., to New Orleans, La., and branches.
Cincinnati, Ohio, via Livingston, Ky., and Knoxville, Tenn., to Atlanta, Ga.
Maysville, Ky., via Frankfort, Ky., Louisville, Ky., and Evansville, Ind., to St. Louis, Mo.

Maine Central
St. Johnsbury, Vt., to Portland, Me., to Eastport, Me., and various branches.

Michigan Central
(*New York Central*)
Chicago, Ill., via Hammond, Ind., Detroit, Mich., and St. Thomas, Ont., to Buffalo, N. Y.
Detroit, Mich., to Mackinaw City, Mich., and other branches.

Missouri-Kansas-Texas
St. Louis, Mo., via Parsons, Kan., and McAlester, Okla., to Denison, Texas.
Kansas City, Kan., via Paola, Kan., and Parsons, Kan., to Oklahoma City, Okla., and Junction City, Kan.
Devol to Forgan, Okla., and other branches.

Missouri Pacific
St. Louis, Mo., via Kansas City and Atchison, Kan., to Omaha, Neb., with branches.
Kansas City, Mo., to Pueblo, Colo.
St. Louis, Mo., via Thebes, Ill., to Cairo, Ill., and other branches.

Mobile & Ohio
St. Louis, Mo., via Cairo, Ill., Jackson, Tenn., and Meridian, Miss., to Mobile, Ala.
Starkville, Miss., to Montgo. ery, Ala.
Corinth, Miss., to Birmingham, Ala. (trackage), and other branches.

Nashville, Chattanooga & St. Louis
Atlanta, Ga., via Chattanooga and Nashville, Tenn., to Memphis, Tenn., with branches.

Newfoundland
St. Johns, N. F., to Port-aux-Basques.

New York Central
New York City, N. Y., via Buffalo and Cleveland, Ohio, to Chicago, Ill.
New York, N. Y., via Albany and Rochester to Niagara Falls.
Utica, N. Y., to Montreal, Que.
Chicago, Ill., via Indiana Harbor, Ind., to Danville, Ill.
Toledo, Ohio, to Detroit, Mich.
Toledo, Ohio, to Nallen, W. Va. (freight), and other branches.

New York, New Haven & Hartford
New York, N. Y., via New Haven, Conn., and Providence, R. I., to Boston, Mass.
New Haven, Conn., via Willimantic, Conn., to Boston, Mass.
Danbury, Conn., via Hartford, to Providence, R. I.
Boston, Mass., to Provincetown.
New London, Conn., to Worcester, Mass., and other branches.

New York, Ontario & Western
New York, N. Y., via Weehawken, N. J., to Oswego, N. Y.
Kingston, N. Y., via Summitville, to Port Jervis and Monticello, N. Y.
Randallsville, N. Y., to Utica, and Rome, N. Y.
Cadosia, N. Y., to Scranton, Pa., and other branches.

Norfolk Southern
Norfolk, Va., via Raleigh, N. C., to Charlotte, N. C., and branches.
Norfolk, Va., to Cape Henry, and Virginia Beach, Va. (Electric Div.).

Norfolk and Western
Norfolk, Va., via Roanoke, Va., Bluefield, W. Va., and Portsmouth, Ohio, to Cincinnati.
Hagerstown, Md., via Roanoke, Va., to Winston-Salem, N. C., also branches.

Northern Pacific
St. Paul, Minn., via Bismarck, N. D., Butte, Mont., and Spokane, Wash., to Portland, Ore.
Wadena, Minn., via Oakes to Leeds, N. D.
Manitoba Junction, Minn., to Winnipeg, Man.
Duluth, Minn., to Ashland, Wis., and other branches.

Pennsylvania
Philadelphia, Pa., to Pittsburgh.
Philadelphia, Pa., to New York, N. Y.
Pittsburgh, Pa., to Buffalo, N. Y.
Philadelphia, Pa., via Baltimore, Md., to Washington, D. C.
Camden, N. J., to Atlantic City.
Pittsburgh, Pa., via Mansfield, Ohio, and Fort Wayne, Ind., to Chicago, Ill.
Pittsburgh, Pa., via Columbus, Ohio, and Logansport, Ind., to Chicago, Ill.
Cincinnati, Ohio, via Columbus, to Sandusky.
Cincinnati, Ohio, to Logansport, Ind.
St. Louis, Mo., to Indianapolis, Ind.
Indianapolis, Ind., to Vincennes, and other branches.

Pere Marquette
Chicago, Ill., via Grand Rapids and Detroit, Mich., St. Thomas, Ont., to Buffalo, N. Y.
Bay City, Mich., to Toledo, Ohio.
Ludington, Mich., to Erieau, Ont., and other branches.

Reading Company
Philadelphia, Pa., via Reading, Pa., to Harrisburg, Allentown, and Newberry Junction, Pa.
Philadelphia, Pa., to Bound Brook, N. J., with trackage to New York, N. Y.
Port Clinton, Pa., via Auburn to Harrisburg, and Lykens, Pa., and other branches.
Wilmington, Del., via Reading, Pa., to Columbia and Slatington, Pa., and other branches.

Saint Louis-San Francisco
St. Louis, Mo., via Fort Smith, Ark., to Paris, Tex.
Kansas City, Mo., via Memphis, Tenn., to Birmingham, Ala.
Sapulpa, Okla., to Denison, Tex., and other branches.

Saint Louis Southwestern
St. Louis, Mo., via Texarkana, Ark.-Tex., to Fort Worth, Tex., and branches.
Caruthersville, Mo., via Hornersville, Mo., to Leachville and Caraway, Ark., and Trumann.

Seaboard Air Line
Portsmouth, Va., via Raleigh, N. C., Columbia, S. C., Savannah, Ga., to Jacksonville, Fla.
Montgomery, Ala., to Savannah, Ga.
Savannah, Ga., to Charleston, S. C., with other branches.

Southern
Washington, D. C., via Lynchburg, Va., Greensboro, N. C., Atlanta, Ga., and Birmingham, Ala., to Columbus, Miss.
Chattanooga, Tenn., to Brunswick, Ga.
Rome, Ga., to Mobile, Ala.
Memphis, Tenn., to Bristol, via Tuscumbia, Ala.
Knoxville, Tenn., to Middlesboro, Ky.
St. Louis, Mo., to Lexington, Ky.

Southern Pacific
Portland, Ore., via Sacramento, Calif., and Willow, Calif., to El Paso, Tex.
San Francisco, Calif., to Ogden, Utah.
El Paso, Tex., to Tucumcari, to Dawson, N. M.

Union Pacific
Kansas City, Mo., to Denver, Colo.
Council Bluffs, Iowa, via Cheyenne, Wyo., to Ogden, Utah, and Butte, Mont.
O'Fallon, Neb., to Torrington, Wyo.
Salt Lake City, Utah, to Los Angeles.
Cheyenne, Wyo., to Denver, Colo., also other branches.

Wabash
Chicago, Ill., via Detroit, Mich., and Windsor, Ont., to Buffalo, N. Y.
Toledo, Ohio, via Logansport, Ind., and Springfield, Ill., to Kansas City, Mo.
Toledo, Ohio, via Montpelier, to New Haven, Ind.
Moberly, Mo., via St. Louis, to Decatur, Ill.
Des Moines, Ia., to Moberly, Mo.
Brunswick, Mo., to Omaha, Neb., and other branches.

Western Pacific
Salt Lake City, Utah, via Elko, Nev., to San Francisco, Calif., and branches.

uct, a large part of the State being underlain with beds of soft coal, which is readily mined. Cement rock, sandstone, limestone, fluorspar, and freestone are quarried in large amounts. Illinois is also a producer of petroleum. Natural gas was discovered in several counties. Some lead is produced, but the lead and zinc mines in northwestern Illinois have not been worked for several years. There are large deposits of iron ores, but these must be mixed with higher grade ores from other States in order to be used in pig-iron production. Brick and pottery clays abound.

Agriculture.—Illinois is one of the chief states in agricultural production. The fertile soil of its immense prairie region is easily cultivated. Corn, hay, oats, and wheat are the principal crops. Broom corn, barley, rye, sorghum, buckwheat, and sweet potatoes are also raised. Dairying is an important industry. Live stock raising for the market contributes largely to the State's wealth. In the number of hogs and horses Illinois ranks high among the States. Sheep raising is an important industry, and there is a large production of mutton and wool. The wool clip was 5,553,000 pounds in 1938. Fruits form a strong factor in the State's agricultural wealth. Total acreage was 18,980,400 in 1938, and the cash income from principal farm crops was $178,471,000.

Manufactures.—This State holds a high place in manufacturing, the leading articles including iron and steel, foundry and machine shop products, woodenware, farm implements and machines, watches and clocks, soap, leather, distilled liquors, clothing, motor vehicles and tank cars. In 1937 the output of manufacturing establishments totaled $5,304,282,629. Slaughtering and meat packing is the most valuable industry.

Fisheries.—Lake Michigan and the rivers supply large quantities of valuable food fish. Whitefish, carp and Buffalo fish form the most important items of the catch.

Commerce.—The State is gridironed with railroads. Fleets of steamers ply between Chicago and all the other prominent ports on the Great Lakes. These vessels usually carry cargoes of raw material, as grain, lumber and iron ore. There is also direct water communication between Chicago and ports on the Atlantic. Steamers now pass through the Welland Canal to the St. Lawrence River and thence down to the ocean.

History.—The French explorer, Joliet, visited this region in 1673, when descending the Mississippi. In 1675 the French Jesuit, Father Marquette, established a mission among the Kaskaskia Indians. La Salle, a French trader, coming from Canada, built Fort Crevecoeur on the Illinois River, and was followed in a few years by other French traders, who founded Kaskaskia, the first permanent settlement by whites in the Mississippi Valley, in 1720; other settlements were made at Cahokia and Fort Chartres about the same time. In 1763, at the close of the French and Indian War, when Canada was ceded by France to England, the Illinois region was included in the transfer. It again formed part of the territory ceded by England to the United States in the treaty of 1783. The Northwest Territory, organized in 1787, comprised what is now Illinois, and this district also was made part of the Indiana Territory, formed in 1800. But in 1809 the Territory of Illinois was created. It extended north to Canada. In 1818 the Territory was admitted to statehood. The fertility of the region, and the ease with which the soil could be cultivated, attracted thousands of immigrants. The Mormons, who attempted to make a permanent settlement at Nauvoo, were driven out of the State in 1848. Chicago, which rose rapidly from a mere frontier settlement to be a great emporium of commerce, suffered severely by the great fire of 1871, but was rapidly rebuilt. The Columbian Exposition, or World's Fair was held there in 1893, and the Century of Progress in 1933 and 1934. The city has had a remarkably rapid growth.

INDIANA.—Physiography.—Near the rivers the surface is hilly, but elsewhere it is level or undulating prairie, sloping toward the southwest. In the northwest there is a long, large sandy tract, interspersed with marshes. Considerable beds of peat are found here. Small lakes are numerous in the northeast. The Lake Michigan shore line, about 50 miles long, is bordered by sand dunes. An extensive area in the State is forested. Oak, ash, hickory, maple and other hardwoods are common. The soil is fertile, especially in the river bottoms. The principal rivers, besides the

Ohio River, which forms the southern boundary, are the Wabash and the White. Lesser streams are the Whitewater, the St. Joseph and the Kankakee.

Minerals.—Limestone and sandstone, both of high grade, fictile and fire-brick clays and kaolin are abundant. The cement-rock beds are very extensive. The coal fields underlie about 20% of the State's area and yield about 20,000,000 tons annually. Indiana's block coal is especially well adapted to the manufacture of iron and steel. For some years the natural gas yield was larger than that in any other State, but it has been decreasing in later years. Petroleum is found in various parts of the State. There are several medicinal springs, the most noted, perhaps, being the French Lick Mineral Springs.

THE BOARD OF TRADE BUILDING, CHICAGO, ILLINOIS

Agriculture.—Most of the State's area is cultivated. Indiana is one of the leading States in grain production and stock raising. Corn, hay, wheat, and oats are the most valuable crops. Rye, barley, potatoes and tobacco are also extensively raised. Maple sugar and sirup, butter, sweet potatoes, honey and beeswax are other valuable products. Immense quantities of fruits and vegetables, especially tomatoes, are grown. Live stock —cattle, hogs, sheep, and horses—contribute largely to the State's wealth. The cash income from principal crops in 1938 was $65,486,000. The poultry industry also is important. The wool clip was 4,900,000 pounds in 1938.

Manufacturing.—The chief manufactures are products of steel works, rolling mills and petroleum refineries. The canning of fruits and vegetables, especially of tomatoes, employs thousands of hands. Meat packing has long been a leading industry. Native timber trees furnish material for lumbering and wood-working. Glass, cement, electrical machinery, agricultural implements, coke-oven products, furniture and leather goods are manufactured. The iron and steel industry has assumed vast proportions in recent years, the city of Gary, a lake port, founded in 1906, now being the largest center of steel and pig-iron production in the

United States. Indiana ranks high in the production of automobiles, this manufacturing interest having rapidly risen to a position of great importance. The value of manufactured products in 1937 was $2,497,547,946.

Commerce.—Transportation facilities are ample, several trunk railroads crossing the State and having branches extending in all directions. Lake Michigan and the Ohio and Wabash Rivers afford extensive facilities for water communication, while land traffic is provided for by 7,052 miles of steam railroads and 789 miles of electric lines. Several important railroads running east and west pass through Indiana. The mileage of good highways is greater than in any other State.

History.—A Frenchman, the Sieur de la Salle, was probably the first white man to visit what is now Indiana. He crossed the northwestern corner of the State in 1670. French traders established in 1731 a settlement at Vincennes. After the French and Indian War, by the Treaty of Paris, concluded in 1763, the region was surrendered to Great Britain by France. During the Revolutionary War, George Rogers Clark, commanding a force of American troops, marched from Virginia to Vincennes, captured the latter place and brought under American rule the Wabash country, as it was then called. In 1783 all the territory east of the Mississippi River and north of Florida was ceded by England to the United States. The first American settlement was made at Clarksville in 1784. The Northwest Territory, organized in 1787, comprised a vast area, which included all the United States territory north of the Ohio River. Indiana Territory was organized in 1800. In 1805, Michigan Territory was cut off and Illinois Territory in 1809. A war with several Indian tribes broke out in 1811, but they were crushed by General Harrison in the decisive battle of Tippecanoe, near the present village of Battle Ground. In 1816, Indiana was admitted as a State into the Union. A strong tide of emigration set into this new and fertile region. After the close of our second war with England (1812-15), settlements multiplied rapidly, and agriculture, manufacturing and commerce developed. Natural gas, discovered in various parts of the State in the last quarter of the 19th century, provided an ideal fuel at low cost and gave a great impetus to manufacturing industries.

IOWA.—Physiography.—Iowa is a prairie State with undulating surface, sloping gently to the southeast. The highest part is the northwest. Bluffs border most of the rivers, and in the northern section there are many hills which are topped with groves of oak and hazel. There are small forests located here and there along the banks of the numerous tributaries of the two great rivers, the Mississippi and the Missouri, between which the central part of the State forms a watershed. Elm, cottonwood, hickory, oak and hazel are the most common trees.

In some districts the surface has been eroded by torrents, giving the land a broken appearance. But there is not much waste land, most of the soil being a deep loam, very fertile, especially in the river valleys. Wild grasses furnish pasturage. Even in the northern part, where the land is not so rich, it can be cultivated with profit. Several of the rivers have falls capable of generating immense hydro-electric power. The climate is healthful, although extremes of heat and cold are not unknown. The annual rainfall averages 32.2 inches and is well distributed throughout the growing season.

Minerals.—Beds of bituminous coal underlie about one-third of the State, and are of great value to the manufacturing interests. Gypsum, lime, cement rock, sandstone, limestone and clay for brick making and pottery are abundant. Lead occurs in the galena limestone.

Agriculture.—Iowa is one of the foremost States in all field crops. Corn is the leading crop; oats and hay follow in value; wheat, potatoes, and barley are extensively cultivated. Iowa is first among the States in the production of corn (1938). Native grasses furnish much cheap hay, over $4,000,000 worth being cured annually. Rye, buckwheat, sorghum, and flaxseed are other important crops. In cash income from all crops grown in 1938, Iowa ranked seventh. Much butter, cheese, and condensed milk is sent to Eastern markets. In the value of live stock, Iowa ranks first among the States, Illinois being second. In 1938 wool clip yielded 9,701,000 pounds. Vast numbers of hogs are raised for food

purposes. The State is also first in poultry and in egg production. Fruits and vegetables are shipped in immense quantities to Chicago and other centers of trade.
Manufacturing.—Meat packing is the foremost industry. The value of the output of pottery and brick increases yearly. In recent years manufactures have developed rapidly; especially in prepared cereals, corn sirup, woodenware, woolen goods, and farm implements. In dairy products the State also ranks high.
Commerce.—The State is covered with a network of railroads, affording ample shipping facilities. The total railroad mileage is 9,474. Water transportation is furnished by the Missouri, Mississippi and Des Moines Rivers, and there is an active traffic on these streams throughout the year.
History.—The French trader, Joliet, and the famous Jesuit missionary, Father Marquette, were the first white men to visit this region, coming in 1673. Hennepin was the next visitor in 1680. A trading post was established near the present site of Dubuque by French fur traders in 1788, who also worked a lead mine near by. France, in 1682, claimed Iowa as part of the Mississippi Valley. In 1762 it was ceded to Spain, retroceded to France in 1800, and, as part of the Louisiana Purchase, came under the American flag in 1803. It belonged in turn to Louisiana, Missouri, Michigan and Wisconsin Territories. In 1838 Wisconsin Territory was divided; the western part was organized as Iowa Territory, and from it was carved the present State. Admission into the Union took place in 1846, and up to the depression of 1929, Iowa enjoyed uninterrupted prosperity through the rapid development of the State's great natural resources.

KANSAS.—Physiography.—Most of the surface of the State is undulating prairie, sloping to the south and east; it is highest in the northwest (4,135 feet above sea level). A belt of sandhills crosses the State in the southwest. The Flint and Cypress Ranges are low hills in the south. There are no mountains and few lakes, and these are small and shallow. The marshes are also few and are salt and of considerable value. The soil of the river valleys and table lands is a rich loam. In the western part the land is sandy and has been given up to stock raising; but irrigation is now making this section productive. Most streams are fringed with trees, the more common species being cottonwoods, elms, oaks, willows, hickories, sycamores, locusts and box elders. In the western half of the State there is but very little timber. Judicious forestry has, however, increased the area of woodland.

The winters are short, and it is only occasionally that the mercury falls below zero. The rainfall in the eastern section is sufficient for farming purposes, but it is more scanty in the west. The summers are hot.

The Missouri River, which bounds Kansas on the northeast, is navigable for steamers. The Arkansas, Republican, Kansas, Smoky Hill and several smaller streams are also navigable to some extent, and all afford opportunities for developing great hydro-electric power. Many species of food fish are found in these rivers.

Kansas is the central State of the Union.
Minerals.—Petroleum and bituminous coal are the chief mineral products of the State in value. About $3,000,000 worth of salt is made yearly from the salines. Other minerals of commercial value are gypsum, sandstone, flagstone, limestone, cement rock, firebrick clay and chalk. Natural gas is found in the southeast, and has become a highly valuable product. Some lead is mined.
Agriculture.—Fruit trees, such as apple, plum, and cherry, have been extensively planted in late years. In the extreme west the rainfall, though slight, is sufficient for stock raising. The irrigated farms there are very productive. Kansas is leader in the production of wheat, 152,184,000 bushels being grown in 1938. Corn is the crop next in value. Other important products are hay, broom corn, oats, sorghum, potatoes, barley, rye, flax and tobacco. The growing of alfalfa has become a prominent industry, and alfalfa hay is shipped East in immense quantities. Alfalfa meal is now largely used as a cattle food. Cattle raising has long been an important interest. Sheep farming is increasing. The wool clip was 3,126,000 pounds in 1938. Dairying and bee-keeping are remunerative industries.
Manufacturing.—Meat packing is the chief industry. Dairy products contribute largely to the State's wealth. Condensed milk, beet sugar, cement, flour, furniture, lubricating greases, ground plaster, lime, salt, bricks, leather and brooms are other important manufactures. The increasing number of natural gas wells in the south are doing much to aid in developing the State's manufacturing interests.
History.—Coronado's expedition crossed this region in 1541. Most of the territory remained unexplored, however, until 1719, when some French fur traders from Louisiana visited it. Fort Leavenworth was built in 1827. The Louisiana Purchase in 1803 included the greater part of what is now Kansas. This area, explored by Lewis and Clark in 1804, became a portion of the Missouri Territory and remained in it till 1821. The "Santa Fé Trail" was established in 1824, marking the beginning of the development and growth of the State. The Kansas region was unorganized until 1854, when it became Kansas Territory. The Missouri Compromise of 1820, restricting the northward extension of slavery, having been repealed, the Territory was made a battle field by violent struggles between advocates of slavery and its opponents. In 1861 Kansas was admitted as a free State.

KENTUCKY.—Physiography.—The surface slopes to the northwest in a series of plateaus, through which channels have been eroded by the rivers. In the east and southeast there are several nearly parallel ranges of the Appalachian system. Between them are deep valleys, with rich soil. The picturesque Cumberland Valley, lying between the Cumberland River and the Pine Mountains, is about 1,000 feet above sea level. In the northwest is the Blue Grass region, a rich, rolling tract of 10,000 square miles. A somewhat similar tract is found in the southwest. West of Green River are the so-called "barrens." These areas are really quite productive prairie land with oak-crowned knolls here and there. Several large marshy tracts are known as "salt licks," on account of their saline incrustation. All the arable land of the State is remarkably fertile. On all the mountain foothills and ridges there are forests of cedar, hemlock, holly, beech and other trees. Bluffs and river bottoms, with deep, loamy soil, are found in the west. In the southwest there are many large shallow lakes. Swamps covered with cypress trees are common here. Among the State's natural attractions are the Blue Grass region's beautiful open forests, interspersed with glades; some lakes in the southwest; the Mammoth Cave, and the mounds and fortifications constructed by aboriginal tribes long extinct. There are many mineral springs. The climate is mild and healthful, and the rainfall is abundant.
Minerals.—Kentucky is one of the principal coal-producing States, having vast deposits of bituminous, block and cannel coals. There is a plentiful supply of iron ore of good quality. Natural gas is obtained to a limited extent. Limestone and sandstone are quarried in large amounts. Brick and pottery clays are abundant. Other mineral products are petroleum, fluorspar, barytes, lime, cement rock, asphalt, natural gas, mineral waters, iron and lead.
Agriculture.—Tobacco is the chief agricultural product, 339,550,000 pounds being grown in 1938. Corn ranks second with 74,547,000 bushels. Other important crops are wheat, potatoes, oats, and rye. The hay crop was 1,748,000 tons in 1938. Live stock raising is an active industry. The State has long had a high reputation for thoroughbred horses. Immense numbers of hogs, sheep, cattle and mules are raised. The wool clip is large and of good quality, 5,309,000 pounds in 1938. Dairying is also an important industry. Timber is plentiful, but much of it is second-growth. The forests are largely hardwood.
Manufactures.—Flour and grist mill products, liquors, lumber and tobacco goods are important manufactures. Much salt is made from the numerous saline springs. Cotton and woolen mills and other textile plants are increasing. Considerable capital is employed in the making of clothing, rope, bagging, furniture and machinery. An increasing amount of pig iron is produced yearly, the raw materials, coal, iron and limestone, being found in the State. Bricks, tile and pottery goods are also manufactured. Kentucky is a leading state in the producing of distilled liquors.
Commerce.—The rail transportation facilities comprise 3,743 miles of steam railroads. Water transport is furnished by the Ohio and Mississippi Rivers.
History.—The first white men known to have discovered this territory were Marquette and Joliet in 1673. Among the early explorers of the State was also Thomas Walker, who, in 1750, crossed the Alleghenies through the wide pass which he named the Cumberland Gap. He was followed by Christopher Gist and John Finley, both, like Walker, from North Carolina. In May, 1767, a party of North Carolina farmers, among them Daniel Boone, made an exploring trip through this new region. The first permanent settlement was made at Harrodsburg by John Harrod in 1774. In 1775 Boone started a trading post there, which he called Boonesborough. A local government was instituted by the settlers in 1775, who named the region Transylvania; but in 1776 Virginia laid claim to the district, and, a year later, it was organized as Kentucky County. During the Revolution British and Indians from beyond the Ohio harassed the settlers. Kentucky, after a long contest with Virginia, became a State in 1792. Attempts were made in 1861 to pass an ordinance of secession, as State laws sanctioned slavery, but the opposition was too strong, and Kentucky remained in the Union.

LOUISIANA.—Physiography.—The surface consists mainly of two parts, the upland region and the coast plain. It is highest in the north, and slopes southeast to the Mississippi Delta. A low range of sandstone hills extends along the northwest. The average elevation is 75 feet. The alluvial regions, including low swamps back of the coast, cover an area of 20,000 square miles. The coast region extends inland for about 30 miles. On the smaller streams the alluvial tract is about 10 miles wide. The Mississippi flows along the ridge formed by its own deposit of silt, from which the land inclines toward low swamps beyond. In the southwest part of the State, north of the coast belt, there are well-watered prairies, with rich soil. Many of the rivers are navigable, and the total length of inland navigation is estimated at 3,700 miles. Dikes or levees from 5 feet to 20 feet high border the lower courses of the river in order to protect the surrounding country from inundation. In the northern part of the State there are rolling tracts of hilly ground. The great delta of the Mississippi is made up of swampy land slightly elevated above the sea level and subject to occasional overflow. The marshy portions of the State are traversed by wide, dry ridges of cultivable land, which are generally inhabited. Much of the State is covered by forests of cypress and hardwoods. The great yellow pine belt enters from southern Mississippi and stretches westward across the State. The soil, except in the extreme north, is exceedingly fertile. The climate is semi-tropical, and the rainfall is abundant.
Minerals.—There are vast deposits of sulphur and of rock salt. The western part of the State has numerous rich petroleum wells, producing millions of barrels yearly. A rapid development of manufacturing in the southeast is the result of the discovery of extensive natural gas fields there.
Agriculture.—Much of the soil seems to be of inexhaustible fertility. This is the principal cane-sugar State, the cane being grown on the alluvial lands. In 1938 Louisiana produced 5,832,000 short tons of sugar. Cotton is a standard crop, but the amount varies from year to year. Louisiana leads in the production of rice with 20,748,000 bushels in 1938. Corn, hay, white potatoes, sweet potatoes, peanuts and garden vegetables are grown extensively. Much attention is given to the raising of hogs, horses and cattle.
Manufacturing.—Refined sugar is the chief manufacture. Much capital is invested in the production of lumber from yellow pine, cypress, oak, ash and other hardwoods. Naval stores, cotton goods, cottonseed oil, flour, clothing and machinery are made in large quantities. Rice is milled extensively.
Commerce.—Louisiana has ample facilities for oversea trade as well as for commercial intercourse with other States. The Mississippi affords a broad waterway extending far into the interior of the country, and several of its tributaries are navigable for long distances. In addition to its many thousand miles of water highway the State has 4,454 miles of railroad, connecting the principal cities with all the important centers of traffic in other sections of the Union. The chief seaport, New Orleans, is the terminal for several foreign steamship lines, and it has a large international trade. It is surpassed in the value of its exports by only three other cities in the United States.
Fisheries.—The State has valuable fisheries. More oysters are marketed than in any other Gulf State, oyster beds extending for hundreds of miles along the

coast. It is estimated that the area suitable for oyster cultivation comprises 7,000 square miles.

History.—Some members of De Soto's expedition visited this region in 1542. La Salle, the French explorer, coming down the Mississippi in 1682, claimed the valley for Louis XIV of France. A French colony was founded in 1699 by the Sieur d'Iberville at Biloxi, now in Mississippi. The first permanent settlement was founded on the site of New Orleans in 1718 and this became the capital in 1720. Louisiana, west of the Mississippi, was transferred to Spain in 1762, and in 1763 Great Britain received the territory east of the river. In 1869 Louisiana was transferred to Spain, and Spain ceded it back to France in 1800. The whole vast region, now represented by several States, was purchased from France by President Jefferson in 1803 for $15,000,000. A portion of Louisiana, east of the Mississippi, belonging then to the Spanish Province of West Florida, did not become United States territory till 1819. The Territory of Orleans was formed in 1804-5, and was admitted as a State in 1812. Louisiana seceded from the Union in 1861. Readmission was granted in 1868.

MAINE.—Physiography.—Maine, the most northeasterly State in the Union, has a hilly surface in the north and central parts. A chain of hills, diverging from the White Mountains, crosses the State in a northeasterly direction. Mount Katahdin (5,267 feet) is the highest elevation in the State. Only about one-third of the State is below 800 feet. A striking feature of the topography is the large number of small lakes, there being over 1,500. Many are well stocked with pickerel, bass, trout and other game fish. The northern part is still largely a forest wilderness interspersed with high hills. Much of the most valuable timber has been cut off, but there are left many stands of pine, spruce, hemlock, balsam, and various species of deciduous trees. This section is a noted hunting ground and resort for sportsmen. The southern part of the State has a number of tracts of great fertility. The seacoast, measured along its numerous narrow indentations, is about 2,000 miles in length, and contains several fine harbors. Maine has many rivers, some of them broken by falls capable of furnishing immense water power for manufacturing purposes.

Minerals.—Building stone, including granite of high grade, lime and roofing slate are exported in large quantities. Maine is a leading State in the production of feldspar. There are several noted medicinal springs in the State, and mineral waters are bottled and shipped to all parts of the country. Poland Spring is especially well known.

Agriculture.—Potatoes and hay are the most valuable crops. Oats, sweet corn, wheat, buckwheat, and barley are cultivated. Much attention is given to dairying and to poultry farming. Horses, cattle and sheep are raised in large numbers. The wool clip is of high quality. Agriculture in Maine, as in the other New England States, declined somewhat in importance after the products of the fertile and easily tilled prairie States began to reach the Eastern markets; but truck farming has increased, and tomatoes and other vegetables are extensively grown for the canneries. Orchard fruits, especially apples, are harvested in large amounts. In 1938, Maine produced 858,000 bushels of apples. The vast forest region furnishes the basic materials for potash, tanbark, spruce gum, and charcoal. Considerable maple sugar is made.

Manufacturing.—An abundance of water power has stimulated manufacturing. Cotton and woolen goods, paper, leather, boots and shoes, foundry and machine shop products and agricultural implements are made. There is an active lumber trade. Granite working employs thousands of hands. Ice is cut and shipped to the large cities in New England and the Middle States. Maine was long famous for its wooden ships. Steel vessels are now constructed in former centers of wooden shipbuilding. Maine has almost a monopoly of the making of spools for the thread factories of the United States. The lumber interest is still large, and the State has hundreds of wood-making mills. Both soft and hard woods are utilized.

Fisheries.—Maine's fishing interests afford employment to many thousands of hands. Cod, mackerel, haddock, halibut, and herring are the chief food fishes. Salmon is taken in the Penobscot in large quantities, but the numbers are lessening every season. Lobster catching and sardine canning are very extensive indus-

tries. Menhaden, caught in vast numbers, are utilized in the manufacture of oil and fertilizer material.

Commerce.—Shipping is facilitated by the number of excellent harbors and by several large navigable rivers. Portland, the largest city, has a great coastwise trade and is connected with Europe by lines of steamships. Steam railroads connect Maine with all parts of the United States and Canada. Within the State there are 2,011 miles of railways.

History.—It is believed that Gaspar Corte-Real, sailing under the Portuguese flag, visited the Maine coast in 1500, while searching for the Northwest Passage. Giovanni da Verrazano, under the order of Francis I of France, skirted the American coast in 1524 and cast

PHOTO BY WARREN BOYER FROM R. I. NESMITH AND ASSOCIATES

A BEAUTIFUL COLONIAL DOORWAY, SALEM, MASSACHUSETTS

anchor in several of the harbors of Maine. Among other explorers who visited it were Estéban Gomez, 1525; Gosnold, 1602; Martin Pring, 1603; Pierre du Guast and Sieur de Monts, 1604; George Weymouth, 1605; and John Smith in 1614. Andre Thevet in 1556 led a French expedition that explored Penobscot Bay. A colony was established by Frenchmen in 1604 on an island in the St. Croix River, but it had only a temporary existence. An English settlement, made in 1607, at the mouth of the Kennebec River was equally short-lived. But under the Mason and Gorges grant the first permanent settlement was made in 1630 at Saco. Settlements at Pemaquid, Sheepscot, Monhegan, Damariscotta, and other places followed rapidly. At the close of the Revolution, British claims were ceded to the United States. In 1652 Maine was added to Massachusetts and remained part of it till 1820, when the "District of Maine" was admitted into the Union as a State.

MARYLAND. — Physiography. — Chesapeake Bay and the Susquehanna River divide Maryland into two unequal parts, called the Eastern and Western Shores. There are three main divisions of the surface—the coast plain, the Piedmont Plateau and the Appalachian Mountain region. The Western Shore's surface is somewhat uneven, and the northwest is traversed by ridges of the Alleghenies. Between these ridges lie wide valleys having exceedingly fertile soil. In the extreme west there are several elevated parklike areas known as "glades." These are noted for their scenic beauty. The "Great Valley" crosses the State and is continued northward by the Cumberland Valley of Pennsylvania and southward by the Shenandoah Valley in Virginia. Dense woods cover the mountain slopes. The Eastern

Shore is a low plain composed largely of aqueous deposit, sand and clay. Swamps and wooded areas, the trees being commonly oaks, cypresses and cedars, are found in the south. There are only 33 miles of Atlantic coast, and the State's harbors are reached by Chesapeake Bay and a number of navigable rivers flowing into it. The climate is mild and healthful, and there is an abundant rainfall.

Minerals.—Coal is the most valuable mineral product. It is mined in the western part of the State. Here, too, are found iron ores of fair quality. Fire clays are plentiful. Marble, granite and serpentine are quarried for building purposes. Kaolin, chromium, cement rock, sand, lime, talc and slate occur in paying quantities.

Agriculture.—Four-fifths of the land is included in farms. The principal products are corn, wheat, hay, potatoes, oats, rye, and barley. These crops are grown largely on the rich land of central and northern Maryland, west of Chesapeake Bay. Fruit cultivation and truck gardening have become important interests on the Eastern Shore and in the lower sections of the Western. Northern markets take most of the products. Large quantities of tomatoes are grown in Maryland; 659,000 bu. in 1938. The crop is absorbed principally by canneries. Dairying and poultry farming are industries of steadily increasing importance. In the lower counties of the Western Shore there are many thousands of acres devoted to the cultivation of tobacco.

Fisheries.—The oyster fishing of Maryland, though limited to Chesapeake Bay, is more extensive than that of any other State except Virginia, and is regulated by law on account of its great value. Clams, shad, menhaden, soft-shelled crabs, and the State's famous terrapin, add to the wealth of the fisheries.

Manufacturing.—Maryland ranks high in the production of canned vegetables (tomatoes, peas, corn). Meats and oysters are also canned in large amounts and exported to all parts of the country. Clothing, tobacco articles, flour, leather, lumber, boots and shoes, bricks, cement, chemicals, metallic wares and cotton goods are manufactured. The iron and steel industry has increased in late years. Steel steamers of the largest tonnage are built at Sparrow's Point.

Commerce.—Chesapeake Bay affords ample harbor accommodation for even the large transatlantic liners, and several lines of steamers connect the chief port, Baltimore, with various European seaports. There is also much coastwise traffic. The Chesapeake and Delaware Canal forms a valuable commercial highway for steamboats plying between Philadelphia and Baltimore.

History.—The first white man to visit the region was Captain John Smith, who sailed up Chesapeake Bay in 1608. A trader's post was established in 1631 on Kent Island, but the first permanent settlement was made in 1634 at St. Mary's by English colonists under Leonard Calvert, a brother of Lord Baltimore, the proprietor of the province. In 1638 the right to initiate legislation was conceded to the people by Lord Baltimore. The colony grew but slowly. In 1652 the colony was seized by the commissioners of Parliament, but it was restored to Lord Baltimore in 1657. In 1689 an association of Protestants, under the leadership of John Coode, seized St. Mary's and assumed control of the government in the name of William and Mary of England. In 1694 the capital was removed from St. Mary's to Annapolis. In 1715 the Province was restored to the fifth Lord Baltimore. Baltimore was founded in 1729. Maryland took up enthusiastically the American fight for independence against British rule in 1776. In 1861 the State refused to join the Confederacy, and thus helped to save Washington. It remained a slave State till 1863, when slavery was abolished in the United States.

MASSACHUSETTS.—Physiography.—The western part is traversed by the Berkshire Hills and hence the surface there is more rugged than in the east. There is, however, but little level land in the State. In the river valleys the soil is fertile. Elsewhere it is generally barren or poor. The southeast has a sandy surface and many swamps covered with second-growth timber. Extensive marshes along the coast yield excellent hay. Careful cultivation and the use of fertilizers have made much of the barren land productive.

Numerous bays and inlets indent the coast line. Several form excellent harbors. Immense water power is available through falls in the Connecticut, Merrimac, Blackstone, Miller's, Nashua, Chicopee and many other smaller streams. In winter the climate is generally cold and humid, but the summers are hot, and the growing season is long. The rainfall is abundant, as in all the Eastern States.

Minerals.—Granite and basalt, the principal mineral products, are extensively quarried. Marble and limestone are found in the Berkshire region. Soapstone, mica, glass sand, lime, and potters' clay are other valuable mineral products.

Agriculture.—Much of the surface is stony, and there is also much waste land, suitable only for pasturage or second-growth timber. But the Connecticut and Housatonic valleys are fertile, and many large areas among the Berkshire Hills have a generous soil well adapted to general farming. Hay is the principal crop, 583,000 tons being grown in 1938. Tobacco grown in the Connecticut Valley brings a high price, the leaf being surpassed only by Cuban tobacco. The crop is worth about $2,000,000 annually. Dairying is carried on in the midland part of the State. Potatoes, corn, rye, and oats are other farm products of economic value. Market gardening for the cities has become an important industry. The cranberry harvest of the Cape Cod district amounts to over 400,000 barrels annually.

Fisheries.—Massachusetts is the leading State in the taking and curing of sea fish, including cod, halibut, swordfish, herring, haddock, bluefish, mackerel and other food fish. Menhaden are seined for oil and fertilizing materials. Shad, alewives and smelts are taken in several rivers. Fishing for clams and other shellfish is a remunerative occupation along the whole coast. Many thousands of men and a large fleet of vessels, a number of them steamers, are engaged in the fishing industries.

Manufacturing.—Massachusetts is a great manufacturing State. It is the leading State in the making of cotton and woolen goods, boots, shoes, and leather and ranks high in the manufacture of paper and cotton goods. Other important manufactures are metal wares, machinery, wire, clothing, electrical apparatus, rubber goods, carpets, refined sugar and canned goods. The shipbuilding interests are very extensive. Large quantities of packed and cured meats are put on the market by packing-house establishments in the eastern part of the State.

Commerce.—A network of railroads covers this commonwealth, connecting it with all parts of the Union and Canada. These lines, 1,960 miles in length, together with excellent highways, greatly facilitate inland traffic. The Cape Cod Canal, completed in 1914, shortens by 70 miles the sea trip between Boston and New York. In the value of foreign commerce Massachusetts ranks high among the States. Lines of steamers link the chief commercial city, Boston, with other ports in all parts of the civilized world, bring in cargoes of raw materials and carry away manufactured goods to the value of hundreds of millions of dollars annually.

History.—Bartholomew Gosnold attempted in 1602 to found a settlement on Cuttyhunk Island. After a few weeks the colony was abandoned. The region was included in grants made in the patent of "Arcadie" to the Sieur de Monts in 1603, the first charter of Virginia, 1606, and the charter of New England in 1620. Plymouth was the first permanent settlement. It was founded in 1620 by a company of Pilgrims, English people, who, to escape persecution on account of their religious beliefs, had left England and had settled in Leyden, Holland. In 1628 another colony was established at Salem by Puritans from England. They came under the auspices of an English company that had obtained a royal patent for the "Governor and Company of the Massachusetts Bay." The colony's growth was rapid, many Puritans coming from England to the new country, where they were free to worship God as they chose. Between 1630 and 1640 about 20,000 persons came from England to the colony. In 1643 Massachusetts Bay united with Plymouth, Connecticut and New Haven for protection against the Indians and Dutch. This was the first confederation formed in North America. Charles II., angered by the spirit of independence shown by the Massachusetts colony, declared its charter forfeited in 1684, and two years later appointed, as Governor of it, Sir Edmund Andros. But in 1689, when the people learned of the English revolution, they drove Andros out. William and Mary granted, in 1691, a new charter, which united the colonies of Massachusetts Bay and Plymouth, and restored to the people the election of members of the Assembly. Massachusetts led the colonies in the Revolutionary War, measures of taxation by England having led to an increasing spirit of resistance among the colonists. The battles of Lexington and Concord, the first contests against British troops sent here to overawe the Americans, took place on her soil. In the Civil War, 1861-65, Massachusetts took a foremost part in preserving the Union. It was one of the original thirteen states.

MICHIGAN.—Physiography.—Michigan consists of two peninsulas, one north, the other south, or, as they are sometimes termed, an upper peninsula and a lower. The upper one has many hills and low mountain ranges covered with forests and rich in iron and copper ores. The highest point does not exceed 2,023 feet above the lake level. In the lower peninsula the surface is undulating, with occasional hills. Nowhere here is the elevation more than 900 feet above the lake surface. In the north there are forests of coniferous and deciduous trees. Along the western lake-coast there

immense quantities of early vegetables, including beans, peas and celery. Peaches, strawberries, raspberries, and other fruits are grown for city markets. The potato harvest is very large, and hay is a most important crop. Corn, potatoes, wheat, oats, rye, barley, and buckwheat follow in value. Dairying has become an extensive industry. Butter and cheese are leading products. Much capital is invested in the live stock industry, and the number of domestic farm animals runs into millions. There are 1,290,000 sheep in the State and the wool clip reached 8,031,000 pounds in 1938. The area devoted to growing sugar beets is about 150,000 acres annually, and Michigan now ranks third in their production. Apples, pears, peaches, grapes and plums are the most valuable orchard crops. More peppermint and chicory are grown here than in any other State.

Fisheries.—The lake fisheries employ about 10,000 men, and the product is very valuable. Whitefish, trout, sturgeon, and pickerel are taken in large numbers.

COURTESY AMERICAN AIRLINES
AN AIR VIEW OF THE UNIVERSITY OF MICHIGAN STADIUM AND THE CAMPUS, ANN ARBOR, MICHIGAN

are extensive sand dunes. Bluffs border Lake Huron. About 200 islands belong to Michigan, the largest being Isle Royale on Lake Superior. Thousands of ponds and small lakes dot the State. The rivers afford little navigation, but are the sources of much water power utilizable for manufacturing purposes. In both peninsulas the rainfall is ample. The climate of the northern one is rigorous and the soil is poor; but the southern peninsula has a milder climate and is noted for its heavy harvests of grain, fruit and root crops. Much lumber is cut, though Michigan no longer leads the Union in timber production. Hardwoods and hemlock are the most common timber trees. Of the hardwoods, maple, birch, and beech are the most important.

Minerals.—Michigan ranks second in the output of iron ores, Minnesota being first. For many years Michigan was the foremost State in the production of copper, and the yield is still very great. Both the iron and copper are mined in the upper peninsula. In the lower there is a large area underlain with bituminous coal. This is used chiefly for local purposes. There are large deposits of salt in the Saginaw district and around Manistee, from which has developed an extensive industry in the production of salt. It is obtained as brine from artesian wells. The salt-yielding territory is estimated to comprise 10,000 square miles. Michigan is a leading State in the yield of bromine. Gypsum, building stone, glass sand, fire clay, and cement rock are found in abundance.

Agriculture.—For years the farming area has been spreading, the cutting off of the forests opening up new lands. Proximity to large cities has favored truck gardening and fruit culture; and the State produces

Manufacturing.—The manufactures are numerous and varied. Automobile construction has been first among the State's industries for a number of years. The lumber interests are still of high value, planing mills utilizing most of the timber cut. Other leading products are iron and steel goods, refined salt, woodenware, farming implements and foundry and machine-shop products. Flour milling and beet sugar refining are now highly important interests. Furniture manufacturing is an extensive industry.

Commerce.—With regard to lake transportation Michigan is the most favorably situated of all the States, as it borders on all the Great Lakes, except Lake Ontario. Railroads reach nearly every county, and trunk lines connect the State with the rest of the Union.

History.—French missionaries and fur traders are believed to have visited southern Michigan as early as 1610. In 1634, Nicollet, a French explorer, discovered Lake Michigan. Father Marquette established a mission post at Sault Sainte Marie in 1668. In 1671 Michilimackinac was founded. A settlement was made at Detroit in 1701 by Antoine de la Motte-Cadillac. Population increased but slowly, for the territory was harassed by Indian warfare. In 1763 this region passed into the possession of Great Britain. The Quebec Act (1774) incorporated the territory with Canada, but little progress was made under English government. At the close of the Revolution the British surrendered the region, though they did not withdraw all their troops until 1796. It was part of the Northwest Territory till 1805, when it was set off as a separate Territory. Prior to that event Ohio had been delimited from the Northwest Territory in 1800, and the lower

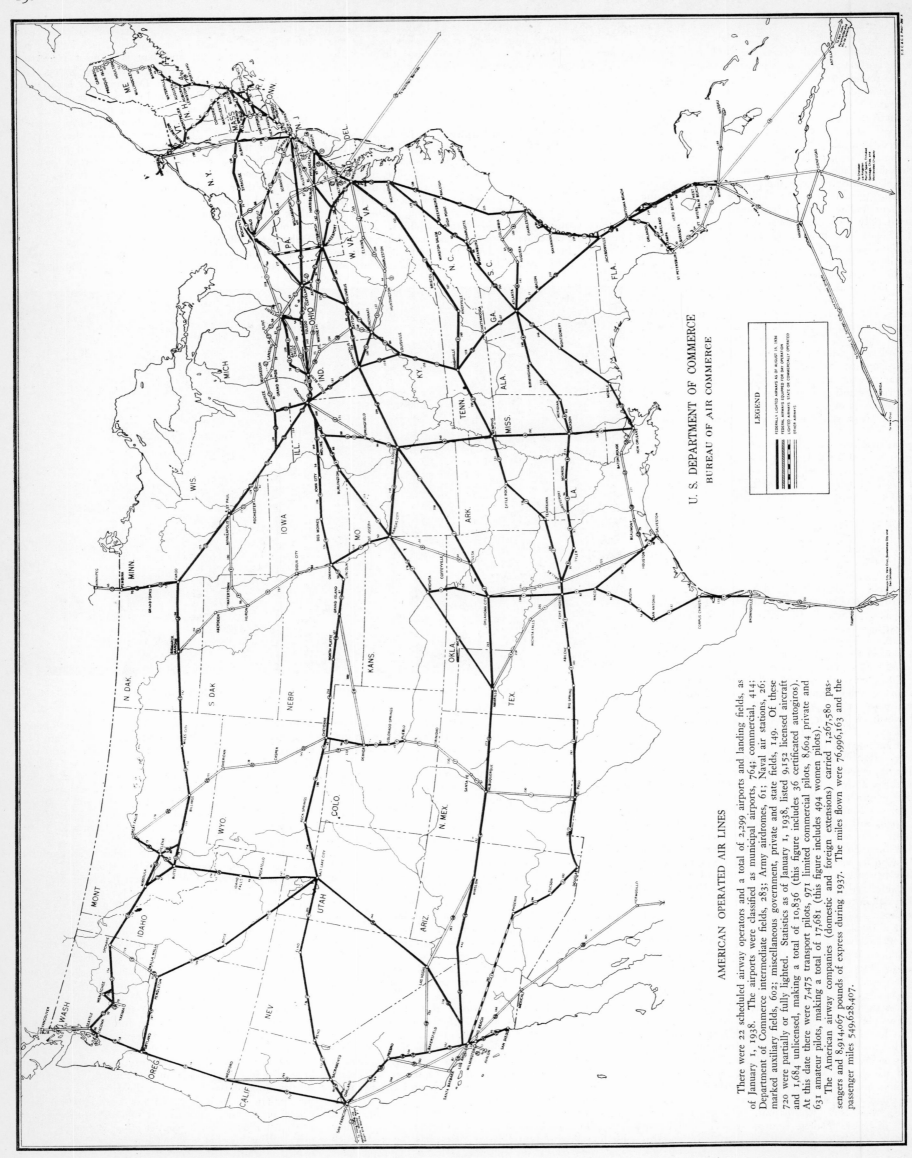

U. S. DEPARTMENT OF COMMERCE
BUREAU OF AIR COMMERCE

LEGEND

AMERICAN OPERATED AIR LINES

There were 22 scheduled airway operators and a total of 2,299 airports and landing fields, as of January 1, 1938. The airports were classified as municipal airports, 764; commercial, 414; Department of Commerce intermediate fields, 283; Army airdromes, 61; Naval air stations, 26; marked auxiliary fields, 602; miscellaneous government, private and state fields, 149. Of these 720 were partially or fully lighted. Statistics as of January 1, 1938, listed 9,152 licensed aircraft and 1,684 unlicensed, making a total of 10,836 (this figure includes 36 certificated autogiros). At this date there were 7,475 transport pilots, 971 limited commercial pilots, 8,604 private and 631 amateur pilots, making a total of 17,681 (this figure includes 494 women pilots). The American airway companies (domestic and foreign extensions) carried 1,267,580 passengers and 8,914,067 pounds of express during 1937. The miles flown were 76,996,163 and the passenger miles 549,628,407.

AIRWAY MAP OF THE UNITED STATES, SHOWING BOTH THE AIRWAYS IN OPERATION AND THOSE UNDER CONSTRUCTION. THE NUMBERS IN CIRCLES ARE THE ROUTE NUMBERS. THESE ARE LISTED ON PAGE 151, WITH THE NAMES OF THE AIRWAY OPERATORS, THE ROUTES OPERATED, THE ROUTE MILEAGE AND THE CLASS OF SERVICE. THE NUMBERS WITHOUT CIRCLES INDICATE THE MILEAGE BETWEEN THE CITIES.

Scheduled Airway Operators and Routes

Route No.	Operator	Routes Operated	Route Mileage	Class of *Service
①	Airline Feeder System, Inc.	New York to Springfield	127	PE
②	American Airlines, Inc.	New York to Los Angeles (via Washington, Nashville and Dallas)	2,649	MPE
		New York to Boston (direct)	192	MPE
		New York to Boston (via Hartford and Providence)	219	MPE
		Boston to Buffalo (via Albany)	414	MPE
		New York to Chicago (via Buffalo and Detroit)	779	MPE
		Detroit to Chicago (via Battle Creek)	261	MPE
		Buffalo to Cleveland	177	MPE
		Chicago to Fort Worth (via St. Louis and Tulsa)	968	MPE
		Chicago to St. Louis (direct)	257	MPE
		Cleveland to Nashville	469	MPE
		Washington to Cleveland (via Cincinnati)	684	MPE
③	Boston-Maine Airways, Inc.	Boston to Bangor	220	MPE
		Boston to Montreal	261	MPE
		Bangor to Caribou	164	MPE
④	Braniff Airways, Inc.	Chicago to Dallas (via Kansas City and Wichita)	965	MPE
		Amarillo to Dallas	345	MPE
		Dallas to Galveston	273	MPE
		Dallas to Brownsville	546	MPE
⑤	Canadian-Colonial Airways, Inc.	New York to Montreal	332	MPE
⑥	Chicago and Southern Air Lines, Inc.	Chicago to New Orleans	892	MPE
⑦	Continental Airlines, Inc.	Denver to El Paso	595	MPE
⑧	Delta Air Corporation	Charleston, South Carolina to Dallas	1,065	MPE
⑨	Hanford Airlines, Inc.	Tulsa to Omaha	383	MPE
		Minneapolis to Kansas City (via Huron)	682	MPE
		Huron to Bismarck	221	MPE
⑪	National Airlines, Inc.	St. Petersburg to Daytona Beach	149	MPE
		St. Petersburg to Miami	204	MPE
⑫	North American Aviation, Inc. (Eastern Air Lines Division)	New York to Miami (via Charleston, S. C.)	1,209	MPE
		New York to New Orleans (via Atlanta)	1,218	MPE
		Chicago to Miami (via Atlanta and Jacksonville)	1,267	MPE
		New Orleans to Houston	329	MPE
⑬	Northwest Airlines, Inc.	Chicago to St. Paul (via Milwaukee and Rochester)	416	MPE
		Chicago to Pembina (via Milwaukee)	769	MPE
		Chicago to St. Paul (direct)	364	MPE
		Fargo to Seattle	1,264	MPE
⑭	Pan American Airways, Inc.	Miami to Havana	229	MPE
		Miami to San Juan	1,161	MPE
		San Juan to Rio de Janeiro	4,571	MPE
		Rio de Janeiro to Buenos Aires	1,471	MPE
⑭	Pan American Airways, Inc.	Miami to Cristobal (via Kingston and Barranquilla)	1,713	MPE
		Barranquilla to Port of Spain	1,021	MPE
		Brownsville to Mexico City (via Tampico)	466	MPE
		Miami to Nassau	188	MPE
		Havana to Belize	742	MPE
		San Francisco to Hong Kong (via Manila, P. I., Honolulu, Midway, Wake and Guam)	8,748	MPE
		Mexico City to Cristobal (via Guatemala)	1,764	MPE
		San Juan to Kingston	817	PE
		Baltimore, Md., to Hamilton, Bermuda	726	MPE
		Port Washington, L. I., to Hamilton, Bermuda	773	MPE
⑮	Pan American Airways, Inc. (Cia Mexicana de Aviacion, S. A.)	Mexico City to Merida	736	PE
		Los Angeles to Mexico City	1,684	PE
⑯	Pan American-Grace Airways, Inc.	Cristobal, Canal Zone to Montevideo, Uruguay (via Santiago, Chile)	4,552	MPE
		Arica, Chile to Villazon, Bolivia (via Tacna, Peru)	872	PE
⑰	Pennsylvania-Central Airlines Corporation	Washington to Detroit (via Pittsburgh and Cleveland)	469	MPE
		Detroit to Milwaukee	259	MPE
		Washington to Buffalo (via Harrisburg)	318	MPE
⑱	Transcontinental and Western Air, Inc.	New York to Los Angeles (via St. Louis)	2,555	MPE
⑲	United Air Lines Transport Corporation	New York to Chicago	717	MPE
		Philadelphia to Cleveland	415	MPE
		Chicago to San Francisco	1,935	MPE
		Salt Lake City to Seattle	816	MPE
		Pendleton to Spokane	154	MPE
		San Diego to Seattle (via Bakersfield and Fresno)	1,198	MPE
⑳	Western Air Express Corporation	Los Angeles to San Francisco (direct)	348	MPE
		Los Angeles to San Francisco (via Santa Barbara and Fresno)	413	MPE
		Cheyenne to Denver	96	MPE
		Chicago to Cheyenne	917	MPE
		San Diego to Salt Lake City	702	MPE
		Salt Lake City to Great Falls	489	MPE
㉑	Wilmington-Catalina Airline, Ltd.	Wilmington to Avalon	31	PE
㉒	Wyoming Air Service, Inc.	Cheyenne to Great Falls	572	MPE

*M—Mail   P—Passenger   E—Express

	Albuquerque, N. Mex.	Atlanta, Ga.	Baltimore, Md.	Boise, Idaho	Boston, Mass.	Brownsville, Tex.	Buffalo, N. Y.	Chicago, Ill.	Cincinnati, Ohio	Cleveland, Ohio	Denver, Colo.	Des Moines, Iowa	Detroit, Mich.	El Paso, Tex.	Fargo, N. Dak.	Fort Worth, Tex.	Galveston, Tex.	Hastings, Nebr.	Hot Springs, Ark.	Houghton, Mich.	Jacksonville, Fla.	Kansas City, Mo.	Los Angeles, Calif.	Louisville, Ky.	Memphis, Tenn.	Miami, Fla.	Minneapolis, Minn.	Missoula, Mont.	Nashville, Tenn.	New Orleans, La.	New York, N. Y.	Norfolk, Va.	Oklahoma City, Okla.	Omaha, Nebr.	Philadelphia, Pa.	Phoenix, Ariz.	Pittsburgh, Pa.	Portland, Me.	Portland, Ore.	Richmond, Va.	St. Louis, Mo.	Salt Lake City, Utah	San Francisco, Calif.	Schenectady, N. Y.	Seattle, Wash.	Shreveport, La.	Spokane, Wash.	Springfield, Mass.	Vermilion, S. Dak.	Washington, D. C.
Albuquerque. N. Mex.		1273	1670	774	1967	838	1577	1126	1248	1417	332	833	1360	228	968	561	803	588	773	1252	1492	717	663	1174	938	1710	980	895	1117	1030	1810	1696	518	718	1748	330	1498	2015	1107	1628	938	483	893	1823	1178	764	1028	1889	742	1648
Atlanta . . . . Ga.	1273		575	1830	933	960	695	583	368	550	1208	738	595	1293	1112	750	688	901	498	947	286	675	1935	317	335	610	905	1790	218	427	747	507	753	815	663	1592	520	1022	2172	470	467	1580	2133	840	2180	548	1960	863	917	542
Baltimore . . . . Md.	1670	575		2055	358	1525	273	603	423	305	1505	913	398	1750	1143	1239	1245	1154	964	808	682	962	2313	498	792	958	948	1947	597	1001	170	167	1173	1026	90	2002	194	446	2367	128	731	1858	2451	278	2341	1064	2110	282	1083	33
Boise . . . . Idaho	774	1830	2055		2266	1610	1872	1453	1663	1754	637	1155	1671	969	975	1263	1538	934	1384	1367	2098	1158	663	1623	1506	2368	1140	252	1631	1713	2153	2137	1138	1044	2113	733	1863	2282	349	2060	1389	292	516	2120	405	1433	290	2196	973	2045
Boston . . . . Mass.	1967	933	358	2266		1881	398	849	737	550	1766	1159	613	2067	1304	1574	1598	1415	1302	922	1015	1250	2590	823	1133	1258	1125	2124	941	1359	188	467	1490	1280	268	2295	478	100	2553	471	1036	2099	2696	150	2508	1410	2279	79	1314	392
Brownsville . . . . . Tex.	838	960	1525	1610	1881		1575	1234	1184	1402	1047	1102	1398	682	1445	471	287	1013	650	1543	1025	923	1370	1093	777	1100	1335	1706	952	536	1695	1465	659	1061	1614	1023	1424	1961	1944	1428	975	1317	1675	1770	2015	510	1852	1805	1161	1493
Buffalo . . . . N. Y.	1577	695	273	1872	398	1575		454	392	175	1368	762	218	1690	923	1221	1289	1019	956	560	880	862	2195	483	802	1184	733	1740	626	1087	291	435	1117	883	278	1904	178	438	2167	375	662	1701	2298	249	2130	1080	1900	325	916	290
Chicago . . . . Ill.	1126	583	603	1453	849	1234	454		249	307	918	310	236	1249	571	820	954	566	585	367	861	413	1741	268	481	1190	356	1348	394	831	711	696	689	432	664	1451	411	892	1765	618	259	1260	1855	702	1743	725	1514	774	479	594
Cincinnati . . . . . . Ohio	1248	368	423	1663	737	1184	392	249		218	1090	509	234	1333	818	839	897	742	569	589	628	541	1892	92	410	957	603	1578	239	708	568	474	755	620	501	1578	258	802	1987	399	308	1450	2037	605	1974	688	1746	659	694	403
Cleveland . . . . . . Ohio	1417	550	305	1754	550	1402	175	307	218		1223	617	94	1521	838	1046	1116	871	787	518	768	700	2044	309	627	1088	632	1640	456	922	404	429	946	738	343	1745	115	603	2063	353	490	1567	2163	408	2035	904	1804	473	785	303
Denver . . . . Colo.	332	1208	1505	637	1766	1047	1368	918	1090	1223		607	1153	554	642	643	925	353	749	970	1468	555	828	1035	878	1732	699	670	1018	1079	1628	1562	503	485	1575	585	1320	1803	985	1488	793	372	946	1618	1020	799	827	1692	468	1490
Des Moines . . . . . Iowa	833	738	913	1155	1159	1102	762	310	509	617	607		545	980	397	640	851	256	488	458	1024	180	1433	477	485	1338	235	1074	523	825	1023	983	469	122	972	1154	718	1197	1479	905	270	952	1547	1012	1470	624	1243	1085	187	895
Detroit . . . . Mich.	1360	595	398	1671	613	1398	218	236	234	94	1153	545		1475	745	1018	1111	800	761	427	832	643	1976	315	621	1156	542	1552	468	938	483	522	905	666	444	1685	208	657	1975	445	452	1490	2087	467	1945	891	1715	540	705	397
El Paso . . . . Tex.	228	1293	1750	969	2067	682	1690	1249	1333	1521	554	980	1475		1161	543	723	757	802	1422	1481	836	702	1253	978	1662	1156	1115	1169	986	1902	1755	578	875	1834	347	1592	2126	1286	1695	1033	689	993	1930	1373	752	1238	1990	920	1726
Fargo . . . . N. Dak.	968	1112	1143	975	1304	1445	923	571	818	838	642	397	745	1161		973	1218	440	875	393	1400	548	1426	818	882	1721	219	819	900	1221	1213	1258	786	390	1186	1225	952	1313	1248	1180	658	865	1447	1157	1206	1002	976	1240	284	1141
Fort Worth . . . . . Tex.	561	750	1239	1263	1574	471	1221	820	839	1046	643	640	1018	543	973		283	544	273	1093	943	460	1212	751	448	1150	870	1312	643	470	1398	1226	188	590	1324	858	1097	1642	1612	1170	568	977	1454	1445	1658	209	1470	1495	689	1210
Galveston . . . . . . Tex.	803	688	1245	1538	1598	287	1289	954	897	1116	925	851	1111	723	1218	283		808	375	1277	799	677	1423	807	492	941	1087	1595	666	288	1415	1195	456	828	1335	1065	1140	1678	1885	1154	697	1249	1693	1487	1938	233	1753	1524	938	1214
Hastings . . . . . . Nebr.	588	901	1154	934	1415	1013	1019	566	742	871	353	256	800	757	440	544	808		513	666	1178	226	1177	693	591	1468	399	891	697	870	1275	1216	357	135	1222	901	967	1454	1271	1142	455	708	1297	1267	1288	615	1061	1340	167	1139
Hot Springs . . . . Ark.	773	498	964	1384	1302	650	956	585	569	787	749	488	761	802	875	273	375	513		901	728	326	1437	480	176	983	722	1385	370	358	1125	955	260	490	1051	1094	825	1371	1733	897	325	1116	1648	1175	1759	142	1552	1224	605	936
Houghton . . . . . Mich.	1252	947	808	1367	922	1543	560	367	589	518	970	458	427	1422	393	1093	1277	666	901		1216	633	1787	636	830	1545	272	1208	760	1187	849	946	926	547	827	1550	630	924	1638	870	591	1242	1833	776	1588	1043	1360	860	510	813
Jacksonville . . . . . Fla.	1492	286	682	2098	1015	1025	880	861	628	768	1468	1024	832	1481	1400	943	799	1178	728	1216		952	2153	595	591	328	1192	2070	502	511	838	548	988	1098	758	1800	703	1113	2442	953	755	1840	2375	960	2450	733	2239	957	1203	647
Kansas City . . . . . Mo.	717	675	962	1158	1250	923	862	413	541	700	555	180	643	836	548	460	677	226	326	633	952		1352	480	370	1247	413	1117	472	678	1097	1009	293	165	1037	1045	784	1300	1397	937	238	922	1500	1107	1505	326	1286	1173	280	943
Los Angeles . . . Calif.	663	1935	2313	663	2590	1370	2195	1741	1892	2044	828	1433	1976	702	1426	1212	1423	1177	1437	1787	2153	1352		1825	1602	2355	1522	910	1777	1675	2446	2352	1182	1312	2388	357	2135	2631	825	2283	1585	577	345	2445	956	1420	939	2515	1291	2295
Louisville . . . . Ky.	1174	317	498	1623	823	1093	483	268	92	309	1035	477	315	1253	818	751	807	693	480	636	595	480	1825		319	923	605	1550	153	623	650	528	675	579	580	1512	345	892	1953	457	242	1400	1983	695	1945	598	1720	745	663	473
Memphis . . . . . . Tenn.	938	335	792	1506	1133	777	802	481	410	627	878	485	621	978	882	448	492	591	176	830	591	370	1602	319		878	700	1483	195	358	953	778	422	529	878	1264	660	1205	1852	722	242	1250	1800	1010	1867	279	1652	1055	642	763
Miami . . . . Fla.	1710	610	958	2368	1258	1100	1184	1190	957	1088	1732	1338	1156	1662	1721	1150	941	1468	983	1545	328	1247	2355	923	878		1516	2359	821	681	1095	802	1233	1402	1023	1998	1014	1357	2716	831	1067	2098	2603	1229	2740	950	2528	1210	1510	927
Minneapolis . . . Minn.	980	905	948	1140	1125	1335	733	356	603	632	699	235	542	1156	219	870	1087	399	722	272	1192	413	1522	605	700	1516		1010	695	1050	1019	1047	692	291	985	1279	745	1145	1435	968	464	988	1585	975	1403	859	1173	1056	238	936
Missoula . . . . . . Mont.	895	1790	1947	252	2124	1706	1740	1348	1578	1640	670	1074	1552	1115	819	1312	1595	891	1385	1208	2070	1117	910	1550	1483	2359	1010		1582	1733	2030	2045	1162	978	1997	932	1754	2133	430	1967	1331	435	762	1978	395	1457	170	2060	887	1940
Nashville . . . . . . Tenn.	1117	218	597	1631	941	952	626	394	239	456	1018	523	468	1169	900	643	666	697	370	760	502	472	1777	153	195	821	695	1582		470	758	586	602	604	683	1445	472	1015	1970	526	253	1390	1958	820	1973	470	1752	863	704	567
New Orleans . . . . . La.	1030	427	1001	1713	1359	536	1087	831	708	922	1079	825	938	986	1221	470	288	870	358	1187	511	678	1675	623	358	681	1050	1733	470		1173	932	575	845	1090	1318	923	1445	2063	899	599	1433	1923	1259	2098	280	1898	1287	960	968
New York . . . . . N. Y.	1810	747	170	2153	188	1695	291	711	568	404	1628	1023	483	1902	1213	1398	1415	1275	1125	849	838	1097	2446	650	953	1095	1019	2030	758	1173		293	1324	1144	83	2142	313	277	2455	287	873	1972	2568	142	2419	1230	2190	120	1189	204
Norfolk . . . . Va.	1696	507	167	2137	467	1465	435	696	474	429	1562	983	522	1755	1258	1226	1195	1216	955	946	548	1009	2352	528	778	802	1047	2045	586	932	293		1186	1095	220	2027	316	565	2458	79	771	1925	2510	426	2440	1037	2211	411	1166	145
Oklahoma City . Okla.	518	753	1173	1138	1490	659	1117	689	755	946	503	469	905	578	786	188	456	357	260	926	988	293	1182	675	422	1233	692	1162	602	575	1324	1186		405	1256	843	1013	1550	1488	1122	456	862	1386	1354	1523	297	1324	1412	502	1150
Omaha . . . . Nebr.	718	815	1026	1044	1280	1061	883	432	620	738	485	122	666	875	390	590	828	135	490	547	1098	165	1312	579	529	1402	291	978	604	845	1144	1095	405		1094	1032	837	1318	1373	1020	352	833	1425	1133	1372	617	1149	1205	115	1012
Philadelphia . . . . . Pa.	1748	663	90	2113	268	1614	278	664	501	343	1575	972	444	1834	1186	1324	1335	1222	1051	827	758	1037	2388	580	878	1023	985	1997	683	1090	83	220	1256	1094		2079	254	360	2419	205	808	1923	2518	205	2388	1153	2159	201	1143	122
Phoenix . . . . Ariz.	330	1592	2002	733	2295	1023	1904	1451	1578	1745	585	1154	1685	347	1225	858	1065	901	1094	1550	1800	1045	357	1512	1264	1998	1279	932	1445	1318	2142	2027	843	1032	2079		1829	2345	1007	1960	1270	504	652	2152	1112	1067	1020	2220	1043	1980
Pittsburgh . . . . Pa.	1498	520	194	1863	478	1424	178	411	258	115	1320	718	208	1592	952	1097	1140	967	825	630	703	784	2135	345	660	1014	745	1754	472	923	313	316	1013	837	254	1829		545	2174	242	561	1670	2264	350	2145	939	1918	400	891	188
Portland . . . . Me.	2015	1022	446	2282	100	1961	438	892	802	603	1803	1197	657	2126	1313	1642	1678	1454	1371	924	1113	1300	2631	892	1205	1357	1145	2133	1015	1445	277	565	1550	1318	360	2345	545		2563	565	1094	2127	2725	197	2513	1484	2285	159	1345	480
Portland . . . . Ore.	1107	2172	2367	349	2553	1944	2167	1765	1987	2063	985	1479	1975	1286	1248	1612	1885	1271	1733	1638	2442	1397	825	1953	1852	2716	1435	430	1970	2063	2455	2458	1488	1373	2419	1007	2174	2563		2381	1723	636	536	2405	143	1783	295	2488	1293	2360
Richmond . . . . Va.	1628	470	128	2060	471	1428	375	618	399	353	1488	905	445	1695	1180	1170	1154	1142	897	870	953	937	2283	457	722	831	968	1967	526	899	287	79	1122	1020	205	1960	242	565	2381		699	1850	2436	406	2362	985	2133	407	1089	96
St. Louis . . . . Mo.	938	467	731	1389	1036	975	662	259	308	490	793	270	452	1033	658	568	697	455	325	591	755	238	1585	242	242	1067	464	1331	253	599	873	771	456	352	808	1270	561	1094	1723	699		1158	1738	898	1722	466	1500	958	450	710
Salt Lake City . Utah	483	1580	1858	292	2099	1317	1701	1260	1450	1567	372	952	1490	689	865	977	1249	708	1116	1242	1840	922	577	1400	1250	2098	988	435	1390	1433	1972	1925	862	833	1923	504	1670	2127	636	1850	1158		592	1950	697	1155	548	2027	785	1845
San Francisco . . Calif.	893	2133	2451	516	2696	1675	2298	1855	2037	2163	946	1547	2087	993	1447	1454	1693	1297	1648	1833	2375	1500	345	1983	1800	2603	1585	762	1958	1923	2568	2510	1386	1425	2518	652	2264	2725	536	2436	1738	592		2548	680	1655	730	2625	1383	2437
Schenectady . . . N. Y.	1823	840	278	2120	150	1770	249	702	605	408	1618	1012	467	1930	1157	1445	1487	1267	1175	776	960	1107	2445	695	1010	1229	975	1978	820	1259	142	426	1354	1133	205	2152	350	197	2405	406	898	1950	2548		2363	1290	2139	86	1165	313
Seattle . . . . Wash.	1178	2180	2341	405	2508	2015	2130	1743	1974	2035	1020	1470	1945	1373	1206	1658	1938	1288	1759	1588	2450	1505	956	1945	1867	2740	1403	395	1973	2098	2419	2440	1523	1372	2388	1112	2145	2513	143	2362	1722	697	680	2363		1820	229	2445	1282	2335
Shreveport . . . . La.	764	548	1064	1433	1410	510	1080	725	688	904	799	624	891	752	1002	209	233	615	142	1043	733	326	1420	598	279	950	859	1457	470	280	1230	1037	297	617	1153	1067	939	1484	1783	985	466	1155	1655	1290	1820		1621	1333	726	1035
Spokane . . . . . . Wash.	1028	1960	2110	290	2279	1852	1900	1514	1746	1804	827	1243	1715	1238	976	1470	1753	1061	1552	1360	2239	1286	939	1720	1652	2528	1173	170	1752	1898	2190	2211	1324	1149	2159	1020	1918	2285	295	2133	1500	548	730	2139	229	1621		2216	1055	2105
Springfield . . . . Mass.	1889	863	282	2196	79	1805	325	774	659	473	1692	1085	540	1990	1240	1495	1524	1340	1224	860	957	1173	2515	745	1055	1210	1056	2060	863	1287	120	411	1412	1205	201	2220	400	159	2488	407	958	2027	2625	86	2445	1333	2216		1242	321
Vermilion . . . . S. Dak.	742	917	1083	973	1314	1161	916	479	694	785	468	187	705	920	284	689	938	167	605	510	1203	280	1291	663	642	1510	238	887	704	960	1189	1166	502	115	1143	1043	891	1345	1293	1089	450	785	1383	1165	1282	726	1055	1242		1073
Washington . . . . D. C.	1648	542	33	2045	392	1493	290	594	403	303	1490	895	397	1726	1141	1210	1214	1139	936	813	647	943	2295	473	763	927	936	1940	567	968	204	145	1150	1012	122	1980	188	480	2360	96	710	1845	2437	313	2335	1035	2105	321	1073	

AIR-LINE DISTANCES BETWEEN THE PRINCIPAL CITIES OF THE UNITED STATES

DISTANCES ARE GIVEN IN STATUTE MILES

peninsula was annexed in 1802 to the Territory of Indiana. In 1805 Michigan was organized as a Territory, retaining this status until it was admitted into the Union as a State in 1837.

MINNESOTA.—Physiography.—Most of the surface is an undulating prairie, diversified with low wooded hills. In the northeast is the Mesabi Range, which attains an elevation of 1,920 feet. Thence the land slopes down to 602 feet at the southern boundary. The "Height of Land," a wide watershed in the northwest part of the State, divides the streams among the basins of the St. Lawrence, Hudson's Bay, Missouri and Mississippi. By far the largest area drains into the last-named river. Most of the Red River Valley is quite flat. A striking feature of Minnesota's topography is the number of lakes, about 7,000. Most of them are small, but there are several that, singly, cover hundreds of square miles. Some have no apparent outlet. A number of small streams flow into Lake Itasca, in which the Mississippi rises. Many rivers are broken by falls. These can furnish enormous water power. Northeast of the Mississippi stretches a vast belt of white pine forest covering nearly one-fourth of the State. This yields much softwood lumber; birch, ash, elm and maple are obtained from the "Big Woods," which extend south from Crow Wing River to within a few miles of the Iowa line. The climate, though severe in winter, is invigorating, the air being free from the excessive humidity found in the Northeast States. In summer the weather is often very hot, but spring and fall are pleasant seasons. The rainfall, though not copious, is well distributed through the growing season. Most of the soil is a rich dark loam.
Minerals.—In the northeast, in the Mesabi, Cuyuna, and Vermilion Ranges, are located the richest iron deposits in the world. The ore is chiefly red hematite of high grade and suitable for steel making. As it absorbs but little moisture, it can be shipped profitably by way of the Great Lakes to the blast furnaces of various cities on the shores of these lakes. For some years Minnesota has been the leading State in the production of iron ore. There is no coal, but apparently inexhaustible beds of peat are found in the Lake Superior district. Building stones, such as granite, gneiss, sandstone, limestone, and quartzite, are quarried in various sections. Cement rock and fire clay are common.
Agriculture.—The deep fertile soil enables the State to grow cereals extensively, though much of the arable land is not cultivated. Wheat is the staple crop. Red River Valley wheat is unexcelled, the land there being of remarkable fertility. Corn grows well over most of the State, and is first in value; oats second. Other very important crops are hay, wheat, potatoes, rye, barley, and flaxseed. The dairying interests are extensive, there being hundreds of creameries and cheese factories. The number has increased rapidly in late years. Cattle, horses and hogs are raised in large numbers. Sheep farming is an important industry in the south part of the State, and the wool clip amounted to 8,354,000 pounds in 1938. Minnesota has a forest area of about 50,000 square miles, birch, cottonwood, spruce and pine being the most common trees. Much timber is cut every year, but the State has an excellent system of forest supervision, and tree planting is encouraged.
Manufacturing.—The manufactures are various and active, motive power being readily obtainable from river falls. Meat packing is the most important industry, followed by flour production, Minnesota's immense crop of wheat being supplemented by the wheat harvests of North Dakota, South Dakota, and other States. Lumbering is important but production is decreasing. Dairy products, condensed milk, woodenware, boots and shoes, bricks and leather goods are also manufactured.
Commerce.—A network of railroads and a waterway to the Atlantic by way of the Great Lakes and the St. Lawrence River afford ample shipping facilities for the export of the State's products. Minneapolis, the center of the milling interests, sends flour to every civilized country on the globe. Iron ores and timber are shipped by way of the Great Lakes to Eastern industrial centers.
History.—Radisson and Groseilliers may have reached this region about 1655-59. One of the first Europeans to visit it was the French explorer, Duluth, and it is believed that in 1678 he built a fort near the present site of the city of Duluth. A Franciscan priest, Father Hennepin, discovered in 1680 the Falls of St. Anthony, and in 1686 Nicholas Perrot took formal possession of the region in the name of the French King. French fur traders before 1700 had established posts on Lake Pepin and on the Minnesota River. Part of Minnesota was included in Canada until the latter province was ceded by France to Great Britain in 1763 and by Great Britain to the United States in 1783. Captain Carver of Connecticut explored this region in 1766. Western Minnesota was included in the Territory of Louisiana, and later in the Territories of Missouri, Michigan, Wisconsin, Iowa and Minnesota. In 1819 the United States erected Fort Snelling. In 1849 the Territory of Minnesota was organized. Its area was nearly double the area of the present State. Minnesota, with its present limits, was admitted into the Union in 1858. A serious Indian war broke out in the year 1862, but was suppressed in a few months by United States regular army troops.

MISSISSIPPI.—Physiography.—Mississippi is in the basin of the Gulf of Mexico. The northern and central parts have a rolling surface, but the northeast, which is forested, is an upland region, attaining near Iuka a height of 780 feet above sea level. The State as a whole slopes gently to the south and west. Along the Mississippi River, north of Vicksburg, the land is low and somewhat swampy, and subject to inundation. This land is very fertile, and much of it is undergoing reclamation. There is no better cotton-growing land in the world. The bottom lands of the Mississippi and other rivers are protected from overflows by levees, which are built by the State. The forest area is very large. Spanish moss, a fibrous material much used in the upholstery trade, is a product of the Gulf Coast forests. Much of Southern Mississippi is level and covered with long-leafed pine woods, which yield immense quantities of tar and turpentine, as well as lumber. In the northern part of the State deciduous trees are common; over 100 species have been officially listed. Cypress is abundant in the swamp regions; oaks, tupelos, sycamores, persimmons, magnolias, sweet gums, hickories, elms and maples in other sections. Three-fourths of the lumber cut consists of yellow pine. Oak is the principal hardwood. As fast as the timber is cut off, the land is utilized for truck farming, being very well adapted for this purpose. The climate is semi-tropical, especially in the south, although frosts are not unknown. The rainfall averages 50 inches annually.
Minerals.—There is not much mineral wealth in the State. Lignite coal measures occupy a small area in the northeast. Fire clays are distributed throughout the State and are of good quality for brick and tile making. Some building stone, gypsum, lime, marls and phosphate rock have been found. There are several mineral springs of high repute.
Agriculture.—Mississippi is chiefly an agricultural State and has a very large number of farms in proportion to its cultivated area. The cash income from field crops in 1938 was $119,381,000. Cotton and corn are the chief staples. Oats, hay, white potatoes, and sweet potatoes are other important products. Some sugar cane and rice are grown in the south. Diversified farming has been introduced, and its benefits are seen in the successful cultivation of nuts and semi-tropical fruits, as well as in the growing of cereals and sorghum. Cattle, horses, mules and hogs are raised in great numbers. The native fruits comprise persimmons, papaws, plums and grapes.
Fisheries.—Mississippi's fishing interests are of minor importance. The oyster and shrimp fisheries are the most valuable.
Manufacturing.—Although Mississippi is not important as a manufacturing State the number of industrial plants is increasing. Lumber, naval stores, wood preserving, and grist-mill products are important products. Cottonseed oil and cake and cotton goods are also among the most valuable manufactures. The deposits of clays are utilized in the making of drain pipe and of pottery.
Commerce.—Bordering on both the Mississippi River and the Gulf of Mexico, the State has the double advantage of river and sea transportation. Pearl River and Vicksburg are the chief customs districts. Several trunk railroads link the commercial centers of the State with all the larger cities of the Union.
History.—Hernando de Soto's expedition reached Mississippi in 1540, and Marquette and Joliet in 1673. Formal possession of the lands adjoining the Mississippi was taken in the name of the King of France by the French explorer, La Salle, when he descended the river in 1682. He gave the name of Louisiana to this new territory. Fortifications were constructed on the present site of Biloxi in 1699, and a permanent settlement was made there in 1712. Natchez, originally called Rosalie, was founded in 1716. The growth of the French settlements was slow, however. New Orleans, founded in 1718, attracted many colonists from the upper districts. In 1763 this region was ceded by France to Great Britain, but in 1783 it passed into the possession of the United States, a part of it rejoining West Florida, a Spanish province. In 1798 the Mississippi Territory was organized. It included a wide area on the east and north not belonging to the present State, but the Territory was not given any part of the Gulf Coast. Much of Alabama was annexed to the Mississippi Territory in 1804. Congress added in 1813 the Gulf counties to the Territory. These were taken from the Spanish province of Florida during the War of 1812, and formally ceded by Spain in 1819. The Territory was admitted as a State with its present boundaries in 1817. With the other Southern States it joined the Confederacy in 1861. Readmission into the Union was granted in 1870, after the State legislature had ratified the 15th amendment.

MISSOURI.—Physiography.—The Missouri River forms part of the western boundary and also crosses the State. North of the river the surface is generally rolling. There is much prairie land toward the west and in the east is a large forested area. South of the Missouri the country is more undulating, and it becomes rougher and more hilly toward the southwest, where the Ozark Mountains form a series of peaks. The southeast is somewhat swampy but has a fertile soil. Levees here protect the low-lying land from inundation by the Mississippi. Severe earthquakes occurred in this district in 1811-12. Highlands, limestone bluffs, border the Mississippi River, but west of these the surface becomes more nearly level. Most of Missouri drains into the Mississippi River or into its great tributary, the Missouri, which crosses the State from west to east. A small portion of the southwest is drained by the Arkansas River. Missouri, being in the central part of the United States, has a continental climate, and therefore is subject to greater varieties of temperature than are experienced in seaboard States within the same lines of latitude. The southeast of the State has the mildest climate. The average July temperature is 80° F. in the extreme south and 75° F. along the northern boundary. The average temperature for January ranges from 35° F. in the south to 20° F. in the north. The rainfall is abundant.
Minerals.—There are large deposits of iron ores and the coal fields cover about 14,000 square miles. But the competition of the Lake Superior district, supplying iron ores which are transported cheaply to points near Pennsylvania coal and the development of southern iron industries, have checked the progress of Missouri's pig-iron output. This State is first, however, in the production of lead. Cobalt and nickel are found in some of the lead ores. Limestone, granite, glass sand, barytes, grindstones, and sandstones are other mineral products obtained in large amounts. Kaolin, fire clays, potter's clay, and cement rock are found in various sections. Petroleum and natural gas have been drilled for successfully in some of the western counties.
Agriculture.—Owing to the varieties of good soil, ample rainfall and temperate climate, the State raises nearly all the chief agricultural staples. The principal crops are corn and hay. Wheat, oats, potatoes, cotton, and sorghum are also grown. The live-stock industry receives much attention; and mules, horses, cattle, and hogs are raised largely in excess of home needs. Missouri sheep contributed 8,711,000 pounds of wool in 1938 to the State's wealth. Poultry products are of great value. There were 21,127,000 chickens on farms in 1939. Dairying is important, large quantities of dairy products being shipped out of the State. Missouri ranks high in the yield of watermelons, tomatoes and garden vegetables. Thousands of acres are devoted to the cultivation of small fruits; and orchard products, apples especially, are grown in immense quantities. Peach and pear culture is also important.
Manufacturing.—Among the more important manufactures are motor vehicles, tobacco goods, paints, boots and shoes, and packed meats. Other valuable products, dependent on the State's agricultural, mineral or timber

resources, are chemicals, paints, bricks, drain tiles, and wagons. Missouri has grown rapidly in population and wealth and has increased her manufactures until she is now the second manufacturing State west of the Mississippi. Foundries and machine shops have multiplied; and flour milling, lumber working, printing and publishing, and the manufacture of clothing and electrical apparatus now employ, each, many thousands of hands.

Commerce.—The State is well supplied with railroads, especially in the northern part, which is traversed by great trunk lines. St. Louis, Kansas City, St. Joseph and Joplin are the principal railroad centers. Much of the trade in grain and cattle passes through Missouri. Railways connect the State with ports on the Gulf, and traffic on the Mississippi by means of large steamers is increasing.

History.—Missouri was included in the vast province of Louisiana, France claiming it on the ground that

the southern boundary northwest across the State and separates the State into two main drainage systems, the Missouri and the Columbia. In the east the surface is rolling but is interrupted by a number of small mountain chains and high hills. Canyons abound, eroded by rivers many of whose upper courses are broken by cataracts. The Great Falls of the Missouri descends, in a series of cascades, 160 feet. In the southwest one of the peaks reaches an altitude of 12,850 feet, and their tops are perpetually snow-capped. The river valleys have a deep loamy soil. The rainfall is not sufficient for general farming, but irrigation reservoirs have been constructed in various parts of the State. The climate is dry and healthful, and the winters are cold and dry. The warm and dry Chinook winds do much toward moderating the excessive cold. The summers are hot, but the heat is not too great for outdoor labor. The average July temperature is 70° F. and the average temperature for January is 11° F. Much of the eastern

The live stock industry has long been the chief interest, cattle ranging the valleys in vast numbers the year round. In 1938, Montana produced 24,510,000 pounds of wool, being surpassed in order by Texas, Wyoming and California. Dry farming is practiced in some sections, but irrigation has been extensively introduced where needed, and 2,600,000 acres have been reclaimed by its aid. There are numerous forested areas in the west and northwest, the trees being mainly conifers, and great lumbering interests have been developed there. Western white pine, western larch, Douglas fir and lodgepole pine are the more common species of trees.

Manufacturing.—Manufactures are increasing, due to the utilization of hydroelectric power, but they are still rather small in volume. Copper refining is the most important industry. Others connected with mining, as quartz crushing and smelting, are carried on. Woodworking, flour milling, petroleum refining, lumbering and other industries intended to supply local needs are numerous. Railway car construction and repair are also important. There is abundant water power still to be developed.

Commerce.—Three great lines of railroad, the Northern Pacific, the Great Northern, and the Chicago, Milwaukee, St. Paul & Pacific, traverse the State, each line having a number of branches. Other railways afford other parts of the State ample transportation facilities. The Missouri and Yellowstone Rivers are navigable for short distances.

History.—French trappers, in 1743, were the first Europeans to enter what is now Montana. Eastern Montana was part of the Louisiana Purchase, but remained unexplored by white men till the Lewis and Clark expedition crossed the State in 1804. The western portion was part of the Oregon country and held jointly by the United States and Great Britain until 1846. Trading posts were established on the Yellowstone in 1809, 1822 and 1829, and in 1846 Fort Benton was built. A discovery of gold in 1858 attracted little attention, but there was a large influx of prospectors in 1863 at Bannack, Virginia City, and Helena. Montana was made a Territory in 1864, being set off from the Territory of Idaho. The Indians were very troublesome and troops were sent against them. A long campaign culminated in the extermination of General Custer's command near the Little Big Horn River in 1876. Shortly after, the Indians were defeated and most of them captured or driven out of the region. The wealth of precious minerals drew many settlers, and the completion of the Northern Pacific Railroad in 1883 brought Montana into communication with the rest of the Union. The Territory became a State in 1889.

COPYRIGHT 1910 BY KISER PHOTO CO. FOR GREAT NORTHERN RAILWAY
GOULD MOUNTAIN, GRINNELL GLACIER AND LAKE, GLACIER NATIONAL PARK

it was discovered by La Salle, who sailed down the Mississippi to its mouth in 1681-1682. Marquette and Joliet had even earlier (1673) descended the great river as far as the mouth of the Arkansas, and it is thought that De Soto, too, may have founded the State in 1541. The first settlement was made by French colonists at St. Genevieve in 1735. French fur traders founded in 1764 a trading post on the present site of St. Louis. About 1720, lead was discovered; and at about the same time the mine La Motte was opened. With the purchase of Louisiana Territory from France in 1803 by the United States the Missouri region passed to the United States. Immigration into the State was rapid and it was organized as a Territory in 1812, and part of the Territory became a State in 1821. Its admission involved the question of extending slavery into new States. Missouri was finally admitted as a slave State under the terms of the famous "Missouri Compromise."

The name Missouri had been applied to the part of the former Louisiana Territory north of what is now the State of Louisiana, and the present boundaries of Missouri were not defined until 1835. Missouri stayed with the Union in the War Between the States, but contained many southern sympathizers.

MONTANA. — Physiography. — The Bitter Root Mountains form the western boundary. East of them the Rocky Mountains traverse the State and between these ranges lies a vast basin. The most striking topographical feature is the high and broad ridge of the Rockies called the Main Divide. This extends from

half of the State is treeless prairie, though cottonwoods, willows and a few other species of trees fringe the rivers. The western section, however, is heavily forested with western white and yellow pine, larch, Engelmann spruce, Douglas fir, lodgepole pine and cedar.

Minerals.—Montana has immense mineral resources. Copper, silver, coal, zinc, gold, and lead are the chief products. It is one of the leading copper-yielding States. The value of gold, silver, copper, lead, and zinc produced in 1936 was $41,587,700. It ranks high in the production of manganese ore. Much bituminous coal is mined and used in local industries. Tungsten, corundum, and grindstones are obtained in paying quantities. Mineral springs have also been found. Iron is found in several counties. Petroleum deposits are situated in the northern part of the State and the wells produced 5,868,000 barrels in 1936. A number of natural gas wells supply gas for industrial purposes. The sapphire mines have produced some gem stones. Building materials, such as granite, marble, slate, and limestone, are abundant. There are large deposits of fire clays and glass sands.

Agriculture.—West of the main range of the Rocky Mountains the rainfall is sufficient for farming purposes. East of this range, however, irrigation is essential for successful agriculture. The area of farm land is steadily increasing, though as yet but a small percentage of the State's tillable land is under the plow. Wheat, hay, oats and corn are the chief crops. Fruit growing has become a very valuable pursuit, the apple harvest amounting to over 500,000 bushels annually.

NEBRASKA.—Physiography.—Nebraska is in the Great Plains region and its surface, a vast plain, slopes gently upward toward the Rocky Mountain foothills. In the extreme west the surface is about 5,000 feet above sea level. The alluvial land of the river valleys is exceedingly fertile. More than half of the State is covered with glacial loess, which also forms a very rich soil. Along the Missouri there are some bluffs; and the hills known as the "Bad Lands," with lower sandhills, are found in the northwest. The State is well watered, three large rivers cross it, and the Missouri borders it on the northeast and east. There are some pine forest areas in the upper Niobrara Valley, but the State is not well supplied with timber. In the east the rainfall averages 30 inches, but only 15 inches in the west where irrigation or "dry farming" is essential to successful agriculture. The climate is dry and temperate but subject to extremes, as Nebraska lies far inland.

Minerals.—Building stone, limestone, chalk, sandstone, and gypsum are quarried in various counties. Cement, fire clays, and potter's clays are common. Salt is obtained from salines by evaporation. Some potash also occurs in the State.

Agriculture.—Nebraska ranks high in agriculture. A deep and rich loam covers most of the eastern half of the State, and all farm crops of temperate latitudes can be grown there. Wild grasses afford pasturage to horses and sheep, and there are extensive cattle ranches in the western part of the State. The wool clip amounted to 2,604,000 pounds in 1938. Corn is the leading crop. Next in value is wheat. Hay, oats and potatoes follow in importance in the order named. Sugar-beet growing is a highly valuable industry, 30 tons to the acre being sometimes obtained without irrigation. Sorghum, flaxseed, tobacco, vegetables and orchard fruits, especially apples, are raised. Large numbers of swine are fattened for the market. Dairy products also contribute largely to the State's wealth.

Manufacturing.—Lack of cheap fuel has somewhat retarded the State's growth in manufacturing. Most of the manufactures are associated with the State's products. The largest industry is meat packing. Dairy products and flour milling come next in value. Agricultural implements, flour, wagons, bricks, cars, smelting products, tiles and salt are important items. The output of beet sugar has steadily increased.

Commerce.—There are ample facilities for transportation, the State having about 6,103 miles of railways. Trunk lines connect the principal cities with other commercial points in all parts of the Union.

History.—It is possible that Coronado's expedition, which left Mexico in search of the Seven Cities of Cibola, reached the southern part of Nebraska in 1541. Later Spanish explorers claim to have gone as far up north as Coronado, but there is no trustworthy account of their journeys. Marquette, descending the Mississippi, passed the mouth of the Missouri in 1673. French fur traders visited this region as early as 1700, and in 1739-40, the Mallet brothers crossed the region from east to west, naming the Platte River. France ceded the country to Spain in 1762. As a part of the Louisiana Purchase it passed to the United States in 1803 and was traversed by various American exploring parties shortly thereafter. A trading post, established at Bellevue in 1807 by Manuel Lisa, a Spaniard, became the first settlement. From then on, until 1854, a number of forts and depots for supplies were established to support the great rush across the State of gold seekers and Mormons. The Nebraska district was afterward a part of the Missouri Territory. When Missouri became a State in 1821 Nebraska was left without organization. In 1834, however, it was made a part of the Indian country. In 1854 Nebraska was organized as a Territory and was admitted to statehood in 1867. Settlement was greatly stimulated by the Homestead Act of 1862, and by 1867 the Union Pacific Railway was extended across the State.

NEVADA.—Physiography.—Nevada is in the great plateau region of western North America. This region includes the "Great Basin," much of whose surface is occupied by this State, and which is really a series of long narrow basins separated by nearly parallel mountain ranges running generally north and south. In some cases only narrow canyons intervene between the ranges. The surface of the valleys is arid, the only plants being sagebrush, greasewood or other desert vegetation. Here and there are shallow lakes. The general surface elevation of the State is from 6,000 to 8,000 feet above sea level. In the south there is an abrupt slope down to the Colorado River, which is 470 feet above the sea. This stream affords navigation to the Gulf of California. The longest river wholly within the State is the Humboldt, which rises near the eastern boundary and flows west and south until, greatly reduced by evaporation, it spreads out in the large swamp known as Humboldt Lake. The valley through which the Humboldt flows is the only east and west one in the State and forms the route of one of the transcontinental railroads. The climate is dry, as most of the west winds lose their moisture passing over the Sierras. Winter temperature often falls below zero, and in summer the thermometer has recorded 100° F. The annual rainfall averages ten inches only and is unevenly distributed, most of it falling in the winter months.

Minerals.—The State is rich in minerals. In 1875 it produced more gold and silver than all the rest of the United States. In 1936 copper was the most valuable product, 135,650,000 lbs. being produced; gypsum and silver follow in commercial importance in the order named. Zinc, tungsten, and quicksilver are other valuable products found. Antimony, salt, sulphur, lead, and borax are obtained in paying quantities; and deposits of building stone, anthracite, and lignite are worked. The total value of principal metals mined in 1936 was $28,950,190.

Agriculture.—All the temperate-zone staple crops are produced in Nevada wherever the soil is watered. Hay is the most valuable crop. Large harvests of wheat, potatoes, barley, oats, and corn are obtained in the irrigated districts. In the bottom land of the Colorado cotton and subtropical fruits grow well. The grazing of cattle and sheep is next in value to the mineral production. The native grasses afford excellent pasturage, even in winter, cattle fattening on them readily. Nevada is one of the great wool-producing States, the wool clip amounting to 5,756,000 pounds in 1938. Several large irrigation projects are under way.

Manufacturing.—The manufacturing establishments are not numerous, but they are steadily increasing and their output shows a high percentage of gain since the census of 1930. Flour milling, car building, ore smelting and refining and lumbering are the principal industries. Considerable manufacturing is done to supply local needs.

Commerce.—The State has 2,114 miles of railway. The Southern Pacific and the Western Pacific cross Nevada, and there are several long branch line connections.

History.—It is believed that the first white person to visit this region was the Franciscan friar, Francisco Garcés, from Mexico, who, in 1775, passed through it on his way to California. In 1825, Ogden of the Hudson's Bay Company entered Nevada, visiting the Humboldt River, and Fremont's exploring expedition spent some time there in 1843-1844. By the Guadalupe Hidalgo treaty, which in 1848 closed the Mexican War, the territory became part of the United States. Next year a company of Mormons settled in the Carson River valley at Mormon Station, now called Genoa. Utah Territory, organized in 1850, comprised all the territory between 37° north latitude and 45° north latitude, extending from the Rocky Mountains to California. Nevada Territory was organized in 1861, and was admitted as a State in 1864, but the present State boundaries were not defined until 1866.

NEW HAMPSHIRE.—Physiography.—The surface is generally rough and hilly, an Appalachian ridge extending along the west side of the State and culminating in the White Mountains. The highest peak of these is Mt. Washington (6,288 feet). The southeastern part is low but is diversified with small rounded hills of glacial drift—drumlins. There are numerous beautiful lakes, the largest being Lake Winnepesaukee, which is about 16 miles long and 6 miles wide. The White Mountains, called the Alps of America, are noted for their wild and romantic scenery. They are the summer resort of thousands of pleasure seekers from all parts of the country. Ample water power is supplied by the rivers, of which the Merrimac is the most important. It turns more spindles than any other stream in the world. Much of New Hampshire's soil is stony. In the valleys of the Saco and the Connecticut, however, the land is fertile and well cultivated. There is an abundant rainfall, and the climate is healthful, though the winters are severe on account of the elevation of the land. The State was originally heavily forested, but most of the merchantable timber—white pine—has been cut down. Lumbering is the oldest industry in New England.

Minerals.—Granite, quarried at several points, comprises one-half of the value of the mineral output. Other mineral products are soapstone, mica, scythe stones and fictile clays. Small deposits of iron, tin ore, lead, silver and zinc have been found.

Agriculture.—Only one-third of the State's acreage is in farms, the rest being too stony for profitable cultivation. Hay is the most valuable crop, followed by potatoes and corn. Oats, barley, and buckwheat are also raised. Orchard fruits are grown, apples being the chief market product. Dairying is an important industry, much milk being shipped to Boston and other cities.

Manufacturing.—Most of the manufactures are carried on in cities and towns in the southern part of the State, where the extensive water power of the Merrimac can be utilized. Cotton and woolen goods, boots and shoes, paper and paper pulp are the chief products. Metal goods, machinery, woodenware, leather, and other manufactures also employ large numbers of workers. Shipbuilding is an important industry.

Commerce.—Two trunk railroad lines connect New Hampshire with the rest of the Union, and shorter railways offer transportation facilities to all sections of the State. The Grand Trunk Railway affords direct connection with Canada's chief centers of trade.

History.—An English navigator, Martin Pring, entered the mouth of the Piscataqua River in 1603, coasted south from there and returned to England, where he made known his discoveries. The famous French explorer, Samuel de Champlain, touched at the Isle of Shoals in 1605, and Captain John Smith sailed along the New Hampshire coast in 1614. New Hampshire was part of the land grant given by the Council for New England in 1622 to Mason and Gorges, and the next year a settlement was made by David Thompson at Little Harbor, now in the town of Rye. In 1643 the territory was annexed to Massachusetts and was made a royal province in 1679, but the boundaries were not defined until some years later. New Hampshire was part of the "Dominion of New England," governed by Andros, the tyrant, who was driven out of the province in 1689. Indian raids retarded the territory's development until the close of the French and Indian war. New Hampshire early entered into the Revolutionary struggle for independence and was well represented in the patriot army at Bunker Hill. It was also New Hampshire troops under their Scotch-Irish leader, General Stark, that won the battle of Bennington, defeating a strong detachment of British troops sent by Burgoyne to ravage the country. In 1788 the Federal Constitution was adopted.

NEW JERSEY.—Physiography.—This is one of the smaller States of the Union, only three others, Connecticut, Delaware and Rhode Island, being of lesser area. New Jersey lies wholly within the Atlantic slope. In the south the surface is low, and slightly rolling, while in the northwestern section of the State, where it is traversed by low mountain ranges of the Appalachian system, it is hilly. The highest point is only 1,805 feet above sea level. The Orange Mountains are three short parallel ridges in the north central part of the State. Along the New Jersey shore of the Hudson River there runs for some miles a ridge of trap rock known as the Palisades, famous for its scenic beauty. Marshes occupy a considerable area in the northeast. The western part of the State drains into the Delaware River. Most of the soil in the coastal plain is sandy, while in the Piedmont district it is a rich loam composed chiefly of clays and marls. The annual rainfall ranges from 42 inches to 50 inches. Between the northern part of the State and the southern there is considerable variation in temperature. Owing to its higher elevation, the north is colder than the south. Ocean influences also help to moderate the winters of southern New Jersey, which lies much lower than the rest of the State. The mean winter temperature of the southern part is 35° F. and of the northern 25° F. The mean summer temperatures are, respectively, 75° F. and 67° F. The State has several noted summer resorts, as Atlantic City, Asbury Park, Long Branch, and Ocean Grove. Lakewood, surrounded by pine woods, is a famous winter resort for invalids.

Minerals.—Building stones, iron ores, roofing slates and zinc are worked in the northern part of the State. Cement rock is quarried in large amounts. Fire-brick clays, potter's clays, glass sand and franklinite are abundant and of high grade. Granite, limestone, sandstone and infusorial earths are found, and there are extensive deposits of marl. This is utilized in the manufacture of fertilizer.

Agriculture.—The soil, a red sandy loam, is easily cultivated, but its needs fertilizing everywhere except in the river valleys. Market gardening and commercial floriculture are extensively pursued in the central and southern parts of the State, New York, Philadelphia and other large cities near by furnishing ready markets for the products. Potatoes, hay, corn, wheat, and rye form the chief farm crops. The tomato pack is large. Orchard cultivation receives much attention, and apples, peaches, pears and small fruits are grown. The cranberry harvest is of considerable value. The State's dairy interests are very active. The cash income from field crops in 1938 was $39,424,000.

Fisheries.—The State's oyster and sea fisheries are of great value. Menhaden are taken for oil and fish guano. Clams are dug in large amounts for city markets. The Delaware River has been stocked with black bass and shad; and perch and trout are also taken in the streams and lakes. Bluefish, sheepshead, butterfish and perch are the other products of the State's fisheries.

Manufacturing.—New Jersey has become one of the leading States in manufacturing. The yearly output includes a wide range of goods. Oil refining, copper refining, silk weaving and making of wire goods, machinery, chemicals, dyeing and finishing of textiles, foundry and machine-shop products, rubber articles and woolen goods are prominent industries. There is also a large production of canned fruits and vegetables, glass, electrical apparatus and high explosives. New Jersey is the leading State in the manufacture of pottery and chinaware. Portland cement, brick, terra cotta and tiling are also produced.

Commerce.—The two principal railroads traversing the State, the Pennsylvania and the Central Railroad of New Jersey, supply ample facilities for passenger and freight transportation. On December 31, 1937, there were 2,133 miles of railway in the State of New Jersey. The chief seaports, Jersey City and Hoboken, have an extensive commerce, both foreign and domestic. Lines of ocean-going steamers connect them with the principal ports of Europe and Asia.

History.—Verrazano, Florentine navigator, sailing under the French flag, is credited with having dropped anchor in New York Bay in 1524. Hudson explored a part of eastern New Jersey in 1609. During 1614 Cornelis Jacobson Mey explored the lower Delaware River. The first permanent settlement was made in 1617 at Bergen by Dutch colonizers from New Amsterdam, the region being then regarded as belonging to New Netherland. In 1623 a settlement was also founded at Fort Nassau, near Gloucester City. Lord Berkeley and Sir George Carteret were granted the country in 1664 by the Duke of York, who afterward became James II. of England. Carteret had been governor of the Isle of Jersey and he called the newly granted province New Jersey. In 1676 it was separated into two provinces, East New Jersey and West New Jersey, the latter section being kept under the proprietorship of Carteret, while the western province passed to the Society of Friends (Quakers) who had settled there some time before. William Penn bought West New Jersey and afterward, in 1682, East New Jersey. In 1702 New Jersey became a royal province, but it was not until 1738 that a separate governorship was established, the province before that year having a separate legislature but being under the jurisdiction of New York. New Jersey promptly took sides with the patriots at the beginning of the Revolution and was the scene of many battles before the war closed. It accepted the Constitution in 1787, thus becoming one of the original thirteen states of the Union.

NEW MEXICO.—Physiography.—The State is a high plateau traversed by mountain ranges. The only part of the State less than 4,000 feet in height above sea level is in the south. The ranges extend in detached series from north to south. The northwest mountain chains are divided by many canyons. There are large forests of cedar, spruce and pine in the mountainous districts, while such deciduous trees as sycamores, cottonwoods and oaks are found in the river valleys. Pine and spruce are cut for lumber. In the southeast is the Llano Estacado, or Staked Plain, a broad tract with scanty vegetation. Nutritious natural grasses cover the mountain basins and afford excellent pasturage. The valleys are generally level, and their soil is noted for its fertility when irrigated. The long plateau, called the Continental Divide, crosses the western part of the State. New Mexico's climate is very dry, the air is clear, and respiratory diseases are almost unknown. The mean temperature for the year is, at Santa Fe, 50° F. The rainfall, which is but slight, comes in summer. In the mountain districts the winter cold is severe.

Minerals.—Mining is the State's chief industry. Large deposits of copper, zinc, gold, silver, and lead are extensively worked. Coal fields underlie thousands of square miles, both bituminous and anthracite, but they are, as yet, not greatly developed. Excellent building stones, including granite, sandstone, limestone and marble are quarried. Turquoises are obtained in four localities within the State. Other important mineral products are molybdenum, potash, cement rock and fire clays. The value of mineral production in 1936 was $45,858,089.

Agriculture.—The soil is rich, but the scanty rains do not supply water enough. Irrigation is practiced with excellent results, the continual sunshine being very favorable to plant life. With the completion of the various irrigation projects now under way, agriculture will become of greater importance. Cotton has in recent years become a profitable crop. Wherever "dry farming" is in operation its success is unquestionable. Potatoes, beans, hay, corn, wheat, sweet potatoes, and

rye are grown. Such fruits as apples, peaches, figs, apricots, pomegranates and grapes flourish in the irrigated sections. The cash income from field crops in 1938 was $13,748,000. Stock-raising is a very important industry, the wild grasses affording rich pasturage, no hand feeding or sheltering being necessary for the stock. New Mexico ranks high in the production of wool, the clip being 14,966,000 pounds in 1938 against 10,100,000 pounds in 1921. The arid areas are noted for many picturesque species of cactus and yucca.

Manufacturing.—The more important manufactures include lumber and timber products, the output of the petroleum refineries, butter, non-alcoholic beverages, and flour and grain-mill products.

COURTESY OF NEW YORK CENTRAL RAILROAD

LOOKING DOWN THE HUDSON RIVER VALLEY BELOW WEST POINT

Commerce.—There are 2,866 miles of railway, including trunk lines and branches. These afford ready transportation to all parts of the Union. Mine products form the largest item of shipment.

History.—Cabeza de Vaca, coming from Mexico, visited this region as early as 1536, while Fray Marcos de Niza is believed to have entered it three years later. Coronado, heading an exploring expedition, traversed the country in 1540 and Espejo in 1582. By 1630 the Franciscans had founded ten missions in Arizona and New Mexico. In 1598, Don Juan de Oñate led 400 colonists into the country and settled at the junction of the Rio Chama and the Rio Grande. The year of Santa Fe's founding is variously estimated as falling between 1598 and 1616. The natives were then living in huge communal houses (*casas grandes*), wore cotton garments of their own manufacture and had mastered the art of pottery making. They also practiced irrigation and raised large crops of corn and vegetables. The Franciscan monks established a rigid rule over the Indians until 1680, when they revolted and drove out the Spaniards. Spanish domination was not reestablished until 1692-96, but was then maintained until the Mexican Revolution in 1821. The territory was surrendered to the United States in 1848 by Mexico under the terms of the treaty of Guadalupe Hidalgo. It then included, besides New Mexico, parts of Arizona, Nevada and Colorado. New Mexico Territory was organized in 1850. In 1853 by the Gadsden Purchase a large strip was annexed in the south. The northwest corner was transferred to Colorado in 1861, and the western half of New Mexico was formed in 1863 into the Territory of Arizona. Statehood was conferred on New Mexico in 1912. Santa Fe is capital of the State as formerly of colony and territory.

NEW YORK.—Physiography.—The Adirondack Mountains, geologically a part of the Laurentian Highlands of Canada, occupy much of the northeastern part. The western section of the State is undulating, descending in rolling terraces to Lake Ontario. The Catskills form another dissected mountain mass, noted for its picturesque scenery. These low mountains slope abruptly to the Hudson; and on their west side the descent to the Mohawk valley is equally steep. Central New York is a plateau whose streams belong to the St. Lawrence system. Its soil is fertile and this region, with its remarkable series of long narrow lakes, the "Finger Lakes," is noted for its scenic beauty. Many of the rivers furnish water power for manu-

facturing purposes, and Niagara Falls in the west supplies one of the world's largest hydro-electric systems. The rivers belong to five main systems, the St. Lawrence, Mississippi, Delaware, Susquehanna and Hudson. The Hudson River is the only large one flowing entirely within the State. To the drainage basin of the Hudson and its large western branch basin of the Mohawk much of New York's commercial supremacy is due. The depressions of the Hudson valley and the Mohawk valley were early utilized as highways to the west, and the latter valley made possible the construction through it of a large canal connecting Lake Erie with the Hudson River, which is navigable from Albany to the sea.

The climate varies somewhat with the locality. In the extreme southeast and in Long Island the January mean temperature is 30° F., but is as low as 15° F. in the Adirondacks region. The corresponding July figures are 72° F. and 66° F. Compared with these two sections, the central and western parts of the State have a climate less subject to extremes. There is an abundant rainfall in all sections.

Minerals.—The State is noted for its immense deposits of rock salt. Some of these are estimated to be 150 feet thick. Granite, marble, sandstone, and limestone are abundant. There are large beds of slate and extensive deposits of iron ore, hydraulic cement, talc, graphite, gypsum, fire-brick, and potter's clays. Petroleum and natural gas are found in the southern part of the State. Minor mineral products are emery, garnets, infusorial earths, and crystalline quartz. Saratoga has famous mineral springs.

Agriculture.—Dairy farming is the leading agricultural industry, the cash income from live stock and livestock products in 1938 being $199,968,000. Hay was the most important crop in 1938, producing 5,501,000 tons. New York produced during this year 26,588,000 bushels of oats; 26,840,000 bushels of potatoes, 25,345,000 bushels of corn; 16,380,000 bushels of apples; 7,533,000 bushels of wheat; 4,307,000 bushels of barley; 2,496,000 bushels of buckwheat; 1,955,000 bushels of tomatoes; 16,360 tons of cherries and a great variety of truck and canning crops.

Forests.—Forestry practices are carried out on all State forest land, the bulk of which is in the Adirondacks. Hemlock and spruce furnish most of the timber cut.

Fisheries.—Many thousands of fishermen are employed in the river, lake and deep-sea fisheries. Whitefish, shad, cod, mackerel and other food fish are taken in immense numbers for the New York markets. Long Island has extensive menhaden fishing interests that supply fish oil and fish fertilizer. Oysters and clams are other important products.

Manufacturing.—New York is the foremost manufacturing State. This position it has long held, although the State lacks coal mines. There is ample water power; Niagara Falls alone can supply millions of hydro-electric horsepower. The State's supremacy in manufacturing, however, arises from the large number of shops and factories making high-grade products. The industries are numerous and widely distributed. Clothing is the most important manufacture; printing and publishing next. Other industrial products are foundry and machine-shop products, boots and shoes, sugar, musical instruments, creamery products, tobacco goods, chemicals, coffee roasting, knit goods, flour, packed meats, leather, electrical apparatus, men's furnishings, lumber products, and furniture. In 1936, the value of the State's manufactured products was $6,094,393,038.

Commerce.—New York is the leading commercial State. Nearly half the imports and exports of the whole country pass through the customs district of New York City. This is now the most important seat of commerce on the globe. New York's coastwise trade is also very large, and much of the traffic of the Great Lakes finds its way eventually to this great commercial emporium. A railway mileage of 8,166 miles and an electric trackage of 343 miles connect the State's principal cities with one another and with all the active trading points in the United States and Canada. The longer railroads are the New York Central, the Erie, the Lehigh Valley and the Delaware and Hudson. The canals have a total length of 525 miles, the longest and most important one, the Erie, being 340 miles long and 12 feet deep. It connects Lake Erie with the Hudson River. Buffalo is the western terminal and Albany the eastern.

History.—Verrazano probably cast anchor in New York harbor in 1524. In the interest of some Dutch merchants Henry Hudson explored in 1609 New York Bay and the river which has been named after him. In the same year Samuel de Champlain, coming from Quebec, visited the northern part of the present State. A number of Dutch sailors passed part of the winter of 1613-14 on the tip of Manhattan Island, and in 1613 some Dutch adventurers established near the present site of Albany a trading post which they called Fort Nassau. This was abandoned in 1617. Permanent settlements were begun on Manhattan Island in 1623 by companies of Walloons, and they also established a trading post, Fort Orange, near Albany. Peter Minuit was in 1626 made director general of the Dutch West India Company, and in that year he bought Manhattan Island from the Indians for goods valued at $24. As the Dutch West India Company desired only to trade with the Indians for furs, the emigration of permanent settlers was not encouraged. But as the acquisition of land from the Indians presented but few difficulties, settlements continued to increase in number. In a few years, however, the company was forced to surrender its monopoly of trade, and then colonists from various countries adventured to New Netherland, as the country was called by the Dutch, and in a few years the chief town, New Amsterdam, had a cosmopolitan population. According to the French Jesuit missionary, Father Jacques, who visited New Amsterdam in 1643, the 500 inhabitants were divided into various religious denominations, including Calvinists, Puritans, Baptists, Lutherans and Catholics, and eighteen different languages were spoken in the town. In 1664 an English squadron of war ships anchored in the harbor, seized the town and renamed it New York in honor of the Duke of York (afterward James II), to whom Charles II, his brother, had granted the country. New York was the theatre of several battles during the Revolution and it was near Saratoga in this State that the British general Burgoyne and his army surrendered in the field. This decisive victory by the Americans encouraged France to come openly to the aid of the Colonies. Slavery was abolished in 1817. The Erie Canal was opened in 1825 and furnished New York a direct water route to the West, which gave a start to the city's immense foreign trade. Since then, progress has been very rapid, and New York is now first among the States in population, manufacturing, commerce and wealth; hence it is called "The Empire State."

NORTH CAROLINA. — Physiography. — The western part is mountainous, the high Great Smoky (or Iron) Mountain range bordering the State. Southeastward extends the Allegheny chain, and between these two mountain ranges there are various ridges. Mitchell's peak in the Black Mountains is the highest peak (6,684 feet) east of the Rocky Mountains. Several lower peaks are over 6,000 feet in height. The State is usually divided by geographers into three belts —the Atlantic coast plain, the Piedmont plain and the Appalachian Mountain district in the west. The central part of the State, the Piedmont plain, is much lower, has a rolling surface and excellent soil, and is the best developed section. There are many fertile valleys and rounded hills in this belt. Eastward to the Atlantic the surface is still lower and has large areas of marsh land. There is the "Tidewater" section. When reclaimed, this swamp land is very fertile. The climate of western North Carolina is healthful and here there are several noted health resorts. The rainfall averages 52 inches annually and is well distributed through the growing season. Severe frosts occur but seldom. In the coastal plain the forests consist mainly of long-leaf pines, loblolly pines and scrub oaks. Cedars, cypresses and live oaks are found in the swamp districts. Palmettos occur in the south. Oaks, chestnuts, and hemlocks are found in the mountain districts. As the climate is varied from subtropical in the southern lowland to the sub-arctic in the Appalachians, the flora shows a wealth of species unequaled in any other area of equal size. Here are the famous carnivorous plants, the Venus flytrap and the pitcher plant, composites, leguminous plants, many kinds of shrubs and berries and wild grapes.

Minerals.—The first gold mine operated in the United States was located in North Carolina, but the gold yield has always been small. Granite is extensively quarried. Clay products contribute one-half of the State's mineral wealth. Mica is mined in several counties. Corundum, coal, feldspar, talc, phosphate rock, iron and barytes are worked.

Agriculture.—Farming is the chief occupation. Fruits are grown in the eastern part. Tobacco is the most important crop, 519,230,000 pounds being produced in 1938. Cotton is second. Corn, hay, sweet potatoes, wheat, peanuts, white potatoes, oats, and buckwheat are grown extensively. In the production of tobacco, North Carolina and Kentucky excel all other States. Truck growing has developed into a very important industry in recent years.

Fisheries.—Along the Atlantic coast fishing is an important industry. Seining is the method most often employed, especially in Albemarle Sound, the most valuable fishing district on the State's seashore. The yearly fish catch is valued at about $2,000,000 annually. Shad, oysters, and clams form the most prominent items. Alewives, bass, perch, mullet, bluefish, weakfish and other varieties of food fish are also taken.

Manufacturing.—There are enormous supplies of water power readily available for manufacturing purposes. It is estimated that the rivers of the State can furnish 3,500,000 horsepower. Only a fraction of it is as yet utilized. Cotton goods, tobacco, furniture and lumber are the most important manufactures. The pine forests yield large quantities of naval stores, which are exported to various parts of the globe. North Carolina has made notable and rapid increase since 1920 in its output of tobacco manufactures, and of hosiery, knit goods, other cotton goods and furniture and has great industrial possibilities.

Commerce.—The estuaries and large rivers of the Atlantic plain and 4,783 miles of railroad track—trunk lines and branches—afford ample facilities for communication.

History.—It is believed that John Cabot saw, in 1497, the North Carolina coast, but no attempt at settlement was made till Sir Walter Raleigh in 1585 sent over from England a company of emigrants who founded a colony on Roanoke Island, which, however, they soon abandoned. He sent a second colony in 1587, but it also failed. Emigrants from the colony of Virginia made the first permanent settlement at Albemarle in 1660. Charles II. in 1663 granted the province of Carolina to eight "lords proprietors," and later it was divided into North Carolina and South Carolina. An Indian war broke out in 1711, but the savages—the Tuscarora tribe—were defeated with the aid of volunteers from Virginia and South Carolina. North Carolina became a royal province in 1728. It very early took the patriot side in the uprising of the colonies in 1774 against England and was the first State to order her delegates in Congress to vote for independence. During the Revolution the State was invaded twice. It was a slave State and joined the other Southern States in seceding from the Union in 1861. At Durham Station Johnston surrendered to Sherman on April 26, 1865. This event practically closed the Civil War. North Carolina was readmitted into the Union in 1868.

NORTH DAKOTA. — Physiography. — Immense rolling prairies occupy the surface east of the Missouri River, which drains much of the State, while in the west there are extensive broken plateaus. There are no mountains, the so-called Turtle Mountains being merely a plateau covered with woods. In the southeast are the "Bad Lands," so termed on account of the difficulty of traveling in this district, which contains many deeply eroded clay hills of fantastic shape. In the southwest the land gradually rises toward the grassy plateau of the Coteau du Missouri. This extends to the extreme southwest corner, where it attains the highest elevation in the State—3,468 feet above sea level. The valley of the Red River of the North is noted for its fertility, the soil being a deep alluvium. The surface soil of much of the State is a rich, dark loam. Though there are great extremes of temperature, the climate is healthful. The rainfall is sufficient for farming in some districts, and irrigation works have been constructed in the drier parts. The principal river is the Missouri. Its chief tributaries are the Cannon Ball, the Knife, the Little Missouri and the Heart. The Yellowstone flows into the Missouri near the Montana boundary. All these streams have their banks lined with high bluffs. A large number of lakes and ponds are scattered throughout the State. There are no forests, but along the river bottoms belts of cottonwoods or poplars are found. Wild grasses and other prairie herbage, excellent cattle food, cover many thousands of square miles.

Minerals.—Coal is the most valuable mineral. Most of the coal beds are lignite, but this is rapidly coming into use for various industrial purposes. Brick and pottery clays, lime, salt, and cement rock are other valuable products. Natural gas has been found in several districts, and some building stone is quarried.

Agriculture.—The soil is not only unusually fertile but readily cultivated. It retains moisture well and thus favors "dry farming." Yet occasionally severe droughts occur. The chief crop is wheat. Oats, flaxseed, hay, barley, corn, rye, and potatoes are raised. Although many of the immense ranches are being divided into farms, the live-stock interests are still very active. Wool is an important product. Dairying has become a very valuable industry. Butter, cheese and condensed mik are shipped East in large amounts.

Manufacturing.—The output of creamery and dairy products is very high, the value of products being over $36,000,000 in 1935. Much flour is milled, and there is considerable manufacturing to meet local needs.

Commerce.—The Northern Pacific Railroad traverses the State. Other long railways are the Great Northern, and the Minneapolis, St. Paul and Sault Sainte Marie. All three connect with Canadian lines. The branch railroads act as feeders to the trunk lines, and the State is thus enabled to ship its products to all parts of the country. The Missouri and the Red River are navigable during part of the year.

History.—Traders of the Hudson's Bay Company and the North West Fur Company were the first to attempt settlement in the region. Some of them lived there for a time but no permanent settlement resulted. North Dakota formed part of the Louisiana Purchase, and shortly after its acquisition by the United States in 1803 it was named the Missouri Territory. The Lewis and Clark expedition wintered in 1805 near Mandan. Lord Selkirk aided a number of emigrants from Scotland to erect a trading post at Pembina in 1810. He mistakenly supposed the site to be Canadian territory. Near this trading station some French Canadians had also made a temporary settlement in 1780. In 1604 Lewis and Clark entered the region; Fremont reached the Territory in 1839; and in 1855 Lieutenant Warner led an exploring party and made a report thereon to the Government. That part of North Dakota east of the Missouri River was in 1849 added to the Minnesota Territory, and the western portion became Nebraska Territory. Dakota was organized in 1861. At that time it included what is now South Dakota and parts of Montana and Wyoming. Indian hostility retarded settlement until the savages were subdued in 1866, and then the stream of immigration into the Territory rapidly increased. Dakota was divided in 1889 into two States—North Dakota and South Dakota, and both were admitted to the Union during the same year.

OHIO.—Physiography.—The surface is a low plateau ranging from 425 to 1,550 feet above sea level. A watershed averaging 1,160 feet in height crosses the State from northeast to west. On the northern side the slope, which is toward Lake Erie, is more abrupt than the southern one, a much larger slope, declining to the Ohio River. There are more streams flowing into the Ohio than into Lake Erie, and as they have cut deep valleys the country has an undulating or rolling character. The largest river in the State is the Muskingum. This is navigable for 100 miles. Steep bluffs border many miles of the Ohio and the other rivers. The northwest has a well-wooded area, partly swampy. The rainfall is abundant in the growing season and the climate is healthful, though sudden changes of temperature occur, especially in the southern portion. Variable winds prevent any prolonged extremes of heat or cold. Temperatures of —39° F. and of 113° F. have been experienced, but the mean temperature for January is 26° F. and for July 73° F.

Minerals.—Ohio is rich in mineral wealth. Bituminous coal underlies about 12,000 square miles, and the State ranks high in coal production. Fire and brick clays are abundant. The value of Ohio's clay output exceeds that of any other State. There are iron-ore deposits in the south. Salt, lime, gypsum, cement rock and mineral waters are important products. The State's output of petroleum and of natural gas is very large. Ohio has long been a leading State in the yield of oilstones, grindstones, scythe stones and sandstone. Limestone and marble are also quarried extensively.

Agriculture.—Ohio is one of the leading farming States. Most of the land is tillable. Corn is the principal crop; wheat is next in value. Hay, oats, potatoes, and tobacco are other crops of importance, the cash income from field crops in 1938 being $85,448,000. Orchard fruits, apples, peaches, pears and plums are produced in large amounts, especially in the Lake Erie district, which also is noted for its numerous vineyards. Flax is a staple crop. Much attention is given to truck gardening and to the growing of sugar beets. The live-stock industry is very important—horses, mules, horned cattle, hogs and sheep being raised in very large numbers. The wool clip amounted to about 17,753,000 pounds in 1938. Poultry farms market every year goods valued at over forty millions of dollars. A large part of Ohio was formerly covered with forests of hardwood, largely white oak. But there is now left scarcely any of this valuable timber. In earlier days, when lumber was easily obtained, the State had several important industries based on the ready supply of wood. Some of these continue, though now all their lumber stock has to be procured from the South and the Northwest.

Manufacturing.—The State ranks fourth in the value of manufactures. Coal and other raw materials together with an abundance of water power gave Ohio opportunity to become a great manufacturing State. The woodworking interests are active and varied, planing-mill products and fine furniture being the most important items of this type of manufacture. Ohio is the leading State in tires, foundry and machine shop products, pottery, and sandstone products. Dairy products are of great value. Packed meats, cement, clothing, flour and gristmill products contribute largely to the State's wealth. In output of iron and steel goods the State ranks next to Pennsylvania, the iron ores of the Lake Superior district being easily transported by way of the Great Lakes to the lake shore of Ohio. It also ranks second in the production of motor vehicles, this being the third most important industry in the State. The construction of steel steamers is an industry of importance. Electrical apparatus and supplies, agricultural implements, tobacco goods, and miscellaneous rubber goods are manufactured in immense quantities. Glass, clothing, and boots and shoes are other important manufactures.

Commerce.—The State is favored with direct water communication by means of the Ohio River with the Mississippi Valley States and by Lake Erie with Canada and the States bordering on the Great Lakes. Canals connecting the Ohio with Lake Erie afford unusual facilities for transportation and the Erie and Welland Canals enable vessels to reach the Atlantic. Ohio has six ports of entry for foreign commerce—Cleveland, Sandusky, Toledo, Columbus, Dayton and Cincinnati. Owing to the State's inland location, the foreign trade is small compared with the vast domestic traffic. Ohio ranks high in total steam railroad mileage, being 8,574. Electrical railroad tracks to the extent of nearly 953 miles greatly aid passenger transport.

History.—Probably the first white visitor to this region was La Salle in 1669, when he discovered the Ohio River and followed its course as far as the Louisville Rapids. Governor Dongan of New York sent in 1686 a trading expedition, but it met with no success. The district was early claimed by both France and England. A French explorer, Celoron, crossed Lake Erie in 1749 from the Canadian side and, pushing through the wilderness to the Allegheny River, sailed down that stream to the Ohio. The region remained under the control of France until after the French and Indian War when the Treaty of Paris in 1763 vested possession in Great Britain. During the Revolution George Rogers Clark took possession of the land as far west as the Mississippi River, and the region passed to the United States. In 1783 it became part of the Northwest Territory. The oldest town in the State, Marietta, was settled by New Englanders in 1788, two earlier settlements having been totally destroyed by Indian tribes. Losantiville, now Cincinnati, was also founded in 1788. Indian warfare raged in the last decade of the 18th century till the red warriors were crushed by General Wayne at Fallen Timbers in 1794. In 1800 the region was organized as a separate territory, and it entered the Union in 1803 as a state. Commodore Perry's great victory in 1813 over a fleet of British warships was won not far from Put-in-Bay, which indents the Ohio shore. Direct water communication between Lake Erie and the Atlantic was established by the construction of the Erie Canal in 1825. This gave a strong impetus to Ohio's development in agriculture, and immigration into this comparatively new and fertile region rapidly increased.

OKLAHOMA.—Physiography.—A rolling prairie from 900 feet to 2,500 feet in elevation occupies most of the surface. The eastern part is well timbered. The highest land is in the extreme west. A range of hills, called the Chautauqua Mountains, extends through the northwestern part and the low Wichita Mountains, noted for their scenic attractions, rise above the plains in the south. North of Texas the State is mostly a plateau. Agriculture is the chief occupation of the people, for the land is generally cultivable. Red clay and finely decomposed sandstone materials constitute much of the soil of the plains. In the river valleys the soil is alluvial, deep and of almost inexhaustible fertility. The climate is generally mild, though the summers are sometimes hot, and severe cold waves are not unknown. The rainfall averages about 31 inches and is sufficient for successful farming. The Red River drains the southern part of the State and the Arkansas the northern.

Minerals.—Oklahoma is the second State in petroleum and natural-gas gasoline production. There is an abundance of coal of high quality. Building stone, including granite and marble, is plentiful. Large deposits of lead and zinc ores are being worked. There are extensive beds of asphalt and gypsum.

Agriculture.—Agriculture has developed with extraordinary rapidity in the last decade and the State ranked high in 1938 in income from chief crops, $76,430,000. Cotton is the most valuable crop. Hay, oats, white potatoes, sweet potatoes, orchard fruits, broom corn, barley, peanuts, and rye are grown extensively. Oklahoma is first in the production of broom corn among the States, having produced in 1938, 12,500 tons. The raising of livestock is a profitable industry. The number of cattle on farms in 1939 was 2,182,000; horses, 372,000; mules, 175,000; sheep, 351,000; swine, 954,000. Poultry products contribute much to the State's wealth. Though the plains here, as elsewhere, are treeless, they are generally covered with nutritious grasses for cattle feeding. Sagebrush, yucca, and cactus are plants found only in a small strip of the extreme western part of the State. In the east there are forests of valuable hardwoods, oak, walnut, and hickory.

Manufacturing.—Petroleum refining, meat packing and the manufacture of flour and grist-mill products are the chief industries in the order named. Dairy products are next in value. Many factories have been started to supply local needs. Brickyards, tile works, dairies, machine shops and foundries, and planing mills are also among the most important.

Commerce.—The State is well supplied with railroads, their trackage being 6,655 miles, and new roads are being planned. Complete shipping facilities are afforded to all parts of the Union.

History.—Coronado's troop of horsemen is said to have crossed this region in 1541, and the State may also have been touched by De Soto during that year. In 1803 the region became part of the United States through the acquisition of the Louisiana country. Congress, in 1834, set apart most of the present State for an Indian reservation and named it Indian Territory. The principal tribes who have inhabited it are the Creeks, Choctaws, Cherokees, Chickasaws, Seminoles and Quapaws. Some of these owned slaves, brought with them from the south, and these tribes sided with the Confederacy in the Civil War. White persons were forbidden by law to purchase land held by any tribe. In 1886 the entry of other Indians was permitted. The Creeks and Seminoles sold most of their lands to the United States in 1889, and these were thrown open to settlers. The first white settlement was made at Oklahoma City in the same year. A mad rush to secure homesteads resulted, and population increased at a remarkable rate. In 1891 and 1893 the Government purchased the land owned by the other Indian tribes and opened it to settlement. Gradually the whites permeated the entire region. The loose system of authority made the country a refuge for fugitives from justice; and it was evident that steps had to be taken toward the formation of a stronger government. Each of the five tribes in the Indian Territory exercised its own form of local self-government. With a view to improving the conditions, the Dawes Commission was appointed in 1893, to prepare the Indians for individual allotment of land. In 1898 the work was completed, and the allotment legally established by the Curtis Act. In 1906 the Territory of Oklahoma and Indian Territory united to draw up a constitution, and in 1907 they were admitted to the Union as the single State of Oklahoma.

OREGON.—Physiography.—The State is separated by the Cascade Mountains into two great divisions, known as Western Oregon and Eastern Oregon, each having distinct climatic and agricultural conditions. From the steep cliffs of the Pacific Coast the surface rises eastward until the Coast Range, averaging 6,000 feet high, is reached. Between this range and the Cascade Mountains, which run parallel with the Coast Range, lie the fertile valleys of the Willamette and Umpqua Rivers. Two-thirds of the eastern part of the State is a rolling plateau with an average elevation of about 3,000 feet above sea level. In the northeast some of the rivers have cut deep canyons. The valleys, watered by the Snake River, the Columbia River and their tributaries, have deep, rich alluvial soils, but most of the southeast is desert through lack of rain. Irrigation has done much to develop this district, nearly 1,500,000 acres being under enterprises. The rainfall varies from the tremendous downpour of from 50 to 100 inches annually on the Pacific Coast to 10 inches in the southeast plateau. The rainy season along the coast lasts from October to the end of April, but is shorter in the Willamette Valley, the largest fertile area in the State. The rivers have immense latent power waiting to be turned into hydro-electric energy. Western Oregon has a mild climate owing to the fact that the prevailing winds blow from the Pacific Ocean, but the eastern district, being more elevated, is cooler. Extremes of temperature, however, are not unknown. All the mountain ranges are heavily forested. It is estimated that one-seventh of the standing merchantable timber of the United States is in Oregon. The most common tree, the Douglas fir, sometimes attains the great height of 300 feet. Oak is the principal hardwood. Other important trees are hemlock, western yellow pine, white fir, spruce, and cedar.

Minerals.—Gold is the chief metal mined, about 52,662 oz., valued at $1,843,170, being mined in 1937. Deposits of copper, lead, silver, platinum, and quicksilver are also worked. Granite, marble, limestone, sandstone and other building stones are quarried. Other nonmetallic minerals found are fire clays, coal, gypsum, borax, niter, potash, and asbestos.

Agriculture.—Oregon is mainly an agricultural State and the cash income from principal crops in 1938 was $46,659,000. In the valleys wheat, potatoes, oats, corn, barley, and rye are produced. Hops have long formed a valuable crop here. Exceptionally fine orchard fruits and grapes are grown in various sections. Oregon apples and plums bring the highest prices in Eastern markets, Hood River apples being especially sought after by dealers. Other important fruits are pears, cherries, plums, loganberries, and strawberries. Hay and sugar beets are leading crops. The live-stock interests are large and varied. Oregon is one of the great wool States, the wool clip being 17,115,000 pounds in 1938.

Fisheries.—Much capital is invested in the fishing industry. Salmon, caught in the rivers flowing into the Pacific, form the most valuable item of the fishing catch. Several State fish hatcheries aid in increasing the supply of young salmon. Herring, oysters and halibut are also caught.

Manufacturing.—For many years manufacturing was limited to turning into finished products raw materials found here in abundance—timber and grain. Now the State has entered on the secondary stage of manufacturing, and minerals and metallic ores are being used as bases of manufacturing. Lumber and lumber products are as yet the most important manufactures. During the World War Oregon sent to eastern shipyards thousands of masts and spars made from trees cut in the State's forests. Flour and grist-mill products, creamery products, copper, tin and sheet-iron goods, packed meats, furniture, machine-shop products, paper and canned goods are also important manufactures.

Commerce.—Oregon is well provided with transportation facilities. Ocean-going steamships reach Portland by way of the Columbia and Willamette Rivers. The Columbia River is one of the largest and deepest in the Union. At certain seasons of the year steamboats go from Portland, on the Willamette River, to Lewiston, Idaho, a city on the Snake River. The Lewis and Cowlitz Rivers, branches of the Columbia, are also navigable for steamers. Long trunk lines, with numerous branch railroads, carry Oregon's exports to all parts of the country.

History.—The region was first visited in 1543 by Bartolomé Ferrelo, a Spaniard. In 1579, Sir Francis Drake came to the Oregon coast, seeking a way home to England by the Northwest Passage. The Spaniards, Aguilar and Vizcaino, also touched the coast of this region in 1603. Another Spaniard, Perez, acting under orders of Charles III., King of Spain, sailed as far as 55° north latitude and on his return anchored in Nootka Sound. Heceta, with Perez second in command, led an exploring expedition in 1775 and landed near the present Port Grenville. There several members of his crew were killed in an attack by Indians. In 1778 the English navigator, Cook, touched at Nootka Sound. La Pérouse, a French commander, sailed along the Oregon coast in 1786. Explorations along the coast of Oregon were made by Ferrelo in 1543 and by Drake in 1579. Kendrick and Gray were sent by Boston merchants in 1792 to learn the opportunities for fur trading in this part of the Northwest. The Lewis and Clark expedition explored the country in 1805-06 and the Pacific Fur Company founded Astoria in 1811 at the mouth of the Columbia River. Russia, Spain, England, and the United States all laid claim to the region; but Spain and Russia soon relinquished their claims by treaty, and England and the United States agreed to occupy the region jointly. Many settlers and missionaries entered the country, which was held in control by the Hudson's Bay Company, the successor of the Pacific Fur Company. By 1844, American settlement had become so thick that demand for a definite location of boundary between Canada and the United States became the Democratic campaign slogan. The Democratic candidate Polk was elected; and tension between the two countries caused them to enter into a compromise placing the boundary approximately at the 49th parallel. In 1848, Oregon was organized as a Territory; and on February 14, 1859, admitted as a State.

PENNSYLVANIA.—Physiography.—The surface is varied. Three belts may be readily distinguished. First the Piedmont plain, about 60 miles wide, occupies the southeastern portion of the State. It rises from nearly sea level at Delaware Bay to a height of about 500 feet at the base of the mountains. The Appalachian Mountain region is the second belt. It extends northeast and southwest, is from 60 miles to 80 miles wide and is traversed by several nearly parallel ridges. Its average elevation is about 1,500 feet above sea level. This section is cut through only by the Susquehanna River. Most of the western half of the State forms the third belt, generally known as the Allegheny plateau. It is not level, being crossed in various directions by river valleys. Prominent topographical features are the parallel mountain ranges which, trending northeast and southwest, cross the State. These form part of the Appalachian chain. The lowland between them is a fine farming section. The valleys are very fertile. The southeast part of the State, which is comparatively level and low-lying, also has a rich soil. The State is drained mainly by three river systems, the Susquehanna, the Ohio, and the Delaware. The climate is milder in the southeast than on the western upland. South of the Blue Mountains the summer is long and the winter short and mild; but on the high plateau section snow falls sometimes to a depth of several feet and the mercury often sinks below zero. An abundant rainfall, averaging 38 inches annually, and evenly distributed through the seasons, renders farming successful in all parts of the State where the soil is tillable.

Minerals.—Pennsylvania's mineral output exceeds in value that of any other State. Its mineral riches form the basis of the State industrial life. The chief product is coal. Coal fields cover two-thirds of the State and more anthracite is mined here than in all the rest of the Union. Pennsylvania leads in production of coke, ferroalloys, pig iron, and slate. The State once produced most of the iron smelted in the Union and still mines large quantities of iron ore, mainly of the magnetite variety. Now, however, much iron ore is imported from the apparently inexhaustible deposits of the Lake Superior district. Petroleum and natural gas are other sources of great wealth. In 1859 petroleum was first discovered in Pennsylvania, and the yield constantly increased until 1882, when it reached 30,000,000 barrels. This amount was exceeded only once. In 1893 the petroleum output totaled 33,009,236 barrels. Since then the decline has been steady, and several other States now outrank Pennsylvania in the production of this mineral oil. Limestone, marble and sandstone are quarried in large quantities in the south and east. There are several salt springs and medicinal springs. Iron and corundum, nickel, zinc, and galena are found.

Agriculture.—All the agricultural staples of the Northern States grow well in Pennsylvania. Much of the soil in the valleys consists of decomposed limestone and yields large harvests of grain and forage crops. Hay and corn are the most valuable crops. Potatoes, wheat, oats, orchard fruits, buckwheat, and rye are also produced in great abundance. Tobacco is an important crop in the southeastern part of the State. Pennsylvania ranks high in the production of buckwheat. The livestock industry is very valuable, the number of farm animals being exceeded in but few States. The wool clip amounted to 3,008,000 pounds in 1938. Considerable areas in both the western plateau and in the northeast are densely wooded, but the trees are small. Oak, maple, ash, elm, and hickory abound in the lowlands. On the mountain sides flourish pine, beech, maple, and birch, while higher up grow spruce, fir, and larch. The plateau woods are mostly deciduous, chestnut and oak predominating, and in the southwest the locust and Kentucky coffee tree are found. The best of the merchantable timber has been cut down. Hemlock, however, is still abundant and furnishes much wood for the lumber market and bark for the tanneries. Some commercial hardwoods are still left, oak and maple being the most important.

Manufacturing.—Pennsylvania is second only to New York in the value of its manufactures. It is the leading State in the production of iron, steel, foundry and machine-shop products and plate glass. Hemlock bark being readily obtainable from the State's forests, the tanning interests here are very extensive. Locomotives, cars, flour, steel goods, planing-mill products and tobacco goods also add largely to the State's industrial wealth. Many thousands of hands are employed in producing woolen goods, worsteds, hosiery, carpets and thrown silk. Pennsylvania is one of the leading states in the manufacture of textiles and clothing. The Delaware shipyards have long been foremost in the construction of steel steamers. Important industries are sugar refining and the manufacture of chemicals.

Commerce.—The Delaware is navigable for ocean-going steamers to Philadelphia and to Trenton, N. J., for small vessels. During high water the Ohio and its constituent streams, the Allegheny and the Monongahela, can be navigated for considerable distances. Having Lake Erie on its northwestern border, Pennsylvania participates in the vast commerce carried on by means of the Great Lakes and the canals connecting them. Philadelphia and Erie are ports of entry and centers of considerable commerce, foreign and domestic. Pittsburgh controls an immense inland trade, and its shipyards build steamers for use on Western waters. There are 10,943 miles of railroad within the State. Several of the lines belong to extensive railroad systems—the Pennsylvania, the Erie, the New York Central, the Baltimore and Ohio, the Lehigh Valley, and the Delaware, Lackawanna and Western Railroads.

History.—Henry Hudson in the *Half Moon,* sailing under the Dutch flag, cast anchor in Delaware Bay in 1609. The voyage of Hudson was the basis of the Dutch claim of sovereignty over the country adjoining the river and the bay. The first settlement of Europeans in Pennsylvania was established in 1643 at New Gottenburg by John Printz, governor of New Sweden, though prior to their advent some Dutch traders had started posts for trading with the Indians. Claiming the whole of the Delaware River Valley under the discoveries of Henry Hudson, Governor Stuyvesant of New Netherland with a fleet of seven vessels captured in 1655 the Swedish trading posts. When New Netherland was surrendered to the English in 1664, the Delaware River settlements also became English territory. In 1681 William Penn, an English Quaker, obtained by royal patent the territory of Pennsylvania and in that year sent over some settlers from England. Next year Penn himself came with more settlers to the colony, and made a treaty with the Indians. Penn's laws were very liberal for the 17th century, and the colony prospered greatly. There was a large immigration of Scotch-Irish, whose descendants promptly ranged themselves on the patriot's side at the outbreak of the Revolutionary War. Many German immigrants, seeking religious freedom, added to the colony's growth. Delaware (then called the "Lower Counties") formed part of Pennsylvania till the Revolution, but had its own legislature. Mason and Dixon's Line was established in 1763-1767. Pennsylvania resisted the Stamp Act, which was Great Britain's last attempt to force taxation without representation on the American colonies, and a Provincial Congress met in Philadelphia in 1774 and adopted resolutions denouncing the tyrannous acts of England. Pennsylvania, after the battles of Lexington and Concord, raised troops for the defense of American liberty and during the Revolutionary struggle for independence the "Pennsylvania Line," as the province's volunteer force was called, was noted for loyalty and valor. The State was the theater of several important battles during the Revolutionary War, and was one of the thirteen original states of the Union. During the Civil War Pennsylvania took a very active part in aiding the Union cause, furnishing 336,000 men for the struggle.

RHODE ISLAND.—Physiography.—The surface is rough and hilly except near the seashore, where there are swamps and level tracts covered with second-growth trees. There are no mountains. The highest elevation, Durfee Hill, rises only 805 feet above sea level. Narragansett Bay reaches northward into the State about 30 miles. It contains a number of islands, one of which, Rhode Island, or Aquidneck, gives its name to the State. The soil is not rich, except on the islands. The climate is agreeable and milder than is the climate of the northern New England States. The Pawtuxet River, the Pawcatuck, the Wood and several other streams afford immense water power, of which much is utilized for manufacturing purposes.

Minerals.—Granite is the most important mineral, and there are several extensive quarries of this stone. Considerable lime is produced. At several points copper ores, iron, coal, graphite, and mica have been found, but the deposits are not extensive enough to repay mining.

Agriculture.—Rhode Island is not now a farming state and does not raise foodstuffs enough to feed its own population. Most of the land is better adapted to grazing than to tillage. Dairying is the most important industry connected with agriculture. Market gardening is carried on near the cities. Hay, corn, potatoes, and oats are the chief farming crops. Much attention is paid to orchard fruits, especially pears, peaches and apples.

Fisheries.—A large number of small vessels and about 1,000 men are employed in taking cod, haddock, bluefish, mackerel, and other food fish for Providence and New York markets. The lobster catch is important. Menhaden are caught for their oil and for fish guano. Porgies, shad and alewives are taken in Narragansett Bay. Providence River oysters and the Bay clams are of high grade.

Manufacturing.—Rhode Island is preeminently a manufacturing State and produces a great variety of articles. The chief manufactures are woolen, cotton and rayon goods, jewelry, rubber articles, bread and bakery products, electrical machinery and appliances, and textile machinery and parts.

Commerce.—Ocean liners call regularly at Providence, which is located on the Providence River, an estuary of Narragansett Bay. The Pawtucket (or Seekonk) River is navigable as far as the city of Pawtucket. Providence receives much coal, cotton and wool for use by the manufacturing establishments in the State and exports large quantities of finished goods. There is also an active coasting trade.

History.—It is believed that Verrazano visited Narragansett Bay in 1524. In 1614 Adriaen Block, a Dutch navigator, also explored the Bay, and in 1636 Roger Williams, a fugitive from the religious intolerance of the authorities of Massachusetts Bay Colony, settled with five companions at Providence. There he founded the first community in the world permitting freedom of religious opinions, political equality and separation of church and State. Other settlements were made at Portsmouth in 1638, at Newport in 1639, and at Warwick in 1643, and a union of the scattered towns was effected in 1644. A royal charter was secured in 1663, and so advanced and liberal were its provisions that it was retained as the fundamental law until 1842. Despite many troubles with the neighboring colonies of Massachusetts and Connecticut, and with savage Indian tribes, the little State prospered. At the beginning of the Revolutionary War, Rhode Island threw off the British yoke and took an active part in the struggle for independence. General Nathaniel Greene, next to Washington the ablest commander in the patriot army, was a Rhode Islander of Quaker descent. The settlements of Rhode Island were characterized by strong political individualism. Afraid that the establishment of a strong federal government would interfere with local privileges, it was with much reluctance that the State finally ratified the Federal Constitution, May 29, 1790. During the Civil War the State furnished to the Union armies more men than her quota demanded.

SOUTH CAROLINA.—Physiography.—For about 100 miles inland from the coast the surface is generally level, the soil is sandy and there are numerous pine forests and extensive swamps. This section is known as the Coastal Plain. Sandy islands, called Sea Islands, fringe the shore in the south. On the western side there is a wide sandy belt partly covered with pine woods. This belt is known as the Pine Barrens or the Sand Hills. West of this section the country becomes somewhat hilly and farther on the Piedmont plateau slopes up to the Appalachian system. The top of Sassafras Mountain, the highest peak in the State, is 3,548 feet above sea level. The chief rivers, including the Savannah, Great Pedee and Santee, are navigable

COURTESY OF U. S. GEOLOGICAL SURVEY
THE BAD LANDS OF SOUTH DAKOTA, FORMED BY WIND AND EROSION

for many miles. At the "fall line," where these streams and several others pass from the hard rock of the upland country down to the sandy coastal plain, falls or rapids occur and furnish much water power. The mountain region has a delightful winter climate, and the climate of the pine barrens district is dry and equable in all seasons. The rainfall averages about 45 inches yearly. Along the coast the climate is semi-tropical and the tree life differs much from that of the northern Atlantic States. Here palmettos, magnolias and live oaks abound. In the swamps the cypress flourishes and the loblolly and long-leaf pine grows on the coastal plain. But in the cooler upland oaks, hickories, elms, maples, chestnuts and other deciduous trees form the forests. Persimmon trees, plane trees and locusts also grow in this State. Wild grapes, raspberries, strawberries and other small fruits abound.

Minerals.—Brick and pottery clays, and stone, sand, and gravel are the most valuable mineral products. Moderate amounts of phosphate rock are quarried. Gold, silver, manganese, lime and monazite have been found in small quantities, but none is being produced in paying amounts at present.

Agriculture.—South Carolina is an agricultural State. Cotton is the predominant crop, about 650,000 bales being produced in 1938. Corn, the second crop in importance, yielded 26,767,000 bushels. Tobacco, hay, sweet potatoes, white potatoes, oats, wheat, peanuts, strawberries, tomatoes and peaches are large crops. Stock raising and wool growing are increasing. The valuable long-staple cotton was first grown on the islands along the Atlantic Coast. Rice is produced in the wet lands; and figs, pomegranates, peaches and grapes are grown extensively in the coast belt. Naval stores come from the pine barrens; and fruits and vegetables are also now raised there.

Manufacturing.—Cotton goods and lumber products are the most important manufactures. Cottonseed oil, flour, machinery and fertilizer are other valuable products. The output of naval stores is steadily decreasing owing to the continued cutting down of the pine trees.

Commerce.—The Savannah, Pedee, Congard, Wateree and Santee are all navigable for many miles, affording ample transportation facilities for trade. Railroad mileage has increased from 973 miles in 1860 to 3,588 in 1935. The longest roads are the Southern Railway, the Atlantic Coast Line and the Seaboard Air Line.

Some foreign trade is carried on by Charleston, cotton being the chief export by water.

History.—The first Europeans to visit the coast of what is now South Carolina were a party of Spaniards from Cuba in 1521. Jean Ribault attempted to found a colony in 1562 at Port Royal, but in a year it was abandoned. Charles II granted in 1663 the province of Carolina (then comprising the two Carolinas) to eight lords proprietors, court favorites. The first permanent settlement was made in 1670 at Albemarle Point on the Ashley River, and 10 years later it was moved to the present site of Charleston. The English philosopher, Locke, drew up for the new province a fantastic scheme of government which the settlers threw aside after a very brief trial. Various constitutions were tried, some almost feudal in nature, most of them leading to dissatisfaction and revolt. In 1729 North Carolina and South Carolina were made royal provinces. When the Revolutionary War began, South Carolina espoused the cause of the patriots, and in the latter years of the war several fierce battles were fought on her soil, including King's Mountain, the Cowpens, Camden and Eutaw Springs. It was one of the original thirteen states. The Nullification movement was started in South Carolina in 1832, but was crushed by President Andrew Jackson. In 1861 the State joined the Confederacy, and the first gun in the Civil War was fired in Charleston harbor by Confederates bombarding Fort Sumter. South Carolina was readmitted to the Union in 1868.

SOUTH DAKOTA.-—Physiography.—East of the Missouri River the land is gently rolling, the valley of the James River extending here north and south across half the State. The elevation of the State is about 2,000 feet with the exception of the extreme northeast corner. The soil is a sandy loam with heavy clay subsoil. West of the Missouri there are many buttes and ridges caused by water erosion. The highest elevation is in the west. Harney Peak (7,242 feet) is the highest point in the State. The Black Hills region is a good grazing country, but irrigation is needed to render it agriculturally productive. The Bad Lands section, which lies east of the Black Hills, is so named on account of the difficulty of traversing it. Deep ravines, high bluffs formed by eroding forces, steep hills—all destitute of vegetation—constitute the predominant features of this singular area. The climate is dry, and bracing, and the rainfall is usually sufficient to insure the growth of crops.

Minerals.—Gold is the principal mineral product, $20,-354,040 worth being produced in 1937. Tin ore is found, but is not mined extensively owing to the difficulty of reducing it. Silver, lead, copper and fictile clays are also obtained. Petroleum and natural gas have been found; and marble, cement rocks, sandstone and other building stones are quarried. Gypsum, lime, coal and mica are worked to some extent.

Agriculture.—Farming is the State's chief industry. Corn is the chief crop. Wheat, oats, hay, barley, flaxseed, rye, and potatoes are important field crops. Flax is raised for its seed. Vegetables and orchard fruits are raised for shipment to Eastern cities. Stock raising is a very important industry, the number of cattle in 1939 being 1,567,000; horses, 358,000; swine, 849,000; sheep, 1,392,000. The wool clip amounted to 8,947,000 pounds in 1938. Dairying is increasing in importance. There are some forested areas in the southwest, and the streams are fringed with trees, but lumbering is not important.

Manufacturing.—The principal manufactures are meat packing, dairy products, printing and publishing, car shop construction, and flour and grist-mill products. There are many small manufacturing establishments which supply local demands.

History.—French fur traders had visited this region prior to its transfer to the United States as part of the Louisiana Purchase in 1803. It was also traversed by the Lewis and Clark expedition in 1804 and 1806. The first permanent settlement was made at Bad River, near the present site of Pierre, in 1817 by fur traders. Indian raids and Civil War troubles delayed for years the growth of this section of the Northwest. In 1861 the Territory of Dakota was created, including North and South Dakota, most of Montana and half of Wyoming. Discoveries of gold in the Black Hills in 1874 caused an inflow of settlers into that district. By popular vote the territory (established 1861) was divided in 1887 at the forty-sixth parallel into two parts, and each of them was admitted as a State into the Union in 1889, one as North Dakota and the other as South Dakota.

TENNESSEE.—Physiography.—East Tennessee is hilly and in parts mountainous. It includes half the Cumberland plateau, which averages 2,000 feet above sea level. Middle Tennessee has an undulating surface with fertile soil and west Tennessee is low and level. The tract along the Mississippi is rich alluvial land. Here are many marshes and lakes abounding in wild fowl, and swamps covered with cypress trees. Everywhere the hills and mountainsides are heavily wooded, and forests of various kinds of timber trees are found in the alluvial plain along the Mississippi River. The climate is mild and healthful, especially on the Cumberland plateau, and there is an abundant rainfall, varying from 42 inches to 52 inches annually.

Minerals.—The State has great mineral wealth. Over forty different kinds of minerals useful in manufacturing industries have been found. Coal is the most important. Iron ores, zinc, copper, cement rock, glass sand and building stone (marble, limestone and sandstone) are other valuable mineral products. There are large deposits of phosphate rock and of clays—pottery and firebrick. Mineral springs are numerous.

Agriculture.—Corn is the chief crop. Cotton and hay follow in value. The variety of soils permits the growing of different products, and such staples as tobacco, wheat, sweet potatoes and white potatoes, oats, hemp, sorghum and peanuts are raised in very large quantities. Fruits are cultivated. The lumber interests are active, millions of feet of lumber being cut every year in the State's 27,000 square miles of woodland. Most of the timber is hardwood. Stock raising is of great importance, and in 1938 there were 1,125,000 cattle; 157,000 horses; 1,012,000 swine and 379,000 sheep in the State. The wool clip amounted to 1,536,000 pounds in 1938.

Manufacturing.—Rayon, knit goods, chemicals, meat-packing products, iron and steel goods, lumber, cars, cottonseed oil, leather, foundry and machine-shop products and tobacco goods are important manufactures. Immense quantities of spring wheat are ground.

Commerce.—The State has 3,799 miles of railroad trackage. Water transportation is afforded by the Mississippi and Tennessee Rivers. Memphis is the most important commercial center.

History.—The Spanish expedition under De Soto crossed the Mississippi near Memphis in 1541. In 1682 Marquette camped on the Tennessee bank of the Mississippi River; and, a short time after, La Salle built a fort where Memphis now stands. The English entered the region about 1748; but no permanent settlement was established before 1756, when Fort Loudon was built. The province of North Carolina once included the region now Tennessee, but in 1790 North Carolina ceded it to the United States Government. Other white settlements were made before the beginning of the Revolution; and in 1784 the settlers in convention proclaimed the district to be a State, to which they gave the name of Franklin. It, however, had a life of only four years. During the Revolution, the State did valiant service under the leadership of John Sevier. Congress organized the Territory "south of the Ohio" in 1790 and admitted it as a State in 1796. Tennessee voted to join the Confederacy in 1861; but east Tennessee, despite the presence of Confederate troops, remained loyal to the national government and contributed many men to the Union armies.

TEXAS.—Physiography.—The surface of Texas, the largest State in the Union, slopes gently from northwest to southeast, all the State's rivers flowing into the Gulf of Mexico. In the northwest is the "Staked Plain" (Llano Estacado), a plateau rising from an elevation of 1,000 feet in the south to 5,000 feet in the north. A large part of the western half of the State is in the Great Plains. There are several low mountain ranges in the western part, south of New Mexico. El Capitan, 8,700 feet high, is the highest point in the State. The coast region is flat and alluvial and fringed with swamps. The land here is rich and produces large crops. Along the coast there are numerous lagoons, cut off from the sea by narrow sandy islands. Western Texas is drier and is a cattle-raising district. In the north there are extensive forests, post oaks and blackjacks, and in the northwest is the mesquite timber region. The coast belt has a long and hot summer, but it is tempered by sea breezes. A delightful climate prevails throughout the inland part, the prairie region. In the northern highland district frosts are not unknown and even zero temperatures have been recorded. The rainfall is abundant in the southeast and in most of the coast tract, but decreases rapidly toward the west. Productive agriculture is not possible without irrigation west of 100° longitude. The whole State is remarkably healthful, except the swamp sections of the coast. The "northers," cool storm winds, which occur occasionally in winter, are seldom destructive.

Minerals.—Petroleum is the most valuable product. Natural-gas gasoline, natural gas, cement rock, zinc, clay products, asphalt, coal, and gypsum are mined with a large yearly output. Texas ranks high in the production of mercury, and is second in the output of asphalt, and sulphur. Some silver is also produced. Granite, sandstone, slate, and limestone are quarried. There are numerous mineral springs.

Agriculture.—Texas is the leading State in the value of agricultural products. It leads in the production of grain, sweet sorghums, and cotton. Among the chief crops are corn, wheat, oats, hay, peanuts, sweet potatoes, and rice. Sea Island cotton is cultivated in the coast districts and sugar cane in the river bottom lands. The hay harvest is large. Broom corn, barley, rye and onions are raised, but in minor quantities. Dairying is another industry in which the State ranks high, and stock raising is extensively carried on. In 1939, the number of cattle on farms was 6,955,000. Horses, mules, sheep and hogs are raised in great numbers, the figures for 1939 being: horses, 679,000; mules, 687,000; sheep, 9,856,000; hogs, 1,820,000. The yearly wool clip is larger than that of any other state, being 76,903,000 pounds in 1938. Much attention is given to the breeding of angora goats, and Texas contributes a great portion of the yearly mohair clip of the country. Poultry raising is very important and the State is famous for its turkeys. Orchard fruits, including peaches and apples, plums and prunes, figs, oranges and grape fruit, are grown. In the pine barrens the long-leaf pine is the predominant tree in the coastal plain and the short-leaf pine in the upland region. Deciduous trees prevail in the forests of the central part of the State. These comprise oaks, hickories, maples, elms, sycamores, mulberries, sweet gums, walnut and ash trees. The ornamental Osage orange tree also flourishes here. In the southeast the palmetto is a prominent figure in the landscape. It has been found profitable to cultivate the pecan tree—first found here wild—and groves of this valuable nut tree are now flourishing in various sections of the State. Along the rivers cottonwoods, live oaks and cypresses flourish. A noted lumber district is the Cross Timbers. It is covered with hardwood forests, principally oak. In the west and northwest there are large areas covered with mesquite, a characteristic tree of the southwest. It has a small trunk but very large roots. These are much used for fuel. Prairie grasses, nutritious cattle food, cover thousands of square miles of prairie. The arid region of the northwest is marked by the presence of the common desert plants, cactuses and yuccas.

Fisheries.—The fisheries are of minor importance. Oysters, trout, bass and red snapper represent the principal items of the catch.

Manufacturing.—Manufacturing was gaining rapidly in variety and output, but received a setback during the financial depression. Petroleum refining is the most important manufacturing industry. The manufacture of cottonseed oil, meat packing, flour milling, foundry and machine-shop production, lumber production and manufacture, railway car construction, the making of artificial ice, and textile manufacturing are among the most important industries. Since the discovery of petroleum some years ago, the refining of that oil gives employment to many thousands of wage earners and has placed the State in the lead as a producer of refinery products. Manufacturing here has the advantage of vast supplies of certain raw materials, as sulphur, petroleum, timber, grain and cotton.

Commerce.—Texas has the largest railway mileage in the Union, 16,641. There are several fine harbors on the Gulf Coast and these afford bases for both foreign and domestic commerce. Houston's export trade is second only to that of New York.

History.—The Spaniard Cabeza de Vaca with three companions, survivors of the ill-fated Narvaez expedition, wandered, in 1528, over a part of what is now Texas. Other Spanish explorers, the friar Marcos de Niza and the explorer Coronado, visited this region in 1540-42. During the next century several other expeditions essayed the alluring task of finding the Seven Cities of Cibola. The French, under the Sieur de la Salle, established a colony on Matagorda Bay in 1685, but soon abandoned it. Several missions were founded by Spanish Franciscans, beginning with the year 1690. Most of them were short-lived, however, and San Antonio, founded in 1714, is generally considered as being the first permanent settlement. After Mexico achieved independence in 1821, a tide of emigration from the United States set in to this northern Mexican province. American influence steadily became stronger and a revolt against the tyranny of the Mexican Government broke out in 1835. Houston's decisive victory over the Mexican commander, Santa Anna, at San Jacinto in 1836, freed Texas. The country's independence was recognized by the United States, Belgium, France, and Great Britain. In 1845 Texas was admitted into the Union as a State. A dispute over the question of boundaries was one of the causes of the Mexican War (1846-48). In 1861 the governor of Texas, Sam Houston, supported by the German settlers, attempted to hold the State for the Union, but the Secessionist sentiment was too strong, and Texas sided with the Confederacy. The last battle of the Civil War was fought on Texan soil—near the Rio Grande on May 13, 1865. In 1870 the State was readmitted into the Union.

UTAH.—Physiography.—The surface has an average elevation of 6,000 feet above sea level and is generally mountainous. The lofty Wasatch Range, forest-clad and extending nearly north and south, divides the State into two unequal parts, which are interspersed with plains and valleys. The larger eastern part is occupied mostly by a series of plateaus cut by river canyons. The west forms part of the Great Basin and most of it is a desert having an elevation of 5,000 feet. There are many small mountain ranges. Great Salt Lake, the most prominent natural feature, is 80 miles long and from 25 miles to 35 miles wide. The Great American Desert lies southwest of this lake. Utah's soil is, in general, a sedimentary loam which is very productive when watered. Sagebrush on the arid plains and grasses on the higher slopes form the chief features of the vegetation. The rainfall is not abundant enough to insure crops; but the soil, no matter how arid, when

THE FAMOUS MORMON TEMPLE, SALT LAKE CITY, UTAH. AT THE LEFT IS THE CAPITOL

irrigated, proves to be extremely rich and yields immense crops. Irrigation reservoirs are increasing in number and rapidly enlarging the productive area of the State. The climate is healthful, though extreme temperatures have been recorded, 116° F. and —50° F.

Minerals.—Utah is rich in minerals. There are immense deposits of coal, copper, and lead. Gold and silver are also found. Asphalt, salt, gypsum, zinc, and lime are also largely produced. Building stone and fictile clays are found in several counties. In 1936, Utah had an output of mineral products valued at $61,103,970.

Agriculture.—The chief crops are hay, wheat, potatoes, oats, barley, and sugar beets. Other important products are alfalfa, rye, corn, and orchard fruits, especially apples and peaches, the conditions being very favorable for their culture. The live-stock industry is a major industry, the lands available for grazing comprising about one-third of the State. Sheep grazing is prominent, and the wool clip in 1938 was 19,473,000 pounds. The acreage of tillable land has been steadily enlarged by dry farming as well as by irrigation. In 1930 over 1,700,000 acres were under irrigation enterprises. Dairying has become a profitable industry, a large amount of creamery products being shipped to eastern markets.

Manufacturing.—Manufactures have steadily grown in importance, but received a setback during the depression of 1929. Beet-sugar refining, ore smelting, flour milling, meat packing, dairy products, car shop construction, and the canning of fruits and vegetables are the principal industries.

Commerce.—The longest railroads serving the State are the Denver and Rio Grande and the Union Pacific. The total railway mileage is more than 2,100.

History.—A detachment from Coronado's exploring expedition is said to have visited this region in 1540, but the first authentic explorations were made in the summer of 1776 when a party of Franciscan friars reached Utah Lake. James Bridger, a trapper, discovered Great Salt Lake in 1824. William Ashley established a fur-trading post on Utah Lake in 1825. Fremont visited this territory in 1843, and Mormons under Brigham Young made the first permanent settlement in 1847 at Salt Lake City, and organized the so-called State of Deseret. By 1848 there were over 5,000 Mormons in the State. The territory within the present boundaries of Utah was part of the Spanish and Mexican possessions until the war with Mexico, in 1848, when it was ceded to the United States with other territory. Congress refused to recognize Deseret, however, and organized the Territory of Utah in 1850, in-

cluding what is now Nevada. Utah was admitted as a State into the Union in 1896.

VERMONT.—Physiography.—The Green Mountain Range, extending north and south, divides Vermont into two sections, known as the Champlain and Connecticut valleys. The range is cut through by four rivers which flow into Lake Champlain. All the larger streams are fed by many smaller tributaries so that the acreage of level or river bottom meadow is considerable. There are many plateaus, hundreds of acres in extent, hence much of the tillage land of the State is comparatively level or slightly rolling. The valley of Lake Champlain comprises a large area of tillable land of great fertility. Hillsides, often extending to the summits of the lower mountains, are covered with grasses. The climate is agreeable, especially in summer. The winters are cold but healthful. At Burlington, which is one of the coldest spots in the State, the highest mean temperature for July is 68° and the lowest mean temperature for January is 16°. The annual rainfall is 33 inches, usually enough to provide sufficient moisture for all crops. The surface is in general somewhat stony and the underlying soil varies from a stiff clay to a light sandy loam. The soils of the lake and river valleys, however, are fertile and repay cultivation.

Minerals.—Vermont is the leading State in marble quarrying. Marble from several districts is whiter and more lasting than the best Carrara marble. Granite ranks next in importance to marble. Slate is also produced in large amounts. Limestone quarries are operated in the western part of the State. Deposits of kaolin, asbestos and soapstone are worked.

Agriculture.—Hay is the chief field crop and in 1938, 1,106,000 tons were produced. The yield of other important crops was: corn, 3,120,000 bushels; potatoes, 1,884,000 bushels; oats, 1,736,000 bushels; apples, 475,000 bushels; barley, 145,000 bushels. Alfalfa has been grown very successfully in many parts of the State on well-drained soils. Clover and timothy mixed claim the largest acreage of the forage crops. Tobacco is grown extensively in the Connecticut valley. Potatoes lead all other crops in average per acre value. The hardy fruits do well in Vermont. Large commercial apple orchards are found in the Champlain valley, in the southern part of the State. Truck crops and small fruits are grown near the larger towns and cities for local supply and for shipment to the Boston and New York markets. Considerable acreages of sweet corn and string beans are grown for canning. The making of maple sugar is an important industry, the yearly production amounting to over 600,000 pounds.

Over 1,000,000 gallons of sirup are produced annually. Dairying is a leading occupation. Milk and cream are sent daily by fast freight trains to Boston and New York. Butter and cheese and canned milk are also exported. As reported in 1939 there were 448,000 cattle on farms, including cows and heifers kept for milk. The value of cattle has more than doubled since the census of 1909.

Manufacturing.—After stone products, woolen goods, wood pulp, grist mill and dairy products, foundry and machine-shop products, planing-mill products, hosiery and knit goods, fire brick and agricultural implements are the chief manufactures. Several rivers are broken by falls well suited for the development of hydroelectric power.

Commerce.—There is considerable trade with Canada. Burlington, the principal city of Vermont, is a United States port of entry. Newport is also the headquarters of a customs district. Steamboats ply on Lake Champlain and the Richelieu River which flows into the St. Lawrence, and convey cargoes between Vermont towns and Montreal. Canals permit vessels to pass from Lake Champlain to the Hudson River. The State has 1,017 miles of railroad track.

History.—Champlain in 1609 entered what is now Vermont. French traders built a fort on Isle la Motte in 1665, but the first permanent settlement was made at Fort Dummer near the site of Brattleboro in 1724. The French erected forts at Crown Point and Chimney Point in 1730-31 and harassed the settlers by using these forts as headquarters for raiders. All the French posts were captured by the settlers before 1759.

New York claimed jurisdiction over part of the Vermont Region commonly known as the New Hampshire Grants. This claim was resented by the people of this section, and a convention held at Bennington decided to resist any process of New York courts. The decision of the controversy was finally left to the King of England who decided in favor of New York in 1764. The settlers resisted, and in 1777 called a convention at Westminster which declared the Grants, as the settlements were called, an independent State.

Vermont early espoused the cause of the Revolutionary patriots. A company of Vermonters, "Green Mountain Boys," led by the famous Ethan Allen, and aided by some Connecticut volunteers, captured Ticonderoga and its British garrison on May 10, 1775. New York persisted in claiming Vermont territory for several years, but finally yielded and Vermont was admitted into the Union in 1791. This State was the first one to abolish slavery.

VIRGINIA.—Physiography.—The surface is divided into three distinct topographical regions—the Coastal plain, the Piedmont plain and the Appalachian Mountain district. These divisions cross the State from southwest to northeast in nearly parallel belts. The tidewater region is a low marshy section traversed by a large number of creeks and rivers and with a coast indented by estuaries of the York, James, Rappahannock and Potomac Rivers. In this tidewater section, the Virginia part of the Eastern shore is included.

The Piedmont plain is a higher and more rolling section, extending to the Blue Ridge Mountains. As these mountains form the most prominent feature of the State's topography, some geologists consider them and the adjacent country a distinct division of the State's surface. The plateau extending west from them falls sharply into the Cumberland valley. West of the Shenandoah valley lies the Appalachian region, a series of broken ridges inclosing narrow valleys.

The middle of the State is an undulating plain with an elevation from 200 feet to 500 feet. The "Valley of Virginia" is a broad belt of rolling country between the Blue Ridge and the Alleghenies. The forests comprise a variety of trees, including pine, oak, hickory, elm, poplar, birch, cedar, locust, juniper, cypress, and chestnut. The climate is mild and equable, except in the mountain districts, where the winters are cold. The rainfall is sufficient for farming in any part of the State and is well distributed throughout the growing season.

The greater part of the State drains into Chesapeake Bay or into the Atlantic, the largest river being the James. The estuaries indenting the coast from Cape Henry to the mouth of the Potomac are navigable.

Minerals.—Coal is the chief mineral product. Granite, clays, slate, limestone, iron and pyrite, mica, talc, soapstone, phosphate rock, and titanium are also found. Manganese is widely distributed. In the southwest there are large deposits of gypsum and rock salt. The mineral output is increasing with the general recovery from depression. Many of Virginia's mineral resources are not yet developed. The State has several mineral springs and watering places.

Agriculture.—The soil varies in fertility, the richest being in the Shenandoah valley. Fertilizers are now coming into general use and the crop yield per acre is augmenting. Market gardening has become a prominent industry. Corn and tobacco are the most valuable crops. Hay, potatoes, wheat, peanuts, oats, cotton, sweet potatoes, and rye are raised. Stock raising is carried on extensively; and creamery products are sent to northern cities. The wool clip was 1,709,000 pounds in 1938. Apple orchards are numerous, their product being much sought after in the markets of large cities.

Fisheries.—For many years the fishing industry has been of high value. Oysters represent the most important item of the catch. A noted food fish, the shad, is captured in large numbers every season. Clams, crabs, squeteagues, and alewives are also taken. Valued for oil and for commercial fertilizer, menhaden are seined in immense numbers.

Manufacturing.—Tobacco products (especially cigarettes and chewing and snuff tobacco), textiles (including rayon, cotton and woolen and hair goods), furniture, chemicals, paper and knit goods are leading manufactures. The state has large railroad repair shops, flour mills and iron works. Lumber products, cars and leather add to the manufactured wealth.

Commerce.—Practicable waterways are afforded by the estuaries and navigable streams, and there are numbers of safe harbors. Norfolk, which has one of the finest harbors in the United States, and Newport News carry on most of the foreign commerce. The Kanawha canal, the Albemarle canal and the Dismal Swamp canal aid traffic. Railroads connect all the principal cities of the State with the rest of the country. The chief exports are flour, corn, cattle, and tobacco.

History.—Virginia was the first colony to be permanently settled by immigrants from England, that country basing its claim to the region by virtue of John Cabot's visit in 1497. Following the visit of Sir Walter Raleigh's fleet in 1584, Virginia remained unsettled until colonists sent by the London Company founded Jamestown in 1607. Other settlements were soon made and in 1619 a colonial assembly was convened in Jamestown. This was the first body of representatives of the people called together in the New World. Negro slavery was introduced into the colony in the same year. In 1624, Virginia became a Crown Colony. A succession of tyrannical governors delayed the progress of the province. After Charles I was executed there was a large wave of Cavalier immigration. Under the rule of the Commissioners sent over by the Commonwealth there was religious and political toleration. But with the accession of Charles II the colony was hampered by navigation acts, was forced to bear the burdens of the slave traffic, and the frontier settlers had to suffer Indian atrocities, while the royal governors refused to heed the people's just complaints. In 1699 a large number of Huguenots came to the colony, and some years later a number of German emigrants settled therein. By 1756 the population had grown to 292,000. Most of the new settlers sought the west, and differences of opinion were frequent between these new settlers and the old "tidewater" plantation owners. Virginia took an early and active part in the colonies' struggle for independence. The State was the scene of many battles during the Civil War, having joined the Confederacy in April, 1861. The western part of the State, however, refused to secede, and was then organized as the State of West Virginia. Virginia was granted readmission into the Union in 1870.

WASHINGTON.—Physiography.—The State is divided by the Cascade Range, extending north and south. The western section is well timbered, has many fertile valleys and a moist and equable climate. The rainfall is heavy. The Cascade Mountains form a high rugged plateau about 100 miles broad. Many peaks rise from it, notably the three great volcanic cones of Mt. Rainier (Mt. Tacoma), Mt. St. Helens and Mt. Adams. Mt. Rainier is the highest (14,408 feet). It has several glaciers. The north central and northeastern parts of the State are mountainous. The Blue Ridge, a mountain range averaging 5,000 feet in altitude, occupies the southeastern corner. Puget Sound abounds in islands, some of them of considerable size, and has many fine harbors. The mountains encircling the sound are heavily forested. East Washington is mainly a great lava plateau, cut by numerous canyons and having but few forests. The rainfall there averages only 16 inches annually. The winters are short but cold and the summers hot and dry. The warm Chinook winds help to moderate the cold. Irrigation is essential to productive farming. The Columbia and Snake Rivers afford steamboat navigation for hundreds of miles. The State's timber wealth is very great.

Western Washington is noted for its forests of giant trees, such as Douglas fir, red cedar, white fir, and western hemlock. Spruce and pine also abound.

Minerals.—Extensive coal beds are worked, the coal affording a high grade of coke. Clays, cement rock, copper, silver, lead, zinc, and magnesite are mined. Gold is obtained from quartz veins. Granite, limestone, marble, and sandstone are quarried in large amounts. Antimony, arsenic, molybdenum, tungsten, and platinum have been found, but not in deposits large enough to pay for mining. The total value of mineral production in 1936 was $23,092,607.

Agriculture.—The most valuable crop is wheat. High in value are apples, hay, potatoes, oats, corn, and barley. Washington is noted for the production of garden vegetables of fine quality. Much attention is given to fruit culture, especially to apple, plum, prune, and peach raising. Dairying is an important interest, and there is a large exportation of butter, cheese and condensed milk. The waterless sections in parts have been reclaimed by irrigation. Stock raising is extensively carried on. The wool clip in 1938 was 5,856,000 pounds.

Fisheries.—Halibut, salmon, smelt, and crabs are caught in vast numbers. Washington oysters are well known. Among other food fish taken are the herring, turbot, sole, rockfish, and fish resembling the bass, perch, and cod of the Atlantic.

Manufacturing.—Lumber products are the most valuable, Washington leading the States in this line of manufacture. Shingles form a most important item. Thousands of masts and spars were sent from here to Government shipyards in the United States and in Europe during the World War. Flour and grist-mill products are shipped to Asiatic ports. Canned fruits, vegetables, shellfish and other fish are important products. Salmon canning employs many thousands of hands, and in this industry Washington surpasses any other State. Slaughtering and meat packing are important. Shipbuilding is extensively carried on in several Puget Sound cities.

Commerce.—Washington has unusually good facilities for carrying on foreign and domestic trade by water. Puget Sound's estuaries and bays offer several safe and commodious harbors. Most of Alaska's seaborne traffic is controlled by Seattle and Tacoma. Port Townsend is the port of entry for the Puget Sound commerce. The Columbia and Snake Rivers have been made navigable for steamboats by means of canals. Large vessels go up the Columbia as far as Vancouver. In 1935 the railway mileage of the State was 5,278. The longest roads are the Great Northern, the Union Pacific, and the Northern Pacific. The transcontinental line of the Chicago, Milwaukee, St. Paul & Pacific crosses the State to Puget Sound.

History.—The region of the present State of Washington was visited in 1592 by Juan de Fuca, who commanded an exploring expedition under the Spanish flag. Robert Gray discovered the Columbia River in 1792, and Lewis and Clark entered the Oregon Territory in 1805 and established their winter quarters at Fort Clatsop, on the north side of the Columbia River, near its mouth. The John Jacob Astor Fur Company founded Astoria in 1811. Settlers were encouraged to enter, and the number of Americans in the country increased rapidly. During the War of 1812 the British Government forced the Astor Company to give way to the Northwest Company, an English trading concern. After the War of 1812 the country was occupied jointly by the Northwest Company and by the early American settlers and pioneer missionaries. The northwest boundary was long a subject of dispute between the United States and Great Britain. The Americans claimed the country as far north as the parallel of latitude 54° 40′. War seemed imminent but the Webster-Ashburton treaty fixed in 1846 the boundary from the Rocky Mountains to the Pacific along the 49th parallel of latitude. In 1848 Oregon Territory was formed, extending from 42° to 49° N. lat., and from the Pacific Ocean to the Rocky Mountains, thus including the present Washington. In 1853 Washington Territory was formed, including the present State and that portion of Idaho and Montana lying north of parallel 46° and west of the Rocky Mountains. Owing to gold discoveries in Washington and the rush of immigrants into the State, there were serious Indian troubles in 1855-56-57. On the formation of the State of Oregon with its present limits, in 1857, the remainder of Oregon Territory was added to Washington Territory. In 1859 England claimed the Haro archipelago, of which San Juan is the largest island. Clashes between British and American soldiers were avoided with difficulty. The quarrel was referred to the German emperor, who decided in favor of the United States in 1872. On the formation of Idaho Territory in 1863, Washington Territory was reduced to the present State limits. In 1889 it was admitted to the Union as a State.

MT. RAINIER NATIONAL PARK PHOTO

MT. RAINIER, WASHINGTON. PERPETUALLY SNOW-CAPPED AND WITH GLACIERS MOVING DOWN ITS SLOPES

WEST VIRGINIA.—Physiography.—The Allegheny Mountains cross the State northeast to southwest and form part of the boundary dividing the State from Virginia. These mountains are low parallel ranges. River valleys traverse the southern part of the State. From the Alleghenies the surface is rolling but with a definite slope downward to the Ohio River. The high ridges are well wooded and most of them contain wide areas of meadow lands, called "glades." Several of the rivers are tributaries of the Ohio, are navigable to some extent and contain falls that would supply enormous hydro-electric power. Dense forests cover a large part of the State's surface and furnish much merchantable timber. There is spruce enough left to keep the wood-pulp mills supplied with basic material for some years. Hemlock, ash, oak, walnut, poplar, spruce, tulip and chestnut constitute the principal trees. West Virginia has many noted medicinal springs. The climate is agreeable and healthful, the elevation of most of the State securing it from malaria and dampness. The January mean temperature ranges from 30° F. in the high mountain districts of the northeast to 35° F. in the south. The July temperature averages 75° throughout the State. The rainfall is heaviest in the south, reaching 45 inches there yearly and about 33 inches annually in the northeast.

Minerals.—West Virginia has vast mineral resources. Coal is the most valuable item. Large quantities of coke are produced. There are immense deposits of petroleum and natural gas. Natural gasoline is also important. Much of the coal, petroleum and gas is transported to manufacturing centers in other States. Building stone is abundant, especially limestone and sandstone, and the fictile clay beds are extensive and valuable. Some zinc is also produced.

Agriculture.—The great staples are corn and hay; but wheat, potatoes, tobacco, and oats are also important crops. Orchard fruits, as apples, pears and peaches, contribute largely to the State's agricultural wealth. The mountainous regions afford excellent pasture lands, and stock raising is a very profitable industry, especially in the valleys of the southeast where rich blue grass is abundant. The State was long noted for its large wool clip, but the number of sheep has decreased in late years.

Manufacturing.—Iron and steel manufactures rank first, and glass-making second, with the manufacture of pottery (including porcelain) third in value in 1935. Car and general construction, lumber, wood pulp, flour and grist-mill products, leather, crockery, porcelain, fire brick, tobacco and cigars are the chief manufactures. Slaughtering and meat packing is an important industry. The State has abundant water power available for manufacturing purposes.

Commerce.—Immense quantities of coal are shipped down the Great Kanawha and Monongahela Rivers. The National Government has rendered these streams navigable by dredging and by the construction of canals where needed. The Ohio affords water communication with the Gulf of Mexico. There are three long railroads, the Baltimore and Ohio, the Chesapeake and Ohio, and the Norfolk and Western. These railways, with their feeders, bring all the State's points of commercial activity into connection with centers of commerce all over the United States.

History.—It is believed that La Salle, when he sailed down the Ohio River, landed in 1669 at several points in the present limits of West Virginia. In the same year Johann Lederer, a German physician in Governor Berkeley's service, explored portions of the State. In the first half of the 18th century many adventurous Scotch-Irish pioneers crossed the Alleghenies and settled in the fertile valleys of the Great Kanawha and its tributaries. Conflicts with the French and Indians followed. At Point Pleasant a bloody battle was fought between several confederated Indian tribes, led by the famous chief, Cornstalk, and some companies of Virginia settlers. The savages were defeated, and this section of the Virginia colony was then rapidly settled, though King George had issued a proclamation forbidding immigrants from crossing over the mountains. The western part of the Virginia province being peopled by hardy backwoodsmen, farmers and workers, where but few slaves were held, soon found good cause to complain of governmental burdens imposed by the wealthy eastern section, where all the manual labor was done by slaves. When Virginia seceded from the Union in 1861 the western counties protested. Delegates from forty of them met in Wheeling and adopted a provisional government. A new State was finally formed and under the name of West Virginia was admitted into the Union in 1863. A new State constitution was adopted in 1871.

WISCONSIN.—Physiography.—The surface is an elevated rolling plateau. Across the northern part extends a watershed reaching in some places 1,700 feet in height. There is a steep slope toward Lake Superior but a less sharp one to the south. A peculiar geological formation is a valley extending diagonally across the State and guiding the courses of the Fox River and the lower Wisconsin. A number of drumlins, mounds and ridges of glacial drift, are scattered over a large part of the State. Though the winters are long, the climate is healthful. The annual rainfall averages 31 inches, and is greatest during the crop-growing season. With the exception of a sandy area in the central part, the soils are of a good quality. The west and south of the State drain into tributaries of the Mississippi; a smaller area on the east is drained by Lake Michigan; and in the north several streams flow into Lake Superior. The Wisconsin is the largest river in the State. In the north there are extensive woodlands composed generally of pine, hemlock, cedar, and balsam, but in the forests of the south and east, deciduous trees are common. For several years Wisconsin ranked first in lumber production, but much of the merchantable timber has been cut down.

Minerals.—Iron, stone, zinc, mineral waters, mineral paints, sand and gravel, and sulphuric acid (the last a by-product of the zinc smelters) are the most important minerals. There are extensive beds of fire-brick clays. Wisconsin is noted for its output of medicinal spring waters.

Agriculture.—Hay and corn are the principal crops. Oats, potatoes, barley, and rye are produced in large quantities. Sugar beets, maple sugar, tobacco, cranberries, hops and orchard fruits are also important products. Considerable acreage is devoted to flax, which is grown for its seed. Wisconsin surpasses all the other States in the value of its dairy interests, butter, cheese and condensed milk being shipped to all parts of the Union. Horses, hogs and sheep are raised in great numbers.

Manufacturing.—Leading manufactures include dairy products, motor vehicle bodies and parts, malt liquors, boots and shoes, electrical machinery, knit goods, canned goods, foundry and machine-shop products, packed meats, pulp and paper. Blast furnaces are fed with iron ores from the vast deposits of the Lake Superior district and the smelted iron is utilized as the basis of finished steel products. The sole disadvantage is the need for importing coal for these industries. A supply of hemlock bark, procured from the State's forests, gave impetus to the leather manufacture, but now the greater portion of the tanning materials are imported. Farming implements, iron and steel wares, cotton and woolen goods are also made in large quantities.

Commerce.—Traffic is conducted on the Mississippi, Wisconsin, Fox, Chippewa, and other rivers. Lake Michigan affords communication with the Atlantic by way of the Great Lakes system, the Welland canal in Canada and the Erie canal in New York. Milwaukee has an excellent harbor and is the largest port of entry for foreign commerce. Wisconsin is well supplied with railroads, having about 11,500 miles of trackage in 1936. The longest are the Minneapolis, St. Paul & Sault Ste. Marie, the Chicago & North Western and the Chicago, Milwaukee, St. Paul & Pacific.

History.—Jean Nicolet, a French fur trader who reached Green Bay in 1634, was the first white explorer of this region. Radisson and Groseilliers descended the Fox in 1654, crossed the portage to the Wisconsin and canoed down to the Mississippi. In 1661 they erected a fort near the site of the present city of Ashland. It was on this spot also that Father Allouez established a mission post in 1665. Another mission, founded by him on the site of the present city of Green Bay, in 1670, became the nucleus of the first permanent settlement in the State. Joliet, Marquette, La Salle and Du Lhut (after whom Duluth is named) are other noted names connected with the State's early history. The French and Indians of this State took the British side in the Revolutionary War and again in the War of 1812. Population increased but slowly until after the close of the Black Hawk War (1832), because fur trading was the chief occupation. Wisconsin was organized into a Territory in 1836 and was admitted as a State in 1848. Immigrants from New England and New York came in large numbers and the newcomers, being strongly anti-slavery in sentiment, did much to create an enthusiastic support of the Union cause when the Southern States seceded. A strong tide of European immigration, principally German, set into the State after the failure of the revolutionary movement in Prussia and Austria. During the Civil War, Wisconsin, always anti-slavery in sentiment, furnished more than its quota of troops called for to defend the Union.

WYOMING.—Physiography.—The surface is a plateau averaging 5,000 feet to 7,000 feet above sea level, traversed by high mountain ranges. The Continental Divide crosses the State from the middle of the southern boundary to the northwestern corner. Some Wyoming streams flow eventually into the Atlantic, some into the Pacific and some into the Gulf of California. Southern Wyoming has numerous buttes (flat-topped hills). Deep canyons are found in almost all parts of the State. In the northwest lies nearly all Yellowstone Park, a wonderland of geysers, hot springs, marvels of scenic beauty and other natural attractions. The soil of the State is somewhat arid in places, but much of it has been made productive either by irrigation or dry farming. Extremes of temperature occur in both winter and summer, but the climate is dry and there is much sunshine in all seasons of the year. Though the winters are cold, the dryness of the air renders them endurable. The rainfall averages only 13 inches a year, and therefore irrigation is necessary to successful agriculture. There are many large forests; official estimates state that 7,000,000 acres are timbered. Most of the trees are conifers, the principal species being western yellow pine, lodgepole pine, and spruce. As Wyoming is a high plateau, its rivers flow with unusual speed down to lower levels; hence there is a vast amount of water power in the State. Only a few of the numerous power sites have been developed. The Yellowstone River with its tributaries drains the northern part of the State. The Little Missouri, the Cheyenne and the North Platte drain the south and the central parts.

Minerals.—Wyoming has vast mineral wealth, which has become increasingly important as transportation facilities have been made available. Petroleum fields are well developed, the yield amounting in 1935 to 13,755,000 barrels. Coal is the most valuable mineral after petroleum. Copper, lead, gold and silver ores occur in several counties. Graphite, asphaltum, asbestos and pottery clays are found, and building stone and gypsum are worked in vast amounts. Soda, sulphur, tin, salt, and mica occur, though at present the deposits would not repay operation for commercial purposes. Mineral springs are numerous.

Agriculture.—Cattle raising is the foremost agricultural industry, as well as the oldest in the State. The wild grasses are very nutritious for feeding live stock. Hog and horse-raising rank high in importance among the stock raising industries. Wyoming ranks high among the other States in the production of wool. The annual wool clip is over one-twelfth of all the wool produced in the Union, totaling over 31,389,000 pounds in 1938. Horses are raised for the Eastern markets, and there are immense herds of dairy cows. More than half the State is pasture land, the rich natural grasses curing into hay without being cut. Crop farming is extensive, especially since the large irrigation projects have been completed, and vegetables, cereals and orchard fruits are grown. Irrigation is practiced on an immense scale and, where the soil is watered, the returns are very large. "Dry" farming is employed in sections where the rainfall averages 15 inches per year or more. Crop yields are not so large as they are on irrigated land, but less capital is required. Drought-resisting grains, as Siberian wheat, barley, oats, rye, flax, millet, Kaffir corn and certain forage plants, as broom grass, Sudan grass, sweet clover and some varieties of alfalfa, yield well on dry-farmed land. Sugar beets, garden vegetables and small fruits are grown very successfully. Wheat, oats, barley and potatoes do well. Hay is an important crop.

Manufacturing.—Except for petroleum refining, Wyoming's manufactures are of little importance. Lumber, meat packing, flour and creamery products are the leaders. The State's resources, if utilized, would support manufacturing on a very large scale. There is an almost limitless amount of hydro-electric energy awaiting development.

Transportation.—Several great railroad systems connect all Wyoming cities with the markets of the East and also of the Pacific Coast. The long railways are the Union Pacific; Chicago, Burlington & Quincy; Chicago & North Western, and the Colorado & Southern. These lines have many feeders, which extend into nearly every county in the State.

History.—The Sieur de la Verendrye and his companions, who passed through this region in 1743-1744, were the first white explorers. In 1803 the region became part of the United States through the Louisiana Purchase. Fur traders and trappers in increasing numbers ranged the northern part in the first quarter of the 19th century. A permanent fort was built on the Laramie River in 1834. Fremont's expedition visited the country in 1842. The discovery of gold in 1867 brought about a rush of settlers. South Pass City was founded in that year, and Cheyenne was laid out about the same time. The region was much disturbed by Indian troubles culminating in the massacre of General Custer and all his troopers in Montana in 1876. A territorial government was organized in 1868, and the suffrage was granted to women. The Territory was admitted to statehood in 1890.

ALASKA.—Physiography.—Alaska is situated at the northwestern extremity of North America. Much of the northern part is swampy and traversed by numerous streams, which begin in hills far back from the coast. The Yukon River divides Alaska into two nearly equal parts, a northern part and a southern. The Coast Range extends through the southern part and continues in the Aleutian Islands. There are many detached peaks and several active volcanoes. Large glaciers, of which Muir and Malaspina are the most remarkable, descend from the mountains to the Pacific. Portions of the Territory, as the Kuskokwim district and the southwest, are capable of growing vegetables and such cereals as barley and oats. In the warmer valleys wheat can be brought to maturity. In the southern half of the Territory there are many large forests. Birch, spruce, cedar, fir, and hemlock abound. Poplars, willows and alders, aspens and larches are found farther north. Grass grows everywhere. The winters are very cold in the interior, but are much milder along the Pacific Coast and in the southeast, the average winter temperature there being only 35° F. There is a copious rainfall along the coast, and fogs are common. Throughout most of the Territory the summers are hot, and vegetation is early and luxuriant. There are several distinct volcanic areas, the most noted being the Valley of Ten Thousand Smokes. Here numerous fumaroles emit gases so hot that they set fire to logs of wood placed across them.

Minerals.—The most valuable mineral output is that of gold, followed by copper, silver, and coal. Tin, platinum, and lead are also worked. Coal beds on the Kenai peninsula have long been utilized by steamers, and there are other deposits of bituminous coal along the coast, and new fields covering more than a thousand square miles have been recently found. Deposits of anthracite of an excellent grade are known to exist in various parts of the Territory. Gypsum, antimony, and graphite occur in various localities, and several petroleum wells have been sunk. Marble is quarried on Prince of Wales Island. Silver and lead occur as galena ore in the Katinsha district. Elsewhere they are by-products of gold and copper mines.

The total value of minerals produced in Alaska for the year 1938 amounted to $27,036,000, and the total mineral output of the Territory since 1880 reached a value of $776,000,000, about $511,000,000 of which was due to gold, Alaska's most valuable mineral product. The gold output for 1938 was valued at $21,917,000, at the current high rate of $35 an ounce. The copper output for the year was valued at $2,932,000; coal, which is used locally, had an output valued at $570,000. Platinum metals (including palladium), silver, tin and lead were produced in considerable quantities. There was a renewal of mining for antimony. Limestone quarries in southeastern Alaska were actively worked and the product shipped to Seattle for use in making cement.

Agriculture.—Truck gardening is carried on near the larger towns, and oats, barley, and wheat are grown in the southeast and in the Kuskokwim valley. Though to no very great extent, cattle and sheep are raised on the Aleutian Islands. Reindeer were introduced several years ago into the northern part of the Territory, and the experiment has proved successful. Siberian wheat is grown extensively in the Tanana valley. Truck farms are increasing in the Matanuska district, and vegetables from there are shipped to the coast towns. Homesteads are being taken up in various sections of the Territory, the land and climate being well adapted to temperate-zone farming.

Fisheries.—Fish are very abundant in salt water as well as in the rivers. Several species of salmon are caught. Herring, halibut, cod (not the Atlantic cod), and the oulachan, a smelt affording much oil, are taken in large numbers. Whales are hunted in the Arctic Ocean and Bering Sea. Food fish is the most important of Alaska's products, being far more valuable than all the gold extracted from the Territory's mines. The total value of the fishery products in 1937 was $51,743,220. Salmon constitutes approximately 90% of the catch. The Pribilof Islands, the home of the fur seal, are administered by the United States Bureau of Fisheries, and the seals, protected by agreement of the United States with Great Britain and other nations, are increasing in number.

Wild Animals.—When the United States acquired Alaska, the Territory was supposed to be valuable to the fur trade only. Then the seals were slaughtered recklessly both in the sea and on the Pribilof Islands. Other fur-bearing animals, as the much-prized sea-otter, the mink, beaver, fox, wolverine, lynx, ermine, and marten, were common. All these are getting scarcer every year. Only Government regulations preserve the seals from extinction by sea robbers. Caribou

and musk oxen are still to be found in the far north, but only in lessening numbers. There are but few species of reptiles in Alaska. Mosquitos and other insects are numerous everywhere from the Arctic Ocean to Dixon's Entrance. Hunters and trappers of wild animals are still allowed to carry on their vocations in the Territory, and shipments of pelts are made every season, though in steadily lessening quantities. Pelts of foxes (including the rare blue fox), bears, minks, ermines, muskrats (the most numerous), otters, and martens are shipped in thousands every spring to Seattle and San Francisco. Fox farming is now an industry. New conservation laws have been passed.

Manufacturing.—The refining of gold ore and of the ores of other metals is carried on to some extent. Many million dollars' worth of salmon is yearly canned for export. Planing mills are in operation in various forested localities, and several flour and grist mills have been erected in the districts producing Siberian wheat and other hardy grains.

Commerce.—Alaska's coastwise commerce is increasing rapidly. At present, most of the Territory's trade is with the United States, the exports consisting mainly of copper, gold, silver, furs, and canned salmon. The most valuable imports are steel rails and tin plate. The latter is used in making cans for the fish-canning industries.

ALASKA'S TRADE WITH THE UNITED STATES

Year	Exports to United States	Imports from United States
1905	$10,801,446	$11,504,255
1910	12,440,380	18,670,339
1920	69,911,422	38,418,473
1930	48,996,962	31,303,291
1938	81,906,036	42,701,222

Population.—Alaska's population in 1920 was 55,036, a decrease of 14.9 per cent on the census of 1910, when the number was 64,356. In 1920 there were 29,371 white residents and 25,666 natives. The 1930 census figure for the Territory is 59,278.

The Natives.—Early explorers found the native population of Eskimos and Aleut Indians apparently much larger than it is now. At any rate, the past half century has seen their numbers greatly diminished by the change in their environment caused by the inrush of gold seekers, and the consequent loss of their accustomed food supplies on land and sea. Contagious diseases, especially the influenza, carried to natives by white man destroyed whole villages. On the other hand, introduction of reindeer into Alaska proved most advantageous for natives who exchanged the uncertain lot of the hunter for the surer life of the herdsman. In 1926, natives owned 235,000 reindeer and were marketing surplus meat. The Alaskan aborigines are intelligent and likely to gain from industrial developments and educational opportunities.

History.—There is some evidence to show that Alaska was known as far back as 1576. A Russian sailor named Popof, exploring East Cape (Siberia), discovered the narrow Strait between Alaska and Asia and learned from the natives of the existence of a great continent toward the east. Vitus Bering, commissioned by Peter the Great of Russia, sailed north through Bering Strait in 1731 but did not touch Alaska. In 1731 a Russian sailor, Gwosdef, was blown on to the Alaskan coast. In 1741 Bering, on a second expedition with Chirikov, reached Alaska. Various exploring parties, Russian, English, Spanish, and French, visited Alaskan territory during the last half of the 18th century, Captain Cook surveying part of the coast in 1776. In 1799 the Russian American Company secured a monopoly of the fur trade, and in 1821 Russia attempted to exclude foreigners from the Bering Sea. English and Russian fur-trading companies explored the country from 1793 down to 1867, the year in which Russian America, as Alaska was then called, was purchased by the United States for $7,200,000 in gold.

Until 1877 authority was vested in the War Department, after which the Treasury Department assumed control. In 1884 the "Organic Act" provided civil government under a governor appointed by the President. In 1912 Alaska was organized as a Territory with a legislative assembly of 8 senators and 16 representatives. But as Congress reserved itself the right to legislate on certain subjects, Alaska is now governed conjointly by Congress and the Territorial assembly.

Juneau is the capital. The Governor of Alaska is appointed by the President and serves four years.

With the discovery of gold an old dispute regarding boundaries was revived. In 1825 Russian America's eastern boundary was fixed by treaty between England and Russia. England, seeking a Pacific outlet for her fur trade, had made strenuous efforts to force Russia to yield to her demands. But Russia refused to surrender any boundary right, and England was compelled to sign the treaty as outlined by Russia. An outlet to the coast became more desirable to Canada, as gold hunters began to swarm into the Klondike, and that country then resurrected the old boundary contentions of England. Three representatives from the United States, two from Canada and one from England, met in London in 1903, and, by a vote of 4 to 2, decided in favor of the claims of the United States.

BAKER ISLAND.—Baker Island (1 mile long, ¾ mile wide) lies in the Pacific Ocean in longitude 176° 33′ W. and latitude 0° 13′ 30″ N., approximately 1,650 miles southwest of Honolulu. It was discovered in 1832. It is expected to serve as an airport.

CANAL ZONE.—By treaty with the republic of Panama on November 18, 1903, the United States was granted in perpetuity the use of a strip of land 5 miles wide on each side of the Panama Canal, which cuts through the Isthmus of Panama. It has an area of 554 square miles, and a population of 39,467. Some islands in Panama Bay were included in the grant. The cities of Panama and Colon are not subject to United States authority, except in matters pertaining to sanitation and quarantine. For this perpetual lease the United States paid $10,000,000 and agreed to pay yearly $250,000. The Canal Zone has an excellent free public school system, including both grammar and high schools. The zone is administered by a Governor appointed by the War Department.

A decidedly tropical climate and a heavy rainfall have fostered a forest growth, rank and luxuriant, comprising much valuable timber. The soil is fertile, but is not well cultivated. Fevers once prevailed here the year round, but the sanitary measures enforced by the Government officials have rendered the district unusually healthful.

The Panama Canal, stretching from ocean to ocean, is about 50 miles long, 85 to 86 feet high, and has a channel that varies in depth from 45 feet to 87 feet, and in width at bottom from 500 feet to 1,000 feet, except where the various canal locks narrow this width to 110 feet. It is a lake canal as well as a lock canal, its dominating feature being Gatun Lake, a great artificially made body of water that covers about 164 square miles and occupies the northern half of that portion of the isthmus through which the canal passes.

The Gatun dam, which forms Gatun Lake by impounding the waters of the Chagres and its tributaries, is nearly 1½ miles long, measured on its crest, nearly ½ mile wide at its base, about 400 feet wide at the water surface, about 100 feet wide at the top, and its crest is finished at an elevation of 105 feet above mean sea level, or 20 feet above the normal level of the lake. Of the total length of the dam only 500 feet, or one-fifteenth, is exposed to the maximum water level. The entire dam contains about 23,000,000 cubic yards.

Gatun Lake impounds the waters of a basin comprising 1,320 square miles. When the surface of the water is at 85 feet above sea level, the lake has an area of about 164 square miles, and contains about 183,000,000,000 cubic feet of water. The surface of the lake is maintained during the rainy season at 87 feet above sea level, making the minimum channel depth in the canal 47 feet.

There are six double locks in the canal; three pairs at Gatun with a combined lift of 85 feet; one pair at Pedro Miguel, with a lift of 30 feet, and two pairs at Miraflores, with a combined lift of 55 feet at mean tide. The usable dimensions of each are the same—a length of 1,000 feet and a width of 110 feet. Each lock is a chamber with walls and floor of concrete and with mitering gates at each end. The lock gates are steel structures 7 feet thick, 65 feet long and from 47 to 82 feet high. They weigh from 390 tons to 730 tons each. Ninety-two leaves are required for the entire canal, the total weighing 60,000 tons. Intermediate gates are used in all except one pair of the locks, in order to save water and time in locking.

The total amount of material excavated for the complete canal was 238,845,587 cubic yards.

CANTON ISLAND.—This island is in latitude 3° S. and longitude 172° W. It is a low strip of land enclosing a lagoon some nine miles long and three miles wide. The island was colonized by the United States early in 1938 for an airplane base and meteorological station.

GUAM.—Guam (or San Juan), the largest of the Marianne or Ladrone Islands, was ceded by Spain to the United States in 1898. It is situated in the Pacific Ocean at latitude 13° 27' N. and longitude 144° 45' E. The island, which contains about 206 square miles, is hilly in the south and low and level in the north. It is well-wooded, has a fertile soil and grows corn, rice, coffee, sweet potatoes, sugar cane, etc.

Guam has a tropical climate, and coconut palm trees grow all over the island. A radio station and cable telegraphs keep the island in communication with the chief Pacific ports. It has a trans-Pacific airport.

The natives are of the Chamorro tribe, and have increased steadily in number during the past 20 years. The total population in 1930 was 18,509.

Elementary education is compulsory. The island, together with other near-by islets, is a naval station, and is therefore under the jurisdiction of the Navy Department. A naval officer is the appointed Governor. Agaña, the largest town, is the seat of government.

For the year ending June 30, 1936, the imports were valued at $532,195 and the exports at $110,981. The principal export items are copra and coconut oil. The chief imports are lumber, rice, flour, canned provisions, kerosene, and cotton goods.

History.—Magellan discovered Guam in 1521. The island was frequently visited by vessels seeking a water supply but no attempt at settlement was made before the founding of a Spanish mission in 1668. The Spanish held Guam until June, 1898, when it was taken by an American cruiser. By the Treaty of Paris, December 10, 1898, Guam became a possession of the United States.

ENDERBURY ISLAND.—Enderbury Island is in latitude 3° S., longitude 171° W. It is about 3½ miles long by 1½ miles wide and is surrounded by a coral reef. The United States colonized it in 1938 for air route and meteorological uses.

HAWAII.—Physiography.—The territory of Hawaii, formerly called the Sandwich Islands, comprises an island chain extending for about 400 miles southeast and northwest which is situated in the Pacific Ocean at about latitude 20° N., longitude 157° W. There are nine inhabited islands—Hawaii (4,016 sq. miles); Oahu (598 sq. miles); Maui (728 sq. miles); Molokai (261 sq. miles); Lanai (139 sq. miles); Kauai (547 sq. miles); Niihau (73 sq. miles); Kahoolawe (44 sq. miles), and Midway (1.5 sq. miles). The coasts are steep and afford but few good harbors. All the islands are of volcanic origin and contain enormous volcanoes. Most of these are extinct, but two of them, Mauna Loa and Kilauea, offer the most appalling examples of volcanic energy to be seen on the globe.

The estimated population in 1930 was: Hawaiian, 22,636; part-Hawaiian, 28,224; Portuguese, 27,588; Porto Rican, 6,671; Spanish, 1,219; Chinese, 27,179; Japanese, 139,631; Filipino, 63,052; Korean, 6,461; Americans, British, German, and Russian, 44,895; all others, 780. Total, 368,336; estimate 1936, 393,277.

Hawaii is noted for its rich and varied scenery—wide valleys, green with tree ferns, deep gorges, cut by torrents, densely wooded mountain sides and level coast lands covered with coconut palms and breadfruit trees. A fertile soil, composed of lava and scoria, a tropical climate and a rainfall averaging 50 inches produce luxuriant vegetation. For nearly three-fourths of the year the northeast trade winds blow across the islands. There are two seasons, the rainy and the dry. The mean temperature for the year is 74.3° F. at Honolulu.

Agriculture.—Sugar is the principal crop. Thousands of tons of raw sugar are exported every year to the United States to be refined. Fruit raising and the canning of fruits, especially pineapples, are steadily growing industries. The taro is an important native food plant. Introduced fruits, as strawberries and raspberries, flourish. Various species of palms, acacias and pandanus trees, including the candle nut, are widely distributed. Cattle and hogs thrive, though not native to any of the islands. There are extensive irrigation works on the four principal islands.

Commerce.—The islands have a railway system (in addition to tracks owned by planters) and there is

THE BRAZILIAN CLIPPER, WEIGHING 19 TONS AND WITH A WING SPREAD OF 114 FEET, MAINTAINS A REGULAR MAIL SERVICE BETWEEN NORTH AND SOUTH AMERICAN POINTS.

regular inter-island service of steamers and airplanes. Honolulu, chief port and commercial center, is in touch with the world by radio and telegraph cable. Steamships connect with the chief Pacific ports. It is on the new trans-Pacific air route. Overseas trade is largely with the United States. Exports include sugar, pineapples, canned fruits, coffee, hides and rice.

History.—Some Spaniards were shipwrecked near Kona, Hawaii, in 1527, and there is little doubt that a Spanish vessel commanded by Juan Gaetano touched at the islands in 1555; but they were not really made known to Europeans till the English navigator, Cook, visited them in 1778. At the time, and for some years thereafter, each island had its own king, or chief. During the last decade of the 18th century, however, Kamehameha I brought all the islands under his rule. *Tabu*, the familiar Polynesian sacred system, enabled him to govern despotically. His son, Kamehameha II, discarded this superstition and invited American missionaries to convert his people. Under Kamehameha III the people were granted a constitutional form of government, which was recognized by various Christian nations. His successor, Queen Liliuokalani, was deposed in 1893. A republic was established in 1894. Formal annexation of the islands by the United States took place in 1898. In 1900 the Territory of Hawaii was organized by Congress.

The Hawaiians are a Polynesian race, but of fairer complexion than most of the people of the South Pacific Islands. Portuguese, Chinese and Japanese now do much of the labor.

HOWLAND ISLAND.—Howland Island (2 miles long, ½ mile wide) lies in the Pacific Ocean in longitude 176° 43' W. and latitude 0° 49' N., approximately 1,620 miles southwest of Honolulu. It was discovered in 1842. It is a station for aircraft.

JARVIS ISLAND.—Jarvis Island (3 miles long, 2 miles wide) lies in the Pacific Ocean in longitude 160° 01" W. and latitude 0° 22' 30" W., approximately 1,500 miles south of Honolulu. It was discovered in 1835. It is a station for aircraft.

MIDWAY ISLANDS.—This group, consisting of two small islands (Sand, 850 acres; and Eastern, 328 acres) with several islets, is about 1,149 miles northwest of Honolulu in longitude 177° 23' W. and latitude 28° 13' N. The group, with a lagoon, lies inside a circular reef about five miles across, the islands being near the southern rim. On July 5, 1859, Captain N. C. Brooks discovered them and claimed the group for the United States, which took formal possession of them on August 28, 1867.

Although unproductive, Midway Islands have some importance as a cable station and are a naval reservation. In 1935, arrangements were in progress for establishing on them an airport (in service in 1936) for aircraft crossing the Pacific.

PHILIPPINE ISLANDS.—Physiography.—These islands form an archipelago shaped like an inverted "Y" and lie between latitudes 4° 41' N. and 20° 10' N. and longitudes 116° 40' E. and 126° 34' E. The most northern island is Y'Ami of the Batanes group, and the most southern is Balut Island of the Sarangani group, which lie south of Mindanao. The nearest foreign territory north is Taiwan (Formosa), 93 miles north of Y'Ami. Balut is only 31 miles from Balamangan, a British islet near Borneo. There are said to be more than 7,000 islands having areas of one-tenth of a square mile or more. Most of the islands are very small. Their aggregate area is 114,400 square miles. The land area of the Philippines extends north and south, 1,150 miles; east and west, 650 miles. All the group is of volcanic origin, and a few of the volcanoes are still active. Two of the islands, Luzon and Mindanao, are listed among the larger islands of the world and contain about 70% of the total area of the islands. Nine others, Panay, Negros, Palawan (Paragua), Cebu, Leyte, Masbate, Samar, Mindoro, and Bohol, comprise the remaining islands of geographical importance. Earthquakes are frequent and destructive. Mountain ranges traverse the larger islands, the highest peak in the archipelago, Mt. Apo (or Da'vao), being in Mindanao. As the waters around the archipelago are everywhere shallow, the islands must stand on a broad plateau which is near the surface. The arrangement of the mountain chains in the two large islands, Luzon and Mindanao, permits the formation of rivers of considerable size. The Rio Grande de Cagayan in Luzon drains an area of 16,000 square miles. A still larger stream is the Rio Grande de Cotobato, which drains the central part of Mindanao. The Pasig River connecting Manila Bay with the Laguna de Bay is only 12 miles long but is of much commercial value. Being of lava origin, the soil is very fertile in the valleys and lowlands. Although the rainfall is very heavy and the climate is hot, the death rate among the white inhabitants is remarkably low. March to June are the hottest months, but the variation of the thermometer is slight. The cool season is from November to February inclusive. During this period the thermometer at Manila ranges from 75° F. to 80° F. Typhoons are common.

Population.—The people number 12,082,366 (1930), 99 per cent of whom are native born. It is estimated that 90 per cent are civilized or partly civilized. The remainder are very primitive in their mode of living. Free schools are maintained throughout the islands, but the proportion of illiterates is still large. About half the population is engaged in agricultural pursuits. Probably the most ancient tribe of the archipelago is represented by the Negro pigmies (Negritos). These are rapidly becoming extinct. Polynesian invaders seized the islands in the 15th century and were, later on, conquered by Malays. Many of these newcomers became Christians, but the Moros, who occupy the Sulu islands and part of Mindanao, early embraced the doctrine of Islam and have remained Mohammedans. Probably 90 per cent of the inhabitants are now civilized. The natives are divided into a number of tribes, mostly of Malay origin. The Negritos are the aborigines. Visayans and Tagals constitute the majority of the population. In the southern islands, the Moros, a warlike tribe, predominate.

Minerals.—The Philippines have great mineral wealth, which is, as yet, but very little developed. Coal is the most widely distributed mineral. While not of high grade, it generally can be used for various industrial purposes. A deposit of coal on Batan Island near Luzon is, however, found to equal the best Japanese coal for use on steamers. Iron, zinc, silver, copper (arsenical pyrites), galena, sulphur, asbestos, stone, lime, clay, sand, and gravel are found. Deposits of petroleum, kaolin and gypsum have been worked profitably for some years. There are numerous mineral springs. The gold output for 1936 was valued at $20,987,995, and this amount is likely to increase with the employment of more efficient methods. In 1937, gold ranked third in value among the Philippine exports. Salt is made in considerable quantities. Plans are in progress for more widespread exploration of the islands in search for oil deposits.

Animal Life.—Most of the North American farm animals are now raised in the islands. But the common draft animal is the carabao, or water buffalo, valued by the natives also for its meat and hide. Goats are common and both their milk and flesh are utilized by the Filipinos. Monkeys, bears, antelopes, serpents, crocodiles and wildcats are numerous. The most important fishes are the garfish, shark, wrasse, sea bass, and smelt. Several kinds of edible shellfish are taken along the shores. The pearl-oyster fisheries of the Sulu archipelago are very profitable. There are hundreds of species of birds, including mound turkeys, pigeons, cockatoos, jungle fowl, hornbill, snipes, and curlews.

Agriculture.—Cultivation of the soil is the chief industry of the islands, but the methods pursued are out of date. Only a few farmers use modern agricultural implements and fertilizers are almost unknown. About one-fifth of the tillable land is under cultivation, and the average size of the tilled area is four to six acres. All tropical economic plants can be grown, the high temperature and abundant rain being very favorable to vegetation. Forests cover thousands of square miles. Many valuable woods, as teak, sandalwood and the camphor tree, are native to these islands. There are found here also 60 species of hardwood trees used by shipbuilders and cabinet makers. A Forestry Bureau has charge of all the forests. Some of the principal products raised for export are sugar, rice and tobacco. Coffee of high grade, cotton and cocoa are also produced. Other exported products are copra, dyewood, sago, bananas, cinnamon and tropical fruits. Nipa palms and bamboos are utilized for industrial purposes. A very valuable plant originally found wild in the islands is the abaca, which resembles the banana. This is the famous Manila hemp, which forms the chief item of export from the islands. Its fibers are twisted into Manila rope. Cultivation of rubber is under way, especially in the south.

Manufacturing.—The principal manufactures are Manila hemp rope, sugar, coconut products and tobacco goods. There is also a large foreign trade in rattans, gums, resins, spices, pearl shell, dyewoods, rice, hardwoods, and coconut oil. Hats, soaps, leather, textiles, and mats are made by handwork.

Commerce.—The islands have a large foreign commerce. There is also a coastwise trade of considerable extent. Large ocean-going steamers can now tie up at the Manila wharves instead of being compelled, on account of shallow water, to anchor two miles away, as formerly. The United States Government has dredged out the harbor and built breakwaters. Six ports are open to foreign trade—Manila, Aparri, Zamboanga, Jolo, Cebu, and Iloilo. There are over 800 miles of railroads and more under construction, and 8,905 miles

of public roads. Telegraph cables and radio stations keep the Philippines in communication with America and Asia. About 70 per cent of the exports go to the United States.

History.—The Philippine Islands were discovered by Magellan in 1521 on his voyage around the globe. He was slain in a skirmish with the natives on the island of Maeton, opposite the present city of Cebu. Spain took formal possession of the archipelago in 1569, though temporary Spanish settlements had been made in some of the islands four years before. Manila was founded in 1571. The islands were first called San Lazaro, then Magellania, East Islands and Indias Espanolas (Spanish Indies). They remained Spanish possessions till they were ceded by the treaty of peace concluded between the United States and Spain on April 11, 1899. After that time the Philippines progressed rapidly. Government was through a governor-general appointed by the President of the United States and an elective legislature of two branches.

A Philippine independence law enacted in March, 1934, was accepted, and a Constitutional Convention proceeded to draft a Constitution, which was approved by President Roosevelt in March, 1935, and adopted by vote in the Philippines in May of the same year. The new title of the country is Commonwealth of the Philippines, at first expected to become Republic of the Philippines in 1946, a change which may be delayed till 1960. The Government consists of the President (elected for six years); the National Assembly (one house only); and the Supreme Court. The United States appoints a High Commissioner. Manuel Quezon became the first elected President in November, 1935.

PUERTO RICO.—Physiography.—This island, one of the West Indies, is situated in the Caribbean Sea, latitude 17° 50′ to 18° 30′ N. and longitude 65° 30′ to 67° 15′ W. From east to west through the southern half of Puerto Rico, which is fourth in size of the islands in the West Indies, runs a broken range of hills from 2,000 feet to 3,000 feet high. The highest, Humaco in the Luquillo Mountains, is 3,532 feet above sea level. The land slopes away from this ridge, or watershed, into broad, level, alluvial plains and valleys with a very rich soil. Around nearly all the island, next to the coast, are fertile fluvial valleys. Forests cover most of the hills. Land swept by the northeast trade winds has an abundant rainfall. There are several small rivers, but most are unnavigable except for short distances above their mouths. They afford, however, excellent drainage, so that Puerto Rico unlike many other West India Islands, has hardly any stagnant water. The climate, though hot, is healthful, summer temperature on the coast land reaching often 100° F. It is considerably cooler in the mountain districts.

Minerals.—Gold, copper, iron, quicksilver, bismuth, tin, platinum, nickel and silver are found; but there is, as yet, no mining undertaking of importance. Brick and pottery clays and gypsum are other important minerals. Building stone, such as limestone, marble and sandstone, is quarried in various parts of the island. Considerable salt is made. Phosphates and guano suitable for fertilizers abound, but the deposits are worked only superficially.

Plant Life.—The higher regions are heavily forested. The trees include palms, ausubo, cedar, laurel, mahoe, mahogany, and candlewood. The island flora includes many species of plants used in medicine or in industrial arts. Good pasturage is afforded by the native grasses. Vegetation is very luxuriant in the valleys, where the temperature is high and the rainfall heavy.

Animal Life.—The island fauna is scanty. Mammals are represented by small rodents and by bats. There is only one species of tortoise. Venomous snakes are unknown and there are but few species of insect pests. Water birds are plentiful along the coast. Food fishes of various species are common both in coast waters and in the rivers.

Agriculture.—Most of the people are engaged in agricultural pursuits. Since the American occupation, modern farm machinery has been introduced, but many of the natives still use crude and wasteful methods. The southeast of the island, unreached by the trade winds, needs irrigation to make the land productive; but most of the island's soil, especially the alluvium coast district, is exceedingly rich. Inland the soil is a clayey loam which contains an abundance of plant food. Only 25 per cent of the land is under cultivation. The remainder is either waste land or pasture or forest.

The chief product is sugar. Next in value are tobacco and coffee. The island also exports pineapples, coconuts, oranges, and garden vegetables. All tropical fruits can be grown successfully, and much attention is now given to fruit growing for American markets.

Manufacturing.—There are several large tobacco factories, sugar refineries and salt works. Leather, soap, matches and iron castings are made to supply local needs. Straw hats are woven for export to the United States. But manufacturing is not yet an important industry, and most of the manufactured articles used in the island are imports from the United States.

Commerce.—Commerce was increasing steadily until 1929 when the world financial depression gave it a setback. In 1901 exports from Puerto Rico to the United States were valued at only $5,587,288; in the fiscal year ending June 30, 1936, Puerto Rico exports to the United States amounted to $96,991,639; total exports to $99,133,924. Imports for the same year were valued at $83,591,354, of which $77,176,472 were from the United States. The most important export is sugar, more than half the whole. Leaf tobacco, cigars, fruits, coconuts, and coffee follow in that order. The chief imports are manufactured goods and breadstuffs.

History.—Puerto Rico ("rich port"), the Boriquen of the Arawark Indians, was discovered by Columbus in 1493. He gave it the name of San Juan Bautista. Ponce de Leon conquered it for Spain in 1510. Atrocious treatment of the enslaved natives exterminated them, then the Spaniards brought from Africa Negroes to work on the plantations. West India buccaneers and pirates often visited the coast. San Juan was twice sacked by English fleets under Drake and the Duke of Cumberland. Spain ceded the island to the United States by a treaty signed on December 10, 1898. The island has representative government. By an act of Congress, approved on March 2, 1917, the people of the island of Puerto Rico were made citizens of the United States. In 1932, by an Act of Congress the name was changed from Porto Rico to Puerto Rico.

SAMOA, AMERICAN.—The Samoan Islands, about 2,200 miles south of the Hawaiian Islands, extend from 13° 26′ to 14° 22′ S., and from 168° 10′ to 172° 48′ W. American Samoa includes the islands west of 171° W., in accordance with a treaty of 1899, and is under the jurisdiction of the Secretary of the Navy. American Samoa is mountainous and of volcanic formation, but productive. Copra is exported. Tutuila is the chief island of American Samoa and its harbor, Pagopago, is the best in the South Seas.

Swains Island, 210 miles north of Tutuila, is under the same jurisdiction. The population of American Samoa, chiefly Polynesian, was 10,436 in 1932.

VIRGIN ISLANDS.—The Virgin Islands, a group of the Leeward Islands in the West Indies, comprise three large islands, St. Thomas, St. John and St. Croix (Santa Cruz) and about 50 very small rocky islets. The group was formerly called the Danish West Indies. St. Thomas has a rugged surface. Much of the soil is untilled, owing to its sterile character. The island's chief town, Charlotte Amalie, has an excellent harbor and has long been a noted port of call for many lines of steamers. St. John and St. Croix are flatter and better watered than St. Thomas. The coast waters are prolific in fish, the forests abound in nut trees, and land too poor for cultivation furnishes good pasturage. Sugar, hides, and bay rum are the principal products.

The islands were discovered in 1493 by Columbus on his second voyage. The Dutch colonized St. Croix as early as 1625. St. Thomas was settled in 1666 by the Danes. The United States bought the group for $25,000,000 from Denmark and took possession on March 31, 1917. The population of the islands has steadily declined since the middle of the last century.

The latest census was taken by the United States in 1930, and gave a total population of 22,012, St. Croix having 11,413, Charlotte Amalie, 9,834, and St. John, 765. About 78 per cent of the inhabitants enumerated were Negroes, 13 per cent were mulattoes, 9 per cent whites and the 3 per cent remaining comprised persons of various Asiatic races. The climate is comparatively healthful. There are four seasons, two wet and two dry. Earthquakes and hurricanes occur.

WAKE ISLAND.—Actually a group of three small coral islands around a lagoon, Wake Island (2,600 acres) lies in the Pacific Ocean in longitude 166° 38′ E. and latitude 19° 15′ N. It was discovered in 1796.

Leading Cities of the United States

Rank	Cities	1930	1920	Rank	Cities	1930	1920	Rank	Cities	1930	1920
1	New York, N. Y.	6,930,446	5,620,048	104	Berkeley, Calif.	82,109	56,036	208	Stamford, Conn.	46,346	35,096
2	Chicago, Ill.	3,376,438	2,701,705	105	Altoona, Pa.	82,054	60,331	209	Waterloo, Ia.	46,191	36,230
3	Philadelphia, Pa.	1,950,961	1,823,779	106	Little Rock, Ark.	81,679	65,142	210	Chelsea, Mass.	45,816	43,184
4	Detroit, Mich.	1,568,662	993,678	107	St. Joseph, Mo.	80,935	77,939	211	Lexington, Ky.	45,736	41,534
5	Los Angeles, Calif.	1,238,048	576,673	108	Saginaw, Mich.	80,715	61,903	212	Williamsport, Pa.	45,729	36,198
6	Cleveland, Ohio	900,429	796,841	109	Harrisburg, Pa.	80,339	75,917	213	Portsmouth, Va.	45,704	54,387
7	St. Louis, Mo.	821,960	772,897	110	Sioux City, Ia.	79,183	71,227	214	Jamestown, N. Y.	45,155	38,917
8	Baltimore, Md.	804,874	733,826	111	Lansing, Mich.	78,397	57,327	215	Lorain, Ohio	44,512	37,295
9	Boston, Mass.	781,188	748,060	112	Pawtucket, R. I.	77,149	64,248	216	Chicopee, Mass.	43,930	36,214
10	Pittsburgh, Pa.	669,817	588,343	113	Manchester, N. H.	76,834	78,384	217	Wichita Falls, Tex.	43,690	40,079
11	San Francisco, Calif.	634,394	506,676	114	Binghamton, N. Y.	76,662	66,800	218	Battle Creek, Mich.	43,573	36,164
12	Milwaukee, Wis.	578,249	457,147	115	Shreveport, La.	76,655	43,874	219	Perth Amboy, N. J.	43,516	41,707
13	Buffalo, N. Y.	573,076	506,775	116	Pasadena, Calif.	76,086	45,354	220	Salem, Mass.	43,353	42,529
14	Washington, D. C.	486,869	437,571	117	Lincoln, Neb.	75,933	54,948	221	Amarillo, Tex.	43,132	15,494
15	Minneapolis, Minn.	464,356	380,582	118	Huntington, W. Va.	75,572	50,177	222	Columbus, Ga.	43,131	31,125
16	New Orleans, La.	458,762	387,219	119	Niagara Falls, N. Y.	75,460	50,760	223	Joliet, Ill.	42,993	38,442
17	Cincinnati, Ohio	451,160	401,247	120	Winston-Salem, N. C.	75,274	48,395	224	Cranston, R. I.	42,911	29,407
18	Newark, N. J.	442,337	414,524	121	East St. Louis, Ill.	74,347	66,767	225	Portsmouth, Ohio	42,560	33,011
19	Kansas City, Mo.	399,746	324,410	122	Troy, N. Y.	72,763	71,996	226	Lima, Ohio	42,287	41,326
20	Seattle, Wash.	365,583	315,312	123	Quincy, Mass.	71,983	47,876	227	Council Bluffs, Ia.	42,048	36,162
21	Indianapolis, Ind.	364,161	314,194	124	Springfield, Ill.	71,864	59,183	228	Montclair, N. J.	42,017	28,810
22	Rochester, N. Y.	328,132	295,750	125	Portland, Me.	70,810	69,272	229	Dubuque, Ia.	41,679	39,141
23	Jersey City, N. J.	316,715	298,103	126	Lakewood, Ohio	70,509	41,732	230	Muskegon, Mich.	41,390	36,570
24	Louisville, Ky.	307,745	234,891	127	Roanoke, Va.	69,206	50,842	231	Warren, Ohio	41,062	27,050
25	Portland, Ore.	301,815	258,288	128	Springfield, Ohio	68,743	60,840	232	Kearny, N. J.	40,716	26,724
26	Houston, Tex.	292,352	138,276	129	Mobile, Ala.	68,202	60,777	233	North Bergen tp., N. J.	40,714	23,344
27	Toledo, Ohio	290,718	243,164	130	New Britain, Conn.	68,128	59,316	234	Fitchburg, Mass.	40,692	41,029
28	Columbus, Ohio	290,564	237,031	131	East Orange, N. J.	68,020	50,710	235	Lynchburg, Va.	40,661	30,070
29	Denver, Colo.	287,861	256,491	132	Racine, Wis.	67,542	58,593	236	St. Petersburg, Fla.	40,425	14,237
30	Oakland, Calif.	284,063	216,261	133	Johnstown, Pa.	66,993	67,327	237	Poughkeepsie, N. Y.	40,288	35,000
31	St. Paul, Minn.	271,606	234,698	134	Cicero, Ill.	66,602	44,995	238	Ogden, Utah	40,272	32,804
32	Atlanta, Ga.	270,366	200,616	135	Atlantic City, N. J.	66,198	50,707	239	Oshkosh, Wis.	40,108	33,162
33	Dallas, Tex.	260,475	158,976	136	Montgomery, Ala.	66,079	43,464	240	Anderson, Ind.	39,804	29,767
34	Birmingham, Ala.	259,678	178,806	137	Newton, Mass.	65,276	46,054	241	East Cleveland, Ohio	39,667	27,292
35	Akron, Ohio	255,040	208,435	138	Covington, Ky.	65,252	57,121	242	La Crosse, Wis.	39,614	30,421
36	Memphis, Tenn.	253,143	162,351	139	Pontiac, Mich.	64,928	34,273	243	Butte, Mont.	39,532	41,611
37	Providence, R. I.	252,981	237,595	140	Hammond, Ind.	64,560	36,004	244	Sheboygan, Wis.	39,251	30,955
38	San Antonio, Tex.	231,542	161,379	141	Topeka, Kans.	64,120	50,022	245	Waltham, Mass.	39,247	30,915
39	Omaha, Neb.	214,006	191,601	142	Oak Park, Ill.	63,982	39,858	246	Quincy, Ill.	39,241	35,978
40	Syracuse, N. Y.	209,326	171,717	143	Brockton, Mass.	63,797	66,254	247	Meriden, Conn.	38,481	29,867
41	Dayton, Ohio	200,982	152,559	144	Evanston, Ill.	63,338	37,234	248	Bloomfield, N. J.	38,077	22,019
42	Worcester, Mass.	195,311	179,754	145	Passaic, N. J.	62,959	63,841	249	Rock Island, Ill.	37,953	35,177
43	Oklahoma City, Okla.	185,389	91,295	146	Terre Haute, Ind.	62,810	66,083	250	Cumberland, Md.	37,747	29,837
44	Richmond, Va.	182,929	171,667	147	Glendale, Calif.	62,736	13,536	251	San Bernardino, Calif.	37,481	18,721
45	Youngstown, Ohio	170,002	132,358	148	Charleston, S. C.	62,265	67,957	252	Green Bay, Wis.	37,415	31,017
46	Grand Rapids, Mich.	168,592	137,634	149	Wheeling, W. Va.	61,659	56,208	253	Raleigh, N. C.	37,379	24,418
47	Hartford, Conn.	164,072	138,036	150	Mount Vernon, N. Y.	61,499	42,726	254	Taunton, Mass.	37,355	37,137
48	Fort Worth, Tex.	163,447	106,482	151	Davenport, Ia.	60,751	56,727	255	Santa Monica, Calif.	37,146	15,252
49	New Haven, Conn.	162,655	162,537	152	Charleston, W. Va.	60,408	39,608	256	West New York, N. J.	37,107	29,926
50	Flint, Mich.	156,492	91,599	153	Augusta, Ga.	60,342	52,548	257	Hazleton, Pa.	36,765	32,277
51	Nashville, Tenn.	153,866	118,342	154	Lancaster, Pa.	59,949	53,150	258	Danville, Ill.	36,765	33,776
52	Springfield, Mass.	149,900	129,614	155	Medford, Mass.	59,714	39,038	259	High Point, N. C.	36,745	14,302
53	San Diego, Calif.	147,995	74,361	156	Hoboken, N. J.	59,261	68,166	260	Auburn, N. Y.	36,652	36,192
54	Bridgeport, Conn.	146,716	143,555	157	Chester, Pa.	59,164	58,030	261	Zanesville, Ohio	36,440	29,569
55	Scranton, Pa.	143,433	137,783	158	Union City, N. J.	58,659	20,651	262	Superior, Wis.	36,113	39,671
56	Des Moines, Ia.	142,559	126,468	159	Malden, Mass.	58,036	49,103	263	Arlington, Mass.	36,094	18,665
57	Long Beach, Calif.	142,032	55,593	160	Madison, Wis.	57,899	38,378	264	Norwalk, Conn.	36,019	27,743
58	Tulsa, Okla.	141,258	72,075	161	Bethlehem, Pa.	57,892	50,358	265	Elgin, Ill.	35,929	27,454
59	Salt Lake City, Utah	140,267	118,110	162	Beaumont, Tex.	57,732	40,422	266	Norristown, Pa.	35,853	32,319
60	Paterson, N. J.	138,513	135,875	163	San Jose, Calif.	57,651	39,642	267	White Plains, N. Y.	35,830	21,031
61	Jacksonville, Fla.	135,116	100,176	164	Springfield, Mo.	57,527	39,631	268	Revere, Mass.	35,680	28,823
62	Yonkers, N. Y.	134,646	115,777	165	Decatur, Ill.	57,510	43,818	269	Steubenville, Ohio	35,422	28,508
63	Norfolk, Va.	129,710	91,558	166	Irvington, N. J.	56,733	25,480	270	Orange, N. J.	35,399	33,268
64	Albany, N. Y.	127,412	113,344	167	Holyoke, Mass.	56,537	60,203	271	Lower Merion tp., Pa.	35,166	23,866
65	Trenton, N. J.	123,356	119,289	168	Hamtramck, Mich.	56,268	48,615	272	Alameda, Calif.	35,033	28,806
66	Kansas City, Kans.	121,857	101,177	169	Cedar Rapids, Ia.	56,097	45,566	273	Lewiston, Me.	34,948	31,791
67	Chattanooga, Tenn.	119,798	57,895	170	York, Pa.	55,254	47,512	274	Watertown, Mass.	34,913	21,457
68	Camden, N. J.	118,700	116,309	171	Jackson, Mich.	55,187	48,374	275	Amsterdam, N. Y.	34,817	33,524
69	Erie, Pa.	115,967	93,372	172	Kalamazoo, Mich.	54,786	48,487	276	West Allis, Wis.	34,671	13,745
70	Spokane, Wash.	115,514	104,437	173	East Chicago, Ind.	54,784	35,967	277	New Brunswick, N. J.	34,555	32,779
71	Fall River, Mass.	115,274	120,485	174	McKeesport, Pa.	54,632	46,781	278	Easton, Pa.	34,468	33,813
72	Fort Wayne, Ind.	114,946	86,549	175	New Rochelle, N. Y.	54,000	36,213	279	Plainfield, N. J.	34,422	27,700
73	Elizabeth, N. J.	114,589	95,783	176	Macon, Ga.	53,829	52,995	280	Newport News, Va.	34,417	35,596
74	Cambridge, Mass.	113,643	109,694	177	Greensboro, N. C.	53,569	19,861	281	Santa Barbara, Calif.	33,613	19,441
75	New Bedford, Mass.	112,597	121,217	178	Austin, Tex.	53,120	34,876	282	Paducah, Ky.	33,541	24,735
76	Reading, Pa.	111,171	107,784	179	Highland Park, Mich.	52,959	46,499	283	Mansfield, Ohio	33,525	27,824
77	Wichita, Kans.	111,110	72,217	180	Galveston, Tex.	52,938	44,255	284	Waukegan, Ill.	33,499	19,226
78	Miami, Fla.	110,637	29,571	181	Waco, Tex.	52,848	38,500	285	Joplin, Mo.	33,454	29,902
79	Tacoma, Wash.	106,817	96,965	182	Fresno, Calif.	52,513	45,086	286	Norwood, Ohio	33,411	24,966
80	Wilmington, Del.	106,597	110,168	183	Hamilton, Ohio	52,176	39,675	287	Sioux Falls, S. D.	33,362	25,202
81	Knoxville, Tenn.	105,802	77,818	184	Durham, N. C.	52,037	21,719	288	Colorado Springs, Colo.	33,237	30,105
82	Peoria, Ill.	104,969	76,121	185	Columbia, S. C.	51,581	37,524	289	Belvedere tp., Calif.	33,023	6,339
83	Canton, Ohio	104,906	87,091	186	Cleveland Heights, Ohio	50,945	15,236	290	Elkhart, Ind.	32,949	24,277
84	South Bend, Ind.	104,193	70,983	187	Port Arthur, Tex.	50,902	22,251	291	Kokomo, Ind.	32,843	30,067
85	Somerville, Mass.	103,908	93,091	188	Dearborn, Mich.	50,358	2,470	292	Laredo, Tex.	32,618	22,710
86	El Paso, Tex.	102,421	77,560	189	Kenosha, Wis.	50,262	40,472	293	Tucson, Ariz.	32,506	20,292
87	Lynn, Mass.	102,320	99,148	190	Asheville, N. C.	50,193	28,504	294	Richmond, Ind.	32,493	26,765
88	Evansville, Ind.	102,249	85,264	191	Pueblo, Colo.	50,096	43,050	295	Rome, N. Y.	32,338	26,341
89	Utica, N. Y.	101,740	94,156	192	Pittsfield, Mass.	49,677	41,763	296	Wilmington, N. C.	32,270	33,372
90	Duluth, Minn.	101,463	98,917	193	Woonsocket, R. I.	49,376	43,496	297	Moline, Ill.	32,236	30,734
91	Tampa, Fla.	101,161	51,608	194	Haverhill, Mass.	48,710	53,884	298	Watertown, N. Y.	32,205	31,285
92	Gary, Ind.	100,426	55,378	195	New Castle, Pa.	48,674	44,938	299	Muskogee, Okla.	32,026	30,277
93	Lowell, Mass.	100,234	112,759	196	Everett, Mass.	48,424	40,120	300	Meridian, Miss.	31,954	23,399
94	Waterbury, Conn.	99,902	91,715	197	Jackson, Miss.	48,282	22,817	301	Pensacola, Fla.	31,579	31,035
95	Schenectady, N. Y.	95,692	88,723	198	Phoenix, Ariz.	48,118	29,053	302	Nashua, N. H.	31,463	28,379
96	Sacramento, Calif.	93,750	65,908	199	Stockton, Calif.	47,963	40,296	303	Fort Smith, Ark.	31,429	28,870
97	Allentown, Pa.	92,563	73,502	200	Brookline, Mass.	47,490	37,748	304	Port Huron, Mich.	31,361	25,944
98	Bayonne, N. J.	88,979	76,754	201	Elmira, N. Y.	47,397	45,393	305	Newburgh, N. Y.	31,275	30,366
99	Wilkes-Barre, Pa.	86,626	73,833	202	Bay City, Mich.	47,355	47,554	306	Marion, Ohio	31,084	27,891
100	Rockford, Ill.	85,864	65,651	203	Berwyn, Ill.	47,027	14,150	307	Bloomington, Ill.	30,930	28,725
101	Lawrence, Mass.	85,068	94,270	204	Clifton, N. J.	46,875	26,470	308	Hagerstown, Md.	30,861	28,064
102	Savannah, Ga.	85,024	83,252	206	Aurora, Ill.	46,589	36,397	309	Bellingham, Wash.	30,823	25,585
103	Charlotte, N. C.	82,675	46,338	207	Muncie, Ind.	46,548	36,524	310	Baton Rouge, La.	30,729	21,782

The Counties of the United States

The 3,070 counties in continental United States are listed below alphabetically by states, with the location of each on its state map indicated. Population figures are in accordance with the census.

ALABAMA

TOTAL 67 COUNTIES

Pop.	County	Index
19,694	Autauga	I 13
28,289	Baldwin	P 7
32,425	Barbour	L 21
20,780	Bibb	H 11
28,020	Blount	E 14
20,016	Bullock	K 19
30,195	Butler	L 13
55,611	Calhoun	E 19
39,313	Chambers	H 21
20,219	Cherokee	D 19
24,579	Chilton	H 13
20,513	Choctaw	L 4
26,016	Clarke	L 7
17,768	Clay	G 18
12,877	Cleburne	F 20
32,556	Coffee	N 17
29,860	Colbert	B 7
25,429	Conecuh	N 11
12,460	Coosa	H 16
41,356	Covington	N 15
23,656	Crenshaw	M 15
41,051	Cullman	D 12
23,175	Dale	N 19
55,094	Dallas	K 11
40,104	De Kalb	C 19
34,280	Elmore	I 16
27,963	Escambia	O 10
63,399	Etowah	D 17
18,443	Fayette	E 8
25,372	Franklin	C 7
30,104	Geneva	O 18
19,745	Greene	H 6
26,265	Hale	I 8
22,820	Henry	M 22
45,935	Houston	O 21
36,881	Jackson	A 18
431,493	Jefferson	F 12
18,001	Lamar	E 6
41,130	Lauderdale	A 8
26,942	Lawrence	B 10
36,063	Lee	I 21
36,629	Limestone	A 11
22,878	Lowndes	K 13
27,103	Macon	J 19
64,623	Madison	A 14
36,426	Marengo	J 7
25,967	Marion	D 6
39,802	Marshall	C 15
118,363	Mobile	P 4
30,070	Monroe	M 9
98,671	Montgomery	K 16
46,176	Morgan	C 12
26,385	Perry	I 10
24,902	Pickens	G 6
32,240	Pike	L 18
26,861	Randolph	G 20
27,377	Russell	J 21
24,510	Saint Clair	E 16
27,576	Shelby	G 14
26,929	Sumter	J 5
45,241	Talladega	G 16
31,188	Tallapoosa	H 19
64,153	Tuscaloosa	G 9
59,445	Walker	E 10
16,365	Washington	M 4
24,880	Wilcox	L 9
15,596	Winston	D 10
2,646,248	Total	

ALASKA

TOTAL 4 DISTRICTS

Pop.	District
19,304	First Judicial
10,127	Second Judicial
16,309	Third Judicial
13,538	Fourth Judicial
59,278	Total

ARIZONA

TOTAL 14 COUNTIES

Pop.	County	Index
17,765	Apache	G 23
40,998	Cochise	P 22
14,064	Coconino	E 13
31,016	Gila	K 18
10,373	Graham	L 22
9,886	Greenlee	L 24
150,970	Maricopa	K 11
5,572	Mohave	F 5
21,202	Navajo	F 20
55,676	Pima	O 13
22,081	Pinal	M 16
9,684	Santa Cruz	Q 18
28,470	Yavapai	H 11
17,816	Yuma	L 5
435,573	Total	

ARKANSAS

TOTAL 75 COUNTIES

Pop.	County	Index
22,300	Arkansas	L 16
25,151	Ashley	Q 14
9,519	Baxter	A 12
35,253	Benton	B 4
14,937	Boone	B 9
17,494	Bradley	P 13
9,752	Calhoun	O 11
15,820	Carroll	A 7
22,646	Chicot	Q 17
24,932	Clark	M 9
27,278	Clay	A 20
11,373	Cleburne	E 14
12,744	Cleveland	N 13
27,320	Columbia	Q 8
21,949	Conway	G 11
44,740	Craighead	D 19
22,549	Crawford	E 4
39,717	Crittenden	H 21
25,723	Cross	G 19
14,671	Dallas	M 11
21,814	Desha	O 17
19,928	Drew	O 15
28,381	Faulkner	H 12
15,762	Franklin	E 6
10,834	Fulton	A 14
36,031	Garland	J 9
9,834	Grant	L 12
26,127	Greene	C 20
30,847	Hempstead	O 6
18,105	Hot Spring	L 9
17,489	Howard	M 6
24,225	Independence	E 16
12,872	Izard	C 14
27,943	Jackson	E 17
64,154	Jefferson	L 14
19,289	Johnson	E 8
16,934	Lafayette	Q 7
21,663	Lawrence	C 17
26,637	Lee	I 19
20,250	Lincoln	M 15
15,515	Little River	O 4
24,110	Logan	G 7
33,759	Lonoke	J 14
13,334	Madison	C 7
8,876	Marion	B 11
30,586	Miller	Q 6
69,289	Mississippi	D 22
20,651	Monroe	J 17
10,768	Montgomery	K 7
20,407	Nevada	O 8
10,564	Newton	D 9
29,890	Ouachita	O 10
7,695	Perry	I 10
40,683	Phillips	K 19
11,792	Pike	L 7
29,695	Poinsett	E 19
14,857	Polk	K 5
26,547	Pope	F 9
15,187	Prairie	J 16
137,727	Pulaski	I 12
16,871	Randolph	B 18
33,394	Saint Francis	H 19
15,660	Saline	J 11
11,803	Scott	I 5
11,056	Searcy	D 11
54,426	Sebastian	G 4
16,364	Sevier	M 4
10,715	Sharp	C 16
7,993	Stone	D 13
55,800	Union	Q 11
11,962	Van Buren	E 12
39,255	Washington	C 4
38,269	White	G 15
22,682	Woodruff	G 17
21,313	Yell	H 8
1,854,482	Total	

CALIFORNIA

TOTAL 58 COUNTIES

Pop.	County	Index
474,883	Alameda	I 6, F 22
241	Alpine	G 11
8,494	Amador	H 9
34,093	Butte	F 7
6,008	Calaveras	H 9
10,258	Colusa	F 5
78,608	Contra Costa	I 6, D 22
4,739	Del Norte	B 2
8,325	Eldorado	G 9
144,379	Fresno	K 10
10,935	Glenn	F 6
43,233	Humboldt	D 2
60,903	Imperial	Q 22
6,555	Inyo	K 16
82,570	Kern	M 13
25,385	Kings	L 11
7,166	Lake	G 4
12,589	Lassen	D 9
2,208,492	Los Angeles	N 15, Q 4
17,164	Madera	J 12
41,648	Marin	C 14, H 4
3,233	Mariposa	I 11
23,505	Mendocino	F 3
36,748	Merced	J 9
8,038	Modoc	B 9
1,360	Mono	H 13
53,705	Monterey	K 7
22,897	Napa	G 5, A 18
10,596	Nevada	F 9
118,674	Orange	P 17, R 6
24,468	Placer	G 9
7,913	Plumus	E 9
81,024	Riverside	P 19, R 9
141,999	Sacramento	H 8
11,311	San Benito	K 8
133,900	San Bernardino	N 18, P 9
209,659	San Diego	Q 19
634,394	San Francisco	I 5
102,940	San Joaquin	H 8
29,613	San Luis Obispo	M 10
77,405	San Mateo	I 5, G 17
65,167	Santa Barbara	N 11
145,118	Santa Clara	J 6, H 22
37,433	Santa Cruz	J 5
13,927	Shasta	D 6
2,422	Sierra	F 10
25,480	Siskiyou	B 5
40,834	Solano	H 6, B 22
62,222	Sonoma	G 3, A 15
56,641	Stanislaus	I 9
14,618	Sutter	G 7
13,866	Tehama	E 6
2,809	Trinity	D 4
77,442	Tulare	L 13
9,271	Tuolumne	H 10
54,976	Ventura	N 13
23,644	Yolo	G 6
11,331	Yuba	F 8
5,677,251	Total	

COLORADO

TOTAL 63 COUNTIES

Pop.	County	Index
20,245	Adams	F 17
8,602	Alamosa	P 12
22,647	Arapahoe	G 17
3,204	Archuleta	Q 8
10,570	Baca	Q 23
9,134	Bent	N 21
32,456	Boulder	E 14
8,126	Chaffee	J 11
3,723	Cheyenne	J 23
2,155	Clear Creek	G 13
9,803	Conejos	Q 11
5,779	Costilla	Q 13
5,934	Crowley	L 19
2,124	Custer	M 13
14,204	Delta	J 5
287,861	Denver	F 15
1,412	Dolores	O 3
3,498	Douglas	H 15
3,924	Eagle	G 9
6,580	Elbert	H 17
49,570	El Paso	K 16
18,896	Fremont	L 13
9,975	Garfield	G 4
1,212	Gilpin	F 13
2,108	Grand	E 11
5,527	Gunnison	K 8
449	Hinsdale	O 7
17,062	Huerfano	O 15
1,386	Jackson	C 10
21,810	Jefferson	G 14
3,786	Kiowa	L 23
9,725	Kit Carson	H 23
4,899	Lake	I 10
12,975	La Plata	P 6
33,137	Larimer	B 13
36,008	Las Animas	Q 18
7,850	Lincoln	J 20
19,946	Logan	B 21
25,908	Mesa	I 3
640	Mineral	O 8
4,861	Moffat	B 4
7,798	Montezuma	P 3
11,742	Montrose	L 4
18,284	Morgan	E 19
24,390	Otero	N 19
1,784	Ouray	M 5
2,052	Park	I 12
5,797	Phillips	C 24
1,770	Pitkin	I 8
14,762	Prowers	N 24
66,038	Pueblo	M 16
2,980	Rio Blanco	E 4
9,953	Rio Grande	P 10
9,352	Routt	C 8
6,250	Saguache	N 10
1,935	San Juan	O 6
2,184	San Miguel	N 3
5,580	Sedgwick	B 24
987	Summit	G 11
4,141	Teller	J 14
9,591	Washington	E 21
65,097	Weld	B 17
13,613	Yuma	E 24
1,035,791	Total	

CONNECTICUT

TOTAL 8 COUNTIES

Pop.	County	Index
386,702	Fairfield	N 5
421,097	Hartford	E 13
82,556	Litchfield	D 6
51,388	Middlesex	K 15
463,449	New Haven	K 11
118,966	New London	I 21
28,659	Tolland	D 18
54,086	Windham	D 23
1,606,903	Total	

DELAWARE

TOTAL 3 COUNTIES

Pop.	County	Index
31,841	Kent	H 21
161,032	New Castle	D 21
45,507	Sussex	K 22
238,380	Total	

DISTRICT OF COLUMBIA

DISTRICT

Pop.		Index
486,869	District of Columbia	J 11

FLORIDA

TOTAL 67 COUNTIES

Pop.	County	Index
34,365	Alachua	D 13
6,273	Baker	C 14
12,091	Bay	N 9
9,405	Bradford	C 14
13,283	Brevard	H 21
20,094	Broward	N 22
7,298	Calhoun	B 1
4,013	Charlotte	K 16
5,516	Citrus	G 13
6,859	Clay	C 15
2,883	Collier	N 19
14,638	Columbia	C 12
142,955	Dade	O 22
7,745	De Soto	K 16
6,419	Dixie	D 10
155,503	Duval	C 16
53,594	Escambia	M 2
2,466	Flagler	E 18
6,283	Franklin	D 3
29,890	Gadsden	B 3
4,137	Gilchrist	D 11
2,762	Glades	K 19
3,182	Gulf	P 11
9,454	Hamilton	B 10
10,348	Hardee	J 16
3,492	Hendry	L 19
4,948	Hernando	G 13
9,192	Highlands	K 19
153,519	Hillsborough	I 14
12,924	Holmes	M 9
6,724	Indian River	I 22
31,969	Jackson	A 1
13,408	Jefferson	B 7
4,361	Lafayette	C 10
23,161	Lake	G 16
14,990	Lee	M 16
23,476	Leon	B 5
12,456	Levy	E 12
4,067	Liberty	C 2
15,614	Madison	B 8
22,502	Manatee	J 14
29,578	Marion	E 15
5,111	Martin	K 22
13,624	Monroe	P 19
9,375	Nassau	B 16
9,897	Okaloosa	M 5
4,129	Okeechobee	J 20
49,737	Orange	G 18
10,699	Osceola	I 19
51,781	Palm Beach	L 23
10,574	Pasco	H 13
62,149	Pinellas	I 12
72,291	Polk	I 17
18,096	Putnam	D 16
18,676	Saint Johns	D 18
7,057	Saint Lucie	J 22
14,083	Santa Rosa	M 3
12,440	Sarasota	K 14
18,735	Seminole	G 18
10,644	Sumter	G 15
15,731	Suwannee	C 10
13,136	Taylor	C 8
7,428	Union	C 13
42,757	Volusia	F 18
5,468	Wakulla	C 5
14,576	Walton	M 7
12,180	Washington	M 9
1,468,211	Total	

GEORGIA

TOTAL 159 COUNTIES

Pop.	County	Index
13,314	Appling	M 18
6,894	Atkinson	N 15
7,055	Bacon	M 17
7,818	Baker	N 6
22,878	Baldwin	H 13
9,703	Banks	D 12
12,401	Barrow	E 10
25,364	Bartow	D 4
13,047	Ben Hill	M 13
14,646	Berrien	N 13
77,042	Bibb	I 10
9,133	Bleckley	J 12
6,895	Brantley	O 20
21,330	Brooks	P 11
5,952	Bryan	L 23
26,509	Bulloch	J 21
29,224	Burke	H 20
9,345	Butts	H 9
10,576	Calhoun	M 5
6,338	Camden	O 22
8,991	Candler	K 19
34,272	Carroll	G 3
9,421	Catoosa	B 3
4,381	Charlton	P 19
105,431	Chatham	L 24
8,894	Chattahoochee	K 4
15,407	Chattooga	C 2
20,003	Cherokee	D 6
25,613	Clarke	E 12
6,943	Clay	M 3
10,260	Clayton	G 7
7,015	Clinch	O 16
35,408	Cobb	E 6
19,737	Coffee	M 15
30,622	Colquitt	O 10
8,793	Columbia	G 19
11,311	Cook	O 12
25,127	Coweta	G 4
7,020	Crawford	I 9
17,343	Crisp	L 10
4,146	Dade	B 1
3,502	Dawson	D 8
23,622	Decatur	O 5
70,278	De Kalb	F 8
21,599	Dodge	K 13
18,025	Dooly	K 10
22,306	Dougherty	M 7
9,461	Douglas	F 5
18,273	Early	N 3
2,744	Echols	P 15
10,164	Effingham	K 24
18,485	Elbert	E 15
24,101	Emanuel	J 18
7,102	Evans	K 20
12,969	Fannin	B 7
8,665	Fayette	G 6
48,667	Floyd	D 2
10,624	Forsyth	D 8
15,902	Franklin	D 13
335,220	Fulton	F 7
7,344	Gilmer	C 6
4,388	Glascock	H 16
19,400	Glynn	N 22
16,846	Gordon	C 4
19,200	Grady	P 7
12,616	Greene	G 13
27,853	Gwinnett	E 9
12,748	Habersham	C 11
30,313	Hall	D 10
13,070	Hancock	H 14
13,263	Haralson	F 2
11,140	Harris	I 4
15,174	Hart	D 15
9,102	Heard	G 3
15,924	Henry	G 8
11,280	Houston	J 11
12,199	Irwin	M 13
21,609	Jackson	E 11
8,594	Jasper	G 10
8,118	Jeff Davis	M 16
20,727	Jefferson	H 17
12,908	Jenkins	I 20
12,681	Johnson	I 16
8,992	Jones	H 11
9,745	Lamar	H 8
5,190	Lanier	O 14
32,693	Laurens	J 15
8,328	Lee	M 8
8,153	Liberty	L 22
7,847	Lincoln	F 17
4,180	Long	M 21
29,994	Lowndes	P 13
4,927	Lumpkin	C 9
9,014	McDuffie	G 17
5,763	McIntosh	M 23
16,643	Macon	K 8
14,921	Madison	E 13
6,968	Marion	K 6
22,437	Meriwether	H 5
9,076	Miller	O 4
23,620	Mitchell	N 7
11,606	Monroe	H 9
10,202	Montgomery	K 17
12,488	Morgan	F 12
9,215	Murray	C 5
57,558	Muscogee	J 4
17,290	Newton	G 9
8,082	Oconee	F 12
12,927	Oglethorpe	F 14
12,327	Paulding	E 4
10,268	Peach	J 10
9,687	Pickens	D 6
12,522	Pierce	N 18
10,853	Pike	H 7
25,141	Polk	E 2
9,005	Pulaski	K 11
8,367	Putnam	G 12
3,820	Quitman	L 3
6,331	Rabun	B 12
17,174	Randolph	M 4
72,990	Richmond	G 19
7,247	Rockdale	F 9
5,347	Schley	K 7
20,503	Screven	I 22
7,389	Seminole	O 4
23,495	Spalding	H 7
11,740	Stephens	C 13
11,114	Stewart	L 4
26,800	Sumter	L 8
8,458	Talbot	I 6
6,172	Taliaferro	G 15
15,411	Tattnall	K 19
10,617	Taylor	J 8
14,997	Telfair	L 15
18,290	Terrell	M 6
32,612	Thomas	P 9
16,068	Tift	N 11
17,165	Toombs	K 18
4,346	Towns	B 10
7,488	Treutlen	J 17
36,752	Troup	H 3
11,196	Turner	M 11
8,372	Twiggs	J 12
6,340	Union	B 9
19,509	Upson	I 7
26,206	Walker	C 2
21,118	Walton	F 10
26,558	Ware	O 17
11,181	Warren	G 16
25,030	Washington	I 15
12,647	Wayne	M 20
5,032	Webster	L 6
9,149	Wheeler	L 16
6,056	White	C 10
20,808	Whitfield	C 3
13,439	Wilcox	L 12
15,944	Wilkes	F 16
10,844	Wilkinson	I 13
21,094	Worth	M 10
2,908,506	Total	

IDAHO

TOTAL 44 COUNTIES

Pop.	County	Index
37,925	Ada	O 5
2,867	Adams	K 4
31,266	Bannock	Q 19
7,872	Bear Lake	Q 22
6,371	Benewah	E 4
18,561	Bingham	O 19
3,768	Blaine	O 13
1,847	Boise	M 6
13,152	Bonner	B 5
19,664	Bonneville	N 18
4,555	Boundary	A 5
1,934	Butte	N 15
1,411	Camas	N 10
30,930	Canyon	N 4
2,121	Caribou	P 21
13,116	Cassia	R 14
1,122	Clark	M 18
6,599	Clearwater	F 7
3,162	Custer	L 12
4,491	Elmore	O 8
9,379	Franklin	R 20
9,924	Fremont	M 21
7,419	Gem	M 5
7,580	Gooding	P 10
10,107	Idaho	I 8
9,171	Jefferson	N 18
8,358	Jerome	P 12
19,469	Kootenai	E 5
17,798	Latah	F 4
4,643	Lemhi	J 11
5,238	Lewis	H 4
3,242	Lincoln	P 12
8,316	Madison	N 21
8,403	Minidoka	P 14
17,591	Nez Perce	H 3
5,870	Oneida	Q 17
4,103	Owyhee	Q 6
7,318	Payette	M 3
4,457	Power	Q 17
19,060	Shoshone	D 6
3,573	Teton	N 22
29,828	Twin Falls	Q 11
3,488	Valley	L 7
7,962	Washington	L 3
1	Yellowstone National Park (part)	L 23
445,032	Total	

ILLINOIS

TOTAL 102 COUNTIES

Pop.	County	Index
62,784	Adams	I 5
22,542	Alexander	R 14
14,406	Bond	M 13
15,078	Boone	A 16
7,892	Brown	I 7
38,845	Bureau	D 12
8,034	Calhoun	L 7
18,433	Carroll	B 11
16,537	Cass	I 9
64,273	Champaign	H 19
37,538	Christian	J 14
17,872	Clark	K 21
16,155	Clay	M 18
21,369	Clinton	N 13
37,315	Coles	J 19
3,982,123	Cook	C 21
21,085	Crawford	L 21
10,419	Cumberland	K 19
32,644	De Kalb	C 16
18,598	De Witt	H 16
17,914	Douglas	J 19
91,998	Du Page	C 19
24,966	Edgar	J 21
8,303	Edwards	N 20
19,013	Effingham	L 17
23,487	Fayette	L 15
15,489	Ford	G 19
59,442	Franklin	O 16
43,983	Fulton	G 9
10,091	Gallatin	P 19
20,417	Greene	K 9
18,678	Grundy	E 18
12,995	Hamilton	O 17
26,420	Hancock	G 5
6,955	Hardin	Q 19
8,778	Henderson	F 6
43,851	Henry	D 10
32,913	Iroquois	G 21
35,680	Jackson	P 13
12,809	Jasper	L 19
31,034	Jefferson	N 16
12,556	Jersey	L 8
20,235	Jo Daviess	A 10
10,203	Johnson	Q 16
125,327	Kane	B 18
50,095	Kankakee	E 21
10,555	Kendall	D 18
51,336	Knox	F 9
104,387	Lake	A 20
97,695	La Salle	D 16
21,885	Lawrence	M 21
32,329	Lee	B 14
39,092	Livingston	F 17
28,863	Logan	H 13
27,329	McDonough	H 7
35,079	McHenry	A 18
73,117	McLean	G 16
81,731	Macon	I 15
48,703	Macoupin	K 11
143,830	Madison	M 11
35,635	Marion	M 16
13,023	Marshall	E 13
15,115	Mason	H 11
14,081	Massac	R 17
10,575	Menard	I 11
16,641	Mercer	E 7
12,369	Monroe	O 10
35,278	Montgomery	K 13
34,240	Morgan	J 10
13,247	Moultrie	J 17
28,118	Ogle	B 13
141,344	Peoria	F 11
22,767	Perry	O 13
15,588	Piatt	I 17
24,357	Pike	J 6
7,996	Pope	Q 17
14,834	Pulaski	R 15
5,235	Putnam	E 14
29,313	Randolph	O 11
14,053	Richland	M 20
98,191	Rock Island	D 8
157,775	Saint Clair	N 11
37,100	Saline	P 17
111,733	Sangamon	J 12
11,676	Schuyler	H 7
8,539	Scott	J 8
25,471	Shelby	K 16
9,184	Stark	E 11
40,064	Stephenson	A 12
46,082	Tazewell	G 12
19,883	Union	Q 14
89,339	Vermilion	H 21
13,197	Wabash	N 21
21,745	Warren	F 7
16,286	Washington	N 13
19,130	Wayne	N 18
18,149	White	O 19
39,019	Whiteside	C 11
110,732	Will	D 20
53,880	Williamson	Q 16
117,373	Winnebago	A 14
18,792	Woodford	F 14
7,630,654	Total	

INDIANA

TOTAL 92 COUNTIES

Pop.	County	Index
19,957	Adams	F 21
146,743	Allen	D 21
24,864	Bartholomew	L 16
11,886	Benton	F 7
13,617	Blackford	G 19
22,290	Boone	I 12
5,168	Brown	L 14
15,049	Carroll	F 11
34,518	Cass	E 13
30,764	Clark	O 17
26,479	Clay	K 8
27,329	Clinton	G 12
10,160	Crawford	P 12
25,832	Daviess	N 8
21,056	Dearborn	M 22
17,308	Decatur	L 18
24,911	De Kalb	C 21
67,270	Delaware	H 19
20,553	Dubois	P 9
68,875	Elkhart	B 16
19,243	Fayette	J 20
34,655	Floyd	P 16
17,971	Fountain	H 7
14,498	Franklin	K 21
15,038	Fulton	D 13
29,202	Gibson	P 5
51,066	Grant	G 17
31,481	Greene	M 9
23,444	Hamilton	I 15
16,605	Hancock	J 16
17,254	Harrison	P 15
19,725	Hendricks	J 12
35,238	Henry	I 18
46,696	Howard	G 14
29,073	Huntington	E 18
23,731	Jackson	N 15
13,388	Jasper	E 8
20,846	Jay	G 21
19,182	Jefferson	N 19
11,800	Jennings	M 18
21,706	Johnson	K 14
43,813	Knox	N 6
27,488	Kosciusko	C 16
13,780	Lagrange	B 18
261,310	Lake	C 7
60,490	La Porte	B 10
35,583	Lawrence	N 12
82,888	Madison	H 17
422,666	Marion	J 14
25,077	Marshall	C 13
10,103	Martin	O 10
29,032	Miami	E 15
35,974	Monroe	L 12
26,980	Montgomery	I 10
19,424	Morgan	K 12
9,841	Newton	E 7
22,404	Noble	C 18
3,747	Ohio	M 22
17,459	Orange	O 12
11,351	Owen	L 10
16,561	Parke	J 8
16,625	Perry	Q 11
16,361	Pike	P 7
22,821	Porter	C 8
17,853	Posey	Q 3
11,195	Pulaski	D 10
20,448	Putnam	J 10
24,859	Randolph	H 21
18,078	Ripley	M 20
19,412	Rush	J 18
160,033	Saint Joseph	B 13
6,664	Scott	N 17
26,552	Shelby	K 17
16,713	Spencer	Q 9

Pop.	County	Index
10,620	Starke	C 10
13,386	Steuben	B 21
28,133	Sullivan	M 6
8,432	Switzerland	N 22
47,535	Tippecanoe	G 9
15,208	Tipton	G 15
5,880	Union	J 22
113,320	Vanderburg	Q 5
23,238	Vermillion	I 6
98,861	Vigo	K 6
25,170	Wabash	E 16
9,167	Warren	G 7
18,230	Warrick	Q 7
16,285	Washington	O 14
54,809	Wayne	I 21
18,411	Wells	F 20
15,831	White	F 9
15,931	Whitley	D 18
3,238,503	Total	

IOWA

TOTAL 99 COUNTIES

Pop.	County	Index
13,891	Adair	M 8
10,437	Adams	N 7
16,328	Allamakee	C 20
24,835	Appanoose	O 15
12,264	Audubon	K 7
22,851	Benton	I 18
69,146	Black Hawk	G 17
29,271	Boone	J 10
17,046	Bremer	E 17
19,550	Buchanan	G 19
18,667	Buena Vista	F 6
17,617	Butler	F 15
17,605	Calhoun	H 8
22,326	Carroll	I 7
19,422	Cass	M 7
16,760	Cedar	J 21
38,476	Cerro Gordo	D 13
18,737	Cherokee	F 4
14,637	Chickasaw	C 17
10,384	Clarke	O 11
16,107	Clay	D 6
24,559	Clayton	E 20
44,377	Clinton	J 24
21,028	Crawford	I 5
25,493	Dallas	K 10
11,150	Davis	P 17
14,903	Decatur	P 11
18,122	Delaware	G 21
38,162	Des Moines	O 21
10,982	Dickinson	B 6
61,214	Dubuque	G 22
12,856	Emmet	B 8
29,145	Fayette	E 19
19,524	Floyd	D 15
16,382	Franklin	F 13
15,533	Fremont	P 4
16,528	Greene	I 9
14,133	Grundy	G 15
17,324	Guthrie	K 8
20,978	Hamilton	H 11
14,802	Hancock	D 11
22,947	Hardin	G 13
24,897	Harrison	K 3
17,660	Henry	N 20
13,082	Howard	B 17
13,202	Humboldt	E 9
11,933	Ida	G 4
17,332	Iowa	K 18
18,481	Jackson	H 23
32,936	Jasper	K 14
16,241	Jefferson	N 18
30,276	Johnson	K 20
19,206	Jones	I 21
19,148	Keokuk	M 18
25,452	Kossuth	C 10
41,268	Lee	P 21
82,336	Linn	I 20
11,575	Louisa	M 21
15,114	Lucas	N 13
15,293	Lyon	B 2
14,331	Madison	M 10
25,804	Mahaska	M 16
25,727	Marion	M 14
33,727	Marshall	I 14
15,866	Mills	N 4
14,065	Mitchell	B 15
18,213	Monona	I 2
15,010	Monroe	N 15
16,752	Montgomery	N 6
29,385	Muscatine	L 22
18,409	O'Brien	D 4
10,182	Osceola	B 4
25,904	Page	P 5
15,398	Palo Alto	D 8
24,159	Plymouth	E 2
15,687	Pocahontas	F 8
172,837	Polk	K 12
69,888	Pottawattamie	M 4
18,727	Poweshiek	K 16
11,966	Ringgold	P 9
17,641	Sac	G 6
77,332	Scott	K 24
17,131	Shelby	K 5
26,806	Sioux	C 2
31,141	Story	I 12
21,987	Tama	I 16
14,859	Taylor	P 7
17,435	Union	O 10
12,603	Van Buren	P 18
40,480	Wapello	O 17
17,700	Warren	M 12
19,822	Washington	M 19
13,787	Wayne	P 13
40,425	Webster	H 10
13,143	Winnebago	B 11
21,630	Winneshiek	B 19
101,669	Woodbury	G 2
11,164	Worth	B 13
20,216	Wright	F 11
2,470,939	Total	

KANSAS

TOTAL 105 COUNTIES

Pop.	County	Index
21,391	Allen	L 23
13,355	Anderson	J 23
23,945	Atchison	E 23
10,178	Barber	O 12
19,776	Barton	I 11
22,386	Bourbon	L 24
20,553	Brown	D 22
35,904	Butler	L 18
6,952	Chase	J 19
10,352	Chautauqua	O 20
31,457	Cherokee	N 24
6,948	Cheyenne	D 2
4,796	Clark	N 8
14,556	Clay	F 16
18,006	Cloud	E 15
13,653	Coffey	J 21
5,238	Comanche	O 10
40,903	Cowley	O 18
49,329	Crawford	M 24
8,866	Decatur	D 6
25,870	Dickinson	H 17
14,063	Doniphan	D 23
25,143	Douglas	H 23
7,295	Edwards	L 10
9,210	Elk	M 20
15,907	Ellis	G 10
10,132	Ellsworth	I 13
11,014	Finney	K 5
20,647	Ford	M 8
22,024	Franklin	I 23
14,366	Geary	G 18
5,643	Gove	H 6
7,772	Graham	F 8
3,092	Grant	M 3
6,211	Gray	M 6
1,712	Greeley	I 2
19,235	Greenwood	L 20
3,328	Hamilton	K 2
12,823	Harper	O 14
22,120	Harvey	K 16
2,805	Haskell	M 5
4,157	Hodgeman	K 8
14,776	Jackson	F 21
14,129	Jefferson	F 22
14,462	Jewell	D 13
27,179	Johnson	G 24
3,196	Kearny	K 3
11,674	Kingman	M 13
6,035	Kiowa	M 10
31,346	Labette	N 23
3,372	Lane	I 6
42,673	Leavenworth	F 24
9,707	Lincoln	G 13
13,534	Linn	J 24
4,145	Logan	G 4
29,240	Lyon	I 20
23,588	McPherson	J 15
20,739	Marion	J 17
23,056	Marshall	D 19
6,858	Meade	O 6
21,243	Miami	I 24
12,774	Mitchell	F 13
51,411	Montgomery	O 21
11,859	Morris	H 18
4,092	Morton	N 2
18,342	Nemaha	D 20
22,665	Neosho	M 23
8,358	Ness	I 8
11,701	Norton	D 8
17,538	Osage	H 21
11,568	Osborne	F 12
9,819	Ottawa	G 15
10,510	Pawnee	K 10
12,159	Phillips	D 10
15,862	Pottawatomie	F 19
13,312	Pratt	M 11
7,362	Rawlins	D 4
47,785	Reno	L 13
14,745	Republic	D 15
13,800	Rice	J 13
19,882	Riley	F 18
9,534	Rooks	F 10
9,093	Rush	I 10
11,045	Russell	H 11
29,337	Saline	H 15
3,976	Scott	I 5
136,330	Sedgwick	M 16
8,075	Seward	N 4
85,200	Shawnee	G 21
6,038	Sheridan	F 6
7,400	Sherman	E 2
13,545	Smith	D 11
10,460	Stafford	K12
2,152	Stanton	M 2
4,655	Stevens	O 3
28,960	Sumner	O 16
7,334	Thomas	F 4
6,470	Trego	H 8
10,830	Wabaunsee	G 20
2,882	Wallace	G 2
17,112	Washington	D 17
2,579	Wichita	I 3
18,646	Wilson	M 21
8,526	Woodson	L 21
141,211	Wyandotte	F 25
1,880,999	Total	

KENTUCKY

TOTAL 120 COUNTIES

Pop.	County	Index
16,401	Adair	I 15
15,180	Allen	K 12
8,494	Anderson	F 16
9,910	Ballard	I 4
25,844	Barren	J 13
11,075	Bath	E 19
38,747	Bell	K 20
9,595	Boone	C 17
18,060	Bourbon	E 18
43,849	Boyd	E 23
16,282	Boyle	H 16
9,616	Bracken	D 19
21,143	Breathitt	H 21
17,368	Breckinridge	G 12
8,868	Bullitt	F 14
12,620	Butler	I 11
13,781	Caldwell	I 8
17,662	Calloway	K 6
73,391	Campbell	C 18
7,363	Carlisle	J 4
8,155	Carroll	D 15
23,839	Carter	E 21
16,747	Casey	I 16
34,283	Christian	J 9
17,640	Clark	F 18
18,526	Clay	I 20
9,004	Clinton	K 15
11,931	Crittenden	H 7
10,204	Cumberland	K 15
43,779	Daviess	G 10
11,475	Edmonson	I 12
7,571	Elliott	F 21
17,079	Estill	G 19
68,543	Fayette	F 17
12,931	Fleming	E 20
41,942	Floyd	H 22
21,064	Franklin	E 16
14,927	Fulton	K 4
4,437	Gallatin	C 16
11,562	Garrard	G 17
9,876	Grant	D 17
30,778	Graves	K 5
17,055	Grayson	H 12
11,401	Green	I 14
24,554	Greenup	D 22
6,147	Hancock	G 11
20,913	Hardin	G 13
64,557	Harlan	J 21
14,859	Harrison	D 18
16,169	Hart	I 13
26,295	Henderson	G 9
12,564	Henry	D 15
8,725	Hickman	K 4
37,449	Hopkins	I 8
10,467	Jackson	H 19
355,350	Jefferson	F 14
12,431	Jessamine	G 17
22,968	Johnson	G 22
93,534	Kenton	C 17
15,230	Knott	H 22
26,266	Knox	J 19
9,093	Larue	H 14
21,109	Laurel	I 19
16,713	Lawrence	F 22
9,729	Lee	G 20
10,765	Leslie	I 21
35,702	Letcher	J 22
14,315	Lewis	D 21
17,687	Lincoln	H 17
8,608	Livingston	I 6
21,875	Logan	J 11
8,530	Lyon	I 7
46,271	McCracken	J 5
14,627	McCreary	K 18
11,072	McLean	H 10
27,621	Madison	G 18
15,719	Magoffin	G 21
15,499	Marion	H 15
12,889	Marshall	J 6
8,584	Martin	G 23
18,862	Mason	D 19
8,042	Meade	F 12
4,958	Menifee	F 20
14,471	Mercer	G 16
9,373	Metcalfe	J 14
13,077	Monroe	K 14
11,660	Montgomery	F 19
15,130	Morgan	F 21
37,784	Muhlenberg	I 10
16,551	Nelson	G 15
8,571	Nicholas	E 19
24,469	Ohio	H 10
7,402	Oldham	E 14
10,710	Owen	D 17
7,223	Owsley	H 20
10,876	Pendleton	C 18
42,186	Perry	I 21
63,267	Pike	H 24
5,800	Powell	G 19
35,640	Pulaski	I 17
3,344	Robertson	D 19
15,149	Rockcastle	I 18
10,893	Rowan	F 21
11,930	Russell	J 16
14,400	Scott	E 17
17,679	Shelby	F 15
11,336	Simpson	K 11
6,606	Spencer	F 15
12,047	Taylor	H 15
13,520	Todd	J 10
12,531	Trigg	K 8
5,348	Trimble	D 15
17,053	Union	G 7
33,676	Warren	J 12
12,623	Washington	G 15
15,848	Wayne	J 16
20,534	Webster	H 8
29,730	Whitley	J 18
8,425	Wolfe	G 20
10,981	Woodford	F 17
2,614,589	Total	

LOUISIANA

TOTAL 64 PARISHES

Pop.	Parish	Index
39,326	Acadia	M 10
15,261	Allen	K 8
18,438	Ascension	M 15
15,990	Assumption	N 15
34,926	Avoyelles	I 11
14,569	Beauregard	K 6
23,789	Bienville	D 7
28,388	Bossier	B 5
124,670	Caddo	C 4
41,963	Calcasieu	M 6
10,430	Caldwell	E 11
6,054	Cameron	N 5
12,451	Catahoula	G 12
32,285	Claiborne	A 7
12,778	Concordia	G 13
31,016	De Soto	E 4
68,208	East Baton Rouge	K 15
15,815	East Carroll	B 14
17,449	East Feliciana	J 15
25,483	Evangeline	K 9
30,530	Franklin	E 12
15,709	Grant	G 9
28,192	Iberia	N 12
24,638	Iberville	M 14
13,808	Jackson	D 9
40,032	Jefferson	O 18
19,765	Jefferson Davis	L 8
38,827	Lafayette	M 11
32,419	Lafourche	O 16
11,668	La Salle	F 10
22,822	Lincoln	C 8
18,206	Livingston	L 16
14,829	Madison	D 14
23,689	Morehouse	A 12
38,477	Natchitoches	F 7
458,762	Orleans	N 19
54,337	Ouachita	C 10
9,608	Plaquemines	O 19
21,007	Pointe Coupee	J 12
65,455	Rapides	I 9
16,078	Red River	E 6
26,374	Richland	D 12
24,110	Sabine	G 5
6,512	Saint Bernard	N 20
12,111	Saint Charles	N 17
8,492	Saint Helena	J 16
15,338	Saint James	M 16
14,078	Saint John the Baptist	M 17
60,074	Saint Landry	K 11
21,767	Saint Martin	M 12
29,397	Saint Mary	O 13
20,929	Saint Tammany	K 19
46,227	Tangipahoa	J 17
15,096	Tensas	E 13
29,816	Terrebonne	P 15
20,731	Union	A 9
33,684	Vermilion	N 9
20,047	Vernon	I 6
29,904	Washington	J 18
29,458	Webster	B 6
9,716	West Baton Rouge	L 13
13,895	West Carroll	B 13
10,924	West Feliciana	I 13
14,766	Winn	E 9
2,101,593	Total	

MAINE

TOTAL 16 COUNTIES

Pop.	County	Index
71,214	Androscoggin	N 6
87,843	Aroostook	D 16
134,645	Cumberland	O 5
19,941	Franklin	K 4
30,721	Hancock	L 17
70,691	Kennebec	M 9
27,693	Knox	N 13
15,498	Lincoln	O 10
41,483	Oxford	L 3
92,379	Penobscot	J 15
18,231	Piscataquis	G 12
16,927	Sagadahoc	O 8
39,111	Somerset	H 7
20,286	Waldo	M 13
37,826	Washington	J 21
72,934	York	Q 3
797,423	Total	

MARYLAND

TOTAL 24 COUNTIES

Pop.	County	Index
79,098	Allegany	L 6
55,167	Anne Arundel	H 14
124,565	Baltimore	D 13
804,874	Baltimore City	F 14
9,528	Calvert	M 14
17,387	Caroline	I 20
35,978	Carroll	C 10
25,827	Cecil	C 18
16,166	Charles	M 11
26,813	Dorchester	M 18
54,440	Frederick	D 8
19,908	Garrett	N 2
31,603	Harford	C 16
16,169	Howard	F 12
14,242	Kent	F 18
49,206	Montgomery	G 9
60,095	Prince Georges	J 12
14,571	Queen Annes	G 19
15,189	Saint Marys	O 14
23,382	Somerset	P 20
18,583	Talbot	J 18
65,882	Washington	B 4
31,229	Wicomico	N 21
21,624	Worcester	O 23
1,631,526	Total	

MASSACHUSETTS

TOTAL 14 COUNTIES

Pop.	County	Index
32,305	Barnstable	M 24
120,700	Berkshire	F 3
364,590	Bristol	L 19
4,953	Dukes	P 23
498,040	Essex	C 20
49,612	Franklin	C 7
335,496	Hampden	I 7
72,801	Hampshire	F 7
934,924	Middlesex	D 17
3,678	Nantucket	R 14
299,426	Norfolk	H 18
162,311	Plymouth	J 22
879,536	Suffolk	F 19
491,242	Worcester	F 12
4,249,614	Total	

MICHIGAN

TOTAL 83 COUNTIES

Pop.	County	Index
4,989	Alcona	J 21
9,327	Alger	F 10
38,974	Allegan	P 12
18,574	Alpena	J 21
9,979	Antrim	J 15
8,007	Arenac	L 20
9,168	Baraga	E 4
20,928	Barry	P 14
69,474	Bay	M 19
6,587	Benzie	J 12
81,066	Berrien	Q 10
23,950	Branch	R 15
87,043	Calhoun	Q 16
20,888	Cass	Q 12
11,981	Charlevoix	I 16
11,502	Cheboygan	H 17
25,047	Chippewa	F 16
7,032	Clare	L 16
24,174	Clinton	O 17
3,097	Crawford	I 17
32,280	Delta	G 9
29,941	Dickinson	F 5
31,728	Eaton	P 16
15,109	Emmet	H 16
211,641	Genesee	O 21
7,424	Gladwin	L 18
31,577	Gogebic	C 22
20,011	Grand Traverse	J 14
30,252	Gratiot	N 17
27,417	Hillsdale	R 17
52,851	Houghton	D 2
31,132	Huron	L 23
116,587	Ingham	P 18
35,093	Ionia	O 16
7,517	Iosco	K 21
20,805	Iron	F 3
21,126	Isabella	M 16
92,304	Jackson	Q 18
91,368	Kalamazoo	Q 13
3,799	Kalkaska	J 15
240,511	Kent	O 14
5,076	Keweenaw	C 4
4,066	Lake	L 13
28,348	Lapeer	N 22
8,206	Leelanau	I 12
49,849	Lenawee	R 19
19,274	Livingston	P 20
6,528	Luce	E 13
8,783	Mackinac	F 15
77,146	Macomb	P 23
17,409	Manistee	K 12
44,076	Marquette	F 6
18,756	Mason	L 11
15,738	Mecosta	M 15
23,652	Menominee	H 7
19,150	Midland	M 18
6,992	Missaukee	K 15
52,485	Monroe	R 21
27,471	Montcalm	N 15
2,814	Montmorency	I 19
84,630	Muskegon	N 11
17,029	Newaygo	M 13
211,251	Oakland	P 22
13,805	Oceana	M 11
6,595	Ogemaw	K 19
11,114	Ontonagon	B 23
12,806	Osceola	L 15
1,728	Oscoda	J 19
5,554	Otsego	J 18
54,858	Ottawa	O 12
11,330	Presque Isle	H 19
2,055	Roscommon	K 17
120,717	Saginaw	N 20
67,563	Saint Clair	O 25
30,618	Saint Joseph	R 14
27,751	Sanilac	N 24
8,451	Schoolcraft	F 11
39,517	Shiawassee	O 19
32,934	Tuscola	N 22
32,637	Van Buren	Q 12
65,530	Washtenaw	Q 20
1,888,946	Wayne	Q 22
16,827	Wexford	K 13
4,842,325	Total	

MINNESOTA

TOTAL 87 COUNTIES

Pop.	County	Index
15,009	Aitkin	I 15
18,415	Anoka	M 16
22,503	Becker	H 6
20,707	Beltrami	E 10
15,056	Benton	L 13
9,838	Big Stone	L 3
33,847	Blue Earth	Q 13
23,428	Brown	P 10
21,232	Carlton	I 18
16,936	Carver	N 14
15,591	Cass	H 11
15,762	Chippewa	N 6
13,189	Chisago	L 18
23,120	Clay	H 3
9,546	Clearwater	F 8
2,435	Cook	B 21
14,782	Cottonwood	Q 8
25,627	Crow Wing	I 13
34,592	Dakota	O 17
12,127	Dodge	P 18
18,813	Douglas	K 7
21,642	Faribault	R 13
24,748	Fillmore	R 21
28,741	Freeborn	R 16
31,317	Goodhue	O 18
9,558	Grant	K 5
517,785	Hennepin	M 15
13,845	Houston	R 23
9,596	Hubbard	H 9
12,081	Isanti	L 16
27,224	Itasca	F 14
15,863	Jackson	R 8
8,558	Kanabec	K 16
23,574	Kandiyohi	N 9
9,688	Kittson	B 2
14,078	Koochiching	D 14
15,398	Lac qui Parle	N 4
7,068	Lake	F 23
4,194	Lake of the Woods	B 10
17,990	Le Sueur	P 14
11,303	Lincoln	O 4
19,326	Lyon	P 6
20,522	McLeod	N 12
6,153	Mahnomen	G 6
17,003	Marshall	C 4
22,401	Martin	R 11
17,914	Meeker	M 11
14,076	Mille Lacs	K 14
25,442	Morrison	K 12
28,065	Mower	R 18
13,902	Murray	Q 6
16,550	Nicollet	P 12
18,618	Nobles	R 6
14,061	Norman	G 3
35,426	Olmsted	P 20
51,006	Otter Tail	J 6
10,487	Pennington	D 5
20,264	Pine	J 18
12,238	Pipestone	Q 4
36,019	Polk	F 4
13,085	Pope	L 7
286,721	Ramsey	N 17
6,887	Red Lake	E 5
20,620	Redwood	O 8
23,645	Renville	O 9
29,974	Rice	P 16
10,962	Rock	R 4
12,621	Roseau	B 6
204,596	Saint Louis	F 19
14,116	Scott	O 15
9,709	Sherburne	L 14
15,865	Sibley	O 12
62,121	Stearns	L 11
18,475	Steele	Q 16
10,185	Stevens	L 5
14,735	Swift	M 6
26,170	Todd	K 9
7,938	Traverse	K 3
17,613	Wabasha	P 20
10,990	Wadena	I 9
14,412	Waseca	Q 15
24,753	Washington	N 17
12,802	Watonwan	Q 10
9,791	Wilkin	J 3
35,144	Winona	Q 22
27,119	Wright	M 13
16,625	Yellow Medicine	O 5
2,563,953	Total	

MISSISSIPPI

TOTAL 82 COUNTIES

Pop.	County	Index
23,564	Adams	N 4
23,653	Alcorn	A 21
19,712	Amite	O 7
26,035	Attala	H 15
9,813	Benton	A 17
71,051	Bolivar	E 7
18,080	Calhoun	D 16
19,765	Carroll	F 13
20,835	Chickasaw	D 19
12,339	Choctaw	F 17
12,152	Claiborne	L 6
19,679	Clarke	L 20
17,931	Clay	F 20
46,327	Coahoma	C 8
31,614	Copiah	L 10
15,028	Covington	M 15
25,438	De Soto	A 13
30,115	Forrest	O 17
12,268	Franklin	N 6
7,523	George	P 21
10,644	Greene	O 21
16,802	Grenada	E 13
11,415	Hancock	R 15
44,143	Harrison	R 18
85,118	Hinds	K 9
38,534	Holmes	G 12
24,729	Humphreys	G 9
5,734	Issaquena	I 6
18,225	Itawamba	C 22
15,973	Jackson	Q 21
18,634	Jasper	L 18
14,291	Jefferson	M 6
14,281	Jefferson Davis	N 13
41,492	Jones	M 17
21,881	Kemper	I 20
19,978	Lafayette	C 15
12,848	Lamar	O 16
52,748	Lauderdale	J 20
12,471	Lawrence	N 11
21,803	Leake	I 15
35,313	Lee	C 20
53,506	Leflore	F 10
26,357	Lincoln	N 9
29,987	Lowndes	G 22
35,796	Madison	I 12
19,923	Marion	O 13
24,869	Marshall	A 15
36,141	Monroe	E 21
15,009	Montgomery	F 14
26,691	Neshoba	I 18
22,910	Newton	J 18
25,560	Noxubee	G 21
19,119	Oktibbeha	G 19
28,648	Panola	C 12
19,405	Pearl River	Q 15
8,197	Perry	O 19
32,201	Pike	O 9
22,034	Pontotoc	C 18
19,265	Prentiss	B 21
25,304	Quitman	C 10
20,353	Rankin	K 12
20,914	Scott	J 15
13,877	Sharkey	I 7
20,897	Simpson	L 13
18,405	Smith	L 15
5,704	Stone	Q 18
66,364	Sunflower	F 8
35,568	Tallahatchie	D 11
17,671	Tate	B 12
18,658	Tippah	A 19
16,411	Tishomingo	A 23
21,233	Tunica	B 10
21,268	Union	B 18
13,871	Walthall	P 12
35,785	Warren	J 7
54,310	Washington	G 7
15,295	Wayne	M 20
12,128	Webster	F 17
13,957	Wilkinson	O 4
21,239	Winston	H 18
17,750	Yalobusha	D 14
37,262	Yazoo	I 10
2,009,821	Total	

MISSOURI

TOTAL 115 COUNTIES

Pop.	County	Index
19,436	Adair	C 12
13,469	Andrew	C 5
13,421	Atchison	A 3
22,077	Audrain	G 15
22,803	Barry	Q 8
14,560	Barton	N 6
22,068	Bates	J 6
11,708	Benton	J 10
12,269	Bollinger	O 21
30,995	Boone	H 13
98,633	Buchanan	E 5
23,697	Butler	H 22, Q 20
12,509	Caldwell	E 8
19,923	Callaway	H 14
9,142	Camden	L 11
33,203	Cape Girardeau	N 22
19,940	Carroll	F 9
5,503	Carter	P 18
20,962	Cass	I 6
11,136	Cedar	M 8
19,588	Chariton	E 11
13,169	Christian	P 10
10,254	Clark	B 15
26,811	Clay	F 6
13,505	Clinton	E 6
30,848	Cole	J 13
19,522	Cooper	H 12
11,287	Crawford	K 17
11,764	Dade	N 8
10,541	Dallas	M 11
14,424	Daviess	C 8
10,270	De Kalb	D 6
10,974	Dent	M 16
13,959	Douglas	P 12
35,799	Dunklin	J 24, R 21
30,519	Franklin	J 17
12,172	Gasconade	J 16
14,348	Gentry	B 6
82,929	Greene	N 9
16,135	Grundy	C 9
17,233	Harrison	B 8
22,931	Henry	J 8
6,430	Hickory	L 10
12,720	Holt	C 4
13,490	Howard	G 12
19,672	Howell	Q 14
9,642	Iron	M 18
470,454	Jackson	H 6
73,810	Jasper	O 6
27,563	Jefferson	J 19
22,413	Johnson	H 8
9,658	Knox	C 14
16,320	Laclede	M 12
29,259	Lafayette	G 8
23,774	Lawrence	O 8
12,093	Lewis	C 15
13,929	Lincoln	G 18
23,339	Linn	D 11
18,615	Livingston	D 9
13,936	McDonald	Q 6
23,070	Macon	D 12
9,418	Madison	N 20
8,368	Maries	K 14
33,493	Marion	D 16
9,350	Mercer	A 9
16,728	Miller	K 13
15,762	Mississippi	P 24
12,173	Moniteau	I 12
13,466	Monroe	E 14
13,011	Montgomery	H 16
10,968	Morgan	J 11
30,262	New Madrid	R 23
26,959	Newton	Q 6
26,371	Nodaway	A 5
12,220	Oregon	Q 16
12,462	Osage	J 15
9,537	Ozark	Q 13
37,284	Pemiscot	J 24
13,707	Perry	M 22
34,664	Pettis	I 10
15,308	Phelps	L 15
18,001	Pike	F 17
13,819	Platte	F 5
17,803	Polk	M 9
10,755	Pulaski	M 13
11,503	Putnam	A 11
10,704	Ralls	F 16
26,431	Randolph	F 12
19,846	Ray	F 8
8,923	Reynolds	N 18
11,176	Ripley	Q 18
24,354	Saint Charles	I 18
13,289	Saint Clair	K 8
35,832	Saint Francois	M 20
10,097	Sainte Genevieve	L 21
211,593	Saint Louis	I 20
821,960	Saint Louis City	I 20
30,598	Saline	G 10
6,951	Schuyler	A 12
8,853	Scotland	B 14
24,913	Scott	P 23
10,894	Shannon	O 16
11,983	Shelby	D 14
27,452	Stoddard	P 21
11,614	Stone	Q 9
15,212	Sullivan	B 11
8,867	Taney	Q 11
18,580	Texas	O 14
25,031	Vernon	L 6
8,082	Warren	I 17
14,450	Washington	L 18
12,243	Wayne	O 20
16,148	Webster	O 11
6,535	Worth	A 6
16,741	Wright	O 12
3,629,367	Total	

MONTANA

TOTAL 56 COUNTIES

Pop.	County	Index
6,654	Beaverhead	M 6
8,543	Big Horn	M 17
9,006	Blaine	D 15
2,738	Broadwater	J 9
12,571	Carbon	N 14
4,136	Carter	L 24
41,146	Cascade	H 9
8,635	Chouteau	F 11
11,242	Custer	J 22
5,553	Daniels	C 21
9,881	Dawson	G 23
16,293	Deer Lodge	K 6
4,568	Fallon	J 24
16,531	Fergus	H 14
19,200	Flathead	D 4
16.124	Gallatin	M 10
4,252	Garfield	G 18
5,297	Glacier	C 6
2,126	Golden Valley	J 14
3,013	Granite	J 5
13,775	Hill	D 12
4,133	Jefferson	K 8
5,238	Judith Basin	H 12
9,541	Lake	F 4
18,224	Lewis and Clark	H 8
2,198	Liberty	D 11
7,089	Lincoln	C 2
4,790	McCone	F 21
6,323	Madison	N 8
2,272	Meagher	J 11
1,626	Mineral	H 2
21,782	Missoula	H 4

Pop.	County	Index
7,242	Musselshell	J 16
10,922	Park	M 11
2,045	Petroleum	H 16
8,208	Phillips	E 17
6,964	Pondera	E 8
3,909	Powder River	M 22
6,202	Powell	H 6
3,941	Prairie	H 22
10,315	Ravalli	K 4
9,633	Richland	F 24
10,672	Roosevelt	D 22
7,347	Rosebud	I 19
5,692	Sanders	F 2
9,869	Sheridan	C 23
56,969	Silver Bow	L 7
6,253	Stillwater	M 14
3,944	Sweet Grass	L 13
6,068	Teton	F 8
6,714	Toole	C 9
1,661	Treasure	J 13
11,181	Valley	E 20
3,751	Wheatland	J 13
2,767	Wibaux	H 25
30,785	Yellowstone	K 16
52	Yellowstone National Park (part)	N 11
537,606	Total	

NEBRASKA

TOTAL 93 COUNTIES

Pop.	County	Index
26,275	Adams	N 17
15,206	Antelope	G 18
1,344	Arthur	I 8
1,676	Banner	J 2
1,584	Blaine	H 12
14,738	Boone	I 18
11,861	Box Butte	G 4
7,169	Boyd	E 16
5,772	Brown	G 13
24,338	Buffalo	L 15
13,062	Burt	H 22
14,410	Butler	K 20
17,684	Cass	L 24
16,427	Cedar	F 20
5,484	Chase	M 7
10,898	Cherry	F 9
10,187	Cheyenne	J 4
13,571	Clay	N 18
11,434	Colfax	I 20
14,327	Cumming	H 21
26,189	Custer	J 13
9,505	Dakota	G 22
11,493	Dawes	E 3
17,875	Dawson	L 13
3,992	Deuel	K 6
11,586	Dixon	F 21
25,273	Dodge	J 22
232,982	Douglas	K 23
5,610	Dundy	N 7
12,971	Fillmore	N 19
9,094	Franklin	O 15
8,114	Frontier	M 11
12,140	Furnas	O 13
30,242	Gage	N 22
5,099	Garden	J 6
3,207	Garfield	H 15
4,287	Gosper	N 13
1,427	Grant	H 8
8,442	Greeley	J 16
27,117	Hall	L 16
12,159	Hamilton	M 18
8,957	Harlan	N 14
3,603	Hayes	N 9
7,269	Hitchcock	O 9
16,509	Holt	G 15
1,180	Hooker	H 9
10,020	Howard	K 16
16,409	Jefferson	O 20
9,157	Johnson	N 23
8,094	Kearney	N 15
6,721	Keith	K 8
3,203	Keyapaha	E 13
4,675	Kimball	K 2
19,110	Knox	F 18
100,324	Lancaster	M 22
25,627	Lincoln	L 10
2,014	Logan	J 11
1,818	Loup	H 14
1,358	McPherson	J 9
26,037	Madison	I 20
10,619	Merrick	K 18
9,950	Morrill	I 4
8,718	Nance	J 18
12,356	Nemaha	N 24
12,629	Nuckolls	O 18
19,901	Otoe	M 23
9,423	Pawnee	O 23
5,834	Perkins	L 8
9,261	Phelps	M 14
11,080	Pierce	G 19
21,181	Platte	J 19
10,092	Polk	K 19
13,859	Redwillow	O 11
19,826	Richardson	O 25
3,366	Rock	F 14
16,356	Saline	N 20
10,402	Sarpy	K 23
20,167	Saunders	K 22
28,644	Scotts Bluff	H 2
15,938	Seward	L 20
10,793	Sheridan	F 6
9,122	Sherman	K 15
4,667	Sioux	E 2
7,809	Stanton	H 20
13,684	Thayer	O 19
1,510	Thomas	H 11
10,462	Thurston	G 22
9,533	Valley	J 15
12,095	Washington	J 23
10,566	Wayne	G 20
10,210	Webster	O 17
2,335	Wheeler	H 16
17,239	York	L 19
1,377,963	Total	

NEVADA

TOTAL 17 COUNTIES

Pop.	County	Index
5,075	Churchill	G 8
8,532	Clark	O 21
1,840	Douglas	I 3
9,960	Elko	B 18
1,077	Esmeralda	K 10
1,333	Eureka	F 16
3,795	Humboldt	B 9
1,714	Lander	G 13
3,601	Lincoln	L 21
3,810	Lyon	H 5
1,863	Mineral	I 7
3,989	Nye	J 16
2,221	Ormsby	H 3
2,652	Pershing	E 8
667	Storey	G 4
27,158	Washoe	D 3
11,771	White Pine	G 21
91,058	Total	

NEW HAMPSHIRE

TOTAL 10 COUNTIES

Pop.	County	Index
22,623	Belknap	M 15
14,277	Carroll	J 16
33,685	Cheshire	Q 7
38,959	Coös	E 16
42,816	Grafton	J 12
140,165	Hillsborough	P 12
56,152	Merrimack	N 13
53,750	Rockingham	P 18
38,580	Strafford	N 18
24,286	Sullivan	N 8
465,293	Total	

NEW JERSEY

TOTAL 21 COUNTIES

Pop.	County	Index
124,823	Atlantic	N 13
364,977	Bergen	C 19
93,541	Burlington	L 13
252,312	Camden	L 10
29,486	Cape May	R 11
69,895	Cumberland	P 9
833,513	Essex	E 18
70,802	Gloucester	M 8
690,730	Hudson	E 20
34,728	Hunterdon	G 11
187,143	Mercer	H 13
212,208	Middlesex	G 16
147,209	Monmouth	I 18
110,445	Morris	D 14
33,069	Ocean	K 17
302,129	Passaic	C 18
36,834	Salem	N 7
65,132	Somerset	G 14
27,830	Sussex	B 14
305,209	Union	F 17
49,319	Warren	D 10
4,041,334	Total	

NEW MEXICO

TOTAL 31 COUNTIES

Pop.	County	Index
45,430	Bernalillo	G 10
3,282	Catron	J 3
19,549	Chaves	K 20
19,157	Colfax	C 18
15,809	Curry	I 24
2,893	De Baca	I 19
27,455	Dona Ana	O 9
15,842	Eddy	N 20
19,050	Grant	M 4
7,027	Guadalupe	H 18
4,421	Harding	E 21
5,023	Hidalgo	P 2
6,144	Lea	M 24
7,198	Lincoln	K 15
6,247	Luna	O 6
20,643	McKinley	F 4
10,322	Mora	E 18
9,779	Otero	N 13
10,828	Quay	G 23
21,381	Rio Arriba	C 9
11,109	Roosevelt	I 23
11,144	Sandoval	F 10
14,701	San Juan	C 3
23,636	San Miguel	F 18
19,567	Santa Fe	F 13
5,184	Sierra	L 7
9,611	Socorro	J 9
14,394	Taos	C 14
9,269	Torrance	H 13
11,036	Union	D 23
16,186	Valencia	H 4
423,317	Total	

NEW YORK

TOTAL 62 COUNTIES

Pop.	County	Index
211,953	Albany	O 23
38,025	Allegany	P 7
1,265,258	Bronx	H 6
147,022	Broome	Q 16
72,398	Cattaragus	P 5
64,751	Cayuga	M 13
126,457	Chautauqua	P 3
74,680	Chemung	Q 12
34,665	Chenango	O 16
46,687	Clinton	D 23
41,617	Columbia	A 6 Q 24
31,709	Cortland	O 15
41,163	Delaware	A 2, Q 10
105,462	Dutchess	C 6, R 23
762,408	Erie	O 5
33,959	Essex	G 23
45,694	Franklin	E 21
46,560	Fulton	L 21
44,468	Genesee	M 7
25,808	Greene	A 4, P 22
3,929	Hamilton	I 20
64,006	Herkimer	J 19
83,574	Jefferson	H 15
2,560,401	Kings	I 5
23,447	Lewis	I 17
37,560	Livingston	N 8
39,790	Madison	N 16
423,881	Monroe	L 9
60,076	Montgomery	N 21
303,053	Nassau	H 7
1,867,321	New York	H 5
149,329	Niagara	L 5
198,763	Oneida	L 17
291,606	Onondaga	M 14
54,276	Ontario	N 10
130,383	Orange	E 3
28,795	Orleans	L 7
69,645	Oswego	K 15
46,710	Otsego	O 19
13,744	Putnam	E 6
1,079,129	Queens	H 6
119,781	Rensselaer	N 24
158,346	Richmond	I 5
59,599	Rockland	F 5
90,960	Saint Lawrence	F 17
63,314	Saratoga	L 23
125,021	Schenectady	N 22
19,667	Schoharie	O 21
12,909	Schuyler	P 12
24,983	Seneca	N 12
82,671	Steuben	Q 10
161,055	Suffolk	H 9
35,272	Sullivan	C 2, R 20
25,480	Tioga	Q 14
41,490	Tompkins	P 13
80,155	Ulster	C 4, R 21
34,174	Warren	J 22
46,482	Washington	K 24
49,995	Wayne	L 11
520,947	Westchester	F 6
28,764	Wyoming	N 7
16,848	Yates	O 11
12,588,066	Total	

NORTH CAROLINA

TOTAL 100 COUNTIES

Pop.	County	Index
42,140	Alamance	D 11
12,922	Alexander	E 4
7,186	Alleghany	C 4
29,349	Anson	I 8
21,019	Ashe	B 3
11,803	Avery	D 2
35,026	Beaufort	G 20
25,844	Bertie	D 20
22,389	Bladen	K 14
15,818	Brunswick	M 15
97,937	Buncombe	O 7
29,410	Burke	F 2
44,331	Cabarrus	G 6
28,016	Caldwell	E 3
5,461	Camden	C 23
16,900	Carteret	J 20
18,214	Caswell	C 11
43,991	Catawba	F 4
24,177	Chatham	F 11
16,151	Cherokee	Q 2
11,282	Chowan	D 21
5,434	Clay	R 3
51,914	Cleveland	G 3
37,720	Columbus	M 14
30,665	Craven	H 19
45,219	Cumberland	I 13
6,710	Currituck	C 23
5,202	Dare	F 24
47,865	Davidson	F 8
14,386	Davie	E 6
35,103	Duplin	I 16
67,196	Durham	D 13
17,894	Edgecombe	E 17
111,681	Forsyth	D 8
29,456	Franklin	D 15
78,093	Gaston	H 4
10,551	Gates	C 21
5,841	Graham	P 3
28,723	Granville	C 14
18,656	Greene	G 17
133,010	Guilford	E 9
53,246	Halifax	D 17
37,911	Harnett	H 13
28,273	Haywood	O 6
23,404	Henderson	P 8
17,542	Hertford	C 20
14,244	Hoke	I 11
8,550	Hyde	G 23
46,693	Iredell	E 5
17,519	Jackson	Q 6
57,621	Johnston	G 15
10,428	Jones	I 18
16,996	Lee	G 12
35,716	Lenoir	H 17
22,872	Lincoln	G 4
20,336	McDowell	F 1
13,672	Macon	Q 4
20,306	Madison	N 7
23,400	Martin	F 19
127,971	Mecklenburg	H 6
13,962	Mitchell	M 9
16,218	Montgomery	H 9
28,215	Moore	H 11
52,782	Nash	E 16
43,010	New Hanover	M 17
27,161	Northampton	C 18
15,289	Onslow	J 18
21,171	Orange	D 12
9,299	Pamlico	I 20
19,143	Pasquotank	C 22
15,686	Pender	K 16
19,668	Perquimans	D 22
22,039	Person	C 12
54,466	Pitt	G 18
10,216	Polk	P 9
36,259	Randolph	F 9
34,016	Richmond	I 10
66,512	Robeson	J 12
51,083	Rockingham	C 9
56,665	Rowan	F 7
40,452	Rutherford	G 1
40,082	Sampson	J 15
20,174	Scotland	J 11
30,216	Stanly	H 8
22,290	Stokes	C 8
39,749	Surry	C 6
11,568	Swain	O 4
9,589	Transylvania	Q 7
5,164	Tyrrell	F 22
40,979	Union	J 7
27,294	Vance	C 15
94,757	Wake	E 14
23,364	Warren	C 16
11,603	Washington	F 21
15,165	Watauga	D 3
53,013	Wayne	H 16
36,162	Wilkes	C 4
44,914	Wilson	F 16
18,010	Yadkin	D 6
14,486	Yancey	N 9
3,170,276	Total	

NORTH DAKOTA

TOTAL 53 COUNTIES

Pop.	County	Index
6,343	Adams	Q 6
18,804	Barnes	M 20
13,327	Benson	H 16
3,140	Billings	L 3
14,853	Bottineau	D 11
5,119	Bowman	Q 2
9,998	Burke	D 6
19,769	Burleigh	M 13
48,735	Cass	M 23
14,554	Cavalier	D 19
10,877	Dickey	Q 19
9,636	Divide	D 3
9,566	Dunn	K 6
6,346	Eddy	I 17
12,467	Emmons	P 13
6,353	Foster	K 18
4,122	Golden Valley	L 2
31,956	Grand Forks	H 22
10,134	Grant	P 9
6,889	Griggs	K 20
8,796	Hettinger	O 6
8,031	Kidder	M 15
11,517	La Moure	O 19
8,089	Logan	O 16
5,439	McHenry	G 12
9,621	McIntosh	Q 16
9,709	McKenzie	I 3
17,991	McLean	J 10
9,516	Mercer	K 8
19,647	Morton	O 11
13,544	Mountrail	G 6
10,203	Nelson	H 20
4,262	Oliver	L 10
14,757	Pembina	D 22
9,074	Pierce	G 14
16,252	Ramsey	G 18
10,983	Ranson	O 22
7,263	Renville	E 9
81,008	Richland	P 24
10,760	Rolette	D 15
9,298	Sargent	Q 22
7,373	Sheridan	J 13
4,687	Sioux	R 9
4,150	Slope	O 3
15,340	Stark	N 5
6,972	Steele	J 21
26,100	Stutsman	M 17
8,393	Towner	E 16
12,600	Traill	J 24
20,047	Walsh	F 21
13,597	Ward	G 10
13,285	Wells	J 15
19,553	Williams	F 3
680,845	Total	

OHIO

TOTAL 88 COUNTIES

Pop	County	Index
20,381	Adams	P 9
69,419	Allen	G 7
36,867	Ashland	G 14
68,361	Ashtabula	C 20
44,175	Athens	N 15
28,034	Auglaize	H 7
94,719	Belmont	K 19
20,148	Brown	P 8
114,084	Butler	N 6
16,057	Carroll	H 19
24,103	Champaign	J 9
90,936	Clark	K 9
29,786	Clermont	O 7
21,547	Clinton	N 9
86,484	Columbiana	G 20
28,976	Coshocton	I 15
35,345	Crawford	G 12
1,201,455	Cuyahoga	D 17
38,009	Darke	J 6
23,714	Defiance	D 6
26,016	Delaware	I 12
42,133	Erie	D 13
44,010	Fairfield	L 13
20,755	Fayette	M 10
361,055	Franklin	K 11
23,477	Fulton	C 8
23,050	Gallia	P 14
15,414	Geauga	D 18
33,259	Greene	L 8
41,486	Guernsey	J 17
589,356	Hamilton	N 5
40,404	Hancock	F 8
27,635	Hardin	G 9
18,844	Harrison	I 19
22,524	Henry	E 8
25,416	Highland	O 9
20,407	Hocking	M 13
16,726	Holmes	H 15
33,700	Huron	E 13
25,040	Jackson	O 14
88,307	Jefferson	I 20
29,338	Knox	I 14
41,674	Lake	C 18
44,541	Lawrence	R 13
59,962	Licking	J 13
8,981	Logan	I 9
109,206	Lorain	E 15
347,709	Lucas	C 9
20,253	Madison	K 10
236,142	Mahoning	F 20
45,420	Marion	H 11
29,677	Medina	F 15
23,961	Meigs	O 15
25,096	Mercer	H 5
51,301	Miami	J 7
18,426	Monroe	L 19
273,481	Montgomery	L 7
13,583	Morgan	M 16
14,489	Morrow	H 12
67,398	Muskingum	K 15
14,961	Noble	L 17
24,109	Ottawa	C 11
15,301	Paulding	E 6
31,445	Perry	L 14
27,238	Pickaway	L 11
13,876	Pike	O 11
42,682	Portage	E 18
22,455	Preble	L 5
25,074	Putnam	F 7
65,902	Richland	G 13
45,181	Ross	N 11
39,731	Sandusky	D 11
81,221	Scioto	P 12
47,941	Seneca	E 11
24,924	Shelby	I 7
221,784	Stark	G 18
344,131	Summit	E 17
123,063	Trumbull	E 20
68,193	Tuscarawas	H 17
19,192	Union	I 10
26,273	Van Wert	G 6
10,287	Vinton	N 13
27,348	Warren	M 7
42,437	Washington	M 17
47,024	Wayne	G 15
24,316	Williams	C 6
50,320	Wood	D 9
19,036	Wyandot	G 10
6,646,697	Total	

OKLAHOMA

TOTAL 77 COUNTIES

Pop.	County	Index
14,756	Adair	G 24
15,228	Alfalfa	B 9
14,533	Atoka	O 18
11,452	Beaver	Q 8
28,991	Beckham	J 2
20,452	Blaine	G 8
32,277	Bryan	Q 17
50,779	Caddo	K 8
28,115	Canadian	I 10
41,419	Carter	O 12
17,470	Cherokee	F 22
24,142	Choctaw	P 20
5,408	Cimarron	Q 2
24,948	Cleveland	J 12
11,521	Coal	M 17
34,317	Comanche	N 8
15,442	Cotton	O 8
18,052	Craig	B 21
64,115	Creek	G 17
27,517	Custer	H 6
15,370	Delaware	D 23
13,250	Dewey	F 5
10,541	Ellis	E 2
45,588	Garfield	D 10
31,401	Garvin	M 13
47,638	Grady	K 11
14,150	Grant	B 10
20,282	Greer	L 3
13,834	Harmon	M 2
7,761	Harper	B 3
16,216	Haskell	J 22
30,334	Hughes	K 17
28,910	Jackson	M 3
17,392	Jefferson	P 10
13,082	Johnston	O 15
50,186	Kay	B 14
15,960	Kingfisher	G 10
29,630	Kiowa	L 5
11,184	Latimer	L 21
42,896	Le Flore	L 24
33,738	Lincoln	H 14
27,761	Logan	F 12
9,639	Love	Q 13
21,575	McClain	K 12
34,759	McCurtain	P 23
24,924	McIntosh	I 20
12,206	Major	E 7
11,026	Marshall	P 15
17,883	Mayes	D 22
12,410	Murray	N 13
66,424	Muskogee	H 21
15,139	Noble	D 13
13,611	Nowata	B 20
29,016	Okfuskee	I 17
221,738	Oklahoma	H 12
56,558	Okmulgee	H 18
47,334	Osage	C 16
38,542	Ottawa	B 23
19,882	Pawnee	E 15
36,905	Payne	F 13
50,778	Pittsburg	L 19
32,469	Pontotoc	M 15
66,572	Pottawatomie	K 14
14,744	Pushmataha	N 21
14,164	Roger Mills	H 2
18,956	Rogers	D 20
79,621	Seminole	J 16
19,505	Sequoyah	I 24
33,069	Stephens	N 10
14,100	Texas	Q 5
24,390	Tillman	N 6
187,574	Tulsa	E 19
22,428	Wagoner	F 20
27,777	Washington	C 19
29,435	Washita	J 5
17,005	Woods	B 6
15,844	Woodward	D 4
2,396,040	Total	

OREGON

TOTAL 36 COUNTIES

Pop.	County	Index
16,754	Baker	G 22
16,555	Benton	H 5
46,205	Clackamas	E 8
21,124	Clatsop	B 5
20,047	Columbia	B 6
28,373	Coos	M 3
3,336	Crook	I 14
3,257	Curry	P 2
14,749	Deschutes	J 11
21,965	Douglas	M 6
3,467	Gilliam	D 14
5,940	Grant	H 18
5,920	Harney	M 18
8,938	Hood River	D 10
32,918	Jackson	Q 6
2,291	Jefferson	G 12
11,498	Josephine	Q 4
32,407	Klamath	O 10
4,833	Lake	O 13
54,493	Lane	J 5
9,903	Lincoln	H 4
24,700	Linn	H 8
11,269	Malheur	M 22
60,541	Marion	F 8
4,941	Morrow	D 16
338,241	Multnomah	D 8
16,858	Polk	F 5
2,978	Sherman	E 13
11,824	Tillamook	D 4
24,399	Umatilla	D 18
17,492	Union	E 20
7,814	Wallowa	C 23
12,646	Wasco	E 11
30,275	Washington	C 6
2,799	Wheeler	G 15
22,036	Yamhill	E 5
953,786	Total	

PENNSYLVANIA

TOTAL 67 COUNTIES

Pop.	County	Index
37,128	Adams	P 15
1,374,410	Allegheny	L 3
79,298	Armstrong	L 5
149,062	Beaver	L 2
37,309	Bedford	O 9
231,717	Berks	M 20
139,840	Blair	M 10
49,039	Bradford	E 17
96,727	Bucks	N 23
80,480	Butler	K 3
203,146	Cambria	M 8
5,307	Cameron	H 11
63,380	Carbon	J 21
46,294	Centre	K 12
126,629	Chester	P 21
34,531	Clarion	I 6
86,727	Clearfield	J 9
32,319	Clinton	H 13
48,803	Columbia	J 18
62,980	Crawford	F 3
68,236	Cumberland	O 14
165,231	Dauphin	M 16
280,264	Delaware	P 23
33,431	Elk	G 8
175,277	Erie	E 3
198,542	Fayette	Q 4
5,180	Forest	G 6
65,010	Franklin	P 13
9,231	Fulton	P 11
41,767	Greene	Q 2
39,021	Huntingdon	M 12
75,395	Indiana	L 6
52,114	Jefferson	I 7
14,325	Juniata	M 14
310,397	Lackawanna	G 21
196,882	Lancaster	O 19
97,258	Lawrence	J 2
67,103	Lebanon	M 18
172,893	Lehigh	L 22
445,109	Luzerne	I 20
93,421	Lycoming	H 15
55,167	McKean	E 9
99,246	Mercer	H 2
40,335	Mifflin	L 13
28,286	Monroe	I 23
265,804	Montgomery	N 22
14,517	Montour	J 17
169,304	Northampton	K 23
128,504	Northumberland	J 16
21,744	Perry	N 14
1,950,961	Philadelphia	P 24
7,483	Pike	H 23
17,489	Potter	F 12
235,505	Schuylkill	K 19
18,836	Snyder	L 15
80,764	Somerset	P 7
7,499	Sullivan	G 18
33,806	Susquehanna	E 20
31,871	Tioga	E 14
17,468	Union	J 15
63,226	Venango	H 4
41,453	Warren	F 6
204,802	Washington	O 2
28,420	Wayne	F 23
294,995	Westmoreland	M 5
15,517	Wyoming	G 19
167,135	York	P 17
9,631,350	Total	

RHODE ISLAND

TOTAL 5 COUNTIES

Pop.	County	Index
25,089	Bristol	G 20
51,390	Kent	H 9
41,668	Newport	J 20
540,016	Providence	D 8
29,334	Washington	L 10
687,497	Total	

SOUTH CAROLINA

TOTAL 46 COUNTIES

Pop.	County	Index
23,323	Abbeville	F 6
47,403	Aiken	I 10
13,294	Allendale	M 11
80,949	Anderson	D 5
19,410	Bamberg	L 13
21,221	Barnwell	K 11
21,815	Beaufort	Q 14
22,236	Berkeley	L 18
16,707	Calhoun	I 14
101,050	Charleston	N 19
32,201	Cherokee	A 10
31,803	Chester	C 12
34,334	Chesterfield	C 17
30,036	Clarendon	I 17
25,821	Colleton	M 14
41,427	Darlington	E 18
25,733	Dillon	E 21
18,956	Dorchester	L 16
19,326	Edgefield	H 9
23,287	Fairfield	E 13
61,027	Florence	G 19
21,738	Georgetown	J 21
117,009	Greenville	C 7
36,078	Greenwood	F 8
17,243	Hampton	N 12
39,376	Horry	G 23
9,988	Jasper	P 13
32,070	Kershaw	E 15
27,980	Lancaster	C 14
42,094	Laurens	E 8
24,096	Lee	F 17
36,494	Lexington	H 12
11,471	McCormick	H 7
27,221	Marion	G 21
31,634	Marlboro	D 19
34,681	Newberry	E 10
33,368	Oconee	C 3
63,864	Orangeburg	J 14
33,709	Pickens	B 5
87,667	Richland	G 14
18,148	Saluda	G 9
116,323	Spartanburg	B 8
45,902	Sumter	G 16
30,920	Union	C 10
34,914	Williamsburg	I 19
53,418	York	B 12
1,738,765	Total	

SOUTH DAKOTA

TOTAL 69 COUNTIES

Pop.	County	Index
80	Armstrong	G 11
7,139	Aurora	L 18
22,917	Beadle	I 19
4,590	Bennett	N 9
11,737	Bon Homme	O 21
16,847	Brookings	I 24
31,458	Brown	C 19
7,416	Brule	L 17
1,931	Buffalo	J 16
8,589	Butte	G 3
5,629	Campbell	C 13
16,703	Charles Mix	N 19
11,022	Clark	G 21
10,088	Clay	O 23
17,457	Codington	F 23
9,535	Corson	D 10
5,353	Custer	L 3
16,821	Davison	L 20
14,606	Day	E 21
8,732	Deuel	H 24
6,476	Dewey	E 11
7,236	Douglas	M 19
8,712	Edmunds	E 16
8,741	Fall River	N 2
6,895	Faulk	F 16
10,729	Grant	E 24
11,420	Gregory	N 16
4,679	Haakon	I 9
8,299	Hamlin	H 22
9,485	Hand	I 17
6,131	Hanson	L 21
3,589	Harding	D 3
7,009	Hughes	I 14
13,904	Hutchinson	N 21
3,690	Hyde	H 15
2,636	Jackson	K 9
5,816	Jerauld	K 18
3,177	Jones	K 12
12,805	Kingsbury	I 22
12,379	Lake	J 23
13,920	Lawrence	H 2
13,918	Lincoln	N 24
6,335	Lyman	K 14
10,316	McCook	L 22
8,774	McPherson	C 16
9,540	Marshall	C 21
11,482	Meade	H 5
5,293	Mellette	M 11
8,376	Miner	J 21
50,872	Minnehaha	L 24
9,603	Moody	J 24
20,079	Pennington	K 4
8,717	Perkins	D 6
5,762	Potter	F 14
15,782	Roberts	C 23
7,326	Sanborn	K 20
4,058	Shannon	N 6
15,304	Spink	G 19
2,381	Stanley	I 11
3,852	Sully	H 13
5,898	Todd	N 12
12,712	Tripp	N 14
14,891	Turner	N 23
11,480	Union	O 25
8,791	Walworth	E 14
2,474	Washabaugh	M 8
1,827	Washington	M 5
16,589	Yankton	O 22
4,039	Ziebach	G 9
692,849	Total	

TENNESSEE

TOTAL 95 COUNTIES

Pop.	County	Index
19,722	Anderson	M 18
21,077	Bedford	O 12
11,237	Benton	M 7
7,128	Bledsoe	O 15
33,989	Blount	O 19
22,870	Bradley	Q 16
26,827	Campbell	L 18
8,935	Cannon	N 13
26,132	Carroll	N 6
29,223	Carter	M 24
9,025	Cheatham	L 10
10,603	Chester	P 5
24,313	Claiborne	L 20
9,577	Clay	L 14
21,775	Cocke	N 22
16,801	Coffee	P 13
17,359	Crockett	N 4
11,440	Cumberland	N 16
222,854	Davidson	M 11
10,106	Decatur	O 7
14,213	De Kalb	N 13
18,491	Dickson	M 9
31,405	Dyer	M 3

Pop.	County	Index
28,891	Fayette	P 3
11,036	Fentress	M 16
21,796	Franklin	Q 12
46,528	Gibson	M 4
28,016	Giles	P 10
12,737	Grainger	M 20
35,119	Greene	M 22
9,717	Grundy	P 13
16,616	Hamblen	M 21
159,497	Hamilton	P 15
9,673	Hancock	L 21
22,193	Hardeman	P 4
16,213	Hardin	Q 6
24,117	Hawkins	L 22
26,063	Haywood	O 3
17,655	Henderson	O 6
26,432	Henry	L 6
13,613	Hickman	N 9
5,555	Houston	M 8
12,039	Humphreys	N 8
13,589	Jackson	M 14
17,914	Jefferson	M 20
12,209	Johnson	L 25
155,902	Knox	M 19
10,486	Lake	L 3
23,406	Lauderdale	N 2
26,776	Lawrence	P 9
5,258	Lewis	O 9
25,422	Lincoln	Q 11
17,805	Loudon	O 18
29,019	McMinn	P 17
19,901	McNairy	Q 5
13,872	Macon	L 13
51,059	Madison	O 5
17,549	Marion	Q 14
15,574	Marshall	P 11
34,016	Maury	O 10
6,127	Meigs	O 17
21,377	Monroe	P 18
30,882	Montgomery	L 9
4,037	Moore	P 12
13,603	Morgan	M 17
29,086	Obion	L 4
18,079	Overton	M 15
7,147	Perry	O 7
5,615	Pickett	K 16
15,686	Polk	Q 17
23,759	Putnam	M 14
13,871	Rhea	O 16
24,477	Roane	N 17
28,191	Robertson	L 11
32,286	Rutherford	N 12
14,080	Scott	L 17
4,047	Sequatchie	P 15
20,480	Sevier	N 20
306,482	Shelby	P 2
15,473	Smith	M 13
13,278	Stewart	L 8
51,087	Sullivan	K 24
28,622	Sumner	L 12
27,498	Tipton	O 2
5,629	Trousdale	L 13
12,678	Unicoi	M 23
11,371	Union	L 19
3,516	Van Buren	O 15
20,209	Warren	O 13
45,805	Washington	L 23
12,134	Wayne	P 8
29,262	Weakley	L 5
15,543	White	N 15
22,845	Williamson	N 10
23,929	Wilson	M 12
2,616,556	Total	

TEXAS

TOTAL 254 COUNTIES

Pop.	County	Index
34,643	Anderson	G 21
736	Andrews	F 8
27,803	Angelina	H 24
2,219	Aransas	O 19
9,684	Archer	C 15
3,329	Armstrong	D 4
15,654	Atascosa	N 16
18,860	Austin	K 20
5,186	Bailey	B 8
3,784	Bandera	L 15
23,888	Bastrop	K 18
7,418	Baylor	C 14
15,721	Bee	O 18
50,030	Bell	I 18
292,533	Bexar	L 16
3,842	Blanco	J 16
1,505	Borden	E 10
15,750	Bosque	G 17
48,563	Bowie	C 23
23,054	Brazoria	M 22
21,835	Brazos	I 20
6,624	Brewster	K 7
5,590	Briscoe	A 11
5,901	Brooks	E 4
26,382	Brown	G 15
19,848	Burleson	J 20
10,355	Burnet	I 17
31,397	Caldwell	K 18
5,385	Calhoun	N 20
12,785	Callahan	F 14
77,540	Cameron	P 5
10,053	Camp	D 22
7,745	Carson	C 4
30,030	Cass	D 24
4,720	Castro	A 9, E 2
5,710	Chambers	K 24
43,180	Cherokee	G 22
16,044	Childress	A 12, E 6
14,545	Clay	C 16
1,963	Cochran	C 8
5,253	Coke	G 12
23,669	Coleman	G 14
46,180	Collin	D 19
14,461	Collingsworth	D 6
19,129	Colorado	L 20
11,984	Comal	L 16
18,430	Comanche	G 16
7,645	Concho	H 13
24,136	Cooke	C 18
19,999	Coryell	H 17
9,395	Cottle	B 13
2,221	Crane	H 8
2,590	Crockett	I 10
11,023	Crosby	C 11
1,228	Culberson	G 4
7,830	Dallam	A 2
325,691	Dallas	E 19
13,573	Dawson	E 10
5,979	Deaf Smith	D 2
13,138	Delta	C 21
32,822	Denton	D 18
27,441	De Witt	M 18
8,601	Dickens	C 12
8,828	Dimmit	O 14
10,262	Donley	D 5
12,191	Duval	P 16
34,156	Eastland	F 15
3,958	Ector	F 8
2,764	Edwards	K 12
53,936	Ellis	F 10
131,597	El Paso	F 1
20,804	Erath	F 16
38,771	Falls	H 19
41,163	Fannin	C 20
30,708	Fayette	K 19
13,563	Fisher	E 12
12,409	Floyd	B 11
6,315	Foard	B 14
29,718	Fort Bend	L 22
8,494	Franklin	D 22
22,589	Freestone	G 20
9,411	Frio	N 15
2,800	Gaines	E 8
64,401	Galveston	L 23
5,586	Garza	D 11
11,020	Gillespie	J 15
1,263	Glasscock	G 10
10,093	Goliad	N 18
28,337	Gonzales	L 18
22,090	Gray	C 5
65,843	Grayson	C 19
15,778	Gregg	E 23
22,642	Grimes	I 21
28,925	Guadalupe	L 17
20,189	Hale	B 10
16,966	Hall	A 12, E 5
13,523	Hamilton	G 16
3,548	Hansford	A 4
14,532	Hardeman	A 13
13,936	Hardin	J 24
359,328	Harris	K 22
48,937	Harrison	E 24
2,185	Hartley	B 2
16,669	Haskell	D 13
14,915	Hays	K 17
4,637	Hemphill	B 6
30,583	Henderson	F 21
77,004	Hidalgo	P 4
43,036	Hill	G 18
9,298	Hockley	C 9
6,779	Hood	E 17
29,410	Hopkins	D 21
30,017	Houston	H 22
22,888	Howard	F 10
3,728	Hudspeth	G 2
49,016	Hunt	D 20
14,848	Hutchinson	B 4
2,049	Irion	H 11
9,046	Jack	D 16
10,980	Jackson	M 20
17,064	Jasper	I 25
1,800	Jeff Davis	I 5
133,391	Jefferson	K 25
4,919	Jim Hogg	R 16
13,456	Jim Wells	P 17
33,317	Johnson	F 18
24,233	Jones	E 13
23,316	Karnes	N 17
40,905	Kaufman	E 20
4,970	Kendall	K 16
701	Kenedy	R 18
3,851	Kent	D 12
10,151	Kerr	K 14
4,119	Kimble	J 14
1,193	King	C 12
3,980	Kinney	L 12
12,451	Kleberg	Q 18
11,368	Knox	C 13
48,529	Lamar	C 21
17,452	Lamb	B 9
8,677	Lampasas	H 16
8,228	La Salle	O 15
27,550	Lavaca	L 19
13,390	Lee	J 19
19,898	Leon	H 21
19,868	Liberty	J 23
39,497	Limestone	H 20
4,512	Lipscomb	A 6
8,956	Live Oak	O 17
5,538	Llano	I 16
195	Loving	G 6
39,104	Lubbock	C 10
12,372	Lynn	D 10
13,883	McCulloch	H 14
98,682	McLennan	G 18
1,351	McMullen	O 16
12,227	Madison	I 21
10,371	Marion	D 24
5,785	Martin	F 10
5,511	Mason	I 15
17,678	Matagorda	N 21
6,120	Maverick	N 12
13,989	Medina	L 15
4,447	Menard	I 14
8,005	Midland	G 9
37,915	Milam	I 19
8,293	Mills	H 16
14,183	Mitchell	F 11
19,159	Montague	C 17
14,588	Montgomery	J 22
1,555	Moore	B 3
10,028	Morris	D 23
6,812	Motley	A 12
30,290	Nacogdoches	G 23
60,507	Navarro	F 20
12,524	Newton	I 25
19,323	Nolan	F 12
51,779	Nueces	P 18
5,224	Ochiltree	A 5
1,404	Oldham	C 2
15,149	Orange	J 25
17,576	Palo Pinto	E 16
24,063	Panola	F 24
18,759	Parker	E 17
5,869	Parmer	A 8, E 1
7,812	Pecos	I 8
17,555	Polk	I 23
46,080	Potter	C 3
10,154	Presidio	J 5
7,114	Rains	D 21
7,071	Randall	D 3
3,028	Reagan	H 10
2,197	Real	K 13
30,923	Red River	C 22
6,407	Reeves	H 6
7,691	Refugio	O 19
1,457	Roberts	B 5
27,240	Robertson	I 20
7,658	Rockwell	D 20
21,821	Runnels	G 13
32,484	Rusk	F 23
11,998	Sabine	G 25
12,471	San Augustine	H 24
9,711	San Jacinto	J 22
23,836	San Patricio	P 18
10,273	San Saba	I 16
3,166	Schleicher	I 12
12,188	Scurry	E 11
6,695	Shackelford	E 14
28,627	Shelby	G 25
2,314	Sherman	A 3
53,123	Smith	E 22
3,016	Somervell	F 17
11,409	Starr	P 3, R 16
16,560	Stephens	E 15
1,431	Sterling	G 11
5,667	Stonewall	D 13
2,807	Sutton	J 12
7,343	Swisher	A 10, E 3
197,553	Tarrant	D 18
41,023	Taylor	F 13
2,660	Terrell	J 9
8,883	Terry	D 9
5,253	Throckmorton	D 14
16,003	Titus	D 22
36,033	Tom Green	H 12
77,777	Travis	J 18
13,637	Trinity	H 22
11,448	Tyler	I 24
22,297	Upshur	D 23
5,968	Upton	H 9
12,945	Uvalde	L 14
14,924	Val Verde	K 11
32,315	Van Zandt	E 21
20,048	Victoria	N 19
18,528	Walker	I 22
10,014	Waller	K 21
4,599	Ward	G 7
25,394	Washington	K 20
42,128	Webb	P 14
29,681	Wharton	M 20
15,555	Wheeler	C 6
74,416	Wichita	B 15
24,579	Wilbarger	B 14
10,499	Willacy	P 5
44,146	Williamson	I 18
17,606	Wilson	M 17
6,784	Winkler	G 7
19,178	Wise	D 17
24,183	Wood	D 22
1,263	Yoakum	D 8
20,128	Young	D 15
2,867	Zapata	R 15
10,349	Zavala	N 14
5,824,715	Total	

UTAH

TOTAL 29 COUNTIES

Pop.	County	Index
5,136	Beaver	M 5
17,810	Box Elder	C 7
27,424	Cache	B 12
17,798	Carbon	I 18
411	Daggett	E 23
14,021	Davis	D 11
8,263	Duchesne	G 18
7,042	Emery	K 17
4,642	Garfield	O 14
1,813	Grand	L 23
7,227	Iron	O 4
8,605	Juab	I 6
2,235	Kane	Q 11
9,945	Millard	K 6
2,536	Morgan	D 13
1,956	Piute	M 10
1,873	Rich	C 14
194,102	Salt Lake	F 11
3,496	San Juan	O 23
16,022	Sanpete	J 12
11,199	Sevier	L 12
9,527	Summit	E 17
9,413	Tooele	F 5
9,035	Uintah	G 23
49,021	Utah	G 12
5,636	Wasatch	G 15
7,420	Washington	Q 3
2,067	Wayne	M 16
52,172	Weber	D 12
507,847	Total	

VERMONT

TOTAL 14 COUNTIES

Pop.	County	Index
17,952	Addison	H 7
21,655	Bennington	P 7
27,253	Caledonia	E 17
47,471	Chittenden	E 8
7,067	Essex	C 21
29,975	Franklin	B 9
3,944	Grand Isle	B 5
10,947	Lamoille	D 11
16,694	Orange	I 14
23,036	Orleans	C 16
48,453	Rutland	L 8
41,733	Washington	F 12
26,015	Windham	P 7
37,416	Windsor	L 12
359,611	Total	

VIRGINIA

TOTAL 100 COUNTIES

Pop.	County	Index
35,834	Accomac	L 24
*42,226	Albemarle	K 12
*27,027	Alleghany	L 7
8,979	Amelia	N 14
19,020	Amherst	M 10
8,402	Appomattox	N 11
*50,764	Arlington	F 18
*50,153	Augusta	J 10
8,137	Bath	J 8
29,091	Bedford	N 8
6,031	Bland	O 2
15,457	Botetourt	M 7
20,486	Brunswick	Q 15
16,740	Buchanan	B 7
13,315	Buckingham	M 12
*63,546	Campbell	O 10
15,263	Caroline	K 17
22,141	Carroll	Q 3
4,881	Charles City	N 18
16,061	Charlotte	P 12
26,049	Chesterfield	N 16
7,167	Clarke	E 14
3,562	Craig	M 6
13,306	Culpeper	H 14
7,535	Cumberland	M 13
16,163	Dickenson	C 6
*47,056	Dinwiddie	O 16
*26,217	Elizabeth City	O 21
6,976	Essex	K 19
25,264	Fairfax	F 17
21,071	Fauquier	G 15
11,698	Floyd	P 5
7,466	Fluvanna	L 13
24,337	Franklin	P 7
*24,022	Frederick	E 13
12,804	Giles	N 4
11,019	Gloucester	M 20
7,953	Goochland	L 15
20,017	Grayson	Q 1
5,980	Greene	I 13
13,388	Greensville	Q 16
41,283	Halifax	Q 11
17,009	Hanover	L 17
*213,239	Henrico	M 17
*27,793	Henry	Q 7
4,525	Highland	I 8
13,409	Isle of Wight	Q 19
*7,579	James City	N 19
7,618	King and Queen	L 19
5,297	King George	I 18
7,929	King William	L 18
8,896	Lancaster	L 21
30,419	Lee	E 3
19,852	Loudoun	F 16
14,309	Louisa	K 14
14,058	Lunenburg	P 13
8,952	Madison	I 13
7,884	Mathews	M 21
32,622	Mecklenburg	Q 13
7,273	Middlesex	L 20
*25,832	Montgomery	O 5
*32,801	Nansemond	Q 20
16,345	Nelson	L 11
4,300	New Kent	M 19
*213,353	Norfolk	Q 21
18,565	Northampton	N 23
11,081	Northumberland	K 21
14,866	Nottoway	O 14
12,070	Orange	J 14
14,852	Page	H 12
15,787	Patrick	Q 5
*83,671	Pittsylvania	Q 9
6,143	Powhatan	M 15
14,520	Prince Edward	N 13
*21,638	Prince George	O 17
16,282	Princess Anne	Q 22
13,951	Prince William	G 16
20,566	Pulaski	O 3
7,717	Rappahannock	G 14
6,878	Richmond	K 19
*104,495	Roanoke	N 6
*24,904	Rockbridge	L 9
*36,941	Rockingham	H 11
25,957	Russell	D 7
24,181	Scott	E 5
20,655	Shenandoah	G 12
25,125	Smyth	D 9
26,870	Southampton	Q 18
*16,875	Spotsylvania	J 16
8,050	Stafford	I 16
7,096	Surry	O 19
12,100	Sussex	P 17
32,477	Tazewell	C 9
8,340	Warren	G 13
*43,246	Warwick	O 20
*42,690	Washington	E 8
8,497	Westmoreland	J 19
51,167	Wise	C 5
20,704	Wythe	P 2
7,615	York	N 20
2,421,851	Total	

*Includes pop. for Indep. Cities.

WASHINGTON

TOTAL 39 COUNTIES

Pop.	County	Index
7,719	Adams	K 20
8,136	Asotin	N 24
10,952	Benton	N 16
31,634	Chelan	G 13
20,449	Clallam	F 3
40,316	Clarke	P 7
5,325	Columbia	N 22
31,906	Cowlitz	N 6
7,561	Douglas	H 16
4,292	Ferry	D 20
6,137	Franklin	M 18
3,662	Garfield	M 23
5,666	Grant	J 17
59,982	Grays Harbor	I 3
5,369	Island	E 7
8,346	Jefferson	G 3
463,517	King	H 9
30,776	Kitsap	H 6
18,154	Kittitas	J 13
9,825	Klickitat	P 13
40,034	Lewis	M 8
11,876	Lincoln	H 20
10,060	Mason	I 5
18,519	Okanogan	D 16
14,970	Pacific	M 3
7,155	Pend Oreille	D 23
163,842	Pierce	K 8
3,097	San Juan	D 6
35,142	Skagit	D 9
2,891	Skamania	O 9
78,861	Snohomish	F 10
150,477	Spokane	H 22
18,550	Stevens	D 22
31,351	Thurston	K 6
3,862	Wahkiakum	N 4
28,441	Walla Walla	N 20
59,128	Whatcom	C 10
28,014	Whitman	K 23
77,402	Yakima	M 13
1,563,396	Total	

WEST VIRGINIA

TOTAL 55 COUNTIES

Pop.	County	Index
18,628	Barbour	F 14
28,030	Berkeley	D 24
24,586	Boone	M 5
22,579	Braxton	I 10
24,663	Brooke	O 24
90,786	Cabell	K 2
10,866	Calhoun	H 8
13,125	Clay	J 9
10,488	Doddridge	E 10
72,050	Fayette	M 8
10,641	Gilmer	H 10
8,441	Grant	F 18
35,878	Greenbrier	M 12
11,836	Hampshire	E 21
28,511	Hancock	N 24
9,816	Hardy	G 20
78,567	Harrison	E 12
16,124	Jackson	H 5
15,780	Jefferson	E 25
157,667	Kanawha	L 6
21,794	Lewis	G 11
19,156	Lincoln	L 3
58,534	Logan	O 4
90,479	McDowell	Q 5
66,655	Marion	D 13
39,831	Marshall	B 11
20,788	Mason	H 4
61,323	Mercer	Q 9
20,084	Mineral	D 19
38,319	Mingo	O 3
50,083	Monongalia	C 13
11,949	Monroe	P 11
8,406	Morgan	D 22
20,686	Nicholas	L 10
72,077	Ohio	P 24
9,660	Pendleton	I 17
6,545	Pleasants	E 8
14,555	Pocahontas	L 14
29,043	Preston	D 16
16,737	Putnam	J 4
68,072	Raleigh	D 8
25,049	Randolph	H 15
15,594	Ritchie	F 9
19,478	Roane	I 7
20,468	Summers	P 10
19,114	Taylor	E 14
13,374	Tucker	F 16
12,785	Tyler	D 10
17,944	Upshur	H 13
31,206	Wayne	L 1
14,216	Webster	K 12
22,334	Wetzel	C 11
6,358	Wirt	G 7
56,521	Wood	F 6
20,926	Wyoming	P 6
1,729,205	Total	

WISCONSIN

TOTAL 71 COUNTIES

Pop.	County	Index
8,003	Adams	J 16
21,054	Ashland	G 6
34,301	Barron	D 10
15,006	Bayfield	E 5
70,249	Brown	O 14
15,330	Buffalo	D 14
10,233	Burnett	B 8
16,848	Calumet	O 15
37,342	Chippewa	E 11
34,165	Clark	G 13
30,503	Columbia	K 18
16,781	Crawford	F 19
112,737	Dane	K 20
52,092	Dodge	M 19
18,182	Door	Q 12
46,583	Douglas	C 5
27,037	Dunn	C 12
41,087	Eau Claire	E 13
3,768	Florence	N 8
59,883	Fond du Lac	N 17
11,118	Forest	M 9
38,469	Grant	G 21
21,870	Green	J 22
13,913	Green Lake	L 16
20,039	Iowa	I 20
9,933	Iron	H 6
16,468	Jackson	G 15
36,785	Jefferson	M 20
17,264	Juneau	I 16
63,277	Kenosha	O 22
16,037	Kewaunee	P 14
54,455	La Crosse	G 16
18,649	Lafayette	I 22
21,544	Langlade	L 10
21,072	Lincoln	J 10
58,674	Manitowoc	P 15
70,629	Marathon	J 12
33,530	Marinette	O 10
9,388	Marquette	K 17
725,263	Milwaukee	O 20
28,739	Monroe	G 16
26,386	Oconto	N 11
15,899	Oneida	J 9
62,790	Outagamie	N 14
17,394	Ozaukee	O 19
7,450	Pepin	C 13
21,043	Pierce	B 13
26,567	Polk	B 9
33,827	Portage	K 14
17,284	Price	H 9
90,217	Racine	O 21
19,525	Richland	H 19
74,206	Rock	L 21
16,081	Rusk	F 9
25,455	Saint Croix	B 11
32,030	Sauk	I 19
8,878	Sawyer	F 8
33,516	Shawano	M 12
71,235	Sheboygan	O 17
17,685	Taylor	H 11
23,910	Trempealeau	E 14
28,537	Vernon	G 18
7,294	Vilas	K 7
31,058	Walworth	N 22
11,103	Washburn	D 8
26,551	Washington	O 19
52,358	Waukesha	N 20
33,513	Waupaca	L 14
14,427	Waushara	K 15
76,622	Winnebago	M 15
37,865	Wood	I 14
2,939,006	Total	

WYOMING

TOTAL 23 COUNTIES

Pop.	County	Index
12,041	Albany	N 19
11,222	Big Horn	C 11
6,720	Campbell	D 19
11,391	Carbon	O 15
7,145	Converse	I 19
5,333	Crook	C 22
10,490	Fremont	J 9
11,754	Goshen	N 23
5,476	Hot Springs	G 10
4,816	Johnson	E 16
26,845	Laramie	P 22
10,894	Lincoln	K 2
24,272	Natrona	J 15
4,723	Niobrara	I 22
8,207	Park	D 7
9,695	Platte	M 21
16,875	Sheridan	B 14
1,944	Sublette	K 5
18,165	Sweetwater	O 8
2,003	Teton	F 3
6,572	Uinta	P 3
4,109	Washakie	F 12
4,673	Weston	F 22
200	Yellowstone National Park (part)	C 3
225,565	Total	

States, Capitals, and Order and Date of Entering Union

State and Order of Entering Union		Date of Entering Union	Capital	State and Order of Entering Union		Date of Entering Union	Capital	State and Order of Entering Union		Date of Entering Union	Capital
Alabama	22	Dec. 14, 1819	Montgomery	Maine	23	March 15, 1820	Augusta	Ohio	17	Feb. 19, 1803	Columbus
Arizona	48	Feb. 14, 1912	Phoenix	Maryland	7	April 28, 1788	Annapolis	Oklahoma	46	Nov. 16, 1907	Oklahoma City
Arkansas	25	June 15, 1836	Little Rock	Massachusetts	6	Feb. 6, 1788	Boston	Oregon	33	Feb. 14, 1859	Salem
California	31	Sept. 9, 1850	Sacramento	Michigan	26	Jan. 26, 1837	Lansing	Pennsylvania	3	Dec. 22, 1787	Harrisburg
Colorado	38	Aug. 1, 1876	Denver	Minnesota	32	May 11, 1858	St. Paul	Rhode Island	13	May 29, 1790	Providence
Connecticut	5	Jan. 9, 1788	Hartford	Mississippi	20	Dec. 10, 1817	Jackson	South Carolina	8	May 23, 1788	Columbia
Delaware	1	Dec. 7, 1787	Dover	Missouri	24	Aug. 10, 1821	Jefferson City	*South Dakota	40	Nov. 2, 1889	Pierre
Florida	27	March 3, 1845	Tallahassee	Montana	41	Nov. 8, 1889	Helena	Tennessee	16	June 1, 1796	Nashville
Georgia	4	Jan. 2, 1788	Atlanta	Nebraska	37	March 1, 1867	Lincoln	Texas	28	Dec. 29, 1845	Austin
Idaho	43	July 3, 1890	Boise	Nevada	36	Oct. 31, 1864	Carson City	Utah	45	Jan. 4, 1896	Salt Lake City
Illinois	21	Dec. 3, 1818	Springfield	New Hampshire	9	June 21, 1788	Concord	Vermont	14	March 4, 1791	Montpelier
Indiana	19	Dec. 11, 1816	Indianapolis	New Jersey	2	Dec. 18, 1787	Trenton	Virginia	10	June 25, 1788	Richmond
Iowa	29	Dec. 28, 1846	Des Moines	New Mexico	47	Jan. 6, 1912	Santa Fe	Washington	42	Nov. 11, 1889	Olympia
Kansas	34	Jan. 29, 1861	Topeka	New York	11	July 26, 1788	Albany	West Virginia	35	June 20, 1863	Charleston
Kentucky	15	June 1, 1792	Frankfort	North Carolina	12	Nov. 13, 1789	Raleigh	Wisconsin	30	May 29, 1848	Madison
Louisiana	18	April 30, 1812	Baton Rouge	*North Dakota	39	Nov. 2, 1889	Bismarck	Wyoming	44	July 10, 1890	Cheyenne

* North Dakota and South Dakota, 39 and 40, were admitted on the same day.

Physical and Commercial Analysis of Canada, Newfoundland and Labrador

GOVERNMENT.—The Dominion of Canada is a federal union of Provinces and Districts within the British Empire. It occupies all continental North America north of the United States except Alaska (American territory), and Labrador, governed by Newfoundland, an adjacent British colony which has remained outside the confederation. Greenland, an island north of Labrador, belongs to Denmark. The two small islands of Miquelon and St. Pierre, near Newfoundland's southern coast, belong to France.

Canada is self-governing, with a chief executive, called the governor-general, appointed by the British Cabinet. He is assisted by a Privy Council. The Canadian Parliament, which is the supreme legislative power, consists of the governor-general, representing the British Crown, a Senate and a House of Commons. Senators are nominated for life by the governor-general, but the members of the House of Commons are elected by the people. A Parliament lasts five years unless dissolved sooner. Each province has also a legislature called the Legislative Assembly, which is empowered to deal with local matters. The Province of Quebec has a second legislative chamber called the Legislative Council. The provincial chief executives, each known as lieutenant-governor, are chosen by the governor-general. Federal and provincial powers are defined by the British North America Act of 1867, which enabled the colonies of British North America to form a federal union under the name of the Dominion of Canada. The Dominion Parliament has exclusive power over all matters except those specifically delegated to the provincial legislatures.

The British North America Act provided for the first time a constitution for a federal system adaptable to British principles and methods of government. The measure had its genesis during the American Civil War and aimed to avoid certain features of the American federal system which were deemed to be defective in practice. The Provinces were conceded less power than that enjoyed by American States, the federal government reserving to itself all other authority not so conceded. Bills passed by any provincial legislature require the assent of the lieutenant-governor before they can become laws, and may be annulled within the year by the governor-general. Bills passed by the Dominion Parliament require, to become laws, the signature of the governor-general and may be disallowed by the British King in Council within a period of two years. This prerogative, however, has fallen into disuse.

In practice, there is no such thing as Imperial control over Dominion affairs by the governor-general acting in the King's name, though theoretically the veto power of the Crown remains unimpaired. The British dominions are not "subject" but "sister" nations in the Empire, connected with the Crown by the governor-general. Lord Tweedsmuir of Elsfield (John Buchan) was appointed governor-general in 1935.

In 1912 the Dominion Parliament enlarged the provinces of Manitoba, Quebec and Ontario by adding to them portions of the Northwest Territories. By these arrangements Manitoba gained 178,000 square miles; Quebec, 354,961 square miles and Ontario 145,400 square miles of additional territory. Quebec is now the largest of all the Canadian Provinces; Ontario is second in area and British Columbia third.

AREAS, BOUNDARIES, AND POPULATION. —Canada is bounded on the east by the Atlantic Ocean, the Gulf of St. Lawrence, Davis Strait and Baffin Bay; on the north by the Arctic Ocean; on the west by Alaska and the Pacific Ocean and on the south by the United States.

All the Arctic islands from Canada north to the Pole, except Greenland, are claimed by the Dominion, as are also the islands of Anticosti, Prince Edward Island and Cape Breton on the east, and Vancouver and Queen Charlotte Islands off the Pacific Coast.

The area of the Dominion is officially computed to be 3,694,863 square miles, of which 228,307 are water, excluding tidal waters, gulfs and Hudson Bay. At the formation of the Dominion in 1867 it comprised only four Provinces, Quebec, Ontario, New Brunswick, and Nova Scotia, and their total area was only 377,945

square miles. The census of 1931 credited the country with a population of 10,376,786.

Physiography.—Canada is divided into four large drainage areas: the Atlantic basin, the chief river being the St. Lawrence; the Hudson Bay basin, whose principal stream is the Nelson; the Arctic area, drained largely by the Mackenzie; and the Pacific basin, whose most important draining rivers are the Yukon and the Fraser.

The eastern border is a highland formed by the Appalachian Mountain system. On the western side of

COURTESY CANADIAN NATIONAL RAILWAYS

MOUNT KERKESLIN AND ATHABASKA FALLS, JASPER NATIONAL PARK, ALBERTA

Canada the lofty Cordilleran chain trends northwest and southeast from the southern boundary to the Arctic Ocean. Between these two mountain systems lies the vast Laurentian plateau. Near the center of it is Hudson Bay. Between the plateau and the high Cordilleran system lie the vast plains of western Canada. In the north from Davis Strait there are thousands of square miles of level country covered with tundra. West of the Rocky Mountains the surface comprises high ridges, valleys and tablelands. Southwestern Canada east of the Rockies is mostly prairie. The soil is fertile.

The lowlands of Ontario and Quebec, draining into the Great Lakes and the St. Lawrence River, form an important farming section. Gaspé peninsula with the neighboring maritime provinces constitutes another section with an undulating surface broken by wide valleys and interspersed with woods.

Climate.—Canada ranges from 42° N. to Arctic regions of perpetual snow and ice and also touches three oceans. The climate shows great variations. In the south and east the rainfall is ample, and there is a great range of temperature. Those sections are the forest regions. The prairie Provinces, Alberta, Saskatchewan and Manitoba, are subject to severe winters and hot summers. The rainfall in these Provinces is much less than in the southeast section, and irrigation or "dry" farming is in many places necessary for successful agriculture. Yet the great plains are overspread with native grasses highly nutritious for live stock and capable of being cured into valuable hay; the Pacific Coast region—that is, the seaward side of the Rocky Mountains—has an oceanic climate, the range of

temperature being small and the rainfall heavy. British Columbia has, for the most part, a milder climate than Nova Scotia, though the former province is in the latitude of Labrador.

Minerals.—Canada has enormous mineral wealth. Coal fields cover many thousands of square miles, though at present the principal mines supply only about 50% of the consumption. The leading coal producing provinces are Nova Scotia, Alberta, British Columbia and Saskatchewan. Alberta contains the chief oil fields. Ontario and New Brunswick produce some oil. Clays (brick and fictile), Portland cement rock, asbestos, building stone, lime, salt, magnesite and pyrites are worked. Natural gas is found in Alberta, Ontario and New Brunswick. Copper, silver, gold, lead, are mined extensively. Most of the world's nickel supplies and more than half the asbestos are obtained from Canadian mines. Yet there can be no doubt that the country's enormous mineral riches have hardly been touched. During the year 1936 the Dominion produced minerals to the following amounts: coal, 15,299,-182 tons; copper, 421,027,732 pounds; gold, 3,748,028 fine ounces; lead, 383,180,909 pounds; nickel, 169,739,-393 pounds; silver, 18,334,487 fine ounces; and cement, 4,508,718 barrels. Other valuable products are: arsenic, asbestos, gypsum, pyrites, and salt. The output of natural gas was 28,113,348,000 cubic feet. Structural materials and clay products are also important.

Fisheries.—Canada's fisheries are the most extensive and the best stocked in the world. They comprise 5,000 miles of Atlantic coast; 7,000 miles of Pacific, and 220,000 square miles of fresh water. The principal food fishes taken in Canadian territorial waters are salmon, cod, lobsters, herring, halibut, haddock, mackerel, hake, sardines, and whitefish. Salmon is the most valuable. Much of the Dominion's vast fish catch is exported, salted, canned, dried, or smoked. The total value of Canadian fisheries production for 1936 was $39,165,055. The number of persons employed was 86,973. The value of the fisheries of the leading Provinces was, in 1936: British Columbia, $17,231,534; Nova Scotia, $8,905,268; New Brunswick, $4,399,735.

In 1936 the values marketed of the chief commercial fishes were: salmon, $13,867,513; lobsters, $4,383,428; cod, $3,331,750; halibut, $1,441,310; herring, $2,576,533; whitefish, $1,525,700; haddock, $1,291,905; smelts, $655,656; trout, $842,738; sardines, $1,598,562; and pickerel, $1,109,397.

Agriculture.—Farming has always been one of the Dominion's main industries. Homesteads may be obtained by intending settlers in various sections of the west and north. About 50 per cent of the population is engaged in the various branches of agriculture. Canada is known throughout the world as a great cereal-producing territory, ranking respectively third and fourth among the countries of the world in the yield of wheat and oats. Modern farm machines have enabled the production of foodstuffs to outstrip the growth of population; hence the Dominion is able to export immense quantities of grains and root crops. The principal products are wheat, oats, barley, flax, rye, buckwheat, corn, hay, and clover. Immense quantities of potatoes, turnips and other root crops are grown. A vast acreage is devoted to peas, beans, alfalfa and fodder corn. Grapes and orchard fruits flourish in the Great Lakes region. The census report of the yield of field crops for 1937 is (bushels): wheat, 182,410,000; oats, 268,442,000; barley, 83,124,000; rye, 5,771,000; flaxseed, 697,600; mixed grains, 36,129,000; potatoes, 42,-547,000 cwt.: hay and clover, 13,030,000 tons. The yield of fodder corn is 3,927,500 tons; of beans, 1,295,500 bushels. Within a comparatively few years the alfalfa product has increased from a few hundred tons grown for experimental purposes to 2,107,000 tons in 1937. The aggregate value of all field crops in 1937 was $553,823,100. This sum shows a decrease of about $59,-000,000 from the year 1936. Canada, like the United States, suffered from successive years of drought. Canada's most important crop, wheat, had an average yield per acre of about 9 bushels. Alberta led the provinces with an average yield of 20 bushels per acre.

The dairy industry has become increasingly profitable, and butter and cheese are exported in large amounts. Most of the creameries and cheese factories are located in the southeast Provinces, but dairy interests are expanding in Manitoba, British Columbia, Saskatchewan and Alberta. Canada ranks fourth among the countries of the world in the output of cheese. In 1937 Canada produced 129,676,600 pounds of factory and farm-made cheese and 359,471,300 pounds of dairy and creamery butter. The total value of butter and cheese in 1937 was $104,958,627.

Live Stock.—Much attention has always been given in the Dominion to the raising of cattle, horses, sheep and hogs. Herds of milch cows and of horses have been much improved in recent years. There were (1937) in the Dominion, by official estimate, 8,840,500 cattle, 3,963,300 swine, 3,339,900 sheep, and 2,882,990 horses. The wool clip in Canada for 1937 was 18,946,-000 pounds. Poultry products add considerably to the country's wealth. Canada possessed 42,954,000 hens, turkeys, geese and ducks. Rabbits are raised in British Columbia in large numbers for the market.

Forests.—The forest central line, starting from the shore of the Straits of Belle Isle, runs west, passing a little south of James Bay and thence northwest to where parallel 67 N. crosses Alaska's eastern boundary. The forest belt's average breadth is about 700 miles, and it is about 3,700 miles long. It is officially calculated that 250,000,000 acres are covered with merchantable timber of high grade. Much of the remainder can be utilized for pulpwood. The total forested area is about 736,000,000 acres. Forest products stand second in the list of Canada's most valuable resources, farm products being the first. The most common saw-timber trees are spruce (the pulp-paper tree), pine, fir, poplar, balsam, birch, tamarack, basswood, beech, ash, hickory and maple. (The Dominion's emblem is the maple leaf.) Spruce furnishes the larger part of the annual lumber cut, for the manufacture of wood pulp is rapidly increasing. White spruce trees are found in commercial timber size as far as 68° N. In the Queen Charlotte Islands there are large areas covered with Sitka spruce. This wood is especially desirable for airplane construction. Vast quantities of manufactured lumber, such as boards, laths and shingles, are exported yearly to various countries of Europe. Next to the United States and the Soviet Union the Dominion has the world's largest forest resources. Warned by many destructive fires in the past, the government takes care now to preserve the timber supply by utilizing airplanes in fire detection and the wireless telegraph to warn forest wardens of any conflagration. Portable fire pumps and other means are used to stop the fire's progress; and lastly, replanting is enforced in many cases. In 1936 the gross value of Canada's wood and paper products was $497,103,666. The total cut of pulpwood in 1936 was estimated at 7,002,057 cords.

Manufacturing.—The Dominion's manufactures increased rapidly after the World War. Within those years the amount of capital invested was largely augmented and the value of Canadian manufactures increased by over 100 per cent. Flour, canned fish, meats and vegetables, wood pulp, planing-mill products, iron and steel goods, leather, paper, chemicals, boots and shoes, clay products, steamers and automobiles are the most important items of manufacture. Canada controls the world's wood pulp trade. Spruce, balsam, fir, hemlock, jack pine and poplar are the woods used in making wood pulp. In 1937 Canada exported to the United States wood pulp to the value of $28,602,029 and newsprint valued at $89,166,874. In addition, Canada sent to this country in 1937 1,166,466 cords of wood to be turned into pulp. The value of this amount of cordwood was $8,544,006.

Water Power.—Canada had about 8,112,751 water horsepower developed or under construction in 1938 out of 20,347,400 horsepower of hydro-electric energy available at minimum yearly flow, under which a turbine installation of 43,700,000 horsepower is available. No other country possesses so much readily available water power. Many of the rivers have falls located near existing commercial centers, and vast hydro-electric power can be supplied at low cost for manufacturing purposes, as well as for city street lighting and household use. For instance, the Gouin dam across the St. Maurice River, Quebec, permits the storage of 160,-000,000 cubic feet of water for hydro-electric use. This dam renders about 1,000,000 horsepower available for

industrial uses, the flow of water being over 12,000 cubic feet a second. Numerous other large water-power developments are under way.

Canals.—Under the control of the Dominion Government there are six canal systems which connect navigable rivers and lakes. These canals have a total length of about 509 statute miles. One of the most important of the canals is the Welland Canal, which connects Lakes Ontario and Erie and makes it possible for ocean traffic to reach the Great Lakes. Usually the steamboats and barges that use the canals carry only bulky merchandise—lumber, coal, grain and iron ore. Vessels from even Lake Superior ports can reach the Atlantic Ocean without breaking bulk. Up to the end of March, 1937, Canada had spent $261,867,311 on her canals. In the year 1937 the total volume of traffic through the canal system of the Dominion amounted to 23,351,000 tons.

Transportation and Commerce.—Canada has an internal navigation system unequaled by any other country. Seagoing vessels may pass from the Gulf of St. Lawrence to the heart of the continent by means of the St. Lawrence River, short canals, and the Great Lakes—over 2,700 miles of waterway. Port Arthur, the Lake Superior terminus of the Canadian Pacific Railway, is 1,915 miles from Vancouver, the Pacific terminus of that railroad. Besides the St. Lawrence there are various other navigable rivers, the Ottawa, which flows into the St. Lawrence, the North Saskatchewan, the Assiniboine and the Red, which belong to the Lake Winnipeg basin. Lake Winnipeg's outlet, the Nelson River, which flows into Hudson Bay, is obstructed by rapids, but canals are to be constructed around these. A short water route from the grain districts of Canada to Europe will then be afforded by the Nelson River, Hudson Bay, Hudson Strait and the Atlantic Ocean.

The Dominion is well supplied with railroads. Two trunk lines run from ocean to ocean, the Canadian Pacific and the Canadian National. Railroads are being built in the prairie Provinces, and there is a network of railways in the older sections of the country. The railway mileage in operation on Dec. 31, 1936, was 58,764. In the Canadian National Railway System, the Government now operates a trackage of about 24,000 miles.

ties. In the Catholic districts education is under control of the authorities of the Catholic Church. In Ontario Protestants, Roman Catholics and Negroes have the right to establish separate schools for elementary education, the local taxes for the support of these schools being separately levied and applied. In Quebec the religious minority in any municipality, whether Protestant or Catholic, may maintain its own schools, the taxation of the minority being separate from that of the majority. In the other Provinces there is also special provision for the education of Catholic children. Each Province regulates educational matters within its own borders. There are numerous high schools, universities, agricultural colleges and technical training institutions which furnish higher education.

History.—There is some evidence that a Norse exploring expedition under Bjarni Herjulfson touched the Labrador coast in 986 A. D. In 1000 A. D., according to the Icelandic sagas, Leif Ericson sailed along a North American shore which some historians have identified as the coast of Nova Scotia. John Cabot discovered the Gulf of St. Lawrence in 1497. As he sailed under the English flag, England based her claim to the ownership of all North America on Cabot's vague description of his discoveries. Verrazano in 1524 visited the coast of southeastern Canada.

The authentic history of Canada begins with the expedition of Cartier, who, under a commission from the French king, reached, in 1534, the land bordering the present Esquimaux Bay, an arm of the Gulf of St. Lawrence. In the name of the King of France he took formal possession of the country. On a second voyage, made in 1535, he ascended the St. Lawrence River as far as the Indian village of Hochelaga, near the present site of Montreal. The first permanent settlement in Canada was made in 1605 at Port Royal (now Annapolis, Nova Scotia) by an expedition led by a French officer, De Monts. Samuel de Champlain, "the father of Canada," visited the country first in 1603, landing near the present site of Quebec. In 1608 he made a second visit and founded Quebec that year. This was long the chief city of "New France," as Canada was afterward called. French explorers had pushed through the untrodden wilderness as far as Lake Superior even before the Pilgrim Fathers touched Plymouth Rock.

CANADA'S EXPORTS, 1937

Classes	United States	United Kingdom	Other Countries	Totals
Vegetable products (except wood, fibers, and chemicals)...	$73,603,221	$197,083,567	$346,450,628	$617,137,416
Animals and their products.............................	46,431,986	73,350,911	133,940,776	253,723,673
Fibers and textiles....................................	3,003,772	2,508,340	12,830,212	18,342,324
Wood, wood products, and paper........................	153,717,675	36,064,065	223,918,476	413,700,216
Iron and its products.................................	6,072,255	13,032,283	53,173,175	72,277,713
Nonferrous metals and their products...................	117,328,297	75,819,787	230,152,314	423,300,398
Nonmetallic minerals and their products................	17,080,392	2,730,516	26,081,028	45,891,936
Chemicals	8,699,580	4,191,193	19,237,697	32,128,470
All other commodities	9,077,366	3,216,036	15,397,600	27,691,002
Totals (including other items not specified)...........	$435,014,544	$407,996,698	$1,061,181,906	$1,904,193,148

Immigration.—Nearly every civilized country in the world has contributed immigrants to Canada. Asiatics—Chinese, Japanese, and Hindus—have found their way into the Dominion. Oriental immigration since 1901 has totaled about 93,000. Government statistics show over 50 nationalities represented in Canadian immigration during the past 30 years; but the British Isles and the United States have sent over two-thirds of the immigrants. Most of the English-speaking immigrants from across the Atlantic came from England and Scotland. About one-fifth of the number were natives of Ireland. Other nationalities represented in recent Canadian immigration are Italians, Germans, Hungarians, Austrians, Russians, Galicians, Swedes, Norwegians, French, Ruthenians and Syrians. Many of the newcomers sought homes in the prairie Provinces and in British Columbia. The Dominion has about 157,000 Hebrews and, despite a head tax, over 46,000 Chinese have settled in Canada.

The immigration into Canada between 1929 and 1937 comprised 116,681 Americans, 121,144 British, and 144,974 emigrants from other countries. Most of the emigrants from the United States were drawn into Canada by the lure of cheap land in the Provinces of Manitoba, Alberta, and Saskatchewan.

Education.—A system of free public schools is maintained by local taxation and government grants. Attendance is compulsory in all provinces except Quebec. The schools are nonsectarian in Protestant communi-

Although the country's population increased but slowly, the French settlements along the St. Lawrence introduced early there the forms of European civilization. Schools were opened at Trois Rivières (Three Rivers) and Tadoussac in 1616. In 1620 the population of Quebec numbered only 60 souls. Yet the very next year the Province adopted a code of laws and established a registry of marriages, births and deaths.

During the seventeenth century French Jesuit missionaries and French fur traders opened up the immense territory north and west. To this they gave the name of New France.

Acadia, settled by the French, was taken from them in 1654 by an expedition from New England but was restored to France in 1655 by the Treaty of Westminster. Canada (New France) prospered under the energetic rule of the Comte de Frontenac (1672-82, and 1689-98). Sir William Phipps headed a force of New England troops which captured Port Royal in 1690, but in 1697 it was restored to France by the Treaty of Ryswick.

By the treaty of Utrecht, concluded in 1713, the Hudson Bay territory, Acadia and Newfoundland, were ceded to Great Britain. An estimate of the population made then gave New France 18,119 white inhabitants. Louisburg on Cape Breton Island, regarded as the strongest fortress in America, was taken in 1745 by a combined force of British and New England ships and soldiers, but was returned to France in

1748 in exchange for Madras, India. The year 1756 saw the beginning of the Seven Years' War, which was closed by the Treaty of Paris, concluded in 1763.

Canada and its dependencies were then ceded to Great Britain. In 1775 the Quebec Act was passed. The outbreak of the American Revolution followed. Montgomery captured Montreal, but his attack on Quebec was made in a blinding snowstorm, and it failed. While leading his troops he was killed by a musket ball.

In 1791 the Province of Quebec was divided into Upper and Lower Canada, each one of the new Provinces having its own legislature and lieutenant-governor.

In the War of 1812-15, waged by the United States against Great Britain, Canada was invaded at several places by American troops, and indecisive battles were fought at Lundy's Lane, Frenchtown and Queenstown Heights, but no permanent lodgment was effected. British and Canadian fleets during this war suffered two defeats from American squadrons, one on Lake Erie by Commodore Perry, the other by Macdonough on Lake Champlain. The war was closed by the Treaty of Ghent, signed on December 24, 1814.

In 1837 there were uprisings in Upper and Lower Canada against the dominance of the ruling officialdom, and, while they failed, they stimulated the movement for full self-government that was eventually realized. Peace was restored, and the two Provinces of Upper Canada (Ontario) and Lower Canada (Quebec) were united in 1841. The advantages of this Union led to the formation of the Dominion of Canada in 1867, comprising all the Canadian Provinces. Newfoundland refused to join the Dominion.

During the last thirty years Canada has prospered greatly, although the depression of 1930 had a marked effect on international trade. The country contributed liberally in men and money to the cause of the Allies in the World War.

SUBDIVISIONS OF CANADA

ALBERTA.—In 1905 parts of former Territories of Athabaska, Assiniboia, Alberta and Saskatchewan were formed into the Province of Alberta. The Province is bounded on the north by the District of Mackenzie; on the east by Saskatchewan; on the south by the United States, and on the west by British Columbia. Area, 255,285 square miles, of which 6,485 are water.
Population.—The population was officially given as 731,605 in 1931. The principal towns are Calgary, 83,761; Edmonton, on the north bank of the Saskatchewan, the Provincial capital, 79,197; Lethbridge, 13,489; and Medicine Hat, 10,300.
Physiography.—The northern region is heavily timbered, broken by patches of prairie, but is more hilly than the rest of the Province. The central and southern portions are open, rolling country, not timbered except along the foothills of the Rocky Mountains. But the vast plains there are covered with prairie grasses, which form an important resource for the raising of stock. Two large drainage systems, the Mackenzie and the Saskatchewan, are represented in Alberta. The Milk River, which flows through 60 miles of Canadian territory, is connected with the Missouri system. The north part of the Province is well watered, the principal rivers there, the Peace and the Athabaska, having many tributaries. The largest lake is Athabaska, 2,062 square miles, of which 1,700 square miles are in Saskatchewan. There are 14,410 square miles of forest reserves.
Climate.—The climate is continental. In winter the mercury frequently stays below zero for days. But the Chinook winds—warm, dry winds from the west —blow often during the cold season and raise the temperature. Heavy snow disappears in a few hours, leaving the prairies dry. Summers are hot but short.
Mineral Resources.—The mineral resources of Alberta are very large. Vast areas are underlain with rich deposits of anthracite, bituminous, and semi-bituminous coal and lignite. The coal mines of Alberta already discovered are of sufficient extent to supply Canada for hundreds of years. Natural gas is obtained in the southeast of the Province. The most important anthracite deposit is at Bankhead, where the Canadian Pacific Railroad has developed a mine of the best grade of hard coal. In 1936, the Province yielded 5,696,960 tons of coal of all kinds. Clays,

gravel, and lime are also important. The total value of all the mineral output for the fiscal year 1937 was $25,328,640.
Soil.—Central Alberta is an immense territory of fertile, finely ground glacial drift topped by accumulated deposits of humus. The upper soil consists of from one to three feet of black vegetable mold, with little, or no mixture of sand or gravel.
Agriculture.—While the Province has been pre-eminently a ranching country, ranching is rapidly giving way to model farming, with an extending system of irrigation. More than half the area of the Province is arable land, readily adaptable to the growing of grain—especially wheat, oats, barley, and rye. Peas and flax are also extensively cultivated. The cereals, being grown well north, are of the hard varieties and bring the highest market price. Alfalfa is a profitable crop in the irrigated areas. Other successful forage crops are timothy, blue grass and clover. Heavy production of field roots crops, as turnips, carrots, mangolds, and sugar beets is the rule. In 1937 Alberta produced (bushels): wheat, 74,000,000; oats, 77,000,000; barley, 22,100,000; rye, 1,185,000; mixed grains, 311,000; flaxseed, 124,000 (cwt.): potatoes, 2,790,000; root crops, 313,000. Of hay and clover the yield was 438,000 tons; fodder corn, 15,000 tons.

Poultry farming has become a highly successful industry. Census returns show that the annual value of its products is much greater than the value of the annual wool clip.

Although grain is the most profitable crop and the easiest of cultivation, diversified farming is also practiced, and potatoes, turnips, carrots, cabbages, hay and alfalfa grow as well as wheat and oats. Potatoes are of fine quality and the average yield is 125 bushels per acre. The sugar-beet industry is prominent.

Next to ranching the most important branch of agriculture is the raising of sheep, hogs, and poultry. The live stock on the farms of Alberta in 1937 numbered: cattle, 1,457,300; sheep, 768,500; horses, 661,200; swine, 773,700; poultry, 6,793,500.
Manufactures.—Alberta is steadily increasing its list of manufactures. Flour mills, beet-sugar factories, breweries, oatmeal mills, and meat-packing plants have been established. There are numerous creameries in operation. In 1936 there were 905 factories with an aggregate capital of $70,224,578; the employees numbered 11,756; the wages paid amounted to $12,328,471 and the gross value of the products was $74,052,010.
Transportation.—Alberta is well served with railways, roads and means of communication. The Canadian National and Canadian Pacific Railroads cross the Province and have branch lines connecting with important places.

There is an extensive telephone system, which is owned by the Provincial Government, and a telegraph service under control of the railroads.

BRITISH COLUMBIA.—Situated on northwest coast of North America, is bounded on the north by the District of Mackenzie and Yukon Territory; on the east by Alberta Province; on the south by the United States, and on the west by the Pacific Ocean and Alaska. Average breadth, about 450 miles; length of coast line, over 1,000 miles. Area, including Vancouver and Queen Charlotte Islands, 366,255 square miles of which 6,975 are water.

The population is given as 694,263. The principal towns are: Victoria, the capital, 39,082; Vancouver, the largest city situated on coast of mainland, 246,593; Nanaimo, 6,745; Nelson, 5,992; Prince Rupert, 6,326; and New Westminster, 17,524.

The Province is traversed from south to north by four principal mountain ranges: the Rocky Mountains, the Selkirk, the Cascade and the Coast Range. The most important rivers are the Fraser, the Stikine, the Skeena, and the Columbia. These rivers flow into the Pacific Ocean. Two other large streams, the Liard and the Peace, belong to the Arctic Ocean system. There are numerous lakes. These, as well as the rivers, occur in wide valleys between the mountain chains. The Pacific Coast is deeply indented with many fine harbors.
Climate.—The moisture-laden winds blowing from the Pacific Ocean and the Japanese current exercise a moderating influence on the climate of the province as far as the Coast Range. Heavy rainfalls are common in this section. High air currents carry some moisture to the Selkirk Range whereon it falls in snow. Beyond

these mountains there is but little rainfall, and irrigation is necessary.
Minerals.—The mineral wealth is enormous. Coal is the chief mineral and its output in 1936 was 1,489,171 tons. It has been computed that the coal reserves of British Columbia total 75,000,000,000 metric tons. Copper mines produced 21,169,343 lbs. of ore in 1936, and about 376,645,367 lbs. of lead were recovered.

Other minerals found are asbestos, arsenic, building stone (granite, sandstone and marble), brick clays and gypsum. Large deposits of iron occur on Vancouver Island. The estimated value of British Columbia's total mineral production for 1937 was $73,143,717.
Forests.—No other area of equal size contains so much forest wealth as the woodland of this Province. The merchantable lumber is estimated at 367,000,000,000 board feet. The coast forests contain the heaviest stands of timber. The principal trees are the Douglas fir, red cedar, balsam, spruce, white pine and western hemlock, a wood much superior to the hemlock of the East. Smaller trees and of slower growth form most of the interior forests. These include western soft pines, western larches, hemlocks, lodgepole pines, spruces, balsams and cedars. But little hardwood is cut.

The value of the lumber and all saw mill products of British Columbia in 1936 amounted to $45,546,430.
Fisheries.—The waters of the long and deeply indented coast line teem with fish. Salmon is by far the most valuable, though the British Columbia species is not a true salmon. Fish of chief commercial value, in addition to salmon, are halibut, herring, cod, black cod, pilchards, clams, crabs, sole, and oysters. Other food fish in British Columbia are trout, shad, bass, sturgeon, oulachan, perch, etc. Value, 1936, $17,231,534.
Agriculture.—There are about 25,000,000 acres of arable land, all of which may be utilized for agricultural production, and an equal number of acres unsuitable at present for farming activities but available for grazing purposes. Some of the best of the farming land is still covered with timber. Where irrigation is practiced, the yield of grain is doubled. On irrigated land the harvest of root crops and alfalfa is also surprisingly large. Wild grasses grow profusely on open ground and afford good grazing for live stock, but the most nutritious cultivated forage crops—clover, timothy, alsike, brome grass and sainfoin, as well as alfalfa, are easily grown and repay cultivation for silo purposes. In the valleys there is considerable alluvial land, especially along the Fraser River. Here dykes have drained the soil and rendered many thousands of acres fit for tillage. The total value of field crops in British Columbia in 1937 was $16,592,500.
Fruit Growing.—Fruit growing is an important industry. In 1930 over 2,000,000 acres were officially estimated to be available for the successful culture of orchard fruits. The principal produce is apples, followed by plums, prunes, peaches, pears, crab apples, apricots and cherries. Raspberries, strawberries and other small fruits are raised.
Live Stock.—Sheep are profitably reared on Vancouver Island and on the lower mainland. Practically all the cattle in the Province are raised under range conditions. But the days of huge cattle ranches are over. Small herds of high-grade animals are preferred now.

In 1937 there were in British Columbia 333,800 cattle (including 121,200 dairy cattle); 183,200 sheep; 55,700 hogs; 62,090 horses and about 3,957,400 poultry.
Dairying.—This industry is making steady progress. In 1937 British Columbia produced more than 8,002,800 pounds of butter; the value of all dairy products for the Province being $9,465,800.
Manufacturing.—British Columbia's manufactures are many and varied. Sawmill products were valued at $45,546,430 in 1936; fishery products, $17,231,534 and pulp and paper, $13,141,602, in 1936. Others of importance include meat, electric power, petroleum, printing and food products. In 1936 the employees (including the Yukon territory) numbered 39,796 and the gross value of the manufactured goods was $216,136,078. This Province has great water power available with a turbine installation of 719,972 h.p. in Jan. 1938.
Commerce.—Vancouver is the chief shipping port. Lines of steamers connect it with other cities on the Pacific Coasts of America and Asia. By means of the Canadian Pacific Railway it has transportation facilities for sending goods to Dominion ports on the Atlantic. This railroad is also connected with the railway

system of the Pacific Coast of the United States. There are several branch lines. Prince Rupert, the western terminus of Canada's other great transcontinental line, the Canadian National, is also a seaport of British Columbia and a shipping point of importance. Steamers ascend the Fraser River as far as Fort Yale, but the other rivers are not navigable for traffic purposes.

Education.—The British Columbia University, opened at Port Grey, Vancouver, in 1915, has an endowment of 2,000,000 acres set aside by the Legislature. It confers degrees in Arts, Applied Science and Agriculture and has power to grant degrees in all branches except theology. Colleges in Victoria and Vancouver are affiliated with McGill University, Montreal, and have high school and university departments.

DISTRICTS OF FRANKLIN, KEEWATIN, AND MACKENZIE.

—Franklin, consisting of all of Canada's Arctic islands, is bounded on the north by the Arctic Ocean; on the east by Kennedy Channel, Kane Basin, Smith Sound, Baffin Bay and Davis Strait; on the south by Quebec, Keewatin, Mackenzie and Yukon; and on the west by the Arctic Ocean. Much of this district remains to be explored. Its area is 554,032 square miles, including 7,500 of water.

Keewatin is bounded on the north by Franklin; on the east by Quebec; and the south by Quebec, Ontario and Manitoba; and on the west by Manitoba and Mackenzie. It contains Hudson Bay, which comprises more than half the district. A few Indians and fur traders are the only inhabitants. The district is believed to be rich in minerals. It has an area of 228,160 square miles, including 9,750 of water.

Mackenzie is bounded on the north by the Arctic Ocean, Dolphin and Union Strait, Coronation Gulf and Dease Strait; on the east by Keewatin; on the south by Saskatchewan, Alberta and British Columbia; and on the west by the Territory of Yukon. It includes the Mackenzie River and several large lakes, among them Great Slave Lake and Great Bear Lake. The so-called "Barren Grounds" have large herds of caribou, musk oxen and valuable fur-bearing animals. Much of the southern part is forested. The area of Mackenzie is 527,490 square miles, including 34,365 of water.

On January 1, 1920, Franklin, Keewatin and Mackenzie were constituted Districts out of the Northwest Territories. They are governed from Ottawa. Population in 1931 was 9,723.

MANITOBA.—Manitoba was created a Province with representative institutions by Act of the Canadian Parliament, taking effect July 25, 1870. Its boundaries were greatly extended in 1912. Manitoba is bounded on the north by the District of Keewatin, on the east by Hudson Bay and Ontario, on the south by the United States, and on the west by Saskatchewan. Total area, 246,512 square miles, of which 26,789 square miles are lake surface.

Population.—In 1931, Manitoba had a population of 700,139 (711,216 by census of 1936). Winnipeg, its chief city, had, in 1931, a population of 218,785; Brandon, 17,082; St. Boniface, 16,305; Portage la Prairie, 6,597.

Physiography.—The southern portion is a perfectly level plain, the bed of a former lake, through which flows the Red River. It is bounded on the east by the Laurentian plateau, which covers the eastern portion of Manitoba beyond Lake Winnipeg. Westward arises another prairie steppe, never more than 500 feet above the southern plain, and running in a northwesterly direction. To the north is a small belt of forest. Manitoba is about two-thirds prairie land. The water area includes Lake Winnipeg (260 miles long by 60 miles wide), and Lake Manitoba, Winnipegosis, and several others. The chief river is the Red River, which enters Manitoba from the south and flows into Lake Winnipeg; it is navigable as far north as the city of Winnipeg, and was in former days the only means of communication between the Province and the outer world. The Nelson River flows into Hudson Bay.

Mineral Resources.—Large deposits of copper sulphide ores have been found in several sections of the Province. Zinc, lead, gold and silver mines are being operated. Structural materials—sand, stone, and cement,—are produced to a value of nearly $2,500,000 annually. Iron, molybdenum, salt, tungsten, and natural gas also occur. The total value of Manitoba's mineral output for 1937 was $16,055,743.

Climate.—The extreme range is from 40° below zero to 95° above. Average annual rainfall is over 17 inches, and snowfall (from November to March) 53 inches.

Soil and Agriculture.—Manitoba is preëminently agricultural. Its soil is rich, black loam with a high percentage of nitrogen, phosphoric acid and potash. To a great extent farming is done by machinery. The soil is peculiarly adapted to the growth of cereal grains, especially wheat. "Manitoba No. 1 Hard" wheat, because of its superior milling qualities, has made the Province famous as a wheat producer. Other prominent crops are oats, barley, rye and potatoes. The estimated area of arable land is 25,000,000 acres. Stock raising and dairying have become important industries. In 1937 the number of live stock on the farms in the Province was: cattle, 847,000; horses, 324,700; sheep, 216,200; swine, 228,900; poultry, 4,333,000.

COURTESY CANADIAN PACIFIC RAILWAY

GRAND PRÉ MEMORIAL PARK, GRAND PRÉ, NOVA SCOTIA, SHOWING THE CHAPEL AND STATUE OF EVANGELINE

Manufactures.—The number of manufacturing establishments in Manitoba in 1936 was 1,011. The amount of capital invested was $118,515,841, the number of employees was 22,507, salaries and wages amounting to $24,490,299. $74,374,078 worth of material was used, and the finished products were valued at $122,050,502.

Winnipeg is the great fur market for western Canada. Millions of dollars' worth of furs are brought down each spring from the northland, and the dealers in Winnipeg, representing the great fur trade of the world, bid upon the packs offered. The fur catch of the Province alone is valued at about $2,000,000 annually.

Education.—In Winnipeg is the University of Manitoba, with affiliated colleges of St. John (Episcopal), St. Boniface (Roman Catholic), Manitoba (Presbyterian), Wesley (Wesleyan), and Manitoba (medical). At Brandon is Brandon College (Baptist).

NEW BRUNSWICK.—This Province is bounded on the north by the Province of Quebec and the Bay of Chaleur; on the east by the Gulf of St. Lawrence, Nova Scotia, and the Bay of Fundy; on the south by the Bay of Fundy, and the State of Maine; and on the west by the State of Maine and the Province of Quebec. It is about 250 miles in extreme length and 190 in breadth, and has a total area of 27,985 square miles, of which 512 square miles are water. It is the second in importance of the Canadian Maritime Provinces.

Population.—The 1931 Canadian census gave New Brunswick a population of 408,219, an increase of about 5.25 per cent above the figures for 1921. The chief towns are St. John (the largest), 47,514; Moncton, 20,689; Fredericton (capital), 8,830; Chatham, 4,017; and Woodstock, 3,259.

Physiography.—Two lines of hills traverse the Province, one following the coast line of the Bay of Fundy, the other starting from the same southwestern district and running diagonally across the Province to the northeast. Between the two lies a low plain, sloping down to the east coast. The northwest region of the Province is a rolling country, fertile, and suited for agriculture. There are many fine rivers in the Province. The principal ones are the St. John River, which flows south from the extreme northwest corner and enters the Bay of Fundy near the boundary line of the United States; the St. Croix, which forms part of the boundary, falling into the Bay of Fundy; the Restigouche, flowing into the Bay of Chaleur; the Miramichi, into Miramichi Bay in the Gulf of St. Lawrence; and the Richibucto, into Northumberland Strait.

A dense forest, principally of spruce and balsam, but often with an admixture of white pine, hemlock, yellow birch, maple, and beech, still covers much of the north, although the land is steadily being brought under cultivation. The forest area is over 21,000 square miles.

There are many small lakes. The coast line is 545 miles long, indented by numerous bays.

Mineral Resources.—Extensive areas of granite, limestone and sandstone have been mapped. Coal, gypsum, natural gas, bituminous shale and salt are found and also rich deposits of bituminous coal of high grade. The amount of coal mined in 1936 was 368,618 tons. Total value of mineral products in 1937 was about $2,788,439.

Climate.—The climate is healthful and dry (except on the coast) and one of great extremes. Temperature ranges from —30° to 95° F. Rainfall averages 40 inches. The northern part of New Brunswick has an annual snowfall of more than 100 inches.

Soil and Agriculture.—The soil, especially in the valleys, is fertile, and at the head of the Bay of Fundy the fertility is of a high grade. As lumbering has proved more remunerative than farming, the agricultural interests have been slower to develop.

The total value of field crops in 1937 was $13,589,000 on an acreage of 907,300. The crops consisted chiefly of oats, barley, hay, potatoes, turnips and buckwheat.

The number of live stock on the farms in 1937 was: horses, 52,300; cattle, 214,500; swine, 95,200; sheep, 107,100. The total number of poultry was 1,339,300.

Forestry.—Forest products to the amount of 213,564,-000 ft. b.m. were cut in the year 1936. They were valued at about $4,720,350. The chief wood is spruce, the most commonly used basis of wood pulp.

Fisheries.—The fisheries, both sea and river, are extensive. Some of the finest salmon fishing in the world is to be had in the Province; the fishing on the Restigouche River being especially celebrated. Cod, lobster, haddock, mackerel, halibut, pollock, herring, and sardines are abundant. Smelt fishing is an important industry. Fish packing has developed on an extensive scale. The total value of the fisheries in 1936 amounted to $4,399,735.

Manufactures.—The manufacture of wood pulp is a leading industry. There are also in New Brunswick manufactures of cotton and woolen goods, paper, machinery, and canned goods. Preserving, drying, and canning of fish are important.

NOVA SCOTIA.—This Province is a peninsula connected with New Brunswick by an isthmus. It is bounded on the north by Northumberland Strait and the Gulf of St. Lawrence; on the east and south by the Atlantic Ocean; on the west by New Brunswick, the Gulf of St. Lawrence, and the Bay of Fundy. Length about 300 miles; breadth about 100 miles, with much variation. The island of Cape Breton, separated from Nova Scotia by the Strait of Canso, forms part of the Province. The total area, including a water area of 325 square miles, is 21,068 square miles.

Population.—The 1931 census gave Nova Scotia a total population of 512,846. Halifax, the capital and leading city, had a population of 59,275, and Sydney, on Cape Breton Island, 23,089. Other principal towns are Glace Bay, 20,706; Yarmouth, 7,055; New Glasgow, 8,858; Truro, 7,901; Dartmouth, 9,100; Amherst, 7,450; Lunenburg, 2,727; and Kentville, 3,033.

Physiography.—The southern side of the Province is wild and rocky, covered with forests and dotted with small lakes. The cities and villages are situated on the coast at the heads of numerous bays indenting it. The surface of the peninsula is undulating, and although there are no mountains, there are several ridges of hills which traverse the country in an easterly and westerly direction. The plateau along the east coast rises from 600 to 1,000 feet high. The Cobequid Hills form the highest elevated land in the Province. Short, small streams are numerous, and there are numerous lakes. In Minas Basin, which penetrates the coast for 60 miles, the flow of the tide from the Bay of Fundy is very strong, and during the equinoxes the rise is often 50 feet. On the opposite shore, at Halifax Harbor, it does not exceed 8 feet.

Mineral Resources.—Minerals abound, embracing ores of gold, silver, lead, antimony, manganese, iron, and tungsten, as well as vast deposits of freestone, granite, porphyry, lime-burning rock, marls, and limestone suitable for cement, fluxing materials, such as silica and colomite, baryte, infusorial earth, porcelain, brick, and fire clays. In addition to these and transcending all other sources of wealth are its deposits of coal and gypsum. Gypsum is found in several counties. The quantity is inexhaustible. Some of the deposits have been operated for nearly a century. In 1936 the coal output was 6,649,102 tons; gypsum—729,019 tons; salt—38,774 tons; gold—11,960 ounces. The total value of mineral output in Nova Scotia was $30,309,665 in 1937.

Climate.—On account of ocean influences there are no great extremes. The average temperature in summer is 45.6°; in winter, 25° F., and rarely reaches zero. Average rainfall is 38.1 inches; and snowfall, 75.4 inches. Fogs prevail along the coast. The climate is remarkably healthful and is the most temperate of all the Provinces of Canada.

Soil and Agriculture.—The Province is well adapted to agriculture and especially to the growth of fruit. The soils, with the exception of hilly districts, are alluvial and fertile. In the valleys, fruit and cereals are cultivated, oats, hay, barley, buckwheat, wheat and rye being the principal cereals, and apples the principal fruit. The value of field crops in 1937 was $10,570,000; dairy products $7,194,600. In 1937 the number of live stock on the farms in Nova Scotia was 42,500 horses; 115,700 milch cows; 113,200 other cattle; 137,600 sheep; 50,000 swine and 1,244,100 poultry.

Forestry.—Nova Scotia holds fifth place in the Dominion's lumber production. Spruce and pine are the principal trees found in the Province, and their shipments to Europe and the United States form a considerable trade. Other important species are hemlock,

birch, maple, and balsam. The value of forest products in 1936 was $2,049,412.

Fisheries.—In 1936 the fisheries of the Province, including lobsters, brought $8,905,268. The chief catches were cod, haddock, hake and cusk, pollock, halibut, herring, and mackerel.

Manufactures.—Wood pulp, manufactured here, is exported in large quantities to England. There are numerous shipyards. Canning, drying, and preserving fish are important industries. The number of manufacturing establishments in 1936 was 1,158; capital invested, $87,888,353; number of employees, 15,944; wages, $13,784,556; gross value of products, $67,784,970.

Education.—Colleges in the Province are: King's College, Windsor; Dalhousie College, Halifax; Acadia University, Wolfville; University of St. Francis Xavier, Antigonish; Presbyterian College, Halifax; Agricultural College, Truro; St. Anne's College, Church Point; and the Technical College, Halifax.

ONTARIO.—This Province, the most populous and wealthy section of Canada, is bounded on the north by Manitoba and Hudson Bay; on the east by Hudson Bay, James Bay, and the Province of Quebec; on the south by Lakes Superior, Huron, Erie and Ontario; on the west by the Province of Manitoba. Its area is 412,582 square miles, of which 49,300 are water.

Population.—In 1931 the population of Ontario was 3,431,683. Toronto, its chief city and capital, is the second city in size in the Dominion, with a population in 1931 of 631,201, according to the census of city officials. Other cities are (1931) Ottawa, capital of the Dominion of Canada, 126,872; Hamilton, 155,547; London, 71,148; Brantford, 32,274; Kingston, 23,439; Windsor, 63,108; Kitchener, 30,793; Guelph, 21,075; Peterboro, 22,327; St. Catherines, 24,753; Port Arthur, 19,818; Stratford, 17,742.

Physiography.—There are no ranges of mountains in Ontario, and the surface is undulating. The Laurentian Hills, including the Laurentian plateau, are to the north of the Province. The plateau, sometimes called the Laurentian Highlands, rises to a height of 1,200 feet. The southern half of the Province is part of the St. Lawrence lowlands. These lowlands, especially the western portion, the peninsula between Lakes Huron, Erie, and Ontario, form the chief agricultural district.

The principal rivers are the Ottawa, which forms the boundary between Ontario and Quebec and flows into the St. Lawrence, and, in the northwest, the Moose and the Albany, flowing into James Bay, and the Severn and Winisk into Hudson Bay. In the southern half of the Province there are no large lakes, but in the western part there are several—the largest being Lakes Nipigon, Nipissing, Simcoe and Lake of the Woods.

Mineral Resources.—In 1936 Ontario was the chief mineral-producing Province, supplying more than two-fifths of Canada's total. The value of the year's output from Ontario mines and quarries was $184,532,892 Gold was in the lead, with an output valued at $49,168,019. Nickel production reached $43,876,525. The silver output was valued at $2,355,343; cement at $2,180,895; copper at $26,898,920; clay products, $1,573,936; natural gas, $6,052,294; platinum, $5,319,922; palladium, $2,483,075; petroleum, $350,767; cobalt, $804,676; salt, $1,557,078. The total value of the non-metallic minerals in 1936 was $8,890,544.

Climate.—The range of mean temperature is from 10° below to 90° above zero. The average temperature for January is 21°; minimum, 10° below zero; the average for July is 68°; maximum, 90°. The mean temperature at Toronto is 45° and the annual rainfall 26 inches.

Soil and Agriculture.—The soils are fertile loams and sand clays in the south; the black loam is of excellent quality and highly productive. The richest and most cultivated portion of the Province is the peninsula between the Ottawa River and Lakes Ontario, Erie and Huron.

The agricultural wealth of the Province has increased rapidly. In 1937 the number of live stock on the farms of Ontario was: 557,900 horses; milch cows, 1,175,900; other cattle, 1,278,300; sheep, 874,700; hogs, 1,487,900; and 22,536,200 poultry.

Principal crops 1937 were: oats, 73,803,000 bushels; potatoes, 10,090,000 cwt.; wheat, 20,290,000 bushels; and fodder corn, 3,081,000 tons. Ontario is the principal Province in the Dominion which can grow the garden vegetables raised in the United States. Fruits

are abundant, especially apples, pears, peaches, plums, and grapes.

In 1937 the total number of acres of field crops in Ontario was over 9,000,000 and the value of the crops $150,367,000.

Forestry.—Ontario ranks second and British Columbia first in the lumber production of Canada. The lumber cut of the Province for 1936 was a total number of 411,526,000 board feet, valued at $10,289,514, principally pine and hemlock.

Over 1,200,000 tons of pulp were produced in 1936. The woods cut for this paper comprised principally spruce and balsam fir.

Fisheries.—Ontario shares with the United States in the fishing advantages of four of the Great Lakes, and her smaller lakes are well stocked with fish. The total value of the fisheries in 1936 was $3,209,422.

Manufactures.—This is the chief manufacturing Province of Canada. The principal articles produced are iron and steel, railway cars, cotton and woolen goods, flour, lumber, doors, sashes, window frames. There is a considerable meat-packing industry. The number of manufacturing establishments in 1936 was 9,753; capital invested, $1,588,484,130; employees, 288,992; wages, $314,872,843; cost of materials, $822,884,081; value of products, $1,547,551,931. The available water power is about 5,330,000 horsepower at minimum flow. Turbine installation produces 2,577,380 horsepower.

Education.—There are several institutions for higher education: Toronto University with affiliated colleges; McMaster University at Toronto; Victoria University, Toronto; Trinity College, Toronto; Queen's College, Kingston; Western University, London; Ottawa University Agricultural College, Guelph; Royal Military College, Kingston.

PRINCE EDWARD ISLAND.—This is the smallest and most densely populated of all the Provinces of Canada. It lies in the Gulf of St. Lawrence, and is separated from Nova Scotia and New Brunswick by Northumberland Strait. Area, 2,184 square miles; length about 130 miles; greatest breadth, 34 miles. The population at the 1931 census was 88,038. Charlottetown (12,361) is the capital.

Physiography.—The coast line presents a succession of large bays and projecting headlands. The surface is undulating, nowhere over 400 feet high. Numerous streams and springs afford abundant water supply.

Climate.—The climate is much milder than the climate of the mainland. During summer the temperature ranges from 75° F. to 88° F. The average mean temperature is 43° F., and the range from 10° F. to 80° F.

Soils and Agriculture.—The country is well adapted to agriculture. The land is generally level; the soil, generally red loam, is rich and of good depth. About 85 per cent of the people are engaged in farming. The total value of the field products for 1937 was $7,475,000, on an acreage of 490,300. Dairying is an important industry. In 1937 the creameries and dairy establishments produced 3,846,700 pounds of butter, valued at $966,400, and 456,300 pounds of cheese, valued at $64,727. The number of live stock on Prince Edward Island in 1937 was as follows: Horses, 28,800; milch cows, 46,100; other cattle, 53,400; sheep, 49,600; hogs, 43,900. Prince Edward Island, the original home of the fur-farming industry, no longer holds its supremacy, being surpassed by the provinces of Quebec and Ontario.

Fisheries.—The fisheries are valuable, and for the year 1936 were valued at $953,029, the principal items being canned lobsters, salt herring, oysters, mackerel, and dried codfish.

Manufactures.—The manufactures are, with the exception of canning, principally confined to supplying local wants, and are chiefly linen and flannels. There are also flour mills, tanneries, pork-packing establishments, shipbuilding and ship-repairing yards. Education is free and compulsory. For higher education there are Prince of Wales College, St. Dunstan's University, and a normal school at Charlottetown.

QUEBEC.—This is the oldest Province and the largest one of the Dominion. It is bounded on the north by Hudson Strait and Ungava Bay; on the east by Labrador and the Gulf of St. Lawrence; on the south by the Bay of Chaleur, the Province of New Brunswick, the States of Maine, New Hampshire, Vermont, and New York, and the Province of Ontario; on the west by Ontario, Hudson Bay and James Bay. The area is 594,534 square miles, including water surface of 71,000 square miles. The island of Anticosti and the Magdalen group in the Gulf of St. Lawrence, belong to the Province.

Population.—The census (1931) gave the Province of Quebec a population of 2,874,255. The province contains Montreal, the largest city in the Dominion, with a population officially reported at (1931) 818,578, composed of a large number of racial elements. Quebec (130,588), the capital, has a population mostly French. The other principal towns in order of population are: Hull, 29,433; Trois Rivieres, 35,450; Sherbrooke, 28,933; St. Hyacinth, 13,448; Shawinigan Falls, 15,345.

Physiography.—The Notre Dame Mountains, a continuation of the Appalachian Range, extend along the whole south side of the St. Lawrence River. The Laurentian Mountains skirt the northern bank of the same river, finally running westward to the shores of Lakes Huron and Superior. The Province abounds in rivers, bays, and lakes. The St. Lawrence, the principal river, is navigable as far as Montreal. Above Montreal the St. Lawrence receives the waters of the Ottawa River, whose length is over 600 miles. The St. Maurice, which rises in Lake Oskelaneo and flows into the St. Lawrence, is over 350 miles long and remarkable for its flow of water and its falls. The Saguenay, rising in Lake St. John, flowing into the St. Lawrence at Tadousac, is one of the most noted streams in the world, and varies in depth from 100 feet to 1,000 feet. The largest lake in the Province is Lake Mistassini, area 975 square miles.

The principal islands of the St. Lawrence are the Island of Montreal and the Island of Orleans.

Mineral Resources.—Quebec has beds of limestone and iron ore, cement rock and building stone and large deposits of graphite, molybdenum, magnesite, copper and sulphur ores, asbestos, and potter's clays. Asbestos, valued at $9,958,183 in 1936, is one of the most important. Other values were: cement, $2,945,074; stone, $1,728,512; clay products, $691,765; lime, $718,585; gold, $13,786,150; sand and gravel, $1,418,231. The mineral output for 1937 was estimated at $65,043,971.

Climate.—The cold in winter is generally steady, the thermometer often registering 20° below zero; the snow lies on the ground from November to April. The mean temperature at Montreal is 42°, and the extreme range is from 20° below zero to 91° above, F.

Soil and Agriculture.—The soil is rich and loamy, in the large valleys of the St. Lawrence, the Ottawa, Matapedia, and Richelieu Rivers, and in the whole region of Lake St. John, and here farming is the chief industry. The lands adjoining the north of Vermont are given to stock raising.

Dairying has become an important branch of agriculture. Butter production in 1937 amounted to 88,577,500 pounds, valued at $22,450,700; cheese, 30,041,200 pounds, valued at $4,146,400.

The principal crops are wheat, oats, rye, barley, peas, beans, buckwheat, clover, hay, corn, fruit, and vegetables.

The total value of all field crops in the Province for 1937 amounted to $81,629,000, on an acreage of 6,042,300. Apples, cherries, plums, and pears are produced in large quantities in the southern part of the Province. Maple sugar and sugar products were valued at $1,308,000 in 1937.

Live Stock.—There were in the Province in 1937 milch cows, 962,400; other cattle, 801,700; sheep, 658,000; hogs, 773,900; horses, 279,900. The poultry was given as 7,603,100.

Forestry.—Quebec stands third in the production of lumber in the Dominion. The area of land on which lumber of merchantable value is to be found is about 203,490 square miles, of which 30,000 are covered with red and white pine. In 1936 Quebec produced 467,670,000 bd. ft. of lumber valued at $8,859,711. In 1936 there was produced 2,236,376 tons of pulp, and 1,960,905 tons of paper, having a total value of $117,992,663.

The fur trade is important, $2,470,998 worth of skins being taken in 1935-1936.

Manufactures.—Quebec has an abundance of water power. The Lachine Rapids above Montreal furnish power for large electrical works. Power is also furnished from the Richelieu River at Chambly. From these sources the power is derived for the operation of street railways, and also for the lighting of the city of Montreal. Shawinigan Falls, on the river St.

Maurice, furnishes like service to the city of Quebec. The estimated available water power of the Province is 8,459,000 h.p. The water power developed amounts to 3,999,686 h.p. The chief manufacturers are wood pulp, paper, cotton goods, dairy products, boots and shoes and tobacco articles. The number of manufacturing establishments in Quebec in 1936 was 7,969; capital invested, $1,029,546,039; number of employees, 194,876; salaries and wages, $182,319,454. Materials costing $455,027,759 were used, producing finished products at a gross value of $863,687,389.

Fisheries.—The fisheries of Quebec are important, the principal fish caught being cod, herring, lobsters, mackerel and smelts. The total value of the fisheries for 1936 was $2,108,404.

There are numerous agricultural, commercial and classical schools, four universities: University of Montreal, at Montreal; McGill University, at Montreal; Laval University, at Quebec; University of Bishop's College, at Lennoxville.

SASKATCHEWAN.—In 1905 parts of the territories of Assiniboia, Saskatchewan, and Athabaska were formed into the Province of Saskatchewan, with a total area of 251,700 square miles, of which 13,725 square miles is water. It is bounded on the north by the Provincial District of Mackenzie, east by Manitoba, south by the United States, and west by Alberta.

Population.—In (1931) Saskatchewan had a population of 921,785. In 1901 there were but 91,279 inhabitants. The principal towns are Regina (1931), 53,209, the capital of the Province, on the main line of the Canadian Pacific, and the terminus of the Arcola branch from the southwest; Moosejaw, 21,299, situated in one of the best wheat sections; Saskatoon, 43,291, at the junction point of the line running from Regina to Prince Albert; Prince Albert, 9,905, on the Saskatchewan River, near the center of the Province: Yorkton, 5,027; North Battleford, 5,986; and Swift Current, 5,296.

Physiography.—Most of Saskatchewan is undulating prairie, with abundant streams and lakes. Reindeer Lake has an area of 2,436 square miles and is 1,150 feet above sea level. Lake Athabaska, part of which is in Alberta 690 feet above sea level, with an area of 2,842 square miles, is the largest. The principal rivers are the Saskatchewan, about 900 miles long, and the Churchill River, in the northern part, 900 miles long.

Mineral Resources.—The region is drift-covered, the soils being drift and alluvial. Coal in abundance is found in the south, in districts drained by the Souris River. In 1936, 1,020,792 tons were produced, as against 25,000 tons in 1898. The estimated total mineral output for 1937 was valued at $10,280,180. The mineral resources of northern Saskatchewan are undeveloped, but are being increasingly exploited by systematic prospecting. Brick clays, glass sand, gold, iron, mineral pigments, natural gas, petroleum, peat and salt are found in the Province.

Climate.—The atmosphere is dry and clear. Winters long and cold, summers short and hot. The mean summer temperature at Battleford is 61.4°, winter 7.1°. The central portion of the Province is much colder.

Soil and Agriculture.—The southern half of the Province may be divided into agricultural and grazing sections. The eastern portion, for a distance of 120 miles west of its eastern boundary, is a continuation westward of the grain-growing areas of Manitoba. The soil is rich, the climate matures plant life rapidly. There is an absence of rust, due to dryness of climate, and also an almost total absence of insect foes. Wheat is the staple cereal; oats, barley, and root crops are also grown in large quantities.

In 1937 the acreage and yield of the principal field crops were as follows: Wheat, 13,893,000 acres, 37,000,000 bushels; oats, 4,380,000 acres, 22,338,000 bushels; barley, 1,174,000 acres, 5,518,000 bushels; flaxseed, 175,000 acres, 123,000 bushels; potatoes, 48,600 acres, 1,312,000 cwt.; hay and clover, 242,400 acres, 128,000 tons; rye, 518,000 acres, 635,000 bushels; turnips, etc., 2,400 acres, 43,000 cwt. The value of farm crops in 1937 was estimated at $52,187,600, on an acreage of 20,483,600.

Dairying is another branch of agriculture that has proved most successful, especially in the eastern and northeastern districts, where mixed farming is eminently suitable. Value, 1937, $16,281,700.

Fisheries.—The series of lakes north of the Saskatchewan River are well stocked with fish. Pike, lake trout, sturgeon, and whitefish abound. The value of the fisheries for 1936 was $367,025.

Manufactures.—The number of manufacturing establishments in Saskatchewan in 1936 was 694; the amount of capital invested, $42,055,557; number of employees, 5,782; wages, $6,013,378; cost of materials, $35,311,152, and the gross value of the finished products, $51,604,510.

Live Stock.—In 1937 there were in the Province 563,700 milch cows, 877,500 other cattle; 873,600 horses; 345,000 sheep; 454,100 hogs, and 8,825,300 poultry. This is a leading Province in horse breeding.

YUKON TERRITORY.—This is the most northwesterly Territory in the Dominion of Canada, and is bounded on the north by the Arctic Ocean; on the east by the District of Mackenzie; on the south by British Columbia and Alaska, and on the west by Alaska. The area is 207,076 square miles, of which 1,730 is water. The discovery of gold in the western part (Klondike region) in 1896 stimulated development. The Territory had a population of 27,219 (in 1901). With the exhaustion of the placer gold the population declined to 8,512 in 1911. Population (1931) 4,230. The principal towns are Dawson and White Horse. The Klondike region is the most productive of all the mining localities. Six-sevenths of the gold discovered comes from placer mining, the richest deposits lying well toward bedrock in gravel solidly frozen. The output of gold in 1897 amounted to $2,500,000; in 1900, $22,275,000; in 1912, $5,549,296; in 1936, $1,764,076. In 1918 a new vein of rich silver ore was found at Mayo. The silver output in 1936 was valued at $496,591; lead was also a valuable mineral product. Furs to a value of $276,946 were taken in 1935-1936. The products of the fisheries were valued at $13,385 in 1936.

The climate is extremely cold, sometimes reaching a temperature of 50 degrees below zero in winter.

NEWFOUNDLAND AND LABRADOR

The island of Newfoundland is situated off the eastern coast of North America between lat. 46° 37' and 51° 39' N., and long. 52° 25' and 59° 25' West. It lies directly northeast of the Gulf of St. Lawrence. Labrador, from which the island is separated by the Strait of Belle Isle on the northwest, is included in the administrative territory of Newfoundland. The length of Newfoundland from north to south is 317 miles, and the average breadth is 130 miles. The area is 42,734 square miles, and that of Labrador 112,400, making a total of 155,134 square miles. The population of Newfoundland in 1935 was 284,800; of Labrador 4,716, totaling 289,516. The Eskimo population numbers about 1,300.

The capital, St. John's, had a population in 1935 of 39,886. Other chief towns and their populations are Corner Brook, 6,374; Grand Falls, 4,244; Bona Vista, 4,022; Carbonear, 3,367; Twillingate, 3,203; Burin, 2,277; Harbour Grace, 2,214; Grand Bank, 2,203; Bay Roberts, 1,911.

The Governor is assisted by an executive council of not exceeding 12 members. The legislative bodies are known as the Legislative-Council and the House of Assembly. The Council is made up of not exceeding 24 members, and House of 27.

Fishing is the most important industry in Newfoundland, the most important catches being those of cod, whale, seal, lobster, herring, salmon, haddock, trout, and mackerel. Total value of the annual catch is about $16,000,000.

The mineral resources of Newfoundland are considerable. Large beds of iron and copper ore are worked. Newfoundland's wealth of timber resources contributes largely to the volume of the colony's exports. In 1936, Newfoundland exported 312,879 short tons of newsprint paper.

In Labrador, surveys disclosed immense resources of timber suitable for pulp and paper manufacture. These discoveries led to a revival of efforts to determine the boundary line between the Labrador territory of Newfoundland and the Canadian Province of Quebec, and in 1927 it was finally established. Fish and furs are valuable products, and the as yet undeveloped mineral resources are believed to be of great value.

Other Nations of the World and Their Chief Possessions and Mandates

ABYSSINIA. See **ITALIAN EAST AFRICA.**

AFGHANISTAN, an Asiatic kingdom, borders Soviet Union, India, and Iran (Persia). *People,* Afghans, Tajiks and independent tribes. *Religion,* Islam. *Products,* grains, fruits, hides, wool. *Capital,* Kábul. *King,* Mohammed Zahir Shah (1933). *Area,* 245,000 sq. m. *Population,* 9,000,000 (est.).

ALBANIA, a European kingdom, is bordered by Yugoslavia, Greece, and the Adriatic. Independence was declared in 1912 and recognized in 1920. Seized by Italy in April, 1939. *People,* Albanians. *Religions,* Moslem and Christian. *Occupations,* grazing and agriculture. *Capital,* Tiranë. *King,* Zog I (1928. Fled April, 1939). *Area,* 10,629 sq. m. Population, 1,003,077.

ALGERIA, a French Colony in northwest Africa, bordered by the Mediterranean Sea, Morocco, Tunisia, Libya, Rio de Oro, and French West Africa. *Government,* by a Governor-General residing at the *capital,* Alger. *Area,* 847,818 sq. m. *Population,* 6,553,451. *People,* chiefly Mussulmen. *Products,* grain, tobacco, tropical fruits, wine, iron, lead, copper, zinc, fish.

ANDORRA, tiny republic in the French Pyrénées, has an area of 191 square miles and a population of 5,231. *Language,* Catalan. *Religion,* Roman Catholic.

ANGLO-EGYPTIAN SUDAN, an Anglo-Egyptian condominium south of Egypt, watered by White Nile and Blue Nile. *Exports,* cotton, gum arabic, ivory. *Governor-General,* Sir George Stewart Symes. *Capital,* Khartoum. *Area,* 972,600 sq. m. *Population,* 5,816,376.

ANGOLA (PORTUGUESE WEST AFRICA), on the western coast of Africa, bounded by Belgian Congo, Northern Rhodesia, Southwest Africa, and the Atlantic Ocean. *Government,* by a Governor-General. *Capital,* Nova Lisboa. *Area,* 484,729 sq. m. *Population,* 3,098,281. *Products,* coffee, maize, sugar, cotton, diamonds, gold, and iron.

ARABIA, great arid peninsula in southwestern Asia, has an estimated *area* of 1,000,000 square miles and a *population* estimated at 7,000,000. Included within it are The Kingdom of Saudi Arabia (Hejaz and Nejd); the Hadramaut; the Imamate of Yemen; the Sultanate of Kuweit; the Sultanate of Oman; Aden and several Sheikdoms. *People,* Arabians. *Religion,* Moslem. *Capitals,* Mecca and Riyadh. *King of Saudi Arabia,* Abdul Aziz ibn Abdur-Rahman Al Faisal Al Sa'ud (1927).

ARGENTINA (ARGENTINE REPUBLIC) occupies a major part of southern South America and is bordered by Bolivia, Paraguay, Brazil, Uruguay, Atlantic Ocean and Chile. Forest, field and animal products are exported. *People,* chiefly Spanish descent. *Language,* Spanish. *Capital,* Buenos Aires. *President,* Roberto M. Ortiz (1938). *Area,* 1,079,965 sq. m. *Population,* 12,228,000.

AUSTRALIA (THE COMMONWEALTH OF AUSTRALIA), a British self-governing dominion occupying the continent of Australia, with Tasmania. Its mandates include New Guinea and (to some degree) Nauru. Papua and the British territories are under the administration of Australia. The six states of Australia are: New South Wales, Victoria, Queensland, South Australia, Western Australia, and Tasmania. There are also the Northern Territory and the Federal Capital Territory in Australia proper. *People and Language.* The people are British and speak English. *Products,* diversified animal and agricultural, also minerals, lumber, fish. *Capital,* Canberra. *Governor-General,* Lord Gowrie (1936). *Prime Minister,* Rt. Hon. Sir Earle C. G. Page. *Area,* 2,974,581 sq. m. *Population,* 6,629,839 (1933); (1935) 6,706,438. Aborigines not included, about 60,000.

AUSTRIA. See **GERMANY.**

BASUTOLAND, a British Colony (transferred to the Union of South Africa) northeast of Cape of Good Hope province. *Government,* by a Resident Commissioner, residing at the *capital,* Maseru, and under the High Commissioner for South Africa. *Area,* 11,716 sq. m. *Population,* 603,150. *People,* Asiatics and colored predominate. *Chief products,* wool, wheat, maize, Kaffir corn, iron, copper, and coal.

BECHUANALAND, a British Protectorate (transferred to the Union of South Africa) bounded by Southwest Africa, Northern Rhodesia, Southern Rhodesia, and the Union of South Africa. *Government,* under the High Commissioner of South Africa by a Resident Commissioner living at the *capital,* Mafeking (in Cape Province). *Area,* 275,000 sq. m. *Population,* 152,983. *People,* Asiatic, colored, native and a few Europeans. *Chief industries,* cattle raising and dairying.

BELGIAN CONGO, a colony in West Central Africa belonging to Belgium and surrounded by French Equatorial Africa, Anglo-Egyptian Sudan, Uganda Protectorate, Tanganyika, Northern Rhodesia, and Angola. *Government,* by a Governor-General. *Capital,* Leopoldville. *Area,* 920,656 sq. m. *Population,* 10,000,000, chiefly native blacks. *Chief products,* cotton, rice, coffee, rubber, ivory, fine hardwoods, copper, diamonds, coal, iron, cobalt, radium, and uranium.

BELGIUM, KINGDOM OF, in western Europe, is bordered by The Netherlands, Germany, Luxembourg, France and the North Sea. Languages of Belgium are French and Flemish. *Products,* iron and steel, motor cars, glass, lace, artificial silk. *Capital,* Bruxelles (Brussels). *King,* Leopold III (1934). *Area,* 11,752 sq. m. *Population,* 8,275,552.

BHUTAN, Himalayan kingdom between Tibet and India. *People,* Mongols. *Religion,* Buddhist. *Products,* rice, corn, musk, elephants, ponies. *Capital,* Punakha. *Maharajah,* Jig-me Wang-chuk (1926). *Area,* about 18,000 sq. m. *Population,* 300,000.

BOLIVIA (BOLIVIAN REPUBLIC) is an inland country of South America, lying across the Andes and bordered by Brazil, Paraguay, Argentina, Chile and Peru. *People,* Indians, mixed races, Spanish. *Religion,* Roman Catholic. *Products,* rubber, hides, cocoa, alpaca wool, oil, tin, lead, copper, silver. *Capitals,* Sucre and La Paz. *President,* Germán Busch (1938). *Area,* 514,464 sq. m. *Population,* 3,077,531.

BRAZIL, UNITED STATES OF, the largest South American country, occupies the eastern and central part of the continent and is bordered by every South American nation except Chile. Near the Equator in northern Brazil, the Amazon, greatest of rivers, drains a vast forest region. *People and Language,* largely Portuguese, except Indians. *Religion,* chiefly Roman Catholic. *Products,* coffee, cotton, sugar, rubber, hides, woods, manganese, gold. *Capital,* Rio de Janeiro. *President,* Dr. Getulio Vargas (Elected 1930, 1934, 1938). *Area,* 3,285,319 sq. m. *Population,* 45,332,660.

BRITISH EMPIRE, THE, includes British Isles, India, dominions, protectorates, dependencies, mandates and possessions over the globe. The Imperial Conference of November, 1926, made Great Britain and the self-governing dominions—Australia, Canada, Irish Free State, Newfoundland, New Zealand, Union of South Africa—equal under the King. The King's official title no longer refers to "The United Kingdom," but reads "George VI, by the Grace of God, of Great Britain, Ireland, and the British Dominions Beyond the Seas King, Defender of the Faith, Emperor of India." *Capital,* London. *King and Emperor,* George VI. Britain had three kings in 1936; George V died on January 20 and was succeeded by Edward VIII, who abdicated on December 10; the reign of George VI began on that date. *Area,* 13,355,426 sq. m. (est.). *Population,* 495,764,000. The British Isles, Atlantic Ocean off northwestern Europe, include Great Britain (England, Scotland, Wales), Ireland (Northern Ireland and Irish Free State), Isle of Man and Channel Islands. Though a region of intensive agriculture, chief industries base on commerce, mining and manufacture. Coal, iron, steel, machinery and textiles are important in a great and varied output. **England,** 50,874 sq. m., 38,173,950 pop.; **Scotland,** 30,405 sq. m., 4,916,000 pop.; **Wales,** 7,466 sq. m., 2,176,050 pop.; **Northern Ireland,** 5,237 sq. m., 1,280,000 pop.

BRITISH GUIANA, a British Colony in northeast South America, bordered by Venezuela, Brazil, Netherland Guiana, and the Atlantic Ocean. *Government,* by a Legislative Council. *Capital,* Georgetown. *Area,* 89,480 sq. m. *Population,* 323,171. *Products,* live stock, sugar cane, rice, coconuts, coffee, cocoa, rubber, limes, gold, diamonds, and bauxite.

BRITISH HONDURAS, a Crown Colony in the Caribbean Sea south of Yucatan Peninsula of Mexico. *Government,* by a Governor, an Executive Council, and a Legislative Council. *Capital,* Belize. *Area,* 8,598 sq. m. *Population,* 54,744. *Products,* bananas, coconuts, cocoa, plantains, citrus fruits, logwood and mahogany.

BRITISH NORTH BORNEO, a territory occupying the northeastern part of the island of Borneo. It is under the British North Borneo Company, *government* being by a Governor, and a Court of Directors in London. *Capital,* Sandakan. *Area,* 31,106 sq. m. *Population,* 277,367. Mohammedan settlers, aborigines, Chinese, and a few Europeans. *Products,* rice, coconuts, gums, sago, nutmegs, gutta-percha, rubber, camphor, coffee, coal, iron, gold, and mineral oil.

BRITISH SOMALILAND, a British Protectorate, in eastern Africa. *Government,* administered by a Governor and Commander-in-chief, who resides at the *capital,* Berbera. *Area,* 68,000 sq. m. *Population,* 344,768, chiefly Mohammedan. *Products,* skins, hides, gum and resins, cattle, goats, sheep, and specie.

BRUNEI, a coastal strip of British territory on the northwest coast of Borneo, adjoining British North Borneo. *Government,* under a Sultan, but by a British Resident. *Capital,* Brunei. *Area,* 2,500 sq. m. *Population,* 33,500. *People,* Europeans, Malays, natives, Chinese, and Indians. *Products,* cutch, rubber, sago, jelutong, brass and silver work, crude oil and natural gas.

BULGARIA, a kingdom in the Balkan Peninsula, southeastern Europe, is bordered by Rumania, Black Sea, Turkey, Greece and Yugoslavia. Agriculture is the chief industry. *People,* Bulgars. *Religion,* Orthodox Greek Catholic. *Capital,* Sofija (Sofia). *King,* Boris III (1918). *Area,* 39,814 sq. m. *Population,* 6,090,215.

CAMEROONS, a French mandate, bounded by the South Atlantic Ocean, Nigeria, French Equatorial Africa, and Spanish Guinea. *Government,* by a Commissioner. *Capital,* Yaoundé. *Area,* 166,489 sq. m. *Population,* 2,232,300 natives and including about two thousand Europeans. *Chief products,* almonds, palm oil, hides, timber, tobacco, bananas, peanuts, and ivory.

CHILE, REPUBLIC OF, extends for some 2,485 miles along the southwest coast of South America. *People,* chiefly of Spanish descent. *Language,* Spanish. *Products,* nitrates, copper, iron ore, gold, silver, coal, grains and fruits. *Capital,* Santiago. *President,* Pedro Aguirre Cerda (1938). *Area,* 286,322 sq. m. *Population,* 4,626,508.

CHINA, REPUBLIC OF. This ancient nation of eastern and central Asia became a republic February 12, 1912. It is bordered by the Soviet Union, India, Nepal, Bhután, French Indo-China, Pacific Ocean, and Manchukuo. *Capital,* Nanking. *People,* Mongols and related races. *Products,* highly varied, include tea, silk and porcelain. *President,* Lin Shen (1935). *Area* (China proper, Tibet, Mongolia and Sinkiang), 3,806,051 sq. m. *Population,* 428,687,000. Much Chinese territory, including Nanking, is now (1939) occupied by the Japanese.

CHOSEN (KOREA), annexed to Japan in 1910. *Government,* by a Governor-General. *Capital,* Keijo. *Area,* 85,206 sq. m. *Population,* 22,898,695. *People,* natives, with some Japanese and Chinese. *Products,* rice, grains, cotton, tobacco, sugar beets, fruit, copper, gold, iron and coal.

COLOMBIA, THE REPUBLIC OF. This South American country lies in the northwestern part of the continent and is bordered by Panama, Caribbean Sea (640 miles), Venezuela, Brazil, Ecuador, Peru, Pacific Ocean (465 miles). *Language,* Spanish. *Products,* precious metals, emeralds, tropical fruits, coffee, hides, rubber. *Capital,* Bogotá. *President,* Eduardo Santos (1938). *Area,* 441,651 sq. m. *Population,* 9,018,000.

COSTA RICA, REPUBLIC OF, a small Central American country, bordered by Nicaragua, Caribbean Sea, Panama and Pacific Ocean. *People,* Spanish descent. *Language,* Spanish. *Products,* bananas, coffee, cattle, gold and silver. *Capital,* San José. *President,* Don Leon Cortes (1936-1940). *Area,* 23,000 sq. m. *Population,* 577,833.

CUBA, a republic occupying the largest island of the West Indies, discovered in 1492, independent since 1898. *People,* of Spanish descent or mixed race. *Religion,* Roman Catholic. Cuba is the largest producer of cane sugar. Habana tobacco is famous. *Capital,* Habana. *President,* Federico Laredo Brú (1936). *Area,* 44,164 sq. m. *Population,* 4,011,088.

CURAÇAO, formed of two groups of islands, in the West Indies, belonging to The Netherlands. *Capital,* Willemstad. *Government,* by a Governor and Council. *Area,* 403 sq. m. *Population,* 83,254. *Products,* beans, pulse, maize, salt, lime phosphate, refined oil.

CYPRUS, a British island in the Mediterranean Sea, fifty miles from Asia Minor. *Government,* by a Governor and Executive Council. *Capital,* Nicosia. *Area,* 3,584 sq. m. *Population,* 347,959. *Products,* grains, olives, raisins, wine, olive oil, silk and marble.

CZECHOSLOVAKIA, central Europe, is bordered by Germany, Poland, Rumania and Hungary. *Exports,* beet sugar, glass textiles. *Capital,* Praha (Prague). *Area,* 54,192 sq. m. *Population,* 15,096,025. (Before partition and annexation.) In October, 1938, and March, 1939, Germany took a large part of the country. Carpathian Ruthenia, in the south, was claimed by Hungary, 1939.

DANZIG, FREE CITY OF. The Treaty of Versailles established the Free City of Danzig, located on the Baltic Sea adjacent to Germany and Poland, under the protection of the League of Nations. *High Commissioner,* C. J. Burckhardt de Reynold. *President of Senate,* Arthur Greiser. *Area,* 754 sq. m. *Population,* 407,517.

DENMARK, KINGDOM OF, on the Peninsula of Jutland and adjacent islands, western Europe, is bordered by Skagerrak, Baltic Sea, Germany and North Sea. Greenland and Faroe Islands belong to Denmark. Iceland, otherwise independent, has the same king. Agriculture and dairying are chief industries, with manufacturing also important. *King,* Christian X (1912). *Area,* 16,571 sq. m. *Population,* 3,656,000.

DOMINICAN REPUBLIC (SANTO DOMINGO), occupies the eastern two-thirds of the island of Hispaniola, West Indies. *People,* whites, Indian, and Negroes, many mulattoes. *Language,* Spanish. *Religion,* Roman Catholic. *Exports,* sugar, cacao, coffee, tobacco. *Capital,* Ciudad Trujillo (formerly Santo Domingo). *President,* Jacinto Peynado (1938). *Area,* 19,332 sq. m. *Population,* 1,478,121.

ECUADOR, REPUBLIC OF, on the west coast of South America, is crossed by the Equator. People are largely Indian, or of mixed race. *Products,* tropical, include cocoa, cagua, ivory, nuts, coffee, hides and rubber. *Capital,* Quito. *President,* Aurelio Mosquera (1938). *Area.* Claimed, 276,000 sq. m. Administered 176,155 sq. m. *Population,* 2,646,645.

EGYPT, kingdom and ancient land of northeastern Africa, borders the Mediterranean and the Red Sea. Population is along the Nile, where yearly overflow, regulated by the Aswan Dam and canals, gives fertility. Proclaimed independent March 15, 1922. *Capital,* Cairo. *King,* Farouk I (1936). *Area,* 383,000 sq. m. Cultivated Area, 13,600 sq. m. *Population,* 15,546,000.

EIRE. See IRELAND.

ERITREA AND ITALIAN SOMALILAND (ITALIAN EAST AFRICA), on the eastern coast of Africa and bordered by the Red Sea, Anglo-Egyptian Sudan, Ethiopia, French and British Somaliland, and Kenya. *Governments,* by Civil Governors named by the King and under the Italian Minister for the Colonies. **Eritrea.**—*Area,* 45,783 sq. m. *Population,* 621,776, mostly natives. *Capital,* Asmara. *Religion,* Mohammedan and Christian. *Products,* camels, sheep, goats, oxen, palm nuts and pearls. **Italian Somaliland.**—*Area,* 190,000 sq. m. *Population,* 1,210,000. *Capital,* Mogadiscio. *Products,* maize, cotton, rice, cattle, sheep.

ESTONIA, established 1918, is bordered by Gulf of Finland, Soviet Union, Latvia and the Baltic Sea. There are beds of oil shale, but products are chiefly those of forests, agriculture and dairying. *People,* Estonian (Finnish-Ugrian origin). *Religion,* chiefly Lutheran. *Capital,* Tallinn. *State Head,* Konstantin Päts (1933). *Area,* 18,354 sq. m. (est.). *Population,* 1,126,413.

ETHIOPIA (ABYSSINIA) is in northeastern Africa. *People,* Semitic and Hamitic. *Religion,* Coptic sect. *Industries,* agriculture and grazing. *Capital,* Addis Ababa. *Emperor,* Haile Silassie I (1928 till Italian occupation, 1936. *Viceroy,* Duke of Aosta). *Area,* 350,000 sq. m. *Population,* 7,500,000 (est.). See **ITALIAN EAST AFRICA.**

FINLAND, a European republic independent since 1919, is bordered by Norway, Arctic Ocean, Soviet Union, Gulf of Finland, Baltic Sea, Gulf of Bothnia and Sweden. Lumbering, agriculture and dairying are basic industries. *People,* Finns. *Religion,* Lutheran. *Capital,* Helsinki (Helsingfors). *President,* Kyosti Kallio (1937). *Area,* 149,954 sq. m. (17,314 sq. m. water). *Population,* 3,762,000.

FRANCE. This European republic is bordered by Belgium, Luxembourg, Germany, Switzerland, Italy, Mediterranean Sea, Spain, Bay of Biscay, Atlantic Ocean, English Channel. France has a mandate for Syria and exercises a protectorate over part of Morocco. Her great colonial possessions include Algeria, Tunisia, French West Africa, French Equatorial Africa, Madagascar and other African territories (more than four million square miles in Africa), besides Indo-China in Asia, French Guiana in South America, islands and bits of land over the globe. Natural resources, particularly in the colonial possessions, are of great diversity and include timber, water power, and nearly every known mineral. Manufactures are notable for variety, quantity, and quality. Textiles (especially silks and laces), wines, automobiles and fancy goods are among the exports. *Capital,* Paris. *President,* Albert Lebrun (1932). *Area,* 212,681 sq. m. *Population,* 41,905,968 (1936). *Area of Possessions, Dependencies, etc.,* 4,681,789 sq. m. (est.). *Population,* 63,849,000.

FRENCH EQUATORIAL AFRICA, in northwest Africa and bordered by Cameroons, French West Africa, Libya, Anglo-Egyptian Sudan, Belgian Congo, the South Atlantic Ocean, and Spanish Guinea. Composed of four colonies, Gabon, Middle Congo, Ubangi-Shari, and Chad. *Government,* by a Governor-General, assisted by an Administrative Council. *Capital,* Brazzaville. *Area,* 912,049 sq. m. *Population,* 3,226,940. *Products,* coffee, cotton, cocoa, palm oil, ivory, camels, sheep, horses, zinc, lead and copper.

FRENCH GUIANA AND ININI, on the northeast coast of South America, and bordered by the Atlantic Ocean, Netherland Guiana, and Brazil. *Government,* by a Governor, assisted by a Privy Council and a Council General. *Capital,* Cayenne. *Area,* 34,740 sq. m. *Population,* 32,596, exclusive of the penal settlement of Maroni. *Products,* rice, maize, cocoa, coffee, sugar cane, timber, gold, phosphates, glue, hides, balata, fish, rum, and rosewood essence.

FRENCH INDO-CHINA, bounded by the China Sea, Gulf of Tonking, Gulf of Siam, Siam and Burma, consists of five states, Cochin-China, Cambodia, Annam, Tonking, and Laos. *Government,* by a Governor-General, assisted by a Secretary-General; a Governor (in Cochin-China) and the Residents-Superior of each remaining state. *Capital,* Hanoi. *Area,* 284,522. *Population,* 21,452,000. *Products,* rice, pepper, coconuts, cinnamon, sugar, tea, tobacco, coffee, fruits, cotton, gold, coal, zinc, graphite, lead, tin, fish, hides, dyewoods, teak, bamboo, and rubber.

FRENCH OCEANIA, groups of islands in the East Pacific Ocean. Principal groups, Society (Tahiti, Moorea, etc.), Marquesas, Tuamotu, Leeward, Gambia, Tubuai, and Rapa Islands. *Government,* by a Governor, assisted by an Administrative Council. *Capital,* Papeete. *Area,* 1,544 sq. m. *Population,* 39,713, mostly French and Chinese. *Products,* coconuts, copra, bananas, sugar cane, vanilla, tropical fruits, pearls, phosphates, and mother-of-pearl.

FRENCH SOMALILAND, a French Colony in Eastern Africa on the Gulf of Aden. *Government,* by a Governor and an Administrative Council. *Capital,* Djibouti. *Area,* 5,790 sq. m. *Population,* 69,782. *Products,* ivory, hides, coffee, butter, skins, sugar, fish and salt.

FRENCH WEST AFRICA, includes Senegal, French Guinea, Ivory Coast, Dahomey, French Sudan, Mauritania, Niger, and Circonscription de Dakar with dependencies. *Government,* by a Governor-General and Council, each colony having a Lieutenant-Governor. *Capital,* Dakar. *Area,* 1,604,159 sq. m. *Population,* 14,468,828. *Products,* peanuts, cocoa, cotton, coffee, fruit, cattle, oils, oil seeds, timber, mahogany and rubber.

GERMANY, now a central European republic, is a federation of the republics that replaced the kingdoms of the former German Empire. Germany is bordered by Denmark, Baltic Sea, Lithuania, Poland, Czechoslovakia, Austria, Switzerland, France, Belgium, The Netherlands and North Sea. By the Treaty of Versailles, German colonies were transferred to nations of the Allies as mandates or possessions. Territorial adjustments in Europe included cession of Alsace-Lorraine to France; Eupen-Malmedy to Belgium; part of Upper Silesia to Poland; Memel (now in Lithuania); Danzig, as a free city; northern Schleswig to Denmark; part of Silesia to Czechoslovakia. The German Republic was proclaimed November 9, 1918. Friedrich Ebert, first President, was elected February 6, 1919; he died February 28, 1925, after re-election. Field-Marshal Paul von Hindenburg was elected President in April, 1925, and held office until his death August 2, 1934, since which time Adolf Hitler has headed the government. On March 1, 1935, the Saar region was restored. In April, 1938, Austria was declared a part of Germany; in October, 1938 and March, 1939, most of Czechoslovakia was annexed; in 1939, Memel. *Language,* German. *Religion,* Protestant (German Evangelical Union) and Roman Catholic. *Exports,* varied. Iron and steel manufactures, textiles and beet sugar are important. *Capital,* Berlin. *Chancellor and Reichsführer,* Adolf Hitler (1934). *Area,* 224,973 sq. m. *Population,* 77,028,-433. (Without Czechoslovakia and later annexations.)

GOLD COAST, on the Gulf of Guinea and belonging to the English, includes Ashanti, Gold Coast Colony, Northern Territories, and Togoland (under British Mandate). *Government,* by a Governor with an Executive and Legislative council. *Capital,* and largest city, Accra. *Area,* 91,843 sq. m. *Population,* 3,441,100, mostly natives. *Products,* cocoa, palm kernels, kola nuts, rubber, copra, maize, yams, fruits, timber, live stock, gold, diamonds, and manganese ores.

GREECE, KINGDOM OF, situated on a peninsula extending from southern Europe into the Mediterranean and bounded on the north by Albania, Yugoslavia, Bulgaria and Turkey. *Products,* olive oil, wine, textiles, cereals, leather. King Constantine died in exile, January, 1923. In December, 1923, George II departed. Recalled October 10, 1935. *King,* George II. *Capital,* Athenai (Athens). *Area,* 54,092 sq. m. *Population,* 6,750,000.

GREENLAND, a large island off northeastern North America, mostly within the Arctic Circle, and buried under ice sheets, is a colonial possession of Denmark. *Government,* by a Council of Ministers and two Resident Councils (one for each District). *Capital,* Godhavn. *Area,* 837,620 sq. m. *Population,* 17,486, natives with a few hundred Danes. *Exports,* seal and whale oil, cod liver oil, eider-down, reindeer skins, seal and fox furs, and walrus ivory.

GUADELOUPE AND DEPENDENCIES, a French Colony in the Lesser Antilles, consisting of two islands, Guadeloupe proper (western) and Grande-Terre (eastern), with five smaller islands—Marie Galante, Les Saintes, Désirade, St. Bartholomy, and St. Martin (northern part). *Government,* by a Governor and Council. *Capital,* Basse-Terre. *Area,* 688 sq. m. *Population,* 267,407. *Products,* coffee, cocoa, sugar, bananas, corn, sweet potatoes, tobacco, salt, sulphur, rum, and canned goods.

GUATEMALA, REPUBLIC OF, in Central America, is bordered by Mexico, British Honduras, Salvador and Pacific Ocean. *People,* Indians and mixed races. *Products,* coffee, sugar, bananas, timber, chicle. *Capital,* Guatemala. *President,* General Jorge Ubico (1931. Reelected 1937). *Area,* 45,452 sq. m. *Population,* 2,245,553.

HAITI, REPUBLIC OF, lies in the western part of the fertile island of Hispaniola, West Indies. *Products,* coffee, tobacco, sugar, fruits. *People,* largely Negroes. *Language,* French. *Capital,* Port-au-Prince. *President,* Sténio Vincent (1930. Reelected 1936). *Area,* 10,204 sq. m. *Population,* 2,550,000.

HONDURAS, REPUBLIC OF, a Central American country, bordered by Caribbean Sea, Nicaragua, Salvador and Guatemala. *People,* of Indian and Spanish descent. *Exports,* bananas, sugar, cattle products. *Capital,* Tegucigalpa. *President,* Dr. Tiburcio Carias Andino (1937). *Area,* 44,275 sq. m. *Population,* 859,761.

HONG KONG, a Crown Colony consisting of an island at the mouth of the Canton River, is a British commercial center and an important military and naval station. *Government,* by a Governor, an Executive Council and a Legislative Council. *Area,* 391 sq. m. *Population,* 944,492, mostly Chinese. *Capital,* Victoria. *Chief industries,* deep sea fishing, ship-building, tin and sugar refining; manufacture of rope, knit-goods, cement, and tobacco.

HUNGARY, KINGDOM OF, formerly united with Austria in the Austro-Hungarian Empire. Hungary became a republic November 16, 1918. Since March 23, 1920, the country has been a monarchy with a regent. Hungary lost part of Transylvania to Rumania; Croatia and Slavonia to Yugoslavia. *People,* Magyars. *Language,* Hungarian. *Religion,* Roman Catholic. *Capital,* Budapest. *Regent,* Admiral Nicholas Horthy de Nagybánya (1920). *Area,* 35,875 sq. m. *Population,* 8,898,367.

ICELAND, KINGDOM OF, occupies an island in the North Atlantic. *People,* Icelandic (chiefly of Scandinavian descent). *Language,* Icelandic, differing from Norwegian. *Industries,* dependent on agriculture. *Exports,* domestic animals and animal products. *Capital,* Reykjavik. *King,* Christian X. of Denmark (1912). *Area,* 39,709 sq. m. *Population,* 114,743.

INDIA, of which the British King is Emperor, is bordered by Afghanistan, China, Siam, Bay of Bengal, Indian Ocean, Arabian Sea. *Chief Industry,* agriculture. *Minerals,* coal, iron, petroleum, gold, silver, precious stones. *Viceroy,* Marquess of Linlithgow (Victor Alexander John Hope (1936). *Religions,* Hindusism, Islam, others. *Area,* 1,808,679 sq. m. *Population,* 352,837,778.

IRAN (PERSIA) is a kingdom in southwestern Asia, on the Plateau of Iran. It is bordered by Soviet Union, Caspian Sea, Afghanistan, Baluchistan, Arabian Sea, Persian Gulf and Iraq. It is a land of ancient history. *People,* Persian. *Religion,* Islam, Shi'a sect. *Exports,* petroleum, carpets, fruits, skins, tobacco. *Capital,* Teheran. *Shah,* Riza Khan Pahlevi (Dec. 16, 1925). *Area,* 628,000 sq. m. (est.). *Population,* 15,055,115.

IRAQ, an Arab kingdom in Asia, occupies historic Mesopotamia. It has valuable oil wells and a fertile soil. *People and Language,* chiefly Arabian. *Religion,* Islam predominant. *Capital,* Baghdad. *King,* Feisal II. (1939). *Area,* 143,240 sq. m. *Population,* 3,300,000 (est.).

IRELAND (EIRE), former **Irish Free State (Saorstat Eireann),** a republic (proclaimed in 1937) and British self-governing dominion (proclaimed December 6, 1922, in accordance with a treaty signed in December, 1921). The republic occupies the southern part of the island of Ireland. *People,* Irish. *Religion,* Roman Catholic. *President,* Dr. Douglas Hyde (1938). *Prime Minister,* Eamon de Valera. *Area,* 27,137 (including water). *Population,* 2,965,854.

ITALIAN EAST AFRICA. By a law passed in June, 1936, Eritrea, Italian Somaliland, and the conquered Empire of Ethiopia became provinces of Italian East Africa, with some readjustment of boundaries between them. Italian East Africa is bounded by the Red Sea, French Somaliland, British Somaliland, Indian Ocean, Kenya and Anglo-Egyptian Sudan. See **ERITREA AND ITALIAN SOMALILAND and ETHIOPIA.**

ITALIAN SOMALILAND. See **ERITREA AND ITALIAN SOMALILAND.**

ITALY, KINGDOM OF, occupies the central peninsula of southern Europe, the islands of Sicily and Sardinia, various smaller islands and part of the mainland northeast of the Adriatic. Italy is bordered by Switzerland, Austria, Yugoslavia, Adriatic Sea, Ionian Sea, Mediterranean Sea, Tyrrhenian Sea and France. In Africa are the colonies of Eritrea, Somaliland and Libya. Italy claims Ethiopia also by conquest. *Capital,* Roma (Rome), in which is located **Vatican City,** center of the Roman Catholic Church. *Industries,* largely dependent on agriculture. *King,* Victor Emanuele III (1900). *Premier,* Benito Mussolini. *Area,* 119,703 sq. m. *Population,* 41,176,671. *Area of Colonies,* 869,053 sq. m. (est.). *Population of Colonies,* 2,429,000.

JAMAICA, a British Crown Colony. *Government,* by a Governor, a Privy Council, and a Legislative Council. *Capital,* Kingston. *Area,* 4,450 sq. m. *Population,* 1,095,000, mostly natives. *Products,* sugar cane, coffee, bananas, coconuts, cocoa, and pimentos; also cattle, sheep, horses, and mules. **Dependencies of Jamaica,** the Turks, Caicos, and Cayman Islands, the Morant Cays and the Pedro Cays, have an area of 224 sq. m. *Products,* sponges, fibers, salt (on the Turks and Caicos Islands), and green turtles (on the Cayman Islands).

JAPAN, EMPIRE OF, covers the five large islands east of Asia—**Honshu, Kyushu, Shikoku, Hokkaido (Yezo),** and **Taiwan (Formosa); Pescadores,** the southern part of **Sakhalin,** called **Karafuto,** and **Chosen (Korea)** on the mainland. Japan controls the former German Pacific possessions north of the Equator (Marshall, Caroline, Marianas, and Pelew Islands) and has a 99-year lease of the Kwantung Peninsula, where are Port Arthur and Dairen. *Religion,* Shintoism and Buddhism (except Taiwan, which follows Chinese doctrines). *Products,* cotton yarn and textiles, silk, iron, coal, tea, rice. *Capital,* Tokyo. *Emperor,* Hirohito acceded December 26, 1926. *Area,* Japan proper, 147,889 sq. m. *Total,* 260,911 sq. m. *Population,* Japan proper, 69,251,900. *Total,* 98,219,812.

KENYA, a British Colony and Protectorate in East Africa, bordered by Ethiopia, Anglo-Egyptian Sudan, Italian Somaliland, the Indian Ocean, Uganda Protectorate, and Tanganyika. *Government,* by a Governor, an Executive Council and a Legislative Council. *Capital,* Nairobi. *Area,* 224,960 sq. m. *Population,* 3,094,300. *Religion,* Pagan beliefs and Mohammedanism. *Products,* coffee, wheat, tea, maize, wattle, sugar, coconuts, cotton, sisal, hardwoods, camphor and cedar.

LATVIA (LATVIAN REPUBLIC), established in November, 1918, from Russian territory, borders Estonia, Soviet Union, Lithuania, and Baltic Sea. *People,* Letts. *Exports,* flax, timber, furniture. *President,* and *Prime Minister,* Karlis Ulmanis (1934). *Capital,* Riga. *Area,* 25,395 sq. m. *Population,* 1,950,502.

LEEWARD ISLANDS, a British Colony southeast of Puerto Rico in the Caribbean Sea, divided into five Presidencies—Antigua, with Barbuda and Redonda; St. Kitts, with Nevis and Anguilla; Dominica; Montserrat; and the Virgin Islands with Sombrero. *Government,* by a Governor and Commander-in-chief, aided in each Presidency by an Executive and a Legislative Council. *Capital,* and largest city, St. John. *Area* for the group, 715 sq. m. *Population,* 135,528. *Chief products,* sugar cane, molasses, limes, tomatoes, cotton, coconuts, tobacco, and salt.

LIBERIA, a republic on the west coast of Africa, was settled by freed slaves from North America in 1822, and became independent in 1847. *People,* Negroes. *Language,* English. *Capital,* Monrovia. *President,* Edwin Barclay (1932. Reëlected, 1936). *Area,* 43,000 sq. m. (est.). *Population,* 2,250,000.

LIBYA, an Italian possession on the northern coast of Africa; bordered by Egypt, Tunisia, Algeria, French West Africa, French Equatorial Africa, and Anglo-Egyptian Sudan. Libya (Tripolitania and Cyrenaica) is divided into Tripoli, Misurata, Benghasi and Derna. Made part of Italy proper in October, 1938. *Governor,* Marshal Italo Balbo. *Capital,* Tripoli, also the largest city. *Official language,* Italian and Arabic. *Total area,* 632,500 sq. m. *Total population,* 717,000. **Tripolitania.** *Area,* 347,400 sq. m. *Population,* 552,920, principally Mussulmen and Jews. **Cyrenaica.** *Area,* 285,640 sq. m. *Population,* 164,080. *Chief products,* sponges, tunny fish, tobacco and tobacco products, salt, matting, carpet, leather goods, gold and silver embroidered fabrics.

LIECHTENSTEIN, a principality between Austrian Vorarlberg and the Swiss cantons of St. Gallen and Graubunden. *People,* Germans. *Religion,* Roman Catholic. *Capital,* Vaduz. *Prince,* Francis Joseph. *Administrator,* Dr. Joseph Hoop. *Area,* 65 sq. m. *Population,* 10,213.

LITHUANIA, formerly a grand duchy of Russia, became a republic and independent, February 16, 1918, receiving recognition June 28, 1919. Acquired Klaipeda (Memel) in 1923, but lost Wilno to Poland. *Products,* agricultural and forest. *People,* chiefly Lithuanians. *Religion,* Roman Catholic predominating. *Capital,* Kaunas (Kovno). *President,* Antanas Smetona (1932. Reelected 1938). *Area,* 21,683 sq. m. *Population,* 2,542,200.

LUXEMBOURG, a grand duchy bordered by Germany, France and Belgium, has economic union with Belgium. Iron mines are very important. *Capital,* Luxembourg. *Grand Duchess,* Charlotte. *Area,* 998 sq. m. *Population,* 304,900.

MADAGASCAR, a large Island Colony belonging to France, off the southeast coast of Africa. *Government,* by a Governor-General, assisted by a Consultative Council. *Capital,* Tananarive. *Area,* 228,707 sq. m. *Population,* 3,853,300, mostly native tribes. *Products,* cattle, sheep, goats, horses, pigs, ostriches, rice sugar, cotton, vanilla, tobacco, butter, lima beans, coffee, timber, plants for textile, dyeing, tanning, and medicinal purposes, cotton and silk goods, and Panama hats.

MALAY STATES. Federated Malay States, Perak, Selangor, Negri Sembilan, and Pahang, in Asia on and adjacent to the Malay Peninsula, are under British protection. *Government,* of each state by a State Council consisting of the Sultan, the British Resident Advisor, and the principal Malay chiefs. The State Councils are under a Federal Council whose President is the High Commissioner of all the Malay States, assisted by the Chief Secretary, and four British Advisors, and other department officials. (The High Commissioner is also Governor of the Straits Settlement.) *Capital,* Kuala-Lumpur. *Area,* 27,506 sq. m. *Population,* 1,777,400. *People,* Chinese and Malays, about equally divided, with a few Indians. *Religion,* Mohammedan. *Products,* rice, coconuts, tapioca, palm oil, rubber, pineapples, timber, gutta-percha, gums, resins, cane, oils, gold, tin, lead, copper, silver, and arsenic.

Non-federated Malay States, Johore, Kelantan, Trengganu, Kedah, and Perlis. *Government.* Under British suzerainty, administered by the Sultan, assisted by a British General Advisor, an Executive Council, and a Legislative Council. *Area,* 23,486 sq. m. *Population,* 1,576,351. *Religion,* Mohammedan. *Products,* rubber, rice, coconuts, palm oil, pepper, maize, gold, tin, galena, silk, boats, and bricks.

MANCHUKUO. Composed principally of the former Chinese territory of Manchuria. Secured its independence with the help of Japan and set up a provisional republic on February 18, 1932. Preliminary constitution drawn up, March 10, 1932. Recognized by Japan, September 15, 1932. In 1933 Jehol was occupied and made part of Manchukuo. In March, 1934, the Chinese Prince, Pu Yi, who had been serving as Chief Executive, was crowned as Emperor Kang Teh. Bordered by China, Soviet Union, Chosen, Yellow Sea, and Sea of Japan. *People,* Mongols. *Religion,* principally Buddhist and Mohammedan. *Products,* soy beans, millet, wheat, rice, lumber, meat, iron, coal, stone. *Capital,* Hsinking. *Emperor,* Kang Teh (1934). *Area,* 446,000 sq. m. *Population,* 30,290,000.

MARTINIQUE, a French Island Colony in the Caribbean Sea, south of the Leeward Islands. *Government,* administered by a Governor, assisted by a Privy Council. *Capital,* Fort de France. *Area,* 385 sq. m. *Population,* 238,600. *Products,* sugar, rum, cocoa, pineapples, bananas, tobacco, and coffee.

MAURITIUS, a British Island in the Indian Ocean, east of Madagascar. *Government,* administered by a Governor, assisted by an Executive Council, residing at Port Louis, the *capital. Area,* 720 sq. m. *Population,* 404,190. *Products,* sugar, copra, poonac, aloe fibre, and rum.

MEXICO (MEXICAN REPUBLIC), immediately south of the United States, is bordered by United States, Gulf of Mexico, Br. Honduras, Guatemala and the Pacific Ocean. *People,* Indians, mixed races, whites of Spanish descent. *Language,* Spanish. *Religion,* Roman Catholic predominating. *Products,* silver, gold, copper, lead, oil, coal and other minerals, henequen, coffee, rubber, hides, guayule, cattle, sugar. Natural resources are great. *Capital,* Mexico, D.F. *President,* Gen. Lázaro Cárdenas (1934). *Area,* 760,290 sq. m. *Population,* 16,552,722.

MONACO, a principality on the Mediterranean, borders the French Department of Alpes-Maritimes. Revenue comes from the Casino of Monte Carlo. *Capital,* Monaco. *Prince,* Louis II. *Area,* 370 acres. *Population,* 22,994.

MONGOLIA, in Asia between China and the Soviet Union. *Government,* similar to the Soviet form and called the People's Revolutionary Government. A Parliament (the Great Huruldan) elected by universal suffrage (males and females over eighteen years of age) meets once a year. They in turn elect an Executive Committee (the Little Huruldan) which is responsible to them. *Capital*, Ulan Bator Khoto (Urga). *Area*, 558,054 sq. m. *Population*, 6,160,000. *Religion*, Lamaism. *Products*, horses, sheep, camels, oxen, wool, skins, furs, and gold.

MOROCCO, northwestern Africa, nominally a sultanate, has a French protectorate, a Spanish protectorate, and Tangier Zone (internationalized). Boundaries are Mediterranean Sea, Algeria, Atlantic Ocean and Rio de Oro. *Industries*, agriculture and sheep raising. *People*, Arabs and Berbers. *Religion*, Mohammedan. *Capitals*, Rabat (French), Tetuan (Spanish). *Sultan*, Sidi Mohammed acceded Nov. 18, 1927. *Total Area*, 213,350 sq. m. *Total Population*, 5,867,271.

MOZAMBIQUE (Portuguese East Africa). A colony belonging to Portugal, on the southeastern coast of Africa, bounded by Tanganyika, Nyasaland, Rhodesia, Swaziland, and the Union of South Africa. *Government*, administered by a Governor-General, assisted by a Government Council and an Executive Council. *Capital*, Lourenço Marques. *Area*, 297,917 sq. m. *Population*, 4,006,000. *Chief products*, copra, sisal, sugar, cotton, and maize.

NEJD, SULTANATE OF. See **ARABIA.**

NEPAL, a kingdom between Tibet and India, containing Mt. Everest. *People*, Gurkhas (Aryan) and Mongolic groups (Bhotias, Gurungs and Magars). *Religion*, Hinduism, Buddhism. *Maharajad Hiraja*, Tribhubana Bir Bikram. *Capital*, Katmandu. *Area*, 54,000 sq. m. (est.). *Population*, 5,600,000 (est.).

NETHERLAND GUIANA (SURINAM), in northeast South America, bordered by British Guiana, the Atlantic Ocean, French Guiana, and Brazil. *Government*, by a Governor and Council composed of the Governor, as President, and three members, all appointed by the Queen of The Netherlands, and an elected representative body called the "Colonial States." *Capital*, Paramaribo. *Area*, 54,291 sq. m. *Population*, 164,100. *Religion*, chiefly Christian, but much Mohammedanism and Hinduism. *Products*, sugar, bananas, coffee, cocoa, rum, rice, maize, and gold.

NETHERLAND INDIA, in the East Indies belonging to the Dutch, and including Java and Madura, Sumatra, Bangka, Billiton, Riau, Borneo, Celebes Island, Molucca Islands (including New Guinea) and Timor Archipelago, and several smaller islands. *Government*, by a Governor-General assisted by a Council, all appointed by the Queen. *Capital*, Batavia. *Area*, 733,642 sq. m. *Population*, 60,731,025. *Products*, coffee, rice, maize, Cassava, sweet potatoes, soy beans, sugar cane, indigo, capsicum, native rubber, tobacco, oil palms, cocoa, cinchona, tea, and live stock (chiefly horses, cattle, and buffaloes), tin and coal.

NETHERLANDS, THE (HOLLAND), a kingdom of western Europe, bordered by North Sea, Germany and Belgium. Possessions include Netherland India (Java, Sumatra, part of Borneo, Celebes, other islands), Curaçao and Netherland Guiana in South America. *People and Language*, Dutch. *Religion*, Dutch Reformed, Roman Catholic, other Christian, Mohammedan, and Buddhist. *Capital*, Gravenhage (The Hague). *Queen*, Wilhelmina (1890). *Area*, 13,202 sq. m. *Population*, 8,392,102.

NEWFOUNDLAND AND LABRADOR, are British Colonies located east of Canada. *Government*, by Governor and Commissioners. *Governor and Commander-in-Chief*, Vice-Admiral Sir Humphrey Thomas Walwyn (1935). **Newfoundland**—*Capital*, St. John's. *Area*, 42,734 sq. m. *Population*, 284,800. *Industries*, fishing; cod, salmon, lobster, halibut, seal, and caplin. Paper and pulp mills furnish a large income. *Minerals*. The resources are extensive, with iron, copper, gold, and silver found in large deposits. **Labrador,** a dependency of Newfoundland and under the same government, has an *area* of 112,400 sq. m. *Population*, 4,716, many Eskimos.

NEW GUINEA, MANDATED TERRITORY OF, an Australian mandate made up of northeastern New Guinea, the Bismarck Archipelago, and the Solomon Islands. *Government*, under an Administrator of the Territory who is appointed by the Australian Government; the laws of Australia, with local modifications, being applied to these territories. *Capital*, Rabaul. *Area*, 91,000 sq. m. *Population*, 462,571. *Chief products*, coconuts, coffee, cocoa, kapok, tropical fruits, yams, sago, taro. Large mineral deposits are still undeveloped. Gold is mined in the Morobe District.

NEW ZEALAND, a British self-governing dominion, South Pacific, consists of two large islands (North and South) and various small ones. About 1,200 miles east of Australia, New Zealand extends from 35° S. to 46° S. Agricultural, forest and mineral resources are of great value. *Exports*, wool, dairy products, frozen meats, other animal products. *People (except Maoris)*, British. *Language*, English. *Capital*, Wellington. *Governor-General*, Viscount Galway (1935). *Area* (*total*), 103,862 sq. m. *Population*, 1,573,810 (1936).

NICARAGUA, REPUBLIC OF, in Central America, is bordered by Honduras, Caribbean Sea, Costa Rica and Pacific Ocean. *People*, Spanish, Indian, Negro. *Language*, Spanish. *Religion*, Roman Catholic predominant. *Products*, coffee, sugar, bananas, hides, woods, gold, silver. *Capital*, Managua. *President*, Anastasio Somoza (1936). *Area*, 51,660 sq. m. *Population*, 829,700.

NIGERIA, a British Protectorate and Colony on the southwest coast of Africa, bounded by French West Africa, French Equatorial Africa, and Cameroons. *Government*, by a Governor, an Executive Council, and a Legislative Council. The Colony is divided into Northern Provinces with a Chief Commissioner, and Southern Provinces with a Lieutenant-Governor. *Capital*, Lagos. *Area*, 372,674 sq. m. *Population*, 19,928,171. *Religion*, chiefly pagan. *Products*, valuable woods, palm oil, palm kernels, cocoa, tin ore, cotton lint, mahogany, tanned sheep and goat skins, iron, lead, coal, silver, lignite, and manganese.

NORWAY, a European monarchy occupying the western part of the Scandinavian Peninsula, is bordered by Finland, Sweden, Skagerrak, North Sea and Atlantic Ocean. *People and Language*, Norwegian. *Religion*, Evangelical Lutheran. *Resources*, forests, fisheries, water power. *Exports*, canned fish, undressed furs, wood pulp, ship propellers, hydroelectric power. *Capital*, Oslo (Christiania). *King*, Haakon VII (1905). *Area*, 124,984 sq. m. (besides Svalbard, 24,142 est.). *Population*, 2,871,400.

NYASALAND, a British Protectorate in East Central Africa, on the west and south shores of Lake Nyasa, and bounded by Tanganyika, Northern Rhodesia, and Mozambique. *Government*, by a Governor and Commander-in-chief, and an Executive and a Legislative Council. *Capital*, Zomba. *Area*, 37,596 sq. m. *Population*, 1,603,914. *Products*, coffee, tobacco, cotton, tea, and live stock.

OMAN, SULTANATE OF, in southeastern Arabia, is on the Persian Gulf. *People*, Arabs and Negroes. *Religion*, Islam. *Products*, camels, dates, pomegranates, limes, dried fish. *Capital*, Masqat. *Sultan*, Saiyid Said bin Taimur. *Area*, 82,000 sq. m. (est.). *Population*, 500,000 (est.).

PALESTINE (HOLY LAND). The British mandate includes also Trans-Jordan (q.v.). Present-day Palestine is bordered by Syria (a French mandate), Trans-Jordan, Saudi Arabia and Mediterranean Sea. *People*, chiefly Arabs; Jewish colonies growing. *Exports*, wine, soap, olive oil, oranges, lemons. *Capital*, Jerusalem. *High Commissioner*, Lieut.-Gen. Sir Arthur G. Wauchope (1931). *Area*, 10,155 sq. m. *Population*, 1,261,000.

PANAMA, REPUBLIC OF, is bordered by Costa Rica, Caribbean Sea, Colombia and Pacific Ocean, and crossed by Canal Zone. *People*, Spanish, Negroes, Indians. *Language*, Spanish. *Religion*, chiefly Roman Catholic. *Products*, bananas, cacao, coconuts, caoutchouc, coffee, sugar, tobacco, woods, hides, pearl shell, tortoise shell. *Capital*, Panama. *President*, Juan Demostenes Arosemena (1936). *Area*, 29,065 sq. m. *Population*, 483,800 (not including Canal Zone).

PAPUA TERRITORY, a British Protectorate belonging to Australia, in the southeastern part of the Island of Papua or New Guinea. *Government*, by a Lieutenant-Governor and Judge, and a Legislative Council, all appointed by the Governor-General of Australia. *Capital*, Port Moresby. *Area*, 90,540 sq. m. *Population*, 276,366. *Chief products*, copra, sago, rubber, gold, silver, and osmiriduin.

PARAGUAY, REPUBLIC OF, an inland country of South America, is bordered by Bolivia, Brazil, and Argentina. Paraguay River gives access to the sea. *People*, of Indian, Spanish, some Negro, origin. *Language*, Spanish. *Religion*, Roman Catholic. *Exports*, cattle products, yerba, tobacco, cotton. *Capital*, Asuncion. *President*, Dr. Felix Paiva (1937). *Area*, 173,700 sq. m., inclusive of disputed area of about 100,000 sq. m. *Population*, 901,768.

PERU, REPUBLIC OF, on the west coast of South America, is bordered by Ecuador, Colombia, Brazil, Bolivia, Chile and Pacific Ocean. It was the land of the Incas. *People*, Indians, mestizos, whites. *Exports*, petroleum, copper, silver, coffee, sugar, cotton, cinchona, wool, hides. *Capital*, Lima. *President*, Gen. Don O. R. Benavides (1933. Reëlected, 1937). *Area*, 482,258 sq. m. *Population*, 6,237,000.

POLAND (POLISH REPUBLIC), established in November, 1918, includes Russian Poland and parts of East Prussia, Upper Silesia, Galicia, Posen and Lithuania. It is bordered by Baltic Sea, Lithuania, Latvia, Soviet Union, Rumania, Czechoslovakia and Germany. *People*, Slavs and Jews. *Religion*, chiefly Roman Catholic. *Exports*, coal, petroleum, iron and steel, zinc, timber, grains, animal products. *Capital*, Warszawa. *President*, Ignatz Moscicki (1933). *Area*, about 149,915 sq. m. *Population*, 33,418,000.

PORTUGAL (PORTUGUESE REPUBLIC), in the western part of the Iberian Peninsula, is bordered by Spain and Atlantic Ocean. *People and Language*, Portuguese. *Religion*, Roman Catholic. *Exports*, sardines, cork, olive oil, resin, planks, hides, chemicals, wool. *Capital*, Lisboa (Lisbon). *President*, Marshal Antonio Carmona (1926. Reëlected, 1928 and 1935). *Area*, 35,490 sq. m. *Population*, 6,826,000. *Area of Colonies*, 812,606 sq. m. *Population of Colonies*, 8,915,705.

REUNION, a French Island in the Indian Ocean east of Madagascar. *Government* by a Governor, a Privy Council and a Council-General. *Capital*, Saint Denis. *Area*, 970 sq. m. *Population*, 197,933. *Chief Products*, sugar, rum, manioc, vanilla, tapioca, and essences. *Chief Industries*, production of spirits and sugar. Forests cover a large acreage.

RHODESIA, NORTHERN, a British Colony on a high plateau in southern Africa. Bounded by Belgian Congo, Mozambique, Nyasaland, Tanganyika, Southern Rhodesia and Angola. *Government*, by a Governor, an Executive Council and a Legislative Council. *Capital*, Lusaka. *Area*, 290,320 sq. m. *Population*, 1,393,258, mostly natives. *Products*, tobacco, wheat, coffee, maize, cattle, gold, silver, lead, zinc, copper, vanadium and coal.

RHODESIA, SOUTHERN, a British colony lying south of Northern Rhodesia in southern Africa. *Government*, by a Governor and Commander-in-Chief, an Executive Council and a Legislature. *Capital*, Salisbury. *Area*, 150,354 sq. m. *Population*, 1,258,860. *Products*, maize, tobacco, legumes, ground nuts, lemons, oranges and other fruits, gold, coal, chrome ore, and asbestos.

RUMANIA (ROMÂNIA), a kingdom in the Balkans, Southeastern Europe, is bordered by Czechoslovakia, Poland, Soviet Union, Black Sea, Bulgaria, Yugoslavia and Hungary. *People and Language*, Rumanian, Magyars, German, Jews, and various Slavic groups. *Religion*, Orthodox Church predominant. *Exports*, grain, petroleum, timber. *Capital*, Bucuresti (Bucharest). *King*, Carol II., acceded June 8, 1930. *Area*, 122,282 sq. m. *Population*, 19,013,363.

RUSSIA. See **SOVIET UNION.**

ST. HELENA, a British Island west of the coast of Angola, in the South Atlantic Ocean. *Government*, by a Governor and an Executive Council. *Capital*, Jamestown. *Area*, 47 sq. m. *Population*, 4,170. *Exports*, fiber, twine and rope.

SALVADOR, EL, is bordered by Guatemala, Honduras and Pacific Ocean. *People*, Indians, mixed races, whites. *Language*, Spanish. *Religion*, Roman Catholic. *Exports*, coffee, sugar, balsam, woods, hides. *Capital*, San Salvador. *President*, Gen. Maximiliano H. Martínez (1931. Reëlected 1935, 1939). *Area*, 13,176 sq. m. *Population*, 1,574,500.

SAN MARINO, a tiny republic in the Apennines, surrounded by Italy, is called the oldest state in Europe.

Capital, San Marino. *Government*, Great Council of 60. *Exports*, wine, cattle, building stone. *Area*, 38 sq. m. *Population*, 14,170.

SARAWAK, on the northwest coast of Borneo (Dutch), adjoining Brunei, is an independent state under the protection of Great Britain. *Government*, administered by a Rajah. *Capital*, Kuching. *Area*, 42,000 sq. m. *Population*, 475,000. *Exports*, sago flour, plantation rubber, jelutong, pepper, gutta-percha, benzine, crude oil, kerosene, rattan and fish.

SAUDI ARABIA, KINGDOM OF. See **ARABIA.**

SERBS, CROATS AND SLOVENES, KINGDOM OF. See **YUGOSLAVIA.**

SEYCHELLES AND DEPENDENCIES, consisting of ninety-two small islands, belong to the British and are located about five hundred miles northeast of Madagascar in the Indian Ocean. *Government*, by a Governor and Commander-in-Chief, an Executive Council and a Legislative Council. *Capital*, Victoria. *Area*, 156 sq. m. *Population*, 29,406. *Products*, coconuts, cinnamon, patchouli, essential oils, mangrove bark, phosphate, live stock and fish.

SIAM, a kingdom of southeastern Asia, is bordered by Burma (in British India), French Indo-China, Gulf of Siam, and Federated Malay States. *Religion*, Buddhist. *Exports*, rice, teak, tin. *Capital*, Bangkok. *King*, Ananda Mahidol (Mar. 2, 1935). *Area*, 200,148 sq. m. *Population*, 14,464,489.

SOUTHWEST AFRICA, in southwestern Africa, is bounded by Angola, Bechuanaland, Union of South Africa, and the Atlantic Ocean. *Government*, as a mandate, by Union of South Africa. An Administrator, deriving his authority from the Governor-General of the Union of South Africa, is aided by an Executive Committee and an Advisory Council. *Capital*, Windhoek. *Area*, 322,393 sq. m. *Population*, 266,930, principally natives. *Products*, live stock, dairy products, diamonds, copper, lead, tin and vanadium.

SOVIET UNION (UNION OF SOVIET SOCIALIST REPUBLICS). This new type of federation replaces the Russian Empire, overthrown in March, 1917, the Soviets coming into power in November, 1917. A new constitution was adopted in December, 1936, in accordance with which the U.S.S.R. consists of eleven member republics: **Russian Soviet Federated Socialist Republic (R.S.F.S.R.)**, which includes Great Russia, various autonomous states, and Siberia to the Pacific Ocean; **White Russian S.S.R.**, in the southwest, bordering Poland; **Ukrainian S.S.R.**, in the southwest, bordering Poland and the Black Sea; three Transcaucasian republics—**Armenian S.S.R., Azerbaijan S.S.R.**, and **Georgian S.S.R.; Turcoman S.S.R.** in Asia, east of the Caspian Sea and touching Persia, Afghanistan, Uzbek and Kazakh; **Uzbek S.S.R.**, east of Turcoman; **Tadzhik S.S.R.**, bordered by Uzbek, Kirghiz, Afghanistan and Sinkiang; **Kazakh S.S.R.**, extending from the Caspian Sea to China and Mongolia; and **Kirghiz S.S.R.**, between Tadzhik and Kazakh. These major divisions include autonomous areas and districts. *People*, Slavs most numerous; many others. *Language*, Russian, others. Decrees are published in six—Russian, Ukrainian, White Russian, Georgian, Armenian, Turkish-Tatar. *Products and Resources*, great and varied. Include grains, timber, furs, petroleum, gold, platinum, coal and iron. *Capital*, Moskva (Moscow). *Chairman of the Council of People's Commissars*, V. M. Molotov. *Area*, 8,241,921 sq. m. *Population*, 165,768,400.

SPAIN, a republic of southwestern Europe, is bordered by Atlantic Ocean, France, Portugal, Mediterranean Sea, Strait and fortress of Gibraltar. *Religion*, Roman Catholic. *Exports*, olives, oranges, wine, quicksilver, minerals, cork, flax, cotton goods. *Capital*, Madrid. *Area*, European, 195,010 sq. m.; of colonies, 128,696 sq. m. *Population*, European, 24,583,096; of colonies, 934,-686. Canary Is.—*Area*, 2,807 sq. m. *Population*, 574,789, and Balearic Is.—*Area*, 1,935 sq. m. *Population*, 370,-853, Canaries and Balearics included with Spain proper.

STRAITS SETTLEMENT, a British Crown Colony made up of Singapore Settlement (including Cocos and Christmas Islands), Penang, Malacca, and Labuan. *Government*, by a Governor, an Executive Council and a Legislative Council. *Capital*, Singapore, a free port of

call for most of the steamers en route from Europe to the Orient, also the world's greatest rubber market. *Area*, 1,600 sq. m. *Population*, 1,059,122. *Religion*, Mohammedan. *Products*, coconuts, pineapples, fruit, rice, rubber, tobacco. *Exports*, tin, rubber, spices, sago, rattan, and preserved fruits.

SVALBARD (SPITSBERGEN), an archipelago belonging to Norway and situated due north of that country at latitude 79° north. The principal islands composing it are West Spitsbergen, or Mainland; North East Land; Prince Charles Foreland; Edge Island; and Bear Island. *Government*, by a Governor appointed by the King. *Capital*, Longyearbyen. *Area*, 24,142 sq. m. *Population*, 2,415.

SWEDEN, a European kingdom in the eastern part of the Scandinavian Peninsula, is bordered by Finland, Gulf of Bothnia, Baltic Sea, Kattegat, and Norway. *Religion*, Lutheran. *Products*, timber, paper pulp, dairy products, iron and steel, machinery. *Capital*, Stockholm. *King*, Gustav V. (1907). *Area*, 173,105 sq. m. *Population*, 6,233,100.

SWITZERLAND. The Swiss Confederation, a republic in the Alps, is bordered by Germany, Austria, Italy and France. It originated August 1, 1291. *People*, Swiss. *Languages*, German, French, Italian, Romansh. *Religion*, Protestant, Roman Catholic. *Exports*, dairy products, salt, machinery, clocks, watches. Hydroelectric power is developed. *Capital*, Bern. *President for 1939*, Philippe Etter. *Area*, 15,940 sq. m. *Population*, 4,066,400.

SYRIA, a mandate of France in Asia Minor, is bordered by Turkey, Iraq, Arabia, Trans-Jordan, Palestine and Mediterranean Sea. Consists of the republics of Syria, Lebanon, Latakia, and Djebel Druze. *Religion*, Sunni Moslem. *Capital*, Beyrouth (Beirut). *High Commissioner*, M. le Comte de Martel (1933). *Area*, 57,460 sq. m. *Population*, 3,130,100.

TAIWAN (FORMOSA), an island belonging to Japan and located north of the Philippines. *Government*, by a Governor-General appointed by Japan and assisted by a Council. *Capital*, Taihoku. *Area*, 13,836 sq. m. *Population*, 5,212,719. *Language*, official, Japanese; but Chinese most frequently spoken. *Products*, rice, sweet potatoes, sugar, tea, jute, live stock, fish, flour, tobacco, glass, bricks, spirits, gold, copper, silver and coal.

TANGANYIKA TERRITORY, a British Mandate, is on the eastern coast of Africa, bounded by Mozambique, Northern Rhodesia, Belgian Congo, Uganda, Kenya, and Indian Ocean. *Government*, by a Governor, an Executive Council and a Legislative Council. *Capital*, Dar es Salaam. *Area*, 363,548 sq. m. *Population*, 4,988,338. *Products*, cotton, coffee, sesame, beeswax, groundnuts, grains, valuable woods, gold, diamonds, tin, mica, red ochre, and salt.

TANGIER ZONE, a neutralized and demilitarized zone in Africa at the western end of the Mediterranean Sea. *Government*, by an Administrator and Assistant Administrators; the Sultan is represented by a Mendoub. *Area*, 225 sq. m. *Population*, 65,000. *Official Languages*, French, Spanish and Arabic. *Products*, wheat, barley, cigarettes, fish and canned goods.

TANNU-TUVA, an independent republic northwest of Mongolia, with the Soviet Union bounding it on the north, east and west. *Government*, socialistic in form. *Capital*, Kysylchoto. *Area*, 63,690 sq. m. *Population*, 62,000. Grazing is the chief occupation. *Exports*, hair, hides and wool. Gold and asbestos are found.

TRANS-JORDAN, bounded by Palestine, Syria, Saudi Arabia, and Iraq, is part of the British Palestine Mandate. *Industries*, agriculture and sheep raising. *Capital*, Amman. *King*, Amir Abdullah Ibn Hussein (1921). *Area*, 16,220 sq. m. *Population*, 325,000.

TRINIDAD AND TOBAGO, a British Colony located northwest of Venezuela. *Government*, by a Governor, an Executive Council and a Legislative Council. *Capital*, Port of Spain. *Area*, 1,976 sq. m. *Population*, 432,058. *Products*, coconuts, cocoa, asphalt, petroleum, copra, kerosene, molasses, sugar and rum.

TUNISIA, a French Protectorate on the northern coast of Africa, bounded on the north and east by the Mediterranean Sea and on the south and west by Libya and Algeria. *Government*, by a Resident-General and

a ministry of eleven heads. *Capital*, Tunis. *Area*, 48,300 sq. m. *Population*, 2,410,692. Some Europeans, but mostly Arabs and Bedouins. *Products*, oranges, lemons and other citrus fruits, wheat, barley, almonds, pistachios, cork, henna, olives, live stock, woolen goods, leather and leather goods, pottery, sardines and tunny, phosphate, iron ore and lead ore.

TURKEY (THE REPUBLIC OF), in southwestern Asia and southeastern Europe, is bordered by Greece, Bulgaria, Black Sea, Soviet Union, Persia, Iraq, Syria, Mediterranean Sea, Aegean Sea. *People and Language*, Turkish. *Resources*, minerals, timber. *Exports*, tobacco, cereals, textiles, cotton, fruits. *Capital*, Ankara (Angora). *President*, General Ismet Inonu (1938). *Area*, 294,415 sq. m. *Population*, 16,188,800.

UGANDA, a British Protectorate in the central part of East Africa, bordered by Anglo-Egyptian Sudan, Kenya, Lake Victoria and Tanganyika Territory, and Belgian Congo. *Government*, by a Governor and Commander-in-Chief, a Legislative Council and an Executive Council, with native chiefs and kings conducting government in their own provinces under the Governor. *Capital*, Entebbe. *Area*, 93,981 sq. m. *Population*, 3,640,638. *Products*, cotton, oil seeds, coffee, tin ore, hides, ivory, tobacco and sugar.

UNION OF SOUTH AFRICA, one of the self-governing dominions of the British Empire, includes **Cape of Good Hope, Natal, Transvaal** and **Orange Free State.** It is remarkable for mineral production, with gold, diamonds, platinum, coal, tin and copper. *People*, Dutch, British, Negroes. *Languages*, English, Dutch. *Capitals*, Pretoria and Capetown. *Governor-General*, Hon. Patrick Duncan (1936). *Prime Minister*, General J. B. M. Hertzog. *Area*, 472,550 sq. m. *Population*, 9,479,985. **Southwest Africa**, a mandate, borders the Atlantic and extends from Orange River to Angola. *Area*, 322,393 sq. m. *Population*, 266,930.

URUGUAY, REPUBLIC OF, in southeastern South America, is bordered by Brazil, Atlantic Ocean and Argentina. *People*, of Spanish descent. *Language*, Spanish. *Religion*, Roman Catholic. *Products*, grains, live-stock, animal products. *Capital*, Montevideo. *President*, Gen. Alfredo Baldomir (1938). *Area*, 72,153 sq. m. *Population*, 2,020,040.

VATICAN CITY, the seat of the Papacy, is situated in Roma, Italy. It has an area of 0.17 sq. m. and a population of 1,025. Vatican City constitutes a tiny state in which the Pope exercises sovereignty, assisted by a Governor. *Supreme Pontiff*, Pius XII. (Eugenio Pacelli), elected as successor of Piux XI, March 2, 1939.

VENEZUELA, UNITED STATES OF, a republic on the northern coast of South America, is bordered by Caribbean Sea, British Guiana, Brazil and Colombia, and crossed by the Orinoco River. Agriculture and cattle raising are chief industries. *Language*, Spanish. *Religion*, Roman Catholic. *Products*, coffee, cacao, balata, cattle, hides, petroleum. *Capital*, Caracas. *President*, General Eleazar Lopez Contreras (1935). *Area*, 352,051 sq. m. *Population*, 3,291,442.

WINDWARD ISLANDS, a British Colony, composed of Grenada, St. Vincent, the Grenadines and St. Lucia Islands. *Government*, by a Governor and Commander-in-Chief. Each island has its own institutions, but there is a common Court of Appeal. *Capital*, St. George's. *Area*, 516 sq. m. *Population*, 185,344. *Products*, cotton, sugar, molasses, rum, cocoa, arrowroot, spices, peanuts, fruits and vegetables. The Sea Island cotton grown here is exceptionally good.

YUGOSLAVIA, or **KINGDOM OF THE SERBS, CROATS AND SLOVENES**, is a European kingdom in the Balkans, bordered by Austria, Hungary, Rumania, Bulgaria, Greece, Albania, Adriatic Sea and Italy. *People*, Slavs. *Resources*, coal, iron, copper and other minerals, forest products, tobacco, silk, cattle. *Capital*, Beograd (Belgrade). *King*, Peter II (1934). *Area*, 95,551 sq. m. *Population*, 14,513,706.

ZANZIBAR, a large coralline island off the coast of Tanganyika, Africa. With the island of Pemba it forms a British Protectorate. *Government*, by a British Resident, Executive and Legislative Councils, and the Sultan. *Capital*, Zanzibar. *Area*, 640 sq. m.; Pemba, 380 sq. m. *Population*, Zanzibar, 137,741; Pemba, 97,687. *Religion*, Mohammedan. *Products*, cloves (world's largest supply), rope, copra, coconut and sesame oil, jewelry and mats.

Population of the Principal Foreign Cities

Important Physical Features of the World

MOUNTAINS (Cont.)

Page	Index	Name	Location
15	F 14	San Francisco Mts. (12,611 ft.)	Ariz.
18	M 12	Sangre de Cristo Mts.	Colo.
18	P 8	San Juan Mts.	Colo.
41	G 6	San Mateo Mts	N. M.
18	N 4	San Miguel Mts.	Colo.
38	B 11	Santa Rosa Mts.	Nev.
18	J 9	Sawatch Mts.	Colo.
17	L 18	Sentinel Peak	Calif.
17	C 6	Shasta, Mt. (14,161 ft.)	Calif.
55	H 10	Shenandoah Mts.	Va.
38	I 11	Shoshone Mts.	Nev.
59	Q 14	Sierra Madre	Wyo.
71	Q 21	Sierra Madre	Mex.
71	C 7	Sierra Madre Occidental	Mex.
91	L 10	Sierra Morena	Spain
12	J 5	Sierra Nevada	N. Am.
91	O 13	Sierra Nevada	Spain
17	B 4	Siskiyou Mts.	Calif.
41	J 9	Socorro Mts.	N. M.
78	O 15	Solimana, Mt.	Peru
80	G 3	Sorata, Mt. (21,276 ft.)	Bol.
111	M 8	Southern Alps	N. Z.
98	E 18	Stanovoi Mts.	Asia
38	G 8	Stillwater Mts.	Nev.
101	K 24	Sulaiman Range	Baluch.
59	O 7	Table Mts.	Wyo.
31	E 2	Taconic Mts.	Mass.
99	H 4	Taurus Mts.	Asia Minor
17	K 18	Telescope Peak	Calif.
9	.....	Terror, Mt.	S. Polar Reg.
59	F 2	Teton Range (Mt. Hayden or Gr. Teton, 13,747 ft.)	Wyo.
92	G 4	Teutoburger Wald	Ger.
91	J 10	Toledo, Montes de	Spain
95	J 19	Transylvanian Alps	Rum.
41	E 15	Truchas Peaks (13,306 ft.)	N. M.
103	F 10	Tsin-Ling Shan	China
15	N 16	Tucson Mts	Ariz.
44	D 13	Turtle Mts.	N. Dak.
53	F 17	Uintah Mts.	Utah
29	P 19	Unaka Mts.	N. C.
27	P 19	Unaka Mts.	Tenn.
18	L 2	Uncompahgre Plateau,	Colo.
83	D 23	Ural Mts	Europe
97	H 8	Valdai Hills (1,100 ft.)	Sov. Un.
94	J 15	Vesuvius, Mt. (vol. 3,891 ft.)	Italy
38	F 3	Virginia Range	Nev.
90	I 22	Vosges Mts.	France
47	E 23	Wallowa Mts.	Ore.
53	F 14	Wasatch Mts.	Utah
39	H 16	Washington, Mt. (6,288 ft.)	N. H.
17	P 5	Waterman, Mt.	Calif.
98	P 10	Western Ghats	Asia
93	J 13	Wetterhorn (12,166 ft.)	Switz.
39	G 16	White Mts	N. H.
17	K 15	Whitney, Mt. (14,496 ft.)	Calif.
46	L 7	Wichita Mts.	Okla.
87	K 21	Wicklow Mts.	Ir. Fr. State
59	I 6	Wind River Range	Wyo.
108	G 17	Witwaters Berg.	U. of S. Afr.
60	K 16	Wrangell, Mt. (14,005 ft.)	Alaska
108	B 20	Zoutpansberg Mts.	U. of S. Afr.
41	G 4	Zuni Buttes	N. M.

OCEANS (O) and SEAS (S)

Page	Index	Name	Location
83	O 12	Adriatic (S)	Europe
83	Q 15	Aegean (S)	Europe
9	.....	Antarctic (O)	S. Pol. Reg.
98	O 8	Arabian (S)	Asia
109	J 9	Arafura (S)	Oceania
9	.....	Arctic (O)	N. Pol. Reg.
10	B 5	Arctic (O)	World
10	I 17	Atlantic (O), N.	World
10	N 19	Atlantic (O), S.	World
97	N 10	Azov (S)	Sov. Un.
83	H 12	Baltic (S)	Europe
109	I 7	Banda (S)	Oceania
10	D 23	Barents (S)	World
9	.....	Beaufort (S)	N. Pol. Reg.
9	.....	Bellingshausen (S)	S. Pol. Reg.
11	B 1	Bering (S)	N. Am.
83	N 18	Black (S)	Europe
10	K 15	Caribbean (S)	World
83	M 24	Caspian (S)	Europe
109	H 6	Celebs (S)	Oceania
109	L 13	Coral (S)	Oceania

OCEANS (O) and SEAS (S) (Cont.)

Page	Index	Name	Location
100	O 11	Dead (S), 1,292 ft. below sea level	Palestine
103	L 20	East China (S)	Asia
100	H 13	Galilee (S)	Palestine
100	.....	Gennesaret (S), see Galilee (S).	
10	C 20	Greenland (S)	World
10	M 1	Indian (O)	World
104	M 9	Inland (S)	Japan
83	Q 12	Ionian (S)	Europe
83	H 6	Irish (S)	Europe
98	I 21	Japan (S)	Asia
109	I 4	Java (S)	Oceania
98	C 12	Kara (S)	Asia
83	P 16	Marmora (S)	Europe
83	Q 9	Mediterranean (S)	Europe
63	M 17	Mindanao (S)	P. I.
9	.....	Nordenskiöld (S)	N. Pol. Reg.
83	H 8	North (S)	Europe
98	E 20	Okhotsk (S)	Asia
10	I 8	Pacific (O), N.	World
10	N 11	Pacific (O), S.	World
105	G 21	Red (S)	Africa
9	.....	Ross (S)	S. Pol. Reg.
17	P 22	Salton (S), about 200 ft. below sea level and falling 4 ft. yearly	Calif.
98	P 19	South China (S)	Asia
63	O 9	Sulu (S)	P. I.
63	M 21	Surigao (S)	P. I.
100	.....	Tiberias (S), see Galilee (S)	
109	K 7	Timor (S)	Oceania
83	P 10	Tyrrhenian (S)	Europe
9	.....	Weddell (S)	S. Pol. Reg.
83	C 17	White (S)	Europe
98	J 19	Yellow (S)	Asia

RIVERS

Page	Index	Name	Location
14	M 8	Alabama	Ala.
65	M 15	Albany	Can.
48	J 5	Allegheny	Pa.
21	M 18	Altamaha	Ga.
75	E 12	Amazon (length 3,900 m.)	Brazil
98	G 19	Amur	Asia
20	O 12	Apalachicola	Fla.
55	M 14	Appomattox	Va.
75	G 15	Araguaye	S. Am.
16	G 9	Arkansas	Ark.
26	M 9	Arkansas	Kan.
46	B 9	Arkansas	Okla.
69	Q 14	Assiniboine	Man.
65	K 7	Athabaska	Can.
20	G 21	Banana	Fla.
67	K 19	Batiscan	Que.
70	I 22	Beaver	Alta.
82	G 16	Bermejo	Arg.
34	L 9	Big Black	Miss.
36	N 17	Bighorn	Mont.
51	J 24	Big Sioux	S. D.
50	J 19	Black	S. C.
58	F 15	Black	Wis.
14	H 8	Black Warrior	Ala.
102	G 23	Brahmaputra	India
52	J 21	Brazos	Tex.
50	E 11	Broad	S. C.
95	D 16	Bug	Poland
20	L 15	Caloosahatchee	Fla.
46	J 12	Canadian	Okla.
43	K 13	Cape Fear	N. C.
25	H 18	Cedar	Iowa
21	M 3	Chattahoochee	Ga.
51	H 8	Cheyenne	S. D.
58	D 13	Chippewa	Wis.
43	D 21	Chowan	N. C.
65	K 9	Churchill	Can.
46	E 9	Cimarron	Okla.
86	M 13	Clyde	Scot.
12	K 4	Colorado (length 1,650 m.)	U. S.
52	I 16	Colorado (length 650 m.)	Tex.
12	C 4	Columbia (length 1,270 m.)	U. S.
105	K 15	Congo (length 2,900 m.)	Africa
13	F 23	Connecticut	U. S.
14	I 15	Coosa	Ala.
50	N 12	Coosawhatchie	S. C.
60	L 16	Copper	Alaska
27	J 16	Cumberland	Ky.
27	L 9	Cumberland	Tenn.
76	I 24	Cuyuni	Venez.

RIVERS (Cont.)

Page	Index	Name	Location
83	N 16	Danube (length 1,725 m.)	Europe
110	N 18	Darling	Australia
40	C 9	Delaware	N. J.
28	R 22	Delta of the Mississippi	La.
106	D 14	Delta of the Nile	Egypt
47	K 10	Deschutes	Ore.
25	J 11	Des Moines	Iowa
32	Q 22	Detroit	Mich.
83	K 17	Dnieper (length 1,400 m.)	Europe
83	L 16	Dniester (length 800 m.)	Europe
97	M 13	Don (length 1,100 m.)	Sov. Un.
91	G 5	Douro	Spain
95	I 10	Drava	Yugoslavia
97	E 14	Dvina	Sov. Un.
91	G 15	Ebro	Spain
50	K 13	Edisto	S. C.
92	I 11	Elbe (length 700 m.)	Ger.
95	H 6	Enns	Austria
20	M 2	Escambia	Fla.
78	A 3	Esmeraldas	Ecuador
79	C 7	Essequibo	Brit. Gu.
99	E 16	Euphrates	Iraq
21	O 6	Flint	Georgia
65	L 4	Fraser (length 695 m.)	Can.
68	B 9	French	Ont.
98	N 12	Ganges (length 1,455 m.)	Asia
90	O 10	Garonne	France
35	L 14	Gasconade	Mo.
67	L 9	Gatineau	Que.
42	P 7	Genesee	N. Y.
15	M 4	Gila	Ariz.
32	N 12	Grand	Mich.
15	D 10	Grand Canyon of the Colorado	Ariz.
40	N 11	Great Egg	N. J.
53	L 20	Green	Utah
91	N 9	Guadalquiver	Spain
91	L 6	Guadiana	Spain
80	E 14	Guapore	Bolivia
19	K 7	Housatonic	Conn.
42	P 24	Hudson (length 315 m.)	N. Y.
38	D 8	Humboldt	Nev.
98	L 18	Hwang-ho (length 2,700 m.)	Asia
23	J 8	Illinois	Ill.
20	H 21	Indian	Fla.
102	C 7	Indus	India
25	E 12	Iowa	Iowa
102	N 21	Irawadi	India
44	L 18	James	N. D.
51	J 20	James	S. D.
55	N 15	James	Va.
100	K 12	Jordan	Palestine
102	E 10	Jumna	India
48	N 12	Juniata	Pa.
75	F 9	Jurua	S. Am.
32	P 12	Kalamazoo	Mich.
57	I 4	Kanawha	W. Va.
23	E 21	Kankakee	Ill.
26	G 18	Kansas (Kaw)	Kan.
29	K 8	Kennebec	Me.
27	E 16	Kentucky	Ky.
36	C 2	Kootenay	Mont.
60	K 7	Kuskokwim	Alaska
98	E 17	Lena	Asia
108	B 18	Limpopo	U. of S. Afr.
15	F 14	Little Colorado	Ariz.
44	L 2	Little Missouri	N. D.
90	J 9	Loire	France
37	K 18	Loup	Neb.
65	F 5	Mackenzie (length 2,525 m.)	Can.
75	F 11	Madeira	S. Am.
75	C 5	Magdalena	S. Am.
78	H 6	Marañon	Peru
95	M 20	Maritsa	Bulgaria
90	G 17	Marne	France
103	O 7	Mekong	Siam
92	A 24	Memel	Ger.
103	O 3	Menam	Siam
58	O 8	Menominee	Wis.
39	N 13	Merrimack	N. H.
90	E 19	Meuse	France
45	N 6	Miami	Ohio
36	D 16	Milk	Mont.
33	M 6	Minnesota	Minn.
66	F 9	Miramichi	N. B.
12	I 15	Mississippi (length 2,495 m.)	U. S.
12	E 11	Missouri (length, 2,945 m.)	U. S.
42	M 19	Mohawk	N. Y.
48	R 3	Monongahela	Pa.
95	K 13	Morava	Yugoslavia

RIVERS (Cont.)

Page	Index	Name	Location
90	H 21	Moselle	France
44	F 9	Mouse	N. D.
110	O 17	Murrumbidgee	Australia
40	E 11	Musconetcong	N. J.
32	L 14	Muskegon	Mich.
45	L 16	Muskingum	Ohio
82	R 11	Negro	Arg.
69	G 16	Nelson	Man.
43	H 16	Neuse	N. C.
42	L 3	Niagara	N. Y.
68	N 13	Niagara	Ont.
105	I 8	Niger (length 2,600 m.)	Africa
105	F 18	Nile (length 4,000 m.)	Africa
37	E 12	Niobrara	Neb.
59	L 22	North Platte	Wyo.
69	J 3	North Saskatchewan	Sask.
98	D 11	Ob	Sov. Un.
20	C 7	Ocilla	Fla.
21	L 13	Ocmulgee	Ga.
21	I 15	Oconee	Ga.
92	F 13	Oder	Ger.
21	J 21	Ogeechee	Ga.
13	J 17	Ohio (length 1,283 m.)	U. S.
108	K 5	Orange	U. of S. Afr.
75	C 8	Orinoco	S. Am.
35	K 12	Osage	Mo.
42	K 14	Oswego	N. Y.
68	B 17	Ottawa (length 690 m.)	Ont.
28	B 11	Ouachita	La.
43	H 20	Pamlico	N. C.
75	I 13	Paraguay	S. Am.
75	L 12	Paraná	S. Am.
34	P 21	Pascagoula	Miss.
40	E 17	Passaic	N. J.
30	G 14	Patapsco	Md.
70	F 17	Peace	Alta.
34	K 13	Pearl	Miss.
52	G 6	Pecos	Tex.
50	E 19	Pee Dee	S. C.
29	K 15	Penobscot	Me.
20	M 1	Perdido	Fla.
75	M 13	Plata, La	S. Am.
37	L 12	Platte	Neb.
94	D 7	Po	Italy
55	D 16	Potomac	Va.
75	F 9	Purús	S. Am.
33	C 13	Rainy	Minn.
55	I 15	Rappahannock	Va.
40	G 16	Raritan	N. J.
12	M 11	Red	U. S.
13	D 12	Red, of the North	U. S.
37	O 15	Republican	Neb.
83	L 9	Rhine	Europe
90	N 19	Rhône	France
12	O 8	Rio Grande	U. S.
43	D 18	Roanoke	N. C.
23	D 10	Rock	Ill.
28	F 4	Sabine	La.
17	F 5	Sacramento	Calif.
67	F 23	Saguenay	Que.
29	I 21	St. Croix	Me.
58	A 11	St. Croix	Wis.
16	C 21	St. Francis	Ark.
66	E 4	St. John	N. B.
20	C 16	St. Johns	Fla.
24	A 13	St. Joseph	Mich.
24	D 21	St. Joseph of Maumee	Ind.
65	N 20	St. Lawrence (length 2,150 m.)	Can.
21	P 20	St. Marys	Ga.
67	J 17	St. Maurice	Que.
49	J 21	Sakonnet	R. I.
22	I 5	Salmon	Idaho
15	K 16	Salt	Ariz.
50	E 6	Saluda	S. C.
23	H 10	Sangamon	Ill.
17	J 9	San Joaquin	Calif.
72	L 14	San Juan	Cen. Am.
50	K 16	Santee	S. C.
90	L 19	Saône	France
65	M 10	Saskatchewan (length 1,205 m.)	Can.
95	J 11	Sava	Yugoslavia
89	O 5	Scheldt	Bel.
48	L 20	Schuylkill	Pa.
45	L 12	Scioto	Ohio
90	G 12	Seine	France
87	K 13	Shannon	Ir. Fr. State
55	G 12	Shenandoah	Va.
32	N 19	Shiawassee	Mich.
70	C 21	Slave	Alta.
22	H 3	Snake (length 940 m.)	Idaho
75	E 9	Solimões	S. Am.
90	F 14	Somme	France
18	H 14	South Platte	Colo.
37	L 4	South Platte	Neb.
92	G 13	Spree	Ger.

RIVERS (Cont.)

Page	Index	Name	Location
48	E 18	Susquehanna	Pa.
20	E 11	Suwannee	Fla.
91	J 6	Tagus	Portugal
14	I 19	Tallapoosa	Ala.
60	I 14	Tanana	Alaska
75	F 13	Tapajoz	S. Am.
44	F 18	Tar	N. C.
85	D 15	Tees	England
13	K 18	Tennessee	U. S.
28	G 12	Tensas	La
85	L 22	Thames	Eng
94	H 11	Tiber	Italy
99	I 17	Tigris	Iraq
24	E 11	Tippecanoe	Ind.
95	H 13	Tisza (Theiss)	Hungary
75	F 17	Tocantins	S. Am.
52	G 21	Trinity	Tex.
38	G 3	Truckee	Nev.
85	A 13	Tweed	Eng.
85	C 14	Tyne	Eng.
97	L 21	Ural (length 1,400 m.)	Sov. Un.
75	L 13	Uruguay	S. Am.
108	I 15	Vaal	U. of S. Afr.
95	M 15	Vardar	Greece
95	C 11	Vistula (length 630 m.)	Pol.
97	K 18	Volga (length 2,300 m.)	Sov. Un.
24	G 8	Wabash	Ind.
50	K 22	Waccamaw	S. C.
92	G 14	Wartha	Ger.
95	D 10	Wartha	Pol.
46	H 3	Washita	Okla.
50	D 14	Wateree	S. C.
92	F 6	Weser	Ger.
16	K 16	White	Ark.
24	M 9	White	Ind.
51	L 12	White	S. D.
47	H 6	Willamette	Ore.
69	P 17	Winnipeg	Man.
54	F 8	Winooski	Vt.
58	H 19	Wisconsin	Wis.
43	G 8	Yadkin	N. C.
56	J 13	Yakima	Wash.
103	H 17	Yangtze-Kiang (length 3,100 m.)	China
34	J 8	Yazoo	Miss.
...	.....	Yellow, see Hwang-ho.	
36	J 18	Yellowstone	Mont.
98	D 13	Yenesei	Asia
55	N 19	York	Va.
48	R 5	Youghiogheny	Pa.
60	J 6	Yukon (length 2,300 m.)	Alaska
105	O 18	Zambezi (length 1,600 m.)	Africa

SOUNDS

Page	Index	Name	Location
43	D 21	Albemarle	N. C.
49	P 9	Block Island	R. I.
28	P 22	Breton	La.
28	N 22	Chandeleur	La.
42	G 9	Long Island	N. Y.
65	C 10	Melville	Can.
34	R 20	Mississippi	Miss.
31	O 25	Nantucket	Mass.
60	H 7	Norton	Alaska
43	H 23	Pamlico	N. C.
56	H 8	Puget	Wash
20	J 23	St. Lucie	Fla.
31	O 22	Vineyard	Mass.

STRAITS

Page	Index	Name	Location
60	F 4	Bering	Alaska
94	I 4	Bonifacio	Italy
65	D 19	Davis	Can.
10	F 18	Denmark	World
85	M 24	Dover	Eng.
73	D 4	Florida	W. Ind.
70	P 11	Georgia	B. C.
91	P 9	Gibraltar	Spain
70	K 6	Hecate	B. C.
65	G 17	Hudson	Can.
56	E 3	Juan de Fuca	Wash.
32	G 16	Mackinac	Mich.
66	H 15	Northumberland	N. S.
101	Q 11	Ormuz	Persia
94	K 24	Otranto	Italy
98	N 19	Taiwan	Asia
98	G 20	Tatar	Asia
98	J 20	Tsushima	Asia

COURTESY OF THE SWISS FEDERAL RAILWAYS. PHOTO BY KERN, LAUSANNE

THE PICTURESQUE ISLAND OF SALAGNON NEAR MONTREUX ON THE LAKE OF GENEVA, SWITZERLAND. A FAVORITE ABODE OF ARTISTS AND WRITERS

COURTESY OF THE LACKAWANNA RAILROAD

THE DELAWARE WATER GAP NEAR STROUDSBURG, PENNSYLVANIA. THE STEEP MOUNTAIN SIDES RISE 1,400 FEET ABOVE THE DELAWARE RIVER

Illustrated Gazetteer of Cities and Towns of the World

This Gazetteer includes cities, towns and villages of the United States of over five hundred inhabitants and a large proportion of incorporated places throughout the world with a population exceeding ten thousand inhabitants. Numerous villages of smaller size have also been included on account of their historical, geographical and literary significance. Population figures are taken from the latest government censuses or, when it seemed advisable, from later reliable estimates and returns. Spellings of all city names are in accordance with the local official form. The important railroad lines that serve American cities and villages have been noted in all cases.

A

AACHEN (Aix-la-Chapelle), Rhenish Prussia, Germany, 162,774.
The city consists of an outer or new town and the inner or old town; is modern, with handsome residences, broad, well paved streets, and many large public squares.
The city is noted for its hot sulphur and chalybeate springs of Aachen. The springs were visited by the Romans, who called the place Aquisgranum. Pepin le Bref and Charlemagne made Aachen their residence and capital.
Its railroad facilities and its proximity to Belgium made Aachen an important military station during the European War.
AALBORG, Amt of Aalborg, Denmark, 48,132.
Port of entry; fisheries.
AALEN, Württemberg, Germany, 12,171.
AARAU, capital of Canton of Aargau, Switzerland, 11,612.
Silk, cotton, mathematical instruments.
AARHUS, Amt of Aarhus, Denmark, 95,644.
Good harbor, active commerce, manufactures.
ABADEH, Iran (Persia), 40,100.
ABBEVILLE, Dept. Somme, France, 19,345.
A very old town. Industrial center. Manufactures: textiles, sugar.
–c. s., Henry Co., Ala., 2,047.
On Atl. Coast Line (R. R.).
–c. s., Wilcox Co., Ga., 1,018.
On Seab. Air Line (R. R.).
–c. s., Vermilion Parish, La., 4,356.
On Sou. Pac. (R. R.).
–c.s., Abbeville Co., S. C., 4,414.
On Seab. Air Line; Sou. (R. Rs.).
ABBIATEGRASSO, Prov. of Milano, Italy, 6,214.
ABBOTSFORD, Clark and Marathon Cos., Wis., 781.
On Mpls., St. P., & S. Ste. M. (R. R.).
ABBOT VILLAGE, Piscataquis Co., Maine, 200.
On Bangor & Aroostook (R. R.).
ABEOKUTA, Nigeria, 45,697.
A former fortified town. Important trading center.
ABERCARN, Monmouthshire, England, 20,554.
Coal mining town.
ABERDARE, Glamorganshire, Wales, 48,751.
Coal and iron mines.
ABERDEEN, Aberdeenshire, Scotland, 167,259.
Aberdeen covers the territory between the Dee and the Don Rivers; the main town, or New Aberdeen, is mostly built from granite, quarried near by, and is sometimes called the "Granite City." Old Aberdeen possesses an interesting granite cathedral. Four bridges span the Dee River. Among the monuments is one to Lord Gordon. Important educational institutions are the University of Aberdeen, Gordon's College, a Latin school (founded in 1263), and the Free Church Divinity College. A granite pier, 2,000 feet long, has made Aberdeen's harbor one of the finest in Scotland, and greatly facilitates maritime trade.
The manufactures of the city include cotton, linen, and woolen goods, rope, leather, paper, soap, candles, chemicals, agricultural implements, iron vessels, and sail-cloth, with extensive foundries, breweries, and distilleries. The granite polishing works are on a large scale. The charter of Aberdeen was granted in 1179 by William the Lion, and extended by Robert Bruce. The town was burnt by the English in 1336, rebuilt and named New Aberdeen. A period of great prosperity began in 1818 with the rediscovery of the art of granite polishing.
–Bingham Co., Idaho, 646.
On Un. Pac. (R. R.).
–Harford Co., Md., 1,240.
On Balt. & Ohio; Penna. (R. Rs.) and Un. States Govt.
–c. s., Monroe Co., Miss., 3,925.
On Ill. Cen.; Mob. & Ohio; St. Lou.-San Fran. (R. Rs.).
In black prairie belt.
–Moore Co., N. C., 1,382.
On Norf. Sou.; Aberd. & Rockf.; Seab. Air Line (R. Rs.).
–c. s., Brown Co., S. D., 16,725.
On Chi. & Nor. West.; Chi., Mil., St. P. & Pac.; Gt. Nor.; Mpls. & St. Lou. (R. Rs.).
Has a manufacturing area of 10½ miles.
–Grays Harbor Co., Wash., 21,723.
On Nor. Pac.; Chi., Mil., St. P. & Pac.; Un. Pac. (R. Rs.).

Lumber industries and fish canneries.
ABERGAVENNY, Monmouthshire, England, 8,608.
On the river Usk, 13 miles west of Monmouth.
ABERNATHY, Hale & Lubbock Cos., Tex., 858.
On Panh. & Santa Fe (R. R.).
ABERSYCHAN, Monmouthshire, England, 25,627.
Rich mines of iron, and oil.
ABERTILLERY, Monmouthshire, England, 31,799.
ABERYSTWITH, Cardiganshire, Wales, 9,474.
Seat of University College of Wales.
ABIDJAN, Ivory Coast. See BINGERVILLE.
ABILENE, c. s., Dickinson Co., Kans., 5,824.
On Atch., Top. & Santa Fe; Chi., Rk. Isl. & Pac.; Un. Pac. (R. Rs.).
–c. s., Taylor Co., Texas, 23,175.
On Abil. & Sou.; Tex. & Pac.; Wich. Val. (R. Rs.).
Dairy and grain industries.
ABINGDON, Berkshire, England, 7,240.
–Knox Co., Ill., 2,771.
On Chi., Burl. & Quincy; Mpls. & St. L. (R. Rs.).
–Harford Co., Md., 1,300.
–c. s., Washington Co., Va., 2,877.
On Norf. & West. (R. R.).
ABINGTON, Plymouth Co., Mass., 5,696.
On N. York, N. Hav. & Hart. (R. R.).
ABIQUIU, Rio Arriba Co., N. Mex., 530.
ABO, Finland. See TURKU.
ABOMEY, Dahomey, Fr. W. Africa, 11,205.
Trading center for an agricultural region.
ABONY, Hungary, 15,777.
Distributing center in farming region.
ABOUKIR, Egypt.
On western extremity of bay of Aboukir, the scene of Nelson's victory over French fleet, Aug. 1-2, 1798. The town is 15 miles northeast of Alexandria.
ABSECON, Atlantic Co., N. J., 2,158.
On Penna.-Read. Seashore (R. R.).
ACADIA, Aroostook Co., Me., 700.
ACAMBARO, State of Guanajuato, Mexico, 15,899.
On National of Mexico (R. R.).
ACANCEH, Yucatan, 2,171.
On Un. Rys. of Yucatan.
ACAPULCO, State of Guerrero, Mexico, 5,768.
Port of call between San Francisco and South American ports; exports hides, timber, and fruit. The harbor is cooled by the well-known cut through the mountains called the Abra de San Nicolas.
ACATLAN, State of Puebla, Mexico, 6,042.
ACATZINGO, State of Puebla, Mexico, 3,385.
On Mexican (R. R.).
ACCOMAC, Accomac Co., Va., 750.
ACCOVILLE, Logan Co., W. Va., 1,000.
On Chesa. & Ohio (R. R.).
ACCRA, capital of Gold Coast, Africa, 60,726.
Port and educational center.
ACCRINGTON, Lancashire, England, 42,973.
Textile mills, dye works, machine shops.
ACERRA, Prov. of Napoli, Italy, about 16,000.
ACIREALE, Prov. of Catania, Sicily, 22,956.
Site of medicinal springs.
ACKERMAN, c. s., Choctaw Co., Miss., 1,169.
On Gulf, Mob. & Nor.; Ill. Cen. (R. Rs.).
ACKLEY, Hardin and Franklin Cos., Iowa, 1,524.
On Ill. Cen.; Mpls. & St. Lou. (R. Rs.).
ACME, Westmoreland Co., Pa., 1,300.
–Kanawha Co., W. Va., 515.
On Chesa. & Ohio (R. R.).
ACQUI, Prov. of Alessandria, Italy, 9,904.
Famous for sulphur springs and baths.
ACRE, Palestine, 7,893.
Historical town of the Crusades.
ACRI, Prov. of Cosenza, Italy, 4,346.
ACTON, Marion Co., Ind., 510.
On Clev., Cin., Chi. & St. Lou. (R. R.).
–Middlesex Co., Mass., 2,635.
On N. York, N. Hav. and Hart. (R. R.).
–Halton Co., Ontario, Canada, 1,855.
On Can. Nat. (R. R.).
–Middlesex, England, 70,523.
Residential suburb of London.
ACTONVALE, Bagot Co., Quebec, Canada, 1,753.
On Can. Pac.; Can. Nat. (R. Rs.).
ACUSHNET, Bristol Co., Mass., 3,951.
On N. York, N. Hav. & Hart. (R. R.).
ACWORTH, Cobb Co., Ga., 1,163.
On Nashville, Chatt. & St. Lou. (R. R.).
ADA, c. s., Norman Co., Minn., 1,285.
On Gt. Nor. (R. R.).
–Hardin Co., Ohio, 2,499.
On Penna. (R. R.).
–c. s., Pontotoc Co., Okla., 11,261.

On Atch., Top. & Santa Fe; Okla. City-Ada-Atoka; St. Lou.-San Fran. (R. Rs.).
Industrial center; oil, zinc, lead and asphalt mines.
ADAIR, Adair and Guthrie Cos., Iowa, 950.
On Chi., Rk. Isl. & Pac. (R. R.).
ADAIRSVILLE, Bartow Co., Ga., 765.
On Nashville, Chatt. & St. Lou. (R. R.).
ADAIRVILLE, Logan Co., Ky., 763.
ADALIA, Turkey. See ANTALYA.
ADAMS, Berkshire Co., Mass., 12,858.
On Bost. & Alb. (R. R.).
Has large paper mills, cotton and woolen factories.
–Mower Co., Minn., 574.
On Chic., Mil., St. P. & Pac. (R. R.).
–Gage Co., Neb., 535.
On Chic., Burl. & Quincy. (R. R.).
–Jefferson Co., N. Y., 1,613.
On N. York Cen. (R. R.).
–Robertson Co., Tenn., 512.
On Lou. & Nash. (R. R.).
–Sumner Co., Tenn., 643.
–Adams Co., Wis., 1,231.
On Chi. & Nor. West (R. R.).
ADAMS CENTER, Jefferson Co., N. Y., 670.
On N. York Cen. (R. R.).
ADAMSTON, Harrison Co., W. Va. (Pop. incl. in Clarkesburg).
On Balt. & Ohio (R. R.).
ADAMSTOWN, Lancaster Co., Pa., 909.
ADAMSVILLE, Jefferson Co., Ala., 710.
On Ill. Cen.; St. Lou.-San Fran. (R. Rs.).
–Newport Co., R. I., 530.
ADANA, capital of Adana Vilayet, Turkey in Asia, 72,652.
Center of agricultural and stock-raising region.
ADDICKS, Harris Co., Tex., 500.
On Mo.-Kan.-Tex. of Tex. (R. R.).
ADDIS ABEBA, Italian East Africa, 109,000.
Trading center.
ADDISON, Winston Co., Ala., 500.
–Du Page Co., Ill., 916.
On Ill. Cen. (R. R.).
–Steuben Co., N. Y., 1,538.
On Balt. & Ohio; Erie (R. Rs.).
–Webster Co., W. Va., 976.
ADDYSTON, Hamilton Co., Ohio, 1,768.
On Balt. & Ohio; Cleve., Cin., Chi. & St. Lou. (R. Rs.).
ADEL, c. s., Cook Co., Ga., 1,796.
On Ga. & Fla.; Ga. So. & Fla.; Sou. Ga. (R. Rs.).
–c. s., Dallas Co., Iowa, 1,669.
On Chi., Mil., St. P. & Pac. (R. R.).
ADELAIDE, capital of South Australia, Australia. Pop. (incl. suburbs) 316,860.
On both sides of the river Torrens, 8 miles from its entrance into the Gulf of St. Vincent. Founded in 1836, and named after Queen Adelaide, consort of William IV. It has a heavy trade in copper, ores, grain and wool. Its chief public buildings are the Government buildings, Parliament House, town hall, post office, the South Australian Institute, and the Governor's residence.
–Fayette Co., Pa., 515.
On Pittsb. & L. Erie (R. R.).
ADELPHIA, Monmouth Co., N. J., 525.
ADEN, Arabia, 32,490.
A British settlement, strongly fortified; important coaling station on steamer route to the East; large transshipment trade.
ADENA, Jefferson Co., Ohio, 1,286.
On Wheel. & L. Erie (R. R.).
ADERNO, Prov. of Catania, Sicily, 39,637.
Town at foot of Mt. Etna.
ADI UGRI, Eritrea, 5,133.
ADJUNTAS, Municipality of Adjuntas, Puerto Rico, 2,612.
ADLAN, Delaware Co., Pa., 2,269.
ADONI, Madras Presidency, India, 31,640.
Textile manufactures.
ADRIA, Prov. of Rovigo, Italy, 13,817.
ADRIAN, Emanuel and Johnson Cos., Ga., 685.
–c. s., Lenawee Co., Mich., 13,064.
On the Det., Tol. & Iron.; N. York Cen.; and the Wab. Railroads.
Shipping point for grain, live stock, and dairy products. Has factories for making woven wire, furniture, auto accessories, electrical appliances, and cement blocks. Commission government. Seat of Adrian College, State Industrial School for Girls, and St. Joseph's Academy.

–Nobles Co., Minn., 1,000.
On Chi., St. P., Mpls. & Oma. (R. R.).
–Bates Co., Mo., 934.
On Mo. Pac. (R. R.).
–Upshur Co., W. Va., 653.
On Balt. & Ohio (R. R.).
ADRIANOPLE, Turkey. See EDIRNE.
ADVANCE, Stoddard Co., Mo., 579.
On St. Lou.-San Fran. (R. R.).
AERSCHOT, South Brabant, Belgium, 8,755.
AFFINITY, Raleigh Co., W. Va., 500.
On Chesa. & Ohio; Virginian (R. Rs.).
AFFTON, St. Louis Co., Mo., 500.
AFRAGOLA, Prov. of Napoli, Italy, 23,018.
Manufactures of straw bonnets.
AFTON, Union Co., Iowa, 1,013.
On Chi., Burl. & Quincy (R. R.).
–Chenango Co., N. Y., 812.
On Del. & Hud. (R. R.).
–Ottawa Co., Okla., 1,219.
On St. Lou.-San Fran. (R. R.).
–Lincoln Co., Wyo., 807.
AGADIR, Morocco, 5,730.
AGANA, capital of Guam Island (U. S.), 8,690.
A naval base in the Pacific.
AGAWAM, Hampden Co., Mass., 7,206.
AGDE, Dept. of Hérault, France, 9,360.
AGEN, Dept. of Lot-et-Garonne, France, 27,152.
AGOO, Prov. of La Union, Luzon, P. I., 12,150.
AGORDAT, Eritrea, 3,056.
AGOUE, Dahomey, Fr. W. Africa, 20,009.
AGRA, capital of Agra, India, 229,764.
Site of the beautiful Taj Mahal, famed tomb of the Emperor Shah Jahan and his queen.
AGRAM, Yugo. See ZAGREB.
AGUADA, Municipality of Aguada, Puerto Rico, 1,992.
AGUADILLA, Municipality of Aguadilla, Puerto Rico, 11,133.
Largest and most important town in southwestern Puerto Rico.
AGUAS BUENAS, Municipality of Aguas Buenas, Puerto Rico, 2,515.
AGUASCALIENTES, State of Aguascalientes, Mexico, 62,244.
On National of Mexico (R. R.).
Health resort, hot springs.
AGUILAR, Las Animas Co., Colo., 1,383.
On Colo. & Sou. (R. R.).
AGUILAR DE LA FRONTERA, Prov. of Cordoba, Spain, 15,000.
Celebrated for its wines and olives.
AGUILAS, Prov. of Murcia, Spain, 17,078.
Grain, smelting works.
AGYROCASTRA, Albania. See GJINONKASTER.
AHMADNAGAR, India, 42,900.
Military station and trading center. Textiles, leather goods, brass and copper pots.
AHMEDABAD, Dist. of Ahmedabad, Bombay, India, 313,789.
Trading and manufacturing center. Textiles, jewelry, and metal handicraft.
AHMEEK, Keweenaw Co., Mich., 624.
AHOSKIE, Hertford Co., N. C., 1,940.
On Atl. Coast Line; Carol. Sou. (R. Rs.).
AIBONITO, Municipality of Aibonito, Puerto Rico, 3,877.
At elevation of 3,000 ft.; surrounded by coffee plantations.
AIDIN, Turkey. See AYDIN.
AIGUN, Manchukuo, 38,112.
Port and shipping center for large farming district.
AIKEN, c. s., Aiken Co., S. C., 6,033.
On Sou. (R. R.).
Popular winter resort; has the Aiken Institute, Normal and Industrial School and factories.
AINSWORTH, c. s., Brown Co., Neb., 1,378.
On Chi. & Nor. West. (R. R.).
AINTAB, Turkey. See GAZI ANTEP.
AIRDRIE, Lanarkshire, Scotland, 25,954.
Iron and Brass foundries.
AITKIN, c. s., Aitkin Co., Minn., 1,545.
On Mpls., St. P. & S. Ste. M.; Nor. Pac. (R. Rs.).
AIX, Dept. of Bouches-du-Rhône, France, 42,615.
Famous for its thermal springs.
AIX-LA-CHAPELLE, Germany. See AACHEN.
AIX-LES-BAINS, Dept. of Savoie, France, 12,889.
Celebrated thermal waters.
AJACCIO, capital of Dept. of Corse (Corsica), France, 37,146.
Birthplace of Napoleon Bonaparte.

Ajmer, capital of Prov. of Ajmer-Merwara, India, 119,524.
Seat of Mayo College; subterranean aqueduct.
Ajo, Pima Co., Ariz., 1,100.
On Tucson, Cor. & Gila Bend (R. R.).
Akamagaseki, Japan. See Shimonoseki.
Akeley, Hubbard Co., Minn., 514.
On Gt. Nor. (R. R.).
–Warren Co., Pa., 585.
On N. York Cen. (R. R.).
Akhaltsikh, Transcaucasia, Sov. Union, 13,600.
A trading center on a caravan route.
Akhisar, Manisa Vilayet, Turkey in Asia, 18,050.
Exports cotton, wool, silk, opium, and cereals.
Akhmyn, Egypt, 24,000.
Akhtirka, Ukraine, Soviet Union, 26,995.
Trade center for agricultural products.
Akita, Japan, 51,069.
A port in northern Japan.
Akmolinsk, Kirghiz, Sov. Union, 35,800.
Akola, Dist. of Akola, India, 47,632.
Cotton trade center.
Akron, c. s., Hale Co., Ala., 793.
On Ala. Gt. Sou.; Sou. (R. Rs.).
–Washington Co., Colo., 1,135.
On Chi., Burl. & Quincy (R. R.).
–Fulton Co., Indiana, 932.
On Erie; Winona (El.) (R. Rs.).
–Plymouth Co., Iowa, 1,304.
On Chi., Mil., St. P. & Pac. (R. R.).
–Erie Co., N. Y., 2,188.
On West Shore (R. R.).
–Lancaster Co., Pa., 747.
On Reading (R. R.).
–c. s., Summit Co., Ohio, 255,040.
On the Akr. & Barb. Belt; Balt. & Ohio; the Akr., Can. & Youngst.; Penna.; Erie (R. Rs.).
This manufacturing and railroad center was founded in 1825.
There are many manufacturing establishments, among them printing and lithographing, cereal products, dirigibles, steel products, electric motors and matches. Coal is mined in the vicinity, and there is an active trade in grain. The largest rubber works in the country are located here.
Akron is the seat of Akron University.
Aksu (Wensuh), Sinkiang, China, 80,000.
Important center of caravan trade in Sinkiang.
Akyab, Burma, India, 37,890.
Leading rice exporting port. Fine harbor; large export trade.
Alabama City, Etowah Co., Ala., 8,544.
On Lou. & Nash.; Nash., Chatt. & St. Louis; Sou. (R. Rs.).
Steel and textile mills.
Alachua, Alachua Co., Fla., 1,004.
On Atl. Coast Line, and Seab. Air Line (R. Rs.).
Alais, France. See Ales.
Alajuela, Province of Alajuela, Costa Rica, 10,282.
Center of important coffee district.
Alameda, Alameda Co., Cal., 35,033.
On Alameda Belt; Atch., Top. & Santa Fe; Sou. Pac.; West Pac. (R. Rs.).
Fish canning, boat manufacturing, machinery, and potteries.
–Bernalillo Co., N. Mex., 506.
On Atch., Top. & Santa Fe (R. R.).
–Bannock Co., Idaho, 1,885.
Alaminos, Luzon, P. I., 14,410.
Alamo, Wheeler Co., Ga., 613.
On Seab. Air Line (R. Rs.).
–c. s., Crockett Co., Tenn., 907.
On Gulf, Mob. & Nor. (R. R.).
–Hidalgo Co., Tex., 1,018.
On Mo. Pac. (R. R.).
Alamogordo, c. s., Otero Co., N. Mex., 3,096.
Situated on the Southern Pacific Railroad.
It is in an agricultural district.
Alamos, State of Sonora, Mexico, 3,008.
Alamosa, Alamosa Co., Colo., 5,107.
On Den. & Rio Gde. West. (R. R.).
Alassio, Prov. of Savona, Italy, 4,521.
Seaport town, 4 miles southwest of Albenga.
Alatir, Soviet Union, 28,500.
Grain and flour-milling center.
Alba, Wood Co., Tex., 662.
On Mo.-Kan.-Tex. of Tex.; Tex. Short Line (R. Rs.).
Albacete, Prov. of Albacete, Spain, 43,892.
Steel products.
Alban, Portage Co., Wis., 515.
Albano, Prov. of Rome, Italy, 10,000.
Favorite summer resort.
Albany, Sta. Decatur P. O., Morgan Co., Ala. (Pop. incl. in Decatur).
–Alameda Co., Cal., 8,569.
–c. s., Dougherty Co., Ga., 14,507.
On Atl. Coast Line; Cen. of Ga.; Ga. Nor.; Ga., Southw. & Gulf; Seab. Air Line (R. Rs.).
On Flint River. Navigation center for shipping cotton.
–Delaware Co., Ind., 1,413.
On N. York, Chi. & St. Lou. (R. R.).
–c. s., Clinton Co., Ky., 852.
–Stearns Co., Minn., 851.
On Gt. Nor.; Mpls., St. P. & S. Ste. M. (R. Rs.).
–c. s., Gentry Co., Mo., 1,858.
On Chi., Burl. & Quincy (R. R.).
–c. s., Albany Co., N. Y., State Capital, 127,412.
Situated on the west bank of the Hudson, 145 miles north of New York City and 164 miles (201 miles by railroad) west of Boston, Mass.
On the Bost. & Alb., the Del. & Hud., the N. York Cen., and the West Shore Railroads.
The city has a river frontage of 4 miles. It is the terminus of the State Barge Canals and a center of river traffic.
The Capitol is of drilled granite, 4 stories high, 300 feet at the highest point, 400 feet long. It is built on a site 155 feet above the Hudson River. Other prominent buildings are the marble State Hall, City Hall, Custom-house, Post-office, Dudley Astronomical Observatory, State Museum of Natural History (1797), State Armory, State Education Building, State Office Building, Cathedral of the Immaculate Conception (Roman Catholic), and Cathedral of All Saints (Episcopal).
Besides its public schools, Albany has academies for boys and girls, a medical college, a law school and a school of pharmacy (departments of Union University), a State normal college, Albany Institute and Historical and Art Society, and Dana Natural History Society. The State Library with the law department has over 506,000 volumes, 265,000 manuscripts, and 473,950 pamphlets. The city has several hospitals and many parks.
Manufactures include skirts, knit goods, pianos, stoves, railroad signals, paper, iron wares, gas meters, toys, chemicals, beds, packing cases, automobiles and parts, bakery products, etc. There is a large lumber trade.
Visited by Henry Hudson in the year 1609, Albany was first occupied by the Dutch in 1614 as a trading post. In May, 1624, on the arrival of eighteen Walloon families, the permanent settlement began, and a small fort, called Orange, or Aurania, was built. In 1626 the settlement was broken up by the war between the Mohawks and the Mohegans, and the families of the town were removed to New Amsterdam (New York). In 1630 a new settlement was made, several Dutch families renting their lands of the patroons, or lords of the manor. The village was then called Beverwyck, afterward Williamstadt, and in 1664 Albany, after the Duke of York and Albany, afterward James II., of England. It was incorporated as the city of Albany in 1686.
Albany continued to be a center for Indian trade, and was inhabited chiefly by Dutch, until the Revolution broke out. In 1787 feudal tenure was abolished. It became the capital of New York in 1807.
–c. s., Linn Co., Ore., 5,325.
On Sou. Pac.; Spok., Port. & Seattle (R. Rs.)
In Willamette Valley. Tourist, game, and fishing section.
–c. s., Shackelford Co., Texas, 2,422.
On Mo.-Kan.-Tex. of Tex. (R. R.).
–Green Co., Wis., 728.
On Chi., Mil., St. P. & Pac. (R. R.).
Albemarle, c. s., Stanly Co., N. C., 3,493.
On Winst.-Sal. Southb.; Yadkin (R. Rs.).
Albert, Tucker Co., W. Va., 500.
Albert City, Buena Vista Co., Iowa, 563.
On Chi., Mil., St. P. & Pac. (R. R.).
Albert Lea, c. s., Freeborn Co., Minn., 10,169.
On Chi., Mil., St. P. & Pac.; Chi., Rk. Isl. & Pac.; Ill. Cen.; Mpls. & St. Lou. (R. Rs.).
Alberton, Howard Co., Md., 570.
On Balt. & Ohio (R. R.).
Albertson, Nassau Co., N. Y., 892.
On Long Isl. (R. R.).
Albertville, Marshall Co., Ala., 2,716.
On Nash., Chatt. & St. Lou. (R. R.).
Albi, capital of Dept. of Tarn, France, 30,293.
On the Tarn River.
Albia, c. s., Monroe Co., Iowa, 4,425.
On Chi., Burl. & Quincy; Ia. Sou. Utilities; Mpls. & St. Lou.; Wab. (R. Rs.).
Albion, c. s., Edwards Co., Ill., 1,666.
On Southern (R. R.).
–c. s., Noble Co., Ind., 1,108.
On Balt. & Ohio (R. R.).
–Kennebec Co., Maine, 840.
–c. s., Calhoun Co., Mich., 8,324.
On Mich. Cen.; N. York Cen. (R. Rs.).
Metal factories mainly for automobile parts.
Albion College (Methodist).
–c. s., Boone Co., Neb., 2,172.
On Chi. & Nor. West.; Un. Pac. (R. Rs.).
–c. s., Orleans Co., N. Y., 4,878.
On Intern. (El.); N. York Cen. (R. Rs.).
In fruit and produce section.
–Erie Co., Pa., 1,681.
On Besse. & L. Erie; Penna. (R. Rs.).
–Providence Co., R. I., 1,175.
On N. York, N. Hav. & Hart. (R. R.).
Albona, Prov. of Pona, Italy, 1,410.
Albrights, Lehigh Co., Pa., 500.
Albunol, Prov. of Granada, Spain, 7,685.
Albuquerque, Prov. of Bohol, Bohol, P. I., 6,361.
–c. s., Bernalillo Co., N. Mex., 26,570.
On Atch., Top. & Santa Fe (R. R.).
Five thousand feet above sea level. Health resort.
Seat of University of New Mexico; shipping point; center of farming district.
Alburgh (Alburgh P. O.), Grand Isle Co., Vt., 1,609.
On Cen. Ver.; Rut. (R. Rs.).
Alburtis, Lehigh Co., Pa., 823.
On Reading (R. R.).
Alcala de Henares, Prov. of Madrid, Spain, 11,142.
An educational center.
Alcamo, Prov. of Trapani, Sicily, 63,051.
Alcantara, Prov. of Caceres, Spain, 3,954.
Alcazar de San Juan, Prov. of Ciudad Real, Spain, 16,117.
Railway center, wines, soap, gunpowder, and chocolate.
Alcester, Union Co., S. D., 546.
On Chi. & Nor. West. (R. R.).
Alcira, Prov. of Valencia, Spain, 20,839.
Fine bridges; in vicinity a stalactitic cavern.
Alcoa, Blount Co., Tenn., 5,255.
On Lou. & Nash.; Sou. (R. Rs.).
Alcoy, Prov. of Alicante, Spain, 36,463.
Industrial center. Textiles, machinery, cigarette paper.
Aldeia Galega, Prov. of Estremadura, Portugal, 9,182.
Alden, Hardin Co., Iowa, 793.
On Chi. & Nor. West.; Ill. Cen. (R. Rs.).
–Freeborn Co., Minn., 532.
On Chi., Mil., St. P. & Pac. (R. R.).
–Erie Co., N. Y., 846.
On Erie; Del., Lack. & West. (R. Rs.).
–Luzerne Co., Pa., 1,800.
On Cen. New Jer. (R. R.).
Aldershot, Southampton, England, 34,281.
Important army station.
Alderson, Luzerne Co., Pa., 600.
On Leh. Val. (R. R.).
–Monroe and Greenbrier Cos., West Va., 1,458.
On Chesa. & Ohio (R. R.).
Aldora, Lamar Co., Ga., 595.
Aldrich, Shelby Co., Ala., 1,013.
On Sou. (R. R.).
Aledo, c. s., Mercer Co., Ill., 2,203.
On Chi., Burl. & Quincy; Rk. Isl. Sou. (R. Rs.).
–Parker Co., Tex., 517.
On Tex. & Pac. (R. R.).
Alençon, capital of Dept. of Orne, France, 17,731.
To the production of point d'Alençon lace the town owes its reputation.
Alep (Aleppo), capital of Sanjak of Alep, Syria, 261,605.
Situated about 80 miles east of the Mediterranean Sea, surrounded by hills. The citadel stands on a high hill, surrounded by a moat and surmounted by minarets and domes.
Alep is believed to be of great antiquity. In 1517 it passed under the dominion of the Turks. It is now controlled by the French.
Alés, Dept. of Gard, France, 41,385.
Important as a silk market.
Alessandria, capital of Prov. of Alessandria, Italy, 43,810.
The city was founded in 1168 by the inhabitants of Cremona, Milano and Placentia as a defense against Emperor Frederick Barbarossa, and named for Pope Alexander III.
Alesund, Norway, 18,373.
Alex, Grady Co., Okla., 598.
On Chi., Rk. Isl. & Pac. (R. R.).
Alexander, Rutherford Co., N. C., 700.
On Sou. (R. R.).
Alexander City, Tallapoosa Co., Ala., 4,519.
On Cen. of Ga. (R. R.).
Alexander Mills, Rutherford Co., N. C., 831.
Alexandrette, Syria, 19,277.
Alexandria, Egypt, 699,400.
A seaport founded by Alexander the Great. After Cairo the largest city of Egypt. Situated at the mouth of the river Nile, on a low ridge of land separating Lake Mareotis from the Mediterranean Sea. Alexandria has two harbors, of which the eastern, or new, port is poorly sheltered. The western, or old, port is the principal marine station of Egypt. There is an outer harbor, protected by a mole two miles long. Railroads and many boat lines aid in making the present Alexandria the commercial emporium of the country. The principal exports are corn, cotton, gums, dates, beans, and senna. It is connected with Cairo not only by rail, but by the Mahmudiye Canal. The Alexandrian library, said to have contained at one time some 700,000 rolls, was pillaged by Christians in the fourth century and destroyed by Arabs in the seventh. The gymnasium and two obelisks (Cleopatra's needles) were near by. One of the obelisks was taken to London in 1878; the other, to Central Park, New York, in 1881.
During the nineteenth century the city prospered under the Turkish viceroys. It was bombarded by the British fleet in 1882, as a result of the rebellion of Arabi Pasha and the Nationalist party.
–Prov. of Walachia, Rumania, 19,387.
–Madison Co., Ind., 4,408.
On Cleve., Cin., Chi. & St. Lou.; N. York, Chi. & St. Lou. (R. Rs.).
–c. s., Rapides Parish, La., 23,025.
On Chi., Rk. Isl. & Pac.; La. & Ark.; Sou. Pac.; Mo. Pac.; Tex. & Pac. (R. Rs.).
Lumber center. In gas oil field.
–c. s., Douglas Co., Minn., 3,876.
On Gt. Nor.; Mpls., St. P. & S. Ste. M. (R. Rs.).
–Clark Co., Mo., 631.
On Chi., Burl. & Quincy (R. R.).
–c. s., Hanson Co., S. Dak., 812.
On Chi., Mil., St. P. & Pac. (R. R.).
–(Ind. City), Arlington Co., Va., 24,149.
On Chesa. & Ohio; Rich., Fred. & Pot.; Sou.; Wash. & Old Dom. (El.) (R. Rs.). Also served by steamship lines.
Airports near. Tourist resort, farming region, manufacturing.
–Glengarry Co., Ontario, Canada, 2,006.
On Canadian National (R. R.).
Alexandria Bay, Jefferson Co., N. Y., 1,952.
Summer resort opposite the Thousand Islands, St. Lawrence River. Seven miles from New York Central Railroad.
Alexandropol (Gymri), Soviet Union. See Leninakan.
Alexandrovsk, Soviet Union. See Zaporozhie.
Alexis, Mercer and Warren Cos., Ill., 786.
On Chi., Burl. & Quincy (R. R.).
Alfaro, Prov. of Logrono, Spain, 6,920.
Alfortville, Dept. of Seine, France, 30,078.
A suburb of Paris.
Alfred, Allegany Co., N. Y., 639.
On Erie (R. R.).
Seat of Alfred University.
–York Co., Maine, 600.
On Bost. & Me. (R. R.).
–La Moure Co., N. Dak., 500.
On Nor. Pac. (R. R.).
Alfredton, Tazewell Co., Va., 515.
Alfreton, Derbyshire, England, 21,232.
Important collieries, potteries, and iron works.
Alger (Algiers), capital of Algeria, 264,232.
Situated on the Bay of Alger.
The number and tonnage of vessels which frequent the port place it close to Marseille and Havre in importance, among French ports. This harbor was first built by Barbarossa in the sixteenth century. Jetties, quays, and docks have been added by the French for shipping purposes. Owing to its mild climate and picturesque location, Alger is fast becoming a popular resort. Over 40 per cent of the present inhabitants are French, about 24 per cent Moors, and many are Jews. Alger is the residence of the Governor-General and of the officers of the Algerian colony. Alger was a dependency of the Turkish Empire until the French conquered Algeria in 1830.
–Arenac Co., Mich., 500.
On Mich. Cen. (R. R.).
–Hardin Co., Ohio, 857.
On Erie (R. R.).
Alghero, Prov. of Sassari, Sardinia, Italy, 11,799.
Exports wines, grains, wool, skins.
Algiers, Algeria. See Alger.
Algoma, Kewaunee Co., Wis., 2,202.
On Green Bay & Western (R. R.).
Algona, c. s., Kossuth Co., Iowa, 3,985.
On Chi. & Nor. West.; Chi., Mil., St. P. & Pac. (R. Rs.).
Algonac, St. Clair Co., Mich., 1,736.
Algonquin, McHenry Co., Ill., 866.
On Chi. & Nor. West. (R. R.).
Algood, Putnam Co., Tenn., 643.
On Tenn. Cen. (R. R.).
Alhambra, Los Angeles Co., Cal., 29,472.
On Pac. Elec.; Sou. Pac. (R. Rs.).
Airport, residential city; some farming and manufacturing.
Aliaga, Prov. of Nueva Ecija, Luzon, P. I., 12,701.
Alicante, capital of Prov. of Alicante, Spain, 69,793.
One of the most important seaports of Spain.
Alice, c. s., Jim Wells Co., Tex., 4,239.
On Sou. Pac.; Tex. Mex. (R. Rs.).
Aliceville, Pickens Co., Ala., 1,066.
On Ala., Tenn. & Nor.; St. Lou.-San. Fran. (R. Rs.).
Alicia, Fayette Co., Pa., 300.
On Monongahela (R. R.).
Aligarh, United Provinces, India, 66,963.
Aliquippa, Beaver Co., Pa., 27,116.
On Aliquippa & Sou.; Pitts. & L. Erie (R. Rs.).
Manufacturing.
Alisal, Monterey Co., Calif., 750.
Aliwal, North, Un. of South Africa, 7,645.
On Orange River, and connected by rail with East London, its harbor.
Alix, Franklin Co., Ark., 500.
On Mo. Pac. (R. R.).
Aljojuca, State of Puebla, Mexico, about 1,985.
Alkmaar, North Holland, Netherlands, 28,294.
Manufactures cheese and sail-cloth.

Allahabad, India, 173,895.
Allegan, c. s., Allegan Co., Mich., 3,941.
On N. York Cen.; Pere Marq. (R. Rs.).
Allegany, Cattaraugus Co., N. Y., 1,411.
On Erie; Penna. (R. Rs.).
–Sierra Co., Calif., 519.
Allen, Pontotoc and Hughes Cos., Okla., 1,438.
On Kan., Okla. & Gulf (R. R.).
–Collin Co., Tex., 500.
On Sou. Pac.; Tex. Elec. (R. Rs.).
Allendale, Bergen Co., N. J., 1,730.
On Erie (R. R.).
–c. s., Allendale Co., S. C., 2,066.
On Charl. & W. Car.; Sou. (R. Rs.).
Allendorf, Kassel, Germany, 3,000.
Allenhurst, Monmouth Co., N. J., 573.
On Cen. of N. Jer.; N. York & L. Br.; Penna. (R. Rs.).
Allen Park, Wayne Co., Mich., 944.
Allenstein, Prussia, Germany, 43,043.
Center of a farming region.
Allenstown, Merrimack Co., N. H., 1,540.
On Suncook Val. (R. R.).
Allenton, Washington Co., R. I., 962.
Allentown, Monmouth Co., N. J., 706.
–c. s., Lehigh Co., Pa., 92,563.
On Cen. of N. Jer.; Leh. Val.; Leh. & N. Eng.; Read. (R. Rs.).
Cement center. Manufactures motor trucks, silks, etc. Seat of Muhlenberg College (Lutheran), Cedar Crest College for Women.
Allerton, Wayne Co., Iowa, 784.
On Chi., Rk. Isl. & Pac. (R. R.).
Alliance, c. s., Boxutte Co., Neb., 6,669.
On Chi., Burl. & Quincy (R. R.).
Agriculture, cattle, and railroad shops.
–Pamlico Co., N. C., 500.
–Stark Co., Ohio, 23,047.
On N. York Cen.; Penna. (R. Rs.).
Foundry products, paving brick, machinery.
Allison, c. s., Butler Co., Iowa, 603.
On Chi. Gt. West. (R. R.).
–McKinley Co., N. Mex., 500.
–Fayette Co., Pa., 1,200.
On Monongahela (R. R.).
Allison Park, Allegheny Co., Pa., 828.
On Balt. & Ohio (R. R.).
Alliston, Simcoe Co., Ontario, Canada, 1,355.
On Can. Pac.; Can. Nat. (R. Rs.).
Shipping point for grain; has flour and woolen mills.
Alloa, Clackmannanshire, Scotland, 18,244.
Seaport and market town.
Allouez, Keweenaw Co., Mich., 1,424. (Includes Ahmeek village.)
–Douglas Co., Wis. (Ind. Sta., Superior P. O.).
On Chi., St. P., Mpls. & Oma.; Gt. Nor.; Nor. Pac.; Duluth, South Shore & Atlantic (R. Rs.).
Alloway, Salem Co., N. J., 600.
On Pa.-Read. Seashore (R. R.).
Allyndale (East Canaan P. O.), Litchfield Co., Conn., 581.
On N. York, N. Hav. & Hart. (R. R.).
Alma, Crawford Co., Ark., 731.
On Mo. Pac. (R. R.).
–Bacon Co., Ga., 1,235.
On Atla., Birm. & Coast (R. R.).
–c. s., Wabaunsee Co., Kans., 730.
On Atch., Top. & Santa Fe; Chi., Rk. Isl. & Pac. (R. Rs.).
–Gratiot Co., Mich., 6,734.
On Ann Arbor; Pere Marq. (R. Rs.).
Motor truck manufacturing center. Seat of Alma College.
–c. s., Harlan Co., Neb., 1,235.
On Chi., Burl. & Quincy (R. R.).
–c. s., Buffalo Co., Wis., 1,009.
On Chi., Burl. & Quincy (R. Rs.).
Alma Ata, Kirghiz, Sov. Union, 161,600.
Almada, Estremadura, Portugal, 11,582.
Almadén, Prov. of Ciudad Real, Spain, 9,829.
Rich mercury mines.
Almagro, Pittsylvania Co., Va., 952.
Almena, Norton Co., Kans., 720.
On Chi., Burl. & Quincy; Chi., Rk. Isl. & Pac. (R. Rs.).
Almeria, Prov. of Almeria, Spain, 54,736.
Important harbor.
Almodovar del Campo, Ciudad Real, Spain, 12,635.
Almont, Lapeer Co., Mich., 844.
On Pere Marquette (R. R.).
Almonte, Lanark Co., Ontario, Canada, 2,415.
On Can. Pac. (R. R.).
Iron works, woolen factories, water-power.
Alnwick, Northumberland, England, 6,882.
Aloguinsah, Cebu Prov., Cebu, P. I., about 15,000.
Alost, East-Flanders, Belgium, 37,852.
Alpaugh, Tulare Co., Calif., 500.
On Atch., Top. & Santa Fe (R. R.).
Alpena, c. s., Alpena Co., Mich., 12,166.
On Detroit & Mackinac (R. R.).
Limestone quarries and cement works.
Alpha, Iron Co., Mich., 560.
On Chi. & Nor. West. (R. R.).
–Warren Co., N. J., 2,374.
On Leh. Val. (R. R.).
Alpine, Bergen Co., N. J., 521.
–c. s., Brewster Co., Texas, 3,495.
On Panh. & Santa Fe; Sou. Pac. (R. Rs.).
–Utah Co., Utah, 509.
Alsager, Cheshire, England, 2,852.
Alta, Buena Vista Co., Iowa, 1,297.
On Ill. Cen. (R. R.).
Alta Loma, San Bernardino Co., Calif., 1,500.
On Pac. Elec.; Sou. Pac. (R. Rs.).
Altamont, Effingham Co., Ill., 1,225.
On Balt. & Ohio; Chi. & East. Ill.; Penna. (R. Rs.).
–Labette Co., Kans., 622.
On St. Lou.-San Fran. (R. R.).
–Albany Co., N. Y., 858.
On Del. & Hud. (R. R.).
Altamura, Prov. of Bari, Italy, 26,877.
Alta Vista, Wabaunsee Co., Kans., 519.
On Chi. Rk. I. & Pac. (R. R.).
Altavista, Campbell Co., Va., 2,367.
On Sou.; Virginian (R. Rs.).
Altdorf, capital of Canton of Uri, Switzerland, 4,254.
Legendary birthplace of William Tell.
Altena, Westphalia, Germany, 16,000.
Altenburg, Thüringen, Germany, 91,074.
Kid gloves, hats, machinery.
Alto, Cherokee Co., Texas, 1,053.
On St. Lou. Southw. (R. R.).
Altofts, Yorkshire, West Riding, England, 4,980.
Alton, Southampton, England, 6,172.
Madison Co., Ill., 30,151.
On Alton; Chi., Burl. & Quincy; Cle., Cin., Chi. & St. Lou.; Mo. & Ill. Bridge & Belt.; Illinois Terminal; Chi., Springf. & St. Lou.; Mo.-Kan.-Tex. (R. Rs.). A belt line connects seven other main roads. River terminal for Mississippi traffic with eight miles of waterfront.
–Sioux Co., Iowa, 1,014.
On Chi., St. P., Mpls. & Oma.; Chi. & Nor. West. (R. Rs.).
–Belknap Co., N. H., 700.
On Bost. & Me. (R. R.).
Altona, Schleswig-Holstein, Germany, 242,006. A suburb of Hamburg, important manufacturing center and port (now part of Hamburg).
–Clinton Co., N. Y., 500.
On Rutland (R. R.).
Alton Park, Hamilton Co., Tenn. (Sta. Chattanooga P. O.).
On Tenn., Ala. & Ga. (R. R.).
Altoona, Etowah Co., Ala., 1,098.
On Lou. & Nash. (R. R.).
–Polk Co., Iowa, 514.
On Chic., Rk. Isl. & Pac.; Des Moines & Cen. Ia. (El.) (R. Rs.).
–Wilson Co., Kansas, 794.
On Mo. Pac. (R. R.).
–Blair Co., Pa., 82,054.
On Penna.; E. Brd. Top Trans. (R. Rs.).
Large railroad shops, textile and knitting mills.
–Eau Claire Co., Wis., 1,044.
On Chi., St. P., Mpls. & Oma. (R. R.).
Altrincham, Cheshire, England, 21,356.
A suburb of Manchester.
Alturas, c. s., Modoc Co., Cal., 2,338.
On Sou. Pac. (R. R.).
Altus, Franklin Co., Ark., 595.
–c. s., Jackson Co., Okla., 8,439.
On Atch., Top. & Santa Fe; Mo.-Kan.-Tex.; Panh. & Santa Fe; St. Lou.-San Fran. (R. Rs.).
Alva, Lee Co., Fla., 540.
On Seab. Air Line (R. R.).
–Harlan Co., Ky., 700.
On Lou. & Nash. (R. R.).
–c. s., Woods Co., Okla., 5,121.
On Atch., Top. & Santa Fe; Chi., Rk. Isl. & Pac. (R. Rs.).
–Clackmannan Co., Scotland, 4,853.
Alvarado, Alameda Co., Calif., 1,800.
On Sou. Pac. (R. R.).
–Johnson Co., Texas, 1,210.
On Gulf, Colo. & Santa Fe; Mo.-Kan.-Tex. of Tex. (R. Rs.).
In an agricultural region.
Alvaro Obregon (Frontera), Tabasco, Mexico, 6,636.
Alverda, Indiana Co., Pa., 500.
Alverton (Stoner), Westmoreland Co., Pa., 500.
On Penna. (R. R.).
Alvin, Brazoria Co., Texas, 1,511.
On Gulf, Colo. & Santa Fe (R. R.).
Alvord, Wise Co., Texas, 754.
On Ft. Worth & Denv. Cy. (R. R.).
Alwar, capital of Alwar, Rajputana, India, 44,760.
Trading place and military station.
Ama, St. Charles Par., La., 815.
On Tex. & Pac. (R. R.).
Amagansett, Suffolk Co., N. Y., 900.
On Long Isl. (R. R.).
Amalfi, Prov. of Salerno, Italy, 3,970.
Amanda, Fairfield Co., Ohio, 557.
On Penna. (R. R.).
Amarillo, c. s., Potter Co., Potter and Randall Cos., Texas, 43,132.
On Chi., Rk. Isl. & Gulf; Ft. Worth & Den. Cy.; Panh. & Santa Fe (R. Rs.).
Grain, live stock and natural gas.
Amasa, Iron Co., Mich., 1,000.
On Chi. & Nor. West.; Chi., Mil., St. P. & Pac. (R. Rs.).
Amasya, Vilayet, Turkey in Asia, 12,481.
Trade center of farming region.
Amatillán, Guatemala, 8,400.
Ambala, Punjab, India, 76,326.
Trade center and military station.
Ambato, Prov. of Tunguragua, Ecuador, 16,600.
Extensive shoe manufactories and agave cordage.
Amberg, Bavaria, Germany, 27,000.
Enamels, machinery and furniture.
Amble, Northumberland, England, 4,208.
Amblecote, Staffordshire, England, 3,099.
Ambler, Montgomery Co., Pa., 3,944.
On Reading (R. R.).
Amboina, capital of Amboina island and of Dutch Residency of Amboina, Moluccas, Netherland India, about 10,000.
Amboy, Lee Co., Ill., 1,972.
On Chi., Burl. & Quincy; Ill. Cen. (R. Rs.).
–Ashtabula Co., Ohio, 500.
On N. York Cen.; N. York, Chi. & St. Lou. (R. Rs.).
–Blue Earth Co., Minn., 593.
On Chi., St. P., Mpls. & Oma. (R. R.).
Ambridge, Beaver Co., Pa., 20,277.
On Penna. (R. R.).
Industrial and farming section.
Iron and steel products.
Amealco, State of Queretaro, Mexico, 1,674.
Ameca, State of Jalisco, Mexico, 11,034.
On National of Mexico (R. R.).
Amenia, Dutchess Co., N. Y., 725.
On N. York Cen. (R. R.).
American Falls, c. s., Power Co., Idaho, 1,280.
On Un. Pac. (R. R.).
American Fork, Utah Co., Utah, 3,047.
On Den. & Rio Gde. West.; Un. Pac.; Salt L. & Utah (El.) (R. Rs.).
Americus, c. s., Sumter Co., Ga., 8,760.
On Cen. of Ga.; Seab. Air Line (R. Rs.).
Amerongen, Netherlands, 2,706.
Amersfoort, Utrecht, Netherlands, 41,287.
Chemical and tobacco industries.
Amery, Polk Co., Wis., 1,354.
On Mpls., St. P. & S. Ste. M. (R. R.).
Ames, Story Co., Iowa, 10,261.
On Chi. & Nor. West.; Ft. Dodge, Des Moines & Sou. (R. Rs.).
Corn, garden tools and college goods. Seat of Iowa State College of Agriculture.
–Dodge Co., Neb., 500.
On Un. Pac. (R. R.).
Amesbury, Essex Co., Mass., 10,514.
On Bost. & Me. (R. R.).
Automobile parts and supplies, shoes, abrasives.
Amherst, Hampshire Co., Mass., 6,473.
On Bost. & Me.; Cen. Ver. (R. Rs.).
Amherst College, and Massachusetts State Agricultural College.
–Lorain Co., Ohio, 2,844.
On N. York Cen. (R. R.).
–Lamb Co., Tex., 964.
On Panh. & Santa Fe (R. R.).
–c. s., Amherst Co., Va., 876.
On Sou. (R. R.).
–Portage Co., Wis., 577.
On Mpls., St. P. & S. Ste. M. (R. R.).
–Cumberland Co., Nova Scotia, 7,450.
On Canadian National Railways.
Port of entry; lumber, shipbuilding.
Amherstburg, Essex Co., Ontario, Canada, 2,759.
On Mich. Cen. (R. R.).
Amherstdale, Logan Co., W. Va., 1,500.
On Chesa. & Ohio (R. R.).
Amiens, Capital of Dept. of Somme (Picardy), France, 93,773.
Situated on the river Somme, and on the Paris and Boulogne Railway.
The Cathedral of Notre Dame of Amiens is one of the most perfect constructions of Gothic architecture, and among the most important cathedrals of Europe.
In 1802 was concluded the treaty called the "Peace of Amiens," when the powers of Europe officially recognized the territorial changes made in Europe by the wars of Napoleon. The city was an important point which the Germans sought to capture in the European war, but it was successfully defended by the Anglo-French forces.
Amite, c. s., Tangipahoa Parish, La., 2,536.
On Ill. Cen. (R. R.).
Amity, Clark Co., Ark., 608.
On Mo. Pac. (R. R.).
Amityville, Suffolk Co., N. Y., 4,437.
On Long Isl. (R. R.).
Amman (Philadelphia), capital of Transjordan, 15,000.
Amol, Masenderan, Iran (Persia), 20,000.
Amory, Monroe Co., Miss., 3,214.
On Mississippian; St. Lou.-San Fran. (R. Rs.).
Amoy, Prov. of Fukien, China, 234,200.
Important exports of native products.
Amritsar, Punjab, India, 264,840.
Manufactures of shawls, silks, and cotton cloth.
Amsterdam, the largest city and legislative capital of the Netherlands, 781,665.
Situated on the western arm of the Zuider Zee, and has an area of 18½ square miles. The city is built in a semicircle. It stands on marshy ground, much of it constructed on ground piles, 50 feet long, driven into the ground at great cost. Traversed by canals, the city is cut up into 90 islands, crossed by 300 bridges. Amsterdam has been a center of Dutch industry for many centuries.
It is an important money market; the Bank of Netherlands is one of the great financial institutions of Europe. The city ranks first among the ports of the Netherlands.
–Montgomery Co., N. Y., 34,817.
On Fonda, Johnst. & Glov. (El.); N. York Cen. (R. Rs.).
One of world's chief manufacturing centers in carpets, fresh-water pearls, and brooms.
–Jefferson Co., Ohio, 1,171.
On N. York Cen. (R. R.).
Amy, Oakland Co., Mich., 900.
Anaconda, c. s., Deer Lodge Co., Mont., 12,494.
On Butte, Ana. & Pac. (R. R.).
Famous for copper smelters.
Anacortes, Skagit Co., Wash., 6,564.
On Gt. Nor. (R. R.).
Puget Sound fishery and timber products.
Anadarko, c. s., Caddo Co., Okla., 5,036.
On Chi., Rk. Isl. & Pac. (R. R.).
Anagni, Prov. of Frosinone, Italy, 6,274.
Anaheim, Orange Co., Cal., 10,995.
On Atch., Top. & Santa Fe; Sou. Pac.; Pac. Elec.; Un. Pac. (R. Rs.).
Anahuac, c. s., Chambers Co., Tex., 513.
Citrus fruits, walnuts, dairying.
Anamosa, c. s., Jones Co., Iowa, 3,579.
On Chi., Mil., St. P. & Pac.; Chi. & Nor. West. (R. Rs.).
Ananiev, Govt. of Ukraine, Soviet Union, 19,000.
Anapa, Soviet Union, 16,565.
Trade center for a farming region.
Añasco, Añasco, Puerto Rico, 3,050.
Anchorage, Alaska, 2,277.
On Alaska (R. R.).
–Jefferson Co., Ky., 564.
On Chesa. & Ohio; Lou. & Nash. (R. Rs.).
Ancona, capital of Prov. of Ancona, Italy, 66,750.
Seaport; famous Arch of Trajan.
Ancud, Prov. of Chiloe, Chile, 3,341.
Anda, Prov. of Bohol, Bohol, P. I., 6,712.
Andalusia, c. s., Covington Co., Ala., 5,154.
On Cen. of Ga.; Lou. & Nash. (R. Rs.).
–Bucks Co., Pa., 1,200.
On Penna. (R. R.).
Anderlecht, Brabant, Belgium (Suburb of Bruxelles), 77,479.
Andernach, Prussia, Germany, 10,111.
10 miles northwest of Koblenz.
Anderson, Shasta Co., Calif., 1,445.
On Sou. Pac. (R. R.).
–c. s., Madison Co., Ind., 39,804.
On Cen. Ind.; Cleve., Cin., Chi. & St. Lou.; Ind. R. R. Sys. (El.); Penna. (R. Rs.).
Automobile parts, stoves and shipping cartons.
–McDonald Co., Mo., 857.
On Kan. Cy. Sou. (R. R.).
–Washington Co., Pa., 512.
On Balt. & Ohio (R. R.).
–c. s., Anderson Co., S. C., 14,383.
On Blue Ridge; Charl. & West. Car.; Pied. & Nor. (El.) (R. Rs.).
Textiles and other manufactures. In agricultural district.
Andorra, Andorra, Europe, 600.
Capital of the little semi-independent country Andorra, located in the Pyrenees.
Andover, Southampton, England, 9,692.
–Oxford Co., Maine, 788.
–Essex Co., Mass., 10,542.
On Bost. & Me. (R. R.).
Seat of Phillips Andover Academy.
–Merrimack Co., N. H., 500.
On Bost. & Me. (R. R.).
–Allegany Co., N. Y., 1,241.
On Erie (R. R.).
–Ashtabula Co., Ohio, 906.
On N. York Cen. (R. R.).
–Wise Co., Va., 535.
On Interstate (R. R.).
Andrews, Huntington Co., Ind., 883.
On Wabash; Ind. R. R. Sys. (El.) (R. Rs.).
–Cherokee Co., N. C., 1,748.
On Sou.; Tenn. & No. Carol. (R. Rs.).
–Georgetown and Williamsburg Cos., S. C., 1,712.
On Seab. Air Line (R. R.).
Andria, Bari, Italy, 55,786.
Andujar, Prov. of Jäen, Spain, 17,950.
Aneta, Nelson Co., N. Dak., 568.
On Gt. Nor. (R. R.).
Angangueo, State of Michoacan, Mexico, 7,431.
On National of Mexico (R. R.).
Angeles, Pampanga Prov., Luzon, P. I., 17,919.
Angelica, Allegany Co., N. Y., 838.
On Pitts., Shawmut & Nor. (R. R.).
Angels, Calaveras Co., Cal., 915.
Angers, Dept. of Maine-et-Loire, France, 87,988.

Situated on the Maine River and on the railway from Nantes to Tours.
Angier, Harnett Co., N. C., 760.
On Durh. & Sou. (R. R.).
Angleton, c. s., Brazoria Co., Texas, 1,229.
On Mo. Pac. (R. R.).
Angol, Prov. of Malleco, Chile, 10,288.
Angola, c. s., Steuben Co., Ind., 2,665.
On N. York Cen. (R. R.).
In a beautiful lake country.
–Erie Co., N. Y., 1,543.
On N. York Cen.; N. York, Chi. & St. Lou.; Penna. (R. Rs.).
Angora, Turkey. See Ankara.
Angouleme, capital of Dept. of Charente, France, 38,915.
Angra, capital city of the Azores, 11,000.
Anita, Cass Co., Iowa, 1,106.
On Chi., Rk. Isl. & Pac. (R. R.).
–Jefferson Co., Pa., 1,000.
On Balt. & Ohio; Penna. (R. Rs.).
Ankara (Angora), Vilayet of Ankara, Turkey, 123,699.
Capital of the Republic. Exports mohair, wool, and grain.
Ankeny, Polk Co., Iowa, 632.
On Chi. & Nor. West.; Ft. Dodge, Des Moines & Sou. (R. Rs.).
Anking, capital of Anhwei, China, 40,000.
Anklam, Prussia, Germany, 16,000.
Anmore, Harrison Co., W. Va., 1,200.
Anna, Union Co., Ill., 3,436.
On Ill. Cen. (R. R.).
Annaberg, Saxony, Germany, 20,000.
Braid and lace center.
Annandale, Wright Co., Minn., 663.
On Mpls., St. P. & S. Ste. M. (R. R.).
–Hunterdon Co., N. J., 500.
On Cen. of N. Jer. (R. R.).
Annapolis, c. s., Anne Arundel Co., Md., State capital, 12,531.
Port of entry, on the south bank of the Severn, 2 miles from the river's entrance into Chesapeake Bay, and on the Baltimore & Annapolis (El.) Railroad. The city is about 22 miles east from Washington.
Annapolis is the seat of the United States Naval Academy, founded in 1845 by George Bancroft, Secretary of the Navy under President Polk. Previous to this, midshipmen prepared themselves at the Naval Asylum at Philadelphia. At the outbreak of the Civil War in 1861, the academy was removed to Newport, R. I., and was reestablished at Annapolis in 1865. Since 1898 the Government has spent $11,000,000 in rebuilding the Naval Academy, making it the finest in the world. John Paul Jones is buried here in the New Memorial Chapel.
Annapolis contains a State-house (in front of which stands the bronze statue of Chief Justice Taney), a governor's mansion, a courthouse, land offices, controller's and treasurer's buildings, and jail; gas works and water works. It is the seat of the Court of Appeals. The harbor, called Annapolis Roads, has a depth of 60 feet in the channel up to Round Bay in the Severn River, 7 miles from the city. From Annapolis Roads a channel 31 feet deep has been dredged to the Naval Academy wharf.
Ann Arbor, c. s., Washtenaw Co., Mich., 26,944.
On the Huron River and on the Michigan Central and the Ann Arbor Railroads. The seat of the University of Michigan, founded in 1837, one of the largest state universities in the Union. Chief manufactures are agricultural implements, automobile accessories, engines, and boilers, radios, balers, etc.
Annecy, Dept. of Haute-Savoie, France, 23,293.
Textiles, leather goods, and paper.
Anniston, c. s., Calhoun Co., Ala., 22,345.
On Lou. & Nash.; Sou. (R. Rs.).
Iron, steel and textile industries.
Annonay, Dept. of Ardèche, France, 15,669.
Industrial center, paper, leather and silk.
Anoka, c. s., Anoka Co., Minn., 4,851.
On Gt. Nor.; Nor. Pac.; Mpls., Anoka & Cuy. Range (El.) (R. Rs.).
Ans, Liége, Belgium, 12,580.
Suburb of Liége.
Ansbach, Bavaria, Germany, 23,000.
Manufacturing town, cardboard, buttons, combs, and automobiles.
Ansley, Jackson Par., La., 619.
On Chi., Rk. Isl. & Pac. (R. R.).
–Custer Co., Neb., 817.
On Chi., Burl. & Quincy (R. R.).
Anson, Somerset Co., Maine, 950.
On Me. Cen. (R. R.).
–c. s., Jones Co., Texas, 2,093.
On Wich. Val. (R. R.).
Ansonia, New Haven Co., Conn., 19,898.
On N. York, N. Hav. & Hart. (R. R.).
Important industrial center, manufacturing wire, copper and brass products.
–Darke Co., Ohio, 651.
On Cle., Cin., Chi. & St. Lou. (R. R.).
Ansonville, Anson Co., N. C., 532.
On Winst.-Sal. Southb. (R. R.).
Ansted, Fayette Co., W. Va., 1,404.
On Chesa. & Ohio (R. R.).
Antalya (Adalia), Vilayet of Antalya, Asia Minor, Turkey, 17,635.
Seaport, Gulf of Adalia.
Antananarivo, Madagascar. See Tananarive.
Antequera, Prov. of Malaga, Spain, 31,526.
Woolen fabrics and sugar.
–Prov. of Bohol, P. I., 10,927.
Anthon, Woodbury Co., Iowa, 826.
On Ill. Cen. (R. R.).
Anthony, c. s., Harper Co., Kans., 2,892.
On Atch., Top. & Santa Fe; Mo. Pac. (R. Rs.).
–Dona Ana Co., N. Mex., 1,200.
Antibes, Alpes-Maritimes, France, 25,014.
A Mediterranean seaport.
Antigo, c. s., Langlade Co., Wis., 8,610.
On Chi. & Nor. West. (R. R.).
Antigua, Guatemala, 12,200.
Antioch, Contra Costa Co., Cal., 3,563.
On Atch., Top. & Santa Fe; Sou. Pac. (R. Rs.).
–Lake Co., Ill., 1,101.
On Mpls., St. P. & S. Ste. M. (R. R.).
Antioche, Syria, Asia Minor, about 38,520.
One of the chief centers of early Christianity.
Antlers, c. s., Pushmataha Co., Okla., 2,246.
On St. Lou.-San Fran. (R. R.).
Antofagasta, capital of Dept. of Antofagasta, Chile, 53,591.
Exports nitrates.
Antonito, Conejos Co., Colo., 858.
On Den. & Rio. Grde. West. (R. R.).
Antram (Palmer Mine), Fayette Co., Pa., 1,200.
On Monongahela (R. R.).
Antrim, Hillstone Co., N. H., 1,102.
On Bost. & Me. (R. R.).
Antung, Manchukuo, 189,435.
Antwerp, Belgium. See Anvers.
Antwerp, Jefferson Co., N. Y., 868.
On N. York Cen. (R. R.).
–Paulding Co., Ohio, 1,024.
On Wabash (R. R.).
Anvers (Antwerp), capital of Prov. of Antwerp, Belgium, 277,929.
Chief commercial city of Belgium, situated on the right bank of the river Scheldt. The principal manufactures are silks and velvets, soap, cigars, serges, and leather. It is the world center for diamond-cutting. Shipbuilding also important. The French obtained possession of the city in 1794, and prosperity revived. After Anvers had been restored to Belgium, its trade increased rapidly till 1914. In that year a German army occupied the city.
Anvil Location, Gogebic Co., Mich., 500.
Aomori, Honshu, Japan, 77,100.
Aosta, Prov. of Aosta, Italy, 12,600.
Vicinity celebrated for its forests of pine, its mines, and mineral springs.
Apache, Caddo Co., Okla., 1,302.
On Chi., Rk. Isl. & Pac. (R. R.).
Apalachicola, c. s., Franklin Co., Fla., 3,370.
On Apalachi. Nor. (R. R.).
Has oyster and other fisheries.
Apalit, Prov. of Pampanga, Luzon, P. I., 11,888.
Aparri, Prov. of Cagayan, Luzon, P. I., 20,601.
Center of tobacco producing region.
Apeldoorn, Gelderland, Netherlands, 67,080.
Chief manufacture: paper.
Apex, Wake Co., N. C., 863.
On Durh. & Sou.; Seab. Air Line (R. Rs.).
Apia, capital of Western Samoa, 3,500.
Aplington, Butler Co., Iowa, 622.
On Ill. Cen. (R. R.).
Apolda, Saxe-Weimar, Germany, 28,000.
Industrial center. Silk products, woolen goods, bells, cardboard, and machinery.
Apollo, Armstrong Co., Pa., 3,406.
On Penna. (R. R.).
Apopka, Orange Co., Fla., 1,450.
On Atl. Coast Line; Seab. Air Line (R. Rs.).
Appalachia, Wise Co., Va., 3,595.
On Interst.; Lou. & Nash.; Sou. (R. Rs.).
Appleton, Swift Co., Minn., 1,625.
On Chi., Mil., St. P. & Pac.; Gt. Nor. (R. Rs.).
–c. s., Outagamie Co., Wis., 25,267.
On Chi. & Nor. West.; Chi., Mil., St. P. & Pac.; Mpls., St. P. & S. Ste. M. (R. Rs.).
Paper mills, lumber, machinery.
Appleton City, c. s., St. Clair Co., Mo., 1,136.
On Mo.-Kan.-Tex. (R. R.).
Appomattox, Appomattox Co., Va., 704.
On Norf. & West. (R. R.).
Apponaug, Kent Co., R. I., 1,410.
On N. York, New Hav. & Hart. (R. R.).
Aqsu (Aksu), Sinkiang. See Wensuh.
Aquila degli Abruzzi, capital of Prov. of Aquila degli Abruzzi, Italy, 38,730.
A summer resort.
Aracajú, Sergipe, Brazil, 53,600.
Arad, capital of Dist. of Arad, Rumania, 77,255.
Aragon, Polk Co., Ga., 909.
On Seab. Air Line; Sou. (R. Rs.).
Aransas Pass, San Patricio and Aransas Cos., Tex., 2,482.
On Arans. Harb. Term.; Sou. Pac. (R. Rs.).
Arapahoe, Furnas Co., Neb., 1,017.
On Chi., Burl. & Quincy (R. R.).
Ararat, Susquehanna Co., Pa., 510.
Arauco, Prov. of Arauco, Chile, 2,680.
Arayat, Luzon, P. I., 12,311.
Arbroath, Forfarshire, Scotland, 17,637.
Manufactures jute, flax, linen, canvas, boots.
Arbuckle, Colusa Co., Calif., 1,000.
On Sou. Pac. (R. R.).
Arbutus, Baltimore Co., Md., 500.
On Penna. (R. R.).
Arcade, Wyoming Co., N. Y., 1,643.
On Arcade & Attica; Penna. (R. Rs.).
Arcadia, Los Angeles Co., Cal., 5,216.
On Atch., Top. & Santa Fe; Sou. Pac.; Pac. Elec. (R. Rs.).
–c. s., De Soto Co., Fla., 4,077.
On Atl. Coast Line; Seab. Air Line (R. Rs.).
–Hamilton Co., Ind., 912.
On Ind. R. R. Sys. (El.); N. York, Chi. & St. Lou. (R. Rs.).
–Crawford Co., Kans., 984.
On St. Lou.-San Fran. (R. R.).
–c. s., Bienville Parish, La., 1,809.
On Ill. Cen. (R. R.).
–Valley Co., Neb., 711.
On Chi., Burl. & Quincy (R. R.).
–Indiana Co., Pa., 500.
On N. York Cen. (R. R.).
–Spartanburg Co., S. Car., 1,800.
On Sou. (R. R.).
–Trempealeau Co., Wis., 1,499.

ORIENT AND OCCIDENT PHOTO
LES ARÈNES, OLD ROMAN AMPHITHEATER, AT ARLES, SOUTHERN FRANCE, DATING FROM THE 2ND CENTURY, A. D. IT HAS A SEATING CAPACITY OF 26,000 PERSONS

On Gr. Bay & West. (R. R.).
Arcanum, Darke Co., Ohio, 1,149.
On Balt. & Ohio; Clev., Cin., Chi. & St. Lou. (R. Rs.).
Arcata, Humboldt Co., Cal., 1,709.
On Arcata & Mad Riv.; Northw. Pac. (R. Rs.).
Archangel, Soviet Union. See Arkhangelsk.
Archbald, Lackawanna Co., Pa., 9,587.
On Del. & Hud.; N. Y., Ont. & West. (R. Rs.).
Archbold, Fulton Co., Ohio, 1,185.
On N. York Cen.; Tol. & Ind. (El.) (R. Rs.).
Archdale, Randolph Co., N. C., 628.
On Southern (R. R.).
Archer, Alachua Co., Fla., 576.
On Atl. Coast Line; Seab. Air Line (R. Rs.).
Archer City, c. s., Archer Co., Texas, 1,512.
On Wich. Fs. & Sou. (R. R.).
Arco, c. s., Butte Co., Idaho, 572.
On Ore. Short Line (R. R.).
Arcola, Douglas Co., Ill., 1,686.
On Ill. Cen.; Penna. (R. Rs.).
Arcos de la Frontera, Prov. of Cadiz, Spain, 15,748.
Center of a horse-raising section.
Arcot, Madras, India, 12,000.
Ardebil, Azerbaijan, Iran (Persia), 44,808.
Arden, Richland Co., S. C., 987.
Ardmore, c. s., Carter Co., Okla., 15,741.
On St. Lou.-San Fran.; Gulf, Colo. & Santa Fe (R. Rs.).
Distributing center for oil fields of southern Oklahoma and part of northern Texas. Near producing oil fields and natural gas fields. Manufactures include refined petroleum, cigars, stoves, firearms, asphalt paint and automobile tires.
–Giles Co., Tenn., 700.
Ardsley, Westchester Co., N. Y., 1,135.
On N. York Cen. (R. R.).
–Montgomery Co., Pa., 1,420.
On Reading (R. R.).
Ardsley-on-Hudson, Westchester Co., N. Y., 500.
On N. York Cen. (R. R.).
Arecibo, Mun. of Arecibo, Puerto Rico, 14,332.
Arendal, Prov. of Aust.-Agder, Norway, 10,403.
An important seaport. Chief exports: timber, wood pulp, aluminum.
Arequipa, capital of Dept. of Arequipa, Peru, 70,000.
Chief industrial city of southern Peru. Textiles, chocolate, flour, machinery.
Arezzo, capital of Prov. of Arezzo, Italy, 19,000.
Interesting for its historical landmarks.
Argao, Prov. of Cebu, Cebu, P. I., 42,000.
Argenta, Lander Co., Nev., 1,053.
On Sou. Pac.; West. Pac. (R. Rs.).
Argenteuil, France, 59,314.
Argentine, Wyandotte Co., Kansas. (Ind. Sta. of Kansas City.)
On Atch., Top. & Santa Fe (R. R.).
Argonia, Sumner Co., Kans., 503.
On Atch., Top. & Santa Fe; Mo. Pac. (R. Rs.).
Argos, Province of Argolis, Greece, 10,504.
Considered by many to be the most ancient Greek city; formerly famous.
–Marshall Co., Ind., 1,211.
On N. York, Chi. & St. Lou. (R. R.).
Argyle, Marshall Co., Minn., 700.
On Gt. Nor. (R. R.).
–Lafayette Co., Wis., 692.
On Ill. Cen. (R. R.).
Ariano di Puglia, capital of Avellino Prov., Italy, 8,438.
Arica, Dept. of Arica, Chile, 13,140.
Port important in Chilean and Bolivian export.
Arista, Mercer Co., W. Va., 520.
On Norf. & West. (R. R.).
Aristes, Columbia Co., Pa., 500.
On Leh. Val. (R. R.).
Ariton, Dale Co., Ala., 611.
On Atl. Coast Line; Cen. of Ga. (R. Rs.).
Arkadelphia, c. s., Clark Co., Ark., 3,380.
On Mo. Pac. (R. R.).
Henderson State Teachers College and Ouachita College.
Arkansas City, c. s., Desha Co., Ark., 1,432.
On Mo. Pac. (R. R.).
–c. s., Cowley Co., Kans., 13,332.
On Atch., Top. & Santa Fe; Midl. Val.; Mo. Pac.; St. Lou.-San Fran. (R. Rs.).
Oil refineries, machine shops, flour mills, gasoline plant, ice plant, and meat packing plant. Center of rich agricultural and dairying district.
Arkhangelsk (Archangel), Soviet Union, 194,300.
An important seaport on the White Sea.
Arkport, Steuben Co., N. Y., 575.
On Erie; Pitts., Shawmut & Nor. (R. Rs.).
Arkville, Delaware Co., N. Y., 650.
On Del. & Nor.; West Shore (R. Rs.).
Arkwright, Spartanburg Co., S. C., 518.
Arles, Dept. of Bouchet-du-Rhône, France, 29,165.
St. Trophimus Cathedral and Hôtel de Ville; libraries and schools; shipbuilding; carshops.
Arlington, Duval Co., Fla., 500.
–Calhoun and Early Cos., Ga., 1,232.
On Cen. of Ga.; Seab. Air Line (R. Rs.).
–Fayette Co., Iowa, 706.
On Chi., Mil., St. P. & Pac. (R. Rs.).
–Reno Co., Kansas, 523.
On Chi., Rk. Isl. & Pac. (R. R.).
–Carlisle Co., Ky., 685.
On Ill. Cen. (R. R.).
–Middlesex Co., Mass., 38,539.
On Bost. & Me. (R. R.).
Manufacturing and market gardening.
–Sibley Co., Minn., 915.
On Mpls. & St. Lou. (R. R.).
–Washington Co., Neb., 622.

On Chi. & Nor. West. (R. R.).
–Dutchess Co., N. Y., 1,500.
On Staten Isl. Rap. Trans. (El.) (R. R.).
–Hancock Co., Ohio, 701.
On N. York Cen.; Nor. Ohio (R. Rs.).
–Gilliam Co., Oregon, 601.
On Un. Pac. (R. R.).
–Kingsbury Co., S. Dak., 1,060.
On Chi. & Nor. West.; Gt. Nor. (R. Rs.).
–Tarrant Co., Texas, 3,661.
On Tex. & Pac. (R. R.).
–Bennington Co., Vt., 1,441.
On Rutland (R. R.).
–Snohomish Co., Wash., 1,439.
On Nor. Pac. (R. R.).
Arlington Heights, Cook Co., Ill., 4,997.
On Chi. & Nor. West. (R. R.).
–Hamilton Co., Ohio, 1,214.
On Clev., Cin., Chi. & St. Lou. (R. R.).
Arlon, Prov. of Luxembourg, Belgium, 11,634.
Arma, Crawford Co., Kansas, 1,910.
On Jop. & Pitts. (El.); Mo. Pac. (R. Rs.).
Armada, Macomb Co., Mich., 840.
On Gd. Trunk (R. R.).
Armavir, Soviet Union, 90,200.
Armentières, Dept. du Nord, France, 24,049.
Partly destroyed in World War. It was occupied by Germans, but given up Oct. 1, 1918.
Armour, c. s., Douglas Co., S. D., 1,008.
On Chi., Mil., St. P. & Pac. (R. R.).
Armstrong, Emmet Co., Iowa, 767.
On Chi., Rk. Isl. & Pac. (R. R.).
–Howard Co., Mo., 548.
On Alton (R. R.).
Armuchee, Floyd Co., Ga., 800.
Arnhem, Gelderland, Netherlands, 83,999.
Manufactures include cabinet-ware, mirrors, and mathematical instruments.
Arnold, Custer Co., Neb., 899.
On Un. Pac. (R. R.).
–Westmoreland Co., Pa., 10,575.
On Penna. (R. R.).
A manufacturing town.
Arnold City, Fayette Co., Pa., 500.
On Pittsb. & L. Erie (R. R.).
Arnolds Park, Dickinson Co., Iowa, 597.
On Chi., Mil., St. P. & Pac. (R. R.).
Arnot, Tioga Co., Pa., 648.
On Erie (R. R.).
Arnprior, Renfrew Co., Ontario, Canada, 4,033.
On Can. Pac.; Can. Nat. (R. Rs.).
Arnstadt, Thüringen, Germany, 22,000.
Mining machinery and chemicals.
Arolsen, Waldeck, Germany, 2,418.
Aronimink, Delaware Co., Pa., 1,900.
Aronimink Heights, Delaware Co., Pa., 1,150.
Arp, Smith Co., Tex., 2,000.
On Mo. Pac. (R. R.).
Arrah, Dist. of Shahabad, India, 48,922.
Agricultural center.
Arras, Dept. of Pas-de-Calais, France, 31,488.
Manufactures beet-sugar and lace; birthplace of Robespierre.
Arroyo, Mun. of Arroyo, Puerto Rico, 4,446.
Arroyo Grande, San Luis Obispo Co., Cal., 892.
On Pac. Coast (R. R.).
Arroyo Hondo, Taos Co., N. Mex., 500.
Arroyoseco, Taos Co., N. Mex., 662.
Arta, Prov. of Epirus, Greece, 7,468.
Artemisa, Prov. of Pinar del Rio, Cuba, 6,996.
Artemovsk, Ukraine, Sov. Union, 52,000.
Artesia, Lowndes Co., Miss., 612.
On Mob. & Ohio (R. R.).
–Eddy Co., N. M., 2,427.
On Atch., Top. & Santa Fe (R. R.).
Artesian, Sanborn Co., S. Dak., 556.
On Chi., Mil., St. P. & Pac. (R. R.).
Arthur, Moultrie and Douglas Cos., Ill., 1,361.
On Chi. & East Ill.; Penna. (R. Rs.).
–Wellington Co., Ontario, Canada, 1,021.
On Can. Pac. (R. R.).
Arvada, Jefferson Co., Colo., 1,276.
On Den. & Interm. (El.); Colo. & Sou. (R. Rs.).
Arvin, Kern Co., Calif., 707.
On Atch., Top. & Santa Fe; Sou. Pac. (R. Rs.).
Aš, Germany. See Asch.
Manufactures silks, woolen and cotton goods, hosiery, and wire.
Asbury, Warren Co., N. J., 580.
R. R. Sta. at Ludlow-Asbury; on Cen. of N. Jer. (R. R.).
Asbury Park, Monmouth Co., N. J., 14,981.
On Cen. of N. Jer.; N. Y. & Long Br.; Penna. (R. Rs.).
Seaside summer resort, 50 miles from New York. City owns beach front.
Aschaffenburg, Bavaria, Germany, 36,000.
Chemical, paper, cellulose, electrical machinery.
Asch (As), Germany, 22,943.
Aschersleben, Prussia, Germany, 28,000.
Potash mines, iron goods, chemicals.
Ascoli Piceno, Prov. of Ascoli Piceno, Italy, 18,500.
The ancient city of Asculum.
Ashaway, Washington Co., R. I., 620.
Ashburn, Turner Co., Ga., 2,073.
On Ga.; Ashb., Sylv. & Cam.; Ga. Sou. & Fla. (R. Rs.).
Ashburnham, Worcester Co., Mass., 800.
On Bost. & Me. (R. R.).
Ashby, Middlesex Co., Mass., 978.
Ashdown, Little River Co., Ark., 1,607.
On Grays., Nashv. & Ashd.; Kans. Cy., Sou.; St. Lou.-San Fran. (R. Rs.).
Asheboro, c. s., Randolph Co., N. C., 5,021.
On High Pt., Rand., Asheb. & Sou.; Norf. Sou. (R. Rs.).
Asher, Pottawatomie Co., Okla., 653.
On Chi., Rk. Isl. & Pac. (R. R.).
Asherton, Dimmit Co., Tex., 1,858.
On Asherton & Gulf (Mo. Pac.) (R. R.).
Asheville, c. s., Buncombe Co., N. C., 50,193.
Situated among the Blue Ridge Mountains at an elevation of nearly 2,500 feet; is well known as a health and pleasure resort. Adjoining the town is Biltmore Park and chateau (now a museum). Asheville is reached by the Southern Railroad and is near Great Pisgah National Forest, Smoky Mountains National Park and Mount Mitchell.
Wood products, cotton products and blankets.
Ashfield, Franklin Co., Mass., 918.
Ashford, Houston Co., Ala., 910.
On Atl. Coast Line (R. R.).
–Windham Co., Conn., 726.
Ash Grove, Greene Co., Mo., 1,107.
On St. Lou.-San Fran. (R. R.).
Ashkhabad, Turcoman, Sov. Union, 79,000.
Important wool and cotton trading center.
Ashland, c. s., Clay Co., Ala., 1,476.
On Ashland (R. R.).
–Cass Co., Ill., 1,007.
On Alton; Balt. & Ohio (R. Rs.).
–c. s., Clark Co., Kans., 1,325.
On Atch., Top. & Santa Fe (R. R.).
–Boyd Co., Ky., 29,074.
On Chesa. & Ohio (R. R.).
Steel, oil, coal and gas.
–Aroostook Co., Maine, 2,100.
On Bangor & Aroostock (R. R.).
–Middlesex Co., Mass., 2,497.
On Bost. & Alb. (R. R.).
Center of a hunting and fishing region.
–Saunders Co., Neb., 1,786.
On Chi., Burl. & Quincy (R. R.).
–Camden Co., N. J., 1,000.
On Penna.-Read. Seashore (R. R.).
–Grafton Co., N. H., 1,200.
On Bost. & Me. (R. R.).
–c. s., Ashland Co., Ohio, 11,141.
On Erie (R. R.).
Ashland College; diverse manufactures.
–Jackson Co., Ore., 4,544.
On Sou. Pac. (R. R.).
Southern Oregon State Normal School.
–Schuylkill Co., Pa., 7,164.
On Leh. Val.; Read. (R. Rs.).
Anthracite coal mining center.
–Hanover Co., Va., 1,297.
On Rich., Fred. & Potomac (R. R.).
–c. s., Ashland Co., Wis., 10,622.
On Chi. & Nor. West.; Chi., St. P., Mpls. & Oma.; Dul., Sou. Sh. & Atl.; Mpls., St. P. & S. Ste. M.; Nor. Pac. (R. Rs.).
Situated on Chequamegon Bay.
Coal and iron ore docks.
Ashland City, c. s., Cheatham Co., Tenn., 712.
On Tenn. Cen. (R. R.).
Ashley, Washington Co., Ill., 772.
On Ill. Cen.; Lou. & Nash. (R. Rs.).
–c. s., McIntosh Co., N. Dak., 1,033.
On Mpls., St. P. & S. Ste. M. (R. R.).
–Delaware Co., Ohio, 734.
On Cle., Cin., Chi. & St. Lou. (R. R.).
–Ashley, Luzerne Co., Pa., 7,093.
On Cen. of N. Jer. (R. R.).
Ashley Falls, Berkshire Co., Mass., 500.
On N. York, N. Hav. & Hart. (R. R.).
Ashley-Hudson, Steuben Co., Ind., 700.
On Wabash (R. R.).
Ashtabula, Ashtabula Co., Ohio, 23,301.
On N. York Cen.; N. York, Chi. & St. Lou.; Penna. (R. Rs.).
Lake Erie port for iron and coal.
Ashton, Fremont Co., Idaho, 1,003.
On Un. Pac. (R. R.).
–Lee Co., Ill., 868.
On Chi. & Nor. West. (R. R.).
–Osceola Co., Iowa, 568.
On Chi., St. P., Mpls. & Oma. (R. R.).
–St. Charles Par., La., 800.
On Tex. & Pac. (R. R.).
–Providence Co., R. I., 2,218.
On N. York, N. Hav. & Hart. (R. R.).
Ashton-Under-Lyne, Lancashire, England, 51,573.
Textile mills, foundries, hat-making.
Ashuelot, Cheshire Co., N. H., 600.
On Bost. & Me. (R. R.).
Ashville, Pickaway Co., Ohio, 1,085.
On Norf. & West. (R. R.).
Askam, Luzerne Co., Pa., 2,500.
Asmara, capital of Italian Colony of Eritrea, Italian East Africa, 21,771.
Trading center in a rich agricultural region.
Asnières, Dept. of Seine, France, 71,831.
A suburb of Paris.
Asola, Prov. of Mantova, Italy, 2,340.

COURTESY SOUTHERN RAILWAYS

A VIEW OF THE CENTRAL SECTION OF ASHEVILLE, NORTH CAROLINA, FROM BEAUCATCHER MOUNTAIN

Asotin, c. s., Asotin Co., Wash., 697.
Aspen, c. s., Pitkin Co., Colo., 705.
On Den. & Rio Grande Western (R. R.).
Aspermont, c. s., Stonewall Co., Texas, 769.
On Wich. Val. (R. R.).
Aspinwall, Allegheny Co., Pa., 4,263.
On Penna. (R. R.).
Assen, capital of Province of Drenthe, Netherlands, 17,652.
An important market town.
Assisi, Prov. of Perugia, Italy, 5,353.
Noted as a pilgrim city.
Assonet, Bristol Co., Mass., 1,500.
On N. York, N. Hav. & Hart. (R. R.).
Assumption, Christian Co., Ill., 1,554.
On Ill. Cen. (R. R.).
Asti, Prov. of Alessandria, Italy, 25,042.
Famous for its wines.
Astoria, Fulton Co., Ill., 1,189.
On Chi., Burl. & Quincy (R. R.).
–c. s., Clatsop Co., Ore., 10,349.
On Spok., Port. & Seattle (R. R.), and steamship connection with U. P. system at Seattle. Founded in 1811 by John Jacob Astor as a fur trading settlement.
Freshwater seaport on Columbia River.
Salmon fisheries, canning, timber, grain.
Astrakhan, Soviet Union, 225,400.
Important fishing and commercial center.
Asturias, Cebu, P. I., 14,827.
Asuncion, capital of Paraguay, South America, 95,651.
A busy port and trading center. The city has excellent streets, hotels and buildings.
Asyût, Egypt, 62,400.
Atchison, c. s., Atchison Co., Kans., 12,538.
Railroad and shipping center on the Atchison, Topeka and Santa Fe, the Chicago, Burlington and Quincy, the Chicago, Rock Island and Pacific, and the Missouri Pacific railroads.
Flour milling, grain, foundry and hardware, seeds and agricultural implements.
Atco, Bartow Co., Ga., 1,603.
–Camden Co., N. J., 1,500.
On Penna.-Read. Seashore (R. R.).
Ath, Prov. of Hainaut, Belgium, 10,186.
Atglen, Chester Co., Pa., 620.
On Pennsylvania (R. R.).
Athena, Umatilla Co., Ore., 504.
On Nor. Pac.; Un. Pac. (R. Rs.).
Athēnai (Athens), capital of Greece, 495,490.
Situated on an extensive and well-watered plain, surrounded on all sides by hills, very near the Gulf of Aegina. The highest of the limestone ridges which break the plain forms the Acropolis or Citadel. The clusters of houses at the foot of the Acropolis occupy the site of ancient Athens. Outside of this extends the Neapolis or New City. Among the public buildings of note the most important are the National University, and the National Library. There are also the Academy, Polytechnic Institute, and National Museum.
The chief interest in Athēnai, however, attaches to her antiquities. Foremost among them is the Parthenon, now in ruins, which crowns the Acropolis. It is Doric, built of white marble, 228 feet in length, and is considered the most perfect model of Grecian architecture. Other buildings of note are the temple of the Wingless Victory, the theater of Dionysius, the ruins of the Odeon or theater of Herodes Atticus, and the Erechtheum. Other places of interest are Mars Hill, the Pnyx, the Prison of Socrates, the Grotto of Apollo, and the Roman baths. The Arch of Hadrian, the Temple of Jupiter, and the Stadium are just outside the city.
Athēnai was named for her tutelary deity, Pallas Athena. The beginning of the history of the city is involved in obscurity, but its first appearance was as the head of a territory called Attica. In the sixth century B.C. Solon drew up the famous Athenian code of laws, and in the fifth Athēnai reached her zenith of glory under Pericles. This was the golden age, and made Athēnai the center of the intellectual and artistic world. This position the city sustained for centuries, until it passed under Roman rule, 146 B.C. It became a part of the Byzantine Empire. In 1456 it was captured by the Turks, and in 1822, at the achievement of Greek independence, fell into the hands of the Greeks. The Turkish garrison was not withdrawn until 1833.
Immediately after that period Athēnai became the seat of the Greek Government.
Athens, Greece. See Athenai.
Athens, c. s., Limestone Co., Ala., 4,238.
On Lou. & Nash. (R. R.).
Seat of Athens College for Women (Methodist).
–c. s., Clarke Co., Ga., 18,192.
On Cen. of Ga.; Gainesv. Mid.; Ga.; Seab. Air Line; Sou. (R. Rs.).
Industrial center; lumber products, textiles.
Seat of the University of Georgia.
–Menard Co., Ill., 1,019.
On Chi. & Ill. Midl. (R. R.).
–Calhoun Co., Mich., 622.
–Greene Co., N. Y., 1,618.
–c. s., Athens Co., Ohio, 7,252.
On Balt. & Ohio; Chesa. & Ohio; N. York Cen. (R. Rs.).
–Bradford Co., Pa., 4,372.
On Leh. Val. (R. R.).
–c. s., McMinn Co., Tenn., 5,385.
On Lou. & Nash.; Sou. (R. Rs.).
–c. s., Henderson Co., Texas, 4,342.
On St. Lou. Southw.; Sou. Pac. (R. Rs.).
–Mercer Co., West Va., 628.
–Marathon Co., Wis., 935.
On Mpls., St. P. & S. Ste. M. (R. R.).
Atherton, San Mateo Co., Calif., 1,324.
On Sou. Pac. (R. R.).
–Lancashire, England, 19,985.
Textile mills, coal-mines, foundries.
Athol, Worcester Co., Mass., 10,751.
On Bost. & Me. (R. R.).
On Mohawk Trail. Farming, manufacturing.
Atimonan, Luzon, P. I., 13,098.
Atkins, Pope Co., Ark., 1,364.
On Mo. Pac. (R. R.).
Atkinson, Henry Co., Ill., 689.
On Chi., Rk. Isl. & Pac. (R. R.).
–Holt Co., Neb., 1,144.
On Chi. & Nor. West. (R. R.).
Atlanta, c. s., De Kalb and Fulton Cos., Ga., State capitol, 270,366.
Situated near the Chattahoochee River; elevation, over 1,000 feet, healthful climate.
Several railroads—the Atlanta & West Point; the Seaboard Air Line; the Southern; the Central of Georgia; the Georgia; the Louisville & Nashville; the Nashville, Chattanooga & St. Louis, and the Atlanta, Birmingham & Coast, converging at Atlanta, greatly facilitate the city's extensive and rapidly increasing trade.
Atlanta is the trade center of the State.
The city's area is about 34.27 square miles. It possesses a fine public library, a State library, and numerous educational institutions: notably Georgia School of Technology, Emory University and Oglethorpe University. Atlanta University, a famous educational institution for Negroes, is located here.
Atlanta has a large export trade. Manufactures include agricultural implements, fertilizers, cotton goods, and general foundry and machine products, paper boxes, soft drinks, stationery, brushes, terra cotta, candy, furniture, lumber, and patent medicines. Atlanta was an important city in the Confederacy and the objective point of General Sherman's campaign. In September, 1864, the city was made a military camp by Sherman, who in November left it in flames, and started on his march to the sea. The city was almost destroyed, but recovered rapidly after the war, and in 1878 became the capital of Georgia.
–Logan Co., Ill., 1,169.
On Alton; Penna. (R. Rs.).
–Hamilton Co., Ind., 551.
On Ind. R. R. Sys. (El.), N. York, Chi. & St. Lou. (R. Rs.).
–Steuben Co., N. Y., 500.
On Del., Lack. & West.; Erie (R. Rs.).
–Cass Co., Texas, 1,685.
On Tex. & Pac. (R. R.).

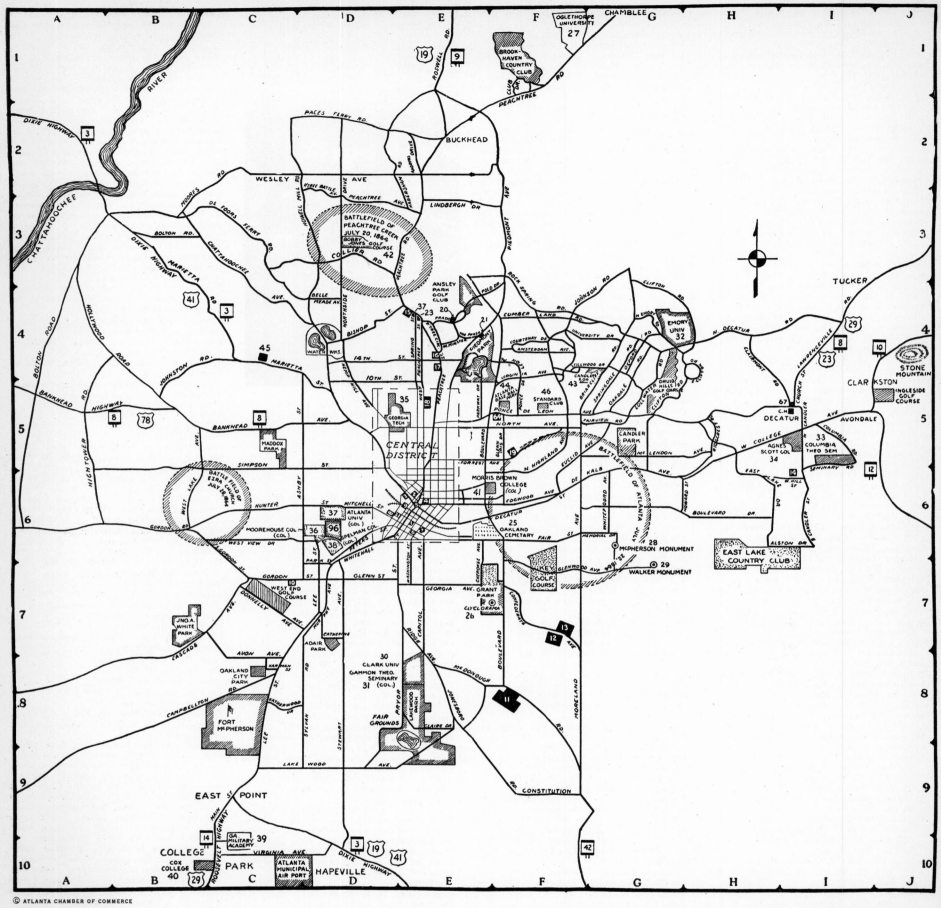

© ATLANTA CHAMBER OF COMMERCE

MAP OF ATLANTA, CAPITAL OF GEORGIA AND LARGEST CITY OF THE SOUTH BETWEEN WASHINGTON AND NEW ORLEANS. ATLANTA IS THE COMMERCIAL
CENTER OF THE SOUTHEAST. STONE MOUNTAIN, ON WHICH A HUGE MEMORIAL TO THE CONFEDERACY IS BEING CHISELED, IS 15 MILES EAST OF ATLANTA

ATLANTIC, c. s., Cass Co., Iowa, 5,585.
  On Chi., Rk. Isl. & Pac. (R. R.).
 —Houghton Co., Mich., 1,100.
  On Copper Range (R. R.).
 —Rockingham Co., N. H., 500.
  On Bost. & Me. (R. R.).
 —Carteret Co., N. C., 685.
ATLANTIC CITY, Atlantic Co., N. J., 66,198.
  One of most popular pleasure and health re-
  sorts in America, situated 60 miles east of
  Philadelphia on an island. Ten miles long
  and ¾ of a mile wide, and about 8 miles
  from the mainland. The beach is one of the
  finest in the country, and is known as the
  Absecon Beach. The streets of the city are
  wide and named after the States of the Union.
  The famous boardwalk is 5 miles in length
  and extends along the ocean front. Boating,
  bathing, and fishing provide popular forms of
  recreation, and many thousands of people en-

joy sea bathing. The transient population dur-
ing the summer is about 500,000. Reached by
Central of New Jersey, Pennsylvania, and
Pennsylvania-Reading Seashore Lines.
ATLANTIC HIGHLANDS, Monmouth Co., N. J.,
  2,000.
  On Cen. of N. Jer. (R. R.).
  Summer resort.
ATLAS, Northumberland Co., Pa., 2,400.
  On Penna. (R. R.).
ATLASBURG, Washington Co., Pa., 600.
  On Penna. (R. R.).
ATLIXCO, State of Puebla, Mexico, 11,989.
  On National of Mexico (R. R.).
ATMORE, Escambia Co., Ala., 3,035.
  On Lou. & Nash.; St. Lou.-San Fran. (R. Rs.).
ATOKA, c. s., Atoka Co., Okla., 1,856.
  On Mo.-Kan.-Tex. of Tex.; Okla. Cy.-Ada-
  Atoka (R. Rs.).
ATTALLA, Etowah Co., Ala., 4,585.

On Ala. Gt. Sou.; Lou. & Nash.; Nash. Chatt.,
  & St. Lou.; Sou. (R. Rs.).
ATTICA, Fountain Co., Ind., 3,700.
  On Chi., Attica & Sou.; Wab. (R. Rs.).
 —Harper Co., Kans., 740.
  On Atch., Top. & Santa Fe (R. R.).
 —Wyoming Co., N. Y., 2,212.
  On Arcade & Attica; Erie; N. York Cen.
  (R. Rs.).
 —Seneca Co., Ohio, 783.
  On Penna. (R. R.).
ATTLEBORO, Bristol Co., Mass., 21,835.
  On N. York, N. Hav. & Hart. (R. R.).
  Jewelry and silverware center.
ATTLEBORO FALLS, Bristol Co., Mass., 1,200.
ATWATER, Merced Co., Calif., 917.
  On Sou. Pac. (R. R.).
 —Kandiyohi Co., Minn., 694.
  On Gt. Nor. (R. R.).
ATWOOD, Piatt and Douglas Cos., Ill., 683.

On Balt. & Ohio (R. R.).
 —c. s., Rawlins Co., Kans., 1,476.
  On Chi., Burl. & Quincy (R. R.).
AUBERVILLIERS, Dept. of Seine, France, 55,871.
AUBURN, Lee Co., Ala., 2,800.
  On West. of Ala. (R. R.).
 —c. s., Placer Co., Cal., 2,661.
  On Sou. Pac. (R. R.).
 —Sangamon Co., Ill., 2,242.
  On Alton; Chi. & Ill. Midl.; Ill. Term. (El.)
  (R. Rs.).
 —c. s., De Kalb Co., Ind., 5,088.
  On Balt. & Ohio; N. York Cen.; Penna.
  (R. Rs.).
 —Logan Co., Ky., 821.
  On Lou. & Nash. (R. R.).
 —c. s., Androscoggin Co., Maine, 18,571.
  On Gd. Tr.; Me. Cen. (R. Rs.).
  Chief industry, shoemaking.
  Worcester Co., Mass., 6,535.

On N. York, N. Hav. & Hart. (R. R.).
–c. s., Nemaha Co., Neb., 3,068.
On Chi., Burl. & Quincy; Mo. Pac. (R. Rs.).
–c. s., Cayuga Co., N. Y., 36,652.
It is on the New York Central and Lehigh Valley Railroads. Auburn has many fine public buildings, handsome residences, and in Seward Park stands a bronze statue of William H. Seward.
One of the two State prisons is located here, and within the same inclosure a State insane asylum. The city is also the seat of Auburn Theological Seminary (founded by the Presbyterians in 1820), and has a State armory. Founded in 1792 as Hardenburg's Corners. Incorporated as a city in 1848.
–Schuylkill Co., Pa., 1,170.
On Penna.; Read. (R. Rs.).
–King Co., Wash., 3,906.
On Chi., Mil., St. P. & Pac.; Gt. Nor.; Nor. Pac.; Un. Pac. (R. Rs.).
Auburndale, Polk Co., Fla., 1,669.
On Atl. Coast Line; Seab. Air Line (R. Rs.).
Auburn Heights, Oakland Co., Mich., 900.
On Gd. Tr. (R. R.).
Auch, capital of Dept. of Gers, France, 13,313.
Brandies and wines.
Auckland (with suburbs), New Zealand, 214,200.
Largest city of the Dominion. A thriving port, magnificent parks, drives, and suburbs.
Audenried, Carbon Co., Pa., 750.
On Cen. of N. Jer.; Leh. Val.; Penna. (R. Rs.).
Audley, Staffordshire, England, 13,619.
Audubon, c. s., Audubon Co., Iowa, 2,255.
On Chi. & Nor. West.; Chi., Rk. Isl. & Pac. (R. Rs.).
–Camden Co., N. J., 8,904.
On Penna.-Read. Seashore (R. R.).
Aue, Saxony, Germany, 25,837.
Manufacturing town. Principal products are machinery and metal ware.
Augsburg, Bavaria, Germany, 176,575.
A leading manufacturing center situated at the confluence of the Wertach and Lech Rivers. An outer and inner city, which formerly possessed extensive fortifications, now removed and replaced by new buildings and streets. Several of these streets retain the old sixteenth and seventeenth century edifices, among them the Rathhaus (1615), still used as the town hall, with its "Golden Hall," famous as one of the finest in Germany. The former palace of the bishops, in which the Augsburg Confession was presented to the Emperor Charles V, the Fugger Palace and the Maximilian Museum are notable buildings. Founded about 9 B. C. by the Romans. Made a free city in 1276, Augsburg was an important trade mart between northern and southern Europe. Seat of the Fuggers, merchants and bankers. Active in the Reformation. Part of Bavaria since 1806.
Augusta, Prov. of Siracusa, Italy, 17,672.
–c. s., Woodruff Co., Ark., 2,243.
On Augusta (R. R.).
–c. s., Richmond Co., Ga., 60,342.
At the head of steamboat navigation on the Savannah River, and on the Atlantic Coast Line; Central of Georgia; Augusta and Summerville; Charleston and Western Carolina; the Georgia; the Georgia and Florida, and the Southern railroads. The Augusta Canal, 9 miles long, contributed to the prosperity of the city. Seat of Medical Department of the University of Georgia, Richmond Academy, and Paine College (colored).
Augusta is one of the largest markets for cotton, cotton seed and cotton seed oil in the South. The city is also a large jobbing center and has extensive floral nurseries. Numerous railroad shops, iron foundries and woodworking industries are located here, and there is an extensive lumber and fruit trade. Much of the gunpowder used by the Confederate armies was made in Augusta. The city was founded by Oglethorpe in 1735.
–Hancock Co., Ill., 1,011.
On Chi., Burl. & Quincy (R. R.).
–Butler Co., Kans., 3,634.
On Atch., Top. & Santa Fe; St. Lou.-San Fran. (R. Rs.).
–Bracken Co., Ky., 1,675.
On Chesa. & Ohio (R. R.).
–c. s., Kennebec Co., Maine, State capital, 17,198.
On the Kennebec River at the head of navigation. The city is traversed by the Maine Central Railroad. The chief part of the city is on the west bank. It has a State-house, a hospital for the insane, a United States Arsenal, and the Maine State Library. A national building for postoffice, pension-office, and United States Court was erected in 1889. The abundant water-power of Augusta is employed in manufactures of cotton goods, paper, woodpulp, boots and shoes, and lumber. Site of old Fort Western.
–Kalamazoo Co., Mich., 711.
On Mich. Cen. (R. R.).
–Oneida Co., N. Y., 1,739.
–Eau Claire Co., Wis., 1,359.
On Chi., St. P., Mpls. & Oma. (R. R.).
Aulander, Bertie Co., N. C., 1,041.
On Atl. Coast Line (R. R.).
Aulnay-sous-Bois, Seine-et-Oise, France, 31,763.
Ault, Weld Co., Colo., 737.
On Un. Pac. (R. R.).
Aurelia, Cherokee Co., Iowa, 723.
On Ill. Cen. (R. R.).
Aurillac, Cantal, France, 19,041.
A trading center in a live-stock raising region.
Aurora, Adams and Arapahoe Cos., Colo., 2,295.
–Kane Co., Ill., 46,589.
On Chi. & Nor. West.; Chi., Burl. & Quincy; Chi., Mil., St. P. & Pac.; Chi., Aur. & Elg. (El.); Elg., Jol. & East. (R. Rs.).
Fine water power; manufactures of pumps, stoves, textiles and furnaces. Aurora College.
–Dearborn Co., Ind., 4,386.
On Balt. & Ohio; Cle., Cin., Chi. & St. Lou. (R. Rs.).
–St. Louis Co., Minn., 1,463.
On Dul., Missabe & Ir. Rge. (R. R.).
–Lawrence Co., Mo., 3,875.
On Mo. Pac.; St. Lou.-San Fran. (R. Rs.).
–c. s., Hamilton Co., Neb., 2,715.
On Chi., Burl. & Quincy (R. R.).
–Portage Co., Ohio, 750.
On Erie (R. R.).
–Sevier Co., Utah, 568.
On Den. & Rio Gde. West. (R. R.).
–York Co., N., Ontario, Canada, 2,587.
On Can. Nat. (R. R.).
Ausable Forks, (Postoffice), Essex Co., N. Y., 1,009.
On Del. & Hud. (R. R.).
Aussig, Germany. See Usti.
Austell, Cobb Co., Ga., 963.
On Sou. (R. R.).
Austin, c. s., Mower Co., Minn., 12,276.
On Chi. Gt. West.; Chi., Mil., St. P. & Pac. (R. Rs.).
Packing plant, flour mills, etc.
–c. s., Lander Co., Nev., 661.
–Potter Co., Pa., 1,116.
On Balt. & Ohio (R. R.).
–Scott Co., Ind., 650.
On Penna.; Ind. R. R. Sys. (El.) (R. Rs.).
–c. s., Travis Co., Texas, State capital, 53,120.
An important railroad center on the Missouri Pacific; and the Missouri, Kansas, Texas of Tex., and the Southern Pacific Railroads and the Colorado River.
The city became the capital of the Republic of Texas in 1839. The old capital was destroyed by fire. The present fine granite edifice was erected on the proceeds derived from the sale of 3,000,000 acres of State land. Besides the Capitol there are the Governor's Mansion, University of Texas, State Library, and asylums for lunatics, mutes, and blind. Manufactures are cottons, stone finishing, furniture, engines, extracts, brick, and Mexican foods.
Austinville, Morgan Co., Ala., 818.
On Lou. & Nash. (R. R.).
Autlán, State of Jalisco, Mexico, 10,723.
Autun, Dept. of Saône-et-Loire, France, 14,863.
Commercial center of a rich agricultural region.
Auxerre, capital of Dept. of Yonne, France, 24,282.
Trade center in famous wine region.
Auxier, Floyd Co., Ky., 500.
On Chesa. & Ohio (R. R.).
Ava, Jackson Co., Ill., 615.
On Mob. & Ohio (R. R.).
–c. s., Douglas Co., Mo., 1,041.
Avalon, Los Angeles Co., Cal., 1,897.
–Livingston Co., Mo., 516.
–Allegheny Co., Pa., 5,940.
On Penna. (R. R.).
Avant, Osage Co., Okla., 696.
On Midl. Val. (R. R.).
Aveiro, Portugal, 12,735.
Port. Brisk trade in wine, oil and fruit.
Avellaneda, Argentina, 214,566.
Important industrial suburb of Buenos Aires.
Avellino, Avellino, Italy, 18,300.
Has old historical landmarks.
Avenal, Kings Co., Calif., 750.
Avenel, Middlesex Co., N. J., 627.
On Penna. (R. R.).
Averill Park, Rensselaer Co., N. Y., 900.
Aversa, Prov. of Napoli, Italy, 22,692.
A suburb of Naples.
Avery, Red River Co., Tex., 1,540.
On Tex. & Pac. (R. R.).
Avigliano, Potenza, Italy, 11,374.
Avignon, Vaucluse, France, 59,472.
Situated on the Rhône River, and about 30 miles from the Mediterranean.
The industries of Avignon include cotton-spinning, paper-making, manufacture of agricultural implements and hardware, silk, and other textiles. The city is the center wheat market of the province, and has an extensive trade in brandy and wines.
Avignon was a Roman city, then a part of Burgundy, and later a republic. Seat of the popes, 1309-1377, it belonged to Rome until 1701, when the French seized it.
Avilla, Noble Co., Ind., 559.
On Penna.; Balt. & Ohio (R. Rs.).
Avinger, Cass Co., Tex., 650.
On La. & Ark. (R. R.).
Avis, Clinton Co., Pa., 1,268.
On N. York Cen. (R. R.).
Avoca, Lawrence Co., Ind., 500.
On Chi., Ind., & Lou. (R. R.).
–Pottawattamie Co., Iowa, 1,673.
On Chi., Rk. Isl. & Pac. (R. R.).
–Assumption Par., La., 814.
–Steuben Co., N. Y., 940.
On Del., Lack. & West.; Erie (R. Rs.).
–Luzerne Co., Pa., 4,943.
On Cen. of N. Jer.; Del. & Hud.; Erie; Lack. & Wyo. Val. (El.); Leh. Val. (R. Rs.).
Avon, Hartford Co., Conn., 1,000.
On N. York, N. Hav. & Hart. (R. R.).
–Fulton Co., Ill., 799.
On Chi., Burl. & Quincy (R. R.).
–Norfolk Co., Mass., 2,362.
On N. York, N. Hav. & Hart. (R. R.).
Shoe manufactures.
–Livingston Co., N. Y., 2,403.
On Erie (R. R.).
–Lorain Co., Ohio, 1,826.
On N. York, Chi. & St. Lou. (R. R.).
–Lebanon Co., Pa., 550.
On Reading (R. R.).
–Bon Homme Co., S. Dak., 661.
On Chi., Mil., St. P. & Pac. (R. R.).
Avon-by-the-Sea, Monmouth Co., N. J., 1,220.
On Cen. of N. Jer.; N. York & Long Br.; Penna. (R. Rs.).
Avondale, Jefferson Co., Ala. (Station of Birmingham).
On Ala., Gt. Sou.; Birm. Belt.; Seab. Air Line; Sou. (R. Rs.).
–Bibb Co., Ga., 535.
On Ga. Sou. & Fla. (R. R.).
–Rutherford Co., N. C., 600.
On Cliffside (R. R.).
–Chester Co., Pa., 763.
On Penna (R. R.).
–Luzerne Co., Pa., 1,042.
On Del., Lack. & West. (R. R.).
Avon Lake (Beach Park Sta.), Lorain Co., Ohio, 1,610.
Avonmore, Westmoreland Co., Pa., 1,240.
On Penna. (R. R.).
Avon Park, Highlands Co., Fla., 3,869.
On Atl. Coast Line; Seab. Air Line (R. Rs.).
Awosting, Ulster Co., N. Y., 505.
Axleton, Washington Co., Pa., 500.
Axtell, Marshall Co., Kans., 604.
On Un. Pac. (R. R.).
Ayacucho, Peru, 20,000.
A commercial and marketing center.
Ayden, Pitt Co., N. C., 1,607.
On Atl. Coast Line (R. R.).
Aydin (Aidin), Aydin Vilayet, Turkey, 11,987.
Trade in figs, cotton and fruit.
Ayer, Middlesex Co., Mass., 3,861.
On Bost. & Me. (R. R.).
Aylmer, Elgin Co., West Ontario, Canada, 2,283.
On Can. Nat.; Mich. Cen.; Wab. (R. Rs.).
–Gatineau Co., East Quebec, Canada, 2,835.
On Can. Pac. (R. R.).
Ayr, Ayrshire, Scotland, 40,412.
Important port. Shipbuilding and foundries.
Azov, North Caucasian Area, Soviet Union, 17,000.
A fishing town on the Don River.
Aztec, c. s., San Juan Co., N. Mex., 740.
On Den. & Rio Gde. West. (R. R.).
Azua, Dominican Republic, 5,704.
Azucar, Palm Beach Co., Fla., 500.
Azusa, Los Angeles Co., Cal., 4,808.
On Atch., Top. & Santa Fe; Pac. Elec.; Sou. Pac. (R. Rs.).

B

Babol (Barfrush), Iran (Persia), 30,000.
A flourishing trade center.
Babylon, Suffolk Co., N. Y., 4,342.
On Long Island (R. R.).
A popular summer resort on Long Island Sound.
Bacacay, Luzon, P. I., 19,846.
Bacarra, Luzon, P. I., 14,470.
Baccarat, Dept. of Meurthe-et-Moselle, France, 5,605.
Partly destroyed in World War.
Back Bay, Princess Co., Va., 829.
On Norf. Sou. (R. R.).
Baclayon, Prov. of Bohol, Bohol, P. I., 8,848.
Bacolod, Negros, P. I., 47,250.
Bacolor, Luzon, P. I., 15,224.
Bacoor, Luzon, P. I., 11,089.
Bacup, Lancashire, England, 20,606.
Industrial center. Textiles and metal working.
Badajoz, Spain, 41,982.
City enjoys much transit trade with Portugal.
Badalona, Barcelona, Spain, 29,361.
Bad Axe, c.s., Huron Co., Mich., 2,332.
On Gd. Tr.; Pere Marq. (R. Rs.).
Baden, Austria, Germany, 22,217.
–Beaver Co., Pa., 1,924.
On Penna. (R. R.).
–Republic of Baden, Germany, 31,000.
A popular watering place in the valley of the Oosbach, close to the Black Forest.
Badian, Cebu, P. I., 17,317.
Bad Ischl (Isehl), Germany, 10,224.
Badoc, Luzon, P. I., 17,586.
Baeza, Jaen, Spain, 15,326.
Famous for red dye.
Bagamoyo, Tanganyika Territory, East Africa, 5,000.
A coast town which has an important mission.
Bagdad, Santa Rosa Co., Fla., 500.
Baggaley, Westmoreland Co., Pa., 1,050.
Baghdad, Iraq, Asia Minor, capital of Iraq, and seat of near-eastern culture, 400,000. Formerly in Turkish territory, passed under British control as a result of the World War.
Once a magnificent Mohammedan city, the capital of the Arabian empire, it is situated on both banks of the Tigris, surrounded by a ruined wall and dry moat.
Baghdad was built from the ruins of Ctesiphon and Seleucia (762 A.D.), enlarged, and attained great magnificence under the Calif Harun-al-Raschid of "Arabian Nights" fame. In 1258, the caliphate was destroyed.
Bagheria, Palermo, Sicily, Italy, 19,051.
Bagley, c. s., Clearwater Co., Minn., 885.
On Gt. Nor. (R. R.).
Bagnolet, Seine, France, 28,052.
Bahawalpur, Punjab, India, 20,943.
Center of agricultural region.
Bahia, Brazil. See São Salvador.
Bahia Blanca, Prov. of Buenos Aires, Argentine Republic, 100,434.
Important seaport and naval station. Ships wheat, oats, cattle, and wool.
Baie St. Paul, Charlevoix Co., Quebec, Canada, 2,916.
Baile Atha Cliath (Dublin), capital of Ireland (Eire), 467,691.
On the east coast of the Irish Free State, at the mouth of the Liffey, on Dublin Bay. Built on land reclaimed from the sea. The river divides the city into nearly equal parts, joined by bridges.
Notable buildings include St. Patrick's Cathedral (Protestant), built in 1190; Christ Church (Protestant), 1038; the Catholic churches, St. Mary's St. Saviour's, St. Augustine's, and St. Kelvin's; the House of Parliament; Trinity College; the Custom-house; the Four Courts; Dublin Castle. Seat of Trinity College and National University.
Manufactures porter, whiskey, poplin, glass, cotton and linen goods, and foundry products. Has a large import trade in grain, raw cotton, timber, petroleum and sugar.
The Danes held the city from the ninth century until 1170, when the Anglo-Norman Conquest by Henry II dispossessed them. The first parliament here was held by James II in 1689. In 1798 and 1803, insurgents failed in attempts to take the city. It was the theater of a fierce, but brief revolt against the British in 1916.
Baileys, Nash Co., N. C., 631.
Bainbridge, c. s., Decatur Co., Ga., 6,141.
On Atl. Coast Line; Seab. Air Line (R. Rs.).
In a lumbering and farming region.
–Chenango Co., N. Y., 1,324.
On Del. & Hud. (R. R.).
–Ross Co., Ohio, 735.
On Det., Tol. & Iron. (R. R.).
–Lancaster Co., Pa., 827.
On Penna. (R. R.).
Baird, c. s., Callahan Co., Tex., 1,965.
On Tex. & Pac. (R. R.).
Bairdford, Allegheny Co., Pa., 1,000.
On Bess. & L. Erie (R. R.).
Baker, c. s., Fallon Co., Montana, 1,212.
On Chi., Mil., St. P. & Pac. (R. R.).
–c. s. Baker Co., Ore., 7,858.
On Un. Pac.; Sumpter Val. (R. Rs.).
Lumber milling and farming.
Bakersfield, c. s., Kern Co., Cal., 26,015.
On Atch., Top. & Santa Fe; Sou. Pac. (R. Rs.).
Oil refineries and fruit packing establishments.
Bakerton, Cambria Co., Pa., 1,200.
On Penna. (R. R.).
–Jefferson Co., W. Va., 518.
On Balt. & Ohio (R. R.).
Baku, capital of Azerbaijan, Transcaucasia, Soviet Union, 709,500.
Situated on the west coast of the Caspian Sea, on the peninsula of Aspheron. It is the center of the Soviet Union's petroleum trade. Azerbaijan submitted to Soviet rule in 1920.
Bala, Montgomery Co., Pa., 611.
On Penna. (R. R.).
Balamban, Prov. of Cebu, Cebu, P. I., 19,004.
Balanga, Prov. of Bataan, Luzon, P. I., 8,141.
Balaon, Luzon, P. I., 12,000.
Balasan, Prov. of Batangas, Luzon, P. I., 22,822.
Balashov, Soviet Union, 26,846.
Balasore, Bengal, India, 21,000.
Trade center in rice producing region.
Balaton, Lyon Co., Minn., 605.
On Chi. & Nor. West. (R. R.).
Balboa, Orange Co., Calif., 810.

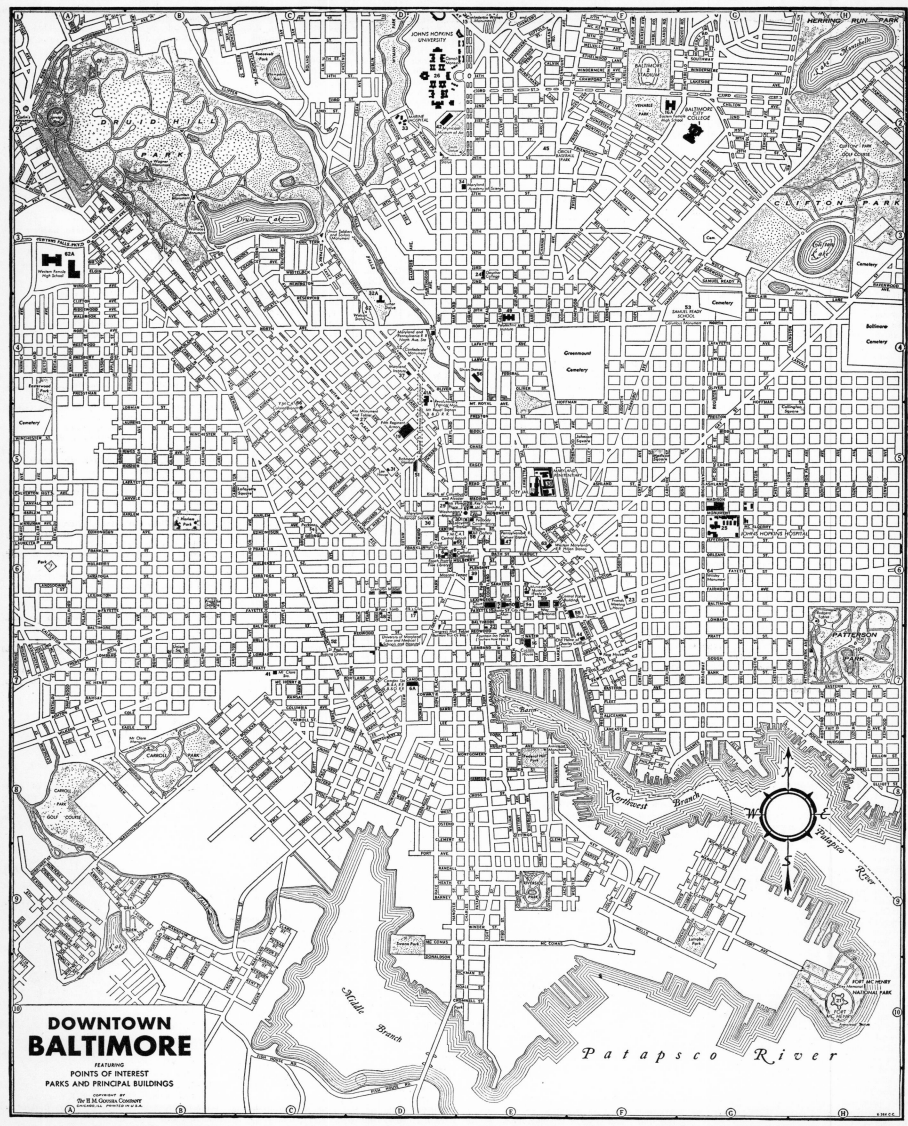

DOWNTOWN BALTIMORE

FEATURING
POINTS OF INTEREST
PARKS AND PRINCIPAL BUILDINGS

COPYRIGHT BY
The H.M.Gousha Company
CHICAGO, ILL. PRINTED IN U.S.A.

MAP OF BALTIMORE, THE PRINCIPAL CITY AND PORT OF ENTRY OF MARYLAND, SITUATED AT THE TIDEWATER HEAD OF THE PATAPSCO RIVER. AMONG ITS HIGHER EDUCATIONAL INSTITUTIONS ARE JOHNS HOPKINS UNIVERSITY, THE UNIVERSITY OF MARYLAND AND GOUCHER COLLEGE.

On Pac. Elec. (R. R.).
–Panama Canal Zone, 3,199.
Balboa Island, Orange Co., Calif., 1,800.
Bald Knob, White Co., Ark., 1,273.
On Mo. Pac. (R. R.).
Bald Mountain, Yancey Co., N. C., 500.
Baldwin, Duval Co., Fla., 849.
On Atl. Coast Line; Seab. Air Line (R. Rs.).
–(Baldwin City P. O.), Douglas Co., Kans., 1,221.
On Atch., Top. & Santa Fe (R. R.).
Site of Baker University (Methodist).
–St. Mary Parish, La., 822.
On Sou. Pac. (R. R.).
–c. s., Lake Co., Mich., 518.
On Pere Marq. (R. R.).
–St. Croix Co., Wis., 808.
On Chi., St. P., Mpls. & Oma. (R. R.).
Baldwinsville, Onondaga Co., N. Y., 3,845.
On Del., Lack. & West. (R. R.).
Baldwinville, Worcester Co., Mass., 2,200.
On Bost. & Alb.; Bost. & Me. (R. Rs.).
Baldwyn, Lee and Prentiss Co., Miss., 1,106.
On Mob. & Ohio (R. R.).
Balfour, Henderson Co., N. C., 500.
Balikessir, Balikessir Vilayet, Turkey in Asia, 26,430.
Center of a mining region.
Balilihan, Prov. of Bohol, Bohol, P. I., 10,044.
Baliuag, Luzon, P. I., 18,403.
Hats, silks, fish, furniture, rice, and sugar.
Balkh, Afghanistan, 15,000.
Ballarat, Victoria, Australia, 37,409.
An important commercial center of the State of Victoria, divided into three municipalities, Ballarat East, Ballarat West, and Sebastopol.
Ballard, King Co., Wash. (Sta. Seattle P. O.).
On Gt. Nor.; Nor. Pac. (R. Rs.).
Ballard Vale, Essex Co., Mass., 1,000.
On Bost. & Me. (R. R.).
Ballast Point, Hillsborough Co., Fla., 1,000.
Ball Ground, Cherokee Co., Ga., 706.
On Lou. & Nash. (R. R.).
Ballinger, c. s., Runnels Co., Texas, 4,187.
On Abil. & Sou.; Gulf, Colo. & Santa Fe (R. Rs.).
Ball Play, Etowah Co., Ala., 650.
Ballston, Arlington Co., Va., 1,250.
Ballston Spa, c. s., Saratoga Co., N. Y., 4,591.
On Del. & Hud. (R. R.).
Popular health resort.
Bally, Berks Co., Pa., 579.
Balnew (Turner), Baltimore Co., Md., 1,350.
Balta, Moldavia Rep., Soviet Union, 21,400.
Chief town in a live stock raising section. Soap, tile, and beer brewing establishments.
Baltic, New London Co., Conn., 2,300.
On N. York, N. Hav. & Hart. (R. R.).
–Houghton Co., Mich., 550.
On Copper Range (R. R.).
–Tuscarawas Co., Ohio, 545.
On Wheel. & L. Erie (R. R.).
Baltimore, Md., 804,874.
Situated on an estuary of the Patapsco River, at the head of navigation, about 14 miles from Chesapeake Bay, on the Baltimore & Ohio; Baltimore & Annapolis (El.); the Pennsylvania; the Western Maryland; the Maryland & Pennsylvania; Baltimore & Eastern railroads. A good harbor and fine geographical situation give Baltimore unusual trade advantages.
The Peabody Institute, endowed by George Peabody, contains a large library, and a conservatory of music; the Roman Catholic Cathedral, remarkable for its fine architecture; the Enoch Pratt free library, the City Hall, Masonic Temple and Post-Office are other notable buildings.
Baltimore ranks as one of the foremost educational centers of the country. The leading institutions are Johns Hopkins University, the University of Maryland, Goucher College, Morgan College (colored), Loyola College, Notre Dame College, and others. There are many charitable institutions, headed by the Johns Hopkins Hospital, ranking in equipment as one of the finest in the world. A Pasteur Institute is also in operation here. Many monuments, and Druid Hill Park, covering 700 acres, add much to the beauty of the city.
The principal industries are the manufacturing of ready-made clothing, copper, tin and iron goods, tobacco products, electrical goods, sugar, packed meats, chemicals, drugs, fertilizer and the canning of fruits and oysters. Shipbuilding has become important and there is a large steel plant at Sparrow's Point. Baltimore is a center of straw hat manufacturing.
Steamship lines connect the city with foreign countries, and the export trade, especially that in grain, meats, cattle, flour, oysters, and petroleum, is very great.
Baltimore was founded in 1729. The construction of the first important line of railway in the United States was commenced at Baltimore in 1828. The first telegraph line was constructed to, and the first message received in, Baltimore.
–Fairfield Co., Ohio, 720.
On N. York Cen. (R. R.).

Bamberg, Bavaria, Germany, 54,000.
Industrial and religious center. Textile mills.
–c. s., Bamberg Co., S. C., 2,450.
On Bamb., Ehr. & Waterb.; Sou. (R. Rs.).
Banbury, Oxfordshire, England, 13,953.
Center of a rich agricultural district. Farm machinery.
Bancroft, Kossuth Co., Iowa, 854.
On Chi. & Nor. West. (R. R.).
–Cuming Co., Neb., 660.
On Chi., St. P., Mpls. & Oma. (R. R.).
Banda, United Provinces, India, 22,600.
Bandar Abu Shehr (Bushire), Faristan, Iran (Persia), 19,000.
Important port. Ships rugs, silk, tobacco, hides, raw cotton and rosewater.
Bandjermasin, chief town of Borneo, Netherland India, 64,223.
Spices, precious stones, gold-dust, rattan, drugs.
Bandon, Coos Co., Ore., 1,516.

COURTESY OF SPANISH TOURIST INFORMATION OFFICE

THE PASEO DE SAN JUAN, BARCELONA, SPAIN. IN THE DISTANCE IS THE TRIUMPHAL ARCH WITH THE COURT HOUSE AT ITS RIGHT

Banff, Prov. of Alberta, Canada, 2,519.
On Can. Pac. (R. R.).
–Banff Co., Scotland, 4,136.
Bangalore, Mysore, British India, 306,470.
A fortified city and military station.
Bangkok, capital of Siam, 681,214.
Chief commercial city of Siam, situated on the Menam River; one of the most picturesque cities of the East. It is divided into numerous islands by canals; many of the inhabitants live in houses built on rafts. A great many of the buildings are of wood or bamboo, and erected on poles. The high wall inclosing the royal palace incloses also the royal library, temples and theater. The Buddhist temples, roofed with gorgeously colored tiles, supported by gilded pillars, are extremely beautiful. The most magnificent temples are at Sekkat, Wat Nun, and Wat Sutat. Electric lines of railway and electric lights have been introduced and modernization is making rapid strides. The commerce of Bangkok is chiefly carried on by Europeans and Chinese. The principal exports are rice and teak and other woods.
Bangkok was an insignificant village in 1776, when it became the capital.
Bangor, Carnarvonshire, Wales, 10,959.
Trade in slate; seat of University College of North Wales.
–c. s., Penobscot Co., Maine, 28,749.
Situated at the head of navigation on the Penobscot River, at the mouth of the Kenduskeag, and on the Maine Central Railroad.
A State Insane Asylum, the Bangor Theological Seminary and the Northern Conservatory of Music are located here.
There are foundries, machine shops, saw mills, planing mills, packing houses, boot and shoe factories, paper and pulp mills.
The city was settled in 1769, and known as Kenduskeag Plantation until 1787, and as Sunbury until 1791, when it was incorporated under its present name.
–Van Buren Co., Mich., 1,274.
On Pere Marq. (R. R.).
–Northampton Co., Pa., 5,824.
On Del., Lack. & West.; Leh. & N. Eng. (R. Rs.).
–La Crosse Co., Wis., 835.
On Chi. & Nor. West.; Chi., Mil., St. P. & Pac. (R. Rs.).
Bangs, Brown Co., Texas, 717.
Gulf, Colo. & Santa Fe (R. R.).
Bangued, Luzon, P. I., 13,895.
Bangui, Fr. Equatorial Africa, 23,674.
Bani Suef, Bani Suef, Egypt, 39,478.
Commercial center for farm region.

Banjaluka, Yugoslavia, 22,177.
Banjarmassin, chief town of Dutch Borneo, about 70,000.
Spices, precious stones, gold-dust, rattan, drugs.
Banjoewangi, Java, Netherland India, 25,066.
Port and military station.
Bankhead, Walker Co., Ala., 800.
On Nor. Ala. (R. R.).
Banksville, Allegheny Co., Pa., 1,400.
Bankura, capital of the District of Bankura, Bengal, India, 20,000.
Banning, Riverside Co., Calif., 2,752.
On Sou. Pac. (R. R.).
Bannockburn, Stirling, Scotland, 4,000.
Scene of Bruce's victory.
Bantam, Litchfield Co., Conn., 545.
On N. York, N. Hav. & Hart. (R. R.).
Bantayan, Cebu, P. I., 16,672.
Bapaume, Pas de Calais, France, 1,907 (pre-war pop.—about 4,000).
About 14 miles S.S.E. of Arras. Occupied by the Germans in the World War and taken by the British, Aug. 29, 1918.
Bapchule, Pinal Co., Ariz., 500.
Baraboo, c. s., Sauk Co., Wis., 5,545.
On Chi. & Nor. West. (R. R.).
Baracoa, Prov. of Oriente, Cuba, 5,205.
One of the oldest settlements in the New World, founded by Diego Columbus in 1514.
Baraga, Baraga Co., Mich., 1,045.
On Dul., Sou. Sh. & Atl. (R. R.).
Barahona, Dominican Republic, 8,359.
Baras, Prov. of Albay, Luzon, P. I., 6,134.
Barataria, Tangipanoa Par., La., 610.
Barberton, Summit Co., Ohio, 23,934.
On Akr. & Barb. Belt; Akr., Can. & Youngs.; Balt. & Ohio; Erie; Penna. (R. Rs.).
Matches, boilers, and rubber products.
Barbizon, Dept. of Seine-et-Marne, France, 540.
Home of the Barbizon School of Painters.
Barboursville, Cabell Co., W. Va., 1,508.
On Chesa. & Ohio (R. R.).
Barbourville, c. s., Knox Co., Ky., 2,380.
On Lou. & Nash. (R. R.).
Barcelona, capital of Prov. of Barcelona, Spain, 1,148,129.
This seaport, the largest city of the Republic, was an old walled city, and still contains many relics of its antiquity.
The University of Barcelona was founded in 1430, and has a large library. Other educational institutions include the Academy of Belles-Lettres, and the Academy of Arts and Sciences. Barcelona is an important cotton manufacturing center, and also produces silk and woolen goods, metal articles, glass, chemicals, paper, and leather.
Barceloneta, Municipality of Barceloneta, Puerto Rico, 1,618.
On Manati River, 12 miles east of Arecibo.
Bardstown, c. s., Nelson Co., Ky., 1,767.
On Lou. & Nash. (R. R.).
Bardwell, c. s., Carlisle Co., Ky., 1,139.
On Ill. Cen. (R. R.).
Bareilly, United Provinces, India, 144,031.
Industrial center and military station. Furniture and upholstery.
Barfrush, Iran (Persia). See Babol.
Bar Harbor, Hancock Co., Maine, 4,486.
Bari, capital of Prov. of Bari, Italy, 164,340.
Important industrial town. Olive-oil, soap, carpets, flour, foundries.
Barili, Prov. of Cebu, P. I., 33,481.
Commercial center of greatest corn-producing region in the Islands.
Barker (Feltonville), Delaware Co., Pa., 500.
Barking, Essex, England, 51,277.

Manufacturing town near London.
Barlad, capital of Dist. of Tutova, Rumania, 25,500.
Soap, candles, lumber. Has an annual horse fair.
Bar-le-Duc, capital of the Department of Meuse, France, 16,697.
A center of the wine industry.
Barletta, Prov. of Bari, Italy, 50,055.
A center of the wine trade.
Barlow, Ballard Co., Ky., 614.
On Ill. Cen. (R. R.).
Barmen, Germany. See Wuppertal.
Barnardsville, Buncombe Co., N. C., 500.
Barnaul, Siberia, Sov. Union, Asia, 109,200.
Mining town, coal, gold, iron, copper, silver, lead, zinc. In center of farming region.
Barnegat, Ocean Co., N. J., 1,100.
On Cen. of N. Jer.; Sou. N. Jer. (R. Rs.).
Barnes, Surrey, England, 42,439.
A residential suburb of London.
Barnesboro, Cambria Co., Pa., 3,506.
On Penna. (R. R.).
Barnesville, c. s., Lamar Co., Ga., 3,236.
On Cen. of Ga. (R. R.).
–Clay Co., Minn., 1,279.
On Gt. Nor. (R. R.).
–Belmont Co., Ohio, 4,602.
On Balt. & Ohio (R. R.).
Barnsboro, Gloucester Co., N. J., 500.
Barnsdall, Osage Co., Okla., 2,001.
On Mid. Val. (R. R.).
Barnsley, Yorkshire, England, 71,522.
Manufactures: textiles, iron, steel, glass, lumber.
Barnstable, c. s., Barnstable Co., Mass., 8,037.
On N. York, N. Hav. & Hart. (R. R.).
Barnwell, c. s., Barnwell Co., S. C., 1,834.
On Atl. Coast Line; Sou. (R. Rs.).
Baroda, capital of State of Baroda, India, 112,862.
Trade and educational center.
Barquisimeto, capital of Lara, Venezuela, 23,109.
Center of rich plantation region.
Barrackpore, Bengal, India, 41,800.
Military station and suburban residence of governors of Bengal.
Barrackville, Marion Co., W. Va., 2,000.
On Balt. & Ohio (R. R.).
Barranquilla, Colombia, 150,000.
Commercial city in petroleum region.
Barranquitas, Municipality of Barranquitas, Puerto Rico, 1,698.
Barre, Worcester Co., Mass., 3,509.
On Bost. & Alb.; Bost. & Me. (R. Rs.).
–Washington Co., Vt., 11,307.
On Barre & Chelsea; Cen. Ver.; Mont. & Wells Riv. (R. Rs.).
Noted for its granite quarries.
Barre Plains, Worcester Co., Mass., 900.
On Bost. & Alb.; Bost. & Me. (R. Rs.).
Barrenfork, McCreary Co., Ky., 515.
Barrie, capital of Simcoe Co., Ontario, Canada, 7,776.
On Canadian National (R. R.).
Railway shops, planing mills, tannery, and manufactures of wool.
Barrington, Cook and Lake Cos., Ill., 3,213.
On Chi. & Nor. West.; Elg., Jol. & East. (R. Rs.).
–Camden Co., N. J., 2,252.
On Penna.-Read. Seashore (R. R.).
–Bristol Co., R. I., 5,501.
On N. York, N. Hav. & Hart. (R. R.).
Barron, c. s., Barron Co., Wis., 1,863.
On Mpls., St. P. & S. Ste. M. (R. R.).
Barrow-in-Furness, Lancashire, England, 73,490.
Has been a manufacturing center of great importance since 1840, when rich ore was discovered and mines and smelters were put in. It has fine docks and some of the largest iron and steel works in England.
Barry, Pike Co., Ill., 1,506.
On Wab. (R. R.).
Barstow, San Bernardino Co., Calif., 2,000.
On Atch., Top. & Santa Fe; Un. Pac. (R. Rs.).
Bartlesville, c. s., Washington Co., Okla., 14,763.
On Atch., Top. & Santa Fe; Mo.-Kan.-Tex. (R. Rs.).
An oil center of the state.
Bartlett, Cook Co., Ill., 504.
On Chi., Mil., St. P. & Pac. (R. R.).
–Carroll Co., N. H., 1,119.
On Me. Cen. (R. R.).
–Bell and Williamson Cos., Texas, 1873.
On Mo.-Kan.-Tex. of Tex. (R. R.).
Bartley, McDowell Co., W. Va., 500.
On Norf. & West. (R. R.).
Barton, Allegany Co., Maryland, 689.
On Cumb. & Penna. (R. R.).
–Belmont Co., Ohio, 1,200.
On Balt. & Ohio (R. R.).
–Orleans Co., Vt., 1,363.
On Can. Pac. (R. R.).
–Washington Co., Wis., 811.
On Chi. & Nor. West. (R. R.).
Barton Heights, Henrico Co., Va. (Suburb of Richmond).
Bartonville, Peoria Co., Ill., 1,886.
Bartow, c. s., Polk Co., Fla., 5,835.

On Atl. Coast Line; Seab. Air Line (R. Rs.). Has fruit groves and phosphate mines.
Barugo, Prov. of Leyte, P. I., 16,187.
Basel (Basle, Bâle), capital of Canton of Basel-stadt, Switzerland, 200,900.
Important manufacturing and commercial town. Divided by the Rhine River into Gross Basel and Klein Basel, connected by bridges. The University of Basel is renowned; founded in 1459 by Pope Pius II. There is also a famous Bible Institute and mission house.
Of its manufactures, that of silk is the most extensive. Others include jewelry, paper, gloves, linen, leather-goods, and printed cottons. Basel was the Roman town Basilia, and early became German.
The Council of Basel, which convened here from 1431 to 1440, was held for the purpose of conciliating Pope Eugenius IV and the followers of Huss.
Base Line, Macomb Co., Mich., 600.
Basey, Samar, P. I., 18,111.
Basford, Nottinghamshire and Derbyshire, England, 52, 101.
Suburb of Nottingham.
Basic, Augusta Co., Va. See Waynesboro.
Basil, Fairfield Co., Ohio, 716.
On N. York Cen. (R. R.).
Basin, c. s., Big Horn Co., Wyo., 903.
On Chi., Burl. & Quincy (R. R.).
Basking Ridge, Somerset Co., N. J., 1,500.
On Del., Lack & West. (R. R.).
Basra, Iraq, estimated, 46,732.
A river port at the head of the Persian Gulf, formerly in Turkish territory and now under the control of Iraq.
Bassano, Vincenza, Italy, 10,111.
Bassein, Lower Burma, India, 45,662.
Center of the rice trade.
Bassett, c. s., Rock Co., Neb., 635.
On Chi. & Nor. West. (R. R.).
–(Bassetts P. O.), Henry Co., Va., 2,050.
On Norf. & West. (R. R.).
Bastia, Corsica, France, 52,208.
Mediterranean seaport town; wealthiest and most populous on island of Corsica.
Bastrop, c. s., Morehouse Parish, La., 5,121.
On Ark. & La. Mo.; Mo. Pac. (R. Rs.).
–c. s., Bastrop Co., Texas, 1,895.
On Mo.-Kans.-Tex. of Tex. (R. R.).
Batac, Prov. of Illocos Notre Luzon, P. I., 26,207.
Batangas, Luzon, P. I., 41,182.
Trade center of an agricultural region.
Batavia, Java, capital and chief city of Netherland, India, 533,015.
Situated on the Bay of Batavia.
Batavia is the most important commercial city in Netherland India. The exports consist mainly of coffee, rice, hides, sugar, pepper, teak, tobacco, indigo, and spices. The European history of Batavia dates from 1610, when the Governor-General, Pieter Both, founded a factory which grew into an important town known as Jaccatra. In 1619 the city took its present name.
–Kane Co., Ill., 5,045.
On Chi., Burl. & Quincy; Chi. & Nor. West.; Chi., Aur. & Elg. (R. Rs.).
–c. s., Genesee Co., N. Y., 17,375.
On Erie; Leh. Val.; N. York Cen. (R. Rs.).
Iron and steel products.
–c. s., Clermont Co., Ohio, 1,119.
On Norf. & West. (R. R.).
Bates, Oxford Co., Me., 513.
On Gd. Tr. (R. R.).
Batesburg, Lexington and Saluda Cos., S. C., 2,839.
On Sou. (R. R.).
Batesville, c. s., Independence Co., Ark., 4,484.
On Mo. Pac. (R. R.).
Site of Arkansas College (Presbyterian).
–Ripley Co., Ind., 2,838.
On Cle., Cin., Chi. & St. Lou. (R. Rs.).
–Panola Co., Miss., 1,062.
On Ill. Cen. (R. R.).
–Zavalla Co., Texas, 625.
Bath, Somerset, England, 68,801.
A noted health resort.
–c. s., Sagadahoc Co., Maine, 9,110.
On Me. Cen. (R. R.).
Important shipbuilding industry; foundries.
First explored in 1605; deeded by an Indian sachem in 1660. Incorporated in 1781; a city in 1848.
–Grafton Co., N. H., 500.
On Bost. & Me. (R. R.).
–c. s., Steuben Co., N. Y., 4,015.
On Bath & Hammonds; Del., Lack. & West.; Erie (R. Rs.).
–Northampton Co., Pa., 1,625.
On Del., Lack. & West.; Leh. & N. Eng., Northamp. & Bath (R. Rs.).
–Aiken Co., S. C., 1,250.
On Sou. (R. R.).
Bathgate, West Lothian Co., Scotland, 10,097.
Industrial town.
Batley, Yorkshire, England, 34,573.
Textiles and artificial silk.
Bato, Prov. of Albay, Luzon, P. I., 12,888.
–Prov. of Ambos-Camarines, Luzon, P. I., 7,937.
Baton Rouge, c. s., East Baton Rouge Parish, La., State capital, 30,729.
Situated on the east bank of the Mississippi, on the line of the Louisiana & Arkansas; the New Orleans, Texas & Mexico; Missouri Pacific, and the Yazoo & Mississippi Valley railroads.
The city stands on a bluff 25 feet above the highest inundations; below the city the river is bordered by plantations of sugar cane and handsome villas. Site of State prison, State institutions for deaf, dumb, and blind, and University of Louisiana.
Manufactures lumber, cottonseed products, chemicals.
It was here on January 26, 1861, that the State ordinance of secession was adopted. On the 7th of May, 1862, the city was taken by the United States forces. Baton Rouge was the State capital from 1849 to 1864, and again from 1880 to the present time. New Orleans was the capital during the intervening 16 years (1864-80).
Batson, Hardin Co., Tex., 650.
Battle Creek, Ida Co., Iowa, 804.
On Chi. & Nor. West. (R. R.).
–Calhoun Co., Mich., 43,573.
Situated at confluence of the Kalamazoo River with Battle Creek, on the Michigan Central and the Grand Trunk Railroads.
It is the home of the Battle Creek Sanatorium and Battle Creek College.
Battle Creek has a world-wide reputation for health foods and cereals, and possesses important manufactures of flour, iron products, wagons, aluminum and brass goods, soft drinks, automobile parts, dog foods, steam pumps, threshing machines, agricultural implements, and hose fixtures. Battle Creek was settled in 1832 and incorporated in 1859.
–Madison Co., Neb., 755.
On Chi. & Nor. West. (R. R.).
Battle Lake, Otter Tail Co., Minn., 552.
On Nor. Pac. (R. R.).
Battle Mountain, Lander Co., Nev., 1,120.
On Nev. Cen.; Sou. Pac.; West. Pac. (R. Rs.).
Batum, Soviet Union, 48,149.
After the World War the city became included in Georgia, a new republic of the Soviet Union.
Bauan, Prov. of Batangas, Luzon, P. I., 27,727.
Market town, cloth embroidery.
Bauang, Prov. of La Union, Luzon, P. I., 12,944.
Baudette, c. s., Lake of the Woods Co., Minn., 822.
On Can. Nat. (R. R.).
Bausman, Lancaster Co., Pa., 500.
Bautzen, Saxony, Germany, 41,000.
Manufactures of machinery, textiles and leather; scene of great battle, 1813.
Bauxite, Saline Co., Ark., 1,500.
On Baux. & Nor.; Chi., Rk. Isl. & Pac. (R. Rs.).
Baxley, c. s., Appling Co., Ga., 2,122.
On Sou. (R. R.).
Baxter, Jasper Co., Iowa, 569.
On Chi. Gt. West. (R. R.).
–Harlan Co., Ky., 550.
On Lou. & Nash. (R. R.).
–Putnam Co., Tenn., 541.
On Tenn. Cen. (R. R.).
–Marion Co., W. Va., 670.
On Monongahela; Balt. & Ohio (R. Rs.).
Baxter Springs, Cherokee Co., Kans., 4,248.
On the Kans. Cy. Sou.; Kan., Okla. & Gulf; St. Lou.-San Fran.; Southw. Mo. (El.) (R. Rs.).
Center of lead and zinc mining district.
Bayambang, Prov. of Pangasinan, Luzon, P. I., 15,310.
Bayamo, Prov. of Santiago, Cuba, 7,423.
Bayamon, Municipality of Bayamon, Puerto Rico, 13,873.
Fruits, sugar, tobacco.
Bayard, Guthrie Co., Iowa, 681.
On Chi., Mil., St. P. & Pac. (R. R.).
–Morrill Co., Neb., 1,559.
On Chi., Burl. & Quincy (R. R.).
–Grant Co., W. Va., 743.
On West Md. (R. R.).
Baybay, Prov. of Leyte, Leyte, P. I., 36,934.
Rice, corn, copra, sugar.
Bay City, c. s., Bay Co., Mich., 47,355.
Situated on Saginaw River at point where river flows into Saginaw Bay, and on the Detroit & Mackinac, the Grand Trunk, the Michigan Central, and the Pere Marquette railroads.
Shipbuilding, both steel and wood, is an important industry. Principal manufactures: automobile parts, clothing, lumber products, electrical machinery, beet sugar, and cigars. The fishing on Saginaw Bay gives employment to many persons. Close to city limits large deposits of coal are found.
–c. s., Matagorda Co., Texas, 4,070.
On Gulf, Colo. & Santa Fe; St. Lou., Brownsv. & Mex.; Tex. & New Orl. (R. Rs.).
Bayfield, Bayfield Co., Wis., 1,195.
On Chi., St. P., Minn. & Oma. (R. R.).
Bay Minnette, c. s., Baldwin Co., Ala., 1,545.
On Lou. & Nash. (R. R.).
Bayonne, Dept. of Basses-Pyrénées, France, 31,350.
Commercial center. Leather goods and chocolate.
–Hudson Co., N. J., 88,979.
On Cen. of N. Jer.; E. Jer. R. R. & Term.; Leh. Val.; Penna. (R. Rs.).
Important manufacturing city on Newark and New York Bays, south of Jersey City and opposite Staten Island, to which it is connected by the Kill Van Kull bridge. Has petroleum refineries and manufactures of radiators, electric launches, insulated wire and cable, structural steel, metal castings, chemicals and silks.
Bayou Goula, Iberville Par., La., 1,031.
On Tex. & Pac. (R. R.).
Bayou La Batre, Mobile Co., Ala., 964.
On Mob. & Ohio (R. R.).
Bay Port, Huron Co., Mich., 534.
On Pere Marq. (R. R.).
Bayport, Washington Co., Minn., 2,590.
On Chi., Mil., St. P. & Pac.; Chi., St. P., Minn. & Oma.; Nor. Pac. (R. Rs.).
–Suffolk Co., N. Y., 1,273.
On Long Isl. (R. R.).
Bayreuth, Bavaria, Germany, 37,000.
Bay St. Louis, c. s., Hancock Co., Miss., 3,724.
On Lou. & Nash. (R. R.).
Port of entry.
Bayside, Humboldt Co., Calif., 500.
–Princess Anne Co., Va., 500.
Bay Springs, Jasper Co., Miss., 927.
On Gulf, Mob. & Nor. (R. R.).
Baytown, Harris Co., Texas., 5,194.
On Mo. Pac. & So. Pac. (R. Rs.).
Bay Village, Cuyahoga Co., Ohio, 2,294.
Railroad name North Dover.
Bayville, Ocean Co., N. J., 850.
–Nassau Co., N. Y., 1,042.
Beach, Golden Valley Co., N. Dak., 1,263.
On Nor. Pac. (R. R.).
Beach Bluff, Essex Co., Mass., 600.
Bost. & Me. (R. R.).
Beach City, Stark Co., Ohio, 725.
On Balt. & Ohio; Wheel. & L. Erie (R. Rs.).
Beach Haven, Ocean Co., N. J., 715.
On Penna. (R. R.).
Beach Park, Lorain Co., Ohio, 1,610.
On Lake Shore Elec. (R. R.).
Beacon, Dutchess Co., N. Y., 11,933.
On N. York Cen.; N. York, N. Hav. & Hart. (R. Rs.).
Seat of Matteawan State Hospital for Criminally Insane.
Beacon Falls, New Haven Co., Conn., 1,300.
On N. York, New Hav. & Hart. (R. R.).
Beaconsfield, Cape Colony, Un. of S. Africa, 20,264.
Beallsville, Washington Co., Pa., 581.
Bearden, Ouachita Co., Ark., 1,147.
St. Lou. Southw. (R. R.).
Beards Fork, Fayette Co., W. Va., 500.
On Virginian (R. R.).
Beardstown, Cass Co., Ill., 6,344.
On Balt. & Ohio; Chi., Burl. & Quincy (R. Rs.).
Beatrice, c. s., Gage Co., Neb., 10,297.
On Chi., Burl. & Quincy; Chi., Rk. Isl. & Pac.; Un. Pac. (R. Rs.).
Agricultural machinery, mirrors, windmills, silos, gasoline engines. Farming and dairying.
Beattyville, c. s., Lee Co., Ky., 906.
On Lou. & Nash. (R. R.).
Beaufort, c. s., Carteret Co., N. C., 2,957.
On Norf. Sou. (R. R.).
Port of entry.
–c. s., Beaufort Co., S. C., 2,776.
On Charl. & W. Car. (R. R.).
Good harbor; cotton, lime, phosphates, and lumber exported; resort.
Beauharnois, Beauharnois Co., Quebec, Canada, 3,729.
On Can. Nat.; N. York Cen. (R. Rs.).
Beaumont, Riverside Co., Cal., 1,332.
On Sou. Pac. (R. R.).
–c. s., Jefferson Co., Texas, 57,732.
On Beau., Sour Lk. & West.; Beau., Wharf & Term.; Gulf, Col. & Santa Fe; Kan. Cy. Sou.; Tex. & N. Orl. (R. Rs.).
Oil refineries. Also a lumber center. Located in extensive rice area, being tributary to three rice irrigating systems.
Beaune, Dept. of Côte d'Or, France, 12,161.
Site of an agricultural school.
Beauvais, capital of Dept. of Oise, France, 18,869.
Textiles, oil, vinegar, casks, jewelry.
Beaver, c. s., Beaver Co., Okla., 1,028.
On Beav., Meade & Englew. (R. R.).
–c. s., Beaver Co., Pa., 5,665.
On Penna.; Pitts. & L. Erie, Steub., E. Liverp. & Beav. Val. Trac. Co. (El.) (R.Rs.).
–c. s., Beaver Co., Utah, 1,673.
Beaver City, c. s., Furnas Co., Neb., 1,024.
On Chi., Burl. & Quincy (R. R.).
Beaver Crossing, Seward Co., Neb., 522.
On Chi. & Nor. West. (R. R.).
Beaverdale, Cambria Co., Pa., 1,643.
Beaver Dam, Ohio Co., Ky., 1,036.
On Ill. Cen. (R. R.).
–Dodge Co., Wis., 9,867.
On Chi., Mil., St. P. & Pac. (R. R.).
–(Beaver Dams P. O.), Schuyler Co., N. Y., 535.
On N. York Cen. (R. R.).
Beaver Falls, Lewis Co., N. Y., 840.
On Lowv. & Beaver Riv. (R. R.).
–c. s., Beaver Co., Pa., 17,147.
On Pennsylvania; Pitts. & Lake Erie (R. Rs.).
Geneva College (Presbyterian).
Beaver Meadow, Carbon Co., Pa., 1,890.
On Beav. Meadow, Tresck & N. Bost.; Lehigh Valley (R. Rs.).
Beaverton, Gladwin Co., Mich., 528.
On Pere Marq. (R. R.).
–Washington Co., Oregon, 1,138.
On Ore. El.; Sou. Pac. (R. Rs.).
Beavertown, Snyder Co., Pa., 604.
On Penna. (R. R.).
Beaver Valley, Columbia Co., Pa., 512.
Bechtelsville, Berks Co., Pa., 549.
On Read. (R. R.).
Beckemeyer, Clinton Co., Ill., 850.
On Balt. & Ohio (R. R.).
Becket, Berkshire Co., Mass., 773.
On Boston & Albany (R. R.).
Beckley, Raleigh Co., W. Va., 9,357.
On Chesa. & Ohio; Virginian (R. Rs.).
Bedford, c. s., Bedfordshire, England, 40,573.
Farm implements; large engineering works.
–c. s., Lawrence Co., Ind., 13,208.
On Chi., Ind. & Lou.; Chi., Mil., St. P. & Pac. (R. Rs.).
Airport. Limestone, fruit, corn, and wheat.
–c. s., Taylor Co., Iowa, 2,100.
On Chi., Burl. & Quincy (R. R.).
–Middlesex Co., Mass., 3,815.
On Bost. & Me. (R. R.).
–Hillsboro Co., N. H., 1,000.
–Westchester Co., N. Y., 1,000.
–Cuyahoga Co., Ohio, 6,814.
On Penna.; Wheel. & L. Erie (R. Rs.).
–c. s., Bedford Co., Pa., 2,953.
On Huntingdon & Broad Top Mt.; Penna (R. Rs.).
–c. s., Bedford Co., Va., 3,713.
On Norf. & West. (R. R.).
–Missisquoi Co., Quebec, Canada, 1,570.
On Canadian Pacific (R. R.).
Bedford Hills, Westchester Co., N. Y., 1,500.
On N. York Cen. (R. R.).
Bedias, Grimes Co., Tex., 750.
On Internat.-Gt. Nor. (R. R.).
Bedminster, Bucks Co., Pa., 1,500.
Bedzin, Dist. of Kielce, Poland, 47,812.
Beebe, White Co., Ark., 1,108.
On Mo. Pac. (R. R.).
Beechbottom, Brooke Co., W. Va., 1,200.
On Penna. (R. R.).
Beech Creek, Muhlenberg Co., Ky., 900.
On Lou. & Nash. (R. R.).
–Clinton Co., Pa., 590.
On N. York Cen.; Penna. (R. Rs.).
Beecher, Will Co., Ill., 772.
On Chi. & East. Ill. (R. R.).
Beech Grove, Marion Co., Indiana, 3,552.
On Clev., Cin., Chi. & St. Lou. (R. R.).
Beechhurst, Nassau Co., N. Y., 2,100.
Beechwood, Norfolk Co., Mass., 510.
On N. York, N. Hav. & Hart. (R. R.).
–Chautauqua Co., N. Y., 500.
–Monongalia Co., W. Va., 650.
Beechwood Park, Delaware Co., Pa., 600.
Beeck, Prussia, Germany, united with Duisburg (1905).
Beemer, Cuming Co., Neb., 571.
On Chi. & Nor. West. (R. R.).
Beeston, Nottinghamshire, England, 16,016.
Beggs, Okmulgee Co., Okla., 1,531.
On St. Lou.-San Fran. (R. R.).
Bègles, Gironde, France, 20,989.
Beirut, Seminole Co., Okla., 1,500.
–Syria. See Beyrouth.
Beja, Portugal, 13,104.
Cloth, pottery, and olive oil.
Bejucal, Prov. of Habana, Cuba, 5,389.
Békés, Hungary, 28,835.
Important railroad and trade center.
Bel Air, c. s., Harford Co., Md., 1,650.
On Md. & Penna. (R. R.).
Belcher, Caddo Par., La., 500.
On Tex. & Pac. (R. R.).
Belchertown, Hampshire Co., Mass., 3,863.
On Bost. & Me.; Cen. Ver. (R. Rs.).
Belding, Ionia Co., Mich., 4,140.
On Pere Marq. (R. R.).
Belém (Para), Brazil, 311,253.
Important commercial city and port.
Belen, Valencia Co., N. Mex., 2,116.
On Atch., Top. & Santa Fe (R. R.).
Belfast, capital of N. Ireland, 415,151.
Situated on the river Lagan at its débouché into Belfast Lough, an arm of the Irish Sea. Belfast is a comparatively modern city and well-built. Its public buildings include the City Hall and museums. The chief educational institution is Queen's University. The botanical gardens of the Natural History Society cover many acres. Belfast is the center of a very large linen trade dating from 1867.

There are extensive shipyards, foundries, and machine shops, manufactures of rope and sail cloth, breweries, distilleries, and dyehouses. The chief exports are cattle, linen goods, and agricultural products. In the fourteenth century Belfast was destroyed by Edward Bruce in 1316, was rebuilt, and became an important town in 1604.
–c. s., Waldo Co., Maine, 4,993.
On Belfast & Moosehead Lake (R. R.).
–Allegany Co., N. Y., 890.
On Penna. (R. R.).
Belfield, Stark Co., N. Dak., 653.
On Nor. Pac. (R. R.).
Belford, Monmouth Co., N. J., 1,304.
On Cen. of N. Jer. (R. R.).
Belfort, capital of territory of Belfort, France, 42,511.
Locomotives, machinery, wire, textiles.
Belgaum, capital of Dist. of Belgaum, India, 45,625.
Center of rich farming region.
Belgrade, Yugoslavia. See Beograd.
–Stearns Co., Minn., 508.

COURTESY OF THE GERMAN TOURIST INFORMATION OFFICE

THE HAUS DES RUNDFUNKS (HOUSE OF BROADCASTING), IN BERLIN, A STRIKING EXAMPLE OF MODERN BUSINESS ARCHITECTURE IN THE GERMAN CAPITAL

On Minn., St. P. & S. Ste. M. (R. R.).
–Washington Co., Mo., 979.
–Gallatin Co., Mont., 533.
On Chi., Mil., St. P. & Pac.; Nor. Pac. (R. Rs.).
Belhaven, Beaufort Co., N. C., 2,458.
On Norf. Sou. (R. R.).
Belington, Barbour Co., W. Va., 1,571.
On Balt. & Ohio; West. Md. (R. Rs.).
Belize, capital of British Honduras, 16,687.
Exports valuable cabinet woods.
Bellaire, c. s., Antrim Co., Mich., 517.
On E. Jordan & Sou.; Pere Marq. (R. Rs.).
–Belmont Co., Ohio, 13,327.
On Balt. & Ohio; Penna.; Wheel. & L. Erie (R. Rs.).
Clay, limestone, iron and steel products, caskets, enamelware.
Bellary, Madras Presidency, India, 47,573.
Cotton cloth and sugar.
Belle, Maries Co., Mo., 630.
On Chi., Rk. Isl. & Pac. (R. R.).
Belle Alliance, Assumption Par., La., 831.
On Tex. & Pac. (R. R.).
Belle Center, Logan Co., Ohio, 861.
On Cle., Cin., Chi. & St. Lou. (R. R.).
Belle Ellen, Bibb Co., Ala., 500.
On Lou. & Nash.; Sou. (R. Rs.).
Bellefontaine, c. s., Logan Co., Ohio, 9,543.
On Cin. & L. Erie. (El.); Cle., Cin., Chi. & St. Lou.; N. York Cen. (R. Rs.).
Manufactures bridges and other metal products.
Bellefonte, New Castle Co., Del., 761.
–c. s., Centre Co., Pa., 4,804.
On Bellef. Cen.; Penna. (R. Rs.).
Belle Fourche, c. s., Butte Co., S. Dak., 2,314.
On Chi. & Nor. West. (R. R.).
Belle Glade, Palm Beach Co., Fla., 1,646.
Belle Plaine, Benton Co., Iowa, 3,239.
On Chi. & Nor. West. (R. R.).
–Sumner Co., Kans., 875.
On Atch., Top. & Santa Fe; Mo. Pac.; Mid. Val. (R. Rs.).
–Scott Co., Minn., 1,236.
On Chi., St. P., Minn. & Oma. (R. R.).
Belle Point, St. John the Baptist Par., La., 2,500.
On La. & Ark.; Yazoo & Miss. Val. (R. Rs.).
Bellerose, Nassau Co., N. Y., 1,202.
On Long Isl. (R. R.).
Belle Valley, Noble Co., Ohio, 603.
On Penna. (R. R.).
Bellevernon, Fayette Co., Pa., 2,489.
On Pitts. & L. Erie (R. Rs.).

–(Spears), Washington Co., Pa., 645.
On Penna. (R. R.).
Belleville, c. s., St. Clair Co., Ill., 28,425.
On Ill. Cen.; Lou. & Nash.; St. Lou. & Ohio Riv.; Sou. (R. Rs.).
Bituminous coal, stove and foundry manufactures. Scott Aviation Field.
–c. s., Republic Co., Kans., 2,720.
On Chi., Rk. Isl. & Pac.; Un. Pac. (R. Rs.).
–Wayne Co., Mich., 758.
On Wabash (R. R.).
–Essex Co., N. J., 26,974.
On Erie (R. R.).
Residential suburb of Newark. Some manufacturing.
–(Belleville P. O.), Richland Co., Ohio, 987.
On Balt. & Ohio (R. R.).
–Capital of Hastings Co., Ontario, Canada, 13,790.
On Can. Nat. (R. R.).
–Mifflin Co., Pa., 1,156.
On Kishacoquillas Val. (R. R.).
–Dane Co., Wis., 564.
On Ill. Cen. (R. R.).
Bellevue, Jackson Co., Iowa, 1,717.
On Bellevue & Cascade; Chi., Mil., St. P. & Pac. (R. Rs.).
–Campbell Co., Ky., 8,497.
On Chesa. & Ohio (R. R.).
–Eaton Co., Mich., 1,029.
On Gd. Tr. (R. R.).
–Sarpy Co., Neb., 1,017.
On Chi., Burl. & Quincy (R. R.).
–Huron and Sandusky Cos., Ohio, 6,256.
On Lake Shore El.; N. York Cen.; N. York, Chi. & St. Lou.; Penna.; L. Erie (R. Rs.).
–Allegheny Co., Pa., 10,252.
On Pennsylvania (R. R.).
Coal mines and gas wells.
–Clay Co., Tex., 546.
On Ft. Worth & Denv. Cy. (R. R.).
Bellewood (Bellwood P. O.), Cook Co., Ill., 4,991.
On Chi. Gt. West. (R. R.).
Bellingham, Norfolk Co., Mass., 3,056.
Railroad name Midland.
–c. s., Whatcom Co., Wash., 30,823.
Is situated on Bellingham Bay and on the Northern Pacific; the Chicago, Milwaukee, St. Paul & Pacific, the Great Northern and the Northern Pacific Railroads. Shipping trade extensive. The city has some of the largest saw mills on the Pacific Coast, a large cedar shingle mill and one of the largest salmon canneries in the world.
Bello Horizonte, Brazil, 167,700.
A commercial center.
Bellows Falls, Windham Co., Vt., 3,930.
On Bost. & Me.; Rut. (R. Rs.).
Bellport, Suffolk Co., N. Y., 633.
On Long Isl. (R. R.).
Bells, Crockett Co., Tenn., 919.
On Gulf, Mob. & Nor.; Lou. & Nash. (R. Rs.).
Belluno, Venezia, Italy, 10,500.
On the Piave River.
Bellville, Richland Co., Ohio, 987.
Railroad name Belleville. On Balt. & Ohio (R. R.).
–c. s., Austin Co., Tex., 1,533.
On Gulf, Colo. & Santa Fe (R. R.).
Bell Ville, Argentine, 20,000.
Bellmawr, Camden Co., N. J., 1,123.
On Penna.-Read. Seashore (R. R.).
Bellwood, Cook Co., Illinois, 4,991.
On Chi. & Nor. West.; Chi., Aur. & Elg. (El.); Ind. Harb. Belt (R. Rs.).
–Blair Co., Pa., 2,560.
On Penna. (R. R.).

Belmar, Monmouth Co., N. J., 3,491.
On Cen. of N. Jer.; N. York & Long Br.; Penna. (R. Rs.).
Summer resort.
Belmond, Wright Co., Iowa, 1,733.
On Chi. Gt. West.; Chi., Rk. Isl. & Pac.; Minn. & St. Lou. (R. Rs.).
Belmont, San Mateo Co., Calif., 984.
On Sou. Pac. (R. R.).
–Middlesex Co., Mass., 24,831.
On Bost. & Me. (R. R.).
Market gardening.
–Tishomingo Co., Miss., 703.
On Ill. Cen. (R. R.).
–Belknap Co., N. H., 800.
On Bost. & Me. (R. R.).
–Allegany Co., N. Y., 1,085.
On Erie (R. R.).
–Gaston Co., N. C., 4,121.
On Piedmont & Nor. (El.); Sou. (R. Rs.).
Cotton yarns.
–Belmont Co., Ohio, 674.
On Balt. & Ohio (R. R.).
–Pleasants Co., W. Va., 500.
On Balt. & Ohio (R. R.).
Beloeil, Verchères Co., Quebec, Canada, 1,434.
On Can. Nat. (R. R.).
Beloit, c. s., Mitchell Co., Kans., 3,256.
On Mo. Pac.; Un. Pac. (R. Rs.).
–Mahoning Co., Ohio, 694.
On Penna. (R. R.).
–Rock Co., Wis., 23,611.
On Chi., Mil., St. P. & Pac.; Chi. & Nor. West. (R. Rs.).
Chief manufactures: oil engines, woodwork machinery, paper-making machinery, and disk grinding. Seat of Beloit College.
Belper, Derbyshire, England, 13,023.
Coal mining town. Wire, hosiery, and lace.
Belpre, Washington Co., Ohio, 1,724.
On Balt. & Ohio (R. R.).
Belt, Cascade Co., Mont., 810.
On Gt. Nor. (R. R.).
Belton, Cass Co., Mo., 992.
On St. Lou.-San Fran. (R. R.).
–Anderson Co., S. C., 1,765.
On Blue Ridge; Piedmont & Nor. (El.); Sou. (R. Rs.).
–c. s., Bell Co., Texas, 3,779.
On Gulf, Colo. & Santa Fe; Mo.-Kan.-Tex. of Tex. (R. Rs.).
Belvedere, Marin Co., Cal., 500.
Belvidere, c. s., Boone Co., Ill., 8,123.
On Chi. & Nor. West. (R. R.).
–c. s., Warren Co., N. J., 2,073.
On Leh. & Hud. Riv.; Penna. (R. Rs.).
Belzoni, c. s., Humphreys Co., Miss., 2,735.
On Yazoo & Miss. Val. (R. R.).
Bement, Piatt Co., Ill., 1,517.
On Ill. Term. (El.); Wab. (R. Rs.).
Bemidji, c. s., Beltrami Co., Minn., 7,202.
On Gt. Nor.; Minn. & Internat., Minn., Red L. & Man.; Minn., St. P. & S. Ste. M. (R. Rs.).
Farming and lumbering, and center of the lake districts.
Bemis, Madison Co., Tenn., 675.
On Gulf, Mob. & Nor.; Ill. Cen. (R. Rs.).
Benares, capital of Dist. of Benares, India, 205,315.
Situated on the north bank of the Ganges and one of the most ancient cities in the Orient. It is the center of Hindu religion and learning, and a holy place for both Brahmanical and Buddhistic pilgrims.
Benavides, Duval Co., Tex., 1,000.
On Tex. Mex. (R. R.).
Ben Avon, Allegheny Co., Pa., 2,472.
On Penna. (R. R.).
Bend, Deschutes Co., Ore., 8,848.
On Gt. Nor.; Ore. Tr.; Ore.-Wash. R. R. & Nav. Co.; Shevlin-Hixon (R. Rs.).
Ben Davis, Marion Co., Ind., 800.
On Ind. R. R. Sys. (El.); Penna. (R. Rs.).
Bendigo, Victoria, Australia, 29,131.
Gold mining town.
Benevento, capital of Prov. of Benevento, Campania, Italy, 30,700.
Many antiquities, including the Arch of Trajan.
Benfeldside, Durham, England, 9,193.
Bengasi, Libya, Italian North Africa, 33,794.
Seaport. Exports barley and ivory.
Benha, Kalyubiye, Egypt, 18,607.
Benholm, Kincardine Co., Scotland, 1,092.
Benicia, Solano Co., Cal., 2,913.
On Sou. Pac. (R. R.).
Benkelman, Dundy Co., Neb., 1,154.
On Chi., Burl. & Quincy (R. R.).
Benld, Macoupin Co., Ill., 2,980.
On Chi. & Nor. West.; Ill. Term. (El.); Litchf. & Mad. (R. Rs.).
Bennettsville, c. s., Marlboro Co., S. C., 3,667.
On Atl. Coast Line; Bennettsv. & Cheraw; Rockingham (R. Rs.).
Bennington, c. s., Bennington Co., Vt., 7,390.
On Rutland (R. R.).
Industries mainly underwear and dress goods. Site of highest battle monument in the world and of Vermont Soldiers' Home.

Bensalem, Bucks Co., Pa., 2,000.
Bensenville, Du Page Co., Ill., 1,680.
On Chi., Mil., St. P. & Pac. (R. R.).
Benson, Cochise Co., Ariz., 925.
On Sou. Pac. (R. R.).
–c. s., Swift Co., Minn., 2,095.
On Gt. Nor. (R. R.).
–Johnston Co., N. C., 1,522.
On Atl. Coast Line (R. R.).
–Rutland Co., Vt., 636.
Bentley and Arksey, Yorkshire, West England, 16,458.
Bentleyville, Washington Co., Pa., 3,609.
On Penna. (R. R.).
Benton, c. s., Saline Co., Ark., 3,445.
On Chi., Rk. Isl. & Pac.; Mo. Pac. (R. Rs.).
–c.s., Franklin Co., Ill., 8,219.
On Chi. & East. Ill.; Ill. Cen.; Mo. Pac. (R. Rs.).
–c. s., Marshall Co., Ky., 1,021.
On Nashv., Chatt. & St. Lou. (R. R.).
–Columbia Co., Pa., 733.
On Reading (R. R.).
–c. s., Polk Co., Tenn., 508.
On Lou. & Nash. (R. R.).
–Lafayette Co., Wis., 869.
On Chi. & Nor. West. (R. R.).
Benton Harbor, Berrien Co., Mich., 15,434.
On Mich. Cen.; Cle., Cin., Chi. & St. Lou.; Pere Marq. (R. Rs.).
Steel and iron castings and machinery construction, loose leaf and steel filing equipment.
Benton Heights, Union Co., N. C., 715.
Bentonville, c. s., Benton Co., Ark., 2,203.
On St. Lou.-San Fran. (R. R.).
Benwood, Marshall Co., W. Va., 3,950.
On Balt. & Ohio, Benw. & Wheel.; Penna.; Wheel. & L. Erie (R. Rs.).
Benzonia, Benzie Co., Mich., 623.
Beograd (Belgrade), capital of Yugoslavia (Serb-Croat-Slovene Kingdom), 289,272.
Largest and best built city of Yugoslavia. Important river port on the Danube. Manufactures not greatly developed. Has a library and several museums.
Berat, Janina Vilayet, Albania, 10,403.
In rich agricultural region.
Berber, Nubia, Ang.-Egypt. Sudan, Est., 20,000.
Berbera, capital of British Somaliland, 20,000.
Berchem, Belgium, 44,486.
Berdichev, Ukraine, Soviet Union, 53,100.
A commercial center.
Berdyansk, Ukraine, Soviet Union, 35,900.
Berea, Madison Co., Ky., 1,827.
On Lou. & Nash. (R. R.).
–Cuyahoga Co., Ohio, 5,697.
On Balt. & Ohio; Cle., Cin., Chi. & St. Lou.; N. York Cen. (R. Rs.).
Beresford, Union and Lincoln Cos., S. Dak., 1,618.
On Chi. & Nor. West. (R. R.).
Bergamo, capital of Prov. of Bergamo, Italy, 21,600.
Manufactures of silk, wool, linen, and iron goods.
Bergen, Norway, 98,546.
A fortified city and walled seaport, located at the head of Vaagen Bay and almost surrounded by water. Bergen lies in a semicircle around the harbor and is a well-built and picturesque city. There are extensive shipbuilding yards. A large proportion of the trade of Norway passes through Bergen. It is the chief fish market in Norway.
–Genesee Co., N. Y., 724.
On N. York Cen. (R. R.).
Bergenfield, Bergen Co., N. J., 8,816.
On West Shore (R. R.).
Bergen-op-Zoom, North Brabant, Netherlands, 21,618.
Considerable trade in anchovies, oysters, and sugar beets.
Bergerac, Dept. of Dordogne, France, 18,902.
Bergholz, Jefferson Co., Ohio, 918.
On N. York Cen. (R. R.).
Bergland, Ontonagon Co., Mich., 600.
On Dul., Sou. Sh. & Atl. (R. R.).
Berkeley, Alameda Co., Cal., 82,109.
On Atch., Top. & Santa Fe; Key Sys. (El.); Sou. Pac. (R. Rs.).
State institution for deaf, dumb, and blind; seat of University of California.
Berkeley Heights, Union Co., N. J., 900.
On Del., Lack. & West. (R. R.).
Berkeley Springs, c. s., Morgan Co., W. Va., 1,039.
On Balt. & Ohio (R. R.).
Berkley, Bristol Co., Mass., 1,156.
Berlin, capital, Republic of Germany, 4,242,501.
Situated on both sides of the Spree River. It is built on a flat, sandy plain. Its geographical position has made it the railway center of northern Germany. Berlin occupies an area of 339 square miles. The principal streets are the famous Unter den Linden, the Wilhelmstrasse, the Königstrasse, and the Leipzigerstrasse. Scattered about the city are a number of notable statues, including the one of Frederick the Great at the head of Unter den Linden. The Brandenburg gate

presents on each face six lofty columns; surmounted by an attic, upon which is a bronze "Victory." In the Belle Alliance Platz is a "Column of Peace," commemorating the peace of 1815. The triumphs of German arms are further typified in the great "Monument of Victory," dedicated in 1875. In the center of the city is the old Royal Palace, containing nearly 700 apartments, part of which is now a museum. Near by are the former palaces of the Emperor and Crown Prince, the Prussian State Library, which contains 2,000,000 volumes, the old and new museums, the National Art Gallery, the arsenal, the Royal Theater, the opera house, and the guardhouse. Other notable structures are the building of the Imperial Reichstag, the palace of the Imperial Chancellor, the old Museum (Hohenzollern) and the New Museum. The Tiergarten is the great pleasure ground of the Berliners.
Berlin is the greatest center of intellectual development in Germany. The Friedrich Wilhelm University, founded in 1809, is the largest in the Reich. Other educational institutions are the Academy of Science, the School of Mining, and the Technical, and Engineering Colleges.
Berlin is the first city in Germany in respect to the variety and importance of its manufactured products. The chief articles are cloths, linen, silks, cottons, iron wares, bronze ware, scientific instruments, pianos, German silverware, chemicals, porcelain, artificial flowers, and beer.
In 1871 Berlin became the capital of the German Empire.
–Hartford Co., Conn., 4,875.
–Worcester Co., Mass., 1,091.
On Bost. & Me. and N. Y., N. H. & H. (R. Rs.).
–Worcester Co., Md., 1,480.
On Balt. & East.; Penna. (R. Rs.).
–Coos Co., N. H., 20,018.
On Bost. & Me.; Gd. Tr. (R. Rs.).
Pulp and paper manufactures.
–Camden Co., N. J., 1,955.
On Penna.-Read. Seashore (R. R.).
–Rensselaer Co., N. Y., 1,200.
On Rutland (R. R.).
–Somerset Co., Pa., 1,393.
On Balt. & Ohio (R. R.).
–Green Lake and Waushara Cos., Wis., 4,106.
On Chi., Mil., St. P. & Pac. (R. R.).
Glove manufacturing center.
Berlin Heights, Erie Co., Ohio, 569.
On L. Shore El.; N. York, Chi. & St. Lou. (R. Rs.).
Bern (or Berne), capital of Canton of Bern, Switzerland, 151,200.
Situated on a promontory 1,800 feet above sea level. The river Aar surrounds it on three sides and is crossed by several bridges. There are numerous fountains, promenades, and monuments. The cathedral, the theater, the natural history and art museums, the library, and the federal council halls are all imposing buildings. The University of Bern was founded in 1834.
The peninsula and town were first fortified by Berchtold, Duke of Zahringen. At his death, in 1218, it became a free imperial city, and in 1353, a part of the Swiss Confederacy. Bern received its name from the city of Verona, called Bern by the Germans.
Bernalillo, c. s., Sandoval Co., N. Mex., 2,100.
On Atch., Top. & Santa Fe; Santa Fe North W. (R. Rs.).
Bernardstown, Franklin Co., Mass., 975.
On Boston & Maine (R. R.).
Bernay, Dept. of Eure, Normandy, France, 7,587.
Bernburg, Anhalt, Germany, 38,000.
Agricultural machinery, salt, paper, chemicals.
Berne, Adams Co., Ind., 1,883.
On Pennsylvania (R. R.).
Bernharts, Berks Co., Pa., 900.
Bernice, Union Parish, La., 965.
Chi., Rk. Isl. & Pac. (R. R.).
–Sullivan Co., Pa., 618.
On Leh. Val. (R. R.).
Bernie, Stoddard Co., Mo., 1,031.
On St. Lou. Southw. (R. R.).
Berrien Springs, Berrien Co., Mich., 1,413.
Berry, Fayette Co., Ala., 500.
On Southern (R. R.).
Berryville, c. s., Carroll Co., Ark., 1,286.
On Mo. & No. Ark. (R. R.).
–c. s., Clarke Co., Va., 1,094.
On Norf. & West. (R. R.).
Berthier, Berthier Co., Quebec, Canada, 2,431.
On Can. Pac. (R. R.).
Berthold, Ward Co., N. Dak., 511.
On Gt. Nor. (R. R.).
Berthoud, Larimer Co., Colo., 811.
On Colo. & Sou. (R. R.).
Bertram, Burnet Co., Tex., 600.
On Tex. & N. Orl. (R. R.).
Bertrand, Phelps Co., Neb., 645.
On Chi., Burl. & Quincy (R. R.).
Berwick, St. Mary Parish, La., 1,679.
On Tex. & N. Orl. (R. R.).
–York Co., Maine, 1,500.
–Columbia Co., Pa., 12,660.
On Del., Lack. & West.; Penna. (R. Rs.).
Steel manufactures.
Berwind, McDowell Co., W. Va., 2,000.
On Norf. & West. (R. R.).
Berwyn, Prince Georges Co., Md., 1,000.
On Balt. & Ohio (R. R.).
–Cook Co., Ill., 47,027.
On Chi., Burl. & Quincy; Ill. Cen. (R. Rs.).
Residential city.
–Chester Co., Pa., 1,800.
On Pennsylvania (R. R.).
Besançon, capital of Dept. of Doubs, France, 65,022.
Situated on the river Doubs, on a promontory topped by a citadel constructed by Vauban. Among the numerous interesting Roman remains is the Gate of Mars built by Marcus Aurelius, 167 A.D. The cathedral dates from the eleventh century.
The city is an important industrial center, especially noted for its watch making and also for its artificial silk manufacture. Besançon was the ancient Veisontium, capital of the Sequani. Caesar conquered it and made of it a Roman stronghold.
Bessemer, Jefferson Co., Ala., 20,721.
On Ala. Gt. Sou.; Atla., Birm. & Coast; Birm. Sou.; Ill. Cen.; Lou. & Nash.; Seab. Air Line; Sou.; St. Lou.-San Fran. (R. Rs.).
Iron and steel foundries, lumber mills, and brick works.
–c. s., Gogebic Co., Mich., 4,035.
On Chi. & Nor. West.; Minn., St. P. & S. Ste. M. (R. Rs.).
–Lawrence Co., Pa., 2,001.
Railroad name Walford.
Bessemer City, Gaston Co., N. C., 3,739.
On Southern (R. R.).
Bessmay, Jasper Co., Tex., 858.
On Gulf, Colo. & Santa Fe; Orange & Northw. (R. Rs.).
Bethalto, Madison Co., Ill., 687.
On Clev., Cin., Chi. & St. Lou. (R. R.).
Bethany, Moultrie Co., Ill., 802.
On Ill. Cen. (R. R.).
–c. s., Harrison Co., Mo., 2,209.
On Chi., Burl. & Quincy (R. R.).
–Lancaster Co., Neb. (Sta. Lincoln P. O.).
–Oklahoma Co., Okla., 2,032.
Bethel, Fairfield Co., Conn., 3,200.
On N. York, N. Hav. & Hart. (R. R.).
–Oxford Co., Maine, 964.
On Gd. Tr. (R. R.).
–Pitt Co., N. C., 1,149.
On Atl. Coast Line (R. R.).
–Clermont Co., Ohio, 1,312.
On Cin., Georgetown (R. R.).
–Windsor Co., Vt., 1,500.
On Cen. Ver. (R. R.).
Bethel Springs, McNairy Co., Tenn., 573.
On Mob. & Ohio (R. R.).
Bethesda, Belmont Co., Ohio, 1,159.
On Balt. & Ohio (R. R.).
Bethlehem, Palestine, 6,817.
Birthplace of the Saviour; Church of the Nativity and several large convents.
–Grafton Co., N. H., 500.
–Lehigh and Northampton Cos., Pa., 57,892.
On Central of New Jersey; Lehigh & New Eng.; Lehigh Valley; Philadelphia, Bethlehem & New England; Reading (R. Rs.).
Consolidated with South Bethlehem. First settled in 1741 by the Moravians, some of whose old buildings remain. Home of the Bethlehem Steel Company. Lehigh University and the Moravian College and Theological Seminary are also located here.
Bethune, Kershaw Co., S. C., 522.
On Seab. Air Line (R. R.).
Betsy Layne, Floyd Co., Ky., 750.
On Chesa. & Ohio (R. R.).
Bettendorf, Scott Co., Iowa, 2,768.
Chi., Burl. & Quincy; Chi., Mil., St. P. & Pac.; Clin., Davenp. & Musc.; Davenp., Rk. Isl. & Northw. (R. Rs.).
Bettsville, Seneca Co., Ohio, 656.
On Pennsylvania (R. R.).
Beulah, Bolivar Co., Miss., 506.
On Yazoo & Miss. Val. (R. R.).
–Mercer Co., N. Dak., 913.
On Nor. Pac. (R. R.).
–Clearfield Co., Pa., 500.
Beulah Heights, Saline Co., Ill., 508.
Beury, Fayette Co., W. Va., 521.
On Chesa. & Ohio (R. R.).
Beuthen, Prussia, Germany, 100,584.
Chemical and machine industries.
Bevelle, Tallapoosa Co., Ala., 1,276.
Beverley, Yorkshire, England, 14,011.
Beverly, Burlington Co., N. J., 2,864.
On Pennsylvania (R. R.).
–Washington Co., Ohio, 600.
–Essex Co., Mass., 25,871.
On Bost. & Me. (R. R.).
Beverly Hills, Los Angeles Co., Cal., 17,429.
On Pac. Elec.; Sou. Pac. (R. Rs.).
Residential suburb of Los Angeles.
–Delaware Co., Pa., 575.
Bevier, Muhlenberg Co., Ky., 600.
On Lou. & Nash. (R. R.).
–Macon Co., Mo., 1,229.
On Bev. & Sou.; Chi., Burl. & Quincy (R. Rs.).
Bexhill, Sussex East, England, 21,229.
Summer resort.
Bexley, Franklin Co., Ohio, 7,396.
–Kent, England, 32,940.
Tools, fitting, and chemicals.
Beyer, Indiana Co., Pa., 515.
Beyrouth (Beirut), Syria, 160,716.
Capital and chief seaport of Syria, also capital of the Republic of Lebanon.
The town has large bazaars, a college, schools (chiefly missions), mosques, and Christian churches. It is the center of the Oriental book trade, and has manufactures of silk, and gold and silver thread. Raw silk is an important commodity. The growth of the city has been very rapid. Beyrouth is very ancient, was mentioned by the Egyptians as early as 1,500 B.C. Formerly in Turkish territory it passed under the control of France following the Great War.
Beziers, Dept. of Hérault, France, 73,305.
Center of wine growing district.
Bhagalpur, Bihar and Orissa, India, 83,847.
Silk industry.
Bhopal, Central India, India, 61,037.
Biala, Siedlce, Poland, 17,549.
Bialystok, Grodno West, Poland, 105,000.
Woolen, silk, distilling and tobacco industries.
Biarritz, Dept. of Basses-Pyrénées, France, 20,691.
A leading seaside resort.
Bibb City, Muscogee Co., Ga., 1,707.
Bicknell, Knox Co., Ind., 5,212.
On Pennsylvania (R. R.).
Biddeford, York Co., Maine, 17,633.
On Bost. & Me. (R. R.).
Manufactures of lumber, cottons, machinery, boots and shoes. Granite is quarried in the vicinity.
Bideford, Devonshire, England, 8,782.
Biel (Bienne), Switzerland, 37,861.
Watch-making, chain-making, and machine industries.
Bielefeld, Prussia, Germany, 121,031.
Silk manufactures.
Biella, Prov. of Vercelli, Italy, 22,146.
Bienne. See Biel.
Bigaa, Prov. of Bulucan, Luzon, P. I., 9,847.
Big Bay, Marquette Co., Mich., 700.
On L. Sup. & Ishpem. (R. R.).
Big Bear City, San Bernardino Co., Calif., 500.
Big Clifty, Grayson Co., Ky., 500.
On Ill. Cen. (R. R.).
Big Four, McDowell Co., W. Va., 500.
On Norf. & West. (R. R.).
Biggar, Saskatchewan, Canada, 1,953.
Big Lake, c. s., Reagan Co., Tex., 832.
On Panh. & Santa Fe (R. R.).
Biglerville, Adams Co., Pa., 659.
On Reading (R. R.).
Big Rapids, c. s., Mecosta Co., Mich., 4,671.
On Penna.; Pere Marq. (R. Rs.).
The Muskegon River furnishes water power to the city's industries, chief of which are furniture and wood products.
Big Run, Jefferson Co., Pa., 795.
On Balt. & Ohio (R. R.).
Big Sandy, Chouteau Co., Mont., 633.
On Gt. Nor. (R. R.).
–Benton Co., Tenn., 603.
On Lou. & Nash. (R. R.).
–Upshur Co., Texas, 579.
On St. Lou. Southw.; Tex. & Pac. (R. Rs.).
Big Spring, c. s., Howard Co., Texas, 13,735.
On Tex. & Pac. (R. R.).
Trade center for nearby oil fields; shipping market for farm products and livestock.
Big Springs (Big Springs P. O.), Deuel Co., Neb., 595.
On Un. Pac. (R. R.).
Big Stone City, Grant Co., S. Dak., 675.
On Chi., Mil., St. P. & Pac. (R. R.).
Big Stone Gap, Wise Co., Va., 3,908.
On Lou. & Nash.; Sou. (R. Rs.).
Big Timber, c.s., Sweet Grass Co., Mont., 1,224.
On Nor. Pac. (R. R.).
Big Wells, Dimmit Co., Tex., 500.
On San Ant., Uvalde. & Gulf (R. R.).
Bisk, Sov. Union in Asia, 62,500.
Bikaner, Rajputana, India, 85,927.
Carpets, sugar, and blanket manufactures.
Bilar, Prov. of Bohol, Bohol, P. I., 6,240.
Bilbao, Prov. of Vizcaya, Spain, 175,898.
Picturesquely situated on both banks of the river Nervion, within encircling hills.
The city owes its importance to its large commerce and to the vast deposits of iron and copper ore in the vicinity.
Billerica, Middlesex Co., Mass., 6,650.
On Bost. & Me. (R. R.).
Settled since 1643-4, and incorporated since 1655.
Billings, c. s., Yellowstone Co., Mont., 16,380.
On Chi., Burl. & Quincy; Gt. Nor.; Nor. Pac. (R. Rs.).
Shipping point for farm produce, livestock and dairy products.
–Noble Co., Okla., 658.
On Chi., Rk. Isl. and Pac. (R. R.).
Biloxi, Harrison Co., Miss., 14,850.
On Lou. & Nash. (R. R.).
Resort. Packing and shipping of sea food.
Bilston, Staffordshire, England, 31,248.
Iron and steel mills.
Binalonan, Prov. of Pangasinan, Luzon, P. I., 17,400.
Binche, Hainaut, Belgium, 10,550.
Bingen, Republic of Hesse, Germany, 9,100.
Bingen-White Salmon, Klickitat Co., Wash., 798.
On Spok., Port. & Seattle (R. R.).
Binger, Caddo Co., Okla., 849.
On Chi., Rk. Isl. & Pac. (R. R.).
Bingerville (formerly Adjame, now Abidjan), capital of Ivory Coast, French West Africa, estimated 1,358.
Bingham, Somerset Co., Maine, 950.
On Me. Cen. (R. R.).
–(Bingham Canyon P. O.), Salt Lake Co., Utah, 3,248.
On Bingh. & Garf.; Den. & Rio Gde. West. (R. Rs.).
Binghamton, c. s., Broome Co., N. Y., 76,662.
On Del. & Hud.; Del., Lack. & West.; Erie (R. Rs.).
New York State Hospital for the Insane. Manufactures of boots and shoes, silks, cigars, photographic products and furniture.
Binh-dinh, French Indo-China, 74,400.
Binmaley, Luzon, P. I., 18,243.
Fisheries, wine, salt, and pottery.
Birch Run, Saginaw Co., Mich., 600.
On Pere Marq. (R. R.).
Birch Tree, Shannon Co., Mo., 505.
On St. Lou.-San Fran. (R. R.).
Birchwood, Washburn Co., Wis., 565.
On Chi., St. P., Minn. & Oma.; Minn., St. P. & S. Ste. M. (R. Rs.).
Bird City, Cheyenne Co., Kan., 742.
On Chi., Burl. & Quincy (R. R.).
Bird Island, Renville Co., Minn., 1,004.
On Chi., Mil., St. P. & Pac. (R. R.).
Bird Mills (East Walpole), Norfolk Co., Mass., 2,000.
On N. York, N. Hav. & Hart. (R. R.).
Birdsboro, Berks Co., Pa., 3,542.
On Penna.; Read. (R. Rs.).
Birdville, Tarrant Co., Tex., 800.
Birkenhead, Cheshire, England, 147,946.
A seaport town opposite Liverpool that has had a remarkable growth since the opening of its shipbuilding yards in 1824. In 1847 magnificent docks were begun which now have a total quayage of 10 miles.
Birmingham, Warwickshire, England, 1,012,700.
In the center of England, on the river Rea, it fulfills the triple functions of a city, a civic county, and a parliamentary and municipal borough.
The center of the city, once an overcrowded district, has been rebuilt and improved and now contains many fine buildings, among them Queen's College, connected with London University, the grammar school of Edward VI., Birmingham and Midland Institute, free library, and theater. The chief ecclesiastical edifices are St. Martin's Church, dating from the thirteenth century, the Roman Catholic Cathedral of Saint Chad, and the Baptist Wyclif Chapel (fourteenth-century Gothic).
The immense coal and iron beds near Birmingham are the principal source of its importance and have made the city the chief seat of British metallic manufactures and an important hardware center of the world. Besides steel and iron wares, including guns, rifles and swords, the city manufactures gold and silver wares, toys, jewelry, glass, buttons, chemicals, and beer. The city's transportation facilities have been greatly increased by numerous canals.
Birmingham was originally the Anglo-Saxon town Beormings Ham, and even in the Middle Ages it was a busy place. Its great industrial and commercial importance began in the sixteenth and seventeenth centuries with its manufactures of metal ornaments, swords, and guns. Its prosperity was greatly increased by the opening of the Lancashire coal and iron fields, and by the middle of the eighteenth century its manufactures were celebrated.
–c. s., Jefferson Co., Ala., 259,678.
On the Central of Georgia; the Louisville and Nashville; the Southern; the St. Louis-San Francisco; Illinois Central; Alabama Great Southern; Atlanta, Birmingham and Coast; Mobile and Ohio; Birmingham Southern; Seaboard Air Line and the Birmingham Belt railroads. The city has 185 miles of street railways.
The city was founded in 1871 and named after Birmingham, the iron and steel manufacturing center of England. It is situated

in a rich mineral-producing section. Extensive deposits of iron ore and beds of coal, limestone and pottery clay are found in the district, and in close proximity to one another. The city is the largest in Alabama. Red Mountain, near the city limits, contains enormous deposits of hematite ore. Three-fourths of the entire iron output of the State is obtained from the Birmingham district. The city has numerous blast furnaces, rolling mills, ship plate mills, foundries, pipe plants, clay working industries, cement plants, lumber mills, factories producing chemicals, textiles, explosives, and a variety of other diversified industries, numbering (1930) 685.
Birmingham has fine parks, a Municipal Auditorium, city-owned golf courses and handsome buildings, among the last-named being the new $3,000,000 court house. Birmingham-Southern and Howard colleges are located here. The "platoon" system of public schools is in effect.
Birmingham was laid out in 1871 and in a few months chartered as a city.
–Van Buren Co., Iowa, 507.
On Chi., Burl. & Quincy (R. R.).
–Oakland Co., Mich., 9,539.
On Gd. Trk. (R. R.).
Birnamwood, Shawano Co., Wis., 557.
On Chi. & Nor. West. (R. R.).
Bisbee, c. s., Cochise Co., Ariz., 8,023.
–Towner Co., N. Dak., 531.
On Gt. Nor.; Minn., St. P. & S. Ste. M. (R. Rs.).
Bisceglie, Prov. of Bari, Italy, 33,905.
Seaport. Many antiquities, including Church of St. Margherita.
Biscoe, Montgomery Co., N. C., 819.
On Norf. Sou. (R. R.).
Bishnupur, Bengal, India, 20,500.
Bishop, Inyo Co., Cal., 1,159.
–Worcester Co., Md., 763.
On Pennsylvania (R. R.).
–Nueces Co., Tex., 953.
On St. Lou., Brownsv. & Mex. (R. R.).
Bishopville, c. s., Lee Co., S. C., 2,249.
On Atl. Coast Line; Seab. Air Line (R. Rs.).
Biskra, Prov. of Constantine, Algeria, 11,231.
A North African winter resort.
Bismarck (formerly Braubauerschaft), Prussia, Germany, united with Gelsenkirchen.
–St. Francois Co., Mo., 1,185.
On Mo.-Ill.; Mo. Pac. (R. Rs.).
–c. s., Burleigh Co., N. Dak., State capital, 11,090.
On the east bank of the Missouri River, on the Northern Pacific and the Minneapolis; St. Paul and Sault Sainte Marie Railroads. The river is navigable for boats 250 to 700 tons for 1,200 miles above Bismarck.
The town contains an immense river warehouse. The bridge across the Missouri River cost about one and a half million dollars. Chief public buildings are the Capitol, the penitentiary, court-house, high school building, etc. There are also waterworks, an electric-light plant, and flour mills.
Bitlis, Bitlis Vilayet, Turkey, 9,050.
Bitolj (Monastir), Yugoslavia, 32,982.
Bitonto, Prov. of Bari, Italy, 26,841.
Wine and olive oil.
Bitterfeld, Prussia, Germany, 21,000.
Biwabik, St. Louis Co., Minn., 1,383.
On Dul., Missabe & Nor. (R. R.).
Bixby, Tulsa Co., Oklahoma, 1,251.
Midl. Val. (R. R.).
Blaby, Leicestershire, England, 32,761.
Black Betsey, Putnam Co., W. Va., 550.
On N. York Cen. (R. R.).
Blackburn, Lancashire, England, 124,500.
Has some handsome public buildings, among them a town hall, Gothic exchange, and draper's hall. The educational institutions include a grammar school, founded by Queen Elizabeth, a municipal technical school, a public library, a museum, and an art gallery. Blackburn is an advanced municipality and one of the greatest cotton manufacturing centers of the world. Manufactures also include machinery and iron products. The town is celebrated as the home of James Hargreaves, the inventor of the spinning-jenny (1767).
Black Creek, Outagamie Co., Wis., 526.
On Gr. Bay & West.; Minn., St. P. & S. Ste. M. (R. Rs.).
Black Diamond, King Co., Wash., 1,400.
On Pacific Coast (R. R.).
Blackduck, Beltrami Co., Minn., 704.
On Minn. & Internat. (R. R.).
Blackfoot, c. s., Bingham Co., Idaho, 3,199.
On Ore. Short Line (R. R.).
Black Hammer, Houston Co., Minn., 696.
Black Horse, Montgomery Co., Pa., 1,000.
Blackinton, Berkshire Co., Mass., 1,000.
On Bost. & Me. (R. R.).
Black Lake, Megantic Co., Quebec, Canada, 2,167.
On Queb. Cen. (R. R.).
Black Lick, Indiana Co., Pa., 1,500.
On Penna. (R. R.).
Blackmount, Grafton Co., N. H., 650.
On Bost. & Me. (R. R.).
Black Mountain, Buncombe Co., N. C., 737.
On Southern (R. R.).
Blackpool, Lancashire, England, 101,543.
One of the most frequented resorts in England.
Black River, Jefferson Co., N. Y., 923.
On N. York Cen. (R. R.).
Black River Falls, c. s., Jackson Co., Wis., 1,950.
On Chi., St. P., Minn. & Oma. (R. R.).
Blackrock, Lawrence Co., Ark., 751.
On St. Lou.-San Fran. (R. R.).
Blacksburg, Cherokee Co., S. C., 1,747.
On Southern (R. R.).
–Montgomery Co., Va., 1,406.
On Norf. & West. (R. R.).
Blackshear, c. s., Pierce Co., Ga., 1,817.
On Atl. Coast Line (R. R.).
Blackstone, Worcester Co., Mass., 4,588.
On N. York, New Hav. & Hart. (R. R.).
Manufactures of cotton goods.
–Nottoway Co., Va., 1,772.
On Norf. & West. (R. R.).
Blackville, Barnwell Co., S. C., 1,284.
On Southern (R. R.).
Blackwater, Cooper Co., Mo., 506.
On Mo. Pac. (R. R.).
Blackwell, Kay Co., Okla., 9,521.
On Atch., Top. & Santa Fe; St. Lou. & San Fran. (R. Rs.).
Adjacent to productive oil and gas fields.
Blackwood, Camden Co., N. J., 1,000.
On Penn.-Read. Seashore (R. R.).
–Wise Co., Va., 600.
On Inters.; Lou. & Nash. (R. R.).
Bladenboro, Bladen Co., N. C., 587.
On Seab. Air Line (R. R.).
Bladensburg, Prince Georges Co., Maryland, 816.
On Balt. & Ohio (R. R.).
Blagoveshchensk, Soviet Union, 63,500.
A trade center in a mining and agricultural region.
Blaine, Aroostook Co., Maine, 500.
–Whatcom Co., Wash., 1,642.
On Gt. Nor. (R. R.).
Blainsburg, Washington Co., Pa., 1,000.
Blair, c. s., Washington Co., Neb., 2,791.
On Chi. & Nor. West.; Chi., St. P., Minn. & Oma. (R. Rs.).
–Jackson Co., Okla., 585.
On Atch., Top. & Santa Fe (R. R.).
–Trempealeau Co., Wisconsin, 702.
On Ettrick; Gr. Bay & West. (R. Rs.).
Blairmore, Alberta, Canada, 1,682.
Blairstown, Warren Co., N. J., 900.
On Del., Lack. & West.; N. York, Susq. & West. (R. Rs.).
Blairsville, Indiana Co., Pa., 5,296.
On Penna. (R. R.).
Blakely, c. s., Early Co., Ga., 2,106.
On Cen. of Ga. (R. R.).
–Lackawanna Co., Pa., 8,260.
On Wilk.-Bar. & East. (R. R.).
Blakeney, Red River Co., Tex., 600.
Blanchard, McClain Co., Oklahoma, 1,040.
On Atch., Top. & Santa Fe (R. R.).
–Centre Co., Pa., 531.
Blanchardville, Lafayette Co., Wis., 651.
On Ill. Cen. (R. R.).
Blanchester, Clinton Co., Ohio, 1,597.
Blanco, San Juan Co., N. Mex., 1,505.
–Blanco Co., Tex., 719.
Bland, Gasconade Co., Mo., 577.
On Chi., Rk. Isl. & Pac. (R. R.).
–c. s., Bland Co., Va., 630.
Blandburg, Cambria Co., Pa., 1,821.
On Penna. (R. R.).
Blanding, San Juan Co., Utah, 555.
Blandinsville, McDonough Co., Ill., 952.
On Tol., Peor. & West. (R. R.).
Blandon, Berks Co., Pa., 800.
On Reading (R. R.).
Blanford, Vermillion Co., Ind., 1,000.
On Chi., Mil., St. P. & Pac. (R. R.).
Blankenburg, Prussia, Germany, 12,003.
A health resort.
Blarney, County Cork, Irish Free State, 700.
Seat of Blarney Castle and its famous stone.
Blasdell, Erie Co., N. Y., 2,015.
On Erie; N. York Cen.; Penna. (R. Rs.).
Blauvelt, Rockland Co., N. Y., 500.
On Erie; West Shore (R. Rs.).
Blenheim, So. Island, New Zealand, 5,530.
-Kent Co., Ontario, Canada, 1,737.
On Pere Marq. (R. R.).
Blessing, Matagorda Co., Tex., 500.
On St. L., Brownsv. & Mex.; Tex. & N. Orl. (R. Rs.).
Blewett, Uvalde Co., Tex., 500.
Blida, Algeria, 29,735.
Trade center in a fruit raising region.
Blissfield, Lenawee Co., Mich., 2,103.
On N. Y. Cen.; Tol. & West. (El.) (R. Rs.).
Block Island, Newport Co., R. I., 1,427.
Blockton, Taylor Co., Iowa, 537.
On Chi. Gt. West. (R. R.).
Blocton, Bibb Co., Ala., 1,013.
On Ala. Gt. Sou.; Lou. & Nash.; Mob. & Ohio; Sou. (R. Rs.).
Bloemfontein, Capital of the Orange Free State, a province of Union of South Africa, 50,656.
A trade and educational center in an agricultural section of the Union.
Blofield, Norfolk, England, 14,407.
Blois, capital of Dept. of Loir-et-Cher, France, 26,025.
Important trade center. Manufactures: shoes, furniture, vinegar, machinery.
Bloomdale, Wood Co., Ohio, 578.
On Balt. & Ohio (R. R.).
Bloomer, Chippewa Co., Wisc., 1,865.
On Chi., St. P., Minn. & Oma. (R. R.).
Bloomfield, Hartford Co., Conn., 3,247.
On N. York, N. Hav. & Hart. (R. R.).
–c. s., Green Co., Ind., 2,298.
On Chi., Ind. & Lou.; Ill. Cen. (R. Rs.).
–c. s., Davis Co., Iowa, 2,226.
On Chi., Burl. & Quincy; Wab. (R. Rs.).
–c. s., Stoddard Co., Mo., 1,023.
–Knox Co., Neb., 1,435.
On Chi., St. P., Minn. & Oma. (R. R.).
–Essex Co., N. J., 38,077.
On Del., Lack. & West.; Erie (R. Rs.).
Direct highway connects with Holland Tunnel. Textiles, paper, thread, motors.
–Perry Co., Pa., 730.
Bloomfield Hills, Oakland Co., Mich., 1,127.
Bloomingburg, Fayette Co., Ohio, 543.
On Balt. & Ohio (R. R.).
Bloomingdale, Passaic Co., N. J., 2,543.
On N. York, Susq. & West. (R. R.).
Blooming Grove, Navarro Co., Tex., 771.
On St. Lou. Southw. (R. R.).
Blooming Prairie, Steele Co., Minn., 1,046.
On Chi., Mil., St. P. & Pac. (R. R.).
Bloomington, San Bernardino, Calif., 1,000.
On Los Ang. & Salt L.; Pac. Elec.; Sou. Pac. (R. Rs.).
–c. s., McLean Co., Ill., 30,930.
On Alton; Clev., Cin., Chi. & St. Lou.; Ill. Cen.; N. York, Chi. & St. Lou.; Ill. Term. (El.) (R. Rs.).
Seat of State Normal School, the Soldiers' Orphans' Home, and Illinois Wesleyan University. In Illinois coal area. Its industries include the building of freight cars, passenger coaches, furnaces, medicines, extracts, oil burners, and washing and ironing machines, and elevators.
–c. s., Monroe Co., Ind., 18,227.
On Chi., Ind. & Lou.; Ill. Cen. (R. Rs.).
Seat of Indiana University, founded in 1920.
–Grant Co., Wisconsin, 591.
Bloomsburg, c. s., Columbia Co., Pa., 9,093.
On Del., Lack. & West.; Read. (R. Rs.).
Seat of Bloomsburg State Normal School. Manufacturing center.
Bloomsbury, Hunterdon Co., N. J., 639.
On Cen. of N. Jer.; Leh. Val. (R. Rs.).
Bloomville, Seneca Co., Ohio, 700.
On Penna. (R. R.).
Blossburg, Tioga Co., Pa., 1,696.
On Erie (R. R.).
Blossom, Lamar Co., Texas, 650.
On Tex. & Pac. (R. R.).
Blountstown, c. s., Calhoun Co., Fla., 1,620.
On Marianna & Blountstown (R. R.).
Blowing Rock, Watauga Co., N. Car., 503.
Blox, Jasper Co., Texas, 721.
On Gulf, Colo. & Santa Fe (R. R.).
Blue Ball, Clearfield Co., Pa., 900.
On Penna. (R. R.).
Blue Bell, Montgomery Co., Pa., 500.
Blue Diamond, Perry Co., Ky., 2,000.
On Lou. & Nash. (R. R.).
Blue Earth, c. s., Faribault Co., Minn., 2,884.
On Chi. & N. West.; Chi., St. P., Minn. & Oma. (R. Rs.).
Bluefield, Tazewell Co., Va., and Mercer Co., W. Va., 23,245.
On Norf. & West. (R. R.).
Railroad shops. Traffic and selling center for Virginian coal fields production.
Blue Hill, Hancock Co., Maine, 800.
–Webster Co., Neb., 669.
On Chi., Burl. & Quincy (R. R.).
Blue Island, Cook Co., Ill., 16,534.
On Balt. & Ohio Chi. Term.; Chi., Mil., St. P. & Pac.; Chi., Rk. Isl. & Pac.; Gd. Tr.; Ill. Cen.; Ind. Harb. Belt; Mich. Cen.; N. York Cen. (R. Rs.).
Canning plants, wire manufactures.
Blue Jay, Raleigh Co., W. Va., 521.
On Chesa. & Ohio (R. R.).
Blue Lake, Humboldt Co., Calif., 555.
On Arcata & Mad Riv. (R. R.).
Blue Mound, Macon Co., Ill., 817.
On Wabash (R. R.).
–Linn Co., Kans., 461.
On Mo. Pac. (R. R.).
Blue Mountain, Calhoun Co., Ala., 1,134.
On Lou. & Nash.; Sou. (R. Rs.).
–Tippah Co., Miss., 569.
On Gulf, Mob. & Nor. (R. R.).
Blue Pennant, Boone Co., W. Va., 500.
On Chesa. & Ohio (R. R.).
Blue Point, Suffolk Co., N. Y., 979.
On Long Isl. (R. R.).
Blue Rapids, Marshall Co., Kans., 1,657.
On Mo. Pac.; Un. Pac. (R. Rs.).
Blue Ridge, c. s., Fannin Co., Ga., 1,190.
On Lou. & Nash. (R. R.).
Blue Springs, Jackson Co., Mo., 706.
On Alton (R. R.).
–Gage Co., Neb., 700.
On Chi., Burl. & Quincy; Un. Pac. (R. Rs.).
Bluff City, Sullivan Co., Tenn., 671.
On Southern (R. R.).
Bluffs, Scott Co., Ill., 953.
On Wabash (R. R.).
Bluffton, c. s., Wells Co., Ind., 5,074.
On Ind. R. R. Sys. (El.); N. York, Chi. & St. Lou. (R. Rs.).
–Allen Co., Ohio, 2,035.
On N. York, Chi. & St. Lou.; Nor. Ohio (R. Rs.).
–Beaufort Co., S. C., 570.
Bluford, Jefferson Co., Ill., 517.
On Ill. Cen.; Sou. (R. Rs.).
Blumbergs, Guadalupe Co., Tex., 600.
On Tex. & N. Orl. (R. R.).
Blumenau, Brazil, 111,794.
Trade center in an agricultural region.
Blyth, Northumberland, England, 31,808.
Coal port. Shipbuilding.
Blythe, Riverside Co., Cal., 1,020.
On Atch., Top. & Santa Fe (R. R.).
Blythedale, Allegheny Co., Pa., 1,000.
On Pitts. & L. Erie (R. R.).
Blytheville, c. s., Mississippi Co., Ark., 10,098.
On St. Lou.-San Fran.; St. Lou. Southw. (R. Rs.).
Wood products among chief manufactures.
Boac, Prov. of Marinduque, Luzon, P. I., 16,000.
Boaz, Marshall Co., Ala., 1,691.
On Nash., Chatt. & St. Lou. (R. R.).
Bobruisk, White Russia, Sov. Union, 64,800.
Bobtown, Greene Co., Pa., 2,000.
Boca Raton, Palm Beach Co., Fla., 784.
On Fla. E. Coast and Seab. Air. L. (R. Rs.).
Bocaue, Prov. of Bulacan, Luzon, P. I., 8,761.
Bocholt, Prussia, Germany, 33,000.
A center of the cotton industry.
Bochum, Prussia, Germany, 314,546.
Coal, iron and steel industries.
Bode, Humboldt Co., Iowa, 507.
On Chi., Rk. Isl. & Pac. (R. R.).
Boerne, c. s., Kendall Co., Texas, 1,117.
On Tex. & N. Orl. (R. R.).
Bogalusa, Washington Parish, La., 14,029.
On Gulf, Mob. & Nor. (R. R.).
In pine timber region. Important industrial center.
Bogata, Red River Co., Tex., 1,000.
On Paris & Mt. Pleasant (R. R.).
Bogo, Prov. of Cebu, Cebu, P. I., 23,367.
Trade center for rich farming district.
Bogotá, capital of Colombia, 251,604.
Situated on a plain, 8,500 feet above sea-level. Bogotá possesses a university, the Colegio Nacionale de San Bartolomé, a military academy, a national library of 50,000 volumes, a museum, a botanical garden, and an observatory. There are many churches and convents.
Bogotá is the trade emporium of this district. The manufactures are not numerous. Near the city are coal, iron, and salt mines.
–Bergen Co., N. J., 7,341.
On N. York, Susq. & West.; West Shore (R. Rs.).
Bohemia, Suffolk Co., N. Y., 788.
Boiling Springs, Cleveland Co., N. Car., 672.
–Cumberland Co., Pa., 1,000.
On Reading (R. R.).
Bois-Colombes, Seine, France, 26,562.
Boise, Ada Co., Idaho, State capital, 21,544.
Situated in a rich mining district, on the Boise River and on the Boise & Western; and Oregon Short Line Railroads. Center of a productive agricultural district. An important wool market.
Boise is a military post, and contains a prison, a penitentiary, United States assay office, United States court, United States land office, and soldiers' home.
The industrial establishments include factories, foundries and lumber mills. It is a wholesale and retail shopping district.
Boise was settled in 1863, and in 1864, with a population of only 300, became a city and State capital.
Boise City, c.s., Cimarron Co., Okla., 1,256.
On Atch., Top. & Santa Fe; Panh. & Santa Fe (R. Rs.).
Bois-le-Duc, Netherlands. See s'Hertogenbosch.
Bokoshe, Le Flore Co., Okla., 715.
On Ft. Smith & West.; Mid. Val. (R. Rs.).
Bolbec, Dept. of Seine-Inférieure, France, 10,209.
Boley, Okfuskee Co., Okla., 874.
On Ft. Smith & West. (R. R.).
Bolivar (Ciudad Bolivar), State of Bolivar, Venezuela, 25,134.
–c. s., Polk Co., Mo., 2,256.
On St. Lou.-San Fran. (R. R.).
–Allegany Co., N. Y., 1,725.
On Pitts., Shawmut & Nor. (R. R.).
–Tuscarawas Co., Ohio, 506.
On Wheel. & L. Erie (R. R.).
–Westmoreland Co., Pa., 783.

On Penna. (R. R.).
–c. s., Hardeman Co., Tenn., 1,217.
On Ill. Cen. (R. R.).
–Jefferson Co., W. Va., 616.
Bolkhov, Soviet Union, 20,700.
A trade center in an orchard region.
Bologna, capital of Prov. of Bologna, Italy, 199,000.
The architecture of Bologna, for the most part medieval, renders it one of the notable cities of Europe. The streets are overhung by the upper stories of the buildings, thus forming miles of shop-lined arcades, dating from the thirteenth century.
It is of great industrial importance. Commerce is extensive, and railway communications are excellent.
Bolondron, Matanzas, Cuba, 3,708.
Bolton, Lancashire, England, 177,253.
On the Croal River, and one of the chief seats of the cotton manufactures of England. There are also paper mills, chemical works, foundries, and dye works.
From early times, Bolton has been an industrial center, and in the reign of Henry VIII. possessed flourishing woolen factories.
–Fulton Co., Ga., 500.
On Nash., Chatt. & St. Lou. (R. R.).
–Worcester Co., Mass., 739.
On N. York, N. Hav. & Hart. (R. R.).
–Columbus Co., N. C., 976.
On Atl. Coast Line (R. R.).
Bolton Landing, Warren Co., N. Y., 775.
Boma, former capital of the Belgian Congo, Africa, 5,127.
Bombay, capital of Bombay Presidency, British India, 1,161,383.
A seaport on the island of Bombay. Since the increase of its railway and industrial facilities it has developed rapidly. Bombay now surpasses all other cities of India as a center of distribution, and since the opening of the Suez Canal has steadily increased in wealth and importance. The chief export articles are cotton, grain, opium, coffee, carpets, rugs, pepper and ivory. The manufactures include yarn, cotton-cloth, lacquer work, and leather.
–Franklin Co., N. Y., 800.
On Gd. Tr. (R. R.).
Bonaparte, Van Buren Co., Iowa, 678.
On Chi., Rk. Isl. & Pac. (R. R.).
Bond, Jackson Co., Ky., 910.
Bondsville, Hampden Co., Mass., 1,500.
On Bost. & Alb.; Bost. & Me. (R. Rs.).
Bonduel, Shawano Co., Wis., 534.
On Chi. & Nor. West. (R. R.).
Bône, Dept. of Constantine, Algeria, 86,332.
A naval station, situated on a bay of the Mediterranean. There are many bazaars, markets, shops, and cafés; manufactures of tapestry and saddlery, and there is an active trade in cattle, sheep, wool, hides, corn, olive oil, tobacco, and wax. Near Bône are the remains of a once famous Numidian city. Hippo Regius, the Episcopal see of St. Augustine, died there in 430.
Bonesteel, Gregory Co., S. Dak., 547.
On Chi. & Nor. West. (R. R.).
Bonham, c. s., Fannin Co., Texas, 5,655.
On Tex. & Pac. (R. R.).
Flour mills and manufactures of furniture.
Bonifay, c. s., Holmes Co., Fla., 1,505.
On Lou. & Nash. (R. R.).
Bonita, Morehouse Par., La., 507.
On Mo. Pac. (R. R.).
Bonn, Rhenish Prussia, Germany, 98,700.
On the left bank of the Rhine, with unusually attractive and picturesque surroundings. The town is very ancient, and contains a venerable cathedral, dating from the eleventh century, and other fine medieval churches. The house in which Beethoven was born, now contains the Beethoven Museum. Bonn is celebrated as the seat of the present Bonn University, founded in 1818. Connected with the university are a library of 300,000 volumes, a museum of Rhenish antiquities, a botanical garden, and a school of agriculture. Bonn was a Roman fortress, and is frequently mentioned by Tacitus as Bonna or Castra Bonensia.
Bonners Ferry, c. s., Boundary Co., Idaho, 1,418.
On Gt. Nor.; Spok. Internat. (R. Rs.).
Bonner Springs, Wyandotte Co., Kans., 1,813.
On Atch., Top. & Santa Fe.; Kans. Cy., Kaw Val. & West. (El.); Un. Pac. (R. Rs.).
Bonne Terre, St. Francois Co., Mo., 4,021.
On Mo.-Ill. (R. R.).
Bonnyman, Perry Co., Ky., 520.
On Lou. & Nash. (R. R.).
Bon Secour, Baldwin Co., Ala., 550.
Boom, Anvers, Belgium, 19,288.
Boomer, Fayette Co., W. Va., 1,213.
On N. York Cen. (R. R.).
Boone, c. s., Boone Co., Iowa, 11,886.
On Chi., Mil., St. P. & Pac.; Chi. & Nor. West., Ft. Dodge, Des Moines & Sou. (R. Rs.).
Airport. Trade market and industrial center.
–c. s. Watauga Co., N. C., 1,295.
On Linville River (R. R.).
Booneville, Logan Co., Ark., 2,099.
On Chi., Rk. Isl. & Pac. (R. R.).
–c. s., Prentiss Co., Miss., 1,703.
On Mob. & Ohio (R. R.).
Boonsboro, Washington Co., Md., 894.
Boonton, Morris Co., N. J., 6,866.
On Del., Lack. & West.
Boonville, Mendocino Co., Calif., 534.
–c. s., Warrick Co., Ind., 4,208.
On Evansv. Suburb & Newb.; Sou. (R. Rs.).
–Cooper Co., Mo., 6,435.
On Mo.-Kan.-Tex.; Mo. Pac. (R. Rs.).
–Oneida Co., N. Y., 2,090.
On N. York Cen. (R. R.).
Boothbay, Lincoln Co., Maine, 525.
Boothbay Harbor, Lincoln Co., Maine, 2,000.
Boothton, Shelby Co., Ala., 1,200.
On Lou. & Nash.; Sou. (R. Rs.).
Bootle, Lancashire, England, 84,970.
A suburb of Liverpool.
Boras, Älvsborg, Sweden, 45,663.
Textile industries.
Bordeaux, capital of Dept. of Gironde, France, 258,348.
In a plain, on the Garonne, about 60 miles from the river's mouth in the Atlantic.
Bordeaux is one of the most important cities of France. Among the public buildings may be mentioned the Cathedral of St. André, consecrated in 1096; the Church of St. Croix of the tenth century; the Church of St. Michel; the Hôtel de Ville; the Palais de Justice, and the great theater built by Louis XVI. The University of Bordeaux is largely attended.
Next to Havre and Marseilles, the city is the country's chief port for transatlantic trade. The first sittings of the National Assembly were held at Bordeaux in 1871. For several weeks it was the seat of government of France when the German armies were threatening Paris in 1914. Rosa Bonheur was born here.
Borden City, Bristol Co., Mass., 2,500.
Bordentown, Burlington Co., N. J., 4,405.
On Penna. (R. R.).
Borgerhout, Anvers, Belgium, 54,479.
A suburb of Anvers.
Borisoglyebsk, Soviet Union, 49,900.
Trade center in farming region.
Borisov, White Russia, Soviet Union, 25,842.
A trade center.

COURTESY OF INDIA STATE RAILWAYS

THE MUNICIPAL OFFICE IN BOMBAY, INDIA, ONE OF THE PRINCIPAL BUILDINGS OF THE CITY AND AN EXAMPLE OF ONE TYPE OF INDIAN ARCHITECTURE

Borongon, Prov. of Samar, Samar, P. I., 17,420.
Borovichi, Soviet Union, 9,500.
Boscawen, Merrimack Co., N. H., 1,359.
On Bost. & Me. (R. R.).
Boscobel, Grant Co., Wisc., 1,762.
On Chi., Mil., St. P. & Pac. (R. R.).
Bossier City, Bossier Parish, La., 4,003.
On La. & Ark.; St. Lou. Southw.; Yazoo & Miss. Val. (R. Rs.).
Boston, Lincolnshire, England, 16,597.
A busy seaport and a center of the fishing industry.
–Marion Co., Ala., 522.
–Thomas Co., Ga., 1,243.
On Atl. Coast Line; Ga. Nor. (R. Rs.).
–c. s., Suffolk Co., Mass., State capital and commercial metropolis of New England, 817,713.
Situated at the west end of Massachusetts Bay. Terminus of the Boston and Albany; Boston and Maine; New York, New Haven and Hartford and Union Freight Railroads. Area 44 square miles. Extending about 2 miles along the harbor, is south Boston, containing large docks and warehouses. The harbor is an indentation of Massachusetts Bay, embracing about 75 square miles. Tunnels, subway and surface lines in Boston are directly connected. The city built the first municipal subway (Tremont Street opened in 1897) in the United States. Commonwealth Avenue, 240 feet wide, is one of the handsomest thoroughfares in the country. The largest boot and shoe markets in the world are on High Street and adjacent streets.
Among the attractive parks are the Common, a park of forty-eight acres in the heart of the city; the Public Garden, the Back Bay Fens, Franklin Park, Bussey Park, the Arnold Arboretum, Marine Park at City Point, and the Charles River Embankment.
The State-House, on Beacon Hill, is now one of the largest capitols in the Union, but retains its old Bulfinch front. Other noted buildings are the Masonic Temple, the Museum of Fine Arts, the court house, stock exchange, chamber of commerce, Trinity Church, the Catholic Cathedral, the Opera House, Christian Science Church and Faneuil Hall. The Public Library faces Copley Square, and with its branches, has more than one and one-half million volumes. The United States customhouse is an immense structure, its tower being especially noteworthy. The old state-house, erected in 1748, contains in its upper floors an historical museum. The city hall, one of the most striking buildings of the city, is built of white Concord granite in the Italian Renaissance style. Old South Church, on Washington Street, is now used as a museum of historical relics. Occupying the site of the old redoubt on Bunker Hill is the famous Bunker Hill Monument. In the Charlestown district is located the United States Navy Yard.
Boston is the commercial metropolis of New England, the leading wool and leather market in the United States, and the center of the greatest shoe and textile community in the world, as well as being preëminent as a fish mart. It ranks next to New York as a commercial port. Its manufactures, like its shipments and jobbing trade, are very diverse. They include printing and publishing, confectionery, electrical machinery, patent medicines, cosmetics, foundry and machine-shop products, iron ware, boots and shoes, brass and rubber goods, musical instruments, clothing, etc.
Boston is widely noted for the number and high character of its educational institutions. Among the institutions for higher education are Boston College (Roman Catholic), Boston University (Methodist), Simmons College, Northeastern University, Boston Normal School, Massachusetts Normal Art School, Kindergarten Training School, music schools, and training schools for nurses at several hospitals. There are over 300 churches in the city. Boston is rich in historic interest. It was settled in 1630 by a party of Puritans from England. It was named after Boston, England, from which many of the colonists had come. A memorable massacre was perpetrated by British soldiers here in 1770, and in 1773 several cargoes of English tea were thrown overboard in the harbor by patriotic citizens. The battle of Bunker Hill was fought on Breed's Hill (now called Bunker Hill) within the present city limits, June 17, 1775.
The city charter was granted in 1822.
–Allegheny Co., Pa., 600.
On Pittsb. & L. Erie (R. R.).
Boswell, Benton Co., Ind., 817.
On N. York, Chi. & St. Lou. (R. R.).
–Choctaw Co., Okla., 934.
On St. Lou.-San Fran. (R. R.).
–Somerset Co., Pa., 1,775.
On Balt. & Ohio (R. R.).
Bosworth, Carroll Co., Mo., 612.
On Atch., Top. & Santa Fe (R. R.).
Bothell, King Co., Wash., 818.
On Nor. Pac. (R. R.).
Botosani, Rumania, 33,000.
A commercial center in a rich agricultural region.
Bottineau, c. s., Bottineau Co., North Dakota, 1,322.
On Gt. Nor. (R. R.).
Bottrop, Prussia, Germany, 77,197.
Industrial center. Iron and steel.
Bougie, Prov. of Constantine, Algeria, 25,261.
Port and commercial center.
Boulder, c. s., Boulder Co., Colo., 11,223.
On Colo. & Sou.; Un. Pac. (R. Rs.).
In mining section. Has a large electric smelter for the production of tungsten. Other important products are lumber, radios, brooms, gold and coal.
University of Colorado located here.
–c. s., Jefferson Co., Mont., 926.
On Gt. Nor. (R. R.).
Boulder Creek, Santa Cruz Co., Calif., 500.
On Sou. Pac. (R. R.).
Boulogne-sur-Mer, Dept. of Pas-de-Calais, 52,374.
One of the most important parts for French-English commerce, shipbuilding.
Boulogne-sur-Seine, Dept. of Seine, France, 97,379. A suburb of Paris.
Bound Brook, Somerset Co., N. J., 7,372.
On Cen. of N. Jer.; Read., Leh. Val. (R. Rs.).
Productions: moving picture films and chemicals.
Bountiful, Davis Co., Utah, 2,571.
On Bamb. Elec. (R. R.).
Bourbon, Marshall Co., Ind., 1,193.
On Penna. (R. R.).
Bourbonnaise, Kankakee Co., Ill., 685.
Bourg-en-Bresse, Dept. of Ain, France, 24,746.
Bourges, Dept. of Cher, France, 49,263.
On the Canal du Berry and at the junction of several rivers. The town is very ancient, and possesses many interesting medieval buildings. The Cathedral of St. Étienne is one of the finest in Europe. Other notable edifices are the archbishop's palace, the Palais de Justice, and the Hôtel de Ville.
Bourges has an arsenal and cannon foundry. Manufactures cloth and cutlery.
Bourne, Barnstable Co., Mass., 3,336.
On N. Y., N. Hav. & Hart. (R. R.).
Bournemouth, Southampton, England, 116,780.
A popular resort.
Boussu-lez-Mons, Hainaut, Belgium, 12,487.
Bovey, Itasca Co., Minn., 1,248.
On Dul., Missabe & Nor.; Gt. Nor. (R. Rs.).
Bovill, Latah Co., Idaho, 572.
On Chi., Mil., St. P. & Pac.; Wash., Ida. & Mont. (R. Rs.).
Bow, Merrimack Co., N. H., 500.
On Bost. & Me. (R. R.).
Bowbells, Burke Co., N. Dak., 695.
On Gt. Nor.; Minn., St. P. & S. Ste. M. (R. Rs.).
Bowdle, Edmunds Co., S. Dak., 818.
On Chi., Mil., St. P. & Pac. (R. R.).
Bowdon, Carroll Co., Ga., 1,024.
On Bowdon (R. R.).
Bowen, Hancock Co., Ill., 643.
On Wabash (R. R.).
Bowenville, Bristol Co., Mass., 2,300.
Bower Hill, Allegheny Co., Pa., 500.

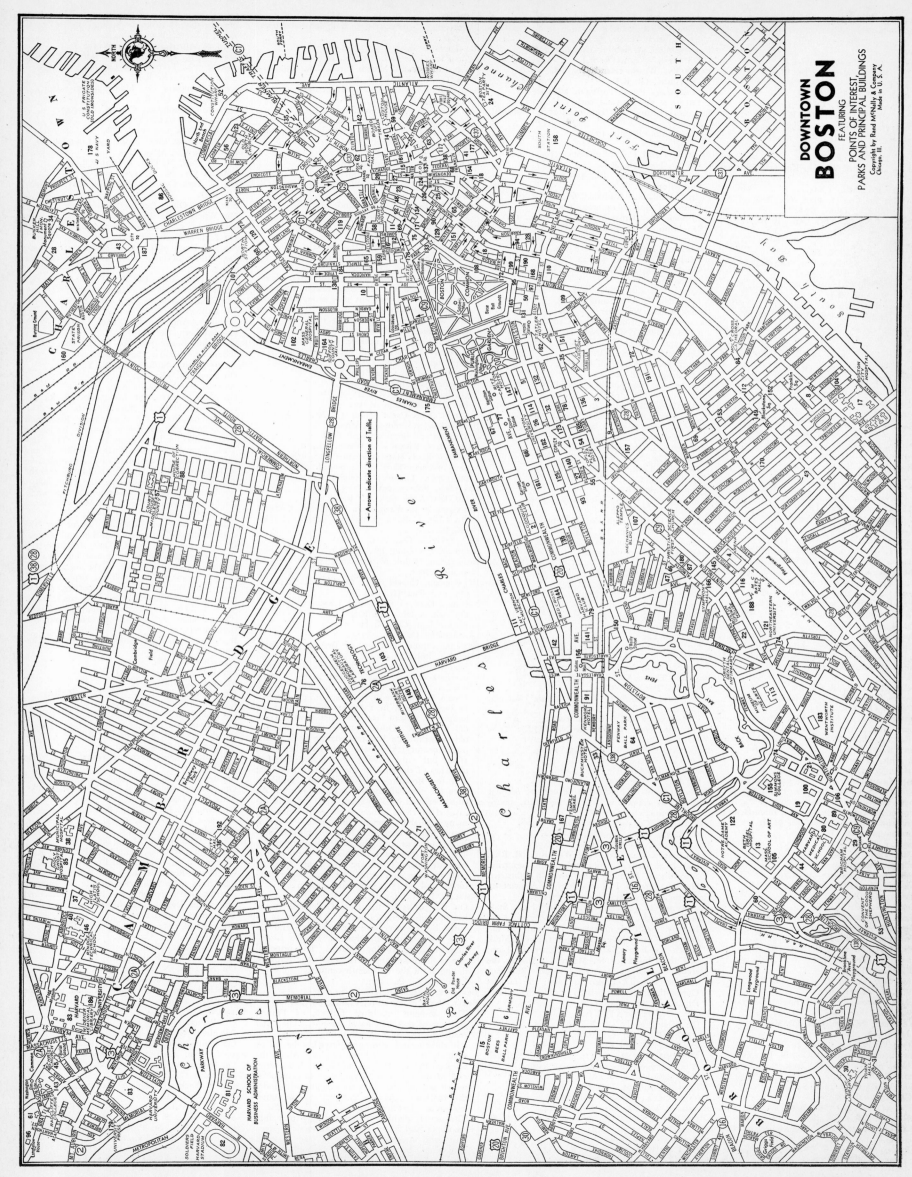

DOWNTOWN
BOSTON
FEATURING
POINTS OF INTEREST,
PARKS AND PRINCIPAL BUILDINGS
Copyright by Rand McNally & Company
Chicago, Ill.
Made in U.S.A.

← Arrows indicate direction of Traffic

MAP OF BOSTON, CAPITAL OF MASSACHUSETTS. BOSTON IS THE SHOE AND LEATHER CENTER OF THE WORLD AND THE LARGEST WOOL MARKET IN THE UNITED STATES, AS WELL AS THE HUB OF HISTORIC INTEREST. ACROSS THE CHARLES RIVER FROM BOSTON IS CAMBRIDGE IN WHICH ARE LOCATED HARVARD UNIVERSITY AND THE MASSACHUSETTS INSTITUTE OF TECHNOLOGY

On Penna.; Pitts., Chart. & Yough.; Pitts. & W. Va. (R. Rs.).
BOWIE, Prince Georges Co., Md., 694.
On Penna. (R. R.).
–Montague Co., Texas, 3,131.
On Chi., Rk. Isl. & Gulf.; Ft. Worth & Denv. Cy. (R. Rs.).
BOW LAKE, Stafford Co., N. H., 500.
BOWLEGS, Seminole Co., Okla., 1,500.
On Chi., Rk. Isl. & Pac. (R. R.).
BOWLING GREEN, Hardee Co., Fla., 1,025.
On Atl. Coast Line (R. R.).
–c. s., Warren Co., Ky., 12,348.
On Lou. & Nash. (R. R.).
In oil area. Seat of Western Kentucky Normal College.
–c. s., Pike Co., Mo., 1,855.
On Alton; St. Lou. & Han. (R. Rs.).
–c. s., Wood Co., Ohio, 6,688.
On Balt. & Ohio; N. York Cen. (R. Rs.).
BOWMAN, Elbert Co., Ga., 604.
On Southern (R. R.).
–c. s., Bowman Co., N. Dak., 888.
On Chi., Mil., St. P. & Pac. (R. R.).
–Orangeburg Co., S. C., 754.
BOWMANS, Carbon Co., Pa., 902.
On Leh. Val. (R. R.).
BOWMANSTOWN, Carbon Co., Pa., 843.
On Cen. of N. Jer.; Leh. Val. (R. Rs.).
BOWMANSVILLE, Erie Co., N. Y., 500.
On West Shore (R. R.).
BOWMANVILLE, Durham Co., Ontario, Canada, 4,080.
On Can. Nat.; Can. Pac. (R. Rs.).
BOWNEMONT, Kanawha Co., W. Va., 1,000.
BOYCE, Rapides Parish, La., 820.
On Tex. & Pac. (R. R.).
BOYCEVILLE, Dunn Co., Wis., 573.
On Minn., St. P. & S. Ste. M. (R. R.).
BOYD, Chippewa Co., Wis., 540.
On Minn., St. P. & S. Ste. M. (R. R.).
BOYERTOWN, Berks Co., Pa., 3,943.
On Reading (R. R.).
BOYKINS, Southampton Co., Va., 636.
On Seab. Air Line (R. R.).
BOYLE, Bolivar Co., Miss., 678.
On Yazoo & Miss. Val. (R. R.).
BOYLES, Jefferson Co., Ala., 1,364.
On Lou. & Nash. (R. R.).
BOYLSTON, Worcester Co., Mass., 1,361.
BOYNE CITY, Charlevoix Co., Mich., 2,650.
On Boyne Cy., Gay. & Alp. (R. R.).
Leather, chemicals, pig iron, lumber, and allied industries. In fruit region.
BOYNTON, Palm Beach Co., Fla., 1,000.
On Fla. East Coast; Seab. Air Line (R. Rs.).
–Muskogee Co., Okla., 1,204.
On St. Lou.-San Fran. (R. R.).
BOYNTON BEACH, Palm Beach Co., Fla., 1,053.
BOZEMAN, c. s., Gallatin Co., Mont., 6,855.
On Chi., Mil., St. P. & Pac.; No. Pac. (R. Rs.).
BRACEBRIDGE, Muskoka Co., Ontario, Canada, 2,436.
On Can. Nat. (R. R.).
BRACKENRIDGE, Allegheny Co., Pa., 6,250.
On Penna. (R. R.).
BRACKETTVILLE, c. s., Kinney Co., Tex., 1,822.
BRADDOCK, Allegheny Co., Pa., 19,329.
On Balt. & Ohio; Penna.; Pittsb. & L. Erie; Union (R. Rs.).
Steel mills.
BRADENTON, c. s., Manatee Co., Fla., 5,986.
On Atl. Coast Line; Seab. Air Line (R. Rs.).
BRADENVILLE, Westmoreland Co., Pa., 1,400.
BRADFORD, Yorkshire, England, 300,900.
The principal seat of the worsted manufactures in England. Cotton, silk, and plush are also important products.
–White Co., Ark., 675.
On Mo. Pac. (R. R.).
–Stark Co., Ill., 951.
On Chi., Burl. & Quincy (R. R.).
–Darke and Miami Cos., Ohio, 1,732.
On Penna. (R. R.).
–McKean Co., Pa., 19,306.
On Balt. & Ohio; Erie; Penna. (R. Rs.).
Airport. Productive oil region.
–Washington Co., R. I., 700.
On N. York, N. Hav. & Hart. (R. R.).
–Gibson Co., Tenn., 570.
On Ill. Cen. (R. R.).
–Orange Co., Vt., 598.
On Bost. & Me. (R. R.).
BRADFORD-ON-AVON, Wiltshire, England, 4,735.
BRADLEY, Kankakee Co., Ill., 3,048.
On Ill. Cen.; N. York Cen. (R. Rs.).
–Penobscot Co., Maine, 500.
–Jefferson Co., Ohio, 1,200.
BRADLEY BEACH, Monmouth Co., N. J., 3,306.
On Cen. of N. Jer.; N. York & Long Br.; Penna. (R. Rs.).
BRADNER, Wood Co., Ohio, 836.
On Chesa. & Ohio (R. R.).
BRADSHAW (Dan), McDowell Co., W. Va., 650.
On Norf. & West. (R. R.).
BRADY (Ranshaw P. O.), Northumberland Co., Pa., 2,000.
On Penna. (R. R.).
–c. s., McCulloch Co., Texas, 3,983.
On Ft. Worth & Rio Gde.; Gulf, Colo. & Santa Fe (R. Rs.).
Local cotton center.
BRADYS BEND, Armstrong Co., Pa., 800.
On West. Allegh. (R. R.).
BRAEBURN, Westmoreland Co., Pa., 1,300.
On Penna. (R. R.).
BRAGA, Braga Prov., Portugal, 26,962.
Firearms, jewelry, and cutlery industries.
BRAGANCA, Prov. of Traz-os-Montes, Portugal, 6,089.
–São Paulo, Brazil, 17,936.
Sugar mills.
BRAHAM, Isanti Co., Minnesota, 579.
On Gt. Nor. (R. R.).
BRAIDWOOD, Will Co., Ill., 1,161.
On Alton (R. R.).
BRÂILA, Wallachia, Rumania, 68,310.
Center of Rumanian grain trade.
BRAINERD, c. s., Crow Wing Co., Minn., 10,221.
On Minn. & Internat.; Nor. Pac. (R. Rs.).
Airport. Center of iron mining region.
BRAINTREE, Essex, England, 8,912.
–Norfolk Co., Mass., 17,122.
On N. York, N. Hav. & Hart. (R. R.).
Shoes and rubber.
BRAMAN, Kay Co., Okla., 507.
On Atch., Top. & Santa Fe (R. R.).
BRAMANVILLE, Worcester Co., Mass., 500.
BRAMPTON, Peel Co., Ontario, Canada, 5,532.
On Can. Pac.; Can. Nat. (R. Rs.).
BRAMWELL, Mercer Co., W. Va., 1,574.
On Norf. & West. (R. R.).
BRANCH DALE, Schuylkill Co., Pa., 813.
On Reading (R. R.).
BRANCHLAND (Branchfield), Lincoln Co., W. Va., 518.
On Chesa. & Ohio (R. R.).
BRANCHVILLE, Fairfield Co., Conn., 501.
On N. York, N. Hav. & Hart. (R. R.).
–Prince Georges Co., Md., 750.
On Balt. & Ohio (R. R.).
–Sussex Co., N. J., 665.
On Del., Lack. & West. (R. R.).
–Orangeburg Co., S. C., 1,689.
On Southern (R. R.).
BRANDENBURG, Prussia, Germany, 63,000.
A suburb of Berlin.
BRANDON, Hillsborough Co., Fla., 600.
On Seab. Air Line (R. R.).
–Brandon Co., Manitoba, Canada, 16,461.
Grain mills and creameries.
On Can. Nat.; Can. Pac.; Gt. Nor. (R. Rs.).
–c. s., Rankin Co., Miss., 692.
On Yazoo & Miss. Val. (R. R.).
–Greenville Co., S. S., 1,500.
On Piedmont & Nor. (El.) (R. R.).
–Rutland Co., Vt., 1,731.
On Rutland (R. R.).
–Fond du Lac Co., Wis., 646.
On Chi., Mil., St. P. & Pac. (R. R.).
BRANFORD, New Haven Co., Conn., 2,365.
On N. York, N. Hav. & Hart. (R. R.).
BRANSON, Tanney Co., Mo., 958.
On Mo. Pac. (R. R.).
BRANTFORD, Brantford Co., Ontario, Canada, 132,274.
Port of entry and industrial center.
On Can. Nat.; L. Erie & Nor. (El.); Tor., Ham. & Buf. (R. Rs.).
BRANTLEY, Crenshaw Co., Ala., 1,053.
On Cen. of Ga. (R. R.).
BRASHEAR, Hopkins Co., Tex., 500.
On La., Ark. & Tex. (R. R.).
BRASOV (Brasso) (Kronstadt), Rumania, 60,694.
Iron and copper works, textile mills, petroleum refineries.
BRATENAHL, Cuyahoga Co., Ohio, 1,308.
BRATISLAVA, Czechoslovakia, 133,000.
BRATTLEBORO, Windham Co., Vt., 8,709.
On Bost. & Me.; Cen. Ver.; West Riv. (R. Rs.).
Has large power plants and granite quarries. Also organ, furniture, and overall industries. Headquarters of Holstein-Friesian Association.
BRAUNSBERG, Prussia, Germany, 15,325.
BRAUNSCHWEIG (Brunswick), capital of the State of Brunswick, Germany, 166,800.
Is very medieval in aspect. Among its old churches may be mentioned the cathedral, which was begun in 1173 by Henry the Lion; and the Church of St. Magnus. Among the secular buildings are the Alstadt Rathhaus (old town hall), begun in 1250; the famous Gewandhaus (trades hall); and the Ducal Palace, erected in 1831-36.
BRAVE, Greene Co., Pa., 641.
On Monongahela (R. R.).
BRAWLEY, Imperial Co., Cal., 10,439.
On Sou. Pac. (R. R.).
Municipal airport. Is 119 ft. below sea level. Alfalfa, vegetables, cantaloupes, lettuce.
BRAYMER, Caldwell Co., Mo., 933.
On Chi., Mil., St. P. & Pac. (R. R.).
BRAYTONVILLE, Berkshire Co., Mass., 1,000.
BRAZIL, c. s., Clay Co., Ind., 8,744.
On Balt. & Ohio; Chi. & East. Ill.; Ind. R. R. Sys. (El.); Penna. (R.Rs.).
–Appanoose Co., Iowa, 525.
On Chi., Burl. & Quincy (R. R.).
BRAZORIA, Brazoria Co., Tex., 816.
On St. Lou., Brownsv. & Mex. (R. R.).
BRAZZAVILLE, capital of French Equatorial Africa, 24,341.
BREA, Orange Co., Cal., 2,435.
On Pac. Elec.; Sou. Pac. (R. Rs.).
BREAUX BRIDGE, St. Martin Parish, La., 1,399.
On Tex. & N. Orl. (R. R.).
BRECKENRIDGE, Gratiot Co., Mich., 685.
On Pere Marq. (R. R.).
–c. s., Wilkin Co., Minn., 2,264.
On Gt. Nor.; Nor. Pac. (R. Rs.).
Great Northern division headquarters with round house and shops.
–Caldwell Co., Mo., 828.
On Chi., Burl. & Quincy (R. R.).
–Stephens Co., Texas, 7,569.
On Cisco & Northeast.; Wichita Fs. & Sou. (R. Rs.).
BREDA, N. Brabant, Netherlands, 44,866.
Woolens, carpets, foundries.
BREESE, Clinton Co., Ill., 1,957.
On Balt. & Ohio (R. R.).
BREEZY HILL, Crawford Co., Kans., 716.
BREISACH, Baden, Germany, 3,131.
BREMEN, Germany, 323,628.
An important city located on the river Weser. Bremen joined the Hanseatic League in 1276, and was one of its most prosperous members. The citizens became Protestants, and the diocese was ceded to Sweden in 1648. In 1710 it was recognized as a free imperial town. Bremen, in 1815, became a member of the German Confederation. See BREMERHAVEN.
–Haralson Co., Ga., 1,030.
On Cen. of Ga.; Sou. (R. Rs.).
–Marshall Co., Ind., 2,105.
On Balt. & Ohio (R. R.).
–Fairfield Co., Ohio, 1,232.
On N. York Cen.; Penna. (R. Rs.).
BREMERHAVEN, Bremen, Germany, 24,000.
The port of Bremen; great docks.
BREMERTON, Kitsap Co., Wash., 10,170.
Nearest R. R. Sta. via steamer to Seattle, Wash. Seat of Navy Yard, Puget Sound. Ship-building yards. Gateway to Olympia Peninsula.
BREMOND, Robertson Co., Tex., 1,025.
On Tex. & N. Orl. (R. R.).
BRENHAM, c. s., Washington Co., Texas, 5,974.
On Gulf, Colo. & Santa Fe; Tex. & N. Orl. (R. Rs.).
BRENT, Bibb Co., Ala., 586.
On Mob. & Ohio; Bir. (R. R.).
BRENTFORD, Middlesex, England, 17,039.
Trade center.
BRENTWOOD, Contra Costa Co., Calif., 500.
On Sou. Pac. (R. R.).
–Prince Georges Co., Md., 1,842.
On Balt. & Ohio (R. R.).
–Rockingham Co., N. H., 500.
–Allegheny Co., Pa., 5,381.
BRESCIA, capital of Prov. of Brescia (in Lombardy), Italy, 78,433.
Beautifully situated on the Mella and Garza, overlooked by a citadel known as the Falcone d'Italia. In the center of the town is the Piazza Vecchia, with the magnificent city hall or loggia begun in 1489 on the ruins of the temple of Vulcan, and the clock tower, Torre del Orologio. Other notable edifices are the old cathedral, La Rotunda, dating back to the ninth century; the new cathedral, begun in 1604, but only recently completed; sixty-five churches of the time of the Venetian Republic; and the Broletto, a twelfth-century building, once the city hall, now a court of justice. An edifice erected by Vespasian, A. D. 72, and excavated in 1822, is now a museum containing many valuable Roman antiquities. There is also a library containing 80,000 volumes, several academies and charitable institutions.
The most important manufactures are of iron and firearms. There are also many spinning and weaving industries, oil and paper factories, and an extensive trade in wine.
BRESLAU, Prussia, Germany, 625,198.
On the banks of the river Oder and at the junction of several railways. The town is divided by the river into the old town and the new town, and five suburbs. Breslau is distinguished for its fine squares. The principal one is the Ring, and on it stands the Rathaus, dating from the fourteenth century.
–Luzerne Co., Pa., 972.
BRESSOUX, Liége, Belgium, 14,903.
BREST, Dept. of Finistère, France, 79,342.
The strongest maritime fortress of France, and one of the chief naval stations. The outer roadstead is very fine, admitting 400 war vessels abreast, and communicates with the sea by a single passage called the Goulet. Along the sides of the channel are numerous lighthouses and in the center of it rise the Mingau rocks, which compel the ships to pass directly under the batteries. At the entrance to the inner harbor are fortifications.
The city is divided by the military port into an upper and lower town, connected by steep stairs and streets. Brest has a large arsenal, magazines, barracks, a naval school, and a school of hydrography. There is also a botanical garden and an observatory. Industries include the repairing and supplying of naval ships, fisheries, flour-mills, and breweries.
Used by Americans in the World War.
BREST-LITOVSK, Poland. See BRZESC' NA BUGU.
BREVARD, c. s., Transylvania Co., N. C., 2,339.
On Southern (R. R.).
BREWER, Penobscot Co., Maine, 6,329.
On Me. Cen. (R. R.).
BREWERTON, Onondaga Co., N. Y., 650.
On N. York Cen. (R. R.).
BREWSTER, Polk Co., Fla., 766.
On Atl. Coast Line; Seab. Air Line (R. Rs.).
–Barnstable Co., Mass., 715.
On N. York, N. Hav. & Hart. (R. R.).
–Putnam Co., N. Y., 1,664.
On N. York Cen.; N. York, N. Hav. & Hart. (R. Rs.).
–Stark Co., Ohio, 1,464.
On Wheel. & L. Erie (R. R.).
BREWTON, c. s., Escambia Co., Ala., 2,818.
On Lou. & Nash. (R. R.).
BRIANÇON, Dept. of Hautes-Alpes, France, 5,636.
BRIAR CLIFF MANOR, Westchester Co., N. Y., 1,794.
On N. York Cen. (R. R.).
BRICELYN, Faribault Co., Minn., 509.
On Chi., Rk. Isl. & Pac.; Chi. & Nor. West. (R. Rs.).
BRICEVILLE, Anderson Co., Tenn., 1,435.
On Southern (R. R.).
BRIDGEBORO, Burlington Co., N. J., 500.
BRIDGEBURG, Canada. See FORT ERIE.
BRIDGEHAMPTON, Suffolk Co., N. Y., 1,500.
On Long Isl. (R. R.).
BRIDGEPORT, Jackson Co., Ala., 2,124.
On Nash., Chatt. & St. Lou.; Sou. (R. Rs.).
–c. s., Fairfield Co., Conn., 146,716.
At the mouth of the Pequonnock River and on an inlet of Long Island Sound. Its harbor is accessible for fairly large vessels. The New York, New Haven and Hartford Railroad, and daily steamboat lines afford easy communication with New York. Notable buildings are the custom-house and post-office, the court-house, the Barnum Memorial Institute, the Burroughs Public Library, and the Young Men's Christian Association building.
The city was an important center for the manufacture of arms, ammunition and submarines during the World War. Its industries are very diversified without any one product leading, but largely relate to the metal trades. Among them are automobiles, airplanes, firearms, cutlery, fittings, drugs, corsets, sewing machines, machines and machine tools, hardware, artillery, toys, electrical supplies, graphophones, steam gauges, asbestos and brake linings, silverware.
Bridgeport was first settled in 1639 and became a city in 1836.
–Lawrence Co., Ill., 2,315.
On Balt. & Ohio (R. R.).
–Marion Co., Ind., 500.
On Penna.; Ind. R. R. Sys. (El.) (R. Rs.).
–c. s., Morrill Co., Neb., 1,421.
On Chi., Burl. & Quincy (R. R.).
–Gloucester Co., N. J., 642.
On Penna.-Read. Seashore (R. R.).
–Belmont Co., Ohio, 4,655.
On Balt. & Ohio; Penna.; Wheel. & L. Erie (R. Rs.).
–Montgomery Co., Pa., 5,595.
On Reading (R. R.).
–Wise Co., Texas, 2,464.
On Chi., Rk. Isl. & Gulf (R. R.).
–Harrison Co., W. Va., 1,567.
On Balt. & Ohio (R. R.).
BRIDGER, Carbon Co., Mont., 567.
On Mont., Wyo. & Sou.; Nor. Pac. (R. Rs.).
BRIDGETON, c. s., Cumberland Co., N. J., 15,699.
On Penna.-Read. Seashore (R. R.).
The city's main industries include the canning of fruits and vegetables, and glass manufacture, one of the largest bottle-blowing plants in the East being located here.
Founded in 1754.
–Craven Co., N. C., 721.
On Norf. Sou. (R. R.).
–Providence Co., R. I., 532.
On N. York, N. Hav. & Hart. (R. R.).
BRIDGETOWN, Barbados, West Indies, 15,200.
Principal commercial center situated in a fine plantation section.
BRIDGEVILLE, Sussex Co., Del., 987.
On Penna. (R. R.).
–Allegheny Co., Pa., 3,939.
On Penna.; Pittsb. & W. Va. (R. Rs.).
BRIDGEWATER, Aroostook Co., Maine, 925.
On Bangor & Aroostook (R. R.).
–Plymouth Co., Mass., 9,201.
On N. York, N. Hav. & Hart. (R. R.).
–Beaver Co., Pa., 1,192.
On Beav. Val.; Pitts. & L. Erie (R. Rs.).
–McCook Co., S. Dak., 762.
On Chi., Mil., St. P. & Pac. (R. R.).
–Rockingham Co., Va., 951.
On Chesa. West. (R. R.).
BRIDGE WATER, Rice Co., Minn., 815.

On Chi. Gt. West.; Minn., Northf. & Sou. (R. Rs.).
BRIDGMAN, Berrien Co., Mich., 848.
On Pere Marq. (R. R.).
BRIDGTON, Cumberland Co., Me., 1,625.
On Bridgton & Harrison (R. R.).
BRIDLINGTON, Yorkshire, England, 19,704.
A frequented watering place or resort.
BRIEG, Prussia, Germany, 28,000.
BRIELLE, Monmouth Co., N. J., 684.
On Cen. of N. Jer.; N. York & Long Br.; Penna. (R. Rs.).
BRIERFIELD, Bibb Co., Ala., 2,040.
On Southern (R. R.).
BRIERLEY HILL, Staffordshire, England, 14,344.
An agricultural center with cattle markets.
BRIGGS, Burnet Co., Tex., 520.
BRIGGSVILLE, Berkshire Co., Mass., 1,200.
BRIGHAM, c. s., Box Elder Co., Utah, 5,093.
On Ore. Short Line; Sou. Pac.; Utah-Idaho Central (El.) (R. Rs.).
BRIGHOUSE, Yorkshire, West Riding, England, 19,756.
Woolen and worsted factories.
BRIGHTON, Sussex, England, 147,427.
A popular watering place on the English Channel, 47 miles from London; the city extends for about 4 miles along the sea coast, fronted by a sea wall 60 feet high. On this wall is a fine promenade, called the Front.
–Victoria, Australia, 29,707.
A watering place near Melbourne.
–Jefferson Co., Ala., 1,708.
c. s., Adams Co., Colo., 3,394.
On Un. Pac. (R. R.).
–Jersey and Macoupin Cos., Ill., 548.
On Alton; Chi., Burl. & Quincy (R. Rs.).
–Washington Co., Iowa, 800.
On Chi., Burl. & Quincy; Chi., Rk. Isl. & Pac.; Minn. & St. Louis (R. Rs.).
–Livingston Co., Mich., 1,287.
On Pere Marq. (R. R.).
–Northumberland Co., Ontario, Canada, 1,580.
On Can. Pac.; Can. Nat. (R. R.).
–Monroe Co., N. Y., 900.
On N. York Cen. (R. R.).
BRIGHTSVILLE, Marlboro Co., S. C., 800.
BRIGHTWATERS, Suffolk Co., N. Y., 1,061.
BRILLIANT, Marion Co., Ala., 600.
On Ill. Cen. (R. R.).
–Jefferson Co., Ohio, 1,682.
On Penna.; Wheel. & L. Erie (R. Rs.).
BRILLION, Calumet Co., Wis., 1,167.
On Chi. & Nor. West. (R. R.).
BRIMFIELD, Peoria Co., Ill., 572.
On Chi., Burl. & Quincy (R. R.).
–Hampden Co., Mass., 892.
BRINDISI, Prov. of Brindisi, Italy, 34,700.
Important seaport and railway terminal.
BRINKLEY, Monroe Co., Ark., 3,046.
On Chi., Rk. Isl. & Pac.; Mo.-Pac.; St. Lou. Southw. (R. Rs.).
BRISBANE, capital of Queensland, Australia, pop. (including suburbs), 313,430.
A seaport near the mouth of the Brisbane River. The wharfs admit large steamers, and several railways terminate here. The Victoria Bridge, which is about 1,100 feet in length, connects North and South Brisbane. The city has fine buildings, including the Government buildings, the postoffice, a technical college, and a school of art. There are two cathedrals, a museum, and botanical gardens.
Brisbane was settled as a penal colony by Sir Arthur Brisbane in 1825, abandoned in 1839, and resettled in 1842. It was incorporated as a city in 1850.
–San Mateo Co., Calif., 1,200.
BRISTOL, Gloucestershire, England, 410,870.
An important railway center at the junction of the rivers Avon and Frome. Bristol has numerous fine public buildings, among them the cathedral erected in 1148 by St. Augustine, St. James's Church (Norman), the Church of St. Mary Redcliffe, notable for its handsome architecture, University College, Clifton College, a grammar school founded in 1532, a school of art, a municipal library, museums, and botanical and zoological gardens, its higher educational facilities. Bristol is one of the prominent commercial ports of England, and has extensive quays. The *Great Western,* the first steamship to cross the Atlantic from England, was built in Bristol.
At the time of the Norman Conquest, Bristol was a walled city, by the name of Briegstow. It was an important commercial place during the Middle Ages. From the port of Bristol John Cabot started on his voyage of discovery in 1497.
–Hartford Co., Conn., 28,451.
On N. York, N. Hav. & Hart. (R. R.).
–c. s., Liberty Co., Fla., 800.
Airport. Industrial center. Famous for clock making.
–Elkhart Co., Indiana, 699.
On N. York Cen. (R. R.).
–Grafton Co., N. H., 1,200.
On Bost. & Me. (R. R.).
–Morgan Co., Ohio, 710.
–Bucks Co., Pa., 11,799.
On Penna. (R. R.).
Airport. Agricultural region.
–c. s., Bristol Co., R. I., 10,855.
On N. York, N. Hav. & Hart. (R. R.).
Founded in 1680 and incorporated since 1747. Has a fine harbor and long water front. Seat of Herreshoff yacht-building plant. Rubber and worsted goods are the principal industries.
–Day Co., S. Dak., 624.
On Chi., Mil., St. P., & Pac. (R. R.).
–Sullivan Co., Tenn., 12,005. Washington Co. (Ind. City), Va., 8,840. Combined population, 20,845.
On Nor. & West.; Sou. (R. Rs.).
Crosses boundary of Tennessee and Virginia. In iron and coal fields, the raw materials of which are used in the manufacture of glass. There are also paper pulp mills, tanneries, woodwork and chemical factories, etc. Location of King College (Presb.) and Southwest Virginia Institute.
–Addison Co., Vt., 1,190.
BRISTOW, Creek Co., Okla., 6,619.
On St. Lou.-San Fran. (R. R.).
In oil and cotton section.
BRITT, Hancock Co., Iowa, 1,593.
On Chi., Mil., St. P. & Pac.; Minn. & St. Lou. (R. Rs.).
BRITTON, Oklahoma Co., Okla., 2,214.
On Atch., Top. & Santa Fe (R. R.).
–c. s., Marshall Co., S. Dak., 1,473.
On Chi., Mil., St. P. & Pac. (R. R.).
BRIVE, Dept. of Corrèze, France, 29,074.
Commercial center of a farming region.
BRNO (Brunn), capital of Moravia, Czechoslovakia, estimated 288,000.
At the confluence of the Schwarzawa and the Zwittawa. Among the interesting buildings are the Cathedral of St. Peter and St. Paul, built in the fifteenth century; St. James, a Gothic church; the Museum of Industrial Arts, and a polytechnic institute. Brno dates back to the ninth century, and has stood some famous sieges.
BROACH (or Bharuch), Bombay Prov., India, 34,276.
Cotton manufacturing center.
BROADALBIN, Fulton Co., N. Y., 1,341.
On Fonda, Johnst. & Glovers. (R. R.).
BROAD BROOK, Hartford Co., Conn., 1,386.
On N. York, N. Hav. & Hart. (R. R.).
BROADMOOR, El Paso Co., Colo., 643.
BROAD MOUNTAIN, Schuylkill Co., Pa., 817.
On Reading (R. R.).
BROADSTAIRS, and St. Peters, Kent, England, 12,748.
A summer resort.
BROAD TOP CITY, Huntingdon Co., Pa., 511.
On Hunt. & Broad Top Mt. (R. R.).
BROADVIEW, Cook Co., Ill., 2,334.
On Ill. Cen.; Ind. Harb. Blt. (R. Rs.).
BROADVIEW HEIGHTS, Cuyahoga Co., Ohio, 689.
BROCKPORT, Monroe Co., N. Y., 3,511.
On N. York Cen. (R. R.).
BROCKTON, Plymouth Co., Mass., 62,407.
On N. York, N. Hav. & Hart. (R. R.).
Has important manufactures, especially of boots and shoes, for which it is one of the great centers of the United States. Also has manufactures of wood and paper boxes, shoe tools, rubber goods, sewing machines, etc. Brockton was formed in 1700.
–Chautauqua Co., N. Y., 1,301.
On N. York Cen.; N. York, Chi. & St. Lou.; Penna. (R. Rs.).
–Schuylkill Co., Pa., 500.
On Reading (R. R.).
BROCKVILLE, Leeds Co., Ontario, Canada, 9,736.
On Can. Nat.; Can. Pac. (R. Rs.).
BROCKWAY, Jefferson Co., Pa., 2,690.
On Balt. & Ohio; Erie; Penna.; Pitts. & Shawmut; Pitts., Shawmut & Nor. (R. Rs.).
BRODERICK, Yolo Co., Calif., 1,500.
BRODHEAD, Rockcastle Co., Ky., 630.
On Lou. & Nash. (R. R.).
–Green Co., Wis., 1,533.
On Chi., Mil., St. P. & Pac. (R. R.).
BRODY, East Galicia, Poland, 12,401.
A trade center.
BROKAW, Marathon Co., Wis., 514.
On Chi., Mil., St. P. & Pac. (R. R.).
BROKEN ARROW, Tulsa Co., Okla., 1,964.
On Mo.-Kan.-Tex. (R. R.).
BROKEN BOW, c. s., Custer Co., Neb., 2,715.
On Chi., Burl. & Quincy (R. R.).
–McCurtain Co., Okla., 2,291.
On Tex., Okla. & East. (R. R.).
BROKEN HILL, New South Wales, Australia, 26,921.
Famous mining town.
BROMBERG, Poland. See BYDGOSZCZ.
BROMLEY, Kent, England, 45,348.
A suburb of London.
–Kenton Co., Ky., 1,017.
BRONSON, c. s., Levy Co., Fla., 694.
–Branch Co., Mich., 1,651.
On N. York Cen. (R. R.).
BRONTE, Coke Co., Texas, 671.
On Panh. & Santa Fe (R. R.).
BRONXVILLE, Westchester Co., N. Y., 6,387.
On N. York Cen. (R. R.).
BROOK, Newton Co., Ind., 815.
On Chi., Attica & Sou. (R. R.).
BROOKELAND, Sabine Co., Tex., 813.
On Gulf, Colo. & Santa Fe (R. R.).
BROOKFIELD, Cook Co., Ill., 10,035.
On Chi., Burl. & Quincy (R. R.).
Suburb of Chicago. Residential. Site of Cook County Zoo.
–Worcester Co., Mass., 700.
On Bost. & Alb. (R. R.).
–Linn Co., Mo., 6,428.
On Chi., Burl. & Quincy (R. R.).
BROOKFORD, Catawba Co., N. C., 694.
BROOKHAVEN, c. s., Lincoln Co., Miss., 5,288.
On Ill. Cen.; Miss. Cen.; (R. Rs.).
–Suffolk Co., N. Y., 510.
On Long Isl. (R. R.).
BROOK HAVEN, Delaware Co., Pa., 500.
BROOKINGS, c. s., Brookings Co., S. Dak., 5,311.
On Chi. & Nor. West. (R. R.).
Seat of Agricultural College.
BROOKLAND, Lexington Co., S. C., 1,722.
BROOKLANDS, Manitoba, Canada, 2,246.
BROOKLAWN, Camden Co., N. J., 1,753.
On Penna.-Read. Seashore (R. R.).
BROOKLET, Bulloch Co., Ga., 536.
On Shearwood (R. R.).
BROOKLIN, Hancock Co., Maine, 700.
BROOKLINE, Norfolk Co., Mass., 50,319.
On Bost. & Alb. (R. R.).
Suburb of Boston. Principally residential.
BROOKLYN, BOROUGH OF. See NEW YORK.
–Windham Co., Conn., 600.
–(Lovejoy P. O.) St. Clair Co., Ill., 2,063.
On Term. R. R. Assn.; Wab. (R. Rs.).
–Poweshiek Co., Iowa, 1,345.
On Chi., Rk. Isl. & Pac. (R. R.).
–Morgan Co., Indiana, 545.
On Penna. (R. R.).
–Jackson Co., Mich., 733.
On N. York Cen. (R. R.).
–Cuyahoga Co., Ohio, 784.
On Balt. & Ohio; Wheel. & L. Erie (R. Rs.).
BROOKLYN CENTER, Hennepin Co., Minn., 1,344.
BROOKLYN JUNCTION (Brooklyn), Wetzel Co., West Va., 779.
On Balt. & Ohio (R. R.).
BROOKNEAL, Campbell Co., Va., 1,692.
On Norf. & West.; Virginian (R. Rs.).
BROOK PARK, Cuyahoga Co., Ohio, 837.
BROOKPORT, Massac Co., Ill., 1,336.
On Ill. Cen. (R. R.).
BROOKSHIRE, Waller Co., Tex., 600.
On Mo.-Kan.-Tex. of Tex. (R. R.).
BROOKSIDE, Hennepin Co., Minn., 848.
On Minn., Northf. & Sou. (R. R.).
–Belmont Co., Ohio, 882.
–Luzerne Co., Pa., 2,000.
BROOKSTON, White Co., Ind., 844.
On Chi., Ind. & Lou. (R. R.).
–Forest Co., Pa., 517.
On Tionesta Val. (R. R.).
BROOKSVILLE, c. s., Hernando Co., Fla., 1,547.
On Atl. Coast Line; Seab. Air Line (R. Rs.).
–c. s., Bracken Co., Ky., 615.
–Hancock Co., Maine, 810.
–Noxubee Co., Miss., 875.
On Mob. & Ohio (R. R.).
BROOKVILLE, c. s., Franklin Co., Ind., 2,148.
On Cle., Cin., Chi. & St. Lou. (R. R.).
–Norfolk Co., Mass., 600.
–Montgomery Co., Ohio, 1,403.
On Balt. & Ohio; Penn. (R. Rs.).
–c. s., Jefferson Co., Pa., 4,387.
On Penna.; Pitts. & Shawmut (R. Rs.).
BROOMALL, Delaware Co., Pa., 1,200.
BROOTEN, Stearns Co., Minn., 604.
On Minn., St. P. & S. Ste. M. (R. R.).
BROUGHTON, Allegheny Co., Pa., 2,200.
BROUSSARD, Lafayette Parish, La., 806.
On Tex. & N. Orl. (R. R.).
BROWERVILLE, Todd Co., Minn., 709.
On Gt. Nor. (R. R.).
BROWN CITY, Sanilac Co., Mich., 785.
On Pere Marq. (R. R.).
BROWN DEER, Milwaukee Co., Wis., 600.
On Chi., Mil., St. P. & Pac.; Mil. Elec. (R. Rs.).
BROWNDELL, Jasper Co., Tex., 519.
On Gulf, Colo. & Santa Fe. (R. R.).
BROWNFIELD, Oxford Co., Maine, 689.
On Me. Cen. (R. R.).
–Fayette Co., Pa., 1,521.
On Balt. & Ohio (R. R.).
–c. s., Terry Co., Tex., 1,907.
On Panh. & Santa Fe (R. R.).
BROWNING, Linn and Sullivan Cos., Mo., 590.
On Chi., Burl. & Quincy (R. R.).
–Glacier Co., Mont., 1,172.
BROWNSBURG, Hendricks Co., Ind., 1,042.
On Cle., Cin., Chi. & St. Lou. (R. R.).
BROWNSTOWN, c. s., Jackson Co., Ind., 1,758.
On Balt. & Ohio (R. R.).
–Cambria Co., Pa., 1,586.
–Lancaster Co., Pa., 800.
BROWNS VALLEY, Traverse Co., Minn., 981.
On Gt. Nor. (R. R.).
BROWNSVILLE, Linn Co., Ore., 746.
On Sou. Pac. (R. R.).
–Fayette Co., Pa., 2,869.
On Monong.; Penna.; Pitts. & L. Erie (R. Rs.).
–Schuylkill Co., Pa., 1,000.
–c. s., Haywood Co., Tenn., 3,204.
On Lou. & Nash. (R. R.).
Cotton and lumber mills.
–c. s., Cameron Co., Texas, 22,021.
On Port Isab. & Rio Gde. Val.; St. Lou., Browns. & Mex.; Tex. & N. Orl. (R. Rs.).
In productive irrigated area.
BROWNTON, McLeod Co., Minn., 632.
On Chi., Mil., St. P. & Pac. (R. R.).
BROWNVILLE, Tuscaloosa Co., Ala., 500.
On Mob. & Gulf (R. R.).
–Piscataquis Co., Maine, 1,500.
On Bangor & Aroostook (R. R.).
–Jefferson Co., N. Y., 842.
On N. York Cen. (R. R.).
BROWNWOOD, Brown Co., Texas, 12,789.
On Ft. Worth & Rio Gde.; Gulf, Colo. & Santa Fe (R. Rs.).
In natural gas and oil fields. Horse and mule market for Southwest.
–Fayette Co., W. Va., 516.
On Chesa. & Ohio (R. R.).
BROXTON, Coffee Co., Ga., 830.
On Ga. & Fla. (R. R.).
BRUAY-EN-ARTOIS, Pas-de-Calais, France, 30,125.
BRUCE, Calhoun Co., Miss., 946.
On Miss. & Skuna Val. (R. R.).
–Rusk Co., Wisconsin, 548.
On Minn., St. P. & S. Ste. M. (R. R.).
BRUCETON, Carroll Co., Tenn., 1,112.
On Nash., Chatt. & St. Lou. (R. R.).
BRUGES, capital of Prov. of West Flanders, Belgium, 51,220.
Medieval in character, with many notable edifices of the Middle Ages until the place was bombarded by the Germans in 1915. Among the famous buildings damaged or destroyed by German cannon were Hôtel de Ville, a fourteenth-century Gothic structure; the building known as Les Halles (cloth and meat halls), with its famous belfry containing chimes reputed to be the finest in Europe; the Palais de Justice, containing many statues and portraits, and the ancient Hospital of St. John (twelfth century), in which are preserved some of the best works of Memling.
The manufactures include lace, textiles, and tobacco and liquors, while horticulture is extensive in the vicinity.
Baldwin of the Iron Arm fortified the place in the ninth century; it was a commercial city with 200,000 inhabitants during the Middle Ages, and a leading emporium of the Hanseatic League from 1240 to 1426. In 1430 Philip the Good established here the Order of the Golden Fleece. After the rebellion of Bruges against Maximilian in the fifteenth century the city began to decline.
BRUIN, Butler Co., Pa., 622.
On Balt. & Ohio. (R. R.).
BRUNDIDGE, Pike Co., Ala., 1,434.
On Atl. Coast Line (R. R.).
BRUNN, Czech. See BRNO.
BRUNSON, Hampton Co., S. C., 675.
On Charl. & W. Car. (R. R.).
BRUNSWICK, Germany. See BRAUNSCHWEIG.
–c. s., Glynn Co., Ga., 14,022.
On Atl., Birm. & Coast; Atl. Coast Line; Sou. (R. Rs.).
A port of entry with a growing water-borne commerce. The industries include oil refining, naval stores and fish canning.
–Cumberland Co., Maine, 6,144.
On Me. Cen. (R. R.).
Seat of Bowdoin College.
–Frederick Co., Md., 3,671.
On Balt. & Ohio (R. R.).
–Chariton Co., Mo., 1,715.
On Wab. (R. R.).
BRUSA, Turkey. See BURSA.
BRUSH, Morgan Co., Colorado, 2,312.
On Chi., Burl. & Quincy (R. R.).
BRUSHY MOUNTAIN, Morgan Co., Tenn., 750.
BRUSSELS, Belgium. See BRUXELLES.
BRÜX, Czechoslovakia, 25,000.
BRUXELLES (Brussels), capital of Prov. of Brabant and of Belgium, 194,268.
The most important city of Belgium, and remarkable for the great number of its ancient buildings and for the beauty of its modern quarter.
The city consists of an upper town, which is the fashionable quarter, and contains the Government buildings, and the lower town, devoted to commerce. Among the ecclesiastical buildings the most prominent are the Gothic Cathedral of St. Gudule, begun in 1220; and St. Jacques sur Caudenberg. The Hôtel de Ville, the most important public building of Bruxelles, Gothic in style, was begun in the fifteenth century and completed in the eighteenth. The Palais d'Arenberg has a valuable gallery of paintings. The educational institutions are an academy of medicine, a veterinary school, a military school, a conservatory of music, and an academy of art. The Royal

Library has 375,000 volumes, and the Palais des Beaux Arts is devoted mainly to paintings and sculptures.
The lace made at Bruxelles is considered the finest in the world. Other manufactures are linen, woolen, and cotton goods, gold and silver embroidery, gloves, paper, jewelry and mathematical and musical instruments.
Near Bruxelles is the battlefield of Waterloo, where Napoleon met his final defeat.
The capital was taken and occupied by the Germans on August 20, 1914, and held till near the close of the Great War in 1918.
Bryan, c. s., Williams Co., Ohio, 4,689.
On Cin. Nor.; N. York Cen.; Tol. & Ind. (El.) (R. Rs.).
–c. s., Brazos Co., Texas, 7,814.
On Internat. Gt. Nor.; Tex. & N. Orl. (R. Rs.).
Texas Agricultural and Mechanical School.
Bryansk, R.S.F.S.R. Sov. Union, 67,000.
Bryant, Hamlin Co., S. D., 656.
On Chi., Mil., St. P. & Pac. (R. R.).
Bryantville, Plymouth Co., Mass., 500.
Bryn Athyn, Montgomery, Pa., 766.
On Reading (R. R.).
Bryn Mawr, Montgomery Co., Pa., 10,206.
On Penna. (R. R.).
Bryn Mawr College for Women.
Bryson City, c. s., Swain Co., N. C., 1,806.
On Southern (R. R.).
Brzesc'na Bugu (Brest-Litovsk), Poland, 48,435.
Belonged to Russia between 1795 and 1921. Peace Treaty between Russia and Central Powers was signed here March 2, 1918, but annulled by Great War.
Brzezany, East Galicia, Poland, 13,045.
Brzeziny, Dist. of Lodz, Poland, 11,715.
Bucaramanga, Santander, Colombia, 80,000.
In a mining and agricultural region.
Bucay, Prov. of Abra, Luzon, P. I., 5,222.
Buchanan, Berrien Co., Mich., 3,922.
On Mich. Cen. (R. R.).
–Westchester Co., N. Y., 1,346.
–Botetourt Co., Va., 825.
On Chesa. & Ohio; Norf. & West. (R. Rs.).
Bucharest, Rumania. See Bucuresti.
Buchtel, Athens Co., Ohio, 799.
On Chesa. & Ohio (R. R.).
Coal mining.
Bückeburg, capital of the German Principality of Schaumburg-Lippe, 6,690.
Buckeye, Maricopa Co., Ariz., 1,077.
On Sou. Pac. (R. R.).
Buckeystown, Frederick Co., Md., 1,425.
On Balt. & Ohio (R. R.).
Buckhannon, c. s., Upshur Co., W. Va., 4,374.
On Balt. & Ohio (R. R.).
Seat of West Virginia Conference Seminary.
Buckhead, Fulton Co., Ga., 2,500.
Buck Hill Falls, Monroe, Pa., 1,500.
Buckholts, Milam Co., Tex., 515.
Buckingham, Labelle Co., Que., Canada, 4,638.
On Can. Pac. (R. R.).
Buckland, Franklin Co., Mass., 1,540.
Buckley, Pierce Co., Wash., 1,052.
On Nor. Pac. (R. R.).
Bucklin, Ford Co., Kans., 939.
On Chi., Rk. Isl. & Pac. (R. R.).
–Linn Co., Mo., 932.
On Atch., Top. & Santa Fe; Chi., Burl. & Quincy (R. Rs.).
Bucknell, Monroe Co., Iowa, 911.
Buckner, Franklin Co., Ill., 1,409.
On Ill. Cen. (R. R.).
–Jackson Co., Mo., 529.
On Mo. Pac. (R. R.).
Buck Run, Schuylkill Co., Pa., 800.
On Reading (R. R.).
Bucksport, Hancock Co., Maine, 1,500.
On Me. Cen. (R. R.).
Bucoda, Thurston Co., Wash., 703.
On Gt. Nor.; Nor. Pac.; Ore.-Wash. R. R. & Nav. (R. Rs.).
Bucuresti (Bucharest), capital of Rumania, 639,789.
On both sides of the river Dimbovitza. The two parts of the town are connected by several bridges of iron and stone.
The chief streets of the city are attractive and are lined with fine buildings. Among these are many Greek churches, a royal palace, a national theater, a palace of justice, and a number of other Government buildings. A university, the Veterinary Institute, the Rumanian Academy, and numerous museums compose the educational institutions. Bucuresti is of little industrial importance. Its trade, however, is considerable. The city was occupied by the Germans in their invasion of Rumania in 1916.
Bucyrus, c. s., Crawford Co., Ohio, 10,027.
On N. York Cen.; Penna. (R. Rs.).
Has foundries and stone plants.
Bud, Wyoming Co., W. Va., 500.
On Virginian (R. R.).
Buda, Bureau Co., Ill., 794.
On Chi., Burl. & Quincy; Chi. & Nor. West. (R. Rs.).
Budapest, capital of Hungary, 1,051,804.
Situated on the Danube River, consists of two cities, Pest (Pesth) on the left bank of the river, and Buda on the right, which were united in 1873 under the official name of Budapest. The towns are connected by several bridges.
Bude, Franklin Co., Miss., 1,378.
On Miss. Cen. (R. R.).
Budweis, Czechoslovakia. See Ceské Budejovice.
Buena Park, Orange Co., Calif., 2,000.
On Atch., Top. & Santa Fe; Sou. Pac. (R. Rs.).
Buena Vista, c. s., Chaffee Co., Colo., 751.
On Denv. & Rio Gde., West. (R. R.).
–c. s., Marion Co., Ga., 1,097.
On Cen. of Ga. (R. R.).
–Allegheny Co., Pa., 600.
On Pitts. & L. Erie (R. R.).
–(Ind. City) Rockbridge Co., Va., 4,002.
On Chesa. & Ohio; Norf. & West. (R. Rs.).
Buenos Aires, capital of Argentine Republic, South America, 2,290,731.
Largest and most important city of South America, situated in a plain on the south bank of the La Plata River. The city has an area of 71 square miles. It is the most modern in appearance of any South American city. The principal square is the Plaza de la Victoria, surrounded by handsome buildings. Among them are the Government palace, the hall of justice, the cathedral (in the style of the Madeleine in Paris), and the archbishop's palace. There are also the Teatro de la Opera and about twenty other theaters. Palermo Park is a fashionable race course.
The National University was founded in 1821. The commercial importance of Buenos Aires is improving with the establishment of new docks, and the use of the Riachuelo Channel. The manufactures of the city include furniture, carriages, machinery, leather, shoes, hats, woven goods, tobacco and liquors. The principal exports are cattle products, wool, and live stock. Buenos Aires was founded in 1535 by Don Pedro de Mendoza, and was named Puerto de Santa Marie de Buenos Aires, after St. (the Virgin) Mary of the Good Airs, or Winds.
Buffalo, Scott Co., Iowa, 547.
On Chi., Mil., St. P. & Pac.; Chi., Rk. Isl. & Pac. (R. Rs.).
–Wilson Co., Kans., 634.
On Mo. Pac. (R. R.).
–c. s., Wright Co., Minn., 1,409.
On Minn., St. P. & S. Ste. M. (R. R.).
–c. s., Dallas Co., Mo., 835.
–Guernsey Co., Ohio, 900.
On Balt. & Ohio (R. R.).
–c. s., Harper Co., Okla., 990.
On Atch., Top. & Santa Fe (R. R.).
–Union Co., S. Car., 1,620.
On Buf., Un.-Car. (R. R.).
–c. s., Johnson Co., Wyo., 1,749.
On Wyoming (R. R.).
–c. s., Erie Co., N. Y., second city of the State, 573,076.
One of the most important commercial ports of the Great Lakes, located at the eastern end of Lake Erie, at the head of the Niagara River. It is on the lines of the Baltimore & Ohio, the Buffalo Creek, the Delaware, Lackawanna & Western, the Erie, International (El.); the Lehigh Valley, the Michigan Central, the New York Central, the New York Chicago & St. Louis; Pennsylvania; and the Pere Marquette; South Buffalo; the Wabash and the West Shore railroads. The river is here crossed by two international bridges, the railroad bridge completed in 1873 and the Peace Bridge, for road traffic, dedicated in 1927. Two-thirds of the more than 37 miles of waterfront is developed. The city has two municipal airports—Buffalo Airport and Buffalo Marine Airport—and a commercial airport (Becker).
Main Street is the chief business thoroughfare; Delaware Avenue, a street of fashionable residences, also found in the Central Park, North Buffalo and other areas.
Among notable buildings are the Buffalo Public Library, City Hall, two state Armories, Buffalo Historical Society Museum, Buffalo Museum of Science, Albright Art Gallery, Grosvenor Library, St. Paul's Church, Trinity Church, St. Joseph's Cathedral, and a fine synagogue. At the Ansley Wilcox house Theodore Roosevelt took the oath of office on the death of President William McKinley.
Educational institutions include State Teachers College, University of Buffalo, Canisius College, D'Youville College, academies, high schools, and comprehensive night schools.
A State insane asylum and Erie County Penitentiary are located here.
For some years Buffalo has made rapid commercial development, due to facilities for steamship connection with the Great Lakes and with New York, and to interstate transportation effected by means of the great eastern railroads and by a belt-line railroad which encircles the city. In 1843 Joseph Dart built the first grain elevator in the world in Buffalo. The city is one of the great Eastern distributors of Western grain. Its many large elevators have a storage capacity of more than 40,000,000 bushels. Its mills have turned out 12,000,000 barrels of flour in a year. The city is also one of the country's most important live-stock markets and a killing and packing center. Enormous quantities of lumber and ores pass through this distributing point of the lake traffic. Through its facilities for obtaining ore, coal and limestone from their source, Buffalo is becoming a leader in the production of pig iron and steel by the growth of new plants for the manufacture of these raw materials. Other leading products are automobiles and parts, aircraft, chemicals, clothing, and printing and publishing manufactures. The city uses electric power generated near Niagara Falls, 31 miles distant.
In 1812, Buffalo was a military post. It was incorporated as a city in 1832.
Buffalo Center, Winnebago Co., Iowa, 768.
On Chi., Rk. Isl. & Pac. (R. R.).
Buffalo Lake, Renville Co., Minn., 545.
On Chi., Mil., St. P. & Pac. (R. R.).
Buford, Gwinnett Co., Ga., 3,357.
On Southern (R. R.).
Bugasong, Antique Prov., Panay, P. I., 10,925.
Buhl, Tuscaloosa Co., Ala., 600.
On Mob. & Gulf; Mob. & Ohio (R. Rs.).
–Twin Falls Co., Idaho, 1,883.
On Ore. Short Line.
–St. Louis Co., Minn., 1,634.
On Dul., Missabe & Nor.; Gt. Nor. (R. Rs.).
Buhler, Reno Co., Kans., 603.
On St. Lou.-San Fran. (R. Rs.).
Bukhara, Uzbek, Sov. Union, Asia, 46,778.
Bulacan, Bulacan Prov., Luzon, P. I., 10,419.
A trade center.
Bulan, Sorsogón Prov., Luzon, P. I., 19,266.
Bulger, Washington Co., Pa., 500.
On Penna. (R. R.).
Bullard, Smith Co., Tex., 500.
On St. Lou. Southw. (R. R.).
Bulli, New South Wales, Austialia, 2,257.
Bullion, Venango Co., Pa., 500.
Bulls Gap, Hawkins Co., Tenn., 1,500.
On Southern (R. R.).
Bulmke, Germany, part of Gelsenkirchen, 1,903.
Bulnes, Prov. of Nuble, Chile, 4,122.
Bunceton, Cooper Co., Mo., 693.
On Mo. Pac. (R. R.).
Bunker Hill, Macoupin Co., Ill., 947.
On Cle., Cin., Chi. & St. Lou. (R. R.).
–Miami Co., Ind., 528.
On N. York, Chi. & St. Lou.; Penna.; Ind. R. R. Sys. (El.) (R. Rs.).
Bunkie, Avoyelles Parish, La., 2,464.
On Tex. & Pac. (R. R.).
Bunnell, c. s., Flagler Co., Fla., 1,111.
On Fla. East Coast (R. R.).
Bunola, Allegheny Co., Pa., 500.
On Pitts. & L. Erie (R. R.).
Buntyn, Shelby Co., Tenn., 523.
On Southern (R. R.).
Bunzlau, Prussia, Germany, 19,000.
Pottery and textile manufactures.

EWING GALLOWAY PHOTO

THE PARLIAMENT BUILDINGS, BUDAPEST, HUNGARY, FROM ACROSS THE DANUBE RIVER

Buras, Plaquemines Par., La., 750.
On N. Orl. & Lower Coast (R. R.).
Burauen, Leyte Prov., Leyte, P. I., 25,647.
Center of abaca growing region.
Burbank, Los Angeles Co., Cal., 16,662.
On Pac. Elec.; Sou. Pac. (R. Rs.).
Oil, motion pictures. Suburb of Los Angeles.
Burden, Cowley Co., Kans., 555.
On Atch., Top. & Santa Fe (R. R.).
Bureau, Bureau Co., Ill., 552.
On Chi., Rk. Isl. & Pac. (R. R.).
Burgas, Bulgaria, 36,099.
Burgaw, c. s., Pender Co., N. C., 1,209.
On Atl. Coast Line (R. R.).
Burgdorf, (Fr. Berthud), Bern Canton, Switzerland, 9,778.
Burgettstown, Washington Co., Pa., 2,266.
On Penna. (R. R.).
Burgin, Mercer Co., Ky., 791.
On Cin., N. Orl. & Tex. Pac.; Sou. (R. Rs.).
Burgos, Burgos Prov., Spain, 33,430.
Agricultural center. Manufactures of woolens, leather goods and chemicals.
Burkburnett, Wichita Co., Texas, 3,281.
On Mo.-Kans.-Tex. of Tex. (R. R.).
Burke, Shoshone Co., Idaho, 876.
On Nor. Pac.; Ore.-Wash. R. R. & Nav. Co. (R. Rs.).
–c. s., Gregory Co., S. Dak., 591.
On Chi. & Nor. West. (R. R.).
Burkesville, c. s., Cumberland Co., Ky., 886.
Burkeville, Nottoway Co., Va., 755.
On Norf. & West.; Sou. (R. Rs.).
Burleson, Johnson Co., Tex., 591.
On Mo.-Kan.-Tex. of Tex. (R. R.).
Burley, Cassia Co., Idaho, 3,826.
On Ore. Short Line (R. R.).
Burlingame, San Mateo Co., Cal., 13,270.
On Sou. Pac. (R. R.).
Residential suburb. Motion picture studios.

MAP OF BUFFALO, THE SECOND LARGEST CITY OF THE STATE OF NEW YORK. BUFFALO IS SITUATED AT THE EASTERN END OF LAKE ERIE AND AT THE HEAD OF THE NIAGARA RIVER. DELAWARE PARK WAS THE SITE OF THE PAN-AMERICAN EXPOSITION HELD IN 1901

–Osage Co., Kans., 1,140.
On Atch., Top. & Santa Fe (R. R.).
–Kent Co., Mich., 700.
Burlington, c. s., Kit Carson Co., Colo., 1,280.
On Chi., Rk. Isl. & Pac. (R. R.).
–Hartford Co., Conn., 700.
On N. York, N. Hav. & Hart. (R. R.).
–Carroll Co., Ind., 615.
–c. s., Des Moines Co., Iowa, 26,755.
On the Mississippi River, and on the Chi., Burl. & Quincy, and the Chi., Rk. Isl. & Pac. railroads.
A railroad, manufacturing and merchandising center and the location of the Burlington railroad shops. Its industries include various products of wood (especially furniture), iron, leather, stone, soap, baskets, gloves, candy and cookies. The city is near extensive coal fields. It was settled in 1832 and incorporated in 1837.
–c. s., Coffey Co., Kans., 2,735.
On Atch., Top. & Santa Fe; Mo.-Kan.-Tex. (R. Rs.).
Trading center.
–c. s., Boone Co., Ky., 600.
–Middlesex Co., Mass., 2,146.
–Burlington Co., N. J., 10,844.
On Penna. (R. R.).
Principally residential city. Foundries and silk mills.
–Alamance Co., N. C., 9,737.
On Southern (R.R.).
Airport. Tobacco, wheat, corn, furniture and hosiery.
–c. s., Chittenden Co., Vt., 24,789.
Beautifully located on the east shore of Lake Champlain, on the Rutland and Central Vermont railroads.
The city is built around a central square, near which are the United States custom-house and post-office, the court-house, the Young Men's Christian Association building, and the city hall. Other notable edifices are the Masonic Temple, the Fletcher Free Library, the Howard Opera House, the Catholic Cathedral, and St. Paul's Church; the University of Vermont, founded in 1791, is located here, and has in connection with it the Billings Library, containing 70,000 volumes.
The harbor is rendered safe by means of an artificial breakwater; the city has steamer lines to other ports on Lake Champlain.
Burlington was settled in 1764, organized as a town in 1797, and granted a city charter in 1865.
–Halton Co., Ontario, Canada, 3,046.
On Can. Nat.; Can. Pac. (R. Rs.).
–Skagit Co., Wash., 1,407.
On Gt. Nor.; Puget Sd. & Casc. (R. Rs.).
–Racine Co., Wis., 4,114.
On Chi., Mil., St. P. & Pac.; Mil. Elec.; Minn., St. P. & S. Ste. M. (R. Rs.).
Burlington Junction, Nodaway Co., Mo., 813.
On Chi., Burl. & Quincy; Wab. (R. Rs.).
Burmont (Gladstone), Delaware Co., Pa., 600.
Burnet, c. s., Burnet Co., Texas, 1,055.
On Tex. & N. Orl. (R. R.).
Burnham, Cook Co., Ill., 994.
On Balt. & Ohio, Chi. Term.; Chi. & Cal. Riv.; Chi. S. Shore & S. Bend (El.); Ind. Har. Blt.; N. York, Chi. & St. Lou.; Penna. (R. Rs.).
–Mifflin Co., Pa., 3,089.
On Kishacoquillas Val.; Penna. (R. Rs.).
Burnley, Lancashire, England, 98,259.
Textile manufactures.
Burns, c. s., Harney Co., Ore., 2,599.
On Ore. & Northw.; Ore. Short Line (R. Rs.).
–Anoka Co., Minn., 899.
–Dickson Co., Tenn., 500.
On Nash., Chatt. & St. Lou. (R. R.).
Burnside, Pulaski Co., Ky., 914.
On Cin., Orl. & Tex. Pac. (R. R.).
Burnsville, c. s., Yancey Co., N. C., 866.
On Black Mt. (R. R.).
–Braxton Co., West Va., 868.
On Balt. & Ohio (R. R.).
Burrage, Plymouth Co., Mass., 525.
On N. York, N. Hav. & Hart. (R. R.).
Burrillville, Providence Co., R. I., 7,355.
Burr Oak, Cook Co., Ill., 1,429.
On Chi., Rk. Isl. & Pac. (R. R.).
–Jewell Co., Kans., 617.
On Mo. Pac. (R. R.).
–St. Joseph Co., Mich., 680.
On N. York Cen. (R. R.).
Burrton, Harvey Co., Kans., 816.
On Ark. Val. Interurb. (El.); Atch., Top. & Santa Fe; St. Lou.-San Fran. (R. Rs.).
Burrville, Litchfield Co., Conn., 689.
On N. York, N. Hav. & Hart. (R. R.).
Bursa (Brusa), Bursa Vilayet, Turkey, 72,271.
Silk and carpet manufactures.
Burt, Kossuth Co., Iowa, 580.
On Chi. & Nor. West. (R. R.).
Burton, Geauga Co., Ohio, 597.
On Balt. & Ohio (R. R.).
Burton-upon-Trent, Staffordshire, England, 49,485.
Center of brewing industry.
Burtscheid, Prussia, Germany, part of Aachen.
Burujird, Iran (Persia), 35,000.

Burwell, c. s., Garfield Co., Neb., 1,156.
On Chi., Burl. & Quincy (R. R.).
Bury, Lancashire, England, 56,186.
Center of woolen trade.
Bury St. Edmunds, Suffolk, England, 16,708.
Trade center of agricultural region.
Bush, Williamson Co., Ill., 589.
On Mo. Pac. (R. R.).
Bushire, Iran. See Bandar Abu Shehr.
Bushnell, c. s., Sumter Co., Fla., 477.
On Seab. Air Line (R. R.).
–McDonough Co., Ill., 2,850.
On Chi., Burl. & Quincy; Tol., Peoria & West. (R. Rs.).
Bussey, Marion Co., Iowa, 546.
On Chi., Burl. & Quincy; Wab. (R. Rs.).
Bute (W. Leisenring P. O.), Fayette Co., Pa., 1,000.
On Penna. (R. R.).
Butler, c. s., Choctaw Co., Ala., 501.
–c. s., Taylor Co., Ga., 857.
On Cen. of Ga. (R. R.).
–De Kalb Co., Ind., 1,643.
On N. York Cen.; Penna.; Wab. (R. Rs.).
–c. s., Bates Co., Mo., 2,706.
On Mo. Pac. (R. R.).
–Morris Co., N. J., 3,392.
On N. York, Susq. & West. (R. R.).
–Richland Co., Ohio, 634.
On Balt. & Ohio (R. R.).
–c. s., Butler Co., Pa., 23,568.
On Balt. & Ohio; Bess. & L. Erie; Penna. (R. Rs.).
In coal, natural gas, limestone and oil section. Industries include railroad cars, plate glass, oil well supplies, steam and gas engines, etc.
–Johnson Co., Tenn., 706.
On Southern (R. R.).
–Waukesha Co., Wis., 800.
On Chi. & Nor. West. (R. R.).
Butte, c. s., Silver Bow Co., Mont., 39,532.
On a slope of the Rocky Mountains, and on the Butte, Anaconda & Pacific; the Chicago, Milwaukee, St. Paul & Pacific; the Great Northern; the Northern Pacific; and the Oregon Short Line railroads.
Home of several of the largest gold, silver, and copper mining companies in the United States. The famous Anaconda copper and silver mines are located here. Most of the industries of Butte are connected with the mines. Butte was incorporated in 1879.
–c. s., Boyd Co., Neb., 569.
Butterfield, Barry Co., Mo., 673.
On St. Lou.-San Fran. (R. R.).
Butternut, Ashland Co., Wis., 604.
On Minn., St. P. & S. Ste. M. (R. R.).
Buttonwood (Christopher), Luzerne Co., Pa., 900.
On Cen. of N. Jer.; Wilk.-Bar. Connect.; Penna. (R. Rs.).
Buttzville, Warren Co., N. J., 500.
On Leh. & Hud. Riv. (R. R.).
Buturlinovka, Soviet Union, 28,089.
Buxton, Derbyshire, England, 15,353.
Watering place famous for its mineral springs.
–York Co., Maine, 1,574.
On Bost. & Me. (R. R.).
Buzau, Rumania, 36,115.
Market for timber, petroleum, grain.
Byars, McClain Co., Okla., 502.
On Atch., Top. & Santa Fe (R. R.).

PHOTO BY GARDNER WELLS FROM R. I. NESMITH AND ASSOCIATES

HASSAN REFA MOSQUES, CAIRO, EGYPT. MINARETS ARE A DISTINCTIVE AND BEAUTIFUL FEATURE OF MOSLEM MOSQUE ARCHITECTURE

Bydgoszcz (Bromberg), Posnania, Poland, 137,000.
Byesville, Guernsey Co., Ohio, 2,638.
On Penna. (R. R.).

Byfield, Essex Co., Mass., 600.
Byhalia, Marshall Co., Miss., 565.
On St. Lou.-San Fran. (R. R.).
Bylas, Graham Co., Ariz., 500.
On Sou. Pac. (R. R.).
Byrnedale, Elk Co., Pa., 619.
On Pitts., Shawmut & Nor. (R. R.).
Byron, Ogle Co., Ill., 915.
On Chi. Gt. West.; Chi., Mil., St. P. & Pac. (R. Rs.).
–Harrison Co., W. Va., 522.
On Balt. & Ohio (R. R.).
Bywood, Delaware Co., Pa., 2,000.

C

Caazapá, Caazapá, Paraguay, 17,711.
Cabatuan, Iloilo Prov., Panay, P. I., 14,784.
Cabin John, Montgomery Co., Md., 1,500.
Cabool, Texas Co., Mo., 908.
On St. Lou.-San Fran. (R. R.).
Cabo Rojo, Puerto Rico, 4,690.
Cabot, Lonoke Co., Ark., 684.
On Mo. Pac. (R. R.).
–Butler Co., Pa., 500.
On Penna. (R. R.).
Cabra, Cordova, Spain, 14,951.
Marble quarries nearby.
Caceres, Caceres Prov., Spain, 24,648.
Center of a sheep-raising region.
Caddo, Bryan Co., Okla., 933.
On Mo.-Kan.-Tex. (R. R.).
Cadereyta, State of Queretaro, Mexico, 2,960.
Cadillac, c. s., Wexford Co., Mich., 9,570.
On Ann Arbor; Penna. (R. Rs.).
Cadiz, Prov. of Cadiz, Spain, 78,986.
On a narrow neck of land on the isle of Leon, and almost surrounded by water.
Its chief articles of export are sherry wine, olive oil, salt, lead ore, and fruit.
Cadiz is said to be the most ancient town in Europe and to have been founded by the Phoenicians about the year 1000 B. C.
–Prov. of Negros Occidental, Negros, P. I., 21,730.
–c. s., Trigg Co., Ky., 1,114.
On Cadiz (R. R.).
–c. s., Harrison Co., Ohio, 2,597.
On Penna. (R. R.).
Cadott, Chippewa Co., Wis., 631.
On Minn., St. P. & S. Ste. M. (R. R.).
Caen, Dept. of Calvados, France, 61,334.
Is noted for its fine specimens of Norman architecture. Among them may be mentioned the Cathedral of St. Étienne, founded by William the Conqueror in 1006; the Church of the Trinity, founded by his wife Matilda, and the Churches of St. Nicholas and St. Pierre.
The chief industries are the raising of flowers and manufactures of Angora gloves, lace, cutlery, linen and cotton goods, and hosiery. Brewing and shipbuilding are also carried on.
Cagliari, Cagliari Prov., Sardinia, Italy, 81,500.
Seat of university; many convents, remains of Roman amphitheater and aqueduct; exports grain, cheese, flax, and wine.
Caguas, Puerto Rico, 22,599.
Sugar mills and tobacco factories.
Cahors, Dept. of Lot, France, 13,269.
Tanning and distilling.
Caibarien, Santa Clara Prov., Cuba, 12,088.

Cainesville, Harrison Co., Mo., 765.
On Chi., Burl. & Quincy (R. R.).
Cairnbrook, Somerset Co., Pa., 1,500.
On Penna. (R. R.).

Cairo, capital and largest city of Egypt, 1,311,200.
Is situated on the right bank of the Nile and is separated into different quarters according to the nationality of the inhabitants. The modern portion of Cairo is built in the European style, and has wide streets, electric cars, and fine hotels. The Ezbekieh Garden separates new Cairo from the old. Cairo is noted for its hundreds of beautiful mosques and magnificent old palaces.
Southeast of the city is the citadel which encloses the arsenal, mint, public offices, and palace of the King.
Cairo is the chief center of Mohammedan learning. The most important educational institution is the Mohammedan University, El-Hazar, founded in 957, and attended by thousands of students. It is said to be the oldest university in the world. Cairo is the great emporium of central African trade, and is connected with other important towns by the Nile and several railways.
Many interesting monuments of former greatness still survive, such as the Pyramids of Giza, which are near the city, the tombs of the Mamelukes, and the obelisk of the Heliopolis.
–c. s., Grady Co., Ga., 3,169.
On Atl. Coast Line (R. R.).
–c. s., Alexander Co., Ill., 13,532.
On Cleveland, Cincinnati, Chicago & St. Louis; Illinois Central; Missouri Pacific; Mobile & Ohio (R. Rs.).
A lumber and grain distributing point and a wholesale jobbing center in many lines of trade. The city's central location and transit facilities enable it to draw from many regions the principal raw materials and supplies needed for the manufacture of iron and steel products. At junction of Mississippi and Ohio Rivers.
–Ritchie Co., W. Va., 607.
On Balt. & Ohio (R. R.).
Cajamarca, Dept. of Cajamarca, Peru, 15,000.
Manufactures of woolen and linen goods, metal-work, leather.
Calabanga, Prov. of Ambos-Camarines, Luzon, P. I., 7,918.
Calais, Dept. of Pas-de-Calais, France, 67,568.
Historic town, fortified, and possesses an important embarkation port; manufactures tulles and laces. It was an objective point (never reached) of extensive German offensive operations during the World War.
–Washington Co., Maine, 5,470.
On Me. Cen. (R. R.).
Head of navigation; lumber, shoes, ships, cotton and plaster are the chief manufactures; the Calais Academy is located here.
Calape, Bohol Prov., Bohol, P. I., 18,391.
Calasiao, Luzon, P. I., 16,438.
Manufactures of hats and woolen fabrics.
Calatayud, Saragossa, Spain, 12,001.
Calbayog, Prov. of Samar, Samar, P. I., 25,415.
Center of timber and coconut region.
Calcutta, capital of Prov. of Bengal, British India, 1,193,651.
The largest city of India. Calcutta was until December, 1911, the capital of India when Delhi was made the capital. Calcutta is located on an arm of the Ganges, and, until surpassed by Bombay, was the chief commercial center of India. The port is deep enough to admit large steamers. A system of underground drainage and excellent water supply have done much for sanitary conditions.
The European quarter is called the "City of Palaces," from the number of fine edifices it contains. The most interesting of these are the Government offices, the mint, and the custom-house. The Bishop's College, schools of mining and engineering, an Indian museum, a university and a botanical garden may be noted as the leading educational establishments. Calcutta is also the seat of the Bengal branch of the Asiatic Society and other learned societies. Near the river lies Fort William, the largest fortress in India. The native portion of the town is mostly built of mud or bamboo, and is called "Black Town."
The principal exports consist of opium, rice, indigo, cotton, tea, lumber, and hides, while the chief imports are linen, silks, hardware, liquors, and salt. There are many native manufactures.
Caldwell, c. s., Canyon Co., Idaho, 4,974.
On Ore. Short Line (R. R.).
–Sumner Co., Kans., 2,087
On Atch., Top. & Santa Fe; Chi., Rk. Isl. & Pac. (R. Rs.).
–Essex Co., N. J., 5,144.
On Erie (R. R.).
Residential, no manufacturing.
–c. s., Noble Co., Ohio, 1,778.
On Penna. (R. R.).
–c. s., Burleson Co., Texas, 1,724.
On Gulf, Colo. & Santa Fe; Tex. & N. Orl. (R. Rs.).
Caledonia, c. s., Houston Co., Minn., 1,554.
On Chi., Mil., St. P. & Pac. (R. R.).

–Livingston Co., N. Y., 1,487.
On Erie; Genesee & Wyoming; Leh. Val.; N. York Cen. (R. Rs.).
–Marion Co., Ohio, 526.
On Cle., Cin., Chi. & St. Lou.; Erie (R. Rs.).
–Ontario, Canada, 1,396.
On Can. Nat. (R. R.).
CALERA, Shelby Co., Ala., 975.
On Lou. & Nash.; Sou. (R. Rs.).
–(Sterrett), Bryan Co., Okla., 503.
On Mo.-Kan.-Tex. (R. R.).
CALEXICO, Imperial Co., Cal., 6,299.
On Inter.-Calif.; Sou. Pac. (R. Rs.).
CALGARY, Alberta, Canada, 83,407.
On Can. Nat.; Can. Pac. (R. Rs.).
Center of a large cattle trade; grain shipping point, very rapid growth.
CALHOUN, Lowndes Co., Ala., 1,000.
On Lou. & Nash. (R. Rs.).
–c. s., Gordon Co., Ga., 2,371.
On Nashv., Chatt. & St. Lou. (R. R.).
–c. s., McLean Co., Ky., 683.
–Henry Co., Mo., 501.
On Mo.-Kan.-Tex. (R. R.).
–Pickens Co., S. C., 816.
On Southern (R. R.).
CALHOUN CITY, Calhoun Co., Miss., 1,012.
On Okol., Houst. & Calh. Cy. (R. R.).

COURTESY OF THE INDIA STATE RAILWAYS

THE VICTORIA MEMORIAL, CALCUTTA, ONE OF THE FINEST BUILDINGS IN THE EAST, USED AS A MUSEUM OF EUROPEAN LIFE IN INDIA

CALHOUN FALLS, Abbeville Co., S. C., 1,759.
On Charl. & W. Car.; Seab. Air Line (R. Rs.).
CALI, Dept. del Valle, Colombia, 131,291.
A commercial center for a large region.
CALICO ROCK, Izard Co., Ark., 659.
On Mo. Pac. (R. R.).
CALICUT, capital of Malabar, Madras, India, 99,273.
A seaport and commercial center.
CALIENTE, Lincoln Co., Nev., 1,026.
On Los Ang. & Salt L. (R. R.).
CALIFON, Hunterdon Co., N. J., 534.
On Cen. of N. Jer. (R. R.).
CALIFORNIA, c. s., Moniteau Co., Mo., 2,384.
On Mo. Pac. (R. R.).
–Hamilton Co., Ohio, 1,000.
–Washington Co., Pa., 2,362.
On Penna. (R. R.).
CALION, Union Co., Ark., 924.
On Chi., Rk. Isl. & Pac. (R. R.).
CALIPATRIA, Imperial Co., Cal., 1,554.
On Sou. Pac. (R. R.).
CALISTOGA, Napa Co., Cal., 1,000.
On San Fran., Napa & Cal. (El.); Sou. Pac. (R. Rs.).
CALIVO, Capiz Dept., Panay, P. I., 13,985.
CALL, Newton Co., Tex., 997.
On Orange & Northw. (R. R.).
CALLAHAN, Nassau Co., Fla., 615.
On Atl. Coast Line; Seab. Air Line (R. Rs.).
CALLAO, Macon Co., Mo., 468.
On Chi., Burl. & Quincy (R. R.).
–Province of Callao, Peru, 75,000.
The seaport for Lima.
CALLAWAY, Custer Co., Neb., 833.
On Un. Pac. (R. R.).
CALLICOON, Sullivan Co., N. Y., 850.
On Erie (R. R.).
CALMAR, Winneshiek Co., Iowa, 915.
On Chi., Mil., St. P. & Pac. (R. R.).
CALOLBON, Prov. of Albay, Luzon, P. I., 8,955.
CALOTO, Dept. del Cuaca, Colombia, 8,907.
CALPINE, Sierra Co., Calif., 600.
On West. Pac. (R. R.).
CALTAGIRONE, Sicily, Italy, 30,805.
Majolica potteries.
CALTANISSETTA, Prov. of Caltanissetta, Italy, 35,200.
Center of sulphur industry.
CALUMET, Houghton Co., Mich., 1,557.
On Cop. Rge.; Min. Rge. (R. Rs.), connecting with Chi., Mil., St. P. & Pac. system.
Metropolis of Michigan's copper district.
–Itasca Co., Minn., 805.
On Dul., Missabe & Nor.; Gt. Nor. (R. Rs.).
CALUMET CITY, Cook Co., Ill., 12,298.
On Balt. & Ohio Chi. Term.; Ind. Harb. Blt. (R. Rs.).
A suburb of Chicago. Residential and manufacturing.
CALUMET PARK, Cook Co., Ill., 1,429.
On Ind. Harb. Blt.; Mich. Cen.; Penna. (R. Rs.).
CALUMPIT, Bulacan Prov., Luzon, P. I., 14,502.
Center of fertile farming district.
CALVERT, Robertson Co., Texas, 2,103.
On Tex. & N. Orl. (R. R.).
CALVIN, Hughes Co., Okla., 626.
On Chi., Rk. Isl. & Pac.; Kan., Okla. & Gulf (R. Rs.).
CALVINIA, Cape of Good Hope, Un. of S. Africa, 2,000.
CALYPSO, Duplin Co., N. C., 538.
On Atl. Coast Line (R. R.).
CAMAGUEY, (Puerto Principe), Puerto Principe Prov., Cuba, 133,309.
Trade center of a stock-raising district.
CAMAJUANI, Santa Clara Prov., Cuba, 7,628.
CAMALIG, Albay Prov., Luzon, P. I., 19,772.
CAMANCHE, Clinton Co., Iowa, 728.
On Chi., Burl. & Quincy; Chi., Mil., St. P. & Pac.; Clin., Davenp. & Musc. (El.); Davenp., Rk. Isl. & Northw.; Chi., Rk. Isl. & Pac. (R. Rs.).
CAMAS, Clark Co., Wash., 4,239.
On Spok., Port. & Seattle (R. R.).
CAMBAY, capital of Prov. of Cambay, British India, 31,877.
Famous for stone-cutting.
CAMBRAI, Dept. of Nord, France, 29,655.
Fortified town, famous before the Great War for its manufacture of linen fabrics called cambric. On August 26, 1914, the Allies retreated from Cambrai following the defeat of the Belgians at Namur, of the British at Mons and the French at Charleroi. The town remained in German hands until the final stage of the war, and was almost destroyed in the frequent conflicts which took place in the vicinity. It was retaken by British and Canadian troops in the Cambrai-St. Quentin Battle, August 26-October 5, 1918.
CAMBRIA, San Luis Obispo Co., Calif., 500.
–(Reeves), Williamson Co., Ill., 815.
On Ill. Cen. (R. R.).
–Montgomery Co., Va., 673.
R. R. name Christiansburg, Va.
–Columbia Co., Wisc., 671.
On Chi., Mil., St. P. & Pac. (R. R.).
CAMBRIDGE, Cambridgeshire, England, 66,803.
Seat of Cambridge University. While less picturesque than Oxford, Cambridge possesses a great beauty in its college buildings and its lawns and gardens, traversed by the river Cam. Some notable buildings of Cambridge are St. Mary's, Trinity, St. Sepulchre's, and St. Clement's churches. The chief interest in the town centers in Cambridge University, founded in the Middle Ages, and consisting of 19 colleges. Among these are Peterhouse (1284), Pembroke (1347), Corpus Christi (1352), King's (1440), and Trinity, St. John's, Magdalen, Caius, Jesus, and Christ's. The university library contains over 600,000 volumes, and the students number about 5,000. Girton and Newnham are associated colleges for women. Cambridge is a very ancient town. In 1200 King John granted the town a charter.
–c. s., Henry Co., Ill., 1,355.
On Chi., Rk. Isl. & Pac. (R. R.).
–Story Co., Iowa, 639.
On Chi., Mil., St. P. & Pac.; Chi., Rk. Isl. & Pac. (R. Rs.).
–c. s., Dorchester Co., Md., 8,544.
On Penna. (R. R.).
–c. s., Middlesex Co., Mass., 118,075.
On Boston & Albany, Boston & Maine (R. Rs.). Is on the Charles River opposite Boston, with which it is connected by several bridges. It comprises Old Cambridge, the seat of Harvard University; North Cambridge, East Cambridge, Cambridgeport, and Mount Auburn. The streets are broad and shaded with elms, and there are many places of historical and literary interest, among these the Craigie House and Elmwood, the homes of Longfellow and Lowell, and Mount Auburn Cemetery, containing the graves of Longfellow, Lowell, Prescott, Motley, Agassiz, Holmes, and other noted men. A principal distinction of Cambridge is Harvard University, the oldest university in the United States, which includes, besides Harvard College, the Bussey Institution (agriculture), the Peabody Museum, the Agassiz Museum, the schools of law, medicine, theology, and dental science. Radcliffe College for Women is connected with the university. Another famous educational institution is the Massachusetts Institute of Technology.
Among Cambridge's industrial establishments are foundries, machine shops, and other extensive manufactories. The Riverside, Athenaeum, and University Presses are well-known printing establishments, and the "Bay Psalm Book," the first book printed in America, was published in Cambridge in 1640.
Cambridge was settled in 1630 by Governor Winthrop. It was called Newtowne. In 1636 Harvard College was founded at Newtowne, and in 1638 Newtowne became Cambridge.
–c. s., Isanti Co., Minn., 1,183.
On Gt. Nor. (R. R.).
–Furnas Co., Neb., 1,203.
On Chi., Burl. & Quincy (R. R.).
–Washington Co., N. Y., 1,762.
On Del. & Hud. (R. R.).
–c. s., Guernsey Co., Ohio, 16,129.
Manufactures of iron, steel, tin, glass and pottery.
On Balt. & Ohio; Penna. (R. Rs.).
Adjacent to some of the largest coal mines in Ohio.
–Dane Co., Wis., 500.
CAMBRIDGE CITY, Wayne Co., Ind., 2,113.
On Ind. R. R. Sys. (El.); N. York, Chi. & St. Lou.; Penna. (R. Rs.).
CAMBRIDGE SPRINGS, Crawford Co., Pa., 1,665.
On Erie (R. R.).
CAMDEN, c. s., Wilcox Co., Ala., 697
On Lou. & Nash. (R. R.).
–c. s., Ouachita Co., Ark., 7,273.
On Chi., Rk. Isl. & Pac.; Mo. Pac.; St. Lou. Southw. (R. Rs.).
Center of an oil field, timber areas and lignite deposits.
–Carroll Co., Ind., 538.
On Penna. (R. R.).
–Knox Co., Maine, 3,000.
Summer resort.
–c. s., Camden Co., N. J., 118,700.
Port of entry, is situated on the Delaware River, opposite Philadelphia, and is the terminus of important railroads—the Pennsylvania-Reading Seashore; and the Pennsylvania lines. Chartered as a city in 1828. An important shipping and manufacturing center. The city's industries are widely diversified and include the most important in the country, some of them the largest of their kind. In the shipbuilding plants on the river front, some of the largest United States battleships have been built. The city is pre-eminent in the manufacture of pens, soaps, talking machines, automobile supplies, electrical equipment, licorice, paper boxes, steam-heating systems, radios, oil cloth and linoleum, and leather.
–Oneida Co., N. Y., 1,912.
On Leh. Val.; N. York Cen. (R. Rs.).
–Preble Co., Ohio, 888.
On Penna. (R. R.).
–c. s., Kershaw Co., S. C., 5,183.
On. Northw. of So. Car.; Seab. Air Line; Sou. (R. Rs.).
–c. s., Benton Co., Tenn., 955.
On the Nash., Chatt. & St. Lou. (R. R.).
–Polk Co., Tex., 1,000.
On Mosc., Cam. & San Aug. (R. R.).
CAMERON, Huerfano Co., Colo., 500.
On Colo. & Sou. (R. R.).
–Clinton and De Kalb Cos., Mo., 3,507.
On Chi., Burl. & Quincy; Chi., Rk. Isl. & Pac. (R. Rs.).
–Calhoun Co., S. C., 620.
On the Atl. Coast Line (R. R.).
–c. s., Milam Co., Texas, 4,565.
On Gulf, Colo. & Santa Fe; Tex. & N. Orl. (R. Rs.).
–Marshall Co., W. Va., 2,281.
On Balt. & Ohio (R. R.).
–Barron Co., Wis., 760.
On Chi., St. P., Minn. & Oma.; Minn., St. P. & S. Ste. M. (R. Rs.).
CAMILING, Tarlac Prov., Luzon, P. I., 23,375.
A trade center. Rice, corn, sugar, timber.
CAMILLA, c. s., Mitchell Co., Ga., 2,025.
On Atl. Coast Line; Ga., Ashb., Sylv. & Cam. (R. Rs.).
CAMILLUS, Onondaga Co., N. Y., 1,036.
On N. York Cen. (R. R.).
CAMINO, Eldorado Co., Calif., 516.
On Cam., Placerv. & L. Tahoe (R. R.).
CAMPAIGN, Warren Co., Tenn., 600.
On Nash., Chatt. & St. Lou.; Nash. & Atl. (R. Rs.).
CAMPBELL, Santa Clara Co., Calif., 1,800.
On Sou. Pac. (R. R.).
–Dunklin Co., Mo., 1,592.
On St. Lou.-San Fran.; St. Lou. Southw. (R. Rs.).
–Franklin Co., Neb., 565.
On Chi., Burl. & Quincy. (R. R.).
–Mahoning Co., Ohio, 14,673.
On Balt. & Ohio (R. R.).
CAMPBELLFORD, Northumberland Co., Ontario, Canada, 2,722.
On Can. Nat. (R. R.).
CAMPBELLSBURG, Washington Co., Ind., 558.
On Chi., Ind. & Lou. (R. R.).
CAMPBELLSPORT, Fond du Lac Co., Wis., 789.
On Chi. & Nor. West. (R. R.).
CAMPBELLSVILLE, c. s., Taylor Co., Ky., 1,923.
On Lou. & Nash. (R. R.).
CAMPBELLTON, Restigouche Co., New Brunswick, Canada, 6,505.
CAMPBELLTOWN, Lebanon Co., Pa., 500.
CAMPECHE, capital of Campeche State, Mexico, 20,125.
On United Railroads of Yucatan.
CAMPECHUELA, Prov. of Santiago, Cuba, 4,817.
CAMP HILL, Tallapoosa Co., Ala., 1,131.
On Cen. of Ga. (R. R.).
–Cumberland Co., Pa., 3,111.
On Penna.-Read. (R. Rs.).
CAMPINAS, São Paulo, Brazil, 166,324.
Commercial center of a coffee-growing district.
CAMPOBASSO, Campobasso Prov., Italy, 18,000.
Manufactures of arms and cutlery.
CAMPOS, State of Rio de Janeiro, Brazil, 225,191.
A trade center in a sugar producing region.
CAMP POINT, Adams Co., Ill., 1,000.
On Chi., Burl. & Quincy (R. R.).
CAMP SEVIER, Greenville Co., S. C., 1,000.
On Southern (R. R.).
CAMPTI, Natchitoches Parish, La., 999.
On La. & Ark. (R. R.).
CAMPWOOD, Real Co., Tex., 800.
On Uvalde & Nor. (R. R.).
CAMROSE, Alberta, Canada, 2,263.
CAMUY, Mun. of Camuy, Puerto Rico, 2,098.
CANAAN, Litchfield Co., Conn., 1,500.
On N. York, N. Hav. & Hart. (R. R.).
–Grafton Co., N. H., 500.
On Bost. & Me. (R. R.).
CANADIAN, c. s., Hemphill Co., Texas, 2,068.
On Panh. & Santa Fe (R. R.).
CANAJOHARIE, Montgomery Co., N. Y., 2,519.
On West Shore (R. R.).
CANAL FULTON, Stark Co., Ohio, 1,160.
On Balt. & Ohio; Penna. (R. Rs.).
CANAL POINT, Palm Beach Co., Fla., 926.
On Fla. East Coast (R. R.).
CANAL WINCHESTER, Franklin Co., Ohio, 906.
On Chesa. & Ohio (R. R.).
CANANDAIGUA, c. s., Ontario Co., N. Y., 7,541.
On N. York Cen.; Penna. (R. Rs.).
CANASERAGA, Allegany Co., N. Y., 620.
On Erie; Pitts., Shawmut & Nor. (R. Rs.).
CANASTOTA, Madison Co., N. Y., 4,235.
On Leh. Val.; N. York Cen.; West Shore (R. Rs.).
CANBERRA, capital of Australia, 7,535.
Established as seat of the Government in 1900.
CANBY, Yellow Medicine Co., Minn., 1,738.
On Chi. & Nor. West. (R. R.).
–Clackamas Co., Oregon, 744.
On Sou. Pac. (R. R.).
CANDIA, Greece. See ERAKLEION.
CANDIJAY, Prov. of Bohol, Bohol, P. I., 8,361.
CANDO, c. s., Towner Co., N. Dak., 1,164.
On Gt. Nor. (R. R.).
CANDON, Ilocos Sur Prov., Luzon, P. I., 19,950.
Trade center in a rice and tobacco region.
CANDOR, Tioga Co., N. Y., 669.
On Del., Lack. & West. (R. R.).
CANEA, Greece, See KHANIA.
CANEBRAKE, McDowell Co., W. Va., 521.
On Norf. & West. (R. R.).
CANETE, Prov. of Arauco, Chile, 2,181.
CANEY, Montgomery Co., Kans., 2,623.
On Atch., Top. & Santa Fe; Mo. Pac. (R. Rs.).
CANFIELD, Mahoning Co., Ohio, 1,015.
On Erie (R. R.).
CANISTEO, Steuben Co., N. Y., 2,548.
On Erie; N. York & Penna. (R. Rs.).
CANISTOTA, McCook Co., South Dakota, 611
On Chi. & Nor. West. (R. R.).
CANJILON, Rio Arriba, N. Mex., 644.

Cannelton, c. s., Perry Co., Ind., 2,265.
On Southern (R. R.).
–Fayette Co., W. Va., 521.
Cannes, Dept. of Alpes-Maritimes, France, 49,032.
Famous winter resort.
Cannington, Ontario Co., Ontario, Canada, 779.
On Can. Nat. (R. R.).
Cannon City, Rice Co., Minn., 931.
Cannon Falls, Goodhue Co., Minn., 1,358.
On Chi. Gt. West.; Chi., Mil., St. P. & Pac. (R. Rs.).
Cannstadt, Württemburg, Germany, united with Stuttgart.
Canoe, Escambia Co., Ala., 500.
On Lou. & Nash. (R. R.).
Canon, Hart and Franklin Cos., Georgia, 568.
On Southern (R. R.).
Canon City, c. s., Fremont Co., Colo., 5,938.
On Atch., Top. & Santa Fe; Den. & Rio Gde. West. (R. Rs.).
Agricultural center in Rocky Mountains, developing industrially coal and oil fields are in the vicinity, and mineral springs. Seat of State Penitentiary.
Canonsburg, Washington Co., Pa., 12,558.
On Penna. (R. R.).
In a rich farming region. Principal manufactures: steel, tin products, pottery, and novelties.
Canora, Saskatchewan, Canada, 1,179.
Canosa, Bari Prov., Italy, 26,172.
Canterbury, Kent, England, 24,450.
Is the ecclesiastical metropolis of England. The chief object of interest of the town is the famous Canterbury Cathedral, erected between the eleventh and fifteenth centuries. It is of Gothic architecture, is 545 feet long and 156 feet across the transept. Here is the chapel of the Holy Trinity where is the shrine of Thomas à Becket placed on the spot of his martyrdom. There are many interesting monuments, cloisters, a chapter house, a deanery, and libraries connected with the cathedral. Canterbury has a number of other ancient churches, and old Chequers Inn contains what is left of the Inn of Chaucer's "Canterbury Tales."
Canterbury was the Roman Durovernum and the Saxon Cantervarough (burg of the men of Kent). After the martyrdom of Thomas à Becket it became notable for pilgrimages.
–Windham Co., Conn., 500.
On N. York, N. Hav. & Hart. (R. R.).
Canthe, Fr. Indochina, 36,000.
Canton, capital of Prov. of Wangtung, 861,000.
Is a great commercial city, located on the Si Kiang (River), about 80 miles from its debouchment into the China Sea. Silk manufacture is an important industry, while cotton goods, embroideries, paper, and porcelain are also manufactured. The foreign trade is mostly carried on by English, American and German commercial houses.
–c. s., Cherokee Co., Ga., 2,892.
On Lou. & Nash (R. R.).
–Fulton Co., Ill., 11,718.
On Chi., Burl. & Quincy; Tol., Peor. & West. (R. Rs.).
Center of agricultural and coal section.
–McPherson Co., Kans., 928.
On Atch., Top. & Santa Fe; Chi., Rk. Isl. & Pac. (R. Rs.).
–Norfolk Co., Mass., 6,505.
On N. York, N. Hav. & Hart. (R. R.).
–c. s., Madison Co., Miss., 4,725.
On Cant. & Carth.; Ill. Cen. (R. Rs.).
–Lewis Co., Mo., 2,044.
On Chi., Burl. & Quincy (R.R.).
–c. s., St. Lawrence Co., N. Y., 2,822.
On N. York Cen. (R. R.).
–Haywood Co., N. C., 5,117.
On Southern (R. R.).
–c. s., Stark Co., Ohio, 104,906.
On Balt. & Ohio; Penna.; Wheel. & L. Erie (R. Rs.).
An important industrial point of Northeastern Ohio. Has large plants of the International Harvester Company, many cigar factories, machine shops and foundries. Near coal mines.
–Blaine Co., Okla., 797.
On Atch., Top. & Santa Fe (R. R.).
–Bradford Co., Pa., 1,904.
On Penna. (R. R.).
–c. s., Lincoln Co., S. Dak., 2,542.
On Chi., Mil., St. P. & Pac. (R. R.).
–Van Zandt Co., Texas, 704.
Canutillo, El Paso Co., Tex., 700.
On Atch., Top. & Santa Fe (R. R.).
Canyon, c. s., Randall Co., Texas, 2,821.
On Panh. & Santa Fe (R. R.).
Capac, St. Clair Co., Mich., 837.
On Gd. Tr. (R. R.).
Capannori, Prov. of Lucca, Italy, 895.
Cape Charles, Northampton Co., Va., 2,527.
On Penna. (R. R.).
Cape Coast, Gold Coast, West Africa, 17,685.
Cape Girardeau, Cape Girardeau Co., Mo., 16,227.
On the Mississippi River, and on Mo. Pac.; St. Lou.-San Fran. (R. Rs.).
Manufactures of shoes, cement, machinery, rock products, and wood products. Center of an important agricultural district.
Cape May, Cape May Co., N. J., 2,637.
On Penna.-Read. Seashore (R. R.).
Seashore resort and naval station.
Cape Porpoise, York Co., Me., 650.
Capetown, legislative seat of the Union of South Africa (British), 352,000.
Is situated 30 miles north of the Cape of Good Hope. It is a modern town, and possesses a government house, a museum, library, Roman Catholic cathedral, Mohammedan mosques, and the University of Capetown, which is located at Groote Schuur, once the home of Cecil Rhodes.
The entrance to the harbor is protected by a military castle, and has been improved by a long breakwater. The commerce of Capetown is important, and the city is the terminus of several railways.
Capetown was founded in 1652 by the Dutch, and was in their possession until 1806, when it was taken by the English. It lies at the foot of Table Mountain, 3,816 feet high.
Capetown is also a hot season (October to March) pleasure resort for South Africa.
Cape Vincent, Jefferson Co., N. Y., 898.
On N. Y. Cen. (R. R.).
Cap Haitien, Haiti, 20,000.
Capistrano, Orange Co., Calif., 1,200.
On Atch., Top. & Santa Fe (R. R.).
Capitol Heights, Prince Georges Co., Md., 1,611.
Capiz, Panay, P. I., 21,996.
Trade center in a rice and sugar-growing district.
Caples, McDowell Co., W. Va., 800.
Norf. & West. (R. R.).
Capodistria, Pola, Italy, 8,192.
Capps, Huerfano Co., Colo., 800.
On Den. & Rio Gde. West. (R. R.).
Capreol, Ontario, Canada, 1,684.
Capron, Boone Co., Ill., 397.
On Chi. & Nor. West. (R. R.).
–Oneida Co., N. Y., 616.
Capua, Prov. of Napoli, Italy, 9,832.
Caracas, capital of Federal Dist. and of Venezuela, 202,342.
Is situated 6 miles south of its port of La Guaira, at an elevation of 4,017 feet.
The city is an export center of petroleum, cacao, coffee, and tobacco.
Caraguatay, Caraguatay, Paraguay, 11,722.
Caramoan, Prov. of Ambos-Camarines, Luzon, P. I., 13,167.
Carapegua, Paraguay, 17,387.
Situated in fertile farming region.
Caratinga, Minas Geraes, Brazil, 137,017.
Trade center in a mining region.
Caravaca, Murcia Prov., Spain, 18,753.
Iron works, tanneries, paper and chocolate factories.
Carberry, Portage la Prairie Co., Manitoba, Canada, 807.
On Can. Nat.; Can. Pac. (R. Rs.).
Carbon, Eastland Co., Texas, 463.
On Mo.-Kans.-Tex. of Texas (R. R.).
–Pittsburgh Co., Okla., 510.
On Mo.-Kans.-Tex. (R. R.).
Carbondale, Jackson Co., Ill., 7,528.
On Ill. Cen. (R. R.).
Seat of Southern Illinois Normal University.
–Athens Co., Ohio, 600.
On Balt. & Ohio (R. R.).
–Lackawanna Co., Pa., 20,061.
On Del. & Hud.; Erie; N. York, Ont. & West. (R. Rs.).
Coal center. Has large machine shops.
Carbon Hill, Walker Co., Ala., 2,519.
On St. Lou.-San Fran. (R. R.).
Carcajente, Valencia, Spain, 13,834.
Agricultural products, silk and linen factories.
Carcar, Cebu Prov., Cebu, P. I., 37,401.
A market community.
Carcassonne, Dept. of Aude, France, 33,441.
Important wine market. Cooperage, cork, and canning industries.
Cardale, Fayette Co., Pa., 750.
Cardenas, Matanzas Prov., Cuba, 29,304.
Sugar exporting center.
Cardiff, Glamorganshire, Wales, 223,648.
Seat of the University of South Wales; great shipping point for coal.
–Cambria Co., Pa., 500.
On Camb. & Ind. (R. R.).
Cardinal, Grenville Co., Ontario, Canada, 1,319.
On Can. Nat. (R. R.).
Cardington, Morrow Co., Ohio, 1,192.
On Cle., Cin., Chi. & St. Lou. (R. R.).
Cardston, Alberta Co., Alberta, Canada, 1,711.
On Can. Pac. (R. R.).
Cardwell, Dunklin Co., Mo., 861.
On St. Lou. Southw. (R. R.).
Carencro, Lafayette Parish, La., 684.
Tex. & N. Orl. (R. R.).
Caretta, McDowell Co., W. Va., 575.
Carey, Wyandot Co., Ohio, 2,722.
On Chesa. & Ohio; Cle., Cin., Chi. & St. Lou.; Nor. Ohio (R. Rs.).
Caribou, Aroostook Co., Maine, 8,500.
On Bangor & Aroostook; Can. Pac. (R. Rs.).
Carigara, Leyte, P. I., 17,709.
Principal exports: abaca, rice, corn, and cotton fabrics.
Carleton, Monroe Co., Mich., 837.
On Det., Tol. & Iron.; Penna.; Pere Marq. (R. Rs.).
Carleton Place, Lanark Co., Ontario, Canada, 4,105.
Carlin, Elko Co., Nev., 825.
On Sou. Pac.; West. Pac. (R. Rs.).
Carlinville, c. s., Macoupin Co., Ill., 4,144.
On Alton; Ill. Term. (El.) (R. Rs.).
Carlisle, Lonoke Co., Ark., 907.
On Chi., Rk. Isl. & Pac. (R. R.).
–c. s., Cumberland, England, 57,107.
Stands at the confluence of three rivers.
Its most celebrated edifice is a cathedral founded by William Rufus. An old castle, founded in 1092, in which Mary Queen of Scots was once imprisoned, is still preserved. Carlisle was a Roman town by the name of Luguvallum, later the British Caerluel, whence Carlisle.
–Sullivan Co., Ind., 852.
On Chi. & East. Ill. (R. R.).
–Warren Co., Iowa, 663.
On Chi., Rk. Isl. & Pac. (R. R.).
–c. s., Nicholas Co., Ky., 1,469.
On Lou. & Nash. (R. R.).
–Middlesex Co., Mass., 569.
On N. York, N. Hav. & Hart. (R. R.).
–c. s., Cumberland Co., Pa., 12,596.
On Penna.; Read. (R. Rs.).
Seat of Dickinson College. Notable in revolutionary times as a military center, and the first town named after Washington. It was the prison of Major André, the home of Molly Pitcher and the first West Point.
–Rusk Co., Tex., 1,000.
–Trinity Co., Tex., 519.
On Waco, Beau., Trin. & Sab. (R. R.).
Carl Junction, Jasper Co., Mo., 1,042.
On Jop.-Pitts. (El.); St. Lou.-San Fran. (R. Rs.).
Carlos, Allegany co., Md., 515.
Carlsbad, Germany. See Karlsbad.
–c. s., Eddy Co., N. Mex., 3,708.
On Atch., Top. & Santa Fe (R. R.).
Adjacent to extensive farming country under irrigation, principally for cotton.
Carlsruhe, Germany. See Karlsruhe.
Carlstadt, Bergen Co., N. J., 5,425.
On N. Jer. & N. York (R. R.).
Carlton, c. s., Carlton Co., Minn., 687.
On Chi., Mil., St. P. & Pac.; Gt. Nor.; Nor. Pac. (R. Rs.).
–Yamhill Co., Ore., 749.
On Carl. & Coast; Sou. Pac. (R. Rs.).
Carlton Hill, Bergen Co., N. J., 506.
On Erie (R. R.).
Carlyle, c. s., Clinton Co., Ill., 2,078.
On Balt. & Ohio (R. R.).
Carman, Macdonald Co., Manitoba, Canada, 1,418.
On Can. Nat.; Can. Pac. (R. Rs.).
–Schenectady Co., N. Y., 500.
Carmarthen, Carmathenshire, Wales, 10,310.
Iron smelters, printing shops, and tinplate works.
Carmel, Hamilton Co., Indiana, 682.
On Chi., Ind. & Lou.; Ind. R. R. Sys. (El.) (R. Rs.).
Carmel-by-the-Sea, Monterey Co., Cal., 2,260.
Carmen, Alfalfa Co., Okla., 904.
On Atch., Top. & Santa Fe; St. Lou.-San Fran. (R. Rs.).
Carmi, c. s., White Co., Ill., 2,932.
On Cle., Cin., Chi. & St. Lou.; Lou. & Nash. (R. Rs.).
Carmichael, Sacramento Co., Calif., 550.
Carmichaels, Greene Co., Pa., 708.
Carmine, Fayette Co., Tex., 500.
On Tex. & N. Orl. (R. R.).
Carnegie, Allegheny Co., Pa., 12,497.
On Penna.; Pitts., Chart. & Yough.; Pitts. & W. Va. (R. Rs.).
Center of Pittsburgh coal district.
–Caddo Co., Okla., 2,063.
On Chi., Rk. Isl. & Pac. (R. R.).
Carnforth, Lancashire, England, 3,193.
Carnot, Allegheny Co., Pa., 500.
Caro, c. s., Tuscola Co., Mich., 2,554.
On Det., Caro & Sand.; Mich. Cen. (R. Rs.).
Caroleen, Rutherford Co., N. C., 1,478.
On Seab. Air Line (R. R.).
Carolina, Mun. of Carolina, Puerto Rico, 5,214.
–Washington Co., R. I., 651.
–Marion Co., W. Va., 850.
On West. Md. (R. R.).
Carona, Cherokee Co., Kansas, 764.
On Mo. Pac.; Northe. Okla (El.) (R. Rs.).
Carouge, Geneva Canton, Switzerland, 8,073.
Carpentertown, Westmoreland Co., Pa., 518.
Carpentersville, Kane Co., Ill., 1,461.
On Chi. & Nor. West. (R. R.).
Carpi, Prov. of Modena, Italy, 11,272.
Carpinteria, Santa Barbara Co., Calif., 1,000.
On Sou. Pac. (R. R.).
Carrabelle, Franklin Co., Fla., 1,035.
On Seab. Air Line (R. R.).
Carrara, Prov. of Massa e Carrara, Italy, 23,951.
Famous for marble quarries and cutting and polishing of marble; academy of sculpture.
Carrboro, Orange Co., N. C., 1,242.
Carrick, Allegheny Co., Pa., 8,305.
Carrickfergus, County Antrim, No. Ireland, 4,608.
Carrier Mills, Saline Co., Ill., 2,140.
On Cle., Cin., Chi. & St. Lou. (R. R.).
Carrington, c. s., Foster Co., N. Dakota, 1,717.
On Minn., St. P. & S. Ste. M.; Nor. Pac. (R. Rs.).
Carrizo Springs, c. s., Dimmit Co., Texas, 2,171.
On San Ant., Uvalde & Gulf (R. R.).
Carrizozo, c. s., Lincoln Co., N. Mex., 1,171.
On Sou. Pac. (R. R.).
Carroll, c. s., Carroll Co., Iowa, 4,691.
On Chi. & Nor.; West. (R. Rs.).
Carrollton, c. s., Pickens Co., Ala., 569.
On Ala., Tenn. & Nor. (R. R.).
–c. s., Carroll Co., Ga., 5,052.
On Cen. of Ga. (R. R.).
–c. s., Green Co., Ill., 2,075.
On Alton (R. R.).
–c. s., Carroll Co., Ky., 2,409.
On Carrollton (R. R.).
–Saginaw Co., Mich., 1,200.
On Gd. Tr.; Pere Marq. (R. Rs.).
–c. s., Carroll Co., Miss., 523.
On Columbus & Greenville (R. R.).
–c. s., Carroll Co., Mo., 4,058.
On Atch., Top. & Santa Fe; Chi., Burl. & Quincy; Wab. (R. Rs.).
–c. s., Carroll Co., Ohio, 2,286.
On Wheel. & L. Erie (R. R.).
–Dallas Co., Texas, 689.
On Mo.-Kan.-Tex. of Tex.; St. Lou.-San Fran.; St. Lou., Southw. (R. Rs.).
Carrolltown, Cambria Co., Pa., 1,227.
On N. York Cen. (R. R.).
Carrollville, Milwaukee Co., Wis., 1,220.
On Chi. & Nor. West.; Mil. Elec. (R. Rs.).
Carson, Mississippi Co., Ark., 1,500.
–Pottawattamie Co., Iowa, 617.
On Chi., Burl. & Quincy; Chi., Rk. Isl. & Pac. (R. Rs.).
Carson City, Montcalm Co., Mich., 972.
On Gd. Tr. (R. R.).
–c. s., Ormsby Co., Nev., 1,596.
State capital. Is on the Virginia and Truckee Railroad, west of Carson River, and situated in a plain surrounded by rugged mountains, some of them snow-capped during the entire year. It contains the Capitol, Federal Building, a United States mint, a State prison (in the quarries of which fossil footprints of gigantic animals have been found), and Government Indian school. Gold and silver are found in the vicinity, as well as valuable hot springs. Carson City is mainly engaged in mining lumbering, and agriculture. It was founded in 1858.
Carson Lake, St. Louis Co., Minn., 1,200.
Cartagena, Murcia, Spain, 102,705.
Large port and principal naval base of Spain.
–Capital of Bolivar, Colombia, 98,851.
Important port. Exports raw products: minerals, timber, etc.
Cartago, Costa Rica, 14,161.
Carter, Beckham Co., Okla., 642.
On Mo.-Kan.-Tex. (R. R.).
Carteret (Roosevelt), Middlesex Co., N. J., 13,339.
On Cen. of N. Jer. (R. R.).
Industrial suburb of Elizabeth.
Cartersville, c. s., Bartow Co., Ga., 5,250.
On Lou. & Nash.; Nash., Chatt. & St. Lou.; Seab. Air Line (R. Rs.).
Carterville, Williamson Co., Ill., 2,866.
On Ill. Cen. (R. R.).
–Jasper Co., Mo., 1,600.
On Mo. Pac.; St. Lou.-San Fran.; Southw. Mo. (El.) (R. Rs.).
In zinc and lead mining district.
Carthage, Dallas Co., Arkansas, 558.
On Chi., Rk. Isl. & Pac. (R. R.).
–c. s., Hancock Co., Ill., 2,240.
On Chi., Burl. & Quincy; Wab. (R. Rs.).
–Rush Co., Ind., 931.
On Cle., Cin., Chi. & St. Lou. (R. R.).
–c. s., Leake Co., Miss., 998.
On Cant. & Carth. (R. R.).
–c. s., Jasper Co., Mo., 9,736.
On Mo. Pac.; St. Lou.-San Fran.; Southw. Mo. (El.) (R. Rs.).
Center of lead and zinc district. Manufactures of shoes, flour, etc. Quarries of Carthage marble.
–Jefferson Co., N. Y., 4,460.
On N. York Cen. (R. R.).
–c. s., Moore Co., N. C., 1,129.
On Moore Cen. (R. R.).
–Hamilton Co., Ohio (Annexed to Cincinnati since 1910.).
On Balt. & Ohio; Cle., Cin., Chi. & St. Lou.; Cin. Nor.; Erie (R. Rs.).
–Miner Co, S. Dak., 537.
On Chi. & Nor. West. (R. R.).
–c. s., Smith Co., Tenn., 1,068.
On Tenn. Cen. (R. R.).

–c. s., Panola Co., Texas, 1,651.
On Gulf, Colo. & Santa Fe (R. R.).
Carupano, Bermudez, Venezuela, 16,088.
Exports coffee, cocoa, sugar, cotton.
Caruthersville, c. s., Pemiscot Co., Mo., 4,781.
On St. Lou.-San Fran.; St. Lou. Southw. (R. Rs.).
Carver, Plymouth Co., Mass., 1,559.
Carverton, Luzerne Co., Pa., 500.
Cary, McHenry Co., Ill., 731.
On Chi. & Nor. West. (R. R.).
–Wake Co., N. C., 909.
On Seab. Air Line; Sou. (R. Rs.).
Caryville, Washington Co., Fla., 1,025.
On Lou. & Nash. (R. R.).
Casablanca, Prov. of Schavich, Morocco, 258,567.
One of the busiest ports in Northern Africa.
Casa Grande, Pinal Co., Arizona, 1,351.
On Sou. Pac. (R. R.).
Casale, Monferrato, Prov. of Alessandria, Italy, 22,700.
Trade center. Has cement factories.
Cascade, c. s., Valley Co., Idaho, 726.
On Ore. Short Line (R. R.).
–Dubuque and Jones Cos., Iowa, 1,221.
On Bellev. & Casc. (R. R.).
–Cascade Co., Mont., 520.
On Gt. Nor. (R. R.).
–Coos Co., N. H., 1,000.
On Gd. Tr. (R. R.).
Caserta, Prov. of Napoli, Italy, 21,637.
Educational center. Silk factories.
Casey, Clark Co., Ill., 2,200.
On Penna.; Westfield (R. Rs.).
–c. s., Adair and Guthrie Cos., Iowa, 785.
On Chi., Rk. Isl. & Pac. (R. R.).
Caseyville, St. Clair Co., Ill., 743.
On Balt. & Ohio; Penna. (R. Rs.).
Cashmere, Chelan Co., Washington, 1,473.
On Gt. Nor. (R. R.).
Cashton, Monroe Co., Wis., 680.
On Chi., Mil., St. P. & Pac. (R. R.).
Casino, New South Wales, Australia, 5,287.
Cason, Morris Co., Tex., 515.
On La., Ark. & Tex. (R. R.).
Casper, c. s., Natrona Co., Wyo., 16,619.
On Chi. & Nor. West.; Chi., Burl. & Quincy (R. Rs.).
Oil refineries. Wood shipping center.
Caspian, Iron Co., Mich., 1,888.
On Chi. & Nor. West. (R. R.).
Cass, Pocahontas Co., West Va., 708.
On Chesa. & Ohio (R. R.).
Cass City, Tuscola Co., Mich., 1,261.
On Gd. Tr. (R. R.).
Cassel, Germany. See Kassel.
Casselton, c. s., Cass Co., N. Dak., 1,253.
On Gt. Nor.; Nor. Pac. (R. Rs.).
Cass Lake, Cass Co., Minn., 1,409.
On Gt. Nor.; Minn., St. P. & S. Ste. M. (R. Rs.).
Cassopolis, c. s., Cass Co., Mich., 1,448.
On Gd. Tr.; Mich. Cen. (R. Rs.).
Cassville, c. s., Barry Co., Mo., 1,016.
On Cassville & Exeter (R. R.).
–(Fort Gay P. O.), Wayne Co., West Va., 850.
–Grant Co., Wis., 875.
On Chi., Burl. & Quincy (R. R.).
Castalia, Erie Co., Ohio, 800.
On Cle., Cin., Chi. & St. Lou.; N. York, Chi. & St. Lou.; Lake Shore (El.) (R. Rs.).
Castanea, Clinton Co., Pa., 725.
Castella, Shasta Co., Calif., 500.
On Sou. Pac. (R. R.).
Castellammare del Golfo, Prov. of Trapani, Italy, 15,746.
Castellammare di Stabia, Prov. of Napoli, Italy, 28,340.
Seaport and industrial center. Dockyards, ironworks, cotton, macaroni, and flour mills.
Castellon-de-la-Plana, Castellon Prov., Spain, 36,657.
Manufactures porcelain, leather, rope, paper, and clothing.
Castile, Wyoming Co., N. Y., 900.
On Erie (R. R.).
Castine, Hancock Co., Maine, 700.
Castle Dale, c. s., Emery Co., Utah, 713.
Castlegate, Carbon Co., Utah, 923.
On Den. & Rio Gde. West. (R. R.).
Castlehill, Aroostook Co., Maine, 75.
Castlemaine, Victoria, Australia, 5,221.
Castlerock, Cowlitz Co., Wash., 1,239.
On Gt. Nor.; Longv., Portl. & Nor.; Nor. Pac.; Ore.-Wash. R. R. & Nav. Co. (R. Rs.).
Castle Shannon, Allegheny Co., Pa., 3,810.
On Pitts. & W. Va. (R. R.).
Castleton, Derbyshire, England, 2,000.
Here stands the Peak Castle, erected by William Peveril, son of the Conqueror. See Scott's "Peveril of the Peak."
–Rutland Co., Vt., 500.
On Del. & Hud. (R. R.).
Castleton-on-Hudson, Rensselaer Co., N. Y., 1,506.
On N. York Cen. (R. R.).
Castletown, Isle of Man, 1,965.
Castlewood, Hamlin Co., S. Dak., 500.
On Chi. & Nor. West. (R. R.).
Castres, Dept. of Tarn, France, 29,133.
Textile center.
Castro del Rio, Prov. of Cordova, Spain, 11,930.
Castrogiovanni, Prov. of Caltanissetta, Sicily, 26,415.
Is chiefly celebrated for its old feudal citadels, the cathedral, founded in 1307, a castle built by Frederick II. of Aragon, a public library, and a museum.
Castronville, Medina Co., Tex., 865.
Castroville, Monterey Co., Calif., 600.
On Sou. Pac. (R. R.).
Caswell, Aroostook Co., Maine.
Catania, capital of Prov. of Catania, Sicily, 199,200.
Is situated at the foot of Mt. Etna. The town is very handsome in appearance, and has many fine buildings. The surrounding country, sometimes called the "granary of Italy," is very fertile, and produces grain, hemp, flax, silk, fruit, wine, and oil. There are also salt mines. The fisheries are extensive. Catania was founded by the Greeks about 729 B. C. Few cities have suffered so frequently from volcanic eruptions and earthquakes.
Cataño, Mun. of Bayamon, Puerto Rico, 6,845.
Catanzaro, Catanzaro Prov., Italy, 26,900.
Residential city.
Catarina, Dimmit Co., Tex., 592.
On Ash. & Gulf (R. R.).
Catasauqua, Lehigh Co., Pa., 4,851.
On Cen. of N. Jer.; Leh. & N. Eng.; Leh. Val.; Read. (R. Rs.).
Catawissa, Columbia Co., Pa., 2,023.
On Del., Lack. & West.; Penna.; Read. (R. Rs.).
Cateechee, Pickens Co., S. C., 800.
Cathlamet, c. s., Wahkiakum Co., Wash., 537.
Catlettsburg, c. s., Boyd Co., Ky., 5,025.
On Chesa. & Ohio (R. R.).
Catlin, Vermilion Co., Ill., 813.
On Wabash (R. R.).
Catsburg, Washington Co., Pa., 2,000.
Catskill, c. s., Greene Co., N. Y., 5,082.
On West Shore (R. R.).
Summer resort; in Rip Van Winkle country.
Cattaraugus, Cattaraugus Co., N. Y., 1,236.
On Erie (R. R.).
Caudéran, Gironde, France, 22,990.
Cauquenes, Maule Prov., Chile, 12,007.
Cava, Prov. of Salerno, Italy, 8,691.
Cavalier, c. s., Penbina Co., N. Dak., 850.
On Gt. Nor. (R. R.).
Cavalla, Greece. See Kavalla.
Cave City, Barren Co., Ky., 773.
On Lou. & Nash. (R. R.).
Cavendish, Windsor Co., Vt., 539.
On Rutland (R. R.).
Cave Spring, Floyd Co., Ga., 723.
On Southern (R. R.).
Cavite, Cavite Prov., Luzon, P. I., 22,163.
Cawker City, Mitchell Co., Kans., 780.
On Mo. Pac. (R. R.).
Cawnpore, capital of Dist. of Cawnpore, British India, 219,189.
Is situated on the Ganges, at the junction of the Jumna. Since 1888 it has been one of the principal railway centers of India. It has an active trade, due to its commercial facilities. Its manufactures include leather goods and cotton and jewelry. Is noted as the scene of a massacre of European residents during the Sepoy rebellion in 1857.
Cayce, Lexington Co., S. C., 1,267.
On Seab. Air Line; Sou. (R. Rs.).
Cayenne, capital of French Guiana, 10,744.
Seaport and chief commercial center of French Guiana. Modern town.
Cayey, Mun. of Cayey, Puerto Rico, 5,984.
Cayuga, Vermillion Co., Ind., 968.
On Chi. & East. Ill.; N. York, Chi. & St. Lou. (R. Rs.).
Cayuga Heights, Tompkins Co., N. Y., 507.
Cazenovia, Madison Co., N. Y., 1,788.
On Leh. Val. (R. R.).
Ceara, Brazil. See Fortaleza.
Cebu, Cebu, P. I., 141,000.
Port and thriving trade center for one of the most populous sections of the Philippines.
Cecil, Washington Co., Pa., 1,000.
On Penna.; Pitts. & W. Va. (R. Rs.).
Cecilia, Hardin Co., Ky., 500.
On Ill. Cen. (R. R.).
Cedar Bluff, Cherokee Co., Ala., 500.
On Southern (R. R.).
–Tazewell Co., Va., 590.
On Norf. & West. (R. R.).
Cedar Bluffs, Saunders Co., Neb., 517.
On Chi. & Nor. West. (R. R.).
Cedarburg, Ozaukee Co., Wis., 2,055.
On Chi., Mil., St. P. & Pac.; Mil. El. (R. Rs.).
Cedar City, Iron Co., Utah, 3,615.
On Los Ang. & Salt L. (R. R.).
Cedar Falls, Black Hawk Co., Iowa, 7,362.
On Chi. Gt. West.; Chi., Rk. Isl. & Pac.; Ill. Cen.; Waterl., Ced. Fs. & Nor. (R. Rs.).
Cedar Grove, Caddo Parish, La.
On Kan. Cy., Sou. (R. R.).
–Essex Co., N. J., 1,887.
Erie (R. R.).
–Kanawha Co., W. Va., 1,110.
On Kelly's Cr. & Northw.; N. York Cen. (R. Rs.).
–Sheyboygan Co., Wis., 814.
On Chi. & Nor. West.; Mil. Elec. (R. Rs.).
Cedar Hill, Robertson Co., Tenn., 800.
On Lou. & Nash. (R. R.).
Cedarhurst, Nassau Co., N. Y., 5,065.
On Long Isl. (R. R)
Cedar Keys, Levy Co., Fla., 1,012
Cedar Knolls, Morris Co., N. J., 650.
Cedar Lake, Lake Co., Ind., 500.
On Chi., Ind. & Lou. (R. R.).
Cedar Lodge, Davidson Co., N. C., 500.
On High Pt., Thomasv. & Dent. (R. R.).
Cedar Rapids, c. s., Linn Co., Iowa, 56,097.
Is located on the Ced. Rap. & Ia. Cy. (El.); Chi. & Nor. West.; Chi., Mil., St. P. & Pac.; Chi., Rk. Isl. & Pac.; the Illinois Central, and the Waterloo, Cedar Falls and Northern Railroads.
The city has extensive pork-packing industries. The manufactures include machinery, agricultural implements, carriages, cereal foods, furniture, and dairy supplies.
Cedar Rapids is the seat of Coe College, founded in 1881. The town was settled in 1845 and incorporated in 1856.
–Boone Co., Neb., 743.
On Un. Pac. (R. R.).
Cedar Springs, Kent Co., Mich., 1,104.
On Gd. Tr.; Penna. (R. Rs.).
Cedartown, c. s., Polk Co., Ga., 8,124.
On Cen. of Ga.; Seab. Air Line (R. Rs.).
Cedarvale, Chautauqua Co., Kans., 1,008.
On Atch., Top. & Santa Fe; Mo. Pac. (R. Rs.).
Cedarville, Cumberland Co., N. J., 1,500.
On Cen. of N. Jer. (R. R.).
–Greene Co., Ohio, 940.
On Penna. (R. R.).
Cefalu, Palermo Prov., Sicily, Italy, 10,799.
A seaport.
Cegléd, Hungary, 37,413.
Ceiba, Mun. of Ceiba, Puerto Rico, 1,627.
Celaya, Guanajuato, Mexico, 24,379.
On National of Mex. (R. R.).
Celeste, Hunt Co., Texas, 803.
On Gulf, Colo. & Santa Fe; Mo.-Kan.-Tex. of Tex. (R. Rs.).
Celina, c. s., Mercer Co., Ohio, 4,664.
On Cin. Nor.; N. York, Chi. & St. Lou. (R. Rs.).
–c. s., Clay Co., Tenn., 756.
–Collin Co., Texas, 948.
On St. Lou., San Fran. & Tex. (R. R.).
Celle, Hannover, Germany, 26,000.
Manufactures timber, leather, sugar, umbrellas, dyes, paper, and wax.
Celoron, Chautauqua Co., N. Y., 1,182.
Cement, Caddo Co., Okla., 1,117.
On St. Lou.-San Fran. (R. R.).
–Dallas Co., Texas, 609.
Cement City, Lenawee Co., Mich., 525.
On Cin. Nor.; N. York Cen. (R. Rs.).
Cementon, Greene Co., N. Y., 500.
On West Shore (R. R.).
–Lehigh Co., Pa., 2,030.
On Leh. Val. (R. R.).
Center, Saguache Co., Colorado, 1,011.
On San Luis Cen. (R. R.).
–Ralls Co., Mo., 516.
On St. Lou. & Han. (R. R.).
–Allegheny Co., Pa., 500.
–c. s., Shelby Co., Texas, 2,510.
On Gulf, Colo. & Santa Fe (R. R.).
Center Belpre, Washington Co., Ohio, 500.
Centerburg, Knox Co., Ohio, 761.
On N. York Cen.; Penna. (R. Rs.).
Centerfield, Sanpete Co., Utah, 554.
Center Hill, Sumter Co., Fla., 673.
On Atl. Coast Line; Seab. Air Line (R. Rs.).
–Fulton Co., Ga., 500.
Centerline, Macomb Co., Mich., 2,604.
On Mich. Cen. (R. R.).
Center Moriches, Suffolk Co., N. Y., 1,451.
On Long Isl. (R. R.).
Center Ossipee, Carroll Co., N. H., 500.
Center Point, Linn Co., Iowa, 812.
On Chi., Rk. Isl. & Pac.; Waterl., Ced. Fls. & Nor. (R. Rs.).
–Kerr Co., Tex., 500.
On Tex. & N. Orl. (R. R.).
Center Rutland, Rutland Co., Vt., 700.
On Clar. & Pittsf.; Del. & Hud.; Rut. (R. Rs.).
Center Sandwich, Carroll Co., N. H., 550.
Center Valley, Lehigh Co., Pa., 700.
On Reading (R. R.).
Centerville, c. s., Bibbs Co., Ala., 791.
On Mob. & Ohio (R.R.).
–Alameda Co., Calif., 1,700.
On Sou. Pac. (R. R.).
–Wayne Co., Ind., 993.
On Ind. R. R. Sys. (Elec.); Penna. (R. Rs.).
–c. s., Appanoose Co., Iowa, 8,147.
On Chi., Burl. & Quincy; Chi., Rk. Isl. & Pac.; Ia. Sou. Utilities (El.) (R. Rs.).
–c. s. (Centreville Sta.), Queen Annes Co., Md., 1,291.
On Balt. & East.; Penna. (R. Rs.).
–c. s., St. Joseph Co., Mich., 820.
On Mich. Cen. (R. R.).
–Silver Bow Co., Mont., 997.
–Washington Co., Pa., 6,467.
–Turner Co., S. Dak., 1,506.
On Chi. & Nor. West. (R. R.).
–c. s. (Centreville Sta.), Hickman Co., Tenn., 943.
On Nash., Chatt. & St. Lou. (R. R.).
–Davis Co., Utah, 670.
On Ore. Short Line (R. R.).
Central, Grant Co., N. Mex., 750.
–Pickens Co., S. C., 1,440.
On Sou. (R. R.).
Central City, c. s., Gilpin Co., Colo., 572.
In gold mining section.
–Marion Co., Ill., 1,148.
On Ill. Cen.; Mo.-Ill. (R. Rs.).
–Linn Co., Iowa, 780.
On Ill. Cen. (R. R.).
–Muhlenberg Co., Ky., 4,321.
On Ill. Cen.; Lou. & Nash. (R. Rs.).
–c. s., Merrick Co., Neb., 2,474.
On Chi., Burl. & Quincy; Un. Pac. (R. Rs.).
–Somerset Co., Pa., 2,107.
On Penna. (R. R.).
Central Falls, Randolph Co., N. C., 510.
–Providence Co., R. I., 44,533.
On N. York, N. Hav. & Hart. (R. R.).
Industrial center; chiefly textiles.
Central Islip, Suffolk Co., N. Y., 1,598.
On Long Isl. (R. R.).
Centralia, Marion and Clark Cos., Ill., 12,583.
On Chi., Burl. & Quincy; Ill. Cen.; Mo.-Ill.; Sou. (R. Rs.).
Transportation center, with large railroad yards and shops. In extensive coal and oil region.
–Nemah Co., Kans., 611.
On Mo. Pac. (R. R.).
–Boone Co., Mo., 2,009.
On Alton; Wabash (R. Rs.).
–Columbia Co., Pa., 2,446.
On Leh. Val. (R. R.).
–Lewis Co., Wash., 8,058.
On Chi., Mil., St. P. & Pac.; Gt. Nor.; Nor. Pac.; Ore.-Wash. R. R. & Nav. Co.; Twin Cy. (El.) (R. Rs.).
Industries: lumber manufacturing, farm produce, dairying, and coal mining.
Central Lake, Antrim Co., Mich., 607.
On Pere Marq. (R. R.).
Central Point, Jackson Co., Ore., 821.
On Sou. Pac. (R. R.).
Central Square, Oswego Co., N. Y., 542.
On N. York Cen.; N. York., Ont. & West. (R. Rs.).
Central Valley, Orange Co., N. Y., 1,049.
On Erie (R. R.).
Central Village, Windham Co., Conn., 1,529.
On N. York, N. Hav. & Hart. (R. R.).
Centre Hall, Centre Co., Pa., 658.
On Penna. (R. R.).
Centreville, Amite and Wilkinson Cos., Miss., 1,344.
On Yazoo & Miss. Val. (R. R.).
Century, Escambia Co., Fla., 1,250.
On Escambia; Lou. & Nash. (R. Rs.).
–Ottawa Co., Okla., 2,040.
On Northe. Okla. (El.); St. Lou.-San Fran. R. Rs.).
–Barbour Co., W. Va., 525.
On Balt. & Ohio (R. R.).
Ceredo, Wayne Co., W. Va., 1,164.
On Balt. & Ohio; Chesa. & Ohio; Norf. & West. (R. Rs.).
Ceres, Stanislaus Co., Cal., 981.
On Sou. Pac. (R. R.).
Cerignola, Foggia Prov., Italy, 36,017.
Cernaŭti (Czernowitz), Rumania, 111,122.
Trading center. Timber, livestock, cattle, spirits, and agricultural produce market.
Cerro, Taos Co., N. Mex., 555.
Cerro de Pasco, Junin Dept., Peru, 18,000.
Copper, silver, gold and lead mining town.
Cerro Gordo, Piatt Co., Ill., 965.
On Ill. Term. (El.); Wab. (R. Rs.).
Cesena, Prov. of Forli, Italy, 15,943.
Ceské Budejovice (Budweis), Czechoslovakia, 43,886.
Timber, iron, chemicals, beer, machinery.
Cetinje, capital of Montenegro (now part of Yugoslavia), about 6,367.
Cette, France. See Sete.
Ceylon, Martin Co., Minn., 475.
On Chi. & Nor. West. (R. R.).
Chadbourn, Columbus Co., N. C., 1,311.
On Atl. Coast Line (R. R.).
Chadderton, Lancashire, England, 27,455.
Textiles and metal working.
Chadron, c. s., Dawes Co., Neb., 4,606.
On Chi. & Nor. West. (R. R.).
Chadwick, Carroll Co., Ill., 558.
On Chi., Burl. & Quincy (R. R.).
–(Chadwicks P. O.), Oneida Co., N. Y., 1,000.
On Del., Lack. & West. (R. R.).
Chaffee, Scott Co., Mo., 2,902.
On Chi. & E. Ill.; St. Lou.-San Fran. (R. Rs.).
Chagrin Falls, Cuyahoga Co., Ohio, 2,739.
On Wheel. & L. Erie (R. R.).
Chalchicomula, State of Puebla, Mexico, 6,668.
Chalco, State of Mexico, Mexico, 3,208.

Chalfant, Allegheny Co., Pa., 1,192.
Chalfont, Bucks Co., Pa., 550.
On Reading (R. R.).
Chalmers, White Co., Ind., 510.
On Chi., Ind. & Lou. (R. R.).
Chalonnes-sur-Loire, Dept. of Maine-et-Loire, France, 3,516.
Chalon-sur-Marne, capital of Dept. of Marne, France, 35,530.
Famed for the defeat of Attila, 451 B.C.
Chalon-sur-Saône, Dept. of Saône-et-Loire, France, 33,204.
Principal industry is founding and working of copper and iron.
Chama, Rio Arriba Co., N. Mex., 700.
On Den. & Rio Gde. West. (R. R.).
Chamberlain, c. s., Brule Co., S. Dak., 1,506.
On Chi., Mil., St. P. & Pac. (R. R.).
Seat of Columbus College.
Chambersburg, c. s., Franklin Co., Pa., 13,788.
On the Pennsylvania and the Western Maryland Railroads.
Woolen and silk mills, stocking factory, several large machine shops, and foundries; main offices and repair shops of Cumberland Valley Railroad. Seat of Wilson College for Women.
Chambery, Dept. of Savoie, France, 28,073.
Manufactures of lace, silk gauze, leather, hats and aluminum products.
Chamblee, De Kalb Co., Ga., 893.
On Southern (R. R.).
Chamois, Osage Co., Mo., 675.
On Mo. Pac. (R. R.).
Chamonix, Dept. of Haute-Savoie, France, 3,811.
Champaign, Champaign Co., Ill., 20,348.
On Cle., Cin., Chi. & St. Lou.; Ill. Cen.; Ill. Term. (El.); Wab. (R. Rs.).
In rich farming region. Manufactures structural iron and steel, castings, tools, refrigerators, and textiles.
Champigny-sur-Marne, Seine, France, 28,883.
Champion, Trumbull Co., Ohio, 800.
On Penna. (R. R.).
Champion Heights, Trumbull Co., Ohio, 500.
Champlain, Clinton Co., N. Y., 1,197.
On Rutland (R. R.).
Chanaral, Prov. of Atacama, Chile, 2,930.
Chance, Somerset Co., Md., 711.
Chandler, Maricopa Co., Ariz., 1,378.
On Sou. Pac. (R. R.).
–Warrick Co., Ind., 650.
On Evansv. Suburb & Newb.; Sou. (R. Rs.).
–c. s., Lincoln Co., Okla., 2,717.
On St. Lou.-San Fran. (R. R.).
–Henderson Co., Tex., 630.
On St. Lou. Southw. (R. R.).
Chandlerville, Cass Co., Ill., 824.
On Jacksonv. & Hav. (R. R.).
Changchow, Fukien, China, 100,000.
Changsha, capital of Hunan, China, 607,000.
Treaty port; silk industry; college of Yo-lo.
Channing, Dickinson Co., Mich., 575.
On Chi., Mil., St. P. & Pac.; Escan. & L. Sup. (R. Rs.).
Chantilly, Dept. of Oise, France, about 6,000.
Chanute, Neosho Co., Kans., 9,536.
On Atch., Top. & Santa Fe; Mo.-Kan.-Tex. (R. Rs.).
Division headquarters of Santa Fe R. R. Surrounded by oil and gas wells.
Chapel Hill, Washington Co., Tex., 600.
On Tex. & N. Orl. (R. R.).
Chapel Hill Station (Chapel Hill P. O.), Orange Co., N. C., 2,699.
On State University (R. R.).
Seat of University of North Carolina.
Chapin, Morgan Co., Ill., 500.
On Chi., Burl. & Quincy; Wab. (R. Rs.).
Chapman, Butler Co., Ala., 1,189.
On Lou. & Nash. (R. R.).
–Dickinson Co., Kans., 831.
On Un. Pac. (R. R.).
Chappaqua, Westchester Co., N. Y., 2,500.
On N. York Cen. (R. R.).
Chappell, Deuel Co., Neb., 1,061.
On Un. Pac. (R. R.).
Chardon, c. s., Geauga Co., Ohio, 1,818.
On Balt. & Ohio (R. R.).
Charenton le Pont, Seine, France, 20,946.
Chariton, c. s., Lucas Co., Iowa, 5,365.
On Chi., Burl. & Quincy; Chi., Rk. Isl. & Pac. (R. Rs.).
Charlemont, Franklin Co., Mass., 923.
On Boston & Maine (R. R.).
Charleroi, Washington Co., Pa., 11,260.
On Penna. (R. R.).
Has iron foundries, glass factories, and coal.
–Hainaut, Belgium, 28,069.
Has metal and glass industries.
Charles City, c. s., Floyd Co., Iowa, 8,039.
On Charl. Cy. West. (El.); Chi., Mil., St. P. & Pac.; Ill. Cen. (R. Rs.).
Charleston, Franklin Co., Ark., 851.
On Mo. Pac. (R. R.).
–c. s., Coles Co., Ill., 8,012.
On Cle., Cin., Chi. & St. Lou.; N. York, Chi. & St. Lou. (R. Rs.).
State Normal School.
–c. s., Tallahatchie Co., Miss., 2,014.
On Yazoo & Miss. Val. (R. R.).
–c. s., Mississippi Co., Mo., 3,357.
On Mo. Pac. (R. R.).
A farming community.
–c. s., Charleston Co., S. C., 62,265.
Largest city of South Carolina. Port of entry, located 7 miles from the ocean. Through a ship channel, with a water front of 15 miles, the city has extensive Government port terminals, livestock sheds and coaling facilities. The harbor is land locked and one of the safest on the coast. It is defended by Forts Sumter, Moultrie, and Battinson on Sullivan's Island.
Charleston is a town of great beauty, and retains many of its old Southern characteristics. The prominent buildings are St. Philip's Church, founded with the city; St. Michael's Church (1761), the cathedral, the customhouse, and the Charleston Museum. The educational institutions comprise the College of Charleston, founded in 1785; South Carolina Medical College, The Citadel (military college), Avery Normal School (for colored students), the Charleston Library, founded in 1748, and a museum of natural history.
Charleston is the chief commercial center of South Carolina, and is connected with other Eastern and Southern ports by steamship lines, and by the Atlantic Coast Line, Seaboard Air Line and Southern Railroads. The chief exports are rice, fertilizers, chemicals, canned goods, cotton goods, lumber, and naval stores.
Charleston was settled by the English in 1670, and was named in honor of Charles II.
Charleston was the first Southern city to join the revolutionary forces. In 1780 it was captured by the British. The first gun of the Civil War was fired at Fort Sumter, and in 1865, the Federals took possession of the evacuated city. In 1886 Charleston was devastated by a severe earthquake, which destroyed property valued at $8,000,000.
–Orleans Co., Vt., 895.
–Penobscot Co., Maine, 150.
–c. s., Kanawha Co., W. Va., State capital, 60,408.
On the Kanawha River (at the confluence of the Elk), 65 miles from its mouth. Steamboats navigate the Kanawha River 23 miles above Charleston. The city is on the Baltimore & Ohio; Chesapeake and Ohio; New York Central; Virginian (via New York Central trackage) railroads.
There is a fine Capitol here, besides other public buildings. The city has natural gas in abundance. Besides the Kanawha and Michigan machine shops, the city has ice factories, woolen mills, planing mills, chemical plants, pulp and paper mills, furniture factories, foundries, engine-building works, and very large ax factories. There is a large trade in lumber and coal.
Charleston became the seat of government in 1869. In 1875 the government removed to Wheeling, and in May, 1885, back to Charleston again, the present capital.
Charlestown, Washington Co, R. I., 1,260.
–Clark Co., Ind., 859.
On Balt. & Ohio (R. R.).
–Sullivan Co., N. H., 1,200.
On Bost. & Me.; Springf. Term. (El.) (R. Rs.).
Charles Town, c. s., Jefferson Co., W. Va., 2,434.
On Balt. & Ohio; Norf. & West. (R. Rs.).
Charleville, Ardennes, France, 22,557.
The city was almost destroyed in the Great War.
–Queensland, Australia, 3,205.
Charlevoix, c. s., Charlevoix Co., Mich., 2,247.
On Pere Marq. (R. Rs.).
Charlotte, c. s., Eaton Co., Mich., 5,307.
On Gd. Tr.; Mich. Cen. (R. Rs.).
–Monroe Co., N. Y.
On Balt. & Ohio; N. York Cen. (R. Rs.).
–c. s., Mecklenburg Co., N. C., 82,675.
On Seab. Air Line; Southern; Norf. Sou.; Piedmont & Nor. (El.) (R. Rs.).
A textile center of the South, containing the plants and offices of large American and British companies. Also a water power center and telegraph relay point. Home of Queen's College (Presbyterian).
–Atascosa Co., Tex., 1,700.
On San Ant., Uvalde & Gulf (R. R.).
–Chittenden Co., Vt., 83.
On Rutland (R. R.).
Charlotte Amalie, St. Thomas, V. I. See St. Thomas. Present name Charlotte Amalie.
Charlottenburg, Prussia, Germany, 353,000.
A suburb of Berlin.
Charlottesville (Ind. City), Albemarle Co., Va., 15,245.
On Chesapeake & Ohio; Southern (R. Rs.).
Seat of University of Virginia and home of Thomas Jefferson. In apple orchard section. Textiles, tan and bark extracts, lumber.
–Hancock Co., Ind., 900.
On Penna. (R. R.).
Charlottetown, Queens Co., capital of Prince Edward Island, 12,361.
On Can. Nat. (R. R.).
Has the Prince of Wales, St. Dunstan's, and Methodist colleges, normal school, and convent; woolen factories, iron foundries, shipbuilding yards.
Charlton, Worcester Co., Mass., 2,366.
Charter Oak, Crawford Co., Iowa, 688.
On Chi., Mil., St. P. & Pac. (R. R.).
Charters Towers, Queensland, Australia, 6,978.
Chartley, Bristol Co., Mass., 525.
Chartres, capital of Dept. of Eure-et-Loire, France, 27,077.
Manufactures include flour, beer, spirits, leather, furniture, and stained glass.
Chase, Rice Co., Kans., 836.
On Atch., Top., & Santa Fe (R. R.).
Chase City, Mecklenburg Co., Va., 1,590.
On Southern (R. R.).
Mecklenburg Springs (medicinal waters) in the vicinity. In a rich agricultural district.
Chaska, c. s., Carver Co., Minn., 1,901.
On Chi., Mil., St. P. & Pac.; Minn. & St. Lou. (R. Rs.).
A manufacturing town in farm region. It has large brick yards and a sugar factory. One of the oldest towns in the State.
Chassell, Houghton Co., Mich., 500.
On Dul., So. Sh. & Atl.; Miner. Rge. (R. Rs.).
Chateaugay, Franklin Co., N. Y., 1,169.
On Rutland (R. R.).
Châteauroux, Dept. of Indre, France, 28,578.
Textiles, machinery, and tobacco products.
Château-Thierry, Dept. of Aisne, France, 8,266.
Scene of intense fighting between the Americans and Germans in Franco-American offensive, June, 1918.
Châtelet, Hainaut, Belgium, 15,124.
Châtelineau, Hainaut, Belgium, 18,193.
Châtellerault, Dept. of Vienné, France, 19,369.
Firearms and cutlery manufactures.
Chatfield, Fillmore and Olmstead Cos., Minn., 1,269.
Chatham, New Brunswick, Canada, 4,017.
On Chi. & Nor. West. (R. R.).
–capital of Kent Co., Ontario, Canada, 14,569.
On Can. Pac.; Can. Nat.; Pere Marq.; Wab. (R. Rs.).
Manufactures wagons, carriages, wheels, flour, woven-wire goods, sugar; has large export trade in grain, pork, country produce, and lumber.
–Kent, England, 42,996.
A naval and military center containing large barracks, school of engineering, and military hospital. The royal dockyard was first established by Queen Elizabeth, and contains shipbuilding and floating docks.
–Sangamon Co., Ill., 883.
On Alton; Ill. Term. (El.) (R. Rs.).
–Barnstable Co., Mass., 2,050.
On N. York, N. Hav. & Hart. (R. R.).
Summer resort. Fishing is the chief industry.
–Morris Co., N. J., 3,869.
On Del., Lack. & West. (R. R.).
–Columbia Co., N. Y., 2,424.
On Bost. & Alb.; N. York Cen.; Rut. (R. Rs.).
–c. s., Pittsylvania Co., Va., 1,143.
On Southern (R. R.).
Chatom, c. s., Washington Co., Ala., 500.
On Ala., Tenn. & Nor. (R. R.).
Chatsworth, c. s., Murray Co., Ga., 607.
On Lou. & Nash. (R. R.).
–Livingston Co., Ill., 981.
On Ill. Cen.; Tol., Peor. & West. (R. Rs.).
Chattanooga, Comanche Co., Okla., 362.
On Chi., Rk. Isl. & Pac. (R. R.).
–c. s., Hamilton Co., Tenn., 119,798.
Is located on the Tennessee River, and on the Central of Georgia; Tennessee, Alabama and Georgia; the Nashville, Chattanooga and St. Louis; the Southern; the Cincinnati; New Orleans and Texas Pacific; and the Alabama Great Southern Railroads. It is very near Lookout Mountain, and is noted for its picturesque scenery.
The principal buildings are a marble customhouse, a public library, a county court-house, and the Erlanger Hospital. Chattanooga is the seat of the University of Chattanooga.
The Chickamauga and Chattanooga National Military Park, Chattanooga-Lookout Mountain Park, and the National Cemetery are features of interest accessible over the Chattanooga Scenic Loop.
The principal trade is in cotton, iron, coal, wheat, and lumber. The manufacturing and industrial establishments are important, and include manufactures of iron and steel, machinery, lumber, textiles and clothing, fittings, furniture, leather, railroad cars and fertilizers.
Chattanooga was settled in 1836 and was then called Ross's Landing. It was incorporated in 1851. An important point in the Civil War, it was the scene of the battles of Chattanooga, Lookout Mountain, and Missionary Ridge.
Chattaroy, Mingo Co., W. Va., 526.
On Norf. & West. (R. R.).
Chaumont, Dept. of Haute-Marne, France, 18,069.
A commercial center. Headquarters of the A. E. F. during the World War.
–Jefferson Co., N. Y., 596.
On N. York Cen. (R. R.).
Chauncey, Athens Co., Ohio, 1,269.
On N. York Cen. (R. R.).
–Luzerne Co., Pa., 655.
Chautauqua, Chautauqua Co., N. Y., 540.
Seat of the Chautauqua Institution. No trade or manufactures.
Chautauqua Park, Daviess Co., Ky., 500.
Cheb (Eger), Czechoslovakia, 31,549.
An agricultural market-center. Manufactures of wine, flour, candles, and tobacco products.
Chebanse, Iroquois and Kankakee Cos., Ill., 523.
On Ill. Cen. (R. R.).
Chebeague Island, Cumberland Co., Md., 529.
Cheboygan, c. s., Cheboygan Co., Mich., 4,923.
On Det. & Mack.; Mich. Cen. (R. Rs.).
Summer resort.
Checotah, McIntosh Co., Okla., 2,110.
On Mo.-Kan.-Tex. (R. R.).
Chefoo (or Chifu), Shantung, China, 132,000.
Chehalis, c. s., Lewis Co., Wash., 4,907.
On Chi., Mil., St. P. & Pac.; Cowl., Cheh. & Cas.; Gt. Nor.; Nor. Pac.; Ore.-Wash. R. R. & Nav. Co., Twin City (El.) (R. Rs.).
Chelan, Chelan Co., Washington, 1,403.
On Gt. Nor. (R. R.).
Chelmsford, Essex, England, 26,537.
Iron foundries, electrical and engineering works.
–Middlesex Co., Mass., 7,595.
On N. York, N. Hav. & Hart. (R. R.).
Chelsea, Tama Co., Iowa, 575.
On Chi. & Nor. West. (R. R.).
–Kennebec Co., Maine, 600.
–Suffolk Co , Mass., 42,673.
On Bost. & Alb.; Bost. & Me. (R. Rs.).
Has manufactures of rubber goods, shoes, and machinery. Seat of a United States marine hospital and of a soldiers' home.
–Washtenaw Co., Mich., 2,268.
On Mich. Cen. (R. R.).
–Rogers Co., Okla., 1,527.
On St. Lou.-San Fran. (R. R.).
Cheltenham, Gloucestershire, England, 49,385.
Situated in the valley of the Chelt. Its mineral springs (saline) have made it a fashionable resort. Of its many churches St. Mary's is the most noteworthy.
Cheltenham is the seat of two colleges.
–Montgomery Co., Pa., 3,500.
On Read. (R. R.).
Chelyabinsk, Soviet Union, 217,000.
Trading center for coal and Siberian grain. Manufactures of agricultural machinery and leather goods.
Chelyan, Kanawha Co., W. Va., 800.
On Chesa. & Ohio (R. R.).
Chemawa, Riverside Co., Calif., 500.
On Pac. Elec. (R. R.).
Chemnitz, Saxony, Germany, 350,657.
Important industrial town. Locomotive and engineering works. Cotton-spinning, hosiery, textiles, dyes, and chemicals.
Chenango Bridge, Broome Co., N. Y., 500.
On Del., Lack. & West. (R. R.).
Chenango Forks, Broome Co., N. Y., 536.
On Del., Lack. & West. (R. R.).
Cheney, Sedgwick Co., Kansas, 720.
On Atch., Top. & Santa Fe (R. R.).
–Spokane Co., Wash., 1,335.
On Chi., Mil., St. P. & Pac.; Nor. Pac.; Ore.-Wash. R. R. & Nav. Co. (R. Rs.).
Large flour mill and a farm implement plant.
Cheneyville, Rapides Parish, La., 835.
On Tex. & N. Orl.; Tex. & Pac. (R. Rs.).
Chengte (Jehol), Manchukuo, 650,000.
Chengtu, Szechuan Prov., China, 800,000.
Chenoa, McLean Co., Ill., 1,325.
On Alton; Tol., Peor. & West. (R. Rs.).
Chepping Wycombe, Buckinghamshire, England, 27,987.
Furniture factories.
Cheraw, Chesterfield Co., S. C., 3,573.
On Atl. Coast Line; Chesterf. & Lancas.; Seab. Air Line (R. Rs.).
Cherbourg, Dept. of Manche, France, 39,105.
Naval station and transatlantic port; important engineering works celebrated for the dike or breakwater; has arsenals, machine shops, and forges; seaside resort.
Cheriton, Northampton Co., Va., 531.
On Penna. (R. R.).
Cherkasi, Soviet Union, 39,673.
Industrial and trade center of a farming region.
Chernigov, Ukraine, Sov. Union, 43,200.
Spirits, leather goods, and flour.
Cherokee, Colbert Co., Ala., 659.
On Southern (R. R.).
–c. s., Cherokee Co., Iowa, 6,443.
On Ill. Cen. (R. R.).
–Crawford Co., Kans., 1,198.
On Jop.-Pitts. (El.); Mo.-Pac.; St. Lou.-San Fran. (R. Rs.).
–c. s., Alfalfa Co., Okla., 2,236.
On Atch., Top. & Santa Fe (R. R.).
–Charleston Co., S. C., 500.

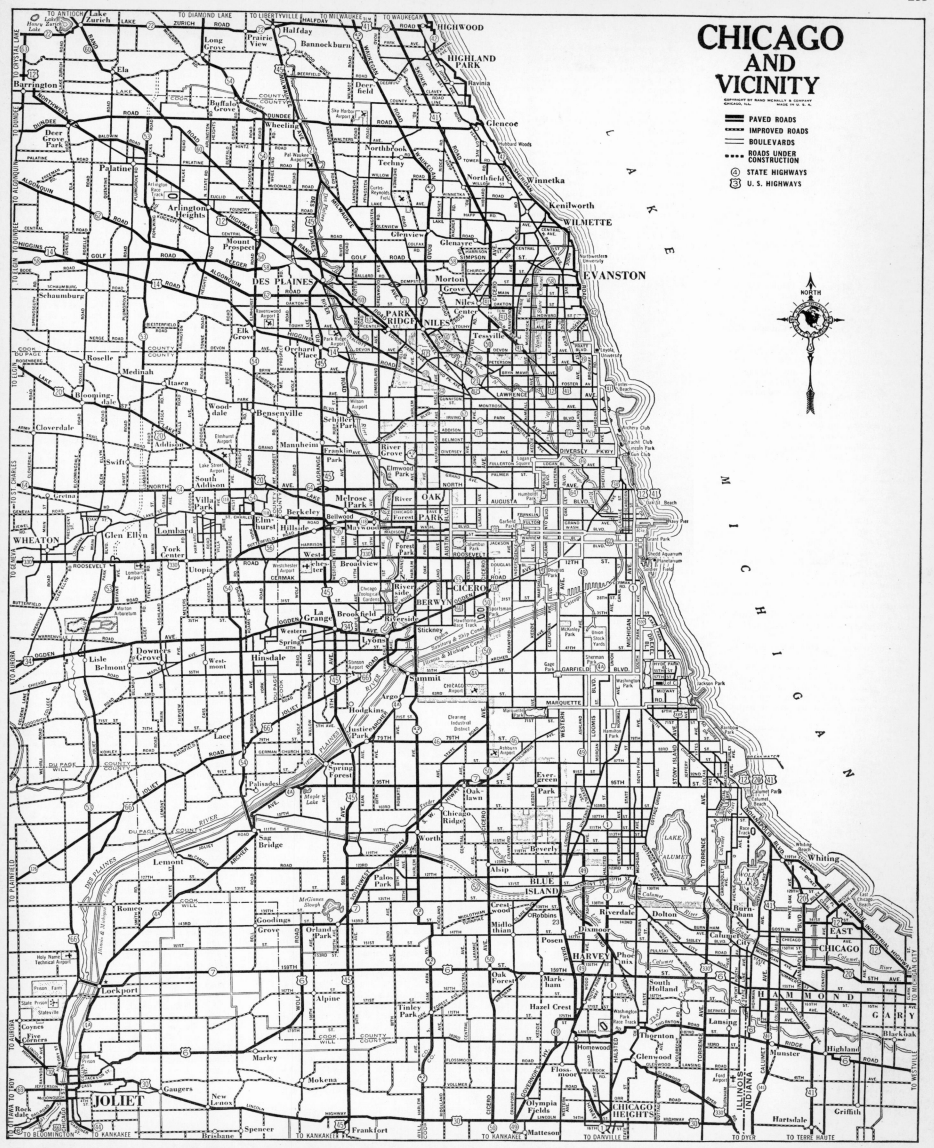

CHICAGO
AND
VICINITY

COPYRIGHT BY RAND McNALLY & COMPANY
CHICAGO, ILL.   MADE IN U.S.A.

PAVED ROADS
IMPROVED ROADS
BOULEVARDS
ROADS UNDER
CONSTRUCTION
STATE HIGHWAYS
U. S. HIGHWAYS

MAP OF CHICAGO AND VICINITY. CHICAGO IS THE SECOND LARGEST CITY OF THE UNITED STATES AND THE THIRD LARGEST CITY IN THE WORLD. IT IS NOTABLE
FOR ITS FINE PARK SYSTEMS AS A RESULT OF EXTENSIVE CIVIC AND RECLAMATION PROJECTS ALONG ITS WATERFRONT ON LAKE MICHIGAN. THIS MAP SHOWS
PARTICULARLY WELL THE RELATION TO THE CITY PROPER OF THE NEIGHBORING TOWNS ON THE NORTH AND SOUTH SHORES AND WEST OF CHICAGO

Cherokee Falls, Cherokee Co., S. C., 725.
On Southern (R. R.).
Cherry, Bureau Co., Ill., 636.
On Chi., Mil., St. P. & Pac. (R. R.).
Cherry Creek, Chautauqua Co., N. Y., 539.
On Erie (R. R.).
Cherryfield, Washington Co., Maine, 1,011.
On Me. Cen. (R. R.).
Cherrytree, Indiana Co., Pa., 519.
On N. York Cen.; Penna. (R. Rs.).
Cherryvale, Montgomery Co., Kans., 3,580.
On Atch., Top. & Santa Fe; St. Lou.-San Fran.; Un. Tract. (El.) (R. Rs.).
Surrounded by oil and gas wells.
Cherry Valley, Winnebago Co., Ill., 587.
On Chi. & Nor. West. (R. R.).
–Otsego Co., N. Y., 707.
On Del. & Hud. (R. Rs.).
–Washington Co., Pa., 1,425.
Cherryville, Gaston Co., N. C., 2,756.
On Seab. Air Line (R. R.).
Chesaning, Saginaw Co., Mich., 1,594.
On Mich. Cen. (R. R.).
Chesapeake, Lawrence Co., Ohio, 1,094.
Chesapeake City, Cecil Co., Md., 1,016.
Cheshire, New Haven Co., Conn., 1,000.
On N. York, N. Hav. & Hart. (R. R.).
–Berkshire Co., Mass., 1,660.
On Bost. & Alb. (R. R.).
Chesley, Bruce Co., Ontario, Canada, 1,699.
On Can. Nat. (R. R.).
Chesnee, Spartanburg Co., S. C., 764.
On Clinchfield (R. R.).
Chester, Middlesex Co., Conn., 1,200.
On N. York, N. Hav. & Hart. (R. R.).
Industries: wire specialties, manicure goods, woodwork.
–Cheshire, England, 41,438.
Railroad and industrial center. Summer resort. Metal working and food production.
–c. s., Randolph Co., Ill., 3,922.
On Mo.-Ill.; Mo. Pac.; St. Lou.-Southw. (R. Rs.).
–Hampden Co., Mass., 1,362.
On Bost. & Alb. (R. R.).
Granite and emery mills.
–Thayer Co., Neb., 579.
On Chi., Burl. & Quincy (R. R.).
–Rockingham Co., N. H., 653.
–Morris Co., N. J., 700.
–Orange Co., N. Y., 1,154.
On Erie; Leh. & Hud. Riv. (R. Rs.).
–Delaware Co., Pa., 59,164.
Is situated on the Delaware River, and on the Baltimore & Ohio, the Pennsylvania, and Reading railroads.
It is the seat of the Crozer Theological Seminary (Baptist) and the Pennsylvania Military College. It has a free library, a city hall, a custom-house, and the house built by William Penn.
The city has important manufactures, including automobile assembling and shipping.
Chester was settled by the Swedes in the year 1644 and was called Upland until 1682, when William Penn gave it its present name.
–c. s., Chester Co., S. C., 5,528.
On Car. & Nor. West.; Lancas. & Chest.; Seab. Air Line; Sou. (R. Rs.).
–Windsor Co., Vt., 684.
On Rutland (R. R.).
–Chesterfield Co., Va., 1,050.
On Atl. Coast Line; Seab. Air Line (R. Rs.).
–Hancock Co., W. Va., 3,701.
On Penna. (R. R.).
Industries: white ware potteries, porcelain, rolling mills, etc.
Chesterfield, Derbyshire, England, 61,146.
Manufactures of cotton, silk, pottery, machinery, and tobacco.
–New London Co., Conn., 700.
–c. s., Chesterfield Co., S. C., 1,030.
On Chesterf. & Lancas. (R. R.).
Chester Hill, Clearfield Co., Pa., 786.
Chester le Street, Durham, England, 16,639.
A suburb of Durham.
Chesterton, Porter Co., Ind., 2,231.
On N. York. Cen. (R. R.).
Chestertown, c. s., Kent Co., Md., 2,809.
On Penna. (R. R.).
–Warren Co., N. Y., 500.
Chestnut Ridge, Fayette Co., Pa., 775.
Cheswick, Allegheny Co., Pa., 1,053.
On Penna. (R. R.).
Chetek, Barron Co., Wis., 1,076.
On Chi., St. P., Minn. & Oma. (R. R.).
Chetopa, Labette Co., Kans., 1,707.
On Mo.-Kan.-Tex.; Mo. Pac. (R. Rs.).
Cheviot, Hamilton Co., Ohio, 8,046.
On Chesa. & Ohio (R. R.).
Chewelah, Stevens Co., Wash., 1,315.
On Gt. Nor. (R. R.).
Cheyenne, c. s., Roger Mills Co., Okla., 826.
On Panh. & Santa Fe (R. R.).
–c. s., Laramie Co., Wyo., State capital, 17,361.
On Chicago, Burlington & Quincy; Colorado & Southern; and Union Pacific railroads. Is 106 miles north of Denver, at an elevation of 6,050 feet, and on the Lincoln and Yellowstone Highways.
The noteworthy buildings are the Capitol, Federal Building, Carnegie Library, Union Pacific Railroad station and car shops, Temple of Scottish Rite Masons, Elks' Home, and Catholic cathedral. There is a large military reservation near the city at Fort F. E. Warren and a municipal aerial field. Cheyenne, settled in 1867, became the capital of Wyoming in 1869.
Cheyenne is the headquarters for representatives of large cattle and sheep interests, and is a shipping point for live stock to Eastern markets: also a distributing point for jobbers of merchandise, and an important banking center. The International Harvester Company has an immense plant here.
Cheyenne Wells, c. s., Cheyenne Co., Colo., 595.
On Un. Pac. (R. R.).
Chiautla, State of Puebla, Mexico, 2,556.
Mining and trade center.

COURTESY NEW YORK CENTRAL R.R.

A GLIMPSE OF THE SKYLINE ALONG MICHIGAN AVENUE, CHICAGO, ILLINOIS

Chicago, c. s., Cook Co., Ill., 3,376,438.
Second city in the United States, and port of entry. Is situated on the southwestern shore of Lake Michigan, and is the terminus of twenty-three trunk-line railroad systems. Embraces all the important lines, making it the foremost transportation center of the country. The city has also a large system of belt lines. When the Great Lakes-St. Lawrence-to-the-ocean-Canal has been built, the city will be practically an inland seaport.
It is the center of western and Great Lakes commerce, and has a water front of 101 miles. The lake shore is protected by breakwaters, forming a splendid harbor at the mouth of the Chicago River. To handle its water-borne commerce, the city has added to its dock and rail facilities (extending 52 miles on the water front) by constructing a municipal pier (Navy Pier) at a cost of $5,000,000. At the mouth of the Calumet River, in South Chicago, is another harbor. The Erie Canal, terminating at Buffalo, and the Welland Canal, connecting Lakes Erie and Ontario, provide commercial communication with Atlantic ports. The Chicago River traverses the city, and by its peculiar course divides it into three sections, known as the North, South, and West Sides.
Chicago's large parks include Lincoln, Humboldt, Garfield, Douglas, Washington, Jackson, Columbus, Grant and Marquette, all connected by boulevards traversing the most beautiful sections of the city.
Chicago is noted for the number, size, and height of its public and business buildings. Among them are the Auditorium, containing a theater seating 7,000 persons; the Civic Opera Building, with two theaters; Board of Trade Building; Chicago Stock Exchange; the Field Building; the Palmolive Building; Merchandise Mart; Wrigley Building; Tribune Tower; Daily News Building; Willoughby Tower; Medinah Temple Building; New York Life Building; Title and Trust Building; Chicago Public Library, costing $2,000,000 and containing 1,700,000 volumes; John Crerar Library; the Northwestern Railroad Station; the Union Station; and the New Post Office.
Other features of the city include the new Navy Pier, the Field Museum, Museum of Science and Industry; the Planetarium; Soldier Field; the Aquarium; Chicago Historical Society; and the Art Institute. On the north shore just outside the city, is Fort Sheridan, and at Great Lakes is the new naval training station with an unrivaled modern equipment. The University of Chicago, founded in 1892, is one of the foremost institutions of learning in the country. Other large schools are the Rush Medical College (now part of the Univ. of Chicago), Univ. of Illinois Medical College, Chicago College of Pharmacy, the Armour Institute of Technology, Lewis Institute, and Northwestern University.
Chicago is the greatest livestock and grain market in the world, as well as the greatest railroad center. Its lumber interests are enormous. It has the world's largest packing and slaughtering plants. Union Stock Yards cover 400 acres and receive more than 10,000,000 head of cattle yearly. Canned meats are sent to all parts of the world.
The water supply of the city is obtained by means of nine tunnels, running from seven cribs four miles into the Lake. The Chicago Sanitary and Ship Canal protects Chicago's water supply from Lake Michigan against pollution by the city's sewerage by providing an outlet to the Mississippi River.
Chicago's wholesale trade and bank resources run into the billions. There were more than 20,000 factories in the Chicago industrial zone in 1930. Its chief industries, ranked according to magnitude and value, are slaughtering and packing, printing and publishing, steel works products, electrical machinery, foundry and machine shop products, clothing, bread and bakery products, confectionery, gas and coke, furniture, paints and varnishes, radios, railway cars, canned goods, chemicals, etc.
The city covers an area of 212.8 square miles. The site of Chicago was first visited by Joliet and Marquette in 1673. The United States Government established there the frontier post of Fort Dearborn in 1804. The village of Chicago was incorporated in 1833, and became a city March 4, 1837. On October 8 and 9, 1871, occurred the great fire which reduced much of the city to ashes. In 1893, the World's Columbian Exposition and in 1933 and 1934, the Century of Progress Exposition, were held in Chicago.
Chicago Heights, Cook Co., Ill., 22,321.
On Balt. & Ohio, Chi. Term.; Chi. & East. Ill.; Chi. Hgts. Term.; Chi., Mil., St. P. & Pac.; Elg., Jol. & East.; Mich. Cen. (R. Rs.).
On the Lincoln and Dixie highways, 27 miles south of Chicago. A city of factories, manufacturing especially steel, steel parts, freight cars, locomotives, and railroad supplies.
Chichester, Sussex, England, 13,911.
Has large agricultural trade.
Chickamauga, Walker Co., Ga., 1,715.
On Cen. of Ga. (R. R.).
Chickasaw, Mobile Co., Ala., 1,200.
On Ala., Tenn. & Nor.; Sou. (R. Rs.).
Chickasha, c. s., Grady Co., Okla., 14,099.
On Atch., Top. & Santa Fe; Chi., Rk. Isl. & Pac.; St. Lou.-San Fran. (R. Rs.).
Extensive cotton and stock feeding point in Oklahoma. Seat of State College for Women.
Chick Springs, Greenville Co., S. C., 1,500.
On Piedmont & Nor. (El.) (R. R.).
Chico, Butte Co., Cal., 7,961.
On Southern Pac.; Sacramento North (El.) (R. Rs.).
Seat of State Normal School and U. S. (Department of Agriculture) Plant and Seed Station. In large rice and fruit section. Chico has a large match factory and other wood working plants.
–Wise Co., Texas, 500.
On Chi., Rk. Isl. & Gulf (R. R.).
Chicopee, Hampden Co., Mass., 41,952.
On the Boston and Maine Railroad and on the Chicopee River which here falls several feet and furnishes power for factories, making cotton goods, rubber wares, farm tools, sporting goods, firearms and ammunitions.
Chicora (Millerstown), Butler Co., Pa., 1,052.
On Balt. & Ohio (R. R.).
Chicora Place, Charleston Co., S. C., 800.
Chicoutimi, Chicoutimi Co., Quebec, Canada, 11,877.
On Can. Nat. (R. R.).
Paper mills.
Chieti, Chieti Prov., Italy, 22,700.
Chihuahua, State of Chihuahua, Mexico, 44,646.
On Chihuahua, Min.; Kan. Cy.; Mex. & Or.; Mex. Nor. West; Nat. of Mex. (R. R.).
Childress, c. s., Childress Co., Texas, 7,163.
On Ft. Worth & Denv. Cy. (R. R.).
Chilhowie, Smyth Co., Va., 712.
On Norf. & West. (R. R.).
Chillan, capital of Nuble Prov., Chile, 54,566.
A busy center of a rich farming and grazing region.
Chillicothe, Peoria Co., Ill., 1,978.
On Atch., Top. & Santa Fe; Chi., Rk. Isl. & Pac. (R. Rs.).
–c. s., Livingston Co., Mo., 8,177.
On Chi., Burl. & Quincy; Chi., Mil., St. P. & Pac.; Wab. (R. Rs.).
An interior town of Missouri upon which many highways converge.
–c. s., Ross Co., Ohio, 18,340.
On Balt. & Ohio; Norf. & West. (R. Rs.).
On Scioto River and Ohio Canal.
Its site is a fertile plain 500 feet high. A trading center of Ross County, with a high annual output of agricultural produce.
–Hardeman Co., Tex., 1,610.
On Ft. Worth & Denv. Cy.; Panh. & Santa Fe (R. Rs.).
In a wheat belt.
Chilliwack, British Columbia, Canada, 2,461.
Chilton, Falls Co., Texas, 884.
On Tex. & New Orl. (R. R.).
–c. s., Calumet Co., Wis., 1,945.
On Chi., Mil., St. P. & Pac. (R. R.).
Chimayo, Santa Fe Co., N. Mex., 500.
Chimbarongo, Colchagua Prov., Chile, 3,090.
Chimkent, Soviet Union, 55,000.
China Grove, Rowan Co., N. C., 1,258.
On Southern (R. R.).
Chinandega, Chinandega, Nicaragua, 17,697.
Center of a sugar producing region.
Chinchilla, Lackawanna Co., Pa., 600.
Chinchow, Manchukuo, 128,541.
Chincoteague Island, Accomac Co., Va., 2,130.
Chingford, Essex, England, 22,051.
A suburb of London.
Chingkiang, Prov. of Kiangsu, China, 200,000.
A river port and commercial town.
Chinnampo, Chosen, 40,568.
A port and active commercial center.
Chino, San Bernardino Co., Cal., 3,118.
On Sou. Pac. (R. R.).
Has a large beet sugar factory and ranch.
Chinook, c. s., Blaine Co., Mont., 1,320.
On Gt. Nor. (R. R.).
Chinwangtao, Prov. of Hopeh, China, 20,000.
Chioggia, Prov. of Venezia, Italy, 22,225.
Picturesque fishing town.
Chipley, c. s., Washington Co., Fla., 1,827.
On Ala. & West. Fla.; Lou. & Nash. (R. Rs.).
–Harris Co., Ga., 583.
On Cen. of Ga. (R. R.).
Chippewa Falls, c. s., Chippewa Co., Wis., 9,539.
On Chi., Mil., St. P. & Pac.; Chi., St. P., Minn. & Oma.; Minn., St. P. & S. Ste. M. (R. Rs.).
Provided with water power resources.
Chiquimula, Guatemala, 21,100
Chireno, Nacogdoches Co., Tex., 521.
Chisholm, Franklin Co., Me., 850.
On Me. Cen. (R. R.).
–St. Louis Co., Minn., 8,308.
On Dul., Missabe & Nor.; Gt. Nor. (R. Rs.).
Chief industry: Iron mining.
Chisimaio, Italian Somaliland, 38,541.
Chisinau (Kishinev), Rumania, 114,954.
Chiswick and Brentford, Middlesex, England, 62,617.
A residential suburb of London.
Chita, Sov. Union in Asia, 81,900.
Chittenango, Madison Co., N. Y., 815.
On West Shore (R. R.).
Chocorua, Carroll Co., N. H., 500.
Choisy-le-Roi, Seine, France, 28,476.
Cholet, Dept. of Maine-et-Loire, France, 23,385.
Manufactures of linen and preserved foods, cattle market.
Cholon, French Ind.-China, 145,000.
The great market town of French Indo-China. Center of the rice trade.
Cholula, State of Puebla, Mexico, 7,197.
On Ind. of Puebla, Nat. of Mex. (R. R.).
Chomutov, Czech., 52,993.

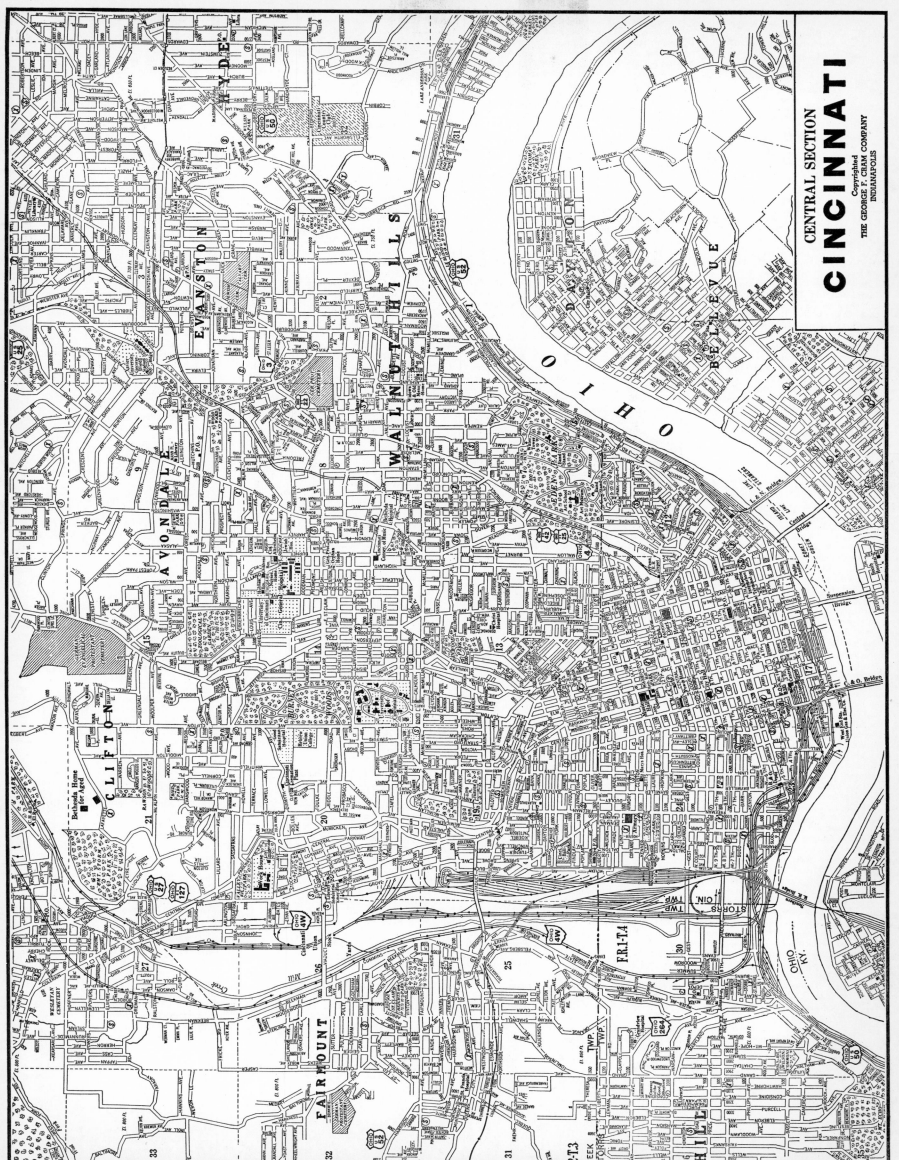

CENTRAL SECTION
CINCINNATI
Copyrighted
THE GEORGE F. CRAM COMPANY
INDIANAPOLIS
OHIO
BELLEVUE
WALNUT HILLS
EVANSTON
AVONDALE
CLIFTON
FAIRMOUNT

MAP OF CENTRAL CINCINNATI, SECOND LARGEST CITY OF OHIO. CINCINNATI IS SITUATED ON THE NORTH BANK OF THE OHIO RIVER AND IS BUILT ON TWO TERRACES, THE HIGHEST BEING 112 FEET AND THE OTHER 60 FEET ABOVE THE RIVER AT LOW WATER. THE UNIVERSITY OF CINCINNATI IS LOCATED HERE

Chorley, Lancashire, England, 30,795.
Textiles, railway cars and metal working.
Choteau, c. s., Teton Co., Mont., 926.
On Chi., Mil., St. P. & Pac.; Gt. Nor. (R. R.).
Chotin, Rumania. See Hotin.
Chowchilla, Madera Co., Calif., 847.
On Sou. Pac. (R. R.).
Chriesman, Burleson Co., Tex., 750.
On Gulf, Colo. & Santa Fe (R. R.).
Chrisman, Edgar Co., Ill., 1,092.
On Balt. & Ohio; Cle., Cin., Chi. & St. Lou. (R. Rs.).
Christchurch (with suburbs), Canterbury Prov., New Zealand, 133,200.
A modern town and trade center. Wool and meat industries.
Christiana, Lancaster Co., Pa., 959.
On Penna. (R. R.).
Christiania, Norway. See Oslo.
Christiansand, Norway. See Kristiansand.
Christiansburg, c. s., Montgomery Co., Va., 1,970.
On Norf. & West. (R. R.).
Christianstad, Sweden. See Kristianstad.
Christiansted, Virgin Islands, on island of Santa Cruz, 3,767.
Christiansund, Norway. See Kristiansund.
Christine, Atascosa Co., Tex., 524.
Christopher, Franklin Co., Ill., 4,244.
On Chi., Burl. & Quincy; Ill. Cen. (R. Rs.).
–(Button Wood), Luzerne Co., Pa., 900.
Christoval, Tom Green Co., Tex., 600.
On Panh. & Santa Fe (R. R.).
Chrudim, Bohemia, Czechoslovakia, 13,292.
Chula Vista, San Diego Co., Cal., 3,869.
On San Diego & Ariz. East. (R. R.).
Chungking, Prov. of Szechwan, China, 635,000.
An important commercial center of the interior of China.
Chur, Canton of Grisons, Switzerland, 15,578.
Center of an active trade, particularly in wine.
Churchill, Trumbull Co., Ohio, 500.
Churchland, Norfolk Co., Va., 1,050.
On Atl. Coast Line; Sou. (R. Rs.).
Church Point, Acadia Parish, La., 1,037.
On Tex. & Pac. (R. R.).
Churchville, Monroe Co., N. Y., 652.
On N. York Cen.; West Shore (R. Rs.).
Churdan, Greene Co., Iowa, 616.
On Chi., Mil., St. P. & Pac. (R. R.).
Churubusco, Whitley Co., Ind., 1,095.
On Pennsylvania (R. R.).
Ciales, Mun. of Ciales, Puerto Rico, 1,830.
Cicero, Cook Co., Ill., 66,602.
On Balt. & Ohio, Chi. Term.; Belt Ry. of Chi.; Chi., Burl. & Quincy; Manufact. Jct. (R. Rs.).
Manufactures electrical supplies, hardware, castings, machine-shop products, rubber, and washing machines.
–Hamilton Co., Ind., 933.
On N. Y., Chi. & St. L.; Ind. R. R. Sys. (Elec.) (R. Rs.).
Cidra, Mun. of Cidra, Puerto Rico, 2,500.
Ciego de Avilla, Puerto Principe, Cuba, 16,408.
Cienfuegos, Prov. of Santa Clara, Cuba, 39,946.
Center of the south coast sugar trade.
Cill Airne (Killarney), Ireland (Eire, former Irish Free State), 5,328. See Killarney.
Cill Choinnigh (Kilkenny), Ireland (Eire, former Irish Free State), 10,046.
Industrial and commercial center. Gristmills, tanneries, and breweries. Coal mines and marble quarries near by.
Cimarron, c. s., Gray Co., Kans., 913.
On Atch., Top. & Santa Fe (R. R.).
–Colfax Co., N. Mex., 698.
On Atch., Top. & Santa Fe (R. R.).
Cincinnati, Appanoose Co., Iowa, 911.
On Chi., Burl. & Quincy (R. R.).
–c. s., Hamilton Co., Ohio, 451,160.
Second city in the State in population. Is situated on the right bank of the Ohio River. The greater part of the city is built upon two terraces or plains, and occupies a position 400 or 450 feet above sea level. It is surrounded by a semicircle of hills.
Cincinnati has decided commercial advantages from its situation on the Ohio River, and from the many railroads which serve it. Among the latter are the Baltimore & Ohio; Cincinnati, Georgetown (El.); Cincinnati & Lake Erie, Chesapeake & Ohio; Cincinnati Northern; Cincinnati & New Orleans & Texas Pacific; Cleveland, Cincinnati, Chicago & St. Louis; Erie; Louisville & Nashville; Norfolk & Western; Pennsylvania railroads.
Cincinnati covers an area of 72.5 square miles, and has a river frontage extending nearly 15 miles. The lowest or "bottom" streets are mainly devoted to manufacturing and wholesale trade. These streets are sometimes flooded at stages of high water. The central and business part of the city has numerous fine stores and is compactly built. Fort Thomas, a picturesque hill-station, and one of the most important depots of the United States Army, is within a short distance. One of the bridges connecting Cincinnati with Covington, Ky., across the Ohio River is a suspension bridge. It is 2,252 feet long with a span of 1,057 feet. Two bridges of wrought-iron connect with Newport, Ky. A bridge of the Cincinnati Southern Railroad unites the city with Ludlow, Ky.
The notable buildings of a public character, are the United States Government Building, erected at a cost of $6,000,000, which contains the post office, custom-house, court-rooms, and various offices; the City Hall, with a tower 250 feet high; County Courthouse, which occupies a whole square; the Springer Music Hall; Art Museum; Chamber of Commerce; Public Library; and the Union Central Life Building, 34 stories high. Among the notable churches are St. Peter's Cathedral (Roman Catholic), St. Paul's Cathedral (Episcopal), the Jewish Synagogue and leading Methodist, Presbyterian and Congregational churches. The Tyler Davidson Fountain, in Fountain Square, is considered one of the finest specimens of monumental art in the United States. The City Hospital consists of eight separate buildings. The zoological gardens and the Rookwood Pottery on Mount Adams, famous for its wares, are features of especial interest.
Cincinnati is favorably situated as a distributing point for all sections of the country, both by rail and river. It has a great variety of manufactures and (1930) nearly 2,400 establishments. Its principal industries are machine tools, foundry and printing products, slaughtering and meat packing, beverages, tobacco products, patent medicines, paint and varnish, radios, paper, wood and metal containers, clothing, woodwork, furniture, washing machines, leather, printing inks, etc.
The educational institutions include the University of Cincinnati, which has associated with it the Cincinnati Hospital and the Cincinnati Observatory, the Lloyd Museum, St. Xavier's College, the Hebrew Union College for the training of Rabbis, the Cincinnati Conservatory of Music, the Ohio Mechanics' Institute, and the Museum and Art School. There are numerous libraries. The parks are extensive, the most famous being Eden Park, of about 400 acres. Cincinnati is noted for its musical societies, and holds an annual musical festival. Among the City's monuments is Barnard's statue of Lincoln, in Lytle Park, unveiled in 1917, the gift of Mr. and Mrs. Charles P. Taft. The statue is an idealistic and symbolic portrayal of Lincoln.
The city was laid out in 1788, by Colonel Israel Ludlow, and named Losantville. In 1789 Fort Washington was built here and the settlement was then renamed Cincinnati, in honor of the Society of the Cincinnati. In 1802 it was incorporated as a village, and as a city in 1819.
Cincinnatus, Cortland Co., N. Y., 645.
On Del., Lack. & West. (R. R.).
Cinnaminson, Philadelphia Co., Pa., 1,817.
On Penna. (R. R.).
Ciotat, La Bouches-du-Rhone, France, 11,604.
Circle, c. s., McCone Co., Mont., 519.
On Nor. Pac. (R. R.).
Circleville, c. s., Pickaway Co., Ohio, 7,369.
On Norf. & West.; Penn. (R. Rs.).
–Pendleton Co., W. Va., 600.
Cisco, Eastland Co., Texas, 6,027.
On Cisco & Northeast; Mo.-Kan.-Tex. of Tex.; Tex. & Pac. (R. Rs.).
Cisne, Wayne Co., Illinois, 467.
On Balt. & Ohio (R. R.).
Cissna Park, Iroquois Co., Ill., 588.
On Chi. & East. Ill. (R. R.).
Citronelle, Mobile Co., Ala., 1,082.
On Mob. & Ohio (R. R.).
City View, Greenville Co., S. Car., 1,200.
Ciudad Bolivar. See Bolivar.
Ciudad Trujillo (Santo Domingo), Dominican Republic, 71,297.
Clacton, Essex, England, 15,851.
An important watering place.
Claflin, Barton Co., Kansas, 586.
On Mo. Pac. (R. R.).
Clairton, Allegheny Co., Pa., 15,291.
On Balt. & O.; Bess. & L. Erie; Pennsylvania; Pitts. & W. Va.; Union (R. Rs.).
Iron, steel, boiler-tubes, boats, and coke products.
Clamart, Seine, France, 32,427.
Clanton, c. s., Chilton Co., Ala., 1,847.
On Louisv. & Nash. (R. R.).
Clara City, Chippewa Co., Minn., 730.
On Gt. Nor.; Minn. West. (R. Rs.).
Clare, Clare Co., Mich., 1,491.
On Ann Arbor; Pere Marq. (R. Rs.).
Claremont, Los Angeles Co., Cal., 2,719.
On Atch., Top. & Santa Fe; Pac. Elec.; Sou. Pac. (R. Rs.).
In the heart of the citrus belt. Notable for its orange crop. Seat of Pomona College.
–Sullivan Co., N. H., 11,000.
On Bost. & Me. (R. R.).
Shoes, paper, textiles, and machinery.
Claremore, c. s., Rogers Co., Okla., 3,720.
On St. Lou.-San Fran.; Mo. Pac. (R. Rs.).
Clarence, Cedar Co., Iowa, 659.
On Chi. & Nor. West. (R. R.).
–Shelby Co., Mo., 1,286.
On Chi., Burl. & Quincy (R. R.).
–Erie Co., N. Y., 600.
On N. York Cen. (R. R.).
–Centre Co., Pa., 800.
Clarendon, c. s., Monroe Co., Ark., 2,149.
On Mo. Pac.; St. Lou. Southw. (R. Rs.).
–Warren Co., Pa., 938.
On Penna.; Tionesta Val. (R. Rs.).
–c. s., Donley Co., Tex., 2,756.
On Ft. Worth & Denv. Cy. (R. R.).
–Rutland Co., Vt., 883.
On Rutland (R. R.).
Clarendon Hills, Du Page Co., Ill., 933.
On Chi., Burl. & Quincy (R. R.).
–Suffolk Co., Mass., 1,000.
On N. York, N. Hav. & Hart. (R. R.).
Claridge, Westmoreland Co., Pa., 1,200.
On Penna. (R. R.).
Clarinda, c. s., Page Co., Iowa, 4,962.
On Chi., Burl. & Quincy (R. R.).
Clarington, Monroe Co., Ohio, 506.
Clarion, c. s., Wright Co., Iowa, 2,578.
On Chi. Gt. West.; Chi., Rk. Isl. & Pac. (R. Rs.).
–c. s., Clarion Co., Pa., 3,201.
On Balt. & Ohio; Lake Erie, Franklin & Clarion (R. Rs.).
Clark, Coshocton Co., Ohio, 1,435.
–c. s., Clark Co., S. Dakota, 1,273.
On Chi. & Nor. West. (R. R.).
–McDowell Co., W. Va., 787.
Clarkdale, Yavapai Co., Ariz., 2,800.
On Atch., Top. & Santa Fe; Un. Verde Ext Min.; Verde Tun. & Smelt. (R. Rs.).
Clarkesville, c. s., Habersham Co., Ga., 617.
Clarkfield, Yellow Medicine Co., Minn., 802
On Minn. & St. Lou. (R. R.).
Clark Mills, Oneida Co., N. Y., 1,266.
On N. York, Ont. & West; West Shore (R. Rs.).
Clarks, Caldwell Par., La., 2,000.
On Mo. Pac.; Ouach. & Nor. West. (R. Rs.).
–Merrick Co., Neb., 540.
On Un. Pac. (R. R.).
Clarksboro, Gloucester Co., N. J., 500.
On Penna.-Read. Seashore (R. R.).
–Monmouth Co., N. J., 850.
Clarksburg, Berkshire Co., Mass., 1,333.
–Rankin Co., Mississippi.
On Yazoo & Miss. Val. (R. R.).
–c. s., Harrison Co., W. Va., 28,866.
On Balt. & Ohio (R. R.).
In the center of a great gas field and adjacent to coal region. Its outstanding industry is glassware, for which there are several factories. There are also zinc smelter plants and a tinplate mill.
Clarksdale, c. s., Coahoma Co., Miss., 10,043.
On Yazoo & Miss. Val. (R. R.).
In the heart of the Mississippi delta, notable for its production of long-staple cotton.
Clarks Green, Lackawanna Co., Pa., 694.
Clarkson, Colfax Co., Neb., 918.
On Chi. & Nor. West. (R. R.).
Clarks Summit, Lackawanna Co., Pa., 2,604.
On Del., Lack. & West. (R. R.).
Clarkston, De Kalb Co., Ga., 606.
On Ga. (R. R.).
–Oakland Co., Mich., 639.
–Cache Co., Utah, 570.
–Asotin Co., Wash., 2,870.
Clarksville, c. s., Johnson Co., Ark., 3,031.
On Mo. Pac. (R. R.).
–c. s., Habersham Co., Ga., 617.
On Tallulah Fs. (R. R.).
–Clark Co., Ind., 2,243.
On Penna. (R. R.).
–Butler Co., Iowa, 1,143.
On Chi. Gt. West.; Chi., Rk. Isl. & Pac. (R. Rs.).
–Pike Co., Mo., 739.
On Chi., Burl. & Quincy (R. Rs.).
–c. s., Montgomery Co., Tenn., 9,242.
On Lou. & Nash.; Tenn. Cen. (R. Rs.).
An important tobacco market.
–c. s., Red River Co., Texas, 2,952.
On Tex. & Pac. (R. R.).
–Mecklenburg Co., Va., 781.
On Southern (R. R.).
Clator (Mt. de Chantel), Ohio Co., W. Va., 523.
Clatskanie, Columbia Co., Ore., 739.
On Spok., Port. & Seattle (R. R.).
Claude, c. s., Armstrong Co., Texas, 1,041.
On Ft. Worth & Denv. Cy. (R. R.).
Clawson, Oakland Co., Mich., 3,377.
Claxton, c. s., Evans Co., Ga., 1,584.
On Seab. Air Line; Shearw. (R. Rs.).
Clay, Webster Co., Ky., 1,551.
On Lou. & Nash.; Ill. Cen. (R. Rs.).
–Onondaga Co., N. Y., 2,500.
On N. York Cen. (R. R.).
–Burleson Co., Texas, 500.
On Gulf, Colo. & Santa Fe (R. R.).
Clay Center, c. s., Clay Co., Kans., 4,317.
On Chi., Rk. Isl. & Pac.; Un. Pac. (R. Rs.).
–c. s., Clay Co., Neb., 933.
On Chi., Burl. & Quincy (R. R.).
Clay City, Clay Co., Ill., 707.
On Balt. & Ohio (R. R.).
–Clay Co., Ind., 1,079.
On Chi., Ind. & Lou.; Cle., Cin., Chi. & St. Lou. (R. Rs.).
–Powell Co., Ky., 528.
On Lou. & Nash. (R. R.).
Claypool, Gila Co., Ariz., 1,500.
On Sou. Pac. (R. R.).
Claysburg, Clark Co., Ind., 615.
–Blair Co., Pa., 1,400.
On Penna. (R. R.).
Claysville, Washington Co., Pa., 912.
On Balt. & Ohio (R. R.).
Clayton, c. s., Barbour Co., Ala., 1,717.
On Cen. of Ga. (R. R.).
–Kent Co., Del., 824.
On Penna. (R. R.).
–c. s., Rabun Co., Ga., 798.
On Tallulah Fs. (R. R.).
–Adams Co., Ill., 965.
On Wabash (R. R.).
–Hendricks Co., Ind., 561.
On Ind. R. R. Sys. (El.); Penna. (R. Rs.).
–c. s., St. Louis Co., Mo., 9,613.
On Chi., Rk. Isl. & Pac. (R. R.).
–Gloucester Co., N. J., 2,351.
On Penna.-Read. Seashore (R. R.).
–c. s., Union Co., N. Mex., 2,518.
On Atch., Top. & Santa Fe; Colo. & Sou. (R. Rs.).
–Jefferson Co., N. Y., 1,940.
On N. York Cen. (R. R.).
Resort for visitors to the Thousand Islands, to which it is a gateway.
–Johnston Co., N. C., 1,533.
On Southern (R. R.).
Clayville, Oneida Co., N. Y., 801.
On Del., Lack. & West. (R. R.).
Clear Creek, Chautauqua Co., N. Y., 801.
Clearfield, Ringgold and Taylor Cos., Iowa, 607.
On Chi., Burl. & Quincy (R. R.).
–c. s., Clearfield Co., Pa., 9,221.
On Balt. & Ohio; N. York Cen.; Penna. (R. Rs.).
–Davis Co., Utah, 799.
On Den. & Rio Gd. West.; Ore. Short Line (R. Rs.).
Clear Fork, Wyoming Co., W. Va., 500.
Clear Lake, Cerro Gordo Co., Iowa, 3,066.
On Chi., Mil., St. P. & Pac.; Mason Cy. & Clear L. (El.) (R. Rs.).
–c. s., Deuel Co., S. Dak., 929.
On Chi., Rk. Isl. & Pac. (R. R.).
–Skagit Co., Wash., 1,019.
On Nor. Pac.; Puget Sd. Casc. (R. Rs.).
–Polk Co., Wisc., 733.
On Chi., St. P., Minn. & Oma. (R. R.).
Clear Spring, Washington Co., Md., 539.
Clearwater, Los Angeles Co., Calif., 2,000.
On Los Ang. & Salt L.; Pac. Elec. (R. Rs.).
–c. s., Pinellas Co., Fla., 9,044.
On Atl. Coast Line; Seab. Air Line (R. Rs.).
Chief industry is citrus fruit growing and fruit packing.
–Sedgwick Co., Kans., 688.
On Atch., Top. & Santa Fe; Mo. Pac. (R. Rs.).
–Antelope Co., Neb., 504.
On Chi. & Nor. West (R. R.).
–Aiken Co., So. Car., 1,000.
On Southern (R. R.).
Cleburne, c. s., Johnson Co., Texas, 11,539.
On Gulf, Colo. & Santa Fe (R. R.).
Railroad shops, foundry, peanut and cotton industries.
Cle Elum, Kittitas Co., Wash., 2,508.
On Chi., Mil., St. P. & Pac.; Nor. Pac. (R. Rs.).
Clemenceau, Yavapai Co., Ariz., 800.
On Un. Verde Ext. Minn. (R. R.).
Clementon, Camden Co., N. J., 2,605.
On Pa.-Read. Seashore (R. R.).
Clemons, Perry Co., Ky., 500.
On Lou. & Nash. (R. R.).
–Washington Co., N. Y., 510.
On Del. & Hud. (R. R.).
Clendenin (Clendenin P. O.), Kanawha Co., W. Va., 1,217.
On Balt. & Ohio (R. R.).
Cleona, Lebanon Co., Pa., 968.
On Reading (R. R.).
Clermont, Lake Co., Fla., 1,321.
On Atl. Coast Line; Tav. & Gulf (R. Rs.).
–Fayette Co., Iowa, 631.
On Chi., Rk. Isl. & Pac. (R. R.).
–Columbia Co., N. Y., 600.
Clermont-Ferrand. Dept. of Puy-de-Dome, France, 101,128.
Chief market for extensive farming region. Clothing, tires, chemicals.
Cleveland, c. s., Cuyahoga Co., Ohio, 900,429.
The largest city in the State. Located on Lake Erie, at the mouth of the Cuyahoga River, and on the lines of the Baltimore and Ohio; the N. Y. Central; the Cleveland, Cincinnati, Chicago & St. Louis; Cuyahoga Valley; the Erie; the Lake Shore Electric; the Newburgh & South Shore; the New York, Chicago & St. Louis; the Pennsylvania; the River Terminal and the Wheeling & Lake Erie Railroads.

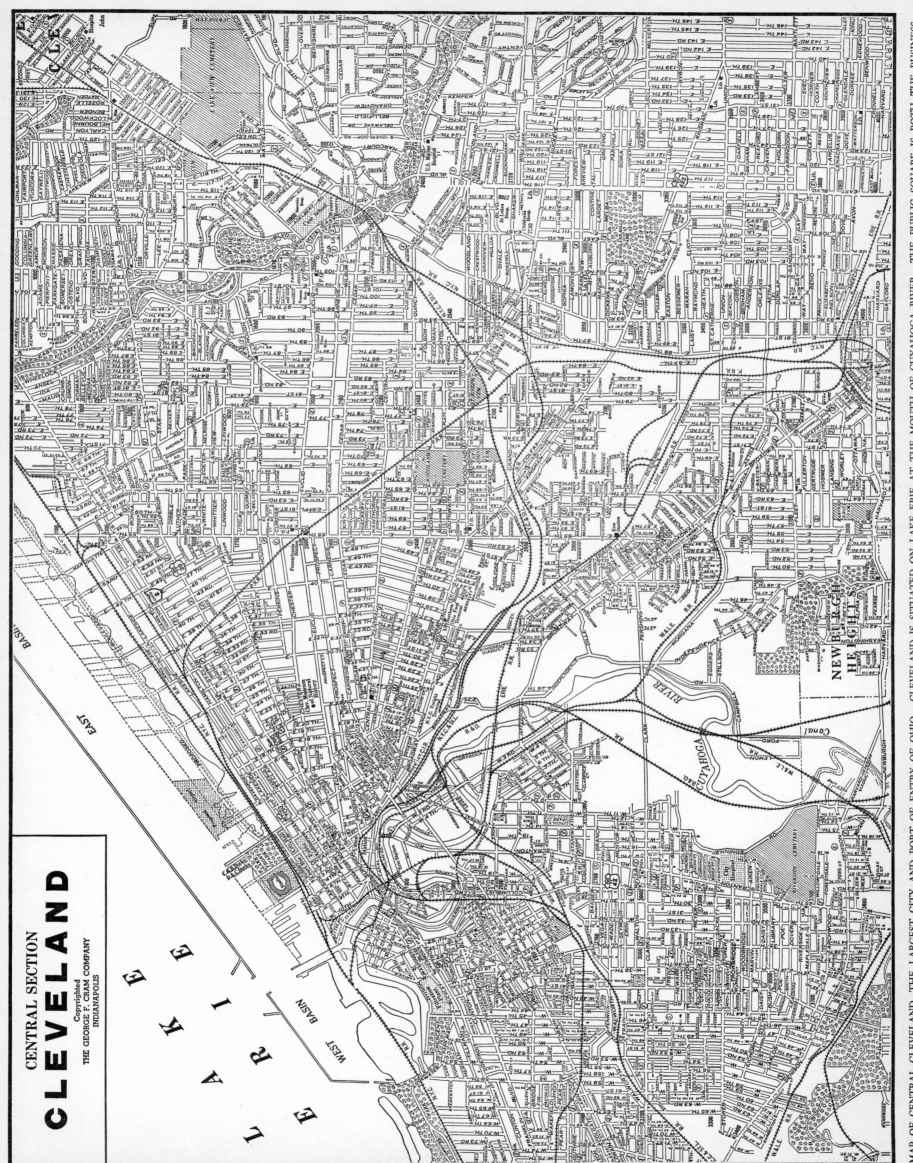

CENTRAL SECTION
CLEVELAND
Copyrighted
THE GEORGE F. CRAM COMPANY
INDIANAPOLIS

MAP OF CENTRAL CLEVELAND, THE LARGEST CITY AND PORT OF ENTRY OF OHIO. CLEVELAND IS SITUATED ON LAKE ERIE AT THE MOUTH OF CUYAHOGA RIVER. THE PUBLIC SQUARE IS BOTH THE BUSINESS CENTER AND ARCHITECTURAL CENTER OF THE GROUP PLAN OF PUBLIC BUILDINGS.

The harbor is protected by a breakwater. The city covers an area of more than 71 square miles with lake frontage of 10 miles. The Cuyahoga River and various tributaries, called "runs," intersect the city unevenly, and are spanned by numerous bridges and viaducts. The city radiates from the Public Square, the principal streets extending like the ribs of an open fan. Lower Superior Avenue and lower Euclid Avenue are the principal business streets. Upper Euclid Avenue is the leading residence thoroughfare.
With the Mesaba iron ranges situated just to the north, and bituminous coal deposits just to the south, Cleveland serves as an outstanding center both for the transit and manufacture of raw materials. Its main industrial importance lies in its diversified fabrications of steel and iron, especially automobiles, trucks, and innumerable automobile accessories, printing presses, hardware, tools, refrigerators, stoves, radios, confectionery, vacuum sweepers, sewing machines, astronomical appliances, electric batteries, confectionery, etc. Among other industries, the most prominent is women's garments. Cleveland also contains the largest paint and varnish factories in the country.
Among prominent business buildings are: Williamson, Garfield, Cleveland Athletic, Citizens' Bank, Chamber of Commerce, Leader-News, the Terminal Group, Rockefeller, Guardian, and Kirby Buildings. There are many fine hotels, among which are Hotel Cleveland, Statler, Colonial, Hollenden, Olmsted, Winton, Fenway and Auditorium. The city has many beautiful churches, Trinity Cathedral, Euclid Avenue Temple, Euclid Avenue Presbyterian Church, First Methodist Church, and St. Agnes being among the most prominent. The Cleveland "Group Plan" is composed of the City Hall, Cuyahoga County Court House, Federal Building, Municipal Auditorium, and Public Library.
In the city are Western Reserve University, John Carroll University, the Case School of Applied Science, and St. Ignatius College (Roman Catholic).
The parks include 2,875 acres. There are more than 44 miles of boulevards.
Cleveland was founded in 1796 by a survey party under the direction of General Moses Cleaveland. In 1814 the village of Cleaveland was incorporated with less than 100 inhabitants. Cleveland (a simplified spelling) was incorporated as a city in 1836, and Ohio City (west of the river) was absorbed in 1854. The first great impetus received by the city was furnished by the completion of the Ohio Canal in 1832. Additional growth followed the railroad connection with the East and the development of the coal fields of Southern Ohio, Pennsylvania, and West Virginia, and of the iron-mining region of the upper lakes.
–c. s., Bolivar Co., Miss., 3,240.
On Yazoo & Miss. Val. (R. R.).
–Mora Co., N. Mex., 600.
–Pawnee Co., Okla., 2,959.
On Mo.-Kan.-Tex. (R. R.).
–c. s., Bradley Co., Tenn., 9,136.
On Southern (R. R.).
–Liberty Co., Tex., 1,422.
On Gulf, Colo. & Santa Fe; Tex. & N. Orl. (R. Rs.).
–Emery Co., Utah, 509.
Cleveland Heights, Cuyahoga Co., Ohio, 50,945.
A residential suburb of Cleveland.
Cleves, Hamilton Co., Ohio, 1,711.
On Cle., Cin., Chi. & St. Lou. (R. R.).
Clewiston, Hendry Co., Fla., 949.
On Atlantic Coast Line (R. R.).
Clichy, Dept. of Seine, France, 56,475.
A manufacturing suburb of Paris.
Clifford, Bristol Co., Mass., 500.
Cliffside, Rutherford Co., N. Car., 1,654.
On Cliffside (R. R.).
Cliffside Park, Bergen Co., N. J., 15,267.
Cliffwood, Monmouth Co., N. J., 550.
On Cen. of N. Jer.; N. York & Long Br.; Penna. (R. Rs.).
Clifton, c. s., Greenlee Co., Ariz., 2,305.
On Sou. Pac. (R. R.).
–Iroquois Co., Ill., 589.
On Ill. Cen. (R. R.).
–Clay and Washington Cos., Kans., 709.
On Chi., Rk. Isl. & Pac.; Mo. Pac.; Un. Pac. (R. Rs.).
–Campbell Co., Ky., 3,080.
–Essex Co., Mass., 610.
On Bost. & Me. (R. R.).
–Passaic Co., New Jersey, 46,875.
On Del., Lack. & West.; Erie (R. Rs.).
Steel, woolen and leather goods, chemicals.
–Spartanburg Co., S. C., 2,380.
–Wayne Co., Tenn., 800.
–Bosque Co., Texas, 1,367.
On Gulf, Colo. & Santa Fe (R. R.).
Clifton Forge (Ind. City), Allegheny Co., Va., 6,839.
On Chesa. & Ohio (R. R.).
Clifton Heights, Delaware Co., Pa., 5,057.
Clifton Springs, Ontario Co., N. Y., 1,819.
On Leh. Val.; N. York Cen. (R. Rs.).
Clinchco, Dickenson Co., Va., 1,050.
On Clinchfield (R. R.).
Clinchfield, Russell Co., Va., 560.
On Clinchfield (R. R.).
Clint, El Paso Co., Tex., 600.
Tex. & N. Orl.; Tex. & Pac. (R. Rs.).
Clinton, c. s., Van Buren Co., Ark., 658.
–Middlesex Co., Conn., 1,200.
On N. York, N. Hav. & Hart. (R. R.).
–c. s., DeWitt Co., Ill., 5,920.
On Ill. Cen.; Ill. Term. (R. Rs.).
–Vermillion Co., Ind., 7,936.
On Chi. & East. Ill. (R. R.).
–c. s., Clinton Co., Iowa, 25,726.
On Chi., Burl. & Quincy; Chi., Mil., St. P. & Pac.; Chicago, R. I. & Pac.; Chi. & Nor. West.; Clin., Davenp. & Musc. (El.); Davenp., Rk. Isl. & Northw. (R. Rs.).
Manufacturing and jobbing center. Corn products, structural iron, sash and door, boilers, and tanks.
–c. s., Hickman Co., Ky., 1,204.
On Ill. Cen. (R. R.).
–c. s., East Feliciana Parish, La., 702.
On Yazoo & Miss. Val. (R. R.).
–Kennebec Co., Maine, 600.
On Me. Cen. (R. R.).
–Worcester Co., Mass., 12,373.
On Bost. & Me.; N. York, N. Hav. & Hart. (R. Rs.).
Manufactures carpets, cotton goods, woolens, and wire cloth.
–Lenawee Co., Mich., 1,026.
On N. York Cen. (R. R.).
–Big Stone Co., Minn., 537.
On Chi., Mil., St. P. & Pac. (R. R.).
–Hinds Co., Miss., 912.
On Yazoo & Miss. Val. (R. R.).
–c. s., Henry Co., Mo., 5,744.
On St. Lou.-San Fran., Mo.-Kan.-Tex. (R. Rs.).
–Hunterdon Co., N. J., 932.
On Leh. Val. (R. R.).
–Oneida Co., N. Y., 1,475.
On N. York, Ont. & West. (R. R.).
–c. s., Sampson Co., N. C., 2,712.
On Atl. Coast Line (R. R.).
–Custer Co., Okla., 7,512.
On Atch., Top. & Santa Fe; Chi., Rk. Isl. & Pac.; Panh. & Santa Fe; St. Lou.-San Fran. (R. Rs.).
–Laurens Co., S. C., 5,643.
On Colum., Newb. & Laur.; Seab. Air Line (R. Rs.).
–c. s., Anderson Co., Tenn., 1,927.
On Southern (R. R.).
–Davis Co., Utah, 625.
–Rock Co., Wis., 902.
R. R. name Clinton Junction.
–Huron Co., Ontario, Canada, 1,789.
On Can. Nat. (R. R.).
Clintondale, Ulster Co., N. Y., 603.
On N. York, N. Hav. & Hart. (R. R.).
Clinton Junction (Clinton P. O.), Rock Co., Wis., 902.
On Chi. & Nor. West.; Chi., Mil., St. P. & Pac. (R. Rs.).
Clintonville, Waupaca Co., Wis., 3,572.
On Chi. & Nor. West (R. R.).
Clintwood, c. s., Dickenson Co., Va., 729.
Clio, Barbour Co., Ala., 867.
On Cen. of Ga. (R. R.).
–Genesee Co., Mich., 1,548.
On Pere Marq. (R. R.).
–Marlboro Co., S. Car., 808.
On Atl. Coast Line; Seab. Air Line (R. Rs.).
Clitheroe, Lancashire, England, 12,008.
Cloquet, Carlton Co., Minn., 6,782.
On Chi., Mil., St. P. & Pac.; Dul. & Northe.; Gt. Nor.; Nor. Pac. (R. Rs.).
Manufactures: Paper and woodwork.
Closter, Bergen Co., N. J., 2,502.
On Erie (R. R.).
Clover, York Co., S. C., 3,111.
On Car. & Nor. West. (R. R.).
Cloverdale, Sonoma Co., Cal., 759.
On Northw. Pac. (R. R.).
–Putnam Co., Indiana, 627.
On Chi., Ind. & Lou. (R. R.).
Cloverport, Breckenridge Co., Ky., 1,324.
On Lou. & Nash. (R. R.).
Clovis, Fresno Co., Cal., 1,316.
On Sou. Pac. (R. R.).
–c. s., Curry Co., N. M., 8,027.
On Atch., Top. & Santa Fe; Panh. & Santa Fe (R. Rs.).
Cluj, Transylvania, Rumania, 98,550.
Textile, paper, sugar, and pottery works. Breweries.
Clune, Indiana Co., Pa., 750.
Clyde, Cloud Co., Kans., 1,157.
On Chi., Rk. Isl. & Pac.; Mo. Pac.; Un. Pac. (R. Rs.).
–Wayne Co., N. Y., 2,374.
On N. York Cen. (R. R.).
–Sandusky Co., Ohio, 3,159.
On Cle., Cin., Chi. & St. Lou.; Lake Shore Elec.; N. York Cent.; Wheel. & L. Erie (R. Rs.).
–Callahan Co., Texas, 706.
On Tex. & Pac. (R. R.).
Clydebank, Dumbarton Co., Scotland, 46,963.
Shipbuilding and engineering works.
Clymer, Chautauqua Co., N. Y., 535.
–Indiana Co., Pa., 2,672.
On N. York Cen.; Penna. (R. Rs.).
Coahoma, Howard Co., Tex., 620.
On Tex. & Pac. (R. R.).
Coal Bluff, Washington Co., Pa., 526.
On Penna. (R. R.).
Coal Centre (Coal Center P. O.), Washington Co., Pa., 629.
On Penna. (R. R.).
Coal City, Grundy Co., Ill., 1,637.
On Alton; Atch., Top. & Santa Fe; Elg., Jol. & East. (R. Rs.).
Coal Creek, Anderson Co., Tenn., 1,116.
On Lou. & Nash.; Sou. (R. Rs.).
Coaldale, Jefferson Co., Ala., 515.
On Lou. & Nash. (R. R.).
–Schuylkill Co., Pa., 6,921.
On Cen. of New Jer.; Leh. & N. Eng. (R. Rs.).
Coalgate, Coal Co., Okla., 2,064.
On Chi., Rk. Isl. & Pac.; Okla. Cy.-Ada-Atoka (R. Rs.).
Coal Grove, Lawrence Co., Ohio, 2,181.
On Norf. & West. (R. R.).
Coal Hill, Johnson Co., Ark., 1,169.
On Mo. Pac. (R. R.).
Coalinga, Fresno Co., Cal., 2,851.
On Sou. Pac. (R. R.).
Coalmont, Clay Co., Ind., 780.
On Chi., Mil., St. P. & Pac. (R. R.).
Coalport, Clearfield Co., Pa., 1,222.
On Penna. (R. R.).
Coalridge, Luzerne Co., Pa., 1,000.
Coalton, Montgomery Co., Ill., 611.
–Jackson Co., Ohio, 646.
On Balt. & Ohio; Chesa. & Ohio (R. Rs.).
Coalville, c. s., Summit Co., Utah, 938.
On Un. Pac. (R. R)
Coamo, Mun. of Coamo, Puerto Rico, 7,639.
Coatesville, Chester Co., Pa., 14,582.
On Penna.; Read. (R. Rs.).
Steel manufactures.
Coaticook, Stanstead Co., Quebec, Canada, 4,044.
On Can. Nat. (R. R.).
Coats, Harnett Co., N. C., 562.
On Durh. & Sou. (R. R.).
Coban, Alta Vera Paz Dept., Guatemala, 26,774.
Center of a coffee growing region.
Cobden, Union Co., Ill., 1,036.
On Ill. Cen. (R. R.).
Cobh (Queenstown), Cork Co., Ireland (Eire, former Irish Free State), 6,075.
Cobleskill, c. s., Schoharie Co., N. Y., 2,594.
On Del. & Hud. (R. R.).
Cobourg, Northumberland Co., Ontario, Canada, 5,834.
Cochabamba, capital of Dept. of Cochabamba, Bolivia, 37,519.
Important commercial town.
Cochin, Madras, India, 22,818.
Seaport and industrial center.
Cochituate, Middlesex Co., Mass., 1,350.
Cochran, Bleckley Co., Ga., 2,267.
On Southern (R. R.).
–Dearborn Co., Ind., 875.
On Balt. & Ohio (R. R.).
Cochranton, Crawford Co., Pa., 727.
On Erie (R. R.).
Cockermouth, Cumberland, England, 4,789.
Cockeysville, Baltimore Co., Md., 1,515.
On Penna. (R. R.).
Cockrell Hill, Dallas Co., Texas, 800.
Cocoa, Brevard Co., Fla., 2,809.
The Railroad name is Cocoa-Rockledge.
Coconut Grove, Dade Co., Fla. (Station of Miami).
On Fla. East Coast (R. R.).
Cody, Jefferson Co., Fla., 530.
On Atl. Coast Line (R. R.).
–c. s., Park Co., Wyo., 1,800.
On Chi., Burl. & Quincy (R. R.).
Coeburn, Wise Co., Va., 784.
On Norf. & West. (R. R.).
Coeur D'Alene, c. s., Kootenai Co., Idaho, 8,297.
On Chi., Mil., St. P. & Pac.; Nor. Pac.; Spok., Coe. D'Ale. & Pal.; Spokane Internat. (R. Rs.).
Coeymans, Albany Co., N. Y., 1,000.
Coffeen, Montgomery Co., Ill., 703.
On N. York, Chi. & St. L. (R. R.).
Coffeyville, Montgomery Co., Kans., 17,636.
On Atch., Top. & S. Fe; Mo.-Kan.-Tex.; Mo. Pac.; Un. Tract. (El.); Mo. Pacific (R. Rs.).
In the heart of the Mid-Continent oil and gas field. Has a number of oil refineries and oil well equipment plants.
Cogdell, Clinch Co., Ga., 600.
Coggon, Linn Co., Iowa, 503.
On Ill. Cen. (R. R.).
Cognac, Dept. of Charente, France, 16,305.
Brandy distilleries.
Cohasset, Norfolk Co., Mass., 3,418.
On N. York, N. Hav. & Hart. (R. R.).
Cohay, Smith Co., Miss., 1,092.
Cohocton, Steuben Co., N. Y., 860.
On Del., Lack. & West.; Erie (R. Rs.).
Cohoes, Albany Co., N. Y., 23,226.
On Del. & Hud.; N. York Cen. (R. Rs.). On Erie Canal.
Extensive manufactures of hosiery and knit goods.
Coihueco, Chile, 1,816.
Coimbatore, Madras, India, 95,198.
Textile, tanning and sugar industries.
Coimbra, Beira, Portugal, 27,333.
An educational center.
Coin, Page Co., Iowa, 536.
On Chi., Burl. & Quincy; Wab. (R. Rs.).
Cojutepeque, Dept. of Tuscatlan, Salvador, 19,914.
Cokato, Wright Co., Minn., 1,125.
On Gt. Nor. (R. R.).
Cokeburg, Washington Co., Pa., 1,550.
On Penna. (R. R.).
Cokedale, Las Animas Co., Colo., 500.
On Colo. & Sou.; Den. & Rio Gde. West (R. Rs.).
Cokeville, Westmoreland Co., Pa., 540.
Colborne, Northumberland Co., Ontario, Canada, 1,015.
On Can. Pac.; Can. Nat. (R. Rs.).
Colby, c. s., Thomas Co., Kans., 2,564.
On Chi., Rk. Isl. & Pac.; Un. Pac. (R. Rs.).
–Clark and Marathon Cos., Wis., 849.
On Minn., St. P. & S. Ste. M. (R. R.).
Colchester, New London Co., Conn., 937.
On N. York, N. Hav. & Hart. (R. R.).
–Essex, England, 48,607.
Site of first Roman colony in Britain.
–McDonough Co., Ill., 1,342.
On Chi., Burl. & Quincy (R. R.).
–Chittenden Co., Vt., 1,515.
On Cen. Ver. (R. R.).
Colden, Erie Co., N. Y., 920.
On Balt. & Ohio (R. R.).
Cold Spring (Cold Spring Sta.), Stearns Co., Minn., 1,147.
On Gt. Nor. (R. R.).
–Putnam Co., N. Y., 1,784.
On N. York Cen. (R. R.).
–San Jacinto Co., Tex., 550.
Cold Spring Harbor, Suffolk Co., N. Y., 982.
Coldwater, c. s., Comanche Co., Kans., 1,294.
On Atch., Top. & Santa Fe (R. R.).
–c. s., Branch Co., Mich., 6,735.
On N. York Cen. (R. R.).
–Tate Co., Miss., 664.
On Ill. Cen. (R. R.).
–Mercer Co., Ohio, 1,787.
On Cin. North.; N. York, Chi. & St. Lou. (R. Rs.).
Coleanor, Bibb Co., Ala., 750.
On Lou. & Nash.; Sou. (R. Rs.).
Colebrook, Coos Co., N. H., 1,500.
On Me. Cen. (R. R.).
–Ashtabula Co., Ohio, 739.
Cole Camp, Benton Co., Mo., 932.
On Chi., Rk. Isl. & Pac.; Mo. Pac. (R. Rs.).
Coleman, Alberta, Canada, 2,129.
–Sumter Co., Fla., 862.
On Seab. Air Line (R. R.).
–Midland Co., Mich., 667.
On Pere Marq. (R. R.).
–c. s., Coleman Co., Texas, 6,078.
On Gulf, Colo. & Santa Fe (R. R.).
Coleraine, Itasca Co., Minn., 1,243.
On Dul., Missabe & Nor.; Gt. Nor. (R. Rs.).
Coleridge, Cedar Co., Neb., 616.
On Chi., St. P., Minn. & Oma. (R. R.).
Colfax, Placer Co., Cal., 912.
On Nev. Co., Nar. Gauge; Sou. Pac. (R. Rs.).
–McLean Co., Ill., 803.
On Ill. Cen. (R. R.).
–Clinton Co., Ind., 690.
On Cle., Cin., Chi. & St. L.; Penna. (R. Rs.).
–Jasper Co., Iowa, 2,213.
On Chi., Rk. Isl. and Pac.; Des Moines & Cen. Ia. (El.) (R. Rs.).
–c. s., Grant Parish, La., 1,141.
On Louisiana & Arkansas (R. R.).
–c. s., Whitman Co., Wash., 2,782.
On Ore.-Wash. R. R. & Nav. Co.; Spoka., Coe. D'Ale. & Pal. (R. Rs.),
–Dunn Co., Wis., 919.
On Minn., St. P. & S. Ste. M. (R. R.).
College Corner, Union Co., Ind., 1,000.
On Balt. & Ohio; Erie (R. Rs.).
College Hill, Hamilton Co., Ohio (Station of Cincinnati).
On Cin. & L. Erie (El.) (R. R.).
–(College) Beaver Co., Pa., 2,643.
College Park, Clayton and Fulton Cos., Ga., 6,604.
On Atl. & West. P. (R. R.).
College Place (Arden), Richland Co., S. C., 987.
College Station, Brazos Co., Tex., 1,500.
On Internat.-Gt. Nor.; Tex. & N. Orl. (R. Rs.).
College View, Lancaster Co., Neb. (Pop. incl. in Lincoln).

On Chi., Burl. & Quincy; Chi., Rk. Isl. & Pac. (R. Rs.).
Collegeville, Montgomery Co., Pa., 878.
On Reading (R. R.).
Collier, Fayette Co., Pa., 619.
On Balt. & Ohio (R. R.).
Collierville, Shelby Co., Tenn., 1,008.
On Southern (R. R.).
Collingdale, Delaware Co., Pa., 7,857.
On Balt. & Ohio (R. R.).
Collingswood, Camden Co., N. J., 12,723.
On Penna.-Read. Seashore (R. R.).
A residential suburb of Camden.
Collingwood, Simcoe Co., Ontario, Canada, 5,809.
On Can. Nat. (R. R.).
Collins, Tattnall Co., Ga., 510.
On Col. & Glennv.; Sea. Air Line (R. Rs.).
–Covington Co., Miss., 935.
On Gulf & Ship Isl. (R. R.).
–Erie Co., N. Y., 500.
On Erie (R. R.).
Collinsville, De Kalb Co., Ala., 892.
On Ala. Gt. Sou. (R. R.).
–Madison Co., Ill., 9,235.
On Penn. (R. R.).
–Middlesex Co., Mass., 2,000.
–Tulsa Co., Okla., 2,249.
On Atch., Top. & Santa Fe (R. R.).
–Grayson Co., Texas, 670.
On Mo.-Kan.-Tex.; Tex. & Pac. (R. Rs.).
Collinwood, Wayne Co., Tennessee, 573.
On Lou. & Nash. (R. R.).
Colma, San Mateo Co., Calif., 2,063.
On Sou. Pac. (R. R.).
Colmar, Upper Alsace, France, 49,448.
Textiles, sugar, machinery and wines.
–Montgomery Co., Pa., 500.
On Reading (R. R.).
Colmar Manor, Prince Georges Co., Md., 1,225.
Colmesneil, Tyler Co., Tex., 500.
On Tex. & N. Orl.; Waco, Beau., Trin. & Sab. (R. Rs.).
Colne, Lancashire and Yorkshire, England, 23,790.
Has important textile manufactures.
Colo, Story Co., Iowa, 532.
On Chi. & Nor. West. (R. R.).
Cologne, Germany. See Köln.
Coloma, Berrien Co., Mich., 826.
On Pere Marq. (R. R.).
Colombes, Seine, France, 61,944.
Colombo, capital of Ceylon, 308,000.
Chief seaport and business center of Ceylon.
Colome, Tripp Co., S. Dak., 531.
On Chi. & Nor. West. (R. R.).
Colon, Matanzas Prov., Cuba, 8,046.
–St. Joseph Co., Mich., 781.
On Mich. Cen. (R. R.).
–Panama, 29,765.
Seaport and railroad terminus; the Gulf of Mexico terminus of the Panama Canal.
Colonia, Middlesex Co., N. J., 500.
On Penna.-Read., Seashore (R. R.).
Colonial Beach, Westmoreland Co., Va., 928.
Colonial Heights, Chesterfield Co., Va., 2,331.
Colonie, Albany Co., N. Y., 1,176.
Colony, Anderson Co., Kansas, 473.
On Atch., Top. & Santa Fe (R. R.).
Colorado, c. s., Mitchell Co., Texas, 4,671.
On Tex. & Pac. (R. R.).
Colorado City, El Paso Co., Colo.
On Den. & R. Gde. West.; Mid. Term. (R. Rs.).
Colorado Springs, c. s., El Paso Co., Colo., 33,237.
Is situated near the foot of Pike's Peak, at an elevation of 6,000 feet. It is on the Atchison, Topeka & Santa Fe; the Chicago, Rock Island & Pacific; the Colorado and Southern; the Denver & Rio Grande Western and the Midland Terminal railroads. A famous resort.
Colp, Williamson Co., Illinois, 1,250.
Colquitt, c. s., Miller Co., Ga., 832.
On Seab. Air Line (R. R.).
Colrain, Franklin Co., Mass., 1,554.
Colton, San Bernardino Co., Cal., 8,014.
On Atch., Top. & Santa Fe; Los Ang. & Salt L.; Pac. Elec.; Sou. Pac. (R. Rs.).
–St. Lawrence Co., N. Y., 500.
–Minnehaha Co., S. Dak., 564.
On Chi., Mil., St. P. & Pac.; Gt. Nor. (R. Rs.).
Columbia, Houston Co., Ala., 926.
On Cen. of Ga. (R. R.).
–Monroe Co., Ill., 1,791.
On E. St. Lou., Colu. & Water. (El.); Mo. & Ohio (R. Rs.).
–c. s., Adair Co., Ky., 1,195.
–c. s., Caldwell Par., La., 760.
On Mo. Pac. (R. R.).
–c. s., Marion Co., Miss., 4,833.
On Fernwood, Columbia & Gulf; Gulf & Ship Islands; Gulf, Mobile & Northern (R. Rs.).
In hardwood and pine timber belt. Has a sawmill and several wood working factories.
–c. s., Boone Co., Mo., 14,967.
On Mo.-Kans.-Tex.; Wabash (R. Rs.). Primarily a school town, its local trade serving student needs. Seat of University of Missouri and Missouri Bible College among other educational institutions.
–c. s., Tyrrell Co., N. C., 864.
On Norf. Sou. (R. R.).
–Lancaster Co., Pa., 11,349.
On Pennsylvania; Reading (R. Rs.).
–c. s., Richland Co., S. C., State capital, 51,581.
Is situated on the Congaree River at the junction of the Broad and Saluda Rivers, and on the Southern, the Atlantic Coast Line, the Seaboard Air Line, and the Columbia, Newberry and Laurens railroads.
The most imposing buildings are the United States court-house, the granite State Capitol Building; Farm Credit Administration Building, and Veterans Hospital. The Columbia College for women, Southern Theological Seminary (Lutheran), Allen University (colored), Benedict College (colored), and the University of South Carolina are located here. Columbia also has a state penitentiary.
–c. s., Maury Co., Tenn., 7,882.
On Lou. & Nash., Chatt. & St. Lou. (R. Rs.).
–Carbon Co., Utah, 500.
On Carbon Co. (R. R.).
Columbia City, c. s., Whitley Co., Ind., 3,805.
On Penn. (R. R.).
Columbia Falls, Flathead Co., Mont., 637.
On Gt. Nor. (R. R.).
Columbia Heights, Anoka Co., Minn., 5,613.
Columbiana, c. s., Shelby Co., Ala., 1,180.
On Lou. & Nash.; Sou. (R. Rs.).
–Columbiana Co., Ohio, 2,485.
On Penna.; Youngst. & Suburb. (El.) (R. Rs.).
Columbiaville, Columbia Co., N. Y., 530.
Columbus, c. s., Muscogee Co., Ga., 43,131.
On Cen. of Ga.; Seab. Air Line; Sou. (R. Rs.).
Large cotton mills and manufactures of cotton goods; there are also iron works, show case factories, planing mills, fertilizer plants, syrup refineries, etc., and extensive water power resources.
–c. s., Bartholomew Co., Ind., 9,935.
On Cle., Cin., Chi. & St. Lou.; Ind. R. R. Sys. (El.); Pennsylvania (R. Rs.).
Situated in a fine farming region. Tanneries, machine shops and woodworking plants.
–Cherokee Co., Kans., 3,503.
On Mo.-Kan.-Tex.; Northe., Okla. (El.); St. Lou.-San Fran. (R. Rs.).
–Hickman Co., Ky., 513.
On Mobile & Ohio (R. R.).
–c. s., Lowndes Co., Miss., 10,743.
On Col. & Greenv.; Mob. & Ohio; St. Lou.-San Fran.; Sou. (R. Rs.).
Seat of Mississippi State College for women. There are foundries, machine shops and extensive railroad shops.
–c. s., Stillwater Co., Mont., 834.
On Nor. Pac. (R. R.).
–c. s., Platte Co., Neb., 6,898.
On Chi., Burl. & Quincy; Un. Pac. (R. Rs.).
–Burlington Co., N. J., 535.
On Penna. (R. R.).
–c. s., Franklin Co., Ohio, State capital, 290,564.
Is situated on the Scioto River, and on the Baltimore & Ohio; the Cincinnati and Lake Erie (El.); the Cleveland, Cincinnati, Chicago, St. Louis; the Chesapeake and Ohio; the Norfolk & Western; the Pennsylvania; and the New York Central railroads. Port Columbus is a finely-equipped airport.
The State Capitol, in a public square, is a fine building of limestone. The Civic Center includes New Federal Building, City Hall, State Office Building, and other important units. Columbus Gallery of Fine Arts houses a valuable collection. The city is the seat of Ohio State University, Capital University and Franklin University. Among state institutions are Central Insane Asylum and the State Penitentiary. The annual Ohio State Fair is held in Columbus.
The manufactures are considerable. There are foundries and machine shops, iron and steel furnaces, flour mills, packing houses, and lumber and planing mills. Other large industries are boots and shoes, furniture, ticket registers, automobile parts, scales, paints and varnishes, and printing and publishing.
Columbus was laid out in 1812, in the midst of an unbroken forest, on the high banks of the Scioto River; incorporated in 1816, and became the State capital in 1817.
–c. s., Colorado Co., Tex., 2,054.
On Tex. & N. Orl. (R. R.).
–Columbia Co., Wis., 2,514.
On Chi., Mil., St. P. & Pac. (R. R.).
Columbus Grove, Putnam Co., Ohio, 1,633.
On Cin. & L. Erie (El.); Balt. & Ohio; Det., Tol. & Iron.; Nor. Ohio (R. Rs.).
Columbus Junction, Louisa Co., Iowa, 867.
On Chi., Rk. Isl. & Pac. (R. R.).
Colusa, c. s., Colusa Co., Cal., 2,116.
On Sacramento No. (El.); Sou. Pac. (R. Rs.).
Colver, Cambria Co., Pa., 1,800.
On Camb. & Ind. (R. R.).
Colville, c. s., Stevens Co., Wash., 1,803.
On Gt. Nor. (R. R.).
Colwyn, Delaware Co., Pa., 2,064.
Comanche, Stephens Co., Okla., 1,704.
On Chi., Rk. Isl. & Pac. (R. R.).
–c. s., Comanche Co., Texas, 2,435.
On Ft. Worth & Rio Gde. (R. R.).
Comayagua (formerly Valladolid), Dept. of Comayagua, Honduras, 8,778.
Formerly capital of Honduras.
Combaconum, India. See Kumbakonam.
Combarbala, Prov. of Coquimbo, Chile, 1,532.
Combined Locks, Outagamie Co., Wis., 545.
On Chi. & Nor. West. (R. R.).
Combs (Doland), Perry Co., Ky., 861.
On Lou. & Nash. (R. R.).
Comer, Madison Co., Ga., 900.
On Seab. Air Line (R. R.).
Comerio, Mun. of Comerio, Puerto Rico, 2,322.
Comfort, Kendall Co., Texas, 713.
On Tex. & N. Orl. (R. R.).
Comfrey, Brown Co., Minn., 535.
On Chi. & Nor. West. (R. R.).
Comines, Dept. of West Flanders, Belgium, 6,080.
The city was destroyed in the World War.
Comiso, Prov. of Ragusa, Italy, 32,166.
Comitan, Chiapas, Mexico, 8,517.
Commack, Suffolk Co., N. Y., 500.
Commerce, Jackson Co., Ga., 3,002.
On Southern (R. R.).
–Ottawa Co., Okla., 2,608.
On Northe. Okla. (El.) (R. R.).
–Hunt Co., Texas, 4,267.
On St. Lou., Southw.; Tex. & N. Orl. (R. Rs.).
Commodore, Indiana Co., Pa., 800.
On N. York Cen.; Penna. (R. Rs.).
Como, capital of Prov. of Como, Lombardy, Italy, 40,600.
Is delightfully situated at the southern extremity of Lake Como, the most celebrated for beauty of all the lakes of Italy. Como was a place of importance among the Romans, and was the birthplace of the elder Pliny.
–Panola Co., Miss., 851.
On Ill. Cen. (R. R.).
–Hertford Co., N. Car., 500.
Compiegne, Dept. of Oise, France, 18,885.
Industrial town. Boat-building, iron and copper founding and cooperage.
Compton, Los Angeles Co., Cal., 12,516.
On Pac. El.; Sou. Pac. (R. Rs.).
In truck farming region. A residential suburb of Los Angeles which also has large manufacturing industries.
Comstock, Kalamazoo Co., Mich., 1,200.
On Mich. Cen. (R. R.).
–Washington Co., N. Y., 1,800.
On Del. & Hud. (R. R.).
Comstock Park, Kent Co., Mich., 1,500.
On Penna.; Pere Marq. (R. Rs.).
Concarneau, Dept. of Finistère, France, 5,995.
Fortified seaport; chief industry, pilchard fishery.
Concepción, Prov. of Concepción, Chile, 85,682.
The chief manufacturing center of the republic; trades in grain, hides, wine, beef; extensive coal deposits in vicinity.
–Luzon, P. I., 17,483.
Conception (Conception Junction P. O.), Nodaway Co., Mo., 514.
On Chi., Gt. West.; Wab. (R. Rs.).
Concord, Contra Costa Co., Cal., 1,125.
On Sacramento Nor. (El.); Sou. Pac. (R. Rs.).
–Middlesex Co., Mass., 7,723.
On Bost. & Me. (R. R.).
Famous as the home of Emerson, Thoreau, Hawthorne, and other writers; the scene of the first battle of the American Revolution.
–Jackson Co., Mich., 603.
On Mich. Cen. (R. R.).
–c. s., Merrimack Co., N. H., State capital, 25,228.
On the west bank of the Merrimac River, 75 miles by rail north-northwest from Boston, and on the Boston & Maine Railroad. The city covers an area of over 60 square miles. The Boston & Maine Railroad has here large car manufactory and repair shops. The city is a channel for the lumber, granite, mineral and agricultural resources of the district. It has silver factories, granite quarries, and cutlery and electrical instrument works, woolen mills and a large printing establishment.
The principal buildings are the State House, and the State Library Building, containing the chambers of the Supreme Court and educational and agricultural State offices, and the New Hampshire Historical Society Library. There are also a State asylum for the insane; a State prison, a government building for post-office, pension office and United States courts. In 1765 it was incorporated. In 1816 became State capital; in 1823 shire town of Merrimack County; in 1853 adopted a city charter.
–c. s., Cabarrus Co., N. C., 11,820.
On Southern (R. R.).
In cotton growing region. Has large textile mills.
–Lake Co., Ohio, 710.
On Balt. & Ohio (R. R.).
Concordia, c. s., Cloud Co., Kans., 5,914.
On Atch., Top. & Santa Fe; Chi., Burl. & Quincy; Mo. Pac.; Un. Pac. (R. Rs.).
The Nazareth Academy is located here. Is the seat of a Catholic bishopric and cathedral.
–Lafayette Co., Mo., 1,140.
On Mo. Pac. (R. R.).
Concrete, Skagit Co., Washington, 736.
On Gt. Nor. (R. R.).
Condon, Gilliam Co., Ore., 940.
On Con., Kinz. & Sou.; Ore.-Wash. R. R. & Nav. Co. (R. Rs.).
Conestee, Greenville Co., S. Car., 500.
Conestoga, Lancaster Co., Pa., 600.
Conesville, Coshocton Co., Ohio, 500.
On Penna.; Wheel. & L. Erie (R. Rs.).
Coney Island, Kings Co., N. Y.
On South Brooklyn (El.) (R. R.).
A popular pleasure resort, and a part of the city of New York.
Confluence, Somerset Co., Pa., 989.
On Balt. & Ohio; West Maryland (R. Rs.).
Congers, Rockland Co., N. Y., 700.
On West Shore (R. R.).
Congleton, Cheshire, England, 12,885.
Lace, silk and tobacco industries.
Conifer, Jefferson Co., Pa., 1,224.
On Pitts. & Shawmut (R. R.).
Conimicut, Kent Co., R. I., 1,500.
On United El. (R. R.).
Conjeeveram, Chingleput Dist., Madras, British India, 61,376.
Silk and cotton weaving.
Connaughton, Montgomery Co., Pa., 708.
Conneaut, Ashtabula Co., Ohio, 9,691.
On Bess. & L. Erie; N. York Cen.; N. York, Chi. & St. Lou. (R. Rs.).
Conneautville, Crawford Co., Pa., 927.
On Bess. & L. Erie; Penna. (R. Rs.).
Connellsville, Fayette Co., Pa., 13,290.
On Balt. & Ohio; Penna.; Pitts. & L. Erie; Pitts. & W. Va.; West. Md. (R. Rs.).
Most important manufacture is coke.
Connelly, Ulster Co., N. Y., 850.
Connersville, c. s., Fayette Co., Ind., 12,795.
On Balt. & Ohio; Cle., Cin., Chi. & St. Lou.; Erie; N. York, Chi. and St. Lou. (R. Rs.).
A busy manufacturing center, auto parts, furniture and electrical goods.
Conover, Catawba Co., N. C., 973.
On Car. & Nor. West.; Sou. (R. Rs.).
Conrad, Grundy Co., Iowa, 536.
On Chi. & Nor. West. (R. R.).
–c. s., Pondera Co., Montana, 1,499.
On Gt. Nor.; Mont. West. (R. Rs.).
Conroe, c. s., Montgomery Co., Texas, 2,457.
On Gulf, Colo. & Santa Fe; Internat.-Gt. Nor. (R. Rs.).
Consett, Durham, England, 12,251.
Metal working and cutlery manufacture.
Conshohocken, Montgomery Co., Pa., 10,815.
On Pennsylvania and Reading (R. Rs.).
A manufacturing town with iron and steel mills, textile, rubber tire and glass works predominating.
Consol, Monroe Co., Ia., 502.
On Chi. & Nor. West. (R. R.).
Constance, Germany. See Konstanz.
Constanţa, Rumania, 60,261.
The chief Rumanian seaport on the Black Sea. Center of iron and petroleum industries.
Constantia, Oswego Co., N. Y., 500.
On N. York, Ont. & West. (R. R.).
Constantine, capital of Dept. of Constantine, Algeria, 113,777.
Is finely situated on an elevation of 2,170 feet above the sea, and surrounded on three sides by a deep ravine, crossed by bridges. It has manufactures of slippers, fezzes, wine, leather novelties, and flour.
Constantine was in ancient times a great city and capital of Numidia. It was destroyed at the beginning of the Christian era and rebuilt by Constantine. It now possesses extensive Roman remains, a citadel, a fortress, barracks, colleges, a Mohammedan seminary and museums.
–St. Joseph Co., Mich., 1,259.
On N. York Cen. (R. R.).
Constantinople, Turkey. See Istanbul.
Constitucion, Prov. of Maule, Chile, 8,379.
Continental, Putnam Co., Ohio, 897.
On N. York, Chi. & St. Lou. (R. R.).
Contoocook, Merrimack Co., N. H., 500.
On Bost. & Me. (R. R.).
Converse, Miami Co., Ind., 931.
On Chesa. & Ohio; Penna. (R. Rs.).
–Spartanburg Co., S. C., 1,025.
On Sou. (R. R.).
Convoy, Van Wert Co., Ohio, 876.
On Penna. (R. R.).
Conway, c. s., Faulkner Co., Ark., 5,534.
On Mo. Pacific (R. R.).
–Orange Co., Fla., 600.
–Franklin Co., Mass., 952.

–Laclede Co., Missouri, 576.
On St. Lou.-San Fran. (R. R.).
–Carroll Co., N. H., 1,150.
On Bost. & Me. (R. R.).
–Beaver Co., Pa., 2,014.
On Penna. (R. R.).
–c. s., Horry Co., S. C., 3,011.
On Atl. Coast Line (R. R.).
–Carnarvonshire, Wales (1921), 8,769.
CONWAY SPRINGS, Sumner Co., Kans., 878.
On Mo. Pac. (R. R.).
CONYERS, c. s., Rockdale Co., Ga., 1,495.
On Ga.; Milstead (R. Rs.).
CONYNGHAM, Luzerne Co., Pa., 522.
On Leh. Val.; Penna. (R. Rs.).
COOKEVILLE, c. s., Putnam Co., Tenn., 3,738.
On Tenn. Cen. (R. R.).
COOKVILLE, Titus Co., Tex., 518.
On St. Lou. Southw. (R. R.).
COOLEEMEE, Davie Co., N. C., 1,842.
On Southern (R. R.).
COOLIDGE, Pinal Co., Ariz., 1,200.
On Sou. Pac. (R. R.).
–Limestone Co., Texas, 1,169.
On Burl.-Rk. Isl. (R. R.).
COON RAPIDS, Carroll Co., Iowa, 1,303.
On Chi., Mil., St. P. & Pac. (R. R.).
COOPER, c. s., Delta Co., Texas, 2,023.
On Tex. & N. Orl. (R. R.).
COOPERSBURG, Lehigh Co., Pa., 1,057.
On Reading (R. R.).
COOPERSTOWN, c. s., Otsego Co., N. Y., 2,909.
On Delaware & Hudson; South. New York (El.) (R. Rs.).
Situated among scenes described in the Leatherstocking tales of James Fenimore Cooper. One of General Clinton's camps in the Revolutionary War.
–c. s., Griggs Co., N. Dak., 1,053.
On Nor. Pac. (R. R.).
COOPERSVILLE, Ottawa Co., Mich., 1,004.
On Gd. Tr. (R. R.).
COPAKE, Columbia Co., N. Y., 550.
On N. York, N. Hav. & Hart. (R. R.).
COPAN, Washington Co., Okla., 521.
On Atch., Top. & Santa Fe (R. R.).
COPAS, Washington Co., Minn., 500.
On Minn., St. P. & S. Ste. M. (R. R.).
COPENHAGEN, Denmark. See KÖBENHAVN.
–Lewis Co., N. Y., 539.
COPIAGUE, Suffolk Co., N. Y., 2,000.
On Long Isl. (R. R.).
COPIAPO, Prov. of Atacama, Chile, 10,141.
COPLAY, Lehigh Co., Pa., 3,279.
On Ironton; Leh. Val. (R. Rs.).
COPPARO, Prov. of Ferrara, Italy, 5,317.
COPPER CITY, Houghton Co., Mich., 587.
On Cop. Rge. (R. R.).
COPPERHILL, Polk Co., Tenn., 1,050.
On Lou. & Nash. (R. R.).
COQUILLE, c. s., Coos Co., Ore., 2,732.
On Sou. Pac. (R. R.).
COQUIMBO, Dept. of Coquimbo, Chile, 7,121.
CORAL, Indiana Co., Pa., 725.
On Balt. & Ohio; Penna. (R. Rs.).
CORAL GABLES, Dade Co., Fla., 6,747.
On Seaboard Air Line (R. R.).
CORAOPOLIS, Allegheny Co., Pa., 10,724.
On Pitts. & L. Erie (R. R.).
Oil, gas, iron, steel and glass works.
CORATO, Prov. of Bari, Italy, 47,930.
Chief center of an agricultural region.
CORBIN, Knox and Whitley Cos., Ky., 8,036.
On Lou. & Nash. (R. R.).
CORCORAN, Kings Co., Cal., 1,768.
On Atch., Top. & Santa Fe (R. R.).
CORDAVILLE, Worcester Co., Mass., 500.
On Bost. & Alb. (R. R.).
CORDELE, c. s., Crisp Co., Ga., 6,880.
On Alta., Birm. & Coast; Ga. Sou. & Fla.; Ga., Southw. & Gulf; Seab. Air Line (R. Rs.).
CORDELL, c. s., Washita Co., Okla., 2,936.
On St. Lou.-San Fran. (R. R.).
CORDER, Lafayette Co., Mo., 610.
On Alton (R. R.).
CORDOBA, capital of Prov. of Cordoba, Argentina, 309,232.
An industrial and trade center.
–capital of Prov. of Cordoba, Andalucia, Spain, 117,919.
Is located on the Guadalquivir River, and is an important railway junction. The city has many interesting Moorish remains.
CORDOVA, Alaska, Dist. of Cordova, 980.
–Walker Co., Ala., 1,830.
On St. Lou.-San Fran.; Ill. Cen.; Sou. (R. Rs.).
CORFU, Greece. See KERKYRA.
CORINNA, Penobscot Co., Maine, 1,400.
On Maine Central (R. R.).
CORINTH, Greece. See KORINTHOS.
–c. s., Alcorn Co., Miss., 6,220.
On Ill. Cen.; Mob. & Ohio; Sou. (R. Rs.).
–Saratoga Co., N. Y., 2,613.
On Del. & Hud. (R. R.).
CORK, c. s., County Cork, Ireland (Eire), 80,700.
Second city of Irish Free State in population situated on the river Lee, about 11 miles from Cork Harbor, and a railway terminus.
The cathedral, Protestant, several other churches and monasteries, Queen's College, and Cork Royal Institution comprise the most important public buildings. Cork was founded about 600 A.D.
CORLISS, Racine Co., Wis. See STURTEVANT.
CORNELIA, Habersham Co., Ga., 1,542.
On Sou.; Tallulah Fs. (R. Rs.).
CORNELIUS, Mecklenburg Co., N. C., 1,230.
On Southern (R. R.).
CORNELL, Chippewa Co., Wis., 1,510.
On Chi., St. P., Minn. & Oma. (R. R.).
CORNING, c. s., Clay Co., Ark., 1,550.
On Mo. Pac. (R. R.).
–Tehama Co., Cal., 1,377.
On Sou. Pac. (R. R.).
–c. s., Adams Co., Iowa, 2,026.
On Chi., Burl. & Quincy (R. R.).
–Steuben Co., N. Y., 15,777.
On Del., Lack. & West.; Erie; N. York Cen. (R. Rs.).
New York Central division headquarters with roundhouses and shops. A manufacturing center near Pennsylvania coal region.
–Perry Co., Ohio, 1,411.
On N. York Cen. (R. R.).
CORNWALL, capital of Stormont Co., Ontario, Canada, 11,126.
On Can. Pac.; Can. Nat.; Mich. Cen. (R. Rs.).
A lake port. Cotton, woolen, grist and saw mills.
–Orange Co., N. Y., 1,910.
On N. Y., Ont. & West.; West Shore (R. Rs.).
–Lebanon Co., Pa., 1,837.
On Cornwall; Penna. (R. Rs.).
CORNWALL ON THE HUDSON, Orange Co., N. Y., 2,500.
On N. York, Ont. & West.; West Shore (R. Rs.).
CORONA, Riverside Co., Cal., 7,018.
On Atch., Top. & Santa Fe; Pac. Elec. (R. Rs.).
Fruit shipping point with large citrus by-product plants.
–Lincoln Co., N. Mex., 550.
On Sou. Pac. (R. R.).
CORONADO, San Diego Co., Cal., 5,425.
On San Diego & Ariz. East. (R. R.).
CORONEL, Prov. of Concepcion, Chile, 9,019.
COROZAL, Mun. of Corozal, Puerto Rico, 3,305.
CORPUS CHRISTI, c. s., Nueces Co., Texas, 27,741.
On Tex. & N. Orl.; San Ant., Uvalde & Gulf; Tex., Mexican (R. Rs.).
Agricultural trading point and tourist resort.
CORRECTIONVILLE, Woodbury Co., Iowa, 1,058.
On Chi. & Nor. West.; Ill. Cen. (R. Rs.).
CORRIENTES, Prov. of Corrientes, Argentina, 52,-716.
A river port. Exports include timber, grain, tobacco, maté, and meat.
CORRIGAN, Polk Co., Tex., 1,200.
On Tex. & N. Orl.; Waco, Beau., Trin. & Sab. (R. Rs.).
CORRIGANVILLE, Allegany Co., Md., 600.
CORRY, Erie Co., Pa., 7,152.
On Erie; Penna. (R. Rs.).
CORSICA, Douglas Co., S. Dak., 486.
On Chi., Mil., St. P. & Pac. (R. R.).
CORSICANA, c. s., Navarro Co., Texas, 15,202.
On Burl.-Rk. Isl.; Chi., Rk. Isl. & Gulf; Ft. Worth & Denv. Cy.; St. Lou. Southw.; Tex. & N. Orl., Tex. Elec. (R. Rs.).
In a productive oil section. Has an extensive refinery and oil-well equipment plant and is also a cotton-mill center. Commission Government.
CORTE MADERA, Marin Co., Cal., 1,027.
On Northw. Pac. (R. R.).
CORTES, Prov. of Bohol, Bohol, P. I., 7,877.
CORTEZ, c. s., Montezuma Co., Colo., 921.
CORTLAND, c. s., Cortland Co., N. Y., 15,043.
On Del., Lack. & West.; Leh. Val. (R. Rs.).
Principal manufactures: wire, cloth and netting.
–Trumbull Co., Ohio, 940.
On Erie (R. R.).
CORTONA, Prov. of Arezzo, Italy, 3,597.
Noted for the number of its Etruscan and Roman antiquities: has cyclopean walls, supposed to be 3,000 years old.
CORUÑA, Spain. See LA CORUÑA.
CORUNNA, c. s., Shiawassee Co., Mich., 1,936.
On Ann Arbor; Gd. Tr. (R. Rs.).
CORVALLIS, c. s., Benton Co., Ore., 7,585.
On Sou. Pac. (R. R.).
CORYDON, c. s., Harrison Co., Ind., 2,009.
On Louisv., New Alb. & Cory. (R. R.).
–c. s., Wayne Co., Iowa, 1,768.
On Chi., Burl. & Quincy; Chi., Rk. Isl. & Pac. (R. Rs.).
–Henderson Co., Ky., 721.
On Ill. Cen. (R. R.).
COS COB, Fairfield Co., Conn., 591.
On N. York, N. Hav. & Hart. (R. R.).
COSENZA, Prov. of Cosenza, Italy, 24,000.
Center of wine district. Some trade in wool.
COSHOCTON, c. s., Coshocton Co., Ohio, 10,908.
On Penna.; Wheel. & L. Erie (R. Rs.).
Commercial and industrial center. Manufactures advertising novelties.
COSMOPOLIS, Grays Harbor Co., Wash., 1,493.
On Chi., Mil., St. P. & Pac.; Ore.-Wash. R. R. & Nav. Co. (R. Rs.).
COSTA MESA, Orange Co., Calif., 1,800.
On Sou. Pac. (R. R.).
COTE DES NEIGES, Jacques-Cartier Co., Quebec, Canada, 2,447.
COTTAGE CITY, Prince Georges Co., Md., 938.
COTTAGE GROVE, Lane Co., Ore., 2,473.
On Ore., Pac. & East.; Sou. Pac. (R. Rs.).
COTTER, Baxter Co., Ark., 1,064.
On Mo. Pac. (R. R.).
COTTONDALE, Jackson Co., Fla., 743.
On Atl. & St. And. Bay; Lou. & Nash. (R. Rs.).
COTTON PLANT, c. s., Woodruff Co., Ark., 1,689.
On Chi., Rk. Isl. & Pac.; Mo. & No. Ark. (R. Rs.).
COTTONPORT, Avoyelles Parish, La., 1,015.
On Tex. & Pac. (R. R.).
COTTON VALLEY, Webster Par., La., 1,133.
On La. & Ark. (R. R.).
COTTONWOOD, Yavapai Co., Ariz., 800.
–Idaho Co., Idaho, 519.
On Camas Prairie. Nor. Pac.; Un. Pac. Sys. (R. R.).
–Lyon Co., Minn., 615.
On Gt. Nor. (R. R.).
COTTONWOOD FALLS, c. s., Chase Co., Kans., 1,133.
On Atch., Top. & Santa Fe (R. R.).
COTULLA, c. s., LaSalle Co., Texas, 3,175.
On Internat. Gt. Nor. (R. R.).
COUDERSPORT, c. s., Potter Co., Pa., 2,740.
On Coudersp. & Port Alleg. (R. R.).
COULTERVILLE, Randolph Co., Ill., 1,337.
On Ill. Cen.; Mo.-Ill. (R. Rs.).
COUNCIL BLUFFS, c. s., Pottawattamie Co., Iowa, 42,048.
Is a railroad center, at the junction of the Chicago, Rock Island & Pacific; the Chicago & North Western; the Chicago, Burlington & Quincy; the Union Pacific; the Chicago Great Western; the Chicago, Milwaukee, St. Paul & Pacific; the Illinois Central; the Union Pacific and the Wabash railroads.
Council Bluffs is an important trade center, and has large cattle yards and grain elevators.
COUNCIL GROVE, c. s., Morris Co., Kans., 2,764.
On Mo. Pac.; Mo.-Kans.-Tex. (R. Rs.).
COUPON, Cambria Co., Pa., 500.
COURBEVOIE, Dept. of Seine, France, 58,638.
Suburb of Paris. Some manufacturing.
COURCELLES, Hainaut, Belgium, 18,071.
COURTDALE, Luzerne Co., Pa., 1,007.
COURTLAND, Sacramento Co., Calif., 500.
COURTNEY, Washington Co., Pa., 617.
On Penna. (R. R.).
COURTRAI, West Flanders, Belgium, 38,569.
Lace and linen manufactures.
COURVILLE, Quebec Co., Quebec, Canada, 1,680.
COUSHATTA, c. s., Red River Parish, La., 959.
On La. & Ark. (R. R.).
COUTANCES, Manche, Lower Normandy, France, 6,401.
COVELO, Mendocino Co., Calif., 600.
COVENTRY, Warwick, England, 184,700.
A historic town, still possessing some remains of medieval architecture. Among these are St. Michael's Church (Gothic in style), Christ Church and St. Mary's Hall, erected during the reign of Henry VI.
Early famous for caps, bonnets, and metal work, and still has extensive factory industries. The city was surrounded by a wall, entered by twelve gates, and had many magnificent pageants and processions. The Lady Godiva procession is still celebrated every three years.
–Tolland Co., Conn.
–Kent Co., R. I., 6,430.
On N. York, N. Hav., & Hart. (R. R.).
COVILHA, Castellobranco, Portugal, 15,640.
The principal industry is the manufacture of saragoça, a heavy brown cloth.
COVINA, Los Angeles Co., Cal., 2,774.
On Pac. Elec.; Sou. Pac. (R. Rs.).
COVINGTON, c. s., Newton Co., Ga., 3,203.
On Cen. of Ga.; Ga. (R. Rs.).
–c. s., Fountain Co., Ind., 2,008.
On Cle., Cin., Chi. & St. Lou. (R. R.).
–c. s., Kenton Co., Ky., 65,252.
Is located opposite Cincinnati, on the Ohio River, and on the Louisville and Nashville and the Chesapeake and Ohio railroads. Covington is connected with Cincinnati and Newport by five bridges.
As an industrial city, Covington has extensive plants for manufacturing X-ray machines, iron fences, tiles, inlaid furniture and carved woodwork, cigars, dyes, sheet metal, engines and boilers, etc. It is an important tobacco market. It has a number of fine buildings.
–c. s., St. Tammany Parish, La., 3,208.
On Gulf, Mob. & Nor. (R. R.).
–Miami Co., Ohio, 1,807.
On Penna. (R. R.).
—Garfield Co., Okla., 927.
On St. Lou.-San Fran. (R. R.).
–Tioga Co., Pa., 500.
On Erie (R. R.).
–c. s., Tipton Co., Tenn., 3,397.
On Ill. Cen. (R. R.).
–c. s., Alleghany Co., Va., 6,538.
On Chesa. & Ohio (R. R.).
COWAN, Franklin Co., Tenn., 1,367.
On Nash., Chatt. & St. Lou. (R. R.).
COWARD, Florence Co., S. C., 500.
On Atl. Coast Line (R. R.).
COWDEN, Shelby Co., Ill., 616.
On Balt. & Ohio; N. York, Chi. & St. Lou. (R. Rs.).
COWDENBEATH, Fife Co., Scotland, 12,731.
Coal mining.
COWETA, Wagoner Co., Okla., 1,274.
On Mo.-Kan.-Tex. (R. R.).
COWLEY, Big Horn Co., Wyo., 526.
On Chi., Burl. & Quincy (R. R.).
COWPENS, Spartansburg Co., S. C., 1,115.
On Southern (R. R.).
COXSACKIE, Greene Co., N. Y., 2,195.
On West Shore (R. R.).
COYTESVILLE, Bergen Co., N. J., 2,000.
COZAD, Dawson Co., Neb., 1,813.
On Un. Pac. (R. R.).
CRAB ORCHARD, Lincoln Co., Ky., 576.
On Lou. & Nash.. (R. R.).
–Cumberland Co., Tenn., 700.
On Tenn. Cen. (R. R.).
CRABTREE, Westmoreland Co., Pa., 1,106.
On Penna. (R. R.).
CRADOCK, Cape of Good Hope, Un. of S. Africa, 9,268.
CRAFTON, Allegheny Co., Pa., 7,004.
On Penna. (R. R.).
CRAIG, c. s., Moffat Co., Colorado, 1,418.
On Den. & Salt L. (R. R.).
–Holt Co., Mo., 626.
On Chi., Burl. & Quincy (R. R.).
CRAINVILLE, Williamson Co., Ill., 413.
On Ill. Cen. (R. R.).
CRAIOVA, Dolju, Rumania, 63,063.
Trade center of farm and timber region.
CRAIRE, c. s., Crane Co., Tex., 2,200.
CRAMER, Jefferson Co., Pa., 620.
On Balt. & Ohio (R. R.).
CRAMERTON, Gaston Co., N. C., 2,000.
On Southern (R. R.).
CRANBERRY JUNCTION, Luzerne Co., Pa., 600
On Leh. Val.; Penna. (R. Rs.).
CRANBURY, Middlesex Co., N. J., 650.
CRANDALL, Clarke Co., Miss., 500.
On Miss. East. (R. R.).
–Kaufman Co., Tex., 750.
On Tex. & N. Orl. (R. R.).
CRANDON, c. s., Forest Co., Wis., 1,679.
On Minn., St. P. & S. Ste. M.; Chi. & Nor. West. (R. Rs.).
CRANE, Stone Co., Mo., 1,030.
On Mo. Pac. (R. R.).
–c. s., Crane Co., Texas, 2,200.
CRANECO, Logan Co., W. Va., 840.
Chesa. & Ohio (R. R.).
CRANESVILLE, Erie Co., Pa., 554.
On Bess. & L. Erie (R. R.).
CRANSTON, Providence Co., R. I., 42,911.
On N. Y., N. H. & H. (R. R.).
CRAWFORD, Oglethorpe Co., Ga., 538.
On Georgia (R. R.).
–Dawes Co., Neb., 1,703.
On Chi., Burl. & Quincy; Chi. & Nor. West. (R. Rs.).
CRAWFORDSVILLE (Crawfordville), Crittenden Co., Ark., 612.
On Mo. Pac. (R. R.).
–c. s., Montgomery Co., Ind., 10,355.
On Chi., Ind. & Lou.; Clev., Cin., Chi. & St. Lou.; Penna. (R. Rs.).
Home of General Lew Wallace, author of "Ben Hur," and seat of Wabash College.
CRAWFORDVILLE, c. s., Taliaferro Co., Ga., 840.
On Georgia (R. R.).
CREAL SPRING, Williamson Co., Ill., 766.
On Ill. Cen. (R. R.).
CREASY, Columbia Co., Pa., 613.
On Penna. (R. R.).
CREEKSIDE, Indiana Co., Pa., 500.
On Balt. & Ohio (R. R.).
CREIGHTON, Knox Co., Neb., 1,388.
On Chi. & Nor. West. (R. R.).
–Allegheny Co., Pa., 1,600.
On Penna. (R. R.).
CRELLIN, Garrett Co., Md., 600.
On Preston (R. R.).
CREMONA, capital of Prov. of Cremona, Italy, 42,000.
A commercial center. Has many historical landmarks.
CRENSHAW, Panola Co., Miss., 575.
On Yazoo & Miss. Val. (R. R.).
–Jefferson Co., Pa., 500.
On Erie; Pitts., Shawmut & Nor. (R. Rs.).
CRESCENT, Logan Co., Okla., 1,190.
On Atch., Top. & Santa Fe (R. R.).
CRESCENT CITY, c. s., Del Norte Co., Cal., 1,720.
–Putnam Co., Fla., 966.
On Atl. Coast Line (R. R.).
CRESCO, c. s., Howard Co., Iowa, 3,069.
On Chi., Mil., St. P. & Pac. (R. R.).
CRESSKILL, Bergen Co., N. J., 1,924.
On Erie (R. R.).
CRESSON, Cambria Co., Pa., 2,317.
On Penna. (R. R.).
CRESSONA, Schuylkill Co., Pa., 1,946.
On Reading (R. R.).

CRESTED BUTTE, Gunnison Co., Colo., 1,251.
On Den. & Rio Gde. West. (R. R.).
CRESTLINE, Crawford Co., Ohio, 4,425.
On Cle., Cin., Chi. & St. Lou.; Penna. (R. Rs.).
CRESTON, c. s., Union Co., Iowa, 8,615.
On Chi., Burl. & Quincy (R. R.).
–Wayne Co., Ohio, 1,029.
On Balt. & Ohio; Erie; Wheel. & L. Erie (R. Rs.).
CRESTVIEW, c. s., Okaloosa Co., Fla., 1,078.
On Lou. & Nash. (R. R.).
CRETE, Will Co., Ill., 1,429.
On Chi. & East. Ill. (R. R.).
–Saline Co., Neb., 2,865.
On Chi., Burl. & Quincy; Mo., Pac. (R. Rs.).
CREVE COEUR, St. Louis Co., Mo., 650.
CREWE, Cheshire, England, 46,061.
Locomotive and car works.
–Nottoway Co., Va., 2,152.
On Norf. & West. (R. R.).
CRICHTON, Mobile Co., Ala., 4,000.
On Mob. & Ohio (R. R.).
CRICKET, Wilkes Co., N. C., 600.
CRIDERSVILLE, Auglaize Co., Ohio, 559.
On Balt. & Ohio (R. R.).
CRIMMITSCHAU, Saxony, Germany, 27,120.
Yarn spinning, dyeing, and machine construction.
CRIPPLE CREEK, c. s., Teller Co., Colo., 1,427.
Is situated on the Midland Terminal Railroad, at an altitude of 10,400 feet.
In a large gold-bearing region, most of Colorado's gold output being mined near here.
CRISFIELD, Somerset Co., Md., 3,850.
On Penna. (R. R.).
CROCKER, Pulaski Co., Mo., 522.
On St. Lou.-San Fran. (R. R.).
CROCKETT, Contra Costa Co., Cal., 3,885.
On Sou. Pac. (R. R.).
–Houston Co., Texas, 4,441.
On Internat.-Gt. Nor. (R. R.).
CROCKETTSVILLE, Breathitt Co., Ky., 500.
CROFTON, Christian Co., Ky., 461.
On Lou. & Nash. (R. R.).
–Knox Co., Nebr., 733.
On Chi., St. P., Minn. & Oma. (R. R.).
CROGHAN, Lewis Co., N. Y., 732.
On Lowv. & Beaver Riv. (R. R.).
CROMWELL, Middlesex Co., Conn., 2,700.
On N. York, N. Hav. & Hart. (R. R.).
CRONSTADT, Soviet Union. See KRONSTADT.
CROOK, Durham, England, 11,690.
CROOKSTON, c. s., Polk Co., Minn., 6,321.
On Great Northern; Northern Pacific (R. Rs.).
Grain and live-stock center of a rich agricultural region in the Red River Valley. Seat of State Agriculture School.
CROOKSVILLE, Perry Co., Ohio, 3,251.
On N. York Cen.; Penna. (R. Rs.).
CROPSEYVILLE, Rensselaer Co., N. Y., 500.
CROSBY, Crow Wing Co., Minn., 3,451.
On Minn., St. P. & S. Ste. M. (R. R.).
–c. s., Divide Co., N. Dak., 1,271.
On G. Nor.; Minn., St. P. & S. Ste. M. (R. Rs.).
–Harris Co., Texas, 750.
On Tex. & N. Orl. (R. R.).
CROSBYTON, c. s., Crosby Co., Texas, 1,250.
On Panh. & Santa Fe (R. R.).
CROSS CITY, c. s., Dixie Co., Fla., 1,097.
On Atl. Coast Line (R. R.).
CROSSETT, Ashley Co., Arkansas, 2,811.
On Ark. & La. Mo.; Ash., Drew & Nor.; Chi., Rk. Isl. & Pac.; Mo. Pac. (R. Rs.).
CROSS HILL, Laurens Co., S. C., 678.
On Seab. Air Line (R. R.).
CROSS PLAINS, Callahan Co., Texas, 1,507.
On Mo.-Kans.-Tex. of Tex. (R. R.).
CROSSVILLE, White Co., Ill., 508.
On Cle., Cin., Chi. & St. Lou. (R. R.).
–c. s., Cumberland Co., Tenn., 1,128.
On Tenn. Cen. (R. R.).
CROSSWICKS, Burlington Co., N. J., 550.
CROSWELL, Sanilac Co., Mich., 1,470.
On Pere Marq. (R. R.).
CROTHERSVILLE, Jackson Co., Ind., 979.
On Ind. R. R. Sys. (Elec.); Penna. (R. Rs.).
CROTON FALLS, Westchester Co., N. Y., 600.
On N. York Cen. (R. R.).
CROTON-ON-HUDSON, Westchester Co., N. Y., 2,447.
On N. York Cen. (R. R.).
CROTTY (Seneca), La Salle Co., Ill., 1,185.
CROWEBURG, Crawford Co., Kans., 250.
CROWELL, c. s., Foard Co., Texas, 1,946.
On Panh. & Santa Fe (R. R.).
CROWLEY, c. s., Acadia Parish, La., 7,656.
On N. Orl., Tex. & Mex.; Tex. & N. Orl.; Tex. & Pac. (R. Rs.).
Known as the "Rice City," one-fifth of the country's production of rice being raised in the district.
CROWN POINT, Lake Co., Ind., 4,046.
On Erie; Penna. (R. Rs.).
–Essex Co., N. Y., 900.
On Del. & Hud. (R. R.).
–Montgomery Co., Ohio, 1,500.
CROWS NEST, Westmoreland Co., Pa., 500.
On Penna. (R. R.).
CROYDON, Surrey, England, 239,960.
Famous for having one of the world's busiest airports.
CROZET, Albemarle Co., Va., 762.
On Chesa. & Ohio (R. R.).
CRUCES, Prov. of Santa Clara, Cuba, 5,671.
CRUCIBLE, Greene Co., Pa., 1,800.
On Monongahela (R. R.).
CRUM LYNNE, Delaware Co., Pa., 1,400.
On Penna. (R. R.).
CRUMPLER, Ashe Co., N. C., 600.
CRYSTAL, Hennepin Co., Minn., 1,865.
On Minn., St. P. & S. Ste. M. (R. R.).
CRYSTAL CITY, Jefferson Co., Mo., 3,057.
On Mo.-Ill.; St. Lou.-San Fran. (R. Rs.).
–c. s., Zavala Co., Tex., 6,609.
On San Ant., Uvalde & Gulf (R. R.).
CRYSTAL FALLS, c. s., Iron Co., Mich., 2,295.
On Chi., Mil. & St. P. & Pac.; Chi. & Nor. West. (R. Rs.).
District chiefly noted for its iron deposits.
CRYSTAL LAKE, McHenry Co., Ill., 3,732.
On Chi. & Nor. West. (R. R.).
CRYSTAL RIVER, Citrus Co., Fla., 860.
On Atl. Coast Line (R. R.).
CRYSTAL SPRINGS, Copiah Co., Miss., 2,257.
On Ill. Cen. (R. R.).
CUAUTEPEC, State of Guerrero, Mexico, 1,880.
CUAUTLA, State of Morelos, Mexico, 5,318.
CUBA, Sumter Co., Alabama, 542.
On Ala. Gt. Sou. (R. R.).
–Fulton Co., Ill., 1,479.
On Chi., Burl. & Quincy; Tol., Peor. & West.; (R. Rs.).
–Crawford Co., Mo., 814.
On St. Lou.-San Fran. (R. R.).
–Allegany Co., N. Y., 1,422.
On Erie; Penna. (R. Rs.).
CUBA CITY, Grant Co., Wis., 1,157.
On Chi. & Nor. West. (R. R.).
CUCUTA, SAN JOSÉ DE, Santander del Norte, Colombia, 70,000.
An important coffee center.
CUDAHY, Milwaukee Co., Wis., 10,631.
On Chi. & Nor. West.; Mil. El. (R. Rs.).
Suburb of Milwaukee. Packing plants, machine shops, tanneries.
CUDDALORE, Madras, India, 59,057.
Seaport. Exports sugar, cotton goods, oil seeds.
CUDDY, Allegheny Co., Pa., 800.
CUENCA, capital of Azuay Prov., Ecuador, 45,497.
Industrial and commercial center. Sugar, woolens and pottery.
–Prov. of Batangas, Luzon, P. I., 7,106.
–c. s., Cuenca Prov., Spain, 13,727.
Situated in a timber region.
CUERO, c. s., DeWitt Co., Texas, 4,672.
On Tex. & N. Orl. (R. R.).
CUIABÁ, capital of Matto Grosso, Brazil, 43,900.
Commercial center and military station.
CULASI, Prov. of Antique, Panay, P. I., 15,776.
CULBERTSON, Hitchcock Co., Neb., 820.
On Chi., Burl. & Quincy (R. R.).
–Roosevelt Co., Mont., 536.
On Gt. Nor. (R. R.).
CULLERA, Prov. of Valencia, Spain, 13,075.
Fishing port, also exports fruits and rice.
CULLMAN, c. s., Cullman Co., Ala., 2,786.
On Lou. & Nash. (R. R.).
CULLOWHEE, Jackson Co., N. C., 1,200.
On Tuckaseegee & Southe. (R. R.).
CULPEPER, c. s., Culpeper Co., Va., 2,379.
On Chesa. & Ohio; Sou. (R. Rs.).
CULVER, Marshall Co., Ind., 1,502.
On Penna. (R. R.).
CULVER CITY, Los Angeles Co., Cal., 5,669.
On Pac. Elec. (R. R.).
CUMANA, Sucre, Venezuela, 21,623.
Oldest European city in the Western Hemisphere.
CUMBERLAND, Cass Co., Iowa, 595.
On Chi., Burl. & Quincy (R. R.).
–Harlan Co., Ky., 2,639.
On Lou. & Nash. (R. R.).
–Cumberland Co., Maine, 705.
On Gd. Tr. (R. R.).
–c. s., Allegany Co., Md., 37,747.
On Balt. & Ohio; Cumberld. & Penna.; Penna.; West. Md. (R. Rs.).
Has large plants for manufacturing tires, tinplate, ground steel shafting, rails, dyes, glassware, silk goods, etc. The Baltimore & Ohio and Western Maryland have large shops here. Made a town in 1785; a city since 1850.
–Guernsey Co., Ohio, 556.
On Balt. & Ohio (R. R.).
–Barron Co., Wis., 1,532.
On Chi., St. P., Minn. & Omaha (R. R.).
CUMBERLAND CENTER, Cumberland Co., Me., 705.
On Me. Cen. (R. R.).
–Providence Co., R. I., 10,160.
CUMBOLA, Schuylkill Co., Pa., 1,385.
On Reading (R. R.).
CUMBY, Hopkins Co., Texas, 646.
On La., Ark. & Tex. (R. R.).
CUMMING, c. s., Forsyth Co., Ga., 648.
CUMMINGTON, Hampshire Co., Mass., 610.
CUNARD, Fayette Co., W. Va., 600.
On Chesa. & Ohio (R. R.).
CUNEO, Piedmont, Italy, 21,600.
CUPERTINO, Santa Clara Co., Calif., 2,500.
CURICO, Prov. of Curico, Chile, 19,094.
CURITYBA, Brazil, 116,632.
Located in a timber and farming region.
CURTIS, Clark Co., Ark., 520.
On Mo. Pac. (R. R.).
–Frontier Co., Neb., 960.
On Chi., Burl. & Quincy (R. R.).
CURTISVILLE, Allegheny Co., Pa., 1,800.
On Bess. & L. Erie (R. R.).
CURWENSVILLE, Clearfield Co., Pa., 3,140.
On Balt. & Ohio; Penna. (R. Rs.).
CUSHING, Payne Co., Okla., 9,301.
On Atch., Top. & Santa Fe; Mo.-Kan.-Tex. (R. Rs.).
–Nacagdoches Co., Tex., 800.
On Tex. & New Orl. (R. R.).
CUSTER, c. s., Custer Co, S. Dak., 1,239.
On Chi., Burl. & Quincy (R. R.).
CUSTER CITY, Custer Co., Okla., 698.
On Atch., Top. & Santa Fe; St. Lou.-San Fran. (R. Rs.).
CUT BANK, Glacier Co., Mont., 845.
On Gt. Nor. (R. R.).
CUTCHOGUE, Suffolk Co., N. Y., 1,300.
On Long Isl. (R. R.).
CUTHBERT, c. s., Randolph Co., Ga., 3,235.
On Cen. of Ga.; Seab. Air Line (R. Rs.).
CUTLER, Perry Co., Ill., 521.
On Mo. Pac. (R. R.).
CUTLER CITY, Lincoln Co., Ore., 500.
CUTTACK, British India, 65,263.
Silver filigree work and tanning.
CUYAHOGA FALLS, Summit Co., Ohio, 19,797.
On Balt. & Ohio; Penna. (R. Rs.).
Manufactures iron and rubber goods.
CUYAHOGA HEIGHTS, Cuyahoga Co., Ohio, 710.
CUYAPO, Nueva Ecija Prov., Luzon, P. I., 19,251.
Center of a rice producing district.
CUYO, Prov. of Paragua, Cuyo, P. I., 14,768.
CUZCO, capital of Dept. of Cuzco, Peru, 40,000.
Is the most ancient city of Peru and according to tradition, was founded in 1020 by the first of the Incas, and was captured by Pizarro.
Its public buildings are among the finest in South America, and include a Dominican convent, which contains many interesting relics of ancient Peru; a cathedral and Augustinian convent, both magnificent buildings, and a university founded in the seventeenth century.
CYCLONE (Simpson), McKean Co., Pa., 750.
CYGNET, Wood Co., Ohio, 523.
On N. York Cen. (R. R.).
CYNTHIANA, Posey Co., Indiana, 556.
On Chi. & East. Ill.; Cle., Cin., Chi. & St. Lou. (R. Rs.).
–c. s., Harrison Co., Ky., 4,386.
On Lou. & Nash. (R. R.).
CYNWYD, Montgomery Co., Pa., 1,040.
On Penna. (R. R.).
CYPRESS, Orange Co., Calif., 610.
On Pac. Elec. (R. R.).
CYRIL, Caddo Co., Okla., 922.
On St. Lou.-San Fran. (R. R.).
CZERNOWITZ, Rumania. See CERNAŬTI.
CZESTOCHOWA, Dept. of Kielce, Poland, 136,000.

D

DABROWICA, Poland, 41,681.
DACCA, Bengal, British India, 138,518.
A commercial center. Carving of shells is a famous industry.
DADE CITY, c. s., Pasco Co., Fla., 1,718.
On Atl. Coast Line; Seab. Air Line (R. Rs.).
In tobacco and citrus fruit section.
DADEVILLE, c. s., Tallapoosa Co., Ala., 1,549.
On Cen. of Ga. (R. R.).
DAET, Camarines Norte Prov., Luzon, P. I., 14,218.
Important commercial center. Rice milling.
DAGAMI, Leyte Prov., Leyte, P. I., 17,802.
DAGUPAN, Pangasinan Prov., Luzon, P. I., 22,612.
DAGUS MINES, Elk Co., Pa., 1,500.
DAHLGREN, Hamilton Co., Illinois, 625.
On Lou. & Nash. (R. R.).
–King George Co., Va., 500.
DAHLONEGA, c. s., Lumpkin Co., Ga., 905.
DAINGERFIELD, c. s., Morris Co., Texas, 818.
On Ark. & Tex. (R. R.).
DAIREN, capital of Kwangtung (Japan), 481,379.
Important port in Manchukuoan commerce.
DAISETTA, Liberty Co., Texas, 1,200.
DAISYTOWN, Washington Co., Pa., 1,500.
DAKAR, capital of Fr. W. Africa, 76,100.
Modern seaport and commercial center of Western Africa.
DALAGUETE, Cebu, P. I., 26,896.
DALE, Spencer Co., Ind., 770.
On Southern (R. R.).
–Cambria Co., Pa., 3,364.
DALHART, Dallam and Hartley Cos., Texas, 4,691.
On Chi., Rk. Isl. & Gulf; Ft. Worth & Denv. Cy. (R. Rs.).
DALLAS, c. s., Paulding Co., Ga., 1,412.
On Seab. Air Line; Sou. (R. Rs.).
–Marion Co., Iowa, 717.
–Gaston Co., N. C., 1,489.
On Car. & Nor. West. (R. R.).
–c. s., Polk Co., Ore., 2,975.
On Sou. Pac. (R. R.).
–Luzerne Co., Pa., 1,188.
On Leh. Val. (R. R.).
–c. s., Dallas Co., Texas, 260,475.
Is located on Trinity River, and on the Chicago, Rock Island & Gulf; Dallas Terminal; Ft. Worth & Denver City; Gulf; Colorado & Santa Fe; Louisiana, Arkansas & Texas; Missouri-Kansas & Texas of Texas; St. Louis-San Francisco & Texas; Texas & New Orleans; St. Louis Southwestern; Texas & Pacific railroads.
Is an important manufacturing and commercial city, a grain and cotton market. Many oil companies have their headquarters here, the city being in the heart of the oil fields of the vicinity, and the manufacture of oil tanks and oil well and refining machinery are among its industries. Cotton goods, machinery for cotton gins and mills, dairy stock and products, saddlery and leather goods, cement refinery machinery, are also turned out in great quantities. The State Fair and Dallas Exposition are held here annually.
DALLAS CENTER, Dallas Co., Iowa, 852.
On Minn. & St. Lou. (R. R.).
DALLAS CITY, Hancock and Henderson Cos., Ill., 1,114.
On Atch., Top. & Santa Fe; Chi., Burl. & Quincy (R. Rs.).
DALLAS MILLS, Madison Co., Ala., 2,000.
DALLASTOWN, York Co., Pa., 2,849.
On Md. & Penna. (R. R.).
DALTON, c. s., Whitfield Co., Ga., 8,160.
On Nash., Chatt. & St. Lou.; South. (R. Rs.).
–Berkshire Co., Mass., 4,282.
On Bost. & Alb. (R. R.).
–Livingston Co., N. Y., 540.
On Erie (R. R.).
–Wayne Co., Ohio, 656.
On Wheel. & L. Erie (R. R.).
–Lackawanna Co., Pa., 1,072.
On Del., Lack. & West. (R. R.).
DALY CITY, San Mateo Co., Cal., 7,838.
On Sou. Pac. (R. R.).
DALZELL, Bureau Co., Ill., 577.
On Chi. & Nor. West.; Chi., Burl. & Quincy (R. Rs.).
DAMANHUR, capital of Prov. of Behera, Egypt, 58,700.
Is on the site of the ancient Hermopolis, or "City of Horus."
DAMAO, City in Portuguese India, 7,000.
DAMARISCOTTA, Lincoln Co., Maine, 800.
DAMAS (Damascus), Syria, Asia Minor, 318,922.
Is situated in the midst of a large valley which opens into the desert of Syria. The waters of the Barade traverse the town. The appearance of Damas is very pleasing from a distance on account of its many cupolas, minarets, and gardens; but the narrow and crooked streets prove a disappointment. There are, however, some beautiful buildings. A citadel dates from 1219 A.D., and two gates, Bab-el Clarki and Bab-el Saghir, from Roman times. Damas derives great importance from its commerce. The manufactures include cotton fabrics, perfumes, and carpets.
Damas is said to be the oldest city in the world. It passed to the Hebrews, the Assyrians, and Romans in turn, and in 1516 fell into the hands of the Turks. In 1832 it was taken by Ibrahim Pasha, but reverted again to the Turks. It has some modern improvements, including electric street railroads and electric lights. Turkey lost Syria as a result of the Great War, and it passed to French control.
DAMASCUS, Washington Co., Va., 1,610.
On Norfolk & Western (R. R.).
DAMIETTA, Egypt. See DUMIÂT.
DAMPREMY, Hainaut, Belgium, 13,274.
DANA, Vermillion Co., Ind., 859.
On Balt. & Ohio (R. R.).
–Worcester Co., Mass., 387.
DANAO, Cebu Prov., Cebu, P. I., 24,600.
Center of an agricultural region producing rice, corn, sugar, copra, and cocoa.
DAN-BATAYAN, Cebu Prov., Cebu, P. I., 21,334.
DANBURY, c. s., Fairfield Co., Conn., 22,261.
On N. York, N. Hav. & Hart. (R. R.).
First settled in 1684. Foremost as the hat manufacturing city of the country, the industry beginning here as early as 1780. Other industries relating to hat making have also developed—mills for making silk bands, leather for linings, preparing furs, and foundries for producing the special hat machines required. Other products include glue, ball bearings, clothing, and surgical instruments.
–Woodbury Co., Iowa, 656.
On Chi. & Nor. West. (R. R.).
DANFORTH, Washington Co., Maine, 1,400.
On Can. Pac.; Me. Cen. (R. Rs.).
DANIA, Broward Co., Fla., 2,469.
On Fla. East Coast; Seab. Air Line (R. Rs.).
DANIELSON, Windham Co., Conn., 4,210.
On N. York, N. Hav. & Hart. (R. R.).
DANIELSVILLE, Northampton Co., Pa., 1,184.
On Leh. & N. Eng. (R. R.).

DANNEMORA, Clinton Co., N. Y., 3,348.
On Del. & Hud. (R. R.).
DANSVILLE, Livingston Co., N. Y., 4,928.
On Dans. & Mt. Mor.; Del., Lack. & West. (R. Rs.).
DANTE, Russell Co., Va., 811.
On Clinchfield (R. R.).
DANTUMADEEL, Friesland, Netherlands, 13,311.
DANVERS, McLean Co., Ill., 601.
On Cle., Cin., Chi. & St. Lou.; Ill. Term. (El.) (R. Rs.).
–Essex Co., Mass., 13,884.
On Bost. & Me. (R. R.).
A residential suburb of Boston.
DANVILLE, c. s., Yell Co., Ark., 761.
On Chi., Rk. Isl. & Pac. (R. R.).
–Contra Costa Co., Calif., 600.
On Sou. Pac. (R. R.).
–c. s., Vermilion Co., Ill., 36,765.
On Chi. & East. Ill.; Cle., Cin., Chi. & St. Lou.; Wabash; N. York Cen.; Ill. Term. (El.) (R. Rs.).
Location of C. & E. I. railroad shops, and among numerous manufactures, has an extensive brick making plant.
–c. s., Hendricks Co., Ind., 1,930.
On Cle., Cin., Chi. & St. Lou. (R. R.).
Is the site of Central Normal College.
–c. s., Boyle Co., Ky., 6,729.
On Cin., N. Orl. & Tex. Pac.; Sou. (R. Rs.).
–Knox Co., Ohio, 764.
On Penna. (R. R.).
–c. s., Montour Co., Pa., 7,185.
On Del., Lack. & West.; Penna.; Read. (R. Rs.).
–Richmond Co., Quebec, Canada, 1,354.
On Can. Nat. (R. R.).
–(Ind. City), Pittsylvania Co., Va., 22,247.
On Danv. & West.; Sou. (R. Rs.).
Tobacco market and cotton mills.
DANZIG, on the Baltic (formerly in Germany), 407,517.
Important seaport, manufacturing center, and fortress. Is on the left bank of the Vistula, fortified by detached forts, and surrounded by a moat. In addition there are contrivances for flooding the city approaches.
The most noteworthy buildings are the Church of St. Mary, begun in 1343, finished two centuries later, containing Memling's "Last Judgment"; the Church of St. Catherine, Trinity Church, and the Rathhaus, fourteenth century.
Danzig was a member of the Hanseatic League. In 1466 it declared itself a free imperial city under Poland; in 1772 became Prussian; in 1807 was taken by Marshal Lefebvre, and in 1814 was retaken by the Allies and restored to Prussia. Its manufactures include machinery, paper, glass and firearms. There are large shipbuilding plants. The exports are principally lumber and farm products.
Under the terms of the Peace Treaty following the Great War, Danzig became a free city in international territory. Since Poland's establishment of the seaport, Gdynia, the commerce of Danzig has greatly decreased.
DAO, Prov. of Antique, Panay, P. I., 15,922.
DAPHNE, Baldwin Co., Ala., 582.
DAPITAN, Sub-Dist. of Dapitan, Mindanao, P. I., 12,865.
DARBHANGA, capital of Dist. of Darbhanga, India, 60,676.
A trade center in a rich farming region.
DARBY, Delaware Co., Pa., 9,899.
On Balt. & Ohio; Penna. (R. Rs.).
DARDANELLE, c. s., Yell Co., Ark., 1,832.
On Chi., Rk. Isl. & Pac.; Dardan. & Russellv.; Ft. Smith, Sub. & Rk. Isl. (R. Rs.).
DAR ES SALAAM, capital of Tanganyika, 22,732.
Seaport and commercial center.
DARIEN, Fairfield Co., Conn., 3,000.
On N. York, N. Hav. & Hart. (R. R.).
–c. s., McIntosh Co., Ga., 937.
DARLASTON, Staffordshire, England, 19,736.
DARLINGTON, Durham, England, 72,093.
Manufacturing center. Coal, iron, castings, locomotives, engines, and shells.
–Montgomery Co., Ind., 690.
On Penna. (R. R.).
–c. s., Darlington Co., S. C., 5,556.
On Atl. Coast Line; Seab. Air Line (R. Rs.).
–c. s., Lafayette Co., Wis., 1,764.
On Chi., Mil., St. P. & Pac. (R. R.).
DARMSTADT, Hessen, Germany, 90,000.
Industrial and educational center.
DARTFORD, Kent, England, 28,928.
DARTMOUTH, Devonshire, England, 6,709.
–Bristol Co., Mass., 9,424.
–Halifax Co., Nova Scotia, 9,100.
On Can. Nat. (R. R.).
DARWEN, Lancashire, England, 36,010.
An industrial suburb of Manchester.
DASSEL, Meeker Co., Minn., 785.
On Gt. Nor. (R. R.).
DATIA, Bundelkhand, India, 24,100.
A walled city of small importance.
DAUFUSKIE ISLAND, Beaufort Co., S. C., 650.
DAUGAVPILS (Dvinsk), Latvia, 43,226.
A strongly fortified city. The city of much fighting during the World War (1914-1918).
DAUIS, Prov. of Bohol, Bohol, P. I., 10,824.
DAUPHIN, Dauphin Co., Pa., 600.
On Penna.; Read. (R. Rs.).
–Dauphin Co., Manitoba, Canada, 4,147.
On Can. Nat. (R. R.).
DAVENPORT, Santa Cruz Co., Calif., 550.
On Sou. Pac. (R. R.).
–Polk Co., Fla., 618.
On Atl. Coast Line (R. R.).
–c. s., Scott Co., Iowa, 60,751.
Is located on the west bank of the Mississippi River, and is connected with Rock Island by two iron bridges. It is on the Chicago, Rock Island & Pacific; the Chicago, Milwaukee, St. Paul & Pacific; the Clinton, Davenport & Muscatine (El.); the Davenport, Rock Island & Northwestern railroads, and has additional transportation facilities by river. The notable buildings are a Public Library, Academy of National Sciences, Academy of Immaculate Conception, St. Ambrose College, St. Katherine's Hall, St. Luke's and Mercy Hospitals, and the State Orphan Home. The manufactures include machinery, steel car gears, carriages, lumber, flour, breakfast foods, ready-cut houses, brooms, cut stone, motor trucks, woolen goods, pottery, cigars. Coal is mined extensively near by, and large quantities of agricultural produce are shipped.
–Lincoln Co., Okla., 1,072.
On Atch., Top. & Santa Fe; St. Lou.-San Fran. (R. Rs.).
–c. s., Lincoln Co., Wash., 987.
On Nor. Pac. (R. R.).
DAVID CITY, c. s., Butler Co., Neb., 2,333.
On Chi., Burl. & Quincy; Chi. & Nor. West.; Un. Pac. (R. Rs.).
DAVIDSON, Mecklenburg Co., N. C., 1,445.
On Southern (R. R.).
–Tillman Co., Okla., 572.
On St. Lou.-San Fran. (R. R.).
–Fentress Co., Tenn., 550.
On Tenn. Cen. (R. R.).
DAVIS, Yolo Co., California, 1,243.
On Sou. Pac. (R. R.).
–Carteret Co., N. C., 525.
–Murray Co., Okla., 1,075.
On Gulf, Colo. & Santa Fe (R. R.).
–Tucker Co., W. Va., 1,656.
On West. Md. (R. R.).
DAVISBORO, Washington Co., Ga., 654.
On Cen. of Ga. (R. R.).
DAVIS CITY, Decatur Co., Ia., 548.
On Chi., Burl. & Quincy (R. R.).
DAVISON, Genesee Co., Mich., 1,298.
On Gd. Tr. (R. R.).
DAVY, McDowell Co., W. Va., 1,000.
Norf. & West. (R. R.).

COURTESY SOCIETY FOR PRESERVATION OF NEW ENGLAND ANTIQUITIES
THE FAIRBANKS HOUSE, DEDHAM, MASSACHUSETTS, DATING BACK TO THE SETTLEMENT OF THE COMMONWEALTH

DAWLISH, Devonshire, England, 4,578.
DAWSON, c. s., Terrell Co., Ga., 3,827.
On Cen. of Ga.; Seab. Air Line (R. Rs.).
–Lac qui Parle Co., Minn., 1,386.
On Minn. & St. Lou. (R. R.).
–Colfax Co., N. Mex., 2,000.
On Sou. Pac. (R. R.).
–Tulsa Co., Okla., 842.
On St. Lou.-San Fran. (R. R.).
–Fayette Co., Pa., 800.
On Balt. & Ohio (R. R.).
–Navarro Co., Texas, 1,131.
On St. Lou.-Southw. (R. R.).
DAWSON SPRINGS, Hopkins Co., Ky., 2,311.
On Ill. Cen. (R. R.).
DAYHOIT (Wilhoit), Harlan Co., Ky., 616.
DAYTON, Tippecanoe Co., Ind., 503.
On N. York, Chi. & St. Lou. (R. R.).
–Webster Co., Iowa, 713.
On Chi. & Nor. West.; Minn. & St. Lou. (R. Rs.).
–Campbell Co., Ky., 9,071.
On Chesa. & Ohio (R. R.).
–c. s., Montgomery Co., Ohio, 200,982.
Is located on the east bank of the Miami River at its confluence with Mad River, and on the Miami and Erie Canal. The railroad connections are furnished by the Erie; the Baltimore and Ohio; the Pennsylvania; the Cleveland, Cincinnati, Chicago and St. Louis; and the Cincinnati & Lake Erie (El.).
The principal buildings are the Steele High School, the Dayton State Hospital, Arcade Market, and St. Elizabeth's Hospital. The court-house is a handsome building, modeled after the Parthenon. There is also a public library of 300,000 volumes. In the western suburbs is the National Military Home for disabled volunteers of the Civil War. The city has also a large college and two theological seminaries.
Notable for the production of automobile tires, autographic registers, automatic toys, automobile lighting, starting and ignition systems, bicycles and motorcycles, bookbinders' machinery, computing scales, electrical plants for farms and homes, electrolyte bleaching machines, fare and cash registers, tobacco machinery, hoisting jacks, golf clubs, toys, electric refrigerators, fire extinguishers, sewing machines, torpedo air compressors, and U. S. Government stamped envelopes. The city's plants include many devoted entirely to the manufacture of other special machines as well as tools requiring delicacy and precision of make. Dayton was settled in 1796, incorporated as a town in 1805, and as a city in 1841. The city has been subject to destructive floods.
–Armstrong Co., Pa., 875.
On Balt. & Ohio (R. R.).
–c. s., Rhea Co., Tenn., 2,006.
On Cin., N. Orl. & Tex. Pac. (R. R.).
–Liberty Co., Tex., 1,207.
On Tex. & N. Orl. (R. R.).
–Rockingham Co., Va., 537.
On Chesa. West. (R. R.).
–c. s., Columbia Co., Wash., 2,528.
On Nor. Pac.; Ore., Wash. R. R. & Nav. Co. (R. Rs.).
DAYTONA BEACH, Volusia Co., Fla., 20,099.
On Fla. East Coast (R. R.).
A popular winter resort.
DEADWOOD, c. s., Lawrence Co., S. Dak., 3,662.
Is situated among the Black Hills, and is the commercial metropolis of the western half of South Dakota. It is on the Chicago & Northwestern and Chicago, Burlington & Quincy railroads.
It is a great ore-producing center, and has smelters and chlorination and cyanide works, and is also an important trade and supply point.
DEAL, Kent, England, 13,680.
A market town and seaport. Frequented as a resort.
–Monmouth Co., N. J., 800.
DEARBORN, Wayne Co., Mich., 50,358.
On Det., Tol. & Iron.; Mich. Cen.; Penna. (R. Rs.).
A residential suburb of Detroit and site of the Ford Museum and Historical Village.
–Platte Co., Mo., 549.
On Chi. Gt. West. (R. R.).
DEBRECEN, Haiduk Comitat, Hungary, 119,901.
The agricultural center of Hungary. Fairs and markets held regularly.
DECATUR, c. s., Morgan Co., Alabama, 15,593.
On Lou. & Nash.; Sou. (R. Rs.).
Cotton mills, steel works, and woodworking plants.
–c. s., De Kalb Co., Ga., 13,276.
On Georgia (R. R.).
Residential suburb of Atlanta.
–c. s., Macon Co., Ill., 57,510.
On Baltimore & Ohio; Illinois Central; Illinois Terminal (El.); Wabash; Pennsylvania (R. Rs.). Served by four railroads and three interurban lines.
A manufacturing and jobbing center. Steel and iron products are among its chief manufactures. Notable also as a large producer of brass plumbing goods, and soda fountains. Its corn and soy bean products are important.
–c. s., Adams Co., Ind., 5,156.
On Erie; N. York, Chi. & St. Lou.; Penna. (R. Rs.).
–Van Buren Co., Mich., 1,582.
On Mich. Cen. (R. R.).
–c. s., Newton Co., Miss., 654.
On Gulf, Mob. & Nor. (R. R.).
–Burt Co., Neb., 683.
–c. s., Wise Co., Texas, 2,037.
On Ft. Worth & Denv. Cy. (R. R.).
DECHERD, Franklin Co., Tenn., 876.
On Nash., Chatt. & St. Lou. (R. R.).
DECKERVILLE, Sanilac Co., Mich., 523.
On Pere Marq. (R. R.).
DECORAH, c. s., Winneshiek Co., Iowa, 4,581.
On Chi., Mil., St. P. & Pac.; Chi., Rk. Isl. & Pac. (R. Rs.).
DECOTO, Alameda Co., Calif., 519.
On Sou. Pac.; West. Pac. (R. Rs.).
DEDHAM, c. s., Norfolk Co., Mass., 15,371.
On N. York, N. Hav. & Hart. (R. R.).
An industrial and residential suburb of Boston.
DEEMSTON, Washington Co., Pa., 648.
DEEPHAVEN, Hennepin Co., Minn., 530.
On Minn. & St. Lou. (R. R.).
DEEP RIVER, Middlesex Co., Conn., 1,916.
On N. York, N. Hav. & Hart. (R. R.).
DEEPWATER, Henry Co., Mo., 1,093.
On St. Lou.-San Fran. (R. R.).
DEEP WATER POINT, Salem Co., N. J., 537.
DEERFIELD, Broward Co., Fla., 1,366.
On Fla. & East Coast; Seab. Air Line (R. Rs.).
–Lake Co., Illinois, 1,852.
On Chi., Mil., St. P. & Pac. (R. R.).
–Franklin Co., Mass., 2,963.
On Bost. & Me.; N. York, N. Hav. & Hart. (R. Rs.).
–Lenawee Co., Mich., 512.
On N. York Cen. (R. R.).
–Dane Co., Wis., 501.
On Chi. & Nor. West. (R. R.).
DEERLODGE, c. s., Powell Co., Mont., 3,510.
On Chi., Mil., St. P. & Pac.; Nor. Pac. (R. Rs.).
DEER PARK, Hamilton Co., Ohio, 2,642.
On Penna. (R. R.).
–Spokane Co., Wash., 1,009.
On Deer Park; Gt. Nor. (R. Rs.).
DEER RIVER, Itasca Co., Minn., 832.
On Gt. Nor. (R. R.).
DEERWOOD, Crow Wing Co., Minn., 552.
On Nor. Pac. (R. R.).
DEFERIET, Jefferson Co., N. Y., 739.
DEFIANCE, c. s., Defiance Co., Ohio, 8,818.
On Balt. & Ohio; Wab. (R. Rs.).
DE FOREST, Dane Co., Wis., 540.
On Chi., Mil., St. P. & Pac. (R. R.).
DE FUNIAK SPRINGS, c. s., Walton Co., Fla., 2,646.
On Lou. & Nash. (R. R.).
DEGRAFF, Logan Co., Ohio, 849.
On Cle., Cin., Chi. & St. Lou. (R. R.).
DE KALB, De Kalb Co., Ill., 8,545.
On Chi. & Nor. West.; Chi. Gt. West.; Chi., Mil., St. P. & Pac. (R. Rs.).
–c. s., Kemper Co., Miss., 888.
On De Kalb & West. (R. R.).
–Bowie Co., Texas, 1,023.
On Tex. & Pac. (R. R.).
DE KOVEN, Union Co., Ky., 486.
On Ill. Cen. (R. R.).
DELAGUA, Las Animas Co., Colo., 1,021.
On Colo. & Southe. (R. R.).
DELANCO, Burlington Co., N. J., 1,272.
On Penna. (R. R.).
DE LAND, c. s., Volusia Co., Fla., 6,241.
On Atl. Coast Line (R. R.).
DELANO, Kern Co., Cal., 2,632.
On Sou. Pac. (R. R.).
–Wright Co., Minn., 914.
On Gt. Nor. (R. R.).
–Schuylkill Co., Pa., 800.
On Leh. Val.; Penna. (R. Rs.).
DELAVAN, Tazewell Co., Ill., 1,084.

On Alton; Ill. Cen. (R. Rs.).
–Walworth Co., Wis., 3,301.
On Chi., Mil., St. P. & Pac. (R. R.).
DELAWANNA, Passaic Co., N. J., 511.
On Del., Lack. & West. (R. R.).
DELAWARE, c. s., Delaware Co., Ohio, 8,675.
On Chesa. & Ohio; Cle., Cin., Chi. & St. Lou.; Penna. (R. Rs.).
–Nowata Co., Okla., 526.
On Mo. Pac.; Un. Tract. (El.) (R. Rs.).
DELAWARE CITY, Newcastle Co., Del., 1,005.
On Penna. (R. R.).
DELCAMBRE, Vermilion & Iberia Pars., La., 640.
On Tex. & N. Orl. (R. R.).
DE LEON, Comanche Co., Texas, 1,766.
On Mo.-Kans.-Tex. of Texas (R. R.).
DELEVAN, Cattaraugus Co., N. Y., 558.
On Penna. (R. R.).
DELFORD, Bergen Co., N. J., 2,500.
P. O. and R. R. name Oradell.
DELFT, South Holland, Netherlands, 50,609.
Is located on the Schie River, and is divided into various sections by canals.
The chief buildings are the Prinsenhof, now a museum, the scene of the assassination of William I. of Orange. The Nieuwe Kerk contains the tombs of William I. and of Hugo Grotius. A town hall, erected in 1618, is an interesting edifice. Among the educational institutions are a polytechnic school and a training school for colonial officials. The city was formerly noted for its delft ware.
DELHI, capital of India, 347,539.
At Delhi, on Dec. 12, 1911, King George V. and Queen Mary of England were crowned as Emperor and Empress of India.
The city is located on the right bank of the Jumna; the Jumma Masjid is the principal mosque. The government buildings have been grouped in an area called New Delhi.
Delhi has an extensive trade in grain, shawls, embroidered stuffs and jewelry. The city is an important railway and financial center. The authentic history of Delhi begins in 1193, when it was taken by the Mohammedans.
–Richland Parish, La., 1,043.
On Mo. Pac.; Yazoo & Miss. Val. (R. Rs.).
–c. s., Delaware Co., N. Y., 1,840.
On N. York, Ont. & West. (R. R.).
–Hamilton Co., Ohio, 1,200.
On Balt. & Ohio; Cle., Cin., Chi. & St. Lou. (R. Rs.).
DELICETO, Prov. of Foggia, Italy, 5,227.
DELITZSCH, Prussia, Germany, 14,878.
Manufactures of beer, tobacco, chemicals, shoes, and hosiery. Coal mines nearby.
DELL RAPIDS, Minnehaha Co., S. Dak., 1,636.
On Chi., Mil., St. P. & Pac. (R. R.).
DELMAR, Sussex Co., Delaware, 2,018.
On Penna. (R. R.).
–Wicomico Co., Maryland. See DELMAR, Del.
–Albany Co., N. Y., 2,500.
On Del. & Hud. (R. R.).
DELMENHORST, Oldenburg, Germany, 31,284.
A suburb of Bremen.
DELMONT, Westmoreland Co., Pa., 721.
On Penna. (R. R.).
–Douglas Co., S. Dak., 518.
DEL NORTE, c. s., Rio Grande Co., Colo., 1,410.
On Den. & Rio Gde. West. (R. R.).
DELORAINE, Souris Co., Manitoba, Canada, 815.
DELORME, Mingo Co., W. Va., 650.
On Norf. & West. (R. R.).
DELPHI, c. s., Carroll Co., Ind., 1,929.
On Chi., Ind. & Lou.; Wab. (R. Rs.).
DELPHOS, Ottawa Co., Kans., 763.
On Un. Pac. (R. R.).
–Allen and Van Wert Cos., Ohio, 5,672.
On N. York, Chi. & St. Lou.; Nor. Ohio; Penna. (R. Rs.).
DELRAY, Wayne Co., Mich. (Sta. Detroit P. O.).
On Delray Conn.; Det. & Tol. Sh. Line; Mich. Cen.; Pere Marq.; Wab. (R. Rs.).
DELRAY BEACH, Palm Beach Co., Fla., 2,708.
On Fla. East Coast; Seab. Air Line (R. Rs.).
DEL REY, Fresno Co., Calif., 600.
On Atch., Top. & Santa Fe (R. R.).
DEL RIO, c. s., Val Verde Co., Texas, 11,693.
On Tex. & N. Orl. (R. R.).
A large wool center in stock-raising section.
DELROY, York Co., Pa., 500.
DELTA, c. s., Delta Co., Colo., 2,938.
On Den. & Rio Gde. West. (R. R.).
–Keokuk Co., Iowa, 588.
On Chi., Rk. Isl. & Pac. (R. R.).
–Fulton Co., Ohio, 1,778.
On Det., Tol. & Iron.; Tol. & Ind. (El.); N. York Cen.; Wab. (R. Rs.).
–York Co., Pa., 762.
On Md. & Penna. (R. R.).
–Millard Co., Utah, 1,183.
On Los Ang. & Salt L. (R. R.).
DELTAVILLE, Middlesex Co., Va., 750.
DEMAREST, Bergen Co., N. J., 1,013.
On Erie (R. R.).
DEMING, c. s., Luna Co., N. Mex., 3,377.
On Atch., Top. & Santa Fe; Sou. Pac. (R. Rs.).
DEMMIN, Prussia, Germany, 12,783.
Textile manufactures.
DEMOPOLIS, Marengo Co., Ala., 4,037.
On Sou.; St. Lou.-San Fran. (R. Rs.).
DEMOREST, Habersham Co., Ga., 730.
On Tallulah Fs. (R. R.).
DENAIN, Dept. of Nord, France, 26,478.
Iron and steel works; breweries.
DENBIGH, c. s., Warwick Co., Va., 1,000.
DENDRON, Surry Co., Va., 671.
DENHAM SPRINGS, Livingston Parish, La., 1,002.
On Yazoo & Miss. Val. (R. R.).
DENIA, Alicante, Spain, 12,612.
Trade center of thriving farming region.
DENISON, c. s., Crawford Co., Iowa, 3,905.
On Chi. & Nor. West.; Ill. Cen. (R. Rs.).
–Grayson Co., Texas, 13,850.
On Kan., Okla. & Gulf of Tex.; Mo.-Kans.-Tex. of Tex.; St. Lou.-San Fran.; Tex. & New Orl.; Tex. El.; Tex. & Pac. (R. Rs.).
Headquarters of Mo.-Kan.-Tex. mechanical department, with machine and car shops. Principal industries are textiles, cotton-seed products, peanuts and pecan shelling, etc., cotton, cotton-seed oil, and flour mills.
DENMARK, Bamberg Co., S. C., 1,713.
On Atl. Coast Line; Seab. Air Line; Sou. (R. Rs.).
–Brown Co., Wis., 779.
On Chi. & Nor. West. (R. R.).
DENNING, Franklin Co., Ark., 384.
On Mo. Pac. (R. R.).
DENNIS, Barnstable Co., Mass., 2,017.
DENNISON, Tuscarawas Co., Ohio, 4,529.
On Penna. (R. R.).
DENNIS PORT, Barnstable Co., Mass., 750.
DE NOYA, Osage Co., Okla., 1,055.
On Atch., Top. & Santa Fe (R. R.).
DENTON, c. s., Caroline Co., Md., 1,604.
On Md. & Del. Seacoast (R. R.).
–Davidson Co., N. C., 540.
On High Pt., Thomasv. & Dent. (R. R.).
–c. s., Denton Co., Texas, 9,587.
On Mo.-Kan.-Tex. of Tex.; Tex. & Pac. (R. Rs.).
Seat of North Texas State Normal College. Industries include an extensive brick plant and flour mills.
DENVER, c. s., Denver Co., Colo., State capital, 287,861.
Is located 5,200 feet above sea level, at the confluence of the South Platte River and Cherry Creek; is an important railroad center at the junction of the Atchison, Topeka & Santa Fe; the Chicago, Burlington & Quincy; the Chicago, Rock Island & Pacific; the Colorado & Southern; Denver & Intermountain (El.); the Denver & Rio Grande Western; the Denver & Salt Lake; and the Union Pacific.
It has many noteworthy buildings, among them the Capitol, constructed of Colorado granite at a cost of $2,000,000; the United States Custom-house and Post-office, the United States Mint, the County Court-house, the Chamber of Commerce, the Mining Exchange, Auditorium, City Hall, and the Union Depot. Other interesting features are the Colorado Museum of Natural History (in City Park); the Civic Center, containing a Greek open-air theater, and municipal golf courses, tennis courts, and baseball diamonds. A favorable climate has made the city a popular resort for both summer and winter.
It is a leading stock market, and has large sheep pens, stock-yard plants, and packing houses. Among its manufactures is mining machinery, which is shipped to all parts of the world. Other products include refined ores, clay products, beet sugar, tents, and confectionery.

COURTESY METROPOLITAN MUSEUM OF ART

THE JUMMA MUSJID MOSQUE AND QUADRANGLE, DELHI, INDIA

–Bremer Co., Ia., 500.
On Waterl., Ced. Fs. & Nor. (R. R.).
–Lancaster Co., Pa., 1,203.
On Reading (R. R.).
DENVILLE, Morris Co., N. J., 1,500.
On Del., Lack. & West. (R. R.).
DE PERE, Brown Co., Wis., 5,521.
On Chi., Mil., St. P. & Pac.; Chi. & Nor. West. (R. Rs.).
DEPEW, Erie Co., N. Y., 6,536.
On Del., Lack. & West.; Erie; Leh. Val.; N. York Cen. (R. Rs.).
–Creek Co., Okla., 1,126.
On St. Lou.-San Fran. (R. R.).
DEPORT, Lamar Co., Texas, 819.
On Paris & Mt. Pleasant (R. R.).
DEPOSIT, Broome and Delaware Cos., N. Y., 1,887.
On Erie (R. R.).
DEPUE, Bureau Co., Ill., 2,200.
On Chi., Mil., St. P. & Pac.; Chi., Rk. Isl. & Pac.; N. York Cen. (R. Rs.).
DE QUEEN, c. s., Sevier Co., Ark., 2,938.
On De Queen & East.; Kan. Cy. Sou. (R. Rs.).
DE QUINCY, Calcasieu Parish, La., 3,589.
On Kan. Cy. Sou.; N. Orl., Tex. & Mex. (R. Rs.).
DERBENT, Daghestan, Soviet Union, 31,200.
Center of a rich agricultural region.
DERBY, c. s., Derbyshire, England, 142,406.
Seat of silk and metal industries.
–New Haven Co., Conn., 10,788.
On N. York, N. Hav. & Hart. (R. R.).
A suburb of New Haven.
–Erie Co., N. Y., 800.
On N. York Cen. (R. R.).
DERBY LINE, Orleans Co., Vermont, 683.
On Queb. Cen. (R. R.).
DE RIDDER, Beauregard Parish, La., 3,747.
On Gulf, Colo. & Santa Fe; Kan. Cy. Sou.; Tex. & N. Orl. (R. Rs.).
DERMOTT, Chicot Co., Ark., 2,942.
On Mo. Pac. (R. R.).
DERRY, Rockingham Co., N. H., 5,131.
On Bost. & Me. (R. R.).
–Westmoreland Co., Pa., 3,046.
On Penna. (R. R.).
DERRY CHURCH, Dauphin Co., Pa., 1,000.
DE RUYTER, Madison Co., N. Y., 466.
On Leh. Val. (R. R.).
DERWENT, Guernsey Co., Ohio, 500.
On Penna. (R. R.).
DES ALLEMANDS, St. Charles Par., La., 518.
On Tex. & N. Orleans (R. R.).
DES ARC, c. s., Prairie Co., Ark., 1,348.
On Chi., Rk. Isl. & Pac. (R. R.).
DESCHAILLONS, Lotbinière Co., Quebec, Canada, 1,650.
DESDEMONA, Eastland Co., Texas, 609.
On Wichita Fs. & Sou. (R. R.).
DESERONTO, Hastings Co., Ontario, Can., 1,476.
On Can. Nat. (R. R.).
DESHLER, Thayer Co., Neb., 1,177.
On Chi., Rk. Isl. & Pac. (R. R.).
–Henry Co., Ohio, 1,538.
On Balt. & Ohio; Cin. & L. Erie (El.) (R. Rs.).
DESLOGE, St. Francois Co., Mo., 1,394.
On Mo.-Ill. (R. R.).
DESMET, Benewah Co., Idaho, 525.
DE SMET, c. s., Kingsbury Co., S. Dak., 988.
On Chi. & Nor. West. (R. R.).
DES MOINES, c. s., Polk Co., Iowa, 142,559. State capital.
It is situated on the Des Moines River and at the mouth of Raccoon River, 357 miles west of Chicago, and on the Chicago & North Western; the Chicago, Burlington & Quincy; the Chicago Great Western; the Chicago, Milwaukee, St. Paul & Pacific; the Chicago, Rock Island & Pacific; the Des Moines & Central Iowa (El.); the Des Moines Western; the Des Moines Union; the Ft. Dodge, Des Moines & Southern (El.); the Minneapolis & St. Louis; the Wabash and other railroads.
It has many important buildings, among them the Capitol, built at a cost of $3,000,000; the United States Government Building, the State Arsenal, and the State and city libraries.
Vast bituminous coal-fields near by have contributed to the growth of extensive industries of which textiles, printing and publishing, silos, incubators, and woodworking are the principal. The annual volume of production is nearly $100,000,000. In 1930 there were 330 establishments, large and small. It is also notable as an important insurance center, there being about fifty companies—life, fire, casualty, accident, etc. It is the seat of two educational institutions of reputation—Drake University, and Des Moines College. Des Moines was settled in 1846, incorporated as the town of Fort Des Moines, 1851, chartered as a city and became the capital of the State in 1857.
DE SOTO, Jackson Co., Ill., 673.
On Ill. Cen.; Mo. Pac. (R. Rs.).
–Jefferson Co., Mo., 5,069.
On Mo. Pac. (R. R.).
DES PLAINES, Cook Co., Ill., 8,798.
On Chi. & Nor. West.; Minn., St. P. & S. Ste. M. (R. Rs.).
DESSAU, capital of Anhalt, Germany, 91,423.
City has manufactures of sugar, chocolate, chemicals, small iron goods, machinery, and some textiles.
DESSUK, Charbieh, Egypt, about 10,000.
DETMOLD, capital of Principality of Lippe, Germany, 18,000.
Has manufactures of furniture, gloves, and agricultural machinery.
DETOUR, Chippewa Co., Mich., 616.
DETROIT, c. s., Wayne Co., Mich., 1,568,662.
It is situated on the Detroit River, 18 miles from Lake Erie, altitude 600 feet, and on the lines of the Canadian Pacific; the Detroit, Toledo & Ironton; Delray Connecting; Detroit Terminal; the Grand Trunk; the Detroit & Toledo Shore Line; New York Central; the Michigan Central; the Pere Marquette; the Wabash; and Pennsylvania. The Detroit River, sometimes called the "Dardanelles of the New World," is here the boundary between the United States and Canada. It affords a splendid harbor, with a water-front of about 9 miles.
The most prominent buildings in the city are the Detroit Public Library, Museum of Art, Masonic Temple, City Hall, Municipal Building, General Motors Building, Penobscot Building, D. Stott Building, Book Tower, Union Trust Building, First National Bank, Statler, Book-Cadillac, Detroit-Leland, Henry Clay, Webster Hall, Barlum, Fort Shelby, and Tuller Hotels, Henry Ford Hospital, and the Michigan Central Station. Belle Isle Park, 825 acres, has a bathing beach, bath house, casino, and luncheon pavilion, a horticultural building, a zoo of 15 acres, and a large aquarium. Detroit leads all other cities in the manufacture of automobiles and automobile accessories. The Detroit River is one of the great commercial waterways of the world; the vessels that pass through in one season carrying nearly one hundred million tons of freight. The remarkable growth of the city's population has been due to the rapid development of the automobile industry. Other important manufactures are iron and steel wares, adding machines, wire cloth, stoves, coin machines, railroad and street cars, airplanes, packed meats, tobacco goods, soda ash, salt, drugs, and clothing.
Tunnels and ferries connect the city with Windsor and other Canadian ports. The Ambassador Bridge links Detroit with Sandwich, Ontario.
–Red River Co., Tex., 850.
On Tex. & Pac. (R. R.).
DETROIT LAKES, c. s., Becker Co., Minn., 3,675.
On Minn., St. P. & S. Ste. M.; Nor. Pac. (R. Rs.).
DE VALLS BLUFF, c. s., Prairie Co., Ark., 672.
On Chi., Rk. Isl. & Pac. (R. R.).
DEVENTER, Overijssel, Netherlands, 36,227.
An agricultural center. Has carpet factories and other textile industries.
DEVIL'S LAKE, c. s., Ramsey Co., N. Dak., 5,451.
On Farmers' Gr. & Ship; Gt. Nor.; Minn., St. P. & S. Ste. M. (R. Rs.).
DEVINE, Medina Co., Texas, 1,093.
On Internat.-Gt. Nor. (R. R.).
DEVOL, Cotton Co., Okla., 328.
On Mo.-Kan.-Tex. (R. R.).
DEVONPORT, Devonshire, England (included in Plymouth).
–Tasmania, 5,153.
DEWAR, Okmulgee Co., Okla., 994.
On Kan., Okla. & Gulf (R. R.).
DEWEY, Washington Co., Okla., 2,095.

MANNING BROS. PHOTO

GRISWOLD STREET, THE FINANCIAL CENTER OF DETROIT, SHOWING THE MODERN, TOWERING BUSINESS STRUCTURES OF THE AUTOMOBILE CITY

On Atch., Top. & Santa Fe; Mo.-Kan.-Tex. (R. Rs.).

DEWEYVILLE, Newton Co., Tex., 1,500.
On Sab. & Neches Val. (R. R.).

DE WITT, c. s., Arkansas Co., Ark., 1,853.
On St. Lou. Southw. (R. R.).
–Saline Co., Neb., 534.
On Chi., Burl. & Quincy; Chi., Rk. Isl. & Pac. (R. Rs.).
–Onondaga Co., N. Y., 500.

DEWITT, Clinton Co., Iowa, 2,041.
On Chi., Mil., St. P. & Pac.; Chi. & Nor. West. (R. Rs.).

DEWSBURY, Yorkshire, England, 54,303.
Market and industrial town. Textiles, iron castings, and machinery. Coal mines nearby.

DEXTER, Dallas Co., Iowa, 748.
On Chi., Rk. Isl. & Pac. (R. R.).
–Penobscot Co., Maine, 3,500.
On Me. Cen. (R. R.).
–Washtenaw Co., Mich., 894.
On Mich. Cen. (R. R.).
–Stoddard Co., Mo., 2,714.
On Mo. Pac.; St. Lou. Southw. (R. Rs.).
–Jefferson Co., N. Y., 1,020.
On Dext. & Nor.; N. York Cen. (R. Rs.).

D'HANIS, Medina Co., Tex., 700.
On Tex. & N. Orl. (R. R.).

DHAR, Central India, India, 18,400.

DIAGONAL, Ringgold Co., Iowa, 577.
On Chi., Burl. & Quincy; Chi. Gt. West. (R. Rs.).

DIAMOND SPRINGS, Eldorado Co., Calif., 550.
On Diam. & Cald.; Sou. Pac. (R. Rs.).

DIAMONDVILLE, Lincoln Co., Wyo., 812.
On Ore. Short Line (R. R.).

DIARBEKR, Turkey. See DIYARBEKIR.

DIBOLL, Angelina Co., Tex., 1,363.
On Tex. & N. Orl.; Tex. Southe. (R. Rs.).

DICKENS, c. s., Dickens Co., Tex., 500.

DICKINSON (Port Dickinson), Broome Co., N. Y., 1,000.
On Del. & Hud. (R. R.).
–c. s., Stark Co., N. Dak., 5,025.
On Nor. Pac. (R. R.).

DICKSON, Lackawanna Co., Pa., 12,395.
On Del. & Hud.; N. York, Ont. & West.; Wilk.-Bar. & East. (R. Rs.).
In center of anthracite region.
–Dickson Co., Tenn., 2,902.
On Nash., Chatt. & St. Lou. (R. R.).

DIEGO SUAREZ, Madagascar, 16,756.

DIEPPE, Dept. of Seine Inférieure, France, 25,500.
It is situated at the mouth of the river Arques,

on the English Channel, between two high ranges of chalk cliffs. The principal buildings are the churches of St. Jacques and St. Remy, the museum and picture gallery, and the theater. The principal manufactures are lace, fine linen, paper, tobacco, and carved articles of horn, bone, and ivory. There are also shipbuilding yards, sugar refineries, distilleries and a fishing fleet. Dieppe is a popular seaside resort.

DIERKS, Howard Co., Ark., 1,544.
On De Queen & East. (R. R.).

DIGHTON, Bristol Co., Mass., 3,116.
On N. York, New Hav. & Hart. (R. R.).
–c. s., Lane Co., Kansas, 797.
On Atch., Top. & Santa Fe (R. R.).

DIGNE, capital of Dept. of Basses-Alpes, France, 6,737.

DIJON, capital of Dept. of Côte d'Or, France, 96,257.
Situated on the right bank of the Ouche. The most interesting buildings are the Church of Notre Dame, the Church of St. Michel, the theater, and the palace of the dukes of Burgundy, now used as a town hall. It is the seat of a university of law, science, and letters, a royal college, a theological seminary, and an academy of art. Has salt refineries, distilleries, and breweries.
Dijon dates from the Roman times. It came into the possession of the Burgundians in the fifth century, and from them passed to the Franks. In the eleventh century it was united to the Duchy of Burgundy and became the capital. On the death of Charles the Bold, 1477, it was annexed to France.

DILLE (Dilles Bottom P. O.), Belmont Co., Ohio, 500.
On Penna. (R. R.).

DILLEY, Frio Co., Texas, 929.
On Internat.-Gt. Nor. (R. R.).

DILLI, Timor, 14,021.

DILLON, c. s., Beaverhead Co., Mont., 2,422.
On Ore. Short Line (R. R.).
–s. c., Dillon Co., S. C., 2,731.
On Atl. Coast Line; Seab. Air Line (R. Rs.).

DILLONVALE, Jefferson Co., Ohio, 1,434.
On N. York Cen.; Wheel. & L. Erie (R. Rs.).

DILLSBORO, Dearborn Co., Ind., 502.
On Balt. & Ohio (R. R.).

DILLSBURG, York Co., Pa., 983.

DILLY, capital of Portuguese Timor, 10,829.

DILWORTH, Clay Co., Minn., 983.
On Nor. Pac. (R. R.).

DIMIAO, Prov. of Bohol, Bohol, P. I., 10,496.

DIMMITT, c. s., Castro Co., Texas, 829.
On Ft. Worth & Denv. Cy. (R. R.).

DIMONDALE, Eaton Co., Mich., 545.
On N. York Cen. (R. R.).

DINAN, Dept. of Côtes-du-Nord, France, 11,822.
Center of a farming region.

DINANT, Prov. of Namur, Belgium, 6,612.

DINAPUR, Bengal, India, 33,699.
A military station.

DINARD, Dept. of Ille-et-Vilaine, France, 7,567.

DINGLE, Iloilo Prov., Panay, P. I., 13,345.

DINGRAS, Ilocos Norte Prov., Luzon, P. I., 21,320.

DINKEY CREEK, Fresno Co., Calif., 800.

DINUBA, Tulare Co., Cal., 2,968.
On Sou. Pac. (R. R.).

DISON, Prov. of Liége, Belgium, 10,501.
Has woolen mills.

DIVERNON, Sangamon Co., Ill., 1,170.
On Ill. Cen. (R. R.).

DIVIDING CREEK, Cumberland Co., N. J., 791.

DIXFIELD, Oxford Co., Maine, 900.
On Me. Cen. (R. R.).

DIXIANA, Jefferson Co., Ala., 2,500.

DIXMOOR (Specialville), Cook Co., Ill., 944.

DIXMUDE, West Flanders, Belgium, 3,234.

DIXON, Solano Co., Cal., 1,000.
On Sou. Pac. (R. R.).
–c. s., Lee Co., Ill., 9,908.
On Chi. & Nor. West.; Ill. Cen. (R. Rs.).
–c. s., Webster Co., Ky., 650.
On Ill. Cen. (R. R.).
–Pulaski Co., Mo., 721.
On St. Lou.-San Fran. (R. R.).
–Rio Arriba Co., N. Mex., 800.

DIXONVILLE, Indiana Co., Pa., 1,500.
On N. York Cen.; Penna. (R. Rs.).

DIYARBEKIR (Diarbekr), Turkey, 34,874.
A commercial center. Gold and silver filigree work.

DIZFUL, Prov. of Khuzistan, Iran (Persia), 50,000.
Preparation of indigo. Making of felt and dyed cloth.

DJIBOUTI, capital of French Somaliland, 9,914.

DJOKJAKARTA, Netherland India, 121,979.
A trade center and watering-place.

D'LO, Simpson Co., Miss., 514.
On Gulf & Ship Isl. (R. R.).

DNEPROPETROVSK (Ekaterinoslav), Soviet Union, 379,200.
Location of an immense water-power development, which has attracted many industries. Has iron and steel mills, flour mills, breweries, and many small factories.

DOBBS FERRY, Westchester Co., N. Y., 5,741.
On N. York Cen. (R. R.).

DÖBELN, Saxony, Germany, 23,000.
Industries include wool spinning, iron founding, and the manufacture of farm implements and machinery.

DODGE, Dodge Co., Neb., 693.
On Chi. & Nor. West. (R. R.).

DODGE CENTER, Dodge Co., Minn., 854.
On Chi. Gt. West.; Chi. & Nor. West. (R. Rs.).

DODGE CITY, c. s., Ford Co., Kans., 9,071.
On Atch., Top. & Santa Fe; Chi., Rk. Isl. & Pac. (R. Rs.).
Famous frontier town. Has car works, flour mills, and creameries.

DODGEVILLE, Bristol Co., Mass., 550.
On N. York, N. Hav. & Hart. (R. R.).
–Houghton Co., Mich., 510.
–c. s., Iowa Co., Wis., 1,937.
On Ill. Cen.; Chi. & Nor. West. (R. Rs.).

DOERUN, Colquitt Co., Ga., 719.
On Ga. Nor. (R. R.).

DOE RUN JUNCTION, St. Francois Co., Mo., 962.
On Mo.-Ill. (R. R.).

DOHENY, PARK, Orange Co., Calif., 549.

DOLAN, Perry Co., Ky., 861.

DOLAND, Spink Co., S. Dak., 510.
On Chi. & Nor. West. (R. R.).

DÔLE, Dept. of Jura, France, 18,117.
Has manufactures of pumps, castings, chemicals, and machinery.

DOLGEVILLE, Herkimer and Fulton Cos., N. Y., 3,309.
On N. York Cen. (R. R.).

DOLLAR BAY, Houghton Co., Mich., 1,000.
On Cop. Rge.; Min. Rge. (R. Rs.).

DOLOMITE, Jefferson Co., Ala., 1,249.
On Woodw. Iron Co. (R. R.).

DOLON-Nor, China, 30,000.

DOLORES, Buenos Aires, Argentina, 27,155.
A trade center.
–Montezuma Co., Colo., 557.
On Rio Gde. Sou. (R. R.).

DOLTON, Cook Co., Ill., 2,923.
On Chi. & East. Ill.; Chi. & West. Ind.; Ind. Harb. Belt; Penna. (R. Rs.).

DONA ANA, Dona Ana Co., N. Mex., 500.
On Atch., Top. & Santa Fe (R. R.).

DONALDSON, Schuylkill Co., Pa., 965.
On Reading (R. R.).

DONALDSONVILLE, c. s., Ascension Par., La., 3,788.
On Tex. & Pac. (R. R.).

DONALSONVILLE, c. s., Seminole Co., Ga., 1,183.
On Atl. Coast Line (R. R.).

DONAUESCHINGEN, Baden, Germany, 5,002.

DONAUWORTH, Germany, 4,821.

DONCASTER, Yorkshire, England, 63,308.

Has an extensive agricultural trade and some industries.

DONGOLA, Union Co., Ill., 635.
On Ill. Cen. (R. R.).

DONIPHAN, c. s., Ripley Co., Mo., 1,398.
On Mo. Pac. (R. R.).

DONNA, Hidalgo Co., Texas, 4,103.
On St. Lou., Browns. & Mex. (R. R.).

DONNELLSON, Lee Co., Ia., 581.
On Chi., Burl. & Quincy (R. R.).

DONNER, Terrebonne Par., La., 1,000.
On Tex. & N. Orl. (R. R.).

DONORA, Washington Co., Pa., 13,905.
On Donora Sou.; Pitts. & W. Va.; Penna. (R. Rs.).
Has mills that produce acid, zinc, wire, nails and steel goods. Extensive coal mines in vicinity.

DONWOOD, Kanawha Co., W. Va., 527.

DOON, Lyon Co., Iowa, 576.
On Chi., St. P., Minn. & Oma.; Gt. Nor. (R. Rs.).

DORA, Walker Co., Ala., 1,143.
On Ill. Cen.; St. Lou.-San Fran. (R. Rs.).

DORADO, Mun. of Dorado, Puerto Rico, 2,328.

DORCHESTER, Dorsetshire, England, 10,030.
A market town in an agricultural region.
–Saline Co., Neb., 579.
On Chi., Burl. & Quincy (R. R.).

DORDRECHT, South Holland, Netherlands, 57,059.
A picturesque town with sawmills, sugar factories, shipyards, and tobacco factories.

DORMONT, Allegheny Co., Pa., 13,190.
A residential suburb of Pittsburgh.

DOROTHEENDORF, Prussia, Germany, united with Zabrze (1905).

DORPAT, Estonia. See TARTU.

DORRIS, Siskiyou Co., Calif., 762.
On Sou. Pac. (R. R.).

DORRISVILLE, Saline Co., Ill., 800.

DORSET, Bennington Co., Vt., 500.

DORTMUND, Prov. of Westphalia, Germany, 540,-875.
It is an important railway center. Dortmund dates from 900. It became eventually a free imperial city, and joined the Hanseatic League. It began to decline in the Thirty Years' War, but is now a busy manufacturing center. It has breweries, flour mills and zinc works. Its most important manufactures are locomotives, cars and heavy machinery.

DOS PALOS, Merced Co., Calif., 1,000.

DOTHAN, c. s., Houston Co., Ala., 16,046.
On Atl. & St. And. Bay; Atl. Coast Line; Cen. of Ga. (R. Rs.).
Diversified agricultural products, grain elevator, mixed feed mill, syrup refinery, peanut mill.

DOUAI, Dept. of Nord, France, 41,598.
Damaged in the World War.

DOUALA, Cameroon (Kamerun), Africa, 42,021.
A market center.

DOUARNENEZ, Finistère, France, 10,556.
A fishing port.

DOUCETTE, Tyler Co., Tex., 519.
On Tex. & N. Orl. (R. R.).

DOUGLAS, Dist. of Juneau, Alaska, 593.
–Cochise Co., Ariz., 9,828.
On Sou. Pac. (R. R.).
An important copper smelting point.
–c. s., Coffee Co., Ga., 4,206.
On Atla., Birm. & Coast; Ga. & Fla. (R. Rs.).
–Isle of Man, 25,000.
–Worcester Co., Mass., 2,403.
–Tucker Co., W. Va., 500.
On Western Maryland (R. R.).
–c. s., Converse Co., Wyo., 1,917.
On Chi., Burl. & Quincy; Chi. & Nor. West. (R. Rs.).

DOUGLASS, Butler Co., Kans., 668.
On Atch., Top. & Santa Fe (R. R.).

DOUGLASSVILLE, Berks Co., Pa., 575.
On Penna.; Read. (R. Rs.).

DOUGLASVILLE, c. s., Douglas Co., Ga., 2,316.
On Southern (R. R.).

DOUR, Hainaut, Belgium, 11,890.

DOVER, Pope Co., Ark., 510.
–Kent Co., England, 41,095.
One of the chief ports of communication between England and the Continent; shipbuilding; sail, rope, and paper making; has thriving coasting trade and fisheries; the castle is a collection of formidable works occupying 35 acres; the harbor, of 3 basins, is a harbor of refuge.
–c. s., Kent Co., Del., State capital, 4,800.
On Jones Creek, and on the Pennsylvania Railroad, 48 miles south of Wilmington, and about 5 miles west of Delaware Bay.
It is the center of a great fruit-growing section. The principal buildings face an open square planted with fine elms. The Statehouse has a fine library. There is a handsome monument to Colonel John Haslett, M.D., who fell at the battle of Princeton.
The chief industries are fruit-drying and flour milling. There are foundry and machine shops, a carriage factory, and a stocking factory.
The town was settled in 1687, and incorpo-

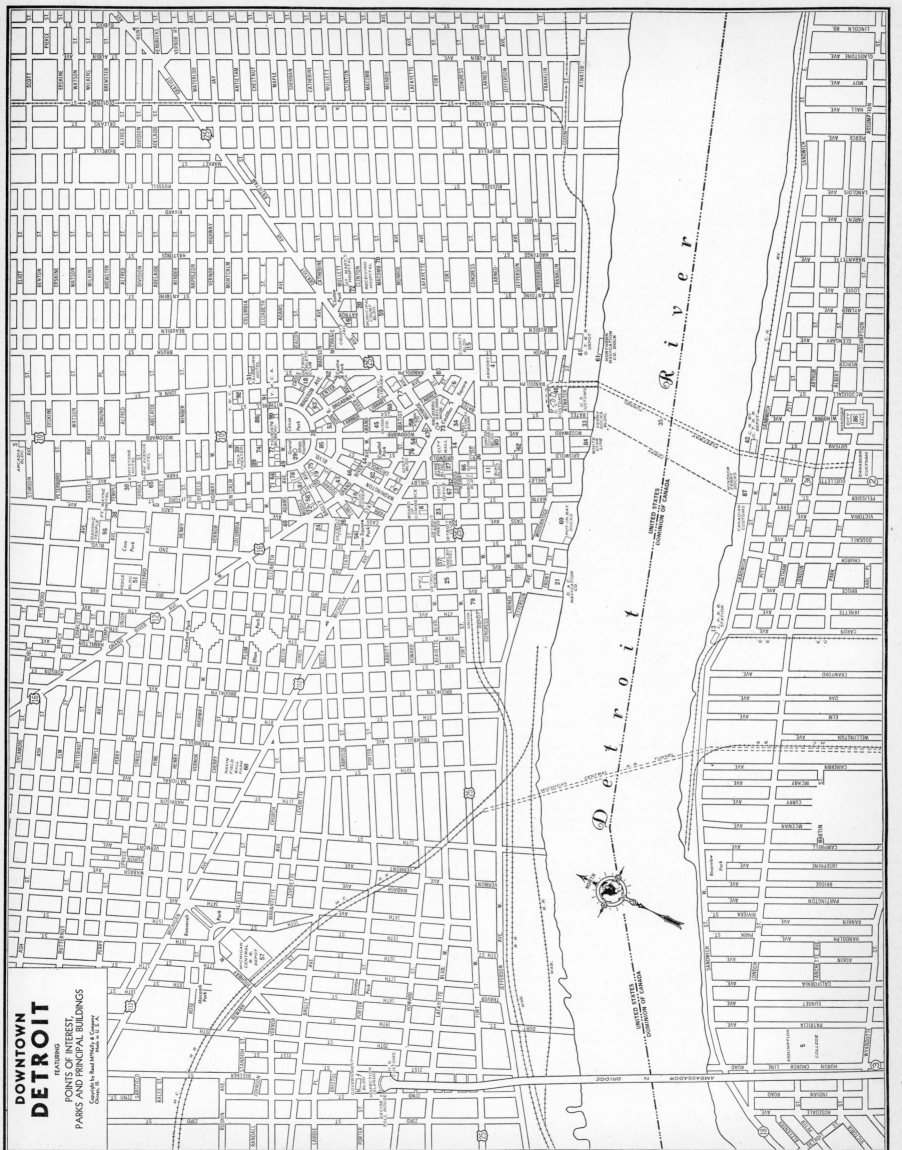

DOWNTOWN DETROIT

FEATURING

POINTS OF INTEREST,
PARKS AND PRINCIPAL BUILDINGS

Copyright by Rand McNally & Company
Chicago, Ill.
Made in U.S.A.

MAP OF THE CENTRAL PART OF DETROIT, THE CHIEF CITY OF MICHIGAN AND THE FOURTH LARGEST CITY OF THE UNITED STATES. DETROIT LEADS ALL OTHER CITIES IN THE MANUFACTURE OF AUTOMOBILES AND RANKS HIGH IN THE PRODUCTION OF AIRPLANES. ACROSS THE DETROIT RIVER IS SHOWN A PART OF WINDSOR, ONTARIO, CONNECTED TO DETROIT BY FERRIES, TUNNELS AND THE AMBASSADOR BRIDGE

rated about 1720, and at the outbreak of the Revolution became the State capital.
–Norfolk Co., Mass., 1,305.
On N. York, N. Hav. & Hart. (R. R.).
–c. s., Strafford Co., N. H., 13,573.
On Bost. & Me. (R. R.).
Has woolen mills, machinery, cotton goods, leather belting, shoes, printing presses, etc.
–Morris Co., N. J., 10,031.
On Cen. of N. Jer.; Del., Lack. & West. (R. Rs.).
An industrial town with manufactures of hosiery, silk, stoves and furnaces, drills, air compressors, and bridges. Iron mines nearby.
–Craven Co., N. C., 621.
On Norf. Sou. (R. Rs.).
–Tuscarawas Co., Ohio, 9,716.
On Balt. & Ohio; Penna. (R. Rs.).
–York Co., Pa., 676.
–c. s., Stewart Co., Tenn., 763.
DOVER CENTER, Cuyahoga Co., Ohio, 2,453.
DOVER-FOXCROFT, c. s., Piscataquis Co., Maine, 3,890.
On Bangor & Aroostook; Me. Cen. (R. Rs.).
DOVER PLAINS, Dutchess Co., N. Y., 1,000.
On N. York Cen. (R. R.).
DOWAGIAC, Cass Co., Mich., 5,550.
On Dowagiac River and 35 miles S. W. of Kalamazoo.
On Mich. Cen. (R. R.).
DOW CITY, Crawford Co., Iowa, 558.
On Ill. Cen.; Chi. & Nor. West. (R. Rs.).
DOWELL, Jackson Co., Ill., 832.
On Ill. Cen. (R. R.).
DOWLING PARK, Suwannee Co., Fla., 500.
On Live Oak, Perry & Gulf (R. R.).
DOWNER'S GROVE, Du Page Co., Ill., 8,977.
On Chi., Burl. & Quincy (R. R.).
DOWNEY, Bannock Co., Idaho, 553.
On Ore. Short Line (R. R.).
–Los Angeles Co., Cal., 5,476.
On Sou. Pac. (R. R.).
DOWNING, Schuyler Co., Mo., 514.
On Chi., Burl. & Quincy (R. R.).
DOWNINGTOWN, Chester Co., Pa., 4,548.
On Penna.; Reading (R. Rs.).
DOWNS, Osborne Co., Kans., 1,285.
On Mo. Pac. (R. R.).
DOWNSVILLE, Delaware Co., N. Y., 532.
DOWS, Franklin and Wright Cos., Iowa, 926.
On Chi., Rk. Isl. & Pac. (R. R.).
DOYLE, Erie Co., N. Y., 750.
DOYLESTOWN, Wayne Co., Ohio, 1,150.
–c. s., Bucks Co., Pa., 4,577.
On Reading (R. R.).
Location of an interesting historical museum.
DOYLINE, Webster Par., La., 600.
On Yazoo & Miss. Val. (R. R.).
DRACUT, Middlesex Co., Mass., 6,500.
DRAKE, McHenry Co., N. Dak., 644.
On Minn., St. P. & S. Ste. M. (R. R.).
DRAKES BRANCH, Charlotte Co., Va., 583.
On Sou. (R. R.).
DRAKESBORO, Muhlenberg Co., Ky., 1,242.
On Lou. & Nash. (R. R.).
DRAMA, Greece, 34,000.
DRAMMEN, Amt of Buskerud, Norway, 25,399.
Engineering works, sawmills, and large pulp and paper plants.
DRANEY, Seine, France, 42,938.
DRAPER, Rockingham Co., N. C., 1,020.
On Danv. & West. (R. R.).
–Salt Lake Co., Utah, 1,250.
On Los Ang. & Salt L. (R. R.).
DRAVOSBURG, Allegheny Co., Pa., 2,391.
On Penna. (R. R.).
DRAYTON, Pembina Co., N. Dak., 502.
On Nor. Pac. (R. R.).
–Spartanburg Co., S. C., 1,000.
DRAYTON PLAINS, Oakland Co., Mich., 1,000.
On Gd. Tr. (R. R.).
DRESDEN, capital of Saxony, Germany, 642,143.
Situated on both banks of the Elbe. The largest park, the Grosse Garten, contains numerous statues, a museum of antiquities, and a zoological and a botanical garden. The most prominent building is the former royal palace, begun in 1534 and enlarged by Augustus the Strong. It has a tower 331 feet high. The Zwinger is the vestibule of an uncompleted palace begun during the reign of Augustus the Strong. Its northwest wing forms the museum, in which is located the Dresden Picture Gallery, for which the city is best known. The city is famous for its china.
–Muskingum Co., Ohio, 1,362.
On Penna.; Wheel. & L. Erie (R. Rs.).
Has paper, woolen and basket mills.
–Kent Co., Ontario, Canada, 1,529.
On Pere Marq. (R. R.).
–c. s., Weakley Co., Tenn., 1,047.
On Nash., Chatt. & St. Lou. (R. R.).
DREW, Sunflower Co., Miss., 1,373.
On Yazoo & Miss. Val. (R. R.).
DREXEL, Cass Co., Mo., 553.
On Kan. Cy. Sou. (R. R.).
–Burke Co., N. Car., 781.
On Southern (R. R.).
DREXEL HILL, Delaware Co., Pa., 1,197.
DRIFTON, Luzerne Co., Pa., 1,400.
On Leh. Val. (R. R.).
DRIGGS, Teton Co., Idaho, 719.
On Ore. Short Line (R. R.).
DROGHEDA, Ireland. See DROIEHEAD ATHA.
Is situated on both sides of the Boyne River, 26 miles north of Baile Atha Cliath (Dublin). Some remains of the old wall by which it was inclosed still exist. Among the architectural attractions of the town are an obelisk, commemorating the victory of William of Orange; Magdalen's Steeple, a fragment of an old Dominican convent, and Lawrence Gate.
The industries include flax-spinning, cotton-weaving, tanning, brewing, the extraction of salt, and iron-casting. There is an active shipping trade.
Drogheda was a political and ecclesiastical center as early as the twelfth century. In 1649 the town was stormed by Cromwell, who massacred its defenders, and in 1690, a few miles away, was fought the battle of the Boyne.
DROHOBYCZ, East Galicia, Poland, 32,622.
The center of a petroleum producing region. Has oil refineries.
DROIEHEAD ATHA (Drogheda), Counties Louth and Meath, Ireland (Eire), 12,716.
DRUMMONDVILLE, Drummond and Arthabaska Cos., Quebec, Canada, 6,609.
DRUMRIGHT, Creek Co., Okla., 4,972.
On Atch., Top. & Santa Fe (R. R.).
DRYBRANCH, Kanawha Co., W. Va., 506.
On Chesa. & Ohio (R. R.).
DRYDEN, Tompkins Co., N. Y., 666.
On Leh. Val. (R. R.).
DUARTE, Los Angeles Co., Calif., 1,500.
On Atch., Top. & Santa Fe; Pac. Elec.; Sou. Pac. (R. Rs.).
DUBACH, Lincoln Parish, La., 608.
On Chi., Rk. Isl. & Pac. (R. R.).
DUBLIN, Irish Free State. See BAILE ATHA CLIATH.
–c. s., Laurens Co., Ga., 6,681.
On Macon, Dub. & Sav.; Wrightsv. & Tennille (R. Rs.).
–Wayne Co., Indiana, 727.
On Penna.; Ind. R. R. Sys. (El.) (R. Rs.).
–Erath Co., Texas, 2,271.
On Mo.-Kans.-Tex. of Texas; St. Lou.-San Fran.; Wichita Fs. & Sou. (R. Rs.).
DUBOIS, Dubois Co., Ind., 504.
On Southern (R. R.).
DU BOIS, Clearfield Co., Pa., 11,595.
On Balt. & Ohio; Penna. (R. Rs.).
An important coal and lumber center. Has coal-tar shops, foundries, machine shops, silk mills, and glass-making plants.
DUBOISTOWN, Lycoming Co., Pa., 1,049.
On Penna. (R. R.).
DUBOVKA, Soviet Union, 16,400.
DUBUQUE, c. s., Dubuque Co., Iowa, 41,679.
A port of entry situated on the west bank of the Mississippi River, at the foot of a picturesque bluff. The railways entering the city are the Chicago Great Western; the Chicago, Burlington & Quincy; the Chicago, Milwaukee, St. Paul & Pacific; and the Illinois Central.
It is the seat of Warburg Seminary (Lutheran), Clarke College, Columbia College, and University of Dubuque.
The city's principal industries are metal manufactures covering a wide field, woodenware (especially sashes and doors) and clothing. Other products include steel hulls for boats, tanks, pumps and fittings. It is the headquarters of the lumber trade for northern Iowa. Its packing industry is of growing importance.
Dubuque is the oldest city in the State and was named in honor of Julien Dubuque. The first permanent settlement dates from 1833.
DUCHESNE, c. s., Duchesne Co., Utah, 590.
DUCK HILL, Montgomery Co., Miss., 553.
On Ill. Cen. (R. R.).
DUCKTOWN, Polk Co., Tenn., 1,526.
DUDLEY, Worcestershire (a detached piece surrounded by Staffordshire), England, 59,579.
–Worcester Co., Mass., 4,568.
DUENWEG, Jasper Co., Mo., 500.
On Mo. Pac. (R. R.).
DUERO, Prov. of Bohol, Bohol, P. I., 8,228.
DUE WEST, Abbeville Co., S. C., 620.
On Due West (R. R.).
DUGGER, Sullivan Co., Ind., 1,383.
On Ill. Cen. (R. R.).
DUISBURG-HAMBORN, Rhenish Prussia, Germany, 440,419.
Is situated on the Rhine, between the Ruhr and Anger, and connected with both by canals. It became a possession of Prussia at the end of the Napoleonic wars. It contains the handsome Gothic church of St. Salvator, also the tomb of the great geographer, Mercator.
An important manufacturing center.
DUKE, Jackson Co., Okla., 543.
On Mo.-Kan.-Tex. (R. R.).
DUKINFIELD, Cheshire, England, 19,309.
An industrial suburb of Manchester.
DULAG, Leyte Prov., Leyte, P. I., 22,550.
Market center of a fertile agricultural region.
DULUTH, Gwinnett Co., Ga., 608.
On Sou. (R. R.).
–c. s., St. Louis Co., Minn., 101,463.
Situated at the western end of Lake Superior, it is the terminus of the Chicago, St. Paul, Minneapolis & Omaha; the Great Northern; the Northern Pacific; Duluth; Winnipeg & Pacific; Duluth, Missabe & Northern; Duluth, South Shore & Atlantic; Chicago, Milwaukee, St. Paul & Pacific; Minneapolis, St. Paul & Sault Ste. Marie railroads, and thirteen steamship lines.
Duluth is one of the leading shipping points in the United States. The principal buildings are the U. S. Custom-house, the U. S. Fisheries Building, the Board of Trade Building, and the Carnegie Library. The industries include blast furnaces, iron works, machine shops, match factories, lumber and flour mills. Its most important exports are lumber, flour, iron ore, coal, and grain.
It was first settled in 1853, and in 1870 was incorporated as a city.
DUMAGUETE, Negros Oriental, P. I., 16,227.
An important commercial town.
DUMANGAS, Iloilo Prov., Panay, P. I., 19,894.
DUMANJUG, Cebu Prov., Cebu, P. I., 23,635.
Center of a farming region.
DUMAS, Desha Co., Ark., 1,669.
On Mo. Pac. (R. R.).
–c. s., Moore Co., Tex., 700.
On Panh. & Santa Fe (R. R.).
DUMBARTON, capital of Dumbartonshire, Scotland, 21,546.
Principal industry is shipbuilding.
DUMFRIES, capital of Dumfriesshire, Scotland, 19,359.
Situated on the river Nith. Among the objects of interest are the mausoleum of Robert Burns and the house in which he lived.
The principal manufactures are tweeds and hosiery. Dumfries is said to have grown up about an ancient British fortress.
DUMIÂT (Damietta), Egypt, 34,812.
A trade center on the lower Nile. Some textiles are manufactured.
DUMONT, Butler Co., Iowa, 698.
On Chi. Gt. West.; Chi. & Nor. West. (R. Rs.).
–Bergen Co., N. J., 5,861.
On West Shore (R. R.).
–Harris Co., Tex., 612.
On Galv., Houst. & Hend.; Internat. Gt. Nor.; Mo.-Kan.-Tex. of Tex. (R. Rs.).
DUNBAR, Fayette Co., Pa., 1,357.
On Balt. & Ohio; N. Hav. & Dunb.; Penna. (R. Rs.).
–Kanawha Co., W. Va., 4,189.
On N. York Cen. (R. R.).
DUNCAN, Greenlee Co., Ariz., 1,050.
On Sou. Pac. (R. R.).
–c. s., Stephens Co., Okla., 8,363.
On Chi., Rk. Isl. & Pac. (R. R.).
–British Columbia, Canada, 1,843.
DUNCANNON, Perry Co., Pa., 1,732.
On Penna.; Susq. Riv. & West. (R. Rs.).
DUNCANSVILLE, Blair Co., Pa., 1,379.
On Penna. (R. R.).
DUNCANWOOD, Harrison Co., Ohio, 1,000.
DUNDALK, Ireland (Eire). See DUN DEALGAN.
–Baltimore Co., Md., 2,210.
On Balt. & Ohio; Penna. (R. Rs.).
DUNDAS, Wentworth Co., Ontario, Canada, 5,026.
On Can. Nat.; Tor., Ham. & Buf. (R. Rs.).
DUN DEALGAN (Dundalk), capital of County Louth, Ireland (Eire), 13,996.
DUNDEE, Forfarshire, Scotland, 175,933.
The third city in Scotland, situated on the left bank of the Firth of Tay, 10 miles from the sea. The Tay is crossed here by a railway bridge, 77 feet above high water.
The most conspicuous object in the city is the old tower, 156 feet high, erected in the twelfth century by David, Earl of Huntingdon. Other buildings are the town hall (18th century), the modern Royal Exchange, Albert Institute and University College.
Dundee, the principal seat of the linen, hemp, and jute manufactures of Great Britain, manufactures also machinery. Shipbuilding is carried on. It has a large harbor, with docks extended at great cost.
The town, originally walled, was created a royal burgh by William the Lion.
–Polk Co., Fla., 722.
On Atl. Coast Line (R. R.).
–Monroe Co., Mich., 1,364.
On Ann Arbor (R. R.).
–Douglas Co., Neb.
–Yates Co., N. Y., 1,086.
On N. York Cen. (R. R.).
DUNEDIN (with suburbs), capital of Dist. of Otago, New Zealand, 82,100.
Principal commercial place of colony.
–Pinellas Co., Fla., 1,570.
On Atl. Coast Line (R. R.).
DUNELLEN, Middlesex Co., N. J., 5,148.
On Cen. of N. Jer. (R. R.).
DUNFERMLINE, Fife, Scotland, 40,918.
Manufacture of table linen.
DUNKERQUE (Dunkirk), Dept. of Nord, France, 31,017.
Situated on the Strait of Dover, and is one of the most important commercial towns of the Republic. Dunkerque was a fortified place of importance in the Middle Ages. In 1658 it was given up to the English, in whose possession it continued until 1662, when Charles II. sold it to Louis XIV., who made it a fortified naval station.
DUNKIRK, France. See DUNKERQUE.
–Blackford and Jay Cos., Ind., 2,583.
On Penna. (R. R.).
–Chautauqua Co., N. Y., 17,802.
On Erie; N. York Cen.; N. York, Chi. & St. Lou.; Penna. (R. Rs.).
Harbor on Lake Erie.
–Hardin Co., Ohio, 905.
On N. York Cen.; Penna. (R. Rs.).
Center of grape production.
DUN LAOGHAIRE (Dunleary), County Dublin, Ireland (Eire), 35,000.
DUNLAP, Harrison Co., Iowa, 1,522.
On Ill. Cen.; Chi. & Nor. West. (R. Rs.).
–Iredell Co., N. C., 680.
–c. s., Sequatchie Co., Tenn., 1,295.
On Nash., Chatt. & St. Lou. (R. R.).
DUNLEARY, Ireland. See DUN LAOGHAIRE.
DUNLO, Cambria Co., Pa., 2,000.
On Penna. (R. R.).
DUNLOOP, Fayette Co., W. Va., 524.
On Kanaw., Gl. Jean & East. (R. R.).
DUNMORE, Lackawanna Co., Pa., 22,627.
On Del., Lack. & West.; Erie; Lack. & Wyo. Val. (El.) (R. Rs.).
An industrial suburb of Scranton. Car shops, silk mills, and stove factories.
DUNN, Harnett Co., N. C., 4,558.
On Atl. Coast Line; Durh. & Sou. (R. Rs.).
DUNNELLON, Marion Co., Fla., 1,068.
On Atl. Coast Line; Seab. Air Line (R. Rs.).
DUNNVILLE, Haldimand and Monck Cos., Ontario, Canada, 3,405.
On Can. Nat.; Tor., Ham. & Buf. (R. Rs.).
DUNSBACK FERRY (Emerick), Albany Co., N. Y., 529.
On N. York Cen. (R. R.).
DUNSMUIR, Siskiyou Co., Cal., 2,610.
On Sou. Pac. (R. R.).
DUPO, St. Clair Co., Ill., 2,082.
On E. St. Lou., Colu. & Water. (El.); Penna.; Mo. Pac. (R. Rs.).
DUPONT, Luzerne Co., Pa., 5,161.
DUQUESNE, Allegheny Co., Pa., 21,396.
On Bess. & L. Erie; Balt. & Ohio; Penna.; Pitts. & L. Erie; Union (R. Rs.).
An industrial city near Pittsburgh. Iron and steel plants.
DU QUOIN, Perry Co., Ill., 7,593.
On Ill. Cen. (R. R.).
DURAND, Winnebago Co., Ill., 554.
On Chi., Mil., St. P. & Pac. (R. R.).
–Shiawassee Co., Mich., 3,081.
On Ann Arbor; Gd. Tr. (R. Rs.).
–c. s., Pepin Co., Wis., 1,590.
On Chi., Mil., St. P. & Pac. (R. R.).
DURANGO, c. s., La Plata Co., Colo., 5,400.
On Den. & Rio Gde. West.; Rio Gde. Sou. (R. Rs.).
–Capital of State of Durango, Mexico, 34,709.
On Nat. of Mex. (R. R.).
An important mining and commercial center.
DURANT, Cedar Co., Iowa, 733.
On Chi., Rk. Isl. & Pac. (R. R.).
–Holmes Co., Miss., 2,480.
On Ill. Cen.; Yazoo & Miss. Val. (R. Rs.).
–c. s., Bryan Co., Okla., 7,463.
On Kans., Okla. & Gulf; Mo.-Kan.-Tex.; St. Lou.-San Fran. (R. Rs.).
DURANT CITY (James City), Elk Co., Pa., 1,000.
On Balt. & Ohio; Kane & Elk (R. Rs.).
DURAZZO, Albania. See DURRËS.
DURBAN (or Port Natal), Natal, Union of South Africa, 270,000.
Situated at the head of a land-locked harbor. Is connected by railroads with Johannesburg and other cities in the interior. It is one of the chief seaports of the colony.
DURHAM, capital of Durham, England, 16,223.
Situated on a steep hill, and nearly encircled by the Wear. The most noteworthy buildings are the cathedral, begun in 1093, and the castle, founded by William the Conqueror in 1072, and which is now the seat of the University of Durham.
The manufactures include mustard, carpets, and iron ware.
–Butte Co., Calif., 1,500.
On Sacramento Nor. (El.); Sou. Pac. (R. Rs.).
–Middlesex Co., Conn., 800.
–Strafford Co., N. H., 900.
On Bost. & Me. (R. R.).
–c. s., Durham Co., N. C., 52,037.
On Durham & Sou.; Norf. Sou.; Norf. & West.; Seab. Air Line; Sou. (R. Rs.).
Seat of Duke University.
Tobacco and cotton manufactures.
–Grey Co., Southeast Ontario, Canada, 1,750.
On Can. Pac.; Can. Nat. (R. Rs.).
DURHAMVILLE, Oneida Co., N. Y., 625.
On N. York, Ont. & West. (R. R.).
DURLACH, Baden, Germany, 18,016.

Has manufactures of brushes, chemicals, machinery, and gloves.
Durrës (Durazzo), Albania, 8,739.
Duryea, Luzerne Co., Pa., 8,503.
On Del., Lack. & West. (R. R.).
Dushore, Sullivan Co., Pa., 715.
On Leh. Val. (R. R.).
Düsseldorf, Rhenish Prussia, Germany, 498,600.
On the right bank of the Rhine. The principal buildings are the town hall, the Academy of Art, and the palace of justice. The most interesting of the churches is the Church of St. Lambert, a Gothic structure of the fourteenth century. Düsseldorf is the home of the famous Düsseldorf school of painting.
It has blast furnaces, textile mills, breweries, and distilleries.
Dustin, Hughes Co., Okla., 537.
On Ft. Smith & West.; Kan., Okla. & Gulf (R. Rs.).
Duxbury, Plymouth Co., Mass., 2,244.
On N. York, New Hav. & Hart. (R. R.).
–Washington Co., Vt., 500.
Dvinsk, Latvia. See Daugavpils.
Dvur Králove, Czechoslovakia, 16,588.
Dwight, Livingston Co., Ill., 2,534.
On Alton; N. York Cen. (R. R.).
Dyer, Lake Co., Ind., 672.
On Chi., Ind. & Lou.; Elg., Jol. & East.; Mich. Cen. (R. Rs.).
–Gibson Co., Tenn., 1,214.
On Mob. & Ohio (R. R.).
Dyersburg, c. s., Dyer Co., Tenn., 8,733.
On Gulf, Mob. & Nor.; Ill. Cen. (R. Rs.).
Dyersville, Dubuque and Delaware Cos., Iowa, 2,046.
On Chi. Gt. West.; Ill. Cen. (R. Rs.).
Dysart, Tama Co., Iowa, 971.
On Chi., Rk. Isl. & Pac. (R. R.).

E

Eads, c. s., Kiowa Co., Colo., 518.
On Mo. Pac. (R. R.).
Eagle, Fayette Co., W. Va., 1,536.
On Chesa. & Ohio (R. R.).
Eagle Bend, Todd Co., Minn., 575.
On Gt. Nor. (R. R.).
Eagle Grove, Wright Co., Iowa, 4,071.
On Chi. Gt. West.; Chi. & Nor. West. (R. Rs.).
Eagle Lake, Polk Co., Fla., 590.
On Atl. Coast Line (R. R.).
–Aroostook Co., Maine, 1,200.
On Bangor & Aroostook (R. R.).
–Colorado Co., Texas, 2,343.
On Gulf, Colo. & Santa Fe; Tex. & N. Orl. (R. Rs.).
Eagle Pass, c. s., Maverick Co., Texas, 5,059.
On Tex. & N. Orl. (R. R.).
Eagle River, Vilas Co., Wis., 1,386.
On Chi. & Nor. West. (R. R.).
Eagle Rock, Botetourt Co., Va., 526.
Eagle Valley, Elk Co., Pa., 500.
Eagleville, Rutherford Co., Tenn., 504.
Earle (Earl P. O.), Crittenden Co., Ark., 2,062.
On Mo. Pac. (R. R.).
Earley, Hertford Co., N. C., 525.
On Atl. Coast Line (R. R.).
Earlham, Madison Co., Iowa, 897.
On Chi., Rk. Isl. & Pac. (R. R.).
Earlington, Hopkins Co., Ky., 3,309.
On Lou. & Nash. (R. R.).
Earl Park, Benton Co., Ind., 501.
On Cle., Cin., Chi. & St. Lou. (R. R.).
Earlsboro, Pottawatomie Co., Okla., 1,950.
On Chi., Rk. Isl. & Pac. (R. R.).
Earlston Furnace, Bedford Co., Pa., 1,000.
On Hunt. & Broad Top Mt. (R. R.).
Earlville, La Salle Co., Ill., 1,028.
On Chi. & Nor. West.; Chi., Burl. & Quincy (R. Rs.).
–Delaware Co., Iowa, 615.
On Ill. Cen. (R. R.).
–Madison and Chenango Cos., N. Y., 868.
On Del., Lack. & West.; N. York, Ont. & West.; West Shore (R. Rs.).
Early, Sac Co., Iowa, 632.
On Chi. & Nor. West. (R. R.).
Easley, Pickens Co., S. C., 4,886.
On Pickens; Sou. (R. Rs.).
East Alton, Madison Co., Ill., 4,502.
On Chi., Burl. & Quincy; Cle., Cin., Chi. & St. Lou.; Ill. Term. Sys. (El.) (R. Rs.).
East Arlington, Bennington Co., Vt., 500.
East Aurora, Erie Co., N. Y., 4,815.
On Penna. (R. R.).
East Bangor, Northampton Co., Pa., 991.
On Del., Lack. & West.; Leh. & N. Eng. (R. Rs.).
East Berlin, Hartford Co., Conn., 835.
On N. York, N. Hav. & Hart. (R. R.).
–Adams Co., Pa., 790.
On East Berlin (R. R.).
East Bernard, Wharton Co., Tex., 500.
On Tex. & N. Orl. (R. R.).
East Bernstadt, Laurel Co., Ky., 950.
On Lou. & Nash. (R. R.).
East Blackstone, Worcester Co., Mass., 2,000.
On N. York, N. Hav. & Hart. (R. R.).
East Boothbay, Lincoln Co., Me., 535.
Eastbourne, Sussex, England, 57,435.
A popular resort and watering place.
East Brady, Clarion Co., Pa., 1,563.
On Penna. (R. R.).
East Brewton, Escambia Co., Ala., 1,002.
East Bridgewater, Plymouth Co., Mass., 2,244.
On N. York, N. Hav. & Hart. (R. R.).
East Brookfield, Worcester Co., Mass., 945.
On Bost. & Alb. (R. R.).
East Butler, Butler Co., Pa., 521.
On Balt. & Ohio; Bess. & L. Erie (R. Rs.).
East Canaan, Litchfield Co., Conn., 581.
East Canon, Fremont Co., Colo., 595.
East Canton, Stark Co., Ohio, 962.
On Wheel. & L. Erie (R. R.).
East Chattanooga, Hamilton Co., Tenn. (Sta. Chattanooga P. O.).
East Chicago, Lake Co., Ind., 54,784.
On Elg., Jol. & East.; Balt. & Ohio Chi. Term.; Chi. So. Shore & So. Bend (El.); Ind. Harb. Blt.; Penna.; Wab. (R. Rs.).
East Cleveland, Cuyahoga Co., Ohio, 39,667.
On N. York Cen.; N. York, Chi. & St. Lou. (R. Rs.).
A residential suburb of Cleveland.
East Columbia, Brazoria Co., Tex., 525.
On Internat. Gt. Nor. (R. R.).
East Columbus, Franklin Co., Ohio, 1,958.
On Balt. & Ohio; N. York Cen.; Penna. (R. Rs.).
East Conemaugh, Cambria Co., Pa., 4,979.
East Corinth, Penobscot Co., Me., 599.
East Dennis, Barnstable Co., Mass., 800.
East Douglas, Worcester Co., Mass., 1,650.
On N. York, N. Hav. & Hart. (R. R.).
East Downingtown, Chester Co., Pa., 2,500.
On Penna. (R. R.).
East Dubuque, Jo Daviess Co., Ill., 1,395.
On Chi., Burl. & Quincy; Chi. Gt. West.; Ill. Cen. (R. Rs.).
East Duke (Duke), Jackson Co., Okla., 543.
East Eddington, Penobscot Co., Me., 650.
East Ellsworth, Pierce Co., Wis., 500.
East Ely, White Pine Co., Nev., 695.
On Nev. Nor. (R. R.).
East Falmouth, Barnstable Co., Mass., 500.
East Flat Rock, Henderson Co., N. C., 1,062.
East Fort Myers, Lee Co., Fla., 1,376.
East Foxboro, Norfolk Co., Mass., 500.
On N. York, N. Hav. & Hart. (R. R.).
East Frankfort, Herkimer Co., N. Y., 500.
East Freetown, Bristol Co., Mass., 800.
East Fultonham, Muskingum Co., Ohio, 621.
On Penna. (R. R.).
East Gaffney (Limestone), Cherokee Co., S. C., 700.
East Galesburg (Randall P. O.), Knox Co., Ill., 587.
On Atch., Top. & Santa Fe (R. R.).
East Gary, Lake Co., Indiana, 2,409.
On Mich. Cen. (R. R.).
East Granby, Hartford Co., Conn., 500.
On N. York, N. Hav. & Hart. (R. R.).
East Grand Forks, Polk Co., Minn., 2,922.
On Gt. Nor.; Nor. Pac. (R. Rs.).
East Grand Rapids, Kent Co., Mich., 4,024.
East Greenbush, Rensselaer Co., N. Y., 616.
East Greenville, Montgomery Co., Pa., 1,749.
On Reading (R. R.).
East Greenwich, Kent Co., R. I., 3,518.
On N. York, N. Hav. & Hart. (R. R.).
East Haddam, Middlesex Co., Conn., 1,000.
Eastham, Essex, England, 146,900.
An industrial suburb of London.
–Barnstable Co., Mass., 606.
On N. York, N. Hav. & Hart. (R. R.).
East Hampton, Middlesex Co., Conn., 2,616.
On N. York, N. Hav. & Hart. (R. R.).
–Suffolk Co., N. Y., 1,934.
On Long Isl. (R. R.).
Easthampton, Hampshire Co., Mass., 10,486.
On Bost. & Me.; N. York, N. Hav. & Hart. (R. Rs.).
East Hartford, Hartford Co., Conn., 17,125.
On N. York, N. Hav. & Hart. (R. R.).
An important industrial suburb of Hartford. Paper, tools, machinery.
East Haven, New Haven Co., Conn., 6,000.
On N. York, N. Hav. & Hart. (R. R.).
East Helena, Lewis and Clarke Cos., Mont., 1,039.
On Nor. Pac. (R. R.).
East Houghton, Houghton Co., Mich., 1,000.
On Dul., So. Sh. & Atl. (R. Rs.).
East Islip, Suffolk Co., N. Y., 1,619.
East Jaffrey, Cheshire Co., N. H., 2,110.
On Bost. & Me. (R. R.).
East Jordan, Charlevoix Co., Mich., 1,523.
On East Jor. & So. (R. R.).
East Kane, McKean Co., Pa., 600.
On Kane & Elk. (R. R.).
East Killingly, Windham Co., Conn., 1,670.
Eastlake, c. s., Eastland Co., Texas, 4,648.
On E. Wich. Fs. & Gulf; Tex. & Pac. (R. Rs.).
East Lansdowne, Delaware Co., Pa., 3,168.
East Lansing, Ingham Co., Mich., 4,389.
On Pere Marq. (R. R.).
East Lauringburg, Scotland Co., N. C., 813.
East Liverpool, Columbiana Co., Ohio, 23,329.
On Penna. (R. R.).
East Liverpool is known as one of the pottery centers of America. Numerous bottle kilns project over its roofs. The products are general white ware and electrical porcelain.
East London, Union of S. Africa, 46,631.
One of the principal summer resorts.
East Long Meadow, Hampden Co., Mass., 3,375.
On N. York, N. Hav. & Hart. (R. R.).
East Lumberton, Robeson Co., N. C., 1,111.
East Lyme (Niantic), New London Co., Conn., 1,312.
On N. York, N. Hav. & Hart. (R. R.).
East Machias, Washington Co., Maine, 1,257.
On Me. Cen. (R. R.).
East Madison, Somerset Co., Me., 575.
Eastman, c. s., Dodge Co., Ga., 3,022.
On Sou.; Wrightsville & Tennille (R. Rs.).
East Mauch Chunk, Carbon Co., Pa., 3,739.
East Mayfield, Sabine Co., Texas, 1,179.
East McKeesport, Allegheny Co., Pa., 2,922.
East Milford, Hillsboro Co., N. H., 520.
On Bost. & Me. (R. R.).
East Millinocket, Penobscot Co., Maine, 1,500.
On Bangor & Aroostook (R. R.).
East Moline, Rock Island Co., Ill., 10,107.
On Chi., Burl. & Quincy; Chi., Mil., St. P. & Pac.; Chi., Rk. Isl. & Pac.; Davenp., Rk. Isl. & Northw. (R. Rs.).
An industrial suburb of Moline with similar industries.
Eastmont, Cambria Co., Pa., 500.
East Moriches, Suffolk Co., N. Y., 1,100.
On Long Isl. (R. R.).
East Newark, Hudson Co., N. J., 2,686.
East Northport, Suffolk Co., N. Y., 2,120.
East Norton, Bristol Co., Mass., 525.
East Norwich, Nassau Co., N. Y., 731.
Easton, c. s., Talbot Co., Md., 4,092.
On Balt. & East.; Penna. (R. Rs.).
–Bristol Co., Mass., 5,294.
On N. York, N. Hav. & Hart. (R. R.).
–c. s., Northampton Co., Pa., 34,468.
On Central of New Jersey; Lehigh & Hudson River; Lehigh Valley; Pennsylvania; Delaware, Lackawanna & Western (R. Rs.).
It has textile and knitting mills and large foundries (steel, iron, bronze, brass, aluminum), and machine shops. Near by are great cement plants and slate quarries. Seat of Lafayette College.
Eastondale, Bristol Co., Mass., 500.
On N. York, N. Hav. & Hart. (R. R.).
East Orange, Essex Co., N. J., 68,020.
On Del., Lack. & West.; Erie (R. Rs.).
East Orwell, Ashtabula Co., Ohio, 600.
On Penna. (R. R.).
East Palatka, Putnam Co., Fla., 1,000.
On Fla. E. Coast (R. R.).
East Palestine, Columbiana Co., Ohio, 5,215.
On Penna. (R. R.).
East Palo Alto, San Mateo Co., Calif., 1,200.
East Paterson, Bergen Co., N. J., 4,779.
On N. York, Susq. & West.; Ill. Cen. (R. Rs.).
East Pembroke, Merrimack Co., N. H., 1,540.
–Genesee Co., N. Y., 500.
On N. York Cen. (R. R.).
East Peoria, Tazewell Co., Ill., 5,027.
On Chi. & Nor. West.; Cle., Cin., Chi. & St. Lou.; Ill. Term. Sys. (El.); N. York, Chi. & St. Lou.; Penna.; Tol., Peoria & West. (R. Rs.).
East Pepperell, Middlesex Co., Mass., 2,000.
East Petersburg, Lancaster Co., Pa., 918.
On Reading (R. R.).
East Pittsburgh, Allegheny Co., Pa., 6,214.
On Balt. & Ohio; Bess. & L. Erie; Penna.; Pittsb. & L. Erie; Union (R. Rs.).
East Point, Fulton Co., Ga., 9,512.
On Atl. & West Pt.; Cen. of Ga. (R. Rs.).
Eastport, Washington Co., Maine, 3,466.
On Me. Cen. (R. R.).
–Suffolk Co., N. Y., 964.
On Long Isl. (R. R.).
East Prairie, Mississippi Co., Mo., 1,385.
On St. Lou. Southw. (R. R.).
East Providence, Providence Co., R. I., 30,113.
On N. York, N. Hav. & Hart. (R. R.).
An industrial town opposite Providence. Chemical manufactures and oyster shipping.
East Quogue, Suffolk Co., N. Y., 500.
East Rainelle, Greenbrier Co., W. Va., 1,272.
East Randolph, Cattaraugus Co., N. Y., 502.
East Retford, Nottinghamshire, England, 14,228.
East Ridge, Hamilton Co., Tenn., 2,152.
East Rochester, Strafford Co., N. H., 1,303.
–Monroe Co., N. Y., 6,627.
On N. Y. Central (R. R.).
–Beaver Co., Pa., 715.
East Rockaway, Nassau Co., N. Y., 4,348.
On Long Isl. (R. R.).
East Rockingham, Richmond Co., N. C., 559.
East Rutherford, Bergen Co., N. J., 7,080.
East St. Louis, St. Clair Co., Ill., 74,347.
Situated on the Mississippi River, opposite St. Louis, Mo., with which it is connected by four bridges. One of the largest transportation centers in the country, being entered by twenty-three railroads, including all the main lines, the whole trackage connected by four belt lines, which also serve the docks on the river front. The Illinois coal regions begin at the city's limits. Nineteen carriers haul the coal into East St. Louis. It is the center of a hog and cattle producing district, and also important as a horse, mule and lumber market. Its industries are large and diverse. Important among them are meat packing, oil refining and storage, car building, and the manufacture of chemicals, roofing, aluminum, steel castings, zinc, railroad supplies, paints and pigments and valves.
East San Diego, San Diego Co., Cal. (Ind. Sta. San Diego).
East Saugus, Essex Co., Mass., 2,500.
On Bost. & Me. (R. R.).
East Setauket, Suffolk Co., N. Y., 1,000.
Eastside, Coos Co., Ore., 556.
East Spencer, Rowan Co., N. C., 2,098.
East Stonehouse, Devonshire, England (included in Plymouth).
East Stroudsburg, Monroe Co., Pa., 6,099.
On Del., Lack. & West.; Del. Val. (R. Rs.).
East Syracuse, Onondaga Co., N. Y., 4,646.
On N. York Cen. (R. R.).
East Tallassee, Tallapoosa, Ala., 2,198.
East Tawas, Iosco Co., Mich., 1,455.
On Det. & Mack.; Erie & Mich. (R. Rs.).
East Templeton, Worcester Co., Mass., 1,000.
East Thomas, Jefferson Co., Ala., 1,589.
East Thomaston, Upson Co., Ga., 3,061.
East Troy, Walworth Co., Wis., 800.
On Mil. El. (R. R.).
Eastvale, Beaver Co., Pa., 601.
East Vandergrift, Westmoreland Co., Pa., 2,441.
On Penna. (R. R.).
Eastview, Westchester Co., N. Y., 1,000.
On N. York Cen. (R. R.).
East Walpole, Norfolk Co., Mass., 2,000.
East Wareham, Plymouth Co., Mass., 675.
East Washington, Washington Co., Pa., 1,859.
East Windsor, Hartford Co., Conn., 200.
On N. York, N. Hav. & Hart. (R. R.).
–Ontario, Canada, 14,251.
A suburb of Windsor.
Eastwood, Onondaga Co., N. Y. (Sta. Syracuse P. O.).
East Woodstock, Windham Co., Conn., 598.
East Worcester, Otsego Co., N. Y., 500.
On Del. & Hud. (R. R.).
Eaton, Weld Co., Colo., 1,221.
On Gt. West.; Un. Pac. (R. Rs.).
–Delaware Co., Ind., 1,273.
On Ind. R. R. Sys. (El.); N. York, Chi. & St. Lou. (R. Rs.).
–Madison Co., N. Y., 500.
On N. York, Ont. & West. (R. R.).
–c. s., Preble Co., Ohio, 3,347.
On Penna. (R. R.).
Eaton Rapids, Eaton Co., Mich., 2,822.
On Mich. Cen.; N. York Cen. (R. Rs.).
Eatonton, c. s., Putnam Co., Ga., 1,876.
On Cen. of Ga. (R. R.).
Eatontown, Monmouth Co., N. J., 1,938.
On Cen. of N. Jer. (R. R.).
Eatonville, Pierce Co., Washington, 912.
On Chi., Mil., St. P. & Pac. (R. R.).
Eau Claire, Richland Co., S. C., 2,915.
–c. s., Eau Claire Co., Wis., 26,287.
On Chi., Mil., St. P. & Pac.; Minn., St. P. & S. Ste. M.; St. P., Minn. & Oma. (R. Rs.).
Favorably situated at the mouth of the Chippewa River for the production of hydro-electric power. Has many industries.
Eau Gallie, Brevard Co., Florida, 1,055.
On Fla. East Coast (R. R.).
Eaux Bonnes, Dept. of Basses-Pyrénées, France, 684.
Ebenezer, Erie Co., N. Y., 2,000.
On Penna. (R. R.).
Ebensburg, c. s., Cambria Co., Pa., 3,063.
On Penna. (R. R.).
Ebersach, Saxony, 9,274.
Eberswalde, Brandenburg, Germany, 31,000.
Ebervale, Luzerne Co., Pa., 580.
On Leh. Val. (R. R.).
Eccles, Lancashire, England, 44,415.
Textile mills and engine works.
–(Admiralty), Raleigh Co., W. Va., 1,027.
On Chesa. & Ohio; Virginian (R. Rs.).
Echternach, Luxembourg, 3,031.
Ecija, Prov. of Sevilla, Spain, 29,934.
Center of a fertile agricultural district.
Eckley, Luzerne Co., Pa., 825.
On Leh. Val. (R. R.).
Eclectic, Elmore Co., Ala., 678.
On Birm. & Southe. (R. R.).
Ecorse, Wayne Co., Mich., 12,716.
On Det. & Tol. Sh. Line; Detroit, Tol. & Iron.; Mich. Cen.; N. York Cen.; Delray Connecting (R. Rs.).
An industrial suburb of Detroit. Castings, steel, and engines.
Ecru, Pontotoc Co., Miss., 560.
On Gulf, Mob. & Nor. (R. R.).
Edcouch, Hidalgo Co., Tex., 914.
On Tex. & New Orl.; St. Lou., Browns. & Mex. (R. Rs.).
Eddington, Penobscot Co., Maine, 487.

–Bucks Co., Pa., 1,000.
On Penna. (R. R.).
Eddystone, Delaware Co., Pa., 2,414.
On Balt. & Ohio; Penna.; Read. (R. Rs.).
Eddyville, Mahaska and Wapello Cos., Iowa, 888.
On Chi., Rk. Isl. & Pac.; Minn. & St. Lou. (R. Rs.).
–c. s., Lyon Co., Ky., 1,990.
On Ill. Cen. (R. R.).
–Ulster Co., N. Y., 640.
Ede, Gelderland, Netherlands, 30,604.
A suburb of Arnheim.
Eden, Erie Co., N. Y., 870.
–Concho Co., Texas, 1,194.
Gulf, Colo. & Santa Fe (R. R.).
–Lamoille Co., Vt., 568.
Edenborn, Fayette Co., Pa., 1,224.
On Monongahela (R. R.).
Edenburg, Clarion Co., Pa., 1,037.
P. O. and R. R. name Knox.
–Lawrence Co., Pa., 650.
On Balt. & Ohio; Penna.; Pitts. & L. Erie (R. Rs.).
Eden Center, Erie Co., N. Y., 870.
On Erie (R. R.).
Edenton, c. s., Chowan Co., N. C., 3,563.
On Norf. Sou. (R. R.).
Eden Valley, Meeker and Stearns Cos., Minn., 612.
On Minn., St. P. & S. Ste. M. (R. R.).
Edessa, capital of Pella, Greece, 13,115.
Edgar, Clay Co., Neb., 987.
On Chi., Burl. & Quincy; St. Jos. & Gd. Isl. (R. Rs.).
–Marathon Co., Wis., 667.
On Chi. & Nor. West. (R. R.).
Edgarton, Mingo Co., W. Va., 650.
Edgartown, c. s., Dukes Co., Mass., 1,399.
Edgefield, c. s., Edgefield Co., S. C., 2,132.
On Ga. & Fla.; Sou. (R. Rs.).
Edge Hill, Montgomery Co., Pa., 900.
Edgeley, La Moure Co., N. Dak., 821.
On Chi., Mil., St. P. & Pac.; Midl. Continent; Nor. Pac. (R. Rs.).
Edgely, Bucks Co., Pa., 1,200.
On Penna. (R. R.).
Edgemont, Fall River Co., S. Dak., 947.
On Chi., Burl. & Quincy (R. R.).
Edgemoor, Montgomery Co., Md., 500.
Edge Moor, New Castle Co., Del., 1,008.
On Penna. (R. R.).
Edgerton, Pipestone Co., Minn., 627.
On Chi., Mil., St. P. & Pac. (R. R.).
–Williams Co., Ohio, 989.
On N. York Cen. (R. R.).
–Rock Co., Wis., 2,906.
On Chi., Mil., St. P. & Pac. (R. R.).
Edgewater, Jefferson Co., Colo., 1,473.
–Bergen Co., N. J., 4,089.
On N. York, Susq. & West.; West Shore (R. Rs.).
Edgewood, Clayton and Delaware Cos., Iowa, 638.
On Chi., Mil., St. P. & Pac. (R. R.).
–Allegheny Co., Pa., 4,821.
On Penna. (R. R.).
–Tarrant Co., Tex., 600.
–Van Zandt Co., Texas, 761.
On Tex. & Pac. (R. R.).
Edgeworth, Allegheny Co., Pa., 1,679.
On Penna. (R. R.).
Edgwood, Harrison Co., W. Va. (Pop. incl. in Wheeling, W. Va.).
Edina, Hennepin Co., Minn., 3,138.
–c. s., Knox Co., Mo., 1,532.
On Quincy, Oma. & Kan. Cy. (R. Rs.).
Edinboro, Erie Co., Pa., 789.
Edinburg, Christian Co., Ill., 799.
On Balt. & Ohio (R. R.).
–Johnson Co., Ind., 2,209.
On Ind. R. R. Sys. (El.); Penna. (R. Rs.).
–Leake Co., Miss., 500.
On Cant. & Carth. (R. R.).
–c. s., Hidalgo Co., Texas, 4,821.
On St. Lou., Brownsv. & Mex.; Tex. & N. Orl. (R. Rs.).
Edinburgh, Midlothian Co., capital of Scotland, 438,998.
Situated 2 miles from the south shore of the Firth of Forth, on lofty parallel ridges. It is divided into an Old Town and a New Town, through which stretches Prince's Street, one of the finest promenades in the world.
Edinburgh contains numerous buildings of note. Among the most important are the castle; the famous royal palace of Holyrood; St. Giles' Church, dating from the fifteenth century; the Episcopal Cathedral of St. Mary's (1879); the Parliament House, built in 1633; Heriot's Hospital (seventeenth century), now the seat of a technical school; the house of John Knox, National Gallery, Royal Institution, Museum of Science and Art, National Portrait Gallery and Antiquarian Museum, and the Blackford Observatory. The Gothic spire erected in 1844, in memory of Walter Scott and the memorial to the Prince Consort (1876) are beautiful monuments. The University, founded in 1582, is one of the most famous in Europe.
The name Edinburgh is supposed to be derived from Edwin, King of Northumbria. Edinburgh rose into importance in the twelfth century. In the fifteenth century it became the capital of Scotland.
Edirne (Adrianople), Turkey, 34,669.
Founded by the Emperor Hadrian, and from 1361 to 1453 the capital of the Ottoman Empire. Captured by the Balkan Allies, March 26, 1913; recaptured by Turkey, July 20, 1913. Edirne is included in the territory west of Istanbul and bordering on the Black and Aegean Seas; assigned to Greece by the Treaty of Sèvres (which was never ratified) and restored to Turkey by the Treaty of Lausanne, July, 1923.
Edison, Calhoun Co., Ga., 1,321.
Edisto Island, Charleston Co., S. C., 1,675.
Edmeston, Otsego Co., N. Y., 650.
On N. York, Ont. & West. (R. R.).
Edmond, Oklahoma Co., Okla., 3,576.
On Atch., Top. & Santa Fe (R. R.).
Edmonds, Snohomish Co., Wash., 1,165.
On Gt. Nor. (R. R.).
Edmonston, Prince Georges Co., Md., 717.
Edmonton, Edmonton Co., Alberta, Canada, 85,774.
On Nor. Alb.; Can. Nat.; Can. Pac. (R. Rs.).
Center of the cattle industry, grain shipping.
–Middlesex, England, 77,652.
An industrial suburb of London. Market gardening nearby.
Edmore, Montcalm Co., Mich., 897.
On Pere Marq. (R. R.).
Edmundston, New Brunswick, Canada, 6,430.
Edna, Labette Co., Kans., 524.
On Mo. Pac. (R. R.).
–c. s., Jackson Co., Texas, 1,752.
On Tex. & N. Orl. (R. R.).
Edon, Williams Co., Ohio, 581.
On Wabash (R. R.).
Edri, Indiana Co., Pa., 515.
On Penna. (R. R.).
Edwards, St. Lawrence Co., N. Y., 562.
On N. York Cen. (R. R.).
Edwardsport, Knox Co., Ind., 850.
On Penna. (R. R.).
Edwardsville, c. s., Madison Co., Ill., 6,235.
On Ill. Term. Sys. (El.); Litchf. & Mad.; N. York, Chicago & St. Lou.; Wab. (R. Rs.).
–Luzerne Co., Pa., 8,847.
Effingham, c. s., Effingham Co., Ill., 4,978.
On Ill. Cen.; Penna.; Wab. (R. Rs.).
–Atchison Co., Kans., 674.
On Mo. Pac. (R. R.).
Egan, Fulton Co., Ga., 1,200.
R. R. name Fernside.
Eger, Czechoslovakia. See Cheb.
Eggertsville, Erie Co., N. Y., 520.
Egg Harbor City, Atlantic Co., N. J., 3,478.
On Penna.-Read. Seash. (R. R.).
Egham, Surrey, England, 15,915.
Egremont, Berkshire Co., Mass., 569.
Egypt, Plymouth Co., Mass., 600.
On N. York, N. Hav. & Hart. (R. R.).
–Lehigh Co., Pa., 1,489.
On Ironton (R. R.).
Ehrenbreitstein, Rhenish Prussia, 2,925.
Ehrenfeld, Cambria Co., Pa., 1,100.
On Penna. (R. R.).
Ehrenfriedersdorf, Saxony, 5,518.
Eichstätt, Germany, 8,006.
Eickel, Prussia, Germany, 34,470.
Eilenburg, Prussian Saxony, Germany, 19,000.
Chemicals, cotton, machinery.
Eindhoven, Brabant, Netherlands, 100,458.
Einsiedeln, of Schwyz, Switzerland, 8,028.
Eisenach, Saxe-Weimar, Germany, 45,000.
Industrial center. Site of the Wartburg where Luther translated the Bible.
Eisk (Yeisk), Soviet Union, 44,800.
Eisleben, Prussian Saxony, Germany, 25,000.
Chemicals and machinery.
Ekaterinburg, Soviet Union. See Sverdlovsk.
Ekaterinodar, Soviet Union. See Krasnodar.
Ekaterinoslav, Soviet Union. See Dnepropetrovsk.
Elaine, Phillips Co., Ark., 511.
On Mo. Pac. (R. R.).
El-Araish, Spanish Morocco. See Larache.
El-Arish, Egypt, 19,000.
Seaport and market center for farm products.
Elba, c. s., Coffee Co., Ala., 2,523.
On Atl. Coast Line (R. R.).
Elbasan, Albania, 13,796.
Agricultural center.
Elberfeld, Germany. See Wuppertal.
–Warrick Co., Ind., 546.
On Cle., Cin., Chi. & St. Lou. (R. R.).
Elberon, Monmouth Co., N. J., 500.
On Cen. of N. Jer.; N. York & Long Br.; Penna. (R. Rs.).
Elbert, McDowell Co., W. Va., 1,200.
On Norf. & West. (R. R.).
Elberta, Benzie Co., Mich., 609.
On Ann Arbor (R. R.).
Elberton, c. s., Elbert Co., Ga., 4,650.
On Seab. Air Line; Sou. (R. Rs.).
Elbeuf, Dept. of Seine-Inférieure, France, 18,379.
A river port and suburb of Rouen.
Elbing, East Prussia, Germany, 71,000.
Site of a large locomotive works.
Elbow Lake, c. s., Grant Co., Minn., 903.
On Gt. Nor.; Minn., St. P. & S. Ste. M. (R. Rs.).
Elburn, Kane Co., Ill., 548.
On Chi. & Nor. West. (R. R.).
El Cajon, San Diego Co., Calif., 1,050.
On San Diego & Ariz. East. (R. R.).
El Campo, Wharton Co., Tex., 2,034.
On Tex. & N. Orl. (R. R.).
El Centro, c. s., Imperial Co., Cal., 8,434.
On Holton Inter-Urb.; San Diego & Ariz. East.; Sou. Pac. (R. Rs.).
El Cerrito (Cerrito), Contra Costa Co., Calif., 3,870.
On Atch., Top. & Santa Fe (R. R.).
Elche, Prov. of Alicante, Spain, 33,167.
An agricultural center. Manufactures of oil, soap, flour, fabrics, and leather goods.
Elco (Wood Run), Washington Co., Pa., 704.
On Penna. (R. R.).
Eldon, Wapello Co., Iowa, 1,788.
On Chi., Rk. Isl. & Pac. (R. R.).
–Miller Co., Mo., 3,171.
On Chi., Rk. Isl. & Pac.; Mo. Pac. (R. Rs.).
Eldora, c. s., Hardin Co., Iowa, 3,200.
On Chi. & Nor. West.; Minn. & St. Lou. (R. Rs.).
El Dorado, c. s., Union Co., Ark., 16,421.
On Chi., Rk. Isl. & Pac.; El Dor. & Wes.; Mo. Pac. (R. Rs.).
The metropolis of a petroleum field.
–c. s., Butler Co., Kans., 8,705.
On Atch., Top. & Santa Fe; Mo. Pac. (R. Rs.).
Oil refineries; oil well supplies.
Eldorado, Saline Co., Ill., 4,482.
On Cle., Cin., Chi. & St. Lou.; Ill. Cen.; Lou. & Nash. (R. Rs.).
–Jackson Co., Okla., 1,183.
On St. Lou.-San Fran. (R. R.).
–c. s., Schleicher Co., Tex., 1,404.
On Panh. & Santa Fe (R. R.).
Eldorado Springs, Cedar Co., Mo., 1,917.
On Mo.-Kan.-Tex. (R. R.).
Eldred, McKean Co., Pa., 1,118.
On Penna. (R. R.).
Eldridge Park, Mercer Co., N. J., 500.
Electra, Wichita Co., Texas, 6,712.
On Ft. Worth & Denv. Cy. (R. R.).
Electric Mills, Kemper Co., Miss., 1,084.
On DeKalb & West.; Mob. & Ohio (R. Rs.).
Elets (Yelets), Soviet Union, 52,300.
Iron foundries, tanneries and tobacco factories.
Elgin, Fayette Co., Iowa, 610.
On Chi., Rk. Isl. & Pac. (R. R.).
–Kane and Cook Cos., Ill., 35,929.
On Chi. & Nor. West.; Chi., Aur. & Elg.; Chi., Mil., St. P. & Pac. (R. Rs.).
Noted watch-making center. Ships immense quantities of dairy products.
–Antelope Co., Neb., 917.
On Chi. & Nor. West. (R. R.).
–Grant Co., N. Dak., 505.
On Chi., Mil., St. P. & Pac.; Nor. Pac. (R. Rs.).
–Union Co., Ore., 728.
On Ore., Wash. R. R. & Nav. Co. (R. R.).
–Bastrop Co., Tex., 1,823.
On Mo.-Kan.-Tex. of Tex.; Tex. & N. Orl. (R. Rs.).
–Capital of Elgin Co., Scotland, 10,192.
Eliasville, Young Co., Tex., 750.
On Wichita Fs. & Sou. (R. R.).
Elida, Allen Co., Ohio, 542.
On Penna. (R. R.).
Eliot, York Co., Maine, 1,200.
On Bost. & Me. (R. R.).
Elisabethville, Belgian Congo, 16,888.
Elisavetgrad, Soviet Union. See Zinovievsk.
Elisavetopol, Soviet Union. See Gandzha.
Elizabeth, Cobb Co., Ga., 922.
On Lou. & Nash.; Nash., Chatt. & St. Lou. (R. Rs.).
–Daviess Co., Ill., 651.
On Chi. Gt. West. (R. R.).
–c. s., Union Co., N. J., 114,589.
Situated 14 miles southwest of New York City, on the Baltimore & Ohio; Central of New Jersey; and the Pennsylvania railroads, and on Staten Island Sound and Newark Bay, and is served by the New York & New Jersey Steamboat Company line.
There are also extensive iron, steel, shipbuilding, chemical, automobile and oil-refining plants.
The city was first settled in 1664, incorporated as a town in 1796, and chartered in 1855. In it were the homes of Alexander Hamilton, Aaron Burr, and General Winfield Scott, hero of the Mexican War.
–Allegheny Co., Pa., 2,939.
On Pitts. & L. Erie (R. R.).
–c. s., Wirt Co., W. Va., 716.
Elizabeth City, c. s., Pasquotank Co., N. C., 10,037.
On Norf. Sou. (R. R.).
It has cotton and hosiery mills, barrel and crate factories, ship and lumber yards.
Elizabethton, c. s., Carter Co., Tenn., 8,093.
On E. Tenn. & W. Nor. Car.; Sou. (R. Rs.).
Elizabethtown, c. s., Hardin Co., Ky., 2,590.
On Ill. Cen.; Lou. & Nash. (R. Rs.).
–c. s., Essex Co., N. Y., 636.
–c. s., Bladen Co., N. C., 765.
On Va. & Car. Sou. (R. R.).
–Lancaster Co., Pa., 3,940.
On Penna. (R. R.).
Elizabethville, Dauphin Co., Pa., 1,341.
On Penna. (R. R.).
Elk, Kanawha Co., W. Va., 1,000.
On Chesa. & Ohio (R. R.).
Elkader, c. s., Clayton Co., Iowa, 1,382.
On Chi., Mil., St. P. & Pac. (R. R.).
Elk City, Montgomery Co., Kans., 599.
On Atch., Top. & Santa Fe (R. R.).
–Beckham Co., Okla., 5,666.
On Chi., Rk. Isl. & Pac.; Mo.-Kans.-Tex. (R. Rs.).
Elk Grove, Sacramento Co., Calif., 895.
On Sou. Pac. (R. R.).
Elkhart, Elkhart Co., Ind., 32,949.
On Cle., Cin., Chi. & St. Lou.; N. York Cen. (R. Rs.).
Manufacturing center. Band instruments, auto parts, paper, iron and steel.
–Morton Co., Kans., 1,076.
On Atch., Top. & Santa Fe (R. R.).
–Anderson Co., Tex., 551.
On Internat.-Gt. Nor. (R. R.).
Elkhart Lake, Sheboygan Co., Wis., 571.
On Chi., Mil., St. P. & Pac. (R. R.).
Elkhorn, Shelby Co., Iowa, 513.
On Atl. Nor. (R. R.).
–McDowell Co., W. Va., 1,285.
On Norf. & West. (R. R.).
–c. s., Walworth Co., Wis., 2,340.
On Chi., St. P., Minn. & Oma. (R. R.).
Elkhorn City, Pike Co., Ky., 996.
On Chesa. & Ohio; Clinchfield (R. Rs.).
Elkin, Surry Co., N. C., 2,357.
On Southern (R. R.).
Elkins, c. s., Randolph Co., W. Va., 7,345.
On Balt. & Ohio; West. Md. (R. Rs.).
Elkland, Tioga Co., Pa., 1,978.
On Balt. & Ohio; N. York Cen. (R. Rs.).
Elk Mills, Cecil Co., Md., 500.
On Balt. & Ohio (R. R.).
Elk Mountain, Buncombe Co., N. C., 700.
On Ashev. & Crag. Mtn. (R. R.).
Elko, c. s., Elko Co., Nev., 3,217.
On Sou. Pac.; West. Pac. (R. Rs.).
Elk Point, c. s., Union Co., S. Dak., 1,425.
On Chi., Mil., St. P. & Pac. (R. R.).
Elk Rapids, Antrim Co., Mich., 615.
On Pere Marq. (R. R.).
Elk River, Clearwater Co., Idaho, 862.
On Chi., Mil., St. P. & Pac. (R. R.).
–c. s., Sherburne Co., Minn., 1,026.
On Gt. Nor.; Nor. Pac. (R. Rs.).
Elkton, c. s., Todd Co., Ky., 951.
On Lou. & Nash. (R. R.).
–c. s., Cecil Co., Md., 3,331.
On Penna. (R. R.).
–Huron Co., Mich., 538.
On Pere Marq. (R. R.).
–Brookings Co., S. Dak., 807.
On Chi. & Nor. West.; Chi., Rk. Isl. & Pac. (R. Rs.).
–Rockingham Co., Va., 965.
On Chesa. West.; Norf. & West. (R. Rs.).
Elkville, Jackson Co., Ill., 1,133.
On Ill. Cen. (R. R.).
Ellamore, Randolph Co., W. Va., 519.
On Middle Fork (R. R.).
Ellaville, c. s., Schley Co., Ga., 764.
On Cen. of Ga. (R. R.).
Ellendale, c. s., Dickey Co., N. Dak., 1,264.
On Chi., Mil., St. P. & Pac.; Gt. Nor. (R. Rs.).
Ellensburg, c. s., Kittitas Co., Wash., 4,621.
On Chi., Mil., St. P. & Pac.; Nor. Pac. (R. Rs.).
Ellenton, Manatee Co., Fla., 840.
On Seab. Air Line (R. R.).
–Aiken Co., S. C., 620.
On Charl. & W. Car. (R. R.).
Ellenville, Ulster Co., N. Y., 3,280.
On N. York, Ont. & West. (R. R.).
Ellerbe, Richmond Co., N. C., 615.
On Norf. Sou. (R. R.).
Ellerslie, Harris Co., Ga., 550.
On Southern (R. R.).
–Allegany Co., Md., 650.
On Balt. & Ohio; Cumb. & Penna. (R. Rs.).
Ellettsville, Monroe Co., Ind., 767.
On Chi., Ind. & Lou. (R. R.).
Ellichpur, Dist. of Amraoti, Berar, India, 26,100.
Timber and cotton center.
Ellicott City, c. s., Howard Co., Md., 1,216.
On Balt. & Ohio (R. R.).
Ellicottville, Cattaraugus Co., N. Y., 978.
On Balt. & Ohio (R. R.).
Ellijay, c. s., Gilmer Co., Ga., 657.
On Lou. & Nash. (R. R.).
Ellington, Chautauqua Co., N. Y., 500.
Ellinwood, Barton Co., Kans., 1,551.

On Atch., Top. & Santa Fe (R. R.).
ELLIOTT, Montgomery Co., Iowa, 556.
On Chi., Burl. & Quincy (R. R.).
ELLIS, Ellis Co., Kans., 1,643.
On Un. Pac. (R. R.).
ELLISVILLE, c. s., Jones Co., Miss., 2,127.
On N. Orl. & Northe. (R. R.).
ELLORE, Godaveri Dist., Madras, India, 37,800.
Carpets, hosiery, leather, cotton and oil, and saltpeter.
ELLOREE, Orangeburg Co., S. C., 1,098.
Atl. Coast Line (R. R.).
ELLPORT, Lawrence Co., Pa., 1,009.
ELLSWORTH, Hamilton Co., Iowa, 520.
On Chi. & Nor. West. (R. R.).
–c. s., Ellsworth Co., Kans., 2,106.
On St. Lou.-San Fran.; Un. Pac. (R. Rs.).
–c. s., Hancock Co., Maine, 3,557.
On Me. Cen. (R. R.).
–Nobles Co., Minnesota, 644.
On Chi., Rk. Isl. & Pac. (R. R.).
–Washington Co., Pa., 2,274.
On Penna. (R. R.).
–c. s., Pierce Co., Wis., 1,124.
On Chi., St. P., Minn. & Oma. (R. R.).
ELLWOOD CITY, Lawrence and Beaver Cos., Pa., 12,323.
On Balt. & Ohio; Pitts. & L. Erie (R. Rs.).
A manufacturing center with products characteristic of the Pittsburgh area.
ELMA, Howard Co., Iowa, 771.
On Chi. Gt. West. (R. R.).
–Erie Co., N. Y., 800.
–Grays Harbor Co., Wash., 1,545.
On Nor. Pac. (R. R.).
ELM CITY, Wilson Co., N. C., 905.
On Atl. Coast Line (R. R.).
ELM CREEK, Buffalo Co., Neb., 708.
On Un. Pac. (R. R.).
ELMER, Salem Co., N. J., 1,219.
On Penna.-Read. Seashore (R. R.).
ELM GROVE, Ohio Co., W. Va. (Pop. incl. in Wheeling).
On Balt. & Ohio (R. R.).
–Waukesha Co., Wis., 500.
On Chi., Mil., St. P. & Pac. (R. R.).
ELMHURST, Du Page Co., Ill., 14,055.
On Chi. & Nor. West.; Chi., Aur. & Elg.; Chi. Gt. West.; Ill. Cen. (R. Rs.).
A residential and educational suburb of Chicago.
–Lackawanna Co., Pa., 841.
On Del., Lack. & West.; Erie (R. Rs.).
ELMINA, Walker Co., Tex., 517.
On Internat.-Gt. Nor. (R. R.).
ELMIRA, c. s., Chemung Co., N. Y., 47,397.
Situated on the Chemung River, and on the Erie, the Delaware, Lackawanna & Western, the Lehigh Valley, and the Pennsylvania railroads.
It is the seat of Elmira College, and the Elmira Free Academy. Among its other features are the Federation Building, Steele Memorial Library, and Arnot Art Gallery. Here is also located the New York State Reformatory, and a state armory. The city has large rolling mills, railroad car shops, iron and steel bridge works.
It is incorporated as the village of Newton in 1815, then re-incorporated as the village of Elmira in 1828, and became a chartered city in 1864.
–Waterloo Co., Ontario, Canada, 2,170.
On Can. Pac.; Can. Nat. (R. Rs.).
ELMIRA HEIGHTS, Chemung Co., N. Y., 5,061.
On Del., Lack. & West.; Erie; Leh. Val. (R. Rs.).
EL MODENA, Orange Co., Calif., 600.
On Sou. Pac. (R. R.).
EL MONTE, Los Angeles Co., Cal., 3,479.
On Pac. El.; Sou. Pac. (R. Rs.).
ELMORA, Cambria Co., Pa., 1,200.
ELMORE, Faribault Co., Minn., 744.
On Chi. & Nor. West.; Chi., St. P., Minn. & Oma. (R. Rs.).
–Ottawa Co., Ohio, 1,107.
On N. York Cen.; Ohio Pub. Serv. (El.) (R. Rs.).
ELMSFORD, Westchester Co., N. Y., 2,935.
On N. York Cen. (R. R.).
ELMSHORN, Holstein, Germany, 16,000.
Weaving, dyeing, and brewing plants.
ELMWOOD, Hartford Co., Conn., 1,500.
On N. York, N. Hav. & Hart. (R. R.).
–Peoria Co., Ill., 1,166.
On Chi., Burl. & Quincy (R. R.).
–Cass Co., Neb., 515.
On Mo. Pac. (R. R.).
–Pierce Co., Wis., 737.
On Chi., St. P., Minn. & Oma. (R. R.).
ELMWOOD PARK, Cook Co., Ill., 11,270.
On Chi., Mil., St. P. & Pac. (R. R.).
A residential suburb of Chicago.
ELMWOOD PLACE, Hamilton Co., Ohio, 4,562.
On Balt. & Ohio; Cle., Cin., Chi. & St. Lou.; Erie; Norf. & West.; Penna. (R. Rs.).
ELNORA, Daviess Co., Ind., 856.
On Chi., Mil., St. P. & Pac.; Cle., Cin., Chi. & St. Lou. (R. Rs.).
EL OBEID, Anglo-Egyptian Sudan, 88,870.
An important trade center.
ELOISE, Wayne Co., Mich., 806.
On Mich. Cen. (R. R.).
ELORA, Wellington Co., South Ontario, Canada, 1,195.
On Can. Pac.; Can. Nat. (R. Rs.).
–Lincoln Co., Tenn., 600.
On Nash., Chatt. & St. Lou. (R. R.).
EL PASO, Woodford Co., Ill., 1,578.
On Ill. Cen.; Tol., Peor. & West. (R. Rs.).
–c. s., El Paso Co., Texas, 102,421.
On the Atchison, Topeka & Santa Fe, the El Paso Southern, the Mexican North Western, the National of Mexico, the Southern Pacific, the Texas & New Orleans, the Texas & Pacific (R. Rs.).
The largest city on the Mexican border of the United States. An important travel center for tourists and health seekers, and known as the "Gateway to Mexico." Its industries include brick manufacturing, cotton ginning, meat packing, wood working and ore smelting. El Paso is a prominent wholesale center for a large territory. Among its notable buildings are the high school, County Court-House, and the Federal Building. The State College of Mines is located here.
ELRAMA, Washington Co., Pa., 1,500.
On Penna. (R. R.).
EL RENO, c. s., Canadian Co., Okla., 9,384.
On Chi., Rk. Isl. & Pac.; Okla. El. (R. Rs.).
EL RIO, Ventura Co., Calif., 500.
On Sou. Pac. (R. R.).
EL RITO, Rio Arriba Co., N. Mex., 500.
ELROD, Tuscaloosa Co., Ala., 500.
On Mob. & Ohio (R. R.).
ELROY, Juneau Co., Wis., 1,546.
On Chi. & Nor. West.; Chi., St. P., Minn. & Oma. (R. Rs.).
ELSA, Hidalgo Co., Tex., 500.
On Tex. & N. Orl. (R. R.).
ELSBERRY, Lincoln Co., Mo., 1,204.
On Chi., Burl. & Quincy (R. R.).
EL SEGUNDO, Los Angeles Co., Cal., 3,503.
On Atch., Top. & Santa Fe; Pac. El.; Sou. Pac. (R. Rs.).
ELSIE, Clinton Co., Mich., 664.
On Ann Arbor (R. R.).
ELSINORE, Riverside Co., Cal., 1,350.
On Atch., Top. & Santa Fe (R. R.).
–Sevier Co., Utah, 654.
On Den. & Rio Gde. West. (R. R.).
ELSINORE, Denmark. See HELSINGÖR.
ELSMERE, New Castle Co., Del., 1,323.
–Kenton Co., Ky., 2,917.
On Cin., N. Orl. & Tex. Pac. (R. R.).
–Albany Co., N. Y., 1,200.
ELTON, Jefferson Davis Parish, La., 742.
On N. Orl., Tex. & Mex. (R. R.).
–Langlade Co., Wis., 500.
On Chi. & Nor. West. (R. R.).
ELVAS, Dist. of Portalegre, Portugal, 11,747.
EL VERANO, Sonoma Co., Calif., 518.
ELVINS, St. Francois Co., Mo., 2,403.
On Mo.-Ill. (R. R.).
ELWOOD, Madison Co., Ind., 10,685.
On N. York, Chi. & St. Lou.; Penna. (R. Rs.).
Industrial and commercial center. Glass and tinplate factories.
–Doniphan Co., Kans., 1,170.
On Chi., Rk. Isl. & Pac.; St. Jos. & Gd. Isl. (R. Rs.).
–c. s., Gosper Co., Nebr., 509.
On Chi., Burl. & Quincy (R. R.).
–Erie Co., N. Y., 1,010.
ELWYN, Allegheny Co., Pa., 500.
ELY, England, Isle of Ely, 8,382.
–St. Louis Co., Minn., 6,156.
On Dul., Missabe & Nor. (R. R.).
–c. s., White Pine Co., Nev., 3,045.
On Nev. Nor. (R. R.).
ELYRIA, c. s., Lorain Co., Ohio, 25,633.
On Balt. & Ohio; Lorain (El.); N. York Cen. (R. Rs.).
Industrial town manufacturing glass, enameled steel, bicycles, invalid chairs, machine screw products, springs and golf balls.
ELYSBURG, Northumberland Co., Pa., 625.
EMAUS, Lehigh Co., Pa., 6,419.
On Reading (R. R.).
EMBREEVILLE, Chester Co., Pa., 500.
On Reading (R. R.).
EMDEN, Hannover, Germany, 33,000.
Seaport. Has school of commerce and navigation.
EMEIGH, Cambria Co., Pa., 1,750.
EMERICK (Dunsbach Ferry), Albany Co., N. Y., 529.
EMERSON, Mills Co., Iowa, 512.
On Chi., Burl. & Quincy (R. R.).
–Bergen Co., N. J., 1,394.
On N. Jer. & N. York (R. R.).
–St. Louis Co., Mo., 650.
On Mo. Pac. (R. R.).
–Dakota, Dixon and Thurston Cos., Neb., 891.
On Chi., St. P., Minn. & Oma. (R. R.).
EMERY, Hanson Co., S. Dak., 485.
On Chi., Mil., St. P. & Pac. (R. R.).
–Emery Co., Utah, 637.
EMERYVILLE, Alameda Co., Cal., 2,336.
On Atch., Top. & Santa Fe; Sou. Pac. (R. Rs.).
EMIGSVILLE, York Co., Pa., 516.
On Penna. (R. R.).
EMINENCE, Henry Co., Ky., 1,323.
On Lou. & Nash. (R. R.).
EMLENTON, Venango Co., Pa., 1,137.
On Penna. (R. R.).
EMMEN, Drenthe, Netherlands, 40,961.
A trade center in a farming area.
EMMENDINGEN, Baden, Germany, 8,835.
EMMERICH, Rhenish Prussia, Germany, 13,562.
EMMETSBURG, c. s., Palo Alto Co., Iowa, 2,865.
On Chi., Mil., St. P. & Pac.; Chi., Rk. Isl. & Pac. (R. Rs.).
EMMETT, Gem Co., Idaho, 2,763.
On Ore. Short Line (R. R.).
EMMITSBURG, Frederick Co., Md., 1,235.
On Emmitsburg (R. R.).
EMORY GAP, Roane Co., Tenn., 500.
On Cin., N. Orl. & Tex. Pac.; Tenn. Cen. R. Rs.).
EMPHAL (Imphal) (Manipur), capital of British Protectorate of Manipur, Assam, India, 104,640.
EMPIRE, Jefferson Co., Ohio, 703.
On Penna. (R. R.).
–Luzerne & Wilkes-Barre Cos., Pa., 1,200.
EMPOLI, Prov. of Firenze, Italy, 8,120.
EMPORIA, c. s, Lyon Co., Kans., 13,138.
On Atch., Top. & Santa Fe; Mo.-Kan.-Texas (R. Rs.).
Agricultural center, especially for stock raising. Seat of Kansas State Normal and Emporia colleges.
–c. s., Greensville Co., Va., 2,144.
On Atl. Coast Line; Sou. (R. Rs.).
EMPORIUM, c. s., Cameron Co., Pa., 2,929.
On Penna. (R. R.).
EMS (Bad Ems), Hesse-Nassau, Germany, 7,121.
EMSWORTH, Allegheny Co., Pa., 2,709.
On Penna. (R. R.).
ENCARNACION, VILLA, Paraguay, 9,475.
ENCINAL, La Salle Co., Tex., 963.
On Internat.-Gt. Nor. (R. R.).
ENCINITAS, San Diego Co., Calif., 500.
On Atch., Top. & Santa Fe (R. R.).
ENCINO, Brooks Co., Tex., 510.
On Tex. & New Orl. (R. R.).
ENDERLIN, Ransom Co., N. Dak., 1,839.
On Minn., St. P. & S. Ste. M. (R. R.).
ENDICOTT, Broome Co., N. Y., 16,231.
On Erie (R. R.).
A trade and industrial town near Binghamton.
–Norfolk Co., Mass., 2,000.
On N. York, N. Hav. & Hart. (R. R.).
–Whitman Co., Wash., 512.
On Ore., Wash. R. R. & Nav. Co. (R. R.).
ENDWELL, Broome Co., N. Y., 2,404.
ENERGY (Fordville), Williamson Co., Ill., 554.
On Ill. Cen. (R. R.).
ENFIELD, Hartford Co., Conn., 1,000.
–Middlesex, England, 67,869.
–White Co., Ill., 744.
On Balt. & Ohio; Lou. & Nash. (R. Rs.).
–Penobscot Co., Maine, 1,138.
On Me. Cen. (R. R.).
–Grafton Co., N. H., 550.
On Bost. & Me. (R. R.).
–Halifax Co., N. C., 2,234.
On Atl. Coast Line (R. R.).
ENGELBERG, Unterwalden, Switzerland, 2,457.
ENGELS, Volga German Republic, Sov. Union, 55,200.
ENGLAND, Lonoke Co., Ark., 2,130.
On St. Lou. Southw. (R. R.).
ENGLEWOOD, Arapahoe Co., Colo., 7,980.
On Atch., Top. & Santa Fe; Den. & Rio Gde. West. (R. Rs.).
–Bergen Co., N. J., 17,805.
On Erie (R. R.).
A delightful residential suburb of New York.
–McMinn Co., Tennessee, 1,471.
On Lou. & Nash. (R. R.).
ENGLEWOOD CLIFFS, Bergen Co., N. J., 809.
ENGLISH, c. s., Crawford Co., Ind., 704.
On Southern (R. R.).
ENGLISHTOWN, Monmouth Co., N. J., 797.
On Penna. (R. R.).
ENHAUT, Dauphin Co., Pa., 2,500.
ENID, c. s., Garfield Co., Okla., 26,399.
On Atch., Top. & Santa Fe; Chi., Rk. Isl. & Pac.; St. Lou.-San Fran. (R. Rs.).
Leading grain market of the state and center of a fertile farming region.
ENKA, Buncombe Co., N. C., 800.
On Southern (R. R.).
ENNIS, Madison Co., Mont., 1,234.
–Ellis Co., Texas, 7,069.
On Tex. El.; Tex. & N. Orl. (R. Rs.).
ENOREE, Spartanburg Co., S. C., 1,500.
On Charl. & W. Car. (R. R.).
ENOSBURG FALLS, Franklin Co., Vt., 1,195.
On Cen. Ver. (R. R.).
ENSCHEDE, Overijssel, Netherlands, 86,766.
A center of weaving and cotton spinning industries. Has a trade school.
ENTERPRISE, c. s., Coffee Co., Ala., 3,702.
On Atl. Coast Line (R. R.).
–Dickinson Co., Kans., 702.
On Atch., Top. & Santa Fe; Chi., Rk. Isl. & Pac.; Un. Pac. (R. Rs.).
–Clarke Co., Miss., 792.
On Mob. & Ohio; N. Orl. & Northe. (R. Rs.).
–Haskell Co., Okla., 519.
–c. s., Wallowa Co., Ore., 1,379.
On Ore., Wash. R. R. & Nav. Co. (R. R.).
–Harrison Co., W. Va., 800.
On Balt. & Ohio (R. R.).
ENUMCLAW, King Co., Wash., 2,084.
On Chi., Mil., St. P. & Pac.; Nor. Pac. (R. Rs.).
ENVILLE, Chester Co., Tenn., 500.
EPERNAY, Dept. of Marne, France, 20,406.
Partially destroyed in the European War, 1914-18.
EPHRAIM, Sanpete Co., Utah, 1,966.
–On Den. & Rio Gde. West. (R. R.).
EPHRATA, Lancaster Co., Pa., 4,988.
On Reading (R. R.).
–Grant Co., Wash., 516.
On Gt. Nor. (R. R.).
EPINAL, Dept. of Vosges, France, 27,708.
A center of cotton spinning, weaving and printing industries.
EPPING, Essex, England, 4,956.
–Rockingham Co., N. H., 900.
On Bost. & Me. (R. R.).
EPPS, West Carroll Par., La., 500.
On Mo. Pac. (R. R.).
EPSOM, Surrey, England, 27,089.
A residential town and site of a famous horse race-track.
EQUALITY, Gallatin Co., Ill., 830.
On Lou. & Nash. (R. R.).
ERAKLEION (Candia), Crete, Greece, 40,900.
The chief commercial center of the island. Principal trade is in olive oil and soap.
ERATH, Vermilion Parish, La., 895.
On Tex. & N. Orl. (R. R.).
ERDENHEIM, Montgomery Co., Pa., 1,000.
ERFURT, Prussian Saxony, Germany, 140,000.
Most noted industry is culture of flowers and vegetables, also manufactures of machinery, clothing, shoes, farm implements, chemicals and beer.
ERICK, Beckham Co., Okla., 2,231.
On Chi., Rk. Is. & Pac. (R. R.).
ERICO (Soppitt), Butler Co., Pa., 520.
ERIE, Whiteside Co., Ill., 888.
On Chi., Burl. & Quincy (R. R.).
–c. s., Neosho Co., Kans., 1,205.
On Atch., Top. & Santa Fe; Mo.-Kan.-Tex. (R. Rs.).
–Monroe Co., Mich., 590.
On Pere Marq. (R. R.).
–c. s., Erie Co., Pa., 115,967.
On Bess. & L. Erie; N. York Cen.; N. York, Chi. & St. Lou.; Penna. (R. Rs.).
On a natural, land-locked harbor of Lake Erie. An important Lake shipping center. It is the port of the Pennsylvania Railroad, which has large storage yards, docks, warehouses and grain elevators there. It has many manufactures. Seat of the St. Benedict's, Villa Marie and Mercyhurst Academies, and the Pennsylvania Soldiers' and Sailors' Home.
ERIN, c. s., Houston Co., Tenn., 819.
On Lou. & Nash. (R. R.).
ERITH, Kent, England, 32,780.
A residential suburb of London.
ERIVAN, Soviet Union, 68,900.
ERLANGEN, Franconia, Bavaria, 30,000.
ERLANGER, Kenton Co., Ky., 1,853.
On Cin., N. Orl. & Tex. Pac. (R. R.).
–Davidson Co., N. C., 500.
ERNEST, Indiana Co., Pa., 1,500.
On Balt. & Ohio (R. R.).
ERSKINE, Polk Co., Minn., 511.
On Gt. Nor.; Minn., St. P. & S. Ste. M. (R. Rs.).
ERVING, Franklin Co., Mass., 1,283.
On Bost. & Me. (R. R.).
ERWIN, Harnett Co., N. C., 1,875.
On Durh. & Sou. (R. R.).
–Unicoi Co., Tenn., 3,623.
On Clinchfield (R. R.).
ERZERUM, Turkey, 33,127.
A commercial and industrial center. Famous for iron and brass work.
ESBJERG, Jutland, Denmark, 28,700.
Seaport for export trade with England.
ESCALANTE, Occidental Negros, P. I., 29,396.
A trade center and port. Some household industries.
–Garfield Co., Utah, 862.
ESCALON, San Joaquin Co., Calif., 785.
On Atch., Top. & Santa Fe; Tidew. Sou. (R. Rs.).
ESCANABA, c. s., Delta Co., Mich., 14,524.
On Chi. & Nor. West.; Chi., Mil., St. P. & Pac.; Escan. & L. Sup. (R. Rs.).
Large veneer plants; manufactures woodenware.
ESCHWEGE, Prussia, Germany, 12,748.
Weaving, cotton spinning, metal founding, and cooperage.
ESCHWEILER, Rhenish-Prussia, Germany, 33,090.
Manufactures of iron, steel and zinc goods.
ESCONDIDO, San Diego Co., Cal., 3,421.
On Atch., Top. & Santa Fe (R. R.).

Escuintla, Dept. of Escuintla, Guatemala, 21,-840.
Center of a cocoa, sugar and coffee producing region.
Eskdale, Kanawha Co., W. Va., 800.
On Chesa. & Ohio (R. R.).
Eskilstuna, Södermanland, Sweden, 36,801.
Iron, steel and cutlery.
Eskisehir, Turkey, 47, 045.
Eskridge, Waubaunsee Co., Kans., 743.
On Atch., Top. & Santa Fe (R. R.).
Esmond, Providence Co., R. I., 542.
On N. York, N. Hav. & Hart. (R. R.).
Esmont, Albemarle Co., Va., 515.
On Chesa. & Ohio; Nelson & Albe. (R. Rs.).
Esperanza, Prov. of Santa Clara, Cuba, 3,524.
Espy, Columbia Co., Pa., 700.
On Del., Lack. & West. (R. R.).
Essen, Rhenish Prussia, Germany, 654,461.
Among the notable buildings are the cathedral, dating from the 12th century, and a gymnasium and Realschule.
Essen derives its trade and industries from its great steel plants, made possible by neighboring coal mines, from its proximity to both the Ruhr and the Rhine, and its situation on three lines of railroads. Before the Great War, its chief industries were connected with the immense works established by the Krupps.
Essex, Essex Co., South, Ontario, Canada, 1,954.
On Mich. Cen. (R. R.).
–Middlesex Co., Conn., 1,500.
On N. York, N. Hav. & Hart. (R. R.).
–Page Co., Iowa, 806.
On Chi., Burl. & Quincy (R. R.).
–Baltimore Co., Md., 2,454.
–Essex Co., Mass., 1,486.
On Bost. & Me. (R. R.).
–Stoddard Co., Mo., 578.
On Mo. Pac. (R. R.).
Essex Fells, Essex Co., N. J., 1,115.
On Erie; Morrist. & Erie (R. Rs.).
Essex Junction, Chittenden Co., Vt., 1,621.
On Cen. Ver. (R. R.).
Essexville, Bay Co., Mich., 1,880.
Essington, Delaware Co., Pa., 1,500.
On Penna.; Read. (R. Rs.).
Esslingen, Württemberg, Germany, 41,000.
Famous for its wines. Also has textile mills and metal works.
Estacada, Clackamas Co., Ore., 524.
Estancia, c. s., Torrance Co., N. M., 634.
On Atch., Top. & Santa Fe (R. R.).
Este, Prov. of Padova, Italy, in Lombardy, 8,874.
Estelline, Hamlin Co., S. Dak., 551.
On Chi. & Nor. West. (R. R.).
–Hall Co., Tex., 950.
On Ft. Worth & Den. Cy. (R. R.).
Esterly, Berks Co., Pa., 790.
Estevan, Saskatchewan, Canada, 2,854.
Esther, St. Francois Co., Mo., 817.
On Mo.-Ill. (R. R.).
Estherville, c. s., Emmet Co., Iowa, 4,940.
On Chi., Rk. Isl. & Pac.; Minn. & St. Lou. (R. Rs.).
Estherwood, Acadia Par., La., 572.
On Tex. & N. Orl. (R. R.).
Estill, Hampton Co., S. C., 1,412.
On Seab. Air Line (R. R.).
Eston, Yorkshire, England, 31,142.
Center of iron mining region. Has blast furnace and foundries.
Eszek, Yugoslavia. See Osijek.
Ethel, Attala Co., Miss., 571.
On Ill. Cen. (R. R.).
Etiwanda, San Bernardino Co., Calif., 500.
On Atch., Top. & Santa Fe; Pac. El.; Sou. Pac. (R. Rs.).
Etna, Allegheny Co., Pa., 7,493.
On Balt. & Ohio; Etna & Montr.; Penna. (R. Rs.).
Eton, Buckinghamshire, England, 2,005.
Etowah, McMinn Co., Tenn., 4,209.
On Lou. & Nash. (R. R.).
Etterbeek, Brabant, Belgium, 44,704.
A suburb of Bruxelles.
Ettrick, Chesterfield Co., Va., 1,010.
Euclid, Cuyahoga Co., Ohio, 12,751.
On N. York, Chi. & St. Lou. (R. R.).
A suburb of Cleveland.
Eudora, Douglas Co., Kans., 653.
On Atch., Top. & Santa Fe (R. R.).
Eufaula, c. s., Barbour Co., Ala., 5,208.
On Cen. of Ga. (R. R.).
–c. s., McIntosh Co., Okla., 2,073.
On Mo.-Kan.-Tex. (R. R.).
Eugene, c. s., Lane Co., Ore., 18,901.
On Ore. El.; Sou. Pac. (R. R.).
Seat of Oregon State University.
Eunice, St. Landry Par., La., 3,597.
On Chi., Rk. Isl. & Pac.; New Orl., Tex. & Mex.; Tex. & N. Orl.; Tex. & Pac. (R. Rs.).
Eupen, Belgium, 12,729.
Forest and farm industries near by.
Eupora, Webster Co., Miss., 1,092.
On Columbus & Greenville (R. R.).
Eureka, c. s., Humboldt Co., Cal., 15,752.
On Northw. Pac. (R. R.).
–c. s., Woodford Co., Ill., 1,534.
On Atch., Top. & Santa Fe; Tol., Peor. & West. (R. Rs.).
–c. s., Greenwood Co., Kans., 3,832.
On Atch., Top. & Santa Fe; Mo. Pac. (R. Rs.).
–St. Louis Co., Mo., 550.
On Mo. Pac.; St. Lou.-San Fran. (R. Rs.).
–c. s., Eureka Co., Nev., 711.
On Eureka Nev. (R. R.).
–Lincoln Co., Mont., 860.
On Gt. Nor. (R. R.).
–McPherson Co., S. Dak., 1,430.
On Chi., Mil., St. P. & Pac. (R. R.).
–Juab Co., Utah, 3,041.
On Den. & Rio Gde. West.; Los Ang. & Salt Lake (R. Rs.).
Eureka Mills, Chester Co., S. C., 1,000.
Eureka Springs, c. s., Carroll Co., Ark., 2,276.
On Mo. & Nor. Ark. (R. R.).
In the Ozark Mountains. A health resort, notable for its many mineral springs.
Euskirchen, Prussia, Germany, 14,549.
Textile mills, breweries, foundries and metal works.
Eustace, Henderson Co., Tex., 513.
On Tex. & N. Orl. (R. R.).
Eustis, Lake Co., Fla., 3,449.
On Atl. Coast Line (R. R.).
Eutaw, c. s., Greene Co., Ala., 1,721.
On Ala. Gt. Sou. (R. R.).
Eutin, Germany, 7,034.
Evadale, Jasper Co., Tex., 515.
On Gulf, Colo. & Santa Fe (R. R.).
Evans, Weld Co., Colo., 540.
On Un. Pac. (R. R.).
Evans City (Evansburg), Butler Co., Pa., 1,561.
On Balt. & Ohio (R. R.).
Evanston, Cook Co., Ill., 63,338.
On Chi., Mil., St. P. & Pac.; Chi., No. Shore & Mil. (El.); Chi. & Nor. West. (R. Rs.).
Seat of Northwestern University.
–c. s., Uinta Co., Wyo., 3,075.
On Un. Pac. (R. R.).
Evansville, Randolph Co., Ill., 543.
On Mo.-Ill. (R. R.).
–c. s., Vanderburg Co., Ind., 102,249.
A port of entry on the Ohio River, and on the Chicago & Eastern Illinois; the Cleveland, Cincinnati, Chicago & St. Louis; the Evansville, Suburban & Newburgh; the Louisville & Nashville; the Illinois Central and the Southern Railroads. It is an important manufacturing town and has an extensive river commerce. One of the largest hardwood markets in the country. Its leading industries are furniture and cigar making, for which here are extensive factories. Seat of Evansville College. Evansville was founded in 1816 by General Robert M. Evans; it was incorporated in 1847.
–Rock Co., Wis., 2,269.
Chi. & Nor. West. (R. R.).
Evart, Osceola Co., Mich., 1,301.
On Pere Marq. (R. R.).
Evarts, Harlan Co., Ky., 1,438.
On Lou. & Nash. (R. R.).
Eveleth, St. Louis Co., Minn., 7,484.
On Dul., Missabe & Nor. (R. R.).
Chief industry: iron mining.
Everett, Middlesex Co., Mass., 47,228.
On Bost. & Alb.; Bost. & Me. (R. Rs.).
Residential and industrial suburb of Boston. Manufactures: Coke and petroleum products.
–Bedford Co., Pa., 1,874.
On Hunt. & Broad Top Mt. (R. R.).
–c. s., Snohomish Co., Wash., 30,567.
Subport of entry. Is situated on Puget Sound, and on the Northern Pacific; Great Northern; Chicago, Milwaukee, St. Paul & Pacific railroads, 33 miles north by east from Seattle. Has fine harbor and markets flour, lead, paper, creosote, timber and lumber throughout Alaska, South America, and the Orient.
Everglades, c. s., Collier Co., Florida, 573.
On Atl. Coast Line (R. R.).
Evergreen, c. s., Conecuh Co., Ala., 2,007.
On Lou. & Nash. (R. R.).
–San Jacinto Co., Tex., 500.
Evergreen Park, Cook Co., Ill., 1,594.
On Gd. Tr. (R. R.).
Everson, Fayette Co., Pa., 1,900.
On Balt. & Ohio; Penna.; Pitts. & L. Erie (R. R.).
Everton, Dade Co., Mo., 368.
On St. Lou.-San Fran. (R. R.).
Evesham, Worcestershire, England, 8,799.
Evora, Prov. of Alemtejo, Portugal, 22,061.
An agricultural center. Region is famous for its mules. Cork-oak forests and mines near by.
Evpatorya, Crimea, Sov. Union, 27,700.
Evreux, capital of Dept. of Eure, France, 20,116.
Metal founding and glass factories.
Ewing, Jackson Co., Ind., 500.
–Holt Co., Neb., 588.
On Chi. & Nor. West. (R. R.).
Excelsior, Hennepin Co., Minn., 1,072.
On Minn. & St. Lou. (R. R.).
–Northumberland Co., Pa., 857.
On Reading (R. R.).
–McDowell Co., W. Va., 529.
On Norf. & West. (R. R.).
Excelsior Springs, Clay Co., Mo., 4,565.
On Chi., Mil., St. P. & Pac.; Chi., Rk. Isl. & Pac.; Wab. (R. Rs.).
Exeter, Devonshire, England, 66,039.
A city, river port, and parliamentary and municipal borough of England, in the county of Devon, on the left bank of the Exe. By means of a canal, vessels of 300 tons can reach the city. Exeter was a British settlement long prior to the invasion of the Romans.
–Tulare Co., Cal., 2,685.
On Atch., Top. & Santa Fe; Sou. Pac.; Visalia (El.) (R. Rs.).
–Filmore Co., Neb., 941.
On Chi. & Nor. West.; Chi., Burl. & Quincy (R. Rs.).
–c. s., Rockingham Co., N. H., 4,506.
On Bost. & Me. (R. R.).
Seat of Philips Exeter Academy.
–Huron Co., South, Ontario, Canada, 1,666.
On Can. Nat. (R. R.).
–Luzerne Co., Pa.
On Leh. Val. (R. R.).
–Washington Co., R. I., 1,617.
Exira, Audubon Co., Iowa, 937.
On Chi., Rk. Isl. & Pac. (R. R.).
Exmouth, Devonshire, England, 14,584.
Experiment, Spalding Co., Ga., 1,600.
On Cen. of Ga.; Sou. (R. Rs.).
Export, Westmoreland Co., Pa., 2,184.
On Penna. (R. R.).

F

Fabriano, Prov. of Ancona, Italy, 8,679.
Faceville, Decatur Co., Ga., 900.
On Atl. Coast Line (R. R.).
Factoryville, Wyoming Co., Pa., 863.
On Del., Lack. & West. (R. R.).
Faenza, Prov. of Ravenna, Italy, 22,469.
Famous for its faience, a variety of pottery.
Fairacres, Dona Ana Co., N. Mex., 500.
Fairbank, Buchanan and Fayette Cos., Iowa, 629.
On Chi. Gt. West. (R. R.).
–Fayette Co., Pa., 500.
On Monongahela (R. R.).
Fairbanks, Alaska, 2,101.
On Alaska (R. R.).
Shipping point for miners' supplies.
Fair Bluff, Columbus Co., N. C., 806.
On Atl. Coast Line (R. R.).
Fairburn, c. s., Campbell Co., Ga., 1,372.
On Atl. & West. Pt. (R. R.).
Fairbury, Livingston Co., Ill., 2,310.
On Tol., Peor. & West.; Wab. (R. Rs.).
–c. s., Jefferson Co., Neb., 6,192.
On Chi., Burl. & Quincy; Chi., Rk. Isl. & Pac.; St. Jos. & Gd. Isl. (R. Rs.).
Fairchance, Fayette Co., Pa., 1,804.
On Balt. & Ohio; Penna. (R. Rs.).
Fairchild, Eau Claire Co., Wis., 634.
On Chi., St. P., Minn. & Oma. (R. R.).
Fairfax, Renville Co., Minn., 916.
On Minn. & St. Lou. (R. R.).
–Atchison Co., Mo., 852.
On Chi., Burl. & Quincy (R. R.).
–Osage Co., Okla., 2,134.
On Atch., Top. & Santa Fe (R. R.).
–Allendale Co., S. C., 1,376.
On Charl. & W. Car.; Seab. Air Line (R. Rs.).
–Fairfax Co., Va., 640.
Fairfield, Jefferson Co., Ala., 11,059.
On Birm. Sou.; Lou. & Nash.; Sou. (R. Rs.).
An industrial suburb of Birmingham. Coke, steel, railway cars, wire, brick, and chemicals.
–c. s., Solano Co., Cal., 1,131.
R. R. name Suisun-Fairfield. On Sacramento Nor. (El.); Sou. Pac. (R. Rs.).
–Fairfield Co., Conn., 5,000.
On N. York, N. Hav. & Hart. (R. R.).
–c. s., Wayne Co., Ill., 3,280.
On Balt. & Ohio; Sou. (R. Rs.).
–c. s., Jefferson Co., Iowa, 6,619.
On Chi., Burl. & Quincy; Chi., Rk. Isl. & Pac. (R. Rs.).
–Somerset Co., Maine, 3,529.
On Me. Cen. (R. R.).
–Clay Co., Neb., 757.
On Chi., Burl. & Quincy; St. Jos. & Gd. Isl. (R. Rs.).
–c. s., Freestone Co., Texas, 712.
Fair Forest, Spartanburg Co., S. C., 600.
On Southern (R. R.).
A summer resort.
Fairhaven, Bristol Co., Mass., 11,005.
On N. York, N. Hav. & Hart. (R. R.).
–St. Clair Co., Mich., 800.
–Monmouth Co., N. J., 2,260.
–Cayuga Co., N. Y., 562.
On Leh. Val. (R. R.).
–Rutland Co., Vt., 2,289.
On Del. & Hud. (R. R.).
Fairhope, Baldwin Co., Ala., 1,549.
Fairland, Shelby Co., Ind., 650.
On Cle., Cin., Chi. & St. Lou. (R. R.).
–Ottawa Co., Okla., 679.
On Kan., Okla. & Gulf; St. Lou.-San Fran. (R. Rs.).
Fairmont, c. s., Martin Co., Minn., 5,521.
On Chi. & Nor. West.; Chi., St. P., Minn. & Oma.; Chi., Mil., St. P. & Pac. (R. Rs.).
–Fillmore Co., Neb., 740.
On Chi., Burl. & Quincy (R. R.).
–Robeson Co., N. C., 1,314.
On Atl. Coast Line (R. R.).
–c. s., Marion Co., W. Va., 23,159.
On Balt. & Ohio; Monongahela (R. Rs.).
A coal-shipping point. Also has manufactures of chemicals, glass, powder, and textiles. Seat of a State Normal School.
Fairmont Mills, Spartanburg Co., S. C., 1,000.
On Piedmont & Nor. (El.) (R. R.).
Fairmount, Richland Co., N. D., 611.
On Chi., Mil., St. P. & Pac.; Gt. Nor.; Minn., St. P. & S. Ste. M. (R. Rs.).
–Vermilion Co., Ill., 741.
On Wabash (R. R.).
–Grant Co., Ind., 2,056.
On Cle., Cin., Chi. & St. Lou. (R. Rs.).
Fairmount City, Clarion Co., Pa., 500.
R. R. name Hepler. On Penna. (R. R.).
Fair Oaks, Sacramento Co., Calif., 1,000.
On Sou. Pac. (R. R.).
–Jasper Co., Ind., 500.
On Chi., Attica & Sou.; Chi., Ind. & Lou. (R. Rs.).
Fairpoint, Belmont Co., Ohio, 1,000.
On Balt. & Ohio (R. R.).
Fairport, Monroe Co., N. Y., 4,604.
On N. Y. Cen.; West Shore (R. Rs.).
Fairport Harbor, Lake Co., Ohio, 4,972.
On Balt. & Ohio; Fairp., Painesv. & East. (R. Rs.).
Fairview, Fulton Co., Ill., 522.
On Chi., Burl. & Quincy (R. R.).
–Richland Co., Mont., 576.
On Gt. Nor. (R. R.).
–Bergen Co., N. J., 9,067.
On Erie (R. R.).
–c. s., Major Co., Okla., 1,887.
On Atch., Top. & Santa Fe (R. R.).
–Cuyahoga Co., Ohio, 3,689.
–Sanpete Co., Utah, 1,120.
On Den. & Rio Gde. West. (R. R.).
–Marion Co., West Va., 836.
Fairview Park, Indiana, 1,106.
Faison, Duplin Co., N. C., 589.
On Atl. Coast Line (R. R.).
Faith, Meade Co., S. Dak., 574.
On Chi., Mil., St. P. & Pac. (R. R.).
Fajardo, Mun. of Fajardo, Puerto Rico, 6,511.
Falaise, Dept. of Calcados, Normandy, France, 6,374.
Falconer, Chautauqua Co., N. Y., 3,579.
On Erie; N. York Cen. (R. Rs.).
Falfurrias, c. s., Brooks Co., Texas, 2,641.
On Tex. & N. Orl. (R. R.).
Falkirk, Stirling, Scotland, 36,000.
Center of a coal and iron district. Foundries, breweries, tanneries, and chemical plants.
Falkville, Morgan Co., Ala., 543.
On Lou. & Nash. (R. R.).
Fallbrook, San Diego Co., Calif., 887.
On Atch., Top. & Santa Fe (R. R.).
Fall Creek, Eau Claire Co., Wis., 528.
On Chi., St. P., Minn. & Oma. (R. R.).
Fallon, Churchill Co., Nevada, 1,758.
On Sou. Pac. (R. R.).
Fall River, c. s., Bristol Co., Mass., 117,414.
Situated at the mouth of the Taunton River, and on Mt. Hope Bay. It is on the New York, New Haven & Hartford (R. R.), and is reached by several lines of steamboats.
The chief manufactures are cotton goods, machinery (including textile machinery), leather belting, trunks and valises, wooden ships, varnish, rayon products, brass and iron goods, hats, shirts and dresses.
Fall River was incorporated in 1803 and chartered as a city in 1834.
Falls Church, Fairfax Co., Va., 2,019.
On Wash. & Old Dom. (El.) (R. R.).
Falls City, c. s., Richardson Co., Neb., 5,787.
On Chi., Burl. & Quincy; Mo. Pac. (R. Rs.).
Falls Creek, Clearfield and Jefferson Cos., Pa., 1,231.
On Balt. & Ohio; Penna. (R. Rs.).
Fallsington, Bucks Co., Pa., 600.
On Penna. (R. R.).
Fallston, Beaver Co., Pa., 665.
On Pitts. & L. Erie (R. R.).
Falls Village, Litchfield Co., Conn., 625.
On N. York, N. Hav. & Hart. (R. R.).
Falmouth, Cornwall, England, 13,492.
Seaport and market town.
–c. s., Pendleton Co., Ky., 1,876.
On Lou. & Nash. (R. R.).
–Barnstable Co., Mass., 6,537.
On N. York, N. Hav. & Hart. (R. R.).
Falun, capital of Kopparberg, Sweden, 13,370.
Copper mines and smelters.
Fano, Prov. of Pesaro and Urbino, Italy, 11,687.
Fanwood, Union Co., N. J., 1,681.
On Cen. of N. Jer. (R. R.).
Fargo, c. s., Cass Co., N. Dak., 28,619.
On Chi., Mil., St. P. & Pac.; Gt. Nor.; Nor. Pac. (R. Rs.).

Is a distributing point for farm products and farm implements.

FAR HILLS (Far Hills-Bedminster Sta.), Somerset Co., N. J., 560.
On Del., Lack. & West. (R. R.).

FARIBAULT, c. s., Rice Co., Minn., 12,767.
On Chi. Gt. West.; Chi., Mil., St. P. & Pac.; Chi., Rk. Isl. & Pac. (R. Rs.).
Center of a farming and dairying region.

FARINA, Fayette Co., Ill., 694.
On Ill. Cen. (R. R.).

FARLEY, Dubuque Co., Iowa, 657.
On Chi. Gt. West.; Ill. Cen. (R. Rs.).

FARMER, Defiance Co., Ohio, 930.

FARMER CITY, DeWitt Co., Ill., 1,621.
On Cle., Cin., Chi. & St. Lou.; Ill. Cen. (R. Rs.).

FARMERSBURG, Sullivan Co., Ind., 993.
On Chi. & East. Ill. (R. R.).

FARMERSVILLE, Montgomery Co., Illinois, 553.
On Ill. Cen. (R. R.).
—Collin Co., Texas, 1,817.
On Gulf, Colo. & Santa Fe; La., Ark. & Tex. (R. Rs.).

FARMERVILLE, c. s., Union Par., La., 1,137.
On Mo. Pac. (R. R.).

FARMINGDALE, Monmouth Co., N. J., 629.
On Cen. of N. Jer.; Penna. (R. Rs.).
—Nassau Co., N. Y., 3,373.
On Long Isl. (R. R.).

FARMINGTON, Hartford Co., Conn., 1,131.
On N. York, N. Hav. & Hart. (R. R.).
—Fulton Co., Ill., 2,269.
On Chi., Burl. & Quincy; Minn. & St. Lou. (R. Rs.).
—Van Buren Co., Iowa, 1,012.
On Chi., Burl. & Quincy; Chi., Rk. Isl. & Pac. (R. Rs.).
—c. s., Franklin Co., Me., 1,737.
On Me. Cen.; Sandy Riv. & Rang. Lks. (R. Rs.).
—Oakland Co., Mich., 1,243.
—Dakota Co., Minn., 1,342.
On Chi., Mil., St. P. & Pac.; Chi., Rk. Isl. & Pac. (R. Rs.).
—c. s., St. Francois Co., Mo., 3,001.
On St. Francois Co. (El.).
—Strafford Co., N. H., 2,200.
On Bost. & Me. (R. R.).
—San Juan Co., N. Mex., 1,350.
On Den. & Rio Gde. West. (R. R.).
—Trumbull Co., Ohio, 650.
—c. s., Davis Co., Utah, 1,339.
On Bamb. (El.); Den. & Rio Gde. West.; Ore. Short Lines (R. Rs.).
—Marion Co., W. Va., 819.
On Balt. & Ohio (R. R.).

FARMLAND, Randolph Co., Ind., 853.
On Cle., Cin., Chi. & St. Lou. (R. R.).

FARMVILLE, c. s., Pitt Co., N. C., 2,056.
On E. Carol.; Norf. Sou. (R. Rs.).
—c. s., Prince Edward Co., Va., 3,133.
On Norf. & West. (R. R.).

FARNBOROUGH, Southampton, England, 16,359.
A military station.

FARNHAM, Missisquoi Co., Quebec, Canada, 4,205.
On Can. Nat.; Can. Pac. (R. Rs.).
—Surrey, England, 18,294.
A marketing center in a rich agricultural region.

FARNWORTH, Lancashire, England, 28,711.
Collieries, iron foundries, and brickyards.

FARO, Prov. of Algarve, Portugal, 14,721.
Seaport and trade center.

FARR (Capps), Huerfano Co., Colo., 800.

FARRAGUT, Fremont Co., Iowa, 523.
On Chi., Burl. & Quincy (R. R.).

FARRELL, Mercer Co., Pa., 14,359.
On Erie; N. York Cen.; Penna.; Pitts. & L. Erie (R. Rs.).
Industries all iron and steel.

FARUKHABAD, United Provinces, India, 51,567.
An important trade center.

FARWELL, c. s., Parmer Co., Tex., 647.
On Panh. & Santa Fe (R. R.).

FASANO, Prov. of Brindisi, Italy, 11,277.

FATEHPUR, United Provinces, India, 19,300.
Trade is principally agricultural.

FAULKTON, c. s., Faulk Co., S. Dak., 713.
On Chi. & Nor. West.; Chi., Mil., St. P. & Pac. (R. Rs.).

FAURESMITH, Orange Free State, Union of S. Africa, South Africa, 1,900.

FAVARA, Prov. of Girgenti, Sicily, 21,155.
Agricultural center. Sulphur mines near by.

FAVERSHAM, Kent, England, 10,091.
A market town and river port.

FAYETTE, c. s., Fayette Co., Ala., 2,109.
On Mob. & Gulf; Sou. (R. Rs.).
—Fayette Co., Iowa, 1,083.
On Chi., Mil., St. P. & Pac. (R. Rs.).
Upper Iowa University is located here.
—c. s., Jefferson Co., Miss., 848.
On Yazoo & Miss. Val. (R. R.).
—c. s., Howard Co., Mo., 2,630.
On Mo.-Kans.-Tex. (R. R.).
—Fulton Co., Ohio, 847.
On N. York Cen. (R. R.).

FAYETTE CITY, Fayette Co., Pa., 1,594.
On Pitts. & L. Erie (R. R.).

COURTESY OF RED STAR LINE
PONTE VECCHIO, THE FAMOUS AND PICTURESQUE BRIDGE IN FLORENCE (FIRENZE), ITALY

FAYETTEVILLE, c. s., Washington Co., Ark., 7,394.
On St. Lou.-San Fran. (R. R.).
—c. s., Fayette Co., Ga., 796.
On Southern (R. R.).
—Onondaga Co., N. Y., 2,008.
On West Shore (R. R.).
—c. s., Cumberland Co., N. C., 13,049.
On Aberd. & Rockf.; Atl. Coast Line; Norf. Sou. (R. Rs.).
Has textile mills. Large shipping trade in naval stores, cotton and lumber.
—(W. Fayetteville), Franklin Co., Pa., 800.
On Penna. (R. R.).
—c. s., Lincoln Co., Tenn., 3,822.
On Nash., Chatt. & St. Lou. (R. R.).
—Fayette Co., W. Va., 1,143.

FAYÛM, capital of Fayûm, Egypt, 58,200.
The center of a fertile agricultural region.

FAYVILLE, Worcester Co., Mass., 525.
On N. York, N. Hav. & Hart. (R. R.).

FÉCAMP, Dept. of Seine-Inférieure, France, 17,708.
A seaport and summer resort.

FEDERAL, St. Francois Co., Mo. See FLAT RIVER.

FEDERALSBURG, Carolina Co., Md., 1,369.
On Penna. (R. R.).

FELICITY, Clermont Co., Ohio, 580.
On Cin., Georgetown (R. R.).

FELLING, Durham, England, 27,041.
Collieries and attendant industries.

FELTONVILLE (Barker), Delaware Co., Pa., 500.
On Balt. & Ohio (R. R.).

FELTS MILLS, Jefferson Co., N. Y., 500.
On N. York Cen. (R. R.).

FENELON FALLS, Victoria Co., Ontario, Canada, 963.
On Can. Nat. (R. R.).

FENNIMORE, Grant Co., Wis., 1,341.
On Chi. & Nor. West. (R. R.).

FENNVILLE, Allegan Co., Mich., 622.
On Pere Marq. (R. R.).

FENTON, Genesee Co., Mich., 3,171.
On Gd. Tr. (R. R.).

FENWICK, Nicholas Co., W. Va., 550.
On Balt. & Ohio (R. R.).

FEODOSIYA, Soviet Union, 28,656.

FERDINAND, Dubois Co., Indiana, 846.
On Ferdinand (R. R.).

FERGUS, Wellington Co., Ontario, Canada, 2,594.
On Can. Pac.; Can. Nat. (R. Rs.).

FERGUS FALLS, c. s., Otter Tail Co., Minn., 9,389.
On Gt. Nor.; Nor. Pac. (R. Rs.).

FERGUSON, St. Louis Co., Mo., 3,798.
On Wabash (R. R.).

FERMO, Prov. of Ascoli-Piceno, Italy, 7,818.

FERNANDINA, c. s., Nassau Co., Fla., 2,692.
On Seab. Air Line (R. R.).

FERNDALE, Humboldt Co., Cal., 889.
—Oakland Co., Mich., 20,855.
A suburb of Detroit.
—Cambria Co., Pa., 2,742.
On Balt. & Ohio; Johnst. & Stony Cr. (R. Rs.).
—Whatcom Co., Wash., 752.
On Gt. Nor. (R. R.).

FERN GLEN, Luzerne Co., Pa., 800.
On Penna. (R. R.).

FERNIE, British Columbia, Canada, 2,732.

FERNSIDE (Egan P. O.), Fulton Co., Ga., 1,200.
On Cen. of Ga. (R. R.).

FERNWOOD, Pike Co., Miss., 500.
On Fernw., Colum. & Gulf; Ill. Cen. (R. Rs.).

—Delaware Co., Pa., 700.
On Penna. (R. R.).

FEROSEPORE, Punjab, India, 54,351.
A grain trade center.

FERRARA, capital of Prov. of Ferrara, Italy, 70,415.

FERRIDAY, Concordia Parish, La., 2,502.
On La. & Ark.; Mo. Pac.; Tex. & Pac. (R. Rs.).

FERRIS, Ellis Co., Texas, 1,438.
On Tex. & N. Orl.; Tex. El. (R. Rs.).

FERROL, EL, Prov. of Corunna, Spain, 30,350.
A principal naval station of Spain.

FERRON, Emery Co., Utah, 508.

FERRUM, Franklin Co., Va., 521.
On Norf. & West. (R. R.).

FERRYSBURG, Ottawa Co., Mich., 500.
On Gd. Trunk; Pere Marq. (R. Rs.).

FERTILE, Polk Co., Minn., 800.
On Nor. Pac. (R. R.).

FÉS (Fez), one of the capitals of Morocco, 144,313.
Chief commercial center of French Morocco, situated on both banks of a tributary of the Sebu. Fés was founded in 793. In the thirteenth century it became the capital of an independent State, and in the sixteenth, of Morocco. Since 1912, the seat of government has been at Rabat.
The industries are numerous, including leather, rugs, silks, and the red "Fez" caps.

FESSENDEN, c. s., Wells Co., N. Dak., 738.
On Minn., St. P. & S. Ste. M. (R. R.).

FESTINIOG, Merionethshire, Wales, 9,072.

FESTUS, Jefferson Co., Mo., 4,085.
On Mo.-Ill.; St. Lou.-San Fran. (R. Rs.).

FEZ, French Morocco. See FÉS.

FIANARANTSOA, Madagascar, 56,797.

FIELD, Curry Co., N. Mex., 511.

FIELDS CORNER, Suffolk Co., Mass., 1,000.

FIERRO, Grant Co., N. Mex., 500.
On Atch., Top. & Santa Fe (R. R.).

FIESOLE, Prov. of Firenze, Italy, 2,786.

FIGUERAS, Prov. of Gerona, Spain, 13,192.

FILBERT, Fayette Co., Pa., 900.

FILER, Twin Falls Co., Idaho, 1,011.
On Ore. Short Line (R. R.).

FILLMORE, Ventura Co., Cal., 2,893.
On Sou. Pac. (R. R.).
—c. s., Millard Co., Utah, 1,374.
On Los Ang. & Salt L. (R. R.).
In irrigated area.

FINCASTLE, c. s., Botetourt Co., Va., 517.

FINDLAY, Shelby Co., Illinois, 682.
On Chi. & East. Ill. (R. R.).
—c. s., Hancock Co., Ohio, 19,363.
Situated on the Blanchard River. It is on the Baltimore & Ohio; the New York Central and the New York, Chicago & St. Louis railroads.
The most notable buildings are Findlay College, the public library, and the city hospital. The chief manufacturing establishments are brick and tile works, foundries and machine shops, rolling mills, flour mills, tire and rubber goods plants, sugar refineries, oil plants and potteries. Findlay was settled in the early part of the nineteenth century and was incorporated as a city in 1837.

FINLEY, c. s., Steele Co., N. Dak., 587.
On Gt. Nor. (R. R.).

FINLEYVILLE, Washington Co., Pa., 595.

On Balt. & Ohio (R. R.).

FINSTERWALD, Prussia, Germany, 13,434.
Sawmills, machine shops, textile mills and rubber factories.

FIREBAUGH, Fresno Co., Calif., 600.
On Sou. Pac. (R. R.).

FIRENZE (Florence), capital of Prov. of Firenze, Tuscany, Italy, 285,000.
Situated on the river Arno. The river divides it into two unequal parts, and is crossed by bridges, two of which the Ponte della Santa Trinità and the Ponte Vecchio (1362, by Taddeo Gaddi), are famous.
Firenze is remarkable for its well-preserved and handsome medieval edifices. There are many magnificent palaces (Strozzi, Pitti, Vecchio, and the Medici-Riccardi). The Pitti and the Uffizi art treasures are world-famous. Among the notable squares, or piazzas, are the Piazza della Signoria, and Loggia dei Lanzi, where Savonarola was burned at the stake.
The most striking building in Firenze, and perhaps in Europe, is the Duomo (begun in 1298), with the largest dome in the world, executed by Brunelleschi, and a campanile, begun by Giotto in 1334.

FIRMINY, Dept. of Loire, France, 20,257.
Coal mines, and manufactures of iron and steel.

FIRTHCLIFFE, Orange Co., N. Y., 500.
On N. York, Ont. & West. (R. R.).

FISHER, Champaign Co., Ill., 709.
On Ill. Cen. (R. R.).

FISHING CREEK, Dorchester Co., Md., 893.

FISHKILL LANDING, Dutchess Co., N. Y., united with Mattewan to form the city of Beacon.
On New York Central; New York, New Haven & Hartford (R. Rs.).

FISKDALE, Worcester Co., Mass., 650.

FISMES, Dept. of Marne, France, 2,109.
Taken by Americans from Germans Aug. 4, 1918. Almost destroyed by shelling.

FITCHBURG, c. s., Worcester Co., Mass., 41,700.
Situated on a branch of the Nashua River, and on the Fitchburg division of the Boston & Maine, and the New York, New Haven & Hartford railroads.
The most notable buildings are the Fitchburg State Teachers College, the Burbank Hospital and the public library. The industrial interests include manufacture of toys, tools, saws, arms, bicycles, shoes, locks, cotton yarns and woolens. Fitchburg was chartered as a city in 1872.

FITCHVILLE, New London Co., Conn., 587.
On Cen. Ver. (R. R.).
—Huron Co., Ohio, 537.

FITZGERALD, c. s., Benn Hill Co., Ga., 6,412.
On Atla., Birm. & Coast; Seab. Air Line (R. Rs.).
Location of Atla., Birm. & Coast railroad shops.

FITZPATRICK, Raleigh Co., W. Va., 620.
On Chesa. & Ohio; Virginian (R. Rs.).

FIUME, Fiume Prov., Italy, 52,900.
A seaport situated at the head of the Bay of Guarnero on the Adriatic.
The most notable buildings are the cathedral, the Church of St. Vitus, the Naval Academy, the Roman triumphal arch, the town hall, and the Government buildings.
The chief industrial establishments are the

Government tobacco factory, the Whitehead torpedo works, the petroleum refinery, the rice-shelling factory, the paper and the saw mills. In 1471 it came into the possession of Austria, and in 1799 was attached to the crown of Fiume, was claimed both by Italy and Yugoslavia after the World War, but in 1924 was finally annexed to Italy, with a Free Zone provided in 1927.
FIVE POINTS, Chambers Co., Ala., 1,010.
On Cen. of Ga. (R. R.).
–Wayne Co., Mich., 1,000.
FLAGLER, Kit Carson Co., Colo., 540.
On Chi., Rk. Isl. & Pac. (R. R.).
FLAGSTAFF, c. s., Coconino Co., Ariz., 3,891.
On Atch., Top. & Santa Fe (R. R.).
Seat of State Normal School.
FLANAGAN, Livingston Co., Ill., 631.
On Ill. Cen. (R. R.).
FLANDREAU, c. s., Moody Co., S. Dak., 2,474.
On Chi., Mil., St. P. & Pac. (R. R.).
FLAT LICK, Knox Co., Ky., 500.
On Lou. & Nash. (R. R.).
FLATONIA, Fayette Co., Texas, 966.
On Tex. & N. Orl. (R. R.).
FLAT RIVER, St. Francois Co., Mo., 3,337.
On Mo.-Ill. (R. R.).
FLAT ROCK, Crawford Co., Ill., 584.
On Cle., Cin., Chi. & St. Lou. (R. R.).
–Henderson Co., N. C., 1,062.
On Southern (R. R.).
FLEETWOOD, Berks Co., Pa., 2,150.
On Reading (R. R.).
FLEMING, Letcher Co., Ky., 1,389.
On Lou. & Nash. (R. R.).
FLEMINGSBURG, c. s., Fleming Co., Ky., 1,265.
On Flemingsb. & Nor. (R. R.).
FLEMINGTON, c. s., Hunterdon Co., N. J., 2,729.
On Cen. of N. Jer.; Leh. Val.; Penna. (R. Rs.).
–Clinton Co., Pa., 1,191.
On Penna. (R. R.).
–Taylor Co., W. Va., 617.
On Balt. & Ohio (R. R.).
FLENSBURG, Schleswig, Germany, 67,000.
FLERS, Dept. of Orne, France, 12,900.
A manufacturing town. Textiles, dyes, and chemicals.
FLETCHER, Henderson Co., N. C., 500.
On Southern (R. R.).
–Comanche Co., Okla., 739.
On St. Lou.-San Fran. (R. R.).
FLINT, c. s., Genesee Co., Mich., 156,492.
Situated on both banks of the Flint River and on the Grand Trunk, and Pere Marquette Railroads. Manufactures automobiles, wagons, carriages, wheels, bodies, axles, paints, and varnishes. Other industries are cigar factories, flouring and woolen mills, and brick and tile works. Seat of Michigan School for the Deaf. Fine public library, court-house, and hospital.
–Flintshire, Wales, 7,635.
FLOMATON, Escambia Co., Ala., 915.
On Lou. & Nash. (R. R.).
FLORA, Clay Co., Ill., 4,393.
On Balt. & Ohio (R. R.).
–Carroll Co., Ind., 1,449.
On Penna. (R. R.).
–Madison Co., Miss., 513.
On Yazoo & Miss. Val. (R. R.).
FLORALA, Covington Co., Ala., 2,580.
On Cen. of Ga.; Lou. & Nash. (R. Rs.).
FLORAL PARK, Nassau Co., N. Y., 10,016.
On Long Isl. (R. R.).
A residential suburb of New York.
FLORENCE, Italy. See FIRENZE.
–c. s., Lauderdale Co., Ala., 11,729.
On Lou. & Nash.; Sou. (R. Rs.).
At foot of Muscle Shoals, Tennessee River.
–c. s., Pinal Co., Ariz., 1,318.
–Fremont Co., Colo., 2,475.
On Atch., Top. & Santa Fe; Den. & Rio Gde. West. (R. Rs.).
–Marion Co., Kans., 1,663.
On Atch., Top. & Santa Fe (R. R.).
–Douglas Co., Neb. (Sta. Omaha P. O.).
On Chi., St. P., Minn. & Oma. (R. R.).
–c. s., Florence Co., S. C., 14,774.
On Atl. Coast Line; Seab. Air Line (R. Rs.).
Cotton, corn, and tobacco. Has railroad shops, cottonseed oil mills, mines, etc.
–Florence Co., Wis., 1,341.
On Chi. & Nor. West. (R. R.).
FLORENCE VILLA, Polk Co., Fla., 928.
On Atl. Coast Line (R. R.).
FLORESVILLE, c. s., Wilson Co., Texas, 1,581.
On Tex. & N. Orl. (R. R.).
FLORHAM PARK, Morris Co., N. J., 1,269.
FLORIANOPOLIS, Santa Catharina, Brazil, 48,300.
FLORIDA, Orange Co., N. Y., 822.
On Erie; Leh. & N. Engl. (R. Rs.).
FLORIDA CITY, Dade Co., Fla., 633.
On Fla., East Coast (R. R.).
FLORINA, Greece, 10,585.
FLORISSANT, St. Louis Co., Mo., 787.
FLOSSMOOR, Cook Co., Ill., 808.
On Ill. Cen. (R. R.).
FLOYDADA, Floyd Co., Texas, 2,637.
On Panh. & Santa Fe; Quan., Acme & Pac. (R. Rs.).
FLUSHING, Netherlands. See VLISSINGEN.
–Genesee Co., Mich., 1,723.
On Gd. Tr. (R. R.).
–Queens Co., N. Y., former village, now Fourth Ward of Queens Borough, New York City.
On Long Island (R. R.).
–Belmont Co., Ohio, 1,119.
On Balt. & Ohio (R. R.).
FOCSANI, Moldavia, Rumania, 32,799.
Oil, soap, leather, and wines.
FOGELSVILLE, Lehigh Co., Pa., 513.
FOGGIA, capital of Prov. of Foggia, Italy, 50,000.
A grain center and wool market.
FOLEY, Baldwin Co., Ala., 791.
On Lou. & Nash. (R. R.).
–Benton Co., Minn., 798.
On Gt. Nor. (R. R.).
FOLIGNO, Prov. of Perugia, Italy, 12,888.
An agricultural center.
FOLKESTONE, Kent, England, 35,890.
FOLKSTON, c. s., Charlton Co., Ga., 506.
On Atl. Coast Line (R. R.).
FOLLANSBEE, Brooke Co., W. Va., 4,841.
On Penna. (R. R.).
FOLLETT, Lipscomb Co., Tex., 658.
On Panh. & Santa Fe (R. R.).
FOLSOM, Sacramento Co., Calif., 1,000.
On Sou. Pac. (R. R.).
FONDA, Pocahontas Co., Iowa, 1,027.
On Chi., Mil., St. P. & Pac.; Ill. Cen. (R. Rs.).
–c. s., Montgomery Co., N. Y., 1,170.
On Fonda, Johnst. & Gloversv.; N. York Cen. (R. Rs.).
FONDE, Bell Co., Ky., 800.
On Lou. & Nash.; Sou. (R. Rs.).
FOND-DU-LAC, c. s., Fond-du-Lac Co., Wis., 26,449.
On Chi. & Nor. West.; Chi., Mil., St. P. & Pac.; Minn., St. P. & S. Ste. M. (R. Rs.).
Lumber, grain, flour, paper and carriages.
FONTAINEBLEAU, Dept. of Seine-et-Marne, France, 17,724.
The residence of Kings of France; contains famous park (45,000 acres).
FONTANA, San Bernardino Co., Cal., 5,600.
On Atch., Top. & Santa Fe; Pac. El.; Sou. Pac. (R. Rs.).
FONTANELLE, Adair Co., Iowa, 833.
On Chi., Burl. & Quincy (R. R.).
FONTENAY-LE-COMTE, Vendée, France, 9,423.
FONTENAY-SOUS-BOIS, Seine, France, 31,546.
FOOCHOW, capital of Fukien Prov., China, 322,700.
A seaport for coasting trade.
FOOTEDALE, Fayette Co., Pa., 500.
On Monongahela (R. R.).
FORBES ROAD, Westmoreland Co., Pa., 695.
On Penna. (R. R.).
FORD, Clark Co., Ky., 792.
On Lou. & Nash. (R. R.).
FORD CITY, Armstrong Co., Pa., 6,127.
On Penna. (R. R.).
–Ontario, Canada. See EAST WINDSOR.
FORD CLIFF, Armstrong Co., Pa., 607.
FORDSVILLE, Ohio Co., Ky., 573.
On Ill. Cen.; Lou. & Nash. (R. Rs.).
FORDVILLE, Williamson Co., Ill. See ENERGY.
FORDWICK, Augusta Co., Va., 620.
On Chesa. & Ohio (R. R.).
FORDYCE, c. s., Dallas Co., Ark., 3,206.
On Chi., Rk. Isl. & Pac.; Fordy. & Prince; St. Lou. Southw. (R. Rs.).
FOREST, c. s., Scott Co., Miss., 2,176.
On Yazoo & Miss. Val. (R. R.).
–Hardin Co., Ohio, 1,103.
On Cle., Cin. & St. Lou.; Penna. (R. Rs.).
–Lambton Co., West, Ontario, Canada, 1,480.
On Can. Nat. (R. R.).
–Cherokee Co., Tex., 500.
On St. Lou. Southw. (R. R.).
FOREST CITY, c. s., Winnebago Co., Iowa, 2,016.
On Chi., Rk. Isl. & Pac.; Minn. & St. Lou. (R. Rs.).
–Holt Co., Mo., 504.
On Chi., Burl. & Quincy (R. R.).
–Rutherford Co., N. C., 4,069.
On Clinchfield; Seab. Air Line; Sou. (R. Rs.).
–Susquehanna Co., Pa., 5,209.
On Del. & Hud.; Erie; N. York, Ont. & West. (R. Rs.).
FORESTDALE, Providence Co., R. I., 765.
On N. York, N. Hav. & Hart. (R. R.).
FORESTER, Scott Co., Ark., 1,000.
On Ark. West. (R. R.).
FOREST GROVE, Washington Co., Ore., 1,859.
On Ore. El.; Sou. Pac.; Spok., Port. & Seattle (R. Rs.).
Seat of Pacific University.
FOREST HILL, Shelby Co., Tenn., 670.
On Southern (R. R.).
FOREST KNOLLS, Marin Co., Calif., 500.
FOREST LAKE, Washington Co., Minn., 916.
On Nor. Pac. (R. R.).
FOREST PARK, Cook Co., Ill., 14,555.
On Balt. & Ohio; Chi. Term.; Chi., Aur. & Elg.; Chi. Gt. West.; Ill. Cen.; Minn., St. P. & S. Ste. M. (R. Rs.).
A residential suburb of Chicago.
–Lawrence Co., Mo., 598.
FORESTVILLE, Sonoma Co., Calif., 500.
On Northw. Pac.; Petaluma & St. Rosa (El.) (R. Rs.).
–Chautauqua Co., N. Y., 677.
On Erie (R. R.).
FORFAR, Forfarshire, Scotland, 10,062.
Textiles and bleaching industries.
FORGAN, Beaver Co., Okla., 605.
On Beav., Mead & Englew.; Mo.-Kan.-Tex. (R. Rs.).
FORKED RIVER, Ocean Co., N. J., 512.
On Cen. of N. Jer. (R. R.).
FORK RIDGE, Claiborne Co., Tenn., 500.
On Lou. & Nash. (R. R.).
FORLI, Prov. of Forli, Italy, 30,400.
An agricultural trade center. Has felt manufactures.
FORNEY, Kaufman Co., Tex., 1,216.
On Tex. & Pac. (R. R.).
FORNFELT, Scott Co., Mo., 1,500.
On St. Lou. Southw. (R. R.).
FORREST, Livingston Co., Ill., 915.
On Tol., Peor. & West.; Wab. (R. Rs.).
FORREST CITY, c. s., St. Francis Co., Ark., 4,594.
On Chi., Rk. Isl. & Pac.; Mo. Pac.; St. Lou. Southw. (R. Rs.).
FORRESTON, Ogle Co., Ill., 908.
On Chi., Mil., St. P. & Pac.; Ill. Cen. (R. R.).
FORST, Brandenburg, Germany, 38,000.
Manufactures of woolen cloth.
FORSYTH, c. s., Monroe Co., Ga., 2,277.
On Cen. of Ga. (R. R.).
–c. s., Rosebud Co., Mont., 1,591.
On Chi., Mil. St. P. & Pac.; No. Pac. (R. Rs.).
FORSYTHE, Shelby Co., Tenn., 550.
On St. Lou.-San Fran. (R. R.).
FORTALEZA, Ceara, Brazil, 143,300.
A seaport. Exports coffee, rubber, sugar, cotton, rum and rice.
FORT APACHE, Navajo Co., Ariz., 600.
FORT ATKINSON, Jefferson Co., Wis., 5,793.
On Chi. & Nor. West. (R. R.).
FORT BAYARD, Grant Co., N. Mex., 1,000.
FORT BENTON, c. s., Chouteau Co., Mont., 1,109.
On Gt. Nor. (R. R.).
FORT BRAGG, Mendocino Co., Cal., 3,022.
On Cal. West. R. R. & Nav. Co. (R. R.).
FORT BRANCH, Gibson Co., Ind., 1,341.
On Chi. & East. Ill. (R. R.).
FORT COBB, Caddo Co., Okla., 827.
On Chi., Rk. Isl. & Pac. (R. R.).
FORT COLLINS, c. s., Larimer Co., Colo., 11,489.
On Colo. & Sou.; Un. Pac. (R. Rs.).
Seat of State Agricultural College.
FORT COVINGTON, Franklin Co., N. Y., 764.
On Gd. Tr. (R. R.).
FORT DAVIS, c. s., Jeff Davis Co., Tex., 666.
FORT DEFIANCE, Apache Co., Ariz., 600.
FORT DE FRANCE, capital of Martinique, West Indies, 48,395.
FORT DEPOSIT, Lowndes Co., Ala., 1,092.
On Lou. & Nash. (R. R.).
FORT DES MOINES, Polk Co., Iowa, 2,000.
FORT DODGE, c. s., Webster Co., Iowa, 21,895.
On Chi. Gt. West.; Ft. Dodge, Des Moines & Sou.; Ill. Cen.; Minn. & St. Lou. (R. Rs.).
Manufactures gypsum and clay products, etc.
–Ford Co., Kans., 515.
FORT EDWARD, Washington Co., N. Y., 3,850.
On Del. & Hud. (R. R.).
Site of Fort Edward Collegiate Institute.
FORT ERIE (Bridgeburg), Welland Co., Ontario, Canada, 3,521.
On Can. Nat.; Mich. Cen.; Wab. (R. Rs.).
FORT FAIRFIELD, Aroostook Co., Maine, 2,616.
On Bangor & Aroostook; Can. Pac. (R. Rs.).
FORT FRANCES, Ontario, Canada, 5,470.
On Can. Nat.; Dul., Winnip. & Pac., Intern. Bridge Term. (R. Rs.).
FORT GAINES, Clay Co., Ga., 1,272.
On Cen. of Ga. (R. R.).
FORT GAY, Wayne Co., W. Va., 850.
On Norf. & West. (R. R.).
FORT GIBSON, Muskogee Co., Okla., 1,159.
On Mo. Pac.; Muskog. El.; St. Lou.-San Fran. (R. Rs.).
FORT JOHNSON, Montgomery Co., N. Y., 833.
FORT KENT, Aroostook Co., Maine, 2,245.
On Bangor & Aroostook (R. R.).
FORT LAUDERDALE, c. s., Broward Co., Fla., 9,222.
On Fla. East Coast; Seab. Air Line (R. Rs.).
FORT LEE, Bergen Co., N. J., 8,759.
FORT LOGAN, Arapahoe Co., Colo., 800.
On Den. & Rio Gde. West. (R. R.).
FORT LUPTON, Weld Co., Colo., 1,578.
R. R. name Lupton. On Un. Pac. (R. R.).
FORT MADISON, c. s., Lee Co., Iowa, 13,779.
On Atch., Top. & Santa Fe; Chi., Burl. & Quincy (R. Rs.).
Santa Fe railroad shops. First fort in what is now Iowa. Famous in Black Hawk wars.
FORT MEADE, Polk Co., Fla., 1,997.
On Atl. Coast Line (R. R.).
–Meade Co., S. Dak., 850.
FORT MILL, York Co., S. C., 2,112.
On Southern (R. R.).
FORT MONTGOMERY, Orange Co., N. Y., 700.
On West Shore (R. R.).
FORT MORGAN, c. s., Morgan Co., Colo., 4,423.
On Chi., Burl. & Quincy; Un. Pac.
FORT MYERS, c. s., Lee Co., Fla., 10,312.
On Atl. Coast Line; Seab. Air Line (R. Rs.).
FORT PAYNE, c. s., De Kalb Co., Ala., 3,375.
On Ala. Gt. Sou. (R. R.).
FORT PIERCE, c. s., St. Lucie Co., Fla., 6,376.
On Fla. East Coast (R. R.).
FORT PIERRE, c s., Stanley Co., S. Dak., 777.
On Chi. & Nor. West. (R. R.).
FORT PLAIN, Montgomery Co., N. Y., 2,906.
R. R. name South St. Plain. On N. York Cen. (R. R.).
FORT RECOVERY, Mercer Co., Ohio, 1,118.
On New York, Chi. & St. Lou. (R. R.).
FORT SCOTT, c. s., Bourbon Co., Kans., 9,802.
On Mo.-Kan.-Tex.; Mo. Pac.; St. Lou.-San Fran. (R. Rs.).
Dairy and industrial center.
FORT SHERIDAN, Lake Co., Ill., 2,000.
On Chi. & Nor. West.; Chi. No. Shore & Mil. (El.) (R. Rs.).
FORT SMITH, c. s., Sebastian Co., Ark., 31,429.
On Mo. Pac.; Ft. Smith & West.; Kan. Cy. Sou.; Mid. Val.; St. Lou.-San Fran. (R. Rs.).
Situated in the midst of a fertile farming region; ships much grain. Second city of the State; manufactures bricks, furniture, leather, glass; territory adjacent has gas fields and coal, zinc, and lead ores.
FORT STOCKTON, c. s., Pecos Co., Texas, 2,695.
On Panh. & Santa Fe (R. R.).
FORT SUMNER, De Baca Co., N. Mex., 839.
On Atch., Top. & Santa Fe (R. R.).
FORT THOMAS, Campbell Co., Ky., 10,008.
A trade center near Covington.
FORTUNA, Humboldt Co., Cal., 1,239.
On Northw. Pac. (R. R.).
FORT VALLEY, Peach Co., Ga., 4,560.
On Cen. of Ga.; Sou. (R. Rs.).
FORTVILLE, Hancock Co., Ind., 1,289.
On Cle., Cin., Chi. & St. Lou.; Ind. R. R. Sys. (El.) (R. Rs.).
FORT WASHINGTON, Montgomery Co., Pa., 800.
On Reading (R. R.).
FORT WAYNE, c. s., Allen Co., Ind., 114,946.
Situated at the junction of the St. Joseph and St. Mary Rivers. It is on the New York Central railroad; the Indiana Railroad System (El.); the New York, Chicago and St. Louis; the Wabash; and the Pennsylvania railroads.
There are a great many substantial industries, their varied productions including oil pumps and tanks, lisle hose, knit goods, agricultural implements, handles, fittings, car wheels, copper wire, electrical equipment, cigars, etc. Four railroads (including the Penna. and Wabash) have large shops here, which employ thousands. Fort Wayne was at first a fort, built by General Anthony Wayne in 1794. It was chartered as a city in 1839.
FORT WILLIAM, Thunder Bay Co., Ontario, Canada, 26,277.
On Can. Nat.; Can. Pac. (R. Rs.).
Large shipments of grain; grain elevators, saw and planing mills.
FORT WORTH, c. s., Tarrant Co., Texas, 163,447.
On. Burl.-Rk. Isl.; Chi., Rk. Isl. & Gulf; Ft. Worth Blt.; Ft. Worth & Denv. Cy.; Ft. Worth & Rio Gde.; Gulf, Colo. & Santa Fe; Internat.-Gt. Nor.; Mo.-Kan.-Tex. of Tex.; St. Lou. Southw.; St. Lou., San Fran. & Tex.; Tex. & N. Orl.; Tex. & Pac. (R. Rs.). Several roads have their general offices here and have greatly extended their terminal facilities.
In addition to being the manufacturing center of the Southwest, Fort Worth, owing to the discovery of vast oil fields within its trade territory in 1917, has become an oil metropolis. Several hundred companies, including the great corporations, have offices here, and there are numerous oil supply houses and refineries. It is also an important cotton, grain and cattle market. Its spacious manufactories include rolling, flour and feed and cotton-oil mills, packing factories, and electric power.
Seat of Texas Christian University, Southwestern Baptist Theological Seminary and Texas Wesleyan College. The city is noted for its handsome church structures and as a Southern center of art and music.
FORT YATES, c. s., Sioux Co., N. Dak., 800.
FORTY FORT, Luzerne Co., Pa., 6,224.
On Del., Lack. & West. (R. R.).
FOSS, Washita Co., Okla., 524.
On Chi., Rk. Isl. & Pac. (R. R.).
FOSSIL, c. s., Wheeler Co., Ore., 538.
FOSSTON, Polk Co., Minn., 978.
On Gt. Nor. (R. R.).
FOSTER, Providence Co., R. I., 1,167.
Contains village of Foster Center.
FOSTORIA, Hancock and Seneca Cos., Ohio, 12,790.
On Balt. & Ohio; Chesa. & Ohio; Cle., Cin., Chi. & St. Lou.; N. York Cen.; N. York, Chi. & St. Lou. (R. Rs.).
A commercial center in a rich farming and petroleum district.
FOUGÈRES, Dept. of Ill-et-Vilaine, France, 20,432.
FOUNTAIN, El Paso Co., Colo., 577.
On Atch., Top. & Santa Fe; Den. & Rio Gde. West. (R. Rs.).

FOUNTAIN CITY, Knox Co., Tenn., 510.
–Buffalo Co., Wis., 880.
On Chi., Burl. & Quincy (R. R.).
FOUNTAIN GREEN, Sanpete Co., Utah, 982.
On Den. & Rio Gde. West. (R. R.).
FOUNTAIN HILL, Lehigh Co., Pa., 4,568.
FOUNTAIN INN, Greenville Co., S. C., 1,264.
On Charl. & W. Car. (R. R.).
FOUR OAKS, Johnston Co., N. C., 684.
On Atl. Coast Line (R. R.).
FOUSTWELL, Somerset Co., Pa., 700.
On Balt. & Ohio (R. R.).
FOWLER, Fresno Co., Cal., 1,171.
On Sou. Pac. (R. R.).
–Otero Co., Colorado, 968.
On Atch., Top. & Santa Fe (R. R.).
–c. s., Benton Co., Ind., 1,564.
On Cle., Cin., Chi. & St. Lou. (R. R.).
–Meade Co., Kans., 620.
On Chi., Rk. Isl. & Pac. (R. R.).
–Clinton Co., Mich., 561.
On Gd. Tr. (R. R.).
–Trumbull Co., Ohio, 500.
On N. York Cen. (R. R.).
FOWLERVILLE, Livingston Co., Mich., 1,141.
On Pere Marq. (R. R.).
FOXBORO, Norfolk Co., Mass., 5,834.
On N. York, N. Hav. & Hart. (R. R.).
–Douglas Co., Wis., 565.
On Gt. Nor. (R. R.).
FOXCROFT, Piscataquis Co., Maine. See DOVER-FOXCROFT.
FOX HILL, Elizabeth City Co., Va., 750.
FOX LAKE, Lake Co., Ill., 880.
–Dodge Co., Wis., 901.
On Chi., Mil., St. P. & Pac. (R. R.).
FRACKVILLE, Schuylkill Co., Pa., 8,034.
On Penna.; Read. (R. Rs.).
FRAMINGHAM, Middlesex Co., Mass., 22,651
On Bost. & Alb.; N. York, N. Hav. & Hart. (R. Rs.).
An industrial suburb of Boston. Manufactures include hats, rubber goods, shoes, auto parts, medicines and stoves.
FRANCESVILLE, Pulaski Co., Ind., 712.
On Chi., Ind. & Lou. (R. R.).
FRANCIS, Pontotoc Co., Okla., 607.
On St. Lou.-San Fran. (R. R.).
FRANCISCO, Gibson Co., Indiana, 728.
On Southern (R. R.).
FRANCONIA, Grafton Co., N. H., 6,576.
On Bost. & Me. (R. R.).
FRANEKER, Friesland, Netherlands, 8,155.
FRANK, Allegheny Co., Pa., 575.
FRANKENBERG, Saxony, Germany, 14,764.
FRANKENHAUSEN, Schwarzburg-Rudolstadt, Germany, 7,010.
FRANKENMUTH, Saginaw Co., Mich., 925.
FRANKENTHAL, Bavaria, Germany, 26,000.
Industrial center. Manufactures include machinery, cooperage, toys, soaps, and castings.
FRANKFORD, Pike Co., Mo., 546.
On St. Lou. & Han. (R. R.).
FRANKFORT, Will Co., Ill., 590.
On Elg., Jol. & East.; Mich. Cen. (R. Rs.).
–c. s., Clinton Co., Ind., 12,196.
On Chi., Ind. & Lou.; N. York, Chi. & St. Lou.; Penna. (R. Rs.).
A railroad center close to the great jobbing and distributing points of the Middle West.
–Marshall Co., Kans., 1,275.
On Mo. Pac.; Un. Pac. (R. Rs.).
–c. s., Franklin Co., Ky., State capital, 11,626.
Situated on the Kentucky River, and on the Louisville & Nashville; the Frankfort & Cincinnati and the Chesapeake & Ohio railroads. The river is navigable by steamboats below and above the city. The city is placed amid picturesque scenery in the heart of the famous "Blue Grass" region of the State. The prominent buildings include the State House, Governor's Mansion, State Arsenal, and State Penitentiary. The State Library has over 146,000 volumes. Water power is furnished by means of a local dam. Frankfort is in a very productive tobacco area and an exclusive market for the weed, with a number of large tobacco warehouses. Its chief manufactures are hemp, shoes, shirts and brooms. Near by are pure-bred Hereford cattle farms. Also noted for horse breeding. Frankfort was founded in 1786 by General James Wilkinson.
–c. s., Benzie Co., Mich., 1,468.
On Ann Arbor (R. R.).
–Herkimer Co., N. Y., 4,203.
On West Shore (R. R.).
–Ross Co., Ohio, 764.
On Balt. & Ohio (R. R.).
FRANKFORT HEIGHTS, Franklin Co., Ill. (Pop. incl. in West Frankfort).
On Ill. Cen. (R. R.).
FRANKFURT-AM-MAIN, Hesse-Nassau, Germany, 555,071.
Situated on the right bank of the Main. The most prominent squares are the Rossmarkt, with the Gutenberg monument; the Goetheplatz, with Schwanthaler's statue of Goethe; the Kaiserplatz, and the Borsenplatz. Among its most notable buildings are the Cathedral of St. Bartholomew (870), built in the Gothic

style (the place of the election and coronation of the German emperors); the Wahlkapelle; the Paulskirche, the seat of the German National Parliament of 1848-49; the Kaisersaal, where emperors held their public banquets. Important in commerce and industry. Manufactures chemicals, gold and silver wire, machinery, carpets, drugs, tobacco, and electric supplies. Home of some of the strongest moneyed institutions in the world. In 1816 it became the capital of the German Confederation. In 1866 it was incorporated with Prussia.
FRANKFURT-AM-ODER, Brandenburg, Germany, 75,000.
FRANKLIN, Macon Co., Ala., 500.
On West. of Ala. (R. R.).
–Franklin Co., Idaho, 531.
On Ore. Short Line (R. R.).
–Morgan Co., Ill., 528.
On Chi., Burl. & Quincy (R. R.).
–c. s., Johnson Co., Ind., 5,682.
On Cle., Cin., Chi. & St. Lou.; Ind. R. R. Sys. (El.); Penna. (R. Rs.).
Seat of Franklin College, chief products, furniture and athletic underwear.
–Crawford Co., Kans., 853.
On Joplin-Pitts (R. R.).
–c. s., Simpson Co., Ky., 3,056.
On Lou. & Nash. (R. R.).
–c. s., St. Mary Parish, La., 3,271.
On N. Iberia & Nor.; Tex. & N. Orl. (R. Rs.).
–Hancock Co., Maine, 500.
On Me. Cen. (R. R.).
–Norfolk Co., Mass., 7,494.
On N. York, N. Hav. & Hart. (R. R.).
–Renville Co., Minn., 535.
On Minn. & St. Lou. (R. R.).
–St. Louis Co., Minn., 625.
On Dul., Missabe & Nor. (R. R.).
–c. s., Franklin Co., Neb., 1,103.
On Chi., Burl. & Quincy (R. R.).
–Merrimack Co., N. H., 6,576.
On Bost. & Me. (R. R.).
–Sussex Co., N. J., 4,176.
On Del., Lack. & West.; Leh. & Hud. Riv.; N. York, Susq. & West. (R. Rs.).
–c. s., Macon Co., N. C., 1,094.
On Tallulah Fs. (R. R.).
–Warren Co., Ohio, 4,491.
On Cin. & L. Erie (El.); Cle., Cin., Chi. & St. Lou.; Cin. Nor. (R. Rs.).
–Cambria Co., Pa., 2,323.
–c. s., Venango Co., Pa., 10,254.
In petroleum region. Has refineries and manufactures of machinery, cranes, engines, tools, paints, and printing.
On Erie; N. York. Cen.; Penna. (R. Rs.).
–c. s., Williamson Co., Tenn., 3,377.
On Lou. & Nash.; Nash.-Frank. (El.) (R. Rs.).
–c. s., Robertson Co., Texas, 961.
On Inter-Gt. Nor. (R. R.).
–Southampton Co., Va., 2,930.
On Seab. Air Line; Sou. (R. Rs.).
FRANKLIN GROVE, Lee Co., Ill., 625.
On Chi. & Nor. West. (R. R.).
FRANKLIN LAKES, Bergen Co., N. J., 893.
FRANKLIN PARK, Cook Co., Ill., 2,425.
On Chi., Mil., St. P. & Pac.; Ind. Harb. Belt; Minn., St. P. & S. Ste. M. (R. Rs.).
FRANKLINTON, Washington Parish, La., 963.
On Gulf, Mob. & Nor. (R. R.).
–Franklin Co., N. C., 1,320.
On Seab. Air Line (R. R.).
FRANKLINVILLE, Gloucester Co., N. J., 500.
On Pa.-Read. Seashore (R. R.).
–Cattaraugus Co., N. Y., 2,021.
On Penna. (R. R.).
–Randolph Co., N. C., 676.
On Atl. & Yadk. (R. R.).
FRANKSTON, Anderson Co., Texas, 1,109.
On Tex. & N. Orl. (R. R.).
FRANKTON, Madison Co., Ind., 829.
On Penna. (R. R.).
FRASCATI, Prov. of Roma, Italy, 10,024.
A residential suburb of Roma.
FRASER, Macomb Co., Mich., 600.
On Gd. Tr. (R. R.).
FRAY BENTOS, Dept. of Rio Negro, Uruguay, 7,000.
Large exports of cattle products.
FRAZEE, Becker Co., Minn., 1,041.
On Nor. Pac. (R. R.).
FRAZERBURGH, Aberdeen, Scotland, 10,203.
FRAZEYSBURG, Muskingum Co., Ohio, 679.
On Penna. (R. R.).
FREDERIC, Polk Co., Wis., 680.
On Minn., St. P. & S. Ste. M. (R. R.).
FREDERICA, Kent Co., Del., 589.
FREDERICIA, Jutland, Denmark, 20,100.
A busy port and industrial center. Has manufactures of cotton goods, tobacco, and chicory.
FREDERICK, Weld Co., Colo., 596.
On Un. Pac. (R. R.).
–c. s., Frederick Co., Md., 14,434.
Center of the finest farming section in the State, on the Baltimore & Ohio; Hagerstown & Frederick (El.), and the Pennsylvania railroads. Brick and brush making are leading

industries. Other industries include canned goods, pumps, cream tubs, and clothing.
–c. s., Tillman Co., Okla., 4,568.
On Mo.-Kan.-Tex.; St. Lou.-San Fran. (R. Rs.).
FREDERICKSBURG, Chickasaw Co., Iowa, 567.
On Chi. Gt. West. (R. R.).
–Crawford Co., Pa., 500.
–Lebanon Co., Pa., 700.
–c. s., Gillespie Co., Texas, 2,416.
On Fredericks. & Nor. (R. R.).
–(Ind. City) Spotsylvania Co., Va., 6,819.
On Richm., Fred. & Pot.; Va. Cen. (R. Rs.).
FREDERICKTOWN, c. s., Madison Co., Mo., 2,954.
On Mo. Pac. (R. R.).
–Knox Co., Ohio, 1,257.
On Balt. & Ohio (R. R.).
FREDERICTON, capital of New Brunswick, Canada, 8,830.
FREDERIKSBERG, Denmark, 109,189.
A suburb of Köbenhavn.
FREDONIA, c. s., Wilson Co., Kans., 4,017.
On Atch., Top. & Santa Fe; St. Lou.-San Fran.; Mo. Pac. (R. Rs.).
–Caldwell Co., Ky., 517.
On Ill. Cen. (R. R.).
–Chautauqua Co., N. Y., 5,814.
On N. York Cen. (R. R.).
–Department of Antioquia, Colombia, 23,754.
A marketing center. Coal mines near by.
FREDRIKSHALD, Norway. See HALDEN.
FREDRIKSTAD, Ostfold Prov., Norway, 14,101.
A center of the timber export trade.
FREEBURG, St. Clair Co., Ill., 1,434.
On Ill. Cen. (R. R.).
FREEDOM, Beaver Co., Pa., 3,227.
On Penna. (R. R.).
FREEHOLD, c. s., Monmouth Co., N. J., 6,894.
On Cen. of N. Jer.; Penna. (R. Rs.).
FREELAND, Saginaw Co., Mich., 780.
On Pere Marq. (R. R.).
–Luzerne Co., Pa., 7,098.
On Leh. Val. (R. R.).
FREELANDVILLE, Knox Co., Ind., 500.
FREEMAN, Hutchison Co., S. Dak., 942.
On Chi., Mil., St. P. & Pac. (R. R.).
–Mercer Co., W. Va., 800.
FREEMANSBURG, Northampton Co., Pa., 1,777.
On Cen. of N. Jer.; Leh. Val. (R. Rs.).
FREEPORT, c. s., Stephenson Co., Ill., 22,045.
On Chi. & Nor. West.; Chi., Mil., St. P. & Pac.; Ill. Cen. (R. Rs.).
A trade and commercial center in a rich farming and dairying region.
–Cumberland Co., Maine, 973.
On Me. Cen. (R. R.).
–Nassau Co., N. Y., 15,467.
On Long Isl. (R. R.).
A residential suburb of New York.
–Harrison Co., Ohio, 578.
On Balt. & Ohio (R. R.).
–Wood Co., Ohio, 606.
–Armstrong Co., Pa., 2,772.
On Penna.; Pitts. & Shawmut (R. Rs.).
–Brazoria Co., Texas, 3,162.
On Hous. & Braz. Val. (R. R.).
FREETOWN, Bristol Co., Mass., 1,813.
–Capital of Sierra Leone, West Africa, 59,523.
An important seaport and commercial center.
FREEWATER, Umatilla Co., Oregon, 732.
On Un. Pac.; Walla Walla Val. (El.) (R. Rs.).
FREIBERG, Saxony, Germany, 36,000.
Center of mining district, on the northern slope of the Erzgebirge.
FREIBURG, capital of Dist. of Freiburg, Germany, 99,122.
Principal trade center of the Black Forest region. Manufactures of buttons, tobacco, silk, paper, and instruments.
FREISING, Bavaria, Germany, 17,000.
A suburb of München.
FREMANTLE, Western Australia, Australia, 17,566.
A seaport and industrial town. Shipbuilding, iron founding, wood working, brewing and tanning.
FREMONT, Steuben Co., Ind., 802.
On N. York Cen. (R. R.).
–Newaygo Co., Mich., 2,157.
On Pere Marq. (R. R.).
–c. s., Dodge Co., Neb., 11,407.
On Chi., Burl. & Quincy; Chi. & Nor. West.; Un. Pac. (R. Rs.).
An important grain and live-stock market.
–Wayne Co., N. Car., 1,316.
On Atl. Coast Line (R. R.).
–c. s., Sandusky Co., Ohio, 13,422.
On Lake Shore (El.); N. York Cen.; N. York, Chi. & St. Lou.; Wheel. & L. Erie (R. Rs.).
A great cutlery manufacturing center.
FRENCH GULCH, Shasta Co., Calif., 618.
FRENCH LICK, Orange Co., Ind., 2,462.
On Chi., Ind. & Lou.; Sou. (R. Rs.).
FRENCH SETTLEMENT, Livingston Par., La., 600.
FRENCHTOWN, Hunterdon Co., N. J., 1,189.
On Penna. (R. R.).
FRENCHVILLE, Aroostook Co., Maine, 1,500.
On Bangor & Aroostook (R. R.).
FRESNILLO, Zacatecas, Mexico, 16,188.
Center of an agricultural region.
FRESNO, c. s., Fresno Co., Cal., 52,513.
On Atch., Top. & Santa Fe; Sou. Pac. (R. Rs.).

The town is surrounded by irrigated lands of great fertility. Has lumber mills, flour mills, machine shops, brick yards, and foundries. Its airport is a very busy one.
FRIAR POINT (Friars Point Sta.), c. s., Coahoma Co., Miss., 988.
On Yazoo & Miss. Val. (R. R.).
FRIBOURG, capital of Canton of Fribourg, Switzerland, (1920) 20,649.
FRIDAY HARBOR, c. s., San Juan Co., Wash., 601.
FRIDLEY, Anoka Co., Minn., 693.
On Gt. Nor.; Minn., Anoka & Cuy. Range (El.); Nor. Pac. (R. Rs.).
FRIEDENSBURG, Berks Co., Pa., 720.
FRIEDLAND, Silesia, Germany, 4,598.
FRIEDRICHRODA, Saxe-Coburg-Gotha, Germany, 5,683.
FRIEDRICHSHAFEN, Württemberg, 11,289.
Site of Zeppelin factory and airport.
FRIEND, Saline Co., Neb., 1,214.
On Chi., Burl. & Quincy (R. R.).
FRIENDSHIP, Lincoln Co., Miss., 800.
–c. s., Allegany Co., N. Y., 1,154.
On Erie; Pitts., Shawmut & Nor. (R. Rs.).
–Scioto Co., Ohio, 500.
FRIES, Grayson Co., Va., 2,205.
On Norf. & West. (R. R.).
FRINTON ON SEA, Essex, England, 2,196.
FRIONA, Parmer Co., Tex., 731.
On Panh. & Santa Fe (R. R.).
FRISCO, Collin Co., Texas, 618.
On St. Lou., San Fran. & Tex. (R. R.).
FRISCO CITY, Monroe Co., Ala., 1,021.
On Man. & Rept.; St. Lou.-San Fran. (R. Rs.).
FRITCH, Hutchinson Co., Tex., 500.
On Chi., Rk. Isl. & Gulf (R. R.).
FROMBERG, Carbon Co., Montana, 550.
On Chi., Burl. & Quincy; Nor. Pac. (R. Rs.).
FROME, Somerset, England, 10,738.
FRONTENAC, Crawford Co., Kans., 2,051.
On Atch., Top. & Santa Fe; Kan. Cy. Sou. (R. Rs.).
FRONTERA, Mexico. See ALVARO OBREGON.
FRONT ROYAL, c. s., Warren Co., Va., 2,424.
On Norf. & West.; Sou. (R. Rs.).
FROST, Navarro Co., Texas, 748.
On St. Lou. Southw. (R. R.).
FROSTBURG, Allegany Co., Md., 5,588.
On Cumb. & Penna.; West. Md. (R. Rs.).
FROSTPROOF, Polk Co., Fla., 1,632.
On Atl. Coast Line (R. R.).
FRUITA, Mesa Co., Colo., 1,053.
On Den. & Rio Gde. West (R. R.).
FRUITLAND, Payette Co., Idaho, 970.
On Ore. Short Line (R. R.).
FRUNZE, Kirghiz, Sov. Union, 71,700.
FRYDEK, Austin Co., Tex., 525.
FRYE (Ivanhoe), Washington Co., Pa., 513.
On Penna. (R. R.).
FRYEBURG, Oxford Co., Maine, 789.
On Me. Cen. (R. R.).
FUKUI, Kyushu, Japan, 64,200.
Chief industry: papermaking.
FUKUOKA, Kyushu, Japan, 299,700.
A trade point and seat of the silk industry.
FULDA, Hesse-Nassau, Germany, 27,000.
Weaving, dyeing, carpets, linen, and felt.
–Murray Co., Minn., 818.
On Chi., Mil., St. P. & Pac. (R. R.).
FULFORD, Dade Co., Fla., 935.
FULLERTON, Orange Co., Cal., 10,860.
On Atch., Top. & Santa Fe; Pac. El.; Los Ang. & Salt L. (R. Rs.).
Fruit and general farm crops comprise the chief industries. Oil and gas fields are near.
–c. s., Nance Co., Nebr., 1,680.
On Un. Pac. (R. R.).
FULTON, Clarke Co., Ala., 766.
On Southern (R. R.).
–Hempstead Co., Ark., 593.
On Mo. Pac. (R. R.).
–Whiteside Co., Ill., 2,656.
On Chi. & Nor. West.; Chi., Burl. & Quincy; Chi., Mil., St. P. (R. Rs.).
–Fulton Co., Ky., 3,502.
On Ill. Cen. (R. R.).
–Keweenaw Co., Mich., 700.
On Cop. Rge. (R. R.).
–c. s., Itawamba Co., Miss., 927.
On Mississippian (R. R.).
–c. s., Callaway Co., Mo., 6,105.
On Alton (R. R.).
–Oswego Co., N. Y., 12,462.
On N. York Cen.; N. York, Ont. & West. (R. Rs.).
Manufactures of woolen goods and paper.
FULTONVILLE, Montgomery Co., N. Y., 831.
On West Shore (R. R.).
FUMAY, Dept. of Ardennes, France, 5,339.
FUNCHAL, capital of Madeira, 67,580.
Center of wine and coal trade. Famous as a winter resort.
FÜNFKIRCHEN, Hungary. See PÉCS.
FUNKSTOWN, Washington Co., Md., 700.
On Balt. & Ohio; Hagerst. & Fred. (El.) (R. Rs.).
FUQUAY SPRINGS, Wake Co., N. C., 963.
On Norf. Sou. (R. R.).
FURCHES, Ashe Co., N. C., 500.
FÜRSTENBERG, Brandenburg, Prussia, 7,310.

Fürstenwalde, Brandenburg, Prussia, 24,000.
Trade and industrial town near Berlin.
Fürth, Bavaria, Germany, 77,000.
A manufacturing town; leading products are mirrors, books, optical instruments, pencils, furniture and toys.
Fusan, Chosen, 206,386.
A seaport and leading commercial center.
Fyffe, De Kalb Co., Ala., 500.
Fyzabad, Oudh, India, 56,620.
An agricultural center and military station.

G

Gaastra, Iron Co., Mich., 755.
Gadsden, c. s., Etowah Co., Ala., 24,042.
On Ala. Gt. Sou.; Lou. & Nash.; Nash., Chatt. & St. Lou.; Sou.; Tenn., Ala. & Ga. (R. Rs.).
Has large steel and iron mills. Coal and iron ores are extensively mined in the vicinity.
Gaeta, Prov. of Roma, Italy, 6,393.
Gaffney, c. s., Cherokee Co., S. C., 6,827.
On Southern (R. R.).
Gage, Ellis Co., Okla., 856.
On Atch., Top. & Santa Fe (R. R.).
Gaillimh (Galway), capital of County Galway, Ireland (Eire), 18,285.
A seaport and commercial center. Exports, woolens, linen, black marble, and agricultural produce.
Gainesboro, c. s., Jackson Co., Tenn., 556.
Gainsborough, Lincolnshire, England, 18,684.
Gainesville, c. s., Alachua Co., Fla., 12,274.
On Atl. Coast Line; Jacksonv., Gainesv. & Gulf; Seab. Air Line (R. Rs.).
Lumbering and phosphate mining center. Seat of the University of Florida.
–c. s., Hall Co., Ga., 8,624.
On Gainesv. Mid.; Sou. (R. Rs.).
–c. s., Cooke Co., Texas, 8,915.
On Gulf, Colo. & Santa Fe; Mo.-Kan.-Tex. of Tex. (R. Rs.).
Gaithersburg, Montgomery Co., Md., 1,068.
On Balt. & Ohio (R. R.).
Galashiels, Selkirk, Scotland, 13,478.
Center of woolen industry.
Galati, Rumania, 101,148.
Commercial center. Industries produce lumber, candles, wire, chemicals, and refined petroleum.
Galatia, Saline Co., Ill., 933.
On Ill. Cen. (R. R.).
Galax, Carroll and Grayson Cos., Va., 2,544.
On Norf. & West.
Galena, c. s., Jo Daviess Co., Ill., 4,656
On Chi. & Nor. West.; Chi., Burl. & Quincy; Ill. Cen. (R. Rs.).
–Cherokee Co., Kans., 4,736.
On St. Lou.-San Fran.; Mo.-Kans.-Tex.; Southw. Mo. (El.) (R. Rs.).
–c. s., Stone Co., Mo., 508.
On Mo. Pac. (R. R.).
Galesburg, c. s., Knox Co., Ill., 28,830.
On Atch., Top. & Santa Fe; Chi., Burl. & Quincy; Rk. Isl. Sou. (R. Rs.).
A college town and a manufacturing center.
–Kalamazoo Co., Mich., 936.
On Mich. Cen. (R. R.).
Gales Ferry, New London Co., Conn., 500.
On N. York, N. Hav. & Hart. (R. R.).
Galesville, Trempealeau Co., Wis., 1,069.
On Chi. & Nor. West. (R. R.).
Galeton, Potter Co., Pa., 2,200.
On Balt. & Ohio (R. R.).
Galion, Crawford Co., Ohio, 7,674.
On Cle., Cin., Chi. & St. Lou.; Erie (R. Rs.).
Gallatin, c. s., Daviess Co., Mo., 1,504.
On Chi., Rk. Isl. & Pac.; Wab. (R. Rs.).
–Allegheny Co., Pa., 900.
On Pitts. & Erie (R. R.).
–c. s., Sumner Co., Tenn., 3,050.
On Lou. & Nash. (R. R.).
Galle, Ceylon, 38,424.
A seaport and secondary trade center.
Gallina, Rio Arriba Co., N. Mex., 588.
Gallipolis, c. s., Gallia Co., Ohio, 7,106.
On Chesa. & Ohio; N. York Cen. (R. Rs.).
Gallitzin, Cambria Co., Pa., 3,458.
On Penna. (R. R.).
Gallup, c. s., McKinley Co., N. Mex., 5,992.
On Atch., Top. & Santa Fe (R. R.).
Galt, Sacramento Co., Calif., 700.
On Sou. Pac. (R. R.).
–Waterloo, South Co., Ontario, Canada, 14,006.
On Can. Pac.; Gd. Riv. (El.); Can. Nat.; L. Erie & Nor. (El.) (R. Rs.).
An industrial center near Hamilton.
Galva, Henry Co., Ill., 2,875.
On Chi., Burl. & Quincy; Chi., Rk. Isl. & Pac. (R. Rs.).
–Ida Co., Iowa, 530.
On Chi. & Nor. West (R. R.).
Galveston, Cass Co., Indiana, 666.
Galveston, c. s., Galveston Co., Texas, 52,938.
One of the most important commercial ports of the Gulf States. Situated on Galveston Island, which is bounded by the Gulf of Mexico on the south and Galveston Bay on the north; joined by causeway with the mainland. The terminus of the Burlington-Rock Island; Galveston Wharf; the International-Great Northern; the Missouri-Kansas-Texas of Texas; the Gulf, Colorado & Santa Fe; the Galveston, Houston & Henderson, and the Texas & New Orleans railroads. It has regular steamship communications with European, Asiatic, Mexican and Cuban ports, and all important American ports by coastwise lines.
Galveston ranks high in exports of cotton and cottonseed products, and in value of foreign exports. Its chief manufactured products are cement, iron, ice, doors, sashes, leather goods, ships, and beer. Its most important buildings are the State Medical College, St. Mary's University, Ball High School, Scottish Rite Cathedral, and Cotton Exchange.
On its southern exposure it is protected from the Gulf by a granite sea-wall, 17 feet above the level of the sea, which is supported by earthen filling, extending two miles in width and five miles in length. This was erected after the disastrous storm of September, 1900, in which thousands of lives were lost, and property valued at over $10,000,000 was destroyed. The sea wall is two feet above the highest water of the 1900 storm.
The island was the resort of pirates until 1827. A charter of incorporation was granted in 1839.
Galway, Ireland. See Gaillimh.
Gambrills, Anne Arundel Co., Md., 500.
On Wash., Balt. & Annap. (El.) (R. R.).
Gamerco, McKinley Co., N. Mex., 600.
Ganado, Jackson Co., Tex., 626.
On Tex. & N. Orl. (R. R.).
Gananoque, Leeds Co., Ontario, Canada, 3,592.
On Thous. Isl. (R. R.).
Gand (Ghent), capital of East Flanders, Belgium, 167,084.
Situated at the confluence of the Lys with the Scheldt. The most notable buildings are the Cathedral of St. Bavon, the Churches of St. Nicholas, St. Michael, and St. Peter, the Château des Comtes, the university buildings, and the Institut des Sciences. Gand is famous for its linen; manufactures iron products, lace, machinery; exports grain, oil, and flax.
Gandara, Samar Prov., Samar, P. I., 14,231.
Gandzha (Elisavetopol), Soviet Union, 84,000.
Textile mills.
Gano, Payne Co., Okla., 500.
On Mo.-Kan.-Tex. (R. R.).
Gap, Hautes-Alpes, France, 13,600.
Gapan, Nueva Ecija Prov., Luzon, P. I., 14,144.
Garber City, Garfield Co., Okla., 1,356.
On Chi., Rk. Isl. & Pac. (R. R.).
Garcias (Garciasville P. O.), Starr Co., Tex., 650.
On St. Lou., Browns. & Mex. (R. R.).
Gardena, Los Angeles Co., Cal., 4,200.
On Pac. El.; Sou. Pac. (R. Rs.).
Garden City, c. s., Finney Co., Kans., 5,925.
On Atch., Top. & Santa Fe; Gard. Cy. West. (R. Rs.).
–St. Mary Par., La., 531.
On N. Iberia & Nor.; Tex. & N. Orl. (R. Rs.).
–Cass Co., Mo., 632.
On St. Lou.-San Fran. (R. R.).
–Nassau Co., N. Y., 7,180.
On Long Isl. (R. R.).
Garden Grove, Decatur Co., Iowa, 558.
On Chi., Burl. & Quincy (R. R.).
Gardenville, Erie Co., N. Y., 737.
On N. York Cen. (R. R.).
Gardiner, Kennebec Co., Maine, 5,609.
On Me. Cen. (R. R.).
Gardner, Grundy Co., Ill., 869.
On Alton (R. R.).
–Johnson Co., Kans., 541.
On Atch., Top., & Santa Fe (R. R.).
–Worcester Co., Mass., 20,397.
Noted for its chair and furniture factories.
On Bost. & Me. (R. R.).
Gardnerville, Douglas Co., Nev., 658.
Garfield, Bergen Co., N. J., 29,739.
On Erie (R. R.).
–Salt Lake Co., Utah, 2,010.
On Bingh. & Garf.; Den. & Rio Gde. West.; Un. Pac.; West. Pac. (R. Rs.).
–Whitman Co., Wash., 703.
On Gt. Nor.; Nor. Pac.; Ore.-Wash. R. R. & Nav. Co. (R. Rs.).
Garfield Heights, Cuyahoga Co., Ohio, 15,589.
A suburb of Cleveland.
Garland, Sampson Co., N. C., 509.
On Alt. Coast Line (R. R.).
–Dallas Co., Texas, 1,584.
On Gulf, Colo. & Santa Fe; Mo.-Kans.-Tex. of Tex. (R. Rs.).
–Box Elder Co., Utah, 824.
On Ore. Short Line (R. R.).
Garner, Hancock Co., Iowa, 1,241.
On Chi., Mil., St. P. & Pac.; Chi., Rk. Isl. & Pac. (R. Rs.).
Garnett, c. s., Anderson Co., Kans., 2,780.
On Atch., Top. & Santa Fe; Mo. Pac. (R. Rs.).
Garretson, Minnehaha Co., S. Dak., 677.
On Gt. Nor. (R. R.).
Garrett, De Kalb Co., Ind., 4,428.
On Balt. & Ohio; Ind. R. R. Sys. (El.) (R. Rs.).
–Floyd Co., Ky., 1,000.
On Chesa. & Ohio (R. R.).
–Somerset Co., Pa., 878.
On Balt. & Ohio; West. Md. (R. Rs.).
Garrettford, Delaware Co., Pa., 950.
Garrettsville, Portage Co., Ohio, 1,179.
Garrettsville-Hiram R. R. name. On Erie (R. R.).
Garrison, Baltimore Co., Md., 550.
–Putnam Co., N. Y., 530.
On N. York Cen. (R. R.).
–McLean Co., N. Dak., 1,024.
On Minn., St. P. & S. Ste. M. (R. R.).
–Nacogdoches Co., Texas, 527.
On Tex. & N. Orl. (R. R.).
Garwood, Union Co., N. J., 3,344.
On Cen. of N. Jer. (R. R.).
–Colorado Co., Tex., 600.
On Gulf, Colo. & Santa Fe (R. R.).
Gary, Lake Co., Ind., 100,426.
Seat of the largest steel industry in the U. S. Founded in 1906 in a wilderness of swamp and dunes on Lake Michigan. Traversed by river Calumet and located on the Balt. & Ohio; Chi. So. Shore & So. Bend (El.); the Elg., Jol. & East.; the Ind. Harbor Blt.; the Mich. Cen.; the N. York Cen.; the Penna.; and the Wab. railroads. Much iron ore is brought into the city, and much steel and coke go out. The plants occupy seven miles of the water front. Has excellent system of public schools.
–Deuel Co., S. Dak., 546.
On Chi. & Nor. West. (R. R.).
–Panola Co., Tex., 530.
On Gulf, Colo. & Santa Fe (R. R.).
Gas City, Grant Co., Ind., 3,087.
On Penna. (R. R.).
–Stephens Co., Okla., 500.
Gaskin City, Saline Co., Ill., 900.
Gasport, Niagara Co., N. Y., 600.
On N. York Cen. (R. R.).
Gassaway, Braxton Co., W. Va., 1,618.
On Balt. & Ohio (R. R.).
Gaston, Delaware Co., Indiana, 654.
On Chesa. & Ohio (R. R.).
Gastonia, c. s., Gaston Co., N. C., 17,093.
On Car. & Nor. West.; Piedmont & Nor. (El.); Sou. (R. Rs.).
Cotton yarn manufacturing center of the South.
Gastonville, Washington Co., Pa., 500.
Gate City, c. s., Scott Co., Va., 1,216.
On Southern (R. R.).
Gateshead, Durham, England, 122,379.
Industries include shipbuilding, iron founding, locomotive works, machine shops, and chemical plants.
Gates Mills, Cuyahoga Co., Ohio, 581.
Gatesville, c. s., Coryell Co., Texas, 2,601.
On St. Lou. Southw. (R. R.).
Gatewood, Ripley Co., Mo., 731.
Gauffs Hill, Lehigh Co., Pa., 650.
Gävle, Gävleborg, Sweden, 38,868.
Chief exports: iron and timber.
Gay, Logan Co., W. Va., 516.
On Chesa. & Ohio (R. R.).
Gaya, British India, 88,005.
A celebrated place of Hindu pilgrimage.
Gaylord, c. s., Otsego Co., Mich., 1,627.
On Mich. Cen. (R. R.).
–c. s., Sibley Co., Minn., 812.
On Minn. & St. Lou. (R. R.).
–Beaufort Co., N. C., 750.
Gay Mills, Crawford Co., Wisconsin, 579.
On Chi., Mil., St. P. & Pac. (R. R.).
Gaysport, Blair Co., Pa.
Gaza, Palestine. See Ghuzzeh.
Gaziantep (Aintab), Vilayet of Gaziantep, Turkey, 50,965.
Chief manufactures are haircloth, cotton goods, leather, and soap.
Gdynia, Poland, 114,000.
Established since 1920 and is now one of the chief seaports on the Baltic Sea.
Geary, Blaine and Canadian Cos., Okla., 1,892.
On Chi., Rk. Isl. & Pac. (R. R.).
Gebo, Hot Springs Co., Wyo., 894.
On Chi., Burl. & Quincy (R. R.).
Ged, Calcasieu Par., La., 500.
Geddes, Charles Mix Co., S. Dak., 609.
On Chi., Mil., St. P. & Pac. (R. R.).
Geelong, Victoria, Australia, 39,225.
A manufacturing center. Textiles, leather, flour, paper, and salt.
Geistown, Cambria Co., Pa., 871.
Gelsenkirchen, Westphalia, Germany, 336,227.
An important manufacturing center in the coal region of Westphalia.
Gembloux, Prov. of Namur, Belgium, 5,280.
Genazzano, Roma, Italy, 4,458.
Genesee, Latah Co., Idaho, 555.
On Nor. Pac. (R. R.).
Geneseo, Henry Co., Ill., 3,406.
On Chi., Rk. Isl. & Pac. (R. R.).
–Rice Co., Kansas, 516.
On Atch., Top. & Santa Fe; Mo. Pac. (R. Rs.).
–c. s., Livingston Co., N. Y., 2,261.
On Erie (R. R.).
Geneva, c. s., Geneva Co., Ala., 1,593.
On Lou. & Nash. (R. R.).
–c. s., Kane Co., Ill., 4,607.
On Chi. & Nor. West. (R. R.).
–Adams Co., Ind., 895.
On Penna. (R. R.).
–c. s., Fillmore Co., Neb., 1,662.
On Chi., Burl. & Quincy; Chi. & Nor. West. (R. Rs.).
–Ontario Co., N. Y., 16,053.
On Leh. Val.; N. York Cen. (R. Rs.).
In the heart of the Finger Lakes region of N. Y. State. Seat of Geneva and William Smith Colleges.
–Ashtabula Co., Ohio, 3,791.
On N. York Cen.; N. York, Chi. & St. Lou. (R. Rs.).
Genève (Geneva), capitol of Canton of Genève, Switzerland, 144,000.
Situated at the southwestern end of Lake Geneva, where the Rhone joins it. The wealthiest city of the country and third in population. The cathedral, consecrated in 1024, is marred by a Corinthian portico of the last century. The flamboyant Chappelle des Macchabees belongs to the fifteenth century. A fine monument erected to Duke Charles II. of Brunswick is 66 feet high. Other interesting objects are the town hall, the university, the Rath Musée (picture gallery), the Musée de l'Ariana, and the opera house. Genève was the birthplace of Rousseau. The city has a large trade, and manufactures watches, jewelry, toys, novelties, and musical boxes.
Genève became a center of the Reformation under the lead of John Calvin (1536-1564), who died here. In 1798 it was incorporated with France. In 1815 it entered with its canton into the Swiss Confederation. Under the Versailles Peace Treaty of 1919, following the World War, Genève was selected as the seat of the League of Nations.
Gennevilliers, Dept. of Seine, France, 29,369.
Genoa, De Kalb Co., Ill., 1,168.
On Chi., Mil., St. P. & Pac.; Ill. Cen. (R. Rs.).
–Nance Co., Neb., 1,089.
On Un. Pac. (R. R.).
–Ottawa Co., Ohio, 1,437.
On Lake Shore El.; N. York Cen.; Ohio Pub. Serv. (El.) (R. Rs.).
–Harris Co., Tex., 610.
On Galv., Houst. & Hend.; Internat.-Gt. Nor.; Mo.-Kan.-Tex. (R. Rs.).
Genoa City, Walworth Co., Wisc., 683.
On Chi. & Nor. West. (R. R.).
Genova (Genoa), Prov. of Genova, Italy, 347,483.
Seaport and commercial center, situated at the head of the Gulf of Genova, between the rivers Bisagno and Polcevera.
The most notable buildings are the ducal palace, one of the finest architectural structures now existing; the Doria, the Serra, the Palazzo Reale, the Cathedral of San Lorenzo, the Church of Carignano, Santa Stefano, L'Annunziata, and the Theatro Carlo Felice.
Long noted for fine velvets and silks.
Gensan, Chosen, 52,563.
Gentian, Muscogee Co., Ga., 500.
On Southern (R. R.).
Gentofte, Denmark, 62,471.
Gentry, Benton Co., Ark., 779.
On Kan. Cy. Sou. (R. R.).
George, Lyon Co., Iowa, 907.
On Ill. Cen. (R. R.).
Georgetown, capital of British Guiana, 64,931.
Seaport. Exports large quantities of sugar, gold, rum, balata, and rice.
–Malay States, 148,400.
–Halton Co., Ontario, Canada, 2,288.
On Can. Nat. (R. R.).
–Fairfield Co., Conn., 910.
On N. York, N. Hav. & Hart. (R. R.).
–District of Columbia (Sta. of Washington, D. C.).
On Balt. & Ohio (R. R.).
–c. s., Sussex Co., Del., 1,763.
On Penna. (R. R.).
–Vermilion Co., Ill., 3,407.
On Cle., Cin., Chi. & St. Lou.; Ill. Term. Sys. (El.) (R. Rs.).
–c. s., Scott Co., Ky., 4,229.
On Cin., N. Orl. & Tex. Pac.; Frankf. & Cin.; Sou. (R. Rs.).
–Essex Co., Mass., 2,009.
On Bost. & Me. (R. R.).
–c. s., Brown Co., Ohio, 1,531.
On Cin., Georgetown (R. R.).
–Kings Co., Prince Edward Island, Canada, 812.
–c. s., Georgetown Co., S. C., 5,082.
On Seab. Air Line (R. R.).
–c. s., Williamson Co., Texas, 3,583.
On Internat.-Gt. Nor.; Mo.-Kan.-Tex. of Tex. (R. Rs.).
George West, c. s., Live Oak Co., Tex., 500.
On San Ant., Uvalde & Gulf (R. R.).
Georgiana, Butler Co., Ala., 1,480.
On Lou. & Nash. (R. R.).
Gera, Germany, 83,000.
Gerardmer, Dept. of Vosges, France, 7,577.
Gerber, Tehama Co., Calif., 1,000.
On Sou. Pac. (R. R.).
Gering, c. s., Scotts Bluff Co., Neb., 2,531.
On Un. Pac. (R. R.).
Germantown, Clinton Co., Ill., 776.

On Southern (R. R.).
–Montgomery Co., Ohio, 2,029.
On Cin. Nor. (R. R.).
Germiston, Transvaal, U. So. Afr., 68,129.
Gerona, Tarlac Prov., Luzon, P. I., 14,856.
–Capital of Prov. of Gerona, Spain, 18,807.
Paper, cotton, and woolen goods.
Gettysburg, c. s., Potter Co., S. Dak., 1,400.
On Chi. & Nor. West. (R. R.).
–c. s., Adams Co., Pa., 5,584.
On Reading; West. Md. (R. Rs.).
Gettysburg battle, July 1-3, 1863, fought here.
Gevelsberg, Westphalia, Prussia, 20,688.
A manufacturing town near Hagen.
Geyserville, Sonoma Co., Calif., 619.
On Northw. Pac. (R. R.).
Ghazipur, United Provinces, India, 27,498.
Opium poppy growing in vicinity. Rose scent distilleries.
Gheel, Antwerp, Belgium, 18,545.
Center of a farming region.
Gheens, Lafourche Par., La., 500.
Ghent, Belgium. See Gand.
Ghuznigik, Afghanistan, estimated 10,000.
Ghuzzeh (Gaza), Palestine, 17,069.
A port exporting principally grain; some weaving.
Giarre, Prov. of Catania, Sicily, 9,321.
Gibara, Santiago Prov., Cuba, 6,868.
Gibbon, Sibley Co., Minn., 612.
On Minn. & St. Lou. (R. R.).
–Buffalo Co., Neb., 825.
On Un. Pac. (R. R.).
Gibbsboro, Camden Co., N. J., 622.
Gibraltar, 21,372.
A fortified rock and town in the possession of Great Britain since 1704. Situated at the southern extremity of the Spanish peninsula, and connected with the continent by a sandy isthmus.
Gibraltar, or the Pillar of Hercules, was regarded by the ancients as the western boundary of the world.
Gibsland (Gibbsland), Bienville Parish, La., 1,090.
On La. & Nor. West.; Yazoo & Miss. Val. (R. Rs.).
Gibson, Terrebonne Par., La., 500.
On Tex. & N. Orl. (R. R.).
Gibsonburg, Sandusky Co., Ohio, 2,129.
On Lake Shore El.; Penna. (R. Rs.).
Gibson City, Ford Co., Ill., 2,163.
On Ill. Cen.; N. York, Chi. & St. Lou.; Wab. (R. Rs.).
Gibsonville, Guilford and Alamance Cos., N. C., 1,605.
On Sou. (R. R.).
Giddings, c. s., Lee Co., Texas, 1,835.
On Tex. & N. Orl. (R. R.).
Gideon, New Madrid Co., Mo., 1,315.
On St. Lou.-San Fran.; St. Lou. Southw. (R. Rs.).
Giessen, Hesse, Germany, 34,000.
An educational and industrial center. Manufactures include castings, rubber goods, machinery, and beer.
Gifford, Indian River Co., Fla., 500.
On Fla. East Coast (R. R.).
Gifu, Honshu, Japan, 90,114.
Chief manufactures are silk and paper.
Gijon, Prov. of Oviedo, Spain, 78,239.
A seaport and industrial center. Exports coal, iron, zinc, and agricultural produce.
Gilbert, Maricopa Co., Ariz., 791.
On Sou. Pac. (R. R.).
–St. Louis Co., Minn., 2,722.
On Dul., Missabe & Nor. (R. R.).
Gilberton, Schuylkill Co., Pa., 4,227.
On Penna.; Read. (R. Rs.).
Gilbertsville, Montgomery Co., Pa., 521.
Gile, Iron Co., Wis., 500.
On Chi. & Nor. West. (R. R.).
Gill, Franklin Co., Mass., 995.
Gillespie, Macoupin Co., Ill., 5,111.
On Cle., Cin., Chi. & St. Lou.; Ill. Term. (El.) (R. Rs.).
–Fayette Co., Pa., 500.
Gillett, Arkansas Co., Arkansas, 870.
On St. Lou. Southw. (R. R.).
–Oconto Co., Wis., 1,076.
On Chi. & Nor. West. (R. R.).
Gillette, c. s., Campbell Co., Wyoming, 1,340.
On Chi., Burl. & Quincy (R. R.).
–Morris Co., N. J., 500.
On Del., Lack. & West. (R. R.).
Gilly, Prov. of Hainaut, Belgium, 25,301.
Coal mines in vicinity.
Gilman, Iroquois Co., Ill., 1,620.
On Ill. Cen.; Tol., Peor. & West. (R. Rs.).
–Harrison Co., Mo., 535.
On Quincy, Oma. & Kan. Cy. (R. R.).
–Essex Co., Vt., 750.
On Me. Cen. (R. R.).
Gilmanton, Belknap Co., N. H., 676.
Gilmer, c. s., Upshur Co., Texas, 1,963.
On St. Lou. Southw. (R. R.).
Gilmerton, Norfolk Co., Va., 628.
On Norf. & West. (R. R.).
Gilmore City, Pocahontas and Humboldt Cos., Ia., 896.
On Minn. & St. Lou. (R. R.).
Gilroy, Santa Clara Co., Calif., 3,502.
On Sou. Pac. (R. R.).
Ginatilan, Cebu Prov., P. I., 12,012.
Gioja Dal Colle, Prov. of Bari, Italy, 22,075.
A market town in a farming region.
Girard, Russell Co., Ala. (Pop. incl. in Phenix City).
On Cen. of Ga. (R. R.).
–Macoupin Co., Ill., 1,760.
On Alton; Chi. & Nor. West.; Chi., Burl. & Quincy; Ill. Term. (El.) (R. Rs.).
–c. s., Crawford Co., Kans., 2,598.
On Atch., Top. & Santa Fe; St. Lou.-San Fran.; Jop.-Pitts. (El.) (R. Rs.).
–Trumbull Co., Ohio, 9,859.
On Balt. & Ohio; Erie; Penna.; Youngst. & Nor. (R. Rs.).
–Erie Co., Pa., 1,554.
On Bess. & L. Erie; N. York, Chi. & St. Lou. (R. Rs.).
–Kent Co., Tex., 500.
Girardville, Schuylkill Co., Pa., 4,891.
On Leh. Val.; Read. (R. Rs.).
Girgenti, capital of Prov. of Girgenti, Sicily, 23,712.
Trade in olive oil, grain, and sulphur.
Gisborne, New Zealand, 15,885.
Seaport and commercial center.
Gisors, Dept. of Eure, France, 5,564.
Giurgiuo, Wallachia, Rumania, 24,503.
Principal exports are timber, grain, salt, and petroleum.
Gjinokaster (Agyrocastra), Albania, 10,836.
Famous for its snuff.
Glace Bay, Nova Scotia, Canada, 20,706.
Port and center of a coal-producing district.
Gladbach, Rhenish Prussia, Germany, 193,529.
Industrial town. Produces paper, castings, machinery, clay products, and nets.
Gladbrook, Tama Co., Iowa, 891.
On Chi. & Nor. West.; Chi. Gt. West. (R. Rs.).
Gladden, Dent Co., Mo., 670.
Glade Spring, Washington Co., Va., 669.
On Norf. & West. (R. R.).
Gladeville, Wise Co., Va. See Wise.
Gladewater, Gregg Co., Texas, 6,000.
On Tex. & Pac. (R. R.).
Gladstone, Delta Co., Mich., 5,170.
On Minn., St. P. & S. Ste. M. (R. R.).
–Clackamas Co., Oregon, 1,348.
–(Burmont), Delaware Co., Pa., 600.
Gladwin, c. s., Gladwin Co., Mich., 1,248.
On Mich. Cen. (R. R.).
Glasco, Cloud Co., Kans., 658.
On Un. Pac. (R. R.).
Glasford, Peoria Co., Ill., 671.
On Tol., Peor. & West. (R. R.).
Glasgow, Lanarkshire, Scotland, 1,088,417.
Situated on the river Clyde, is the most important and populous manufacturing and commercial city of Scotland. Noteworthy buildings are the Cathedral of St. Mungo, a splendid specimen of Gothic architecture, begun in 1123; the court-house, Royal Exchange, Traders' Hall, town hall and the Royal Infirmary. The University was founded in 1450, and has a library of 175,000 volumes. There are, besides the Andersonian University, the College of Physicians and the Mechanics' Institute. The great industries of the town are shipbuilding and engineering. The manufactures include steam tubes, boilers, locomotives, textiles, chemicals, sugar, tobacco, and beer.
Glasgow came into existence in 560, when St. Kentigern built an abbey there.
–c. s., Barren Co., Ky., 5,042.
On Lou. & Nash. (R. R.).
–Howard Co., Mo., 1,409.
On Alton; Wab. (R. Rs.).
–c. s., Valley Co., Mont., 2,216.
On Gt. Nor. (R. R.).
–Rockbridge Co., Va., 507.
On Chesa. & Ohio; Norf. & West. (R. Rs.).
–Kanawha Co., W. Va., 614.
On N. York Cen. (R. R.).
Glassport, Allegheny Co., Pa., 8,390.
On Pitts. & L. Erie (R. R.).
Glastonbury, Somerset, England, 4,515.
–Hartford Co., Conn., 4,000.
Nearest R. R. Sta. Hartford.
Glatz, Prussia, Germany, 18,000.
Center for a rich agricultural region.
Glauchau, Saxony, Germany, 29,000.
An industrial center producing textiles, paper, dyes, aluminum, thread, and machinery.
Glazov, R.S.F.S.R., Sov. Union, 11,300.
Gleason, Weakley Co., Tenn., 760.
On Nash., Chatt. & St. Lou. (R. R.).
Gleasonton, Clinton Co., Pa., 500.
Gleiwitz, Silesia, Germany, 111,082.
Trade and industrial center of a mining region.
Glen Alpine, Burke Co., N. C., 529.
On Southern (R. R.).
Glenbrook, Fairfield Co., Conn., 800.
On N. York, N. Hav. & Hart. (R. R.).
Glenburn, Lackawanna Co., Pa., 520.
On Del., Lack. & West. (R. R.).
Glen Campbell, Indiana Co., Pa., 588.
On N. York Cen.; Penna. (R. Rs.).
Glen Carbon, Madison Co., Ill., 1,340.
On Ill. Cen.; Litchf. & Mad.; N. York, Chi. & St. Lou. (R. Rs.).
Glencoe, Etowah Co., Ala., 800.
On Lou. & Nash. (R. R.).
–Cook Co., Ill., 6,295.
On Chi. & Nor. West.; Chi., Nor. Shore & Mil. (El.) (R. Rs.).
–c. s., McLeod Co., Minn., 1,925.
On Chi., Mil., St. P. & Pac. (R. R.).
–Lincoln Co., N. Mex., 575.
–Belmont Co., Ohio, 500.
On Balt. & Ohio (R. R.).
–Middlesex Co., West, Ontario, Canada, 788.
On Can. Pac.; Can. Nat.; Wab. (R. Rs.).
Glen Cove, Nassau Co., N. Y., 11,430.
On Long Isl. (R. R.).
Residential suburb of New York.
Glendale, Maricopa Co., Arizona, 3,665.
On Atch., Top. & Santa Fe (R. R.).
–Los Angeles Co., Cal., 62,736.
On Los Ang. & Salt L.; Pac. El.; Sou. Pac. (R. Rs.).
A residential suburb of Los Angeles. Has large potteries.
–St. Louis Co., Mo., 1,451.
On St. Lou.-San Fran.; Mo. Pac. (R. Rs.).
–Hamilton Co., Ohio, 2,360.
On Balt. & Ohio; Erie (R. Rs.).
–Douglas Co., Oregon, 516.
On Sou. Pac. (R. R.).
Glendive, c. s., Dawson Co., Mont., 4,629.
On Nor. Pac. (R. R.).
Glendon, Northampton Co., Pa., 615.
On Cen. of N. Jer. (R. R.).
Glendora, Los Angeles Co., Cal., 2,761.
On Atch., Top. & Santa Fe; Pac. El. (R. Rs.).
Glen Elder, Mitchell Co., Kans., 609.
On Mo. Pac. (R. R.).
Glen Ellyn, Du Page Co., Ill., 7,680.
On Chi., Aur. & Elg.; Chi. & Nor. West. (R. Rs.).
Glenfield, Allegheny Co., Pa., 950.
On Penna. (R. R.).
Glen Flora, Wharton Co., Tex., 500.
On Gulf, Colo. & Santa Fe (R. R.).
Glen Garden, Tarrant Co., Tex., 500.
Glen Gardner, Hunterdon Co., N. J., 554.
On Cen. of N. Jer. (R. R.).
Glenham, Dutchess Co., N. Y., 500.
On N. York, N. Hav. & Hart. (R. R.).
Glen Jean, Fayette Co., W. Va., 1,000.
On Chesa. & Ohio; Kanaw., Gl. Jean & East. (R. Rs.).
Glenmora, Rapids Parish, La., 1,875.
On Mo. Pac. (R. R.).
Glennie, Alcona Co., Mich., 500.
Glenns Ferry, Elmore Co., Idaho, 1,414.
On Ore. Short Line.
Glennville, Tattnall Co., Ga., 1,503.
On Col. & Glennv. (R. R.).
Glenolden, Delaware Co., Pa., 4,482.
On Balt. & Ohio; Penna. (R. Rs.).
Glen Park, Jefferson Co., N. Y., 559.
Glen Ridge, Essex Co., N. J., 7,365.
On Del., Lack. & West.; Erie (R. Rs.).
Glen Rock, Bergen Co., N. J., 4,369.
On Erie (R. R.).
–York Co., Pa., 1,309.
On Penna. (R. R.).
–Converse Co., Wyo., 819.
On Chi. & Nor. West.; Chi., Burl. & Quincy (R. Rs.).
Glen Rose, c. s., Somervell Co., Texas, 983.
Glens Falls, Warren Co., N. Y., 18,531.
On Del. & Hud. (R. R.).
Manufactures paper, shirts, collars, cement, etc. A summer resort for Adirondack tourists.
Glenshaw, Allegheny Co., Pa., 500.
On Balt. & Ohio (R. R.).
Glen Ullin, Morton Co., N. Dak., 950.
On Nor. Pac. (R. R.).
Glenview, Cook Co., Ill., 1,886.
On Chi., Mil., St. P. & Pac.; Chi., No. Shore & Mil. (El.) (R. Rs.).
Glenville, Fairfield Co., Conn., 999.
–c. s., Gilmer Co., W. Va., 799.
Glen White, Raleigh Co., W. Va., 519.
On Chesa. & Ohio; Virginian (R. Rs.).
Glenwillard, Allegheny Co., Pa., 650.
On Pitts. & L. Erie (R. R.).
Glenwood, Pike Co., Ark., 1,310.
On Mo. Pac. (R. R.).
–Wheeler Co., Ga., 569.
On Seab. Air Line (R. R.).
–Cook Co., Illinois, 603.
On Balt. & Ohio Chi. Term.; Chi. & East Ill. (R. Rs.).
–c. s., Mills Co., Iowa, 4,269.
On Chi., Burl. & Quincy (R. R.).
–c. s., Pope Co., Minn., 2,220.
On Minn., St. P. & S. Ste. M.; Nor. Pac. (R. Rs.).
Glenwood City, St. Croix Co., Wis., 771.
On Minn., St. P. & S. Ste. M. (R. R.).
Glenwood Springs, c. s., Garfield Co., Colo., 1,825.
On Den. & Rio Gde. West. (R. R.).
Noted for its mineral waters. A health and pleasure resort.
Glidden, Carroll Co., Iowa, 854.
On Chi. & Nor. West. (R. R.).
–Ashland Co., Wis., 760.
On Minn., St. P. & S. Ste. M. (R. R.).
Globe, c. s., Gila Co., Ariz., 7,157.
On Sou. Pac. (R. R.).
Glocester, Providence Co., R. I., 1,901.
Glogau, Prussia, Germany, 27,000.
Important industrial town. Castings, machinery, printing, tobacco, and sugar.
Glomawr, Perry Co., Ky., 650.
On Lou. & Nash. (R. R.).
Gloryetta, Orange Co., Calif., 700.
Glossop, Derbyshire, England, 19,510.
A market town. Has manufactures of woolen goods, paper, dyes, and printing.
Gloster, De Soto Par., La., 500.
On Tex. & Pac. (R. R.).
–Amite Co., Miss., 1,139.
On Yazoo & Miss. Val. (R. R.).
Gloucester, capital of Gloucestershire, England, 52,937.
A seaport and commercial center. Chief industries produce matches, rope, lumber, chemicals, agricultural implements, and boats.
–Essex Co., Mass., 24,164.
On Bost. & Me. (R. R.).
A summer resort and artists' mecca. First settled in 1623; incorporated a town in 1643; a city since 1873. The creed of Universalism was established here in 1770. The city has granite quarries, boatbuilding plants and manufactures fish products, glue, shoes, machinery, nets, and twine.
Gloucester City, Camden Co., N. J., 13,796.
On Penna.-Read. Seashore (R. R.).
An industrial suburb of Camden.
Glouster, Athens Co., Ohio, 2,903.
On N. York Cen. (R. R.).
Gloversville, Fulton Co., N. Y., 23,099.
Chief industry is glove-making.
On Fonda, Johnst. & Glovers. (R. R.).
Glückstadt, Prussia, Germany, 6,823.
Gmünd, Württemberg, Germany, 21,000.
Clocks, watches, and optical instruments.
Gnadenhutten, Tuscarawas Co., Ohio, 870.
On Penna. (R. R.).
Gniezno (Gnesen), Poznan, Poland, 29,924.
A trade and industrial town. Textiles, beer, and spirits.
Gôa, Portuguese Prov. of Gôa, India, 23,000.
Gobles, Van Buren Co., Mich., 519.
On Mich. Cen. (R. R.).
Goderich, Ontario, Canada, 4,491.
On Can. Pac.; Can. Nat. (R. Rs.).
Godhavn, capital of Danish possession of Greenland, 301.
Godth, Greenland, 588.
Goffstown, Hillsborough Co., N. H., 850.
On Bost. & Me. (R. R.).
Golconda, c. s., Pope Co., Ill., 1,184.
On Ill. Cen. (R. R.).
Golden, c. s., Jefferson Co., Colo., 2,426.
Situated on Clear Creek, 14 miles west of Denver, and on the Colorado & Southern and Denver & Intermountain (Electric) railroads. Leading industries are porcelain and brick making. Seat of Colorado School of Mines.
–Adams Co., Ill., 567.
On Chi., Burl. & Quincy; Wab. (R. Rs.).
–Tishomingo Co., Miss., 569.
On Ill. Cen. (R. R.).
Golden City, Barton Co., Mo., 828.
On St. Lou.-San Fran. (R. R.).
Goldendale, c. s., Klickitat Co., Wash., 1,116.
On Spok., Port. & Seattle (R. R.).
Goldens Bridge, Westchester Co., N. Y., 500.
On N. York Cen. (R. R.).
Golden Valley, Hennepin Co., Minn., 1,326.
Goldfield, Wright Co., Iowa, 700.
On Chi. & Nor. West.; Chi., Rk. Isl. & Pac. (R. Rs.).
Gold Hill, Jackson Co., Ore., 502.
On Sou. Pac. (R. R.).
Goldsboro, c. s., Wayne Co., N. C., 14,985.
On Alt. Coast Line; Norf. Sou.; Sou. (R. Rs.).
Lumber and tobacco are the principal products.
Goldthwaite, c. s., Mills Co., Texas, 1,324.
On Gulf, Colo. & Santa Fe (R. R.).
Goleta, Santa Barbara Co., Calif., 582.
On Sou. Pac. (R. R.).
Goliad, c. s., Goliad Co., Texas, 1,428.
On Tex. & N. Orl. (R. R.).
Gomel, White Russia, Sov. Union, 121,200.
Iron foundries and machine shops.
Gonaives, Haiti, 10,000.
Gondar, Ethiopia, 3,000.
Gonzales, c. s., Gonzales Co., Texas, 3,859.
On Tex. & N. Orl. (R. R.).
Gonzalez, Escambia Co., Fla., 500.
On Lou. & Nash. (R. R.).
Good Hope, St. Charles Par., La., 500.
On La. & Ark.; Yazoo & Miss. Val. (R. Rs.).
Gooding, c. s., Gooding Co., Idaho, 1,592.
On Oregon Short Line (R. R.).
Seat of Gooding College.
Goodland, Newton Co., Ind., 978.
On Chi., Attica & Sou.; Penna. (R. Rs.).

–c. s., Sherman Co., Kans., 3,212.
On Chi., Rk. Isl. & Pac. (R. R.).
GOODLETTSVILLE, Davidson Co., Tenn., 919.
On Lou. & Nash. (R. R.).
GOODMAN, Holmes Co., Miss., 608.
On Ill. Cen. (R. R.).
GOOD PINE, La Salle Par., La., 1,000.
On La. & Ark. (R. R.).
GOODRICH, Polk Co., Tex., 500.
On Tex. & N. Orl. (R. R.).
GOODWATER, Coosa Co., Ala., 996.
On Cen. of Ga. (R. R.).
GOODWELL, Texas Co., Okla., 501.
On Chi., Rk. Isl. & Pac. (R. R.).
GOODWINS MILLS, York Co., Me., 575.
GOOLE, Yorkshire, West, England, 20,238.
A river port near Hull.
GOOSE CREEK, Harris Co., Texas, 5,208.
On Mo. Pac.; Southern Pac. (R. Rs.).
GÖPPINGEN, Württemberg, Germany, 22,000.
GORAKHPUR, capital of Dist. of Gorakhpur, British India, 57,985.
An agricultural center and military station.
GORDO, Pickens Co., Ala., 811.
On Mob. & Ohio (R. R.).
GORDON, Wilkinson Co., Ga., 1,199.
On Cen. of Ga. (R. R.).
–Sheridan Co., Neb., 1,958.
On Chi. & Nor. West. (R. R.).
–Schuylkill Co., Pa., 1,069.
On Reading (R. R.).
–Palo Pinto Co., Tex., 510.
On Tex. & Pac. (R. R.).
GOREVILLE, Johnson Co., Ill., 531.
On Chi. & East. Ill.; Chi., Burl. & Quincy (R. Rs.).
GORHAM, Cumberland Co., Maine, 1,088.
On Bost. & Me. (R. R.).
–Coos Co., N. H., 2,763.
On Bost. & Me.; Gd. Tr. (R. Rs.).
GORI, Georgian Republic, Sov. Union, 13,100.
GORINCHEM, South Holland, Netherlands, 14,034.
Agricultural trade center.
GORIZIA (Gorz), Italy, 32,800.
In the World War of 1914-18 the city was captured by the Italians (1916), to whom it passed from Austria after the peace.
GORKI (Nizhni-Novgorod), R.S.F.S.R. Soviet Union, 451,500.
A river port and very important commercial center. Site of a large annual trade fair.
GÖRLITZ, Silesia, Germany, 92,000.
On the left bank of the Neisse. Among its Gothic churches is that of St. Peter and St. Paul (1423-1497). Outside the town is the Kreuzkapelle (1481-1489), an imitation of the Holy Sepulchre. A railway viaduct, 2,720 feet in length and 118 feet high, here crosses the valley of the Neisse. Görlitz manufactures textile wares; there are also iron foundries and machine shops, glass works and tobacco factories. Görlitz was taken and held alternately by the Swedes and the Imperialists during the Thirty Years' War.
GORMAN, Eastland Co., Tex., 1,154.
On Mo.-Kan.-Tex. of Tex. (R. R.).
GORZ, Italy. See GORIZIA.
GOSHEN, c. s., Orange Co., N. Y., 2,891.
On Erie; Leh. & N. Eng. (R. Rs.).
–c. s., Elkhart Co., Ind., 10,397.
On Cle., Cin., Chi. & St. Lou.; N. York Cen.; Winona (El.) (R. Rs.).
Manufactures chiefly woodwork.
–Utah Co., Utah, 669.
On Den. & Rio Gde. West. (R. R.).
GOSLAR, Prussia, Germany, 22,000.
Situated in a mining region of the Harz Mountains.
GOSPORT, Southampton, England, 37,928.
–Owen Co., Ind., 722.
On Chi., Ind. & Lou.; Penna. (R. Rs.).
GOTEBO, Kiowa Co., Oklahoma, 827.
On Chi., Rk. Isl. & Pac. (R. R.).
GOTEBORG (Gothenburg), capital of Län of Goteborg, Sweden, 262,676.
A seaport, the second in importance in Sweden. A well-built town. Situated at the mouth of the Gota. The manufactures include sail-cloth, cotton, and other goods. There are shipbuilding yards, iron works, breweries, and sugar refineries. The trade is very extensive. The harbor is defended by forts, and there is a dry dock cut in the solid rock. The completion of the Gota Canal and railway facilities have increased the city's importance.
GOTHA, capital of Saxe-Coburg-Gotha, Germany, 48,000.
Industries produce rubber goods, machinery, furniture, toys, porcelain, and printing.
GOTHENBURG, Sweden. See GOTEBORG.
–Dawson Co., Neb., 2,322.
On Un. Pac. (R. R.).
GÖTTINGEN, Hannover, Germany, 47,149.
Seat of the University of Göttingen, founded by George II.; royal academy of sciences.
GOUDA, Prov. of South Holland, Netherlands, 29,162.
Famous for its cheeses.
GOULBURN, New South Wales, Australia, 14,849.
An agricultural trade center.

GOULD, Lincoln Co., Ark., 827.
On Ark.; Mo. Pac. (R. Rs.).
GOULDSBORO (Sand Cut), Wayne Co., Pa., 621.
On Del., Lack. & West. (R. R.).
GOUROCK, Renfrew Co., Scotland, 8,844.
GOUVERNEUR, St. Lawrence Co., N. Y., 4,015.
On N. York Cen. (R. R.).
GOWANDA, Cattaraugus and Erie Cos., N. Y., 3,042.
On Erie (R. R.).
GOWRIE, Webster Co., Iowa, 1,059.
On Chi. & Nor. West.; Chi., Rk. Isl. & Pac.; Ft. Dodge, Des Moines & Sou.; Minn. & St. Lou. (R. Rs.).
GOYAZ, capital of Goyaz, Brazil, 21,223.
An inland trade center.
GRAAF-REYNET, Un. of S. Africa, Africa, 9,222.
GRACE, Bannock Co., Idaho, 626.
On Ore. Short Line (R. R.).
GRACETON, Indiana Co., Pa., 500.
On Penna. (R. R.).
GRACEVILLE, Jackson Co., Fla., 1,165.
On Lou. & Nash. (R. R.).
–Big Stone Co., Minn., 969.
On Chi., Mil., St. P. & Pac.; Gt. Nor. (R. Rs.).
GRACEWOOD, Richmond Co., Ga., 500.
On Ga. & Fla. (R. R.).
GRAETTINGER, Palo Alto Co., Iowa, 777.
On Chi., Rk. Isl. & Pac. (R. R.).
GRAFTON, Jersey Co., Ill., 1,026.
On Ill. Term. (El.) (R. R.).
–Worcester Co., Mass., 7,686.
On Graf. & Upton (El.) (R. R.).
–Rensselaer Co., N. Y., 572.
–c. s., Walsh Co., N. Dak., 3,136.
On Gt. Nor.; Nor. Pac. (R. Rs.).
–Lorain Co., Ohio, 935.
On Balt. & Ohio; Cle., Cin., Chi. & St. Lou. (R. Rs.).
–c. s., Taylor Co., W. Va., 7,737.
On Balt. & Ohio (R. R.).
–Ozaukee Co., Wis., 1,065.
On Chi., Mil., St. P. & Pac.; Mil. El. (R. Rs.).
GRAHAM, c. s., Alamance Co., N. C., 2,972.
On Southern (R. R.).
–c. s., Young Co., Texas, 4,981.
On Chi., Rk. Isl. & Gulf; Wichita Fs. & Sou. (R. Rs.).
–Tazewell Co., Va. See BLUEFIELD.
GRAHAMSTOWN, capital of Albany Dist., Cape of Good Hope, Union of S. Africa, 19,768.
GRAMMICHELE, Prov. of Catania, Italy, 24,000.
A trade center.
GRAMMONT, Prov. of East Flanders, Belgium, 12,664.
GRAMPIAN, Clearfield Co., Pa., 533.
On Penna. (R. R.).
GRANADA, capital of Prov. of Granada, Andalusia, Spain, 118,179.
Formerly the Moorish capital. The Alhambra, a Moorish palace, the finest extant specimen of Moorish architecture. Other fine edifices are the unfinished palace of Charles V., the Generalife, the Puerta Judicaria, the Alcazaba, and the cathedral.
In 1235 Granada was a splendid city. After the expulsion of the Moors from Spain it declined rapidly.
–Capital of Dept. of Granada, Nicaragua, 27,120.
GRANBURY, c. s., Hood Co., Texas, 996.
On Ft. Worth & Rio Gde. (R. R.).
GRANBY, Hartford Co., Conn., 625.
On N. York, N. Hav. & Hart. (R. R.).
–Hampshire Co., Mass., 956.
–Newton Co., Mo., 1,445.
On Mo. Pac.; St. Lou.-San Fran. (R. Rs.).
–Shefford Co., Quebec, Canada, 10,587.
On Can. Nat.; Montr. & So. Cos. (El.) (R. Rs.).
A suburb of Montreal.
GRAND BLANC, Genesee Co., Mich., 917.
On Pere Marq. (R. R.).
GRAND CANYON, Coconino Co., Ariz., 550.
On Atch., Top. & Santa Fe (R. R.).
GRAND COTEAU, St. Landry Par., La., 580.
GRANDFIELD, Tillman Co., Okla., 1,416.
On Chi., Rk. Isl. & Pac.; Mo.-Kans.-Tex. (R. Rs.).
GRAND FORKS, British Columbia, Canada, 1,298.
On Can. Pac.; Gt. Nor. (R. Rs.).
–c. s., Grand Forks Co., N. Dak., 17,112.
On Great Northern; Northern Pacific (R. Rs.).
Location of University of North Dakota and Wesley Colleges.
Manufactures flour, sashes and doors, packing plant products, dairy products, brick, etc. Distributing center.
GRAND GORGE, Delaware Co., N. Y., 600.
On West Shore (R. R.).
GRAND HAVEN, c. s., Ottawa Co., Mich., 8,345.
On Gd. Tr.; Pere Marq. (R. Rs.).
GRAND ISLAND, c. s., Hall Co., Neb., 18,041.
On Chi., Burl. & Quincy; St. Jos. & Gd. Isl.; Un. Pac. (R. Rs.).
An extensive horse market.
–Erie Co., N. Y., 500.
GRAND ISLE, Aroostook Co., Maine, 600.
On Bangor & Aroostook (R. R.).
–Grand Isle Co., Vt., 500.
On Rutland (R. R.).

INTERIOR OF THE ALHAMBRA, GRANADA, SPAIN

GRAND JUNCTION, c. s., Mesa Co., Colo., 10,247.
On Den. & Rio Gde. West. (R. R.).
The center of an extensive irrigated region.
–Greene Co., Iowa, 1,025.
On Chi. & Nor. West.; Minn. & St. Lou. (R. Rs.).
–Hardeman Co., Tenn., 524.
On Ill. Cen.; Sou. (R. Rs.).
GRAND LEDGE, Eaton Co., Mich., 3,572.
On Pere Marq. (R. R.).
GRAND MARAIS, Alger Co., Mich., 650.
–Cook Co., Minn., 618.
GRAND MEADOW, Mower Co., Minn., 585.
On Chi., Mil., St. P. & Pac. (R. R.).
GRAND MÈRE, Champlain Co., Quebec, Canada, 6,461.
On Can. Nat.; Can. Pac. (R. Rs.).
GRAND NARROWS, Cape Breton Co., Nova Scotia, Canada, 302.
GRAND PRAIRIE, Dallas Co., Texas, 1,529.
On Tex. & Pac. (R. R.).
GRAND RAPIDS, c. s., Kent Co., Mich., 168,592.
Situated on both sides of the Grand River, and on the Michigan Central, the New York Central, the Grand Trunk, the Pere Marquette, the Pennsylvania railroads.
The Grand River supplies excellent water-power for the city's extensive manufactures, comprising furniture, flour, machinery, automobiles, band instruments, flypaper, printing, paper boxes, knit goods, asphalt shingles, carpet sweepers, auto bodies, etc. The gypsum quarries of Grand Rapids have a large output. The manufacture of furniture is the principal industry, the value of the yearly output amounting to millions of dollars. Another important manufacture is plaster.
The noteworthy structures include the City Hall, Grand Rapids Savings Bank, Michigan Trust Building, Blodgett Memorial Hospital, Masonic Temple, Pantlind Hotel, Rowe Hotel, and Morton House.
Grand Rapids was the site of an Indian village in 1760, was settled in 1833, and incorporated as a city in 1850.
–c. s., Itasca Co., Minn., 3,206.
On Gt. Nor. (R. R.).
–Wood Co., Ohio, 589.
On N. York, Chi. & St. Lou. (R. R.).
–Wood Co., Wis. See WISCONSIN RAPIDS.
GRAND SALINE, Van Zandt Co., Tex., 1,799.
On Tex. & Pac.; Tex. Short Line (R. Rs.).
GRAND TOWER, Jackson Co., Ill., 953.
On Ill. Cen. (R. R.).
GRAND VIEW, Spencer Co., Ind., 588.
–Johnson Co., Texas, 892.

On Mo.-Kan.-Tex. of Tex. (R. R.).
–Yakima Co., Wash., 1,085.
On Nor. Pac.; Ore.-Wash. R. R. & Nav. Co. (R. Rs.).
GRANDVIEW, Jackson Co., Mo., 707.
On Kan. Cy. Sou.; St. Lou.-San Fran. (R. Rs.).
GRANDVIEW HEIGHTS, Franklin Co., Ohio, 6,358.
GRANDVILLE, Kent Co., Mich., 1,346.
On Pere Marq. (R. R.).
GRANGER, Williamson Co., Texas, 1,703.
On Mo.-Kan.-Tex. of Tex. (R. R.).
–Yakima Co., Wash., 568.
On Nor. Pac.; Ore.-Wash. R. R. & Nav. Co. (R. Rs.).
GRANGEVILLE, c. s., Idaho Co., Idaho, 1,360.
On Camas Prairie Nor. Pac.; Un. Pac. Sys. (R. Rs.).
GRANITE, Greer Co., Okla., 1,341.
On Chi., Rk. Isl. & Pac. (R. R.).
GRANITE CITY, Madison Co., Ill., 25,130.
On Alton; Alton & Sou.; Balt. & Ohio; Chi., Burl. & Quincy; Chi. & East. Ill.; Cle., Cin., Chi. & St. Lou.; Ill. Term. (El.); Litchf. & Mad.; Lou. & Nash.; Penna.; N. York, Chi. & St. Lou.; Term. R. R. Assn.; Wab. (R. Rs.).
A busy manufacturing suburb of St. Louis, Mo.
GRANITE FALLS, c. s., Yellow Medicine and Chippewa Cos., Minn., 1,791.
On Chi., Mil., St. P. & Pac.; Gt. Nor. (R. Rs.).
–Caldwell Co., N. C., 2,147.
On Car. & Nor. West. (R. R.).
GRANITE QUARRY, Rowan Co., N. C., 507.
On Yadkin (R. R.).
GRANITEVILLE, Iron Co., Mo., 600.
–Washington Co., Vt., 1,200.
GRANT, c. s., Perkins Co., Neb., 798.
On Chi., Burl. & Quincy (R. R.).
–Grant Co., W. Va., 700.
On West. (R. R.).
GRANT CITY, c. s., Worth Co., Mo., 1,126.
On Chi., Burl. & Quincy (R. R.).
GRANTHAM, Lincolnshire, England, 19,709.
The market center of an agricultural region.
GRANT PARK, Kankakee Co., Ill., 508.
On Chi. & East. Ill. (R. R.).
GRANTS, Valencia Co., N. Mex., 800.
On Atch., Top. & Santa Fe (R. R.).
–Pamlico Co., N. C., 500.
On Norf. Sou. (R. R.).
GRANTSBORO, Pamlico Co., N. C., 500.
GRANTSBURG, c. s., Burnett Co., Wis., 777.
On Nor. Pac. (R. R.).
GRANTS PASS, c. s., Josephine Co., Ore., 4,666.
On Cal. & Ore. Coast; Sou. Pac. (R. Rs.).

noteworthy of the public buildings. Cocoa is the chief export. Other items are coffee, ivory, nuts, rubber, hides, and Panama hats. The city was founded by Orellana in 1537.

GUAYMAS, Sonora, Mexico, 8,786.
On Sou. Pac. of Mex. (R. R.).

GUAYNABO, Mun. of Guaynabo, Puerto Rico, 1,181.

GUBAT, Sorsogon Prov., Luzon, P. I., 19,483.

GUBBIO, Prov. of Perugia, Italy, 6,284.

GUBEN, Germany, 44,000.
Weaving, dyeing, and papermaking.

GUELMA, Dept. of Constantine, Algeria, 9,390.

GUELPH, c. s., Willington, Ontario, 21,075.
On Can. Pac.; Can. Nat. (R. Rs.).
A busy agricultural center.

GUERNEVILLE, Sonoma Co., Calif., 800.
On Northw. Pac. (R. R.).

GUERNSEY, Platte Co., Wyo., 656.
On Colo. & Wyo.; Chi., Burl. & Quincy (R. Rs.).

GUERRERO, State of Coahuila, Mexico, 1,029.

GUEYDAN, Vermilion Parish, La., 1,313.
On Tex. & N. Orl. (R. R.).

GUFFEY, Westmoreland Co., Pa., 612.
On Balt. & Ohio (R. R.).

GUIDE ROCK, Webster Co., Neb., 690.
On Chi., Burl. & Quincy (R. R.).

GUILFORD, c. s., Surrey, England, 30,753.
A grain market.
—New Haven Co., Conn., 1,880.
On N. York, N. Hav. & Hart. (R. R.).
—Piscataquis Co., Maine, 1,500.
On Bangor & Aroostook (R. R.).

GUILFORD COLLEGE, Guilford Co., N. C.
On Southern (R. R.).

GUIN, Marion Co., Ala., 1,099.
On St. Lou.-San Fran. (R. R.).

GUINDULMAN, Bohol Prov., Bohol, P. I., 13,347.

GUINES, Prov. of Habana, Cuba, 13,679.
The center of a rich tobacco-growing region.

GUINOBATAN, Albay Prov., Luzon, P. I., 26,740.
Abaca and rice growing.

GUIUAN, Samar Prov., Samar, P. I., 15,435.

GULF HAMMOCK, Levy Co., Fla., 600.
On Atl. Coast Line (R. R.).

GULFPORT, Pinellas Co., Fla., 1,036.
On Seab. Air Line (R. R.).
—c. s., Harrison Co., Miss., 12,547.
On Gulf & Ship Isl.; Lou. & Nash. (R. Rs.).
A port of entry with extensive exports of southern yellow pine lumber. It has a U. S. naval training station, and the Gulf Coast Military and Naval Academy.

GUMBINNEN, Prussia, Germany, 19,000.
An industrial and agricultural center.

GUMMERSBACH, Prussia, Germany, 18,000.

GUM RUN, Luzerne Co., Pa., 500.
On Leh. Val.; Penna. (R. Rs.).

GUNNISON, c. s., Gunnison Co., Colo., 1,415.
On Den. & Rio Gde. West. (R. R.).
—Sanpete Co., Utah, 1,057.
On Den. & Rio Gde. West. (R. R.).

GUNTERSVILLE, c. s., Marshall Co., Ala., 2,826.
On Nash., Chatta. & St. Lou. (R. R.).

GURABO, Mun. of Gurabo, Puerto Rico, 3,242.

GURDON, Clark Co., Ark., 2,172.
On Mo. Pac. (R. R.).

GURLEY, Madison Co., Ala., 581.
On Southern (R. R.).

GURNEE, Lake Co., Ill., 503.
On Chi., Mil., St. P. & Pac. (R. R.).

GUSTINE, Merced Co., Cal., 1,016.
On Sou. Pac. (R. R.).

GÜSTROW, Mecklenburg-Schwerin, Germany, 22,464.

GUTHRIE, Todd Co., Ky., 1,272.
On Lou. & Nash. (R. R.).
—c. s., Logan Co., Okla., 9,582.
On Cottonwood Creek, and on the Atchison, Topeka & Santa Fe; the Fort Smith & Western and the Oklahoma railroads.
The city has an extensive trade in wholesale merchandise; among the industrial establishments are cottonseed oil, planing, and flouring mills, mattress factory, foundry and machine shops, and basket and broom works. The oil industry is also developing in the vicinity. The city has curative mineral waters derived from artesian wells, and has established a novel bath house—the only municipal institution of its kind—for visitors seeking hydrotherapeutic treatment.
Guthrie was founded in 1889, became the territorial capital in 1890 and the State capital in 1907. Capital changed to Oklahoma City in 1913. First constitutional convention was held in Guthrie, November 20, 1906.

GUTHRIE CENTER, c. s., Guthrie Co., Iowa, 1,813.
On Chi., Rk. Isl. & Pac. (R. R.).

GUTTENBURG, Clayton Co., Iowa, 1,918.
On Chi., Mil., St. P. & Pac. (R. R.).
—Hudson Co., N. J., 6,535.

GUYANDOTTE, Cabell Co., W. Va. (Sta. Huntington P. O.).
On Balt. & Ohio; Chesa. & Ohio (R. Rs.).

GUYMON, c. s., Texas Co., Okla., 2,181.
On Chi., Rk. Isl. & Pac. (R. R.).

GUYTON, Effingham Co., Ga., 583.
On Cen. of Ga. (R. R.).

GWALIOR, Gwalior Prov., India, 21,999.

An industrial center in a cotton growing region.

GWYNN, Mathews Co., Va., 540.

GYMPIE, Queensland, Australia, 9,131.

GYMRI, Soviet Union. See LENINAKAN.

GYOR (or Raab), Hungary, 50,977.
An agricultural center. Has textile mills.

GYPSUM, Saline Co., Kans., 657.
On Mo. Pac. (R. R.).
—Ottawa Co., Ohio, 740.
On N. York Cen. (R. R.).

GYULA, Rumania, 25,221.

H

HAARLEM, North Holland, Netherlands, 129,126.
An industrial suburb of Amsterdam.

HAARLEMMERMEER, Netherlands, 26,793.

HABANA (Havana), Prov. of Habana, Cuba, capital of Cuban Republic, 589,079.
An important commercial point. Its harbor is one of the finest in the world. The city is divided into two sections, the older one of which has narrow, crooked streets, while the modern Habana has broad avenues, lined with palm trees. Among the notable buildings are the opera house (Teatro Tacon); the cathedral, built in 1724; the Government buildings, and the celebrated fortresses, Morro Castle and Punta, at the mouth of the harbor; and La Cabana, a fortress southeast of Morro. The city has a university and large botanical gardens.
The manufactures include chocolate, sugar, liquors, woolens, and straw hats. The cigars made in Habana are world famous. Sugar, tobacco, molasses, and beeswax are exported. Habana was founded by Velasquez in 1519.

HACKBERRY, Cameron Par., La., 800.

HACKENSACK, c. s., Bergen Co., N. J., 24,568.
On N. Jer. & N. York; N. York, Susq. & West. (R. Rs.).
A residential suburb of New York. Has textile and paper mills.

HACKETT, Washington Co., Pa., 525.
On Balt. & Ohio (R. R.).

HACKETTSTOWN, Warren Co., N. J., 3,038.
On Del., Lack. & West. (R. R.).
Seat of Centenary Collegiate Institute (Methodist) and State Fish Hatchery.

HACKLEBURG, Marion Co., Ala., 628.
On Ill. Cen. (R. R.).

HADDAM, Middlesex Co., Conn., 700.
On N. York, N. Hav. & Hart. (R. R.).

HADDINGTON, capital of East Lothian, Scotland, 4,405.

HADDONFIELD, Camden Co., N. J., 8,857.
On Penna.-Read. Seash. (R. R.).

HADDON HEIGHTS, Camden Co., N. J., 5,394.
On Penna.-Read. Seash. (R. R.).

HADJIN, Turkey, 1,200.

HADLEY, Hampshire Co., Mass., 2,711.
On Bost. & Me. (R. R.).

HAGAMAN, Montgomery Co., N. Y., 867.

HAGAN JUNCTION, Sandoval Co., N. Mex., 647.
On Atch., Top. & Santa Fe (R. R.).

HAGEN, Westphalia, Germany, 148,300.
Has extensive iron and steel works; paper mills; cotton-print, tobacco, and sugar factories; breweries, and quarries.

HAGERMAN, Chaves Co., N. Mex., 609.

HAGERSTOWN, Wayne Co., Ind., 1,262.
On Penna. (R. R.).
Manufactures piston-rings.
—c. s., Washington Co., Md., 30,861.
On Balt. & Ohio; Norf. & West.; West. Md.; Penna. (R. Rs.).
Has large railroad shops and yards. Furniture, pipe organs, automobile parts, airplanes, chemicals, shoes and underwear, are the leading industries.

HAGERSVILLE, Haldimand Co., Ontario, Canada, 1,385.
On Can. Nat.; Mich. Cen. (R. Rs.).

HAGUE, THE, Netherlands. See SGRAVENHAGE.
—Warren Co., N. Y., 550.

HAGUENAU, Bas-Rhin, France, 22,523.

HAHIRA, Lowndes Co., Ga., 941.
On Ga. Sou. & Fla. (R. R.).

HAHNTOWN, Westmoreland Co., Pa., 514.
On Pennsylvania (R. R.).

HAIFA, Palestine, 99,000.

HAIGLER, Dundy Co., Neb., 535.
On Chi., Burl. & Quincy (R. R.).

HAIL, Saudi Arabia, 20,000.

HAILEY, c. s., Blaine Co., Idaho, 973.
On Ore. Short Line (R. R.).

HAILEYVILLE, Pittsburg Co., Okla., 1,801.
On Chi., Rk. Isl. & Pac. (R. R.).

HAINES, Tarrant Co., Tex., 500.

HAINES CITY, Polk Co., Fla., 3,430.
On Atl. Coast Line (R. R.).

HAINES FALLS, Greene Co., N. Y., 590.
On West Shore (R. R.).

HAIPHONG, Fr. Indo-China, 80,000.
A seaport. Has cotton-spinning, oil, soap, and cement factories.

HAJDUBOSZORMENY, Comitat of Hajdu, Hungary, 28,861.

HAJDUNANAS, Comitat of Hajdu, Hungary, 17,085.

HAJDUSZOBOSZLO, Comitat of Hajdu, Hungary, 17,029.

HAJIPUR, Bihar and Orissa, India, 21,400.

HAKODATE, island of Hokkaido, Japan, 207,480.
Situated at the base of a rocky cliff on the island of Hokkaido. It has a capacious and fortified harbor with extensive docks. The city is clean, symmetrically laid out, and contains some attractive buildings. It is the seat of a naval school.

HAL, Brabant, Belgium, 17,308.
A suburb of Bruxelles.

HALBERSTADT, Magdeburg, Germany, 48,000.
Sugar, cigars, gloves, paper, and machinery.

HALDEN (Fredrikshald), Ostfold Prov., Norway, 10,278.
A center of the lumber industry.

HALE, Cheshire, England, 10,669.
—Carroll Co., Mo., 574.
Chi., Burl. & Quincy (R. R.).

HALE CENTER, Hale Co., Tex., 1,007.
On Panh. & Santa Fe (R. R.).

HALEDON, Passaic Co., N. J., 4,812.

HALES CORNERS, Milwaukee Co., Wis., 700.
On Mil. El. (R. R.).

HALESITE, Suffolk Co., N. Y., 500.

HALEYVILLE, Winston Co., Ala., 2,115.
On Ill. Cen.; Nor. Ala. (R. Rs.).
The Illinois Central repair shops are located here. Cotton and lumber market.

HALF MOON BAY, San Mateo Co., Calif., 800.

HALIFAX, Plymouth Co., Mass., 817.
On N. York, N. Hav. & Hart. (R. R.).
—Dauphin Co., Pa., 757.
On Penna. (R. R.).
—Halifax Co., Nova Scotia, Canada, 59,275.
On the Dominion Atlantic; Halifax and Southwestern, and the Intercolonial railroads.
Capital of Nova Scotia; excellent harbor, strongly fortified; fine docks; manufactures machinery, boots, shoes, cordage, cotton and woolen goods; numerous fine buildings; seat of Dalhousie University and an engineering school.
—Yorkshire, England, 98,122.
Has large cotton and woolen industries and manufactures of iron, steel, and chemicals.

HALL (or Schwabisch Hall), Württemberg, Germany, 8,978.

HALLAM, York Co., Pa., 771.

HALLANDALE, Broward Co., Fla., 957.
On Fla. East Coast; Seab. Air Line (R. Rs.).

HALLE-ON-SAALE, Prussian Saxony, Germany, 209,200.
Attained commercial importance in the eleventh century, and during the twelfth and thirteenth centuries was a member of the Hanseatic League. From 1806-14, became part of the Kingdom of Westphalia. By the treaty of Vienna was restored to Prussia.
Halle has a famous university founded in 1694. Its library, founded in 1696, contains over 350,000 volumes and many thousand manuscripts.

HALLETTSVILLE, c. s., Lavaca Co., Texas, 1,406.
On Tex. & N. Orl. (R. R.).

HALLOCK, c. s., Kittson Co., Minn., 869.
On Gt. Nor. (R. R.).

HALLOWELL, Kennebec Co., Maine, 2,675.
On Me. Cen. (R. R.).

HALLS, Lauderdale Co., Tenn., 1,474.
On Ill. Cen. (R. R.).

HALLS SUMMIT, Red River Par., La., 750.
On Sib., L. Bisten & Sou. (R. R.).

HALLSTEAD, Susquehanna Co., Pa., 1,254.
On Del., Lack. & West. (R. R.).

HALLSVILLE, Harrison Co., Tex., 600.
On Tex. & Pac. (R. R.).

HALLUIN, Dept. of Nord, France, 13,278.
Textiles, rubber goods, and leather.

HALMSTAD, capital of Halland, Sweden, 23,866.

HÄLSINGBORG, Malmöhus, Sweden, 60,015.
One of the chief manufacturing towns and ports of Sweden.

HALSTAD, Norman Co., Minn., 535.
On Gt. Nor. (R. R.).

HALSTEAD, Harvey Co., Kans., 1,367.
On Atch., Top. & Santa Fe (R. R.).

HAMA, Syria, 36,000.
A center of trade for the Bedouin.

HAMADAN, capital of Prov. of Hamadan, Iran (Persia), 99,852.
A trade and distributing center.

HAMAMATSU, Shizuoku, Japan, 109,475.
A port and industrial town.

HAMBORN, Germany. See DUISBURG.

HAMBURG, capital of Hamburg, Germany, 1,647,000.
One of the free cities of Germany. It is situated about 80 miles from the North Sea, on the northern branch of the Elbe. The town of Altona adjoins it on the west. From the Elbe proceed canals which intersect the eastern and lower part of the city in all directions, and it is also intersected by the Alster, which here forms two fine streams, the Binnenalster and Aussenalster. The quays and harbor accommodation are very extensive. After the destructive fire of 1842 whole streets were rebuilt

---

in a magnificent and expensive style. The most important public buildings are the Church of St. Nicholas, a noble Gothic structure, with a lofty tower and spire, built between 1845 and 1874; St. Peter's, another lofty Gothic edifice; St. Michael's, the largest of the churches; an elegant Jewish temple; an exchange, a noble edifice, consisting chiefly of a magnificent hall, surrounded by a fine colonnade. There are also the Johanneum Institution, containing an ancient college, museums, and the city library, several well-endowed hospitals; zoological and botanical gardens; the Kunsthalle, a large collection of pictures and sculpture, theaters, etc. Hamburg's immense industries and trade which made it the greatest commercial port on the European continent, almost disappeared as a result of the Great War of 1914-18. Since peace was declared the city has renewed its activities and will probably recover its former preeminence. Hamburg was founded by the Emperor Charlemagne, who (808-811) built a citadel and a church on the heights between the Elbe and the eastern bank of the Alster. It became important as a commercial city in the twelfth century, and in the thirteenth it combined with Lübeck in forming the Hanseatic League. The rapid commercial development of Hamburg was checked by the World War, but is again in evidence.

—c. s., Ashley Co., Ark., 1,517.
On Mo. Pac. (R. R.).
—Fremont Co., Iowa, 2,103.
On Chi., Burl. & Quincy (R. R.).
—Sussex Co., N. J., 1,160.
On Leh. & Hud. Riv.; N. York, Susq. & West. (R. Rs.).
—Erie Co., N. Y., 4,731.
On Erie (R. R.).
—Berks Co., Pa., 3,637.
On Penna. (R. R.).

HAMDEN, New Haven Co., Conn., 19,020.
—Vinton Co., Ohio, 883.
On Balt. & Ohio; Chesa. & Ohio (R. Rs.).

HAMELM, Hannover, Germany, 28,000.
Paper, leather, tobacco, sugar, and ships. Site of the legend of the Pied Piper.

HAMILTON, capital of Bermuda, 3,259.
—c. s., Marion Co., Ala., 695.
—Hancock Co., Ill., 1,687.
On Tol., Peor. & West.; Wab. (R. Rs.).
—Greenwood Co., Kans., 549.
On Atch., Top. & Santa Fe (R. R.).
—Essex Co., Mass., 2,235.
On Bost. & Me. (R. R.).
—Allegan Co., Mich., 500.
On Pere Marq. (R. R.).
—Caldwell Co., Mo., 1,572.
On Chi., Burl. & Quincy (R. R.).
—c. s., Ravalli Co., Mont., 1,839.
On Nor. Pac. (R. R.).
—Madison Co., N. Y., 1,700.
On N. York, Ont. & West. (R. R.).
Seat of Colgate University.
—Martin Co., N. Car., 508.
—c. s., Butler Co., Ohio, 52,176.
On Balt. & Ohio; Erie; Cin. & L. Erie (El.); Penna. (R. Rs.).
Has extensive paper mills.
—Hamilton Co., Ontario, 155,547.
On Can. Pac.; Can. Nat.; Tor., Ham. & Buff. (R. R.).
The "Birmingham of Canada." Center of a fruit growing region. Manufactures of farm machinery are especially important.
—Lanarkshire, Scotland, 44,224.
—c. s., Hamilton Co., Texas, 2,084.
On St. Lou. Southw. (R. R.).
—(Montreal) Fond du Lac Co., Wis., 1,819.

HAMLER, Henry Co., Ohio, 535.
On Balt. & Ohio; Det., Tol. & Iron. (R. Rs.).

HAMLET, Richmond Co., N. C., 4,801.
On Seab. Air Line (R. R.).

HAMLIN, Aroostook Co., Maine, 486.
—Monroe Co., N. Y., 500.
On N. York Cen. (R. R.).
—Jones Co., Tex., 2,328.
On Abil. & Sou.; Hamlin & Northw.; Mo.-Kan.-Tex. of Texas; Panh. & Santa Fe (R. Rs.).
—Lincoln Co., W. Va., 844.

HAMM, Westphalia, Germany, 52,000.
Machinery, wire, leather goods, and beer.

HAMME, East Flanders, Belgium, 15,016.

HAMMON, Roger Mills Co., Okla., 736.
On Mo.-Kan.-Tex.; Panh. & Santa Fe (R. Rs.).

HAMMOND, Lake Co., Ind., 64,560.
On Balt. & Ohio, Chi. Term.; Chesa. & Ohio; Chi., Ind. & Lou.; Chi. So. Shore & So. Bend (El.); Elg.; Jol. & East.; Erie; Ind. Harb. Belt; Mich. Cen.; N. York Cen.; N. York, Chi. & St. Lou.; Penna.; Wab. (R. Rs.).
Industrial center near Chicago. Chief products are railroad cars, steel, petroleum products, chemicals, pianos, surgical instruments, castings, and printing.
—Tangipahoa Parish, La., 6,072.
On Ill. Cen.; Yazoo & Miss. Val. (R. Rs.).

HAMMONDSPORT, Steuben Co., N. Y., 1,063.
On Erie (R. R.).

A center of the domestic champagne industry with extensive vineyards and wine cellars.
Hammonton, Atlantic Co., N. J., 7,656.
On Penna.-Read. Seash. (R. R.).
Hampden, Hampden Co., Mass., 854.
–Geauga Co., Ohio, 604.
Hampshire, Kane Co., Ill., 656.
On Chi., Mil., St. P. & Pac. (R. R.).
Hampstead, Carroll Co., Md., 905.
On West. Md. (R. R.).
–Rockingham Co., N. H., 700.
On Bost. & Me. (R. R.).
Hampton, c. s., Calhoun Co., Ark., 669.
On Thorn. & Alex. (R. R.).
–Henry Co., Ga., 1,002.
On Cen. of Ga. (R. R.).
–c. s., Franklin Co., Iowa, 3,473.
On Chi. Gt. West.; Chi., Rk. Isl. & Pac.; Minn. & St. Lou. (R. Rs.).
–Rockingham Co., N. H., 1,200.
On Bost. & Me. (R. R.).
–Hunterdon Co., N. J., 861.
On Cen. of N. Jer.; Del., Lack. & West. (R. Rs.).
–c. s., Hampton Co., S. C., 811.
On Charl. & West. Car.; Hampt. & Branchv. (R. Rs.).
–c. s., Elizabeth City Co., Va., 6,382.
On Chesa. & Ohio (R. R.).
Seat of Hampton Institute (colored and Indian).
–Middlesex, England, 13,053.
A residential suburb of London.
Hamtramck, Wayne Co., Mich., 56,268.
An industrial town completely surrounded by Detroit. Automobile manufacturing.
Hanaford (Logan), Franklin Co., Ill., 617.
Hanau, Prussia, Germany, 40,000.
Hanceville, Cullman Co., Ala., 780.
On Lou. & Nash. (R. R.).
Hancock, Washington Co., Md., 947.
On West. Md. (R. R.).
–Houghton Co., Mich., 5,795.
On Copr. Rge.; Dul., So. Sh. & Atl.; Min. Rge. (R. Rs.)
–Stevens Co., Minn., 798.
On Gt. Nor. (R. R.).
–Hillsborough Co., N. H., 515.
On Bost. & Me. (R. R.).
–Delaware Co., N. Y., 1,427.
On Erie; N. York, Ont. & West. (R. Rs.).
Handsboro, Harrison Co., Miss., 1,200.
Hanford, c. s., Kings Co., Cal., 7,028.
On Atch., Top. & Santa Fe; Sou. Pac. (R. Rs.).
Hangchow, capital of Prov. of Chekiang, China, 506,900.
An important commercial center and river port. Famous for its silk industries.
Hanging Rock, Lawrence Co., Ohio, 550.
On Norf. & West. (R. R.).
Hankinson, Richland Co., N. Dak., 1,400.
On Gt. Nor.; Minn., St. P. & S. Ste. M. (R. Rs.).
Hankow, Prov. of Hupeh, China, 777,993.
Chief commercial center of central China.
Hanley, Staffordshire, England, now included in Stoke-upon-Trent.
Hanna City, Peoria Co., Ill., 563.
On Minn. & St. Louis (R. R.).
Hannastown, Westmoreland Co., Pa., 950.
On Penna. (R. R.).
Hannibal, Marion Co., Mo., 22,761.
On Chi., Burl. & Quincy; Han. Connect.; St. Lou. & Han.; Wab. (R. Rs.).
Hannover, capital of Prov. of Hannover, Prussia, Germany, 438,922.
Lies on both sides of the Leine. The old city is surrounded on the north and east by a new and modern city, built since 1840, and noted for its handsome buildings which include the museum, the Polytechnic School, the Lyceum, and the royal palace (an extensive edifice on the Leine), with various institutions for higher education.
Hanoi, capital of French Indo-China, 149,000.
Industries include cotton spinning, brewing, and distilling and the manufacture of tobacco. Native industries also important.
Hanover, Grafton Co., N. H., 2,200.
Seat of Dartmouth College.
–Jo Daviess Co., Ill., 806.
On Hanover (R. R.).
–Washington Co., Kans., 894.
On Chi., Burl. & Quincy; St. Jos. & Gd. Isl. (R. Rs.).
–Plymouth Co., Mass., 2,709.
On N. Y., N. H., & H. (R. R).
–York Co., Pa., 11,805.
Trade center for a farming region.
On Penna.; West. Md. (R. Rs.).
–Grey Co., Southeast, Ontario, Canada, 3,077.
On Can. Pac.; Can. Nat. (R. R.).
Hansi, Hissar Dist., Punjab, India, 15,200.
Has cotton industries.
Hanson, Plymouth Co., Mass., 2,417.
Hapeville, Fulton Co., Ga., 4,224.
On Cen. of Ga. (R. R.).
Happy, Swisher Co., Tex., 724.
On Panh. & Santa Fe (R. R.).
Harahan, Jefferson Par., La., 892.
On Yazoo & Miss. Val. (R. R.).
Harar, Ethiopia, 50,000.
A caravan trade center.
Harbin, Manchukuo, 482,452.
The chief city of central Manchukuo. Has machine shops, soybean factories, grain mills, and tanneries.
Harbinger, Currituck Co., N. Car., 525.
Harbor Beach, Huron Co., Mich., 1,892.
On Pere Marq. (R. R.).
Harbor Grace, Newfoundland, 2,215.
On west side of Conception Bay.
Harbor Springs, Emmett Co., Mich., 1,429.
On Penna. (R. R.).
Harburg, Prussia, Germany. See Hamburg.
Harco, Saline Co., Ill., 650.
On Cle., Cin., Chi. & St. Lou. (R. R.).
Hardaway, Macon Co., Ala., 500.
On Seab. Air Line (R. R.).
Hardeeville, Beaufort & Jasper Cos., S. C., 728.
On Atl. Coast Line; Sou. (R. Rs.).
Hardenberg, Netherlands, 2,494.
Hardin, c. s., Calhoun Co., Ill., 733.
–Ray Co., Mo., 821.
On Atch., Top. & Santa Fe; Wab. (R. Rs.).
–Big Horn Co., Mont., 1,169.
On Chi., Burl. & Quincy (R. R.).
Hardinsburg, c. s., Breckinridge Co., Ky., 805.
On Lou. & Nash. (R. R.).
Hardwar, United Provinces, India, 28,700.
A Hindu place of pilgrimage.
Hardwick, Worcester Co., Mass., 2,379.
–Caledonia Co., Vt., 1,667.
On Hardwick & Woodbury (R. R.).
Hardy, c. s., Sharp Co., Ark., 508.
On St. Lou.-San Fran. (R. R.).
–Pike Co., Ky., 809.
On Norf. & West. (R. R.).
Harkers Island, Carteret Co., N. C., 700.
Harlan, Allen Co., Ind., 500.
–c. s., Shelby Co., Iowa, 3,145.
On Chi. & Nor. West.; Chi. Gt. West.; Chi., Rk. Isl. & Pac. (R. Rs.).
–c. s., Harlan Co., Ky., 4,327.
On Lou. & Nash. (R. R.).
Harleigh, Luzerne Co., Pa., 585.
Harlem, Columbia Co., Ga., 784.
On Georgia (R. R.).
–Blaine Co., Montana, 708.
On Gt. Nor. (R. R.).
Harleton, Harrison Co., Tex., 513.
Harlingen, Friesland, Netherlands, 10,443.
–Cameron Co., Texas, 12,124.
On St. Lou., Brownsv. & Mex.; Tex. & N. Orl. (R. Rs.).
Center of an irrigation district.
Harlowton, c. s., Wheatland Co., Mont., 1,473.
On Chi., Mil., St. P. & Pac. (R. R.).
Harmony, Clay Co., Ind., 2,100.
On Penna.; Ind. R. R. Sys. (El.) (R. Rs.).
–Fillmore Co., Minn., 821.
On Chi., Mil., St. P. & Pac. (R. R.).
–Butler Co., Pa., 786.
On Balt. & Ohio (R. R.).
Harper, Harper Co., Kans., 1,660.
On Atch., Top. & Santa Fe (R. R.).
Harper's Ferry, Jefferson Co., W. Va., 705.
On Balt. & Ohio (R. R.).
Scene of John Brown's raid.
Harrah, Oklahoma Co., Okla., 693.
On Chi., Rk. Isl. & Pac. (R. R.).
Harriman, Roane Co., Tenn., 4,588.
On Cin., N. Orl. & Tex. Pac.; Har. & Northe.; Lou. & Nash.; Sou.; Tenn. Cen. (R. Rs.).
–Orange Co, N. Y., 657.
On Erie (R. R.).
Harrington, Kent Co., Del., 1,812.
On Penna. (R. R.).
–Lincoln Co., Wash., 519.
On Gt. Nor. (R. R.).
Harrington Park, Bergen Co., N. J., 1,251.
On West Shore (R. R.).
Harris, Chisago Co., Minn., 584.
On Nor. Pac. (R. R.).
Harrisburg, c. s., Poinsett Co., Ark., 1,111.
On Mo. Pac. (R. R.).
–c. s., Saline Co., Ill., 11,625.
On Cle., Cin., Chi. & St. Lou. (R. R.).
Center of an agricultural and mining region. Has flour mills, brick yards, and sawmills.
–Linn Co., Ore., 575.
On Ore. Elec.; Sou. Pac. (R. Rs.).
–Dauphin Co., Pa., State capital and county seat, 80,339.
On the Susquehanna River, 105 miles west and north of Philadelphia, and on the following railroads: the Pennsylvania, and the Reading. The situation of Harrisburg is most picturesque. The river, almost a mile wide at this point, is spanned by several fine bridges. The river-front forms a most attractive public park. In a beautiful park of thirteen acres stands the new Capitol, one of the most palatial and costly steel, brick, and marble structures in the country, replacing the old one which was burned in 1897. In Capitol Park is a monument to the soldiers who fell in the Mexican War, the statue of General John F. Hartranft. The Dauphin County Soldiers' Monument is a shaft 100 feet high, raised to the soldiers of the county who died in the Civil War. Across the Susquehanna is Fort Washington, marking the most northern advance of the Confederate Army. A great Memorial Bridge, in honor of the soldiers, sailors and marines of Pennsylvania who served in the World War has been erected at the east end of the Capitol, and is an architectural accession to its Capitol Park. Besides the Capitol, and the State Library, founded in 1790, Harrisburg contains a court-house, governor's residence, State arsenal, State Insane Hospital, county court-house, prison, theaters, high schools, a public library, Board of Trade Building, Conservatory of Music, two Masonic buildings, city hospital, Home for the Friendless, and the Children's Industrial Home. The town is the seat of a Protestant Episcopal and of a Roman Catholic bishopric.
Harrisburg is notable for its public parks and parkways. The latter girdle the city, and total about 1,100 acres in area. The former include playground and athletic facilities, a golf course, and public baths. Owing to its exceptional railroad facilities, Harrisburg is also important in the commercial world. The principal industries are: iron and steel products, leather and rubber goods, book-keeping machines, hosiery, silk, shoes, bookbinding machines, women's and children's clothing, and cigars. Settled in 1726 by John Harris, an English trader, who secured grants of 800 acres. In 1753 was known as Harris's Ferry. In 1785 the town was laid out and called first Harrisburg and then Louisburg in honor of Louis XVI. In 1791 incorporated as Harrisburg, in 1812 became the State capital, and in 1860 chartered as a city. It was here in 1828 that the Harrisburg Convention met that led to the high protective tariff of that year.
–Harris Co., Texas, 1,461.
On Galv., Houst. & Hend.; Internat.-Gt. Nor.; Mo.-Kan.-Tex. of Tex.; Tex. & N. Orl. (R. Rs.).
Harrison, c. s., Boone Co., Ark., 3,626.
On Mo. & Nor. Ark. (R. R.).
–Hudson Co., N. J., 15,601.
On Del., Lack. & West.; Erie; Penna. (R. Rs.).
–Westchester Co., N. Y., 10,195.
On N. York, N. Hav. & Hart. (R. R.).
–Hamilton Co., Ohio, 1,449.
On Cle., Cin., Chi. & St. Lou. (R. R.).
Harrisonburg (Ind. City), c. s., Rockingham Co., Va., 7,232.
On Balt. & Ohio; Chesa. West.; Sou. (R. Rs.).
Harrison City, Westmoreland Co., Pa., 500.
On Penna. (R. R.).
Harrisonville, Richmond Co., Ga.
On Georgia (R. R.).
–c. s., Cass Co., Mo., 2,306.
On Mo.-Kan.-Tex.; Mo. Pac.; St. Lou.-San Fran. (R. Rs.).
Harriston, Wellington Co., Ontario, Canada, 1,296.
On Can. Pac.; Can. Nat. (R. R.).
Harrisville, Lewis Co., N. Y., 896.
On N. York Cen. (R. R.).
–Butler Co., Pa., 583.
–c. s., Ritchie Co., W. Va., 1,192.
Harrodsburg, c. s., Mercer Co., Ky., 4,029.
On Southern (R. R.).
Harrogate, Yorkshire, England, 39,785.
An inland resort and tourist center.
–Claiborne Co., Tenn., 700.
On Lou. & Nash. (R. R.).
Harrow-on-the-Hill, Middlesex, England, 26,378.
Hart, Oceana Co., Mich., 1,690.
On Pere Marq. (R. R.).
Hartford, Geneva Co., Ala., 1,419.
On Cen. Ga. (R. R.).
–Sebastian Co., Ark., 1,210.
On Chi., Rk. Isl. & Pac.; Midl. Val. (R. Rs.).
–c. s., Hartford Co., Conn., State capital, 164,072.
Port of entry, situated at the head of navigation for large vessels on the Connecticut River, 50 miles from Long Island Sound and at the mouth of Park River, that flows through the city and is crossed by several bridges. The city is on the New York, New Haven & Hartford railroad. The Capitol, a fine building of white marble, contains valuable portraits and statues. The present city hall was once the old State house, where the Hartford Convention met in 1814-15. Other buildings are the Travellers Tower, Morgan Memorial, State Arsenal, post office, St. Joseph's Cathedral (Roman Catholic), Young Men's Christian Association, Hartford and St. Joseph's Hospitals, Hartford Orphan Asylum, Retreat for the Insane, Hartford American Asylum for the Deaf and Asylum for the Blind, Trinity College, and Hartford Theological Seminary (Congregational). The Public Library, known as the Wadsworth Atheneum, is a castellated structure of Tudor architecture. It is also the headquarters of the Connecticut Historical Society. The Colt Gallery, which houses memorials of the Colt family, adjoins it. Besides Bushnell Park, covering about fifty acres, and Charter Oak Park, there are Kenney, Goodwin, Riverside, Pope, Elizabeth and other parks. A notable memorial is the Soldiers' and Sailors' Arch, erected in memory of Connecticut men who fell in the Great War.
Hartford is the home of vast insurance capital. Its chief manufactures are bicycles, firearms, machine guns, airplanes, auto parts, tools, telephone parts, brushes, typewriters, clocks, organs, mattresses, screws, nails, pins, envelopes, steam boilers and engines, machinery, car wheels, hosiery, knit goods, and electric vehicles. The city is the center of an extensive trade in Connecticut tobacco.
In 1635 and 1636 the Rev. Thomas Hooker and Samuel Stone came with colonists from Newtown (Cambridge), Mass., and called the place Newtown, and in 1637 Hartford, after Hertford, England, the birthplace of Stone. On January 14, 1630, was adopted here the first of all written Government constitutions, the famous "Fundamental Orders of Connecticut." It was here in 1687 that the Royal Governor, Andros, attempted to seize the Connecticut charter, which, tradition says, the colonists saved by concealing in an oak, afterward called the Charter Oak. Here in 1780 the Yorktown campaign was planned. From 1701 to 1873 New Haven was co-capital with Hartford, but in 1875 the latter became again sole capital.
–Madison Co., Ill., 1,566.
On Ill. Term. (El.) (R. R.).
–Lyon Co., Kans., 507.
On Mo.-Kan.-Tex. (R. R.).
–c. s., Ohio Co., Ky., 1,106.
On Lou. & Nash. (R. R.).
–Van Buren Co., Mich., 1,484.
On Pere Marq. (R. R.).
–Minnehaha Co., S. Dak., 643.
On Chi., St. P., Minn. & Oma. (R. R.).
–Windsor Co., Vt., 550.
On Cen. Ver.; Woodstock (R. Rs.).
–Washington Co., Wis., 3,754.
On Chi., Mil., St. P. & Pac. (R. R.).
Hartford City, c. s., Blackford Co., Ind., 6,613.
On Ind. R. R. Sys. (El.); N. York, Chi. & St. Lou.; Penna. (R. Rs.).
Hartington, c. s., Cedar Co., Neb., 1,568.
On Chi., St. P., Minn. & Oma. (R. R.).
Hartland, Somerset Co., Maine, 800.
On Me. Cen. (R. R.).
–Waukesha Co., Wis., 945.
On Chi., Mil., St. P. & Pac. (R. R.).
Hartlepool, Durham, England, 20,545.
A busy North Sea port and commercial center, with shipyards, engineering works, sawmills, and flour mills.
Hartly, O'Brien Co., Iowa, 1,272.
On Chi., Mil., St. P. & Pac.; Chi., Rk. Isl. & Pac. (R. Rs.).
Hartman, Johnson Co., Ark., 542.
On Mo. Pac. (R. R.).
Hartselle, Morgan Co., Ala., 2,204.
On Lou. & Nash. (R. R.).
Hartshorne, Pittsburg Co., Okla., 3,587.
On Chi., Rk. Isl. & Pac. (R. R.).
Hartsville, Darlington Co., S. C., 5,067.
On Atl. Coast Line; Seab. Air Line (R. Rs.).
–c. s., Trousdale Co., Tenn., 1,015.
On Lou. & Nash. (R. R.).
Hartwell, c. s., Hart Co., Ga., 2,048.
On Hartwell (R. R.).
Harvard, McHenry Co., Ill., 2,988.
On Chi. & Nor. West. (R. R.).
–Worcester Co., Mass., 952.
On Bost. & Me. (R. R.).
–Clay Co., Neb., 865.
On Chi., Burl. & Quincy; Chi. & Nor. West. (R. Rs.).
Harvey, Cook Co., Ill., 16,374.
On Balt. & Ohio Chi. Term.; Chi., Mil., St. P. & Pac.; Gd. Tr.; Ill. Cen. (R. Rs.).
A residential and industrial suburb of Chicago. Road machinery, railroad cars, stoves, and aluminum ware.
–Wells Co., N. Dak., 2,157.
On Minn., St. P. & S. Ste. M. (R. R.).
Harveyton, Perry Co., Ky., 700.
On Lou. & Nash. (R. R.).
Harwich, Essex, England, 12,700.
An important port and commercial center. Has large fishing industry.
–Barnstable Co., Mass., 2,373.
On N. York, N. Hav. & Hart. (R. R.).
Harwick Port, Barnstable Co., Mass., 500.
Harwood Mines, Luzerne Co., Pa., 960.
Hasbrouck Heights, Bergen Co., N. J., 5,658.
On N. Jer. & N. York (R. R.).
Haskell, Passaic Co., N. J., 845.
On Erie (R. R.).
–Muskogee Co., Okla., 1,682.
On Midl. Val. (R. R.).
–c. s., Haskell Co., Texas, 2,632.
On Wichita Val. (R. R.).
Haslam, Shelby Co., Tex., 527.
On Tex. & N. Orl. (R. R.).
Haslingden, Lancashire, England, 16,637.
Cotton textiles.

Haspe, Westphalia, Germany, 25,636.
Has iron foundries and rolling mills.
Hasselt, capital of Prov. of Limburg, Belgium, 25,840.
Famous for its breweries and distilleries.
Hastings, St. Johns Co., Fla., 673.
On Fla. East Coast (R. R.).
–c. s., Barry Co., Mich., 5,227.
On Chi., Kalam. & Sag.; Mich. Cen. (R. Rs.).
–c. s., Dakota Co., Minn., 5,086.
On Chi., Mil., St. P. & Pac. (R. R.).
–Cambria Co., Pa., 2,011.
On Penna. (R. R.).
–c. s., Adams Co., Neb., 15,490.
On Chi., Burl. & Quincy; Mo. Pac.; Chi. & Nor. West.; Un. Pac.; St. Jos. & Gd. Isl. (R. Rs.).
Seat of Hastings College (Presbyterian).
–Sussex, England, 65,199.
The Battle of Hastings was fought near here in 1066.
New Zealand, 18,300.
Hastings-on-Hudson, Westchester Co., N. Y., 7,097.
On N. York Cen. (R. R.).
Hatboro, Montgomery Co., Pa., 2,651.
On Reading (R. R.).
Hatfield, Hampshire Co., Mass., 2,433.
On Bost. & Me.; N. York, N. Hav. & Hart. (R. Rs.).
–Montgomery Co., Pa., 1,149.
On Reading (R. R.).
Hathras, United Prov., India, 37,900.
A rapidly developing commercial center.
Hatillo, Mun. of Hatillo, Puerto Rico, 2,611.
Hatteras, Dare Co., N. C., 500.
Hattiesburg, c. s., Forrest Co., Miss., 18,601.
On Bonhomie & Hattiesburg Sou.; Gulf & Ship Island; Miss.-Cen.; N. Orl. & Northe. (R. Rs.).
Yellow pine lumber provides the chief industry. Agriculture and stock raising are also important industries.
Hatton, Traill Co., N. Dak., 804.
On Gt. Nor. (R. R.).
Haubstadt, Gibson Co., Ind., 674.
On Chi. & East Ill. (R. R.).
Haugesund, Norway, 17,217.
An important fishing port.
Hauppauge, Suffolk Co., N. Y., 538.
Hautmont, Dept. of Nord, France, 14,636.
Damaged in the World War.
Havana, Cuba. See Habana.
–Gadsden Co., Fla., 1,036.
On Seab. Air Line; Jacksonv. & Hav. (R. Rs.).
–c. s., Mason Co., Ill., 3,451.
On Chi. & Ill. Midl.; Ill. Cen. (R. Rs.).
Havant, Southampton, England, 4,264.
Havelock, Lancaster Co., Neb. (Pop. incl. in Lincoln).
On Chi., Burl. & Quincy; Chi., Rk. Isl. & Pac. (R. Rs.).
Haven, Reno Co., Kans., 578.
On Mo. Pac. (R. R.).
Haverhill, Essex Co., Mass., 49,516.
On Bost. & Me. (R. R.).
Chief product is women's shoes and kindred articles—wood heels, etc., in the manufacture of which it is preeminent. Incorporated in 1645. Birthplace of the poet Whittier.
Haverstraw, Rockland Co., N. Y., 5,621.
On N. Jer. & N. York; West Shore (R. Rs.).
Haviland, Kiowa Co., Kans., 656.
On Chi., Rk. Isl. & Pac. (R. R.).
Havre, France. See Le Havre.
–c. s., Hill Co., Mont., 6,372.
On Gt. Nor. (R. R.).
Havre de Grace, Hartford Co., Md., 3,985.
On Balt. & Ohio; Penna. (R. Rs.).
Hawarden, Sioux Co., Iowa, 2,459.
On Chi. & Nor. West.; Chi., Mil., St. P. & Pac. (R. Rs.).
Hawesville, c. s., Hancock Co., Ky., 790.
On Lou. & Nash. (R. R.).
Hawick, Roxburghshire, Scotland, 18,214.
Manufactures hosiery and tweeds.
Hawk, Mitchell Co., N. C., 500.
Hawkesbury, Prescott Co., Ontario, Canada, 5,177.
On Can. Nat. (R. R.).
Hawkeye, Fayette Co., Iowa, 530.
On Chi., Mil., St. P. & Pac. (R. R.).
Hawkinsville, c. s., Pulaski Co., Ga., 2,484.
On Sou.; Wrights. & Tennille (R. Rs.).
Hawk Run, Clearfield Co., Pa., 663.
On N. York Cen. (R. R.).
Hawley, Clay Co., Minn., 958.
On Nor. Pac. (R. R.).
–Wayne Co., Pa., 1,811.
On Erie (R. R.).
Haworth, Bergen Co., N. J., 1,042.
On West Shore (R. R.).
Haws, Somerset Co., Pa., 500.
On Balt. & Ohio (R. R.).
Hawthorn, Alachua Co., Fla., 618.
On Atl. Coast Line; Seab. Air Line (R. Rs.).
–Clarion Co., Pa., 571.
On Penna. (R. R.).
Hawthorne, Passaic Co., N. J., 11,868.
On Erie; N. York, Susq. & West. (R. Rs.).
A suburb of Paterson.
–Los Angeles Co., Cal., 6,596.
On Pac. El. (R. R.).
–c. s., Mineral Co., Nev., 757.
Haxtun, Phillips Co., Colo., 1,027.
On Chi., Burl. & Quincy (R. R.).
Hayden, Routt Co., Colo., 554.
On Den. & Salt L. (R. R.).
Haydenville, Hampshire Co., Mass., 1,000.
On N. York, N. Hav. & Hart. (R. R.).
–Hocking Co., Ohio, 1,000.
On Chesa. & Ohio (R. R.).
–Westmoreland Co., Pa., 518.
Hayfield, Dodge Co., Minn., 730.
On Chi. Gt. West. (R. R.).
Haynesville, Claiborne Parish, Louisiana, 2,541.
On La. & Nor. West. (R. R.).
Hayneville, c. s., Lowndes Co., Ala., 525.
Hays, Ellis Co., Kans, 5,357.
On Un. Pac. (R. R.).
–Allegheny Co., Pa., (Br. Homestead P. O.).
On Penna.; Pitts. & L. Erie; Union (R. Rs.).
Hay Springs, Sheridan Co., Neb., 853.
On Chi. & Nor. West. (R. R.).
Hayti, Pemiscot Co., Mo., 1,620.
On St. Lou.-San Fran. (R. R.).
Hayward, Nacogdoches Co., Tex., 600.
On Nacog. & Sou. East. (R. R.).
–c. s., Sawyer Co., Wis., 1,207.
On Chi., St. P., Minn. & Oma. (R. R.).
–Alameda Co., Cal., 5,530.
On Sou. Pac.; West. Pac. (R. Rs.).
Hazard, c. s., Perry Co., Ky., 7,021.
On Lou. & Nash. (R. R.).
Hazaribagh, Bengal, British India, 20,977.
A farming and mining center.
Hazebrouk, Dept. of Nord, France, 15,462.
Partly destroyed in the World War.
Hazel Crest, Cook Co., Ill., 1,162.
On Ill. Cen. (R. R.).
Hazel Green, Grant Co., Wis., 601.
On Chi. & Nor. West. (R. R.).
Hazelhurst, c. s., Copiah Co., Miss., 2,447.
On Ill. Cen. (R. R.).
–McKean Co., Pa., 650.
Hazelwood, Hayworth Co., N. C., 1,168.
On Southern (R. R.).
Hazen, Prairie Co., Ark., 787.
On Chi., Rk. Isl. & Pac.; St. Lou. Southw. (R. Rs.).
–Mercer Co., N. Dak., 689.
On Nor. Pac. (R. R.).
Hazlehurst, c. s., Jeff Davis Co., Ga., 1,378.
On Ga. & Fla.; Sou. (R. Rs.).
Hazleton, Gibson Co., Ind., 507.
On Chi. & East. Ill. (R. R.).
–Luzerne Co., Pa., 36,765.
Located in the anthracite region. Has manufactures of silk, knit-goods, iron, steel, and pumps.
On Leh. Val.; Penna. (R. Rs.).
Headland, Henry Co., Ala., 1,811.
On Atl. Coast Line (R. R.).
Healdsburg, Sonoma Co., Cal., 2,296.
On Northw. Pac. (R. R.).
Healdton, Carter Co., Okla., 2,017.
On Gulf, Colo. & Santa Fe (R. R.).
Heanor, Derbyshire, England, 22,386.
Has knitting mills and collieries.
Hearne, Robertson Co., Texas, 2,956.
On Tex. & N. Orl.; Internat.-Gt. Nor. (R. Rs.).
Heath Springs, Lancaster Co., S. C., 520.
On Southern (R. R.).
Heaton, Avery Co., N. C., 500.
Heavener, Le Flore Co., Okla., 2,269.
On Ark. West.; Kan. Cy. Sou. (R. Rs.).
Hebburn, Durham, England, 24,125.
An industrial suburb of Newcastle.
Heber, c. s., Wasatch Co., Utah, 2,477.
On Den. & Rio Gde. West. (R. R.).
Heber Springs, c. s., Cleburne Co., Ark., 1,401.
On Mo. & No. Ark. (R. R.).
Hebron, McHenry Co., Ill., 608.
On Chi. & Nor. West. (R. R.).
–Porter Co., Ind., 693.
On Penna. (R. R.).
–Wicomico Co., Md., 805.
On Balt. & East. (R. R.).
–c. s., Thayer Co., Neb., 1,804.
On Chi., Burl. & Quincy; Chi., Rk. Isl. & Pac. (R. Rs.).
–Morton Co., N. D., 1,348.
On Nor. Pac. (R. R.).
–Licking Co., Ohio, 757.
On N. York Cen. (R. R.).
–Palestine, 17,532.
A trade center with many native industries.
Hebronville, Bristol Co., Mass., 650.
On N. York, N. Hav. & Hart. (R. R.).
Hecla, Brown Co., S. Dak, 568.
On Chi. & Nor. West. (R. R.).
Hector, Renville Co., Minn., 864.
On Chi., Mil., St. P. & Pac. (R. R.).
Hedley, Donley Co., Texas, 807.
On Ft. Worth & Denv. Cy. (R. R.).
Hedrick, Keokuk Co., Iowa, 810.
On Chi., Burl. & Quincy; Chi., Mil., St. P. & Pac.; Minn. & St. Lou. (R. Rs.).
Heerlen, Netherlands, 46,885.
A center in a coal mining area.
Heflin, c. s., Cleburne Co., Ala., 1,231.
On Southern (R. R.).
Hegins, Schuylkill Co., Pa., 900.
Heidelberg, Baden, Germany, 84,650.
Situated on the left bank of the Neckar, at the foot of the Geisberg and Königstuhl.
The principal buildings are the Church of St. Peter, the Church of the Holy Ghost, and the castle, begun in the end of the thirteenth century. The University of Heidelberg, founded in 1386, is the oldest in Germany.
The principal industry is brewing. One of the greatest curiosities of the place is the Heidelberg tun, a huge wine cask, kept in a cellar under the castle. In the sixteenth century Heidelberg was prominent as the seat of Calvinism.
–Jasper Co., Miss., 653.
On N. Orl. & N. East. (R. R.).
–Allegheny Co., Pa., 2,130.
Heijo, Chosen, 172,746.
An industrial and commercial center.
Heilbronn, Württemberg, Germany, 60,308.
A commercial center, with industries producing automobiles, chemicals, iron and steel goods, paints, and machinery.
Heilwood, Indiana Co., Pa., 1,000.
On N. York Cen.; Penna. (R. R.).
Helder, North Holland, Netherlands, 29,339.
A naval and military station.
Helena, Shelby Co., Ala., 549.
On Atl., Birm. & Coast (R. R.).
–c. s., Phillips Co., Ark., 8,316.
On Mo. & No. Ark.; Mo. Pac.; Yazoo & Miss. Val. (R. Rs.).
–Telfair Co., Ga., 963.
On Seab. Air Line; Sou. (R. Rs.).
–c. s., Lewis and Clark Co., Mont., State capital, 11,803.
This commercial center of the State is on the Great Northern and Northern Pacific railroads, 4,200 feet above sea level. It lies in the fertile Prickly Pear Valley, surrounded by a highly productive mineral region; engages extensively in gold, silver, and iron mining. Has ore refineries, foundries and machine shops, and large biscuit, confectionery, farm implements, tobacco and milling plants.
Seat of Montana Wesleyan University, St. Vincent's Academy, and St. Aloysius's College.
The chief buildings are the Capitol, the United States Assay Office, the Cathedral (Catholic), and public, State, and other libraries. The town was settled in 1864 as a mining camp, and incorporated in 1881.
–Alfalfa Co., Okla., 735.
On St. Lou.-San Fran. (R. R.).
–Newberry Co., S. C., 596.
On Southern (R. R.).
Helensburg, Dumbarton, Scotland, 8,893.
Helenwood, Scott Co., Tenn., 500.
On Cin., N. Orl. & Tex. Pac. (R. R.).
Hellam (Hallam), York Co., Pa., 771.
On Penna. (R. R.).
Hellertown, Northampton Co., Pa., 3,851.
On Reading (R. R.).
Hellier, Pike Co., Ky., 2,112.
On Chesa. & Ohio (R. R.).
Hellin, Prov. of Albacete, Spain, 12,558.
Helmetta, Middlesex Co., N. J., 801.
On Penna. (R. R.).
Helmond, Netherlands, 25,410.
Helmstedt, Brunswick, Germany, 18,000.
An industrial city near Magdeburg.
Helper, Carbon Co., Utah, 2,707.
On Rio Gde. West. (R. R.).
Helsingör, Denmark, 15,841.
Helsinki (Helsingfors), Govt. of Uusimaa, capital of Finland, 283,598.
A busy seaport and the educational center of Finland.
Heltonville, Lawrence Co., Ind., 602.
On Chi., Mil., St. P. & Pac. (R. R.).
Helvetia Mines, Clearfield Co., Pa., 500.
On Balt. & Ohio (R. R.).
Hemel Hempstead, Hertfordshire, England, 15,122.
Paper and iron industries.
Hemet, Riverside Co., Cal., 2,235.
On Atch., Top. & Santa Fe (R. R.).
Hemingford, Box Butte Co., Neb., 1,025.
On Chi., Burl. & Quincy (R. R.).
Hempfield, Westmoreland Co., Pa., 500.
Hemphill, c. s., Sabine Co., Tex., 731.
On Lufk. Hemp. & Gulf (R. R.).
–McDowell Co., W. Va., 500.
On Norf. & West. (R. R.).
Hempstead, Nassau Co., N. Y., 12,650.
A residential and resort suburb of New York.
On Long Isl. (R. R.).
–c. s., Waller Co., Texas, 1,942.
On Tex. & N. Orl. (R. R.).
Henderson, c. s., Henderson Co., Ky., 11,668.
On Ill. Cen.; Lou. & Nash. (R. Rs.).
Has coal mines within city limits, and a number of tobacco factories. Other products include furniture, pickles, nicotine, boxes, and baskets.
–c. s., Sibley Co., Minn., 672.
On Chi., St. P., Minn. & Oma. (R. R.).
–c. s., Vance Co., N. C., 6,345.
On Seab. Air Line; Sou. (R. Rs.).
–c. s., Chester Co., Tenn., 1,503.
On Mob. & Ohio (R. R.).
–c. s., Rusk Co., Texas, 2,932.
On Internat.-Gt. Nor. (R. R.).
Hendersonville, c. s., Henderson Co., N. C., 5,070.
On Southern (R. R.).
Hendricks, Lincoln Co., Minn., 702.
On Chi. & Nor. West. (R. R.).
Hengelo, Overysser, Netherlands, 34,328.
Important for its textile industries.
Henin-Liétard, Pas-de-Calais, France, 21,946.
Hennessey, Kingfisher Co., Okla., 1,271.
On Chi., Rk. Isl. & Pac. (R. R.).
Henniker, Merrimack Co., N. H., 780.
On Bost. & Me. (R. R.).
Henning, Otter Tail Co., Minn., 731.
On Minn., St. P. & S. Ste. M.; Nor. Pac. (R. Rs.).
–Lauderdale Co., Tenn., 639.
On Ill. Cen. (R. R.).
Henrietta, Ray County, Mo., 632.
On Atch., Top. & Santa Fe (R. R.).
–Rutherford Co., N. C., 1,384.
On Seab. Air Line (R. R.).
–c. s., Clay Co., Texas, 2,020.
On Ft. Worth & Denv. Cy.; Mo.-Kan.-Tex. of Texas (R. Rs.).
Henry, Marshall Co., Ill., 1,658.
On Chi., Rk. Isl. & Pac. (R. R.).
Henryetta, Okmulgee Co., Okla., 7,694.
On Kan., Okla. & Gulf; St. Lou.-San Fran. (R. Rs.).
Hephzibah, Richmond Co., Ga., 646.
On Ga. & Fla. (R. R.).
Heppner, c. s., Morrow Co., Ore., 1,190.
On Ore.-Wash. R. R. & Nav. Co. (R. R.).
Herat, Afghanistan; 100,000.
Situated in a plain near the Herirood River. Is a post of commercial and military importance, where the great roads leading to India meet.
Herbert, Fayette Co., Pa., 550.
Hereford, c. s., Herefordshire, England, 24,159.
An interesting historical town and trade center.
–c. s., Deaf Smith Co., Texas, 2,458.
On Panh. & Santa Fe (R. R.).
Herford, Westphalia, Germany, 37,000.
Leading products are textiles.
Hericourt, Dept. of Haute-Saône, France, 5,552.
Herington, Dickinson Co., Kans., 4,207.
On Chi., Rk. Isl. & Pac.; Mo. Pac. (R. Rs.).
Herisau, Canton of Appenzell Rh.-Int., Switzerland, 13,601.
Noted for its embroideries.
Herkimer, c. s., Herkimer Co., N. Y., 10,446.
On N. York Cen. (R. R.).
Famous as the center of a dairy region. Industries are principally creamery products.
Herman, Grant Co., Minn., 518.
On Gt. Nor. (R. R.).
Hermann., c. s., Gasconade Co., Mo., 2,063.
On Mo. Pac. (R. R.).
Hermannstadt, Rumania. See Sibiu.
Hermiston, Umatilla Co., Ore., 608.
On Ore.-Wash. R. R. & Nav. Co. (R. R.).
Hermleigh, Scurry Co., Tex., 544.
On Panh. & Santa Fe; Rosc., Snyd. & Pac. (R. Rs.).
Hermon, St. Lawrence Co., N. Y., 527.
Hermon Center, Penobscot Co., Maine.
Hermosa Beach, Los Angeles Co., Cal., 4,796.
On Atch., Top. & Santa Fe; Pac. El. (R. Rs.).
Hermupolis, Greece, 21,156.
Hernando, c. s., De Soto Co., Miss., 938.
On Ill. Cen. (R. R.).
Herndon, Northumberland Co., Pa., 699.
On Penna.; Read. (R. Rs.).
–Fairfax Co., Va., 887.
On Wash. & Old Dom. (El.) (R. R.).
Herne, Westphalia, Germany, 66,510.
Has coal mines and boiler works.
Hernösand, capital of län of Västernorrland, Sweden, 11,461.
Seaport. Exports forest products.
Heron Lake, Jackson Co., Minn., 786.
On Chi., St. P., Minn. & Oma. (R. R.).
Herreid, Campbell Co., S. Dak., 594.
On Minn., St. P. & S. Ste. M. (R. R.).
Herrin, Williamson Co., Ill., 9,708.
On Chi., Burl. & Quincy; Ill. Cen.; Mo. Pac. (R. Rs.).
Hershey, Dauphin Co., Pa., 2,700.
On Reading (R. R.).
Hersfeld, Prussia, 11,269.
Herstal, Prov. of Liége, Belgium, 24,832.
An industrial suburb of Liége.
Herten, Westphalia, Germany, 19,167.
Hertford, Hertfordshire, England, 11,376.
Agricultural trade, breweries, glove factories.
–c. s., Perquimas Co., N. C., 1,914.
On Nor. Sou. (R. R.).
Hespeler, Waterloo Co., South, Ontario, Canada, 2,752.
On Grand River; Can. Nat. (R. Rs.).
Hessmer, Avoyelles Par., La., 500.
On La. & Ark. (R. R.).

On Erie (R. R.).
Honeybrook, Chester Co., Pa., 654.
On Penna. (R. R.).
Honey Grove, Fannin Co., Texas, 2,475.
On Tex. & Pac. (R. R.).
Honolulu, capital of the Hawaiian Islands, on the island of Oahu on Oahu Bay, 137,582.
The most important city in the Pacific islands, and an important entrepôt for vessels plying between the United States and Asiatic countries. Its harbor, one of the finest in the world, is formed by a deep basin in the coral reef which surrounds the island. The city has ship-repair yards, machine works, and large pineapple canneries.
Noteworthy structures are the palace, the Government buildings, Roman Catholic cathedral, post office, and the Bishop Museum. Seat of the University of Hawaii.
Hood River, c. s., Hood River Co., Ore., 2,757.
On Mount Hood; Oregon-Wash., R. R. & Nav. Co. (R. Rs.).
Fruit and lumber are the chief industries.
Hooghly, India, 30,000.
Jute manufactures.
Hooker, Texas Co., Okla., 1,628.
On Beav., Meade & Englew.; Chi., Rk. Isl. & Pac. (R. Rs.).
Hooksett, Merrimack Co., N. H., 800.
On Bost. & Me. (R. R.).
Hooper, Dodge Co., Neb., 985.
On Chi. & Nor. West. (R. R.).
–Weber Co., Utah, 1,100.
On Den. & Rio Gde. West. (R. R.).
Hoopeston, Vermilion Co., Ill., 5,613.
On Chi. & East. Ill.; N. York, Chi. & St. Lou. (R. Rs.).
Hoorn, North Holland, Netherlands, 12,026.
A seaport and trade center.
Hoosick Falls, Rensselaer Co., N. Y., 4,755.
On Bost. & Me. (R. R.).
Hooversville, Somerset Co., Pa., 1,448.
On Balt. & Ohio (R. R.).
Hopatcong, Sussex Co., N. J., 534.
On Cen. of N. Jer. (R. R.).
Hope, Hempstead Co., Ark., 6,008.
On La. & Ark.; Mo. Pac.; St. Lou.-San Fran. (R. Rs.).
–Bartholomew Co., Ind., 1,085.
On Cle., Cin., Chi. & St. Lou. (R. R.).
–Dickinson Co., Kans., 561.
On Atch., Top. & Santa Fe; Mo. Pac. (R. Rs.).
–Steele Co., N. Dak., 535.
On Gt. Nor. (R. R.).
–Providence Co., R. I., 1,269.
On N. York, N. Hav. & Hart. (R. R.).
Hopedale, Worcester Co., Mass., 3,068.
–Harrison Co., Ohio, 742.
On N. York Cen.; Pitts. & W. Va. (R. Rs.).
Hope Mills, Cumberland Co., N. C., 971.
On Atl. Coast Line; Va. & Car. Sou. (R. Rs.).
Hopewell, Mercer Co., N. J., 1,467.
On Reading (R. R.).
–(Ind. City), Prince George Co., Va., 11,327.
On Norf. & West.; Seab. Air Line (R. Rs.).
Hopkins (West Minneapolis), Hennepin Co., 3,834.
On Chi., Mil., St. P. & Pac.; Gt. Nor.; Minn. & St. Lou. (R. Rs.).
–Nodaway Co., Mo., 815.
On Chi., Burl. & Quincy (R. R.).
–Richland Co., S. Car., 925.
On Southern (R. R.).
Hopkinsville, c. s., Christian Co., Ky., 10,746.
On Ill. Cen.; Lou. & Nash.; Tenn. Cen. (R. Rs.).
A tobacco market and site of Bethel Woman's College.
Hopkinton, Delaware Co., Iowa, 758.
On Chi., Mil., St. P. & Pac. (R. R.).
–Middlesex Co., Mass., 2,616.
On N. York, N. Hav. & Hart. (R. R.).
–Merrimack Co., N. H., 500.
–St. Lawrence Co., N. Y., 750.
–Washington Co., R. I., 3,277.
Hopland, Mendocino Co., Calif., 860.
On Northw. Pac. (R. R.).
Hopwood, Fayette Co., Pa., 821.
Hoquiam, Grays Harbor Co., Wash., 12,766.
On Nor. Pac.; Chi., Mil., St. P. & Pac.; Ore.-Wash. R. R. & Nav. Co. (R. Rs.).
Furthermost western city on Pacific coast. In important standing timber section. Has extensive saw mills.
Horatio, Sevier Co., Ark., 1,028.
On Kan. Cy. Sou. (R. R.).
Horde, Westphalia, Germany, 34,575.
A manufacturing suburb of Dortmund.
Horicon, Dodge Co., Wis., 2,214.
On Chi., Mil., St. P. & Pac. (R. R.).
Hormigueros, Mun. of Hormigueros, Puerto Rico, 1,959.
Hornell, Steuben Co., N. Y., 16,250.
On Erie; Pitts., Shawmut & Nor. (R. Rs.).
Principal shops of Erie System. Has silk mills and woodworking plant.
Hornersville, Dunklin Co., Mo., 877.
On St. Lou. Southw. (R. R.).
Horning, Allegheny Co., Pa., 675.
On Pitts. & W. Va. (R. R.).
Hornsbyville (Tampico), York Co., Va., 561.
Hornsey, Middlesex, England, 95,524.
A suburb of London.
Hornu, Hainaut, Belgium, 12,029.
Horodenka, East Galicia, Poland, 12,303.
Horse Cave, Hart Co., Ky., 1,259.
On Lou. & Nash. (R. R.).
Horseheads, Chemung Co., N. Y., 2,430.
On Del., Lack. & West.; Erie; Leh. Val.; Penna. (R. Rs.).
Horsens, Amt of Aarhus, Jutland, Denmark, 28,300.
Manufactures of tobacco, soap, textiles, organs, condensed milk, and engines.
Horsham, Sussex, England, 13,579.
Horst, Limburg, Netherlands, 7,131.
Horten, Norway, 10,797.
Horton, Brown Co., Kans., 3,573.
On Chi., Rk. Isl. & Pac. (R. R.).
–Randolph Co., W. Va., 528.
Hortonville, Bristol Co., Mass., 800.
–Outagamie Co., Wis., 906.
On Chi. & Nor. West. (R. R.).
Horwich, Lancashire, England, 15,680.
Hosford, Liberty Co., Fla., 650.
On Apalach. Nor. (R. R.).
Hoshangabad, Central Provinces, India, 13,500.
Hosmer, Edmunds Co., S. Dak., 529.
On Chi., Mil., St. P. & Pac. (R. R.).
Hospers, Sioux Co., Iowa, 548.
On Chi., St. P., Minn. & Oma. (R. R.).
Hosston, Caddo Par., La., 500.
On Tex. & Pac. (R. R.).
Hostetter, Westmoreland Co., Pa., 948.
On Penna. (R. R.).
Hotchkiss, Delta Co., Colo., 541.
On Den. & Rio Gde. West. (R. R.).
Hotien (Khotan), Sinkiang, 50,000.
Hotin (Chotin), Rumania, 15,287.
Hot Springs, National Park, c. s., Garland Co., Ark., 20,238.
A health resort, situated on Hot Springs Creek, and on the Missouri Pacific and the Chicago, Rock Island & Pacific Railroads. The name was acquired from the presence of thermal springs containing valuable medicinal qualities. These springs constitute a much frequented resort for invalids. Forty-four hot springs; daily flow, about 1,000,000 gallons; temperature, 145° F. On Government reservation, springs owned by United States Government, and under its direct supervision.
–Sierra Co., N. Mex., 1,336.
–Madison Co., N. C., 637.
On Southern (R. R.).
–c. s., Fall River Co., S. Dak., 3,263.
On Chi. & Nor. West.; Chi., Burl. & Quincy (R. Rs.).
Houghton, c. s., Houghton Co., Mich., 3,757.
On Cop. Rge.; Dul., So. Sh. & Atl.; Min. Rge. (R. Rs.).
Houghton-le-Springs, Durham, England, 10,492.
Houlka, Chickasaw Co., Miss., 579.
On Gulf, Mob. & Nor. (R. R.).
Houlton, c. s., Aroostook Co., Maine, 6,000.
On Bangor & Aroostook; Can. Pac. (R. Rs.).

COURTESY SOUTH MANCHURIAN RAILWAY

HSI-AN, MANCHUKUO, TYPICAL OF THE COUNTRY, WITH UNPAVED STREETS SWARMING WITH MEN AND ANIMALS

Houma, c. s., Terrebonne Parish, La., 6,531.
On Tex. & N. Orl. (R. R.).
Houston, Houston Co., Minn., 794.
On Chi., Mil., St. P. & Pac. (R. R.).
–c. s., Chickasaw Co., Miss., 1,477.
On Gulf, Mob. & Nor.; Okol., Houst. & Calh. Cy. (R. Rs.).
–c. s., Texas Co., Mo., 690.
–c. s., Harris Co., Texas, 292,352.
Situated on Buffalo Bayou at the head of deep sea navigation of the Houston Ship Channel, fifty miles inland from the Gulf of Mexico. It is served by the Burlington-Rock Island; the Galveston, Houston & Henderson; the Gulf, Colorado & Santa Fe; the Houston Belt & Terminal; the Missouri-Kansas-Texas of Texas; the Missouri Pacific and the Southern Pacific railroads.
Built on both sides of Buffalo Bayou, which is crossed by several bridges. Houston is a great cotton and lumber market and a leading center for oil refining, with many refineries on its water front. Large deposits of sulphur are located in accessible areas.
The Ship Channel, made by widening and deepening Buffalo Bayou, was opened in 1915 and has played a part in making Houston a world port, especially important in the shipping of cotton and petroleum.
The city has a notable museum of Fine Arts and a university, Rice Institute.
Houston, named for General Sam Houston, was settled in 1836 and was capital of the Republic of Texas in 1837.
–Washington Co., Pa., 1,742.
On Penna. (R. R.).
Houston Heights, Harris Co., Texas (Sta. Houston P. O.).
On Mo.-Kan.-Tex. of Tex.; Tex. & N. Orl. (R. Rs.).
Houtzdale, Clearfield Co., Pa., 1,351.
On Penna.; Pitts. & Susq. (R. Rs.).
Hove, East Sussex, England, 54,994.
A suburb of Brighton.
Howard, c. s., Elk Co., Kans., 1,191.
On Atch., Top. & Santa Fe (R. R.).
–Centre Co., Pa., 664.
On Penna. (R. R.).
–c. s., Miner Co., S. Dak., 1,191.
On Chi., Mil., St. P. & Pac. (R. R.).
Howard City, Montcalm Co., Mich., 872.
On Penna.; Pere Marq. (R. Rs.).
Howard Lake, Wright Co., Minn., 763.
On Gt. Nor. (R. R.).
Howe, Lagrange Co., Ind., 810.
On Penna. (R. R.).
–Le Flore Co., Okla., 692.
On Chi., Rk. Isl. & Pac.; Kan. Cy. Sou. (R. Rs.).
–Grayson Co., Texas, 565.
On Tex. & N. Orl. (R. R.).
Howell, c. s., Livingston Co., Mich., 3,615.
On Ann Arbor; Pere Marq. (R. Rs.).
–Colfax Co., Neb., 952.
On Chi. & Nor. West. (R. R.).
Howland, Penobscot Co., Maine, 950.
Howrah, Bengal, India, 224,873.
A center of the jute industry.
Hoxie, Lawrence Co., Ark., 1,448.
On Mo. Pac.; St. Lou.-San Fran. (R. Rs.).
–Sheridan Co., Kans., 933.
On Un. Pac. (R. R.).
Hoytville, Tioga Co., Pa., 572.
On Erie (R. R.).
Hradec Kralove, Czech., 17,818.
The market center of a fertile region.
Hsi-an, Prov. of Mukden, Manchukuo, 20,000.
An agricultural center.
Hsinking, capital of Manchukuo, 201,293.
Huaraz, Dept. of Ancachs, Peru, 20,000.
Huatabampo, State of Sonora, Mexico, 4,508.
Hubbard, Hardin Co., Iowa, 795.
On Chi. & Nor. West. (R. R.).
–Trumbull Co., Ohio, 4,080.
On Erie; N. York Cen. (R. Rs.).
–Hill Co., Texas, 1,855.
On Burl.-Rk. Isl.; St. Lou. Southw. (R. Rs.).
Hubbardston, Worcester Co., Mass., 1,000.
On Bost. & Me. (R. R.).
Hubbell, Houghton Co., Mich., 1,400.
On Cop. Rge.; Min. Rge. (R. Rs.).
Hubli, Bombay Presidency, India, 89,495.
Huddersfield, Yorkshire, England, 113,467.
A center of the manufacture of woolen goods.
Hudson, Middlesex Co., Mass., 8,495.
On Bost. & Me. (R. R.).
–Lenawee Co., Mich., 2,361.
On Cin. Nor.; N. York Cen. (R. Rs.).
–Hillsborough Co., N. H., 2,000.
On Bost. & Me. (R. R.).
–c. s., Columbia Co., N. Y., 12,337.
On Bost. & Alb.; N. York Cen. (R. Rs.).
Manufactures cement, ice tools, ginger ale, knitted goods, and power presses.
–Caldwell Co., N. C., 650.
On Car. & Nor. West. (R. R.).
–Summit Co., Ohio, 1,324.
On Penna. (R. R.).
–Lincoln Co., S. Dak., 528.
On Chi., Mil. & St. P. (R. R.).
–c. s., St. Croix Co., Wis., 2,725.
On Chi., St. P., Minn. & Oma. (R. R.).
–Fremont Co., Wyo., 328.
On Chi. & Nor. West. (R. R.).
Hudson Falls, c. s., Washington Co., N. Y., 6,449.
On Del. & Hud. (R. R.).
Hudsonville, Ottawa Co., Mich., 643.
On Pere Marq. (R. R.).
Hué, capital of Annam, Fr. Indo-China, 34,000.
A commercial center in an agricultural region.
Huejutla, State of Hidalgo, Mexico, 2,843.
Huelva, Spain, 44,058.
Oil, wine, cork and esparto grass.
Hueneme, Ventura Co., Calif., 600.
On Ventura Co. (R. R.).
Huesca, capital of Prov. of Huesca, Spain, 14,105.
Huffs Station, Westmoreland Co., Pa., 675.
Hughes, St. Francis Co., Ark., 815.
On Mo. Pac. (R. R.).
Hughesdale, Providence Co., R. I., 918.
Hughes Springs, Cass Co., Texas, 736.
On La., Ark. & Tex. (R. R.).
Hughestown, Luzerne Co., Pa., 2,252.
Hughesville, Charles Co., Md., 500.
On Wash., Brandyw. & Pt. Lookout (R. R.).
–Lycoming Co., Pa., 1,868.
On Williamsp. & Nor. Br. (R. R.).
Hughson, Stanislaus Co., Calif., 500.
On Atch., Top. & Santa Fe (R. R.).
Hugo, c. s., Lincoln Co., Colo., 712.
On Un. Pac. (R. R.).
–c. s., Choctaw Co., Okla., 5,272.
On St. Lou.-San Fran. (R. R.).
Hugoton, c. s., Stevens Co., Kans., 1,426.
On Atch., Top. & Santa Fe (R. R.).
Hull (or Kingston-on-Hull), Yorkshire, England, 313,366.
A parliamentary, municipal, and county borough, and third port in the kingdom; outlet for woolen and cotton goods from the midland counties, and entrepôt for oversea trade with Germany and Scandinavia; has vast docks.
In 1298 Edward I. named it Kingston-upon-Hull and gave it a charter.
–Wright Co., Quebec, Canada, 29,433.
On Can. Pac. (R. R.).
Pulp, paper, and match factories.
–Pike Co., Ill., 554.
On Chi., Burl. & Quincy; Wab. (R. Rs.).
–Sioux Co., Iowa, 905.
On Chi., Mil., St. P. & Pac. (R. R.).
–Plymouth Co., Mass., 2,619.
On N. York, N. Hav. & Hart. (R. R.).
–Liberty Co., Tex., 727.
On Beau., Sour L. & West. (R. R.).
Hulmeville, Bucks Co., Pa., 582.
Humacao, Mun. of Humacao, Puerto Rico, 8,407.
Humansville, Polk Co., Mo., 1,022.
On St. Lou.-San Fran. (R. R.).
Humble, Harris Co., Texas, 3,527.
On Tex. & N. Orl. (R. R.).
Humboldt, Humboldt Co., Iowa, 2,251.
On Minn. & St. Lou. (R. R.).
–Allen Co., Kans., 2,464.
On Atch., Top. & Santa Fe; Mo.-Kan.-Tex. (R. Rs.).
–Richardson Co., Neb., 1,435.
On Chi., Burl. & Quincy (R. R.).
–Pershing Co., Nev., 564.
On Sou. Pac. (R. R.).
–Gibson Co., Tenn., 4,613.
On Lou. & Nash.; Mob. & Ohio (R. Rs.).
Hume, Edgar Co., Ill., 585.
On Balt. & Ohio; Kan. & Sidell (R. Rs.).
–Bates Co., Mo., 595.
On Kan. Cy. Sou. (R. R.).
Humeston, Wayne Co., Iowa, 924.
On Chi., Burl. & Quincy (R. R.).
Hummelstown, Dauphin Co., Pa., 3,036.
On Reading (R. R.).
Hummels Wharf, Snyder Co., Pa., 500.
Humphrey, Jefferson Co., Ark., 595.
On St. Lou. Southw. (R. R.).

COURTESY NEW YORK CENTRAL R. R.

LOOKING NORTH ON MERIDIAN STREET, INDIANAPOLIS, INDIANA. THE $10,000,000
WORLD WAR MEMORIAL IS SEEN AT THE RIGHT

I

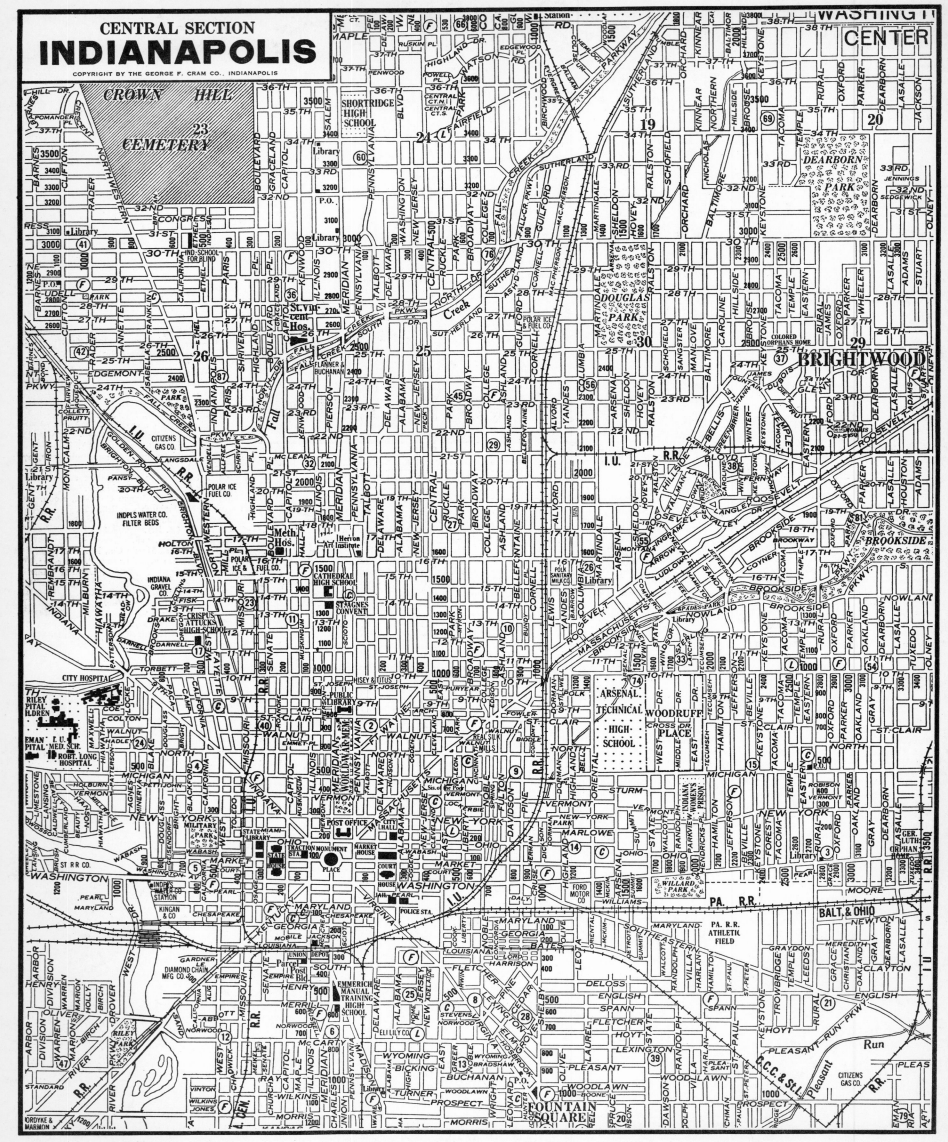

CENTRAL SECTION
INDIANAPOLIS
COPYRIGHT BY THE GEORGE F. CRAM CO., INDIANAPOLIS

MAP OF CENTRAL INDIANAPOLIS, THE CAPITAL AND LARGEST CITY OF INDIANA. THE CITY IS SITUATED ON THE WHITE RIVER. AN ARCHITECTURAL FEATURE OF INDIANAPOLIS IS THE $10,000,000 WORLD WAR MEMORIAL PLAZA, SITUATED AT THE INTERSECTION OF SEVERAL OF THE MAIN STREETS OF THE CITY

On Green Bay & Western (R. R.).
IONE, Amador Co., Calif., 950.
On Amador Cen.; Sou. Pac. (R. Rs.).
–Pend Oreille Co., Wash., 594.
On Chi., Mil., St. P. & Pac. (R. R.).
IONIA, c. s., Ionia Co., Mich., 6,562.
On Gd. Tr.; Pere Marq. (R. Rs.).
IOTA, Acadia Parish, La., 827.
On Sou. Pac. (R. R.).
IOWA CITY, c. s., Johnson Co., Iowa, 15,340.
On Ced. Rap. & Ia. Cy. (El.); Chi., Rk. Isl. & Pac. (R. Rs.).
At junction of leading highways. Former State capital. Seat of Iowa University.
IOWA FALLS, Harden So., Iowa, 4,112.
On Chi., Rk. Isl. & Pac.; Chi. & Nor. West.; Ill. Cen. (R. Rs.).
IOWA PARK, Wichita Co., Texas, 2,009.
On Ft. Worth & Denv. Cy. (R. R.).
IPAVA, Fulton Co., Ill., 635.
On Chi., Burl. & Quincy (R. R.).
IPSWICH, Suffolk, England, 87,557.
An important industrial town.
–Queensland, Australia, 22,498.
Center of a mining and agricultural region.
–Essex Co., Mass., 6,217.
On Bost. & Me. (R. R.).
–Edmunds Co., S. D., 943.
On Chi., Mil., St. P. & Pac. (R. R.).
IQUIQUE, capital of Prov. of Tarapaca, Chile, 52,203.
A seaport from which much nitrate is shipped.
IRETON, Sioux Co., Iowa, 612.
On Chi. & Nor. West. (R. R.).
IRIGA, Prov. of Ambos Camarines, Luzon, P. I., 23,598.
A farming and lumbering center.
IRKUTSK, Siberia, Soviet Union in Asia, 158,500.
On the Trans-Siberian Railroad. One of the most important commercial cities of the Asiatic Soviet Union. Immense tea trade.
IRON BELT, Iron Co., Wis., 800.
On Mpls., St. P. & S. Ste. M. (R. R.).
IRONDALE, Jefferson Co., Ala., 1,517.
On Ala. Gt. Sou.; Cen. of Ga.; Seab. Air Line; Sou. (R. Rs.).
IRON GATE, Alleghany Co., Va., 777.
On Chesa. & Ohio (R. R.).
IRON MOUNTAIN, c. s., Dickinson Co., Mich., 11,652.
On Chi. & Nor. West.; Chi., Mil., St. P. & Pac. (R. Rs.).
Located in an iron and timber district.
IRON RIVER, Iron Co., Mich., 4,665.
On Chi. & Nor. West.; Chi., Mil., St. P. & Pac. R. Rs.).
–Bayfield Co., Wis., 800.
On Dul., So. Sho. & Atl.; Nor. Pac. (R. Rs.).
IRON SPRINGS, Adams Co., Pa., 600.
IRONTON, c. s., Iron Co., Mo., 974.
On Mo. Pac. (R. R.).
–Crow Wing Co., Minn., 1,033.
On Mpls., St. P. & S. Ste. M.; Nor. Pac. (R. Rs.).
–c. s., Lawrence Co., Ohio, 16,621.
On Det., Tol. & Iron.; Norf. & West., Chesa. & Ohio (R. Rs.).
Has extensive mining and lumbering industries.
IRONWOOD, Gogebic Co., Mich., 14,299.
On Chi. & Nor. West.; Mpls., St. P. & S. Ste. M. (R. Rs.).
Industries; hydro-electric power supply, iron ore, mining and lumbering.
IROQUOIS, Dundas Co., Ontario, Canada, 937.
On Can. Nat. (R. R.).
–Beadle and Kingsbury Cos., S. Dak., 470.
On Chi. & Nor. West. (R. R.).
IRVINE, c. s., Estill Co., Ky., 3,640.
On Lou. & Nash. (R. R.).
–Ayre Co., Scotland, 8,318.
IRVING, Montgomery Co., Ill., 553.
On Chi. & East. Ill.; Cle., Cin., Chi. & St. Lou. (R. Rs.).
–Dallas Co., Tex., 731.
On Chi., Rk. Isl. & Gulf; St. Lou.-San Fran. (R. Rs.).
IRVINGTON, Alameda Co., Calif., 1,000.
On Sou. Pac.; West. Pac. (R. Rs.).
–Marion Co., Ind. (Sta. of Indianapolis).
On Balt. & Ohio; Erie (R. Rs.).
–Breckinridge Co., Ky., 764.
On Lou. & Nash. (R. R.).
–Essex Co., N. J., 56,733.
On Leh. Val. (R. R.).
–Westchester Co., N. Y., 3,067.
On N. York Cen. (R. R.).
–Lancaster Co., Va., 735.
IRVONA, Clearfield Co., Pa., 1,213.
On N. York Cen.; Penna. (R. Rs.).
IRWIN, Westmoreland Co., Pa., 3,443.
On Penna. (R. R.).
IRWINTON, Wilkinson Co., Ga., 561.
ISABAN, McDowell Co., W. Va., 612.
On Norf. & West. (R. R.).
ISABELA, Occidental Negros, Negros, P. I., 19,653.
–Mun. of Isabela, Puerto Rico, 2,810.
ISABELLA, Polk Co., Tenn., 850.
ISCHL, Germany. See BAD ISCHL.

ISEGHEM, Prov. of West Flanders, Belgium, 14,738.
ISELIN, Middlesex Co., N. J., 710.
On Penna. (R. R.).
ISERLOHN, Westphalia, Germany, 32,000.
A steel manufacturing town near Wuppertal.
ISFAHAN, Iran (Persia), 100,100.
Ancient capital of Persia; center of commerce; seat of Roman Catholic bishop and a bishop of the Gregorian National Armenians. Isfahan is famous in Persian poetry and history.
ISHPEMING, Marquette Co., Mich., 9,238.
On Chi. & Nor. West.; Dul., So. Sh. & Atl.; L. Sup. & Ishpem. (R. Rs.).
ISLAND, McLean Co., Ky., 694.
On Lou. & Nash. (R. R.).
ISLAND FALLS, Aroostook Co., Maine, 800.
On Bangor & Aroostook (R. R.).
ISLAND GROVE, Sangamon Co., Ill., 500.
On Wabash (R. R.).
ISLAND PARK, Nassau Co., N. Y., 1,002.
On Long Isl. (R. R.).
ISLAND POND, Essex Co., Vt., 1,837.
On Gd. Tr. (R. R.).
ISLE, Mille Lacs Co., Minn., 523.
On Mpls., St. P. & S. Ste. M. (R. R.).
ISLESBORO, Waldo Co., Maine, 697.
ISLETA, Bernalillo Co., N. M., 1,000.
On Atch., Top. & Santa Fe (R. R.).
ISLETON, Sacramento Co., Cal., 2,090.
On Sou. Pac. (R. R.).
ISLINGTON, Norfolk Co., Mass., 700.
On N. York, N. Hav. & Hart. (R. R.).
ISLIP TERRACE, Suffolk Co., N. Y., 946.
ISMAIL, Bessarabia, Rumania, 26,123.
An agricultural trade center.
ISOLA, Humphreys Co., Miss., 519.
On Ill. Cen. (R. R.).
ISSAQUAH, King Co., Wash., 763.
On Nor. Pac. (R. R.).
ISSOUDUN, Dept. of Indre, France, 11,511.
ISSY, Dept. of Seine, France, 44,091.
About 5 miles S. W. of Paris.
ISTANBUL (Constantinople), former capital of the Ottoman Empire, and the largest city of Turkey, 741,148.
Is located on a promontory bounded by the Sea of Marmora, the Bosporus, and the Golden Horn, an inlet of the Bosporus. On the one side not surrounded by water is a strong wall. The city has been modernized, and most of its quaint but dirty picturesqueness has disappeared. On the site of the ancient Byzantium is the seraglio, in which was until 1863, the great gate known as the "Sublime Porte."
The most magnificent structure of the city is the celebrated Mosque of St. Sophia, which was built originally for a Christian church by Justinian in the sixth century, and was converted into a mosque by Mohammed II. in the fifteenth. Other famous mosques are those of Achmed, Suleiman, and of Bajazet. The public schools of Istanbul are of three grades; the mosque colleges for the study of theology and law, the provincial schools for boys, and the primary schools for both sexes. A university founded in 1900 and a lyceum established in 1867 furnish higher educational facilities. There are also numerous libraries, museums, and literary societies. Robert College is under American management.
During the last decade a great effort has been made by the government to educate the people. Istanbul has a fine harbor. The trade is chiefly in the hands of foreigners, and the exports consist of silks, carpets, wool, filigree work, hides, and embroideries. The city has railway connection with Edirne (Adrianople), Beograd (Belgrade) and Paris.
Istanbul is the ancient Byzantium founded by the Dorians in the seventh century B. C. In 330 A. D. it was rebuilt by Constantine who made it the capital of the Roman Empire under the name of Constantinople. It was changed to Istanbul in 1928. In 1453 Mohammed II. created it the capital of the Ottoman Empire.
ITÁ, Paraguay, 30,252.
ITALY, Ellis Co., Texas, 1,230.
On Mo. Pac.; Mo-Kan.-Tex. of Tex.; Texas Electric (R. Rs.).
ITANGUA, Paraguay, 11,317.
ITASCA, Du Page Co., Ill., 594.
On Chi., Mil., St. P. & Pac. (R. R.).
–Hill Co., Texas, 1,665.
On Mo.-Kan.-Tex. of Tex. (R. R.).
ITHACA, c. s., Gratiot Co., Mich., 1,780.
On Ann Arbor (R. R.).
–c. s., Tompkins Co., N. Y., 20,708.
On Del., Lack. & West.; Leh. Val. (R. Rs.).
Situated at head of Cayuga Lake on N. Y. State Barge Canal System.
Has a number of industries, but is chiefly noted as the seat of Cornell University.
ITTA BENA, Leflore Co., Miss., 1,370.
On Columbus & Greenville (R. R.).
ITZEHOE, Holstein, Germany, 21,000.
Iron founding, ship building, and wool spinning.
IUKA, c. s., Tishomingo Co., Miss., 1,441.

On Southern (R. R.).
IVA, Anderson Co., S. C., 1,273.
On Charl. & W. Car. (R. R.).
IVANHOE, c. s., Lincoln Co., Minn., 556.
On Chi. & Nor. West. (R. R.).
–(Frye), Washington Co., Pa., 513.
–Wythe Co., Va., 650.
On Norf. & West. (R. R.).
IVANOVO, Vosnesensk, Soviet Union, 188,500.
IVERSON, Carlton Co., Minn., 556.
On Nor. Pac. (R. R.).
IVORYTON, Middlesex Co., Conn., 820.
IVRY-SUR-SEINE, Dept. of Seine, France, 44,859.
An industrial and residential suburb of Paris.
IXELLES, Brabant, Belgium, 87,113.
IZMIR (Smyrna), Turkey, 170,959.
Has a magnificent harbor.

J

JACKMAN, Somerset Co., Maine, 900.
On Can. Pac. (R. R.).
JACKSBORO, c. s., Campbell Co., Tenn., 834.
On Lou. & Nash.; Sou. (R. Rs.).
–c. s., Jack Co., Texas, 1,837.
On Chi., Rk. Isl. & Gulf; St. Lou., San Fran. & Tex. (R. Rs.).

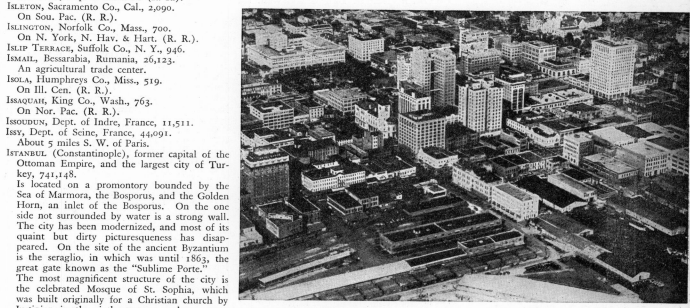

AN AERIAL VIEW OF THE CENTRAL PORTION OF JACKSONVILLE, THE GATEWAY TO FLORIDA AND THE CENTER OF A LARGE WINTER TOURIST POPULATION

JACKSON, Clarke Co., Ala., 1,828.
On Southern (R. R.).
–c. s., Amador Co., Cal., 2,005.
–c. s., Butts Co., Ga., 1,776.
On Southern (R. R.).
–c. s., Breathitt Co., Ky., 2,109.
On Lou. & Nash. (R. R.).
–East Feliciana Parish, La., 3,966.
–c. s., Jackson Co., Mich., 55,187.
On Cle., Cin., Chi. & St. Lou.; Gd. Tr.; N. York Cen.; Mich. Cen. (R. Rs.).
Chief manufactures: automobile and related industries. There are large plants for making electric refrigerators, radios, clothing, automotive wheels, axles, springs, gears, shafts and horns.
–c. s., Jackson Co., Minn., 2,206.
On Chi., Mil., St. P. & Pac. (R. R.).
–c. s., Hinds Co., Miss., State capital, 48,282.
On the Pearl River and on the Illinois Central, the Gulf, Mobile and Northern Railroads, 45 miles east of Vicksburg and 183 miles north of New Orleans.
The old capitol houses the noted State Library, the largest in the south. Seat of Millsaps and Belhaven Colleges, also of a college for colored students. Manufactures are mostly confined to timber, cotton-seed oil, and foundry products.
Jackson was settled about 1830 and incorporated 1840. During the Civil War it was occupied by General Grant, 1863, and in 1864 was nearly destroyed by General Sherman.
–c. s., Cape Girardeau Co., Mo., 2,465.
On Mo. Pac. (R. R.).
–c. s., Northampton Co., N. C., 677.
–c. s., Jackson Co., Ohio, 5,922.
On Balt. & Ohio; Chesa. & Ohio; Det., Tol. & Iron. (R. Rs.).
–c. s., Madison Co., Tenn., 22,172.
On Gulf, Mob. & Nor.; Ill. Cen.; Mob. & Ohio.; Nash., Chatt. & St. Lou. (R. Rs.).
Center of a farming region. Site of Union University and a state Agricultural College.
–Teton Co., Wyo., 533.
JACKSON CENTER, Shelby Co., Ohio, 526.
On Det., Tol. & Iron. (R. R.).
JACKSONS, Schuylkill Co., Pa., 575.

On Southern (R. R.).
JACKSONVILLE, Calhoun Co., Ala., 2,840.
On Seab. Air Line; Sou. (R. Rs.).
Seat of State Normal School.
–c. s., Duval Co., Fla., 146,259.
On Atl. Coast Line; Fla. East Coast; Ga. Sou. & Fla.; Jacksonv. Term.; Seab. Air Line; Sou. (R. Rs.).
A growing port with extensive wharf and terminal facilities. Its water-borne traffic is large—lumber, flour, naval stores and cotton being the chief exports. A general distributing point for wholesale trade.
–c. s., Morgan Co., Ill., 17,747.
On Chi., Burl. & Quincy; Alton; Wab. (R. Rs.).
Noted for its manufactures of Ferris Wheels and steel bridges. Site of Illinois Women's College.
–c. s., Onslow Co., N. C., 783.
On Atl. Coast Line (R. R.).
–Athens Co., Ohio, 880.
On N. York Cen. (R. R.).
–Jackson Co., Ore., 706.
–Cherokee Co., Texas, 6,748.
On Mo. Pac.; St. Lou. Southw.; Sou. Pac. (R. Rs.).
JACKSONVILLE BEACH, Duval Co., Fla., 1,094.
JACMEL, South Coast, Haiti, 7,500.
JACOBABAD, Sindh, British India, 10,800.
A grain trade center.
JACOBS CREEK, Westmoreland Co., Pa., 550.
On Balt. & Ohio; Pitts. & L. Erie (R. Rs.).
JAEN, capital of Prov. of Jaen, Spain, 36,233.
Has a picturesque location on the slopes of the Jabalcuz Mountains.
JAFFA, Palestine, Asia Minor, 71,000.
The Joppa of the Bible. It was taken in 1799 by Napoleon.
JAFFNA, island of Jaffna, Ceylon, 45,708.
A trade center in an agricultural section.
JAGERNDORF, Germany. See KRNOV.
JAGNA, Bohol, P. I., 14,210.
JAIPUR, capital of State of Jaipur, India, 144,179.
Famous for its gem cutting industries.
JALAPA, capital of Veracruz, Mexico, 36,812.
On Nat'l of Mex.; Jalapa & Teocelo (R. Rs.).
Frequented by tourists during hot seasons.
–Guatemala, 16,600.
On Int. of Cen. Amer. (R. R.).
JALONG, Person Co., N. Car., 783.
JALPAN, State of Querétaro, Mexico, 1,389.
JAMESBURG, Middlesex Co., N. J., 2,048.
On Penna. (R. R.).
JAMES CITY, Craven Co., N. C., 600.
On Atl. & Nor. Car. (R. R.).
JAMESPORT, Daviess Co., Mo., 839.
On Chi., Rk. Isl. & Pac. (R. R.).
JAMESTOWN, Tuolumne Co., Calif., 815.
On Sierra Ry. of Calif. (R. R.).
–Boone Co., Ind., 552.
On Cle., Cin., Chi. & St. Lou. (R. R.).
–Chautauqua Co., N. Y., 45,155.
On Erie; Jamest., Westf. & Northw. (El.) (R. R.).
Site of the Chautauqua Institution. Manufactures: furniture and building trim. Many dairy farms in the vicinity.
–c. s., Stutsman Co., N. Dak., 8,187.
On Nor. Pac.; Midl. Continent (R. Rs.).
Seat of Jamestown College.
–Greene Co., Ohio, 944.
On Balt. & Ohio (R. R.).
–Mercer Co., Pa., 710.
On N. York Cen.; Penna. (R. Rs.).
–Newport Co., R. I., 1,897.
–c. s., Fentress Co., Tenn., 857.
On Oneida & West. (R. R.).

Jamesville, Onondaga Co., N. Y., 800.
On Del., Lack. & West. (R. R.).
Janesville, Waseca Co., Minn., 1,184.
On Chi. & Nor. West. (R. R.).
–c. s., Rock Co., Wis., 21,628.
On Chi., Mil., St. P. & Pac.; Chi. & Nor. West. (R. Rs.).
Manufacturing center of various commodities such as fountain pens, fencing, auto parts, canned vegetables, furniture, clothing, and tools.
Janiuay, Panay, P. I., 25,075.
Jarales, Valencia Co., N. Mex., 700.
On Atch., Top. & Santa Fe (R. R.).
Jaro, Leyte, P. I., 24,572.
Has large sugar mills.
Jaroslaw, Galicia, Poland, 22,330.
Textiles, pottery, and brandy.
Jarrow, Durham, England, 32,018.
An industrial suburb of Newcastle.
Jarvisburg, Currituck Co., N. C., 550.
Jasonville, Greene Co., Ind., 3,536.
On Chi., Mil., St. P. & Pac. (R. R.).
Jasper, c. s., Walker Co., Ala., 5,313.
On Ala. Cen.; Ill. Cen.; Nor. Ala.; St. Lou.-San Fran. (R. Rs.).
–c. s., Hamilton Co., Fla., 1,748.
On Atl. Coast Line; Ga. Sou. & Fla. (R. Rs.).
–c. s., Pickens Co., Ga., 563.
On Lou. & Nash. (R. R.).
–c. s., Dubois Co., Ind., 3,905.
On Southern (R. R.).
–Pipestone and Rock Cos., Minn., 769.
On Gt. Nor. (R. R.).
–Jasper Co., Mo., 754.
On Mo. Pac. (R. R.).
–c. s., Marion Co., Tenn., 1,251.
On Nash., Chatt. & St. Lou. (R. R.).
–c. s., Jasper Co., Texas, 3,393.
On Gulf, Colo. & Santa Fe (R. R.).
Jassy, Rumania. See Iasi.
Jaszapati, Jasz-Nag.-Szolnok, Comitat, Hungary, 12,378.
Jaszbereny, Jasz-Nag.-Szolnok, Hungary, 29,874.
An agricultural distributing point.
Jativa, Prov. of Valencia, Spain, 14,148.
Jauer, Prussia, Germany, 12,158.
Java, Walworth Co., S. Dak., 529.
On Chi., Mil., St. P. & Pac. (R. R.).
Jayton, Kent Co., Tex., 623.
On Wichita Val. (R. R.).
Jayuya, Mun. of Jayuya, Puerto Rico, 6,361.
Jeanerette, Iberia Parish, La., 2,228.
On Mo. Pac.; Sou. Pac. (R. Rs.).
Jeanesville, Luzerne Co., Pa., 500.
On Leh. Val. (R. R.).
Jeannette, Westmoreland Co., Pa., 15,126.
On Penna. (R. R.).
An industrial town near Pittsburgh. Noted for its glass manufactures.
Jefferson, c. s., Jackson Co., Ga., 1,869.
On Gainesv. Midl. (R. R.).
–c. s., Greene Co., Iowa, 3,431.
On Chi., Mil., St. P. & Pac.; Chi. & Nor. West. (R. Rs.).
–Worcester Co., Mass., 861.
On Bost. & Me. (R. R.).
–c. s., Ashtabula Co., Ohio, 1,601.
On N. York Cen. (R. R.).
–Greene Co., Pa., 528.
–c. s., Marion Co., Texas, 2,329.
On Jef. & Northw.; La., Ark. & Tex.; Tex. & Pac. (R. Rs.).
–c. s., Jefferson Co., Wis., 2,639.
On Chi. & Nor. West. (R. R.).
Jefferson City, c. s., Cole Co., Mo., State capital, 21,596.
Situated on the Missouri River, and on the Mo. Pac., and the Mo.-Kan.-Texas railroads. Jefferson City is 125 miles west of St. Louis, in a rich agricultural, timber, and mining region.
–Jefferson Co., Tenn., 1,898.
On Southern (R. R.).
Jeffersontown, Jefferson Co., Ky., 614.
On Southern (R. R.).
Jeffersonville, Twiggs Co., Ga., 692.
On Macon, Dub. & Sav. (R. R.).
–c. s., Clark Co., Ind., 11,946.
On Balt. & Ohio; Cle., Cin., Chi. & St. Lou.; Penna.; Ind. R. R. Sys. (El.) (R. Rs.).
Site of an Army supply depot.
–Fayette Co., Ohio, 656.
On Det., Tol. & Iron. (R. R.).
Jehol, Manchukuo, 650,000.
A thriving commercial center and former summer residence of the Manchu emperors.
Jelgava (Mitau), Courland, Latvia, 33,048.
Occupied by the Bolshevists Jan. 18, 1918; recaptured by the Letts, March 19, 1919.
Jellico, Campbell Co., Tenn., 1,530.
On Lou. & Nash.; Sou. (R. Rs.).
Jemappes, Prov. of Hainaut, Belgium, 14,573.
Site of a famous battle in 1792.
Jemeppe, Liége, Belgium, 13,725.
Jemez (Jemes P. O.), Sandoval Co., N. Mex., 650.
Jena, Saxe-Weimar, Germany, 57,000.
Seat of a famous university. The city has various manufactures; especially noted for its optical goods.
–c. s., La Salle Parish, La., 1,007.
On La. & Ark. (R. R.).
Jenkinjones, McDowell Co., W. Va., 800.
On Norf. & West. (R. R.).
Jenkins, Letcher Co., Ky., 8,465.
On Chesa. & Ohio (R. R.).
Jenkintown, Montgomery Co., Pa., 4,797.
On Reading (R. R.).
Seat of Beaver College.
Jenks, Tulsa Co., Okla., 1,110.
On Midl. Val. (R. R.).
Jennings, Hamilton Co., Fla., 536.
On Ga. Sou. & Fla. (R. R.).
–c. s., Jefferson Davis Parish, La., 4,036.
On Sou. Pac. (R. R.).
–Pawnee Co., Okla., 653.
On Mo.-Kans.-Tex.; (R. R.).
Jenny Lind, Sebastian Co., Ark., 517.
On Mo. Pac. (R. R.).
Jerez de la Frontera, Prov. of Cadiz, Andalusia, Spain, 64,861.
Jerez de Los Caballeros, Prov. of Badajoz, Spain, 14,991.
Noted as the birthplace of Balboa.
Jericho, Nassau Co., N. Y., 500.
Jermyn, Lackawanna Co., Pa., 3,519.
On Del. & Hud.; N. York, Ont. & West. (R. Rs.).
Jerome, Yavapai Co., Ariz., 4,932.
On Verde Tun. & Smelt. (R. R.).
–c. s., Jerome Co., Idaho, 1,976.
On Un. Pac. (R. R.).
Jersey City, c. s., Hudson Co., N. J., 316,715.
Situated on the Hudson River, and the Pennsylvania; the Erie; the Lehigh Valley; the Central of New Jersey; Delaware, Lackawanna & Western; the Baltimore and Ohio; the New York Central; Hudson and Manhattan; the New Jersey and New York; New York, Ontario & Western; the New York, Susquehanna and Western Railroads; opposite New York City with which it is connected by steam ferries and tunnels under the Hudson River.
The business interests of Jersey City are closely allied with those of New York City. Being the terminus of several large railroad and steamship lines, the commercial trade is very extensive. It has large stockyards, slaughter-houses, grain elevators, and meat-packing establishments, also varied and extensive manufactures. Jersey City was formerly known as Paulus Hook; was laid out in 1804; chartered as the city of Jersey in 1820; incorporated as Jersey City in 1838.
Jersey Shore, Lycoming Co., Pa., 5,781.
On N. York Cen.; Penna. (R. Rs.).
Jerseyville, c. s., Jersey Co., Ill., 4,309.
On Alton; Chicago, Springfield & St. Louis (R. Rs.).
Jerusalem, Palestine, 125,000.
Situated on an elevated site within the fork of two ravines, the Valley of Jehoshaphat and the Valley of Hinnom. On the eastern side of this valley is Mt. Moriah, where stood the palace and temple of Solomon. Immediately south of this stood the mountain fortress of Zion, known as the City of David. Ancient Jerusalem possessed three walls, and the present limits of the city are much the same as those indicated by the third wall. Of the seven gates only five are now used. The interior of the city has many mosques, churches, and convents. The houses are substantially built of stone, and in most cases without windows. The streets are merely long lanes with dead walls on each side of them. The Church of the Holy Sepulchre, built by Helena, the mother of Constantine the Great, is remarkable for its decorations and the number of pilgrims by whom it is visited. The inclosure known as El Haram-Esh-Sherif (The Noble Sanctuary) is in the form of a parallelogram surrounded by a lofty wall.
Jerusalem surrendered December 10, 1917. The British, under General Allenby, entered December 11, 1917.
Jessore, capital of Jessore Dist., Bengal, British India, 8,300.
Jesup, c. s., Wayne Co., Ga., 2,303.
On Atl. Coast Line; Sou. (R. Rs.).
–Buchanan Co., Iowa, 736.
On Ill. Cen. (R. R.).
Jetmore, c. s., Hodgeman Co., Kansas, 964.
On Atch., Top. & Santa Fe (R. R.).
Jewell, Jewell Co., Kans., 686.
On Mo. Pac. (R. R.).
–Hamilton Co., Iowa, 950.
On Chi. & Nor. West. (R. R.).
–Tazewell Co., Va., 521.
On Norf. & West. (R. R.).
Jewett, Harrison Co., Ohio, 876.
On Penna.; Wheel. & L. Erie (R. Rs.).
–Leon Co., Tex., 516.
On Mo. Pac.; Burl.-Rk. Isl. (R. Rs.).
Jewett City, New London Co., Conn., 4,436.
On N. York, New Hav. & Hart. (R. R.).
Jhansi, United Provinces, India, 66,432.
Center for agricultural trade.
Jiddah, Saudi Arabia, 25,000
On the Red Sea, chief port of Saudi Arabia. The chief seaport of the country.
Jihlava (Iglau), Czechoslovakia, 31,031.
A mining and commercial center.
Jimenez, State of Chihuahua, Mexico, 6,033.
On Nat. of Mex. (R. R.).
Jinotega, Nicaragua, 19,990.
Jinotepe, Nicaragua, 13,984.
Jinsen, Chosen, 100,303.
The seaport of Keijo.
Joachimsthal, Czechoslovakia. See Jachymov.
João Pessoa (Parahiba), Brazil, 101,300.
A port and market center.
Jodhpur, capital of Jodhpur Dist., Rajputana, India, 94,736.
A fortified commercial town with manufactures of leather and embroideries.
Joe, Madison Co., N. C., 550.
Joffre, Washington Co., Pa., 750.
Johannesburg, Transvaal Province, Union of South Africa, 554,000.
The central point of the gold fields of the district stretching southwest from Pretoria to Potchefstrom, and known as the Witwatersrand. Founded in September, 1886, on a desolate plateau at the height of 5,600 feet above sea level, it has grown with remarkable rapidity.
–Otsego Co., Mich., 721.
John Sevier, Knox Co., Tenn., 700.
On Southern (R. R.).
Johnson, c. s., Stanton Co., Kans., 582.
On Atch., Top. & Santa Fe (R. R.).
–Lamoille Co., Vt., 659.
On St. Johns & L. Champ. (R. R.).
Johnsonburg, Elk Co., Pa., 4,737.
On Balt. & Ohio; Erie; Penna. (R. Rs.).
Johnson City (formerly Lestershire), Broome Co., N. Y., 13,567.
On Del., Lack. & West.; Erie (R. Rs.).
A suburb of Binghampton.
–c. s., Washington Co., Tenn., 25,080.
On Clinchfield; E. Tenn. & West. Nor. C.; Sou. (R. Rs.).
In mining and timber section.
Chief industries: woodworking, chemical, iron (including the Cranberry pig iron for armor plate), silk, hosiery, flour, dye, leather, tannic acid, flooring, drugs, fabricated steel, and brick.
Seat of East Tennessee State Normal School and U. S. Government Soldiers' Home.
Johnsonville, Rensselaer Co., N. Y., 575.
On Bost. & Me. (R. R.).
Johnston, Providence Co., R. I., 9,768.
–Edgefield Co., S. C., 1,072.
On Southern (R. R.).
Johnston City, Williamson Co., Ill., 5,955.
On Chi. & East. Ill.; Mo. Pac. (R. Rs.).
Johnstone, Renfrew, Scotland, 12,837.
Flax spinning, paper making, iron founding, and machine shops.
Johnstown, Weld Co., Colo., 767.
On Gt. West. (R. R.).
–c. s., Fulton Co., N. Y., 10,801.
On Fonda, Johnst. & Glovers (R. R.).
An important glove-making center.
–Licking Co., Ohio, 1,006.
On N. York Cen. (R. R.).
–Cambria Co., Pa., 66,993.
On Balt. & Ohio; Penna. (R. Rs.).
Steel plants are famous. Manufactures include radios, silk, stoves, paints, motor trucks, mine cars, and electrical machinery.
Joliet, c. s., Will Co., Ill., 42,993.
On the Illinois Waterway (connecting Lake Michigan with the Mississippi River), and on the Alton, Atchison, Topeka and Santa Fe; the Chicago, Rock Island and Pacific; the Elgin, Joliet and Eastern; the Chicago, Milwaukee, St. Paul and Pacific, and the Michigan Central railroads.
It has manufactures of steel and barbed wire, stove and boiler works, machine shops, tin plate and horseshoe works, bridge and farm implement plants.
Site of State Penitentiary.
Joliette, Joliette Co., Quebec, Canada, 10,765.
On Can. Nat.; Can. Pac. (R. Rs.).
Jonesboro, Jefferson Co., Ala.
On Lou. & Nash. (R. R.).
–c. s., Craighead Co., Ark., 10,326.
On St. Lou.-San Fran.; St. Lou. Southw. (R. Rs.).
Center of a lumbering and agricultural region.
–c. s., Clayton Co., Ga., 1,065.
On Cen. of Ga. (R. R.).
–c. s., Union Co., Ill., 1,241.
On Mob. & Ohio (R. R.).
–Grant Co., Ind., 1,496.
On Chesa. & Ohio; Clev., Cin., Chi. & St. Lou. (R. Rs.).
–c. s., Jackson Parish, La., 1,949.
On Chi., Rk. Isl. & Pac. (R. R.).
–Lee Co., N. C., 838.
On Atl. Coast Line; Atl. & West. (R. Rs.).
–c. s., Washington Co., Tenn., 981.
On Southern (R. R.).
Jones Mill, Monroe Co., Ala. See Frisco City.
Jonesport, Washington Co., Maine, 1,200.
Jonestown, Coahoma Co., Miss., 506.
On Ill. Cen. (R. R.).
–Lebanon Co., Pa., 624.
On Reading (R. R.).
Jonesville, Catahoula Parish, La., 1,123.
On La. & Ark. (R. R.).
–Hillsdale Co., Mich., 1,316.
On N. York Cen. (R. R.).
–Yadkin Co., N. C., 1,306.
–Union Co., S. C., 1,153.
On Southern (R. R.).
Jönköping, capital of Län of Jönköping, Sweden, 30,908.
Famous for its match factories.
Joplin, Jasper & Newton Cos., Mo., 33,454.
On Atch., Top. & Santa Fe; Joplin-Pittsb. (El.); Kan. Cy. Sou.; Mo. & Ark.; Mo.-Kan.-Tex.; Mo. Pac.; St. Lou.-San Fran. (R. Rs.).
A noted center of the lead and zinc industry.
Jordan, Scott Co., Minn., 1,119.
On Chi., St. P., Mpls. & Oma.; Mpls. & St. Lou. (R. Rs.).
–Onondaga Co., N. Y., 1,145.
On West Shore; N. York Cen. (R. Rs.).
Joseph, Wallowa Co., Oregon, 504.
On Un. Pac. (R. R.).
Josephine, Indiana Co., Pa., 500.
On Balt. & Ohio; Penna. (R. Rs.).
Joshua, Johnson Co., Tex., 550.
On Gulf, Colo. & Santa Fe (R. R.).
Jourdanton, c. s., Atascosa Co., Tex., 767.
On Mo. Pac. (R. R.).
Jovellanos, Prov. of Matanzas, Cuba, 7,282.
Jovellar, Prov. of Albay, Luzon, P. I., 6,798.
Joy, Mercer Co., Ill., 524.
On Chi., Burl. & Quincy (R. R.).
Juana Diaz, Mun. of Juana Diaz, Puerto Rico, 2,717.
Juarez, State of Chihuahua, Mexico, 43,138.
Largest city and main port of entry on the United States and Mexican border.
Jubbulpore, India, 104,317.
Important as a military station.
Judsonia, White Co., Ark., 1,123.
On Mo. Pac. (R. R.).
Juiz de Fora, Menas Geraes, Brazil, 70,000.
An important mining and commercial center.
Julesburg, Sedgwick Co., Colo., 1,467.
On Un. Pac. (R. R.).
Juliette, Monroe Co., Ga., 500.
On Southern (R. R.).
Jumet, Hainaut, Belgium, 30,183.
Has noted glass works.
Juncos, Mun. of Juncos, Puerto Rico, 5,581.
Junction, Kimble Co., Tex., 1,415.
Junction City, Union Co., Ark., 814.
On Chi., Rk. Isl. & Pac. (R. R.).
–c. s., Geary Co., Kans., 8,313.
On Mo.-Kan.-Tex.; Un. Pac. (R. Rs.).
–Boyle Co., Ky., 731.
On Cin., N. Orl. & Tex. Pac.; Lou. & Nash. (R. Rs.).
–Perry Co., Ohio, 860.
On Balt. & Ohio; N. York Cen.; Penna. (R. Rs.).
–Lane Co., Ore., 922.
On Sou. Pac.; Spok., Port. & Seattle (R. Rs.).
Juneau, capital of Alaska, 4,043.
Has steamship connections with Seattle and Canadian points. Local industries include lumber, salmon canning, gold quartz milling, and other mining work. No railroad connections.
Juneau, c. s., Dodge Co., Wis., 1,154.
On Chi. & Nor. West. (R. R.).
Junedale, Carbon Co., Pa., 595.
Jung Bunzlau, Germany. See Mladá Boleslav.
Juniata, Blair Co., Pa. (pop. incl. in Altoona).
Junin, Argentina, 55,854.
Center of a rich mining region.
Junior, Barbour Co., West Virginia, 560.
On West. Md. (R. R.).
Juno, McDowell Co., W. Va., 575.
On Norf. & West. (R. R.).

K

Kabul, capital of Afghanistan, 200,000.
A trade center and distributing point.
Fruit growing center.
Kagi, Taiwan, 66,853.
Kagoshima, Kagoshima Ken, Japan, 181,736.
A seaport and industrial center.
Kahoka, c. s., Clark Co., Mo., 1,507.
On Chi., Burl. & Quincy (R. R.).
Kaifeng, Honan, China, 223,000.
One of the most historic cities of China and the center of an extensive agricultural region.
Kaijo, Chosen, 50,570.
Kairwan, Tunisia, 21,532.
The sacred city of the colony.
Kaisarieh, Turkey. See Kayseri.
Kaiserslautern, Bavaria, Germany, 61,000.
Textiles, castings, and beer.
Kalama, c. s., Cowlitz Co., Wash., 940.
On Gt. Nor.; Nor. Pac.; Un. Pac. (R. Rs.).
Kalamai, Morea, Greece, 28,955.
A seaport and commercial town.

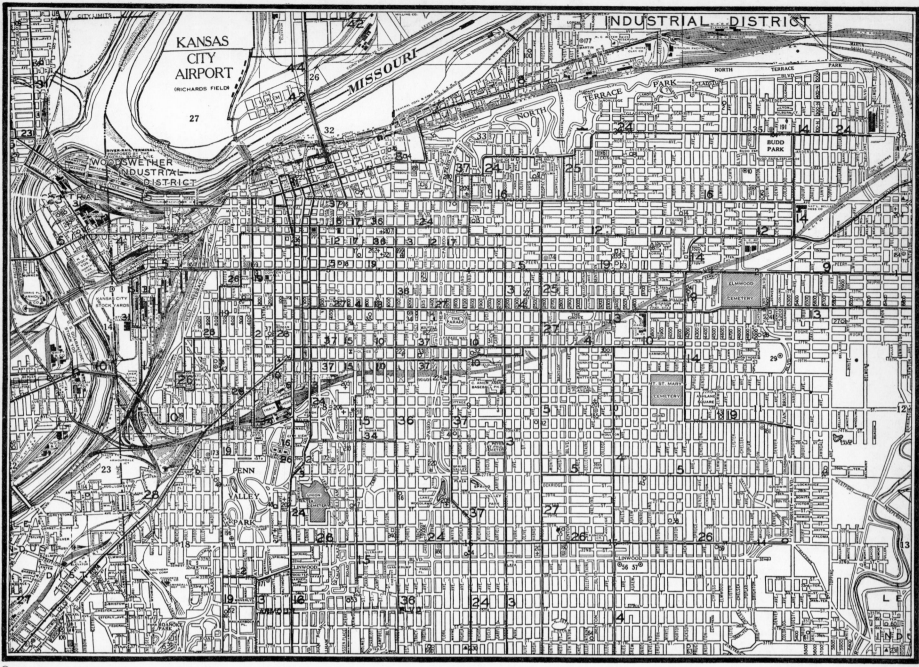

© GALLUP MAP & SUPPLY CO.

MAP OF AN OUTSTANDING SECTION OF KANSAS CITY, THE SECOND CITY OF MISSOURI IN SIZE AND IMPORTANCE. IT IS CONTIGUOUS WITH KANSAS CITY, KANSAS, AND THE TWO CITIES ARE PRACTICALLY A SINGLE COMMUNITY INDUSTRIALLY AND RESIDENTIALLY. GREATER KANSAS CITY IS THE LARGEST MARKETING AND WHOLESALING CENTER FOR HAY, STOCK HOGS AND STOCK AND FEED CATTLE IN THE UNITED STATES

Olive industry in vicinity.

KALAMAZOO, c. s., Kalamazoo Co., Mich., 54,786. On west bank of Kalamazoo River and on the Chicago, Kalamazoo and Saginaw; the Pennsylvania; the New York Central; Grand Trunk; and the Michigan Central Railroads. Paper is the main manufacture. Other industries include automobiles, trunks, boilers, etc.

KALGAN, Prov. of Chahar, China, 60,000. The "gateway" city to northern China. A military and commercial center.

KALGOORLIE, Western Australia, Australia, 9,088.

KALININ (Tver), Soviet Union, 146,000. An important industrial and trade center. Situated in a rich farming and grazing area.

KALISPELL, c. s., Flathead Co., Mont., 6,094. On Gt. Nor. (R. R.).

KALISZ, Poland, 55,125. An industrial town and one of the oldest cities in Poland.

KALKASKA, c. s., Kalkaska Co., Mich., 861. On Penna. (R. R.).

KALMAR, Sweden, 19,801. A seaport. Exports timber and oils.

KALOCSA, Pest-Pilis-Solt-Kiskún, Comitat, Hungary, 11,877.

KALONA, Washington Co., Iowa, 704. On Chi., Rk. Isl. & Pac. (R. R.).

KALUGA, Soviet Union, 60,600. Sawmilling, smelting, brewing, tanning, and sausage making.

KAMENETS-PODOLSK, Ukraine, Soviet Union, 32,041.

KAMENSKAYA, Soviet Union, 34,151.

KAMPEN, Overijssel, Netherlands, 19,838. Principal trade is in hay and dairy products.

KAMSACK, Saskatchewan, Canada, 1,810.

KANAB, c. s., Kane Co., Utah, 1,195.

KANAGAWA, Honshu, Japan, 12,000.

KANAWHA, Hancock Co., Iowa, 609. On Mpls. & St. Lou. (R. R.).

KANAZAWA, island of Honshu, Japan, 163,733. Bronze, porcelain, and silk manufactures.

KANDAHAR, Afghanistan, 60,000. The leading commercial center of the country.

KANDY, Ceylon, 37,147. Has beautiful botanical gardens and a famous Buddhist temple.

KANE, Greene Co., Ill., 511. On Alton (R. R.).
—McKean Co., Pa., 6,232. On Balt. & Ohio; Penna. (R. Rs.).

KANKAKEE, c. s., Kankakee Co., Ill., 20,620. On Cle., Cin., Chi. & St. Lou.; Ill. Cen.; N. York Cen. (R. Rs.). A shipping point on the Kankakee River. Manufactures agricultural implements, furniture, clothing.

KANNAPOLIS, Cabarrus Co., N. C., 12,661. On Southern (R. R.). A marketing center in a farming section.

KANO, Nigeria, 89,462. Chief industry is weaving and embroidery of cotton cloth. Formerly a slave market.

KANOPOLIS, Ellsworth Co., Kansas, 906. On Mo. Pac.; Un. Pac. (R. Rs.).

KANOSH, Millard Co., Utah, 570.

KANSAS, Walker Co., Ala., 500. On St. Lou.-San. Fran. (R. R.).
—Edgar Co., Ill., 900. On Cle., Cin., Chi. & St. Lou. (R. R.).

KANSAS CITY, c. s., Wyandotte Co., Kans., 124,568. Situated at the junction of the Missouri and Kansas Rivers, separated from Kansas City, Mo., only by the State line. Is on the Atchison, Topeka & Santa Fe; Chicago Great Western; Chicago, Rock Island and Pacific; Kansas & Missouri Terminal, Kansas City, Kaw Valley & Western; Kansas City Southern; Missouri Pacific; and Union Pacific railroads. Is the second meat-packing center of the

United States, and, together with Kansas City, Mo., is second in livestock receipts and in flour output. Its other products include soap, flour, cooperage, boxes, wagons, condensed milk, structural steel, railroad iron, car wheels, scales, etc. Shops of the Missouri Pacific, the Union Pacific, and the Rock Island Railroads are located here.
—Jackson Co., Mo., 399,746. Situated on the Missouri River, and is the trade center of the Missouri Valley. The most important railroads in the country serve the city, namely, the Atchison, Topeka & Santa Fe; the Chicago, Burlington & Quincy; the Chicago, Rock Island & Pacific; Alton; the Chicago Great Western; the Chicago, Milwaukee, St. Paul & Pacific; the Kansas City, Kaw Valley & Western; The Missouri & Kansas (El.); the North Kansas City Bridge (El.); the Kansas City Public Service (El.); the St. Louis-San Francisco; the Kansas City Connecting; the Kansas City Southern; the Mo.-Kans.-Texas; the Missouri Pacific; the Quincy, Omaha and Kansas City; the Union Pacific and the Wabash railroads.
The city's packing house products were valued at nearly $250,000,000 in 1930. Other leading industries with a great output are soap and heavy chemicals, flour and grist mill products, and oils. Its jobbing trade is enormous, leading with hay, grain and straw, automobiles, and lumber. It has numerous grain elevators.
Features of the city are the park and boulevard system, Union Station, the Municipal Auditorium, Liberty Memorial, William Rockhill Nelson Gallery of Art, the Fine Arts Institute and the Conservatory of Music.
Originally settled about 1821.

KAPLAN, Vermilion Parish, La., 1,653. On Sou. Pac. (R. R.).

KARACHI, Presidency of Bombay, British India, 247,791. Has large manufactures of rugs and carpets.

KARBALA, Iraq, 35,000. A place of pilgrimage.

KARCAG, Hungary, 24,269.

KARIKAL, French establishment in India, 18,944.

KARLSBAD (Karlovy Very), Germany, 24,029. Situated on the Tepl River. Noted for its widely celebrated hot mineral springs. The whole town of Karlovy Very appears to stand on a vast caldron of boiling water, which is kept from bursting only by the safety-valves the springs provide.

KARLSKRONA, Sweden, 25,492.

KARLSRÜHE (Carlsruhe), capital of Baden, Germany, 154,902.

KARLSTAD, Sweden, 27,081. A seaport and naval station.

KARNAK, 2,000.
—Pulaski Co., Ill., 771. On Chi. & East. Ill.; Cle., Cin., Chi. & St. Lou. (R. Rs.).

KARNES CITY, c. s., Karnes Co., Texas, 1,141. On Sou. Pac. (R. R.).

KARS, Turkey, 13,735. Textiles.

KARTAH, Chattooga Co., Ga., 750.

KARTHAUS, Clearfield Co., Pa., 550. On N. York Cen. (R. R.).

KARWIN, Prussia (formerly Austrian), 14,326.

KASHGAR, Sinkiang. See SHUFU.

KASKA, Schuylkill Co., Pa., 600.

KASOTA, Le Sueur Co., Minn., 593. On Chi., Mil., St. P. & Pac.; Chi., St. P., Minn. & Oma.; Chi. & Nor. West. (R. Rs.).

KASSALA, Anglo-Eg., Sudan, 51,183. A military station.

KASSEL (Cassel), capital of the province of Hesse-Nassau, Prussia, Germany, 175,018.

Situated on the Fulda River about eight miles below the mouth of the Eder.
Consists of the Alstadt, or old town, the Oberneustadt, the Hohenzollern quarter, and Welheiden. Kassel is one of the handsomest towns in Germany and has fine squares and streets. Near Kassel, on the slopes of the Habichtswald, is the famous estate of Wilhelmshöhe where Napoleon III was confined after the fall of Sedan.
Kassel dates from 913, when it was Chassala. It became a Prussian possession in 1866.
Kasson, Dodge Co., Minn., 1,019.
On Chi. & Nor. West. (R. R.).
Kaswin, Iran (Persia). See Qasvin.
Katernberg, Prussia, Germany, 22,392.
Katmandu, capital of Kingdom of Nepal, 108,800.
Possesses numerous temples.
Katowice, Poland, 133,000.
Iron works, foundries, and machine shops.
Kaufbeuren, Bavaria, 9,160.
Kaufman, c. s., Kaufman Co., Texas, 2,279.
On Sou. Pac. (R. R.).
Kaukauna, Outagamie Co., Wis., 6,581.
On Chi. & Nor. West. (R. R.).
Kaunas (Kovno), capital of Lithuania, 130,000.
On right bank of the Nieman River.
Kavalla (Cavalla), Macedonia, Greece, 54,980.
A seaport and walled town.
Kaw, Kay Co., Okla., 1,001.
On Atch., Top. & Santa Fe (R. R.).
Kayford, Kanawha Co., W. Va., 750.
On Chesa. & Ohio (R. R.).
Kaymoor, Fayette Co., W. Va., 700.
On Chesa. & Ohio (R. R.).
Kayseri (Kaisarieh), Turkey in Asia, 46,491.
Kaysville, Davis Co., Utah, 992.
On Bamberger Elec.; Den. & Rio Gde. West.; Un. Pac. (R. Rs.).
Kazan, capital of Tartar Rep., Soviet Union, 258,700.
The leading industrial, commercial, and educational center of the region.
Keansburg, Monmouth Co., N. J., 2,190.
On Cen. of N. Jer. (R. R.).
Kearney, Clay Co., Mo., 523.
On Chi., Burl. & Quincy (R. R.).
–c. s., Buffalo Co., Neb., 8,575.
On Chi., Burl. & Quincy; Un. Pac. (R. Rs.).
Seat of State Normal School and Kearney Military Academy.
Kearneysville, Jefferson Co., W. Va., 500.
On Balt. & Ohio (R. R.).
Kearny, Hudson Co., N. J., 40,716.
On Cen. of N. Jer.; Erie (R. Rs.).
A residential and industrial suburb of New York.
Kearsarge, Houghton Co., Mich., 1,000.
Kecskemet, Pest Comitat, Hungary, 79,505.
The market center of a rich farming region.
Keegan, Aroostook Co., Me., 730.
On Bangor & Aroostook (R. R.).
Keelung, Tarwan. See Kiirun.
Keen, Polk Co., Iowa, 500.
Keene, Jessamine Co., Ky., 500.
–c. s., Cheshire Co., N. H., 13,794.
On Bos. & Me. (R. R.).
In a summer tourist district. Seat of State Normal School.
–Essex Co., N. Y., 600.
–Johnson Co., Tex., 500.
On Gulf, Colo. & Santa Fe (R. R.).
Keeseville, Essex and Clinton Cos., N. Y., 1,794.
Keewatin, Itasca Co., Minn., 2,134.
On Gt. Nor. (R. R.).
Keighley, Yorkshire, England, 40,440.
Keijo (Seoul), capital of Chosen (Korea), 677,-241.
Situated on the Han River. It lies among granite hill ranges. Has wide streets and modern facilities for communication.
Keiser, Mississippi Co., Ark., 600.
On St. Lou.-San Fran. (R. R.).
Keisterville, Fayette Co., Pa., 600.
Keithsburg, Mercer Co., Ill., 1,081.
On Chi., Burl. & Quincy; Mpls. & St. Lou. (R. Rs.).
Keller, Accomac Co., Va., 530.
On Penna. (R. R.).
Kellerton, Ringgold Co., Iowa, 540.
On Chi., Burl. & Quincy (R. R.).
Kellettville, Forest Co., Pa., 839.
On Shef. & Tion. (R. R.).
Kelleys Island, Erie Co., Ohio, 638.
Kellogg (Kellogg-Wardner), Shoshone Co., Idaho, 4,124.
On Un. Pac. (R. R.).
–Jasper Co., Iowa, 580.
On Chi., Rk. Isl. & Pac. (R. R.).
Kellyville, Creek Co., Okla., 548.
On St. Lou.-San Fran. (R. R.).
Kelso, Cowlitz Co., Wash., 6,260.
On Gt. Nor.; Nor. Pac.; Un. Pac. (R. Rs.).
Kemmerer, c. s., Lincoln Co., Wyo., 1,884.
On Un. Pac. (R. R.).
Kemp, Kaufman Co., Tex., 990.
On Sou. Pac. (R. R.).
Kempten, Bavaria, Germany, 26,097.
Textiles and paper making.
Kempton, Preston Co., W. Va., 750.
On West. Md. (R. R.).
Kemptville, Grenville Co., North, Ontario, Canada, 1,286.
On Can. Pac. (R. R.).
Kena (or Keneh), Egypt. See Qena.
Kenbridge, Lunenburg Co., Va., 753.
On Virginian (R. R.).
Kendal, Westmoreland, England, 15,575.
Kendal Green, Middlesex Co., Mass., 560.
On Bost. & Me. (R. R.).
Kendall, Monroe Co., Wis., 517.
On Chi. & Nor. West. (R. R.).
Kendallville, Noble Co., Ind., 5,439.
On N. York Cen.; Penna. (R. Rs.).
Kendrick, Marion Co., Fla., 500.
On Atl. Coast Line (R. R.).
Kenedy, Karnes Co., Tex., 2,610.
On Sou. Pac. (R. R.).
Has hot mineral wells.
Kenesaw, Adams Co., Neb., 614.
On Chi., Burl. & Quincy (R. R.).
Kenilworth, Warwickshire, England, 7,592.
–Cook Co., Ill., 2,501.
On Chi. & Nor. West.; Chi. Nor. Shore & Mil. (El.) (R. Rs.).
–Union Co., N. J., 2,243.
On Rahway Valley (R. R.).
Kenilworth (Madison), Chester Co., Pa., 500.
Kenley, Houston Co., Tex., 610.
Kenly, Johnston Co., N. C., 965.
On Atl. Coast Line (R. R.).
Kenmare, Ward Co., N. Dak., 1,494.
On Mpls., St. P. & S. Ste. M. (R. R.).
Kenmore, Erie Co., N. Y., 16,482.
A suburb of Buffalo.
–Summit Co., Ohio (St. Akron P. O.).
On Balt. & Ohio; Erie (R. Rs.).
Kennebunk, York Co., Maine, 2,200.
On Bost. & Me. (R. R.).
Kennebunkport, York Co., Maine, 750.
A resort formerly known for its ships.
Kennedy, Chautauqua Co., N. Y., 625.
On Erie (R. R.).
Kenner, Jefferson Parish, La., 2,440.
On Ill. Cen.; La. & Ark.; Mo. Pac. (R. Rs.).
Kennett, c. s., Dunklin Co., Mo., 4,128.
On St. Lou.-San Fran. (R. R.).
Kennett Square, Chester Co., Pa., 3,091.
On Penna. (R. R.).
Kennewick, Benton Co., Wash., 1,519.
On Nor. Pac.; Spok., Port. & Seattle; Un. Pac. (R. Rs.).
Kenney, De Witt Co., Ill., 485.
On Ill. Cen.; Penna. (R. Rs.).
Kennywood Park, Allegheny Co., Pa., 500.
Kenosha, c. s., Kenosha Co., Wis., 50,262.
On Chi. & Nor. West.; Chi. Nor. Shore & Mil. (El.); Mil. El. (R. Rs.).
A lake port and important manufacturing town. Automobile parts, hosiery, underwear, brass and iron beds. Has a beautiful civic center.
Kenova, Wayne Co., W. Va., 3,680.
On Balt. & Ohio; Ches. & Ohio; Norf. & West. (R. Rs.).
Kensett, White Co., Ark., 889.
On Doniph., Kens. & Searcy; Mo. Pac.; Mo. & Ark. (R. Rs.).
Kensington, Montgomery Co., Md., 948.
On Balt. & Ohio (R. R.).
–Hartford Co., Conn., 2,443.
–Smith Co., Kansas, 540.
On Chi., Rk. Isl. & Pac. (R. R.).
–Nassau Co., N. Y., 824.
Kent, Litchfield Co., Conn., 1,054.
On N. York, N. Hav. & Hart. (R. R.).
–Portage Co., Ohio, 8,375.
On Balt. & Ohio; Erie; Wheel. & L. Erie (R. Rs.).
The Erie has shops and yards here. Seat of State Normal College.
–King Co., Wash., 2,320.
On Chi., Mil., St. P. & Pac.; Gt. Nor.; Nor. Pac.; Un. Pac. (R. Rs.).
Kentland, c. s., Newton Co., Ind., 1,355.
On N. York Cen.; Penna. (R. Rs.).
Kenton, c. s., Hardin Co., Ohio, 7,069.
On Erie; Cle., Cin., Chi. & St. Lou.; N. York Cen. (R. Rs.).
Chief products: tools, electrical cranes, mechanical toys, advertising novelties.
–Obion & Gibson Cos., Tenn., 810.
On Mob. & Ohio (R. R.).
Kentville, capital of Kings Co., Nova Scotia, 3,033.
On Dom. Atl. (R. R.).
Kentwood, Tangipahoa Parish, La., 1,726.
On Ill. Cen. (R. R.).
Kenvil, Morris Co., N. J., 1,000.
On Del., Lack. & West. (R. R.).
Kenwood Park, Linn Co., Iowa.
On Chi., Mil., St. P. & Pac. (R. Rs.).
Kenyon, Goodhue Co., Minn., 1,382.
On Chi., Gt. West.; Chi., Mil., St. P. & Pac. (R. Rs.).
Keokee, Lee Co., Va., 575.
On Southern (R. R.).
Keokuk, Lee Co., Iowa, 15,106.
On Chi., Burl. & Quincy; Chi., Rk. Isl. & Pac.; Tol., Peor. & West.; Wab. (R. Rs.).
Site of the great Mississippi hydro-electric plant.
Keosauqua, c. s., Van Buren Co., Iowa, 855.
On Chi., Rk. Isl. & Pac. (R. R.).
Keota, Keokuk Co., Iowa, 955.
On Chi., Rk. Isl. & Pac. (R. R.).
Kepples, Armstrong Co., Pa., 540.
On Winfield (R. R.).
Kerch, Crimean Rep., Sov. Union, 66,700.
An important grain port.
Kerens, Navarro Co., Texas, 1,435.
On St. Lou. Southw. (R. R.).
Kerhonkson, Ulster Co., N. Y., 560.
On N. York, Ont. & West. (R. R.).
Kerkhoven, Swift Co., Minn., 553.
On Gt. Nor. (R. R.).
Kerkyra, Corfu, Greece, 32,221.
Kerman, Iran (Persia), 59,500.
Famous for its shawls and rugs.
Kermanshan, Kurdistan, Iran (Persia), 70,200.
A distributing point for the farm produce of a very fertile region.
Kermit, Mingo Co., W. Va., 749.
On Norf. & West. (R. R.).
Kern (Kern Junction), Kern Co., Cal.
On Atch., Top. & Santa Fe; Sou Pac.; Sunset (R. Rs.).
Kernersville, Forsyth Co., N. C., 1,754.
On Southern (R. R.).
Kerrville, c. s., Kerr Co., Texas, 4,546.
On Sou. Pac. (R. R.).
Kersey, Elk Co., Pa., 700.
On Pitts., Shawmut & Nor. (R. R.).
Kershaw, Kershaw and Lancaster Cos., S. C., 1,120.
On Southern (R. R.).
Ketchikan, Alaska, 3,796.
Salmon and halibut fishing.
Ketona, Jefferson Co., Ala., 500.
On Lou. & Nash. (R. R.).
Kewanee, Henry Co., Ill., 17,093.
On Chi., Burl. & Q. (R. R.).
Has important manufactures. Coal is mined nearby.
Kewanna, Fulton Co., Ind., 682.
On Chesa. & Ohio; Penna. (R. Rs.).
Kewaskum, Washington Co., Wis., 799.
On Chi. & Nor. West. (R. R.).
Kewaunee, c. s., Kewaunee Co., Wis., 2,409.
On Ann Arbor; Gr. Bay & West (R. Rs.).
Keyport, Monmouth Co., N. J., 4,940.
On Cen. of N. Jer. (R. R.).
Keyser, c. s., Mineral Co., W. Va., 6,248.
On Balt. & Ohio; West. Md. (R. Rs.).
In a fruit growing district.
Keystone, McDowell Co., W. Va., 1,897.
On Norf. & West. (R. R.).
Keysville, Charlotte Co., Va., 589.
On Southern (R. R.).
Keytesville, c. s., Chariton Co., Mo., 738.
On Wabash (R. R.).
Key West, Monroe Co., Fla., 12,317.
The southernmost city of the U. S. Has a chain of islands extending 100 miles from tip of Florida peninsula and joined to the mainland by a road crossing the Keys. Cigar making is the chief industry. A large trade is done in fish and sponges. Has a growing sea commerce with Cuba, West Indies, and South America.
Kezar Falls, York and Oxford Cos., Me., 883.
Khabarovsk, Siberia, Soviet Union, Asia, 102,000.
Center of fur trade and marketing town. Has a fine airport.
Khania (Canea), Capital of Crete, Greece, 25,-484.
Principal seaport and commercial center of the island.
Kharkov, Ukraine, Soviet Union, 654,300.
Center of a region which is being intensively developed. Industries are principally metallurgical. Has a large annual trade fair.
Khartoum, capital of Anglo-Egyptian Sudan, Africa, 49,741.
Commercial and political center. Gen. Gordon was killed here in 1884.
Khaskovo, Bulgaria, 26,622.
Kherson, Ukraine Soviet Union, 82,900.
A grain trade center.
Khiva, Soviet Union, Asia, 23,700.
Khoi, Iran (Persia), 25,000.
Khotan. See Hotien.
Khotin, Rumania. See Hotin.
Khurja, United Provinces, India, 27,400.
Grain and indigo trade center.
Kiaochow, Shantung, China, 35,000.
Former German territory.
Kickapoo, Polk Co., Tex., 510.
On Waco, Beau., Trin. & Sab. (R. R.).
Kidderminster, Worcestershire, England, 29,914.
Kiefer, Creek Co., Okla., 606.
On St. Lou.-San Fran. (R. R.).
Kiefertown (Kifertown), Fayette Co., Pa., 600.
Kiel, Prussia, Germany, 218,000.
Situated at the head of a deep fiord of the Baltic. Before the World War the headquarters of the German navy. The seat of a university, founded in 1665.
Kiel is the eastern terminus of the Kaiser Wilhelm Canal, connecting the Baltic and the North Sea. Under the Peace Treaty the canal became an internationalized free waterway.
–Calumet and Manitowoc Cos., Wis., 1,803.
On Chi., Mil., St. P. & Pac. (R. R.).
Kielce, Poland, 58,397.
Hemp spinning, cotton printing, and cement works.
Kiev, Ukraine, Soviet Union, 538,600.
One of the oldest towns of Soviet Union, situated on the Dnieper. Founded before the Christian era. In 1882 it was made the capital of the Russian principality. Here in 988 Christianity was first preached in Russia by St. Vladimir. The city formerly was a most important ecclesiastic center and was visited by more than 250,000 pilgrims annually. The university, removed here from Vilna in 1833, is largely attended. The fortress of Kiev, begun by Peter the Great in 1706, occupies a commanding site on the right bank of the Dnieper. Kiev was the scene of much fighting between the Bolshevists and Ukrainians following the Russian Revolution.
Kiirun (Keelung), Taiwan, 87,400.
An important port and trade center on the northern end of the island.
Kilbourn, Columbia Co., Wis. See Wisconsin Dells.
Kilkenny, Irish Free State. See Cill Choinnigh.
Killarney, County Kerry, Ireland (Eire), 5,328.
Situated near the famous lakes of Killarney, and particularly noted for its Catholic cathedral. The Lakes of Killarney are three connected lakes near the center of Kerry, a coast county in the southwest of Munster Province, Irish Free State, 45 miles west of Cork. The beautiful scenery around the Lakes, the shores of which have rich colorings, is the chief attraction, while Carrantuel, the highest mountain in Ireland, towers among the MacGillicuddy Reeks above the lakes to a height of 3,414 feet. Now Cill Airne.
–Souris Co., Manitoba, Canada, 1,003.
On Can. Pac. (R. R.).
–Raleigh Co., W. Va., 500.
On Chesa. & Ohio; Virginian (R. Rs.).
Killbuck, Holmes Co., Ohio, 703.
On Penna. (R. R.).
Killeen, Bell Co., Texas, 1,260.
On Gulf, Colo. & Santa Fe (R. R.).
Killingly (Dayville), Windham Co., Conn., 700.
On N. York, N. Hav. & Hart. (R. R.).
Kilmarnock, Ayr Co., Scotland, 36,393.
A manufacturing town. Machinery, textiles, cheese, and shoes.
–Lancaster Co., Va., 521.
Kilmichael, Montgomery Co., Miss., 577.
On Columbus & Greenville (R. R.).
Kilwa, Tanganyika, 1,734.
Kimball, c. s., Kimball Co., Neb., 1,711.
On Un. Pac. (R. R.).
–Brule Co., S. Dak., 1,150.
On Chi., Mil., St. P. & Pac. (R. R.).
–McDowell Co., W. Va., 1,467.
On Norf. & West. (R. R.).
Kimberley, Cape of Good Hope, Un. of S. Africa, 38,941.
Center of diamond industry.
–Outagamie Co., Wis., 2,256.
On Chi. & Nor. West. (R. R.).
Kimberly, Jefferson Co., Ala., 547.
On Lou. & Nash. (R. R.).
–Twin Falls Co., Idaho, 648.
On Ore. Short Line (R. R.).
Kinard, Calhoun Co., Fla., 500.
Kincaid, Christian Co., Ill., 1,583.
On Chi. & Ill. Midl. (R. R.).
Kincardine, Bruce North Co., Ontario, Canada, 2,465.
On Can. Nat. (R. R.).
Kinder, Allen Parish, La., 962.
On Mo. Pac. (R. R.).
Kinderhook, Columbia Co., N. Y., 822.
Kineshma, Soviet Union, 63,500.
King City, Monterey Co., Cal., 1,483.
On Sou. Pac. (R. R.).
–Gentry Co., Mo., 1,101.
On Chi., Burl. & Quincy (R. R.).
Kingfield, Franklin Co., Maine, 972.
Kingfisher, c. s., Kingfisher Co., Okla., 2,726.
On Chi., Rk. Isl. & Pac. (R. R.).
Kingman, Fountain Co., Ind., 502.
On Chi., Attica & Sou. (R. R.).
–c. s., Mohave Co., Ariz., 2,200.
On Atch., Top. & Santa Fe (R. R.).
–c. s., Kingman Co., Kans., 2,812.
On Atch., Top. & Santa Fe; Mo. Pac. (R. Rs.).
Kingmine, Carbon Co., Utah, 939.
On Utah (R. R.).
Kingsburg, Fresno Co., Cal., 1,322.
On Sou. Pac. (R. R.).
Kingsford, Dickinson Co., Mich., 5,526.
Kingsley, Plymouth Co., Iowa, 1,093.
On Chi. & Nor. West. (R. R.).
King's Lynn, Norfolk, England, 20,580.
Seaport, manufacturing and fishing town.
Kings Mills, Warren Co., Ohio, 800.

On Penna. (R. R.).
King's Mountain, Cleveland Co., N. C., 5,632. On Southern (R. R.).
Kings Point, Nassau Co., N. Y., 1,294.
Kingsport, Sullivan Co., Tennessee, 11,914. On Clinchfield (R. R.).
Kingston, Surrey Co., capital and principal city of Jamaica, West Indies, 71,704.
A seaport located on a fine harbor. The town is strongly fortified. It has various charitable and collegiate institutions, a workhouse, penitentiary, and theaters. The suburbs are remarkable for their natural beauty, and many of the wealthier residents, including the Governor, have their homes outside the city limits. Kingston harbor admits the largest vessels. It is inclosed by a long tongue of land, at the extremity of which is Port Royal, and the entrance is defended by forts. The railways of the island center here. The foreign commerce is considerable.
On January 14, 1907, the island of Jamaica suffered an earthquake shock which laid Kingston in ruins and destroyed 1,700 lives and millions of dollars' worth of property.
–Bartow Co., Ga., 553.
On Nash., Chatt. & St. Lou. (R. R.).
–Plymouth Co., Mass., 2,743.
On N. York, N. Hav. & Hart. (R. R.).
–Rockingham Co., N. H., 750.
–c. s., Ulster Co., N. Y., 28,088.
On N. York, Ont. & West.; West Shore (R. Rs.).
Railroad repair shops, shirt and cigar factories, and brick yards.
Kingston is located in midst of beautiful mountain scenery.
–Ross Co., Ohio, 857.
On Norf. & West. (R. R.).
–Marshall Co., Okla., 552.
On St. Lou.-San Fran. (R. R.).
–Luzerne Co., Pa., 21,600.
On Del., Lack. & West.; Leh. Val. (R. Rs.).
Anthracite mining is leading industry. Clothing factories.
–Washington Co., R. I., 580.
On Narra. Pier; N. York, N. Hav. & Hart. (R. Rs.).
–c. s., Roane Co., Tenn., 827.
–Ontario, Canada, 23,439.
Built on the site of Old Fort Frontenac.
On Can. Pac.; Can. Nat. (R. Rs.).
Kingston-on-Hull. See Hull.
Kingston-upon-Thames, Surrey, England, 39,052.
Kingstree, c. s., Williamsburg Co., S. C., 2,392.
On Atl. Coast Line (R. R.).
A tobacco and cotton market.
Kingsville, Essex Co., South Ontario, Canada, 2,174.
On Pere Marq. (R. R.).
–Ashtabula Co., Ohio, 750.
On N. York Cen.; N. York, Chi. & St. Lou. R. Rs.).
–(North Kingsville), Ashtabula Co., Ohio, 853.
On N. York Cen.; N. York, Chi. & St. Lou. R. Rs.).
–Kleberg Co., Texas, 6,815.
On Mo. Pac. (R. R.).
Kingwood, c. s., Preston Co., W. Va., 1,709.
On Balt. & Ohio; W. Va. Nor. (R. Rs.).
Kinmundy, Marion Co., Ill., 813.
On Chi. & East. Ill.; Ill. Cen. (R. Rs.).
Kinney, St. Louis Co., Minn., 737.
Kinsley, c. s., Edwards Co., Kans., 2,211.
On Atch., Top. & Santa Fe; Wich. Northw. (R. Rs.).
Kinsman, Trumbull Co., Ohio, 600.
On N. York Cen. (R. R.).
Kinston, c. s., Lenoir Co., N. C., 11,362.
On Atl. Coast Line; Atl. & Nor. Car. (R. Rs.)
Principal industries: lumber, hosiery, cotton yarns and tobacco.
Kioto, Japan. See Kyoto.
Kiowa, Barber Co., Kans., 1,491.
On Atch., Top. & Santa Fe; Mo. Pac. (R. Rs.).
–Pittsburg Co., Okla., 689.
On Mo.-Kan.-Tex. (R. R.).
Kirbyville, Jasper Co., Texas, 1,184.
On Gulf, Colo. & Santa Fe (R. R.).
Kirchhörde, Westphalia, Germany, 14,725
Kirin, Manchukuo, 142,960.
Kirkcaldy, Fife, Scotland, 46,019.
Principal products: textiles, castings, machinery, pottery, linoleum and oil cloth.
Kirkland, De Kalb Co., Ill., 526.
On Chi., Mil., St. P. & Pac. (R. R.).
–Childress Co., Tex., 524.
On Ft. Worth & Denv. Cy. (R. R.).
–King Co., Wash., 1,714.
On Nor. Pac. (R. R.).
Kirklin, Clinton Co., Ind., 644.
On Chi., Ind. & Lou. (R. R.).
Kirksville, c. s., Adair Co., Mo., 8,293.
On Quincy, Oma. & Kan. Cy.; Wab. (R. Rs.).
Kirkwood, De Kalb Co., Ga.
On Seab. Air Line; Ga. (R. Rs.).
–Warren Co., Ill., 693.
On Chi., Burl. & Quincy (R. R.).
–St. Louis Co., Mo., 9,169.
On Mo. Pac.; St. Lou.-San Fran. (R. Rs.).
Kirov (Vyatka), Sov. Union, 85,600.
A trade and manufacturing center.
Kirovo (Zinovievsk), Sov. Union, 68,800.
Manufactures: lumber, tobacco, brick and liquors.
Kirriemuir, Forfarshire, Scotland, 4,755.
Kirwin, Phillips Co., Kans., 497.
On Mo. Pac. (R. R.).
Kishena, Shawano Co., Wis., 500.
Kishinev, Rumania. See Chisinau.
Kiskunfelegyhaza, Hungary, 38,204.
Noted for its great cattle markets.
Kispest, Hungary, 67,819.
A suburb of Budapest.
Kissimmee, c. s., Osceola Co., Fla., 3,379.
On Atl. Coast Line (R. R.).
Kistler, Mifflin Co., Pa., 518.
–Logan Co., W. Va., 519.
On Chesa. & Ohio (R. R.).
Kitchener, capital of Waterloo Co., North, Ontario, Canada, 30,793.
On Grand Riv. (El.); Can. Nat. (R. Rs.).
A port and center of a farming region.
Kittanning, c. s., Armstrong Co., Pa., 7,808.
On Penna.; Pitts. & Shawmut (R. Rs.).
Kittery, York Co., Maine, 3,000.
On Bos. & Me. (R. R.).
Kitzmiller, Garrett Co., Md., 827.
Kiukiang, Kiangsi Prov., China, 80,200.
A river port noted for its tea trade.
Kiungchow, Hainan Prov., China, 46,000.
A seaport and distributing center.
Kladno, Bohemia, Czechoslovakia, 20,671.
A coal mining town.
Klagenfurt, capital of Carinthia, Austria, 29,909.
Situated in a rich mining and farming region.
Klaipeda (Memel), 40,000. Lithuania.
With contiguous territory Klaipeda was renounced by Germany to the Allied Powers under the Peace Treaty of Versailles. It was assigned to Lithuania in 1923.
Klamath Falls, c. s., Klamath Co., Ore., 16,093.
On Gt. Nor.; Ore., Calif. & East.; Sou. Pac. (R. Rs.).
A lumber manufacturing center.
Klausenburg, Rumania. See Cluj.
Kleve, Prussia, Germany, 20,288.
Chief manufactures are boots, shoes, tobacco and machinery.
Klotzville, Assumption Par., La., 530.
Knights Landing, Yolo Co., Calif., 600.
On Sou. Pac. (R. R.).
Knightstown, Henry Co., Ind., 2,209.
On Cle., Cin., Chi. & St. Lou.; Penna. (R. Rs.).
Knightsville, Clay Co., Ind., 704.
On Penna. (R. R.).
Knightville, Cumberland Co., Me., 645.
Knobnoster, Johnson Co., Mo., 683.
On Mo. Pac. (R. R.).
Knox, Knox Co., Ill., 587.
On Atch., Top. & Santa Fe (R. R.).
–c. s., Starke Co., Ind., 1,815.
On N. York Cen.; N. York, Chi. & St. Lou. (R. Rs.).
Knox City, Knox Co., Texas, 906.
On Panh. & Santa Fe (R. R.).
Knoxville, Johnson Co., Ark., 520.
On Mo. Pac. (R. R.).
–Knox Co., Ill., 1,867.
On Chi., Burl. & Quincy (R. R.).
–c. s., Marion Co., Iowa, 4,697.
On Chi., Burl. & Quincy (R. R.).
–Tioga Co., Pa., 608.
On Balt. & Ohio; N. York Cen. (R. R.).
–c. s., Knox Co., Tenn., 105,802.
Situated on the Tennessee River, and on the Louisville & Nashville and the Southern railroads.
Knoxville is at the head of the steamboat navigation of the river and has a very large trade in general commodities. It is one of the largest industrial centers of the South, containing (in 1930) over 180 manufacturing plants. The Southern railroad shops, the largest in the South, are located here. The city is in a productive region of natural resources, including lumber, coal, iron ore, copper, zinc and marble. Noted for the number and beauty of its churches. Seat of the University of Tennessee, with an agricultural experiment station; the Knoxville College for colored students (United Presbyterians).
The city was founded in 1792; State capital in 1796-1811; chartered as a city in 1816.
Kobe, Ken of Osaka, Japan, 938,200.
Important seaport on the island of Hondo.
Köbenhavn (Copenhagen), capital of Denmark, 686,343 (approximately 873,044 with suburbs).
Situated on the coast of Zealand and partly on the island of Amager. The harbor is the naval station of Denmark. The city is protected from invasion of the Baltic by high embankments.
Among the noteworthy buildings are the royal palace of Christianborg, the royal library, the Thorwaldsen Museum, the ministries, and the arsenal. The most imposing churches are the Frühe Kirke, adorned by Thorwaldsen; St. Peter's (German); Trinity Church, and the Church of Our Saviour.
Köbenhavn is the center of Scandinavian art, science, and literature. The University, founded in 1478, has a library of 600,000 volumes and 20,000 manuscripts. Connected with it is a polytechnic institute.
Shipbuilding is an important industry, and there are manufactures of textiles, machinery, porcelain, and sugar. The city has an active shipping trade.
Bishop Absalon founded Köbenhavn in 1168 as a refuge from the northern pirates, under the name of Axelhaus. The present name, Köbenhavn, means Merchant's Haven.
Koblenz (Coblenz), Rhenish Prussia, Germany, 65,300.
Situated at the confluence of the Moselle and the Rhine, with beautiful surroundings. The city is commercially and industrially important with considerable shipping and varied manufactures. Among its remarkably fine old buildings are the fortress of Ehrenbreitstein and the Church of St. Castor. Koblenz was founded in 9 B.C. by the Romans, who called it "Confluentes". It was headquarters for American troops of occupation from 1919 to 1923.
Koburg, Saxe-Coburg-Gotha, Germany, 29,038.
Machinery, lumber, glass, porcelain, and colors.
Koch, St. Louis Co., Mo., 700.
On Mo. Pac. (R. R.).
Kochi, capital of Kochi prefecture, Japan, 96,991.
Noted for its coral.
Kochville, Saginaw Co., Mich., 765.
Kofu, capital of Yamanishi prefecture, Japan, 79,446.
Silk weaving industry.
Kohler, Sheboygan Co., Wis., 1,748.
Kokand, Sov. Union, Asia, 84,800.
Commercial center for a large region.
Kokomo, c. s., Howard Co., Ind., 32,843.
On Ind. R. R. Sys. (El.); N. York, Chi. & St. Lou.; Penna. (R. Rs.).
Principal industries: steel, radios, pottery and glass wares, furnaces, automobile accessories, and wire products.
Kokura, Ken of Fukuoka, Japan, 88,049.
A seaport and trade center.
Kolburg, Prussia, Germany, 33,000.
A seaport and trade center. Tourist resort.
Kolding, Jutland, Denmark, 22,400.
Cattle export center.
Kolhapur, India, 69,860.
Kolin, Bohemia, Czechoslovakia, 18,509.
Köln (Cologne), Ger., 756,605.
Situated on the left (West) bank of the Rhine and connected by magnificent bridges with its suburbs on the right bank. Excellent railway, bus and steamship connections.
Köln is the leading commercial center of the Rhineland. Fairs are held in spring and autumn, and the Exhibition Halls, on the right bank, are an important modern feature.
The great university, 1388-1918, was refounded in 1919. Köln's most noted edifice is the Dom or cathedral, begun in the thirteenth century and finished in the nineteenth. It is considered the finest example of Gothic architecture in the world, and has a length of 444 feet and a tower 512 feet high. Other structures of interest are the Rathaus, the Church of St. Gereon, the court of justice, and the municipal museum, and the stadium.
The city has great historical interest. A Roman colony was established here in 50 A.D. Köln was a member of the Hanseatic League. It was British headquarters during the period of occupation following the World War.
Kolomyja, East Galicia, Poland, 33,385.
Has active trade in farm products.
Kom, Iran (Persia), 35,000.
Komotau, Czechoslovakia. See Chomutov.
Konawa, Seminole Co., Okla., 2,070.
On Okla. Cy.-Ada-Atoka (R. R.).
Kongmoon, Prov. of Kwantung, China, 32,000.
Seaport. Distributing point for farm produce.
Konia, Turkey. See Konya.
Königgratz, Czechoslovakia. See Hradec Kralove.
Königinhof, Czechoslovakia. See Dvur Králove.
Königsberg, capital of East Prussia, Germany, 315,651.
Situated 20 miles from the Baltic Sea on the Pregel, whose two arms, the old and the new Pregel, unite within the city. It consists of three towns, Alstadt, Lobenicht, and Kneiphof, which in 1724 were incorporated into the present city. Built as a fortress in 1255 against the pagan Samlaender, it rose to importance through its corn trade. In 1523 it became the capital of the Duchy of Prussia.
Königshütte, Prussia. See Krolewska Huta.
Konin, Poland, 10,390.
Konnarack, Washington Co., Va., 517.
Konstanz (Constance), Baden, Germany, 32,950.
A very old town, full of interesting buildings. Among these is the seat of the Council of Constance, the Barrosa Inn, where the treaty of Constance with the Lombard League was signed. Another is the home of John Huss. Konstanz has an active trade and various manufactures.
Konya (Konia), Turkey, 52,486.
Koppel, Beaver Co., Pa., 1,057.
On Penna.; Pitts. & L. Erie (R. Rs.).
Korcë, Albania, 22,787.
A marketing center in a grain area.
Korinthos (Corinth), Greece, 9,944.
One of the greatest cities of ancient Greece; destroyed by the Romans in 142 B.C. and rebuilt by them; conquered by the Venetians, then by Mohammed II; destroyed by earthquake in 1858, then rebuilt.
Kortkamp, Montgomery Co., Ill., 500.
Kosciusko, c. s., Attala Co., Miss., 3,237.
On Ill. Cen. (R. R.).
Kosice, Czechoslovakia, 70,232.
Wool and lumber center.
Koslin, Prussia, Germany, 30,000.
Kosse, Limestone Co., Texas, 805.
On Sou. Pac. (R. R.).
Kostroma, Soviet Union, 90,700.
Has flour mills, sawmills, and clothing factories.
Köthen (or Cöethen), Anhalt, Prussian Saxony, 26,695.
Kouts, Porter Co., Ind., 583.
On Erie; Penna. (R. Rs.).
Kovno, Lithuania. See Kaunas.
Kozlov, Soviet Union. See Michurinsk.
Kragujevac, Serbia, Yugoslavia, 27,249.
Has government powder factory.
Krakow (Cracow), Galicia, Poland, 255,000.
Situated on the left bank of the Vistula River.
Krakow consists of an old town, a castle quarter, and a number of suburbs.
Krakow is a center of Polish nationality and is reputed to have been founded about the year 700. It was the capital of Poland until the seat of government was transferred to Warsaw.
Krasnodar (Ekaterinodar), No. Caucasian Area, Soviet Union, 218,900.
The center of a farming and naphtha region.
Krasnoyarsk, Siberia Soviet Union, Asia, 101,500.
Important manufacturing town situated in a gold mining region.
Krebs, Pittsburg Co., Okla., 1,375.
On Mo.-Kans.-Texas; Pittsb. (El.) (R. Rs.).
Krefeld, Rhenish Prussia, Germany, 165,300.
Famous for its textile schools. Has numerous varied industries.
Kreigbaum, Allegany Co., Md., 600.
On Cumb. & Penna. (R. R.).
Kremenchug, Ukraine, Soviet Union, 68,700.
Kremnica, Czechoslovakia, 5,389.
Krems, Germany, 14,587.
Kremsier, Czechoslovakia. See Kroměřiz.
Kreuzburg, Germany, 12,264.
Kreuznach, Rhenish Prussia, Germany, 26,000.
A watering place.
Kristianssand (Christianssand), Norway, 18,700.
Fortified port and fishing center.
Kristianstad, capital of Christianstads-Län, Sweden, 13,515.
A seaport. Exports granite and wood pulp.
Kristiansund (Christiansund), Norway, 44,028.
A seaport and fishing town.
Krnov (Jagerndorf), Germany, 23,465.
One of the country's woolen-working centers.
Krolewska Huta, East Silesia, Poland, 80,734.
A center of Poland's iron industry.
Kroměřiz (Kremsier), Czechoslovakia, 18,583.
Situated in a farming and grazing region.
Kronstadt, Rumania. See Brasov.
Kronstadt (Cronstadt), Soviet Union, 43,800.
Situated on Kotlin Island, about 30 miles west of Leningrad. Founded by Peter the Great. Fortified in 1710.
Krotoszyn, Poland, 12,969.
Kuala Lumpur, capital of Federated Malay States, 111,800.
A modern city and administrative center.
Kuching, capital of Sarawak, on island of Borneo, 25,000.
Kuibishev (Samara), Sov. Union, 183,200.
Center of a fertile farming region.
Kulm, La Moure Co., N. Dak., 742.
On Minn., St. P. & S. Ste. M. (R. R.).
Kulmbach, Germany, 11,874.
Kulpmont, Northumberland Co., Pa., 6,120.
On Penna. (R. R.).
Kumamoto, Prov. of Hiogo, island of Kiushiu, Japan, 195,000.
An important rice market.
Kumbakonam (Combaconum), Madras, British India, 62,317.
Ancient capital of the Chola dynasty and one of the sacred places of the Hindus.
Kuopio, Finland, 24,341.
Kure, Hiroshima Dist., Japan, 239,900.
A seaport and naval station.
Kursk, Soviet Union, 102,500.
A railway and grain center.
Kurthwood, Vernon Par., La., 850.
On Red Riv. & Gulf (R. R.).
Kurume, Fukuoka Dist., Japan, 83,008.
Important commercial town.

Kustrin, Prussia, Germany, 19,355.
Kutais, Georgia, Soviet Union, 70,100.
Agricultural produce, silk, and cloth.
Kutna Hora, Czech., 13,900.
Kuttawa, Lyon Co., Ky., 883.
On Ill. Cen. (R. R.).
Kuttenberg, Czechoslovakia. See Kutna Hora.
Kutztown, Berks Co., Pa., 2,841.
On Reading (R. R.).
Kuweit, capital of Kuweit Sultanate, 30,000.
Market center. Famous for boat-building.
Kyle, Hays Co., Texas, 606.
On Mo. Pac. (R. R.).
–McDowell Co., W. Va., 525.
On Norf. & West. (R. A.).
Kylertown, Clearfield Co., Pa., 500.
Kyoto, Japan, 1,080,593.
A center of fine art industries and former capital of Japan.
Kyrock, Edmonson Co., Ky., 631.

L

Labadieville, Assumption Par., La., 600.
On Sou. Pac. (R. R.).
La Belle, Hendry Co., Fla., 671.
On Seab. Air Line (R. R.).
–Lewis Co., Mo., 820.
On Quincy, Omaha & Kan. Cy. (R. R.).
Labo, Ambos-Camarines, Luzon, P. I., 7,699.
La Carlota, Negros, P. I., 23,200.
A sugar center.
Lac Du Flambeau, Vilas Co., Wis., 888.
La Center, Ballard Co., Ky., 537.
On Ill. Cen. (R. R.).
Lachine, Jacques-Cartier Co., Quebec, Canada, 18,630.
On Can. National (R. R.).
At the head of Lachine Rapids.
Lachute, Argenteuil Co., Quebec, Canada, 3,906.
On Can. Nat.; Can. Pac. (R. Rs.).
Lackawanna, Erie Co., N. Y., 23,948.
On Balt. & Ohio; Penna; South Buffalo (R. Rs.).
Steel is the chief industry.
Lackawaxen, Pike Co., Pa., 500.
On Erie (R. R.).
Lackey, Floyd Co., Ky., 522.
On Chesa. & Ohio (R. R.).
Laclede, Linn Co., Mo., 644.
On Chi., Burl. & Quincy (R. R.).
Lacombe, Red Deer Co., Alberta, Canada, 1,259.
On Can. Pac. (R. R.).
–St. Tammany Par., La., 615.
On Gulf, Mob. & Nor. (R. R.).
Lacon, c. s., Marshall Co., Ill., 1,548.
On Alton (R. R.).
Lacona, Warren Co., Iowa, 443.
On Chi., Burl. & Quincy (R. R.).
–Oswego Co., N. Y., 546.
On N. York Cen. (R. R.).
Laconia, c. s., Belknap Co., N. H., 12,471.
On Bost. & Me. (R. R.).
In lake district and a resort for summer vacationists. Railroad cars and hosiery are principal industries.
La Conner, Skagit Co., Wash., 549.
Lacoochee, Pasco Co., Fla., 1,000.
On Atl. Coast Line; Seab. Air Line (R. Rs.).
La Coruña, capital of Coruña Dist., Spain, 67,-093.
Lacoste, Medina Co., Tex., 521.
On Sou. Pac. (R. R.).
La Crescent, Houston Co., Minn., 520.
On Chi., Mil., St. P. & Pac. (R. R.).
La Crescenta, Los Angeles Co., Cal., 6,000.
La Crosse, La Porte Co., Ind., 568.
On Chesa. & Ohio; Chi., Attica & Sou.; Chi., Ind. & Lou.; Penna.; Pere Marq. (R. Rs.).
–c. s., Rush Co., Kans., 1,553.
On Mo. Pac. (R. R.).
–c. s., La Cross Co., Wis., 39,614.
On Chi., Burl. & Quincy; Chi., Mil., St. P. & Pac.; Chi. & Nor. West. (R. Rs.).
Agricultural, manufacturing, jobbing and tourist center. State Teachers' College and Vocational School. On Mississippi River.
La Cygne, Linn Co., Kans., 1,055.
On St. Lou.-San Fran. (R. R.).
Ladd, Bureau Co., Ill., 1,318.
On Chi. & Nor. West.; Chi., Burl. & Quincy; Chi., Mil., St. P. & Pac.; N. York Cen. (R. Rs.).
Laddonia, Audrian Co., Mo., 576.
On Alton (R. R.).
Ladoga, Montgomery Co., Ind., 829.
On Chi., Ind. & Lou. (R. R.).
Ladonia, Fannin Co., Texas, 1,199.
On Gulf, Colo. & Santa Fe (R. R.).
Ladue, St. Louis Co., Mo., 780.
On Mo.-Kans.-Tex. (R. R.).
Ladysmith, capital of Klip River Co., Natal, Un. of S. Africa, 9,701.
–Rusk Co., Wis., 3,493.
On Mpls., St. P. & S. Ste. M. (R. R.).
Laeken, Brabant, Belgium, 3,800.
La Esperanza, Honduras, 1,780.
La Farge, Vernon Co., Wis., 756.
On Chi., Mil., St. P. & Pac. (R. R.).
Lafayette, c. s., Chambers Co., Ala., 2,119.
On Cen. of Ga. (R. R.).
–Contra Costa Co., Calif., 750.
On Sacramento Nor. (El.) (R. R.).
–Boulder Co., Colo., 1,842.
On Chi., Burl. & Quincy; Colo. & Sou. (R. Rs.).
–c. s., Walker Co., Ga., 2,811.
On Cen. of Ga. (R. R.).
–c. s., Tippecanoe Co., Ind., 26,240.
On Chi., Ind & Lou.; Cle., Cin., Chi. & St. Lou.; N. York, Chi. & St. Lou.; Wab. (R. Rs.).
Important grain market; meat packing; manufactures machinery and diversified products. Seat of Purdue University.
–c. s., Lafayette Parish, La., 14,635.
On Sou. Pac. (R. R.).
Sugar cotton, and lumber center. Seat of Southwestern Louisiana Institute.
–Sussex Co., N. J., 600.
On Del., Lack. & West. (R. R.).
–c. s., Macon Co., Tenn., 577.
La Fayette, Washington Co., R. I., 700.
On N. York, N. Hav. & Hart. (R. R.).
La Fère, Dept. of Aisne, France, 1,833.
Almost destroyed in the Great War. Flank of great German offensive, March 21, 1918.
La Feria, Cameron Co., Tex., 1,594.
On Mo. Pac. (R. R.).
La Fleche, Dept. of Sarthe, France, 10,101.
An important agricultural market.
La Follette, Campbell Co., Tenn., 2,637.
On Lou. & Nash. (R. R.).
La Fontaine, Wabash Co., Ind., 604.
On Cle., Cin., Chi. & St. Lou. (R. R.).
La Garenne-Colombes, Seine, France, 24,734.
Lagonoy, Camarines Norte, Luzon, P. I., 12,675.
Lagos, capital of Nigeria, 126,108.
A leading west-African seaport, and trade center for Nigeria. Has excellent buildings.
La Grande, c. s., Union Co., Ore., 8,050.
On Un. Pac. (R. R.).
La Grange, c. s., Troup Co., Ga., 20,131.
On Atl. & West. Pt.; Atla., Birm. & Coast (R. Rs.).
An important manufacturing center. Products: cotton, rugs, canvas, bagging, cotton seed oil and cake. Seat of La Grange College for Women.
–Cook Co., Ill., 10,103.
On Chi., Burl. & Quincy; Ind. Harb. Blt. (R. Rs.).
A residential suburb of Chicago.
–c. s., Oldham Co., Ky., 1,121.
On Lou. & Nash. (R. R.).
–Lewis Co., Mo., 1,160.
On Chi., Burl. & Quincy (R. R.).
–Lenoir Co., N. C., 1,500.
On Norf. Sou. (R. R.).
–c. s., Fayette Co., Texas, 2,354.
On Mo.-Kan.-Tex. of Tex.; Sou. Pac. (R. Rs.).
Commercial center for a farming region.
Lagrange, Lorain Co., Ohio, 498.
On Cle., Cin., Chi. & St. Lou. (R. R.).
–c. s., Lagrange Co., Ind., 1,640.
On Penna. (R. R.).
La Grange Park, Cook Co., Ill., 2,939.
La Grulla, Starr Co., Tex., 800.
On St. Lou., Browns. & Mex. (R. R.).
La Guaira, Carácas Dist., Venezuela, 8,323.
Laguna, Valencia Co., N. Mex., 500.
On Atch., Top. & Santa Fe (R. R.).
Laguna Beach, Orange Co., Cal., 1,981.
Lagunitas, Marin Co., Calif., 512.
La Habra, Orange Co., Cal., 2,273.
On Sou. Pac.; Un. Pac. (R. Rs.).
La Harpe, Hancock Co., Ill., 1,175.
On Tol., Peor. & West. (R. R.).
–Allen Co., Kans., 719.
On Mo.-Kans.-Tex.; Mo. Pac. (R. Rs.).
Lahore, capital of Punjab, India, 400,075.
A railroad and military center. Chief products; silks, gold and silver lace, rugs, metal goods. Has numerous educational institutions.
Lahr, Baden, Germany, 14,075.
Laibach, Yugoslavia. See Ljubljana.
Laingsburg, Shiawassee Co., Mich., 767.
On Mich. Cen. (R. R.).
La Jara, Conejos Co., Colo., 602.
On Den. & Rio. Gde. West. (R. R.).
Lajas, Mun. of Lajas, Puerto Rico, 3,183.
La Jolla, San Diego Co., Cal., 3,857.
La Junta, c. s., Otero Co., Colo., 7,193.
On Atch., Top. & Santa Fe (R. R.).
Lake Alfred, Polk Co., Fla., 629.
On Atl. Coast Line (R. R.).
Lake Andes, Chas. Mix Co., S. Dak., 845.
On Chi., Mil., St. P. & Pac. (R. R.).
Lake Arthur, Jefferson Davis Parish, La., 1,602.
On Sou. Pac. (R. R.).
Lake Benton, c. s., Lincoln Co., Minn., 903.
On Chi. & Nor. West. (R. R.).
Lake Bluff, Lake Co., Ill., 1,452.
On Chi. & Nor. West.; Chi. No. Shore & Mil. (El.) (R. Rs.).
Lake Burien City, King Co., Wash., 1,030.
Lake Butler, c. s., Union Co., Fla., 886.
On Atl. Coast Line; Ga. Sou. & Fla. (R. Rs.).
Lake Charles, c. s., Calcasieu Parish, La., 15,-791.
On Kan. Cy. Sou.; Mo. Pac.; Sou. Pac. (R. Rs.).
Leading manufactures: petroleum products, cellulose, and lumber. Situated in a rice growing region.
Lake City, c. s., Craighead Co., Ark., 760.
On St. Lou.-San Fran. (R. R.).
–c. s., Columbia Co., Fla., 4,416.
On Atl. Coast Line; Ga. Sou. & Fla.; Seab. Air Line (R. Rs.).
–Calhoun Co., Iowa, 2,012.
On Chi. & Nor. West. (R. R.).
–c. s., Missaukee Co., Mich., 610.
On Penna. (R. R.).
–Wabasha Co., Minn., 3,210.
On Chi., Mil., St. P. & Pac. (R. R.).
–Florence Co., S. C., 1,942.
On Atl. Coast Line (R. R.).
Lake Crystal, Blue Earth Co., Minn., 1,173.
On Chi., St. P., Mpls. & Oma. (R. R.).
Lakefield, Peterborough West, Ontario, Canada, 1,332.
On Can. Nat. (R. R.).
–Jackson Co., Minn., 1,349.
On Chi., Mil., St. P. & Pac. (R. R.).
Lake Forest, Lake Co., Ill., 6,554.
On Chi. & Nor. West.; Chi. No. Shore & Mil. (El.) (R. Rs.).
Seat of Lake Forest College.
Lake Garfield, Polk Co., Fla., 500.
On Seab. Air Line (R. R.).
Lake Geneva, Walworth Co., Wis., 3,073.
On Chi. & Nor. West. (R. R.).
Lake George, Warren Co., N. Y., 848.
On Del. & Hud. (R. R.).
Lake Grove, Clackamas Co., Ore., 800.
Lake Helen, Volusia Co., Fla., 850.
Lakehurst, Ocean Co., N. J., 947.
On Cen. of New Jer. (R. R.).
Lakeland, Polk Co., Fla., 18,554.
On Atl. Coast Line (R. R.).
A center of Florida phosphate industry.
Seat of Florida Southern College (Methodist).
–c. s., Lanier Co., Ga., 1,006.
On Lakeland (R. R.).
Lake Linden, Houghton Co., Mich., 1,714.
On Cop. Rge.; Min. Rge. (R. Rs.).
Lake Lynn, Fayette Co., Pa., 500.
On Balt. & Ohio (R. R.).
Lake Maitland, Orange Co., Fla., 511.
Lake Mills, Winnebago Co., Iowa, 1,474.
On Chi. & Nor. West.; Minn. & St. Lou. (R. Rs.).
–Jefferson Co., Wis., 2,007.
On Chi. & Nor. West. (R. R.).
Lake Milton, Mahoning Co., Ohio, 500.
Lakemore, Summit Co., Ohio, 1,670.
Lake Odessa, Ionia Co., Mich., 1,220.
On Pere Marq. (R. R.).
Lake Orion, Oakland Co., Mich., 1,369.
On Mich. Cen. (R. R.).
Lake Park, Dickinson Co., Iowa, 708.
On Chi., Rk. Isl. & Pac. (R. R.).
–Becker Co., Minn., 624.
On Nor. Pac. (R. R.).
Lake Placid, Highlands Co., Fla., 582.
On Atl. Coast Line (R. R.).
–Essex Co., N. Y., 2,930.
On Del. & Hud.; N. York Cen. (R. Rs.).
Lakeport, c. s., Lake Co., Cal., 1,318.
Lake Preston, Kingsbury Co., S. Dak., 1,009.
On Chi., Mil., St. P. & Pac.; Chi. & Nor. West. (R. Rs.).
Lake Providence, c. s., East Carroll Parish, La., 2,867.
On Mo. Pac. (R. R.).
Lake View, Sac. Co., Iowa, 993.
On Chi. & Nor. West. (R. R.).
Lakeview, Montcalm Co., Mich., 850.
On Pere Marq. (R. R.).
–Logan Co., Ohio, 586.
On N. Y. Cen. (R. R.).
–c. s., Lake Co., Ore., 1,799.
On Sou. Pac. (R. R.).
Lake Village, Chicot Co., Ark., 1,582.
On Mo. Pac. (R. R.).
Lakeville, St. Joseph Co., Ind., 522.
On Penna.; Wab. (R. Rs.).
–Plymouth Co., Mass., 1,443.
–Dakota Co., Minn., 522.
On Chi., Mil., St. P. & Pac.; Mpls., Northf. & Sou. (R. Rs.).
Lake Wales, Polk Co., Fla., 3,401.
On Atl. Coast Line; Seab. Air Line (R. Rs.).
Lakewood, Ocean Co., N. J., 5,000.
On Cen. of N. Jer. (R. R.).
A popular health and winter resort.
–Chautauqua Co., N. Y., 1,837.
On Erie (R. R.).
–Cuyahoga Co., Ohio, 70,509.
–Kent Co., R. I., 985.
Lake Worth, Palm Beach Co., Fla., 5,940.
On Fla. East Coast; Seab. Air Line (R. Rs.).
Lakin, c. s., Kearny Co., Kansas, 719.
On Atch., Top. & Santa Fe (R. R.).
Lakota, c. s., Nelson Co., N. Dak., 860.
On Gt. Nor. (R. R.).
La Linea, Prov. of Cadiz, Spain, 63,236.
La Madeleine, Nord, France, 21,501.
Lamar, c. s., Prowers Co., Colo., 4,233.
On Atch., Top. & Santa Fe (R. R.).
–c. s., Barton Co., Mo., 2,381.
On Mo. Pac.; St. Lou.-San Fran. (R. Rs.).
–Darlington Co., S. Car., 915.
On Atl. Coast Line; Seab. Air Line (R. Rs.).
La Marque, Galveston Co., Tex., 740.
On Galv., Houst. & Hend.; Mo. Pac.; Mo.-Kan.-Tex. of Tex. (R. Rs.).
Lambert, Quitman Co., Miss., 800.
On Ill. Cen. (R. R.).
–Fayette Co., Pa., 600.
Lamberton, Redwood Co., Minn., 782.
On Chi. & Nor. West. (R. R.).
–Fayette Co., Pa., 600.
Lambertville, Hunterdon Co., N. J., 4,518.
On Penna. (R. R.).
La Mesa, San Diego Co., Cal., 2,513.
On San Diego & Ariz. East. (R. R.).
–Dona Ana Co., N. Mex., 600.
Lamesa, c. s., Dawson Co., Texas, 3,528.
On Panh. & Santa Fe (R. R.).
Lamia, capital of Phthiotis and Phocis, Greece, 14,205.
Lamoille, Bureau Co., Ill., 504.
On Chi., Burl. & Quincy (R. R.).
Lamoni, Decatur Co., Iowa, 1,739.
On Chi., Burl. & Quincy (R. R.).
Lamont, Buchanan Co., Iowa, 521.
On Chi. Gt. West. (R. R.).
–Grant Co., Okla., 554.
On St. Lou.-San Fran. (R. R.).
Lamonte, Pettis Co., Mo., 515.
On Mo. Pac. (R. R.).
La Moure, c. s., La Moure Co., N. Dak., 889.
On Nor. Pac. (R. R.).
Lampasas, c. s., Lampasas Co., Texas, 2,709.
On Gulf, Colo. & Santa Fe; Sou. Pac. (R. Rs.).
Lampeter, Lancaster Co., Pa., 500.
Lanark, Carroll Co., Ill., 1,208.
On Chi., Mil., St. P. & Pac. (R. R.).
–Raleigh Co., W. Va., 525.
On Chesa. & Ohio (R. R.).
Lancaster, Los Angeles Co., Calif., 1,000.
On Sou. Pac. (R. R.).
–c. s., Garrard Co., Ky., 1,630.
On Lou. & Nash. (R. R.).
–Worcester Co., Mass., 2,590.
On Bost. & Me. (R. R.).
–c. s., Schuyler Co., Mo., 807.
On Chi., Burl. & Quincy (R. R.).
–c. s., Coos Co., N. H., 2,200.
On Bost. & Me.; Me. Cen. (R. Rs.).
–Erie Co., N. Y., 7,040.
On Del., Lack. & West.; Erie; N. York Cen. (R. Rs.).
–c. s., Fairfield Co., Ohio, 18,716.
On Chesa. & Ohio; Penna. (R. Rs.).
The commercial center of a rich agricultural region. Coal and gas fields in the vicinity.
–c. s., Lancaster Co., Pa., 59,949.
Situated on the Pennsylvania, and the Reading railroads. It is located in a fertile tobacco and grain region and is an important tobacco market. The most important industries are cigar manufactures, boiler and engine works, and the making of linoleum, watches, toys, confectionery, chemicals, umbrellas, and soap. Lancaster was settled in 1729, was the State capital in 1799-1812, and received its city charter in 1818.
Seat of Franklin and Marshall College.
–c. s., Lancaster Co., S. C., 3,545.
On Lancas. & Chest.; Sou. (R. Rs.).
–Dallas Co., Texas, 1,133.
On Mo.-Kan.-Tex. of Texas; Tex. & N. Orl. (R. Rs.).
–c. s., Grant Co., Wis., 2,432.
On Chi. & Nor. West. (R. R.).
–Lancashire, England, 43,396.
A market and industrial town. Textiles, cabinet making, railroad cars, and oil cloth.
Lanchow, capital of Prov. of Kansu, China, 500,-000.
Lanciano, Prov. of Chieti, Italy, 10,076.
Of interest historically.
Landau, Bavaria, Germany, 15,000.
Has large cattle market.
Lander, c. s., Fremont Co., Wyo., 1,826.
On Chi. & Nor. West. (R. R.).
Landgraff, McDowell Co., W. Va., 700.
On Norf. & West. (R. R.).
Landis, Rowan Co., N. C., 1,388.
On Sou. (R. R.).
Landisville, Atlantic Co., N. J., 790.
On Cen. of New Jer. (R. R).
–Lancaster Co., Pa., 632.
On Penna.; Read. (R. Rs.).
Lando, Chester Co., S. Car., 800.
On Edgmoor & Manetta (R. R.).
Landrum, Spartanburg Co., S. C., 1,212.
On Sou. (R. R.).
Landsberg, Brandenburg, Germany, 46,000.
Engine and boiler works, iron foundries, and cigars, sugar, oil, jute, and carriage factories.
Landshut, Bavaria, Germany, 32,000.
Principal industries: brewing, tanning and iron founding.

Landskrona, Lan of Malmöhus, Sweden, 18,534.
On a little island (Hven), opposite this port, Tycho Brahe built his observatory of Uranienborg.
Lanesboro, Berkshire Co., Mass., 1,237.
–Fillmore Co., Minn., 1,014.
On Chi., Mil., St. P. & Pac. (R. R.).
–Susquehanna Co., Pa., 731.
On Del. & Hud.; Erie (R. Rs.).
Lanett, Chambers Co., Ala., 5,204.
On Chattah. Val.; West. of Ala. (R. Rs.).
Langaran, Mindanao, P. I., 11,318.
Langdale, Chambers Co., Ala., 650.
On Chattah. Val. (R. R.).
Langdon, c. s., Cavalier Co., N. Dak., 1,221.
On Gt. Nor. (R. R.).
Langenbielau, Silesia, Germany, 17,693.
Textile industries.
Langendreer, Prussia, Germany, 27,557.
A suburb of Bochum.
Langensalza, Prussian Saxony, 11,969.
An industrial center. Has sulphur springs near by.
Langhorne, Bucks Co., Pa., 1,147.
On Penna.; Read. (R. Rs.).
Langley, Aiken Co., S. C., 1,688.
On Southern (R. R.).
Langres, Dept. of Haute-Marne, France, 7,868.
Lansdale, Montgomery Co., Pa., 8,379.
On Reading (R. R.).
Lansdowne, Delaware Co., Pa., 9,542.
On Penna. (R. R.).
L'Anse, c. s., Baraga Co., Mich., 2,421.
On Dul., So. Sh. & Atl. (R. R.).
Lansford, Carbon Co., Pa., 9,632.
On Cen. of N. Jer.; Leh. & N. Eng. (R. Rs.).
Lansing, Cook Co., Ill., 3,378.
On Penna. (R. R.).
–Allamakee Co., Iowa, 1,321.
On Chi., Mil., St. P. & Pac. (R. R.).
–Leavenworth Co., Kans., 988.
On Atch., Top. & Santa Fe; Un. Pac. (R. Rs.).
–c. s., Ingham Co., Mich., capital of the State, 78,397.
Situated on the Grand River, which at this point is crossed by several bridges, and on the Grand Trunk; Pere Marquette; New York Central; and Michigan Central Railroads. The manufactures include agricultural implements, flour, stoves, machinery, awning and tents, oil burners, sugar, tools, dies, cigars, flour, wagons, and automobiles.
Laoag, Ilocos Norte, Luzon, P. I., 38,469.
A busy port. Rice, sugar, cotton, and tobacco shipping point.
Laon, Dept. of Aisne, France, 20,254.
In fighting zone during the Great War.
La Paloma, Cameron Co., Tex., 500.
On Mo. Pac. (R. R.).
La Paz, Dept. of La Paz, Bolivia, one of the capitals of Bolivia, 202,000.
While Sucre is the constitutional capital, La Paz is the actual one. Distributing point for much farm produce and center of a mining region.
Lapeer, c. s., Lapeer Co., Mich., 5,008.
On Gd. Tr.; Mich. Cen. (R. Rs.).
Lapel, Madison Co., Ind., 1,140.
On Cen. Ind. (R. R.).
La Plata, capital of Prov. of Buenos Aires, Argentine Republic, 179,587.
An important meat packing center.
–Macon Co., Mo., 1,406.
On Atch., Top. & Santa Fe; Wab. (R. Rs.).
La Porte, c. s., La Porte Co., Ind., 15,755.
On N. York Cen.; N. York, Chi. & St. Lou.; Pere Marq. (R. Rs.).
Has an airport. Chief manufactures: water heaters, steel doors, woolen goods, machinery, and band instruments.
–Harris Co., Texas, 1,280.
On Sou. Pac. (R. R.).
La Porte City, Blackhawk Co., Iowa, 1,470.
On Chi., Rk. Isl. & Pac.; Waterl., Ced. Fs. & Nor. (El.) (R. Rs.).
La Prairie, La Prairie and Napierville Cos., Quebec, Canada, 2,774.
On Can. Nat. (R. R.).
La Pryor, Zavalla Co., Tex., 702.
On Un. Pac. (R. R.).
Larache (El Araish), Sp. Morocco, 32,010.
Situated in a rich orchard and market garden region.
Laramie, c. s., Albany Co., Wyo., 8,609.
On Laramie, Nor. Pk. & West; Un. Pac. (R. Rs.).
Larchmont, Westchester Co., N. Y., 5,282.
On N. York, N. Hav. & Hart. (R. R.).
Laredo, Grundy Co., Mo., 578.
On Chi., Mil., St. P. & Pac. (R. R.).
–c. s., Webb Co., Texas, 32,618.
On Mo. Pac.; Natl. of Mex.; Rio Gde. & Eag. Pass; Tex. Mex. (R. Rs.).
A port of entry and commercial center. Situated in a rich truck-farming and fruit growing region. Cannel coal is mined near by.
Lares, Mun. of Lares, Puerto Rico, 3,205.
Largo, Pinellas Co., Fla., 958.
On Atl. Coast Line; Seab. Air Line (R. Rs.).
Larimore, Grand Forks Co., N. Dak., 979.
On Gt. Nor. (R. R.).
Larissa, capital of Nomarchy of Larissa, Thessaly, Greece, 24,125.
A marketing center. Of great interest historically.
Larkspur, Marin Co., Cal., 1,241.
On Northw. Pac. (R. R.).
Larksville, Luzerne Co., Pa., 9,322.
Larned, c. s., Pawnee Co., Kans., 3,495.
On Atch., Top. & Santa Fe; Mo. Pac.; Wich. Northw. (R. Rs.).
La Rochelle, Dept. of Charente Inférieur, France, 47,737.
A seaport and distributing point.
La Roche-sur-Yon, Dept. of Vendée, France, 14,538.
La Rue, Marion Co., Ohio, 698.
On Cle., Cin., Chi. & St. Lou. (R. R.).
Larvik, Norway, 10,383.
La Salle, Weld Co., Colo., 564.
On Un. Pac. (R. R.).
–La Salle Co., Ill., 13,149.
On Chi., Burl. & Quincy; Chi., Rk. Isl. & Pac.; Ill. Cen.; La Salle & Bureau Co. (R. Rs.).
Has extensive manufactures of zinc, sulphuric acid, cement, brick, and clocks. Coal mines and stone quarries near by.
–Niagara Co., N. Y. (Sta. Niagara Falls P. O.).
On Erie; N. York Cen.; West Shore (R. Rs.).
Las Animas, c. s., Bent Co., Colo., 2,517.
On Atch., Top. & Santa Fe (R. R.).
Las Cruces, c. s., Dona Ana Co., N. Mex., 5,811.
On Atch., Top. & Santa Fe (R. R.).
La Serena, Chile, 32,743.
Located in a fruit growing region.
La Seyne-sur-Mer, Var, France, 27,073.
Las Palmas, Canary Islands, 83,553.
A busy seaport and exporting point.
Las Piedras, Dept. of Las Piedras, Puerto Rico, 2,032.
L'Assomption, L'Assomption Co., Quebec, Canada, 1,576.
On Can. Nat. (R. R.).
Las Vegas, c. s., Clark Co., Nevada, 5,165.
On Un. Pac. (R. R.).
–c. s., San Miguel Co., N. Mex., 4,719.
On Atch., Top. & Santa Fe (R. R.).
–(town) San Miguel Co., N. Mex., 4,378.
Latacunga, Prov. of Leon, Ecuador, 15,600.
Population largely Indian.
Lathrop, Clinton Co., Mo., 940.
On Atch., Top. & Santa Fe; Chi., Burl. & Quincy (R. Rs.).
Latouche, Alaska, 339.
Latrobe, Westmoreland Co., Pa., 10,644.
On Ligonier Val.; Penna. (R. Rs.).
Collieries, steel works, and woolen mills.
Latta, Dillon Co., S. C., 1,166.
On Atl. Coast Line (R. R.).
Lattaquie, capital of Latakia, Syria, 20,000.
Center of the Latakia tobacco trade.
Lauban, Prussia, Germany, 16,000.
Machinery, textiles, and flour.
Lauenburg, Prussia, Germany, 20,000.
A marketing center in a farming region.
Lauingen, Swabia, Bavaria, 4,838.
Laun, Czechoslovakia. See Louny.
Launceston, (and suburbs), Tasmania, 27,532.
A tourist and health resort. Has tin smelteries, woolen mills, and potteries.
La Union, Dept. of Union, Chile, 5,735.
Laurel, Sussex Co., Del., 2,277.
On Penna. (R. R.).
–Franklin Co., Ind., 516.
On Cle., Cin., Chi. & St. Lou. (R. R.).
–Prince Georges Co., Md., 2,532.
On Balt. & Ohio (R. R.).
–c. s., Jones Co., Miss., 18,017.
On Gulf, Mob. & Nor.; Ill. Cen.; N. Orl. & Northe. (R. Rs.).
Large shipping point for yellow pine lumber.
–Yellowstone Co., Montana, 2,558.
On Chi., Burl. & Quincy; Gt. Nor.; Nor. Pac. (R. Rs.).
–Cedar Co., Neb., 864.
On Chi., Burl. & Quincy; Chi., St. P., Mpls. & Oma. (R. Rs.).
Laureldale, Berks Co., Pa., 3,209.
On Reading (R. R.).
Laurel Hill, Okaloosa Co., Fla., 749.
On Lou. & Nash. (R. R.).
Laurel Run, Luzerne Co., Pa., 944.
On Cen. of N. Jer. (R. R.).
Laurel Springs, Camden Co., N. J., 1,343.
On Penna.-Read.-Seashore (R. R.).
Laurens, Pocahontas Co., Iowa, 1,071.
On Chi., Rk. Isl. & Pac.; Chi. & Nor. West. (R. Rs.).
–c. s., Laurens Co., S. C., 5,443.
On Charl. & West. Car.; Colum., Newb. & Laur. (R. Rs.).
Laurinburg, c. s., Scotland Co., N. C., 3,312.
On Laurinburg & Sou.; Seab. Air Line (R. Rs.).
Laurium, Houghton Co., Mich., 4,916.
On Copper Range (R. R.).
Lausanne, capital of Canton of Vaud, Switzerland, 99,900.
A famous educational center, and the place where the Lausanne Treaty was drawn up.
Lauzon, Levis Co., Quebec, Canada, 7,084.
Lava Hot Springs, Bannock Co., Idaho, 544.
On Un. Pac. (R. R.).
Laval, Dept. of Mayenne, France, 28,380.
Textile manufactures.
Lavelle, Schuylkill Co., Pa., 800.
La Verne, Los Angeles Co., Cal., 2,860.
On Atch., Top. & Santa Fe; Pac. El.; Sou. Pac. (R. Rs.).
–Harper Co., Okla., 903.
On Mo.-Kan.-Tex. (R. R.).
La Veta, Huerfano Co., Colo., 782.
On Den. & Rio Gde. West. (R. R.).
Lavonia, Franklin Co., Ga., 1,511.
On Southern (R. R.).
Lawndale, Cleveland Co., N. C., 728.
On Lawndale Ry. & Indus. Co. (R. R.).
Lawnside, Camden Co., N. J., 1,379.
On Penna.-Read. Seashore (R. R.).
Lawrence, c. s., Douglas Co., Kans., 13,902.
On Atch., Top. & Santa Fe; Kans. Cy., Kaw Val. & West.; Un. Pac. (R. Rs.).
Seat of the University of Kansas.
–Marion Co., Ind., 840.
On Cle., Cin., Chi. & St. Lou.; Ind. R. R. Sys. (El.) (R. R.).
–c. s., Essex Co., Mass., 86,785.
On the Merrimac River, 26 miles north by west of Boston, and 10 miles northeast of Lowell, and on the Boston & Maine Railroad. An important manufacturing center for worsted and woolen goods, chemicals, coated paper, shoes, bobbins and shuttles, hair combs, rugs, shoe laces, and paper mill machinery.
Lawrence was incorporated a town in 1847 and a city in 1853.
–Van Buren Co., Mich., 570.
On Pere Marq. (R. R.).
–Nuckolls Co., Neb., 528.
On Chi., Burl. & Quincy; Mo. Pac. (R. Rs.).
–Nassau Co., N. Y., 3,041.
On Long Isl. (R. R.).
Lawrenceburg, c. s., Dearborn Co., Ind., 4,072.
On Balt. & Ohio; Cle., Cin., Chi. & St. Lou. (R. Rs.).
–c. s., Anderson Co., Ky., 1,763.
On Southern (R. R.).
–c. s., Lawrence Co., Tenn., 3,102.
On Lou. & Nash. (R. R.).
Lawrence Mills (South Gardner), Kennebec Co., Me., 500.
Lawrenceville, c. s., Gwinnett Co., Ga., 2,156.
On Seab. Air Line (R. R.).
–c. s., Lawrence Co., Ill., 6,303.
On Balt. & Ohio; Cle., Cin., Chi. & St. Lou. (R. Rs.).
–Mercer Co., N. J., 750.
On Trenton-Princeton Trac. Co. (R. R.).
–c. s., Brunswick Co., Va., 1,629.
On Southern (R. R.).
Lawson, Ray Co., Mo., 590.
On Atch., Top. & Santa Fe; Chi., Mil., St. P. & Pac.; Chi., Rk. Isl. & Pac. (R. Rs.).
Lawsonia, Somerset Co., Md., 800.
Lawtey, Bradford Co., Fla., 444.
On Seab. Air Line (R. R.).
Lawton, Van Buren Co., Mich., 1,164.
On Mich. Cen.; Pere Marq. (R. Rs.).
–c. s., Comanche Co., Okla., 12,121.
On Chi., Rk. Isl. & Pac.; St. Lou.-San Fran. (R. Rs.).
Near by are oil and gas fields; also Fort Sill military reservation.
–Fayette Co., W. Va., 516.
Layland, Fayette Co., W. Va., 500.
On Chesa. & Ohio (R. R.).
Layton, Davis Co., Utah, 597.
On Den. & Rio Gde. West.; Un. Pac. (R. Rs.).
Leachville, Mississippi Co., Ark., 1,157.
On St. Lou.-San Fran.; St. Lou. Southw. (R. Rs.).
Lead, Lawrence Co., S. D., 5,733.
On Chi., Burl. & Quincy; Chi. & Nor. West. (R. Rs.).
Leadville, c. s., Lake Co., Colo., 3,771.
On Colo. & Sou.; Den. & Rio Gde. West. (R. Rs.).
Leakesville, c. s., Greene Co., Miss., 662.
On Miss. & Ala. (R. R.).
Leaksville, Rockingham Co., N. C., 1,814.
On Danv. & West. (R. R.).
Leamington, Warwickshire, England, 29,662.
Noted for its scenic beauty.
–Essex South, Ontario, Canada, 4,902.
On Mich. Cen.; Pere Marq. (R. Rs.).
Leary, Calhoun Co., Ga., 531.
On Cen. of Ga. (R. R.).
Leavenworth, c. s., Leavenworth Co., Kans., 19,486.
Situated on the west bank of the Missouri River, and on the Atchison, Topeka and Santa Fe; the Chicago, Burlington & Quincy; the Missouri Pacific; the Union Pacific; the Chicago Great Western; and the Leavenworth Terminal Railway and Bridge Company railroads. Has diversified industries. Coal deposits underlie city.
The Soldiers' Home houses veterans of the Civil War. Fort Leavenworth is a regimental headquarters, and here are located the United States Infantry and Cavalry School and the United States military prison.
–Chelan Co., Wash., 1,415.
On Great Northern (R. R.).
Leavittsburg, Trumbull Co., Ohio, 2,500.
On Balt. & Ohio; Erie (R. Rs.).
Lebanon, St. Claire Co., Ill., 1,828.
On Balt. & Ohio (R. R.).
–c. s., Boone Co., Ind., 6,445.
On Cen. Ind.; Cle., Cin., Chi. & St. Lou.; Penna. (R. Rs.).
–Smith Co., Kans., 733.
On Chi., Rk. Isl. & Pac. (R. R.).
–c. s., Marion Co., Ky., 3,248.
On Lou. & Nash. (R. R.).
–York Co., Maine, 1,148.
–c. s., Laclede Co., Mo., 3,562.
On St. Lou.-San Fran. (R. R.).
–Grafton Co., N. H., 5,500.
On Bost. & Me. (R. R.).
–Hunterdon Co., N. J., 550.
On Cen. of N. Jer. (R. R.).
–c. s., Warren Co., Ohio, 3,222.
On Penna. (R. R.).
–Linn Co., Ore., 1,851.
On Spok., Port. & Seattle; Sou. Pac. (R. Rs.).
–c. s., Lebanon Co., Pa., 25,561.
On Cornwall; Penna.; Read. (R. Rs.).
Near the most productive magnetite mines in the world. Has extensive iron and steel works.
–c. s., Wilson Co., Tenn., 4,656.
On Tenn. Cen. (R. R.).
–c. s., Russell Co., Va., 560.
Lebanon Independent, Lebanon Co., Pa., 2,252.
Lebanon Junction, Bullitt Co., Ky., 1,267.
On Lou. & Nash. (R. R.).
Le Blanc-Mesnil, Seine-et-Oise, France, 21,660.
Lebo, Coffey Co., Kans., 591.
On Atch., Top. & Santa Fe (R. R.).
Lebu, capital of Prov. of Arauco, Chile, 3,393.
Lecce, capital of Prov. of Lecce, Italy, 40,000.
Le Center, (Le Sueur Center), c. s., Le Sueur Co., Minn., 948.
On Chi., Mil., St. P. & Pac. (R. R.).
Leckrone, Fayette Co., Pa., 700.
On Balt. & Ohio; Monong. (R. Rs.).
Le Claire, Scott Co., Iowa, 691.
On Chi., Mil., St. P. & Pac.; Chi., Burl. & Quincy; Clin., Davenp. & Musc.; Davenp., Rk. Isl. & Northw. (R. Rs.).
Lecompte, Rapides Parish, La., 1,247.
On Chi., Rk. Isl. & Pac.; Red Riv. & Gulf; Tex. & Pac. (R. Rs.).
Le Creusot (or Creusot), Saône-et-Loire, France, 29,417.
Headquarters of the iron and steel works of Schneider & Co., covering 750 acres.
Ledeberg, East Flanders, Belgium, 13,359.
Ledford, Saline Co., Ill., 462.
On Cle., Cin., Chi. & St. Lou. (R. R.).
Ledyard, New London Co., Conn., 200.
Lee, Penobscot Co., Maine, 3,000.
–Berkshire Co., Mass., 4,178.
On N. York, N. Hav. & Hart. (R. R.).
Leechburg, Armstrong Co., Pa., 4,489.
On Penna. (R. R.).
Leedey, Dewey Co., Okla., 646.
On Missouri-Kansas-Texas (R. R.).
Leeds, Yorkshire, England, 482,789.
Situated on the River Aire. The Leeds and Liverpool Canal communicates with the Aire. Leeds is the center of the woolen and iron industry of England. Its history extends over more than 1,200 years, the town being mentioned by the Venerable Bede as the capital of a small British kingdom about 616. Seat of Leeds University.
–Jackson Co., Mo., 515.
On Kan. Cy. Sou.; Mo. Pac.; St. Lou.-San Fran. (R. Rs.).
–Benson Co., N. Dak., 725.
On Gt. Nor.; Nor. Pac. (R. Rs.).
Leeper, Wayne Co., Mo., 530.
On Mo. Pac.; Mo. Sou. (R. Rs.).
Leer, Prussia, Germany, 12,232.
An industrial center and river port.
Leesburg, Lake Co., Fla., 4,326.
On Atl. Coast Line; Seab. Air Line (R. Rs.).
–c. s., Lee Co., Ga., 691.
On Cen. of Ga. (R. R.).
–Cumberland Co., N. J., 605.
On Penna.-Read. Seashore (R. R.).
–Highland Co., Ohio, 830.
On Balt. & Ohio (R. R.).
–c. s., Loudoun Co., Va., 1,640.
On Wash. & Old Dom. (El.) (R. R.).
Leesport, Berks Co., Pa., 615.
On Penna.; Read. (R. Rs.).
Lees Summit, Jackson Co., Mo., 2,035.
On Mo. Pac. (R. R.).
Leesville, c. s., Vernon Parish, La., 3,291.
On Kan. Cy Sou. (R. R.).
–Lexington Co., S. C., 1,340.
On Southern (R. R.).
Leetonia, Columbiana Co., Ohio, 2,332.
On Erie; Penna.; Youngst. & Sub. (R. Rs.).
Leetsdale, Allegheny Co., Pa., 2,774.

On Penna. (R. R.).
LEEUWARDEN, Friesland Prov., Netherlands, 48,-482.
Important as a commercial town. Manufactures boats, lumber, castings, furniture, organs and cigars.
LEE VALLEY, Hawkins Co., Tenn., 880.
LEFORS, Gray Co., Tex., 952.
On Ft. Worth & Denv. Cy. (R. R.).
LEGASPI, Prov. of Albay, Luzon, P. I., 52,756.
A trade center. Abaca, corn, sugar, rice and tobacco grown in region.
LEGHORN, Italy. See LIVORNO.
LEH, capital of Ladakh, Kashmir, India, 3,500.
LE HAVRE (Havre), Dept. of Seine-Inférieure, France, 164,083.
A fortified town and busy seaport. Is situated on a low alluvial tract of land, and is divided into unequal parts by its outward port and basins. The port is the best and most accessible on the coast. The principal buildings are the Church of Notre Dame, the Exchange, Palace of Justice, and Musée Bibliothèque. There are also schools of navigation and industrial arts.
Le Havre ranks second among the commercial ports of France. The manufactures include steam engines, cotton goods, and glassware. The exports consist of cottons and silks, woolens, leather, copper, hides, and wine. There are gun factories, chemical and glass works, sugar refineries and shipbuilding yards.
Le Havre, originally named Villa Françoise, was founded by Francis I. in the sixteenth century.
LEHI, Utah Co., Utah., 2,826.
On Den. & Rio Gde. West.; Salt. L. & Utah (El.); Un. Pac. (R. Rs.).
LEHIGH, Webster Co., Iowa, 996.
On Ft. Dodge, Des Moines & Sou. (R. R.).
–Coal Co., Okla., 497.
On Okla. City-Ada-Atoka (R. R.).
LEHIGHTON, Carbon Co., Pa., 6,490.
On Cen. of N. Jer.; Leh. Val. (R. Rs.).
LEICESTER, capital of Leicestershire, England, 239,111.
A busy commercial and industrial town. Principal industry is hosiery. Also beer, woolen goods, shoes, rubber goods, lace, printing, and tobacco.
–Worcester Co., Mass., 4,426.
LEIDEN (Leyden), Prov. of South Holland, Netherlands, 70,860.
Situated on the Rhine. Leyden University, founded by the Prince of Orange in 1575, was at one time one of the most celebrated in Europe.
LEIGH, Lancashire, England, 45,313.
A market town near Manchester.
–Colfax Co., Neb., 692.
On Chi. & Nor. West. (R. R.).
LEIGHTON, Colbert Co., Ala., 670.
On Sou. (R. R.).
LEIPSIC, Putnam Co., Ohio, 1,571.
On Balt. & Ohio; Det., Tol. & Iron.; N. York, Chi. & St. Lou. (R. Rs.).
LEIPZIG, Saxony, Germany, 717,000.
Situated on the White Elster River. Many of the houses are very lofty, exhibiting the carved masonry which characterized the old German style of building. Leipzig is the site of the famous conservatory of music. It is a great publishing and industrial center. A great commercial fair, held twice a year, is visited by buyers from all parts of the world.
Leipzig dates from the eleventh century. In 1813 was fought here the "Battle of Nations," when Napoleon was defeated by the combined forces of Austria, Prussia, Russia, and Sweden, under the command of Schwarzenberg, Blücher, and Bernadotte.
LEISENRING, Fayette Co., Pa., 850.
On Balt. & Ohio; Penna. (R. Rs.).
LEITCHFIELD, c. s., Grayson Co., Ky., 950.
On Ill. Cen. (R. R.).
LEITH, seaport of Edinburgh, Midlothian Co., Scotland. (United to Edinburgh, 1920.)
LEITMERITZ, Czechoslovakia. See LITOMERICE.
LEJUNIOR, Hardin Co., Ky., 1,000.
LELAND, La Salle Co., Ill., 548.
On Chi., Burl. & Quincy (R. R.).
–Washington Co., Miss., 2,426.
On Ill. Cen. (R. R.).
LE MANS, capital of Dept. of Sarthe, France, 84,525.
Manufactures tobacco, leather, bells, hemp, machinery, stained glass, motors, and textiles.
LE MARS, c. s., Plymouth Co., Iowa, 4,788.
On Chi., St. P., Mpls. & Oma.; Ill. Cen. (R. Rs.).
Seat of Western Union College.
LEMBERG, Poland. See LWÓW.
LEMERY, Luzon, P. I., 15,647.
Situated in a rich agricultural region.
LEMMON, Perkins Co., S. Dak., 1,785.
On Chi., Mil., St. P. & Pac. (R. R.).
LEMONT, Cook Co., Ill., 2,582.
On Alton; Atch., Top. & Santa Fe (R. Rs.).
LEMOORE, Kings Co., Cal., 1,399.
On Sou. Pac. (R. R.).
LEMOYNE, Cumberland Co., Pa., 4,171.
On Penna.; Read. (R. Rs.).
LENA, Stephenson Co., Ill., 1,145.
On Ill. Cen. (R. R.).
LENINAKAN (Gymri), Transcaucasia, Soviet Union, 49,000.
A port of entry and important trade center.
LENINGRAD, Sov. Union, formerly St. Petersburg and Petrograd, capital of Russia until 1918, 2,776,400.
Situated at the head of the Gulf of Finland and the mouth of the Neva. Before entering the sea the Neva subdivides into many branches, thus giving origin to 100 islands of various sizes. One single line of railway connects Leningrad with the head of the Volga and Moskva; another with Poland and Western Europe; a third with the Baltic Provinces; and a fourth with Finland. The real connection between the former Russian Empire and its capital was established through the Neva. Owing to this connection, the city became, and has remained for more than 150 years, the chief commercial port of the country.
The great Neva has within the city itself so great a depth that large ships can lie alongside its granite embankments. But it is shallow at the mouth, with a narrow and sinuous channel, so that Kronstadt, built on an island 16 miles to the west of Leningrad, is the real port of the city.
The main body of the city stands on the mainland, on the left bank of the Neva and has a beautiful granite quay. Only two permanent bridges cross the Neva. The island of Vassili, between the Great and Little Nevas, has at its head the Stock Exchange, surrounded by spacious storehouses, and the Academy of Sciences, the University, and the Academy of Arts. On the Peterburgski Island stands the old fortress of St. Peter and St. Paul, facing the Winter Palace, and containing the mint and the cathedral wherein the members of the former imperial family were buried; its old-fashioned casemates are used as political prisons, the deposed Czar (Nicholas II.) and some of his ministers having been incarcerated there following the Revolution of 1917. Farther up the mainland the right bank of the Neva is covered by the poorer parts of the city, but contains some public buildings and a great number of industrial establishments. The main part of Leningrad has for its center the Old Admiralty. Three important streets radiate from it; the first of them is the famous Nevski Prospect. A spacious square, planted with trees, encloses the Old Admiralty on three sides. To the east of it rise the huge mass of the Winter Palace, the Hermitage Gallery of Art, and the semicircular buildings of the former General Staff, which surround a square facing the palace, and are adorned by the Alexandra columns, a shaft of red granite 84 feet high. West of the Admiralty is the Petrovski Square. The Cathedral of St. Isaac of Dalmatia, the most magnificent structure in the city, was erected by Nicholas I. Its interior decorations are very rich, and it contains paintings by the best representatives of Russian art. The Nevski Prospect is one of the finest streets in the world. It runs for 3,200 yards, with a width of 130 feet, from the Admiralty to the Moskva Railway station. It passes by the Kazan Cathedral, the Gostinoi Dvor—a two-story building containing numerous shops—the public library, the Square of Catherine II., and the Anitchkoff Palace. Before the World War of 1914-18, Leningrad was one of the great industrial centers of Russia. It was also surpassed by few cities as an educational and scientific center. Leningrad was the center of the March and November revolutions of 1917. Population and trade declined after Moskva became the capital. The city has been largely rebuilt and rehabilitated.
LENINSK, R.S.F.S.R., Soviet Union, 66,300.
LENNI, Delaware Co., Pa., 500.
On Penna. (R. R.).
LENNI MILLS, Delaware Co., Pa., 500.
LENNOX, Lincoln Co., S. Dak., 1,178.
On Chi., Mil., St. P. & Pac.; Gt. Nor. (R. Rs.).
A farm trade center.
LENNOXVILLE, Sherbrooke Co., Quebec, 1,927.
On Can. Pac.; Can. Nat.; Queb. Cen. (R. Rs.).
LENOIR, c. s., Caldwell Co., N. C., 6,532.
On Car. & Nor. West. (R. R.).
–Loudon Co., Tenn., 4,470.
On Southern (R. R.).
LENORA, Norton Co., Kans., 600.
On Mo. Pac. (R. R.).
LENOX, Taylor Co., Iowa, 1,171.
On Chi., Burl. & Quincy (R. R.).
–Berkshire Co., Mass., 2,706.
On N. York, N. Hav. & Hart. (R. R.).
–Macomb Co., Mich., 575.
–Dyer Co., Tenn., 525.
On Ill. Cen. (R. R.).
LENOX DALE, Berkshire Co., Mass., 700.
On N. York, N. Hav. & Hart. (R. R.).
LENS, Pas-de-Calais, France, 32,730.
Scene of heavy fighting in the World War. Almost destroyed. Held by Germans and finally evacuated by them Sept. 4, 1918.
LEOBEN, Styria, Austria, 11,438.
Has large iron smelteries.
LEOBSCHÜTZ, East Silesia, Germany, 12,696.
Textiles, carriages, and machinery.
LEOLA, c. s., McPherson Co., S. Dak., 812.
On Mpls. & St. Lou.; Mound Cy. & East. (R. Rs.).
LEOMINSTER, Worcester Co., Mass., 21,810.
On N. York, N. Hav. & Hart. (R. R.).
LEON, c. s., Decatur Co., Iowa, 2,006.
On Chi., Burl. & Quincy (R. R.).
–Butler Co., Kans., 550.
On St. Lou.-San Fran. (R. R.).
–Guanajuato, Mexico, 69,279.
On Nat. of Mex. (R. R.).
The center of a grain raising region.
–capital of Leon Dept., Nicaragua, 58,957.
Largest city and chief commercial center of a rich agricultural district.
–Panay, P. I., 25,000.
–capital of Prov. of Leon, Spain, 24,155.
Of interest historically.
LEONARD, Fannin Co., Texas, 1,131.
On Mo.-Kans.-Tex. (R. R.).
LEONARDTOWN, c. s., St. Mary's Co., Md., 697.
LEONETH, St. Louis Co., Minn., 500.
LEONIA, Bergen Co., N. J., 5,350.
On Erie (R. R.).
LEOPOLDVILLE, capital of Belgian Congo, 35,946.
LEOTI, c. s., Wichita Co., Kans., 762.
On Mo. Pac. (R. R.).
LEPANTO, Poinsette Co., Ark., 1,195.
On St. Lou.-San Fran. (R. R.).
LE PUY, Dept. of Haute-Loire, France, 21,660.
Lace industry is important.
LERICI, Prov. of Specia, Italy, 4,053.
LERIDA, capital of Prov. of Lerida, Spain, 42,566.
Thriving trade in wine, olive oil, timber, cattle, horses and sheep.
LE ROY, McLean Co., Ill., 1,595.
On Cle., Cin., Chi. & St. Lou.; Ill. Cen. (R. Rs.).
–Coffey Co., Kans., 822.
On Mo. Pac. (R. R.).
–Mower Co., Minn., 661.
On Chi. Gt. West.; Chi., Mil., St. P. & Pac. (R. Rs.).
–Genesee Co., N. Y., 4,474.
On Balt. & Ohio; Erie; N. Y. Cen. (R. Rs.).
–Lake Co., Ohio, 683.
LESCOVAZ, Yugoslavia, 17,615.
Center of the flax and hemp growing region.
LESLIE, Searcy Co., Ark., 657.
On Mo. & Ark. (R. R.).
–Sumter Co., Ga., 620.
On Seab. Air Line (R. R.).
–Ingham Co., Mich., 1,105.
On Mich. Cen. (R. R.).
LESSINES, Hainaut, Belgium, 10,380.
LESTER, Raleigh Co., W. Va., 609.
On Chesa. & Ohio; Virginian (R. Rs.).
LE SUEUR, Le Sueur Co., Minn., 1,897.
On Chi., St. P., Mpls. & Oma. (R. R.).
LETHBRIDGE, Medicine Hat Co., Alberta, Canada, 13,523.
In agricultural and coal mining region.
On Can. Pac. (R. R.).
LETOHATCHEE, Lowndes Co., Ala., 500.
On Lou. & Nash. (R. R.).
LETTSWORTH, Pointe Coupee Par., La., 725.
On Tex. & Pac. (R. R.).
LEVALLOIS-PERRET, Seine, France, 65,186.
LEVAN, Juab Co., Utah, 611.
On Un. Pac. (R. R.).
LEVELLAND, c. s., Hockley Co., Tex., 1,661.
On Panh. & Santa Fe (R. R.).
LEVERETT, Franklin Co., Mass., 726.
On Cent. Vt. (R. R.).
LEVIS, Levis Co., Quebec, Canada, 11,724.
On Can. Nat.; Queb. Cen.; Can. Pac. (R. Rs.).
Port and distributing point opposite Quebec.
LEVISTON, Carbon Co., Pa., 595.
On Leh. Val. (R. R.).
LEVY, Pulaski Co., Ark., 1,197.
On Mo. Pac. (R. R.).
LEWES, Sussex, England, 10,785.
The market center for a rich farming region.
–Sussex Co., Del., 1,923.
On Penna. (R. R.).
LEWIS, Cass Co., Iowa, 589.
On Chi., Rk. Isl. & Pac. (R. R.).
–Edwards Co., Kans., 490.
On Atch., Top. & Santa Fe (R. R.).
LEWISBURG, Preble Co., Ohio, 936.
On Cle., Cin., Chi. & St. Lou. (R. R.).
–c. s., Union Co., Pa., 3,308.
On Penna.; Read. (R. Rs.).
–c. s., Marshall Co., Tenn., 3,112.
On Lou. & Nash.; Nash., Chatt. & St. Lou. (R. Rs.).
–c. s., Greenbrier Co., W. Va., 1,293.
LEWISPORT, Hancock Co., Ky., 574.
On Lou. & Nash. (R. R.).
LEWIS RUN, McKean Co., Pa., 837.
On Balt. & Ohio; Erie (R. Rs.).
LEWISTON, c. s., Nez Perce Co., Idaho, 9,403.
On Nor. Pac.; Un. Pac. (R. Rs.).
Important lumber and mining center. With foundries, machine shops, etc.
–Androscoggin Co., Maine, 34,948.
On Gd. Tr.; Me. Cen. (R. Rs.).
Trade center; "twin" city of Auburn. Manufactures textiles, shoes and woolens. Bates College is located here.
–Winona Co., Minn., 656.
On Chi. & Nor. West. (R. R.).
–Niagara Co., N. Y., 1,013.
On N. York Cen.; Lewist. & Youngst. Front. (R. Rs.).
–Cache Co., Utah, 1,783.
On Utah-Idaho Cen. (El.); Un. Pac. (R. Rs.).
LEWISTOWN, c. s., Fulton Co., Ill., 2,249.
On Chi., Burl. & Quincy (R. R.).
–c. s., Fergus Co., Mont., 5,358.
On Chi., Mil., St. P. & Pac.; Gt. Nor. (R. Rs.).
–c. s., Mifflin Co., Pa., 13,357.
On Kishacoquillas Val.; Penna. (R. Rs.).
One of the earliest iron manufacturing centers of the State.
LEWISVILLE, Lafayette Co., Ark., 1,061.
On St. Lou. Southw. (R. R.).
–Chester Co., Pa., 514.
–Potter Co., Pa., 514.
–Denton Co., Tex., 853.
On Mo.-Kan.-Tex. of Tex. (R. R.).
LEXINGTON, McLean Co., Ill., 1,292.
On Alton (R. R.).
–c. s., Fayette Co., Ky., 45,736.
On Chesa. & Ohio; Cin., New Orl. & Tex. Pac.; Lou. & Nash.; Sou. (R. Rs.).
The largest tobacco market in the country. Noted for its thoroughbred horse raising.
–Middlesex Co., Mass., 10,813.
On Bost. & Me. (R. R.).
–c. s., Holmes Co., Miss., 2,590.
On Ill. Cen. (R. R.).
–c. s., Lafayette Co., Mo., 4,595.
On Mo. Pac. (R. R.).
–c. s., Dawson Co., Neb., 2,962.
On Un. Pac. (R. R.).
–c. s., Davidson Co., N. C., 9,652.
On Sou.; Winst.-Sal. Southb. (R. Rs.).
–Richland Co., Ohio, 614.
On Balt. & Ohio (R. R.).
–Cleveland Co., Okla., 836.
–c. s., Lexington Co., S. C., 1,152.
On Southern (R. R.).
–c. s., Henderson Co., Tenn., 1,823.
On Nash., Chatt. & St. Lou. (R. R.).
–Lee Co., Texas, 519.
On Sou. Pac. (R. R.).
–c. s., Rockbridge Co., Va., 3,752.
On Balt. & Ohio; Chesa. & Ohio (R. Rs.).
Seat of Virginia Military Institute.
LEYDEN, Netherlands. See LEIDEN.
LEYTON, Essex, England, 128,920.
Numerous cathedrals and monasteries.
LHASA, capital of Tibet, 18,000.
LIAOYANG, Manchuria, 38,638.
LIBAU, Latvia. See LIEPAJA.
LIBBY, c. s., Lincoln Co., Montana, 1,752.
On Gt. Nor. (R. R)
LIBERAL, c. s., Seward Co., Kans., 4,509.
On Chi., Rk. Isl. & Pac. (R. Rs.).
–Barton Co., Mo., 848.
On Mo. Pac.; St. Lou.-San Fran. (R. Rs.).
LIBERTY, Adams Co., Ill., 500.
–c. s., Union Co., Ind., 1,241.
On Balt. & Ohio; Erie (R. Rs.).
–c. s., Casey Co., Ky., 549.
–c. s., Amite Co., Miss., 551.
–c. s., Clay Co., Mo., 3,516.
On Chi., Burl. & Quincy; Chi., Mil., St. P. & Pac.; Chi. Rk. Isl. & Pac. (R. Rs.).
Seat of William Jewell College (Baptist).
–Sullivan Co., N. Y., 3,427.
On N. York, Ont. & West. (R. R.).
–Randolph Co., N. C., 873.
On Atl. & Yadk. (R. R.).
–Allegheny Co., Pa., 906.
–Fayette Co., Pa., 1,000.
–Pickens Co., S. C., 2,128.
On Southern (R. R.).
–De Kalb Co., Tenn., 500.
–c. s., Liberty Co., Texas, 2,187.
On Sou. Pac. (R. R.).
LIBERTY CENTER, Henry Co., Ohio, 748.
On Wabash (R. R.).
LIBERTY HILL, Williamson Co., Tex., 604.
On Sou. Pac. (R. R.).
LIBERTYVILLE, Lake Co., Ill., 3,791.
On Chi., Mil., St. P. & Pac.; Chi. No. Shore & Mil. (El.) (R. Rs.).
LIBMANAN, Luzon, P. I., 12,277.
LIBOG, Prov. of Albay, Luzon, P. I., 6,972.
LIBON, Prov. of Albay, Luzon, P. I., 8,745.
LIBOURNEE, Dept. of Gironde, France, 19,491.
Wine and brandy trade center.
LICHFIELD, Staffordshire, England, 8,508.
LICHTENBERG, Saxony, Germany, 2,081.
LICK BRANCH, Morgan Co., Ky., 9,019.
LIDGERWOOD, Richland Co., N. Dak., 1,029.
On Gt. Nor.; Mpls., St. P. & S. Ste. M. (R. Rs.).
LIÉGE, capital of Prov. of Liége, Belgium, 165,634.
Situated on the Meuse River. Liége was one

of the largest manufacturing towns of Europe, owing to its situation in a district abounding in coal, iron, lead, copper, and marble, and its industries are still of major importance. The city was taken by the Germans in 1914, at the outbreak of the Great War.

LIEGNITZ, Silesia, Germany, 76,544.
An important trade center in a farming area.

LIEPAJA (Libau), Latvia, 57,098.
An important seaport with coal and oil facilities. Exports much grain and farm produce.

LIERRE, Prov. of Anvers, Belgium, 28,584.
Cutlery industry leads.

LIÉVIN, Pas-de-Calais, France, 25,127.

LIGAO, Albay Prov., Luzon, P. I., 21,467.
Abaca, rice and coconuts.

LIGNY, Prov. of Namur, Belgium, 2,045.

LIGONIER, Noble Co., Ind., 2,064.
On N. York Cen. (R. R.).
–Westmoreland Co., Pa., 1,978.
On Ligonier Val. (R. R.).

LIGUA, Dept. of Ligua, Chile, 3,227.

LILBOURN, New Madrid Co., Mo., 1,154.
On St. Lou.-San Fran.; St. Lou. Southw. (R. Rs.).

LILLE, capital of Dept. of Nord, France, 200,575.
Partly destroyed in the World War, 1914-18. Occupied by Germans, who were driven out by British, Oct. 17, 1918.

LILLINGTON, c. s., Harnett Co., N. C., 752.
On Atl. & West.; Norf. Sou. (R. Rs.).

LILLY, Cambria Co., Pa., 2,162.
On Penna. (R. R.).

LILOAN, Cebu Prov., Cebu, P. I., 19,827.
Fishing is the principal industry.

LIMA, capital of Peru, capital of Dept. of Lima, 284,827.
Situated at the foot of granitic hills, on the Rimac River. The numerous domes and spires give Lima a fine appearance from a distance. Among the public buildings and institutions are the cathedral, the convent of San Francisco, the exhibition palace, and the University of San Marcos. The manufactures are relatively unimportant but there is a considerable import and export trade through the port of Callao. Its manufactures include textiles, leather goods, furniture and pottery. Lima was founded in 1535 by Pizarro.
–Livingston Co., N. Y., 897.
On Leh. Val. (R. R.).
–c. s., Allen Co., Ohio, 42,287.
On Det., Tol. & Iron.; Penna.; Balt. & Ohio; N. York, Chi. & St. Lou.; Erie (R. Rs.). Makes locomotives, electric refrigerators, cigars, neon signs, busses, etc.
–Delaware Co., Pa., 500.

LIMACHE, Prov. of Valparaiso, Chile, 8,697.

LIMASOL, Cyprus, 15,349.

LIMBACH, Saxony, Germany, 17,004.
A manufacturing suburb of Chemnitz.

LIMBURG, Prov. of Liége, Belgium, 4,330.

LIMBURG-AN-DER-LAHN, Prussia, Germany, 11,552.

LIMERICK, Irish Free State. See LUIMNEACH.
–York Co., Maine, 800.

LIME ROCK, P. O., Litchfield Co., Conn., 650.
On N. York, N. Hav. & Hart. (R. R.).
–Providence Co., R. I., 527.

LIME SPRINGS, Howard Co., Iowa, 539.

On Chi., Mil., St. P. & Pac. (R. R.).

LIMESTONE, Alger Co., Mich., 671.
–Aroostook Co., Maine, 1,953.
On Bangor & Aroostook (R. R.).
–Cattaraugus Co., N. Y., 599.
On Balt. & Ohio; Erie; Penna. (R. Rs.).

LIMINGTON, York Co., Maine, 747.

LIMOGES, capital of Haute-Vienne, France, 95,217.
Noted for its fine porcelains.

LIMON, Lincoln Co., Colorado, 1,100.
On Chi., Rk. Isl. & Pac.; Un. Pac. (R. Rs.).

LIMÓN, capital of Limón Prov., Costa Rica, 16,540.

LIMONAR, Matanzas, Cuba, 2,398.

LINARES, Prov. of Jaen, Spain, 40,010.
–Prov. of Linares, Chile, 15,074.
Center of an irrigation district.

LINCOLN, Washington Co., Ark., 687.
On St. Lou.-San Fran. (R. R.).
–Placer Co., Cal., 2,094.
On Sou. Pac. (R. R.).
–c. s., Logan Co., Ill., 12,855.
On Alton; Ill. Cen.; Ill. Term. (El.) (R. Rs.). Shipping point for grain and numerous other farm products. Coal mines in the vicinity.
–(Lincoln Center), c. s., Lincoln Co., Kans., 1,638.
On Atch., Top. & Santa Fe; Un. Pac. (R. Rs.).
–Penobscot Co., Maine, 2,161.
On Me. Cen. (R. R.).
–Middlesex Co., Mass., 1,573.
On Bost. & Me. (R. R.).
–c. s., Lancaster Co., Neb., State capital, 79,592.
Situated on the Chicago, Burlington & Quincy; the Chicago & North Western; the Union Pacific; the Chicago, Rock Island & Pacific; and Missouri Pacific (R. Rs.). A transportation, manufacturing and commercial center for an extensive territory, especially for grain and milling. Leading products include chemicals, machinery, leather goods, stone and clay products, printing and publishing. Seat of University of Nebraska (including the College of Agriculture), Nebraska Wesleyan University, Cotner University, and Union College.
–Grafton Co., N. H., 1,200.
On Bost. & Me. (R. R.).
–Middlesex Co., N. J., 3,504.
On Cen. of N. J.; Leh. Val. (R. Rs.).
–Providence Co., R. I., 10,453.
A suburb of Providence.
–Addison Co., Vt., 800.
–Lincolnshire, England, 66,246.
Manufactures agricultural implements.

LINCOLNDALE, Westchester Co., N. Y., 500.
On N. York Cen. (R. R.).

LINCOLN PARK, Wayne Co., Mich., 12,336.
On Penna. (R. R.).
A suburb of Detroit.
–Norris Co., N. J., 1,831.
On Del., Lack. & West. (R. R.).

LINCOLNTON, Lincoln Co., Ga., 916.
–c. s., Lincoln Co., N. C., 3,781.
On Car. & Nor. West.; Seab. Air Line (R. Rs.).

LINCOLNVILLE, Charleston Co., S. C., 600.
On Southern (R. R.).

LIND, Adams Co., Wash., 730.
On Chi., Mil., St. P. & Pac.; Nor. Pac. (R. Rs.).

LINDALE, Floyd Co., Ga., 3,380.

On Cen. of Ga.; Sou. (R. Rs.).
–Smith Co., Texas, 743.
On Mo. Pac. (R. R.).

LINDAU, Bavaria, Germany, 13,582.
A pleasure resort.

LINDEN, c. s., Marengo Co., Ala., 982.
On Lou. & Nash.; St. Lou.-San Fran. (R. Rs.).
–Montgomery Co., Ind., 541.
On Chi., Ind. & Lou.; N. York, Chi. & St. Lou. (R. Rs.).
–Genesee Co., Mich., 717.
On Gd. Tr. (R. R.).
–Union Co., N. J., 21,206.
On Penna. (R. R.).
A residential town near Elizabeth.
–c. s., Perry Co., Tenn., 539.
–c. s., Cass Co., Texas, 718.
On Jeff. & Northw. (R. R.).

LINDENHURST, Suffolk Co., N. Y., 4,040.
On Long Isl. (R. R.).

LINDENOLD, Camden Co., N. J., 2,523.
On Penna.-Read.-Seashore (R. R.).

LINDON, Utah Co., Utah, 589.
On Salt L. & Utah (El.) (R. R.).

LINDSAY, Tulare Co., Cal., 3,878.
On Atch., Top. & Santa Fe; Sou. Pac. (R. Rs.). In fruit section, with a large olive acreage.
–Garvin Co., Okla., 1,713.
On Chi., Rk. Isl. & Pac.; Atch., Top. & Santa Fe (R. Rs.).
–Victoria Co., Ontario, Canada, 7,505.
On Can. Pac.; Can. Nat. (R. Rs.).

LINDSBORG, McPherson Co., Kans., 2,004.
On Mo. Pac.; Un. Pac. (R. Rs.).

LINDSTROM, Chisago Co., Minn., 561.
On Nor. Pac. (R. R.).

LINE LEXINGTON, Bucks Co., Pa., 519.

LINESVILLE, Crawford Co., Pa., 963.
On Bess. & L. Erie; Penna. (R. Rs.).

LINEVILLE, Clay Co., Ala., 1,329.
On Atla., Birm. & Coast (R. R.).
–Wayne Co., Iowa, 531.
On Chi., Rk. Isl. & Pac. (R. R.).

LINFIELD, Montgomery Co., Pa., 750.
On Reading; Penna. (R. Rs.).

LINGAYEN, Pangasinan Prov., Luzon, P. I., 22,780.
Rice growing and fishing are most important.

LINGLESTOWN, Dauphin Co., Pa., 718.

LINHART, Allegheny Co., Pa., 500.
On Bess. & L. Erie; Un. (R. Rs.).

LINKÖPING, Sweden, capital of Län of Ostergötland, 32,919.
Has tobacco, cloth, and hosiery factories.

LINN, c. s., Osage Co., Mo., 555.

LINN CREEK, Camden Co., Mo., 553.

LINNEUS, Aroostook Co., Maine, 753.
–c. s., Linn Co., Mo., 760.
On Chi., Burl. & Quincy (R. R.).

LINTHICUM HEIGHTS, Anne Arundel Co., Md., 3,000.
On Balt. & Annap. (El.) (R. R.).

LINTON, Greene Co., Ind., 5,085.
On Chi., Mil., St. P. & Pac.; Penna.; Ill. Cen. (R. Rs.).
–c. s., Emmons Co., N. Dak., 1,192.
On Chi., Mil., St. P. & Pac.; Nor. Pac. (R. Rs.).

LINVILLE, Avery Co., N. C., 500.
On Linville River (R. R.).

LINWOOD, Walker Co., Ga., 828.
–Atlantic Co., N. J., 1,514.
On Penna.-Read. Seashore (R. R.).
–Delaware Co., Pa., 4,000.

LINZ, capital of Upper Austria, 108,970.
Has an active transit trade and manufactures of boats, cloth, and agricultural implements.

LIPA, Batangas Prov., Luzon, P. I., 46,677.

LIPPSTADT, Westphalia, Germany, 9,000.
Cigars, spirits, and carriages.

LIPSCOMB, Jefferson Co., Ala., 1,774.

LISBÔA (Lisbon), Prov. of Estremadura, capital of Portugal, 594,390.
Situated on the Tagus, near its entrance into the Atlantic. The city is built on several small hills, and presents a picturesque appearance from the harbor. Of architectural curiosities the most important is the Alcantara aqueduct, which supplies all the public fountains and wells of the city. Lisbôa contains a large number of educational and scientific institutions, among which are the Royal Academy of Science, founded in 1778, a naval academy, and an academy of engineering. Lisbôa was captured in 716 by the Saracens, who held it until 1147, when it was taken by Alfonso I. In 1755 occurred the historic earthquake, by which over half the city was destroyed and more than 30,000 lives were lost.

LISBON, New London Co., Conn.
–Linn Co., Iowa, 795.
On Chi. & Nor. West. (R. R.).
–Androscoggin Co., Maine, 4,002.
On Me. Cen. (R. R.).
–Grafton Co., N. H., 1,700.
On Bost. & Me. (R. R.).
–c. s., Ransom Co., N. Dak., 1,650.
On Nor. Pac. (R. R.).
–c. s., Columbiana Co., Ohio, 3,405.
On Erie; Pitts., Lisb. & West. (R. Rs.).

LISBON FALLS, Androscoggin Co., Maine, 2,666.
On Me. Cen. (R. R.).

LISBURN, County Antrim, No. Ireland, 12,388.
A market town, about six miles from Belfast.

LISIEUX, Dept. of Calvados, France, 16,032.
Woolen manufactures are important.

LISMAN, Choctaw Co., Ala., 521.
On Ala., Tenn. & Nor. (R. R.).

LISMORE, New South Wales, Australia, 11,762.

LISTIE, Somerset Co., Pa., 650.
On Balt. & Ohio (R. R.).

LISTOWEL, Perth Co., North, Ontario, Canada, 2,676.
On Can. Pac.; Can. Nat. (R. Rs.).

LITCHFIELD, c. s., Litchfield Co., Conn., 1,075.
On N. York, N. Hav. & Hart. (R. R.).
–Montgomery Co., Ill., 6,612.
On Chi., Burl. & Quincy; Cle., Cin., Chi. & St. Lou.; Ill. Cen.; Wab.; Ill. Term. (El.) (R. Rs.).
–Hillsdale Co., Mich., 634.
On N. York Cen. (R. R.).
–c. s., Meeker Co., Minn., 2,880.
On Gt. Nor. (R. R.).
–Medina Co., Ohio, 838.
On Nor. Ohio (R. R.).

LITCHFIELD CORNERS, Kennebec Co., Maine, 773.

LITHERLAND, Lancashire, England, 15,967.

LITHGOW, New South Wales, Australia, 13,444.

WESTMINSTER ABBEY, WHERE ENGLAND'S KINGS AND QUEENS ARE CROWNED. BURIAL HERE IS THE GREATEST HONOR TO THE FAMOUS DEAD

THE PICTURESQUE DAILY CEREMONY OF THE MOUNTING OF THE GUARD AT HORSE GUARDS (BARRACKS), WHITEHALL, LONDON, ENGLAND

LITHONIA, De Kalb Co., Ga., 1,457.
  On Georgia (R. R.).
LITITZ, Lancaster Co., Pa., 4,368.
  On Reading Co. (R. R.).
LITOMERITZ, Bohemia, Germany, 18,509.
LITTLE CHUTE, Outagamie Co., Wis., 2,833.
  On Chi. & Nor. West. (R. R.).
LITTLE COMPTON, Newport Co., R. I., 1,589.
LITTLE FALLS, c. s., Morrison Co., Minn., 5,014.
  On Nor. Pac. (R. R.).
  —Passaic Co., N. J., 4,500.
  On Erie; Del., Lack. & West. (R. Rs.).
  —Herkimer Co., N. Y., 11,105.
  On N. York Cen. (R. R.).
  Manufactures knit goods, bicycles, paper, etc.
LITTLE FERRY, Bergen Co., N. J., 4,155.
  On West Shore; N. York, Susq. & West. (R.
  Rs.).
LITTLEFIELD, Lamb Co., Tex., 3,218.
  On Panh. & Santa Fe (R. R.).
LITTLE RIVER, Rice Co., Kansas, 626.
  On Atch., Top. & Santa Fe (R. R.).
LITTLE ROCK, c. s., Pulaski Co., Ark., State capi-
  tal, 81,679.
  On Arkansas River, and the Chicago, Rock
  Island & Pacific; the Missouri Pacific; and the
  St. Louis Southwestern Railroads.
  It is the largest city and the trade center of
  the State. Its manufactures include cotton-
  seed oil, cotton goods, furniture, stoves, cooper-
  age, brick, caskets, clothing, fertilizer, and
  cement. There are several foundries, machine
  shops, bauxite mines, and granite quarries.
  It is the seat of St. Johns Seminary and the
  Medical School of the University of Arkansas.
  —Lyon Co., Iowa, 585.
  On Chi., Rk. Isl. & Pac. (R. R.).
LITTLESTOWN, Adams Co., Pa., 2,001.
  On Penna. (R. R.).
LITTLETON, c. s., Arapahoe Co., Colo., 2,019.
  On Atch., Top. & Santa Fe; Den. & Rio Gde.
  West. (R. Rs.).
  —Aroostook Co., Maine, 1,035.
  On Bangor & Aroostook (R. R.).
  —Middlesex Co., Mass., 1,530.
  On Bost. & Me. (R. R.).
  —Grafton Co., N. H., 4,000.
  On Bost. & Me. (R. R.).
  A summer resort of the White Mountains.
  Has glove, whetstone and knitting plants.
  —Halifax and Warren Cos., N. C., 1,133.
  On Seab. Air Line (R. R.).
  —Wetzel Co., W. Va., 648.
  On Balt. & Ohio (R. R.).
LITTLETON COMMON, Middlesex Co., Mass., 1,000.
LITTLE VALLEY, c. s., Cattaraugus Co., N. Y.,
  1,196.
  On Erie (R. R.).
LITTORIA, Littoria, Italy, 19,339.
LIVE OAK, Sutter Co., Calif., 800.
  On Sacramento Nor. (El.); Sou. Pac. (R. Rs.).
  —c. s., Suwannee Co., Fla., 2,995.
  On Atl. Coast Line; Live Oak, Perry & Gulf;
  Seab. Air Line (R. Rs.).
LIVERMORE, Alameda Co., Cal., 3,119.
  On Sou. Pac.; West. Pac. (R. Rs.).
  —Humboldt Co., Iowa, 666.
  On Chi., Rk. Isl. & Pac.; Mpls. & St. Lou. (R.
  Rs.).
  —McLean Co., Ky., 1,573.
  On Lou. & Nash. (R. R.).

situated on the estuary of the Mersey. Noteworthy buildings are town hall, rebuilt in 1795,
exchange building, customhouse, post office,
dock office, St. George's Hall, Free Public
Library and Museum. The University of Liverpool and Liverpool College are the principal
educational institutions.
The leading industries are ship repairing,
sugar refining, corn mills, and iron and steel
working. The docks of Liverpool are among
the greatest of the world's engineering works.
A great landing stage for passengers, covering
four acres, extends along the river beyond the
docks. Liverpool has a large trade with North
and South America.
  —Onondaga Co., N. Y., 2,244.
  On N. York Cen. (R. R.).
  —Perry Co., Pa., 586.
  —c. s., of Queens Co., Nova Scotia, 2,669.
  On Can. Nat. (R. R.).
  Seventy-five miles southwest of Halifax.
LIVINGSTON, c. s., Sumter Co., Ala., 1,072.
  On Ala. Gt. Sou. (R. R.).
  —Merced Co., Calif., 803.
  On Sou. Pac. (R. R.).
  —Madison Co., Ill., 1,447.
  On Chi. & East Ill.; Cle., Cin., Ch. & St. Lou.
  (R. Rs.).
  —Rockcastle Co., Ky., 912.
  On Lou. & Nash. (R. R.).
  —c. s., Park Co., Mont., 6,391.
  On No. Pac. (R. R.).
  A tourist point for Yellowstone Park. In a
  developing mineral and farming section. The
  Nor. Pac. has offices, shops and yards here.
  —Essex Co., N. J., 1,000.
  —Overton Co., Tenn., 1,526.
  —c. s., Polk Co., Texas, 1,165.
  On Waco, Beau., Trin. & Sab.; Sou. Pac. (R.
  Rs.).
LIVINGSTONE, N. Rhodesia, 5,600.
LIVONIA, Livingston Co., N. Y., 774.
  On Erie; Leh. Val. (R. Rs.).
  —Pointe Coupee Par., La., 500.
  On Mo. Pac.; Tex. & Pac. (R. Rs.).
LIVORNO (Leghorn), Prov. of Livorno, Italy,
  123,618.
  A seaport and leading industrial town. Ships,
  castings, glass, and textiles.
LIZEMORES, Clay Co., W. Va., 521.
LJUBLJANA (Laibach), Yugoslavia, 59,768.
  An important road center and industrial town.
LLANELLY, Carmarthenshire, Wales, 38,393.
  A seaport and industrial town. Lead-smelting,
  shipbuilding and woolen factories.
LLANFAIR, Cambria Co., Pa., 500.
LLANO, c. s., Llano Co., Texas, 2,124.
  On Sou. Pac. (R. R.).
LLEWELLYN, Schuylkill Co., Pa., 526.
  On Reading (R. R.).
LLOYDELL, Cambria Co., Pa., 875.
  On Penna. (R. R.).
LOAY, Prov. of Bohol, Bohol, P. I., 10,519.
LOANDA, Angola. See SÃO PAULO DE LUANDA.
LOBOC, Prov. of Bohol, Bohol, P. I., 11,348.
LOCH GARMAN, Ireland (Eire). See WEXFORD.
LOCK No. 4, Washington Co., Pa., 618.
LOCKE, Cayuga Co., N. Y., 650.
  On Leh. Val. (R. R.).
LOCKEFORD, San Joaquin Co., Calif., 619.
  On Sou. Pac. (R. R.).
LOCKESBURG, c. s., Sevier Co., Ark., 747.

ST. PAUL'S CATHEDRAL, LONDON, ONE OF THE FINEST EXAMPLES OF RENAISSANCE
ARCHITECTURE IN ENGLAND

  On Sou. Pac.; Mo.-Kan.-Tex. of Tex. (R. Rs.).
LOCK HAVEN, c. s., Clinton Co., Pa., 9,668.
  On N. York Cen.; Penna. (R. Rs.).
  Has silk, paper, brick plants, etc.
LOCKLAND, Hamilton Co., Ohio, 5,703.
  On Balt. & Ohio; Erie; Cle., Cin., Chi. & St.
  Lou. (R. Rs.).
LOCKMOOR, Wayne Co., Mich., 961.
LOCKNEY, Floyd Co., Texas, 1,466.
  On Ft. Worth & Denver City; Panh. & Santa
  Fe (R. Rs.).
LOCKPORT, Will Co., Ill., 3,383.
  On Alton; Atch., Top. & Santa Fe (R. Rs.).
  —Lafourche Parish, La., 866.
  On Sou. Pac. (R. R.).
  —St. Joseph Co., Mich., 835.
  —c. s., Niagara Co., N. Y., 23,160.
  On Intern. (El.); Erie; N. York Cen. (R. Rs.).
  Also on State Barge Canal, which has five
  large locks here. Has many industries and is
  in a fruit and grain raising section.
LOCKWOOD, Dade Co., Mo., 823.
  On St. Lou.-San Fran. (R. R.).
LOCLE, LE, Canton of Neuchâtel, Switzerland,
  12,075.
  The town is important for its manufactures of
  clocks, watches, jewelry and lace.
LOCUST GROVE, Mayes Co., Okla., 510.
  On Kan., Okla. & Gulf (R. R.).
LOCUST VALLEY, Nassau Co., N. Y., 937.
  On Long Isl. (R. R.).
LODA, Iroquois Co., Ill., 499.
  On Ill. Cen. (R. R.).
LODI, San Joaquin Co., Cal., 6,788.
  On Sou. Pac.; Cen. Calif. Trac. (El.) (R. Rs.).
  —Bergen Co., N. J., 11,549.
  On N. York, Susq. & West. (R. R.).
  A manufacturing suburb of Hackensack.
  —Medina Co., Ohio, 1,273.
  On Balt. & Ohio; Wheel. & L. Erie (R. Rs.).
  —Columbia Co., Wis., 1,065.
  On Chi. & Nor. West. (R. R.).
  —Prov. of Milan, Italy, 21,661.
  At the bridge of Lodi, May 10, 1796, Napoleon
  gained a victory over the Austrians.
LODZ, Govt. of Lodz, Poland, 665,000.
  Noted for its large textile mills.
LOGAN (Hanaford), Franklin Co., Ill., 617.
  On Ill. Cen. (R. R.).
  —c. s., Harrison Co., Iowa, 1,654.
  On Ill. Cen.; Chi. & Nor. West. (R. Rs.).
  —Phillips Co., Kans., 726.

  On Mo. Pac. (R. R.).
  —c. s., Hocking Co., Ohio, 6,080.
  On Chesa. & Ohio (R. R.).
  —c. s., Cache Co., Utah, 9,979.
  On Un. Pac.; Utah-Ida. Cen. (El.) (R. Rs.).
  —c. s., Logan Co., W. Va., 4,396.
  On Chesa. & Ohio (R. R.).
  In center of coal fields.
LOGANSPORT, c. s., Cass Co., Ind., 18,508.
  On Penna.; Wab. (R. R.).
  An important shipping point for farm prod-
  ucts. Leading manufactures are fire fighting
  equipment, furniture, clothing, fishing tackle,
  brooms, silos, and electric refrigerators.
  —De Soto Parish, La., 1,040.
  On Sou. Pac. (R. R.).
LOGANVILLE, Walton Co., Ga., 631.
LOGTOWN, Hancock Co., Miss., 500.
LOHRVILLE, Calhoun Co., Iowa, 776.
  On Chi. Gt. West.; Chi., Mil., St. P. & Pac.;
  Chi. & Nor. West. (R. Rs.).
LOIZA, Mun. of Loiza, Puerto Rico, 1,892.
LOJA, Prov. of Loja, Ecuador, 17,000.
  —Prov. of Granada, Spain, 20,493.
  Woolens, silk, paper, and leather.
LOKEREN, East Flanders, Belgium, 24,267.
LOMAS DE ZAMORA, Argentina, 84,177.
LOMBARD, Du Page Co., Ill., 6,197.
  On Chi. Gt. West.; Chi. & Nor. West.; Chi.,
  Aur. & Elg. (R. Rs.).
LOME, capital of Togo, Africa, 10,400.
LOMETA, Lampasas Co., Texas, 865.
  On Gulf, Colo. & Santa Fe (R. R.).
LOMIRA, Dodge Co., Wis., 603.
  On Mpls., St. P. & S. Ste. M. (R. R.).
LOMITA, Los Angeles Co., Cal., 7,052.
LOMITA PARK, San Mateo Co., Calif., 800.
  On Sou. Pac. (R. R.).
LOMME, Nord, France, 21,583.
LOMPOC, Santa Barbara Co., Cal., 2,845.
  On Sou. Pac. (R. R.).
LOMZA, Prov. of Bialystok, Poland, 25,065.
LONACONING, Allegany Co., Md., 2,426.
  On Cumberl. & Penna.; West. Md. (R. Rs.).
LONDON, London Co., England, capital of the
  British Empire, and one of the most populous
  cities in the world; administrative county,
  4,230,200, "Greater London," 8,401,000.
  London, or "Greater London," on both sides
  of the Thames, in the counties of Surrey,
  Middlesex, Kent, and Essex, is composed of
  (a) Registration London, called the "Inner

THE HISTORIC TOWER OF LONDON AS SEEN FROM THE THAMES RIVER

  —Androscoggin Co., Maine, 1,113.
LIVERMORE FALLS, Androscoggin Co., Maine,
  3,148.
  On Me. Cen. (R. R.).
LIVERPOOL, Lancashire, England, 856,850.
  The second commercial port of Great Britain,

  On De Queen & East. (R. R.).
LOCKHART, Covington Co., Ala., 500.
  On Cen. of Ga.; Lou. & Nash. (R. Rs.).
  —Union Co., S. C., 1,858.
  On Southern (R. R.).
  —c. s., Caldwell Co., Texas, 4,367.

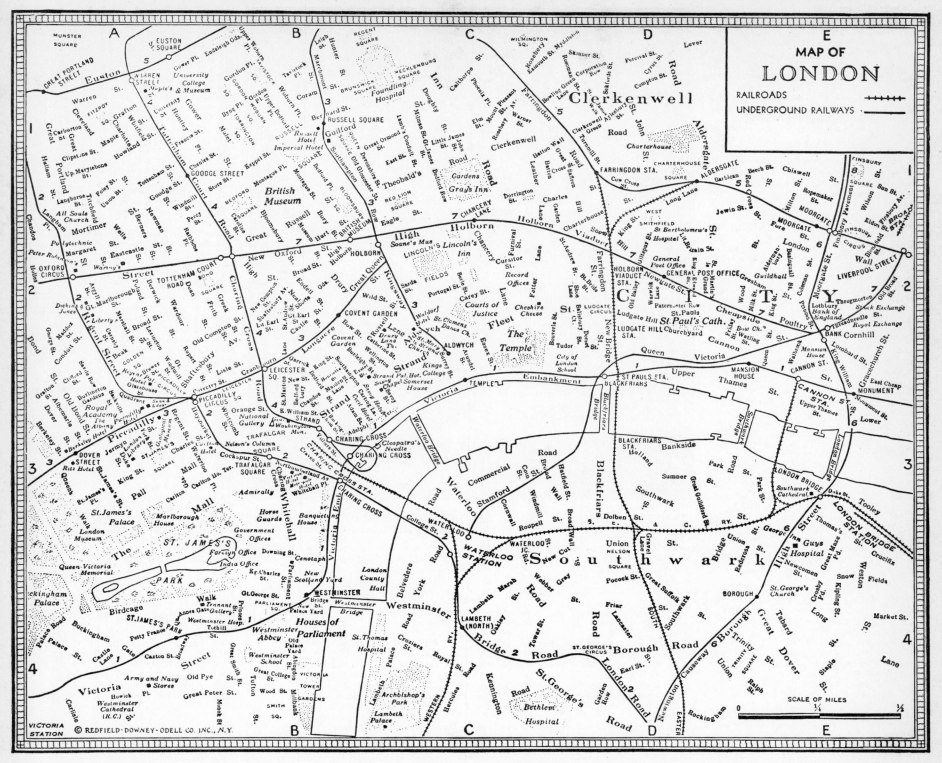

MAP OF CENTRAL LONDON, CAPITAL OF ENGLAND AND THE HEART OF THE BRITISH COMMONWEALTH OF NATIONS. "THE CITY," COVERING 675 ACRES, IS THE ECONOMIC CENTER OF LONDON. ITS STREETS, SUCH AS PICCADILLY, BOND, HOLBORN, THE STRAND AND OTHERS, AND SUCH BUILDINGS AS WESTMINSTER ABBEY, ST. PAUL'S, THE TOWER AND THE HOUSES OF PARLIAMENT, ARE FAMILIAR TO EVERY READER OF HISTORY AND LITERATURE

Ring," with a population of 4,298,000 and (b) the Suburban Districts, called the "Outer Ring," with a population of 3,904,218.

Registration London is composed of (1) the city of London, called "the City," strictly speaking, a city within the city, with a distinct administration under the Lord Mayor, who has no jurisdiction beyond its limits and (2) the Administrative County of London, under control of the London County Council, and divided into 28 municipal boroughs; viz.: Battersea, Bermondsey, Bethnal Green, Camberwell, Chelsea, Deptford, Finsbury, Fulham, Greenwich, Hackney, Hammersmith, Hampstead, Holborn, Islington, Kensington, Lambeth, Lewisham, Paddington, Poplar, St. Marylebone, St. Pancras, Shoreditch, Southwark, Stepney, Stoke-Newington, Wandsworth, Woolwich, and the city of Westminster.

The registration County of London coincides with the Administrative County of London and very nearly with the collective parliamentary boroughs of London.

The north and south portions of London are connected by bridges, and communication is also maintained subterraneously by the Thames Tunnel and subways. London is divided into several hundred parishes. The portion known as the city may be termed the financial center of the British Empire. What is legally termed the port of London extends about 7 miles below London Bridge beyond Blackwall; though the actual port, consisting of the upper, middle, and lower pools, does not reach

beyond Limehouse. Independent of the river accommodation thus afforded for shipping, a series of vast inland docks extends from the Tower to nearly opposite Greenwich. There is also here an export and import dock, with room for 500 large merchantmen. The London docks, about 1½ miles below London Bridge, cover a large area. The tobacco warehouses are also very extensive. The city was formerly walled, with large entrances or gates. It may be divided into the City, and the East End, or commercial part, lying east of the Temple, and the West End, containing the clubs, museums, and residences.

London has many parks and gardens and squares. The most noted among these are Trafalgar Square, St. James Park, adjoining the royal residences; Hyde Park, covering 390 acres, the fashionable recreation park; Kensington Gardens, covering 240 acres; Regents Park, 472 acres, and containing famous zoological gardens; Battersea Park, and Victoria Park. Among the principal streets are Pall Mall, Oxford Street, Piccadilly, Regent Street, containing the finest shops; the Strand, a business thoroughfare; Fleet Street, Whitechapel, Leicester Square, and Lombard Street.

London has more buildings of historical, literary, and scientific importance than any other city in the world. The most interesting of these are St. Paul's Cathedral (1675-1710), 500 feet in length and 364 feet in height; Westminster Abbey, dating from the thirteenth century and one of the most famous churches

in the world; the Houses of Parliament; the Mansion House; the Guildhall; the Royal Courts of Justice; Buckingham Palace; the British Museum, with a library of 3,500,000 volumes; the Natural History Museum; the South Kensington Museum; the National Gallery, one of the largest galleries of paintings in the world; Christ's Hospital, formerly a boys' school; Charterhouse Asylum; and the Tower, the most noted historic structure in England. London stands among the first in the number of its institutions of learning. First among these is the University of London, including University College and King's College; Imperial College of Science and Technology; Royal College of Music, the London School of Economics, and many other schools and learned societies.

The industrial interests of London are on a large scale, being the largest manufacturing city in Great Britain. Chief products are clothing and apparel, machinery, printing and publishing, food products, rubber goods, chemicals and drugs, brushes, leather goods and paper products. There are large manufactories in other lines.

Nothing is known of London previous to the invasion of the Romans; but we learn from Tacitus that so early as the reign of Nero it was an important emporium. Eventually it became the capital of England, and after the Norman conquest, received a charter. The history of London thenceforward is one of continual progression, though at different

periods severely visited by fires and pestilence. In 1381 Wat Tyler's rebellion was suppressed by the citizens.

In the fifteenth century London began to make marvelous strides, and in the sixteenth it vied with Venezia, Genova, and Amsterdam, both in extensive foreign commerce and in the opulence of its citizens. During the reign of Charles II., the city was partly desolated, first by the ravages of the Great Plague, and shortly after, in 1660, by what is known in history as the "Great Fire of London," which almost entirely destroyed the old city.

—c. s., Middlesex Co., Ontario, 71,148.
An important distributing center for a rich agricultural region. Manufactures petroleum products and farm machinery.
On Can. Pac.; Can. Nat.; London & Port Stan. (El.); Mich. Cen. (R. Rs.).
—c. s., Laurel Co., Ky., 1,950.
On Lou. & Nash. (R. R.).
—c. s., Madison Co., Ohio, 4,141.
On Cle., Cin., Chi. & St. Lou.; Penna. (R. Rs.).

LONDONDERRY, chief town of County Londonderry, Northern Ireland, 45,159.
Principal manufactures are linen, ships, liquors, and flour. Fisheries are also important.
—Rockingham Co., N. H., 750.
On Bost. & Me. (R. R.).

LONE OAK, Hunt Co., Texas, 720.
On Mo.-Kan.-Tex. of Tex. (R. R.).
LONE TREE, Johnson Co., Iowa, 627.
On Chi., Rk. Isl. & Pac. (R. R.).

LONE WOLF, Kiowa Co., Okla., 1,023.
On Atch., Top. & Santa Fe; Chi., Rk. Isl. & Pac. (R. Rs.).
LONGACRE, Fayette Co., W. Va., 500.
On N. York Cen. (R. R.).
LONG BEACH, Los Angeles Co., Cal., 142,032.
On Pac. Elec.; Sou. Pac.; Union Pac. (R. Rs.). Popular resort. Rich oil field. Truck garden products. Manufactures: machinery, automobiles, petroleum products.
—Harrison Co., Miss., 1,346.
On Lou. & Nash. (R. R.).
—Nassau Co., N. Y., 5,817.
On Long Isl. (R. R.).
On the South Shore of Long Island.
LONG BRANCH, Monmouth Co., N. J., 18,399.
Situated on the Atlantic Ocean and the Shrewsbury River, and on the Pennsylvania; New York & Long Branch; Central of New Jersey (R. Rs.).
Long Branch is a noted summer resort.
LONG LAKE, Hamilton Co., N. Y., 750.
LONGMEADOW, Hampden Co., Mass., 5,105.
On N. York, N. Hav. & Hart. (R. R.).
LONGMONT, Boulder Co., Colo., 6,029.
On Chi., Burl. & Quincy; Colo. & Sou.; Gt. West. (R. Rs.).
Industries, vegetable canning, sugar refining.
LONG PINE, Brown Co., Neb., 937.
On Chi. & Nor. West. (R. R.).
LONG PRAIRIE, c. s., Todd Co., Minn., 1,854.
On Gt. Nor. (R. R.).
LONG RIDGE, Fairfield Co., Conn., 679.
LONG RUN, Allegheny Co., Pa., 500.
On Leh. Val. (R. R.).
LONGTON, Elk Co., Kans., 700.
On Atch., Top. & Santa Fe (R. R.).
LONGUEIL, Chambly Co., Quebec, Canada, 5,407.
On Can. Nat. (R. R.).
LONG VALLEY, Morris Co., N. J., 500.
On Cen. of N. Jer. (R. R.).
LONGVIEW, Catawba Co., N. C., 1,262.
—c. s., Gregg Co., Texas, 5,036.
On Gulf, Colo. & Santa Fe; Mo. Pac.; Tex. & Pac. (R. Rs.).
—Cowlitz Co., Wash., 10,652.
On Chi., Mil., St. P. & Pac.; Gt. Nor.; Longv., Portl. & Nor.; Nor. Pac.; Un. Pac. (R. Rs.).
LONOKE, c. s., Lonoke Co., Ark., 1,674.
On Chi., Rk. Isl. & Pac. (R. R.).
A farm trade center.
LONSDALE, Rice Co., Minn., 508.
On Chi., Mil., St. P. & Pac. (R. R.).
LONS-LE-SAUNIER, capital of Dept. of Jura, France, 14,661.
Wines are famous. Salt mines near by.
LOOGOOTEE, Martin Co., Ind., 2,203.
On Balt. & Ohio (R. R.).
LOOKOUT, Fayette Co., W. Va., 500.
On Chesa. & Ohio (R. R.).
LOOKOUT MOUNTAIN, Hamilton Co., Tenn., 1,031.
LOOMIS, Placer Co., Calif., 500.
On Sou. Pac. (R. R.).
—Sullivan Co., N. Y., 500.
LOON, Bohol Prov., Bohol, P. I., 23,713.
Coconuts, cotton, tobacco, and corn.
LOPEZ, Sullivan Co., Pa., 800.
On Leh. Val. (R. R.).
LORAIN, Lorain Co., Ohio, 44,512.
On Balt. & Ohio; Lake Term.; Lorain & W. Va.; N. York Cen.; N. York, Chi. & St. Lou. (R. Rs.).
Shipping point for farm products, lumber, coal and iron ore.
—Cambria Co., Pa., 1,360.
LORAINE, Mitchell Co., Texas, 750.
On Tex. & Pac. (R. R.).
LORBERRY JUNCTION, Schuylkill Co., Pa., 550.
On Reading (R. R.).
LORCA, Prov. of Murcia, Spain, 75,021.
Trade center with manufactures of wool, leather, chemicals, and porcelain. Sulphur, silver, and lead mines in vicinity.
LORDSBURG, c. s., Hidalgo Co., N. M., 2,069.
On Sou. Pac. (R. R.).
LORE CITY, Guernsey Co., Ohio, 580.
On Balt. & Ohio (R. R.).
LORENZO, Alameda Co., Calif., 500.
On Sou. Pac.; West. Pac. (R. Rs.).
—Crosby Co., Texas, 739.
On Panh. & Santa Fe (R. R.).
LORETO, Prov. of Ancona, Italy, 2,897.
LORETTO, Dickinson Co., Mich., 500.
On Chi. & Nor. West. (R. R.).
—Lawrence Co., Tenn., 1,000.
On Lou. & Nash. (R. R.).
LORIENT, Dept. of Morbihan, France, 45,817.
A strongly fortified seaport with many manufactures.
L'ORIGINAL, Prescott Co., Ontario, Canada, 1,121.
On Can. Nat. (R. R.).
LORIMOR, Union Co., Iowa, 577.
On Chi. & Gt. West. (R. R.).
LORING, Worcester Co., Mass., 500.
LORIS, Horry Co., S. C., 900.
On Atl. Coast Line (R. R.).
LORRACH, Baden, Germany, 18,000.
Textile and allied manufactures.
LORRAINE, Harrison Co., Texas, 500.
On La.; Ark. & Tex.; Ill. Cen. (R. Rs.).

LOS ALAMITOS, Orange Co., Calif., 800.
On Sou. Pac. (R. R.).
LOS ANDES, Prov. of Aconcagua, Chile, 12,352.
LOS ANGELES, c. s., Los Angeles Co., Cal., 1,238,048.
On the Los Angeles River, 345 miles southeast from San Francisco, and on the Southern Pacific; the Atchison, Topeka & Santa Fe; Pacific Electric; Los Angeles Junction; and the Union Pacific System (R. Rs.) and steamship lines connecting with the ports of the world. The commercial metropolis and the most progressive city of southern California. Its seaborne trade is increasing rapidly. It is favorably situated for the great markets of the Orient, Australasia and Latin-America. Being near vast oil supplies, it ships great quantities of lubricants and by-products. Has large imports of lumber for transit. Industries: shipbuilding, meat packing, canning, rubber goods, furniture, machinery, food products, clothing, chemicals, tires, automobile accessories and assembling, and kindred lines. It has become especially prominent as a center of the motion picture industry. The municipal aqueduct, the longest one in the world, brings water a distance of 250 miles.
Seat of the University of Southern California, Loyola College, University of California at Los Angeles and Occidental College.
Among the chief buildings are the City Hall, Hall of Justice, California State Building, and Los Angeles Public Library.
—La Salle Co., Tex., 500.
On Mo. Pac. (R. R.).
LOS BANOS, Merced Co., Cal., 1,875.
On Sou. Pac. (R. R.).
LOS GATOS, Santa Clara Co., Cal., 3,168.
On Sou. Pac. (R. R.).
LOS LUNAS, c. s., Valencia Co., N. Mex., 513.
On Atch., Top. & Santa Fe (R. R.).
LOS NIETOS, Los Angeles Co., Calif., 1,000.
On Atch., Top. & Santa Fe; Pac. El.; Sou. Pac. (R. Rs.).
LOS SAENZ, Starr Co., Tex., 600.
LOST CREEK, Schuylkill Co., Pa., 550.
On Leh. Val.; Read. (R. Rs.).
LOST NATION, Clinton Co., Iowa, 493.
On Chi., Mil., St. P. & Pac. (R. R.).
LOTA, Chile, 31,707.
Coal mines, smelters, and brickyards.
LOTT, Falls Co., Texas, 921.
On Sou. Pac. (R. R.).
LOUANN, Ouachita Co., Ark., 910.
On Mo. Pac. (R. R.).
LOUDON, Merrimack Co., N. H., 675.
—c. s., Loudon Co., Tenn., 2,578.
On Southern (R. R.).

COURTESY AMERICAN AIRLINES, INC.

CHURCHILL DOWNS, LOUISVILLE, KENTUCKY, THE SCENE OF THE ANNUAL RUNNING OF THE AMERICAN TURF CLASSIC, THE KENTUCKY DERBY

Site of old Fort Loudon.
LOUDONVILLE, Albany Co., N. Y., 527.
—Ashland Co., Ohio, 2,068.
On Penna. (R. R.).
LOUGHBOROUGH, Leicestershire, England, 26,945.
Hosiery is the principal product. Others are bells, and dyes.
LOUGHMAN, Polk Co., Fla., 750.
On Atl. Coast Line (R. R.).
LOUIN, Jasper Co., Miss., 583.
On Gulf, Mob. & Nor. (R. R.).
LOUISA, c. s., Lawrence Co., Ky., 1,961.
On Chesa. & Ohio (R. R.).
LOUISBURG, Miami Co., Kans., 625.
On Mo.-Kan.-Tex. (R. R.).
—c. s., Franklin Co., N. C., 2,182.
On Seab. Air Line (R. R.).
LOUISE, Humphreys Co., Miss., 514.
On Ill. Cen. (R. R.).
LOUISEVILLE, Maskinonge Co., Quebec, Canada, 2,365.
On Can. Pac. (R. R.).
LOUISIANA, Pike Co., Mo., 3,549.
On Alton; Chi., Burl. & Quincy (R. Rs.).
LOUISVILLE, Barbour Co., Ala., 587.
On Cen. of Ga. (R. R.).
—Boulder Co., Colo., 1,681.
On Colo. & Sou. (R. R.).
—c. s., Jefferson Co., Ga., 1,650.
On Lou. & Wadley (R. R.).
—c. s., Clay Co., Ill., 803.
—c. s., Jefferson Co., Ky., 307,745.
Situated at the falls of the Ohio River, 400 miles from its mouth and 130 miles southwest of Cincinnati; on the Baltimore and Ohio; the Chesapeake and Ohio; the Chicago, Indianapolis and Louisville; the Cleveland, Cincinnati, Chicago and St. Louis; the Illinois Central; the Kentucky and Indiana Terminal; the Indiana Railroad System Electric; the Louisville and Nashville; the Pennsylvania; and the Southern Railroads. Has extensive water-front of 7 miles on Ohio River, and is connected by fine bridges with the cities of New Albany and Jeffersonville, on the right bank of the river.
The principal public buildings are the post office, custom-house, court-house, city hall, Columbia Building, Kentucky Home Life Building, Heyburn Building, Starks Building, Louisville Trust Company Building and the buildings of the University of Louisville. The Memorial Auditorium, costing $1,250,000, commemorates the Jefferson County soldiers and sailors who served in the World War. Louisville has numerous churches; the most prominent, as specimens of ecclesiastical architecture, are Warren Memorial, Calvary, St. Paul's, the cathedral, and Broadway Baptist.

There are many excellent schools, both public and private, and for higher education there are several medical colleges and theological seminaries, a law school, school of dentistry, schools of pharmacy; art school, in addition to the University of Louisville, the latter with a museum and library of about 100,000 volumes. The commerce of the city is important not only an account of its many railway connections, but also on account of its river traffic—the Ohio River being made navigable here around the rapids by a canal. Its manufactures include tobacco products, flour, packed meats, machinery, fittings, printing and publishing, lumber and veneer, auto parts, cooperage, brooms, medicines, chemicals, clothing, cars and leather. Louisville is the largest leaf tobacco market in the country. The city has extensive trade in corn, pork, and wheat. It is also noted for its horse racing.
Settled on April 17, 1779, by a party of forty-nine led by George Rogers Clark. Received a charter in 1828, to be superseded by charters of 1851, 1870, and 1892.
—c. s., Winston Co., Miss., 3,013.
On Gulf, Mob. & Nor. (R. R.).
—Cass Co., Neb., 969.
On Chi., Burl. & Quincy; Chi., Rk. Isl. & Pac.; Mo. Pac. (R. Rs.).
—Stark Co., Ohio, 3,130.
On Penna. (R. R.).
LOUNY (Laun), Czech., 11,884.
LOUP CITY, c. s., Sherman Co., Neb., 1,446.
On Chi., Burl. & Quincy; Un. Pac. (R. Rs.).
LOURDES, Hautes-Pyrénées, France, 11,529.
Site of a famous shrine.
LOURENCO MARQUES, capital of Mozambique, Portuguese East Africa, 47,390.
Seaport and coaling station.
LOUVAIN, Brabant, Belgium, 40,028.
Burnt by the Germans, August, 1914.
LOUVIERS, Dept. of Eure, France, 10,239.
LOVELADY, Houston Co., Texas, 502.
On Mo. Pac. (R. R.).
LOVELAND, Larimer Co., Colo., 5,506.
On Colo. & Sou.; Gt. West. (R. Rs.).
—Clermont, Hamilton and Warren Cos., Ohio, 1,954.
On Balt. & Ohio; Penna. (R. Rs.).
LOVELL, Big Horn Co., Wyo., 1,857.
On Chi., Burl. & Quincy (R. R.).
LOVELOCK, c. s., Pershing Co., Nev., 1,263.
On Sou. Pac. (R. R.).
LOVILIA, Monroe Co., Iowa, 727.
On Chi., Burl. & Quincy; Wab. (R. Rs.).
LOVING, Eddy Co., N. Mex., 600.
On Atch., Top. & Santa Fe (R. R.).
LOVINGTON, Moultrie Co., Ill., 1,121.
On Penna.; Wab. (R. Rs.).
—c. s., Lea Co., N. Mex., 961.
On Tex.-N. Mex. (R. R.).
LOW (Twila), Harlan Co., Ky., 516.
On Lou. & Nash. (R. R.).
LOWBER, Westmoreland Co., Pa., 718.
LOWDEN, Cedar Co., Iowa, 697.
On Chi. & Nor. West. (R. R.).
—Walla Walla Co., Wash., 503.
On Un. Pac. (R. R.).
LOWELL, Lake Co., Ind., 1,274.
On Chi., Ind. & Lou. (R. R.).
—c. s., Middlesex Co., Mass., 100,114.
Situated on the Merrimack River and the Boston and Maine, and the New York, New Haven and Hartford railroads.
The city derives immense water power from the falls of the river, and is a large producer of cotton, shoes and hosiery goods. It also makes paper products, artificial limbs, needles, thread, woolen goods, plush and bunting. Also has large patent medicine plants.
Lowell was incorporated as a town in 1826, and as a city in 1836. Seat of Lowell Textile Institute.
—Kent Co., Mich., 1,919.
On Gd. Tr.; Pere Marq. (R. Rs.).
—Gaston Co., N. C., 1,664.
On Piedmont & Nor. (El.); Sou. (R. Rs.).
—Washington Co., Ohio, 545.
On Balt. & Ohio (R. R.).
—Snohomish Co., Washington, 740.
On Chi., Mil., St. P. & Pac.; Nor. Pac.; Gt. Nor. (R. Rs.).
LOWELLVILLE, Mahoning Co., Ohio, 2,550.
On Balt. & Ohio; Penna.; Pitts. & L. Erie (R. Rs.).
LOWER LAKE, Lake Co., Calif., 870.
LOWRY CITY, St. Clair Co., Mo., 549.
On St. Lou.-San Fran. (R. R.).
LOWVILLE, c. s., Lewis Co., N. Y., 3,424.
On Lowv. & Beaver Riv.; N. York Cen. (R. Rs.).
LOYAL, Clark Co., Wis., 862.
On Mpls., St. P. & S. Ste. M. (R. R.).
—Harlan Co., Ky., 1,468.
On Lou. & Nash. (R. R.).
LOYALHANNA, Westmoreland Co., Pa., 800.
On Penna. (R. R.).
LOYALTON, Sierra Co., Calif., 837.
On West. Pac. (R. R.).
LOYSVILLE, Perry Co., Pa., 700.

MAP OF METROPOLITAN LOS ANGELES, CALIF., THE FIFTH LARGEST CITY OF THE UNITED STATES AND WITH THE LARGEST AREA OF ANY CITY IN THE WORLD.
LOS ANGELES LIES IN THE VALLEY OF THE LOS ANGELES RIVER WHICH BISECTS IT

Lubao, Pampanga Prov., Luzon, P. I., 21,614.
In a rice and sugar district.
Luanda, Angola. See São Paulo de Luanda.
Lubbock, c. s., Lubbock Co., Texas, 20,520.
On Ft. Worth & Denv. Cy.; Panh. & Santa Fe (R. Rs.).
A commercial center in a fine farming region.
Lubec, Washington Co., Maine, 1,500.
Lübeck, Germany, 137,700.
A seaport with Baltic and Scandinavian trade.
Lublin, Poland, 120,000.
A textile center. Also trade in grain and cattle.
Lucas, Lucas Co., Iowa, 514.
On Chi., Burl. & Quincy (R. R.).
–Russell Co., Kans., 634.
On Un. Pac. (R. R.).
Lucasville, Scioto Co., Ohio, 933.
On Norf. & West. (R. R.).
Lucban, Taybas Prov., Luzon, P. I., 12,868.
Lucca, capital of Prov. of Lucca, Italy, 54,500.
Jute and silk manufactures.
Lucedale, c. s., George Co., Miss., 834.
On Gulf, Mob. & Nor. (R. R.).
Lucerne, Switzerland. See Luzern.
Luck, Poland, 35,700.
A trading center.
–Polk Co., Wis., 560.
On Mpls., St. P. & S. Ste. M. (R. R.).
Luckenwalde, Prussia, Germany, 26,000.
Cloth and hat factories.
Luckey, Wood Co., Ohio, 720.
On N. York Cen. (R. R.).
Lucknow, United Provinces, India, 251,097.
A commercial and military center. Manufactures paper, printing, metal products, textiles, and gold and silver brocades.
–Bruce South, Ontario, Canada, 973.
On Can. Nat. (R. R.).
Lucy, St. John the Baptist Par., La., 500.
Ludington, c. s., Mason Co., Mich., 8,898.
On Lud. & Nor.; Pere Marq. (R. Rs.).
Ludlow, Kenton Co., Ky., 6,485.
On Cin., N. Orl. & Tex. Pac. (R. R.).
–Hampden Co., Mass., 8,569.
On Bost. & Alb. (R. R.).
–Windsor Co., Vt., 1,642.
On Rutland (R. R.).
Ludowici, c. s., Long Co., Ga., 615.
On Atl. Coast Line (R. R.).
Ludwigsburg, Württemberg, Germany, 32,000.
A suburb of Stuttgart.
Ludwigshaven-am-Rhein, Bavaria, Germany, 106,000.
An industrial suburb of Mannheim.
Lufkin, c. s., Angelina Co., Texas, 7,311.
On Angel. & Nech. Riv.; St. Lou. Southw.; Tex. Southe.; Sou. Pac. (R. Rs.).
Lugansk, Ukraine, Sov. Union, 119,400.
Refined ore, flour, saws, ball-bearings, and beer. Now Vorochilovgrad.
Lugerville, Price Co., Wis., 510.
Lugo, capital of Prov. of Lugo, Spain, 35,987.
The principal industries are tanning, and the weaving of linen and woolens.
Luimneach (Limerick), capital of Limerick Co., Ireland (Eire), 39,448.
A port and commercial center. Bacon, flour, beer, leather, and milk.
Luke, Alleghany Co., Md., 1,064.
On Balt. & Ohio; West. Md. (R. Rs.).
Luling, St. Charles Par., La., 950.
On Tex. & Pac. (R. R.).
–Caldwell Co., Texas, 5,970.
On Sou. Pac. (R. R.).
Lumber City, Telfair Co., Ga., 1,043.
On Southern (R. R.).
Lumberport, Harrison Co., W. Va., 1,289.
On Balt. & Ohio (R. R.).
Lumberton, Lamar Co., Miss., 2,374.
On New Orl. & Northe. (R. R.).
–Burlington Co., N. J., 700.
On Penna. (R. R.).
–c. s., Robeson Co., N. C., 4,140.
On Seab. Air Line; Virginia & Car. So. (R. Rs.).
Lumpkin, c. s., Stewart Co., Ga., 1,103.
On Seab. Air Line (R. R.).
Lund, Län of Malmohus, Sweden, 24,512.
Sugar, iron, furniture and gloves.
Lundale, Logan Co., W. Va., 525.
On Chesa. & Ohio (R. R.).
Lüneberg, Hanover, Germany, 31,000.
A trade center with manufactures of chemicals, ironware, carpets, and haircloth.
Lunenberg, c. s., Lunenberg Co., Nova Scotia, 2,727.
On Can. Nat. (R. R.).
–Worcester Co., Mass., 1,500.
–Essex Co., Vt., 1,400.
On Me. Cen. (R. R.).
Lunéville, Dept. of Meurthe-et-Moselle, France, 23,665.
Partly destroyed in the World War.
Lungchow, Dept. of Kwangsi, China, 20,000.
A river port and marketing town.
Lupton (Ft. Lupton P. O.), Weld Co., Colo., 1,578.
On Un. Pac. (R. R.).
Luque, Paraguay, 16,206.
Near Asuncion.
Luquillo, Mun. of Luquillo, Puerto Rico, 1,926.
Luray, c. s., Page Co., Va., 1,459.
On Norf. & West. (R. R.).
Nearby the famous Luray cavern.
Lurgan, County Armagh, Northern Ireland, 12,553.
Lushun. See Riojun.
Lusk, Westmoreland Co., Pa., 515.
–c. s., Niobrara Co., Wyo., 1,218.
On Chi. & Nor. West. (R. R.).
Lutcher, St. James Parish, La., 1,481.
On Ill. Cen.; Mo. Pac. (R. Rs.).
Lutesville, Bollinger Co., Mo., 582.
On Mo. Pac. (R. R.).
Lutgendortmund, Westphalia, Germany, 15,216.
Luther, Oklahoma Co., Okla., 613.
On Mo.-Kan.-Tex.; St. Lou.-San Fran. (R. Rs.).
Lutherville, Baltimore Co., Md., 500.
On Penna. (R. R.).
Lutie, Latimer Co., Okla., 519.
On Chi., Rk. Isl. & Pac. (R. R.).
Luton, Bedfordshire, England, 68,526.
Chief seat of straw-plaiting industry.
Lutsk. See Luck.
Luttringhausen, Prussia, Germany, 13,673.
Iron and textiles.
Lutz, Hillsborough Co., Fla., 600.
On Seab. Air Line (R. R.).
Lützen, Prussian Saxony, Germany, 4,469.
Luverne, c. s., Crenshaw Co., Ala., 1,874.
On Atl. Coast Line (R. R.).
–Humboldt and Kossuth Cos., Iowa, 570.
On Mpls. & St. Lou.; Chi. & Nor. West. (R. Rs.).
–c. s., Rock Co., Minn., 2,644.
On Chi., St. P., Minn. & Oma.; Chi., Rk. Isl. & Pac. (R. Rs.).
Luxemburg, capital of Luxemburg, 57,740.
Luxor, Westmoreland Co., Pa., 725.
Luxora, Mississippi Co., Ark., 1,074.
On St. Lou.-San Fran. (R. R.).
Luzern (Lucerne), capital of Canton of Luzern, Switzerland, 74,700.
A noted center for tourists and summer visitors in Switzerland.
Luzerne, Luzerne Co., Pa., 6,950.
On Del., Lack. & West.; Leh. Val. (R. Rs.).
Luzon, Sullivan Co., N. Y., 800.
On N. York, Ont. & West. (R. R.).
Lwów (Lemberg), East Galicia, Poland (1921), 316,177.
Lwow has numerous churches, monasteries, and noteworthy museums. In the seventeenth century and earlier was called the "town of the monks." Several of the churches are fine buildings, as the Greek cathedral, in the Italian style; the Gothic Roman Catholic cathedral (1350-1640); the Armenian cathedral, dating from the fourteenth century; also, the university, founded in 1784.
Founded in 1259, Lemberg was an important city of Poland from 1340. It fell to Austria at the first partition of Poland. In the World War (1914-18) it was the scene of heavy fighting between Russian and Austro-German forces. Captured by Russians, who later yielded it to Austro-German forces.
Lyck, East Prussia, Germany, 15,000.
Brick, leather, flour, and machinery.
Lyford, Willacy Co., Tex., 795.
On Un. Pac. (R. R.).
Lykens, Dauphin Co., Pa., 3,033.
On Penna.; Read. (R. Rs.).
Lyman, Scotts Bluff Co., Neb., 656.
On Un. Pac. (R. R.).
Lyme, New London Co., Conn. See Old Lyme.
Lynbrook, Nassau Co., N. Y., 11,993.
On Long Isl. (R. R.).
A residential suburb of New York.
Lynch, Boyd Co., Neb., 498.
On Chi. & Nor. West. (R. R.).
Lynchburg, Highland Co., Ohio, 792.
On Balt. & Ohio (R. R.).
–Lee Co., S. C., 512.
On Atl. Coast Line (R. R.).
–(Ind. City) Campbell Co., Va., 40,661.
On Chesa. & Ohio; Norf. & West.; Sou. (R. Rs.).
Important as a tobacco market, and shoe manufacturing center. Situated in a picturesque location in a mountain pass.
Lynden, Whatcom Co., Wash., 1,564.
On Chi., Mil., St. P. & Pac. (R. R.).
Lyndhurst, Cuyahoga Co., Ohio, 1,922.
Lyndon, c. s., Osage Co., Kans., 830.
On Mo. Pac. (R. R.).
Lyndonville, Orleans Co., N. Y., 708.
On N. York Cen. (R. R.).
–Caledonia Co., Vt., 1,559.
On Can. Pac. (R. R.).
Lyndora, Butler Co., Pa., 3,057.
On Balt. & Ohio (R. R.).
Lynn, Randolph Co., Ind., 936.
On Cle., Cin., Chi. & St. Lou.; Penna. (R. Rs.).
–Essex Co., Mass., 100,909.
Seaport on Massachusetts Bay 13 miles northeast of Boston, and on the Boston & Maine Railroad. Noted center of boot and shoe manufacture. Has also an immense plant for making electric apparatus.
"Lynn Woods," a natural pleasure ground, covers more than 2,000 acres.
Lynnfield Center, Essex Co., Mass., 1,896.
On Bost. & Me. (R. R.).
Lynn Haven, Bay Co., Fla., 1,340.
Lynnhurst, Essex Co., Mass., 500.
Lynwood, Los Angeles Co., Cal., 7,323.
On Pac. El.; Sou. Pac. (R. Rs.).
Lyon Station, Berks Co., Pa., 511.
Lyons, Boulder Co., Colo., 567.
On Chi., Burl. & Quincy (R. R.).
–c. s., Toombs Co., Ga., 1,445.
On Seab. Air Line (R. R.).
–Cook Co., Ill., 4,787.
–Greene Co., Ind., 806.
On Penna. (R. R.).
–c. s., Rice Co., Kans., 4,144.
On Atch., Top. & Santa Fe; Mo. Pac.; St. Lou.-San Fran. (R. Rs.).
–Ionia Co., Mich., 592.
On Pere Marq. (R. R.).
–Burt Co., Neb., 985.
On Chi., Burl. & Quincy; Chi., St. P., Mpls. & Oma. (R. Rs.).
–c. s., Wayne Co., N. Y., 3,956.
On N. York Cen.; West Shore (R. Rs.).
–Capital of Dept. of Rhone, France, 570,622.
Third city of the republic. Situated on a peninsula between the rivers Rhône and Saône, and on the Paris and Marseille and other railroads.
The cathedral and church of St. Nizier, the Hotel de Ville, the finest edifice of the kind in the country, the hospital, the public library, and the Palais des Arts are among the most notable institutions. The silk industry of Lyons is the most important in the world. It is the great trade entrepôt for the north and south of France. Lyons, the ancient Lugdunum, was founded about 42 B.C.
–Berks Co., Pa., 511.
On Reading (R. R.).
Lyons Falls, Lewis Co., N. Y., 882.
On N. York Cen. (R. R.).
Lyons View, Knox Co., Tenn., 500.

M

Maasin, Leyte, P. I., 22,314.
Native cloth and pottery.
Maastricht, capital of Limburg, Netherlands, 60,533.
A commercial and trade center.
Mabank, Kaufman Co., Tex., 963.
On Sou. Pac. (R. R.).
Mabel, Fillmore Co., Minn., 686.
On Chi., Mil., St. P. & Pac. (R. R.).
Maben, Oktibbeha & Webster Cos., Miss., 508.
On Col. & Greenv.; Gulf., Mob. & Nor. (R. Rs.).
Mabscott, Raleigh Co., W. Va., 1,260.
On Chesa. & Ohio; Virginian (R. Rs.).
Macabebe, Luzon, P. I., 16,082.
In a rice and sugar growing region.
Macahé, Rio de Janeiro, Brazil, 60,280.
A marketing and industrial town near Rio de Janeiro.
Macao, Prov. of Kwangtung, China, 74,000.
A Portuguese port and colony. Chief manufactures are cement, fire-crackers, preserves, and metal working. Noted as a fishing center. Has a large annual industrial fair.
Macclenny, Baker Co., Fla., 616.
On Seab. Air Line (R. R.).
Macclesfield, Cheshire, England, 34,902.
Has silk and cotton mills.
Macdonald, Fayette Co., W. Va., 1,175.
On Chesa. & Ohio; Kanaw., Glen Jean. & East. (R. Rs.).
Macedon, Wayne Co., N. Y., 566.
On West Shore (R. R.).
Macedonia, Summit Co., Ohio, 734.
On Penna. (R. R.).
Maceio, capital of Alagoas, Brazil, 129,105.
A port and trade center.
Macerata, Prov. of Macerata, Italy, 13,200.
Machias, c. s., Washington Co., Maine, 1,800.
On Me. Cen. (R. R.).
–Cattaraugus Co., N. Y., 585.
On Balt. & Ohio; Penna. (R. Rs.).
Mackay, Queensland, Australia, 10,665.
–Custer Co., Idaho, 777.
On Un. Pac. (R. R.).
Mackinac Island, Mackinac Co., Mich., 566.
Mackinaw, Tazewell Co., Ill., 760.
On Cle., Cin., Chi. & St. Lou.; Ill. Term. Sys. (El.); Penna. (R. Rs.).
Mackinaw City, Cheboygan and Emmet Cos., Mich., 875.
On Mich. Cen.; Penna. (R. Rs.).
Macksville, Stafford Co., Kans., 763.
On Atch., Top. & Santa Fe (R. R.).
Macleod, Macleod Co., Alberta, Canada, 1,447.
On Can. Pac. (R. R.).
Macomb, c. s., McDonough Co., Ill., 8,509.
On Chi., Burl. & Quincy (R. R.).
Mâcon, capital of Dept. of Saône-et-Loire, Burgundy, France, 19,324.
Varied manufactures and an important wine trade.
–c. s., Bibb Co., Ga., 53,829.
On Cen. of Ga.; Ga.; Ga. So. & Fla.; Macon, Dub. & Sav.; Sou. (R. Rs.).
Market and mill center of Georgia cotton belt. Has large cotton mills, also ceramics, clay and brick plants, packing houses, noted nurseries, wood work factories and railroad shops.
Site of Ocmulgee National Monument. Seat of Wesleyan College and Mercer University.
–Macon Co., Ill., 800.
On Ill. Cen. (R. R.).
–c. s., Noxubee Co., Miss., 2,198.
On Mob. & Ohio (R. R.).
–c. s., Macon Co., Mo., 3,851.
On Chi., Burl. & Quincy; Wab. (R. Rs.).
Macungie, Lehigh Co., Pa., 842.
On Reading (R. R.).
Madawaska, Aroostook Co., Maine, 3,300.
On Bangor & Aroostook (R. R.).
Maddock, Benson Co., N. Dak., 631.
On Nor. Pac. (R. R.).
Madeira, Hamilton Co., Ohio, 1,162.
On Balt. & Ohio (R. R.).
Madelia, Watonwan Co., Minn., 1,397.
On Chi., St. P., Mpls. & Oma. (R. R.).
Madera, c. s., Madera Co., Cal., 4,665.
On Atch., Top. & Santa Fe; Sou. Pac. (R. Rs.).
Fruit, grain, cotton, livestock. Chief manufactures, lumber products.
Madill, c. s., Marshall Co., Okla., 2,203.
On St. Lou.-San Fran. (R. R.).
Madison, St. Francis Co., Ark., 634.
On Chi., Rk. Isl. & Pac. (R. R.).
–New Haven Co., Conn., 1,155.
On N. York, N. Hav. & Hart. (R. R.).
–c. s., Madison Co., Fla., 2,515.
On Ga. & Fla.; Seab. Air Line (R. Rs.).
–c. s., Morgan Co., Ga., 1,966.
On Cen. of Ga.; Ga. (R. Rs.).
–Madison Co., Ill., 7,661.
On Alton; Alton & Sou.; Balt. & Ohio; Chi. & East. Ill.; Chi., Burl. & Quincy; Cle., Cin., Chi. & St. Lou.; Ill. Cen.; Ill. Term. (El.); Litchf. & Mad.; Lou. & Nash.; N. York, Chi. & St. Lou.; Penna.; Term. R. R. Assn.; Wab. (R. Rs.).
–c. s., Jefferson Co., Ind., 6,530.
On Penna. (R. R.).
–Greenwood Co., Kans., 1,316.
On Atch., Top. & Santa Fe; Mo. Pac. (R. Rs.).
–Somerset Co., Maine, 3,036.
On Me. Cen. (R. R.).
–c. s., Lac qui Parle Co., Minn., 1,916.
On Minn. & St. Lou. (R. R.).
–Monroe Co., Mo., 664.
On Wabash (R. R.).
–c. s., Madison Co., Neb., 1,842.
On Un. Pac. (R. R.).
–Morris Co., N. J., 7,481.
On Del., Lack. & West. (R. R.).
–Rockingham Co., N. C., 1,497.
On Atl. & Yadk.; Norf. & West. (R. Rs.).
–Lake Co., Ohio, 927.
On N. York Cen.; N. York, Chi. & St. Lou. (R. Rs.).
–(Kenilworth), Chester Co., Pa., 500.
–c. s., Lake Co., S. Dak., 5,024.
On Chi., Mil., St. P. & Pac. (R. R.).
–Davidson Co., Tenn., 850.
On Lou. & Nash. (R. R.).
–c. s., Boone Co., W. Va., 1,156.
On Chesa. & Ohio (R. R.).
–c. s., Dane Co., Wis., State capital, 57,899.
Situated on a strip of land between Lakes Mendota and Monona. It is on the Chicago, Milwaukee, St. Paul and Pacific; the Chicago and North Western; and the Illinois Central railroads; 82 miles west of Milwaukee.
It contains the Capitol, University of Wisconsin, United States Government building, and U. S. Forest Products Laboratory. The city is a well-known summer resort. It has a large trade in agricultural products, farming implements, wagons, etc.
Madisonville, c. s., Hopkins Co., Ky., 6,908.
On Ill. Cen.; Lou. & Nash. (R. Rs.).
–St. Tammany Parish, La., 837.
–Hamilton Co., Ohio (Sta. Cincinnati P. O.).
On Balt. & Ohio; Penna. (R. Rs.).
–c. s., Monroe Co., Tenn., 926.
On Lou. & Nash. (R. R.).
–c. s., Madison Co., Texas, 1,294.
On Mo. Pac. (R. R.).
Madoc, Hastings Co., Ontario, Canada, 1,059.
On Can. Nat. (R. R.).
Madras, capital of Madras Presidency, British India, 647,230.
Situated on the Bay of Bengal. A number of noteworthy buildings, among them Fort St. George (1639); Government House; St. Thomé Cathedral; Chepauk Palace; Engineering College; and Luz Church. The city possesses an important maritime trade, and exports chrome and magnesite, cotton, and hides. "Madras"

cotton is produced here. The site of Madras was acquired by the English in 1640.

MADRID, Prov. of Madrid, capital of Spain, 1,048,-072.

Situated near the heart of the country, on the left bank of the Manzanares, and on a hilly, sandy, treeless plateau. One of the handsomest of European cities, it has a very modern aspect, but is partly surrounded by a brick wall 20 feet high. On the east side is the famous Prado. Madrid has numerous public squares, of which the chief are the Puerta del Sol, the center of pleasure and business; the Plaza Mayor, the scene of the autos-da-fé; the Plaza del Oriente, in front of the royal palace, and the Plaza de las Cortes. The largest building in Madrid is the Palacio Real, built of white marble, and occupying an area of 220,-000 square feet. Madrid has also many churches, several decorated by old masters; many monasteries, used since 1836 for secular purposes, and nunneries. The educational institutions comprise the University of Madrid, Schools of architecture, agriculture, the fine arts and music, several museums, a botanical

COURTESY OF THE SPANISH TOURIST INFORMATION OFFICE

THE PALACIO REAL IN MADRID, SPAIN, LATER THE HOME OF THE PRESIDENT

garden, an observatory, and the National Library. The royal museum in the Prado contains one of the richest collections of paintings in the world. The city has manufactures of jewelry, leather, chemicals, pottery, fans, perfumes, dried fruits, clothing, hats, printing and publishing, distilled liquors, and food products. There is an active commerce.

Madrid, or Majerit, is first mentioned in history in the year 932, when it was taken by Romiro II. of Leon. A strong outpost of the Arabs, it was captured by Alfonso VI. of Castile in 1083. Philip II. made it his capital in 1560. From this time it grew rapidly until it became the chief city of Spain.

—Boone Co., Iowa, 2,061.
On Chi., Mil., St. P. & Pac. (R. R.).

MADURA, Madras Presidency, British India, 182,-018.
Famous for its wonderful temples.

MAEBASHI, Japan, 84,925.
An important center of the silk trade.

MAESTEG, Glamorganshire, South Wales, 25,552.
Coal mining center.

MAGALAN, Luzon, P. I., 9,777.

MAGALLANES, Magallanes, Chile, 31,254.

MAGARAO, Ambos-Camarines, Luzon, P. I., 5,746.

MAGAZINE, Logan Co., Ark., 560.
On Chi., Rk. Isl. & Pac. (R. R.).

MAGDA, Rapides Par., La., 570.
On La. & Ark. (R. R.).

MAGDALENA, Socorro Co., N. Mex., 1,371.
On Atch., Top. & Santa Fe (R. R.).
—Argentina, 25,507.
An agricultural trade center.

MAGDEBURG, capital of Prussian Saxony, Germany, 306,894.
Important manufacturing city; distinguished champion of the Reformation; the scene of massacre by Tilly in 1631. Center of the beet sugar industry. Manufactures machinery, refined sugar, chemicals, cigars, and pottery.

MAGEE, Simpson Co., Miss., 964.
On Gulf & Ship Isl. (R. R.).

MAGNITOGORSK, Ural Area, Soviet Union, 155,000.
A manufacturing center, established within recent years.

MAGNOLIA, c. s., Columbia Co., Ark., 3,008.
On La. & Nor. West. (R. R.).
—c. s., Pike Co., Miss., 1,660.
On Ill. Cen. (R. R.).
—Camden Co., N. J., 1,522.
On Penna.-Read. Seashore (R. R.).
—Duplin Co., N. C., 802.

On Atl. Coast Line (R. R.).
—Carroll and Stark Cos., Ohio, 685.
On Penna. (R. R.).

MAGNOLIA SPRINGS, Jasper Co., Tex., 500.

MAGOG, Stanstead Co., Quebec, Canada, 6,302.
On Can. Pac. (R. R.).

MAHAFFEY, Clearfield Co., Pa., 667.
On N. York Cen.; Penna. (R. Rs.).

MAHANOY CITY, Schuylkill Co., Pa., 14,784.
On Leh. Val.; Read. (R. Rs.).
Anthracite mines, iron works, and shirt factories.

MAHÉ, French possession on west coast of India, 11,000.

MAHNOMEN, c. s., Mahnomen Co., Minn., 989.
On Mpls., St. P. & S. Ste. M. (R. R.).

MAHOMET, Champaign Co., Ill., 729.
On Cle., Cin., Chi. & St. Lou. (R. R.).

MAHOPAC FALLS, Putnam Co., N. Y., 800.

MAHRISCH OSTRAU, Czechoslovakia. See MORAVSKA OSTRAVA.

MAHRISCH SCHONBERG, Czechoslovakia. See SUMPERK.

MAHWAH, Bergen Co., N. J., 874.
On Erie (R. R.).

MAIDEN, Catawba Co., N. C., 1,628.
On Car. & Nor. West. (R. R.).

MAIDENHEAD, Berkshire, England, 17,520.
A residential town and boating center.

MAIDSTONE, Kent, England, 42,259.
The principal buildings are the medieval Church of All Saints, St. Peter's Church, and School of Science and Art. Cement and limeworks, and paper mills.

MAIKOP, North Caucasian Area, Soviet Union, 54,400.

MAIMANA, Afghanistan, 25,000.

MAINZ, Hesse, Germany, 142,627.
Situated on the left bank of the Rhine, opposite the mouth of the Main, and is one of the principal fortresses of Germany. Among the more interesting buildings are St. Martin's cathedral, the old electoral palace, now containing the City Library, picture gallery, museum, and the Church of St. Stephen, a fine specimen of Gothic architecture. The city is noted for the excellence of its leather goods. Furniture, chemicals, and musical instruments are also made here.
Mainz was for long the first ecclesiastical city of Germany.
Its history during the sixteenth century is of interest in connection with the Reformation. It was occupied by French Troops in 1918, after the Armistice ending the World War.

MAIQUETIA, Venezuela, 11,854.
On the N. E. coast, just west of La Guaira.

MAISONS-ALFORT, Seine, France, 34,384.

MAITLAND, New South Wales, Australia, 12,960.
Center of a very rich farming area. Coal mines in the vicinity.
—Orange Co., Fla., 552.
—Holt Co., Mo., 576.
On Chi., Burl. & Quincy (R. R.).
—McDowell Co., W. Va., 500.
On Norf. & West. (R. R.).

MAJUNGA, Madagascar, 22,444.
Has a good harbor and exports principally livestock products.

MAKASSER, Celebes, Netherland India, 86,662.
Leading seaport and distributing point for native products and raw materials.

MAKO, capital of Csanad Co., Hungary, 35,814.
Located in a vegetable raising district.

MALABUYOC, Cebu, P. I., 15,224.

MALACCA, Malay States, 45,000.
An agricultural settlement. Rubber plantation near by.

MALAD (Malad City P. O.), c. s., Oneida Co., Idaho, 2,535.
On Un. Pac. (R. R.).

MALAGA, capital of Prov. of Malaga, Spain, 203,-844.
Seaport town on the Mediterranean Sea, 68 miles northeast of Gibraltar. An important manufacturing city.
—Eddy Co., N. Mex., 701.
On Atch., Top. & Santa Fe (R. R.).

MALAKOFF, Seine, France, 28,439.

MALASIQUI, Luzon, P. I., 25,721.
A marketing town in a farming district.

MALATIA (Malatya), Turkey, 27,233.
The center of a district noted for its luscious fruits.

MALDEN, Middlesex Co., Mass., 57,277.
On Bost. & Me. (R. R.).
A residential and industrial suburb of Boston.
—Dunklin Co., Mo., 2,025.
On St. Lou.-San Fran.; St. Lou. Southw. (R. Rs.).

MALILOPOT, Prov. of Albay, Luzon, P. I., 7,533.

MALINAO, Prov. of Albay, Luzon, P. I., 13,631.

MALINES (Mechelen), Prov. of Anvers, Belgium, 60,438.
Has a large trade in linen, needles, furniture, and oil.

MALITBOG, Province of Leyte, Leyte, P. I., 15,723.

MALLAWI, Prov. of Asyut, Egypt, 19,842.

MALMESBURY, Cape of Good Hope, Un. of South Africa, 4,085.

MALMÖ, Län of Malmöhus, Sweden, 144,482.
An important seaport, industrial town, and fishing center. Has a large export trade in textiles, pulp, machinery, rubber goods, sugar, and tobacco products.

MALOLOS, Bulacan Prov., Luzon, P. I., 26,444.
The trade center of a rice growing region.

MALONE, c. s., Franklin Co., N. Y., 8,657.
On N. York Cen.; Rut. (R. Rs.).
A manufacturing town in a scenic region.

MALTA, c. s., Phillips Co., Mont., 1,342.
On Gt. Nor. (R. R.).
—Morgan Co., Ohio, 932.
On Balt. & Ohio (R. R.).

MALVERN, c. s., Hot Spring Co., Ark., 5,115.
On Chi., Rk. Isl. & Pac.; Mo. Pac. (R. Rs.).
—Mills Co., Iowa, 1,320.
On Chi., Burl. & Quincy; Wab. (R. Rs.).
—Carroll Co., Ohio, 1,100.
On Penna. (R. R.).
—Chester Co., Pa., 1,551.
On Penna. (R. R.).
—Worcestershire, England, 15,632.
An inland watering place.

MALVERNE, Nassau Co., N. Y., 2,256.
On Long Isl. (R. R.).

MAMARONECK, Westchester Co., N. Y., 11,766.
On N. York, N. Hav. & Hart. (R. R.).
Some manufacturing but largely suburban in attractive and historical location on Long Island Sound.

MAMBAJAO, Misamis Prov., Mindanao, P. I., 21,382.

MAMIE, Currituck Co., N. C., 518.

MAMMOTH, Westmoreland Co., Pa., 550.
On Penna. (R. R.).
—Juab Co., Utah, 650.
On Den. & Rio Gde. West.; Un. Pac. (R. Rs.).

MAMMOTH SPRINGS, Fulton Co., Ark., 600.
On St. Lou.-San Fran. (R. R.).

MAMOU, Evangeline Parish, La., 800.
On Chi., Rk. Isl. & Pac. (R. R.).

MAN, Logan Co., W. Va., 835.
On Chesa. & Ohio (R. R.).

MANAGUA, State of Managua and capital of Nicaragua, 61,679.
The political and commercial center of the republic.

MANAHAWKEN, Ocean Co., N. J., 825.
On Sou. N. Jer. (R. R.).

MANAMEH, capital of Bahrein Islands, Persian Gulf (British), about 25,000.
The commercial center of the islands.

MANANJARY, Madagascar, 17,284.

MANAOAG, Pangasinan, Luzon, P. I., 22,279.
The marketing center for a farming region.

MANAPLA, Prov. of Negros Occidental, Negros, P. I., 10,041.

MANASQUAN, Monmouth Co., N. J., 2,320.
On Cen. of New Jer.; N. York & Long Br.; Penna. (R. Rs.).

MANASSA, Conejos Co., Colo., 953.

MANASSAS, c. s., Prince William Co., Va., 1,215.
On Chesa. & Ohio; Sou. (R. Rs.).

MANATEE, Manatee Co., Fla., 3,278.
On Atl. Coast Line; Seab. Air Line (R. Rs.).

MANATI, Manati, Puerto Rico, 7,447.

MANAÚS (Manaos), capital of State of Amazonas, Brazil, 86,500.
A busy inland port on the Amazon River. The principal exports are rubber, nuts, cocoa, dried fish, hides, and piassava fiber.

MANAWA, Waupaca Co., Wis., 711.
On Gr. Bay & West (R. R.).

MANCELONA, Antrim Co., Mich., 1,143.
On Penna. (R. R.).

MANCHESTER, Lancashire, England, 758,140.
The greatest industrial town of the kingdom, situated on the Irwell, Irk and Medlock Rivers. The principal among its public buildings are the Exchange, built in the Doric style; the town hall, an elegant building of Ionic architecture, and the Royal Hospital. It has also several educational institutions, among them Victoria University. It is as a manufacturing city that Manchester derives its importance, being the center of the cotton manufacture of England. The spinning trade is extensive and considerable quantities of yarn are annually exported. Other leading industries include dyeing, bleaching, machine manufacturing and engineering. Derives considerable advantages from the coal-fields in its neighborhood, and from the canals and railways which connect it with different parts of the country.
—Walker Co., Ala., 518.
On Ala. Cen. (R. R.).
—Hartford Co., Conn., 23,000.
On N. York, N. Hav. & Hart. (R. R.).
A silk manufacturing center.
—Meriwether and Talbot Cos., Ga., 3,745.
On Atla., Birm. & Coast (R. R.).
—c. s., Delaware Co., Iowa, 3,413.
On Ill. Cen.; Manch. & Oneida (R. Rs.).
—c. s., Clay Co., Ky., 900.
On Lou. & Nash. (R. R.).
—Carroll Co., Md., 643.
—Essex Co., Mass., 2,509.

COURTESY OF THE INDIA STATE RAILWAYS

THE GATEWAYS TO THE TEMPLE OF MENAKSHA AT MADURA, ONE OF THE CHIEF HINDU CITIES OF SOUTHERN INDIA

On Bost. & Me. (R. R.).
–Washtenaw Co., Mich., 1,037.
On N. York Cen. (R. R.).
–St. Louis Co., Mo., 600.
–c. s., Hillsborough Co., N. H., 76,834.
Situated on the Merrimac River, and on Boston and Maine Railroad. The chief industrial plants are those of cotton, woolen goods, cigars, and shoes.
–Ontario Co., N. Y., 1,429.
On Leh. Val. (R. R.).
–Adams Co., Ohio, 2,009.
R. R. Sta. via Ferry, at Trinity, Ky.; Chesa. & Ohio (R. R.).
–York Co., Pa., 940.
–c. s., Coffee Co., Tenn., 1,227.
On Nash., Chatt. & St. Lou. (R. R.).
–Red River Co., Tex., 500.
Manchester Centre, Bennington Co., Vt., 765.
Mancos, Montezuma Co., Colo., 646.
On Rio Gde. Sou. (R. R.).
Mandalay, capital of British Upper Burma, 134,950.
Mandan, c. s., Morton Co., N. Dak., 5,037.
On Nor. Pac. (R. R.).
Mandaue, Cebu, P. I., 21,464.
Manufacturers of corn products, sugar, and salt.
Mandeville, St. Tammany Parish, La., 1,069.
On Gulf, Mob. & Nor. (R. R.).
Mangalore, Madras Presidency, British India, 66,756.
A seaport. Exports coffee, lumber and pepper.
Mangatarem, Pangasinan Prov., Luzon, P. I., 16,582.
Mangham, Richland Par., La., 714.
On Mo. Pac. (R. R.).
Mangum, c. s., Greer Co., Okla., 4,806.
On Chi., Rk. Isl. & Pac.; Mo.-Kan.-Tex. (R. Rs.).
Manhattan, Will Co., Ill., 628.
On Chi., Mil., St. P. & Pac.; Wab. (R. Rs.).
–c. s., Riley Co., Kans., 10,738.
On Chi., Rk. Isl. & Pac.; Un. Pac. (R. Rs.).
Home of Kansas State Agricultural College.
–Gallatin Co., Montana, 501.
On Chi., Mil., St. P. & Pac.; Nor. Pac. (R. Rs.).
Manhattan Beach, Los Angeles Co., Cal., 1,891.
On Atch., Top. & Santa Fe; Pac. El. (R. Rs.).
Manheim, Lancaster Co., Pa.
On Reading Co. (R. R.).
Manila, Mississippi Co., Ark., 1,226.
On St. Lou.-San Fran. (R. R.).
–capital of Philippine Islands, 488,000.
Situated on the Pasig River, on east shore of Manila Bay and 32 miles from its entrance. There are fine plazas, public squares, gardens, and promenades. The University of the Philippines and the University of Santo Tomas are located here. The population of Manila is made up of Filipinos, Japanese, Chinese and Spaniards.
The River Pasig divides Manila in two parts, that on the south being occupied by the military defenses and foreign residential district, and on the north by the commercial, mercantile, manufacturing, and residential quarters and suburbs. Two parallel dikes for breakwaters define the entrance of the Pasig River from Manila Bay. The city's manufactures include tobacco articles, cotton goods, clothing, rope, lumber, rubber, and furniture. Besides hemp, the exports include sugar, tobacco, coffee, and dyewoods.
Manila was founded by Legaspi in 1571. In 1762 it was taken and held for some months by a British fleet. The Bay was the scene of the first naval battle of the Spanish-American war, and the city surrendered to the United States, August 13, 1898.
Manilla, Crawford Co., Iowa, 1,032.
On Chi., Mil., St. P. & Pac. (R. R.).
Manipur, India. See Emphal.
Manisa, Turkey, 30,746.
Manistee, c. s., Manistee Co., Mich., 8,078.
On Man. & Northe.; Pere Marq. (R. Rs.).
Machine and boiler works.
Manistique, c. s., Schoolcraft Co., Mich., 5,198.
On Mpls., St. P. & S. Ste. M.; Manis. & L. Sup. (R. Rs.).
Manito, Prov. of Albany, Luzon, P. I., 4,876.
–Mason Co., Ill., 711.
On Chi. & Ill. Midl. (R. R.).
Manitou, c. s., El Paso Co., Colo., 1,205.
A tourist and health resort, situated at the base of Pike's Peak, 80 miles south of Denver, on the Manitou and Pike's Peak; Midland Terminal; the Denver and Rio Grande West. railroads. Elevation 6,300 feet above the level of the sea. Manitou is surrounded by magnificent mountain scenery and is noted for its iron and soda springs, which have various medicinal qualities. Manitou has been called "The Saratoga of the West."
A mountain (cog) railway runs from Manitou Iron Springs to the summit of Pike's Peak. In the vicinity are Monument Park and the Garden of the Gods.
Manitowoc, c. s., Manitowoc Co., Wis., 22,963.
On Mpls., St. P. & S. Ste. M.; Chi. & Nor. West.; Pere Marq.; Ann Arbor (R. Rs.).
A lake harbor and industrial town. Shipbuilding and aluminum working are important.
Manizales, Caldes, Colombia, 85,146.
Mankato, c. s., Jewell Co., Kans., 1,417.
On Chi., Rk. Isl. & Pac.; Mo. Pac. (R. Rs.).
–c. s., Blue Earth Co., Minn., 14,038.
On Chi. Gt. West.; Chi., Mil., St. P. & Pac.; Chi., St. P., Mpls. & Omaha; Chi. & Nor. West. (R. Rs.).
Notable for its stone, lime and cement products and other building materials; tools, machinery, and flour.
Manlius, Onondaga Co., N. Y., 1,538.
On West Shore (R. R.).
Manly, Worth Co., Ia., 1,447.
On Mpls. & St. Lou.; Chi., Rk. Isl. & Pac.; Chi. Gt. West. (R. Rs.).
Mannheim, Province of Baden, Germany, 275,132.
Situated at the confluence of the Neckar and the Rhine. The principal buildings are the palace, containing museums of antiquities, natural history, etc., and the Jesuit Church. Chief commercial center of Baden, to which it was annexed in 1802.
Manning, Carroll Co., Iowa, 1,817.
On Chi. & Nor. West.; Chi. Gt. West.; Chi., Mil., St. P. & Pac. (R. Rs.).
–c. s., Clarendon Co., S. C., 1,884.
On Atl. Coast Line (R. R.).
–Angelina Co., Tex., 715.
Mannington, Marion Co., W. Va., 3,261.
On Balt. & Ohio (R. R.).
Manor, Westmoreland Co., Pa., 1,305.
On Penna. (R. R.).
–Travis Co., Texas, 654.
On Sou. Pac. (R. R.).
Manorville, Suffolk Co., N. Y., 500.
On Long Isl. (R. R.).
–Armstrong Co., Pa., 608.
On Penna. (R. R.).
Manresa, Prov. of Barcelona, Spain, 27,305.
Casting, textiles, paper, chemicals, and soap.
Mansfield, Scott & Sebastian Cos., Ark., 919.
On Chi., Rk. Isl. & Pac.; St. Lou-San Fran. (R. Rs.).
–Nottinghamshire, England, 46,075.
Mining and manufacturing.
–Piatt Co., Ill., 681.
On Cle., Cin., Chi. & St. Lou.; Wab. (R. Rs.).
–c. s., De Soto Parish, La., 3,837.
On Kan. Cy. So.; Mansf. Ry. & Transp.; Tex. & Pac. (R. Rs.).
–Bristol Co., Mass., 6,543.
On N. York, N. Hav. & Hart. (R. R.).
–Wright Co., Mo., 861.
On St. Lou.-San Fran. (R. R.).
–c. s., Richland Co., Ohio, 33,525.
On Balt. & Ohio; Erie; Penna. (R. Rs.).
Mansfield is in the heart of a fertile agricultural district. It possesses many fine residences as well as imposing public buildings. It has manufactures of rolled steel sheets, farm implements, electrical devices, stoves and candles. Seat of Ohio State Reformatory.
–Tioga Co., Pa., 1,755.
On Erie (R. R.).
–Tarrant Co., Texas, 635.
On Sou. Pac. (R. R.).
Manson, Calhoun Co., Iowa, 1,382.
On Chi., Rk. Isl. & Pac.; Ill. Cen. (R. Rs.).
Mansura, Avoyelles Parish, La., 1,067.
On La. & Ark.; Tex. & Pac. (R. Rs.).
Mansura, El, capital of Prov. of Dakalieh, Egypt, 72,200.
Cotton, textile mills are leading industry.
Manteca, San Joaquin Co., Cal., 1,614.
On Sou. Pac.; Tidew. Sou. (R. Rs.).
Manteno, Kankakee Co., Ill., 1,149.
On Ill. Cen. (R. R.).
Manteo, c. s., Dare Co., N. C., 547.
Manti, c. s., Sanpete Co., Utah, 2,200.
On Den. & Rio Gde. West (R. R.).
Manton, Wexford Co., Mich., 1,008.
On Penna. (R. R.).
Mantova, Italy. See Mantua.
Mantua, capital of Prov. of Mantova, Italy, 39,600.
A trade center and military station.
–Portage Co., Ohio, 777.
On Erie (R. R.).
Manville, Somerset Co., N. J., 5,441.
On Cen. of N. Jer.; Leh. Val.; Read. (R. Rs.).
Many, c. s., Sabine Parish, La., 1,239.
On Kan. Cy. Sou. (R. R.).
Manzanillo, Manzanillo Prov., Cuba, 63,560.
A seaport. Leading exports are sugar, tobacco, and hides.
Manzano, Torrance Co., N. Mex., 500.
Manzanola, Otero Co., Colo., 578.
On Atch., Top. & Sante Fe (R. R.)
Maple Heights, Cuyahoga Co., Ohio, 5,950.
Maple Lake, Wright Co., Minn., 660.
On Mpls., St. P. & S. Ste. M. (R. R.).
Maple Shade, Burlington Co., N. J., 5,048.
On Penna. (R. R.).
Mapleton, Monona Co., Iowa, 1,622.
On Chi. & Nor. West.; Chi., Mil., St. P. & Pac. (R. Rs.).
–Iron Co., Mich., 500.
–Blue Earth Co., Minn., 862.
On Chi., Mil., St. P. & Pac. (R. R.).
–Huntingdon Co., Pa., 804.
On Penna. (R. R.).
–Utah Co., Utah, 663.
On Den. & Rio Gde. West (R. R.).
Mapleville, Providence Co., R. I., 556.
Maplewood, St. Louis Co., Mo., 12,657.
On Mo. Pac. (R. R.).
A residential suburb of St. Louis.
Maplewood Park, St. Clair Co., Ill., 760.
Maquoketa, c. s., Jackson Co., Iowa, 3,595.
On Chi. & Nor. West.; Chi., Mil., St. P. & Pac. (R. Rs.).
Maracaibo, State of Zulia, Venezuela, 110,010.
Principal seaport of Venezuela.
Maragha, Prov. of Aserbeidshan, Persia, 1,500.
Maranhão, Brazil. See São Luiz.
Maras, Turkey, 25,672.
Has considerable trade in carpets and embroideries.
Marathon, Buena Vista Co., Iowa, 573.
On Chi., Mil., St. P. & Pac.; Chi. & Nor. West. (R. Rs.).
–Cortland Co., N. Y., 860.
On Del., Lack. & West. (R. R.).
–Brewster Co., Tex., 750.
On Sou. Pac. (R. R.).
–Marathon Co., Wis., 808.
On Chi. & Nor. West. (R. R.).
Marble, Itasca Co., Minn., 738.
On Dul., Missabe & Nor.; Gt. Nor. (R. Rs.).
Marble Falls, Burnet Co., Tex., 865.
On Tex. & N. Orl. (R. R.).
Marblehead, Essex Co., Mass., 10,173.
On Bost. & Me. (R. R.).
–Ottawa Co., Ohio, 1,027.
On Lakeside & Marbleh.; Ohio Pub. Serv. (El.) (R. Rs.).
Marblehill, Pickens Co., Ga., 500.
Marburg, Hesse-Nassau, Germany, 26,000.
A university town and famous for its pottery.
Marbury, Charles Co., Md., 500.
Marceline, Linn Co., Mo., 3,555.
On Atch., Top. & Santa Fe (R. R.).
Marcellus, Cass Co., Mich., 944.
On Gd. Tr. (R. R.).
–Onondaga Co., N. Y., 1,083.
On Mar. & Otisco (R. R.).
Marchena, Prov. of Seville, Spain, 15,309.
Mineral baths near by.
Marchienne-au-Pont, Hainaut, Belgium, 22,952.
Has iron and glass works.
Marcinelle, Hainaut, Belgium, 21,907.
In a coal mining region.
Marco, Natchitoches Par., La., 500.
Marcus, Cherokee Co., Iowa, 1,138.
On Ill. Cen. (R. R.).
–Stevens Co., Washington, 583.
On Gt. Nor. (R. R.).
Marcus Hook, Delaware Co., Pa., 4,867.
On Penna.; Read. (R. Rs.).
Marcy, Oneida Co., N. Y., 2,604.
On N. York Cen. (R. R.).
Marcy-en-Baroeul, Nord, France, 21,322.
Mardin, Vilayet Mardin, Turkey, 22,249.
Mare Island, Solano Co., Calif., 500.
Marengo, McHenry Co., Ill., 1,948.
On Chi. & Nor. West. (R. R.).
–Crawford Co., Ind., 806.
On Southern (R. R.).
–c. s., Iowa Co., Iowa, 2,112.
On Chi., Rk. Isl. & Pac. (R. R.).
Marfa, c. s., Presidio Co., Texas, 3,909.
On Sou. Pac. (R. R.).
Marfork, Raleigh Co., W. Va., 600.
On Chesa. & Ohio (R. R.).
Marfrance, Greenbriar Co., W. Va., 1,066.
On Chesa. & Ohio; N. York Cen. (R. Rs.).
Margaret, Armstrong Co., Pa., 500.
On Balt. & Ohio (R. R.).
Margaretville, Delaware Co., N. Y., 771.
On Del. & Nor. (R. R.).
Margate, Kent, England, 31,312.
A seaside resort.
Margate City, Atlantic Co., N. J., 2,913.
On Penna.-Read. Seashore (R. R.).
Marguerite, Westmoreland Co., Pa., 600.
On Penna. (R. R.).
Marianao, Marianao Prov., Cuba, 32,285.
A suburb of Habana.
Marianna, c. s., Lee Co., Ark., 4,314.
On Mo. Pac. (R. R.).
–c. s., Jackson Co., Fla., 4,023.
On Lou. & Nash.; Marian. & Blountst. (R. Rs.).
–Washington Co., Pa., 1,762.
On Penna. (R. R.).
–Minas Geraes, Brazil, 66,947.
In a mining region.
Mariánské Lázné, Germany. See Marienbad.
Maribojoc, Bohol, P. I., 13,623.
Maricao, Mun. of Maricao, Puerto Rico, 1,197.
Maricopa, Kern Co., Cal., 1,071.
On Atch., Top. & Santa Fe (R. R.).
Marienbad, Germany, 7,177.
A watering place.
Marienburg, East Prussia, Germany, 24,000.
Manufactures agricultural machinery, lumber and sugar.
Marienville, Forest Co., Pa., 700.
On Balt. & Ohio (R. R.).
Marietta, c. s., Cobb Co., Ga., 7,638.
On Lou. & Nash.; Nash., Chatt. & St. Lou. (R. Rs.).
Marietta has various mills, marble works, and foundries. The climate is healthful, and the city is a popular winter resort. A national cemetery is located here.
–c. s., Washington Co., Ohio, 14,285.
On Balt. & Ohio; Penna. (R. Rs.).
On the Ohio River at the mouth of the Muskingum. The oldest town in the State, founded in 1788 by General R. Putnam. The city ships considerable garden produce and has numerous manufactures: safes, furniture, machinery, baskets, and paint. Also a great oil center. Seat of Marietta College.
–c. s., Love Co., Okla., 1,505.
On Gulf, Colo. & Santa Fe (R. R.).
–Lancaster Co., Pa., 1,969.
On Penna. (R. R.).
Marieville, Rouville Co., Quebec, Canada, 1,986.
On Montr. & So. Cos. (El.) (R. R.).
Marine, Madison Co., Ill., 537.
On Ill. Cen. (R. R.).
Marine City, St. Clair Co., Mich., 3,462.
On Port Hur. & Detr. (R. R.).
Marinette, c. s., Marinette Co., Wis., 13,734.
On Chi., Mil., St. P. & Pac.; Chi. & Nor. West. (R. Rs.).
A port of entry. Has large sawmills, paper mills, and grist mills.
Maringouin, Iberville Par., La., 518.
On Tex. & Pac. (R. R.).
Marion, c. s., Perry Co., Ala., 2,141.
On Southern (R. R.).
–c. s., Williamson Co., Ill., 9,033.
On Chi. & East. Ill.; Ill. Cen.; Mar. & East.; Mo. Pac. (R. Rs.).
–c. s., Grant Co., Ind., 24,496.
On Chesa. & Ohio; Cle., Cin., Chi. & St. Lou.; N. York, Chi. & St. Lou.; Penna. (R. Rs.).
A trade center for a farming region. Manufactures: radios, glass, motors, stoves, brick, paper, and flour.
–c. s., Linn Co., Iowa, 4,348.
On Chi., Mil., St. P. & Pac. (R. R.).
–c. s., Marion Co., Kans., 2,069.
On Atch., Top. & Santa Fe; Chi., Rk. Isl. & Pac. (R. Rs.).
–c. s., Crittenden Co., Ky., 1,892.
On Ill. Cen. (R. R.).
–Somerset Co., Md., 600.
On Penna. (R. R.).
–Plymouth Co., Mass., 1,867.
On N. York, N. Hav. & Hart. (R. R.).
–Osceola Co., Mich., 607.
On Ann Arbor (R. R.).
–Wayne Co., N. Y., 700.
On Penna. (R. R.).
–c. s., McDowell Co., N. C., 2,467.
On Clinchfield; Sou. (R. Rs.).
–c. s., Marion Co., Ohio, 31,084.
On Chesa. & Ohio; Cle., Cin., Chi & St. Lou.; Erie; Penna. (R. Rs.).
Fine farms and quarries nearby. Leading products are steel, glass, steam shovels, tractors, and agricultural machinery.
–Franklin Co., Pa., 500.
On Penna. (R. R.).
–c. s., Marion Co., S. C., 4,921.
–Turner Co., S. Dak., 786.
On Atl. Coast Line; Ral. & Charl. (R. Rs.).
–c. s., Smyth Co., Va., 4,156.
On Norf. & West. (R. R.).
Manufactures: Woodwork, foundry products, etc. Seat of Marion College.
–Waupaca Co., Wis., 992.
On Chi. & Nor. West. (R. R.).
Marion Heights, Northumberland Co., Pa., 2,001.
Marion Junction (Marion P. O.), Turner Co., S. Dak., 704.
On Chi., Mil., St. P. & Pac. (R. R.).
Marionville, Lawrence Co., Mo., 1,227.
On St. Lou.-San Fran. (R. R.).
Marissa, St. Clair Co., Ill., 1,630.
On Ill. Cen. (R. R.).
Mariupol, Ukraine, Soviet Union, 152,800.
Center of a grain raising region. Has smelters and textile mills.
Marked Tree, Poinsett Co., Ark., 2,276.
On St. Lou.-San Fran. (R. R.).
Markesan, Green Lake Co., Wis., 872.
On Chi., Mil., St. P. & Pac. (R. R.).
Markle, Huntington and Wells Co., Ind., 621.
On Erie (R. R.).
Marks, c. s., Quitman Co., Miss., 1,258.
On Ill. Cen. (R. R.).
Marksville, c. s., Avoyelles Parish, La., 1,527.
On Tex. & Pac. (R. R.).
Marlboro, Middlesex Co., Mass., 15,781.
On Bost. & Me.; N. York, N. Hav. & Hart. (R. Rs.).

Located near Boston. Has large boot and shoe manufactures.
–Cheshire Co., N. H., 1,200.
On Bost. & Me. (R. R.).
–Monmouth Co., N. J., 500.
On Cen. of N. Jer. (R. R.).
–Ulster Co., N. Y., 3,000.
On West Shore (R. R.).
Marlette, Sanilac Co., Mich., 990.
On Pere Marq. (R. R.).
Marlin, c. s., Falls Co., Texas, 5,338.
On Mo. Pac.; Sou. Pac. (R. Rs.).
Noted health resort, with hot mineral wells.
Marlinton, c. s., Pocahontas Co., W. Va., 1,586.
On Chesa. & Ohio (R. R.).
Marlow, Stephens Co., Okla., 3,084.
On Chi., Rk. Isl. & Pac. (R. R.).
Marmaduke, Greene Co., Ark., 894.
On St. Lou. Southw. (R. R.).
Marmarth, Slope Co., N. Dak., 721.
On Chi., Mil., St. P. & Pac. (R. R.).
Marmet, Kanawha Co., W. Va., 1,200.
On Chesa. & Ohio (R. R.).
Maroa, Macon Co., Ill., 1,154.
On Ill. Cen.; Ill. Term. (El.); Penna. (R. Rs.).
Marque-en-Baroeul, Nord, France, 21,322.
Marquette, Clayton Co., Iowa, 814.
On Chi., Mil., St. P. & Pac. (R. R.).
–McPherson Co., Kans., 645.
On Mo. Pac. (R. R.).
–c. s., Marquette Co., Mich., 14,789.
Situated on south shore of Lake Superior on inlet named Marquette Bay, 170 miles west of Sault Ste. Marie, and on the Duluth, South Shore & Atlantic; and the Lake Superior & Ishpeming railroads.
Shipping point for iron ore. Mining and lumbering town.
Marquez, Leon Co., Tex., 518.
On Mo. Pac. (R. R.).
Marrakech, French Morocco, 191,936.
A busy marketing center.
Mars, Butler Co., Pa., 1,302.
On Balt. & Ohio (R. R.).
Marsala, Prov. of Trapani, Sicily, 30,788.
Fortified seaport; noted for wines.
Marseille, Dept. of Bouches du Rhône, France, 914,232.
Second city in population in France, situated on the Gulf of Lions. Though a handsome city as a whole, Marseille is not rich in public edifices. The harbor is one of the finest in France, and is strongly defended by various works. Owing to the conquest of Algeria, and the opening of the Suez Canal, the foreign commerce exceeds that of every other port of France. Marseille has immense soap factories, iron and copper smelters, engine works, and automobile factories.
Marseilles, La Salle Co., Ill., 4,292.
On Chi., Rk. Isl. & Pac. (R. R.).
Marshall, c. s., Searcy Co., Ark., 638.
On Mo. & Ark. (R. R.).
–c. s., Clark Co., Ill., 2,368.
On Penna.; Cle., Cin., Chi. & St. Lou. (R. Rs.).
–c. s., Calhoun Co., Mich., 5,019.
On Mich. Cen. (R. R.).
–c. s., Lyon Co., Minn., 3,250.
On Chi. & Nor. West.; Gt. Nor. (R. Rs.).
–c. s., Saline Co., Mo., 8,103.
On Alton; Mo. Pac. (R. Rs.).
Seat of Missouri Valley College.
–Madison Co., N. C., 1,132.
On Southern (R. R.).
–Logan Co., Okla., 695.
On Atch., Top. & Santa Fe (R. R.).
–c. s., Harrison Co., Tex., 16,203.
On Marsh., Elys. Flds. & Sou. East.; Tex. & Pac. (R. Rs.).
A cotton growing and industrial center. Manufactures include car wheels, fertilizer, brick, baskets, chairs, crates, and dairy products. Gas fields near by.
Marshallberg, Carteret Co., N. C., 500.
Marshalls, Digby Co., Nova Scotia, 989.
Marshallton, Chester Co., Pa., 528.
Marshalltown, c. s., Marshall Co., Iowa, 17,373.
On Chi. Gt. West.; Mpls. & St. Lou.; Chi. & Nor. West. (R. Rs.).
Chief products are machinery, engines, furnaces, auto accessories, and canned goods. Center of a grain and livestock region.
Marshallville, Macon Co., Ga., 931.
On Cen. of Ga. (R. R.).
Marshfield, Plymouth Co., Mass., 2,073.
On N. York, N. Hav. & Hart. (R. R.).
–c. s., Webster Co., Mo., 1,378.
On St. Lou.-San Fran. (R. R.).
–Coos Co., Ore., 5,287.
On Sou. Pac. (R. R.).
–Wood Co., Wis., 8,778.
On Chi. & Nor. West.; Chi., St. P., Mpls. & Oma.; Mpls., St. P. & S. Ste. M. (R. Rs.).
Mars Hill, Aroostook Co., Maine, 1,000.
On Bangor & Aroostook (R. R.).
Marshville, Union Co., N. C., 933.
On Seab. Air Line (R. R.).
Marshwood, Lackawanna Co., Pa., 556.
On Erie (R. R.).
Marstons Mills, Barnstable Co., Mass., 600.

Mart, McLennan Co., Tex., 2,853.
On Mo. Pac. (R. R.).
Martaban, Tuscaloosa Co., Ala., 525.
On Lou. & Nash. (R. R.).
Martin (Smalley), Floyd Co., Ky., 799.
On Chesa. & Ohio (R. R.).
–c. s., Bennett Co., S. Dak., 942.
–Weakley Co., Tenn., 3,300.
On Ill. Cen.; Nash., Chatt. & St. Lou. (R. Rs.).
Martina Franca, Prov. of Taranto, Italy, 24,355.
A trade center near Taranto.
Martindale, Caldwell Co., Tex., 550.
Martinez, c. s., Contra Costa Co., Cal., 6,569.
On Sou. Pac. (R. R.).
Martinsburg, Audrain Co., Mo., 530.
On Chi., Burl. & Quincy; Wab. (R. Rs.).
–Blair Co., Pa., 1,295.
On Penna. (R. R.).
–c. s., Berkeley Co., W. Va., 14,857.
On Balt. & Ohio; Penna. (R. Rs.).
Located in a fruit-growing region. Manufactures include cider, apple butter, vinegar, hosiery, clothing, and clay products.
Martins Ferry, Belmont Co., Ohio, 14,524.
On Balt. & Ohio; Penna.; Wheel. & L. Erie (R. Rs.).
Industries: coal, sheet metal ware and castings, heating equipment, glassware.
Martinsville, Clark Co., Ill., 1,206.
On Penna. (R. R.).
–c. s., Morgan Co., Ind., 4,962.
On Cle., Cin., Chi. & St. Lou.; Penna. (R. Rs.).
Has mineral springs. Health resort.
–(Ind. City), c. s., Henry Co., Va., 7,705.
On Danv. & West.; Norf. & West. (R. Rs.).
A Virginia tobacco center, with factories and warehouses.
Marvell, Phillips Co., Ark., 624.
On Mo. Pac. (R. R.).
Maryborough, Victoria, Australia, estimated 6,000.
Center of a rich farming region. Coal mines and forests near by.
–March Co., Queensland, Australia, 12,000.
Maryd Station, Schuylkill Co., Pa., 500.
On Reading (R. R.).
Marysville, c. s., Yuba Co., Cal., 5,763.
On Sou. Pac.; West. Pac.; Sacramento Nor. (El.) (R. Rs.).
–Vermilion Co., Ill. See Potomac.
–c. s., Marshall Co., Kans., 4,201.
On Un. Pac. (R. R.).
–St. Clair Co., Mich., 1,405.
On Port Hur. & Det. (R. R.).
–York Co., N. B., Canada, 1,512.
On Can. Nat.; Can. Pac. (R. Rs.).
–c. s., Union Co., Ohio, 3,639.
On Cle., Cin., Chi. & St. Lou.; N. York Cen. (R. Rs.).
–Perry Co., Pa., 1,922.
On Penna. (R. R.).
–Snohomish Co., Wash., 1,354.
On Gt. Nor. (R. R.).
Maryville, Madison Co., Ill., 602.
On Ill. Term. (El.) (R. R.).
–c. s., Nodaway Co., Mo., 5,217.
On Chi., Burl. & Quincy; Wab. (R. Rs.).
–c. s., Blount Co., Tenn., 4,958.
On Lou. & Nash.; Sou. (R. Rs.).
Masan, Chosen, 23,243.
Masardis, Aroostook Co., Maine, 300.
On Bangor & Aroostook (R. R.).
Masaya, capital of Dept. of Masaya, Nicaragua, 18,000.
Situated in a fertile agricultural region.
Mascara, Prov. of Oran, Algeria, 31,449.
Mascoutah, St. Clair Co., Ill., 2,311.
On Lou. & Nash. (R. R.).
Maseru, capital of Basutoland, Africa, 2,320.
Mash-Had (Meshed), Prov. of Khorassan, Iran (Persia), 139,300.
An important trade center with large wool industry and rug factories.
Mason, c. s., Ingham Co., Mich., 2,575.
On Mich. Cen. (R. R.).
–Warren Co., Ohio, 854.
On Penna. (R. R.).
–c. s., Mason Co., Texas, 1,535.
Mason City, c. s., Cerro Gordo Co., Iowa, 23,304.
On Chi. Gt. West.; Chi., Rk. Isl. & Pac.; Mpls. & St. Lou.; Chi. & Nor. West.; Chi., Mil., St. P. & Pac.; Mason Cy. & Clear L. (El.) (R. Rs.).
The commercial metropolis of a fertile agricultural region. Meat packing, sugar mills, and clay products factories.
–Mason Co., Ill., 1,941.
On Alton; Ill. Cen. (R. Rs.).
–(Mason P. O.), Mason Co., W. Va., 691.
On Balt. & Ohio (R. R.).
Masontown, Fayette Co., Pa., 3,873.
On Monongahela (R. R.).
–Preston Co., W. Va., 924.
On Balt. & Ohio (R. R.).
Masqat (Muscat), capital of Oman, Arabian Pen., 10,000.
Massa, Prov. of Massae, Carrara, Italy, 16,906.
Massaua, Eritrea, Africa, 20,480.
The leading seaport.

Massena, St. Lawrence Co., N. Y., 10,637.
On Gd. Tr.; Mass. Term.; N. York. Cen. (R. Rs.).
Located in a dairying region.
Massillon, Stark Co., Ohio, 26,400.
On Balt. & Ohio; Penna.; Wheel. & L. Erie (R. Rs.).
Alloy and cold drawn steel products.
Masson, Hull Co., Quebec, Canada, 2,015.
Masters, Fayette Co., W. Va., 800.
On Chesa. & Ohio (R. R.).
Matador, c. s., Motley Co., Texas, 1,302.
Matagalpa, Nicaragua, 39,271.
In a coffee producing region.
Matagorda, Coahoma Co., Miss., 510.
On Ill. Cen. (R. R.).
–Matagorda Co., Tex., 805.
On Gulf, Colo. & Santa Fe (R. R.).
Matamoras, Pike Co., Pa., 1,784.
Matamoros, State of Tamaulipas, Mexico, 9,733.
On Nat. of Mex. (R. R.).
Matanzas, Cuba, 46,717.
It ranks next to Habana in commerce.
Matara, Ceylon, 18,893.
Mataro, Prov. of Barcelona, Spain, 24,125.
Matawan, Monmouth Co., N. J., 2,496.
On Cen. of N. Jer.; Penna.; N. York & Long Branch (R. Rs.).
Matewan, Mingo Co., W. Va., 932.
On Norf. & West. (R. R.).
Mathews, Lafourche Par., La., 500.
On Sou. Pac. (R. R.).
Mathis, San Patricio Co., Tex., 915.
On Mo. Pac.; Sou. Pac. (R. Rs.).
Matoaka, Mercer Co., W. Va., 929.
On Norf. & West.; Virginian (R. Rs.).
Matsue, Prov. of Shimane, Japan, 44,496.
Paper mills.
Matsumoto, Prov. of Nagano, Japan, 72,141.
A marketing center.
Matsuyama, Prov. of Ehime, Japan, 82,479.
Famous thermal baths in the vicinity.
Mattapan, Suffolk Co., Mass., 5,000.
On N. York, N. Hav. & Hart. (R. R.).
Mattapoisett, Plymouth Co., Mass., 1,682.
On N. York, N. Hav. & Hart. (R. R.).
Resort town on Buzzard's Bay.
Mattawa, Nipissing Co., Ontario, Canada, 1,616.
On Can. Pac. (R. R.).
Matteson, Cook Co., Ill., 736.
On Elg., Jol. & East.; Ill. Cen.; Mich. Cen. (R. Rs.).
Matthews, Grant Co., Indiana, 513.
On Penna. (R. R.).
Mattoon, Coles Co., Ill., 14,631.
On Cle., Cin., Chi. & St. Lou.; Ill. Cen. (R. Rs.).
An important shipping point for corn, wheat, oats, and broom corn. Engine and pump manufactures.
–Shawano Co., Wis., 508.
On Chi. & Nor. West. (R. R.).
Mauban, Prov. of Tayabas, Luzon, P. I., 12,499.
Maubeuge, Dept. of Nord, France, 23,622.
Almost destroyed in the World War, 1914-18.
Mauch Chunk, c. s., Carbon Co., Pa., 3,206.
On Cen. of N. Jer.; Leh. Val. (R. Rs.).
Industrial center.
Mauck, Page Co., Va., 1,000.
Maud, Seminole and Pottawatomie Cos., Okla., 4,326.
On Okla. Cy.-Ada-Atoka (R. R.).
Mauldin, Montgomery Co., Ark., 896.
Maumee, Lucas Co., Ohio, 4,588.
On Cin. & L. Erie (El.); Wab.; N. York, Chi. & St. Lou. (R. Rs.).
Maunabo, Mun. of Maunabo, P. R., 1,344.
Mauston, c. s., Juneau Co., Wis., 2,107.
On Chi., Mil., St. P. & Pac. (R. R.).
Max, McLeon Co., N. Dak., 500.
On Mpls., St. P. & S. Ste. M. (R. R.).
Max Meadows, Wythe Co., Va., 778.
On Norf. & West. (R. R.).
Maxton, Robeson Co., N. C., 1,386.
On Atl. Coast Line; Seab. Air Line (R. Rs.).
Maxwell, Colusa Co., Calif., 506.
On Sou. Pac. (R. R.).
–Story Co., Iowa, 721.
On Chi., Mil., St. P. & Pac. (R. R.).
Mayaguez, Mun. of Mayaguez, Puerto Rico, 44,907.
Textile and garment manufactures.
Maybrook, Orange Co., N. Y., 1,159.
On Erie; Leh. & Hud. Riv.; N. York, N. Hav. & Hart. (R. Rs.).
Maydelle, Cherokee Co., Tex., 500.
On Sou. Pac. (R. R.).
Mayen, Rhenish Prussia, Germany, 14,287.
Mayenne, Dept. of Mayenne, France, 8,751.
Mayesville, Sumter Co., S. C., 649.
On Atl. Coast Line (R. R.).
Mayfield, Santa Clara Co., Cal., 1,150.
On Sou. Pac. (R. R.).
–c. s., Graves Co., Ky., 8,177.
On Ill. Cen. (R. R.).
A tobacco market.
–Fulton Co., N. Y., 722.
–Lackawanna Co., Pa., 3,774.
On Del. & Hud.; N. York, Ont. & West. (R. Rs.).

Mayfield Heights, Cuyahoga Co., Ohio, 2,612.
Maynard, Middlesex Co., Mass., 7,107.
On Bost. & Me. (R. R.).
–Chippewa Co., Minn., 504.
On Gt. Nor. (R. R.).
–Belmont Co., Ohio, 600.
On Balt. & Ohio; Wheel. & L. Erie (R. Rs.).
Maynardville, c. s., Union Co., Tenn., 500.
Mayo, c. s., Lafayette Co., Fla., 708.
–Anne Arundel Co., Md., 700.
Mayodan, Rockingham Co., N. C., 1,948.
On Norf. & West. (R. R.).
Mayport, Duval Co., Fla., 511.
Maysville, Banks and Jackson Cos., Ga., 619.
On Southern (R. R.).
–c. s., Mason Co., Ky., 6,557.
On Chesa. & Ohio; Lou. & Nash. (R. Rs.).
–c. s., De Kalb Co., Mo., 946.
On Chi., Rk. Isl. & Pac. (R. R.).
–Jones Co., N. C., 797.
On Atl. Coast Line (R. R.).
–Garvin Co., Okla., 875.
On Atch., Top. & Santa Fe (R. R.).
Maytown, Lancaster Co., Pa., 520.
Mayville, Tuscola Co., Mich., 654.
On Pere Marq. (R. R.).
–c. s., Chautauqua Co., N. Y., 1,273.
On Jamest., Westf. & Northw. (El.); Penna. (R. Rs.).
–Traill Co., N. Dak., 1,199.
On Gt. Nor. (R. R.).
–Dodge Co., Wis., 2,521.
On Chi., Mil., St. P. & Pac. (R. R.).
Maywood, Cook Co., Ill., 25,829.
On Chi. & Nor. West.; Chi., Aur. & Elg. (El.); Ind. Harb. Bt.; Chi. Gt. West. (R. Rs.).
Manufactures mainly metal products. Seat of Lutheran Theological Seminary.
–Los Angeles Co., Cal., 6,794.
–Marion Co., Ind., 900.
On Penna. (R. R.).
–Frontier Co., Neb., 525.
On Chi., Burl. & Quincy (R. R.).
–Bergen Co., N. J., 3,398.
On N. York, Susq. & West. (R. R.).
Mazamet, Dept. of Tarn, France, 15,447.
Mazatenango, Guatemala, 12,900.
Mazomanie, Dane Co., Wis., 747.
On Chi., Mil., St. P. & Pac. (R. R.).
Mazon, Grundy Co., Ill., 526.
On Atch., Top. & Santa Fe (R. R.).
Mbabane, capital of Swaziland, Africa, 1,550.
McAdenville, Gaston Co., N. C., 914.
On Piedmont & Nor. (El.) (R. R.).
McAdoo, Schuylkill Co., Pa., 5,239.
On Leh. Val.; Penna. (R. Rs.).
McAlester, c. s., Pittsburg Co., Okla., 11,804.
On Chi., Rk. Isl. & Pac.; Mo.-Kan.-Tex.; Pittsb. Co. (El.) (R. Rs.).
Coal center of southwest. Also has cotton gins.
McAllen, Hidalgo Co., Texas, 9,074.
On Mo. Pac.; Sou. Pac. (R. Rs.).
Situated in a fruit-growing region.
McArthur, c. s., Vinton Co., Ohio, 1,188.
On Chesa. & Ohio (R. R.).
McBee, Chesterfield Co., S. C., 514.
On Charl., Monr. & Col.; Seab. Air Line (R. Rs.).
McCall, Valley Co., Idaho, 651.
On Un. Pac. (R. R.).
–Ascension Par., La., 710.
On Tex. & Pac. (R. R.).
McCamey, Upton Co., Texas, 3,446.
On Panh. & Santa Fe (R. R.).
McCaysville, Fannin Co., Ga., 1,969.
McCleary, Grays Harbor Co., Wash., 1,320.
On Nor. Pac. (R. R.).
McClellandtown, Fayette Co., Pa., 821.
McClellanville, Charleston Co., S. C., 502.
McClenny, c. s., Baker Co., Fla., 610.
On Seab. Air Line (R. R.).
McCloud, Siskiyou Co., Calif., 1,000.
On McCloud River (R. R.).
McClure, Snyder Co., Pa., 700.
On Penna. (R. R.).
McClusky, Sheridan Co., N. Dak., 719.
On Nor. Pac. (R. R.).
McColl, Marlboro Co., S. C., 1,657.
On Atl. Coast Line; Seab. Air Line (R. Rs.).
McComb, Pike Co., Miss., 10,057.
On Ill. Cen. (R. R.).
Shipping point for garden truck, cotton and cattle.
–Hancock Co., Ohio, 932.
On Balt. & Ohio; N. York, Chi. & St. Lou. (R. Rs.).
McConnellsburg, c. s., Fulton Co., Pa., 768.
McConnelsville, c. s., Morgan Co., Ohio, 1,754.
Natural Bridge and Council Rock are located nearby.
McCook, c. s., Redwillow Co., Neb., 6,688.
On Chi., Burl. & Quincy (R. R.).
McCool, Attala Co., Miss., 562.
On Ill. Cen. (R. R.).
McCormick, c. s., McCormick Co., S. C., 1,304.
On Charl. & W. Car. (R. R.).
McCracken, Rush Co., Kans., 551.
On Mo. Pac. (R. R.).
McCrory, c. s., Woodruff Co., Ark., 924.
On Mo. Pac. (R. R.).

McCUNE, Crawford Co., Kans., 577.
On St. Lou.-San Fran. (R. R.)
McCURTAIN, Haskell Co., Okla., 934.
On Fort Smith & West. (R. R.).
McDERMITT, Humboldt Co., Nev., 2,000.
McDERMOTT, Scioto Co., Ohio, 850.
On Norf. & West. (R. R.).
McDONALD, Trumbull Co., Ohio, 1,714.
—Washington and Allegheny Cos., Pa., 3,281.
On Montour; Penna. (R. Rs.).
McDONOUGH, c. s., Henry Co., Georgia, 1,068.
On Southern (R. R.).
McDOWELL, Floyd Co., Ky., 500.
On Chesa. & Ohio (R. R.).
McEWEN, Humphreys Co., Tenn., 620.
On Nash., Chatt. & St. Lou. (R. R.).
McFARLAND, Kern Co., Calif., 750.
On Sou. Pac. (R. R.).
McGEHEE, Desha Co., Ark., 3,488.
On Mo. Pac. (R. R.).
McGILL, White Pine Co., Nev., 3,000.
On Nev. Nor. (R. R.).
McGRANN, Armstrong Co., Pa., 500.
McGRAW (McGrawville), Cortland Co., N. Y., 1,082.
On Del., Lack. & West. (R. R.).
McGREGOR, Clayton Co., Iowa, 1,299.
On Chi., Mil., St. P. & Pac. (R. R.).
—McLennan Co., Texas, 2,041.
On Gulf, Colo. & Santa Fe; St. Lou. Southw. (R. Rs.).
McGUFFEY, Hardin Co., Ohio, 710.
McHENRY, McHenry Co., Ill., 1,354.
On Chi. & Nor. West. (R. R.).
—Ohio Co., Ky., 608.
On Ill. Cen. (R. R.).
—Stone Co., Miss., 630.
On Ill. Cen. (R. R.).
McINTOSH, Polk Co., Minn., 688.
On Gt. Nor. (R. R.).
—c. s., Corson Co., S. Dak., 663.
On Chi., Mil., St. P. & Pac. (R. R.).
McINTYRE, Indiana Co., Pa., 600.
On Balt. & Ohio (R. R.).
McKEESPORT, Allegheny Co., Pa., 54,632.
On Balt. & Ohio; McKeesp. Connect.; Penna.; Pitts. & L. Erie (R. Rs.).
In the heart of a rich natural gas field. Coal mines in vicinity. Has huge tube plants, blast furnaces, tin-plating works, railroad construction works. Seat of Douglas Business College.
McKEES ROCKS, Allegheny Co., Pa., 18,116.
On Pitts., Alleg. & McK. Rks.; Pitts. & L. Erie; Pitts., Chart. & Yough. (R. Rs.).
A suburb of Pittsburgh. Has coal mines and large iron and steel plants.
McKENZIE, Carroll Co., Tenn., 1,858.
On Lou. & Nash.; Nash., Chatt. & St. Lou. (R. Rs.).
McKINNEY, c. s., Collin Co., Texas, 7,307.
On La., Ark. & Tex.; Sou. Pac.; Tex. El. (R. Rs.).
Live stock, grain and cotton market.
McKOWNVILLE, Albany Co., N. Y., 506.
McLAUGHLIN, Corson Co., S. Dak., 678.
On Chi., Mil., St. P. & Pac. (R. R.).
McLAURIN, Forrest Co., Miss., 510.
On Ill. Cen. (R. R.).
McLEAN, McLean Co., Ill., 676.
On Alton (R. R.).
—Gray Co., Texas, 1,521.
On Chi., Rk. Isl. & Pac. (R. R.).
McLEANSBORO, c. s., Hamilton Co., Ill., 2,162.
On Lou. & Nash. (R. R.).
McLOUD, Pottawatomie Co., Okla., 812.
On Chi., Rk. Isl. & Gulf (R. R.).
McLOUTH, Jefferson Co., Kans., 535.
McMECHEN, Marshall Co., W. Va., 3,710.
On Balt. & Ohio (R. R.).
McMINNVILLE, c. s., Yamhill Co., Ore., 2,917.
On Sou. Pac. (R. R.).
—c. s., Warren Co., Tenn., 3,914.
On Nash., Chatt. & St. Lou. (R. R.).
McPHERSON, c. s., McPherson Co., Kans., 7,048.
On Atch., Top. & Santa Fe; Chi., Rk. Isl. & Pac.; Mo. Pac.; Un. Pac. (R. Rs.).
McRAE, c. s., Telfair Co., Ga., 1,314.
On Seab. Air Line; Sou. (R. Rs.).
McROBERTS, Letcher Co., Ky., 2,146.
On Lou. & Nash. (R. R.).
McSHERRYSTOWN, Adams Co., Pa., 2,050.
McVEIGH, Pike Co., Ky., 1,298.
On Norf. & West. (R. R.).
McVEYTOWN, Mifflin Co., Pa., 566.
On Penna. (R. R.).
McVILLE, Nelson Co., N. Dak., 513.
On Gt. Nor. (R. R.).
MEADE, c. s., Meade Co., Kans., 1,330.
On Chi., Rk. Isl. & Pac. (R. R.).
MEADOWBROOK, Montgomery Co., Pa., 800.
On Reading (R. R.).
MEADOW CREEK, Summers Co., W. Va., 600.
On Chesa. & Ohio; N. York Cen. (R. Rs.).
MEADOW VIEW, Washington Co., Va., 618.
On Norf. & West. (R. R.).
MEADVILLE, Linn Co., Mo., 540.
On Chi., Burl. & Quincy (R. R.).
—c. s., Crawford Co., Pa., 16,698.
On Bess. & L. Erie; Erie (R. Rs.).
Erie railroad shops are located here. Manu-

factures metal products. Allegheny College.
MEAFORD, Grey Co., N., Ont., Can., 2,624.
On Can. Nat. (R. R.).
MEARS, Oceana Co., Mich., 912.
On Pere Marq. (R. R.).
MEAUX, Dept. of Seine-et-Marne, France, 14,429.
Has considerable trade in agricultural products.
MEBANE, Alamance and Orange Cos., N. C., 1,568.
On Southern (R. R.).
MECCA, Hejaz, Saudi Arabia, 70,000.
A holy Mohammedan city, situated in a long, narrow, sandy valley, running north and south; called in the Koran "the valley without seeds." The only public building of consequence is the Beitullah, or El-Haram, the famous mosque of Mecca, in the interior of which is the Caaba, or Holy House, its doors being coated with silver, embellished with gold ornaments, in which is the celebrated "black stone," said to have been brought by the angel Gabriel to form the foundation. The Holy Well of Zemzem, said to have been found by Hagar when her son Ishmael was dying of thirst, supplies the city with water for drinking and ablution. About 15 miles east of Mecca is the hill of Arafat, where Mohammed used to retire to pray, and which is much frequented by pilgrims. Mecca is celebrated as the birthplace of Mohammed. Only Mussulmans are permitted to enter the city.
—Riverside Co., Calif., 500.
On Sou. Pac. (R. R.).
—Parke Co., Ind., 1,000.
On Balt. & Ohio (R. R.).
MECHANIC FALLS, Androscoggin Co., Maine, 1,650.
On Can. Nat.; Me. Cen. (R. Rs.).
MECHANICSBURG, Champaign Co., Ohio, 1,424.
On Cle., Cin., Chi. & St. Lou. (R. R.).
—Cumberland Co., Pa., 5,647.
On Penna. (R. R.).
—Lancaster Co., Pa., 600.
MECHANICSVILLE, Windham Co., Conn., 609.
On N. York, N. Hav. & Hart. (R. R.).
—Cedar Co., Iowa, 781.
On Chi. & Nor. West. (R. R.).
—Schuylkill Co., Pa., 706.
MECHANICVILLE, Saratoga Co., N. Y., 7,924.
On Bost. & Me.; Del. & Hud. (R. Rs.).
Manufactures paper, knit goods, bricks, etc.
MECHELEN, Belgium. See MALINES.
MEDARYVILLE, Pulaski Co., Indiana, 610.
On Chi., Ind. & Lou. (R. R.).
MEDELLIN, capital of Dept. of Antioquia, Colombia, 128,295.
Gold and silver mining center. Coffee and cattle raising in the vicinity are also important.
—Cebu Prov., Cebu, P. I., 15,274.
MEDFIELD, Norfolk Co., Mass., 4,162.
On N. York, N. Hav. & Hart. (R. R.).
MEDFORD, Middlesex Co., Mass., 61,444.
On Bost. & Me. (R. R.).
Seat of Tufts College.
—Burlington Co., N. J., 1,000.
On Penna. (R. R.).
—c. s., Grant Co., Okla., 1,084.
On Atch., Top. & Santa Fe; Chi., Rk. Isl. & Pac. (R. Rs.).
—c. s., Jackson Co., Ore., 11,007.
On Sou. Pac. (R. R.).
Center of a lumbering and ranching region.
—c. s., Taylor Co., Wis., 1,918.
On Mpls., St. P. & S. Ste. M. (R. R.).
MEDIA, c. s., Delaware Co., Pa., 5,372.
On Penna. (R. R.).
MEDIAPOLIS, Des Moines Co., Iowa, 793.
On Chi., Burl. & Quincy; Chi., Rk. Isl. & Pac. (R. Rs.).
MEDICAL LAKE, Spokane Co., Wash., 1,671.
On Nor. Pac. (R. R.).
MEDICINE HAT, Medicine Hat Co., Alberta, Canada, 9,592.
On Can. Pac. (R. R.).
Ranching, coal mining, and gas fields near by.
MEDICINE LODGE, c. s., Barber Co., Kans., 1,624.
On Atch., Top. & Santa Fe (R. R.).
MEDINA, Orleans Co., N. Y., 6,071.
On N. York Cen. (R. R.).
—c. s., Medina Co., Ohio, 4,071.
On Balt. & Ohio; Nor. Ohio (R. Rs.).
—Kingdom of Hejaz, Arabia, about 30,000.
One of Arabia's holy cities containing the tomb of Mohammed.
MEDOMAK, Lincoln Co., Maine, 630.
On Me. Cen. (R. R.).
MEDORA, Jackson Co., Indiana, 654.
On Balt. & Ohio (R. R.).
MEDWAY, Norfolk Co., Mass., 3,268.
On N. York, N. Hav. & Hart. (R. R.).
MEEKER, c. s., Rio Blanco Co., Colo., 1,069.
—Lincoln Co., Okla., 562.
On Atch., Top. & Santa Fe (R. R.).
MEERANE, Saxony, Germany, 25,000.
Leading city for woolen industries.
MEERUT, United Provinces, India, 91,181.
Center of a fertile agricultural region.
MEGANTIC, Compton Co., Quebec, Canada, 3,911.
MEGARA, Dept. of Central Greece, Nomarchy of Attica, Greece, 10,441.

MEGARGEL, Archer Co., Tex., 813.
On St. Lou., San Fran. & Tex. (R. R.).
MEHALLET EL KEBIR, Gharbiya, Egypt, 51,900.
Commercial town with cotton manufactures.
MEIGS, Mitchell and Thomas Cos., Ga., 1,000.
On Atl. Coast Line (R. R.).
MEININGEN, Thüringen, Germany, 20,000.
Chemicals, paper, and pottery.
MEISSEN, Saxony, Germany, 46,000.
Famous for its Dresden China.
MEKNES (Meguinez), Morocco, 75,131.
MELBOURNE, capital of Victoria and second city of Australia (incl. suburbs), 1,016,500.
Situated on the Yarra River, 9 miles from its mouth. A great commercial city. Exports much wheat, wool, fruits, and refrigerated meat. Melbourne has extensive manufactures and is the financial center of Australia.
—Brevard Co., Fla., 2,753.
On Fla. East Coast (R. R.).
MELCHER, Marion Co., Iowa, 1,673.
On Chi., Rk. Isl. & Pac. (R. R.).
MELCROFT, Fayette Co., Pa., 500.
On Balt. & Ohio (R. R.).
MELENA, Prov. of Habana, Cuba, 2,608.
MELILLA, Spanish Zone, Morocco, 50,170.
MELIPILLA, Prov. of Santiago, Chile, 8,730.
MELITOPOL, Ukraine, Sov. Union, 32,200.
MELLEN, Ashland Co., Wis., 1,629.
On Mpls., St. P. & S. Ste. M. (R. R.).
MELROSE, Middlesex Co., Mass., 24,256.
On Bost. & Me. (R. R.).
A residential suburb of Boston.
—Stearns Co., Minn., 1,801.
On Gt. Nor. (R. R.).
—Curry Co., N. Mex., 655.
On Atch., Top. & Santa Fe (R. R.).
MELROSE PARK, Cook Co., Ill., 10,741.
On Ind. Harb. Blt.; Chi. & Nor. West. (R. Rs.).
A suburb of Chicago.
MELUN, Dept. of Seine-et-Marne, France, 17,499.
An agricultural marketing town.
MELVILLE, St. Landry Parish, La., 1,541.
On Tex. & Pac. (R. R.).
—Saskatchewan, Canada, 3,923.
On Canadian National (R. R.).
MELVINDALE, Wayne Co., Mich., 4,053.
On Det., Tol. & Iron. (R. R.).
MEMMINGEN, Bavaria, Germany, 14,049.
Textile industries.
MEMPHIS, Lower Egypt.
Twelve miles south by west of Cairo; little is left to attest the former importance of the ancient city save the pyramids, the tombs of Sakhara, and the statue of Rameses II.
—c. s., Shelby Co., Tenn., 253,143.
Is a port of entry, situated on the Mississippi River, and on the Chicago, Rock Island and Pacific; the Illinois Central; the Mobile and Ohio; the Union; the Southern; the Louisville and Nashville; the Nashville, Chattanooga and St. Louis; the Missouri Pacific; the St. Louis-San Francisco and the St. Louis Southwestern railroads.
This city is a leading market for inland cotton, hardwood lumber, cottonseed and oil, and drugs, and a distributing point for automobiles. It contains a custom-house, Cotton Exchange, Merchants' Exchange, Builders' Exchange, Industrial Bureau, Freight Bureau. Other features embrace several colleges and professional schools, an art gallery, two libraries, and a large auditorium. The city is the seat of Southwestern (Presbyterian) University.
—Macomb and St. Clair Cos., Mich., 574.
On Pere Marq. (R. R.).
—c. s., Scotland Co., Mo., 1,728.
On Chi., Burl. & Quincy (R. R.).
—c. s., Hall Co., Texas, 4,257.
On Gulf, Colo. & Santa Fe (R. R.).
MENA, c. s., Polk Co., Ark., 3,118.
On Kan. Cy. Sou. (R. R.).
MENANDS, Albany Co., N. Y., 1,522.
On Del. & Hud. (R. R.).
MENARD, Menard Co., Texas, 1,969.
On Ft. Worth & Denv. Cy. (R. R.).
MENASHA, Winnebago Co., Wis., 9,062.
On Chi., Mil., St. P. & Pac.; Mpls., St. P. & S. Ste. M.; Chi. & Nor. West. (R. Rs.).
Has extensive paper and woodworking plants.
MENDENHALL, Simpson Co., Miss., 919.
On Gulf & Ship Isl. (R. R.).
MENDHAM, Morris Co., N. J., 1,278.
MENDOCINO, Mendocino Co., Calif., 500.
MENDON, Adams Co., Ill., 580.
On Chi., Burl. & Quincy (R. R.).
—Worcester Co., Mass., 1,265.
—St. Joseph Co., Mich., 692.
On Penna. (R. R.).
—Mercer Co., Ohio, 502.
MENDOTA, La Salle Co., Ill., 4,008.
On Chi., Burl. & Quincy; Chi., Mil., St. P. & Pac.; Ill. Cen. (R. Rs.).
MENDOZA, capital of Prov. of Mendoza, Argentina, 76,780.
A cattle raising center.
MENGTSZ, Yunnan, China, 193,000.
MENIN, West Flanders, Belgium, 19,723.
Linen and flannel manufactures.

MENLO, Guthrie Co., Iowa, 500.
On Chi., Rk. Isl. & Pac. (R. R.).
MENLO PARK, San Mateo Co., Cal., 2,254.
On Sou. Pac. (R. R.).
MENNO, Hutchinson Co., S. Dak., 978.
On Chi., Mil., St. P. & Pac. (R. R.).
MENOMINEE, c. s., Menominee Co., Mich., 10,320.
On Ann Arbor; Chi. & Nor. West.; Chi., Mil., St. P. & Pac. (R. Rs.).
Manufactures lumber, furniture, printing, candy, electrical appliances, stained glass, machinery.
MENOMONEE FALLS, Waukesha Co., Wis., 1,291.
On Chi., Mil., St. P. & Pac. (R. R.).
MENOMONIE, c. s., Dunn Co., Wis., 5,595.
On Chi., Mil., St. P. & Pac.; Chi., St. P., Mpls. & Oma. (R. Rs.).
Seat of Stout Institute.
MENTON, Dept. of Alpes-Maritimes, France, 21,703.
A popular resort.
MENTONE, San Bernardino Co., Calif., 510.
On Atch., Top. & Santa Fe; Sou. Pac. (R. Rs.).
—Kosciusko Co., Ind., 704.
On N. York, Chi. & St. Lou.; Winona (El.) (R. Rs.).
—(Porterville), Loving Co., Tex., 600.
MENTOR, Lake Co., Ohio, 1,589.
On N. York Cen.; N. York, Chi. & St. Lou. (R. Rs.).
MENUF, Prov. of Menufieh, Egypt, 22,316.
MEPPEL, Prov. of Drenthe, Netherlands, 12,133.
An agricultural marketing center.
MERANO, Prov. of Bolzano, Italy, 19,185.
Frequented by lung-trouble sufferers.
MERCED, c. s., Merced Co., Cal., 7,066.
On Atch., Top. & Santa Fe; Sou. Pac.; Yosemite Val. (R. Rs.).
MERCEDES, Uruguay, 30,000.
Has a large trade in wool and livestock products.
—Hidalgo Co., Tex., 6,608.
On Mo. Pac. (R. R.).
MERCER, Muhlenberg Co., Ky., 800.
On Ill. Cen. (R. R.).
—c. s., Mercer Co., Pa., 2,125.
On Bess. & L. Erie; Penna. (R. Rs.).
MERCERSBURG, Franklin Co., Pa., 1,634.
On Penna. (R. R.).
MERCHANTVILLE, Camden Co., N. J., 3,592.
On Penna. (R. R.).
MEREDITH, Belknap Co., N. H., 1,200.
On Bost. & Me. (R. R.).
MEREDOSIA, Morgan Co., Ill., 820.
On Wabash (R. R.).
MERGENTHEIM, Württemberg, Germany, 5,430.
MERIDA, capital of Yucatan, Mexico, 95,015.
On United Rys. of Yucatan.
A center of the sisal fibre industry.
—capital of the State of Mérida, Venezuela, 12,006.
MERIDEN, New Haven Co., Conn., 38,481.
On N. York, N. Hav. & Hart. (R. R.).
Particularly noted for its silverware manufactures.
MERIDIAN, Ada Co., Idaho, 1,004.
On Un. Pac. (R. R.).
—c. s., Lauderdale Co., Miss., 31,954.
On Ala. Gt. Sou.; Gulf, Mob. & Nor.; Ill. Cen.; Merid. & Bigb. Riv.; Mob. & Ohio; N. Orl. & Northe.; Sou. (R. Rs.).
Cotton gins, brickyards, canneries, and knitting mills.
—c. s., Bosque Co., Texas, 759.
On Gulf, Colo. & Santa Fe (R. R.).
MERIGOLD, Bolivar Co., Miss., 804.
On Ill. Cen. (R. R.).
MERION STATION, Montgomery Co., Pa., 4,000.
On Penna. (R. R.).
MERKEL, Taylor Co., Tex., 1,848.
On Tex. & Pac. (R. R.).
MERRIAM, Johnson Co., Kan., 2,500.
On St. Lou.-San Fran. (R. R.).
MERRICK, Nassau Co., N. Y., 3,662.
On Long Isl. (R. R.).
MERRICKVILLE, Grenville-Dundas Co., Ontario, Canada, 812.
On Can. Pac. (R. R.).
MERRILL, Plymouth Co., Iowa, 605.
On Chi., St. P., Mpls. & Oma.; Chi. & Nor. West.; Gt. Nor.; Ill. Cen. (R. Rs.).
—Saginaw Co., Mich., 616.
On Pere Marq. (R. R.).
—c. s., Lincoln Co., Wis., 8,458.
On Chi., Mil., St. P. & Pac. (R. R.).
MERRILLAN, Jackson Co., Wis., 554.
On Chi. & Nor. West.; Gr. Bay & West. (R. Rs.).
MERRIMAC, Essex Co., Mass., 2,209.
On Bost. & Me. (R. R.).
MERRITTON, Lincoln and Niagara Cos., Ontario, Canada, 2,523.
On Can. Nat.; Niag., St. Cath. & Tor. (El.) (R. Rs.).
MER ROUGE, Morehouse Parish, La., 669.
On Mo. Pac. (R. R.).
MERRYVILLE, Beauregard Parish, La., 2,626.
On Gulf, Colo. & Santa Fe (R. R.).
MERSEBURG, Prussian Saxony, Germany, 29,000.
Machinery, leather and beer.

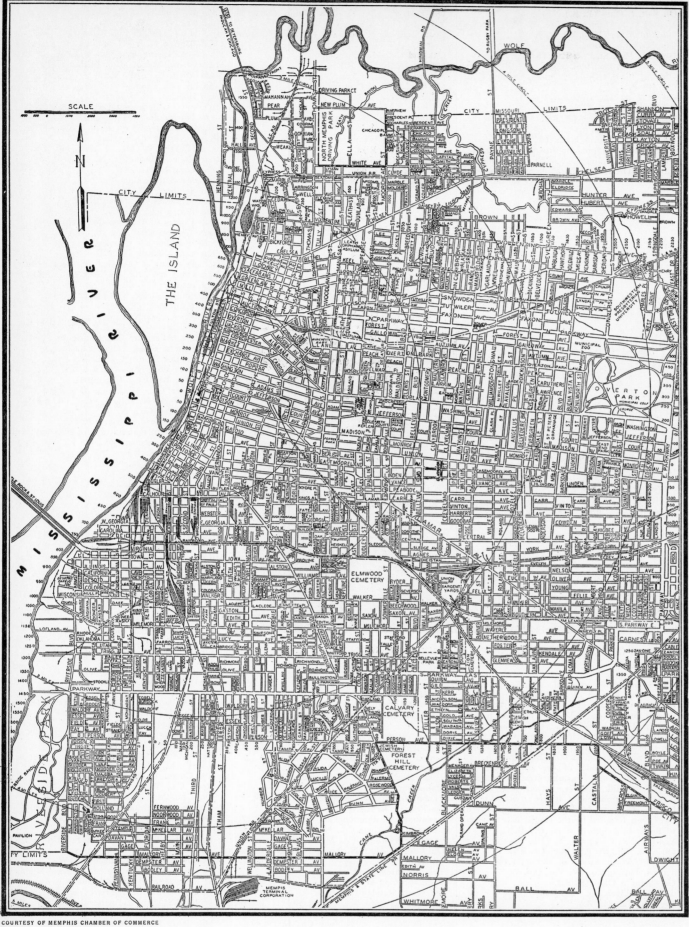

MAP OF MEMPHIS, THE LARGEST CITY IN TENNESSEE AND THE MOST IMPORTANT COMMERCIAL CENTER ON THE MISSISSIPPI RIVER BETWEEN ST. LOUIS AND NEW ORLEANS. MEMPHIS IS THE LARGEST HARDWOOD LUMBER AND INLAND COTTON MARKET IN THE UNITED STATES

7,400 feet above sea-level, near several lakes. Wonderful climate.

The principal public buildings are the cathedral, palace of government, and College of Mines. Among important educational institutions are the University of Mexico City, a school of law, a school of medicine, technical schools, teachers' training schools, an academy of art, a conservatory of music, the National Library, the National Museum and the National Observatory.

The manufacturers are of comparatively limited extent, and trade is largely in the hands of foreigners. The manufactures include iron products, textiles, tobacco articles, leather goods and flour.

—Miami Co., Ind., 510.
On Penna. (R. R.).
—Oxford Co., Maine, 2,100.
—c. s., Audrain Co., Mo., 8,290.
On Alton; Chi., Burl. & Quincy; Wab. (R. Rs.).
—Oswego Co., N. Y., 1,297.
On N. York Cen. (R. R.).
—Pampanga Prov., Luzon, P. I., 16,023.
MEYCAUAYAN, Prov. of Bulacan, Luzon, P. I., 11,186.
MEYERSDALE, Somerset Co., Pa., 3,065.
On Balt. & Ohio; West. Md. (R. Rs.).
MEZOTUR, Hungary, 27,645.
A trade center in a grain and cattle raising country.
MIAGO, Iloilo Prov., Panay, P. I., 26,940.
Abaca and pina fabrics are leading products.
MIAMI, Gila Co., Arizona, 7,693.
On Sou. Pac. (R. R.).
—c. s., Dade Co., Fla., 127,600.
On Fla. East Coast; Seab. Air Line (R. Rs.).
A popular winter resort. Its beach is separated from the city by Biscayne Bay, across which connecting causeways have been built. The ocean front has been greatly extended and harbor and dock improvements have been made. Leading manufactured products are boats, canned goods, lumber, novelties, clothing, auto parts, glass, and cigars.
—Colfax Co., N. Mex., 530.
—c. s., Ottawa Co., Okla., 8,064.
On Kans., Okla. & Gulf; Northe. Okla. (El.); St. Lou.-San Fran. (R. Rs.).
—c. s., Roberts Co., Texas, 953.
On Panh. & Santa Fe (R. R.).
MIAMI BEACH, Dade Co., Fla., 13,330.
MIAMISBURG, Montgomery Co., Ohio, 5,518.
On Cin. & L. Erie (El.); Cle., Cin., Chi. & St. Lou.; Erie; Balt. & Ohio (R. Rs.).
MIAMI SHORES, Dade Co., Fla., 693.
MIANUS, Fairfield Co., Conn., 900.
MICANOPY, Alachua Co., Fla., 722.
On Atl. Coast Line; Jacksonv., Gainesv. & Gulf (R. Rs.).
MICCO, Logan Co., West Va., 250.
On Chesa. & Ohio (R. R.).
MICCOSUKEE, Leon Co., Fla., 500.
On Atl. Coast Line (R. R.).
MICHIGAN CITY, Laporte Co., Ind., 26,735.
On Chi., Ind. & Lou.; N. York, Chi. & St. Lou.; Mich. Cen.; Chi. Sou. Shore & Sou. Bend (El.); Pere Marq. (R. Rs.).
Lake port and industrial town. Wire specialties, bicycles, castings, metal furniture.
MICHURINSK (Kazlov), Soviet Union, 65,900.
Machinery; trade in cattle and their products.
MIDDELBURG, Zeeland, Netherlands, 18,389.
Principally of historical interest.
—Transvaal Prov., Union of South Africa, 2,694.
MIDDLEBORO, Plymouth Co., Mass., 8,865.
On N. York, N. Hav. & Hart. (R. R.).
MIDDLEBOURNE, c. s., Tyler Co., W. Va., 769.
MIDDLE BRANCH (Middlebranch P. O.), Stark Co., Ohio, 525.
On Wheel. & L. Erie (R. R.).
MIDDLEBURG, Schoharie Co., N. Y., 948.
—c. s., Snyder Co., Pa., 1,024.
On Penna. (R. R.).
—Cape of Good Hope, Un. of South Africa, 5,371.
MIDDLEBURGH HEIGHTS, Cuyahoga Co., Ohio, 874.
MIDDLEBURY, New Haven Co., Conn., 1,100.
—Elkhart Co., Ind., 656.
On N. York Cen. (R. R.).
—c. s., Addison Co., Vt., 2,003.
On Rutland (R. R.).
MIDDLEFIELD, Middlesex Co., Conn., 1,204.
On N. York, N. Hav. & Hart. (R. R.).
—Geauga Co., Ohio, 726.
On Balt. & Ohio (R. R.).
MIDDLE GRANVILLE, Washington Co., N. Y., 650.
On Del. & Hud. (R. R.).
MIDDLEPOINT, Van Wert Co., Ohio, 574.
On Penna. (R. R.).
MIDDLEPORT, Niagara Co., N. Y., 1,596.
On N. York Cen. (R. R.).
—Meigs Co., Ohio, 3,505.
On Chesa. & Ohio; N. York Cen. (R. Rs.).
—Schuylkill Co., Pa., 1,225.
On Reading (R. R.).
MIDDLESBORO, Bell Co., Ky., 10,350.
On Lou. & Nash.; Sou. (R. Rs.).
A popular summer resort.

MERTHYR, Tydfil, Glamorganshire, Wales, 71,099.
Iron, smelting and coal-mining.
MERTZON, Irion Co., Tex., 684.
On Panh. & Santa Fe (R. R.).
MERV, Turcoman, Rep., Sov. Union, 30,600.
MERXEM, Anvers, Belgium, 27,174.
MESA, Maricopa Co., Ariz., 3,711.
On Sou. Pac. (R. R.).
MESHANTICUT, Providence Co., R. I., 725.
On N. York, N. Hav. & Hart. (R. R.).
MESHED, Iran (Persia). See MASH-HAD.
MESHOPPEN, Wyoming Co., Pa., 525.
On Leh. Val. (R. R.).
MESILLA, Dona Ana Co., N. Mex., 2,000.
MESQUITE, Dallas Co., Texas, 729.
On Tex. & Pac. (R. R.).

MESSICK, York Co., Va., 517.
MESSINA, capital of Province of Messina, Italy, 114,051.
A busy port and commercial center.
METAMORA, Woodford Co., Ill., 707.
On Alton (R. R.).
—Fulton Co., Ohio, 552.
On Ohio & Morenci (El.).
METHUEN, Essex Co., Mass., 21,073.
On Bost. & Me. (R. R.).
Adjoins Lawrence, and is mainly residential. Has cotton and woolen mills.
METLAKATLA, Alaska, 466.
METROPOLIS, c. s., Massac Co., Ill., 5,573.
On Chi., Burl. & Quincy; Ill. Cen.; Nashv., Chatt. & St. Lou.; Paduc. & Ill. (R. Rs.).

METTER, c. s., Cadler Co., Ga., 1,424.
On Cen. of Ga. (R. R.).
METUCHEN, Middlesex Co., N. J., 5,748.
On Leh. Val.; Penna. (R. Rs.).
METZ, Moselle, France, 83,119.
A fortified town. Manufactures shoes, metal goods, preserves, and tobacco.
MEXIA, Limestone Co., Texas, 6,579.
On Burl.-Rk. Isl.; Sou. Pac. (R. Rs.).
MEXICO, Distrito Federal, capital of Republic of Mexico, 1,029,068.
On Mexican; National of Mex.; San Raf. & Atlixco; Mex. Valley Sanitary Dist.; Mayo River; Toluca, Tenanzo & San Juan (R. Rs.).
Situated within the State of Mexico, about

MIDDLESBROUGH, Yorkshire, England, 138,489.
An industrial center in one of the world's greatest iron districts.
MIDDLESEX (Lincoln), Middlesex Co., N. J., 3,504.
 —Nash Co., N. C., 559.
 On Norf. Sou. (R. R.).
 —Washington Co., Vt., 751.
 On Cen. Vir. (R. R.).
MIDDLETON, Lancashire, England, 29,189.
An industrial suburb of Manchester.
 —Essex Co., Mass., 1,975.
 —Dane Co., Wis., 983.
 On Chi., Mil., St. P. & Pac. (R. R.).
MIDDLETOWN, c. s., Middlesex Co., Conn., 24,554.
 On N. York, N. Hav. & Hart. (R. R.).
Has diversified manufactures. Its location on the Connecticut River is exceedingly picturesque.
 —New Castle Co., Del., 1,247.
 On Penna. (R. R.).
 —Logan and Menard Cos., Ill., 507.
 On Alton (R. R.).
 —Henry Co., Ind., 1,348.
 On Penna. (R. R.).
 —Frederick Co., Md., 818.
 On Hagerst. & Fred. (R. R.).
 —Monmouth Co., N. J., 9,209.
 On Cen. of N. Jer.; N. York & Long Br.; Penna. (R. Rs.).
 —Orange Co., N. Y., 21,276.
 On Erie; N. York, Ont. & West.; Middletown & Union (R. Rs.).
A residential town and the center of a fertile farming region. Has railroad shops and numerous small industries.
 —Butler Co., Ohio, 29,992.
 On Balt. & Ohio; Cin. & L. Erie (El.); Cle., Cin., Chi. & St. Lou.; Penna. (R. Rs.).
A leading manufacturing center for miscellaneous paper products. The tobacco industry has also developed here.
 —Dauphin Co., Pa., 6,085.
 On Penna.; Read. (R. Rs.).
 —Newport Co., R. I., 3,007.
 On N. York, N. Hav. & Hart. (R. R.).
MIDDLEVILLE, Barry Co., Mich., 804.
 On Mich. Cen. (R. R.).
 —Herkimer Co., N. Y., 760.
 On N. York Cen. (R. R.).
MIDLAND, Sebastian Co., Ark., 373.
 On Mid. Val.; St. Lou.-San Fran. (R. Rs.).
 —Allegany Co., Md., 865.
 On Cumb. & Penna.; West. Md. (R. Rs.).
 —(Bellingham P. O.), Norfolk Co., Mass., 800.
 On N. York, N. Hav. & Hart. (R. R.).
 —c. s., Midland Co., Mich., 8,038.
 On Mich. Cen.; Pere Marq. (R. Rs.).
 —Beaver Co, Pa., 6,007.
 On Penna.; Steub., E. Liv. & Beav. Val. Tr. (R. Rs.).
 —c. s., Midland Co., Texas, 5,484.
 On Tex. & Pac. (R. R.).
 —Simcoe Co., East, Ontario, Canada, 6,920.
 On Can. Nat.; Can. Pac. (R. Rs.).
MIDLAND CITY, Dale Co., Ala., 755.
 On Atl. Coast Line (R. R.).
MIDLAND PARK, Bergen Co., N. J., 3,638.
 On N. York, Susq. & West. (R. R.).
MIDLOTHIAN, Ellis Co., Texas, 1,168.
 On Gulf, Col. & Santa Fe; Sou. Pac. (R. Rs.).
 —Cook Co., Ill., 1,775.
 On Chi., Rk. Isl. & Pac. (R. R.).
MIDVALE, Tuscarawas Co., Ohio, 667.
 On Balt. & Ohio (R. R.).
 —Luzerne Co., Pa., 500.
 On Lac. & Wyo. Val. (El.) (R. R.).
 —Salt Lake Co., Utah, 2,451.
 On Den. & Rio Gde. West.; Un. Pac. (R. Rs.).
MIDVALLEY, Columbia Co., Pa., 900.
 On Leh. Val. (R. R.).
MIDVILLE, Burke Co., Ga., 853.
 On Cen. of Ga.; Ga. & Fla.; Statesb. Nor. (R. Rs.).
MIDWAY, Bullock Co., Ala., 710.
 On Cen. of Ga. (R. R.).
 —Crawford Co., Kans., 525.
 On St. Lou.-San Fran. (R. R.).
 —Woodford Co., Ky., 808.
 On Lou. & Nash.; Sou. (R. Rs.).
 —Washington Co., Pa., 951.
 On Penna. (R. R.).
 —Madison Co., Tex., 530.
 —Wasatch Co., Utah, 745.
MIFFLIN, Juniata Co., Pa., 913.
 On Penna. (R. R.).
MIFFLINBURG, Union Co., Pa., 1,959.
 On Penna. (R. R.).
MIFFLINTOWN, c. s., Juniata Co., Pa., 1,027.
MIFFLINVILLE, Columbia Co., Pa., 613.
MIGNON, Talladega Co., Ala., 2,407.
MIKESKA, Live Oak Co., Tex., 518.
 On Mo. Pac. (R. R.).
MILACA, c. s., Mille Lacs Co., Minn., 1,318.
 On Gt. Nor. (R. R.).
MILAM, Sabine Co., Tex., 750.
MILAN, Dodge and Telfair Cos., Ga., 630.
 On Seab. Air Line (R. R.).
 —Rock Island Co., Ill., 888.
 On Chi., Rk. Isl. & Pac.; Rk. Isl. Sou. (R. Rs.).

 —Ripley Co., Indiana, 877.
 On Balt. & Ohio (R. R.).
 —Monroe and Washtenaw Cos., Mich., 1,947.
 On Ann Arbor; Wab. (R. Rs.).
 —Chippewa Co., Minn., 548.
 On Chi., Mil., St. P. & Pac. (R. R.).
 —c. s., Sullivan Co., Mo., 2,002.
 On Chi., Burl. & Quincy; Quincy, Oma. & Kan. Cy. (R. Rs.).
 —Coos Co., N. H., 719.
 —Erie Co., Ohio, 678.
 On Wheel. & L. Erie (R. R.).
 —Gibson Co., Tenn., 3,155.
 On Ill. Cen.; Lou. & Nash. (R. Rs.).
MILANO (Milan), capital of Prov., Italy, 712,844.
Second city of Italy. One of the finest cities of Europe. The most remarkable among its public buildings are the cathedral, an imposing

NORTON & PEEL AND HIBBARD STUDIO PHOTO.

A VIEW OF THE SKYLINE OF MINNEAPOLIS, MINNESOTA, WITH ITS CONCENTRATION OF MODERN OFFICE BUILDINGS

Gothic structure, adorned with over 4,500 statues; the Church of St. Ambrose, in which the German emperors received the Lombard crown; the Palazzo del Corte, or royal palace, and the Teatro della Scala. The city is entered by ten gates, of which the Porta Orientale is the richest and most remarkable. In the Piazzi di Castello is an arena built by Napoleon I in 1806, on the model of the amphitheater at Rome. The city manufactures locomotives, machinery, silk, leather, cotton and woolen goods and automobiles. It has an active trade. Milano (ancient Mediolanum), supposed to have been founded by the Gauls, was annexed to Rome by Scipio Nascica, 191 B. C.
MILBANK, c. s., Grant Co., S. Dak., 2,549.
 On Chi., Mil., St. P. & Pac. (R. R.).
MILBRIDGE, Washington Co., Maine, 1,150.
MILBURN, Fayette Co., W. Va., 550.
 On Chesa. & Ohio (R. R.).
MILDRED, Sullivan Co., Pa., 728.
 On Leh. Val. (R. R.).
MILES, Centre Co., Pa., 600.
 —Runnels Co., Tex., 972.
 On Gulf, Colo. & Santa Fe (R. R.).
MILESBURG, Centre Co., Pa., 644.
 On Penna. (R. R.).
MILES CITY, c. s., Custer Co., Mont., 7,175.
 On Chi., Mil., St. P. & Pac.; Nor. Pac. (R. Rs.).
MILFORD, New Haven Co., Conn., 11,300.
 On N. York, N. Hav. & Hart.
A popular summer resort. Seed-raising is a leading agricultural industry.
 —Kent and Sussex Cos., Del., 3,719.
 On Penna. (R. R.).
 —Iroquois Co., Ill., 1,442.
 On Chi. & East. Ill. (R. R.).
 —Kosciusko Co., Ind., 869.
 On Cle., Cin., Chi. & St. Lou.; Winona (El.) (R. Rs.).
 —Dickinson C., Iowa, 1,062.
 On Chi., Mil., St. P. & Pac. (R. R.).
 —Penobscot Co., Maine, 900.
 On Me. Cen. (R. R.).

 —Worcester Co., Mass., 15,008.
 On Bost. & Alb.; Graf. & Upton (El.); N. York, N. Hav. & Hart (R. Rs.).
Boot and shoe factories. Granite quarries near by.
 —Oakland Co., Mich., 1,364.
 On Pere Marq. (R. R.).
 —Seward Co., Neb., 832.
 On Chi., Burl. & Quincy (R. R.).
 —Hillsborough Co., N. H., 3,000.
 On Bost. & Me. (R. R.).
 —Hunterdon Co., N. J., 933.
 On Penna. (R. R.).
 —Clermont and Hamilton Cos., Ohio, 1,915.
 On Penna. (R. R.).
 —c. s., Pike Co., Pa., 886.
 —Ellis Co., Texas, 747.
 On Mo.-Kan.-Tex.; Tex. Elec. (R. Rs.).
 —Beaver Co., Utah, 1,517.
 On Un. Pac. (R. R.).
MILFORD CENTER, Union Co., Ohio, 647.
 On Cle., Cin., Chi. & St. Lou.; Penna. (R. Rs.).
MILFORD HAVEN, Pembrokeshire, Wales, 10,116.
A seaport and fishing center.
MILIANA, Dept. of Algiers, Algeria, 13,521.
MILITARY JUNCTION, Pulaski Co., Ark., 673.
MILLAU, Dept. of Aveyron, France, 16,437.
Manufactures of kid gloves.
MILLBOURNE MILLS, Delaware Co., Pa., 525.
 On Penna. (R. R.).
MILLBRIDGE, Washington Co., Mo., 1,150.
MILLBROOK, Dutchess Co., N. Y., 1,296.
MILLBURY, Worcester Co., Mass., 6,879.
 On Bost. & Alb.; N. York, N. Hav. & Hart. (R. Rs.).
Textiles, thread, hardware.
 —Randolph Co., W. Va., 723.
 On West. Maryland (R. R.).
MILLDALE, Hartford Co., Conn., 781.
 On N. York, N. Hav. & Hart. (R. R.).
MILLEDGEVILLE, c. s., Baldwin Co., Ga., 5,534.
 On Cen. of Ga.; Ga. (R. Rs.).
 —Carroll Co., Ill., 807.
 On Chi., Burl. & Quincy (R. R.).
MILLEN, c. s., Jenkins Co., Ga., 2,527.
 On Cen. of Ga. (R. R.).
MILLER, Lawrence Co., Mo., 576.
 On St. Lou.-San Fran. (R. R.).
 —c. s., Hand Co., S. Dak., 1,468.
 On Chi. & Nor. West. (R. R.).
MILLER GROVE, Hopkins Co., Tex., 600.
MILLERS, Carroll Co., Md., 600.
 On West. Md. (R. R.).
MILLERSBURG, Bourbon Co., Ky., 770.
 On Lou. & Nash. (R. R.).
 —c. s., Holmes Co., Ohio, 2,203.
 On Penna. (R. R.).
 —Dauphin Co., Pa., 2,909.
 On Penna. (R. R.).
MILLERSTOWN, Ferry Co., Pa., 689.
 On Penna. (R. R.).
 —(Chicora P. O.), Butler Co., Pa., 1,052.

MILLERTON, Dutchess Co., N. Y., 919.
 On N. York Cen. (R. R.).
MILLETT, Nye Co., Nevada, 513.
MILL HALL, Clinton Co., Pa., 1,421.
 On Penna.; N. York Cen. (R. Rs.).
MILLHEIM, Centre Co., Pa., 659.
MILLINGTON, Tuscola Co., Mich., 678.
 On Mich. Cen. (R. R.).
 —Shelby Co., Tenn., 662.
 On Ill. Cen. (R. R.).
MILLINOCKET, Penobscot Co., Me., 5,350.
 On Bangor and Aroostook (R. R.).
In the lake region of the Penobscot River.
MILLIS, Norfolk Co., Mass., 2,098.
 On N. York, N. Hav. & Hart. (R. R.).
MILL NECK, Nassau Co., N. Y., 516.
 On Long Isl. (R. R.).
MILLPORT, Lamar Co., Ala., 714.
 On Southern (R. R.).
MILLSAP, Parker Co., Tex., 815.
 On Tex. & Pac. (R. R.).
MILLS COLLEGE, Alameda Co., Calif., 978.
MILLSTADT, St. Clair Co., Ill., 1,014.
MILLSTONE, Letcher Co., Ky., 1,000.
 On Lou. & Nash. (R. R.).
MILLTOWN, Lanier Co., Ga. See LAKELAND.
 —Crawford and Harrison Cos., Ind., 795.
 On Southern (R. R.).
 —Charlotte Co., N. B., Canada, 1,735.
 On Can. Pac. (R. R.).
 —Middlesex Co., N. J., 2,994.
 On Raritan Riv. (R. R.).
MILLVALE, Allegheny Co., Pa., 8,166.
 On Balt. & Ohio; Penna. (R. Rs.).
MILL VALLEY, Marin Co., Calif., 4,164.
 On Nor. West. Pac. (R. R.).
MILLVILLE, Bay Co., Fla., 2,020
 —Worcester Co., Mass., 1,901.
 On N. York, N. Hav. & Hart. (R. R.).
 —Cumberland Co., N. J., 14,705.
 On Penna.-Read. Seash. (R. R.).
Has important manufactures of glass and textiles.
 —Columbia Co., Pa., 666.
 On Penna. (R. R.).
MILNOR, Sargent Co., N. D., 564.
 On Nor. Pac. (R. R.).
MILO, Warren Co., Iowa, 542.
 On Chi., Burl. & Quincy (R. R.).
 —Piscataquis Co., Maine, 1,600.
 On Bangor & Aroostook (R. R.).
 —Carter Co., Okla., 550.
MILROY, Rush Co., Ind., 650.
 On Cle., Cin., Chi. & St. Lou. (R. R.).
MILTON, Sussex Co., Del., 1,130.
 On Penna. (R. R.).
 —c. s., Santa Rosa Co., Fla., 1,537.
 On Lou. & Nash. (R. R.).
 —Wayne Co., Ind., 612.
 On N. York, Chi. & St. Lou. (R. R.).
 —Van Buren Co., Iowa, 771.
 On Chi., Burl. & Quincy (R. R.).
 —Norfolk Co., Mass., 18,147.
 On N. York, N. Hav. & Hart. (R. R.).
Has granite quarries.
 —Strafford Co., N. H., 1,000.
 On Bost. & Me. (R. R.).
 —Umatilla Co., Ore., 1,576.
 On Un. Pac.; Walla Walla Val. (El.) (R. Rs.).
 —Northumberland Co., Pa., 8,552.
 On Penna.; Read. (R. Rs.).
 —Chittenden Co., Vt., 641.
 On Cen. Ver. (R. R.).
 —Pierce Co., Wash., 559.
 —Cabell Co., W. Va., 1,305.
 On Chesa. & Ohio (R. R.).
 —Rock Co., Wis., 1,128.
 On Chi., Mil., St. P. & Pac. (R. R.).
 —Halton Co., Ontario, Canada, 1,839.
 On Can. Pac.; Can. Nat. (R. Rs.).
MILTONVALE, Cloud Co., Kans., 734.
 On Atch., Topeka & Santa Fe; Union Pacific (R. Rs.).
MILWAUKEE, c. s., Milwaukee Co., Wisc., 578,249.
Situated on the western end of Lake Michigan; at the mouth of the Milwaukee River; on the Chicago & North Western, the Chicago, Milwaukee, St. Paul & Pacific, the Chicago, North Shore & Milwaukee (El.), the Grand Trunk, the Milwaukee Electric, the Minneapolis, St. Paul & Sault Ste. Marie, and the Pere Marquette railroads. It has a fine harbor and a large commerce. The manufactures are varied and extensive, the principal ones being iron and steel goods, flour, auto bodies and parts, shoes, electrical goods, furniture, printing, beer, candy, leather, packed meats, and machinery. It has extensive grain elevators. The chief public buildings are the County Courthouse, the City Hall, the Northwestern Soldiers' National Home; the Federal Building containing the post office and custom-house; the Public Library adjoining the new Civic Center, and the Municipal Auditorium; the Layton Art Gallery, and the Industrial Exposition Building. Marquette University is located here. Milwaukee was founded in 1835.
MILWAUKIE, Clackamas Co., Ore., 1,767.
 On Portland (El.); Sou. Pac. (R. Rs.).
MIMS, Brevard Co., Fla., 700.
 On Fla. East Coast (R. R.).

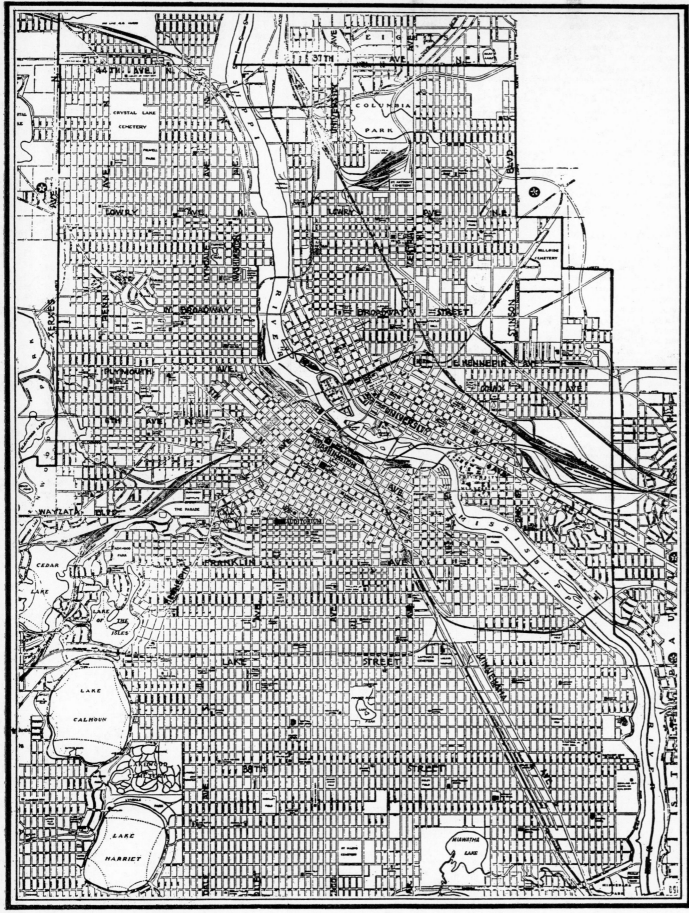

MAP OF CENTRAL MINNEAPOLIS, THE LARGEST CITY OF MINNESOTA. THE GREAT WATER POWER OF THE FALLS OF ST. ANTHONY AND THE TRANSPORTATION FACILITIES OF THE CITY HAVE MADE MINNEAPOLIS THE MOST IMPORTANT MANUFACTURING AND DISTRIBUTING CENTER OF THE NORTHWEST. THE CITY IS THE LARGEST WHEAT MARKET AND FLOUR PRODUCER OF THE COUNTRY

MINEVILLE, Essex Co., N. Y., 787.
  On L. Champ. & Moriah (R. R.).
MINGLANILLA, Cebu Prov., Cebu, P. I., 12,723.
MINGO JUNCTION, Jefferson Co., Ohio, 5,030.
  On Penna.; Pitts. & W. Va.; Wheel. & L. Erie (R. Rs.).
MINIA (Minieh), Egypt. See MINYA, EL.
MINIER, Tazewell Co., Ill., 726.
  On Alton; Pennsylvania (R. Rs.).
MINNEAPOLIS, c. s., Ottawa Co., Kans., 2,028.
  On Atch., Top. & Santa Fe; Un. Pac. (R. Rs.).
  —c. s., Hennepin Co., Minn., 464,356.
  Situated on both banks of the Mississippi River, 10 miles west by north of St. Paul. The Falls of St. Anthony are in the heart of the city. It is on the Chicago, Burlington and Quincy; the Chicago Great Western; the Chicago, St. Paul, Minneapolis and Omaha; the Great Northern; the Northern Pacific; the Chicago, Rock Island and Pacific; the Minneapolis and St. Louis; the Chicago, Milwaukee, St. Paul and Pacific; Minnesota Western; the Minneapolis, Anoka and Cuyuna Range (El.); the Minneapolis, Northfield and Southern; the Minneapolis Eastern; the Minnesota Transfer; and the Minneapolis, St. Paul and Sault Ste. Marie railroads.
  Among the more notable buildings of the city are the city hall and court-house, the Northwestern Guaranty Loan Company, the post office, the Municipal Auditorium, the Masonic Temple; Pillsbury Science Hall.
  Minneapolis is foremost in flour and lumber products. Other important industries are the manufacture of agricultural implements and machinery. The city is the seat of the University of Minnesota.
  Minneapolis was settled in 1849. It received its charter as a city in 1867.
MINNEDOSA, Marquette Co., Manitoba, Canada, 1,680.
  On Can. Pac. (R. R.).
MINNEOLA, Clark Co., Kans., 548.
  On Chi., Rk. Isl. & Pac. (R. R.).
MINNEOTA, Lyon Co., Minn., 918.
  On Chi. & Nor. West. (R. R.).
MINNEQUA, Pueblo Co., Colo., 500.
  On Colo. & Wyo.; Den. & Rio Gde. West.; Atch., Top. & Santa Fe; Colo. & Sou. (R. Rs.).
MINOA, Onondaga Co., N. Y., 899.
  On N. York Cen.; West Shore (R. Rs.).
MINOCQUA, Oneida Co., Wis., 800.
  On Chi., Mil., St. P. & Pac. (R. R.).
MINONK, Woodford Co., Ill., 1,910.
  On Atch., Top. & Santa Fe; Ill. Cen. (R. Rs.).
MINOOKA-TAYLOR, Lackawanna Co., Pa., 9,000.
  On Del. & Hud.; Cen. of N. Jer. (R. Rs.).
MINOT, c. s., Ward Co., N. Dak., 16,099.
  On Gt. Nor.; Mpls., St. P. & S. Ste. M. (R. Rs.).
  The chief trading center in the northern part of the State. Wheat, cattle, and poultry farming region.
MINOTOLA, Atlantic Co., N. J., 530.
  On Cen. of N. Jer.; Penna.-Read. Seash. (R. Rs.).
MINSK, capital of White Russia, Soviet Union, 180,900.
  Smelters, machine shops, breweries, tanneries, and paper mills.
MINSTER, Auglaize Co., Ohio, 1,381.
  On N. York, Chi. & St. Lou. (R. R.).
MINTO, Walsh Co., N. Dak., 565.
  On Gt. Nor. (R. R.).
MINYA, EL, Egypt, 34,694.
MIRANDO CITY, Webb Co., Tex., 981.
  On Tex. Mex. (R. R.).
MIRZAPUR, Dist. of Mirzapur, India, 54,904.
  Lac factories and rug makers.
MISHAWAKA, St. Joseph Co., Ind., 28,630.
  On Gd. Tr.; N. York Cen. (R. Rs.).
  Rubber goods and machinery.
MISHICOT, Manitowoc Co., Wis., 600.
MISKOLCZ, Borsod Comitat, Hungary, 62,208.
  Marketing town in a farming region.
MISSION, Hidalgo Co., Texas, 5,120.
  On Mo. Pac. (R. R.).
  In a fertile district producing garden crops and citrus fruits. Oil occurs in the region.
MISSION SAN JOSE, Alameda Co., Calif., 531.
MISSISSIPPI CITY, Harrison Co., Miss., 1,000.
  On Lou. & Nash. (R. R.).
MISSOLONGHI, Capital of Sub-Dept. of Acarnania and Aetolia, Greece, 9,270.
MISSOULA, c. s., Missoula Co., Mont., 14,657.
  On Chi., Mil., St. P. & Pac.; Nor. Pac. (R. Rs.).
  Site of University of Montana.
MISSOURI VALLEY, Harrison Co., Iowa, 4,230.
  On Chi. & Nor. West. (R. R.).
MITAU, Latvia. See JELGAVA.
MITCHELL, Lawrence Co., Ind., 3,226.
  On Balt. & Ohio; Chi., Ind. & Lou. (R. Rs.).
  —Perth Co., South, Ontario, Canada, 1,588.
  On Can. Nat. (R. R.).
  —Scotts Bluff Co., Neb., 2,058.
  On Chi., Burl. & Quincy (R. R.).
  —c. s., Davison Co., S. Dak., 12,834.
  On Chi., Mil., St. P. & Pac.; Chi., St. P., Mpls. & Oma. (R. Rs.).
  A center of the State corn region.

MINALABAC, Prov. of Camarines Sur, Luzon, P. I., 4,099.
MINAS, capital of La Valleja, Uruguay, 28,000.
  An agricultural center.
MINAS NOVAS, Brazil, 48,533.
  An important mining town.
MINATARE, Scotts Bluff Co., Neb., 1,079.
  On Chi., Burl. & Quincy (R. R.).
MINCO, Grady Co., Okla., 962.
  On Chi., Rk. Isl. & Pac. (R. R.).
MINDEN, Westphalia, Germany, 28,000.
  Beer, ships, tobacco, chocolate, leather, cement, and chemicals.
  —c. s., Webster Parish, La., 5,623.
  On La. & Ark. (R. R.).
  —c. s., Kearney Co., Neb., 1,716.

On Chi., Burl. & Quincy (R. R.).
MINDENMINES, Barton Co., Mo., 787.
  On Mo. Pac.; St. Lou.-San Fran. (R. Rs.).
MINEOLA, c. s., Nassau Co., N. Y., 8,155.
  On Long Isl. (R. R.).
  —Wood Co., Texas, 3,304.
  On Mo. Pac.; Mo.-Kan.-Tex.; Tex. & Pac. (R. Rs.).
MINERAL CITY, Tuscarawas Co., Ohio, 840.
  On Balt. & Ohio; Penna. (R. Rs.).
MINERAL POINT, Iowa Co., Wis., 2,274.
  On Chi., Mil., St. P. & Pac. (R. R.).
MINERAL RIDGE, Trumbull Co., Ohio, 1,600.
  On Erie (R. R.).
MINERAL SPRINGS, Howard Co., Ark., 712.
  On Grays., Nashv. & Ashd. (R. R.).

MINERAL WELLS, Palo Pinto Co., Texas, 5,986.
  On St. Lou.-San Fran. & Tex.; Weatherf., Min. Ws. & Northw. (R. Rs.).
MINERS MILLS, Luzerne Co., Pa., 3,000.
  On Cen. of N. Jer.; Del. & Hud.; Leh. Val. (R. Rs.).
MINERSVILLE, Schuylkill Co., Pa., 9,392.
  On Penna.; Read. (R. Rs.).
  —Beaver Co., Utah, 800.
MINERVA, Carroll and Stark Cos., Ohio, 2,675.
  On N. York Cen.; Penna.; Wheel. & L. Erie (R. Rs.).
MINERVINO MURGE, Prov. of Bari, Italy, 18,816.
  An agricultural center.
MINETTO, Oswego Co., N. Y., 750.
  On N. York, Ont. & West. (R. R.).

Mitchellville, Polk Co., Iowa, 702.
On Chi., Rk. Isl. & Pac.; Des Moines & Cen. Ia. (El.) (R. Rs.).
Mito, capital of Ibarki Prefecture, Japan, 50,647.
Paper textiles, and cigarettes.
Mittweida, Saxony, Germany, 20,000.
Has cotton spinning and weaving mills.
Mizpah, Atlantic Co., N. J., 500.
On Pa.-Reading Seashore (R. R.).
Mladá Boleslav (Jung Bunzlau), Bohemia, Germany, 19,604.
A railroad center with sugar, soap, and candle factories. The city has fine buildings and was once a center for the Bohemian Brethren.
Moab, c. s., Grand Co., Utah, 853.
Moalboal, Prov. of Cebu, Cebu, P.I., 14,959.
A marketing town.
Mobeetie, Wheeler Co., Tex., 667.
On Panh. & Santa Fe (R. R.).
Moberly, Randolph Co., Mo., 13,772.
On Mo.-Kan.-Tex.; Wab. (R. Rs.).
Mobile, c. s., Mobile Co., Ala., 68,202.
Port of entry. Situated on the Mobile River, near Mobile Bay, and on the Alabama, Tenn. and Northern; the Southern; the Louisville and Nashville; the Mobile and Ohio; and the Gulf, Mobile & Northern railroads.
The city has extensive docks and does an important export trade having regular steamship connections with Europe, Latin America, and the Orient. The principal buildings are the United States Government Building, United States Marine Hospital, City Hospital, the Battle House, Masonic Temple, Knights of Columbus Hall, and the Cathedral of the Immaculate Conception. Mobile was founded by the French in 1710.
Mobridge, Walworth Co., S. Dak., 3,425.
On Chi., Mil., St. P. & Pac. (R. R.).
Moca, Dominican Republic, 5,704.
–Mun. of Moca, Puerto Rico, 2,585.
Mocambique, capital of Mozambique (Portuguese East Africa), 6,898.
Mocksville, c. s., Davie Co., N. C., 1,503.
On Southern (R. R.).
Modena, capital of Prov. of Modena, Italy, 51,320.
Trade center of an agricultural region.
–Chester Co., Pa., 599.
On Reading (R. R.).
Modesto, c. s., Stanislaus Co., Cal., 13,842.
On Sou. Pac.; Tidew. Sou.; Modesto & Emp. (El.) (R. Rs.).
Situated in a great irrigation project. Dairy products, poultry and fruit raising. Has a fine airport.
Modica, Prov. of Raguso, Sicily, 55,817.
Has interesting caves.
Mödling, Lower Austria, 18,736.
A popular summer resort.
Mogadiscio, capital of Italian Somaliland, 20,501.
Seaport and leading commercial town.
Mogador, Morocco, 14,491.
A seaport and market center.
Mogadore, Portage and Summit Cos., Ohio, 1,502.
On Wheel. & L. Erie; Ak., Can. & Youngst. (R. Rs.).
Mogilev, White Russia, Soviet Union, 58,100.
A trade and industrial center in a fertile farming region.
Mohall, c. s., Renville Co., N. Dak., 676.
On Gt. Nor. (R. R.).
Mohawk, Herkimer Co., N. Y., 2,835.
On West Shore (R. R.).
Mohnton, Berks Co., Pa., 1,824.
Mohrland, Emery Co., Utah, 512.
On Utah (R. R.).
Mojave, Kern Co., Calif., 750.
On Atch., Top. & Santa Fe; Sou. Pac. (R. R.).
Moji, Ken of Fukuoka, Japan, 108,127.
Located in a coal-mining region.
Mokane, Callaway Co., Mo., 575.
On Mo.-Kan.-Tex. (R. R.).
Mokena, Will Co., Ill., 562.
On Chi., Rk. Isl. & Pac. (R. R.).
Molalla, Clackamas Co., Ore., 655.
On Sou. Pac. (R. R.).
Molenbeek, suburb of Bruxelles, Belgium, 67,410.
Molfetta, Prov. of Bari, Italy, 45,407.
Has interesting neolithic ruins.
Molina, Prov. of Talca, Chile, 4,541.
Moline, Rock Island Co., Ill., 32,236.
On Chi., Burl. & Quincy; Chi., Mil., St. P. & Pac.; Chi., Rk. Isl. & Pac.; Davenp., Rk. Isl. & Northw. (R. Rs.).
Noted as the premier farm implement manufacturing center. East of the city are the Rock Island railroad plants.
–Elk Co., Kans., 901.
On Atch., Top. & Santa Fe (R. R.).
Mollenauer, Allegheny Co., Pa., 700.
Mombasa, Kenya, 18,800.
Leading seaport and commercial center.
Momence, Kankakee Co., Ill., 2,236.
On Chi. & East. Ill.; N. York Cen.; Chi., Mil., St. P. & Pac. (R. Rs.).
Monaca, Beaver Co., Pa., 4,641.
On Pitts. & L. Erie (R. R.).
Monaco, principality of Monaco, within Dept. of Alpes-Maritimes, France, 2,020.
Monaco forms the larger part of the Principality of Monaco, the smallest state in Europe; on Monaco Bay opposite Monte Carlo.
Monahans, Ward Co., Tex., 816.
On Tex. & Pac.; Tex.-N. Mex. (R. Rs.).
Monarch, Fayette Co., Pa., 700.
–Sheridan Co., Wyo., 500.
On Chi., Burl. & Quincy (R. R.).
Monastir, Yugoslavia. See Bitolj.
Moncada, Prov. of Tarlac, Luzon, P. I., 10,503.
Moncks Corner, c. s., Berkeley Co., S. C., 623.
On Atl. Coast Line (R. R.).
Monclo, Logan Co., W. Va., 620.
On Chesa. & Ohio (R. R.).
Monclova, State of Coahuila, Mexico, 6,877.
On Nat. of Mex. (R. R.).
Moncton, Westmoreland Co., N. B., Canada, 20,689.
On Can. Nat. (R. R.).
Stoves, engines, boilers, and lumber mills.
Mondamin, Harrison Co., Iowa, 534.
On Chi. & Nor. West. (R. R.).
Mondovi, Buffalo Co., Wis., 1,623.
On Chi., St. P., Mpls. & Oma. (R. R.).
Monessen, Westmoreland Co., Pa., 20,268.
On Pitts. & L. Erie; Pitts. & W. Va. (R. Rs.).
An industrial city about thirty miles south of Pittsburgh. It manufactures steel, tin plate, wire fencing and other metal products.
Monett, Barry Co., Mo., 4,099.
On St. Lou.-San Fran. (R. R.).
Monette, Craighead Co., Ark., 1,111.
On St. Lou.-San Fran. (R. R.).
Monghyr, capital of Monghyr Dist., Bihar, India, 52,863.
Chief manufacture is cigarettes.
Mongtse, Yünnan, China. See Mengtsz.
Monkton, Addison Co., Vt., 683.
Monmouth, c. s., Warren Co., Ill., 8,666.
On Chi., Burl. & Quincy; Mpls. & St. Lou.; Rk. Isl. Sou. (R. Rs.).
–Kennebec Co., Maine, 500.
On Me. Cen. (R. R.).
–Polk Co., Ore., 906.
Monmouth Junction, Middlesex Co., N. J., 500.
On Penna. (R. R.).
Monon, White Co., Ind., 1,374.
On Chi., Ind. & Lou. (R. R.).
Monona, Clayton Co., Iowa, 1,163.
On Chi., Mil., St. P. & Pac. (R. R.).
Monongah, Marion Co., W. Va., 1,909.
On Balt. & Ohio (R. R.).
Adjacent to large coal mines. A coke manufacturing center.
Monongahela, Washington Co., Pa., 8,675.
On Penna.; Pitts. & L. Erie (R. Rs.).
Monopoli, Prov. of Bari, Italy, 14,884.
Textiles, wine, and olives.
Monreale, Prov. of Palermo, Italy, 16,486.
Oranges, olives, and almonds raised near by.
Monroe, Fairfield Co., Conn., 1,221.
On N. York, N. Hav. & Hart. (R. R.).
–c. s., Walton Co., Ga., 3,706.
On Georgia; Gainesv. Midland; Greene Co. (R. Rs.).
–Jasper Co., Iowa, 936.
On Chi., Rk. Isl. & Pac. (R. R.).
–c. s., Ouachita Parish, La., 26,028.
On Ark. & La. Mo.; La. & Pine Bluff; Mo. Pac.; Ill. Cen. (R. Rs.).
Center of the world's largest gas field. Manufactures pulp and paper, ink, brick, and lumber.
–Waldo Co., Maine, 650.
–c. s., Monroe Co., Mich., 18,110.
On Det. & Tol. Sh. Line; Penna.; Mich. Cen.; Pere Marq.; N. York Cen. (R. Rs.).
–Orange Co., N. Y., 1,621.
On Erie (R. R.).
–c. s., Union Co., N. C., 6,100.
On Seab. Air Line (R. R.).
–Fayette Co., Pa., 622.
–Sevier Co., Utah, 1,247.
–Snohomish Co., Wash., 1,570.
On Gt. Nor.; Chi., Mil., St. P. & Pac. (R. Rs.).
–c. s., Green Co., Wis., 5,015.
On Chi., Mil., St. P. & Pac.; Ill. Cen. (R. Rs.).
Center of cheese industry.
Monroe-Cedar Knoll, Morris Co., N. J., 650.
On Morrist. & Erie (R. R.).
Monroe City, Knox Co., Ind., 544.
–Monroe & Marion Cos., Mo., 1,820.
On Chi., Burl. & Quincy; Wab. (R. Rs.).
Monroe Hall, Westmoreland Co., Va., 518.
Monroeton, Bradford Co., Pa., 500.
On Leh. Val.; Susq. & N. York (R. Rs.).
Monroeville, c. s., Monroe Co., Ala., 1,355.
On Man. & Rept. (R. R.).
–Allen Co., Ind., 897.
On Penna. (R. R.).
–Huron Co., Ohio, 1,080.
On Balt. & Ohio; N. York Cen.; Wheel. & L. Erie (R. Rs.).
Monrovia, Los Angeles Co., Cal., 10,890.
On Atch., Top. & Santa Fe; Pac. El.; Sou. Pac. (R. Rs.).
–Capital of Republic of Liberia, 10,000.
Mons, capital of Hainaut, Belgium, 27,719.
Scene of heavy fighting in the early stages of the Great War of 1914-18.
Monsey, Rockland Co., N. Y., 500.
On Erie (R. R.).
Monson, Piscataquis Co., Maine, 1,070.
On Monson (R. R.).
–Hampden Co., Mass., 5,193.
On Cen. Ver. (R. R.).
Montagnana, Prov. of Padova, Italy, 7,871.
Montague, Siskiyou Co., Calif., 507.
On Sou. Pac.; Yreka (R. Rs.).
–Franklin Co., Mass., 7,967.
On Bost. & Me. (R. R.).
–(Whitehall-Montague), Muskegon Co., Mich., 887.
On Pere Marq. (R. R.).
Montague City, Franklin Co., Mass., 635.
On N. York, N. Hav. & Hart. (R. R.).
Mont Alto, Franklin Co., Pa., 606.
On Penna. (R. R.).
Montauban, Dept. of Tarn-et-Garonne, France, 32,025.
It was a fortress of the Huguenots.

COURTESY OF THE CANADIAN PACIFIC RAILWAYS
WINDSOR STATION, A LANDMARK IN MONTREAL, CANADA. BESIDE THE STATION STANDS ST. GEORGES AND ON THE LEFT ST. JAMES CATHEDRAL

Montauk, Suffolk Co., N. Y., 608.
On Long Isl. (R. R.).
Montceau-les-Mines, Dept. of Saône-et-Loire, France, 26,902.
The center of the Blanzy Coal Basin. Textile mills, foundries, and machine shops.
Montclair, Essex Co., N. J., 42,017.
On Del., Lack. & West.; Erie (R. Rs.).
A residential suburb of New York.
Mont Clare, Montgomery Co., Pa., 900.
On Penna. (R. R.).
Montdidier, Dept. of Somme, France, 4,706.
Taken from Germans by French in August, 1918. Almost destroyed.
Monteagle, Grundy Co., Tenn., 1,000.
On Nash., Chatt. & St. Lou. (R. R.).
Montebello, Los Angeles Co., Cal., 5,498.
On Un. Pac. (R. R.).
Monte Carlo, Principality of Monaco, France, 9,428.
Noted for its gaming tables.
Montello, c. s., Marquette Co., Wis., 1,245.
On Mpls., St. P. & S. Ste. M. (R. R.).
Monterey, Monterey Co., Cal., 9,141.
On Sou. Pac. (R. R.).
–Putnam Co., Tenn., 1,731.
On Tenn. Cen. (R. R.).
Monterey Park, Los Angeles Co., Cal., 6,406.
A residential suburb of Los Angeles.
Monte Rio, Sonoma Co., Calif., 500.
Monterrey, capital of Nuevo Leon, Mexico, 132,577.
On Nat. of Mex. (R. R.).
A distribution and trade center for a ranching region.
Montesano, c. s., Grays Harbor Co., Wash., 2,460.
On Nor. Pac.; Un. Pac.; Chi., Mil., St. P. & Pac. (R. Rs.).
Montevallo, Shelby Co., Ala., 1,245.
On Southern (R. R.).
Montevideo, capital of Uruguay, 674,000.
Chief port and commercial center. Exports meat, hides, wheat, corn and flour. Has beautiful suburbs and a fine university.
–c. s., Chippewa Co., Minn., 4,319.
On Chi., Mil., St. P. & Pac. (R. R.).
Monte Vista, Rio Grande Co., Colo., 2,610.
On Den. & Rio Gde. West.; San Luis Cen. (R. Rs.).
Montezuma, Macon Co., Ga., 2,284.
On Atla., Birm. & Coast; Cen. of Ga. (R. Rs.).
–Parke Co., Ind., 1,292.
On Balt. & Ohio (R. R.).
–c. s., Poweshiek Co., Iowa, 1,257.
On Chi., Rk. Isl. & Pac.; Minn. & St. Lou. (R. Rs.).
Montfort, Grant Co., Wis., 554.
On Chi. & Nor. West. (R. R.).
Montgomery, c. s., Montgomery Co., Ala. State capital, 66,079.
Situated on the Alabama River, and on the Louisville and Nashville; the Belt Line; the Western of Alabama; Central of Georgia; Seaboard Air Line; Atlantic Coast Line; Mobile and Ohio railroads.
Owing to its accessibility to timber, and deposits of coal and iron is an important commercial center, and shipping point for cotton. Its leading industries include textiles, railroad repairs, fertilizer, lumber, and woodworking products.
Montgomery was founded in 1817 and was chartered in 1837. Montgomery was made State capital in 1847.
–Kane Co., Ill., 546.
On Chi., Burl. & Quincy (R. R.).
–Le Sueur Co., Minn., 1,570.
On Chi., Mil., St. P. & Pac.; Mpls. & St. Lou. (R. Rs.).
–Orange Co., N. Y., 884.
On Erie; West Shore (R. Rs.).
–Lycoming Co., Pa., 1,903.
On Penna.; Read. (R. Rs.).
–Fayette and Kanawha Cos., W. Va., 2,906.
On Chesa. & Ohio (R. R.).
–Franklin Co., Vt., 1,386.
Montgomery City, c. s., Montgomery Co., Mo., 1,510.
On Wab. (R. R.).
Monticello, c. s., Drew Co., Ark., 3,076.
On Mo. Pac.; Ash., Drew & Nor. (R. Rs.).
Seat of State Agricultural and Mechanical College.
–c. s., Jefferson Co., Fla., 2,042.
On Atl. Coast Line; Seab. Air Line (R. Rs.).
–c. s., Jasper Co., Ga., 1,593.
On Cen. of Ga. (R. R.).
–c. s., Piatt Co., Ill., 2,378.
On Ill. Cen.; Ill. Term. (El.); Wab. (R. Rs.).
–c. s., White Co., Ind., 2,331.
On Chi., Ind. & Lou.; Penna. (R. Rs.).
–Jones Co., Iowa, 2,259.
On Chi., Mil., St. P. & Pac. (R. R.).
–c. s., Wayne Co., Ky., 1,503.
–c. s., Aroostook Co., Maine, 1,000.
On Bangor & Aroostook (R. R.).
–Wright Co., Minn., 924.
On Gt. Nor. (R. R.).
–c. s., Lawrence Co., Miss., 606.
On Gulf, Mob. & Nor. (R. R.).
–c. s., Sullivan Co., N. Y., 3,450.
On N. York, Ont. & West. (R. R.).
–Green Co., Wis., 644.
On Chi., Mil., St. P. & Pac.; Ill. Cen. (R. Rs.).
Montlucon, Dept. of Allier, France, 42,515.
Glass, chemicals, machinery, pottery, stone, textiles, and rubber goods. Coal mines near by.
Montmagny, Montmagny Co., Quebec, Canada, 3,927.
On Can. Nat. (R. R.).
Montoro, Cordova, Spain, 18,140.
Olive oil and timber.

Montour Falls, Schuyler Co., N. Y., 1,489.
On Penna. (R. R.).
Montoursville, Lycoming Co., Pa., 2,710.
On Reading (R. R.).
Montpelier, Bear Lake Co., Idaho, 2,436.
On Un. Pac. (R. R.).
–Blackford Co., Ind., 1,859.
On Ind. R. R. Sys. (El.); N. York, Chi. & St. Lou. (R. Rs.).
Williams Co., Ohio, 3,677.
On Wabash (R. R.).
–c. s., Washington Co., Vt., State capital, 7,837.
On Winooski River, and on Central Vermont and Montpelier & Wells River railroads.
The principal industry is quarrying granite. The town was made the State capital in 1805.
Montpellier, Dept. of Hérault, France, 90,787.
Has considerable trade in wine, brandy and fruit. Manufactures include chemicals, cooperage, and soap.
Montreal, Prov. of Quebec, Canada, 818,578.
Situated on an island of the same name, in the Province of Quebec, at the head of ocean navigation on the St. Lawrence River. It is on the Canadian National; Canadian Pacific; New York Central; Delaware & Hudson; Montreal & Southern Counties; and Rutland Railroads. The twin towers of the Roman Catholic Church of Notre Dame, built 1824-29, are 227 feet high, in one of them is one of the largest bells on the continent, the "Gros Bourdon," 24,780 pounds. The Roman Catholic Cathedral of St. James is modeled after St. Peter's at Rome. There are about 100 churches in Montreal, the oldest being Notre Dame de Bonsecours (1771). Among its educational institutions are McGill University; a branch of Laval University, Quebec; the medical school of Bishop's College University; St. Mary's College and the Seminary of St. Sulpice.
In 1535 Jacques Cartier found here an Indian village named Hoche-laga. In 1642 the city named Ville Marie de Montreal, was laid out as a missionary center. In 1760 it was taken by the English, and during our Revolutionary War by an American expedition.
–(Hamilton), Iron Co., Wis., 1,819.
Montreuil-sous-Bois, Seine, France, 71,803.
An industrial suburb of Paris.
Montrose, c. s., Montrose Co., Colo., 3,566.
On Den. & Rio Gde. West. (R. R.).
–Lee Co., Iowa, 621.
On Chi., Burl. & Quincy (R. R.).
–Natchitoches Par., La., 500.
On Tex. & Pac. (R. R.).
–Genesee Co., Mich., 621.
On Gr. Tr. (R. R.).
–Henry Co., Mo., 531.
On Mo.-Kan.-Tex. (R. R.).
–c. s., Susquehanna Co., Pa., 1,909.
On Del., Lack. & West.; Leh. Val. (R. Rs.).
–McCook Co., S. Dak., 564.
On Chi., Mil., St. P. & Pac. (R. R.).
–Forfar Co., Scotland, 11,889.
Montrouge, Seine, France, 33,260.
Mont St. Amand, E. Flanders, Belgium, 17,754.
Montvale, Bergen Co., N. J., 1,243.
On N. Jer. & N. York (R. R.).
Montville, Waldo Co., Maine, 664.
–New London Co., Conn., 3,970.
On Cen. Ver. (R. R.).
–Morris Co., N. J., 900.
On Del., Lack. & West. (R. R.).
Monument Beach, Barnstable Co., Mass., 500.
On N. York, N. Hav. & Hart. (R. R.).
Monza, Prov. of Milano, Italy, 37,388.
Moody, McLennan Co., Texas, 1,014.
On Gulf, Colo. & Santa Fe (R. R.).
Moonachie, Bergen Co., N. J., 1,465.
On N. Jer. & N. York (R. R.).
Moore, Cleveland Co., Okla., 538.
On Atch., Top. & Santa Fe; Okla. El. (R. Rs.).
–(Prospect Park), Delaware Co., Pa., 4,623.
On Penna. (R. R.).
–Frio Co., Tex., 575.
On Mo. Pac. (R. R.).
Moorefield, c. s., Hardy Co., W. Va., 734.
On Balt. & Ohio (R. R.).
Moore Haven, c. s., Glades Co., Fla., 751.
On Atl. Coast Line (R. R.).
Mooreland, Woodward Co., Okla., 706.
On Atch., Top. & Santa Fe (R. R.).
Moorestown, Burlington Co., N. J., 6,500.
On Penna. (R. R.).
Mooresville, Morgan Co., Ind., 1,910.
On Penna. (R. R.).
–Iredell Co., N. C., 5,619.
On Southern (R. R.).
Moorhead, c. s., Clay Co., Minn., 7,651.
On Gt. Nor.; Nor. Pac. (R. Rs.).
Seat of State Normal School.
–Sunflower Co., Miss., 1,553.
On Ill. Cen.; Col. & Greenv. (R. Rs).
Mooringsport, Caddo Parish, La., 802.
On Kan. Cy. Sou. (R. R.).
Moorpark, Ventura Co., Calif., 500.
On Sou. Pac. (R. R.).
Moose Jaw, Moosejaw Co., Saskatchewan, Canada, 19,805.
On Can. Pac.; Can. Nat. (R. Rs.).
Lumber, flour, and farm machinery.
Moose Lake, Carlton Co., Minn., 742.
On Mpls., St. P. & S. Ste. M.; N. Pac. (R. Rs.).
Moosic, Lackawanna Co., Pa., 4,557.
On Cen. of N. Jer.; Del. & Hud.; Lack. & Wyo. Val. (El.); Wilk.-Bar. & East. (Erie) (R. Rs.).
Moosomin, Qu'Appelle Co., Saskatchewan, Canada, 1,119.
On Can. Pac. (R. R.).
Moosup, Windham Co., Conn., 3,481.
On N. York, N. Hav. & Hart. (R. R.).
Mora, c. s., Kanabec Co., Minn., 1,014.
On Gt. Nor. (R. R.).
–c. s., Mora Co., N. Mex., 1,000.
Moradabad, United Provinces, British India, 110,562.
Has manufactures of cotton weaving, printing and making ornamental brassware.
Moran, Portage Co., Ohio, 500.
On Wheel. & L. Erie (R. R.).
–Allen Co., Kans., 612.
On Mo.-Kan.-Tex.; Mo. Pac. (R. Rs.).
–Shackelford Co., Texas, 907.
On Mo.-Kan.-Tex. of Tex. (R. R.).
Moratalla, Prov. of Murcia, Spain, 13,412.
In a wine and olive oil producing district.
Moravia, Appanoose Co., Iowa, 684.
On Chi., Mil., St. P. & Pac.; Ia. Sou. Utilities (El.); Wab. (R. Rs.).
–Cayuga Co., N. Y., 1,295.
On Leh. Val. (R. R.).
Moravská Ostrava, Silesia, Czechoslovakia, 125,-347.
An important industrial center with iron and steel works. Coal is mined in the vicinity.
Morden, Lisgar Co., Manitoba, Canada, 1,416.
On Can. Pac.; Gt. Nor. (R. Rs.).
Morea Colliery, Schuylkill Co., Pa., 850.
On Lehigh Val. (R. R.).
Moreauville, Avoyelles Parish, La., 600.
On La. & Ark.; Tex. & Pac. (R. Rs.).
Morehead, c. s., Rowan Co., Ky., 825.
On Chesa. & Ohio; Morehead & Nor. Fk. (R. Rs.).
Morehead City, Carteret Co., N. C., 3,483.
On Atl. & Nor. Car.; Beauf. & Morehead (R. Rs.).
Morehouse, New Madrid Co., Mo., 1,165.
On Mo. Pac.; St. Lou.-San Fran. (R. Rs.).
Morelia, capital of State of Michoacán, Mexico, 39,916.
On Nat. of Mex. (R. R.).
A manufacturing and educational center. Chief products are textiles, tobacco, and candies.
Morenci, Greenlee Co., Ariz., 1,500.
–Lenawee Co., Mich., 1,773.
On N. York Cen.; Ohio & Mor. (El.) (R. Rs.).
Morewood, Westmoreland Co., Pa., 500.
A coke works.
Morgan, Redwood Co., Minn., 640.
On Chi. & Nor. West. (R. R.).
–Allegheny Co., Pa., 1,000.
On Penna. (R. R.).
–Bosque Co., Texas, 509.
On Gulf, Colo. & Santa Fe; Mo.-Kan.-Tex. (R. Rs.).
–c. s., Morgan Co., Utah, 953.
On Un. Pac. (R. R.).
Morgan City, St. Mary Parish, La., 5,985.
On Sou. Pac. (R. R.).
Morganfield, c. s., Union Co., Ky., 2,551.
On Ill. Cen.; Lou. & Nash. (R. Rs.).
Morgan Hill, Santa Clara Co., Cal., 908.
On Sou. Pac. (R. R.).
Morgan Park, Cook Co., Ill. (Sta. Chicago P. O.).
On Balt. & Ohio Chi. Term.; Chi., Rk. Isl. & Pac. (R. Rs.).
Morganton, c. s., Burke Co., N. C., 6,001.
On Southern (R. R.).
Morgantown, c. s., Butler Co., Ky., 551.
–Morgan Co., Ind., 748.
On Cle., Cin., Chi. & St. Lou.; Ill. Cen. (R. Rs.).
–c. s., Monongalia Co., W. Va., 16,186.
On Balt. & Ohio; Monong. (R. Rs.).
Morganza, Pointe Coupee Par., La., 608.
On Tex. & Pac. (R. R.).
Moriah, Essex Co., N. Y., 500.
Morioka, Ken of Iwate, Japan, 62,255.
A commercial and marketing town in northern Japan.
Morlaix, Dept. of Finistère, France, 13,944.
Morley, Yorkshire, England, 23,397.
A suburb of Leeds.
–Las Animas Co., Colo., 600.
On Atch., Top. & Santa Fe (R. R.).
Morningside, Hennepin Co., Minn., 903.
Morning Sun, Louisa Co., Iowa, 856.
On Chi., Rk. Isl. & Pac.; Mpls. & St. Lou. (R. Rs.).
Morocco, Newton Co., Ind., 1,006.
On Chi., Attica & Sou.; N. York Cen. (R. Rs.).
Moron, Prov. of Moron, Cuba, 9,650.
Moroni, Sanpete Co., Utah, 1,218.
On Den. & Rio Gde. West. (R. R.).
Morovis, Mun. of Morovis, Puerto Rico, 2,013.
Morrill, Brown Co., Kansas, 535.
On Un. Pac. (R. R.).
–Scotts Bluff Co., Neb., 756.
On Chi., Burl. & Quincy (R. R.).
Morrillton, c. s., Conway Co., Ark., 4,043.
On Mo. Pac. (R. R.).
Morris, c. s., Grundy Co., Ill., 5,568.
On Chi., Rk. Isl. & Pac.; Fox & Ill. Un. (El.) (R. Rs.).
–c. s., Stevens Co., Minn., 2,474.
On Gt. Nor.; Nor. Pac. (R. Rs.).
–Otsego Co., N. Y., 554.
–Okmulgee Co., Okla., 1,706.
On St. Lou.-San Fran. (R. R.).
Morrisburg, Dundas Co., Ont., Can., 1,420.
On Can. Nat. (R. R.).
Morrison, c. s., Whiteside Co., Ill., 3,067.
On Chi. & Nor. West. (R. R.).
–Warwick Co., Va., 521.
On Chesa. & Ohio (R. R.).
Morrisonville, Christian Co., Ill., 968.
On Wabash (R. R.).
–Clinton Co., N. Y., 750.
On Del. & Hud. (R. R.).
Morris Plains, Morris Co., N. J., 1,713.
On Del., Lack. & West. (R. R.).
Morris Run, Tioga Co., Pa., 2,352.
On Erie; N. York Cen. (R. Rs.).
Morristown, Shelby Co., Ind., 608.
On Balt. & Ohio; Erie (R. Rs.).
–Rice Co., Minn., 613.
On Chi. Gt. West. (R. R.).
–c. s., Morris Co., N. J., 15,197.
On Del., Lack. & West.; Morrist. & Erie (R. Rs.).
A trading center and beautiful residential town with historic sites and buildings, some of which are included in Morristown National Monument (established in 1933).
–St. Lawrence Co., N. Y., 505.
On N. York Cen. (R. R.).
–c. s., Hamblen Co., Tenn., 7,305.
On Southern (R. R.).
Morrisville, Madison Co., N. Y., 583.
–Bucks Co., Pa., 5,368.
On Penna. (R. R.).
–Lamoille Co., Vt., 1,822.
On St. Johns. & L. Champ. (R. R.).
Morro Bay, San Luis Obispo Co., Calif., 800.
Morrow, Clayton Co., Ga., 500.
On Cen. of Ga. (R. R.).
–Warren Co., Ohio, 738.
On Penna. (R. R.).
Morse, Acadia Par., La., 549.
On Sou. Pac. (R. R.).
Morton, Tazewell Co., Ill., 1,501.
On Atch., Top. & Santa Fe; Ill. Term. (El.); Penna. (R. Rs.).
–Renville Co., Minn., 756.
On Mpls. & St. Lou. (R. R.).
–Scott Co., Miss., 955.
On Ill. Cen. (R. R.).
–Delaware Co., Pa., 1,341.
On Penna. (R. R.).
–c. s., Cochran Co., Tex., 725.
Morton Grove, Cook Co., Ill., 1,974.
On Chi., Mil., St. P. & Pac. (R. R.).
Morton's Gap, Hopkins Co., Ky., 1,068.
On Lou. & Nash. (R. R.).
Morven, Anson Co., N. C., 590.
On Atl. Coast Line (R. R.).
Moscow, Soviet Union. See Moskva.
–c. s., Latah Co., Idaho, 4,476.
On Gt. Nor.; Nor. Pac.; Un. Pac. (R. Rs.).
Seat of the University of Idaho, a state coeducational institution.
–Hillsdale Co., Mich., 788.
–Lackawanna Co., Pa., 892.
On Del., Lack. & West. (R. R.).
Mosinee, Marathon Co., Wis., 1,229.
On Chi., Mil., St. P. & Pac. (R. R.).
Moskva (Moscow), capital of the Soviet Union, 3,663,300.
Situated on the Moskva River. The Kremlin (formerly containing the Czar's palace, palaces of the nobility, and many cathedrals) forms the center of the city. Within its walls are now many political bureaus, the most important of which are the Council of People's Commissars, the Central Executive Committee of the Soviet Union and the All-Russian Central Executive Committee. In the Red Square adjoining the Kremlin is Lenin's mausoleum of black basalt. The city is now being systematically beautified; many new public structures are planned, among them the Palace of the Soviets, which is to be surmounted by a huge statue of Lenin. Moskva abounds in museums and libraries. The Lenin State Public Library, containing about 3,000,000 volumes, is one of the largest in the world. Moskva's subway, recently completed, is considered superior to any other in the world. The city dates from 1147. It became the capital of Muscovy and afterwards of the whole Russian Empire but was deprived of this honor in 1703, when St. Petersburg (now Leningrad) was founded. Moskva became the capital of the Soviet Union after the Revolution of 1917.
Mossamedes, Angola, 10,578.
Mossley, Lancashire, England, 12,041.
Moss Point, Jackson Co., Miss., 2,453.
On Miss. Exp. (R. R.).
Mostaganem, Oran, Algeria, 38,555.
A marketing center.
Mosul, Iraq, Asia, 100,000.
The center of a great petroleum region.
Motherwell, Lanark Co., Scotland, 64,708.
Has large iron and steel works.
Mott, c. s., Hettinger Co., N. Dak., 1,036.
On Chi., Mil., St. P. & Pac.; Nor. Pac. (R. Rs.).
Mottville, Onondaga Co., N. Y., 500.
On Skaneateles (R. R.).
Moulins, Dept. of Allier, France, 22,365.
A commercial center. Produces beer, textiles, chemicals, and furniture.
Moulmein, Lower Burma, India, 61,301.
Seaport, shipping point, rice and teakwood.
Moulton, c. s., Lawrence Co., Ala., 639.
–Appanoose Co., Iowa, 1,476.
On Chi., Burl. & Quincy; Wab. (R. Rs.).
–Lavaca Co., Tex., 850.
On Sou. Pac. (R. R.).
Moultrie, St. Johns Co., Fla., 500.
On Fla. East Coast (R. R.).
–c. s., Colquitt Co., Ga., 8,027.
On Atla., Birm. & Coast; Ga. Nor.; Ga. & Fla. (R. Rs.).
Moultrieville, Charleston Co., S. C., 515.
Mound, Hennepin Co., Minn., 668.
On Gt. Nor. (R. R.).
Mound Bayou, Bolivar Co., Miss., 834.
On Ill. Cen. (R. R.).
Mound City, c. s., Pulaski Co., Ill., 2,548.
On Cle., Cin., Chi. & St. Lou.; Ill. Cen. (R. Rs.).
–c. s., Linn Co., Kans., 771.
On Mo. Pac. (R. R.).
–Holt Co., Mo., 1,525.
On Chi., Burl. & Quincy (R. R.).
Moundridge, McPherson Co., Kans., 854.
On Mo. Pac. (R. R.).
Mounds, Pulaski Co., Ill., 2,129.
On Ill. Cen. (R. R.).
–Creek Co., Okla., 740.
On St. Lou.-San Fran. (R. R.).
Moundsville, c. s., Marshall Co., W. Va., 14,-411.
On Balt. & Ohio (R. R.).
A coal-mining center. Has manufactures of glass, zinc, and airplanes.
Mound Valley, Labette Co., Kans., 658.
On Mo.-Kan.-Tex.; St. Lou.-San Fran. (R. Rs.).
Moundville, Hale Co., Ala., 757.
On Ala. Gt. Sou. (R. R.).
Mountainair, Torrance Co., N. Mexico, 1,027.
On Atch., Top. & Santa Fe (R. R.).
Mountain Ash, Whitley Co., Ky., 500.
On Lou. & Nash. (R. R.).
Mountain City, c. s., Johnson Co., Tenn., 1,058.
On Southern (R. R.).
Mountain Grove, Wright Co., Mo., 2,229.
On St. Lou.-San Fran. (R. R.).
Mountain Home, c. s., Baxter Co., Ark., 585.
–c. s., Elmore Co., Idaho, 1,243.
On Un. Pac. (R. R.).
Mountain Iron, St. Louis Co., Minn., 1,349.
On Dul., Missabe & Nor. (R. R.).
Mountain Lake, Cottonwood Co., Minn., 1,388.
On Chi., St. P., Minn. & Oma. (R. R.).
Mountain Lakes, Morris Co., N. J., 2,132.
On Del., Lack. & West. (R. R.).
Mountain Pine, Garland Co., Ark., 1,000.
On Mo. Pac. (R. R.).
Mountainside, Union Co., N. J., 965.
Mountain View, Santa Clara Co., Cal., 3,308.
On Sou. Pac. (R. R.).
–Jefferson Co., Colo., 664.
–Howell Co., Mo., 783.
On St. Lou.-San Fran. (R. R.).
–Kiowa Co., Okla., 1,025.
On Chi., Rk. Isl. & Pac. (R. R.).
Mountainview, Carroll Co., N. H., 500.
On Bost. & Me. (R. R.).
Mount Airy, Frederick and Carroll Cos., Md., 860.
On Balt. & Ohio (R. R.).
–Surry Co., N. C., 6,045.
On Atl. & Yadk. (R. R.).
Mount Angel, Marion Co., Ore., 979.
On Sou. Pac. (R. R.).
Mount Ayr, c. s., Ringgold Co., Iowa, 1,704.
On Chi., Burl. & Quincy (R. R.).
Mount Bethel, Somerset Co., N. J., 500.
Mount Braddock, Fayette Co., Pa., 800.
On Balt. & Ohio (R. R.).
Mount Calm, Hill Co., Texas, 603.
On St. Lou. Southw. of Tex. (R. R.).
Mount Calvary, Fond du Lac Co., Wis., 500.
Mount Carmel, New Haven Co., Conn., 603.
On N. York, N. Hav. & Hart. (R. R.).
–c. s., Wabash Co., Ill., 7,132.
On Cle., Cin., Chi. & St. Lou.; Sou. (R. Rs.).
–Northumberland Co., Pa., 17,967.
On Leh. Val.; Penna.; Read. (R. Rs.).
Among anthracite mines.
Mount Carroll, c. s., Carroll Co., Ill., 1,775.
On Chi., Mil., St. P. & Pac. (R. R.).
Mount Claire, Macoupin Co., Ill., 650.
Mount Clare, Harrison Co., W. Va., 522.

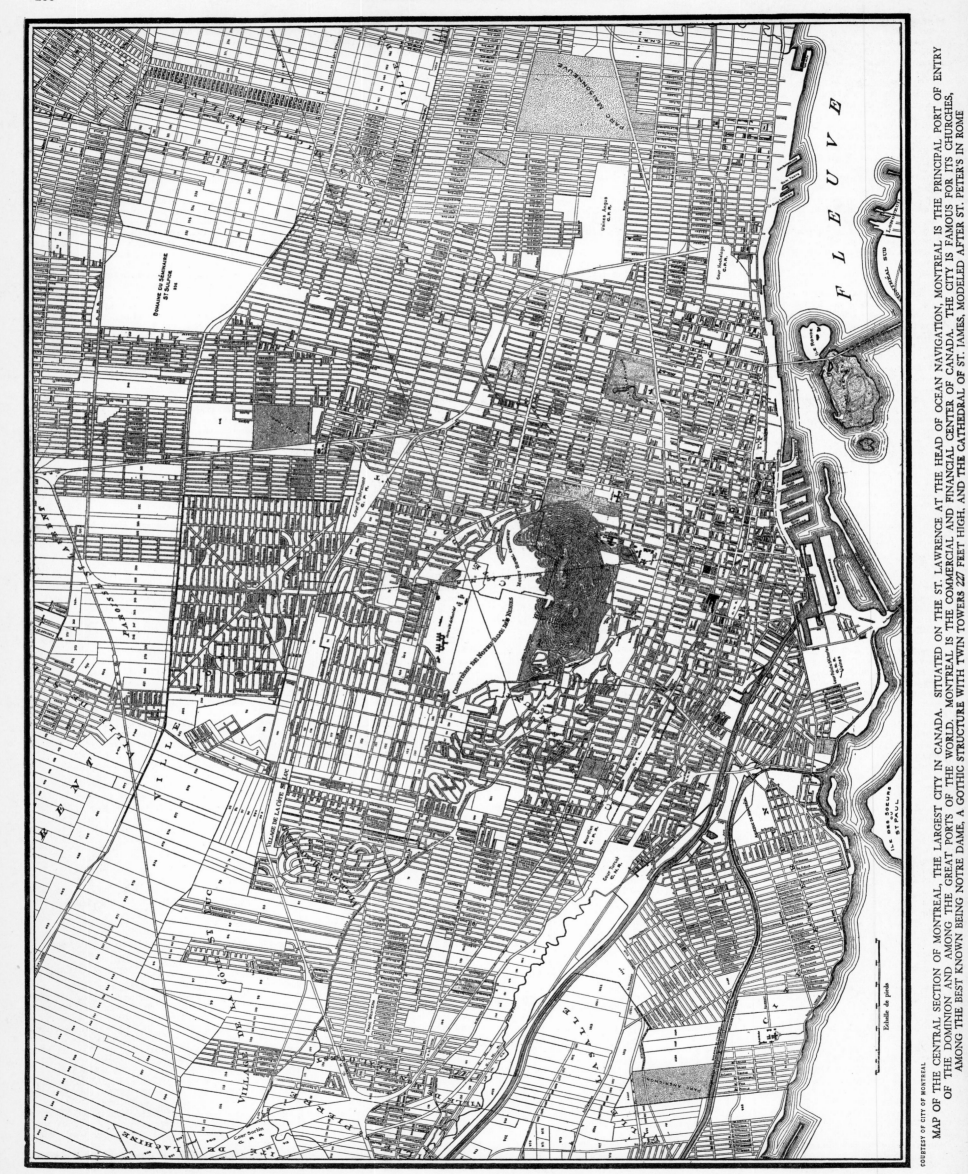

MAP OF THE CENTRAL SECTION OF MONTREAL, THE LARGEST CITY IN CANADA. SITUATED ON THE ST. LAWRENCE AT THE HEAD OF OCEAN NAVIGATION, MONTREAL IS THE PRINCIPAL PORT OF ENTRY OF THE DOMINION AND AMONG THE GREAT PORTS OF THE WORLD. MONTREAL IS THE COMMERCIAL AND FINANCIAL CENTER OF CANADA. THE CITY IS FAMOUS FOR ITS CHURCHES, AMONG THE BEST KNOWN BEING NOTRE DAME, A GOTHIC STRUCTURE WITH TWIN TOWERS 227 FEET HIGH, AND THE CATHEDRAL OF ST. JAMES, MODELED AFTER ST. PETER'S IN ROME

MOUNT CLEMENS, c. s., Macomb Co., Mich., 13,-
497.
On Gd. Tr. (R. R.).
Noted for its mineral baths. A health resort.
MOUNT DE CHANTAL, W. Va., 523.
On Balt. & Ohio (R. R.).
MOUNT DORA, Lake Co., Fla., 1,613.
On Atl. Coast Line (R. R.).
MOUNT EDEN, Alameda Co., Calif., 500.
On Sou. Pac. (R. R.).
MOUNT ENTERPRISE, Rusk Co., Tex., 625.
On Sou. Pac. (R. R.).
MOUNT EPHRAIM, Camden Co., N. J., 2,319.
On Penna.-Read. Seash. (R. R.).
MOUNT FOREST, Wellington Co., North, Ontario,
Canada, 1,801.
On Can. Pac.; Can. Nat. (R. Rs.).
MOUNT GAY, Logan Co., W. Va., 516.
MOUNT GILEAD, Montgomery Co., N. C., 1,011.
On Norf. Sou. (R. R.).
-c. s., Morrow Co., Ohio, 1,871.
On Cle., Cin., Chi. & St. Lou.; N. York Cen.
(R. Rs.).
MOUNT GREENWOOD, Cook Co., Ill., 1,441.
On Gd. Tr. (R. R.).
MOUNT HEALTHY, Hamilton Co., Ohio, 3,530.
On Cin. & L. Erie (El.) (R. R.).
MOUNT HERMON, Franklin Co., Mass., 600.
On Bost. & Me. (R. R.).
MOUNT HOLLY, Gaston Co., N. C., 2,254.
On Seab. Air Line; Piedmont & Nor. (El.) (R.
Rs.).
-c. s., Burlington Co., N. J., 6,573.
On Penna. (R. R.).
MOUNT HOLLY SPRINGS, Cumberland Co., Pa.,
1,140.
MOUNT HOPE, Morris Co., N. J., 1,000.
On Mt. Hope Miner. (R. R.).
-Fayette Co., W. Va., 2,361.
On Chesa. & Ohio; Kanaw., Gl. Jean & East.;
Virginian (R. Rs.).
MOUNT HOREB, Dane Co., Wis., 1,425.
On Chi. & Nor. West. (R. R.).
MOUNT IDA, c. s., Montgomery Co., Ark., 512.
-Arlington Co., Va., 500.
MOUNT JACKSON, Shenandoah Co., Va., 575.
On Southern (R. R.).
MOUNT JEFFERSON, Carbon Co., Pa., 700.
MOUNT JEWETT, McKean Co., Pa., 1,379.
On Balt. & Ohio; Erie (R. Rs.).
MOUNT JOY, Lancaster Co., Pa., 2,716.
On Penna. (R. R.).
MOUNT JULIET, Wilson Co., Tenn., 500.
On Tenn. Cen. (R. R.).
MOUNT KISCO, Westchester Co., N. Y., 5,127.
On N. York Cen. (R. R.).
MOUNT McGREGOR, Saratoga Co., N. Y., 500.
MOUNT MORRIS, Ogle Co., Ill., 1,902.
On Chi., Burl. & Quincy (R. R.).
-Genesee Co., Mich., 1,982.
On Pere Marq. (R. R.).
-Livingston Co., N. Y., 3,238.
On Dansv. & Mt. Mor.; Del., Lack. & West.;
Erie; Penna. (R. Rs.).
MOUNT OLIVE, Macoupin Co., Ill., 3,079.
On Ill. Cen.; Ill. Term. (El.); Litchf. & Mad.;
Wab. (R. Rs.).
-Covington Co., Miss., 812.
On Ill. Cen. (R. R.).
-Wayne Co., N. C., 2,685.
On Atl. Coast Line (R. R.).
MOUNT OLIVER, Allegheny Co., Pa., 7,071.
MOUNT ORAB, Brown Co., Ohio, 541.
On Norf. & West. (R. R.).
MOUNT PENN, Berks Co., Pa., 3,017.
MOUNT PLEASANT, c. s., Henry Co., Iowa, 3,743.
On Chi., Burl. & Quincy (R. R.).
Seat of Iowa Wesleyan College.
-c. s., Isabella Co., Mich., 5,211.
On Ann Arbor; Pere Marq. (R. Rs.).
-Cabarrus Co., N. C., 838.
-Jefferson Co., Ohio, 674.
On Wheel. & L. Erie (R. R.).
-Westmoreland Co., Pa., 5,869.
On Balt. & Ohio; Penna. (R. Rs.).
-Charleston Co., S. C., 1,415.
-Maury Co., Tenn., 2,010.
On Lou. & Nash. (R. R.).
-c. s., Titus Co., Texas, 3,541.
On St. Lou. Southw.; Paris & Mt. Pleasant (R.
Rs.).
-Sanpete Co., Utah, 2,284.
On Den. & Rio Gde. West. (R. R.).
MOUNT PROSPECT, Cook Co., Ill., 1,225.
On Chi. & Nor. West. (R. R.).
MOUNT PULASKI, Logan Co., Ill., 1,445.
On Ill. Cen. (R. R.).
MOUNT RAINIER, Prince Georges Co., Md., 3,832.
MOUNT ROYAL, Gloucester Co., N. J., 500.
On Penna.-Read. Seash. (R. R.).
MOUNT ST. JOSEPH, Jefferson Co., Ohio, 550.
MOUNT SAVAGE, Allegany Co., Md., 2,087.
On Cum. & Penna.; West. Md. (R. Rs.).
MOUNT SHASTA (Sisson), Siskiyou Co., Cal.,
1,009.
On McLoud River; Sou. Pac. (R. Rs.).
MOUNT STERLING, c. s., Brown Co., Ill., 1,724.
On Wabash (R. R.).
-c. s., Montgomery Co., Ky., 4,350.

On Chesa. & Ohio (R. R.).
-Madison Co., Ohio, 1,090.
On Balt. & Ohio (R. R.).
MOUNT TABOR, Morris Co., N. J., 500.
On Del., Lack. & West. (R. R.).
MOUNT UNION, Huntingdon Co., Pa., 4,892.
On E. Broad Top; Penna. (R. Rs.).
MOUNT VERNON, Mobile Co., Ala., 810.
On Ala., Tenn. & Nor.; Sou. (R. Rs.).
-c. s., Montgomery Co., Ga., 779.
On Seab. Air Line (R. R.).
-Jefferson Co., Ill., 12,375.
On Chi. & E. Ill.; Lou. & Nash.; Mo. Pac.;
Sou. (R. Rs.).
A trading center and shipping point in a rich
agricultural region.
-c. s., Posey Co., Ind., 5,035.
On Chi. & E. Ill.; Lou. & Nash. (R. Rs.).

-Linn Co., Iowa, 1,441.
On Chi. & Nor. West. (R. R.).
-c. s., Rockcastle Co., Ky., 939.
On Lou. & Nash. (R. R.).
-c. s., Lawrence Co., Mo., 1,342.
On St. Lou.-San Fran. (R. R.).
-Westchester Co., N. Y., 61,499.
On N. York Cen.; N. York, N. Hav. & Hart.
(R. Rs.).
Adjoins the Bronx borough of New York City.
Has some industries, but mainly residential.
-c. s., Knox Co., Ohio, 9,370.
On Balt. & Ohio; Penna. (R. Rs.).
-c. s., Franklin Co., Texas, 1,222.
On St. Lou. Southw. (R. R.).
-c. s., Skagit Co., Wash., 3,690.
On Gt. Nor. (R. R.).
MOUNT VICTORY, Hardin Co., Ohio, 597.
On Cle., Cin., Chi. & St. Lou. (R. R.).
MOUNTVILLE, Lancaster Co., Pa., 954.
On Penna. (R. R.).
MOUNT WASHINGTON, Hamilton Co., Ohio (Sta.
of Cincinnati).
MOUNT WOLF, York Co., Pa., 999.
On Penna. (R. R.).
MOUSCRON, West Flanders, Belgium, 31,835.
A commercial and industrial town.
MOVILLE, Woodbury Co., Iowa, 911.
On Chi. & Nor. West. (R. R.).
MOWEAQUA, Shelby Co., Ill., 1,478.
On Ill. Cen. (R. R.).
MOYLAN, Delaware Co., Pa., 1,000.
On Penna. (R. R.).

MOYOCK, Currituck Co., N. C., 500.
On Norf. Sou. (R. R.).
MOZAMBIQUE. See MOCAMBIQUE.
MUHLENBURG, Berks Co., Pa., 6,000.
On Read. (R. R.).
MUIR, Schuylkill Co., Pa., 750.
MUKDEN, Manchukuo, 543,638.
Chief commercial and educational center. A
distributing point for raw materials—mineral
and agricultural. Rapidly growing city.
MUKWONAGO, Waukesha Co., Wis., 846.
On Mil. El.; Mpls., St. P. & S. Ste. M. (R.
Rs.).
MULBERRY, Crawford Co., Ark., 895.
On Mo. Pac. (R. R.).
-Polk Co., Fla., 1,774.
On Atl. Coast Line; Seab. Air Line (R. Rs.).
-Clinton Co., Ind., 960.

On N. York, Chi. & St. Lou. (R. R.).
-Crawford Co., Kans., 1,405.
On Jop. & Pitts. (El.); Kan. Cy. Sou.; St. Lou.-
San Fran. (R. Rs.).
MULBERRY GROVE, Bond Co., Ill., 596.
On Penna. (R. R.).
MULCHEN, Prov. of Bio-Bio, Chile, 6,826.
MULDROW, Sequoyah Co., Okla., 557.
On Mo. Pac. (R. R.).
MULESHOE, c. s., Bailey Co., Tex., 779.
On Panh. & Santa Fe (R. R.).
MÜLHEIM-AM-RHEIN, Prussia, Germany, 131,000.
An industrial suburb of Köln.
MÜLHEIM-AN-DER-RUHR, Prussia, 127,295.
MULHOUSE, Alsace, France, 96,697.
Textiles, chemicals, and machinery.
MULLAN, Shoshone Co., Idaho, 1,891.
On Nor. Pac. (R. R.).
MULLDOON (Muldoon), Fayette Co., Tex., 600.
On Sou. Pac. (R. R.).
MULLEN, c. s., Hooker Co., Neb., 524.
On Chi., Burl. & Quincy (R. R.).
MULLENS, Wyoming Co., W. Va., 2,356.
On Virginian (R. R.).
MULLICA HILL, Gloucester Co., N. J., 600.
On Penna.-Read. Seashore (R. R.).
MULLINS, Marion Co., S. C., 3,158.
On Atl. Coast Line; Seab. Air Line (R. Rs.).
MULTAN, capital of Dist. of Multan, Punjab,
India, 108,351.
MULVANE, Sedgwick and Sumner Cos., Kans.,
923.
On Atch., Top. & Santa Fe (R. R.).

MÜNCHEN (Munich), capital of Bavaria, Germany,
736,000.
Situated on an extensive plateau about 1,700
feet above sea level, on the bank of the Isar.
The former Royal Palace forms a very extensive series of buildings, chiefly in the Italian
style, and contains many magnificent apartments and rich artistic and other treasures.
Connected with it are the Court Church and
the Court and National Theatre. The city is
celebrated for its fine galleries of sculpture
(Glyptothek) and painting (Old and New
Pinakothek), and for the picture collection in
the Bavarian National Museum. One of its
most famous institutions is the Deutsches Museum, a great industrial museum with moving
machines, models, and demonstrations of phenomena. The Library has upward of 1,300,000
volumes. The university was founded in 1472.
In addition there are schools of science, arts,
and engineering, and many fine churches, including the cathedral, founded in 1488.
München has many foundries for iron and
bronze work and for bell casting, also breweries, cotton and woolen factories, tanneries,
and machine shops.
MÜNCHEN-GLADBACH. See GLADBACH.
MUNCIE, c. s., Delaware Co., Ind., 46,548.
On Cle., Cin., Chi. & St. Lou.; Chesa. & Ohio;
Ind. R. R. Sys. (El.); Penna.; N. York, Chi. &
St. Lou.; Munc. & West. (R. Rs.).
A trade and industrial center in a fine agri-
cultural region. Manufactures are auto parts,
fruit jars, wire, cable, insulators, castings,
storage batteries, and glass building blocks.
MUNCY, Lycoming Co., Pa., 2,413.
On Penna.; Read. (R. Rs.).
MUNDAY, Knox Co., Texas, 1,318.
On Wich. Val. (R. R.).
MUNDELEIN, Lake Co., Ill., 1,011.
On Chi. No. Shore & Mil. (El.); Mpls., St.
P. & S. Ste. M. (R. Rs.).
MÜNDEN, Prussia, Germany, 11,983.
MUNFORD, Talladega Co., Ala., 515.
On Lou. & Nash.; So. (R. Rs.).
MUNFORDVILLE, c. s., Hart Co., Ky., 649.
On Lou. & Nash. (R. R.).
MUNHALL, Allegheny Co., Pa., 12,995.
On Bess. & L. Erie; Balt. & Ohio; Penna.; Pitts.
& L. Erie; Union (R. Rs.).
MUNISING, c. s., Alger Co., Mich., 3,956.
On Lake Superior & Ishpeming (R. R.).
MUNROE, Middlesex Co., Mass., 800.
On Bost. & Me. (R. R.).
MUNSON, Clearfield Co., Pa., 650.
On N. York Cen. (R. R.).
MÜNSTER, Lake Co., Indiana, 975.
On Chi., Ind. & Lou. (R. R.).
-capital of Westphalia, Prussia, Germany,
122,210.
An educational and industrial center. Famous
for its cathedral.
MURCIA, capital of Prov. of Murcia, Spain,
166,341.
Famous for its silks and citrus fruits.
MURDO MACKENZIE (Murdo P. O.), Jones Co.,
S. Dak., 625.
On Chi., Mil., St. P. & Pac. (R. R.).
MURFREESBORO, c. s., Pike Co., Ark., 733.
On Murfreesb.-Nashv. (R. R.).
-Hertford Co., N. C., 1,000.
-c. s., Rutherford Co., Tenn., 7,993.
On Nash., Chatt. & St. Lou. (R. R.).
MURPHY, Calaveras Co., Calif., 600.
-c. s., Cherokee Co., N. C., 1,612.
On Lou. & Nash.; Sou. (R. Rs.).
MURPHYSBORO, c. s., Jackson Co., Ill., 8,182.
On Ill. Cen.; Mob. & Ohio; Mo. Pac. (R. Rs.).
MURRAY, Clarke Co., Iowa, 828.
On Chi., Burl. & Quincy (R. R.).
-c. s., Calloway Co., Ky., 2,891.
On Nash., Chatt. & St. Lou. (R. R.).
-Salt Lake Co., Utah, 5,172.
On Den. & Rio Gde. West.; Un. Pac. (R. Rs.).
MURRAY CITY, Hocking Co., Ohio, 1,048.
On Chesa. & Ohio (R. R.).
MURRAY HILL, Union Co., N. J., 500.
On Del., Lack. & West. (R. R.).
MURRAYSVILLE, Westmoreland Co., Pa., 800.
On Penna. (R. R.).
MURRAYVILLE, Morgan Co., Ill., 502.
On Alton (R. R.).
MUSCAT, Arabia. See MASQAT.
MUSCATINE, c. s., Muscatine Co., Iowa, 16,778.
On Chi., Mil., St. P. & Pac.; Chi., Rk. Isl. &
Pac.; Clin., Davenp. & Musc. (R. Rs.).
Famous as a center of the pearl button industry.
MUSCLE SHOALS, Colbert Co., Ala., 719.
R. R. Sta. at Sheffield.
MUSCODA, Grant Co., Wis., 900.
On Chi., Mil., St. P. & Pac. (R. R.).
MUSKEGON, c. s., Muskegon Co., Mich., 41,390.
On Musk. Ry. & Nav. Co.; Gd. Tr.; Pere
Marq.; Penna. (R. Rs.).
A lake port and commercial center. Is center
of fruit and dairying region. A summer resort.
MUSKEGON HEIGHTS, Muskegon Co., Mich.,
15,584.
On Musk. Ry. & Nav. Co.; Gd. Tr.; Penna.;
Pere Marq. (R. Rs.).

MUNICH, BAVARIA'S GAY AND BEAUTIFUL CAPITAL AND ONE OF THE WORLD'S
ART CENTERS. THIS VIEW SHOWS MARIEN-PLATZ WITH THE CITY HALL ON
THE RIGHT AND THE MIGHTY FRAUEN-KIRCHE IN THE BACKGROUND

Muskogee, c. s., Muskogee Co., Okla., 32,026.
On Kan., Okla. & Gulf; Midl. Val.; Mo.-Kan.-Tex.; St. Lou.-San Fran. (R. Rs.).
Manufactures oil, cotton, iron products.
Musselborgh, Edinburgh, Scotland, 16,996.
Muttra, capital of Dist. of Muttra, United Provinces, India, 60,590.
Mutual, Westmoreland Co., Pa., 810.
On Penna. (R. R.).
Muzaffarnagar, capital of Muzaffarnagar Dist., India, 35,347.
Myers, Charleston Co., S. C., 500.
Myerstown, Lebanon Co., Pa., 2,593.
On Reading (R. R.).
Myrtle Point, Coos Co., Ore., 1,362.
On Sou. Pac. (R. R.).
Myrtlewood, Marengo Co., Ala., 500.
On Lou. & Nash.; Mer. & Bigbee Riv. (R. Rs.).
Mysore, capital of Mysore, India, 107,142.
Mystic, New London Co., Conn., 2,547.
On N. York, N. Hav. & Hart. (R. R.).
–Appanoose Co., Iowa, 1,953.
On Chi., Mil., St. P. & Pac.; Ia. Sou. Utilities (El.) (R. Rs.).
Mytilini, Mytilini (Lesbos) Island, Greece, 33,000.
Chief town of the island.

N

Nabua, Prov. of Camarines Sur, Luzon, P. I., 19,314.
An agricultural marketing center.
Nacogdoches, c. s., Nacogdoches Co., Tex., 5,687.
On Nacog. & Sou. East.; Sou. Pac. (R. Rs.).
Naga, Prov. of Cebu, P. I., 20,599.
Located in a fertile farming area.
Nagano, capital of Ken of Nagano, Japan, 73,912.
A commercial center. Has Buddhist temple with magnificent carvings.
Nagaoka, Japan, 57,866.
A commercial town in an agricultural region.
Nagasaki, Ken of Nagasaki, Japan, 210,700.
One of the country's important harbors and commercial centers. Has a large naval station.
Nagcarlan, Luzon, P. I., 14,853.
Nagor Rajasima, Siam, 599,165.
Nagoya, capital of Prefecture of Aichi, Japan, 1,082,816.
A commercial and industrial town. Noted for its manufactures of cotton and silk embroideries.
Nagpur, Central Provinces, India, 215,165.
A commercial and educational center. Chief manufactures are hand woven and embroidered textiles.
Naguabo, Mun. of Naguabo, Puerto Rico, 4,109.
Nagulian, Prov. of Isabela, Luzon, P. I., 14,828.
Nagybecskerek, Yugoslavia. See Veliky Beckerek.
Nagykörös, Pest Comitat, Hungary, 28,584.
A leading trade and marketing town a short distance south of Budapest.
Nahant, Essex Co., Mass., 1,748.
Nairobi, capital of Kenya, British E. Africa, 20,400.
A modern town on a beautiful location. Native bazaars and markets cover nearly ten acres. An outfitting point for big-game hunters.
Nakchichevan, capital of Nakchichevan, Soviet Union, 55,438.
The chief industries are silk and cotton weaving and wine making.
Namagpacan, Prov. of La Union, Luzon, P. I., 13,641.
Namangan, Soviet Union in Asia, 90,900.
Cotton ginning and considerable trade in agricultural products.
Nambe, Santa Fe Co., N. Mex., 534.
Nameoki, Madison Co., Illinois, 2,257.
On Alton; Chi. & E. Ill.; Cle., Cin., Chi. & St. Lou.; Ill. Term. (El.); Wab. (R. Rs.).
Nampa, Canyon Co., Idaho, 8,206.
On Un. Pac. (R. R.).
In center of Boise irrigation project.
Seat of Northwest Nazarene College.
Namur, capital of the Prov. of Namur, Belgium, 30,389.
Cutlery, glass, and leather manufactures.
Nanaimo, Nanaimo Co., B. C., Can., 6,745.
On Can. Nat.; Can. Pac.; Esquimalt & Nanaimo (R. Rs.).
Nancy, Dept. of Meurthe, France, 121,301.
An educational center and commercial town in northeastern France.
Nanking, capital of China, 633,500.
On the Yangtze River; the chief seat of literature of the country; important manufactures. Capital was moved here from Peiping (Peking) in 1928.
Nanterre, Dept. of Seine, France, 46,065.
Suburb of Paris and scene of an annual pilgrimage.
Nantes, capital of Dept. of Loire-Inférieure, France, 195,185.
Situated on the right bank of the Loire. An important commercial and industrial city.
Nantes was the Portus Namnetum of the Romans, and the former capital of Brittany.
Nanticoke, Luzerne Co., Pa., 26,043.
On Cen. of N. Jer.; Penna. (R. Rs.).
Anthracite mines and manufactures of silk yarn, hosiery and cigars.
Nantucket, c. s., Nantucket Co., Mass., 3,495.
Nanty Glo, Cambria Co., Pa., 5,598.
On Camb. & Ind.; Penna. (R. Rs.).
Napa, c. s., Napa Co., Cal., 6,437.
On Sou. Pac. (R. R.).
Napanee, c. s., Lennox Co., Ontario, Can., 3,497.

COURTESY CANADIAN PACIFIC

A PANORAMA OF THE CITY OF NAPLES WITH ITS HISTORIC HARBOR AND VESUVIUS IN ERUPTION IN THE DISTANCE

On Can. Nat. (R. R.).
Napanoch, Ulster Co., N. Y., 642.
On N. York, Ont. & West. (R. R.).
Naperville, Du Page Co., Ill., 5,118.
On Chi., Burl. & Quincy (R. R.).
Napier, North Isl., New Zealand, 15,550.
Naples, Italy. See Napoli.
–Collier Co., Fla., 517.
On Atl. Coast Line; Seab. Air Line (R. Rs.).
–Cumberland Co., Maine, 185.
–Ontario Co., N. Y., 1,070.
On Leh. Val. (R. R.).
–Morris Co., Tex., 843.
On St. Lou. Southw. (R. R.).
Napoleon, c. s., Henry Co., Ohio, 4,545.
On Det., Tol. & Iron.; Wab. (R. Rs.).
–c. s., Logan Co., N. Dak., 709.
On Mpls., St. P. & S. Ste. M. (R. R.).
Napoleonville, c. s., Assumption Parish, La., 1,180.
On Sou. Pac.; Tex. & Pac. (R. Rs.).
Napoli (Naples), capital of Prov. of Naples, Italy, 757,251.
The largest city of Italy, situated on the north shore of the Bay of Naples. Its site is magnificent, being on the side of a nearly semicircular bay, partly along the shore, and partly climbing the adjacent slopes, bounded on one side by the Heights of Posilipo, and on the other by Vesuvius, while the background is rich in natural beauty. The city is divided into two unequal parts by a steep ridge proceeding from the height on which stands the Castle of St. Elmo, and terminated by a rocky islet surmounted by the Castello dell' Ovo. The largest and most ancient part of Napoli lies to the southeast of these heights. This now forms the business quarter. The western and more modern part of the city is the fashionable quarter, and commands magnificent views.
Nappanee, Elkhart Co., Ind., 2,957.
On Balt. & Ohio (R. R.).
Nara, Prov. of Nara, Japan, 52,781.
A religious center.
Naranjito, Mun. of Naranjito, Puerto Rico, 1,839.
Narberth, Montgomery Co., Pa., 4,669.
On Penna. (R. R.).
Narbonne, Aude, France, 30,047.
Narragansett, Washington Co., R. I., 1,593.
On Narrag. Pier (R. R.).
Narrows, Giles Co., Va., 1,345.
On Norf. & West.; Virginian (R. Rs.).
Narrowsburg, Sullivan Co., N. Y., 605.
On Erie (R. R.).
Narva, Estonia, 24,970.
A manufacturing center.
Narvacan, Prov. of Ilocos Sur, Luzon, P. I., 23,069.
Rice, corn, cotton, sugar, and tobacco raised in vicinity.
Nash, Bowie Co., Tex., 500.
On Tex. & Pac. (R. R.).
Nashua, Chickasaw Co., Iowa, 1,363.
On Ill. Cen. (R. R.).
–c. s., Hillsboro Co., N. H., 31,463.
On Bost. & Me. (R. R.).
Cotton goods, paper, asbestos shingles, and refrigerators.
Nashville, c. s., Howard Co., Ark., 2,469.
On Grays.; Murfreesb.-Nash.; Mo. Pac. (R. Rs.).
–c. s., Berrien Co., Ga., 1,672.
On Ga. & Fla. (R. R.).
–c. s., Washington Co., Ill., 2,243.
On Mo. Ill.; Lou. & Nash. (R. Rs.).
–Barry Co., Mich., 1,249.
On Mich. Cen. (R. R.).
–c. s., Nash Co., N. C., 1,137.
On Atl. Coast Line (R. R.).
–c. s., Davidson Co., Tenn., State capital, 153,866.
It is situated on the Cumberland River, 200 miles from its mouth. On the Louisville & Nashville; the Nashville, Chattanooga & St. Louis; the Nashville-Franklin (El.) and the Tennessee Central railroads.
It has the largest white population of any city in the State. The city is one of the most important educational centers in the country. It is the seat of Vanderbilt University, the Peabody College for Teachers, the medical and law departments of the University of Tennessee. The institutions for colored students are Fisk University, and Mehary Medical College. There are several public libraries, among them the Carnegie and the Board of Trade Library.
Nashville is a large manufacturer of fertilizers, candy, iron goods, crackers, harnesses and trunks, printing and publishing, hosiery, shoes, furniture, and grinds immense quantities of winter wheat.
Nashville was named for General Francis Nash of North Carolina, an American soldier of the War of the Revolution, who was mortally wounded at the battle of Germantown, Pa.
Nashwauk, Itasco Co., Minn., 2,555.
On Gt. Nor. (R. R.).
Nasik, capital of Dist. of Nasik, Bombay Presidency, India, 48,703.
Has manufactures of brass and copper wares.
Nassau, Rensselaer Co., N. Y., 670.
–Capital of the Bahama Islands, 20,538.
The commercial and tourist center.
Nasugbu, Prov. of Batangas, Luzon, P. I., 12,672.
Natal, Rio Grande de Norte, Brazil, 46,100.
Natchez, c. s., Adams Co., Miss., 13,422.
On Miss. Cen.; Natchez & Sou.; Ill. Cen.; Mo. Pac. (R. Rs.).
Cotton-shipping center. Has sawmills, woodwork plants and foundries.
Natchitoches, c. s., Natchitoches Parish, La., 4,547.
On Tex. & Pac. (R. R.).
Natick, Middlesex Co., Mass., 14,394.
On Bost. & Alb. (R. R.).
A residential and commercial town near Boston.
–Kent Co., R. I., 5,488.
On N. York, N. Hav. & Hart. (R. R.).
National City, San Diego Co., Cal., 7,301.
On Atch., Top. & Santa Fe; San Diego & Ariz. East. (R. Rs.).
National Park, Gloucester Co., N. J., 1,828.
Natoma, Osborne Co., Kansas, 599.
On Un. Pac. (R. R.).
Natrona, Allegheny Co., Pa., 7,200.
On Penna. (R. R.).
Natural Bridge (Post Office), Jefferson Co., N. Y., 500.
Nauck, Arlington Co., Va., 520.
Naugatuck, New Haven Co., Conn., 14,315.
On N. York, N. Hav. & Hart. (R. R.).
The principal manufactures are rubber goods, safety pins, airplanes, and candy.
Naumburg-on-the-Saale, Prussian Saxony, Germany, 31,000.
Of interest historically.
Nauplia, Greece. See Navplion.
Nauvoo, Walker Co., Ala., 648.
On Nor. Ala. (R. R.).
–Hancock Co., Ill., 966.
Ferry connection with Chi., Burl. & Quincy (R. R.), at Montrose, Ia.
Navanagar, State of Nawanagar, India, 50,000.
Silks, locomotives, pearls, and dyeing.
Navarre, Stark Co., Ohio, 1,593.
On Wheel. & L. Erie (R. R.).
Navasota, c. s., Grimes Co., Texas, 5,128.
On Gulf, Colo. & Santa Fe; Mo. Pac.; Sou. Pac. (R. Rs.).
Navesink, Monmouth Co., N. J., 608.
Navojoa, on the Rio Mayo, State of Sonora, Mexico, 9,254.
On South. Pac. of Mex. (R. R.).
Navotas, Rizal Prov., Luzon, P. I., 13,309.
Navplion, Greece, 7,163.
Naylor, Ripley Co., Missouri, 553.
On Mo. Pac.; St. Lou.-San Fran. (R. Rs.).
Nazareth, Palestine, 8,719.
–Northampton Co., Pa., 5,505.
On Del., Lack. & West.; Leh. & N. Eng. (R. Rs.).
Neath, Glamorganshire, Wales, 33,322.
Copper, tin, steel, and galvanized iron works.
Nebraska City, c. s., Otoe Co., Neb., 7,230.
On Chi., Burl. & Quincy; Mo. Pac. (R. Rs.).
Necedah, Juneau Co., Wis., 761.
On Chi. & Nor. West.; Chi., Mil., St. P. & Pac. (R. Rs.).
Neche, Pembina Co., N. D., 502.
On Gt. Nor. (R. R.).
Needham, Norfolk Co., Mass., 11,828.
On N. York, N. Hav. & Hart. (R. R.).
Manufactures: knit wear, sweaters, infants' wear and surgical goods.
Needles, San Bernardino Co., Cal., 3,144.
On Atch., Top. & Santa Fe (R. R.).
Neenah, Winnebago Co., Wis., 9,151.
On Chi. & Nor. West.; Chi., Mil., St. P. & Pac.; Mpls., St. P. & S. Ste. M. (R. Rs.).
Neepawa, Portage la Prairie Co., Manitoba, Canada, 2,068.
On Can. Nat.; Can. Pac. (R. Rs.).
Neffsville, Lancaster Co., Pa., 700.
Negapatam, Madras Presidency, India, 48,527.
Has large railway car shops and several technical institutes.
Negaunee, Marquette Co., Mich., 6,552.
On Chi. & Nor. West.; Dul., So. Sh. & Atl.; L. Sup. & Ishpem. (R. Rs.).
Mining center in heart of iron and timber belt.
Neillsville, c. s., Clark Co., Wis., 2,118.
On Chi., St. P., Mpls. & Oma. (R. R.).
Neisse, Silesia, Germany, 36,000.
A marketing center in a farming and cattle raising region.
Nekoosa, Wood Co., Wis., 2,005.
On Chi. & Nor. West.; Chi., Mil., St. P. & Pac.; Mpls., St. P. & S. Ste. M. (R. Rs.).
Neligh, c. s., Antelope Co., Neb., 1,649.
On Chi. & Nor. West. (R. R.).
Nelliston, Montgomery Co., N. Y., 553.
Nellore, capital of Dist. of Nellore, Madras Presidency, India, 45,895.
Millet, rice, and cattle are raised in the vicinity.
Nelson, Lancashire, England, 38,306.
Cotton and silk weaving.
–Pickens and Cherokee Cos., Ga., 798.
On Lou. & Nash. (R. R.).
–Muhlenberg Co., Ky., 513.
On Ill. Cen. (R. R.).
–c. s., Nuckolls Co., Neb., 903.
On Chi., Burl. & Quincy. (R. R.).
Nelsonville, Athens Co., Ohio, 5,322.
On Chesa. & Ohio (R. R.).
A coal-mining center. Manufactures clay products.
Nemacolin, Greene Co., Pa., 2,600.
On Monongahela (R. R.).

NENANA, Alaska, 291.
On Alaska (R. R.).

NEODESHA, Wilson Co., Kans., 3,321.
On Mo. Pac.; St. Lou.-San Fran. (R. Rs.).

NEOGA, Cumberland Co., Ill., 995.
On Ill. Cen.; N. York, Chi. & St. Lou. (R. Rs.).

NEOLA, Pottawattamie Co., Iowa, 944.
On Chi., Mil., St. P. & Pac.; Chi., Rk. Isl. & Pac. (R. Rs.).

NEON, Letcher Co., Ky., 1,077.
On Lou. & Nash. (R. R.).

NEOSHO, c. s., Newton Co., Mo., 4,485.
On Kan. Cy. Sou.; Mo. & Ark.; St. Lou.-San Fran. (R. Rs.).
An industrial center in the Ozark region.

NEPHI, c. s., Juab Co., Utah, 2,573.
On Den. & Rio Gde. West.; Un. Pac. (R. Rs.).

NEPONSET, Bureau Co., Ill., 520.
On Chi., Burl. & Quincy (R. R.).

NEPTUNE (Neptune City), Monmouth Co., N. J., 2,258.

NESCOPECK, Luzerne Co., Pa., 1,614.
On Penna. (R. R.).

NESHAMINY FALLS, Bucks Co., Pa., 500.
On Reading (R. R.).

NESHANNOCK FALLS, Lawrence Co., Pa., 537.
On Penna. (R. R.).

NESQUEHONING, Carbon Co., N. J., 4,176.
On Cen. of N. Jer.; Leh. & N. Eng. (R. Rs.).

NESS CITY, c. s., Ness Co., Kans., 1,620.
On Atch., Top. & Santa Fe (R. R.).

NETCONG, Morris Co., N. J., 2,097.
On Del., Lack. & West. (R. R.).

NETTLETON, Craighead Co., Ark., 748.
On St. Lou.-San Fran.; Mo. Pac. (R. Rs.).
—Lee and Monroe Cos., Miss., 834.
On St. Lou.-San Fran. (R. R.).
—Cambria Co., Pa., 500.

NEUBRANDENBURG, Mecklenburg-Strelitz, Germany, 13,675.

NEUBURG, Bavaria, Germany, 7,564.

NEUCHÂTEL, Neuchâtel Canton, Switzerland, 22,775.
Cattle and cheese; asphalt. Railway center.

NEUGERSDORF, Saxony, Germany, 11,168.

NEUILLY-SUR-SEINE, Dept. of Seine, France, 56,938.
A fashionable suburb west of Paris.

NEUMUNSTER, Holstein, Germany, 40,000.
An industrial town near Hamburg.

NEURUPPIN, Brandenburg, Prussia, Germany, 20,000.
Textiles, starch, and machinery.

NEUSALZ, Silesia, Germany, 14,212.
Famous for its thread manufactures.

NEUSATZ, Yugoslavia. See NOVI SAD.

NEUSS, Düsseldorf, Rhenish Prussia, Germany, 55,800.
An industrial suburb of Düsseldorf.

NEUSTADT, Silesia, Prussia, Germany, 22,000.
A marketing center of an agricultural region.
—Saxe-Coburg-Gotha, Bavaria, Germany, 8,761.

NEUSTADT-ON-THE-HARDT, Bavaria, Germany, 20,726.
One of the centers of the Rhenish "grape cure."

NEUSTADT-ON-THE-ORLA, Saxony, Germany, 7,660.

NEUSTETTIN, Pomerania, Prussia, Germany, 16,000.

NEUSTRELITZ, capital of Mecklenburg-Strelitz, Germany, 19,400.

NEUTITSCHEIN, Czechoslovakia. See NOVY JICIN.

NEUTRA, Czechoslovakia. See NITRA.

NEUWIED, Rhenish Prussia, Germany, 21,000.
Manufactures porcelain stoves.

NEVADA, c. s., Story Co., Iowa, 3,133.
On Chi. & Nor. West.; Chi., Rk. Isl. & Pac. (R. Rs.).
—c. s., Vernon Co., Mo., 7,448.
On Mo.-Kans.-Tex.; Mo. Pac. (R. Rs.).
—Wyandot Co., Ohio, 741.
On Penna. (R. R.).

NEVADA CITY, c. s., Nevada Co., Cal., 1,701.
On Nev. Co., Nar. Gauge (R. R.).

NEVERS, Dept. of Nièvre, France, 33,699.
Of great historical interest.

NEW ALBANY, c. s., Floyd Co., Ind., 25,819.
On Balt. & Ohio; Chi., Ind. & Lou.; Ky. & Ind. Term.; Penna.; Sou. (R. Rs.).
An industrial town with manufactures of plywood, furniture, tools, engines, textiles, and leather. Coal mines in the vicinity.
—c. s., Union Co., Miss., 3,187.
On Gulf, Mob. & Nor.; St. Lou.-San Fran. (R. Rs.).

NEW ALBIN, Allamakee Co., Iowa, 556.
On Chi., Mil., St. P. & Pac. (R. R.).

NEW ALEXANDRIA, Westmoreland Co., Pa., 615.
On Penna. (R. R.).

NEWARK, Independence Co., Ark., 897.
On Mo. Pac. (R. R.).
—New Castle Co., Dela., 3,899.
On Balt. & Ohio; Penna. (R. Rs.).
Seat of Univ. of Delaware.
—c. s., Licking Co., Ohio, 30,596.
On Balt. & Ohio; Penna. (R. Rs.).
A commercial town. Near by may be found many earth-works of the Mound-builders.
—Nottinghamshire, England, 18,055.

The trade center of a fine farming area. Various industries.
—c. s., Essex Co., N. J., 442,337.
Situated on the Passaic River, and Baltimore & Ohio; Central of New Jersey; Delaware, Lackawanna & Western; Erie; Hudson & Manhattan (El.); Lehigh Valley and Pennsylvania railroads, 9 miles west of New York City.
The chief public buildings are the Catholic Cathedral, County Court House, City Hall, Federal Building, Public Library, New Jersey State Bank, the Prudential, Fireman's Insurance, Chamber of Commerce, and Mutual Benefit buildings.
Among the leading industries are smelting and refining, leather, foundry and machine-shop products, jewelry, radio supplies, paints and varnishes, incandescent lamps, chemicals, clothing, dies, and printing. The city is an important insurance center.
It is the seat of Newark Academy, State Normal School, Newark Technical College, New Jersey Law School, and New Jersey Historical Society.
The city was first settled in 1666; incorporated in 1693 as a township; in 1836 as a city.
—Wayne Co., N. Y., 7,649.
On N. Y. Cen.; Penna.; West Shore (R. Rs.).

NEWARK VALLEY, Tioga Co., N. Y., 795.
On Leh. Val. (R. R.).

NEW ATHENS, St. Clair Co., Ill., 1,269.
On Ill. Cen. (R. R.).

NEW AUGUSTINE, St. Johns Co., Fla. (Sta. St. Augustine P. O.).

NEWAYGO, c. s., Newaygo Co., Mich., 1,227.
On Pere Marq. (R. R.).

NEW BADEN, Clinton Co., Ill., 1,243.
On Southern (R. R.).

NEW BALTIMORE, Macomb and St. Clair Cos., Mich., 1,148.
—(Post Office), Greene Co., N. Y., 550.

NEW BEDFORD, c. s., Bristol Co., Mass., 110,022.
Situated on the Acushnet River, N. York, N. Hav. & Hart. (R. R.).
There are numerous industrial establishments, mainly those of cotton and yarn, which are among the largest in the world, and have made New Bedford a great producer of the finer grade of cotton. Other leading products are golf balls, soap, tools, boats, beer, silk goods, silverware, rubber goods and paper goods.
Its public library is said to be one of the oldest in the country.

NEWBERG, Yamhill Co., Ore., 2,951.
On Sou. Pac. (R. R.).

NEW BERLIN, Sangamon Co., Ill., 661.
On Wabash (R. R.).
—Chenango Co., N. Y., 1,076.
On N. York, Ont. & West.; Unadilla Val. (R. Rs.).
—Union Co., Pa., 650.

NEWBERN, Dyer Co., Tenn., 1,621.
On Ill. Cen. (R. R.).

NEW BERN, c. s., Craven Co., N. C., 11,981.
On Atl. & Nor. Car.; Atl. Coast Line; Norf. Sou. (R. Rs.).
A lumber manufacturing town.

NEWBERRY, Alachua Co., Fla., 778.
On Atl. Coast Line (R. R.).
—c. s., Luce Co., Mich., 2,465.
On Duluth, South Shore & Atl. (R. R.).
—c. s., Newberry Co., S. C., 7,298.
On Colum., Newb. & Laur.; Sou. (R. Rs.).
Has textile mills.

NEW BETHEL, Marion Co., Ind., 500.

NEW BETHLEHEM, Clarion Co., Pa., 1,590.
On Penna. (R. R.).

NEW BLOOMFIELD (Bloomfield), c. s., Perry Co., Pa., 730.
On Susq. Riv. & West. (R. R.).

NEW BOSTON, Mercer Co., Ill., 736.
On Chi., Burl. & Quincy (R. R.).
—Hillsboro Co., N. H., 500.
On Bost. & Me. (R. R.).
—Scioto Co., Ohio, 5,931.
On Balt. & Ohio; Norf. & West. (R. Rs.).
—Schuylkill Co., Pa., 648.
On Penna. (R. R.).
—Bowie Co., Texas, 949.
On Tex. & Pac. (R. R.).

NEW BRAUNFELS, c. s., Comal Co., Texas, 6,242.
On Mo. Pac.; Mo.-Kan.-Tex. of Tex. (R. Rs.).

NEW BREMEN, Auglaize Co., Ohio, 1,485.
On N. York, Chi. & St. Lou. (R. R.).

NEW BRIGHTON, Ramsey Co., Minn., 500.
On Mpls., St. P. & S. Ste. M.; Chi, Burl. & Quincy; Chi., Mil., St. P. & Pac.; Chi., Rk. Isl. & Pac.; Gt. Nor.; Mpls. Transf.; Mpls. & St. Lou.; Chi., St. P., Mpls. & Oma.; Nor. Pac. (R. Rs.).
—Beaver Co., Pa., 9,950.
On Penna.; Pitts. & L. Erie (R. Rs.).

NEW BRITAIN, Hartford Co., Conn., 68,128.
On N. York, N. Hav. & Hart. (R. R.).
A leading industrial center with a large output of hardware, cutlery, tools, castings, and machinery.

NEW BROCKTON, Coffee Co., Ala., 727.
On Atl. Coast Line (R. R.).

NEW BRUNSWICK, c. s., Middlesex Co., N. J., 34,555.
On Penna.; Raritan Riv. (R. Rs.).
Manufacturing center with prosperous industries. Seat of Rutgers College and Sage Library.

NEW BUFFALO, Berrien Co., Mich., 1,051.
On Mich. Cen.; Pere Marq. (R. Rs.).

NEWBURG, Phelps Co., Mo., 1,036.
On St. Lou.-San Fran. (R. R.).
—(Newburgh), Cuyahoga Co., Ohio (Sta. Cleveland P. O.).
On Balt. & Ohio; Newburgh & So. Shore; Wheel. & L. Erie (R. Rs.).
—Preston Co., W. Va., 745.
On Balt. & Ohio (R. R.).

NEWBURGH, Warwick Co., Ind., 1,262.
On Evans. & Ohio Val. (El.); Ev. Sub. & Newburgh (R. Rs.).
—Orange Co., N. Y., 31,275.
On Erie; West Shore (R. Rs.).
A river port and commercial town. Ships a large quantity of orchard, farm, and dairy products.

NEWBURGH HEIGHTS, Cuyahoga Co., Ohio, 4,152.

NEWBURY, Berkshire, England, 13,336.
Trade is principally agricultural.
—Essex Co., Mass., 1,576.
On Bost. & Me. (R. R.).

NEWBURYPORT, c. s., Essex Co., Mass., 14,815.
On Bost. & Me. (R. R.).
An important port and manufacturing town, with many historical landmarks.

NEW BUTLER, Waukesha Co., Wis. See BUTLER.

NEW CANAAN, Fairfield Co., Conn., 2,372.
On N. York, N. Hav. & Hart. (R. R.).

NEW CANADA, Aroostook Co., Maine.

NEW CARLISLE, St. Joseph Co., Ind., 718.
On Chi. So. Shore & So. Bend (El.); N. York Cen. (R. Rs.).
—Clark Co., Ohio, 1,089.
On Cle., Cin., Chi. & St. Lou. (R. R.).

NEWCASTLE, Northumberland, England, 283,145.
Situated on the Tyne River, about 8 miles above its mouth in the North Sea. It is connected with Gateshead on the opposite side of the river by five bridges.
Newcastle owes its importance to its location in the center of the great coal fields of Durham and Northumberland. Its industries are locomotive and iron works and shipbuilding yards.
—Placer Co., Calif., 750.
On Sou. Pac. (R. R.).
—New South Wales, Australia (incl. suburbs), 104,491.
An important port and commercial town. Industries include shipbuilding, chemical, coke, fertilizer, cement, and wood-working plants. Has a very fine harbor.
—Young Co., Texas, 1,157.
On Wichita Fs. & Sou. (R. R.).
—c. s., Weston Co., Wyo., 1,201.
On Chi., Burl. & Quincy (R. R.).

NEW CASTLE, Jefferson Co., Ala., 850.
On Lou. & Nash. (R. R.).
—New Castle Co., Del., 4,131.
On Penna. (R. R.).
—c. s., Henry Co., Ind., 14,027.
On Cle., Cin., Chi. & St. Lou.; Ind. R. R. Sys. (El.); N. York, Chi. & St. Lou.; Penna. (R. Rs.).
Famous for its rose nurseries.
—c. s., Lawrence Co., Pa., 48,674.
On Balt. & Ohio; Erie; Penna.; Pitts. & L. Erie (R. Rs.).
Leading products are tin plate and steel.

NEWCASTLE-UNDER-LYME, Staffordshire, England, 23,246.

NEW CHURCH, Accomac Co., Va., 675.
On Penna. (R. R.).

NEWCOMER, Fayette Co., Pa., 700.
On Penna. (R. R.).

NEWCOMERSTOWN, Tuscarawas Co., Ohio, 4,265.
On Penna. (R. R.).

NEW CONCORD, Muskingum Co., Ohio, 1,087.
On Balt. & Ohio (R. R.).

NEW CUMBERLAND, Cumberland Co., Pa., 4,283.
On Penna. (R. R.).
—c. s., Hancock Co., W. Va., 2,300.
On Penna. (R. R.).

NEW DELHI, Delhi Province, India, 64,855.

NEW DERRY, Westmoreland Co., Pa., 550.

NEW DURHAM, Hudson Co., N. J., 6,025.
On Erie; N. York, Susq. & West. (R. Rs.).

NEW EAGLE, Washington Co., Pa., 1,793.

NEW EGYPT, Ocean Co., N. J., 500.
On Penna. & Atl. (R. R.).

NEWELL, Buena Vista Co., Iowa, 812.
On Ill. Cen. (R. R.).
—Butte Co., S. Dak., 580.
On Chi. & Nor. West. (R. R.).

NEWELLTON, Tensas Parish, La., 627.
On Mo. Pac. (R. R.).

NEW ENGLAND, Hettinger Co., N. D., 911.
On Chi., Mil., St. P. & Pac. (R. R.).

NEWFIELD, Gloucester Co., N. J., 880.
On Penna.-Read. Seashore (R. R.).

NEW FLORENCE, Westmoreland Co., Pa., 796.
On Penna. (R. R.).
—Montgomery Co., Mo., 571.
On Wabash (R. R.).

NEWFOUNDLAND, Morris Co., N. J., 600.
On N. York, Susq. & West. (R. R.).
—Wayne Co., Pa., 500.

NEW FRANKLIN, Howard Co., Mo., 1,210.
On Mo.-Kan.-Tex. (R. R.).

NEW FREEDOM, York Co., Pa., 1,125.
On Penna.; Stewartstown (R. Rs.).

NEW GLARUS, Green Co., Wis., 1,010.
On Chi., Mil., St. P. & Pac. (R. R.).

NEW GLASGOW, Nova Scotia, Canada, 8,858.
On Can. Nat. (R. R.).

NEW GOSHEN, Vigo Co., Ind., 500.
On Chi., Mil., St. P. & Pac. (R. R.).

NEW GRETNA, Burlington Co., N. J., 958.

NEW HAMBURG, Waterloo South Co., Ontario, Canada, 1,436.
On Can. Nat. (R. R.).

NEW HAMPTON, c. s., Chickasaw Co., Iowa, 2,458.
On Chi. Gt. West.; Chi., Mil., St. P. & Pac. (R. Rs.).

NEW HARMONY, Posey Co., Ind., 1,022.
On Ill. Cen. (R. R.).

NEW HARTFORD (Landers), Litchfield Co., Conn., 1,834.
On N. York, N. Hav. & Hart. (R. R.).
—Butler Co., Iowa, 500.
On Ill. Cen. (R. R.).
—Oneida Co., N. Y., 1,885.
On Del., Lack. & West.; N. York, Ont. & West. (R. Rs.).

NEW HAVEN, c. s., New Haven Co., Conn., 162,655.
Situated at the head of New Haven Harbor, and on the New York, New Haven and Hartford Railroad.
It is the seat of Yale University, one of the foremost institutions of learning in the United States, chartered as a collegiate school in 1701. The city has also a number of features of historic interest, including Central Green, where the city was first settled in 1638; Grove Street Cemetery, where Noah Webster and other notable men are buried, etc.
Prominent landmarks are the County Court House, Public Library, City Hall, Soldiers' Monument (in East Rock Park), and the "Bowl," Yale's celebrated athletic field.
The city's industries are varied, the better known being firearms, clocks, sporting goods, musical instruments, hardware, and wire products.
—Allen Co., Ind., 1,702.
On N. York, Chi. & St. Lou.; Wab. (R. Rs.).
—Macomb Co., Mich., 774.
On Gd. Tr. (R. R.).
—Franklin Co., Mo., 876.
On Mo. Pac. (R. R.).
—Mason Co., W. Va., 750.
On Balt. & Ohio (R. R.).

NEW HOLLAND, Fayette and Pickaway Cos., Ohio, 741.
On Penna. (R. R.).
—Lancaster Co., Pa., 1,725.
On Penna. (R. R.).

NEW HOLSTEIN, Calumet Co., Wis., 1,274.
On Chi., Mil., St. P. & Pac. (R. R.).

NEW HOPE, Bucks Co., Pa., 1,113.
On Penna.; Reading (R. Rs.).

NEW IBERIA, c. s., Iberia Parish, La., 8,003.
On Mo. Pac.; Sou. Pac. (R. Rs.).
Ships cotton, sugar, corn and rice.

NEWINGTON, Hartford Co., Conn., 4,572.
On N. York, N. Hav. & Hart. (R. R.).

NEW HYDE PARK, Nassau, N. Y., 3,314.
On Long Isl. (R. R.).

NEW KENSINGTON, Westmoreland Co., Pa., 16,762.
On Penna. (R. R.).
A coal mining center with manufactures of glass, aluminum, iron, white lead, tin plate, and springs.

NEWKIRK, c. s., Kay Co., Okla., 2,135.
On Atch., Top. & Santa Fe (R. R.).

NEW KNOXVILLE, Auglaize Co., Ohio, 528.

NEW LEBANON, Montgomery Co., Ohio, 509.

NEW LENOX, Will Co., Ill., 652.
On Chi., Rk. Isl. & Pac.; Wab. (R. Rs.).

NEW LEXINGTON, c. s., Perry Co., Ohio, 3,901.
On Penna.; N. York Cen. (R. Rs.).

NEW LISBON, Juneau Co., Wis., 1,076.
On Chi., Mil., St. P. & Pac. (R. R.).

NEW LONDON, New London Co., Conn., 29,640.
On Cen. Ver.; N. York, N. Hav. & Hart. (R. Rs.).
A summer and yachting resort. Seat of Connecticut College for Women.
—Henry Co., Iowa, 1,336.
On Chi., Burl. & Quincy (R. R.).
—c. s., Ralls Co., Mo., 900.
On St. Lou. & Han. (R. R.).
—Merrimack Co., N. H., 600.
—Huron Co., Ohio, 1,527.
On Cle., Cin., Chi. & St. Lou.; Nor. Ohio (R. Rs.).
—Outagamie and Waupaca Cos., Wis., 4,661.
On Chi. & Nor. West.; Gr. Bay & West. (R. Rs.).

NEW LYME STATION (New Lyme), Ashtabula Co., Ohio, 627.
On Penna. (R. R.).

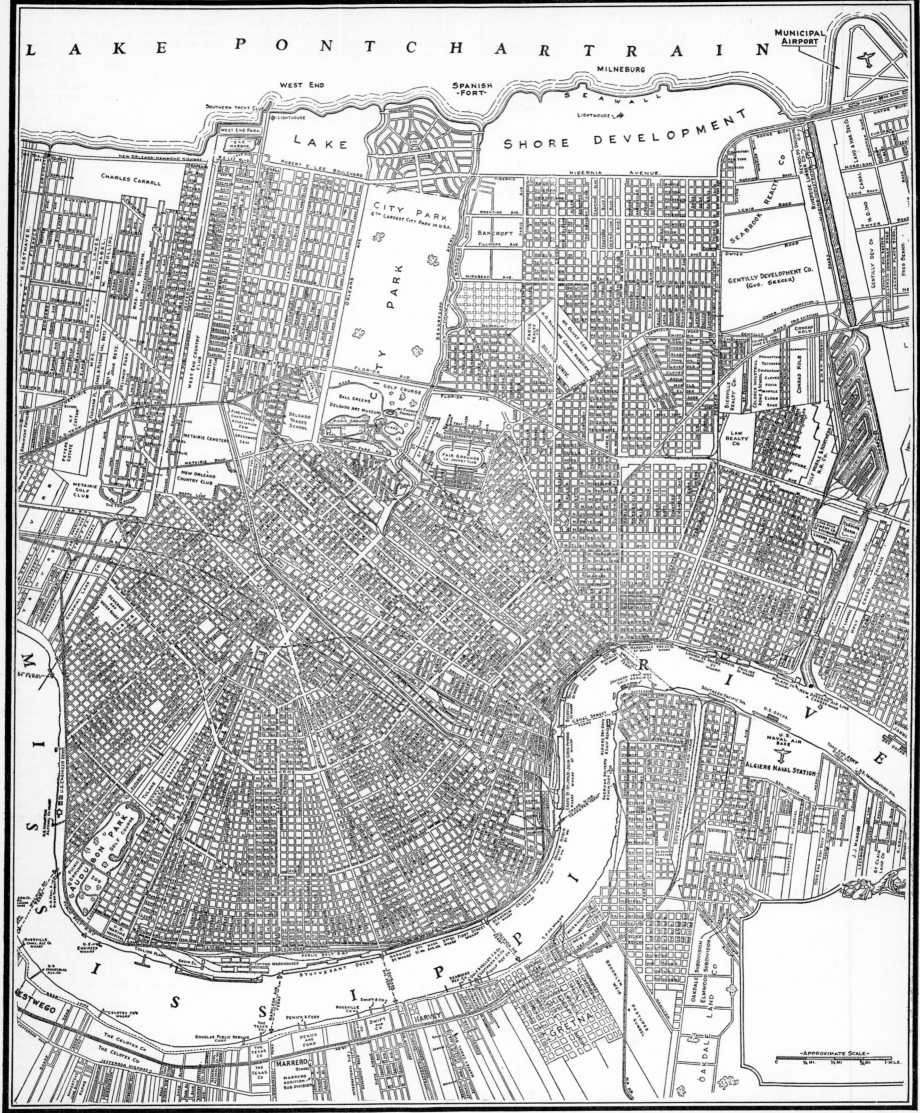

MAP OF THE PRINCIPAL SECTION OF NEW ORLEANS. CHIEF CITY OF LOUISIANA AND THE GATEWAY TO THE MISSISSIPPI. ONE HUNDRED STEAMSHIP LINES USE ITS SPACIOUS WHARVES. RICH IN HISTORY AND ROMANCE, WITH ITS FRENCH TRADITION, NEW ORLEANS IS ONE OF THE MOST COLORFUL AND PICTURESQUE OF OUR CITIES

New Madison, Darke Co., Ohio, 516.
On Penna. (R. R.).
New Madrid, c. s., New Madrid Co., Mo., 2,309.
On St. Lou. Southw. (R. R.).
Newman, Stanislaus Co., Cal., 1,269.
On Sou. Pac. (R. R.).
–Douglas Co., Ill., 1,054.
On Balt. & Ohio (R. R.).
–Essex Co., N. Y., 800.
Newman Grove, Madison Co., Neb., 1,146.
On Chi. & Nor. West. (R. R.).
New Market, Madison Co., Ala., 500.
On Nash., Chatt. & St. Lou. (R. R.).
–Taylor Co., Iowa, 630.
On Chi., Burl. & Quincy (R. R.).
–Jefferson Co., Tenn., 500.
On Southern (R. R.).
–Shenandoah Co., Va., 640.
On Southern (R. R.).
Newmarket, Rockingham Co., N. H., 2,500.
On Bost. & Me. (R. R.).
–York Co., Ont., Can., 3,748.
On Can. Nat. (R. R.).
New Marlboro, Berkshire Co., Mass., 921.
New Marshall, Logan Co., Okla., 695.
New Martinsville, c. s., Wetzel Co., W. Va., 2,814.
On Balt. & Ohio (R. R.).
New Matamoras, Washington Co., Ohio, 781.
New Miami, Butler Co., Ohio, 1,289.
New Milford, Litchfield Co., Conn., 3,000.
On N. York, N. Hav. & Hart. (R. R.).
–Bergen Co., N. J., 2,556.
On N. Jer. & N. York (R. R.).
–Susquehanna Co., Pa., 782.
On Del., Lack. & West. (R. R.).
Newnan, Coweta Co., Ga., 6,386.
On Atl. & West Pt.; Cen. of Ga. (R. Rs.).
New Orleans, c. s., Orleans Parish, La., 458,762.
Situated on both sides of the Mississippi River, 106 miles above its mouth in the Gulf of Mexico. It is on the Gulf, Mobile & Northern; the Illinois Central; the Louisiana & Arkansas; the Louisiana Southern; the Louisville & Nashville; the Missouri Pacific; the New Orleans & Lower Coast; the New Orleans & Northeastern; the Southern Pacific; the Texas & Pacific; and the Texas-Pacific-Missouri Pacific Terminal of New Orleans railroads.
A considerable portion of the city is below the high-water level of the river. To protect it from annual inundations, a high, broad embankment, or levee, has been constructed along the city front and for a long distance up and down the river.
Tulane University, founded in 1884, is located here. Other collegiate institutions are the Ursuline College, Loyola University, the H. Sophie Newcomb Memorial College for Women, the Dillard Memorial University for Negroes, Xavier University for Negroes, and Dominican College.
The French market is celebrated and is one of the sights of the city. The area of public squares is about 1,700 acres, the chief parks being the City Park and Audubon Park. A unique feature of New Orleans is the annual carnival, which takes place on Shrove Tuesday, or Mardi Gras. New Orleans is one of the world's great cotton markets. Manufacturing industries include sugar refining, canning, papermaking, rice cleaning, woodworking, iron and steel works.
The city was founded in 1718 by Sieur de Bienville, and named in honor of the Duke of Orléans. It passed into the hands of the Spanish in 1763, was reconveyed to France in 1800, and became a part of the United States by the Louisiana Purchase in 1803. At this time it had a population of 8,000. On January 8, 1815, the British, under General Packenham, attacked the city and were defeated by a much smaller number of Americans under General Jackson. In 1862 New Orleans was blockaded by the Federal fleet under Admiral Farragut, who succeeded in passing the forts in the Mississippi River, and on April 25 anchored in front of the city. After a few days it was surrendered to the Union forces.
New Oxford, Adams Co., Pa., 1,138.
On West. Md. (R. R.).
New Paltz, Ulster Co., N. Y., 1,362.
On West Shore (R. R.).
New Paris, Elkhart Co., Ind., 634.
On Cle., Cin., Chi. & St. Lou.; Wab.; Winona (El.) (R. Rs.).
–Preble Co., Ohio, 925.
On Penna. (R. R.).
New Philadelphia, c. s., Tuscarawas Co., Ohio, 12,365.
On Balt. & Ohio; Penna. (R. Rs.).
–Schuylkill Co., Pa., 2,557.
On Reading (R. R.).
New Plymouth, Payette Co., Idaho, 510.
on Un. Pac. (R. R.).
New Port Richey, Pasco Co., Fla., 797.
On Seab. Air Line (R. R.).
Newport, c. s., Jackson Co., Ark., 4,547.
On Chi., Rk. Isl. & Pac.; Mo. Pac. (R. Rs.).
–New Castle Co., Del., 947.
On Penna. (R. R.).
–Madison Co., Ill., 500.
–c. s., Vermillion Co., Ind., 777.
On Chi. & East. Ill. (R. R.).
–Monmouthshire, England, 89,198.
A seaport and marketing town with an increasing trade.
–c. s., Campbell Co., Ky., 29,744.
On Chesa. & Ohio; Lou. & Nash. (R. Rs.).
Manufacturing and residential city.
–(Newport Junction), Penobscot Co., Maine.
On Maine Cen. (R. R.).
–c. s., Sullivan Co., N. H., 4,200.
On Bost. & Me. (R. R.).
–Washington Co., Minn., 541.
On Chi., Burl. & Quincy; Chi., Mil., St. P. & Pac.; Chi., Rk. Isl. & Pac. (R. Rs.).
–Herkimer Co., N. Y., 696.
On N. York Cen. (R. R.).
–Washington Co., Ohio, 500.
–Lincoln Co., Oregon, 1,530.
–Perry Co., Pa., 1,891.
On Penna. (R. R.).
–c. s., Newport Co., R. I., 29,202.
Port of entry, situated on the island of Rhode Island, in Narragansett Bay, and on the New York, New Haven & Hartford Railroad. It is a fashionable summer resort. There are beautiful summer residences, owned by persons of wealth from Boston and New York.
Newport is the seat of the United States Naval War College, United States Training Station, Torpedo Station, and the Naval Hospital.
–c. s., Cocke Co., Tenn., 2,989.
On Southern (R. R.).
–Giles Co., Va., 983.
–c. s., Orleans Co., Vt., 5,094.
On Can. Pac.; Queb. Cen. (R. Rs.).
–c. s., Pend Oreille Co., Wash., 1,080.
On Gt. Nor.; Chi., Mil., St. P. & Pac. (R. Rs.).
Newport Beach, Orange Co., Cal., 2,203.
On Pac. El. (R. R.).
Newport News (Ind. City), Warwick Co., Va., 34,417.
On Chesa. & Ohio (R. R.).
A seaport and commercial center. Exports tobacco and coal. Resorts and beaches near by; also Fort Monroe and Langley Field.
New Prague, Scott and Le Sueur Cos., Minn., 1,543.
On Mpls. & St. Lou. (R. R.).
New Preston (Post Office), Litchfield Co., Conn., 798.
New Providence, Union Co., N. J., 1,918.
On Del., Lack. & West. (R. R.).
–Montgomery Co., Tenn., 904.
New Richland, Waseca Co., Minn., 777.
On Mpls. & St. Lou. (R. R.).
New Richmond, Clermont Co., Ohio, 1,830.
On Chesa. & Ohio (R. R.).
–St. Croix Co., Wis., 2,112.
On Chi., St. P., Mpls. & Oma.; Mpls., St. P. & S. Ste. M. (R. Rs.).
New River, Pulaski Co., Va., 550.
On Norf. & West. (R. R.).
New Roads, c. s., Pointe Coupee Parish, La., 1,473.
On Tex. & Pac. (R. R.).
New Rochelle, Westchester Co., N. Y., 54,000.
On N. York., N. Hav. & Hart. (R. R.).
Founded by Huguenot refugees in 1687. Is mainly a residential section. Seat of College of New Rochelle (Catholic) for women.
New Rocky Comfort (Foreman), Little River Co., Ark., 1,056.
New Rockford, c. s., Eddy Co., N. D., 2,195.
On Nor. Pac.; Gt. Nor. (R. Rs.).
Newry, Counties Down and Armagh, Northern Ireland, 11,963.
New Salem, Morton Co., N. Dak., 804.
On Nor. Pac. (R. R.).
–Fayette Co., Pa., 900.
On Monongahela (R. R.).
–(Delmont P. O.), Westmoreland Co., Pa., 721.
New San Salvador, Salvador, 31,450.
A marketing center situated in a fertile valley.
New Sharon, Mahaska Co., Iowa, 1,052.
On Mpls. & St. Lou. (R. R.).
New Shoreham, Newport Co., R. I., 1,044.
New Smyrna, Volusia Co., Fla., 4,470.
On Fla. East Coast (R. R.).
New Straitsville, Perry Co., Ohio, 1,718.
On Chesa. & Ohio (R. R.).
New Suffolk, Suffolk Co., N. Y., 600.
New Tazewell, Claiborne Co., Tenn., 821.
Newton, Dale Co., Ala., 661.
On Atl. Coast Line (R. R.).
–c. s., Baker Co., Ga., 517.
–c. s., Jasper Co., Ill., 2,076.
On Ill. Cen. (R. R.).
–c. s., Jasper Co., Iowa, 11,560.
On Chi., Rk. Isl. & Pac.; Mpls. & St. Lou. (R. Rs.).
Manufactures washing machines, trenching machines, show cases, and advertising novelties.
–c. s., Harvey Co., Kans., 10,581.
On Ark. Val. Interurban (El.); Atch., Top. & Santa Fe; Mo. Pac. (R. Rs.).
Flour, threshing machines, brooms, ice, and dairy products. Seat of Bethel College.
–Middlesex Co., Mass., 66,144.
On Bost. & Alb. (R. R.).
A residential suburb of Boston. Some manufacturing.
–Newton Co., Miss., 2,011.
On Gulf, Mob. & No.; Ill. Cen. (R. Rs.).
–c. s., Sussex Co., N. J., 5,401.
On Del., Lack. & West. (R. R.).
–c. s., Catawba Co., N. C., 4,394.
On Car. & Nor. West.; Sou. (R. Rs.).
–c. s., Newton Co., Tex., 1,000.
On Gulf & Nor.; Nor. Pac. (R. Rs.).
–Cache Co., Utah, 555.
Newton Falls, St. Lawrence Co., N. Y., 750.
On N. York Cen. (R. R.).
–Trumbull Co., Ohio, 3,458.
On Balt. & Ohio; N. York Cen.; Penna. (R. Rs.).
Newtown, Fairfield Co., Conn., 2,635.
On N. York, N. Hav. & Hart. (R. R.).
–Hamilton Co., Ohio, 939.
On Norf. & West. (R. R.).
–Bucks Co., Pa., 1,824.
On Read. (R. R.).
New Ulm, c. s., Brown Co., Minn., 7,308.
On Mpls. & St. Lou.; Chi. & Nor. West. (R. Rs.).
New Vienna, Clinton Co., Ohio, 628.
On Balt. & Ohio (R. R.).
Newville, Henry Co., Ala., 528.
On Atl. Coast Line (R. R.).
–Cumberland Co., Pa., 1,482.
On Penna. (R. R.).
New Washington, Crawford Co., Ohio, 921.
On Nor. Ohio; Penna. (R. Rs.).
New Washington, P. I., 24,453.
A marketing center. Rice, sugar, tobacco, corn, abaca, and cattle are raised in the vicinity.
New Westminster, New Westminster Co., British Columbia, Canada, 17,524.
On Can. Pac.; Gt. Nor.; Can. Nat.; British Col. El.; Vanc. & Lulu Is. (R. Rs.).
A commercial and manufacturing center. Lumber, iron, canned fruit and fish, are the chief industries.
In 1898 the city was almost destroyed by fire.
New Willard, Polk Co., Tex., 518.
On Sou. Pac. (R. R.).
New Wilmington, Lawrence Co., Pa., 907.
On Penna. (R. R.).
New Windsor, Carroll Co., Md., 503.
On West. Md. (R. R.).
New York, the commercial metropolis of the State of New York and of the United States, largest city in the world, has an area of 320 sq. mi., 6,930,446.
New York has five boroughs:
Manhattan, the original New York City (an island which is 13½ mi. long and 2 mi. wide and separated from the mainland by the Harlem River and Spuyten Duyvil Creek) and Welfare, Ward's, Governor's and Randall's Islands, has a total area of 22 sq. mi., 1,867,312. Bronx, the mainland north of Manhattan Island, and North Brother, South Brother, Rikers, City, Rodman, Hunter, and Harts islands, have a total area of 42 sq. mi., 1,265,258.
Brooklyn, a portion of Long Island, Coney Island (on which are located the Brighton Beaches and Manhattan Beach) and a number of islands in Jamaica Bay, has a total area of 81 sq. mi., 2,560,401. Queens, a portion of Long Island, which includes Rockaway Beach and numerous small islands in Jamaica Bay, has a total area of 117 sq. mi., 1,079,129.
Richmond, Staten Island, has an area of 57 sq. mi., 158,346. The strikingly beautiful landlocked harbor of New York includes the lower bay, the upper bay, the East River, and the North, or Hudson River. Steamships enter it from the sea by Sandy Hook through the Narrows, or through Hell Gate which connects the East River with Long Island Sound. Hudson River here averages a mile wide and is navigable for 150 miles; the East River is not so wide, but both are deep enough for the large ships, and furnish many miles of wharfage. The Harlem River and a ship canal at the north end of Manhattan Island connect the two great rivers. The total water front of Greater New York is 578 miles. New York has ranked first in the U. S. in population since the taking of the first Federal census. In 1790 it was first with 33,131; in 1800, with 60,515; in 1810, with 96,373; in 1820, with 123,706; in 1830, with 202,589; in 1840, with 312,710; in 1850, with 515,547; in 1860, with 813,669; in 1870, with 942,292; in 1880, with 1,206,299; in 1890, with 1,515,-301; in 1900, with 3,437,202 for the Greater city; in 1910, with 4,766,883; in 1916, with 5,528,750, in 1920 with 5,621,151, and in 1930 with 6,930,446 respectively.
The main portion of Manhattan, from 8th Street north to 155th Street, is laid out with severe regularity, the numbered avenues running north and south and cross streets at right angles, east and west. Broadway, the principal thoroughfare, runs north from the Battery, until at 10th Street it deflects to the west, crossing the rectangular streets diagonally. Below 10th Street the streets are irregular and narrow. In this portion of the city, in what is known as the "Lower East Side," is concentrated a large portion of the foreign resident population, living mainly in densely packed tenement houses.
The most southerly mile of Manhattan is given over to the financial district, shipping offices and a great variety of other business and professional offices. In this small area are many tall buildings, and there is a greater concentration of business than in any other equal area in the world. From 23rd Street to 59th Street is an area the center of which is given over primarily to hotels, theaters and large retail department stores, flanked on both sides with residential property and industrial plants. Centering on 42nd Street is the new midtown skyscraper zone.
The 125th Street region is known as Harlem. The high ground above Harlem on the west side is known as Washington Heights. Central Park, 2½ miles long, about ½ mile wide, 840 acres, between 59th and 110th Streets, and Fifth Avenue and Central Park West, is the chief city park. It contains lakes, a menagerie, an Egyptian obelisk, "Cleopatra's Needle" (1500 B.C.), many statues, and the Metropolitan Museum of Art. Other parks are Van Cortlandt Park, 1,132 acres; Pelham Bay Park, 1,788 acres; and Bronx Park, 719 acres, containing the Botanical and Zoological Gardens. On Morningside Heights are located the buildings of Columbia University, St. Luke's Hospital, and the great Cathedral of St. John the Divine. The Croton and the Catskill aqueducts supply the city's water.
The architecture of New York exhibits great contrasts and diverse styles. The steel frame building or "sky-scraper," is characteristic of New York, where there are more edifices of this style of structure than in any other city. Notable among them may be mentioned: Empire State, 102 stories, 1,250 feet; Chrysler, 77 stories, 1,046 feet; Cities Service, 67 stories, 950 feet; Manhattan Company, 70 stories, 927 feet; Radio City—Central Tower, 70 stories, 850 feet; Woolworth, 60 stories, 792 feet; City Bank Farmers' Trust, 60 stories, 760 feet; Metropolitan Life, 52 Stories, 700 feet; 500 Fifth Avenue, 58 stories, 699 feet; Chanin, 56 stories, 680 feet; Lincoln, 53 stories, 673 feet; Irving Trust, 51 stories, 654 feet; 10 East Fortieth Street, 48 stories, 632 feet; Waldorf-Astoria, 47 stories, 625 feet; RCA-Victor, 50 stories, 622 feet; New York Life, 34 stories, 617 feet; Singer, 41 stories, 612 feet; Ritz Tower, 42 stories, 592 feet; Municipal, 42 stories, 584 feet; Sherry Netherland, 38 stories, 570 feet; Continental Bank, 35 stories, 560 feet.
Other notable buildings are the Custom-house and the Produce Exchange at the foot of Broadway, the Stock Exchange on Broad Street; the City Hall dating from 1803; the County Court House, 1861; the Federal Building; the Appellate Division of the Supreme Court in Madison Square, a white marble structure in Corinthian style; the "Flatiron" building on a triangular lot at Broadway, Fifth Avenue, and 23rd Street; the Grand Central Station, at 42nd Street and Fourth Avenue; the Pennsylvania Railroad Station, between Seventh and Eighth Avenues and 31st and 33rd Streets; the Post-office building at 8th Avenue and 32nd Street, facing Pennsylvania Station; the Museum of Natural History at 77th Street, with the Planetarium at 81st and Central Park West; the buildings of Columbia University at 116th Street, and of the College of the City of New York, at 138th Street and Amsterdam Avenue.
Among the educational institutions of New York, first place is held by Columbia University (chartered in 1754 as King's College). Associated with it are Barnard College (for women); the Teachers College, and the College of Physicians and Surgeons. Among other educational institutions are the New York University (1831); the College of the City of New York; Cooper Union, in which nearly all the courses are free; Fordham University, Manhattan, and St. Francis Xavier, Roman Catholic Colleges; besides numerous professional schools.
Notable churches are St. Patrick's Cathedral (Roman Catholic); Riverside Church (Baptist); Cathedral of St. John the Divine, St. Paul's Chapel; Trinity, Grace, St. Thomas's, St. George's, and St. Bartholomew's (Episcopal); the Fifth Avenue Presbyterian; Madison Avenue Methodist Episcopal; the Broadway Tabernacle (Congregational); All Souls (Unitarian); the Divine Paternity (Universalist); the First and Second Churches of Christ; Scientist, the Temples Emanu-El, and Israel (Jewish).
The Astor and Lenox Libraries, with the aid of the Tilden Trust, were consolidated into the New York Public Library, for which a new building was built at a cost of $9,000,000.

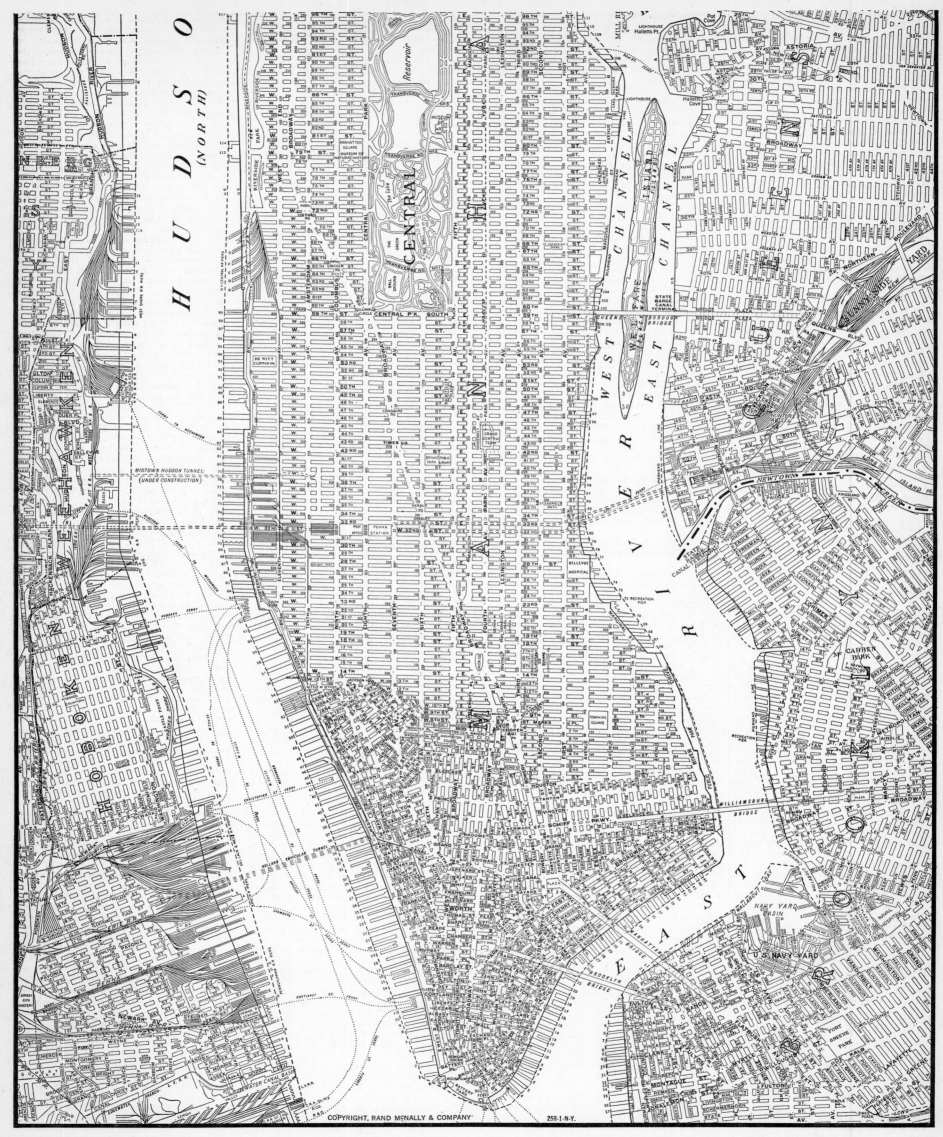

MAP OF LOWER MANHATTAN, AN ISLAND IN NEW YORK BAY BOUNDED BY THE HUDSON, THE EAST, AND THE HARLEM RIVERS, AND COMPRISING THE BOROUGH OF MANHATTAN OF GREATER NEW YORK. NEW YORK IS THE MOST IMPORTANT PORT ON THE ATLANTIC SEABOARD, AND IS LINED BY GREAT PIERS

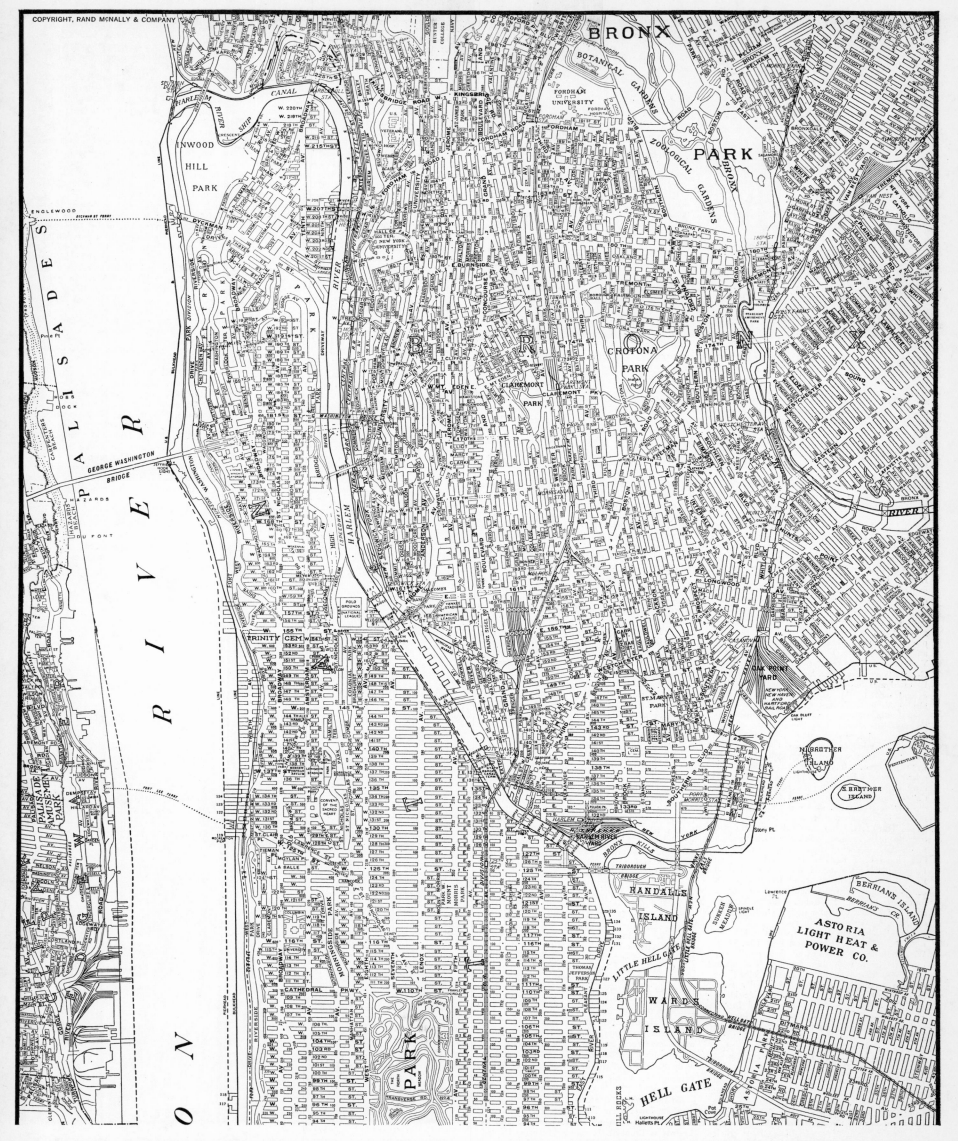

MAP OF UPPER MANHATTAN AND THE BRONX, TWO OF THE FIVE BOROUGHS OF GREATER NEW YORK. THE BRONX IS NORTHEAST OF MANHATTAN ACROSS THE HARLEM RIVER AND IS A RAPIDLY GROWING BUSINESS CENTER. THE NEW YORK ZOOLOGICAL AND BOTANICAL GARDENS ARE LOCATED IN BRONX PARK

WILLIAM FRANGE PHOTO

THE NEW YORK MEDICAL CENTER, NEW YORK CITY, LARGEST IN THE WORLD. INCORPORATING ELEVEN SCHOOLS AND HOSPITALS

and which possesses more than 3,400,000 volumes. It maintains numerous branch circulating libraries throughout Greater New York. The Metropolitan Museum of Art, in Central Park, near 82d Street, contains paintings, statuary, ivories, tapestries, porcelains, Greek, Roman, and Egyptian antiquities. The American Museum of Natural History, 77th Street and Central Park West, contains collections of natural history, paleontology, and ethnology. Pertaining to it are the Planetarium and the Theodore Roosevelt Memorial Building. There are nearly 200 theaters, music halls, and similar first-class amusement places in the city.

As a business center, New York has long been not only the first city of this continent, but the first or second city of the world, London being its only rival. It is the greatest seaport of the world. The port of New York receives two-thirds of the imports into the United States, and one-third of the exports pass out of it. The principal exports are grain, flour, cotton, tobacco, petroleum, dairy products, iron, and steel goods, fruits, cattle and frozen meat. The manufactures of New York cover a wide range of products.

Greater New York has a large mileage of Street, Elevated and Subway tracks. Northward they extend near to the city line at Yonkers and Mount Vernon. Tubes under the East River extend the subway system with connections through Brooklyn and outlying points. There are also tubes under that river for local traffic. In addition, the Long Island railroad tunnels connect with the Penn. R. R. system in Manhattan. The Manhattan and Bronx subway system has west and east routes (running north and south) connected by a "shuttle" cross-town line at Times Square. There are two sets of tubes under the Hudson, connecting Manhattan with Jersey City.

Three (formerly four) elevated lines still run over the main avenues, south and north through Manhattan. Many of the numerous surface car lines have been replaced by bus lines. The Holland Tunnel extends under the Hudson River between Manhattan and Jersey City. It consists of twin tubes which accommodate four lanes of vehicular traffic. Lincoln Tunnel, at 38th Street, a vehicular tunnel passing under the Hudson, was opened in 1938.

George Washington Bridge spans the Hudson River between Manhattan and Fort Lee, N. J. West Side Express Highway is a partly elevated roadway, with three lanes each of north and south motor traffic. It extends along the Hudson from Duane Street (eventually from the Battery) to connect with Riverside Drive and Henry Hudson Parkway at 72nd Street. The Triborough Bridge was completed in 1936 and connects the Boroughs of Manhattan, Bronx and Queens.

Among the great railways that start from New York are the New York Central; Central of New Jersey; the New York, New Haven and Hartford; the Pennsylvania; the Baltimore and Ohio; the Delaware, Lackawanna and Western; the New York, Ontario and Western; the Erie; the Lehigh Valley; the West Shore; the Long Island; the New York, Susquehanna and Western. Most of these have their termini at Jersey City or Hoboken, being connected with Manhattan by ferries and by the two extensive tunnel systems under the Hud-

son River. The Pennsylvania Railroad has a large terminal station in the heart of the city, trains running through tunnels under the Hudson River to the South and West, and under the East River to points on the Long Island Railroad.

The New York World's Fair, 1939, occupies a site near Flushing Bay on the northwest shore of Long Island. It commemorates the one hundred and fiftieth anniversary of the inauguration of George Washington as first President of the United States, and the grounds will become a permanent formal park for the citizens of Greater New York when the vast celebration comes to an end.

The approaches to the harbor of New York are defended by strong fortifications at Sandy Hook, the Narrows, and at the head of Long Island Sound. On both sides of the lower sections of the city the river front presents a succession of piers crowded with shipping and local ferries.

Near the head of New York Bay are two islands belonging to the United States. These are Governors Island, a military station, and Bedloes Island, not now fortified, and site of Bartholdi's Statue of Liberty. Blackwell's Island, connected by bridge with Manhattan and Queens, contains city institutions. Connecting Manhattan and Brooklyn are three magnificent suspension bridges: Brooklyn Bridge, 5,900 feet long; Williamsburg Bridge, with a total 7,200 feet, and Manhattan Bridge, with a total length of 6,855 feet. A still larger bridge, supported on piers near its central part, connects Manhattan with Queens.

Verrazano probably entered New York Bay in 1524. In 1609 Henry Hudson sailed up New York Bay and the Hudson River, and four years later the Dutch began the establishment of trading posts on Manhattan Island, where a settlement soon rose which received the name of New Amsterdam. In 1664 the town was surrendered to the English, and was given the name of New York. New York was the meeting-place of Congress from 1785 to 1790, and Washington was inaugurated President here in 1789. In 1807 the first steamboat, starting from this city, navigated the Hudson. Steam communication with the Old World was inaugurated in 1838. In 1873 the limits of the city were extended beyond Manhattan Island to include Morrisania, West Farms, and Kingsbridge, and in 1898 New York, Brooklyn and the rest of what are now the city's five boroughs, united to make a greater New York.

Brooklyn Borough is situated on the western extremity of Long Island, on New York Bay, and the East River, extending from the ocean at Coney Island to the East River and New York Harbor. The northern part of Brooklyn consists of the former city of Williamsburg and the town of Greenpoint. It occupies the whole of Kings County. In the west central part, on Wallabout Bay, is located the United States Navy Yard. The shore opposite lower New York is an irregular bluff, with an elevation of about 90 feet, and is known as Brooklyn Heights, where are located many fashionable residences and club-houses. The main business street is Fulton Street, from Fulton Ferry to East New York, and contains

some of the largest retail establishments in the United States. Clinton Street (on the Heights) is the handsomest street in the city, and is lined with fine residences surrounded by ornamental grounds and shade trees. Other fashionable residence streets are Remsen, Montague and Pierrepont. The favorite drive is through Prospect Park and along the Ocean Parkway, a boulevard 210 feet wide, extending to the seashore at Coney Island. About one-half mile southeast of Prospect Park is Greenwood Cemetery.

Prospect Park, with 526 acres, is the second largest park in Brooklyn. (The largest is Marine Park, 1,767 acres.) Prospect Park is situated on an elevated ridge, commands a magnificent view, and is one of the most picturesque parks in the United States.

The principal public buildings of Brooklyn are grouped together about the Borough Hall. This building is of white marble in the Ionic style. The Kings County Court-house stands east of the Borough Hall, and has a marble front with a Corinthian portico and an iron dome over 100 feet high. Near the courthouse are the Municipal Building and the Hall of Records, both of marble. The Federal Building is the finest structure in the borough, built of granite at a cost of $5,000,000. It is in the Romanesque style, with numerous turrets and a tall tower. It is occupied by the post office and the United States courts. Other notable buildings and institutions are the Academy of Music, Pratt Institute (technical school), the Brooklyn Library, still unfinished, the Art Association Building, the Brooklyn Polytechnic Institute, Long Island Historical Society, Packer Collegiate Institute (women), Brooklyn College of Pharmacy, and the museum of the Brooklyn Institute. The most important hospitals are the Long Island College, Brooklyn Homeopathic, St. Mary's and St. Peter's. Of Brooklyn's 575 ecclesiastical edifices, the best known is Plymouth Church. The Atlantic Dock, and the Erie and Brooklyn Basins are among the most extensive works of

the kind in the country. The former embraces 40 acres, while the latter occupy 60 and 40 acres respectively. Over $200,000,000 has been spent on Brooklyn's shore line, which extends 200 miles, and with the completion of pending improvements on Jamaica Bay, will extend 150 miles more. More than half of New York's foreign commerce is handled at the Brooklyn docks, which are used by more than 40 steamship lines, with a fleet of 700 vessels. Associated with the navy yard are two drydocks, 465 and 307 feet long.

The manufactures are legion. In 1932 Brooklyn had 6,704 factories, employing 130,031 persons. The Borough also contains one terminus of the Long Island Railroad system. There are several lines of subway and elevated roads and suburban trolleys.

Brooklyn was settled by the Dutch in 1636, and in 1646 was incorporated by the authorities of New Amsterdam under the name of Breukelen. It came into the possession of the English in 1666. In 1776 the Battle of Long Island was fought upon the site of Prospect Park. Brooklyn was incorporated as a village in 1816 and as a city in 1834. In 1894 the city was made coextensive with Kings County, and in 1898 united with the city of New York to constitute the borough of Brooklyn. It is now considerably more populous than Manhattan, having at the last census a population of 2,560,401.

—(Mills, P. O.), Otter Tail Co., Minn., 667.

On Nor. Pac. (R. R.).

—Oneida Co., N. Y., 4,006.

On West Shore (R. R.).

NEZHIN, Soviet Union. See NYEZHIN.

NIAGARA, Marinette Co., Wis., 2,033.

NIAGARA FALLS, Niagara Co., N. Y., 75,460. Situated on the Niagara River, and on the Erie; Lehigh Valley; Michigan Central; New York Central; Niagara Junction; Niagara, St. Catharines & Toronto (El.) railroads.

Niagara Falls has long been famous as a scenic resort and is visited by tourists from all parts of the world. It is developing also into

COURTESY ROCKEFELLER CENTER

A GROUP VIEW OF ROCKEFELLER CENTER, NEW YORK CITY. THE TOWERING STRUCTURE IN THE BACKGROUND HAS THE GREATEST FLOOR AREA OF ANY OFFICE BUILDING IN THE WORLD

COURTESY EMPIRE STATE INC.

THE TOWERING EMPIRE STATE BUILDING, NEW YORK CITY, STANDING ON THE SITE OF THE OLD WALDORF-ASTORIA HOTEL. IT IS THE TALLEST OFFICE BUILDING IN THE WORLD, ITS 102 STORIES EXTENDING 1,247 FEET ABOVE THE SIDEWALK

an important manufacturing place, its growth being due to the utilization of the extraordinary power of Niagara River and Falls. Hydro-electric power generated here is transmitted to many points. Among the industries are flour and paper mills, foundries and machine shops, aluminum, carbide, and carborundum works and electro-chemical works.

NIAGARA FALLS, Welland Co., Ontario, Canada, 19,046.
On Can. Nat.; Mich. Cen.; Niag., St. Cath. & Tor. (El.); Wab. (R. Rs.).
The city is situated on the Niagara River opposite the Falls. The river is here crossed by two bridges. The Falls View Bridge, crushed by ice, will eventually be replaced.

NIAGARA-ON-THE-LAKE, Lincoln Co., Ontario, Canada, 1,228.
On Mich. Cen. (R. R.).

NIANTIC, Macon Co., Ill., 589.
On Wab.; Ill. Term. (El.) (R. Rs.).

NICE, Dept. of Alpes-Maritimes, France, 241,916.
Situated on the coast of the Mediterranean, 98 miles east-northeast of Toulon. Owing to the advantages of its situation, Nice has long been celebrated as a winter resort. The city consists of three parts—the New Town on the west, the Old Town, and the Port on the east. The first of these is the part frequented by foreigners, and has beautiful promenades stretching along the seashore, and overlooked by villas and hotels. The Old or Upper Town clusters at the foot of a rocky height, the Castle Hill, an isolated mass of limestone 318 feet high, formerly crowned by a strong castle. Nice was ceded to France by Victor Emmanuel in 1860. It was the birthplace of Garibaldi.

NICHOLASVILLE, c. s., Jessamine Co., Ky., 3,128.
On Cin., N. Orl. & Tex. Pac. (R. R.).

NICHOLLS, Coffee Co., Ga., 651.
On Atl., Birm. & Coast (R. R.).

NICHOLS, Tioga Co., N. Y., 533.
On Del., Lack. & West. (R. R.).

NICHOLSON, Wyoming Co., Pa., 932.
On Del., Lack. & West. (R. R.).

NICKERSON, Reno Co., Kans., 1,061.
On Atch., Top. & Santa Fe; Mo. Pac. (R. Rs.).

NICOLET, Nicolet Co., Quebec, Canada, 2,868.
On Can. Nat. (R. R.).

NICOSIA, capital of Cyprus, 23,700.
Tanning and hand weaving.
—Prov. of Castrogiovanni, Sicily, 12,519.
This town still retains a medieval appearance.

NICTHEROY, Brazil. See NITEROI.

NIEDERHERMSDORF, Silesia, Germany, 11,713.

NIIGATA, Echigo, Ken Niigata, Japan, 125,106.
A port and commercial center situated in a petroleum producing district. Leading manufacture is lacquer-ware.

NIJMEGEN, Gelderland, Netherlands, 89,534.
A trade and marketing center in a rich agricultural district. Has manufactures of Prussian blue, beer, pottery, leather, cigars, and gold and silver work.

NIKOLAEV, Soviet Union, 141,400.

NIKOLAISTED, Finland. See VAASA.

NIKOLSK-USSURIISK, Eastern Territory, Siberia, Sov. Union, 60,000.

NILAND, Imperial Co., Calif., 500.
On Sou. Pac. (R. R.).

NILES, Cook Co., Ill., 2,137.
—Berrien Co., Mich., 11,326.
On Cle., Cin., Chi. & St. Lou.; Mich. Cen. (R. Rs.).
A trade and shipping point for a rich farming region. Has diversified manufactures.
—Trumbull Co., Ohio, 16,314.
On Balt. & Ohio; Erie; Penna. (R. Rs.).
The city is situated on the Mahoning River. Sheet steel and products comprise the chief industry. Rubber tires, incandescent lamp bulbs, fire brick, steel barrels, and dishes are also produced. Birthplace of President William McKinley.

NILES CENTER, Cook Co., Ill., 5,005.
On Chi. & Nor. West.; Chi., No. Shore & Mil. (El.) (R. Rs.).

NIMES, capital of Dept. of Gard, France, 93,758.
A very old city and famous for its cathedral.

NINETY SIX, Greenwood Co., S. C., 1,381.

On Southern (R. R.).

NING PO, Prov. of Chekiang, China, 213,000.
Treaty port, situated in a fertile plain, 16 miles from the mouth of the Yung River, and about 100 miles south of Shanghai.

NINGUTA, Prov. of Kirin, Manchukuo, 30,000.
A trade center and distributing point.

NIOBRARA, c. s., Knox Co., Neb., 761.
On Chi. & Nor. West. (R. R.).

NIORT, Dept. of Deux-Sèvres, France, 27,830.
Glove and brush making are principal industries.

NIPOMO, San Luis Obispo Co., Calif., 750.
On Pac. Coast. (R. R.).

NIS (Nish), Servia, Yugoslavia, 35,384.
An important trade center. The chief manufactures are iron casting, engines, flour, packed meats, and trucks.

NISKAYUNA, Schenectady Co., N. Y., 500.
On N. York Cen. (R. R.).

NITEROI (Nictheroy), capital of State of Rio de Janeiro, Brazil, 125,247.
A residential suburb of Rio de Janeiro.

NITRA, Czech., 21,259.

NIUCHWANG, China. See YINKOW.

NIVELLES, Brabant, Belgium, 12,794.
Parchment, cardboard, and paper.

NIXON, Gonzales Co., Texas, 1,037.
On Sou. Pac. (R. R.).

NIZHNI-NOVGOROD, Soviet Union. See GORKI.

NIZHNI-TAGIL, Soviet Union, 54,483.
Gold, platinum and copper mines near by. Has a large wagon works.

NOBLESTOWN, Allegheny Co., Pa., 600.
On Penna. (R. R.).

NOBLESVILLE, c. s., Hamilton Co., Ind., 4,811.
On Cen. Ind.; Ind. R. R. Sys. (El.); N. York, Chi. & St. Lou. (R. Rs.).

NOCATEE, De Soto Co., Fla., 900.
On Atl. Coast Line; Seab. Air Line (R. Rs.).

NOCONA, Montague Co., Texas, 2,352.
On Mo.-Kan.-Tex. of Texas (R. R.).

NOGALES, c. s., Santa Cruz Co., Ariz., 6,006.
On Sou. Pac. (R. R.).
Port of entry on American-Mexican border. In rich mineral zone. Center for mining, land and cattle interests in Mexico.

NOGENT-SUR-MARNE, Seine, France, 21,056.

NOISY-LE-SEC, Seine, France, 22,359.

NOKOMIS, Montgomery Co., Ill., 2,454.
On Chi. & East Ill.; Cle., Cin., Chi. & St. Lou. (R. Rs.).

NOME, Alaska, 1,213.

NORA SPRINGS, Floyd Co., Iowa, 1,070.
On Chi., Mil., St. P. & Pac.; Chi., Rk. Isl. & Pac. (R. Rs.).

NORBORNE, Carroll Co., Mo., 1,190.
On Atch., Top. & Santa Fe; Wab. (R. Rs.).

NORCATUR, Decatur Co., Kans., 496.
On Chi., Burl. & Quincy (R. R.).

NORCROSS, Gwinnett Co., Ga., 892.
On Southern (R. R.).

NORFIELD, Lincoln Co., Miss., 1,399.
On Ill. Cen. (R. R.).

NORFOLK, Litchfield Co., Conn., 1,280.
—Norfolk Co., Mass., 2,073.
On N. York, N. Hav. & Hart. (R. R.).
—Madison Co., Neb., 10,717.
On Chi. & Nor. West.; Chi., St. P., Mpls. & Oma.; Un. Pac. (R. Rs.).
A trade and distributing center for various manufactured products.
—(Ind. City), Norfolk Co., Va., 129,710.
Situated on the Elizabeth River, and on the Seaboard Air Line; Atlantic Coast Line; Chesapeake & Ohio; Norfolk & Western; Southern; Pennsylvania; Norfolk Southern; and Virginian railroads. Second largest city in Virginia, and with Portsmouth, on the opposite bank of the river, constitutes one of the largest naval stations in the United States. The harbor is large and safe. The city is the shipping point for garden truck, lumber, fertilizer, cotton, peanuts, naval stores, tobacco, auto parts, and machinery.

NORLINA, Warren Co., N. C., 761.
On Seab. Air Line (R. R.).

NORMA, Scott Co., Tenn., 500.
On Tennessee (R. R.).

NORMAL, McLean Co., Ill., 6,768.
On Alton; Ill. Cen. (R. Rs.).
—Shelby Co., Tenn., 595.
On Southern (R. R.).

NORMAN, c. s., Cleveland Co., Okla., 9,603.
On Atch., Top. & Santa Fe (R. R.).

NORMANGEE, Leon and Madison Cos., Texas, 869.
On Burl., Rk. Isl. (R. R.).

NORMAN PARK, Colquitt Co., Ga., 748.
On Atla., Birm. & Coast (R. R.).

NOROTON, Fairfield Co., Conn., 2,000.
On N. York, N. Hav. & Hart. (R. R.).

NORRIDGEWOCK, Somerset Co., Maine, 800.
On Me. Cen. (R. R.).

NORRIS CITY, White Co., Ill., 1,109.
On Balt. & Ohio; Cle., Cin., Chi. & St. Lou. (R. Rs.).

NORRISTOWN, c. s., Montgomery Co., Pa., 35,853.
On Penna.; Read. (R. Rs.).
A residential suburb of Philadelphia. Has textile industries.

NORRKÖPING, Län Linköping, Ostergotland, Sweden, 67,727.
The fourth town of Sweden. Manufactures textiles, sugar, paper, printing, tobacco, carpets, and beer.

NORTH, Orangeburg Co., S. C., 755.
On Seab. Air Line (R. R.).
—Mathews Co., Va., 551.

NORTH ABINGTON, Plymouth Co., Mass., 3,000.
On N. York, N. Hav. & Hart. (R. R.).

NORTH ACTON, Middlesex Co., Mass., 600.
On N. York, N. Hav. & Hart. (R. R.).

NORTH ADAMS, Berkshire Co., Mass., 22,085.
On Bost. & Alb.; Bost. & Me. (R. Rs.).

NORTH AMHERST, Hampshire Co., Mass., 750.

NORTHAMPTON, Northamptonshire, England, 92,314.
On the Nene, about 60 miles N.W. of London. Center of English shoemaking industry; breweries, paper mills, foundries and brickworks are also important.
—c. s., Hampshire Co., Mass., 24,525.
On Bost. & Me.; N. York, N. Hav. & Hart. (R. Rs.).
Seat of Smith College. Industries: silk products, brushes, filtration machinery, etc. First settled in 1654.
—Northampton Co., Pa., 9,839.
On Cen. of N. Jer.; Northamp. & Bath (R. R.).

NORTH HAMPTON, Rockingham Co., N. H., 695.
On Bost. & Me. (R. R.).

NORTH ANDOVER, Essex Co., Mass., 7,164.
On Bost. & Me. (R. R.).

NORTH ARLINGTON, Bergen Co., N. J., 8,263.

NORTH ASHEBORO (Spero), Randolph Co., N. C., 526.

NORTH ATTLEBORO, Bristol Co., Mass., 10,202.
On N. York, N. Hav. & Hart. (R. R.).

NORTH AUGUSTA, Aiken Co., S. C., 2,003.
On Ga. & Fla. (R. R.).

NORTH AURORA, Kane Co., Ill., 682.
On Chi. & Nor. West.; Chi., Burl. & Quincy (R. Rs.).

NORTH BALTIMORE, Wood Co., Ohio, 2,402.
On Balt. & Ohio (R. R.).

NORTH BATON ROUGE, East Baton Rouge Parish, La., 8,000.
On La. & Ark.; Ill. Cen.; Nor. Pac. (R. Rs.).

NORTH BATTLEFORD, Saskatchewan, Canada, 4,719.
On Can. Nat.; Can. Pac. (R. Rs.).

NORTH BAY, Ontario, Canada, 15,528.
On Can. Pac.; Can. Nat.; Temisk & Nor. Ont. (R. Rs.).
A lumber and mining town on Lake Nipissing. Also a summer tourist resort.

NORTH BELLE VERNON, Westmoreland Co., Pa., 3,072.

NORTH BEND, Dodge Co., Neb., 1,108.
On Un. Pac. (R. R.).
—Hamilton Co., Ohio, 597.
On Balt. & Ohio; Cle., Cin., Chi. & St. Lou. (R. Rs.).
—Coos Co., Ore., 4,012.
On Sou. Pac. (R. R.).
—Clinton Co., Pa., 816.
On Pennsylvania (R. R.).
—King Co., Wash., 548.
On Chi., Mil., St. P. & Pac.; Nor. Pac. (R. Rs.).

NORTH BENNINGTON, Bennington Co., Vt., 933.
On Rutland (R. R.).

NORTH BERGEN, Hudson Co., N. J., 40,714.
On Erie; N. York, Ont. & West.; N. York, Susq. & West.; West Shore (R. Rs.).
A residential suburb of New York.

NORTH BERWICK, York Co., Maine, 1,442.
On Bost. & Me. (R. R.).

NORTH BILLERICA, Middlesex Co., Mass., 2,700.
On Bost. & Me. (R. R.).

NORTHBORO, Worcester Co., Mass., 2,396.
On N. York, N. Hav. & Hart. (R. R.).

NORTH BRADDOCK, Allegheny Co., Pa., 16,782.
Primarily a residential suburb of Pittsburgh, but has a large steel plant.

NORTH BRANCH, Lapeer Co., Mich., 658.
On Gd. Tr. (R. R.).
—Chisago Co., Minn., 800.
On Nor. Pac. (R. R.).

NORTH BRENTWOOD, Prince George Co., Md., 641.

NORTHBRIDGE, Worcester Co., Mass., 10,577.
On N. York, N. Hav. & Hart. (R. R.).

NORTH BROOKFIELD, Worcester Co., Mass., 3,186.
On Bost. & Alb. (R. R.).

NORTH CANTON, Stark Co., Ohio, 2,648.
On Balt. & Ohio (R. R.).

NORTH CATASAUQUA, Northampton Co., Pa., 2,700.

NORTH CHARLEROI, Washington Co., Pa., 2,879.

NORTH CHARLESTON, Charleston Co., S. C., 2,000.
On Atl. Coast Line; Seab. Air Line (R. Rs.).

NORTH CHELMSFORD, Middlesex Co., Mass., 3,000.
On Bost. & Me. (R. R.).

NORTH CHICAGO, Lake Co., Ill., 8,466.
On Elg., Jol. & East. (El.); Chi. No. Shore & Mil. (El.); Chi. & Nor. West. (R. Rs.).

NORTH CHILLICOTHE, Peoria Co., Ill., 1,004.

NORTH CITY (Coello), Franklin Co., Ill., 900.

NORTH COLLEGE HILL, Hamilton Co., Ohio, 4,139.

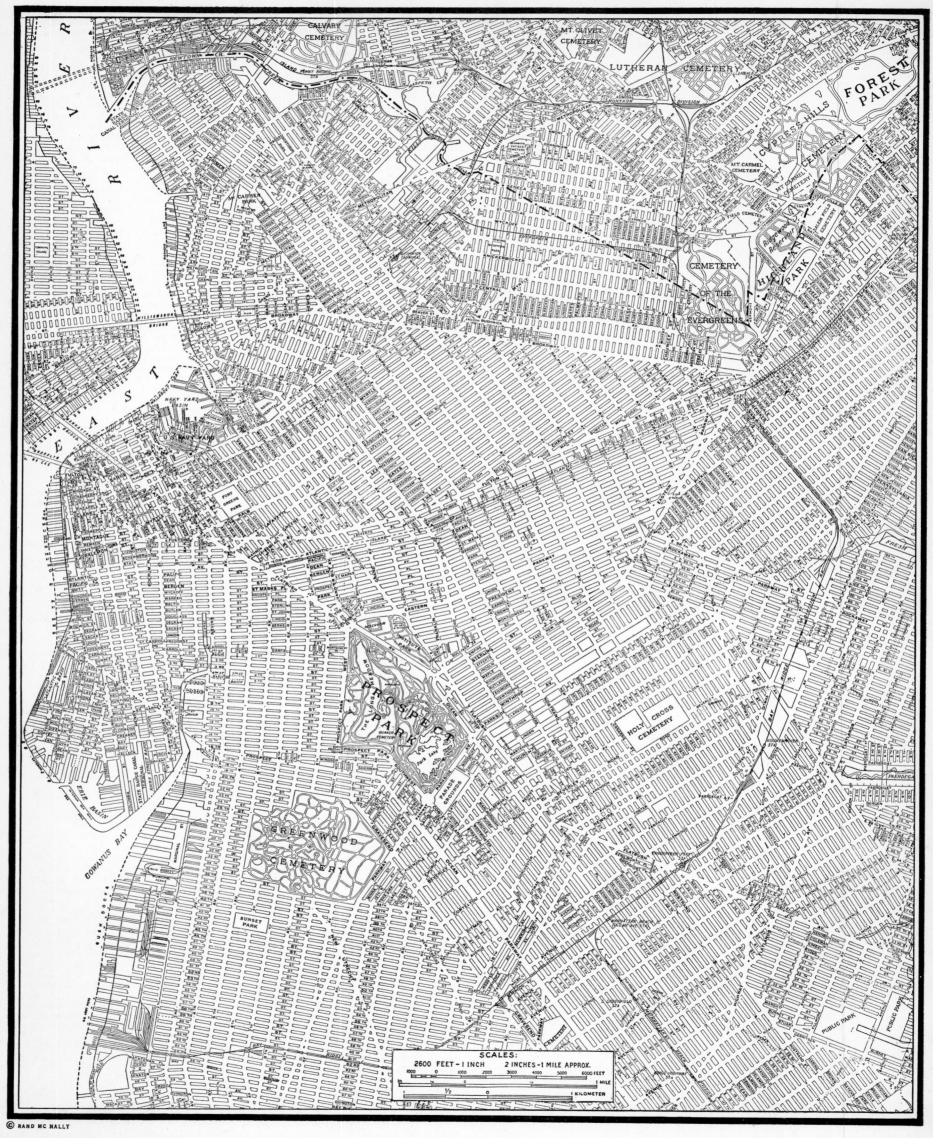

© RAND MC NALLY

MAP OF BROOKLYN, A BOROUGH OF NEW YORK CITY SITUATED ON THE SOUTHWESTERN END OF LONG ISLAND WITH A WATERFRONT OF APPROXIMATELY 36 MILES. THE BOROUGH IS CONNECTED WITH MANHATTAN BY BRIDGES AND SUBWAYS. BROOKLYN IS THE SEAT OF THE BROOKLYN NAVY YARD, THE LARGEST IN THE WORLD

North Collins, Erie Co., N. Y., 1,165.
On Erie (R. R.).
North Conway, Carroll Co., N. H., 900.
On Bost. & Me.; Me. Cen. (R. Rs.).
North Dana, Worcester Co., Mass., 565.
North Dover (Bay Village P. O.), Cuyahoga Co., Ohio, 2,294.
On N. York, Chi. & St. Lou.; Lake Shore (El.) (R. Rs.).
North East, Erie Co., Pa., 3,670.
On N. York Cen.; N. York, Chi. & St. Lou. (R. Rs.).
Northeast, Cecil Co., Md., 1,412.
On Penna. (R. R.).
Northeast Harbor, Hancock Co., Me., 625.
North Easton, Bristol Co., Mass., 3,000.
On N. York, N. Hav. & Hart. (R. R.).
North English, Iowa Co., Iowa, 780.
On Chi., Mil., St. P. & Pac. (R. R.).
North Ferrisburg (Post Office), Addison Co., Vt., 825.
Northfield, Franklin Co., Mass., 1,950.
On Cen. Ver. (R. R.).
Seat of Northfield Seminary for girls.
–Rice Co., Minn., 4,153.
On Chi. Gt. West.; Chi., Mil., St. P. & Pac.; Chi., Rk. Isl. & Pac.; Minn., Northf. & Sou. (R. Rs.).
–Merrimack Co., N. H., 1,336.
On Bost. & Me. (R. R.).
–Atlantic Co., N. J., 2,804.
On Penna.-Read.-Seashore (R. R.).
–Summit Co., Ohio, 1,750.
–Washington Co., Vt., 2,075.
On Cen. Ver. (R. R.).
Seat of Norwich University.
North Fond du Lac, Fond du Lac Co., Wis., 2,244.
On Mpls., St. P. & S. Ste. M. (R. R.).
North Freedom, Sauk Co., Wis., 554.
On Chi. & Nor. West. (R. R.).
North Greenwood, Leflore Co., Miss. See Greenwood.
North Guilford, New Haven Co., Conn., 570.
North Hackensack, Bergen Co., N. J., 593.
On N. Jer. & N. York (R. R.).
North Haledon, Passaic Co., N. J., 2,157.
North Hampton, Rockingham Co., N. H., 695.
On Bost. & Me. (R. R.).
North Haven, New Haven Co., Conn., 3,502.
On N. York, N. Hav. & Hart. (R. R.).
North Haverhill, Grafton Co., N. H., 650.
North Hudson, St. Croix Co., Wis., 625.
North Industry, Stark Co., Ohio, 650.
On Balt. & Ohio (R. R.).
North Irwin, Westmoreland Co., Pa., 1,064.
North Isleboro, Waldo Co., Me., 650.
North Judson, Starke Co., Ind., 1,348.
On Chesa. & Ohio; N. York Cen.; Penna.; Erie (R. Rs.).
North Kansas City, Clay Co., Mo., 2,574.
On Chi., Burl. & Quincy; No. Kas. Cy. Bridge (El.); Wab.; Quincy, Oma. & Kan. Cy. (R. Rs).
North Kemmerer, Lincoln Co., Wyo., 522.
On Un. Pac. (R. R.).
North Kennebunkport, York Co., Maine, 500.
North Kingstown, Washington Co., R. I., 4,767.
North Kingsville, Ashtabula Co., Ohio, 853.
On N. York Cen. (R. R.).
North Las Vegas, Clark Co., Nev., 1,000.
North Lewisburg, Champaign Co., Ohio, 686.
On Erie (R. R.).
North Liberty, St. Joseph Co., Ind., 823.
On N. York Cen.; Wab. (R. Rs.).
North Little Rock, Pulaski Co., Ark., 19,418.
On Chi., Rk. Isl. & Pac.; Mo. Pac.; St. Lou. Southw. (R. Rs.).
An individual suburb of Little Rock.
North Loup, Valley Co., Neb., 657.
On Un. Pac. (R. R.).
North Madison, Jefferson Co., Ind., 573.
On Penna. (R. R.).
North Manchester, Wabash Co., Ind., 2,765.
On Cle., Cin., Chi. & St. Lou.; Penna. (R. Rs.).
Seat of Manchester College.
North Mankato, Nicollet Co., Minn., 2,822.
North Menominee, Dunn Co., Wis., 500.
North Miami, Dade Co., Fla., 1,354.
On Fla. & East Coast (R. R.).
–Ottawa Co., Okla., 503.
On Northe. Okla. (El.) (R. R.).
North Miami Beach, Dade Co., Fla., 522.
On Fla. East Coast (R. R.).
North Milwaukee, Milwaukee Co., Wis. (Pop. incl. in Milwaukee).
On Chi., Mil., St. P. & Pac.; Mpls., St. P. & S. Ste. M. (R. Rs.).
North Muskegon, Muskegon Co., Mich., 1,370.
On Pere Marq. (R. R.).
North New Portland, Somerset Co., Me., 570.
North Nyssa, Malheur Co., Ore., 520.
North Olmsted, Cuyahoga Co., Ohio, 2,624.
North Parsonfield, York Co., Me., 731.
North Pelham, Westchester Co., N. Y., 4,890.
North Plainfield, Somerset Co., N. J., 9,760.
North Platte, c. s., Lincoln Co., Neb., 12,061.
On Un. Pac. (R. R.).
Agriculture, livestock, icing plant. Airport.
Northport, Suffolk Co., N. Y., 2,528.
On Long Isl. (R. R.).
–Tuscaloosa Co., Ala., 2,173.
On Mob. & Ohio (R. R.).
–Leelanau Co., Mich., 577.
On Man. & Northe. (R. R.).
North Portland Junction, Multnomah Co., Ore., 500.
On Nor. Pac.; Un. Pac.; Spok., Port. & Seattle (R. Rs.).
North Powder, Union Co., Ore., 553.
On Un. Pac. (R. R.).
North Pownal, Bennington Co., Vt., 680.
On Bost. & Me. (R. R.).
North Providence, Providence Co., R. I., 11,104.
North Reading, Middlesex Co., Mass., 2,321.
On Bost. & Me. (R. R.).
North Ridgeville, Lorain Co., Ohio, 600.
North Rochester, Beaver Co., Pa., 800.
On Penna. (R. R.).
North Rose, Wayne Co., N. Y., 750.
On N. York Cen. (R. R.).
North St. Paul, Ramsey Co., Minn., 2,915.
On Mpls., St. P. & S. Ste. M. (R. R.).
North Salem, Westchester Co., N. Y., 600.
North Salt Lake, Davis Co., Utah, 515.
On Bamb. El.; Den. & Rio Gde. West.; Un. Pac. (R. Rs.).
North Scituate, Plymouth Co., Mass., 528.
On N. York, N. Hav. & Hart. (R. R.).
North Smithfield, Providence Co., R. I., 3,945.
North Springfield, Windsor Co., Vt., 790.
North Star (Tyre), Allegheny Co., Pa., 750.
North Stonington, New London Co., Conn., 1,135.
North Sydney, Cape Breton Co., Nova Scotia, 6,139.
On Can. Nat. (R. R.).
North Tarrytown, Westchester Co., N. Y., 7,417.
North Tazewell, Tazewell Co., Va., 600.
North Terre Haute, Vigo Co., Ind., 800.
On Chi. & East Ill.; Penna. (R. Rs.).
North Tonawanda, Niagara Co., N. Y., 19,019.
On Erie; Intern. (El.); Leh. Val.; N. York Cen.; West Shore (R. Rs.).
An industrial town. Lumber, paper, iron, petroleum products, musical instruments, and radiators.
North Troy, Orleans Co., Vt., 1,045.
On Can. Pac. (R. R.).
Northumberland, Coos Co., N. H., 2,360.
On Bost. & Me. (R. R.).
–Northumberland Co., Pa., 4,483.
On Del., Lack. & West.; Penna.; Read. (R. Rs.).
North Utica, La Salle Co., Ill., 1,120.
Northvale, Bergen Co., N. J., 1,144.
On Erie (R. R.).
North Vassalboro, Kennebec Co., Me., 575.
North Vernon, Jennings Co., Ind., 2,989.
On Balt. & Ohio; Cle., Cin., Chi. & St. Lou.; Penna. (R. Rs.).
Northville, Wayne and Oakland Cos., Mich., 2,566.
On Pere Marq. (R. R.).
–Fulton Co., N. Y., 1,250.
–Suffolk Co., N. Y., 618.
North Wales, Montgomery Co., Pa., 2,393.
On Reading Co. (R. R.).
North Walpole, Cheshire Co., N. H., 1,425.
North Warren, Warren Co., Pa., 900.
On N. York Cen. (R. R.).
North Webster, Kosciusko Co., Ind., 500.
North Weymouth, Norfolk Co., Mass., 3,045.
North Wildwood, Cape May Co., N. J., 2,049.
On Penna.-Read.-Seashore (R. R.).
North Wilkesboro, Wilkes Co., N. C., 3,668.
Northwood, c. s., Worth Co., Iowa, 1,554.
On Chi., Rk. Isl. & Pac.; Mpls. & St. Lou. (R. Rs.).
–Grand Forks Co., N. Dak., 971.
On Gt. Nor. (R. R.).
North Woodstock (Post Office), Grafton Co., N. H., 530.
On Bost. & Me. (R. R.).
North Yarmouth (Dunns), Cumberland Co., Maine, 569.
On Gd. Tr. (R. R.).
North York, York Co., Pa., 2,416.
Norton, c. s., Norton Co., Kans., 2,688.
On Chi., Burl. & Quincy; Chi., Rk. Isl. & Pac. (R. Rs.).
–Bristol Co., Mass., 2,925.
On N. York, N. Hav. & Hart. (R. R.).
Seat of Wheaton College.
–Wise Co., Va., 3,077.
On Interst.; Lou. & Nash.; Norf. & West. (R. Rs.).
Nortonville, Jefferson Co., Kans., 622.
On Atch., Top. & Santa Fe (R. R.).
–Hopkins Co., Ky., 829.
On Ill. Cen.; Lou. & Nash. (R. Rs.).
Norwalk, Los Angeles Co., Cal., 5,111.
On Sou. Pac.; Pac. Elec. (R. Rs.).
–Fairfield Co., Conn., 36,019.
On N. York, N. Hav. & Hart. (R. R.).
Men's and women's wear, foundry products, tires, etc.
–c. s., Huron Co., Ohio, 7,776.
On N. York Cen.; Wheel. & L. Erie (R. Rs.).
A residential city with some manufactures.
–Monroe Co., Wis., 565.
On Chi. & Nor. West. (R. R.).
Norway, Oxford Co., Maine, 2,446.
On Can. Nat. (R. R.).
–Dickinson Co., Mich., 4,016.
On Chi. & Nor. West. (R. R.).
In an iron mining district.
Norwell, Plymouth Co., Mass., 1,666.
Norwich, Norfolk, England, 126,207.
Manufactures shoes, chemicals, table spices, and iron goods.
–New London Co., Conn., 23,021.
On Cen. Ver.; N. York, N. Hav. & Hart. (R. Rs.).
Principal manufactures are fire-arms, textiles, thermos bottles, locks, rubber goods, buttons, trunks, and machinery.
–c. s., Chenango Co., N. Y., 8,378.
On Del., Lack. & West.; N. York, Ont. & West. (R. Rs.).
Pharmaceutical products, knitted goods, hammers.
–Windsor Co., Vt., 800.
On Bost. & Me. (R. R.).
–Oxford Co., S., Ontario, Canada, 1,158.
On Can. Nat. (R. R.).
Norwichtown, New London Co., Conn. (Ind. Branch Norwich P. O.).
On Cen. Ver. (R. R.).
Norwood, Norfolk Co., Mass., 15,574.
On N. York, New Hav. & Hart. (R. R.).
A residential and industrial suburb of Boston.
–Carver Co., Minn., 607.
On Chi., Mil., St. P. & Pac.; Mpls. & St. Lou. (R. Rs.).
–Bergen Co., N. J., 1,358.
On Erie (R. R.).
–St. Lawrence Co., N. Y., 1,880.
On N. York Cen.; Norw. & St. Lawr.; Rutland (R. Rs.).
–Stanly Co., N. C., 1,452.
On Winst. Sal. Southb.; Norf. Sou. (R. Rs.).
–Hamilton Co., Ohio, 33,411.
On Balt. & Ohio; Norf. & West.; Penna. (R. Rs.).
A suburb of Cincinnati with manufactures of playing cards, safes, furniture, pianos, tools, and electrical products.
–Kent Co., R. I., 930.
On N. York, N. Hav. & Hart. (R. R.).
–(Norwood Station), Delaware Co., Pa., 3,878.
On Penna. (R. R.).
Notasulga, Macon Co., Ala., 756.
On West. of Ala. (R. R.).
Notre-Dame de Graces, Jacques-Cartier Co., Quebec, Can.
On Can. Nat. (R. R.).
Nottingham, Nottinghamshire, England, 283,030.
An important industrial town with large manufactures of hosiery, silk, cotton, drugs, rubber goods, furniture, bicycles, and machinery.
–Cuyahoga Co., Ohio (annexed to Cleveland).
On N. York Cen. (R. R.).
Nouméa, capital of New Caledonia, Melanesia, 10,708.
Seaport and chief trade center.
Novara, capital of Prov. of Novara, Piedmont, Italy, 44,564.
Silk textiles, iron castings, cotton and rice mills, organs, and maps.
Novato, Marin Co., Calif., 700.
On Northw. Pac. (R. R.).
Novgorod, R.S.F.S.R. Soviet Union, 38,000.
Lumber, shoes, bricks, beer and spirits. One of the oldest cities in Russia.
Novinger, Adair Co., Mo., 846.
On Chi., Burl. & Quincy; Quincy, Oma. & Kan. Cy. (R. Rs.).
Novi Sad (Neusatz), Yugoslavia, 63,966.
Pottery and cotton manufactures.
Novocherkassk, Transcaucasia, Soviet Union, 63,300.
Center for wine, corn and timber exports.
Novorossiisk, North Caucasian Dist., R.S.F.S.R., Soviet Union, 100,100.
Important seaport on the Black Sea.
Novo-Sibirsk, Siberia, Soviet Union, 278,000.
A commercial and distributing center.
Novy Jičin, Czech., 13,785.
Nowata, c. s., Nowata Co., Okla., 3,531.
On Mo. Pac.; Un. Elec. (El.) (R. Rs.).
Nowrytown, Indiana Co., Pa., 518.
Noxapater, Winston Co., Miss., 526.
On Gulf, Mob. & Nor. (R. R.).
Nueva Caceres, Prov. of Ambos, Camarines, Luzon, P. I., 9,396.
Nueva Imperial, Prov. of Cantin, Chile, 6,118.
Nuevitas, Prov. of Nuevitas, Cuba, 6,143.
Nuevo de Julio, Buenos Aires, Argentina, 57,424.
A commercial center.
Nuevo Laredo, Tamaulipas, Mexico, 21,636.
On Nat. of Mex. (R. R.).
Exports hides, wool, and corn.
Nukha, Transcaucasia, Soviet Union, 26,300.
Silk worm culture and spinneries.
Nunda, Livingston Co., N. Y., 1,085.
On Penna. (R. R.).
Nuneaton, Warwickshire, England, 46,305.
Iron goods, pipes, clothing, and bricks.
Nunnelly, Hickman Co., Tenn., 520.
On Nash., Chatt. & St. Lou. (R. R.).
Nürnberg, Prov. of Middle Franconia, Bavaria, Germany, 410,438.
On the Pegnitz River. It is one of the quaintest and most interesting towns of Germany. Historical buildings are The Church of St. Lorenz (1224-1477), with two towers 233 feet high; Church of St. Sebald (1225-1377), with the shrine executed by Peter Vischer; the Italian Renaissance town hall (1622); the gymnasium, founded by Melanchthon (1526) and Albrecht Dürer's house.
Nuroad, St. Louis Co., Mo., 1,000.
Nutley, Essex Co., N. J., 20,572.
On Erie (R. R.).
A residential suburb of Newark.
Nutwood, Trumbull Co., Ohio, 500.
Nyack, Rockland Co., N. Y., 5,392.
On Erie (R. R.).
On the west bank of the Hudson River.
Nyezhin (Nezhin), Ukraine, Soviet Union, 29,116.
Center of a tobacco raising district.
Nyiregyhaza, Hungary, 52,776.
An agricultural, manufacturing and railroad center.
Nyköbing, Denmark, 13,919.
A fishing port.
Nyköping, Sweden, 11,953.
A port and marketing town.
Nyssa, Malheur Co., Oregon, 821.
On Un. Pac. (R. R.).

O

Oak Bluffs, Dukes Co., Mass., 1,657.
Oak Creek, Routt Co., Colo., 1,211.
On Den. & Salt L. (R. R.).
Oakdale, Stanislaus Co., Cal., 2,112.
On Sierra; So. Pac.; Atch., Top. & Santa Fe (R. Rs.).
–Allen Parish, La., 3,188.
On Gulf, Colo. & Santa Fe; Mo. Pac. (R. Rs.).
–Antelope Co., Neb., 663.
On Chi. & Nor. West. (R. R.).
–Allegheny Co., Pa., 1,703.
On Pennsylvania (R. R.).
–Morgan Co., Tenn., 1,123.
On Cin., N. Orl. & Tex. Pac.; Sou. (R. Rs.).
Oakes, Dickey Co., N. Dak., 1,709.
On Mpls., St. P. & S. Ste. M.; Chi. & Nor. West.; Nor. Pac. (R. Rs.).
Oakesdale, Whitman Co., Wash., 637.
On Gt. Nor.; No. Pac.; Un. Pac. (R. Rs.).
Oakfield, Aroostook Co., Maine, 600.
On Bangor & Aroostook (R. R.).
–Genesee Co., N. Y., 1,919.
On West Shore (R. R.).
–Fond du Lac Co., Wis., 577.
On Chi. & Nor. West. (R. R.).
Oakford (Neshaminy Falls), Bucks Co., Pa., 500.
On Reading (R. R.).
Oak Grove, c. s., West Carroll Parish, La., 1,241.
On Mo. Pac. (R. R.).
–Jackson Co., Mo., 702.
On Alton (R. R.).
Oakharbor, Ottawa Co., Ohio, 1,849.
On N. York Cen.; Ohio Pub. Ser. Co. (R. Rs.).
Oak Hill, Jackson Co., Ohio, 1,578.
On Balt. & Ohio; Det., Tol. & Iron. (R. Rs.).
–Allegheny Co., Pa., 1,200.
On Balt. & Ohio; Union; Penna., Bessemer & L. Erie (R. Rs.).
–Fayette Co., W. Va., 2,076.
On Virginian (R. R.).
Oakhurst, Monmouth Co., N. J., 900.
–San Jacinto Co., Tex., 750.
Oakland, c. s., Alameda Co., Cal., 284,063.
On Oakland Harbor, with a western frontage on San Francisco Bay.
It is the western terminus of the Atchison, Topeka & Santa Fe; Sacramento Northern (El.); Key System; Southern Pacific; and the Western Pacific railroads. The San Francisco-Oakland Bridge is nine miles long and represents unique features of engineering.
One of the largest manufacturing centers of the Pacific Coast, especially in shipbuilding. It is also a great fruit center.
Noted for its Skyline Boulevard, Lake Merritt (a salt water lake in the heart of the city), and its City Hall, 433 feet high, built on the office building plan.
–Coles Co., Ill., 1,036.
On N. York, Chi. & St. Lou.; Penna. (R. Rs.).
–Pottawattamie Co., Iowa, 1,181.
On Chi., Rk. Isl. & Pac. (R. R.).
–Kennebec Co., Maine, 2,000.
On Me. Cen. (R. R.).
–c. s., Garrett Co., Md., 1,583.
On Balt. & Ohio (R. R.).
–St. Louis Co., Mo., 557.
On Mo. Pac.; St. Lou.-San Fran. (R. Rs.).
–Burt Co., Neb., 1,433.

On Chi., St. P., Mpls. & Oma.; Chi., Burl. & Quincy (R. Rs.).
–Bergen Co., N. J., 735.
On N. York, Susq. & West. (R. R.).
–Susquehanna Co., Pa., 1,040.
–Providence Co., R. I., 500.
On N. York, N. Hav. & Hart. (R. R.).
Oakland Beach, Kent Co., R. I., 1,600.
Oakland City, Gibson Co., Ind., 2,842.
On Cle., Cin., Chi. & St. Lou.; Sou. (R. Rs.).
Oak Lane, Philadelphia Co., Pa., 13,200.
A residential suburb of Philadelphia.
Oak Lawn, Providence Co., R. I., 722.
On N. York, N. Hav. & Hart. (R. R.).
Oakley, Cassia Co., Idaho, 882.
On Un. Pac. (R. R.).
–Contra Costa Co., Cal., 761.
On Atch., Top. & Santa Fe (R. R.).
–Cook Co., Ill., 2,045.
On Ill. Term. (El.); Wabash (R. Rs.).
–Logan Co., Kans., 1,202.
On Un. Pac. (R. R.).
–Lincoln Co., Wyo., 558.
Oaklyn, Camden Co., N. J., 3,843.
On Penna.-Read.-Seashore (R. R.).
Oakman, Walker Co., Ala., 927.
On Southern (R. R.).
Oakmont, Allegheny Co., Pa., 6,027.
On Penna. (R. R.).
Oak Park, Cook Co., Ill., 63,982.
On Chi., Aur. & Elg. (El.); Chi. & Nor. West.; Balt. & Ohio Chi. Term. (R. Rs.).
A residential suburb of Chicago.
–Oakland Co., Mich., 1,079.
Oak Ridge, Armstrong Co., Pa., 500.
On Penna. (R. R.).
Oaks, Montgomery Co., Pa., 700.
On Reading (R. R.).
Oaktown, Knox Co., Ind., 771.
On Chi. & East. Ill. (R. R.).
Oakview, Delaware Co., Pa., 650.
Oakville, Halton Co., Ont., Can., 3,857.
On Can. Pac.; Can. Nat. (R. Rs.).
–Litchfield Co., Conn., 923.
On N. York, N. Hav. & Hart. (R. R.).
–St. Louis Co., Mo., 536.
(Forsythe), Shelby Co., Tenn., 550.
On St. Lou.-San. Fran. (R. R.).
Oakwood, Vermilion Co., Ill., 537.
On Cle., Cin., Chi. & St. Lou.; Ill. Term. (El.) (R. Rs.).
–Cecil Co., Md., 853.
–Marion Co., Mo., 1,500.
On Chi., Burl. & Quincy; St. Lou. & Han. (R. Rs.).
–Montgomery Co., Ohio, 6,494.
–Leon Co., Texas, 888.
On Mo. Pac. (R. R.).
Oas, Prov. of Albay, Luzon, P. I., 16,489.
Oaxaca, capital of State of Oaxaca, Mexico, 31,-348.
On Nat. of Mex. (R. R.).
A general trade and marketing town.
Obando, Prov. of Bulacan, Luzon, P. I., 7,612.
Oberammergau, Bavaria, Germany, 2,281.
Noted for the "Passion Play" performed every ten years, fulfilling a vow of 1634.
Oberhausen, Prussia, Germany, 192,300.
Oberlin, c. s., Decatur Co., Kans., 1,880.
On Chi., Burl. & Quincy (R. R.).
c. s., Allen Parish, La., 790.
On Mo. Pac. (R. R.).
–Lorain Co., Ohio, 4,292.
On N. York Central (R. R.).
Seat of Oberlin College and Conservatory.
–Dauphin Co., Pa., 564.
Obion, Obion Co., Tenn., 1,100.
On Ill. Cen. (R. R.).
Oblong, Crawford Co., Ill., 1,427.
On Ill. Cen. (R. R.).
Ocala, c. s., Marion Co., Fla., 8,110.
On Atl. Coast Line; Seab. Air Line (R. Rs.).
Ocate, Mora Co., N. M., 833.
Occum, New London Co., Conn., 600.
Ocean Beach, San Diego Co., Cal., 713.
Ocean City, Worcester Co., Md., 946.
On Balt. & Eastern (R. R.).
–Cape May Co., N. J., 5,525.
On Penna.-Read. Seashore (R. R.).
Oceanco, Westmoreland Co., Pa., 500.
On Penna. (R. R.).
Ocean Grove, Bristol Co., Mass., 650.
–Monmouth Co., N. J., 1,182.
On N. York & Long Br.; Cen. of N. Jer.; Penna. (R. Rs.).
Ocean Park, Los Angeles Co., Cal. (Pop. incl. in Santa Monica).
On Pacific El.; Sou. Pac. (R. Rs.).
Oceanport, Monmouth Co., N. J., 1,872.
On Cen. of New Jer. (R. R.).
Oceanside, San Diego Co., Cal., 3,508.
On Atch., Top. & Santa Fe (R. R.).
Ocean Springs, Jackson Co., Miss., 1,663.
On Lou. & Nash. (R. R.).
Ocean View, Cape May Co., N. J., 500.
–Norfolk Co., Va., 881.
Ocheyedan, Osceola Co., Iowa, 627.
On Chi., Rk. Isl. & Pac. (R. R.).
Ocilla, Irwin Co., Ga., 2,034.
On Seab. Air Line (R. R.).
Ocoee, Orange Co., Fla., 664.
On Atl. Coast Line; Tav. & Gulf (R. Rs.).
Oconomowoc, Waukesha Co., Wis., 4,190.
On Chi., Mil., St. P. & Pac.; Mil. El. (R. Rs.).
Oconto, c. s., Oconto Co., Wis., 5,030.
On Chi., Mil., St. P. & Pac.; Chi. & Nor. West. (R. Rs.).
Oconto Falls, Oconto Co., Wis., 1,921.
On Chi. & Nor. West. (R. R.).
Ocumare de Tuy, capital of Miranda, Venezuela, 6,175.
Odanah, Ashland Co., Wis., 600.
On Chi. & Nor. West. (R. R.).
Odebolt, Sac Co., Iowa, 1,388.
On Chi. & Nor. West (R. R.).
Odell, Livingston Co., Ill., 908.
On Alton (R. R.).
Odem, San Patricio Co., Tex., 842.
On Mo. Pac. (R. R.).
Odenkirchen, Prussia, Germany, 20,023.
Cotton spinning, weaving, tanning, and dyeing.
Odense, capital of Odense, Denmark, 74,119.
A very old town. Exports mostly agricultural produce.
Odessa, Ukraine, Soviet Union, 459,400.
Seaport and important city, situated on the Black Sea, halfway between the mouths of the Dniester and Bug Rivers. Produces salt, glass, metal, and machinery.
Fierce fighting between the Bolshevists and Ukrainians took place at Odessa following the Russian revolution.
–Lafayette Co., Mo., 1,861.
On Alton (R. R.).
–c. s., Ector Co., Tex., 2,407.
On Tex. & Pac. (R. R.).
–Lincoln Co., Wash., 830.
On Gt. Nor. (R. R.).
Odin, Marion Co., Ill., 1,204.
On Balt. & Ohio; Ill. Cen. (R. Rs.).
Odon, Daviess Co., Ind., 981.
On Chi., Mil., St. P. & Pac. (R. R.).
O'Donnell, Lynn and Dawson Cos., Tex., 1,026.
On Panh. & Santa Fe (R. R.).
Oedenburg. See Sopron.
Oella, Baltimore Co., Md., 660.
On Balt. & Ohio (R. R.).
Oels, Prussia, Germany, 14,447.
Shoes, furniture and machinery.
Oelsnitz, Saxony, Germany, 17,000.
Has a large carpet factory.
Oelwein, Fayette Co., Iowa, 7,794.
On Chi. Gt. West.; Chi., Rk. Isl. & Pac. (R. Rs.).
O'Fallon, St. Clair Co., Ill., 2,373.
On Balt. & Ohio; Ill. Term. (El.); Lou. & Nash. (R. Rs.).
–St. Charles Co., Mo., 594.
On Wabash (R. R.).
Offenbach, Hesse, Germany, 82,000.
Fancy leather goods, celluloid, chemicals, boilers, and machinery are the leading manufactures.
Offenburg, Baden, Germany, 16,613.
Textiles and machinery.
Ogallala, Keith Co., Neb., 1,631.
On Un. Pac. (R. R.).
Ogden, Boone Co., Iowa, 1,429.
On Chi. & Nor. West. (R. R.).
–c. s., Weber Co., Utah, 40,272.
Second largest city in State. Situated on the Weber River, on the Sou. Pac.; Un. Pac.; Den. & Rio Gde. West.; Bamb (El.); and Utah-Ida. Cen. (El.) (R. Rs.).
Shipping point for fruit and farm products.
Ogdensburg, Sussex Co., N. J., 1,138.
On N. York, Susq. & West. (R. R.).
–St. Lawrence Co., N. Y., 16,915.
On N. York Cen.; Rutland (R. Rs.).
A commercial and industrial center. Leading products are shade rollers, paper, pulp, and silk. Near the Thousand Islands.
Oglesby, La Salle Co., Ill., 3,910.
On Chi., Mil., St. P. & Pac.; Ill. Cen. (R. Rs.).
Oglethorpe, c. s., Macon Co., Ga., 953.
On Atla., Birm. & Coast; Cen. of Ga. (R. Rs.).
Seat of Oglethorpe University.
Ogontz, Montgomery Co., Pa., 500.
Ogunquit, York Co., Me., 600.
Ohio, Bureau Co., Ill., 510.
On Chi., Burl. & Quincy (R. R.).
Ohio City, Van Wert Co., Ohio, 879.
On Cle., Cin., Chi. & St. Lou.; Erie; N. York, Chi. & St. Lou. (R. Rs.).
Ohio Falls, Clark Co., Ind., 1,200.
Ohligs (formerly Merscheid), Prussia, Germany, 29,768.
A railroad and industrial center near Solingen.
Oil City, Venango Co., Pa., 22,075.
On Erie; N. York Cen.; Penna. (R. Rs.).
Has oil refineries and machine shops.
–Caddo Par., La., 1,030.
On Kan. Cy. Sou. (R. R.).
–(Oilcenter), Kern Co., Cal., 500.
On Atch., Top. & Santa Fe; Sou. Pac. (R. Rs.).
Oildale, Kern Co., Cal., 2,000.
Oilfield, Caldwell Co., Tex., 1,000.
On Sou. Pac.; Mo. Pac. (R. Rs.).
Oilton, Creek Co., Okla., 1,518.
On Atch., Top. & Santa Fe (R. R.).
–Webb Co., Tex., 500.
On Tex. Mex. (R. R.).
Ojai, Ventura Co., Cal., 1,468.
On Sou. Pac. (R. R.).
Ojus, Dade Co., Fla., 600.
On Fla. East Coast (R. R.).
Okanogan, c. s., Okanogan Co., Washington, 1,519.
On Gt. Nor. (R. R.).
Okawville, Washington Co., Ill., 634.
On Lou. & Nash. (R. R.).
Okayama, capital of Okayama Ken, Japan, 154,500.
Okeechobee, c. s., Okeechobee Co., Fla., 1,914.
On Fla. East Coast; Seab. Air Line (R. Rs.).
Okeene, Blaine Co., Okla., 1,035.
On Chi., Rk. Isl. & Pac.; St. Lou.-San Fran. (R. Rs.).
Okemah, c. s., Okfuskee Co., Okla., 4,002.
On Fort Smith & West. (R. R.).
Oklahoma City, Oklahoma Co., Okla., State capital, 185,389.
Situated on the Canadian River, and on the Atchison, Topeka & Santa Fe; the Chicago, Rock Island & Pacific; the Missouri-Kansas-Texas; the Oklahoma City-Ada-Atoka; the Fort Smith & Western; the Oklahoma City Junction; the Oklahoma (El.); and the St. Louis-San Francisco railroads.
In 1890 the population was 4,151; in 1900, 10,037; and in 1910, 64,205; 1920, 91,295.
It is the most important city in the State.
The jobbing interests are very large, and the city has cotton and cottonseed-oil industries, flouring mills, sash and door factories, oil refineries, packing houses, and manufactories of threshers, engines, scales and hay presses.
Okmulgee, c. s., Okmulgee Co., Okla., 17,097.
On Okmulgee Northern; St. Louis-San Francisco (R. Rs.).
Operating center of Okmulgee oil field, which has a huge output, with extensive refineries.
Okolona, c. s., Chickasaw Co., Miss., 2,235.
On Okol., Houst. & Calh. Cy.; Mob. & Ohio (R. Rs.).
Ola, Yell Co., Ark., 648.
On Chi., Rk. Isl. & Pac.; Ft. Smith, Sub. & Rk. Isl. (R. Rs.).
Olar, Bamberg Co., S. C., 540.
On Seab. Air Line (R. R.).
Olathe, c. s., Johnson Co., Kans., 3,555.
On Atch., Top. & Santa Fe; St. Lou.-San Fran.; Mo. & Kans. (El.) (R. Rs.).
–Montrose Co., Colo., 593.
On Den. & Rio Gde. West. (R. R.).
Olcott, Kanawha Co., W. Va., 511.
On Kanaw. Cen. (R. R.).
Old Albuquerque, Bernalillo Co., N. M., 2,000.
Old Bridge, Middlesex Co., N. J., 1,020.
On Penna. (R. R.).
Oldbury, Worcestershire, England, 35,918.
An industrial suburb of Birmingham.
Olden, Eastland Co., Tex., 1,026.
On Tex. & Pac. (R. R.).
Oldenburg, capital of Oldenburg, Germany, 66,951.
A trade and commercial center for a fertile agricultural region.
–Franklin Co., Indiana, 575.
Old Forge (Thendara), Herkimer Co., N. Y., 840.
On N. York Cen. (R. R.).
–Lackawanna Co., Pa., 12,661.
On Del., Lack. & West.; Erie; Wilk.-Bar. & East. (R. Rs.).
Coal mines.
Old Fort, McDowell Co., N. C., 866.
On Southern (R. R.).
Old Greenwich, Fairfield Co., Conn., 2,368.
On N. York, N. Hav. & Hart. (R. R.).
Oldham, Lancashire, England, 140,309.
On the Medlock, near Manchester.
A manufacturing center, famous for its cotton spinning, textiles, and machine shops. It is near an extensive coal-producing area.
Old Hickory, Davidson Co., Tenn., 8,164.
On Tenn. Cen. (R. R.).
Old Lyme (Lyme), New London Co., Conn., 600.
Old Orchard Beach (Old Orchard), York Co., Maine, 1,000.
On Bost. & Me. (R. R.).
Old Point Comfort, Elizabeth City Co., Va., 1,500.
On Chesa. & Ohio; Penna. (R. Rs.).
Old Saybrook (Saybrook), Middlesex Co., Conn., 1,643.
Old Tappan, Bergen Co., N. J., 600.
Old Town, Penobscot Co., Maine, 7,266.
On Me. Cen. (R. R.).
Old Westbury, Nassau Co., N. Y., 1,264.
Olean, Cattaraugus Co., N. Y., 21,790.
On Erie; Penna.; Pitts., Shawmut & Nor. (R. Rs.).
In an oil and gas region.
Oley, Berks Co., Pa., 720.
Olin, Jones Co., Iowa, 632.
On Chi., Mil., St. P. & Pac. (R. R.).
Oliphant Furnace, Fayette Co., Pa., 500.
On Balt. & Ohio; Penna. (R. Rs.).
Olive, Orange Co., Cal., 600.
On Atch., Top. & Santa Fe (R. R.).
Olive Hill, Carter Co., Ky., 1,484.
On Chesa. & Ohio (R. R.).
Olivers Mills, Luzerne Co., Pa., 500.
On Leh. Val. (R. R.).
Oliver Springs, Anderson and Roane Cos., Tenn., 660.
On Lou. & Nash.; Sou. (R. Rs.).
–Fayette Co., Pa., 1,057.
Olivet, Eaton Co., Mich., 566.
On Gd. Tr. (R. R.).
Olivia, c. s., Renville Co., Minn., 1,475.
On Chi., Mil., St. P. & Pac. (R. R.).
Olla, La Salle Par., La., 740.
On Mo. Pac.; Natchez, Urania & Ruston (R. Rs.).
Olmsted, Pulaski Co., Ill., 560.
On Cle., Cin., Chi. & St. Lou. (R. R.).
Olmsted Falls, Cuyahoga Co., Ohio, 673.
On N. York Cen. (R. R.).
Olmutz, Czechoslovakia. See Olomouc.
Olney, c. s., Richland Co., Ill., 6,140.
On Balt. & Ohio; Ill. Cen. (R. Rs.).
–Young Co., Tex., 4,138.
On Wich. Fs. & Sou.; St. Lou.-San Fran. (R. Rs.).
Olomouc, Moravia, Czechoslovakia, 65,989.
An important market for farm products grown in the vicinity—cereals and cattle especially.
Olton, c. s., Lamb Co., Tex., 687.
Olustee, Baker Co., Fla., 452.
On Seab. Air Line (R. R.).
–Jackson Co., Okla., 651.
On St. Lou.-San Fran. (R. R.).
Olympia, Thurston Co., Wash., State capital, 11,733.
On Deschutes River at the southern extremity of Puget Sound, on the Northern Pacific and the Union Pacific railroads, in a timber, coal, and sandstone region.
The principal manufactures are connected with the lumber industry, but there are also breweries, canneries, and knitting mills.
There was a small settlement a mile south of Olympia in 1846. The town was laid out in 1851, chartered as a city in 1859.
Olympia Mills, Richland Co., S. C., 1,300.
Olyphant, Lackawanna Co., Pa., 10,743.
On Del. & Hud.; Del., Lack. & West.; N. York, Ont. & West.; Wilk.-Bar. & East. (R. Rs.).
Extensive collieries.
Omaha, c. s., Douglas Co., Neb., 214,006.
Situated on the Missouri River, and on the Chicago, Rock Island & Pacific; Chicago, Burl. & Quincy; Chicago Great Western; Illinois Central; Chicago & Northwestern; Wabash; Chicago, Milwaukee, St. Paul & Pacific; the Chicago, St. Paul, Minneapolis & Omaha; Missouri Pacific; and the Union Pacific railroads.
Industrial and commercial center of the state.
Its annual factory output is valued at more than $300,000,000. It does a huge grain and live stock business. Among its leading products are butter, meat and flour. Creighton University and the Municipal University of Omaha are located here.
–Morris Co., Tex., 506.
On St. Lou. Southw. (R. R.).
Omak, Okanogan Co., Wash., 2,547.
On Gt. Nor. (R. R.).
Omar, Logan Co., W. Va., 1,800.
On Chesa. & Ohio (R. R.).
Omdurman, Anglo-Egyptian Sudan, 110,436.
The headquarters of native traders of the region. Ivory, ostrich feathers, and gum arabic.
Omro, Winnebago Co., Wis., 1,255.
On Chi., Mil., St. P. & Pac. (R. R.).
Omsk, Siberian Area, Soviet Union, 277,000.
A commercial and industrial center. Chief products are farm machinery, vodka, beer, clothing, and sausage.
Onaga, Pottawatomie Co., Kans., 829.
On Un. Pac. (R. R.).
Onalaska, La Crosse Co., Wis., 1,408.
On Chi. & Nor. West.; Chi., Burl. & Quincy; Chi., Mil., St. P. & Pac. (R. Rs).
–Lewis Co., Wash., 1,200.
On Cowl., Cheh. & Cas.; Newauk. Val. (R. Rs.).
Onamia, Mille Lacs Co., Minn., 514.
On Mpls., St. Paul & S. Ste. Marie (R. R.).
Onancock, Accomac Co., Va., 1,245.
Onarga, Iroquois Co., Ill., 1,469.
On Ill. Cen. (R. R.).
Onawa, c. s., Monona Co., Iowa, 2,538.
On Chi. & Nor. West.; Ill. Cen. (R. Rs.).
Onaway, Presque Isle Co., Mich., 1,492.
On Det. & Mack. (R. R.).
Oneco, Windham Co., Conn., 650.
On N. York, N. Hav. & Hart. (R. R.).
Oneida, Knox Co., Ill., 560.
On Chi., Burl. & Quincy (R. R.).
–Madison Co., N. Y., 10,558.
On N. York Cen.; N. York, Ont. & West. (R. Rs.).
Famous for its silver-plated ware.
–Schuylkill Co., Pa., 1,068.
On Leh. Val. (R. R.).

–Scott Co., Tenn., 1,382.
On Oneida & West.; Cin., N. Orl. & Tex. Pac.; Tenn. (R. Rs.).
O'NEILL, c. s., Holt Co., Neb., 2,019.
On Chi. & Nor. West.; Chi., Burl. & Quincy (R. Rs.).
ONEONTA, c. s., Blount Co., Ala., 1,387.
On Lou. & Nash. (R. R.).
–Otsego Co., N. Y., 12,536.
On Del. & Hud.; Sou. N. York (El.); West Shore (R. Rs.).
Center of a rich agricultural region. Chief manufactures are silks, gloves, flour, and railway repairs.
ONIDA, c. s., Sully Co., S. Dak., 605.
On Chi. & Nor. West. (R. R.).
ONOMICHI, Ken of Hiroshima, Japan, 29,084.
On Inland Sea.
ONONDAGA CASTLE, Onondaga Co., N. Y., 622.
ONONDAGA VALLEY, Onondaga Co., N. Y., 540.
ONOVILLE, Cattaraugus Co., N. Y., 500.
ONSET, Plymouth Co., Mass., 1,000.
On N. York, N. Hav. & Hart. (R. R.).
ONSTWEDDE, Groningen, Netherlands, 18,110.
An agricultural center.
ONTARIO, San Bernardino Co., Cal., 13,583.
On Un. Pac.; Pac. Elec.; Sou. Pac. (R. Rs.).
A suburb of Pomona.
–Malheur Co., Ore., 1,941.
On Un. Pac. (R. R.).
ONTONAGON, c. s., Ontonagon Co., Mich., 1,937.
On Chi., Mil., St. P. & Pac. (R. R.).
OOLITIC, Lawrence Co., Ind., 1,210.
On Chi., Mil., St. P. & Pac. (R. R.).
OOLTEWAH, Hamilton Co., Tenn., 524.
On Southern (R. R.).
OOSTBURG, Sheboygan Co., Wis., 671.
On Chi. & Nor. West.; Mil. Elec. (R. Rs.).
OPAVA, Germany. See TROPPAU.
OPELIKA, c. s., Lee Co., Ala., 6,136.
On Cen. of Ga.; West. of Ala. (R. Rs.).
OPA LOCKA, Dade Co., Fla., 522.
On Seab. Air Line (R. R.).
OPELOUSAS, c. s., St. Landry Parish, La., 6,299.
On N. Orl., Tex. & Mex.; Tex. & Pac.; Sou. Pac. (R. Rs.).
OPHEIM, Valley Co., Mont., 510.
On Gt. Nor. (R. R.).
OPON, Prov. of Cebu, P. I., 21,003.
OPORTO, Portugal. See PORTO.
OPP, Covington Co., Ala., 2,918.
On Lou. & Nash. (R. R.).
OPPELN, East Silesia, Germany, 44,000.
Cement, beer, soap, cigars, chemicals, and lime.
OPPORTUNITY, Spokane Co., Wash., 1,500.
On Chi., Mil., St. P. & Pac.; Gt. Nor. (R. Rs.).
OQUAWKA, c. s., Henderson Co., Ill., 777.
On Chi., Burl. & Quincy (R. R.).
ORADEA, Mare, Crisana, Rumania, 82,355.
An important railway and industrial center. Leading products are spirits, pottery. Has brisk agricultural products trade.
ORADELL (Delford), Bergen Co., N. J., 2,500.
On N. Jer. & N. York (R. R.).
ORAN, capital of Dept. of Oran, Algeria, 200,671.
A seaport and distributing center for a large area. Exports farm produce and native textiles.
–Scott Co., Mo., 940.
On Mo. Pac.; St. Lou.-San Fran. (R. Rs.).
ORANGE, Orange Co., Cal., 8,066.
On Pac. Elec.; Atch., Top. & Santa Fe (R. Rs.).
Products: Lima beans, fruit, gasoline (from natural gas); crude oil, beet sugar, etc.
–New Haven Co., Conn., 1,200.
On N. York, N. Hav. & Hart. (R. R.).
–Franklin Co., Mass., 5,383.
On Bost. & Me. (R. R.).
–Essex Co., N. J., 35,399.
On Del., Lacka. & West.; Erie (R. Rs.).
Including East Orange, West Orange and South Orange, the district is known as the "Oranges." Orange has a large hatting industry; East Orange, electrical plants; West Orange, the Edison works, phonographs, etc.
–New South Wales, Australia, 9,634.
–c. s., Orange Co., Texas, 7,913.
On Mo. Pac.; Sou. Pac. (R. Rs.).
Oil and gas fields; pine and cypress forests; truck gardening.
–c. s., Orange Co., Va., 1,381.
On Chesa. & Ohio; Sou. (R. Rs.).
ORANGEBURG, c. s., Orangeburg Co., S. C., 8,776.
On Atl. Coast Line; Sou. (R. Rs.).
–(Orangeburgh), Rockland Co., N. Y., 750.
On Erie; West Shore (R. Rs.).
ORANGE CITY, c. s., Sioux Co., Iowa, 1,727.
On Chi. & Nor. West. (R. R.).
–Volusia Co., Fla., 572.
On Atl. Coast Line (R. R.).
ORANGE COVE, Fresno Co., Cal., 500.
On Atch., Top. & Santa Fe (R. R.).
ORANGEFIELD, Orange Co., Tex., 930.
On Sou. Pac. (R. R.).
ORANGE PARK, Clay Co., Fla., 716.
On Atl. Coast Line (R. R.).
ORANGEVILLE, Dufferin Co., Ontario, Canada, 2,614.
On Can. Pac. (R. R.).
–Baltimore City Co., Md., 1,520.
On Penna. (R. R.).
–Emery Co., Utah, 532.
ORAS, Samar Prov., Samar, P. I., 12,058.
ORBISONIA, Huntingdon Co., Pa., 741.
On E. Broad Top (R. R.).
ORCHARD, Antelope Co., Neb., 505.
On Chi., Burl. & Quincy (R. R.).
ORCHARD PARK, Erie Co., N. Y., 1,144.
On Balt. & Ohio (R. R.).
ORCUTT, Santa Barbara Co., Cal., 719.
On Pac. Coast (R. R.).
ORD, c. s., Valley Co., Neb., 2,226.
On Chi., Burl. & Quincy; Un. Pac. (R. Rs.).
ORDWAY, c. s., Crowley Co., Colo., 1,139.
On Mo. Pac. (R. R.).
ORDZHONIKIDZE (Vladikavkaz), capital of Ingush, Soviet Union, 113,200.
A commercial and trade center. Is of considerable historical interest.
ÖREBRO, capital of Län of Örebro, Sweden, 45,663.
The center of the Swedish shoe industry.
OREGON, c. s., Ogle Co., Ill., 2,376.
On Chi., Burl. & Quincy (R. R.).
–c. s., Holt Co., Mo., 922.
–Dane Co., Wis., 857.
On Chi. & Nor. West. (R. R.).
OREGON CITY, c. s., Clackamas Co., Ore., 5,761.
On Sou. Pac.; Portland (El.) (R. Rs.).
OREL, Soviet Union, 91,300.
Trade center for a fertile grain-raising region.
OREM, Utah Co., Utah, 1,915.
On Salt L. & Utah (El.) (R. R.).
ORENBURG, Soviet Union, 144,600.
A railroad and industrial center. Chief manufactures are lumber, beer, metal goods, and bricks. Trading caravans from Asia bring rugs, silk, cotton, skins, and dried fruits.
ORENSE, capital of Province of Orense, Spain, 18,315.
Chocolate and leather are chief manufactures.
ORFORDVILLE, Rock Co., Wis., 502.
On Chi., Mil., St. P. & Pac. (R. R.).
ORIENT, Franklin Co., Ill., 1,267.
On Chi. & East. Ill. (R. R.).
–Suffolk Co., N. Y., 650.
–Fayette Co., Pa., 1,625.
On Monongahela (R. R.).
ORIENTAL, Pamlico Co., N. C., 601.
On Norf. Sou. (R. R.).
ORIHUELA, Prov. of Alicante, Spain, 37,529.
A trade center and site of Orihuela University.
ORILLIA, Simcoe Co., Ontario, Canada, 8,183.
On Can. Nat.; Can. Pac. (R. R.).
ORION, Henry Co., Illinois, 620.
On Chi., Burl. & Quincy; Chi., Rk. Isl. & Pac. (R. Rs.).
–Oakland Co., Mich. See LAKE ORION.
–Prov. of Bataan, Luzon, P. I., 7,887.
ORISKANY, Oneida Co., N. Y., 1,142.
On N. York Cen. (R. R.).
ORISKANY FALLS, Oneida Co., N. Y., 853.
On N. York, Ont. & West. (R. R.).
ORIZABA, State of Veracruz, Mexico, 42,977.
On Mexican (R. R.).
Center of a rich farming region which produces sugar, rum, tobacco, and corn. Has large cotton factories.
ORIZATLAN, State of Hidalgo, Mexico, about 9,772.
ORLAND, Glenn Co., Cal., 1,195.
On Sou. Pac. (R. R.).
ORLANDO, c. s., Orange Co., Fla., 30,481.
On Atl. Coast Line; Seab. Air Line (R. Rs.).
Winter resort with fine residential section. Shipping point for citrus fruits and garden truck. Rollins College is situated at Winter Park, four miles northeast.
ORLAND PARK, Cook Co., Ill., 571.
On Wab. (R. R.).
ORLÉANS, Dept. of Loiret, France, 73,155.
On the right bank of the Loire. The house in which Joan of Arc, the "Maid of Orléans," is supposed to have lived is now a museum.
ORLEANS, Orange Co., Ind., 1,422.
On Chi., Ind. & Lou. (R. R.).
–Barnstable Co., Mass., 1,425.
On N. York, N. Hav. & Hart. (R. R.).
–Harlan Co., Neb., 985.
On Chi., Burl. & Quincy (R. R.).
–Orleans Co., Vt., 1,301.
On Can. Pac. (R. R.).
ORMOC, Leyte Prov., Leyte, P. I., 38,247.
ORMOND, Volusia Co., Fla., 1,904.
On Fla. East Coast (R. R.).
OROFINO, c. s., Clearwater Co., Idaho, 1,078.
On Nor. Pac.; Un. Pac. (R. Rs.).
ORONO, Penobscot Co., Maine, 2,100.
On Me. Cen. (R. R.).
Seat of University of Maine.
ORONOGO, Jasper Co., Mo., 551.
On Mo. Pac.; St. Lou.-San Fran. (R. Rs.).
OROQUIETA, Prov. of Misamis, Mindanao, P. I., 17,960.
A marketing town in a farming region.
OROSHAZA, Békés Comitat, Hungary, 25,871.
Located in a wine-growing, and cattle raising district.
OROSI, Tulare Co., Cal., 1,200.
On Atch., Top. & Santa Fe (R. R.).
OROVILLE, c. s., Butte Co., Cal., 3,698.
On Sou. Pac.; West. Pac.; Sacramento Nor. (El.) (R. Rs.).
A center of California olive industry.
–Okanogan Co., Wash., 800.
On Gt. Nor. (R. R.).
ORRICK, Ray Co., Missouri, 689.
On Wabash (R. R.).
ORRVILLE, Wayne Co., Ohio, 4,427.
On Penna.; Wheel. & L. Erie (R. Rs.).
ORTING, Pierce Co., Wash., 1,109.
On Nor. Pac. (R. R.).
ORTONVILLE, c. s., Bigstone and Lac qui Parle Cos., Minn., 2,017.
On Chi., Mil., St. P. & Pac. (R. R.).
–Oakland Co., Mich., 553.
ORURO, capital of Dept. of Oruro, Bolivia, 41,410.
The center of a tin mining district.
ORVISTON, Centre Co., Pa., 528.
On N. York Cen. (R. R.).
ORWELL, Oswego Co., N. Y., 500.
–Ashtabula Co., Ohio, 599.
ORWIGSBURG, Schuylkill Co., Pa., 2,031.
On Leh. Val. (R. R.).
ORWIN, Schuylkill Co., Pa., 600.
OSAGE, c. s., Mitchell Co., Iowa, 2,964.
On Ill. Cen.; Chi. Gt. West. (R. Rs.).
–Osage Co., Oklahoma, 627.
On Mo.-Kan.-Tex. (R. R.).
–Monongalia Co., W. Va., 500.
On Monongahela (R. R.).
OSAGE CITY, Osage Co., Kans., 2,277.
On Atch., Top. & Santa Fe; Mo. Pac. (R. Rs.).
OSAKA, Japan, 3,101,900.
Situated at the mouth of the Yodo River. The city lies on a plain opening on the Gulf of Osaka, and is intersected with canals.
Osaka has a very large number of places of worship. It is the headquarters of the rice and tea trade; has sugar refineries, ship yards, machine shops, steel and glass works, cotton and woolen mills. There is a foreign settlement, mostly occupied by missionaries.
–Wise Co., Va., 500.
On Interstate (R. R.).
OSAKIS, Douglas and Todd Cos., Minn., 1,155.
On Gt. Nor. (R. R.).
OSAWATOMIE, Miami Co., Kans., 4,701.
On Mo. Pac. (R. R.).
Railroad shops, oil refineries, and candy factory. Seat of State Hospital.
OSBORN, Greene Co., Ohio, 1,271.
On Cle., Cin., Chi. & St. Lou.; Erie (R. Rs.).
OSBORNE, c. s., Osborne Co., Kans., 2,074.
On Atch., Top. & Santa Fe; Mo. Pac. (R. Rs.).
–Allegheny Co., Pa., 506.
OSBORNSVILLE, Ocean Co., N. J., 550.
OSCEOLA, c. s., Mississippi Co., Ark., 2,573.
On St. Lou.-San Fran. (R. R.).
–c. s., Clarke Co., Iowa, 2,871.
On Chi., Burl. & Quincy (R. R.).
–c. s., St. Clair Co., Mo., 1,043.
On St. Lou.-San Fran. (R. R.).
–c. s., Polk Co., Neb., 1,054.
On Un. Pac. (R. R.).
–Tioga Co., Pa., 568.
On Balt. & Ohio; N. York Cen. (R. Rs.).
–Hill Co., Tex., 500.
–Polk Co., Wisconsin, 607.
On Mpls., St. P. & S. Ste. M. (R. R.).
OSCEOLA MILLS, Clearfield Co., Pa., 2,002.
On Penna. (R. R.).
OSCHATZ, Saxony, Germany, 10,439.
Sugar, felt, and clothing industries.
OSCHERSLEBEN, Prussian Saxony, Germany, 13,489.
Has manufactures of sugar, castings, brick, beer, and machinery.
OSCODA, Iosco Co., Mich., 600.
On Det. & Mack (R. R.).
OSGOOD, Ripley Co., Ind., 1,173.
On Balt. & Ohio (R. R.).
OSHAWA, Ontario Co., Ontario, Canada, 23,437.
On Can. Nat.; Can. Pac.; Oshawa (El.) (R. Rs.).
A lake port and industrial town. Motor cars, flour, woollens, farm machinery, and leather.
–Nicollet Co., Minn., 516.
On Chi. & Nor. West. (R. R.).
OSHKOSH, c. s., Garden Co., Neb., 843.
On Un. Pac. (R. R.).
–c. s., Winnebago Co., Wis., 40,108.
On Chi. & Nor. West.; Chi., Mil., St. P. & Pac.; Mpls., St. P. & S. Ste. M. (R. Rs.).
In lake district. Has many woodworking, metal and textile factories. Seat of State Teachers College and State Asylum.
OSIJEK (Eszik), Yugoslavia, 40,339.
Has a thriving trade in grain, livestock, and other farm products. Leading manufactures include textiles, leather, sugar, glass, and hats.
OSKALOOSA, c. s., Mahaska Co., Iowa, 10,123.
On Chi., Rk. Isl. & Pac.; Mpls. & St. Lou. (R. Rs.).
Surrounded by coal mines and clay beds. Has flour and feed mills, iron and brass foundries.
–c. s., Jefferson Co., Kans., 862.
OSLO (Christiania), capital of Norway, 253,124.
Situated on Oslo Fjord and on the Aker River, it is Norway's chief seaport. It is a well-built city with fine squares and promenades, among which that of St. John's Hill is notable. It has interesting and fast-growing suburbs. Among Oslo's old churches are the Gamle Akers Kieke, known prior to 1150. Trinity Church (Modern Gothic), and the Church of Our Saviour (1697). Other noteworthy buildings are the Parliament House, the Royal Palace, the Art Museum, and the University, which was founded by Frederick VI in 1811-1812, and has connected with it a library of some 500,000 volumes, a museum, a botanical garden, and an observatory. There are also military schools and a technical school.
In recent years, port improvements and hydro-electric developments have added to the city's importance.
Oslo was renamed Christiania in 1624 and held that title for 300 years. In 1925, the old name of Oslo was restored.
OSMANJIK, Turkey in Asia, 4,132.
OSMOND, Pierce Co., Neb., 750.
On Chi., Burl. & Quincy (R. R.).
OSNABRÜCK, Hanover, Germany, 94,000.
Seat of a famous university.
OSORNO, Prov. of Llanquihue, Chile, 16,229.
A marketing center in a mining region.
OSSEO, Trempealeau Co., Wis., 933.
On Chi., St. P., Mpls. & Oma. (R. R.).
–Hennepin Co., Minn., 561.
On Gt. Nor. (R. R.).
OSSETT, Yorkshire, England, 14,838.
Coal mines and woolen mills.
OSSIAN, Wells Co., Ind., 788.
On N. York, Chi. & St. Lou.; Ind. R. R. Sys. (El.) (R. Rs.).
–Winneshiek Co., Iowa, 740.
On Chi., Mil., St. P. & Pac.; Chi., Rk. Isl. & Pac. (R. Rs.).
OSSINING, Westchester Co., N. Y., 15,241.
On N. York Cen. (R. R.).
Site of Sing Sing State prison.
OSTEND, Prov. of West Flanders, Belgium, 49,621.
Held by Germans during the World War. Ostend harbor was blocked by British naval forces April 22, 1918; occupied by Allies the following October.
OSTERODE, East Prussia, Germany, 17,000.
Center of a farming region.
OSTERVILLE, Barnstable Co., Mass., 800.
OSTRAU, Czechoslovakia. See MORAVSKA-OSTRAVA.
OSTROG, Govt. of Volhynia, Poland, 12,975.
Famous for its leather.
OSTROWO, Poland, 17,306.
It has manufactures of woolen cloth.
OSTUNI, Prov. of Brindisi, Italy, 19,298.
A picturesque walled city.
OSWEGO, Kendall Co., Ill., 932.
On Chi., Burl. & Quincy (R. R.).
–c. s., Labette Co., Kans., 2,410.
On Mo.-Kan.-Tex.; St. Lou.-San Fran. (R. Rs.).
–c. s., Oswego Co., N. Y., 22,652.
On Del., Lack. & West.; N. York Cen.; N. York, Ont. & West. (R. Rs.).
A center of Great Lakes commerce. Has manufactures of steel wares, matches, rayon, paper products, candy, foundry products, shoes, and woolen goods.
–Clackamas Co., Oregon, 1,285.
On Sou. Pac. (R. R.).
OSYKA, Pike Co., Miss., 750.
On Ill. Cen. (R. R.).
OTARU, Ken of Yezo, Japan, 144,884.
A leading fisheries center.
OTEEN, Buncombe Co., N. C., 600.
OTEGO, Otsego Co., N. Y., 555.
On Del. & Hud. (R. R.).
OTISVILLE, Orange Co., N. Y., 809.
On Erie (R. R.).
OTON, Prov. of Iloilo, Panay, P. I., 15,370.
OTSEGO, Allegan Co., Mich., 3,245.
On N. York Cen. (R. R.).
OTSU, capital of Shiga Ken, Japan, 34,380.
The ancient capital of the mikados.
OTTAWA, c. s., Carleton Co., Ontario, capital of the Dominion of Canada, 126,872.
Situated at the confluence of the Ottawa and Rideau Rivers, on the Rideau Canal, and on the Canadian Pacific; the Canadian National; New York Central railroads.
Seat of the University of Ottawa.
–c. s., La Salle Co., Ill., 15,094.
On Chi., Burl. & Quincy; Chi., Rk. Isl. & Pac. (R. Rs.).
Manufactures plate glass, fire brick, farm implements, etc.
–c. s., Franklin Co., Kans., 9,530.
On Atch., Top. & Santa Fe; Mo. Pac. (R. Rs.).
Seat of Ottawa University.
–c. s., Putnam Co., Ohio, 2,169.
On Balt. & Ohio; Det., Tol. & Iron. (R. Rs.).
OTTAWA HILLS, Lucas Co., Ohio, 1,185.
OTTERBEIN, Benton Co., Ind., 616.
On Cle., Cin., Chi. & St. Lou.; N. York, Chi. & St. Lou. (R. Rs.).
OTTER CREEK, Levy Co., Fla., 989.
On Atlantic Coast Line (R. R.).
OTTUMWA, c. s., Wapello Co., Iowa, 28,075.
On Chi., Burl. & Quincy; Chi., Mil., St. P. & Pac.; Chi., Rk. Isl. & Pac.; Wab. (R. Rs.).

THE PARLIAMENT BUILDINGS, OTTAWA, CANADA. AN IMPOSING ARCHITECTURAL GROUP OF GOTHIC STRUCTURES SITUATED
AT THE SUMMIT OF PARLIAMENT HILL

Located in a bituminous coal region, and in
the heart of a grain and livestock district.

OUDTSHOORN, Cape of Good Hope, Union of
South Africa, 13,225.

OUGREE, Prov. of Liège, Belgium, 19,763.
A suburb of Seraing.

OULU (Uleaborg), Finland, 24,924.
Seaport and export center.

OURAY, c. s., Ouray Co., Colo., 707.
Near the base of Mount Hayden, on the Denver and Rio Grande Western Railway.

OURO PRETO, capital of Minas Geraes, Brazil.
The center of a gold and silver mining region.
Seat of a school of mines.

OUTREMONT, Laurier-Outremont Dist., Quebec,
Canada, 28,641.
On Can. Pac.; N. York Cen. (R. Rs.).
A residential suburb of Montreal.

OVALLE, Prov. of Coquimbo, Chile, 11,795.

OVERBROOK, Philadelphia Co., Pa., 2,200.
On Penna (R. R.).

OVERLAND, St. Louis Co., Mo., 830.

OVERLEA, Baltimore Co., Md., 1,212.

OVERPECK, Butler Co., Ohio, 500.
On Balt. & Ohio; Erie (R. Rs.).

OVERTON, Dawson Co., Neb., 600.
On Un. Pac. (R. R.).

OVID, Clinton Co., Mich., 1,131.
On Gd. Tr. (R. R.).
—c. s., Seneca Co., N. Y., 537.
On Leh. Val. (R. R.).

OVIEDO, capital of Prov. of Oviedo, Spain, 76,048.
—Seminole Co., Fla., 1,163.
On Atl. Coast Line; Seab. Air Line (R. Rs.).

OWATONNA, c. s., Steele Co., Minn., 7,654.
On Chi., Mil., St. P. & Pac.; Chi., Rk. Isl. &
Pac.; Chi. & Nor. West. (R. Rs.).

OWEGO, c. s., Tioga Co., N. Y., 4,742.
On Del., Lack. & West.; Erie; Leh. Val. (R.
Rs.).

OWEN, Clark Co., Wis., 1,102.
On Mpls., St. P. & S. Ste. M. (R. R.).

OWENS (Kanawha City), Kanawha Co., W. Va.,
1,000.
On Chesa. & Ohio (R. R.).

OWENSBORO, c. s., Daviess Co., Ky., 22,765.
On Ill. Cen.; Lou. & Nash. (R. Rs.).
Center of a gas and oil region and a leading
agricultural region.

OWEN SOUND (formerly Sydenham), capital of
Grey Co., Ontario, Canada, 12,839.
On Can. Pac.; Can. Nat. (R. Rs.).
An industrial lake port. Manufactures ships,
machinery, farm implements, flour, and lum-
ber.

OWENSVILLE, Gibson Co., Ind., 1,056.
On Chi. & East. Ill. (R. R.).
—Gasconade Co., Mo., 1,424.
On Chi., Rk. Isl. & Pac. (R. R.).

OWENTON, c. s., Owen Co., Ky., 975.

OWINGSVILLE, c. s., Bath Co., Ky., 933.

OWOSSO, Shiawassee Co., Mich., 14,496.
On Ann Arbor; Gd. Tr.; Mich. Cen. (R. Rs.).

Situated in a sugar beet district. Manufactures
motor cars, furniture, flour, and sugar.

OXFORD, Oxfordshire, England, 80,540.
Situated on a gentle acclivity between the
Cherwell and the Thames, here called the Isis.
It is the seat of one of the most celebrated universities in the world, an English university
that lays claim to great antiquity, tradition
assigning its foundation to King Alfred in 972.
The earliest charter was granted by King John,
and its privileges were confirmed and extended
by subsequent monarchs, the act by which it
was created a corporate body having been
passed during the reign of Elizabeth in 1570.
The constitution of the university was changed
in August, 1854, and amended in June, 1856.
Attached to the University is the Bodleian
Library, founded by Sir Thomas Bodley, containing more than 700,000 printed volumes,
and more than 50,000 valuable manuscripts.
The oldest building is the castle keep, built in
the time of William the Conqueror. Among
the most noteworthy churches are the Christ
Church, 1524; the Cathedral, 12th century; St.
Mary Magdalen, 1320, and St. Giles's (twelfth
and thirteenth centuries). The principal build-
ings are Sheldonian Theater, the University
buildings, Ashmolean Museum, Municipal
Building and Radcliffe Library.
—Calhoun Co., Ala., 1,206.
On Southern (R. R.).
—Newton Co., Ga., 537.
—Benton Co., Ind., 853.
On Chi., Attica & Sou.; N. York, Chi. & St.
Lou. (R. Rs.).
—Johnson Co., Iowa, 521.
On Chi., Rk. Isl. & Pac. (R. R.).
—Sumner Co., Kans., 1,150.
On Atch., Top. & Santa Fe; Mo. Pac.; Midl.
Val. (R. Rs.).
—Talbot Co., Md., 915.
On Penna. (R. R.).
—Worcester Co., Mass., 4,249.
On N. York, N. Hav. & Hart. (R. R.).
—Oakland Co., Mich., 2,052.
On Gd. Tr.; Mich. Cen. (R. Rs.).
—c. s., Lafayette Co., Miss., 2,890.
On Ill. Cen. (R. R.).
Seat of University of Mississippi.
—Furnas and Harlan Cos., Neb., 1,155.
On Chi., Burl. & Quincy (R. R.).
—(Oxford Furnace), Warren Co., N. J., 1,723.
On Del., Lack. & West. (R. R.).
—Chenango Co., N. Y., 1,601.
On Del., Lack. & West.; N. York, Ont. & West.
(R. Rs.).
—c. s., Granville Co., N. C., 4,101.
On Seab. Air Line; Sou. (R. Rs.).
John Penn, signer of the Declaration of Inde-
pendence, was born in Oxford.
—Butler Co., Ohio, 2,588.
On Balt. & Ohio; Erie (R. Rs.).
Seat of Miami University and Western College
for Women.

—Chester Co., Pa., 2,606.
On Penna. (R. R.).

OXFORD JUNCTION, Jones Co., Iowa, 759.
On Chi., Mil., St. P. & Pac. (R. R.).

OXNARD, Ventura Co., Cal., 6,285.
On Sou. Pac.; Ventura Co. (R. Rs.).

OYSTER BAY, Nassau Co., N. Y., 5,314.
On Long Isl. (R. R.).
One of the oldest towns on Long Island; principal industry is oyster cultivation; home of
the late ex-President Theodore Roosevelt.

OZARK, c. s., Dale Co., Ala., 3,103.
On Atl. Coast Line; Cen. of Ga. (R. Rs.).
—c. s., Franklin Co., Ark., 1,564.
On Mo. Pac. (R. R.).
—c. s., Christian Co., Mo., 885.
On St. Lou.-San Fran. (R. R.).

OZONA, c. s., Crockett Co., Tex., 2,128.

P

PAARL, Cape of Good Hope, Union of South
Africa, 18,580.
Located in a fine fruit country.

PACHUCA, capital of State of Hidalgo, Mexico,
41,220.
On Mexican; Nat. of Mex. (R. Rs.).
The center of a silver mining region.

PACIFIC, Franklin Co., Mo., 1,456.
On Mo. Pac.; St. Lou.-San Fran. (R. Rs.).

PACIFIC GROVE, Monterey Co., Cal., 5,558.
On Sou. Pac. (R. R.).

PACIFIC JUNCTION, Mills Co., Ia., 594.
On Chi., Burl. & Quincy (R. R.).

PACKERTON, Carbon Co., Pa., 590.
On Leh. Val. (R. R.).

PADANG, Sumatra, Neth. Indies, 51,976.
The chief port on the west coast of Sumatra.

PADEN, Okfuskee Co., Okla., 595.
On Ft. Smith & West. (R. R.).

PADEN CITY, Wetzel and Tyler Cos., W. Va.,
2,281.
On Balt. & Ohio (R. R.).

PADERBORN, Westphalia, Germany, 35,000.
Glass, soap, tobacco, shoes.

PADOVA (Padua), capital of Prov. of Padova,
Italy, 83,086.
Situated at the junction of the Brenta and
Bacchiglione Rivers. Has a celebrated univer-
sity, founded in the thirteenth century.

PADUCAH, c. s., McCracken Co., Ky., 33,541.
On Ill. Cen.; Nash., Chatt. & St. Lou.; Paduc.
& Ill. (R. Rs.).
A leading tobacco and strawberry market.
—c. s., Cottle Co., Tex., 2,802.
On Quan., Acme & Pac. (R. R.).

PAGANI, Prov. of Salerno, Italy, 13,552.

PAGELAND, Chesterfield Co., S. C., 707.
On Chester. & Lancas. (R. R.).

PAGOSA SPRINGS, c. s., Archuleta Co., Colo., 804.

PAGUATE, Valencia Co., N. M., 515.

PAHLEVI, Iran (Persia), 16,900.

PAHOKEE, Palm Beach Co., Fla., 3,421.
On Fla. East Coast (R. R.).

PAHUATLAN, State of Puebla, Mexico, 15,372.

PAINESDALE, Houghton Co., Mich., 2,647.
On Cop. Rge. (R. R.).

PAINESVILLE, c. s., Lake Co., Ohio, 10,944.
On Balt. & Ohio; N. York Cen.; Fairp.,
Painesv. & East.; N. York, Chi. & St. Lou.
(R. Rs.).
Famous for its large nurseries.

PAINT CREEK (Paint), Somerset Co., Pa., 1,336.
On Balt. & Ohio (R. R.).

PAINTED POST, Steuben Co., N. Y., 2,328.
On Del., Lack. & West.; Erie (R. Rs.).

PAINTSVILLE, c. s., Johnson Co., Ky., 2,411.
On Chesa. & Ohio (R. R.).

PAISLEY, Renfrewshire, Scotland, 120,268.
Noted for its thread manufactures. Formerly
famous for the manufacture of Paisley shawls.
—Bruce Co., Ontario, Canada, 724.
On Can. Nat. (R. R.).

PAKHOI, Prov. of Kwangtung, China, 35,000.
A seaport and local trade center.

PALACIOS, Matagorda Co., Tex., 1,318.
On Sou. Pac. (R. R.).

PALANPUR, States of Western India, India, 20,347.
A railway junction and marketing town.

PALATINE, Cook Co., Ill., 2,118.
On Chi. & Nor. West. (R. R.).

PALATINE BRIDGE, Montgomery Co., N. Y., 503.
On N. York Cen. (R. R.).

PALATKA, c. s., Putnam Co., Fla., 6,543.
On Atl. Coast Line; Fla. East Coast; Ga. Sou.
& Fla. (R. Rs.).
Cypress mills. Shipping center.

PALEMBANG, Sumatra, Netherland India, 108,145.

PALERMO, capital of island of Sicily and of the
Prov. of Palermo, Italy, 317,735.
A seaport and commercial center surrounded
by a very fertile farming area. Much citrus
fruit raising. Exports varied and large.

PALESTINE, Crawford Co., Ill., 1,670.
On Ill. Cen. (R. R.).
Situated in a petroleum and farming region.
Has important salt works.
—c. s., Anderson Co., Texas, 11,445.
On Mo. Pac.; Sou. Pac. (R. Rs.).

PALESTRINA, Prov. of Roma, Italy, 6,208.

PALISADE, Mesa Co., Colo., 851.
On Den. & Rio Gde. West. (R. R.).
—Hitchcock Co., Neb., 731.
On Chi., Burl. & Quincy (R. R.).
—Bergen Co., N. J., 1,400.

PALISADES PARK, Bergen Co., N. J., 7,065.
On Erie (R. R.).

PALMA, capital of the Balearic Isles, Spain, 88,262.
A favorite tourist resort.

PALM BEACH, Palm Beach Co., Fla., 1,836.
On Fla. East Coast (R. R.).

PALMER, Hampden Co., Mass., 9,437.
On Bost. & Alb.; Cen. Ver. (R. Rs.).
A manufacturing town on the Chicopee River.
—Marquette Co., Mich., 650.
—Merrick Co., Neb., 588.
On Chi., Burl. & Quincy (R. R.).
—Grundy Co., Tenn., 1,158.
On Nash., Chatt. & St. Lou. (R. R.).
—Ellis Co., Texas, 758.
On Sou. Pac.; Tex. Elec. (R. Rs.).

PALMERSTON, Wellington Co., Ontario, Canada,
1,543.
On Can. Nat. (R. R.).

PALMERTON, Carbon Co., Pa., 7,678.
On Cen. of N. Jer.; Chesa. Rdge.; Leh. & N.
Eng. (R. Rs.).

PALMETTO, Manatee Co., Fla., 3,092.
On Seab. Air Line; Atl. Coast Line (R. Rs.).
—Campbell and Coweta Cos., Ga., 964.
On Atl. & West Pt. (R. R.).

PALMIRA, Valle del Cauca, Colombia, 27,032.
Marketing center for farm and native produce.
—Santa Clara Prov., Cuba, 4,954.

PALMYRA, Macoupin Co., Ill., 760.
On Chi., Springf. & St. Lou. (R. R.).
—c. s., Marion Co., Mo., 1,967.
On Chi., Burl. & Quincy (R. R.).
—Burlington Co., N. J., 496.
On Penna. (R. R.).
—Wayne Co., N. Y., 2,592.
On N. York Cen. (R. R.).
—Lebanon Co., Pa., 4,377.
On Reading (R. R.).
—Jefferson Co., Wis., 642.
On Chi., Mil., St. P. & Pac. (R. R.).

PALO, Leyte Prov., Leyte, P. I., 20,518.

PALO ALTO, Santa Clara Co., Cal., 13,652.
On Sou. Pac. (R. R.).
Educational and residential, near San Fran-
cisco. Seat of Stanford University.
—Schuylkill Co., Pa., 1,908.
On Read. (R. R.).

PALOMPON, Leyte Prov., Leyte, P. I., 16,220.
A port and native trading center.

PALOUSE, Whitman Co., Wash., 1,151.
On Nor. Pac.; Wash., Ida. & Mont.; Gt. Nor.
(R. Rs.).

PAMIERS, Dept. of Ariège, France, 14,035.

PAMPA, c. s., Gray Co., Texas, 10,470.
On Ft. Worth & Denv. Cy.; Panh. & Santa Fe
(R. Rs.).

A busy agricultural center in the Panhandle.

Pamplona, capital of Prov. of Navarra, Spain, 33,163.
Has a flourishing agricultural trade and manufactures of textiles, flour, leather, paper, and pottery.

Pana, Christian Co., Ill., 5,835.
On Balt. & Ohio; Chi. & East. Ill.; Cle., Cin., Chi. & St. Lou.; Ill. Cen. (R. Rs.).

Panama, Bond and Montgomery Cos., Ill., 1,026.
On N. York, Chi. & St. Lou. (R. R.).
–Dept. of Panama, Panama Republic, capital city, 74,409.
On the Gulf of Panama and on the Pacific Coast of the Isthmus of Panama. It lies on a strip of land, across which its streets stretch from sea to sea. Panama is important as the terminus of the inter-oceanic railway and of the Panama Canal.
–LeFlore Co., Okla., 754.
On Kan. Cy. Sou.; Midl. Val. (R. Rs.).

Panama City, c. s., Bay Co., Fla., 8,701.
On Atl. & St. And. Bay (R. R.).

Panay, Capiz Prov., Panay, P. I., 13,411.

Pandan, Prov. of Antique, Panay, P. I., 16,202.
A port and commercial town.

Pandora, Putnam Co., Ohio, 588.
On Nor. Ohio (R. R.).

Pangburn, White Co., Ark., 634.
On Mo. & Ark. (R. R.).

Panglao, Prov. of Bohol, Bohol, P. I., 9,115.

Panguitch, c. s., Garfield Co., Utah, 1,541.

Panhandle, c. s., Carson Co., Texas, 2,035.
On Panh. & Santa Fe (R. R.).

Panipat, Punjab, India, 32,915.
A town of great antiquity.

Paniqui, Panay, P. I., 16,593.
Situated in an agricultural region.

Panjim, Gôa, Portuguese India, Malabar Coast, 10,000.

Panora, Guthrie Co., Iowa, 1,014.
On Chi., Mil., St. P. & Pac. (R. R.).

Pantin, Dept. of Seine, France, 37,716.
An industrial suburb of Paris.

Paoay, Prov. of Ilocos Norte, Luzon, P. I., 16,622.

Paola, c. s., Miami Co., Kans., 3,825.
On Mo.-Kan.-Tex.; Mo. Pac.; St. Lou.-San Fran. (R. Rs.).

Paoli, c. s., Orange Co., Ind., 2,016.
On Chi., Ind. & Lou. (R. R.).
–Chester Co., Pa., 3,500.
On Penna. (R. R.).

Paombong, Prov. of Bulacan, Luzon, P. I., 9,221.

Paonia, Delta Co., Colo., 958.
On Den. & Rio Gde. West. (R. R.).

Pápa, Veszprém Comitat, Hungary, 21,352.
Potteries, tobacco factories and trade in farm produce.

Papeete, capital of Tahiti, French Polynesia, 7,061.

Papillion, c. s., Sarpy Co., Neb., 718.
On Un. Pac. (R. R.).

Paragould, c. s., Greene Co., Ark., 5,966.
On Mo. Pac.; St. Lou. Southw. (R. Rs.).

Paraguari, Paraguay, 10,980.

Paramaribo, capital of Netherland Guiana, or Surinam, South America, 51,554.
A port and commercial center.

Paramus, Bergen Co., N. J., 2,649.

Paraná, capital of Entre Rios, Argentina, 66,204.
A port and trade center on the Paraná River. Located in a rich farming region.

Parchim, Mecklenburg-Schwerin, Germany, 11,857.

Parco, Carbon Co., Wyo., 727.
On Un. Pac. (R. R.).

Pardeeville, Columbia Co., Wis., 873.
On Chi., Mil., St. P. & Pac. (R. R.).

Pardubice (Pardubitz), Bohemia, Czechoslovakia, 28,841.
Iron machinery, sugar, and beer. Located in a livestock raising region.

Paris, Dept. of Seine, capital of France, 2,829,746.
It occupies an area of about 20,000 acres, of which 12,000 are covered by buildings. By accessions of both territory and population it increased from about 200,000 at the end of the 13th century; 415,000 in 1637; 500,000 in 1680; 547,756 in 1800; 909,126 in 1836; 1,696,141 in 1861; 1,825,274 in 1870; 2,239,928 in 1881; 2,447,957 in 1891; to 2,714,068 in 1901; to 2,763,393 in 1906, being then the third city in the world in point of population.
Situated in the Seine Valley, surrounded by the heights of Charonne la Villette, the Buttes-Chaumont, Montmartre, Ste. Geneviève, Montrouge, and the Batte-aux-Cailles. Through the valleys between these heights the river runs from east to west, enclosing two islands, upon which part of the city is built. It is navigable by small steamers. The quays or embankments, which extend along the Seine on both sides, protect the city from inundation and form excellent promenades. The river is crossed by numerous bridges, the more important being Pont Neuf, Pont des Arts, Pont Sully, Pont Austerlitz, Pont National, Pont du Carrousel, Pont Royal, and Pont de l'Alma. The city is surrounded by lines of fortifications. Paris is divided into 20 arrondissements, at the head of each of which is a maire. Each arrondissement contains four quarters. Some of the wide streets are known as "boulevards," the one specifically called "the Boulevard" extends, in an irregular arc on the north side of the Seine, from the Place de la Bastille in the east to the Place de la Madeleine in the west. It includes the Boulevards Du Temple, St. Martin, St. Denis, Des Italiens, Capucines, Madeleine, etc., and its length of nearly 3 miles forms a magnificent avenue. Here may be noted also the triumphal arches of Porte St. Denis and Porte St. Martin, the former of which is 72 feet in height. On the south side of the Seine the boulevards are neither so numerous nor so extensive, the best known being the Boulevard St. Germain. The exterior boulevards are outside the old city limits; and the military boulevards, still farther out, extend round the old fortifications. After the boulevards mentioned some of the best known streets are the Rue de Rivoli, Rue Castiglione, Rue de la Paix, Rue de la Chaussée d'Antin, Rue de Lafayette, Avenue des Champs Élysées, Avenue de la Grande Armée, Boulevard de Sébastopol, and the Rue des Pyramides.
The most notable public squares or places are the Place de la Concorde, one of the largest and most striking squares in Europe. It is adorned by an Egyptian obelisk, fountains, and statues; the Place de l'Étoile in which is situated the Arc de Triomphe, a splendid structure, 152 feet in height; the Place Vendôme, with column to Napoleon I; the Place des Victoires, with equestrian statue of Louis XIV; the Place de la Bastille, with colossal statue of the Republic, and the Place des États-Unis. Within the city are situated the gardens of the Tuileries, and of the Luxembourg, in which are fine conservatories of rare plants; the Jardin des Plantes, in which are the zoological gardens, hot-houses, museums, and laboratories, the Buttes-Chaumont Gardens, the Parc de Monceaux, and the Champs-Élysées, the latter being a favorite resort of all classes. But the most extensive parks are outside the city. Of these the Bois de Boulogne covers an area of 2,150 acres, and comprises the race courses of Longchamps and Auteuil. The Bois de Vincennes offers a fine view over the surrounding country. The most celebrated cemetery in Paris is Père Lachaise (106½ acres), which has many important monuments. The Catacombs extend under a portion of the southern part of the city. Of the churches of Paris the most famous is the Cathedral of Notre-Dame (12th and 13th centuries). It is a cruciform structure, with two square towers. The whole length of the church is 426 feet, its breadth 164 feet. The church of La Madeleine, a modern structure, stands fronting the Rue Royale; St. Eustache (1532-1637), a mixture of degenerate Gothic and Renaissance architecture; St. Germain l'Auxerrois; St. Gervais; St. Roch; St. Sulpice; Notre Dame de Lorette; St. Vincent de Paul; and the Church of the Sacred Heart, on the heights of Montmartre, a vast structure in medieval style, and the Panthéon, now a shrine of memorial to the great dead of France.
Notable among the public buildings of Paris are its palaces. The Louvre, a great series of buildings within which are two large courts, is now a museum which comprises splendid collections of sculpture, paintings, engravings, bronzes, pottery, and antiquities; the palace of the Tuileries, the Palais du Luxembourg, which contains the Musée du Luxembourg. The Palais Royale is a famed resort; the Palais d'Élysée, situated on the Rue St. Honoré, with a large garden, is now the residence of the President of the Republic; the Palais de l'Industrie is used for the annual salon of modern paintings. The Hôtel de Ville, used as a town hall, is a very fine example of Renaissance architecture. The Hôtel des Invalides is now used as a retreat for disabled soldiers and contains the sarcophagus of the first Napoleon. The mint (Hôtel des Monnaies) contains an immense collection of coins and medals. The other principal Government buildings are the Bourse de Commerce in front of the Halles Centrales. The Eiffel Tower, built in connection with the Paris Exhibition of 1889, is the highest steel tower in the world.
Paris is a great center of music, art, and learning. The chief institutions for higher education are the Sorbonne, the University of Paris and the Collège de France. Among other Parisian schools are the secondary schools or lycées, technical and professional schools. Of the libraries the most important is the Bibliothéque Nationale, one of the largest in the world, containing over 3,000,000 volumes. Among the museums, besides the Louvre and the Luxembourg, there may be noted the Musée d'Artillerie, in the Hôtel des Invalides, containing suits of ancient armor and arms; the Conservatoire des Arts et Métiers; the Trocadero Palace, and the Cluny Museum. The noted society of eminent authors and scientists is the Institute of France.
The theaters of Paris are exceedingly numerous. The most important are the Opera House, a gorgeous edifice of great size, the Opéra Comique, the Théâtre Français, the Odéon, and the Théâtre des Varieties.
Some of the manufactures are leather goods, metal products, jewelry, fine hardware, paper hangings, cabinet-work, carriages, automobiles, fans, glass and pottery, silk and woolen goods, shawls and carpets, Gobelin tapestry, lace embroidery, artificial flowers, machines, scientific instruments, books, engravings, refined sugar, tobacco, chemicals, gloves and perfumes.
At the time of Caesar's conquest of Gaul, the small tribe of the Parisii were found inhabiting the banks of the Seine. It was a fortified town A.D. 360. In the beginning of the fifth century it fell into the hands of Clovis, who made it his capital. In 987 a new dynasty was established by Hugh Capet, from whose reign downward Paris was the residence of the kings of France. The English occupied Paris from 1420-1436. The Germans took the city in 1871 after a siege. During the Commune, 1871, Paris suffered another siege and a great fire. The city was not taken at any time during the World War.
–c. s., Logan Co., Ark., 3,234.
On Mo. Pac.; Ft. Smith, Sub. & Rk. Isl. (R. Rs.).
–c. s., Bear Lake Co., Idaho, 825.
On Un Pac. (R. R.).
–c. s., Edgar Co., Ill., 8,781.
On Cle., Cin., Chi. & St. Lou.; Penna. (R. Rs.).
–c. s., Bourbon Co., Ky., 6,204.
On Lou. & Nash.; Frankf. & Cin. (R. Rs.).
–c. s., Monroe Co., Mo., 1,367.
On Wabash (R. R.).
–c. s., Henry Co., Tenn., 8,164.
On Lou. & Nash.; Nash., Chatt. & St. Lou. (R. Rs.).
–c. s., Lamar Co., Texas, 15,649.
On Gulf, Colo. & Santa Fe; St. Lou., San Fran. & Tex.; Sou. Pac.; Tex. & Pac.; Paris & Mt. Pleasant (R. Rs.).
An important cotton market, and distributing point for varied agricultural produce.
–Brant Co., South Ontario, Canada, 4,137.
On Can. Nat.; L. Erie & Nor. (El.) (R. Rs.).

Parish, Oswego Co., N. Y., 508.
On N. York Cen. (R. R.).

Park City, Summit Co., Utah, 4,281.
On Den. & Rio Gde. West; Un. Pac. (R. Rs.).
Mining center.

Parker, c. s., Turner Co., S. Dak., 1,225.
On Chi., Mil., St. P. & Pac.; Chi. & Nor. West. (R. Rs.).

Parker City (Parker), Randolph Co., Ind., 794.
On Cle., Cin., Chi. & St. Lou. (R. R.).

Parkersburg, Butler Co., Iowa, 1,046.
On Chi. & Nor. West.; Ill. Cen. (R. Rs.).
–c. s., Wood Co., W. Va.; (1920) 29,623.
On Balt. & Ohio (R. R.).
In a gas and oil region. Petroleum products, glass, lumber, steel, porcelain and rayon.

Parkers Landing (Parker City), Armstrong Co., Pa., 1,300.
On Balt. & Ohio; Penna. (R. Rs.).

Parkers Prairie, Otter Tail Co., Minn., 631.
On Minn., St. P. & S. Ste. M. (R. R.).

Parkesburg, Chester Co., Pa., 2,288.
On Penna. (R. R.).

Park Falls, Price Co., Wis., 3,036.
On Chi., St. P., Mpls. & Oma.; Mpls., St. P. & S. Ste. M. (R. Rs.).

Parkhill, Middlesex Co., West, Ontario, Canada, 1,030.
On Can. Nat. (R. R.).
–Cambria Co., Pa., 700.

Parkin, Cross Co., Ark., 1,676.
On Mo. Pac. (R. R.).

Parkland, Bucks Co., Pa., 500.
On Reading (R. R.).
–Pierce Co., Wash., 750.

Park Lane, Arlington Co., Va., 1,500.
On Wash. & Old Dom. (El.) (R. R.).

Park Rapids, c. s., Hubbard Co., Minn., 2,081.
On Gt. Nor. (R. R.).

Park Ridge, Cook Co., Ill., 10,417.
On Chi. & Nor. West. (R. R.).
A residential suburb of Chicago.
–Bergen Co., N. J., 2,229.
On N. Jer. & N. York (R. R.).

Park River, Walsh Co., N. Dak., 1,131.
On Gt. Nor. (R. R.).

Parkrose, Multnoma Co., Ore., 500.

Parks, Stephens Co., Tex., 750.
On Cisco & Nor. East. (R. R.).

Parkside, Delaware Co., Pa., 1,497.

Parksley, Accomac Co., Va., 697.
On Penna. (R. R.).

Parkston, Hutchinson Co., S. D., 1,272.
On Chi., Mil., St. P. & Pac. (R. R.).

EWING GALLOWAY PHOTO

THE EAST FAÇADE OF THE MUSEUM DE LOUVRE, PARIS, THE FAMOUS GALLERY CONTAINING THE ART TREASURES OF FRANCE VISITED YEARLY BY MANY THOUSANDS OF AMERICAN TOURISTS

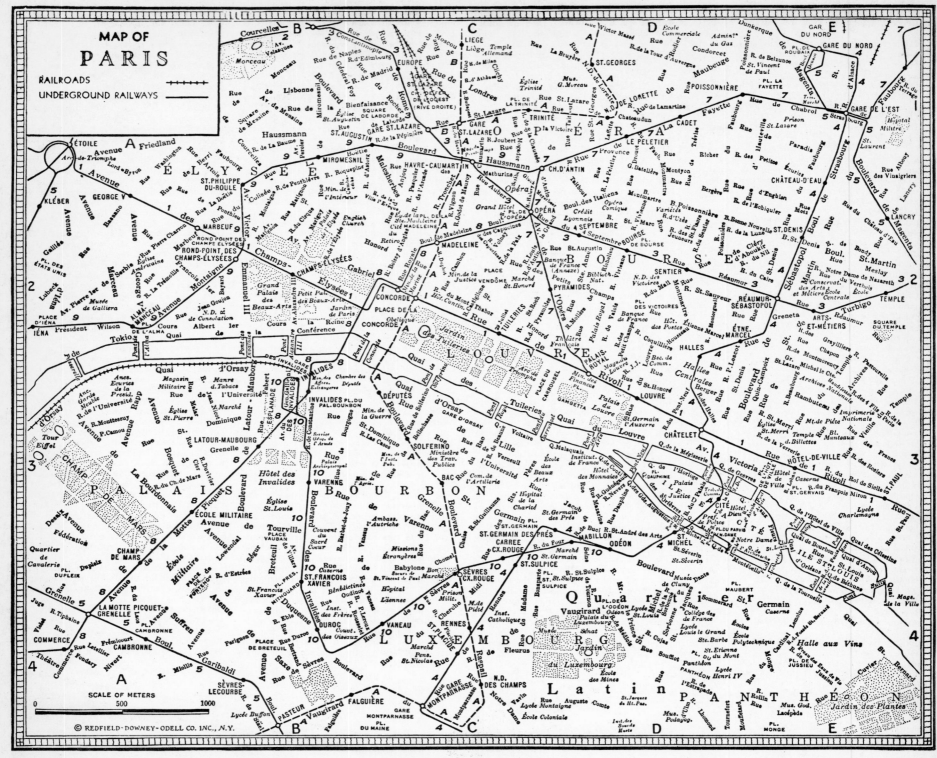

MAP OF PARIS, THE CAPITAL OF FRANCE AND CENTER OF FRENCH NATIONAL LIFE. FOUNDED BEFORE THE CHRISTIAN ERA, IT HAS RANKED THROUGH THE CEN-
TURIES AS THE FOREMOST CULTURAL CENTER OF EUROPE. ITS FAMOUS BUILDINGS, AMONG THEM THE CATHEDRAL OF NOTRE DAME, THE PANTHÉON, THE
EIFFEL TOWER AND OTHERS, AS WELL AS ITS CELEBRATED GALLERIES, THE LOUVRE AND LUXEMBOURG, ARE VISITED BY THOUSANDS OF TOURISTS YEARLY

PARKSVILLE, Sullivan Co., N. Y., 500.
    On N. York, Ont. & West. (R. R.).
PARK VIEW, Rio Arriba Co., N. M., 500.
PARKVILLE, Platte Co., Mo., 636.
    On Chi., Burl. & Quincy (R. R.).
    —St. Louis Co., Minn., 600.
PARLIN, Middlesex Co., N. J., 1,200.
    On Raritan Riv. (R. R.).
PARMA, capital of Prov. of Parma, Italy, 69,200.
    An agricultural center and famous for its
    cheese.
    —Canyon Co., Idaho, 750.
    On Un. Pac. (R. R.).
    —Jackson Co., Mich., 613.
    On Mich. Cen. (R. R.).
    —New Madrid Co., Mo., 1,051.
    On St. Lou.-San Fran.; St. Lou. Southw. (R.
    Rs.).
    —Cuyahoga Co., Ohio, 13,899.
    On Balt. & Ohio (R. R.).
    A suburb of Cleveland.
PARMA HEIGHTS, Cuyahoga Co., Ohio, 960.
PARNASSUS, Westmoreland Co., Pa., 6,240.
    On Penna. (R. R.).
PARNU (Pernau), Estonia, 20,660.
    A seaport and resort. Fishing center.
PAROWAN, c. s., Iron Co., Utah, 1,474.
PARRAL (Hidalgo Del), Chihuahua, Mexico, 18,-
    583.
    On Nat. of Mex.; Par. & Dur. (R. Rs.).
    A gold and silver mining center.
PARRAMATTA, New South Wales, Australia, 18,-
    076.

A suburb of Sydney.
PARRAS, State of Coahuila, Mexico, 7,284.
    On Nat. of Mex. (R. R.).
PARRSBORO, Cumberland Co., Nova Scotia, 1,919.
    On Cumberland (R. R.).
PARRY SOUND, Parry Sound Co., Ontario, Canada,
    3,512.
    On Can. Nat.; Can. Pac. (R. Rs.).
PARRYVILLE, Carbon Co., Pa., 553.
    On Cen. of N. J. (R. R.).
PARSONS, Labette Co., Kans., 14,962.
    On Mo.-Kan.-Tex.; St. Lou.-San Fran.; Un.
    Elec. (R. Rs.).
    Located in a coal and oil region. Also an
    agricultural center.
    —Decatur Co., Tenn., 915.
    —c. s., Tucker Co., W. Va., 2,012.
    On West. Md. (R. R.).
PARTANNA, Prov. of Trapani, Sicily, Italy, 17,313.
PASADENA, Los Angeles Co., Cal., 76,086.
    On the Atch., Top. & Santa Fe; Pac. El.; Sou.
    Pac.; and Union Pac. (R. Rs.).
    A residential suburb near Los Angeles. Has
    many beautiful buildings and parks. Site of
    the Huntington Library and Art Gallery. The
    famous Rose Bowl amphitheater is also here.
    Seat of Pasadena College.
    —Harris Co., Tex., 1,647.
    On Sou. Pac. (R. R.).
PASCAGOULA, c. s., Jackson Co., Miss., 4,339.
    On Miss. Exp.; Lou. & Nash. (R. Rs.).
PASCO, c. s., Franklin Co., Wash., 3,496.
    On Nor. Pac.; Spok., Port. & Seattle (R. Rs.).

PASEWALK, Prussia, Germany, 11,743.
PASIG, Prov. of Rizal, Luzon, P. I., 16,174.
    The trade center of a rice growing region.
PASO ROBLES, San Luis Obispo Co., Cal., 2,573.
    On Sou. Pac. (R. R.).
PASSAIC, Passaic Co., N. J., 62,959.
    On Del., Lack. & West.; Erie; N. York, Susq.
    & West. (R. Rs.).
    Has a large production of woolens, silks and
    cotton goods; also shatter-proof glass, metal,
    and leather plants.
PASSAU, Bavaria, Germany, 25,000.
    Tobacco, beer, porcelain, and machinery are
    leading manufactures.
PASSCHENDALE, W. Flanders, Belgium, 2,065.
PASS CHRISTIAN, Harrison Co., Miss., 3,004.
    On Lou. & Nash.; Ill. Cen. (R. Rs.).
PASSO FUNDO, Rio Grande do Sul, Brazil, 113,460.
    The center of a mining and agricultural region.
PASTO, capital of Narino, Colombia, 43,162.
    A trade center. Has some woolen mills.
PATASKALA, Licking Co., Ohio, 787.
    On Balt. & Ohio; Penna. (R. Rs.).
PATCHOGUE, Suffolk Co., N. Y., 6,860.
    On Long Isl. (R. R.).
PATERNO, Prov. of Catania, Sicily, Italy, 31,436.
    A suburb of Catania.
PATERSON, c. s., Passaic Co., N. J., 138,513.
    Situated on the Passaic River, on the Erie; the
    Delaware, Lackawanna & West.; and the New
    York, Susquehanna & Western railroads.
    The chief industry is silk production, in which
    it leads the country. Other important prod-

ucts are airplane motors, textile, and general
machinery.
    Paterson was founded in 1791 by a cotton-
    manufacturing society which owed its origin to
    Alexander Hamilton. The city was named in
    honor of Governor William Paterson of New
    Jersey. Incorporated as a city in 1851.
PATERSON HEIGHTS, Beaver Co., Pa., 639.
PATIALA, Patiala State, India, 55,129.
PATILLAS, Mun. of Patillas, Puerto Rico, 2,265.
PATNA, capital of Patna Div., Bihar and Orissa
    Prov., India, 159,690.
    Situated on the Ganges River. Contains a fa-
    mous oriental museum.
PATNONGON, Prov. of Antique, Panay, P. I., 15,-
    571.
PATOKA, Marion Co., Ill., 546.
    On Ill. Cen. (R. R.).
    —Gibson Co., Ind., 634.
    On Chi. & East. Ill. (R. R.).
PATOUTVILLE, Iberia Par., La., 500.
    On Sou. Pac. (R. R.).
PATRAI (Patras), capital of Nomarchy of Achaia,
    Greece, 73,300.
    The chief seaport on the west coast of Greece.
PATTEN, Penobscot Co., Maine, 800.
    On Bangor & Aroostook (R. R.).
PATTERSON, Stanislaus Co., Cal., 905.
    On Sou. Pac. (R. R.).
    —St. Mary Parish, La., 2,206.
    On Sou. Pac. (R. R.).
    —Putnam Co., N. Y., 800.
    On N. York Cen. (R. R.).

Patton, San Bernardino Co., Cal., 4,100.
On Atch., Top. & Santa Fe; Pac. El. (R. Rs.).
–Allegheny Co., Pa., 2,000.
–Cambria Co., Pa., 2,988.
On N. York Cen.; Penna. (R. Rs.).
Pattonsburg, Daviess Co., Mo., 1,009.
On Quincy, Oma. & Kan. Cy.; Wab. (R. Rs.).
Paturages, Hainaut, Belgium, 11,793.
Pau, Dept. of Basses-Pyrénées, France, 40,151.
Famous as a winter health resort.
Paulding, c. s., Paulding Co., Ohio, 1,904.
On Cle., Cin., Chi. & St. Lou. (R. R.).
Paullina, O'Brien Co., Iowa, 1,013.
On Chi. & Nor. West. (R. R.).
Paulsboro, Gloucester Co., N. J., 7,121.
On Penna.-Read. Seash. (R. R.).
Pauls Valley, c. s., Garvin Co., Okla., 4,235.
On Atch., Top. & Santa Fe; Gulf, Colo. & Santa Fe (R. Rs.).
Pavia, capital of Prov. of Pavia, Italy, 35,724.
An important agricultural center. Has iron foundries and artificial silk factories.
Pavlograd, Soviet Union, 41,000.
Pavo, Brooks and Thomas Cos., Ga., 750.
On Ga. Nor. (R. R.).
Paw Creek (Thrift), Mecklenburg Co., N. C., 600.
On Piedmont Nor. (El.); Seab. Air Line (R. Rs.).
Pawhuska, c. s., Osage Co., Okla., 5,931.
On Atch., Top. & Santa Fe; Midl. Val. (R. Rs.).
Pawling, Dutchess Co., N. Y., 1,204.
On N. York Cen. (R. R.).
Pawnee, Sangamon Co., Ill., 959.
On Chi. & Ill. Midl. (R. R.).
–c. s., Pawnee Co., Okla., 2,562.
On Atch., Top. & Santa Fe; St. Lou.-San Fran. (R. Rs.).
Pawnee City, c. s., Pawnee Co., Neb., 1,573.
On Chi., Burl. & Quincy; Chi., Rk. Isl. & Pac. (R. Rs.).
Paw Paw, Lee Co., Ill., 559.
On Chi., Burl. & Quincy (R. R.).
–c. s., Van Buren Co., Mich., 1,684.
On Pere Marq. (R. R.).
–Morgan Co., W. Va., 800.
On Balt. & Ohio (R. R.).
Pawtucket, Providence Co., R. I., 72,820.
Situated on the Pawtucket River, and on the New York, New Haven and Hartford Railroad. The city has manufacturing establishments of airplane parts, radio tubes, sporting goods, cotton, woolen, silk, plush, webbing, and rayon mills and thread factories. The first cotton factory in the United States was built here by Samuel Slater in 1790.
Pax, Fayette Co., W. Va., 608.
On Kanaw., Gl. Jean & East.; Virginian (R. Rs.).
Paxinos, Northampton Co., Pa., 500.
Paxtang, Dauphin Co., Pa., 1,594.
Paxton, c. s., Ford Co., Ill., 2,892.
On Ill. Cen.; N. Y., Chi. & St. Lou. (R. Rs.).
–Worcester Co., Mass., 731.
–Keith Co., Neb., 507.
On Un. Pac. (R. R.).
Payette, c. s., Payette Co., Idaho, 2,618.
On Ore. Short Line (Un. Pac.) (R. R.).
Payne, Paulding Co., Ohio, 1,014.
On N. York, Chi. & St. Lou. (R. R.).
Paynesville, Stearns Co., Minn., 1,121.
On Mpls., St. P. & S. Ste. M.; Gt. Nor. (R. Rs.).
Paysandu, capital of Dept. of Paysandu, Uruguay, 37,000.
The second town of Uruguay. A center of the meat packing industry and has sawmills, breweries, creameries, tanneries, and canning plants.
Payson, Utah Co., Utah, 3,045.
On Den. & Rio Gde. West; Salt L. & Utah; Un. Pac. (R. Rs.).
Peabody, Marion Co., Kans., 1,576.
On Atch., Top. & Santa Fe; Chi., Rk. Isl. & Pac. (R. Rs.).
–Essex Co., Mass., 22,082.
On Bost. & Me. (R. R.).
Leather goods and textiles.
Peach Creek, Logan Co., W. Va., 500.
On Chesa. & Ohio (R. R.).
Peapack, Somerset Co., N. J. (Pop. incl. in Peapack-Gladstone).
On Del., Lack. & West. (R. R.).
Peapack-Gladstone, Somerset Co., N. J., 1,273.
Pearisburg, Giles Co., Va., 668.
On Norf. & West.; Va. (R. Rs.).
Pearl River, Rockland Co., N. Y., 2,575.
On N. Jer. & N. York (Erie) (R. R.).
Pear Ridge, Jefferson Co., Tex., 1,500.
Pearsall, c. s., Frio Co., Texas, 2,536.
On Mo. Pac. (R. R.).
Pearson, c. s., Atkinson Co., Ga., 712.
On Atl. Coast Line (R. R.).
Peason, Sabine Co., La., 1,500.
Pecan Gap, Delta Co., Tex., 625.
On Gulf, Colo. & Santa Fe (R. R.).
Pecatonica, Winnebago Co., Ill., 1,152.
On Chi. & Nor. West. (R. R.).
Peckville, Lackawanna Co., Pa., 8,000.
On Del. & Hud.; N. York, Ont. & West.; Wilk.-Bar. & East. (Erie) (R. Rs.).
Peconic, Suffolk Co., N. Y., 647.
On Long Isl. (R. R.).
Pecos, c. s., Reeves Co., Texas, 3,304.
On Pecos Val. Sou.; Tex. & Pac.; Panh. & Santa Fe (R. Rs.).
–San Miguel Co., N. M., 1,029.
Pecs, Hungary, 64,391.
A trade center in an agricultural region.
Peebles, Adams Co., Ohio, 1,235.
On Norf. & West. (R. R.).
–Capital of Peebles Co., Scotland, 6,432.
Peekskill, Westchester Co., N. Y., 17,125.
On N. York Cen. (R. R.).
Industries include dairying, poultry farming, stoves, underwear, dress goods, foundry products, yeast, vinegar, oilcloth, gin, firebrick, etc.
Pe Ell, Lewis Co., Wash., 891.
On Nor. Pac. (R. R.).
Pegram, Greenwood Co., S. C., 2,000.
On Southern (R. R.).
Peiping (Peking), Prov. of Hopen, China, 811,000.
Former capital of China, situated on a vast sandy plain, between the Pei-ho and the Hoang-ho. It consists of two contiguous cities, each separately surrounded by walls, and together entered by sixteen gates. The inner enclosure, or "forbidden city," surrounded by walls of yellow tiles, hence called the "Yellow Wall," contains the palaces of the former emperor and empress. The southern city, called the Wai-ching, or "outer city," is occupied by the Chinese, and is both the seat of business and the residence of most of the population. The wall is 30 feet high, 25 feet thick at the base, and 12 feet at the top. That of the imperial city is 40 feet high.
Peiraievs (Piraeus), Nomarchy of Attica, Greece, 284,500.
The port of Athenai, with which it communicates by a railway. The city was planned by Themistocles and laid out by Hippodamus of Miletus, and was built in the days of Pericles; this ruler and Cimon before him built the three "long walls" that connected Athenai with its port.
Pekin, c. s., Tazewell Co., Ill., 16,129.
On the Illinois River, and the Alton; Atch., Top. & Santa Fe; Chi. & Ill. Midl.; Cle., Cin., Chi. & St. Lou.; Ill. Cen.; Peor. & Pek. Un.; Peor. Term. (R. Rs.).
Grain and agricultural market. Industries: corn products, leather goods, alcohol, yeast, coal mining.
Pelahatchie, Rankin Co., Miss., 1,599.
On Canton & Carthage; Ill. Cen. (R. Rs.).
Pelham, Hampshire Co., Mass., 504.

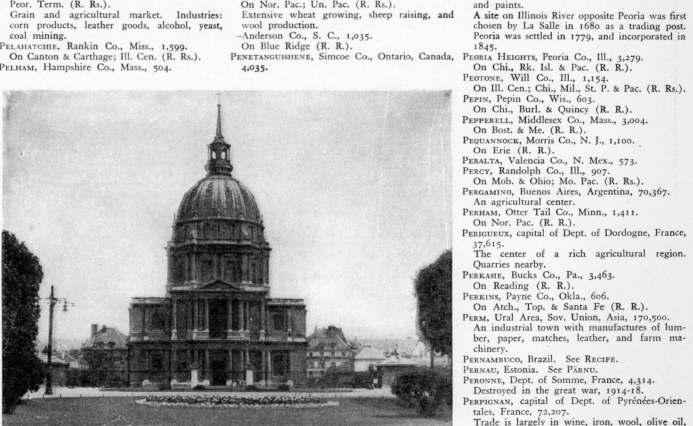

COURTESY RAILWAYS OF FRANCE

L'HOTEL DES INVALIDES, PARIS, FRANCE, THE TOMB OF NAPOLEON AND ONE OF THE PRINCIPAL POINTS OF INTEREST IN THE FRENCH CAPITAL

–Westchester Co., N. Y., 2,053.
On N. York, N. Hav. & Hart. (R. R.).
–Mitchell Co., Ga., 2,762.
On Atl. Coast Line; Flint Riv. & N.E. (R. Rs.).
–Hillsboro Co., N. H., 814.
–Caswell Co., N. C., 750.
On Southern (R. R.).
Pelham Manor, Westchester Co., N. Y., 4,908.
On N. York, N. Hav. & Hart. (R. R.).
A residential suburb of New York, on Pelham Bay.
Pelican Rapids, Otter Tail Co., Minn., 1,365.
On Gt. Nor. (R. R.).
Pella, Marion Co., Iowa, 3,326.
On Chi., Rk. Isl. & Pac. (R. R.).
Pell City, St. Clair Co., Ala., 835.
On Seab. Air Line; Sou. (R. Rs.).
Pellston, Emmet Co., Mich., 810.
On Penna. (R. R.).
Pelly, Harris Co., Texas, 3,452.
Pelotas, Rio Grande do Sul, Brazil, 60,000.
The center of a cattle raising region.
Pelzer, Anderson Co., S. C., 3,315.
On Piedmont & Nor. (El.); Sou. (R. Rs.).
Pemberton, Burlington Co., N. J., 783.
On Penna.; Penna. & Atl. (R. Rs.).
–Raleigh Co., W. Va., 521.
On Chesa. & Ohio; Virginian (R. Rs.).
Pemberville, Wood Co., Ohio, 960.
On Chesa. & Ohio; N. York Cen. (R. Rs.).
Pembina, c. s., Pembina Co., N. Dak., 551.
On Nor. Pac. (R. R.).
Pembroke, Pembrokeshire, Wales, 12,008.
–Capital of Renfrew Co., Ontario, Canada, 9,368.
On Can. Pac.; Can. Nat. (R. Rs.).
–Bryan Co., Ga., 788.
On Seab. Air Line (R. R.).
–Christian Co., Ky., 775.
On Lou. & Nash. (R. R.).
–Plymouth Co., Mass., 1,621.
–Genesee Co., N. Y., 2,209.
On N. York Cen. (R. R.).
–Robeson Co., N. C., 524.
On Atl. Coast Line; Seab. Air Line (R. Rs.).
–Giles Co., Va., 800.
On Norf. & West.; Virginian (R. Rs.).
Penablanca, Sandoval Co., N. Mex., 1,006.
Pen Argyl, Northampton Co., Pa., 4,310.
On Del., Lack. & West.; Leh. & N. Eng. (R. Rs.).
Penarth, Glamorganshire, Wales, 17,710.
A coal shipping port near Cardiff. It is also a watering place.
Penasco, Taos Co., N. Mex., 600.
Penbrook, Dauphin Co., Pa., 3,567.
Pencoyd, Montgomery Co., Pa., 832.
On Penna.; Read. (R. Rs.).
Pender, c. s., Thurston Co., Neb., 1,006.
On Chi., St. P., Mpls. & Oma. (R. R.).
Pendleton, Madison Co., Ind., 1,538.
On Cle., Cin., Chi. & St. Lou.; Ind. R. R. Sys. (El.) (R. Rs.).
–c. s., Umatilla Co., Ore., 6,621.
On Nor. Pac.; Un. Pac. (R. Rs.).
Extensive wheat growing, sheep raising, and wool production.
–Anderson Co., S. C., 1,035.
On Blue Ridge (R. R.).
Penetanguishene, Simcoe Co., Ontario, Canada, 4,035.
On Can. Nat. (R. R.).
Penfield, Monroe Co., N. Y., 700.
–Clearfield Co., Pa., 700.
On Balt. & Ohio; Penna. (R. Rs.).
Peninsula, Summit Co., Ohio, 510.
On Balt. & Ohio (R. R.).
Penn, Westmoreland Co., Pa., 926.
On Penna. (R. R.).
Pennington, Mercer Co., N. J., 1,335.
On Reading (R. R.).
Pennington Gap (Pennington), Lee Co., Va., 1,553.
On Lou. & Nash. (R. R.).
Pennsboro, Ritchie Co., W. Va., 1,616.
On Balt. & Ohio (R. R.).
Pennsburg, Montgomery Co., Pa., 1,494.
On Reading (R. R.).
Pennsgrove, Salem Co., N. J., 5,895.
On Penna.-Read. Seash. (R. R.).
Pennside, Berks Co., Pa., 1,500.
Penns Park, Bucks Co., Pa., 1,000.
Pennsylvania Furnace, Huntingdon Co., Pa., 500.
On Bellef. Cen. (R. R.).
Penn Valley, Montgomery Co., Pa., 1,000.
Pennville, Jay Co., Ind., 578.
–York Co., Pa., 507.
Penn Yan, c. s., Yates Co., N. Y., 5,329.
On N. York Cen.; Penna. (R. Rs.).
Penobscot, Hancock Co., Maine, 700.
Penowa, Washington Co., Pa., 1,187.
On Pitts. & West Va. (R. R.).
Pensacola, c. s., Escambia Co., Fla., 30,806.
On Lou. & Nash.; St. Lou.-San Fran. (R. Rs.).
Situated on the Gulf of Mexico. Its landlocked harbor has a United States Naval Air Station. An important market for naval stores and fish. It has large shipbuilding plants. A summer and winter resort.
Pensauken, Camden Co., N. J., 2,000.
On Penna. (R. R.).
Pentwater, Oceana Co., Mich., 772.
Penuelas, Mun. of Penuelas, Puerto Rico, 1,421.
Penza, R.S.F.S.R. Soviet Union, 119,000.
Has sawmills, paper mills, and match factories.
Penzance, Cornwall, England, 11,342.
A seaport. Leading exports are tin, copper, and stone.
Peoria, c. s., Peoria Co., Ill., 104,969.
Situated on the Illinois River and on the Alton; the Chicago, Burlington & Quincy, the Chicago & Illinois Midland; Chicago, Rock Island & Pacific; the Cleveland, Cincinnati, Chicago & St. Louis; the Illinois Central; Pennsylvania; New York, Chicago & St. Louis; Minneapolis & St. Louis; Chicago & North Western; Illinois Terminal (El.); the Toledo, Peoria & Western; Peoria & Pekin Union; and the Peoria Terminal.
In the rich agricultural section and close to coal region. Has nearly 200 factories. Chief products, distilled liquors, tractors, farm implements, furnaces, chemicals, structural iron, and paints.
A site on Illinois River opposite Peoria was first chosen by La Salle in 1680 as a trading post. Peoria was settled in 1779, and incorporated in 1845.
Peoria Heights, Peoria Co., Ill., 3,279.
On Chi., Rk. Isl. & Pac. (R. R.).
Peotone, Will Co., Ill., 1,154.
On Ill. Cen.; Chi., Mil., St. P. & Pac. (R. Rs.).
Pepin, Pepin Co., Wis., 603.
On Chi., Burl. & Quincy (R. R.).
Pepperell, Middlesex Co., Mass., 3,004.
On Bost. & Me. (R. R.).
Pequannock, Morris Co., N. J., 1,100.
On Erie (R. R.).
Peralta, Valencia Co., N. Mex., 573.
Percy, Randolph Co., Ill., 907.
On Mob. & Ohio; Mo. Pac. (R. Rs.).
Pergamino, Buenos Aires, Argentina, 70,367.
An agricultural center.
Perham, Otter Tail Co., Minn., 1,411.
On Nor. Pac. (R. R.).
Perigueux, capital of Dept. of Dordogne, France, 37,615.
The center of a rich agricultural region. Quarries nearby.
Perkasie, Bucks Co., Pa., 3,463.
On Reading (R. R.).
Perkins, Payne Co., Okla., 606.
On Atch., Top. & Santa Fe (R. R.).
Perm, Ural Area, Sov. Union, Asia, 170,500.
An industrial town with manufactures of lumber, paper, matches, leather, and farm machinery.
Pernambuco, Brazil. See Recife.
Pernau, Estonia. See Pärnu.
Peronne, Dept. of Somme, France, 4,314.
Destroyed in the great war, 1914-18.
Perpignan, capital of Dept. of Pyrénées-Orientales, France, 72,207.
Trade is largely in wine, iron, wool, olive oil, and cork.
Perrine, Dade Co., Fla., 1,054.
On Fla. East Coast (R. R.).
Perry, c. s., Taylor Co., Fla., 2,400.
On Atl. Coast Line; Live Oak, Perry & Gulf; Sou. Ga. (R. Rs.).
–c. s., Houston Co., Ga., 1,398.
On Cen. of Ga. (R. R.).
–Dallas Co., Iowa, 5,881.
On Chi., Mil., St. P. & Pac.; Mpls. & St. Lou.; Des Moines & Cen. Ia. (El.) (R. Rs.).
In a farming district.
Washington Co., Maine, 500.
On Me. Cen. (R. R.).
–(South Hanover), Plymouth Co., Mass., 541.
–Shiawassee Co., Mich., 835.
On Gd. Tr. (R. R.).

–Ralls Co., Mo., 976.
On St. Lou. & Han. (R. R.).
–Wyoming Co., N. Y., 4,231.
On Balt. & Ohio (R. R.).
Condensed milk, knitted goods, other factory products.
–Lake Co., Ohio, 602.
On Fairp., Painesv. & East.; N. York Cen.; N. York, Chi. & St. Lou. (R. Rs.).
–c. s., Noble Co., Okla., 4,206.
On Atch., Top. & Santa Fe; St. Lou.-San Fran. (R. Rs.).
PERRYOPOLIS, Fayette Co., Pa., 825.
On Pitts. & L. Erie (R. R.).
PERRYSBURG, Wood Co., Ohio, 3,182.
On Balt. & Ohio (R. R.).
PERRYSVILLE, Ashland Co., Ohio, 615.
On Penna. (R. R.).
–Allegheny Co., Pa., 1,000.
PERRYTON, c. s., Ochiltree Co., Tex., 2,824.
On Panh. & Santa Fe (R. R.).
PERRYVILLE, Cecil Co., Md., 704.
On Penna. (R. R.).
–c. s., Perry Co., Mo., 2,964.
PERSHING (Stauffer), Westmoreland Co., Pa., 1,000.
On Balt. & Ohio (R. R.).
PERTH, capital of Western Australia, Australia (incl. suburbs), 212,150.
The center of trade, commerce, banking, and politics of the State. A terminus of the railroads running to the inland gold fields.
–Capital of Perth Co., Scotland, 34,807.
Situated on the right bank of the river Tay. Celebrated for its bleachfields and dye works; also an extensive center for manufactures of textiles. Probably of Roman origin. Its earliest known charter is dated 1106.
–Lanark Co., Ontario, Can., 4,099.
On Can. Pac. (R. R.).
PERTH AMBOY, Middlesex Co., N. J., 43,516.
On Cen. of N. Jer.; Leh. Val.; Penna.; N. York & Long Br.; Stat. Isl. Rap. Tr. (R. Rs.).
An industrial town in the New York area. Copper smelting and ceramics.
PERU, La Salle Co., Ill., 9,121.
On Chi., Burl. & Quincy; Chi., Rk. Isl. & Pac. (R. Rs.).
Coal mines and zinc works.
–c. s., Miami Co., Ind., 12,730.
On Chesa. & Ohio; Ind. R. R. Sys. (El.); N. Y., Chi. & St. L.; Wab.; Winona (El.) (R. Rs.).
Has a large alarm clock factory and zinc works. Coal mines in the vicinity.
–Chautauqua Co., Kans., 569.
On Mo. Pac. (R. R.).
–Nemaha Co., Neb., 835.
On Chi., Burl. & Quincy (R. R.).
–Clinton Co., N. Y., 560.
On Del. & Hud. (R. R.).
PERUGIA (ancient Perusia), capital of Prov. of Perugia, Italy, 24,133.
Situated on an eminence above the Tiber and is surrounded by walls. It is rich in art and literary treasures, and has many remarkable buildings, including Gothic cathedral of the fifteenth century.
Perugia was an old Etruscan city, and was conquered by Rome in 310 B.C.
PESARO, capital of Prov. of Pesaro e Urbino, Italy, 18,506.
An agricultural center; a seaport. Frequented by tourists.
PESHAWAR, Peshawar Dist., British India, 87,440.
A trade center and entry point for goods from inner Asia.
PESHTIGO, Marinette Co., Wis., 1,579.
On Chi. & Nor. West. (R. R.).
PETALUMA, Sonoma Co., Cal., 8,245.
On Northw. Pac.; Petaluma & Santa Rosa (El.) (R. Rs.).
PETERBORO, Hillsboro Co., N. H., 2,347.
On Bost. & Me. (R. R.).
PETERBOROUGH, Peterborough, England, 22,445.
An industrial and commercial center. Chief manufactures are agricultural implements and clay products.
–Capital of Peterborough Co., Ontario, Canada, 22,327.
On Can. Pac.; Can. Nat. (R. Rs.).
Electrical machinery, bridges, farm implements, lumber, flour, and woolens.
PETERHEAD, Aberdeen Co., Scotland, 15,285.
PETERSBURG, Petersburg Co., Alaska, 1,252.
–c. s., Menard Co., Ill., 2,319.
On Alton; Chi. & Ill. Midl. (R. Rs.).
–c. s., Pike Co., Ind., 2,609.
On Cle., Cin., Chi. & St. Lou. (R. R.).
–Monroe Co., Mich., 705.
On N. York Cen.; Det., Tol. & Iron. (R. Rs.).
–Boone Co., Neb., 585.
On Chi. & Nor. West. (R. R.).
–Mahoning Co., Ohio, 500.
–Huntingdon Co., Pa., 627.
On Penna. (R. R.).
–Lincoln and Marshall Cos., Tenn., 556.
On Nash., Chatt. & St. Lou. (R. R.).
–Hale Co., Tex., 548.
On Ft. Worth & Denv. Cy. (R. R.).
–(Ind. City), Dinwiddie Co., Va., 28,564.
On Atl. Coast Line; Norf. & West.; Seab. Air Line (R. Rs.).
Extensive market for tobacco and peanuts. Was headquarters of Cornwallis, Lafayette and Lee.
–c. s., Grant Co., W. Va., 1,410.
On Balt. & Ohio (R. R.).
PETERSHAM, Worcester Co., Mass., 718.
PETERSON, Clay Co., Iowa, 598.
On Chi. & Nor. West. (R. R.).
PETOSKEY, c. s., Emmet Co., Mich., 5,740.
On Penna.; Pere Marq. (R. Rs.).

EWING GALLOWAY PHOTO

TRIPLE ARCHED GATEWAY IN FRONT OF THE HALL OF CLASSICS IN PEKING, CHINA

PETROGRAD, Sov. Union. See LENINGRAD.
PETROLIA, Lambton Co., Ontario, Canada, 2,596.
On Can. Nat.; Mich. Cen. (R. Rs.).
–Clay Co., Texas, 806.
On Wich. Val. (R. R.).
PETROPAVLOVSK, Soviet Union in Asia, 65,800.
Center of the caravan trade from the Kirghiz Steppe region.
PETROS, Morgan Co., Tenn., 1,015.
On Har. & Northe. (R. R.).
PEUMO, Prov. of Colchagua, Chile, 3,081.
PEWAUKEE, Waukesha Co., Wis., 1,067.
On Chi., Mil., St. P. & Pac. (R. R.).
PEWEE VALLEY, Oldham Co., Ky., 582.
On Lou. & Nash. (R. R.).
PEWSEY, Wiltshire, England, 14,292.
A marketing town.
PFLUGERVILLE, Travis Co., Tex., 500.
On Mo.-Kan.-Tex. of Tex. (R. R.).
PFORZHEIM, Baden, Germany, 79,000.
Gold and silver ornament industry.
PHARR, Hidalgo Co., Texas, 3,225.
On Mo. Pac. (R. R.).
PHELPS, Ontario Co., N. Y., 1,397.
On Leh. Val.; N. York Cen. (R. Rs.).
–Vilas Co., Wis., 500.
On Chi. & Nor. West. (R. R.).
PHENIX CITY, Lee and Russell Cos., Ala., 13,862.
On Cen. of Ga. (R. R.).
A residential and industrial suburb of Columbus, Ga., and located in a cotton-growing district.
PHILADELPHIA, Philadelphia Co., Pa., 1,950,961.
Situated on the Delaware and Schuylkill Rivers, and on the Pennsylvania; the Pennsylvania-Reading Seashore; the Reading and the Baltimore & Ohio railroads.
It is the largest city of Pennsylvania, and the third largest in the United States. It has always stood among the first cities of the country, having ranked as high as second and never lower than fourth. It was second in 1790, with a population of 28,522; second in 1800 with 41,220; second in 1810, with 53,722; second in 1820, with 63,802; third in 1830, with 80,462; third in 1840, with 93,665; fourth in 1850, with 121,376; second in 1860, with 565,529; second in 1870, with 674,022; second in 1880, with 847,170; third in 1890, with 1,046,964; in 1900, with 1,293,697; in 1910, with 1,549,008, and in 1920, with 1,823,779. The city is built chiefly on a low peninsula between the two rivers, and there is a water frontage on the Delaware River of over 16 miles, with 5 miles of docks. The harbor in front of the wharfs has an average depth of 50 feet. The Schuylkill River, which runs through the city, is navigable for large vessels to Walnut Street, and is crossed by many bridges. The section of the city west of the Schuylkill is locally called West Philadelphia; another noted section is known as Germantown. League Island is the site of the United States Navy Yard.
Fairmount Park is one of the largest public parks in the world. It extends more than 7 miles on both banks of the Schuylkill River, and has an area of over 3,000 acres.
At the intersection of Market and Broad Streets stands the City Hall. The total cost of the building was $25,000,000. There are other noted buildings, including the Pennsylvania Art Museum, costing $20,000,000; the Rodin Museum, a reproduction of the Musée at Meudon, France; the United States mint; the post office, costing nearly $8,000,000; the Pennsylvania Hospital, covering an entire square; the building of the Historical Society of Pennsylvania; the Philadelphia Library, containing upward of 700,000 volumes; the Academy of Fine Arts, containing one of the most extensive collections of paintings, engravings, bronzes, and sculptures in the United States; the custom-house, copied from the Parthenon, and considered one of the best samples of Doric architecture in the world. Among the city's historical features are Independence Hall, famous as the State House of the Colonial period; Betsy Ross House (birthplace of the American flag); and Franklin's grave.
In its manufacturing products Philadelphia ranks next to New York. There are about 5,567 manufacturing establishments. The great Cramp shipbuilding yards are on the Delaware River. The Baldwin Locomotive Works are the largest in the world. In addition to ships and locomotives, the city has an enormous production of refined petroleum, printing and publishing, knit goods, clothing, electrical machinery, packed meats, confectionery, chemicals, hats, cigars, glazed kid, bed sheetings, paper boxes, carpets, and street cars. The institutions for higher education include Temple University; the University of Pennsylvania; the Jefferson Medical College; the Woman's Medical College; the Hahnemann Medical College; and Drexel Institute. There are colleges of dentistry, pharmacy, osteopathy, and veterinary surgery. Girard College, founded by the great philanthropist, Stephen Girard, is devoted to the education of orphan boys.
Philadelphia was founded by William Penn in 1682. It was incorporated a city in 1789 and enlarged in 1854.
–c. s., Neshoba Co., Miss., 2,560.
On Gulf, Mob. & Nor. (R. R.).
–Jefferson Co., N. Y., 817.
On the N. York Cen. (R. R.).
PHILIP, c. s., Haakon Co., S. Dak., 887.
On Chi. & Nor. West. (R. R.).
PHILIPP, Tallahatchie Co., Miss., 530.
On Ill. Cen. (R. R.).
PHILIPPEVILLE, Dept. of Constantine, Algeria, 66,112.
A seaport and trade center. The French founded the modern city in 1838, but ruins of Roman structures exist.
PHILIPPI, c. s., Barbour Co., W. Va., 1,767.
On Balt. & Ohio (R. R.).
PHILIPPOPOLIS, Bulgaria. See PLOVDIV.
PHILIPSBURG, c. s., Granite Co., Mont., 1,300.
On Nor. Pac. (R. R.).
–Centre Co., Pa., 3,600.
On N. York Cen.; Penna. (R. Rs.).
PHILLIPS, Franklin Co., Maine, 734.
–c. s., Price Co., Wis., 1,901.
On Mpls., St. P. & S. Ste. M. (R. R.).
PHILLIPSBURG, c. s., Phillips Co., Kans., 1,781.
On Chi., Rk. Isl. & Pac. (R. R.).
–Warren Co., N. J., 19,255.
On Cen. of N. Jer.; Del., Lack. & West.; Leh. & Hudson Riv., Leh. Val.; Penna. (R. Rs.).
Has silk, cement, chemical plants, foundries, railroad shops.
PHILMONT, Columbia Co., N. Y., 1,868.
On N. York Cen. (R. R.).
PHILO, Champaign Co., Ill., 512.
On Wabash (R. R.).
–(Taylorsville) Muskingum Co., Ohio, 1,810.
On Balt. & Ohio (R. R.).
PHILOMATH, Benton Co., Ore., 694.
On Sou. Pac. (R. R.).
PHIPPSBURG, Sagadahoe Co., Maine, 500.
On the Kennebec River, near Bath.
PHOEBUS, c. s., Elizabeth City Co., Va., 2,956.
On Chesa. & Ohio (R. R.).
PHOENIX, c. s., Maricopa Co., Ariz., State Capital, 48,118.
On the Atchison, Topeka & Santa Fe, and the Southern Pacific railroads.
The city is situated in the heart of the Salt River Valley, notable for the vast Government irrigation system known as the Salt River project, comprising 252,000 acres, at the head of which are the famous Roosevelt Dam and Lake (25 miles in length). The main crops are cotton, for which there are a large number of gins in the Phoenix district; citrus fruits, and farm produce. Tourist center.
Phoenix was settled in 1870 and incorporated in 1881; it was made the state capital in 1889.
–Cook Co., Ill., 3,033.
On Balt. & Ohio Chi. Term. (R. R.).
–Baltimore Co., Md., 515.
On Penna. (R. R.).
–Oswego Co., N. Y., 1,758.
On N. York Cen. (R. R.).
PHOENIXVILLE, Chester Co., Pa., 12,029.
On Penna.; Read. (R. Rs.).
An industrial center. Manufactures iron, steel, bridges, boilers, and textiles.
PIACENZA, capital of Prov. of Piacenza, Italy, 43,277.
Ancient city with many fine historic buildings.
PIATRA-NEAMT, Moldavia, Rumania, 26,511.
Has sawmills and textile factories. Also a popular resort.
PIAVE, Greene Co., Miss., 1,000.
PIAZZA ARMERINA, Prov. of Castrogiovanni, Italy, 27,429.
A marketing town.
PICAYUNE, Pearl River Co., Miss., 4,698.
On N. Orl. & Northe. (R. R.).
PICHER, Ottawa Co., Okla., 7,773.
On Northe. Okla. (El.); Southw. Mo. (El.); St. Lou.-San. Fran. (R. Rs.).
PICKENS, c. s., Pickens Co., S. C., 1,130.
On Pickens (R. R.).
–Holmes Co., Miss., 635.
On Ill. Cen. (R. R.).
PICKTON, Hopkins Co., Tex., 500.
On La., Ark. & Tex. (R. R.).
PICTON, Prince Edward Co., Ontario, Canada, 3,580.
On Can. Nat. (R. R.).
PICTOU, Pictou Co., Nova Scotia, 3,152.
On Can. Nat. (R. R.).
Lobster fishing and canning.
PICTURE ROCKS, Lycoming Co., Pa., 548.
PIEDMONT, Calhoun Co., Ala., 3,668.
On Seab. Air Line; Sou. (R. Rs.).
–Alameda Co., Cal., 9,333.
On Key System (R. R.).
A beautiful suburb of Oakland.
–Wayne Co., Mo., 916.
On Mo. Pac. (R. R.).
–Greenville Co., S. C., 1,374.
On Piedmont & Nor. (El.); Sou. (R. Rs.).
–Mineral Co., W. Va., 2,241.
On Balt. & Ohio; Cumb. & Penna.; West. Md. (R. Rs.).
PIERCE, c. s., Pierce Co., Neb., 1,271.
On Chi. & Nor. West. (R. R.).
–Tucker Co., W. Va., 500.
On West. Md. (R. R.).
PIERCE CITY (Peirce City), Lawrence Co., Mo., 1,135.
On St. Lou.-San Fran. (R. R.).
PIERCEFIELD, St. Lawrence Co., N. Y., 750.
On N. York Cen. (R. R.).
PIERCETON, Kosciusko Co., Ind., 878.
On Penna. (R. R.).
PIERMONT, Rockland Co., N. Y., 1,765.
On Erie (R. R.).
PIERRE, c. s., Hughes Co., S. Dak., State capital, 4,013.
On the Missouri River, and on the Chicago & North Western (R. R.).
The commercial center of extensive stock-raising and farming district. Principal trading point for the Black Hills section.
The town settled in 1880 and incorporated three years later; obtained a charter in 1900.
PIERREVILLE, Yamaska Co., Quebec, Canada, 1,352.
On Can. Nat. (R. R.).

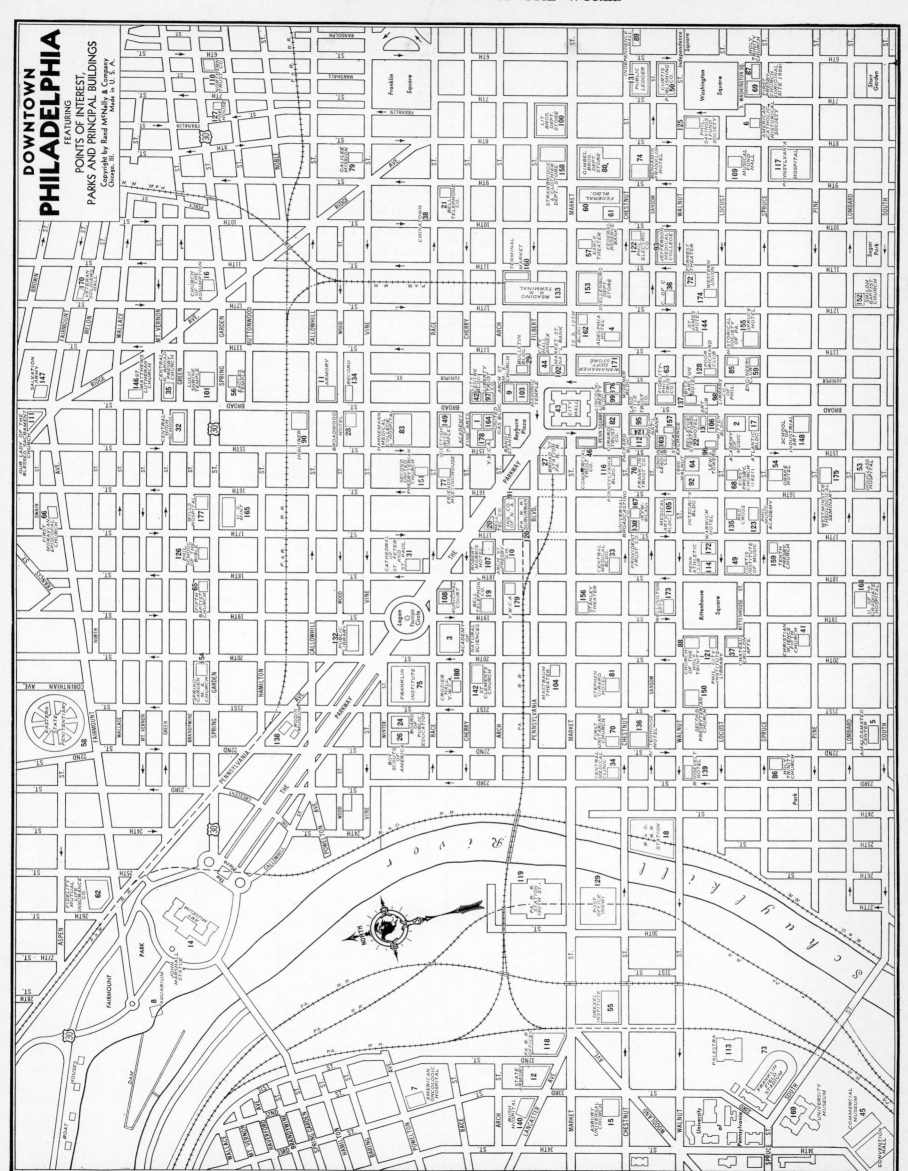

DOWNTOWN PHILADELPHIA

FEATURING
POINTS OF INTEREST,
PARKS AND PRINCIPAL BUILDINGS

Copyright by Rand McNally & Company
Made in U.S.A.
Chicago, Ill.

MAP OF THE CENTRAL PART OF PHILADELPHIA, CHIEF CITY OF PENNSYLVANIA, THIRD LARGEST CITY IN THE UNITED STATES AND SECOND TO NEW YORK IN IMPORTANCE AS A PORT ON THE ATLANTIC SEABOARD. PHILADELPHIA IS A CENTER OF HISTORIC INTEREST. THE DECLARATION OF INDEPENDENCE WAS ENACTED HERE IN INDEPENDENCE HALL, WHICH CONTAINS THE LIBERTY BELL.

Pierson, Volusia Co., Fla., 673.
On Atlantic Coast Line (R. R.).
–Woodbury Co., Iowa, 551.
On Chi. & Nor. West. (R. R.).
Pierz, Morrison Co., Minn., 634.
Pietermaritzburg, capital of Natal, Union of South Africa, 47,421.
Center of an extensive agricultural region.
Pigeon, Huron Co., Mich., 836.
On Pere Marq.; Gd. Tr. (R. Rs.).
Pigeon Cove, Essex Co., Mass., 1,306.
Pigeon Creek, Butler Co., Ala., 590.
Piggott, c. s., Clay Co., Ark., 1,885.
On St. Lou.-San Fran.; St. Lou. Southw. (R. Rs.).
Piketon, Pike Co., Ohio, 713.
On Norf. & West. (R. R.).
Pikeville, c. s., Pike Co., Ky., 3,376.
On Chesa. & Ohio (R. R.).
–c. s., Bledsoe Co., Tenn., 551.
On Nash., Chatt. & St. Lou. (R. R.).
Pilar (Villa Del), Paraguay, 6,800.
On Paraguay River.
Pilger, Stanton Co., Neb., 578.
On Chi. & Nor. West. (R. R.).
Pilot Grove, Cooper Co., Mo., 654.
On Mo.-Kan.-Tex. (R. R.).
Pilot Mountain, Surry Co., N. C., 1,010.
On Atl. & Yadk. (R. R.).
Pilot Point, Denton Co., Texas, 1,108.
On Mo.-Kan.-Tex. of Tex.; Tex. & Pac. (R. Rs.).
Pilsen, Czechoslovakia. See Plzen.
Pima, Graham Co., Ariz., 980.
On Sou. Pac. (R. R.).
Pinar del Rio, capital of Prov. of Pinar del Rio, Cuba, 15,600.
An important tobacco market.
Pinckard, Dale Co., Ala., 633.
On Atl. Coast Line (R. R.).
Pinckneyville, c. s., Perry Co., Ill., 3,046.
On Ill. Cen.; Mo. Pac. (R. Rs.).
Pinconning, Bay Co., Mich., 826.
On Det. & Mack.; Mich. Cen. (R. Rs.).
Pine Bluff, c. s., Jefferson Co., Ark., 20,760.
On the Arkansas River and the Mo. Pac.; St. Lou. Southw. (R. Rs.).
A wholesale jobbing, and industrial center.
Pine Bluffs, Laramie Co., Wyo., 670.
On Un. Pac. (R. R.).
Pine Bush, Orange Co., N. Y., 800.
On Erie (R. R.).
Pinecastle, Orange Co., Fla., 564.
On Atl. Coast Line (R. R.).
Pine City, c. s., Pine Co., Minn., 1,343.
On Nor. Pac. (R. R.).
Pine Grove, Schuylkill Co., Pa., 2,257.
On Reading (R. R.).
–Wetzel Co., W. Va., 820.
On Balt. & Ohio (R. R.).
Pine Hill, Camden Co., N. J., 1,392.
Pinehurst, Dooly Co., Ga., 519.
On Ga. Sou. & Fla. (R. R.).
–Moore Co., N. C., 1,600.
On Norf. Sou. (R. R.).
–Snohomish Co., Wash., 1,200.
Pine Island, Goodhue Co., Minn., 961.
On Chi. Gt. West.; Chi. & Nor. West. (R. Rs.).
Pineland, Sabine Co., Texas, 1,500.
On Gulf, Colo. & Santa Fe (R. R.).
Pine Ridge, Shannon Co., S. Dak., 618.
Pine Valley, LeFlore Co., Okla., 1,700.
On Okla. & Rich Mtn. (R. R.).
Pineville, c. s., Bell Co., Ky., 3,567.
On Lou. & Nash. (R. R.).
–Rapides Parish, La., 3,612.
On La. & Ark. (R. R.).
–Mecklenburg Co., N. C., 1,108.
On Southern (R. R.).
Pinewood, Hickman Co., Tenn., 615.
Piney Fork, Jefferson Co., Ohio, 1,000.
On N. York Cen. (R. R.).
Pingyangfu, Shansi, China, 173,000.
An ancient and holy city.
Pinole, Contra Costa Co., Cal., 781.
On Atch., Top. & Santa Fe; Sou. Pac. (R. Rs.).
Pinsk, Poland, 31,913.
A commercial and industrial center. Chief products are pottery, leather, oil, soap, and beer. Located in a rich farming region.
Pioneer, Williams Co., Ohio, 686.
On Pioneer & Fayette (R. R.).
Piotrkow, District of Lotz, Poland, 51,281.
Situated in an agricultural district. Flour, lumber, leather, and farm implements.
Piper City, Ford Co., Ill., 650.
On Tol., Peor. & West. (R. R.).
Pipers Gap, Carroll Co., Va., 650.
Pipestone, c. s., Pipestone Co., Minn., 3,489.
On Chi., Mil., St. P. & Pac.; Chi., Rk. Isl. & Pac.; Chi., St. P., Mpls. & Oma.; Gt. Nor. (R. Rs.).
Piqua, Miami Co., Ohio, 16,009.
On Balt. & Ohio; Penna. (R. Rs.).
Manufactures furniture, textiles, diversified wood products, heating systems, etc.
Piraeus, Greece. See Peiraievs.
Pirano, Pola, Italy, 5,587.
Pirmasens, Palatinate, Bavaria, Germany, 47,200.
Chief industry is shoe manufacturing.
Pirna, Saxony, Germany, 33,703.
Glass, machinery, cigars, pottery, slate, cotton yarn, and enamelled goods.
Pirot, Serbia, Yugoslavia, 11,238.
Manufactures of jewelry, rugs, and woolen braid.
Pisa, capital of Prov. of Pisa, Italy, 51,774.
Situated on the Arno River. It is the seat of the ancient University of Pisa, a college of nobles, and an Episcopal seminary. The historical features are the famous Campanile or leaning tower; the baptistry and cathedral.
Pisagua, Prov. of Tarapaca, Chile, 1,788.
Piscataway, Middlesex Co., N. J., 2,011.
Pisek, Bohemia, Czechoslovakia, 16,973.
The marketing center of cereal and cattle raising region.
Pisino, Pola, Italy, 3,271.
Pistoia, Prov. of Pistoia, Italy, 29,967.
Has numerous old architectural masterpieces.
Pitcairn, Allegheny Co., Pa., 6,317.
On Penna. (R. R.).
–St. Lawrence Co., N. Y., 570.
Pitman, Gloucester Co., N. J., 5,411.
On Penna.-Read. Seash. (R. R.).
Pittock, Allegheny Co., Pa., 2,000.
Pittsboro, c. s., Chatham Co., N. C., 675.
On Seab. Air Line (R. R.).
Pittsburg, Contra Costa Co., Cal., 9,610.
On Atch., Top. & Santa Fe; Sou. Pac.; Sacramento Nor. (Elec.) (R. Rs.).
–Crawford Co., Kans., 19,339.
On Atch., Top. & Santa Fe; Kan. Cy. Sou.; Mo. Pac.; Jop. & Pitts. (El.); St. Lou.-San Fran. (R. Rs.).
In coal section. Railroad shops, iron foundries.
–Williamson Co., Ill., 809.
On Marion & Eastern (R. R.).
–Coos Co., N. H., 600.
–Pittsburg Co., Okla., 873.
On Chi., Rk. Isl. & Pac.; Mo.-Kan.-Tex. (R. Rs.).
–c. s., Camp Co., Texas, 2,640.
On La., Ark. & Tex.; St. Lou. Southw. (R. Rs.).
Pittsburgh, c. s., Allegheny Co., Pa., 669,817.
Port of entry, situated at the confluence of the Monongahela and Allegheny Rivers, at the head of the Ohio River, on the Monongahela Connecting; the Pittsburgh, Allegheny & McKees Rock; the Allegheny & South Side; the Baltimore & Ohio; the Pittsburgh & Lake Erie; the Pennsylvania; the Pittsburgh & West Virginia railroads.
Among the chief buildings are the Allegheny Courthouse, the United States Post Office and Federal Court Building, dedicated in October, 1934, and the Chamber of Commerce, Gulf, Koppers, Grant and Clark buildings.
Pittsburgh is known as the workshop of the world, especially in relation to its iron and steel industry, which embraces the leading products of bulk in those metals, such as bridges, locomotives, and other railroad equipment. The city is also the seat of many of America's other dominating industries on account of its situation in one of the richest mineral sections. It is preëminent in the production of glass, wire, air brakes, mill machinery, aluminum, pickles, preserves, radium, vanadium, electrical, tube and pipe equipment, tin plate, fire brick, white lead, cork petroleum products, electrical machinery, alloys, paint and varnish.
The city has many educational institutions; the University of Pittsburgh, the Carnegie Institute of Technology, the Pennsylvania College for Women and the Duquesne University.
In 1754, at the suggestion of George Washington, the English began to erect a blockhouse on the present site of the city. They, however, were driven away by the French, who built a fort at the junction of the two rivers and named it Du Quesne. In 1758, after two unsuccessful attempts to retake the place, the English, under General Forbes, made a third attempt, and the French burned and evacuated the fort. In the following year another fort was erected here, named in honor of William Pitt. Shortly after a village was established by some English and Scotch settlers, and in 1770 it numbered 200 inhabitants. The British garrison abandoned the fort in 1772, and with the outbreak of the Revolution in 1775 it was occupied by Virginia Colonial troops till 1779. The place was incorporated as a city March 18, 1816. It was visited by a destructive fire April 10, 1845, when property worth nearly $10,000,000 was destroyed.
The consolidation of Allegheny with Pittsburgh was effected in 1909.
Pittsfield, c. s., Pike Co., Ill., 2,356.
On Wabash (R. R.).
–Somerset Co., Maine, 2,075.
On Me. Cen. (R. R.).
–c. s., Berkshire Co., Mass., 47,516.
On Bost. & Alb.; N. York, N. Hav. & Hart. (R. Rs.).
Has a large plant of the General Electric Co.; paper and textile mills. A resort and manufacturing city.
–Merrimack Co., N. H., 1,300.
On Suncock Val. (R. R.).
Pittsford, Hillsdale Co., Mich., 550.
On N. York Cen. (R. R.).
–Monroe Co., N. Y., 1,460.
On N. York Cen.; West Shore (R. Rs.).
–Rutland Co., Vt., 860.
On Rutland (R. R.).
Pittston, Luzerne Co., Pa., 18,246.
On Cen. of N. Jer.; Del. & Hud.; Del., Lack. & West.; Erie; Lack. & Wyo. Val. (El.); Leh. Val. (R. Rs.).
In the anthracite coal region. Manufactures paper, textiles, terra-cotta, cut-glass, brass castings, and cigars.
Pittsville, Wood Co., Wis., 508.
On Chi., Mil., St. P. & Pac. (R. R.).
Placerville, c. s., Eldorado Co., Cal., 2,322.
On Cam., Placerv. & L. Tahoe; Sou. Pac. (R. Rs.).
Placetas, Santa Clara Prov., Cuba, 9,402.
Plain City, Madison and Union Cos., Ohio, 1,288.
On Penna. (R. R.).
Plain Dealing, Bossier Parish, La., 1,412.
On St. Lou. Southw. (R. R.).
Plainfield, Windham Co., Conn., 2,500.
On N. York, N. Hav. & Hart. (R. R.).
–Will Co., Ill., 1,428.
On Elg., Jol. & East. (R. R.).
–Hendricks Co., Ind., 1,617.
On Penna.; Ind. R. R. Sys. (Elec.) (R. Rs.).
–Union Co., N. J., 34,422.
On Balt. & Ohio; Cen. of N. Jer. (R. Rs.).
A commercial center of a large trade area.
–Waushara Co., Wis., 537.
On Mpls., St. P. & S. Ste. M. (R. R.).
Plains, Sumter Co., Ga., 609.
On Seab. Air Line (R. R.).
–Sanders Co., Mont., 522.
On Nor. Pac. (R. R.).
Plainview, Yell Co., Ark., 654.
–Wabasha Co., Minn., 1,233.
On Chi. & Nor. West. (R. R.).
–Pierce Co., Neb., 1,216.
On Chi., Burl. & Quincy; Chi. & Nor. West. (R. Rs.).
–c. s., Hale Co., Texas, 8,834.
On Ft. Worth & Denv. Cy.; Panh. & Santa Fe (R. Rs.).
In an agricultural and cattle-raising district.
Plainville, Hartford Co., Conn., 6,301.
On N. York, N. Hav. & Hart. (R. R.).
Electrical supplies, ball-bearings, machines.
–Rooks Co., Kans., 974.
On Un. Pac. (R. R.).
–Norfolk Co., Mass., 1,606.
Plainwell, Allegan Co., Mich., 2,279.
On N. York Cen.; Penna. (R. Rs.).
Plaistow, Rockingham Co., N. H., 700.
On Bost. & Me. (R. R.).
Plandome, Nassau Co., N. Y., 769.
On Long Isl. (R. R.).
Plankinton, c. s., Aurora Co., S. Dak., 715.
On Chi., Mil., St. P. & Pac. (R. R.).
Plano, Kendall Co., Ill., 1,785.
On Chi., Burl. & Quincy (R. R.).
–Collin Co., Texas, 1,554.
On St. L. Southw.; Sou. Pac.; Tex. Elec. (R. Rs.).
Plant City, Hillsborough Co., Fla., 7,094.
On Atl. Coast Line; Seab. Air Line (R. Rs.).
Plantsville, Hartford Co., Conn., 3,000.
On N. York, N. Hav. & Hart. (R. R.).
Plaquemine, c. s., Iberville Parish, La., 5,124.
On Tex. & Pac. (R. R.).
Platte, Charles Mix Co., S. Dak., 1,139.
On Chi., Mil., St. P. & Pac. (R. R.).
Platte Center, Platte Co., Neb., 525.
On Un. Pac. (R. R.).
Platte City, c. s., Platte Co., Mo., 587.
On Chi., Rk. Isl. & Pac. (R. R.).
Platteville, Grant Co., Wis., 4,047.
On Chi., Mil., St. P. & Pac.; Chi. & Nor. West. (R. Rs.).
Plattsburg, c. s., Clinton Co., Mo., 1,672.
On Atch., Top. & Santa Fe; Chi., Rk. Isl. & Pac.; Quincy, Oma. & Kan. Cy. (R. Rs.).
–c. s., Clinton Co., N. Y., 13,349.
On Del. & Hud. (R. R.).
Manufactures lumber and paper. Has an army post, and is the site of a large annual citizens' military training camp.
Plattsmouth, c. s., Cass Co., Neb., 3,793.
On Chi., Burl. & Quincy; Mo. Pac. (R. Rs.).
Plauen, Prov. of Zwickau, Saxony, Germany, 113,000.
A textile and machinery manufacturing town.
Pleasant City, Guernsey Co., Ohio, 627.
On Penna. (R. R.).
Pleasantdale, Cumberland Co., Me., 867.
Pleasant Gap, Centre Co., Pa., 900.
On Penna. (R. R.).
Pleasant Grove, Utah Co., Utah, 1,754.
On Salt L. & Utah (El.); Un. Pac. (R. Rs.).
Pleasant Hill, Sabine Parish, La., 807.
On Tex. & Pac. (R. R.).
–Cass Co., Mo., 2,330.
On Chi., Rk. Isl. & Pac.; Mo. Pac. (R. Rs.).
–Miami Co., Ohio, 746.
–Lancaster Co., S. C., 2,000.
On Southern (R. R.).
Pleasant Hill Junction, Lebanon Co., Pa., 5,000.
Pleasanton, Alameda Co., Cal., 1,237.
On Sou. Pac.; West. Pac. (R. Rs.).
–Linn Co., Kans., 1,203.
On Mo. Pac.; St. Lou.-San Fran. (R. Rs.).
–Atascosa Co., Texas, 1,154.
On San Ant., Uvalde & Gulf (Mo. Pac.) (R. R.).
Pleasant Ridge, Hamilton Co., Ohio, 4,500.
On Penna. (R. R.).
–Oakland Co., Mich., 2,885.
On Gd. Tr. (R. R.).
Pleasant Unity, Westmoreland Co., Pa., 800.
On Penna. (R. R.).
Pleasantville, Marion Co., Iowa, 757.
On Chi., Burl. & Quincy (R. R.).
–Atlantic Co., N. J., 11,580.
On Penna.-Reading Seashore (R. R.).
A suburb of Atlantic City.
–Westchester Co., N. Y., 4,540.
On N. York Cen. (R. R.).
–Venango Co., Pa., 750.
Plentywood, c. s., Sheridan Co., Mont., 1,226.
On Gt. Nor. (R. R.).
Plessisville, Megantic Co., Que., Can., 2,536.
On Can. Nat. (R. R.).
Pleven, Bulgaria, 30,200.
An agricultural center.
Plock, Prov. of Warsaw, Poland, 32,777.
A river port and trade center with considerable trade in agricultural produce.
Ploesti, capital of Dist. of Prahova, Rumania, 76,873.
Center of petroleum industry.
Plovdiv (Philippopolis), capital of Plovdiv, Bulgaria, 100,485.
Here, in 1878, the Turks were defeated by the Russians. An earthquake in 1928 destroyed a part of the town.
Plum Bayou, Jefferson Co., Ark., 5,405.
Plumerville (Plummerville), Conway Co., Ark., 613.
On Mo. Pac. (R. R.).
Plumsteadville, Bucks Co., Pa., 750.
Plumville, Indiana Co., Pa., 518.
On Balt. & Ohio (R. R.).
Plymouth, Devonshire, England, 208,166.
Situated at the head of Plymouth Sound, between the rivers Plym and Tamar. Between it and the Sound is the Hoe, an open space, surmounting a cliff on which is the citadel, a bastioned fortress, containing a governor's residence and extensive barracks. The port is chiefly important as a naval station.
–Litchfield Co., Conn., 500.
–Hancock Co., Ill., 745.
On Chi., Burl. & Quincy (R. R.).
–c. s., Marshall Co., Ind., 5,290.
On N. York, Chi. & St. Lou.; Penna. (R. Rs.).
–c. s., Plymouth Co., Mass., 13,183.
On N. York, N. Hav. & Hart. (R. R.).
Port of entry; oldest town in New England; site of landing of the "Mayflower," 1620.
–Wayne Co., Mich., 4,484.
On Pere Marq. (R. R.).
–Grafton Co., N. H., 1,800.
On Bost. & Me. (R. R.).
–c. s., Washington Co., N. C., 2,139.
On Atl. Coast Line; Norf. Sou. (R.Rs.).
–Huron and Richland Cos., Ohio, 1,339.
On Balt. & Ohio; Nor. Ohio (R. Rs.).
–Luzerne Co., Pa., 16,543.
On Del., Lack. & West.; Del. & Hud. (R. Rs.).
–Sheboygan Co., Wis., 3,882.
On Chi. & Nor. West.; Chi., Mil., St. P. & Pac.; Wis. Pwr. & Light (El.) (R. Rs.).
Plympton, Plymouth Co., Mass., 558.
Plzen (Pilsen), Czechoslovakia, 114,150.
Famous for its beer. In a farming region.
Pnom Penh, capital of Cambodia, French Indo-China, 103,000.
Pocahontas, c. s., Randolph Co., Ark., 1,896.
On St. Lou.-San Fran. (R. R.).
–Bond Co., Ill., 976.
On Penna. (R. R.).
–c. s., Pocahontas Co., Iowa, 1,308.
On Chi., Rk. Isl. & Pac. (R. R.).
–Tazewell Co., Va., 2,293.
On Norf. & West. (R. R.).
Pocantico Hills, Westchester Co., N. Y., 500.
Pocatello, c. s., Bannock Co., Idaho, 16,471.
On Un. Pac. (R. R.).
Situated in a fertile irrigation region. Chief industries are dairying and railroad car repairs.
Pocomoke (Pocomoke City P. O.), Worcester Co., Md., 2,609.
On Penna. (R. R.).
Podgorica, Montenegro, Yugoslavia, 10,651.
Sawmills and tobacco factories.
Point Breeze, Tarrant Co., Tex., 750.
Point de Galle (or Punta Gallo), Ceylon. See Galle.
Pointe à la Hache, c. s., Plaquemines Parish, La., 515.
Pointe à Pitre, Island of Guadeloupe, West Indies, 30,465.
Chief seaport and commercial town.

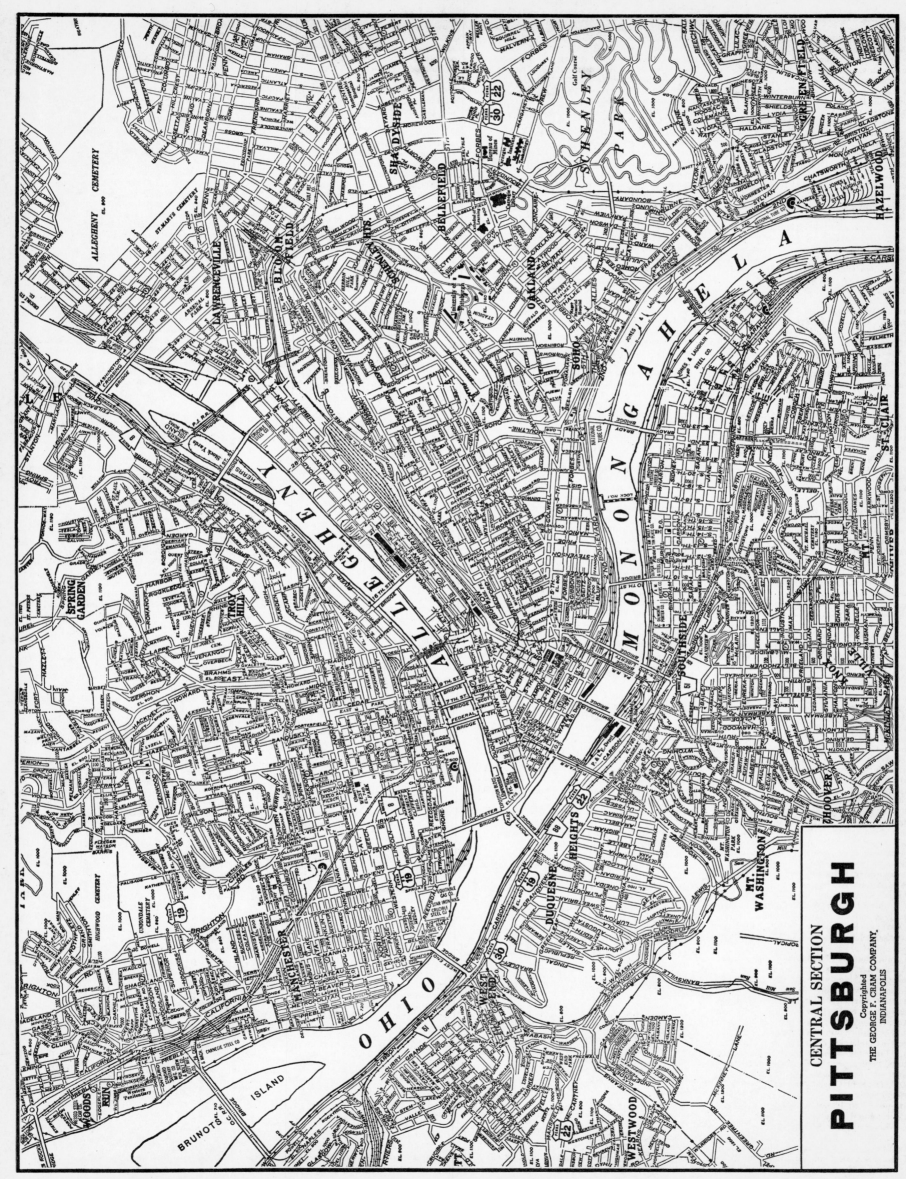

CENTRAL SECTION
PITTSBURGH

Copyrighted
THE GEORGE F. CRAM COMPANY,
Indianapolis

MAP OF CENTRAL PITTSBURGH, THE SECOND LARGEST CITY AND PORT OF ENTRY OF PENNSYLVANIA. THE CITY IS SITUATED AT THE UNION OF THE OHIO, ALLEGHENY AND MONONGAHELA RIVERS. AMONG THE HIGHER EDUCATIONAL INSTITUTIONS LOCATED HERE ARE CARNEGIE INSTITUTE OF TECHNOLOGY, THE UNIVERSITY OF PITTSBURGH AND DUQUESNE UNIVERSITY

Point Isabel, Cameron Co., Tex. See Port Isabel.
Point Marion, Fayette Co., Pa., 2,039.
On Balt. & Ohio (R. R.).
Point of Rocks, Frederick Co., Md., 500.
On Balt. & Ohio (R. R.).
Point Pleasant, Ocean Co., N. J., 2,058.
On Cen. of N. Jer.; N. York & Long Br.; Penna. (R. Rs.).
–c. s., Mason Co., W. Va., 3,301.
On Balt. & Ohio; N. York Cen. (R. Rs.).
Point Pleasant Beach, Ocean Co., N. J., 1,844.
Poissy, Dept. of Seine-et-Oise, France, 12,502.
A suburb of Paris.
Poitiers, capital of Dept. of Vienne, France, 44,235.
A commercial and industrial town.
Pojuaque, Santa Fe Co., N. Mex., 539.
Pola, Pola Prov., Italy, 36,047.
A seaport and marketing center.
Poland, Androscoggin Co., Maine, 1,503.
On Me. Cen. (R. R.).
–Mahoning Co., Ohio, 968.
Polangui, Prov. of Albay, Luzon, P. I., 13,330.
Polk, Venango Co., Pa., 3,337.
On N. York Cen. (R. R.).
–Polk Co., Neb., 532.
On Un. Pac. (R. R.).
Polkton, Anson Co., N. C., 534.
On Seab. Air Line (R. R.).
Pollock, Campbell Co., S. Dak., 520.
On Mpls., St. P. & Sault Ste. Marie (R. R.).
Polo, Prov. of Bulacan, Luzon, P. I., 9,330.
–Ogle Co., Ill., 1,871.
On Chi., Burl. & Quincy; Ill. Cen. (R. Rs.).
–Caldwell Co., Mo., 584.
On Chi., Mil., St. P. & Pac.; Chi., Rk. Isl. & Pac. (R. Rs.).
Polson, c. s., Lake Co., Mont., 1,455.
On Nor. Pac. (R. R.).
Poltava, Ukraine, Soviet Union, 98,600.
Pomeroy, Calhoun Co., Iowa, 826.
On Ill. Cen. (R. R.).
–c. s., Meigs Co., Ohio, 3,563.
On Chesa. & Ohio; N. York Cen. (R. Rs.).
–Chester Co., Pa., 600.
On Penna. (R. R.).
–c. s., Garfield Co., Wash., 1,600.
On Un. Pac. (R. R.).
Pomfret, Windham Co., Conn., 1,500.
On N. York, N. Hav. & Hart. (R. R.).
Pomona, Los Angeles Co., Cal., 20,804.
On Un. Pac.; Sou. Pac.; Pac. Elec.; Atch., Top. & Santa Fe (R. Rs.).
In fruit section. Seat of Pomona College.
–Franklin Co., Kans., 515.
On Atch., Top. & Santa Fe; Mo. Pac. (R. Rs.).
–Guilford Co., N. C., 1,500.
On Sou. (R. R.).
Pomonkey, Charles Co., Md., 600.
Pompano, Broward Co., Fla., 2,309.
On Fla. East Coast; Seab. Air Line (R. Rs.).
Pompton Lakes, Passaic Co., N. J., 3,104.
On N. York, Susq. & West. (R. R.).
Pompton Plains, Morris Co., N. J., 1,200.
On Erie (R. R.).
Ponca, c. s., Dixon Co., Neb., 920.
Ponca City, Kay Co., Okla., 16,136.
On Atch., Top. & Santa Fe; Chi., Rk. Isl. & Pac. (R. Rs.).
Center of production and pipe line connection of oil fields, with refineries and gasoline plants.
Ponce, Mun. of Ponce, Puerto Rico, 60,867.
Ponchatoula, Tangipahoa Parish, La., 2,898.
On Ill. Cen. (R. R.).
Pond Creek, Grant Co., Okla., 857.
On Chi., Rk. Isl. & Pac. (R. R.).
Pondichery, French settlement in India, 46,667.
Trade center of an agricultural region.
Ponta Delgada, Azores Islands, 18,022.
A seaport and the colony's chief trade center.
Pontefract, Yorkshire, England, 19,053.
Has foundries, tanneries, breweries, brickyards, and terra-cotta works.
Pontiac, c. s., Livingston Co., Ill., 8,272.
On Alton; Ill. Cen.; Wab. (R. Rs.).
–c. s., Oakland Co., Mich., 64,928.
On Gr. Tr. (R. R.).
Manufactures automobiles, trucks and accessories.
Pontianak, Borneo, Netherland India, 45,440.
Has an active export trade.
Pontotoc, c. s., Pontotoc Co., Miss., 2,018.
On Gulf, Mob. & Nor. (R. R.).
Pontypridd, Glamorganshire, Wales, 42,737.
Located in a coal region and has some manufactures.
Poole, Dorsetshire, England, 57,258.
A seaport and trade center.
Poona, Dist. of Poona, Bombay, India, 198,078.
Cotton, paper, rice, and sugar mills. Several educational institutions.
Popayan, Dept. of Cauca, Colombia, 31,832.
A trade center.
Poperinghe, West Flanders, Belgium, 11,554.
An agricultural center.
Poplar, Roosevelt Co., Mont., 1,046.
On Gt. Nor. (R. R.).
Poplar Bluff, c. s., Butler Co., Mo., 7,551.
On Mo. Pac.; St. Lou.-San Fran. (R. Rs.).
Poplarville, c. s., Pearl River Co., Miss., 1,498.
On N. Orl. & Northe. (R. R.).
Pori (Björneborg), Finland, 18,395.
A lumber shipping port.
Poros, Island of Poros, Argolis, Greece, 4,593.
Port Adelaide, So. Australia, Australia, 29,850.
Portage, Aroostook Co., Me., 516.
On Bang. & Aroostook (R. R.).
–Cambria Co., Pa., 4,432.
On Penna. (R. R.).
–c. s., Columbia Co., Wis., 6,308.
On Chi., Mil., St. P. & Pac.; Mpls., St. P. & S. Ste. M. (R. Rs.).
Portage la Prairie, Portage La Prairie Co., Manitoba, Canada, 6,538.
On Can. Nat.; Can. Pac. (R. Rs.).
Portageville, New Madrid Co., Mo., 1,262.
On St. Lou.-San Fran. (R. R.).
Portal, Burke Co., N. Dak., 512.
On Mpls., St. P. & S. Ste. M. (R. R.).
Port Alberni, B. C., Canada, 2,356.
On Esquimalt & Nanaimo (R. R.).
Portalegre, Capital of Dist. of Portalegre, Prov. of Alentejo, Portugal, 11,005.
Interesting Roman and prehistoric remains near by.
Portales, Roosevelt Co., N. Mex., 2,519.
On Atch., Top. & Santa Fe (R. R.).
Port Alfred, Quebec, Canada, 2,342.
On Roberval Saguenay (R. R.).
Port Allegany, McKean Co., Pa., 2,193.
On Coudersp. & Pt. Alleg.; Penna. (R. Rs.).
Port Allen, c. s., West Baton Rouge Parish, La., 1,524.
On Tex. & Pac. (R. R.).
Port Angeles, c. s., Clallam Co., Wash., 10,188.
On Chi., Mil., St. P. & Pac. (R. R.).
A lumber and fish port.
Port Arthur, Kwangtung. See Riojun.
–Thunder Bay Co., Ont., Can., 19,818.
On Can. Nat.; Can. Pac. (R. Rs.).
–Jefferson Co., Texas, 50,902.
On Kan. Cy. Sou.; Sou. Pac. (R. Rs.).
Growing seaport on Gulf of Mexico, with shipbuilding plants; also has large oil refineries.
Port au Prince, capital of Republic of Haiti, estimated 120,000.
Principal seaport and trade center.
Port Austin, Huron Co., Mich., 503.
On Pere Marq. (R. R.).
Port Barre, St. Landry Parish, La., 674.
On Mo. Pac.; Sou. Pac.; Tex. & Pac. (R. Rs.).
Port Byron, Rock Island Co., Ill., 587.
On Chi., Mil., St. P. & Pac. (R. R.).
–Cayuga Co., N. Y., 890.
On N. York Cen.; West Shore (R. Rs.).
Port Carbon, Schuylkill Co., Pa., 3,225.
On Reading (R. R.).
Port Chester, Westchester Co., N. Y., 22,662.
On N. York, N. Hav. & Hart. (R. R.).
Manufactures heating apparatus, electrical products, machinery, bolts and nuts, wire, stoves, clothing, etc.
Port Chicago (Bay Point), Contra Costa Co., Cal., 1,032.
On Atch., Top. & Santa Fe; Bay Pt. & Clay.; Sacramento Nor. (El.); Sou. Pac. (R. Rs.).
Port Clinton, c. s., Ottawa Co., Ohio, 4,408.
Located on Lake Erie, and on the N. York Cen.; Ohio Pub. Serv. (El.) (R. Rs.).
Port Colborne, Welland Co., Ontario, Canada, 6,503.
On Can. Nat.; Niag., St. Cath. & Tor. (El.); Tor., Ham. & Buf. (R. Rs.).
Port Dalhousie, Lincoln and Niagara Cos., Ontario, Canada, 1,547.
On Can. Nat.; Niag., St. Cath. & Tor. (El.) (R. Rs.).
Port de Paix (or Port-a-Paix), Haiti, 8,000.
Port Deposit, Cecil Co., Md., 963.
On Penna. (R. R.).
Port Dickinson, Broome Co., N. Y., 1,902.
On Susquehanna River.
Port Dover, Norfolk Co., South, Ontario, Canada, 1,707.
On Can. Nat.; L. Erie & Nor. (El.) (R. Rs.).
Port Edwards, Wood Co., Wis., 988.
On Chi., Mil., St. P. & Pac.; Chi. & Nor. West.; Mpls., St. P. & S. Ste. M. (R. Rs.).
Port Elgin, Bruce Co., West, Ontario, Canada, 1,305.
On Can. Nat. (R. R.).
Port Elizabeth, Cape of Good Hope, Un. of S. Africa, 118,000.
An important seaport and commercial center. Principal export is wool.
Porter, Porter Co., Ind., 805.
On Elg., Jol. & East. (El.); Mich. Cen.; N. York Cen.; Pere Marq. (R. Rs.).
–Oxford Co., Maine, 883.
–Wagoner Co., Okla., 525.
On Mo.-Kan.-Tex. (R. R.).
Porterdale, Newton Co., Ga., 3,002.
On Cen. of Ga. (R. R.).
Porterfield (Center Belpre), Washington Co., Ohio, 500.
On Balt. & Ohio (R. R.).
Porterville, Tulare Co., Cal., 5,303.
On Atch. Top. & Santa Fe; Sou. Pac. (R. Rs.).
Port Ewen, Ulster Co., N. Y., 1,100.
On West Shore (R. R.).
Port Fulton, Clark Co., Ind., 1,100.
Port Gamble, Kitsap Co., Wash., 500.
Port Gibson, c. s., Claiborne Co., Miss., 1,861.
On Ill. Cen. (R. R.).
Port Glasgow, Renfrew Co., Scotland, 19,616.
Shipbuilding, engineering works, and sawmills.
Port Henry, Essex Co., N. Y., 2,040.
On Del. & Hud.; L. Champ. & Moriah (R. Rs.).
Port Hope, Durham Co., East, Ontario, Canada, 4,723.
On Can. Nat.; Can. Pac. (R. Rs.).
Port Huron, c. s., St. Clair Co., Mich., 31,361.
Is situated at foot of Lake Huron and at head of St. Clair River, 57 miles northeast of Detroit, on Grand Trunk; Pere Marquette; Port Huron & Detroit railroads. Has drydocks and shipyards. Ferry lines and a tunnel connect the city with Sarnia on Canadian side.
Manufactures are food, beverages, paper, printing, chemicals, oils, ship and dock building, stone and clay products, textiles, water, light and power, woodwork products.
Port Isabell (Point Isabel), Cameron Co., Tex., 1,177.
On Port Isab. & Rio Gde. Val. (R. R.).
Portishead, Somersetshire, England, 3,908.
Port Jefferson, Suffolk Co., N. Y., 2,679.
Has station on Long Isl. (R. R.).
Port Jervis, Orange Co., N. Y., 10,243.
On Erie; N. York, Ont. & West. (R. Rs.).
The Erie has extensive railroad shops here.
Manufactures: Glass, silver, underwear, silk.
Port Lairge, Ireland (Eire). See Waterford.
Portland, Ashley Co., Ark., 543.
On Mo. Pac. (R. R.).
–Middlesex Co., Conn., 2,500.
On N. York, N. Hav. & Hart. (R. R.).
–La Salle Co., Ill. See Oglesby.
–c. s., Jay Co., Ind., 5,276.
On Penna.; N. York, Chi. & St. Lou. (R. Rs.).
–c. s., Cumberland Co., Maine, 70,810.
Port of entry, situated on Casco Bay, and on Boston & Maine; Grand Trunk; Maine Central, and Portland Terminal railroads.
It has direct steamship connections with many coast cities of the United States and Canada.
The principal buildings are a custom-house, United States Marine Hospital, the Maine General Hospital, headquarters of the Maine Historical Society, and the Portland Society of Natural History.
A shipping point for fruit, wheat, garden produce, live-stock, lumber, cooperage, etc. Among a variety of industries are canned goods, shoes, chemicals, and wood work. Noted for its fisheries.
Portland was first settled by the English in 1630.
–Ionia Co., Mich., 1,902.
On Pere Marq. (R. R.).
–Traill Co., N. Dak., 500.
On Gt. Nor. (R. R.).
–c. s., Multnomah Co., Ore., 301,815.
Port of entry, on Willamette River, 12 miles from its union with Columbia River, and on the Great Northern; Northern Pacific; Portland Electric; Southern Pacific; Spokane, Portland & Seattle and Union Pacific railroads.
The city of Portland has direct steamship connection not only with San Francisco and other points on the coast, Puget Sound and Columbia River, but more than 60 lines connect it with ports throughout the world. There is a fine municipal airport. Modern docks along its 30-mile waterfront on the Willamette accommodate the largest sea-going vessels.
Lumber is the chief industry. The City also does an immense trade as a meat packing and fish center, and is the second largest wheat shipping port, with great flour mills, as well as one of the largest wool centers of the country.
The manufacture of lumber, furniture, paper, ready-cut houses, machinery, auto bodies, woolen goods, and ships and boats are prominent among the large industries. The inhabitants cultivate rose gardens and hedges and a rose festival is held annually.
It is the seat of Reed College, Northwestern College of Law, and Portland University.
Portland was settled in 1845 and received its city charter in 1851.
–Northampton Co., Pa., 551.
On Del., Lack. & West.; Leh. & N. Eng.; Penna. (R. Rs.).
–Sumner Co., Tenn., 1,030.
On Lou. & Nash. (R. R.).
Port Lavaca, c. s., Calhoun Co., Texas, 1,367.
On Tex. & N. Orl. (R. R.).
Port Leyden, Lewis Co., N. Y., 717.
On N. York Cen. (R. R.).
Port Louis, capital of the island of Mauritius, Indian Ocean, 54,459.
A seaport and the chief commercial center.
Port Matilda, Centre Co., Pa., 508.
On Penna. (R. R.).
Port Monmouth, Monmouth Co., N. J., 1,500.
On Cen. of N. Jer. (R. R.).
Port Morris, Morris Co., N. J., 565.
On Del., Lack. & West.; Leh. & Hud. Riv. (R. Rs.).
Port Neches, Jefferson Co., Texas, 2,327.
On Kan. Cy. Sou. (R. R.).
Port Norris, Cumberland Co., N. J., 2,000.
On Cen. of N. Jer. (R. R.).
Porto (Oporto), capital of Dist. of Porto, Portugal, 232,280.
Important city and seaport, situated on the right bank of the Douro River. The manufactures are textiles, rope, leather, pottery, wine and tobacco. Porto occupies the site of the ancient Portus Cole, from which the name Portugal is derived.
Porto Alegre, capital of Rio Grande do Sul, Brazil, 327,628.
Commercial port and industrial center with manufactures of ships, textiles, shoes, stoves, carriages, and dairy products.
Port of Spain, capital of island of Trinidad, 73,623.
A busy seaport and the leading trade center of the island.
Porto Novo, Dahomey, French W. Africa, 27,000.
A seaport with considerable export trade in palm oil, kola nuts, timber, and other raw materials.
Port Orange, Volusia Co., Fla., 754.
On Fla. East Coast (R. R.).
Port Orchard, c. s., Kitsap Co., Wash., 1,145.
Port Perry, Ontario, Canada, 1,163.
On Can. Nat. (R. R.).
–Allegheny Co., Pa., 1,031.
On McKeesp. Connect. (R. R.).
Port Pirie, So. Australia, Australia, 11,677.
Port Republic, Rockingham Co., Va., 500.
On Norf. & West. (R. R.).
Port Royal, Juniata Co., Pa., 579.
On Penna. (R. R.).
Port Said, Egypt, 121,200.
In the governorship of Suez Canal; coaling station; the main harbor has a depth of 26 feet and area of 570 acres, protected by piers of concrete laid in the sea; the inner harbor consists of the "commercial" harbor, the "arsenal" harbor, and the Basin Cherif, the last with a military depot and barracks.
Port St. Joe, Gulf Co., Fla., 798.
On Apalach. Nor. (R. R)
Portsmouth, Southampton, England, 249,288.
Chief naval station. It consists of four districts, Portsmouth proper, Portsea, Landport, and Southsea. Portsmouth proper is a garrison town. Portsea is the seat of the naval dockyard, Landport is an artisan quarter, and Southsea is a favorite seaside resort. Southsea Castle with its adjacent earthworks, the batteries of the Gosport side, and the circular forts built out in the roadstead, command the entrance to Portsmouth Harbor. The Royal dockyard is considered one of the largest establishments of its kind in the world.
–c. s., Rockingham Co., N. H., 14,495.
Port of entry, situated on the Piscataqua River, and the Boston & Maine Railroad.
First settled in 1623; incorporated in 1653; a city in 1849. Due to President Theodore Roosevelt, the treaty of peace between Russia and Japan was signed here in 1905. The U. S. Navy Yard is located near by. The chief industries are buttons, shoes, agricultural byproducts, gypsum board, shipbuilding, and coal transportation. The city has a deep and commodious harbor.
–c. s., Scioto Co., Ohio, 42,560.
On Balt. & Ohio; Chesa. & Ohio; Norf. & West. (R. Rs.).
In corn belt, near large sandstone quarries. Railroad shops, steel, ceramics, shoes.
–Kingston Co., Ont., Can., 2,741.
–Newport Co., R. I., 3,603.
On N. York, N. Hav. & Hart. (R. R.).
–(Ind. City), c. s., Norfolk Co., Va., 45,704.
On Chesa. & Ohio; Atl. Coast Line; Norf. & West.; Norf. & Ports. Belt; Penna.; Seab. Air Line; Sou. & Virginian (R. Rs.).
Port of entry.
Port Sudan, Anglo-Egyptian Sudan, 19,135.
A seaport and chief exporting center for raw materials and native products.
Port Tampa, Hillsborough Co., Fla., 1,090.
On Atl. Coast Line (R. R.).
Port Townsend, c. s., Jefferson Co., Wash., 3,979.
On Port Towns. Sou. (R. R.).
Portville, Cattaraugus Co., N. Y., 969.
On Penna.; Pitts., Shawmut & Nor. (R. Rs.).
Port Vue, Allegheny Co., Pa., 3,510.
On Pitts. & L. Erie (R. R.).
Port Washington, Nassau Co., N. Y., 3,000.
On Long Isl. (R. R.).
–Tuscarawas Co., Ohio, 499.
On Penna. (R. R.).
–c. s., Ozaukee Co., Wis., 3,693.
On Chi. & Nor. West.; Mil. El. (R. Rs.).
Posen, Poland. See Poznan.
–Cook Co., Ill., 1,329.

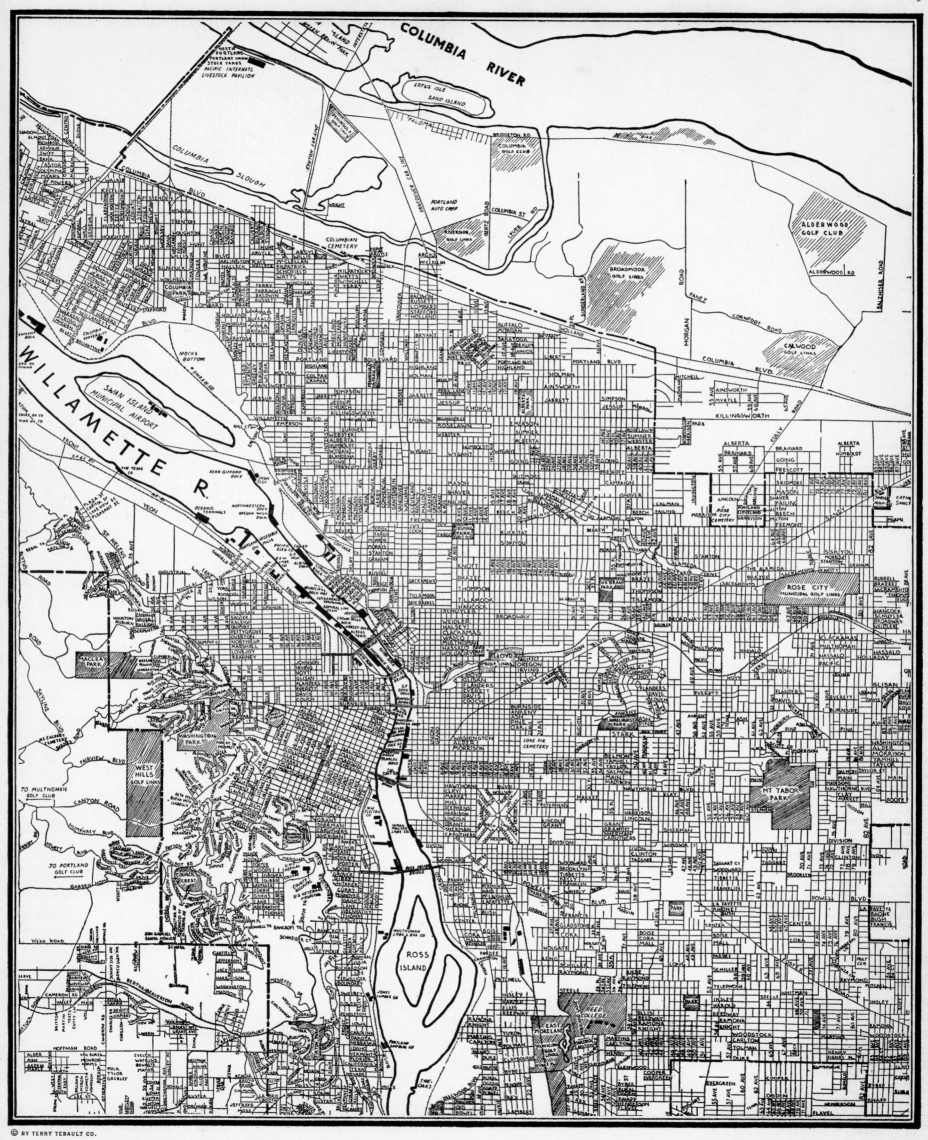

MAP OF PORTLAND, ORE. THE CITY IS SITUATED ON THE WILLAMETTE RIVER NEAR ITS JUNCTION WITH THE COLUMBIA. PORTLAND IS LAID OUT IN TERRACES FROM BOTH SIDES OF THE WILLAMETTE. THE UNIVERSITY OF OREGON MEDICAL SCHOOL IS LOCATED HERE

On Ind. Har. Belt Line (R. R.).
Poseyville, Posey Co., Ind., 810.
On Chi. & East Ill.; Ill. Cen. (R. Rs.).
Possneck, Thüringen, Germany, 14,625.
Manufactures woolens, leather, and porcelain.
Post, c. s., Garza Co., Texas, 1,668.
On Panh. & Santa Fe (R. R.).
Post Falls, Kootenai Co., Idaho, 509.
On Chi., Mil., St. P. & Pac.; Nor. Pac.; Spok., Coe. D'Ale. & Pal. (Gt. Nor.) (R. Rs.).
Postville, Allamakee Co., Iowa, 1,060.
On Chi., Mil., St. P. & Pac.; Chi., Rk. Isl. & Pac. (R. Rs.).
Potchefstroom, Transvaal, Un. of So. Africa, 19,099.
Poteau, c. s., Le Flore Co., Okla., 3,169.
On Kan. Cy. Sou.; St. Lou.-San Fran. (R. Rs.).
Poteet, Atascosa Co., Texas, 1,231.
On Mo. Pac. (R. R.).
Potenza, capital of Potenza, Italy, 13,895.
Potomac (Marysville), Vermilion Co., Ill., 643.
On Ill. Cen. (R. R.).
Potosi, capital of Dept. of Potosi, Bolivia, 36,429.
The center of a rich silver mining region.
–c. s., Washington Co., Mo., 1,279.
On Mo. Pac. (R. R.).
–Grant Co., Wis., 447.
On Chi., Burl. & Quincy (R. R.).
Pototan, Panay, P. I., 28,000.
The center of a fertile farming region. Has sugar mills and native manufactures.
Potsdam, capital of Prov. of Brandenburg, Prussia, Germany, 70,000.
Situated at the confluence of the Nuthe and the Havel. Seat of a seminary, a school for military cadets and a geographical school.
–St. Lawrence Co., N. Y., 4,136.
On N. York Cen. (R. R.).
Potter, Cheyenne Co., Nebr., 515.
On Un. Pac. (R. R.).
Potter Valley, Mendocino Co., Cal., 512.
Pottstown, Montgomery Co., Pa., 19,430.
On Penna.; Read. (R. Rs.).
Has large iron and steel plants.
Pottsville, c. s., Schuylkill Co., Pa., 24,300.
On Leh. Val.; Penna.; Read. (R. Rs.).
In anthracite coal region. Has foundries among other industries, and railroad shops.
Poughkeepsie, c. s., Dutchess Co., N. Y., 40,288.
Situated on the east bank of the Hudson River, and on the New York, New Haven & Hartford and the New York Central railroads. It has daily steamboat connections with New York and Albany. The Hudson is here crossed by a celebrated bridge which cost nearly $5,000,000. In a fruit growing section. The city has numerous manufactures, including machinery, clothing, tools, chemicals, buttons, and furniture. The seat of Vassar College.
Poulan, Worth Co., Ga., 611.
On Atl. Coast Line (R. R.).
Poulsbo, Kitsap Co., Wash., 584.
Poultney, Rutland Co., Vt., 1,570.
On Del. & Hud. (R. R.).
Powell, Park Co., Wyo., 1,156.
On Chi., Burl. & Quincy (R. R.).
–Navarro Co., Tex., 521.
On St. Lou. Southw. (R. R.).
Powellton, Fayette Co., W. Va., 800.
On Chesa. & Ohio (R. R.).
Power, Brooke Co., W. Va., 1,532.
Powhatan, Natchitoches Par., La., 500.
On Tex. & Pac. (R. R.).
–(Powhatan Point P. O.), Belmont Co., Ohio, 2,329.
On Penna. (R. R.).
Pownal, Bennington Co., Vt., 1,425.
On Bost. & Me. (R. R.).
Poynette, Columbia Co., Wis., 672.
On Chi., Mil., St. P. & Pac. (R. R.).
Pozarevac, Serbia, Yugoslavia, 14,055.
An agricultural center.
Poznan (Posen), capital of Prov. of Posnania, Poland, 269,000.
Situated 90 miles north of Breslau, on the Varta River. Is one of the oldest cities of Poland, was a member of the Hanseatic League, and reached great prosperity in the sixteenth century. In former Prussian Poland, ceded to Poland after the World War.
Pozorrubio, Luzon, P. I., 15,368.
Prague, Czechoslovakia. See Praha.
–Lincoln Co., Okla., 1,299.
On Ft. Smith & West. (R. R.).
Praha (Prague), formerly capital of Bohemia, now capital of Czechoslovakia, 945,000.
Situated on the slope of the hills which skirt both sides of the Vltava. The royal Burg, on the Hradcany (240 feet), the ancient residence of the Dukes of Bohemia, dates from the sixteenth and seventeenth centuries. The neighboring cathedral of St. Vitus (1344) is still unfinished. Here are the mausoleum (1589) and the shrine of St. John of Nepomuk.
The university, founded in 1348, possesses a library of over 500,000 volumes, a fine observatory, museums of zoology and anatomy. Praha is the great center of the commerce of Czechoslovakia, and has an important transit trade.
Praha was founded about 1100. On Nov. 14, 1918, the Assembly met in Praha and declared the existence of the Czechoslovak Republic.
Prairie City, McDonough Co., Ill., 531.
On Chi., Burl. & Quincy (R. R.).
–Jasper Co., Iowa, 793.
On Chi., Rk. Isl. & Pac. (R. R.).
Prairie du Chien, c. s., Crawford Co., Wis., 3,943.
On Chi., Burl. & Quincy; Chi., Mil., St. P. & Pac. (R. Rs.).
Manufactures woolen goods, cement and building material.
Prairie du Rocher, Randolph Co., Ill., 510.
On Mo. Pac. (R. R.).
Prairie du Sac, Sauk Co., Wis., 949.
On Chi., Mil., St. P. & Pac. (R. R.).
Prairie Grove, Washington Co., Ark., 743.
On St. Lou.-San Fran. (R. R.).
Prato, Prov. of Firenze, Tuscany, Italy, 19,926.
Manufactures of woolens and straw plaitings.
Pratt, c. s., Pratt Co., Kans., 6,162.
On Atch., Top. & Santa Fe; Chi., Rk. Isl. & Pac.; Wich. Northw. (R. Rs.).
Prattsburgh (Prattsburgh P. O.), Steuben Co., N. Y., 584.
On Prattsburgh (R. R.).
Prattville, c. s., Autauga Co., Ala., 2,331.
On Mob. & Ohio (R. R.).
–Greene Co., N. Y., 500.
Premont, Jim Wells Co., Tex., 1,100.
On Sou. Pac. (R. R.).
Prenter, Boone Co., W. Va., 600.
On Chesa. & Ohio (R. R.).
Prentiss, c. s., Jeff Davis Co., Miss., 655.
On Miss. Cen. (R. R.).
Prenzlau, Brandenburg, Germany, 22,000.
Machinery, castings, beer and sugar.
Prerov (Prerau), Moravia, Czechoslovakia, 22,362.
Prescott, c. s., Yavapai Co., Ariz., 5,517.
On Atch. Top. & Santa Fe (R. R.).
Mining, stock raising and farming.
–c. s., Nevada Co., Ark., 3,033.
On Presc. & Northw.; Mo. Pac. (R. Rs.).
–Grenville Co., South, Ontario, Canada, 2,984.
On Can. Pac.; Can. Nat. (R. Rs.).
–Pierce Co., Wis., 755.
On Chi., Burl. & Quincy (R. R.).
Presho, Lyman Co., S. Dak., 517.
On Chic., Mil. & St Paul (R. R.).
Presidio, Presidio Co., Texas, 1,202.
On Panh. & Santa Fe (R. R.).
Presque Isle, Aroostook Co., Maine, 4,662.
On Bangor & Aroostook; Can. Pac. (R. Rs.).
Pressburg, Czechoslovakia. See Bratislava.
Preston, Lancashire, England, 118,839.
A commercial and industrial town at the head of Ribble estuary. It has extensive docks. Cotton, textiles, iron castings, chemicals, soap, and boats.
–New London Co., Conn., 3,928.
–c. s., Franklin Co., Idaho, 3,381.
On Un. Pac.; Utah Ida. Cen. (El.) (R. Rs.).
–Jackson Co., Iowa, 596.
On Chi., Mil., St. P. & Pac. (R. R.).
–Caroline Co., Md., 315.
On Balt. & East. (R. R.).
–c. s., Fillmore Co., Minn., 1,214.
On Chi., Mil., St. P. & Pac. (R. R.).
–Allegheny Co., Pa., 2,000.
On Pitts., Allegh. & McK. Rks. (R. R.).
–Waterloo Co., So., Ontario, Can., 6,280.
On Can. Nat.; Gd. Riv. (El.) (R. Rs.).
Prestonburg, c. s., Floyd Co., Ky., 2,105.
On Chesa. & Ohio (R. R.).
Prestwich, Lancashire, England, 23,876.
Pretoria, Transvaal Province, administrative capital of the Union of South Africa, 138,000.
A beautiful, modern town, with many parks and drives. Has several educational institutions and manufactures of cement and iron.
Pribram, Bohemia, Czechoslovakia, 10,468.
Silver, lead, zinc, bismuth, and antimony mines near by.
Price, c. s., Carbon Co., Utah, 4,084.
On Den. & Rio Gde. West. (R. R.).
Pricedale (Somers R. R. name), Westmoreland Co., Pa., 1,036.
On Pitts. & L. Erie (R. R.).
Price Hill, Raleigh Co., W. Va., 500.
On Chesa. & Ohio; Kanaw., Gl. Jean & East.; Virginian (R. Rs.).
Prichard, Mobile Co., Ala., 4,580.
On Mob. & Ohio (R. R.).
Priest River, Bonner Co., Idaho, 949.
On Gt. Nor. (R. R.).
Primghar, c. s., O'Brien Co., Iowa, 962.
On Ill. Cen. (R. R.).
Primos, Delaware Co., Pa., 500.
On Penna. (R. R.).
Prince Albert, Prince Albert Co., Saskatchewan, Canada, 11,049.
On Can. Nat.; Can. Pac. (R. Rs.).
–Cape of Good Hope, Un. of S. Africa, 1,778.
Prince George, c. s., Prince George Co., Va., 35.
Princess Anne, c. s., Somerset Co., Md., 975.
On Penna. (R. R.).
Prince Rupert, British Columbia, Canada, 6,350.
Pacific terminus of the Canadian National Railway.
Princeton, c. s., Bureau Co., Ill., 4,762.
On Chi., Burl. & Quincy (R. R.).
–c. s., Gibson Co., Ind., 7,505.
On Chi. & East. Ill.; Sou. (R. Rs.).
–c. s., Caldwell Co., Ky., 4,764.
On Ill. Cen. (R. R.).
–Washington Co., Maine, 500.
–(Princeton Depot), Worcester Co., Mass., 707.
On Bost. & Me. (R. R.).
–Marquette Co., Mich., 600.
On L. Sup. & Ishpem. (R. R.).
–c. s., Mille Lacs Co., Minn., 1,636.
On Gt. Nor. (R. R.).
–c. s., Mercer Co., Mo., 1,509.
On Chi., Rk. Isl. & Pac. (R. R.).
–Mercer Co., N. J., 6,992.
On Penna.; Trent.-Princ. Trac. (R. Rs.).
Seat of Princeton University.
–Johnston Co., N. C., 509.
On Southern (R. R.).
–c. s., Mercer Co., W. Va., 6,955.
On Virginian (R. R.).
–Green Lake Co., Wis., 1,183.
On Chi. & Nor. West. (R. R.).
Princeville, Peoria Co., Ill., 994.
On Atch., Top. & Santa Fe; Chi., Rk. Isl. & Pac. (R. Rs.).
–Edgecombe Co., N. C., 614.
Prineville, c. s., Crook Co., Ore., 1,027.
On City of Prineville (R. R.).
Pringle, Luzerne Co., Pa., 2,372.
Prizren, Vardar Banat, Yukoslavia, 18,952.
A marketing town.
Proctor, Rutland Co., Vt., 2,515.
On Clare. & Pittsf.; Rut. (R. Rs.).
–(Proctorknott), St. Louis Co., Minn., 2,521.
On Dul., Missabe & Nor. (R. R.).
Proctorsville, Windsor Co., Vt., 669.
On Rutland; Clare. & Pittsf. (R. Rs.).
Proctorville, Lawrence Co., Ohio, 675.
Progreso, Hidalgo Co., Tex., 500.
On San Ben. & Rio Gde. Val. (Mo. Pac.) (R. R.).
Progress, Dauphin Co., Pa., 1,550.
Prophetstown, Whiteside Co., Ill., 1,353.
On Chi., Burl. & Quincy (R. R.).
Proskurov, Ukraine, Soviet Union, 31,990.
A trade center and river port.
Prospect, Marion Co., Ohio, 1,013.
On Chesa. & Ohio (R. R.).
Prospect Park, Passaic Co., N. J., 5,909.
–(Moores), Delaware Co., Pa., 4,623.
On Penna. (R. R.).
Prosperity, Newberry Co., S. C., 844.
On Colum., Newb. & Laur.; Sou. (R. Rs.).
Prosser, c. s., Benton Co., Wash., 1,569.
On Nor. Pac. (R. R.).
Prostejov (Prossnitz), Czechoslovakia, 33,487.
The center of a fertile agricultural region.
Protection, Comanche Co., Kans., 1,022.
On Atch., Top. & Santa Fe (R. R.).
Providence, Webster Co., Ky., 4,742.
On Ill. Cen.; Lou. & Nash. (R. Rs.).
–c. s., Providence Co., R. I., State capital, 243,006.
Situated on the Providence River, and on the N. York, N. Hav. & Hart. (R. R.).
A leading port of entry in New England, with a great coastwise commerce, also overseas traffic with Latin-America, West Indies, Cape Verde Islands and Canadian ports. It has extensive coaling and fuel oil facilities. It is noted for its cotton, woolen and jewelry industries, and has a very large shoe-lace factory. Among its products are machinery and rubber goods. Prominent buildings include the State House, Federal Building, City Hall, Union Station, State Armory and Providence County Court House. Seat of Brown University and Pembroke College. First settled in 1636 by Roger Williams. Incorporated in 1832.
–Cache Co., Utah, 1,088.
On Utah, Ida. Cen. (El.) (R. R.).
Provincetown, Barnstable Co., Mass., 4,071.
On N. York, N. Hav. & Hart. (R. R.).
Provo, c. s., Utah Co., Utah, 14,766.
On Den. & Rio Gde. West.; Salt. L. & Utah (El.); Utah; Un. Pac. (R. Rs.).
Located in a rich agricultural and horticultural district. Seat of Brigham Young University.
Prudence, Fayette Co., W. Va., 525.
On Chesa. & Ohio (R. R.).
Pryor (Pryor Creek), c. s., Mayes Co., Okla., 1,828.
On Mo.-Kan.-Tex. (R. R.).
Przemysl, Galicia, Poland, 51,379.
A trade and industrial town. Manufactures include refined naphtha, machinery, lumber, and flour. Fell to the Russians March 15, 1915; retaken by Austro-German forces June 2, the same year.
Pskov, R.S.F.S.R., Soviet Union, 52,600.
A port on the Velikaya River.
Puebla, capital of State of Puebla, Mexico, 114,793.
On Nat. of Mex.; Mexican (R. Rs.).
Fourth city of Mexico, situated on a fruitful plain, 7,120 feet above sea level. In the vicinity are Orizaba, Popocatepetl, and other lofty mountains. It was founded in 1531, and is one of the handsomest towns in the republic. On the great square stands the cathedral, a Doric building with two towers, the interior of which is sumptuously decorated.
Pueblo, c. s., Pueblo Co., Colo., 50,096.
Situated on the Arkansas River, at the junction of the Fontaine qui Bouille, and on the Colorado & Southern; the Missouri Pacific; Atchison, Topeka & Santa Fe; the Denver & Rio Grande Western; and the Colorado railroads.
In an extensive single-farm irrigation district. Colorado's chief manufacturing center. Has huge steel plants and zinc and gold and silver smelters. A natural location for raw material (coal, ore, etc.) of the Rocky Mountain region.
Puerta Plata, Dominican Rep., 11,277.
Puerto Cabello, Carabobo, Venezuela, 20,622.
A seaport and trade center. Exports include coffee, cocoa, dyewoods, hides, and copper ore.
Puerto de Santa Maria, Prov. of Cadiz, Spain, 18,839.
A seaport and industrial town.
Puerto Principe, Cuba. See Camaguey.
Puerto Real, Prov. of Cadiz, Spain, 9,198.
Pulaski, Pulaski Co., Ill., 521.
On Ill. Cen. (R. R.).
–Oswego Co., N. Y., 2,046.
On N. York Cen. (R. R.).
–c. s., Giles Co., Tenn., 3,367.
On Lou. & Nash. (R. R.).
–c. s., Pulaski Co., Va., 7,168.
On Norf. & West. (R. R.).
–Brown Co., Wis., 839.
On Chi. & Nor. West. (R. R.).
Pullman, Whitman Co., Wash., 3,322.
On Nor. Pac.; Un. Pac. (R. Rs.).
Pumphrey, Anne Arundel Co., Md., 500.
On Balt. & Annap. (El.) (R. R.).
Punaka, capital of Bhutan, 5,000.
Punta Arenas, Chile. See Magallanes.
Punta Gorda, c. s., Charlotte Co., Fla., 1,578.
On Atl. Coast Line (R. R.).
Punxsutawney, Jefferson Co., Pa., 9,266.
On Balt. & Ohio; Penna. (R. Rs.).
A center for coal, coke and farm products.
Purcell, c. s., McClain Co., Okla., 2,817.
On Atch., Top. & Santa Fe; Gulf, Colo. & Santa Fe (R. Rs.).
Purcellville, Loudoun Co., Va., 747.
On Wash. & Old Dom. (El.) (R. R.).
Puritan, Gogebic Co., Mich., 500.
Purvis, c. s., Lamar Co., Miss., 881.
On N. Orl. & Northe. (R. R.).
Putaendo, Prov. of Aconcagua, Chile, 1,948.
Puteaux, Seine, France, 43,829.
A suburb of Paris.
Putnam, c. s., Windham Co., Conn., 7,318.
On N. York, N. Hav. & Hart. (R. R.).
–Callahan Co., Tex., 601.
On Tex. & Pac. (R. R.).
Puxico, Stoddard Co., Mo., 766.
On St. Lou.-San Fran. (R. R.).
Puyallup, Pierce Co., Wash., 7,094.
On Nor. Pac.; Gt. Nor.; Un. Pac. (R. Rs.).
Pyne Breaker, Lackawanna Co., Pa., 500.
Pyote, Ward Co., Tex., 1,097.
On Tex. & Pac. (R. R.).
Pyrgos, capital of Nomarchy of Elio, Greece, 19,206.
Pyrites, St. Lawrence Co., N. Y., 500.
On N. York Cen. (R. R.).

Q

Qazvin, Iran (Persia), 60,000.
Qena, Egypt, 27,523.
Center of the grain trade. Water jars and bottles.
Quakake, Schuylkill Co., Pa., 525.
On Leh. Val.; Read. (R. Rs.).
Quaker City, Guernsey Co., Ohio, 613.
On Balt. & Ohio (R. R.).
Quakertown, Bucks Co., Pa., 4,883.
On Read. (R. R.).
Quanah, c. s., Hardeman Co., Texas, 4,464.
On Ft. Worth & Denv. Cy.; Quan., Acme & Pac.; St. Lou.-San Fran. (R. Rs.).
Quantico, Prince William Co., Va., 538.
On Rich., Fred. & Pot. (R. R.).
Quapaw, Ottawa Co., Okla., 1,340.
On Kan., Okla. & Gulf; St. Lou.-San Fran. (R. Rs.).
Quarryville, Lancaster Co., Pa., 1,028.
On Penna. (R. R.).
Quebec, capital of Prov. of Quebec, Canada, 130,588.
Located at the confluence of the St. Lawrence and St. Charles Rivers, and on the Canadian Pacific; Canadian National; Quebec Light & Power Company's Railroad; the Quebec Central Railroads. It is divided into two parts, called the Upper and Lower Towns. The former is built on the highest part of the Plateau, and is surrounded with a wall and strongly protected in other ways. The latter,

chiefly given to trade, occupies the base of Cape Diamond, the extreme point of the table-land. Sometimes called the "Gibraltar of America." Shipping is the principal industry. Seat of Laval University.

The site of Quebec, originally occupied by an Indian village named Stadacona, was discovered by Jacques Cartier in 1535, but the city was founded by Champlain in 1608. It continued to be the center of French trade and civilization, as well as of Roman Catholic missions in North America, till 1759, when it was captured by the British under General Wolfe. A monument on the "Plains of Abraham" is erected on the spot where Wolfe fell. The city was unsuccessfully attacked by Americans, December 31, 1775.

QUEBRADILLAS, Mun. of Quebradillas, Puerto Rico, 2,113.
QUECREEK, Somerset Co., Pa., 600.
QUEDLINBURG, Prussia, Germany, 27,000.
A commercial center of an agricultural district.
QUEEN CITY, Schuyler Co., Mo., 619.
On Wabash (R. R.).
QUEENSTOWN, Ireland (Eire). See COBH.
–Cape of Good Hope, Un. of S. Africa, 18,254.
In a wheat and wool producing area.
QUENEMO, Osage Co., Kans., 612.
On Atch., Top. & Santa Fe; Mo. Pac. (R. Rs.).
QUENTIN, Lebanon Co., Pa., 500.
QUERÉTARO, capital of State of Querétaro, Mexico, 31,648.
On Nat. of Mex. (R R.).
Cottons, woolens, pottery, and iron wares.
QUESTA, Taos Co., N. Mex., 900.
QUETTA, capital of Baluchistan, British India, 60,272.
An important commercial and trade center.
QUEZALTENANGO, Dept. of Quezaltenango, Guatemala, 23,449.
Has a large agricultural trade and textile manufactures.
QUIBERON, Dept. of Morbihan, on the peninsula of Quiberon, France, 3,556.
QUICHE (or Santa Cruz Quiche), Dept. of Quiche, Guatemala, 17,073.
An agricultural marketing town.
QUILLOTA, Prov. of Valparaiso, Chile, 14,859.
A center of the fruit and wine industry.
QUIMPER, capital of Dept. of Finistère, France, 18,814.
Noted for its pottery.
QUINCY, c. s., Gadsden Co., Fla., 4,064.
On Seab. Air Line (R. R.).
–c. s., Adams Co., Ill., 39,241.
Situated on the Mississippi River, and on the Chicago, Burlington & Quincy; the Quincy, Omaha & Kansas City and the Wabash railroads. Its industrial establishments include stove foundries, cereal mills, machine shops and tobacco factories.
–Norfolk Co., Mass., 76,909.
On N. York, N. Hav. & Hart. (R. R.).
Shipbuilding and granite quarrying.
–Branch Co., Mich., 1,265.
On N. York Cen. (R. R.).
–Logan Co., Ohio, 500.
On Cle., Cin., Chi. & St. Lou.; Det., Tol. & Iron. (R. Rs.).
–Franklin Co., Pa., 800.
On Penna. (R. R.).
QUINGUA, Prov. of Bulacan, Luzon, P. I., 8,224.
QUINLAN, Hunt Co., Texas, 512.
On Tex. & N. Orl. (Sou. Pac.) (R. R.).
QUINNESEC, Dickinson Co., Mich., 800.
On Chi. & Nor. West.; Chi., Mil., St. P. & Pac. (R. Rs.).
QUINNIMONT, Fayette Co., W. Va., 500.
On Chesa. & Ohio (R. R.).
QUINTER, Gove Co., Kan., 530.
On Un. Pac. (R. R.).
QUINTON, Pittsburg Co., Okla., 1,804.
On Ft. Smith & West. (R. R.).
–Salem Co., N. J., 525.
On Penna.-Read. Seash. (R. R.).
QUIRIEGO, State of Sonora, Mexico, on the Rio Mayo, 3,568.
QUIRIHUE, Prov. of Maule, Chile, 2,918.
QUITAQUE, Briscoe Co., Tex., 945.
On Ft. Worth & Denv. Cy. (R. R.).
QUITMAN, c. s., Brooks Co., Ga., 4,149.
On Atl. Coast Line; Sou. Ga. (R. Rs.).
–c. s., Clarke Co., Miss., 1,872.
On Miss. East.; Mob. & Ohio (R. Rs.).
–c. s., Wood Co., Tex., 1,027.
QUITO, capital of Prov. of Pichincha and of the Republic of Ecuador, 118,350.
Situated on the eastern slope of the western branch of the Andes and at the base of the volcanic mountain of Pichincha. Cocoa, hat-straw, and food products.
QUM, Iran (Persia), 39,200.
QUOGUE, Suffolk Co., N. Y., 758.
Has a station on Long Isl. (R. R.).

R

RAAB, Hungary. See GYÖR.
RABAT, capital of French Morocco, 83,698.

Primarily a residential town.
RACCOON (Joffre), Washington Co., Pa., 750.
On Penna. (R. R.).
RACELAND, Lafourche Par., La., 500.
On Tex. & N. Orl. (Sou. Pac.). (R. R.).
RACELAND JUNCTION (Raceland P. O.), Greenup Co., Ky., 1,088.
On Chesa. & Ohio (R. R.).
RACINE, Meigs Co., Ohio, 513.
–c. s., Racine Co., Wis., 67,542.
Situated on Lake Michigan at the mouth of the Root River, and on the Chicago, Milwaukee, St. Paul & Pacific; the Chicago &

COURTESY CANADIAN PACIFIC
QUEBEC, CANADA, SHOWING A GLIMPSE OF THE PICTURESQUE LOWER TOWN, THE HISTORIC HEIGHTS AND THE FAMOUS CHATEAU FRONTENAC

North Western; the Chicago, North Shore & Milwaukee (El.); and the Milwaukee (El.) railroads.
A manufacturing and transportation center. Settled in 1834 as Port Gilbert.
RADAUTI, Bukovina, Rumania, 16,808.
RADCLIFFE, Lancashire, England, 24,674.
A suburb of Manchester.
–Hardin Co., Iowa, 627.
On Chi. & Nor. West. (R. R.).
RADEBERG, Saxony, Germany, 16,000.
Located near Dresden.
RADFORD (Ind. City), Montgomery Co., Va., 6,227.
On Norf. & West. (R. R.).
RADHANPUR, capital of Radhanpur State, Bombay Presidency, India, 17,000.
RADNOR, Delaware Co., Pa., 1,000.
On Penna. (R. R.).
RADOM, Kielce, Poland, 78,063.
Has iron and machine works, and tanneries.
RAEFORD, c. s., Hoke Co., N. C., 1,303.
On Aberd. & Rockf.; Laurinburg & Sou. (R. Rs.).
RAGAZ, Canton of St. Gall, Switzerland, 2,159.
Noted for its mineral waters; one of the most frequented watering-places in Europe.
RAGLAND, St. Clair Co., Ala., 981.
On Seab. Air Line (R. R.).
RAGUSA, Prov. of Ragusa, Sicily, 33,072.
Stone quarries.
–Yugoslavia. See DUBROVNIK.
RAHWAY, Union Co., N. J., 16,011.
On Penna. (R. R.).
An industrial town in the New York area.
RAINELLE, Greenbrier Co., West Va., 920.
On Chesa. & Ohio; N. York Cen. (R. Rs.).
RAINIER, Columbia Co., Ore., 1,353.
On Spok., Port. & Seattle (R. R.).
–Thurston Co., Wash., 500.
On Chi., Mil., St. P. & Pac.; Gt. Nor.; Nor. Pac. (R. Rs.).
RAIPUR, India, 45,390.
A commercial and educational center.
RAJHMUNDRY, Madras Presidency, India, 63,526.
A marketing town in an agricultural region.

RALEIGH, c. s., Wake Co., N. C., State capital, 37,379.
Situated on the Sou.; Seab. Air Line; Norf. & Sou. (R. Rs.).
It has a large trade in cotton and tobacco. Industries: textile mills, foundries and brick works.
–Raleigh Co., W. Va., 500.
On Chesa. & Ohio (R. R.).
RALLS, Crosby Co., Texas, 1,365.
On Panh. & Santa Fe (R. R.).
RALPHTON, Somerset Co., Pa., 600.
On Balt. & Ohio (R. R.).
RALSTON, Pawnee Co., Okla., 725.
On Atch., Top. & Santa Fe (R. R.).
–Douglas Co., Neb., 809.
On Chi., Burl. & Quincy; Mo. Pac. (R. Rs.).
RAMEY, Clearfield Co., Pa., 803.
On Penna. (R. R.).
RAMONA, Washington Co., Okla., 617.
On Atch., Top. & Santa Fe (R. R.).
RAMPUR, capital of native State of Rampur, India, 73,156.
An agricultural and industrial center. Manufactures damask, pottery, steel, and sugar.
RAMSAY, Gogebic Co., Mich., 1,500.
On Chi. & Northw. (R. R.).
RAMSEUR, Randolph Co., N. C., 1,220.
On Atl. & Yadk. (R. R.).
RAMSEY, Fayette Co., Ill., 807.
On Ill. Cen.; N. York, Chi. & St. Lou. (R. Rs.).
–Bergen Co., N. J., 3,258.
On Erie (R. R.).
RAMSGATE, Kent, England, 33,597.
A seaport and popular resort.
RANCAGUA, capital of Prov. of Colchagua, Chile, 32,478.
Situated in a rich farming district.
RANCHES OF TAOS (Ranchos de Taos), Taos Co., N. Mex., 1,035.
RANCHUELO, Prov. of Santa Clara, Cuba, 3,789.
RANDALLSTOWN, Baltimore Co., Md., 500.
RANDERS, Denmark, 30,254.
An industrial town with manufactures of spirits, gloves, railroad cars, and machinery.
RANDLEMAN, Randolph Co., N. C., 1,863.
On High Pt., Rand., Asheb. & Sou. (R. R.).
RANDOLPH, Norfolk Co., Mass., 7,580.
On N. York, N. Hav. & Hart. (R. R.).
–Cedar Co., Neb., 1,145.
On Chi., Burl. & Quincy; Chi., St. P., Mpls. & Omaha (Chi. & Nor. West.) (R. Rs.).
–Cattaraugus Co., N. Y., 1,308.
On Erie (R. R.).
–Orange Co., Vt., 1,957.
On Cen. Ver. (R. R.).
–Columbia and Dodge Cos., Wis., 1,161.
On Chi., Mil., St. P. & Pac. (R. R.).

RANDOLPH FIELD, Bexar Co., Tex., 1,200.
On Tex. & N. Orl. (Sou. Pac.) (R. R.).
RANDOM LAKE, Sheboygan Co., Wis., 576.
On Chi., Mil., St. P. & Pac. (R. R.).
RANGELEY, Franklin Co., Maine, 866.
On Rangeley Lake, in a famous vacation region.
RANGER, Eastland Co., Texas, 6,208.
On Tex. & Pac.; Wichita Fs. & Sou. (R. Rs.).
RANGOON, Pegu Division, capital and the chief seaport of Burma, 400,415.
Situated at the junction of the Pegu, Hlaing, or Rangoon, and Pazundaung Rivers. Since its occupancy by the British in 1852, Rangoon is practically a new town, and its population has increased many times.
A large and increasing commerce is carried on with British, Indian, and Chinese ports. It also has an extensive inland trade.
RANGPUR, capital of Rangpur Dist., Bengal, India, 20,749.
The marketing center for a fertile farming area. Jute, rice, tobacco, and oil seeds.
RANKIN, Vermilion Co., Ill., 840.
On N. York, Chi. & St. Lou. (R. R.).
–Allegheny Co., Pa., 7,956.
On Balt. & Ohio; Penna.; Pitts. & L. Erie; Union; Bessemer & L. Erie (R. Rs.).
–c. s., Upton Co., Tex., 935.
On Panh. & Santa Fe (R. R.).
RANSHAW, Northumberland Co., Pa., 2,000.
R. R. name, Brady.
RANSOMVILLE, Niagara Co., N. Y., 750.
On N. York Cen. (R. R.).
RANSON, Jefferson Co., W. Va., 1,002.
RANTOUL, Champaign Co., Ill., 1,555.
On Ill. Cen. (R. R.).
RAPID CITY, c. s., Pennington Co., S. D., 11,346.
On Chi., Mil., St. P. & Pac.; Chi. & Nor. West.; Rap. Cy., Black Hs. & West. (R. Rs.).
In the Black Hills alfalfa region and contiguous to seven fertile valleys. Has extensive water power and lumber industry. Seat of State School of Mines.
RAPIDES, Rapides Par., La., 2,805.
On Tex. & Pac. (R. R.).
RAPURAPU, Prov. of Albay, Luzon, P. I., 6,709.
RARITAN, Somerset Co., N. J., 4,751.
On Cen. of N. Jer. (R. R.).
RASCHID (Rosetta), Egypt, 22,758.
Famous as being the place where the Rosetta Stone, a basal rock with inscriptions in Greek, hieroglyphs, and demotic, was found.
RASTATT, Baden, Germany, 14,003.
Chief manufactures are stoves, beer, paper, sugar, tobacco, and woodworking products.
RASTENBURG, Prussia, Germany, 16,021.
Flour, sugar, oil, and machinery.
RATHBUN, Appanoose Co., Ia., 299.
On Chi., Mil., St. P. & Pac. (R. R.).
RATHBURN (Soddy), Hamilton Co., Tenn., 2,250.
On Cin., N. Orl. & Tex. Pac. (R. R.).
RATHENOW, Prussia, Germany, 28,000.
RATHMINES, County of Dublin, Irish Free State, 40,367.
A suburb of Baile Atha Cliath (Dublin).
RATIBOR, East Silesia, Germany, 50,000.
A river port and commercial center.
RATINGEN, Prussia, Germany, 14,000.
RATISBON, Germany. See REGENSBERG.
RATLAM, Central Indian States, India, 28,000.
RATON, c. s., Colfax Co., N. Mex., 6,090.
On Atch., Top. & Santa Fe (R. R.).
Large coal deposits, also gold, silver, copper.
RAVENA, Albany Co., N. Y., 1,963.
On West Shore (R. R.).
RAVENNA, capital of Prov. of Ravenna, Italy, 23,063.
An active agricultural center. The city was founded long before the Christian era. Scene of a great battle in 1512.
–Estill Co., Ky., 1,189.
On Lou. & Nash. (R. R.).
–Buffalo Co., Neb., 1,559.
On Chi., Burl. & Quincy (R. R.).
–c. s., Portage Co., Ohio, 8,019.
On Balt. & Ohio; Erie; Penna. (R. Rs.).
RAVENSBURG, Württemberg, Germany, 18,000.
A trade center.
RAVENSCROFT, White Co., Tenn., 626.
RAVENSWOOD, Jackson Co., W. Va., 1,189.
On Balt. & Ohio (R. R.).
RAVINE (Lorberry Junction), Schuylkill Co., Pa., 550.
On Reading (R. R.).
RAWAL PINDI, Punjab, India, 75,767.
The largest military station in India. Manufactures of locomotives, castings, tents, refined oil, and beer.
RAWICZ, Poland, 11,127.
A commercial center with diversified manufactures.
RAWLINGS, Allegany Co., Md., 1,795.
On West. Md.; Balt. & Ohio (R. Rs.).
RAWLINS, c. s., Carbon Co., Wyo., 4,868.
On Un. Pac. (R. R.).
RAWTENSTALL, Lancashire, England, 28,575.
A suburb of Manchester.
RAY, Williams Co., N. Dak., 621.
On Gt. Nor. (R. R.).
–(Clune), Indiana Co., Pa., 750.

On Balt. & Ohio (R. R.).
Ray City, Berrien Co., Ga., 602.
On Ga. & Fla. (R. R.).
Raymond, Medicine Hat Co., Alberta, Canada, 1,849.
On Can. Pac. (R. R.).
–Montgomery Co., Ill., 726.
On Wabash (R. R.).
–c. s., Hinds Co., Miss., 547.
On Ill. Cen. (R. R.).
–Rockingham Co., N. H., 900.
On Bost. & Me. (R. R.).
–Pacific Co., Wash., 3,828.
On Nor. Pac.; Chi., Mil., St. P. & Pac. (R. Rs.).
Raymondville, c. s., Willacy Co., Texas, 2,050.
On Mo. Pac. (R. R.).
Rayne, Acadia Parish, La., 3,710.
On Sou. Pac.; Tex. & Pac. (R. Rs.).
Raynham, Bristol Co., Mass., 2,208.
On N. York, N. Hav. & Hart. (R. R.).
Raynham Center, Bristol Co., Mass., 1,225.
Raytown, Jackson Co., Mo., 500.
On Chi., Rk. Isl. & Pac. (R. R.).
Rayville, c. s., Richland Parish, La., 2,076.
On Mo. Pac.; Ill. Cen. (R. Rs.).
Readfield, Kennebec Co., Maine, 300.
On Me. Cen. (R. R.).
Reading, Berkshire, England, 97,153.
A railway and agricultural center. Famous for its nurseries. Manufactures of castings, farm machinery, biscuits, pottery, tin-boxes, velvet, silk, and sauces.
–Middlesex Co., Mass., 10,703.
On Bost. & Me. (R. R.).
–Hillsdale Co., Mich., 954.
On N. York Cen. (R. R.).
–Hamilton Co., Ohio, 5,723.
On Penna. (R. R.).
–c. s., Berks Co., Pa., 111,171.
On the Schuylkill River, the Pennsylvania, and the Reading railroads.
On account of its location near a rich iron and coal region, Reading has unusual industrial facilities. The chief manufactures are foundry and machine shop products, iron and steel, textiles, paint, paper, and hosiery.
Reading was settled in 1748, became a borough in 1783, and a city in 1847.
Readsboro, Bennington Co., Vt., 722.
On Hoosac Tun. & Wilm. (R. R.).
Readstown, Vernon Co., Wis., 544.
On Chi., Mil., St. P. & Pac. (R. R.).
Reagan, Falls Co., Tex., 500.
On Sou. Pac. (R. R.).
Reamstown, Lancaster Co., Pa., 700.
Rebeirão Preto, São Paulo, Brazil, 50,000.
Recife (Pernambuco), capital of Pernambuco, Brazil, 472,800.
Situated on the east coast, and of three distinct parts: Recife, on a small peninsula; San Antonio on an island; and Boa Vista, on the mainland.
Boa Vista is the fashionable residential quarter. The principal exports are sugar and cotton. Recife was founded by the Portuguese in the sixteenth century. It is now the third largest city in Brazil and the second in point of commercial importance.
Recklinghausen, Westphalia, Prussia, Germany, 87,000.
Located in a coal region. Has foundries, brick yards, and textile plants.
Rector, Clay Co., Ark., 1,617.
On St. Lou. Southw. (R. R.).
Red Ash, Tazewell Co., Va., 500.
On Norf. & West. (R. R.).
Red Bank, Monmouth Co., N. J., 11,622.
On Cen. of N. Jer.; N. York & Long Br.; Penna. (R. Rs.).
A residential suburb of New York.
Red Bay, Franklin Co., Ala., 1,297.
On Ill. Cen. (R. R.).
Red Bluff, c. s., Tehama Co., Cal., 3,517.
On Sou. Pac. (R. R.).
Redboiling Springs, Macon Co., Tenn., 800.
Red Bud, Randolph Co., Ill., 1,208.
On Mob. & Ohio (R. R.).
Red Cliff, Eagle Co., Colo., 544.
On Den. & Rio Gde. West. (R. R.).
Red Cloud, c. s., Webster Co., Neb., 1,519.
On Chi., Burl. & Quincy (R. R.).
Red Creek, Wayne Co., N. Y., 560.
On N. York Cen. (R. R.).
Red Deer, Red Deer Co., Alb., Can., 2,384.
On Can. Nat. (R. R.).
Reddell, Evangeline Co., La., 1,500.
On Chi., Rk. Isl. & Pac. (R. R.).
Redding, c. s., Shasta Co., Cal., 4,188.
On Sou. Pac. (R. R.).
–Fairfield Co., Conn., 500.
On N. York, N. Hav. & Hart. (R. R.).
Redditch, Worcestershire, England, 19,280.
Needles, fish-hooks, and engines.
Red Dragon (Blue Pennant), Boone Co., W. Va., 500.
On Chesa. & Ohio (R. R.).
Redfield, Dallas Co., Iowa, 870.
On Chi., Mil., St. P. & Pac. (R. R.).
–c. s., Spink Co., S. Dak., 2,573.
On Chi. & Nor. West.; Chi., Mil., St. P. & Pac. (R. Rs.).
Red Granite (Redgranite), Waushara Co., Wis., 977.
On Chi. & Nor. West. (R. R.).
Red Hill, Montgomery Co., Pa., 851.
On Reading (R. R.).
Red Hook, Dutchess Co., N. Y., 996.
Red Jacket, Houghton Co., Mich., 1,657.
–Mingo Co., W. Va., 1,237.
On Norf. & West. (R. R.).
Redkey, Jay Co., Ind., 1,370.
On N. York, Chi. & St. Lou.; Penna. (R. Rs.).
Red Lake Falls, c. s., Red Lake Co., Minn., 1,386.
On Gt. Nor.; Nor. Pac. (R. Rs.).
Redlands, San Bernardino Co., Cal., 14,177.
On Atch., Top. & Santa Fe; Pac. Elec.; Sou. Pac. (R. Rs.).
Chief industry: citrus and deciduous fruits. Seat of University of Redlands.
Red Lion, York Co., Pa., 4,757.
On Md. & Penna. (R. R.).
Red Lodge, c. s., Carbon Co., Mont., 3,206.
On Nor. Pac. (R. R.).
Redman Mills, Allegheny Co., Pa., 515.
Redmond, Sevier Co., Utah., 577.
On Den. & Rio Gde. West. (R. R.).
–Deschutes Co., Oregon, 994.
On Spok., Port. & Seat.; Un. Pac. (R. Rs.).
Red Oak, c. s., Montgomery Co., Iowa, 5,778.
On Chi., Burl. & Quincy (R. R.).
Redondo Beach, Los Angeles Co., Cal., 9,347.
On Atch., Top. & Santa Fe; Pac. El.; Sou. Pac. (R. Rs.).
Red River, York Co., S. C., 685.
On Sou. (R. R.).
Redruth, Cornwall, England, 9,904.
Red Springs, Robeson Co., N. C., 1,300.
On Atl. Coast Line (R. R.).
Red Star, Fayette Co., W. Va., 600.
On Chesa. & Ohio (R. R.).
Red Wing, c. s., Goodhue Co., Minn., 9,629.
On Chi. Gt. West.; Chi., Mil., St. P. & Pac. (R. Rs.).
Redwood, Jefferson Co., N. Y., 524.
On N. York Cen. (R. R.).
Redwood City, c. s., San Mateo Co., Cal., 8,962.
On Sou. Pac. (R. R.).
Redwood Falls, c. s., Redwood Co., Minn., 2,552.
On Chi. & Nor. West. (R. R.).
Reed City, c. s., Osceola Co., Mich., 1,792.
On Penna.; Pere Marq. (R. Rs.).
Reedley, Fresno Co., Cal., 2,589.
On Atch., Top. & Santa Fe; Sou Pac. (R. Rs.).
Reedsburg, Sauk Co., Wis., 2,967.
On Chi. & Nor. West. (R. R.).
Reeds Lake (E. Gd. Rapids), Kent Co., Mich., 4,024.
Reedsport, Douglas Co., Ore., 1,178.
On Sou. Pac. (R. R.).
Reedsville, Manitowoc Co., Wis., 617.
On Chi. & Nor. West. (R. R.).
–Mifflin Co., Pa., 1,700.
On Penna.; Kishacoquillas Val. (R. Rs.).
Reedville, Northumberland Co., Va., 500.
Reeves, Williamson Co., Ill. See Cambria.
Reform, Pickens Co., Ala., 898.
On Mob. & Ohio; Ala., Tenn. & Nor. (R. Rs.).
Refugio, c. s., Refugio Co., Texas, 2,019.
On Mo. Pac. (R. R.).
Regensburg (Ratisbon), Bavaria, Germany, 81,000.
Chief manufactures include pottery, flooring, musical instruments, furniture, sugar, pencils, and chemicals.
Reggio, capital of Prov. of Reggio di Calabria, Italy, 122,728.
Destroyed by an earthquake in 1908.
–Capital of Prov. of Reggio nell' Emilia, Italy, 93,606.
Locomotives, railroad cars, and cheese.
Regina, c. s., Regina Co., capital of Saskatchewan, Canada, 53,354.
On Can. Nat.; Can. Pac. (R. Rs.).
A market and distributing center for an agricultural region. The headquarters of the Royal Canadian Mounted Police.
Regla, Cuba, now part of Habana.
Rehoboth, Bristol Co., Mass., 2,777.
Rehoboth Beach, Sussex Co., Del., 795.
On Penna. (R. R.).
Reichenbach, Silesia, Prussia, Germany, 17,000.
Dyes, beer, machinery, gas buttons, and chemicals. Considerable trade in grain and cattle.
–Saxony, Germany, 32,000.
Textile mills.
Reichenberg (Liberec), Germany, 38,525.
Reidsville, Tattnall Co., Ga., 631.
On Collins & Glennv. (R. R.).
–Rockingham Co., N. C., 6,851.
On Southern (R. R.).
Reigate, Surrey, England, 30,830.
A marketing town near London.
Reims, Dept. of Marne, France, 116,687.
Situated on the Vesle River, strongly fortified with detached forts, is well built, and has a picturesque appearance. The cathedral (1212) is one of the finest specimens of Gothic architecture. The Romanesque Church of St. Remy, with the saint's shrine, is nearly of equal size. Also noteworthy are the Porta Marris, a Roman triumphal arch, and the Lycée. Reims is one of the principal entrepôts for the wines of Champagne. It is one of the great centers of the woolen manufacture in France. Both city and cathedral suffered from bombardment in the World War, restorations after the war taking some years to complete. Reims was built on the site of an ancient capital of the Remi.
Reinbeck, Grundy Co., Iowa, 1,425.
On Chi. Gt. West.; Chi., Rk. Isl. & Pac. (R. Rs.).
Reiner (Reinerton), Schuylkill Co., Pa., 550.
On Reading (R. R.).
Reinholds, Lancaster Co., Pa., 750.
On Reading (R. R.).
Reisterstown, Baltimore Co., Md., 1,635.
Relay, Baltimore Co., Md., 2,016.
On Balt. & Ohio (R. R.).
Reliance (Reliance Mine), Sweetwater Co., Wyo., 600.
On Un. Pac. (R. R.).
Remedios, Santa Clara Prov., Cuba, 8,541.
Remington, Jasper Co., Ind., 879.
On Penna. (R. R.).
Remlig, Jasper Co., Tex., 761.
Remscheid, Rhenish Prussia, Germany, 101,200.
A center of the hardware industry.
Remsen, Plymouth Co., Iowa, 1,181.
On Ill. Cen. (R. R.).
Renaix, East Flanders, Belgium, 24,085.
Textile center.
Rendsburg, Holstein, Germany, 18,000.
Commercial and marketing town. Dyes, iron, and machine manufactures.
Renfrew, Renfrew Co., S. Ont., Can., 5,296.
On Can. Pac.; Can. Nat. (R. Rs.).
–Butler Co., Pa., 518.
On Balt. & Ohio (R. R.).
–Renfrew Co., Scotland, 14,986.
An industrial suburb of Glasgow.
Rengo, Prov. of Colchagua, Chile, 6,049.
Rennes, capital of Dept. of Ille-et-Vilaine (Brittany), France, 98,538.
Situated at the confluence of the Ille and Vilaine Rivers. Several bridges connect the upper (new) town and the lower (old) town. Rennes is favorably situated for commerce, and carries on a considerable trade in its own manufactures, which include sail-cloth, table linen, etc. Rennes was the capital of the Gallic tribe of the Redones.
Reno, c. s., Washoe Co., Nev., 18,529.
On West. Pac.; Sou. Pac.; Va. & Truck. (R. Rs.).
The city is a jobbing center for Nevada and Eastern California. Seat of State University.
–Venango Co., Pa., 800.
On Erie; N. York Cen. (R. Rs.).
Renovo, Clinton Co., Pa., 3,947.
On Penna. (R. R.).
Rensselaer, c. s., Jasper Co., Ind., 2,798.
On Chi., Ind. & Lou. (R. R.).
–Rensselaer Co., N. Y., 11,223.
On Bost. & Alb.; N. York Cen. (R. Rs.).
Has railroad shops and manufactures of felt, pharmaceutical products, dyes and chemicals.
Renton, King Co., Wash., 4,062.
On Chi., Mil., St. P. & Pac. No. P.; Pac. Coast (R. Rs.).
Renville, Renville Co., Minn., 1,064.
On Chi., Mil., St. P. & Pac. (R. R.).
Republic, Greene Co., Mo., 841.
On St. Lou.-San Fran. (R. R.).
–Seneca Co., Ohio, 512.
On Balt. & Ohio (R. R.).
–Marquette Co., Mich., 1,090.
On Chi., Mil., St. P. & Pac. (R. R.).
–Fayette Co., Pa., 2,500.
On Monongahela (R. R.).
–c. s., Ferry Co., Wash., 710.
On Gt. Nor. (R. R.).
Requena, Prov. of Valencia, Spain, 18,818.
The center of an agricultural region.
Reserve, St. John the Baptist Par., La., 2,500.
On La. & Ark.; Yazoo & Miss. Val. (Ill. Cen.) (R. Rs.).
–Erie Co., N. Y., 637.
Resht, capital of Gilan, Iran (Persia), 89,900.
Center of silk and rice trade.
Retalhuleu, Guatemala, 12,500.
Retreat, Luzerne Co., Pa., 2,000.
On Penna. (R. R.).
Retsil, Kitsap Co., Wash., 700.
Reus, Prov. of Tarragona, Spain, 30,266.
Woolens, leather, wine, and liquors.
Reutlingen, Württemberg, Germany, 32,000.
Textiles, leather, and machinery.
Revel, Estonia. See Tallinn.
Revere, Suffolk Co., Mass., 35,319.
On Bost. & Me. (R. R.).
A resort on Massachusetts Bay.
Revloc, Cambria Co., Pa., 1,600.
On Camb. & Ind.; Penna. (R. Rs.).
Rexburg, c. s., Madison Co., Idaho, 3,048.
On Un. Pac. (R. R.).
Rexford, Saratoga Co., N. Y., 500.
Rexmont, Lebanon Co., Pa., 500.
Reykjavik, capital of Iceland, 34,231.
Principal seaport and commercial center, with near-by fisheries. The city has government buildings, museums, a national library and a university.
Reynolds, Taylor Co., Ga., 880.
On Cen. of Ga. (R. R.).
–Grand Forks and Traill Cos., N. D., 351.
On Gt. Nor. (R. R.).
Reynoldsburg, Franklin Co., Ohio, 562.
Reynoldsville, Jefferson Co., Pa., 3,480.
On Penna. (R. R.).
Rezaiah (Urmia), Iran, 49,800.
Rheydt, Germany. See Gladbach.
Rhinebeck, Dutchess Co., N. Y., 1,569.
Rhinecliff, Dutchess Co., N. Y., 500.
On N. York Cen. (R. R.).
Rhinelander, c. s., Oneida Co., Wis., 8,019.
On Chi. & Nor. West.; Mpls., St. P. & S. Ste. M.; Robbins (R. Rs.).
Has lumber mills.
Rhodell, Raleigh Co., W. Va., 518.
On Virginian (R. R.).
Rhodes, Rhodes. See Rodi.
Rhodhiss (Rhodhiss Junction), Burke and Caldwell Cos., N. C., 954.
On Car. & Nor. West. (R. R.).
Rhondda, Glamorganshire, Wales, 144,344.
Center of iron industries.
Rhone, Luzerne Co., Pa., 1,692.
Rialto, San Bernardino Co., Cal., 1,642.
On Atch., Top. & Santa Fe; Sou. Pac.; Un. Pac.; Pac. El. (R. Rs.).
Ribeirão Preto, São Paulo, Brazil, 68,838.
A trade center in a coffee-growing region.
Rib Lake, Taylor Co., Wis., 1,180.
On Mpls., St. P. & S. Ste. M. (R. R.).
Rice, Navarro Co., Texas, 591.
On Sou. Pac. (R. R.).
Rice Lake, Barron Co., Wis., 5,177.
On Chi, St. P., Mpls. & Omaha; Mpls., St. P. & S. Ste. M.; Chi. & Nor. West. (R. Rs.).
Rices Landing, Green Co., Pa., 977.
On Monongahela (R. R.).
Riceville, Howard and Mitchell Cos., Iowa, 807.
On Chi. Gt. West. (R. R.).
Richard City, Marion Co., Tenn., 522.
On Nash., Chatt. & St. Lou. (R. R.).
Richards, Grimes Co., Tex., 800.
On Burl.-Rk. Isl. (R. R.).
Richardson, Dallas Co., Tex., 629.
On Sou. Pac.; Tex. Elec. (R. Rs.).
Richardson Park, New Castle Co., Del., 4,200.
Richardton, Stark Co., N. D., 710.
On Nor. Pac. (R. R.).
Richburg, Allegany Co., N. Y., 580.
On Pitts., Shawmut & Nor. (R. R.).
Richeyville, Washington Co., Pa., 1,600.
Richfield, Hennepin Co., Minn., 3,344.
–c. s., Sevier Co., Utah, 3,067.
On Den. & Rio Gde. West. (R. R.).
Richfield Springs, Otsego Co., N. Y., 1,333.
On Del., Lack. & West.; Sou. N. York (El.) (R. Rs.).
–Summit Co., Ohio, 600.
Richfol, Washington Co., Pa., 2,300.
On Penna. (R. R.).
Richford, Franklin Co., Vt., 1,783.
On Can. Pac.; Cen. Ver. (R. Rs.).
Rich Hill, Bates Co., Mo., 2,118.
On Mo. Pac. (R. R.).
Richland, Stewart Co., Ga., 1,577.
On Seab. Air Line (R. R.).
–Keokuk Co., Iowa, 713.
On Chi., Mil., St. P. & Pac. (R. R.).
–Pulaski Co., Mo., 945.
On St. Lou.-San Fran. (R. R.).
–Oswego Co., N. Y., 600.
On N. York Cen. (R. R.).
–Lebanon Co., Pa., 952.
On Reading (R. R.).
–Navarre Co., Tex., 541.
On Sou. Pac. (R. R.).
Richland Center, c. s., Richland Co., Wis., 3,632.
On Chi., Mil., St. P. & Pac. (R. R.).
Richlands, Tazewell Co., Va., 1,355.
On Norf. & West. (R. R.).
–Onslow Co., N. C., 503.
Richlandtown, Bucks Co., Pa., 642.
Richmond, Surrey, England, 37,791.
A suburb of London.
–Contra Costa Co., Cal., 20,093.
On Atchison, Topeka & Santa Fe; Southern Pacific (R. Rs.).
The industrial center of San Francisco's "Eastbay District." Has a large petroleum refinery and railroad repair shops.
–McHenry Co., Ill., 514.
On Chi. & Nor. West. (R. R.).
–c. s., Wayne Co., Ind., 32,493.
On the Whitewater River, and on the Chesa. & Ohio; Penna. (R. Rs.).
Seat of Earlham College.
A commercial and distributing center.
–c. s., Madison Co., Ky., 6,495.
On Lou. & Nash. (R. R.).
–Sagadahoc Co., Maine, 600.
On Me. Cen. (R. R.).
–Berkshire Co., Mass., 628.

On Bost. & Alb. (R. R.).
–Macomb Co., Mich., 1,493.
On Gd. Tr. (R. R.).
–Stearns Co., Minn., 603.
On Gt. Nor. (R. R.).
–c. s., Ray Co., Mo., 4,129.
On Atch., Top. & Santa Fe (R. R.).
–Washington Co., R. I., 1,667.
–c. s., Fort Bend Co., Texas, 1,432.
On Gulf, Colo. & Santa Fe; Tex. & N. Orl. (Sou. Pac.) (R. Rs.).
–Cache Co., Utah, 1,140.
On Un. Pac.; Utah-Ida. Cen. (R. Rs.).
–Chittenden Co., Vt., 718.
On Cen. Ver. (R. R.).
–(Ind. City), c. s., Henrico Co., Va., state capital, 182,929.
On the James River, and on the Southern; the Richmond, Fredericksburg & Potomac; the Atlantic Coast Line; the Chesapeake & Ohio; and Seaboard Air Line Railroads.
Noted as tobacco manufacturing city with huge plants for making cigars and cigarettes. It also has extensive paper, publishing, and lithographing industries; also woodwork, cellophane, rayon, chemical, printing, locomotive and baking-powder plants.
The Capitol, which stands on Shockoe Hill, dates from 1785. In the Central Hall are a bust of Lafayette, Houdon's statue of Washington and busts of other Virginian presidents. The original Senate Chamber housed the Confederate House of Representatives in the Civil War. The original House of Delegates, restored, has sculptures of great Virginians and was the scene of Aaron Burr's trial in 1807. The executive mansion of the Confederate States, now a museum, contains many relics of the Civil War. First settled about 1609 and established as a town in 1742, Richmond became capital of the state in 1779 and was incorporated as a city in 1782. From 1861 to 1865 it was capital of the Confederate States.
–Richmond Co., Quebec, Canada, 2,596.
On Can. Nat. (R. R.).
Richmond Beach, King Co., Wash., 780.
On Gt. Nor. (R. R.).
Richmond Heights, St. Louis Co., Mo., 9,150.
Richmond Highlands, King Co., Wash., 600.
Richmondville, Schoharie Co., N. Y., 618.
On Del. & Hud. (R. R.).
Rich Square, Northampton Co., N. C., 800.
On Seab. Air Line (R. R.).
Richton, Perry Co., Miss., 950.
On Gulf, Mob. & Nor. (R. R.).
Richwood, Union Co., Ohio, 1,573.
On Erie (R. R.).
–Nicholas Co., W. Va., 5,720.
On Balt. & Ohio (R. R.).
Riddlesburg, Bedford Co., Pa., 610.
On Hunt., Broad Top Mt. (R. R.).
Riderwood, Choctaw Co., Ala., 737.
On Ala., Tenn. & Nor. (R. R.).
Ridge Farm, Vermilion Co., Ill., 888.
On Cle., Cin., Chi. & St. Lou.; N. York, Chi. & St. Lou. (R. Rs.).
Ridgefield, Fairfield Co., Conn., 2,050.
On N. York, N. Hav. & Hart. (R. R.).
Residential town near New York border.
–Bergen Co., N. J., 4,671.
On Erie (R. R.).
–Clarke Co., Wash., 607.
On Nor. Pac.; Gt. Nor.; Un. Pac. (R. Rs.).
Ridgefield Park, Bergen Co., N. J., 10,764.
On West Shore; N. York, Susq. & West. (R. Rs.).
A residential suburb of New York.
Ridgeland, c. s., Jasper Co., S. C., 715.
On Atl. Coast Line (R. R.).
Ridgeley, Mineral Co., W. Va., 1,972.
On West. Md. (R. R.).
Ridgely, Caroline Co., Md., 703.
On Penna. (R. R.).
–Lake Co., Tenn., 979.
On Ill. Cen. (R. R.).
–Mineral Co., W. Va., 1,972.
On West. Md. (R. R.).
Ridge Spring, Saluda Co., S. C., 628.
On Southern (R. R.).
Ridgetown, Kent Co., Ontario, Canada, 1,952.
On Mich. Cen.; Pere Marq. (R. Rs.).
Ridgeville, Randolph Co., Ind., 909.
On Penna. (R. R.).
–Lorain Co., Ohio, 570.
Ridgeway, Harrison Co., Mo., 676.
On Chi., Burl. & Quincy (R. R.).
Ridgewood, Bergen Co., N. J., 12,188.
On Erie (R. R.).
A residential suburb of Paterson.
–Richland Co., S. C., 600.
Ridgway, c. s., Elk Co., Pa., 6,313.
On Balt. & Ohio; Penna. (R. Rs.).
–Gallatin Co., Ill., 930.
On Balt. & Ohio (R. R.).
Ridley Park, Delaware Co., Pa., 3,356.
On Balt. & Ohio; Penna. (R. Rs.).
Ridlonville, Oxford Co., Me., 2,500.
Riegelsville, Warren Co., N. J., 510.
On Penna. (R. R.).

–Bucks Co., Pa., 725.
Rienzi, Alcorn Co., Miss., 500.
On Mob. & Ohio (R. R.).
Riesa, Saxony, Germany, 26,000.
A river port and distributing point. There are rolling-mills, sawmills, and iron works.
Riesel, McLennan Co., Tex., 567.
On Sou. Pac. (R. R.).
Rieti, Prov. of Rieti, Italy, 10,052.
The center of a fertile agricultural district.
Rifle, Garfield Co., Colo., 1,287.
On Den. & Rio Gde. West. (R. R.).
Riga, capital of Latvia, 385,063.
Situated on the Dwina River. The chief edifices are the cathedral, built in 1204; St. Peter's Church (1406), with a steeple 460 feet high; the castle of the old Knights of the Sword (1494-1515), and several old guild houses and Hanseatic halls.
Its industries include lumber, machinery, dairy products, canned goods, textiles, metal ware and glass.
Riga was founded in 1201 by Albert, Bishop of Livonia, and soon became a commercial town and member of the Hanseatic League.
Latvia resisted control by the Russian Bolshevists, who occupied Riga in January, 1919. Lettish troops took possession the following May. Latvia afterwards was recognized as an independent republic.
Rigby, Jefferson Co., Idaho, 1,531.
On Un. Pac. (R. R.).
–Lawrence Co., Pa., 1,000.
Rijswijk, Prov. of S. Holland, Netherlands, 15,929.
Treaty of Ryswick (1697) was signed here.
Rillton, Westmoreland Co., Pa., 600.
On Penna. (R. R.).
Rimersburg, Clarion Co., Pa., 1,319.
On the Penna. (R. R.).
Rimini, Prov. of Forli, Italy, 21,306.
A favorite resort and of interest historically.
Rimouski, Rimouski Co., Quebec, Can., 5,589.
On Can. Nat. (R. R.).
Rincon, Mun. of Rincon, Puerto Rico, 1,531.
Rindgemere (E. Rochester), Stafford Co., N. H., 1,303.
On Bost. & Me. (R. R.).
Ringgold, Bienville Par., La., 618.
On Sib., L. Bisten. & Sou. (R. R.).

with which it is interspersed being crowned with artillery.
Rio Grande, Rio Grande do Sul, Brazil, 47,600.
A seaport, and industrial center. Meat packing, woollens, and food products.
–Mun. of Rio Grande, Puerto Rico, 2,297.
Rio Grande (Rio Grande City), c. s., Starr Co., Texas, 2,283.
On Mo. Pac. (R. R.).
Rio Hondo, Cameron Co., Tex., 713.
On San Ben. & Rio Gde. Val. (R. R.).
Riojun (Port Arthur) (Lushun), Kwantung, 31,059.
A port at the southwestern extremity of Liaotung Peninsula, Asia. Formerly held by Russia, to whom China leased it in 1898. It was strongly fortified and became a great Russian naval station. In Russo-Japanese War was besieged by Japanese, and after a defense lasting 210 days capitulated; the entire peninsula came under Japanese rule.
Rio Negro, Dept. of Antioquia, Colombia, 15,814.
A trade and marketing center with some native industries.
Rio Piedras, Mun. of Rio Piedras, Puerto Rico, 16,849.
A residential suburb of San Juan.
Rio Vista, Solano Co., Cal., 1,309.
Ripley, c. s., Tippah Co., Miss., 1,468.
On Gulf, Mob. & Nor. (R. R.).
–Chautauqua Co., N. Y., 1,200.
On N. York Cen.; N. York, Chi. & St. Lou. (R. Rs.).
–Brown Co., Ohio, 1,556.
–c. s., Lauderdale Co., Tenn., 2,330.
On Ill. Cen. (R. R.).
–c. s., Jackson Co., W. Va., 669.
On Balt. & Ohio (R. R.).
Ripon, Fond du Lac Co., Wis., 3,984.
On Chi., Mil., St. P. & Pac.; Chi., St. P., Mpls. & Oma. (R. Rs.).
Ripon College.
Ripraps (Fox Hill), Elizabeth City Co., Va., 750.
Rising City, Butler Co., Nebr., 1,000.
On Un. Pac. (R. R.).
Rising Star, Eastland Co., Texas, 1,160.
On Mo.-Kan.-Tex. of Tex. (R. R.).
Rising Sun, c. s., Ohio Co., Ind., 1,379.
–Cecil Co., Md., 565.
On Penna. (R. R.).
–Wood Co., Ohio, 628.

COURTESY MUNSON STEAMSHIP LINES

A PANORAMA OF RIO DE JANEIRO, BRAZIL, AND ITS HARBOR, WHICH IS ONE OF THE MOST BEAUTIFUL IN THE WORLD

–Catoosa Co., Ga., 684.
On Nash., Chatt. & St. Lou. (R. R.).
Ringling, Jefferson Co., Okla., 1,002.
On Gulf, Colo. & Santa Fe (R. R.).
Ringtown, Schuylkill Co., Pa., 899.
On Reading (R. R.).
Ringwood (Ringwood Manor), Passaic Co., N. J., 1,038.
On Erie (R. R.).
Rio, Columbia Co., Wis., 641.
On Chi., Mil., St. P. & Pac. (R. R.).
Riobamba, capital of Prov. of Chimborazo, Ecuador, 21,900.
Rio Branco, Rio Grande do Sul, Brazil, 26,200.
Rio Cuarto, Cordoba, Argentina, 89,600.
Situated in a stock-raising region.
Rio de Janeiro, Federal Dist. and capital of Brazil, 1,700,500.
The largest and most important commercial city of South America and located on the Guanabara Bay. Parallel with the beach runs the main street, the Avenida Rio Branco. The imperial palace skirts the beach. The harbor is one of the finest known. The entrance is commanded by heavy batteries—all islands

On Chesa. & Ohio (R. R.).
Rison, Cleveland Co., Ark., 876.
On St. Lou. Southw. (R. R.).
Rittman, Wayne Co., Ohio, 2,785.
On Erie; Balt. & Ohio (R. Rs.).
Ritzville, c. s., Adams Co., Wash., 1,777.
On Nor. Pac. (R. R.).
Riva, Trento, Italy, 4,355.
Rivas, capital of Dept. of Rivas, Nicaragua, 9,349.
The center of a coffee and cocoa district.
Rive-de-Gier, Dept. of Loire, France, 14,483.
Has coal mines, glass and iron works, and textile manufactures.
Riverbank, Stanislaus Co., Cal., 803.
On Atch., Top. & Santa Fe (R. R.).
Riverdale, Cook Co., Ill., 2,504.
On Ill. Cen.; Penna.; Balt. & Ohio. Chi. Term. (R. Rs.).
–Prince George Co., Md., 1,533.
On Balt. & Ohio (R. R.).
–Morris Co., N. J., 1,052.
On Erie (R. R.).
River Falls, Covington Co., Ala., 556.
On Lou. & Nash. (R. R.).

–Pierce and St. Croix Cos., Wis., 2,363.
On Chi., St. P., Mpls. & Oma. (R. R.).
River Forest, Cook Co., Ill., 8,829.
On Chi. & Nor. West. (R. R.).
River Grove, Cook Co., Ill., 2,741.
On Chi., Mil., St. P. & Pac. (R. R.).
Riverhead, c. s., Suffolk Co., N. Y., 6,000.
On Long Isl. (R. R.).
River Junction, Gadsden Co., Fla., 2,563.
On Apalach. Nor.; Atl. Coast Line; Lou. & Nash.; Seab. Air Line (R. Rs.).
Rivermines, St. Francois Co., Mo., 721.
On Mo.-Ill. (R. R.).
River Park, St. Joseph Co., Ind. See South Bend.
River Rouge, Wayne Co., Mich., 17,314.
On Det. & Tol. Sh. Line; Mich. Cen.; N. York Cen. (R. Rs.).
Riverside, c. s., Riverside Co., Cal., 29,696.
On Pac. El.; Los Ang. & Salt L. (Un. Pac.); Atch., Top. & Santa Fe; Sou. Pac. (R. Rs.).
In great citrus fruit district. Has packing houses, canneries and a huge cement plant.
–Fairfield Co., Conn., 3,200.
On N. York, N. Hav. & Hart. (R. R.).
–Cook Co., Ill., 6,770.
On Chi., Burl. & Quincy (R. R.).
–Washington Co., Iowa, 638.
On Chi., Rk. Isl. & Pac. (R. R.).
–Bergen Co., N. J., 2,210.
–Burlington Co., N. J., 4,000.
On Penna. (R. R.).
–Steuben Co., N. Y., 671.
–Monongalia Co., W. Va., 940.
Riverton, Sangamon Co., Ill., 1,582.
On Wab.; Ill. Term. (El.) (R. Rs.).
–Fremont Co., Iowa, 590.
On Chi., Burl. & Quincy (R. R.).
–Burlington Co., N. J., 2,483.
On Penna. (R. R.).
–Salt Lake Co., Utah, 1,025.
On Den. & Rio Gde. West.; Salt Lk. & Utah (R. Rs.).
–Warren Co., Va., 500.
On Norf. & West.; Sou. (R. Rs.).
–Fremont Co., Wyo., 1,608.
On Chi. & Nor. West. (R. R.).
Riverview (Anson), Somerset Co., Me., 950.
On Me. Cen. (R. R.).
–Wayne Co., Mich., 743.
Rivesville, Marion Co., W. Va., 1,700.
On Balt. & Ohio; Monon. (R. Rs.).
Riviera, Palm Beach Co., Fla., 1,629.
On Fla. East Coast (R. R.).
Rivière du Loup, Temiscouata Co., Quebec, Canada, 8,499.
On Can. Nat.; Temisc. (R. Rs.).
Rixford, McKean Co., Pa., 518.
Riyadh, one of capitals of Saudi, Arabia, 30,000.
A large oasis. A focus for desert trade.
Roachdale, Putnam Co., Ind., 631.
On Balt. & Ohio; Chi., Ind. & Lou. (R. Rs.).
Roanne, Dept. of Loire, France, 41,460.
The starting point of Loire River navigation.
Roanoke, Randolph Co., Ala., 4,373.
On Atla., Birm. & Coast; Cen. of Ga. (R. Rs.).
–Woodford Co., Ill., 1,088.
On Atch., Top. & Santa Fe (R. R.).
–Huntington Co., Ind., 849.
On Wab. (R. R.).
–(Ind. City), Roanoke Co., Va., 69,206.
On Norf. & West.; Virginian (R. Rs.).
Railroad equipment, foundry products, textiles, furniture, steel fabricating products.
Roanoke Rapids, Halifax Co., N. C., 3,404.
On Seab. Air Line (R. R.).
Roaring Spring, Blair Co., Pa., 2,724.
On Penna. (R. R.).
Robbins, Scott Co., Tenn., 500.
On Cin., New Orl. & Tex. Pac. (R. R.).
–Cook Co., Ill., 753.
Robbinsdale, Hennepin Co., Minn., 4,427.
On Gt. Nor. (R. R.).
Roberdell (East Rockingham), Richmond Co., N. C., 559.
On Seab. Air Line (R. R.).
Robersonville, Martin Co., N. C., 1,181.
On Atl. Coast Line (R. R.).
Robertsdale, Baldwin Co., Ala., 678.
On Lou. & Nash. (R. R.).
–Lake Co., Ind., 9,500.
On N. York Cen.; Penna. (R. Rs.).
–Huntingdon Co., Pa., 651.
On E. Broad Top. (R. R.).
Robertson, Cape of Good Hope, Union of South Africa, 4,945.
–St. Louis Co., Mo., 500.
On Wabash (R. R.).
Roberval, Lake St. John Co., Que., Can., 2,770.
On Can. Nat. (R. R.).
Robeson, Berks Co., Pa., 500.
On Reading (R. R.).
Robesonia, Berks Co., Pa., 1,468.
On Reading (R. R.).
Robinson, c. s., Crawford Co., Ill., 3,668.
On Cle., Cin., Chi. & St. Lou.; Ill. Cen. (R. Rs.).
–Indiana Co., Pa., 900.
Robstown, Nueces Co., Tex., 4,183.
On Mo. Pac.; Tex. Mex. (R. Rs.).

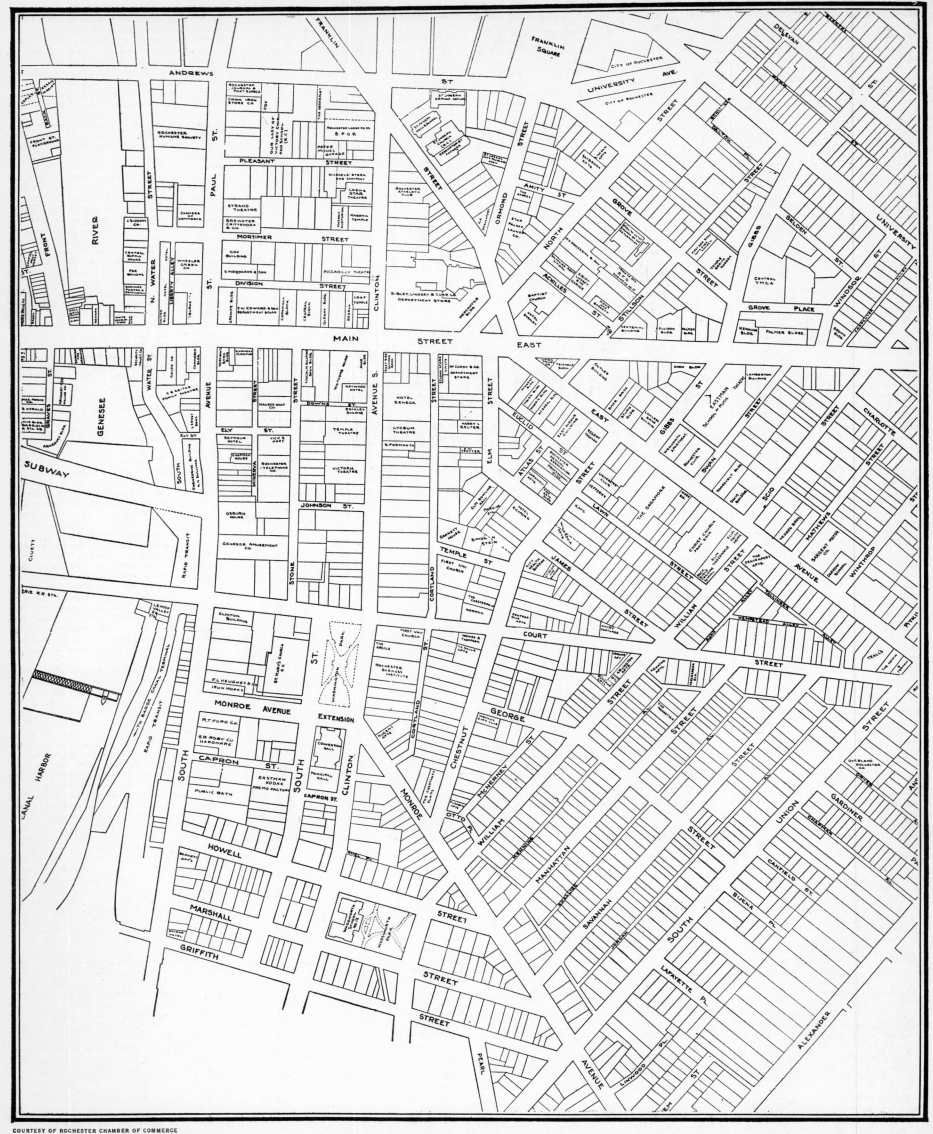

MAP OF THE BUSINESS CENTER OF ROCHESTER, N. Y. THE CITY IS SITUATED ON THE FALLS OF GENESEE RIVER, THE BARGE CANAL AND LAKE ONTARIO. ROCHESTER
IS THE SEAT OF THE UNIVERSITY OF ROCHESTER, WHICH INCLUDES THE EASTMAN SCHOOL OF MUSIC

Roby, c. s., Fisher Co., Texas, 801.
On Roby & Nor. (R. R.).
Rochdale, Lancashire, England, 90,278.
A place of considerable antiquity, and was early noted for its woolen manufactures, which have remained a chief staple. Cotton goods are extensively manufactured.
–Worcester Co., Mass., 1,200.
On Bost. & Alb. (R. R.).
Rochefort-sur-Mer, Dept. of Charente-Inférieure, France, 29,482.
Seaport, naval arsenal, and fortress of the first class, situated on the Charente. It was founded in 1665 as a naval station by Colbert. Birthplace of Pierre Loti.
Rochelle, Wilcox Co., Ga., 1,053.
On Seab. Air Line (R. R.).
–Ogle Co., Ill., 3,785.
On Chi. & Nor. West.; Chi., Burl. & Quincy; Chi., Mil., St. P. & Pac. (R. Rs.).
–Grant Par., La., 620.
On Mo. Pac.; Trem. & Gulf (R. Rs.).
–McCulloch Co., Tex., 515.
On Gulf. Colo. & Santa Fe (R. R.).
Rochelle Park, Bergen Co., N. J., 1,200.
On N. York, Susq. & West. (R. R.).
Rochester, Kent, England, 31,196.
–c. s., Fulton Co., Ind., 3,518.
On Erie; N. York, Chi. & St. Lou. (R. Rs.).
–Plymouth Co., Mass., 1,229.
–Oakland Co., Mich., 3,554.
On Gd. Tr.; Mich. Cen. (R. Rs.)
–c. s., Olmsted Co., Minn., 20,621.
On Chi. Gt. West.; Chi. & Nor. West. (R. Rs.).
Home of the noted Mayo Clinic.
–Strafford Co., N. H., 10,209.
On Bost. & Me. (R. R.).
Has shoe, woolen and lumber mills.
–c. s., Monroe Co., N. Y., 328,132.
Situated on the Genesee River, and on the West Shore; the New York Central; the Lehigh Valley; the Erie; the Baltimore & Ohio; and Pennsylvania railroads and the Barge Canal. In the center of the city are the Main Falls of the Genesee.
The city is the trade center of a large and rich agricultural region. Three falls of the Genesee River give abundant water power for manufacturing. There is a drop of more than 200 feet within the city's limits from which thousands of horse power is developed. It is one of the most important manufacturing cities of New York State. Rochester is the seat of the University of Rochester (including the Eastman School of Music), Colgate-Rochester Divinity School, Nazareth College and St. Bernard's Seminary.
Occupied as early as 1788, the first permanent settlement was made by Nathaniel Rochester in 1810. The place was incorporated in 1817 and received its city charter in 1834.
–Beaver Co., Pa., 7,726.
On Penna. (R. R.).
–Haskell Co., Tex., 562.
On Panh. & Santa Fe (R. R.).
–Windsor Co., Vt., 750.
Roche-sur-Yon, France. See La Roche-sur-Yon.
Rock, Mercer Co., W. Va., 600.
On Norf. & West.; Virginian (R. Rs.).
Rockaway, Morris Co., N. J., 3,132.
On Cen. of N. Jer., Del., Lack. & West. (R. Rs.)
Rockdale, Will Co., Ill., 1,701.
On Chi., Rk. Isl. & Pac.; Elg., Jol. & East. (R. Rs.).
–Delaware Co., Pa., 1,537.
On Penna. (R. R.).
–Milam Co., Texas, 2,204.
On Mo. Pac.; Sou. Pac. (R. Rs.).
Rock Falls, Whiteside Co., Ill., 3,893.
On Chi., Burl. & Quincy; Chi. & Nor. West. (R. Rs.).
Rockford, c. s., Winnebago Co., Ill., 85,864.
Situated on the Rock River, and on the Illinois Central; Chicago, Milwaukee, St. Paul & Pacific; Chicago, Burlington & Quincy; Chicago & North Western Railroads.
Chief manufactures: Machine tools, furniture, dog food, foundry and machine shop products, stoves, textiles, fabricated metal products.
–Floyd Co., Iowa, 996.
On Chi., Rk. Isl. & Pac. (R. R.).
–Kent Co., Mich., 1,613.
On Penna. (R. R.).
–Mercer Co., Ohio, 887.
On Cle., Cin., Chi. & St. Lou. (R. R.).
Rock Hall, Kent Co., Md., 714.
Rockhampton, Queensland, Australia, 30,000.
Rock Hill, York Co., S. C., 11,322.
On Southern (R. R.), which has shops here. Cotton market. Seat of Winthrop College.
–St. Louis Co., Mo., 1,309.
On Mo. Pac. (R. R.).
Rockhill Furnace (Rockhill), Huntingdon Co., Pa., 502.
Rockingham, Scott Co., Ia. (Pop. incl. in Davenport).
–c. s., Richmond Co., N. C., 2,906.
On Seab. Air Line; Rockingham (R. Rs.).

Rock Island, c. s., Rock Island Co., Ill., 37,953.
Situated on the Mississippi River, and on the Chicago, Burlington & Quincy; Chicago, Milwaukee, St. Paul & Pacific; Chicago, Rock Island & Pacific; Davenport, Rock Island & Northwestern; and Rock Island Southern railroads.
Here the Mississippi is spanned by two wrought-iron bridges. The city derives its name from an island in the river which belongs to the United States and is used by the Federal Government for a great central arsenal, a large armory and foundry, and military headquarters. Manufactures include farm implements, steel and iron products, lumber, oil. Augustana College and Theological Seminary is located here.
Rockland, c. s., Knox Co., Maine, 9,075.
On Me. Cen. (R. R.).
Lime and cement, shipbuilding, fisheries.

PUBLISHERS' PHOTO SERVICE, N. Y.

THE EXTERIOR OF THE COLISEUM, ROME, ITALY. THIS STRUCTURE, THE LARGEST THEATER IN THE WORLD, WAS BEGUN BY VESPASIAN AND COMPLETED BY TITUS IN 80 A. D.

–Plymouth Co., Mass., 7,890.
On N. York, N. Hav. & Hart. (R. R.).
–Ontonagon Co., Mich., 700.
On Chi., Mil., St. P. & Pac. (R. R.).
–Russell Co., Ontario, Canada, 2,118.
On Can. Nat. (R. R.).
Rockland Lake, Rockland Co., N. Y., 580.
Rockledge, Montgomery Co., Pa., 1,920.
–Brevard Co., Fla., 567.
On Fla. East Coast (R. R.).
Rocklin, Placer Co., Cal., 724.
On Sou. Pac. (R. R.).
Rockmart, Polk Co., Ga., 3,264.
On Seab. Air Line; Sou. (R. Rs.).
Rock Point, Charles Co., Md., 500.
Rockport, c. s., Spencer Co., Ind., 2,396.
On Evansv. & Ohio Val. (El.); Sou. (R. Rs.).
–Ohio Co., Ky., 671.
On Ill. Cen. (R. R.).
–Knox Co., Maine, 1,000.
–Essex Co., Mass., 3,634.
On Bost. & Me. (R. R.).
–c. s., Atchison Co., Mo., 1,162.
On Rk. Port, Langd. & Nor. (R. R.).
–c. s., Arkansas Co., Texas, 1,140.
On Tex. & N. Orl. (Sou. Pac.). (R. R.).
Rock Rapids, c. s., Lyon Co., Iowa, 2,221.
On Chi., Rk. Isl. & Pac.; Ill. Cen. (R. Rs.).
Rock Springs, Sweetwater Co., Wyo., 8,440.
On Un. Pac. (R. R.).
Rocksprings, c. s., Edwards Co., Tex., 998.
Rockton, Winnebago Co., Ill., 1,077.
On Chi., Mil., St. P. & Pac. (R. R.).
Rockvale, Fremont Co., Colo., 710.
On Atch., Top. & Santa Fe (R. R.).
Rock Valley, Sioux Co., Iowa, 1,204.
On Chi., Mil., St. P. & Pac. (R. R.).
Rockville, Tolland Co., Conn., 7,445.
On N. York, N. Hav. & Hart. (R. R.).
–c. s., Parke Co., Ind., 1,832.
On Penna. (R. R.).
–c. s., Montgomery Co., Md., 1,422.
On Balt. & Ohio (R. R.).
Rockville Centre, Nassau Co., N. Y., 13,718.
On Long Isl. (R. R.).
A residential suburb of New York.
Rockwall, c. s., Rockwall Co., Texas, 1,071.
On Mo.-Kan.-Tex. (R. R.).
Rockwell, Cerro Gordo Co., Iowa, 750.
On Mpls. & St. Lou. (R. R.).
–Rowan Co., N. C., 696.
On Yadkin (R. R.).
Rockwell City, c. s., Calhoun Co., Iowa, 2,108.
On Chi., Mil., St. P. & Pac.; Ft. Dodge, Des Moines & Sou.; Ill. Cen. (R. Rs.).
Rockwood, Somerset Co., Pa., 1,176.
On Balt. & Ohio; West. Md. (R. Rs.).
–Wayne Co., Mich., 953.
On Det., Tol. Sh. Line; Mich. Cen.; N. York Cen. (R. Rs.).
–Roane Co., Tenn., 3,898.
On Cin., N. Orl. & Tex. Pac.; Tenn. Cen. (R. Rs.).
Rocky, Washita Co., Okla., 518.
On St. Lou.-San Fran. (R. R.).
Rocky Ford, Otero Co., Colo., 3,426.
On Atch., Top. & Santa Fe (R. R.).
Rockygrove, Venango Co., Pa., 2,000.
Rocky Hill, Hartford Co., Conn., 1,000.
On N. York, N. Hav. & Hart. (R. R.).
–Somerset Co., N. J., 512.
On Penna. (R. R.).
Rocky Mount, Edgecombe and Nash Cos., N. C., 21,412.
On Atl. Coast Line (R. R.).
An important cotton and tobacco market.
Rockymount, c. s., Franklin Co., Va., 1,339.
On Norf. & West. (R. R.).
Rocky Mount Mills, Nash Co., N. C.
Rocky River, Cuyahoga Co., Ohio, 5,632.
On N. York, Chi. & St. Lou. (R. R.).
Rodas, Prov. of Santa Clara, Cuba, 3,408.
Rodez, capital of Aveyron, France, 18,450.
Textile manufactures.
Rodi (Rhodes), capital of island of Rhodes, Mediterranean Sea, 20,000.
Rodosto, Turkey. See Tekirdagi.
Roebling, Burlington Co., N. J., 3,403.
On Penna. (R. R.).
Roermond, Limburg, Netherlands, 16,599.
A commercial center with manufactures of textiles, paper, flour, and beer.
Roff, Pontotoc Co., Okla., 772.
On St. Lou.-San Fran. (R. R.).
Rogers, Benton Co., Ark., 3,554.
On St. Lou.-San Fran. (R. R.).
–Bell Co., Texas, 1,032.
On Gulf, Colo. & Santa Fe (R. R.).
Rogers City, c. s., Presque Isle Co., Mich., 3,278.
On Det. & Mack. (R. R.).
Rogersville, c. s., Hawkins Co., Tenn., 1,590.
On Southern (R. R.).
Rohrersville, Washington Co., Md., 1,447.
On Balt. & Ohio (R. R.).
Roland, Story Co., Iowa, 759.
On Mpls. & St. Lou. (R. R.).
Rolfe, Pocahontas Co., Iowa, 1,012.
On Mpls. & St. Lou.; Chi.. & Nor. West. (R. Rs.).
Rolla, c. s., Phelps Co., Mo., 3,670.
On St. Lou.-San Fran. (R. R.).
Seat of State School of Mines and Metallurgy.
–c. s., Rolette Co., N. Dak., 852.
On Gt. Nor. (R. R.).
Rollingbay, Kitsap Co., Wash., 530.
Rolling Fork, c. s., Sharkey Co., Miss., 902.
On Yazoo & Miss. Val. (Ill. Cen.) (R. R.).
Rollinsford, Strafford Co., N. H., 901.
On Bost. & Me. (R. R.).
Roma (Rome), the capital of Italy and of the spiritual empire of the Popes, 1,062,861.
Situated on both sides of the Tiber, the river here making two nearly equal bends, the upper of which encloses a large alluvial flat, known by the ancient name of Campus Martius. A large part of the modern city stands on this flat, but the ancient city lay mostly to the east and southeast of this, occupying a series of eminences known as the "Seven Hills" of Rome (the Capitoline, the Palatine, the Aventine, the Quirinal, the Viminal, the Esquiline, and the Caelian Hill). It has lost much of its ancient picturesque appearance, and is rapidly acquiring the appearance of a great modern city. The extensive excavations carried out have laid completely bare the remains of many of the grandest monuments of ancient Roma, notably the whole of the Forum Romanum and the Via Sacra, the remains of the Temples of Saturn, Castor and Pollux, Vespasian, Faustina, and the so-called Temple of Vesta; the Catacombs; the Colosseum, and the Arches of Titus and Constantine. There are seven bridges across the Tiber within the city.
Among the principal streets and squares of modern Roma are the Piazza del Popolo, immediately within the Porta del Popolo, with a fine Egyptian obelisk in its center, and from which diverge the three principal streets, the Via di Ripetta, the Corso, and the Via del Babuino. The Corso stretches for upward of a mile in a direct line, and is the finest street in the city. The Via del Babuino contains a large number of handsome edifices. The whole of the city to the east of this street, included between it and the Corso, is regarded as the aristocratic quarter. The Ghetto, or Jews' quarter, was cleared away in 1889. The chief open spaces besides the Piazza del Popolo are the Piazza S. Pietro, the Piazza Navona, the Piazza di Spagna, the Piazza Barberini, beside the palace of the same name; the Piazza Colonna, in the center of the city, with column of Marcus Aurelius; near it, in the Piazza di Monte Citoria, is the spacious Chamber of Deputies. The Pincio, or "hill of gardens," is a fashionable drive. At a short distance outside the walls on the north of the city is the Villa Borghese, forming a finely planted and richly decorated park.
The most remarkable church is the Cathedral of St. Peter, the largest and most imposing in the world, which now is part of the "free" Vatican City. Another remarkable church is that of San Giovanni in Laterano, built by Constantine the Great, restored and decorated by Giotto. Other churches are those of Santa Maria Maggiore (352), Santa Croce, San Clement, containing a number of interesting frescoes by Masaccio; Il Gesu, the principal church of the Jesuits (1577); Sta. Maria degli Angeli, originally a part of Diocletian's Baths, converted into a church by Michelangelo, one of the most imposing which Roma possesses; Sta. Maria in Ara Coeli, on the Capitoline, a very ancient church, containing the figure of the infant Christ called the "santissimo bambino"; Sta. Maria in Cosmedin, remarkable for its lofty and beautiful campanile of the eighth century; Sta. Maria sopra Minerva, so-called from occupying the site of a temple of that goddess, the only Gothic church in Roma; Sta. Maria in Dominica or della Navicella, on the Caelian, is remarkable for its porphyry columns and the frieze of the nave painted by Romano and Del Vago.
The Vatican and the immediate territory in the vicinity of St. Peter's was relinquished by Italy to the Catholic Church in 1929, and is now an independent division. The palace of the Quirinal is now occupied by the King of Italy. The Palazzo della Cancelleria was designed by Bramante, and is one of the finest in Roma. On the southeast side of the piazza is the Senatorial Palace, in which the senate holds its meetings. The building also contains the offices of the municipal administration and an observatory. Its façade was constructed by Giacoma della Porta, under the direction of Michelangelo. On the southwestern side of the piazza is the palace of the Conservatori. Opposite is the museum of the Capitol. A recent construction is the magnificent Mussolini Forum, seating 100,000 spectators.
Among private palaces may be noted the Palazzo Barberini with a collection of paintings. The Palazzo Borghese is chiefly celebrated for its picture gallery. The Palazzo Farnese is one of the finest in Rome. The Palazzo Rospigliosi, erected in 1603, contains the celebrated fresco of Aurora by Guido; Villa Farnesina contains Raphael's "Cupid and Psyche."
Among educational institutions the first place is claimed by the university, founded in 1303. The Collegio Romano, formerly a Jesuit college, now contains the Archeological Museum and the recently established library, Biblioteca Vittorio Emanuele, consisting of about a million volumes. The Collegio de Propaganda Fide is the establishment where Roman Catholic missionaries are trained. The Accademia di San Luca, for the promotion of the fine arts, was founded in 1595. Other associations and institutions connected with art, science, or learning are numerous; one of them, the Accademia de' Lincei, founded in 1603 by Galileo, is the earliest scientific society of Italy. Besides the Vatican and Vittorio Emanuele libraries, the chief are the Biblioteca Casanatense, the Biblioteca Angelica and the Biblioteca Barberini.
–Starr Co., Tex., 700.

ROMANS, Dept. of Drôme, France, 19,489.
 On Isère River.
ROMBLON, Romblon, P. I., 10,457.
 Famous for its beautiful buri mats.
ROME, Italy. See ROMA.
 —c. s., Floyd Co., Ga., 21,843.
 On Cen. of Ga.; Nash., Chatt. & St. Lou.; Sou. (R. Rs.).
 A cotton market. Seat of Shorter College.

ROSBORO, Pike Co., Ark., 581.
 On Mo. Pac. (R. R.).
ROSCOE, Coshocton Co., Ohio, 650.
 On Penna. (R. R.).
 —Washington Co., Pa., 1,310.
 On Penna. (R. R.).
 —Sullivan Co., N. Y., 900.
 On N. York, Ont. & West. (R. R.).
 —Nolan Co., Texas, 1,250.

ROSENHEIM, Bavaria, Germany, 18,000.
 A popular watering place.
ROSETO, Northampton Co., Pa., 1,746.
 On Leh. & N. Eng. (R. R.).
ROSETON, Orange Co., N. Y., 700.
 On West Shore (R. R.).
ROSETTA, Egypt. See RASCHID.
ROSEVILLE, Placer Co., Cal., 6,425.
 On Sou. Pac. (R. R.).

On Chi., Rk. Isl. & Pac.; Den. & Rio Gde. West. (R. Rs.).
 —c. s., Chaves Co., N. Mex., 11,173.
 On Atch., Top. & Santa Fe (R. R.).
 In irrigated area. Seat of New Mexico Military Institute.
ROTAN, Fisher Co., Tex., 1,632.
 On Mo.-Kan.-Tex. of Tex. (R. R.).
ROTHENBURG, Bavaria, Germany, 8,828.
ROTHERHAM, Yorkshire, England, 69,689.
 An industrial town near Sheffield. Has manufactures of iron, steel, brass, pottery, cutlery, beer, lumber, rope, and railroad cars.
ROTHESAY, Bute Co., Scotland, 9,346.
ROTHSVILLE, Lancaster Co., Pa., 800.
 On Reading (R. R.).
ROTTERDAM, Prov. of South Holland, Netherlands, 594,948.
 Situated on the Nieuwe Maas, or Meuse, at its junction with the Rotte; about 14 miles from the North Sea, with which it is also directly connected by a ship canal (Nieuwe Waterweg), admitting the largest vessels. The town is intersected by numerous canals, which permit large vessels to moor alongside the warehouses in the very center of the city. These canals, which are crossed by innumerable drawbridges and swing bridges, are in many cases lined with rows of trees; and the handsome quay on the river front, 1¼ miles long, is known as the Boompjes ("little trees"), from a rows of elms planted in 1615. The houses are quaint edifices, having their gables to the street, with overhanging upper stories. The principal buildings are the old and new town halls, stock exchange, old East India House, Boyman's Museum, containing chiefly Dutch and modern paintings, and the Government dockyards and arsenal, besides the numerous churches, of which the most conspicuous is the Groote Kerk or Church of St. Laurens.
 Rotterdam contains shipbuilding yards, sugar refineries, distilleries, tobacco factories, and large machine works; but its mainstay is commerce. It not only carries on a very extensive and active trade with Great Britain, Netherland India, and other transoceanic countries, but has developed an important commerce with Germany, Switzerland, and Central Europe. Rotterdam received town rights in 1340, and in 1573 it obtained a vote in the Estates of the Netherlands; but its modern prosperity has been chiefly developed since 1830.
ROTTERDAM JUNCTION, Schenectady Co., N. Y., 1,000.
 On West Shore (R. R.).
ROTTWEIL, Wurtemberg, Germany, 10,556.
ROUBAIX, Dept. of Nord, France, 107,105.
 A highly important seat of the French textile industry, remarkable for its rapid growth.
ROUEN, capital of Dept. of Seine-Inférieure, France, 122,832.
 Situated on the right bank of the Seine. The public buildings of interest are the cathedral, containing many old monuments, and one of the finest specimens of Gothic architecture in France; the Church of St. Ouen, also Gothic, and that of St. Maclou. A modern monument to Joan of Arc stands in the market place at the spot where she was burned at the stake in 1431. Two bridges over the Seine, one of stone, another of iron, connect the town with the suburb of St. Sever. The important manufactures are textiles, machinery, soap, iron products and pottery. Dyeing, both of woolens and cotton, is also carried on.
ROULERS (Roeselare), West Flanders, Belgium, 27,690.
 Lace, carpet, and linen factories.
ROULETTE, Potter Co., Pa., 500.
 On Coudersp. & Pt. Alleg. (R. R.).
ROUNDHEAD, Hardin Co., Ohio, 802.
ROUND LAKE, Saratoga Co., N. Y., 600.
 On Del. & Hud. (R. R.).
ROUND ROCK, Williamson Co., Texas, 1,173.
 On Mo. Pac. (R. R.).
ROUNDUP, c. s., Musselshell Co., Mont., 2,577.
 On Chi., Mil., St. P. & Pac. (R. R.).
ROUSES POINT, Clinton Co., N. Y., 1,920.
 On Cen. Ver.; Del. & Hud.; Gd. Tr.; Napierv. Jct.; Rut. (R. Rs.).
ROUSEVILLE, Venango Co., Pa., 1,059.
 On Penna. (R. R.).
ROUZERVILLE, Franklin Co., Pa., 950.
ROVERETO, Trento, Italy, 11,836.
 An industrial town. Much damaged in World War.
ROVIGNO, Pola, Italy, 9,453.
ROVIGO, capital Prov. of Rovigo, Italy, 13,191.
 Has interesting buildings and ruins and a library notable for its rare editions.
ROVNO, Soviet Union, 45,000.
 An active commercial town.

A COMPREHENSIVE VIEW OF ST. PETER'S AND VATICAN CITY WITH THE MANY-BRIDGED TIBER IN THE BACKGROUND. THE FOUNDATION STONE OF ST. PETER'S WAS LAID BY POPE JULIUS II IN 1506

—Oneida Co., N. Y., 32,338.
 On the N. York Cen.; the N. York, Ont. & West. (R. Rs.), and State Barge Canal. Industries: copper, brass and steel products.
 —Franklin Co., Ohio, 500.
 On Cin. & L. Erie (El.) (R. R.).
ROMEO, Macomb Co., Mich., 2,283.
 On Gd. Tr. (R. R.).
ROMNEY, c. s., Hampshire Co., W. Va., 1,441.
 On Balt. & Ohio (R. R.).
ROMULUS, Wayne Co., Mich., 755.
 On Pere Marq.; Wab. (R. Rs.).
RONAN, Lake Co., Mont., 537.
 On Nor. Pac. (R. R.).
RONCEVERTE, Greenbrier Co., W. Va., 2,254.
 On Chesa. & Ohio (R. R.).
RONCO, Fayette Co., Pa., 1,054.
 On Monongahela (R. R.).
RONDA, Prov. of Malaga, Spain, 30,393.
 An agricultural center with considerable trade in leather, horses, soap, wine, flour, and hats.
RONKONKOMA, Suffolk Co., N. Y., 1,000.
 On Long Isl. (R. R.).
RONSDORF, Rhenish Prussia, Germany, 15,365.
 An active center of the iron industry.
ROODHOUSE, Greene Co., Ill., 2,621.
 On Alton (R. R.).
ROOSENDAAL, North Brabant, Netherlands, 22,053.
 An agricultural center.
ROOSEVELT, Middlesex Co., N. J. See CARTERET.
 —Nassau Co., N. Y., 5,826.
 —Kiowa Co., Okla., 721.
 On St. Lou.-San Fran. (R. R.).
 —Duchesne Co., Utah, 1,051.
ROPER, Washington Co., N. Car., 660.
ROSALIA, Whitman Co., Wash., 633.
 On Chi., Mil., St. P. & Pac.; Nor. Pac.; Spok., Coe. D'Ale. & Pal. (Gt. Nor.). (R. Rs.).
ROSARIO, Prov. of Santa Fe, Argentine Republic, 509,300.
 Situated on the west bank of the Parana River. It has an excellent harbor, and carries on a large commerce direct with Europe. The city is laid out, on a smaller scale, on the lines of Buenos Aires.
 —Prov. of Batangas, Luzon, P. I., 22,174.

On Roscoe, Snyder & Pac.; Tex. & Pac. (R. Rs.).
ROSEAU, c. s., Roseau Co., Minn., 1,028.
 On Gt. Nor. (R. R.).
ROSEBORO, Sampson Co., N. C., 768.
 On Atl. Coast Line (R. R.).
ROSE BUD, Clearfield Co., Pa., 1,000.
 On Penna. (R. R.).
 Coal port.
ROSEBUD, Falls Co., Tex., 1,565.
 On Sou. Pac. (R. R.).
ROSEBURG, c. s., Douglas Co., Ore., 4,362.
 On Sou. Pac. (R. R.).
ROSEDALE, Parke Co., Ind., 657.
 On Balt. & Ohio; Penna. (R. Rs.).
 —c. s., Bolivar Co., Miss., 2,117.
 On Ill. Cen. (R. R.).
ROSE HILL, Duplin Co., N. C., 554.
 On Atl. Coast Line (R. R.).
 —Lee Co., Va., 500.
 On Lou. & Nash. (R. R.).
ROSELAND, Essex Co., N. J., 1,058.
 On Morrist. & Erie (R. R.).
 —St. Joseph Co., Ind., 777.
 —Tangipahoa Parish, La., 1,139.
 On Ill. Cen. (R. R.).
ROSELLE, Union Co., N. J., 13,021.
 On Cen. of N. Jer.; Rahw. Val.; Leh. Val. (R. Rs.).
 —Du Page Co., Ill., 807.
 On Chi., Mil., St. P. & Pac. (R. R.).
ROSELLE PARK, Union Co., N. J., 8,969.
 On Cen. of N. Jer.; Leh. Val.; Rahw. Val. (R. Rs.).
ROSEMEAD, Los Angeles Co., Cal., 4,500.
 On Pac. El. (R. R.).
ROSEMONT, Montgomery Co., Pa., 2,600.
 On Penna. (R. R.).
 —Taylor Co., W. Va., 800.
 On Balt. & Ohio (R. R.).
ROSENBURG, East Silesia, Germany, 5,877.
 —Fort Bend Co., Texas, 1,941.
 On Gulf, Colo. & Santa Fe; Sou. Pac. (R. Rs.).
ROSENDALE, Ulster Co., N. Y., 539.
 On West Shore (R. R.).
ROSENHAYN, Cumberland Co., N. J., 850.
 On Cen. of N. Jer. (R. R.).

—Warren Co., Ill., 975.
 On Chi., Burl. & Quincy (R. R.).
 —Macomb Co., Mich., 6,836.
 —Muskingum and Perry Cos., Ohio, 1,412.
 On Penna. (R. R.).
ROSHOLT, Portage Co., Wis., 515.
 On Chi. & Nor. West. (R. R.).
ROSICLARE, Hardin Co., Ill., 1,794.
 On Ill. Cen. (R. R.).
ROSLYN, Kittitas Co., Wash., 2,603.
 On Nor. Pac. (R. R.).
 —Nassau Co., N. Y., 2,500.
 On Long Isl. (R. R.).
 —Montgomery Co., Pa., 2,500.
 On Reading (R. R.).
ROSS, Marin Co., Cal., 1,355.
 On Northw. Pac. (R. R.).
 —Lake Co., Ind., 1,000.
ROSSANO, Prov. of Cosenza, Italy, 10,787.
 Marble and alabaster quarries in vicinity.
ROSSITER, Indiana Co., Pa., 2,000.
 On Balt. & Ohio (R. R.).
ROSSLAU, Anhalt, Germany, 12,000.
 Has iron foundries and machine shops.
ROSSLYN, Arlington Co., Va., 3,000.
 On Arl. & Fairfax; Penna.; Wash. & Old Dom. (El.) (R. Rs.).
ROSSVILLE, Walker Co., Ga., 3,230.
 On Cen. of Ga. (R. R.).
 —Vermilion Co., Ill., 1,453.
 On Chi. & East. Ill. (R. R.).
 —Clinton Co., Ind., 626.
 On Chi., Ind. & Lou. (R. R.).
 —Shawnee Co., Kans., 603.
 On Un. Pac. (R. R.).
ROSTOCK, Mecklenburg-Schwerin, Ger., 93,501.
 An important commercial port and seat of the famous University of Rostock.
ROSTOV, R.S.F.S.R., Soviet Union, 20,864.
 Situated on Lake Nero, near Yaroslavl.
ROSTOV-NA-DONU, North Caucasian Area, Soviet Union, 323,700.
 Principal shipping point of wheat and other products of southeastern Soviet Union.
ROSWELL, Cobb Co., Ga., 1,432.
 —El Paso Co., Colo., 500.

ROWAYTON, Fairfield Co., Conn., 1,500.
 On N. York, N. Hav. & Hart. (R. R.).
ROWES RUN, Fayette Co., Pa., 2,000.
 On Penna. (R. R.).
ROWLAND, Robeson Co., N. C., 915.
 On Atl. Coast Line (R. R.).
ROWLESBURG, Preston Co., W. Va., 1,573.

On Balt. & Ohio (R. R.).
Rowley, Essex Co., Mass., 1,495.
On Bost. & Me. (R. R.).
Rowley Regis, Staffordshire, England, 41,238.
A suburb of Birmingham.
Rowne, Wolhynia, Poland, 40,788.
Region is famous for its horses and cattle.
Roxana, Madison Co., Ill., 1,139.
On Alton; Cle., Cin., Chi. & St. Lou.; Ill. Term. (El.) R. Rs.).
Roxboro, c. s., Person Co., N. C., 3,657.
On Norf. & West. (R. R.).
Roy, Harding Co., N. Mex., 713.
On Sou. Pac. (R. R.).
–Weber Co., Utah, 557.
On Bamberger Elec.; Den. & Rio. Gde. West.; Un. Pac. (R. Rs.).
Royal, Beaufort Co., N. C., 600.
On Atl. Coast Line (R. R.).
Royal Center, Cass Co., Ind., 777.
On Penna. (R. R.).
Royal Oak, Oakland Co., Mich., 22,904.
On Gd. Tr. (R. R.).
A residential suburb of Detroit.
Royalston, Worcester Co., Mass., 841.
On Bost. & Me. (R. R.).
Royalton, Franklin Co., Ill., 2,108.
On Ill. Cen.; Mo. Pac. (R. Rs.).
–Morrison Co., Minn., 518.
On Nor. Pac. (R. R.).
–Dauphin Co., Pa., 1,117.
On Penna. (R. R.).
Royersford, Montgomery Co., Pa., 3,719.
On Penna.; Read. (R. Rs.).
Royse City, Rockwall and Collins Cos., Texas, 1,128.
On Mo.-Kan.-Tex. of Tex. (R. R.).
Royston, Yorkshire, West Riding, England, 7,156.
–Franklin, Hart and Madison Cos., Ga., 1,447.
On Southern (R. R.).
Ruckersville, Greene Co., Va., 550.
Rudolstadt, Thüringen, Germany, 15,925.
Porcelain, chemicals and machinery.
Rueil, Dept. of Seine-et-Oise, France, 26,796.
Has photographic works.
Ruffs Dale, Westmoreland Co., Pa., 500.
On Penna. (R. R.).
Rugby, Warwickshire, England, 23,824.
Site of celebrated public school, founded in 1567.
–c. s., Pierce Co., N. Dak., 1,512.
On Great Northern (R. R.).
Ruhport, now part of Duisburg, Germany.
Ruidoso, Lincoln Co., N. Mex., 549.
–Presidio Co., Tex., 530.
Rule, Haskell Co., Texas, 1,094.
On Panh. & Santa Fe (R. R.).
Ruleville, Sunflower Co., Miss., 1,181.
On Yazoo & Miss. Val. (Ill. Cen.) (R. R.).
Rulo, Richardson Co., Neb., 719.
On Chi., Burl. & Quincy (R. R.).
Rumford, Oxford Co., Maine, 8,726.
On Me. Cen. (R. R.).
Has large paper mills.
–Providence Co., R. I., 625.
On N. York, N. Hav. & Hart. (R. R.).
Rumford Falls, Oxford Co., Maine. See Rumford.
Rumson, Monmouth Co., N. J., 2,073.
A summer resort on Shrewsbury River.
Runcorn, Cheshire, England, 18,158.
A suburb of Liverpool.
Runge, Karnes Co., Texas, 1,136.
On Tex. & N. Orl. (Sou. Pac.) (R. R.).
Runnemede, Camden Co., N. J., 2,436.
On Penna.-Read. Seash. (R. R.).
Rupert, c. s., Minidoka Co., Idaho, 2,250.
On Un. Pac. (R. R.).
Rural Hall, Forsyth Co., N. C., 600.
On Atl. & Yadk.; Sou. (R. Rs.).
Rural Retreat, Wythe Co., Va., 500.
On Norf. & West. (R. R.).
Rural Ridge, Alleghany Co., Pa., 700.
On Bess. & L. Erie (R. R.).
Rural Valley, Armstrong Co., Pa., 948.
Rush City, Chisago Co., Minn., 908.
On Nor. Pac. (R. R.).
Rushford (City), Fillmore Co., Minn., 1,125.
On Chi., Mil., St. P. & Pac. (R. R.).
–(village), Fillmore Co., Minn., 633.
Rush Springs, Grady Co., Okla., 1,340.
On Chi., Rk. Isl. & Pac. (R. R.).
Rushsylvania, Logan Co., Ohio, 507.
On Cle., Cin., Chi. & St. Lou. (R. R.).
Rushville, c. s., Schuyler Co., Ill., 2,388.
On Chi., Burl. & Quincy (R. R.).
–c. s., Rush Co., Ind., 5,709.
On Balt. & Ohio; N. York, Chi. & St. Lou.; Erie; Penna.; Cle., Cin., Chi. & St. Lou. (R. Rs.).
–Sheridan Co., Neb., 1,006.
On Chi. & Nor. West. (R. R.).
Rusk, c. s., Cherokee Co., Texas, 3,859.
On St. Lou. Southw.; Sou. Pac. (R. Rs.).
Ruskin, Hillsborough Co., Fla., 600.
On Atl. Coast Line (R. R.).
Russe (Rustchuk), Bulgaria, 50,300.
An important commercial town with manufactures of pottery, tobacco, and food products.
Russell, Lucas Co., Iowa, 571.
On Chi., Burl. & Quincy (R. R.).
–c. s., Russell Co., Kans., 3,260.
On Un. Pac. (R. R.).
–Greenup Co., Ky., 2,084.
On Chesa. & Ohio (R. R.).
–Hampden Co., Mass., 1,283.
On Bost. & Alb. (R. R.).
–St. Lawrence Co., N. Y., 500.
–Warren Co., Pa., 500.
On N. York Cen. (R. R.).
Russell Springs, Russell Co., Ky., 500.
Russellton, Allegheny Co., Pa., 4,000.
On Bess. & L. Erie (R. R.).
Russellville, c. s., Franklin Co., Ala., 3,146.
On Nor. Ala. (R. R.).
–c. s., Pope Co., Ark., 5,628.
On Dardan. & Russellv.; Mo. Pac. (R. Rs.).
–c. s., Logan Co., Ky., 3,297.
On Lou. & Nash. (R. R.).
Russiaville, Howard Co., Ind., 800.
On N. York, Chi. & St. Lou. (R. R.).
Rustchuk, Bulgaria. See Russe.
Ruston, c. s., Lincoln Parish, La., 4,400.
On Chi., Rk. Isl. & Pac.; Yazoo & Miss. Val. (Ill. Cen.) (R. Rs.).
–Pierce Co., Wash., 818.
On Un. Pac. (R. R.).
Ruth, White Pine Co., Nev., 2,000.
On Nev. Nor. (R. R.).
Rutherford, Bergen Co., N. J., 14,915.
On Erie (R. R.).
A residential suburb of Jersey City.
–Gibson Co., Tenn., 747.
On Mob. & Ohio (R. R.).
Rutherford Heights, Dauphin Co., Pa., 580.
On Reading (R. R.).
Rutherfordton, c. s., Rutherford Co., N. C., 2,020.
On Seab. Air Line; Sou. (R. Rs.).
Rutherglen, Lanark Co., Scotland, 25,157.
An industrial suburb of Glasgow.
Ruthven, Palo Alto Co., Iowa, 739.
On Chi., Mil., St. P. & Pac.; Mpls. & St. Lou. (R. Rs.).
–Wilcox Co., Ala., 523.
On Lou. & Nash. (R. R.).
Rutland, Bibb Co., Ga., 560.
On Cen. of Ga. (R. R.).
–Worcester Co., Mass., 2,406.
On Bost. & Me. (R. R.).
–Meigs Co., Ohio, 570.
On N. York Cen. (R. R.).
–c. s., Rutland Co., Vt., 17,315.
On Clare. & Pitts.; Del. & Hud.; Rut. (R. Rs.).
Notable as a marble center; also for scale-making. Has big railroad shops and lumber mills. Settled in 1761.
Rutland Heights, Worcester Co., Mass., 800.
Rutledge, Morgan Co., Ga., 523.
On Georgia (R. R.).
–Delaware Co., Pa., 789.
–c. s., Grainger Co., Tenn., 518.
On Southern (R. R.).
Ruvo di Puglia, Prov. of Bari, Italy, 26,628.
Has an early 13th century cathedral.
Ryan, Jefferson Co., Okla., 1,258.
On Chi., Rk. Isl. & Pac. (R. R.).
Ryazan, R.S.F.S.R., Sov. Union, 62,700.
A trade and marketing center. Agricultural machinery, shoes, leather goods, bricks, and spirits.
Rybinsk, R.S.F.S.R., Sov. Union, 86,700.
A busy port and trade center on the Volga River.
Ryde, Isle of Wight, England, 10,519.
A popular resort.
Rye, Rockingham Co., N. H., 1,081.
–Westchester Co., N. Y., 8,712.
On N. York, N. Hav. & Hart. (R. R.).
Ryegate, Caledonia Co., Vt., 1,216.
Rzeszow, East Galicia, Poland, 27,499.
An agricultural center.

S

Saalfeld, Saxe-Meiningen, Germany, 19,000.
Industrial center near ochre and iron mines.
Saarbrücken, Rhenish Prussia, Germany, 129,085.
Situated in a coal mining region and has large iron works and glass factories.
Saargemund, France. See Sarreguemines.
Saarlautern (Saarlouis), Saar-Pfalz, Germany, 32,000.
Saaz (Zatec), Germany, 16,211.
Sabac, Yugoslavia, 12,563.
A busy port on the Sava River.
Sabadell, Prov. of Barcelona, Spain, 37,529.
Cloth, linen, paper, flour, castings, and lumber.
Sabana Grande, Mun. of Sabana Grande, Puerto Rico, 4,119.
Sabanilla, Prov. of Matanzas, Cuba, 2,391.
Sabattus, Androscoggin Co., Me., 900.
On Me. Cen. (R. R.).
Sabetha, Nemaha Co., Kans., 2,220.
Chi., Rk. Isl. & Pac.; St. Jos. & Gd. Isl. (Un. Pac.). (R. Rs.).
Sabina, Clinton Co., Ohio, 1,296.
On Balt. & Ohio; Penna. (R. Rs.).
Sabinal, Uvalde Co., Texas, 1,586.
On Tex. & N. Orl. (Sou. Pac.) (R. R.).
Sabraton (Sturgiss City), Monongalia Co., W. Va., 1,717.
On Balt. & Ohio (R. R.).
Sabula, Jackson Co., Iowa, 759.
On Chi., Mil., St. P. & Pac. (R. R.).
Sac City, c. s., Sac Co., Iowa, 2,854.
On Chi., Mil., St. P. & Pac.; Chi. & Nor. West. (R. Rs.).
Sackets Harbor, Jefferson Co., N. Y., 742.
On N. York Cen. (R. R.).
Saco, York Co., Maine, 7,233.
On Bost. & Me. (R. R.).
–Phillips Co., Mont., 506.
On Gt. Nor. (R. R.).
Sacramento, c. s., Sacramento Co., Cal., State capital, 93,750.
Situated at the confluence of the Sacramento and American Rivers, on the Southern Pacific; Western Pacific; Central California Traction, and the Sacramento Northern Electric Railroads. At the head of navigation for large steamboats and sailing vessels, it is a great commercial center.
The most important buildings are the State Capitol, the exposition buildings of the State Agricultural Society, the court-house, United States Government Building and the Crocker Art Gallery. Here are the Southern Pacific and Western Pacific shops. In center of extensive asparagus, pear, and hop-producing area. Has large fruit canneries, packing houses, publishing houses, machine shops, rice mills, and milk-product plants. Other industries: railroad and automobile equipment. Captain John A. Sutter built a fort here in 1839, but the city was not settled till 1848. Sacramento was made the State capital in 1854, and received its city charter in 1863.
Sacred Heart, Renville Co., Minn., 685.
On Chi., Mil., St. P. & Pac. (R. R.).
Saddle River, Bergen Co., N. J., 657.
Sadieville, Scott Co., Ky., 527.
On Cin., N. Orl. & Tex. Pac. (R. R.).
Saegerstown, Crawford Co., Pa., 645.
On Erie (R. R.).
Safety Harbor, Pinellas Co., Fla., 583.
On Seab. Air Line (R. R.).
Safford, c. s., Graham Co., Ariz., 1,706.
On Sou. Pac. (R. R.).
Safi, Morocco, 26,065.
A seaport and trade center.
Saga, Kyushu I., Japan, 46,178.
A commercial town near Nagasaki.
Sagamore, Armstrong Co., Pa., 1,750.
On Balt. & Ohio (R. R.).
–Barnstable Co., Mass., 790.
On N. York, N. Hav. & Hart. (R. R.).
Sagan, Prov. of Sagan, Silesia, Germany, 18,000.
Chief industries are wool-spinning and cloth weaving.
Sagasik, Egypt. See Zagazig.
Sag Harbor, Suffolk Co., N. Y., 2,773.
On Long Isl. (R. R.).
Saginaw, c. s., Saginaw Co., Mich., 80,715.
Situated on the Saginaw River, and on the Michigan Central; the Grand Trunk, and the Pere Marquette railroads.
Center of rich agricultural section. Its lumber trade is important, and it has a large beet-sugar factory. Other important products are tapes and rules, glass products, foundry products, machinery, and auto parts. Within and near city limits are a number of coal mines, and salt, oil and gas wells. Saginaw was incorporated in 1859.
Sagnay, Prov. of Camarines, Sur, Luzon, P. I., 5,437.
Saguache, c. s., Saguache Co., Colo., 1,010.
Sagua la Grande, Santa Clara Prov., Cuba, 17,487.
A sugar center.
Saharanpur, Northwest Province, India, 78,655.
Has a large wood carving industry.
Saïgon, capital of Cochin China, French Indo-China, 109,000.
A river port and rice trade center.
St. Agatha, Aroostook Co., Maine., 1,000.
Ste. Agathe des Monts, Terrebonne Co., Quebec, Canada, 2,949.
On Can. Pac. (R. R.).
St. Albans, c. s., Franklin Co., Vt., 8,020.
On Cen. Ver. (R. R.).
–Kanawha Co., W. Va., 3,254.
On Chesa. & Ohio (R. R.).
Coal field outlet.
St. Andrew, Bay Co., Fla., 1,247.
St. Andrews, Fife Co., Scotland, 8,269.
Ste. Anne de Beaupré, Montgomery Co., Quebec, Canada, 1,901.
On Queb. Ry., Lght. & Pow. (R. R.).
A Roman Catholic place of pilgrimage.
Ste. Anne de Bellevue, Jacques-Cartier Co., Quebec, Canada, 2,417.
On Can. Nat. (R. R.).
St. Anne, Kankakee Co., Ill., 1,078.
On Chi. & East. Ill.; Cle., Cin., Chi. & St. Lou. (R. Rs.).
St. Ansgar, Mitchell Co., Iowa, 964.
On Ill. Cen. (R. R.).
St. Anthony, c. s., Fremont Co., Idaho, 2,778.
On Un. Pac. (R. R.).
St. Augustine, c. s., St. John Co., Fla., 10,418.
On Fla. East Coast (R. R.).
Oldest permanent settlement in the United States. Coast resort. Industries: cigar-making and fisheries.
St. Benedict, Cambria Co., Pa., 600.
On N. York Cen. (R. R.).
St. Bernard, Hamilton Co., Ohio, 7,487.
On Balt. & Ohio; Cle., Cin., Chi. & St. Lou.; Cin. Nor.; Norf. & West.; Penna. (R. Rs.).
–c. s., St. Bernard Par., La., 520.
St. Bernice, Vermillion Co., Ind., 1,000.
On Chi., Mil., St. P. & Pac. (R. R.).
St. Boniface, Provencher Co., Manitoba, Canada, 16,305.
On Can. Nat.; Can. Pac.; Gter. Win. Water Dist. (R. Rs.).
Situated near Winnipeg.
St. Brieuc, capital of Dept. of Côtes-du-Nord, France, 31,640.
An agricultural trade center.
St. Catharines, capital of Lincoln Co., Ontario, Canada, 24,753.
On Can. Nat.; Niag., St. Cath. & Tor. (El.) (R. Rs.).
A commercial town south of Toronto.
St. Chamond, Dept. of Loire, France, 14,711.
A manufacturing town near St. Étienne.
St. Charles, Kane Co., Ill., 5,377.
On Chi. Gt. West.; Chi. & Nor. West.; Chi., Aur. & Elg. (R. Rs.).
–Hopkins Co., Ky., 634.
On Ill. Cen. (R. R.).
–Saginaw Co., Mich., 1,463.
On Mich. Cen. (R. R.).
–Winona Co., Minn., 1,311.
On Chi. & Nor. West.; Chi. Gt. West. (R. Rs.).
–c. s., St. Charles Co., Mo., 10,491.
On Mo.-Kan.-Tex.; Wab. (R. Rs.).
A commercial center in a farming district.
St. Clair, St. Clair Co., Mich., 3,389.
On Port Hur. & Det. (R. R.).
–Franklin Co., Mo., 1,135.
On St. Lou.-San Fran. (R. R.).
–Schuylkill Co., Pa., 7,296.
On Penna.; Read. (R. Rs.).
St. Clair Heights, Wayne Co., Mich.
St. Clair Shore, Macomb Co., Mich., 6,745.
St. Clairsville, c. s., Belmont Co., Ohio, 2,440.
On Balt. & Ohio; Wheel. & L. Erie (R. Rs.).
St. Cloud, Osceola Co., Fla., 1,972.
On Atl. Coast Line (R. R.).
–Dept. of Seine-et-Oise, France, 16,597.
–c. s., Stearns, also in Benton and Sherburne Cos., Minn., 21,000.
On Gt. Nor.; Nor. Pac. (R. Rs.).
Situated in a grain-raising and dairying section. Quarries near by.
St. Croix Falls, Polk Co., Wis., 952.
On Mpls., St. P. & S. Ste. M. (R. Rs).
St. David, Fulton Co., Ill., 977.
On Chi., Burl. & Quincy (R. R.).
–Aroostook Co., Maine, 1,200.
On Bangor & Aroostook (R. R.).
–Delaware Co., Pa., 1,000.
On Penna. (R. R.).
St. Denis, Dept. of Seine, France, 78,401.
An industrial suburb of Paris.
–Capital of Réunion Island, 26,807.
A busy seaport and the commercial center of the Colony.
St. Die, Dept. of Vosges, France, 20,345.
A commercial town located in an agricultural and lumbering region.
St. Dizier, Dept. of Haute-Marne, France, 19,149.
An important center of the iron trade.
St. Edward, Boone Co., Neb., 1,030.
On Un. Pac. (R. R.).
St. Elmo, Fayette Co., Ill., 1,329.
On Chi. & East. Ill.; Penna. (R. Rs.).
–Mobile Co., Ala., 550.
On Lou. & Nash. (R. R.).
–Hamilton Co., Tenn. (Sta. Chattanooga P. O.).
On Tenn., Ala. & Ga. (R. R.).
Ste. Genevieve, c. s., Ste. Genevieve Co., Mo., 2,662.
On Mo. Ill.; St. Lou.-San Fran. (R. Rs.).
Saintes, Charente Inférieure, France, 21,160.
A trade center with manufactures of brick and tile.
St. Étienne, Loire, France, 190,236.
Situated on the Furens, a small tributary of the Loire River, and in the center of one of the most valuable coal fields of France. It is the seat of a national college, a school of mines, a chemical laboratory, public library, a gallery of art and a commercial museum.
The first railways in France were built from St. Étienne, one in 1828 to Andrézieux, the other in 1831 to Lyon.
St. Eustache, Two Mountains Co., Quebec, Canada, 1,187.
On Can. Pac.; Can. Nat. (R. Rs.).
St. Ferdinand, St. Louis Co., Mo., 1,039.
St. Francis, c. s., Cheyenne Co., Kans., 1,103.
On Chi., Burl. & Quincy (R. R.).

—Aroostook Co., Maine, 1,000.
On Bangor & Aroostook (R. R.).
St. Francisville, Lawrence Co., Ill., 1,202.
On Cle., Cin., Chi. & St. Lou. (R. R.).
—c. s., West Feliciana Parish, La., 830.
On La. & Ark.; Ill. Cen. (R. Rs.).
St. Francois, St. Francois Co., Mo., 500.
On Mo. Ill. (R. R.).
St. Gabriel, Iberville Par., La., 768.
On Ill. Cen.; Mo. Pac. (R. R.).
St. Gabriel de Brandon, Berthier Co., Quebec, Canada, 1,530.
On Can. Pac. (R. R.).
St. Gallen, St. Gallen Canton, Switzerland, 64,020.
A rural center with embroidery industries.
St. George, Knox Co., Maine, 2,108.
—c. s., Dorchester Co., S. C., 1,639.
On Southern (R. R.).
—c. s., Washington Co., Utah, 2,434.
—Charlotte Co., N. B., Canada, 1,087.
On Can. Pac. (R. R.).
St. Germain, Dept. of Seine-et-Loire, France, 22,539.
A residential suburb of Paris.
St. Gilles, Brabant, Belgium, 65,298.
A suburb of Bruxelles.
St. Helena, Napa Co., Cal., 1,582.
On Sou. Pac.; San Fran., Napa & Cal. (R. Rs.).
St. Helens, Lancashire, England, 106,793.
An industrial suburb of Liverpool, notable for its glass manufactures.
—Columbia Co., Ore., 3,994.
On Spok., Port. & Seattle (R. R.).
St. Helier, capital of island of Jersey, Great Britain, 27,000.
Seaport and commercial center.
St. Henry, Mercer Co., Ohio, 571.
On Cle., Chi., Cin. & St. Lou. (R. R.).
St. Hyacinthe, St. Hyacinthe Co., Quebec, Canada, 13,448.
On Can. Nat.; Can. Pac. (R. Rs.).
Organs, leather, woolens, and farm implements.
St. Ignace, c. s., Mackinac Co., Mich., 2,109.
On Dul., Sou. Ch. & Atl. (R. R.).
St. Ignatius, Lake Co., Mont., 727.
St. Ingbert, Saar-Pfalz, Germany, 21,978.
St. James, c. s., Watonwan Co., Minn., 2,808.
On Mpls. & St. Lou.; Chi., St. P., Mpls. & Oma. (R. Rs.).
—Phelps Co., Mo., 1,294.
On St. Lou.-San Fran. (R. R.).
—Suffolk Co., N. Y., 1,167.
On Long Isl. (R. R.).
St. Jean (St. Johns), St. Jean Co., Que., Can., 11,256.
On Can. Nat.; Can. Pac.; Cen. Ver. (R Rs.).
St. Jerome, Terrebonne Co., Que., Can., 8,967.
On Can. Nat.; Can. Pac. (R. Rs.).
St. Jo, Montague Co., Texas, 960.
On Mo.-Kan.-Tex. of Tex. (R. R.).
St. Johann, Saar, Rhenish Prussia, 26,500.
Has iron foundries and machine shops.
St. John, St. John Co., Prov. of New Brunswick, Canada, 47,514; with county, 61,613.
Situated on the St. John River, at its entrance into the Bay of Fundy, and on the Canadian Pacific, and the Canadian National railroads. St. John is the winter port of Canada, and the commercial center of New Brunswick. Lumber, fish, furs, and agricultural produce being the chief exports.
—Capital of island of Antigua, British West Indies, 10,000.
—c. s., Stafford Co., Kans., 1,646.
On Atch., Top. & Santa Fe (R. R.).
—Whitman Co., Wash., 471.
On Un. Pac. (R. R.).
St. John Plantation, Aroostook Co., Me., 700.
St. John's, capital of Newfoundland, 39,886.
Situated near the eastern extremity of the peninsula, and on the Newfoundland Railroad. The harbor is inclosed by two mountains, affording a perfect shelter for vessels.
The principal buildings are the Government House, House of Assembly, poor-house, penitentiary, hospital, and several banks. The industries are foundries, tanneries, oil refineries, a net factory, boot and shoe plant, and gas works. The trade of St. John's consists chiefly in supplying fishermen with clothing, provisions, fishing and hunting gear.
St. Johns, c. s., Apache Co., Ariz., 1,300.
—c. s., Clinton Co., Mich., 3,929.
On Grand Trunk (R. R.).
—Quebec, Can. See St. Jean.
St. Johnsbury, c. s., Caledonia Co., Vt., 7,920.
On Can. Pac.; St. Johns. & L. Champ.; Me. Cen. (R. Rs.).
St. Johnsville, Montgomery Co., N. Y., 2,273.
On N. York Cen. (R. R.).
St. Joseph, Beauce Co., Que., Can., 1,625.
On Que. Cen. (R. R.).
—Champaign Co., Ill., 777.
On Cle., Cin. Chi. & St. Lou.; Ill. Term. (El.) (R. Rs.).
—c. s., Tensas Parish, La., 864.
On Mo. Pac. (R. R.).
—c. s., Berrien Co., Mich., 8,349.

On Mich. Cen.; Pere Marq. (R. Rs.).
Has metal, woodwork, paper, hosiery, electrical equipment, plants, etc.
—Stearns Co., Minn., 1,009.
On Gt. Nor. (R. R.).
—c. s., Buchanan Co., Mo., 80,935.
Situated on the Missouri River, and on the Atchison, Topeka & Santa Fe; Chicago, Burlington & Quincy; Chicago Great Western; Missouri Pacific; Chicago, Rock Island & Pacific; St. Joseph & Grand Island (Union Pacific); St. Joseph Terminal; and Union Terminal railroads.
The chief manufactures are packing house, and grain mill products, men's clothing, shoes, candies, writing tablets, dairy and brewery products, saddlery, etc. Large stock yards.
The city was established by Joseph Robidoux in 1843, and chartered as a city in 1885.
St. Laurent, Jacques-Cartier Co., Quebec, Canada, 5,348.
On Can. Nat. (R. R.).
St. Lawrence, Berks Co., Pa., 760.
St. Lô, capital of Dept. of Manche, France, 11,814.
Has important textile industries.
St. Louis, St. Louis City Co., Mo., 821,960.
Chief city of the State, situated on the west bank of the Mississippi River, 20 miles south of the mouth of the Missouri, and on the Alton; Alton & Southern; Baltimore & Ohio; Chicago, Burlington & Quincy; Chicago & Eastern Illinois; Chicago, Rock Island & Pacific; Cleveland, Cincinnati, Chicago & St. Louis; Illinois Central; Illinois Terminal (El.); Litchfield & Madison; Louisville & Nashville; Manufacturers; Missouri-Kansas-Texas; Missouri Pacific; Mobile & Ohio; New York, Chicago & St. Louis; Pennsylvania; St. Louis & O'Fallon; St. Louis-San Francisco; St. Louis Southwestern; Southern; Terminal Association of St. Louis; and Wabash railroads.

COURTESY FLORIDA EAST COAST RAILWAY

CATHEDRAL, ST. AUGUSTINE, FLORIDA, SAID TO BE THE OLDEST CATHOLIC CHURCH IN THE UNITED STATES

The river front is mostly a levee, lined with docks and warehouses. The Eads Bridge, a massive structure, was completed in 1874. Since then four other bridges have been built. St. Louis has a park system which constitutes one of its most attractive features. The largest are Forest Park, which comprises 1,380 acres; Tower Grove Park, covering 276 acres; the Shaw Missouri Botanical Garden, 75 acres, and the Fair Grounds, with 141 acres. The principal public buildings are the postoffice; the custom-house; the city hall; the public library; the court-house; the Civil Courts Building; the Union Railroad Station, with a trainhouse covering 30 tracks and used by 25 railroad companies; the Chamber of Commerce Building; the Railway Exchange Building; the Auditorium; the Mercantile Club Building; and a number of tall, modern office buildings.
Manufacturing represents about 60 per cent of the business of the city. In 1929 the value of its products was estimated at over one billion dollars. The principal industries are machinery, foundry products, woodenware, airplanes and parts, motors, boots and shoes, lumber, tobacco and cigars, meat packing, furs, chemicals, furniture, stoves, etc.
The institutions of higher education are Washington University and St. Louis University, several medical colleges, dental college, and theological seminaries. St. Louis was incorporated as a town in 1809, and as a city in 1822. In 1896 the city was swept by a destructive tornado. In 1904 an exposition was held to celebrate the Louisiana Purchase.
—Gratiot Co., Mich., 2,494.
On Pere Marq. (R. R.).
—Capital of Senegal, French West Africa, 30,817.
A commercial center and distributing point near Dakar.
St. Louis Park, Hennepin Co., Minn., 4,710.

On Chi., Mil., St. P. & Pac.; Mpls. & St. Lou.; Minn., Northf. & Sou. (R. Rs.).
St. Luce (Upper Frenchville), Aroostook Co., Maine, 1,500.
On Bangor & Aroostook (R. R.).
St. Malo, Dept. of Ille-et-Vilaine, France, 13,836.
A seaport and fisheries town.
St. Mande, an eastern suburb of Paris, France, adjoining the Bois de Vincennes, 22,253.
St. Maries, Benewah Co., Idaho, 1,996.
On Chi., Mil., St. P. & Pac. (R. R.).
St. Martin, Worcester Co., Md., 1,374.
St. Martinsville, c. s., St. Martin Parish, La., 2,455.
On Sou. Pac. (R. R.).
St. Marys, Camden Co., Ga., 732.
On St. Marys (R. R.).
—St. Joseph Co., Ind., 800.
—Pottawatomie Co., Kans., 1,216.
On Un. Pac. (R. R.).
—Ste. Genevieve Co., Mo., 554.
On St. Lou.-San Fran. (R. R.).
—Auglaize Co., Ohio, 5,433.
On N. York Cen.; N. York, Chi. & St. Lou. (R. Rs.).
—Elk Co., Pa., 7,433.
On Pitts., Shawmut & Nor.; Penna. (R. Rs.).
—c. s., Pleasants Co., W. Va., 2,182.
On Balt. & Ohio (R. R.).
—Perth Co., South, Ontario, Canada, 3,802.
On Can. Pac.; Can. Nat. (R. Rs.).
St. Marys College, Contra Costa Co., Cal., 750.
On Sacramento Nor. (El.) (R. R.).
St. Marys of the Lake, Lake Co., Ill., 500.
On Chi. No. Shore & Mil. (El.) (R. R.).
St. Matthews, c. s., Calhoun Co., S. C., 1,750.
On Southern (R. R.).
St. Maur-des-Fossés, Dept. of Seine, France, 56,740.
An industrial suburb of Paris.
St. Meinrad, Spencer Co., Ind., 439.
St. Michael, Cambria Co., Pa., 521.
On Penna. (R. R.).
St. Michaels, Talbot Co., Md., 1,308.
St. Mihiel, Dept. of Meuse, France, 4,581.
Tip of celebrated salient in the German lines which was assaulted and reduced by American forces in September, 1918.
St. Moritz, Canton of Grisons, Switzerland, 3,823.
St. Nazaire, Dept. of Loire-Inférieure, France, 43,281.
An important seaport and distributing center.
St. Nicholas, Schuylkill Co., Pa., 819.
On Reading (R. R.).
St Nicolas, East Flanders, Belgium, 41,527.
Linen manufactures.
St. Omer, Dept. of Pas-de-Calais, France, 18,373.
Linen, soap, sugar, briar-pipes, dyes, and liquors.
St. Ouen, Seine, France, 51,106.
An industrial suburb of Paris and a busy river port.
St. Paris, Champaign Cc., Ohio, 1,177.
On Det., Tol. & Iron.; Penna. (R. Rs.).
St. Paul, Neosho Co., Kans., 904.
On Mo.-Kan.-Tex. (R. R.).
—Decatur and Shelby Cos., Ind., 678.
On Cle., Cin., Chi. & St. Lou. (R. R.).
—c. s., Ramsey Co., Minn., State capital, 271,606.
Port of entry, situated on the Mississippi River, and on the Northern Pacific; the Great Northern; the Chicago, Milwaukee, St. Paul and Pacific; the Chicago, Rock Island and Pacific; the Chicago, St. Paul, Minneapolis and Omaha; the Minneapolis and St. Louis; the Chicago, Burlington and Quincy; the Minneapolis, St. Paul and Sault Ste. Marie; Chicago Great Western; and the Minnesota Transfer railroads.
It is the seat of Hamline University (Methodist Episcopal), Concordia College (Lutheran), Macalester College (Presbyterian), St. Paul's and St. Thomas's Seminaries (Roman Catholic), College of St. Catherine, St. Paul College of Law, several medical colleges, and an academy of natural sciences.
The principal buildings are the Capitol, State Historical Society Building, Court House and City Hall, Custom-house, Post-office, State Office Building, St. Paul's Cathedral, St. Paul Public Library, J. J. Hill Reference Library, State Law Library, and the Municipal Auditorium. Como Park, one of the beauty spots of St. Paul, covers over 400 acres.
Manufactures meat packing and dairy products, printing and publishing products, railway cars, paints, foundry products, fur goods, boots and shoes, and paper boxes.
St. Paul was first settled by French Canadians in 1838. It received its city charter in 1854.
—c. s., Howard Co., Neb., 1,621.
On Chi., Burl. & Quincy; Un. Pac. (R. Rs.).
—Robeson Co., N. C., 2,080.
On Va. & Car. Sou. (R. R.).
—Réunion Island, 22,679.
A seaport and commercial center.
—Wise Co., Va., 716.
On Clinchfield; Norf. & West. (R. Rs.).
St. Paul Park, Washington Co., Minn., 982.

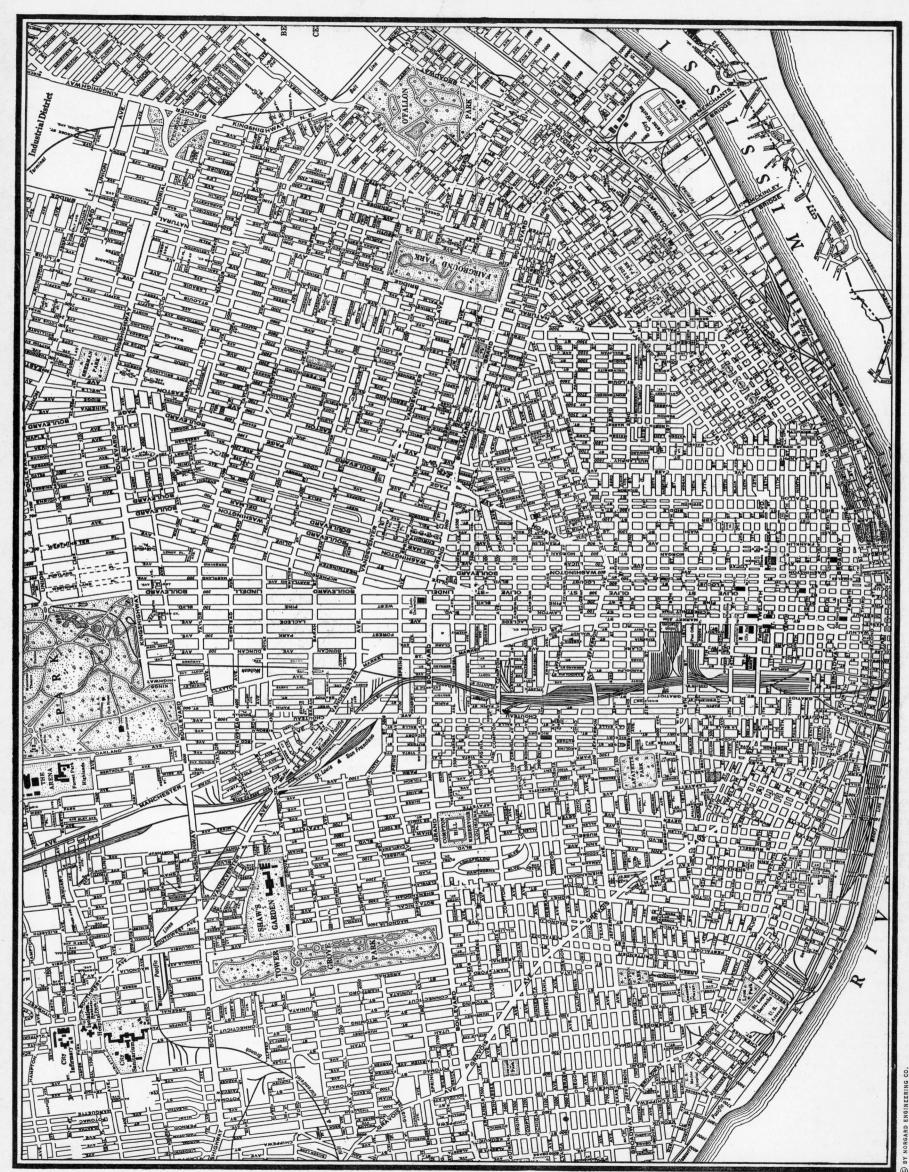

MAP OF THE CENTRAL SECTION OF ST. LOUIS, THE CHIEF CITY OF MISSOURI AND SEVENTH LARGEST CITY IN THE UNITED STATES. THE LOCATION OF ST. LOUIS NEAR THE ILLINOIS COAL FIELDS AND NEARNESS TO OTHER RAW MATERIALS, TOGETHER WITH ITS VAST ELECTRIC POWER AND TRANSPORTATION FACILITIES, HAVE MADE THE CITY A CENTER FOR MANUFACTURING AND DISTRIBUTION

On Chi., Burl. & Quincy (R. R.).
St. Pauls, Robeson Co., N. C., 2,080.
On Va. & Car. Sou. (R. R.).
St. Peter, Nicollet Co., Minn., 4,811.
On Chi. & Nor. West.; Chi., St. P., Mpls. & Oma. (R. Rs.).
St. Peter Port, capital of the island of Guernsey, Great Britain, 18,900.
Seaport and trade center.
St. Petersburg, Pinellas Co., Fla., 40,856.
On Atl. Coast Line; Seab. Air Line (R. Rs.).
Winter resort. A port and trade center as well as a popular resort.
—Capital of old Russia. See Leningrad.
St. Pierre, French island of Réunion, Indian Ocean, 22,048.
Has sugar and canning industries.
St. Pölten, Lower Austria, Germany, 31,619.
Railroad and industrial town with manufactures of cotton yarn, iron, and hardware.
St. Quentin, Aisne, France, 49,028.
Partly destroyed in the World War. In its vicinity bitter and prolonged fighting occurred between Anglo-American and German forces in the summer of 1918. Scene of great battles in earlier wars.
St. Raymond, Portneuf Co., Quebec, Canada, 1,772.
On Can. Nat. (R. R.).
St. Regis Falls, Franklin Co., N. Y., 1,080.
St. Remi, Napierville Co., Quebec, Canada, 1,201.
On Can. Nat. (R. R.).
St. Rose, Laval Co., Quebec, Canada, 1,661.
On Can. Pac. (R. R.).
St. Servan, Dept. of Ille-et-Vilaine, France, 12,323.
A fishing town.
St. Simons Island, Glynn Co., Ga., 1,000.
St. Stephen, Charlotte Co., N. B., Canada, 3,437.
On Can. Pac. (R. R.).
St. Stephens, Washington Co., Ala., 1,312.
—Berkeley Co., S. C., 911.
On Atl. Coast Line; Car. West. (R. Rs.).
Ste. Therese, Terrebonne Co., Quebec, Canada, 3,292.
On Can. Pac. (R. R.).
St. Thomas, capital of Elgin Co., West Ontario, Canada, 15,430.
On Can. Pac.; Can. Nat.; London & Pt. Stan. (El.); Mich. Cen.; Pere Marq.; Wab. (R. Rs.).
An industrial and educational center.
—Pembina Co., N. Dak., 595.
On Gt. Nor. (R. R.).
—(now again Charlotte Amalie), situated on the island of St. Thomas, Virgin Islands, 7,036.
Built chiefly on three hills which are the spurs of a mountain.
Charlotte Amalie has one of the finest harbors in the West Indies and is an important coaling and oil-fueling station. The United States government has constructed many new buildings, including Bluebeard Castle Hotel, to make this city a tourist winter resort.
St. Tite, Champlain Co., Quebec, Canada, 1,969.
On Can. Nat. (R. R.).
St. Trond (or Sanct Truijen), Prov. of Limburg, Belgium, 16,494.
Sakai, Ken of Osaka, Japan, 120,347.
A seaport and fishing center with varied manufactures.
Sakata, Prov. of Ugo, Ken of Akita, Japan, 31,700.
A seaport and trade center.
Salada Beach, San Mateo Co., Cal., 500.
Salamanca, Cattaraugus Co., N. Y., 9,577.
On Balt. & Ohio; Erie; Penna. (R. Rs.).
—Salamanca Prov., Spain, 49,801.
A railroad and commercial center. Seat of the famous University of Salamanca.
Salé, Morocco, 25,821.
A seaport and distribution point.
Sale City, Mitchell Co., Ga., 506.
On Flint Riv. & Northe. (R. R.).
Salem, c. s., Marion Co., Ill., 4,420.
On Balt. & Ohio; Chi. & East. Ill.; Mo.-Ill. (R. Rs.).
—c. s., Washington Co., Ind., 3,194.
On Chi., Ind. & Lou. (R. R.).
—c. s., Essex Co., Mass., 43,472.
Port of entry, on Massachusetts Bay and on the Boston & Maine railroad. A manufacturing center. Is also interesting for its rich and varied historical associations.
Salem was founded in 1626 by Roger Conant, and was in existence on the arrival of John Endicott and his Colonists in 1628.
—c. s., Dent Co., Mo., 2,250.
On St. Lou.-San Fran. (R. R.).
—Rockingham Co., N. H., 600.
On Bost. & Me. (R. R.).
—c. s., Salem Co., N. J., 8,047.
On Penna.-Read. Seash. (R. Rs.).
—Washington Co., N. Y., 1,081.
On Del. & Hud. (R. R.).
—Columbiana Co., Ohio, 10,622.
On Penna. (R. R.).
An agricultural center with manufactures of engines, stoves, organs, auto parts, rubber

products, and china. Situated in a gas and coal region.
—c. s., Marion Co., Ore., State capital, 26,266.
On the Willamette River, and the Oregon Electric, and Southern Pacific railroads, 53 miles south from Portland. In an agricultural and fruit-growing region. Water for manufacturing purposes is brought to the town from the Willamette and Santiam Rivers by an 18 mile canal. Manufactures dried and canned fruit. Seat of Willamette University. Salem was laid out in 1844 near a Methodist mission established in 1834; incorporated, 1853; permanent State capital, 1864.
—c. s., McCook Co., S. Dak., 1,171.
On Chi. & Nor. West.; Chi., St. P., Mpls. & Omaha (R. Rs.).
—c. s., Roanoke Co., Va., 4,833.
On Nor. & West.; Virginian (R. Rs.).
Seat of Roanoke College.
—Utah Co., Utah, 610.
On Salt L. & Utah (El.) (R. R.).
—Harrison Co., W. Va., 2,943.
On Balt. & Ohio (R. R.).

—Presidency of Madras, India, 102,181.
A river port and trade center with important weaving industries.
Salem Depot, Rockingham Co., N. H., 775.
On Bost. & Me. (R. R.).
Salerno, capital of Prov. of Salerno, Italy, 34,125.
Situated on the Gulf of Salerno, at the foot and on the side of a hill crowned by the remains of an ancient citadel. It is the seat of a seminary and a lyceum.
The city produces cotton goods, macaroni and cement. The foundation of Salerno is attributed to the Greeks.
Salford, Lancashire, England, 223,442.
An important manufacturing and commercial town. Chief products include cotton goods, iron, chemicals, furniture, rubber goods, engines, and machinery.
Salida, c. s., Chaffee Co., Colo., 5,065.
On Den. & Rio Gde. West. (R. R.).
—Stanislaus Co., Cal., 600.
On Sou. Pac. (R. R.).
Salina, c. s., Saline Co., Kans., 19,136.

On Atch., Top. & Santa Fe; Chi., Rk. Isl. & Pac.; Mo. Pac.; Un. Pac. (R. Rs.).
A leading trade center with large flour mills.
—Mayes Co., Okla., 582.
On Kans., Okla. & Gulf (R. R.).
—Westmoreland Co., Pa., 1,200.
On Penna. (R. R.).
—Sevier Co., Utah, 1,383.
On Den. & Rio Gde. West. (R. R.).
Salinas, c. s., Monterey Co., Cal., 10,263.
On Sou. Pac. (R. R.).
Situated in one of the richest agricultural regions in the country.
—Mun. of Salinas, Puerto Rico, 2,512.
Saline, Washtenaw Co., Mich., 1,009.
On Mich. Cen. (R. R.).
Saline, Perry Co., Mo., 1,069.
Salineville, Columbiana Co., Ohio, 2,133.
On Penna. (R. R.).
Salisbury, capital of Southern Rhodesia, 32,974.
A trade and commercial center located in a gold-mining region.
—Litchfield Co., Conn., 1,000.
On N. York, N. Hav. & Hart. (R. R.).

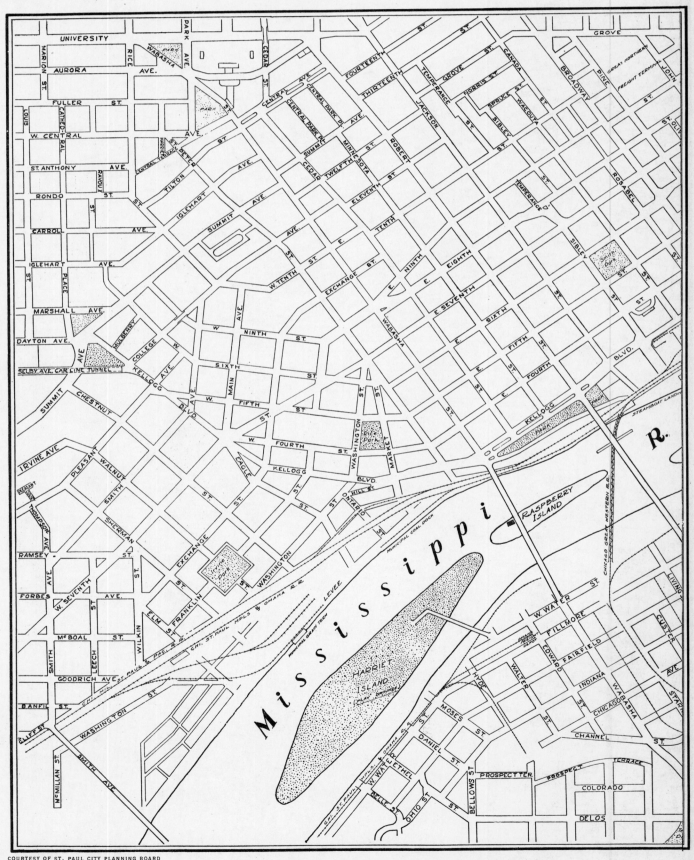

MAP OF THE CITY OF ST. PAUL, CAPITAL OF MINNESOTA. ST. PAUL JOINS MINNEAPOLIS AT THE NORTHWEST. THE TWO CITIES ARE CALLED THE "TWIN CITIES" AND FORM THE PRINCIPAL DISTRIBUTING CENTER FOR THE NORTHWEST

–c. s., Wicomico Co., Md., 10,997.
On Balt. & East.; Penna. (R. Rs.).
A wholesale distributing center for the "eastern shore."
–Essex Co., Mass., 2,245.
On Bost. & Me. (R. R.).
–Chariton Co., Mo., 1,768.
On Wabash (R. R.).
–c. s., Rowan Co., N. C., 16,951.
On Sou.; Yadkin (R. Rs.).
Has large textile mills. Granite quarries and iron deposits near by.
–Somerset Co., Pa., 710.
–capital of Wiltshire, England, 26,456.
A residential town with numerous places of historical interest.

Sallisaw, c. s., Sequoyah Co., Okla., 1,785.
On Kan. Cy. Sou.; Mo. Pac. (R. Rs.).

Salmon, c. s., Lemhi Co., Idaho, 1,371.
On Gilm. & Pitts. (R. R.).

Salmon Creek, Clark Co., Wash., 500.

Salmon Falls, Strafford Co., N. H., 500.
On Bost. & Me. (R. R.).

Salona, Greece. See Amphissa.

Salonika, Greece. See Thessalonike.

Salta, Salta Prov., Argentina, 34,236.
The center of an extensive farming and stock-raising region.

Saltcoats, Ayr, Scotland, 10,173.

Saltillo, capital of State of Coahuila, Mexico, 45,272.
On Nat. of Mexico (R. R.).
An active commercial and industrial town. Has several textile and flour mills.
–Hardin Co., Tenn., 500.

Salt Lake City, c. s., Salt Lake Co., Utah, State capital, 140,267.
Situated on the Jordan River and on the Bamberger Electric; Denver & Rio Grande Western; Los Angeles & Salt Lake (Un. Pac.); Union Pacific; and Western Pacific; Salt Lake & Utah (El.); Salt Lake, Garfield & Western (El.) (R. Rs.). At the base of the Wasatch Mountains, 4,334 feet above sea level. Contributes half of Utah's total manufactures of $150,000,000 annually. Center for the production of salt, sugar, candy, potash, and mineral; also for live stock and wool.
The important buildings are Mormon Temple, built at a cost of $5,000,000, the marble and granite State Capitol, Museum of Pioneer Relics, and many other buildings associated with the Mormons. Seat of University of Utah. The city was founded by 143 Mormons under Brigham Young in 1847.

Salto, Uruguay, 35,000.
The center of a stock-raising region.

Saltsburg, Indiana Co., Pa., 1,036.
On Penna. (R. R.).

Saltville, Smyth and Wash. Cos., Va., 2,964.
On Norf. & West. (R. R.).

Saluda, Polk Co., N. C., 558.
On Southern (R. R.).
–c. s., Saluda Co., S. C., 1,381.
On Aug. Nor. (R. R.).

Saluzzo, Prov. of Cuneo, Piedmont, Italy, 9,786.

Salvisa, Mercer Co., Ky., 500.

Salzburg, capital of Salzburg, Austria, 63,231.
A manufacturing and market town. It has a university and many interesting buildings, which include a cathedral.

Salzwedel, Prussian Saxony, Germany, 16,000.
Textiles, leather, and needles.

Samara, Sov. Union. See Kuibishev.

Samarkand, Uzbek Rep., Soviet Un., Asia, 154,600.
On the Zeravshan River and the Central Asiatic Railroad, the city is the trade and industrial center of Central Asia.

Sambor, East Galicia, Poland, 22,110.
A river port and trade center.

Samoa, Humboldt Co., Cal., 600.
On Northw. Pac. (R. R.).

Sampsel, Livingston Co., Mo., 500.
On Wabash (R. R.).

Samshui, Prov. of Kwangtung, China, 7,400.

Samson, Geneva Co., Ala., 1,656.
On Cen. of Ga.; Lou. & Nash. (R. Rs.).

Samsun, Vilayet of Samsun, Turkey, 33,839.
The center of a tobacco and cereal-growing district.

Sana, Yemen, Arabia, 20,000.
Marketing center for a fruit and farming region.

San Andreas, c. s., Calaveras Co., Cal., 1,082.

San Angelo, c. s., Tom Greene Co., Texas, 25,308.
On Gulf, Colo. & Santa Fe; Panh. & Santa Fe (R. Rs.).
In live stock and wool-growing region.

San Anselmo, Marin Co., Cal., 4,650.
On Northw. Pac. (R. R.).

San Antonio, c. s., Bexar Co., Texas, 231,542.
Situated on the San Antonio River, and on the International-Great Northern (Mo. Pac.); the Missouri-Kansas-Texas of Texas; the San Antonio, Uvalde and Gulf (Mo. Pac.), and the Texas and New Orleans (Sou. Pac.) Railroads. It is the seat of several collegiate and academic institutions and a military reservation. Notable buildings are the Federal building, courthouse, city hall, Cathedral of San Fernando, and the Alamo, part of the structure of an old Franciscan mission. It is a great retail and jobbing center for Southwest Texas and a large portion of Mexico. Also a live stock, wool and hide market. Noted for its mineral waters.
One mile north is Fort Houston, one of the most important military posts of the United States. San Antonio received a city charter in 1873.

San Antonio de los Banos, Prov. of Habana, Cuba, 10,645.
A tobacco town near Habana.

Sanatoga, Montgomery Co., Pa., 500.
On Reading (R. R.).

San Augustine, c. s., San Augustine Co., Texas, 1,247.
On Gulf, Colo. & Santa Fe (R. R.).

San Benito, Cameron Co., Texas, 10,753.
On San Ben. & Rio Gde. Val. (Mo. Pac.); St. Lou., Browns. & Mex. (Mo. Pac.) (R. Rs.).

San Bernardino, c. s., San Bernardino Co., Cal., 37,481.
Situated on the Atchison, Topeka & Santa Fe; Los Angeles & Salt Lake (Un. Pac.); and Southern Pacific; Union Pacific; and Pacific Electric railroads. The vicinity is noted for its beautiful scenery and healthful climate and for its mud, hot water, and sulphur baths. The industries include foundries and machine shops, mining, canning, and fruit and stock-raising. The annual National Orange Show is held here. The Santa Fe Railroad has large shops here. San Bernardino was founded in 1851 by Mormons.

San Bernardo, Prov. of Santiago, Chile, 14,464.
A suburb of Santiago.

Sanborn, O'Brien Co., Iowa, 1,213.
On Chi., Mil., St. P. & Pac. (R. R.).
–Redwood Co., Minn., 518.
On Chi. & Nor. West. (R. R.).

Sanbornville, Carroll Co., N. H., 850.
On Bost. & Me. (R. R.).

San Bruno, San Mateo Co., Cal., 3,610.
On Sou. Pac. (R. R.).

San Carlos, San Mateo Co., Cal., 1,132.
On Sou. Pac. (R. R.).
–Prov. of Nuble, Chile, 8,860.
–Prov. of Pangasinan, Luzon, P. I., 41,820.
A center of the sugar industry.

San Cataldo, Prov. of Caltanissetta, Sicily, 19,359.
Sulphur mines in the vicinity.

San Clemente, Orange Co., Cal., 667.
On Atch., Top. & Santa Fe (R. R.).

San Cristobal, Las Casas, Chiapas, Mexico, 16,780.
A marketing center.
–Capital of Táchira, Venezuela, 21,874.

Sancti Spiritus, Santa Clara Prov., Cuba, 87,620.
A trade and marketing town located in a grazing region.

Sand, Liberty Co., Tex., 500.

Sandakan, capital of British North Borneo, 13,826.

Sandborn, Knox Co., Ind., 641.
On Penna. (R. R.).

Sandcoulee, Cascade Co., Mont. (including Stockett), 1,000.

Sanderson, c. s., Terrell Co., Texas, 1,850.
On Tex. & N. Orl. (Sou. Pac.) (R. R.).

Sandersville, c. s., Washington Co., Ga., 3,011.
On Sandersv. (R. R.).
–Jones Co., Miss., 565.
On N. Orl. & Northe. (R. R.).

Sandgate, Queensland, Australia, 18,327.

San Diego, c. s., San Diego Co., Cal., 147,995.
Situated on the San Diego Bay, and on the Atchison, Topeka & Santa Fe and San Diego & Arizona Eastern Railroads. The city's harbor is one of the best in the world.
The first mission in California was founded here in 1769, and the city was laid out in 1867. The monument on the Mexican boundary, La Jolla Cave, Sweetwater Dam, Hotel del Coronado at Coronado Beach, Theosophical headquarters at Point Loma, Scripps Institution of Oceanography at La Jolla, the Stadium in Balboa Park, and the San Diego Mission are objects of local interest.
The industries include fishing, fruit and vegetable canning and packing.
San Diego Bay is the southern headquarters of the Pacific Squadron, United States Navy; the location of the U. S. Marine Corps base, and a Naval Training Station.
–c. s., Duval Co., Texas, 2,262.
On Tex. Mex. (R. R.).

San Dimas, Los Angeles Co., Cal., 2,087.
On Atch., Top. & Santa Fe; Pac. El.; Sou. Pac. (R. Rs.).

Sandoval, Marion Co., Ill., 1,264.
On Balt. & Ohio; Ill. Cen. (R. Rs.).
–Sandoval Co., N. Mex., 596.

Sandpoint, Bonner Co., Idaho, 3,290.
On Gt. Nor.; Nor. Pac.; Spok. Internat. (R. Rs.).

Sand Springs, Tulsa Co., Okla., 6,674.
On Sand Springs; Mo.-Kan.-Tex. (R. Rs.).

Sandston, Henrice Co., Va., 750.

Sandstone, Pine Co., Minn., 1,083.
On Gt. Nor. (R. R.).

Sandusky, c. s., Erie Co., Ohio, 24,622.
Port of entry at the mouth of the Sandusky River, an estuary of Lake Erie, and on the Balt. & Ohio; the Cle., Cin., Chi. & St. Lou.; the N. York Cen.; the N. York, Chi. & St. Lou., and the Penna. (R. Rs.).
There are great railroad terminal docks for lake traffic. Headquarters for fish industry. The city is adjacent to extensive limestone, gypsum marl and sand deposits. Its industries include the manufacture of rubber goods, paper products, artists' materials, precision instruments, tools, machinery, and cement.
–c. s., Sanilac Co., Mich., 1,305.
On Det., Caro. & Sand.; Pere Marq. (R. Rs.).
–Jefferson Co., Ala., 750.

Sandwich, Essex Co., North, Ontario, Canada, (1931) 10,715.
On Essex Terminal (R. R.).
Opposite Detroit, Mich.
–De Kalb Co., Ill., 2,611.
On Chi., Burl. & Quincy (R. Rs.).
–Barnstable Co., Mass., 1,516.
On N. York, N. Hav. & Hart. (R. R.).

Sandy, Salt Lake Co., Utah, 1,436.
On Den. & Rio Gde. West.; Un. Pac. (R. Rs.).

Sandy Creek, Oswego Co., N. Y., 648.

Sandy Hill, Washington Co., N. Y. See Hudson Falls.

Sandy Hook, Fairfield Co., Conn., 1,743.
On N. York, N. Hav. & Hart. (R. R.).

Sandy Lake, Mercer Co., Pa., 679.
On N. York Cen. (R. R.).

San Elizario, El Paso Co., Tex., 550.

San Fabian, Prov. of Pangasinan, Luzon, P. I., 15,998.
A trade and commercial center.

San Felipe, capital of Prov. of Aconcagua, Chile, 11,963.
A commercial town in a fertile valley near Santiago.
–(Hagan Junction), Sandoval Co., N. Mex., 647.
On Atch., Top. & Santa Fe (R. R.).

San Fernando, Los Angeles Co., Cal., 7,567.
On Pac. El.; So. Pac. (R. Rs.).
Citrus fruits, grapes and walnuts.
–capital of Prov. of Colchagua, Chile, 13,016.
–Prov. of La Union, Luzon, P. I., 19,885.
Tobacco, rice, abaca, sugar, and coconuts.
–Prov. of Cebu, Cebu, P. I., 20,029.
Located in a rice and sugar-raising district.
–Prov. of Pampanga, Luzon, P. I., 21,092.
Trade center of an agricultural area.
–Prov. of Cadiz, Spain, 26,953.
A naval port and commercial center.
–Trinidad, W. I., 15,024

Sanford, Covington Co., Ala., 750.
On Lou. & Nash. (R. Rs.).
–Conejos Co., Colo., 597.
–c. s., Seminole Co., Fla., 10,903.
On Atl. Coast Line (R. R.).
A winter resort.
–York Co., Maine, 13,392.
–Lee Co., N. C., 4,253.
On Atl. & West.; Atl. Coast Line; Seab. Air Line; Atl. & Yadk. (R. Rs.).

Sanford and Springvale, York Co., Me., 2,530.
On Bost. & Me. (R. R.).

San Francisco, c. s., San Francisco Co., Cal., 634,394.
Greater San Francisco, which includes Oakland and the Alameda, Berkeley, counties of Marin and San Mateo, contained in 1930 over two million people.
It is the most important commercial and ocean traffic point west of the Missouri River. It is situated on a peninsula with the ocean on one side and the bay of San Francisco on the other, and has an area of 42 square miles. On the site of the city are many hills. The highest of these, known as the "Twin Peaks," form a background to the leading thoroughfares and others are traversed by the fashionable residential streets. The most noted of these is Nob Hill, upon which the men who constructed the first overland railroad built their homes. From the famous Cliff House and the Sutro Heights, on the hills of the west or ocean side, is a magnificent view of the Seal Rocks and Pacific Ocean. The commercial part of the town is fairly level and lies along the bay. The chief business thoroughfare is Market Street, 3½ miles long, with which the streets from the north and west hills intersect. This feature gives the city a striking skyline.
On Atchison, Topeka & Santa Fe; Key System; Northwestern Pacific; Sacramento Northern (El.); Southern Pacific; Western Pacific (R. Rs.).
The harbor of San Francisco is one of the finest in the world, having an area of 450 square miles and navigable by the largest steamers. The entrance to the harbor is the famous Golden Gate, spanned by the now famous Golden Gate Bridge. Regular steamship lines connect the city with Japan, China, and ports in many other foreign countries.
Owing to these facilities, the commercial importance of San Francisco is considerable. Its situation on a peninsula, across which summer trade-winds blow, has given San Francisco a mild and healthful climate. Among the city's many features are the Civic Center, embracing a fine group of buildings, namely, the City Hall, Auditorium, War Memorial buildings, the State Building and Public Library, situated round a spacious plaza adorned with statuary and tropical flora. Other points of interest are the Presidio, Chinatown, Palace of Fine Arts (in Exposition Grounds), Golden Gate Memorial Museum, the Affiliated Colleges (which house the medical, dental and pharmaceutical departments of the University of California), the Museum of Anthropology, California Palace of the Legion of Honor, the Mission Dolores, and the Roman Catholic Cathedral. The largest of the city parks is Golden Gate Park, covering more than 1,000 acres and redeemed from a waste of sand dunes, now one of the most beautiful in the country.
On April 18, 1906, came the great earthquake, which shook down hundreds of houses in all quarters of the city and buried many scores of people under the ruins. Fire followed in the wake of the disaster and destroyed nearly forty square miles, or 508 blocks of the city. The total loss of the fire and earthquake was estimated at about $400,000,000. The rebuilding of the city was at once vigorously begun, and the destroyed portions were replaced. The downtown district, where nearly every building suffered, was completely rebuilt at a cost of $350,000,000.
The Panama-Pacific International Exposition was held here in 1915. This great international exposition covering 625 acres brilliantly celebrated the greatest achievement of the twentieth century—the completion of the Panama Canal, the joining of the Atlantic and the Pacific Oceans.
The first settlement at San Francisco was made by Spaniards, who in October, 1776, established a military post and a mission of Franciscan Friars. The Mexicans secured control of California in 1822, and a small village called Dolores grew up around the mission. In 1836, 3 miles northwest of the mission a village, Yerba Buena, was founded, and from this the modern city was developed. In 1846, when the United States took possession, Yerba Buena changed its old name to that of the mission and bay, San Francisco. The city was incorporated in 1850, and in 1856 the city and county were consolidated.

San Francisco de Macoris, Dom. Rep., 10,305.

San Gabriel, Los Angeles Co., Cal., 7,224.
On Sou. Pac.; Pac. El. (R. Rs.).

Sanger, Fresno Co., Cal., 2,967.
On Sou. Pac. (R. R.).
–Denton Co., Texas, 1,119.
On Gulf, Colo. & Santa Fe (R. R.).

Sangerhausen, Prussia, Germany, 11,079.
A trade and marketing town.

San German, Mun. of San German, Puerto Rico, 6,280.

Sangerville, Piscataquis Co., Maine, 700.
On Bangor & Aroostook (R. R.).

San Ildefonso, Prov. of Bulacan, Luzon, P. I., 8,973.
–Santa Fe Co., N. Mex., 500.
On Atch., Top. & Santa Fe; Den. & Rio Gde. West. (R. Rs.).

Sanitarium, Napa Co., Cal., 500.

San Jacinto, Riverside Co., Cal., 1,346.
On Atch., Top. & Santa Fe (R. R.).

San Javier de Loncomilla, Prov. of Linares, Chile, 6,281.

San Joaquin, Prov. of Iloilo, Panay, P. I., 17,842.
Situated in a timber and dyewoods region.

San José, Prov. of San José, Republic of Costa Rica, Central America, capital city, 63,635.
The center of a rich agricultural region. Has various institutions for higher education.

San Jose, c. s., Santa Clara Co., Cal., 57,651.
On Sou. Pac.; West. Pac. (R. Rs.).
Center for deciduous fruit and dairy products. Has canneries and plants for making cans and fruit-handling machinery.
–Prov. of Matanzas, Cuba, 1,356.
–Prov. of Camarines Sur, Luzon, P. I., 8,711.
–Prov. of Batangas, Luzon, P. I., 11,074.

San Juan, capital of San Juan Prov., Argentina, 20,000.
–San Benito Co., Cal., 772.
–Prov. of La Union, Luzon, P. I., 11,909.
Located in a timber region.
–Mun. of San Juan, capital of Puerto Rico, 137,215.
One of the most important seaports and commercial towns in the West Indies. Sugar, tobacco, coffee, and fruits are exported.
–Hidalgo Co., Texas, 1,615.
On St. L., Browns. & Mex. (Mo. Pac.) (R. R.).

San Juan Bautista de las Minas, Paraguay, 12,345.

San Juan Capistrano, Orange Co., Cal., 1,200.
On Atch., Top. & Santa Fe (R. R.).

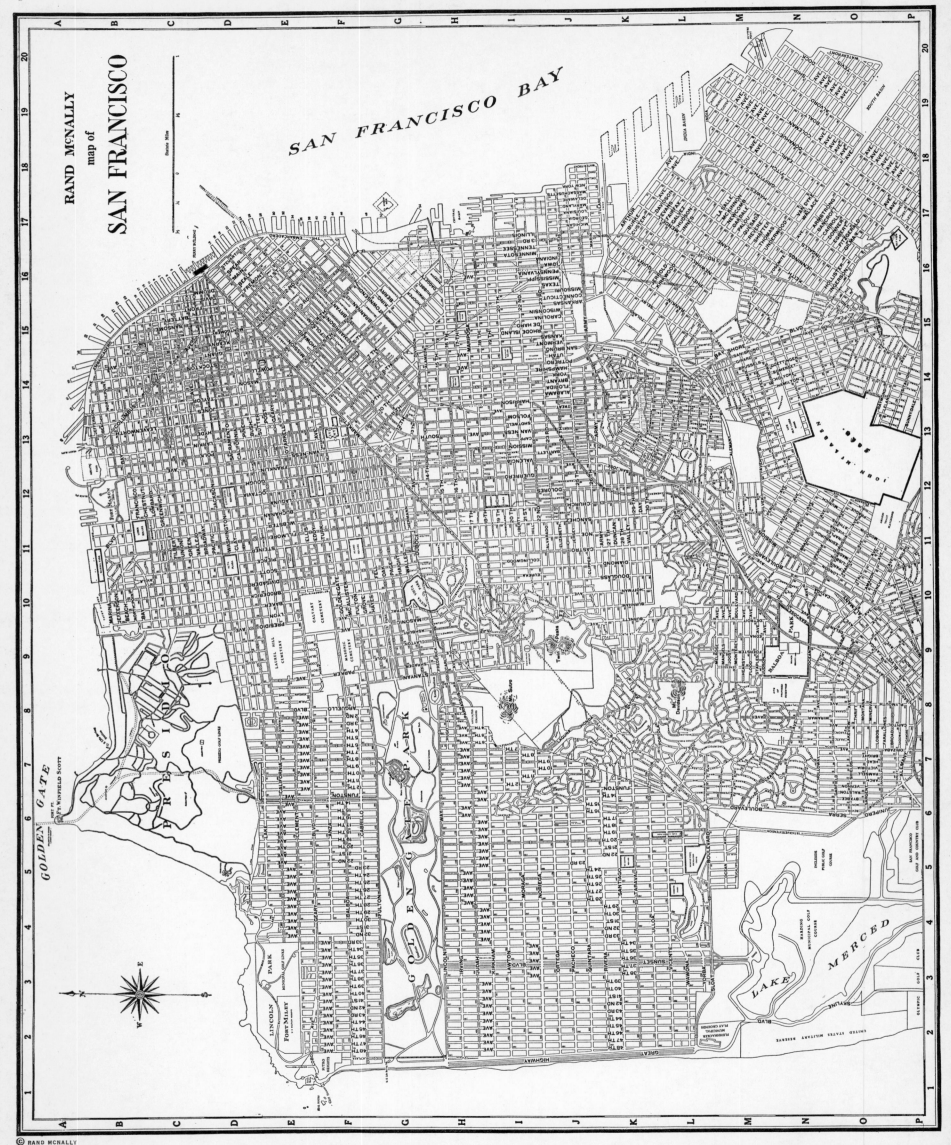

RAND McNALLY
map of
SAN FRANCISCO

SAN FRANCISCO BAY

MAP OF SAN FRANCISCO, THE SECOND LARGEST CITY ON THE PACIFIC COAST. IT IS SITUATED ON A PENINSULA WITH THE PACIFIC OCEAN ON THE WEST AND
SAN FRANCISCO BAY ON THE NORTH AND EAST. THE SITE OF SAN FRANCISCO IS EXTREMELY HILLY WITH EIGHT CHIEF PROMONTORIES OVERLOOKING THE BAY.

San Juan del Rio, State of Durango, Mexico, 1,966.
—Querétaro, Mexico, 7,020.
On Nat. of Mex. (R. R.).
Sankertown, Cambria Co., Pa., 917.
Sankt Polten, Lower Austria, 36,247.
A railroad and industrial center. Manufactures cotton, iron, and hardware.
San Leandro, Alameda Co., Cal., 11,455.
On Sou. Pac.; West. Pac. (R. Rs.).
Caterpillar tractors are manufactured here.
San Lorenzo, Mun. of San Lorenzo, Puerto Rico, 5,292.
—(Lorenzo), Alameda Co., Cal., 500.
On Sou. Pac.; West. Pac. (R. Rs.).
San Lúcar de Barrameda, Cadiz, Spain, 7,103.
San Luis, capital of San Luis Prov., Argentina, 24,870.
A trade center in a mining and agricultural district.
—Prov. of Santiago, Cuba, 5,546.
—Prov. of Pampanga, Luzon, P. I., 9,785.
—Costilla Co., Colo., 750.
San Luis Obispo, c. s., San Luis Obispo Co., Cal., 8,276.
On Pac. Coast; Sou. Pac. (R. Rs.).
San Luis Potosi, San Luis Potosi State, Mexico, 72,561.
On National of Mex.; Potosi & Rio Verde (R. Rs.).
An important distributing point in a mining and agricultural district.
San Marco in Lamis, Prov. of Foggia, Italy, 18,214.
A marketing town.
San Marcos, c. s., Hays Co., Tex., 5,134.
On Mo.-Kan.-Tex. of Tex. (R. R.).
Cotton center. Seat of Southwest Texas State Normal School.
San Marino, Los Angeles Co., Cal., 3,730.
On Pac. El.; Sou. Pac. (R. Rs.).
San Mateo, San Mateo Co., Cal., 13,444.
On Sou. Pac. (R. R.).
A suburb of San Francisco.
San Miguel, San Miguel Dept., Salvador, 41,109.
On Int. of Cen. Amer. (R. R.).
—Prov. of Bulacan, Luzon, P. I., 18,147.
A suburb of Manila.
—State of Guanajuato, Mexico, 8,626.
On National of Mexico (R. R.).
Sannicandro Garganico, Prov. of Foggia, Italy, 12,364.
San Nicholas, Prov. of Ilocos Norte, Luzon, P. I., 12,259.
San Nicolas de los Arroyos, Prov. of Buenos Aires, Argentine Republic, 50,493.
A busy port and distributing point.
San Pablo, Prov. of Lacuna, Luzon, P. I., 31,500.
San Pedro, Honduras, 17,500.
A trade and marketing center for farm produce.
—Los Angeles Co., Cal. (Pop. incl. in Los Angeles P. O.).
On Atch.; Top. & Santa Fe; Pac. El.; Un. Pac.; Sou. Pac. (R. Rs.).
San Pedro de Macoris, Dom. Rep., 18,889.
San Rafael, c. s., Marin Co., Cal., 8,022.
On Northw. Pac. (R. R.).
—Prov. of Bulacan, Luzon, P. I., 8,122.
San Remigio, Antique, Panay, P. I., 6,271.
San Remo, Prov. of Remo, Italy, 19,456.
A winter resort.
San Saba, c. s., San Saba Co., Texas, 2,240.
On Gulf, Colo. & Santa Fe (R. R.).
San Salvador, Capital of Dept. of San Salvador, Salvador, 97,161.
The commercial center and leading industrial town. Manufactures of soap, ice, candles, silks, textiles, cigars, and liquors.
San Sebastian, Mun. of San Sebastian, Puerto Rico, 3,826.
A seaport and industrial town with manufactures of lumber, flour, soap, glass, and paper.
—Capital of Prov. of Guipúzoca, Spain, 86,292.
San Severo, Prov. of Foggia, Italy, 33,237.
Surrounded by vineyards and olive groves.
San Simon, Cochise Co., Ariz., 700.
On Sou. Pac. (R. R.).
Santa Ana, c. s., Orange Co., Cal., 30,322.
On Atch., Top. & Santa Fe; Pac. El.; Sou. Pac. (R. Rs.).
In fruit section. Tourist resort.
—Salvador, 77,316.
Cigars, pottery, sugar, and textiles.
Santa Anna, Coleman Co., Tex., 1,883.
On Gulf, Colo. & Santa Fe (R. R.).
Santa Barbara, c. s., Santa Barbara Co., Cal., 33,613.
Situated on Santa Barbara Channel and on the Southern Pacific Railroad, 270 miles S. S. W. of San Francisco.
Its location is particularly favorable to producing the dry and equable climate that has made it a favorite health resort during the winter months, and won for it the name, "American Mentone." Santa Barbara is in the midst of a fertile grapegrowing district which is also rich in other fruits as well as in nuts and flowers. It is a depot for olive, petroleum, asphaltum and wool. Within the past few years the vicinity of the city has become noted

for the production of petroleum and asphaltum. The first settlement at this point was made by Mexicans in 1782.
—State of Minas Geras, Brazil, 61,403.
A mining and trade center.
—Prov. of Iloilo, Panay, P. I., 32,000.
Sugar, corn, rice, coconuts, and tobacco are cultivated in the vicinity.
—Prov. of Pangasinan, Luzon, P. I., 13,227.
A river port and marketing town.
Santa Clara, Santa Clara Co., Cal., 6,302.
On Southern Pacific (R. R.).
Fruit preserving and packing. In apricot and prune section. Seat of University of Santa Clara (Catholic).
—Prov. of Santa Clara, Cuba, 26,800.
Located in a sugar growing district.
Santa Cruz, capital of Dept. of Sta. Cruz, Bolivia, 30,851.
Located in an agricultural and live stock raising district.
—Island of Tenerife, Capital of Canary Islands, 60,700.
An important coaling port and commercial center.
—c. s., Santa Cruz Co., Cal., 14,395.
On Southern Pacific (R. R.).
Located in the heart of the redwood region. Fruit growing is principal industry.
—Santa Fe Co., N. Mex., 600.
—Laguna Prov. of Luzon, P. I., 14,151.
In a fertile agricultural region.
Santa Cruz Quiché, Guatemala. See Quiché.
Santa Fe, capital of Prov. of Santa Fe, Argentina, 138,428.
A river port, railroad center, and commercial city situated in an agricultural and stock raising region.
—c. s., Santa Fe Co., N. Mex., State capital, 11,176.
On the Atchison, Topeka and Santa Fe and the Denver and Rio Grande Western Railroads. The town is in an agricultural, stock-raising, and mineral region, which contains gold, silver, copper, lead, zinc, coal, marble, building stone, clay, and gypsum.
In the old part of Santa Fe, the oldest settlement in the United States next to St. Augustine, the streets are narrow and crooked, but in the newer part they are wide and regularly laid out. In the plaza is a soldiers' memorial monument and the old Spanish governor's building, now the official residence of the chief executive, containing the treasures of the New Mexico Historical Society. The old Church of San Miguel, said to be the oldest in the United States, built about 1605, was destroyed by the Indians and rebuilt in 1710. The new Cathedral of San Francisco was built around the former one erected in 1622.
The site of Santa Fe was formerly occupied by an Indian pueblo. In 1605 the Spaniards occupied the place and reduced the Indians to slavery. In 1680 the Indians expelled the Spaniards, burned all their archives, and obliterated all traces of the rich mines of the country. In 1692 Vargas again captured the place for the Spaniards who held it until 1821, when Mexico declared its independence. In 1846 United States troops under General S. W. Kearney took the city; in 1848 the territory was ceded to the United States, and in 1851 created the Territory of New Mexico, with Santa Fe as the capital.
Santa Fe de Bogota. See Bogota.
Santa Fe de Guanajuato, Mexico. See Guanajuato.
Santa Fe Springs, Los Angeles Co., Cal., 2,020.
On Atch., Top. & Santa Fe (R. R.).
Santa Isabel, Prov. of Bulacan, Luzon, P. I., 9,000 (estimated).
—Mun. of Ponce, Puerto Rico, 2,053.
Santa Margarita, San Luis Obispo Co., Cal., 700.
On Sou. Pac. (R. R.).
Santa Maria, Prov. of Ilocos Sur, Luzon, P. I., 11,743.
—Santa Barbara Co., Cal., 7,057.
On Pac. Coast; Sta. Maria Val. (R. Rs.).
Santa Maria Capua Vetere, Prov. of Napoli, Italy, 20,591.
Has interesting historical relics.
Santa Marta, Dept. of Magdalena, Colombia, 22,067.
A seaport and trading center.
Santa Monica, Los Angeles Co., Cal., 37,146.
On Mo. Pac.; Pac. El. (R. Rs.).
A seaside resort and suburb of Los Angeles.
Santander, Prov. of Santander, Spain, 90,774.
One of the chief seaports of Spain.
Santa Paula, Ventura Co., Cal., 7,452.
On Sou. Pac. (R. R.).
Santaquin, Utah Co., Utah, 1,115.
On Den. & Rio Gde. West. (R. R.).
Santa Rita, Grant Co., N. Mex., 1,500.
On Atch., Top. & Santa Fe (R. R.).
Santa Rosa, Honduras, 10,807.
—c. s., Sonoma Co., Cal., 10,636.
On Nw. Pac.; Petaluma & Sta. Rosa (R. Rs.).
Shipping center for hops and prunes. Fruit

canning and drying and other industries.
—c. s., Guadalupe Co., N. Mex., 1,127.
On Chi., Rk. Isl. & Pac.; Sou. Pac. (R. Rs.).
—Cameron Co., Tex., 737.
On Tex. & N. Orl. (R. R.).
Santiago, capital of Santiago del Estero, Argentina, 45,875.
An important commercial center in a farming region. Chief products are grain, hides, tobacco, and cotton.
—capital of Prov. of Santiago and of Chile, 829,240.
Situated in a large, fertile plain, on the Mapocho River, near the foot of the Andes.
The city is of Spanish architecture. Attractive promenades, boulevards, and squares have been constructed. The Tajamar, on the banks of the Mapocho, is a vast embankment of solid masonry to protect the city from the inroads of the river. Santiago was founded in 1541.
—Dominican Republic, 35,927.
—Prov. of Coruña, Spain, 25,870.
The city is celebrated for its silversmiths' work.
Santiago de Cuba, capital of Prov. of Santiago de Cuba, 144,975.
Situated on a splendid harbor 5 miles long, and defended by forts.
Santiago is second in population of the cities of the island. It is the center of a rich agricultural region.
Santiago was founded by Velasquez in 1524. It was the objective point of the American land operations during the war with Spain (1898), and outside its harbor occurred the second of the two great naval battles of the war (July 3, 1898). In this engagement the Spanish fleet, consisting of six cruisers, was totally destroyed, 350 men being killed and about 1,700 being made prisoners. The American loss was one killed and ten wounded. Two weeks later the Americans occupied the city, and continued to hold it until the evacuation of Cuba in 1902.
Santiago de Guatemala. See Guatemala.
Santiago de Guayaquil. See Guayaquil.
Santiago de las Vegas, Prov. of Habana, Cuba, 6,287.
Santipur, Prov. of Bengal, India, 24,992.
Situated 50 miles north of Calcutta.
Santo, Palo Pinto Co., Tex., 524.
On Tex. & Pac. (R. R.).
Santo Amaro, Bahia, Brazil, 105,341.
An active trade center and river port.
Santo Domingo, Prov. of Santa Clara, Cuba, 3,244.
—Prov. of Ilocos Sur, Luzon, P. I., 13,019.
—Capital, Dominican Republic, West Indies, See Ciudad Trujillo.
Christopher Columbus was buried here until 1796; his remains were then removed to Habana, Cuba.
Santos, São Paulo, Brazil, 105,000.
Important coffee shipping port.
Santo Tomas, Prov. of Batangas, Luzon, P. I., 13,125.
San Vicente, Salvador, 33,495.
Situated in a volcanic region abounding in hot springs and geysers.
San Ysidro, San Diego Co., Cal., 1,368.
On San Diego & Ariz. East. (R. R.).
São João d'el Rey, State of Minas Geraes, Brazil, 66,747.
A trade and mining center.
São Luiz de Maranhao, capital of State of Maranhao, Brazil, 66,500.
A seaport which exports much cotton, sugar, and rice.
São Paulo, capital of State of São Paulo, Brazil, 1,151,249.
The world's center of the coffee raising industry. Has also an exceedingly large trade in other agricultural products. Manufactures textiles, furniture, clothing, machinery.
São Paulo de Luanda (Loanda), capital of Angola, 17,947.
A seaport and export center for palm oil, coffee, hides, ivory, rubber, and various mineral ores.
São Salvador (Bahia), capital of State of São Salvador (Bahia), Brazil, 363,726.
São Salvador is the seat of the Primate of Brazil and excels all other cities of the republic in the number of its ecclesiastical buildings. The city has a fine harbor and a large shipping trade. Important exports are rosewood, sugar, hides, dyewoods, tobacco, cacao, and coffee.
São Salvador is the oldest city in Brazil. Bahia Bay was entered by Amerigo Vespucci in 1503, and the city was founded in 1510 by a Portuguese navigator, Correa.
Sapporo (or Satsupro), Ken of Yezo, Japan, 196,541.
An agricultural town with manufactures of flour, hemp, flax, beer, and lumber.
Sapulpa, c. s., Creek Co., Okla., 10,533.
On St. Lou.-San Fran.; Sapulpa Un. (El.) (R. Rs.).
Oil center with an extensive refinery, also has glass factories and cotton compresses.
Sara, Prov. of Iloilo, Panay, P. I., 27,100.
A marketing center in a farming district.
Saragossa, Spain. See Zaragoza.

Sarajevo, capital of Drina Banat, Yugoslavia, 78,182.
Site of the murder of Archduke Ferdinand of Austria, an event which led to the World War.
Saranac, Ionia Co., Mich., 729.
On Grand Trunk (R. R.).
Saranac Inn, Franklin Co., N. Y., 500.
On N. York Cen. (R. R.).
Saranac Lake, Franklin and Essex Cos., N. Y., 8,020.
On Del. & Hud.; N. York Cen. (R. Rs.).
Sarasota, c. s., Sarasota Co., Fla., 9,802.
On Atl. Coast Line; Seab. Air Line (R. Rs.).
Saratoga, Santa Clara Co., Cal., 1,091.
—Hardin Co., Tex., 1,525.
—Carbon Co., Wyo., 567.
On Sarat. & Encamp. Val. (R. R.).
Saratoga Springs, Saratoga Co., N. Y., 13,169.
On Bost. & Me.; Del. & Hud. (R. Rs.).
A famous health and pleasure resort, site of world famous mineral springs.
Saratov, Soviet Union, 327,500.
A port and commercial center on the Volga River with manufactures of iron, lumber, and flour. Has various educational institutions.
Saravia, Negros Occidental Prov., Negros, P. I., 13,984.
A commercial and marketing town.
Sarcoxie, Jasper Co., Mo., 1,017.
On St. Lou.-San Fran. (R. R.).
Sardinia, Brown Co., Ohio, 564.
On Norf. & West. (R. R.).
Sardis, c. s., Panola Co., Miss., 1,298.
On Ill. Cen. (R. R.).
—Burke Co., Ga., 580.
On Sav. & Atl. (R. R.).
Sargent, Custer Co., Neb., 834.
On Chi., Burl. & Quincy (R. R.).
Sariaya, Luzon, P. I., 14,045.
Sarnia, capital of Lambton Co., Ontario, Canada, 18,191.
On Can. Nat.; Pere Marq. (R. Rs.).
A town and port of entry on the St. Clair River. Has large petroleum refineries.
Sarno, Prov. of Salerno, Italy, 11,573.
Sarpsborg, Norway, 12,401.
A seaport and industrial town. Has paper and textile mills.
Sarreguemines, Dept. of Moselle, France, 16,001.
Has manufactures of plush, velvet, porcelain, and pottery.
Sartell, Benton and Stearns Cos., Minn., 521.
On Nor. Pac. (R. R.).
Sarver, Butler Co., Pa., 530.
On Penna. (R. R.).
Sasakwa, Seminole Co., Okla., 781.
On St. Lou.-San. Fran. (R. R.).
Sasebo, Nagasaki Ken, Japan, 133,172.
A commercial and trade center near Nagasaki.
Saskatoon, Saskatoon Co., Saskatchewan, Canada, 41,734.
On Can. Nat.; Can. Pac. (R. Rs.).
An agricultural trade center. Has manufactures of flour, tractors, clothing, brick, and cement.
Sassari, capital of Prov. of Sassari, Italy, 35,862.
Has a number of interesting historical landmarks.
Satanta, Haskell Co., Kan., 421.
On Atch., Top. & Santa Fe (R. R.).
Satara, Bombay, India.
Satu-Mare, Maramuresh, Rumania, 51,074.
Saugatuck, Allegan Co., Mich., 606.
—(Westport), Fairfield Co., Conn., 1,500.
On N. York, N. Hav. & Hart. (R. R.).
Saugerties, Ulster Co., N. Y., 4,060.
On West Shore (R. R.).
Chief industry: paper production. Tourist point for Catskills.
Saugus, Essex Co., Mass., 15,076.
On Bost. & Me. (R. R.).
A residential suburb of Boston.
Sauk Center, Stearns Co., Minn., 2,716.
On Gt. Nor.; Nor. Pac. (R. Rs.).
Sauk City, Sauk Co., Wis., 1,137.
On Chi., Mil., St. P. & Pac. (R. R.).
Sauk Rapids, c. s., Benton Co., Minn., 2,656.
On Gt. Nor.; Nor. Pac. (R. Rs.).
Sault Sainte Marie, c. s., Chippewa Co., Mich., 13,755.
Port of call for lake traffic, on the St. Mary's River near outlet of Lake Superior, 350 miles north of Detroit, on the Canadian Pacific; the Duluth, South Shore and Atlantic; and the Minneapolis, St. Paul and Sault Sainte Marie railroads. Has great water power; the fall at the rapids is 20 feet, with a flow of 80,000 cubic feet of water per second.
The Michigan Northern Power Company has a canal and power plant built at a cost of $6,500,000. The canal is two and a half miles long, and 200 feet wide.
The city is noted for its great Government Locks, known as the Soo Locks, which connect Lake Superior and Lake Huron. These locks with the St. Mary's River carry an enormous commerce.
First settled in 1668.
—Capital of Algoma Co., Ontario, Canada, 23,045.

A port of entry and commercial center.
The "Twin" of the America Sault Ste. Marie.
On Alg. Cen. & Hud. Bay; Can. Pac. (R. Rs.).
SAUMUR, Dept. of Maine-et-Loire, France, 17,158.
A wine center.
SAUNDERSVILLE, Worcester Co., Mass., 500.
On N. York, N. Hav. & Hart. (R. R.).
SAUQUOIT, Oneida Co., N. Y., 700.
On Del., Lack. & West. (R. R.).
SAUSALITO, Marin Co., Cal., 3,667.
On Northw. Pac. (R. R.).
On San Francisco Bay, about six miles north
of San Francisco.
SAVAGE, Howard Co., Md., 1,100.
On Balt. & Ohio (R. R.).
SAVANNA, Carroll Co., Ill., 5,086.
On Chi., Burl. & Quincy; Chi., Mil., St. P. &
Pac. (R. Rs.).
-Pittsburg Co., Okla., 525.
On Mo.-Kan.-Tex. (R. R.).
SAVANNAH, Chatham Co., Ga., 85,024.
Port of entry, on the Savannah River, and on
the Central of Georgia; Atlantic Coast Line;
Seaboard Air Line; Southern; and Savannah
and Atlanta railroads.
The industries are cotton and cotton-seed prod-
ucts, boats, lumber, auto tops, sugar refining
and phosphate fertilizers.
Savannah was founded in 1733 by General
Oglethorpe. It was chartered as a city in 1789.
-c. s., Andrew Co., Mo., 1,888.
On Chi., Burl. & Quincy; Chi. Gt. West. (R.
Rs.).
-c. s., Hardin Co., Tenn., 1,129.
-Wayne Co., N. Y., 600.
On N. York Cen.; West Shore (R. Rs.).
SAVIGLIANO, Prov. of Cuneo, Italy, 10,046.
SAVONA, Prov. of Savona, Italy, 51,832.
A seaport and center of Italy's iron industries.
-Steuben Co., N. Y., 545.
On Del., Lack. & West.; Erie (R. Rs.).
SAWTELLE, Cal. See WEST LOS ANGELES.
SAWYER, Door Co., Wis., 1,200.
SAWYERVILLE, Macoupin Co., Ill., 501.
On Ill. Term. (El.) (R. R.).
SAWYERWOOD, Summit Co., Ohio, 507.
SAXIS, Accomac Co., Va., 726.
SAXON, Iron Co., Wis., 948.
On Chi. & Nor. West.; Dul., So. Shore & Atl.
(R. Rs.).
-Spartanburg Co., S. C., 1,650.
On Piedmont & Nor. (El.) (R. Rs.).
SAXTON, Berford Co., Pa., 1,128.
On Hunt. & Broad Top Mt. (R. R.).
SAXTONS RIVER, Windham Co., Vt., 670.
SAYBROOK (Old Saybrook), Middlesex Co., Conn.,
1,643.
On N. York, N. Hav. & Hart. (R. R.).
-McLean Co., Ill., 746.
On N. York, Chi. & St. Lou. (R. R.).
-Ashtabula Co., Ohio, 600.
On N. York Cen.; N. York, Chi. & St. Lou.
(R. Rs.).
SAYLESVILLE, Providence Co., R. I., 1,416.
On Moshas. Val. (R. R.).
SAYRE, c. s., Beckham Co., Okla., 3,157.
On Chi., Rk. Isl. & Pac. (R. R.).
-(Sayre Mines), Jefferson Co., Ala., 640.
On Lou. & Nash. (R. R.).
-Bradford Co., Pa., 7,902.
On Leh. Val. (R. R.).
SAYRETON, Jefferson Co., Ala., 987.
On Sou. (R. R.).
SAYREVILLE, Middlesex Co., N. J., 8,658.
On Raritan Riv. (R. R.).
SAYVILLE, Suffolk Co., N. Y., 3,800.
On Long Isl. (R. R.).
SCALP LEVEL (Windber), Cambria Co., Pa., 1,875.
On Penna. (R. R.).
SCAMMON, Cherokee Co., Kans., 899.
On Northe. Okla. (El.); St. Lou.-San Fran.
(R. R.).
SCANDIA, Republic Co., Kans., 630.
On Chi., Rk. Isl. & Pac.; Mo. Pac. (R. Rs.).
SCANTIC (E. Windsor), Hartford Co., Conn.,
3,815.
On N. York, N. Hav. & Hart. (R. R.).
SCARBORO, Cumberland Co., Maine, 2,445.
On Bost. & Me. (R. R.).
SCARBOROUGH, Yorkshire, England, 41,791.
A tourist resort and fishing port.
SCARBRO, Fayette Co., W. Va., 950.
On Chesa. & Ohio (R. R.).
SCARSDALE, Westchester Co., N. Y., 9,690.
On N. York Cen. (R. R.).
SCHAEFFERSTOWN, Lebanon Co., Pa., 900.
SCHAERBEEK, Prov. of Brabant, Belgium, 122,790.
A suburb of Bruxelles.
SCHAFFHAUSEN, canton of Schaffhausen, Switzer-
land, 34,100.
A lumber and agricultural center. Has watch
and clock factories.
SCHAGHTICOKE, Rensselaer Co., N. Y., 555.
On Bost. & Me. (R. R.).
SCHALLER, Sac Co., Iowa, 724.
On Chi. & Nor. West. (R. R.).
SCHELL CITY, Vernon Co., Mo., 413.
On Mo.-Kan.-Tex. (R. R.).
SCHENECTADY, c. s., Schenectady Co., N. Y.,
95,692.

Situated on the Erie Canal, the Mohawk River,
and the New York Central, the Delaware &
Hudson (R. Rs.), and the Fonda, Johnstown &
Gloversville (R. Rs.).
It is the seat of Union University, founded in
1795, which includes with the college depart-
ment, schools of law, medicine and pharmacy.
The manufactures are mechanical and textile.
The locomotive plant located here is one of
largest of its kind in the country; here are also
the shops and headquarters of the General
Electric Company. Terminal of State Barge
Canal.
Schenectady was settled in 1661. It received a
city charter in 1798.
SCHENEVUS, Otsego Co., N. Y., 562.

On Del. & Hud. (R. R.).
SCHERERVILLE, Lake Co., Ind., 580.
On Penna. (R. R.).
SCHIEDAM, South Holland, Netherlands, 61,038.
Has great gin distilleries.
SCHILLER PARK, Cook Co., Ill., 709.
On Mpls., St. P. & S. Ste. M. (R. R.).
SCHILTIGHEIM, Bas Rhin, France, 22,074.
A suburb of Strasbourg.
SCHIMBARA, Ken of Nagasaki, island of Kiushiu,
Japan, 20,000.
SCHLEISINGERVILLE, Wis. See SLINGER.
SCHLEIZ, Principality of Reuss-Schleiz (Younger
Branch), Germany, 6,120.
SCHLESWIG, Crawford Co., Iowa, 638.
On Chi. & Nor. West. (R. R.).
-capital of Schleswig-Holstein, Germany, 19,000.
Situated in a rich dairying region.
SCHLETTSTADT, France. See SELESTAT.
SCHMALKALDEN, Hesse-Nassau, Prussia, Germany,
10,401.
SCHMÖLLN, Thüringen, Germany, 13,475.
Buttons, cigars, and wooden shoes.
SCHNECKSVILLE, Lehigh Co., Pa., 680.
SCHOFIELD, Marathon Co., Wis., 1,287.
On Chi., Mil., St. P. & Pac.; Chi. & Nor. West.
(R. Rs.).
SCHOHARIE, c. s., Schoharie Co., N. Y., 827.
On Schoh. Val. (R. R.).
SCHÖNEBECK, Prussia, Germany, 35,100.
Has manufactures of chemicals, machinery,
bicycles, rubber, and explosives.
SCHOOLCRAFT, Kalamazoo Co., Mich., 833.
On N. York Cen.; Gd. Tr. (R. Rs.).
SCHRAM CITY, Montgomery Co., Ill., 867.
SCHROON LAKE, Essex Co., N. Y., 500.
SCHULENBURG, Fayette Co., Tex., 1,604.
On Tex. & N. Orl. (Sou. Pac.) (R. R.).
SCHULTER, Okmulgee Co., Okla., 650.
On St. Lou.-San Fran. (R. R.).
SCHUYLER, c. s., Colfax Co., Neb., 2,588.

On Chi., Burl. & Quincy; Un. Pac. (R. Rs.).
-Nelson Co., Va., 700.
On Nelson & Albe. (R. R.).
SCHUYLERVILLE, Saratoga Co., N. Y., 1,411.
On Bost. & Me. (R. R.).
SCHUYLKILL HAVEN, Schuylkill Co., Pa., 6,514.
On Leh. Val.; Penna.; Reading (R. Rs.).
SCHWEIDNITZ, Silesia, Germany, 32,000.
An industrial town near Breslau.
SCHWEINFURT, Bavaria, Germany, 39,000.
Dyes, machinery, and shoes.
SCHWELM, Westphalia, Prussia, Germany, 21,659.
Manufactures of iron, steel, and textiles.
SCHWENNINGEN, Württemberg, Germany, 18,978.
SCHWERIN, capital of Mecklenburg-Schwerin,
Germany, 52,000.

COURTESY OF THE NORTHERN PACIFIC RAILWAY.

A GLIMPSE OF THE OLYMPIC MOUNTAINS ACROSS PUGET SOUND WITH A PORTION
OF THE BUSINESS SECTION OF SEATTLE IN THE FOREGROUND

A marketing and trade center. Most important
manufacture is furniture.
SCHWERTE, Westphalia, Germany, 13,702.
SCIO, Harrison Co., Ohio, 760.
On Penna.; Wheel. & L. Erie (R. Rs.).
SCIOTOVILLE, Scioto Co., Ohio (Sta. Portsmouth
P. O.).
On Balt. & Ohio; Norf. & West. (R. Rs.).
SCIPIO, Millard Co., Utah, 544.
SCITUATE, Plymouth Co., Mass., 3,846.
On N. York, N. Hav. & Hart. (R. R.)
-Providence Co., R. I., 2,729.
SCOBEY, c. s., Daniels Co., Mont., 1,259.
On Gt. Nor. (R. R.).
SCOOBA, Kemper Co., Miss., 933.
On Mob. & Ohio (R. R.).
SCOTCH PLAINS, Union Co., N. J., 3,500.
SCOTIA, Humboldt Co., Cal., 1,000.
On Northw. Pac. (R. R.).
-Schenectady Co., N. Y., 7,437.
On Bost. & Me. (R. R.).
SCOTLAND, Bon Homme Co., S. Dak., 1,203.
On Chi., Mil., St. P. & Pac. (R. R.).
-East Baton Rouge Par., La., 900.
On La. & Ark.; Ill. Cen. (R. Rs.).
SCOTLAND NECK, Halifax Co., N. C., 2,339.
On Atl. Coast Line (R. R.).
-Franklin Co., Pa., 750.
On Penna. (R. R.).
SCOTT CITY, c. s., Scott Co., Kans., 1,625.
On Atch., Top. & Santa Fe; Mo. Pac. (R. Rs.)
SCOTTDALE, Westmoreland Co., Pa., 6,714.
On Balt. & Ohio; Penna. (R. Rs.).
-De Kalb Co., Ga., 700.
On Ga. (R. R.).
SCOTT HAVEN, Westmoreland Co., Pa., 500.
On Balt. & Ohio; Pitts. & L. Erie (R. Rs.).
SCOTTSBLUFF, Scotts Bluff Co., Neb., 8,465.
On Chi., Burl. & Quincy (R. R.).
SCOTTSBORO, c. s., Jackson Co., Ala., 2,304.
On Southern (R. R.).

SCOTTSBURG, c. s., Scott Co., Ind., 1,702.
On Ind. R. R. Sys. (El.); Penna. (R. Rs.).
SCOTTSDALE, Maricopa Co., Ariz., 1,000.
SCOTTSVILLE, Monroe Co., N. Y., 936.
On Balt. & Ohio; Penna. (R. Rs.).
-c. s., Allen Co., Ky., 1,867.
On Lou. & Nash. (R. R.).
SCOTTVILLE, Mason Co., Mich., 1,002.
On Pere Marq. (R. R.).
SCRANTON, Greene Co., Iowa, 1,058.
On Chi. & Nor. West. (R. R.).
-Osage Co., Kans., 566.
On Atch., Top. & Santa Fe (R. R.).
-c. s., Lackawanna Co., Pa., 143,433.
Situated on the Lackawanna River, and on
the New York, Ontario & Western; Delaware
& Hudson; Central of New Jersey; Delaware,
Lackawanna & Western; Lackawanna & Wyom-
ing-Valley; and Erie (R. Rs.). The city is the
third largest in the State, and is in the anthra-
cite coal region. The chief industries are coal
mining, foundries, steel works and a few
textile mills.
The city was established in 1840 by George W.
and Joseph H. Scranton. It was made a bor-
ough in 1854, and received its city charter in
1866.
SCREVEN, Wayne Co., Ga., 505.
On Atl. Coast Line (R. R.).
SCRIBNER, Dodge Co., Neb., 1,066.
On Chi. & Nor. West. (R. R.).
SCUTARI, Albania. See SHKODËR.
SEABOARD, Northampton Co., N. C., 534.
On Seab. Air Line (R. R.).
SEABREEZE, Volusia Co., Fla. (Sta. Daytona Beach
P. O.).
-Monroe Co., N. Y., 1,000.
On N. York Cen. (R. R.).
SEA BRIGHT, Monmouth Co., N. J., 899.
On Cen. of N. Jer. (R. R.).
SEABROOK, Rockingham Co., N. H., 1,000.
On Bost. & Me. (R. R.).
SEA CLIFF, Nassau Co., N. Y., 3,456.
On Long Isl. (R. R.).
SEAFORD, Sussex Co., Del., 2,468.
On Penna. (R. R.).
-York Co., Va., 627.
-Nassau Co., N. Y., 1,723.
On Long Isl. (R. R.).
SEAFORTH, Huron Co., South, Ontario, Canada,
1,686.
On Can. Nat. (R. R.).
SEAGOVILLE, Dallas Co., Tex., 604.
On Tex. & N. Orl. (Sou. Pac.) (R. R.).
SEAGRAVES, Gaines Co., Texas, 505.
On Panh. & Santa Fe (R. R.).
SEA ISLE CITY, Cape May Co., N. J., 850.
On Penna.-Read.-Seash. (R. R.).
SEAL BEACH, Orange Co., Cal., 1,156.
On Pac. El. (R. R.).
SEAL COVE, Hancock Co., Me., 600.
SEALE, c. s., Russell Co., Ala., 713.
On Cen. of Ga. (R. R.).
SEALKOTE, Punjab, India. See SIALKOT.
SEALY, Austin Co., Tex., 1,800.
On Gulf, Colo. & Santa Fe; Mo.-Kan.-Tex. of
Tex. (R. Rs.).
SEAMAN, Adams Co., Ohio, 717.
On Norf. & West. (R. R.).
SEANOR, Somerset Co., Pa., 500.
On Penna. (R. R.).
SEARCY, c. s., White Co., Ark., 3,387.
On Chi., Rk. Isl. & Pac.; Doniph., Ken. &
Searcy; Mo. & Ark. (R. Rs.).
SEARLES, Tuscaloosa Co., Ala., 713.
SEARSMONT, Waldo Co., Maine, 613.
SEARSPORT, Waldo Co., Maine, 1,200.
On Bangor & Aroostook (R. R.).
SEASIDE, Clatsop Co., Ore., 1,565.
On Spok., Port. & Seattle (R. R.).
-Monterey Co., Cal., 1,800.
On Sou. Pac. (R. R.).
SEASIDE PARK, Ocean Co., N. J., 571.
On Penna. (R. R.).
SEAT PLEASANT, Prince George Co., Md., 2,500.
On East Washington (R. R.).
SEATTLE, c. s., King Co., Wash., 365,583.
Port of entry, situated on Puget Sound, and
Chicago, Milwaukee, St. Paul & Pacific; Great
Northern; Northern Pacific; Pacific Coast and
Union Pacific railroads; and has connections
by boat and train with the Canadian Pacific
at Vancouver. It is a leading port in trade and
passenger service to Alaska and has direct
steamship connections with the chief ports of
the Orient.
Located on hills between Puget Sound and
Lake Washington, Seattle overlooks a fine har-
bor and is in a region of great scenic beauty.
The tide-water front on Elliott Bay is over 15
miles long and has a large number of piers
and docks. Lumber, coal and grain are among
the chief local industries. It is the largest
center of fisheries on the continent.
Seat of the University of Washington.
SEBASTOPOL, Sonoma Co., Cal., 1,762.
On Petaluma & Sta. Rosa (El.) (R. R.).
SEBEKA, Wadena Co., Minn., 548.
On Gt. Nor. (R. R.).
SEBEWAING, Huron Co., Mich., 1,441.

On Pere Marq. (R. R.).
SEBOYETA, Valencia Co., N. Mex., 648.
SEBREE, Webster Co., Ky., 940.
On Lou. & Nash. (R. R.).
SEBRING, c. s., Highlands Co., Fla., 3,194.
On Atl. Coast Line; Seab. Air Line (R. Rs.).
–Mahoning Co., Ohio, 3,949.
On Penna. (R. R.).
SECAUCUS, Hudson Co., N. J., 8,950.
On Del., Lack. & West.; Erie (R. Rs.).
A residential and industrial suburb of New York, adjoining Jersey City.
SECO, Letcher Co., Ky., 1,150.
On Lou. & Nash. (R. R.).
SECTION, Jackson Co., Ala., 500.
SEDALIA, c. s., Pettis Co., Mo., 20,806.
On Mo.-Kan.-Tex.; Mo. Pac. (R. Rs.).
Industries: packing houses, railroad shops and flour mills.
SEDAN, Dept. of Ardennes, France, 18,559.
Scene of German victory in War of 1870. Damaged in World War. Entered by Americans in advance along the Meuse, Nov. 6, 1918.
–c. s., Chautauqua Co., Kans., 1,753.
On Mo. Pac. (R. R.).
SEDGWICK, Harvey Co., Kans., 681.
On Ark. Val. Interurb. (El.); Atch., Top. & Santa Fe (R. Rs.).
SEDRO WOOLLEY, Skagit Co., Wash., 2,719.
On Gt. Nor.; Nor. Pac. (R. Rs.).
SEEKONK, Bristol Co., Mass., 5,011.
SEELYVILLE, Vigo Co., Ind., 825.
On Ind. R. R. Sys. (El.); Penna. (R. Rs.).
SEGOVIA, capital of Prov. of Segovia, Spain, 16,336.
SEGUIN, c. s., Guadalupe Co., Texas, 5,225.
On Tex. & N. Orl. (Sou. Pac.) (R. R.).
SEGUNDO, Las Animas Co., Colo., 600.
On Colo. & Wyo. (R. R.).
SEILING, Dewey Co., Okla., 568.
SELAH, Yakima Co., Wash., 767.
On Nor. Pac.; Un. Pac. (R. Rs.).
SELBY, c. s., Walworth Co., S. Dak., 613.
On Chi., Mil., St. P. & Pac. (R. R.).
SELBYVILLE, Sussex Co., Del., 661.
On Penna. (R. R.).
SELDEN, Sheridan Co., Kans., 503.
On Chi., Rk. Isl. & Pac. (R. R.)
SELESTAT, Bas Rhin, France, 11,363.
Has a famous cathedral.
SELIGMAN, Yavapai Co., Ariz., 500.
On Atch., Top. & Santa Fe (R. R.).
SELINSGROVE, Snyder Co., Pa., 2,797.
On Penna. (R. R.).
SELKIRK, Selkirk Co., Manitoba, Can., 4,566.
On Can. Pac. (R. R.).
SELLERS, Marion and Dillon Cos., S. C., 690.
On Atl. Coast Line (R. R.).
SELLERSBURG, Clark Co., Ind., 1,050.
On Ind. R. R. Sys. (El.); Penna. (R. Rs.).
SELLERSVILLE, Bucks Co., Pa., 2,063.
On Reading (R. R.).
SELMA, c. s., Dallas Co., Ala., 18,012.
On Lou. & Nash.; Sou. West. of Ala. (R. Rs.).
Center of cotton and live stock region. Has cotton and oil mills, creameries, railroad repair shops. Jobbing point for West Alabama.
–Fresno Co., Cal., 3,047.
On Sou. Pac. (R. R.).
–Grant Par., La., 812.
On Mo. Pac. (R. R.).
–Bexar Co., Tex., 519.
–Johnston Co., N. C., 1,857.
On Atl. Coast Line; Sou. (R. Rs.).
SELMER, c. s., McNairy Co., Tenn., 925.
On Mob. & Ohio (R. R.).
SEMARANG, Java, Netherland India, 217,775.
One of the leading ports and commercial center of a kapok and sugar raising region.
SEMINOLE, Seminole Co., Okla., 11,459.
On Chi., Rk. Isl. & Pac. (R. R.).
Situated in a farming and stock raising region.
–Armstrong Co., Pa., 500.
SEMIPALATINSK, Kazak Rep., Soviet Union, 120,200.
SENATH, Dunklin Co., Mo., 1,086.
On St. Lou.-San Fran. (R. R.).
SENATOBIA, c. s., Tate Co., Miss., 1,264.
On Ill. Cen. (R. R.).
SENDAI, Ken. of Miyage, Japan, 219,547.
An important marketing and trade center. Formerly a feudal stronghold.
SENECA, c. s., Nemaha Co., Kans., 2,098.
On St. Jos. & Gd. Isl. (Un. Pac.) (R. R.).
–La Salle Co., Ill., 1,186.
On Chi., Rk. Isl. & Pac. (R. R.).
–Newton Co., Mo., 1,063.
On St. Lou.-San Fran. (R. R.).
–Oconee Co., S. C., 1,929.
On Blue Ridge; Sou. (R. Rs.).
–Campbell Co., Va., 2,000.
On Virginian (R. R.).
SENECA FALLS, Seneca Co., N. Y., 6,443.
On Leh. Val.; N. York Cen. (R. Rs.).
SENECAVILLE, Guernsey Co., Ohio, 993.
On Balt. & Ohio (R. R.).
SENOIA, Coweta Co., Ga., 736.
On Atl., Birm. & Coast; Cen. of Ga. (R. Rs.).
SENTA, Yugoslavia, 32,044.
Located near Subotica. A marketing center.
SENTINEL, Washita Co., Okla., 1,269.
On Atch., Top. & Santa Fe (R. R.).
SEOUL, Chosen. See KEIJO.
SEQUIM, Clallam Co., Wash., 534.
On Chi., Mil., St. P. & Pac. (R. R.).
SERAING, Liége, Belgium, 43,310.
Site of the famous Cockerille machine works.
SERAMPORE, Bengal, India, 49,600.
A river port and commercial center. Formerly a Danish possession.
SERENA, LA, capital of Serena, Chile, 20,696.
Principal industries are brewing and the making of fruit conserves.
SERGEANT BLUFF, Woodbury Co., Iowa, 569.
On Chi. & Nor. West. (R. R.).
SERPUKHOV, Soviet Union, 77,500.
The chief manufactures are textiles, chintzes, dyes, iron and copper castings, and lumber.
SESSER, Franklin Co., Ill., 2,315.
On Chi., Burl. & Quincy (R. R.).
SETAUKET, Suffolk Co., N. Y., 2,000.
On Long Isl. (R. R.).
SÈTE, Dept. of Hérault, France, 37,324.
A seaport and busy commercial center with manufactures of liqueurs, cooperage, and chemicals. Also a fishing town.
SETIF, Dept. of Constantine, Algeria, 31,736.
A marketing center and military station.
SETUBAL, Prov. of Estremadura, Portugal, 37,074.
A seaport and trade center. Exports fruit, salt, and fish.
SEVASTOPOL, Crimean Rep., Soviet Union, 78,300.
A seaport and naval station. Has manufactures of machinery, flour, leather, soap, and tiles.
SEVERY, Greenwood Co., Kans., 537.
On Atch., Top. & Santa Fe; St. Lou.-San Fran. (R. Rs.).
SEVIERVILLE, c. s., Sevier Co., Tenn., 882.
On Tenn. & No. Car. (R. R.).
SEVILLA, capital of Prov. of Sevilla, Spain, 238,727.
On left bank of Guadalquivir. The city proper, surrounded by old Moorish walls, has a labyrinth of narrow, crooked streets. The cathedral (1401-1519) is an imposing Gothic edifice. The Giralda is a square Moorish steeple, 350 feet high. The Alcazar was the ancient Moorish palace. The lonja, or Exchange, 100 feet square, contains the American archives and the Cañons de Carmona, an aqueduct on arches, which conveys water from Alcala de Guadaira. Sevilla has a university, founded 1504, with a large library.
Sevilla was the Hispalis of the Romans, in whose time it was of commercial importance. Sevilla suffered in the civil war of 1936.
SEVILLE, Medina Co., Ohio, 785.
On Balt. & Ohio (R. R.).
–Volusia Co., Fla., 585.
On Atl. Coast Line (R. R.).
SÈVRES, Seine-et-Oise, France, 15,501. Famous for its fine porcelain.
SEWANEE, Franklin Co., Tenn., 1,500.
On Nashv., Chatt. & St. L. (R. R.).
SEWARD, Alaska, 835.
On Alaska (R. R.).
–c. s., Seward Co., Neb., 2,737.
On Chi., Burl. & Quincy; Chi. & Nor. West. (R. Rs.).
–Westmoreland Co., Pa., 742.
On Penna. (R. R.).
SEWICKLEY, Allegheny Co., Pa., 5,599.
On Penna. (R. R.).
SEYMOUR, New Haven Co., Conn., 6,100.
On N. York, N. Hav. & Hart. (R. R.).
–Jackson Co., Ind., 7,508.
On Penna.; Balt. & Ohio; Chi., Mil., St. P. & Pac.; Ind. R. R. Sys. (El.) (R. Rs.).
–Wayne Co., Iowa, 1,571.
On Chi., Mil., St. P. & Pac.; Chi., Rk. Isl. & Pac. (R. Rs.).
–Webster Co., Mo., 681.
On St. Lou.-San Fran. (R. R.).
–c. s., Baylor Co., Texas, 2,626.
On St. Lou., San Fran. & Tex.; Wich. Val. (R. Rs.).
–Outagamie Co., Wis., 1,201.
On Grn. Bay & West. (R. R.).
SEYMOURVILLE (Plaquemine), Iberville Par., La., 517.
On Tex. & Pac. (R. R.).
SEYNE-SUR-MER, Dept. of Var, France, 23,168.
An industrial suburb of Toulon.
SFAX, Tunisia, Africa, 39,969.
Port, trade center, and market for phosphates from the interior. Fisheries are important.
S'GRAVENHAGE (The Hague), capital of the Netherlands, 482,397.
Residence of the Queen. The city was the seat of the Second Peace Conference, 1907, and the World Court, 1929-30.
SHABBONA, De Kalb Co., Ill., 546.
On Chi., Burl. & Quincy (R. R.).
SHADYSIDE, Belmont Co., Ohio, 4,098.
On Penna. (R. R.).
SHAFT, Schuylkill Co., Pa., 1,100.
On Read. (R. R.).
SHAFTER, Kern Co., Cal., 500.
On Atch., Top. & Santa Fe (R. R.).
SHAFTON, Westmoreland Co., Pa., 800.
On Penna. (R. R.).
SHAHJAHANPUR, United Provinces, British India, 72,616.
A trade center and military station situated in a fertile farming district.
SHAHRUO, Iran (Persia), 15,100.
SHAKER HEIGHTS, Cuyahoga Co., Ohio, 17,783.
A residential suburb of Cleveland.
SHAKOPEE, c. s., Scott Co., Minn., 2,023.
On Chi., Mil., St. P. & Pac.; Chi., St. P., Mpls. & Omaha (R. Rs.).
SHAMOKIN, Northumberland Co., Pa., 20,274.
On Penna., Reading (R. Rs.).
In anthracite coal region and a shipping point. Manufactures silk underwear, cigars, etc.
SHAMOKIN DAM, Snyder Co., Pa., 738.
SHAMROCK, Creek Co., Okla., 777.
On St. Lou.-San Fran. (R. R.).
–Dixie Co., Fla., 1,200.
–Wheeler Co., Texas, 3,780.
On Chi., Rk. Isl. & Gulf; Ft. Worth & Denv. Cy. (R. Rs.).
SHANGHAI, Prov. of Kiangsu, China, 3,259,100.
Seaport and chief emporium for European commerce, situated near the junction of the Hwang-pu and the Wu-sung Rivers. The Chinese city proper is enclosed within walls 24 feet high. In 1843 Shanghai was opened as one of the five treaty ports; an important foreign settlement is now established (with a separate government) outside the city walls. In the foreign settlement there are a fine cathedral and modern buildings.
SHANNON, Carroll Co., Ill., 575.
On Chi., Mil., St. P. & Pac. (R. R.).
–Lee Co., Miss., 524.
On Mob. & Ohio (R. R.).
SHARON, Litchfield Co., Conn., 500.
–Norfolk Co., Mass., 3,683.
On N. York, N. Hav. & Hart. (R. R.).
–Mercer Co., Pa., 25,908.
On Erie; N. York Cen.; Penna.; Pitts. & L. Erie (R. Rs.).
Industries largely products of steel foundries.
–Weakley Co., Tenn., 596.
On Ill. Cen. (R. R.).
–Walworth Co., Wis., 733.
On Chi. & Nor. West. (R. R.).
SHARON HILL, Delaware Co., Pa., 3,825.
On Penna. (R. R.).
SHARON SPRINGS, c. s., Wallace Co., Kans., 749.
On Un. Pac. (R. R.).
SHARONVILLE, Hamilton Co., Ohio, 1,111.
On Cle., Cin., Chi. & St. Lou. (N. York Cen.) (R. R.).
SHARPSBURG, Washington Co., Md., 818.
–Allegheny Co., Pa., 8,642.
On Penna. (R. R.).
SHARPSVILLE, Mercer Co., Pa., 5,194.
On Erie; Pitts. & L. Erie; N. York Cen.; Penna. (R. Rs.).
–Tipton Co., Ind., 512.
On N. York, Chi. & St. Lou. (R. R.).
SHARPTOWN, Wicomico Co., Md., 727.
SHASI, Prov. of Hupeh, China, 114,200.
A river port and center of the cotton trade.
SHATTUCK, Ellis Co., Okla., 1,490.
On Atch., Top. & Santa Fe; Panh. & Santa Fe (R. Rs.).
SHAW, Bolivar Co., Miss., 1,612.
On Yazoo & Miss. Val. (Ill. Cen.) (R. R.).
SHAWANGUNK, Ulster Co., N. Y., 1,400.
SHAWANO, c. s., Shawano Co., Wis., 4,188.
On Chi. & Nor. West.; Mpls., St. P. & S. Ste. M. (R. Rs.).
SHAWINIGAN FALLS, St. Maurice Co., Quebec, Canada, 15,345.
On Can. Nat.; Can. Pac. (R. Rs.).
Has large hydroelectric plants and paper mills.
SHAWNEE, Johnson Co., Kan., 583.
–Perry Co., Ohio, 1,457.
On N. York Cen.; Balt. & Ohio (R. Rs.).
–c. s., Pottawatomie Co., Okla., 23,283.
On Atch., Top. & Santa Fe; Chi., Rk. Isl. & Pac.; Okla. Cy., Ada-Atoka (R. Rs.).
Railroad center with repair shops. Seat of Oklahoma Baptist University.
SHAWNEETOWN, c. s., Gallatin Co., Ill., 1,440.
On Balt. & Ohio; Lou. & Nash. (R. Rs.).
SHAWOMET, Kent Co., R. I., 500.
SHAWSHEEN VILLAGE, Essex Co., Mass., 900.
On Bost. & Me. (R. R.).
SHEBOYGAN, c. s., Sheboygan Co., Wis., 39,251.
On Chi. & Nor. West.; Mil. El. (R. Rs.).
A lake fishing center and industrial town. Manufactures of chairs, enamel-ware, bookcases, and desks.
SHEBOYGAN FALLS, Sheboygan Co., Wis., 2,934.
On Chi. & Nor. West. (R. R.).
SHEFFIELD, Yorkshire, England, 517,300.
Situated at the junction of the Sheaf and Don. The chief ecclesiastical building is the ancient parish Church of St. Peter. The trade of Sheffield is chiefly connected with cutlery, for which it has long been famous, and the manufacture of all forms of steel, iron, brass work and Britannia ware.
Sheffield is supposed to have been originally a Roman station. Edward I. granted it a charter as a market town in 1296. There is indication in Chaucer's writings that the town was noted for its cutlery in his day.
–Colbert Co., Ala., 6,221.
On Lou. & Nash.; Nor. Ala.; Sou. (R. Rs.).
In a region of agricultural, forest and mineral resources. Has varied industries. Near Shiloh National Military Park.
–Bureau Co., Ill., 941.
On Chi., Rk. Isl. & Pac. (R. R.).
–Franklin Co., Iowa, 1,057.
On Mpls. & St. Lou. (R. R.).
–Berkshire Co., Mass., 1,810.
On N. York, N. Hav. & Hart. (R. R.).
–Lorain Co., Ohio, 1,256.
On N. York, Chi. & St. Lou. (R. R.).
–Warren Co., Pa., 2,500.
On Penna.; Shef. & Tion.; Tionesta Val. (R. Rs.).
SHELBINA, Shelby Co., Mo., 1,826.
On Chi., Burl. & Quincy; Shelby Co. (R. Rs.).
SHELBURN, Sullivan Co., Ind., 1,548.
On Chi. & East. Ill. (R. R.).
SHELBURNE, Franklin Co., Mass., 1,606.
–Dufferin Co., Ontario, Canada, 1,077.
On Can. Pac. (R. R.).
–Shelburne Co., Nova Scotia, 1,474.
On Can. Nat. (R. R.).
SHELBURNE FALLS, Franklin Co., Mass., 3,300.
On Bost. & Me. (R. R.).
SHELBY, Shelby Co., Ala., 790.
On Lou. & Nash. (R. R.).
–Shelby Co., Iowa, 617.
On Chi., Rk. Isl. & Pac. (R. R.).
–Oceana Co., Mich., 1,152.
On Pere Marq. (R. R.).
–Bolivar Co., Miss., 1,811.
On Yazoo & Miss. Val. (Ill. Cen.) (R. R.).
–c. s., Toole Co., Mont., 2,004.
On Gt. Nor. (R. R.).
–Polk Co., Neb., 630.
On Un. Pac. (R. R.).
–c. s., Cleveland Co., N. C., 10,789.
On Seab. Air Line; Sou.; Lawndale (R. Rs.).
A health and pleasure resort.
–Richland Co., Ohio, 6,198.
On Balt. & Ohio; Cle., Cin., Chi. & St. Lou. (R. Rs.).
SHELBYVILLE, c. s., Shelby Co., Ill., 3,491.
On Chi. & East. Ill.; Cle., Cin., Chi. & St. Lou. (R. Rs.).
–c. s., Shelby Co., Ind., 10,618.
On Cle., Cin., Chi. & St. Lou.; Penna. (R. Rs.).
The center of an agricultural area, situated near Indianapolis.
–c. s., Shelby Co., Ky., 4,033.
On Chesa. & Ohio; Sou.; Lou. & Nash. (R. Rs.).
–Shelby Co., Mo., 704.
–c. s., Bedford Co., Tenn., 5,010.
On Nash., Chatt. & St. Lou. (R. R.).
SHELDON, Iroquois Co., Ill., 1,121.
On Cle., Cin., Chi. & St. Lou.; Tol., Peor. & West. (R. Rs.).
–O'Brien Co., Iowa, 3,320.
On Chi., Mil., St. P. & Pac.; Chi., St. P., Mpls. & Omaha; Ill. Cen. (R. Rs.).
–Franklin Co., Vt., 500.
On St. Johns & L. Champ. (R. R.).
SHELF, Yorkshire, West Riding, England, 2,600.
SHELLEY, Bingham Co., Idaho, 1,447.
On Un. Pac. (R. R.).
SHELL LAKE, Washburn Co., Wis., 826.
On Chi., St. P., Mpls. & Omaha (R. R.).
SHELLMAN, Randolph Co., Ga., 1,117.
On Cen. of Ga. (R. R.).
SHELL ROCK, Bulter Co., Iowa, 806.
On Chi. Gt. West.; Chi., Rk. Isl. & Pac. (R. Rs.).
SHELLSBURG, Benton Co., Iowa, 546.
On Chi., Rk. Isl. & Pac. (R. R.).
SHELTON, Fairfield Co., Conn., 10,113.
On N. York, N. Hav. & Hart. (R. R.).
Manufactures women's wear and household goods.
–Dixie Co., Fla., 600.
–Buffalo Co., Neb., 927.
On Un. Pac. (R. R.).
–c. s., Mason Co., Wash., 3,091.
On Nor. Pac. (R. R.).
SHEMAKHA, Soviet Union, 20,000.
A trading and marketing town.
SHENANDOAH, Page Co., Iowa, 6,502.
On Chi., Burl. & Quincy; Wab. (R. Rs.).
–Schuylkill Co., Pa., 21,782.
On Leh. Val.; Penna.; Read. (R. Rs.).
An anthracite coal-mining town.
–Page Co., Va., 1,980.
On Norf. & West. (R. R.).
SHEPARDSVILLE, Vigo Co., Ind., 500.
SHEPHERD, Isabella Co., Mich., 839.
On Ann Arbor (R. R.).
–San Jacinto Co., Tex., 513.
On Tex. & N. Orl. (Sou. Pac.) (R. R.).
SHEPHERDSTOWN, Jefferson Co., W. Va., 888.
On Norf. & West. (R. R.).
SHEPHERDSVILLE, c. s., Bullitt Co., Ky., 633.
On Lou. & Nash. (R. R.).
SHEPPTON, Schuylkill Co., Pa., 1,040.

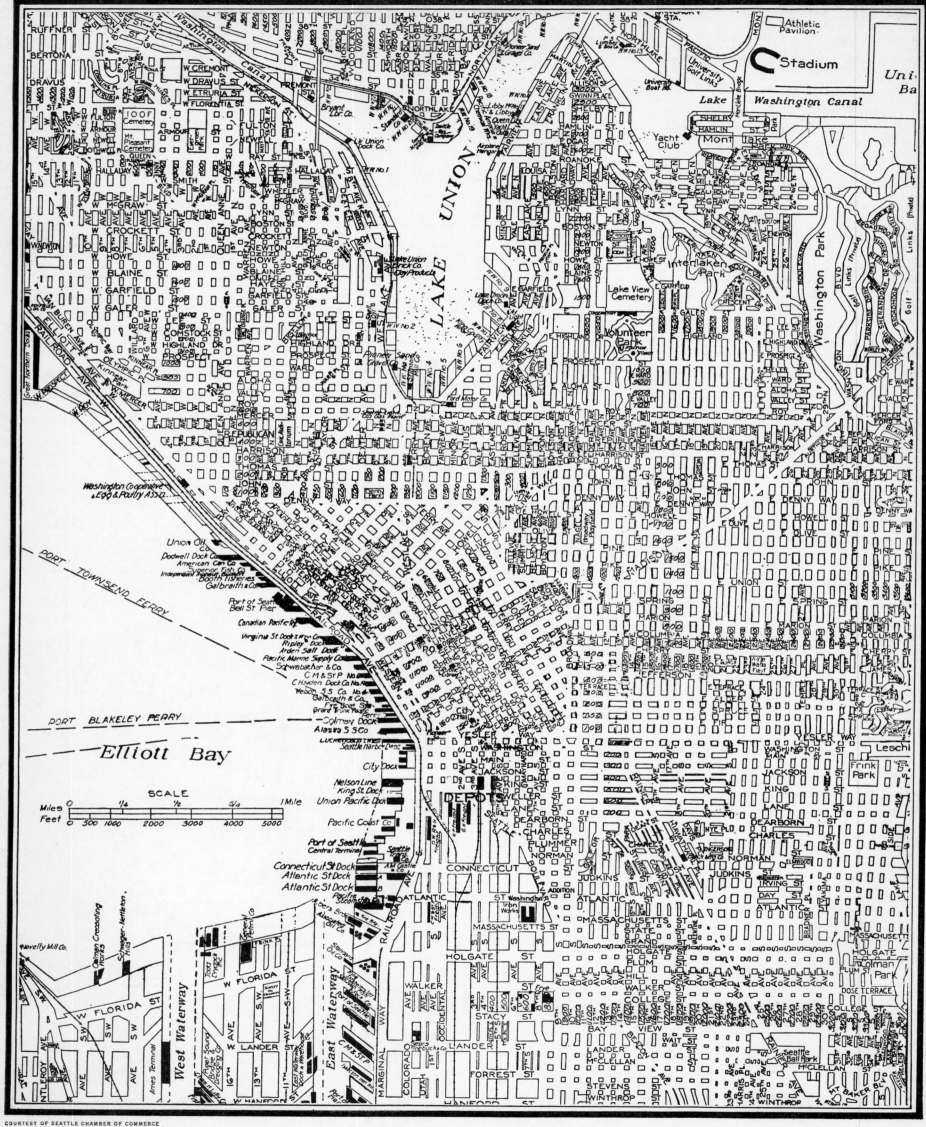

MAP OF CENTRAL SEATTLE, THE CHIEF CITY OF WASHINGTON AND INDUSTRIAL CENTER OF THE PACIFIC NORTHWEST.   SEATTLE HAS DOCKING FACILITIES FOR
OVER 100 STEAMSHIP LINES CONNECTING THE CITY WITH ASIATIC, EUROPEAN AND SOUTH AMERICAN PORTS, AND WITH OTHER PORTS OF NORTH AMERICA

Smithland, c. s., Livingston Co., Ky., 519.
Smithmill, Clearfield Co., Pa., 618.
Smithsburg, Washington Co., Md., 598.
On West. Md. (R. R.).
Smith's Falls, Lanark Co., Ontario, Can., 7,108.
On Can. Pac.; Can. Nat. (R. Rs.).
Smith's Grove, Warren Co., Ky., 718.
On Lou. & Nash. (R. R.).
Smiths Station (Smiths), Lee Co., Ala., 500.
On Cen. of Ga. (R. R.).
Smithton, Westmoreland Co., Pa., 709.
On Balt. & Ohio; Pitts. & L. Erie (R. Rs.).
Smithtown (Atlantic), Rockingham Co., N. H., 500.
On Bost. & Me. (R. R.).
Smithtown Branch, Suffolk Co., N. Y., 700.
Smithville, Lee Co., Ga., 777.
On Cen. of Ga. (R. R.).
–Clay Co., Mo., 902.
On Quincy, Oma. & Kan. Cy. (R. R.).
–Wayne Co., Ohio, 582.
–c. s., De Kalb Co., Tenn., 886.
–Bastrop Co., Texas, 3,296.
On Mo.-Kan.-Tex. of Tex. (R. R.).
Smock, Fayette Co., Pa., 1,036.
On Penna. (R. R.).
Smoke Bend, Ascension Par., La., 620.
On Tex. & Pac. (R. R.).
Smokerun, Clearfield Co., Pa., 592.
On Penna. (R. R.).
Smolensk, Soviet Union, 104,100.
A railroad and commercial center. Chief industries are copper and iron smelting, sawmills, brickyards, machine shops, and textile mills.
Smyrna, Turkey. See Izmir.
–Kent Co., Del., 1,958.
On Penna. (R. R.).
–Cobb Co., Ga., 1,178.
On Nash., Chatt. & St. Lou. (R. R.).
–Rutherford Co., Tenn., 531.
On Nash., Chatt. & St. Lou. (R. R.).
Smyth (Balfour), Henderson Co., N. C., 500.
On Southern (R. R.).
Sneads, Jackson Co., Fla., 740.
On Lou. & Nash. (R. R.).
Sneedville, c. s., Hancock Co., Tenn., 500.
Snohomish, Snohomish Co., Wash., 2,688.
On Gt. Nor.; Nor. Pac.; Chi., Mil., St. P. & Pac. (R. Rs.).
Snoqualmie, King Co., Wash., 752.
On Chi., Mil., St. P. & Pac.; Nor. Pac. (R. Rs.).
Snowflake, Navajo Co., Ariz., 659.
On Apache (R. R.).
Snow Hill, c. s., Worcester Co., Md., 1,604.
On Penna. (R. R.).
–Ouachita Co., Ark., 500.
–c. s., Greene Co., N. C., 826.
Snow Shoe (Clarence P. O.), Centre Co., Pa., 520.
On Penna. (R. R.).
Snyder, Kiowa Co., Okla., 1,195.
On St. Lou.-San Fran. (R. R.).
–Erie Co., N. Y., 612.
–c. s., Scurry Co., Texas, 3,008.
On Rosc., Snyd. & Pac.; Panh. & Santa Fe (R. Rs.).
Soche (Yarkand), Sinkiang, China, 70,000.
A caravan and trade center situated in a rich agricultural region.
Social Circle, Walton Co., Ga., 1,766.
On Georgia (R. R.).
Society Hill, Darlington Co., S. C., 573.
On Atl. Coast Line (R. R.).
Socorro, c. s., Socorro Co., N. Mex., 2,058.
On Atch., Top. & Santa Fe (R. R.).
–El Paso Co., Texas, 600.
Soda Springs, c. s., Caribou Co., Idaho, 831.
On Un. Pac. (R. R.).
Soddy (Rathburn), Hamilton Co., Tenn., 2,250.
On Cin., N. Orl. & Tex. Pac. (R. R.).
Söderhamn, Gävleborg, Sweden, 11,643.
A seaport and trade center on the Baltic Sea.
Södertälje, Sweden, 14,371.
A canal port near Stockholm.
Sodus, Wayne Co., N. Y., 1,444.
On N. York Cen. (R. R.).
Sodus Point, Wayne Co., N. Y., 525.
On Penna. (R. R.).
Soerabaja, Java, Netherland India, 341,675.
Next to Batavia it is the most important commercial port in Netherland India. It is also an important naval base.
Soerakarta, Java, Netherland India, 165,484.
Center of the tobacco growing region.
Soest, Westphalia, Germany, 22,000.
Iron, machinery, soap, sugar, lamps, and cigars.
Sofija (Sofia), capital of Bulgaria, 321,094.
An industrial and commercial center with manufactures of flour, leather, textiles, tobacco, and food products. The city has fine public buildings and is the seat of two universities. There are hot springs in the vicinity.
Soignies, Hainaut, Belgium, 10,599.
A suburb of Bruxelles.
Soissons, Dept. of Aisne, France, 20,090.
Partly destroyed in the European War and captured by Franco-American forces in their drive against the Soissons-Marne-Reims salient in July, 1918.
Sokoto, Nigeria, Africa, 8,000.
Soldiers Grove, Crawford Co., Wis., 710.
On Chi., Mil., St. P. & Pac. (R. R.).
Soledad, Monterey Co., Cal., 594.
On Sou. Pac. (R. R.).
Soledade, Rio Grande do Sul, Brazil, 39,329.
A trade center in an agricultural region.
Solingen, Rhenish Prussia, Germany, 140,200.
Cutlery and hardware manufactures.
Solomon, Dickinson Co., Kans., 985.
On Atch., Top. & Santa Fe; Chi., Rk. Isl. & Pac.; Un. Pac. (R. Rs.).
Solomonsville, Graham Co., Ariz., 800.
On Sou. Pac. (R. R.).
Solon, Cuyahoga Co., Ohio, 1,027.

COURTESY AMERICAN AIRLINES, INC.

AN AERIAL VIEW OF THE UNIVERSITY OF NOTRE DAME, SOUTH BEND, INDIANA, SHOWING THE COLLEGE BUILDINGS AND THE NEW ROCKNE STADIUM IN THE BACKGROUND

On Erie; Wheel. & L. Erie (R. Rs.).
Solothurn, capital of Canton of Solothurn, Switzerland, 21,700.
A railroad and commercial center.
Solvay, Onondaga Co., N. Y., 7,986.
On Del., Lack. & West.; N. York Cen. (R. Rs.).
Sombor, Yugoslavia, 32,256.
A center of the corn and cattle trade.
Sombrerete, State of Zacatecas, Mexico, 4,747.
On Nat. of Mex. (R. R.).
Somerdale, Camden Co., N. J., 1,151.
On Penna.-Read. Seashore (R. R.).
Somers (Pricedale P. O.), Westmoreland Co., Pa., 1,036.
On Pitts. & L. Erie (R. R.).
–Flathead Co., Mont., 1,000.
On Gt. Nor. (R. R.).
Somerset, East, Cape of Good Hope, Union of South Africa, 5,046.
–Gunnison Co., Colo., 600.
On Den. & Rio Gde. West. (R. R.).
–c. s., Pulaski Co., Ky., 5,506.
On Cin., N. Orl. & Tex. Pac. (R. R.).
–Bristol Co., Mass., 5,656.
On N. York, N. Hav. & Hart. (R. R.).
–Perry Co., Ohio, 1,297.
On Balt. & Ohio (R. R.).
–c. s., Somerset Co., Pa., 4,395.
On Balt. & Ohio (R. R.).
Somers Point, Atlantic Co., N. J., 2,073.
On Penna.-Read. Seashore (R. R.).
Somersville, Tolland Co., Conn., 800.
Somersworth, Strafford Co., N. H., 5,680.
On Bost. & Me. (R. R.).
Somerton, Yuma Co., Ariz., 891.
On Yuma Val. (R. R.).
Somerville, Middlesex Co., Mass., 100,773.
On the Mystic River, and on the Boston & Maine (R. R.).
The city is built on seven hills, some of which were fortified during the Revolutionary War.
–c. s., Somerset Co., N. J., 8,255.
On Cen. of N. Jer. (R. R.).
–c. s., Fayette Co., Tenn., 1,333.
On Nash., Chatt. & St. Lou. (R. R.).
–Burleson Co., Texas, 2,287.
On Gulf, Colo. & Santa Fe (R. R.).
Sommerfeld, Brandenburg, Germany, 11,182.
Somonauk, De Kalb Co., Ill., 578.
On Chi., Burl. & Quincy (R. R.).
Sonderbörg, Denmark, 12,100.
Sondershausen, Thüringen, Germany, 9,978.
Sondrio, capital of Prov. of Sondrio, Lombardy, Italy, 6,349.
Sonman, Cambria Co., Pa., 800.
Sonneberg, Thüringen, Germany, 20,000.
Famous for its toy manufactures.
Sonoma, Sonoma Co., Cal., 980.
On Northw. Pac. (R. R.).
Sonora, c. s., Tuolumne Co., Cal., 2,278.
On Sierra of Calif. (R. R.).
–Pinal Co., Ariz., 1,500.
–c. s., Sutton Co., Texas, 1,942.
On Panh. & Santa Fe (R. R.).
Sonsonate, Salvador, 20,553.
A trade center in a very rich farming region.
Sonyea, Livingston Co., N. Y., 2,500.
On Dansv. & Mt. Morris; Penna. (R. Rs.).
Soochow, Kiangsu, China, 260,000.
A large trade and marketing town on the Grand Canal.
Soperton, c. s., Treutlen Co., Ga., 1,081.
On Macon, Dub. & Sav. (R. R.).
Sophia, Raleigh Co., W. Va., 611.
On Virginian (R. R.).
Sopron, Hungary, 35,887.
A trade and commercial town.
Soquel, Santa Cruz Co., Cal., 1,800.
Sorau, Brandenburg, Germany, 19,000.
A railroad and commercial center.
Sorel, Richelieu Co., Quebec, Can., 10,320.
On Can. Nat. (R. R.).
Sorento, Bond Co., Ill., 831.
On Chi., Burl. & Quincy; N. York, Chi. & St. Lou. (R. Rs.).
Soroca, Bessarabia, Rumania, 14,661.
An agricultural town in a region raising corn, wool, fruit, and cattle.
Sorrento, Prov. of Napoli, Italy, 7,121.
–Ascension Par., La., 819.
On La. & Ark. (R. R.).
Sorsogon, Sorsogon Prov., Luzon, P. I., 17,049.
An agricultural center.
Sosnowiec, Poland, 116,000.
Coal mines, textile mills, and iron foundries.
Sotteville-les-Rouen, Dept. of Seine-Inférieure, France, 26,657.
A suburb of Rouen.
Souderton, Montgomery Co., Pa., 3,857.
On Reading (R. R.).
Sour (Tyre), Syria, 4,500.
Souris, Brandon Co., Manitoba, Can., 1,661.
On Can. Pac. (R. R.).
–Prince Edward Island, Canada, 1,063.
On Can. Nat. (R. R.).
Sour Lake, Hardin Co., Texas, 1,199.
On Beaumont, Sour L. & West. (R. R.).
Sousse, Tunisia, 25,324.
A port and trade center. Chief exports: phosphates and olive oil.
South Aberdeen, Grays Harbor Co., Wash., 3,000.
On Nor. Pac.; Chi., Mil., St. P. & Pac. (R. Rs.).
South Acton, Middlesex Co., Mass., 800.
On Bost. & Me. (R. R.).
South Altoona, Blair Co., Pa., 940.
On Penna. (R. R.).
South Amboy, Middlesex Co., N. J., 8,476.
On Cen. of N. Jer.; N. York & Long Br.; Penna.; Raritan Riv. (R. Rs.).
In the midst of clay and sand deposits, which furnish the material for its industries. Also tidewater coal shipping point. The Victory Bridge, opened in 1926 and spanning the Raritan River, connects South Amboy with Perth Amboy.
South Amherst, Lorain Co., Ohio, 914.
On Lorain & Southern (R. R.).
Southampton, Southampton Co., Eng., 176,025.
A seaport on the south coast of England.
–Bruce Co., No., Ont., Can., 1,489.
On Can. Nat. (R. R.).
–Hampshire Co., Mass., 954.
On N. York, N. Hav. & Hart. (R. R.).
–Suffolk Co., N. Y., 3,737.
On Long Isl. (R. R.).
Fashionable resort on South Shore of Long Island.
Southard, Blaine Co., Okla., 500.
On St. Lou.-San Fran. (R. R.).
South Ashburnham, Worcester Co., Mass., 800.
On Bost. & Me. (R. R.).
South Attleboro, Bristol Co., Mass., 5,000.
South Barre, Worcester Co., Mass., 1,500.
On Bost. & Alb. (R. R.).
South Bellingham, Norfolk Co., Mass., 2,000.
South Belmar, Monmouth Co., N. J., 886.
On Reading (R. R.).
South Beloit, Winnebago Co., Ill., 2,361.
On Chi. & Nor. West. (R. R.).
South Bend, c. s., St. Joseph Co., Ind., 104,193.
On the St. Joseph River, and on the Chi., So. Shore & So. Bend (El.); Cle., Cin., Chi. & St. Lou.; Gd. Tr.; Mich. Cen.; N. Jer., Ind. & Ill.; N. York Cen.; and Penna. (R. Rs.).
Leading manufactures: automobiles, sewing machines, farm machinery, toys, electrical goods.
Seat of University of Notre Dame.
–c. s., Pacific Co., Wash., 1,798.
On Chi., Mil., St. P. & Pac.; Nor. Pac. (R. Rs.).
South Berwick, York Co., Me., 1,800.
On Bost. & Me. (R. R.).
South Bethlehem, Northampton Co., Pa. See Bethlehem.
–Albany Co., N. Y., 500.
On West Shore (R. R.).
Southboro, Worcester Co., Mass., 2,109.
On N. York, N. Hav. & Hart. (R. R.).
South Boston, Halifax Co., Va., 4,841.
On Norf. & West.; Sou. (R. Rs.).
South Bound Brook, Somerset Co., N. J., 1,763.
Southbridge, Worcester Co., Mass., 15,786.
On N. York, N. Hav. & Hart. (R. R.).
Optical industry. Shuttle manufacturing plant.
South Brownsville, Fayette Co., Pa., 5,314.
On Monongahela (R. R.).
Southbury, New Haven Co., Conn., 1,100.
On N. York, N. Hav. & Hart. (R. R.).
South Canon, Fremont Co., Colo., 1,471.
South Canonsburg, Washington Co., Pa.
South Charleston, Clark Co., Ohio, 1,208.
On Det., Tol. & Iron.; Penna. (R. Rs.).
–Kanawha Co., W. Va., 5,904.
On Chesa. & Ohio (R. R.).
South Chelmsford, Middlesex Co., Mass., 550.
On N. York, N. Hav. & Hart. (R. R.).
South Chicago Heights, Cook Co., Ill., 1,691.
South Cle Elum, Kittitas Co., Wash., 338.
South Coatesville, Chester Co., Pa., 1,785.
South Connellsville, Fayette Co., Pa., 2,516.
On Balt. & Ohio (R. R.).
South Corning, Steuben Co., N. Y., 714.
South Coventry, Tolland Co., Conn., 900.
South Dayton, Cattaraugus Co., N. Y., 570.
On Erie (R. R.).
South Deerfield, Franklin Co., Mass., 1,333.
On Bost. & Me.; N. York, N. Hav. & Hart. (R. Rs.).
South Duxbury (Standish), Plymouth Co., Mass., 1,692.
On N. York, N. Hav. & Hart. (R. R.).
South Easton, Bristol Co., Mass., 632.
On N. York, N. Hav. & Hart. (R. R.).
South Elgin, Kane Co., Ill., 745.
On Chi. & Nor. West. (R. R.).
South Eliot, York Co., Maine, 963.
South Enola, Cumberland Co., Pa., 1,016.
South Essex, Essex Co., Mass., 700.
South Euclid, Cuyahoga Co., Ohio, 4,399.
Southend-on-Sea, Essex, England, 120,093.
A popular resort for Londoners.
Southern Pines, Moore Co., N. C., 2,524.
On Seab. Air Line (R. R.).
A winter resort.
South Fork, Cambria Co., Pa., 3,227.
On Penna. (R. R.).
South Fort Plain (Ft. Plain P. O.), Montgomery Co., N. Y., 2,906.
On West Shore (R. R.).
South Fort Smith, Sebastian Co., Ark., 625.
On Mo. Pac. (R. R.).
South Frankfort, Benzie Co., Mich.
On Ann Arbor (R. R.).
South Ft. Mitchell, Kenton Co., Ky., 1,617.
South Fulton, Obion Co., Tenn., 1,988.
On Ill. Cen. (R. R.).
South Gardiner, Kennebec Co., Me., 600.
On Me. Cen. (R. R.).
South Gate, Los Angeles Co., Cal., 19,632.
On Los Ang. & Salt L.; Sou. Pac. (R. Rs.).
A suburb of Los Angeles.
Southgate, Campbell Co., Ky., 1,735.
South Glastonbury, Hartford Co., Conn., 1,500.
South Glen Falls, Saratoga Co., N. Y., 2,689.
On Del. & Hud. (R. R.).
South Greensburg, Westmoreland Co., Pa., 2,520.

On Penna. (R. R.).
South Groveton, Trinity Co., Texas, 1,008.
South Hadley, Hampshire Co., Mass., 6,838.
Seat of Mt. Holyoke College for Women.
South Hadley Falls, Hampshire Co., Mass., 5,000.
South Hanover (Perry), Plymouth Co., Mass., 541.
South Hanson, Plymouth Co., Mass., 831.
On N. York, N. Hav. & Hart. (R. R.).
South Haven, Van Buren Co., Mich., 4,804.
On Pere Marq.; Mich. Cen. (R. Rs.).
South Heights, Beaver Co., 549.
On Pitts. & L. Erie (R. R.).
South Hill, Mecklenburg Co., Va., 1,405.
On Southern (R. R.).
South Holland, Cook Co., Ill., 1,873.
On Chi. & East. Ill. (R. R.).
South Houston (Dumont), Harris Co., Tex., 612.
On Galv., Hous. & Hen.; Mo.-Kans.-Tex.; Mo. Pac. (R. Rs.).
South Hutchinson, Reno Co., Kans., 804.
Southington, Hartford Co., Conn., 5,125.
On N. York, N. Hav. & Hart. (R. R.).
South International Falls, Koochiching Co., Minn., 939.
South Jacksonville, Morgan Co., Ill.. 562.
–Duval Co., Fla. (Pop. incl. in Jacksonville).
On Fla. East Coast (R. R.).
South Kingstown, Washington Co., R. I., 6,100.
Seat of Rhode Island State College.
South Lancaster, Worcester Co., Mass., 1,000.
On Bost. & Me. (R. R.).
South Langhorne, Bucks Co., Pa., 789.
South Lebanon, Warren Co., Ohio, 713.
On Penna. (R. R.).
South Lyon, Oakland Co., Mich., 844.
On Gd. Tr.; Pere Marq. (R. Rs.).
South Manchester, Hartford Co., Conn., 2,299.
On N. York, N. Hav. & Hart. (R. R.).
South Meriden, New Haven Co., Conn., 600.
South Miami, Dade Co., Fla., 1,690.
On Fla. East Coast; Seab. Air Line (R. Rs.).
South Milwaukee, Milwaukee Co., Wis., 10,706.
On Chi. & Nor. West. (R. R.).
A suburb of Milwaukee.
Southmont, Cambria Co., Pa., 1,925.
South New Castle, Lawrence Co., Pa., 1,038.
South Norfolk (Ind. City), Norfolk Co., Va., 7,857.
On Norf. & Portsm. Belt; Norf. & West.; Virginian (R. Rs.).
South Nyack, Rockland Co., N. Y., 2,212.
On Erie (R. R.).
Southold, Suffolk Co., N. Y., 1,500.
On Long Isl. (R. R.).
South Orange, Essex Co., N. J., 13,630.
On Del., Lack. & West. (R. R.).
A residential community in the New York-Newark area.
South Paris, c. s., Oxford Co., Maine, 1,961.
On Gd. Tr. (R. R.).
South Pasadena, Los Angeles Co., Cal., 13,730.
On Atch. Top. & Santa Fe; Sou. Pac.; Pac. El. (R. Rs.).
South Peabody, Essex Co., Mass., 3,500.
On Bost. & Me. (R. R.).
South Pekin, Tazewell Co., Ill., 1,222.
On Alton; Ill. Cen.; Chi. & Nor. West. (R. Rs.).
South Pittsburg, Marion Co., Tenn., 2,103.
On Nash., Chatt. & St. Lou. (R. R.).
South Plainfield, Middlesex Co., N. J., 5,047.
South Poland, Androscoggin Co., Me., 765.
On Leh. Val. (R. R.).
Southport, Lancashire, England, 78,927.
A popular pleasure resort.
–Fairfield Co., Conn., 1,480.
On N. York, N. Hav. & Hart. (R. R.).
–c. s., Brunswick Co., N. C., 1,760.
On Wilm., Brunsw. & Sou. (R. R.).
–Marion Co., Ind., 521.
On Ind. R. R. Sys. (El.); Penna. (R. Rs.).
South Portland, Cumberland Co., Me., 13,840.
A suburb of Portland.
South Portsmouth, Greenup Co., Ky., 500.
On Chesa. & Ohio (R. R.).
South Range, Houghton Co., Mich., 1,120.
On Copper Range (R. R.).
South Renovo, Clinton Co., Pa., 1,054.
Southridge, Wyandotte Co., Kans., 900.
South River, Middlesex Co., N. J., 10,759.
On Raritan Riv. (R. R.).
Has large brick and tile works.
South Rockwood, Monroe Co., Mich., 700.
South Royalton, Windsor Co., Vt., 800.
On Cen. Ver. (R. R.).
South St. Paul, Dakota Co., Minn., 10,009.
On Chi., Burl. & Quincy; Chi. Gt. West.; Chi., Mil., St. P. & Pac.; Chi., Rk. Isl. & Pac.; Chi., St. P., Mpls. & Omaha; Gt. Nor.; Mpls., St. P. & S. Ste. M.; Mpls. & St. Lou. (R. Rs.).
Live stock market and packing center.
South San Antonio, Bexar Co., Tex., 2,708.
On Nor. Pac. (R. R.).
South San Francisco, San Mateo Co., Cal., 6,193.
On Sou. Pac. (R. R.).
South Seaville, Cape May Co., N. J., 500.
On Penna.-Read. Seash. (R. R.).

South Shaftsbury, Rutland Co., Vt., 625.
On Rutland (R. R.).
South Shields, Durham, England, 113,452.
Situated near the mouth of the Tyne, opposite North Shields. A shipping point for coal and coke; a center of the ship-building industry.
South Sioux City, Dakota Co., Neb., 3,927.
On Chi., Burl. & Quincy; Chi., St. P., Mpls. & Omaha (R. Rs.).
South Stillwater, Washington Co., Minn. See Bayport.
South Sudbury, Middlesex Co., Mass., 500.
On Bost. & Me.; N. York, N. Hav. & Hart. (R. Rs.).
South Superior, Sweetwater Co., Wyo., 751.
South Swansea, Bristol Co., Mass., 800.
On N. York, N. Hav. & Hart. (R. R.).
South Vineland, Cumberland Co., N. J., 506.
On Penna.-Read. Seash. (R. R.).
South Washington, Arlington Co., Va., 750.
South Waverly, Bradford Co., Pa., 1,336.
South Webster, Scioto Co., Ohio, 697.
On Balt. & Ohio (R. R.).
Southwest (Hecla), Westmoreland Co., Pa., 3,000.
On Penna. (R. R.).
Southwest Greensburg, Westmoreland Co., Pa., 3,105.
Southwest Harbor, Hancock Co., Me., 500.
South Weymouth, Norfolk Co., Mass., 6,500.
On N. York, N. Hav. & Hart. (R. R.).
South Whitely, Whitely Co., Ind., 1,102.
On N. York, Chi. & St. Lou.; Penna. (R. Rs.).
Southwick, Hampden Co., Mass., 1,540.
On N. York, N. Hav. & Hart. (R. R.).
South Williamsport, Lycoming Co., Pa., 6,058.
On Penna. (R. R.).
South Wilmington, Grundy Co., Ill., 722.
On Elg., Jol. & East. (R. R.).
South Windham, Cumberland Co., Me., 900.
On Me. Cen. (R. R.).
South Windsor, Hartford Co., Conn., 900.
On N. York, N. Hav. & Hart. (R. R.).
South Yarmouth, Barnstable Co., Mass., 645.
South Zanesville, Muskingum Co., Ohio, 1,278.
On Penna.; N. York. Cen. (R. Rs.).
Spadra, Johnson Co., Ark., 5,395.
On Mo. Pac. (R. R.).
Spalding, Greeley Co., Neb., 839.
On Un. Pac. (R. R.).
Spangler, Cambria Co., Pa., 2,761.
On Penna. (R. R.).
Spanish Fork, Utah Co., Utah, 3,727.
On Den. & Rio Gde. West.; Los. Ang. & Salt L. (Un. Pac.); Salt L. & Utah (El.) (R. Rs.).
Sparkill, Rockland Co., N. Y., 960.
On Erie (R. R.).
Sparkman, Dallas Co., Ark., 711.
On Chi., Rk. Isl. & Pac. (R. R.).
Sparks, Cook Co., Ga., 635.
On Ga. & Fla.; Ga. Sou. & Fla. (R. Rs.).
–Washoe Co., Nev., 4,508.
On Sou. Pac. (R. R.).
Sparr, Marion Co., Fla., 500.
On Seab. Air Line (R. R.).
Sparrows Point Junction, Baltimore City Co., Md., 1,401.
On Balt. & Ohio (R. R.).
Sparta, c. s., Hancock Co., Ga., 1,613.
On Ga. (R. R.).
–Randolph Co., Ill., 3,385.
On Mo.-Ill.; Mob. & Ohio (R. Rs.).
–Gallatin Co., Ky., 500.
On Lou. & Nash. (R. R.).
–Kent Co., Mich., 1,939.
On Gd. Tr.; Pere Marq. (R. Rs.).
–Sussex Co., N. J., 600.
On N. York, Susq. & West. (R. R.).
–c. s., White Co., Tenn., 2,211.
On Nash., Chatt. & St. Lou. (R. R.).
–c. s., Monroe Co., Wis., 4,949.
On Chi., Mil., St. P. & Pac.; Chi. & Nor. West. (R. Rs.).
Spartanburg, c. s., Spartanburg Co., S. C., 28,723.
On Charl. & W. Car.; Clinchfield; Piedmont & Nor. (El.); Sou. (R. Rs.).
A leading textile center. Seat of Wofford College and Converse College.
Sparté, capital of Laconia, Greece, 5,799.
Spearfish, Lawrence Co., S. D., 1,738.
On Chi., Burl. & Quincy (R. R.).
Spearman, c. s., Hansford Co., Tex., 1,580.
On Panh. & Santa Fe (R. R.).
Spearville, Ford Co., Kans., 654.
On Atch., Top. & Santa Fe (R. R.).
Specialville (Dixmoore), Cook Co., Ill., 944.
Speed, Clark Co., Ind., 800.
On Ind. R. R. Sys. (El.); Penna. (R. Rs.).
Speedway, Cook Co., Ill., 1,600.
–Marion Co., Ind., 1,420.
On Balt. & Ohio; Cle., Cin., Chi. & St. Lou. (R. Rs.).
Speedwell, Claiborne Co., Tenn., 750.
–Wythe Co., Va., 500.
Speers, Washington Co., Pa., 654.
Spencer, c. s., Owen Co., Ind., 2,179.
On Penna. (R. R.).
–c. s., Clay Co., Iowa, 5,019.

On Chi., Mil., St. P. & Pac.; Mpls. & St. Lou. (R. Rs.).
–Worcester Co., Mass., 6,487.
On Bost. & Alb. (R. R.).
–Boyd Co., Neb., 653.
On Chi. & Nor. West. (R. R.).
–Tioga Co., N. Y., 628.
On Leh. Val. (R. R.).
–Rowan Co., N. C., 3,128.
On Southern (R. R.).
–Medina Co., Ohio, 592.
On Nor. Ohio; Wheel. & L. Erie (R. Rs.).
–McCook Co., S. Dak., 608.
On Chi., St. P., Mpls. & Omaha (R. R.).
–c. s., Roane Co., W. Va., 2,493.
On Balt. & Ohio (R. R.).
Spencerport, Monroe Co., N. Y., 1,249.
On N. York Cen. (R. R.).
Spencerville, Allen Co., Ohio, 1,612.
On Erie (R. R.).
Spero (No. Asheboro P. O.), Randolph Co., N. C., 750.
On High Pt., Rand., Asheb. & Sou. (R. R.).
Sperry, Tulsa Co., Okla., 563.
On Midl. Val. (R. R.).
Sperryville, Rappahannock Co., Va., 800.
Speyer, Bavaria, Germany, 26,000.
Manufactures of beer, sugar, machinery, vinegar, paper, and musical instruments.
Spezia, Prov. of Spezia, Italy, 76,061.
The chief naval harbor of Italy. Shipbuilding and allied industries are important.
Spiceland, Henry Co., Ind., 722.
On N. York, Chi. & St. Lou. (R. R.).
Spickard (Spickardsville), Grundy Co., Mo., 569.
On Chi., Rk. Isl. & Pac. (R. R.).
Spindale, Rutherford Co., N. C., 3,066.
On Seab. Air Line; Sou. (R. Rs.).
Spirit Lake, Kootenai Co., Idaho, 1,241.
On Chi., Mil., St. P. & Pac. (R. Rs.).
–c. s., Dickinson Co., Iowa, 1,778.
On Chi., Mil., St. P. & Pac.; Chi., Rk. Isl. & Pac. (R. Rs.).
Spiro, Le Flore Co., Okla., 969.
On Kan. Cy. Sou.; Ft. Smith & West. (R. Rs.).
Split, Yugoslavia, 43,808.
Spokane, c. s., Spokane Co., Wash., 115,514.
On the Spokane River and on the Chi., Mil., St. P. & Pac.; Gt. Nor.; Nor. Pac.; Spok. Internatl.; Spok., Port. & Seattle; and Union Pac. (R. Rs.).
Center of a large lumber trade; also an important center of agricultural, mining, jobbing, and financial interests for the interior northwest. Has extensive stockyards.
Spooner, Lake of the Woods Co., Minn., 214.
–Washburn Co., Wis., 2,426.
On Chi., St. P., Mpls. & Oamha (R. R.).
Spotswood, Middlesex Co., N. J., 921.
On Penna. (R. R.).
Sprague, Lincoln Co., Wash., 639.
On Nor. Pac. (R. R.).
Spray, Rockingham Co., N. C., 3,088.
On Danv. & West. (R. R.).
Spremberg, Brandenburg, Prussia, Germany, 12,669.
Bicycles, woolen cloth, and cigars.
Spring Arbor, Jackson Co., Mich., 500.
On Mich. Cen. (R. R.).
Spring Canyon, Carbon Co., Utah, 1,000.
On Den. & Rio Gde. West.; Utah (R. Rs.).
Spring City, Chester Co., Pa., 2,963.
On Penna. (R. R.).
–Rhea Co., Tenn., 1,090.
On Cin., N. Orl. & Tex. Pac. (R. R.).
–Sanpete Co., Utah, 992.
On Den. & Rio Gde. West. (R. R.).
Spring Creek, Madison Co., N. C., 600.
Springdale, Washington Co., Ark., 2,763.
On St. Lou.-San Fran. (R. R.).
–Fairfield Co., Conn., 4,500.
On N. York, N. Hav. & Hart. (R. R.).
–Allegheny Co., Pa., 4,781.
On Penna.; Reading (R. Rs.).
Springer, Colfax Co., N. Mex., 957.
On Atch., Top. & Santa Fe (R. R.).
Springerville, Apache Co., Ariz., 575.
Springfield, c. s., Sangamon Co., Ill., State capital, 71,864.
On the Alton; Balt. & Ohio; Chi. & Ill. Midl.; Chi., Springf. & St. Lou.; Ill. Cen.; Spring Term.; Ill. Term. (El.) and Wab. (R. Rs.).
The industries of the city are due to the production of coal mines in the vicinity.
Home and burial place of Abraham Lincoln. The city was founded in 1819, and received its city charter in 1840.
–c. s., Baca Co., Colo., 1,393.
On Atch., Top. & Santa Fe (R. R.).
–c. s., Washington Co., Ky., 1,487.
On Lou. & Nash. (R. R.).
–Livingston Par., La., 500.
–c. s., Hampden Co., Mass., 149,642.
Port of entry on the Connecticut River, and on the New York, New Haven & Hartford; the Boston & Maine; and the Boston & Albany railroads.
Seat of the United States Armory and Arsenal established in 1795. The industries include the manufacture of Government rifles, revolvers, skates, motorcycles, automobile tires, radios, refrigerators, games, chemical products, magnetos, matches, paper, etc.
Its principal buildings are the Municipal group (Auditorium, Campanile, and Administration building), the Art and Science Museums, and the City Library. Bay Path Institute and the American International College are located here. Springfield was founded by William Pynchon with colonists from Roxbury in 1636.
–Brown Co., Minn., 2,049.
On Chi. & Nor. West. (R. R.).
–c. s., Greene Co., Mo., 57,527.
On Mo. Pac.; St. Lou.-San Fran. (R. Rs.).
Poultry packing and shipping center. Stoves, wagons, structural steel are manufactured. Drury College and Southwest Teachers' College.
–Union Co., N. J., 3,600.
On Rahway Valley (R. R.).
–c. s., Clark Co., Ohio, 68,743.
On the Mad River, and on the Penna.; the Cle., Cin., Chi. & St. Lou.; the Det., Tol. & Iron.; Erie (R. Rs.).
A magazine publishing center. Manufactures motors, piano plates, farm implements, trucks and advertising novelties. Seat of Wittenberg College. Settled in 1799, incorporated in 1827.
–Lane Co., Ore., 2,364.
On Sou. Pac. (R. R.).
–Orangeburg Co., S. C., 943.
On South. (R. R.).
–Bon Homme Co., S. Dak., 661.
On Chi., Mil., St. P. & Pac. (R. R.).
–c. s., Robertson Co., Tenn., 5,577.
On Lou. & Nash. (R. R.).
–Windsor Co., Vt., 4,943.
On Springfield Term. Ry. Corp. (El.) (R. R.).
–Hampshire Co., W. Va., 1,200.
On Balt. & Ohio (R. R.).
Spring Forest, Cook Co., Ill., 733.
Spring Green, Sauk Co., Wis., 779.
On Chi., Mil., St. P. & Pac. (R. R.).
Spring Grove, Houston Co., Minn., 867.
On Chi., Mil., St. P. & Pac. (R. R.).
–York Co., Pa., 1,236.
On Penna.; West. Md. (R. Rs.).
Spring Hill, Johnson Co., Kans., 494.
On St. Lou.-San Fran. (R. R.).
–Webster Co., La., 1,546.
On La. & Ark. (R. R.).
–Scotland Co., N. C., 500.
On Laurinburg & Sou. (R. R.).
Spring Hope, Nash Co., N. C., 1,222.
On Atl. Coast Line (R. R.).
Spring Lake, Ottawa Co., Mich., 1,271.
On Gd. Tr. (R. R.).
–Monmouth Co., N. J., 1,745.
On Cen. of N. Jer.; N. York & Long Br.; Penna. (R. Rs.).
Spring Lake Heights, Monmouth Co., N. J., 1,221.
Spring Mills, Centre Co., Pa., 550.
Spring Mountain, Carbon Co., Pa., 500.
On Reading (R. R.).
Springport, Jackson Co., Mich., 562.
On Mich. Cen. (R. R.).
Springtown, Parker Co., Tex., 500.
Springvale, York Co., Me., 2,530.
On Bost. & Me. (R. R.).
Spring Valley, Bureau Co., Ill., 5,270.
On Chi. & Nor. West.; Chi., Burl. & Quincy; Chi., Rk. Isl. & Pac. (R. Rs.).
–Fillmore Co., Minn., 1,712.
On Chi. Gt. West.; Chi., Mil., St. P. & Pac. (R. Rs.).
–Rockland Co., N. Y., 3,948.
On Erie; N. Jer. & N. York (R. Rs.).
–Pierce Co., Wis., 896.
On Chi., St. P., Mpls. & Omaha (R. R.).
Springville, Linn Co., Ia., 598.
On Chi., Mil., St. P. & Pac. (R. R.).
–Tulare Co., Cal., 665.
–Erie Co., N. Y., 2,540.
On Balt. & Ohio (R. R.).
–Utah Co., Utah, 3,748.
On Denv. & Rio Gde. West.; Salt L. & Utah (El.); Un. Pac. (R. Rs.).
Springwater, Livingston Co., N. Y., 600.
Spruce Pine, Mitchell Co., N. C., 1,546.
On Clinchfield (R. R.).
Spur, Dickens Co., Texas, 1,899.
On Wich. Val. (R. R.).
Spurger, Tyler Co., Tex., 500.
Srinagar (Kashmir or Cashmere), capital of Kashmir, India, 173,573.
Beautifully situated in the celebrated Vale of Kashmir, scene of Moore's famous poem "Lalla Rookh."
Staatsburg, Dutchess Co., N. Y., 500.
On N. York Cen. (R. R.).
Stacy, Carteret Co., N. C., 610.
Stacyville, Mitchell Co., Iowa, 529.
On Ill. Cen. (R. R.).
–Penobscot Co., Me., 170.
On Bangor & Aroostook (R. R.).
Stade, Hannover, Germany, 11,992.
A river port and marketing center.
Stafford, Tolland Co., Conn., 700.
–Pickens Co., Ala., 519.
On Mob. & Ohio (R. R.).

–capital of Staffordshire, England, 29,485.

–Stafford Co., Kans., 1,860.
On Atch., Top. & Santa Fe; Mo. Pac. (R. Rs.).

STAFFORD SPRINGS (Stafford), Tolland Co., Conn., 3,492.
On Cen. Ver. (R. R.).

STAFFORDVILLE, Tolland Co., Conn., 500.

STALIN (Yuzovka), Soviet Union, 285,500.
An industrial town in a coal and iron region.

STALINGRAD (Tsaritsin), Soviet Union, 383,000.
An important port on the Volga River. Manufactures of machinery, metal goods, lumber, beer, and chemicals.

STALINSK (Kuznetsk), Soviet Union, Asia, 199,500.
A trade center with manufactures of agricultural machinery, leather, and bricks.

STALYBRIDGE, Cheshire, England, 24,823.

STAMBAUGH, Iron Co., Mich., 2,400.
On Chi. & Nor. West.; Chi., Mil., St. P. & Pac. (R. Rs.).

STAMFORD, Fairfield Co., Conn., 46,346.
On N. York, N. Hav. & Hart. (R. R.).
Industries: manufactures of locks, hardware, and diversified products.

–Delaware Co., N. Y., 1,103.
On West Shore (N. York Cen.) (R. R.).

–Jones Co., Tex., 4,095.
On Wich. Val.; Mo.-Kan.-Tex. of Tex. (R. Rs.).

STAMPS, Lafayette Co., Ark., 2,705.
On La. & Ark.; St. Lou. Southw. (R. Rs.).

STANAFORD, Raleigh Co., W. Va., 500.
On Chesa. & Ohio (R. R.).

STANBERRY, Gentry Co., Mo., 2,029.
On Wabash (R. R.).

STANDARD, Putnam Co., Ill., 352.
On Chi., Mil., St. P. & Pac. (R. R.).

–Lehigh Co., Pa., 3,053.
On Balt. & Ohio (R. R.).

STANDARDVILLE, Carbon Co., Utah, 200.
On Den. & Rio Gde. West.; Utah (R. Rs.).

STANDING ROCK, Chambers Co., Ala., 1,839.
On Atl., Birm. & Coast (R. R.).

STANDISH, c. s., Arenac Co., Mich., 803.
On Mich. Cen. (R. R.).

–Cumberland Co., Me., 200.

STANFORD, McLean Co., Ill., 443.
On Alton (R. R.).

–c. s., Lincoln Co., Ky., 1,544.
On Lou. & Nash. (R. R.).

–c. s., Judith Basin Co., Mont., 509.
On Gt. Nor. (R. R.).

STANFORD UNIVERSITY, Santa Clara Co., Cal., 720.

STANHOPE, Sussex Co., N. J., 1,089.

STANISLAWOW (Stanislau), East Galicia, Poland, 60,256.
A commercial town situated in an agricultural and lumbering region.

STANLEY, Gaston Co., N. C., 1,084.
On Seab. Air Line (R. R.).

–c. s., Mountrail Co., N. Dak., 936.
On Gt. Nor. (R. R.).

–Chippewa Co., Wis., 1,988.
On Mpls., St. P. & S. Ste. M. (R. R.).

STANTON, Montgomery Co., Iowa, 607.
On Chi., Burl. & Quincy (R. R.).

–Orange Co., Cal., 800.
On Pac. El.; Sou. Pac. (R. Rs.).

–c. s., Montcalm Co., Mich., 955.
On Pere Marq. (R. R.).

–Franklin Co., Mo., 200.
On St. Lou.-San Fran. (R. R.).

–c. s., Stanton Co., Neb., 1,479.
On Chi. & Nor. West. (R. R.).

–Haywood Co., Tenn., 503.
On Lou. & Nash. (R. R.).

–c. s., Martin Co., Tex., 1,384.
On Tex. & Pac. (R. R.).

STANTONSBURG, Wilson Co., N. C., 607.
On Norf. Sou. (R. R.).

STANWOOD, Cedar Co., Iowa, 531.
On Chi. & Nor. West. (R. R.).

–Snohomish Co., Wash., 715.
On Gt. Nor. (R. R.).

STAPLES, Todd Co., Minn., 2,667.
On Nor. Pac. (R. R.).

STAPLETON, Baldwin Co., Ala., 1,045.
On Lou. & Nash. (R. R.).

STAR, Montgomery Co., N. C., 634.
On Norf. Sou. (R. R.).

STÁRA ZAGORA, Bulgaria, 28,857.

STARBEE, Van Buren Co., Ark., 500.

STARBUCK, Pope Co., Minn., 781.
On Nor. Pac. (R. R.).

–Columbia Co., Wash., 346.
On Union Pacific (R. R.).

STAR CITY, Lincoln Co., Ark., 932.
On Arkansas (R. R.).

–Pulaski Co., Ind., 550.
On Penna. (R. R.).

–Monongalia Co., West Va., 1,121.
On Balt. & Ohio (R. R.).

STARGARD, Pomerania, Germany, 35,000.
A river port and marketing center.

STAR JUNCTION, Fayette Co., Pa., 3,055.
On Pitts. & L. Erie (R. R.).

STARKE, c. s., Bradford Co., Fla., 1,317.
On Seab. Air Line (R. R.).

STARKSBORO, Addison Co., Vt., 150.

STARKVILLE, c. s., Oktibbeha Co Miss., 3,612.

On Ill. Cen.; Mob. & Ohio (R. Rs.).

–Las Animas Co., Colo., 945.
On Atch., Top. & Santa Fe (R. R.).

STASSFURT, Prussian Saxony, Germany, 16,000.
Has important salt and chemical industries.

STATE CENTER, Marshall Co., Iowa, 1,012.
On Chi. & Nor. West. (R. R.).

STATE COLLEGE, Centre Co., Pa., 4,450.
On Bellefonte Cen. (R. R.).
Seat of Pennsylvania State College.

–Craighead Co., Ark., 500.

STATESBORO, c. s., Bulloch Co., Ga., 3,996.
On Cen. of Ga.; Statesb. Nor. (R. R.).

STATESVILLE, c. s., Iredell Co., N. C., 10,491.
On Southern (R. R.).
Industries: flour milling, furniture, textiles, tobacco and lumber.

STATHAM, Barrow Co., Ga., 522.
On Seab. Air Line (R. R.).

STAUFFER (Pershing), Westmoreland Co., Pa., 1,000.
On Balt. & Ohio (R. R.).

STAUNTON, Macoupin Co., Ill., 4,618.
On Ill. Term. (El.); Litch. & Mad.; Wab. (R. Rs.).

–(Ind. City), c. s., Augusta Co., Va., 11,990.
On Balt. & Ohio; Chesa. & Ohio (R. Rs.).
A residential and educational town. The famous Virginia Natural Bridge is near. Seat of Staunton Military Academy.

STAVANGER, capital of Amt of Rogaland, Norway, 46,780.
Noted for its fisheries products.

STAVROPOL, (Vorochilovsk), S. Union, Asia, 61,400.
Has textile and olive-oil industries. A trade center for Turkish and Persian trade.

STAYNER, Simcoe Co., N. Ontario, Can., 1,019.
On Can. Nat. (R. R.).

STAYTON, Marion Co., Ore., 797.

STEAMBOAT SPRINGS, c. s., Routt Co., Colo., 1,198.
On Den. & Salt L. (R. R.).

STEARNS, McCreary Co., Ky., 2,176.
On Cin., N. Orl. & Tex. Pac.; Ky. & Tenn. (R. Rs.).

STEELE, Pemiscot Co., Mo., 1,219.
On St. Lou.-San Fran. (R. R.).

–Kidder Co., N. D., 519.
On Nor. Pac. (R. R.).

STEELEVILLE, Randolph Co., Ill., 909.
On Mo. Pac. (R. R.).

STEELTON, Dauphin Co., Pa., 13,291.
On Penna.; Read.; Steel. & Highsp. (R. Rs.).
Location of Bethlehem steel plant.

STEELVILLE, c. s., Crawford Co., Mo., 854.
On St. Lou.-San Fran. (R. R.).

STEGE, Contra Costa Co., Cal., 520.
On Sou. Pac. (R. R.).

STEGER, Cook and Will Cos., Ill., 2,985.
On Chi. & East. Ill. (R. R.).

STEILACOOM, Pierce Co., Wash., 722.
On Gt. Nor.; Nor. Pac.; Un. Pac. (R. Rs.).

STEINAMANGER, Hungary. See SZOMBATHELY.

STELLARTON, Pictou Co., Nova Scotia, 5,002.
On Can. Nat. (R. R.).

STELLENBOSCH, Cape of Good Hope, Union of South Africa, 8,782.

STEMMERS RUN, Baltimore Co., Md., 630.
On Penna. (R. R.).

STENDAL, Brandenburg, Prussia, Germany, 30,000.
An agricultural center.

STEPHENS, Ouachita Co., Ark., 1,045.
On St. Lou. Southw. (R. R.).

STEPHENS CITY, Frederick Co., Va., 606.
On Balt. & Ohio (R. R.).

STEPHENSON, Wilkinson and Amite Cos., Miss., 715.
On Yazoo & Miss. Val. (Ill. Cen.) (R. R.).

STEPHENVILLE, c. s., Erath Co., Texas, 3,944.
On Gulf, Colo. & Santa Fe (R. R.).

STEPNEY DEPOT (Stepney), Fairfield Co., Conn., 1,200.
On N. York, N. Hav. & Hart. (R. R.).

STERKRADE, Rhenish Prussia, Germany, 50,661.

STERLING, c. s., Logan Co., Colo., 7,195.
On Chi., Burl. & Quincy; Un. Pac. (R. Rs.).

–Windham Co., Conn., 590.
On N. York, N. Hav. & Hart. (R. R.).

–Whiteside Co., Ill., 10,012.
On Chi., Burl. & Quincy; Chi. & Nor. West. (R. Rs.).
Industries: stock farms, builders' hardware, farm implements, and foundry products.

–Rice Co., Kans., 2,266.
On Atch., Top. & Santa Fe; Mo. Pac. (R. Rs.).

–(Loring), Worcester Co., Mass., 1,556.
On N. York, N. Hav. & Hart. (R. R.).

–Johnson Co., Neb., 702.
On Chi., Burl. & Quincy (R. R.).

STERLING CITY, c. s., Sterling Co., Texas, 867.
On Gulf, Colo. & Santa Fe (R. R.).

STERLINGTON, Ouachita Par., La., 600.
On Mo. Pac. (R. R.).

STERNBERG, Moravia, Germany, 12,767.
Has large textile and tobacco factories.

STETTIN, capital of Pomerania, Prussia, Germany, 270,225.
Chief seaport of Prussia. The principal part of the city is built on the left bank of the Oder,

while on the right bank are the suburbs of Lastadie and Silberwiese, connection being maintained by several bridges, one of which is a large railway swing bridge. Notable features are the old royal palace, now occupied as Government offices; the new town hall, two monumental gateways, Gothic churches.

STETTLER, Alberta, Canada, 1,219.
On Can. Nat.; Can. Pac. (R. Rs.).

STEUBENVILLE, c. s., Jefferson Co., Ohio, 35,422.
On Penna.; Wheel. & L. Erie (R. Rs.).
An industrial center with large manufactures of iron, steel, paper, glass, and clay products.

STEVENAGE, Hertfordshire, England, 5,476.

STEVENS (Silver Grove), Campbell Co., Ky., 600.
On Chesa. & Ohio (R. R.).

STEVENSON, Jackson Co., Ala., 733.
On Nash., Chatt. & St. Lou.; Sou. (R. Rs.).

STEVENS POINT, c. s., Portage Co., Wis., 13,623.
On Gr. Bay & West.; Mpls., St. P. & S. Ste. M. (R. Rs.).
Pulp and paper mills and furniture factories.

STEVENSVILLE, Ravalli Co., Mont., 692.
On Nor. Pac. (R. R.).

STEWARDSON, Shelby Co., Ill., 629.
On N. York, Chi. & St. Lou.; Wab. (R. Rs.).

STEWART, McLeod Co., Minn., 541.
On Chi., Mil., St. P. & Pac. (R. R.).

STEWART HEIGHTS, Harris Co., Tex., 545.

STEWART MANOR, Nassau Co., N. Y., 1,291.
On Long Isl. (R. R.).

STEWARTSTOWN, Coos Co., N. H., 1,148.
–York Co., Pa., 863.
On Stewartstown (R. R.).

STEWARTSVILLE, De Kalb Co., Mo., 520.
On Chi., Burl. & Quincy (R. R.).

–Warren Co., N. J., 1,100.
On Del., Lack. & West. (R. R.).

STEWARTVILLE, Olmstead Co., Minn., 793.
On Chi. Gt. West. (R. R.).

STICKNEY, Cook Co., Ill., 2,005.
–Raleigh Co., W. Va., 800.
On Chesa. & Ohio (R. R.).

STIGLER, c. s., Haskell Co., Okla., 1,517.
On Midl. Val. (R. R.).

STILES, Lehigh Co., Pa., 721.

STILLMORE, Emanuel Co., Ga., 618.

STILL RIVER, Litchfield Co., Conn., 511.
On N. York, N. Hav. & Hart. (R. R.).

STILLWATER, c. s., Washington Co., Minn., 7,173.
On Chi., Mil., St. P. & Pac.; Chi., St. P., Mpls. & Omaha; Nor. Pac. (R. Rs.).

–Saratoga Co., N. Y., 1,051.
On Bost. & Me. (R. R.).

–c. s., Payne Co., Okla., 7,016.
On Atch., Top. & Santa Fe (R. R.).

STILWELL, c. s., Adair Co., Okla., 1,366.
On Kan. Cy. Sou. (R. R.).

STIRLING, capital of Stirling, Scotland, 22,897.
Stirling Castle played an important part in Scottish history. Stirling is now a prosperous modern city.

–Morris Co., N. J., 950.
On Del., Lack. & West. (R. R.).

STIRRAT, Logan Co., W. Va., 1,000.
On Chesa. & Ohio (R. R.).

STOCKBRIDGE, Berkshire Co., Mass., 1,921.
On N. York, N. Hav. & Hart. (R. R.).

–Ingham Co., Mich., 715.
On Gd. Tr. (R. R.).

STOCKDALE, Washington Co., Pa., 772.
On Penna. (R. R.).

–Wilson Co., Tex., 696.
On Tex. & N. Orl. (Sou. Pac.) (R. R.).

STOCKERTOWN, Northampton Co., Pa., 602.
On Leh. Val.; Leh. & N. Eng. (R. Rs.).

STOCKETT, Cascade Co., Mont., 500.

STOCKHOLM, Län of Stockholm, Sweden, capital of the kingdom, 514,333.
On several islands and the mainland, between a bay of the Baltic and Lake Mälar, in a situation that is most picturesque. The ancient nucleus of Stockholm is an island in mid-channel, called "the Town"; on it stand the imposing royal palace (1697-1754); the principal church (St. Nicholas's), in which the kings are crowned; the House of the Nobles (1648-1670); the town house; the ministries of the kingdom; and the principal wharf, a fine granite quay, fronting east. Immediately west of the central island lies the Knights' Island (Riddarholm), almost entirely occupied by the old House of Parliament; the old Franciscan Church, in which all the later sovereigns of Sweden have been buried; the royal archives, and law courts. Ship Island is the headquarters of the Swedish navy, and is built over with marine workshops, ship-building yards. Beyond these connected by bridges lies the "Island of the Holy Spirit," containing the new Houses of Parliament, and Bank of Sweden.
Stockholm ranks first among Swedish ports in the value of its imports.

–Aroostook Co., Maine, 900.
On Bangor & Aroostook (R. R.).

STOCKPORT, Cheshire, England, 125,505.
An important industrial and railway town adjacent to Manchester. Industries are similar to those of the larger city.

STOCKTON, c. s., San Joaquin Co., Cal., 47,963.
On Atch., Top. & Santa Fe; Sou. Pac.; West. Pac.; Stock. Term. & East.; Tidew. Sou. (R. Rs.). It is also an inland seaport.
Produces agricultural implements, cereals, leather, engines, canned fruits. Center for staple commodities for San Joaquin County.

–Jo Daviess Co., Ill., 1,505.
On Chi. Gt. West. (R. R.).

–Baldwin Co., Ala., 1,100.

–Luzerne Co., Pa., 742.
On Leh. Val. (R. R.).

–c. s., Rooks Co., Kans., 1,328.
On Mo. Pac. (R. R.).

–c. s., Cedar Co., Mo., 647.

–Hunterdon Co., N. J., 556.
On Penna. (R. R.).

STOCKTON-ON-TEES, Durham, England, 67,724.
A port and commercial center.

STOCKWELL, Tippecanoe Co., Ind., 513.
On Cle., Cin., Chi. & St. Lou. (R. R.).

STOKE-UPON-TRENT, Staffordshire, England, 276,619.
Famous for its pottery manufacture.

STOLP, Pomerania, Germany, 44,000.
A trade and marketing town in a farming region.

STONE, Pike Co., Ky., 996.
On Norf. & West. (R. R.).

STONEBORO, Mercer Co., Pa., 1,189.
On N. York Cen.; Penna. (R. Rs.).

STONEFORT, Saline Co., Ill., 500.
On Cle., Cin., Chi. & St. Lou. (R. R.).

STONEHAM, Middlesex Co., Mass., 10,841.
On Bost. & Me. (R. R.).
A residential town north of Boston.

STONEHURST HILLS, Delaware Co., Pa., 950.

STONE MOUNTAIN, De Kalb Co., Ga., 1,335.
On Georgia (R. R.).

STONEVILLE, Rockingham Co., N. C., 564.
On Norf. & West. (R. R.).

STONEWALL, Selkirk Co., Man., Can., 1,031.
On Can. Pac. (R. R.).

–Clarke Co., Miss., 2,048.
On Mob. & Ohio (R. R.).

STONINGTON, New London Co., Conn., 2,006.
On N. York, N. Hav. & Hart. (R. R.).

–Christian Co., Ill., 1,057.
On Wabash (R. R.).

–Hancock Co., Maine, 800.

STONY BROOK, Suffolk Co., N. Y., 819.
On Long Isl. (R. R.).

STONY CREEK, New Haven Co., Conn., 950.
On N. York, N. Hav. & Hart. (R. R.).

STONY CREEK MILLS, Berks Co., Pa., 600.

STONY POINT, Rockland Co., N. Y., 2,700.
On West Shore (R. R.).

–Alexander Co., N. C., 700.
On Southern (R. R.).

STORM LAKE, c. s., Buena Vista Co., Iowa, 4,157.
On Chi., Mil., St. P. & Pac.; Ill. Cen.; Mpls. & St. Lou. (R. Rs.).

STORRS, Carbon Co., Utah.
On Denv. & Rio Gd. West.; Utah (R. Rs.).

STORY CITY, Story Co., Iowa, 1,434.
On Chi. & Nor. West.; Mpls. & St. Lou. (R. Rs.).

STOTTVILLE, Columbia Co., N. Y., 1,079.

STOUFFVILLE, York Co., Ont., Can., 1,155.
On Can. Nat. (R. R.).

STOUGHTON, Norfolk Co., Mass., 8,478.
On N. York, N. Hav. & Hart. (R. R.).

–Dane Co., Wis., 4,497.
On Chi., Mil., St. P. & Pac. (R. R.).

STOUTSVILLE, Fairfield Co., Ohio, 509.
On Penna. (R. R.).

STOVER, Morgan Co., Mo., 517.
On Chi., Rk. Isl. & Pac. (R. R.).

STOW, Middlesex Co., Mass., 1,190.
–Summit Co., Ohio, 2,500.

STOWE, Lamoille Co., Vt., 531.
–Montgomery Co., Pa., 2,000.
On Penna.; Reading (R. Rs.).

STRABANE, Washington Co., Pa., 1,700.

STRALSUND, Pomerania, Prussia, Germany, 42,000.
A seaport and trade center. Has a school of navigation.

STRASBOURG, Bas-Rhin, France, 193,119.
Situated on the Ill River. By means of canals it is brought into communication with the Atlantic and the Mediterranean. The chief building is the cathedral, a medieval structure. The city's industries are very varied, and include tanning, brewing, machine making, and the preparation of its celebrated *pâtés de foie gras*. Strasbourg, under the name of Argentoratum, is supposed to have been founded by the Romans.

STRASBURG, Emmons Co., N. Dak., 695.
On Chi., Mil., St. P. & Pac. (R. R.).

–Tuscarawas Co., Ohio, 1,305.
On Balt. & Ohio; Penna. (R. Rs.).

–Lancaster, Pa., 975.
On Strasburg (R. R.).

–Shenandoah Co., Va., 1,901.
On Balt. & Ohio; Sou. (R. Rs.).

STRATFORD, capital of Perth Co., North, Ontario, Canada, 17,742.
On Can. Nat. (R. R.).
An industrial town with machine shops, flour

mills, textile plants, and sawmills. Ships a large amount of dairy products.
—Fairfield Co., Conn., 19,212.
　On N. York, N. Hav. & Hart. (R. R.).
—Hamilton and Webster Cos., Iowa, 699.
　On Chi. & Nor. West. (R. R.).
—Camden Co., N. J., 958.
　On Penna.-Read. Seashore (R. R.).
—Garvin Co., Okla., 950.
　On Atch., Top. & Santa Fe (R. R.).
—c. s., Sherman Co., Tex., 873.
　On Chi., Rk. Isl. & Gulf; Panh. & Santa Fe (R. Rs.).
—Marathon Co., Wis., 960.
　On Chi. & Nor. West. (R. R.).
STRATFORD-ON-AVON, Warwickshire, England, 11,616.
　On the right bank of the Avon River, crossed by a fine bridge of fourteen pointed arches, nearly 400 years old. "The Birthplace," the house in which Shakespeare was born, was restored in 1859. In the cruciform parish church are his grave and portrait bust, also the font in which he was baptized.
STRATHAM, Rockingham Co., N. H., 500.
　On Bost. & Me. (R. R.).
STRATHROY, Middlesex Co., West, Ontario, Canada, 2,964.
　On Can. Nat. (R. R.).
STRATTON, Hitchcock Co., Neb., 663.
　On Chi., Burl. & Quincy (R. R.).
—Kit Carson Co., Colo., 507.
　On Chi., Rk. Isl. & Pac. (R. R.).
—Franklin Co., Me., 601.
—Jefferson Co., Ohio, 791.
　On Steub., E. Liv. & Beaver Val. Trac. (El.) (R. R.).
STRAUBING, Bavaria, Germany, 24,000.
STRAWBERRY PLAINS, Jefferson Co., Tenn., 500.
　On Southern (R. R.).
STRAWBERRY POINT, Clayton Co., Iowa, 1,128.
　On Chi., Mil., St. P. & Pac. (R. R.).
STRAWN, Palo Pinto Co., Texas, 1,429.
　On Tex. & Pac. (R. R.).
STREATOR, La Salle Co., Ill., 14,728.
　On Alton; Atch., Top. & Santa Fe; Chi., Burl. & Quincy; N. Y. Cen.; Wabash (R. Rs.).
　A commercial and industrial town situated in the heart of the corn belt. Coal mines near by.
STREETER, Stutsman Co., N. D., 711.
　On Nor. Pac. (R. R.).
STREETMAN, Freestone Co., Tex., 509.
　On Chi., Rk. Isl. & Gulf; Ft. Worth & Denv. Cy. (R. Rs.).
STRIEGAU, Silesia, Germany, 14,135.
　Leather products and machinery.
STRINGTOWN, Atoka Co., Okla., 558.
　On Mo.-Kan.-Tex. (R. R.).
STROMSBURG, Polk Co., Neb., 1,320.
　On Chi., Burl. & Quincy; Union Pac. (R. R.).
STRONG, Union Co., Ark., 740.
　On Mo. Pac. (R. R.).
—Chase Co., Kans., 822.
　On Atch., Top. & Santa Fe (R. R.).
STRONGHURST, Henderson Co., Ill., 734.
　On Atch., Top. & Santa Fe (R. R.).
STRONGS, Chippewa Co., Mich., 762.
　On Dul., Sou. Sho. & Atl. (R. R.).
STRONGSVILLE, Cuyahoga Co., Ohio, 1,349.
　On Balt. & Ohio (R. R.).
STROUD, Lincoln Co., Okla., 1,894.
　On St. Lou.-San Fran. (R. R.).
STROUDSBURG, c. s., Monroe Co., Pa., 5,961.
　On N. York, Susq. & West. (Erie); Penna.; Del., Lack. & West. (R. Rs.).
STRUTHERS, Mahoning Co., Ohio, 11,249.
　On Penna.; Pitts. & L. Erie (R. Rs.).
　A suburb of Youngstown.
STRYJ, East Galicia, Poland, 30,682.
　A port and commercial town situated in a farming section and petroleum field.
STRYKER, Williams Co., Ohio, 817.
　On N. York Cen.; Tol. & Ind. (El.) (R. Rs.).
STRYKERSVILLE, Wyoming Co., N. Y., 600.
STUART, Adair and Guthrie Cos., Iowa, 1,626.
　On Chi., Rk. Isl. & Pac. (R. R.).
—c. s., Martin Co., Fla., 2,070.
　On Fla. East Coast (R. R.).
—Holt Co., Neb., 763.
　On Chi. & Nor. West. (R. R.).
—Hughes Co., Okla., 535.
　On Chi., Rk. Isl. & Pac. (R. R.).
—c. s., Patrick Co., Va., 588.
　On Danv. & West. (R. R.).
STUHLWEISSENBURG, Hungary. See SZEKESFEHÉRVÁR.
STUMP CREEK (Cramer), Jefferson Co., Pa., 620.
　On Balt. & Ohio (R. R.).
STURBRIDGE, Worcester Co., Mass., 1,918.
STURGEON, Boone Co., Mo., 600.
　On Wabash (R. R.).
STURGEON BAY, c. s., Door Co., Wis., 4,983.
　On Ahnapee & West. (Grn. Bay & West.) (R. R.).
STURGEON FALLS, Nipissing Co., Ont., Can., 4,234.
　On Can. Pac. (R. R.).
STURGIS, Union Co., Ky., 2,154.
　On Ill. Cen. (R. R.).
—St. Joseph Co., Mich., 6,950.
　On N. York Cen.; Penna. (R. Rs.).

—c. s., Meade Co., S. Dak., 2,591.
　On Chi. & Nor. West. (R. R.).
STURGISS, Monongalia Co., West Va. See SABRATON.
STURTEVANT (Corliss), Racine Co., Wis., 746.
　On Chi., Mil., St. P. & Pac. (R. R.).
STUTTGART, capital of Württemberg, Germany, 445,000.
　Situated near the left bank of the Neckar, 816 feet above the sea. Stuttgart is the center in south Germany for the book trade, paper mills, type foundries, printing houses, and

A DELIGHTFULLY PICTURESQUE SCENE ON STOCKHOLM'S WATERFRONT SHOWING THE SAILS OF SWEDISH SHIPS DRYING WHILE SAILORS UNLOAD SWEET SMELLING BIRCH BROUGHT DOWN FROM THE NORTHERN PROVINCES

lithographic establishments. Dates from 1229.
—c. s., Arkansas Co., Ark., 4,927.
　On St. Lou. Southw.; Chi., Rk. Isl. & Pac. (R. Rs.).
STUYVESANT FALLS, Columbia Co., N. Y., 600.
SUBLETTE, c. s., Haskell Co., Kans., 643.
　On Atch., Top. & Santa Fe (R. R.).
SUBOTICA, Yugoslavia, 100,058.
　A large commercial center located in a rich farming and cattle-raising region. Has manufactures of iron ware, furniture, shoes, and railroad cars.
SUCCASUNNA, Morris Co., N. J., 618.
　On Del., Lack. & West. (R. R.).
SUCHOW, Prov. of Kiangsu, China, 500,000.
　A treaty port, situated on the Imperial Canal, and numerous islands, separated by canals. Suchow has for generations been a noted center of the silk manufacture and of the printing of cheap Chinese classics.
SUCRE, Dept. of Chuquisaca and one of the official capitals of Bolivia, estimated 29,857.
　A trade and marketing town situated in a fertile agricultural section.
SUDAN, Lamb Co., Tex., 1,014.
　On Panh. & Santa Fe (R. R.).
SUDBURY, Nipissing Co., Ontario, Canada, 18,518.
　On Can. Nat.; Can. Pac. (R. Rs.).
　The center of the nickel mining region.
—Middlesex Co., Mass., 1,638.
　On N. York, N. Hav. & Hart. (R. R.). Also served by N. E. Trans. motor coaches. The "Wayside Inn" attracts tourists.
SUEZ, Egypt, 35,547.
　Red Sea terminus of Suez Canal.

SUFFERN, Rockland Co., N. Y., 3,757.
　On Erie (R. R.).
SUFFIELD, Hartford Co., Conn., 1,150.
　On N. York, N. Hav. & Hart. (R. R.).
SUFFOLK (Ind. City), c. s., Nansemond Co., Va., 10,271.
　On Atl. Coast Line; Norf. & West.; Norf. Sou.; Seab. Air Line; Sou.; Virginian (R. Rs.). Peanut and related industries. Lumber center.
SUGAR CITY, Crowley Co., Colo., 598.
　On Mo. Pac. (R. R.).
—Madison Co., Idaho, 621.

On Ore. Short Line (Un. Pac.) (R. R.).
SUGAR CREEK, Jackson Co., Mo., 1,657.
　On Atch., Top. & Santa Fe; Kan. Cy. Sou. (R. Rs.).
—Tuscarawas Co., Ohio, 895.
　On Wheel. & L. Erie (R. R.).
SUGAR GROVE, Pendleton Co., W. Va., 500.
SUGAR HILL, Grafton Co., N. H., 500.
　On Bost. & Me. (R. R.).
SUGAR LAND, Ft. Bend Co., Tex., 1,840.
　On Sugar Land (Mo. Pac.); Tex. & N. Orl. (Sou. Pac.) (R. Rs.).
SUGARLOAF, Luzerne Co., Pa., 500.
SUGAR NOTCH, Luzerne Co., Pa., 2,768.
　On Cen. of N. Jer.; Leh. Val. (R. Rs.).
SUHAG, Egypt, 22,000.
　A river port and marketing center.
SUHL, Prussian Saxony, Germany, 16,000.
SUISUN CITY (Suisun-Fairfield), Solano Co., Cal., 905.
　On Sou. Pac.; Sacramento Nor. (Ei.) (R. Rs.).
SULLIGENT, Lamar Co., Ala., 1,078.
　On St. Lou.-San Fran. (R. R.).
SULLIVAN, c. s., Moultrie Co., Ill., 2,339.
　On Chi. & East. Ill.; Ill. Cen.; Wab. (R. Rs.).
—c. s., Sullivan Co., Ind., 5,306.
　On Chi. & East. Ill.; Ill. Cen.; Chi., Mil., St. P. & Pac. (R. Rs.).
—Hancock Co., Maine, 120.
—Franklin and Crawford Cos., Mo., 2,013.
　On St. Lou.-San Fran. (R. R.).
SULPHUR, Calcasieu Parish, La., 1,888.
　On Tex. & N. Orl. (Sou. Pac.) (R. R.).
—c. s., Murray Co., Okla., 4,242.
　On St. Lou.-San Fran. (R. R.).

SULPHUR SPRINGS, c. s., Hopkins Co., Texas, 5,417.
　On St. Lou. Southw.; La., Ark. & Tex. (R. Rs.).
SULTAN, Snohomish Co., Wash., 830.
　On Gt. Nor. (R. R.).
SULTANABAD, Iran (Persia), 55,000.
SULZBACH, Rhenish Prussia, Germany, 5,822.
SUMAS, Whatcom Co., Wash., 647.
　On Chi., Mil., St. P. & Pac.; Nor. Pac.; Can Pac. (R. Rs.).
SUMEN, Dept. of Sumen, Bulgaria, 26,600.
　Center for grain and wine. Manufactures clothing, copper and tin wares, embroideries.
SUMITON (Summit), Walker Co., Ala., 800.
　On St. Lou.-San Fran. (R. R.).
SUMMERDALE, Cumberland Co., Pa., 600.
SUMMERHILL, Cambria Co., Pa., 785.
　On Penna. (R. R.).
SUMMER SHADE, Metcalf Co., Ky., 2,839.
SUMMERTON, Clarendon Co., S. C., 812.
SUMMERVILLE, c. s., Chattooga Co., Ga., 933.
　On Cen. of Ga. (R. R.).
—Jefferson Co., Pa., 1,202.
　On Penna.; L. Erie, Frank. & Clar. (R. Rs.).
—Dorchester Co., S. C., 2,579.
　On Southern (R. R.).
—c. s., Nicholas Co., W. Va., 536.
SUMMIT, Cook Co., Ill., 6,548.
　On Alton (R. R.).
—(Yellville) Marion Co., Ark., 750.
　On Mo. Pac. (R. R.).
—Pike Co., Miss., 1,157.
　On Ill. Cen. (R. R.).
—Union Co., N. J., 14,556.
　On Del., Lack. & West.; Rahw. Val. (R. Rs.).
—Lake Co., S. Dak., 503.
　On Chic., Mil. & St. Paul (R. R.).
SUMMIT HILL, Carbon Co., Pa., 5,567.
　On Lehigh & New England (R. R.).
　Located in an important anthracite coal field. The chief industry is coal mining. The Burning Mine has been smoldering for a century.
SUMMITVILLE, Madison Co., Ind., 1,017.
　On Cle., Cin., Chi. & St. Lou. (R. R.).
SUMNER, Lawrence Co., Ill., 967.
　On Balt. & Ohio (R. R.).
—Bremer Co., Iowa, 1,561.
　On Chi. Gt. West. (R. Rs.).
—c. s., Tallahatchie Co., Miss., 618.
　On Yazoo & Miss. Val. (Ill. Cen.) (R. R.).
—Pierce Co., Wash., 1,967.
　On Chi., Mil., St. P. & Pac.; Nor. Pac.; Gt. Nor.; Un. Pac. (R. Rs.).
SUMRALL, Lamar Co., Miss., 1,364.
　On Miss. Cen. (R. R.).
SUMTER, c. s., Sumter Co., S. C., 11,780.
　On Seab. Air Line; Northw. of S. C.; Atl. Coast Line; Sou. (R. Rs.).
SUN, Fayette Co., W. Va., 500.
　On Chesa. & Ohio; Kanaw., Gl. Jean & East. (R. Rs.).
SUNAPEE, Sullivan Co., N. H., 700.
　On Bost. & Me. (R. R.).
SUNBRIGHT, Morgan Co., Tenn., 500.
　On Cin., N. Orl. & Tex. Pac. (R. R.).
SUNBURY, Delaware Co., Ohio, 784.
　On Penna. (R. R.).
—c. s., Northumberland Co., Pa., 15,626.
　On Penna.; Read.; Del., Lack. & West. (R. Rs.). Pennsylvania shops and yards, also silk and dye mills.
SUNCOOK, Merrimack Co., N. H., 3,000.
　On Bost. & Me.; Suncook Val. (R. Rs.).
SUNDERLAND, Durham, England, 185,870.
　The largest town of Durham, including nearly three parishes. Trade interests are shipping, the coal trade—the Pemberton Mine (2,286 deep)—and shipbuilding.
—Franklin Co., Mass., 1,182.
SUNDSVALL, Län of Västernorrland, Sweden, 18,006.
　A seaport and commercial center. Has fisheries.
SUNFLOWER, Sunflower Co., Miss., 530.
　On Yazoo & Miss. Val. (Ill. Cen.) (R. R.).
SUNLAND, Los Angeles Co., Cal., 1,000.
SUNNYSIDE, Carbon Co., Utah, 749.
　On Den. & Rio Gde. West. (R. R.).
—Yakima Co., Wash., 2,113.
　On Nor. Pac.; Un. Pac. (R. Rs.).
SUNNYSLOPE, Los Angeles Co., Cal., 700.
　On Pac. El.; Sou. Pac. (R. Rs.).
SUNNYVALE, Santa Clara Co., Cal., 3,094.
　On Sou. Pac. (R. R.).
SUNOL, Alameda Co., Cal., 600.
　On Sou. Pac.; West. Pac. (R. Rs.).
SUN PRAIRIE, Dane Co., Wis., 1,337.
　On Chi., Mil., St. P. & Pac. (R. R.).
SUNSET, St. Landry Par., La., 520.
　On Tex. & N. Orl. (Sou. Pac.) (R. R.).
—Montague Co., Tex., 665.
　On Ft. Worth & Denv. Cy. (R. R.).
—Davis Co., Utah, 600.
SUPERIOR, Pinal Co., Ariz., 4,000.
　On Magma Ariz. (R. R.).
—Nuckolls Co., Neb., 3,044.
　On Atch., Top. & Santa Fe; Chi., Burl. & Quincy; Mo. Pac.; Chi. & Nor. West. (R. Rs.).
—McDowell Co., W. Va., 500.

On Norf. & West. (R. R.).
–c. s., Douglas Co., Wis., 36,113.
Port of entry, on Lake Superior, and Nor. Pac.; Gt. Nor.; Dul., So. Sh. & Atl.; Chi., Mil., St. P. & Pac.; Chi., St. P., Mpls. & Oma.; Mpls., St. P. & S. Ste. M.; and L. Sup. Term. & Trans. railroads.
It has a fine harbor, well sheltered and deep. The leading industries produce salt, chairs, milk powder, boxes.
–Sweetwater Co., Wyo., 1,156.
On Un. Pac. (R. R.).
Suquamish, Kitsap Co., Wash., 691.
Surabaya, Netherland India. See Soerabaja.
Surakarta, Java, Netherland India. See Soerakarta.
Surat, capital of Surat Dist., Bombay, British India, 98,936.
A center of trade and industry. Has cotton mills, gins, and presses; rice mills. Makes brocades, rugs, soap and inlaid wood products.
Suresnes, Seine, France, 32,018.
Surfside (Nantasket Beach), Plymouth Co., Mass., 1,356.
Surgoinsville, Hawkins Co., Tenn., 500.
On Southern (R. R.).
Susanville, c. s., Lassen Co., Cal., 1,358.
On Sou. Pac. (R. R.).
Susquehanna, Susquehanna Co., Pa., 3,203.
On Erie (R. R.).
Sussex, Sussex Co., N. J., 1,415.
On Leh. & N. Eng.; N. York, Susq. & West. (R. Rs.).
Suterville (Suter), Westmoreland Co., Pa., 918.
On Balt. & Ohio (R. R.).
Sutherland, Lincoln Co., Neb., 753.
On Un. Pac. (R. R.).
–O'Brien Co., Iowa, 802.
On Chi. & Nor. West. (R. R.).
Sutter, Sutter Co., Cal., 500.
On Sacramento Nor. (El.) (R. R.).
Sutter Creek, Amador Co., Cal., 1,013.
Sutton, Worcester Co., Mass., 2,408.
–Clay Co., Neb., 1,540.
On Chi., Burl. & Quincy (R. R.).
–c. s., Braxton Co., W. Va., 1,205.
On Balt. & Ohio (R. R.).
Svendborg, Amt of Svendborg, Denmark, 14,392.
A seaport and marketing town.
Sverdlovsk (Ekaterinburg), Soviet Union, 400,-800.
Scene of the murder of the ex-Czar and his family in 1918.
Swainsboro, c. s., Emanuel Co., Ga., 2,442.
On Ga. & Fla.; Wadley Sou. (R. R.).
Swampscott, Essex Co., Mass., 10,480.
On Bost. & Me. (R. R.).
Swandale, Clay Co., W. Va., 525.
On Buf. Cr. & Gavley (R. R.).
Swannanoa, Buncombe Co., N. C., 1,800.
On Southern (R. R.).
Swans Island, Hancock Co., Me., 190.
Swansea, St. Clair Co., Ill., 1,201.
–Glamorganshire, Wales, 164,825.
An important seaport and smelting town.
–Bristol Co., Mass., 4,327.
–Lexington Co., S. C., 717.
On Seab. Air Line (R. R.).
Swansea Center, Bristol Co., Mass., 800.
Swanton, Fulton Co., Ohio, 1,505.
On N. York Cen.; Tol. & Ind. (El.) (R. Rs.).
–Franklin Co., Vt., 1,558.
On Cen. Ver.; St. Johns & L. Champ. (R. Rs.).
Swarthmore, Delaware Co., Pa., 3,405.
On Penna. (R. R.).
Seat of Swarthmore College.
Swastika, Colfax Co., N. Mex., 550.
On Atch., Top. & Santa Fe (R. R.).
Swatara Station, Dauphin Co., Pa., 500.
On Read. (R. R.).
Swatow, Prov. of Kwangtung, China, 178,600.
A river port and agricultural trade center.
Swayzee, Grant Co., Ind., 604.
On N. York, Chi. & St. Lou. (R. R.).
Swea City, Kossuth Co., Iowa, 695.
On Chi., Rk. Isl. & Pac. (R. R.).
Swedeland, Montgomery Co., Pa., 1,150.
On Penna.; Read.; Up. Mer. & Ply. (R. Rs.).
Swedesboro, Gloucester Co., N. J., 2,123.
On Penna.-Read. Seash. (R. R.).
Sweeney, Brazoria Co., Tex., 510.
On Mo. Pac. (R. R.).
Sweetser, Grant Co., Ind., 735.
On Chesa. & Ohio; Penna. (R. Rs.).
Sweet Springs, Saline Co., Mo., 1,641.
On Mo. Pac. (R. R.).
Sweetwater, Monroe Co., Tenn., 2,271.
On Southern (R. R.).
–c. s., Nolan Co., Texas, 10,848.
On Tex. & Pac.; Panh. & Santa Fe; Gulf, Colo. & Santa Fe (R. Rs.).
The commercial center of a rich stock-raising region. Oil and gas wells in the vicinity.
Swellendam, Cape of Good Hope, Union of South Africa, 3,784.
Swift Current, Saskatchewan, Canada, 5,074.
On Can. Pac. (R. R.).
Swindon, Wiltshire, England, 62,407.
Has a large locomotive and railroad car plant, quarries, clothing factories, grist mills.
Swinemunde, Pomerania, Prussia, Germany, 18,000.
A port and seaside resort.
Swissvale, Allegheny Co., Pa., 16,029.
On Penna. (R. R.).
An industrial suburb of Pittsburgh.
Swoyerville, Luzerne Co., Pa., 9,133.
Sycamore, c. s., De Kalb Co., Ill., 4,021.
On Chi. Gt. West.; Chi. & Nor. West. (R. Rs.).
–Talladega Co., Ala., 631.
On Lou. & Nash. (R. R.).
–Turner Co., Ga., 559.
On Ga. Sou. & Fla. (R. R.).
–Wyandot Co., Ohio, 808.
On Nor. Ohio; N. York Cen. (R. Rs.).
Sydney, capital of New South Wales, Australia, including suburbs, 1,267,350.
Situated on the southern shore of Port Jackson, the shore line being indented by bays or inlets, forming harbors, and lined with wharfs, quays, and warehouses. The city is the outlet for a mining and agricultural region, and its exports of leather, wool, and gold are important. Sydney was founded in 1788.
–Cape Breton Co., Nova Scotia, 23,089.
On Can. Nat.; Syd. & Louisb. (R. Rs.).
A port and commercial center. Has large steel and coal industries.
Sydney Mines, Cape Breton Co., Nova Scotia, 7,769.
On Can. Nat. (R. R.).
Sygan, Allegheny Co., Pa., 500.
On Penna.; Pitts. & W. Va. (R. Rs.).
Sykesville, Carroll Co., Md., 661.
On Balt. & Ohio (R. R.).
–Jefferson Co., Pa., 2,103.
On Balt. & Ohio (R. R.).
Sylacauga, Talladega Co., Ala., 4,115.
On Cen. of Ga.; Lou. & Nash. (R. Rs.).
Sylva, c. s., Jackson Co., N. C., 1,340.
On Tuckaseegee & Southe.; Sou. (R. Rs.).
Sylvan Grove, Lincoln Co., Kans., 502.
On Un. Pac. (R. R.).
Sylvania, c. s., Screven Co., Ga., 1,781.
On Savan. & Atl.; Sylv. Cen. (R. Rs.).
–Lucas Co., Ohio, 2,106.
On N. York Cen. (R. R.).
Sylvan Lake, Oakland Co., Mich., 799.
Sylvester, c. s., Worth Co., Ga., 1,984.
On Atl. Coast Line; Ga., Ashb., Sylv. & Cam. (R. Rs.).
Sylvia, Reno Co., Kans., 524.
On the Atch., Top. & Santa Fe (R. R.).
Syosset, Nassau Co., N. Y., 1,358.
On Long Isl. (R. R.).
Syracuse, Kosciusko Co., Ind., 1,190.
On Balt. & Ohio (R. R.).
–capital of Prov. of Siracusa, Italy. See Siracusa.
–c. s., Hamilton Co., Kans., 1,553.
On Atch., Top. & Santa Fe (R. R.).
–c. s., Onondaga Co., N. Y., 209,326.
On Lake Onondaga, the State Barge Canal (terminal), and the Delaware, Lackawanna & Western, the West Shore; and the New York Central (R. Rs.).
Syracuse is a leading city in manufactures. Among its leading products are tool steel, automobile parts, farm implements, typewriters, silverware, shoes, electrical goods. It is the seat of Syracuse University, as well as of numerous other educational institutions. Syracuse was first visited in 1654 by Jesuit missionaries. The State purchased the tract containing the salt springs from the Onondaga Indians in 1778 and 1795. It was permanently settled in 1797; incorporated as a village in 1826, and received its city charter in 1847.
–Otoe Co., Neb., 947.
On Chi., Burl. & Quincy (R. R.).
–Meigs Co., Ohio, 678.
–Davis Co., Utah, 800.
On Un. Pac. (R. R.).
Szarvas, Comitat of Bekes, Hungary, 25,490.
Center of a farming and stock-raising region.
Szatmar-Nemeti, Rumania. See Satu Mare.
Szeged, Comitat of Csongrad, Hungary, 136,438.
A large and important commercial town. Seat of a university.
Szekesfehérvár, Hungary, 40,731.
Has tanneries and shoe factories and trade in wine, fruit, and horses.
Szentes, Comitat of Csongrad, Hungary, 32,885.
A river port and trade center.
Szepingkai, Manchukuo, 45,000.
Szolnok, capital of Comitat of Jazygia-Great-Cumania-Szolnok, Hungary, 38,764.
A railway center and river port.
Szombathely, Hungary, 35,756.
The center of a wine-producing region. Manufactures textiles, lumber, machinery, flour, and railroad cars.

T

Taal, Batangas Prov., Luzon, P. I., 21,155.
An agricultural center. Has native manufactories.
Tabaco, Prov. of Albay, Luzon, P. I., 25,000.
Abaca is principal product of the region.
Table Rock, Pawnee Co., Neb., 673.
On Chi., Burl. & Quincy (R. R.).
Tabor, Bohemia, Czechoslovakia, 14,251.
–Fremont and Mills Cos., Iowa, 1,017.
–(Mount Tabor) Morris Co., N. J., 500.
On Dela., Lack. & West. (R. R.).
Tabor City (Mount Tabor), Columbus Co., N. C., 1,165.
On Atl. Coast Line (R. R.).
Tabriz, capital of Prov. of Azerbijan, Iran (Persia), 220,000.
Situated on the Agi, 36 miles above the river's entrance into Lake Urmia.
Tabriz has manufactures of silks, cottons, carpets, leather and leather goods, etc., and is the center of a large dried fruit industry. Emporium for the trade of Persia on the west.
Tacloban, Leyte Prov., Leyte, P. I., 15,478.
Tacna, Prov. of Tacna, Chile, 16,776.
A trade and marketing center.
Tacoma, c. s., Pierce Co., Wash., 106,817.
Port of entry on Commencement Bay, at the southern extremity of Puget Sound, on ground 300 feet above the sound. It is on the Northern Pacific; Chicago, Milwaukee, St. Paul & Pacific; Great Northern; and Union Pac. railroads. A lumber port, with timber industries making furniture, sashes and doors, lumber, toys, pulp, box shooks and other woodwork. A flour milling center for export and a smelter center for gold, copper, silver and arsenic. Manufactures chemicals and fish products. Tacoma has a large overseas traffic with all parts of the world.
Tacoma was settled in 1868, and made the terminus of the Northern Pacific Railroad in 1873.
Taconite, Itasca Co., Minn., 485.
On Dul., Missabe & Nor. (R. R.).
Tacubaya, Distrito Federal, Mexico, 54,775.
On Nat. of Mex. (R. R.).
A residential suburb of Mexico, D. F.
Taft, Kern Co., Cal., 3,442.
On Sunset (Sou. Pac.) (R. R.).
–Muskogee Co., Okla., 690.
On Midl. Val. (R. R.).
–San Patricio Co., Tex., 1,792.
On Tex. & N. Orl. (Sou. Pac.) (R. R.).
Taftville, New London Co., Conn., 3,965.
Taganrog, North Caucasian Area, Soviet Union, 149,500.
A seaport and busy shipping point for agricultural produce.
Tagbilaran, Bohol Prov., Bohol, P. I., 12,590.
Tagus Ranch, Tulare Co., Cal., 1,000.
Tahlequah, c. s., Cherokee Co., Okla., 2,495.
On St. Lou.-San Fran. (R. R.).
Tahoka, c. s., Lynn Co., Texas, 1,620.
On Panh. & Santa Fe (R. R.).
Taichu, Taiwan, Japan, 51,572.
A trade and marketing center in a tea-raising region.
Taihoku, capital of Taiwan, Japan, 283,085.
The trade and commercial center of the colony.
Tainan, Taiwan, Japan, 109,887.
Important seaport and trade center.
Taiyuan, Shansi, China, 500,000.
A river port and shipping point for coal.
Takamatsu, capital of Ken of Kagawa, Japan, 79,907.
A maritime town and distributing point.
Takao, Taiwan, 76,380.
A seaport and commercial center.
Takaoka, Ken of Toyama, Japan, 51,760.
Iron foundries, textile mills, and dye works.
Takasaki, Ken of Gumma, Japan, 59,923.
Has textile industries.
Takoma Park, Montgomery and Prince Georges Cos., Md., and D. C., 6,415.
On Balt. & Ohio (R. R.).
Talbotton, c. s., Talbot Co., Ga., 1,064.
On Atl., Birm. & Coast; Talbotton (R. Rs.).
Talca, Prov. of Talca, Chile, 59,364.
An agricultural center. Region produces principally wheat, grapes, and livestock.
Talcahuano, Prov. of Concepción, Chile, 43,085.
The leading naval station.
Talibon, Prov. of Bohol, Bohol, P. I., 12,226.
Talihina, LeFlore Co., Okla., 1,032.
On St. Lou.-San Fran. (R. R.).
Talisay, Prov. of Negros Occidental, Negros, P. I., 14,147.
–Prov. of Cebu, Cebu, P. I., 15,299.
Talladega, c. s., Talladega Co., Ala., 7,596.
On Atl., Birm. & Coast; Lou. & Nash.; Sou. (R. Rs.).
Has cotton, hosiery and oil mills.
Tallahassee, c. s., Leon Co., Fla., State capital, 11,725.
Situated 21 miles north of the Gulf of Mexico, and 165 miles west of Jacksonville on the Seaboard Air Line railroad.
Live stock and dairy market. Also tourist resort. Florida State College for Women.
Tallapoosa, Haralson Co., Ga., 2,417.
On Southern (R. R.).
Tallassee, Elmore Co., Ala., 849.
On Birm. & Southe. (R. R.).
Tallinn (Revel), Estonia, 145,565.
Capital of Estonia and situated on the Bay of Revel, Gulf of Finland.
The Germans in their invasion of Russia in the final stages of the World War, occupied the city for a time in 1918.
Tallmadge, Summit Co., Ohio, 2,000.
On Erie (R. R.).
Tallman, Rockland Co., N. Y., 500.
On Erie (R. R.).
Tallulah, c. s., Madison Parish, La., 3,332.
On Mo. Pac.; Yazoo & Miss. Val. (Ill. Cen.) (R. Rs.).
Taltal, Prov. of Antofagasta, Chile, 7,835.
Tama, Tama Co., Iowa, 2,626.
On Chi., Mil., St. P. & Pac.; Chi. & Nor. West.; Tama & Tol. (El.) (R. Rs.).
Tamaqua, Schuylkill Co., Pa., 12,936.
On Cen. of N. Jer.; Read.; Leh. & N. Eng. (R. Rs.).
Tamaroa, Perry Co., Ill., 881.
On Ill. Cen.; Mo. Pac. (R. Rs.).
Tamatave, Madagascar, 23,207.
Important seaport, former capital.
Tambov, Soviet Union, 101,700.
A trade and mining center in a fertile agricultural region.
Tammerfors, Finland. See Tampere.
Tamms, Alexander Co., Ill., 717.
On Chi. & East. Ill.; Mob. & Ohio (R. Rs.).
Tampa, Hillsborough Co., Fla., 100,151.
On Atl. Coast Line; Seab. Air Line (R. Rs.).
Seat of cigar industry.
Ship building is carried on. A phosphate shipping plant.
Tampere (Tammerfors), Finland, 59,200.
Manufactures of textiles, paper, and leather goods.
Tampico, Tamaulipas, Mexico, 70,183.
On Nat. of Mex. (R. R.).
The leading seaport and distributing point. Is situated near a very rich petroleum region and is a center for that industry.
–Whiteside Co., Ill., 693.
On Chi., Burl. & Quincy; Hoop., York & Tamp. (R. Rs.).
Tams, Raleigh Co., W. Va., 506.
On Chesa. & Ohio; Virginian (R. Rs.).
Tamworth, New South Wales, Australia, 9,913.
Tananarive, capital of Madagascar, 100,893.
In interior, 140 miles southwest of Tamatave.
Tanauan, Prov. of Batangas, Luzon, P. I., 22,-470.
An agricultural center.
–Prov. of Leyte, Leyte, P. I., 19,074.
Tandil, Buenos Aires, Argentina, 52,647.
Situated in a farming and stock raising region.
Taneytown, Carroll Co., Md., 938.
On Penna. (R. R.).
Tangier, Tangier Zone (Morocco), 60,000.
A seaport and international city and zone.
–Accomac Co., Va., 1,120.
Tanjay, Prov. of Negros Oriental, Negros, P. I., 15,038.
Tanjore, Madras, India, 66,880.
The city is famous for its silk brocade, jewelry, inlaid copper work, and rugs.
Tanner, Limestone Co., Ala., 500.
On Lou. & Nash. (R. R.).
Tannersville, Greene Co., N. Y., 656.
On West Shore (N. York Cen.) (R. R.).
Tanta, capital of Prov. of Charbieh, Egypt, 94,421.
The site of several large annual fairs.
Taos, c. s., Taos Co., N. M., 500.
Tappan, Rockland Co., N. Y., 900.
On Erie; West Shore (N. York Cen.) (R. Rs.).
Taranto, Prov. of Taranto, Italy, 89,534.
A seaport and commercial center. Chief industries are shipbuilding, and the making of olive-oil, flour, and beer.
Tarare, Dept. of Rhone, France, 10,395.
A textile center.
Tarascon, Dept. of Bouches du Rhone, France, 5,058.
An ancient town in southeastern France.
Tarbes, capital of Dept. of Hautes-Pyrénées, France, 34,749.
A commercial and industrial center. Manufactures of leather, pottery, and wood products. The region is famous for its fine horses.
Tarboro, c. s., Edgecombe Co., N. C., 6,379.
On Atl. Coast Line; E. Carol. (R. Rs.).
Tarentum, Allegheny Co., Pa., 9,551.
On Penna. (R. R.).
In coal mine section. Industries: iron and steel products, plate glass, glass bottles, mining.
Tarifa, Prov. of Cadiz, Spain, 11,957.
A seaport and marketing town.
Tariffville, Hartford Co., Conn., 1,316.
Tarija, capital of Dept. of Tarija, Bolivia, 17,150.
The center of a stock-raising district.
Tarkio, Atchison Co., Mo., 2,016.
On Chi., Burl. & Quincy (R. R.).
Tarlac, Prov. of Tarlac, Panay, P. I., 25,000.
An important commercial center.
Tarnopol, East Galicia, Poland, 35,831.
Chief industries are corn-milling and the preparation of wax and honey.
Tarnow, Galicia, Poland, 45,235.

Agricultural implements, glass, and chicory.

TARPON SPRINGS, Pinellas Co., Fla., 3,520.
On Atl. Coast Line; Seab. Air Line (R. Rs.).

TARRAGONA, capital of Prov. of Tarragona, Spain, 28,008.
A flourishing seaport and commercial center. Famous for its wines and vinegar. Manufactures of files, soaps, flour, chocolate, paper, and salted fish.

TARRANT (Tarrant City), Jefferson Co., Ala., 7,341.
On Lou. & Nash. (R. R.).

TARRYTOWN, Westchester Co., N. Y., 6,841.
On N. York Cen. (R. R.).

TARSUS, Vilayet of Mersin, Turkey, 22,058.
A port and trade center in a farming region.

TARTU (Dorpat), Estonia, 59,000.
Situated on the Embach. The Domberg, a hill at the northwest extremity of the town, is the seat of Tartu University, founded in 1632 by Gustavus Adolphus of Sweden. It has a library of about 300,000 volumes, an art mu-

TASHKENT, Uzbek Rep., Soviet Union, 491,000.
A commercial and marketing center in an agricultural region. Has manufactures of cotton, tobacco, leather, lumber, cellulose, and machinery.

TATAMY, Northampton Co., Pa., 592.
On Leh. Val. (R. R.).

TATE, Pickens Co., Ga., 1,548.
On Lou. & Nash. (R. R.).

TAUNTON, c. s., Bristol Co., Mass., 37,431.
On the Taunton River, and on the New York, New Haven & Hartford (R. R.). Trading center. Manufactures cotton goods, stoves, furnaces and silverware.

–Somerset, England, 25,177.
A marketing town and distributing point. Manufactures of silk and other textiles.

TAVARES, c. s., Lake Co., Fla., 1,123.
On Atl. Coast Line; Seab. Air Line; Tav. & Gulf (R. Rs.).

TAVIRA, Prov. of Algarve, Portugal, 12,762.

TAWAS CITY, c. s., Iosco Co., Mich., 1,034.
On Det. & Mack.; Erie & Mich. (R. Rs.).

TAYABAS, Prov. of Tayabas, Luzon, P. I., 14,833.
Situated in a rice and coconut producing region.

TAYLOR, Baker Co., Fla., 669.

–Lackawanna Co., Pa., 10,428.
On Cen. of N. Jer.; Del., Lack. & West. (R. Rs.).
Located in an anthracite coal-mining region.

–Greenville Co., S. C., 1,500.
On Piedmont & Nor. (El.); Sou. (R. Rs.).

–Williamson Co., Texas, 7,463.
On Internat.-Gt. Nor. (Mo. Pac.); Mo.-Kan. Tex. of Tex. (R. Rs.).

TAYLOR'S FALLS, Chisago Co., Minn., 527.
On Nor. Pac. (R. R.).

TAYLORS ISLAND, Dorchester Co., Md., 750.

TAYLOR SPRINGS, Montgomery Co., Ill., 774.
On Cle., Cin., Chi. & St. Lou. (R. R.).

TAYLORSVILLE, c. s., Spencer Co., Ky., 729.
On Lou. & Nash. (R. R.).

–c. s., Alexander Co., N. C., 926.

On Southern (R. R.).

–Smith Co., Miss., 805.
On Gulf & Ship Isl. (Ill. Cen.) (R. R.).

TAYLORVILLE, c. s., Christian Co., Ill., 7,316.
On Balt. & Ohio; Chi. & Ill. Midl.; Wab. (R. Rs.).

TAZEWELL, c. s., Claiborne Co., Tenn., 800.
On Southern (R. R.).

–c. s., Tazewell Co., Va., 1,211.
On Norf. & West. (R. R.).

TCHELYABINSK, Soviet Union. See CHELYABINSK.

TCHERKAZY, Soviet Union. See CHERKASI.

TCHULA, Holmes Co., Miss., 907.
On Yazoo & Miss. Val. (Ill. Cen.) (R. R.).

TEAGUE, Freestone Co., Tex., 3,509.
On Chi., Rk. Isl. & Gulf; Ft. Worth & Denv. Cy. (R. Rs.).

TEANECK, Bergen Co., N. J., 16,513.
On West Shore (N. York Cen.) (R. R.).
A residential and marketing town.

TEATICKET, Barnstable Co., Mass., 675.

TECAMACHALCO, State of Puebla, Mexico, 3,143.
On Natl. of Mex. (R. R.).

TECUMSEH, Lenawee Co., Mich., 2,456.
On Det., Tol. & Iron.; N. York Cen. (R. Rs.).

–c. s., Johnson Co., Neb., 1,829.
On Chi., Burl. & Quincy (R. R.).

–Pottawatomie Co., Okla., 2,419.
On Chi., Rk. Isl. & Pac.; Gulf, Colo. & Santa Fe (R. Rs.).

TEGUCIGALPA, capital of Honduras, 22,640.

TEHACHAPI, Kern Co., Cal., 736.
On Atch., Top. & Santa Fe; Sou. Pac. (R. Rs.).

TEHRAN, Prov. of Irakajemi, capital of Iran (Persia), 360,300.
Situated on a wide plain. The old wall and ditch were leveled in 1868, and the space thus gained made into a boulevard. Fortifications consist of a bastioned rampart and ditch. In the vicinity are the ruins of Rei, the birthplace of Harun al-Raschid. Commercial center.

TEHUACAN, State of Puebla, Mexico, 10,679.
On Natl. of Mex. (R. R.).

TEKAMAH, c. s., Burt Co., Neb., 1,804.
On Chi., St. P., Mpls. & Oma. (R. R.).

TEKOA, Whitman Co., Wash., 1,408.
On Chi., Mil., St. P. & Pac.; Un. Pac. (R. Rs.).

TEKONSHA, Calhoun Co., Mich., 595.
On Mich. Cen. (R. R.).

TEL AVIV, Palestine, 140,000.
Distributing center for Jewish colonists.

TELL CITY, Perry Co., Ind., 4,873.
On Southern (R. R.).

TELLICO PLAINS, Monroe Co., Tenn., 902.
On Lou. & Nash. (R. R.).

TELLURIDE, c. s., San Miguel Co., Colo., 512.
On Rio Gde. Sou. (R. R.).

TEMESVAR, Rumania. See TIMISOARA.

TEMPE, Maricopa Co., Ariz., 2,495.
On Sou. Pac. (R. R.).

TEMPERANCE, Monroe Co., Mich., 720.
On Ann Arbor (R. R.).

TEMPLE, Bell Co., Texas, 15,345.
On Gulf, Colo. & Santa Fe; Mo.-Kan.-Tex. of Tex. (R. Rs.).
In agricultural and stock raising region. Has cotton compresses and cotton-seed oil mills.

–Carroll Co., Ga., 573.
On Southern (R. R.).

–Cotton Co., Okla., 1,182.
On Chi., Rk. Isl. & Pac. (R. R.).

–Berks Co., Pa., 1,250.
On Reading; Penna. (R. Rs.).

TEMPLE CITY, Los Angeles Co., Cal., 3,400.
On Pac. El. (R. R.).

TEMPLETON, Worcester Co., Mass., 4,302.
On Bost. & Alb. (R. R.).

–Armstrong Co., Pa., 1,000.
On Penna. (R. R.).

TEMUCO, Prov. of Cautin, Chile, 81,226.
A commercial center.

TENAFLY, Bergen Co., N. J., 5,669.
On Erie (R. R.).

TENAHA, Shelby Co., Texas, 591.
On Gulf, Colo. & Santa Fe; Tex. & N. Orl. (Sou. Pac.) (R. Rs.).

TENINO, Thurston Co., Wash., 938.
On Nor. Pac.; Un. Pac.; Gt. Nor. (R. Rs.).

TEN MILE, Charleston Co., S. C., 1,000.

On Southern (R. R.).

TENNILLE, Washington Co., Ga., 1,666.
On Cen. of Ga.; Sandersville; Wrights. & Tennille (R. Rs.).

TEPEACA, State of Puebla, Mexico, 2,816.
On Nat. of Mex. (R. R.).

TEPIC, Nayarit, Mexico, 15,109.
On Sou. Pac. of Mex. (R. R.).
In a mining and lumbering region.

TEPLITZ-SCHÖNAU (Teplice-Sanov), Bohemia, Germany, 30,911.
A popular spa. Has manufactures of glass, textiles, pottery, and chemicals. Near a deposit of lignite coal.

TERAMO, capital of Prov. of Teramo, Italy, 9,865.

TERERRO, San Miguel Co., N. Mex., 1,000.

TERESZINA (Therazina), Teresina, Brazil, 60,000.
A river port and commercial town. Manufactures include cotton, sugar, castings, and soap.

TERLIZZI, Prov. of Bari, Italy, 23,462.
Region produces almonds and wine.

TERMINAL ISLAND, Los Angeles Co., Cal., 1,046.
On Los Ang. & Salt L. (Un. Pac.) (R. R.).

TERMINI IMERESE, Prov. of Palermo, Sicily, 18,307.
Has much frequented hot springs.

TERMONDE (or Dendermonde), East Flanders, Belgium, 9,997.

TERNI, Prov. of Terni, Italy, 26,775.
Manufactures of iron, steel, naval ordnance, carbide, and woolen yarn.

TERRA ALTA, Preston Co., W. Va., 1,474.
On Balt. & Ohio (R. R.).

TERRACE, Allegheny Co., Pa., 500.

TERRA CEIA, Manatee Co., Fla., 979.
On Seab. Air Line (R. R.).

TERRACE PARK, Hamilton Co., Ohio, 713.
On Penna. (R. R.).

TERRA HILL, Lancaster Co., Pa., 812.

TERRAL, Jefferson Co., Okla., 593.
On Chi., Rk. Isl. & Pac. (R. R.).

TERREBONNE, Terrebonne Co., Que., Can., 1,955.
On Can. Pac. (R. R.).

TERRE HAUTE, c. s., Vigo Co., Ind., 62,810.
On the Wabash River, and on the following railroads: Chi. & East. Ill.; Chi., Mil., St. P. &

Pac.; Cle., Cin., Chi. & St. Lou.; Ind. R. R. Sys. (El.); and Penna.
Center of Indiana coal fields, also of clay and shale deposits. Manufactures alcohol, beer, glass, sanitary cans, clay products, machinery, straw board, baking powder and food products.

TERRE HILL, Lancaster Co., Pa., 812.

TERRELL, Kaufman Co., Texas, 8,795.
On Tex. & Pac.; Sou. Pac. (R. Rs.).
Has railroad shops. In midst of cotton district.

TERRY, c. s., Prairie Co., Mont., 779.
On Nor. Pac.; Chi., Mil., St. P. & Pac. (R. Rs.).

TERRYVILLE, Litchfield Co., Conn., 2,250.
On N. York, N. Hav. & Hart. (R. R.).

TETUAN, Spanish Morocco, 48,347.
A beautiful town and trade center. Region abounds in fruits of all kinds.

TEUTOPOLIS, Effingham Co., Ill., 710.
On Penna. (R. R.).

TEWKSBURY, Middlesex Co., Mass., 6,563.
On Bost. & Me. (R. R.).

TEXARKANA, c. s., Miller Co., Ark., 10,764.
–Bowie Co., Texas, 16,602.
Twin cities of separate municipalities on the Texas-Arkansas State line, on Kansas City Southern; Missouri Pacific; St. Louis Southwestern; and Texas & Pacific (R. Rs.).
Leading industrial products are caskets, cedar chests, baskets, crates, handles, creosoted timbers, clay pipe, pottery, overalls, brooms, fertilizer and cottonseed oil.

TEXAS, Baltimore Co., Md., 1,009.
On Penna. (R. R.).

TEXAS CITY, Galveston Co., Texas, 3,534.
On Burl.-Rk. Isl.; Gulf, Colo. & Santa Fe, Mo.-Kan.-Tex.; Mo. Pac.; Sou. Pac.; Tex. Cy. Term. (R. Rs.).

TEXHOMA, Texas Co., Okla., 819.
On Chi., Rk. Isl. & Pac.; Chi., Rk. Isl. & Gulf (R. Rs.).

TEXICO, Curry Co., N. M., 569.

TEXLA, Orange Co., Tex., 517.
On Orange & Northw. (Mo. Pac.) (R. R.).

TEXLINE, Dallam Co., Texas, 711.
On Ft. Worth & Denv. Cy. (R. R.).

TEXOLA, Beckham Co., Okla., 581.
On Chi., Rk. Isl. & Gulf; Chi., Rk. Isl. & Pac. (R. Rs.).

TEXON, Reagan Co., Tex., 1,200.
On Panh. & Santa Fe (R. R.).

THATCHER, Graham Co., Ariz., 895.
On Sou. Pac. (R. R.).

THAYER, Sangamon Co., Ill., 813.
On Alton; Chi., Burl. & Quincy; Ill. Term. (El.) (R. Rs.).

–Oregon Co., Mo., 1,632.
On St. Lou.-San Fran. (R. R.).

THEALKA, Johnson Co., Ky., 520.
On Chesa. & Ohio (R. R.).

THEBES, Alexander Co., Ill., 751.
On Mo. Pac.; St. Lou. Southw.; Chi. & East Ill. (R. Rs.).

–Dept. of Attica-Boeotia, Greece, 7,113.

THE DALLES, c. s., Wasco Co., Ore., 5,883.
On Un. Pac. (R. R.).

THE FALLS (Ellsworth Falls), Hancock Co., Me., 1,040.
On Me. Cen. (R. R.).

THEODORE, Mobile Co., Ala., 500.
On Lou. & Nash.; Mob. & Ohio (R. R.).

THEODOSIA, Soviet Union. See FEODOSIYA.

THEOPHILO-OTTONI, Brazil, 126,298.

THE PAS, Manitoba, Canada, 3,405.
On Can. Nat.; Hudson Bay (R. Rs.).

THERESA, Jefferson Co., N. Y., 873.
On N. York Cen. (R. R.).

THERMOPOLIS, c. s., Hot Springs Co., Wyo., 2,129.
On Chi., Burl. & Quincy (R. R.).
Hot mineral springs.

THESSALON, Algoma Co., Ont., Can., 1,632.
On Can. Pac. (R. R.).

THESSALONIKĒ (Salonika), capital of Dept. of Salonica, Greece, 265,160.
The Allied forces on the Macedonian front in the World War were centered on Thessalonikē.

THETFORD, Orange Co., Vt., 1,052.
On Bost. & Me. (R. R.).

THETFORD MINES, Megantic Co., Que., Canada, 10,701.
On Queb. Cen. (R. R.).
Has world's largest asbestos mines.

THIBODAUX, c. s., Lafourche Parish, La., 4,442.
On Sou. Pac.; Tex. & Pac. (R. Rs.).

THIEF RIVER FALLS, Pennington Co., Minn., 4,268.
On Gt. Nor.; Mpls., St. P. & S. Ste. M. (R. Rs.).

THIELLS, Rockland Co., N. Y., 700.
On N. Jer. & N. York (R. R.).

THIELT, West Flanders, Belgium, 11,611.

THIENSVILLE, Ozaukee Co., Wis., 500.
On Chi., Mil., St. P. & Pac.; Mil. Elec. Ry. (El.) (R. Rs.).

THIERS, Dept. of Puy de Dome, France, 16,181.
Noted for its fine cutlery.

THOMAS, Custer Co., Okla., 1,256.
On Atch., Top. & Santa Fe; St. Lou.-San Fran. (R. Rs.).

–Jefferson Co., Ala., 1,530.

TAOS, NEW MEXICO, FAMOUS INDIAN TOWN, HAVEN OF THE ARTIST WITH ITS DWELLINGS PRE-DATING THE SPANISH CONQUEST

seum, observatory and botanical garden. The National Museum of Estonia is located here.

On Ala. Gt. Sou.; Birm. Sou.; Lou. & Nash.; Seab. Air Lines; Sou; St. Lou.-San Fran. (R. Rs.).
–Tucker Co., W. Va., 1,660.
On West. Md. (R. R.).
Thomaston, Litchfield Co., Conn., 3,900.
On N. York, N. Hav. & Hart. (R. R.).
–c. s., Upson Co., Ga., 4,922.
On Cen. of Ga. (R. R.).
–Knox Co., Maine, 1,700.
On Me. Cen. (R. R.).
Thomasville, Clarke Co., Ala., 1,504.
On Southern (R. R.).
–c. s., Thomas Co., Ga., 11,733.
On Atla., Birm. & Coast; Atl. Coast Line (R. Rs.).
A popular winter resort.
–Davidson Co., N. C., 10,090.
On High Pt., Thomasv. & Dent.; Sou. (R. Rs.).
An agricultural center.
Thompson, Windham Co., Conn., 4,999.
On N. York, N. Hav. & Hart. (R. R.).
–Winnebago Co., Iowa, 538.
On Chi., Rk. Isl. & Pac. (R. R.).
Thompsonville, Franklin Co., Ill., 569.
On Ill. Cen. (R. R.).
–Hartford Co., Conn., 9,643.
On N. York, N. Hav. & Hart. (R. R.).
Thomson, c. s., McDuffie Co., Ga., 1,914.
On Georgia (R. R.).
–Carroll Co., Ill., 508.
On Chi., Burl. & Quincy; Chi., Mil., St. P. & Pac. (R. Rs.).
Thorn, Poland. See Torun.
Thornaby-on-Tees, Yorkshire, England, 21,233.
An industrial center. Chief products are castings, engines, ships, lumber, and flour.
Thornbury, Ontario, Canada, 764.
On Can. Nat. (R. R.).
Thorndale, Chester Co., Pa., 500.
On Penna. (R. R.).
–Milam Co., Tex., 1,002.
On Internat.-Gt. Nor. (Mo. Pac.) (R. R.).
Thorndike, Hampden Co., Mass., 1,200.
On Bost. & Alb. (R. R.).
Thornton, Cook Co., Ill., 1,012.
On Chi. & East. Ill.; Balt. & Ohio Chi. Term.; Chi., Mil., St. P. & Pac. (R. Rs.).
–Calhoun Co., Ark., 550.
On St. Lou. Southw. (R. R.).
–Providence Co., R. I., 4,000.
–Limestone Co., Texas, 739.
On Tex. & N. Orl. (Sou. Pac.) (R. R.)
Thorntown, Boone Co., Ind., 1,325.
On Cle., Cin., Chi. & St. Lou. (R. R.).
Thornwood, Westchester Co., N. Y., 1,500.
On N. York Cen. (R. R.).
Thorofare, Gloucester Co., N. J., 500.
On Penna.-Read. Seashore (R. R.).
Thorold, Welland Co., Ont., Canada, 5,092.
On Can. Nat.; Niag., St. Cath. & Tor. (El.) (R. Rs.).
Thorp, Clark Co., Wis., 892.
On Mpls., St. P. & S. Ste. M. (R. R.).
–Kittitas Co., Wash., 500.
On Chi., Mil., St. P. & Pac.; Nor. Pac. (R. Rs.).
Thorpe, McDowell Co., W. Va., 500.
On Norf. & West. (R. R.).
Thorsby, Chilton Co., Ala., 771.
On Lou. & Nash. (R. R.).
Thourout, West Flanders, Belgium, 11,074.
A suburb of Bruges.
Thrasher, Prentiss Co., Miss., 600.
On Mob. & Ohio (R. R.).
Three Forks, Gallatin Co., Mont., 884.
On Nor. Pac.; Chi., Mil., St. P. & Pac. (R. Rs.).
Three Lakes, Oneida Co., Wis., 975.
On Chi. & Nor. West. (R. R.).
Three Oaks, Berrien Co., Mich., 1,336.
On Mich. Cen. (R. R.).
Three Rivers, Can. See Trois Rivières.
–Hampden Co., Mass., 1,632.
On Cen. Ver.; Bost. & Alb. (R. Rs.).
–St. Joseph Co., Mich., 6,863.
On N. York Cen.; Mich. Cen. (R. Rs.).
–Live Oak Co., Tex., 1,275.
On San Ant., Uvalde & Gulf (Mo. Pac.) (R. R.).
Three Sands, Kay Co., Okla., 1,698.
Thrift (Paw Creek), Mecklenburg Co., N. C., 600.
On Piedmont & Nor. (El.); Seab. Air Line (R. R.).
Throckmorton, c. s., Throckmorton Co., Texas, 1,135.
On Cisco & Northe. (R. R.).
Throop, Lackawanna Co., Pa., 8,027.
On Del., Lack. & West.; N. York, Ont. & West. (R. Rs.).
Thunderbolt, Chatham Co., Ga., 802.
Thurber, Erath Co., Tex., 500.
On Tex. & Pac. (R. R.).
Thurin, Orange Co., Cal., 500.
Thurmont, Frederick Co., Md., 1,185.
On Hagerst. & Fred. (El.); West. Md. (R. Rs.).
Tice, Lee Co., Fla., 500.
On Atl. Coast Line (R. R.).
Tickfaw, Tangipahoa Par., La., 500.
On Ill. Cen. (R. R.).
Ticonderoga, Essex Co., N. Y., 3,680.
On Del. & Hud. (R. R.).
Tidioute, Warren Co., Pa., 970.
On Penna. (R. R.).
Tiel, Gelderland, Netherlands, 12,370.
Tiehling, Manchukuo, 46,282.
Tientsin, Prov. of Hopei, China, 1,389,000.
Free port; point of landing of allied troops during "Boxer" uprising (1900).
Tierra Amarilla, c. s., Rio Arriba Co., N. Mex., 550.
Tiffin, c. s., Seneca Co., Ohio, 16,428.
On Balt. & Ohio; Cle., Cin., Chi. & St. Lou.; Penna. (R. Rs.).
A railroad and commercial center.
Tiflis, capital of Transcaucasia, Soviet Union, 405,900.
A trade and industrial center. Manufactures bricks, tobacco, soap, leather, lumber, and furniture.
Tifton, c. s., Tift Co., Ga., 3,390.
On Atl., Birm. & Coast; Atl. Coast Line; Ga. Sou. & Fla. (R. Rs.).
Tigard, Washington Co., Ore., 500.
On Ore. El. (Sp., Port. & Seat.); Sou. Pac. (R. Rs.).
Tigerton, Shawano Co., Wis., 831.
On Chi. & Nor. West. (R. R.).
Tignall, Wilkes Co., Ga., 505.
Tihwa, Sinkiang, China, 50,000.
Tilburg, North Brabant, Netherlands, 87,297.
A commercial and industrial center in a dairy and farming region.
Tilden, Antelope and Madison Cos., Neb., 1,106.
On Chi. & Nor. West. (R. R.).
–Randolph Co., Ill., 981.
On Ill. Cen. (R. R.).
–c. s., McMullen Co., Texas, 500.
Tilghman, Talbot Co., Md., 700.
Tillamook, c. s., Tillamook Co., Ore., 2,549.
On Sou. Pac. (R. R.).
Tillsonburg, Oxford Co., Ont., Can., 3,385.
On Can. Pac.; Can. Nat.; Mich. Cen.; Wab. (R. Rs.).
Tilsit, East Prussia, Germany, 57,286.
Iron foundries, machine shops, tanneries.
Tilton, Belknap Co., N. H., 1,500.
On Bost. & Me. (R. R.).
–Vermilion Co., Ill., 1,394.
On Wab.; Ill. Term. (El.) (R. Rs.).
Tiltonsville, Jefferson Co., Ohio, 2,242.
On Penna.; Wheel. & L. Erie (R. Rs.).
Timber Lake, c. s., Dewey Co., S. Dak., 560.
On Chi., Mil., St. P. & Pac. (R. R.).
Timisoara, Rumania, 91,866.
A large and important commercial and industrial center. Manufactures of paper, lumber, tobacco, flour, beer, leather, and textiles.
Timmonsville, Florence Co., S. C., 1,919.
On Atl. Coast Line; Seab. Air Line (R. Rs.).
Timpson, Shelby Co., Texas, 1,545.
On Tex. & N. Orl. (Sou. Pac.) (R. R.).
Tinley Park, Cook Co., Ill., 823.
On Chi., Rk. Isl. & Pac. (R. R.).
Tinnevelly, Madras, India, 57,078.
An agricultural center.
Tioga, Rapides Parish, La., 522.
On Mo. Pac.; La. & Ark. (R. Rs.).
–Grayson Co., Texas, 591.
On Tex. & Pac.; Mo.-Kan.-Tex. of Tex. (R. Rs.).
–Nicholas Co., W. Va., 500.
On Strouds Cr. & Muddlety (R. R.).
Tionesta, c. s., Forest Co., Pa., 670.
On Penna. (R. R.).
Tippecanoe City, Miami Co., Ohio, 2,559.
On Balt. & Ohio (R. R.).
Tipperary, County Tipperary, Ireland (Eire), 5,000.
Tipton, Staffordshire, England, 35,792.
An industrial center. Heavy iron goods.
–c. s., Tipton Co., Ind., 4,861.
On N. York, Chi. & St. Lou.; Ind. R. R. Sys. (El.) (R. Rs.).
–c. s., Cedar Co., Iowa, 2,145.
On Chi., Rk. Isl. & Pac.; Chi. & Nor. West. (R. Rs.).
–Moniteau Co., Mo., 1,067.
On Mo. Pac. (R. R.).
–Tillman Co., Okla., 1,459.
On Mo.-Kan.Tex. (R. R.).
Tiptonville, c. s., Lake Co., Tenn., 1,359.
On Ill. Cen. (R. R.).
Tiranë, capital of Albania, 30,806.
A marketing and trade center. A picturesque town with many parks and mosques.
Tiraspol, Ukraine, Soviet Union, 31,600.
An agricultural center.
Tirlemont, Brabant, Belgium, 20,662.
A suburb of Louvain.
Tirnovo, Bulgaria, 12,802.
A trade and marketing town. Ancient capital of Bulgaria (1186-1393).
Tisbury, Mass. See Vineyard Haven.
Tishomingo, c. s., Johnston Co., Okla., 1,281.
Tiskilwa, Bureau Co., Ill., 893.
On Chi., Rk. Isl. & Pac. (R. R.).
Titusville, c. s., Brevard Co., Fla., 2,360.
On Fla. East Coast (R. R.).
–Mercer Co., N. J., 500.
On Penna. (R. R.).
–Crawford Co., Pa., 8,055.
On N. York Cen.; Penna. (R. Rs.).
Tiverton, Devonshire, England, 9,611.
–Newport Co., R. I., 5,118.
On N. York, N. Hav. & Hart. (R. R.).
Tiverton Four Corners, Newport Co., R. I., 621.
Tivoli, Dutchess Co., N. Y., 713.
On N. York Cen. (R. R.).
Tlemcen, Dept. of Oran, Algeria, 26,384.
Has a large trade and manufactures of cloth, rugs, and leather goods.
Toa Alta, Mun. of Toa Alta, Puerto Rico, 1,126.
Toa Baja, Mun. of Toa Baja, Puerto Rico, 1,817.
Toano, James City Co., Va., 500.
On Chesa. & Ohio (R. R.).
Tobolsk, Soviet Union, Asia, 14,798.
A trade center.
Tobyhanna, Monroe Co., Pa., 526.
On Del., Lack. & West. (R. R.).
Toccoa, c. s., Stephens Co., Ga., 4,602.
On Southern (R. R.).
Tocopilla, Prov. of Antofagasta, Chile, 15,305.
Todmorden, Lancashire, England, 22,223.
A textile center near Manchester.
Togus (Veterans Administration Home), Kennebec Co., Me., 2,350.
Tohatchi, McKinley Co., N. Mex., 2,000.
Tokushima, Tokushima Ken, Japan, 90,633.
A trade center in an agricultural area.
Tokyo, Dist. of Tokyo-fu, capital of Japan, 5,875,667.
On the Bay of Tokyo, on the southeastern coast of Hondo, the largest of the Japanese islands and connected by rail with Yokohama and Kanazawa. Tokyo contains the Imperial University, the leading educational institution of Japan, and is rapidly becoming westernized.
Toledo, capital of Prov. of Toledo, Spain, 26,237.
This city was the capital of the Visigoth realm in Spain in the Mohammedan kingdom in the eleventh century, and of the Castilian realm.
–c. s., Cumberland Co., Ill., 733.
On Ill. Cen. (R. R.).
–c. s., Tama Co., Iowa, 1,825.
On Chi. & Nor. West.; Tama & Tol. Elec. (R. Rs.).
–c. s., Lucas Co., Ohio, 290,718.
On Maumee River near Maumee Bay, Lake Erie, and on the Ann Arbor; Balt. & Ohio; Chesa. & Ohio; Cle., Cin., Chi. & St. Lou.; Det. & Tol. Sh. Line; Det., Tol. & Iron.; Lake Shore (El.); Mich. Cen.; N. York Cen.; N. York, Chi. & St. Lou.; Ohio Pub. Serv. (El.); Penna.; Pere Marq.; Tol. & Ind. (El.); Tol. & West. (El.); Tol. Term.; Wab.; Wheel. & L. Erie (R. Rs.).
A lake shipping port, especially for coal and iron. Also a wheat market, with several elevators. Has great blast furnaces. Industries: oil refining, oil-well supplies, cut and plain glassware, safety glass, plate glass, automobiles, electrical appliances, radios, tools, hats, stoves, malleable castings and scales. Seat of Toledo University. The river is navigable for the largest lake steamers.
–c. s., Lincoln Co., Ore., 2,137.
On Sou. Pac. (R. R.).
–Lewis Co., Wash., 530.
–Prov. of Cebu, P. I., 25,330.
Toliman, State of Querétaro, Mexico, 3,082.
Tolleson, Maricopa Co., Ariz., 910.
On Sou. Pac. (R. R.).
Tolono, Champaign Co., Ill., 790.
On Ill. Cen.; Wab. (R. Rs.).
Toluca, Marshall Co., Ill., 1,413.
On Atch., Top. & Santa Fe. (R. R.).
–State of Mexico, Mexico, 41,234.
On Nat. of Mex.; Toluca & Tenango; Toluca & San Juan (R. Rs.).
An attractive commercial town situated in a picturesque mountain region.
Tomah, Monroe Co., Wis., 3,354.
On Chi., Mil., St. P. & Pac. (R. R.).
Tomahawk, Lincoln Co., Wis., 2,919.
On Chi., Mil., St. P. & Pac.; Marin., Tom. & West. (R. Rs.).
–Searcy Co., Ark., 536.
Tombstone, Cochise Co., Ariz., 849.
On Sou. Pac. (R. R.).
Tomé, Prov. of Tomé, Chile, 5,039.
Tomhicken, Luzerne Co., Pa., 500.
On Leh. Val.; Penna. (R. Rs.).
Tomkins Cove, Rockland Co., N. Y., 1,000.
On West Shore (R. R.).
Tompkinsville, c. s., Monroe Co., Ky., 850.
Toms Creek, Wise Co., Va., 1,500.
On Norf. & West. (R. R.).
Tomsk, Siberia, Soviet Union, Asia, 128,400.
On the Tom River, and great trade route from Tyumen to Irkutsk, near the Siberian Railway.
Toms River, c. s., Ocean Co., N. J., 3,290.
On Cen. of N. Jer.; Penna. (R. Rs.).
Tonasket, Okanogan Co., Wash., 513.
On Gt. Nor. (R. R.).
Tonawanda, Erie Co., N. Y., 12,681.
On N. York Cen. (R. R.).
Western terminus of N. Y. state canal system. Has foundries and woodworking plants.
Tonganoxie, Leavenworth Co., Kans., 1,074.
On Un. Pac. (R. R.).
Tonica, La Salle Co., Ill., 500.
On Ill. Cen. (R. R.).
Tonkawa, Kay Co., Okla., 3,311.
On the Atch., Top. & Santa Fe; Chi., Rk. Isl. & Pac. (R. Rs.).
Tonopah, Nye Co., Nev., 2,115.
On Tonop. & Goldf. (R. R.).
Tooele, c. s., Tooele Co., Utah, 5,135.
On Tooele Val. (R. R.).
Toomsboro, Wilkinson Co., Ga., 665.
On Cen. of Ga. (R. R.).
Toowoomba, Queensland, Australia, 26,145.
A marketing town situated in an agricultural and lumbering region.
Topanga, Los Angeles Co., Cal., 600.
Topeka, Lagrange Co., Ind., 489.
On Wabash (R. R.).
–c. s., Shawnee Co., Kans., State capital, 73,677.
On the Kan. River, and Chi., Rk. Isl. & Pac.; the Un. Pac.; Atch., Top. & Santa Fe; and Mo. Pac. (R. Rs.).
The city has large packing houses, foundries, creameries, railroad and machine shops, printing plants, flour mills, etc.
Topeka was laid out in 1854, incorporated in 1857, and made State capital in 1861.
Toppenish, Yakima Co., Wash., 2,774.
On Nor. Pac. (R. R.).
Topsfield, Essex Co., Mass., 1,113.
On Bost. & Me. (R. R.).
Topsham, Sagadahoc Co., Maine, 1,200.
On Me. Cen. (R. R.).
Topton, Berks Co., Pa., 1,667.
On Reading (R. R.).
Torino (Turin), Torino, Italy, 594,698.
Is situated at junction of the rivers Po and Dora Ripaira, has richly decorated cathedral and many historical edifices, including Royal Palace and ancient palace of dukes of Savoy. Silks, cottons, leather products, and motor cars are among the leading manufactures.
Törökszentmiklós, Comitat of Jász-Nagykun-Szolnok, Hungary, 28,503.
A leading trade and farming center.
Toronto, capital of Prov. of Ontario, Canada, 631,201.
Port of entry and second city in population, situated on Lake Ontario, and on the Canadian Pacific and Canadian National Railroads.
Toronto is one of the leading manufacturing centers of Canada, its industries embracing nearly every field. It also has large facilities for an extensive lake traffic. There are many handsome public buildings, including the residence of the lieutenant-governor, the imposing new Parliament buildings. Osgoode Hall (law courts), the University of Toronto, Trinity College (Anglican), are the best known of the city's many educational institutions.
Toronto was founded in 1794 by Gov. Simcoe.
–Woodson Co., Kans., 674.
On Atch., Top. & Santa Fe; Mo. Pac. (R. Rs.).
–Jefferson Co., Ohio, 7,044.
On Penna. (R. R.).
Torquay, Devonshire, England, 46,165.
A popular resort.
Torrance, Los Angeles Co., Cal., 7,271.
On Atch., Top. & Santa Fe; Pac. El.; Sou. Pac. (R. Rs.).
–Westmoreland Co., Pa., 500.
On Penna. (R. R.).
–Torrance Co., N. Mex., 540.
On Sou. Pac. (R. R.).
Torre del Greco, Prov. of Napoli, Italy, 33,915.
A port and marketing town near Napoli.
Torreon, Coahuila, Mexico, 66,091.
On Nat. of Mex. (R. R.).
Torrington, Litchfield Co., Conn., 26,040.
On N. York, N. Hav. & Hart. (R. R.).
An industrial and commercial town west of Hartford. Is an important center of the brass and needle industries and other manufactures.
–Goshen Co., Wyo., 1,811.
On Chi., Burl. & Quincy (R. R.).
Tortona, Prov. of Alessandria, Italy, 10,391.
Tortosa, Catalonia, Spain, 33,044.
Torun (Thorn), Poland, 54,280.
Totonicapan, capital of Dept. of Totonicapan, Guatemala, 29,970.
Manufactures of cloth, furniture, pottery, and musical instruments. Hot springs near by.
Totowa, Passaic Co., N. J., 4,600.
Tottenham, Middlesex, England, 157,748.
A suburb of London.
Tottori, Ken of Tottori, Japan, 37,189.
A seaport and marketing center.
Touchet, Walla Walla Co., Wash., 500.
On Un. Pac. (R. R.).
Touisset, Bristol Co., Mass., 500.
Toulon, Dept. of Var, France, 150,310.
Situated on a deep inlet of the Mediterranean, formed by the peninsula of Sópet. It is, next to Brest, the principal naval station of France. The port militaire, one of the largest in Eu-

rope, comprises the old Darse (wet-docks), formed under Henri IV, the new under Louis XIV, and the Darse of Castigneau; three repairing docks and three arsenals.
Toulon is said to have been founded by a Roman soldier, Telo Martins, and was known as Telo in the fourth century.
c. s., Stark Co., Ill., 1,203.
On Chicago, Rk. Isl. & Pac. (R. R.).
TOULOUSE, capital of Dept. of Haute-Garonne, France, 213,220.
One of the most important cities of France; is the seat of an archbishop, of a university, with colleges of science, medicine, law, and art. The commercial interests, considerable by reason of its position on the route between the Mediterranean and the Pyrénées, are centered in grain, wine, marbles from the Pyrénées, and wood; its manufacturing interests in textiles and agricultural and general staples. Toulouse was an independent possession of an ancient French family of this name. In 825 the possession was made a dukedom.
TOURCOING, Dept. of Nord, France, 78,393.
One of the leading textile centers of France.
TOURNAI, Hainaut, Belgium, 35,898.
Has a large trade in carpets, clothing, and fancy goods.
TOURNUS, Dept. of Saône-et-Loire, 51,031.
TOURS, capital of Dept. of Indre-et-Loire, France, 83,753.
Manufactures silks, printing, steel, automobiles, machinery, porcelain, and shoes.
TOVEY (Humphrey), Christian Co., Ill., 933.
On Chi. & Ill. Midl. (R. R.).
TOWANDA, c. s., Bradford Co., Pa., 4,104.
On Leh. Val.; Susq. & N. York (R. Rs.).
–Butler Co., Kans., 409.
On Mo. Pac. (R. R.).
TOWER, St. Louis Co., Minn., 801.
On Dul., Missabe & Nor. (R. R.).
TOWER CITY, Schuylkill Co., Pa.
On Reading (R. R.).
TOWER HILL, Shelby Co., Ill., 642.
On Balt. & Ohio; Cle., Cin., Chi. & St. Lou. (R. Rs.).
TOWNER, c. s., McHenry Co., N. D., 622.
On Gt. Nor. (R. R.).
TOWNLEY, Walker Co., Ala., 1,175.
On St. Lou.-San Fran. (R. R.).
TOWNSEND, c. s., Broadwater Co., Mont., 743.
On Nor. Pac. (R. R.).
–Middlesex Co., Mass., 1,942.
On Bost. & Me. (R. R.).
TOWNSEND HARBOR, Middlesex Co., Mass., 500.
On Bost. & Me. (R. R.).
TOWNSVILLE, Queensland, Australia, 31,800.
A port and commercial center.
TOWSON, c. s., Baltimore Co., Md., 2,074.
On Md. & Penna. (R. R.).
TOYAH, Reeves Co., Tex., 553.
On Tex. & Pac. (R. R.).
TOYAMA, capital of Toyama Ken, Japan, 75,099.
TOYOHASHI, Japan, 98,554.
A maritime town and marketing point.
TRABZON, capital of Trabzon Vilayet, Turkey, 28,713.
A seaport on the Black Sea and center of transit trade with Iran (Persia).
TRACY, San Joaquin Co., Cal., 3,829.
On Sou. Pas. (R. R.).
–Lyon Co., Minn., 2,570.
On Chi. & Nor. West. (R. R.).
TRACY CITY, Grundy Co., Tenn., 1,675.
On Nash., Chatt. & St. Lou. (R. R.).
TRAER, Tama Co., Iowa, 1,417.
On Chi. & Nor. West.; Chi., Rk. Isl. & Pac. (R. Rs.).
TRAFFORD, Allegheny and Westmoreland Cos., Pa., 4,187.
On Penna. (R. R.).
TRAIGUEN, Prov. of Cautin, Chile, 8,125.
TRAINER, Delaware Co., Pa., 1,648.
On Penna. (R. R.).
TRALEE, County Kerry, Ireland (Eire), 10,000.
TRANI, Prov. of Bari, Italy, 33,223.
A seaport and trade center.
TRANSCONA, Manitoba, Canada, 5,578.
On Can. Nat. (R. R.).
TRAPANI, Province of Trapani, Italy, 55,532.
Marketing town and seaport.
TRAUTENAU, Bohemia, Germany, 15,923.
Has an important linen industry.
TRAVERSE CITY, c. s., Grand Traverse Co., Mich., 12,539.
On Penna.; Man. & Northe.; Pere Marq. (R. Rs.).
TREBIZOND, Turkey. See TRABZON.
TREDEGAR, Monmouthshire, Eng., 23,195.
Has coal mines and iron works.
TREECE, Cherokee Co., Kans., 613.
On Northe. Okla. (El.) (R. R.).
TREMENTINA, San Miguel Co., N. Mex., 500.
TREMONT, Tazewell Co., Ill., 798.
On Cle., Cin., Chi. & St. Lou. (R. R.).
–Schuylkill Co., Pa., 2,304.
On Reading (R. R.).
TREMONTON, Boxelder Co., Utah, 1,009.
On Ore. Short Line (Un. Pac.) (R. R.).
TREMPEALEAU, Trempeleau Co., Wis., 541.
On Chi. & Nor. West.; Chi., Burl. & Quincy (R. Rs.).
TRENTO (Trent), Prov. of Trento, Italy, 31,146.
Considerable wine trade; scene of the Council of Trent (1545-63).
TRENTON, Hastings Co., South, Ontario, Canada, 6,276.
On Can. Nat.; Can. Pac. (R. Rs.).
–c. s., Gilchrist Co., Fla., 677.
On Atl. Coast Line (R. R.).
–Clinton Co., Ill., 1,271.
On Balt. & Ohio (R. R.).
–Todd Co., Ky., 524.
On Lou. & Nash. (R. R.).
–Wayne Co., Mich., 4,022.
On Det. & Tol. Sh. Line; Det., Tol. & Iron.; N. York Cen.; Mich Cen. (R. Rs.).
–c. s., Grundy Co., Mo., 6,992.
On Chi., Rk. Isl. & Pac.; Quincy, Oma. & Kan. Cy. (R. Rs.).
–c. s., Hitchcock Co., Neb., 865.
On Chi., Burl. & Quincy (R. R.).
–c. s., Mercer Co., N. J., State capital, 123,356.
On the Delaware River (at the head of navigation), the Delaware and Raritan Canal, Reading, Pennsylvania and the Trent.-Princeton Tract. railroads. An iron and steel manufacturing center, specially noted for its wire mills, also for pottery and rubber industries. The State House, Washington's Monument, Soldiers' and Sailors' Memorial, and the old Hessian Barracks are notable features. Settled in 1679. The Battle of Trenton, 1776, was fought here.
c. s., Jones Co., N. C., 500.
–Butler Co., Ohio, 636.
On Erie; Balt. & Ohio; Cin. & L. Erie (El.) (R. Rs.).
–c. s., Gibson Co., Tenn., 2,892.
On Mob. & Ohio (R. R.).
TRESCKOW, Carbon Co., Pa., 1,856.
On Cen. of N. Jer. (R. R.).
TREVES, Germany. See TRIER.
TREVESKYN (Cuddy P. O.), Allegheny Co., Pa., 800.
On Penna.; Pitts. & W. Va. (R. Rs.).
TREVISO, capital of Prov. of Treviso, Italy, 29,840.
Has many historical landmarks.
TREVORTON, Northumberland Co., Pa., 2,600.
On Read. (R. R.).
TREZEVANT, Carroll Co., Tenn., 547.
On Lou. & Nash. (R. R.).
TRIBES HILL, Montgomery Co., N. Y., 800.
On N. York Cen. (R. R.).
TRIBUNE, Greeley Co., Kans., 544.
On Mo. Pac. (R. R.).
TRICHINOPOLY, Madras, India, 141,640.
Manufactures are goldsmiths' work, textiles, soap, cigars, and food products.
TRIER (Treves), Rhenish Prussia, Germany, 76,700.
Iron founding, tanning, dyeing, and wine-making.
TRIESTE, Italy, 228,583.
An important Adriatic seaport.
TRIKKALA, Thessaly, Greece, 18,682.
Trade center of wheat, corn, tobacco, and silk-cocoons.
TRIMBLE, Athens Co., Ohio, 680.
On N. York Cen. (R. R.).
–Dyer Co., Tenn., 723.
On Ill. Cen. (R. R.).
TRIMOUNTAIN, Houghton Co., Mich., 700.
On Cop. Rge. (R. R.).
TRINIDAD, c. s., Las Animas Co., Colo., 11,732.
On Atch., Top. & Santa Fe; Colo. & Sou.; Colo. & So. East.; Den. & Rio Gde. West. (R. Rs.).
Tourist resort in picturesque region.
–Santa Clara Prov., Cuba, 45,930.
A marketing town for sugar, tobacco, honey, and vegetables.
–Capital of Dept. of El Beni, Bolivia, 7,481.
–Henderson Co., Tex., 1,000.
On St. Lou. Southw. (R. R.).
TRINITY, Trinity Co., Texas, 2,036.
On Internat.-Gt. Nor. (Mo. Pac.); Waco, Beau., Trin. & Sab. (R. Rs.).
–Randolph Co., N. C., 554.
On High Pt., Randle., Asheb. & Sou. (R. R.).
TRION, Chattooga Co., Ga., 3,289.
On Cen. of Ga. (R. R.).
TRIPOLI, Bremer Co., Iowa, 891.
On Chi. Gt. West. (R. R.).
–Capital of Libya, 86,137.
A seaport and important commercial center. Trade is largely in agricultural products, and the leading manufactures are tobacco, food supplies, salt, ordnance, and beer.
–Rep. of Lebanon, Syria, 35,000.
Trade center and military station. Manufactures soap and tobacco. Sponge-fishing and fruit growing are important.
TRIPOLIS, Morea, Greece, 14,937.
An agricultural town.
TRIPP, Hutchinson Co., S. Dak., 901.
On Chi., Mil., St. P. & Pac. (R. R.).
TRIVANDRUM, capital of Travancore, India, 96,016.
A residential town and a resort for pilgrims.
TROIS RIVIÈRES (Three Rivers), St. Maurice Co., Quebec, Canada, 35,450.
On Can. Nat.; Can. Pac. (R. Rs.).
An important commercial town with large pulp and paper mills.
TROITSK, Soviet Union, Asia, 41,900.
A supply point for the Ural district.
TRONA, San Bernardino Co., Cal., 775.
On Trona (R. R.).
TRONDHIEM, Prov. of Troms, Norway, 54,135.
A seaport and fishing center. Has sawmills, ship-yards, and machine shops.
TROON, Ayr Co., Scotland, 8,544.
TROPPAU (Opava), Germany, 36,083.
Sugar, clothing, beer, machinery.
TROTTER, Fayette Co., Pa., 950.
On Penna. (R. R.).
TROTWOOD, Montgomery Co., Ohio, 660.
On Balt. & Ohio; Penna. (R. Rs.).
TROUP, Smith and Cherokee Cos., Texas, 1,318.
On Internat.-Gt. Nor. (Mo. Pac.) (R. R.).
TROUT, La Salle Par., La., 850.
On La. & Ark. (R. R.).
TROY, c. s., Pike Co., Ala., 6,814.
On Atl. Coast Line; Cen. of Ga. (R. Rs.).
–Latah Co., Idaho, 619.
On Nor. Pac. (R. R.).
–Perry Co., Ind., 562.
On Southern (R. R.).
–Madison Co., Ill., 1,122.
On Ill. Term. (El.); Penna. (R. Rs.).
–c. s., Doniphan Co., Kans., 1,238.
On Chi., Rk. Isl. & Pac.; St. Jos. & Gd. Isl. (Un. Pac.) (R. Rs.).
–Waldo Co., Me., 651.
–c. s., Lincoln Co., Mo., 1,419.
On St. Lou. & Troy (R. R.).
–Lincoln Co., Mont., 498.
On Gt. Nor. (R. R.).
–Cheshire Co., N. H., 1,000.
On Bost. & Me. (R. R.).
–c. s., Rensselaer Co., N. Y., 72,763.
On Hudson River, and on the New York Central; Boston & Maine; Troy Union, and Delaware & Hudson railroads.
Terminus of the Barge and Champlain Canals. Home of the collar and shirt industry. Other leading manufactures are bells and brushes, valves, and engineering instruments.
Seat of Rensselaer Polytechnic Institute, Russell Sage College, and Emma Willard School.
Troy's first settlement, the village of Van der Heyden, was made about 1786, and in 1789 the name was changed to Troy. Its first charter was received in 1816.
c. s., Montgomery Co., N. C., 1,522.
On Norf. Sou. (R. R.).
–c. s., Miami Co., Ohio, 8,675.
On Balt. & Ohio; Cle., Cin., Chi. & St. Lou. (R. Rs.).
–Bradford Co., Pa., 1,190.
On Penna. (R. R.).
–Obion Co., Tenn., 522.
–Bell Co., Tex., 509.
On Mo.-Kan.-Tex. of Tex. (R. R.).
TROYES, Dept. of Aube, France, 57,961.
Hosiery. Has school for hosiery makers.
TRUCHAS, Rio Arriba Co., N. Mex., 850.
TRUCKEE, Nevada Co., Cal., 1,000.
On Sou. Pac. (R. R.).
TRUJILLO ALTO, Mun. of Trujillo Alto, Puerto Rico, 1,040.
TRUMAN, Poinsett Co., Ark., 2,995.
On St. Lou.-San Fran.; St. Lou. Southw. (R. Rs.).
–Martin Co., Minn., 730.
On Chi., St. P., Mpls. & Oma. (R. R.).
TRUMANSBURG, Tompkins Co., N. Y., 1,077.
On Leh. Val. (R. R.).
TRUMBAUERSVILLE, Bucks Co., Pa., 692.
TRUMBULL, Fairfield Co., Conn., 3,624.
On N. York, N. Hav. & Hart. (R. R.).
TRURO, Cornwall, England, 11,074.
Pottery-making and tinsmelting.
–Barnstable Co., Mass., 541.
On N. York, N. Hav. & Hart. (R. R.).
–Colchester Co., Nova Scotia, 7,901.
On Dom. Atl.; Can. Nat. (R. Rs.).
TRUSCOTT, Knox Co., Tex., 500.
On Panh. & Santa Fe (R. R.).
TRUSSVILLE, Jefferson Co., Ala., 900.
On Ala. Gt. Sou.; Lou. & Nash. (R. Rs.).
TRUTNOV, Germany. See TRAUTENAU.
TRYON, Polk Co., N. C., 1,670.
On Southern (R. R.).
TSARITSIN, Soviet Union. See STALINGRAD.
TSINAN, capital of Shantung Province, China, 250,000.
A river port and trade center. Noted for its silks and glasswares.
TSINGTAO, Shantung, China, 390,000.
A seaport and commercial center.
TSU, Ken of Miye, Japan, 56,088.
A maritime town and marketing point. Has several fine temples.
TUAPSE, Soviet Union, 34,400.
TUBAC, Santa Cruz Co., Ariz., 500.
On Sou. Pac. (R. R.).
TUBIGON, Prov. of Bolhol, P. I., 21,201.
TÜBINGEN, Württemberg, Germany, 28,686.
Famous for its university, founded 1477.
TUBURAN, Prov. of Cebu, P. I., 30,505.
TUCAPAU, Spartanburg Co., S. C., 810.
TUCKAHOE, Westchester Co., N. Y., 6,138.
On N. York Cen. (R. R.).
–Cape May Co., N. J., 680.
On Penna.-Read. Seash. (R. R.).
TUCKERMAN, Jackson Co., Ark., 930.
On Mo. Pac. (R. R.).
TUCKERTON, Ocean Co., N. J., 1,429.
On Sou. N. Jer. (R. R.).
TUCSON, c. s., Pima Co., Ariz., 32,503.
On Sou. Pac. (R. R.).
Large copper mines in vicinity; also gold, silver, and lead workings. Cotton, livestock, and alfalfa are other industries.
Tucson dates from 1692. Famous health resort, and home of State University.
TUCUMAN, Argentina, 126,422.
The metropolis of a rich sugar cane region. Has a number of sugar-mills.
TUCUMCARI, c. s., Quay Co., N. Mex., 4,143.
On Chi., Rk. Isl. & Pac.; Sou. Pac. (R. Rs.).
TUGUEGARAO, Prov. of Cagayan, Luzon, P. I., 19,284.
A river port and tobacco shipping point.
TUJUNGA, Los Angeles Co., Cal., 2,311.
TULA, Soviet Union, 199,500.
Chief manufactures are rifles, samovars, cutlery, sugar, and leather.
TULANCINGO, State of Hidalgo, Mexico, 9,497.
On Nat. of Mex. (R. R.).
TULARE, Tulare Co., Cal., 6,207.
On Atch., Top. & Santa Fe; Sou. Pac. (R. Rs.).
TULAROSA, Otero Co., N. Mex., 1,406.
On Sou. Pac. (R. R.).
TULIA, c. s., Swisher Co., Texas, 2,202.
On Panh. & Santa Fe (R. R.).
TULLAHOMA, Coffee Co., Tenn., 4,023.
On Nash., Chatt. & St. Lou. (R. R.).
TULLE, capital of Dept. of Corrèze, France, 15,617.
The principal industry is the manufacture of small arms.
TULLOS, La Salle Par., La., 707.
On Mo. Pac. (R. R.).
TULLY, Onondaga Co., N. Y., 680.
On Del., Lack. & West. (R. R.).
TULLYTOWN, Bucks Co., Pa., 658.
On Penna. (R. R.).
TULSA, c. s., Tulsa Co., Okla., 141,258.
On Atch., Top. & Santa Fe; Mo.-Kan.-Tex.; Midl. Valley; St. Lou.-San Fran.; Sand Springs; Sapulpa Un. (El.) (R. Rs.).
A leading commercial and industrial town in the heart of a rich oil, mineral and agricultural region. The principal industries converge around the petroleum industry and a large petroleum exposition is held here annually. Founded in 1882. Chartered as a city in 1902. Seat of the University of Tulsa.
TUMWATER, Thurston Co., Wash., 793.
On Nor. Pac.; Un. Pac. (R. Rs.).
TUNBRIDGE WELLS, Kent, England, 16,332.
A residential town and watering place. Famous for "Tunbridge Ware"—novelties and furniture made of wood.
TUNICA, c. s., Tunica Co., Miss., 1,043.
On Yazoo & Miss. Val. (Ill. Cen.) (R. R.).
TUNIS, capital of Tunisia, Africa, 202,405.
A seaport and leading commercial town. It is becoming a favorite resort.
TUNKHANNOCK, c. s., Wyoming Co., Pa., 1,973.
On Leh. Val. (R. R.).
TUNNELHILL, Cambria Co., Pa., 600.
TUNNELTON, Preston Co., W. Va., 595.
On Balt. & Ohio; W. Va. Nor. (R. Rs.).
TUOLUMNE, Tuolumne Co., Cal., 1,250.
On Sierra Ry. of Cal.
TUPELO, c. s., Lee Co., Miss., 6,361.
On Mob. & Ohio; St. Lou.-San Fran. (R. Rs.).
TUPPER LAKE, Franklin Co., N. Y., 5,271.
On N. York Cen. (R. R.).
TURIN, Italy. See TORINO.
TURKEY, Hall Co., Tex., 975.
On Ft. Worth & Denv. Cy. (R. R.).
TURKU (Abo), capital of Govt. of Turku-Pori, Finland, 67,722.
Seaport, manufactures, and shipbuilding.
TURLOCK, Stanislaus Co., Cal., 4,276.
On Sou. Pac.; Tidew. Sou. (R. Rs.).
TURN, Valencia Co., N. Mex., 600.
TURNER, Androscoggin Co., Maine, 600.
–Wyandotte Co., Kans., 600.
On Atch., Top. & Santa Fe (R. R.).
–(Balnew), Baltimore Co., Md., 1,350.
On Balt. & Ohio; Penna. (R. Rs.).
TURNERS FALLS, Franklin Co., Mass., 6,300.
On Bost. & Me.; N. York, N. Hav. & Hart. (R. Rs.).
TURNERSVILLE, Coryell Co., Tex., 796.
TURNHOUT, Prov. of Antwerp, Belgium, 26,792.
Has manufactures of cloth and playing cards, and a breeding establishment for leeches.
TURON, Reno Co., Kans., 650.
On Mo. Pac.; Chi., Rk. Isl. & Pac. (R. Rs.).
TURTLE CREEK, Allegheny Co., Pa., 10,690.
On Penna.; Union; Bess. & L. Erie (R. Rs.).

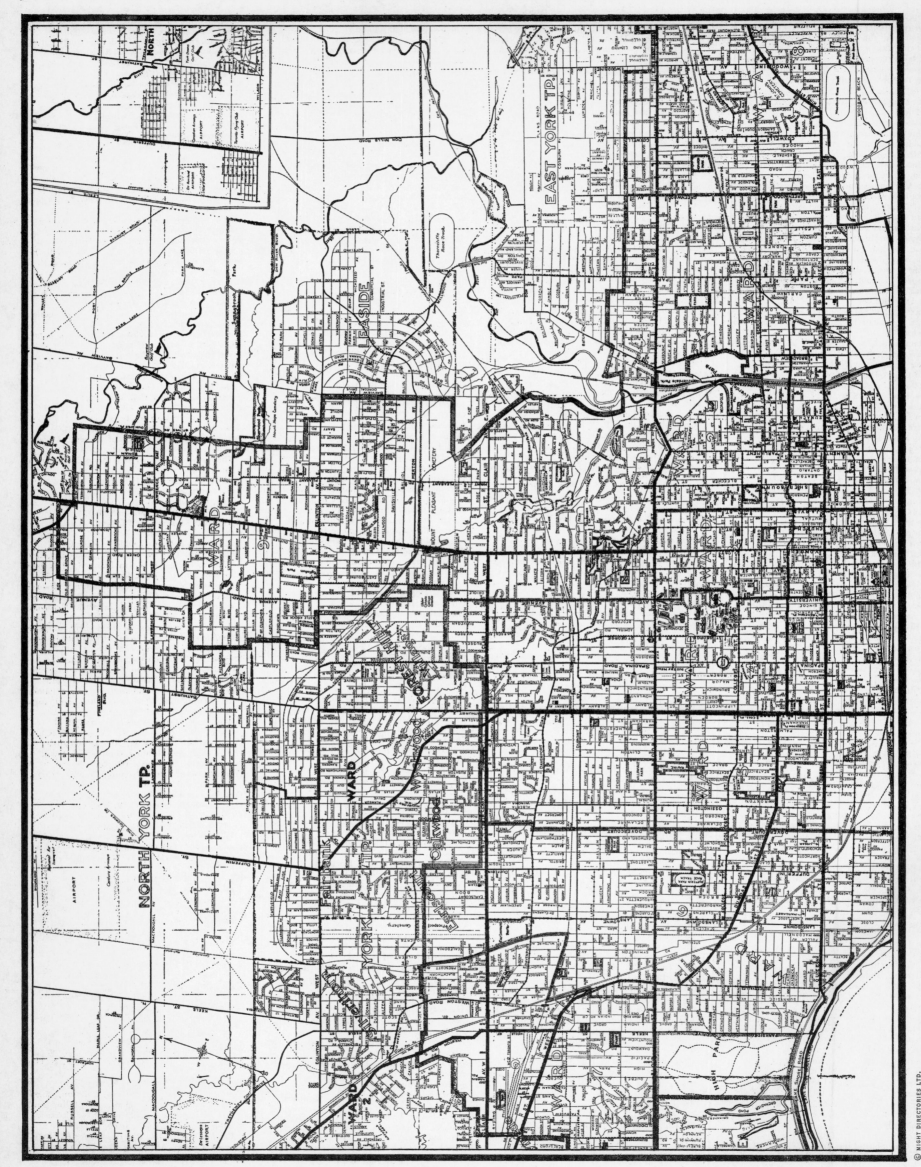

MAP OF CENTRAL TORONTO, CAPITAL OF THE PROVINCE OF ONTARIO AND THE SECOND LARGEST CITY OF CANADA. TORONTO IS THE PUBLISHING CENTER OF THE DOMINION AND ONE OF ITS IMPORTANT INDUSTRIAL CITIES. NIAGARA FALLS FURNISH ABUNDANT HYDROELECTRIC POWER AT A LOW COST FOR MANUFACTURING

In a coal mining region. Has manufactures of electrical products.
Turtle Lake, Barron Co., Wis., 598.
On Chi., St. P., Mpls. & Oma.; Mpls., St. P. & S. Ste. M. (R. Rs.).
–McLean Co., N. D., 579.
On Nor. Pac. (R. R.).
Tuscaloosa, c. s., Tuscaloosa Co., Ala., 20,659.
On Ala. Gt. Sou.; Lou. & Nash.; Mob. & Ohio (R. Rs.).
A trade and commercial center with blast furnaces, foundries, coke ovens, and paper mills. Situated in a fine farming and lumbering region.
Tuscarawas, Tuscarawas Co., Ohio, 631.
Tuscarora, Schuylkill Co., Pa., 790.
On Reading (R. R.).
Tuscola, c. s., Douglas Co., Ill., 2,569.
On Balt. & Ohio; Chi. & East. Ill.; Ill. Cen. (R. Rs.).
Tuscumbia, c. s., Colbert Co., Ala., 4,533.
On Lou. & Nash.; Sou. (R. Rs.).
Tuskegee, c. s., Macon Co., Ala., 3,314.
On Tuskegee (R. R.).
Tustin, Orange Co., Cal., 926.
On Atch., Top. & Santa Fe; Sou. Pac. (R. Rs.).
Tuttle, Grady Co., Okla., 766.
On St. Lou.-San Fran. (R. R.).
Tuttlingen, Württemberg, Germany, 17,000.
Shoes, cutlery, surgical instruments, and woolens.
Tutwiler, Tallahatchie Co., Miss., 873.
On Yazoo & Miss. Val. (Ill. Cen.) (R. R.).
Tuxedo Park (Tuxedo), Orange Co., N. Y., 2,300.
On Erie (R. R.).
–New Castle Co., Del., 525.
Tuxtla Guttierez, capital of State of Chiapas, Mexico, 13,483.
A trade center with tanning and indigo industries.
Tver, Sov. Union. See Kalinin.
Tweed, Hastings Co., Ontario, Canada, 1,271.
On Can. Nat.; Can. Pac. (R. Rs.).
Twila, Harlan Co., Ky., 516.
Twin Bridges, Madison Co., Mont., 671.
On Nor. Pac. (R. R.).
Twin City, Emanuel Co., Ga., 901.
Twin Falls, c. s., Twin Falls Co., Idaho, 8,787.
On Ore. Short Line (Un. Pac.) (R. R.).
Twin Rocks, Cambria Co., Pa., 1,541.
On Penna. (R. R.).
Twinsburg, Summit Co., Ohio, 1,000.
On Wheel. & L. Erie (R. R.).
Twin Valley, Norman Co., Minn., 657.
On Nor. Pac. (R. R.).
Two Harbors, c. s., Lake Co., Minn., 4,425.
On Dul., Missabe & Nor. (R. R.).
Two Rivers, Manitowoc Co., Wis., 10,083.
On Chi. & Nor. West. (R. R.).
Has agricultural and lumbering industries.
Tyler, Lincoln Co., Minn., 905.
On Chi. & Nor. West. (R. R.).
–c. s., Smith Co., Texas, 17,113.
On Internat.-Gt. Nor. (Mo. Pac.); St. Lou. Southw. (R. Rs.).
Pecans, fruits, berries, cotton, and vegetables. In an oil and gas region.
–Clearfield Co., Pa., 1,536.
On Balt. & Ohio; Penna.; Pitts., Shawn. & Nor. (R. Rs.).
Tylerdale, Washington Co., Pa., 1,580.
On Penna. (R. R.).
Tylertown, c. s., Walthall Co., Miss., 1,102.
On Fernw., Colum. & Gulf; Gulf, Mob. & Nor. (R. Rs.).
Tyndall, c. s., Bon Homme Co., S. Dak., 1,303.
On Chi., Mil., St. P. & Pac. (R. R.).
Tynemouth, Northumberland, England, 64,913.
A watering-place and residential town near Newcastle.
Tyngsboro, Middlesex Co., Mass., 1,331.
On Bos. & Me. (R. R.).
Tyre, Syria. See Sour.
–Allegheny Co., Pa., 750.
Tyrone, Blair Co., Pa., 9,042.
On Bellef. Cen.; Penna. (R. Rs.).
Tyronza, Poinsett Co., Ark., 573.
On St. Lou.-San Fran. (R. R.).
Tyumen, Siberia, Soviet Union, Asia, 64,600.
Important industrial center, with tanneries, smelting works, rug making. The oldest town in Siberia.

U

Ubay, Prov. of Bohol, Bohol, P. I., 8,261.
Ubol, Siam, 745,307.
Ucasville, New London Co., Conn., 989.
Udaipur, capital of Udaipur, India, 44,035.
A picturesque residential town and marketing center. Has several fine temples.
Uddevalla, Dept. of Göteborg, Sweden, 15,104.
A seaport and trade center with textile factories.
Udine, capital of Prov. of Udine, Italy, 52,691.
Silk spinning is the leading industry.
Ufa, capital of Bashkir Rep., Soviet Union, 167,900.
Uhrichsville, Tuscarawas Co., Ohio, 6,437.
On Balt. & Ohio; Penna. (R. Rs.).
Uitenhage, Cape of Good Hope, Union of South Africa, 20,584.
Ujpest, Hungary, 69,533.
A suburb of Budapest.
Ukiah, c. s., Mendocino Co., Cal., 3,124.
On Northw. Pac. (R. R.).
Ulan-Bator Khoto, Mongolia, 30,000.
Ulan Ude (Verkhnii Udinsk), Buryat-Mongol Rep., Sov. Union, 55,800.
Uleaborg, Finland. See Oulu.
Ullin, Pulaski Co., Ill., 800.
On Chi. & East. Ill.; Ill. Cen. (R. Rs.).
Ulm, Württemberg, Germany, 62,590.
Borax, wire rope, cheese, jute, leather, lace, and perfumes. Has a famous cathedral.
Ulster Park, Ulster Co., N. Y., 640.
On West Shore (N. York Cen.) (R. R.).
Ulyanovsk (Simbirsk), Soviet Union, 74,000.
A trade and marketing town in a fertile agricultural region.
Ulysses, c. s., Grant Co., Kan., 830.
On Atch., Top. & Santa Fe (R. R.).
–(Lewisville), Potter Co., Pa., 514.
Uman, Soviet Union, 40,600.
An industrial and commercial town near Kiev.
Umatilla, Lake Co., Fla., 953.
On Atl. Coast Line (R. R.).
Umballah, India. See Amballah.
Unadilla, Dooly Co., Ga., 1,203.
On Ga. Sou. & Fla. (R. R.).
–Otsego Co., N. Y., 1,063.
On Del. & Hud. (R. R.).
Unicoi, Unicoi Co., Tenn., 600.
On Clinchfield (R. R.).
Union, St. James Par., La., 740.
On Yazoo & Miss. Val. (Ill. Cen.) (R. R.).
–Knox Co., Me., 500.
–Newton and Neshoba Cos., Miss., 1,705.
On Gulf, Mob. & Nor. (R. R.).
–c. s., Franklin Co., Mo., 2,143.
On Chi., Rk. Isl. & Pac. (R. R.).
–(Unionbury), Hudson Co., N. J., 16,472.
On Rahway Valley (R. R.).
A suburb of Newark.
–Broome Co., N. Y. (Sta. Endicott P. O.).
On Erie (R. R.).
–Union Co., Ore., 1,107.
On Union (R. R.).
–c. s., Union Co., S. C., 7,419.
On Sou.; Buf. Un.-Carol. (R. Rs.).
Union Beach, Monmouth Co., N. J., 1,893.
Union Bridge, Carroll Co., Md., 862.
On West Md.; Penna. (R. Rs.).
Union City, New Haven Co., Conn., 3,500.
On N. York, N. Hav. & Hart. (R. R.).
–Campbell Co., Ga., 776.
On Atl., Birm. & Coast; Atl. & West. Pt. (R. Rs.).
–Hudson Co., N. J., 58,659.
An industrial suburb of New York. Has important silk manufactures.
–Randolph Co., Ind., 3,084.
On Cle., Cin., Chi. & St. Lou.; Balt. & Ohio; Penna. (R. Rs.).
–Branch & Calhoun Cos., Mich., 1,104.
On Mich. Cen. (R. R.).
–Darke Co., Ohio, 1,305.
–Erie Co., Pa., 3,788.
On Erie; Penna. (R. Rs.).
–c. s., Obion Co., Tenn., 5,865.
On Mob. & Ohio; Nash., Chatt. & St. Lou. (R. Rs.).
Uniondale, St. Louis Co., Mo., 226.
–Nassau Co., N. Y., 2,810.
Union Deposit, Dauphin Co., Pa., 525.
Union Furnace, Hocking Co., Ohio, 700.
On Chesa. & Ohio (R. R.).
Union Gap, Yakima Co., Wash., 586.
On Nor. Pac.; Un. Pac. (R. Rs.).
Union Grove, Racine Co., Wis., 755.
On Chi., Mil., St. P. & Pac. (R. R.).
Union Point, Greene Co., Ga., 1,627.
On Georgia (R. R.).
Union Springs, c. s., Bullock Co., Ala., 2,875.
On Cen. of Ga. (R. R.).
–Cayuga Co., N. Y., 794.
On Leh. Val. (R. R.).
Uniontown, Perry Co., Ala., 1,424.
On Southern (R. R.).
–Union Co., Ky., 1,235.
On Ill. Cen. (R. R.).
–Carroll Co., Md., 500.
–Stark Co., Ohio, 500.
–c. s., Fayette Co., Pa., 19,544.
On Balt. & Ohio; Penna. (R. Rs.).
A busy commercial and industrial town near Pittsburgh. Has a fine airport.
Unionville, Hartford Co., Conn., 2,135.
On N. York, N. Hav. & Hart. (R. R.).
–c. s., Putnam Co., Mo., 1,811.
On Chi., Burl. & Quincy (R. R.).
–Ashtabula Co., Ohio, 600.
On N. York Cen.; N. York, Chi. & St. Lou. (R. Rs.).
United, Westmoreland Co., Pa., 716.
On Penna. (R. R.).
Unity, Waldo Co., Me., 892.
On Belfast & Moosehead Lake (R. R.).
–Sullivan Co., N. H., 501.
–Allegheny Co., Pa., 700.
On Penna. (R. R.).
Universal, Allegheny Co., Pa., 2,000.
On Bess. & L. Erie; Balt. & Ohio; Pitts. & L. Erie; Penna.; Union (R. Rs.).
University City, St. Louis Co., Mo., 25,809.
A residential and educational suburb of St. Louis. Seat of Washington University.
University Heights, Ind., 2,237.
–Cuyahoga Co., Ohio, 2,237.
University Place, Lancaster Co., Neb. (Pop. incl. in Lincoln).
On Chi., Rk. Isl. & Pac. (R. R.).
Upland, San Bernardino Co., Cal., 4,713.
On Pac. El.; Atch., Top. & Santa Fe.; Sou. Pac. (R. Rs.).
–Grant Co., Ind., 906.
On Penna. (R. R.).
Seat of Taylor University.
–Delaware Co., Pa., 2,500.
On Balt. & Ohio; Penna. (R. Rs.).
Unley, So. Australia, Australia, 40,999.
Upper Alton, Madison Co., Ill. (annexed to Alton City).
On Alton; Chi., Burl. & Quincy (R. Rs.).
Upper Arlington, Franklin Co., Ohio, 3,059.
Upper Black Eddy, Bucks Co., Pa., 500.
Upper Fairmount, Somerset Co., Md., 510.
Upper Mauch Chunk, Carbon Co., Pa., 2,000.
Upper Musquodoboit, Halifax Co., Nova Scotia, 480.
On Can. Nat. (R. R.).
Upper Nyack, Rockland Co., N. Y., 842.
Upper Sandusky, c. s., Wyandot Co., Ohio, 3,889.
On Chesa. & Ohio; Penna. (R. Rs.).
Upperville (St. Luce), Aroostook Co., Me., 1,500.
Uppsala, capital of Län of Uppsala, Sweden, 30,190.
A publishing center. Has a famous university.
Upton, Worcester, Mass., 2,163.
On Grafton & Upton (El.) (R. R.).
Uralsk, Kazak Rep., Soviet Union, Asia, 52,200.
A trade and industrial center in a rich mining district.
Urania, La Salle Par., La., 500.
On Mo. Pac.; Natch., Uran. & Rust. (R. Rs.).
Urbana, c. s., Champaign Co., Ill., 13,060.
On Cle., Cin., Chi. & St. Lou.; Ill. Term. (El.) Wab. (R. Rs.).
Has foundry and machine and incandescent bulb plants. Seat of Illinois University.
–c. s., Champaign Co., Ohio, 7,742.
On Cin. & L. Erie; Cle., Cin., Chi. & St. Lou.; Penna. (R. Rs.).
Urban Crest, Franklin Co., Ohio, 650.
On Balt. & Ohio (R. R.).
Urbandale, Polk Co., Ia., 596.
Urbino, capital of Prov. of Pesar e Urbino, Italy, 5,231.
Urdaneta, Prov. of Pangasinan, Luzon, P. I., 24,360.
An agricultural center.
Urfa, Vilayet of Urfa, Turkey, 31,255.
The center of a grain and cotton-raising region.
Uriah, Monroe Co., Ala., 700.
Urich, Henry Co., Mo., 507.
Uruapan, State of Michoacan, Mexico, 16,713.
On Nat. of Mex. (R. R.).
A trade and marketing town.
Uruguay, Prov. of Entre Rios, Argentina, 23,394.
The center and distributing point for a fertile farming region.
Uskub, Yugoslavia. See Skoplje.
Uskudar (Skutari), Vilayet of Istanbul, Turkey, 124,555.
An important trade center and industrial town on the east side of Bosporus, opposite Istanbul. Manufactures leather, textiles, metal goods, and food products.
Usti (Aussig), Germany, 43,802.
A river port and coal-shipping point. Has large chemical plants.
Ute, Monona Co., Iowa, 616.
On Chi., Mil., St. P. & Pac.; Chi. & Nor. West. (R. Rs.).
Utica, Macomb Co., Mich., 873.
On Mich. Cen. (R. R.).
–La Salle Co., Ill., 1,250.
On Chi., Rk. Isl. & Pac. (R. R.).
–Clark Co., Ind., 500.
–Hinds Co., Miss., 652.
On Yazoo and Miss. Val. (Ill. Cen.) (R. R.).
–Seward Co., Neb., 566.
On Chi., Burl. & Quincy (R. R.).
–c. s., Oneida Co., N. Y., 101,740.
On the Mohawk R. and Erie Canal; also on Del., Lack. & West.; N. York, Ont. & West.; N. York Cen.; West Shore (R. Rs.).
Manufactures textiles of all kinds, heaters, firearms, brass and iron beds. In rich agricultural section; dairying predominates. Utica was settled by colonists from England and New England. It was incorporated as a village in 1798; received its city charter in 1832.
–Licking Co., Ohio, 1,394.
On Balt. & Ohio (R. R.).
Utrecht, capital of Prov. of Utrecht, Netherlands, 160,798.
The central point of the Netherlands railway system, and carries on an extensive trade in grain and cattle and in Utrecht velvet, carpets, floor cloth, cottons, linens.
Utrecht is the oldest town in Netherlands, and was called by the Romans "Trajectum ad Rhenum," that is, "Ford of the Rhine."
Utsunomiya, capital of Tochigi, Japan, 81,380.
An important commercial center northeast of Tokyo.
Utuado, Municipality of Utuado, Puerto Rico, 5,582.
Uvalda, Montgomery Co., Ga., 513.
On Ga. & Fla. (R. R.).
Uvalde, c. s., Uvalde Co., Texas, 5,286.
On San Ant., Uvalde & Gulf (Mo. Pac.); Sou. Pac. (R. Rs.).
Trade in farm produce, sheep and goats.
Uxbridge, Ontario Co., Ont., Can., 1,325.
On Can. Nat. (R. R.).
–Worcester Co., Mass., 6,397.
On N. York, N. Hav. & Hart. (R. R.).

V

Vaasa (Nikolaistad), Finland, 29,200.
A seaport. Exports forest products.
Vac, Comitat of Pest, Hungary, 21,098.
A river port and industrial town. Has a large wine industry.
Vacaville, Solano Co., Cal., 1,556.
On Sacramento Nor. (El.) Sou. Pac. (R. Rs.).
Vaiden, c. s., Carroll Co., Miss., 648.
On Ill. Cen. (R. R.).
Vail, Crawford Co., Iowa, 622.
On Chi. & Nor. West. (R. R.).
Valatie, Columbia Co., N. Y., 1,246.
Valders, Manitowoc Co., Wis., 504.
On Mpls., St. P. & S. Ste. M. (R. R.).
Valdese, Burke Co., N. C., 1,816.
On Sou. (R. R.).
Valdivia, capital of Prov. of Valdivia, Chile, 50,816.
In a rich farming and lumbering region.
Valdosta, c. s., Lowndes Co., Ga., 13,482.
On Atl. Coast Line; Ga. & Fla.; Ga. So. & Fla. (R. Rs.).
State Woman's College and Emory Junior College.
Vale, c. s., Malheur Co., Ore., 922.
On Ore. Short Line (Un. Pac.) (R. R.).
Valence, Dept. of Drôme, France, 36,582.
An industrial and commercial town on the Rhône River. Has manufactures of silks, wines, leather, and food products.
Valencia, capital of Prov. of Valencia, Spain, 352,802.
On the Mediterranean. The old battlemented walls, erected by Pedro IV in 1346, were removed in 1871. Valencia, or Valentia de Cid, dating from the second century, B.C., was destroyed by Pompey; taken by the Goths, A.D. 413; by the Moors, 715; and by the Cid, 1094.
–Capital of State of Carabobo, Venezuela, 49,214.
Surrounded by a fertile plantation district.
–Prov. of Bohol, Bohol, P. I., 11,084.
Valenciennes, Dept. of Nord, France, 42,564.
Partly destroyed in the World War.
Valentine, Cherry Co., Neb., 1,672.
On Chi. & Nor. West. (R. R.).
Valetta, capital of Malta, 23,855.
Strongly fortified; the military works were constructed by the Knights of Malta; headquarters of the British Mediterranean fleet.
Valhalla, Westchester Co., N. Y., 4,000.
On N. York Cen. (R. R.).
Valier, Franklin Co., Ill., 1,176.
On Chi., Burl. & Quincy (R. R.).
–Pondera Co., Mont., 575.
–On Mont. West. (R. R.).
–Jefferson Co., Pa., 500.
On Balt. & Ohio (R. R.).
Valladolid, in Old Castile, capital of Prov. of Valladolid, Spain, 97,528.
On the left bank of the Pisuerga, and on the Irun-Madrid Railway. It is a fortress, has a cathedral founded in 1585 by Philip II, monasteries and a university founded in 1346.
The old Roman town of Pintia was rebuilt in 625 by the Goths, the name Valladolid was first applied to it after its recovery from the Moors, 1072.
–Prov. of Negros Occidental, Negros, P. I., 10,213.
Vallejo, c. s., Solano Co., Cal., 14,476.
On Sou. Pac.; San Fran., Napa & Cal. (R. Rs.).
A seaport and busy industrial town near San Francisco. Opposite the city is Mare Island Navy Yard.
Vallenar, Prov. of Atacama, Chile, 7,378.
Valley, Douglas Co., Neb., 1,039.
On Un. Pac. (R. R.).
–Stevens Co., Wash., 500.
On Gt. Nor. (R. R.).
Valley Center, Sedgwick Co., Kan., 621.

On Atch., Top. & Santa Fe; St. Lou.-San Fran.; Ark. Val.-Inter. (El.) (R. Rs.).
VALLEY CITY, c. s., Barnes Co., N. Dak., 5,268.
On Mpls., St. P. & S. Ste. M.; Nor. Pac. (R. Rs.).
VALLEY COTTAGE, Rockland Co., N. Y., 650.
On West Shore (R. R.).
VALLEY FALLS, Jefferson Co., Kans., 1,265.
On Atch., Top. & Santa Fe; Un. Pac. (R. Rs.).
–Rensselaer Co., N. Y., 577.
On Bost. & Me. (R. R.).
–Providence Co., R. I., 5,542.
On N. York, N. Hav. & Hart. (R. R.).
VALLEYFIELD, Beauharnois Co., Quebec, Canada, 11,411.
A river port and transit town near Montreal.
On Can. Nat.; N. York Cen. (R. Rs.).
VALLEY JUNCTION (West Des Moines), Polk Co., Iowa, 4,280.
On Chi., Rk. Isl. & Pac.; Mpls. & St. Lou. (R. Rs.).
VALLEY MILLS, Bosque Co., Texas, 936.
On Gulf, Colo. & Santa Fe (R. R.).
VALLEY PARK, St. Louis Co., Mo., 1,772.
On St. Lou.-San Fran.; Mo. Pac. (R. Rs.).
VALLEY STREAM, Nassau Co., N. Y., 11,790.
On Long Isl. (R. R.).
A residential suburb of New York.
VALLEY VIEW, Madison Co., Ky., 524.
–Cuyahoga Co., Ohio, 594.
–Schuylkill Co., Pa., 1,600.
–Cooke Co., Tex., 700.
On Gulf, Colo. & Santa Fe (R. R.).
VALLIANT, McCurtain Co., Okla., 608.
On St. Lou.-San Fran.; Tex., Okla. & East. (R. Rs.).
VALMEYER, Monroe Co., Ill., 528.
On Mo. Pac. (R. R.).
VALPARAISO, Prov. of Aconcagua, Chile, 263,410.
Fortified seaport, situated at the base of steep, bare hills about 1,600 feet high, and round the head of a bay which possesses good anchorage.
–c. s., Porter Co., Ind., 8,079.
On Gd. Tr.; N. York, Chi. & St. Lou.; Penna. (R. Rs.).
–State of Zacatecas, Mexico, 2,546.
–Saunders Co., Neb., 523.
On Un. Pac. (R. R.).
VAN, Van Zandt Co., Tex., 1,000.
On Tex. Short Line (R. R.).
VAN ALSTYNE, Grayson Co., Texas, 1,453.
On Sou. Pac.; Tex. Elec. (R. Rs.).
VAN BUREN, c. s., Crawford Co., Ark., 5,182.
On Mo. Pac.; St. Lou.-San Fran. (R. Rs.).
–Grant Co., Ind., 766.
On N. York, Chi. & St. Lou. (R. R.).
–Aroostook Co., Me., 3,300.
On Bangor & Aroostook (R. R.).
VANCEBORO, Washington Co., Me., 713.
On Can. Pac.; Maine Cen. (R. Rs.).
–Craven Co., N. C., 742.
On Norf. Sou. (R. R.).
VANCEBURG, c. s., Lewis Co., Ky., 1,388.
On Chesa. & Ohio (R. R.).
VANCOUVER, Vancouver Co., British Columbia, Canada, 246,593.
On Can. Pac.; Can. Nat.; British Col. (El.); Gt. Nor.; Vancouv. & Lulu Isl. (R. Rs.).
An important seaport and commercial town. Has a very large grain trade. Also exports timber, canned fish, flour, and apples. Has foundries, canneries, sawmills, paper mills, breweries, and sugar mills.
–c. s., Clarke Co., Wash., 15,766.
On the Columbia River and the Nor. Pac.; Gt. Nor.; Un. Pac.; Spok., Port. & Seattle (R. Rs.).
A port on the Columbia River and an important lumber shipping point. Situated in an agricultural region.
VANDALIA, c. s., Fayette Co., Ill., 4,342.
On Ill. Cen.; Penna. (R. Rs.).
–Audrain Co., Mo., 2,450.
On Alton (R. R.).
VANDERBILT, Fayette Co., Pa., 994.
On Pitts. & L. Erie (R. R.).
VANDERGRIFT, Westmoreland Co., Pa., 11,479.
On Penna. (R. R.).
Located in a farming, coal-mining and petroleum district.
VANDERGRIFT HEIGHTS, Westmoreland Co., Pa.
VANDLING, Lackawanna Co., Pa., 1,169.
VAN DYKE, Macomb Co., Mich., 5,500.
VAN HORN, c. s., Culberson Co., Tex., 853.
On Tex. & Pac. (R. R.).
VAN HORNE, Benton Co., Iowa, 527.
On Chi., Mil., St. P. & Pac. (R. R.).
VAN HOUTEN, Colfax Co., N. Mex., 600.
On Atch., Top. & Santa Fe (R. R.).
VANKLEEK HILL, Prescott Co., Ontario, Canada, 1,380.
On Can. Pac.; Can. Nat. (R. Rs.).
VAN LEAR, Johnson Co., Ky., 2,338.
On Chesa. & Ohio (R. R.).
VAN METER, Westmoreland Co., Pa., 750.
On Pitts. & L. Erie (R. R.).
VANNDALE, Cross Co., Ark., 519.
On Mo. Pac. (R. R.).
VANNES, capital of Dept. of Morbihan, France, 24,068.
Tanning and cotton weaving.
VANOSS, Pontotoc Co., Okla., 518.
On Atch., Top. & Santa Fe (R. R.).
VANPORT, Beaver Co., Pa., 875.
On Beav. Val.; Penna. (R. Rs.).
VAN VOORHIS, Washington Co., Pa., 800.
On Penna. (R. R.).
VAN WERT, c. s., Van Wert Co., Ohio, 8,472.
On Cle., Cin., Chi. & St. Lou.; Penna. (R. Rs.).
VARDAMAN, Calhoun Co., Miss., 627.
On Okol., Houst. & Calh. Cy. (R. R.).
VARINA, Wake Co., N. C., 500.
On Norf. Sou.; Durham & Sou. (R. Rs.).
VARNA, Bulgaria, 72,200.
A port and industrial town. Leading manufactures are iron, machinery, textiles, petroleum, chemicals, and food products.
VARNVILLE, Hampton Co., S. C., 969.
On Charl. & West Car. (R. R.).
VASS, Moore Co., N. C., 602.
On Seab. Air Line (R. R.).
VASSALBORO, Kennebec Co., Me., 100.
On Me. Cen. (R. R.).
VASSAR, Tuscola Co., Mich., 1,816.
On Mich. Cen.; Pere Marq. (R. Rs.).
VÄSTERAS, Sweden, 30,378.
An agricultural center on Lake Mälar.
VÄSTERVIK, Sweden, 12,611.
A port and commercial town on the Baltic Sea.
VATICAN CITY, the seat of the Papacy, Italy, 531.
It occupies an area of half a square mile, wholly within the city of Roma, from which it was relinquished by Italy to the Catholic Church in 1929. It is now an independent division, the "State of Vatican City."
The most celebrated monument within Vatican City is the Church of St. Peter, the largest and most imposing place of worship in the world. Other places of interest include the old and new palaces of the Popes, the Sistine chapel, the Loggia and Stanze, containing picture galleries, museums, and library.
VAUCLUSE, Aiken Co., S. C., 600.
On Southern (R. R.).
VAUGHN, Guadaloupe Co., N. Mex., 968.
On Atch., Top. & Santa Fe; Sou. Pac. (R. Rs.).
VAUXHALL, Union Co., N. J., 1,700.
VAYLAND, Hand Co., S. Dak., 550.
On Chi. & Nor. West. (R. R.).
VEAZIE, Penobscot Co., Me., 568.
On Me. Cen. (R. R.).
VEBLEN, Marshall Co., S. Dak., 505.
On Mpls., St. P. & S. Ste. M. (R. R.).
VEEDERSBURG, Fountain Co., Ind., 1,606.
On Chi., Attica & Sou.; N. York, Chi. & St. Lou.; Cle., Cin., Chi. & St. Lou. (R. Rs.).
VEGA, Oldham Co., Tex., 519.
On Chi., Rk. Isl. & Gulf (R. R.).
VEGA ALTA, Mun. of Vega Alta, Puerto Rico, 3,192.
VEGA BAJA, Mun. of Vega Baja, Puerto Rico, 4,641.
VEGUITA, Socorro Co., N. Mex., 500.
VELARDE, Rio Arriba Co., N. Mex., 600.
On Den. & Rio Gde. West. (R. R.).
VELASCO, Brazoria Co., Tex., 755.
On Hous. & Braz. Val. (Mo. Pac.) (R. R.).
VELIKY BEČKEREK (Nagybecskerek), Yugoslavia, 32,831.
The center of a fertile agricultural region.
VELSEN, North Holland, Netherlands, 43,073.
Situated on the North Sea Canal, forming the port of entry for Amsterdam.
VELVA, McHenry Co., North Dak., 870.
On Minn., St. P. & S. Ste. M. (R. R.).
VENEZIA (Venice), capital of Prov. of Venezia, Italy, 162,695.
Situated near the head of the Adriatic. The city is built almost entirely on piles driven into about eighty small islands in the shallow waters of the Bay of Venice. A modern viaduct, crossing the Lagoons, supported on 222 arches, part of the Verona and Venezia Railway, has lately united the Continent with the Littorale, or protecting beach of the city. The eighty islands on which the city is built are separated from each other by narrow channels, which serve the purpose of thoroughfares, being constantly traversed by gondolas (long narrow boats) and motorboats, answering the purpose of cabs and omnibuses. Some of the islands are large enough to have short streets and piazzas, but in general they present rows of buildings, with canal fronts. The longest and most important street in Venezia, the Mercerie, is only 15 feet wide. Of the few other streets, the Via 22 Marzo and the Corso Vittorio Emanuele are perhaps the most important. Over this canal there are three bridges besides the railroad bridge, that of the Rialto consisting of a single arch 90 feet in span and 24 feet in height, built of marble in 1590.
Venezia was for many centuries the capital of the first maritime and commercial state in the world. It consequently contains a large number of public buildings and palatial residences; among the most celebrated are the cathedral of St. Mark, the Procurators' palaces (Royal Palace), both on the Piazza San Marco, and the palace of the Doges. Venezia was founded, 421 A.D., as a place of refuge during the invasion of Italy by Attila.
VENICE, Los Angeles Co., Cal. (Pop. incl. in Los Angeles).
On Pac. El.; Sou. Pac. (R. Rs.).
–Madison Co., Ill., 5,362.
On Alton; Cle., Cin., Chi. & St. Lou.; Wab.; Ill. Term. (El.) (R. Rs.).
VENLO, Limburg, Netherlands, 25,595.
Manufactures liquors, beer, leather, needles, tobacco, and yarn.
VENTNOR, Atlantic Co., N. J., 6,674.
VENTSPILS (Windau), Latvia, 17,253.
A seaport and seaside resort.
VENTURA, c. s., Ventura Co., Cal., 11,603.
On Sou. Pac. (R. R.).
Trading center and shipping point for a fertile agricultural section and for the oil fields near by.
VENUS, Johnson Co., Texas, 570.
On Gulf, Colo. & Santa Fe; Internat.-Gt. Nor. (Mo. Pac.) (R. Rs.).
VERACRUZ, Veracruz State, Mexico, 67,889.
On Mex.; V. C.-Alva; Nat. of Mex. (R. Rs.).
A seaport and commercial center.
VERBENA, Chilton Co., Ala., 500.
On Lou. & Nash. (R. R.).
VERCELLI, Prov. of Vercelli, Piedmont, Italy, 25,680.
A trade center and shipping point for cereals and rice.
VERDEN, Grady Co., Okla., 587.
On Chi., Rk. Isl. & Pac. (R. R.).
VERDIGRE, Knox Co., Neb., 618.
On Chi. & Nor. West. (R. R.).
VERDUGO CITY, Los Angeles Co., Cal., 1,500.
VERDUN, Dept. of Meuse, France, 19,460.
Almost destroyed in World War, being the object of a big but unsuccessful assault by the Germans in 1916. Its cathedral particularly suffered from German gunners.
Jacques-Cartier Co., Que., Can., 31,605.
A suburb of Montreal.
VERGENNES, Addison Co., Vt., 1,705.
On Rutland (R. R.).
VERKHNII UDINSK, Sov. Union. See ULAN UDE.
VERMILION, Erie Co., Ohio, 1,464.
On N. York Cen.; Lake Shore (El.); N. York, Chi. & St. Lou. (R. Rs.).
VERMILLION, c. s., Clay Co., S. Dak., 2,850.
On Chi., Mil., St. P. & Pac. (R. R.).
VERMONT, Fulton Co., Ill., 948.
On Chi., Burl. & Quincy (R. R.).
VERMONTVILLE, Eaton Co., Mich., 581.
On Mich. Cen. (R. R.).
VERNAL, c. s., Uintah Co., Utah, 1,744.
VERNDALE, Wadena Co., Minn., 424.
On Nor. Pac. (R. R.).
VERNOLENINSK, Sov. Union. See NIKOLAEV.
VERNON, Los Angeles Co., Cal., 1,269.
On Atch., Top. & Santa Fe; Los Ang. & Salt L. (Un. Pac.) (R. Rs.).
–c. s., Lamar Co., Ala., 519.
–Tolland Co., Conn., with Rockville City, 7,695.
On N. York, N. Hav. & Hart. (R. R.).
–Oneida Co., N. Y., 602.
On West Shore (R. R.).
–c. s., Wilbarger Co., Texas, 9,137.
On Ft. Worth & Denv. Cy.; St. Lou.-San Fran. (R. Rs.).
–Windham Co., Vt., 609.
On Cen. Ver. (R. R.).
VERNONIA, Columbia Co., Ore., 1,625.
On United (Spok., Port. & Seat.) (R. R.).
VERO BEACH, c. s., Indian River Co., Fla., 3,056.
On Fla. East Coast (R. R.).
VERONA, capital of Prov. of Verona, Italy, 113,139.
Famous for its historical landmarks, architecture, and art.
–Lee Co., Miss., 554.
On Mob. & Ohio (R. R.).
–Essex Co., N. J., 7,161.
On Erie (R. R.).
–Allegheny Co., Pa., 4,376.
On Penna. (R. R.).
VERPLANCK, Westchester Co., N. Y., 1,267.
VERSAILLES, capital of Dept. of Seine-et-Oise, France, 73,839.
Site of the famous palace and park of Louis XIV, built in 1672, and the two palaces called the Grand and the Petit Trianon, the latter associated with Marie Antoinette; the French Revolution opened here with the assembly of the States-General in 1789, the unification of Germany was consummated here by proclaiming the King of Prussia Emperor of Germany, 1871. Scene of the signing of the Treaty of Peace with Germany, following the World War of 1914-18.
–Brown Co., Ill., 515.
On Wabash (R. R.).
–c. s., Ripley Co., Ind., 523.
–c. s., Woodford Co., Ky., 2,244.
On Southern (R. R.).
–c. s., Morgan Co., Mo., 1,662.
On Chi., Rk. Isl. & Pac. (R. R.).
–Darke Co., Ohio, 1,465.
On Cle., Cin., Chi. & St. Lou. (R. R.).
–Allegheny Co., Pa., 2,473.
On Balt. & Ohio (R. R.).
VERSEC, Yugoslavia. See VRŠAC.
VERVIERS, Prov. of Liége, Belgium, 41,384.
A center for textiles and yarn spinning.
VESTABURG, Washington Co., Pa., 1,062.
On Penna. (R. R.).
VEVAY, c. s., Switzerland Co., Ind., 1,183.
VEVEY, Canton of Vaud, Switzerland, 13,041.
A center of a wine-making region.
VIAN, Sequoyah Co., Okla., 900.
On Mo. Pac. (R. R.).
VIANNA DO CASTELLO, Portugal, 11,819.
A seaport and trade center.
VIBORG, Finland. See VIIPURI.
–Turner Co., S. D., 721.
On Gt. Nor. (R. R.).
VICENZA, capital of Vicenza, Italy, 42,628.
Has masterpieces of historic architecture.
VICHY, Allier, France, 25,074.
Famous for its mineral waters.
VICI, Dewey Co., Okla., 593.
On Mo.-Kan.-Tex. (R. R.).
VICKERY, Dallas Co., Tex., 813.
On Tex. Elec. (R. R.).
VICKSBURG, c. s., Warren Co., Miss., 22,943.
On Yazoo & Miss. Val. (Ill. Cen.) (R. R.).
A river port and shipping point. A center for cotton and lumber industries. Objective in an important campaign of the Civil War.
–Kalamazoo Co., Mich., 1,735.
On Penna.; Gd. Tr. (R. Rs.).
VICTOR, Teller Co., Colo., 1,291.
On Midl. Term. (R. R.).
–Iowa and Poweshiek Cos., Iowa, 794.
On Chi., Rk. Isl. & Pac. (R. R.).
–Ontario Co., N. Y., 1,042.
On N. York Cen.; Leh. Val. (R. Rs.).
VICTORIA, Victoria Co., capital of British Columbia, Canada, 39,082.
On Can. Nat.; Can. Pac.; Esquimalt & Nan. (R. Rs.).
An industrial and commercial center with manufactures of canned fish, lumber, soap, machinery, furniture, shoes, and brick.
–Esperito Santo, Brazil, 32,100.
A seaport and important commercial town. A leading mineral exporting point.
–Ellis Co., Kans., 757.
On Un. Pac. (R. R.).
–Prov. of Tarlac, Luzon, P. I., 15,662.
–c. s., Victoria Co., Texas, 7,421.
On St. Lou., Browns. & Mex. (Mo. Pac.); Tex. & N. Orl. (Sou. Pac.) (R. Rs.).
–Lunenburg Co., Va., 1,568.
On Virginian (R. R.).
–Prov. of Cautin, Chile, 8,585.
VICTORIAVILLE, Arthabaska Co., Quebec, Canada, 6,213.
On Can. Nat. (R. R.).
VICTORVILLE, San Bernardino Co., Cal., 1,800.
On Atch., Top. & Santa Fe; Los Ang. & Salt L. (Un. Pac.) (R. Rs.).
VICTORY MILLS, Saratoga Co., N. Y., 473.
On Bost. & Me. (R. R.).
VIDALIA, Toombs Co., Ga., 3,585.
On Ga. & Fla.; Macon, Dub. & Sav.; Seab. Air Line (R. Rs.).
–c. s., Concordia Parish, La., 1,141.
On La. & Ark.; Mo. Pac. (R. Rs.).
VIDIN, Bulgaria, 19,600.
A river port and commercial center.
VIENNA, Austria. See WIEN.
–c. s., Dooly Co., Ga., 1,832.
On Atla., Birm. & Coast; Ga. Sou. & Fla. (R. Rs.).
–c. s., Johnson Co., Ill., 874.
On Cle., Cin., Chi. & St. Lou. (R. R.).
–Fairfax Co., Va., 903.
On Arl. & Fairfax; Wash. & Old Dom. (El.) (R. Rs.).
VIENNE, Dept. of Isère, France, 25,436.
Textile mills, iron foundries, distilleries.
VIERSEN, Rhenish Prussia, Germany, 33,000.
Silks, cotton, paper, shoes, and cement.
VIGAN, Luzon, P. I., 17,765.
A commercial town with native industries.
VIIPURI (Viborg), Finland, 72,200.
A seaport and popular summer resort.
VILLACH, Austria, 23,831.
Manufactures of timber and lead wares. Numerous resorts in the vicinity.
VILLA GARCIA, State of Zacatecas, Mexico, 1,547.
VILLA GROVE, Douglas Co., Ill., 2,001.
On Chi. & East. Ill. (R. R.).
VILLALBA, Mun. of Villalba, Puerto Rico, 3,527.
VILLANUEVA, San Miguel Co., N. Mex., 600.
VILLA PARK, Du Page Co., Ill., 6,220.
On Chi. Gt. West.; Chi. & Nor. West.; Chi. Aur. & Elg. (R. Rs.).
VILLARICA, Carroll and Douglas Cos., Ga., 1,304.
On Southern (R. R.).
VILLARRICA, Paraguay, 35,769.
Situated in a rich farming section and has a large trade in yerba maté.
VILLASIS, Pagansinan, Luzon, P. I., 14,244.
VILLEJUIF, Seine, France, 27,540.
VILLE PLATTE, c. s., Evangeline Parish, La. 1,722.
On Tex. & Pac. (R. R.).

VILLEURBANNE, Rhône, France, 81,322.
    A manufacturing suburb of Lyons.
VILLISCA, Montgomery Co., Iowa, 2,032.
    On Chi., Burl. & Quincy (R. R.).
VILNA, Poland. See WILNO.
VIÑA DEL MAR, Chile, 49,488.
    A suburb of Valparaiso.
VINALHAVEN, Knox Co., Me., 1,800.
VINCENNES, Seine, France, 48,967.
    A residential suburb of Paris.
    -c. s., Knox Co., Ind., 17,564.
    On Balt. & Ohio; Cle., Cin., Chi. & St. Lou.;
    Chi. & East. Ill.; Penna. (R. R.).
    An industrial and commercial town situated in
    a rich agricultural region. Manufactures in-
    clude structural steel, pearl buttons, monu-
    ments, fertilizer, flour, dairy products, chickens
    and soft drinks. The oldest town in Indiana.
VINCENT, Shelby Co., Ala., 1,192.
    On Cen. of Ga. (R. R.).
VINCENTOWN, Burlington Co., N. J., 865.
VINEGAR BEND, Washington Co., Ala., 556.
    On Miss. & Ala.; Mob. & Ohio (R. Rs.).
VINE GROVE, Hardin Co., Ky., 523.
    On Ill. Cen. (R. R.).
VINELAND, Cumberland Co., N. J., 7,556.
    On Cen. of N. Jer.; Penna.-Read. Seash. (R.
    Rs.).
VINEYARD HAVEN, Dukes Co., Mass., 1,500.
    On island of Martha's Vineyard.
VINITA, c. s., Craig Co., Okla., 4,263.
    On Mo.-Kan.-Tex.; St. Lou.-San Fran. (R. Rs.).
VINNITSA, Soviet Union, 72,800.
    Situated in a grain and cattle raising region.
VINTON, c. s., Benton Co., Iowa, 3,372.
    On Chi., Rk. Isl. & Pac. (R. R.).
    -Calcasieu Parish, La., 1,989.
    On Tex. & N. Orl. (Sou. Pac.) (R. R.).
    -Roanoke Co., Va., 3,610.
    On Norf. & West. (R. R.).
VINTONDALE, Cambria Co., Pa., 1,658.
    On Balt. & Ohio; Penna.; Cambria & Ind. (sta-
    tion Rexis) (R. Rs.).
VIOLA, Mercer Co., Ill., 566.
    On Chi., Burl. & Quincy (R. R.).
    -Richland and Vernon Cos., Wis., 699.
    On Chi., Mil., St. P. & Pac. (R. R.).
VIOLET HILL, York Co., Pa., 500.
VIRAC, Prov. of Albay, Luzon, P. I., 13,441.
VIRDEN, Macoupin Co., Ill., 3,011.
    On Alton; Chi. & Nor. West.; Chi. Burl. &
    Quincy; Ill. Term. (El.) (R. Rs.).
    -Brandon Co., Manitoba, Can., 1,590.
    On Can. Nat.; Can. Pac. (R. Rs.).
VIRGIL, Greenwood Co., Kan., 598.
    On Atch., Top. & Santa Fe (R. R.).
VIRGINIA, c. s., Cass Co., Ill., 1,494.
    On Balt. & Ohio (R. R.).
    -St. Louis Co., Minn., 11,963.
    On Dul., Missabe & Nor.; Dul., Winnip. &
    Pac.; Gt. Nor. (R. Rs.).
    Situated in the heart of the Mesaba iron range.
    Has large open-pit iron mines.
VIRGINIA BEACH, Princess Anne Co., Va., 1,719.
    On Norf. Sou. (R. R.).
VIRGINIA CITY, c. s., Storey Co., Nev., 488.
    On Virginia & Truck. (R. R.).
VIROQUA, c. s., Vernon Co., Wis., 2,792.
    On Chi., Mil., St. P. & Pac. (R. R.).
VISALIA, c. s., Tulare Co., Cal., 7,263.
    On Atch., Top. & Santa Fe; Sou. Pac. (R. Rs.).
VISBY, Sweden, 10,467.
    A seaport and marketing town on the Baltic
    Sea.
VISTA, San Diego Co., Cal., 3,000.
    On Atch., Top. & Santa Fe (R. R.).
VITEBSK, Soviet Union, 127,300.
    An agricultural center with manufactures of
    glass, farm machinery, shoes, clothing, and
    needles.
VITERBO, Prov. of Viterbo, Italy, 18,315.
    Marketing center in an agricultural district.
VITORIA, capital of Prov. of Alava, Spain, 41,245.
    A center of trade in wine, horses, wool, and
    hardware.
VITRY-SUR-SEINE, Seine, France, 46,945.
VITTORIA, Prov. of Ragusa, Italy, 29,888.
    The metropolis of the Sicilian wine trade.
VIVIAN, Caddo Parish, La., 1,646.
    On Kan. Cy. Sou. (R. R.).
    -McDowell Co., W. Va., 650.
    On Norf. & West. (R. R.).
VLAARDINGEN, Prov. of South Holland, Nether-
    lands, 28,570.
    A suburb of Rotterdam and a center of the
    North Sea herring and cod fisheries.
VLADIKAVKAZ, Soviet Union. See ORDZHONI-
    KIDZE.
VLADIMIR, Soviet Union, 45,600.
    Knitted goods, fruit juices, brick, and lumber.
VLADIVOSTOK, Far Eastern Area, Soviet Union,
    190,000.
    The principal Soviet port on the Pacific Ocean.
    Exports mainly agricultural produce and lum-
    ber. Has large ship yards.
VLISSINGEN (Flushing), Netherlands, 21,664.
    An important seaport and commercial center
    situated at the mouth of the West Scheldt.
VOLGA, Brookings Co., S. Dak., 557.
    On Chi. & Nor. West. (R. R.).

VOLOGDA, Soviet Union, 72,400.
    The center of a large agricultural district with
    manufactures of farm implements, leather, pot-
    tery, glass, and cement.
VOLOS, Dept. of Larissa, Thessaly, Greece, 49,400.
    A seaport and trade center.
VOLSK, Soviet Union, 57,000.
    A marketing center and port on the Volga.
VOLUNTOWN, New London Co., Conn., 651.
    On Del. & Hud.; West Shore (R. Rs.).
VOROCHILOVGRAD, Soviet Union. See LUGANSK.
VOROCHILOVSK, Sov. Union. See STAVROPOL.
VORONEZH, Soviet Union, 212,400.
VOTH, Jefferson Co., Tex., 600.
    On Gulf, Colo. & Santa Fe; Tex. & N. Orl.
    (Sou. Pac.) (R. Rs.).
VREDENBURGH, Monroe Co., Ala., 815.

On Wheel. & L. Erie (R. R.).
WACONIA, Carver Co., Minn., 1,291.
    On Mpls. & St. Lou. (R. R.).
WADDINGTON, St. Lawrence Co., N. Y., 679.
    On Norwood & St. Lawr. (R. R.).
WADENA, c. s., Wadena Co., Minn., 2,512.
    On Gt. Nor.; Nor. Pac. (R. Rs.).
WADESBORO, c. s., Anson Co., N. C., 3,124.
    On Atl. Coast Line; Seab. Air Line; Winst.-Sal.
    Southb. (R. Rs.).
WADING RIVER, Suffolk Co., N. Y., 500.
WADLEY, Randolph Co., Ala., 527.
    On Atla., Birm. & Coast (R. R.).
    -Jefferson Co., Ga., 1,055.
    On Cen. of Ga.; Lou. & Wadley; Wadley &
    Sou. (R. Rs.).
WADSWORTH, Medina Co., Ohio, 5,930.
    On Erie (R. R.).

STATUE OF BARTOLOMMEO COLLEONI, IN VENICE, BY ANDREA DEL VERROCCHIO,
CONSIDERED THE FINEST OF EQUESTRIAN SCULPTURE

On Vredenburgh Saw Mill Co. (R. R.).
VRŠAC, Yugoslavia, 29,423.
    Famous for its red wines and brandy.
VULCAN, Dickinson Co., Mich., 1,150.
    On Chi. & Nor. West. (R. R.).
VYATKA, Soviet Union. See KIROV.

W

WABAN, Middlesex Co., Mass., 3,500.
    On Bost. & Alb. (R. R.).
WABASH, c. s., Wabash Co., Ind., 8,840.
    On Cle., Cin., Chi. & St. Lou.; Ind.; Wab. (R.
    Rs.).
WABASHA, c. s., Wabasha Co., Minn., 2,212.
    On Chi., Mil., St. P. & Pac. (R. R.).
WABENO, Forest Co., Wis., 1,800.
    On Chi. & Nor. West. (R. R.).
WACHAPREAGUE, Accomac Co., Va., 585.
WACO, c. s., McLennan Co., Texas, 52,848.
    At the confluence of the Bosque and Brazos
    Rivers, and on the Mo.-Kan.-Tex. of Tex.; the
    Mo.; St. Lou. Southw.; Sou. Pac. and Tex.
    Elec. (R. Rs.).
    An important commercial and industrial cen-
    ter in the heart of a cotton growing district.
    Manufactures textiles, flour, wood products,
    condensed milk, tents, awnings, cement, cof-
    fins, caskets, work clothes, camp furniture.
    Seat of Baylor University.
    -Starke Co., Ohio, 600.

WAELDER, Gonzales Co., Texas, 1,048.
    On Tex. & N. Orl. (Sou. Pac.) (R. R.).
WAGENER, Aiken Co., S. C., 545.
WAGNER, Charles Mix Co., S. Dak., 1,350.
    On Chi., Mil., St. P. & Pac. (R. R.).
WAGONER, c. s., Wagoner Co., Okla., 2,994.
    On Mo.-Kan.-Tex.; Kan., Okla. & Gulf; Mo.
    Pac. (R. Rs.).
WAGON MOUND, Mora Co., N. Mex., 852.
    On Atch., Top. & Santa Fe (R. R.).
WAHJAMEGA, Tuscola Co., Mich., 1,150.
    On Mich. Cen. (R. R.).
WAHOO, c. s., Saunders Co., Neb., 2,689.
    On Chi., Burl. & Quincy; Chi. & Nor. West.;
    Un. Pac. (R. Rs.).
WAHPETON, c. s., Richmond Co., N. Dak., 3,176.
    On Chi., Mil., St. P. & Pac.; Gt. Nor.; Nor.
    Pac. (R. Rs.).
WAITE PARK, Stearns Co., Minn., 1,318.
    On Gt. Nor. (R. R.).
WAITSBURG, Walla Walla Co., Wash., 869.
    On Nor. Pac.; Un. Pac. (R. Rs.).
WAITSFIELD, Washington Co., Vt., 675.
WAITZEN, Hungary. See VÁC.
WAKAMATSU, Ken of Fukushima, Japan, 43,729.
    Noted for its manufactures of lacquer-ware.
WAKARUSA, Elkhart Co., Ind., 973.
    On Wabash (R. R.).
WAKAYAMA, Ken of Wakayama, Japan, 179,732.
    A maritime town with cotton industries.
WAKEENEY, c. s., Trego Co., Kans., 1,846.

On Un. Pac. (R. R.).
WAKEFIELD, Yorkshire, England, 56,010.
    A leading agricultural center with manufac-
    tures of farm implements, flour, and beer.
    -Clay Co., Kans., 578.
    On Un. Pac. (R. R.).
    -Middlesex Co., Mass., 16,494.
    On Bost. & Me. (R. R.).
    A residential suburb of Boston.
    -Gogebic Co., Mich., 3,677.
    On Chi. & Nor. West. (R. R.).
    -Dixon and Wayne Cos., Neb., 1,112.
    On Chi., St. P., Mpls. & Oma. (R. R.).
    -Washington Co., R. I., 4,000.
    On Narrag. Pier (R. R.).
    -Sussex Co., Va., 881.
    On Norf. & West. (R. R.).
WAKE FOREST, Wake Co., N. C., 1,536.
    On Seab. Air Line (R. R.).
    Seat of Wake Forest College.
WAKONDA, Clay Co., S. Dak., 461.
    On Chi. & Nor. West. (R. R.).
WALBRIDGE, Wood Co., Ohio, 905.
    On Ches. & Ohio; Penna.; Tol. Term. (R.
    Rs.).
WALDEN, Orange Co., N. Y., 4,283.
    On West Shore (R. R.).
WALDENBURG, Silesia, Germany, 66,364.
    Machinery, brick, pottery, furniture, textiles.
WALDO, Alachua Co., Fla., 736.
    On Seab. Air Line (R. R.).
    -Columbia Co., Ark., 942.
    On St. Lou. Southw. (R. R.).
WALDOBORO, Lincoln Co., Me., 2,311.
    On Me. Cen. (R. R.).
WALDRON, c. s., Scott Co., Ark., 1,077.
    On Ark. Western (Kans. City Sou.) (R. R.).
    -Shelby Co., Ind., 500.
    On Cle., Cin., Chi. & St. Lou. (R. R.).
WALDWICK, Bergen Co., N. J., 1,728.
    On Erie (R. R.).
WALFORD (Bessemer P. O.), Lawrence Co., Pa.,
    2,001.
    On Penna.; Pitts. & L. Erie (R. Rs.).
WALHALLA, Pembina Co., N. Dak., 700.
    On Gt. Nor. (R. R.).
    -c. s., Oconee Co., S. C., 2,388.
    On Blue Ridge (R. R.).
WALKER, c. s., Cass Co., Minn., 618.
    On Gt. Nor.; Minn. & Internat. (R. Rs.).
    -Livingston Par., La., 524.
    On Yazoo & Miss. Valley (Ill. Cen.) (R. R.).
WALKERSVILLE, Frederick Co., Md., 623.
    On Penna. (R. R.).
WALKERTON, St. Joseph Co., Ind., 1,137.
    On Balt. & Ohio; N. York, Chi. & St. Lou.;
    N. York Cen. (R. Rs.).
    -Bruce Co., South, Ontario, Can., 2,431.
    On Can. Pac.; Can. Nat. (R. Rs.).
WALKERVILLE, Silver Bow Co., Mont., 2,052.
    -Essex Co., East, Ontario, Canada, 10,105.
    On Can. Nat.; Essex Term.; Pere Marq.; Wab.
    (R. Rs.).
WALL, Allegheny Co., Pa., 2,236.
WALLACE, c. s., Shoshone Co., Idaho, 3,634.
    On Nor. Pac.; Un. Pac. (R. Rs.).
    -St. John the Baptist Co., La., 500.
    -Duplin Co., N. C., 734.
    On Atl. Coast Line (R. R.).
    -Harrison Co., W. Va., 500.
    On Balt. & Ohio (R. R.).
WALLACEBURG, Kent Co., Ont., Can., 4,326.
    On Pere Marq. (R. R.).
WALLAGRASS, Aroostook Co., Me., 1,145.
    On Bangor & Aroostook (R. R.).
WALLASEY, Cheshire, England, 97,465.
    A residential town near Liverpool.
WALLA WALLA, c. s., Walla Walla Co., Wash.,
    15,976.
    On the Nor. Pac.; Un. Pac.; Walla Walla Val-
    ley (El.) (R. Rs.).
    Trading center of grain and fruit section. Seat
    of Whitman College.
WALLED LAKE, Oakland Co., Mich., 600.
    On Gd. Tr. (R. R.).
WALLER, Waller Co., Tex., 518.
    On Tex. & N. Orl. (Sou. Pac.) (R. R.).
WALLINGFORD, New Haven Co., Conn., 11,170.
    On N. York, N. Hav. & Hart. (R. R.).
    Located near New Haven. Has manufactures
    of firearms, hardware, silverware, brass goods,
    rubber goods, tools, and wire.
    -Delaware Co., Pa., 1,000.
    On Penna. (R. R.).
    -Rutland Co., Vt., 650.
    On Rutland (R. R.).
WALLINGTON, Bergen Co., N. J., 9,063.
WALLINS (Wallins Cr.), Harlan Co., Ky., 900.
    On Lou. & Nash. (R. R.).
WALLIS, Austin Co., Tex., 690.
    On Gulf, Colo. & Santa Fe; Tex. & N. Orl.
    (Sou. Pac.) (R. R.).
WALLISVILLE, c. s., Chambers Co., Texas, 37.
WALLKILL, Ulster Co., N. Y., 800.
    On West Shore (R. R.).
WALL LAKE, Sac Co., Ia., 749.
    On Ill. Cen.; Chi. & Nor. West. (R. Rs.).
WALLOPSBURG, Indiana Co., Pa., 515.
    On Balt. & Ohio (R. R.).
WALLOWA, Wallowa Co., Ore., 749.

On Un. Pac. (R. R.).
Wallsend, Northumberland, England, 44,582.
Has coal mines, ship-yards, and engineering works.
–Bell Co., Ky., 518.
On Lou. & Nash. (R. R.).
Walnut, Bureau Co., Ill., 833.
On Chi., Burl. & Quincy (R. R.).
–Pottawattamie Co., Iowa, 935.
On Chi., Rk. Isl. & Pac. (R. R.).
–Crawford Co., Kans., 535.
On Mo.-Kan.-Tex.; Atch., Top. & Santa Fe (R. Rs.).
–Madison Co., N. C., 500.
Walnut Cove, Stokes Co., N. C., 1,081.
On Atl. & Yadk.; Norf. & West. (R. Rs.).
Walnut Creek, Contra Costa Co., Cal., 1,014.
On Sacramento Nor. (El.); Sou. Pac. (R. Rs.).
Walnut Grove, Sacramento Co., Cal., 631.
On Sou. Pac. (R. R.).
–Redwood Co., Minn., 586.
On Chi. & Nor. West. (R. R.).
–Leake Co., Miss., 753.
On Gulf, Mob. & Nor. (R. R.).
–Hardin Co., Tenn., 513.
Walnutport, Northampton Co., Pa., 1,151.
On Cen. of N. Jer.; Leh. Val. (R. Rs.).
Walnut Ridge, c. s., Lawrence Co., Ark., 2,007.
On Mo. Pac.; St. Lou.-San Fran. (R. Rs.).
Walnut Springs, Bosque Co., Tex., 765.
On Mo.-Kan.-Tex. of Tex. (R. R.).
Walpole, Norfolk Co., Mass., 7,449.
On N. York, N. Hav. & Hart. (R. R.).
–Cheshire Co., N. H., 950.
On Bost. & Me. (R. R.).
Walsall, Staffordshire, England, 103,102.
The center of a coal mining and quarrying region. Has several annual fairs. Iron and brass foundries and glove factories.
Walsenburg, c. s., Huerfano Co., Colo., 5,503.
On Colo. & Sou.; Den. & Rio Gde. West. (R. Rs.).
Walterboro, c. s., Colleton Co., S. C., 2,592.
On Atl. Coast Line (R. R.).
Walteria, Los Angeles Co., Cal., 536.
Walters, Cotton Co., Okla., 2,262.
On Chi., Rk. Isl. & Pac. (R. R.).
Waltersburg, Fayette Co., Pa., 550.
On Penna. (R. R.).
Waltersville, Warren Co., Miss., 500.
Waltham, Middlesex Co., Mass., 40,557.
On Bost. & Me. (R. R.).
An industrial suburb of Boston. Has one of the largest watch factories in the world.
Walthamstow, Essex, England, 132,965.
A residential and education suburb of London.
Walthill, Thurston Co., Neb., 1,162.
On Chi., Burl. & Quincy (R. R.).
Walton, Boone Co., Ky., 854.
On Cin., N. Orl. & Tex. Pac.; Lou. & Nash. (R. Rs.).
–Cass Co., Ind., 685.
On Penna. (R. R.).
–Delaware Co., N. Y., 3,496.
On N. York, Ont. & West. (R. R.).
–Roane Co., W. Va., 500.
Walville, Lewis Co., Wash., 500.
On Nor. Pac. (R. R.).
Walworth, Walworth Co., Wis., 920.
On Chi., Mil., St. P. & Pac. (R. R.).
–Wayne Co., N. Y., 500.
On N. York Cen. (R. R.).
Wamac, Clinton, Washington and Marion Cos., Ill., 1,232.
Wamego, Pottawatomie Co., Kans., 1,726.
On Un. Pac. (R. R.).
Wampum, Lawrence Co., Pa., 883.
On Penna.; Pitts. & L. Erie (R. Rs.).
Wanamie, Luzerne Co., Pa., 1,536.
On Cen. of N. Jer. (R. R.).
Wanaque, Passaic Co., N. J., 3,119.
On Erie (R. R.).
Wanatah, La Porte Co., Ind., 750.
On Chi., Ind. & Lou.; Penna. (R. Rs.).
Wanchese, Dare Co., N. C., 1,040.
Wandsbeck, Schleswig-Holstein, Germany, 44,000.
A suburb of Hamburg.
Wanette, Pottawatomie Co., Okla., 758.
On Atch., Top. & Santa Fe (R. R.).
Wanganui, New Zealand, 23,200.
A seaport and trade center for a stockraising region.
Wanhsein, Szechwan, China, 208,000.
A commercial and marketing center.
Wanlock, Monroe Co., Ia., 500.
Wanne-Eickel, Prussia, Germany, 92,269.
Situated in a coal mining region.
Wanskuck, Providence Co., R. I., 500.
Wantagh, Nassau Co., N. Y., 1,284.
On Long Isl. (R. R.).
Wapakoneta, c. s., Auglaize Co., Ohio, 5,378.
On Balt. & Ohio; N. York Cen. (R. Rs.).
Wapanucka, Johnston Co., Okla., 553.
On Kan., Okla. & Gulf (R. R.).
Wapato, Yakima Co., Wash., 1,222.
On Nor. Pac. (R. R.).
Wapella, De Witt Co., Ill., 521.
On Ill. Cen.; Ill. Term. (El.) (R. Rs.).
Wapello, c. s., Louisa Co., Iowa, 1,502.
On Chi., Rk. Isl. & Pac. (R. R.).
Wapping, Hartford Co., Conn., 986.
Wappingers Falls, Dutchess Co., N. Y., 3,336.
War, McDowell Co., W. Va., 1,392.
On Norf. & West. (R. R.).
Wardensville, Hardy Co., W. Va., 189.
On Winch. & Wardens. (R. R.).
Wardner, Shoshone Co., Idaho, 903.
Ware, Hampshire Co., Mass., 7,727.
On Bost. & Alb.; Bost. & Me. (R. Rs.).
War Eagle, Mingo Co., W. Va., 1,524.
On Norf. & West. (R. R.).
Wareham, Plymouth Co., Mass., 6,047.
On N. York, N. Hav. & Hart. (R. R.).
Warehouse Point, Hartford Co., Conn., 1,601.
Ware Neck, Gloucester Co., Va., 500.
Ware Shoals, Greenwood Co., S. C., 3,502.
On Ware Shoals (R. R.).
Waretown, Ocean Co., N. J., 511.
On Cen. of N. Jer. (R. R.).
Warm Springs, Deer Lodge Co., Mont., 1,900.
On Mo. Pac. (R. R.).
–c. s., Bath Co., Va., 912.
Warner, Merrimack Co., N. H., 450.
On Bost. & Me. (R. R.).
Warners, Onondaga Co., N. Y., 510.
On N. York Cen.; West Shore (R. Rs.).
Warrnambool, Victoria, Australia, 8,906.
Warren, Cochise Co., Ariz., 2,250.
On Sou. Pac. (R. R.).
–c. s., Bradley Co., Ark., 2,523.
On Mo. Pac.; War. & Ouach. Val.; War. & Saline Riv. (R. Rs.).
–Jo Daviess Co., Ill., 1,179.
On Ill. Cen. (R. R.).
–Huntington Co., Ind., 1,177.
On N. York, Chi. & St. Lou. (R. R.).
–Knox Co., Me., 853.
On Me. Cen. (R. R.).
–Worcester Co., Mass., 3,662.
On Bost. & Alb. (R. R.).
–Macomb Co., Mich., 515.
On Mich. Cen. (R. R.).
–c. s., Marshall Co., Minn., 1,472.
On Gt. Nor.; Minn., St. P. & S. Ste. M. (R. Rs.).
–Grafton Co., N. H., 500.
On Bost. & Me. (R. R.).
–c. s., Trumbull Co., Ohio, 41,062.
On Balt. & Ohio; Erie; Penna. (R. Rs.).
Iron, steel, lamps, sprinkler systems, cable, tools, machinery, and steel drums.
–c. s., Warren Co., Pa., 14,863.
On N. York Cen.; Penna. (R. Rs.).
A commercial and industrial town situated in a rich oil and gas region.
–Bristol Co., R. I., 7,389.
On N. York, N. Hav. & Hart. (R. R.).
–Washington Co., Vt., 325.
Warrendale, Allegheny Co., Pa., 500.
Warrensburg, Macon Co., Ill., 517.
On Ill. Cen. (R. R.).
–c. s., Johnson Co., Mo., 5,146.
On Mo. Pac. (R. R.).

PHOTO. BY CHARLES PHELPS CUSHING. R. I. NESMITH ASSOCIATES.

THE FAÇADE OF THE NEW SUPREME COURT BUILDING, WASHINGTON, D. C., WHERE THE NATION'S HIGHEST TRIBUNAL HOLDS ITS DELIBERATIONS

–Warren Co., N. Y., 2,000.
On Del. & Hud. (R. R.).
Warrensville, Lycoming Co., Pa., 715.
Warrensville Heights, Cuyahoga Co., Ohio, 877.
Warrenton, c. s., Warren Co., Ga., 1,289.
On Georgia (R. R.).
–c. s., Warren Co., Mo., 1,250.
On Wabash (R. R.).
–c. s., Warren Co., N. C., 1,072.
On Warrenton (R. R.).
–Clatsop Co., Ore., 683.
On Spok., Port. & Seattle (R. R.).
–c. s., Fauquier Co., Va., 1,450.
On Southern (R. R.).
Warrington, Lancashire, England, 79,322.
On the Mersey. Though of recent development, it is an ancient place, the Wallington of Domesday. Manufacturing center.
–Escambia Co., Fla., 1,000.
Warrior, Jefferson Co., Ala., 646.
On Lou. & Nash. (R. R.).
Warrior Run, Luzerne Co., Pa., 1,516.
On Cen. of N. Jer.; Leh. Val. (R. Rs.).
Warroad, Roseau Co., Minn., 1,184.
On Dul., Minn. & Pac. (Can. Nat.); Gt. Nor. (R. Rs.).
Warsaw, Poland. See Warszawa.
–Hancock Co., Ill., 1,866.
On Tol., Peor. & West. (R. R.).
–c. s., Kosciusko Co., Ind., 5,730.
On Cle., Cin., Chi. & St. Lou.; Penna.; Winona (El.) (R. Rs.).
–c. s., Gallatin Co., Ky., 800.
–c. s., Benton Co., Mo., 1,102.
On Mo. Pac. (R. R.).
–Duplin Co., N. C., 1,222.
On Atl. Coast Line; Atl. & Car. (R. Rs.).
–c. s., Wyoming Co., N. Y., 3,477.
On Balt. & Ohio; Erie (R. Rs.).
Warszawa (Warsaw), Poland, 1,261,000.
Situated on the Vistula, being connected with Praga, its fortified suburb, by a floating bridge. Warszawa consists of an old and new town, independent of its suburbs; a place of great antiquity, an industrial center.
In the Great War of 1914-18, Warszawa was taken by the Germans in their invasion of Russia. With the restoration of Poland by the Peace Treaty, it became the capital.
Wartrace, Bedford Co., Tenn., 606.
On Nash., Chatt. & St. Lou. (R. R.).
Warwick, Warwickshire, England, 13,459.
The marketing center of a farming region and site of a number of historic places.
–Franklin Co., Mass., 565.
–Orange Co., N. Y., 2,443.
On Leh. & Hud. (R. R.).
–Kent Co., R. I., 27,072.
The center of a number of resorts and beaches.
Wasco, Kern Co., Cal., 2,000.
On Atch., Top. & Santa Fe (R. R.).
Waseca, c. s., Waseca Co., Minn., 3,815.
On Chi. & Nor. West.; Mpls. & St. Lou. (R. Rs.).
Washburn, Aroostook Co., Me., 700.
On Aroostook Val.; Bangor & Aroostook (R. Rs.).
–Marshall and Woodford Cos., Ill., 854.
On Alton (R. R.).
–c. s., McLean Co., N. Dak., 753.
On Minn., St. P. & S. Ste. M. (R. R.).
–Bayfield Co., Wis., 2,238.
On Chi., St. P., Minn. & Oma. (R. R.).
Washington, c. s., Hempstead Co., Ark., 457.
On Mo. Pac. (R. R.).
–(Broderick), Yolo Co., Cal., 1,500.
On Sou. Pac. (R. R.).
–District of Columbia, 493,000.
Capital of the United States. In 1800 the seat of government was removed from Philadelphia to Washington, the new city which was created especially for the purpose of a national capital from the plans of Major Pierre Charles L'Enfant. The city lies on the north bank of the Potomac River. It is on the lines of the Baltimore & Ohio; the Chesapeake & Ohio; the Pennsylvania; the Richmond, Fredericksburg & Potomac; the Washington & Old Dominion (El.); and the Southern railroads, and several interurban electric lines.
The center of the city is Capitol Hill, from which radiate twenty-one wide avenues, intersected by rectangularly disposed and alphabetically named streets running east and west, and numbered streets north and south. Many of the wide avenues, lined with thousands of trees, are named after the States. From the Capitol west to the Washington Monument extend the botanical gardens and the Mall, containing the National Museum, the Army Medical Museum, the Smithsonian Institution, the Freer Gallery, and the Agricultural Department. From the Washington Monument north are the Executive grounds, Corcoran Gallery, the Pan-American Union Building, Continental Hall, and the freestone White House Building, the Commerce Building, State, War, and Navy Building, and Treasury Building. Northeast from this point, is the United States Soldiers' Home. West of this across the Petworth settlement is Rock Creek Park, with the National Zoological Park adjoining it on the south, through which Rock Creek runs south by Washington Heights, southwest by Oak Hill Cemetery, and south into the Potomac River. Northeast of this cemetery, Massachusetts Avenue crosses the creek to the United States Naval Observatory, and beyond to Fairview Heights. East of the Capitol and separated from it by First Street is the Library of Congress, north of which lies the Supreme Court Building. Southeast of this is the United States Navy Yard on the eastern branch of the Potomac, with Anacostia over the bridge. Northwest of the Capitol are the City Hall and Pension Office. The Capitol, 751 feet long and 3½ acres in area, stands 90 feet above the Potomac and faces east. The corner-stone was laid by Washington in 1793. The wings, of pure white marble, were begun in 1851 by President Filmore. Upon the dome of the rotunda (96 feet in diameter) rises 287 feet above the basement Crawford's bronze statue of Liberty. Besides the rotunda with its historical paintings are the Senate Chamber in the north, the House of Representatives in the south wing, and the old Hall of Representatives, now used for historical statues. The whole building cost $16,000,000. The Senate and House office buildings are near by. The Congressional Library was completed in 1897 at a cost of $6,180,000. It is 470 feet long and 340 feet wide and contains over 3,000,000 books. Other Government buildings in Washington are the Land Office Building; the Patent Office, with Doric portico; the Department of Agriculture, and the Bureau of Engraving and Printing.
The Pan-American Building, most of whose cost was donated by the late Andrew Carnegie, is the headquarters of the Pan-American Union (composed of 21 Republics of the Western Hemisphere).
Washington is the seat of several universities. The largest are George Washington (non-secta-

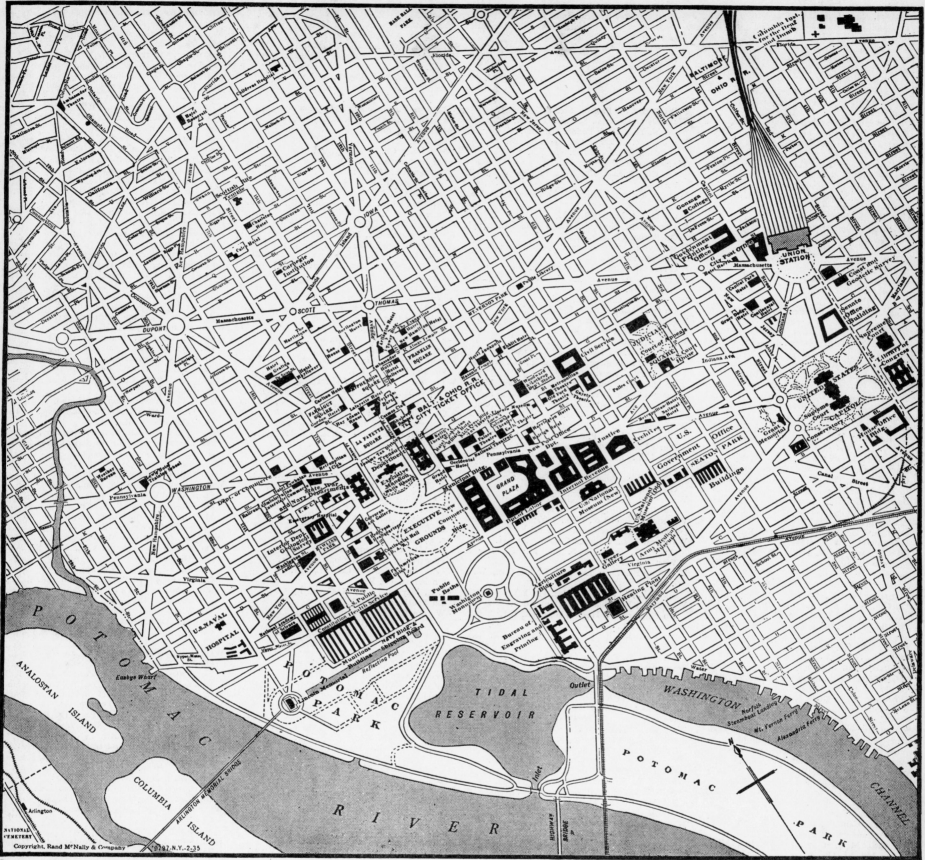

MAP OF WASHINGTON, D. C., CAPITAL OF THE UNITED STATES. THE CAPITOL LOOKS DOWN PENNSYLVANIA AVENUE TO THE WHITE HOUSE. BETWEEN THESE BUILD-INGS AN ENORMOUS CONSTRUCTION PROGRAM IS IN PROGRESS, THE NEW GOVERNMENT BUILDINGS COSTING OVER $200,000,000. THE MAJESTIC LINCOLN MEMORIAL STANDS ON THE BANK OF THE POTOMAC RIVER

rian), Georgetown (Roman Catholic), Howard (non-sectarian, co-educational, and without color distinction), National College, American University, Columbus University, and the Cath-olic University of America.

The Washington Monument is a marble obelisk 555 feet high. It was begun in 1848, finished in 1884. Mount Vernon, Washington's home, is about 15 miles below the city, and Arling-ton, General Lee's Home, now a national cemetery, is on the Virginia shore of the Potomac, overlooking the city.

The government of the city is under the control of three commissioners appointed, two by the President from citizens of the District of three years' residence, and one detailed by the President from the Corps of Engineers of the United States Army.

The District was formed March 30, 1791, by a cession of land (100 square miles) on both sides of the Potomac in two counties, Washing-ton and Alexandria; the latter receded to Vir-

ginia in 1846. In 1814 the British set fire to the Capitol, the White House, and other public buildings.
—Litchfield Co., Conn., 1,200.
—c. s., Wilkes Co., Ga., 3,158.
  On Georgia (R. R.).
—Tazewell Co., Ill., 1,741.
  On Alton; Atch., Top. & Santa Fe; Tol.; Peor. & West. (R. Rs.).
—c. s., Daviess Co., Ind., 9,070.
  On Balt. & Ohio; Cle., Cin., Chi. & St. Lou. (R. Rs.).
—c. s., Washington Co., Iowa, 4,814.
  On Chi., Burl. & Quincy; Chi., Mil., St. P. & Pac.; Chi., Rk. Isl. & Pac. (R. Rs.).
—c. s., Washington Co., Kans., 1,533.
  On Chi., Burl. & Quincy; Mo. Pac. (R. Rs.).
—Mason Co., Ky., 500.
—St. Landry Parish, La., 1,004.
  On Tex. & N. Orl. (Sou. Pac.) (R. R.).
—Knox Co., Me., 100.
—Franklin Co., Mo., 5,918.

On Mo. Pac. (R. R.).
—Warren Co., N. J., 4,410.
  On Del., Lack. & West. (R. R.).
—c. s., Beaufort Co., N. C., 7,035.
  On Atl. Coast Line; Norf. Sou. (R. Rs.).
—c. s., Washington Co., Pa., 24,545.
  On Balt. & Ohio; Penna. (R. Rs.).
  Situated in a coal, oil, and gas region. Manu-factures include annealing boxes, baby car-riages, glass products, tin plate, steel plate and tungsten.
—Kent Co., R. I., 1,000.
  On N. York, N. Hav. & Hart. (R. R.).
—Orange Co., Vt., 200.
WASHINGTON COURT HOUSE, c. s., Fayette Co., Ohio, 8,426.
  On Balt. & Ohio; Penna.; Det., Tol. & Iron. (R. Rs.).
WASHINGTON HEIGHTS, Calhoun Co., Mich. (An-nexed to Battle Creek in 1927).
WASHINGTON LANE, Philadelphia Co., Pa., 1,000.
  On Reading (R. R.).

WASHINGTON MINES, Fayette Co., Pa., 1,300.
  On Pitts. & L. Erie (R. R.).
WASHINGTON PARK, St. Clair Co., Ill., 3,837.
  On Balt. & Ohio (R. R.).
WASHINGTONVILLE, Orange Co., N. Y., 663.
  On Erie (R. R.).
—Columbiana and Mahoning Cos., Ohio, 816.
  On Erie (R. R.).
WASHOUGAL, Clarke Co., Wash., 1,206.
  On Spok., Port. & Seattle (R. R.).
WASHTA, Cherokee Co., Iowa, 448.
  On Ill. Cen. (R. R.).
WASKOM, Harrison Co., Tex., 600.
  On La., Ark. & Tex.; Tex. & Pac. (R. Rs.).
WASSAW, Chatham Co., Ga. See THUNDERBOLT.
WATCHUNG, Somerset Co., N. J., 906.
WATERBORO, York Co., Me., 914.
  On Bost. & Me. (R. R.).
WATERBURY, c. s., New Haven Co., Conn., 99,902.
  An industrial center in western Connecticut at the confluence of the Naugatuck, Great

Brook and Mad Rivers, and on the New York, New Haven & Hartford (R. R.).
Known as the "Brass City" supplying a large proportion of brass in the United States. Also a famous watch and clock center. Incorporated in 1686, received city charter in 1853.
–Washington Co., Vt., 1,776.
On Cen. Ver. (R. R.).
Waterbury Center, Washington Co., Vt., 510.
Waterford (Port Lairge), capital of County Waterford, Ireland (Eire), 26,647.
A port and commercial center on the Suir River. Manufactures beer, salt, flour, and castings. Has extensive fisheries.
–Norfolk Co., Ontario, Can., 1,213.
On Mich. Cen.; Tor., Ham. & Buf.; L. Erie & Nor. (El.) (R. Rs.).
–New London Co., Conn., 4,742.
On N. York, N. Hav. & Hart. (R. R.).
–Oxford Co., Me., 743.
–Camden Co., N. J., 1,500.
On Penna.-Read. Seash. (R. R.).
–Saratoga Co., N. Y., 2,921.
On Del. & Hud. (R. R.).
–Erie Co., Pa., 769.
On Penna. (R. R.).
–Caledonia Co., Vt., 712.
–Racine Co., Wis., 739.
On Mil. El. (R. R.).
Waterford Works (Waterford), Camden Co., N. J., 1,500.
Waterloo, Prov. of Brabant, Belgium, 5,669.
Scene of Napoleon's defeat, June 18, 1815.
–Nevada Co., Ark., 500.
On Reader (R. R.).
–Shefford Co., Quebec, Canada, 2,192.
On Can. Pac.; Can. Nat. (R. Rs.).
–Waterloo Co., N., Ontario, Can., 8,110.
On Can. Nat.; Grand River (El.) (R. Rs.).
–c. s., Monroe Co., Ill., 2,239.
On Mob. & Ohio (R. R.).
–De Kalb Co., Ind., 1,244.
On N. York Cen. (R. R.).
–c. s., Black Hawk Co., Iowa, 46,191.
On Chi. Gt. West.; Chi., Rk. Isl. & Pac.; Ill. Cen.; Waterl., Ced. Fs. & Nor. (El.) (R. Rs.).
In a rich farming region. Has diversified industries, including manufactures of tractors, cream separators and packing plant products.
–c. s., Seneca Co., N. Y., 4,047.
On Leh. Val.; N. York Cen. (R. Rs.).
–Jefferson Co., Wis., 1,272.
On Chi., Mil., St. P. & Pac. (R. R.).
Waterloo-with-Seaforth, Lancashire, England, 31,180.
A resort and suburb of Liverpool.
Waterman, De Kalb Co., Ill., 520.
On Chi., Burl. & Quincy (R. R.).
Watersmeet, Gogebic Co., Mich., 500.
On Chi. & Nor. West. (R. R.).
Watertown, Litchfield Co., Conn., 3,000.
On N. York, N. Hav. & Hart. (R. R.).
–Middlesex Co., Mass., 35,827.
On Bost. & Me. (R. R.).
A residential and industrial suburb of Boston.
–Carver Co., Minn., 594.
On Minn. West. (R. R.).
–c. s., Jefferson Co., N. Y., 32,205.
On N. York Cen. (R. R.).
Manufactures paper mill machinery, air brakes, fancy flowers, paper, textiles, plumbing supplies, clothing, electrical goods, and thermometers. Near the Thousand Islands.
–c. s., Codington Co., S. Dak., 10,246.
On Chi., Rk. Isl. & Pac.; Chi. & Nor. West; Gt. Nor.; Mpls. & St. Lou. (R. Rs.).
Packed meat, flour, and machinery.
–Wilson Co., Tenn., 928.
On Tenn. Cen. (R. R.).
–Jefferson and Dodge Cos., Wis., 10,613.
On Chi., Mil., St. P. & Pac.; Chi. & Nor. West.; Mil. El. (R. Rs.).
A trading and shipping center for a dairying region.
Water Valley, c. s., Yalobusha Co., Miss., 3,738.
On Ill. Cen. (R. R.).
Waterville, Marshall Co., Kans., 733.
On Mo. Pac. (R. R.).
–Kennebec Co., Me., 15,454.
On Me. Cen. (R. R.).
Leading manufactures are pulp, paper, and textiles. Seat of Colby College.
–Le Sueur Co., Minn., 1,419.
On Chi. Gt. West.; Mpls. & St. Lou. (R. Rs.).
–Oneida Co., N. Y., 1,298.
On Del., Lack. & West. (R. R.).
–Lucas Co., Ohio, 973.
On Cin. & L. Erie; N. York, Chi. & St. Lou. (R. Rs.).
–c. s., Douglas Co., Wash., 856.
On Waterville (R. R.).
Watervliet, Berrien Co., Mich., 1,207.
On Pere Marq. (R. R.).
–Albany Co., N. Y., 16,083.
On Del. & Hud. (R. R.).
A suburb of Troy. Manufactures textiles, paper, castings, bells, asbestos products, stoves, ladders, and clothing.
Watford, Lambton Co., Ont., 979.
On Can. Nat. (R. R.).
–Hertfordshire, England, 56,799.
A commercial town with flour mills, breweries and iron foundry.
Watford City, McKenzie Co., N. Dak., 769.
On Gt. Nor. (R. R.).
Wathena, Doniphan Co., Kans., 957.
On Chi., Rk. Isl. & Pac.; St. Jos. & Gd. Isl. (Un. Pac.) (R. Rs.).
Watkins, Meeker Co., Minn., 518.
On Mpls., St. P. & S. Ste. M. (R. R.).
Watkins Glen, c. s., Schuyler Co., N. Y., 2,956.
On N. York Cen.; Penna. (R. Rs.).
Watonga, c. s., Blaine Co., Okla., 2,228.
On Chi., Rk. Isl. & Pac. (R. R.).
Watseka, c. s., Iroquois Co., Ill., 3,144.
On Chi. & East. Ill.; Tol., Peor. & West. (R. Rs.).
Watson (Mineral Sprgs.), Jefferson Co., Ala., 1,013.
On Lou. & Nash. (R. R.).
Watsontown, Northumberland Co., Pa., 2,248.
On Penna. (R. R.).
Watsonville, Santa Cruz Co., Cal., 8,344.
On Sou. Pac. (R. R.).
Wattrelos, Nord, France, 31,084.
Watts, Los Angeles Co., Cal. (In Los Angeles.)
On Pac. El. (R. R.).
Waubay, Day Co., S. D., 926.
On Chi., Mil., St. P. & Pac. (R. R.).
Wauchula, c. s., Hardee Co., Fla., 2,705.
On Atl. Coast Line (R. R.).
Wauconda, Lake Co., Ill., 554.
Waukegan, c. s., Lake Co., Ill., 33,499.
On Chi. No. Shore & Mil.; Elg., Jol. & East.; Chi. & Nor. West. (R. Rs.).
An industrial town north of Chicago. Manufactures pharmaceuticals, wire fence, radios, printing, engines, asbestos products, and clothing. Has a good harbor.
Waukesha, c. s., Waukesha Co., Wis., 17,176.
On Chi., Mil., St. P. & Pac.; Chi. & Nor. West.; Mil. El.; Mpls., St. P. & S. Ste. M. (R. Rs.).
Noted for its medicinal springs and mineral waters.
Waukon, c. s., Allamakee Co., Iowa, 2,526.
On Chi., Mil., St. P. & Pac. (R. R.).
Waunakee, Dane Co., Wis., 640.
On Chi. & Nor. West. (R. R.).
Wauneta, Chase Co., Neb., 793.
On Chi., Burl. & Quincy (R. R.).
Waupaca, c. s., Waupaca Co., Wis., 3,131.
On Mpls., St. P. & S. Ste. M.; Gr. Bay & West. (R. Rs.).
Waupun, Fond du Lac and Dodge Cos., Wis., 5,768.
On Chi., Mil., St. P. & Pac. (R. R.).
Wauregan, Windham Co., Conn., 606.
On N. York, N. Hav. & Hart. (R. R.).
Waurika, c. s., Jefferson Co., Okla., 2,368.
On Chi., Rk. Isl. & Pac.; Wich. Val. (R. Rs)
Wausa, Knox Co., Neb., 754.
On Chi., St. P., Minn. & Oma. (R. R.).
Wausau, c. s., Marathon Co., Wis., 23,758.
On Chi. & Nor. West.; Chi., Mil., St. P. & Pac. (R. Rs.).
The center of a dairying region.
Wausaukee, Marinette Co., Wis., 663.
On Chi., Mil., St. P. & Pac. (R. R.).
Wauseon, c. s., Fulton Co., Ohio, 2,889.
On Det., Tol. & Iron.; N. York Cen.; Wab.; Tol. & Ind. (El.) (R. Rs.).
Wautoma, c. s., Waushara Co., Wis., 1,044.
On Chi. & Nor. West. (R. R.).
Wauwatosa, Milwaukee Co., Wis., 21,194.
On Chi., Mil., St. P. & Pac.; Mpls., St. P. & S. Ste. M.; Mil. El. (R. Rs.).
A suburb of Milwaukee.
Wauzeka, Crawford Co., Wis., 519.
On Chi., Mil., St. P. & Pac. (R. R.).
Waveland, Montgomery Co., Ind., 542.
On Penna. (R. R.).
–Hancock Co., Miss., 663.
On Lou. & Nash. (R. R.).
Waverley, Middlesex Co., Mass., 6,000.
On Bost. & Me. (R. R.).
Waverly, Morgan Co., Ill., 1,390.
On Chi., Burl. & Quincy; Chi., Springf. & St. Lou. (R. Rs.).
–c. s., Bremer Co., Iowa, 3,652.
On Chi. Gt. West.; Chi., Rk. Isl. & Pac.; Ill. Cen.; Waterloo, Ced. Fs. & Nor. (El.) (R. Rs.).
–Coffey Co., Kans., 618.
On Atch., Top. & Santa Fe (R. R.).
–Lafayette Co., Mo., 941.
On Mo. Pac. (R. R.).
–Tioga Co., N. Y., 5,662.
On Del., Lack. & W.; Erie; Leh. Val. (R. Rs.).
–Pike Co., Ohio, 1,603.
On Det., Tol. & Iron.; Norf. & West. (R. Rs.).
–Lackawanna Co., Pa., 520.
–c. s., Humphreys Co., Tenn., 1,152.
On Nash., Chatt. & St. Lou. (R. R.).
–Sussex Co., Va., 1,355.
On Norf. & West. (R. R.).
Waverly Hall, Harris Co., Ga., 515.
On Southern (R. R.).
Waxahachie, c. s., Ellis Co., Texas, 8,042.
On Chi., Rk. Isl. & Gulf; Ft. Worth & Denv. Cy.; Mo.-Kan.-Tex. of Tex.; Tex. & N. Orl. (Sou. Pac.) (R. Rs.).
Waxhaw, Union Co., N. C., 840.
On Seab. Air Line (R. R.).
Waycross, c. s., Ware Co., Ga., 15,510.
On Atla., Birm. & Coast; Atl. Coast Line (R. Rs.).
Center of an agricultural and lumbering region. Ships fruit, corn, sugar, tobacco, lumber, and naval stores.
Wayland, Floyd Co., Ky., 2,436.
On Chesa. & Ohio (R. R.).
–Henry Co., Iowa, 625.
On Mpls. & St. Lou. (R. R.).
–Middlesex Co., Mass., 3,346.
On Bost. & Me. (R. R.).
–Allegan Co., Mich., 1,013.
On Penna. (R. R.).
–Steuben Co., N. Y., 1,814.
On Del., Lack. & W.; Erie; Pitts., Shawn. & Nor. (R. Rs.).
Waymart, Wayne Co., Pa., 902.
Wayne, Wayne Co., Mich., 3,423.
On Mich. Cen.; Pere Marq. (R. Rs.).
–c. s., Wayne Co., Neb., 2,381.
On Chi., St. P., Minn. & Oma. (R. R.).
–Passaic Co., N. J., 500.
On Erie (R. R.).
–Wood Co., Ohio, 600.
On N. York Cen. (R. R.).
–Delaware Co., Pa., 3,000.
On Penna. (R. R.).
–c. s., Wayne Co., W. Va., 675.
On Norf. & West. (R. R.).
Wayne City, Wayne Co., Ill., 577.
On Southern (R. R.).
Waynedale, Allen Co., Ind., 1,210.
On N. York, Chi. & St. Lou.; Ind. (R. Rs.).
Wayne Junction, Philadelphia Co., Pa., 1,200.
On Balt. & Ohio; Reading (R. Rs.).
Waynesboro, c. s., Burke Co., Ga., 3,922.
On Cen. of Ga.; Savann. & Atl. (R. Rs.).
–Franklin Co., Pa., 10,167.
On Penna.; West. Md. (R. Rs.).
–Augusta Co., Va., 6,226.
On Chesa. & Ohio; Norf. & West. (R. Rs.).
–c. s., Wayne Co., Miss., 1,120.
On Mob. & Ohio (R. R.).
–c. s., Wayne Co., Tenn., 908.
Waynesburg, Stark Co., Ohio, 1,186.
On Penna. (R. R.).
–c. s., Greene Co., Pa., 4,915.
On Monong.; Penna. (R. Rs.).
Waynesfield, Auglaize Co., Ohio, 561.
Waynesville, DeWitt Co., Ill., 511.
On Penna. (R. R.).
–c. s., Haywood Co., N. C., 2,414.
On Southern (R. R.).
–Warren Co., Ohio, 697.
On Penna. (R. R.).
Waynetown, Montgomery Co., Ind., 664.
On Cle., Cin., Chi. & St. Lou. (R. R.).
Waynoka, Woods Co., Okla,, 1,840.
On Atch., Top. & Santa Fe (R. R.).
Wayside, Monmouth Co., N. J., 500.
Wayville, Saratoga Co., N. Y., 500.
On Bost. & Me. (R. R.).
Wayzata, Hennepin Co., Minn., 1,100.
On Gt. Nor.; Minn. West. (R. Rs.).
Weatherford, Custer Co., Okla., 2,417.
On Chi., Rk. Isl. & Pac. (R. R.).
–c. s., Parker Co., Texas, 4,912.
On Gulf, Colc. & Santa Fe; St. Lou., San Fran. & Tex.; Tex. & Pac.; Weatherf., Min. Ws. & Northw. (R. Rs.).
Weatherly, Carbon Co., Pa., 2,531.
On Leh. Val. (R. R.).
Weathersfield, Windsor Co., Vt., 1,156.
Weaverville, Buncombe Co., N. C., 848.
–c. s., Trinity Co., Cal., 650.
Webb, Tallahatchie Co., Miss., 531.
On Yazoo & Miss. Val. (Ill. Cen.) (R. R.).
Webb City, Jasper Co., Mo., 6,876.
On Mo. Pac.; St. Lou.-San Fran. (R. Rs.).
Webster, Sumter Co., Fla., 339.
On Atl. Coast Line (R. R.).
–Worcester Co., Mass., 13,837.
On Bost. & Alb.; N. York, N. Hav. & Hart. (R. Rs.).
Cotton textiles and shoes.
–Monroe Co., N. Y., 1,552.
On N. York Cen. (R. R.).
–Westmoreland Co., Pa., 1,800.
On Pitts. & L. Erie (R. R.).
–c. s., Day Co., S. Dak., 2,033.
On Chi., Mil., St. P. & Pac. (R. R.).
–Burnett Co., Wis., 501.
On Minn., St. P. & S. Ste. M. (R. R.).
Webster City, c. s., Hamilton Co., Iowa, 7,024.
On Ft. Dodge, Des Moines & Sou.; Ill. Cen.; Chi. & Nor. West. (R. Rs.).
Webster Groves, St. Louis Co., Mo., 16,487.
On Mo. Pac.; St. Lou.-San Fran. (R. Rs.).
A residential suburb of St. Louis.
Webster Springs (Addison), c. s., Webster Co., W. Va., 976.
On West. Md. (R. R.).
Websterville, Washington Co., Vt., 1,000.
On Barre & Chelsea (R. R.).
Wedgefield, Sumter Co., S. C., 500.
On Atl. Coast Line (R. R.).
Wednesbury, Staffordshire, England, 31,534.
Has large iron and steel works.
Weed, Siskiyou Co., Cal., 4,000.
On Sou. Pac. (R. R.).
Weedsport, Cayuga Co., N. Y., 1,325.
On Leh. Val.; West Shore (R. Rs.).
Weedville, Elk Co., Pa., 600.
On Balt. & Ohio; Penna.; Pitts., Shawmut & Nor. (R. Rs.).
Weehawken, Hudson Co., N. J., 14,807.
On Erie; Hob. Mfrs.; N. York, Ont. & West.; West Shore (R. Rs.).
A suburb of New York.
Weeks (Weeks Island), Iberia Par., La., 500.
On Tex. & N. Orl. (Sou. Pac.) (R. R.).
Weeksbury, Floyd Co., Ky., 1,509.
On Chesa. & Ohio (R. R.).
Weeping Water, Cass Co., Neb., 1,029.
On Mo. Pac. (R. R.).
Wehrun, Indiana Co., Pa., 619.
On Balt. & Ohio; Penna. (R. Rs.).
Weimar, Thüringen, Germany, 49,000.
A famous university town. Noted for its association with the lives of Goethe and Schiller.
–Colorado Co., Texas, 1,256.
On Tex. & N. Orl. (Sou. Pac.) (R. R.).
Weiner, Poinsett Co., Ark., 537.
On St. Lou. Southw. (R. R.).
Weinheim, Baden, Germany, 16,000.
A favorite resort and tourist center.
Weir, Cherokee Co., Kans., 1,158.
On St. Lou.-San. Fran.; North. Okla. (El.) (R. Rs.).
–Choctaw Co., Miss., 570.
On Ill. Cen. (R. R.).
Weirton, Hancock Co., W. Va., 9,658.
On Penna. (R. R.).
Weiser, c. s., Washington Co., Idaho, 2,724.
On Ore. Short Line (Un. Pac.); Pac. & Ida. Nor. (Un. Pac.) (R. Rs.).
Weissenfels, Prussian Saxony, Germany, 40,000.
Has manufactures of cardboard, machinery, shoes, rubber goods, and paper.
Weissport, Carbon Co., Pa., 661.
On Cen. of N. Jer. (R. R.).
Welborn, Wyandotte Co., Kan., 1,000.
Welch, Craig Co., Okla., 448.
On Mo.-Kan.-Tex. (R. R.).
–McDowell Co., W. Va., 5,376.
On Norf. & West. (R. R.).
Welcome, Martin Co., Minn., 519.
On Chi. & Nor. West.; Chi., Mil., St. P. & Pac. (R. Rs.).
Weldon, Halifax Co., N. C., 2,323.
On Atl. Coast Line; Seab. Air Line (R. Rs.).
–Montgomery Co., Pa., 644.
–Houston Co., Tex., 500.
On Waco, Beau., Trin. & Sab. (R. R.).
Weleetka, Okfuskee Co., Okla., 2,042.
On Ft. Smith & West.; St. Lou.-San Fran. (R. Rs.).
Welland, Welland Co., Ont., Can., 10,709.
On Can. Nat.; Mich. Cen.; Niag., St. Cath. & Tor. (El.); Tor., Ham. & Buf.; Wab. (R. Rs.).
Situated on the south end of the Welland Canal. Textile industries and machine shops.
Wellborn, Brazos Co., Tex., 500.
On Tex. & N. Orl. (Sou. Pac.) (R. R.).
Wellesley, Norfolk Co., Mass., 13,376.
On Bost. & Alb. (R. R.).
A residential town and seat of Wellesley College.
Wellesley Hills, Norfolk Co., Mass., 6,000.
On Bost. & Alb. (R. R.).
Wellfleet, Barnstable Co., Mass., 948.
On N. York, N. Hav. & Hart. (R. R.).
Wellingborough, Northampton, England, 21,221.
A center of agricultural trade.
Wellington, Dist. of Wellington, capital of New Zealand, 116,700.
A busy commercial seaport and industrial town with diversified small manufactures, beautiful suburbs and various educational institutions.
–Larimer Co., Colo., 533.
On Colo. & Sou. (R. R.).
–c. s., Sumner Co., Kans., 7,309.
On Atch., Top. & Santa Fe; Chi., Rk. Isl. & Pac. (R. Rs.).
–Middlesex Co., Mass., 800.
On Bost. & Me. (R. R.).
–Lafayette Co., Mo., 756.
On Mo. Pac. (R. R.).
–Lorain Co., Ohio, 2,235.
On Cle., Cin., Chi. & St. Lou.; Lorain & West Va.; Wheel. & L. Erie (R. Rs.).
–Collingsworth Co., Tex., 3,570.
On Ft. Worth & Denv. Cy.; Mo.-Kan.-Tex. of Tex. (R. Rs.).
Wellman, Washington Co., Iowa, 853.
On Chi., Rk. Isl. & Pac. (R. R.).
Wells, York Co., Me., 600.
–Delta Co., Mich., 550.
On Chi., Mil., St. P. & Pac.; Escan. & L. Sup. (R. Rs.).
–Faribault Co., Minn., 1,795.
On Chi., Mil., St. P. & Pac. (R. R.).
–Elko Co., Nev., 655.
On Sou. Pac.; Un. Pac.; West. Pac. (R. Rs.).

–Hamilton Co., N. Y., 400.
–Rutland Co., Vt., 250.
Wellsboro, c. s., Tioga Co., Pa., 3,643.
On N. York Cen. (R. R.).
Wellsburg, c. s., Brooke Co., W. Va., 6,398.
On Penna.; Pitts. & W. Va. (R. Rs.).
–Grundy Co., Iowa, 508.
On Chi., Rk. Isl. & Pac. (R. R.).
–Chemung Co., N. Y., 581.
On Erie (R. R.).
Wells River, Orange Co., Vt., 553.
On Bost. & Me.; Can. Pac.; Mont. & Wells Riv. (R. Rs.).
Wellston, St. Louis Co., Mo., 7,400.
–Jackson Co., Ohio, 5,319.
On Balt. & Ohio; Chesa. & Ohio (R. Rs.).
–Lincoln Co., Okla., 632.
Wellsville, Franklin Co., Kans., 711.
On Atch., Top. & Santa Fe (R. R.).
–Montgomery Co., Mo., 1,525.
On Chi., Burl. & Quincy; Wab. (R. Rs.).
–Allegany Co., N. Y., 5,674.
On Balt. & Ohio; Erie (R. Rs.).
–Columbiana Co., Ohio, 7,956.
On Penna.; Steub., E. Liv. & Beav. Val. Trac. (El.) (R. Rs.).
–Cache Co., Utah, 1,270.
On Ore. Short Line (Un. Pac.); Utah-Ida. Cen. (El.) (R. Rs.).
Wellton, Yuma Co., Ariz., 500.
On Sou. Pac. (R. R.).
Welsh, Jefferson Davis Parish, La., 1,514.
On Tex. & N. Orl. (R. R.).
Wenatchee, c. s., Chelan Co., Wash., 11,627.
On Gt. Nor. (R. R.).
Wenchow, Prov. of Chekiang, China, 631,300.
An important seaport and commercial town situated on the Gow River. A distributing point for agricultural products and raw materials from the interior.
Wendel, Westmoreland Co., Pa., 700.
On Balt. & Ohio (R. R.).
Wendell, Gooding Co., Idaho, 725.
On Ore. Short Line (Un. Pac.) (R. R.).
–Wake Co., N. C., 980.
On Norf. Sou. (R. R.).
Wendling, Lane Co., Ore., 500.
On Sou. Pac. (R. R.).
Wenham, Essex Co., Mass., 1,196.
Wenlock, Shropshire, England, 14,152.
Situated in a district having coal mines and limestone quarries. Has iron works.
Wenona, Marshall Co., Ill.
On Ill. Cen. (R. R.).
–Somerset Co., Md., 650.
Wenonah, Gloucester Co., N. J., 1,245.
On Penna.-Read.-Seash. (R. R.).
Wensuh (Aksu), Sinkiang, 80,000.
A great caravan trading center. Has manufactures of textiles, leather, metal goods, and jasper.
Wentworth, Grafton Co., N. H., 100.
On Bost. & Me. (R. R.).
Wentzville, St. Charles Co., Mo., 596.
On Wab. (R. R.).
Wernersville, Berks Co., Pa., 1,096.
On Reading (R. R.).
Wernigerode, Prussia, Germany, 23,300.
A marketing center in the Harz Mountains.
Wesel, Rhenish Prussia, Germany, 25,000.
A railroad and river traffic center. Has a number of quaint old houses.
Weslaco, Hidalgo Co., Tex., 4,879.
On St. Lou., Browns. & Mex. (Mo. Pac.) (R. R.).
Wesleyville, Erie Co., Pa., 2,854.
On N. York, Chi. & St. L.; N. York Cen. (R. Rs.).
Wessington, Beadle and Hand Cos., S. Dak., 564.
On Chi. & Nor. West. (R. R.).
Wessington Springs, c. s., Jerauld Co., S. Dak., 1,408.
On Chi., Mil., St. P. & Pac. (R. R.).
Wesson, Copiah Co., Miss., 799.
On Ill. Cen. (R. R.).
West, McLennan Co., Tex., 1,801.
On Mo.-Kan.-Tex. of Tex.; Tex. El. (R. Rs.).
West Acton, Middlesex Co., Mass., 731.
On Bost. & Me. (R. R.).
West Albany, Albany Co., N. Y., 1,169.
On N. York Cen. (R. R.).
West Alburgh, Grand Isle Co., Vt., 515.
On Cen. Ver. (R. R.).
West Alexandria, Preble Co., Ohio, 924.
On Cin. Nor. (R. R.).
West Alliance, Pamlico Co., N. C., 500.
On Norf. Sou. (R. R.).
West Alliquippa, Beaver Co., Pa., 2,931.
On Aliquippa & Sou.; Pitts. & L. E. (R. Rs.).
West Allis, Milwaukee Co., Wis., 34,671.
On Chi., Mil., St. P. & Pac.; Chi. & Nor. West.; Mil. El. (R. Rs.).
West Auburn, Worcester Co., Mass., 1,200.
On Bost. & Alb. (N. York Cen.) (R. R.).
West Babylon, Suffolk Co., N. Y., 1,196.
West Baden, Orange Co., Ind., 1,174.
On Chi., Ind. & Lou.; Sou. (R. Rs.).
West Baldwin, Cumberland Co., Me., 500.
On Me. Cen. (R. R.).

West Barrington, Bristol Co., R. I., 2,000.
On N. York, N. Hav. & Hart. (R. R.).
West Bay City, Bay Co., Mich. (Sta. Bay City P. O.).
On Gd. Tr.; Mich. Cen. (R. Rs.).
West Belmar, Monmouth Co., N. J., 2,000.
West Bend, Palo Alto Co., Iowa, 634.
On Chi., Rk. Isl. & Pac. (R. R.).
–c. s., Washington Co., Wis., 4,760.
On Chi. & Nor. West. (R. R.).
West Berlin, Camden Co., N. J., 820.
On Penna.-Read.-Seash. (R. R.).
West Berwick, Columbia Co., Pa. (annexed to Berwick).
On Del., Lack. & West. (R. R.).
West Blocton, Bibb Co., Ala., 1,070.
Westboro, Worcester Co., Mass., 6,073.
On Bost. & Alb. (N. York Cen.) (R. R.).
West Boylston, Worcester Co., Mass., 2,158.
On Bost. & Me. (R. R.).
West Branch, Cedar Co., Ia., 652.
On Chi., Rk. Isl. & Pac. (R. R.).
–c. s., Ogemaw Co., Mich., 1,164.
On Mich. Cen. (R. R.).
West Brattleboro, Windham Co., Vt., 560.
West Bridgewater, Plymouth Co., Mass., 3,356.
On N. York, N. Hav. & Hart. (R. R.).
–(Bridgewater), Beaver Co., Pa., 1,892.
On Beav. Val.; Pitts. & L. Erie; Penna. (R. Rs.).
West Bromwich, Staffordshire, England, 81,281.
A suburb of Birmingham.
Westbrook, Middlesex Co., Conn., 790.
On N. York, N. Hav. & Hart. (R. R.).
–Cumberland Co., Me., 10,807.
On Bost. & Me.; Me. Cen. (R. Rs.).
Has textile and paper mills.
–Cottonwood Co., Minn., 610.
On Chi., St. P., Minn. & Oma. (R. R.).
–Mitchell Co., Tex., 512.
On Tex. & Pac. (R. R.).
West Brookfield, Worcester Co., Mass., 1,258.
On Bost. & Alb. (R. R.).
West Brownsville, Washington Co., Pa., 1,717.
On Penna.; Pitts. & L. Erie (R. Rs.).
West Brownsville Junction, Washington Co., Pa., 500.
On Penna. (R. R.).
West Burlington, Des Moines Co., Iowa, 1,333.
On Chi., Burl. & Quincy (R. R.).
Westby, Vernon Co., Wis., 1,366.
On Chi., Mil., St. P. & Pac. (R. R.).
West Caldwell, Essex Co., N. J., 2,911.
West Cape May, Cape May Co., N. J., 1,048.
West Carrollton, Montgomery Co., Ohio, 2,101.
On Cin. & L. Erie (El.) (R. R.).
West Carthage, Jefferson Co., N. Y., 1,722.
West Catasauqua, Lehigh Co., Pa., 500.
West Chester, c. s., Chester Co., Pa., 12,325.
On Penna. (R. R.).
The center of a well-known horse- and cattle-raising region.
West Chicago, Du Page Co., Ill., 3,477.
On Chi., Burl. & Quincy; Chi. & Nor. West.; Chi., Aur. & Elg. (El.); Elg., Jol. & East. (R. Rs.).
West City, Franklin Co., Ill., 1,091.
West Claremont, Sullivan Co., N. H., 600.
West Clinton, Vermillion Co., Ind., 700.
On Chi., Mil., St. P. & Pac. (R. R.).
West Columbia, Brazoria Co., Tex., 3,525.
West Concord, Dodge Co., Minn., 613.
On Chi. Gt. West. (R. R.).
–Middlesex Co., Mass., 3,500.
On Bost. & Me.; N. York, N. Hav. & Hart. (R. Rs.).
West Conshohocken, Montgomery Co., Pa., 2,579.
On Reading; Upper Merion & Plym. (R. Rs.).
West Covina, Los Angeles Co., Cal., 769.
West Covington, Kent Co., Ky. (annexed to Covington).
West Creek, Ocean Co., N. J., 500.
West Decatur (Blue Ball), Clearfield Co., Pa., 900.
West Dundee, Kane Co., Ill. (Pop. incl. in Dundee).
West Easton, Northampton Co., Pa., 1,564.
West Elizabeth, Allegheny Co., Pa., 1,074.
West Elmhurst, Du Page Co., Ill., 1,000.
On Chi., Aur. & Elg. (R. R.).
West End, Moore Co., N. C., 600.
On Norf. Sou. (R. R.).
–Galveston Co., Tex., 1,000.
On Tex. Cy. Term. (R. R.).
West Enfield, Penobscot Co., Me., 686.
On Me. Cen. (R. R.).
West Englewood, Bergen Co., N. J., 2,700.
On West Shore (R. R.).
Westerly, Washington Co., R. I., 10,999.
On N. York, N. Hav. & Hart. (R. R.).
The center of a resort area.
Western, Saline Co., Neb., 511.
On Chi., Burl. & Quincy (R. R.).
Western Port, Allegany Co., Md., 3,440.
On West. Md.; Cumb. & Penna. (R. Rs.).
Western Springs, Cook Co., Ill., 3,894.
On Chi., Burl. & Quincy (R. R.).
Westerville, Franklin Co., Ohio, 2,879.
On Penna. (R. R.).

West Fairview, Cumberland Co., Pa., 1,794.
On Penna. (R. R.).
West Falmouth, Cumberland Co., Me., 786.
On Me. Cen. (R. R.).
West Fayetteville, Franklin Co., Pa., 800.
Westfield, Clark Co., Ill., 646.
On Westfield (R. R.).
–Hamilton Co., Ind., 688.
On Cen. Ind.; Chi., Ind. & Lou. (R. Rs.).
–Aroostook Co., Me., 312.
On Bangor & Aroostook (R. R.).
–Hampden Co., Mass., 18,788.
On Bost. & Alb.; N. York, N. Hav. & Hart. (R. Rs.).
An industrial town near Springfield. Manufactures paper, boilers, radiators, bicycles, etc.
–Union Co., N. J., 15,801.
On Cen. of N. Jer. (R. R.).
–Chautauqua Co., N. Y., 3,466.
On N. York Cen.; Jamest., Westf. & Northw. (El.) N. York, Chi. & St. Lou. (R. Rs.).
–Tioga Co., Pa., 1,193.
On Balt. & Ohio; N. York Cen. (R. Rs.).
–Marquette Co., Wis., 769.
On Minn., St. P. & S. Ste. M. (R. R.).
Westfir, Lane Co., Ore., 500.
On Sou. Pac. (R. R.).
Westford, Windham Co., Conn., 700.
–Middlesex Co., Mass., 3,789.
On Boston & Maine (R. R.).
West Fort Dodge, Webster Co., Ia., 1,200.
On Chi. Gt. West. (R. R.).
West Frankfort, Franklin Co., Ill., 14,683.
On Chi. & East. Ill.; Chi., Burl. & Quincy; Ill. Cen. (R. Rs.).
A busy coal-mining town.
West Gardiner, Kennebec Co., Me., 300.
West Gloucester, Essex Co., Mass., 2,500.
On Bost. & Me. (R. R.).
West Greenville, Greenville Co., S. C., 1,917.
West Groton, Middlesex Co., Mass., 600.
On Bost. & Me. (R. R.).
West Grove, Chester Co., Pa., 1,375.
On Penna. (R. R.).
West Ham, Essex, England, 276,150.
A residential and industrial suburb of London.
West Hammond, Cook Co., Ill. See Calumet City.
Westhampton Beach, Suffolk Co., N. Y., 994.
West Hanover, Plymouth Co., Mass., 700.
On N. York, N. Hav. & Hart. (R. R.).
West Hartford, Hartford Co., Conn., 24,941.
A residential and industrial suburb of Hartford.
West Hartlepool, Durham, England, 68,134.
An active seaport and commercial town which carries on trade with north European ports.
West Haven, New Haven Co., Conn., 25,808.
On N. York, N. Hav. & Hart. (R. R.).
A residential and industrial suburb of New Haven.
West Haverstraw, Rockland Co., N. Y., 2,834.
On N. Jer. & N. York; West Shore (R. Rs.).
West Hazleton, Luzerne Co., Pa., 7,310.
West Helena, Phillips Co., Ark., 4,489.
On Helena & Southw.; Mo. Pac.; Mo. & Ark. (R. Rs.).
West Hempstead, Nassau Co., N. Y., 1,776.
On Long Isl. (R. R.).
West Hickory, Catawba Co., N. C., 1,706.
West Homestead, Allegheny Co., Pa., 3,552.
On Balt. & Ohio; Pitts. & L. Erie; Union (R. Rs.).
Westhope, Bottineau Co., N. Dak., 521.
On Gt. Nor. (R. R.).
West Jefferson, Madison Co., Ohio, 1,376.
On Cin. & Lake Erie (El.); Penna. (R. Rs.).
–Ashe Co., N. C., 704.
On Norf. & West. (R. R.).
West Jonesport, Washington Co., Me., 1,000.
West Jordan, Salt Lake Co., Utah, 1,220.
On Den. & Rio Gde. West.; Salt Lake & Utah (El.) (R. Rs.).
West Kankakee, Kankakee Co., Ill., 800.
On N. York Cen. (R. R.).
West Kennebunk, York Co., Me., 719.
On Me. Cen. (R. R.).
West Kingston, c. s., Washington Co., R. I., 1,000.
On Narrag. Pier; N. York, N. Hav. & Hart. (R. Rs.).
West Kittanning, Armstrong Co., Pa., 1,005.
West Lafayette, Coshocton Co., Ohio, 1,106.
On Penna. (R. R.).
–Tippecanoe Co., Ind., 5,095.
Westland, Washington Co., Pa., 800.
West Lawn, Berks Co., Pa., 2,069.
West Lebanon, Warren Co., Ind., 595.
On Wab. (R. R.).
–Grafton Co., N. H., 1,725.
On Bost. & Me. (R. R.).
West Leechburg, Westmoreland Co., Pa., 1,044.
On Penna. (R. R.).
West Liberty, Muscatine Co., Iowa, 679.
On Chi., Rk. Isl. & Pac. (R. R.).
–c. s., Morgan Co., Ky., 569.
–Logan Co., Ohio, 1,248.
On Cle., Cin., Chi. & St. Lou. (R. R.).
West Linn, Clackamas Co., Ore., 1,956.
On Sou. Pac. (R. R.).

West Long Branch, Monmouth Co., N. J., 1,686.
West Los Angeles, Los Angeles Co., Cal. (Pop. incl. in Los Angeles).
On Pac. El.; Sou. Pac. (R. Rs.).
West Manayunk, Montgomery Co., Pa., 2,000.
On Penna.; Read. (R. Rs.).
West Mansfield, Logan Co., Ohio, 675.
On N. York Cen. (R. R.).
–Bristol Co., Mass., 565.
On N. York, N. Hav. & Hart. (R. R.).
West Marion, McDowell Co., N. C., 500.
West Mayfield, Beaver Co., Pa., 876.
West Medway (Woodside), Norfolk Co., Mass., 1,625.
West Memphis, Crittenden Co., Ark., 895.
On Chi., Rk. Isl. & Pac.; Mo. Pac.; St. Lou.-San Fran. (R. Rs.).
West Middlesex, Mercer Co., Pa., 1,181.
On Erie; N. York Cen.; Penna.; Pitts. & L. Erie (R. Rs.).
West Milton, Miami Co., Ohio, 1,388.
West Milwaukee, Milwaukee Co., Wis., 4,168.
West Mineral, Cherokee Co., Kans., 531.
On Mo.-Kan.-Tex. (R. R.).
West Minneapolis, Minn. See Hopkins.
Westminster, c. s., Carroll Co., Md., 4,463.
On West. Md. (R. R.).
–Orange Co., Cal., 1,500.
On Sou. Pac. (R. R.).
–Worcester Co., Mass., 1,600.
On Bost. & Me. (R. R.).
–Oconee Co., S. C., 1,774.
On Southern (R. R.).
West Monessen, Washington Co., Pa., 618.
On Penna. (R. R.).
West Monroe, Ouachita Parish, La., 6,566.
On Yazoo & Miss. Val. (Ill. Cen.) (R. R.).
Westmont, Cambria Co., Pa., 3,388.
–Du Page Co., Ill., 2,733.
On Chi., Burl. & Quincy (R. R.).
–Camden Co., N. J., 1,010.
On Penna.-Read. Seash. (R. R.).
West Monterey, Clarion Co., Pa., 610.
On Penna. (R. R.).
Westmoore, Luzerne Co., Pa., 2,000.
Westmoreland, Imperial Co., Cal., 1,300.
On Sou. Pac. (R. R.).
–Pottawatomie Co., Kan., 525.
–Cheshire Co., N. H., 730.
On Bost. & Me. (R. R.).
–Wayne Co., W. Va., 1,000.
On Chesa. & Ohio (R. R.).
Westmoreland City, Westmoreland Co., Pa., 1,200.
West Mystic, New London Co., Conn., 600.
On N. York, N. Hav. & Hart. (R. R.).
West Nanticoke, Luzerne Co., Pa., 1,811.
On Del., Lack. & West.; Penna. (R. Rs.).
West Newbury, Essex Co., Mass., 1,475.
West Newton, Westmoreland Co., Pa., 2,953.
On Balt. & Ohio; Pitts. & L. Erie (R. Rs.).
West New York, Hudson Co., N. J., 37,107.
Weston, Fairfield Co., Conn., 500.
–Middlesex Co., Mass., 3,848.
On Bost. & Me. (R. R.).
–Platte Co., Mo., 1,028.
On Chi., Burl. & Quincy (R. R.).
–Los Animas Co., Colo., 510.
On Colo. & Wyo. (R. R.).
–Wood Co., Ohio, 794.
On Balt. & Ohio; Cin. & L. Erie (El.) (R. Rs.).
–Umatilla Co., Ore., 384.
On Ore.-Wash. R. R. & Nav. Co. (Un. Pac.) (R. R.).
–c. s., Lewis Co., W. Va., 8,646.
On Balt. & Ohio (R. R.).
–York Co., West, Ontario, Can., 4,723.
On Can. Pac.; Can. Nat. (R. Rs.).
Weston-Super-Mare, Somerset, England, 28,-555.
A popular seaside resort.
West Orange, Essex Co., N. J., 24,327.
On Erie (R. R.).
A suburb of New York. In Llewellyn Park is the former home of Thomas A. Edison.
Westover, Clearfield Co., Pa., 520.
On N. York Cen.; Penna. (R. Rs.).
–Monongalia Co., West Va., 1,633.
West Palm Beach, c. s., Palm Beach Co., Fla., 27,248.
On Fla. East Coast; Seab. Air Line (R. Rs.).
A popular winter resort on the eastern coast of Florida. Year-round deep sea fishing.
West Paris (Bates), Oxford Co., Me., 513.
On Grand Trunk (Can. Nat.) (R. R.).
West Park, Cuyahoga Co., Ohio (Sta. Cleveland P. O.).
On N. York Cen. (R. R.).
–Ulster Co., N. Y., 500.
On West Shore (R. R.).
West Paterson, Passaic Co., N. J., 3,101.
On Del., Lack. & West. (R. R.).
West Pawlet, Rutland Co., Vt., 1,050.
On Del. & Hud. (R. R.).
West Peabody, Essex Co., Mass., 1,124.
On Bost. & Me. (R. R.).
West Pembroke, Washington Co., Me., 700.
West Peru, Oxford Co., Me., 600.
West Pittsburgh, Lawrence Co., Pa., 700.

COURTESY NEW YORK CENTRAL SYSTEM

AN IMPOSING VIEW OF THE BUILDINGS OF THE UNITED STATES MILITARY ACADEMY AT WEST POINT, NEW YORK, SHOWING ITS SUPERB SETTING AMONG THE HILLS ALONG THE HUDSON RIVER

On Balt. & Ohio; Pitts. & L. Erie; West. Allegh. (R. Rs.).

West Pittston, Luzerne Co., Pa., 2,940.
On Del., Lack. & West.; Leh. Val.; W. Pitts.-Exe. (R. Rs.).

West Plains, c. s., Howell Co., Mo., 3,335.
On St. Lou.-San Fran. (R. R.).
—Meade Co., Kans., 662.

West Point, Troup Co., Ga., 2,146.
On Atl. & West Pt.; Chattah. Val.; West. of Ala. (R. Rs.).
—Lee Co., Iowa, 536.
On Chi., Burl. & Quincy (R. R.).
—Hardin Co., Ky., 697.
On Ill. Cen.; Lou. & Nash. (R. Rs.).
—c. s., Clay Co., Miss., 4,677.
On Col. & Greenv.; Ill. Cen.; Mob. & Ohio (R. Rs.).
—c. s., Cuming Co., Neb., 2,225.
On Chi. & Nor. West. (R. R.).
—Orange Co., N. Y., 4,530.
On N. Y., Ont. & West.; West Shore (R. Rs.).
—Weber Co., Utah, 630.
—King William Co., Va., 1,844.
On Southern (R. R.).

Westport (Saugatuck), Fairfield Co., Conn., 6,073.
On N. York, N. Hav. & Hart. (R. R.).
—Decatur Co., Ind., 637.
On Cle., Cin., Chi. & St. L.; Chi., Mil., St. P. & Pac. (R. Rs.).
—Bristol Co., Mass., 4,355.
—Essex Co., N. Y., 790.
On Del. & Hudson (R. R.).

West Portsmouth, Scioto Co., Ohio, 2,500.
West Reading, Berks Co., Pa., 4,908.
West Richfield, Summit Co., Ohio, 500.
West Ridgeway, Elk Co., Pa., 1,000.
West Rutland, Rutland Co., Vt., 2,500.
On Clare. & Pitts.; Del. & Hud. (R. Rs.).
West St. Paul, Dakota Co., Minn., 4,463.
On Chi., Rk. Isl. & Pac. (R. R.).
West Salem, Edwards Co., Ill., 825.
On Illinois Central (R. R.).
—Wayne Co., Ohio, 645.
On Erie (R. R.).
—Polk Co., Ore., 974.
On Sou. Pac. (R. R.).
—La Crosse Co., Wis., 1,011.
On Chi., Mil., St. P. & Pac.; Chi. & Nor. West. (R. Rs.).

West Sand Lake, Rensselaer Co., N. Y., 700.
West Sanford, Seminole Co., Fla., 1,500.
West Santa Barbara, Santa Barbara Co., Cal., 1,000.

On Sou. Pac. (R. R.).
West Sayville, Suffolk Co., N. Y., 1,058.
West Seneca, Erie Co., N. Y., 2,000.
On Erie; Leh. Val.; N. York Cen.; N. York, Chi. & St. Lou. (R. Rs.).
West Southern Pines, Moore Co., N. C., 806.
West Spokane, Spokane Co., Wash., 500.
On Ore.-Wash. R. R. & Nav. Co. (Un. Pac.) (R. R.).
West Springfield, Hampden Co., Mass., 17,118.
On Bost. & Alb. (R. R.).
A suburb of Springfield.
West Stockbridge, Berkshire Co., Mass., 1,138.
On N. York, N. Hav. & Hart. (R. R.).
West Suffield, Hartford Co., Conn., 700.
On N. York, N. Hav. & Hart. (R. R.).
West Sullivan, Hancock Co., N. Y., 612.
West Swanzey, Cheshire Co., N. H., 525.
On Bost. & Me. (R. R.).
West Tampa, Hillsborough Co., Fla. (Sta. Tampa P. O.).
West Tatnuck, Worcester Co., Mass., 1,000.
West Telford, Montgomery Co., Pa., 1,252.
West Terre Haute, Vigo Co., Ind., 3,588.
On Penna. (R. R.).
West Townsend, Middlesex Co., Mass., 600.
On Bost. & Me. (R. R.).
West Union, c. s., Fayette Co., Iowa, 2,056.
On Chi., Mil., St. P. & Pac.; Chi., Rk. Isl. & Pac. (R. Rs.).
—c. s., Adams Co., Ohio, 1,094.
—Doddridge Co., West Va., 984.
On Balt. & Ohio (R. R.).
—Clark Co., Ill., 750.
On Cle., Cin., Chi. & St. Lou. (R. R.).
West Unity, Williams Co., Ohio, 825.
On Wab.; Cin. Nor. (R. Rs.).
West University Place, Harris Co., Tex., 1,322.
West Upton, Worcester Co., Mass., 1,190.
West Vernon, Wilbarger Co., Tex., 955.
West View, Allegheny Co., Pa., 6,028.
Westville, Holmes Co., Fla., 500.
On Lou. & Nash. (R. R.).
—Vermilion Co., Ill., 3,901.
On Chi. & East Ill.; Cle., Cin., Chi. & St. Lou.; Ill. Term. (El.) (R. Rs.).
—Gloucester Co., N. J., 3,462.
On Penna.-Read. Seash. (R. R.).
—Adair Co., Okla., 691.
On Kan. Cy. Sou.; St. Lou.-San Fran. (R. Rs.).
—Jefferson Co., Pa., 538.
On Balt. & Ohio (R. R.).
West Warren, Worcester Co., Mass., 1,736.
On Bost. & Alb. (R. R.).
West Warwick (Arctic), Kent Co., R. I., 17,696.

On N. York, N. Hav. & Hart. (R. R.).
—(Centerville), Kent Co., R. I., 1,114.
On N. York, N. Hav. & Hart. (R. R.).
Westwego, Jefferson Par., La., 3,987.
On Mo. Pac.; Tex. & Pac. (R. Rs.).
West Wheeling, Belmont Co., Ohio, 850.
On Balt. & Ohio (R. R.).
West Windsor, Windsor Co., Vt., 512.
West Winfield, Herkimer Co., N. Y., 779.
On Del., Lack. & West. (R. R.).
Westwood, Norfolk Co., Mass., 2,537.
—Lassen Co., Cal., 3,500.
On Sou. Pac.; West. Pac. (R. Rs.).
—Boyd Co., Ky., 3,000.
—Bergen Co., N. J., 4,861.
On N. Jer. & N. York (R. R.).
West Wyoming, Luzerne Co., Pa., 2,769.
West York, York Co., Pa., 5,381.
On Penna.; West. Md. (R. Rs.).
Wetaskiwin, Wetaskiwan Co., Alb., Can., **2,058.**
On Can. Pac. (R. R.).
Wethersfield, Hartford Co., Conn., 7,512.
On N. York, N. Hav. & Hart. (R. R.).
—Henry Co., Ill. See Kewanee.
Wetteren, East Flanders, Belgium, 17,857.
Wetumka, Hughes Co., Okla., 2,153.
On St. Lou.-San Fran. (R. R.).
Wetumpka, c. s., Elmore Co., Ala., 2,357.
On Lou. & Nash. (R. R.).
Wewahitchka, c. s., Gulf Co., Fla., 755.
Wewoka, c. s., Seminole Co., Okla., 10,401.
On Chi., Rk. Isl. & Pac. (R. R.).
A trade and marketing town located in a petroleum and agricultural region.
Wexford (Loch Garman), County Wexford, Ireland (Eire), 11,879.
A seaport and commercial town situated near an agricultural region. Also has fisheries.
Weyauwega, Waupaca Co., Wis., 1,067.
On Minn., St. P. & S. Ste. M. (R. R.).
Weyburn, Saskatchewan, Canada, 5,338.
Weymouth, Norfolk Co., Mass., 21,748.
On N. York, N. Hav. & Hart. (R. R.).
Weymouth and Melcombe Regis, Dorsetshire, England, 21,982.
A seaport and marketing center.
Whaleyville, Nansemond Co., Va., 750.
Wharton, Morris Co., N. J., 3,683.
On Cen. of N. Jer.; Del., Lack. & West.; **Mt.** Hope Miner.; Wharton & Nor. (R. Rs.).
—c. s., Wharton Co., Texas, 2,691.
On Gulf, Colo. & Santa Fe; Tex. & N. Orl. (Sou. Pac.) (R. Rs.).
What Cheer, Keokuk Co., Iowa, 1,310.

On Chi. & Rk. Isl. & Pac.; Chi. & Nor. West. (R. Rs.).
Whately, Franklin Co., Mass., 1,133.
On Boston & Maine & N. York, N. Hav. & Hart. (R. Rs.).
Wheatcroft, Webster Co., Ky., 705.
On Ill. Cen. (R. R.).
Wheatland, Clinton Co., Iowa, 539.
On Chi., Mil., St. P. & Pac.; Chi. & Nor. West. (R. Rs.).
—Knox Co., Ind., 806.
On Balt. & Ohio (R. R.).
—Mercer Co., Pa., 1,518.
On Erie; Pitts. & L. Erie; Penna. (R. Rs.).
—c. s., Platte Co., Wyo., 1,997.
On Colo. & Sou. (R. R.).
Wheaton, c. s., Du Page Co., Ill., 7,258.
On Chi. & Nor. West.; Chi., Aur. & Elg. (El.) (R. Rs.).
—c. s., Traverse Co., Minn., 1,279.
On Chi., Mil., St. P. & Pac. (R. R.).
Wheat Ridge, Jefferson Co., Colo., 500.
Wheeler, c. s., Wheeler Co., Tex., 931.
Wheelersburg, Scioto Co., Ohio, 900.
On Norf. & West. (R. R.).
Wheeling, c. s., Ohio Co., W. Va., 61,659.
On the Ohio River, and on the Wheel. & L. Erie; Penna.; and the Balt. & Ohio (R. Rs.). Natural gas and bituminous coal are near by. Center of the iron and steel industry. Has varied manufactures. Wheeling was settled in 1769. In 1863-70 and in 1875-85 it was the State capital.
Wheelwright, Floyd Co., Ky., 1,822.
On Chesa. & Ohio (R. R.).
Whigham, Grady Co., Ga., 442.
On Atl. Coast Line (R. R.).
Whippany, Morris Co., N. J., 1,970.
On Morris. & Erie (R. R.).
Whistler, Mobile Co., Ala., 2,442.
On Mob. & Ohio (R. R.).
Whitaker, Allegheny Co., Pa., 2,072.
Whitakers, Edgecombe and Nash Cos., N. C., 930.
On Atl. Coast Line (R. R.).
Whitby, Yorkshire, North Riding, England, 11,-441.
A marketing center in an agricultural region.
—Ontario, Ontario, Canada, 5,053.
On Can. Nat.; Can. Pac. (R. Rs.).
White, Brookings Co., S. Dak., 522.
On Chi., Rk. Isl. & Pac. (R. R.).
—Bartow Co., Ga., 544.
On Lou. & Nash. (R. R.).
White Bear Lake, Ramsey Co., Minn., 2,600.
On Nor. Pac. (R. R.).
White Bluffs, Benton Co., Wash., 600.
On Chi., Mil., St. P. & Pac. (R. R.).
White Castle, Iberville Parish, La., 1,499.
On Tex. & Pac. (R. R.).
White City, Morris Co., Kans., 625.
On Chi., Rk. Isl. & Pac.; Mo.-Kan.-Tex. (R. R.).
—San Augustine Co., Tex., 1,200.
White Cloud, Doniphan Co., Kans., 562.
—c. s., Newaygo Co., Mich., 615.
On Pere Marq. (R. R.).
White Deer, Carson Co., Tex., 1,010.
On Panh. & Santa Fe (R. R.).
Whitefield, Lincoln Co., Me., 908.
—Coos Co., N. H., 1,693.
On Bost. & Me.; Me. Cen. (R. Rs.).
Whitefish, Flathead Co., Mont., 2,803.
On Gt. Nor. (R. R.).
Whitefish Bay, Milwaukee Co., Wis., 5,362.
On Mil. Elec. (R. R.).
White Hall, Greene Co., Ill., 2,928.
On Alton; Chi., Burl. & Quincy (R. Rs.).
—Lowndes Co., Ala., 750.
On West. of Ala. (R. R.).
—Livingston Par., La., 550.
—Muskegon Co., Mich., 1,394.
On Pere Marq. (R. R.).
—Jefferson Co., Mont., 553.
On Nor. Pac. (R. R.).
—Washington Co., N. Y., 5,191.
On Del. & Hud. (R. R.).
—c. s., Trempealeau Co., Wis., 915.
On Gr. Bay & West (R. R.).
—Clarke Co., Ga., 547.
On Cen. of Ga. (R. R.).
Whitehaven, Cumberland, England, 21,142.
Exports are coal, pig iron, steel, and stone.
White Haven, Luzerne Co., Pa., 1,537.
On Cen. of N. Jer.; Leh. Val. (R. Rs.).
Whitehouse, Lucas Co., Ohio, 618.
On Wabash (R. R.).
—Smith Co., Tex., 500.
On Int.-Gt. Nor. (Mo. Pac.) (R. R.).
White House Station, Hunterdon Co., N. J., 1,000.
On Cen. of N. Jer. (R. R.).
White Lake, Aurora Co., S. D., 506.
On Chi., Mil., St. P. & Pac. (R. R.).
—Langlade Co., Wis., 530.
On Chi. & Nor. West.; Minn., St. P. & S. Ste. M. (R. R.).
Whitemarsh, Montgomery Co., Pa., 500.
On Penna. (R. R.).
White Mills, Wayne Co., Pa., 650.
On Erie (R. R.).

White Pigeon, St. Joseph Co., Mich., 966.
On N. York Cen. (R. R.).
White Pine, Jefferson Co., Tenn., 516.
On Southern (R. R.).
White Plains, c. s., Westchester Co., N. Y., 35,830.
On N. York Cen. (R. R.).
White River Junction, Windsor Co., Vt., 2,271.
On Bost. & Me.; Cen. Ver. (R. Rs.).
White Salmon, Klickitat Co., Wash., 798.
Whitesboro, Oneida Co., N. Y., 3,375.
On N. York Cen. (R. R.).
–Grayson Co., Texas, 1,535.
On Mo.-Kans.-Tex. of Tex.; Tex. & Pac. (R. Rs.).
Whitesburg, c. s., Letcher Co., Ky., 1,804.
On Lou. & Nash. (R. R.).
Whiteside, Marion Co., Tenn., 540.
On Nash., Chatt. & St. Lou. (R. R.).
White Springs, Hamilton Co., Fla., 683.
On Ga. Sou. & Fla. (R. R.).
White Sulphur Springs, c. s., Meagher Co., Mont., 575.
On White Sulp. Sprgs. & Yellowst. Pk. (R. R.).
–Greenbrier Co., West Va., 1,484.
On Chesa. & Ohio (R. R.).
Whitesville, Ocean Co., N. J., 600.
–Allegany Co., N. Y., 523.
–Boone Co., W. Va., 1,225.
On Chesa. & Ohio (R. R.).
Whiteville, c. s., Columbus Co., N. C., 2,203.
On Atl. Coast Line (R. R.).
–Hardeman Co., Tenn., 692.
On Nash., Chatt. & St. Lou. (R. R.).
Whitewater, Butler Co., Kans., 589.
On Chi., Rk. Isl. & Pac.; Mo. Pac. (R. Rs.).
–Walworth Co., Wis., 3,465.
On Chi., Mil., St. P. & Pac. (R. R.).
Whitewright, Grayton Co., Texas, 1,480.
On Mo.-Kan.-Tex.; St. Lou. Southw. (R. Rs.).
Whiting, Lake Co., Ind., 10,880.
On Balt. & Ohio; Balt. & Ohio Chi. Term.; Elg., Jol. & East.; Ind. Harb. Blt.; Penna.; N. York Cen.; Chi. Short Line (R. Rs.).
Situated near Chicago and noted for its large petroleum refineries.
–Monona Co., Ia., 627.
On Chi. & Nor. West. (R. R.).
Whitins (Linwood), Worcester Co., Mass., 1,550.
On N. York, N. Hav. & Hart. (R. R.).
Whitinsville, Worcester Co., Mass., 7,000.
Whitley City, c. s., McCreary Co., Ky., 1,200.
On Cin., N. Orl. & Tex. Pac. (R. R.).
Whitman, Plymouth Co., Mass., 7,591.
On N. York, N. H. & Hart. (R. R.).
Whitmire, Newberry Co., S. C., 2,763.
On Seab. Air Line (R. R.).
Whitmore Lake, Washtenaw Co., Mich., 575.
On Ann Arbor (R. R.).
Whitney, Hill Co., Texas, 751.
On Mo.-Kans.-Tex. of Tex. (R. R.).
–Westmoreland Co., Pa., 925.
On Penna. (R. R.).
Whitney's Point, Broome Co., N. Y., 639.
On Del., Lack. & West. (R. R.).
Whitsett (Whitsett Jct.), Fayette Co., Pa., 750.
On Pitts. & L. Erie (R. R.).
Whitt, Parker Co., Tex., 527.
Whittemore, Kossuth Co., Iowa, 604.
On Chi., Mil., St. P. & Pac. (R. R.).
Whittier, Los Angeles Co., Cal., 14,822.
On Los Ang. & Salt Lake (Un. Pac.); So. Pac.; Pac. El. (R. Rs.).
A residential suburb of Los Angeles.
Whittle Springs, Knox Co., Tenn., 1,500.
Whitwell, Marion Co., Tenn., 1,568.
On Nash., Chatt. & St. Lou. (R. R.).
Wiarton, Bruce Co., N., Ont., Canada, 1,949.
On Can. Nat. (R. R.).
Wibaux, Wibaux Co., Mont., 619.
On Nor. Pac. (R. R.).
Wichita, c. s., Sedgwick Co., Kans., 103,347.
On the Arkansas and Little Arkansas Rivers, and on the Atch., Top. & Santa Fe; the Mo. Pac.; the Midl. Val.; Ark. Val. Interurb (El.); the Chi., Rk. Isl. & Pac.; and the St. Lou.-San Fran. (R. Rs.).
Adjacent to extensive oil fields. A livestock and meat-packing center and notable for its annual live stock show. Flour milling leads among its diversified industries. Important grain market, especially for wheat and broom corn. Other leading products are airplanes, wood products, novelties, and machinery.
Seat of Friends' University (Quaker), and Municipal University of Wichita.
Wichita Falls, c. s., Wichita Co., Tex., 43,690.
On Ft. Worth & Denv. Cy.; Mo.-Kans.-Tex. of Tex.; Wichita Fs. & Sou.; and Wichita V. (R. Rs.).
A manufacturing, agricultural and oil center of northwest Texas. Has oil refineries.
Wickenburg, Maricopa Co., Ariz., 734.
On Atch., Top. & Santa Fe (R. R.).
Wickford, Washington Co., R. I., 1,065.
On N. York, N. Hav. & Hart. (R. R.).
Wickliffe, Lake Co., Ohio, 2,491.
On N. York Cen.; N. York, Chi. & St. Lou. (R. Rs.).
–c. s., Ballard Co., Ky., 1,108.
On Ill. Cen.; Mob. & Ohio (R. Rs.).
Wiconisco, Dauphin Co., Pa., 1,895.
Widen, Clay Co., W. Va., 1,800.
On Buf. Cr. & Gauley (R. R.).
Widnes, Lancashire, England, 40,608.
Wien (Vienna), Austria, Germany, 1,843,173.
On the Danube Canal, a branch of the Danube. The river Wien flows through the city and joins the canal. Wien consists of the Inner City and ten districts, viz., Leopoldstadt, Landstrasse, Wieden, Margareten, Mariahilf, Neubau, Josefstadt, Alsergrund, Favoriten, Hietzing.
Though Wien contains buildings of the fourteenth and thirteenth centuries nearly all the most pretentious public buildings date from the nineteenth century. The Inner City and the Ringstrasse are the handsomest. In the former are the Cathedral of St. Stephen (1300-1510), with a tower 450 feet in height; and the Hofburg, or palace of the deposed Hapsburgs. On one side or other of the Ringstrasse rise the exchange, the university, the huge Gothic New Rathhaus, the Parliament house, the Supreme Law Courts, the Museums of Natural History and of Art on either side of the imposing monument of the Empress Maria Theresa, the Opera House, the Academy of Art, the Austrian Museum of Art and Industry. Vienna has many large public parks, the largest being the Prater. The university, founded in 1365, was formerly renowned throughout the world as a medical school. The extensive public picture gallery in the Museum of Art is famous for its unrivaled examples of the Venetian school, Rubens and Dürer. The National Library has over 1,000,000 volumes, and was founded in 1444.
Before the Great War, Wien was the chief industrial city of the Austrian empire and a center of finance. But with the disruption of the empire as part of the conditions of peace imposed by the Allied Powers, Wien lost its commercial and social preëminence. Wien occupies the site of the Roman Vindobona, which was established A.D. 14. The beginning of its present importance dates from the Crusades. In 1276 it became the capital of the Hapsburg dynasty. In 1814-15 the Congress of Wien (Vienna) was held to reorganize the political system of Europe. In 1938, Austria was annexed to Germany.
Wiener Neustadt, Prov. of Lower Austria, Austria, 36,751.
An industrial town with manufactures of locomotives, railroad cars, textiles, leather goods, paper, and sugar.

COURTESY OF THE AMERICAN TOURIST INFORMATION OFFICE

THE OPERA HOUSE, IN VIENNA, AUSTRIA, BUILT IN EARLY FRENCH RENAISSANCE STYLE, CONSIDERED THE MOST FAMOUS OPERA HOUSE IN THE WORLD

Wiergate, Newton Co., Tex., 1,521.
On Gulf. & Nor. (R. R.).
Wiesbaden, Prov. of Hesse-Nassau, Prussia, Germany, 159,800.
A noted resort; mineral springs.
Wigan, Lancashire, England, 85,357.
A trade and industrial town. Has coal mines and various manufactures.
Wiggins, c. s., Stone Co., Miss., 1,074.
On Gulf & Ship Isl. (Ill. Cen.) (R. R.).
Wigton, Clearfield Co., Pa., 786.
On Pitts. & Susq. (R. R.).
Wilber, c. s., Saline Co., Neb., 1,352.
On Chi., Burl. & Quincy (R. R.).
Wilbraham, Hampden Co., Mass., 2,969.
Wilbur, Lincoln Co., Wash., 737.
On Nor. Pac. (R. R.).
Wilburton, c. s., Latimer Co., Okla., 1,524.
On Chi., Rk. Isl. & Pac.; Mo.-Kan.-Tex. (R. Rs.).
–Columbia Co., Pa., 550.
On Leh. Val. (R. R.).
Wilcoe, McDowell Co., W. Va., 1,200.
On Norf. & West. (R. R.).
Wilder, Fentress Co., Tenn., 1,200.
On Tenn. Cen. (R. R.).
–Windsor Co., Vt., 1,125.
On Bost. & Me. (R. R.).
Wildrose, Williams Co., N. D., 518.
On Gt. Nor. (R. R.).
Wild Rose, Waushara Co., Wis., 512.
On Chi. & Nor. West. (R. R.).
Wildwood, Cape May Co., N. J., 5,330.
On Penna.-Read. Seashore (R. R.).
–Sumter Co., Fla., 1,345.
On Seab. Air Line (R. R.).
–Allegheny Co., Pa., 850.
On Balt. & Ohio (R. R.).
Wildwood Crest, Cape May Co., N. J., 738.
On Penna.-Read. Seash. (R. R.).
Wiley, Prowers Co., Colo., 589.
On Atch., Top. & Santa Fe (R. R.).
Wilhelmshaven, Hannover, Prussia, Germany, 77,000.
A seaport and naval station.
Wilkes-Barre, c. s., Luzerne Co., Pa., 86,626.
On the Susquehanna River; and on the Leh. Val.; the Penna.; the Del., Lack. & West.; the Del. & Hud.; the Cen. of N. Jer.; the Lack. & Wyo. Val.; Penna. (R. Rs.).
Anthracite coal mining is the principal industry, followed by iron, steel and textiles (especially silks).
The city was founded in 1769, incorporated in 1806, and received its city charter in 1871.
Wilkesboro, c. s., Wilkes Co., N. C., 1,042.
R. R. Sta. at No. Wilkesboro.
On Sou. (R. R.).
Wilkins, Beaufort Co., S. C., 500.
Wilkinsburg, Allegheny Co., Pa., 29,639.
On Penna. (R. R.).
A residential suburb of Pittsburgh.
Wilkinsonville, Worcester Co., Mass., 780.
On N. York, N. Hav. & Hart. (R. R.).
Willacoochee, Atkinson Co., Ga., 1,006.
On Atl. Coast Line; Ga. & Fla. (R. Rs.).
Willamette, Clackamas Co., Ore., 1,100.
On Sou. Pac. (R. R.).
Willard, Huron Co., Ohio, 4,514.
On Balt. & Ohio (R. R.).
–Cumberland Co., Maine, 521.
–Seneca Co., N. Y., 500.
On Leh. Val. (R. R.).
–Box Elder Co., Utah, 561.
On Un. Pac.; Utah Ida., Cen. (R. Rs.).
Willcox, Cochise Co., Ariz., 806.
On Sou. Pac. (R. R.).
Willemstad, Island of Curaçao, Netherland West Indies, 25,848.
The chief port and commercial town of the island.
Willenhall, Staffordshire, England, 21,147.
A suburb of Wolverhampton.
Willesden, Middlesex, England, 184,410.
A suburb of London.
Williams, Coconino Co., Ariz., 2,166.
On Atch., Top. & Santa Fe (R. R.).
–Colusa Co., Cal., 851.
On Sou. Pac. (R. R.).
–Hamilton Co., Ia., 500.
On Ill. Cen. (R. R.).
–Le Flore Co., Okla., 500.
On Midl. Val. (R. R.).
Williams Bay, Walworth Co., Wis., 630.
On Chi. & Nor. West. (R. R.).
Williamsburg, Iowa Co., Iowa, 1,219.
On Chi., Mil., St. P. & Pac. (R. R.).
–c. s., Whitley Co., Ky., 1,826.
On Lou. & Nash. (R. R.).
–Hampshire Co., Mass., 1,899.
On N. York, N. Hav. & Hart. (R. R.).
–Clermont Co., Ohio, 1,147.
On Norf. & West. (R. R.).
–Blair Co., Pa., 1,898.
On Penna. (R. R.).
–c. s., James City Co., Va., 3,778.
On Chesa. & Ohio (R. R.).
Williamsdale, Butler Co., Ohio, 500.
Williams Grove, Clearfield Co., Pa 600.
Williamson, c. s., Mingo Co., W. Va., 9,410.
On Norf. & West. (R. R.).
–Madison Co., Ill., 518.
On Litchf. & Mad. (R. R.).
–Lucas Co., Iowa, 814.
On Chi., Rk. Isl. & Pac. (R. R.).
–Wayne Co., N. Y., 1,000.
On N. York Cen. (R. R.).
Williamsport, c. s., Warren Co., Ind., 1,053.
On Wabash (R. R.).
–Pickaway Co., Ohio, 524.
–Washington Co., Md., 1,775.
On Hagerst. & F'dk.; Penna.; W. Md. (R. Rs.).
–c. s., Lycoming Co., Pa., 45,729.
On the Susquehanna River, and on the Read.; the Penna.; and the N. York Cen. (R. Rs.).
Has furniture, crepe paper, textile, metal working, motor, and wire rope plants.
Williamston, Ingham Co., Mich., 1,458.
On Pere Marquette (R. R.).
–c. s., Martin Co., N. C., 2,731.
On Atl. Coast Line (R. R.).
–Anderson Co., S. C., 2,235.
On Sou.; Piedmont & Nor. (El.) (R. Rs.).
Williamstown, Berkshire Co., Mass., 4,272.
On Bost. & Me. (R. R.).
Seat of Williams College.
–Grant Co., Ky., 917.
On Cin., N. Orl. & Tex. Pac. (R. R.).
–Gloucester Co., N. J., 1,536.
On Penna.-Read. Seash. (R. R.).
–Dauphin Co., Pa., 2,958.
On Penna; Reading (R. Rs.).
–Orange Co., Vt., 500.
On Cen. Ver. (R. R.).
–Wood Co., W. Va., 1,657.
On Balt. & Ohio (R. R.).
Williamsville, Sangamon Co., Ill., 661.
On Alton; Ill. Term. (El.) (R. Rs.).
–Erie Co., N. Y., 3,119.
On Leh. Val. (R. R.).
Willimansett, Hampden Co., Mass., 3,000.
On Bost. & Me. (R. R.).
Willimantic, c. s., Windham Co., Conn., 12,102.
On Cen. Ver.; N. York, N. Hav. & Hart. (R. Rs.).
Manufactures of cotton and silk textiles.
Williston, Levy Co., Fla., 862.
On Atl. Coast Line; Seab. Air Line (R. Rs.).
–c. s., Williams Co., N. Dak., 5,106.
On Gt. Nor. (R. R.).
–Barnwell Co., S. C., 1,024.
On Southern (R. R.).
Williston Park, Nassau Co., N. Y., 4,427.
Willisville, Perry Co., Ill., 506.
On Mob. & Ohio (R. R.).
Willits, Mendocino Co., Cal., 1,424.
On Northw. Pac.; Cal. West. R. R. & Nav. (R. Rs.).
Willmar, c. s., Kandiyohi Co., Minn., 6,173.
On Gt. Nor. (R. R.).
Willoughby, Lake Co., Ohio, 4,252.
On N. York Cen.; N. York, Chi. & St. Lou. (R. Rs.).
Willowbrook, Los Angeles Co., Cal., 2,500.
On Pac. El. (R. R.).
Willow City, Bottineau Co., N. Dak., 577.
On Gt. Nor. (R. R.).
Willow Glen, Santa Clara Co., Cal., 4,167.
Willow Grove, Montgomery Co., Pa., 3,000.
On Reading (R. R.).
Willowick, Lake Co., Ohio, 667.
Willow Lake, Clark Co., S. Dak., 514.
On Gt. Nor. (R. R.).
Willows, c. s., Glenn Co., Cal., 2,024.
On Sou. Pac. (R. R.).
Willow Springs, Howell Co., Mo., 1,430.
On St. Lou.-San Fran. (R. R.).
–Cook Co., Ill., 1,500.
On Alton; Atch., Top. & Santa F. (R. Rs.).
–(Greggton) Gregg Co., Tex., 2,000.
On Tex. & Pac. (R. R.).
Willowvale, Oneida Co., N. Y., 1,100.
Willsboro, Essex Co., N. Y., 725.
On Del. & Hudson (R. R.).
Willshire, Van Wert Co., Ohio, 506.
On N. York, Chi. & St. Lou. (R. R.).
Wills Point, Van Zandt Co., Texas, 2,023.

On Tex. & Pac. (R. R.).
WILMAR, Drew Co., Ark., 627.
On Mo. Pac. (R. R.).
WILMERDING, Allegheny Co., Pa., 6,291.
On Pennsylvania (R. R.).
WILMETTE, Cook Co., Ill., 15,233.
On Chi. & Nor. West.; Chi., No. Shore & Mil. (El.) (R. Rs.).
A residential suburb of Chicago.
WILMINGTON, c. s., Newcastle Co., Del., 106,597.
At the junction of the Delaware, Christiana, and Brandywine Rivers, and on the Reading; the Pennsylvania and the Baltimore & Ohio (R. Rs.).
There are passenger and freight steamship lines to the ports on the Atlantic Coast. Industries: shipbuilding, railroad equipment, leather goods, foundry products, machinery, rubber goods, tobacco, chemicals, paints, explosives and vulcanized fiber.
In 1638 the Swedes built here Fort Christiana. This was captured by the Dutch in 1655, and called Fort Altena, and the place was named Christinaham. In 1731 the village of Willington, named thus in honor of Thomas Willing, was founded. The name was subsequently converted into Wilmington. The place received its city charter in 1822.
–Will Co., Ill., 1,741.
On Alton (R. R.).
–Middlesex Co., Mass., 4,493.
On Bost. & Me. (R. R.).
–c. s., New Hanover Co., N. C., 32,270.
On Cape Fear River, on the Atl. Coast Line; and Seab. Air Line (R. Rs.).
Has fertilizer plants, shipyards, cotton mills, iron works, woodwork factories. As a South Atlantic port of entry has terminal facilities. In strawberry zone and trucking section.
During the Civil War the city was one of the chief ports of the Confederacy, and a notable resort for blockade runners.
–c. s., Clinton Co., Ohio, 5,332.
On Balt. & Ohio; Penna. (R. Rs.).
–Windham Co., Vt., 611.
On Hoosac Tun. & Wilm. (R. R.).
WILMORE, Jessamine Co., Ky., 1,329.
On Cin., New Orl. & Tex. Pac. (R. R.).
WILMOT, Ashley Co., Ark., 777.
On Mo. Pac. (R. R.).
–Roberts Co., South Dak., 604.
On Chi., Mil., St. P. & Pac. (R. R.).
WILNO (WILNA), Poland, 207,000.
An important marketing center in a grain-raising and lumbering region.
WILPEN, Westmoreland Co., Pa., 700.
On Ligonier Val. (R. R.).
WILSEY, Morris Co., Kans., 790.
On Mo. Pac. (R. R.).
WILSON, Ellsworth Co., Kans., 1,107.
On Un. Pac. (R. R.).
–Mississippi Co., Ark., 1,500.
On Delta Val. & Sou.; St. Lou.-San Fran. (R. Rs.).
–Hartford Co., Conn., 600.
On N. York, N. Hav. & Hart. (R. R.).
–Niagara Co., N. Y., 660.
On New York Cen. (R. R.).
–c. s., Wilson Co., N. C., 12,613.
On Atl. Coast Line; Norf. Sou. (R. Rs.).
Noted as a tobacco market.
–Carter Co., Okla., 2,517.
On Gulf, Colo. & Santa Fe (R. R.).
–Allegheny Co., Pa., 3,265.
On Bess. & L. Erie; Balt. & Ohio; Pitts. & L. Erie; Penna.; Union (R. Rs.).
–Northampton Co., Pa., 8,265.
WILSONVILLE, Shelby Co., Ala., 770.
On Southern (R. R.).
–Macoupin Co., Ill., 1,220.
WILTON, Shelby Co., Ala., 562.
On Sou. (R. R.).
–Fairfield Co., Conn., 800.
On N. York, N. Hav. & Hart. (R. R.).
–Muscatine Co., Iowa, 1,104.
On Chi., Rk. Isl. & Pac. (R. R.).
–Franklin Co., Me., 3,266.
On Me. Cen. (R. R.).
–Burleigh and McLean Cos., N. Dak., 1,001.
On Nor. Pac.; Mpls., St. P. & S. Ste. M. (R. Rs.).
–Hillsborough Co., N. H., 1,690.
On Bost. & Me. (R. R.).
WILTON STA. (Dryden), Franklin Co., Maine, 1,100.
On Me. Cen. (R. R.).
WIMBLEDON, Surrey, England, 59,520.
A suburb of London and site of international tennis matches.
WINAMAC, c. s., Pulaski Co., Ind., 1,679.
On Penna. (R. R.).
WINBURNE, Clearfield Co., Pa., 1,285.
On N. York Cen. (R. R.).
WINCHENDON, Worcester Co., Mass., 6,603.
On Bos. & Alb.; Bos. & Me. (R. Rs.).
WINCHESTER, Lewis Co., Idaho, 665.
On Craig Mountain (R. R.).
–Southampton, England, 22,969.
Educational center and site of cathedral.
–c. s., Scott Co., Ill., 1,532.
On Chi., Burl. & Quincy (R. R.).
–c. s., Randolph Co., Ind., 4,487.
On Cle., Cin., Chi. & St. Lou.; Penna. (R. Rs.).
–c. s., Clark Co., Ky., 8,233.
On Chesa. & Ohio; Lou. & Nash. (R. Rs.).
–Middlesex Co., Mass., 13,371.
On Bost. & Me. (R. R.).
A residential suburb of Boston.
–Cheshire Co., N. H., 900.
On Bost. & Me. (R. R.).
–Adams Co., Ohio, 821.
On Norf. & West. (R. R.).
–c. s., Franklin Co., Tenn., 2,210.
On Nash., Chatt. & St. Lou. (R. R.).
–(Ind. City), c. s., Frederick Co., Va., 10,855.
On Balt. & Ohio; Penna.; Winch. & Wardens. (R. Rs.).
A trade and marketing center in the fertile Shenandoah Valley. Fruit and fruit products are shipped.
–Dundas Co., Ontario, Canada, 1,027.
On Can. Pac. (R. R.).
WINDAU, Latvia. See VENTSPILS.
WINDBER, Somerset Co., Pa., 9,205.
On Penna. (R. R.).
WINDER, Barrow Co., Ga., 3,283.
On Gainesv. Midl.; Seab. Air Line (R. Rs.).
WINDGAP, Northampton Co., Pa., 1,388.
On Leh. & N. Eng. (R. R.).
WINDFALL, Tipton Co., Ind., 734.
On Penna. (R. R.).
WINDHAM, Rockingham Co., N. H., 600.
On Bost. & Me. (R. R.).
–Greene Co., N. Y., 765.
WINDHOEK, capital of Southwest Africa, 20,300.
The leading commercial and trade center of the Colony.
WINDOM, c. s., Cottonwood Co., Minn., 2,123.
On Chi., St. P., Mpls. & Oma. (R. R.).
WINDSOR, Nova Scotia, Canada, 3,032.
On Dominion Atlantic (R. R.).
–Weld Co., Colo., 1,852.
On Gt. West.; Colo. & Sou. (R. Rs.).
–North Essex Co., Ont., Can., 63,108.
On Can. Pac.; Can. Nat.; Mich. Cen.; Wab.; Essex Term. (R. Rs.).
A port of entry situated on the east side of the St. Clair River across from Detroit. In a rich agricultural region. Diversified manufactures.
–Hartford Co., Conn., 6,100.
On N. York, N. Hav. & Hart. (R. R.).
–Shelby Co., Ill., 927.
On Cle., Cin., Chi. & St. Lou.; Wab. (R. Rs.).
–Henry Co., Mo., 1,879.
On Chi., Rk. Isl. & Pac.; Mo.-Kan.-Tex. (R. Rs.).
–Broome Co., N. Y., 661.
On Del. & Hudson (R. R.).
–c. s., Bertie Co., N. C., 1,425.
On Carol. Sou. (R. R.).
–York Co., Pa., 1,009.
–Windsor Co., Vt., 3,689.
On Bost. & Me.; Cen. Ver. (R. Rs.).
WINDSOR LOCKS, Hartford Co., Conn., 4,073.
On N. York, N. Hav. & Hart. (R. R.).
WINDSOR MILLS, Richmond Co., Quebec, Canada, 2,720.
On Can. Pac.; Can. Nat. (R. Rs.).
WINDTHORST, Archer Co., Tex., 500.
WINFIELD, Marion Co., Ala., 1,254.
On Ill. Cen.; St. Lou.-San Fran. (R. R.).
–Henry Co., Iowa, 933.
On Chi., Burl. & Quincy; Minn. & St. Lou. (R. Rs.).
–c. s., Cowley Co., Kans., 8,816.
On Atch., Top. & Santa Fe; Mo. Pac.; St. Lou.-San Fran. (R. Rs.).
–Lincoln Co., Mo., 386.
On Chi., Burl. & Quincy (R. R.).
–Titos Co., Tex., 500.
On St. Lou. Southw. (R. R.).
WINGATE, Dorchester Co., Md., 800.
–Union Co., N. C., 526.
On Seab. Air Line (R. R.).
WINGDALE, Dutchess Co., N. Y., 500.
On N. York Cen. (R. R.).
WINGHAM, Huron Co., N. Ont., Canada, 1,959.
On Can. Pac.; Can. Nat. (R. Rs.).
WINK, Winkler Co., Tex., 3,963.
On Tex.-N. Mex. (R. R.).
WINKLEMAN, Gila Co., Ariz., 729.
On Sou. Pac. (R. R.).
WINLOCK, Lewis Co., Wash., 864.
On Chi., Mil., St. P. & Pac.; Gt. Nor.; Nor. Pac.; Un. Pac. (R. Rs.).
WINNEBAGO, Faribault Co., Minn., 1,701.
On Chi., Mil., St. P. & Pac.; Chi., St. P., Minn. & Omaha (R. Rs.).
–Winnebago Co., Ill., 588.
On Chi. & Nor. West. (R. R.).
–Thurston Co., Neb., 653.
On Chi., Burl. & Quincy (R. R.).
WINNECONNE, Winnebago Co., Wis., 821.
On Chi., Mil., St. P. & Pac. (R. R.).
WINNEMUCCA, c. s., Humboldt Co., Nev., 1,989.
On Sou. Pac.; West. Pac. (R. Rs.).
WINNER, Tripp Co., S. Dak., 2,136.
On Chi. & Nor. West. (R. R.).
WINNETKA, Cook Co., Ill., 12,166.
On Chi. & Nor. West.; Chi. No. Shore & Mil. (El.) (R. Rs.).
A residential suburb of Chicago.
WINNFIELD, c. s., Winn Parish, La., 3,721.
On Chi., Rk. Isl. & Pac.; La. & Ark.; Trem. & Gulf (R. Rs.).
WINNIPAUK, Fairfield Co., Conn., 500.
On N. York, N. Hav. & Hart. (R. R.).
WINNIPEG, capital of Prov. of Manitoba, Canada, 215,814.
At the confluence of the Assiniboine and Red Rivers, and on the Can. Pac.; the Can. Nat.; Mid. of Man.; Gt. Nor.; Nor. Pac. (R. Rs.).
Winnipeg is the shipping point for the Canadian territory between Lake Superior and the Rocky Mountains. One of the world's important grain markets. Winnipeg was a trading post of the Hudson Bay Company prior to 1870. It was incorporated by the Provincial Legislature in 1873.
WINNSBORO, c. s., Fairfield Co., S. C., 2,344.
On Southern (R. R.).
–c. s., Franklin Parish, La., 1,965.
On Mo. Pac. (R. R.).
–Wood and Franklin Cos., Texas, 1,905.
On La., Ark. & Tex. (R. R.).
WINNWOOD LAKE, Clay Co., Mo., 500.
WINONA, c. s., Winona Co., Minn., 20,850.
On Chi. & Nor. West.; Chi., Burl. & Quincy; Chi. Gt. West.; Chi., Mil., St. P. & Pac.; Gr. Bay & West. (R. Rs.).
An industrial town situated on the Mississippi River with manufactures of flour, medicines, farm machinery, shoes, fur clothing, spices, and auto accessories.
–c. s., Montgomery Co., Miss., 2,607.
On Ill. Cen.; Col. & Greenv. (R. Rs.).
–Smith Co., Tex., 600.
On St. Lou. Southw. (R. R.).
–(Masters) Fayette Co., W. Va., 800.
On Chesa. & Ohio (R. R.).
WINOOSKI, Chittenden Co., Vt., 5,308.
On Cen. Ver. (R. R.).
WINSLOW, Navajo Co., Ariz., 3,917.
On Atch., Top. & Santa Fe (R. R.).
–Pike Co., Ind., 1,175.
On Southern (R. R.).
–Kennebec Co., Me., 3,000.
On Me. Cen. (R. R.).
–Kitsap Co., Wash., 669.
WINSTED, Litchfield Co., Conn., 7,883.
On N. York, N. Hav. & Hart. (R. R.).
WINSTON-SALEM, c. s., Forsyth Co., N. C., 75,274.
On Norf. & West.; Sou.; Winst.-Sal.-Southb. (R. Rs.).
Manufactures woolen goods, cigarettes, wagons, furniture, boxes, machinery, blankets and air-conditioning machinery. A tobacco center.
WINTER GARDEN, Orange Co., Fla., 2,301.
On Atl. Coast Line; Tav. & Gulf (R. Rs.).
WINTER HARBOR, Hancock Co., Me., 517.
WINTER HAVEN, Polk Co., Fla., 5,527.
On Atl. Coast Line; Seab. Air Line (R. Rs.).
WINTER PARK, Orange Co., Fla., 4,837.
On Atl. Coast Line; Seab. Air Line (R. Rs.).
WINTERPORT, Waldo Co., Me., 600.
On Bangor & Aroostook (R. R.).
WINTER QUARTERS, Carbon Co., Utah, 623.
WINTERS, Runnels Co., Texas, 2,423.
On Abil. & Sou. (R. R.).
–Yolo Co., Cal., 896.
On Sou. Pac. (R. R.).
WINTERSET, c. s., Madison Co., Iowa, 2,921.
On Chi., Rk. Isl. & Pac. (R. R.).
WINTERTHUR, Canton of Zürich, Switzerland, 53,944.
WINTERVILLE, Pitt Co., N. C., 654.
On Atl. Coast Line (R. R.).
–Clarke Co., Ga., 432.
On Ga. (R. R.).
WINTHROP, Kennebec Co., Me., 1,500.
On Me. Cen. (R. R.).
A residential suburb and seaside resort.
–Suffolk Co., Mass., 17,001.
–Sibley Co., Minn., 1,037.
On Mpls. & St. Lou. (R. R.).
WINTHROP HARBOR, Lake Co., Ill., 661.
On Chi. & Nor. West.; Chi. Nor. Shore & Mil. (El.) (R. Rs.).
WINTHROP MINE (National Mine), Marquette Co., Mich., 900.
WINTON, Lackawanna Co., Pa., 8,508.
On Del. & Hud.; Del., Lack. & West.; N. York, Ont. & West. (R. Rs.).
–Hertford Co., N. C., 582.
WINTON PLACE, Hamilton Co., Ohio (station of Cincinnati).
On Balt. & Ohio; Cle., Cin., Chi. & St. Lou.; Erie; Norf. & West.; Penna. (R. Rs.).
WIRT, Carter Co., Okla., 650.
WISCASSET, c. s., Lincoln Co., Me., 850.
On Me. Cen. (R. R.).
WISCONSIN DELLS (Kilbourn), Columbia Co., Wis., 1,489.
On Chi., Mil., St. P. & Pac. (R. R.).
WISCONSIN RAPIDS, c. s., Wood Co., Wis., 8,726.
On Chi. & Nor. West.; Chi., Mil., St. P. & Pac.; Gr. Bay & West.; Minn., St. P. & S. Ste. M. (R. Rs.).
WISE, Edgefield Co., S. C., 1,300.
On Ga. & Fla.; Sou. (R. Rs.).
–c. s., Wise Co., Va., 1,112.
WISHEK, McIntosh Co., N. Dak., 1,146.
On Minne., St. P. & S. Ste. M. (R. R.).
WISMAR, Mecklenburg-Schwerin, Germany, 26,000.
Seaport and trade center. Woolen factories.
WISNER, Cuming Co., Neb., 1,327.
On Chi. & Nor. West. (R. R.).
–Franklin Par. La., 692.
On Mo. Pac. (R. R.).
WISSAHICKON, Philadelphia Co., Pa., 6,000:
On Reading (R. R.).
WISTER, LeFlore Co., Okla., 761.
On Chi., Rk. Isl. & Pac.; St. Lou.-San Fran. (R. Rs.).
WITHERBEE, Essex Co., N. Y., 1,567.
WITT, Montgomery Co., Ill., 1,516.
On Chi. & East. Ill.; Cle., Cin., Chi. & St. Lou. (R. Rs.).
WITTEN, Westphalia, Prussia, Germany, 72,600.
An industrial town in the Ruhr District.
WITTENBERG, Prussian Saxony, Germany, 24,000.
A trade and marketing center in an agricultural region.
–Shawano Co., Wis., 863.
On Chi. & Nor. West. (R. R.).
WLOCLAWEK, Poland, 56,277.
WOBURN, Middlesex Co., Mass., 19,695.
On Bost. & Me. (R. R.).
An industrial suburb of Boston.
WOBURN HIGHLANDS, Middlesex Co., Mass., 1,500.
On Bost. & Me. (R. R.).
WOLBACH, Greeley Co., Neb., 501.
On Chi., Burl. & Quincy (R. R.).
WOLCOTT, New Haven Co., Conn., 972.
–White Co., Ind., 747.
On Penna. (R. R.).
–Wayne Co., N. Y., 1,260.
On N. York Cen. (R. R.).
WOLCOTTVILLE, Lagrange and Noble Cos., Ind., 646.
On Penna.; Wab. (R. Rs.).
WOLFDALE, Washington Co., Pa., 550.
WOLFEBORO, Carroll Co., N. H., 2,000.
On Bost. & Me. (R. R.).
WOLFEBORO FALLS, Carroll Co., N. H., 520.
On Bost. & Me. (R. R.).
WOLFE CITY, Hunt Co., Texas, 1,405.
On Gulf, Colo. & Santa Fe; St. Lou. Southw. (R. Rs.).
WOLFENBÜTTEL, Brunswick, Germany, 20,000.
A trade and commercial town situated near Braunschweig.
WOLF POINT, c. s., Roosevelt Co., Mont., 1,539.
On Gt. Nor. (R. R.).
WOLFVILLE, Kings Co., Nova Scotia, Canada, 1,818.
On Dom. Atl. (R. R.).
WOLLONGONG, New South Wales, Australia, 11,403.
WOLVERHAMPTON, Staffordshire, England, 133,190.
An industrial and commercial center. Iron, steel, machinery, locks, bicycles, rubber goods, chemicals, and papier mache.
WOMELSDORF, Berks Co., Pa., 1,484.
On Reading (R. R.).
WONEWOC, Juneau Co., Wis., 717.
On Chi. & Nor. West. (R. R.).
WOOD (Woodvale Sta.), Huntingdon Co., Pa., 1,500.
On E. Broad Top. (R. R.).
WOODBINE, Harrison Co., Iowa, 1,348.
On Ill. Cen.; Chi. & Nor. West. (R. Rs.).
–Cape May Co., N. J., 2,146.
On Penna.-Read. Seash. (R. Rs.).
WOODBOURNE, Sullivan Co., N. Y., 500.
WOODBRIDGE, Middlesex Co., N. J., 25,266.
On Penna.; Read.; Cen. of N. Jer. (R. Rs.).
A suburb of New York.
WOODBURN, Marion Co., Ore., 1,675.
On Sou. Pac. (R. R.).
WOODBURY, Litchfield Co., Conn., 800.
–Meriwether Co., Ga., 849.
On Sou.; Atla., Birm. & Coast (R. Rs.).
–c. s., Gloucester Co., N. J., 8,172.
On Penna.-Read. Seash. (R. R.).
–c. s., Cannon Co., Tenn., 502.
WOODBURY HEIGHTS, Gloucester Co., N. J., 997.
On Penna.-Read. Seash. (R. R.).
WOODCLIFF LAKE, Bergen Co., N. J., 871.
On N. Jer. & N. York (R. R.).
WOODHULL, Henry Co., Ill., 567.
On Chi., Burl. & Quincy (R. R.).
WOODLAKE, Tulare Co., Cal., 570.
On Atch., Top. & Santa Fe; Visalia El. (R. Rs.).
WOODLAND, c. s., Yolo Co., Cal., 5,542.
On Sou. Pac.; Sacramento Nor. (El.) (R. Rs.).
–Aroostook Co., Me., 600.
–Washington Co., Me., 2,200.
On Me. Cen. (R. R.).
–Northampton Co., N. C., 501.
On Seab. Air Line (R. R.).
–Clearfield Co., Pa., 1,000.
On N. York Cen.; Penna. (R. Rs.).
–Cowlitz Co., Wash., 1,050.
On Gt. Nor.; Nor. Pac.; Un. Pac. (R. Rs.).

Woodlawn, Jefferson Co., Ala. (Sta. of Birmingham).
On Ala. Gt. Sou.; Cen. of Ga.; Lou. & Nash.; Sou.; Seab. Air Line (R. Rs.).
–Erie Co., N. Y., 1,920.
–Beaver Co., Pa. See Aliquippa.
Woodlyne, Camden Co., N. J., 2,878.
–Delaware Co., Pa., 1,000.
Woodmont, New Haven Co., Conn., 531.
On N. York, N. Hav. & Hart. (R. R.).
Wood Ridge, Bergen Co., N. J., 5,159.
On N. Jer. & N. York (R. R.).
Woodridge, Sullivan Co., N. Y., 774.
On N. York, Ont. & West. (R. R.).
Wood River, Madison Co., Ill., 8,136.
On Alton; Cle., Cin., Chi. & St. Lou.; Ill. Term. (El.) (R. Rs.).
–Hall Co., Neb., 751.
On Un. Pac. (R. R.).
Woodruff, Spartanburg Co., S. C., 3,175.
On Charl. & W. Car. (R. R.).
Woodruff Place, Marion Co., Ind., 1,216.
Wood's Run (Elco), Washington Co., Pa., 704.
On Penna. (R. R.).
Woodsboro, Refugio Co., Tex., 1,286.
On St. Lou., Brownsv. & Mex. (R. R.).
Woods Cross, Davis Co., Utah, 1,300.
On Den. & Rio Gde. West.; Ore. Short Line (Un. Pac.) (R. Rs.).
Woodsfield, c. s., Monroe Co., Ohio, 2,317.
Woods Hole, Barnstable Co., Mass., 600.
On N. York, N. Hav. & Hart. (R. R.).
Woodside (West Medway), Norfolk Co., Mass., 1,625.
On N. York, N. Hav. & Hart. (R. R.).
Woodstock, c. s., McHenry Co., Ill., 5,471.
On Chi. & Nor. West. (R. R.).
–Lenawee Co., Mich., 600.
–Grafton Co., N. H., 175.
On Bost. & Me. (R. R.).
–Ulster Co., N. Y., 550.
–c. s., Windsor Co., Vt., 1,312.
–c. s., Shenandoah Co., Va., 1,552.
On Southern (R. R.).
–Carleton Co., N. B., Canada, 3,250.
On Can. Pac.; Can. Nat. (R. Rs.).
–capital of Oxford Co., N. Ont., Canada, 11,395.
On Can. Pac.; Can. Nat. (R. Rs.).
The trade center of a rich agricultural region.
Woodstown, Salem Co., N. J., 1,832.
On Penna.-Read. Seash. (R. R.).
Woodsville, c. s., Grafton Co., N. H., 1,500.
On Bost. & Me.; Mont. & Wells Riv. (R. Rs.).
Woodville, Sandusky Co., Ohio, 1,151.
On Penna.; Lake Shore (El.) (R. Rs.).
–c. s., Wilkinson Co., Miss., 1,113.
On Yazoo & Miss. Val. (Ill. Cen.) (R. R.).
–Allegheny Co., Pa., 4,000.
On Penna.; Pitts., Chart. & Yough. (R. R.).
–c. s., Tyler Co., Tex., 969.
On Tex. & N. Orl. (Sou. Pac.) (R. R.).
Woodward, Dallas Co., Iowa, 901.
On Chi, Mil., St. P. & Pac.; Des M. & Cen. Ia. (R. Rs.).
–Jefferson Co., Ala., 825.
On Ala., Gt. So.; Birm. Sou.; Ill. Cen.; Lou. & Nash.; Seab. Air Line; Sou.; St. Lou.-San Fran. (R. Rs.).
–c. s., Woodward Co., Okla., 5,056.
On Atch., Top. & Santa Fe; Mo.-Kan.-Tex. (R. Rs.).
Wooldridge, Campbell Co., Tenn., 631.
On Sou. (R. R.).
Woonsocket, Providence Co., R. I., 46,822.
On N. York, N. Hav. & Hart. (R. R.).
An important industrial center on the Blackstone River with manufactures of textiles, rubber goods, rayon, and clothes wringers.
–c. s., Sanborn Co., S. Dak., 1,128.
On Chi., Mil., St. P. & Pac. (R. R.).
Wooster, c. s., Wayne Co., Ohio, 10,742.
On Balt. & Ohio; Penna. (R. Rs.).
Located in a gas and oil region. Has a large paint-brush factory.
Worcester, Worcestershire, England, 50,497.
An industrial and commercial center with porcelain and glove factories. Has a number of interesting historical landmarks.
–Cape of Good Hope, Union of South Africa, 12,515.
–Worcester Co., Mass., 190,471.
At the source of the Blackstone River, and on N. York, N. Hav. & Hart.; Bost. & Alb.; Bost. & Me. (R. Rs.).
Manufactures machine tools and rolling-mill construction. There are over 600 manufacturing plants in the Worcester industrial area. Worcester is the seat of Clark University, Clark College, the Worcester Polytechnic Institute, and the College of the Holy Cross. Worcester was founded in 1674, but the settlers were soon driven away by the Indians. It was permanently established in 1713; incorporated in 1822 and chartered as a city in 1848.
Worden, Madison Co., Ill., 1,111.
On Litch. & Mad.; Wabash; Ill. Term. (El.) (R. Rs.).
Workington, Cumberland, England, 24,691.
Has large collieries and blast furnaces.
Worland, c. s., Washakie Co., Wyo., 1,461.
On Chi., Burl. & Quincy (R. R.).
Wormleysburg, Cumberland Co., Pa., 1,404.
Worms, Hesse, Germany, 49,000.
In a wine-producing region near Mannheim.
Woronoco, Hampden Co., Mass., 522.
On Bost. & Alb. (R. R.).
Wortendyke, Bergen Co., N. J., 1,100.
On N. York, Susq. & West. (R. R.).
Wortham, Freestone Co., Texas, 1,404.
On Tex. & N. Orl. (Sou. Pac.) (R. R.).
Worthing, Sussex, West, England, 46,230.
A popular seaside resort.
Worthington, Greene Co., Ind., 1,687.
On Cle., Cin., Chi. & St. Lou.; Penna. (R. Rs.).
–Greenup Co., Ky., 843.
–Hampshire Co., Mass., 530.
–c. s., Nobles Co., Minn., 3,878.
On Chi., Rk. Isl. & Pac.; Chi., St. P., Minn. & Oma. (R. Rs.).
–Franklin Co., Ohio, 1,239.
On Cle., Cin., Chi. & St. L.; Penna. (R. Rs.).
–Armstrong Co., Pa., 661.
On Balt. & Ohio (R. R.).
Wrangell, Alaska, 948.
Wray, c. s., Yuma Co., Colo., 1,785.
On Chi., Burl. & Quincy (R. R.).
Wrens, Jefferson Co., Ga., 1,085.
On Savann. & Atl. (R. R.).
Wrentham, Norfolk Co., Mass., 4,160.
On N. York, N. Hav. & Hart. (R. R.).
Wrexham, Denbighshire, Wales, 18,567.
A marketing town situated a short distance southwest of Chester.
Wright City, McCurtain Co., Okla., 572.
On Tex., Okla. & East. (R. R.).
Wrightstown, Brown Co., Wis., 612.
On Chi. & Nor. West. (R. R.).
Wrightsville, c. s., Johnson Co., Ga., 1,741.
On Wrights. & Tenille (R. R.).
–York Co., Pa., 2,247.
On Penna. (R. R.).
Wrigley, Hickman Co., Tenn., 595.
Wuchang, Prov. of Hupeh, China, 610,000.
A river port opposite Hankow. Has a large trade and some textile and food products industries.
Wuchow, Prov. of Kwangsi, China, 90,000.
A port and trade center on the Si Kiang. Exports sugar, hides, oils, and aniseed.
Wuhu, Prov. of Anhwei, China, 131,000.
The commercial center of a rice, cotton, and tea-growing region.
Wuppertal (Barmen-Elberfeld), Rhenish Prussia, Germany, 408,600.
A leading manufacturing city near Köln.
Würzburg, Bavaria, Germany, 101,000.
Situated on the Main. Its old fortifications have been demolished, but it is still overlooked by the fortress of Marienberg. Once the Prince Bishops of Wurzburg ruled an area ot 1,900 square miles. The see was secularized in 1803.
Wyaconda, Clark Co., Mo., 544.
On Atch., Top. & Santa Fe (R. R.).
Wyalusing, Bradford Co., Pa., 709.
On Leh. Val. (R. R.).
Wyandotte, Wayne Co., Mich., 28,368.
On Det. & Tol. Sh. Line; Det., Tol. & Iron.; Mich. Cent.; N. York Cen.; Wyand. Term. (R. Rs.).
An industrial suburb of Detroit.
Wyanet, Bureau Co., Ill., 859.
On Chi., Burl. & Quincy; Chi., Rk. Isl. & Pac. (R. Rs.).
Wyano, Westmoreland Co., Pa., 1,400.
On Penna. (R. R.).
Wyanoka, Crittenden Co., Ark., 520.
Wyatt, Harrison Co., W. Va., 500.
On West. Md. (R. R.).
Wyckoff, Bergen Co., N. J., 1,500.
On N. York, Susq. & West. (R. R.).
Wylie, Collin Co., Texas, 771.
On Gulf, Colo. & Santa Fe; St. Lou. Southw. (R. Rs.).
Wymore, Gage Co., Neb., 2,680.
On Chi., Burl. & Quincy (R. R.).
Wyncote, Montgomery Co., Pa., 1,500.
Wyndmere, Richland Co., N. Dak., 521.
On Nor. Pac.; Mpls., St. P. & S. Ste. M. (R. Rs.).
Wyndmoor, Philadelphia Co., Pa., 2,500.
On Reading (R. R.).
Wynne, c. s., Cross Co., Ark., 3,505.
On Mo. Pac. (R. R.).
Wynnewood, Garvin Co., Okla., 1,820.
On Gulf, Colo. & Santa Fe (R. R.).
–Montgomery Co., Pa., 1,000.
On Penna. (R. R.).
Wynona, Osage Co., Okla., 1,171.
On Mo.-Kan.-Tex. (R. R.).
Wyoming, Kent Co., Del., 684.
On Penna. (R. R.).
–Stark Co., Ill., 1,408.
On Chi., Burl. & Quincy; Chi., Rk. Isl. & Pac. (R. Rs.).
–Jones Co., Iowa, 634.
On Chi., Mil., St. P. & Pac. (R. R.).
–Kent Co., Mich., 1,800.
On Pere Marq. (R. R.).
–Hamilton Co., Ohio, 3,767.
On Balt. & Ohio; Erie (R. Rs.).
–Luzerne Co., Pa., 4,648.
On Del., Lack. & West.; Leh. Val. (R. Rs.).
Wyomissing, Berks Co., Pa., 3,111.
On Reading (R. R.).
Wytheville, c. s., Wythe Co., Va., 3,327.
On Norf. & West. (R. R.).

X

Xanthe, Greece, 33,712.
A trade and marketing center in Macedonia.
Xenia, Clay Co., Ill., 559.
On Balt. & Ohio (R. R.).
–c. s., Greene Co., Ohio, 10,507.
On Penna.; Balt. & Ohio (R. Rs.).
The trade center of a rich farming and stock raising region. Has manufactures of rope, twine, furniture, and shoes.

Y

Yabucoa, Mun. of Humacao, Puerto Rico, 4,174.
Yadkinville, Yadkin Co., N. C., 590.
Yakima, c. s., Yakima Co., Wash., 22,101.
On Nor. Pac.; Ore.-Wash. R. R. & Nav. Co. (Un. Pac.) (R. Rs.).
Commercial center of the Yakima Valley.
Yakutsk, Yakut Rep., Sov. Union, 23,000.
Yalaha, Lake Co., Fla., 516.
On Atlantic Coast Line (R. R.).
Yale, St. Clair Co., Mich., 1,345.
On Pere Marq. (R. R.).
–Payne Co., Okla., 1,734.
On Atch., Top. & Santa Fe; Mo.-Kan.-Tex. (R. Rs.).
Yalesville, New Haven Co., Conn., 1,000.
On N. York, N. Hav. & Hart. (R. R.).
Yalta, Crimea Rep., R.S.F.S.R., Sov. Union, 25,100.
Yamagata, capital, Yamagata Ken, Japan, 63,423.
A trade and commercial town near Sendai.
Yancey, Medina Co., Tex., 1,000.
Yanceyville, Caswell Co., N. C., 500.
Yankton, Yankton Co., S. Dak., 6,579.
On Chi. & Nor. West.; Chi., Mil., St. P. & Pac.; Gt. Nor. (R. Rs.).
Yaphank, Suffolk Co., N. Y., 3,160.
On Long Isl. (R. R.).
Yardley, Bucks Co., Pa., 1,308.
On Reading (R. R.).
Yardville, Mercer Co., N. J., 2,360.
On Penna. (R. R.).
Yarkand, Sinkiang. See Soche.
Yarmouth, Norfolk, England, 56,769.
A seaport and popular resort.
–Cumberland Co., Me., 1,800.
On Grand Trunk (Can. Nat.) (R. R.).
–Barnstable Co., Mass., 2,095.
On N. York, N. Hav. & Hart. (R. R.).
–Yarmouth Co., Nova Scotia, Can., 7,055.
On Dom. Atl.; Can. Nat. (R. Rs.).
Yarmouth Junction, Cumberland Co., Me., 1,125.
On Grand Trunk (Can. Nat.); Me. Cen. (R. Rs.).
Yaroslavl, Soviet Union, 167,300.
A city on the Volga River with manufactures of textiles, tobacco, leather, and lacquer ware.
Yates, Luzerne Co., Pa., 765.
Yatesboro, Armstrong Co., Pa., 2,067.
On Balt. & Ohio (R. R.).
Yates Center, c. s., Woodson Co., Kans., 2,173.
On Atch., Top. & Santa Fe (R. R.).
Yates City, Knox Co., Ill., 592.
On Chi., Burl. & Quincy (R. R.).
Yatesville, Luzerne Co., Pa., 768.
On Cen. of N. Jer.; Del. & Hud.; Wilk.-Bar. & East. (Erie) (R. Rs.).
Yauco, Ponce Mun., Puerto Rico, 9,491.
Yazoo City, c. s., Yazoo Co., Miss., 5,579.
On Yazoo & Miss. Val. (Ill. Cen.) (R. R.).
Yeadon, Delaware Co., Pa., 5,430.
Yeagertown, Mifflin Co., Pa., 1,900.
On Kishacoquillas Val.; Penna. (R. Rs.).
Yeisk, Soviet Union, Asia. See Eisk.
Yelets, Soviet Union. See Elets.
Yellow Springs, Greene Co., Ohio, 1,427.
On Penna. (R. R.).
Antioch College is located here.
Yemassee, Beaufort and Hampton Cos., S. C., 589.
On Atl. Coast Line; Charl. & W. Car. (R. Rs.).
Yerington, c. s., Lyon Co., Nev., 1,005.
On Nev. Cop. Blt. (R. R.).
Yezd, Iran (Persia), 55,100.
Center of caravan trade; inhabited by Parsees (fire-worshippers).
Yingkow, Manchukuo, 135,110.
Yoakum, DeWitt and Lavaca Cos., Texas, 5,656.
On Tex. & N. Orl. (Sou. Pac.) (R. R.).
Yoe, York Co., Pa., 560.
On Md. & Penna. (R. R.).
Yokkaichi, Ken of Miyé, Japan, 51,811.
Silk, paper, and porcelain manufactures.
Yokohama, Kanagawa Ken, Japan, 704,290.
Important port; chief center of western trade.
Yokosuka, Kanagawa Ken, Japan, 182,871.
A seaport and important naval station.
Yola, Nigeria, 20,000.
The center of an extensive agricultural region.
Yonezawa, Ken of Yamagata, Japan, 44,731.
A trade and marketing center.
Yonges Island, Charleston Co., S. C., 500.
On Atl. Coast Line (R. R.).
Yonkers, Westchester Co., N. Y., 134,646.
Situated on the Hudson River, 15 miles north by east of the Grand Central Station, New York City, on the New York Central (R. R.). The census of 1930 places the number of various manufacturing establishments at 141, with output valued at $113,500,000. Yonkers was first settled about 1650; from 1672 to 1779 was included in the Philipse Manor. Was incorporated a village in 1855 and chartered a city in 1872.
Yorba Linda, Orange Co., Cal., 1,500.
On Pac. El. (R. R.).
York, Sumter Co., Ala., 1,796.
On Ala. Gt. Sou.; Ala., Tenn. & Nor.; Sou. (R. Rs.).
–Yorkshire, England, 84,810.
An important commercial and industrial center. Site of several educational institutions and a famous cathedral.
–York Co., Me., 300.
–c. s., York Co., Neb., 5,712.
On Chi., Burl. & Quincy; Chi. & Nor. West. (R. Rs.).
Seat of York College (United Brethren).
–c. s., York Co., Pa., 55,254.
Situated on Codorus Creek, and on the Penna.; West. Maryland; Maryland & Penna. (R. Rs.). Here are a collegiate institute, county academy, business colleges, and several libraries. It has a number of manufacturing plants, the leading products being ice machines, safes, artificial teeth, paper products, auto parts, clothing, and furniture. Locally notable for its farmers' markets for bringing producers and consumers together. From September, 1777, to June, 1778, the Continental Congress met here while Philadelphia was occupied by the British.
–c. s., York Co., S. C., 2,827.
On Car. & Northw.; Sou. (R. Rs.).
York Haven, York Co., Pa., 770.
On Penna. (R. R.).
Yorkton, Mackenzie Co., Saskatchewan, Canada, 4,931.
On Can. Pac.; Can. Nat. (R. Rs.).
Yorktown, Delaware Co., Ind., 909.
On Cle., Cin., Chi. & St. Lou.; Ind. R. R. Sys. (El.) (R. Rs.).
–De Witt Co., Texas, 1,882.
On Tex. & N. Orl. (Sou. Pac.) (R. R.).
Yorktown Heights, Westchester Co., N. Y., 1,500.
On N. York Cen. (R. R.).
York Village, York Co., Me., 800.
Yorkville, Oneida Co., N. Y., 3,406.
–Belmont and Jefferson Cos., Ohio, 1,963.
On Penna.; Wheel. & L. Erie (R. Rs.).
Yosemite National Park, Mariposa Co., Cal., 1,000.
Youngstown, c. s., Mahoning Co., Ohio, 170,002.
On the Mahoning River, and on the Balt. & Ohio; L. Erie & East.; Erie; N. York Cen.; Penna.; Pitts. & L. Erie; Youngst. & Suburb.; Youngst. & Nor. (R. Rs.).
Has great iron and steel industries.
Youngstown was settled by John Young in 1797. Became county seat in 1876.
–Niagara Co., N. Y., 639.
Youngsville, Warren Co., Pa., 1,907.
On N. York Cen.; Penna. (R. Rs.).
–Lafayette Par., La., 536.
On Tex. & N. Orl. (Sou. Pac.) (R. R.).
Youngwood, Westmoreland Co., Pa., 2,783.
On Penna. (R. R.).
Ypres, West Flanders, Belgium, 15,338.
Destroyed in the World War, 1914-18. Rebuilt since 1920.
Ypsilanti, Washtenaw Co., Mich., 10,143.
On Mich. Cen. (Nor. Pac.) (R. R.).
Seat of State Normal School.
Yreka, c. s., Siskiyou Co., Cal., 2,126.
On Yreka Western (R. R.).
Ysleta, El Paso Co., Tex., 2,446.
On Tex. & N. Orl. (Sou. Pac.); Tex. & Pac. (R. Rs.).
Ystad, Län of Malmöhus, Sweden, 11,444.
A seaport and marketing center near Malmö.
Yuba City, c. s., Sutter Co., Cal., 3,605.
On Sou. Pac.; Sacramento Nor. (El.) (R. Rs.).
Yukon, Canadian Co., Okla., 1,455.
On Chi., Rk. Isl. & Pac.; Okla. (R. Rs.).
–Westmoreland Co., Pa., 2,000.
On Penna. (R. R.).
Yuma, c. s., Yuma Co., Ariz., 4,892.
On Sou. Pac.; Yuma Val. (R. Rs.).
–Yuma Co., Colo., 1,360.
On Chi., Burl. & Quincy (R. R.).
Yumbel, Prov. of Concepción, Chile, 3,592.
Yuriev, Soviet Union. See Dorpat.
Yuzouka, Soviet Union. See Stalin.

Z

ZAANDAM, North Holland, Netherlands, 34,591.
The center of an agricultural region.

ZACATECAS, capital of Zacatecas State, Mexico, 18,801.
On Nat. of Mex. (R. R.).
One of the chief silver-mining centers of the Republic.

ZACHARY, East Baton Rouge Parish, La., 626.
On Yazoo & Miss. Val. (Ill. Cen.) (R. R.).

ZAGREB (Agram), Croatia-Slavonia, Yugoslavia, 185,581.
A commercial and industrial center on the Sava River. Has manufactures of tobacco, leather, rugs, textiles, hats, shoes, paper, and chemicals.

ZAMA, Attala Co., Miss., 707.

ZAMBOANGA, P. I., 99,700.
The center of a rich agricultural district.

ZAMORA, capital of Prov. of Zamora, Spain, 18,136.
Situated in a grain-producing region.

—State of Michoacan, Mexico, 13,208.
On Nat. of Mex. (R. R.).
Situated 75 miles northwest of Morelia.

ZANESVILLE, c. s., Muskingum Co., Ohio, 36,440.
On the Muskingum River, and on the Balt. & Ohio; the Wheel. & L. Erie; the N. York Cen.; and the Penna. (R. Rs.).
In a section rich in glass, molding sands, brick and pottery clays, building stone, iron, steel, and natural gas. Zanesville has long been known as the "Clay City" as it contains the largest art pottery and the two largest tile works in the world, besides other clay industries. There are also shoe factories.

ZANTE, Greece. See XANTHE.

ZANZIBAR, capital of Zanzibar, British protectorate, East Africa, 45,276.
Chief port and commercial center.

ZAPATA, Zapata Co., Tex., 1,041.

ZAPOROZHE (Alexandrovsk), Ukraine, Soviet Union, 192,400.
A port and commercial center on the Dnieper River. Chief manufactures are engines and farm machinery.

ZAQAZIQ, Prov. of Charkieh, Egypt, 57,000.
The center of the Egyptian cotton trade.

COURTESY SWISS FEDERAL R.R.

ZURICH, SWITZERLAND'S LARGEST CITY, A SPOT OF RARE SCENIC BEAUTY,

ZARA, Italian possession on west coast of Yugoslavia, 11,990.

ZARAGOZA, capital of Prov. of Zaragoza, Spain, 189,062.
A trade and marketing center. Leading manufactures are food products.

ZATEC, Germany. See SAAZ.

ZEBULON, c. s., Pike Co., Ga., 576.
On Sou. (R. R.).

—Wake Co., N. C., 860.
On Norf. Sou. (R. R.).

ZEELAND, Ottawa Co., Mich., 2,850.
On Pere Marq. (R. R.).

ZEIGLER, Franklin Co., Ill., 3,816.
On Chi., Burl. & Quincy; Ill. Cen.; Mo. Pac. (R. Rs.).

ZEITUN, Greece. See LAMIA.

ZELIENOPLE, Butler Co., Pa., 1,933.
On Balt. & Ohio (R. R.).

ZELLWOOD, Orange Co., Fla., 700.
On Seab. Air Line (R. R.).

ZENTA, Yugoslavia. See SENTA.

ZEPHYR, Brown Co., Tex., 500.
On Gulf, Colo. & Santa Fe (R. R.).

ZEPHYRHILLS, Pasco Co., Fla., 938.
On Atl. Coast Line; Seab. Air Line (R. Rs.).

ZERBST, Anhalt, Germany, 20,000.
Situated in an agricultural region near Dessau.

ZHITOMIR, Soviet Union, 79,200.

ZILLAH, Yakima Co., Wash., 728.
On Nor. Pac.; Ore.-Wash. R. R. & Nav. Co. (Un. Pac.) (R. Rs.).

ZILWAUKEE, Saginaw Co., Mich., 700.
On Gd. Tr.; Mich. Cen. (N. York Cen.) (R. Rs.).

ZINCVILLE, Ottawa Co., Okla., 500.
On St. Lou.-San Fran. (R. R.).

ZINDER, French West Africa, 10,356.
A trade center and former capital.

ZINOVIEVSK (Elisavetgrad), Sov. Union. See KIROVO.

ZION, Lake Co., Ill., 5,991.
On Chi. & Nor. West.; Chi., No. Sh. & Mil. (El.) (R. Rs.).

ZION GROVE, Schuylkill Co., Pa., 600.

ZIONSVILLE, Boone Co., Ind., 1,131.
On Cle., Cin., Chi. & St. Lou. (R. R.).

ZITTAU, Saxony, Germany, 40,000.

ZLIN, Czechoslovakia, Germany (through seizure of March, 1939), 21,584.

ZOMBOR, Yugoslavia. See SOMBOR.

ZONA, Washington Par., La., 500.
On Gulf, Mob. & Nor. (R. R.).

ZOQUITLAN, State of Puebla, Mexico, 1,332.

ZUFFENHAUSEN, Württemberg, Germany, 15,455.
A trade and marketing town.

ZUMBROTA, Goodhue Co., Minn., 1,350.
On Chi. Gt. West.; Chi., Mil., St. P. & Pac. (R. Rs.).

ZÜRICH, capital of Canton of Zürich, Switzerland, 339,200.
At the point where the Limmat issues from the Lake of Zürich and unites with its tributary the Zihl. Zürich is the most important commercial and industrial town in Switzerland. Center of the silk industry, and has cotton and paper mills.

ZWEIBRÜCKEN, Bavaria, Germany, 17,783.
Silk, machinery, and leather are the leading manufactures.

ZWICKAU, Saxony, Germany, 87,000.
An industrial town near Chemnitz. Chief manufactures are textiles, machinery, chemicals, paper, glass, dyes, aluminum, hosiery, and porcelain.

ZWOLLE, capital of Prov. of Overijssel, Netherlands, 41,706.
An agricultural center. Has large cattle trade.

—Sabine Parish, La., 1,264.
On Kans. City Sou.

Presidents of the United States, Their Chief Opponents, and Their Electoral Vote

Year	President-Elect	Party	State	Electoral Vote	Chief Opponent	Party	State	Electoral Vote	Remarks
1789	George Washington	Federalist	Virginia	69					
1792	George Washington	Federalist	Virginia	132					
1796	John Adams	Federalist	Massachusetts	71	Thomas Jefferson	Democratic Republican	Virginia	68	
1800	Thomas Jefferson	Democratic Republican	Virginia	73	Aaron Burr	Democratic Republican	New York	73	Elected by House of Representatives.
1804	Thomas Jefferson	Democratic Republican	Virginia	162	Charles Pinckney	Federalist	So. Carolina	14	
1808	James Madison	Democratic Republican	Virginia	122	Charles Pinckney	Federalist	So. Carolina	47	
1812	James Madison	Democratic Republican	Virginia	128	DeWitt Clinton	Federalist	New York	89	
1816	James Monroe	Democratic Republican	Virginia	183	Rufus King	Federalist	New York	34	
1820	James Monroe	Democratic Republican	Virginia	231	John Quincy Adams	Democratic Republican	Massachusetts	1	
1824	John Quincy Adams	National Republican	Massachusetts	84	Andrew Jackson	Democrat	Tennessee	99	Elected by House of Representatives.
1828	Andrew Jackson	Democrat	Tennessee	178	John Quincy Adams	National Republican	Massachusetts	83	
1832	Andrew Jackson	Democrat	Tennessee	219	Henry Clay	National Republican	Kentucky	49	
1836	Martin Van Buren	Democrat	New York	170	William H. Harrison	Whig	Ohio	73	
1840	William H. Harrison	Whig	Ohio	234	Martin Van Buren	Democrat	New York	60	
1841	John Tyler	Whig	Virginia						Vice-President until death of Harrison, 1841.
1844	James K. Polk	Democrat	Tennessee	170	Henry Clay	Whig	Kentucky	105	
1848	Zachary Taylor	Whig	Louisiana	163	Lewis Cass	Democrat	Michigan	127	
1850	Millard Fillmore	Whig	New York						Vice-President until death of Taylor, 1850.
1852	Franklin Pierce	Democrat	New Hampshire	254	Winfield Scott	Whig	New Jersey	42	
1856	James Buchanan	Democrat	Pennsylvania	174	John C. Frémont	Republican	California	114	
1860	Abraham Lincoln	Republican	Illinois	180	Stephen A. Douglas / John C. Breckinridge	Democrat / Democrat	Illinois / Kentucky	12 / 72	
1864	Abraham Lincoln	Republican	Illinois	212	George McClellan	Democrat	New Jersey	21	
1865	Andrew Johnson	Republican	Tennessee						Vice-President until assassination of Lincoln, 1865.
1868	Ulysses S. Grant	Republican	D. C.	214	Horatio Seymour	Democrat	New York	30	
1872	Ulysses S. Grant	Republican	D. C.	286	T. A. Hendricks	Democrat	Indiana	42	
1876	Rutherford B. Hayes	Republican	Ohio	185	Samuel Tilden	Democrat	New York	184	
1880	James A. Garfield	Republican	Ohio	214	W. S. Hancock	Democrat	Pennsylvania	155	
1881	Chester A. Arthur	Republican	New York						Vice-President until assassination of Garfield, 1881.
1884	Grover Cleveland	Democrat	New York	219	James G. Blaine	Republican	Maine	182	
1888	Benjamin Harrison	Republican	Indiana	233	Grover Cleveland	Democrat	New York	168	
1892	Grover Cleveland	Democrat	New York	277	Benjamin Harrison	Republican	Indiana	145	
1896	William McKinley	Republican	Ohio	271	William J. Bryan	Democrat	Nebraska	176	
1900	William McKinley	Republican	Ohio	292	William J. Bryan	Democrat	Nebraska	155	
1901	Theodore Roosevelt	Republican	New York						Vice-President until assassination of McKinley, 1901.
1904	Theodore Roosevelt	Republican	New York	336	Alton B. Parker	Democrat	New York	140	
1908	William Howard Taft	Republican	Ohio	321	William J. Bryan	Democrat	Nebraska	162	
1912	Woodrow Wilson	Democrat	New Jersey	435	Theodore Roosevelt / William Howard Taft	Progressive / Republican	New York / Ohio	88 / 8	
1916	Woodrow Wilson	Democrat	New Jersey	277	Charles E. Hughes	Republican	New York	254	
1920	Warren G. Harding	Republican	Ohio	404	James M. Cox	Democrat	Ohio	127	
1923	Calvin Coolidge	Republican	Massachusetts						Vice-President until death of Harding, 1923.
1924	Calvin Coolidge	Republican	Massachusetts	382	John W. Davis	Democrat	New York	136	
1928	Herbert Hoover	Republican	California	444	Alfred E. Smith	Democrat	New York	87	
1932	Franklin D. Roosevelt	Democrat	New York	472	Herbert Hoover	Republican	California	59	
1936	Franklin D. Roosevelt	Democrat	New York	523	Alfred M. Landon	Republican	Kansas	8	